P9-CEP-760

The Encyclopedia of Ireland

EDITED BY **BRIAN LALOR**
FOREWORD BY **FRANK MCCOURT**

Yale University Press
New Haven and London

First published in 2003 by Gill & Macmillan Ltd
with associated companies throughout the world.
First published in the United States in 2003 by
Yale University Press.

Index compiled by Helen Litton
Design by Identikit, Dublin
Visualisation by Joakim Säflund
Print origination by Carole Lynch, Dublin
Colour reproduction by Typeform Repro, Dublin
Printed by Butler & Tanner Ltd, Frome

This book is typeset in Bembo 9 pt on 11.5 pt.

The paper used in this book comes from the wood pulp of managed forests. For every tree felled, at least one tree is planted, thereby renewing natural resources.

Library of Congress Control Number: 2003103834

ISBN 0-300-09442-6 (cloth: alk. paper)

A CIP catalogue record for this book is available
from the British Library.

10 9 8 7 6 5 4 3 2 1

Contents

List of Sponsors

The publishers acknowledge gratefully the generosity of the sponsors who have contributed significantly, both financially and otherwise, to the development of *The Encyclopedia of Ireland*.

THE IRISH TIMES

Foreword

Frank McCourt

The Encyclopedia of Ireland is a hard-to-put-down book. It sits by my elbow making it difficult for me to write these words. I want to get back to it, to go from page to page, topic to topic, so that nothing gets done, the face goes unshaved, work accumulates, the dog starves, dishes pile up in the sink, the lawn is a jungle, the wife talks of packing her bags.

But I'm on my way to Limerick. I want to see what the *Encyclopedia* says about the city of my boyhood and it isn't easy getting to the articles on Limerick because as I turn the pages—going backwards—I happen to see the name "Mackey, Mick (1912–1982)," oh, Lord, hero of my childhood who knew my mother and told her I look like a hurler myself and if I "avoided porter" I might be a great hurler, too.

Porter? Now what was that? It's what my father and the plain people of Ireland drank but, alas, it's not in the *Encyclopedia.* Under "Guinness Brewery" we find stout, "single" and "double," and that, for the moment, will suffice. I've downed my share of pints but I never knew whether they were single or double and am content to remain innocent.

We're on our way to Limerick but the pages fall open to "homosexuality" and how do you expect me to skip three articles occupying five columns on this topic by the hero of the hour, David Norris, himself? Here, and throughout the book, there are nuggets of information that could easily be developed into books, plays, films. In 1634, John Atherton, Anglican Bishop of Waterford and Lismore, is said to have promoted an Act for the Punishment of the Vice of Buggery. Subsequently His Grace was arrested for this very act and "hanged outside Christ Church Cathedral in Dublin . . . the first victim of the legislation he had helped introduce." Isn't that delicious?

Limerick will have to wait while I satisfy my curiosity about the Anglo-Irish, their ballads, their literature, their society. This is rich stuff, especially Terence Brown's short sketch on "Anglo-Irish literature" which warns us of the danger of employing this term. He suggests we shy away from the hyphen to the more "correct" (my word) "Irish literature in English." In "Anglo-Irish society," however, Peter Somerville-Large suggests that in recent times the words "Anglo-Irish" had "finally become an accepted and appreciated aspect of the process of Irish history."

I know, I know, I know Anglo-Irish landlords were brutal and chased innocent foxes and despoiled fair Irish Catholic maidens and were mean to their tenants but when I read William Trevor—all is forgiven. (I know you're as eager to get to Limerick as I am but you'll surely excuse me if I stop a moment to look up Mr. Trevor, chronicler of a sad, disappearing community.) William Butler Yeats celebrated the "Hard-riding country gentlemen" but William Trevor, in his last novel, *The Story of Lucy Gault,* limns the end of that ride into a melancholy fadeout.

Why, when I think of William Trevor, do I couple him with John McGahern? A quick look at John, to make sure he's there and to make sure he gets his due.

More than his due. Selena Guinness describes his work in a phrase for which I would yield up my first-born: "the bare exactitude of his prose." May the First Mover send Selena anything she desires if she keeps on writing like that, but then wasn't she inspired by John McGahern!

Onward. But wait. McGahern to McGladdery, another entry that demands attention. Did you know that the last man in Ireland "to be judicially killed" was Robert McGladdery (1935–1961)? The poor devil was only twenty-six but he had murdered nineteen-year-old Pearl Gamble and was hanged for his sins on 20 December 1961.

This might tempt you to turn to the article "crime" but who is this "Crimea Bob" in the opposite column? A horse, if you don't mind. Took part in the Charge of the Light Brigade, survived, and was buried with military honors in Co. Tipperary. (You won't find this in the *Encyclopedia* but the only survivor of the Little Big Horn disaster was the horse of General Custer's right-hand man, Major Myles Keogh. That horse is buried in Auburn, New York.) You're welcome. Ask me anything.

When you hold this *Encyclopedia* in your hands or on your lap or on a strong board you have every right to be self-indulgent. You want to move on to Limerick but why shouldn't you find out what they're saying about two writers who can't make up their minds as to how they should spell their first names—Tóibín, Colm, and McCann, Colum. Aw, no. I can't stay here. Look at their dates of birth: Tóibín, 1955; McCann, 1965. Striplings—prolific, elegant, diverse, adventurous, courageous. I want to live a long time to witness their accomplishments. Their looming will be large.

If you want to meander joyfully through the *Encyclopedia* you can look at the helpful cross-references to relevant articles attached to most of the entries. Your interest in Chaim Hertzog might lead you to "Jews" and the relevant articles here are:

"Hertzog, Chaim"; "Kernoff, Harry"; "Limerick Pogrom" (Yes, we're getting there);

"Solomons, Estella." (Dear Editor: In a future edition of the *Encyclopedia* please include an article on Estella Solomons' distinguished and accomplished family. I don't ask for much and have I complained?)

You've never heard of the Limerick Pogrom? My *Webster's New World Dictionary* defines "pogrom" as "1. an organized massacre of Jews, as in Czarist Russia. 2. any similar attack." To describe what happened in Limerick in 1904 as a pogrom is to stretch the meaning of the word to the borders of Kerry and beyond. There were demonstrations and threats, fists were clenched and shaken, and the Jews of Collooney Street were invited to emerge and be hanged, an invitation they declined. "A shameful episode," says Dermot Keogh, author of the "Limerick Pogrom" article, "it is unique in the history of twentieth-century Ireland."

We ought to learn from the "episode" but we can't linger. Better to move on to a remarkable and cheering moment in the history of Limerick, namely, "Limerick Soviet."

Limerick Soviet! Read the article and you'll see how the people of Limerick, the workers, took over the city from 9 April to 24 April 1919. The strike received international coverage because of press presence to cover the "proposed transatlantic flight by Major Woods; it was they who nicknamed the general strike a soviet."

Not to cavil but there's a fine long article on Cork City by Kevin Hourihan and no such thing for Limerick City. I bring this up to alert the editors to the possibility of cries of anguish from

Limerick which has already suffered mightily. There are five short articles on Limerick occupying barely two columns while Cork enjoys four and a half columns.

But wait: The drums and fifes will be heard in Belfast which receives seven whole columns.

I'm almost afraid to look at Dublin but in the interest of something or other I must: Twelve and a half columns.

All right. Fair enough. After all, Dublin is the capital. It's where Roddy Doyle lives. Wait. A quick look at the article on Roddy. Aw, for God's sake, the man was born in 1958 and writes a novel every time he gets a new ream of paper.

Be kind to yourself with this *Encyclopedia:* you can't swallow it in one gulp. You might be tempted to travel from front to back, stopping to feast here and there, but don't treat it like a book. It is a treasure. Better to dip and meander and to sing the praises of the contributors for the succinctness and restraint of their writing.

This is a book that will settle many an argument and, I hope, send many a reader off on a journey. I'm on one myself.

Preface

'Be not afeard: the isle is full of noises,
Sounds and sweet airs, that give delight, and hurt not.'

Caliban[1]

In Alain Resnais' film *Hiroshima, Mon Amour,*[2] the opening sequence of documentary footage from 1945 forms a background to a dialogue between the lovers in the film, a French woman and a Japanese man, about the events of the bombing of the city. The more the woman claims that she has read the texts and seen the pictures in the museum, the more the man responds that she cannot truly understand—because she was not there.

The Encyclopedia of Ireland is a work of reference. Its texts and illustrations open a door into the Irish version of that collective unattainable past. We were not there, but a work of this scope and scale provides us with the possibility of understanding. Although individual entries are of necessity brief summaries of their topics, they lead us to that broader coverage which is encompassed by the totality of the *Encyclopedia's* content.

Published in the early years of the twenty-first century, this *Encyclopedia* seeks to present the best of current consensual thought on the wide span of Irish experience. It acknowledges the protracted struggles of Ireland's history, but its principal theme is to celebrate the gift to the culture of the world of a vibrant and irrepressible people. Ireland here stands both as a subject of particular interest and singularity, but also as just another place in the world, a small island off the west coast of Europe, its people sharing with many other societies the griefs and triumphs of human fortune and misfortune. The elasticity of the encyclopedia form is one of its main attractions, the content expanding or contracting under the hands of its editors. This elasticity represents an encyclopedia's strength and, conversely, its greatest difficulty. The issues facing the editors of *The Encyclopedia of Ireland* were to define its scope and establish criteria for inclusion. A geological time-frame from the Pre-Cambrian to the present day, and a concentration within the range of human habitation in Ireland, gives an effective timespan of the last eight thousand years. The enigmatic nature of much prehistory narrows the concentration further to that of contemporarily recorded history, from the fifth century AD, with an ever-expanding coverage into the present, including the twenty-first century.

While the primary focus of the *Encyclopedia* is on movements, events and people now in the past, the needs of a comprehensive reference work would not be served by excluding living persons and present-day concerns. Here the editorial process treads in more difficult territory, since such inclusions lack the sanction of time. The main events and *dramatis personae* of twentieth and early twenty-first-century political and cultural life are included, but this field is disrespectful of attempts to encapsulate: some of its seminal events and pivotal characters may yet be concealed from view. In the context of a single-territory general encyclopedia, the complex grain of the topic has been represented in both major and minor keys, and by an aspiration towards generosity and inclusiveness.

Sixteen senior consultant editors and fifty consultant contributors have guided the standing army of 950 writers, based in more than a hundred universities and institutions in four continents. Independent scholars have also both acted as consultants and contributed to the publication. While the preponderance of contributors are based in Ireland, the combined institutional involvement from North America and the United Kingdom equals that of Irish institutional participation.

Communicating with such a vast team over the four-and-a-half-year timespan of the project was made possible only electronically; without e-mail, years would have been added to the time necessary to commission, receive, edit and collate the million and a quarter words here assembled. The acceptance level among invited contributors from the outset was both impressive and gratifying for the editors, with widespread enthusiasm being shown for the concept of an encyclopedia of Ireland as a publication long overdue in the context of essential general works of reference.

Anybody or anything that is a product of the broad and diverse culture of Ireland is a legitimate subject for consideration in this volume: those who left Ireland, no less than those who went there, and those who define themselves as British in Ireland, as well as those who assert their Irishness in Britain. It is important to state that the encyclopedia was not conceived as an encyclopedia of the Republic of Ireland. Establishing its appropriate territory proved not to be a problem editorially, but it was on this question that the greatest difficulty was experienced by many of its contributors. From its inception, the whole island of Ireland, its islands and seas, its peoples both at home and abroad, were conceived as the geographical territory and historic social milieu of the *Encyclopedia*. Individual contributors experienced considerable difficulty with the concept of being asked to write on a unitary island and tended in their separate scholarly disciplines not to let their critical scrutiny extend either north or south beyond the opaque glass of the border. This phenomenon is not an experience peculiar to *The Encyclopedia of Ireland*, but is the result of seventy years of political, cultural and economic separation between the two regions of the island, during which both territories have led parallel lives, while their peoples developed multiple ambiguities in mutual disregard, ranging from official posturing to private amnesia.

In 1996 the British Academy hosted a three-day conference at Nuffield College, Oxford, the first systematic study of the social, economic and political development of the two Irelands since partition, at which commentators in the social sciences gathered to share their perspectives. In his introduction to the published conference papers,[3] David Rottman begins: 'The obstacles to comparing the two Irelands are formidable,' and continues: 'Scholars in the South do not regard the North as a useful or appropriate point of comparison. And scholars in the North do not regard the South as fruitful point of comparison.' Another contributor, John Bradley, expands on the difficulty: 'Northern researchers tended to look exclusively to Britain, while Southern researchers tended to be more preoccupied with European and world arenas.' The difficulty presented to any scholar wishing to write comprehensively of life on the whole island is further illuminated by the appearance in 2000 of the first publication[4] since 1921 to contain comparative statistics on a wide range of topics

1. William Shakespeare, *The Tempest,* III, 2.
2. *Hiroshima, Mon Amour,* script by Marguerite Duras, directed by Alain Resnais, 1959.
3. Anthony F. Heath, Richard Breen and Christopher T. Whelan (eds.), *Ireland North and South: Perspectives from Social Science,* 1999.
4. Northern Ireland Statistics & Research Agency/Central Statistics Office, *Ireland North and South: A Statistical Profile,* 2000.

from both Northern Ireland and the Republic—on education, economics, agriculture, population and society. (Of the ten most popular babies' names in Northern Ireland and the Republic in 1999, seven were common to both jurisdictions, though in a different order of preference; neither Patrick nor Patricia appeared in either list.) While the difficulty of making island-wide comparisons without appropriate research material may be particularly concentrated in the social sciences, the *Encyclopedia* was faced with the task of convincing many of its academic contributors to cast their intellectual nets wider than their disciplines had for generations been accustomed to do. This publication is a landmark in setting its sights beyond the restricted horizons of the past.

The *Encyclopedia* was conceived as interlocking strata on three levels: textual, visual, and cartographic. While the core of the volume is self-evidently its text, the visual content has been taken no less seriously. Over 700 illustrations not only serve to visually enhance the topics to which they are attached but also convey their own argument. That the illustrations might create resonances across the entirety of the text was a conscious objective, and in many cases an illustration chosen for a specific entry contextualises other topics as well. The richness of visual material, as well as the diverse sources from which they have come, brings together a remarkable body of images which can confirm or challenge received wisdom, or memory. Some iconic images have been selected for their centrality to an event or period; alternatively, oblique angles also have been sought, as well as ephemera from the margins of history, to suggest a point, or to underscore an idea.

The cartography, like the images, is seen as sustaining the geographical and historical narrative, enabling the reader to engage with the localness that is an integral aspect of the Irish mind and landscape. Not since Samuel Lewis's *A Topographical Dictionary of Ireland* in 1837 have the counties received such individual consideration, centre though they are of all local sentiment and sense of belonging. Here their individuality has been exploited, and what curious shapes they are when isolated from their conventional island context.

If inclusiveness and generosity of spirit guided the creating of the *Encyclopedia,* other criteria lay behind its formation in specific directions. The central plank of Irish cultural standing in the world has been for 300 years its writers in English, who, from Jonathan Swift to the many distinguished writers of the present day, have defined a specific linguistic and conceptual territory, witty, satirical, ironic. That segment of Irishry is well represented here, at greater or lesser length. It finds itself among contemporaries of every generation who have achieved much yet occupy little collective presence on the international (or even the local) stage. Irish science from the eighteenth to the twenty-first century is of considerable distinction and deserves to be acknowledged. Literature in Irish, the other voice that exists in parallel to that of Swift and his successors, has been heard less abroad than perhaps any other aspect of Irish life and culture; here it occupies a place equal with those areas already established in the public mind. In these areas alone there is much treasure trove for the exploring reader, as there is in the frequently overlooked contribution of women, to the sciences and to scholarship generally, to political and cultural life, and in a diversity of fields which also receive fitting acknowledgement.

Many smaller fields are also charted, where the Irish intelligence ventured as variously as in other areas, in philosophy and, to remain with the 'p's, in popular music, which have produced singular achievements in their diverse paths: George Berkeley, that great immaterialist, who would have the reader believe that this weighty tome exists only if the reader believes it to do so, here sharing space with the reality of that anthem for children everywhere, Jimmy Kennedy's 'The Teddy Bears' Picnic'.

While the editors strove to maintain proportionality between all categories of entries, from the extended overview essays on individual topics to the briefest of biographical notes, and to impose order on such a heterogeneous mass of information, it was important to ensure that those aspects of culture that are of their nature dominant should not exclude the ephemeral, minor or eccentric inclusions that form an antidote to the surfeit of great deeds and worthy persons, and for these Laurence Sterne will speak in their defence: 'Digressions, incontestably, are the sunshine;—they are the life, the soul of reading! Take them out of this book for instance,—you might as well take this book along with them; one cold external winter would reign in every page of it; restore them to the writer;—and he steps forth like a bridegroom, bids All-hail; brings in variety, and forbids the appetite to fail.'[5]

The Irish diaspora presents a particular dilemma for *The Encyclopedia of Ireland* in that, while it is home to more than 95 per cent of all people of Irish birth or origin, yet the time-frame for the diaspora's actual existence is at its greatest extent from the seventeenth to the twenty-first century, a brief period compared with the eight thousand years of historic human presence on the island of Ireland. The island is the true topic of the *Encyclopedia,* and everything that has happened within its shores. The activities of the Irish people abroad are an essential element of the story, yet one that should not dislodge the core entity of the island itself, defined by its geography and all that transpired within it and around it. The diaspora entries can be no more than a sampling of the second great Irish tale, since the primal narrative, the Ur tale, is securely located on the island in the western sea, the second as firmly scattered to a myriad of Babelonian dispersions.

The idea of publishing an encyclopedia of Ireland was the inspiration of Gill & Macmillan's Publishing Director, Fergal Tobin, who has, over the years of its gestation, focused his considerable determination on ensuring that the concept should be realised in a fitting and scholarly manner. When the elasticity of the project moved it in a relentlessly expanding direction—more content, more personnel, more contributors, more costs—he never lost his sense of vision of the cultural significance of the *Encyclopedia* and the appropriateness of publishing it now, as a testament to Irish achievement, and as a calling-card to the new century. Without Fergal Tobin's courage and encouragement, *The Encyclopedia of Ireland* could not have become the multitudinous textual and visual feast into which it has evolved.

Other staff members without whom the creating and finessing of the entire volume would not have been possible and to whom my profoundest thanks are due, are Myra Dowling for whom no task was too demanding, Sinead McCoole and Carla Briggs who scoured the picture libraries and museums of the world for images, Fiona Markham and Carole Lynch who managed to solve even the most intractable of problems, and Mairead O'Keeffe, Production Director of Gill & Macmillan, whose organizing skills ensured that our collective aspirations were successfully delivered between the covers of this hefty and myriad voiced volume.

Brian Lalor
General Editor

5. Laurence Sterne, *Tristram Shandy,* 1759, book 1, chapter 22.

Consultant Editors

Jonathan Bardon is a lecturer in the School of Modern History, Queen's University, Belfast, and the author of *A History of Ulster* (1992).

Joseph Brady is head of the Geography Department, University College, Dublin, joint editor of *Dublin Through Space and Time* (2001), and editor of the journal *Irish Geography.*

Terence Brown is professor of Anglo-Irish literature at Trinity College, Dublin, a fellow of the college and the author of *The Life of W. B. Yeats: A Critical Biography* (1999).

Tom Garvin is professor of politics at University College, Dublin, and the author of *Nationalist Revolutionaries in Ireland* (1987) and *1922: The Birth of Irish Democracy* (1996).

Janice Holmes is a lecturer in Irish history at the School of History and International Affairs, University of Ulster, Coleraine, and the author of *Religious Revivals in Britain and Ireland, 1859–1905* (2000).

Susan McKenna-Lawlor is emeritus professor at the National University of Ireland, Maynooth, and managing director of Space Technology Ireland Ltd.

Peter Murray is curator of the Crawford Municipal Art Gallery, Cork, and vice-chairperson of the Cultural Relations Committee and has written extensively on Irish art, most recently monograph catalogues on Patrick Swift, John O'Leary, and Michael Warren.

Máirín Nic Eoin is a lecturer in the Department of Irish, St Patrick's College, Dublin, and the author of *An Litríocht Réigiúnach* (1982), *Eoghan Ó Tuairisc: Beatha agus Saothar* (1988), and *B'Ait Leo Bean: Gnéithe den Idé-eolaíocht Inscne i dTraidisiún Liteartha na Gaeilge* (1998).

Dáibhí Ó Cróinín is an associate professor in the Department of History at the National University of Ireland, Galway, and the author of *Early Medieval Ireland, 400–1200* (1995).

Liam O'Dowd is professor of sociology and director of the Centre for International Borders Research at Queen's University, Belfast.

Mary O'Dowd is a senior lecturer in modern history at Queen's University, Belfast, author of *Power, Politics and Land: Early Modern Sligo, 1568–1688* (1991) and joint editor of *The Field Day Anthology of Irish Writing,* vols. IV–V (2002).

Patrick O'Sullivan is the founder of the Irish Diaspora Research Unit at the University of Bradford and general editor of *The Irish World Wide* (six volumes, 1992–7).

Fintan Vallely is a traditional musician and writer, lecturer in traditional music at the Dundalk Institute of Technology, and editor of *The Companion to Irish Traditional Music* (1999).

John Waddell is professor of archaeology at the National University of Ireland, Galway, and the author of *The Prehistoric Archaeology of Ireland* (2000).

Christopher T. Whelan is a research professor at the Economic and Social Research Institute and joint editor of *The Development of Industrial Society in Ireland* (1992) and *Ireland North and South* (1999).

Harry White is professor of music at University College, Dublin, general editor of the Irish Musical Studies series, and the author of *The Keeper's Recital: Music and Cultural History in Ireland, 1770–1970* (1998).

Consultant Contributors

Maura Adshead is lecturer in politics and public administration in the Department of Government and Society, University of Limerick, and the author of *Developing European Regions?: Comparative Governance, Policy Networks and European Integration* (2002).

Myrtle Allen is a founder-member of the European Community of Chefs (Euro-Toques) in Ireland, founder of the Cork Free Choice Consumer Group, managing director of Ballymaloe House, and the author of *The Ballymaloe Cook Book* (1984).

Mark J. Costello is executive director of the Huntsman Marine Science Centre, St Andrews, New Brunswick.

Neville Cox is a lecturer in law at Trinity College, Dublin, and the author of *Blasphemy and the Law in Ireland* (2001).

Ronald Cox is a research fellow and director of the Centre for Civil Engineering Heritage, Trinity College, Dublin, and joint author of *Civil Engineering Heritage: Ireland* (1998).

Anne-Marie Cunningham is projects co-ordinator with Earthwatch.

Ciarán Deane is an editor with a publishing firm and the author of *The Guinness Book of Irish Facts and Feats* (1994).

John de Courcy Ireland is honorary research officer of the Maritime Institute of Ireland, president of Dún Laoghaire lifeboat station, and the author of numerous works on Ireland and the sea.

Stephen Dixon is an artist and journalist and joint author of *Gift of the Gag: The Explosion in Irish Comedy* (1999).

Patricia Donlon is a former director of the National Library of Ireland and the author of *St James Guide to Children's Writers* (1998).

Mairead Dunlevy is keeper emeritus at the National Museum of Ireland and the author of *Dress in Ireland* (2nd edition, 1999), *Jewellery, 17th and 20th Centuries* (2001), and *Dublin Barracks: A Brief History of Collins Barracks, Dublin* (2002).

Deirdre Falvey is arts editor of the *Irish Times* and joint author of *Gift of the Gag: The Explosion in Irish Comedy* (1999).

Michael Fewer is an architect and conservationist, lecturer in architecture at Dublin Institute of Technology, and the author of *The Way-marked Trails of Ireland* (1996), *By Swerve of Shore* (1998), and *A Walk in Ireland* (2001).

Maureen Gaffney is a psychologist, broadcaster, and writer, chairperson of the National Economic and Social Forum, member of the Council of the Economic and Social Research Institute, and the author of *The Way We Live Now* (1996).

Brian Galvin is senior information specialist with the Health Research Board.

Nicola Gordon Bowe is a writer, art and design historian, and lecturer at the National College of Art and Design, author of *The Life and Work of Harry Clarke* (1989), and joint author of *The Arts and Crafts Movements in Dublin and Edinburgh* (1998).

Patrick Hannon is professor of moral theology and director of postgraduate studies at St Patrick's College, Maynooth, and the author of *Church, State, Morality and Law* (1992).

Eddie Holt is a lecturer in the School of Communications at Dublin City University and a weekly columnist for the *Irish Times*.

Alannah Hopkin is a writer and critic, writing about travel, the visual arts, and literature.

Aine Hyland is professor of education at the University College, Cork, and joint editor of a three-volume collection of extracts from educational documents from earliest times to the 1990s.

John Kelly is a writer and broadcaster on popular music and culture.

Mary Kelly is a senior lecturer in the Department of Sociology, University College, Dublin.

Philip R. Lane is a college fellow and associate professor of economics at Trinity College, Dublin, and director of the Institute for International Integration Studies.

Ian Leask is a lecturer in philosophy at the Mater Dei Institute, Dublin.

Brendan Lynch is a former driver and Grand Prix reporter, a member of the Guild of Motoring Writers, and the author of *Green Dust: Ireland's Unique Motor Racing History* (1988).

Donal MacCarron is a military and aviation historian and the author of *A View from Above* (2000).

Dermot McGuinne is senior lecturer and head of the Department of Fine Art at Dublin Institute of Technology and the author of *Irish Type Design: A History of Printing Types in the Irish Character* (1992).

John Minihan is a photographer whose work has been exhibited throughout the world and the author of *Shadows from the Pale* (1995), *Samuel Beckett Photographs* (1996), and *An Unweaving of Rainbows: Images of Irish Writers* (1998).

Christopher Morash is senior lecturer in English at the National University of Ireland, Maynooth, and the author of *A History of Irish Theatre, 1601–2000* (2002) and *Writing the Irish Famine* (1995).

Sinéad ní Shúinéar is an anthropologist specialising in Irish Traveller culture and relations between Traveller and settled people.

David Norris is a member of Seanad Éireann, author of *James Joyce's Dublin* (1984) and *A Beginner's Guide to James Joyce* (1994), and joint editor of *Proceedings of James Joyce International Symposium* (1982 and 1992).

George O'Brien is professor of English at Georgetown University, Washington, and the author of an autobiographical trilogy and two books on Brian Friel.

Mary O'Doherty is archivist of the Mercer Library, Royal College of Surgeons in Ireland.

Brendan O'Donoghue is chief herald and director of the National Library of Ireland.

Colm O'Gaora is the author of a collection of short stories, *Giving Ground* (1993) and two novels, *A Crooked Field* (1999) and *Another Sky* (2003).

Diarmuid Ó Giolláin is statutory lecturer in the Department of Folklore and Ethnology, University College, Cork, and the author of *Locating Irish Folklore: Tradition, Modernity, Identity* (2000).

Diarmaid Ó Muirithe is senior lecturer emeritus at University College, Dublin, and the author of *A Dictionary of Anglo-Irish: Words and Phrases from Irish in the English of Ireland* (1996).

Timothy O'Neill is a historian and calligrapher, secondary school teacher, and the author of *The Irish Hand* (1984).

Richard Pine is director of the Durrell School of Corfu and the author of works on Lawrence Durrell, Brian Friel, Oscar Wilde, Brendan Kennelly, the Gate Theatre, and the Royal Irish Academy of Music.

Jim Power is chief economist and chief investment strategist at Friends First Group, Dublin.

Patrick Purcell is a retired brigadier-general in the Defence Forces.

Kevin Rockett is a lecturer in film studies at Trinity College, Dublin, and joint author of *Cinema and Ireland* (1987).

Bernard Share was the first general secretary of CLÉ (the Irish Book Publishers' Association), former editor of *Books Ireland,* author of *Slanguage: A Dictionary of Slang and Colloquial English in Ireland* (second edition, 2003).

Jim Sherwin is a television producer and principal sports commentator with RTÉ and chairperson of the Rooney Prize for Irish Literature.

Paddy Smith is a farming journalist, writer, and broadcaster.

Ailbhe Smyth is director of the Women's Education, Research and Resource Centre at University College, Dublin, and joint editor of the 'Arts and literature' section of the *Routledge International Encyclopedia of Women* (2000).

Peter Somerville-Large is a writer on travel and social history as well as a fiction writer and the author of *To the Navel of the World* (1986) and *The Irish Country House: A Social History* (1995).

Carolyn Swift (1923–2002) was dance critic of the *Irish Times,* a former member of Bord Scannán na hÉireann and the board of the Abbey Theatre, and the author of *Stage by Stage* (1985) and joint author of *Spiked: Church-State Intrigue and 'The Rose Tattoo'* (2002).

Ríonach uí Ógáin is a lecturer in the Department of Irish Folklore, University College, Dublin, and has published on aspects of folk tradition, especially traditional song.

John Wakeman is founder-editor of *The Shop: A Magazine of Poetry* and former editor of *World Authors, 1950–1970* (1975) and *World Film Directors, 1890–1985* (1987–8).

Contributors and Readers

Thomas Acton is professor of Romani studies at the University of Greenwich and editor of *Scholarship and the Gypsy Struggle* (2000).

Bernard Adams is a journalist and the author of *Denis Johnston: A Life* (2002).

Jean Agnew is an archivist and author and editor of the Drennan-McTier Letters (1998–9).

Pat Ahern is a musician, a lecturer in mathematics at Cork Institute of Technology, and traditional music columnist for the *Irish Examiner.*

Anders Ahlqvist is professor of Old and Middle Irish and Celtic philology at the National University of Ireland, Galway.

Yahya al-Hussein is imam and president of the Islamic Foundation of Ireland.

Cormac Allen is an architectural historian and an associate director of Murray Ó Laoire, architects.

Des Allen is chief executive officer of Tennis Ireland.

Gregory Allen (1927–2001) was a member of the Garda Síochána, archivist at Garda Headquarters and curator of the Garda Museum on its foundation, and the author of *The Garda Síochána: Policing Modern Ireland, 1922–82* (1999).

Nicholas Allen is Government of Ireland postdoctoral research fellow in Trinity College, Dublin, and the author of *George Russell (AE) and the New Ireland, 1905–30* (2002).

Jody Allen Randolph is an independent scholar and poetry critic.

Jonathan Allison is associate professor of English at the University of Kentucky and editor of *Yeats's Political Identities* (1996), *Patrick Kavanagh: A Reference Guide* (1996) and *William Butler Yeats* (2002) and joint editor of *Poetry and Contemporary Culture* (2002).

Rod Alston works at Eden Plants, Rossinver, Co. Leitrim.

J. H. Andrews was formerly associate professor of geography at Trinity College, Dublin.

Martyn Anglesea is keeper of fine art at the Ulster Museum, Belfast, and the author of *The Royal Ulster Academy of Arts: A Centennial History* (1981) and *Portraits and Prospects: British and Irish Drawings and Watercolours from the Ulster Museum, Belfast* (1989).

Éamonn Ansbro is director of Kingsland Observatory of Space Exploration Ltd, Boyle, Co. Roscommon.

Brigitte Anton is a librarian with the Linen Hall Library, Belfast, and the author of articles on the Young Ireland movement.

John Appleby is a senior lecturer in history at Liverpool Hope University College and editor of *A Calendar of Material Relating to Ireland from the High Court of Admiralty Examinations, 1536–1641* (1992).

Jean Archer is a geologist and archivist and has published extensively on Irish geology and the history of geological cartography in Ireland.

Brian Arkins is associate professor of classics at the National University of Ireland, Galway, and the author of *Builders of My Soul: Greek and Roman Themes in Yeats* (1990).

Marie Arndt is the author of *A Critical Study of Sean O'Faolain's Life and Work* (2001).

Ivana Bacik is Reid professor of criminal law, criminology and penology at Trinity College, Dublin, and a practising barrister and has published on criminal law, human rights and equality issues.

Craig Bailey is a research fellow at the Institute for the Study of Civil Society, London.

M. G. L. Baillie is professor of archaeology and palaeoecology at Queen's University, Belfast, and the author of *A Slice Through Time: Dendrochronology and Precision Dating* (1995).

Linda Ballard is executive and policy assistant to the chief executive of the National Museums and Galleries of Northern Ireland and former curator of textiles at the Ulster Folk and Transport Museum.

Joanna Banks is artistic director of the College of Dance and a graduate of the Royal Ballet School, London, and has had an international performing career in dance.

Tony Bareham is the author of *Charles Lever: New Evaluations* (1991).

Alan Barrett is a senior research officer at the Economic and Social Research Institute, Dublin.

Sean Barrett is a senior lecturer in economics at Trinity College, Dublin.

Ruth Barrington is chief executive officer of the Health Research Board and the author of *Health, Medicine and Politics in Ireland* (1987).

Frank Barry lectures at University College, Dublin, and publishes in the fields of macro-economics, international trade, and economic development.

Joe Barry is a farmer, forester, and journalist.

Terry Barry is associate professor of medieval history at Trinity College, Dublin, the author of *The Archaeology of Medieval Ireland* (1987), and editor of *A History of Settlement in Ireland* (2000).

Ursula Barry is a college lecturer in women's studies at the Women's Education, Research and Resource Centre in University College, Dublin, and joint author of *The Equality Research Database* (2001).

Darius Bartlett is a lecturer in the Department of Geography, University College, Cork, and joint editor of *Marine and Coastal Geographical Information Systems* (1999).

Brendan Bartley is a transport and spatial planner and lectures in urban geography at the National University of Ireland, Maynooth.

Kevin Barton works with the Applied Geophysics Unit at the National University of Ireland, Galway, and has been carrying out geophysical surveys on archaeological sites since 1991.

Catherine Bates lectures in design history and theory at Limerick School of Art and Design.

Guy Beiner is a Government of Ireland research fellow in the Department of Modern History, Trinity College, Dublin, and the author of *To Speak of Ninety-Eight: Remembering the Year of the French in Ireland* (2002).

Jacqueline Belanger is a research associate at Cardiff University.

John Belchem is dean of the Faculty of Arts, University of Liverpool, and has published extensively on Liverpool, Irish migration, and popular radicalism.

Jonathan Bell is head of the Curatorial Division at the Ulster Folk and Transport Museum and editor of *Ulster Folklife.*

Douglas Bennett is a lecturer, writer and broadcaster and the author of *Irish Georgian Silver* (1972), *The Encyclopaedia of Dublin* (1991), and *A Dublin Anthology* (1994).

Dorothy Benson is pathology teaching co-ordinator and assistant museum curator at the Royal College of Surgeons in Ireland.

Stefan Bergh is a lecturer in the Department of Archaeology of the National University of Ireland, Galway, and the author of *Landscape of the Monuments: A Study of the Passage Tombs in the Cúil Irra Region, Co. Sligo* (1995).

Edel Bhreathnach is a research fellow in Scoil na Gaeilge, National University of Ireland, Galway, and the author of *Tara: A Select Bibliography* (1995).

Síghle Bhreathnach-Lynch is curator of Irish paintings at the National Gallery of Ireland and has published widely on nineteenth and early twentieth-century Irish painting and sculpture.

Derek Birrell is professor of social administration and head of the School of Policy Studies at the University of Ulster.

Eileen Black is curator of fine art in the Ulster Museum and has published catalogues of the museum's collection and numerous articles on aspects of Irish art.

Allan Blackstock is a lecturer in the School of History and International Affairs, Queen's University, Belfast, and the author of *An Ascendancy Army: The Irish Yeomanry, 1796–1834* (1998).

Marjorie Bloy is a history teacher in Rotherham, England.

Cormac Bourke is curator of medieval antiquities, Ulster Museum, and editor of *From the Isles of the North* (1995) and *Studies in the Cult of Saint Columba* (1997).

Marie Bourke is keeper and head of education at the National Gallery of Ireland and researches, writes and lectures on Irish art and on museum education.

Patrick Bowe is the author of *The Gardens of Ireland* (1986) and joint author of *Irish Gardens and Demesnes from 1830* (1980) and *A History of Gardening in Ireland* (1995).

Barra Boydell is senior lecturer in music at the National University of Ireland, Maynooth.

Finbar Boyle works with Claddagh Records and is a former organiser of the Tradition Club.

John Bradley is senior lecturer in the Department of Modern History, National University of Ireland, Maynooth, and the author of *Irish Historic Towns Atlas: Kilkenny* (2000).

Joseph M. Bradley is a lecturer in the Department of Sports Studies, University of Stirling, and the author of *Ethnic and Religious Identity in Modern Scotland: Culture, Politics and Football* (1995).

Ciaran Brady is senior lecturer in modern history and a fellow of Trinity College, Dublin, and the author of *The Chief Governors: The Rise and Fall of Reform Government in Tudor Ireland, 1536–1588* (1994).

John Brannigan is a teaching assistant in Trinity College, Dublin, and the author of *New Historicism and Cultural Materialism* (1998) and *Brendan Behan* (2002).

Fran Brearton is a lecturer in English at Queen's University, Belfast.

C. S. Breathnach is emeritus professor at the Department of Human Anatomy and Physiology, University College, Dublin.

Diarmuid Breathnach is a librarian and the joint author of the *Beathaisnéis* series (seven volumes, 1986–2002).

Caoimhín Breatnach is a lecturer in the Department of Modern Irish, University College, Dublin, and the author of *Patronage, Politics and Prose* (1996).

Pádraig A. Breatnach is professor of Classical Irish at University College, Dublin, the author of *Téamaí Taighde Nua-Ghaeilge* (1997), and the editor of *Éigse: A Journal of Irish Studies*.

Hugh Bredin is senior lecturer in scholastic philosophy at Queen's University, Belfast.

Helen Brennan is a writer and researcher in the field of Irish dance studies and the author of *The Story of Irish Dance* (1999).

P. B. Brennan is a staff officer at the Military Archives, Dublin.

Rory Brennan is a poet and former broadcaster, arts administrator, and university lecturer.

John Brewer is professor of sociology at Queen's University, Belfast.

A. L. Brindley is an archaeologist at the Department of Archaeology, Rijksuniversiteit, Groningen, Netherlands.

Mícheál Briody is a lecturer at the Language Centre of the University of Helsinki, Finland.

Gabrielle Brocklesby is a librarian who set up the RTÉ Illustrations Archive and is now an independent researcher.

Michael Brown is a lecturer in the Department of History, University College, Dublin, and the author of *Francis Hutcheson in Dublin, 1719–1730: The Crucible of His Thought* (2002).

Michelle P. Brown is curator of illuminated manuscripts at the British Library, London.

Stuart Brown is professor of philosophy at the Open University, Milton Keynes.

Alan Browne is emeritus professor at the Royal College of Surgeons in Ireland and former master of the Rotunda Hospital, Dublin.

Peter Browne is a presenter and producer with RTÉ Radio, lecturer, teacher, record producer, performer on uilleann pipes, and former member of the Bothy Band.

M. T. Brück is an astronomer and the author of *Agnes Mary Clerke and the Rise of Astrophysics* (2002).

Dominic Bryan is a lecturer in the Institute of Irish Studies, Queen's University, Belfast, and the author of *Orange Parades: The Politics of Ritual, Tradition and Control* (2000).

Anthony Buckley is an anthropologist at the Ulster Folk and Transport Museum and the author of *Yoruba Medicine* (1985) and *Negotiating Identity* (1995).

Victor Buckley is senior archaeologist with the Heritage Service and the author of *Burnt Offerings: International Contributions to Burnt Mount Archaeology* (1990).

Michael Bulfin is head of forestry research at Teagasc and the author of *Trees on the Farm* (1992).

Philip J. Bull teaches history at La Trobe University, Melbourne, and is the author of *Land, Politics and Nationalism: A Study of the Irish Land Question* (1996).

Eleanor Burgess is editor of the *Journal of the Butler Society* and a Council member of the British Association for Irish Studies.

James Burke is a military engineer in the Corps of Engineers and former commandant of the School of Military Engineering.

D. Thorburn Burns is professor emeritus of analytical chemistry at Queen's University, Belfast, and research professor of chemistry at Kasesart University, Bangkok.

Sam Burnside is director of the Verbal Arts Centre, Derry, and the author of *Walking the Marches* (1990) and *The Glow upon the Fringe* (1994).

Mervyn Busteed is lecturer in geography at the University of Manchester.

Patricia Butler is an art historian, lecturer and critic and the author of *Three Hundred Years of Irish Watercolours and Drawings* (1990) and *Irish Botanical Illustrators and Flower Painters* (2000).

Cyril Byrne is a professor at St Mary's University, Halifax, Nova Scotia, where he set up the Chair of Irish Studies in 1986.

Paul Byrne is a civil servant in the Department of Finance and the author of *From the Shannon to the Sea: A Study of the Southern Uí Néill* (2003).

Peter Byrne is a sports writer and historian and the author of *The Official History of Irish Football* (1996).

Paul Caffrey lectures in the National College of Art and Design and is the author of *Castletown* (1990), *John Comerford* (1999), and *Treasures to Hold: Irish and English Miniatures, 1650–1850* (2000).

Mary Cahill is an assistant keeper in the Irish Antiquities Division, National Museum of Ireland.

Finbar Callanan is Secretary of The Irish Academy of Engineering and former Director General of the Institution of Engineers of Ireland. He was previously Chief Civil Engineer, Bord Na Mona.

Frank Callanan is a senior counsel and the author of *The Parnell Split* (1992) and *T. M. Healy* (1996).

Julian Campbell is a tutor in the history of art at Crawford College of Art and Design, Cork, and the author of *The Irish Impressionists* (1984).

Matthew Campbell is senior lecturer in English literature at the University of Sheffield.

Anthony Candon is an archaeologist and historian and director of the Ulster History Park, Omagh.

Nicholas Canny is head of the Department of History, National University of Ireland, Galway, director of the Centre for Human Settlement and Historical Change, and the author of *Making Ireland British, 1580 to 1650* (2001).

Tom Cantwell is a squash player and administrator and a former president of Irish Squash.

Margarita Cappock is project development officer of the Francis Bacon Studio at the Hugh Lane Municipal Gallery of Modern Art, Dublin and co-author of *Francis Bacon's Studio at the Hugh Lane* (2001).

Kevin Carey is an assistant professor of economics at American University, Washington.

Nicholas Carolan is director of the Irish Traditional Music Archive, Dublin.

David Caron lectures in visual communication at the National College of Art and Design, Dublin.

Andrew Carpenter is associate professor of English at University College, Dublin, author of *Verse in English from Eighteenth-Century Ireland* (1998) and associate editor of *The Field Day Anthology of Irish Writing,* vols. I–III (1991).

Fionnuala Carragh is a curator at the Ulster Folk and Transport Museum, Cultra, Co. Down.

Patrick Carroll is assistant professor in the Department of Sociology, Science and Technology Studies Program, at the University of California, Davis, and the author of *Colonial Discipline: The Making of the Irish Convict System* (2000).

Fionnuala Carson Williams is a lecturer in the Institute of Irish Studies, Queen's University, Belfast, and the author of *Irish Proverbs from the English of Ireland* (2000).

Marion R. Casey is assistant professor of history and faculty fellow in Irish American Studies at New York University.

Markus Casey is a consultant archaeologist and the author of *Promontory Forts in Ireland* (2003).

Seamas Caulfield is professor of archaeology at University College, Dublin, and a member of the Belderrig Research Centre, Co. Mayo, and has carried out research into the Céide Fields Stone Age settlement.

Mary E. Cawley is a senior lecturer in geography at the National University of Ireland, Galway, and has research interests in rural change and development.

T. C. Champion is professor of archaeology at the University of Southampton.

R. A. Charlton is lecturer in hydrology, fluvial geomorphology and water resource management in the Department of Geography, National University of Ireland, Maynooth, and joint author of *Managing Fluvial and Coastal Environments* (2002).

Jonathan Cherry is senior tutor in the Geography Department, University College, Dublin.

Helena C. G. Chesney was keeper of zoology at the Ulster Museum, Belfast, and joint editor of *Nature in Ireland: A Scientific and Cultural History* (1997).

Martin Clancy is a freelance writer and researcher and a consultant in communications and instructional design.

Heather Clark is an assistant professor of English at Marlboro College, Vermont.

Mary Clark is city archivist, Dublin City Council, and joint editor of *Directory of Historic Dublin Guilds* (1993) and *The Maps of the Archbishops of Dublin* (2001).

Brian Clarke studied metalsmithing in Paris, is a visiting lecturer in the National College of Art and Design, and has his own studio in Co. Wicklow, from where he runs an International School of Silversmithing.

Howard Clarke lectures in medieval history at University College, Dublin.

Tony Clayton-Lea is a journalist and broadcaster and writes on popular culture and the arts for the *Irish Times*.

Brian Cliff is a visiting assistant professor at Emory University, Atlanta.

Michael Clower is a former amateur rider and the author of books on Mick Kinane, Charlie Swan, and Istabraq.

Catriona Clutterbuck lectures in the Department of Anglo-Irish Literature and Drama, University College, Dublin.

Davis Coakley is consultant physician at St James's Hospital, Dublin, professor of medical gerontology at Trinity College, Dublin, and the author of *Irish Masters of Medicine* (1992) and *Oscar Wilde: The Importance of Being Irish* (1994).

John Coakley is a senior lecturer in the Department of Politics at University College, Dublin, and contributing joint editor of *Politics in the Republic of Ireland* (third edition, 1999).

Maurice Colbert is an agricultural economist at the Irish Co-operative Organisation Society Ltd, Dublin.

Marie Coleman is a Government of Ireland postdoctoral scholar in history at University College, Dublin, and the author of *County Longford and the Irish Revolution, 1910–1923* (2002).

Steve Coleman is lecturer in anthropology at the National University of Ireland, Maynooth, an associate of the Humanities Institute of Ireland, and joint editor of *The End of Irish History?: Critical Reflections on the Celtic Tiger* (2003).

Neil Collins is a professor in the Department of Government at University College, Cork, and joint author of *Irish Politics Today* (2001).

Paul Collins is a musicologist and organist, has composed instrumental and vocal works, and lectures in music at Mary Immaculate College, University of Limerick.

Timothy Collins is a chartered librarian at the James Hardiman Library, National University of Ireland, Galway, and the author of *Floreat Hibernia* (1985), *Transatlantic Triumph and Heroic Failure* (2002), and *Decoding the Landscape* (2002).

Anne Colman is a mentor at Mountain Oaks School, Pine Grove, California, and the author of *Dictionary of 19th-Century Irish Women Poets*.

Michelle Comber is a part-time lecturer in the Department of Archaeology, National University of Ireland, Galway.

Patrick Comerford is a priest of the Church of Ireland and a writer and lecturer on theology and church history.

Verena Commins is a traditional musician, ethnomusicologist, composer, and teacher.

Denis Conniffe is research professor at the Economic and Social Research Institute, president of the Irish Statistical Association, and vice-president of the Irish Economic Association.

Claire Connolly is a lecturer in English literature and cultural criticism at Cardiff University.

Anne Connon is a research associate at the Centre for the Study of Human Settlement and Historical Change, National University of Ireland, Galway.

Paul Connors is an officer in the Defence Forces Public Relations Section.

Geoffrey Cook is a lecturer in the Department of Social Policy and Social Work, University College, Dublin.

Patrick Cooke is curator of Kilmainham Gaol Museum, Dublin, and the Pearse Museum, Rathfarnham, Co. Dublin.

Gabriel Cooney is professor of archaeology at University College, Dublin, the author of *Landscapes of Neolithic Ireland* (2001), and joint author of *Irish Prehistory: A Social Perspective* (1994).

Pádraig Corkery lectures in theology at St Patrick's College, Maynooth.

Karen Corrigan is a senior lecturer at the University of Newcastle.

Cathryn Costello is a lecturer in European law at the Law School, Trinity College, Dublin, and director of the Irish Centre for European Law.

Con Costello is the author of *A Most Delightful Station: The British Army on the Curragh of Kildare, 1855–1922* (1966) and *Faith or Fatherhood: John Butler, Catholic Bishop of Cork, 1763–1787* (2000).

Emma Costello is assistant librarian of the Oireachtas.

Peter Costello is a biographer and cultural historian and the author of *The Heart Grown Brutal* (1977) and *James Joyce: The Years of Growth* (1992) and joint author of *John Stanislaus Joyce* (1997).

John Joe Costin is a landscape consultant.

Claire Cotter is director of the Western Stone Forts Project with the Discovery Programme.

Michelle Cotter is a doctoral candidate in the Department of Anthropology, National University of Ireland, Maynooth, where she has taught courses in tourism and heritage.

Patricia Coughlan is a professor in the English Department, University College, Cork, and has published on Spenser, English writings about Ireland, 1590–1660, Samuel Beckett, and twentieth-century women writers.

Damien Courtney is head of the Department of Social and General Studies, Cork Institute of Technology, and has published on many aspects of demography.

Ultan Cowley is an independent historian and the author of *Paddy and the Big Ditch* (1994) and *The Men Who Built Britain: A History of the Irish Navvy* (2001).

Gareth Cox is senior lecturer and head of the Department of Music at Mary Immaculate College, University of Limerick, and the author of *Anton Weberns Studienzeit* (1991).

Rose Mary Craig is a freelance trade and tourism consultant and a former senior development adviser with Enterprise Ireland.

Matt Cranitch is a lecturer in electronic engineering at Cork Institute of Technology, a traditional musician, and a researcher in Sliabh Luachra fiddle music at the University of Limerick.

Leo Creedon is lecturer in mathematics at the University of Regina in Saskatchewan, Canada.

Michael Cronin is director of the Research Centre for Textual Studies and dean of the Joint Faculty of Humanities, Dublin City University, and the author of *Across the Lines: Language, Culture, Translation* (2000).

Mike Cronin is senior research fellow in history at De Montfort University, Leicester, and the author of *A History of Ireland* (2001) and joint author of *The Wearing of the Green: A History of St Patrick's Day* (2002).

Anne Crookshank is former professor of the history of art at Trinity College, Dublin, and joint author of *The Painters of Ireland* (1978) and *Ireland's Painters 1600–1940* (2002).

Frank Crosby is lecturer in sheep husbandry at University College, Dublin.

Virginia Crossman is senior lecturer in history at Staffordshire University and the author of *Politics, Law and Order in Nineteenth-Century Ireland* (1996).

John Crowley lectures in the Department of Geography, University College, Cork.

Nuala Cullen is a freelance food writer and the author of *Savouring Ireland* (1998).

John Cullinane is a lecturer in the Music Department, University College, Cork, and the author of five books in the series 'Aspects of the History of Irish Dancing'.

Glenn Cumiskey is the sound engineer at the Irish Traditional Music Archive, Dublin.

Patrick J. Cummins is a retired nursing officer who has published extensively on Irish aviation history.

Bernadette Cunningham is deputy librarian of the Royal Irish Academy and the author of *The World of Geoffrey Keating: History, Myth and Religion in Seventeenth-Century Ireland* (2000).

George Cunningham is a heritage activist, writer, historian and conference facilitator and the author of *The Anglo-Norman Advance into the South-West Midlands of Ireland, 1185–1221* (1987).

Michael Curran is a former lecturer in liturgy and sacramental theology at Milltown Institute of Theology and Philosophy, Dublin.

Ita Daly was a teacher of English and Spanish before becoming a full-time writer. She has published five novels, one collection of short stories, and three books for children.

John Daly is a former tutor with the Open University and National College of Art and Design, Dublin, the author of *The Scribner Book of Irish Writing* (2001), and consultant editor of the *Irish Journal of Medical Science* and *Journal of Irish Colleges of Physicians and Surgeons*.

Nicholas Daly is a lecturer in the School of English, Trinity College, Dublin.

Graham Davis is course director of the MA in Irish studies at Bath Spa University College, Bath, and the author of *Land!: Irish Pioneers in Mexican and Revolutionary Texas* (2002).

Richard P. Davis is an emeritus professor of history at the University of Tasmania and a fellow of the Australian Academy of Humanities.

William J. Davis is associate lecturer in the history of science at the Open University, Milton Keynes, and joint contributing editor of *Irish Innovators in Science and Technology* (2002).

Gerald Dawe is lecturer in English and director of the Wilde Centre for Irish Writing at Trinity College, Dublin, and has published five collections of poetry and three volumes of essays.

Barbara Dawson is director of the Hugh Lane Municipal Gallery of Modern Art, Dublin, and the author of *Hugh Lane and the Origins of the Dublin Collection* (1993), and co-author of *Francis Bacon's Studio at the Hugh Lane* (2001).

Róisín de Buitléar is a glass artist and lecturer in the National College of Art and Design.

John W. de Courcy is associate professor emeritus of civil engineering at University College, Dublin, and the author of *The Liffey in Dublin* (1996).

Enda Delaney is lecturer in history at Queen's University, Belfast, and the author of *Demography, State and Society: Irish Migration to Britain, 1921–1971* (2000).

Peter Denman lectures in the Department of English at the National University of Ireland, Maynooth.

Gearóid Denvir is senior lecturer in Scoil na Gaeilge, National University of Ireland, Galway, and the author of *Cadhan Aonair: Saothar Liteartha Mháirtín Uí Chadhain* (1987) and *Litríocht agus Pobal* (1997).

Liam de Paor is a marketing consultant and editor of *Forage Guide* (2002) and *Agriculture Review* (2002).

Marie-Annick Desplanques is research co-ordinator in the Department of Folklore and Ethnology, University College, Cork.

Paula Devine is senior social survey officer at the Institute of Governance, Public Policy and Social Research, Queen's University, Belfast.

John Devitt is head of the English Department in the Mater Dei Institute of Education, Dublin, where he lectures on drama.

Robert J. N. Devoy is former director of the Coastal Resources Centre and associate professor in the Department of Geography, University College, Cork.

William Dick is a physicist and a specialist in renewable energy.

Aibhlin Dillane is a traditional musician (flute and piano), graduate of the Irish World Music Centre, University of Limerick, and doctoral candidate in ethnomusicology at the University of Chicago.

John Dillon is regius professor of Greek at Trinity College, Dublin, joint author of *A Classical Lexicon to James Joyce* (1977), and editor of *Plotinus: The Enneads,* translated by Stephen MacKenna (1991).

Gabriel Doherty is a college lecturer in the Department of History, University College, Cork, and joint editor of *Michael Collins and the Making of the Irish State* (1998).

James E. Doherty is joint author of *A Dictionary of Irish History, 1800–2000* (2003).

Liz Doherty is a fiddle player and academic from Co. Donegal.

Richard Doherty is a military historian and joint author of *Irish Winners of the Victoria Cross* (2000).

B. L. Donagh is an officer in the Defence Forces.

Eric Donald is a journalist with the *Farmers Journal.*

Dervilla Donnelly is emeritus professor of organic chemistry at University College, Dublin, a member of the Board of Management and former president of the Royal Dublin Society, chairperson of the Dublin Institute for Advanced Studies.

Margaret Donnelly is a journalist with the *Farming Independent.*

Noreen Doody is lecturer in Irish literature at Boston University and tutor in Irish and English literature at Trinity College, Dublin, and St Patrick's College, Dublin.

Mark Dooley lectures in philosophy and theology at University College, Dublin, and is the author of *The Politics of Exodus* (2001) and *The Catastrophe of Memory* (2002).

Terence Dooley is fellow in the humanities attached to the Department of Modern History, National University of Ireland, Maynooth, and the author of *The Decline of the Big House in Ireland* (2001).

Theo Dorgan is a poet, editor, documentary scriptwriter and broadcaster on radio and television, former director of Poetry Ireland/Éigse Éireann.

J. Glynn Douglas is a Quaker involved in the organisation of the Religious Society of Friends in Ireland and its Historical Committee and the author of *Friends in 1798* (1998).

Martin Dowling is traditional arts officer with the Arts Council of Northern Ireland, a fiddle player and teacher, and the author of *Tenant Right and Agrarian Society in Ulster, 1600–1870* (1998).

Myra Dowling is a graduate in communication studies, has worked in the IT and publishing industries, and was editor and project manager for *The Encyclopaedia of Ireland.*

Linda Dowling Almeida is an adjunct professor at New York University, teaching Irish-American history and literature, and the author of *Irish Immigrants in New York City, 1945–1995* (2001).

David Doyle is a lecturer in history at University College, Dublin, and has taught United States and Irish diaspora studies.

E. D. Doyle is a retired army officer who writes on military affairs.

Eugene J. Doyle has written on nineteenth-century British, Australian and Irish history and is researching a biography of the nineteenth-century British politician Sir William Harcourt.

Elizabeth Drew is a research student in the English Department, Trinity College, Dublin, and managing editor of *Crossings: Electronic Journal of Art and Technology.*

Owen Dudley Edwards is reader in history at the University of Edinburgh.

Patrick Duffy is associate professor of geography at the National University of Ireland, Maynooth, and the author of *Landscapes of South Ulster* (1993).

Seán Duffy is a fellow and head of the Department of Medieval History, Trinity College, Dublin, the author of *Ireland in the Middle Ages* (1997), and general editor of *Atlas of Irish History* (1997).

Carolyn Duggan is head tutor in the Department of English, University College, Cork, lecturing in theatre history, practical drama, and post-colonial literature.

Gerry Dukes is a critic and academic, editor of an annotated edition of Samuel Beckett's novellas, and the author of an illustrated biography of Beckett.

James Dukes is a retired commandant in the FCA and the author of a history of the 44th Battalion, LDF, and FCA (1984).

Robert Dunbar is lecturer in charge of English at the Church of Ireland College of Education, Dublin.

Michael Dunne is a lecturer in the Faculty of Philosophy, National University of Ireland, Maynooth, and editor of the extant works of Peter of Ireland (1993).

Sarah Durcan is an artist and a lecturer in the Faculty of Fine Art, National College of Art and Design, Dublin.

Meaghan Dwyer is a doctoral student in Boston College.

Robert Elgie is Paddy Moriarty professor of government and international studies at Dublin City University and the author of *Political Leadership in Liberal Democracies* (1995).

Ian Elliott is a former assistant professor of the Dublin Institute for Advanced Studies at Dunsink Observatory, Dublin.

William Ellison is a retired naval officer and a consultant in maritime heritage, media, and tourism.

Chris Emblow is a marine ecologist and managing director of Ecological Consultancy Services Ltd, Dublin.

David Emmons is a former professor of history at the University of Montana and the author of *The Butte Irish: Class and Ethnicity in an American Mining Town, 1875–1925* (1989).

Richard English is professor of politics at Queen's University, Belfast, and the author of *Ernie O'Malley: IRA Intellectual* (1998).

Séamus Enright is a Redemptorist priest and a founder of the Irish Religious Houses Heritage Association.

George Eogan is a former professor of archaeology at University College, Dublin, and the author of *Knowth and the Passage Tombs of Ireland* (1986).

Colmán Etchingham is a lecturer in the Department of Modern History, National University of Ireland, Maynooth, and the author of *Church Organisation in Ireland, AD 650 to 1000* (1999).

Tony Fahey is a sociologist with the Economic and Social Research Institute and joint author of *Family Formation in Ireland: Trends, Data Needs and Implications* (2001).

Tony Farmar is a publisher and an author specialising in social and business history.

Jane Fenlon is a consultant with the Heritage Service and the author of *The Ormonde Picture Collection* (2001).

Desmond Fennell is a writer and author of *The Postwestern Condition: Between Chaos and Civilisation* (2002).

Brian Ferran was formerly chief executive of the Arts Council of Northern Ireland.

Denise Ferran is an artist, head of education at the Ulster Museum, and the author of *W. J. Leech: An Irish Painter Abroad* (1966).

Diarmaid Ferriter lectures in Irish history at St Patrick's College, Dublin, and is the author of books on temperance, local government, the Great Famine, and women in Irish history.

Joanne Findon is assistant professor in the Department of English, Trent University, and the author of *A Woman's Words: Emer and Female Speech in the Ulster Cycle* (1997).

John Fingleton is chairman of the Irish Competition Authority.

Alison FitzGerald is a doctoral student at the Victoria and Albert Museum and Royal College of Art, London.

Jennifer FitzGerald is a senior lecturer in English at Queen's University, Belfast.

John Edward FitzGerald is a lecturer in Irish and Newfoundland history in the Department of History, Memorial University of Newfoundland.

Patrick Fitzgerald is lecturer and development officer at the Centre for Migration Studies, Ulster-American Folk Park, Omagh, and joint editor of *Atlantic Crossroads: Historical connections between Scotland, Ulster and North America* (2001).

Ger FitzGibbon is a senior lecturer in the English Department and chairperson of the Board of Drama and Theatre Studies, University College, Cork, joint editor of *Theatre Talk: Voices of Irish Theatre Practitioners* (2001), and author of the play *The Rock Station*.

Elizabeth FitzPatrick is a lecturer in medieval archaeology at the National University of Ireland, Galway, and joint editor of *Gaelic Ireland, c. 1250–c. 1650: Land Lordship and Settlement* (2001).

Marie Therese Flanagan is senior lecturer in the School of Modern History, Queen's University, Belfast, and the author of *Irish Society, Anglo-Norman Settlers and Angevin Kingship* (1989).

Petros Florides is a senior fellow and associate professor of applied mathematics at Trinity College, Dublin.

Richard D. Floyd is a teaching fellow at Washington University, St Louis, Missouri.

Claire Foley is a senior inspector in the Environment and Heritage Service of Northern Ireland with responsibility for the protection of monuments not in state care.

Susan Foran is a doctoral student in the Medieval History Department of Trinity College, Dublin, and joint director of the Galloglass Project.

Michael Fortune is greyhound and horse-racing commentator with RTÉ, greyhound correspondent of the *Irish Examiner and Racing Post,* and editor of *Ireland's Greyhound Weekly* and *Irish Greyhound Review Annual.*

Peter Francis is an author and honorary fellow of the Institute of Irish Studies, Queen's University, Belfast, specialising in Irish ceramic and glass history.

Lyndon Fraser is a lecturer in the Department of Sociology and Anthropology at the University of Canterbury and the author of *To Tara via Holyhead: Irish Catholic Immigrants in Nineteenth-Century Christchurch* (1997).

T. G. Fraser is professor of history and Provost of Magee College, University of Ulster, author of *Ireland in Conflict, 1922–1998* (2000), and editor of *The Irish Parading Tradition: Following the Drum* (2000).

Adrian Frazier is director of the MA course in drama and theatre studies, National University of Ireland, Galway, and the author of *George Moore, 1852–1933* (2000).

Peter Froggatt is a former medical consultant at the Royal Victoria Hospital, Belfast, and former dean of the Faculty of Medicine and president and vice-chancellor of Queen's University, Belfast.

Michael F. Funchion is professor of history at South Dakota State University and editor of *Irish American Voluntary Organizations* (1983).

Daniel Gahan is professor of history at the University of Evansville, Indiana, and the author of *The People's Rising: Wexford, 1798* (1995) and *Rebellion: Ireland in 1798* (1997).

Éamonn Gaines is a doctoral student at the National University of Ireland, Maynooth, seminarist lecturer in philosophy at St Patrick's College, Maynooth, and honorary secretary of the Irish Philosophical Society.

Colman Gallagher lectures in Quaternary geomorphology in the Department of Geography, University College, Dublin.

John J. Gardiner is professor of forestry, University College, Dublin.

Neal Garnham is senior research fellow in the Academy for Irish Cultural Heritages, University of Ulster.

Mary Garrison is a lecturer in the Department of History and the Centre for Medieval Studies, University of York.

Wilbert Garvin is a former lecturer in education at Queen's University, Belfast, author of *The Irish Bagpipes: Their Construction and Maintenance* (2000), joint editor of *His Master's Touch: A Tutor for the Uilleann Pipes by Séamus Ennis* (1998).

Catherine Gaynor is a lecturer in the history of art at University College, Dublin.

Laurence M. Geary is the editor of *Rebellion and Remembrance in Modern Ireland* (2001).

Maeve Ellen Gebruers is printed materials officer with the Irish Traditional Music Archive, Dublin.

Patrick Geoghegan lectures in history in Trinity College, Dublin, is attached to the Royal Irish Academy Dictionary of Irish Biography, and is the author of *The Irish Act of Union* (1999).

Michael Gill is managing director of Gill & Macmillan Ltd.

Dermot Gilleece is golf editor of the *Irish Times.*

Fergus Gillespie is deputy chief herald in the Genealogical Office.

Gordon Gillespie is a political research officer for the Northern Ireland Assembly and joint author of *Northern Ireland: A Chronology of the Troubles, 1968–1999* (1999).

Sheridan Gilley is reader in theology at the University of Durham, author of *Newman and his Age* (1990), and joint editor of *The Irish in the Victorian City* (1985), *The Irish in Britain, 1815–1939* (1989), and *The Irish in Victorian Britain: A Local Dimension* (1999).

William Gillies is professor of Celtic at the University of Edinburgh and has published widely on Irish and Gaelic literary history.

Brian Girvin is professor of comparative politics at the University of Glasgow and the author of *Between Two Worlds* (1989), *The Right in the Twentieth Century* (1994), and *From Union to Union* (2002).

Angela Gleason is a research scholar at the Dublin Institute for Advanced Studies.

Aoife Goodman is a barrister with research interests in the history of medieval Ireland and particularly of the north Munster area.

Michael Gould is a retired senior lecturer, author of *Civil Engineering at Queen's, Belfast, 1849–1999* and *Workhouses of Ulster* (1983), and joint author *Civil Engineering Heritage of Ireland* (1998).

Rod Gow is a lecturer in the Mathematics Department, University College, Dublin, and the author of *Creators of Mathematics: The Irish Connection* (2000).

John Graby is an architect, director of the Royal Institute of the Architects of Ireland, and editor of the *Irish Architectural Review.*

Pierce A. Grace is professor of surgical science at the University of Limerick and consultant vascular surgeon with the Mid-Western Regional Health Board.

Robert J. Grace is lecturer in history at Université Laval, Québec, and the author of *The Irish in Québec: An Introduction to the Historiography* (1993).

Colin Graham is lecturer in Irish writing at Queen's University, Belfast, and the author of *Deconstructing Ireland* (2001).

Len Graham is a professional singer who has recorded twelve albums of traditional songs.

Richard P. Grainger is former chief mechanical engineer with Iarnród Éireann and past president of the Institution of Engineers of Ireland.

John Gray is librarian of the Linen Hall Library, Belfast, a social historian and broadcaster, and the author of *City in Revolt: James Larkin and the Belfast Dock Strike of 1907* (1985).

Peter Gray is a senior lecturer in history at the University of Southampton and the author of two books and numerous articles on the Great Famine.

Philip Graydon is a doctoral student at Queen's University, Belfast.

Jonathan Greer is a former research officer in the School of Policy Studies, University of Ulster, is the author of *Partnership Governance in Northern Ireland: Improving Performance* (2001), and now works in the Department of Finance in Dublin.

Nicholas Grene is professor of English literature at Trinity College, Dublin, and the author of *Synge: A Critical Study of the Plays* (1975), *Bernard Shaw: A Critical View* (1984), and *The Politics of Irish Drama* (1999).

Brian Griffin is co-ordinator of the Irish Studies Centre at Bath Spa University College and the author of *The Bulkies: Police and Crime in Belfast, 1800–1865* (1997).

William D. Griffin is professor of history at St John's University, Jamaica, NY.

Eoin Grogan is director of the Lake Settlement Research Project and a specialist in prehistoric settlement archaeology and social organisation and the application of GIS technology to archaeological analysis and mapping.

Bernadette Grummell is an occasional lecturer in the sociology of communication in the Department of Sociology, University College, Dublin, and is completing a doctorate on the role of education in Irish broadcasting.

Geraldine Guiden is the manager of McCullough-Pigott, Dublin.

Selina Guinness is a lecturer in Irish literature at Dún Laoghaire Institute of Art, Design and Technology.

Gerry Gunning is executive director of the Rural Development Section of the Irish Farmers' Association.

Thomas E. Hachey is chaired professor of history and executive director of the Center for Irish Programs, Boston College.

Valerie Hall is senior lecturer in past environmental studies at the Institute of Irish Studies, Queen's University, Belfast.

Colin Hamilton is a flutemaker, musician and scholar and the author of *The Irish Fluteplayer's Handbook* (1990).

Douglas Hamilton is an economic researcher who has worked for a number of governmental and non-governmental organisations in Ireland and Britain and has written widely on the Irish economy, both North and South.

Ann Hamlin is a specialist in the history and archaeology of the early Irish church. A former lecturer at the University of Exeter, she was director of built heritage in the Department of the Environment for Northern Ireland.

Marie Hammond Callaghan is a research fellow and doctoral candidate in women's studies at the Women's Education, Research and Resource Centre, University College, Dublin, and a member of the Canadian Voice of Women for Peace.

Derek Hand is a lecturer in English at Dún Laoghaire Institute of Art, Design and Technology and the author of *John Banville: Exploring Fictions* (2002).

Robbie Hannan is an uilleann piper and curator of musicology at the Ulster Folk and Transport Museum, Cultra, Co. Down.

Peter Harbison is an archaeologist, honorary academic editor of the Royal Irish Academy, and the author of *Guide to the National and Historic Monuments of Ireland* (1992), *High Crosses of Ireland* (1992), and *The Golden Age of Irish Art* (1999).

Niamh Hardiman is a former fellow of Somerville College, Oxford, a lecturer in the Politics Department of University College, Dublin, and the author of *Pay, Politics and Economic Performance* (1988).

Colin M. Harper is a teacher, researcher, and writer.

Ruth-Ann M. Harris is adjunct professor of history and Irish studies at Boston College, author of *The Nearest Place That Wasn't Ireland: Early Nineteenth-Century Irish Labor Migration* (1994), and editor of the first four volumes of *The Search for Missing Friends*.

Peter Hart holds the research chair in Irish studies at Memorial University of Newfoundland.

Frank Harte is an architect, a singer and collector of traditional songs, and an authority on the song tradition; he has lectured and published, devised radio programmes, issued recordings, and collected a large archive of songs.

Liam Harte is a lecturer in the Academy for Irish Cultural Heritages at the University of Ulster, has published widely on modern Irish fiction and autobiography, and is joint editor of *Contemporary Irish Fiction* (2000).

Barrie Hartwell is senior research officer in the School of Archaeology and Palaeoecology, Queen's University, Belfast.

Anthony Harvey is editor of the Royal Irish Academy Dictionary of Medieval Latin from Celtic Sources.

R. Haslam is an assistant professor of English at Saint Joseph's University, Philadelphia, and a writer on Irish fiction, cinema, and cultural theory.

Richard B. Haslam is a former statutory lecturer and head of the Department of Public Administration, University College, Cork, and former county manager, Limerick County Council.

Moyra Haslett is a lecturer in the School of English, Queen's University, Belfast, and the author of *Byron's 'Don Juan' and the Don Juan Legend* (1997).

Gary Hastings is rector of Aughaval Group of Parishes, Co. Mayo, and a traditional flute-player.

Hugh Haughton is senior lecturer in English and related literature at the University of York.

William Anthony Hay is a senior fellow at the Foreign Policy Research Institute, Philadelphia.

John Hayes is head of the Department of Philosophy and co-ordinating head of the Arts Departments, Mary Immaculate College, University of Limerick.

Mick Heaney is a journalist with the *Sunday Times*.

Dana Hearne is a lecturer in Irish studies and women's studies at the Simone de Beauvoir Institute, Concordia University, Montréal, and editor of *The Tale of a Great Sham* by Anna Parnell (1986).

Peter Hegarty is a writer and radio producer and the author of a biography of Peadar O'Donnell (1999).

Roddy Hegarty is development officer with the Federation for Ulster Local Studies.

Thomas Hennessey is a fellow of the Royal Historical Society and lecturer in history at Canterbury Christ Church University College.

Grainne Henry is a teacher in Presentation Secondary School, Listowel, Co. Kerry, part-time lecturer at the Irish College of Humanities, Tralee.

Kevin Herlihy is a historian with a special interest in religious history and the author of *Propagating the Word of Irish Dissent, 1650–1800* (1998).

Gordon L. Herries Davies is an emeritus fellow of Trinity College, Dublin, and the author of works in the history of the earth sciences, geological cartography, and Irish institutions.

Gareth Higgins is a writer and research consultant, specialising in religion, sectarianism, peace issues, and the cinema.

Judith Hill is the author of *The Building of Limerick* (1991) and *Irish Public Sculpture* (1998).

Myrtle Hill is director of the Centre for Women's Studies, Queen's University, Belfast, author of *Women of Ireland: Image and Experience, c. 1800–1920* (second edition, 1999), and joint author of *Evangelical Protestantism in Ulster, 1740–1900* (1992).

Sophia Hillan (formerly Sophia Hillan King) is associate director of the Institute of Irish Studies, Queen's University, Belfast, and the author of *The Edge of Dark: A Sense of Place in the Writings of Michael McLaverty and Sam Hanna Bell* (2000).

Paddy Hillyard is professor of social administration and policy at the University of Ulster and the author of *Suspect Community* (1993).

P. Frank Hodnett is professor of applied mathematics in the Department of Mathematics and Statistics, University of Limerick.

Rijcklof Hofman is a member of the academic staff of the Titus Brandsma Instituut, Katholieke Universiteit Nijmegen, and the editor of the *Sankt Gall Priscian Commentary* (1996) and the *Gerardi Magni Opera Omnia* for *Corpus Christianorum*.

Gerard Hogan is a senior counsel, lecturer in law at Trinity College, Dublin, and joint editor of Kelly's *The Irish Constitution* (1994).

Jefferson Holdridge is an assistant professor at Wake Forest University, editor of WFU Press, and the author of *Those Mingled Seas: The Poetry of W. B. Yeats, the Beautiful and the Sublime* (2000).

Patrick Honohan is an adviser at the World Bank, former research professor at the Economic and Social Research Institute, and former economic adviser to the Taoiseach.

Michael A. Hopkinson lectures in history at the University of Sterling and is the author of *Green against Green: The Irish Civil War* (1988) and *The Irish War of Independence* (2002).

John Horgan is professor of journalism at Dublin City University.

Michael Hornsby-Smith is emeritus professor of sociology at the University of Surrey and editor of *Catholics in England, 1950–2000* (1999).

Patricia Horton is an editor with Blackstaff Press, Belfast.

Daphne Hosford is a marketing professional and a hockey player.

Kevin Hourihan is statutory lecturer in the Department of Geography, University College, Cork, and joint editor of *Perspectives on Cork* (1998).

Jim Hourihane is a lecturer in geography at St Patrick's College, Dublin, author and editor of geography textbooks, and editor and contributor to the Thomas Davis series *Engaging Spaces* (2002).

David Howlett is editor of the *Dictionary of Medieval Latin from British Sources* (2002) and consultant to the Royal Irish Academy's Dictionary of Medieval Latin from Celtic Sources.

Michael Hurley is a Jesuit, founder of the Irish School of Ecumenics and the Columbanus Community of Reconciliation, and the author of *Christian Unity: An Ecumenical Second Spring?* (1998).

Jacqueline A. Hurtley is a professor of English literature at the University of Barcelona and the author of *José Janés: Editor de Literatura Inglesa* (1992).

Wesley Hutchinson is professor of Irish studies at the Institut d'Anglais Charles V, University of Paris.

Aideen M. Ireland is an archivist with the National Archives and an antiquarian researcher and has written on the history of nineteenth-century Irish museums and collections.

Liam Irwin is head of the Department of History at Mary Immaculate College, University of Limerick, and the author of *Explorations: Centenary Essays, Mary Immaculate College* (1998).

Kenneth W. James is curator of the Department of Geology, Ulster Museum, Belfast.

K. J. James is assistant professor in the Department of History and chair of Scottish studies at the University of Guelph, Ontario.

Bart Jaski is a lecturer in medieval history at the University of Utrecht and the author of *Early Irish Kingship and Succession* (2000).

Richard Jay is senior lecturer in politics at Queen's University, Belfast, acting academic director of Queen's University at Armagh, and the author of *Joseph Chamberlain: A Political Study* (1981).

A. Norman Jeffares has held chairs in various universities and has written on and edited the works of Farquhar, Goldsmith, Sheridan, Moore, Yeats, Gogarty, and Joyce.

Henry A. Jefferies is head of history at Thornhill College, Derry, and the author of *Priests and Prelates of Armagh in the Age of Reformations* (1997).

Keith Jeffery is professor of modern history at the University of Ulster at Jordanstown.

Rod Jenkins is a retired spacecraft project manager and an amateur astronomer.

Elva Johnston is a lecturer in early Irish history, University College, Dublin.

Karl Johnston is a freelance journalist, former rugby correspondent for the *Irish Press,* and the author of *Ireland's Triple Crown* (1985).

Mairead M. Johnston is costume and textile heritage consultant at the Sign of the Golden Fan and the author of *Hidden in the Pile: The Abbey Leix Carpet Factory* (1997).

Micheal Johnston is former president of the Irish Amateur Rowing Union and the author of *The Big Pot: The Story of the Irish Senior Rowing Championship, 1912–1991* (1992).

Roy Johnston is professor of art at Eastern Michigan University and the author of *Roderic O'Conor: Barbican Art Gallery, London, and Ulster Museum, Retrospective Exhibition Catalogue* (1985), and *Roderic O'Conor: Musée de Pont-Aven, Catalogue de l'Oeuvre Gravé* (1999).

Tom Johnstone is the author of *Orange, Green and Khaki: The Story of the Irish Regiments in the Great War, 1914–18* (1992).

E. M. Johnston-Liik was professor of history at Macquarie University, Sydney, and is the author of *History of the Irish Parliament* (2002).

David S. Jones is associate professor in the Department of Political Science, National University of Singapore.

Mary Jones is a social scientist and the author of *These Obstreperous Lassies* (1988).

Donald Jordan is vice-president of academic affairs and professor of history at Menlo College, California, and the author of *Land and Politics in Ireland: County Mayo from the Plantation to the Land War* (1994).

Eamonn Jordan is the author of *The Feast of Famine: The Plays of Frank McGuinness* (1997), editor of *Theatre Stuff* (2000), and joint editor of *Theatre Talk: Voices of Irish Theatre Practitioners* (2001).

Martin Joyce is publisher and editor of *Walking World Ireland.*

Labhrás Joye is curator of military history at the National Museum of Ireland, Dublin.

Fiona Kearney is visual arts officer of University College, Cork, and has published widely on contemporary photography and Irish art.

John Kearon is a master shipwright and wooden ship conservator, formerly of Tyrrell's of Arklow, and head of maritime, industrial and land transport conservation at the National Museums and Galleries on Merseyside, Liverpool.

Michael Keating (1927–2001) worked in the rail, aviation and maritime industries and held a pilot's licence.

Donal Keenan is a former press officer of the GAA and is now a journalist with *Ireland on Sunday.*

Deborah Kelleher is senior lecturer in English at the Royal Irish Academy of Music and a teaching fellow in University College, Dublin.

Margaret Kelleher is a lecturer in the English Department, National University of Ireland, Maynooth, author of *The Feminization of Famine* (1997), and joint editor of *The Cambridge History of Irish Literature.*

Thomas Kelley is adjunct professor of history at Boston University and a research assistant for the *Dictionary of Irish Biography.*

Aaron Kelly is Leverhulme fellow at the University of Edinburgh and joint editor of *Critical Ireland* (2001) and *Cities of Belfast* (2003).

Anne Kelly is director of arts administration studies, University College, Dublin, and joint editor of *From Maestro to Manager: Critical Issues in Arts and Culture Management* (1997).

Éamonn P. Kelly is keeper of Irish antiquities at the National Museum of Ireland, Dublin.

Fergus Kelly is director and senior professor at the School of Celtic Studies, Dublin Institute for Advanced Studies, and the author of *Early Irish Farming* (1997) and *A Guide to Early Irish Law* (1988).

James Kelly is head of the History Department at St Patrick's College, Dublin, and the author of a number of books on eighteenth-century Irish history.

John Kelly is former Registrar, dean of the Faculty of Engineering and Architecture and professor emeritus of chemical engineering, University College, Dublin.

Liam Kelly is professor of Irish visual culture at the School of Art and Design, University of Ulster, Coleraine.

Mary A. Kelly is retired matron of the Rotunda Hospital, Dublin.

Ronan Kelly is joint editor of *New Voices IV* (2003) and is writing a critical biography of Thomas Moore.

Thomas A. F. Kelly is lecturer in philosophy at the National University of Ireland, Maynooth, the author of *Language and Transcendence* (1994) and *Language, World, and God* (1996), and editor of the *IPS Yearbook* and *Maynooth Philosophical Papers*.

Tim Kendall teaches at the University of Bristol, is editor of Thumbscrew Press, and is the author of *Paul Muldoon* (1996) and *Sylvia Plath* (2001).

Patricia Kennedy is a lecturer in the Department of Social Policy and Social Work, University College, Dublin, and has carried out research on maternity policies in Ireland.

Róisín Kennedy is a Government of Ireland Research Scholar attached to the History of Art Department, University College, Dublin, and is the author of *Dublin Castle Art* (1999).

S. B. Kennedy is head of fine and applied art at the Ulster Museum, Belfast.

Kevin Kenny is associate professor of history at Boston College and the author of *Making Sense of the Molly Maguires* (1998) and *The American Irish: A History* (2000).

Michael Kenny is keeper of the Art and Industrial Division of the National Museum of Ireland, Dublin, and the author of numerous articles on the history of Irish coinage and coin hoards.

Daire Keogh lectures in the History Department of St Patrick's College, Dublin, and is the editor of *Acts of Union* (2001).

Dermot Keogh is professor of history and Jean Monnet professor of European integration studies, University College, Cork, a member of the Royal Irish Academy, Fulbright professor at Boston College, and Woodrow Wilson scholar.

Paul J. Kerr is head of music at Rathdown School, Glenageary, Co. Dublin.

Declan Kiberd is professor of Anglo-Irish literature and drama, University College, Dublin, and the author of *Idir Dhá Chultúr* (1993), *Inventing Ireland* (1995), and *Irish Classics* (2000).

M. Alison Kibler is a visiting fellow in history at the Australian National University and the author of *Rank Ladies: Gender and Cultural Hierarchy in American Vaudeville* (1999).

David Kiely is a novelist and biographer and the author of a life of J. M. Synge and *Bloody Women: Ireland's Female Killers* (1999).

Siobhán Kilfeather is a lecturer in English at the University of Sussex and joint editor of *The Field Day Anthology of Irish Writing*, vols. IV–V (2002).

Carla King is a lecturer in history at St Patrick's College, Dublin, author of *Michael Davitt* (1999), and editor of *Famine, Land and Culture in Ireland* (2000) and *Michael Davitt: Collected Writings, 1868–1906* (2001).

Jason King is a Government of Ireland postdoctoral fellow at the Centre for Migration Studies, University College, Cork, and has published articles on migration literature in Ireland and North America.

Séamus J. King is a retired teacher at Rockwell College, Co. Tipperary, and the author of *A History of Hurling* (1996).

Claudia Kinmonth is a senior research fellow at Buckinghamshire Chilterns University College and the author of *Irish Country Furniture, 1700–1950* (1993).

Péter Király is a physicist with the Space Physics Department, Research Institute for Particle and Nuclear Physics, Budapest, and the author of publications on cosmic ray, space, theoretical and astrophysics topics.

Peadar Kirby is a senior lecturer in the School of Communications, Dublin City University, and the author of *The Celtic Tiger in Distress: Growth with Inequality in Ireland* (2002) and *Latin America in a Globalized World* (2003).

Elizabeth M. Kirwan is an assistant keeper in the Department of Manuscripts and former prints and drawings librarian at the National Library of Ireland, Dublin.

Knight of Glin; **Desmond FitzGerald,** 29th Knight of Glin is an art historian and lecturer, president of the Irish Georgian Society, joint author of *The Painters of Ireland* (1978), and *Ireland's Painters 1600–1940* (2002).

Mary Kotsonouris is a former judge of the District Court and the author of *Retreat from Revolution: The Dáil Courts, 1920–24* (1994) and *The Winding-Up of the Dáil Courts* (2004).

Malgorzata Krasnodębska-D'Aughton is a postdoctoral Government of Ireland fellow in the Department of History, University College, Cork, and has published on insular art, manuscript art, Hiberno-Latin, and patristic exegesis.

Peter Kuch is Convenor of the Irish Studies Program, University of New South Wales, author of *Yeats and AE* (1986), and editor of *Russell's Writings on Literature* (2004).

Brian Lacey is chief executive officer of the Discovery Programme.

Brigid Laffan is Jean Monnet professor of European politics and director of the Dublin European Institute, University College, Dublin, and the author of *Organising for a Changing Europe: Irish Central Government and the European Union* (2001).

Michael Laffan is a lecturer in modern Irish history, University College, Dublin, and the author of *The Partition of Ireland, 1911–1925* (1983) and *The Resurrection of Ireland: The Sinn Féin Party, 1916–1923* (Cambridge 1999).

Denise Laing is a doctoral student in Trinity College, Dublin.

Allegra D. Lalor is a photographer, outdoor pursuits instructor, and works in education in Dublin.

Brian Lalor is a printmaker and former director of the Architectural Department of the Temple Mount excavations at Jerusalem. Recent publications include an illustrated edition of *The Ballad of Reading Gaol* (1997) and *The Irish Round Tower* (1999).

Keith Lamb is a former researcher in horticulture with University College, Dublin, and An Foras Talúntais.

Sheila Landy is science librarian and faculty librarian for science and agriculture, Queen's University, Belfast.

Orla Lane is senior research officer in the Policy Institute, Trinity College, Dublin.

Helen Lanigan Wood is curator of Fermanagh County Museum and the author of *Images of Stone: Figure Sculpture of the Lough Erne Basin* (second edition, 1985).

Paul Larmour is reader in architecture and a senior lecturer in the School of Architecture, Queen's University, Belfast, and the author of *Celtic Ornament* (1981), *Belfast: An Illustrated Architectural Guide* (1987), and *The Arts and Crafts Movement in Ireland* (1992).

Joe Larragy lectures in social policy at the National University of Ireland, Maynooth, and has published on the role of community and voluntary organisations in social partnership.

David Latané is associate professor of English at Virginia Commonwealth University, Richmond, editor of *Victorians Institute Journal,* and the author of *Browning's Sordello and the Aesthetics of Difficulty* (1987).

Margarethe Lauber is a former postgraduate student in the School of Sociology and Social Policy, Queen's University, Belfast, researching Belfast peace lines.

Ann Lavan is a lecturer in the Department of Social Policy and Social Work, University College, Dublin, and the author of *Social Need and Community Social Services* (1981) and *Fifty Years of Social Welfare Policy* (2000).

Richard Layte is an economic sociologist and a researcher with the Economic and Social Research Institute, Dublin.

Joep Leerssen is professor of modern European literature at the University of Amsterdam.

C. D. A. Leighton is a priest of the Premonstratensian order and teaches British and Irish history at Bilkent University, Ankara.

Pádraig Lenihan teaches history at the University of Limerick and has published on the Confederation of Kilkenny, early modern Irish military history, and seventeenth-century demographic history.

Colm Lennon is senior lecturer in the Department of Modern History, National University of Ireland, Maynooth, and the author of *Sixteenth-Century Ireland: The Incomplete Conquest* (1994).

Madeleine Leonard is a senior lecturer in the School of Sociology and Social Policy, Queen's University, Belfast, and has published on the sociology of childhood.

Fergus Linehan is the author of two novels and many plays, musicals and comedy revues and a former arts editor of the *Irish Times*.

Declan Little is project ecologist with the People's Millennium Forests, Newtown Mount Kennedy, Co. Wicklow.

John Logan is senior lecturer in history and head of the Department of Government and Society, University of Limerick.

Patrick Long is a historian and heritage consultant and former curator of Monaghan County Museum.

Ann Lynch is senior archaeologist with the Heritage Service.

John Patrick Lynch is a teaching fellow in the Institute of Lifelong Learning, Queen's University, Belfast.

Christopher J. Lynn is Inspector of Historic Monuments, Department of the Environment, Belfast.

Barry Lyons is librarian of Freemasons' Hall, Dublin.

J. B. Lyons is former professor of the history of medicine at the Royal College of Surgeons in Ireland and consultant physician to St Michael's Hospital, Dún Laoghaire, and Mercer's Hospital, Dublin.

Mary Ann Lyons is a lecturer in the Department of History, St Patrick's College, Dublin.

Seán Lysaght lectures in humanities at Galway-Mayo Institute of Technology, Castlebar, and has published several collections of poetry and a biography of Robert Lloyd Praeger.

Mairead McAnallen is a former gallery administrator and editor of *Craft Review* at the Crafts Council of Ireland and now works on a variety of craft development projects.

Breandán Mac Aodha (1934–2001) was head of the Department of Geography at the National University of Ireland, Galway, a specialist in cultural and historical geography, and a member of the Place-Names Commission.

Caoimhín Mac Aoidh is a fiddler and founder-member of Cairdeas na bhFidleírí, chief executive of Donegal Local Development Company, and the author of *Between the Jigs and the Reels: The Donegal Fiddle Tradition*.

Michael McAteer lectures at Carlow College and is the author of *Standish O'Grady, Æ, Yeats: An Imagined History* (2002).

Eve McAulay is a doctoral student in Trinity College, Dublin, and a researcher in the history of art and architecture.

Lawrence W. McBride is professor of history at Illinois State University and editor of *Images, Icons, and the Irish Nationalist Imagination* (1999).

Éanna Mac Cába is a senior lecturer in the Department of Irish, St Patrick's College, Dublin.

Lawrence J. McCaffrey is professor of Irish and Irish American history (Emeritus) at Loyola University of Chicago.

Anthony McCann is a research fellow at the Smithsonian Center for Folklife and Cultural Heritage, Washington.

May McCann is a former lecturer in social anthropology at Queen's University, Belfast, and joint editor of *Irish Travellers: Culture and Ethnicity* (1996).

Críostóir Mac Carthaigh is archivist-collector with the Department of Irish Folklore, University College, Dublin.

Daniel McCarthy is a senior lecturer in the Department of Computer Science and a fellow of Trinity College, Dublin, and has published on computation, chronology, and the Irish annals.

Imelda McCarthy is a lecturer in social work in the Department of Social Policy and Social Work, University College, Dublin, and editor of *Poverty and Social Exclusion* (1994) and *Irish Family Studies* (1995).

Michael McCarthy is head of the Department of History of Art, University College, Dublin, and the author of *The Origins of the Gothic Revival* (1987) and editor of *Lord Charlemont and his Circle* (2001).

Muriel McCarthy is keeper of Marsh's Library, Dublin, and the author of *All Graduates and Gentlemen: Marsh's Library* (1980).

Patricia McCarthy is joint author of *Farmleigh* (2002) and has recently completed a commission to research the history of the buildings of the King's Inns.

Thomas McCarthy is a poet and librarian at Cork City Library and the author of *Mr Dinneen's Careful Parade: New and Selected Poems* (1999).

Donal McCartney is professor emeritus of modern Irish history, University College, Dublin, and the author of *Dawning of Democracy: Ireland, 1800–1870* (1987), *W. E. H. Lecky: Historian and Politician* (1994), and *UCD: A National Idea* (1999).

Michael McCaughan is Keeper of Transport in the National Museums and Galleries of Northern Ireland. He has published widely on maritime themes and is the author of *The Birth of the Titanic* (1998)

John McCavitt is head of politics at Abbey Grammar School, Newry, and the author of *Sir Arthur Chichester, Lord Deputy of Ireland, 1605–16* (1998) and *The Flight of the Earls* (2002).

Don McClenahan is a motorcycle enthusiast and historian.

Nollaig Mac Congáil is professor of Irish at the National University of Ireland, Galway.

Liam Mac Con Iomaire is a teacher and broadcaster and the author of *Camchuairt Chonamara Theas*, and *Breandán Ó hEithir: Iomramh Aonair* (2000).

Sinéad McCoole is a freelance historical and picture researcher and author of *Hazel, A Life of Lady Lavery* (1996).

Dónal P. McCracken is a professor of history and dean of the Faculty of Humanities at the University of Durban-Westville, South Africa, and the author of *MacBride's Brigade* (1999) and *Forgotten Protest* (2002).

Mícheál Mac Craith is a Franciscan priest, professor of Modern Irish at the National University of Ireland, Galway, and the author of *Lorg na hIasachta ar na Dánta Grá* (1989) and *Oileán Rúin agus Muir an Dáin: Staidéar ar Fhilíocht Mháirtín Uí Dhireáin* (1993).

Elizabeth McCrum is keeper of applied art at the Ulster Museum, Belfast, and the author of *Fabric and Form: Irish Fashion since 1950* (1996).

Conor McDermott is director of the Irish Archaeological Wetland Unit at University College, Dublin.

Nicholas McDonald is senior lecturer in the Psychology Department at Trinity College, Dublin.

Piaras Mac Éinrí is director of the Irish Centre for Migration Studies, University College, Cork, has published on migration issues, and is the author of 'Immigration policy in Ireland' in *Responding to Racism in Ireland* (F. Farrell and P. Watt, eds., 2001).

Karen McElrath is a reader in sociology at Queen's University, Belfast, and has published in the areas of drug use and HIV risk behaviour.

Gearóid Mac Eoin is retired professor of Old and Middle Irish and Celtic philology at the National University of Ireland, Galway.

Joseph McEvoy is a chartered engineer and former managing director of ASEA Electric (Ireland) Ltd.

John McFarland is archivist of Armagh Observatory.

Fearghal McGarry is a lecturer in Irish history at Queen's University, Belfast.

Uáitéar Mac Gearailt is a lecturer in Irish language and literature at St Patrick's College, Dublin.

Brian McGinn is a writer and researcher on the history of the Irish in the Americas.

Roger MacGinty is a lecturer in the Department of Politics, University of York, and joint author of *Guns and Government: The Management of the Northern Ireland Peace Process* (2002).

Caoimhín Mac Giolla Léith is a lecturer in the Department of Modern Irish, University College, Dublin, and the author of *Oidheadh Chloinne hUisneach* (1992).

Charles Ivar McGrath is a research fellow in the Department of Modern Irish History, University College, Dublin, and author of *The Making of the Eighteenth-Century Irish Constitution: Government, Parliament and the Revenue, 1692–1714* (2000).

Philip McGuinness is a writer and a lecturer at Dundalk Institute of Technology.

James McGuirk is junior lecturer in philosophy at the National University of Ireland, Maynooth.

John J. N. McGurk is former head of history at Liverpool Hope University College, fellow in Irish studies, University of Liverpool, and the author of *The Elizabethan Conquest of Ireland* (1997).

Patrick McGurk is emeritus reader in mediaeval history at Birkbeck College, University of London.

Niall McKeith is a technical officer in the Department of Experimental Physics, National University of Ireland, Maynooth, and curator of the National Science Museum at St Patrick's College, Maynooth.

Malachy McKenna is a specialist in Celtic languages and professor in the School of Celtic Studies, Dublin Institute for Advanced Studies.

Patrick McKenna works for the Department of Transport and is the author of 'The formation of Hiberno-Argentine society' in *English-Speaking Communities in Latin America* (Oliver Marshall, ed., 2000).

Robert McKim is a professor of religious studies and philosophy at the University of Illinois and the author of *Religious Ambiguity and Religious Diversity* (2001).

Eithne McLaughlin is professor and head of social policy at Queen's University, Belfast, and former vice-chairperson in charge of research at the Standing Advisory Commission on Human Rights during the Employment Equality Review, 1994–7.

Ken McLeod is editor of the *Seán Reid Society Journal*.

Neil McLeod is professor of law at Murdoch University, Western Australia.

Alf Mac Lochlainn is a former director of the National Library of Ireland and former librarian of National University of Ireland, Galway, inaugural holder of the Burns chair of Irish studies, Boston College, and the author of satirical verse and surrealist novellas.

Dympna McLoughlin is a lecturer in modern history at the National University of Ireland, Maynooth.

Deirdre McMahon is a lecturer in history at Mary Immaculate College, University of Limerick.

Gerard McMahon is a lecturer in the Department of Experimental Physics, National University of Ireland, Maynooth, assistant curator of the National Science Museum, Maynooth, and author of *Combined Heat and Power: Towards a Policy for Ireland* (1983).

Damian McManus is associate professor of Irish at Trinity College, Dublin, and the author of *A Guide to Ogam* (1991).

Ruth McManus is a lecturer in the Geography Department, St Patrick's College, Dublin, and the author of *Dublin, 1910–1940: Shaping the City and Suburbs* (2002).

Liam Mac Mathúna is registrar of St Patrick's College, Dublin, and editor of a critical edition of *Séadna* by Peadar Ó Laoghaire (1987).

Séamus Mac Mathúna is professor of Irish at the University of Ulster, Coleraine, and the author of *Immram Brain: Bran's Journey to the Land of the Women* (1985).

Norman McMillan is a senior lecturer in the Institute of Technology, Carlow, optical engineer, inventor, founder of tensiography, a campaigner for the recognition of Irish science and engineering heritage, and the author of *Prometheus's Fire* (2000).

Joseph McMinn is professor of Anglo-Irish studies at the University of Ulster, Jordanstown, and the author of *John Banville: A Critical Study* (1991) and *The Supreme Fictions of John Banville* (1999).

Anna McMullan is director of the master's degree in Irish theatre and film at the School of Drama, Trinity College, Dublin, and the author of *Theatre on Trial: Samuel Beckett's Later Drama* (1993).

Ciarán Mac Murchaidh lectures in the Department of Irish, St Patrick's College, Dublin.

Suzanne McNab is a lecturer and co-ordinator of the joint honours degree in history of art and fine art and design at the National College of Art and Design and writes on early mediaeval and modern Irish art.

Brian McNamara is an uilleann piper and authority on the music of Co. Leitrim and a senior lecturer in Dublin City University.

Paul McNulty is professor of agricultural and food engineering at University College, Dublin, and senior editor of agricultural mechanisation and automation for the *UNESCO Encyclopedia of Life Support Systems* (2002).

Séamas Mac Philib is assistant keeper in the Irish Folklife Division, Museum of Country Life, Castlebar, Co. Mayo.

Aodán Mac Póilín is director of the Ultach Trust, Belfast.

Donald MacRaild is head of history at the University of Northumbria, Newcastle, author of *Irish Migrants in Modern Britain, 1750–1922* (1999), and editor of *The Great Famine and Beyond: Irish Migrants in Britain in the Nineteenth and Twentieth Centuries* (2000).

Louis McRedmond is a journalist, historian and barrister, author of *To the Greater Glory* (1991), and editor of *Modern Irish Lives* (1996).

Ailbhe Mac Shamhráin lectures in medieval Irish studies in the Department of Old Irish, National University of Ireland, Maynooth, and is the author of *Church and Polity in Pre-Norman Ireland* (1996).

Tom MacSweeney is marine correspondent with RTÉ.

Shirley MacWilliam is an artist, writer and lecturer in contemporary arts at Nottingham Trent University.

Brendan McWilliams is a former deputy director of the Meteorological Service and a daily weather columnist with the *Irish Times*.

Angela Madden is orchestral administrator with the Ulster Orchestra, Belfast.

Eoin Magennis is research and information manager of Intertrade Ireland.

Tess Maginess is a tutor and student support officer at Queen's University, Armagh, and the author of *Conjuring Complexities: Essays on Flann O'Brien* (1996) and *Vivarium* (1997).

Antain Mag Shamhráin is an editor with An Gúm, joint publisher and editor of *Oghma* (1989–98), and the author of *Litríocht, Léitheoireacht, Critic* (1986).

Julie Maguire is the projects officer for the Environmental Research Institute, University College, Cork.

Evelyn Mahon is a senior lecturer in sociology at Trinity College, Dublin, has published extensively on the women's movement, and was director and principal author of the 'Women and Crisis Pregnancy' study.

Jack Mahon is a former Galway all-Ireland footballer and a sports writer and columnist.

Elizabeth Malcolm is professor of Irish studies at the University of Melbourne and has published on Irish social history.

J. P. Mallory is professor of prehistoric archaeology at Queen's University, Belfast.

Gerry Mangan is principal officer of the EU and International Unit, Department of Social, Community and Family Affairs.

Conleth Manning is senior archaeologist in charge of the Archaeological Survey of Ireland and the author of *Early Irish Monasteries* (1995).

Catherine Marshall is curator of collections at the Irish Museum of Modern Art, Dublin.

Edward Martin is a retired neurologist.

James Martin is a former senior engineer with Bord na Móna and UNIDO adviser on peat and papyrus briquette production in Rwanda and Burundi.

P. J. Mathews lectures in the Department of English, St Patrick's College, Dublin, and is academic director of the Parnell Summer School.

Patrick Maume is an assistant lecturer in the School of Modern History, Queen's University, Belfast, and the author of *The Long Gestation: Irish Nationalist Political Life, 1891–1918* (1999).

Kim Mawhinney is curator of applied art at the Ulster Museum, Belfast.

Brian Maye is a historian and the author of *Fine Gael, 1923–1987* (1993) and *Arthur Griffith* (1997).

Gerardine Meaney lectures in film studies and English at University College, Dublin, author of *Unlike Subjects: Women, Theory, Fiction* (1993), and joint editor of *The Field Day Anthology of Irish Writing*, vols. IV–V (2002).

Robert Meehan is Quaternary geologist with Teagasc.

Mel Mercier is a performer, composer and a lecturer in music, University College, Cork.

Fionola Meredith teaches philosophy and feminist theory at Queen's University, Belfast.

Robbie Meredith is outreach officer for the Linen Hall Library and teaches Irish prose in the School of English, Queen's University, Belfast.

Austin Mescal is a meat and livestock consultant and former chief inspector of the Department of Agriculture, Food and Rural Development.

David Michaelsen is pursuing a doctorate in Latin American history at the University of Florida, Gainesville.

Robert Miller is senior lecturer in sociology at Queen's University, Belfast, and a member of the ARK Data Archive Project.

Gerald Mills is senior lecturer in the Department of Geography, University College, Dublin, with an interest in the study of climates, particularly those close to the ground.

Michael Mills is a former Ombudsman and political correspondent of the *Irish Press*.

Robert Mills is librarian of the Royal College of Physicians of Ireland.

Kenneth Milne is historiographer for the Church of Ireland, former principal of the Church of Ireland College of Education, Dublin, author of *The Irish Charter Schools* (1996), and editor of *Christ Church Cathedral, Dublin: A History* (2000).

Mike Milotte is a senior reporter and presenter with RTÉ Current Affairs and the author of *Communism in Modern Ireland: The Pursuit of the Workers' Republic since 1916* (1984).

Martin Mitchell is a research fellow at the Research Institute of Irish and Scottish Studies, University of Aberdeen, and the author of *The Irish in the West of Scotland, 1797–1848: Trade Unions, Strikes and Political Movements* (1998).

David Mock teaches at Tallahassee Community College, Florida, and is joint editor of *Dictionary of Obituaries of Modern British Radicals* (1989) and editor of *History and Public Policy* (1991) and *Legacy of the West* (1995).

Paul Mohr is a Connemara geologist.

Charles Mollan is the author of *Irish National Inventory of Historic Scientific Instruments* (1995) and senior editor of *Irish Innovators in Science and Technology* (2001).

Frank Molloy is senior lecturer in English at Charles Sturt University, Wagga Wagga, New South Wales, and the author of *Victor J. Daley: A Comprehensive Bibliography* (2000).

Karen Molloy is a senior researcher in the Palaeoenvironmental Unit, Department of Botany, National University of Ireland, Galway, specialising in palaeo-ecology and long-term human impact on the landscape.

Colette Moloney is a lecturer in music at Waterford Institute of Technology and the author of *The Irish Music Manuscripts of Edward Bunting: An Introduction and Catalogue* (2000).

Mick Moloney is a teacher, musician, arts presenter and advocate, record producer, and professor of Irish studies at New York University.

Michael Monk is a lecturer in archaeology at University College, Cork, and joint editor of *Early Medieval Munster: Archaeology, History and Society* (1998).

Alex Montwill is professor of physics at University College, Dublin.

Christopher Moore is a specialist in historic decoration and course director and lecturer at the Institute of Professional Auctioneers and Valuers, Dublin.

David Mooney is acting head of keyboard studies at the DIT Conservatory of Music and Drama.

Michael Moore is an artist and a member of the International Academy of Ceramics, Geneva.

Josephine Moran is an archaeologist and the author of *Painted and Stained Window Glass from Kells Priory, Co. Kilkenny* (2002).

Jimmy O'Brien Moran is an uilleann piper and is engaged in postgraduate research at the University of Limerick.

Sean Farrell Moran is a professor in the Department of History, Oakland University, Michigan, and the author of *Patrick Pearse and the Politics of Redemption: The Mind of the Easter Rising, 1916* (1994).

Edgar Morgenroth is research officer at the Economic and Social Research Institute, Dublin, working in regional development and growth economics, author of *Analysis of the Economic, Employment and Social Profile of the Greater Dublin Region* (2001).

Christopher Moriarty is an honorary research associate in the Zoology Department, Trinity College, Dublin, and formerly in the Marine Institute and the author of *Eels* (1978), *Down the Dodder* (1991), and *Ireland: Atmosphere and Impressions* (2001).

Vincent Morley has lectured in history at the National University of Ireland, Galway, and is the author of *Irish Opinion and the American Revolution, 1760–1783* (2002).

A. D. Morrison-Low is curator of historic scientific instruments, National Museums of Scotland.

Margaret Morse is a postgraduate student in the University of Southampton.

Karena Morton is a freelance conservator of archaeological finds and wall paintings.

Rachel Moss is an architectural historian and part-time tutor at the School of Architecture, University College, Dublin.

George Mott is a photographer and the joint author of *The Houses of Ireland* (1975) and *Churches and Abbeys of Ireland* (1976).

John Moulden is a researcher at the Centre for the Study of Human Settlement and Historical Change, National University of Ireland, Galway.

Charles Mount is archaeologist of the Irish Heritage Council and has published extensively on Irish archaeology.

Terry Moylan is archivist with na Píobairí Uilleann, a piper and set-dance teacher, and the author of *The Age of Revolution, 1776–1815, in the Irish Song Tradition*.

Rosemarie Mulcahy is honorary senior fellow in the Department of the History of Art, University College, Dublin.

Michael Mullaney is a lecturer in canon law at St Patrick's College, Maynooth, and Milltown Institute, Dublin, and the author of *Incardination and the Universal Dimension of the Priestly Ministry: A Comparison Between CIC 17 and CIC 83* (Rome 2002).

Suzanne Mulligan is a doctoral student in theology and a tutor in the Department of Moral Theology, St Patrick's College, Maynooth.

Tom Munnelly is a collector and archivist with the Folk Music Division of the Department of Irish Folklore, University College, Dublin.

Andrew Murphy is reader in English literature at the University of St Andrews and the author of *But the Irish Sea Betwixt Us: Ireland, Colonialism and Renaissance Literature* (1999) and *Seamus Heaney* (2000).

Clíona Murphy is professor of European history at California State University, Bakersfield, author of *The Women's Suffrage Movement and Irish Society* (1989), and joint editor of *Surviving Women: Studies on Irish Women's History* (1990).

James H. Murphy teaches in the Department of English, De Paul University, Chicago, and is the author of *Abject Loyalty: Nationalism and Monarchy in Ireland During the Reign of Queen Victoria* (2001).

John A. Murphy is emeritus professor of Irish history at University College, Cork.

Matt Murphy is director of Sherkin Island Marine Station, Co. Cork, and editor of *Sherkin Comment*.

Michael Murphy is a lecturer in music in Mary Immaculate College, University of Limerick, and joint editor of *Musical Constructions of Nationalism* (2001).

Paula Murphy is a lecturer in the history of art at University College, Dublin.

Peter Murphy is a freelance music writer and senior contributor to the magazine *Hot Press* and whose work has also appeared in Australia, the United States, and Canada.

Jo Murphy-Lawless is a feminist sociologist and the author of *Reading Birth and Death: A History of Obstetric Thinking* (1998) and *Fighting Back: Women and the Impact of Drug Abuse on Families and Communities* (2002).

Joe Murray is an agricultural journalist, broadcaster and media consultant, former Head of Agriculture at RTÉ and recipient of many broadcasting awards, and former lecturer in crop husbandry at University College, Dublin.

John Nash is a lecturer in the Department of English, Trinity College, Dublin, and editor of *Joyce's Audiences* (2002).

Lindie Naughton is a sports journalist and writer and the author of *Irish Olympians* (1992) and *Lady Icarus* (2003), a biography of Lady Mary Heath.

Kenneth Neill is a magazine publisher in Memphis, Tennessee, a founder-member of the Ireland-Paraguay Friendship Society, and the author of *An Illustrated History of the Irish People* (1979).

Conor Newman is a lecturer in the Department of Archaeology, National University of Ireland, Galway, and the author of *Tara: An Archaeological Survey* (1997).

Stephen Newman is a lecturer in the Department of Irish, Mary Immaculate College, University of Limerick.

Muireann Ní Bhrolcháin is a senior lecturer in medieval Irish and Celtic studies at the National University of Ireland, Maynooth.

Siobhán Ní Chonaráin is a traditional musician and a research student in the area of social history and Irish music at the University of Limerick.

Éilís Ní Dheá is a lecturer in Irish at Mary Immaculate College, University of Limerick, and joint editor of *The Lesser Used Languages and Teacher Education* (1995).

Aisling Ní Dhonnchadha is a lecturer in the Department of Modern Irish at the National University of Ireland, Maynooth, and the author of *An Gearrscéal sa Ghaeilge, 1898–1940* (1981).

Máirín Ní Dhonnchadha is professor of Old and Middle Irish at the National University of Ireland, Galway, and joint editor of *The Field Day Anthology of Irish Writing,* vols. IV–V (2002).

Aoibheann Nic Dhonnchadha is an assistant professor in the School of Celtic Studies, Dublin Institute for Advanced Studies.

Úna Nic Éinrí is a lecturer in Irish in Mary Immaculate College, University of Limerick, and the author of *An Cantaire Siúlach: Tadhg Gaelach* (2001).

Máire Ní Mhaonaigh is a fellow of St John's College and university senior lecturer in the Department of Anglo-Saxon, Norse and Celtic at the University of Cambridge and joint editor of *Ireland and Scandinavia in the Early Viking Age* (1998).

Máire Ní Mhurchú is a librarian and the joint author of the *Beathaisnéis* series (seven volumes, 1986–2002).

Caoilfhionn Nic Pháidín is director of Fiontar at Dublin City University, joint founder of the publishing company Cois Life, and the author of *Fáinne an Lae (1898–1900) agus an Athbheochan* (1998).

Éilís Ní Shúilleabháin is a sean-nós singer and teaches sean-nós singing at University College, Cork.

Pádraigín Ní Uallacháin is a professional singer and broadcaster and editor of *Songs of a Hidden Ulster* (2002).

Dorothy Ní Uigín works in the Department of Spoken Irish at the National University of Ireland, Galway.

Meidhbhín Ní Úrdail is a lecturer in the Department of Modern Irish, University College, Dublin, and the author of *The Scribe in Eighteenth and Nineteenth-Century Ireland: Motivations and Milieu* (2000).

Maarten Nieuwenhuis is senior lecturer in forest management at University College, Dublin.

Brian Nolan is an economist and a research professor at the Economic and Social Research Institute, Dublin, and has published on income inequality, poverty, social policy, and health.

Trevor Norton is professor of marine biology at the University of Liverpool, director of the Port Erin Marine Laboratory, Isle of Man, and the author of *Stars Beneath the Sea* (1999) and *Reflections on a Summer Sea* (2001).

Julia Nunn is environmental recorder at the Centre for Environmental Data and Recording, Ulster Museum, Belfast.

Colm Ó Baoill is professor of Celtic at the University of Aberdeen.

Dónall Ó Braonáin is a journalist with RTÉ.

Máirtín Ó Briain is a lecturer in the School of Irish, National University of Ireland, Galway, and has published articles on aspects of the Ossianic Cycle.

Justin O'Brien is editor of current affairs with UTV and the author of *The Arms Trial* (2000) and *The Modern Prince: Charles J. Haughey and the Quest for Power* (2002).

Kathleen O'Brien is associate professor of fine arts at Concordia University, Montréal, and an artist and writer.

William O'Brien lectures on prehistory in the Department of Archaeology, National University of Ireland, Galway.

Éamonn Ó Bróithe is a singer.

Fiacc O Brolchain is a sailor and marine journalist, editor of *Aquaculture Ireland,* and the author of a history of commercial fishing in Ireland.

Eileen O'Byrne is a founder-member and past president of the Association of Professional Genealogists in Ireland, editor of *The Convert Rolls* (1981), and contributor to *Irish Genealogy: A Record Finder* (1981).

Stiofán Ó Cadhla is college lecturer in the Department of Folklore and Ethnology, University College, Cork, and the author of *Cá bhFuil Éire?: Guth an Ghaisce i bPrós Sheáin Uí Ríordáin* (1998).

Fiacre Ó Cairbre is a senior lecturer in mathematics at the National University of Ireland, Maynooth.

Ciarán O'Carroll is a priest of the Archdiocese of Dublin and a lecturer in ecclesiastical history.

Dónal O'Carroll is president of the Military History Society of Ireland.

Diarmaid Ó Catháin is a solicitor and has published on aspects of eighteenth-century Ireland.

Tomás Ó Cathasaigh is Henry L. Shattuck professor of Irish studies at Harvard University, Massachusetts, and the author of *The Heroic Biography of Cormac mac Airt* (1977).

Seán Ó Cearnaigh is a publisher and the author of *Scríbhneoirí na Gaeilge, 1945–1995* (1995).

Niall Ó Ciosáin teaches in the Department of History, National University of Ireland, Galway, and is the author of *Print and Popular Culture in Ireland, 1750–1850* (1997).

Colmán N. Ó Clabaigh is a monk in Glenstal Abbey, Co. Limerick, lectures in medieval Irish ecclesiastical history, and is the author of *The Franciscans in Ireland, 1400–1534* (2001).

Nellie O'Cleirigh is the author of books on Carrickmacross and Limerick lace.

Ciarán Ó Coigligh is a lecturer in Irish language, literature and civilisation in St Patrick's College, Dublin, and the author of novels, poetry, a collection of short stories, and Irish translations of the *Odyssey* and the *Divine Comedy*.

Micheál Ó Comáin is a herald in the Genealogical Office.

Breandán Ó Conaire is head of the Irish Department, St Patrick's College, Dublin, and former president of the Irish Amateur Boxing Association.

Brian Ó Conchubhair is a visiting assistant professor at the Keough Institute for Irish Studies, University of Notre Dame, Indiana.

Breandán Ó Conchúir is associate professor of Irish, University College, Cork, and the author of *Scríobhaithe Chorcaí, 1700–1850* (1982).

Cathal O'Connell is statutory lecturer in social policy in the Department of Applied Social Studies, University College, Cork, and has published on housing policy and the development of the Irish welfare state.

Daire O'Connell is curator of the outreach programme at the Hugh Lane Municipal Gallery of Modern Art, Dublin, and the author of the catalogues of the retrospective exhibitions *Mainie Jellett* (1991) and *Patrick Swift* (1993) and of *Picture This* (1997).

Philip O'Connell is an associate editor of the *Economic and Social Review* and is engaged in a number of comparative European research projects.

Sandra O'Connell is a doctoral student in the School of English, Trinity College, Dublin, a journalist, and editor of the journal *Irish Architect*.

Anne O'Connor is a lecturer in Irish folklore at the Academy of Irish Cultural Heritages, University of Ulster, and the author of *Child Murderess and Dead Child Traditions: A Comparative Study* (1991).

Anne V. O'Connor is a former teacher at Alexandra College, Dublin, and joint author of *Gladly Learn and Gladly Teach* (1983).

Deirdre O'Connor is lecturer in resource economics in the Department of Agribusiness, Extension and Rural Development, University College, Dublin, and joint author of *The Future of Irish Agriculture* (1999).

Emmet O'Connor lectures in history and politics at Magee College, Derry, and is the author of *A Labour History of Ireland, 1824–1960* (1992).

James P. O'Connor is the entomologist and a former keeper of natural history at the National Museum of Ireland, Dublin, and the author of *Irish Indoor Insects: A Popular Guide* (2000).

Julia S. O'Connor is professor of social policy at the University of Ulster and joint author of *States, Markets, Families: Gender, Liberalism and Social Policy in Australia, Canada, Great Britain and the United States* (1999).

Marie O'Connor is a research sociologist, director of the European Institute of Midwifery, and the author of *Birth Tides: Turning Towards Home Birth* (1995).

Pat J. O'Connor lectures in geography at the University of Limerick and is the author of *People Make Places* (1989) and *Atlas of Irish Place-Names* (2001).

Raymond O'Connor lectures in the Department of Geography, University College, Cork.

Kieran O'Conor is a lecturer in the Department of Archaeology, National University of Ireland, Galway, and the author of *The Archaeology of Medieval Rural Settlement in Ireland* (1998).

Alan O'Day is a fellow in modern history at Greyfriars, University of Oxford, and the author of *Parnell and the First Home Rule Episode* (1986) and *Irish Home Rule, 1867–1921* (1998).

Niall Ó Dochartaigh is a lecturer in the Department of Political Science and Sociology, National University of Ireland, Galway, and the author of *From Civil Rights to Armalites* (1997).

Christopher O'Donnell is a Carmelite priest and associate professor of spirituality at the Milltown Institute of Theology and Philosophy, Dublin.

Godfrey O'Donnell is a deacon of the Romanian Orthodox Church in Ireland and a registered psychotherapist with the Irish Council for Psychotherapy.

Katherine O'Donnell is a lecturer in the Women's Education, Research and Resource Centre, University College, Dublin, and joint editor of *Love, Sex, Intimacy and Friendship Between Men, 1550–1800* (2002).

Ruan O'Donnell lectures in history at the University of Limerick and is the author of *Aftermath: Post-Rebellion Insurgency in Wicklow, 1799–1803* (2000).

Derek O'Donoghue works at Teagasc in Cork.

Jo O'Donoghue is a publisher and the author of a book on the novelist Brian Moore.

Tony O'Donoghue is a sports broadcaster and historian specialising in track and field athletics.

Ite O'Donovan is a lecturer in the DIT Conservatory of Music and Drama and founder-director of the Dublin Choral Foundation.

Anne O'Dowd is assistant keeper in the National Museum of Ireland, and the author of *Meitheal: A Study of Co-Operative Labour in Rural Ireland* (1982) and *Spalpeens and Tattie-Hokers: The History and Folklore of the Irish Migratory Agricultural Labourer* (1991).

Proinsias Ó Drisceoil is the author of *Ar Scaradh Gabhail: An Fhéiniúlacht in 'Cín Lae Amhlaoibh Uí Shúilleabháin'* (2000).

Dennis O'Driscoll is a civil servant and poet and the author of *Troubled Thoughts, Majestic Dreams* (2001).

Tadhg Ó Dúshláine is senior lecturer in Modern Irish and dean of the Faculty of Celtic Studies, National University of Ireland, Maynooth, and the author of *An Eoraip agus Litríocht na Gaeilge, 1600–1650* (1987) and *Where We Sported and Played* (1991).

Dermot W. O'Dwyer is a lecturer in the Department of Civil, Structural and Environmental Engineering, Trinity College, Dublin.

Frederick O'Dwyer is an architect and architectural historian and the author of *The Architecture of Deane and Woodward* (1997).

Maria Cullen O'Dwyer is joint founder of Prehistoric Music Ireland and author of Prehistoricmusic.com (2002).

Riana O'Dwyer is a lecturer in English at the National University of Ireland, Galway, and contributing editor to *Irish Studies: A General Introduction* (1988) and *The Field Day Anthology of Irish Writing*, vols. IV–V (2002).

Simon O'Dwyer is the joint founder of Prehistoric Music Ireland and author of Prehistoricmusic.com (2002).

Patrick O'Farrell is emeritus Scientia professor of history at the University of New South Wales and the author of *The Irish in Australia* (third edition, 2000).

Colette O'Flaherty is an assistant keeper in the National Library of Ireland, Dublin.

Raghnall Ó Floinn is assistant keeper in the Irish Antiquities Division of the National Museum of Ireland, Dublin, and has published on medieval insular metalwork.

Kevin O'Gorman is a member of the Society of African Missions and teaches moral theology at Kimmage Mission Institute, Dublin.

Cormac Ó Gráda is professor of economics, University College, Dublin, author of *Black '47 and Beyond* (1999), and joint author of *Famine Demography: Perspectives from the Past and Present* (2002).

John O'Grady is a retired statutory lecturer in the history of art, University College, Dublin, and the author of *The Life and Work of Sarah Purser* (1996).

John W. O'Hagan is associate professor of economics and college bursar of Trinity College, Dublin, and editor of *The Economy of Ireland* (2002).

Gearóid Ó hAllmhuráin is an ethnomusicologist, Jefferson Smurfit professor of Irish studies at the University of Missouri, St Louis, and the author of *Traditional Music from Clare and Beyond* (1996) and *A Pocket History of Irish Traditional Music* (1998).

Eunan O'Halpin is professor of modern history at Trinity College, Dublin, and the author of *The Decline of the Union: British Government in Ireland, 1892–1920* (1987) and *Defending Ireland: The Irish State and Its Enemies since 1922* (2000).

Eoghan Ó hAnluain is a senior lecturer in the Department of Modern Irish, University College, Dublin.

Deirdre O'Hara is a maritime archaeologist with the Irish Underwater Council.

Patricia O'Hara is senior policy analyst with the Western Development Commission and the author of *Partners in Production?: Women, Farm and Family in Ireland* (1998).

Kathleen O'Higgins is a freelance social researcher, formerly with the Economic and Social Research Institute, Dublin, and the author of studies on drug abuse, children in state care, and housing.

Dáithí Ó hÓgáin is associate professor of Irish folklore, University College, Dublin, the author of numerous books, and a poet and short-story writer.

Margaret Ó hÓgartaigh is a tutor in history at St Patrick's College, Dublin, and has published on the history of education and the history of medicine.

Ruairí Ó hUiginn is professor of Modern Irish at the National University of Ireland, Maynooth, author of several studies on aspects of Irish language and literature, editor of *Léachtaí Cholm Cille,* and former editor of *Ainm.*

Éamonn O'Keeffe is a music teacher and choirmaster and secretary of the Irish RILM Committee.

Máire O'Keeffe is a teacher, fiddle player, and doctoral student at the Irish World Music Centre, University of Limerick.

Hilary O'Kelly is a dress historian who works at the National College of Art and Design, Dublin.

Joe Ó Labhraí is head of the Department of Irish and Irish-Medium Education at St Mary's University College, Belfast.

Lillis Ó Laoire is a lecturer in the Department of Languages and Cultural Studies, University of Limerick, and the author of *Ar Chreag i Lár na Farraige: Amhráin agus Amhránaithe i dToraigh* (2002).

Paul O'Leary is senior lecturer in Welsh history at the University of Wales, Aberystwyth.

Philip O'Leary is an associate professor at Boston College and the author of *The Prose Literature of the Gaelic Revival, 1881–1921: Ideology and Innovation* (1994).

Richard O'Leary is a lecturer in sociology in the School of Sociology and Social Policy, Queen's University, Belfast, a former research fellow at Nuffield College, Oxford, and the author of *Coeducation and Gender Equality* (1996).

Thomas O'Loughlin is senior lecturer in historical theology in the Department of Theology, University of Wales, Lampeter, and joint editor of *Scriptores Latini Hiberniae.*

Nessa O'Mahony is a former head of public affairs with the Arts Council, Dublin.

Pádraig Ó Máille is a priest, poet and essayist and the author of *Dúdúchas* (1972) and *Living Dangerously* (1999).

Eoin O'Malley is an economist with the Economic and Social Research Institute, Dublin.

Nollaig Ó Muraíle is reader in Irish and Celtic studies at Queen's University, Belfast, and the author of *The Celebrated Antiquary: Dubhaltach Mac Fhirbhisigh, His Lineage, Life and Learning* (1996).

Liam P. Ó Murchú is a senior lecturer in the Department of Modern Irish, University College, Cork, and the editor of *Cúirt an Mheonoíche* (1982), from Merriman's autograph copy of the poem.

Máirtín Ó Murchú is senior professor at the Dublin Institute for Advanced Studies and the author of *East Perthshire Gaelic* (1989) and *Cumann Buan-Choimeádta na Gaeilge* (2001).

Seosamh Ó Murchú is senior editor with An Gúm, former editor of *Comhar* and joint editor of *Oghma,* and a founder-member of the independent Dublin radio station Raidió na Life.

Kevin O'Neill is director of the Irish Studies programme at Boston College and the author of *Family and Farm in Pre-Famine Ireland: The Parish of Killeshandra* (1984).

Des O'Rawe lectures in the School of Languages, Literatures and Arts, Queen's University, Belfast, and has published on Irish literature and culture.

Colm O'Reardon is policy adviser to the leader of the Labour Party.

Jennifer O'Reilly is statutory lecturer in medieval history and contributor to the history of art course at University College, Cork.

Peter O'Reilly is an angling adviser with the Central Fisheries Board, the author of several angling books, and a game fishing instructor.

Seán O'Reilly is director of the Architectural Heritage Society of Scotland, author of *Irish Houses and Gardens: From the Archives of Country Life* (1998), and former editor of the journal of the Irish Georgian Society, *Irish Architectural and Decorative Studies.*

Peadar Ó Riada is a musician and conductor of the Cóir Chúil Aodha, Co. Cork.

Pádraig Ó Riain is professor of Early and Medieval Irish at University College, Cork, and editor of *Corpus Genealogiarum Sanctorum Hiberniae* (1985).

Michelle O Riordan is an assistant professor and publications officer at the School of Celtic Studies, Dublin Institute for Advanced Studies, and the author of *The Gaelic Mind and the Collapse of the Gaelic World* (1990).

Patricia O'Riordan is a postgraduate student in philosophy at Trinity College, Dublin.

Charles E. Orser Junior is distinguished professor of anthropology at Illinois State University and editor of *Encyclopedia of Historical Archaeology* (2002).

Peter O'Shaughnessy is a theatre director, actor, playwright and lecturer and the author of three historical works and two children's books.

Finian O'Shea is a primary teacher and lecturer in education at Church of Ireland College of Education, Dublin, and president of the Reading Association of Ireland.

Pádraig Ó Siadhail is associate professor of Irish studies at St Mary's University, Halifax, Nova Scotia.

Séamas Ó Síocháin is a senior lecturer in the Department of Anthropology, National University of Ireland, Maynooth, and joint editor of *Irish Travellers: Culture and Ethnicity* (1994).

Aidan O'Sullivan is a lecturer in the Department of Archaeology, University College, Dublin, and the author of *The Archaeology of Lake Settlement in Ireland* (1998) and *Foragers, Farmers and Fishers in a Coastal Landscape* (2001).

Eoin O'Sullivan is a lecturer in social policy in the Department of Social Studies, Trinity College, Dublin, and joint author of

Suffer the Little Children: The Inside Story of Ireland's Industrial Schools (1999).

Niamh O'Sullivan is a lecturer in the National College of Art and Design, Dublin, and the author of *Re-orientations: Aloysius O'Kelly: Painting, Politics and Popular Culture* (1999).

Oran O'Sullivan is general manager of Birdwatch Ireland, a former editor of the *Irish Bird Report,* and managing editor of *Wings.*

Sara O'Sullivan is a lecturer in the Department of Sociology, University College, Dublin.

William O'Sullivan (1921–2000) was keeper of manuscripts in Trinity College Library, Dublin, and the author of 'Irish manuscripts, 600–1200,' in *New History of Ireland,* vol. 1 (2002).

Francis O'Toole is a lecturer in the Department of Economics, Trinity College, Dublin, and has published on tax reform, tax expenditures, basic income, and unjust enrichment.

Pat O'Toole is a farmer and part-time journalist.

Tina O'Toole is a lecturer in the Department of English, University College, Cork, project researcher at the HEA Munster Women Writers' Project and is engaged in a critical study of the lives and work of Sarah Grand and George Egerton.

Michael Ovchinnikov is a head of division at the Keldysh Institute of Applied Mathematics, Russian Academy of Sciences, and the author of *Magnetic Orientation Systems of Artificial Earth Satellites* (1985) and *Lectures on Space Flight Dynamics* (1997).

Gary Owens is professor of history at Huron University College, Canada.

John Page is artistic director of the Portsmouth Festivities and the author of 'The post-war Irish symphony: Frank Corcoran's Symphony No. 2,' in *Musical Studies,* vol. 7 (2003).

Tony Parker lectures in geography at University College, Dublin, and is director of the Centre for Retail Studies.

Matthew Parkes works on the Irish Geological Heritage Programme at the Geological Survey of Ireland, covering archives and collections as well as sites of importance.

Susan M. Parkes is an emeritus fellow and former senior lecturer in education at Trinity College, Dublin, and the author of *Kildare Place: The History of the Church of Ireland Training College, 1811–1969* (1984).

Eve Patten lectures in English at Trinity College, Dublin, and has published research on nineteenth and twentieth-century Anglo-Irish literature.

Henry Patterson is professor of politics at the University of Ulster, Jordanstown, and the author of *The Politics of the Two Irish States since 1939* (2002).

Alexander Peach is a lecturer in history and sociology at the Centre for Research in Ethnic Relations, University of Warwick.

Peter Pearson is an artist and writer with an interest in architectural history and the applied arts and the author of *Between the Mountains and the Sea* (1998) and *The Heart of Dublin* (2000).

Gary Peatling is a former fellow of the Society of the Humanities, Cornell University, and the author of *British Opinion and Irish Self-Government, 1865–1925* (2001).

Martine Pelletier is a lecturer in the University of Tours and the author of a book on Brian Friel and Field Day.

Juan José Pérez-Camacho is a physicist and former visiting research fellow at Trinity College, Dublin, where he carried out research in the early history of science in Dublin.

Adrian Phillips is an emeritus professor in the Geology Department of Trinity College, Dublin, and the author of papers on the geology of Ireland ranging from the Precambrian to the Tertiary.

Eamon Phoenix is a broadcaster on historical and political issues, senior lecturer in history at Stranmillis University College, Belfast, and the author of *Northern Nationalism, 1890–1940* (1994).

Pierce T. Pigott is a chartered engineer and former director of engineering services at the Office of Public Works.

Emilie Pine is a doctoral student in Trinity College, Dublin.

Vivienne Pollock is curator of historic photographs at the Ulster Museum, Belfast, and joint author of *Women of Ireland: Image and Experience, 1880–1920* (1999).

Homan Potterton is a former director of the National Gallery of Ireland and joint author of *Irish Art and Architecture: From Pre-History to the Present* (1978).

D. G. Pringle is a senior lecturer in geography at the National University of Ireland, Maynooth.

Lindsay Proudfoot is reader in Irish historical geography at the School of Geography, Queen's University, Belfast.

David Quin is a lecturer in journalism and director of the MA in journalism at the Dublin Institute of Technology.

Feargal Quinn is founder and executive chairman of the Superquinn supermarket group, a member of Seanad Éireann, and the author of *Crowning the Customer* (1990).

Oliver P. Rafferty is visiting professor of Irish studies and history at John Carroll University, Cleveland, and the author of *Catholicism in Ulster, 1603–1983* (1994) and *The Church, the State and the Fenian Threat, 1861–75* (1999).

Barry Raftery is professor of Celtic archaeology at University College, Dublin, and the author of *Pagan Celtic Ireland* (1994).

K. J. Rankin is a doctoral candidate in the Department of Geography, University College, Dublin, and research fellow at the Geopolitics and International Research Centre, School of Oriental and African Studies, University of London.

Gunther Rasche is professor of theoretical physics at the Institute of Theoretical Physics, University of Zürich.

Rosemary Raughter is an independent scholar, has published articles on eighteenth-century female philanthropy and on women and religion, and is at present researching a biography of Lady Arbella Denny.

Bob Reece is associate professor in history and director of the Centre for Irish Studies, Murdoch University, Western Australia, and the author of *The Origins of Irish Convict Transportation to New South Wales* (2001).

William Reville is associate professor of biochemistry and director of electron microscopy at University College, Cork, and writes the weekly 'Science Today' column in the *Irish Times.*

Valerie Richardson is a senior lecturer in the Department of Social Policy and Social Work, University College, Dublin, and joint author of *Towards a Standardised Framework for Inter-Country Adoption Assessment Procedures* (1999).

Rosemary Richey is a lecturer in humanities at Lauder College, Dunfermline.

Michael Richter is professor of medieval history at the University of Konstanz, author of *Medieval Ireland: The Enduring Tradition* (1988), and joint author of *Ireland and Europe in the Early Middle Ages: Texts and Transmission* (2002).

Pádraigín Riggs is a senior lecturer in the Department of Modern Irish, University College, Cork, and the author of *Donncha Ó Céileachair* (1978) and *Pádraic Ó Conaire: Deoraí* (1994).

Joseph Robins is a social historian, formerly an assistant secretary of the Department of Health and Children, and the author of *Fools and Mad* (1986), *Custom House People* (1993), *The Miasma* (1995), and *Champagne and Silver Buckles* (2001).

Anthony Roche is a senior lecturer in Anglo-Irish literature and drama at University College, Dublin, editor of *Irish University Review,* and the author of *Contemporary Irish Drama* (1994).

Consilio Rock is a member of the Sisters of Mercy and tutor in moral theology at St Patrick's College, Maynooth.

Emer Rockett is a film lecturer on the New York University programme in Dublin, has lectured at University College, Dublin, and Dún Laoghaire Institute of Art, Design and Technology, and is joint author of *Neil Jordan* (2002).

Cilian Roden is a consultant botanical ecologist with a special interest in algae.

Bill Rolston is professor of sociology at the University of Ulster, Jordanstown, and joint author of *Encounters: How Racism Came to Ireland* (2002).

Brendan Rooney is research fellow at the National Gallery of Ireland, author of *The Life and Work of H. J. Thaddeus* (2003), and joint author of *Irish Paintings in the National Gallery of Ireland, vol. 1* (2001).

Ian Campbell Ross is associate professor of English and a fellow of Trinity College, Dublin, and the author of *Laurence Sterne: A Life* (2001).

Lord Rosse; Brendan Parsons, seventh Earl of Rosse, is founding director of the Birr Scientific and Heritage Foundation.

David Rottman is associate director of research at the National Center for State Courts in Williamsburg, Virginia, and joint author of *Understanding Contemporary Ireland* (1990), *Class Stratification* (1995), and *Dispensing Justice Locally* (1998).

Stephen A. Royle is senior lecturer in the School of Geography, Queen's University, Belfast, and the author of *A Geography of Islands: Small Island Insularity* (2001).

Frances Ruane is associate professor of economics at Trinity College, Dublin, and chairperson of the National Statistics Board.

Clive Ruggles is professor of archaeoastronomy at the School of Archaeology and Ancient History, University of Leicester, and the author of *Astronomy in Prehistoric Britain and Ireland* (1999).

Paul Russell is head of classics at Radley College, Abingdon, Oxfordshire, visiting lecturer in Celtic at the University of Oxford, and the author of *Introduction to the Celtic Languages* (1995).

Eugene Ryan is head of the Rural Environmental Protection Scheme at Teagasc.

Michael Ryan is director of the Chester Beatty Library and an honorary professor of Trinity College, Dublin, joint author of *Reading the Irish Landscape* (2001), and editor of *Ireland and Insular Art* (1987) and *The Illustrated Archaeology of Ireland* (1991).

Raymund Ryan is curator at the Heinz Architectural Center, Pittsburgh, Pennsylvania, and is joint author of *Building Tate Modern* (2000) and author of *Cool Construction* (2001).

Vera Ryan is a lecturer in the history of art at Crawford College of Art and Design, Cork.

Colin Rynne is the author of *At the Sign of the Cow: The Cork Butter Market, 1769–1924* (1998), *The Industrial Archaeology of Cork City and its Environs* (1999), *A Life of Usefulness: Abraham Beale and the Monard Ironworks* (2001) and editor of *The Heritage of Ireland* (2000).

Adrian Scahill is a doctoral student at University College, Dublin.

W. Garrett Scaife is a fellow emeritus and former associate professor in the Department of Mechanical and Manufacturing Engineering, Trinity College, Dublin, and the author of *From Galaxies to Turbines: Science, Technology and the Parsons Family* (2000).

Susan Schreibman is assistant director of Maryland Institute for Technology in the Humanities, University of Maryland, and the author of *Collected Poems of Thomas MacGreevy: An Annotated Edition* (1991).

Alan Scott is a teaching assistant at Queen's University, Belfast.

A. B. Scott is professor emeritus of Late Latin at Queen's University, University.

Derek Scott is a retired wholesale draper and president of the Irish Cricket Union.

Máire Scully is an account manager with a public relations firm and former part-time sports journalist and public relations officer of Irish Basketball.

Rachael Sealy Lynch is associate professor of English at the University of Connecticut.

Regina Sexton is a food historian and food writer and the author of *A Little History of Irish Food* (1998).

Gerald P. Shannon is a lecturer in mathematics in the Faculty of Informatics, University of Ulster at Coleraine, and the author of 'Andrew Young' in *Creators of Mathematics: The Irish Connection* (2000).

Tom Sherlock is a traditional music consultant and former production manager of Claddagh Records.

Ruth Sherry is professor of English literature at the Norwegian University of Science and Technology, Trondheim. She has edited Frank O'Connor's plays *The Invincibles* (1980) and *Moses' Rock* (1984).

Sally Shortall is a reader in sociology at Queen's University, Belfast, and the author of *Women and Farming: Property and Power* (1999).

Séamus Shortall is an international cycling official, a systems analyst, and the author of *Pierce O'Mahony: An Irishman in Bulgaria* (2002).

Anngret Simms is associate professor of geography at University College, Dublin, and joint editor of *Irish Historic Towns Atlas, No. 1–11* (1985–2002).

Katharine Simms is a senior lecturer in the Department of Medieval History, Trinity College, Dublin, and the author of *Irish Warlords: The Changing Political Structure of Gaelic Ireland in the Later Middle Ages* (1987).

Richard Sinnott is professor of politics at University College, Dublin, and the author of *Irish Voters Decide: Voting Behaviour in Elections and Referendums since 1918* (1995).

Peter Sirr is a poet and director of the Irish Writers' Centre; his most recent collection of poems is *Bring Everything* (2000).

Elaine Sisson is a senior lecturer in visual culture at Dún Laoghaire Institute of Art, Design and Technology and the author of *Pearse's Patriots: The Cult of Boyhood at St Enda's* (2002).

Michael Slavin is an equestrian journalist and commentator and the author of *The Book of Tara* (1996) and *Show-Jumping Legends, Ireland, 1868–1998* (1998).

D. Patrick Sleeman studies badgers at University College, Cork.

Brendan Smith is a senior lecturer in history at the University of Bristol and the author of *Colonisation and Conquest in Medieval Ireland: The English in Louth, 1170–1330* (1999).

Emer Smyth is a senior research officer with the Economic and Social Research Institute and the author of *Do Schools Differ?* (1999).

Theo Snoddy is an art historian and the author of *Dictionary of Irish Artists, Twentieth Century* (1996, 2002).

Adrian Somerfield is former senior science master at St Columba's College, Rathfarnham, Co. Dublin, and former president of the Irish Science Teachers' Association.

Joseph Spence is headmaster of Oakham School, Rutland, and was formerly Master in College at Eton College, Windsor.

Clare Stancliffe is an honorary reader in ecclesiastical history in the Departments of History and Theology, University of Durham.

David Stapleton is a former chief of staff of the Defence Forces who served as force commander of the UN force on the Golan Heights and was founding president of the Representative Association of Commissioned Officers.

Julie Anne Stevens is a postdoctoral research fellow at Trinity College, Dublin, and has published on nineteenth and twentieth-century Irish fiction.

Anne Millar Stewart is curator of fine art at the Ulster Museum, Belfast.

Bruce Stewart is lecturer in Irish literary history at the University of Ulster, Coleraine, literary director of the Princess Grace Irish Library, Monaco, and the author of *The Politics of Irish Literary Criticism* (2003).

Norman Storey is an equine specialist adviser with Teagasc at Kildalton College, Piltown, Co. Kilkenny.

Matthew Stout lectures in early and medieval Irish history at St Patrick's College, Dublin, and is the author of *The Irish Ringfort* (1997) and joint editor of *Atlas of the Irish Rural Landscape* (1997).

Eileen Sweeney is a member of the Society of the Holy Child Jesus, a retired teacher of English and African Literature and is the author of *Another Country; the Land of Literature* (1979).

Paul Sweeney is a business and economic adviser and the author of *The Celtic Tiger: Ireland's Continuing Economic Miracle* (2000).

David Sweetman is chief archaeologist of the Heritage Service, general editor of the County Archaeological Inventory Series, and author of *The Medieval Castles of Ireland* (1999).

Donal Synnott is director of the National Botanic Gardens, Dublin, with a particular interest in the ecology of mosses and ferns and the history of Irish botany and horticulture.

Friedrich-Maria Taaffe lectured in the history of science at Comenius University, Bratislava, Slovak Republic.

Tigran Tchrakian is professor of mathematical physics at the National University of Ireland, Maynooth, and a research associate at the Dublin Institute for Advanced Studies.

Virginia Teehan is university archivist and director of the Heritage and Visual Arts Office, University College, Cork.

Armin Thellung is professor of theoretical physics at the Institute of Theoretical Physics, University of Zürich.

F. Glenn Thompson is a uniform researcher, vice-president of the Military History Society of Ireland, and the author of *The Uniforms of 1798–1803* (1988) and *The Flags and Uniforms of the Irish Volunteers and Yeomanry* (1990).

Ken Thompson is a letter-cutter and sculptor in stone from Co. Cork.

Linda Thompson is a company director and administrator and a former associate lecturer with the Open University.

Mary Thompson is a lecturer in the English Department, St Patrick's College, Dublin, and editor of *Selected Plays of Austin Clarke* (2002).

Mark Tierney is a monk of Glenstal Abbey, Co. Limerick, and a writer and historian.

Martin Tierney is parish priest of Kill of the Grange, Co. Dublin, a columnist in the *Irish Catholic,* and the author of *The New Elect: The Church and New Religious Groups* (1985).

Alan Titley is head of the Irish Department, St Patrick's College, Dublin, and the author of *An tÚrscéal Gaeilge* (1990).

Fergal Tobin is publishing director of Gill & Macmillan and the author of *The Best of Decades: Ireland in the 1960s* (1984).

R. B. Tobin is a postgraduate student at the University of Oxford and is writing a study of Hubert Butler.

Hilary Tovey is a senior lecturer in the Sociology Department of Trinity College, Dublin, a fellow of TCD, and joint author of *A Sociology of Ireland* (2000).

Pauric Travers is an educationalist, historian, and author.

Brian Trench is a former journalist and a senior lecturer in the School of Communications, Dublin City University.

Wolfgang Truetzschler is a senior lecture in communications at Dublin Institute of Technology.

Derval Tubridy is a lecturer in English at Goldsmiths College, University of London, and the author of *Thomas Kinsella: The Peppercanister Poems* (2001).

Hugh Tully is officer in charge of the Naval Intelligence Department.

John Turpin is professor of the history of art and head of the Faculty of the History of Art and Design and Complementary Studies, National College of Art and Design.

Bernadette A. Twomey directs an independent Irish dance school in Sheffield and is a full-time school teacher of music.

Maria Tymoczko is professor of comparative literature at the University of Massachusetts. She is the author of a study of James Joyce, *The Irish 'Ulysses'* (1994), and of *Translation in a Postcolonial Context: Early Irish Literature in English Translation* (1999).

Jürgen Uhlich is a lecturer in Early Irish at Trinity College, Dublin, and the author of *Die Morphologie der Komponierten Personennamen des Altirischen* (1993).

Gearóidín Uí Laighléis is a lecturer in Irish at St Patrick's College, Dublin, and the author of *Seán Mac Maoláin agus Ceart na Gaeilge* (2002).

Diane Urquhart is a lecturer in modern Irish history in the Institute of Irish Studies, University of Liverpool, and the author of *Women in Ulster Politics, 1890–1940: A History Not Yet Told* (2000).

Dorothy Walker (1929–2002) was a writer and lecturer on Irish and international art of the twentieth century, one of the founders of the Rosc exhibition, and the author of *Louis Le Brocquy* (1981) and *Modern Art in Ireland* (1997).

Eamonn Wall is associate professor of English at the University of Missouri-St Louis and the author of *From the Sin-e Cafe to the Black Hill* (2000).

Patrick Wallace is director of the National Museum of Ireland, Dublin.

Alison Walsh is fiction editor with Gill & Macmillan.

James Walsh is professor and head of the Department of Geography at the National University of Ireland, Maynooth, and joint author of *Irish Agriculture in Transition: A Census Atlas* (1999).

John Walsh is lecturer in intercultural studies and communication at the Fiontar Centre for Enterprise Education at Dublin City University and the author of *Díchoimisiúnú Teanga: Coimisiún na Gaeltachta, 1926* (2002).

Ned Walsh was pig specialist with the Irish Farmers' Association.

Paul Walsh is a senior archaeologist with the Heritage Service, Department of the Environment and Local Government, and the author of *Discover Galway* (2001).

Bronwen Walter is reader in social and cultural geography at Anglia Polytechnic University, Cambridge, and the author of *Outsiders Inside: Whiteness, Place and Irish Women* (2001).

Philip W. Walton is professor of applied physics at the National University of Ireland, Galway.

Alex Ward is assistant keeper in the Art and Industrial Division, National Museum of Ireland, Dublin.

Andrew Ward is a lecturer in philosophy at the University of York.

Margaret Ward is assistant director of Democratic Dialogue, Belfast, and the author of *Unmanageable Revolutionaries: Women and Irish Nationalism* (1983) and *Hanna Sheehy-Skeffington* (1997).

Geoff Warke is Field Survey Officer at the Geological Survey of Northern Ireland, with responsibility for abandoned mine workings.

Richard Warner is keeper of archaeology and ethnography in the Ulster Museum, Belfast.

Iarfhlaith Watson is a lecturer in sociology at University College, Dublin, managing editor of the *Irish Journal of Sociology,* and member of the board of the Sociological Association of Ireland.

Seosamh Watson is dean of the Faculty of Celtic Studies, University College, Dublin, a member of the editorial board of the UNESCO *Atlas Linguarum Europae,* and the author of *Mac na Míchomhairle* (1979) and *Oidhreacht Ghleann Cholm Cille* (1989).

Denis Weaire is Erasmus Smith professor of natural and experimental philosophy in the Physics Department of Trinity College, Dublin.

David Wheatley lectures at the University of Hull and is the author of two collections of poetry, *Thirst* (1997) and *Misery Hill* (2001).

Kevin Whelan is Michael J. Smurfit Director of the Keough–Notre Dame Centre, Dublin.

Norman White is the author of *Hopkins: A Literary Biography* (1992) and *Hopkins in Ireland* (2002).

Desi Wilkinson is a traditional musician and singer, a teacher, a founder-member of the group Cran, and a postdoctoral research associate at the University of Limerick under the auspices of the Irish Research Council for the Humanities and Social Science.

Jonathan Williams is a literary agent and associate editor of *The Field Day Anthology of Irish Writing*, vols. I–III (1991).

Nicholas J. A. Williams is a senior lecturer in Irish at University College, Dublin.

William H. A. Williams is a professor at the Union Institute and University, Cincinnati, and the author of *'Twas Only an Irishman's Dream: The Image of Ireland and the Irish in American Popular Song Lyrics, 1800–1920* (1996).

Lori Williamson teaches for the Open University, Milton Keynes, and is the author of *Power and Protest: Frances Power Cobbe and Victorian Society* (2002).

Grania Willis is equestrian correspondent of the *Irish Times* and editor of the *Irish Horse World* (sport horse supplement in the *Irish Field*), represented Ireland at senior international level in three-day eventing, and wrote a weekly hunting column for the *Irish Field.*

S. E. Wilmer is a senior lecturer in drama at Trinity College, Dublin, and the author of *Theatre, Society and the Nation: Staging American Identities* (2002).

James G. Wilson is a senior lecturer in environmental science at Trinity College, Dublin, and the author of *Eutrophication in Irish Waters* (1996) and *The Intertidal System* (2002).

Peter Wilson is a former director of Dublin Zoo.

Robin Wilson is director of Democratic Dialogue, Belfast.

Valerie Wilson is assistant curator of textiles at the Ulster Folk and Transport Museum, Holywood, Co. Down, and researches and writes on Irish textiles.

Elizabeth Wincott Heckett is a research associate in the Department of Archaeology, University College, Cork.

Frank Winder is a former professor of biochemistry at Trinity College, Dublin.

Joley Wood teaches English in the United States and has written on George Bernard Shaw.

Jonathan Wooding is a lecturer in the Department of Theology and Religious Studies, University of Wales, Lampeter, and assistant director of the Centre for the Study of Religion in Celtic Societies.

Peter Woodman is professor of archaeology at University College, Cork, and the author of *Excavations at Mount Sandel, 1973–1977* (1985), and *Excavations at Ferriter's Cove: Last Hunters—First Farmers on the Dingle Peninsula* (1999).

C. J. Woods is a researcher on the Royal Irish Academy's *Dictionary of Irish Biography* and an occasional lecturer in modern history at the National University of Ireland, Maynooth.

Gus Worth is chief executive of Earthwatch and Friends of the Earth, Ireland.

Patrick N. Wyse Jackson is curator of the Geological Museum, Trinity College, Dublin.

Gráinne Yeats is a singer and harper, a researcher into the history and music of the Irish harp, and the first professional musician to revive and record the music of the traditional wire-strung instrument.

Susan Youngs is curator in the Department of Medieval and Modern Europe, British Museum, London, and editor of *The Work of Angels: Masterpieces of Celtic Metalwork, AD 600–900.*

Acknowledgements

Almost a thousand people were directly involved in creating *The Encyclopedia of Ireland* and to them we owe a debt of thanks for their support and cooperation over a period of four and a half years. A core group of individuals made themselves available to the *Encyclopedia*'s editorial team and were called upon rather more often than they may have anticipated or wished. For their generosity with their time, advice, expertise and in the resolution of many problems, we are grateful.

To all those other consultants, contributors, advisors and specialist readers, we also convey our thanks for the many services which they provided. To the individuals and institutions in Ireland and abroad who lent precious original and photographic material, and who extended copyright permission for use as illustrations, we express our gratitude.

Personal thanks are due to Jonathan Bardon, Terence Brown, Joe Brady, Nicola Gordon Bowe, Richard Charkin, Martin Clancy, Mary Clarke, Colette Cowlard, Derek Cullen, David and Edwin Davison, Enda Delaney, Michael Diggin, Kate Duffy, Charlotte Fabian, Julia Fairlie, Desmond Fennell, Joanna Finegan, Liz Forster, David Gorry, Patrick Hannon, Ian Jacobs, Simon Lincoln, Helen Litton, Jim McArdle, Marie McFeely, Susan McKenna-Lawlor, Louis McRedmond, Shane Mawe, John Minihan, Jacquie Moore, Christopher Moriarty, Denis Mortell, Peter Murray, Máirín Nic Eoin, Úna Ní Chonchúir, Bairbre Ní Fhloinn, Ríonach uí Ógáin, Sinéad ní Shúinéar, David Norris, Dáibhí Ó Cróinín, Brendan O'Donoghue, Siobhan O'Rafferty, Niamh O'Sullivan, John Peacock, Richard Pine, Letitia Pollard, Maureen Porteous, Aideen Quigley, Zöe Reid, Deirdre Rennison Kunz, Tony Roche, David Rose, Bride Rosney, Barbara Ryan, Joakim Säflund, Regina Sexton, Bernard Share, Dr Michael Solomons, Derek Speirs, Fintan Vallely, Anna MacBride White and Jonathan Williams,

Two pivotal figures in the cultural life of Ireland, Carolyn Swift, co-founder of the Pike Theatre, and Dorothy Walker, co-founder of Rosc, who continued to be involved with the *Encyclopedia* even when seriously ill, died before publication. To the memory of these courageous and bountiful women we dedicate *The Encyclopedia of Ireland.*

Encyclopedia Staff

Editorial

Brian Lalor, general editor
Myra Dowling, editor and project manager
Seamas Ó Brogáin, senior copy-editor
Alison Walsh, managing editor
Tess Tattersall, managing editor
Jim McArdle, proof reader
Emer Ryan, assistant copy-editor
Helen Litton, indexer
Dearbhla Farrell, editorial assistant
Petula Martyn, editorial assistant
Edel Smullen, editorial assistant
Jaimee Biggins, editorial assistant

Picture research

Carla Briggs, picture editor
Sinead McCoole, picture editor
Sarah Durcan, picture editor
Gabrielle Brocklesby, picture researcher
Penny Iremonger, picture researcher
Louis McManus, picture researcher

Administration

Fergal Tobin, publishing director
Fiona Markham, administrative secretary
Siofra Gavin, editorial secretary
Karen O'Donoghue, temporary secretary
Anita Ruane, marketing
Pamela Coyle, marketing

Production

Mairead O'Keeffe, production director
Carole Lynch, typesetter
Mark Loughran, designer
Aoileann O'Donnell, production assistant
Jennifer Brady, production assistant

Cartography

Cartographica Ltd, historical and national cartography
Netmaps, Geografia Cartografia S.A., county maps
David Gorry, cartographic consultant

Notes for Readers

Order of entries. Entries are arranged alphabetically in letter-by-letter order (thus 'Abbeyknockmoy' comes before 'abbeys'), with the following exceptions. Punctuation to identify the primary article will override the strict letter-by-letter system. Thus 'agriculture: changing nature…' will regard 'agriculture' as a stand-alone headword, with the words following the colon disregarded for purposes of alphabetisation. Likewise, minor punctuation to isolate a headword will follow a similar logic: 'Armagh, primacy of' will ignore the part of headword following the comma and will therefore appear before 'Armagh Pipers' Club'. Parts of headwords in parentheses are ignored for purposes of alphabetisation. Abbreviations and contractions in headwords are treated as if fully spelled out: thus 'Dr' is alphabetised as 'Doctor'.

Likewise, all punctuated headings will precede conjuncted ones: thus, 'Antrim, Glens…' precedes 'Antrim and Derry…'. In every case where a county name and the name of the county town/city are identical, the county article precedes the city/town one, being a progression from the greater to the lesser entity. In such cases, the county article always appears before articles bearing the county name as the primary part of the headword. Thus 'Armagh, County' precedes 'Armagh, Book of'.

Surnames beginning with 'Mc' are alphabetised as if this were spelled 'Mac' (thus Macadam, McAleese, Mac Anna); but note that in some individual names (up to about the twelfth century) the element 'mac', meaning 'son (of),' is not part of a hereditary surname and the name is therefore not transposed. (Such names can be identified wherever they occur by the fact that the M of 'mac' is not capitalised.) Entries beginning with 'St' (such as St Patrick's Bell, St Patrick's Cathedral) are arranged as if this were spelled 'saint'; but the saints themselves will be found under their personal names (thus Patrick). Prepositions (such as 'for' and 'of') and conjunctions ('and') are also disregarded.

Entries for battles, manuscripts and other topics named after a geographical location are given with the location as headword (thus Armagh, Book of; Aughrim, Battle of; Avoca, Vale of). The names of features beginning with 'Lough' and 'Mount' are not transposed (thus Lough Erne, Mount Gabriel).

Headwords consisting of the names of literary works in Irish up to about the eighteenth century are followed by an English translation, which is also used as an index entry (thus 'Colloquy of the Old Men' will be found in addition to 'Acallam na Senórach').

Authorship. All entries appear above the name of the author or joint authors, with the exception of statistical entries, which are institutionally credited.

Spelling of Irish names. Proper names from before c. 1200 are generally given in contemporary spelling (Acallam na Senórach, Táin Bó Cuailnge). Tribal names, placenames and mythical names whose use survived into historical times are generally given in Classical Irish spelling (Dál gCais, Maigh Breagha). Generic, technical, literary and folk terms are generally given in Modern Irish spelling (aonach, céilí Dé, Lúnasa, Samhain, tuath). Many exceptions were made to all patterns to accommodate individual names that are better known today in different spellings.

Placenames. The spelling of placenames is standardized according to the usage of the Ordnance Survey of Ireland, although this does not always correspond to the versions in use locally.

Cross-references. Cross-references to other entries by corresponding headword are given in SMALL CAPITALS. Cross-references to related illustrations are given to page numbers.

Terminology. The term 'Ireland' is used to refer to the entire thirty-two-county island, while 'the Irish Free State', 'the Republic of Ireland' and 'the Republic' refer specifically to the southern twenty-six-county state (which was known as the Irish Free State from 1922 to 1937). Under the new constitution adopted in that year, the name of the state was declared to be Éire or, in the English language, Ireland. From 1949 it has more commonly been called the Republic of Ireland. 'Northern Ireland' or 'the North' refer to the northern six-county area of Ulster, which is politically part of the United Kingdom. However, the use of 'Ireland' is neither so simple nor so easily contained. Entries that cover the period before and after 1922 frequently begin with 'Ireland' (referring to the entire island) but continue with 'the Republic', having narrowed the focus to the Southern state. 'Ireland' and 'Irish' have, depending on context, wide usages and occasionally appear when a more precise term would appear awkward.

Parallel or composite entries are generally given where parallel institutions or phenomena exist in both Northern Ireland and the Republic. Where the Northern Ireland situation is not specific to Northern Ireland but common to the United Kingdom, such references are omitted.

Index. There are two indexes at the end of the book. The subject index divides the headwords by topic, enabling the reader to locate related entries. Topics, events or individuals which might legitimately be found under more than one subject heading are, because of constraints of space, only given once, thus Michael Hartnett, whom the reader might expect to find under Literature in English as well as Literature in Irish, is only included in the first category, while Samuel Beckett appears in the Literature in English list, but not under Theatre. The general index will assist the reader in locating references. It lists the principal persons, places and events that are mentioned within entries but do not have their own headwords.

List of Abbreviations

ACNI	Arts Council of Northern Ireland
AOH	Ancient Order of Hibernians
BA	bachelor of arts
BBC	British Broadcasting Corporation
BMus	bachelor of music
BSc	bachelor of science
BSE	bovine spongiform encephalopathy ('mad cow disease')
c.	circa
CBS	Christian Brothers' School
CCÉ	Comhaltas Ceoltóirí Éireann
cd	candela
CEMA	Council for the Encouragement of Music and the Arts
CIE	Córas Iompair Éireann
Co.	County
Cos.	Counties
CSO	Central Statistics Office
cu. ft	cubic feet
DCU	Dublin City University
DIT	Dublin Institute of Technology
DMus	doctor of music
DSc	doctor of science
DUP	Democratic Unionist Party
DUTC	Dublin United Tramway Company (1896) Ltd
EEC	European Economic Community
EMU	European Monetary Union
ESB	Electricity Supply Board
EU	European Union
FÁS	Foras Áiseanna Saothair (Training and Employment Authority)
fl.	flourished
ft	feet
GDP	gross domestic product
GNP	gross national product
GPO	General Post Office
ha	hectares
Hon.	Honourable
hPa	hectopascal
in.	inches
INLA	Irish National Liberation Army
IRA	Irish Republican Army
IRB	Irish Republican Brotherhood
ITGWU	Irish Transport and General Workers' Union (now SIPTU)
km	kilometres
km^2	square kilometres
LittD	doctor of letters
LP	long-playing record
Ltd	Limited
m	metres
m^2	square metres
MA	master of arts
mbar	millibars
miles/h	miles per hour
mm	millimetres
MP	member of Parliament
m/s	metres per second
MSc	master of sciences
MScEcon	master of economic science
MusB	bachelor of music
MusD	doctor of music
NCAD	National College of Art and Design
NICRA	Northern Ireland Civil Rights Association
NIHE	National Institute of Higher Education
NUI	National University of Ireland
NUIG	National University of Ireland, Galway
NUIM	National University of Ireland, Maynooth
NUU	New University of Ulster (now University of Ulster)
OECD	Organisation for Economic Co-operation and Development
OPW	Office of Public Works
PhD	doctor of philosophy
PLC	Public Limited Company
Prof.	Professor
PSNI	Police Service of Northern Ireland (formerly Royal Ulster Constabulary)
QUB	Queen's University, Belfast
RAF	Royal Air Force
RBAI	Royal Belfast Academical Institution
RCSI	Royal College of Surgeons in Ireland
RDS	Royal Dublin Society
Rev.	Reverend
RHA	Royal Hibernian Academy of Arts
RIA	Royal Irish Academy
RIAI	Royal Institute of the Architects of Ireland
RIAM	Royal Irish Academy of Music
RIC	Royal Irish Constabulary
RTC	Regional Technical College
RTÉ	Radio-Telefís Éireann
RUC	Royal Ulster Constabulary (now Police Service of Northern Ireland)
RUI	Royal University of Ireland
SDLP	Social Democratic and Labour Party
SIPTU	Services, Industrial, Professional and Technical Union
sq. ft	square feet
sq. miles	square miles
SS.	Saints
St	Saint
TCD	Trinity College, Dublin (sole college of the University of Dublin)
TD	teachta Dála (member of Dáil Éireann)
Tta	Teoranta [Limited]
UCC	University College, Cork
UCD	University College, Dublin
UCG	University College, Galway (now National University of Ireland, Galway)
UDA	Ulster Defence Association
UN	United Nations
UNESCO	United Nations Educational, Scientific and Cultural Organisation
UTV	Ulster Television
UU	University of Ulster
UUP	Ulster Unionist Party
UVF	Ulster Volunteer Force
UWC	Ulster Workers' Council
VEC	Vocational Education Committee

IRELAND
POLITICAL
Airport
Ferry port
Ferry route
National park
Border
Railways
Main roads
Scotland
North Channel
Campbletown
Rathlin I.
Tory I.
Aran I.
Rathlin O'Birne I.
Achill I.
Clare I.
Inishbofin
Aran Is.
ATLANTIC OCEAN
Great Blasket I.
Skellig Rocks
Clear I.
Fastnet Rock
Celtic Sea
St. George's Channel
Irish Sea
Saltee Is.
Stranraer and Cairnyan
Liverpool
Holyhead and Isle of Man
Fishguard
Pembroke
Le Harve and Cherbourg
Swansea
Roscoff
NORTHERN IRELAND
Ulster
Connacht
Leinster
Munster
REPUBLIC OF IRELAND
DONEGAL
LONDONDERRY
ANTRIM
TYRONE
FERMANAGH
ARMAGH
DOWN
MONAGHAN
CAVAN
LOUTH
MEATH
DUBLIN
KILDARE
WICKLOW
CARLOW
WEXFORD
KILKENNY
LAOIS
OFFALY
WESTMEATH
LONGFORD
ROSCOMMON
LEITRIM
SLIGO
MAYO
GALWAY
CLARE
LIMERICK
TIPPERARY
WATERFORD
KERRY
CORK
Glenveagh National Park
Burren National Park
Wicklow Mts. National Park
Killarney National Park
Buncrana
Letterkenny
Lifford
Strabane
Derry/Londonderry
Portrush
Portstewart
Coleraine
Ballycastle
Ballymoney
Ballymena
Larne
Antrim
Bangor
BELFAST
Newtownards
Lisburn
Cookstown
Omagh
Dungannon
Donegal
Ballyshannon
Bundoran
Enniskillen
Portadown
Lurgan
Armagh
Banbridge
Downpatrick
Newcastle
Monaghan
Newry
Warrenpoint
Dundalk
Sligo
Ballina
Charlestown
Carrick-on-Shannon
Cavan
Ardee
Castlebar
Westport
Ballyhaunis
Castlerea
Longford
Kells
Drogheda
Claremorris
Ballinrobe
Navan
Balbriggan
Roscommon
Trim
Tuam
Mullingar
Athlone
DUBLIN
Dún Laoghaire
Bray
Galway
Ballinsloe
Tullamore
Newbridge
Kildare
Loughrea
Gort
Athy
Portlaoise
Wicklow
Ennistymon
Roscrea
Carlow
Arklow
Ennis
Nenagh
Gorey
Kilrush
Limerick
Thurles
Kilkenny
Foynes
Cashel
Newcastle West
Tipperary
Enniscorthy
Listowel
Clonmel
New Ross
Tralee
Ráth Luirc
Caher
Carrick on-Suir
Wexford
Rosslare
Dingle
Mitchelstown
Waterford
Tramore
Mallow
Fermoy
Killarney
Dungarvan
Cahersiveen
Macroom
Midleton
Youghal
Kenmare
Cork
Cobh
Bandon
Kinsale
Bantry
Clonakilty
Skibberkeen
9°
7°
55°
54°
53°
52°
N
0
40 km
40 miles

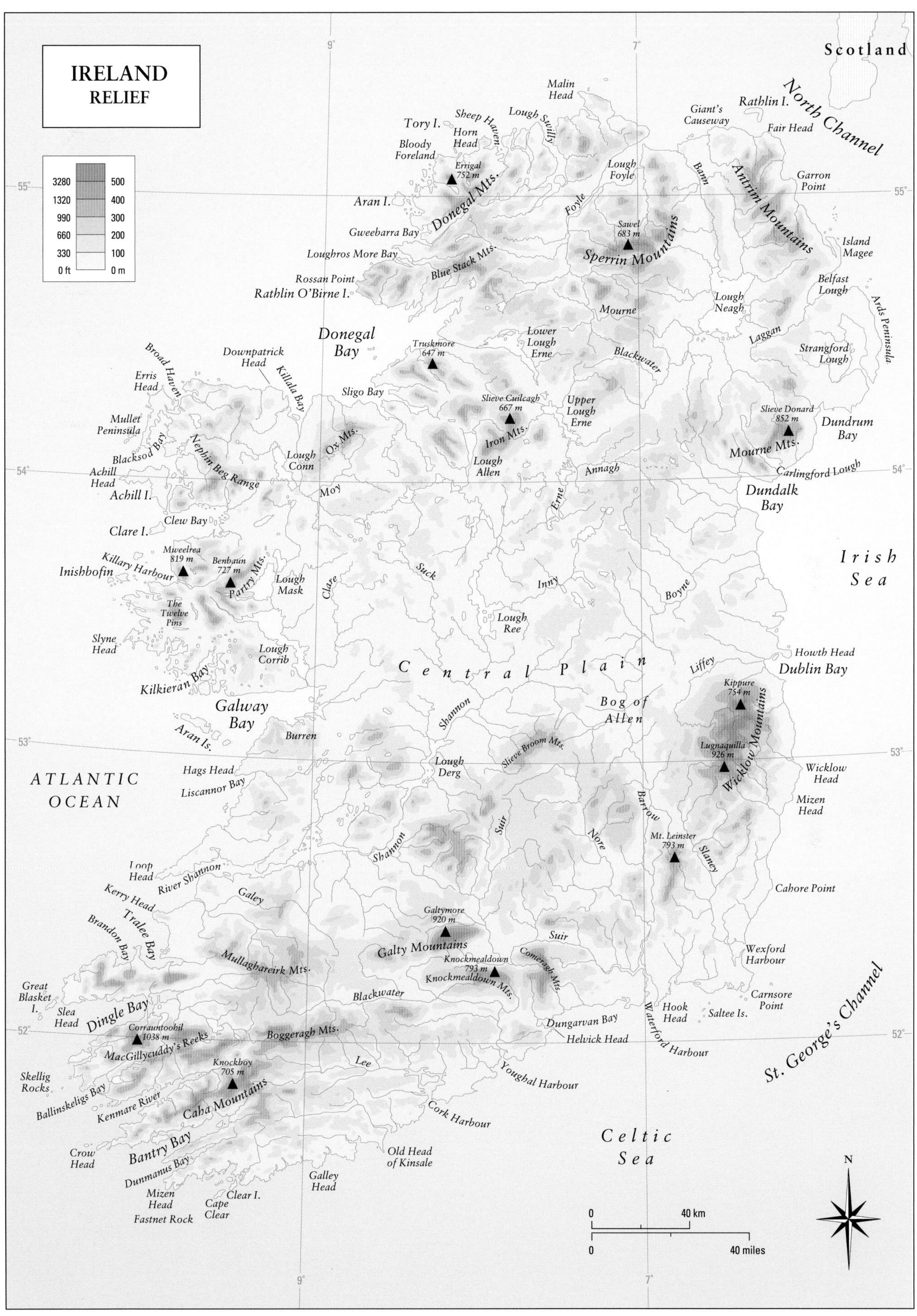
IRELAND
RELIEF
3280
1320
990
660
330
0 ft
500
400
300
200
100
0 m
Scotland
North Channel
Rathlin I.
Giant's Causeway
Fair Head
Malin Head
Lough Swilly
Sheep Haven
Tory I.
Horn Head
Bloody Foreland
Errigal 752 m
Donegal Mts.
Aran I.
Gweebarra Bay
Loughros More Bay
Blue Stack Mts.
Rossan Point
Rathlin O'Birne I.
Lough Foyle
Foyle
Bann
Antrim Mountains
Garron Point
Sawel 683 m
Sperrin Mountains
Island Magee
Belfast Lough
Ards Peninsula
Lough Neagh
Mourne
Laggan
Strangford Lough
Donegal Bay
Lower Lough Erne
Blackwater
Truskmore 647 m
Broad Haven
Erris Head
Downpatrick Head
Killala Bay
Sligo Bay
Slieve Cuilcagh 667 m
Upper Lough Erne
Slieve Donard 852 m
Dundrum Bay
Mullet Peninsula
Blacksod Bay
Nephin Beg Range
Ox Mts.
Iron Mts.
Mourne Mts.
Lough Conn
Lough Allen
Annagh
Carlingford Lough
Achill Head
Achill I.
Moy
Erne
Dundalk Bay
Clew Bay
Clare I.
Irish Sea
Mweelrea 819 m
Benbaun 727 m
Killary Harbour
Inishbofin
Partry Mts.
Lough Mask
Clare
Suck
Inny
Boyne
The Twelve Pins
Lough Ree
Slyne Head
Lough Corrib
Howth Head
Liffey
Dublin Bay
Central Plain
Kilkieran Bay
Bog of Allen
Kippure 754 m
Galway Bay
Shannon
Wicklow Mountains
Aran Is.
Burren
Slieve Bloom Mts.
Lugnaquilla 926 m
Lough Derg
Wicklow Head
ATLANTIC OCEAN
Hags Head
Liscannor Bay
Barrow
Mizen Head
Suir
Nore
Mt. Leinster 793 m
Shannon
Slaney
Loop Head
River Shannon
Cahore Point
Kerry Head
Galey
Tralee Bay
Brandon Bay
Galtymore 920 m
Suir
Galty Mountains
Mullaghareirk Mts.
Knockmealdown 793 m
Comeragh Mts.
Knockmealdown Mts.
Wexford Harbour
Great Blasket I.
Slea Head
Dingle Bay
Blackwater
Carnsore Point
Hook Head
Saltee Is.
St. George's Channel
Corrauntoohil 1038 m
Boggeragh Mts.
Dungarvan Bay
Helvick Head
Waterford Harbour
MacGillycuddy's Reeks
Lee
Knockboy 705 m
Skellig Rocks
Youghal Harbour
Ballinskeligs Bay
Kenmare River
Caha Mountains
Cork Harbour
Bantry Bay
Celtic Sea
Crow Head
Old Head of Kinsale
Dunmanus Bay
Galley Head
Clear I.
Mizen Head
Cape Clear
Fastnet Rock
0
40 km
0
40 miles
N
55°
54°
53°
52°
9°
7°

Aran Islands
(see page 37). Aerial view of Inishmore (Árainn), largest of the three Aran Islands, Co. Galway. Dunbeg promontory fort is in the foreground; the karstic terrain is continued at the Burren, Co. Clare. [Michael Diggin Photography]

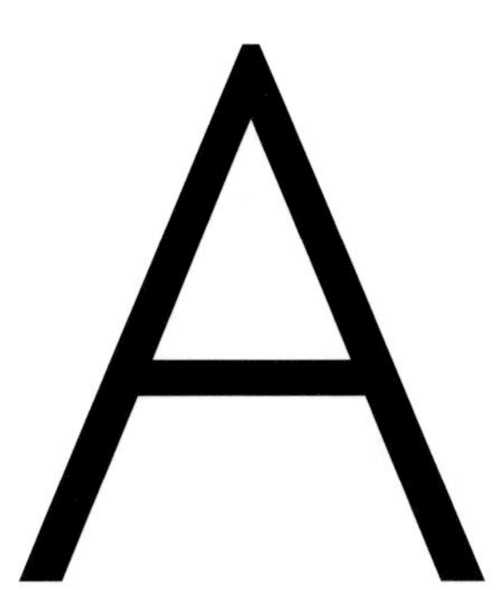

Abbeyknockmoy, Co. Galway, a Cistercian monastery founded by CATHAL CROBHDHEARG Ó CONCHÚIR in 1190. Substantial parts of the fabric remain and demonstrate close links with other abbeys in the west. Traces of late MEDIEVAL WALL PAINTINGS, depicting St Sebastian, a Crucifixion, a Trinity, and the three living and three dead, survive in the presbytery. **Rachel Moss**

abbeys. The introduction to Ireland of the Continental monastic orders, which began in the twelfth century with the CISTERCIANS, Benedictines, and Augustinian Canons, brought about a revolution in MONASTICISM and ecclesiastical architecture. Of these first arrivals the Cistercians, introduced to Ireland by St MALACHY, made the greatest impact. The first monastery was founded at MELLIFONT, Co. Louth, in 1142; by 1228 thirty-four had been established, enjoying either an Irish or an Anglo-Norman patronage.

Cistercian architecture embodied the ideals of the order. The rural simplicity of the monks' way of life was reflected in their architecture, which in theory at least was utilitarian and free from superfluous ornament. As the needs of all Cistercians throughout Europe were more or less the same, the same architectural formula was adopted, in a rational, integrated scheme. Various buildings were grouped around a cloister. The church had a short presbytery, adequate for the simple liturgical requirements of the brethren, and transepts were accommodated with small chapels for private prayer. The nave usually had aisles and was divided approximately in the middle by a screen to separate the monks from the lay brothers. Grouped around the other sides of the cloister were, to the east, the chapter-house, with dormitories above, sometimes linked to the south transept by a night stair. To the south were the refectory and kitchen, and along the west the lay brothers' quarters.

The architecture of the Augustinian Canons was more varied. Many of their earliest foundations were at the site of early Irish monasteries, such as Glendalough, Co. Wicklow, and MOLANA ABBEY, Co. Waterford, and some appear to have made use of existing buildings. A number of early thirteenth-century foundations, including ATHASSEL, Co. Tipperary, BALLINTOBER, Co. Mayo, and Kells, Co. Kilkenny, adopted the general Cistercian model of cruciform church with southern cloister but with some adjustments to suit the particular needs of the community and the site.

The construction of so many large-scale religious houses required organised teams of masons. While there is some evidence that monks oversaw the work, the building itself was carried out by teams of professionals. The same group of sculptors can be traced working at the Cistercian houses of Boyle and ABBEYKNOCKMOY, Co. Galway, for the Augustinians at Cong, Co. Mayo, and Ballintober, and for the cathedral at CLONFERT, Co. Galway (see p. 909).

The Franciscan and Dominican orders, both introduced in the earlier part of the thirteenth century, also made a significant impact on Irish monastic architecture. As preaching orders, dependent on alms, both orders established themselves principally in towns and Anglo-Norman boroughs. The buildings of these mendicant orders, called *friaries*, vary but have a number of characteristic features. Churches were usually divided into two distinct parts: a choir, often quite long, for the friars, and a nave for the laity. From the fourteenth century a central tower generally marked the division. Franciscan towers are characterised by their tall, slender proportions, resting on arches of narrow span, which gave the effect of a tunnel separating nave from choir. As lay congregations expanded, an aisle and sometimes a transept were added to the nave. In the Franciscan friaries this was usually on the south side, as—contrary to Cistercian tradition—domestic ranges were built around a northern cloister.

From the early fourteenth century the Cistercian order went into decline, and construction work was restricted to repairs and rebuilding. In the fifteenth century towers were a particular focus of attention, being built or rebuilt at a number of abbeys, such as TINTERN, Co. Wexford, and JERPOINT, Co. Kilkenny. Extensive rebuilding was undertaken at HOLYCROSS and at Kilcooley, Co. Tipperary. Some of the finest architectural sculpture of the period is found in this work, prime examples being the cloister at Jerpoint, the *sedilia* (altar seats) at Holycross, and the screen at Kilcooley.

The mendicant friars undertook the most prolific building activity in the later Middle Ages. Between 1349 and 1539 sixty new friaries were constructed and forty-four houses of the Third Order, which lived under a less strict rule. Friaries were often built in a piecemeal fashion, as funds became available. On the whole, the architecture is quite plain, and decorative details such as window tracery are simple, particularly compared with contemporary developments in England.

Most of the furniture and decoration of Irish medieval abbeys has been lost. Traces of wall-painting at Clare Abbey, Co. Galway, Abbeyknockmoy, and Holycross suggest that interior walls were decorated with a mixture of religious and secular scenes of varying quality. Decorated floor tiles and fragments of STAINED GLASS have also been recovered from a number of sites. A number of high-quality medieval tombs are preserved, generally commemorating the abbey or friary's patrons. **Rachel Moss**

Abbey Theatre, Dublin. In 1899 W. B. YEATS, LADY GREGORY, and EDWARD MARTYN founded the Irish Literary Theatre, to 'show that Ireland is the home of an ancient idealism.' Their first production, Yeats's THE COUNTESS CATHLEEN, staged in Dublin on 8 May 1899, was an instant *cause célèbre* (see p. 1045). Over the next few years the company staged new plays in various Dublin venues, joining forces in 1902 with two actors, FRANK FAY and Willie Fay, whose production of *Cathleen Ni Houlihan* (credited to Yeats) created an influential parable of self-sacrifice. Renamed the National Theatre Society, the company moved in 1904 to a converted music hall, the former Mechanics' Institute in Abbey Street, Dublin, funded by Yeats's patron Annie E. F. Horniman.

Designed by JOSEPH HOLLOWAY, the Abbey Theatre accommodated 565 patrons in an auditorium with a single balcony facing a small proscenium stage roughly 6 m (20 ft) square. On this stage performers such as SARA ALLGOOD and the FAYS presented fifty-five

Abbey Theatre. *Scene from W. B. Yeats'* The Shadowy Waters, *first performed by the Irish National Theatre Society at the Molesworth Hall, Dublin, 14 January 1904, with Frank Fay as Forgael (bottom left), a role he repeated at the Abbey Theatre, 8 December 1906. The photograph is from Yeats' Abbey Scrapbooks arranged by Lady Gregory. [Council of Trustees of the National Library of Ireland, Ms 19, 844]*

new plays in the period 1904–10, including all of JOHN MILLINGTON SYNGE's work, Yeats's *On Baile's Strand* (1904), and Lady Gregory's *The Rising of the Moon* (1907). Such was the passion attached to the Abbey in those years that Synge's PLAYBOY OF THE WESTERN WORLD (1907) provoked riots with its darkly grotesque view of rural life. Nonetheless there was internal conflict. Most of the original actors had departed by 1910, feeling that the nationalist impulses of *Cathleen Ni Houlihan* had been sacrificed; ironically, Annie Horniman felt that the theatre had become too nationalist, and she withdrew her subsidy in 1910.

In the following decade the running of the Abbey fell largely to Lady Gregory and LENNOX ROBINSON, whose comedy *The Whiteheaded Boy* (1916) was to prove a favourite with audiences. While the Abbey continued to nurture good actors—including F. J. MCCORMICK and RIA MOONEY—it did not find a playwright of Synge's calibre until it staged SEAN O'CASEY's ABBEY TRILOGY, *The Shadow of a Gunman* (1923), *Juno and the Paycock* (1924), and *The Plough and the Stars* (1926). Like Synge's *Playboy*, O'Casey's *Plough and the Stars* provoked a series of riots; and, like Synge's *Playboy*, it quickly settled into the Abbey repertoire after the riots had died down, becoming one of the theatre's most frequently performed plays.

Indeed respectability became one of the Abbey's biggest challenges, particularly after it was granted a Government subsidy in 1926. The situation worsened from 1941 when, after a series of vicious internecine battles in the 1930s, ERNEST BLYTHE became managing director. By this time all the Abbey's original founders were dead, and Blythe became committed to a policy of long runs, which limited the number of new plays. When the original Abbey Theatre burnt down in 1951 and the company moved into the QUEEN'S ROYAL THEATRE, Lennox Robinson remarked that the Abbey 'was like a knife that had had six new blades and five new handles and still called itself the same knife.'

The Abbey company remained at the Queen's until 1966, when a new theatre, designed by MICHAEL SCOTT, opened on the original site. The 1966 Abbey has a fan-shaped 628-seat auditorium facing a wide 12 m (40-ft) stage, with a fly system, hydraulic stage traps, and a computerised lighting system. Tucked under the lobby is the Peacock, a smaller, flexible theatre that can be used as either a proscenium or thrust stage. With these exciting new premises, the emergence of a new generation of playwrights, and Blythe's eventual retirement, the modern Abbey Theatre began to take shape.

With the changes came new structures. The post-1966 Abbey has been defined by the position of artistic director, initiated by Hugh Hunt, 1970–71, and subsequently held by Lelia Doolan, 1971–2, TOMÁS MAC ANNA, 1972–8 and 1984–5, JOE DOWLING, 1978–84, and later GARRY HYNES, 1991–4, PATRICK MASON, 1994–9, and Ben Barnes (1999–). Though the Abbey continues to nurture new playwrights (particularly in the Peacock), it is increasingly a director's theatre, and this has resulted in a steady rise in production values. Indeed by the end of the twentieth century there was a widespread feeling that the Abbey had outgrown its 1966 building, and plans were being discussed for a replacement to allow a further development of the theatre's repertoire. **Christopher Morash**

Abbey Trilogy, three plays by SEAN O'CASEY set in the Dublin tenements and criticising the alleged betrayal of working-class experience in the heroic events of the national independence movement, 1916–22. Davoren, a poet who acts the part of an IRA fugitive, is the anti-hero of *The Shadow of a Gunman* (1923), a two-act tragedy set during the Anglo-Irish War and O'Casey's first Abbey production. *Juno and the Paycock* (1924)—the most popular play in the theatre's twenty-year history—tells the story of the Boyle family during the Civil War, while *The Plough and the Stars* (1926) provoked riots in protest against its satire of the 1916 Rising. **Selina Guinness**

Abbey Trilogy. *Flag of the Irish Citizen Army, based on the Plough constellation (Ursa Major) and suggesting the injunction from Isaiah 'They shall beat their swords into ploughshares ...' The flag provided Sean O'Casey with the title for his play* The Plough and the Stars. *[National Museum of Ireland]*

Abbott, Thomas Kingsmill (1829–1913), clergyman, philosopher, and polymath. Born in Dublin; educated at TCD. He was successively professor of moral philosophy, of Biblical Greek and of Hebrew at TCD and eventually became college librarian. He is perhaps best known for his *Elements of Logic* (1895); he also translated Kant's logical and ethical writings and wrote a critique of BERKELEY's theory of vision. **Ian Leask**

A, B, C Specials (Ulster Special Constabulary), 1920–70. The Ulster Special Constabulary was formed in October 1920 as the British government's response to unionist demands for an auxiliary police force to safeguard Ulster (in practice the six north-eastern counties) against IRA attacks. In September 1920 Sir JAMES CRAIG, the future Prime Minister of Northern Ireland and a junior minister in the Lloyd George coalition, pressed the Cabinet to place the pre-war ULSTER VOLUNTEER FORCE on an official footing to 'curb rebel influences' in the six counties earmarked for partition under the Government of Ireland Bill (1920). The idea won the support of LLOYD GEORGE and Winston Churchill but was opposed by General Macready, commander of British forces in Ireland, and DUBLIN CASTLE officials, who feared an increase in sectarian violence. The new force consisted of three sections: a full-time elite A section, a part-time B section, and an unpaid C reserve force, with 5,500, 19,000 and 7,500 members, respectively. It was financed and equipped by the British government and placed under the control of the ROYAL IRISH CONSTABULARY. Its deployment during the period 1920–22 provided UNIONISM with its own territorial militia for repelling IRA attacks, facilitating the partitioning of Ireland. It was viewed by nationalists as viciously sectarian; but efforts under the

CRAIG–COLLINS PACT of March 1922 to broaden it to include Catholics failed, because of IRA violence and unionist intractability.

With the confirmation of the BORDER in 1925, the A and C sections were disbanded but the B Specials continued as a part-time reserve force and played a decisive part in defeating the IRA BORDER CAMPAIGN of 1956–62. The 'B men' were regarded with suspicion by nationalists in Northern Ireland, and the abolition of the force was a central demand of the CIVIL RIGHTS MOVEMENT in the late 1960s. Finally, in 1970, as a result of the HUNT COMMITTEE Report, the force was disbanded and replaced with a new part-time security force, this time under British military control, the ULSTER DEFENCE REGIMENT. **Eamon Phoenix**

abduction of heiresses. The abduction and forced MARRIAGE of women of fortune emerged as a feature of Irish life in the late seventeenth century. Perpetrated by men of modest means, many of whom were Catholics, it was considered a particularly reprehensible offence by the Protestant authorities, who made it a capital offence in 1707. This little inhibited the practice, but changing social mores and the more ready recourse to the death penalty in the 1780s hastened its decline. [see HAYES, HENRY BROWN.] **James Kelly**

abortion, law of. Under the CONSTITUTION OF IRELAND (article 40.3.3), 'the State acknowledges the right to life of the unborn and, with due regard to the equal right to life of the mother guarantees... to defend and vindicate that right.' Because of the lack of abortion facilities, and despite the legal ban on such abortions by the Offences Against the Person Act (1861), at least 6,000 Irish women annually travel abroad—mainly to England—to have an abortion. In *Attorney-General v. X* (1992) the state sought to prevent an allegedly suicidal fourteen-year-old girl, pregnant as a result of rape, from travelling abroad to have an abortion. The SUPREME COURT ruled that a woman was entitled to an abortion in Ireland where her pregnancy posed a real and substantial risk to her life (as distinct from her health), including the risk of suicide. In November 1992 two amendments were made to article 40.3.3 with regard to abortion, guaranteeing a woman's right to travel and her right to information (the latter subject to Government regulation). In March 2002, a proposed amendment to article 40.3.3 was rejected by the people; the amendment would have had the effect of introducing into Irish law a criminal statute in respect of abortion, and would have removed the maternal suicide justification for abortion.

In Northern Ireland also abortion law is still governed by the Offences Against the Person Act (1861) but is interpreted by the courts as allowing for lawful abortion where there is a risk to the life or the physical or mental health or well-being of the mother, where the pregnancy is the result of rape or incest, where the woman is HIV-positive, or where there is a severe case of fetal abnormality. [see 'X' CASE; 'C' CASE.] **Neville Cox**

abortion referendums. Abortion in the Republic is proscribed under sections 58 and 59 of the Offences Against the Person Act (1861). After a successful campaign by the pro-life lobby, an amendment prohibiting abortion, article 40.3.3, was inserted in the CONSTITUTION OF IRELAND in 1983, which declares: 'The State acknowledges the right to life of the unborn and, with due regard to the equal right to life of the mother, guarantees in its laws to respect and, as far as practicable, by its laws to defend and vindicate that right.' In the 'X' CASE, in 1992, the SUPREME COURT ruled that a sexually abused teenager could go abroad for an abortion, because she had suicidal intentions as a result of her pregnancy (see p. 1155). A combination of this judgment and the Treaty of Maastricht precipitated three related referendums in 1995. Amendments to the Constitution that guaranteed the freedom to travel (so that one could avail of abortion in other member-states of the European Union) and the provision of information on abortion were passed; but a reformulation of article 40.3.3 was rejected. In 1995 the Regulation of Information (Services Outside the State for Termination of Pregnancies) Act (1995) was enacted. In that year a government-sponsored study on crisis pregnancies and abortions estimated an abortion rate of 5.6 per 1,000 women aged between fifteen and forty-four normally resident in the Republic. A Green Paper presenting seven possible legislative options, from an absolute constitutional ban on abortion to abortion on demand, was published in 1998, but the Oireachtas sub-committee failed to reach a consensus on the issue. The Government put the Twenty-Fifth Amendment of the Constitution Bill to the electorate on 6 March, which proposed overruling the Supreme Court judgment on the suicide issue in addition to legalising certain medical practices to safeguard the life of pregnant women, but this amendment was narrowly rejected. A further referendum in 2002, which proposed removing the threat of suicide as grounds for abortion, was rejected by the electorate.

In Northern Ireland abortion is subject to the Offences Against the Person Act (1861), as the (British) Abortion Act (1967) does not apply there. The courts have made a number of judgments permitting abortion where the continuation of the pregnancy would adversely affect the physical or mental health of the mother, and so a limited number of abortions are carried out there; women who seek abortions on other grounds travel to England. **Evelyn Mahon**

a Búrc, Éamon (1866–1942), tailor and storyteller. Born in Carna, Co. Galway; lived in America for part of his childhood. He was perhaps the finest storyteller collected from in the twentieth century. The longest folk-tale ever recorded in Ireland—taking three nights to tell and amounting to more than 30,000 words—was collected from him. **Mícheál Briody**

'Acallamh na Senórach' ('The Colloquy of the Old Men'), the longest and most impressive work of the FIONN CYCLE, dating from c. 1200. It consists of a *frame tale* in which more than 160 anecdotes in prose and verse about Fionn and the Fianna are accommodated; some ecclesiastical lore is also found in it. The old men of the title—Caoilte, the narrator, and OISÍN—survived the alleged destruction of the Fianna in the third century. They meet St PATRICK, who converts them to Christianity; Caoilte journeys with the saint and others throughout Ireland and narrates the legendary lore of places visited by them. **Máirtín Ó Briain**

accordion. The accordion has been played in Ireland since the middle of the nineteenth century, when it first arrived in the form of a one-row, ten-button diatonic instrument. By the turn of the century it had become known as the melodeon. Played in the 'push and draw' style, its adoption into Irish TRADITIONAL MUSIC coincided with the decline of the pipes and the spread of SET-DANCING.

By the late 1920s fully chromatic two-row accordions were common in traditional music; by the 1930s instruments pitched in keys of C/C sharp, C sharp/D, D/D sharp and G/G sharp were available. The addition of the second row of buttons allowed previous 'press and draw' players to play mainly on the inside row but to move to the outside row for semitones, such as C natural and F natural. In America the 'outside in' system was popular, with the Boston accordion-player Joe Derrane being one of the best-known exponents of that system. The 'push and draw' style was especially favoured by dancers because of the staccato, bouncy phrasing achieved through the alternate pressing and drawing of the bellows.

JOE COOLEY and PADDY O'BRIEN became two of the most highly regarded players of the accordion in traditional music during the 1950s. Cooley played the 'push and draw' style on a D/D sharp accordion, while O'Brien is credited with popularising the B and C style of playing. He developed a system that did not require much bellows work and so allowed the player to play smoothly across the rows in a more legato style.

The piano-accordion has been played in Ireland for many years but never acquired the same popularity in traditional music circles as the button accordion and is still not favoured among musicians. The powerful volume and consistency of accordions during the 1950s and 60s ensured that they were commonly used in céilí and marching bands, particularly in Northern counties (see p. 1074). **Máire O'Keeffe**

'ac Dhonncha, Seán (1919–1996), traditional singer. Born in Carna, Co. Galway; won a scholarship to Coláiste Éinde and qualified as a primary teacher in 1940. He taught in Co. Cavan from 1947 and spent twenty-five years as principal teacher in Ahascragh National School near Ballinasloe. He was the first traditional singer to record on the Gael-Linn label, won a gold medal at the 1953 OIREACHTAS, and was awarded Gradam Shean-Nós Cois Life in 1995. On his seventy-fifth birthday in 1994 Cló Iar-Chonnachta issued a CD selection of his songs in Irish and English, *Seán 'ac Dhonncha: An Spailpín Fánach*. **Liam Mac Con Iomaire**

Achill Island, Co. Mayo, the largest Irish island, with an area of 144 km² (56 sq. miles). The island rises to 672 m (2,200 ft) at Slievemore. The traditional economy was based on farming, principally pastoralism, and fishing. In 1834 Protestant evangelists, led by EDWARD NANGLE, set up a missionary settlement at Dugort. Another historic settlement is the deserted village of Slievemore on the flanks of the mountain. Achill's population (4,901 in 1841, before the GREAT FAMINE) remained high (4,825 in 1901), the pressure being relieved by seasonal MIGRATION. Achill 'tatie-hookers' (migratory POTATO-diggers) were once an important labour element of Scottish potato-harvesting. In 1892 thirty-two of them were drowned while leaving the island; in 1937 another ten died in a fire in Scotland. The island, which had a population of 1,692 in 2002, retains some farming and fishing but is also an important tourist destination. It was connected to the mainland by a bridge in 1886. [see MIGRATORY LABOUR.] **Stephen A. Royle**

acting and performance. Since 1700, Ireland has produced a significant number of the leading performers in the English-language theatre. It could be argued that a society in which the future has often been uncertain produces people capable of chameleon-like transformation and the ability to improvise; equally, it has long been observed that Irish culture places a high value on the dexterous use of the spoken word. There is no doubt an element of truth in both these explanations; however, the sustained success of Irish actors over so many diverse historical periods defies any single cultural explanation.

Robert Wilks (1665–1732), who began his acting career in the SMOCK ALLEY THEATRE, Dublin, was the first Irish actor to make an impact, later becoming joint manager of the Drury Lane Theatre, London. He was followed by James Quin (1693–1766), a leading tragic actor with a resounding, declamatory style; Henry Mossop

abortion. *A 'Youth for Choice' demonstration outside the entrance to St Stephen's Green, Dublin, 1992. Since the 1992 referendum, abortion is legal in Ireland when a pregnancy poses a real and substantial risk to the life of the mother, though the 2002 referendum attempted unsuccessfully to reverse this decision. [Derek Speirs/Report]*

(1729–1774); SPRANGER BARRY; and PEG WOFFINGTON. More lasting was the influence of THOMAS SHERIDAN, who introduced the important innovation of banning spectators from sitting on the stage, while his contemporary CHARLES MACKLIN was instrumental in introducing a more naturalistic style of acting with his playing of Shylock in 1741.

Irish contribution to the English stage continued through the nineteenth century with the great Shakespearian actor Barry Sullivan (1821–1891). As plays with an Irish theme became more common it became possible for Irish actors, including TYRONE POWER and later DION BOUCICAULT, to specialise in Irish roles. The broad comic acting style of Power and Boucicault relied on frequent asides to the audience, which made the cavernous theatres of the period seem intimate. Acting in much smaller venues, the original ABBEY THEATRE actors were able to develop a very different style of performance, characterised by stillness and an incantatory manner of speaking. This characteristic Abbey style was nurtured by the company's leading actors, FRANK FAY and W. G. Fay and exemplified by SARA ALLGOOD. However, by 1920, as actors such as BARRY FITZGERALD, F. J. MCCORMICK and RIA MOONEY began to join the company from more expansive performance backgrounds, the Abbey style became less subtle, fusing the more traditional techniques of playing to the audience with the restrained movement of the early Abbey. This new hybrid style was used to particular effect in the early plays of SEAN O'CASEY, such as *Juno and the Paycock* (1924).

When HILTON EDWARDS and MÍCHEÁL MAC LIAMMÓIR founded the GATE THEATRE, Dublin, in 1928 they developed a much more self-conscious, mannered style of performance than was common at the Abbey. However, they were in many ways the exception to the rule, as Irish acting throughout the middle years of the twentieth century was characterised by a lack of affectation, typified by SIOBHÁN MCKENNA's memorable performances as St Joan (1954). There was one obvious reason why Irish actors often seemed natural: almost no formal training was available until the final decades of the twentieth century. CYRIL CUSACK, for instance, learnt his craft by acting in travelling companies from a very early age. Most professional actors simply began working with amateur or university companies, before moving on to professional roles. There were a few exceptions, the Abbey School of Acting and, notably, the heroic (and tiny) Focus Theatre in Dublin, a Stanislavski training studio responsible for training GABRIEL BYRNE (1950–) and Tom Hickey (1948–), among others. The principal change in the formation of actors did not take place until the 1980s, when the Gaiety School of Acting (1986–) opened and TRINITY COLLEGE, Dublin, introduced an actor training course (1984–). Most young actors now have some amount of formal training. Meanwhile the number of Irish performers with an international reputation remains disproportionately high, exemplified in the present generation by FIONA SHAW and KENNETH BRANAGH. **Christopher Morash**

Act of Union. The Union Club *(1801), an annotated, hand-coloured engraving by James Gillray. Opponents of the Act of Union (some with shamrock on their hats) drown their sorrows; the Prince of Wales lies supine beneath the table; Lord Moira (in green coat) sits above him, with Richard Brinsley Sheridan holding a bottle aloft behind Moira; Charles James Fox slumps in the left foreground. [National Gallery of Ireland]*

Adams. *Gerry Adams, MP for West Belfast since 1983, addressing a press conference outside the Sinn Féin offices in Belfast. The republican mural (left) is an essential element of political dialogue in Northern Ireland. [Derek Speirs/Report]*

Act of Union (1800). Following the 1798 REBELLION the British government decided to abolish the Irish Parliament, concentrating parliamentary representation through legislative union in Westminster, but maintained Dublin Castle as the seat of government in Ireland. An initial attempt to pass the Union failed in 1799, but through the ruthless use of patronage, bribery, and intimidation it succeeded in 1800. Skilfully directed through the House of Commons by the CHIEF SECRETARY FOR IRELAND, CASTLEREAGH, the Union came into effect on 1 January 1801, creating the United Kingdom of Great Britain and Ireland. When George III refused to accompany the measure with CATHOLIC EMANCIPATION the British Prime Minister, WILLIAM PITT, and other leading politicians, including Castlereagh, resigned in protest. After 1801 the main political issues in Ireland were Emancipation and Repeal of the Union. The former was achieved in 1829, but Repeal proved far more difficult. Various attempts to secure home rule failed, and it was only with the ANGLO-IRISH TREATY of 1922 that it ceased to apply to what is now the Republic; the Union still connects Great Britain and Northern Ireland. **Patrick Geoghegan**

Acton, Charles (1914–1999), music critic and activist. Born near Bristol of a Co. Wicklow family; studied natural sciences without taking a degree at Cambridge, where he wrote music reviews with BRIAN BOYDELL for *Varsity Weekly*. Later he was a founder of the DUBLIN ORCHESTRAL PLAYERS. In 1955, after several business ventures, he succeeded A. J. POTTER as music critic of the *Irish Times* (retiring in 1987), a position in which he was centrally influential in the public perception of music-making in Ireland, receiving the inaugural Seán O'Boyle Award in 1986 for his services to Irish music. He wrote more than 6,000 reviews, articles, and interviews, including contributions to *Éire-Ireland*, where he conducted a seminal public debate with SEÁN Ó RIADA on the relation of the 'classical' and 'traditional' music genres. A governor of the RIAM from 1954 (receiving a fellowship in 1990 and becoming vice-president in 1998), he was joint editor with RICHARD PINE of the official history of the academy, *To Talent Alone* (1998). **Paul J. Kerr and Richard Pine**

Adams, Gerard (Gerry) (1948–), politician. Born into a republican family in west Belfast; educated by the CHRISTIAN BROTHERS, becoming a barman at seventeen. Radicalised by the Divis Street riots during the 1964 general election campaign, he joined SINN FÉIN and in 1967 the Northern Ireland Civil Rights Association. Following a split in the republican movement in 1970 he aligned himself with the militant Provisional wing. He was interned in March 1972 but dramatically released in June to take part in secret but abortive talks in London between an IRA delegation and the Secretary of State for Northern Ireland, William Whitelaw. Following the failure of these talks he played a central role in planning the bomb blitz on Belfast known as BLOODY FRIDAY. He played an important policy-making role during the HUNGER STRIKES of 1981, which saw the emergence of his party as a political force.

In 1983 he was elected president of Sinn Féin and abstentionist MP for West Belfast, unseating the former SDLP leader GERRY FITT. Though badly wounded by loyalists in Belfast in 1984, he steadily pushed Sinn Féin towards greater political participation, overthrowing the Southern 'old guard' and paving the way for recognition of Dáil Éireann in 1986 and the Hume–Adams dialogue of 1988–94. This led directly to the first IRA ceasefire of 1994. Following the reinstatement of the ceasefire in July 1997, Adams took part in the all-party talks that resulted in the BELFAST AGREEMENT (1998). Sinn Féin won a record 17.5 per cent of the vote in the subsequent Assembly elections, and Adams steered his party into the new power-sharing Executive in 1999, while declining a post himself. Since 1996 he has sought to raise Sinn Féin's political profile in the Republic while insisting that IRA decommissioning and British demilitarisation must go hand in hand. **Eamon Phoenix**

Adeney, Walter Ernest (1857–1935), scientist. Studied chemistry at the ROYAL COLLEGE OF SCIENCE FOR IRELAND. In 1887 he was appointed to the Royal University of Ireland. He ultimately became professor of chemistry in the National University. His early research was with WALTER HARTLEY on the wavelengths of lines of refrangibility in the spectra of elementary substances. Thereafter he moved to applied science, considering in particular problems arising from the discharge of sewage and waste products into rivers and tidal estuaries. He associatively conducted with H. G. Becker classical investigations of the absolute rate of aeration of water. He was awarded the Mullins Gold Medal (1896) and an honorary DSc (1897). He retired from the university in 1923 and was awarded the BOYLE MEDAL in 1928. **Susan McKenna-Lawlor**

administrative divisions, created by state or church to facilitate particular functions. Most were adapted from older territorial units, which had evolved for quite different purposes

Ireland is divided into four historical *provinces*—CONNACHT, LEINSTER, MUNSTER, and ULSTER—a simplified legacy of more complex divisions that existed up to a thousand years ago. These were divisions of the country among dominant population groups at an early stage in history, broadly coinciding with significant environmental regions, Ulster being separated from the midlands by the drumlin hills and lakelands, Connacht from Leinster by the River SHANNON. Modifications were made in the twelfth century: Co. Clare was transferred from Munster to Connacht, Co. Cavan from Connacht to Ulster, and Co. Louth from Ulster to Leinster. The names of Ulster, Leinster, and Munster are NORSE constructions on top of the Irish names: *Ulaidh* or *Cúige Uladh* ('the fifth of the men of Ulaidh'), *Laighin* or *Cúige Laighean*, and *an Mhumhain* or *Cúige Mumhan*; the Irish term *cúige* (literally 'fifth') is evidence of the probable existence of *Midhe* or Meath as a provincial territory. *Tír* (Irish for 'territory') was added by the Norse to make *Laighinster*, etc.

Counties, of which there are thirty-two, are the territorial units of primary social and economic significance today. They were first established by the ANGLO-NORMANS and the English as an arm of LOCAL GOVERNMENT, in most instances based on existing Irish lordships. Most of the counties in Leinster and Munster had been created by the Normans by the thirteenth century; English governments of the sixteenth and seventeenth centuries created the remainder, including Queen's County (Laois) and King's County (Offaly) and the modern counties of Ulster. The administrative importance of the counties was enhanced with the establishment of county councils in 1898; their social and cultural significance was bolstered by their use by the GAELIC ATHLETIC ASSOCIATION from the late nineteenth century.

Baronies, of which there are 324, emerged under the Anglo-Normans as convenient administrative and landholding units between the county and the parish. By the eighteenth century county GRAND JURIES were managed by barony, and in the nineteenth century the principal censuses and valuations were also administered by barony. These functions were subsequently taken over by the newly created county councils.

Rural districts were sub-divisions of counties created in 1898, based on the earlier *poor law unions*, created to administer the POOR LAW. They consisted of aggregates of *district electoral divisions* (DEDs), designed to elect members to the Board of Guardians of workhouses. DEDs continue in use as statistical and data-collection units.

Parishes are territorial units used by church authorities for the religious and fiscal administration of their congregations; they have an enduring social and cultural significance, especially in rural areas. The older medieval units continue in the jurisdiction of the CHURCH OF IRELAND, mostly in unions of parishes. Catholic parishes were formed separately after the eighteenth-century PENAL LAWS, though many are based on the older medieval units. As *civil parishes*, of which there are 2,420, the traditional parishes were used as a vehicle of local government in the eighteenth and nineteenth centuries.

Townlands, of which there are more than 63,000, are the smallest territorial units, averaging 132 ha (326 acres) in area. Originating in early medieval Ireland as basic farmholdings, they have largely survived as an important element of the rural landscape and community and continue to be used as postal addresses and in the census of population. [see ANGLO-NORMAN AND ENGLISH ADMINISTRATION IN IRELAND; BOROUGHS; PARLIAMENT 1200–1700; PARLIAMENT 1692–1800.] **Patrick Duffy**

Adomnán (c. 628–704), abbot and scholar, patron of the diocese of Raphoe. He came from the same Donegal family as COLM CILLE and was IONA's ninth abbot (679–704). He is best remembered today for his life of Colm Cille (see p. 1113), a major source for the history of IONA and of insular MONASTICISM; its account of royal anointing influenced the development of kingship in Europe. His other book, *De Locis Sanctis* ('On the holy places'), deals with places mentioned in the Scriptures. Posing as the account of a pilgrim 'Gallic bishop', Arculf (in addition to what Adomnán knew from books), it is a complex manual for solving exegetical problems using geographical knowledge. Among the many attempts to reconcile such conflicting statements, his is one of the most competent and original in method. His medieval reputation as a scholar rested on this work, and he was one of the few Irish writers who were labelled 'illustrious'. It was one of the first early Irish works in manuscript.

Adomnán's diplomatic and legal work is less well known. His interest in mitigating the effects of war took him to Northumbria on behalf of Irish captives, and he was a central figure at the Synod of Birr (697), which produced the *Lex Innocentium*, his *Cáin* for the protection of women, children, and other non-combatants. In church law he is credited with a series of *Canones* and he is the most recent named authority in some recensions of the *Collectio Canonum Hibernensis*; he possibly had a role in its creation. He also took part in the EASTER CONTROVERSY; but his scholarly legacy is the role he played in the growth of the medieval propositional approach to Scripture. **Thomas O'Loughlin**

adoption, a process whereby a child is incorporated in a new FAMILY, severing all legal connections with the natural parents, whose rights and duties towards the child are extinguished. Legal adoption was introduced originally to deal with the dual issue of infertility and the stigma of unmarried parenthood. However, because of the increased social acceptance of non-married parenthood and the financial supports for single parents, there has been a marked decrease in the availability of babies for adoption. Consequently there has been an increase in inter-country adoption, and the adoption of older children.

Adoption in the Republic was first introduced by the Adoption Act (1952) and in Northern Ireland by the Adoption of Children Act (Northern Ireland) (1929). Both jurisdictions are signatories of the Hague Convention on the Protection of Children and Co-operation in Respect of Inter-Country Adoption. Under the Adoption Act (1952), the Adoption Board is responsible for the regulation of adoption societies and the overseeing and granting of adoption orders. In Northern Ireland, under the Adoption (Northern Ireland) Order (1987), jurisdiction for granting adoption orders lies with the county courts and the High Court. Legislation in both jurisdictions lays down the criteria for eligibility to adopt and for children who may be adopted.

Adoption societies vet the suitability of adopters according to a number of criteria before the placement of a child. In granting an adoption order the Adoption Board or the court must regard the welfare of the child as the paramount consideration. Adopted people in the Republic cannot obtain access to their original birth certificate, but in Northern Ireland they may obtain it after the age of eighteen. An increasing acceptance of 'open adoption' has led to the introduction of conditional adoption orders in Northern Ireland, under the Children (Northern Ireland) Order (1995), providing for contact with the family of origin, where appropriate. A voluntary National Contact Register exists in the Republic, while in Northern Ireland the Registrar-General maintains a Contact Register of natural parents who indicate their wish to be placed on it. **Valerie Richardson**

adventure, tale type: see ECHTRAE.

'Adventure of the Churl of the Grey Coat': see 'EACHTRA BHODAIGH AN CHÓTA LACHTNA'.

AE: see RUSSELL, GEORGE.

Áed Findliath, King of TARA 862–879. Son of Niall Caille of CENÉL NEOGHAIN; he married Máel Muire, daughter of Cináed mac Alpín, King of the Scots. Having subdued the ULAIDH, he succeeded MÁEL SECHNAILL in the kingship of Tara. He defeated the VIKINGS at Lough Foyle, 866, and uprooted their settlements. His successors included his son NIALL GLÚNDUB. **Ailbhe Mac Shamhráin**

aerial photography and remote sensing. Remote sensing is the act of collecting information about something without making direct contact with it. Strictly speaking, any visual or similar observation of a phenomenon through, for example, a telescope or microscope may be regarded as remote sensing; most commonly, however, the term describes the collection of information about the Earth through photographic or digital processes.

Particularly during and since the two world wars of the twentieth century, air photography has become a standard tool for map publishers (including the ORDNANCE SURVEY of Ireland), planners, resource managers, environmental scientists, and a host of other professions and disciplines. Two main classes of aerial photography exist. *Vertical air photographs* are taken from a viewpoint that looks straight down on the land below; traditionally these photographs were taken using black-and-white film, though colour and infra-red films are now frequently used. Slightly overlapping pairs of vertical photographs (*'stereo pairs'*) can make it possible for very detailed measurements of terrain to be made through a process known as *photogrammetry*. In contrast, *oblique air photographs* show the land in perspective, as it would be seen by an observer looking out of an aircraft window: here colour film is most frequently used. The aircraft used for photography typically operate at altitudes of approximately 1,000–1,300 m (3,000–4,000 ft), though some military and other special-purpose planes can fly up to 40 km (25 miles) above the Earth's surface. Aerial photography is now the principal means of providing information for updating Ordnance Survey maps.

Orbiting satellites and craft such as the Space Shuttle provide higher-altitude vantage points, typically hundreds or even thousands of kilometres above the Earth. In the early days of space travel many rolls of film were taken using hand-held cameras. With modern digital scanners, objects as small as 1 m (3 ft) across can be routinely observed from space, with repeat coverage of the same area available up to several times per day.

In Ireland, applications of satellite remote sensing using visible or invisible (infra-red and ultra-violet) light can be considerably hampered by cloud cover, which prevents clear views from space for much of the year. For this reason, many space-borne remote sensing applications in Ireland rely instead on imagery obtained through alternative techniques, such as microwave radar. Despite this handicap, the technology is of great importance in a wide range of disciplines, including meteorology, agriculture, town and country planning, forestry, oceanography, and geological exploration. **Darius Bartlett**

Aer Lingus, an airline incorporated on 22 May 1936 as a joint venture with Blackpool and West Coast Air Services and established as the national carrier under the Air Navigation and Transport Act (1936). (The name is a phonetic spelling of *Aer-Loingeas*, 'air fleet'.) Its first route, from the military aerodrome at Baldonnel, Co. Dublin, to Bristol, was operated under the title Irish Sea Airways; its first aircraft, a De Havilland DH84 Dragon, registration EI-ABA, inaugurated the service on 27 May 1936. Routes were subsequently opened to Liverpool, the Isle of Man, and London, but the onset of the SECOND WORLD WAR curtailed further development until 1946–7, when services to Continental cities from the new Dublin Airport (to which Aer Lingus had moved in 1940) were introduced. Transatlantic services were added by Aerlínte Éireann in 1958.

The cyclical nature of the airline industry from the 1950s to the 70s and the vulnerability of Aer Lingus as a small airline with a limited market encouraged it to diversify into selling its technical and organisational expertise internationally and acquiring hotels in destination cities, particularly in North America. It was also involved in 1975 in the joint creation of the GPA Group, specialising in aircraft leasing, and a number of other ventures. But in 1980–81 the airline sustained the largest deficit in its history, and it sought additional capital from the Government as sole shareholder. The subsequent turnaround, however, proved to be relatively short-lived, and through much of the 1990s the airline, in common with many others, came close to bankruptcy, with the government's stated intention of disposing of 49 per cent of it to private interests being put on hold. Cost-cutting, including a substantial reduction in the work force, contributed to the airline's return to profitability and route expansion in 2001–2. **Bernard Share**

aerodromes and airports. The earliest Irish aerodromes date from 1917, when eight sites were selected for the ROYAL FLYING CORPS by WILLIAM SHOLTO DOUGLAS, subsequently Marshal of the Royal Air Force. Of these, Aldergrove (outside Belfast), Baldonnel (outside Dublin) and Collinstown (now Dublin Airport) were to develop into major airports in later years. A Belfast airport operated briefly at Malone in the 1920s, and the establishment of an aircraft industry by SHORT AND HARLAND led to the development of Sydenham, later Belfast City Airport. The outbreak of the SECOND WORLD WAR saw the construction of some twenty airfields, landing strips, and flying-boat bases, including Castle Archdale on LOUGH ERNE. Most of these were operational by 1941. Eglinton, transferred to the Royal Navy in 1943, became the Derry civil airport after the war; but the majority of the thirty airfields established between 1930 and 1945 have reassumed an agricultural or other role.

The first commercial airport in the Irish Free State was opened in 1931 for IONA NATIONAL AIRWAYS, and in 1936 AER LINGUS operated its first services out of the Air Corps base at Baldonnel, transferring in 1940 to the new Collinstown Airport (Dublin Airport), with its award-winning terminal building by Desmond FitzGerald.

Flying-boats had been using a base at FOYNES (Co. Limerick) since 1939. In 1941 the first land-plane touched down at Rineanna on the opposite bank of the river, now SHANNON AIRPORT. A small airfield was operated at Farmer's Cross in Cork, but this site was considered too restricted, and a full-scale civil airport was opened at Ballygarvan in 1961. In the following years local airports were inaugurated, with varying degrees of success, at Farranfore (Co. Kerry), Galway, Knock (Co. Mayo), Sligo, and Waterford, as well as at Cill Rónáin on the Aran islands, with scheduled services from Galway.

Among the many small private airports the most consistently successful has been Weston, near Leixlip, Co. Kildare, established in the immediate post-war years. In addition to Baldonnel, other military airports were or are operated at Finner (Co. Donegal) and Gormanston (Co. Meath), the latter one of the original 1917 airfields. In recent years Dublin Airport in particular has seen rapid expansion in passenger numbers (some 15 million in 2002), reflected in *ad hoc* building additions and bedevilled by the continuing absence of a rail link with the city. **Bernard Share**

aes dána (men of art), the poetic grades in early Ireland. According to the BREHON LAW texts—dating from between the seventh and ninth centuries—the category that enjoyed the highest prestige was that of the *file* (poet). An *ollam filed* (chief poet) was placed on the same scale as a petty king, with an honour-price (the sum payable for any serious offence against him) of twenty-one cows. A poet's status depended on his technical expertise and on his skill in composing verse in praise of his patron and satirising his patron's enemies. The law texts also recognised a lower category of poet, the *bard*, who had not undergone the professional training of the *file*. There are occasional references to female poets.

The law texts provide information on the social position and qualifications of other 'men of art'. Of these the most highly regarded was the *sáer* (carpenter), qualified in church-building, boat-building, mill construction, and working in yew-wood; his honour-price could reach ten cows. Of somewhat lower status were the blacksmith, silversmith, and coppersmith. The only musician who had free status was the *cruittire* (harpist). [see AOSDÁNA; FILÍ.] **Fergus Kelly**

age structure and dependency, the number of people in each age category in society and the numbers in the dependent age groups, i.e. young and old, relative to the remainder of the population. Age and sex are the two most important demographic variables, affecting the entire social, cultural, economic, and political fabric of a society. They influence FERTILITY and MARRIAGE, mortality, MIGRATION, levels of dependency, the availability of labour, and EMPLOYMENT opportunities.

The population pyramid (see p. 281) provides the best graphical representations of these variables. This is expressed in proportions, to illustrate variations in the age structures of the Republic and Northern Ireland; it does not show, therefore, the difference in POPULATION (3.7 and 1.7 million, respectively). The smaller young-aged populations reflect the decline in fertility, while lower mortality is evident from the number surviving to older ages. The higher number of older women can be attributed to their higher life expectancy compared with men. The impact of migration may be seen especially in the young adult age groups.

Dependency refers to the number of dependants in the population. Economic dependency may be measured using the number of persons not at work relative to those at work. However, it is more usual to relate the number of young and old dependants to those in the 'active' age groups. Age dependency is usually a measure of those under fifteen added to those over sixty-five years relative to the remainder. Young dependency has been higher in Northern Ireland than in the Republic since the 1990s and old dependency has been higher since the 1980s. In 1999 young dependency was 33.3 per cent in the Republic and 35.4 per cent in Northern Ireland. Old dependency was 16.9 per cent in the Republic and 20.3 per cent in Northern Ireland. Young dependency is higher than in any other member-state of the EUROPEAN UNION; old dependency is lower than in any other member-state except for the Netherlands (18.3 per cent). **Damien Courtney**

agrarian protest, a tradition existing throughout the eighteenth and nineteenth centuries and into the early years of the twentieth century. Probably originating with the HOUGHER movement in Connacht during 1708–12, this form of social protest (cattle maiming and driving) reached a peak between 1760 and the beginning of the GREAT FAMINE in the 1840s and ended with the 'cattle drives' of the early 1900s. Beyond the 1840s there was a steady incorporation of this type of activity in broader political campaigns, such as those of the LAND LEAGUE and HOME RULE, which sought to make the question of land reform both a motive force of and also subordinate to NATIONALISM.

In the later eighteenth century, agrarian protest was generally conducted through the mechanism of a secret society. Groups such as the WHITEBOYS, OAKBOYS, HEARTS OF STEEL, and RIGHTBOYS, though differing in certain respects, had many common features. Firstly, all the protests had a regional spread, which made them noteworthy. Secondly, they recurred in areas associated with rapid economic change, such as south Ulster and much of Munster. Thirdly, the protests were often aimed at resisting this change or at the conviction that the LANDLORDS or clergy were exploiting economic success. Fourthly, all the protests were violent, some resulting in deaths; the number of deaths increased dramatically in the 1790s as the government increased its vigilance and as the protesters were now using arms. Fifthly, most of the protests assembled large numbers of people, often at night, to visit and intimidate their targets as well as sending threatening letters and signs. Finally, oaths of secrecy and solidarity, symbols (ribbons, insignia or dress), and mythical leaders (Captain Fearnought or General Right) featured in most groups.

Agrarian protest was based time and again on grievances over changes in land use (especially the introduction of grazing on lands formerly used for tillage), rents or lease conditions, the taxes collected by local and central government, and TITHES. However, the movements were sometimes considered political, either because their demands struck a deeper chord (such as the TITHE WAR of the early 1830s) or because they occurred in periods of political upheaval (as with the DEFENDERS in the 1790s); they could also take on millenarian overtones. Certainly after the 1790s any protest movement was seen as being a threat to the government in Dublin. **Eoin Magennis**

agribusiness, industrialised AGRICULTURE, developed around the two main types of farm enterprise, dairy and beef. Dairy processing began in the farmhouse, developing through local co-operatives that have since become internationally trading food companies. Some larger co-operatives became publicly quoted companies but with the former co-operatives maintaining a shareholding. The three largest milk-processors are Glanbia PLC, Dairygold Co-op, and Kerry PLC, processing 70 per cent of the Irish milk pool.

The beef-processing industry developed more recently. Traditionally most cattle reared in Ireland were exported to England for slaughter; now 95 per cent of the 2 million cattle produced annually are processed in Ireland, though 90 per cent of the beef is exported. The three largest processors are Irish Food Processors, Dawn Meats, and Kepak. All are privately owned companies, operating multiple sites in Ireland and Britain. Up to twenty other single-site private processors export and supply the home market. Dairygold Co-op is the only co-operative involved in beef-processing. Glanbia PLC is the largest processor of pig meat, with three factories; Dawn and Dairygold (Galtee) are the other principal operators. Kepak, Dawn and Slaney Meats dominate the processing of sheep meat, with 75 per cent of lamb produced being exported to France. Two million tonnes of grain is produced annually, used for animal feed, malting, and flour milling. The former state-owned Irish Sugar Company was privatised in the early 1990s and became Greencore PLC; it now has a monopoly in sugar-processing and is also the largest maltster. **Eric Donald**

agricultural labourers, a range of occupational positions in modern Ireland, from hired labourers to family workers, crossing the fluid boundaries between farmer, agricultural labourer, and part-time artisan. In the 1830s the relative decline in the number of agricultural labourers was already detectable: this process was expedited through EMIGRATION in the 1840s and by a subsequent shift in farm labour forces from hired workers to 'assisting relatives' in the second half of the nineteenth century. The imprecise boundary between farmer and labourer may have become even more nebulous during the same period, with the increasing move towards less labour-intensive TILLAGE. The degree of labourers' political power has been a point of historiographical debate and refers to another debate over their relative place in the post-FAMINE social structure, and expressions of their independence as a collective group, with specific class interests, as they were integrated with other groups in rural social structure. **K. J. James**

agriculture. Modern Irish agriculture could be said to have begun in the early 1960s, when the proliferation of combine harvesters completed the MECHANISATION of farming and, in the process, killed off the last of the *meitheal*-type gatherings of friends and neighbours helping out with the cutting, reaping, binding, and threshing of corn crops. In the forty years between then and the end of the twentieth century, Irish farming was to see more changes than it had undergone in the previous two centuries.

By the 1960s, though Ireland was still affected by Britain's cheap food policy, farmers were tantalised by the prospect of a new era for agriculture beginning on the Continent with the establishment of the EEC and a COMMON AGRICULTURAL POLICY. At that time Irish farming was emerging from the dark ages—though mechanisation for many farmers meant an ironic situation where they had a mowing machine to cut hay but it was drawn by a horse. The prospects of joining the EEC (which came about in 1973) would bring Irish farmers a long way from their roots as tenant-farmers during the nineteenth century. In the fifty years from 1881 the ownership of 2 million ha (5 million acres) of agricultural land had changed hands from some 10,000 landlords to 400,000 tenant proprietors as Ireland moved from the landlordism base of farming, which had grown out of the feudal system of the Middle Ages.

Farming had changed little in 6,000 years, except through the development of the plough. About 6,000 years ago, when the early NEOLITHIC people switched from hunting to farming, cattle became very important to the earliest farmers, but they also kept sheep and carried out some cultivation of wheat, oats, and barley. Land was often held in common by a community, though more formal structures began to be imposed with the arrival of the Celtic peoples, who had a hierarchical social structure, which included various classes of farmers and land tenants. In the early Middle Ages—when there was no COINAGE—cattle, grain and white meats were among the valuables used in measuring a person's wealth. CHRISTIANITY and the growth in power of the church brought still further organisation to agriculture, especially in relation to land tenure and ownership.

By the early seventeenth century English law was imposed, and the power of landlords strengthened, leading to the creation of the tenancy system, with its land agents, middlemen, tenants and sub-tenants, often resulting in the sub-division of land into uneconomic holdings. By an act of 1704, Catholics were not allowed to buy land, resulting in a reduction in the number of Catholic

agribusiness. *The harvesting of sugarbeet. When the sugar industry was privatised in 1991, the state-owned Irish Sugar Company was bought by a group of investors, who formed Greencore. Since then it has grown through acquisitions to include malt, milling, bakeries, margarine, and convenience foods. [Greencore Group PLC]* landowners. This served to increase the powers of the mainly Protestant landlords, before their position was eroded by the activities of the LAND LEAGUE and by the Land Law (Ireland) Act (1881), introduced by GLADSTONE, which legalised the 'three Fs'—fair rent, fixity of tenure, and free sale—and at last made it possible, and practical, for farmers to become the owners of their own farms.

By the 1950s the same mechanisation that was beginning to make life easier for farmers—allied to a reduction in the number of holdings and a change from TILLAGE to livestock—had drastically reduced the number of people working on the land. In 1912 there were nearly 650,000 males working on farms in the twenty-six counties that were later to form the Republic; by 1964 this figure had fallen to 343,500. In the whole of Ireland the number of holdings bigger than 0.4 ha (1 acre) had fallen from 552,800 in 1855 to 387,900 in 1955 and to 199,000 by 1991. Big land banks were divided by the Land Commission and distributed to local landowners, former estate workers and local owners of uneconomic smallholdings or allotted to farmers brought from poorer land in the west by the CONGESTED DISTRICTS BOARD and by the LAND COMMISSION so that by the end of the century the few big estates still in existence were being run by a handful of workers. In the eyes of many rural people the satisfaction began to go out of farming in the middle of the twentieth century, as it began its inevitable progress towards becoming the isolated life it would attain by the beginning of the twenty-first century, when it became commonplace to walk the farm and not meet another person in the day's work.

During the 1960s farming began the change to being a business rather than a way of life, with a more intensive approach taken to production, helped by land drainage schemes as well as rural electrification, which saw 71 per cent of the 400,000 homes of rural areas of the Republic connected to the national grid by 1961. The colour of the landscape began to change to the deeper greens of grassland that was heavily fertilised, and silage was made instead of hay as winter feed. Even the colour of the cattle changed, from the different colours of the dual-purpose shorthorn in dairy herds to the black-and-white of the Friesian and from the black whiteheads in beef herds to the softer browns and whites of imported breeds. Farmers, through their own organisations, began to travel abroad, especially to the Continent, where they saw—and then adopted on their own farms—better management and production techniques. Instead of being sold at street fairs after haggling and 'spitting on hands', cattle and sheep were now being sold in LIVESTOCK MARTS, where the big attraction for both buyer and seller was the fact that the animals were weighed beforehand, making it possible for the first time to buy and sell by the hundredweight. Also in the 1960s, more organised marketing was developed by An Bord Bainne (founded 1961), which demonstrated through its exports of Kerrygold-branded butter that the produce of Irish farms could be sold throughout the world for premium prices, rather than cheaply as a non-branded commodity in Britain. Similarly, the processing of cattle and sheep in meat factories brought a new dimension to the business of farming, providing welcome competition to the traditional live export trade that dominated animal production.

Prosperity, however, remained elusive for the farming community until membership of the EEC brought higher prices for farm produce in the 1970s. Land prices soared, both North and South, in response to this new-found wealth, though the upheaval of suddenly being part of a European market was not without its hiccups. In 1974 the cattle market in the Republic slumped to such an extent that one farmer reported that he received so little for a calf at his local livestock mart that he had only a small amount of change after buying a chicken in the supermarket. Prices of the main farm produce were supported by the EEC through intervention; and though this action provided a floor to farm incomes, it soon led to beef, butter, powdered-milk, and grain 'mountains', with ships being pressed into service at one time to store the mounds of intervention BUTTER and beef.

During this period farmers began to specialise. In the first half of the twentieth century a farmer typically had some milking cows, a herd of beef or store cattle and a flock of sheep, some crops, and also pigs and poultry. By the late 1970s and into the 1980s a typical dairy farmer tended to be just that, while many dry-stock, sheep, and tillage farmers had bottled milk delivered to their doorstep, just like a town-dweller. All this was to change again from the late 1980s, when quotas limited production and farmers needed to broaden their range of farm enterprises. Some planted forests on their land, with EU support, to make a decent living.

By the last two decades of the twentieth century things had come full circle in some respects when farmers from Britain and the Continent began to visit Ireland to see how farmers here were doing things and to pick up tips. Cereal-growers had by then become so efficient that they were achieving higher yields than farmers anywhere else in Europe. Farmers had become proficient low-cost producers of milk and beef from grass. However, the rapid technical changes in production techniques were counteracted by the overproduction of food throughout Europe; and Ireland, exporting some 60 per cent of its agricultural output, was particularly vulnerable to world fluctuations in prices, even though farm incomes were strongly supported by direct payments from the EUROPEAN UNION. To compound the problems, land prices were driven upwards by 'hobby' farmers (business people buying up small farms to have a place in the country or somewhere they could keep a few horses for the children); a significant number of full-time farmers became part-time farmers, as they could not afford to buy land that had increased from an average of €5,000 per hectare in 1990 to €9,000 per hectare in 1998; and many farmers were in despair as they discovered that their children, traditional successors to the farm, showed no interest and instead were leaving the land to make careers in the booming non-farming areas.

At the end of the twentieth century, livestock and livestock products in both parts of Ireland accounted for about 90 per cent of the total value of agricultural output, with crops, fruit and horticulture making up the remaining 10 per cent. Generally speaking, intensive pig, poultry, and egg production was higher in Northern Ireland, while the contribution of enterprises based on grassland was higher in the Republic. Cattle and milk products accounted for more than three-quarters of the value of livestock and livestock products in the Republic and about two-thirds in Northern Ireland. Sheep, poultry, and eggs accounted for a higher proportion of the total value of Northern Ireland's output for livestock and livestock products: 25 per cent, compared with 12 per cent in the Republic. Fruit and potatoes were more important to the Northern agricultural economy, with 3 per cent of land devoted to fruit and 13 per cent devoted to potatoes; in the Republic the comparable figures were 0.3 per cent for fruit and 4 per cent for potatoes. During the twentieth century the number of cattle and sheep in Ireland doubled, from 4.6 million to 9 million cattle and from 4.4 million to 10 million sheep; but the number of farms halved, from 515,000 to fewer than 200,000. In 2000, agricultural employment as a proportion of total employment was 7.8 per cent in the Republic and 4.9 per cent in Northern Ireland. [see AGRIBUSINESS.] **Paddy Smith**

agriculture: changing nature and distribution. Traditionally, agriculture has been the most important industry in Ireland, but its relative importance has declined significantly over recent years. In 1989 it accounted for 10.5 per cent of GROSS DOMESTIC PRODUCT and 14.5 per cent of EMPLOYMENT; by 1998 these shares had declined to 4.7 per cent and 8.7 per cent, respectively. Agriculture and food products accounted for 11 per cent of all exports in 1998, down from 21 per cent in 1991.

There are many reasons for the decline in the relative importance of agriculture. Chief among these are the low productivity associated with most of the industry, resulting in comparatively low incomes for many farmers; the shift towards greater reliance on industrial inputs; the continuing transition to an urban society and economy; and, more recently, some reductions in the level of direct financial support provided by the Government and the EUROPEAN UNION for agricultural production.

The changes in agriculture are the outcome of a number of related processes that characterise the so-called 'productivist' phase in the history of agriculture. This phase has applied to Ireland since the late 1950s and especially since membership of the EEC in 1973, after which the mechanisms for modernising agriculture within the framework of the COMMON AGRICULTURAL POLICY became the dominant influence on change in agricultural production.

Three related processes are associated with the production-oriented model of farming that characterised the period from c. 1960: intensification, specialisation, and concentration. Intensification is associated with significant increases in the use of off-farm inputs, such as artificial fertilisers, herbicides, and pesticides, along with a much greater reliance on mechanisation and transfer of research to increase yields of crops and livestock. Intensification not only results in increased levels of productivity but can also have negative impacts through a reduction in the number of farm families that are able to earn a sufficient income from farming, and there may also be environmental and landscape impacts. The removal of hedgerows to facilitate mechanisation has resulted in the loss of habitats for wildlife as well as dramatically altering the appearance of the landscape in some areas. The number of tractors used on Irish farms increased from 43,700 in 1960 to approximately 160,000 at the end of the twentieth century.

Specialisation is the trend by individual farmers towards deriving an increasing share of their income from one dominant enterprise. By 1991 almost four-fifths of all farms could be categorised as specialising in one of the following types of farming: beef cattle (42.1 per cent), dairy farming (24.4 per cent), sheep (8.8 per cent), TILLAGE (2.9 per cent), or other—mainly horticulture or pig or poultry farming (1.4 per cent). In the south-west, 45 per cent of farms are specialist dairy farms, while in the west and north-west more than half the total specialise in the rearing of beef cattle. Specialisation is closely related to intensification and facilitates the achievement of economies of scale in production and also the acquisition of more advanced farm management practices and more efficient linkages between farmers and the AGRIBUSINESSES that purchase their output for processing. On the other hand, specialisation may lead to increased vulnerability to factors affecting particular sectors and also to a disruption of self-regulating systems in the natural ENVIRONMENT. Specialisation and intensification have resulted in an increasing share of the output of different sectors of agriculture coming from fewer farms. Dairy cows were grazed on approximately 56 per cent of all farms in the early 1970s; by 1997 the proportion was less than 30 per cent. Between 1973 and 1997 the average number of cows per dairy farm increased from ten to thirty-two, so that more than two-fifths of all dairy cows are on approximately 18 per cent of all dairy farms.

agriculture. *A modern farmer, his attention divided between office and farmyard, illustrating the changing trend of agriculture from a way of life to a business. [Derek Speirs/Report]*

The trend towards concentration is most marked in the pig and poultry sectors. The average number of animals per pig farm increased from 102 in 1981 to 859 in 1997, with more than 90 per cent of the total concentrated on fewer than 400 farms.

Each of the main sectors of the agriculture industry has a distinctive regional distribution, which can be explained by environmental factors (SOILS and CLIMATE indices), historical influences on farm size, the demographic profile of farmers, and the impact of support systems and other initiatives sponsored by the Government and the European Union under the Common Agricultural Policy. Dairying is the most profitable and most widespread type of farming, accounting for almost 35 per cent of gross agricultural output in 1998; it is strongly concentrated in the lowland parts of Munster, extending eastwards into Co. Kilkenny and also significant in Co. Monaghan and east Cavan. The distribution is strongly influenced by the favourable conditions for grassland in the south-west, together with historical patterns of access to export markets through the ports of Cork and Waterford and, from the late nineteenth century, the distribution of privately owned and co-operative creameries.

The store cattle sector accounts for another 33 per cent of gross agricultural output. It is mostly associated with small farms on poorer-quality lowlands, especially in parts of east Mayo, north Roscommon, south Leitrim, most of Co. Longford and much of Co. Clare, apart from the south-west and east of the country. In many of these areas, where the main emphasis is on rearing young cattle, earnings from farming are supplemented by incomes from non-farm occupations. A tradition of fattening older cattle prevails on the limestone farms of Cos. Westmeath and Meath, usually on relatively large farms.

Mixed grazing occurs on about one-fifth of all farms, mainly in two distinctive areas. Mixed sheep and cattle grazing have been the traditional type of farming throughout most of east Galway and south Roscommon, while in the south-east, especially Cos. Carlow and Wexford, arable farming is frequently combined with some livestock, mainly cattle or sheep. These farms are typically above average in size, operated by younger farmers, and produce relatively high economic returns.

The sheep sector accounts for only 5 per cent of total output. The specialist sheep farmers—in contrast to those who combine the rearing of sheep with other types of farming—are often found concentrated in hill areas, because of the unsuitability of such areas for other types of livestock.

Arable crops grown on about one-fifth of all farms account for approximately 7 per cent of total output. This sector is highly capital-intensive and has been subjected to increasing concentration. Almost 40 per cent of the total area of arable crops is on about 2,000 large farms, mainly on free-draining lowlands of the dryer and sunnier east and south-east, with localised concentrations in east Cork and east Donegal.

The patterns of adjustment in farming over recent decades have resulted in very uneven outcomes. In the mid-1990s there were about 35,300 commercial farms, 23 per cent of the total. More than 40,000 farms, representing almost another 30 per cent, were already operated part-time. The relative importance of this category is due to increase. Another 30 per cent are under pressure to either raise their incomes by availing of alternative employment or run the risk of becoming further marginalised. For the remaining residual group, about 20 per cent of the total, their future in farming is very doubtful. These farms are typically small and operated by elderly farmers.

The future, therefore, is likely to consist of three categories of farms. There will be a core group of perhaps only 20,000 commercial farms operating competitively in a market environment dominated by world prices. A second group will be heavily dependent on direct payments, legitimised as payments for protecting the rural environment and also on the grounds of a political desire to maintain viable rural communities. Many of this group will also be heavily dependent on incomes from non-farming activities. The third group, which is likely to be much smaller, will include farms diversifying into non-conventional lines of production, such as tree farming, alternative livestock enterprises, ORGANIC farming, and agri-tourism. This category is likely to be dispersed, in accordance with resource potential and market opportunities. To plan for these adjustments, agriculture in the future will need to be viewed as a component of integrated multi-sectoral and multi-dimensional strategies for sustainable RURAL DEVELOPMENT, as outlined in the White Paper *Ensuring the Future: A Strategy for Rural Development in Ireland* (1999). **James Walsh**

agriculture and the environment. Mechanisation and the adoption of scientific methods and management revolutionised farming in Ireland from the 1960s. In the 60s and 70s there was large-scale development of farmyards to accommodate the growing numbers of livestock made possible by the increased use of fertiliser and the change to silage for winter feeding. In 1973 Ireland joined the EEC, and European agricultural policy further boosted stock numbers and agricultural output. Cattle numbers in the Republic increased from 7.5 million head in 1978 to 7.9 million in 1998; in the same period sheep numbers increased from 3.3 million to 8.4 million. During the period 1981–98 sales of nitrogen fertiliser increased from 275,000 tonnes to 432,000 tonnes, while phosphate levels have increased to the point where 20 per cent of farms have a level greater than their needs. Excessive use of nitrogen and phosphate causes problems with water quality.

This rapid increase in stock numbers and intensification has had a significant impact on the environment. The point-source pollution that caused large fish kills has been largely rectified but has given way to diffuse pollution. There continues to be pressure on the environment from agricultural waste, eutrophication, overgrazing (especially on the blanket peat soils of the west), and the emission of greenhouse gases. During this period of increased productivity the consequential effects on landscape, habitats, and wildlife were not adequately considered.

Reforms in the COMMON AGRICULTURAL POLICY set about limiting agricultural output in member-states of the European Union; these measures were also to encourage farming practices that would be compatible with the protection of the environment and the landscape. In response to these developments, in 1994 the Department of Agriculture and Food launched the Rural Environmental Protection Scheme. This was open to all farmers with more than 3 ha ($7\frac{1}{2}$ acres) who were prepared to farm within given nutrient limits and to carry out environmental protection work and habitat enhancement. During the period of REPS1 (1994–9) approximately 46,000 farmers participated. In November 2000 a new scheme, REPS2, modelled closely on REPS1, was launched; the objective is to have 70,000 farmers participating.

The Department of Agriculture for Northern Ireland began implementing agri-environmental measures in 1988. The scheme identified two areas of national importance for their landscape, habitat and heritage value; within these areas farmers were offered the opportunity of entering into voluntary five-year management agreements. These areas were subsequently expanded to the point where 20 per cent of Northern Ireland was designated. In May 1999 the department launched the Countryside Management Scheme, and this continues to operate.

The schemes in both parts of Ireland have as their objective to compensate farmers appropriately for moving towards farming in a defined environmentally sustainable manner and for the cost incurred or loss of income sustained in doing so, and to familiarise them with methods of environmentally responsible farming. The quality of the schemes is high, and the amount of checking involved has contributed to the maintenance of a high degree of compliance. These schemes will form the blueprint for future schemes aimed at requiring all farming activities to be compatible with environmental protection and renewal. **Eugene Ryan**

agriculture, future of. The number of people employed in agriculture has declined rapidly over the past century. In the 1950s, 38 per cent of the labour force in the Republic was employed in agriculture, while now that figure is closer to 9 per cent, and 5 per cent in Northern Ireland. The typical size of farm is above the EU average, at 29 ha (72 acres) in the Republic and 36 ha (89 acres) in Northern Ireland. There are pronounced regional differences in farming. The western and north-western regions are characterised by smaller farms and poorer land. Dairying and beef are the primary agricultural enterprises undertaken, but there are regional differences.

Farms in Ireland are largely owner-occupied family businesses. Because of a history of colonial tenancy, Irish farm families have a tenacious hold on their farms. Land is transferred inter-generationally from father to son. Very little land comes on the market, and there is limited long-term leasing. This has resulted in a relatively slow structural change even in the face of enormous economic pressures. The capacity for increasing food consumption is limited, yet technological advances have significantly increased agricultural production. This has deflated farm incomes and placed severe strains on farm families. The implications for small farms are very serious, with many becoming non-viable. In general, the farming sector is now supplementing farm income with off-farm employment, or by relying on EU transfer payments. While previously it was a privilege to inherit a farm, securing succession is now a problem. The future of farming is very uncertain. **Sally Shortall**

agriculture and the environment. *Reaping the corn in Toome, Co. Antrim (early twentieth century), before the widespread use of farm machinery. [Green Collection, Ulster Folk and Transport Museum; reproduced with the kind permission of the Trustees of the National Museums and Galleries of Northern Ireland]*

agriculture: statistical profile. The composition of the total value of agricultural output is very similar in both parts of Ireland. In 1998 livestock and livestock products accounted for just under 90 per cent of the total in both jurisdictions; this situation had been broadly unchanged during the second half of the 1990s. Of the total value of livestock and livestock products, cattle and milk production accounted for more than three-quarters in the Republic in 1998 and for approximately two-thirds in Northern Ireland. On the other hand, sheep, poultry, and eggs account for a higher proportion of the total value of Northern Ireland's output (25 per cent, compared with 12 per cent).

Table 1: Estimated value of agricultural output—livestock and livestock products, 1998

	Republic		Northern Ireland	
	value (million pounds)	proportion	value (million pounds stg)	proportion
Cattle	1,086.7	38.2%	318.6	35.0%
Pigs	212.0	7.5%	67.0	7.4%
Sheep and lambs	162.6	5.7%	95.9	10.6%
Poultry	129.7	4.6%	89.3	9.8%
Milk	1,134.1	39.9%	286.5	31.5%
Eggs	15.9	0.6%	37.2	4.1%
Other livestock/products	102.9	3.6%	14.5	1.6%
Total	2,843.9		909.0	

A higher proportion of land under crops, fruit, and horticulture is devoted to fruit (3 per cent) and potatoes (13 per cent) in Northern Ireland than in the Republic, where fruit accounts for just 0.3 per cent and potatoes 4 per cent. In value, the contribution of mushrooms has been growing and now represents 20 per cent of the total from fruit, crops, and horticulture in the Republic and 26 per cent in the North. By 2000, employment in agriculture (including hunting, forestry, and fishing) accounted for 7.8 per cent of total employment in the Republic and was even lower, at 4.9 per cent, in Northern Ireland.

Table 2: Employment in agriculture as a proportion of total employment, 1997–2000

	Republic	Northern Ireland
1997	10.3%	5.1%
1998	9.0%	5.1%
1999	8.5%	5.1%
2000	7.8%	4.9%

Central Statistics Office/Northern Ireland Statistics & Research Agency

Ahenny, Co. Tipperary, site of two aniconic (non-pictorial) HIGH CROSSES with geometrical decoration, both probably copied from sophisticated wooden prototypes with applied bronze sheets and studs. The bases bear scriptural carvings: Daniel (South Cross), Adam naming animals, the 'Raised Christ', the headless Goliath brought to Jerusalem, and a chariot procession (North Cross). Their date is probably about the first half of the ninth century (see p. 491). **Peter Harbison**

Ahern, Bartholomew (Bertie) (1951–), politician. Born in Dublin; educated St Aidan's CBS, Whitehall, Rathmines College of Commerce (Dublin), and UCD. An accountant, he entered Dáil Éireann as part of the FIANNA FÁIL landslide of 1977. Like many newly elected that year, he was associated with CHARLES HAUGHEY, whose successful bid for the party leadership he supported. He was rewarded with the position of assistant government whip in 1980 and was chief whip in the short-lived Haughey Government of 1982. On the return of Fianna Fáil to office in 1987, he was appointed Minister for Labour, where he developed a considerable reputation as a conciliator. He succeeded ALBERT REYNOLDS as Minister for Finance in November 1991, a position he retained on the fall of Haughey and the succession of Reynolds three months later. Party leader on Reynolds' resignation in 1994, he won the 1997 general election and became Taoiseach in a Fianna Fáil-dominated Coalition Government. It presided over the boom years of the CELTIC TIGER and was rewarded with a decisive election victory in 2002. Ahern played a central part in the negotiations leading to the BELFAST AGREEMENT of 1998. **Tom Garvin**

Ahrends, Burton and Koralek, architects. The partnership consists of Peter Ahrends (1933–), born in Berlin, Richard Burton (1933–), born in London, and Paul Koralek (1933–), born in Vienna; all educated at the Architectural Association, London. They established Ahrends, Burton and Koralek in London, 1961, after Koralek won an international competition for the Berkeley Library for TRINITY COLLEGE, Dublin. Inspired by the 1950s Brutalism of Le Corbusier, this concrete vessel on its ceremonial plinth was completed in 1967. Subsequent Irish buildings include St Andrew's College, Booterstown, Co. Dublin, and the Arts Faculty Building, Trinity College, 1968–79. Their Dublin office, established 1996, designed buildings in Britain and Jerusalem, and the British embassy in Moscow. **Raymund Ryan**

Aibidil Gaoidheilge agus Caiticiosma (1571), the first book published in Irish in Ireland. It consists of an Epistle, rules of spelling, the Anglican catechism, various prayers, and the articles of religion of 1566. It was compiled by Seán Ó Cearnaigh, treasurer of ST PATRICK'S CATHEDRAL, and printed in Dublin at the expense of Alderman John Ussher. **Nicholas J. A. Williams**

Aidan of Lindisfarne (died 651), monk, bishop, and missionary in Northumbria. Born in Ireland. King Oswald asked IONA for missionaries, and Aidan (ordained bishop 635) was sent. From his base in LINDISFARNE he organised preaching, while educating English clergy to continue his missionary work. Our information comes from Bede's *Historia Ecclesiastica Gentis Anglorum*, III. **Thomas O'Loughlin**

aided (pl. *aideda, aitte, oitte*) (literally, death, violent death; slaughter; the act of killing; fate, plight), a narrative genre in Irish literature, the 'death-tale', that has been productive from the Old Irish period to the present day. Perhaps the narrative type most typical of early Irish literature, it is named as a category of tales that poets should know in the tenth-century tale list found in the Book of Leinster, which includes as exemplars 'Aided Con Ruí' (The Death of Cú Roí) and 'Aided Con Culainn' (The Death of CÚ CHULAINN), among others. Still earlier than the tale list are poems, notably those by Flannacán mac Cellaig and CINAED UA HARTACÁIN, from the ninth and tenth centuries, respectively, that also contain mnemonic listings related to the deaths (and presumably death-tales) of heroes.

The death-tales are stories of unnatural and untimely deaths, rather than death by old age, and the stories often function to bring to a close a narrative cycle about a character or group of characters. The *aided* is therefore related to other genres of early Irish literature, including the *orgain* or *orcain* ('slaying, massacre'), TOGAIL ('destruction, ravaging, attack'), and CATH ('battle'), as well as to heroic or epic tales in other literatures that have as their climax the death and apotheosis of a hero (as for example the Iliad and Beowulf). Despite the emphasis on violent and heroic death, *aideda* are not uniformly tragic or sad: they can have humorous, sexual, or scatological elements also, as for example in 'Aided Fergusa maic Roich' (The Death of Fergus mac Roich).

Some of the death-tales were taken up by the Irish LITERARY REVIVAL and achieved currency in English-language versions, notably 'Aided Con Culainn', which furnished the material for Yeats's last play, *The Death of Cuchulain*, and the iconography of OLIVER SHEPPARD's statue *The Death of Cú Chulainn* (1911), placed in the GENERAL POST OFFICE, Dublin, in 1935 to commemorate the 1916 RISING (see p. 1090). If the narrative function of this genre was to close a heroic age or a personal biography, the social functions may have been epitomised by their narration at wakes and the funeral celebrations of heroes and leaders, accentuating the mystery of death and its momentousness. **Maria Tymoczko**

AIDS (acquired immunodeficiency syndrome), a condition, caused by a virus, in which white blood cells are destroyed, resulting in the loss of the immunity to disease. Statistics on HIV (human immunodeficiency virus) and AIDS in Ireland have been officially compiled since the mid-1980s, with almost 3,000 people recorded as testing positive for HIV antibodies and more than 400 AIDS deaths. This official data is criticised by many activists in the fields of social and medical support as being of poor quality and insufficiently representing the full extent of the life-threatening illness. In fact the first efforts to raise public awareness in the early to middle 1980s were undertaken not by governments but by gay health action groups. AIDS has been a largely male disease throughout the country. In Northern Ireland, where 86 per cent of transmission is thought to have occurred sexually, gay sex represents 58 per cent of that total. AIDS has also deeply affected intravenous heroin drug users in the Republic, who constitute the largest group infected—41 per cent of the official total, compared with a mere 3 per cent so infected in Northern Ireland, where heroin use was far less commonplace until recently. Haemophiliacs infected through blood products have been a third vulnerable group. A fourth small group has comprised the children born to HIV-infected mothers. Official and public responses to the illness were marked by initial complacency and then by an often cruel tendency to marginalise and demonise those affected and their families, no matter what the route of transmission. At the same time, public health approaches to limiting the spread of the illness have led gradually to officially endorsed, if far from comprehensive, initiatives to distribute clean needles and condoms and to organise safe-sex schemes for sub-groups perceived as especially at risk, such as male and female prostitutes. However, a reluctance to develop full-scale safe-sex and drugs education for children and young people has resulted in rising rates of transmission of the virus. **Jo Murphy-Lawless**

Aiken, Frank (1898–1983), revolutionary and politician. Born in Co. Armagh; educated at St Colman's College, Newry. He was a leader of the local IRA, 1918–22, and hesitantly anti-Treaty. As newly appointed chief of staff of the IRA he gave the 'dump arms' order of 1923. A FIANNA FÁIL TD for Louth from 1927 to 1973, he was a close colleague of ÉAMON DE VALERA and was Minister for Defence during the SECOND WORLD WAR years, a portfolio that included significant censorship functions. He served as Minister for External Affairs, 1951–4 and 1957–69, becoming well known for his opposition to Cold War policies. **Tom Garvin**

Aikenhead, Mary (1787–1858), founder of the Irish Sisters of Charity. Born in Cork. A convert to Catholicism at sixteen, she determined on the religious life. Following three years in a novitiate in York she returned to Dublin to be professed. Archbishop DANIEL MURRAY suggested that she establish the first congregation of the Irish Sisters of Charity. She established nine houses of the order in her lifetime; the order also established St Vincent's Hospital, Dublin, in 1834, the first Catholic voluntary hospital in the city. The order was an important element in the self-confident Catholic institutional revival of the early nineteenth century. **Fergal Tobin**

Ailwee Cave, Co. Clare, 5 km (3 miles) south of Ballyvaghan, discovered in 1944 by Jack McGann. The original passages measured 204 m (670 ft) in length, but in 1976 access was obtained to St Patrick's Series, and a further 866 m (2,841 ft) of passages were found in 1977. In 1973 the bones of a horse and small mammals were unearthed in Horse Haven, together with the tooth of a bear, later complemented by the discovery of bear bones. In 1979 a bear skull was found in Bear Haven (so called because of the shallow pits made in it by hibernating bears). The newest excavations revealed a sequence of passages, including Midsummer Chamber, containing 5,000-year-old stalagmites; River Cavern, where a stream of unknown source and destination emerges; and Canal Passage, where the route ends in water sumps of undetermined length. The cave was created by water picking a wandering horizontal course eastwards into thin, fossil-rich beds of limestone. These conduits expanded by water dissolving and eroding large horizontal tubes into overlying thick limestone beds and later by seeping downwards through a network of small vertical fissures. The date at which these processes began is unknown, though calcite was being formed within the cave 350,000 years ago. The cave's antiquity is confirmed by the presence of sediments injected inwards from beneath a glacier crossing the entrance of the cave and by numerous thin layers of silt and clay, recording engorgement of the passages by glacial meltwater; these facts show that the cave's dimensions have remained unchanged since glaciers last covered Ireland, about 10,000 years ago. **Colman Gallagher**

Airbertach mac Colsse Dobráln (died 1016), a monk of the monastery of Ros Ailithir (Ross Carbery, Co. Cork). He taught in the MONASTIC SCHOOL and composed verse of a simple kind to help his students memorise their lessons, including a poem on world geography based on classical Latin writings and another on the history of the composition of the Psalms. Two further poems on Biblical topics are probably also his, as the four are found together in the manuscript source. Stylistic similarities and other considerations point to his having been the author also of 'Saltair na Rann', the great epic on the fall and salvation of humankind, written c. 988. In 990 he was taken captive by Scandinavian raiders and brought to their base on Scattery Island in the Shannon Estuary, whence he was ransomed by Brian Bórú. In the record of his death he is described as *airchinnech* or superior of the monastery. **Gearóid Mac Eoin**

aircraft construction. In 1916 the Belfast shipbuilding firm of HARLAND AND WOLFF received a contract for the construction of three hundred small wooden training and coastal patrol biplanes, followed in 1918 by an order for twenty of the large Handley Page V 1500, but only three had been completed when the FIRST WORLD WAR ended. In 1937 a new company, Short and Harland Ltd, began aircraft manufacture at Queen's Island, Belfast, a joint venture between the shipbuilders and SHORT BROTHERS, who had been manufacturing balloons and aircraft in Britain since 1901. The firm was subsequently responsible for the design and production of many notable civil and military aircraft, including the Stirling and Sunderland bombers, the Solent flying-boat, the Canberra, and the Skyvan. The company is now owned by the Canadian firm Bombardier Aerospace, but the aviation downturn following the 11 September 2001 World Trade Center bombing in the United States affected it severely. **Bernard Share**

Airec Menman Uraird maic Coisse ('Urard mac Coisse's Stratagem'), an allegorical tale in which the poet, Urard mac Coisse, complains to the King of TARA, Domnall mac Muirchertaig (died 980), that he had been plundered by the king's kinsmen. The king restores his goods. The tale asserts the privileged position of the poets and may be the work of Urard himself. **Gearóid Mac Eoin**

aisling (eighteenth century), an allegorical poetic form that became especially popular in the political compositions of the Munster poets in the eighteenth century. The term refers to a vision or a dream image, and the eighteenth-century genre draws heavily on the female sovereignty images to be found in medieval allegorical texts such as ECHTRAE MAC NECHACH MUIGMEDÓIN and the praise poetry of the EARLY MODERN period. While negative female images (of harlot, adulteress, or bad mother) are employed in seventeenth-century poetry to depict the breakdown of the Irish political order, Ireland is presented in more sympathetic terms in eighteenth-century JACOBITE POETRY, where she becomes a beautiful young woman or an abused maiden lamenting the absence of her rightful partner. AOGÁN Ó RATHAILLE was an early master of the genre; in his ornate 'Gile na Gile' the image of rape is used to dramatically depict Ireland's plight during the reign of George I.

The genre was an ideal vessel for the expression of the millennial and messianic messages central to Jacobite rhetoric and became highly formalised in the work of EOGHAN RUA Ó SÚILLEABHÁIN, where the political message is depicted as a dramatic encounter between the dream woman and the poet-speaker, culminating in a note of hope with a prophecy of return and Stuart reinstatement. Mid-eighteenth-century examples such as SEÁN CLÁRACH MAC DOMHNAILL's 'Bímse buan ar buairt gach ló' (popularly known as 'Mo ghille mear') emphasise the ill-treatment and abuse meted out to Éire in the absence of her true protector; all examples of the genre are marked by a highly conventional depiction of sex roles and relations.

In popular adaptations of the *aisling* the sovereignty figure is sometimes addressed in vernacular terms as Caitlín Ní Uallacháin, Síle Ní Ghadhra, Cáit Ní Dhuibhir, or Móirín Ní Chuileannáin. Through the employment of the language of personal acquaintance, the allegorical images in such instances become less a metaphorical representation of Ireland and more a substitution for the oppressed Catholic underclass, making the *aisling* a powerfully emotive channel for the expression of social discontent and political disaffection. Another variation on the theme is to be found in the incorporation of 'Gráinne Mhaol'—the name applied in popular tradition to GRACE O'MALLEY—as an image of defiance and resistance. In the aisling poetry of northern poets such as ART MAC CUMHAIGH the Jacobite content is less overt; Mac Cumhaigh's popular 'Úrchill an Chreagáin' presents an image of a fairy woman come to deliver the poet from the desolation accompanying the overthrow of the native nobility.

The *aisling* as a literary form outlived the collapse of Stuart hopes in 1745, becoming more formalised and less specific in focus and context. Aspects of the form were adapted to serve the needs of almost every subsequent national movement of significance. Through the translations of Jacobite poetry by JAMES CLARENCE MANGAN, John D'Alton, and others, Caitlín Ní Uallacháin and her contemporaries entered the literature of the Anglo-Irish LITERARY REVIVAL, providing the source for literary works such as W. B. YEATS's influential play *Cathleen Ni Houlihan*. The genre has been widely critiqued in recent years, and the conventions on which it was founded have been subverted by poets, visual artists, and film-makers. **Máirín Nic Eoin**

aislinge ('vision'), an early Irish prose tale type in which the hero has a dream or vision. The best-known examples are the Old Irish 'Aislinge Óenguso' (the dream of Óengus) and the twelfth-century 'AISLINGE MEIC CONGLINNE' (the dream of Mac Con Glinne). 'Aislinge Óenguso' tells how Óengus of TUATHA DÉ DANANN dreams of a beautiful woman, and falls in love with her. She is Cáer, daughter of the King of the Connacht Tuatha Dé Danann, and she alternates between human and swan form. They meet, transform into swans, and fly away. The tale inspired W. B. Yeats's poem 'The Song of Wandering Aengus'. 'Aislinge Meic Conglinne' satirises both AISLING and IMMRAM (voyage) genres. The scholar-hero, Mac Con Glinne, travels to the monastery of Cork, is treated inhospitably, and is sentenced to death. He is saved when he recounts a vision in which he voyages through a universe of food on a boat of lard. The abbot of Cork realises that Mac Con Glinne should be spared so that he can exorcise a demon of gluttony that has taken hold of Cathal mac Finguine (died 742), King of Munster. Mac Con Glinne succeeds, parodically and triumphantly. **Elva Johnston**

'Aislinge Meic Conglinne' ('The Vision of Mac Conglinne'), a twelfth-century tale of comic genius, in two different versions, about a king physically possessed by a demon of gluttony and an undernourished monastic student turned poet (Mac Con Glinne), who tries to tempt the demon forth by recounting the vision he has had of a paradisiacal Land of Food. This verse-and-prose work parodies incidents from the life of Christ and satirises identifiable church figures of the day and monastic and scholastic institutions. It is a pastiche of many literary genres, including visions, voyage-tales, and wooing-tales, and provides a dense web of intertextual references, some now unidentifiable. It is also uniquely rich in information on the medieval Irish diet. **Máirín Ní Dhonnchadha**

'Aithbe Damsa Bés Marai' ('The Lament of Cailleach Bhéarra'), arguably the greatest surviving medieval Irish poem, and certainly the most frequently edited and translated. Its speaker bears the multiple-meaning title of *cailleach*, which means 'consort', 'nun' or 'old woman' and is associated with the Beara Peninsula, Co. Cork—hence Cailleach Bhéarra. There is a crucial ambivalence in the line 'Is mé Caillech Béirre buí,' which can be interpreted to mean 'I am the former Cailleach Bhéarra.' In Irish tradition Cailleach Bhéarra is said to have enjoyed extraordinary longevity and to have survived serial epochs and historical ruptures. In her function as a witness to events that would otherwise be unknown she is comparable to Tuán mac Stairn, Mongán mac Fiachna, OISÍN, and the CHILDREN OF LIR. In the poem she has become at last an ordinary mortal, living out her final years in a monastery of women. Her bleak vision of the transience of worldly pleasure is tempered by belief in the promise of Christian redemption after death. The poem turns on consideration of different modalities of time: the linear, finite time of humankind, the cyclical time of nature, and the eternity promised to Christians. In a prose introduction the speaker is named as Digde (alias Díge) and is counted among the 'wonderful *cailleachs*' of the people of Corca Dhuibhne (DINGLE PENINSULA, Co. Kerry). This apparent anomaly can be resolved if we accept that the introduction exemplifies the common error of conflating author and speaker. It has been translated by many modern writers, including AUSTIN CLARKE, LADY GREGORY, MICHAEL HARTNETT, BRENDAN KENELLY, THOMAS KINSELLA, and JOHN MONTAGUE. **Máirín Ní Dhonnchadha**

Alcock and Brown. John Alcock (1892–1919), pilot, and Arthur Whitten-Brown (1886–1948), navigator, were the first fliers to make a successful non-stop crossing of the Atlantic Ocean, departing from St John's, Newfoundland, at 1:58 p.m. on 14 June 1919 and landing in Derrygimla Bog, near Clifden, Co. Galway, fifteen hours and fifty-seven minutes later. Their aircraft, a First World War Vickers Vimy bomber, averaged 190 km/h (118 miles/h). Both were knighted and Alcock was killed in an air crash the same year. **Bernard Share**

alcohol and alcoholism. The abuse of alcohol is the principal form of substance abuse in Ireland. The drinking of alcohol is an integral part of social life, and there is an attitude of tolerance towards the consumption, and indeed the abuse, of alcohol not applied to the abuse of other substances. In comparison with other countries the figures for ALCOHOL CONSUMPTION per capita appear low, until adjustment is made for the relatively large number of non-drinkers. The alcohol industry makes a significant contribution to the ECONOMY, in three areas: EMPLOYMENT, tax revenue, and balance of payments. Probably the greatest concern for the future is access by teenagers to alcohol. Despite legislation banning the sale of alcohol to those under the age of eighteen and its consumption

Alcock and Brown. *The Vickers Vimy aircraft powered by two 360-hp Rolls-Royce Eagle VIII engines in which Alcock and Brown made the first transatlantic flight in April 1919, after it had crashlanded in Derrygimla Bog, Co. Galway. [Sean Sexton]*

alcohol. *Members of the 'Pioneers' (Pioneer Total Abstinence Association of the Sacred Heart) pass the Parnell Monument in O'Connell Street, Dublin, before proceeding to Croke Park for their diamond jubilee rally, June 1959. [Lensmen and Associates]*

by them in public, research has shown that under-age drinking is widespread. An increasing number of young people are starting to drink early, a larger proportion are regular drinkers by eighteen, and many abuse alcohol. **Kathleen O'Higgins**

alcohol consumption. In late medieval Ireland the consumption of alcohol was a ritualised activity. Drinking took place only on special occasions: at seasonal and religious festivals, at family and community celebrations, and during the entertainment of important guests. Alcohol was associated with feasting. Drink was expensive, as the production of ale, beer, or spirits used up scarce grain supplies, while wine had to be imported from the Continent. In the coastal towns, among the ANGLO-NORMANS, the regular consumption of alcohol appears to have been more common at this time. Merchants who controlled the wine trade established taverns on their premises, while brewing was largely in the hands of women, working in the home.

This pattern of regular drinking in towns and occasional drinking in the countryside was still evident in Ireland as late as the nineteenth century. Then temperance advocates attacked urban workers for drinking heavily during and after work and on weekends, whereas the rural population was criticised for occasional lengthy bouts of drunkenness during and following fairs and wakes and on saints' days. But urban patterns increasingly influenced rural Ireland as traditional festivals were suppressed and licensed public houses selling commercially produced beer and spirits spread widely. During the nineteenth and early twentieth centuries, however, the temperance movement, strongly supported by the churches, succeeded in creating a large population of total abstainers. Few women drank, neither did most devout Catholics and Protestants; in 1968 it was estimated that 52 per cent of the adult population of the Republic were abstainers. Heavy alcohol consumption tended to be especially common among male urban tradesmen and labourers and among bachelor small farmers; these groups certainly suffered from high levels of alcohol-related physical and mental disease.

Despite the efforts of various successful religious anti-drink organisations, the pub remained a vital centre of Irish social life in both town and country throughout the twentieth century, though increasingly regulated and taxed. Illicit spirits, in the form of POITÍN, continued to be distilled, but not on the same scale as in the previous century. But the Irish were drinking more in the second half of the twentieth century than in the first; studies suggest that it was some time in the early 1970s that Ireland changed from being a country in which the majority of the adult population were teetotallers to one in which the majority were drinkers. This increase partly reflected growing affluence. From the late 1960s also, pubs ceased being largely male domains as more and more women began to drink in public. In addition, drinkers were becoming younger.

Yet while alcohol consumption surged during the 1960s and 70s and again during the 1990s, the Irish were still far down the European league of drinkers. A study in 1998 showed that the Republic was twelfth in a list of European countries according to quantity of alcohol consumed per head per annum, far behind Luxembourg, Portugal, and France though well ahead of Italy, the Netherlands, and Britain. [see ALCOHOL ABUSE; ETHER DRINKING; DISTILLING; TALBOT, MATT.] **Elizabeth Malcolm**

Alcorn, Michael (1962–), composer. Born in Belfast, he graduated from the Universities of Ulster and Durham, studied under John Casken, and holds a doctorate in composition. A senior lecturer at Queen's University, Belfast, he works chiefly in the field of music technology. His works have been broadcast throughout Europe, the Americas, and Asia. He has received commissions from the BBC, IRISH CHAMBER ORCHESTRA, and OPERA THEATRE COMPANY. He is chairman of the Irish Electro-Acoustic Music Association. **Paul J. Kerr**

Aldritt family (fl. 1900s) aircraft builders. Louis Aldritt, his father, Frank Aldritt, and his brothers were the proprietors of a garage in Maryborough (Port Laoise), Co. Laois. In 1912 they built a monoplane with the help of a schoolboy, JAMES FITZMAURICE, later to become an Atlantic pioneer. The aircraft had limited success, and the endeavour was condemned by local clergy of both denominations. Except for a few engine components, all the aircraft's parts were made in Ireland. Its remains were preserved at Aldritts' garage until recently. **Donal MacCarron**

Alexander, Cecil Frances, née Humphries (1818–1895), poet and hymn-writer. Born in Dublin. In 1850 she married William Alexander, subsequently Anglican Bishop of Derry and Raphoe and (after his wife's death) Primate of All Ireland. A friend of such renowned Anglican divines as Keble and Pusey, she published her *Hymns for Little Children* in 1848, which contained hymns that achieved popularity throughout the English-speaking world: 'All Things Bright and Beautiful', 'There Is a Green Hill Far Away', and 'Once in Royal David's City'. **Terence Brown**

Algerian corsairs. Throughout the seventeenth and eighteenth centuries there are frequent references in contemporary accounts to Algerian corsairs harassing traders off the Irish coast. There had long been rivalry between North African and Spanish seamen over control of the Gibraltar Strait and the west Mediterranean trade; and when Spain expelled its large Muslim population early in the seventeenth century many of the refugees took to the seas, later reinforced by adventurers from the African interior, in a counter-offensive against all Spaniards and eventually all Christian European trade. Political and religious upheavals in Ireland drove many people from their land, and some joined the Algerian corsairs, notably a successful Irish mariner, O'Driscoll, from Co. Cork. In 1631 Algerian corsairs carried off the whole population of Baltimore, Co. Cork; when, after years, the British government offered to ransom them back, only a tiny minority accepted, the remainder having settled down happily in North Africa. [see PIRACY; THOMPSON, ELIZABETH.] **John de Courcy Ireland**

Allen, Bog of, an area of peatland between Cos. Kildare, Meath, and Offaly. The bog is not a single entity but a complex that formerly covered 200,000 ha (750 sq. miles), with peat 5 m (15 ft) thick, but now diminished by stripping and drainage.

Its formation began 9,000 years ago in fens along the shores of post-glacial LAKES. With increased biological productivity and the accumulation of organic debris the lakes became shallower and were invaded by water lilies, bulrushes, and reeds. In the acidifying waters dead plants amassed into *fen peat*, which was colonised by willow, alder, and native pine woods. As the peat accumulated, the bog water-table rose, allowing the wood-fen margin to expand between 8,500 and 5,000 years ago. However, with increasing accumulation of peat, between 7,500 and 1,500 years ago the peats became both starved of inorganic nutrients from below and colonised by sphagnum, which flourishes on nutrients from rain alone. This period is represented in the Bog of Allen by highly *humified* or decayed peat more than 3.5 m (12 ft) thick, indicative of warm, dry conditions dominated by aerobic decay processes. However, the uppermost peat in the Bog of Allen is only weakly humidified, indicating wetter, cooler, extremely waterlogged conditions characterised by anaerobic conditions in which organic decomposition was minimal. As a result, preserved in the bog are important records of Ireland's post-glacial environmental and human heritage.

The Bog of Allen has given its name to the *Allen soil series*, the characteristic peaty soil of large tracts of the midlands. **Colman Gallagher**

Allen, Dave, stage name of David Tynan O'Mahony (1936–), comedian. Born in Dublin. A former newspaper clerk and Butlin's holiday camp 'redcoat', he became one of British television's most controversial comics of the 1970s, presenting a relaxed, urbane, articulate image, in contrast to the Irish buffoons of the variety era. Material about sex and religion led to his being banned from Australian television and incurred the wrath of Mary Whitehouse, British television's morals watchdog; nevertheless he became a star, presenting 'Sunday Night at the London Palladium' in 1967, 'Tonight with Dave Allen' the following year, and 'Dave Allen at Large' in the 1970s. **Stephen Dixon and Deirdre Falvey**

Allgood, Sara (1883–1950), actor. Born in Dublin. She was on the stage at the ABBEY THEATRE on its opening night in 1904. She played the Widow Quinn in THE PLAYBOY OF THE WESTERN WORLD, 1907, and when touring Australia with *Peg o' My Heart* made her first film, *Just Peggy* (1918). She also appeared in Alfred Hitchcock's *Blackmail* (1929) and his version of SEAN O'CASEY's *Juno and the Paycock* (1930) (see p. 2). After touring America with the Abbey Theatre in the mid-1930s she settled in Hollywood; while she usually played minor roles as an Irish cook or landlady, there were more substantial appearances in *Jane Eyre* (1943) and *The Lodger* (1944). **Kevin Rockett**

Alliance Party of Northern Ireland, formed in April 1970 by centrist political interests, including members of the liberal-unionist New Ulster Movement, and attracting some adherents who had not previously been involved in politics. Its priority was the elimination of sectarian strife. Its support for the maintenance of Northern Ireland's constitutional position within the United Kingdom so long as that was the majority wish was accompanied by advocacy of action to give all sections of the population a fair deal. It strongly supported, and was part of the coalition that sustained, the power-sharing Executive of 1974, in which it had two representatives. Despite its appeal to Protestant and Catholic moderates it never won more than approximately 13 per cent of the local government vote and 10 per cent of the regional vote, with support concentrated mainly in more prosperous and predominantly urban areas. A slight decline in its electoral fortunes from the early 1980s reflected the impact of the HUNGER STRIKES on the Catholic vote and perhaps owed something to increased fragmentation of party politics, encouraged by the reintroduction from 1973 of proportional representation. A disappointing performance in the 1998 NORTHERN IRELAND ASSEMBLY elections prevented the party from securing an expected ministerial position in the Executive set up under the BELFAST AGREEMENT (1998), although Lord Alderdice became Speaker of the Assembly. **Alan Scott**

Allingham, William (1824–1889), poet and diarist, best remembered for 'The Fairies'. Born in Ballyshannon, Co. Donegal. From 1846 he worked as a customs officer while publishing poems, notably *The Music Master* (1854), illustrated by Rossetti and Millais. In 1854 he left for London to become a full-time writer. Conversations with the pre-Raphaelites, Tennyson and Carlyle, are recorded in his diary (published 1907). *Laurence Bloomfield in Ireland* (1864) is an ambitious narrative poem about land agitation in Co. Donegal. In 1872 he became editor of *Fraser's Magazine* in London. W. B. YEATS selected and edited *Sixteen Poems* (1905) by Allingham, 'my master in Irish verse.' **Matthew Campbell**

Allman, George James (1812–1898), zoologist. Born in Cork; graduated in medicine from TCD in 1843. In the following year he was appointed professor of Botany, in succession to his namesake, William Allman. He became a world authority on two groups of animals, coelenterates and polyzoans. In 1854 he was elected to fellowship of the Royal Society and in 1855 became regius professor of natural history at the University of Edinburgh, retiring in 1870 to live in Weybridge in England. He was an enthusiast for the popularisation of science and a leading light in the British Association for the Advancement of Science. **Christopher Moriarty**

Allman, George Johnston (1824–1904), mathematician. Born in Dublin; graduated in 1844 from TCD, where his father, William Allman, was professor of botany. He was appointed professor of mathematics at Queen's College, Galway, in 1853, and retained this position until his retirement in 1893. His main scholarly interest was ancient Greek mathematics, and his reputation in this subject is based on his book *Greek Geometry from Thales to Euclid* (1889), which remains a valuable reference. **Rod Gow**

Altan, a TRADITIONAL MUSIC group founded by the husband-and-wife duo Frankie Kennedy (FLUTE) and Máiréad Ní Mhaonaigh (FIDDLE and vocals) in the mid-1980s and notable for their promotion of the music and song of Co. Donegal. The fiddle is the predominant instrument in Donegal music and features strongly in Altan's sound. Paul O'Shaughnessy (fiddle) and Ciarán Tourish (fiddle) have played alongside Ní Mhaonaigh; the ACCORDION-player Dermot Byrne joined in 1984, following Kennedy's death. Mark Kelly and Dáithí Sproule (guitar) and Ciarán Curran (bouzouki) are long-time members. A busy touring schedule, especially in North America, and a series of ground-breaking recordings have helped establish Altan as one of the most popular and influential of the traditional bands since the 1980s. **Tom Sherlock**

Altar controversy. In 1847, the worst year of the GREAT FAMINE, Rev. William Allen Fisher (1808–1880), CHURCH OF IRELAND rector of Kilmoe, Co. Cork, erected a new church in the townland of Altar. Because it was built by the local poor he called it Teampall na mBocht (Church of the Poor). It has been a source of contention ever since. Some Catholics claim that Fisher diverted to it funds contributed to the Kilmoe Relief Committee for general famine relief, and further that he employed Catholics in its building, but only on condition that they convert to the Church of Ireland. At that time a number of Anglican clergymen were accused of such bribing of the starving with food or work, a practice known as 'SOUPERISM'. Fisher has been demonised as the arch-souper. Protestants, on the contrary, maintain that the church was built not out of Relief Committee money but with donations solicited directly from well-wishers in Ireland and England, and from Fisher's own income.

The Great Famine coincided with the so-called 'SECOND REFORMATION', a Protestant campaign to promote the mass conversion of the Catholic majority. Fisher undoubtedly committed himself to this campaign and was unashamedly a proselytiser. He certainly made many converts—how many is disputed—but he vehemently denied any sort of bribery or coercion. His defenders insist that he owed his conversions not to 'souperism' but to his compassion for all who suffered; they revere him as a saintly man who worked selflessly for forty years with the hungry, sick, and dying of both faiths until he himself died of famine fever. The anguished letters Fisher wrote to his family in England about the suffering in Kilmoe, and his efforts to alleviate it, give some weight to this view; but in the absence of objective evidence the claims and counter-claims continue. This was demonstrated in 1985 in the controversy that greeted the staging at the ABBEY THEATRE, Dublin, of Eoghan Harris's play *Souper Sullivan*, implying Fisher's complete innocence. [see NANGLE, REV. EDWARD.] **John Wakeman**

Allingham. *William Allingham, author of* The Fairies *and* Laurence Bloomfield in Ireland, *an epic poem dealing with absentee landlordism in his native Co. Donegal. [Council of Trustees of the National Library of Ireland; R.13378]*

amateur and community theatre. As with most European cultures, the earliest forms of Irish theatre were community-based, taking the form of civic pageants paraded through the streets of MEDIEVAL TOWNS. From at least the fifteenth century both Dublin and Kilkenny hosted a regular Corpus Christi procession, involving episodes from the Old and New Testaments. However, by the middle of the seventeenth century (and earlier in Dublin) these traditions had faded.

While the civic pageants were exclusively urban phenomena, the form of folk drama known as mumming was rural, appearing first in the late seventeenth century, possibly imported from Scotland. Using disguises, cross-dressing, and simple scripts based around iconic characters (such as the Doctor and Cromwell), the MUMMERS moved from house to house at particular times of the year, playing in the kitchens of the communities in which they lived. In some parts of rural Ulster and Connacht mumming continued to be practised well into the twentieth century. Over time, the mumming tradition merged with the staging of scripted plays, such as Robert Ashton's *The Battle of Aughrim* (1728), which was performed in barns throughout rural Ulster until the middle of the nineteenth century. At the same time private performances in country houses were common throughout the eighteenth and nineteenth centuries.

In the late nineteenth century a new kind of amateur theatre society came into being, often with an overt political agenda. Such groups provided the early ABBEY THEATRE with many of its personnel. However, in the years leading up to the 1916 RISING the political came to dominate the theatrical, and most of these groups disbanded—though the Dublin Shakespeare Society, originally the Dublin Branch of the British Empire Shakespeare Society (1907–), remains a notable exception.

It was not until the early 1930s that amateur theatre once again began to take hold in towns and villages. It quickly became competitive, and a circuit of festivals was in existence by the early 1940s. By 1953 this was given a focus when the competitive All-Ireland Drama Final was first held in Athlone, administered by the DRAMA LEAGUE OF IRELAND. Providing an early outlet for such playwrights as JOHN B. KEANE and TOM MURPHY, the amateur festival circuit brought amateurs into close contact with professionals, who acted as adjudicators. Indeed until the mid-1970s the amateur movement provided most actors and directors with the experience, training and contacts necessary to make the move into the professional sphere. Meanwhile, outside the competitive festivals, some communities began staging collectively written works, beginning with those created in the late 1970s by the Turf Lodge Fellowship, Belfast, under the guidance of the playwright Martin Lynch. At the beginning of the twenty-first century there were an estimated 500 amateur companies of varying sizes throughout the country, playing to combined annual audiences of half a million. **Christopher Morash**

Amergin Glúngel ('bright-knee'), a mythical poet who accompanied the legendary Milesian invaders to Ireland. He is best known in early traditions for naming Ireland: according to these, he named the country after three goddesses of TUATHA DÉ DANANN: Fódla, Banba, and Ériu. The last of these gives us ÉIRE (later *Éirinn*) and, ultimately, *Ireland*. [see IRELAND, NAMES OF.] **Elva Johnston**

American wake. A distinctive feature of EMIGRATION from Ireland in the nineteenth century was the ritual of departure often referred to as the American wake. The custom developed from the tradition of the WAKE, whereby neighbours and friends sat up overnight in the company of a body before burial. For an emigrant to America, the finality of the departure was symbolised by equating departure for the New World with that for the next world. It is worth noting that those emigrants who left for Britain, either temporarily or permanently, were not generally 'waked'. To put this ritual in context it is useful to observe that estimated rates of return migration from North America to Ireland were significantly lower than the European average during the later nineteenth century.

The custom appears to have had its origins in the later eighteenth century in Ulster, from which emigration was then greatest. Practised by both Presbyterians and Catholics, the ceremony was then more generally known as a *living wake*. From the 1830s onwards, as emigration became increasingly embedded in the culture of Catholic Ireland, the American wake became particularly associated with the more traditional and Irish-speaking areas of the midlands and west.

In the days before departure the emigrant would tour the locality to bid farewell to friends and relatives and to invite them to attend their American wake on their last night at home. The party would gather, normally in the house of the departing emigrant, now generally referred to as 'the Yank'. Gifts or verbal salutations were offered before the older participants gathered around the HEARTH to sing and tell stories, while the younger folk danced to the sound of FIDDLE and pipes; as the night progressed, WHISKEY or POITÍN might be offered to sustain flagging energies. Frequently, as in real wakes, the distinctive sound of women KEENING would be heard. As dawn came, the cabin was cleared to allow the emigrant a private parting from their family. The younger people then accompanied the emigrant at least part of the way on the journey (a ceremony known as the 'convoy'), often to a distant hill or crossroads, from where they watched the figure pass out of sight.

The American wake combined elements of both gaiety and grief, though the latter was almost always predominant. It also served as a reminder to the emigrant of the importance of supporting the home with the remittance of money from wherever they settled. While the tradition of gathering to mark the departure of an emigrant endured into the twentieth century, the occasion less frequently displayed openly the same level of emotional intensity. [see DIASPORA; UNITED STATES, IRISH IN.] **Patrick Fitzgerald**

amhráin saothair, traditional work songs. *Ceapóga*, associated with light work and involving sung dialogue in verse form, are the only surviving form of work songs still sung in Ireland today. The task to be performed may be sharpening a razor, waxing thread, or twisting a *súgán* (straw rope). The songs are of a simple structure, usually a quatrain sung in 6/8 time, and generally of a jocose nature. The first singer sings a line, followed by a nonsense chorus line; this is followed by the second singer singing another line, followed by another nonsense or chorus line.

The LÚIBÍN ('little twister'), originally from the Muskerry, Co. Cork, tradition, is a sung dialogue between two singers with a chorus separating each verse, usually a quatrain or octet; the dialogue is witty and records local events or subjects. These songs have been made popular by the annual OIREACHTAS competitions. **Peadar Ó Riada**

'Amhrán na bhFiann', the national anthem of the Republic. It was written as 'The Soldier's Song' by PEADAR KEARNEY in 1907, with music by his friend Patrick Heeney, in association with

Kearney and Seán Rogan (see p. 927). It was first published in 1912 by Bulmer Hobson in *Irish Freedom* and from c. 1914 became the marching song of the IRISH VOLUNTEERS. The Irish translation by Liam Ó Rinn, first published in 1923, has since become the version generally sung. In 1924 the chorus of 'Amhrán na bhFiann' became the *de facto* anthem of the Irish Free State, officially confirmed in July 1926. **Glenn Cumiskey**

Amlaíb Cuarán, King of Dublin, 945–980. Son of Sitric; he married GORMLAITH, daughter of Murchad, King of Leinster. He was a convert to Christianity, and his plundering of ecclesiastical sites, such as Kells, Co. Meath, and Kildare, was politically motivated. Defeated by MÁEL SECHNAILL, King of Mide, in 980, he abdicated, dying on IONA. His successors included his sons Glúniarainn and Sitric. **Ailbhe Mac Shamhráin**

Amnesty Association, founded in Dublin on 28 June 1869 with the aim of agitating for the release of prisoners who had been involved in Fenian outrages since 1867. Headed by ISAAC BUTT, it had as its most prominent and energetic activist John 'Amnesty' Nolan. It had considerable success in intimidating GLADSTONE's government into releasing prisoners in 1869 and 1871. Without doubt, the activities of the Amnesty Association renewed and intensified nationalist sentiment in Ireland as a whole. The movement's apex was reached with a series of 'monster meetings' in the autumn of 1873. By 1875 the emphasis had largely shifted to the House of Commons, where John O'Connor Power and CHARLES STEWART PARNELL became the leading advocates in demanding amnesty for the few remaining Fenian prisoners. **Oliver P. Rafferty**

Amongst Women (1990), a novel by JOHN MCGAHERN. It studies the rural household of Michael Moran, republican veteran and patriarch, over a period of twenty years in post-independence Ireland. The title comes from the Rosary, recited by Moran every evening. He defines his family as a 'larger self'; his children love and fear him equally as he exercises his authority through a series of domestic rituals that show his resistance to change and to the wider world. The understated tension of the novel and its perceptive characterisation won McGahern the *Irish Times*-Aer Lingus Irish Fiction Prize. It was also dramatised in a joint RTÉ-BBC production narrated by Tony Doyle (1998). **Selina Guinness**

Amory, Thomas (c. 1691–1788), novelist. Probably born in London of planter stock; he claimed to have been brought to Ireland as an infant, to have learnt Irish, and to have been educated at TCD. In his eccentric *Memoirs of Several Ladies of Great Britain* (1755) and THE LIFE OF JOHN BUNCLE, ESQ. (1756–66), he reveals an informed interest in the contemporary Irish-speaking and Gaelic-speaking worlds and their history unusual in English-language writers of the middle of the eighteenth century. An enthusiastic scholar, anti-Trinitarian, and proponent of women's education, Amory is at times difficult to distinguish from his fictional creation John Buncle. **Ian Campbell Ross**

'Amra Choluimb Chille', a lament in Old Irish for COLM CILLE. Attributed to DALLÁN FORGAILL, it was probably composed shortly after the saint's death in 597 and is therefore one of the oldest surviving literary works in Irish. Colm Cille's royal ancestry is repeatedly honoured in the poem, but he is praised as a spiritual rather than a secular leader, a faithful follower of the cross of Christ, ascetic and virtuous in his daily life, and protector of the naked and the poor. Great emphasis is placed on his learning and scholarship, and on his role as a teacher. **Tomás Ó Cathasaigh**

anchoritism. Early Irish MONASTICISM was much influenced by the traditions of the Egyptian desert fathers, and many early Irish saints are described as hermits or anchorites, though little is known of their way of life. Increased contacts with the Continent from the eleventh century and the ANGLO-NORMAN impact on the Irish church influenced the life-style of Irish anchorites in the later Middle Ages. Between the eleventh and seventeenth centuries there are occasional references to Irish anchorites in Dublin, Cork, Cashel, Slane, Fore, and Fulda (Germany), while individual CISTERCIANS, Augustinian Canons, and FRANCISCANS are also recorded as living as hermits. There are two documents on the anchoritic life in a late thirteenth-century manuscript from St Thomas's Court, Dublin. The only definite example of a medieval Irish hermit's dwelling is in Fore, Co. Westmeath; it contains a plaque dated 1616 commemorating Patrick Begley, its last known occupant. **Colmán N. Ó Clabaigh**

Ancient Order of Hibernians (AOH). Founded in New York in 1836, the AOH is rooted in eighteenth-century and perhaps earlier Catholic secret societies. Chapters of the AOH in America protested against anti-Irish Catholic DISCRIMINATION, provided benefits to members, and aided nationalist movements. The Irish organisation merged with the American AOH (Board of Erin) in 1898. In America there was a strong Ulster bias in memberhip (often in competition for jobs against Leinstermen and Munstermen). Membership declined after 1920, though several American chapters remain active. The AOH experienced a rebirth in Ireland after 1907, and it was active in the 1918 general election; in Northern Ireland AOH activities help Catholics maintain a sense of community. **Lawrence W. McBride**

Andrews, Christopher S. ('Todd') (1901–1985), public servant. Born in Dublin; educated at St Enda's School, Synge Street CBS, and UCD. He took part in the WAR OF INDEPENDENCE and the CIVIL WAR on the anti-Treaty side. He subsequently worked in TOURISM and the ESB and pioneered the development of BOGS as sources of fuel, becoming chairman of BORD NA MÓNA in 1946. From 1958 to 1966 he was chairman of CIÉ and closed down many railway lines considered to be uneconomic, including the suburban Harcourt Street line in Dublin, now the path of the LUAS. He was chairman of the RTÉ Authority, 1966–70. Andrews had a reputation for forcefulness. He published two classic autobiographies, *Dublin Made Me* (1979) and *A Man of No Property* (1982). **Tom Garvin**

Andrews, Éamonn (1922–1987), television broadcaster. Born in Dublin; educated at Synge Street CBS. He worked in many areas of Irish cultural life, including THEATRE, commercials, sports, and writing. He became a household name after he joined the BBC, where he presented popular television programmes, including 'What's My Line?,' 'The Eamonn Andrews Show', 'Today' and 'This is Your Life'. He was the chairman of the RTÉ Authority from the introduction of television in Ireland in 1961 until 1966. **Bernadette Grummell**

Andrews, John Miller (1871–1956), politician. Born in Comber, Co. Down; educated in Belfast, and became a director of his family LINEN-bleaching firm and of the Belfast Ropeworks. An MP in the Northern Ireland parliament for Co. Down (1921–9) and for Mid-Down (1929–53), he was a founder-member of the Ulster Unionist Labour Association, which he chaired, and served as Minister of Labour from 1921 to 1937. He was Minister of Finance from 1937 to 1940 when, on the death of Lord Craigavon, he became Northern Ireland's second Prime Minister. The somewhat lethargic response of his ageing Cabinet to the exigencies of the SECOND WORLD WAR, and his unwillingness to replace the old guard with younger, more vigorous ministers, left him open to internal Unionist Party criticism. He was eventually ousted in 1943, when he was succeeded as Prime Minister by the more dynamic BASIL BROOKE. He remained president of the ULSTER UNIONIST COUNCIL, 1940–47. Throughout his life he was noted for his deep involvement in the ORANGE ORDER, in which he occupied the offices of grand master of County Down from 1941, of Ireland, 1948–54, and of the Imperial Grand Council of the World, 1949–54. **Alan Scott**

Andrews, Mary K. (1852–1914), geologist. Born in Belfast, youngest daughter of DR THOMAS ANDREWS. For some years she was honorary secretary of the Geological Section of BELFAST NATURALISTS' FIELD CLUB and, together with SYDNEY MARY THOMPSON and others, she carried out research on the local glacial deposits. She also contributed geological photographs to the collection of the British Association. Among her published papers are 'The Early History of Magnetism' (*Nature*, 1876) and 'Notes on Some Igneous Rocks in Antrim and Down'. **Geoff Warke**

Andrews, Thomas (1813–1885), chemist and university administrator. Born in Belfast, son of a LINEN merchant; he began his study of CHEMISTRY in 1828 at the University of Glasgow and continued it later in Paris. He published the first of his many scientific papers at the age of fifteen. At twenty-three he became a physician in Belfast, as well as professor of chemistry at the Royal Belfast Academical Institution. When the Queen's College, Belfast, opened in 1845, he became its first professor of chemistry, as well as vice-president. An outstanding experimentalist in chemistry, he was the first to show that ozone is another form of oxygen. Using narrow-bore, thick glass capillary tubes to contain gases under great pressure, he showed that Boyle's Law does not describe the behaviour of gases under extreme conditions of temperature and pressure. His discoveries led to the liquefaction of all gases, some of which had previously been thought not to be able to exist as liquids. Internationally recognised, he was elected to many scientific academies and in 1867 became president of the British Association for the Advancement of Science. **William J. Davis**

anemometer. *The anemometer on the East Pier, Dún Laoghaire, Co. Dublin, a small granite building erected in 1852 to house the equipment for charting wind speed, invented by Thomas Romney Robinson of Trinity College, Dublin. [Dún Laoghaire Harbour Company; photo: Denis Mortell]*

anemometer, a device for measuring the strength of the wind, invented to improve the quality of navigation and the safety of seafarers. The anemometer was invented by REV. THOMAS ROMNEY ROBINSON of Trinity College, Dublin, in 1845 and was erected on the East Pier of Kingstown (DÚN LAOGHAIRE) HARBOUR, then nearing completion. The original instrument housed in a small Egyptian revival granite building (1852) was consulted, particularly by yachtsmen and the masters of sailing ships. In time, anemometers came to be widely used, both on shore and on board ship. The original anemometer continued to function until near the end of the twentieth century when, needing cleaning and repairs, it was taken down by the harbour authority, to be replaced, thoroughly renovated, with a weather station on its original site in 1999. **John de Courcy Ireland**

Angelus, the, from *'Angelus Domini'* ('the angel of the Lord'), the opening words of a Latin prayer commemorating the Annunciation and Incarnation, common in Catholic countries and originally (since 1326) said at dawn, noon and sunset and, since the seventeenth century, announced by the ringing of church bells. The practice had its origin in the seven canonical hours for monastic prayer—matins and lauds, prime, terce, sext, nones, vespers, and compline—recited at regular hours throughout the day. The public radio, and later television, broadcasting of the Angelus bell at noon and 6 p.m. on Radio Éireann (now RTÉ) was inaugurated at 6 p.m. on 15 August 1950, at the request of ARCHBISHOP JOHN CHARLES MCQUAID and with the agreement of León Ó Broin, Secretary of the Department of Posts and Telegraphs. The bells, which ring in a 3-3-3-9 sequence, are those of St Mary's Pro-Cathedral, Marlborough Street, Dublin.

Though the practice has been seen by critics of the Irish state as evidence of its triumphalist sectarian character, the events commemorated, the Annunciation and Incarnation, are accepted by all Christian denominations; nor is the Irish practice unique. In Finland YLE, the national broadcasting service, transmits the bells of the Lutheran Turku Cathedral at noon, while Radio Ylen Ykkonen broadcasts church bells at 6 p.m. **Brian Lalor**

Anglade, François (1758–1834), theologian. Born in Milheu, Aveyron, France; studied philosophy at Rodez and theology in Paris, where he was professor in 1789. He left France in 1792, having refused to take the OATH OF ALLEGIANCE. He is believed to have spent six years working as a gardener in Wales. In 1802 he was appointed first professor of logic at ST PATRICK'S COLLEGE,

angling. *An angler casting a dry fly for brown trout on the River Suir, Co. Tipperary. The pursuit of native fish in wild places makes Ireland a prime venue for game angling; there are countless rivers and small loughs where the lone angler can fish in solitude. [Central Fisheries Board]*

Maynooth, and in 1810 professor of moral theology. His main work is *Institutiones Philosophiae* (three volumes, 1813–15). He also took charge of sacred music at Maynooth on his appointment and, after his retirement, took charge of liturgy. **Thomas A. F. Kelly**

angling, coarse. Ireland's limestone-rich and largely unspoilt rivers and lakes hold huge stocks of coarse fish, particularly bream, roach, tench, and pike. Most coarse angling is concentrated in the lakelands of Cos. Cavan, Monaghan, and Leitrim, the River Erne system, and the River Shannon catchment, where the deep and slow-moving rivers and lakes are ideally suited to the gathering of large feeding shoals of bream and roach. However, the main coarse species of bream, roach, rudd, roach-bream hybrid, tench, eel, perch, and pike can be found in waters throughout Ireland, while dace can be found in the Munster Blackwater and carp in the Lough in Cork and a number of small lakes in the midlands. The primary coarse angling waters include Lough Oughter, Lough Gowna, Lough Muckno, Lough Ramor, Lough Garadice, Lough Ree, Lough Major, Lough Erne, Ballinafid Lake, Galmoylestown Lake, Ross Lake, Corstown Lake, Castle Lake, the Rivers Shannon, Erne, Blackwater, Bann, and Suck, Inniscarra Reservoir, Newry Ship Canal, and the Royal Canal and Grand Canal.

Before the 1950s coarse angling was largely undeveloped as a sport; it was then revolutionised by English anglers who, recognising the abundant fishing to be had in the relatively unfished lakes and rivers, began to visit Ireland in increasing numbers. BORD FÁILTE quickly recognised the TOURISM potential of these visitors and took steps to enhance the facilities available to visiting as well as native anglers. Tourism continues to underpin much coarse angling activity, with the principal angling festivals—such as the Guinness Classic at Enniskillen, the Irish Ferries King of Clubs, the Portumna Shannon Festival, and the All-Ireland Open Championship—each attracting 200–300 visiting anglers. It is estimated by Bord Fáilte that coarse angling contributed €18.5 million to national income in 2000.

Coarse angling is administered by the National Coarse Fishing Federation of Ireland, while the Central Fisheries Board and regional fisheries boards are responsible for the promotion and marketing of angling, together with policy research and the administering of national and EU funding schemes. In Northern Ireland the Fisheries Conservancy Board for Northern Ireland and the Foyle Fisheries Commission supervise the issuing of coarse angling licences and the development of angling. **Colm O'Gaora**

angling, game. Ireland's position on the western seaboard of Europe and its proximity to the North Atlantic Drift, together with its wealth of limestone-rich rivers and lakes, provides migratory Atlantic salmon and sea trout, as well as native brown trout, with an ideal habitat. The high alkalinity of some of the largest lakes, such as Lough Conn, Lough Mask, and Lough Corrib, allows the brown trout populations to grow rapidly in both size and number, while the multitude of rivers attract prolific runs of migratory salmon and sea trout. In addition to native salmon, sea trout, brown trout, and the rarely fished-for char, some fisheries, particularly state-owned reservoir fisheries, have introduced rainbow trout to their waters.

Game angling for salmon and sea trout requires the purchase of a state licence, irrespective of venue and method. Game fisheries are owned by a variety of interests, including the state, businesses, angling syndicates, landowners and other individuals, clubs and associations. Many of these controlling interests demand a daily, weekly, monthly or annual fee from anglers, while some do not open their waters to other anglers at all. Game angling is seasonal, depending on the fisheries district, venue, species, and time of year. Game angling contributed €34.8 million to national income in 2000.

Though nearly all Ireland's sea-going rivers have annual runs of salmon and sea trout, and brown trout are to be found in almost every water, game angling is largely concentrated around the fisheries of LOUGH CORRIB AND LOUGH MASK, Lough Conn and the Moy system, the River SUIR, the KILLARNEY LAKES, and the River SHANNON system. With Ireland having some of the best game fishing in Europe, the tourist market for the sport is well developed. The angling season tends to peak with the mayfly hatch on the great western lakes in May and June, when thousands of anglers travel to Ireland from Britain and the Continent. Salmon catches declined dramatically during the 1990s, and in 2000 the Central Fisheries Board introduced a salmon carcase tagging and log-book scheme in an attempt to accurately monitor the changes in salmon numbers. **Colm O'Gaora**

angling, sea. The seas off Ireland provide the most varied and exciting sea angling in Europe. The combination of the warmer waters of the North Atlantic Drift and the cooler waters of the North Atlantic means that species as diverse as bass, cod, monkfish, gurnard and blue and porbeagle shark are regularly caught in Irish waters. In addition, the rugged nature of the Irish coast allows plentiful specimen fish to be caught using shore, inshore and deep-sea angling methods. The varied nature of the coastline offers the sea angler a wide choice of fishing venues, from the long, sweeping and shallow shores of the east coast, home to Ireland's premier shore match angling venues, to the jagged promontories and peninsulas of the south-west, west and north-west, which provide easy access to the deep waters at the edge of the Continental shelf.

Ireland's reputation as Europe's premier sea fishing venue is primarily based on its shore and deep-sea fisheries. Unpolluted beaches, harbours and coastal rocks provide a wide variety of shore fishing, including beach-casting for bass, flounder, and codling, harbour fishing for conger and mullet, and rock fishing for pollack, wrasse, and mackerel. The deep-sea fishing centres of Kinsale, Co. Cork, Fenit, Co. Kerry, Clifden, Co. Galway, and Westport, Co. Mayo, among others, are home to small fleets of charter boats designed and equipped for fishing for blue and porbeagle shark, conger, ling, skate, ray, monkfish, and other deep-sea species. The tourist potential of sea angling has been well developed, and anglers from all over Europe travel to Ireland in great numbers each year, with deep-sea and inshore angling becoming increasingly popular. The development, promotion, and marketing of sea angling is carried out by the Central Fisheries Board, together with the seven regional fisheries boards. In Northern Ireland the Department of Agriculture and Rural Development has responsibility for managing rivers and drainage and for sea fisheries. The largest representative body is the Irish Federation of Sea Anglers. **Colm O'Gaora**

Anglo-Boer Wars. Irishmen fought in the three British imperial campaigns against the Afrikaner republics of South Africa, initially when Captain Smith and two companies of the 27th Regiment (Inniskilling Fusiliers) invaded the Republic of Natalia, 1841–2. The regiment lost the Battle of Congella but successfully withstood an attack on the Old Fort, Durban.

In the First Anglo-Boer War (1880–81) General Sir George Colley of Dublin fell at the Battle of Majuba. On the Boer side was Alfred Aylward from Co. Wexford, a former volunteer commander in the Transvaal Republic. The 94th Regiment (Connaught Rangers) fought in the war, and a detachment was decimated at Bronkhorst Spruit.

The Second Anglo-Boer War (1899–1902) witnessed close to 30,000 Irish soldiers in action from three cavalry and eight infantry regiments, including Hart's 5th (Irish) Brigade. Generals of Irish birth included Roberts, KITCHENER, White, French, and Kelly-Kenny. Irishmen were prominent at the Battles of Colenso, Tugela Heights, Lindley, and Dalmanutha, when there were more than 4,000 casualties. On the Boer side were two Irish Transvaal *commandos* or brigades. One, consisting of some 250 men under John Blake and JOHN MACBRIDE, fought outside Ladysmith, at Colenso, and in the Boer retreat of 1900. Another short-lived commando of about sixty men under Arthur Lynch fought on the Boer retreat out of Natal. In Ireland, the Irish Transvaal Committee campaigned to dissuade Irishmen from enlisting to fight on the British side. **Dónal P. McCracken**

Anglo-Irish Agreement (1985), an agreement between the British and Irish governments, eventually registered with the United Nations and probably the most significant political arrangement for Northern Ireland from the time of the Government of Ireland Act (1920) to the BELFAST AGREEMENT (1998). In spite of glacial relations between the Irish and British governments just a few years earlier, Margaret Thatcher's Conservative government and GARRET FITZGERALD'S Coalition Government were alarmed by the growing electoral support for SINN FÉIN and frustrated by the Unionists' resistance to power-sharing with Catholics. Remembering how the SUNNINGDALE AGREEMENT had been wrecked by the ULSTER WORKERS' COUNCIL strike of 1974, the two prime ministers constructed an arrangement designed to be immune to loyalist protest. The most innovative feature of the accord, which was signed at Hillsborough, Co. Down, on 15 November 1985, was the Intergovernmental Conference, which would meet regularly to promote CROSS-BORDER CO-OPERATION and deal with security and with legal and political matters (including discrimination, electoral arrangements, the status of the Irish language, and the use of flags and emblems). The conference was to be serviced by a permanent secretariat of Northern and Southern civil servants set up at Maryfield, outside Holywood, Co. Down. The first of the twelve articles stated that constitutional change could come about only with the consent of the majority in Northern Ireland but that if a majority sought such change in the future, that change would be given legislative effect. The agreement met with furious reaction from all unionist groupings. **Jonathan Bardon**

Anglo-Irish ballads. 'Ballad' in contemporary parlance means a popular indigenous song in English, frequently lively and often patriotic. The term has had many chronological and regional shifts of meaning. Frequently it was used as a synonym of 'song'; later usage decreed that though all ballads were songs, not all songs were ballads. The popular broadsheet and chapbook presses continued to refer to all their poetry as ballads, but academic and literary figures such as Bishop Thomas Percy in 1765 drew the attention of the public to older traditional narratives; these found popularity with a public who were at the time eagerly absorbing the romantic epics of James Macpherson. The accepted form of the older or classic ballad was agreed to be a narrative told in quatrains or couplets, with or without a chorus or refrain, and related in the third person. Later ballads used various stanzaic patterns and introduced subjectivity and moralising. Even now it is little realised how widespread the classic ballads were in Ireland.

Songwriters in Irish had little fondness for narrative; consequently all the older ballads came from Britain, though their ultimate origin in some instances can be shown to have been in continental Europe or further afield. Still, those that took root in Irish soil can be fairly described as Anglo-Irish. Venerable rarities, such as 'The Maid and the Palmer' and 'Prince Robert', continued to be sung in Ireland long after they had become extinct elsewhere. Some ballads of nineteenth-century Irish origin, such as 'The Lake of Coolfinn', 'Derry Jail', and 'Molly Bawn', have adopted the old ballad form particularly well. The Anglo-Irish ballad shares much with the song tradition of England and Scotland, and much of the repertoire is interchangeable. The large corpus of ballads relating to NAPOLEON Bonaparte is found on both sides of the Irish Sea, though some, such as 'The Green Linnet' and 'The Bonny Bunch of Roses', are of obvious Irish origin. The adventures of Irish highwaymen—'Brave Michael Power' or 'Brennan on the Moor'—are indistinguishable from those of Dick Turpin.

Ireland's history is reflected in its ballads, and their heroes are frequently historical figures, such as DANIEL O'CONNELL. 'The Croppy Boy' and hundreds of other minor figures are elevated to hero status because of their resistance to oppression, a trait that is reflected in songs and tales from every colonised nation. Throughout the nineteenth century, poets such as JAMES CLARENCE MANGAN, THOMAS D'ARCY MAGEE, THOMAS DAVIS, and other contributors to the NATION composed pseudo-heroic ballads in the mode of romantic nationalism then popular throughout Europe. Few if any of these ballads found a permanent place in oral tradition. Journalistic ballads recounting massacres, murders, and more mundane domestic matters follow the general pattern and are distinguishable as Irish only because of their subject matter. These constitute a considerable proportion of the ballad repertoire in Ireland. Many of the STAGE-IRISH songs emanating from nineteenth-century England, showing the Irish people as buffoons, were crude in the extreme, while those originating on the American vaudeville stage were patronising and often equally embarrassing. Nevertheless several humorous American ballads, such as 'Tim Finnegan's Wake' and 'Doran's Ass', were found to be congenial to traditional singers in Ireland and entered the English-language repertoire. [see BALLAD SHEETS AND BROADSIDES.] **Tom Munnelly**

Anglo-Irish Free Trade Area Agreement (AIFTA), an agreement signed in 1965 that provided for the gradual establishment of FREE TRADE in most industrial commodities between the Republic on the one hand and Northern Ireland and Britain on the other. Provision was also made for improving the Republic's access to the British market in agricultural goods. The Agreement further strengthened the Republic's commitment to a policy of free trade, the culmination of this coming in 1973 when the Republic and Britain joined the EEC. While the Republic was in this period in the process of a transition from protection to free trade, Northern Ireland, by contrast, had been fully integrated in an economic sense with Britain, its main trading partner, for 150 years. As a result, much interest attached to the question of how these contrasting experiences influenced the pattern of international trade and payments at this time in the two parts of the country. Surprisingly perhaps, in view of the extremely high initial levels of protection from which the Republic started, the process of adjustment to free trade had by the early 1970s proved relatively smooth. Although industrial imports from the United Kingdom increased relative to non-UK imports and relative to supplies from domestic sources, the effect of the agreement on employment was estimated as involving a net loss of only 2,000 jobs. **John W. O'Hagan**

Anglo-Irish literature (also called Irish writing in English), a term employed in literary and cultural history to characterise literature in English by Irish authors, to distinguish such writing from literature in Irish. One of the earliest surviving English-language texts is 'The Land of Cokaygne', a fantasy of monastic and convent licence, which has been preserved in a fourteenth-century manuscript that also contains at least one piece of verse (by a Franciscan friar named as Michael of Kildare) among its pieces of satirical and religious writings, seventeen of which are in English. Other early writings in English include topographical descriptions and historical and political treatises in prose associated with the English conquest, upon which the English poet Edmund Spenser reflected at the end of the sixteenth century. Literary historians usually identify the emergence of a distinctive Anglo-Irish tradition with the writings of JONATHAN SWIFT and see him as the unconscious progenitor of a line of figures that includes GOLDSMITH, BURKE, EDGEWORTH, YEATS, SYNGE, O'CASEY, JOYCE, and BECKETT, as well as many lesser writers.

The term 'Anglo-Irish literature' has increasingly come to be seen as problematic, however, as it seems to associate all writing by Irish authors in English with the Anglo-Irish caste, which from the WILLIAMITE SETTLEMENT until 1922 exercised near-hegemonic power. Though Irish writing in English has often reflected a dual debt—to indigenous and English literary and linguistic traditions—'Anglo-Irish' has increasingly seemed an inappropriate term for categorising the writings in English of those who are not specifically associated with the Anglo-Irish, and those who came to maturity after PARTITION in 1920 or independence in 1922. Accordingly the term 'Irish literature in English' is now considered to refer to creative writing by Irish men and women of all social origins and political commitments; with the expansion of the idea of 'literature' to include a wide variety of textual practices, the term 'Irish writing in English' is sometimes preferred. **Terence Brown**

Anglo-Irish Agreement. *Garret FitzGerald and Margaret Thatcher sign the Anglo-Irish Agreement in November 1985. In the background are Peter Barry (far left), Dick Spring (third left), and Tom King (fourth right). [Photocall Ireland]*

Anglo-Irish society (seventeenth to twenty-first centuries). The recognition of the PROTESTANT ASCENDANCY and the concept of Anglo-Irish society were first applied in the seventeenth and eighteenth centuries. It derived from a new wave of conquest of Ireland. Previous invaders, largely Welsh ANGLO-NORMANS, had in time reverted to being called 'Old English'. While, for the most part, the 'old English' had been defenders of the Crown, they had assimilated among the CELTS and NORSE settlers and were not divided from them by religion.

Those who came to Ireland with the Elizabethan settlements and the Ulster PLANTATIONS brought division emphasised by the Reformation. For the vanquished, the term 'planter' implied usurper not only in race and language but also in religion. For the newcomers there was continuous struggle involved in retaining the land they had conquered. EDMUND SPENSER in Kilcolman Castle, Co. Cork, did not last, nor did WALTER RALEIGH. CHICHESTER, and the crafty RICHARD BOYLE, Earl of Cork, might acquire lands and splendour in Ulster and in Cork, but their achievements were followed by a long and brutal war. The peace and prosperity of the RESTORATION in 1660 was soon interrupted by the WILLIAMITE WARS. The victory of the BOYNE finally ushered in peace, which would stretch for a hundred years and bring about the golden age of the Ascendancy. But this safety net of peace imposed the PENAL LAWS on the majority of those who lived in Ireland.

In the century that followed the Boyne and ended with the Rebellion of 1798, those who lived in what they considered a Protestant nation achieved a proud standard of civilisation. They enjoyed years of wealth, privilege, and taste in a society where MRS MARY DELANY held her soirées in Delville outside Dublin and Lord CHARLEMONT brought back from his Grand Tour the refinements of classical learning, agreeably symbolised in the architecture of his CASINO at Marino, a villa of great elegance.

The formation, in 1731, of the DUBLIN SOCIETY—the first society of its kind in Europe—was to have important repercussions on Anglo-Irish society. Throughout Ireland, towns and cities were transformed and made handsome. In Dublin a harmonious age of architecture produced not only fine buildings such as Gandon's CUSTOM HOUSE, the FOUR COURTS, the ROTUNDA, and the Duke of Leinster's great house beside a snipe bog, but streets and squares of red-brick houses. 'All there is gaiety pleasure, luxury and extravagance,' ARTHUR YOUNG wrote of Dublin in 1771. Classical education and cultured ideals were apparent in the roll call of seventeenth and eighteenth-century Anglo-Irish achievers, which included Bishop GEORGE BERKELEY, JONATHAN SWIFT, OLIVER GOLDSMITH, RICHARD BRINSLEY SHERIDAN, and WILLIAM CONGREVE.

Elsewhere in the countryside, on vast estates like that of Lord Eyre in Co. Galway, which covered 14,000 ha (35,000 acres), this society indulged in excess. Notorious were the hunting, shooting, ABDUCTION OF HEIRESSES, duelling, drinking, and eating. 'I have not seen less than fourteen dishes of meat for dinner, and seven for supper,' noted Mrs Delany. Claret was an accepted part of the lifestyle; Lord Orrery wrote of how 'drunkenness is the touchstone by which to try every man and he that cannot or will not drink, has a mark set upon him.' Among those whom the historian WILLIAM LECKY described as 'the lower gentry', the behaviour of the Rakes of Mallow was tolerated: 'beauing, belling, dancing, drinking, breaking windows, damning, sinking ...'

It was astonishing how quickly this golden age was shattered by the Rebellion of 1798. Ironically, among those who contributed to its destruction were men like WOLFE TONE and ROBERT EMMET, who had been educated at TRINITY COLLEGE, Dublin, founded to further the aims of the imposed religion. In one decade the Anglo-Irish were still building their great houses, intellectualising, brawling, and defending their short-lived Protestant Parliament with their elaborately costumed VOLUNTEERS. In the following decade their independence was fatally curtailed by rebellion and the decision of their rulers in England to bring a solution to the problems caused by the example of the French Revolution. With the ACT OF UNION, wholesale distribution of peerages encouraged betrayal. Those who resisted were rewarded with a kind of fame. 'You are not going to bribe me,' shouted the fourth Earl of POWERSCOURT to a government emissary before throwing him out of the house. The descendants of Kendal Bushe are still proud that the word 'incorruptible' was written beside his name.

The instincts of Bushe and Powerscourt were correct. Many who transplanted to England following the Act of Union did not return. The German traveller Johannes Kohl noted in 1842 that one indication of the owners' absence was the white window-blinds that were always pulled down. For those who stayed, the act not only destroyed overnight the atmosphere of the golden age but signalled the beginning of power slipping into the hands of the Catholic majority. No longer could Protestants speak for the Irish nation, and, as the years went by, their position became more marginalised. In the years that brought CATHOLIC EMANCIPATION and the DISESTABLISHMENT of the CHURCH OF IRELAND, they were increasingly seen as little more than members of a colonial garrison whose prerogative was loyalty to England. If, as frequently happened, those who opposed the unionist position—such as THOMAS DAVIS, WILLIAM SMITH O'BRIEN, ISAAC BUTT, and CHARLES STEWART PARNELL—came from their own ranks, the wound of perceived betrayal was the more poisoned.

The 'gentry' were expected to live in large houses and have some connection with the land. 'A doomed aristocracy' was how the novelist GEORGE BIRMINGHAM described the Anglo-Irish, ignoring the rest. There were many small farmers and shopkeepers to whom the label of Anglo-Irish was never applied, while most Protestants belonged to the middle classes. If the Union had seen the departure of many wealthy peers who retreated to England, other Protestants dominated commercial and professional life. Dublin squares glistened with the brass plates of doctors and attorneys, while the railway age opened up opportunities for a new prosperity. But many of the opportunities to create wealth were not open to those who saw themselves as aristocratic and denied their children opportunities to join the professional classes, largely limiting their roles to the British armed forces or the weakening Church of Ireland.

The landlord was popularly seen as an ogre who had usurped land rightly belonging to those who paid him rent. The GREAT FAMINE enhanced this image, sometimes justifiably, with the brutal role of EVICTION, but many landlords, helpless in the face of disaster, became bankrupt under the ENCUMBERED ESTATES ACT. The years following the Famine brought a brief period of rural prosperity before the onset of the land wars of the 1870s. Landlords who expected the 'loyalty' of their tenants saw this vanish, not only in the face of the secret ballot but also with the threat of murder. The Wyndham LAND ACTS recompensed them for the loss of rents, but often the money was not wisely used by those who derided 'that scoundrel Gladstone', while the subsequent loss of income was a further threat to the survival of the BIG HOUSE. The twentieth century saw a new dominance of the Anglo-Irish in the world of literature and art. The Celtic Renaissance, the LITERARY REVIVAL, and the establishment of the Abbey Theatre owed much of their force to such figures as DOUGLAS HYDE, WILLIAM BUTLER YEATS, and

LADY GREGORY. Painters who contributed to this cultural legacy included NATHANIEL HONE, WILLIAM ORPEN, and WALTER OSBORNE. Dramatists included OSCAR WILDE and GEORGE BERNARD SHAW, who further enriched the country of his birth and upbringing with his legacy to the National Gallery of Ireland.

Shaw, and Yeats who loftily declared that 'we are not a petty people,' received their NOBEL PRIZES, and DOUGLAS HYDE and ERSKINE CHILDERS both became President of Ireland. Of the others, demoralised by the WAR OF INDEPENDENCE and the burning of some 200 big houses, many fled to England, or remained, observed by Evelyn Waugh as 'quietly receding into their own mists, turning their backs on the world of effort and culture.' They carried on the old way of life unmolested. There was the ROYAL DUBLIN SOCIETY to receive them, the derided Kildare Street Club, hunt balls, draughty houses, and the remnants of walled estates where hunting continued much as it was observed, a century apart, in the work of SOMERVILLE AND ROSS and MOLLY KEANE. But the Big House was an increasing liability, threatened by rats, damp, and dry rot; the age of dereliction had arrived. The very existence of the Anglo-Irish was threatened, not only by economic forces but by such factors as the NE TEMERE decree, which drastically reduced Protestant numbers through mixed marriages. When the IRISH FREE STATE was established in 1921, Protestants made up 10 per cent of the population; by the 1940s they had declined to 6 per cent, and there were fears that they might vanish altogether. That this did not happen was largely because of a wider and more generous view of being Irish. The religious barriers broke down, and ARCHBISHOP MCQUAID's ban on Catholics entering Queen Elizabeth's bastion of Trinity College, Dublin, became meaningless. The words 'Anglo-Irish' had finally become an accepted and appreciated aspect of the process of Irish history. [see GEORGIAN PERIOD; BIG HOUSE, THE; BIG HOUSE NOVEL, THE; PROTESTANT ASCENDANCY.] **Peter Somerville-Large**

Anglo-Irish Treaty (1921). The Articles of Agreement were signed by representatives of the British and Dáil governments in the early hours of 6 December 1921. The terms offered by the British government were represented as the limit of possible concession. A 'Free State' was offered, granting a large measure of independence in domestic concerns, along Canadian lines. This state had to make an imperial contribution to the British exchequer, and the so-called TREATY PORTS were to remain under British jurisdiction. Clause XII made provision for a BOUNDARY COMMISSION to be established if Northern Ireland opted out of membership of the new

Anglo-Irish Society. View of Carton, Co. Kildare, *by William van der Hagan shows the country seat of the FitzGeralds c. 1730, with elaborate formal gardens, radiating avenues, and an artificial mound with viewing tower in the right foreground, all characteristic of the great estates developed during the eighteenth century. [Private collection]*

state. Most controversially, an oath of fidelity had to be sworn to the British Crown by Irish ministers and representatives, a GOVERNOR-GENERAL was to be appointed, and appeals to the British Privy Council were to be permitted. The Treaty followed five months of complex negotiations, culminating in a two-month conference in London.

The official Irish negotiating position was to seek settlement in accordance with DE VALERA's concept of 'external association,' which allowed recognition of the British Crown in foreign policy only and ensured Irish SOVEREIGNTY in domestic affairs. As in so many negotiations, the most important events took place at the final stage. The principal barriers to agreement were the Northern and constitutional status issues: defence and economic matters did not create stumbling-blocks. The terms sidestepped the Northern question but insisted on Irish recognition of the Crown, admittedly in a diluted form. LLOYD GEORGE in the final hours threatened immediate resumption of war if all the Irish delegates did not sign. They were committed to referring any document back to Dublin before signature; his tactic of ultimatum was designed to prevent this. Robert Barton and George Gavan Duffy were opposed to the terms but conceded under intense pressure from their colleagues ARTHUR GRIFFITH, MICHAEL COLLINS, and Eamon J. Duggan. In Dublin, de Valera rejected the terms almost immediately, believing that the delegates had broken their promise, though they had full plenipotentiary powers. De Valera's decision to abstain from the conference had created the chance for Lloyd George to take advantage of divisions in the SINN FÉIN leadership.

For all the melodrama at the end of the negotiations, the Treaty terms were predictable. The Treaty was enthusiastically received in Britain and by the spring of 1922 had been comfortably passed by Parliament. In the twenty-six counties, however, it split all elements of nationalist opinion, only narrowly winning a majority in the Dáil government and in DÁIL ÉIREANN itself. A considerable majority of the IRA opposed what they regarded as a sell-out of the Republic. British insistence on the Treaty terms ended any hope of compromise in the South and led to the outbreak of CIVIL WAR in late June. Despite the relatively easy pro-Treaty victory in the ensuing conflict and electoral support for the Treaty in 1922 and 1923, the document continued to polarise political opinion for most of the twentieth century. After achieving power in 1932, de Valera progressively dismantled the Treaty. **Michael A. Hopkinson**

Anglo-Irish War: see WAR OF INDEPENDENCE.

Anglo-Norman, a term conventionally used to describe the English adventurers and colonists who came to Ireland from the late twelfth century onwards; it is not attested in contemporary Irish or English sources, which invariably describe the incomers as English. Other terms used, such as Cambro-Norman and Anglo-French, serve to emphasise the fact that those who came to Ireland were of mixed background, and many spoke French.

The first generation of incomers were Normans and Flemings who had settled in south Wales in the wake of the Norman conquest of England after 1066 (hence 'Cambro-Normans'), but subsequent immigrants came predominantly from England and were from a wide range of social backgrounds. Some were great magnates who held lands in different parts of England and Wales as well as in the Duchy of Normandy; the majority of these lost their Norman possessions in 1204 when Philip Augustus, King of France, seized the Duchy of Normandy from the English Crown. Consequent on the loss of Normandy the newcomers in Ireland sought to offset Norman losses by a more intensive economic exploitation of their Irish lands, while the English Crown also became more concerned to exploit its recently acquired Irish lordship and to establish political, legal, and administrative structures that conformed to those of England. Inevitably this led to a more predatory and colonial attitude towards Ireland.

In the train of great magnates like STRONGBOW and HUGH DE LACY came settlers of lesser rank, most of whom became tenant landholders; but a significant minority settled in the cities of Dublin and Waterford, in towns such as Drogheda, Kilkenny, and New Ross, or in rural boroughs, which were little more than villages but whose residents enjoyed a privileged legal status. Many of these were landless men and labourers attracted to Ireland by the opportunities for increased wealth and improved status, in some instances attaining thereby the status of free men.

Anglo-Norman immigration was closely linked to the Anglo-Norman military advance but can be distinguished as a separate process. It occurred most densely in Leinster, Meath, and Munster and coincided with a wider European demographic expansion and colonisation of peripheral areas.

There is not enough evidence to calculate the number of immigrants relative to the native population, but it probably reached its maximum in the late thirteenth century, with numbers declining thereafter. The outbreak of the plague known as the BLACK DEATH, which reached Ireland in 1348, particularly affected townspeople and had a greater impact on the settler community than on the Irish. It resulted in a prolonged agricultural depression, with the result that many of the lands held by the Anglo-Norman colonists were abandoned and reverted to the native Irish. The most enduring legacy of the Anglo-Norman incomers on the Irish landscape is the stone castles and earthen fortifications known as mottes, built to facilitate and maintain the original military takeover. [see CASTLES, MEDIEVAL; EARTHWORKS, MEDIEVAL; ECONOMY, 1200–1700; ENGLISH SETTLEMENT IN IRELAND; FOOD, LATE MEDIEVAL; MEDIEVAL LAND OWNERSHIP AND TENURE.] **Marie Therese Flanagan**

Anglo-Norman and English administration. English administration in Ireland between the thirteenth and late seventeenth centuries displayed one simple and deeply flawed pattern by which institutional and procedural developments initiated in England were gradually introduced in an almost identical form in Ireland some time later. The royal exchequer, the first central office of administration to be clearly established in England, was the first to be introduced into Ireland, shortly before 1200; thereafter the development of its dual character, as an office of revenue collection and accounts and as a court dealing with the Crown's fiscal rights, also took place in the Irish office. Chancery, England's second most important administrative office, was also established in Ireland in the early thirteenth century, though it took longer to develop its powers and responsibilities than its English counterpart. In the same way High Courts of Justice—Common Pleas, dealing with civil cases, and King's Bench, dealing with criminal and royal cases—had developed their own particular spheres of business in Ireland by the late fourteenth century, while Parliament, the highest English court of law, which granted a right of royal taxation in exchange for rights of representation and statutory law-making, had begun to develop in a similar manner in Ireland by the end of the thirteenth century. At local level also the English model was faithfully followed: sheriffs and shire courts, manor courts, courts-baron, and assizes were all in operation by the close of the Middle Ages, though never comprehensively and often intermittently.

During the sixteenth century the principal reforms of institutions and practice initiated in England in the 1530s were gradually extended to Ireland, including provincial councils in Munster and Connacht, new law officers (Attorneys-General and Solicitors-General), new modes of practice in exchequer, the reform and extension of Chancery business, the reduction of the Irish Council, and the establishment of a new court of equity, following England's Star Chamber, as Castle Chamber.

Yet the attempt to construct a 'little England in Ireland' simply by adopting England's administrative framework obscured some profound disparities between the two societies, the most important of which resided at the apex of the administrative system in the monarchy itself. Over this period only four English monarchs—John, RICHARD II, JAMES II, and WILLIAM III—visited Ireland (with disastrous personal consequences for the first three); and though Ireland was recognised as a kingdom in its own right in 1541, the country never had a separate monarch. Because there was no Irish king there was, more importantly, no Irish court, and the country therefore lacked that crucial centripetal force that in England drew the great regional magnates towards the monarch for personal gain, rivalry, alliance, or sheer entertainment. The absence of a king and a court bore most heavily on the office intended to serve as the monarch's proxy in Ireland, the Viceroy (Justiciar, later Lord Deputy or LORD LIEUTENANT), who found himself willy-nilly at the centre of two opposing forces. An Englishman appointed through court politics, the Viceroy tended to give priority to English or even court matters, neglecting the needs, interests, and problems of Ireland; alternatively, an Irish-born Viceroy appointed through local influence tended equally to concentrate on defending or extending his own or his supporters' interests, to the neglect of the concerns of the Crown. Few succeeded in controlling such opposing tendencies—with the exception, perhaps, of Sir ANTHONY ST LEGER in the 1540s, or JAMES BUTLER, the first Duke of Ormond in the 1660s—and none succeeded for long. Conflict, corruption, neglect, and failure were consequently the hallmarks of the Irish Viceroyalty; and the tensions that undermined it profoundly affected all the subordinate offices in the Irish administration. The effectiveness of the Irish Council, the chief executive and advisory body, was paralysed by the intrigues of opposing local and English interests. Increasingly from the later sixteenth century the Irish Parliament became a battleground between native and newcomer, which viceroys (such as Wentworth in the 1630s) sometimes chose to exploit but more usually preferred to neglect. Even more seriously, the law courts and the offices of Chancery and Exchequer were transformed by newly arrived English officers into instruments for the extortion of titles, leases, rents, and fines from native landholders made vulnerable by their uncertainty of tenure, their religious conservatism, and their gradual exclusion from administrative office.

The poisoning of the offices of central administration in the early seventeenth century was repeated with even greater rapidity at local level. In the early phases of the period the English Crown had conceded the impossibility of exercising direct jurisdiction over the Irish localities by granting away extensive palatine liberties to the Anglo-Irish magnates, who undertook to maintain the forms and procedures of English law in return for control over the business and personnel of local courts. The abolition of these liberties and the extension of English control over all of Ireland in the late sixteenth and early seventeenth centuries saw the introduction, for the first time in many areas, of conventional means of English county government, the quarter sessions. But far from serving as the vehicles of equitable and uniform local government as they

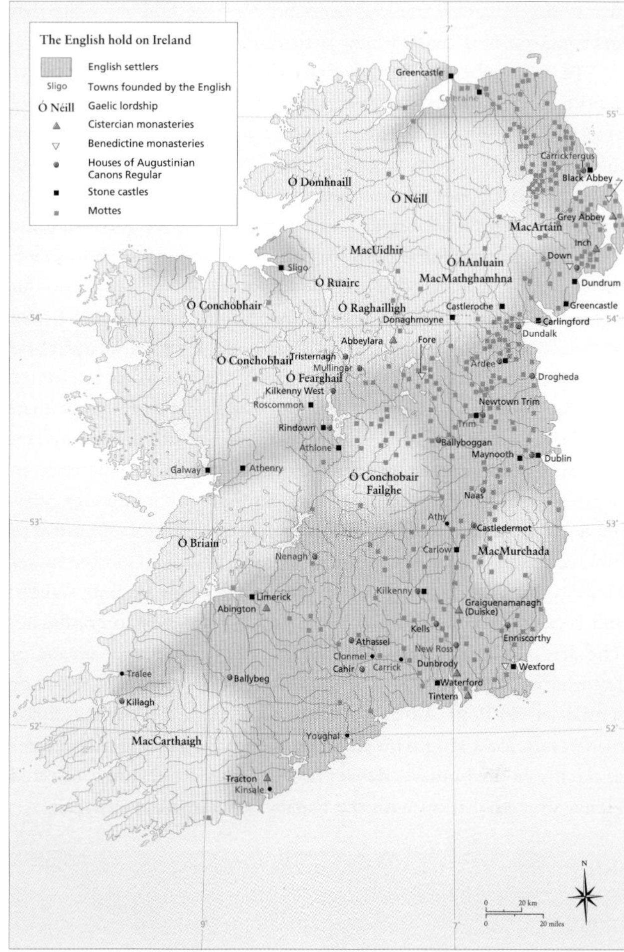

were perceived to function in England, these local magistracies provided a further and more systematic means for newly arrived English officers to continue the struggle for land and power in provincial Ireland. Thus it was that the uncritical introduction of an administrative system intended to give order, stability and uniformity to an Anglicised Ireland had become a source of political and cultural conflict that would persist for centuries. [see PARLIAMENT, 1200–1700.] **Ciaran Brady**

Anglo-Norman conquest. There was no single large-scale invasion of Ireland by the ANGLO-NORMANS such as occurred in the Norman conquest of England in 1066. The first group arrived as mercenaries in the returning party of DERMOT MACMURROUGH, exiled King of Leinster, in the autumn of 1167; in May and August 1169 and August 1170 they were augmented by additional recruits, the most important of whom was STRONGBOW, to whom Dermot offered his daughter, Aoife, in marriage. Until the death of Dermot in 1171 the incomers were under his command. The traditional year of 1169 for the Anglo-Norman 'invasion' derives from an account of the military exploits of the Anglo-Normans, EXPUGNATIO HIBERNICA, by the contemporary commentator GIRALDUS CAMBRENSIS, who accorded a leading role to his relatives and especially to his uncle, ROBERT FITZ STEPHEN, who landed in May 1169.

With the help of his overseas recruits Dermot recovered his kingdom, took control of Waterford and Dublin, and had embarked on expansionist incursions into Meath when he died unexpectedly in May 1171. Following his death Ruaidhrí Ó Conchobhair, King of Connacht and would-be high king, attempted to assert control over Strongbow, who now held Leinster, including Dublin and

Waterford. Ruaidhrí tried unsuccessfully to take Dublin, a city that had long-standing trading links with England.

In September 1171 the character of Anglo-Norman intervention altered dramatically with the military expedition to Ireland of HENRY II of England. The reasons for his intervention have been the subject of controversy. He had received a Papal privilege, 'LAUDABILITER', in 1155 authorising a conquest of Ireland, but he did not act on it until a significant number of his subjects had gone there, of whom Strongbow was by far the most important. Strongbow had succeeded to the Earldom of Pembroke on his father's death in 1148, but Henry, on his accession in 1154, had refused to acknowledge him as earl. The political instability in Ireland consequent on Ruaidhrí Ó Conchobhair's failure to assert control over Strongbow and the destabilising threat that Strongbow then posed to Henry's kingdom, with his resources greatly augmented by his Irish acquisitions, determined the timing of Henry's expedition in September 1171. He was not obliged to fight any military engagements in Ireland: a substantial number of Irish kings submitted to him voluntarily, while Strongbow agreed to hold Leinster under Henry's lordship in return for the retention of his English, Welsh, and Norman holdings, which Henry had threatened to confiscate. The Irish bishops endorsed Henry's intervention as a means of restoring political stability and promoting church reform, and they sent letters to Pope Alexander III to that effect. This was a diplomatic coup for a king who stood accused of instigating the murder of Archbishop Thomas à Becket in December 1170, and it effected Henry's reconciliation with the Papacy. **Marie Therese Flanagan**

Anglo-Norman. *Trim Castle, Co. Meath, the largest medieval castle in Ireland. The original fortification, founded by Hugh de Lacy at this site in c. 1172, was destroyed by Ruaidhrí Ó Conchobhair a year later. The existing castle was built c. 1200. [Dúchas, The Heritage Service]*

Anglo-Norman influence on language. Anglo-Norman gave a new lexicon to Irish. Hundreds of French loanwords were assimilated into Irish, such as *cábla*, cable < Anglo-Norman *cable*; Irish *cailís*, chalice < AN *calis*; Irish *garda*, guard < AN *garde*, guard, ward, guardianship; Irish *póirse*, porch < AN *porche*; Irish *cúirtéis*, courtesy, salute < AN *curteis*; Irish *suipéar*, supper < AN *super*; Irish *tuáille*, towel < AN *toaille*. Legal and administrative terms abound: Irish *aturnae*, attorney, solicitor < AN *aturnee*; Irish *báille*, bailiff < AN *bailli*; Irish *baránta*, warranty < AN *warantie*; Irish *contae*, county < AN *cuntee*; Irish *constábla*, constable < AN *conestable*; Irish *oighre*, heir < AN *eire*; Irish *léas*, lease < AN *les*; Irish *seirbhís*, service < AN *servise*.

The STATUTES OF KILKENNY could not be enforced. By 1541, English had given way to Irish to such a degree that a Dublin parliament, meeting to proclaim HENRY VIII King of Ireland, were relieved when the Earl of Ormond rose to reply to the speeches of the Speaker of the Parliament and the King's Chancellor; immediately afterwards,

> bothe the effecte of the preposicion and answer was briefly and prudentlie declared in the Irysshe tong, to the said Lordes, by the mouthe of the Erle of Ormonde, greatly to their contentation.

The descendants of the Norman war-lords simply did not understand the King's English. Furthermore, they preferred Irish tenants to English tenants, who were, in general, more impoverished. The State Papers for 1537 complained:

> They bring into the hart of the English pale Irishe tenantes, whiche neither can speke the Englishe tonge, ne were capp or bonet, and expulseth ofte the auncient good Englishe tenantes, that therfor the same be likewise provided for; in effecte, by that meanes, the pore Englishe tenantes are dryvin hither into Englande and Wales, and the Irishe tenantes in their roulmes [places] and fermes.

That same year the State Papers tell of Justice Luttrell's annoyance that in Co. Kildare,

> which was more parte Englyshe, as the countye of Dublyne now is, ther is not one husbandman, in effect, that spekeith Englyshe, ne useith any English sort ne maner, and their gentyllmen be after the same sort.

Forty years later, in the 1570s, the Lord Chancellor complained:

> All English, and the most part with delight, even in Dublin, speak Irish, and are greatly spotted in manners, habit and conditions with Irish stains.

This was true of everywhere the Normans had settled, with the exception of the Co. Wexford baronies of Forth and Bargy and the district of Fingall, north of Dublin. The main reasons were the enactment in a Dublin parliament of the Reformation legislation already passed in England: the dissolution of the monasteries, and the Act of Supremacy, which required the acknowledgment of Henry VIII as supreme head of the church. This legislation merely united the 'OLD ENGLISH' (a term used to distinguish the English whose ancestors had settled in Ireland during the Middle Ages from the 'NEW ENGLISH', who came under the Tudors and Stuarts) and the native Irish; and the symbols of their unity were the Catholic religion and the IRISH LANGUAGE. One of the New English, Fynes Moryson, described the developing situation in the early 1600s:

> The meere Irish disdayned to learne or speak the English tounge, yea the English Irish and the very Cittizens (excepting those of Dublin where the lord Deputy resides) though they could speake English as well as wee, yet Commonly speak Irish among themselues, and were hardly induced by our familiar Conversation to speake English with vs, yea Common experience shewed, and my selfe and others often obserued, the Cittizens of Watterford and Corcke hauing wyues that could speake English as well as wee, bitterly to chyde them when they speak English with vs.

Diarmaid Ó Muirithe

annals. The Irish annals constitute a substantial and unique collection of annual records of ecclesiastical and political events accumulated in MONASTERIES from the middle of the sixth century to the end of the sixteenth century. They were inspired by a chronicle assembled by Rufinus of Aquiliea in Italy in the early fifth century, based largely on the historical works of Eusebius of Caesarea, namely his *Chronicle* and *Church History*. Rufinus's work, which distinctively identified the beginning of each year with the notation *K1*, representing *Kalendae Ianuarii* (i.e. 1 January), provided a chronology and epitome of Biblical and Old World history up to the Nativity, followed by Christian history up to the late fourth century.

In the later part of the sixth century COLM CILLE, founder and abbot of the monastery of IONA, used this as the basis for what is now known as the Iona Chronicle. He retrospectively inserted into Rufinus's chronicle entries reflecting Irish prehistory, such as the kings of Eamain Macha and TARA, then continued the chronicle into the fifth century with entries identifying the pioneers of Irish Christianity, such as PATRICK and BRIGID, and political entries principally relating to the UÍ NÉILL. In the sixth century he recorded the development of monasteries, the rise of his own northern branch of the Uí Néill, and terrestrial phenomena. This chronicle was maintained in Iona after Colm Cille's death up to the middle of the eighth century, when it was removed to Ireland. Here it was continued and copies made that form the basis for all the surviving collections of annals, each of which reflects something of the monastery and the district in which it was continued or compiled. For example, the Annals of Tigernach, CLONMACNOISE and Roscrea and the CHRONICUM SCOTORUM all reflect ecclesiastical and political events relevant to the monastery and environs of Clonmacnoise; the Annals of Ulster reflect first Armagh and then Derry, northern Connacht and Fermanagh; the Annals of Inisfallen reflect the monastery of Emly and Munster. In this way, between the eighth and the sixteenth centuries a number of monasteries maintained Colm Cille's tradition of recording annual summaries of events involving themselves and their milieu. With the Tudor-Stuart plantations and suppression of the monasteries this tradition ended, except for one final flourish when, in the 1630s, a group of four Franciscans, led by MÍCHEÁL Ó CLÉIRIGH, compiled many of these annalistic texts into one enormous compendium, now known as the Annals of the FOUR MASTERS (though there may have been as many as seven scribes involved). While in doing this they sometimes modified the chronology and the content of some of these records, they saved for posterity material that would otherwise have been lost. [see CHRONOLOGY OF IRISH HISTORY.] **Daniel McCarthy**

Anthologia Hibernica, *or Monthly Collections of Science, Belles-Lettres and History* (1793–4), a cultural periodical published monthly from January 1793 to December 1794. It can be seen as an academy of the literary talent of late eighteenth-century Ireland; its subscription lists contain the names of the emerging authors SYDNEY OWENSON and THOMAS MOORE, as well as many established figures from the eighteenth-century Irish revival. The six-monthly editorial prefaces convey their own sense of purpose for a journal that, while not always taking Ireland as its topic, conceived of and addressed an audience of educated Irish readers. The declared model was the *Gentleman's Magazine*, and the choice of the miscellany format allowed a free mix of antiquarian, poetical, medical, and legal contributions. **Claire Connolly**

Anti-Divorce Campaign, the main anti-divorce campaigning group in both the 1986 and 1996 constitutional referendums on divorce in the Republic. Launched in April 1986, it was headed by Senator Des Hanafin (FIANNA FÁIL), and its most visible public figures were Prof. William Binchy and Joe McCarroll. Roman Catholic in orientation, it was not officially linked to the CATHOLIC CHURCH, although it had informal connections with FAMILY SOLIDARITY, a parish-based Catholic lay organisation founded in the early 1980s that campaigned to defend Catholic principles in family policy, principally in connection with ABORTION and DIVORCE. Its campaigning methods were highly effective and contributed to the defeat of the pro-divorce REFERENDUM in 1986 and to the narrowness of the margin in support of divorce in the 1995 referendum (see p. 919). **Tony Fahey**

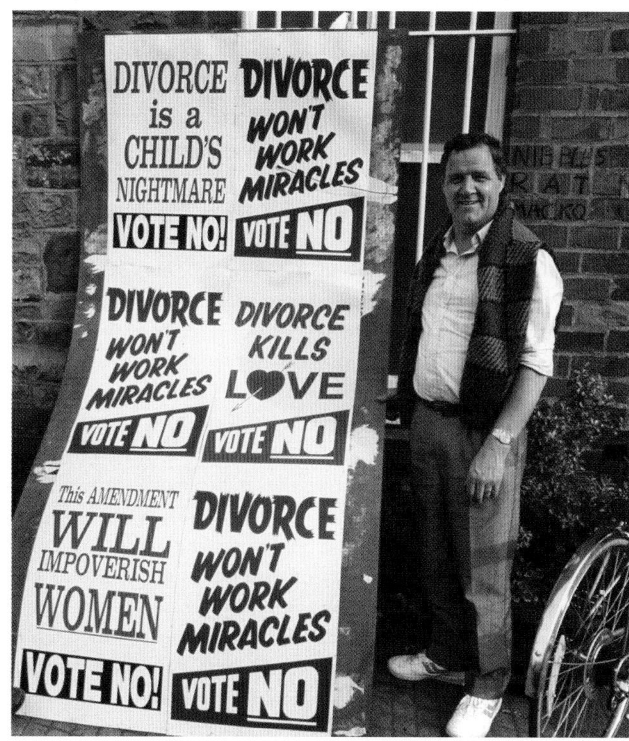

Anti-divorce campaign. *A member of the 1986 Anti-Divorce Campaign. The anti-divorce lobby argued that divorce impoverishes women and children, on the basis of research conducted in other countries on the financial impact of divorce. [Derek Speirs/Report]*

Antient Concert Rooms, a former MUSIC VENUE in Great Brunswick Street (Pearse Street), Dublin. The Antient (*sic.*) Concerts Society (founded 1834) established the venue and promoted large vocal and instrumental concerts there until the society's end in 1863. Classes were held at the Antient Concert Rooms that led to the establishment of the RIAM in 1848. From the 1850s, concerts and chamber recitals at the concert rooms featured many of the RIAM's personnel. Later concerts were given by the Dublin Chamber Music Union (established 1873) and MICHELE ESPOSITO's DUBLIN ORCHESTRAL SOCIETY (established 1899). In 1916 the Antient Concert Rooms closed permanently; the building later became a cinema and is now derelict. **Paul J. Kerr**

Anti-Partition League (APL), the main Nationalist party in Northern Ireland in the decade 1945–55. The return of a Labour Party government in Britain in 1945 was the signal for an upsurge in anti-partitionist activity in Northern Ireland as the various strands of nationalism coalesced in a new mass movement. The league was launched at a conference in Dungannon, Co. Tyrone, in November 1945, with the aim of 'uniting all those opposed to partition.' An executive committee was formed comprising all the Nationalist MPs and senators; branches were established; and James McSparran, a leading Catholic barrister and MP, was elected chairman, with Malachy Conlon MP as secretary.

The APL adopted a policy of active opposition at STORMONT and Westminster after a decade of parliamentary abstention, forging links with the Coalition Government in the South after 1948 and the Friends of Ireland group in the British Labour Party. It conducted a prolific propaganda campaign against partition in Ireland, Britain, and the United States, drawing attention to such practices as GERRYMANDERING and DISCRIMINATION. In January 1949 Dáil Éireann established the All-Party Anti-Partition Committee to assist the APL in the Northern Ireland elections; but the spectacle of Southern interference rebounded to unionism's electoral advantage in the 'Chapel Gates Election' of February 1949. The IRELAND ACT (1949) was a blow to the league and by the early 1950s it was in decline, challenged by a revived IRA. **Eamon Phoenix**

antiquarians and archaeologists. The first record of strictly archaeological antiquarian activity is the visit of the Welsh scholar Edward Lhuyd to Ireland in 1699–1700; his visit and writings left a model that was followed thereafter. Of the many societies established in the late seventeenth and early eighteenth centuries none stand up to scrutiny by present-day standards; however, the work of WILLIAM MOLYNEAUX and later Thomas Molyneux in encouraging the establishment of learned societies, especially the Dublin Philosophical Society and the Dublin Physico-Historical Society, led to much original work. In the eighteenth century the work carried out and encouraged by Burton Conyngham is especially important, while the reports of antiquities made by Pococke to the London Society of Antiquaries are valuable. The recording of antiquities by artists, especially the GROSE family and GABRIEL BERANGER, is important. The establishment of the Dublin Society (1731), now the ROYAL DUBLIN SOCIETY, and the creation of a committee of antiquities (1772) set antiquarian pursuits on a sounder footing, though the work of GEN. CHARLES VALLANCEY in particular remains suspect. With the establishment of the ROYAL IRISH ACADEMY (1785), antiquarianism acquired a more scholarly voice. In tandem with the work of the ORDNANCE SURVEY (1824), modern research came of age, and the work of EUGENE O'CURRY, JOHN O'DONOVAN, and GEORGE PETRIE is exceptional. Unfortunately BETHAM's scholarly rivalry with Petrie led him into serious error.

During the nineteenth century the establishment of local societies and journals encouraged excellent work, in which F. J. Bigger, Thomas Carruthers and William James Knowles in Co. Antrim, M. S. Westropp in Co. Clare, Brash, Robert Day and Thomas Windele in Co. Cork, Frazer, Wakeman and Sir WILLIAM WILDE in Dublin, Robert Graves and Prim in Co. Kilkenny, and Wood-Martin in Co. Sligo must be especially noted. The personal collections of many of these antiquarians eventually enriched national museums in Ireland as well as those abroad. With the introduction of treasure trove legislation (1861) and the establishment of the Dublin Museum of Science and Art (1877), now the NATIONAL MUSEUM OF IRELAND, the death knell of antiquarianism was sounded. University departments of archaeology were established, rigorous scholarship ensued, and archaeology became an academic discipline and no longer an antiquarian pursuit. **Aideen M. Ireland**

Antrim, County (*Contae Aontroma*)

Province:	ULSTER
County town:	BELFAST
Area:	2,838 km^2 (1,092 sq. miles)
Population (1991)*:	642,000
Features:	Antrim Mountains
	GIANT'S CAUSEWAY
	GLENS OF ANTRIM
	LOUGH NEAGH
	River BANN
	River Lagan
Of historical interest:	CARRICKFERGUS CASTLE
	DUNLUCE CASTLE
Industry and products:	DISTILLING
	LINEN
	Oats
	POTATOES
	Synthetic fibre

Petula Martyn

* last year of census by county, [see NORTHERN IRELAND.]

County Antrim, north-easternmost county of Ulster and of Northern Ireland. Co. Antrim's scenery is dominated by the Tertiary basalts of the Antrim Plateau in the east and the fertile lowlands of the Bann valley in the west; the famous GIANT'S CAUSEWAY is near Portrush in the north of the county. Historically the county has maintained close cultural links with south-west Scotland from at least the fourteenth century, with further significant Scots settlement between the sixteenth and eighteenth centuries, leaving a legacy of PRESBYTERIANISM, lowland Scots loanwords, and (until the nineteenth century) shared agricultural technologies. Part of so-called 'inner' or eastern Ulster, Co. Antrim has traditionally shared in the relative prosperity of this area, with generally higher land values, more modern AGRICULTURE, earlier and more extensive URBANISATION and INDUSTRIALISATION, and lower nineteenth-century population losses than areas further west. The modern county remains a complex mosaic of spreading suburbanisation on the fringes of greater Belfast in the south-east, marginal upland farming on the Antrim Plateau, and vigorous prosperity in the market towns along the Bann valley. **Lindsay Proudfoot**

Antrim (*Aontroim*), a town on the north-east shore of LOUGH NEAGH at the mouth of Six Mile Water; population (1991) 20,878. The town may owe its origin to an Early Christian monastery here, of which little is known, though a tenth or eleventh-century ROUND TOWER survives nearby at Steeple. A motte and bailey in the castle grounds adjacent to the town may indicate the presence of early ANGLO-NORMAN settlement, and Antrim was listed as a borough in 1333. Its later medieval history is obscure, but in 1605 Sir James Hamilton was granted a market charter for the site. In 1613 Sir Hugh Clotworthy built the first castle (rebuilt in 1662 and 1813, burnt in 1922), and the town grew slowly under the patronage of the Clotworthys (later Viscounts Massareene). Incorporated in 1665, Antrim became closely associated with the LINEN industry in the eighteenth century and was increasingly influenced by the growth of Belfast in the nineteenth century.

In modern times Antrim was designated a regional growth centre in the Mathew Report (1963) and subsequently attracted considerable, though relatively short-lived, investment in synthetic textiles. It now acts as a dormitory suburb for Belfast, a local

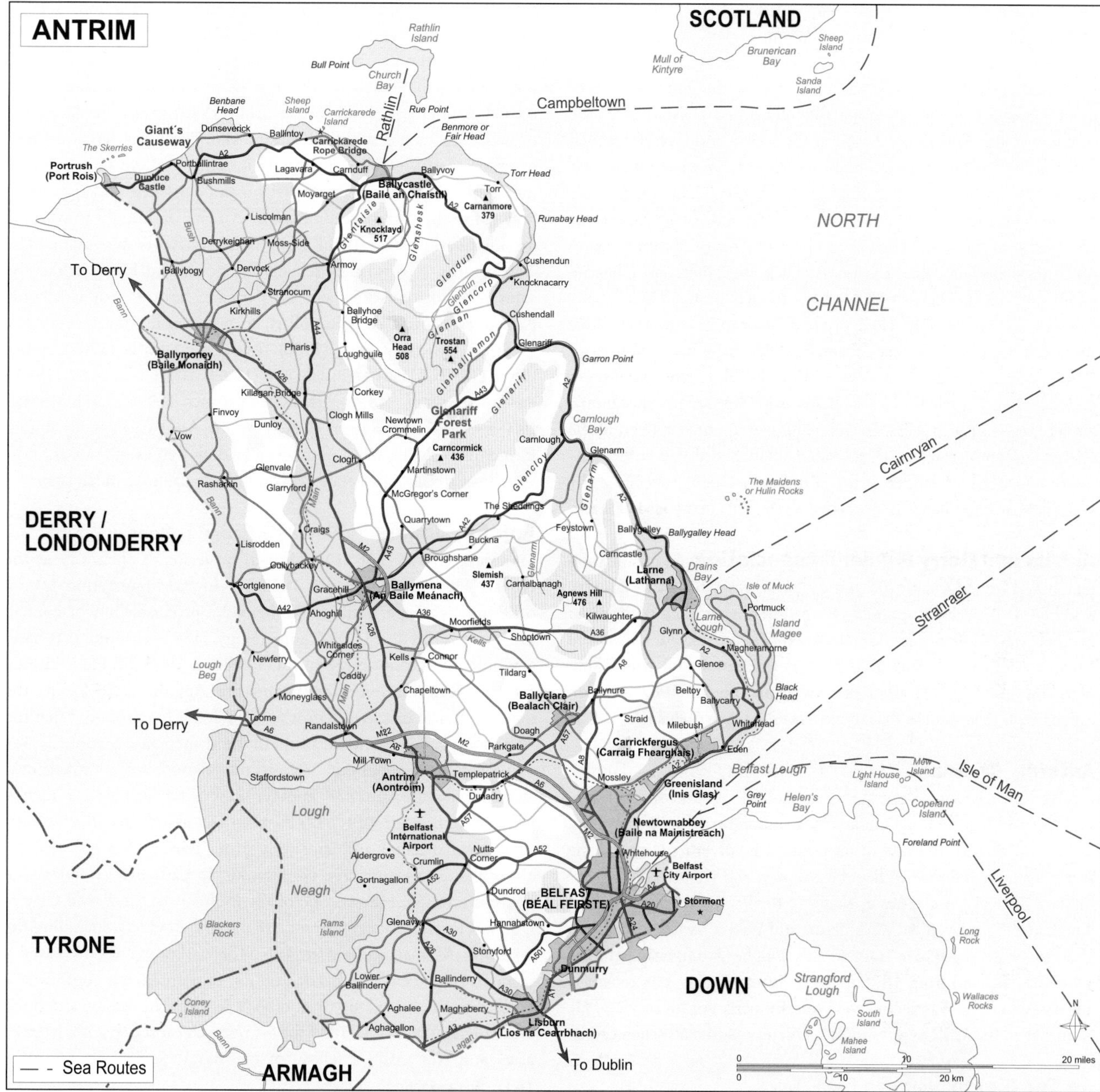

market, and a centre for light engineering and electronics. The town retains its original plantation plan, with the main street aligned on the gates of the demolished castle. **Lindsay Proudfoot**

Antrim, Battle of (1798). Though the rebellion had begun in Leinster on 23 May, northern UNITED IRISHMEN did not rise until HENRY JOY MCCRACKEN raised the standard of revolt on 6 June. McCracken had no intention of attempting to take Belfast, then the second-largest garrison in the country; instead the plan was to seize Antrim, where magistrates were due to meet on 7 June. Three rebel columns converged on the town, one from Randalstown and Toome, another from the Six Mile Water valley, and the third, led by McCracken, from Craigarogan Fort near Roughfort. Major-General George Nugent in Belfast had been kept well informed by spies, and Crown forces sped to the town from both Belfast and Blaris camps. Entering the town by the Scotch Quarter at about 2:30 p.m., McCracken's men achieved some initial successes: a VOLUNTEER gun mounted on an old chaise fired two deadly rounds before it fell off its mounting; and the 22nd Dragoons, charging down a narrow street, impaled themselves on insurgent pikes. As Ballyclare United men were fighting their way down Bow Lane, Lord O'Neill was mortally wounded near the Market House. Poor communications and rumours of defeat caused hesitation in the ranks of the other two columns of insurgents, approaching from the north-east and north-west. Colonel James Durham, leading Crown forces from the Belfast garrison, seized the initiative and bombarded the insurgents from Sentry Hill; his soldiers then scattered the United men, finishing off any wounded they found and summarily putting to death thirty others captured in arms. **Jonathan Bardon**

Antrim, Glens of. 'Glen' (*Gleann*) is a widely used geographical term in both Ireland and Scotland. No precise definition exists, but it is often used to indicate a steeply sided and sometimes rugged valley and is particularly appropriate to glacial landscapes, as in the glacial spillway of the GLEN OF THE DOWNS or the glaciated valley of Glendalough. 'Glen' often appears, therefore, as part of the name of scenic areas, such as Glencar (Co. Kerry), Glennasmole (Co. Wicklow), and Glenveigh (Co. Donegal). Perhaps the best-known glens are the Glens of Antrim. The Antrim Plateau rises to over 360 m (120 ft), and into this are cut nine glens, with a general east-to-west trend. An area of great natural beauty, the glens also facilitated agriculture and so attracted early settlement. Because of the ruggedness of the landscape they remained isolated until the building of the Antrim coast road in the 1830s, and each developed a distinctive character and cultural heritage. Irish was spoken here up to the middle of the nineteenth century. The glens have conjured up images of tradition, tranquillity, and natural beauty, as epitomised in the song 'The Green Glens of Antrim'. From north to south they are Glentaisie, Glenshesk, Glendun, Glencorp, Glenaan, Glenballyeamon, Glenariff, Glencloy, and Glenarm. Their populations vary considerably: Glencorp and Glenaan have no more than fifty occupied houses between them, but Glenariff is home to perhaps 1,000 people, and there are 500–600 in Glencloy. Both Glenshesk and Glentaisie reach the sea at Ballycastle, famous for the annual 'OLD LAMMAS FAIR'. Glenariff has been given the title 'Queen of the Glens', a reference to its steeply sided U-shaped valley with a distinctive pattern of ladder farms and fine scenery, especially the waterfalls on the Glenariff river. [see BALD, WILLIAM.] **Joseph Brady**

Antrim and Derry Fiddlers' Association, an organisation established in 1953 with the aim of 'preserving the art of country fiddling.' It is largely responsible for promoting the rich tradition of north Ulster fiddle music. Founder-members include Alex Kerr and Mickey McIlhatton, both Co. Antrim fiddlers. Frank McColum, who composed 'The Home Ruler', was appointed in 1967 as liaison officer with COMHALTAS CEOLTÓIRÍ ÉIREANN. **Len Graham**

Antsell, Thomas (1817–1893), scientist. Born in Dublin; received a medical degree at the Royal College of Surgeons, London, in 1839 and lectured in Dublin and at different medical schools at home and abroad. Because of his political involvement as a Young Irelander he was forced to flee the country, and went to New York in 1848. In 1854 he acted as geologist to the Pacific Railroad Survey. Thereafter he moved to Washington and held a variety of posts as chemist or geologist. He subsequently taught at universities in the United States and from 1871 to 1877 lived in Japan as a technical adviser, where he was decorated by the Emperor for his services. He is buried in the US Congressional Cemetery. **Susan McKenna-Lawlor**

An Túr Gloine: see TÚR GLOINE, AN.

Anúna, a vocal and instrumental ensemble dedicated to the performance of medieval and contemporary Celtic music. Founded in 1987 as An Uaithne and renamed Anúna in 1992, the group features the compositions of Michael McGlynn (director). Anúna now includes sixteen members. Albums include *Anúna* (1993), *Invocation* (1994), and *Behind the Closed Eye* (1997). Guest appearances include BBC 'Songs of Praise' and the Peace of the World Symposium at the Waterfront, Belfast, as well as singing with RIVERDANCE. **Paul J. Kerr**

aonach, a medieval assembly at which political, social and commercial transactions were made and games and contests were held. Certain gatherings probably originated as funeral games. They were held at a fixed time, and specific rules applied to maintain order. In later periods the *aonach* functioned primarily as a fair. **Bart Jaski**

Aosdána (from AES DÁNA), the controversial academy of letters and the fine arts established by the Government of the Republic through the ARTS COUNCIL in 1981 with the encouragement of the Taoiseach, CHARLES HAUGHEY, whose cultural adviser was ANTHONY CRONIN. Founded in order to publicly honour distinguished achievement in the arts, its membership is confined to those born or resident in Ireland and is drawn from the disciplines of literature, visual arts, and music. Membership is restricted to a maximum of 200 (originally 150), and the election of new members is by their peers, based on the existence of a significant body of original and creative work. A *cnuas* or annuity is available for members to free them from non-creative employment. The Toscaireacht is Aosdána's ten-person governing body, while the supreme rank of Aosdána is the *Saoi* (an honour that is accompanied by a torc-like gold collar), to which role SAMUEL BECKETT (1984), SEAN O'FAOLAIN (1986), PATRICK COLLINS (1987), MARY LAVIN (1992), LOUIS LE BROCQUY (1992), TONY O'MALLEY (1993), BENEDICT KIELY (1996), FRANCIS STUART (1996), and SEAMUS HEANEY (1997) have been elected. While Aosdána includes among its members a substantial number of leading figures in the arts, individuals of similar eminence remain outside its ranks. **Brian Lalor**

Apjohn, James (1796–1886), scientist. Born in Grean, Co. Limerick; educated at TCD. He was professor of chemistry at the Royal College of Surgeons, 1828–50. In the Engineering School of Trinity College, Dublin, he held the professorships of applied CHEMISTRY, 1844–81, and mineralogy, 1845–81, and was later appointed university professor of chemistry, 1850–74. He is known for his work on hygrometry and the Apjohn Dew Point; the meteorological historian Knowles-Middleton has proposed that the Mason hygrometer should properly be named the Apjohn hygrometer. The name apjohnite was given to a South African manganese alum he described in 1838; another mineral he analysed was named jellettite, to honour JOHN JELLETT (who was an inventor of a sophisticated saccharimeter and later provost of Trinity College). Apjohn also investigated inorganic compounds, in particular complexes of potassium oxide. He was one of the founders of the Royal City of Dublin Hospital, Baggot Street. He published widely, including the textbook *Manual of the Metalloids* (1865, 1866); Dickens based a scene in *Bleak House* on his description of spontaneous combustion. Elected to the ROYAL IRISH ACADEMY in 1828, he was awarded the Cunningham Medal in 1839 for his research on the specific heats of gases and was made a fellow of the Royal Society (London) in 1855. **Susan McKenna-Lawlor**

Apjohn, James Henry (1845–1914), engineer and inventor. Born in Dublin, son of JAMES APJOHN; educated at TCD, graduating in arts and engineering. He lived in India, 1869–1901, where he worked at the Indian Public Works Department (ultimately becoming chief engineer) on problems in civil and sanitary engineering, including the construction of the first sewage and purification works at Howrah, Bengal, and the development of a new type of burning ghat. He was awarded the Telford Premium by the Institution of Civil Engineering (London) in 1879. Following his retirement to London, he invented a device for bulking and packing tea. He also invented and patented a new gear system for cars. **Susan McKenna-Lawlor**

Apprentice Boys of Derry. The first organisation with this name was set up in 1813 to celebrate the action of thirteen apprentices who closed the gates of Derry against Jacobite forces in 1688, which began the SIEGE OF DERRY. Membership was small until the decision in 1889 to allow branches to be set up in other parts of Ulster. Membership grew rapidly in the 1920s. The main annual parade took place on 12 August, and an effigy of LUNDY, the governor of Derry, was burned on 18 August. The 1969 parade led directly to the introduction of British troops on active service. After years of bans and conflicts in south Belfast, and Dunloy in particular, the commemorations have been noticeably peaceful since 1997. **Jonathan Bardon**

aquaculture, the commercial breeding of fish and shellfish. The aquaculture industry in Ireland, established during the 1970s, expanded greatly during the 1980s and 90s. In 1990 fin-fish production was 7,352 tonnes (worth €30 million) and shellfish production 19,222 tonnes (€7.1 million); in 1998 these figures had increased to 17,180 tonnes (€60.3 million) and 23,210 tonnes (€60.3 million), respectively. The emergence of salmon-farming is the main contributor to this increase, with salmon production increasing from 3.5 per cent of total fin-fish production in 1980 to 86 per cent in 1998. Other fin-fish species that are farmed include trout, arctic char, and eels, with mussels the most significant species of farmed shellfish, ahead of oysters, clams, and scallops. The most important area for mussel production is Bantry Bay, producing 4,000 tonnes per annum, which is approximately 30 per cent of total national production.

The aquaculture industry is concentrated in coastal areas of the north, west, and south-east, where employment locally can be as high as 25 per cent. Ireland exports 91 per cent of its total marine produce, primarily to member-states of the European Union (80 per cent), the other 20 per cent being exported to the Far East, the Philippines, and Africa (Egypt and Nigeria). Of concern to the industry are 'red tides' or toxic algal blooms, which can close farms for many months, and sea lice, a serious parasite of farmed salmon, which causes substantial losses in the industry each year. **Julie Maguire**

aqueducts. Because of the relatively gentle nature of Ireland's topography, CANAL-builders did not have to contend with any serious physical obstructions, with the exception of deep BOGS. Where a canal was to be carried across a river, an aqueduct was required. The GRAND CANAL is carried over the River LIFFEY by the Leinster Aqueduct, near Sallins, Co. Kildare; designed by Richard Evans, it has five masonry arch spans of 7.6 m (25 ft) and was completed in 1784. Further west the Barrow Line of the Grand Canal crosses the River Barrow near Monasterevin, Co. Kildare, on an aqueduct designed by Hamilton Killaly; it has three spans, each of 12.6 m ($41\frac{1}{2}$ ft) and was completed in 1831. Aqueducts of note on the Royal Canal are the Boyne Aqueduct near Longwood, Co. Meath, which carries the canal over the River Boyne, and the Whitworth Aqueduct, which carries it over the River Inny near Abbeyshrule, Co. Longford, and the Newmills Aqueduct (1777). **Ronald Cox**

Aran crios (*crios*, 'belt'), a traditional multi-coloured woollen belt still made on the Aran Islands but today kept alive mainly by the tourist industry. While woven belts were made in other traditional cultures, the technique employed on the ARAN ISLANDS is unique, as the belt is formed without the use of a loom or tablets: instead the white warp threads are stretched either between two stools or between the maker's hand and foot, while a piece of stick and a loop of woollen thread tag the sheds for the colourful weft threads. [see PAMPOOTIES.] **Anne O'Dowd**

Aran Islands, Co. Galway, three slabs of Carboniferous limestone in Galway Bay forming the islands of Inishmore (also called Inis Mór), with an area of 30.5 km^2 (12 sq. miles), Inishmaan (Inis Meáin), with an area of 9.1 km^2 ($3\frac{1}{2}$ sq. miles), and Inisheer (Inis Oírr), with an area of 5.7 km^2 ($2\frac{1}{4}$ sq. miles). The stone forts on the islands, made from the local stone, are probably Late BRONZE AGE; the most famous is DÚN AONGHASA (Dun Aengus), a semi-circular structure on a magnificent cliff-top site. There are also numerous Early Christian remains, including the oratory of Temple Benen and Tighlath Eany, an early church with antae (see p. 194). The islands' appearance is distinctive, with thousands of kilometres of dry-stone walling enclosing usually tiny fields. The walls served the purpose of removing loose stone from farmland and at the same time protecting the soil of the treeless islands from wind erosion. Much of the soil has been made by placing alternate layers of sand and seaweed on the bare limestone, suggesting former population pressures. In 1841, before the GREAT FAMINE, Inishmore had a population of 2,592 people, Inishmaan 473, and Inisheer 456; in 1901 these figures were 1,941, 421, and 483, respectively; in 1996 the totals were 838, 191, and 274. The population is largely Irish-speaking. Traditional farming and fishing are now supported by TOURISM, particularly on Inishmore and Inisheer. Inishmaan, the central island, remains the most unchanged but has a textile factory. Each island has an airstrip. The islands have attracted writers and artists, including JOHN MILLINGTON SYNGE (see p. 1). **Stephen A. Royle**

Aran knitting. The traditional dress of the Aran Islanders was very uniform for most of the nineteenth century and the first decades of the twentieth century; the introduction of a new element into the almost regimented dress code of both men and women would have been a slow process. Fishermen from the British coast, dressed in their finely knitted jumpers, came into contact with the Aran Islanders throughout the nineteenth century, and by the early years of the twentieth century the gansey or fisherman's jumper had been introduced to the islands. They were at first knitted by women for their own husbands and children, and in a short time the intricate stitches in the raised patterns became extremely elaborate. The knitters relate the different stitches to island life and give them names such as the blackberry, honeycomb, cable, moss, and diamond. Encouraged by competitions held by the COUNTRY SHOP, Dublin, and by the skill and inventiveness of the women, island knitters produced a product that is today known all over the world. [see CLOTHING, TRADITIONAL.] **Anne O'Dowd**

Áras an Uachtaráin ('President's House'), official residence of the President of Ireland, near the centre of the PHOENIX PARK, Dublin, formerly the Viceregal Lodge; designed and built in 1751 by NATHANIEL CLEMENTS, Park Ranger, as a residence for himself. In 1782 it was sold to the state as a 'country seat' for the LORD LIEUTENANT, later becoming the official residence of the Lord Lieutenant and subsequently of the GOVERNOR-GENERAL OF THE IRISH FREE STATE. In 1816 it was extended and improved by FRANCIS JOHNSTON, who added the Ionic portico at the front. **Fergal Tobin**

Arboe, Co. Tyrone, site of a HIGH CROSS dating from the ninth or tenth century, close to the western shore of Lough NEAGH. At 5.7 m (19 ft) it is the second-tallest high cross in Ireland and one of Ulster's few intact specimens. The east face has Old Testament scenes, Christ's second coming and the Last Judgment, while the west face illustrates Christ's public life, passion, and death. The south side has a Paul and Anthony panel, while the north side apparently features a childhood of Christ cycle. **Peter Harbison**

Arbuckle, James (c. 1690–1742), poet and essayist. Born in Belfast; graduated from the University of Glasgow (1720); studied for the ministry but was not ordained. His published poems include 'Glotta', 'Snuff', and 'On the Death of Joseph Addison'. Arbuckle was a friend of the Scottish poet Allan Ramsay. Moving to Dublin, he was patronised by Viscount Molesworth; he edited the *Dublin Weekly Journal* (1725–9), contributing the Hibernicus Letters. In 1729 he edited the *Tribune*. He was also an associate of SWIFT in the 1730s. At the time of his death he was a clerk in the CUSTOM HOUSE. Influenced by the third Earl of Shaftesbury and by Addison, Arbuckle espoused the aesthetic concept of politeness, helping to introduce literary criticism into Ireland. **Michael Brown**

archaeology (general chronology). Chronologies in archaeology are of two types: *relative chronologies*, based on seriation, find association, stratigraphy, typology, and POLLEN ANALYSIS, and *absolute chronology*, nowadays based on DENDROCHRONOLOGY (the most accurate method but applicable only to some wood species) and RADIOCARBON DATING (less accurate but applicable to a wide range of materials containing carbon). The most widely used general chronological framework is the 'three age' system of Stone Age, BRONZE AGE, and IRON AGE, introduced in the nineteenth century. This is a broadly based framework of successive phases of technological development for prehistory, now termed the Palaeolithic Period, MESOLITHIC Period, NEOLITHIC Period, Bronze Age, and Iron Age. In Ireland the Mesolithic Period is defined as approximately 7000–4000 BC, the Neolithic approximately 4000–2400 BC, and the Bronze Age 2400–600 BC, followed by the prehistoric Iron Age, conventionally defined as 600 BC to AD 400. The EARLY HISTORIC PERIOD (sometimes called the early medieval) extends from c. 400 to c. 1100 and is followed by the Middle Ages to c. 1350. Post-medieval archaeology includes aspects of MARITIME ARCHAEOLOGY, INDUSTRIAL ARCHAEOLOGY, and the study of later settlements. **A. L. Brindley**

architectural crafts. The anatomy of any historical building consists of its structure, including walls, roof, and floors, and its main details, such as windows, doors, architraves, and other decorative features. In Ireland there is a long history of skills associated with the building tradition, from the stone carvings at NEWGRANGE to the masonry of the GALLARUS ORATORY and the ornamentation of Cormac's Chapel at the Rock of CASHEL. These are some of the stonemason's great achievements, which were to continue through to the exquisite stonecutting of the eighteenth and nineteenth centuries to be seen on any GEORGIAN doorcase. The joiner's skill can be seen in the solid roof structures, in timber floors, windows, and doors, while the wood-carver's accomplishments are in evidence in many churches and public buildings, such as the ROYAL HOSPITAL, Kilmainham, Dublin. Ireland has a proud tradition of decorative PLASTERWORK, dating particularly from the eighteenth century and visible in Ireland's many fine Georgian houses (see pp. 543, 603). Wrought iron, stained glass, and bricklaying were the product of prized skills; together with stonemasonry and joinery these were for many years controlled by the guild system.

All architectural crafts are perishable, with pollution, vandalism, neglect, and ignorance leading to their destruction. Ireland has lost much, especially since the 1950s, though there is a growing interest in traditional skills, including such once-common practices as THATCHING and limewashing. [see PEARSON COLLECTION.] **Peter Pearson**

architecture. Ireland belongs firmly in the building tradition of continental Europe, with the consideration that its isolated island position frequently led to the delayed arrival of external influences as well as to the development of indigenous ideas peculiar to the society's own social requirements, material wealth, and technical capacity.

The most prevalent form of early architecture in Ireland is that of EARTHWORKS, which in various forms, and over an immense time-span, stretching from prehistory to the late Middle Ages, preceded and paralleled an architecture variously of timber, stone, packed earth, and brick. As architecture may be considered to encompass all three-dimensional answers to structural needs, the funerary structures of the Neolithic, Bronze and Iron Ages are the earliest evidence of building techniques used for human purposes. The Neolithic passage tomb cemeteries at CARROWMORE and CARROWKEEL, Co. Sligo, and the BOYNE VALLEY, Co. Meath, exhibit a continuing interest in the creation of monumental stoneworks, utilising basic materials of available stone, earth, and gravel, allied to a keen understanding of fundamental engineering principles in the manipulation of immense loads. The internalised architecture of the passage tombs of Dowth and NEWGRANGE in the Boyne Valley exhibits an accomplished use of post and lintel principles, corbelling, load-bearing and distribution, and other techniques. From the Late Bronze to the Late Iron Age, defensive and ceremonial stone structures were erected, some of considerable ambition, such as the clifftop complex of DÚN AONGHASA on the ARAN ISLANDS and the hilltop fortress of the Grianán of Aileach, Co. Donegal.

Prior to the advent of Christianity in the fifth century, the majority of buildings were of wattle or timber within single or multiple earthen or stone protective ramparts, the uni-vallate or multi-vallate enclosures that represent the most widespread settlement type over an extensive period. Christianity brought the ecclesiastical need for the construction of churches, initially of timber and, from around the eighth or ninth century, of stone. These remarkable diminutive single-cell oratories, with their steeply pitched gables and stone roofs, were the earliest examples of conventional formal architecture. By the tenth century the ambitions of the ecclesiastical builders had advanced to producing larger churches, such as the Cathedral of CLONMACNOISE (c. AD 909), and the development of the ROUND TOWERS, circular stone ecclesiastical belfries. Little advance was made in church architecture until the twelfth century. English and continental European influence are evident in Cormac's Chapel (1127–34), CASHEL, Co. Tipperary, a nave-and-chancel church built for Cormac Mac Carthy, king and bishop. This intriguing building blends Irish structural forms with a veneer of ROMANESQUE style, possibly the first ecclesiastical building to incorporate extensive surface decoration, figurative sculpture, fresco, and an aspiration towards monumentality.

Continental European contacts brought the monastic orders in the twelfth century, with the Cistercian establishment of MELLIFONT, Co. Louth, in 1142. Here the ordered plan of a cruciform church with aisles and transepts, as well as attendant cloister, chapter house, refectory, and dormitory, all arranged according to strict rules of utility and simplicity, introduced an architectural formalism that was to become the major force of the following centuries. The transition from Romanesque to Gothic can be seen in the stylistic variations of the many Cistercian daughter-houses.

ANGLO-NORMAN military structures include ringworks, earthwork castles, and the motte and bailey, such as those at Knockgraffon, Co. Tipperary, and Granard, Co. Longford, and the great thirteenth-century stone quadrangular castles, composed of a curtain wall between corner drum towers. DUBLIN CASTLE and King John's Castle,

Limerick, are characteristic examples, while that of Trim, Co. Meath, has a substantial keep. The creation of walled towns commenced in the tenth century with the VIKING establishment of DUBLIN, though proto-urban settlements were already in existence at monastic sites like CLONMACNOISE and ARMAGH. The Anglo-Norman medieval walled town was generally linear in plan, with a main street and long, narrow individual house-plots extending to the walls. The fifteenth-century walled town of Galway, with its stone merchants' houses decorated with armorial and decorative sculptures, represented the apogee of confident and prosperous settlement.

HALL-HOUSES and TOWER-HOUSES became the typical residences of the local magnates, and were also built within towns. The majority of individual town dwellings were single-storey and thatched, of timber or stone. Tower-houses were essentially defensive, surrounded by a bawn enclosure wall for dwellings and livestock. From the thirteenth century, churches were built in all the Norman towns, of which few survive unaltered by subsequent ecclesiastical requirements.

From the late sixteenth century, fortified houses begin to replace the castle concept. Of the greater houses, all follow a similar multi-windowed, four-square plan with corner towers. Rathfarnham, Co. Dublin (1585), PORTUMNA, Co. Galway (1618), and BURNCOURT, Co. Tipperary (1641), are impressive in their scale and sense of Renaissance order.

Classicism made slow inroads during the seventeenth century, with rural courthouses and military establishments the principal buildings of interest. The Tholsel or market house common to country towns displays a wide variety of attempts at civic architecture; the MAIN GUARD in Clonmel (1674), the palatinate courthouse built by the Duke of Ormond, is among the more accomplished examples. Star forts and other defences, particularly CHARLES FORT, Kinsale, Co. Cork (1677), reflect an awareness of contemporary Continental military architecture.

Domestic architecture outside the towns and villages remained undeveloped, with CLACHAN nucleated settlements common in the west, and estate villages being created in areas under landlord influence. The dispersed farmsteads, a characteristic of rural occupation, largely follow the mid-eighteenth-century ENCLOSURE policies of landlords.

The building of the ROYAL HOSPITAL, Kilmainham, Dublin (1680), and the Royal Barracks (Collins Barracks), Dublin (1704), by Sir WILLIAM ROBINSON introduced classical principles on the grand scale and established a style for public architecture. From the late seventeenth century, great and more modest houses were built on estates throughout the country, creating the 'BIG HOUSE' element of the landscape, which was to remain a dominant aspect of political, economic, and social influence up to the beginning of the twentieth century. From the eighteenth century, estate and market towns acquired the layout they have retained into the present, linear collections of single-storey thatched dwellings being replaced by two-storey slated ones, with market squares, churches, courthouse, and other public buildings.

In the hands of EDWARD LOVETT PEARCE, classical influence reached a climax in the PARLIAMENT HOUSE, Dublin (1728). Major country houses, such as CASTLETOWN (1719) and CARTON (1739), both in Co. Kildare, established Palladianism as the favoured idiom. Educational and religious architecture prospered throughout the century, as did urban domestic building, particularly in the creation of the imposing residential streets and squares of regular brick-fronted mansions for the gentry and professional classes in Dublin, Limerick, Cork, and Belfast, a style that maintained its influence into the late nineteenth century, though palatial town-houses ceased to be built after 1800. The work of the WIDE STREETS COMMISSIONERS established the rational town planning that gave Dublin its present structure. The late GEORGIAN PERIOD saw the civic buildings of JAMES GANDON in Dublin as well as significant public buildings, the Custom House by DAVIS DUCART in Limerick, followed by Greek revival courthouses in country towns, of which the finest is Carlow by Sir RICHARD MORRISON. Country house building continued unabated on estates throughout the Victorian era.

Classicism was challenged by the Gothic Revival movement. In church building, Catholics favoured the verities of classicism; the Pro-Cathedral, Dublin (1816), is an accomplished Greek Revival composition. Protestants favoured Gothic, as in the austere parish churches of JOHN SEMPLE, a situation that was to change by the end of the nineteenth century, with Gothic being widely adopted for church building of all denominations. Gothic Revival reached its climax in the cathedral-building of the century's end, in such buildings as William Burges's St Finn Barr's, Cork (1862), and those of Armagh (1840–73), Monaghan (1861), Cobh, Co. Cork (1867), and Letterkenny, Co. Donegal (1891), all monumental buildings on a scale unseen since the medieval period. Country houses became more eclectic, with Classical, Gothic, Scots Baronial, Tudor, and other styles remaining popular.

The cultural revival movements of the 1880s introduced the influence of antiquarian research into Ireland's past as a fresh theme and stylistic repertoire for architecture and the applied arts. The

architecture. *The Long Room, Trinity College Library, Dublin, designed by Thomas Burgh in 1712; in 1860 the architects Deane and Woodward added the timber barrel-vaulted ceiling and gallery bookcases. [Board of Trinity College, Dublin]*

Celtic Revival became influential in the decoration of ecclesiastical buildings. The parish churches of Clane, Co. Kildare (1883), and Rathdaire, Co. Laois (1884), and the HONAN CHAPEL, Cork (1916), are exotics of this genre. This movement heralded Arts and Crafts, Art Deco, and early Modern influences, eventually being superseded by them. Cinema architecture achieved particular significance in the Art Deco style, but this influence was short-lived.

Modernist influences began appearing in the architecture of the 1930s, and a small number of important buildings were erected. GERAGH (1937), MICHAEL SCOTT's house in Dublin, Dublin Airport (1941) by Desmond FitzGerald, and Busáras, Dublin (1953), also by Scott, are landmark buildings in a time when classical influence lingered for public buildings, such as STORMONT Parliament House (1932), Cork City Hall (1935), Cavan Cathedral (1941), and Galway Cathedral (1957), and public architecture struggled to find an appropriate voice. R. M. BUTLER, who designed churches and public buildings, brought an individual interpretation to his buildings, derived from Celtic Revival and early Modernism.

Little public architecture of distinction was built in any part of Ireland from the 1940s to the 1980s, with the significant exception of developments in the area of hospitals, schools and cinemas, while domestic housing expanded like an inflatable tyre around all urban settlements which were allowed to decay at the centre. The absence of coherent planning policies was evident throughout the country, with the new towns of Shannon (1961) and Craigavon (1966) isolated examples of attempts to direct urban growth. Throughout the latter half of the twentieth century the church architecture of LIAM MCCORMICK remained singular in its inventiveness and developed sense of location, while buildings such as the Carroll's Factory, Dundalk (1967), by RONALD TALLON, stand out from the dross of commercial office and factory building. Economic resurgence in the late twentieth century brought new creative talents to the fore, with Group 91's TEMPLE BAR FRAMEWORK PLAN for the urban renewal of a Dublin city centre area setting a standard for intelligent contextual development, giving evidence that public and private architecture in Ireland was emerging from an extended period of apathy. **Brian Lalor**

architecture, urban domestic. In Irish towns and cities, domestic architecture includes a wide variety of house types, ranging from the largest detached mansion in its own grounds, such as LEINSTER HOUSE (now the seat of Dáil Éireann) in Kildare Street, Dublin, to the humblest one-roomed cottage. In between are many variations, which can be dated by stylistic features, though caution must be exercised, as earlier houses were often overlaid in the dress of later periods: frequently Georgian brick houses were rendered or stuccoed, their small-paned sash windows removed, and features of later times added, thus confusing attempts to date these structures.

Despite the widespread destruction of historic houses in cities and towns, good examples from most periods survive. In the eighteenth century the terraced brick-built house became the standard type, while outside Dublin stone-built houses are far more common. Though principally found in Dublin, Limerick, and Cork, brick houses were also common in Waterford, Ennis, Drogheda, and many other towns. These houses were two, three, or even four storeys high, usually over a basement, where the kitchens were. The principal reception rooms included two (front and back) on the ground floor, while a generous flight of stairs gave access to the main drawing-room at the front of the house on the first floor. Bedrooms were above; toilets and bathrooms were not usually accommodated, or even considered: outside lavatories were the norm.

The houses of the rich, such as those of Merrion Square in Dublin or Pery Square in Limerick, were often fitted with mahogany doors, ornate marble mantelpieces, and lavish decorative PLASTERWORK. In the late seventeenth and early eighteenth centuries, houses in Dublin and Cork were smaller and more modest. Their gable fronts, similar to houses in the Netherlands, led to their being called 'Dutch Billies'. Few of these houses survive today. They were timber-panelled inside and for the most part had no decorative plasterwork.

Most surviving Georgian houses in Dublin date from the middle of the eighteenth century onwards; outstanding examples of the larger town-house can be seen in St Stephen's Green, while Powerscourt House in South William Street is a perfect town-house of the later eighteenth century. Most terraced houses were equipped with a cellar, with stores and stables to the rear, where horses and coach would be kept. A coal cellar under the footpath supplied fuel for the many fireplaces. The front of a typical Georgian house is characterised by its brick façade, timber sash windows, carved stone doorcase, and delicate leaded fanlight. The staircase is often ornate. Most of these houses, especially the larger ones, have been used as offices since the end of the nineteenth century.

There was no magic date when the Georgian style was suddenly transformed into the Victorian, and even up to the 1840s terraces continued to be built with all the hallmarks of the eighteenth century. Pembroke Road in Dublin and Day Square in Tralee are good examples, both dating from the early nineteenth century during which the SUBURBS grew out from the cities, and house styles changed, but the basic arrangement of rooms remained the same. In domestic architecture there was a move away from brick façades to rendered fronts, especially in some areas, such as Dún Laoghaire, Co. Dublin, and Cobh, Co. Cork. With the invention of plate glass, larger, plainer-looking windows were introduced.

While classical or Italianate detail remained fashionable, houses were sometimes built with Gothic or even Tudor detail. The classical doorcase with its columns gradually gave way to a bold entrance with carved brackets or scrolls. More modest terraced housing was also built, usually two storeys high with a slated roof. In some towns, rows of houses were built to accommodate mill or factory workers; these were usually plain, though well proportioned. Many new houses were built for the nineteenth-century middle classes, and from the 1860s onwards the bay window became a popular feature, with widespread use of smooth red brick. The two-storeyed houses of Rathmines and Drumcondra, Dublin, or any suburb in Cork or Limerick, are typical of the later decades of the nineteenth century. Internally, mass-produced ornament, such as cast-iron fireplaces and other products of the INDUSTRIAL REVOLUTION, such as tiles, washbasins, and toilets, were in evidence. Stained glass also became popular.

In provincial towns, such as Birr, Co. Offaly, and Cashel, Co. Tipperary, the place of residence was often combined with a shop beneath, and there are many good examples of these stucco-fronted terraced houses with shop-front in the typical Irish town. Sometimes a wide carriage arch with wooden doors allowed access to a yard behind. The importance of original timber doors and windows to such streetscapes was not widely recognised until the late twentieth century, when they were beginning to disappear.

It was not until the very end of the nineteenth century that efforts were made to replace slum housing in cities with purpose-built accommodation, often called artisans' dwellings. These small red-brick terraced houses were built by municipal authorities and

architecture. *The purpose-built factory for P. J. Carroll and Company, Dundalk, Co. Louth (1970), designed by Michael Scott and Partners along a cellular concept with exposed steel structure. To the right is a stainless-steel sculpture by Gerda Fromel, the three panels formed to resemble sails, which turn slowly in the wind. [Photo © John Donat, courtesy of Scott Tallon Walker]*

philanthropic bodies, such as the Dublin Artisans' Dwellings Company, from the 1870s onwards.

The character of domestic architecture changed radically in the twentieth century as semi-detached two-storey houses became the norm and housing estates began to spread around cities and towns, evolving into the 'urban sprawl' of twenty-first-century Ireland. **Peter Pearson**

architecture, vernacular, buildings not designed by professionals but created within the informal, oral, communal or 'folk' tradition. As well as farmhouses this can include town architecture, agricultural buildings, workshops, and mills. Town vernacular architecture in Ireland was not as common as the rural, nor has it been subject to the same degree of study.

Because of the denuding of woodland by the eighteenth century, building in stone predominates in the Irish tradition. Mud construction occurs in many parts of the country also, particularly in the east. Unlike many other European countries, very little timber-framing or cruck construction survives in Ireland. Small-scale farming meant that large farm complexes were comparatively rare, traditionally occurring mainly in the east. Otherwise, the twentieth-century corrugated iron hay-shed is ubiquitous.

Frequent rain meant pitched roofs. Roofing in slate or split stone was used traditionally in a few areas only: the usual covering was a thatch of straw or reed. Once the majority house type, thatched houses are now a very small minority, and only a few thousand survive; others have been reroofed in slate or covered with corrugated iron sheeting. Thatched houses have not generally received the same attention by the conservation lobby as rural manor-houses or old urban houses but have often been a source of nostalgia in popular media and in art, projected as a core Irish symbol. However, because thatched and vernacular houses generally do not meet modern standards of comfort, privacy, status, or popular aesthetics, to a large extent they have been demolished or converted to outhouses. Where renovation occurs it is often for use as a holiday home.

The Irish vernacular farmhouse does not exhibit great regional variation. Vernacular houses were mainly one room wide, rectangular, one-storeyed, thatched, and whitewashed, with variation apparent in whether hip or gable-roofed, stone or mud-walled. Other regional features were bed-outshots in Connacht and Ulster and two-storey 'thatched mansions' in Leinster. Nor is the tradition in general very ancient, compared with that of other countries. Most examples are derived from the eighteenth, nineteenth, and early twentieth centuries.

Irish vernacular houses have a similarity with much of the vernacular houses of Scotland, Wales, and the west of England, where the elongated rectangular one-storey stone or mud house is found, as well as in parts of France and other parts of continental Europe. However, there is much more variation of vernacular house types in England and on the Continent than in Ireland.

Though often derided by conservationists, modern bungalows in rural Ireland have been influenced to a certain extent by the vernacular tradition: most are rectangular and one-storeyed, and the kitchen is often the main living-room. Other features, however—such as plastic doors, landscape windows, external arches, classical pillars, and stone facing—derive from a milieu at odds with the earlier tradition and often in discord with the surroundings. This has contributed to a crisis in planning permission for rural houses. Buildings from the vernacular tradition tended to accord well with the surrounding environment, being composed of local and generally organic materials and usually being built to obtain shelter from prevailing winds rather than achieving maximum visibility, which is the modern tendency. There are some signs of attempts to borrow from the vernacular style in re-creating the rectangular house in a more unadorned external style than that of the bungalow of previous decades. [see FARMHOUSE TYPES; IRISH AGRICULTURAL MUSEUM; IRISH FOLKLIFE MUSEUM; ULSTER FOLK AND TRANSPORT MUSEUM.] **Séamas Mac Philib**

Ardagh. *The Ardagh Chalice, dating approximately from the second half of the eighth century, regarded as one of the finest specimens of early medieval metalwork. A communion vessel, it is composed of gold, silver, bronze, brass, copper, and lead and comprises 354 pieces. The names of the twelve apostles are incised on a band running round the outside of the bowl, below the level of the handles. [National Museum of Ireland]*

Ardagh Chalice, a large silver chalice, one of two communion cups from a hoard of metalwork (which also contained four brooches) found at Reerasta Rath, near Ardagh, Co. Limerick, in 1868; the chalice is now in the NATIONAL MUSEUM. The second cup, which is rather smaller, is made of copper alloy. The Ardagh Chalice belongs to an insular (relating to the islands of Britain and Ireland) group of altar vessels that is characterised by a large bowl balanced by a distinctive large splayed circular foot and an elaborate method of construction. It is a ministerial chalice, designed for serving communion wine to the congregation. Made of beaten silver, the bowl is united to the foot by a hollow cast copper-alloy stem, through which passes a stout pin to fasten the assembly together; an elaborate cast gilt copper-alloy disc, in the centre of which is a large rock crystal, disguises the emergence of the pin on the underside and its catchplate. The pin was made too short to function properly, and in ancient times the chalice was disassembled and the stem filled with lead in an effort to stabilise it. The bowl is equipped with two handles with decorative escutcheons and two medallions divided by arcs into crosses. Its rim has an applied copper-alloy beading.

The great glory of the Ardagh Chalice is its elegant filigree and cast-glass ornament. The filigree—in a band below the rim, on the handles and their escutcheons, and on the underside disc—shows a series of patterns composed of interlace and stylised beasts, birds, and serpents. The glass ornaments consist of hemispherical beads and plaques decorated with angular panels in imitation of *cloisonné* gemstone work. Some of the beads have grilles cut from sheet metal set into their surface, in imitation of the *cloisons* or metal cells used in Germanic and Anglo-Saxon jewellery to hold segments of gemstone in place. The ornamental repertoire additionally includes stamped foils, wire mesh, a little amber, and gold granulation. On the surface of the bowl is a lightly incised inscription, somewhat blundered, recording the names of the Apostles in a display script close to that of the great contemporary illuminated manuscripts. This is set as a reserve against a stippled background within incised borders, which expand into animal and human-head ornament below the handle escutcheons and the bowl medallions.

With its elaborate polychrome style and assembly, the chalice belongs clearly to the eighth-century climax of INSULAR ART. Its nearest counterpart is the paten from the DERRYNAFLAN HOARD. The last object in the Ardagh Hoard to be manufactured was a silver penannular 'ball' brooch of a style current in the late ninth and tenth centuries, and so it is likely that the hoard was concealed in VIKING times. **Michael Ryan**

Ardbraccan, Co. Meath, an ecclesiastical settlement associated with Troscán, son of Óengus, and Bishop Ultán (died 657), whose lost 'Life' of St PATRICK was used by the hagiographers Tírechán and Muirchú. Plundered by the Norse kings of Dublin, Gothfrith (951) and Sitric (1031 and 1035), and burnt by Munstermen in 1115, it declined in the twelfth century. **Ailbhe Mac Shamhráin**

Ardfert, Co. Kerry, an early monastic settlement founded by St BRENDAN; by 1117 it had superseded RATASS as the diocesan centre of Kerry. The austere thirteenth-century cathedral retains sections of a twelfth-century west doorway and blind arcade. The south wall of the choir is punctuated by nine lancet windows, an unusual feature, echoed in the nearby Franciscan friary. An aisle and transept were added to the south side of the nave in the fifteenth century. To the north-west of the cathedral is Templenahoe, the nave of which incorporates some examples of high-quality ROMANESQUE sculpture, and Templegriffin, a small fifteenth-century church. **Rachel Moss**

Ardmore, Co. Waterford, an ecclesiastical complex founded about the fifth century by St Declan and the possible site of a pre-Patrician community. The twelfth-century ROUND TOWER is among the tallest and latest to survive. St Declan's Oratory stands to the east. The ruined ROMANESQUE cathedral was enlarged in the thirteenth century and incorporates transitional architectural features. Figurative sculptures narrating Old and New Testament subjects, including the Judgment of Solomon, the Fall of Man, and episodes from Christ's passion, were re-set into the exterior of the west wall. They are very rare examples in Ireland of Romanesque sculptures designed specifically for an architectural context. **Suzanne McNab**

Ardmore Studios, Bray, Co. Wicklow, a film studio established in 1958 by EMMET DALTON and the theatre impresario and film exhibitor Louis Elliman, with the support of ERNEST BLYTHE. Its purpose was to adapt ABBEY THEATRE plays as films; these included

Louis D'Alton's *This Other Eden* (1959) and WALTER MACKEN's *Home Is the Hero* (1959), in which the author was acclaimed for his performance in the title role. This policy quickly gave way to one that sought to encourage foreign producers to make films at the studios, the first and most interesting being *Shake Hands with the Devil* (1959), a drama of the War of Independence starring James Cagney, followed by *A Terrible Beauty* (1960), with Robert Mitchum in the lead. Most subsequent films used Ardmore (and Ireland) simply as another location, such as *The Spy Who Came In from the Cold* (1965), *The Face of Fu Manchu* (1965), and *Excalibur* (1981), which was made while the film's director, John Boorman, was chairman of the studio. The use of state funds to subsidise Ardmore from 1975 to 1982 was a point of contention with independent film-makers in their campaign for an indigenous Irish cinema, which led to the setting up of BORD SCANNÁN NA HÉIREANN. The studios, which now mainly serve Irish and foreign productions and have no direct involvement in the financing of films, are owned by the rock group manager PAUL MCGUINNESS and the media accountant Ossie Kilkenny, with Enterprise Ireland owning 31 per cent. **Kevin Rockett**

Ards Peninsula, Co. Down, a peninsula enclosing STRANGFORD LOUGH, with only the narrow channel between the towns of Portaferry at its southern tip and Strangford providing access to the sea. The landscape is characterised by gently undulating drumlins, with both pasture and arable farmland. There are many archaeological features, reflecting the great antiquity of settlement. The VIKINGS gave Strangford Lough the original of its English name, meaning 'violent fjord', referring to the narrow channel to the sea. After 1606 the peninsula was planted, and many Scottish settlers were attracted to the area. NEWTOWNARDS, begun by Hugh Montgomery, was developed as an important market town, while the existing ports of Strangford and Portaferry were enhanced. The present population within the area of Ards Borough Council is approximately 70,000. Some 25,000 people live in Newtownards, the main town, of whom a sizeable proportion commute to Belfast, the main industrial centre. The remainder of the peninsula is predominantly rural, with a small number of medium-sized coastal towns: Donaghadee (population 4,500), Portaferry (population 2,500), and Portavogie (population 1,500), an important SEA-FISHING centre. There are many fine beaches along the coast, while Strangford Lough is of international importance as a wildlife habitat, particularly for overwintering wildfowl, and is one of the most important breeding sites in Ireland for the common seal. A designated 'area of outstanding natural beauty', the lough also contains several nature reserves. **Joseph Brady**

Argentina, the Irish in. The Irish were a consistent presence in European colonies from the sixteenth century. This contact began through the IRISH COLLEGES in Catholic Europe, and Irish graduates often enrolled in the colonial service of their adopted country as a means of gaining promotion and making their fortune. Consequently, a relatively small number of Irish people were to have an influence on European colonisation out of proportion to their numbers. Irish emigration to Argentina illustrates this point, while the situation was similar throughout Latin America and French Canada.

The first Irish people to set foot in South America, in April 1520, were two cabin boys on Magellan's voyage to circumnavigate the world. In February 1536 a group of colonists, led by Pedro Mendoza, landed on the River Plate (Rio de la Plata) and founded Buenos Aires; among them were John and Thomas Farel and Isabel Farrel. The names Coleman, Lucas, Galvan, and Fays (probably Hayes) appear also.

In 1776 the next phase of Irish emigration to Argentina began. Many emigrants arrived in Buenos Aires in 1777, such as Michael O'Gorman of Co. Clare, who became head of the Sanitary Commission. By 1780 he had founded the Faculty of Medicine. In 1792 his cousin Thomas O'Gorman, a naval captain, arrived from Mauritius, and he became an important merchant. John Thomand O'Brien of Co. Wicklow arrived from Spain with the rank of captain; he was later to become a general in the Argentine army. By 1775 the merchants, realising the value of leather and wool in Europe, began rounding up the wild herds of cattle and sheep roaming the pampas. They recruited a hundred butchers and tanners from Ireland to provide the skilled labour; more were recruited from Ireland over the next twenty-five years. These Irishmen are believed to have founded the Argentine beef industry. Among Irish names listed as substantial merchants by 1800 in Buenos Aires were Cullen, Lynch, Dogan, O'Ryan, and Butler.

The British invaded the River Plate in 1806–7 with soldiers recruited largely from Mullingar and Athlone. Many deserted to the Argentine side and found work with the merchants on their vast *estancias* (estates), improving the quality of the native cattle and sheep. WILLIAM BROWN of Co. Mayo founded the Argentine navy

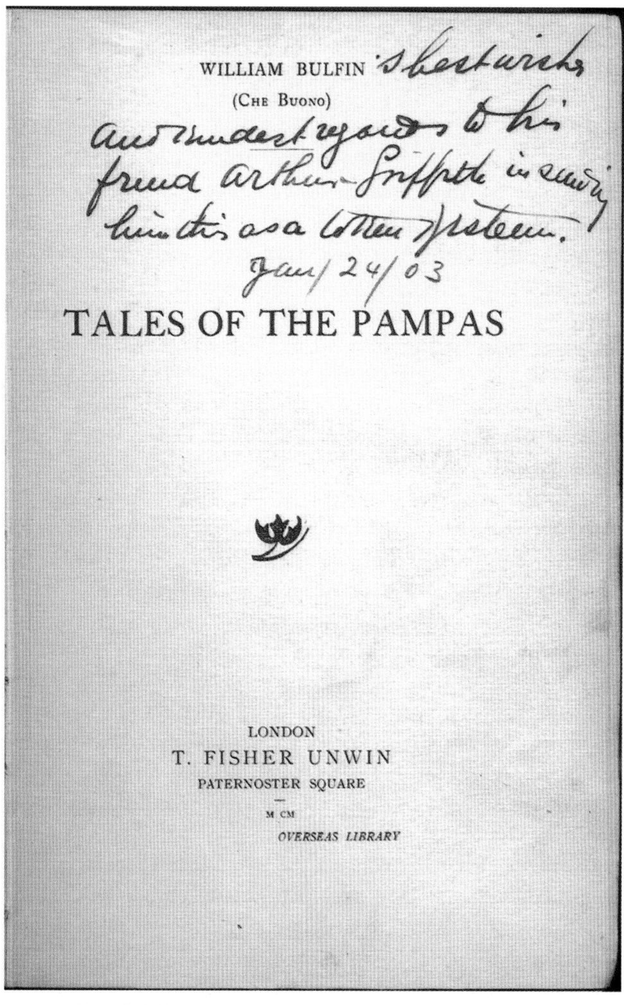
WILLIAM BULFIN
(CHE BUONO)

TALES OF THE PAMPAS

LONDON
T. FISHER UNWIN
PATERNOSTER SQUARE
MCM
OVERSEAS LIBRARY

Argentina, Irish writing in. *Title page of William Bulfin's* Tales of the Pampas, *with an inscription from Bulfin to Arthur Griffith. [Board of Trinity College, Dublin]*

following independence and is honoured today as a national hero. Such was the quality of these ex-soldiers as workers and estancia managers and their popularity with the resident Irish population that General O'Brien returned to Ireland for more emigrants. Supported by knowledge obtained from letters from the ex-soldiers, emigrants from Westmeath responded to O'Brien's call in great numbers. Another merchant, Patrick Browne of Wexford, also brought large numbers from the Rosslare area c. 1824. About 40,000 people were to emigrate from Ireland to Argentina over the next fifty years. Some 10 per cent appear to have settled there permanently, forming a unique Irish community moulded by Father Anthony Fahy. Their descendants, many of whom speak English with an Irish accent, form the basis of the Irish-Argentine community, which today numbers approximately 300,000. **Patrick McKenna**

Argentina, Irish writing in. Little has been written on nineteenth-century Irish emigration to Argentina, and many of the works relevant to the topic are long out of print. One of the most important works on this subject is *Los Irlandeses en la Argentina* (1987) by Eduardo Coghlan, a complete genealogy of almost every nineteenth-century Irish settler and probably the most complete data-base of any Irish emigrant group. Other important sources include the Hiberno-Argentine newspaper *Southern Cross* (all issues of the other Irish owned-newspaper, the *Standard*, are now lost). A very good account of emigration by women is the novel *You'll Never Go Back* (1946) by Kathleen Nevin. **Patrick McKenna**

ARK: see NORTHERN IRELAND SOCIAL AND POLITICAL ARCHIVE.

Arkle (1957–1970), a racehorse. Foaled at Bryanstown, Co. Kildare, in 1957 and bred by Mary Baker in Co. Dublin, he was bought by Anne, Duchess of Westminster, as a three-year-old and trained by Tom Dreaper. The greatest steeplechaser of all time, he won the Cheltenham Gold Cup three years in succession, 1964–6; in his 1966 victory he was carrying 19 kg (3 stone) more than any other horse and still won by thirty lengths. Other victories included the Irish Grand National, 1964, Whitbread Gold Cup, 1965, King George VI Chase, 1965, Hennessy Gold Cup, 1964–5, and Leopardstown Chase, 1964–6. He broke a pedal bone in the 1966 King George VI Chase and was retired early. **Ciarán Deane**

Arklow (*An tInbhear Mór*), Co. Wicklow, an important nodal point on the Avoca River; population (2002) 9,963. The English name derives from a Norse name meaning 'Arnkel's meadow'. The Anglo-Normans built a castle here, which was finally destroyed in 1649. One of the decisive battles of the 1798 REBELLION took place here on 9 June when English forces under General Needham defeated insurgents led by Father Michael Murphy, who was killed in the battle. The town has a great seafaring and boat-building tradition, and Arklow was selected as the base for Ireland's first lifeboat station in 1826. A maritime museum recalls this aspect of Arklow's history.

An attractive town whose linear layout follows the steep contours of the valley, Arklow has benefited from a bypass on the main road to Rosslare, which reduces through traffic by half. A notable feature is the Nineteen Arches Bridge by Andrew Noble (1759), the longest stone-arched bridge in Ireland. Arklow is noted for the production of pottery; Arklow Potteries, which once employed more than a thousand people, closed in 1999, and the town's main industry is the Irish Fertiliser Industries plant. **Ruth McManus**

Armagh, County (*Contae Ard Mhacha*)

Province:	ULSTER
County town:	ARMAGH
Area:	1,254 km^2 (483 sq. miles)
Population (1991)*:	119,000
Features:	LOUGH NEAGH
	River BLACKWATER
	Slieve Gullion
Of historical interest:	Armagh Cathedral
	NAVAN FORT
Industry and products:	Apples, POTATOES, flax
	Chemicals
	food-processing
	Fruit-growing
	LINEN
	Optical equipment

Petula Martyn

* last year of census by county, [see NORTHERN IRELAND.]

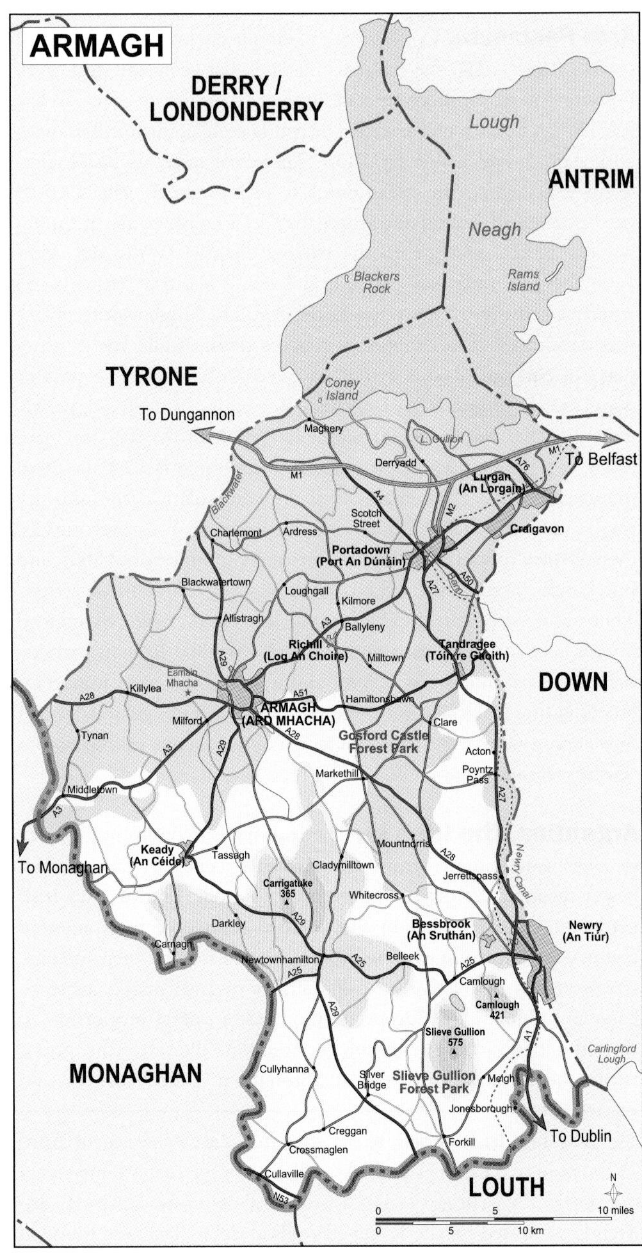

Armagh Observatory. *The observatory with (left to right) the Armagh dome, housing the Troughton Equatorial Telescope (1790), sector tower supporting an anemometer by Monroe (1870), and second round tower (1827); in front are the library and two low-lying domes, one of which houses the Robinson Memorial telescope and the other an 18-in. Calver telescope, later converted into a Schmidt telescope. [Armagh Observatory]*

County Armagh, southern Ulster and Northern Ireland border county. To the west of the town of Armagh is NAVAN FORT, the remains of Emain Macha, ancient capital of Ulster and an important prehistoric site. Co. Armagh displays varied relief, ranging from the fertile claylands of the Lough NEAGH basin in the north to the dryer limestone soils of the BLACKWATER valley in the south-west and the older, more resistant sandstone hills and Pre-Cambrian volcanic intrusion of Slieve Gullion in the south. The county also forms part of the Ulster Drumlin Belt and shares in its highly dissected topography, which in the past formed a barrier with Leinster. Incorporated in the UÍ NÉILL hegemony during the Middle Ages, Co. Armagh was confiscated during the PLANTATIONS and settled by both English and Scots. The county was a centre of LINEN production from the eighteenth century; by 1800 its rural landscape was highly sub-divided and densely populated. Linen production provided a buffer against the worst effects of the GREAT FAMINE, though Co. Armagh shared in the general post-Famine population decline. During the recent 'TROUBLES' south Armagh gained a particular reputation for paramilitary REPUBLICANISM, a modern reflection of the traditionally independent and anti-authoritarian attitudes of the communities living in the southern border uplands. **Lindsay Proudfoot**

Armagh (*Ard Mhacha*), ancient town and primatial seat, county town, and service centre; population (1991) 14,265. Armagh stands at the junction between Co. Armagh's southern uplands and its fertile northern lowlands. Its skyline is dominated by the two cathedrals dedicated to St PATRICK: the Protestant cathedral (largely nineteenth-century) on its hilltop site—itself enclosed within a *bivallate* (double-banked) earthwork that shows evidence of NEOLITHIC occupation—and the twin towers of the Catholic cathedral (1840–73). Armagh first claimed ecclesiastical precedence in the ninth century and was proclaimed an archbishopric at the SYNOD OF RATHBRASSIL in 1111. The modern town dates from the archbishop's acquisition of the site and surrounding barony in 1607 during the PLANTATION OF ULSTER and his subsequent development of the place in the 1620s. The most spectacular improvements occurred during the later eighteenth century. ROCQUE's map of 1760 shows the new streets laid out by Thomas Ogle, the Sovereign, and these provided the basis for Archbishop Robinson's extensive remodelling after 1767. He rebuilt the cathedral, built a bishop's palace, library, observatory, Royal School, and housing, sponsored a new barracks, jail, hospital, and college, encouraged widespread tenant improvements, and was responsible for turning the town commons into a public walk, subsequently remodelled as the Mall by 1810. Robinson's improvements represent the most extensive GEORGIAN remodelling carried out in any Ulster town, and much of what he built survives today to lend Armagh its characteristic sense of place, despite recent losses through bombs, road construction, and insensitive new development. **Lindsay Proudfoot**

Armagh, Book of (c. AD 807), a Latin manuscript of 215 (originally 222) vellum leaves, 195 by 145 mm, now in TRINITY COLLEGE Library, Dublin. It contains two lives of St Patrick by Muirchú (transmitted in two other manuscripts) and Tírechán (not transmitted elsewhere), several texts on and by St Patrick, the only surviving Early Irish complete text of the New Testament, and several texts by Sulpicius Severus, including his Life of St Martin. For centuries it was believed that St Patrick himself was the scribe, hence its Irish name Canóin Pátraicc; however, the main scribe identifies himself as FERDOMNACH (died 846) and indicates that the writing was done at the request of Torbach, abbot of Armagh, 807–8. The Patrician documents were used to establish the prerogatives of Armagh as archiepiscopal see of Ireland and Patrick as apostle of the Irish. During the Middle Ages a hereditary keeper belonging to the MacMoyre family was appointed for the book. The last MacMoyre keeper sold it in 1680; in 1854 it was presented to Trinity College. **Rijcklof Hofman**

Armagh, primacy of. By the seventh century there is documentary evidence that Armagh claimed to have been founded by the fifth-century British missionary PATRICK. Such fifth-century evidence as survives is inconclusive about this; what is certain is that, from the seventh century, Patrick's supposed founding of Armagh underpinned that church's pretensions: a supreme judicial role and the right to exact tribute from Ireland's churches and people. Such aspirations were realised intermittently by Armagh prelates, the 'successors of Patrick', in the eighth, ninth, and tenth centuries, long before Armagh's ecclesiastical primacy over Ireland was officially endorsed by a centralising Papacy in the twelfth century. **Colmán Etchingham**

Armagh Observatory, instituted in 1790 by Archbishop Richard Robinson; it seems initially to have formed part of a scheme for the setting up of a University of Ulster. Ownership is now vested in a Board of Governors, consisting of the Archbishop of Armagh, the Dean and Chapter of St Patrick's (CHURCH OF IRELAND) Cathedral Church, Armagh, a nominee of Queen's University, Belfast, and a nominee of the Department of Culture, Arts, and Leisure. The observatory has been at the forefront of investigations of the Universe, spearheading many novel developments. A wide range of investigations are carried out, including studies of the Solar System and its relations with the Earth and the physics of the stars and galaxies. The Department provides basic funding through a grant in aid, while the British Particle Physics and Astronomy Research Council awards grants for individual research projects. **John McFarland**

Armagh Pipers' Club, formed in 1966 to revive and promote the playing of the uilleann pipes and TRADITIONAL MUSIC generally. It was initiated by the painter and piper J. B. VALLELY and his wife, Eithne (née Carey), a FIDDLE-player from Co. Donegal. Classes were begun in Armagh and neighbouring towns and a series of regular concerts introduced to the locality with such musicians as SÉAMUS ENNIS and WILLIE CLANCY. The club continues to inspire new generations of players, with a hundred and more children taught each year. These have achieved top awards at Slógadh and FLEADH CHEOIL competitions, and many are now professional musicians. From 1980 to 1985 the club hosted the first traditional music summer school in Northern Ireland, at Benburb, Co. Tyrone, and since 1998 it has run the William Kennedy Festival of Piping. **Fintan Vallely**

Armour, James Brown (1841–1928), 'Armour of Ballymoney', Presbyterian minister. Born in Lisboy, Ballymoney, Co. Antrim. Appointed minister at Ballymoney, 1869, he was a political radical, representing the extremity of Presbyterian liberalism, a staunch Gladstonian, and supporter of home rule. As such, he was in a small minority within Ulster PRESBYTERIANISM. An enemy of SECTARIANISM, he also opposed PARTITION. **Fergal Tobin**

armoured trains. The effects of the CIVIL WAR on the RAILWAYS were severe; by November 1922 a third of the Great Southern and Western Railway's mileage was closed because of sabotage. In an attempt to provide some protection, the Railway Defence and Maintenance Corps of the Free State Army deployed four specially armoured LOCOMOTIVES. In addition, it operated petrol-driven Lancia armoured cars fitted with flanged wheels; one of them, named *Grey Ghost*, was ambushed by the IRA when patrolling the Clonmel–Thurles line and its crew forced to surrender. **Bernard Share**

Arms Crisis (1970). On 6 May 1970 the TAOISEACH, JACK LYNCH, sacked two members of his Government, CHARLES HAUGHEY, Minister for Finance, and Neil Blaney, Minister for Agriculture. No explanation was given. A third minister, Kevin Boland, resigned in protest and was joined by a junior minister, Paudge Brennan. The following morning Lynch called a meeting of the FIANNA FÁIL Parliamentary Party to put forward a motion asserting his right as Taoiseach to appoint or dismiss members of the Government. The motion was passed, and a possible rebellion in the party was avoided. Later he told DÁIL ÉIREANN that the sackings were connected with reports of an attempt to import arms illegally.

Three weeks later an army intelligence officer, Captain James Kelly, was arrested and questioned about the operation. Haughey and Blaney were also arrested, together with John Kelly, a prominent Belfast republican, and Albert Luyckx, a Belgian businessman. All were charged with conspiring to illegally import arms. Blaney was discharged by the District Court for lack of evidence; the others were later found not guilty at a trial by jury. The entire event, which became known as the Arms Crisis, rocked the state and created divisions within Fianna Fáil that lasted to the end of the century.

The release of DEFENCE FORCES records early in 2001 threw new light on the events of 1967–70 and confirmed the claim by Captain Kelly during his trial that a directive had been issued to the army in February 1970 by the Minister for Defence, Jim Gibbons, to prepare for incursions into Northern Ireland to help the nationalist population in a 'doomsday' situation. Kelly said he regarded the directive as providing authority for the purchase of arms. Shortly afterwards, in examining the files released by the Department of Justice under the thirty-year rule, he found that considerable sections of the evidence of his superior, Colonel Michael Hefferon, had been deleted from the book of evidence before the trial in 1970. He claimed that this had been done deliberately within the department in order to secure his conviction. DESMOND O'MALLEY, who was Minister for Justice at the time, claimed in a lengthy response that the deletion of sections of Hefferon's evidence was carried out by the prosecution in order to comply with the rules of evidence. Similar deletions had been made in the statements of several other witnesses, he said. In any event, he said these actions had no effect on the outcome, as Colonel Hefferon covered the entire material, including the deleted sections, in his evidence in court. **Michael Mills**

Armstrong, Sir Alexander (1818–1899), explorer. Born in Crahan, Co. Fermanagh; educated at TCD and the University of Edinburgh, where he was awarded an MD in 1841. He entered the Royal Navy as ship's surgeon in 1842 and in 1849 joined the expedition under Sir ROBERT M'CLURE in search of the missing polar explorer Sir John Franklin, who had vanished in 1847 while searching for the North-West Passage. He spent four years in the polar regions as surgeon and naturalist and was commended for preserving the health of the sailors he cared for. His later career included service in the Baltic, North America, and Malta and appointment as director-general of the Naval Medical Corps, 1869–71. He was made a knight commander of the Order of the Bath in 1871 and a fellow of the Royal Society in 1873. **Peter Somerville-Large**

Armstrong, Arthur (1924–1996), painter. Born in Carrickfergus, Co. Antrim; attended QUB and Belfast College of Art. He exhibited at the Grafton Gallery, Dublin, in 1950 and the CEMA Gallery, Belfast, 1956 and 1961, and showed at the IRISH EXHIBITION OF LIVING ART and the OIREACHTAS, and in 1957 won a CEMA travel scholarship to Spain. He moved to London but in 1962 settled in Dublin. He first exhibited at the RHA in 1962 and had an exhibition at the Arts Council Gallery, Belfast, in 1966. He won the DOUGLAS HYDE Gold Medal at the 1968 Oireachtas. In 1969, with GEORGE CAMPBELL and GERARD DILLON, he created the settings for *Juno and the Paycock* at the ABBEY THEATRE, Dublin. He became a member of the RHA in 1972 and in 1973 was a prize-winner at the ACNI 'Art in Context' scheme for play sculpture. He exhibited at Madrid and Washington in 1974 and had a retrospective at the Arts Council Gallery, Belfast, in 1981. **Theo Snoddy**

Armstrong, Reg (1928–1979), racing motorcyclist. One of Ireland's most successful competitors, he was three times a runner-up in the world championship and won seven grand prix races, as well as the 1952 Senior TT. **Brendan Lynch**

army. In 2002 the army in the Republic had an approximate strength of 8,500 personnel, both male and female, relying solely on voluntary enlistment. Its mission and roles are to defend the state against armed aggression, to aid the civil power, to participate in multi-national peace support, crisis management and humanitarian relief operations in support of the UNITED NATIONS and under UN mandate, including regional security missions authorised by the United Nations, and to carry out such other duties as arise from time to time.

The army comprises three brigades, the DEFENCE FORCES Training Centre, a logistics base, and a number of special establishments. The three brigades have distinct geographical areas of responsibility: the 1st (Southern) Brigade is primarily responsible for operational tasks in the south of the country, the 2nd (Eastern) Brigade for the east, and the 4th (Western) Brigade for the west and north-west. Each brigade contains elements of the following corps: Infantry, Artillery, Cavalry, Communications and Information Services, Transport and Vehicle Maintenance, Ordnance, Engineering, Military Police, and Medical. The Defence Forces Training Centre, which is in the CURRAGH, is primarily responsible for the military education of DEFENCE FORCES personnel. Military courses are conducted in the various training institutes, including officer, NCO, cadet and recruit training, as well as specialist training for the various corps. The logistics base, also in the Curragh, has a major stores function and also carries out repairs and maintenance on all types of military equipment, from small hand-held radios to armoured vehicles. Special establishments include the ARMY RANGER WING, ARMY EQUITATION SCHOOL, and DEFENCE FORCES SCHOOL OF MUSIC. **Paul Connors**

army. *Infantry training at the Defence Forces Training Centre, Curragh Camp, Co. Kildare, 2002. [Public Relations Section, Defence Forces, Ireland]*

army corps. The army comprises nine corps: Infantry, Artillery, Cavalry, Engineers, Communications and Information Services, Medical, Military Police, Ordnance, and Transport and Vehicle Maintenance.

Infantry Corps. The major combat corps of the army, with nine regular and eighteen reserve battalions. The Infantry trains soldiers in such military skills as leadership, weapons marksmanship, fieldcraft, map-reading, survival, first aid, and confidence training.

Artillery Corps. Armed with high-calibre long-range weapons, the Artillery Corps is one of the four combat support corps of the army. It includes a directorate in Defence Forces Headquarters and the Artillery School in the Defence Forces Training Centre. Field artillery units consist of three regular and five reserve regiments, equipped with 105 mm and 25-pounder guns and 120 mm heavy mortars. The corps has one air defence regiment, with its headquarters in the DFTC, and four batteries: a regular battery in the DFTC and reserve batteries in Cork, Limerick, and Dublin. Air defence is provided by the RBS 70 missile system and both L60 and L70 AD guns. Since 1962 the Artillery Corps has supported each Irish UN contingent with a heavy mortar troop.

Cavalry Corps. One of the four combat support corps of the army; its main function is to provide the primary reconnaissance resource of the infantry brigade. The corps was originally established as the Armoured Car Corps, employing Rolls-Royce, Lancia and Peerless armoured cars. In 1934 it was renamed the Cavalry Corps, and it was at that time that the distinctive Glengarry cap was introduced. The years of the SECOND WORLD WAR saw the corps at its maximum strength of twenty-five squadrons. On UN missions the corps has contributed armoured car groups to Congo and Cyprus and reconnaissance groups to Lebanon. The present establishment of the corps is six cavalry squadrons, three of which are reserve, and one armoured cavalry squadron. The corps is mainly equipped with Panhard armoured cars and Scorpion tracked combat reconnaissance vehicles.

Corps of Engineers. One of the four combat support corps of the army; its function is to provide engineering services and resources to the Defence Forces. At the foundation of the state in 1922 the Works, Salvage and Railway Protection Repair and Maintenance Corps was set up to salvage materials and repair barracks damaged during the WAR OF INDEPENDENCE and the CIVIL WAR. In 1924 this unit was replaced by the Engineer Corps. In 1931 field engineering companies and the School of Military Engineering were added. Planning and design teams were set up in the 1970s to design and implement the construction of major new engineering works in the DEFENCE FORCES.

Communications and Information Service Corps. Formerly the Signal Corps, it developed from the communications organisation of the Civil War (1922–3), which had established a Headquarters, Training School, Wireless Section and Workshops in Portobello Barracks in 1922. Approximately sixty-five wireless stations were operated in barracks and posts during the Civil War. The Signal Corps was set up in 1924. It grouped its School, Stores and Workshops in the Signals Depot, CURRAGH, during the 1930s. During the Second World War a field forces company, eight field, four garrison, Army Headquarters, and AIR CORPS signal companies provided communications for the Defence Forces. A field company is an integral component of an infantry brigade and is responsible for its communications support. The corps has supplied communications for all units serving overseas on United Nations and EUROPEAN UNION missions. The 1998 defence reorganisation merged the Signal Corps and the Military Information Technology Section to form the Communications and Information Services Corps. **E. D. Doyle**

Medical Corps. Established in 1922 as the Army Medical Service. The Medical Corps is one of the combat service support corps. It comprises a directorate, the Medical School of the Combat Service Support College, the Logistics Base Hospital (St Bricin's, Dublin), a medical detachment in the Defence Forces Training Centre, and three regular and five reserve field medical companies. Medical, dental, and pharmaceutical officers are commissioned as direct entries following professional qualification. Enlisted personnel are trained in the Medical School and with civilian institutions, as appropriate. The corps is responsible for the maintenance of health and the provision of medical services and support to the Defence Forces. Medical personnel have served with every overseas peacekeeping mission to which Ireland has contributed contingents. The Medical Corps badge was the first corps badge to be adopted by the Defence Forces.

Military Police. The Military Police Corps, formed in 1923, is the law enforcement agency within the Defence Forces. It derives its authority from the Provost-Marshal, who is appointed under the Defence Act (1954) 'for the prompt suppression of all offences.' To assist the Provost-Marshal in carrying out his duties a military police company is based in each brigade area, under the command of an assistant provost-marshal. Military police are responsible for the investigation of crimes and misdemeanours in the military and assist in the maintenance of good order and discipline. Personnel of the corps are recognisable by their distinctive red berets.

Ordnance Corps. The Ordnance Corps is responsible for the procurement and maintenance of all ordnance equipment in the Defence Forces, ranging from anti-aircraft missiles and naval armament to the uniforms worn by military personnel. The corps is also responsible for the procurement of food and the provision of commercial catering services. Because of the technical nature of the corps' tasks it incorporates a high number of technicians with appropriate qualifications and expertise in fields such as weapons, ammunition, fire control systems, and night-vision equipment. The Ordnance Corps also provides the state's only explosive ordnance disposal, or bomb disposal, service. To carry out this mission efficiently and safely it keeps abreast of international developments in terrorist devices. The corps has developed its own specific procedures and equipment to deal with unexploded ordnance and regularly conducts courses for its own personnel and also for students from other countries.

Transport and Vehicle Maintenance Corps. The Supply and Transport Corps was established on 2 May 1942. On 1 November 1998 it was re-established as the Transport and Vehicle Maintenance Corps, in line with the recommendations of the Defence Forces reorganisation plan. The corps is responsible for the procurement, management, and maintenance of soft-skinned and armoured vehicles, including the supply of fuel. It is also responsible for driver training, driving standards, and certification. **Paul Connors**

Army Equitation School, established by the Irish Free State in 1926 and based in McKee Barracks, Dublin. The role of the school is to advertise and promote the Irish HORSE and Ireland abroad. In 1928 the Russian instructor Colonel Paul Rodzianko introduced the classical training principles of Federico Caprilli. Since its inception the Army Equitation School has been the backbone of Irish SHOW-JUMPING teams, and its riders have represented Ireland at OLYMPIC, World and European championships. In the 1999/2000 season army riders were members of the Irish team that won a record-breaking ten international team competitions (Nations Cups). **Paul Connors**

Army Ranger Wing, a special forces unit trained to carry out specialist conventional and anti-terrorist operations. Conventional operations include operating behind enemy lines, securing vital objectives, and long-range patrolling. Anti-terrorist operations include VIP protection, aircraft hijackings, and hostage situations. The unit is directly answerable to the Chief of Staff of the Defence Forces. **Paul Connors**

Army School of Music, see DEFENCE FORCES SCHOOL OF MUSIC.

Arnold, Bruce (1936–), critic, novelist, and political journalist. Born in London; educated at TCD. He is the author of pioneering works on WILLIAM ORPEN (1981) and MAINIE JELLETT (1991), a critical biography of JACK YEATS (1998), novels, and two studies of contemporary Irish politics. **Richard Pine**

Arrowsmith, Aaron (1750–1823), cartographer. Born in Winston, Co. Durham; he became a map-publisher in London in 1790 after surveying land in his native county. Beginning ambitiously with an eleven-sheet world map, he spent the rest of his life compiling and publishing maps and atlases of every kind. His map of Ireland at 4 statute miles to the inch (1:253,440), published in 1811, was based mainly on CHARLES VALLANCEY's hitherto unpublished military survey, combined with D. A. BEAUFORT's map of 1792 and all the latest available county surveys. These materials were too variable in quality for Arrowsmith's map to be highly regarded by Irish readers. **J. H. Andrews**

arterial drainage, extensive river drainage to alleviate flooding. As Ireland has a relatively high maritime rim and a flat Central Plain, rivers are sluggish and prone to silting, causing waterlogging of adjacent lands. Five Drainage Acts were passed between 1715 and 1925; however, schemes were piecemeal and poorly maintained. The Browne Drainage Commission (1940), in a fundamental review of drainage, recommended that planning be on a catchment-wide basis, that schemes be maintained at public expense, and that performance be monitored regularly. These recommendations were incorporated in the Arterial Drainage Act (1945). This entails monitoring water levels and discharge measurements at 300 sites. The OFFICE OF PUBLIC WORKS designed, constructed, and maintains drainage schemes in thirty-four catchments, benefiting 260,000 ha (640,000 acres).

A further hundred sites are monitored in Northern Ireland by the Rivers Agency, the statutory authority for drainage and flood relief. It pursues an extensive drainage programme, and where river catchments cross the border, the two jurisdictions co-operate. **Pierce T. Pigott**

Arthurian literature in Irish translation. Arthurian literature has had some influence in the Irish tradition. In prose one encounters Arthurian themes in Early Modern romances (fifteenth to seventeenth centuries) and in folk-tale versions derived from these. In verse there are a few Arthurian allusions in bardic verse; the Ossianic ballad 'Laoi an Bhruit' is based on the Arthurian 'Lay of the Horn' and 'Lay of the Mantle'. There are also intriguing hints of an awareness of Arthur, King of the Britons, before the explosion of Arthurian literature triggered by Geoffrey of Monmouth's *History of the Kings of Britain*. But most references postdate Geoffrey's work, and many belong to the age of Malory's *Morte d'Artur*. It is noteworthy that English versions, rather than French, seem to have been the main intermediary whereby Arthurian literature filtered through into Irish.

Most Irish Arthurian texts are pretty thoroughly assimilated to native tale-telling norms. In some instances the connection with Continental romance is tenuous indeed. 'Eachtra Mhacaoimh an Iolair' and 'Eachtra an Mhadra Mhaoil' are simply Irish romances within an Arthurian frame, and 'Eachtra Mhelóra agus Orlando' is a mere pastiche. The hero of 'Eachtra an Amadáin Mhóir' bears a certain resemblance to Perceval (perhaps through the English Sir Percyvelle). But the idealism and religious charge of Arthurian literature are hard to find, despite some traces in 'Céilidhe Iosgaide Léithe'. The one real exception is 'Lorgaireacht an tSoidhigh Naomhtha', a fifteenth-century translation of a lost English version of 'The Quest for the Holy Grail'. The unknown translator resisted the usual bombastic elaboration and adopted a simple but dignified, slightly archaic idiom in which the edifying tone of the original was allowed to shine through. **William Gillies**

art schools. The DUBLIN SOCIETY Drawing Schools of Figure (1746), Landscape and Ornament (1756), Architecture (1764) and Modelling (1811) provided an education in drawing for the craftsmen who built GEORGIAN Dublin and for landscape and portrait painters. From 1829 the Schools of Antique and Life Drawing of the ROYAL HIBERNIAN ACADEMY provided the main education for artists. The Royal Dublin Society schools became a School of Design in 1849, with instruction relating to pattern drawing for industry. It was taken over by the state in 1877 as the Metropolitan School of Art, which it remained until 1936, when it was renamed the National College of Art, with diploma courses in PAINTING, SCULPTURE, and design.

In Cork a Papal gift of a collection of antique casts in 1818 initiated art education there. The policies and financial support of the Department of Science and Art led to the establishment of schools of design in Cork (1850), Belfast (1850), Waterford (1852), Limerick (1852), Clonmel (1854), and Derry (1874). These became general art schools, open to women, and by 1900 were supported by the local authorities.

After 1922 art schools came under the Departments of Education, North and South. From the 1960s a modernisation process in curriculum and management took place. The Belfast School of Art became a faculty of the Ulster Polytechnic, later University of Ulster. The other schools, including the School of Marketing and Design, Dublin, and Dún Laoghaire School of Art, became part of institutes of technology by the late 1990s. Following student disturbances, the National College of Art was reconstituted by statute in 1971 as the National College of Art and Design (NCAD) and developed the widest range of studio-based degrees in the country, becoming a recognised college of the National University of Ireland in 1996. **John Turpin**

Arts Council, the (An Chomhairle Ealaíon) (1952–), a statutory agency established by the Arts Act (1951) to stimulate public interest in and promote knowledge, appreciation, and practice of the arts. The Arts Act (1973), among other things, made it possible for local authorities to assist the Arts Council or any person organising an exhibition or other event whose effect would stimulate public interest in the arts, promote knowledge, appreciation and practice of the arts, or assist in improving the standards of the arts.

The Arts Council acts as the development agency for the arts; it is the primary source of support for the individual creative and interpretative artist and operates on the principle that everyone is entitled to access to and participation in the arts. It provides advice to Government and non-government bodies, individuals, and arts organisations on artistic matters and provides support and financial assistance for artistic purposes to individuals and organisations. **Nessa O'Mahony**

Arts Council of Northern Ireland, first established in 1943 as the Council for the Encouragement of Music and the Arts (CEMA) and reconstructed as a statutory body in 1994. Initially its funds were provided by the Pilgrim Trust and matched by the Ministry of Education. In 1963 it became the Arts Council, and grant aid was provided by the Department of Education. At present its resources are provided by the NORTHERN IRELAND ASSEMBLY's Department of Culture, Arts and Leisure and by the national lottery. Its functions are to promote the arts, to advise the Government on arts policy, to administer an annual budget, to consult district councils about spending and policy, and to disburse

Northern Ireland's share of Arts Lottery funding. The fifteen-member council is appointed by the Northern Ireland Minister of the Arts through open competition. The administration is directed by a chief executive supported by professional staff responsible for subject and functional areas. **Brian Ferran**

arts and crafts movement (1880s–1930s). The international revival of interest in handicrafts and the arts of design in the later part of the nineteenth century, first inspired by the example of William Morris, was reflected in Ireland from the 1880s. With encouragement from the HOME ARTS AND INDUSTRIES ASSOCIATION and other organisations involved in the development of rural art industries, various minor arts flourished in the 1890s. The founding of the ARTS AND CRAFTS SOCIETY OF IRELAND by the Earl of Mayo in 1894 provided a focus for both rural groups and individual artists. Seven important exhibitions were held by the society in Dublin, and later in Cork, from 1895 until its demise in 1925, while re-organisation in 1909 enabled it to extend its influence by setting up provincial committees and forming a Guild of Irish Art Workers. The movement also provided the impetus for the development of specialist craft facilities in the main art colleges as well as the founding of a number of commercially organised studios, particularly in the fields of FURNITURE and STAINED GLASS.

The movement embraced a large number of people in all parts of Ireland involved in a variety of crafts, including lacemakers and embroiderers in convents and amateur wood-carvers and art metal-workers in rural areas as well as a number of professional artists, working individually or in groups, such as the DUN EMER GUILD, CUALA INDUSTRIES, and AN TÚR GLOINE. The most accomplished artists, notably PERCY OSWALD REEVES, HARRY CLARKE, WILHELMINA GEDDES, and MIA CRANWILL, attracted critical acclaim in Ireland and abroad. **Paul Larmour**

Arts and Crafts Society of Ireland, founded in Dublin by Dermot Wyndham Bourke, seventh Earl of Mayo, and a few enthusiastic pioneers, amateurs, and connoisseurs in 1894, six years after its English namesake and model. Its aim was to invigorate demoralised standards of design, to stimulate skilled craftsmanship and industrial endeavour to equal what it had been in the past, and to inspire individual expression in a contemporary, rather than reproductive, idiom. Its exhibitions—of historic Irish work and English arts and crafts collections as well as of current work—were intended to increase awareness of the need for appropriate native design and inspired national achievement during a period of lively political and cultural aspiration. Commitments to HOUSING, HEALTH, hygiene, EMPLOYMENT, and agricultural reform were as seminal to Ireland's arts and crafts ideology as the parallel, and better-known, revivals of IRISH LANGUAGE and literature that informed the art of the period.

After two didactic exhibitions, in 1895 and 1899, the society's third, more selective exhibition of 1904 showed the effects of superior design education at the reformed Schools of Art in Dublin, Cork, and Belfast; by 1910 individual talents and original skills had emerged. The society's 1917, 1921, and 1925 exhibitions marked the achievements of HARRY CLARKE, WILHELMINA GEDDES, and OSWALD REEVES, among others, in stained glass, graphics, and enamelwork, before its inevitable decline. **Nicola Gordon Bowe**

Ascall mac Torcaill (Höskellr Thorkelssonn) (died 1171), head of the paramount Hiberno-Norse family in twelfth-century Dublin. He became its king in 1160 and in 1166 rebelled against his overlord, DERMOT MACMURROUGH of Leinster. The latter and STRONGBOW reconquered Dublin in 1170, and Ascall fled to the Scottish Isles; he returned following MacMurrough's death in 1171 but was captured and beheaded. **Seán Duffy**

Ascendancy: see ANGLO-IRISH SOCIETY.

Asgard, a 15.5 m (50-ft) wooden yacht, built in 1905 by the Norwegian designer Colin Archer for ERSKINE CHILDERS. In 1914 Childers sailed it into Howth, Co. Dublin, with a cargo of 900 rifles for the IRISH VOLUNTEERS. After Childers' death the yacht was in England and from 1969 to 1974 it was Ireland's first sail training vessel. It was put on display in KILMAINHAM GAOL, Dublin, from 1979 to 2001. Its successor, *Asgard II*, a 25 m (82-ft) wooden brigantine, was designed and built by John Tyrrell of Arklow in 1981 as Ireland's national sail training vessel. An extremely popular vessel, it became a consistent winner in the International Tall Ships races. [see HOWTH GUN-RUNNING.] **John Kearon**

Ash, rock group. Formed in the early 1990s in Downpatrick, Co. Down, by Tim Wheeler, Mark Hamilton, and Rick McMurray, Ash quickly established themselves as one of the best young guitar bands in Europe. In 1994, while still in secondary school, they released their pop-punk mini-album *Trailer.* In 1997 the trio became a quartet with the addition of the guitarist Charlotte Hatherley. The subsequent Ash sound proved to be more textured and harder-edged, as evidenced by their album *Nu-Clear Sounds* (1998). *Free All Angels* (2001) yielded five British hit singles. **Tony Clayton-Lea**

Ashe, Thomas (1885–1917), republican and educator. Born in Lispole, Co. Kerry; active in the GAELIC LEAGUE and IRISH VOLUNTEERS. During the 1916 RISING he led the Volunteers at Ashbourne, Co. Meath. His death sentence was commuted to life imprisonment. Released in 1917, he was later re-arrested and died as a result of forced feeding in Mountjoy Jail. **Seán Farrell Moran**

Ashford, William (1746–1824), artist. Born in Birmingham, he came to Ireland in 1764. He worked for some years in the Board of Ordnance and seems to have had no artistic training, though he may have attended classes in the Dublin Society schools, where he won premiums. His earliest exhibited works were flower pieces, now in the NATIONAL GALLERY OF IRELAND, and still lifes. His first exhibited landscape was in 1772. He exhibited in Dublin and London, making a reputation in both cities, and in 1723 was appointed first president of the ROYAL HIBERNIAN ACADEMY. His landscapes include genre elements, carriages, carts, beggars, fishermen, and haymakers. He did not paint wild nature but worked mostly for the aristocracy and gentry, painting their demesnes. His trees are outstanding; he was also praised for his sea pieces, now rarely found, and occasionally painted subject pictures based on Shakespearian scenes, or contemporary events, such as the opening of the Ringsend dock, now in the National Gallery of Ireland (see p. 155). [see CANALS.] **Anne Crookshank**

Ashlin, George Coppinger (1838–1921), architect. Born at Carrigrenane, Co. Cork, but brought up in England following the death of his father, a London corn factor. He was apprenticed to Edward Pugin in 1856 and also attended the Royal Academy Schools, London. After the break-up of PUGIN AND ASHLIN in 1868 he continued to practise under his own name until 1903, when he

arts and crafts. *Detail of nave capital in St Brendans Cathedral, Loughrea, Co. Galway, carved in 1902–6 by Michael Shorthall. He also carved the baptismal font and corbels. [Courtesy St Brendans Cathedral; photo: Denis Mortell]*

formed a partnership with his assistant Thomas A. Coleman and nephew Stephen Ashlin. He worked on Queenstown (Cobh) Cathedral, Co. Cork, up until its consecration in 1919 and completed A. W. N. PUGIN's Killarney Cathedral in 1914. He designed numerous churches, including Clonakilty, Co. Cork (1869), Delvin, Co. Westmeath (1873), Cahersiveen, Co. Kerry (1882), and Midleton, Co. Cork (1893). For Lord Ardilaun he built the CHURCH OF IRELAND church at Raheny, Dublin (1885). His largest secular work was the asylum (now St Ita's Hospital) at Portrane, Co. Dublin, won in competition in 1895. He was president of the ROYAL INSTITUTE OF THE ARCHITECTS OF IRELAND, 1902–4. [see ST COLMAN'S CATHEDRAL.] **Frederick O'Dwyer**

Askeaton Castle, Co. Limerick, a castle on a small island encircled by two branches of the River Deel, originally an Anglo-Norman castle. It became a fortress of the Earls of Desmond in the fourteenth century, until it was seized by English forces in 1580. It was besieged by the second Earl of Desmond in 1598 for 247 days. The standing remains are mainly fifteenth-century, but there was originally an early thirteenth-century earth-and-timber castle. The central area of high bedrock has a thirteenth-century wall enclosing the upper ward; within this are two fifteenth-century towers and a sixteenth-century hall. There is a fine fifteenth-century hall in the outer ward, built on the remains of the thirteenth-century one, and there is a thirteenth-century *solar* (domestic quarters) attached to the south gable. The curtain-walls enclosing the outer ward date from the fifteenth century. **David Sweetman**

Aston, William (1841–1911), orientalist. Born in Derry; educated at home. He studied classics at Queen's College, Belfast, and served with the British consular service in Japan from 1864, where, with service in Korea, he remained until 1889. He was the author of numerous pioneering works on Japanese grammar, language, and literature, including *Japanese Literature* (1889) and *Ancient Chronicles of Japan* (1896). **Brian Lalor**

astronomy: 5,000 years of observation. Possibly the most convincing evidence for prehistoric astronomical alignment in northern Europe is found in the BOYNE VALLEY, Co. Meath. There, at the megalithic tombs of Brú na Bóinne, NEWGRANGE, built c. 3000 BC, a 19 m (62-ft) passage in the south-eastern side of the monument leads to a central chamber in which, for a few days around the winter solstice, the sun on rising traverses the length of the passage to suffuse the interior with a golden light. This alignment, generally assumed to have been associated with religious ritual carried out to mark the beginning of the solar year, could be made possible only by prolonged studies of the movement of the sun by skilled observers. At the nearby megalithic site of KNOWTH, two passages within the monument are aligned with the rising and setting sun at the spring and autumn equinoxes. A third tomb in the Boyne Valley, that of Dowth, has an alignment with the setting sun at the winter solstice.

Irish sources identify certain orders of learned men in Celtic society, including in particular the FILÍ. Of special interest is an incantation ascribed to AMERGHIN GLÚNGHEAL that refers specifically to his knowledge of lunar and solar cycles:

> Who is it that casts light over the hosting on the mountain top?
> Who is it that proclaims the ages of the Moon?
> Who reveals the spot where the Sun rests?
> Who, if it be not I?

Following the overthrow of pagan society by CHRISTIANITY, sophisticated ecclesiastical schools were quickly set up. These were internally stratified according to seven grades or orders of wisdom, within which system professors of the fifth grade had, among other subjects, to master arithmetic and astronomy.

The cycles of the Sun and Moon that had so occupied the attention of earlier people had a direct bearing in Christian Ireland on the ecclesiastical problem of establishing the date of Easter. From the earliest days of Christian observance, Easter was celebrated in Ireland on the Sunday that fell between the fourteenth and the twentieth day after the first full moon after 25 March (the traditional date of the Crucifixion). This practice, different from that observed in Rome, provoked a profound dispute, the EASTER CONTROVERSY, and Irish monks, such as CUMMIAN FADA, took a particular interest in the mechanism of constructing Easter Tables. The activity of computing these tables gave rise over time to the assembling of related manuscripts, called *computi*, which could include lists of calculations, verses for memorising computational rules, and works on arithmetic, astronomy, chemistry, and medicine. The ANNALS, later compiled by the monks, also came to contain many references to celestial events, such as eclipses and apparitions of comets.

The monks were interested in placing the science of the day within the framework of Christianity. *De Mirabilibus Sacrae Scripturae* (fl. 655) by AUGUSTINE ERIUGENA considers various miracles mentioned in the Scriptures and argues, using analogies, that in each instance the laws of nature were not violated, as existing principles could provide an explanation. He also discussed the 532-year cycle for determining the date of Easter as well as lunar rainbows, the tides, and the action of the sea in forming islands. *Liber de Ordine Creaturarum*, once attributed to Isidore of Seville but now to a seventh-century author in Ireland, describes a layered structure of the Universe, with the Heaven of the Angels at the top, Hell at the bottom, and the material world in between. The ordering principle was the relative weight of the four elements of classical cosmology.

The monks transported their interest in natural science to the Continent during their evangelising missions and contemporary accounts show that during the eighth and ninth centuries Irish intellectuals, such as Fergil the Geometer, the monk DUNGAL, DICUIL THE GEOGRAPHER, and the philosopher JOHN SCOTUS ERIUGENA were considered in the courts of Europe to be authorities on astronomical matters. From c. 850 to 877 Eriugena was at the court of Charles the Bald as a member—some say director—of the palace school. His commentary on a book by Martianus Capella (860) contains ideas developed in his master work, *Periphysicon* (On Nature), written c. 865. In this text he quotes Aristotle, Eratosthenes, Plato, PTOLEMY, and Pythagoras and presents a cosmological system in which the Sun's orbit is equidistant between the surface of the Earth and the sphere of the fixed stars. Though the Sun rotates around the Earth, the planets Mercury, Venus, Mars, and Jupiter (but not Saturn) orbit the Sun. It has been suggested that Eriugena's universe presages that proposed by Tycho Brahe in the sixteenth century, where the Sun and Moon orbit a stationary Earth but all the other planets orbit the Sun. His intellectual approach was, however, qualitative rather than mathematical.

The period of the VIKING invasions (793–1014) saw the plundering of many MONASTERIES and the destruction of their books. In the twelfth century the mendicant orders adopted the system of conventual schools for teaching scripture and theology; courses in natural science and certain of the teachings of Aristotle were later added. Good students could be sent on to one of the newly founded universities, such as those of Oxford, Paris, Bologna, and Montpellier. Ireland's distinguished contribution to the conserving of ancient science and philosophy thereby came to be complemented by contributions at the new European universities. PETER OF IRELAND, an acclaimed logician and master of natural science, taught Thomas Aquinas at Naples, 1239–44. At Oxford, RICHARD FITZRALPH (1299–1360) was associated with the innovative *'calculatores'* of Merton College who first attempted the mathematicisation of physics; the importance of his contribution is seen in his treatment of such topics as time and motion.

The great period for the dissemination of Islamic science in the West was the twelfth and early thirteenth centuries. 'An Irish Astronomical Tract', based in part on an Irish translation of a medieval Latin version of an Arabic work by Messahalah, a Jewish astronomer at Alexandria c. AD 800, survives. The tract contains chapters dealing with the nature and functions of the four elements, the characteristics of the Earth, water, volcanoes, and tides, the heavenly bodies and their movements, the winds, thunder, clouds, rain, and lightning.

Three factors—the translation of Greco-Arabic works on science and natural philosophy into Latin, the emergence of theologians and natural philosophers, and the formation of the medieval universities—are recognised as having provided the intellectual stimulus that led to the Copernican revolution. The lives of its leading figures—Copernicus, Tycho Brahe, Johannes Kepler, Galileo Galilei, and Isaac Newton—spanned the period 1473–1727. Representative of the new thinking, the Irish scholars David Delahide (c. 1529) and Leonard Fitzsimon (c. 1541) were highly respected mathematicians at Oxford, while the much-travelled Bernard O'Connor, a keen Newtonian and author of *Evangelium Medici* (1697), was elected a member of the Royal Society. In the spirit of COUNTER-REFORMATION a Jesuit college was founded in Dublin by CHRISTOPHER HOLYWOOD (John Geraldine), who published the first known scientific book by an Irish writer, *De Meteoris* (1613). In this text, which predates the telescopic observations of Galileo, he provides an overview of astronomy and, against a Ptolemaic background, introduces his own innovative ideas. Among important scientific manuscripts of the time preserved in Dublin is one from c. 1551 dealing with the teachings of the Spanish Jesuit Dominigo de Soto on accelerated motion and falling bodies, as well as *Commentaria in 8 Physicorum Libros Arist. et Magistri Soto* by Cristobal Caberra (1589–1643), which refers to both Aristotle and de Soto.

In the last quarter of the sixteenth century Jesuit schools in Ireland prepared a new generation of Catholic boys for education in the IRISH COLLEGES established in France, Spain, Portugal, Italy, and Spanish Flanders. ELIZABETH I of England, who considered this practice politically undesirable, countered by founding TRINITY COLLEGE in Dublin in 1592 to promote 'religion, civility, and learning.' Fellows of note at the college, in the period when the fruits of the Copernican revolution were challenging previous thinking, included Ambrose Ussher, LUKE CHALLONER, John Winthrop, Anthony Martin, and Thomas Lydyat from Oxford. The latter published, while at Trinity, *De Natura Coeli* (1605), attacking Aristotelian physics against a generally Ptolemaic background. Fellow countryman Nathaniel Carpenter's *Geography Delineated Forth* (1625) provides an account of the Copernican system, with a defence of the Tychonian system. JAMES USSHER showed in his writings a familiarity with both old and new astronomical thinking, and his manuscript *Ad Solarem Hypothesin Concinnandam Requiruntur* (1627) provides the first Irish account of, and support for, Keplerian heliocentric astronomy. In 1774 Provost Andrews bequeathed £3,000 to Trinity College for the erection and equipping of an astronomical observatory, which was constructed in 1783 at DUNSINK, Co. Dublin. Another professional observatory was founded in 1791 at Armagh by Archbishop THOMAS ROMNEY ROBINSON.

The nineteenth century was marked by the founding of a multiplicity of private observatories, whose founders and operators were drawn from the ranks of university graduates, the clergy, and the Anglo-Irish aristocracy (both women and men). Many of these made a significant contribution to the astronomy of the day, in particular WILLIAM PARSONS, third EARL OF ROSSE, at Birr, Co. Offaly. Also, an important technical contribution to the astronomy of the time was provided by the telescope-makers THOMAS and HOWARD GRUBB of Dublin, who developed astronomical instruments of unrivalled excellence.

By the twentieth century the frustrating experience of trying to make observations in a climate essentially unsuitable for stellar astronomy suggested to professional astronomers the solution of making observations at more favourable sites overseas. Following negotiations it was agreed that, from 1950, a 91 cm (36-in.) reflecting telescope at Boyden in South Africa could be jointly used by personnel at Armagh, Dunsink, and Harvard to study nearby and distant galaxies. In 1958 MERVYN ELLISON arranged to obtain films taken with a solar telescope (H-Alpha Lyot Heliograph) at the Cape of Good Hope for analysis at Dunsink Observatory. These arrangements were succeeded in 1997 by an agreement between the National Board for Science and Technology, the DUBLIN INSTITUTE FOR ADVANCED STUDIES, and the Science Research Council in Britain by which Irish astronomers can participate in the use of powerful astronomical instruments located in the Canary Islands. **Susan McKenna-Lawlor**

astronomy, prehistoric. The night sky is a spectacular sight for people living away from the glare of modern street lights, and it is scarcely surprising that prehistoric people became intimately familiar with the heavenly bodies and their movements. The sky was an essential part of their world. However, though there is an understandable modern fascination with the roots of people's interest in the sky, it is a mistake to see prehistoric astronomy as a precursor of modern scientific astronomy. How people perceive the sky—what they notice as important—is highly culture-dependent. People interpret what they see in the celestial realm by weaving a series of interconnections between objects, places, and events in the sky and those in the terrestrial environment, entities in imagined worlds, and the workings of human society itself. This leads to the development of *cosmologies*—shared systems of beliefs about the nature of the world.

Aspects of prehistoric cosmologies may be reflected in the alignment of monuments or houses in relation to astronomical events such as sunrise or sunset at the solstices, or in otherwise inexplicable spatial patterning in various human activities, such as the burial of the dead. Astronomical alignments are merely one sort of symbolic relationship among many that might have reflected cosmological principles, but they are particularly evident to us because we can use modern astronomy to reconstruct the appearance of ancient skies.

A number of NEOLITHIC and BRONZE AGE monuments in Ireland incorporate astronomical alignments, the most famous being the passage tomb at NEWGRANGE, Co. Meath, aligned on the rising midwinter sun. A shaft of sunlight shone in through a *roof-box*, a slot above the tomb entrance, for a few minutes after sunrise on mornings around the winter solstice and would have continued to light up the interior even after access was blocked to the living. This surely reflects a perceived connection between the Sun and the ancestors whose remains were placed in the tomb. More modest monuments also incorporate alignments on the solstices, such as the Bronze Age STONE ALIGNMENT at Gleninagh, Co. Galway. The motivation may have been to make them appear part of the functioning of nature; they would have become especially charged with symbolic power at certain times, when ritualistic activities may well have taken place, their timing regulated by the cycles of the heavens.

The main difficulty is that our perception that a monument is aligned astronomically does not mean that this was intended by, or was meaningful to, the builders. The stone circle at DROMBEG, Co. Cork, is aligned on the winter solstice, but it is one of over fifty similar monuments in the south-west that, as a group, show no consistent astronomical relationships, which raises the suspicion that the Drombeg alignment is unintentional. On the other hand, where we are fortunate enough to have a regional group of monuments with similar astronomical relationships appearing again and again, there is a much higher probability that they were intentional. The Bronze Age stone alignments of Cos. Cork and Kerry seem to be strongly related to the Moon, and many of them are also aligned on prominent summits. This hints at a broader range of cosmological relationships, of which astronomical alignments formed only one part. **Clive Ruggles**

astronomy in early Irish manuscripts. The material associated with astronomy in early Irish manuscripts can be divided into three parts: calendrical material concerned with calculating the date of Easter; accounts of astronomical phenomena and astronomical texts written by Irish monks in Ireland and overseas; and accounts of astronomical matters written by overseas experts. Outstanding in providing a contemporary view of the calendrical complexities of the former is the Paschal Epistle of CUMMIAN FADA (632), in which he first refers to a cycle introduced to Ireland by St PATRICK. Easter tables compiled at various monastic sites came in time to be augmented by examples of calculations, with verses to ease the memorising of computational rules. Interest in solar and lunar cycles caused Irish monks to become familiar with Hellenistic thinking, and this expertise they took with them to Europe.

astronomy. *Howard Grubb (foreground, right) supervising the installation of the Radcliffe Twin Telescope in Oxford, 1902, consisting of a 24-in. photographic refractor and an 18-in. visual refractor in a 32-ft dome with a rising floor. [Ian Elliott, Dunsink Observatory]*

VIRGILIUS, who arrived in France c. 741, taught that the Earth is spherical. In 811 the monk DUNGAL explained to the Emperor Charlemagne why two solar eclipses had occurred in the previous year. In the ninth century DICUIL dedicated an astronomical work in prose and verse to Louis the Pious, while ERIUGENA at the court of Charles the Bald produced a philosophical work in which he discussed the so-called geo-heliocentric system.

To the third category belongs 'An Irish Astronomical Tract', which is based in part on a translation into Irish of a medieval Latin version of an Arabic work by Messahalah, a Jewish astronomer of Alexandria who flourished shortly before AD 800. **Susan McKenna-Lawlor**

Athassel Priory, Co. Tipperary, an Augustinian priory founded towards the end of the twelfth century by William de Burgo. The richly endowed priory became one of the largest and most powerful in Ireland; its prior was a parliamentary peer. The priory buildings, which date from the middle of the thirteenth century, follow the general principles of CISTERCIAN planning, though they were adapted in later centuries for both spiritual and defensive purposes. A well-preserved medieval bridge spanning an old mill-race leads to the gate-house of the priory. A high-quality thirteenth-century tomb from Athassel is now on display at CASHEL. [see ABBEYS.] **Rachel Moss**

athletics, the most popular sport in Ireland in the late nineteenth and early twentieth centuries. A vibrant native tradition of athletic competition may be linked to Irish mythology as well as to the early medieval Aonach Tailteann; that tradition was preserved into the modern era in rudimentary contests of strength, stamina, and agility, the undocumented pastimes of a rural community memorably illustrated by the sledge-throwing contest in CHARLES KICKHAM's *Knocknagow* (1873).

The first formal athletics meeting in Ireland was held in 1857 at TRINITY COLLEGE, Dublin; and with the inauguration of the annual sports of the Cork Amateur Athletic Club in 1862, and the formation of the Civil Service Athletic Club in 1867, the popularity of the sport grew rapidly, with athletics meetings quickly becoming a regular feature in all parts of the country. There was not yet any formal governance of the sport; however, the Irish Champion Athletic Club was formed in 1872, taking a lease on some land at Lansdowne Road, Dublin, where it laid down a cinder path. That club inaugurated an Irish championship meeting, which was held annually from 1873 until 1884.

The most notable performer to emerge in this period was Pat Davin (1857–1949), who established world records in both the high jump (1880) and the long jump (1883). The structure of the sport became formalised with the foundation of the GAELIC ATHLETIC ASSOCIATION in 1884 and the Irish Amateur Athletic Association in 1885, those bodies being generally representative of the nationalist and unionist political constituencies, respectively. National championships were held annually by both associations until a single governing body for the sport, the National Athletic and Cycling Association, was formed in 1922. From 1895 to shortly before the FIRST WORLD WAR a period of co-operation between the two bodies coincided with what has been considered a golden age for the sport. While Irish emigrants were distinguishing themselves abroad, most notably in the United States, a small group of gifted athletes dominated the sport at home while also making their mark on the international stage. The most notable of these—Tom Kiely (1869–1951), Peter O'Connor (1872–1957), and Con Leahy (1876–1921)—not only won OLYMPIC championships but at different times travelled to America 'to uphold', in O'Connor's words, 'the athletics abilities of Irishmen.' In 1901 O'Connor set a world record in the long jump that was to last for twenty years. The strength of this national tradition is attested by the fact that Irish-born athletes won no fewer than thirty-eight Olympic medals in the period between 1896 and 1922: eighteen gold, fifteen silver, and five bronze.

athletics. *Sonia O'Sullivan, world champion athlete, on a training run in her home town of Cobh, Co. Cork, against a background of St Colman's Cathedral and West View, known as the 'Stack of Cards'. [Inpho Photography; photo: Pat Bolger]*

Eventually, however, the impact of EMIGRATION, the rise in popularity of team sports, and the failure of the governing bodies to develop and foster athletics, combined with the disruptive effects of the First World War, brought an end to an era of remarkable achievement. Olympic successes by Pat O'Callaghan (1905–1991) and Robert Tisdall (1907–) in 1928 and 1932 could not disguise the fact that the sport was receding both in popularity and in importance through the inter-war years and beyond, a situation exacerbated by the expulsion of the National Athletic and Cycling Association from the international federation in a dispute over the issue of control in Northern Ireland. The sport is now governed by the Athletic Association of Ireland and the Northern Ireland Athletics Federation.

Something of a revival was sparked when Ronnie Delany (1935–) won the prestigious 1,500 m event at the Melbourne Olympics in 1956, and whereas Irish glory had previously been achieved in field events, this time success was to be achieved on the track. Eamonn Coghlan (1952–), John Treacy (1957–), Marcus O'Sullivan (1961–), and Frank O'Mara (1960–) won a total of eight world championships between 1983 and 1993.

The participation of women in athletics had been only tentatively fostered from the mid-1960s, but by the end of the century two remarkable athletes had emerged. Catherina McKiernan (1969–) won silver medals in four successive world cross-country championships before turning to the marathon to win three major city races—Berlin (1997), London, and Amsterdam (1998)—seeming to be on track to win a major championship until sidelined by injury. Arguably the most successful Irish athlete ever is Sonia O'Sullivan (1969–), who so far has won three world championships, at track and cross-country, three European track titles, and an Olympic silver medal at 5,000 m. She also holds the world record for 2,000 m and the European record for 3,000 m. **Tony O'Donoghue**

Athlone (*Baile Átha Luain*), Co. Westmeath, a town established on both banks of the River SHANNON at a strategic crossing-point; population (2002) 7,479. The first bridge was built by TOIRDHEALBHACH Ó CONCHOBHAIR in 1120, replaced with a stone bridge and castle by the ANGLO-NORMANS c. 1210. Athlone became the headquarters of the English Presidency of Connacht under Sir HENRY SIDNEY, and a new stone bridge was constructed in 1566–7. The town was central to the Williamite campaign of 1690–91, when it was besieged on two occasions. A new military barracks was established in the early eighteenth century, and this role was retained after 1922 when Athlone became the headquarters of the Free State army's Western Command. A stage-coach service to Dublin was established in the eighteenth century. Two railway companies, the Midland Great Western and the Great Southern, served Athlone in the nineteenth century, and the town retains its transport role today as a road and rail junction. A new bridge over the Shannon and a relief road on the northern perimeter of the built-up area (1991) enhanced local communications. The Shannon is important to the town's economy for fishing and river TOURISM; other employers include high-technology firms and the Department of Education and Science. Athlone Institute of Technology has provided third-level education since 1970. Among Athlone's best-known sons is the tenor JOHN MCCORMACK. **Ruth McManus**

Athlone Rail Bridge (1851), erected to carry the main railway line to the west across the River SHANNON. It has bow-string girders and a central opening span. Compressed air was used in forming the piers, the first time in Ireland this technique of excluding water from the workings was employed. **Ronald Cox**

Atkins, William Ringrose (1812–1887), artist. Born in Cork; probably trained by his uncle GEORGE PAIN. His first competition success, a chapel at Mount Jerome Cemetery, Dublin (1845), led to his largest commission, the Cork Lunatic Asylum (1846–57). In 1846 he also built the church at Clonbur, Co. Mayo. These show him a disciple of PUGIN; but stylistic diversity is evident in the next decade, most notably his masterpiece of domestic architecture, Oak Park, Tralee (1856–61), which shows also the influence of John Ruskin. Later works show him alert to the Italianate style introduced by Charles Barry and to William Butterfield's practice. **Michael McCarthy**

Atkins, William Ringrose Golden (1884–1959), plant physiologist. Born in Cork; educated at TCD, where he was assistant to the professor of botany, 1911–20. In 1920 he was employed as indigo research botanist in India but in the following year returned to Europe on his appointment as head of general physiology in the laboratory of the Marine Biological Association in Plymouth, where he served until his retirement in 1955. His research covered a wide range, but his particular interest was in the distribution of animals and crops in relation to light and soil acidity. He was elected a fellow of the Royal Society in 1925 and awarded the RDS BOYLE MEDAL in 1928. **Christopher Moriarty**

Atkinson, G. M. W. [George Mounsey Wheatley] (c. 1806–1884), artist. Born in Cobh, Co. Cork, of English parents. He spent some years at sea as a ship's carpenter before settling in his native town, where he was appointed Inspector of Shipping and Emigrants. Self-taught as an artist, he enjoyed limited success in his lifetime, though paintings such as *The White Squadron in Cork Harbour* (1843) are among the finest Irish marine views. His three sons, George Mounsey, Richard Peterson, and Robert, and his daughter, Sarah, all became painters, while another descendant, George Atkinson, taught at the Metropolitan School of Art, Dublin, in the early twentieth century. Paintings by Atkinson can be seen in the Crawford Municipal Art Gallery, Cork, and the offices of the Port of Cork. **Peter Murray**

Atlantic telegraph cable. The first successful Atlantic telegraph cable was laid in July 1866 by the GREAT EASTERN, then the world's largest steamship, from Valentia Island, Co. Kerry, to Heart's Content, Newfoundland. WILLIAM THOMSON of Belfast was the electrical engineer for the project; ROBERT CHARLES HALPIN of Co. Wicklow was navigating officer (later captain) (see p. 469). The cable could transmit telegraph messages in Morse code at seven words per minute, and a short telegram cost about €25; by the late 1960s telegrams could be sent at more than 2,500 words per minute, and the cost of a short message had fallen to 6c. Two very sensitive instruments invented by Thomson, the mirror galvanometer and the siphon recorder, were essential to the successful operation of the cable. An earlier invention of Thomson's, the sounding machine, played an important role in the accurate charting of the ocean floor in advance of the cable-laying.

By 1883 almost 130,000 km (80,000 miles) of submarine telegraph cables had been laid, at a cost of €38 million, including nine transatlantic cables. The invention of the short-wave wireless system by MARCONI provided the first real technical alternative to these cables. **Gerard McMahon**

Athlone Railway Bridge. *Built in 1850 across the River Shannon, it is over 165 m (540 ft) in length and has a central span of 37 m (120 ft). The engineer was G. W. Hemans, and the contractors were Fox and Henderson. [Council of Trustees of the National Library of Ireland; R.2926]*

atmospheric railway. From 29 March 1844 to 12 April 1854 the extension to Dalkey of the DUBLIN AND KINGSTOWN RAILWAY was operated on the atmospheric principle. One of the few examples ever built and unique to Ireland, it employed a valve consisting of a leather flap that controlled propulsion from a piston working in a 380 mm (15-in.) cast-iron pipe in which a vacuum was created by a pumping-house at the Dalkey terminus. The route was on a rising gradient, and the return to Dún Laoghaire was by gravity. The system proved uneconomic, however; and rats evinced a taste for the leather valves and the lard with which they were lubricated. Atmospheric Road in Dalkey commemorates the short-lived experiment. **Bernard Share**

At Swim-Two-Birds (1939), a novel by FLANN O'BRIEN. This elaborately inventive text concerns a Dubliner, Trellis, who in a seedy environment is at work on a novel about sin; his activities are narrated by an unknown UCD student. This narrative complexity is compounded to a delightfully absurd degree, as Trellis believes he can recruit characters for his book from the existing stock in literature. These characters take on a life of their own when Trellis falls asleep. One character whom he has been involved in creating determines to write a book about Trellis. A *jeu d'esprit* of mingled comic zest and parodic glee, *At Swim-Two-Birds* has been identified by some critics as a post-modernist text *avant la lettre*. **Terence Brown**

Attorney-General, the chief legal officer of the state, leader of the bar, and adviser to the Government on matters of law and legal opinion, as provided for by article 30 of the CONSTITUTION OF IRELAND. The Attorney-General is appointed by the President of Ireland, following nomination by the TAOISEACH, and becomes a member of the Government and therefore retires from office on the resignation of the Taoiseach or the fall of the Government. By convention he or she is a senior counsel (senior barrister) but ceases to engage in private practice while in office. The Attorney-General advises the Government on the constitutionality of bills and represents the state or the public interest in litigation.

The English Attorney-General acts for Northern Ireland but has advisers in respect of Northern Ireland matters. **Neville Cox**

Aud, a German arms ship. Originally a cargo ship, the *Castro*, built in Hull for Ellerman's Wilson line, it traded between English and European ports of the North Sea and the Baltic. It happened to be in German waters when war began in 1914 and was promptly taken over by the German navy. When, thanks largely to ROGER CASEMENT, Germany agreed to send a cargo of arms and ammunition to be picked up by the IRISH VOLUNTEERS in support of the planned 1916 RISING, it was officially registered as a vessel of the Imperial German navy, refitted, and carefully disguised as a Norwegian ship, named *Aud*. It was sent to rendezvous off the

Magharee Islands, Co. Kerry, with the German submarine *U19*, on which Casement was being brought to Ireland, and he was to deal with the discharge of its cargo. Its commander, Spindler, whose lack of objectivity is notable in his account of the voyage (its English translation misleadingly entitled *The Mystery of the Casement Ship*), wasted time, lost his way, and missed the vital rendezvous with *U19*. The *Aud* was captured and instructed to accompany the British sloop *Bluebell* to Cobh; Spindler scuttled it before its arrival in harbour. The wreck has been investigated by divers and some of the arms retrieved. **John de Courcy Ireland**

Audleystown, Co. Down, a dual COURT TOMB overlooking the southern shore of STRANGFORD LOUGH, discovered in 1946 and excavated in 1952 and 1956/7. It consists of a wedge-shaped long cairn, aligned from north-west to south-east, with straight sides revetted with dry-stone walling. At each end a shallow forecourt gives access to a burial gallery, which is divided into four chambers. The remains of at least seventeen bodies, some partly burnt, were found in each gallery, together with plain and decorated NEOLITHIC pottery, flint implements, and animal bones. **Paul Walsh**

Aughrim, Battle of (22 July 1691), between the forces of WILLIAM III and JAMES II, representing the Protestant and Catholic interests, respectively. Following his defeat at ATHLONE on 10 July, the Marquis de SAINT-RUTH decided, with the help of his second in command, the Comte de Tesse, to launch into battle while his JACOBITE army was still intact. He chose as his battleground Aughrim Hill, 26 km (16 miles) south-west of Athlone. The armies were equally matched, with approximately 20,000 men each; the Jacobite line extended for 2.5 km ($1\frac{1}{2}$ miles) from the village of Aughrim along the eastern slope of Kilcommaden Hill to the Tristaun River.

At first the Jacobite army was in the ascendant and GODARD VAN GINKEL's attack was making slow progress, as the Jacobites used a system of defence in depth by means of their improvised breastworks. However, Saint-Ruth had switched forces from the left in order to strengthen his right wing. Van Ginkel then launched an attack on the Irish left centre, ordering ten battalions of infantry to wade through BOG, with mud and water up to their waists. Once over this natural defence they were met with a determined counter-attack as the Jacobite foot guards and Colonel Gordon O'Neill's Ulstermen plied them with pikes and musket butts until 'the blood flowed into their shoes.' At this point Saint-Ruth jubilantly declared that the enemy was broken; but victory was snatched away when a chance cannon shot struck off Saint-Ruth's head. When the Irish cavalry heard the news, war-weariness and demoralisation overcame them, and they offered no resistance to the Williamite advance. Simultaneously the Irish infantry battalion that had been defending the ruins of nearby Aughrim Castle ran short of ammunition. PATRICK SARSFIELD endeavoured to cover the retreat with the cavalry but was unable to save the infantry from wholesale massacre. About 7,000 Irish Jacobites were killed and 450 taken prisoner, compared with 2,000 killed or wounded on WILLIAM III's side.

The Battle of Aughrim was the most decisive battle of the Jacobite wars in Ireland. Only a week after this setback the Irish army stationed at Galway capitulated, leaving Limerick the last important Jacobite stronghold. **Rosemary Richey**

Aughrim Slopes Céilí Band, formed in 1927 as the Aughrim Slopes Trio by Paddy Kelly and Jack Mulcair (fiddle) and Joe Mills (accordion). They were later joined by Garda Jim Drury (fiddle) and Josie O'Halloran (piano), and the band was formed when Father Cummins of Ballinasloe requested céilí music for the opening of a scouts' club. Weekly radio broadcasts on 2RN followed, with 'Lament after the Battle of Aughrim' as their signature tune. The band toured England, Scotland, and Wales, playing to huge emigrant audiences, and won the all-Ireland band competition in 1953. They recorded *Jigs and Reels: The Aughrim Slopes Céilí Band* (1956) as a compilation of their original recordings. **Verena Commins**

Augustine Eriugena (fl. 655), author of the treatise *De Mirabilibus Sacrae Scripturae*. This work is exceptional in that it demonstrates a strictly scientific approach in the matter of making direct observations of nature and subjecting them to logical interpretation. The treatise aims to explain each miracle of the Scriptures as an extreme case of phenomena within the laws of nature. A list of the terrestrial MAMMALS of Ireland is given, solving the problem of how they reached the country after Noah's Flood by proposing that Ireland had been cut off from the European continent by marine erosion. **Christopher Moriarty**

Auraicept na nÉces (the scholars' primer), an OLD IRISH text on language, possibly composed by CENN FÁELAD, towards the end of the seventh century. Its first section is pseudo-historical, dealing with the origin of Irish; this is followed by linguistically more interesting matter, such as the letters in Greek, Irish, and Latin, gender, some verbal forms, and an appendix of extended nominal paradigms. Its extensive manuscript tradition testifies to its perceived value to medieval learned men; modern scholarship has not, until fairly recently, taken it very seriously. **Anders Ahlqvist**

Australia, the Irish in. From 1788, with the establishment of the British penal colony in Sydney, New South Wales, the active and substantial Irish minority has been a founding people in the Australian settlements. The Irish-derived proportion of its population makes Australia the most 'Irish' country in the world outside Ireland, up to a third of its 19 million people having some Irish ancestry. It has been argued that the Irish were the essential dynamic factor: Australia was shaped by the tension and clash between Irish-oriented minority and English-oriented majority, a debate and contest over what kind of country it should be. Irish challenges over the big issues of immigration, religion, education, ownership, government, and authority eventually resulted in compromise, sharing, liberties, and tolerance. The Irish and their descendants rose to integral equality and leadership in Australian society.

From 1791, when the first Irish convicts were transported from Cork, until 1868, when TRANSPORTATION ended in Western Australia, 40,000 Irish prisoners comprised a quarter of the convict total. Most were ordinary criminals, but a significant number were political rebels (see p. 705). Their colonial image, imported from England and confirmed by incidents in Australia, was one of a disloyal, seditious, rebel low-life, a prejudice that lingered in Australian history. In fact from 1810 emancipated Irish convicts were settling on land grants, becoming prosperous, and anxious to identify with their new home. Freedom for their Catholic religion, liberty for its practice and priests, was their initial cause. Many of their early priests were Irish, but authority was vested in the English Benedictine order, a situation productive of tension and difficulty until bishops and priests from Ireland gained control from the 1860s.

The emancipated Irish convict element was soon a dwindling segment in the substantial and continuous free Irish IMMIGRATION from the 1830s to 1880s, attracted by free or assisted passage offered by settler-hungry Australian governments and attractive land provision. The gold rushes, from the 1850s, were a particular incentive. Though met with considerable hostility from establishment and Protestant elements, these Irish people became an accepted, colourful, and widely dispersed aspect of colonial life in both country and city. Ten per cent were Protestants; the Anglo-Irish were a significant element. Several early colonial governors and their officials were Anglo-Irish, liberalising the colonial atmosphere and administration. The professions of law, medicine, and engineering had strong Anglo-Irish representation. Irishmen were notable also in movements of legendary Australian protest, such as the Eureka Stockade incident of 1854, led by PETER LALOR, and the bushranging career of NED KELLY, who was of Irish descent.

A distinctive Irish-Australian sub-culture developed from the 1880s to the 1930s, encouraged and dominated by the Catholic Church, in particular Cardinal Patrick Moran, and by imported Irish teaching orders. Its emphasis was on religion (especially separate Catholic EDUCATION), respectability, and successful participation in all levels of Australian life—ideals then very imperfectly realised. The Catholic education system, with its Irish character, continued to be the basis of social and economic advancement, fostering a culture whose arts, literature, and music were a feature of the Irish-Australian world. A vigorous Irish Catholic challenge to dominant English-Australian loyalist and secular values formed in the period 1914–21. By then Irish Catholics and their descendants, predominantly of the working class, increasingly supported the Australian Labour Party.

The 1916 RISING, in the midst of Australian conscription referendums in the period 1916–17, polarised the Australian community. Spectacularly led by Archbishop Mannix of Melbourne, Irish Catholics were drawn into sectarian conflict; but by the 1920s the Irish cause in Australia had suffered a reverse from which it never recovered. The CIVIL WAR of 1921–3 induced profound disillusionment and revulsion. Where previously Ireland, its subjections and reactions seemed to reflect Irish-Australians' own local predicaments and exclusions, they now turned strictly to their Australian business, though the social atmosphere remained one of subtle division, difference, and hesitation. But a reversal of negative images and reactions developed from the 1980s; it became an asset to be Irish.

At the start of the twenty-first century the Irish-born element of the Australian population is tiny—less than 0.5 per cent—but this is supplemented by almost as many visitors, and the context is one of warm community acceptance. The principal determining factor in the Irish-Australian experience has been the great distance from Ireland, productive of identification, sentiment, and good will but little actual involvement. **Patrick O'Farrell**

Australia, Irish writing in. In the early decades of European settlement in Australia the majority of Irish people were convicts. Their hostility to the penal system was reflected in numerous ballads, which circulated widely; well-known examples are 'Bold Jack Donahue' and 'The Wild Colonial Boy', which dramatised the exploits of bushrangers and celebrated defiance of the British authorities. Francis MacNamara, 'Frank the Poet' (born 1811), is credited with a number of these ballads.

With the increase in the number of settlers, other forms of verse were much in evidence. From the middle of the nineteenth century lyrics full of nostalgia for green fields far away and poems on the quest for Irish liberty filled the columns of newspapers in every colony. A pervasive influence was THOMAS MOORE, whose *Irish Melodies* provided models with their wistful tones and muted demands for freedom. Poetic composition was an emotional release for many, such as MARY EVA KELLY, whose mind and spirit remained in Ireland and who saw the new land as irremediably alien.

Later generations of poets were more likely to seek an accommodation between the old world and the new. Poets at the turn of the century, such as the Irish-born Victor Daley (1858–1905), occasionally looked to the 'CELTIC TWILIGHT' for inspiration, but their imaginative sources were more likely to be Australian, or European, a trend continued into the twentieth century. The Australian-born poets Vincent Buckley (1925–1988) and R. D. FitzGerald (1902–1987), for example, might draw on vestigial influences of their Irish ancestry, but it was only one strand among many in their work. Ballads continued to be popular, the best-known collection being John O'Brien's *Around the Boree Log* (1921), which affectionately portrayed the lives of Irish settlers in the bush.

Writers of fiction in nineteenth-century Australia were more circumscribed by literary circumstances than poets. Novels especially were written mainly for English readers, who were fascinated by the Australian exotic. Irish stereotypes might be acceptable, but not thoughtful studies of Irish responses to the new world. Even a novel such as *Moondyne* (1879) by JOHN BOYLE O'REILLY, a Fenian prisoner who escaped from Western Australia, featured an English hero, despite an undercurrent of Irish-Australian issues in the narrative. Arguably the most significant Irish character in fiction is Richard Mahony in Henry Handel Richardson's trilogy *The Fortunes of Richard Mahony* (1917–29). Here again, while Mahony was born in Dublin and his traumatic mental deterioration results from a conflict between Australia and the old world, the latter is represented by England, not Ireland. Only in recent decades, principally in the novels of Thomas Keneally, has the psyche of the Irish, especially the Catholic Irish, in Australia been explored. *Bring Larks and Heroes* (1967), on the convict era, and *A River Town* (1995), on the rural milieu of the early 1900s, are two such books.

Similarly in drama it is modern plays rather than those of the colonial period that have fully explored the tensions between Irish origins and everyday life in Australia. Two well-regarded examples are Peter Kenna's *A Hard God* (1974) and Ron Blair's *The Christian Brothers* (1976). **Frank Molloy**

Autumn Journal (1939), a long poem by LOUIS MACNEICE. Written between August and December 1938, it is divided into twenty-four sections and contains (in MacNeice's words) reportage, metaphysics, ethics, lyrical emotion, autobiography, and nightmare. One of the seminal poems of the 1930s and indeed of the twentieth century, it weaves together public and private, recording MacNeice's complex response to personal and political crisis in the late 1930s in a London overshadowed by the threat of war. Written with virtuosic brio, it dramatises the poet's feelings about Spain, the FIRST WORLD WAR, his love-hate relation to Ireland, the 'land of ambush', the National Gallery, and teaching the classics. It combines formal variety, journalistic flair, and poignant wit. **Hugh Haughton**

Auxiliaries: see BLACK AND TANS AND AUXILIARIES.

aviation. Following early experiments with lighter-than-air machines and the novelty and challenge of the first aircraft, the development of aviation in Ireland has been governed by two fundamental geographical considerations: its island status and its position on the western rim of Europe. The first factor led to early plans for international connections, at first to Britain (the first crossings of the IRISH SEA were in 1912, and the first air mail was flown from Belfast to Liverpool in 1928) and subsequently further afield. The second factor led the leading aviation powers on both sides of the Atlantic to see Ireland as an important transit stop, first for flying-boats and after 1945 for land-planes, until the introduction of jet aircraft, with their greatly enhanced range, progressively reduced the requirement for refuelling on transatlantic crossings.

Because of Northern Ireland's status as part of the United Kingdom and its consequent involvement in that country's European wars, the development of aviation there was to develop a markedly military orientation. Aircraft construction dates from the FIRST WORLD WAR but reached its apogee during the SECOND WORLD WAR, when many aerodromes, flying-boat bases, and landing fields were brought into use. Men and women from all parts of Ireland served with the ROYAL FLYING CORPS and the Royal Air Force in both wars, many being awarded decorations for their destruction of enemy planes. The Dubliners George McElroy (First World War) and Paddy Finucane (Second World War) were outstanding in this respect.

Military aviation on a lesser scale was inaugurated with the establishment of the IRISH FREE STATE and of the AIR CORPS and has been employed regularly in support of the civil power. Though the state was neutral during the Second World War, there were some 200 crashes or forced landings by American, British, and German aircraft in the state and its territorial waters. The Air Corps provided salvage teams (reimbursed by the Allied authorities as appropriate), and both British and German survivors were interned at the CURRAGH; American combatants were permitted to cross the border to Northern Ireland, and as the war progressed the same leniency was applied to the British. The Government further compromised its neutrality by permitting American and British flights from the North through the 'Donegal Corridor' to the Atlantic and northwards over the Inishowen Peninsula.

The first recorded fatal crash of a civil aircraft was in May 1933 off Dalkey, Co. Dublin, and involved a De Havilland Gypsy Moth, registration EI-AAH. AER LINGUS lost a Douglas DC3 near Shannon in 1946, without loss of life; subsequent fatal crashes involved the DC3 *St Kevin* in Wales, 10 January 1952, and the disappearance of the Vickers Viscount *St Felim* off the Tuskar Rock, 24 March 1968, an event not yet fully explained. The cargo airline Aer Turas lost a Bristol freighter and its crew of two on its approach to Dublin Airport on 12 June 1967. A Transworld Airlines Constellation bound for New York crashed on approach at Shannon in December 1946—the first of several accidents, fatal and non-fatal, involving this aircraft type at or near the airport. Shannon rescue services were also involved in major offshore crashes, including the loss of an Air India Boeing 747 off the Co. Kerry coast on 23 June 1985, the world's worst aviation disaster at that time, in which 329 passengers and crew were lost to a terrorist bomb.

The first search-and-rescue facility was introduced in 1964 in DUBLIN BAY by the Air Corps, employing an Alouette III helicopter. Helicopters have since played an important part in air ambulance services, island relief, and border surveillance.

Pioneer flights with an Irish involvement included that of the *Bremen* and of Charles Kingsford Smith, whose *Southern Cross* took off from Portmarnock strand, near Dublin, on the second successful east-west Atlantic crossing in June 1930 with the Irishman Paddy Saul as navigator. In 1932 the British pioneer Jim Mollison took off from the same site to complete the first solo east-west Atlantic crossing. [see ALCOCK AND BROWN; BALLOONING; BLAND, LILIAN; FERGUSON, HARRY; FITZMAURICE, JAMES; FOYNES; HEATH, LADY MARY.] **Bernard Share**

aviation and the Second World War. More than 200 British, American, and German military aircraft crashed or force-landed in neutral Ireland and its territorial waters during the SECOND WORLD WAR. Virtually all German aircraft were destroyed either accidentally or deliberately by their crews; in Co. Donegal alone there were approximately forty such incidents, because of the proximity of the Northern Ireland bases. Intact Allied aircraft were allowed to depart after refuelling and repair work, and salvaged equipment specifically requested by the Allies was also handed over. The AIR CORPS provided salvage teams that often had to operate in inaccessible sites; their efforts were paid for by the relevant British or American authorities.

At first all surviving British and German crew members were interned at the CURRAGH CAMP, Co. Kildare. Surviving British crew members from crashes after 1942 were repatriated, while those interned in the previous two years were repatriated between October 1943 and June 1944. All surviving German crew members remained interned for the duration of the war. Surviving American crew members were not interned.

The Government granted permission to British military aircraft based in Northern Ireland to fly over its neutral territory in a designated corridor in order to reach the North Atlantic more easily. The corridor, based on the flying-boat base on LOUGH ERNE, was 32 km (20 miles) wide, bounded on the north by the cliffs of Donegal Bay and on the south by INNISHMURRAY. Later the warplanes were allowed to fly over the Inishowen Peninsula directly to the North Channel. **Donal MacCarron**

Avoca, Vale of, a glaciated valley in south Co. Wicklow, extending south-eastwards from where the Avonmore and Avonbeg Rivers meet near Rathdrum, the 'Meeting of the Waters' celebrated in song by THOMAS MOORE. The Avoca River flows to the sea at Arklow. The valley contains the attractive villages of Woodenbridge and Avoca; its superb pastoral landscape is somewhat marred by abandoned copper-mines near Avoca and a fertiliser plant near Arklow at Shelton Abbey, former home of the Earls of Wicklow. **Patrick Duffy**

axes, stone, used in Ireland from the MESOLITHIC PERIOD to the BRONZE AGE but particularly during the NEOLITHIC PERIOD (c. 4000–2400 BC). Research by the Irish Stone Axe Project from 1991 shows that there are at least 20,000 known stone axeheads. Wooden hafts rarely survive. Axeheads were made from a variety of sources, porcellanite being the most important. Both primary sources (outcrop) and secondary sources (boulders and cobbles) were used, TIEVEBULLIAGH, Co. Antrim, being particularly important. Initial working to produce *rough-outs* was by either flaking or hammering and pecking; the rough-outs were then ground and polished. Axeheads of foreign origin also occur, notably from a source at Great Langdale, Cumbria. **Gabriel Cooney**

Aylward, Margaret Louisa (1810–1889), religious founder. Born in Waterford, daughter of a wealthy Catholic merchant; educated at the QUAKER school, Waterford, and the Ursuline Convent, Thurles, Co. Tipperary. Moving to Dublin, she involved herself in Catholic charities, becoming embroiled in a number of sectarian controversies with the Irish Church Mission. In 1857 she founded the Sisters of the Holy Faith, a teaching order subsequently influential, especially in the Archdiocese of Dublin. **Fergal Tobin**

Barry, James *(see page 74)*. Portrait of James Barry and Edmund Burke in the Characters of Ulysses and his Companions Fleeing from the Cave of Polyphemus *(1776), showing Burke (right) and Barry (left) in an incident from Homer's* Odyssey. *[Courtesy of Crawford Municipal Art Gallery, Cork]*

B

Babington, William (1756–1833), physician and chemist. Born at Portglenone, Co. Antrim; studied medicine at Guy's Hospital for Incurables, London, thereafter spending four years at the Naval Hospital in Haslar, Hampshire. In 1785 he returned to Guy's, where he was appointed physician and lectured in Chemistry. While there he published *A Syllabus of a Course of Lectures Read at Guy's Hospital in Chemistry* (1789). In 1795 he published *Systematic Arrangement of Minerals* and also *New System of Mineralogy* (1799). The classification he introduced represented an advance on existing systems. A meeting he called in 1807 led to the foundation of the Geological Society, and he was a founder in 1819 of the Hunterian Society (named for John Hunter, the father of scientific surgery). A mineral first described by the French mineralogist A. Levy was named babingtonite in his honour. **Susan McKenna-Lawlor**

Bachall Íosa ('the staff of Jesus'), a miraculous CROZIER, one of the insignia of St PATRICK and one of the chief treasures of Armagh, first mentioned in 789. Transferred to CHRIST CHURCH, Dublin, in the late twelfth century by the ANGLO-NORMANS, it was destroyed in 1538. **Raghnall Ó Floinn**

Bachelors, the, pop group. Formed in Dublin in 1958 by John Stokes and the brothers Con and Declan Cluskey, the Bachelors were 'discovered' in Scotland three years later by the entrepreneur Phil Solomon. Their style was very much boy-next-door folk and pop. They became extremely successful in the British pop charts, with fourteen top-thirty hit singles between 1963 and 1967, including 'Charmaine' (1963), 'Diane' (1964), and 'The Sound of Silence' (1966), and on the cabaret circuit with their easy-listening reworkings of popular pre-rock ballads. The composition of the group remained stable for twenty-five years, up to the mid-1980s. **Tony Clayton-Lea**

Bacon, Francis (1909–1992), artist. Born in Dublin to English parents; educated at Dean Close School, Cheltenham. He left the family home in Kildare at the age of sixteen and travelled to London, Berlin, and Paris. Having worked briefly as a furniture designer, he began painting c. 1930, with no formal training. His first significant work was *Crucifixion* (1933), a subject that became an obsession. *Three Studies for Figures at the Base of a Crucifixion* (1944) established him as a new force in post-war art. A figurative artist, he was inspired by the work of Velázquez, Michelangelo, van Gogh, and Picasso. Photography, cinema, literature, and medical imagery also provided source materials. Frequently described as violent and disturbing, his paintings concentrate on the human body, injury, and paint as an expressive medium. Apart from periods in Monte Carlo, Tangier, and Paris, he remained in London. In 1961 he moved to 7 Reece Mews, South Kensington, his principal home and studio for the rest of his life. During his lifetime he had major exhibitions at the Grand Palais, Paris, the Metropolitan Museum of Art, New York, and two retrospectives at the Tate Gallery, London, and was the first living Western artist to have a retrospective in the Soviet Union. His work is represented in most major collections, and his reconstructed Reece Mews studio, where he worked from 1961 to 1992, has been installed at the Hugh Lane Municipal Gallery of Modern Art, Dublin, which also holds an archive of the studio contents. **Margarita Cappock**

Bahá'í, an independent worldwide faith founded in Iran by Bahá'u'lláh in the nineteenth century on the spiritual principles common to all major world religions. The first Bahá'í community in Ireland was established in Dublin in 1948; there are now approximately 1,000 Bahá'ís in Ireland, gathered in twenty-five spiritual assemblies. **Gabrielle Brocklesby**

Baile Átha Cliath (Dublin). Dublin's Irish and English names have different roots, both of which take us back to the city's pre-urban origins. *Áth Cliath* (the prefixed *baile*, 'settlement', appears first in the fourteenth century) reflects a prehistoric human-made feature of the River LIFFEY: a ford made passable at low tide by the deposition of rafts of hurdlework on the exposed mudflats. The settlement itself grew up on a low east-west ridge parallel to the river, arranged around a central space represented nowadays by Cornmarket. This included a church site, later that of St Audoën's but possibly linked earlier to the cult of COLM CILLE. By the seventh century there was another ecclesiastical focus, due south of a tidal pool in the River Poddle. This 'dark pool' gave rise to the place-name *Dubhlinn*, which is associated consistently with shadowy abbots and bishops. The double pre-urban nucleus of the later town was the meeting-point of four *slite* (long-distance highways) and no doubt also of sea-lanes across the IRISH SEA.

That this strategic site at the head of DUBLIN BAY proved to be an irresistible attraction to VIKINGS in the ninth century comes as no surprise. After an exploratory plundering raid in 837, Scandinavian men and women, mainly from Norway or from Norwegian colonies in northern and western Scotland, began to settle in 841. Their *longphort* (defended ship enclosure) has not yet been identified archaeologically, but these aggressive foreigners probably occupied a number of sites on both banks of the Liffey. Recent excavations at Exchange Street have uncovered post-and-wattle houses of a type that became standard in the tenth century. From 853, Dublin's Viking leaders are referred to in Irish sources as kings, and their kingdom became the Scandinavians' principal trading base in Ireland. After an enforced exile of fifteen years (902–17) the same dynasty re-established itself, certainly in the vicinity of present-day Exchange Street and the lower part of Fishamble Street. The first defensive enclosure of earth and timber has been dated archaeologically to the middle of the tenth century, from which time written sources employ the epithet *dún*, 'stronghold'. By this stage DUBLIN was a town in the making, as distinct from a pirates' lair and slave-trading emporium.

Following the decisive defeat of King AMLAÍB CUARÁN at the Battle of TARA in 980, Dublin came progressively under the control of Irish kings, starting with MÁEL SECHNAILL II of Mide. Through local economic exchanges and intermarriage its population would have become increasingly Hibernicised, with the result that scholars use the label Hiberno-Norse for the period down to the

Bacon. *Francis Bacon at the Claude Bernard art gallery in Paris, 1977. Bacon's reconstructed London studio is the centrepiece of a permanent Bacon archive, which contains the most significant collection of the artist's works on paper, at the Hugh Lane Municipal Gallery of Modern Art, Dublin. [John Minihan]*

ANGLO-NORMAN takeover in 1170. In NORSE speech the place was called Dyflinn and its territory Dyflinnarskíri ('Dublinshire'). The Scandinavian cultural dimension is well represented by finds of ships' timbers, wood carvings, and runic inscriptions. Physically the eleventh century saw significant expansion westwards from the eastern core, and the enlarged settlement appears to have been enclosed by a stone wall by c. 1100. English influences are indicated by finds of Anglo-Saxon coins and by the establishment of a mint, Ireland's first, c. 997. A generation later CHRIST CHURCH CATHEDRAL was founded, the early bishops being subject to the authority of the Archbishop of Canterbury. By the twelfth century there were over a dozen parish churches inside and outside the walls, serving an estimated population of 5,000. Continental influences, especially from northern France, are reflected in the material culture and in monasteries belonging to reformed orders, notably St Mary's Abbey. This was in the north of the Liffey suburb of Ostmanby, which had its own parish church dedicated to St Michan. Accordingly, by 1170 a thriving town had already come into being. **Howard Clarke**

Bailegangaire (1985), a play by THOMAS MURPHY, first directed by GARRY HYNES at the Druid Theatre, Galway, on 5 December 1985. In her last role, SIOBHÁN MCKENNA played Mommo, a version of Mother Ireland, telling an oft-told (but never completed) tale to her two granddaughters about a laughing competition that went horribly wrong in a town subsequently called Bailegangaire (from Irish *Baile gan Gáire*, 'place without laughter') (see p. 674). But the old woman is senile and foul-mouthed, and the play itself is set amid the chaos of 1984 Ireland, with one of the granddaughters facing an unwanted pregnancy. As the two stories intertwine, the younger women help Mommo bring the story to a redemptive conclusion, and Murphy disproves the criticism that he can write only male characters. **Anthony Roche**

Bailey, Lady Mary, née Westenra (1890–1960), aviator. Born in Co. Monaghan, the daughter of Baron 'Derry' Rossmore. She became a household name in 1928 when she flew solo from London to Cape Town and back in a tiny open-cabin DH Moth. Following her marathon flight, the International Aviation League awarded her a trophy as champion airwoman of the world, and in 1930 she was made a dame of the Order of the British Empire for her services to aviation. **Lindie Naughton**

Bairéad, Riocard (1740–1819), poet. Born and lived in the townland of Barrack on the Mullet Peninsula in Erris, Co. Mayo; in his middle years he moved to Carn, closer to Belmullet. He is said to have been imprisoned in 1798 in Castlebar for his involvement with the UNITED IRISHMEN. He was a hedge schoolmaster for much of his life and is also alleged to have run a SHEEBEEN. He is chiefly remembered for his drinking song 'Preab san Ól' and for 'Eoghan Cóir' ('Generous Eoghan'), an ironic encomium to a pitiless land agent of the Binghams. He is buried in the churchyard at Cross. **Nicholas J. A. Williams**

Bairéad, Tomás (1893–1973), journalist and short-story writer. Born in Moycullen, Co. Galway. He wrote for the *Irish Independent*, 1922–48. His short-story collections include *Cumhacht na Cinniúna* (1936), awarded a prize by the IRISH ACADEMY OF LETTERS, *An Geall a Briseadh* (1938), and *Ór na hAitinne* (1949). He also published *Gan Baisteadh* (1972), a collection of autobiographical essays. **Aisling Ní Dhonnchadha**

Baker, Henry Aaron (1753–1836), architect. Apprenticed to THOMAS IVORY, he worked with JAMES GANDON after Ivory's death, first as pupil, then as partner. When Gandon retired during the building of the KING'S INNS, the supervision of the project was handed over to Baker. On Ivory's death in 1786 Baker became Master of the DUBLIN SOCIETY's School of Architectural Drawing, a position he retained until his own death fifty years later. The laying out of Westmorland Street and D'Olier Street for the WIDE STREETS COMMISSIONERS in the latter years of the eighteenth century was his important contribution to the building of Dublin. **Patricia McCarthy**

balaclava, a close-fitting knitted hood, usually black, with apertures for the eyes and mouth, adopted as headgear by republican and loyalist paramilitaries in Northern Ireland since the 1970s. It originated in the garment worn by British soldiers at Balaklava in Ukraine during the bitter winter conditions of the Crimean War (1853–6). **Brian Lalor**

Balbriggan (*Baile Brigín*), Co. Dublin, a town 30 km (18 miles) north of Dublin; population (2002) 6,619. It is associated in legend with St PATRICK, who is said to have baptised his successor, St Beinneán, in the River Delvin. The expansion of the town in the eighteenth century owed much to the local landlords, the Hamilton family, who were responsible for the building of the harbour and for the introduction of weaving in 1780. The hosiery and underwear firm of Smyth and Company became a household name and remained the biggest employer in the area for 200 years, until its closure in 1980. The principal employer is Wavin (Ireland) Ltd, which manufactures plastic pipes. Balbriggan still has a working harbour; however, it is increasingly seen as a commuter town for both Dublin and Drogheda, particularly because of its position on the Dublin–Belfast railway line. It has one of the highest proportions of workers commuting by train in the country, at more than 12 per cent (1996). It is also on the main Dublin–Belfast road, and the narrowness of its streets caused serious congestion until the opening of a bypass in 1998. **Ruth McManus**

Bald, William (c. 1789–1857), civil engineer, surveyor, and cartographer. Born probably at Buntisland, Fife; educated locally and at Edinburgh. He worked at mapping in Scotland before moving to Ireland in 1807, where he took part in the trigonometrical survey of Co. Mayo and planned and supervised the construction of the Antrim Coast Road for the Board of Public Works. **Ronald Cox**

Balfe, Michael William (1808–1870), composer, violinist, and singer. Born in Dublin; he went to London in 1823 and was deputy leader of the Drury Lane orchestra. He made his stage debut as a baritone in Weber's *Der Freischütz* in Norwich. He composed opera, ballet, cantatas, songs (including sacred songs), and arrangements of MOORE'S *Irish Melodies*. He studied singing and counterpoint in Italy and composed his first ballet, *La Pérouse* (1828), for La Scala. The year 1835 saw his acceptance as a serious English composer with the opera *The Siege of Rochelle*. The simple ballad-like airs of his operas appealed to the English public. His most successful opera was *The Bohemian Girl* (1843). **Paul J. Kerr**

Balfour, Arthur James (1848–1930), Scottish politician. Born in East Lothian, Scotland. A Unionist Conservative MP from 1871 to 1922, he was CHIEF SECRETARY FOR IRELAND from 1887 to 1891, when his repression of LAND LEAGUE agitation earned him the nickname 'Bloody Balfour'. He oversaw the establishment of the CONGESTED DISTRICTS BOARD and other ameliorative measures. From 1902 until 1905 he served as British Prime Minister. He resigned the unionist leadership in 1911 and afterwards became an advocate of HOME RULE for Ireland with protection for Ulster. **Eunan O'Halpin**

Ball, Anne Elizabeth (1808–1872), botanist. Born in Cobh, Co. Cork; she lived in Dublin from 1837. She concentrated on *cryptogams* (non-flowering plants), including marine algae. Through their brother Robert, Anne and her sister MARY BALL came to know notable naturalists of the day, including WILLIAM HARVEY and William Thompson, who published their researches and new records. Harvey in particular assisted Anne and named his new species *Ballia callitricha* and *Cladophora balliana* after her. Records of hydroids and fungi she sent to Thompson were published in *Natural History of Ireland*, vol. 4 (1856). Her collections and illustrations are in the herbaria at UCC and the National BOTANIC GARDENS, Dublin. **Helena C. G. Chesney**

Ball, Sir Charles Bent (1851–1916), surgeon and naturalist. Born in Dublin, son of Robert Ball, the naturalist, and brother of Sir ROBERT BALL, the astronomer; educated at TCD. He was surgeon to several Dublin hospitals and Honorary Surgeon to the King in Ireland. An expert on diseases of the rectum and anus, he wrote several books that remained standard texts for many years. He also served as a Commissioner for education. An amateur naturalist, he participated in marine dredging expeditions in the 1880s off southern and western Ireland, the results of which were published by others. He was knighted in 1902 and created a baronet in 1911. **Patrick N. Wyse Jackson**

Ball, Frances (Teresa) (1794–1861), religious founder. Born in Dublin. She entered the Bar Convent in York, 1814, and introduced the Institute of the Blessed Virgin Mary in Ireland, 1821. She founded ten convents in Ireland and sent sisters to India, Gibraltar, Mauritius, Canada, England, and Spain. **Séamus Enright**

Ball, John (1818–1889), alpinist and politician. Born in Dublin; he entered the University of Cambridge in 1835 and completed his studies with distinction but, as a Roman Catholic, was prevented from taking a degree. After Cambridge he travelled in Europe, studying BOTANY and Alpine glaciology. He was called to the bar in 1845 and appointed a POOR LAW COMMISSIONER in 1846; his work in famine relief led to serious illness. From 1852 to 1858 he was MP for Carlow, taking a progressive liberal stand. On retiring from public life he devoted himself to science and was elected a member of the ROYAL IRISH ACADEMY and a fellow of the Royal Society. He was the first president of the Alpine Club and wrote a three-volume book, *The Alpine Guide* (1870). **Christopher Moriarty**

Ball, Margaret, née Bermingham (c. 1515–c. 1584), recusant. Born at Skreen, Co. Meath. In 1530 she married a wealthy Dublin merchant, Alderman Bartholomew Ball (died 1568), who served as Mayor of Dublin, 1553–4. Margaret refused to conform to Protestantism. She taught Catholic youths in her home, which also served as a refuge for bishops and priests. In the late 1570s she was arrested during a Mass at her home and was briefly imprisoned. Her son, Walter, a staunch Protestant, was Mayor of Dublin in 1580 when James FitzEustace staged the BALTINGLASS REBELLION. Fearing a Catholic conspiracy in the Pale, Walter had his mother, among other recusants, arrested. Unable to walk, she was drawn through the streets on a wooden hurdle to Dublin Castle, where, 'worn out by the filth of the prison, by her sufferings and by her infirmities,' she died c. 1584. She was beatified by Pope John Paul II in 1992. **Mary Ann Lyons**

Ball, Mary (1812–1898), naturalist. Born in Cobh, Co. Cork. She collected insects, shells, and marine invertebrates. Assembling information on insect behaviour, she was the first to identify the phenomenon of *stridulation* (in corixid water bugs); this finding was published by her brother Robert, 1845–6. Like her sister ANNE BALL, she met leading naturalists such as William Thompson, who included Mary's invertebrate collection among thirty important Irish collections in 1834 and named the mollusc *Rissoa balliae* after her. Michel-Edmond de Selys Longchamps, the European authority on dragonflies, visited her collection and published many of her observations and records in 1846. Portions of her collections survive in the NATIONAL MUSEUM, Dublin. **Helena C. G. Chesney**

Ball, Sir Robert Stawell (1840–1913), astronomer. Born in Dublin; educated at TCD. In 1865 he was appointed assistant astronomer to the Earl of ROSSE and tutor to his three younger sons; in 1867 he became professor of applied mechanics at the ROYAL COLLEGE OF SCIENCE, Dublin. His mathematical work on the dynamics of rigid bodies (theory of screws) earned him fellowship of the Royal Society, 1873, and the Cunningham Medal of the ROYAL IRISH ACADEMY, 1879. As director of DUNSINK OBSERVATORY from 1874 he continued the parallax investigations undertaken

Ball, Robert Stawell. *Sir Robert Stawell Ball and the Meridian Circle at the University of Cambridge, where Ball was Lowndean professor of astronomy from 1892 until his death in 1913. [Private collection]*

by his predecessors. He was an accomplished lecturer and author of a text on spherical astronomy and many popular books on astronomy. In 1892 he moved to Cambridge as Lowndean professor of astronomy. He was also president of the Royal Astronomical Society, 1897–9. **Ian Elliott**

Ball, Valentine (1843–1895), geologist. Born in Dublin; studied at TCD. The second son of the naturalist Robert Ball (1802–57), he joined the staff of the Geological Survey of India in 1864. There economic geology became his chief concern, but he was fascinated by all aspects of natural history. In 1881 he returned home to assume the chair of geology and mineralogy at Trinity College, Dublin. His ambition had long been to head a great museum, and in 1883 he resigned his chair to become director of the Dublin Science and Art Museum. **Jean Archer**

ballad-sheets and broadsides. Though the term 'ballad' suggests narrative song, in fact these printed sheets contained every type of song and prose. (They were called *broadsheets* or *broadsides* because their text appeared on one side of the sheet only.) Cambridge University Library houses a unique broadsheet of a poem by PILIB BOCHT Ó HUIGINN, 'Tuar Ferge Foighide', printed in 1571 in an elegant Irish typeface. Later broadsheets in Irish were generally miserable productions in barely intelligible phonetic transcription. Broadsheets in English were far more common; 'Mount Taragh's Triumph' (1626), a Dublin broadsheet in praise of CHARLES I, seems to be the oldest surviving example. Some broadsheets sold by the hundred thousand, with DUBLIN CASTLE keeping a watchful eye on balladmongers suspected of peddling seditious songs. Broadsheets were the romantic novels and the tabloid press of their day, love and murder being among the most popular themes (see p. 527). Many traditional songs found their way onto broadsheets, while a considerable number of songs made first for the broadsheet industry were absorbed into the oral tradition. The most prolific broadsheet presses included those of Nugent and Brereton of Dublin, Haly of Cork, and Nicholson of Belfast. Broadsheet-sellers were still to be seen on Dublin streets up to the early 1960s. **Tom Munnelly**

Ballagh, Robert (1943–), artist. Born in Dublin; trained as an architectural draughtsman. Ballagh has had a varied career as showband musician, theatre set designer, and painter. Apart from his photo-realist portraits, some of them autobiographical, others of cultural and political personalities, he has produced stamp and banknote designs. In 1969 he began a series of paintings that, while paying homage to the appropriations of Roy Lichtenstein and the interiors of Patrick Caulfield, draw their iconography from nineteenth-century history paintings. *The Rape of the Sabines*, based on Jacques-Louis David's painting, is in the Crawford Gallery, Cork. He also designed sets for RIVERDANCE. **Peter Murray**

Ballance, John (1839–1893), New Zealand politician. Born in Glenavy, Co. Antrim, a farmer's son; educated at Glenavy National School. He was apprenticed to a Belfast ironmonger before emigrating to England, thence to Australia, and in 1865 to New Zealand. He worked as a journalist, in time founded the *Wanganui Herald*, and played a pivotal role in the Maori Wars, helping to raise and command a cavalry regiment. He entered politics in 1873 and served in the Grey government of 1878, first as Commissioner of Customs and Minister of Education. When leader of the Liberal Party he took power as Prime Minister in 1890. He died in Wellington while in office. **David Kiely**

ballet. In 1927 W. B. YEATS invited NINETTE DE VALOIS to establish a ballet school at the ABBEY THEATRE, Dublin. In 1934 this closed for lack of funds, but one student, Jill Gregory, became a soloist with Sadler's Wells Ballet, London, and two others, Cepta Cullen and Muriel Kelly, founded their own ballet schools in Dublin. At the same time JOHN REGAN was establishing himself overseas as a dancer, choreographer, and dance director.

It was not until the 1950s that professional ballet companies were established in Ireland. These were Patricia Mulholland's Irish Ballet Company in Belfast, JOAN DENISE MORIARTY's Irish Theatre Ballet in Cork, and Patricia Ryan's National Ballet in Dublin. Ryan was a pupil of Nadine Nicolaeva Legat, widow of Nijinsky's teacher, and her company, founded in 1957, performed in the GAIETY, OLYMPIA, and QUEEN'S THEATRES, using principal dancers from the Royal Ballet in London, the Paris Opera, and the Russian State Ballet of Sverdlovsk. They performed the classics and original work by Ryan, set to the music of Irish composers, such as A. J. POTTER, notably *Careless Love*. Principal dancers with National Ballet were Geraldine Morris (who subsequently danced with the Royal Ballet in London), Joan Wilson (who went on to dance with London Ballet), and Deirdre O'Donoghue (who trained at the Royal Ballet and later became a soloist with Scottish Ballet and the Stuttgart Ballet; because of injury she gave up dancing, becoming ballet mistress to Nederlands Dans Theater and Deutsche Oper, Berlin, and for Rudolf Nureyev). Another principal was Ester Ó Brolcháin, who became assistant artistic director of the College of Dance in 2000.

Patricia Mulholland's company was regularly subsidised by the ARTS COUNCIL OF NORTHERN IRELAND, which enabled it to tour throughout Europe, introducing audiences to her tales from Irish mythology in a unique blend of ballet and traditional dance. In this she was a forerunner of SIAMSA TÍRE, though the latter combined traditional dance with contemporary dance, rather than ballet. At home, Mulholland's company, led by Norman Maen, performed in the Empire Theatre and the Belfast GRAND OPERA HOUSE. She was outraged when, in 1973, Moriarty took the name Irish Ballet Company for her Cork company; but lack of co-operation between the two jurisdictions ensured that nothing was done to prevent the duplication. Moriarty's first professional company, Irish Theatre Ballet, had as its principal the Israeli dancer Domy Reiter-Soffer, later to become chief choreographer for Irish National Ballet with such works as *Yerma* (1977), *Chariots of Fire* (1978), *Medea* (1981), and *Lady of the Camelias* (1984).

In 1963 the ARTS COUNCIL, unable to continue its sporadic subvention of both companies, insisted on Irish Theatre Ballet amalgamating with Ryan's National Ballet; but the joint venture soon failed. Not until 1973 was Moriarty able to found her Irish Ballet Company, later renamed Irish National Ballet. Its ballet master was the former Royal Ballet dancer David Gordon of Belfast; choreographers included Peter Darrell, ANTON DOLIN, Royston Maldoon, Michael Corder, Nils Christies, Charles Czarny, and Michel de Lutry, while Patrick Murray was the designer and, in 1988, artistic director. Irish principals included Anna Donovan, Patricia Crosby, Carol Bryans, and Seán Cunningham, formerly (as John Cunningham) with Western Theatre Ballet and the Gulbenkian Ballet. In 1989, having had its subsidy withdrawn, the company gave its final performance with Reiter-Soffer's *Oscar*.

In 1984 two former principals, Roy Galvin and Joanna Banks, had formed Pas de Deux Company to perform classical highlights and works by John Regan in Dublin venues such as the NATIONAL GALLERY and NATIONAL CONCERT HALL. In 1979 the antique dealer and ballet enthusiast Louis O'Sullivan founded Dublin City Ballet, originally named Oscar Theatre Ballet. Anton Dolin reproduced *Giselle* for the company in the Olympia Theatre for the 1980 Dublin Theatre Festival, and Paula Hinton-Gore reproduced *Les Sylphides* at the GATE THEATRE in 1982; but in May 1985 Peter Brinson, in his report for the Arts Council, *The Dancer and the Dance*, recommended withdrawing funding, and the company closed in 1986. Its ballet master and principal dancer, the Mexican Babil Gandara, immediately formed Irish Theatre Ballet. He had been a principal with Irish National Ballet before joining Dublin City Ballet in 1981, when he also taught at the Irish National College of Dance in Blackrock, Co. Dublin. His company provided ballets for the DUBLIN GRAND OPERA SOCIETY seasons at the Gaiety Theatre and produced small pieces, mostly by Gandara, as well as one by John Scott; but without Arts Council subsidies the company ceased operations in 1988.

It was ten years before another ballet company appeared. Starting on a shoestring, Ballet Ireland was founded by Anne Maher and her Austrian husband Günther Falusy. She had trained with the Irish Ballet Company before dancing with Dublin City Ballet, then won a scholarship to the Académie de Danse Classique de Monte Carlo and went on to dance with British Ballet Theatre and Wiener Ballet Theater, directed by Falusy, where she became a principal in 1987. For three years Ballet Ireland was confined to highlights from the classics and small works, as lack of funds kept casts small. In 2001, however, the company finally obtained long-term funding from the Arts Council. [see DANCE, CONTEMPORARY.] **Carolyn Swift**

Ballina (*Béal an Átha*), Co. Mayo, a town on the River Moy at the head of Killala Bay, the largest town of Co. Mayo; population (2002) 6,918. It is a rail terminus with a district hospital and the site of the cathedral of the Catholic diocese of Killala (dedicated to St Muireadhach). There are ruins of an Augustinian friary (1427) at Ardnaree. The town was founded in 1729 by O'Hara, Lord Tyrawley, and improvements took place in the late eighteenth and early nineteenth centuries. There is an important salmon fishery there, and several small and medium-sized industries. **Mary E. Cawley**

Ballinakill Céilí Band (1926–43). In 1926 the Ballinakill Traditional Dance Players were assembled by a local priest, Father Larkin, to provide music for dancing in a school in Ballinakill, near Loughrea, Co. Galway. The original members were Tommy Whyte and Jerry Moloney (fiddle), Stephen Moloney and Tommy Whelan (flute), and Anna Rafferty (piano). They were the first céilí band to broadcast on 2RN after SÉAMUS CLANDILLON heard them playing at a feis in Athlone in 1928. They recorded nine 78s and toured Ireland, England, and America. Their recordings include *St Patrick's Night in Dublin* and *Leprechauns*. **Verena Commins**

Ballinamore and Ballyconnell Canal, a 62 km (39-mile) waterway linking the River SHANNON at the village of Leitrim with the River Erne north of Belturbet, constructed between 1847 and the late 1850s. A combined drainage and navigation scheme, it was successful in flood prevention but a failure as a commercial waterway: only eight boats passed through it during its short working life. A combination of canalised river, open loughs, and canal proper, it suffered from the beginning from structural defects—including banks caving in and leaks through the stonework of locks—and in 1869 was abandoned. It was reopened to leisure traffic on 26 May 1994 and renamed the Shannon–Erne Waterway following a four-year, €30 million restoration that also involved the rebuilding of thirty-four bridges and sixteen locks, now electronically controlled. The reopening has materially enhanced the economy of a previously disadvantaged area. **Bernard Share**

Ballinasloe (*Béal Átha na Sluaighe*), Co. Galway, a town on the River Suck, near the Co. Roscommon border, the second-largest town in Co. Galway; population (2002) 5,977. The main Dublin–Galway rail and road routes pass through the town. There are two hospitals—St Brigid's Psychiatric Hospital (1838) and Portiuncula—and a limited industrial presence. A long-established horse fair is held annually in October. There are remains of a medieval church at the east end of Church Street and the ruins of the residence of the sixteenth-century English governor of Connacht, Sir Anthony Brabazon, near the River Suck. Ballinasloe was developed primarily in the eighteenth century by the Trench family, Earls of Clancarty, whose residence was Garbally (now St Joseph's College) on the west side of the town. The Catholic parish church of St Michael (1852–8) by J. J. McCarthy (to a design revised by PUGIN) contains works by several well-known early twentieth-century stained-glass artists and sculptors (Joseph Tierney, HARRY CLARKE, Patrick Pollen, ALBERT POWER, and MIA CRANWILL) and vestments, banners, and carpets by the DUN EMER GUILD, designed by JACK B. YEATS. **Mary E. Cawley**

Ballinasloe Fair, a fair with its origins in the early Middle Ages. A charter was granted by George I to the Earl of Clancarty in 1722, and the fair grew to become the largest in Europe. During

Ballinasloe. *Ballinasloe Fair, one of Europe's oldest horse fairs, takes place during the first week of October. In the eighteenth and nineteenth centuries it was the best-known horse fair in Europe, but it declined after the First World War, when cavalry was no longer widely used. [Imagefile]*

the eighteenth century its stock largely consisted of longhorn cattle, but by the early nineteenth century it had evolved into a horse fair. Buyers came from central Europe and Russia to purchase mounts for their armies; NAPOLEON Bonaparte's horse Marengo, on which he rode at the Battle of Waterloo, was bought there. The fair takes place during the first week of October, but since the early twentieth century its primary role—the buying and selling of horses—has dwindled. **Verena Commins**

Ballincollig (*Baile an Chollaigh*), Co. Cork, a satellite town 10 km (6 miles) west of Cork; population (2002) 15,131. In 1794 a gunpowder mill was established by two businessmen near the River LEE, using a weir for power and transport. The raw materials were imported—saltpetre from India and sulphur from Sicily—with charcoal available locally. The enterprise was so successful that it was taken over by the Board of Ordnance in 1805 and expanded to meet increased demands for the Napoleonic wars. It was withdrawn from use in 1815 and returned to private ownership in 1833. It continued to produce gunpowder throughout the nineteenth century, though it became increasingly uncompetitive because of the development of chemical explosives, such as dynamite. It closed in 1903 but is commemorated today in a heritage centre. Ballincollig was also the site of a large artillery barracks (1814), built as security for the gunpowder mills; it was used continuously by the British and Irish armies until 1998 and was the mainstay of the town until the 1960s.

In 1966 Ballincollig's population was 1,000, but in 1967 it was designated by Cork County Council a 'satellite town' for Cork and has since expanded rapidly through the building of many housing estates. Though at first seen by many as only a temporary place of residence, Ballincollig has become a more stable and independent town in recent years. [see CORK GUNPOWDER EXPLOSION.] **Kevin Hourihan**

Ballintober Abbey, Co. Mayo, founded in 1216 for the Augustinian Canons by CATHAL CROBHDHEARG Ó CONCHOBHAIR; the east end of the building was complete by 1225. Detailing on the three east windows links it to a number of other ABBEYS in the west. The nave was rebuilt after a fire in 1265 and is crude by comparison. Further additions, including the cloister and west door, were made in the fifteenth century. Following the Dissolution, the church continued to be used for worship. Restoration was begun in 1846 and again in 1889 but only fully completed in 1963. The abbey now serves as a Catholic parish church. **Rachel Moss**

ballooning. On 4 February 1784, a year after the first successful balloon flight by the Montgolfier brothers in France, an unmanned balloon was successfully flown from the Rotunda Gardens, Dublin, by a Mr Riddick. The following 27 April, *Faulkner's Dublin Journal* recorded: 'Navan—Last Thursday (15th) the long expected Air Balloon was liberated in this town.' The crew were a Mr Rosseau and a ten-year-old drummer-boy.

Ireland's first native aeronaut was Richard Crosbie (born in Co. Wicklow in 1755). His boat-shaped 'aeronautic chariot' was exhibited in Dublin in 1784, and he also experimented with hydrogen-filled balloons, one of which, with a cat as crew, ditched close to the Isle of Man. In January 1785 he attempted a crossing of the IRISH SEA, taking off in his 'grand air balloon and flying barge' from Ranelagh, Dublin, watched by a crowd of 35,000. With night falling, however, he decided to come down to earth in Clontarf, north of the city. He made further attempts the same year, but weight problems caused him to substitute a volunteer, Richard McGwire, a twenty-one-year-old student, who was drifting dangerously out to sea before he succeeded in puncturing the envelope (the release valve having jammed) and landing in the water off Howth, from where he was rescued.

It was not until 1 October 1810 that the British balloonist James Sadleir came close to achieving the crossing, ditching in the sea off Anglesey. His son Windham Sadleir was to succeed in July 1817, taking off from Dublin and landing at Holyhead six hours later. In July 1864 the *Britannia*—at 30.5 m diameter claimed to be the largest balloon in the world—made a successful ascent from the Botanic Gardens, Belfast.

Flights continued until the advent of the aeroplane, c. 1910, relegated the balloon to the realm of leisure activities by such bodies as the Dublin Ballooning Club (1968), a member of the Balloon and Airship Association of Ireland. **Bernard Share**

Ballymena (*An Baile Meánach*), Co. Antrim, an industrial and market town on the River Braid; population (1991) 28,112. A medieval settlement is indicated by a motte and bailey in the suburb of Harryville. The modern town was founded c. 1610 by a Scots planter, William Adair, and became closely associated with the rise of the linen industry. An important LINEN market from the 1730s, Ballymena was nevertheless described in 1846 as 'an antiquated and irregular town undergoing transmutation to modern neatness and order.' Ballymena participated fully in the shift to factory-based linen production in the middle of the nineteenth century, aided by the completion of the Belfast rail link in 1860. The town's growing prosperity was reflected in the construction of various architecturally significant public buildings, including the courthouse (1846), Anglican parish church (1855, 1882), and Catholic church (1860).

Ballymena was designated a growth centre by the Mathew Report (1963), and this encouraged residential and industrial development and infrastructural improvement. In recent years it has maintained its reputation for prosperity, and large retail centres have been completed on the outskirts and at the Fair Hill. **Lindsay Proudfoot**

Ballymote, Book of, one of a number of great Irish MANUSCRIPTS from late medieval Connacht (others being the Books of Uí Maine and of Lecan, the Yellow Book of Lecan, and the Leabhar Breac). This collection of genealogical and quasi-historical literature is the work of three scribes—Magnus Ó Duibhgennáin, Solamh Ó Droma, and Robeartus Mac Síthigh—who produced it c. 1390, partly at the seat of the Mac Donnchaidh lords of Corran and Tirerrill in Ballymote, Co. Sligo, and partly in the house of Domhnall Mac Aedhagáin in Ormond (Co. Tipperary). In 1522 it passed from Mac Donnchaidh ownership to that of Ó Domhnaill of Tír Chonaill; it was acquired by ARCHBISHOP JAMES USSHER in the seventeenth century, was later in TRINITY COLLEGE Library, and in 1785 was presented to the ROYAL IRISH ACADEMY (see p. 818). **Nollaig Ó Muraíle**

Ballynahatty and the Giant's Ring, Co. Down, a Late NEOLITHIC ceremonial complex in the Lagan Valley. The PASSAGE TOMB tradition is represented by at least six cists and a grave. The grave has been used as a nodal point around which to construct one of the best-preserved HENGE monuments, the Giant's Ring, approximately 200 m (650 ft) in diameter. Excavation has linked this to an oval timber enclosure, 100 by 70 m (330 by 230 ft), with grooved ware associations 100 m (330 ft) to the north. An elaborately designed entrance with a façade of massive timbers led through a square structure to an inner enclosure surrounding a probable excarnation platform. The whole structure was ritually burnt. **Barrie Hartwell**

Ballynahinch, Battle of (12–13 June 1798), at Ballynahinch, Co. Down, a decisive conflict in the United Irish REBELLION OF 1798. The mainly Presbyterian rebel force, variously estimated at 5,000–7,000, were led by HENRY MUNRO, while the royal army of approximately 1,500, comprising Irish militia and yeomanry, Scots fencibles, and regular artillery and dragoons, were commanded by General George Nugent. Deficient in firepower, having relatively few musketeers, and only several small ship cannon crudely mounted on farm carts as makeshift gun-carriages, Munro relied on massed pike-men; Nugent, in contrast, had proper field-guns and howitzers. The action began with inconclusive skirmishing and cannonading on the evening of the twelfth, during which many of Munro's men deserted, alarmed by the cannon fire.

Ignoring advice to attack during darkness, Munro began the main battle at dawn on the thirteenth. After several hours of severe fighting in the streets of the town (the cannon-fire was heard in Belfast, 25 km/15 miles away), during which Munro's men fought stoutly, the rebels gave way and were pursued by Nugent's cavalry. More died attempting to escape than in the battle, including BETSY GRAY. The total rebel casualties were about 500, while Nugent's loss was minimal. Munro went into hiding but was betrayed and later hanged and decapitated before his own door in Lisburn. The defeat marked the end of the Ulster rising; the horrendous aftermath gave rise to the popular saying among Co. Down farmers that they would never again be prevailed upon to 'catch cannon balls on the points of pikes and pitchforks.' **Allan Blackstock**

Ballyshannon (*Béal Átha Seanaidh*), Co. Donegal, a town on the north bank of the River Erne at a historically important crossing-site at the head of the estuary; population (2002) 2,273. The crossing was controlled for much of the sixteenth century by the O'Donnells, who had built a castle here. In 1608 the surrounding lands were granted to Sir Henry Folliot, a planter. The site was included in both lists of proposed PLANTATION towns in 1609 and 1611, and the town was finally incorporated in 1613, receiving a second borough charter in 1622. Despite the navigational difficulties of the Erne, the town flourished during the eighteenth and nineteenth centuries as a port (rebuilt in 1834) and market centre for a large and fertile hinterland but suffered from the loss of much of this at partition.

The ESB constructed one of Ireland's few hydro-electric power stations above the town. More recently Ballyshannon has benefited from the growth of TOURISM. Despite recent redevelopment, especially in the Purt, the suburb south of the river, the town retains a late nineteenth-century commercial flavour and remains one of the most architecturally rewarding towns in Co. Donegal. **Lindsay Proudfoot**

Baltinglass Abbey, Co. Wicklow, a CISTERCIAN abbey founded by DERMOT MACMURROUGH, King of Leinster, in 1148 and colonised by monks from MELLIFONT. Standing remains include the church, with typical eastern transept chapels and aisled nave, and some fragments of the early fourteenth-century cloister arcade. Twelfth-century ornamental details on the west window and north cloister door reflect native taste and contravene the austere principles of Cistercian architecture. The presbytery, crossing and eastern part of the nave were walled off to serve as a parish church, to which the existing tower was added in 1815. **Rachel Moss**

Ballynahinch. Battle of Ballynahinch, *1798, by Thomas Robinson. The defeat of the United Irishmen at the Battle of Ballynahinch marked the end of the 1798 Rebellion in Ulster. The battle has been lost by the rebels, and (from right) the English commander, General Nugent, greets dragoons carrying the captured rebel liberty standard. Captain Evatt (centre) of the Monaghan Militia is mortally wounded, while (left) Hugh McColloch, a rebel colonel, is about to be hanged. [By permission of the Office of Public Works]*

Baltinglass Rebellion. James Eustace, third Viscount Baltinglass (died 1585), having recently returned from Rome, displayed the Papal banner in June 1580 and announced a crusade for his 'faith and fatherland,' in sympathy with that initiated by JAMES FITZMAURICE FITZGERALD in 1579. He was joined by FIACH MAC HUGH O'BYRNE of Co. Wicklow. Eustace canvassed in vain for support among the leading families of the Pale, although, significantly, they did not expose his conspiracy. Crown officials were greatly surprised by the revolt. Lord Deputy Grey's army was routed by O'Byrne at GLENMALUR, Co. Wicklow, in August 1580, prompting Irish lords in the north and west to rebel also. On 10 September 1580, 600 Italian and Spanish soldiers landed at SMERWICK, Co. Kerry, to support the crusade led by the Fitzgeralds, but they were overwhelmed by a larger English army.

The Baltinglass Rebellion petered out ignominiously, but it was notable for the harsh response of the government to it. It is now regarded as important in prefiguring a militant Catholic NATIONALISM that embraced members of the Old English community in the Pale as well as the native Irish community. **Henry A. Jefferies**

Bambrick, Joe (1905–1983), soccer player. Born in Belfast. He was a prolific goal-scorer whose ability in the penalty area was such that the catchphrase 'Slip it to Joe' was part of the football vocabulary in Northern Ireland for the greater part of twenty years. Revered in the folklore of Linfield, he is reputed to have scored more than a thousand goals in a career that took in a period with Chelsea. His six goals in Northern Ireland's 7–0 win over Wales in 1930 still survive as a record in international football. In just eleven games for Northern Ireland he grew to legendary status. **Peter Byrne**

Banfield, Gottfried von (1890–1986), naval officer and aviator. Born in Austria, the son of a distinguished Austrian naval captain originally from Castlelyons, Co. Cork; studied at the Austrian naval college at Rijeka under its head, John O'Flanagan. After service in two battleships he became convinced that aircraft were going to participate decisively in future naval warfare, and he became one of the first pilots of Austria's pioneer naval air force. During the FIRST WORLD WAR he was a spectacular success in action against Italian, British, and French ships and aircraft in the Adriatic; having been awarded every distinction of the Austrian armed forces, he was presented with a special new one by Emperor Franz Josef. The people of Trieste gave him a huge silver wreath for his remarkable success in protecting the city from Italian air raids. After the war he studied shipbuilding and inherited through his marriage the largest ship-repairing firm in the Mediterranean. Having become a pacifist as a result of his war experiences, he refused to repair warships for Mussolini. In the late 1960s he visited Ireland as a guest of the MILITARY HISTORY SOCIETY. **John de Courcy Ireland**

Bangor (*Beannchar*), Co. Down, the fourth-largest town in Northern Ireland, now a dormitory suburb of Belfast as well as a day-trippers' seaside resort; population (1991) 52,437. The town's origins are ecclesiastical and lie in St Comhghall's foundation of Bangor Abbey c. 555. For 300 years Bangor was one of the most important Christian sites in Western Europe, but it gradually declined as a result of the combined effects of VIKING raids and local dynastic rivalry. During the Middle Ages it was little more than a village, but its fortunes revived when it was granted borough status in 1612, and a local planter, Sir James Hamilton, made it his seat, investing heavily in the new town. Two important buildings survive from this time: the parish church, rebuilt in 1617 from the remains of the medieval abbey, and the Customs House. The eighteenth and early nineteenth centuries witnessed little further growth until the railway link with Belfast was completed; the population doubled, from 3,000 to 6,000, in the twenty years after 1881.

The town's late Victorian architectural character was established at this time and provides an elegant background for the yacht marina. Much of the town's residential growth has taken place since the 1960s, and the historical core is now surrounded by extensive commuter housing estates and light industry, connected by an arterial ring road system to Belfast. **Lindsay Proudfoot**

Bangor Abbey, Co. Down, founded in the middle of the sixth century by Comhghall (friend of COLM CILLE and teacher of COLUMBANUS). For several centuries it was an important monastery and centre of learning. It had disappeared by the tenth century, having suffered from VIKING raids; MALACHY restored it in the twelfth century and settled it with Augustinian Canons. **Thomas O'Loughlin**

Bangor, Antiphonary of (c. 690), a manuscript of thirty-six leaves, containing 129 Latin prayer-formulas, mostly composed in the sixth and seventh centuries to supplement the Psalter in the liturgical prayer of the monastic community. It illustrates wonderfully the creative encounter between the Latin culture of the Western churches and the native literary tradition of Ireland, issuing in the monasteries in new Latin hymns and prayers, especially in verse. Some of the verse, composed in classical metres or in structural imitations of them (such as *Sancti venite*), is of a high standard. The style of Irish lyrical poetry is here reflected in a hymn of classical form (*Hymnum dicat turba fratrum*), while the native tradition of rhythmic verse gave rise to a new kind of Latin verse (such as *Sacratissimi martyres*). There is abundant evidence of contact with Spain and northern Italy as the source of some of the liturgical prose texts. The hours of prayer at Bangor all have their counterparts in the great tradition of liturgical prayer that had developed in the Western monastic and cathedral churches; many interesting adaptations of that tradition to Irish spiritual needs and creative impulses can be noted. **Michael Curran**

Banim, John (1798–1842), writer. Born in Kilkenny; educated at St John's College and the Dublin Society Drawing Schools. He became a drawing master at St John's College but turned to writing after an unhappy love affair with a pupil. After fluctuating success in poetry, drama, and journalism, he married and moved to London; he eventually returned, poor and unwell, to Kilkenny, where he died. His fame rests principally on his historical novel *The Boyne Water* (1826) and *Tales by the O'Hara Family* (1825, 1826). The *Tales*, written in collaboration with his brother, MICHAEL BANIM, alternate between sensationalising and vindicating the characteristics of the rural farming and labouring classes. **Richard Haslam**

Banim, Michael (1796–1874), writer. Born in Kilkenny. He abandoned the prospect of a legal career to help in his father's shop. After the family business collapsed he became postmaster of Kilkenny, later retiring to Booterstown, Co. Dublin, where he died. He collaborated with his brother, JOHN BANIM, on *Tales by the O'Hara Family* (1825, 1826), contributing the vivid and energetic 'Crohoore of the Bill-Hook' and the less accomplished 'Peter of the Castle'. His solo novels include the historical piece *The Croppy* (1828) and the melodramatic *The Ghost Hunter and His Family* (1833). In 1865 he edited and introduced a collected edition of the brothers' works. **Richard Haslam**

banjo, a plucked or picked fretted lute in which the sound is amplified by the tensioning of the strings over a bridge seated on a fine skin diaphragm stretched over a circular frame. The instrument's early origins are obscure, but the fact that its precursors came from Africa to America in slavery, probably by way of the West Indies, is by now well established. Until c. 1800 the banjo remained essentially an African-American instrument, though at times there was considerable interaction between blacks and whites in pre-Civil War America. The five-string version was carried to Ireland by minstrel groups in the middle of the nineteenth century and was played widely by TRAVELLERS.

In the early twentieth century the four-string tenor banjo was adopted by such musicians as Mike Flanagan and Neil Nolan in Irish-American dance halls. It remained very much a marginal instrument in Ireland until Barney McKenna of the DUBLINERS played it in the early 1960s. The tuning he used was an octave below the fiddle, making the fingering very appropriate for most of the traditional tunes. At that time there were barely a dozen traditional Irish musicians playing the tenor banjo; its popularity has grown to the point where there are now more than 5,000 players.
Mick Moloney

banking. The Bank of Ireland is the oldest Irish bank, founded by act of Parliament in 1783. Under this act no other bank with more than six shareholders or partners could issue its own notes, and this right to issue notes was then the essential characteristic of a bank. Consequently, the Bank of Ireland enjoyed a virtual monopoly, the only competition being provided by the small private banks with fewer than six shareholders. Most of these were forced out of business after the banking crisis of 1820, with the result that the Bank of Ireland's dominance became even stronger.

However, its monopoly position began to come under serious challenge. In Belfast the Northern Bank was founded in 1825, the Belfast Banking Company in 1827, and the Ulster Bank in 1836. In the south the Hibernian Bank and Provincial Bank of Ireland were founded in 1825, the latter having its head office in London. The Hibernian Bank was formed by Catholic businessmen who felt excluded from banking because of the political and religious preferences of the Bank of Ireland. In 1834 DANIEL O'CONNELL established the National Bank, also with its head office in London. The Royal Bank of Ireland was then formed in 1836. In Cork the Munster Bank opened in 1864, but it was forced out of business in 1885. However, it re-emerged the same year as the Munster and Leinster Bank, with its head office in Cork.

In the second half of the nineteenth century the restrictions on banking and the inability to issue notes were gradually dismantled, and the result was the emergence of a widespread branch banking system.

Alongside these developments of banking, a range of other types of financial institution emerged during the nineteenth century. The Post Office Savings Bank was established in 1861, with a wide network of branches throughout the country. A number of savings banks also emerged. The Cork Savings Bank was established in 1817 and the Dublin Savings Bank a year later.

Four building societies were formed between 1861 and 1883, to provide finance for the purchase of private dwellings; but it was

banking. *Head office of the Allied Irish Bank group in Ballsbridge, Dublin (1979), by Robinson Keefe Devane, with Alexandra Wejchert's 12 m high stainless-steel sculpture* Freedom *(1985). [Mark Joyce]* not until the 1960s that the building societies began to provide meaningful competition to the banks. In 1861 the Workingman's Benefit Building Society was formed; it became the First National Building Society in 1961. The Irish Civil Service Building Society was formed in 1864, followed nine years later by the Irish Industrial Benefit Building Society, now the Irish Nationwide. In 1884 the forerunner of the Irish Permanent Building Society, the Irish Temperance Permanent Benefit Building Society, was formed. Finally, the Educational Building Society (now the EBS Building Society) was founded in 1935. In Northern Ireland the major British building societies have a strong presence, while there are just two local building societies. The Progressive is the result of a merger of five Belfast building societies in 1914, while the Londonderry Provident operates in Derry.

The nine banks that existed in Ireland at the end of the nineteenth century were reduced to four over the following eighty years. The Midland Bank in Britain took over the Belfast Bank in 1917; in 1923 it sold its branches in the Free State to the Royal Bank. In 1965 the Midland Bank bought the Northern Bank; it retained its branches in the South and in 1970 merged with the Belfast Bank, at which time the Belfast Bank ceased to operate. The Bank of Ireland acquired the Hibernian Bank in 1958 and the National Bank in 1966. The same year the three remaining independent clearing banks—the Munster and Leinster, the Provincial, and the Royal—amalgamated to form Allied Irish Banks, thereby creating a bank that was comparable in size to the Bank of Ireland. Ulster Bank had been taken over by National Westminster Bank in 1917. The four groups that finally emerged were Bank of Ireland, Allied Irish Banks, Northern Bank, and Ulster Bank, with British parent companies owning the last two.

During the period in which this rationalisation was going on the Government of the Irish Free State/Republic set up a number of state-owned banks. The Agricultural Credit Corporation (now ACC Bank) was set up in 1927 to facilitate the development of agriculture, regarded as an important strategic industry at that time, while the Industrial Credit Corporation (now ICC Bank) was set up in 1933 with the purpose of helping to develop domestic industry.

The face of banking has changed dramatically since the 1960s. AIB and Bank of Ireland have grown dramatically and have significantly expanded their activities. Normal retail and commercial banking are still important elements of their activities, but they have diversified into many other areas, including stockbroking, mortgage lending, corporate finance, life assurance, and fund management. Bank of Ireland bought the ICS Building Society in 1985 to gain a share in the domestic mortgage market. AIB has operations in Britain, Poland, and the United States, while Bank of Ireland, having diversified into the United States for a relatively short period, is now concentrated in Ireland and Britain.

After acquiring the Northern Bank, Midland Bank managed the Northern and Belfast Banking Company under a joint holding company called United Northern Banks. However, the two were merged under the Northern title in 1970. In 1986 the Midland Bank decided to create a separate entity in the South, called Northern Bank (Ireland). In 1987 National Australia Bank acquired Northern Bank and Northern Bank (Ireland), changing the name of the latter to National Irish Bank in 1988. Ulster Bank is now owned by Royal Bank of Scotland.

Since the late 1960s there have been mergers among the various savings banks. Monaghan Savings Bank merged with Dublin Savings Bank in 1977, and Waterford Savings Bank merged with these in 1988. Limerick Savings Bank merged with the Cork Bank in 1986. The two resulting institutions, the Cork and Dublin savings banks, came together to form TSB Bank in 1992. This was subsequently sold to Irish Life and Permanent, itself the result of the merger of the Irish Permanent Building Society and Irish Life and is now known as Permanent TSB.

The building societies have also experienced significant change since the 1960s, faced with increased competition from the associated banks in the mortgage market. The Building Societies Act (1989) significantly broadened the range of services that building societies could offer, and allowed them to be converted into banks. The Irish Permanent was converted into a bank by 1994, and First Active (formerly First National) converted in 1998. ICC Bank was sold to Bank of Scotland in 2000, and the ACC is expected to be sold in the near future.

Competition in domestic banking has increased dramatically. The barriers to entry have been gradually dismantled, and the associated banks now face aggressive competition from smaller financial institutions and from foreign banks, with or without a physical presence in Ireland. Following the creation of the single EUROPEAN MARKET in banking and of EUROPEAN MONETARY UNION, foreign competition is likely to become even more intense over the coming years, while the desirability of maintaining banks with domestic ownership will become an issue of considerable debate. **Jim Power**

banking, central. Though the first COINAGE in Ireland can be traced back to the tenth century, the first separate Irish currency was that established in 1460 by the Irish Parliament in Drogheda. Its evolution thereafter was difficult and unsatisfactory. There was a shortage of coins, there was a lack of uniformity in the coins in circulation, the relationship with the English currency created instability, and the economy still operated to a large extent on a barter system. In 1826 the monetary provisions of the Act of Union (1800) were implemented, and full political and monetary union was established between Ireland and Britain. The Irish currency was abolished, and British notes and coins circulated in Ireland.

On the establishment of the Irish Free State in 1922 the only currency with full legal tender status was that issued by the British government. The Coinage Act (1927) provided for the issue of Irish coins; simultaneously the Government set up a commission of inquiry into banking, the Parker-Willis Commission, to consider whether an Irish central bank should be established. It concluded that one should not, but it proposed that a Currency Commission be established to manage the issue of Irish legal tender notes. This commission was established by the Currency Act (1927). The commission had no powers to act as lender of last resort, or to set reserve requirements for commercial banks, but provisions were made for an IRISH POUND and the issue of Irish legal tender notes in exchange for gold, British legal tender, or British government securities. The act also specified that the value of the Irish pound should be equal to the value of the British pound; in effect the Irish pound was the same as the British pound, backed by sterling assets, but with Irish notes. The first notes were issued in 1928, while Northern Ireland remained within the sterling area, with British currency in circulation.

The Currency Commission remained in existence until 1942, at which time its powers for managing the currency were transferred to the CENTRAL BANK. Until the establishment of the Currency Commission there was no institution of the central-bank type in Ireland, and therefore there was no lender of last resort if commercial banks got into financial trouble. The Bank of Ireland, founded by royal charter in 1783, had performed some of the functions of a central bank, issuing notes and coins and managing the government's account, but it was not always willing to lend money to banks that were in financial trouble. After the abolition of the Irish currency in 1826 the Bank of England was given some supervisory powers over banking in Ireland, but before the Second World War it made it clear that it was not prepared to act as lender of last resort for the Irish banking system.

A second Banking Commission had been set up in 1934 to look into the issue of a fully fledged central bank. The commission's majority report was published in August 1938, recommending that the Currency Commission be replaced by a central bank, with enhanced powers and functions. The Government accepted this recommendation, and after considerable debate the Central Bank Act (1942) was enacted, and the Central Bank of Ireland was duly set up in 1943. However, it was not given many of the traditional powers of a central bank. The Government continued to maintain its account with the Bank of Ireland, the Central Bank did not acquire custody of the reserves of the commercial banks, and it had no statutory power to restrict credit. Its most important function was safeguarding the integrity of the currency.

The face of Irish banking changed dramatically during the 1960s as new banks entered the market and existing banks began to merge. It became clear that the powers of the Central Bank would need to be enhanced to cope with these changes; accordingly the Central Bank Act (1971) was passed, which broadened considerably the powers of the institution. New powers included the licensing and supervision of banks; the transfer of the Government's account from the Bank of Ireland to the Central Bank; the expansion of the monetary policy capability of the Central Bank, including the power to issue primary and secondary reserve ratio requirements; and provision for changes in the exchange rate of the Irish pound by Government order, after consultation with the Central Bank, which created the possibility of breaking the link with the British pound.

The Central Bank Act (1989) further increased the powers of the Central Bank. It strengthened and extended its licensing and supervisory powers in respect of banking business, provided for the establishment and maintenance of a scheme for the protection of small deposits at licence-holders, and gave the bank supervisory powers over a broader range of institutions, including financial institutions associated with the INTERNATIONAL FINANCIAL SERVICES CENTRE, financial futures and options exchanges, and money brokers. The Building Societies Act (1989) and the Trustee Savings Banks Act (1989) gave the Central Bank supervisory powers over building societies and trustee savings banks, respectively.

During the 1990s the powers of the Central Bank evolved further, and it gradually assumed control of other financial institutions, including unit trusts, investment companies with variable capital, the Industrial Credit Corporation, the Agricultural Credit Corporation, and insurance intermediaries. **Jim Power**

Bann, River, a river flowing northwards from the Mountains of Mourne to the Atlantic Ocean, at 129 km (80 miles) the longest and most important river in Ulster. It is divided into upper and lower reaches by LOUGH NEAGH. The Upper Bann rises in south Down and reaches Lough Neagh to the north of Craigavon. The river and the power it could generate facilitated the development of the linen industry in such towns as Banbridge and Portadown. It leaves the northern end of Lough Neagh near Toome and flows towards Coleraine, to reach the ocean between Portstewart and Castlerock, Co. Antrim. Portstewart has been a popular holiday destination since the nineteenth century, and the Bann estuary is an important part of its tourism resources. For most of its course the Lower Bann is mainly a deep, slow, wide and navigable channel draining a large, mainly agricultural, catchment area (4,500 km^2, 1,740 sq. miles). There are four major tributaries—the Clady, Agivey, Macosquin, and Ballymoney Rivers—all but the last joining from the west, having risen in the Sperrin Mountains. Both parts of the river are important fisheries, with the Lower Bann particularly significant for salmon and coarse fishing. Because it virtually bisects Northern Ireland, the Bann has long been regarded as a sociocultural and economic divide. The term 'west of the Bann' is often used to describe the more agricultural and less economically developed area of Northern Ireland with its nationalist demographic, and electoral dominance. **Joseph Brady**

banshee (*bean Sí*, woman of the OTHERWORLD), the supernatural death messenger of Irish FOLKLORE. A solitary being, she heralded the death of a family member with her cry and was believed to follow certain families. The banshee tradition is said to derive from earlier traditions of a goddess or ancestral guardian spirit. More usually experienced aurally, the banshee is depicted as an old woman seen combing her long hair. She is widely attested in folklore, being known by different names throughout the country. **Anne O'Connor**

'Banshenchas' ('lore of women'), a twelfth-century tract that survives in metrical and prose form in manuscripts of the twelfth to the seventeenth centuries. The poem is attributed to the blind poet Gilla Mo-Dutu Ó Caiside; he gives 1147 as the composition date, Meath as his origin, and DEVENISH as the location. The poem may be based on a prose tract; the surviving prose version greatly widens the scope of the poem. The texts, originally structured on the list of high kings, catalogue about 700 women. These are mainly Irish, but the prose version adds Biblical and classical names, beginning with Eve. The husbands and children of most women are included. All the important female characters from the main sagas appear, together with semi-historical and pseudo-historical figures. The historical sections provide an unrivalled source for eleventh and twelfth-century MARRIAGE patterns and behaviour. Most of the major contemporary dynasties are dealt with in detail, and many minor families find mention. Some individuals married six or seven times; it is common for women to have two or three husbands. It does not elaborate on the facts, and no personal details or information on divorce or marriage procedures are given. **Muireann Ní Bhrolcháin**

Bantry (*Beanntraí*), Co. Cork, a town at the head of Bantry Bay; population (2002) 3,147. In the Middle Ages it was the site of a Franciscan abbey, but the town itself was founded by English colonists as part of the PLANTATION OF MUNSTER before 1600. The attraction was the rich pilchard fisheries of Bantry Bay. Fishing was the mainstay of the town's economy throughout its history, with the fish cured locally and exported in huge quantities.

Historically Bantry is most associated with the attempted French invasion in 1796 in support of the UNITED IRISHMEN. A fleet of forty-eight ships with more than 13,000 soldiers sailed from Brest in December; however, storms prevented them from landing, and the fleet scattered and returned to France. The largest local landowner, Richard White, was created Lord Bantry for his part in resisting the invasion. His home, Bantry House, a fine Georgian building, is now one of the chief tourist attractions in west Cork; one of its outbuildings contains a museum devoted to the French armada. In the early nineteenth century Bantry became a substantial market and service town, with a population of 4,000 in 1841. The GREAT FAMINE began a long period of decline, with the population reaching a low point of 2,200 in 1961. Since then the town has recovered and it is now a prosperous service and TOURISM centre with limited manufacturing industry. Its central square, named after THEOBALD WOLFE TONE, was transformed into a pedestrian piazza in 1996. [see GARINISH.] **Kevin Hourihan**

Bantry Bay expedition (1796), expedition by French troops planning to invade Ireland. Some 13,000 seasoned French soldiers, commanded by General Lazare Hoche, left Brest on the west coast of France on 15 December 1796 to invade Ireland. Storms blew Hoche and his flagship out into the Atlantic. Fifteen French ships, carrying 6,400 men, did reach Bantry Bay on 22 December, but a contrary east wind prevented them from landing. Had Hoche's forces succeeded in landing, they would undoubtedly have overwhelmed the inexperienced British forces in Ireland, made up largely of fencibles, MILITIA, and YEOMANRY. [see BLACKWELL, JAMES.] **C. J. Woods**

Banville, John (1945–), novelist. Born in Wexford. His first published collection of short stories was *Long Lankin* (1970). His novels include *Nightspawn* (1971); *Birchwood* (1973); a tetralogy on science: *Doctor Copernicus* (1976), *Kepler* (1981), *The Newton Letter* (1982), and *Mefisto* (1986); a trilogy on art: *The Book of Evidence* (1989), *Ghosts* (1993), and *Athena* (1995); *The Untouchable* (1997); and *Eclipse* (2000). He has also written two plays, *The Broken Jug* (1994) and *God's Gift* (2000), and two screenplays, *Reflections* (1986), a television adaptation of *The Newton Letter*, and THE LAST SEPTEMBER (1999), based on ELIZABETH BOWEN's novel. He was literary editor of the IRISH TIMES, 1988–98, and from 1999 has been its chief literary critic.

Banville has enjoyed a consistently high reputation as a literary, rather than a popular, novelist. His fiction reflects a self-conscious interest in artistic, intellectual, and philosophical history, often weaving these ideas into stories told in a highly subjective, sensuous and dreamlike style. He identifies twentieth-century modernists, especially Marcel Proust and Henry James, and the poets Rilke and Wallace Stevens as important influences on his work. He belongs to the non-realist tradition in the Irish novel, that of JOYCE, FLANN O'BRIEN, and BECKETT. His distinctive blend of an Irish subject matter with a wider, European range of reference and allusion has led many critics to see him as one of Ireland's most innovative and challenging novelists, and a supreme stylist. **Joseph McMinn**

Baptists, a Protestant dissenting sect that emerged in England during the seventeenth century. It stressed congregational independence, lay leadership, and strict personal piety and was most noted for its practice of believer's (adult) baptism. Baptists came to Ireland in the 1650s with Cromwellian forces, where they had their greatest support. With the RESTORATION in 1660 they declined dramatically in numbers until only a few isolated groups remained. Throughout the eighteenth century the Baptists lost members to the CHURCH OF IRELAND, while their increasingly introspective piety kept them isolated from EVANGELICALISM. In 1800 there were only five congregations, all in the south and south-east. It was only in the nineteenth century, under the influence of the revival of 1859, that the community expanded, and then mainly among the rural population of Ulster. In 1895 the Baptist Union of Ireland was formed, and today it represents more than a hundred congregations. **Kevin Herlihy**

barántas ('warrant'), a light composition in verse practised by the Munster poets of the eighteenth and nineteenth centuries. These literary warrants were issued by the poets, in mock imitation of legal warrants, usually for some crime (real or otherwise) committed by another poet or by some member of the community. The author, as *ardsirriam* ('high sheriff'), usually calls for the informant to describe the crime and name its perpetrator; the 'criminal' is then hunted down and brought before the court, where a 'punishment' is proposed. A collection of *barántais* has been edited by Pádraig Ó Fiannachta in *An Barántas* (1978). **Breandán Ó Conchúir**

Barbary ape (*Macaca sylvanus*), a tail-less primate, 65–75 cm (2ft 2 in. to 2 ft 6 in.) in maximum height. In antiquity it was native to north Africa; in classical times it was a popular household pet throughout the Mediterranean region. The remains of a Barbary ape were found in pre-Roman levels of the Titelberg, a hill-fort in Luxembourg. Remains have also been identified from two Roman sites in Britain. Bones of two Barbary apes have been found in excavations in Ireland. The skull and mandible of a young adult (between five and seven years old) were found in excavations under an IRON AGE mound at NAVAN FORT, Co. Armagh, in the 1960s; RADIOCARBON DATING of the mandible confirmed the date of deposition given by the archaeological evidence as about the middle of the second century BC. The ape presumably came to Navan Fort in the Iron Age as a prestige gift or trophy. It may have been brought by traders from Mediterranean lands. Its presence in layers associated with a series of large round buildings further testifies to the prestige of the occupants of the site. In the early 1970s a fragmentary juvenile female skull and skeleton were found in a medieval layer during excavations at Carrickfergus, Co. Antrim. The overseas connections of the port town were also demonstrated by the types of exotic pottery found. **Christopher J. Lynn**

Barber-Surgeons' Guild, Dublin, founded as the Guild of St Mary Magdalene in 1446, when barbers (who practised surgery) were granted a charter by Henry VI. The guild, whose chapel was in CHRIST CHURCH CATHEDRAL, ranked fourth among Dublin's guilds in order of importance. It regulated surgical training and practice until surgeons withdrew and established the College of Surgeons in 1784. The guild was dissolved 1840. **Dorothy Benson**

Barden, Garrett (1939–), philosopher. Born in Dublin; educated at UCD, Heythrop College in Oxfordshire, the University of Oxford, and UCC. Associate professor of philosophy at UCC. One of Ireland's best regarded moral philosophers, Barden is also a noted historian of ideas. Major publications include *Towards Self-Meaning* (with Philip McShane, 1969), *After Principles* (1990), and *Essays on a Philosophical Interpretation of Justice* (1999). **Fionola Meredith**

bardic duanaire. The use of the term *duanaire* to refer to a poem book or a compilation of poems within a larger work derives from the Early Modern period. References to and examples of different types of duanaire attest to the contemporary significance of such compilations and their importance as sources for later generations of scribes and scholars. An individual duanaire may be a collection of works by one poet or a family of poets, a thematic compilation, an anthology composed or compiled for the edification of a particular patron or family, or a miscellany of poems transcribed from various sources by later scribes. Though references exist to collections of the work of renowned poets, such as the thirteenth-century MUIREADHACH ALBANACH Ó DÁLAIGH, there are few surviving examples of the duanaire of individual poets. Examples are the copies of thirty poems from the duanaire of the fourteenth-century GERALD FITZGERALD, Earl of Desmond (Gearóid Iarla), which survive in a fifteenth-century composite manuscript, and the collection of fifty-six poems by three fifteenth-century members of the learned family of Ó hUiginn preserved in the Yellow Book of Lecan, a volume that may have been compiled for use in the Ó hUiginn school of poetry. Examples of thematic compilations include collections of poems on religious or moral subjects, such as the fifteenth-century PILIB BOCHT Ó HUIGINN's *duanaire diadhachta*, material from which can be found in a number of later manuscripts, and the two large anthologies of devotional material entitled *Duanaire Diadha* compiled and written by MÍCHEÁL ÓG Ó LONGÁIN in Cork between 1816 and 1820.

From the point of view of the historian, the compilations of greatest political and cultural interest are the family poem books and the later miscellaneous collections compiled for particular patrons or families. Brian Ó Cuív lists nine families for whose members poem collections were compiled, the earliest example being the collection for fourteenth-century members of the Mág Shamhradháin family to be found in Leabhar Méig Shamhradháin. Typical of this type of duanaire are the conventional poems of praise that were the stock in trade of the classical poet and whose main function was the legitimising of the political and social position of the poet's patron. Though the poems in such collections have been seen as formulaic and politically naïve, recent scholarship uses the evidence of sixteenth and seventeenth-century examples compiled for members of families such as the O'Haras, Maguires, and O'Byrnes to illustrate the potential of conventional bardic idiom to adapt and react to political and cultural change.

Miscellaneous compilations, derived from various sources, become more common from the seventeenth century onwards as the function of transcription itself becomes one of preserving a literary tradition under threat of extinction. Important seventeenth-century examples include the Book of O'Donnell's Daughter, a compilation of poems relating largely to the O'Donnell family written in Flanders in the first half of the seventeenth century, and the compilation now known as the Book of O'Conor Don, a collection of more than 340 poems compiled in Ostend in 1631 by a scribe named Aodh Ó Dochartaigh for the exiled Somhairle MacDonnell. This volume contains religious and didactic poems, numerous examples of conventional bardic eulogy addressed at various times to members of over a dozen well-known families, and seventeenth-century poems on the decline of poetry and Ireland's political misfortunes. Ó Dochartaigh was also responsible for the compilation of DUANAIRE FINN, a collection of sixty-eight Fionn cycle poems. [see CLASSICAL IRISH POETRY.] **Máirín Nic Eoin**

Bardwell, Leland (1928–), writer. Born in India of Irish parents, she spent her childhood in Co. Kildare. She spent time in London but settled in Ireland. She published poetry and fiction, has had her drama produced, and helped to found *Cyphers*, the literary magazine published in Dublin. Among her novels are *Girl on a Bicycle* (1977), *The House* (1984), and *There We Have Been* (1989). **Terence Brown**

Barlow, Jane (1857–1917), writer. Born in Clontarf, Co. Dublin. The daughter of Rev. James William Barlow, vice-provost of Trinity College, she is chiefly known for *Irish Idylls* (1892), a collection of comic stories about peasant life set in the fictional Connemara community of Lisconnel. She was a prolific writer, publishing a further nine collections of stories and several novels, among which are *Kerrigan's Quality* (1894), describing a famine eviction, *The Founding of Fortunes* (1902), and *In Mio's Country* (1917). She produced six collections of verse, including *Bog-land*

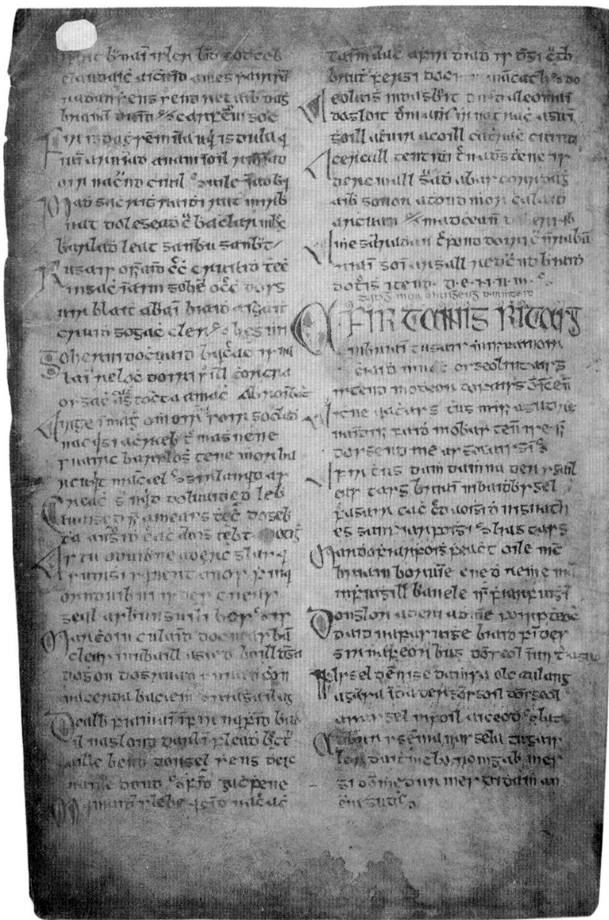

Bardic Dunaire. *Duanaire Mhéig Shamhradháin or The Book of Magauran, a fourteenth-century vellum manuscript of poems in praise of the family of Tomás Mág Shamhradháin. The page shown here is in the hand of the main scribe of the volume, Ruaidhrí Ó Cianáin. [Council of Trustees of the National Library of Ireland; Ms. G1200]*

Studies (1892) and the narrative poem *Ghost-Bereft* (1901). While enjoying popularity in England and America, she was largely overlooked by the Irish Revivalists. **Selina Guinness**

Barnacle, Nora (1884–1951), partner and muse of JAMES JOYCE. Born in Galway, daughter of Thomas Barnacle, a baker, and Annie Barnacle. Having worked variously as a laundress and a chambermaid, she moved to Dublin, where she met Joyce while she was working at Finn's Hotel. She first 'walked out' with him on 16 June 1904, later 'BLOOMSDAY'; they left together for Continental Europe in October the same year, finally settling in Trieste, where their two children, Giorgio and Lucia, were born in 1905 and 1907, respectively. The couple eventually married in England in 1931. Nora Barnacle died in Zürich in 1951, ten years after the death of her husband in the same city. **Brian Galvin**

Barnardo, Thomas John (1845–1905), doctor and philanthropist. Born in Dublin; educated privately. In 1866 he moved to London to study medicine, with the aim of becoming a medical missionary in China, but abandoned his studies to devote himself to helping the thousands of destitute children in the slums of London. He founded the East End Mission in 1867 and a number of homes for destitute children, which became known as Dr Barnardo's Homes. Working on the principle that 'no destitute child was ever turned away,' the homes had up to 800 children in daily care by 1900. It is estimated that in Barnardo's lifetime up to a quarter of a million children were helped by his organisation. **Ciarán Deane**

Barralet, John James (c. 1747–1815), watercolour painter. Born in Dublin; attended DUBLIN SOCIETY Schools, where he received a premium in 1764. He ran schools in London from 1770 to 1779 but returned to Dublin, where he taught at the Dublin Society Schools during the illness of James Mannin. His finest works include *King William Giving Orders to Sir Albert Conyngham, at the Head of the Enniskilliners* (1780) and *The Duchess of Rutland in Her Carriage* (1785). He exhibited at the Society of Artists in Ireland, and worked for topographical engravers. In 1795 he left for America, where he produced prints of patriotic American themes. **Brendan Rooney**

Barret, George (1732–1784), artist. Born in the Liberties of Dublin, son of a clothier; self-taught as an artist, then trained under ROBERT WEST and James Mannin at the DUBLIN SOCIETY's Drawing Schools. He was influenced by the aesthetic theories of EDMUND BURKE to study from nature, rather than copying Old Masters, and painted landscapes in Co. Wicklow. He moved to London in 1762 and two years later exhibited *View of the Waterfall at Powerscourt* and *View in the Dargle* at the Society of Artists. Influential in the formation of the Royal Academy, 1768, he exhibited regularly there until 1782, when he was appointed Master Painter at Chelsea Hospital. He painted a room at Norbury Park and views of Welbeck Abbey, Nottinghamshire, 1765, and also Dalkeith Park, Lothian, 1768. His sons Joseph, James, and George and his daughter Mary all became artists. *View of the Waterfall at Powerscourt*, together with other landscapes, including a decorative cycle of classical landscapes painted for Russborough House, are now in the NATIONAL GALLERY OF IRELAND, Dublin. **Peter Murray**

Barry, Gerald. *Gerald Barry (1952–), composer whose oeuvre, notable for rich instrumental textures and rhythmic articulation, includes orchestral and chamber pieces and vocal and choral works. [Contemporary Music Centre; Eugene Langan]*

Barrington, Sir Jonah (1760–1834), barrister and politician. Member of Parliament for Tuam, 1792–8, and Banagher, 1799–1800, Barrington led the way in bringing charges of corruption against the government during the passing of the ACT OF UNION (1800). He was himself later accused of embezzlement and went into exile in Paris, where he published *Personal Sketches of His Own Times* (1827–32) and *The Rise and Fall of the Irish Nation* (1833), often cited for their vivid if highly subjective account of the tumultuous events he witnessed. Barrington's comments on such figures as MARIA EDGEWORTH, SYDNEY OWENSON, and THOMAS MOORE reflect what was publicly thought about these authors. **Claire Connolly**

Barrow, River, a river whose catchment takes in parts of Cos. Laois, Offaly, Kildare, Carlow, Kilkenny, Wexford, and Waterford and which drains an area of 3,068 km^2 (1,185 sq. miles). It rises in the Slieve Bloom Mountains approximately 6 km ($3\frac{3}{4}$ miles) from Clonaslee, Co. Laois. For much of its upper course it flows across the limestone that underlies the south-eastern part of the Central Lowland before going through the Graiguenamanagh Gap, a gorge incised in older and more resistant rocks between Brandon Hill and the Blackstairs Mountains. It is joined by the River SUIR at Cheekpoint and by the River NORE approximately 4 km ($2\frac{1}{2}$ miles) upstream of New Ross; the three rivers discharge into Waterford Harbour through a common estuary, with the tidal stretch of the Barrow extending far upstream to Saint Mullins, Co. Carlow. The Barrow, in conjunction with stretches of canal constructed between 1756 and 1791, provides a navigable channel between New Ross and the main canal system at Athy. **R. A. Charlton**

Barry, Gerald (1952–), composer. Born in Co. Clare, a graduate of UCD, he studied composition with Stockhausen and Klagel, and organ with Piet Kee. His works include commissions from the BBC, and the production of three operas, *The Intelligence Park* (1990), *The Triumph of Beauty and Deceit* (1994), for Channel 4 Television, and *The Bitter Tears of Petra von Kant* (2002), commissioned by RTÉ. He has collaborated with several music groups, including the New York New Music Ensemble, the Ives Ensemble, the Arditti Quartet, and the IRISH CHAMBER ORCHESTRA, which commissioned *La Jalousie Taciturne* (1996). His works have been performed at numerous music festivals, including the BBC Proms, Warsaw Autumn, and Musik Trienalle Köln. He is a member of AOSDÁNA. **Paul J. Kerr and Richard Pine**

Barry, James (1741–1806), artist. Born in Cork; trained as an artist under John Butts before moving to Dublin. His first major painting, *The Baptism of the King of Cashel by St Patrick*, attracted a prize in 1763 from the DUBLIN SOCIETY and also the patronage of EDMUND BURKE. Burke arranged for him to move to London the following year to work under James 'Athenian' Stuart. In 1765, again under Burke's patronage, he embarked on a lengthy tour of Europe. Having studied the works of Poussin and Le Sueur in Paris, he moved to Rome, where he continued to develop a lifelong passion for classical antiquity and history painting. He also studied in Bologna, receiving a diploma from the Accademia Clementina.

Fired with enthusiasm, he returned to London in 1771 and produced a number of history paintings that quickly won him membership of the Royal Academy. Supported by the sale of prints, he embarked on his most important work, a cycle of six complex allegorical paintings, in the Royal Society of Arts. He was appointed professor at the Royal Academy in 1782 but was expelled in 1799 for his radical political views and his increasingly erratic attacks on other academicians. His later years were marred by paranoia and a severe persecution complex. He died in poverty but is now regarded as the most important neo-classical painter in eighteenth-century Britain (see p. 60). **Peter Murray**

Barry, James Miranda Stuart, (1795–1865), army surgeon. Born in Co. Cork, niece of the painter JAMES BARRY; disguised as a boy, she entered the University of Edinburgh, qualified as a physician in 1812, and studied surgery at Guy's Hospital, London. She joined the British army in 1813 and was posted as assistant surgeon to the Cape Colony (South Africa), where she worked for twelve years. In 1836 she was appointed principal medical officer of St Helena; she later served in the Windward and Leeward Islands, in Malta, Corfu, and finally Canada, where she was appointed inspector-general of British hospitals. She retired in 1859 and settled in London. Only after her death did her gender become widely known, and a planned military funeral was abandoned. She is credited with having carried out one of the first successful Caesarean operations in modern medical history. **Ciarán Deane**

Barry, John (1745–1803), seaman. Born at Ballysampson, near Tacumshin, Co. Wexford. He emigrated to America and in time became a ship-owner in Philadelphia. In April 1776, as master of an ancient brigantine, the *Lexington*, he made the first rebel capture of a British warship, the *Edward*, and later the *Black Prince*. In different ships he made a series of surprise attacks on British naval vessels blockading the rebel-held coast, and in 1782, in the 36-gun frigate *Alliance*, he greatly assisted the rebel cause by a series of captures of British merchant ships with valuable cargoes, culminating in the seizure of richly laden merchant ships on the way to England from Jamaica. He sold these in France for £620,610 in gold and presented the proceeds to the rebel leadership. After the successful conclusion of the American War of Independence he went back to trading for a time and then was made captain of the new republic's first custom-built warship, the 44-gun *United States*, in consequence of which he is considered to be the 'father' of the US navy. There is a statue of him in Wexford by the American sculptor N. A. Wheeler Williams (1955). **John de Courcy Ireland**

Barry, Leanora, née Kearney, 'Mother Lake' (1849–1930), American labour leader and social reformer. Born in Co. Cork. She emigrated with her family in 1852, settling in New York, where she became a teacher. She married W. E. Barry in 1871; he died ten years later, leaving her with two children, whom she supported through working in the clothing industry. So appalling were the working conditions that she thenceforth devoted her life to labour reform. She moved to St Louis, Missouri, married O. R. Lake, yet continued to travel, campaigning for women's suffrage and arousing much public support for prohibition. **David Kiely**

Barry, Sebastian (1955–), playwright. Born in Dublin; educated at TCD. Barry's writing career began with novels such as *Macker's Garden* (1982) and *The Engine of Owl-Light* (1987) and collections of poems such as *The Water-Colourist* (1983) and *The Rhetorical Town* (1985). Following the experimental play *The Pentagonal Dream* (1986), Barry's first play produced at the ABBEY THEATRE, *Boss Grady's Boys* (1988), brought him considerable acclaim. The lives of two old brothers living on a remote hill farm evoke a Beckettian bleakness, but the rich lyricism of the play and its suppression of narrative in favour of mood established the characteristic tone and style of Barry's theatre. Many of his characters share an odd and otherworldly quality, whether they are a fundamentalist sect living on a small island in *Prayers of Sherkin* (1990), a motley gang of cowboys planning to rob a gold-train in *White Woman Street* (1992), a nineteenth-century music-hall dancer marrying an Anglo-Irish gentleman in *The Only True History of Lizzie Finn* (1995), a senile former policeman contemplating the birth of the Irish state in *Steward of Christendom* (1995), or a middle-class couple warring through an alcohol-driven marriage in *Our Lady of Sligo* (1998). While by no means avant-garde, Barry's use of poetic dialogue, suppression of plot and fluidity of theatrical form have had a significant impact in the Irish theatre and beyond. *Hinterland* (2002) provoked considerable public controversy because of its use of material drawn from contemporary political life to explore the meaning of personal and political corruption. Despite gaining numerous awards for his plays, Barry returned to the novel form with *The Whereabouts of Eneas McNulty* (1998) and *Annie Dunne* (2002). **Ger FitzGibbon**

Barry, Spranger (1719–1777), actor and THEATRE manager. Born in Dublin. He was a silversmith until his stage debut at the SMOCK ALLEY THEATRE, 1744. By 1746 he was playing in *Othello* with CHARLES MACKLIN at Drury Lane, London, later moving to

Barry, John. *Statue of Commodore John Barry (1955), known as the 'Father of the American Navy', at Crescent Quay, Wexford, by N. A. Wheeler Williams. In 1956 it was presented to the people of Ireland by President Eisenhower on behalf of the United States of America. [Denis Mortell]*

Covent Garden. He returned to Dublin, opening the Crow Street Theatre in 1761. **Christopher Morash**

Barry, Thomas (Tom) (1897–1980), revolutionary. Born in Killorglin, Co. Kerry. He joined the British army in 1915 and was wounded in the FIRST WORLD WAR. He was training officer of the West Cork Brigade of the IRA from mid-1920; his command of the controversial Kilmichael ambush on 28 November made him a flying column leader. He opposed the ANGLO-IRISH TREATY in arms but later became an advocate of peace negotiations; he subsequently worked as a superintendent for Cork Harbour Commissioners but remained active in the IRA. In 1936 he was appointed chief of staff, but his planned attack on Northern Ireland was abortive, and he resigned in 1938. **Peter Hart**

Barry, Vincent (1908–1975), chemist. Born in Cork; educated at UCD. He became assistant to Prof. Tom Dillon at University College, Galway. His work on sugars there quickly led to an industry based on seaweed. A pure scientist, he had a keen sense of the importance of fundamental work. The Irish state, then barely two decades in existence, was intent on creating organisations to serve the needs of its citizens. One of these, the Medical Research Council of Ireland, turned its attention to the widespread incidence of tuberculosis. From 1950, as director of the Council's new laboratories, Barry led a team that had notable successes in synthesising drugs for use in chemotherapy. The laboratory also discovered a drug, phenazine B663, highly effective against leprosy. **William J. Davis**

Barry family, an Austrian naval family originating in Co. Cork. Captain Richard Barry (1825–1866) took part in the repression of various attempts in mid-nineteenth-century Italy to liberate that country and free those areas ruled by the Austro-Hungarian Empire. His younger brother, Alfred (1829–1907)—a legend to this day along the east coast of the Adriatic—learnt seamanship in the Austrian Lloyd merchant fleet. By 1859 he was commander of the naval frigate *Triton*, and in 1864, as captain of a screw frigate, he took part in an Austro-German fleet in one of the first naval battles between iron-clad steamships, off Heligoland against the Danes. In 1866, off the island of Vis, he played a leading part in the Austrian navy's greatest victory, against an Italian fleet, and is remembered for having, in courtesy, thrown down his pistol when about to shoot the captain of the Italian *Maria Pia*, whose ship had blundered out of a cloud of smoke to within yards of his ship.

Alfred's son, Richard (fl. 1915), also rose to be an admiral. He was in charge of a polar expedition that found and explored the territory named after the Austrian emperor of the time, Franz Josef Land. He was for a time commander-in-chief of the Austrian navy during the FIRST WORLD WAR, in which his son, Harry, won a series of medals in command of destroyers in the Adriatic and gunboats on the Danube. **John de Courcy Ireland**

Barton, Rose (1856–1929), painter. Born in Co. Tipperary into a well-to-do family; privately educated. Accompanied by her friend Mildred Ann Butler she studied art in Paris at the studio of Henri Gervex. She first exhibited at the RHA in 1878 and in the 1880s showed watercolours at exhibitions in Dublin and London. Living mostly in London, she was elected an associate of the Royal Watercolour Society in 1893. Two books illustrated with her atmospheric city views, *Picturesque Dublin Old and New* (1898) and *Familiar London* (1904), made her work known to a wider audience. **Peter Murray**

basketball. Irish Basketball, the national governing body for basketball, was formed in 1947 and affiliated to the international governing body the same year. The association is responsible for the promotion, development, and administration of all basketball activities in Ireland. Its principal objective is to increase the level of participation in basketball and to provide professionally managed courses, competitions, leagues, and services. A National Executive Committee governs policy, and there is a professional staff of ten.

More than 150,000 people actively play basketball at some level in Ireland, making it the second most popular physical activity (after SOCCER) among the twelve to eighteen age group. There are more than 300 clubs, catering for players at all levels, from mini-basketball to senior level. Approximately 1,200 club teams participate in local leagues. The premier competitions are the National League and the National Cup. More than a hundred teams participate at senior and junior level in the National Cup, with more than 9,000 fans attending the finals weekend.

There are 585 post-primary schools registered with the Irish Schools Basketball office and approximately 1,000 primary schools registered with the Irish Mini-Basketball Association. Six national teams compete at international level in European championships and four-country international tournaments; the Irish senior men's team qualified for the semi-final round of the European championship for the first time in 2001.

In association with the ESB and the Irish Sports Council, Irish Basketball launched the Community Hoops Programme in May 1998. Its object is to install vandal-resistant outdoor hoops throughout Ireland, providing free and open access to the sport for everyone. More than 300 have so far been installed. **Máire Scully**

Bastable, Patrick Kevin (1918–1992), philosopher and logician. Born in Dublin; educated at UCD. He lectured at University College, Dublin, 1960–88, and in Massachusetts. He published *Desire for God* (1947), *Logic: A Depth Grammar of Rationality* (1975), and *The Letters of St Patrick* (1993), completing this last after Daniel Conneely's death. He was a founder-member of the PSYCHOLOGICAL SOCIETY OF IRELAND and the Irish Rorschach Forum. He was an admirer of Cardinal Newman; in *The Person of Conscience* he explores Newman's understanding of intellectual, moral, and religious excellence as tasks to be undertaken uniquely by each person. **Thomas A. F. Kelly**

Bates, Sir Richard Dawson (1876–1949), politician. A solicitor by profession, he was appointed secretary to the newly formed ULSTER UNIONIST COUNCIL in 1906, continuing in the post until 1921. He is credited with a major organisational role in co-ordinating successful resistance to the HOME RULE BILL (1912). Knighted in 1921, he served as an MP in the Northern Ireland Parliament for East Belfast, 1921–9, and for Victoria, 1929–43. His ready responsiveness to grass-roots loyalist fears was reflected in his actions as Minister of Home Affairs, 1921–43, and in particular his support for successive Civil Authorities (Special Powers) Acts, introduced in 1922 and renewed periodically thereafter. Considered by critics a somewhat mediocre and unimaginative hard-liner, he remained ever distrustful of the Catholic minority as a potentially subversive fifth column. Having been made a baronet in 1937, his final years as Minister of Home Affairs were marked by relative laxity and ineffectiveness in preparing Northern Ireland for the SECOND WORLD WAR. The resultant unpopularity brought about a parliamentary vote of censure in 1942, which he survived, but his ministerial career did not outlast the change of Prime Minister the following year. **Alan Scott**

battle: see CATH.

Batty (or Betty), William Henry West (1791–1874), actor. Born in Shrewsbury, England, to a Lisburn family; reared on a farm at Ballynahinch, Co. Down. In 1803, at the age of twelve, he made his theatrical debut to a packed house in Belfast. He was immediately invited to play in Dublin, where he is reputed to have learnt the role of Hamlet in three hours. When he played in Covent Garden, London, on 1 December 1804, the military had to be called to control the excited crowd. In 1805 PITT adjourned Parliament to see him play Hamlet. He amassed an enormous fortune and retired at the age of thirty-three. **Ciarán Deane**

Bax, Sir Arnold (1883–1953), composer. Born in London; educated privately and at the Royal Academy of Music, where he won a Macfarren Scholarship. His prolific output includes seven symphonies, ballets, film music, orchestral suites, chamber works, song cycles, works for piano, and choral works. Influenced by 'The Wanderings of Oisin' by W. B. YEATS, he adopted Ireland as his second home, living in Dublin, 1910–14, befriending PÁDRAIC COLUM and GEORGE RUSSELL, publishing poems, plays and short stories under the pseudonym 'Dermot O'Byrne', including *A Dublin Ballad* (1916), which was banned by the British authorities as seditious. Though he had no Irish blood, he became 'more Irish than the Irish,' claiming to have found the 'hidden Ireland' that he stated was beyond the ken of Irish composers such as STANFORD and HARTY. The tone poem *In the Faery Hills* (1909) marked a maturation in his compositional style, which displayed the influence of Celtic mythology, contemporary Irish events and the Irish countryside, of which the most prominent works were 'Roscatha' (1910), 'In the Garden of Fand' (1913–16), 'In Memoriam Patrick Pearse' (1917), and the first and second symphonies (1922, 1924). Ironically, as Master of the King's Musick, 1942–53, he wrote several incidental pieces for British state occasions, including 'Coronation March' (1953). **Paul J. Kerr and Richard Pine**

BBC Northern Ireland Orchestra. Established in 1924 in Belfast, directed by E. Godfrey Brown; promoted classical music concerts and broadcasts. The seventy-piece orchestra continued in existence until 1981 when it amalgamated with the ULSTER ORCHESTRA (founded 1966). The BBC Northern Ireland Light Orchestra, formed in 1949, had sixteen players directed by David Curry. Throughout the 1950s BBC Northern Ireland organised classical music concerts, together with Radio Éireann, the RDS, and the Belfast Philharmonic Society, and sponsored schools broadcasts. **Paul J. Kerr**

BBC Sound Archives, a massive collection documenting almost three-quarters of a century of broadcasting, of particular Irish interest because of its substantial holdings of original TRADITIONAL MUSIC. It was collected mainly between 1947 and 1954, on the initiative of Brian George, by SÉAMUS ENNIS, SEÁN O'BOYLE, and Peter Kennedy. The collection documents English and Irish songs, KEENING, LILTING, solos, duets, and all manner of instrumental groups, as well as dancing, speech, folklore, and local customs, comprising more than a hundred hours of unique performances. **Glenn Cumiskey**

Béal Bocht, An (1941), a popular pseudo-autobiography by 'Myles na gCopaleen' (FLANN O'BRIEN). It satirises aspects of the Irish revival movement and parodies the writings of some well-known authors, such as TOMÁS Ó CRIOMHTHAINN and SÉAMAS Ó GRIANNA. It is informed by an accomplished literary and witty sensibility, allied to a sense of Rabelaisian anarchy. **Breandán Ó Conaire**

Béaloideas (1927–), journal of the Folklore of Ireland Society. It was edited by SÉAMUS Ó DUILEARGA, 1927–70, which period could be described as the golden age of the journal, when a great variety of FOLKLORE texts was made available to the public. Subsequent editors have concentrated on publishing research rather than folklore texts. **Mícheál Briody**

Bealtaine (May Day), one of the QUARTER DAYS in the early Irish calendar, associated with growth and abundance. Many pre-Christian customs were observed to celebrate the arrival of summer. In parts of Ireland a May bush is erected and decorated with colourful ribbons and flowers, and formerly bonfires were lit. Maypoles were associated with towns and cities, but this custom was no longer observed by the middle of the nineteenth century. Dancing and music were part of the celebrations. May Morning dew was said to have particular power to maintain a youthful skin. Supernatural forces were active at this time; dairy produce was particularly vulnerable and had to be protected. May Eve was a time of contact between mortals and the immortal world. The stealing of BUTTER was prevalent, and charms to protect it therefore common. Cattle, crops, land, and water were also vulnerable and were accordingly protected by various means, including charms, holy water, and prayers. [see IMBOLC; LUNASA; SAMHAIN.] **Ríonach uí Ógáin**

Béaslaí, Piaras (1883–1965), journalist, critic, poet, and innovative Irish-language playwright. Born in Liverpool; educated at Francis Xavier College. He was jailed after the 1916 RISING. A Gaelic Leaguer and notable publicist, he supported the ANGLO-IRISH TREATY. A major-general during the CIVIL WAR, his biography of MICHAEL COLLINS (1925) was controversial. **Diarmuid Breathnach and Máire Ní Mhurchú**

Beatha Aodha Ruaidh Uí Dhomhnaill, a life of RED HUGH O'DONNELL by Lughaidh Ó Cléirigh, written between 1616 and 1636. It is written in a florid, archaic style and has been disparaged by historians for perceived inaccuracies. Closer perusal, however, reveals it to be a deliberately crafted work. Despite the traditional annalistic form, the author adopts the role of Renaissance biographer in emphasising character, motivation, and causality. Of particular interest is the importance placed on O'Donnell's youthful imprisonment in DUBLIN CASTLE as the pivotal event of his career and the deliberate recall of his captivity at important moments in his life. **Mícheál Mac Craith**

Beattie, Jack (1886–1960), politician. A Belfast shipyard worker, Beattie first came to prominence in 1918 as a socialist supporter of the British Empire but steadily moved over to an anti-partitionist position. In 1925 he was elected as a candidate of the NORTHERN IRELAND LABOUR PARTY to the Northern Ireland Parliament for East Belfast. He was the only NILP member of Parliament to survive the abolition of proportional representation in 1929, and he continued to represent the Pottinger division of Belfast until 1949, in spite of being expelled from the NILP in 1934 for his republican views. He was elected to represent West Belfast for the Irish Labour Party, 1943–50 and 1951–5. **Jonathan Bardon**

Beatty, Sir Alfred Chester (1875–1968), mining engineer and art collector. Born in New York; attended Princeton University but transferred to Columbia University, from which he graduated as a mining engineer. Working in the south-western United States, he rapidly established himself in his profession and developed significant mining interests. He was associated with the Guggenheims and, both on their behalf and on his own, was instrumental in expanding their mining interests both within and outside the United States. From an early age he was a collector, and he already had a library of note when his first wife died in 1910. Already a wealthy man, he decided, for various reasons, to move his base of operations to London, where by 1911 he took up permanent residence. His second marriage took him on a honeymoon journey to Egypt, where he extended his range of interests to include Arabic manuscripts. A further journey in 1917 to the Far East expanded his interests more widely into Chinese and Japanese works of art. In particular he developed an eye for Nara Ehon and built up an extremely important collection of these. Expert advisers whom he employed not only to assist him in assessing material but also to see to the scholarly publication of his purchases supported his collecting, especially in Islamic manuscripts.

Beatty became a British subject in the 1930s and during the Second World War played an important behind-the-scenes role in the provision of strategic raw materials for the Allies and in helping to unblock obstacles to efficient wartime production of armaments. A combination of factors prompted him to leave his home in Britain as his active business career was coming to an end. Mindful of his Irish ancestry, he explored the possibility of moving to Dublin, and in 1950, with the ready support of Irish diplomats and politicians, he established his collection in Shrewsbury Road, Dublin. There a small purpose-built library was created by him, which he opened to researchers in 1953 and later, in a limited way, to the public. In 1957 a purpose-built exhibition gallery was added to the library; this was expanded in the 1970s. He was knighted in 1954 and in 1957 became the first honorary citizen of Ireland. Beatty found his Irish home congenial, and he decided, in consultation with the Government, that his library would be left in trust for the benefit of the public after his death. He died in 1968 and was accorded a state funeral, the only private citizen to receive such an honour. The CHESTER BEATTY LIBRARY became a public charitable trust in 1969, supported by a grant from the Government of Ireland. It continues to be a trust owned by a Board of Trustees and supported by an annual government subvention. **Michael Ryan**

Beaufort, D. A. [Daniel Augustus] (1739–1821), CHURCH OF IRELAND minister, scholar, and topographer. Born in London; educated at TCD. After graduating in 1759 he spent most of his life in Ireland as rector of Navan, Co. Meath from 1765, and vicar of Collon, Co. Louth, 1789–1821. He played an active part in Irish social and intellectual life, notably as a founder-member and first librarian of the ROYAL IRISH ACADEMY, and took a keen practical interest in farming, architecture, topography, and education. To posterity he is best known for his civil and ecclesiastical map of Ireland (1792), based on a critical examination of all available sources within a framework of astronomically determined latitudes and longitudes. His *Memoir* explaining the construction of this map is a unique source for Irish cartographic history; it also includes a brief geographical account of Ireland, but this does little justice to the extent of Beaufort's knowledge, acquired by first-hand observation throughout the country and recorded with diligence and zest in his unpublished diaries. **J. H. Andrews**

Beaufort, Sir Francis (1774–1857), admiral and hydrographer. Born in Navan, Co. Meath; he joined the British navy in 1787. He served with distinction in the French Revolutionary and Napoleonic wars but grew more and more interested in the safety of life at sea. He became Hydrographer to the Navy in 1829 and held the post for a record twenty-six years, during which he had thorough surveys made of the seas around Ireland and Britain, the Mediterranean, the east coast of Africa, the West Indies, Australia, New Zealand, the China Sea, the Gulf of St Lawrence, and South America. He was also a skilled cryptographer, the inventor of the Beaufort scale of wind velocities, which is still in use, and a member of the Arctic Council, which arranged early scientific voyages to the Arctic. He helped to prove that the screw propeller was more effective than paddles for driving steamships, and invented a semaphore signal system that could send a message within minutes from Galway to Dublin. He is generally considered to have been the greatest hydrographer of all time. Thanks to him, for at least a century British Admiralty charts were universally accepted as the surest guides for navigation of the world's seas and oceans. **John de Courcy Ireland**

Beckett, John (1927–), conductor, teacher, performer, and broadcast researcher. He taught harpsichord and early music at the RIAM, 1971–83. In the 1960s he performed with David Munroe and Doris Keogh in the early music ensemble Musica Reservata. He began the Dublin Harpsichord Ensemble and the Bach Cantata series of concerts in St Anne's Church, Dawson Street, Dublin, which ran from the early 1970s. With the Purcell Consort he performed many RTÉ and BBC broadcasts and wrote incidental music for television programmes. He conducted the RTÉ SYMPHONY ORCHESTRA and was also a producer and researcher with the BBC in the early 1980s. **Paul J. Kerr**

Beckett, Mary (1926–), teacher and writer. Born in Belfast; educated at St Mary's Training College. She moved to Dublin in 1956 after her marriage. Her works include *A Belfast Woman* (1980), *Give Them Stones* (1987), *A Literary Woman* (1990), *A Family Tree* (1992), and *Hannah or Pink Balloons* (1995). She is most poised in the SHORT-STORY form. Her work often deals with the emotional wastage of ordinary women in steady but passionless relationships. In *A Literary Woman* a clever and chilling sub-plot connects the various characters. She has also written for children. **Tess Maginess**

Beckett, Samuel (1906–1989), novelist, dramatist, and poet. Raised in Foxrock, Co. Dublin, the second son of William Beckett and May Roe. Educated at Portora Royal School, Enniskillen, he studied French and Italian at TCD, graduating with a first-class degree. He taught at Campbell College, Belfast, in 1928, then at the École Normale Supérieure in Paris, 1928–30; there he became friends with THOMAS MACGREEVEY and a close admirer of JAMES JOYCE, who proved a strong influence on Beckett's early writing. Beckett's essay 'Dante...Bruno.Vico..Joyce', written in support of Joyce's FINNEGANS WAKE, was published with his first prose piece, 'Assumption', in the journal *Transition* in 1929. *Whoroscope* (1930), his long poem on time narrated by Descartes, won a competition sponsored by Nancy Cunard's Hours Press. Over the summer of 1930 Beckett wrote a study of Proust (1931), before returning from Paris to Dublin to take up a post as lecturer in French at TCD. He lectured there for only four terms before resigning abruptly in January 1932 because he felt he could not bear to teach others what he did not know himself. There followed a period of travel in Germany and France; he settled in Paris, where he wrote his first novel, *Dream of Fair to Middling Women* (1992). The years 1932–7

Beckett, Samuel. *Samuel Beckett with the German theatre director Walter Asmus at the Riverside Studios, London, in February 1984 during rehearsals for a production of* Waiting for Godot. *[John Minihan]*

were a period of travel and turmoil. Moving to and from Germany, France, England, and Ireland, Beckett cultivated a friendship with the painter JACK B. YEATS. In June 1933 his father died.

Beckett's early writing includes the short stories *More Pricks than Kicks* (1934) and a book of poems, *Echo's Bones and Other Precipitates* (1935). In 1937 he left Ireland for Paris, disaffected with what he saw as the parochialism, conservatism, and nationalism of Irish society. There he completed *Murphy* (1938), a comic novel that plays on Descartes' distinction between mind and body. He remained in Paris during the occupation of the SECOND WORLD WAR, working for the French Resistance between 1941 and 1942. When his cell was betrayed to the Nazis he and his companion, Suzanne Deschevaux-Dumesnil, escaped to Roussillon, where Beckett worked as a farm labourer and continued his resistance activities, for which he was awarded the Croix de Guerre. There he finished *Watt* (1953), a novel that explores the relationship between language and reality through a narrative full of repetition and permutations.

After *Watt*, Beckett began writing in French, citing the need to write without style. Certainly his later work exhibits a greater simplicity and objectivity than the earlier, Joyce-influenced prose. *Mercier and Camier*, Beckett's first novel in French, was completed in 1946 but not published until 1970. There followed a number of short stories and novellas in French before he turned to theatre, writing *Eleuthéria* in 1947. In August 1950 Beckett's mother died. His second play, WAITING FOR GODOT (1953), brought him success and security. On a spare stage two characters debate the passage of time and the futility of action while waiting for an unknown person, who never arrives. Subsequent plays—*Endgame* (1957), *Krapp's Last Tape* (1958), and *Happy Days* (1961)—explore the ability to endure under hostile circumstances and the difficulty of self-knowledge. Beckett's theatre work is complemented by plays for radio and television. The trilogy of novels *Molloy* (1951), *Malone Dies* (1951), and *The Unnamable* (1953) explores a diminishing realm of consciousness in a narrative that is reduced to its bare elements. *How It Is* (1961) dispenses with traditional narrative form to tell a story of torment, relationships, and language. These works develop Beckett's distinctive style, which can be described in his own phrase, 'Form is content, content is form.' Beckett was now writing in English and French, and translating his work into both languages. In 1969 he was awarded the NOBEL PRIZE for Literature 'for his writing, in which—in new forms for the novel and drama—the destitution of modern man acquires its elevation.'

His later plays, which he often directed, display a minimalism and visuality that strip theatre to the basics of space and sound, bodies and movement. These include *Play* (1964), *Come and Go* (1966), *Breath* (1969), *Not I* (1973), and *Rockaby* (1981). His late prose is characterised by a spare and rigorous style, culminating in the powerful trilogy of novels *Company* (1980), *Ill Seen Ill Said* (1981), and *Worstward Ho* (1983). Though critics anticipated for decades his retreat into silence, Beckett continued writing until his death. His final work (1988) asks the question fundamental to all his writing: 'What is the Word?' Samuel Beckett remains one of the foremost writers of the twentieth century (see p. 616). **Dervall Tubridy**

Beckett, Walter (1914–1996), composer, arranger, teacher, and music critic. Born in Dublin; studied organ with GEORGE HEWSON and harmony with JOHN F. LARCHET at the RIAM. He wrote many arrangements for the Radio Éireann Light Orchestra and Singers in the 1940s and was music critic for the *Irish Times*, 1946–52. He was appointed professor of harmony at the RIAM; his compositions include *Suite for Orchestra* (1945), *Irish Rhapsody for Orchestra* (1945), a string quartet, a symphony, and a song cycle. **Paul J. Kerr**

bed and breakfast accommodation. Irish hospitality has long been renowned, but the concept of paying for guest accommodation is relatively new. When the number of tourists began to increase in the mid-1960s, bed and breakfast accommodation—where the traveller is offered a bed for the night in a family home and a cooked breakfast (the 'Irish breakfast' or 'Ulster fry') the following morning—was a convenient way of increasing the amount of accommodation available without large-scale capital investment. It also supplemented family income without the need for working outside the home. While such accommodation is to be found in many countries, it was particularly suited to Ireland because of the long tradition of offering hospitality to travellers.

The first bed and breakfast organisation, Irish Farmhouse Holidays, was set up in 1966 with twenty members. Its first chairwoman, Nancy Fitzgerald of Co. Cork, recalls that a problem at the outset was the Irish tradition of offering free hospitality: people were frowned on by their neighbours for charging guests money to stay in their homes; but the attitude changed when it became apparent that visitors expected to pay, and the income was a boon, especially to families struggling to stay on the land. Town and Country Homes was set up a few years later to represent non-farmhouse bed and breakfast providers and by 2002 had more than 2,000 registered members. Both organisations produce annual publications listing members, all of whose premises have been inspected. The provider pays for membership and in return receives publicity. For a small fee, providers can also be included on a computerised information and reservations network.

In 2001 there were 562 providers of farmhouse accommodation registered in the Republic, 1,788 country houses, 1,439 town houses, and 129 providers in other specialist categories; Northern Ireland had 872 providers registered with the NORTHERN IRELAND TOURIST BOARD, which also inspects them and grants operating licences. There is no legal requirement to register with BORD FÁILTE ÉIREANN or the NITB, and some people choose to offer accommodation without registration, thereby operating without the publicity available to registered providers; because of this there is no figure for the total number of providers.

In 1987 the owners of large historic houses formed a marketing group called Hidden Ireland, which now has thirty-nine members offering bed and breakfast accommodation, mainly in large houses, at double the normal price. In 1990 John Colclough of Tourism Resources Ltd formed the Friendly Homes of Ireland group, offering bed and breakfast accommodation in more modest historic or characterful houses.

During the 1980s, investment in TOURISM was encouraged by tax incentives, grants, and support from the EUROPEAN UNION. Many providers used grants to upgrade their facilities. Bord Fáilte established and maintained high standards in the sector, though its approach was frequently criticised for rigid adherence to rules. In 1996 Bord Fáilte licensed organisations representing accommodation groups to become self-regulatory, and the approval of premises is now carried out by an authorised contractor. In the 1990s there was much investment in new houses designed specifically for the bed and breakfast trade. While these offer a uniform standard of comfort, they are in essence professionally run small businesses, and many lack the welcome and the unpredictable appeal of the traditional family home. **Alannah Hopkin**

Bede (672/3–735), monk, scholar, historian, poet, and Christian teacher. Bede spent virtually the whole of his life as a monk at the twin-site monastery of Wearmouth-Jarrow in the Anglo-Saxon kingdom of Northumbria. He was intelligent, learned, and a valued author in many fields: Biblical commentaries, chronology, Latin language and poetry, and above all history and hagiography. He also had an interest in natural phenomena; his work *The Reckoning of Time* incorporated a world chronicle and included important advances in the understanding of tides.

Bede's greatest work is his *Ecclesiastical History of the English People* (731). Though its primary emphasis is on England, it contains valuable material relating to seventh-century Ireland. It includes extracts from original letters addressed to Irish churchmen by Roman bishops in England and by a Pope-elect, and information on the many Anglo-Saxon visitors who came to Ireland, including to the monastery of Rath Melsigi (probably Clonmelsh, Co. Carlow), for which Bede is the main source. He also records the founding of monasteries in Ireland by Colmán of Lindisfarne after his withdrawal from Northumbria following the SYNOD OF WHITBY. Above all, he has valuable information on COLM CILLE's monastic foundations and the position of IONA as the head of its family of MONASTERIES in both Ireland and Britain and on the Irish mission to Northumbria led by AIDAN. Further items of Irish interest include a Northumbrian raid on Brega and the conversion of ADOMNÁN of Iona to the Roman EASTER, as a result of which he persuaded churches in northern Ireland to conform.

Throughout his *History*, Bede shows an impressive concern for accuracy and informative detail. At the same time his selection and presentation of material is tailored to fit his overall theme: how the Britons' sinfulness resulted in their defeat by the pagan Anglo-Saxons; how the latter had been converted by Roman missionaries from Pope Gregory and by Irish missionaries from Iona led by AIDAN; how Northumbria had accepted the Roman Easter at Whitby; and how Iona's evangelisation of Northumbria was repaid when a Northumbrian converted it to the Roman Easter in 716. Bede excelled in many areas of scholarship; in all of them he sought to further Christianity, particularly in Northumbria. His concern that contemporary bishops were not effectively conveying the Gospel to remote peasants emerges in his revealing letter to Bishop Ecgberht of York (735). It also underlies his *History and Life of Cuthbert*, where Aidan and Cuthbert are held up as models of evangelistic simplicity for contemporaries. The same concerns led Bede to translate important texts into English. His writings and agenda were transmitted to the Continent by Anglo-Saxon missionaries and helped to inspire the Carolingian Renaissance.

In 836 Bede was hailed as a 'Father' of the church. His works remained popular and were responsible for spreading the AD dating used in his *History*, which has since become universal. [see EASTER CONTROVERSY.] **Clare Stancliffe**

Bedell, William (1571–1642), scholar and bishop. Born in Essex; educated at the University of Cambridge. He distinguished himself as a scholar at Cambridge, not only in divinity but as a linguist, his repertoire of languages including Hebrew, Syriac, and Arabic. This background was reflected in his career in Ireland, when, as provost of the University of Dublin (TCD), 1627–9, and later as Bishop of Kilmore and Ardagh, 1629 (he resigned Ardagh 1633), he took steps to ensure that CHURCH OF IRELAND clergy were taught Irish to enable them to employ the native tongue of the Catholic masses in an evangelical bid to convert them to Protestantism. In a similar vein he endeavoured to provide religious texts in Irish, completing a catechism in 1631 and setting about the more ambitious task of translating the Old Testament, eventually publishing in 1685. Essentially he adopted a 'persuasive' approach to spreading Protestantism in Ireland, in contrast to many of his contemporaries, who preferred coercive measures. As it turned out, his unaggressive manner of seeking to convert Catholics was reflected in his treatment by the rebels following the outbreak of rebellion in 1641, during which thousands of Protestants were massacred. Unlike many of his fellow-Protestants, who were taken by surprise, Bedell had warning of advancing rebel forces, though he refused to leave his ministry. He was taken prisoner for a short time and later took refuge in the house of a Protestant minister, where he caught a fever and died. [see BIBLE IN IRISH.] **John McCavitt**

Beechey, Richard Brydges (1808–1895), marine painter. Born in London, son of the portrait-painter Sir William Beechey; a naval officer, he received art tuition at the Royal Naval College in Portsmouth and throughout his life was a painter of fine marine views. He exhibited at the Royal Academy, 1832–77, and the British Institution, 1833–59. Engaged in survey work in the west of Ireland, he submitted paintings to the ROYAL HIBERNIAN ACADEMY. He retired from the navy in 1864 and settled at Monkstown, Co. Dublin. Four years later he was elected an honorary member of the Royal Hibernian Academy. In later years he moved to Plymouth. His painting *HM Mail Boat Connaught* is in the NATIONAL GALLERY OF IRELAND. **Peter Murray**

beehive huts or *clocháns*, round mortarless structures built on the *corbel* principle—a traditional and timeless building method applied (with square interior) on SCEILG MHICHÍL in the early Middle Ages and still practised on the DINGLE PENINSULA, Co. Kerry, in the twentieth century. There, hundreds of ruined examples may have served as pilgrims' hostels. They are distributed in coastal areas from the south-west to the north-west of Ireland. **Peter Harbison**

Behan, Brendan (1922–1964), playwright and author. Born in Dublin to a family with strong republican sympathies, a nephew of PEADAR KEARNEY; after a brief education he followed his father's trade of house-painter and sign-writer. He was arrested in Liverpool and sent to Borstal for participating in the IRA bombing campaign in England; he was also jailed in Ireland. His experiences later produced the autobiographical *Borstal Boy* (1958), his finest work. He was active as a journalist, short-story writer and minor poet in both Irish and English. His first plays were THE QUARE FELLOW and AN GIALL; but it was the publication of his book and the quick sequence of the London productions of *The Quare Fellow* (1956) and *The Hostage* (1958) that brought him fame. His reputation depended as much on his own quick-witted personality as on the literary qualities of his work. He was a very uneven writer, and his later books had to be pieced together by an editor; but even his slightest writing sparkles with wit, warmth, and human compassion. *Brendan Behan's Island* (1962) is a miscellany with evocative drawings by Paul Hogarth. Other theatre pieces, such as the unfinished *Richard's Cork Leg*, are of little consequence. Behan's biographers have explored his HOMOSEXUAL leanings; but these, such as they were, would seem to have been a natural consequence for a youth incarcerated at the age of sixteen. He died in Dublin from the complications of alcoholism and diabetes. **Peter Costello**

Behan, John (1938–), sculptor. Born in Dublin; studied at the NCAD and the Royal Academy School, Oslo. A founder-member of the Project Arts Centre, Dublin, 1967, he established the Dublin Art Foundry, 1970, is a founder-member of the Association of Artists in Ireland, 1973, and a member of the ROYAL HIBERNIAN ACADEMY and of AOSDÁNA. His favoured subjects are symbols, motifs, and figures from Irish history and mythology; he is known for his sculptures of bulls, which express a raw and primitive energy. **Suzanne McNab**

Beit, Sir Alfred (1903–1994), politician and philanthropist. Born in London; educated at the University of Oxford. He was a Conservative member of the British Parliament, 1931–46. He moved to Russborough House, near Blessington, Co. Wicklow, in 1952, where he housed the Beit art collection of Old Master works of principally the Dutch, Flemish, and Spanish schools formed by his uncle, Alfred Beit (1853–1906), founder with Cecil Rhodes of the De Beers Diamond Mining Company. The Alfred Beit Foundation was established in 1976 to administer the collection, and in 1987 seventeen of its most significant works, by Goya, Hobbema, Metsu, Velázquez, and Vermeer, were donated to the NATIONAL GALLERY OF IRELAND. Serious thefts of paintings from Russborough occurred in 1974, 1986, 2001, and 2002. Sir Alfred and Lady Beit became honorary Irish citizens in 1993. **Brian Lalor**

Bel, James (1824–1908), chemist. Born at Altnamagham, Newtownhamilton, Co. Armagh. Following early private education he studied chemistry and mathematics at University College, London. In 1846 he joined the chemical section of the Inland Revenue Department, attaining the rank of principal in 1874. He was responsible for many improvements in methodologies relating to the analysing of foodstuffs, some of which passed into legislation. His three-part book *The Analysis and Adulteration of Foods* (1881–3) was translated into German. He also wrote *The Chemistry of Tobacco* (1887). He was elected a fellow of the Royal Society, 1884, and was president of the Institute of Chemistry, 1888–91. **Susan McKenna-Lawlor**

Behan, Brendan. *The playwright and author Brendan Behan working in McDaid's Bar, Dublin, August 1952. His experiences in borstal produced the autobiographical* Borstal Boy *(1958), considered his finest work. [Getty Images/Hulton Archive]*

Belfast (*Béal Feirste*), city and port at the head of Belfast Lough, between Cos. Antrim and Down, and principal city of Northern Ireland. Belfast's site is a flat-floored glacial trough between the Antrim Plateau, which rises to 481 m (1,574 ft) at Divis, overlooking the city, and the lower Castlereagh Hills. The area is drained by the River Lagan and its tributaries. Belfast was a crossing-point of the Lagan, guarded by a castle built in the late twelfth century; but much of the land was boggy, and Belfast consequently was less important in historical times than Carrickfergus.

Modern Belfast is recent by European standards, dating from 1603, when land was granted by the British Crown to Sir ARTHUR CHICHESTER in recognition of military service. He laid out a fortified town on the Co. Antrim shore and settled it mainly with English and Scots. The Irish lived outside the town to the west, the apex of a sector of Catholic housing even now. As sole landowners, the Chichesters (later Earls, then Marquises, of Donegall) influenced Belfast's development. Their castle, built in 1611, burnt down in 1708 at the start of the tenure of the incapable fourth earl (1695–1757), who had inherited in 1706; his long rule saw Belfast described as 'ruinous' by 1752. His nephew, the fifth earl and first marquis (1739–1799), though an absentee landlord, carefully guided Belfast, and a number of decent GEORGIAN buildings were erected, including the Poor House, now Clifton House (1774), and the White LINEN HALL (1785). He was also involved in the Lagan Navigation, from Belfast to LOUGH NEAGH. Belfast became known as the 'Athens of the North'; it did not remain so.

Belfast changed dramatically into an industrial city. There was early INDUSTRIALISATION in the eighteenth century, with small-scale SHIPBUILDING and cotton manufacture (first introduced as a make-work scheme in the Poor House). Cotton became a factory industry; then, from the 1820s, LINEN took over. Linen factories, mainly on the Co. Antrim side of the city, stimulated the growth of engineering and chemical industries, many sited in Ballymacarret, across the Lagan. Industrialisation was aided by the second Marquis of Donegall, who had huge debts and leased much land for development from 1822. He continued to live beyond his means, building a large mansion in Ormeau Park (demolished in 1870), and owed €507,895 (£400,000) on his death. His successor had to let the remainder of the estate go under the ENCUMBERED ESTATES Act.

In 1849 William Hickson opened a shipyard on reclaimed land, later called Queen's Island, created from spoil from dredging for harbour improvements. He employed EDWARD HARLAND as manager, who bought the yard in 1859 and in 1861 took GUSTAV WOLFF as his partner. HARLAND AND WOLFF became successful and employed 9,000 people in 1900, around which time another 35,000 worked in textiles, mainly linen; Belfast had become 'Linenopolis'. Ropeworks and engineering were also significant. The population reached 349,180 in 1901, from 70,308 in 1841, many housed in red-brick terraces. Belfast became a city in 1888.

Belfast has a legacy of fine nineteenth-century buildings, including Queen's University (1849), the Palm House in the BOTANIC GARDENS (completed 1852), the Custom House (1857), the Crown Liquor Saloon (1885), a pub with an ornate interior, now owned by the National Trust, and the GRAND OPERA HOUSE (1895), as well as the City Hall, completed in 1906 on the site of the White Linen Hall.

Belfast's zenith is symbolised by the launching in 1911 of the TITANIC, the world's largest ship (46,328 tons), which famously sank on its first voyage. The roots of Belfast's twentieth-century problems were planted earlier, particularly the divisions between Protestants and Catholics, which had often seen unrest in the nineteenth century. On the larger scale, these divisions were part of the larger divisions which led to the partition of Ireland. Belfast became the capital of Northern Ireland, with a parliament meeting first in the City Hall in 1921 before moving in 1932 to STORMONT, just outside the city. Belfast's industry was hit by the depression; the city's second shipyard, Workman Clark, closed in 1935. The SECOND WORLD WAR saw a revival in orders for Harland and Wolff and also for SHORT BROTHERS, the aircraft manufacturers who had moved from England in 1937.

After the war Belfast's industries became increasingly uncompetitive. Its housing was ageing, and the city's woes were increased by its full participation in the 'TROUBLES', the deadly communal strife that erupted again from 1969. Belfast experienced many bombings and shootings, two of the worst incidents being the bombing by loyalists of McGurk's pub in North Queen Street in 1971, when fifteen people were killed, and the bombing by the IRA of LA MON HOUSE, outside Belfast, in 1978, when twelve died. 'PEACE LINE' barricades were built to separate Catholic and Protestant areas of the city; but thousands just abandoned Belfast, and the city's population fell from 416,679 in 1971 to 279,237 in 1991.

In the 1990s there was a cessation of violence, which encouraged a policy of urban regeneration, including housing renewal. There were new transport facilities too, including new river crossings by road and rail. The site of the former gasworks and redundant dock areas were regenerated by Laganside Corporation, its most notable development being Lanyon Place, with hotel, office blocks, and Waterfront Hall, a new concert hall that opened in 1997 (see p. 790).

Belfast remains an industrial city, though there seem always to be concerns over the future of Harland and Wolff. It became again a political capital as devolved government returned to Northern Ireland in 1999 and 2000, after DIRECT RULE had been imposed in 1972. Belfast is an important port and also has ferries to England and Scotland. There are two airports: the City Airport, the airfield in the harbour originally built for Short Brothers—now Belfast's largest manufacturer—and Belfast International Airport at Aldergrove, to the north-east. **Stephen A. Royle**

Belfast Agreement/Good Friday Agreement (1998), the most significant attempt to resolve the Northern Ireland problem since partition. The scene had been set by the election of a Labour Party government in Britain in May 1997 and the offer of the new Prime Minister, Tony Blair, to admit SINN FÉIN to all-party negotiations without preconditions, provided the IRA reinstated its 1994 ceasefire.

The talks opened on 15 September 1997, under the chairmanship of Senator George Mitchell, and were attended by the ULSTER UNIONIST PARTY, SDLP, SINN FÉIN, ALLIANCE PARTY, and three smaller parties—the WOMEN'S COALITION, PROGRESSIVE UNIONIST PARTY, and the Ulster Democratic Party, as well as the British and Irish governments. The negotiations concentrated on three 'strands'—relationships within Northern Ireland (strand 1), North-South relations (strand 2), and Anglo-Irish relations (strand 3)—while sub-committees dealt with the decommissioning of paramilitary weapons and 'confidence-building measures', including police reform and the release of prisoners. In discussions, the UUP refused to engage directly with Sinn Féin, while, as a result of paramilitary violence, both Sinn Féin and the Ulster Democratic Party were expelled briefly. In January 1998 the governments of the United Kingdom and the Republic of Ireland issued their own document, which envisaged balanced constitutional change, a NORTHERN IRELAND ASSEMBLY, North-South structures, and a British-Irish Council.

The chairman's deadline of 9 April 1998 concentrated minds, and the closing days witnessed an intensive round of bilateral contacts involving Prime Minister Tony Blair and TAOISEACH BERTIE AHERN and intervention by the President of the United States, Bill Clinton. Crucial concessions to Sinn Féin on prisoners and decommissioning required a written assurance by Blair to DAVID TRIMBLE on the issue. The agreement provided for a 108-member Assembly, elected by proportional representation, a power-sharing Executive, a North-South Ministerial Council, a British-Irish Council, and a proviso that major decisions would require a cross-community vote in the Assembly. The Irish Government undertook to recommend the amendment of articles 2 and 3 of the CONSTITUTION OF IRELAND, while the British government agreed to repeal the Government of Ireland Act (1920). An acceptance of the decommissioning of paramilitary weapons was deemed to be 'an indispendable part of this agreement.' Finally, paramilitary prisoners would be released within two years, and an independent commission would report on a new police service.

The agreement was endorsed by 71 per cent of voters in the North and by 94 per cent in the South in referendums held on 22 May 1998, and the institutions were formally established in December 1999 (see pp. 789, 1149). **Eamon Phoenix**

Belfast Blitz (1941). On the afternoon of 30 November 1940 a single German plane flew unobserved high over Belfast. The crew brought back photographs of suitable targets, and the photo-reconnaissance unit of the German Air Force discovered that the city was defended by only seven anti-aircraft batteries, making Belfast the most undefended city in the United Kingdom. Only some houses in the harbour area had domestic air-raid shelters: none had been provided anywhere else. The fall of France earlier in the year brought Northern Ireland within range of the Luftwaffe. On the night of 7/8 April 1941 a small squadron of German bombers destroyed the HARLAND AND WOLFF fuselage factory and delivered damaging blows to the docks. The sky was clearing on the evening of Easter Tuesday, 15 April, as 180 bombers approached Belfast; between 10:45 p.m. and 3:45 a.m. they dropped 203 tonnes of bombs and 800 fire-bomb canisters. At 4:35 a.m. the Northern Ireland government sent an appeal to the Taoiseach, ÉAMON DE VALERA, who sent fire engines north from Dundalk, Drogheda, Dublin, and Dún Laoghaire. But there was little any firefighters could do: at one point 140 fires raged in the city. At least 900 people were killed; no other city, apart from London, lost so many lives in a single air raid.

The Germans returned again in force on 4/5 May 1941, and as it was a clear night with a full moon they inflicted devastating attacks on the docks, shipyard, aircraft factory, and vessels in the harbour. The death toll was 191, comparatively low because so many citizens had evacuated the city or were sleeping in the open air on neighbouring hills. **Jonathan Bardon**

Belfast Boycott, a nationalist BOYCOTT of goods and services produced by Belfast concerns organised in the summer of 1920 in

Belfast Blitz. *British soldiers engaged in rescue work at Alvin's Road, Belfast, April 1941. Between 10:45 p.m. and 3:45 a.m. on 15 April 1941, 180 German bombers dropped 203 tonnes of bombs on Belfast, killing at least 900 people. [Trustees of the Imperial War Museum, London; H8959]*

retaliation for the 'Belfast pogrom'—the expulsion of Catholic workers from Protestant businesses. Originally aimed at Belfast banks and insurance companies, the boycott was later extended to include goods produced in Belfast and the surrounding area. A Department of the Boycott was set up by the Free State Government, under Joseph MacDonagh, to co-ordinate the action, which was enforced by the IRA. Though individual firms suffered quite badly, as did some unionist businesses in the south of Ireland, the boycott did not fundamentally damage the economy of what became Northern Ireland; but it was deeply resented by unionists, whose partitionism was reinforced by the violence and intimidation of the campaign. The action was officially lifted following the Craig-Collins pact of January 1922, though anti-Treaty republicans fitfully tried to continue the boycott for some time afterwards. In fact one of the most dramatic episodes of the campaign occurred in April 1922, when IRA men in Dublin destroyed 660 litres[3] (145,000 gallons) of WHISKEY, worth £50,000, belonging to the Dunville distillery, owned by the family of Sir JAMES CRAIG. **Keith Jeffery**

Belfast Corporation. Granted to Sir ARTHUR CHICHESTER in 1603, Belfast was still a very new town when it was incorporated by JAMES I in 1613. The charter created a corporation made up of a 'sovereign' and twelve burgesses—all appointed by the 'Lord of the Castle' (Chichester)—with powers to create freemen, to pass by-laws, and to elect two members to the Irish Parliament. Under the patronage of the Chichester family the corporation did much to promote the development of Belfast into a thriving centre of commerce in the late seventeenth century. In the eighteenth century, however, the corporation was neglectful, and it was left largely to the initiative of leading Presbyterian families to bring improvements to the town, such as the provision of a water supply, a poorhouse, and quays.

In 1840 the inactive and unrepresentative corporation was replaced by an elected body. Despite bitter party divisions between Conservatives and Liberals (later between Unionists and Nationalists), the corporation was assiduous in promoting the modernisation of the fast-growing town through, for example, street-building, erecting a Town Hall, regulating domestic housing, and laying effective sewers and drains.

In 1888 Belfast became a city; and in 1906, with funds largely raised from the profits of the gasworks, the corporation erected a magnificent City Hall. During the inter-war years the corporation was dominated by a Unionist clique known as the 'City Hall Party', and its record of municipal improvement was wretched. This neglect was exposed by the German air raids in the BELFAST BLITZ of 1941, and the government placed the city in the hands of a commission for three years.

With the help of central government funds, much was achieved in the post-war years. However, outrageous cronyism, lack of transparency in the awarding of contracts, and bitter political division continued to characterise the corporation. The local government reforms of 1972 dissolved the corporation and replaced it with Belfast City Council, a body with much-reduced powers. **Jonathan Bardon**

Belfast dock strike (1907). JAMES LARKIN arrived in Belfast as organiser of the National Union of Dock Labourers in January 1907 and within three months claimed to have recruited 2,900 dockers and all the carters in the city's docks. In response to growing agitation for better pay and conditions the employers locked out their workers on 5 May and brought in 'free labour' from England, with the assistance of the Shipping Federation. The consequence was a summer of ultimately unsuccessful industrial action, which eventually involved several sectors of the labour force—including, at one point, policemen. Though the strike never involved more that 3,500 workers, it generated spontaneous and non-sectarian support on a large scale. Attendance at the daily strike meetings varied between 5,000 and 10,000, and more than 100,000 marched in a demonstration organised by the Trades Council on 26 July. The strike was finally ended in July, essentially on the employers' terms; though the unions claimed a victory, the consequences of the strike for organised labour in the city were disastrous, and serious decline followed. The Workers' Union, which had five branches in Belfast by 1908, declined so much by 1913 that it withdrew its organiser and in effect suspended its activities in the city. Though the strike was an important event in the history of the labour movement, as a purely industrial action it was unsuccessful and even damaging to the trade unions. **John Patrick Lynch**

Belfast Exposed, a photographic organisation established in 1983 by a group of local photographers. It works with groups from both sides of the sectarian divide, offering educational courses in photography, hosting exhibitions, and providing bursaries to support local photographers. The organisation has a library of approximately half a million photographs, an invaluable visual archive of Belfast between 1983 and 2000. **Myra Dowling**

Belfast Harp Festival (1792), a three-day event organised by a committee led by James McDonnell, a member of a distinguished family from Glenariff in the Glens of Antrim. A doctor, with a great interest in cultural affairs, he was a man of patriotic though moderate views who had a particular interest in the HARP, having been taught to play in childhood. His aim in organising the festival was to encourage the few remaining traditional harpers by bringing them together to play and to compete for prizes. Ten Irish harpers and one Welshman attended; six were blind, and their ages ranged from ninety-seven down to fifteen. All were men except for Rose Mooney, who won third prize. First and second prizes went to Charles Fanning and Arthur O'Neill (Dr McDonnell's former teacher); but all who played were given some payment.

The real importance of the festival lay in the presence of EDWARD BUNTING, who was commissioned to write down the music as it was played. As well as the music he took down a mass of information about the harpers and their traditional harp lore; but for him, the greater part of this would have disappeared for ever. Bunting's collection was the catalyst for much nineteenth-century collecting of folk music and provided the basis for MOORE's *Melodies*. **Gráinne Yeats**

Belfast Natural History and Philosophical Society, founded in 1821, with Dr James L. Drummond as first president. The Society's museum opened at 7 College Square, North, in 1831. Natural history lectures were introduced, and the collections expanded rapidly. By 1842 the Society had broadened its scope and assumed its present title. In 1910 its collections, as well as a fine library, were presented to the city of Belfast for a proposed new museum. Following delays resulting from the FIRST WORLD WAR, Belfast Museum (now the ULSTER MUSEUM) opened in the BOTANIC GARDENS in 1921. The Society's numbers remain healthy and the varied lecture programme is well supported. **Helena C. G. Chesney**

Belfast Naturalists' Field Club, founded in 1863, the first such club in Ireland. The field club movement arose in the 1850s from the need to supplement scientific lectures with practical fieldwork. The Department of Science and Art financed Ralph Tate to teach natural sciences in Belfast; the success of his wide-ranging classes led to the founding of Belfast Naturalists' Field Club. Adventurous programmes of field excursions led by enthusiastic naturalists such as Samuel Stewart and ARTHUR STELFOX attracted a large number of members. The club's early field recording expanded into valuable surveys of the North's FLORA, FAUNA, and GEOLOGY, on which current biodiversity research is based. **Helena C. G. Chesney**

Belfast Port. A Ballast Board was established in 1785, and improvements were undertaken. WILLIAM DARGAN completed the first cut of the approach channel in 1841, creating Dargan's Island (later Queen's Island). Belfast Harbour Commissioners were constituted in 1847 and Victoria Channel opened in 1849. EDWARD HARLAND began shipbuilding here in 1858, later joined by GUSTAV WOLFF to form one of the world's largest shipbuilding companies, builders of the TITANIC. An extensive system of docks was created, 1850–1900, including Abercorn Basin (1867) and Alexandra Graving Dock (1889), with Musgrave Channel formed in 1904 and Thompson Graving Dock built in 1911. Belfast Airport was established in the port in 1933. Post-war expansion included the new Belfast Dock (1968) and Building Dock (1970) and roll-on/roll-off container and ferry terminals. **Ronald Cox**

Belfast riots (nineteenth century). The rapid development of the cotton and LINEN industries in Belfast in the first half of the nineteenth century drew tens of thousands of Catholics and Protestants from the impoverished countryside west of the River Bann into the town. These people brought memories of dispossession, massacre, and religious conflict into a largely Presbyterian town where community relations had previously been exemplary. The migrants chose where they settled with care, and conflict frequently erupted along the unstable boundaries of the new enclaves, notably between the (Catholic) Pound Loney and the (Protestant) Sandy Row. The most severe riots, lasting several weeks, occurred in 1857, 1864, 1872, and 1886.

The importing of sectarian politics from other parts of Ulster, coupled with increasingly vociferous street preaching, exacerbated an already volatile situation. Parliamentary and corporation elections often provided the catalyst for conflict, with elections celebrated by chairing the victorious candidate through opposing districts, accompanied at times by bands playing party tunes. The Liberal-Tory and later Nationalist-Unionist split ran largely, though not exclusively, along religious lines, Catholics remaining without a representative until 1856.

The emergence of identifiable single-denomination districts allowed interface areas to develop, for example between the Protestant Sandy Row and the Catholic Pound (Lower Falls). The inquiries following the riots of 1857 and 1864 recognised this patchwork division and drew attention to the practice of hooting at Catholic funerals as they made their way from the Pound through Sandy Row to Friar's Bush graveyard; they also led indirectly to the dissolution of Belfast's partisan, Protestant-dominated police force, the 'Bulkies'. The 1864 inquiry listed 327 killed or injured, 107 by gunshot, 214 cases of contusion, five stabbings, and one death from fright.

The introduction of the first HOME RULE Bill and the founding of the Unionist Party in 1886 were again followed by extensive and prolonged rioting, with seven people killed by the police over a three-day period in June. At least thirty citizens, and perhaps as many as fifty, were killed during the summer of 1886 [see SECTARIANISM; TORIES]. **Roddy Hegarty**

Belfast riots (twentieth century). In the twentieth century, riots in Belfast were overwhelmingly sectarian confrontations sparked by an issue connected to the broader constitutional question. Such was the case in the early 1920s, at the time of partition. During the autumn of 1932 Protestants and Catholics united briefly in Belfast to campaign for increases in outdoor relief (UNEMPLOYMENT assistance), made by the Board of Guardians to the long-term unemployed. Serious rioting had occurred; but this manifestation of working-class solidarity was short-lived. In 1935 Belfast 'reverted to type' with serious inter-COMMUNAL VIOLENCE, sparked by the Twelfth of July celebrations. The continuing high level of unemployment, which had reached 24 per cent in 1934 (compared with a United Kingdom average of 16.5 per cent) had caused mounting tension in the city. The Minister of Home Affairs, RICHARD DAWSON BATES, fearing public disorder, banned all processions but capitulated to demands from the Orange Order to exempt them. Rioting broke out in the York Street area, which was

Belfast Harp Festival. *Engraving by William Brocas of Edward Bunting (1811), musician and collector of Irish music. Bunting's annotation of the music played at the Belfast Harp Festival ensured the survival of old harp music and lore. The Bunting Collection, a rich source of music, texts, and information from the eighteenth and nineteenth centuries, is now in the library of Queen's University, Belfast. [National Gallery of Ireland]*

to last until late August and left thirteen people dead and about 400—mainly Catholics—homeless. An attempt by Westminster MPs to call for an inquiry was frustrated by the Prime Minister, Stanley Baldwin, who refused to act, as the matter lay in the jurisdiction of the Northern Ireland government. The long-term consequence of these events was a hardening of nationalist views towards the Northern Ireland government and a loss of confidence in Westminster. In August 1969 events in Derry lit the fuse that led to the explosion of the sectarian powder-keg in Belfast.

From the 1970s, as the security forces expanded and became more expert in dealing with riots, confrontations between members of one community (usually, but not exclusively, the Catholic community) and the security forces became the norm, rather than inter-community riots. With the massive population movement that occurred after 1968, both within Belfast (as people moved to 'safer' areas inhabited by their co-religionists) and out of Belfast into surrounding areas, the opportunity for confrontations between Protestants and Catholics was reduced. Despite this, 'peace walls' dividing the antagonistic communities were still being expanded in interface areas in north and east Belfast in 2002.

In contrast to the sectarian riots noted above, the riots of October 1932 saw Protestant and Catholic workers united in attacking the police following protests demanding an increase in outdoor relief for the unemployed. These 'cross-community' outdoor relief riots were almost unique in the twentieth century. [see TROUBLES.] **Gordon Gillespie, John Patrick Lynch**

Belfast shipbuilding. The nineteenth century was a period of revolution in sea transport. Shipyards moved from building wooden sailing-ships to ever-larger steamships with iron and steel hulls. This technological change was a vital factor in the expansion of international commerce, as ships became less dependent on winds and currents and began to operate on predictable and regular timetables.

Belfast's first shipyard was established in 1791 when William Ritchie, a Scot from Ayrshire, began building wooden sailing-ships. Other shipbuilders followed; but it was not until the second half of the nineteenth century, when sailing-ships began to be eclipsed by iron steamships, that the city became an international shipbuilding centre. In Belfast the construction of iron ships was not an extension of wooden shipbuilding techniques but a development of the growing industry of boilermaking. Significantly, the first iron vessel built in Belfast, the *Countess of Caledon* (1838), was constructed by the engineering and boilermaking firm of Victor Coates and Company.

The Belfast Harbour Commissioners played a significant role in developing the shipbuilding infrastructure of the port. In 1853 they laid out a shipyard at Dargan Island (later renamed Queen's Island) for Robert Hickson, a partner in a local ironworks. Lacking practical shipbuilding ability, Hickson later sold the business to his yard manager, Edward Harland. In 1861 Harland, in partnership with G. W. Wolff, founded the firm of HARLAND AND WOLFF, which quickly established a reputation as a specialist yard for high-quality, innovative iron and steel ships.

Victor Coates and Company continued in business until the 1860s. MacIlwaine and Lewis, another Belfast engineering and boilermaking firm, also went into shipbuilding c. 1868 and remained in operation until 1894, when, as MacIlwaine and MacColl, they were taken over by the rising shipbuilders Workman Clark and Company. Formed in 1880, Workman Clark established an engine works in 1891 and became specialist shipbuilders from c. 1900. The yard pioneered the refrigerated steamship and built the first turbine-powered transatlantic passenger liner, the *Victorian* (1904). In 1902 Workman Clark headed the list of world shipbuilding tonnage output; but prosperity declined after the FIRST WORLD WAR, and the firm finally went out of business in 1935.

Belfast became an international shipbuilding city for a number of reasons. In addition to business enterprise and the city's importance as a trading port, there was ample space for shipyard expansion on the reclaimed slobland of Queen's Island. Farsighted policies by the Belfast Harbour Commissioners, in building dry docks and generally facilitating shipyards, were also crucial to the industry's successful development. **Michael McCaughan**

Belfast Telegraph, an evening newspaper published in Belfast and the most widely read daily in Northern Ireland. Founded in 1870 as the *Belfast Evening Telegraph* (dropping 'Evening' in 1918), it was mainstream unionist until 1953, when a new editor, Jack Sayer, initiated a more liberal line, seeking common ground with moderate nationalists. By 1957 average daily circulation approached 200,000, making it the biggest-selling daily in Ireland. It was bought by the Thomson Group in 1961, then by the Trinity Group, and in 2000—despite unionist objections—by the Dublin-based INDEPENDENT NEWS AND MEDIA. Its average daily circulation is now 111,000. **David Quin**

Belfast tramways. Horse trams were introduced in Belfast in 1872, running on standard-gauge 1.6 m (5 ft 3 in.) track, though this was reduced to 1.45 m (4 ft 9 in.) a few years later. The first trams ran from Castle Place to Botanic Gardens. Extensions were added in 1875 and 1879, the main routes being operated by the Belfast Street Tramways Company, which also worked systems owned by three smaller companies. In 1896 the company obtained powers to electrify the system, but this did not occur until Belfast Corporation took over the BST in 1904. Work began on 1 February the following year and was completed in seven months, the official opening taking place on 29 November. Some fifty of the 171 horse trams were converted to electric traction, and the addition of new cars brought the fleet up to 220.

A number of new routes were added in 1913; but in the period following the FIRST WORLD WAR the tramways suffered serious competition from buses. Belfast Corporation began introducing buses of its own in 1926, presaging the gradual abandonment of the system as track became unserviceable. Trolley-buses replaced trams on the Falls Road route in March 1936, but the outbreak of the SECOND WORLD WAR brought about a reprieve; two routes, however, were converted in 1941 and 1942, and after 1945 further closures followed. The last trams, from Queen's Road to the Ardoyne depot, ran on 28 February 1954. Horse tram no. 381 and electric trams nos. 249 and 357 are preserved in the ULSTER FOLK AND TRANSPORT MUSEUM. **Bernard Share**

Bell, The (1940–54), a monthly magazine of literature and social comment published in Dublin, founded by SEAN O'FAOLAIN, edited by O'Faolain until 1946 and then by PEADAR O'DONNELL. It acted as a strong, lively focus for liberal voices in challenging the Catholic nationalist consensus of the time, in particular on censorship and clericalism. It published new writers, such as FRANK O'CONNOR, PATRICK KAVANAGH, FLANN O'BRIEN, LOUIS MACNEICE, MARY LAVIN, JOHN MONTAGUE, BRENDAN BEHAN, JAMES PLUNKETT, and MICHAEL MCLAVERTY. Under O'Donnell's editorship it maintained its intellectual challenge while also moving leftwards. **David Quin**

Bell, Derek (1935–2002), harpist and composer. Born in Belfast, he studied music at the Royal College of Music, London, and in Europe and the United States. His other instruments included oboe, cor anglais, horn, hammered dulcimer, and keyboards. He played with the Royal Philharmonic Orchestra and the symphony orchestras of Pittsburgh, Moscow, London, Budapest, and the BBC. His principal compositions include piano sonatas and the *Symphony in E flat*; he wrote his first concerto at the age of twelve. He became professor of harp at the Belfast Academy of Music and joined the CHIEFTAINS full time in 1974. He recorded six solo albums, including *The Mystic Harp* (1 & 2) (1996). **Paul J. Kerr**

Bell, Laura (1829–1894), courtesan, social missionary, and preacher. Born in Co. Antrim. She worked as a shop assistant in Belfast before taking to prostitution in Dublin. Having gained a reputation while still in her teens, she moved to London, where she became the celebrated 'Queen of Whoredom'. She had a religious conversion at the age of thirty-one and became an evangelical preacher and social missionary. For three decades, in co-operation with the Prime Minister, W. E. GLADSTONE, she worked to rescue London prostitutes. She retired to a cottage in Hampshire, where she died. **Ciarán Deane**

Bell, Robert (1864–1934), naturalist. Born in Co. Down; he received only elementary education. From a working-class family, he worked for forty years as a riveter in the Belfast shipyards. As a boy he became interested in fossils and minerals and taught himself geology through visits to Belfast Museum. He became a prominent member of BELFAST NATURALISTS' FIELD CLUB, devoting his spare time to fieldwork. Restricted by circumstances to the district around Belfast, he became an expert on the fossils of the Lias and chalk and the zeolite minerals of the Tertiary basalts. He supplied museums with specimens, became an adviser to the GEOLOGICAL SURVEY, and was made a life member of the Mineralogical Society of London. **Kenneth W. James**

Bell, Sam Hanna (1909–1990), novelist, short-story writer, and radio producer. Born in Glasgow and brought home to Raffrey, Co Down, as a child; educated at Belfast College of Art. His works include *Summer Loanen and Other Stories* (1943), *December Bride* (1951), *Erin's Orange Lily* (1956), *The Hollow Ball* (1961), *Within Our Province* (1972), *The Theatre in Ulster* (1972), *A Man Flourishing* (1973), *Across the Narrow Sea* (1987), and *Tatler Tales* (1981). His critical merit rests arguably on *December Bride*, where lyricism is counterpointed with the dourness of the characters. It was filmed in 1990 by THADEUS O'SULLIVAN, starring DONAL MCCANN. His Ulster Protestants are at best stoical, at worst mordantly bleak. **Tess Maginess**

Bellamont Forest, Cootehill, Co. Cavan. Sir EDWARD LOVETT PEARCE's small masterpiece of a Palladian villa perches on a rolling drumlin between lakes and is one of the most perfect early eighteenth-century houses in Ireland. Begun c. 1728 for Thomas Coote, husband of the architect's aunt, and originally called Coote Hill, its design was inspired by Pearce's direct observation of villas by Andrea Palladio in Italy. Of two storeys over a rusticated basement, the rich red-brick façade offset by bold sandstone quoins gives the house the character of a model. The four-bay entrance front has a Doric portico, with a heavy stringcourse defining the attic storey. In contrast to its cubic exterior, the internal spaces are complexly arranged, with fine coffered ceilings in the principal rooms. It was renamed Bellamont in 1767 on the elevation of Charles Coote as Earl of Bellamont. **Brian Lalor**

Bell Burnell, (Susan) Jocelyn, née Bell (1943–), astronomer. Born in Lurgan, Co. Armagh; educated at the Universities of Glasgow and Cambridge. While a postgraduate student at the Mullard Radio Laboratory, Cambridge, she collaborated with her supervisor, Antony Hewish, in constructing a radio telescope to investigate the scintillation of distant radio sources. With this instrument, and by meticulous analysis of the recorded signals, she discovered in 1967 an astronomical source of short (1.3-second) regular pulses of radio emission. It was the first known pulsar—a rapidly spinning neutron star of about twice the Sun's mass, collapsed to a sphere of only a few kilometres in diameter. The theoretical possibility of such a condensed object had been predicted some thirty years earlier, but its discovery was of great significance to physics. Following research posts at Southampton, 1968–73, and London, 1974–82, she worked at the Royal Observatory, Edinburgh, 1982–91, where she managed the British support team of the international James Clerk Maxwell submillimetre-wave telescope in Hawaii. She was professor of physics at the Open University, 1991–2001 and in 2001 was appointed dean of science at the University of Bath. She has received nine honorary doctorates and numerous other awards, notably commander of the Order of the British Empire, the Michelson Medal, Philadelphia (jointly with Hewish), 1973, the American Astronomical Society's first Beatrice Tinsley Prize, 1987, and the Royal Astronomical Society's Herschel Medal, 1989. **M. T. Brück**

Belleek, fine hard-paste porcelain with iridescent clear glaze produced from the 1860s in Belleek, Co. Fermanagh. Belleek is a definitive product of Irish ceramics, though its most well-known decorative items—shell-form vases, openwork plaited lattice baskets, and allegorical figures such as 'Erin awakening from her slumbers'—represent only a small fraction of its wide product range of earthenware and stoneware. The initiative of the local landlord John Caldwell Bloomfield brought the designer Robert Williams Armstrong and the Dublin businessman David McBirney together to establish the ceramic factory, which was made viable by locally available clays, water power, and turf for firing. Belleek is still in production. **Brian Lalor**

Belleek Singers' Festival, a seminal FESTIVAL of traditional singing financed by the ARTS COUNCIL OF NORTHERN IRELAND. It was conceived in 1978 by CIARÁN CARSON, the Arts Council's traditional arts officer, who believed that, despite a considerable revival in dance music, the singing tradition had been conspicuously ignored. It brought together singers from throughout Ireland, beginning a movement that has seen an increasing profile for traditional singing. The Arts Council of Northern Ireland supported four such annual festivals until similar events (now over a dozen annually) became locally organised. **John Moulden**

Beltany, Co. Donegal, one of the most impressive STONE CIRCLES in Ireland, consisting of sixty-four standing stones (there may originally have been over eighty) forming a circle 44 m (144 ft) in diameter. It has achieved particular notoriety because of an alignment on a hilltop behind which the sun rises about the first of May, corresponding to the Celtic festival of BEALTAINE. Unfortunately the idea that the Celtic calendar had a precursor in a precise 'MEGALITHIC calendar', dividing the year into eight equal parts, remains completely unproved, as does the idea that the modern name of this circle reflects an astronomical alignment intended by the original builders. **Clive Ruggles**

Benbulbin, an isolated part of the Cuilcagh Plateau, its towering limestone escarpments guarding the coastal plain and Atlantic approaches of Co. Sligo. The plateau of Benbulbin, composed of the massive, vertically jointed Dartrey limestone, exhibits classic karstic features, including limestone pavements, as at the BURREN. The Dartrey limestone is underlaid by GLENCAR limestone and then the more erodible Benbulbin shales. The greater erosion of the shales by Quaternary glaciers led to undercutting of the overlying limestones. This, coupled with the impermeability of the shales to groundwaters descending through the limestones, has led to slope instability and the rotational landslides that have given Benbulbin its distinctive scarped profile. In its turn, fluvial erosion has exploited the vertical joints of the limestone, creating deep gorges, vertical cliffs, and isolated monoliths.

Benbulbin boasts 136 plant species, including several rare Alpine varieties that found refuge on the plateau during the last GLACIATION and thrived in its fragile calcareous soils, derived from the weathering of the limestones. In particular, the fringed sandwort grows nowhere else in Ireland. By way of contrast with a GEOLOGY that fosters mountain avens, Alpine saxifrage, and cushion pinks, the Dartrey limestone also plays host to an extensive vein of barytes. The mineral was first mined from Benbulbin in 1878, with production reaching a peak in the middle of the twentieth century at 100,000 tonnes per year, and was mainly used in the manufacture of paint. **Colman Gallagher**

Benbulbin. *Benbulbin, an isolated plateau of the Dartrey Mountains, Co. Sligo, steeped in history and mythology. Its breathtaking beauty and unique landscape provided inspiration for the poet W. B. Yeats, who is buried in Drumcliff churchyard. [Imagefile]*

Benburb, Battle of (1646), the biggest set-piece battle of the wars that raged from 1641 to 1652. The battle is considered the most spectacular military success of native Irish arms against Anglo-Scots opposition, outshining HUGH O'NEILL's victory at the BATTLE OF THE YELLOW FORD in 1598, as the Battle of Benburb was fought along conventional European military lines, whereas that at the Yellow Ford relied to a considerable extent on Irish-style ambuscade tactics. The rebel Irish forces in 1646 were led by OWEN ROE O'NEILL (nephew of Hugh), a highly experienced military commander trained on the Continent. Having assembled an army some 5,000 strong, Owen Roe engaged ROBERT MUNRO's larger force of 6,000 men, which had been raised to defend the Protestant settlers of Ulster. Having strategically positioned himself between three advancing settler columns, O'Neill surprised Munro by opting for a formal engagement instead of for a judicious retreat. Having mounted a 24 km (15-mile) march to cut off O'Neill from retiring to the safety of Charlemont fort, Munro encountered O'Neill's army deployed for battle in conventional formation. In the ensuing fighting the exhaustion of Munro's forces is considered to have contributed to their defeat. Be that as it may, Munro suffered a catastrophic defeat, his casualties being estimated by contemporaries at between 2,000 and 3,000 and possibly more.

Like that of the Yellow Ford, the Battle of Benburb is considered to have been a lost opportunity for the native Irish of Ulster. Instead of driving the remnants of settler forces from the north, Owen Roe O'Neill diverted his attention south. **John McCavitt**

Bennett, Louie (1870–1956), TRADE UNION activist. Born in Dublin into a family of auctioneers; educated in London. She travelled extensively and wrote several novels, including *Prisoner of His Word* (1908). By 1910 she was honorary secretary of the IRISH WOMEN'S SUFFRAGE FEDERATION and organising secretary of the Irish section of the Union of Democratic Control. In 1916 she became sub-editor of the IRISH CITIZEN, and in 1918, with HELEN CHENEVIX, undertook the reorganisation of the IRISH WOMEN WORKERS' UNION. **Mary Jones**

Benson, Sir John (1812–1874), architect and engineer. Born in Collooney, Co. Sligo, where he had the patronage of the local squire, EDWARD COOPER of Markree Castle, who sent him to the DUBLIN SOCIETY's School of Architectural Drawing. His works in Co. Sligo include a number of churches. From 1846 he held a succession of surveyorship appointments in Cork, culminating with that of city surveyor in 1851; he was also harbour engineer. He adapted and extended the Cork Corn Exchange to serve as a National Exhibition Building (1852), subsequently winning the competition to design the Dublin Exhibition Building (1853) on Leinster Lawn, for which he was knighted. **Frederick O'Dwyer**

Beranger, Gabriel (1729–1817), artist. Born in Rotterdam, of Dutch HUGUENOT origin; he came to Ireland in 1750 and earned a living as a print-seller and framer, teacher of drawing, and painter of pastel portraits, still life, and landscapes. He was soon involved in the antiquarian movement and was used by such men as William Burton Conyngham and CHARLES VALLANCEY to tour the country painting antiquities. His clear, wash watercolours and drawings were used as the basis for engravings in Francis Grose's *Antiquities of Ireland* (1791) and are now mainly in the ROYAL IRISH ACADEMY and the NATIONAL LIBRARY OF IRELAND. **Anne Crookshank**

Beresford, Lord John George (1773–1862), Anglican bishop. Born in Dublin, a member of the powerful Beresford family; educated at the University of Oxford. As Archbishop of Armagh from 1822 to 1862 he restored Armagh Cathedral. He opposed CATHOLIC EMANCIPATION, believing 'PROTESTANT ASCENDANCY' to be essential to the constitution, and he strongly opposed the national schools, supporting the rival Church Education Society. He served as both vice-chancellor and chancellor of TRINITY COLLEGE, Dublin, and gave the college its campanile. **Kenneth Milne**

Berger-Hammerschlag, Alice (1917–1969), abstract painter, illustrator, and stage designer. Born in Vienna; trained at Vienna Academy of Arts and School of Arts and Crafts. She settled in Belfast in 1938. One of the first painters in Ireland to adopt an abstract expressionist technique, she ran the New Gallery in Belfast in the 1960s, a time when few commercial galleries existed in the city, and was a set-designer for the Lyric Theatre. In 1970 the Alice Berger-Hammerschlag Trust, making awards to young Irish artists, was established in her memory. The ULSTER MUSEUM has a large holding of her works, much of it donated by her family. **S. B. Kennedy**

Bergin, Patrick (1953–), actor. Born in Dublin. From a theatrical family, Bergin had acted, directed, and produced plays in London before playing the lead in the Irish gangster feature *The Courier* (1988). He played a terrorist who left the IRA in the television film *Act of Betrayal* (1989), the nineteenth-century explorer Sir Richard Burton in *Mountains of the Moon* (1990), and a murderous husband in the commercially successful *Sleeping with the Enemy* (1991). Other films include *Robin Hood* (1991), *The Real Charlotte* (1991), *Frankenstein* (1993), *Map of the Human Heart* (1993), and *Lawnmower Man 2* (1996). **Kevin Rockett**

Berkeley, George (1685–1753), philosopher and Anglican bishop. Born in Kilkenny; he attended Kilkenny College and TCD, graduating in 1704. He was ordained in the Anglican Church in 1709 and spent most of the period 1713–34 abroad, in London, on the Continent, and in America, where he lived in Rhode Island. He had gone to America with the aim of establishing a college in Bermuda but never received the money he had been promised. However, he had a considerable influence on education in America. His later years, from 1734 on, were mostly spent in Ireland, where he was Bishop of Cloyne, carrying out his episcopal duties with generous concern for the well-being of all who lived in his diocese. He died in Oxford, where his son was a student, in 1753.

His works include essays on motion, vision, topics in mathematics, and theology, as well as his contributions in philosophy. His first important philosophical work was *An Essay towards a New Theory of Vision* (1709). This was followed by *A Treatise concerning the Principles of Human Knowledge* (1710) and *Three Dialogues between Hylas and Philonous* (1713). Later important works include *Alciphron* (1732), a largely theological treatise, THE QUERIST (1735–52) (see p. 906), and *Siris* (1744), in which the medicinal properties of tar water are extolled.

Berkeley is an extremely important figure in the history of philosophy, and more broadly in the history of ideas. Lectures on his work are given today in departments of philosophy around the world, and his work is well known far beyond the English-speaking world; in the United States, the city of Berkeley, California and its university are named after him. Though his philosophical views are subtle and ingenious, the main themes are accessible. In the entire universe there are only minds and ideas. The existence of minds consists in perceiving, whereas the existence of ideas, including sensations, consists in being perceived. Physical objects consist of qualities—the very qualities we observe them to have; and qualities are sensations. Hence, the existence of physical objects consists in being perceived. Thus Berkeley endorses the idealist view that the physical world depends upon the mind; consequently there is no need for material substance. (Indeed he argued at length that the very concept of material substance is incoherent.) The sensations that constitute the physical world are given to us by God, the one infinite mind. Since God is their source, we are constantly in intimate contact with God, and we can therefore always reasonably be certain of God's existence. Berkeley is not saying that the world is an illusion: it does not have mind-independent existence, but it is nevertheless real, and we perceive it directly, and accurately. There is no room for the sort of scepticism that is possible if, with many of Berkeley's predecessors, we were to accept that we can never get beyond a veil of ideas through which we perceive a mind-independent material world. Scepticism of this sort cannot get a foothold in Berkeley's system, because the perceived is the real, or, as he put it, 'to be is to be perceived'. **Robert McKim**

Bernal, John Desmond (1901–1971), scientist. Born in Nenagh, Co. Tipperary; educated at the University of Cambridge. An X-ray crystallographer, he was one of the first modern physicists to work at the interface with biology, recognising that the key to many biological problems lies in molecular structure. He is also remembered for his models of liquid structure. Bernal was a leading figure in British Marxism, which coloured his many influential books on science history and policy. He was professor of physics at Birkbeck College, University of London, from 1935 to 1968, a fellow of the Royal Society, and was awarded the Lenin Peace Prize in 1953. **Denis Weaire**

Best, George (1946–), soccer player. Born in Belfast; he joined Manchester United as a boy. He grew into a cult figure on the team that Sir Matt Busby built in the aftermath of the Munich air disaster of 1958. Widely acknowledged as one of the most talented soccer players of the latter half of the twentieth century, his extravagant skills on the pitch were matched only by his excesses off it. He shared in the club's European Cup win over Benfica at Wembley in 1968 when he was the first Irishman to be named as European Footballer of the Year. A charismatic personality who later became a television football analyst, he continued to attract publicity long after his playing career ended. He made the last of his thirty-seven appearances for Northern Ireland in 1978, against Holland. **Peter Byrne**

'Betha Colaim Chille', a life of COLM CILLE produced by MAGHNUS Ó DOMHNAILL in his castle at Lifford, Co. Donegal, in 1532. The distinguishing features of this work—lay authorship, antiquarian character in consulting sources, and simple language that could be understood by all—bear the strong imprint of Renaissance values. **Mícheál Mac Craith**

Betham, Sir William (1779–1853), heraldic official. Born at Stradbrooke, Suffolk. Knighted in 1812, he was appointed Ulster King of Arms in 1820. A Hibernophile, he was particularly interested in early Irish history and the Irish genealogies and made a three-volume copy of Roger O Ferral's *Linea Antiqua* (1709), with additions and indexes.

His great contribution to Ulster's Office was his classification of the manuscript materials there, as well as an explanation of their provenance, such as arms registers, visitations, and funeral entries. Between 1807 and c. 1828 he compiled his monumental index to prerogative wills down to 1800, subsequently edited by Sir Arthur Vicars as *The Prerogative Wills of Ireland* (1897). He made abstracts of the genealogical information found in the wills in notebooks now in the NATIONAL ARCHIVES; on the basis of the abstracts he compiled sketch pedigrees with additions and amendments, now in the Genealogical Office. Also in the Genealogical Office are his manuscript works 'Ancient Anglo-Irish Families', 'Milesian Families', and extensive pedigrees of Hiberno-Norman families compiled from the

Plea and Patent Rolls from the time of Henry III to that of Edward VI. He also made partial transcriptions of the manuscript calendars, abstracts and index of John Lodge, a former Deputy Keeper of the Rolls, compiled from the Patent Rolls and other official records. In 1834 he published *The Gael and the Cymbri, or An Inquiry into the Origin and History of the Irish, Scots, Picts, Britons and Gauls; and of the Caledonians, Picts, Welsh, Cornish and Bretons*. His enthusiasm was greater than his scholarship; he absurdly deduced that Irish was related to 'Iberian' and Phoenician. On the positive side, it was Betham who discovered the CATHACH, the sixth-century psalter of COLM CILLE, when he opened its shrine. He was also an avid collector of Irish manuscripts and was on the governing body of the ROYAL IRISH ACADEMY, where his collection of Irish manuscripts is now housed. [see FAMILY HISTORY; GENEALOGY.] **Fergus Gillespie**

'Betty, Lady' (c. 1750–c. 1807), public executioner. Probably born and raised in Co. Kerry. She ran a lodging house in Roscommon. She apparently murdered a lodger for money before realising that it was her own son, recently returned from his travels. She was sentenced to be hanged, along with a large group of WHITEBOYS, but no hangman could be found. At her suggestion it was agreed that she would act as executioner in exchange for her freedom. She allegedly hanged twenty-five men on that day, earning her instant notoriety. She was public executioner in Connacht for many years. Many UNITED IRISHMEN were hanged by her, in recognition of which the LORD LIEUTENANT lifted her death sentence in 1802. For her own protection she lived permanently inside Roscommon Jail. **Ciarán Deane**

Bewerunge, Heinrich (1862–1923), born in Leitmathe, Westphalia; a German priest and church music scholar. He studied theology at the University of Würzburg, and attended the Royal School of Music and the School of Church Music, Regensburg. A central figure in the Cecilian movement for the revival of church choral music in Ireland, he was appointed professor of sacred music at ST PATRICK'S COLLEGE, Maynooth, a post he held from 1888 until his death. His writings centred on the editing and analysis of Gregorian chant. He held the chair of music at UCD from 1914 until 1916. From 1891 to 1893 he was editor of the Irish Cecilian journal, LYRA ECCLESIASTICA. **Paul J. Kerr**

Bewick, Pauline (1935–), painter. Born in England and raised in Co. Kerry; studied at the NCAD. She has worked in many media, including watercolour, ceramics, tapestry, and stained glass.

Berkeley. The Bermuda Group *(1729–30) by John Smibert, showing the philosopher George Berkeley (right) with his wife, Anne, holding their first child, Henry, next to her companion, Miss Handcock, with the artist (standing, extreme left) and other members of Berkeley's circle: John Wainwright (seated), Richard Dalton (standing second left), and John James. [National Gallery of Ireland]*

Her paintings are figurative and are executed in a clear, linear style that shows accomplished graphic skills. Her subjects often express the joy of life, echoed in her use of vibrant colour. A film on her life, *A Painted Diary* (1985), was made by David Shaw Smith for RTÉ; there is also an illustrated biography by JAMES WHITE, *Painting a Life* (1985). She is a member of the ROYAL HIBERNIAN ACADEMY and of AOSDÁNA. **Suzanne McNab**

Bewley, Charles (1888–1969), diplomat. Born in Dublin into an old QUAKER business family that owned the celebrated Bewley's coffee shops in Dublin; he was awarded a scholarship to the University of Oxford, where he won the Newdigate Prize for English verse, previously won by OSCAR WILDE. Called to the bar in 1914, he built a strong practice on the Western Circuit and was for a time acting professor of law at University College, Galway. A convert to Catholicism, he wrote widely for the Catholic press in England and the United States. He failed to win a seat for SINN FÉIN in 1918 but was a barrister in the Republican Courts and served as a Sinn Féin 'envoy' in Berlin, with responsibility for commercial affairs—a position he held until 1922, when he returned to Ireland to practise law. He was appointed envoy extraordinary and minister plenipotentiary to the Holy See in 1929. A gifted linguist, he knew Italian and German. After ÉAMON DE VALERA and FIANNA FÁIL came to power in 1932 he was transferred to Berlin, where he remained until he parted company with the Irish diplomatic service in 1939. During the war years he remained in Rome, where he is alleged to have worked as a member of the German intelligence service under the cover of being a journalist. Arrested at the end of the war, he was fortunate not to have been hanged as a collaborator. He continued to live in Italy until his death in 1969. **Dermot Keogh**

Bewley family, merchants, caterers, and philanthropists. In the early eighteenth century Mungo Bewley left England to escape the religious intolerance being experienced by the Society of Friends. During the eighteenth and nineteenth centuries the Bewleys were involved in milling, textile importing, banking, brewing, and mining. Charles Bewley was the first family member to engage in the importing of tea from China, c. 1835, leading by 1894 to the establishment of Bewley's Oriental Cafés, which remained a significant feature of Dublin's urban culture throughout the twentieth century. The company's flagship café in Grafton Street opened in 1924 during the 'Tutmania' that followed the discovery of Tutankhamun's tomb in 1922, and its façade, by A. C. C. Miller, reflects the prevailing enthusiasm for all things Egyptian; the interior contains a sequence of HARRY CLARKE windows depicting cakes carried on classical columns. Many writers, from JAMES JOYCE to MARY LAVIN, have patronised Bewley's and mentioned its cafés in their work. Bewley's was absorbed into Campbell Catering, a hotel and catering firm, in 1995, and its Bewley's brand name has become ubiquitous. **Brian Lalor**

Bianconi, Carlo (Charles) (1786–1875), transport operator. Born in Lombardy, he came to Ireland in 1802. While tramping the country as an itinerant pedlar he became aware of the deficiencies of public transport in rural areas. He established himself as a carver and gilder in 1806, first in Carrick-on-Suir and later in Waterford and Clonmel, then conceived the possibility of cheap transport based on regular timetables. In 1815 he opened his first route, between Clonmel and Caher, with one horse and one car; ten years later his cars were travelling more than 1,600 km (1,000 miles) a day throughout south Leinster and Munster. His vehicles, popularly known as 'bians', were innovative in design, with four-wheeled cars carrying up to twenty passengers and built in his own workshops in Clonmel replacing the original two-wheelers (see p. 1068).

Bianconi met the challenge of the railway age by establishing feeder services to railheads and at the same time taking shares in railway companies. A strong supporter of DANIEL O'CONNELL, he became a naturalised citizen in 1831. He retired in 1865 to his estate at Longfield, near Cashel, Co. Tipperary, disposing of his business on generous terms to his employees and agents. His coach-building industry in Clonmel survived into the 1940s. **Bernard Share**

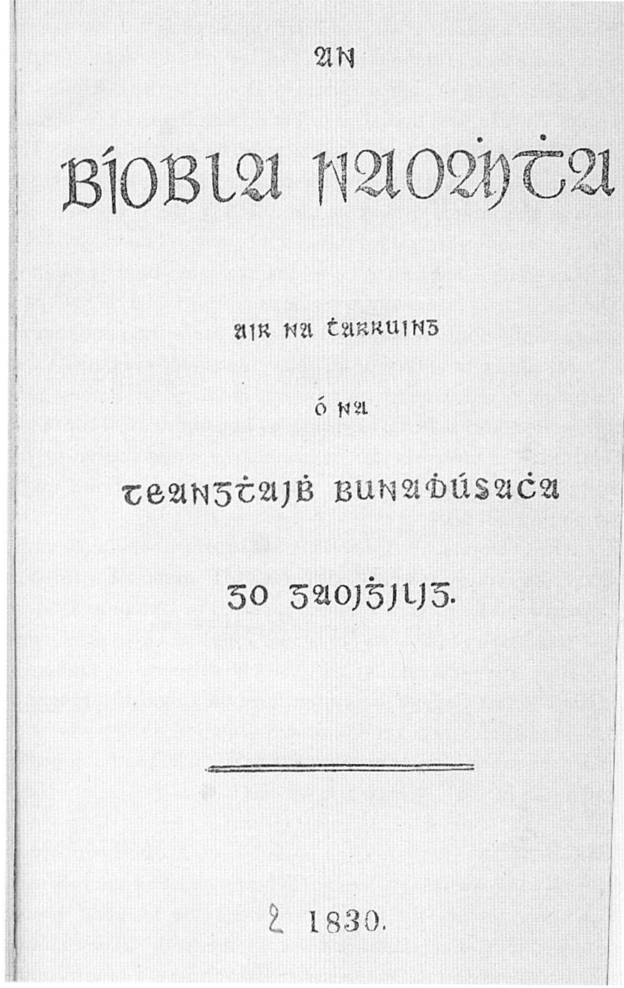
AN

BÍOBLA NAOṀṪA

AIR NA ṪARRUING

Ó NA

TEANGṪAIḂ BUNAḊÚSAĊA

GO GAOIĠILIG.

1830.

Bible. *Title page of the 1830 edition of the Ó Domhnaill-Bedell Bible in Irish. The Bible was first translated into Irish in the late sixteenth century. [Council of Trustees of the National Library of Ireland; LO 2462]*

Bible in Irish. The Irish were familiar with the Scriptures in Latin from the coming of CHRISTIANITY in the fifth century. There was no Irish TRANSLATION, however, until the late sixteenth century, when the authorities of the established church suggested a translation of the New Testament. A Gaelic type was cut for the purpose and was first used by Seán Ó Cearnaigh to print AIBIDIL GAOIDHEILGE AGUS CAITICIOSMA. The translation of the New Testament itself was begun by Ó Cearnaigh and two other clerics, Nicolás Bhailís and Fearganainm Ó Domhnalláin, but it was completed and seen through the press in 1602–3 by Uilliam Ó Domhnaill, later Archbishop of Tuam. The New Testament is claimed to be based on the Greek text, an assertion corroborated by a close reading of the work. Ó Domhnaill went to London to present a copy of his book to ELIZABETH I, but it is not known whether she received it before she died.

The translation of the Old Testament from the English of the King James Bible was undertaken in the 1630s by Muircheartach Ó Cionga at the insistence of WILLIAM BEDELL, who died before the book could be printed. Bedell's manuscript was rescued by Denis Sheridan and Henry Jones and subsequently delivered to Andrew Sall (died 1682). Sall, an erstwhile Jesuit, had recently returned to Ireland from Oxford at the request of ROBERT BOYLE to assist with the publication of the Scriptures in Irish. Boyle first financed a reprint of Ó Domhnaill's New Testament, to which Sall contributed an English introduction based on the preface to the French New Testament of the Jansenists. This second edition of the Irish New Testament, though prepared in Dublin by Irish scholars in Trinity College, was published in London by Robert Everingham in 1682, using a new Gaelic typeface cut by Joseph Moxon. The text of the Old Testament, similarly prepared in Dublin, was sent to London and printed by Everingham in 1685. Both the New and Old Testaments were guided through the press in London by Aodh Ó Raghallaigh, an Irish scholar employed by Boyle as editor. Though Bedell's manuscript contained the Apocrypha, Boyle's puritan sensibilities meant he could not countenance their publication.

An edition of Ó Domhnaill's New Testament and Bedell's Old Testament together in roman type was produced by Robert Kirk and printed, also at Boyle's expense, in London in 1690 for use in Scotland. Unfortunately the translation was unintelligible to the Scots, who did not receive a Gaelic translation of the entire Scriptures until 1801.

The Ó Domhnaill-Bedell Bible was reprinted repeatedly in the nineteenth century and was widely used by Catholics. A revision of Ó Domhnaill by Earnán de Siúnta appeared in Dublin in 1951. A new translation of the New Testament from the Greek by Coslett Ó Cuinn was published for the Church of Ireland in Dublin in 1970. The first Catholic translation from the original languages of the entire Bible (including the deuterocanonical books) was made under the supervision of PÁDRAIG Ó FIANNACHTA and published in Maynooth in 1981. **Nicholas J. A. Williams**

'Big Bertha' (1963–1993), a prolific cow. A *droimeann* (white-backed cow) owned by Jerome O'Leary of Blackwater Bridge, Co. Kerry, she was the most prolific cow ever recorded, having produced thirty-nine calves. She was also the world's oldest known cow when she died on 30 December 1993 at the age of forty-nine. **Ciarán Deane**

Big House, the. From the time of the Elizabethan conquest, the Big House, the residence of the planters, manifested first in fortified castles, subsequently in Palladian mansions, modest rectories or fantasies of the Gothic Revival, was the focus of what was long perceived as an alien landlord class. Fuelled by rents from its tenantry, the life-style of the inhabitants of the Big House, widely condemned by, among others, Frederick Engels, varied between splendid civilised living, extravagance, debt, irresponsibility, and eccentricity, reaching its zenith in the middle of the eighteenth century. In the late nineteenth century the huge disposable income of estates was diminished by the LAND ACTS, triggered by the LAND WAR. Widespread destruction of houses during the 'TROUBLES' of 1919–23 was followed by their steady disappearance. However, recent new wealth has given rise to an appreciation for surviving Big Houses. A difference in attitude accepts that the Big House is an important aspect of Irish culture. [see ANGLO-IRISH SOCIETY.] **Peter Somerville-Large**

'Big House' novel, fictions of the lives of the LANDLORD class and their interaction with the tenantry. One of the great issues in Ireland from the seventeenth to the nineteenth centuries was the division between tenants and landlords, the latter mostly of English descent, having come into possession of their estates through confiscation. Tensions grew in the nineteenth century with the struggle for CATHOLIC EMANCIPATION in the 1820s, the TITHE WAR of the 1830s, and the GREAT FAMINE of the 1840s. The LAND WAR of the 1880s marked the beginning of the end of the control of great estates by the Anglo-Irish ascendancy. From MARIA EDGEWORTH's CASTLE RACKRENT (1800) the topic has been a central one in Irish fiction.

The eighteenth century was notable for the building of great country houses, such as CARTON House, Co. Kildare, seat of the Dukes of Leinster, though of course many landlords lived in much more modest homes. The term 'Big House novel' should be treated with some caution, however, as it places the emphasis on the domestic and personal rather than on the political and social. During the nineteenth century the emphasis was on the political, as Anglo-Irish writers sought to envisage a viable future for their class; Edgeworth's novel was intended as a warning about the dangers they faced. The parlous condition of the rural class structure was a theme taken up by CHARLES LEVER in novels such as *The Martins of Cro' Martin* (1856) and *Lord Kilgobbin* (1872), while SHERIDAN LE FANU added a gothic twist to the Anglo-Irish predicament in his writing. GEORGE MOORE's *A Drama in Muslin* (1886) is a Catholic Big House novel set during the Land War.

After the Land War, the FIRST WORLD WAR—in which many Anglo-Irish soldiers died—and the 'Troubles' of the early 1920s, the power of the landed class was gone, and Big House novels, from SOMERVILLE AND ROSS's *The Big House at Inver* (1925) and ELIZABETH BOWEN's THE LAST SEPTEMBER (1929) to MOLLY KEANE's *Good Behaviour* (1981), both castigate and mourn a departing way of life. The Big House novel, however, continued to be used to interesting effect in the twentieth century by writers from non-landed backgrounds, such as AIDAN HIGGINS in *Langrishe, Go Down* (1966), JENNIFER JOHNSTON in *The Captains and the Kings* (1972), and JOHN BANVILLE in *Birchwood* (1973). **James H. Murphy**

Binchy, Maeve (1940–), novelist and journalist. Born in Dublin; educated at UCD. She worked for many years as a journalist with the IRISH TIMES. Her first novel, *Light a Penny Candle* (1982), was a popular success, inaugurating her career as a writer of skilfully plotted, emotionally engaging bestsellers and winning her a worldwide readership. **Terence Brown**

Bindon, Francis (c. 1690–1765), artist. Born in Co. Clare, son of the MP for Ennis; studied art and architecture at the University of Padua c. 1716 and afterwards in London under the portrait painter Godfrey Kneller. A friend of JONATHAN SWIFT, he was a successful portrait painter in Dublin during the 1720s and in 1733 was elected a member of the DUBLIN SOCIETY. He collaborated with the architect RICHARD CASTLE on designs for Russborough House, 1741, and Belan House, Athy, Co. Kildare, 1743. His portraits of Jonathan Swift (c. 1735) and TURLOUGH CAROLAN (c. 1720, attributed) are in the NATIONAL GALLERY OF IRELAND, Dublin. **Peter Murray**

Bingham, Billy (1931–), soccer player. Born in Belfast. A skilful winger who joined Sunderland from Glentoran in 1950, he was a member of the Northern Ireland team that reached the World Cup finals in Sweden in 1958—the first Irish team to do so. Having made sixty-seven international appearances, he went on to enjoy a successful managerial career, first at club level in England and later in two periods as manager of Northern Ireland. He was widely acclaimed for his stewardship of the teams that reached the 1982 World Cup finals in Spain—an achievement he repeated at Mexico four years later. **Peter Byrne**

Bingham, Sir Richard (1528–1599), soldier and politician. Born in Dorset. A zealous soldier, in 1579 he was sent to Ireland by ELIZABETH I to help suppress the DESMOND REBELLION. He took part in the massacre of Spanish and Italian soldiers at SMERWICK, Co. Kerry. Following the rebellion the queen made him President of Connacht in 1584. He revived the compositions agreements with Irish lords in 1585, which provided the financial basis for effective English government in south Connacht and Co. Clare with the support of the Earls of Clanricarde and Thomond, the leading noblemen west of the Shannon. He governed Connacht with an iron fist and was ardent in his use of the death penalty; he claimed to have put to death a thousand survivors of the ill-fated SPANISH ARMADA who came ashore in Connacht. However, Lord Deputy PERROT was concerned lest Bingham's ruthless style of government might provoke the Irish into a general rebellion. Certainly Bingham's extension of English authority into north Connacht created great difficulties with the MacWilliam Burkes of Co. Mayo and BRIAN O'ROURKE of Co. Leitrim. As the political situation grew increasingly unstable in the early 1590s, Bingham's administration attracted further hostile attention from those seeking to appease HUGH O'NEILL. In 1596 Bingham travelled to London to defend his reputation but was relieved of his post. In 1598, however, he returned to Ireland as marshal of the queen's army in the midst of the Nine Years' War, but he died soon after his arrival in Dublin on 18 January 1599. **Henry A. Jefferies**

biochemistry, the study of the structure and functioning of living things at the molecular level. It covers the structure and biosynthesis of monomers, such as sugars, amino acids, nucleotides and fats, and the study of how they are converted into polymers, how genetic information is stored as DNA, how this is replicated and repaired, and how it is copied into RNA and translated into the sequence of amino acids in polypeptides. It also considers how polypeptides are folded into the higher-order structures that are proteins; how proteins function, particularly as enzymes, and how these catalyse reactions; how energy is captured, stored and made available in cells; the significance of membranes and other units of the structure of organisms; and how the actions of cells and organisms are co-ordinated and controlled, including immune reactions, nerve action, and embryology. Biochemistry overlaps with molecular biology, cell biology, and molecular genetics.

Biochemistry began in the nineteenth century, primarily in Germany, and grew mainly from physiological chemistry; it became a distinct discipline in the twentieth century. In 1909 J. A. Milroy was appointed lecturer in biochemistry in the Department of Physiology of Queen's University, Belfast, and in 1924 to the independent chair of biochemistry. In TRINITY COLLEGE, Dublin, a lectureship in biochemistry in the Department of Physiology was created in 1921, and W. R. Fearon was appointed and subsequently held a personal chair of biochemistry in 1934, but an independent Department of Biochemistry was not created until later. Fearon was noted for developing colorimetric reactions for biological molecules and for a textbook on biochemistry, which had several editions and translations. In UNIVERSITY COLLEGE, DUBLIN, E. J. CONWAY was appointed in 1934 to a chair of biochemistry and pharmacology. He was notable for his work on the distribution of ions in tissues and for inventing microdiffusion analysis which was then very valuable. Departments of Biochemistry, or of overlapping disciplines, appeared later in other third-level institutions. **Frank Winder**

biology, the scientific study of life; it can be divided into *botany* (the study of plants), *zoology* (the study of animals), *genetics* (the study of inheritance), and *ecology* (the study of the relationship between animals and plants and their environment). Like other areas of science, it has progressed from description to the study of processes thereby instigating a rapid growth in biochemistry in the second half of the twentieth century.

The earliest biologists to describe Ireland were the seventh-century monk AUGUSTINE ERIUGENA and the twelfth-century GIRALDUS CAMBRENSIS. Notable biologists who worked in Ireland include G. H. CARPENTER, J. S. FAIRLEY, A. G. MORE, R. F. SCHARFF, and A. E. J. WENT; other prominent names include Arthur Stringer (c. 1664–c. 1728), who wrote *The Experienced Huntsman* (1714); JOHN RUTTY (1697–1775), who wrote *An Essay towards a Natural History of the County of Dublin* (1771); William Thompson (1805–1852), who wrote *The Natural History of Ireland* (1849–65); R. M. Barrington, who financed research and published many papers in addition to *The Migration of Birds as Observed at Irish Lighthouses* (1900); R. J. Anderson, who wrote a number of papers describing whales; R. L. PRAEGER, who wrote *The Way that I Went* (1937) and *A Populous Solitude* (1941); and C. Douglas Deane (1914–1992), who wrote *The Mammals of Strangford Lough* (1971) and a regular newspaper column.

More recent biologists working in Ireland have included Mark Holmes of the NATIONAL MUSEUM, a noted worker on marine invertebrates, and LOUIS RENOUF of the UNIVERSITY COLLEGE, CORK. Renouf pioneered marine biological research at LOUGH HYNE, Co. Cork, a salt-water lake connected to the Atlantic Ocean by narrow rapids. As the entire catchment area for the lough is small, it presents a unique opportunity for conservation. It became an important early marine-protected area and possesses one of the richest arrays of marine plants and animals in temperate waters anywhere in the world; it has also become one of the most important sites for marine biological research, largely as a result of the work of two British biologists, JACK KITCHING and JOHN EBLING. **D. Patrick Sleeman**

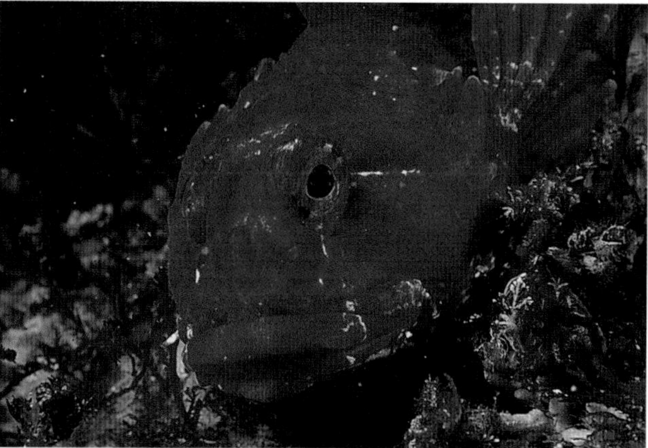

biology. *The long-spined sea scorpion* (Taurulus bubalis) *common all around the coasts of Ireland. Its camouflage colouring changes to blend with its surroundings, often red when living on rocks covered in pink coralline algae. [Nigel Motyer]*

Birmingham, George A., pen-name of Rev. James Owen Hannay (1865–1950), CHURCH OF IRELAND clergyman and satirist. Born in Belfast. As Rector of Westport, 1892–1916, he established himself as a prolific novelist and acute social observer. He combined 'condition of Ireland' novels such as *The Seething Pot* (1905) and *Hyacinth* (1906) with the lighter farces, such as *Spanish Gold* (1908), that established his popularity. Hannay was a nationalist, believing that the Irish gentry should have acted as leaders of their country instead of trusting the treacherous English and seeing the separatists of SINN FÉIN as preferable to the jobbery and clericalism of local parliamentary nationalists. He was active in the GAELIC LEAGUE but resigned because of controversy over his criticisms of Catholic clerical authority; and his lighthearted farce *General John Regan* (1913) caused riots in Westport when it was denounced as an insult to the town. Hannay became a British army chaplain in 1916 and spent the rest of his life in English parishes; he continued to write, but the quality of his work declined. **Patrick Maume**

Birmingham, John (1816–1884), astronomer and poet. Born at Millbrook, Co. Galway, to a line claiming the Barony of Athenry. He was a great favourite with his tenants for his athletic prowess, puns, and pranks. During the 1850s, encouraged by RICHARD GRIFFITH, he surveyed, and published on, the GEOLOGY of south-west Co. Galway. He also surveyed the route for the Tuam–Claremorris railway line. In 1866 he discovered the nova T Coronae Borealis, and thereafter devoted his life to astronomical research, reviews, popular articles, and observatory open-days. He co-operated with Angelo Secchi of the Vatican Observatory and with DUNSINK, Copenhagen and Athens Observatories. In 1883 he was awarded the Cunningham Medal of the ROYAL IRISH ACADEMY for his Catalogue of the Red Stars. Birmingham Crater on the Moon is named after him. His poetry is exemplified by a satire on England's relief programme during the GREAT FAMINE and by the long poem 'Anglicania' (1863). He was active in the campaign for animal rights. His personal papers and library were destroyed after his death. **Paul Mohr**

'Birmingham Six', a name given to six Irishmen wrongly convicted of the bombing of two pubs in Birmingham carried out by the IRA in 1974, which resulted in twenty-two deaths. Hugh Callaghan, Paddy Hill, Gerry Hunter, Richard McIlkenny, Billy Power, and John Walker were imprisoned for more than sixteen years. After a long campaign to prove their innocence, their convictions were eventually quashed in 1991 after it was established that evidence against them had been fabricated. **Martin Clancy**

Birmingham, the Irish in. Irish people are first recorded in the town during the seventeenth century, and by the end of the eighteenth century a small Irish business community is discernible. Though the number of Irish-born residents reached a peak at approximately 11,500 in the 1861 census, contemporary commentators perceived the Irish community as much larger. During this period, reactionary elements were operating in Birmingham, a centre of Catholic revival and Irish nationalist and Fenian activity. Anti-Catholic and anti-Irish agitation reached their height with the 'Murphy Riots' in 1867, when the Park Street area was attacked and suffered considerable damage in a week of disturbances associated with the religious agitator WILLIAM MURPHY.

By the end of the nineteenth century the Birmingham Irish were to be found in all strata of the city, from labourers to professionals and businessmen. The Dunlop Rubber Company was founded in the 1850s by two Irish families, and in 1856 the *Birmingham Evening Mail* was established by an Irishman, William C. Sullivan. An Irish Institute was founded in 1919, and the oldest GAA club in Britain was established there in 1939. The Birmingham Irish were involved in the two world wars, either through enlistment or through work in arms manufacturing and nursing. Irish emigration to Birmingham began to increase greatly during the 1950s and 60s, with many Birmingham firms actively recruiting in Ireland. Discrimination, particularly in housing, was widespread, and specific organisations were established to help the Irish community.

Events in Northern Ireland in this period began to have an impact on the Irish in Birmingham. The IRA bombed two city-centre pubs in 1974, leaving twenty-one people dead and 161 injured. The PREVENTION OF TERRORISM ACT was rushed through Parliament in twenty-four hours, and the 'BIRMINGHAM SIX' were wrongly convicted of the crime. Despite the widespread horror expressed by the Birmingham Irish, the inevitable backlash turned violent, and it took many years for the community to rebuild its confidence in the city. A number of organisations represent the Irish community, estimated in 1991 at 140,000. The ST PATRICK'S DAY parade, revived in 1995, has become the largest in Britain, attracting 75,000 people in 2000. The city council has also embraced Birmingham's cultural diversity and has proposed redeveloping the Digbeth area as an 'Irish quarter'. [see ENGLAND, IRISH IN.] **Alexander Peach**

Birr Castle, Birr, Co. Offaly, home of the Parsons family since 1620 and of BIRR CASTLE OBSERVATORY. In 1807 Sir LAURENCE PARSONS, fifth baronet, inherited the Earldom of Rosse from an uncle in Co. Longford. His son, WILLIAM PARSONS, third earl, and his grandsons LAURENCE PARSONS, fourth earl, and Sir CHARLES PARSONS, continued the scientific tradition of Birr Castle, largely because the boys of the second generation were educated at Birr by tutors who were engaged by their father as assistant astronomers.

Most of the scientific heritage is on display in Birr Castle Demesne, which is open to the public every day of the year. In the centre of the park is the great telescope completed by William Parsons, now fully restored and working. The old coach-house courtyard, through which the demesne is entered, has been converted into Ireland's Historic Science Centre, showing the achievements of the Parsons family in astronomy, photography, engineering, and in the introduction of botanical species.

The surrounding demesne, extending into Co. Tipperary, includes thousands of species of plants grown from seed collected from all over the world on plant-hunting expeditions that members of the family either set up or supported. Particularly noteworthy are the world's oldest and tallest box hedges and the hornbeam cloisters of the recently restored Millennium Gardens. Tree trails and seasonal exhibitions complete the scene in the demesne, whose features have won three all-Ireland awards. [see PARSONS, MARY, COUNTESS OF ROSSE.] **Lord Rosse**

Birr Castle Observatory (1827–78), established at Birr Castle, Co. Offaly, by WILLIAM PARSONS, THIRD EARL OF ROSSE. Possessed of a first-class mathematics degree from Oxford, he began building telescopes in 1827 and, in the following year, constructed his first machine for grinding and polishing mirrors of speculum metal. In 1839 a 900 mm (36-in.) telescope was completed; in 1842 he successfully cast a 1,800 mm (72-in.) mirror; this 'Leviathan of Birr' was inaugurated on 15 February 1845. The epoch-making discovery of the spiral character of the galaxy Messier 51 followed and for some thirty years, until superceded by photographs, drawings made at Birr provided important information on the structures of many galaxies. The Leviathan remained the world's largest telescope until 1917.

In 1868 LAURENCE PARSONS, FOURTH EARL OF ROSSE, used the 900 mm telescope to measure the heat of the Moon. Observations of the satellites of Uranus were made with the Leviathan (1872–4); a catalogue of drawings of Jupiter made at the 900 mm telescope was published in 1889. Following Laurence's death in 1908 the Leviathan was dismantled. It was fully restored in the 1990s.

Among astronomers, physicists, and mathematicians who worked at Birr were MARY WARD, GEORGE J. STONEY, and BINDON STONEY. Astronomical observers included REV. WILLIAM H. RAMBAUT, R. J. Mitchell, and S. Hunter. The latter made an important detailed drawing of the Orion Nebula. ROBERT S. BALL, Charles E. Burton, and Ralph Copeland were assistant astronomers. The Danish astronomer Johan Ludwig Emil Dreyer initiated a comprehensive survey of star clusters, nebulae and galaxies using the Leviathan (1874–8), while the German astronomer Otto Boeddicker made naked-eye observations of the Milky Way from Birr (1880–1916). **Susan McKenna-Lawlor**

Birrell, Augustine (1850–1933), politician. Born in Liverpool, England. A Liberal MP, he served as CHIEF SECRETARY FOR IRELAND from 1907 until 1916, during which period he oversaw the Irish Universities Act (1908) and the Irish Land Act (1909); however, by 1914, he was an amiable and whimsical but ineffectual minister who had wearied of office. He was the main political casualty of the failure to anticipate and prevent the 1916 RISING, and he resigned on 3 May. **Eunan O'Halpin**

Black, Cathal (1952–), film director and writer. His relatively few films stand apart from most Irish productions in their concern with the image over the word, as well as in dealing with the marginalised and oppressed in contemporary Ireland. His first film, *Wheels* (1976), an adaptation of a short story by JOHN MCGAHERN, explored the relationship of a son with his father, who remains on the family farm after the son migrates to the city. *Our Boys* (1981) employed drama and documentary film to explore the harsh regime of CHRISTIAN BROTHERS' education; *Pigs* (1984) featured a disparate group of social outcasts; *Korea* (1995), from another McGahern story, looked at emigration in the early 1950s in relation to the legacy of the CIVIL WAR and the modernising impulse behind the Rural Electrification Scheme; and *Love and Rage* (1999) was about the 'real' Playboy of the Western World. **Kevin Rockett**

Black, Donald Taylor (1951–), documentary film-maker. Formerly a theatre director, he is now head of the Department of Film and Media in Dún Laoghaire Institute of Art, Design, and Technology. He has made films on a range of topics, including the cinema itself in his debut documentary about LIAM O'LEARY, *At the Cinema Palace* (1983), and in *Irish Cinema: Ourselves Alone?* (1995); prisons in *The Joy* (1997); the DIVORCE referendum in *Hearts and Souls* (1995); a portrait of the forensic pathologist Dr John Harbison in *Dead Man's Doctor* (1995); and films on Gaelic games, soccer, rugby, tourism, and archaeology. His films on the arts have included studies of JIMMY O'DEA (1985), SAM THOMPSON (1986), OLIVER ST JOHN GOGARTY (1987), BRIAN FRIEL (1993), and MÍCHEÁL MAC LIAMMÓIR (1999). **Kevin Rockett**

Black, Joseph (1728–1799), chemist and physician. Born in Bordeaux of Belfast parents; educated at home and at the Universities of Belfast and Edinburgh. He made important discoveries about the properties of 'fixed air' (carbon dioxide) and in 1756 was appointed professor of chemistry at the University of Glasgow. Lavoisier developed Black's work and recommended him as an associate member of the Académie Royale des Sciences in Paris. He became professor of chemistry at the University of Edinburgh in 1766. James Watt's first steam engine was partly based on Black's research. His *Lectures on Chemistry* was published in many editions; he is acknowledged as a founder of modern chemistry. **Ciarán Deane**

Black and Tans. The Auxiliaries *by Maurice MacGonigal, showing the second of the two RIC auxiliary forces sent to Ireland in the attempt to break the IRA. Comprising former British military officers, the Auxiliaries were responsible for much of the terror that was unleashed by the two forces. [National Museum of Ireland]*

Black and Tans and Auxiliaries. Because of attacks on the ROYAL IRISH CONSTABULARY and the breakdown of civil authority in 1919, the British government recruited police auxiliaries, largely in Britain during 1920. They became known as the Black and Tans, after their mixture of RIC (bottle-green) and British army (khaki) uniforms and a Limerick hunt known as the 'Black-and-Tans'. By October 1920 they numbered over 2,000 and were associated with a wave of reprisals. In July a separate force, the Auxiliaries, was formed from former British military officers, paid twice the rate of the RIC and sent to troubled areas. Under independent control, they gained a reputation for harsh methods, in particular the burning of the centre of Cork in December 1920. Both forces were more the effect than the cause of the failings of British administration. [see HUNTING.] **Michael A. Hopkinson**

Blackburn, Helen (1842–1903), suffragist. Born in Valentia Island, Co. Kerry, where her father was a civil engineer. The family moved to London in 1859. She was active in the suffrage movement in England for more than twenty years, serving as secretary of the West of England Suffrage Society and editor of the *Englishwoman's Review*, 1881–90. Her active participation ended in 1895, but she continued to write extensively on women's issues. Her published work includes *The Condition of Working Women* (1896), *Women under the Factory Acts* (1903), and *Women's Suffrage: A Record of the Movement in the British Isles* (1902). [see WOMEN'S SUFFRAGE MOVEMENT.] **Brian Galvin**

'Black Death', the name given to a pandemic of bubonic and pneumonic plague that originated in Asia and moved westwards along trade routes, arriving in Europe in 1347. In Ireland it arrived at Howth, Co. Dublin, in August 1348; spreading to Dublin and

Drogheda, it left 14,000 dead by Christmas, according to the pessimistic calculations of the chronicler Friar John Clyn of Kilkenny. It moved rapidly through Ireland, especially the towns, where cramped conditions encouraged the spread of infection and left the impression that the ANGLO-NORMANS in the towns suffered most. It did affect rural Ireland, however, reaching Moylurg, Co. Roscommon, by 1349. After the initial outbreak it recurred periodically, causing social disorder and dislocation; entire villages were deserted and lands laid to waste, leading to an agricultural depression that intensified an economic decline already in progress and further weakened the Anglo-Norman colony. It is estimated that the population of Ireland was reduced by between a third to a half by the close of the fourteenth century. **Susan Foran**

Black Pig's Dyke, the name given in FOLKLORE and in antiquarian speculation to a number of LINEAR EARTHWORKS or prehistoric dykes recorded mainly in Cos. Down, Armagh, Monaghan, Cavan, and Leitrim. Individual sections can have different names, such as the Worm Ditch, the Black Pig's Race, and the Dane's Cast, and the name sometimes changes from one edition of the Ordnance Survey map to another. The Black Pig is explained in local legend as a wicked schoolmaster who was transformed into a pig and banished; the pig created the ditches with its snout as it rampaged angrily across the countryside.

These disparate earthworks have been considered by some writers to form a unified defence system, which they called the Black Pig's Dyke. It has been suggested that in late prehistory it formed a co-ordinated boundary stretching from the area of Dundalk, Co. Louth, to Bundoran, Co. Donegal, thereby forming a defensive southern boundary for ancient Ulster. The large gaps were imagined as being filled by mountains, BOGS, and vanished forests, and it was suggested that the earthworks were principally constructed across existing routeways. This hypothesis was to some extent fuelled by the interest of some who saw in such a defence system a prehistoric parallel with a modern political boundary. Since the separate dykes have not, however, been shown to be of the same age, any discussion of possible relationships between them is speculative.

Linear earthworks said to be part of the Black Pig's Dyke include a 9 km ($5\frac{1}{2}$-mile) stretch in Co. Leitrim between Lough Melvin and Lough Macnean Upper, a 5 km (3-mile) length in Co. Monaghan south of Scotshouse, a 5 km (3-mile) section between Dowra, Co. Cavan, and the north end of Lough Allen, and an earthwork called the Dúnchaladh that runs for 5 km (3 miles) between Lough Kinale and Lough Gowna in Co. Longford. Sections of similar linear earthworks in Cos. Armagh and Down are known as the Dane's Cast, the best preserved of which is the section running south from Scarva, Co. Down, along the east side of the Newry River. The diverse sections of earthworks can comprise two embankments some 2 m ($6\frac{1}{2}$ ft) high and 10 m (33 ft) wide running in parallel with two ditches, or a single bank between two ditches, or a bank with one ditch.

Recent archaeological investigations have shown that two of the earthworks date from the first or second century BC. One of the dated sections said to be part of the dyke, known as the Dorsey, near Silverbridge in south Co. Armagh, was built in the same decade as NAVAN FORT, in the period 100–90 BC. This lends some credibility to the idea that a meeting was intended, perhaps with Navan as the chief site. Even if the separate known lengths of earthwork (perhaps with others since obliterated) were constructed as part of a co-ordinated system, they can hardly have been defended militarily. In addition to defence, the earthworks, perhaps marking the boundaries of individual communities, may have had symbolic, legal or religious purposes. **Christopher J. Lynn**

Blackshaw, Basil (1932–), painter. Born in Glengormley, Co. Antrim; studied at Belfast College of Art. CEMA provided a travel scholarship to Paris; he also held a one-person show in Belfast, 1961. He held an ACNI exhibition with T. P. FLANAGAN in 1967 and a retrospective at the Arts Council Gallery in 1974. In the 1970s portraits of Harry Thompson and Patricia Mulholland were commissioned by the ACNI; he was also awarded a bursary in 1979 and held a solo show in 1981. He was represented in the Rosc exhibitions 'The Irish Imagination, 1959–1971', in Dublin in 1971, 'Irish Art, 1943–1973', in Cork, 1980, and Dublin, 1988. Other portraits include those of BRIAN FRIEL, President MARY ROBINSON, and Archbishops J. W. Armstrong and G. O. SIMMS. A retrospective exhibition opened in Belfast, with ninety-two works, touring 1995–8. **Theo Snoddy**

Blackwater, River, rises on the Cork-Kerry border and flows eastwards through Mallow and Fermoy, Co. Cork, and Lismore and Cappoquin, Co. Waterford. From Cappoquin it abruptly changes direction to flow southwards, to enter the sea at Youghal. At 160 km (100 miles) long the Blackwater is Ireland's fourth-longest river. It flows in a fertile limestone valley separated from the parallel and more southerly River LEE by a sandstone ridge forming the Boggeragh and Nagles Mountains. MESOLITHIC assemblages have been found in the valley, mainly in the vicinity of Cappoquin. The Blackwater is noted for its salmon-fishing. **R. A. Charlton**

Blackwell, James Bartholomew (1763–1820), soldier and revolutionary. Born in Ennis, Co. Clare; having been sent to France at the age of eleven to complete his education, he later studied medicine at the University of Paris. He became a lieutenant in the Regiment of Hussars, befriended the revolutionaries Desmoulins and Danton, and took part in the attack on the Bastille on 14 July 1789. He fought in the early revolutionary campaigns before sailing to BANTRY BAY in December 1796 with WOLFE TONE and General Hoche in the ill-fated attempt to liberate Ireland. He revisited Ireland with NAPPER TANDY but was captured and jailed in Dublin for two years. On his return to France he was appointed *chef de bataillon* of the Irish Legion and served under Napoleon. **Ciarán Deane**

Blades, the, rock group, formed in the late 1970s in Ringsend, Dublin. The band's power-chord pop songs (mostly written by Paul Cleary and his brother Lar) won them a loyal following. Their two albums, *The Last Man in Europe* (1985) and *Raytown Revisited* (1986), met with critical acclaim, containing such gems as 'Ghost of a Chance' and 'Down Market'. The band is regarded as one of the greatest rock and pop acts of 80s Dublin. Cleary subsequently formed the short-lived Partisans in 1986. In 2000 a double CD collection of the Blades, *Those Were the Days,* was released. **Tony Clayton-Lea**

Blake, Liam (1952–), photographer. Born in Dublin. Having trained originally as a lithographic printer, he developed an interest in photography and turned professional in 1978. He is best known for his work for the 'Real Ireland' series of postcard images. Publications include *Real Ireland* (1984), *Portraits of the Irish* (1985), and *Pictures from the Garden* (1999). **Myra Dowling**

Blanchflower, Danny (1926–1993), soccer player. Born in Belfast. He began his illustrious career as a part-time professional with Glentoran. After a short spell with Barnsley he participated in the most successful period in Tottenham Hotspur's history. He captained the team to the FA Cup and First Division championship double in 1961—the year in which he was named as Player of the Year in England for a second occasion. Three years earlier he had filled a similar role for Northern Ireland in Sweden, and in due course became manager of the team. An innovative thinker on the game, he was, at the summit of his career, among the most highly rated half-backs in Europe. **Peter Byrne**

Bland, Lilian Emily (1878–1971), Ireland's first woman pilot and builder of its first biplane. She constructed the plane, unaided, at her home in Carnmoney, near Belfast. Named *May-fly*, it was built as an unpowered craft, but in 1910 Bland acquired a 20-horse-power two-stroke engine, the noise of which she described as 'like a cat fight on a very enlarged scale.' The *May-fly* achieved lift-off from Lord O'Neill's park at Randalstown, Co. Antrim, in September 1910, reaching a height of 9 m (30 ft) on several occasions. Bland planned to build another glider and to offer aircraft for sale ('Irish Biplanes, Improved *May-fly* type ... from £250 without engine'), but her father, fearing both for her safety and her financial stability, brought her AVIATION career to a premature end. **Bernard Share**

'blarney', flattering, untrustworthy, or loquacious talk associated with and in the past considered common to Irish people, or to people of Irish origin. Numerous apocryphal anecdotes connect the term with BLARNEY CASTLE, Co. Cork, and its seventeenth-century owner Cormac MacCarthy, who is said to have deliberately misled Sir GEORGE CAREW, Lord President of Munster, with his talk. Kissing the stone at Blarney Castle (believed to grant 'the gift of the gab') first became common in the nineteenth century. The stone, which forms a lintol of the machicolations on the south side of the castle parapet, requires the individual's head and shoulders to be suspended over a 26 m (85-ft) drop. Performing this once-perilous feat has become a popular tourist attraction. **Brian Lalor**

Blarney Castle, Co. Cork, probably Ireland's most famous castle, the principal residence of the MacCarthys, Lords of Muskerry. It is a large complex TOWER-HOUSE built in two phases, a primary tower four storeys high and a slightly later five-storey addition. It has mainly small slit windows, and this, with its extensive run of machicolations (stone structures overhanging the wall-tops) and its naturally defensive position, makes it a formidable castle. It has a large oriel window, with other large sixteenth-century windows and two large fireplaces on the third floor. The origin of the strange custom of kissing the Blarney Stone is unknown. **David Sweetman**

Blasket Islands, Co. Kerry, an archipelago of six islands off the DINGLE PENINSULA. One of the islands, Tiaracht, is the westernmost part of Ireland and of Europe. A number of the small islands occasionally supported people; but the principal settlement was on the largest, An Blascaod Mór or Great Blasket Island (4.6 km², $1\frac{3}{4}$ sq. miles). This steeply sloping island had its village in the east, where the land flattens out sufficiently to permit arable agriculture, though fishing was the principal activity. The village never had any services, and its people had to visit the mainland even to attend church. Its population was 153 in 1841 (before the GREAT FAMINE) and reached a peak c. 1916 at 176; but the twentieth century saw a steady exodus of young people, mainly to America. The population was officially evacuated in 1953, though some lingered on until the following year; their houses, now largely roofless, are visited by thousands of tourists each summer.

'blarney'. *An early twentieth-century postcard giving a comic representation of 'Kissing the Blarney Stone' from the outside; the ritual is now performed from within the walls. [Mary Evans Picture Library]*

The Great Blasket is noted for its literature, especially the autobiographies of MUIRIS Ó SÚILEABHÁIN, PEIG SAYERS, and TOMÁS Ó CRIOMHTHAINN, which portray a vibrant but declining traditional island society. There is a Blasket heritage centre at Dunquin (Dún Chaoin) on the mainland (see pp. 808, 963). [see FOOD OF THE BLASKET ISLANDS.] **Stephen A. Royle**

Blathmac Son of Cú Brettan (fl. 760), monk and poet, author of two poems to the Blessed Virgin. Possibly intended originally as 150-quatrain sections of a larger work, the poems now consist of 149 and 109 quatrains in *deibhí* metre. They contain references to the Scriptures and to native tradition, which suggests that Blathmac had an education and training typical of ecclesiastics of the era of the Old Irish GLOSSES and Félire Oengussa. His father, Cú Brettan, King of the Fir Roiss (present-day Co. Monaghan), fought in the Battle of Allen (718) and is referred to in the story of that battle, Cath Almaine. **Uáitéar Mac Gearailt**

Blessington Lake: see POLLAPHUCA RESERVOIR.

Bligh, Vice-Admiral William (1754–1817), naval officer. Born in Cornwall. In 1799 he went to Dublin to advise on improving the port's safety; at that time, Dublin had the reputation of being the most dangerous port in the world to approach and to leave. Having made the first and brilliantly accurate chart of Dublin Bay, he gave advice about the Liffey Bar and other problems that were the cause of the port's terrible reputation. He is often referred to as 'Captain Bligh of the *Bounty*', because of a false and sensational account of one episode in a crowded career, while the great service he gave to Ireland in 1799 and 1800, and his other achievements, are largely forgotten. **John de Courcy Ireland**

Blood, Baroness May (1938–), community worker. Born in Belfast; educated at Blyth Street, Belfast, and left school at the age of fourteen to work as a cutter in Blackstaff Mill. During her thirty-nine years there she became an active trade unionist and voluntary community worker. In 1990 she became a full-time community worker for the Greater Shankill Partnership—a community-led regeneration project. She was made a member of the Order of the British Empire in 1996, followed by a life peerage in 1999. A founder-member of the Northern Ireland Women's Coalition, she was a member of the Coalition talks teams at the multi-party peace talks in Belfast, culminating in the BELFAST AGREEMENT (1998). She holds honorary doctorates from the University of Ulster and Queen's University, Belfast. **Alison Walsh**

blood-and-thunder bands, a variety of Ulster FLUTE BAND, often colloquially referred to as 'kick-the-Pope bands', because of their sectarian and aggressive character. They use small B flat flutes, many snare drums, and one or two bass drums. The bands produce a distinctive and provocative sound, but the musicality is secondary to political demonstration and display. There is an emphasis on drums and volume, with an almost exclusively political repertoire of tunes. Preceding the band, the mace-bearer dances and tosses his mace in the air; the bass drummers may also dance. Uniforms may include sun-glasses and paramilitary regalia. [see MARCHING SEASON.] **Gary Hastings**

Bloody Friday, a name given to 21 July 1972, when the PROVISIONAL IRA set off twenty-two bombs in Belfast. The episode marked a sharp intensification of its campaign, following the collapse of a two-week truce on 9 July. The chief of staff of the Provisional IRA, Seán Mac Stiofáin, said it constituted 'a concerted sabotage offensive.' The principal targets were economic and infrastructural, including bus and railway stations and a ferry terminal, as well as shopping centres. The bombs were timed to go off within the space of an hour and a quarter in the early afternoon, and the concentration of attacks succeeded in overstretching the security forces. The confusion was intensified by a large number of hoax warnings; many people who moved away from a suspected device on the Albert Bridge took shelter in the nearby Oxford Street bus station, where a bomb went off, killing six people, including two soldiers and a bus-driver who was an RUC reservist. The injuries caused were so devastating that initial estimates put the number of those killed at eleven, but the final total was nine; some 130 people were wounded. It was one of the most devastating attacks of the 'TROUBLES', and the impact in alienating public opinion—including nationalist opinion—from the Provisionals was considerable, powerfully reinforced by gruesome television pictures of human remains being scooped into plastic bags in Oxford Street. For the British government the pressure to respond was met by 'Operation Motorman' ten days later, which swept away the republican 'no-go' areas that had existed since August 1969. **Keith Jeffery**

Bloody Sunday, Dublin (1920). Early on 21 November 1920 IRA parties under the direction of MICHAEL COLLINS raided the residences of suspected British intelligence agents (known as the Cairo Gang), killing fourteen and wounding six. That afternoon, at the Dublin-Tipperary GAELIC FOOTBALL match in Croke Park, Dublin, twelve spectators were killed as well as Michael Hogan of the Tipperary team and sixty wounded by Auxiliaries, possibly

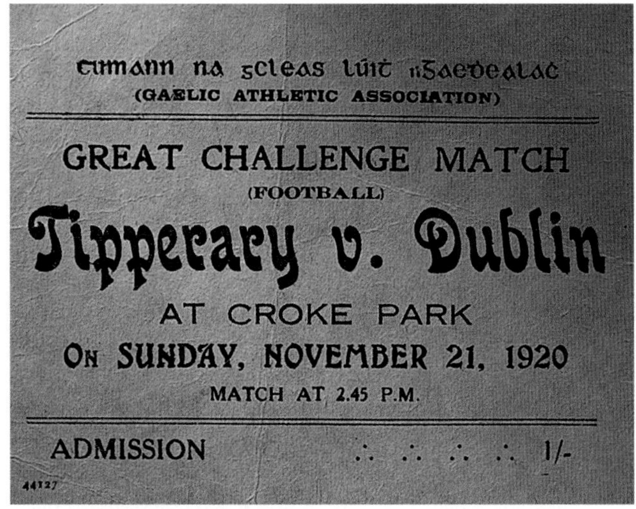

CUMANN NA GCLEAS LÚIT nGAEDEALAC
(GAELIC ATHLETIC ASSOCIATION)
GREAT CHALLENGE MATCH
(FOOTBALL)
Tipperary v. Dublin
AT CROKE PARK
ON SUNDAY, NOVEMBER 21, 1920
MATCH AT 2.45 P.M.
ADMISSION ∴ ∴ ∴ ∴ 1/-
44127

Bloody Sunday, Dublin (1920). *A ticket from the Tipperary v. Dublin match at Croke Park, Dublin, played on Sunday 21 November 1920, when the Auxiliaries drove armoured cars into the football ground and fired at the players and the crowd, killing twelve people and wounding sixty. [GAA Museum; photo: Denis Mortell]*

in reprisal, following a police raid on the grounds. Three republicans —Peadar Clancy, Conor Clune, and Dick McKee—were shot that evening at DUBLIN CASTLE while 'trying to escape'. This infamous day was a microcosm of the whole WAR OF INDEPENDENCE. **Michael A. Hopkinson**

Bloody Sunday, Derry, (1972), a name given to 30 January 1972, when British soldiers of the Parachute Regiment shot dead thirteen unarmed men (and one who died subsequently) taking part in a peaceful, though illegal, civil rights demonstration in Derry. A further twelve people were wounded. The march, 6,000 strong, was to be addressed by BERNADETTE MCALISKEY (then Bernadette Devlin) MP and the veteran British socialist Fenner Brockway at the Guildhall, but the security forces confined the demonstration to the Bogside area, where army units were deployed to arrest 'trouble-makers'. Some soldiers, claiming afterwards that they had first been fired upon, began shooting near Rossville Flats, where most of the fatalities occurred. The killings were widely condemned and prompted a series of protests, including a march on the British embassy in Merrion Square, Dublin, which was attacked and burned (see p. 810). The British government established an inquiry under the Lord Chief Justice of England, Lord Widgery, whose report in April 1972 found that none of the dead was 'proved to have been shot whilst handling a firearm or bomb' yet exonerated the soldiers, though he conceded that some fire had been 'reckless'. The shootings and the report, regarded by many as a cynical white-wash, remained a sharp point of contention between nationalists and the British government, sustained by annual Bloody Sunday commemoration marches, so much so that in January 1998 the British Prime Minister, Tony Blair, announced a new inquiry into the events under another senior English judge, Lord SAVILLE. **Keith Jeffery**

'Bloomsday', a name given to 16 June 1904, the date on which JAMES JOYCE set ULYSSES (1922), his odyssey of Dublin life. The main character, Leopold Bloom, traverses the city before returning in the early hours of 17 June to his home and spouse in 7 Eccles Street. Joyce chose this date because it was the one on which he and his partner, NORA BARNACLE, first 'walked out' together. In 1954

PATRICK KAVANAGH, ANTHONY CRONIN, Brian O'Nolan, and a few others marked the fiftieth anniversary of that day in a visit to the MARTELLO TOWER in Sandycove, where *Ulysses* opens; since then Bloomsday has become a notable Dublin—and increasingly international—festival. **Terence Brown**

Blount, Charles, Baron Mountjoy (1563–1606), English soldier and administrator, responsible for completing the Elizabethan conquest of Ireland in 1603. Mountjoy's early forays against the armies of HUGH O'NEILL, Earl of Tyrone, and his confederates had proved anything but a success. A series of engagements in the Moyry Pass area, Co. Down, during the autumn of 1600 almost proved fatal to Mountjoy and his army. His problems were compounded by the arrival of Spanish forces at Kinsale. Preventing Tyrone's forces from joining with the Spanish during the BATTLE OF KINSALE (1601) became the key to the outcome of the war. Having routed O'Neill's forces and succeeded in securing the departure of the Spanish, Mountjoy was still faced with the problem of inducing the submission of the redoubtable O'Neill, opting for a strategy of planting garrisons in Ulster combined with a ruthless spoliation tactic, which caused widespread famine in the province. With the rebel forces having been reduced to the verge of submission, the imminent death of ELIZABETH I in 1603 prompted Mountjoy to offer terms to O'Neill. Rewarded for his Irish achievements by being created Earl of Devonshire, Mountjoy retained his position as LORD LIEUTENANT of Ireland though domiciled in England. For the remainder of his life he exercised a restraining influence on the militant Protestant officials who dominated the administration in Dublin, not only seeking to ensure that the TREATY OF MELLIFONT was honoured but frowning on the persecuting impulses of CHICHESTER, fearing that they would precipitate renewed conflict. **John McCavitt**

Blueshirts. The Army Comrades' Association, founded in 1932 by army veterans, was a vaguely fascist response to FIANNA FÁIL's victory in the general election of that year. Many pro-Treatyites and ex-servicemen joined, and it became a defender of large-farmer interests against the smaller, 'mixed' arable farmer. It adopted some of the manners of Continental fascist movements—a raised arm salute and blue shirts (hence the popular name). EOIN O'DUFFY, former Commissioner of the GARDA SÍOCHÁNA dismissed by DE VALERA, became leader in July 1933, engaging in *coupiste* rhetoric. His movement, then called the National Guard, was faced down by FIANNA FÁIL in August 1933. Afterwards the Blueshirts joined with Cumann na nGaedheal and the Centre Party to form FINE GAEL. Under other names (the Young Ireland Association, League of Youth), the organisation faded away; O'Duffy and some 700 of his followers went to Spain in 1936 to support Franco in the SPANISH CIVIL WAR. **Tom Garvin**

Blythe, Ernest (Earnán de Blaghd) (1889–1975), revolutionary, politician, and managing director of the ABBEY THEATRE. Born in Magheragall, Co. Antrim; educated locally. He joined the IRB and the GAELIC LEAGUE, and was imprisoned in 1916. He became a member of DÁIL ÉIREANN for North Monaghan, 1918–33, and was successively Minister for Commerce, Finance, and Posts and Telegraphs, a senator, 1933–6, and managing director of the Abbey Theatre, 1941–67. A committed IRISH-LANGUAGE revivalist throughout his life, his management of the Abbey was often criticised; however, he kept it alive during a difficult period. He published two volumes of autobiography, *Trasna na Bóinne* (1957) and *Slán le hUltaibh* (1969). **Christopher Morash**

Boa Island, Co. Fermanagh, site of a *janiform* or two-faced IDOL (from the Roman god Janus) in Caldragh graveyard, consisting of two busts set back to back, each with a large head and crossed limbs cut from a single block of stone. In 2001 a fragment of stone with a hand carved on it was discovered close to the idol, and the hand links up with one of the limbs, evidently an arm, on the north-east side. What was once interpreted as a phallus now looks like a

Bloody Sunday, Derry (1972). *Black-and-white portraits of the victims of the Bloody Sunday shootings being displayed on a hillside in the Creggan area of Derry, 2 February 1997, overlooking the route taken by the civil rights march twenty-five years before. [Photocall Ireland]*

narrow raised band extending downwards to the base of what was once a larger idol. The bottom surface of the stone is irregular, suggesting that the lower part of the idol may be missing. Nearby is another idol brought from Lustymore Island, characterised by a large face above arms with touching hands. All but a few of the surviving stone idols come from the northern part of Ireland, and they were probably carved in the IRON AGE. Similar carvings found throughout the Celtic world provide evidence of the worship of numerous GODS AND GODDESSES. **Helen Lanigan Wood**

Board of First Fruits. The concept of 'first fruits'—the donating of the first year's stipends of a clergyman to a church fund—predates the REFORMATION. Under an act of HENRY VIII the king replaced the Church as beneficiary; it was not until 1704 that the money was redirected to poor Protestant clergy and 1712 when a board was set up in Ireland. The funds raised in Ireland were meagre, notwithstanding the establishment of a supplementary voluntary fund by Archbishop Boulter in 1725. It was only with the advent of substantial parliamentary subventions after 1777 that serious benefits began to flow, in the form of loans and grants for the construction and purchase of churches and glebes. These were increased after the ACT OF UNION (1800). Between 1791 and 1826 almost a million pounds was expended; between 1813 and 1844 more than 200 new churches were erected in Munster alone.

Most of the Board of First Fruits churches of this period are simple gothic boxes with a tower at the west end. A good many, though not all, were designed by the board's retained architects; the first of these was JOHN BOWDEN, c. 1814–22. After his death the work was allocated (by ecclesiastical province) to William Farrell (Armagh), John SEMPLE and Son (Dublin), JAMES PAIN (Cashel), and Joseph Welland (Tuam). Under the CHURCH TEMPORALITIES (IRELAND) ACT (1833) the Board of First Fruits was replaced by the Ecclesiastical Commissioners. **Frederick O'Dwyer**

Board of Works, established in 1831 as the principal agency for promoting ECONOMIC DEVELOPMENT. It was composed of three salaried commissioners and their staff, answerable to the Treasury in London. It took responsibility for inland navigation, the construction and maintenance of public buildings, and making grants and loans for public works, later adding drainage, fisheries, land improvement, workers' and teachers' houses, railway construction, and national monuments. In 1845–7 the board was also given charge of famine relief works, a task that overwhelmed its limited capabilities. [see OFFICE OF PUBLIC WORKS; DÚCHAS.] **Peter Gray**

Boate, Gerard (1604–1649), physician and naturalist. Born in the Netherlands; studied medicine at the University of Leiden. In 1630 he moved to London to work as physician to CHARLES I; in 1642 he subscribed £180 to a fund set up by the Long Parliament for the conquest of Ireland. Using material supplied by his brother Arnold, who had lived in Ireland for several years, he wrote *Irelands Naturall History* (1652), a guide to Ireland 'for the benefit of the Adventurers and Planters therein.' On his first visit to Ireland he died in Dublin soon after his arrival. **Seán Lysaght**

boats, prehistoric. The oldest known Irish craft are LOG-BOATS, such as a MESOLITHIC poplar log-boat found in the Shannon estuary and a NEOLITHIC log-boat found in the River BANN in Co. Armagh, which was used in the middle of the fourth millennium BC. Almost no ancient boats of any other type have been found in Ireland. Ethnographic sources suggest that composite craft, of skin and light framework, and sewn-plank craft or rafts could have provided the earliest forms of water transport. BRONZE AGE sewn-plank craft have been found in British estuaries, and it is likely that they were used in Ireland too. The oldest boat that is not a log-boat is a plank-built oak vessel of Mediterranean type found in Lough Lene, Co. Westmeath, made during the IRON AGE, in the second or third century BC. The BROIGHTER boat, a gold miniature found with other gold objects near Limavady, Co. Derry, is a 184 mm ($7\frac{1}{4}$-in.) long model of a sailing vessel from the first century BC with mast and yard-arm, benches, and oars. The type of boat represented is uncertain but is possibly a large skin boat. [see BROIGHTER HOARD; LURGAN LOG-BOAT; SEVERIN, TIM.] **A. L. Brindley**

boats, traditional. Hollowed log-boats were used from at least the MESOLITHIC AGE up to the seventeenth century, being succeeded by the modern planked *cot* of river and lake. Iconographic and especially literary evidence for the use of the *curach* or skin boat is known from the IRON AGE and Early Christian era. Much archaeological evidence of *clinker-built* boats and ships (with the hull constructed of overlapping planks in shell sequence) and of boatbuilding has been recovered from tenth-century to thirteenth-century settings in the excavations at Wood Quay, Dublin.

A variety of traditional boat types—more than sixty—has survived into modern times. On the north and east coast and on the larger lakes, clinker-built boat types predominate, examples of which are the Greencastle yawl and east coast skiff, while on the south and west coasts a *carvel* or skeleton sequence of boatbuilding (edge-to-edge planking on a pre-erected oak frame) is still favoured; examples include the seine boats of south Kerry, the GALWAY HOOKER, and the Achill yawl. **Críostóir Mac Carthaigh**

bodhrán, the Irish member of the frame-drum family. It is made by stretching a single cured goatskin over one side of a circular wooden frame that measures between 35 and 45 cm (14 and 18 in.) in diameter and 10 to 15 cm (4 to 6 in.) in depth. While the use of a stick (sometimes known as a *cipín* or a *'tipper'*) to strike the skin is most popular today, the older hand-striking style is still practised by some prominent musicians, such as DÓNAL LUNNY and CHRISTY MOORE, and by many players in Co. Sligo and the northern counties. Until the 1950s the bodhrán was principally associated with the annual ritual of the WREN BOYS, which takes place on St Stephen's Day, 26 December. Its popularity increased dramatically with the advent of the fleadhanna ceoil in the early 1950s, and its status began to change significantly from the late 1950s as a result of its dramatic role in JOHN B. KEANE's play SIVE and SEÁN Ó RIADA's effective integration of the instrument into his arrangements of TRADITIONAL MUSIC for CEOLTÓIRÍ CHUALANN. Performance practice changed gradually as the bodhrán's ritual role diminished and players adapted their playing style to the acoustic demands of indoor concert and session environments. Johnny 'Ringo' McDonagh was the first player to make extensive use of timbral variation by manipulating the skin of the instrument; this practice was adopted and continues to be explored by such players as Tommy Hayes, Frank Torpey, John Joe Kelly, Colm Murphy, and Mel Mercier. Parallel innovations in sticking technique have contributed to the expansion of the rhythmic repertoire of the instrument in the last three decades of the twentieth century and have consolidated the position of the bodhrán as the primary traditional percussion instrument. **Mel Mercier**

Bodkin, Thomas Patrick (1887–1961), art critic and administrator. Born in Dublin; educated at Paris, RUI, and KING'S INNS.

He was one of the first to engage with Irish cultural politics; his *Report on the Arts in Ireland* (1949), commissioned by the Government, led to the establishment of the ARTS COUNCIL. Director of the NATIONAL GALLERY OF IRELAND, 1927–35, and subsequently of the Barber Institute, Birmingham, he campaigned for the return of the LANE pictures to Dublin. His *Four Irish Landscape Painters* (1920), on GEORGE BARRET, JAMES A. O'CONNOR, WALTER OSBORNE, and NATHANIEL HONE, remains authoritative. **Richard Pine**

Bodley, Seóirse (1933–), composer and teacher. Born in Dublin. He studied at the RIAM, UCD, and in Stuttgart under Johann Nepomuk David and Hans Müller-Kray. Emeritus professor of music at University College, Dublin, where he has worked since 1959, he teaches composition, electro-acoustic music and aspects of Irish music. His music (which includes five symphonies, two chamber symphonies, and a large range of chamber music and songs) demonstrates many influences, including the European avant-garde, Irish traditional music, serialism, aleatory and modern electronic procedures. **Paul J. Kerr**

Bodley. *Seoirse Bodley's works include symphonies, choral, vocal and orchestral pieces. Symphony No. 2, 'I Have Loved the Lands of Ireland' (1980), was commissioned on the commemoration of the centenary of the birth of Patrick Pearse and had its premiere on 9 January 1981. [Contemporary Music Centre, Eugene Langan]*

Boer Wars: see ANGLO-BOER WARS.

bog bodies, human remains that have survived because of the preservative properties of peat. Most consist of skeletal remains, but in some instances the skin, hair, and nails are also preserved. Some 120 bodies have now been recorded from ninety sites, though physical remains survive from less than a quarter of these.

The earliest bog bodies date from the NEOLITHIC Period; but most fall into one of two categories, the later prehistoric period and the late Middle Ages or early modern period. The earlier group, typically found in blanket BOGS, can be radiocarbon-dated to the early centuries BC and AD, and these are directly comparable to the classic IRON AGE bog bodies of northern Europe. Typically these consist of the deliberate burial of naked or partly clothed individuals, sometimes accompanied by wooden stakes (to fix the bodies physically and metaphorically in place) or animal bones (as food or votive offerings); occasionally there is evidence of violent death. Both sexes and all ages are represented, and multiple burials have been noted occasionally. The best-preserved body was that uncovered at Gallagh, Co. Galway, in 1821. Now desiccated, it was the body of a man in his twenties, clothed only in a leather cape. A twisted rope around his neck allows the possibility that he was strangled, while radiocarbon dating suggests that he lived in the late first millennium BC. Opinions vary on the significance of these deliberate burials. Many believe they represent human sacrifices, while others argue that these were the victims of executions or the punishment killing of social outcasts.

The second group can be dated largely to the later Middle Ages. These bog bodies are of interest because of the preservation of CLOTHING, particularly woollen garments, such as cloaks, jackets, trousers, and dresses; they are therefore a valuable resource for the history of dress. The majority of these later burials are known from upland bogs. While some are deliberate burials, others would appear to be accidental deaths, the remains of those who lost their way or were engulfed in bog slides (a form of peatland avalanche). **Raghnall Ó Floinn**

bogs, biogenic landforms consisting of a mat of living vegetation overlying *peat*, a deposit of partially decayed dead plants. For the bog to grow, the production of new vegetation must proceed faster than the decomposition of dead plants. These conditions exist in areas of high rainfall with poorly drained SOILS low in oxygen. In such circumstances the *aerobic* bacteria (operating in an oxygen environment) and fungi normally responsible for the decomposition of organic matter are rare or absent, and consequently the decay processes are slowed. These conditions exist in many parts of Ireland, with its cool, wet climate, low rates of evaporation, and abundant poorly drained lake basins lying between glacial moraines. About 9,000 years ago aquatic biological productivity increased in the myriad post-glacial lakes; planktonic organic debris began to accumulate; and the lakes filled with calcareous marl deposits. Mosses, pondweeds, water-lilies, and bulrushes then invaded the increasingly shallow calcium-rich and magnesium-rich alkaline waters, and *fens* were created, characterised by waterlogged mineral soils dominated by *anaerobic* bacteria (living without oxygen). In these conditions plant remains were not decomposed by the normal bacterial process of oxidation, in which humus, carbon dioxide, and water are produced: instead, without oxygen, dead plants decomposed only partially, amassing into fen peats, with methane as an anaerobic by-product. As water depths decreased further, the fen peats were colonised by sedges, willow, alder, and native pinewoods. With an increasing accumulation of peat, the wood-fen margin expanded between 8,500 and 5,000 years ago, gradually engulfing the slopes surrounding the fens.

Ireland's most famous peatland, the Bog of ALLEN, developed first in this way across the midlands between the Rivers BOYNE, LIFFEY, BARROW, and SHANNON. Never a single entity but rather a network that reflects the complexity of the underlying glacial landscape, the bog originally covered 2,000 km^2 (770 sq. miles) before being largely destroyed by stripping and drainage. CLARA BOG, part of the Bog of Allen complex in Co. Offaly, developed as a fen in a glacial lake basin until 6,300 years ago. Though intact active fen peatlands are now rare in Ireland, Pollardstown Fen in Co. Kildare is an excellent example.

Between 7,500 and 1,500 years ago changes occurred in many fens that caused a new type of peat to be deposited. Where fen peats had grown thicker than 2 m ($6\frac{1}{2}$ ft), the roots of the vegetation growing at the surface could no longer reach the mineral-rich substrate. In areas receiving between 700 and 1,000 mm of rain over at least 150 days per year the nutrient-starved fens were colonised by *sphagnum* (moss), which flourishes on nutrients from rain alone. By removing calcium and magnesium from rain and releasing hydrogen, sphagnum caused the bog waters to become acidified, further reducing aerobic bacterial activity and accelerating the accumulation of plant remains as peat. Because sphagnum—itself colonised by heathers, sundews (nourished by ingesting insects), and sedges—can hold twenty times its own weight in water, the new bogs were essentially huge sponge-like domes of water raised above the surrounding land. These biological landforms, known as *raised bogs*, are characterised by very thick accumulations of sphagnum peat, largely devoid of tree remains.

The condition of the peat in a raised bog is a useful indicator of a changing climate. For example, the lower 3.5 m (12 ft) of sphagnum peat in the Bog of Allen was relatively highly *humified* or decayed, indicating warm, dry conditions with comparatively abundant aerobic micro-organisms. The uppermost peat, however, was weakly humified, indicating cooler, waterlogged conditions, anaerobic bacterial processes, and minimal decomposition.

In Clara Bog, Ireland's largest intact raised bog, well-humified sphagnum peat began expanding beyond the original fen over forested mineral soils 6,300 years ago in relatively warm, dry conditions. About 2,000 years ago peat humification diminished, reflecting cooler, wetter conditions. About 4,000 years ago Lough Roe and Lough Beag formed within the sphagnum peat on the eastern side of Clara Bog. Late in the nineteenth century Shanley's Lough formed in a depression on the western side of the bog; this is unusual in sustaining a birch woodland in undrained, nutrient-deficient peat.

Clearly, an important consequence of the reduced rate of organic decomposition in bogs is the survival of a rich record of post-glacial changes in the environment. For the same reason, raised bogs have been a plentiful source of archaeological information, with more than 1,600 finds emerging from them, including artefacts and habitations from the Neolithic Period to the Middle Ages, BOG BODIES from the IRON AGE, and wooden trackways and roads from the BRONZE AGE to the Iron Age.

As a consequence of changes in climate, about 4,000 years ago a third type of bog developed, with peat that carpets the underlying topography. These *blanket bogs* are of two types. Along the western seaboard, *Atlantic raised bog* developed in areas receiving more than 1,200 mm of rainfall over at least 235 days per year. Because of the high rainfall at altitudes above 150 m (500 ft) in the west and above 200 m (650 ft) elsewhere, *mountain blanket bogs* also formed. This heavy rainfall caused iron to be leached from the existing mineral soils and to be chemically precipitated lower down the soil profile. The result was the formation of extensive impermeable iron pans that prevented adequate drainage of the soil and led to waterlogging. The peat that formed in these conditions is typically black, 2–6 m ($6\frac{1}{2}$–20 ft) thick, and consists of the remains of grasses and sedges, with small amounts of sphagnum. In the west, pine stumps are commonly found at the base of blanket bogs, indicating a rapid transition from a heavily forested landscape. The remains of the Neolithic CÉIDE FIELDS in Co. Mayo preserved beneath blanket bog confirm that the environmental change associated with the spread of the bogs was both rapid and powerful enough to destroy a highly ordered agricultural community. [see BORD NA MÓNA; CORLEA BOG.] **Colman Gallagher**

Bogside, Battle of the (1969), a name given to the events of 12–14 August 1969 in Derry. At a time of rising tension associated with CIVIL RIGHTS and loyalist marches, the annual loyalist demonstration by the APPRENTICE BOYS of Derry on 12 August sparked off a violent response from nationalists in the Bogside area below the city walls, where the Apprentice Boys marched. Barricades were set up around the area, and fierce fighting broke out between nationalists and loyalists. The RUC, whom nationalists perceived as supporting the loyalists, were attacked with stones, bricks and petrol bombs and responded with CS anti-riot gas. Many buildings, including a police barracks, were set on fire. More than 200 people were injured in the first night's fighting. Defiant Bogsiders proclaimed the establishment of 'Free Derry', a 'no-go' area from which the security forces were excluded and which survived for nearly three years. Throughout the battle the charismatic young radical MP Bernadette Devlin (now MCALISKEY) played a leading part in the events, and striking images of her role were transmitted from Derry by the world's news media. Violence spread to other parts of Northern Ireland, especially Belfast, and the clear inability of the police to cope marked a serious loss of control by the Unionist government. The battle ended on the late afternoon of 14 August, when the RUC were withdrawn and British soldiers were deployed on riot control duties in Northern Ireland for the first time since the 1930s (see p. 883). [see BRITISH ARMY IN NORTHERN IRELAND.] **Keith Jeffery**

Boland, Eavan (1944–), poet. Born in Dublin; after a childhood in London and New York she returned to Dublin at fourteen to attend Holy Child School, Killiney, and later TCD. She began writing poems in early childhood and made her publishing debut at seventeen with *23 Poems*, the first of three pamphlets. Her first book, *New Territory*, was published in 1967 while she was a lecturer in TCD (1967–8). She worked for many years as a literary journalist, primarily for the IRISH TIMES but also for small-circulation magazines such as *This Week*. In 1995 she was appointed professor of English at Stanford University, California.

Boland has been a central voice in both Irish and American poetry. She was born into the 60s generation of Irish poets that includes SEAMUS HEANEY, MICHAEL LONGLEY, and DEREK MAHON, with whom she had considerable contact and camaraderie as a young poet. She also became a leading voice in the generation of American women poets—Sylvia Plath, Adrienne Rich, and Denise Levertov—who had brought radical change to American poetry in the 1960s and 70s. She has been, since the mid-60s, the standard-bearer and critique-maker for the emergence of Irish women poets and has put together a body of work (eight volumes of poetry and one volume of prose essays) that will help to define her generation of Irish poets. **Jody Allen Randolph**

Boland, John Pius (1870–1955), the first Irish person to win an OLYMPIC gold medal. Born in Dublin of a wealthy merchant family; educated in Dublin, Birmingham, Bonn, and at the University of Oxford. A Greek friend at Oxford, Thrasyvoalas Manaos, was on the committee of the inaugural modern Olympic Games in Athens in 1896 and invited him to attend. Boland played some recreational TENNIS while in Athens and was persuaded to enter the Olympic competition. He duly won the men's singles on 30 March by beating Dionysios Kasdaglis of Greece, adding the doubles in partnership with Fritz Traun from Germany. A barrister, he sat as Nationalist MP for South Kerry, 1900–18. He lived most of his life in London, where he died. **Fergal Tobin**

'Bold Thady Quill, The', a satirical song on Quill's athletic prowess (in fact he had none), composed for him in 1888 by Johnny Tom Gleeson of Duhallow, Co. Cork, as payment for reaping. It was popularised in the 1940s by Seán Ó Síocháin and later by Joe Lynch in a recording for the Dublin music pubishers, Walton's. **Fintan Vallely**

Bolger, Dermot (1959–), novelist, dramatist, poet, and publisher. Born in Dublin; educated at Beneavin College. He worked as a factory hand and as a library assistant before becoming a full-time writer and publisher. He founded the Raven Arts Press in 1977 and managed it until 1992, since when he has been executive editor of New Island Books. His large output includes eight plays, seven novels, six volumes of poetry, and seven edited anthologies. His poem and play collections, *Taking My Letters Back: New and Selected Poems* (1998) and *Plays 1* (2000), deal with restless, disaffected personae troubled by the lack of a sense of home and identity. Similar characters inhabit his novels, especially *Night Shift* (1985), *The Woman's Daughter* (1987), and *The Journey Home* (1990), a trilogy set amid the social and moral squalor of contemporary Dublin. His later work is softer in tone: *Father's Music* (1997), set in London, Dublin, and Co. Donegal, has elements of the thriller, while *Temptation* (2000) deals with a middle-aged woman's meditation on the lost passion of her youth. **Liam Harte**

Bolger, Mercedes (1931–), harpist and teacher. She studied harp and cello at the RIAM and later with Ivor James and Gwendoline Mason in London. She joined the Scottish Orchestra as cellist and second harpist in 1951. As solo harp with the Radio Éireann Light Orchestra she toured Europe in 1958. The 'My Gentle Harp' series of broadcasts led to the *Sounding Harps* book series, jointly produced by Bolger and GRÁINNE YEATS in the 1990s. A founder-member of Cairde na Cruite, she has taught at the DIT Conservatory of Music and Drama since 1975. **Paul J. Kerr**

Böll, Heinrich (1917–1985), novelist. Born in Cologne, Germany. Winner of the NOBEL PRIZE for Literature, 1972. His writing, concerned with life in Germany during and after the SECOND WORLD WAR, presents a radical critique of Germany's Nazi past and post-war materialism. In the 1950s Böll and his family came to live in Dugort, ACHILL ISLAND, Co. Mayo, where his house is now run by the Heinrich Böll Foundation as a residence for artists and writers. Böll's *Irish Journey* (1957) depicts the Ireland of the 1950s, seen in spiritual and material terms as not far removed from the Ireland of the 1920s. **Brian Lalor**

bombing campaigns in Britain. From the point of view of republican thinking, bombing campaigns in Britain had certain advantages: they 'brought the war home' to the British and raised the profile of their campaign in Britain through attacks on prominent individuals, government offices, important buildings, economic and military targets, or targets that fell into several of these categories simultaneously. A bombing campaign in Britain also had less potential to provoke loyalist retaliation against Catholics than a similar campaign conducted in Northern Ireland. In the 1880s the Fenians' 'dynamite war' had included a successful attack on the chamber of the House of Commons, while the most notable IRA bombing campaign in Britain prior to the post-1968 Troubles was that of 1939–40, under the direction of the IRA chief of staff Sean Russell. These set a precedent for the more frequent and ambitious campaigns that followed the Troubles of the 1970s.

Military targets, though far from being the object of most attacks, were bombed on a significant number of occasions. In February 1972 an Official IRA car bomb at Aldershot Military Barracks, Hampshire, killed five women workers, a gardener, and a Catholic chaplain. In February 1974 a bomb on a coach carrying soldiers and their families killed eleven people near Bradford. In October 1981 two people were killed and forty injured in an attack on Chelsea Barracks in London. A week later the commandant-general of the Royal Marines was badly injured when an IRA bomb exploded under his car.

In July 1982 eight British soldiers were killed by two IRA bombs at Knightsbridge and Regent's Park, London; three more died later from injuries received in the explosions. In August 1988, in the first bomb attack in Britain for four years, one soldier was killed and nine injured in an attack on Inglis Barracks, London. In September 1989 ten bandsmen were killed and twenty-two injured by an IRA bomb at the barracks of the Royal Marines School of Music in Deal, Kent.

During the 'TROUBLES', republicans often attacked British government or establishment figures. In October 1974 there was an unsuccessful attempt to assassinate Denis Howell, the Minister of Sport, by planting a bomb under his car. In March 1979 Airey Neave, the Conservative Party spokesman on Northern Ireland, died after an INLA bomb exploded under his car as he drove out of an underground car park at the House of Commons. The Conservative MP Ian Gow was killed by an IRA car bomb at his home in July 1990. The best-known attack of this kind came on 12 October 1984 when an IRA bomb exploded at the Grand Hotel, Brighton, where many senior members of the Conservative Party, including the Prime Minister, Margaret Thatcher, were staying during their party conference. Five people were killed, including Sir Anthony Berry MP and Roberta Wakeham, wife of the government chief whip. Another target has been government offices and buildings. In March 1973 IRA car bombs at the Central Criminal Court (the Old Bailey) and the Ministry of Agriculture in London killed one person and injured nearly 250 others. Another attack occurred in February 1991 when an IRA mortar bomb landed in the garden of 10 Downing Street less than 15 yards from where a Cabinet meeting was being held.

Well-known buildings were attacked in an attempt to raise the profile of the republican campaign in Britain. In October 1971 the Post Office Tower in London became an early target of IRA bombers. In June 1974 targets included the 900-year-old Westminster Hall and the Tower of London, where one person was

Boland, Eavan. *Eavan Boland, poet and writer, explores in her poetry issues of Irish significance, the mystery and beauty in the familiar aspects of life, and previously uncharted areas of female experience. [Carcanet Press Ltd]*

killed and forty others injured. In December 1991 a series of incendiary attacks in London included one on the National Gallery, while in April 1997 a bomb scare at the Grand National horse race at Aintree, Lancashire, led to its postponement.

In the wake of the IRA ceasefires, dissident republicans continued to attack government and other buildings. In September 2000 a rocket attack was made on the Secret Intelligence Service ('MI6') building in London, and in March 2001 a bomb exploded in a taxi outside the BBC Television Centre. There have also been attacks on commercial targets: oil terminals and gasworks were bombed on a number of occasions. The IRA also made a series of three separate mortar bomb attacks on Heathrow Airport, near London, in March 1994. Buildings involved in the finance industry were also attacked. In July 1990 an IRA bomb caused extensive damage to the London Stock Exchange; in April 1992 two bombs killed three people at the Baltic Exchange in London; and in April 1993 a bomb at the Nat-West Tower in London killed one person, injured more than thirty, and caused an estimated £1,000 million worth of damage.

In November 1992 an attempt to bomb England's tallest building at Canary Wharf, London, was foiled by security men; but on 9 February 1996 a massive bomb in the same area marked the end of the IRA ceasefire announced in August 1994. This bomb killed two people and injured more than a hundred others. A wave of smaller actual and attempted bombings followed, including an attack on Hammersmith Bridge, London, which had been the object of an IRA bombing in 1939 and would again be attacked, this time by dissident republicans, in June 2000. The culmination of this wave of attacks came in mid-June when a 3,500 lb IRA lorry bomb exploded in Manchester city centre, injuring a hundred people.

Certain bombings, because of their indiscriminate nature, have been seen as terror attacks. On 5 October 1974 IRA bombs exploded at two pubs in Guildford, Surrey, killing five people and injuring fifty-four. In October 1975 the 'GUILDFORD FOUR' were found guilty of causing the explosions, but the convictions were quashed in 1989; in 1976 the 'MAGUIRE SEVEN' were also wrongly convicted of making the Guildford bombs.

On 21 November 1974 nineteen people were killed and 182 injured by bombs planted by the IRA at pubs in Birmingham; two more people died later from their injuries. The bombings led to the introduction of the PREVENTION OF TERRORISM ACT as well as to the wrongful convictions of the 'BIRMINGHAM SIX'. Other significant attacks included a bomb outside Harrod's department store in London in December 1983, which killed six people and injured ninety, and an explosion at Victoria Station, London, during the morning rush hour of 18 February 1991, which killed one person and injured forty-three. Another bombing that caused a wave of revulsion occurred in March 1993 when two boys, three-year-old Jonathan Ball and twelve-year-old Tim Parry, were killed by an IRA bomb in Warrington, Cheshire. In August 2001 seven people were injured in Ealing, London, by a bomb planted by the 'Real IRA', while a further dissident republican bomb was planted in Birmingham in November. **Gordon Gillespie**

Bonar Law, Andrew (1858–1923), Unionist Conservative politician. Born in Canada; educated in Scotland. He was a Unionist MP, 1900–10 and 1911–23. In the House of Commons he led the opposition to the third HOME RULE Bill in 1911–12. An able minister from 1915, he was hard-headed though not entirely inflexible on Ireland; his primary allegiance was to Ulster UNIONISM, not to Irish unionism. He became British Prime Minister in October 1922, but in 1923 he resigned because of illness and died soon afterwards. **Eunan O'Halpin**

Bond, Oliver (c. 1761–1798), UNITED IRISHMAN. Born in Co. Donegal; he trained in Co. Derry. He moved to Dublin and made his fortune in the WOOLLEN industry there in the 1780s. A prominent republican from 1791, he was one of the United Irish leadership seized at a meeting in his home in Bridge Street on 12 March 1798. While his conviction for high treason was set aside by the government, his sudden death in Newgate Prison two months later aroused suspicions of foul play. **Ruán O'Donnell**

bones, rhythm, an early musical instrument, now enjoying a revival on both sides of the Atlantic. With evidence that they were played as long ago as 4000 BC, the bones are among the earliest and most enduring of percussion instruments. Associated primarily with folk music in Ireland, England, Scotland, the United States, and Québec, they can be made from animal bone as well as from various woods, plastic, or slate. The North American two-handed style flourished in the hands of the minstrel show character 'Brother Bones' in the second half of the nineteenth century and again for a period in the middle of the twentieth century, when popular performers, including Theodore Goon (as Mr Goon Bones) and Freeman Davis (as Brother Bones), produced several best-selling records. Most Irish bones-players use the one-handed style of playing in the performance of traditional dance music; influential Irish players have included Peadar Mercier (CEOLTÓIRÍ CHUALANN and the CHIEFTAINS) and his son Mel Mercier, Johnny 'Ringo' McDonagh (DÉ DANANN), and Patrick 'Sport' Murphy from Abbeyfeale, Co. Limerick. **Mel Mercier**

Bonner, Packie (1960–), soccer player. Born in Co. Donegal. Signed by Glasgow Celtic from a local junior club, Keadue Rovers, in 1978, he went on to become one of the club's most influential personalities. Having made his debut against Motherwell on ST PATRICK'S DAY, 1979, he amassed a total of 648 first team appearances over the next fifteen years—a figure exceeded only by Billy McNeill and Roy Aitken. His career with the Republic of Ireland was equally protracted, encompassing eighty appearances before his retirement in 1996. A key member of JACK CHARLTON's squad, he assumed hero status by saving a penalty from Daniel Timofte of Romania to earn the team a place in the quarter-finals of the 1990 World Cup championship in Italy (see p. 1001). **Peter Byrne**

Bonny (or Bonney), Anne (c. 1700–c. 1725), pirate. Born in Co. Cork, probably Kinsale or Baltimore, the illegitimate daughter of an attorney, who took her to Charleston, South Carolina, where she grew up on a plantation. She eloped with a seaman c. 1720. It is thought that her husband later sold her to her lover, the pirate captain 'Calico' Jack Rackham. On Rackham's ship she met another female pirate, the Englishwoman Mary Read. Disguised in male dress, the two women took part in acts of piracy before Rackham and his crew were captured and brought to trial in Jamaica. On 28 November 1720 the entire crew was sentenced to death, but Bonny was released on grounds of her pregnancy. Her fate thereafter remains unknown. Her story is told by Daniel Defoe in his *History of the Pyrates* (1724). **Ciarán Deane**

Bono: see HEWSON, PAUL.

bookbinding. The craft and art of bookbinding dates from ancient times, when it became necessary to protect MANUSCRIPTS with covers. Though none of the original bindings of early Irish manuscripts have survived, they must have been provided with covers to match the beauty of the manuscripts. While there are no examples of Irish bindings from this early period, there are some examples of seventeenth-century gold-tooled presentation bindings from Dublin (now in the Gilbert Library, Dublin, the British Library, London, and the Pierpoint Morgan Library, New York).

Though these bindings are excellent, however, it is not until the eighteenth century that the greatest period of Irish bookbinding arrived, with the splendid series of 149 volumes of the journals of both houses of the Irish Parliament, 1613–1800. Magnificently bound in full crimson leather and lavishly tooled in gold, these volumes were destroyed in the fire in the Public Record Office, Dublin, in 1922. The tradition of producing fine bindings was continued in the eighteenth century by the firms of Joseph Leathley, George Mullen, Samuel Watson, and William McKenzie. In the late nineteenth and early twentieth centuries Sir Edward Sullivan and Eleanor Kelly produced some fine bindings.

With the exception of the work of a few individuals, little fine binding is carried on in Ireland today. The demand for fine bindings requires patronage, and few book-collectors are prepared to commission special bindings for their books. Hand binding also takes time, and the fine leathers and gold required for special bindings have to be imported and are expensive. There is the additional problem of training bookbinders. Dublin Institute of Technology, Bolton Street, teaches a certain amount of hand binding and book restoration as part of its trade printing and management course for senior apprentices, but there is no course devoted entirely to hand binding. Some commercial firms bind books for the printing trade and also bind books for private customers, and there are in addition some independent bookbinders. But there is so little demand for this type of work that no firm or individual can exist on this very specialised work alone.

A feature of the bookbinder's craft that has become important for libraries with collections of rare books and manuscripts is the specialised work of the book conservator, a craft for which a high level of bookbinding skill is required as well as an understanding of ancient methods of bookbinding and a knowledge of the chemistry of leather, vellum, and paper. This work is carried out in the Conservation Laboratory of TRINITY COLLEGE Library, Dublin, and the Delmas Conservation Bindery in MARSH'S LIBRARY. [see GREAT BOOK OF IRELAND.] **Muriel McCarthy**

Book of Common Prayer, official Anglican prayer book. The Book of Common Prayer owes much to Archbishop Thomas Cranmer's restructuring and translation into English of the traditional offices of the church. It first appeared in 1549, followed by a more Protestant edition in 1552; there were further revised editions in 1559 and 1662. The use of the Book of Common Prayer extended to Ireland by successive acts of uniformity. DISESTABLISHMENT of the CHURCH OF IRELAND provided the opportunity for further revision. In 1878, after years of lengthy and sometimes acrimonious debate, those wishing for a book giving more emphasis to Protestant teaching had to be satisfied with the introduction of new regulations that greatly restricted the use of ritual. A new Book of Common Prayer is to be published in 2004, incorporating the traditional forms of service and those approved in 1984 for alternative use. **Kenneth Milne**

Book of the Taking of Ireland: see LEBOR GABÁLA ÉRENN.

Book of Resurrection, the: see LEABHAR NA HAISEIRGHE.

book shrines. *A book shrine of the eighth-century Stowe Missal, made of eleventh-century wood and metal plates. The silver-gilt jewelled cross with rock crystal dates from the fourteenth century. [National Museum of Ireland]*

book shrines, box-like containers made to protect important MANUSCRIPTS. They are to be distinguished from book covers. A book shrine typically takes the form of a rectangular box composed of metal sheets, often (but not always) fastened to a wooden core, its dimensions dictated by the manuscript it was designed to contain. It is not clear whether such book shrines are uniquely Irish, or whether book covers were known in the early Irish church. The later seventh-century *Ordo Romanus Primus* notes that in Rome, GOSPEL books were carried in a *capsa* (case). The Irish term *cumhdach* is often translated as 'book shrine', though it carries the more general meaning of cover or shrine; it is not certain, therefore, whether the cumhdach of the Book of KELLS recorded as stolen in 1007 was an ornamented book cover or a book shrine. ADOMNÁN, writing at the close of the seventh century, was familiar with the concept of book shrines or cases, referring to the miraculous preservation of books recovered from water as being kept *in scrinio* or *in scriniolo* (in a case or cover). This suggests that the primary function of book shrines was to protect their contents.

The earliest surviving example, found in Lough Kinale, Co. Longford, dates from the eighth century. This is also the largest known. It bears on its front face an elaborate cross with raised cast-metal bosses and is fitted with straps at each end to enable it to be carried about—features that are found on most other surviving examples. Book shrines continued to be made until at least the end of the eleventh century, though many were repaired and re-decorated well into the later Middle Ages. Inscriptions and historical associations show that book shrines were commissioned by the most important lay and ecclesiastical patrons of their day. The lost cover of the Book of DURROW recorded that it was ordered by FLANN SINNA, King of Ireland (879–916), while his son Donnchad was responsible for enshrining the Book of ARMAGH in 937. In the later Middle Ages, book shrines were redecorated by the most powerful chieftains, including Philip O'Kennedy, King of Ormond, 1366–77, Tadhg O'Carroll, King of Éile, 1377–1407, and ART MACMURROUGH KAVANAGH, King of Leinster (in 1403). Many of these manuscripts were believed to have been written by saints of the early Irish church. Four are associated with the cult of COLM CILLE (the CATHACH, the Misach, and the lost covers of the Books of Kells and Durrow). Of the nine surviving book shrines, four were certainly made for Gospel books; the presence of a cross on most surviving book shrines shows that Gospel books were most commonly enshrined. [see BENTHAM, WILLIAM.] **Raghnall Ó Floinn**

Boole, George (1815–1864), mathematician. Born in Lincoln, England, son of a poor cobbler; self-taught in mathematics after leaving school at fourteen. In 1844 he was awarded the first gold medal in mathematics of the Royal Society of London and in 1849 became the first professor of mathematics at Queen's College, Cork (now UCC), though he had neither a formal secondary education nor a university degree. He devised a novel mathematical system, now called Boolean algebra, that enabled him to express certain principles governing logical thought and reasoning in symbolic or algebraic form. This appeared in *An Investigation of the Laws of Thought* (1854), which was a breakthrough in mathematics. In 1938 an American engineer, Claude Shannon, discovered that Boolean algebra provides exactly what is required to describe the electronic switching circuits that now lie at the heart of computers; the indispensable binary approach is a direct descendant of Boole's mathematical research, and his ideas can be recognised as having had a profound influence on present-day society. Boole also created a new branch of mathematics, called invariant theory, and made important contributions in differential equations and probability. [see VOYNICH, ETHEL LILIAN.] **Fiacre Ó Cairbre**

booleying (*buaile*, 'summer pasture'), the removal of livestock during the summer to mountain and moorland, where they were tended mainly by young women. It was not only an economically important practice but also had social importance for communities and played a role in the transmission of FOLKLORE. **Mícheál Briody**

Boomtown Rats, The: see GELDOF, BOB.

Booth, Evelyn Mary (1897–1988), botanist. Born in Co. Wicklow. She lived most of her life at Bunclody, on the Carlow-Wexford border, where she cultivated an impressive garden and became an accomplished angler. She was an active member of the Wild Flower Society and of the Botanical Society of the British Isles. In the 1950s she recorded the wild plants of south-east Ireland for an *Atlas of the Flora of Great Britain and Ireland* (1962). She continued to record in Co. Carlow and produced a FLORA of the county in 1979. **Donal Synnott**

border, the. The border that partitioned Ireland in 1920–21 was the product of the protracted struggle over HOME RULE. It was the preferred option of none of the protagonists—the British government, Irish nationalists, or Irish (and Ulster) Unionists—though the Ulster Unionists came to see it as the most practical means of remaining within the United Kingdom. When partition was formally enacted by the Government of Ireland Act (1920), however, it received the votes of none of the Irish members of the House of Commons. The subsequent ANGLO-IRISH AGREEMENT of 1921, negotiated by SINN FÉIN and the British government, contained a provision for the six-county unit of NORTHERN IRELAND (the counties of Antrim, Armagh, Derry/Londonderry, Down, Fermanagh, Tyrone) to opt out of the jurisdiction of the Dublin Parliament, which was immediately availed of by the existing devolved administration in Belfast.

Article 12 of the Anglo-Irish Treaty allowed for a BOUNDARY COMMISSION to 'determine in accordance with the wishes of the inhabitants, so far as may be compatible with economic and geographic conditions, the boundaries between Northern Ireland and the rest of Ireland.' In the event, the commission was not created until 1924, and it interpreted its terms of reference conservatively. No plebiscites were held, and the eventual rectification of the border proposed in its official report (1925) was quickly set aside by the three governments involved. This border remained; and the Council of Ireland proposed in 1920–21 to enable co-operation between the two new Irish jurisdictions was stillborn.

At first partition was seen by Ulster Unionists and British Conservatives merely as a tactic to prevent home rule altogether. Once the permanent House of Lords veto on home rule was ended, a number of options were considered for excluding 'Protestant Ulster' from home rule. These included the exclusion of the nine counties of Ulster, the four counties with Protestant and Unionist majorities, the possibility of 'county option'—i.e. county plebiscites—and the exclusion of Ulster, or part of it, for temporary periods. Ulster Unionists and their Conservative allies in Britain finally settled for the six-county option, which maximised the territorial area within which a permanent pro-Union majority could be sustained. However, the Government of Ireland Act also granted a local 'home rule' parliament to Belfast, not sought at first by unionists but quickly embraced by them as yet another barrier against the creation of an all-Ireland entity.

At the outset the characteristics of the border were those of an imperial rather than a national boundary. A fresh, and arbitrary, division imposed by the Imperial Parliament, it meandered through a 'mixed' border zone for approximately 280 miles, following old county boundaries, cutting through hundreds of agricultural holdings, approximately 180 roads, and twenty railway lines. It bisected villages and, in some instances, houses and shops. Like imperial borders elsewhere, it failed to correspond at local level to linguistic, religious, or economic borders. Though customs posts were established in 1923, the border remained more permeable and more easily crossed than most international boundaries.

Between the 1920s and 1960s the border began to assume more of the characteristics of a national border. The main indicators of this process included the efforts to establish the diplomatic and constitutional independence of the IRISH FREE STATE in the 1920s and 30s, inter-war policies of economic protection, and the impact of the SECOND WORLD WAR, when the border divided a belligerent from a neutral state. In the post-war period the practical significance of the border grew as Britain and Ireland pursued different but expanded roles in the provision of WELFARE, EDUCATION, and the promotion of ECONOMIC DEVELOPMENT.

Episodic IRA attacks along the border led to the closure of many cross-border roads. Locally, however, the border was porous and encouraged a widespread and durable smuggling culture. Membership of the EUROPEAN UNION by both Ireland and the United Kingdom has had ambiguous effects on the border. On the one hand it has encouraged a culture of formal CROSS-BORDER CO-OPERATION, while on the other hand since 1979 the border has marked a boundary between two currency zones, as parity between the Irish and British currencies ended.

From its inception, however, the border suffused politics in Northern Ireland, in that elections tended to be plebiscites on its existence. Long-established sectarian boundaries between Protestant and Catholic were enhanced as quasi-national borders. For much of the period between 1920 and the early 1970s the 'zero-sum' politics of territorial control and sectarian head-count were privileged at the expense of intercommunal negotiation and compromise. The long conflict in Northern Ireland from the late 1960s led to the increased military fortification of the border by the British army; since the BELFAST AGREEMENT (1998), however, there has been an institutionalisation of cross-border co-operation between the two jurisdictions. [see PARTITION.] **Liam O'Dowd**

border campaign (1956–62). On 12 December 1956 the IRA launched 'Operation Harvest', with simultaneous attacks on military targets, a courthouse, three bridges, and a BBC transmitter. Though this campaign was not formally called off until February 1962, it constituted a serious offensive only for the first seven months. The single large-scale engagement was a bungled raid on the RUC barracks at Brookeborough, Co. Fermanagh, in which two IRA men were fatally injured, including 'Seán South of Garryowen', later commemorated by a popular ballad. Over the whole campaign nineteen people died, of whom six were policemen. Reflecting the weakness of the IRA at the time, the campaign was limited in effect to a zone along the border, and most of the attacks were either assassination attempts or bombs planted at fixed targets, such as bridges, telephone exchanges, RUC barracks, and oil depots. This carried its own risks: five people died in November 1957 when an IRA bomb was being moved across the border from Co. Louth. Apart from the absence of any mobilisation in towns, such as Derry and Belfast (where the IRA Army Council did not think it was strong enough to protect nationalists against unionist reprisals), a major factor in the failure of the campaign was the stringent security measures adopted by both the Belfast and Dublin governments. In the North more than 180 IRA suspects were interned under the Special Powers Act, while in the Republic FIANNA FÁIL introduced INTERNMENT in July 1957, eventually detaining over 200 suspects. **Keith Jeffery**

Bord Fáilte Éireann, the state body responsible for monitoring and marketing the tourist industry of the Republic. Its structure and responsibilities have changed as the tourist industry has grown. The board is a successor to Bord Cuartaíochta na hÉireann, set up under the Tourist Traffic Act (1939), which compiled the first register of visitor accommodation. It was dormant throughout the years of the SECOND WORLD WAR. In 1952 the Government established Fógra Fáilte to promote Ireland as a tourist destination, while An Bord Fáilte developed domestic tourism; these were merged in 1955 as Bord Fáilte Éireann, a statutory body financed primarily by annual Government grant. In 2000 it received a Government grant of £49.4 million.

While the image projected to potential visitors is one of Ireland as a quaint, rural backwater, Bord Fáilte in contrast used the latest management and marketing techniques to develop and promote its 'product'—Ireland and its amenities. The board was also responsible for monitoring the standard of accommodation, restaurants, and car hire and coach tour operators, awarding Bord Fáilte's shamrock symbol to those that were approved. Providers of accommodation paid an annual fee in return for inspection and the inclusion of their details in publications distributed to tourists.

In 1958 Bord Fáilte inaugurated the annual NATIONAL TIDY TOWNS COMPETITION. In 1995, as a result of rapid growth in the industry, the Arthur D. Little Report reassessed the role of the

border campaign. *Between 1956 and 1962 the IRA attacked bridges, and a range of civilian and military targets along the border. The campaign ended on 26 February 1962 when a ceasefire was called by the IRA. [Kelvin Boyes Photography]* board, recommending that it concentrate on promoting Ireland overseas and overseeing developments in the industry while decreasing its direct involvement in the domestic market, where the REGIONAL TOURISM AUTHORITIES were already running a network of tourist information offices. Providers of accommodation, car hire operators and coach tour operators were encouraged to become self-regulating. The Tidy Towns Competition passed to the Department of the Environment.

The all-Ireland initiative Tourism Ireland, established in 2001, has the role of selling Ireland abroad as a holiday destination, leaving Bord Fáilte, which was always primarily a marketing organisation, with a greatly reduced role. During 2001 its staff was reduced from about 250 (100 of whom were overseas) to about 120, based at its head office in Dublin. Bord Fáilte continues to be responsible for promoting tourism in the home market. In the four years from 2001 it will administer more than €127 million in grants from the National Development Plan for the physical development of the industry, identifying new attractions for Tourism Ireland to market overseas. It also continues to carry out its research function to keep the industry and the Government fully informed. [see NORTHERN IRELAND TOURIST BOARD.] **Alannah Hopkin**

Bord na Móna, established in 1933 as the Turf Development Board Ltd, re-established in 1946 by the Department of Industry and Commerce. Twenty-five BOGS were to be drained to produce 1 million tons of machine-won turf per year for twenty-five years. A quarter of this was to be supplied at an agreed price to the ESB power stations at Portarlington, Co. Offaly, and Allenwood, Co. Kildare, the remainder to be sold for industrial and domestic use. The board improved Lullymore briquette factory and its bog production of milled peat and erected a moss peat litter factory at Kilberry, Co. Kildare, and an experimental station. From 1952 it began producing 4 million tons of milled peat per year to supply several power stations and a further three briquette factories. Two more moss peat litter factories were built, and methods of controlling industrial pollution with peat were also developed. [see ELECTRICITY SUPPLY; ENERGY SOURCES.] **James Martin**

Bord Scannán na hÉireann (Irish Film Board), established in 1981, the Government agency charged with developing the film industry. During the period of the 'first board', 1981–7, small but significant sums (€600,000 per year) were invested in culturally incisive films; when these fell out of favour with policy-makers the board was closed down by the TAOISEACH, CHARLES HAUGHEY. Reactivated in 1993 by the Minister for Arts and Culture, MICHAEL D. HIGGINS, under Lelia Doolan as chairperson and Rod Stoneman as chief executive, the 'second board's' initial annual budget was €1.4 million, rising to over €5 million by the late 1990s and €16 million by 2002. With attractive tax concessions for wealthy individuals and corporations investing in films introduced in the Finance Act (1987), the twin approach led to a burgeoning of film production during the late 1990s and later. An explicitly commercial policy, already in evidence by the mid-1990s, was adopted under the board's new chairman, Ossie Kilkenny, following a Government review of the industry in 1998; support for a global audiovisual product as well as the creation of jobs, rather than film culture, emerged as its primary objective. The board's membership has included the film director NEIL JORDAN and the actors GABRIEL BYRNE and PATRICK BERGIN. Films supported include Jordan's first feature film, *Angel* (1982), PAT MURPHY's *Anne Devlin* (1984), PAT O'CONNOR's *Circle of Friends* (1995), PADDY BREATHNACH's *I Went Down* (1997), and GERRY STEMBRIDGE's *About Adam* (2000). **Kevin Rockett**

boroughs, self-governing towns, entitled to elect members of Parliament. By 1700, Ireland contained 117 boroughs, exercising local self-government and returning two members to Parliament. The borough franchise varied widely, but all except ten were 'closed' boroughs, controlled by a single patron. The ACT OF UNION (1800) reduced to thirty-three the number entitled to elect members of Parliament; and a uniform franchise was introduced in 1832. Municipal powers were removed from many boroughs, and in 1840 Catholics were admitted to the corporations of the remainder. The Redistribution Act (1885) further reduced the number of parliamentary boroughs to nine. [see ADMINISTRATIVE DIVISIONS.] **Peter Gray**

Boston, the Irish in. Often described as the 'capital of Irish America', Boston, Massachusetts, has been home to Irish emigrants for more than 150 years. While numbers are smaller than in New York and other larger cities, people of Irish birth or descent make up 29 per cent of greater Boston's population—by far the largest national group in the area—compared with 12 per cent in metropolitan New York.

The few Irish people who emigrated to Boston in the eighteenth and early nineteenth centuries were mostly Ulster Presbyterians. The GREAT FAMINE of the 1840s brought large numbers of Catholic Irish for the first time. Initial sympathy for the starving immigrants gave way to dismay as figures rose—from 4,000 in 1820 to 117,000 in 1850. Nearly half arrived directly from Ireland, while countless more travelled down from the quays at QUÉBEC. By 1860, 26 per cent of Boston's population was Irish. Largely unskilled, Irish men became manual labourers, while women found work as domestic servants or in the nearby Lowell and Lawrence textile mills. Their increasing numbers provoked anti-Catholic and anti-Irish hostility from Boston's Protestant population. Work advertisements stated 'No Irish need apply,' while political parties like the 'Know-Nothings' continued to gain power. The worst episode of violence occurred in 1834, when nativist mobs burnt an Ursuline convent in nearby Charlestown.

Such memories persisted in Irish minds, contributing to a separatist mentality long after they achieved success. The Irish quickly established institutions to help them settle into city life. The *Pilot*, a newspaper founded in 1829 and edited by well-known Irishmen such as JOHN BOYLE O'REILLY, helped sustain the community and kept it informed of news from Ireland. But the most important institution was the Catholic Church, which created a network of churches, hospitals, and orphanages. Irish separatism did not extend to education, however. By 1905, 25 per cent of public school teachers were Irish; by 1908, 75 per cent of Irish children attended public schools.

The Irish became more economically mobile by the late 1800s, moving out of North End slums to such districts as South Boston and Dorchester. Yet while many became teachers and lawyers, the community was still heavily concentrated in unskilled labour well into the 1960s. Because of the difficulty of penetrating the rigid Yankee social hierarchy, politics became one of the few ways for the Irish to advance. From Hugh O'Brien, 1885–8, to Raymond L. Flynn, 1984–93, the Irish dominated city government and slowly began to infiltrate the cultural establishment. Politicians such as John 'Honey Fitz' Fitzgerald and James Michael Curley practised ward-based politics, playing on national and racial tensions and

Botanic Gardens. *Glasshouses of the Curvilinear Range at the National Botanic Gardens, Dublin, designed and built by Richard Turner between 1843 and 1868. [National Botanic Gardens, Dublin]*

constructing widespread patronage networks. This local success was duplicated on a national scale with the election in 1963 of President JOHN F. KENNEDY—a symbol to Irish-Americans everywhere that they had finally achieved acceptance.

Boston's Irish-born population decreased during the twentieth century—from 71,441 in 1890 to 57,011 in 1920—but Irish-Americans maintained strong connections with Ireland through FAMILY, TOURISM, and cultural and nationalist movements. At the beginning of the twenty-first century Boston continues to be a popular destination for Irish immigrants, businessmen, and students and remains a centre of Irish culture in America. [see UNITED STATES, THE IRISH IN; CANADA, THE IRISH IN.] **Meaghan Dwyer**

botanic gardens and arboreta contain documented collections of named and labelled plants, often in scientific or geographical groups and with an educational, conservation, or research purpose. Four gardens in Ireland are designated botanic gardens: the National BOTANIC GARDENS (DUBLIN), the BOTANIC GARDENS (BELFAST), the Talbot Botanic Garden (Malahide, Co. Dublin), and Trinity College Botanic Garden, Dublin. A botanic garden established in Cork in 1808 survived until the 1840s, when it was abandoned. All the existing botanic gardens contain collections of trees. The National Botanic Gardens have an area set aside as an arboretum; the John F. Kennedy Memorial Forest Park and Arboretum at Dunganstown, Co. Wexford, is the *de facto* national arboretum while Castlewellan, Co. Down, is the designated national arboretum for Northern Ireland.

Botanic gardens have their origin in the physic gardens of the seventeenth and earlier centuries. The value of growing plants for medicinal use and for demonstration and teaching was realised by the medical institutions, as collecting plants from the wild limited the number and scope of plants available. Horticulture provided a means of having a wide range of plants from far and near and in sufficient quantity readily available. The success of physic gardens prompted the growing of plants for agricultural research and teaching as well as for BOTANY, the study of plants as a science in itself.

Irish gardens and arboreta probably contain about a tenth of the world's plant species. An equable oceanic CLIMATE, particularly in areas close to the south and west coasts, and influenced by the GULF STREAM, enables a wide range of plants from around the world to be grown. Many plants from climatic zone 9 (applied to the plants of the sub-tropics) can be grown outdoors for up to ten years, and some survive for decades through the hardest of Irish winters. Higher-zone plants are generally impossible to grow outdoors in Ireland. Besides the huge genetic pool of plant material in botanic gardens and arboreta and other documented collections, large numbers of species as well as cultivated varieties could be grown in Ireland that are not yet in cultivation.

The realisation in the nineteenth century that Ireland has a climate favourable to the cultivation of plants from a wide range of climatic zones led to a dramatic increase in the importing of plants from around the world. However, as early as the end of the sixteenth century WALTER RALEIGH had grown exotic plants on his estate at Youghal, Co. Cork. A century later Sir Arthur Rawdon imported crates of plants from Jamaica and successfully grew at least some of them for a time in his Co. Down garden. From the middle of the eighteenth century Anthony Foster had a large collection of North American plants on his estate in Collon, Co. Louth. In 1790 his son JOHN FOSTER, Speaker of the Irish Parliament, secured government support for the formation of the Dublin Society's garden at Glasnevin. Plants from the Americas, Australia, and New Zealand as well as from India, China, and Japan found their way to Ireland from private collectors, commercial horticultural firms, and from the growing network of botanic gardens throughout the world. A surprising number of plants were found to be hardy in Ireland or parts of it, while the development of large heated glasshouses in botanic gardens and in the great estates greatly extended the number of species that could be grown.

Plant collectors such as Edward Madden, AUGUSTINE HENRY, Thomas Coulter, and William Burbidge made significant contributions to the store of good plants in botanic gardens. Some of the curators or directors of botanic gardens who made a lasting contribution to plantsmanship were William Ferguson and Charles McKimm at Belfast, Ninian Niven, David Moore and Sir FREDERICK MOORE at Glasnevin, and John Bain and William Burbidge at Trinity College.

In the past, plants were acquired *ad hoc* or in an opportunist manner. The expansion of the collections in Irish gardens and arboreta is now more focused and takes account of conservation, environmental and trade issues and of international conventions, such as those on biological diversity, Agenda 21, and CITES.

In addition to gardens in public ownership, many estates and private gardens have large and interesting collections of trees, shrubs, and herbaceous plants; some have close links with botanic gardens and arboreta. The importance of documented private collections is recognised by botanic gardens and by the principal botanical and horticultural organisations. The scientific value of plants in private collections supplements that of designated botanic gardens and arboreta. Important documented collections of herbaceous plants are held in large and small gardens throughout the country. The gardens of the NATIONAL TRUST in Northern Ireland, Mount Stewart and Rowallane, as well as being aesthetically pleasing contain large and valuable documented collections. There are outstanding collections, particularly of trees and other woody plants, in the gardens at BIRR CASTLE, Co. Offaly; FOTA, Co. Cork; Mount Congreve, Co. Waterford; GARINISH, Co. Cork; Headford, Co. Meath; Kilmacurragh, Co. Wicklow; Glenveagh, Co. Donegal; Earlscliffe, Co. Dublin; Brook Hall, Co. Derry; Muckross House, Co. Kerry; and many other estates. Fingal County Council manages the Talbot Botanic Garden at Malahide, Co. Dublin; the plant collection is particularly rich in Australasian plants. Lord Talbot de Malahide, who created the garden, had a particular interest in the Tasmanian flora, helping to produce a six-volume illustrated account of its most spectacular plants between 1967 and 1978.

Ten major gardens and arboreta are already in state care while others are being acquired. The Forest Service in Northern Ireland manages Castlewellan, Co. Down. The Department of the Environment and Local Government manages the National Botanic Gardens, the J. F. Kennedy Arboretum, Kilmacurragh, Muckross, Garinish, and Glenveagh. Avondale, at Rathdrum, Co. Wicklow, is managed by the Forest Service and has a fine collection of trees associated with Augustine Henry. **Donal Synnott**

Botanic Gardens (Belfast). The Botanic Gardens in Belfast have their origin in the formation of the Belfast Botanic and Horticultural Society in 1827. In the same year the Society established a garden on an acre of ground at Bradbury Place; two years later it was moved to its permanent home on a 6 ha (14-acre) site known as The Course at the junction of Malone Road and Stranmillis Road. The gardens, known as the Royal Botanic Gardens from 1840 to 1893, were transferred in the latter year to the ownership of Belfast City Council.

The first curator of the garden was the botanist THOMAS DRUMMOND, who is commemorated in the name of a number of mosses first reported by him. He remained as curator for only two years, leaving to explore the flora of North America. His successor, John Campbell, also left after a short period, to be followed in 1836 by Daniel Ferguson, who remained until his death in 1864. He published an important guide to the gardens and greatly expanded the collections, and succeeded in flowering the giant Amazon waterlily as early as 1853 in a specially built house. The excellence and popularity of the gardens in the middle of the nineteenth century are due mainly to the work and application of Ferguson. He was succeeded for a four-year term by his son William, who in turn was succeeded by Forsythe Johnston, who had been a gardener at the Duke of Devonshire's estate at Chatsworth, Derbyshire. In 1877 the garden foreman, Charles McKimm, was appointed curator and he remained until his death in 1907, instituting many changes and improvements.

The gardens, which include within them the ULSTER MUSEUM, provide an important public park for Belfast. They also have an extensive botanical collection, especially in the glasshouses; these, including the Palm House designed by CHARLES LANYON, are its chief attraction. The wings of the Palm House were built by RICHARD TURNER of Dublin; building began in 1839, before the construction of the Turner houses at Glasnevin and Kew. Young of Edinburgh completed the central dome of the Palm House to a revised design by Lanyon. The building was restored in the 1980s and contains a well-grown collection of tropical plants and spectacular seasonal displays of decorative flowering plants.

The other significant glasshouse is the tropical Ravine House, also restored in the 1980s. Work on this was begun in 1887 and was largely carried out by the curator, Charles McKimm, and his gardeners. This unique house was constructed as a sunken glen viewed from above from a railed balcony and walkway; a tropical pool was added in 1902 to grow the giant Amazon waterlily. **Donal Synnott**

Botanic Gardens (Dublin). The National Botanic Gardens at Glasnevin, Dublin, cover 20 ha (50 acres) on the south bank of the River Tolka to the north of the city. Much of the gardens are on a gravel ridge, where the soil is limy and free-draining; part is on alluvial soil, the ancient flood plain of the Tolka.

The gardens were founded by the DUBLIN SOCIETY with the financial aid of the Irish Parliament in 1795 and were given into state care in 1878. They house the national herbarium of over half a million specimens as well as a significant collection of economic botany samples. There is a specialist library of botanical and horticultural books and papers and a collection of 2,000 botanical drawings and watercolours.

The first professor of botany, WALTER WADE, and the first head gardener, John Underwood, soon developed the gardens to a stage where they were described as 'the brightest jewel in the crown of the Dublin Society.' Ninian Niven (curator 1834–8) re-landscaped the gardens; features that survive from his time include the chain tent pergola and the rose pergola, as well as the system of paths and roads throughout the gardens. DAVID MOORE (curator 1838–79) was the most illustrious manager of the gardens, developing the collections to a remarkable degree and achieving international recognition for his contributions to botany and horticulture. His son FREDERICK MOORE became curator in 1880 at the early age of twenty-two and expanded the collections, being especially successful with tropical orchids. During his term Glasnevin became a centre of horticultural excellence, rivalling both Kew and Edinburgh. He was knighted in 1911. When he retired in 1922 he and his father between them had been directors of the gardens for eighty-four years.

Moore was succeeded by John Besant, an Englishman trained at Kew Gardens, London. He maintained good standards, as did his successor in 1946, Dr Tom Walsh. When Aidan Brady became director in 1968 he and John Fanning of the Department of Agriculture set about creating a scientific arm at Glasnevin. The herbarium and botany collections at the NATIONAL MUSEUM were transferred to Glasnevin, and three botanists were appointed, the first since the death of Dr W. R. McNab in 1880.

The gardens contain a number of historic glasshouses. The Dublin ironmaster RICHARD TURNER built the Curvilinear Range between 1843 and 1868; this was magnificently restored by the OFFICE OF PUBLIC WORKS in 1995. The Water House was built in 1853 to house the giant Amazon water-lily (*Victoria amazonica*). The Great Palm House, made by Boyd of Paisley, was erected in 1884. [see BOTANIC GARDENS AND ARBORETA.]. **Donal Synnott**

botany. The study of botany in Ireland began with plant recording, a desire to discover what plants grew in the country and where they were to be found. Early plant records were of the useful and the curious. The founding of the DUBLIN SOCIETY in 1731 gave a great impetus to the development of the sciences; it promoted botany by offering premiums for the discovery of new plants. In 1795 it founded a botanic garden at Glasnevin, outside Dublin (now the NATIONAL BOTANIC GARDENS), 'for promoting a scientific knowledge in the various branches of horticulture.'

Developments in the philosophy of science had their effects on botany in Ireland as elsewhere. From the middle of the eighteenth century the Linnaean binomial system of naming plants made for easier communication among scientists and plantspeople. The classification of plants indicated degrees of relationship and led to the theory of evolution by natural selection, proposed by Darwin and Wallace in the middle of the nineteenth century. The rediscovery of Gregor Mendel's work on the mathematics of inherited characteristics provided the scientific basis for genetic studies. **Donal Synnott**

Bothy Band, the, one of the most influential bands in the TRADITIONAL MUSIC revival of the 1970s. The original composition was Tommy Peoples (FIDDLE), MATT MOLLOY (FLUTE), PADDY KEENAN (UILLEANN PIPES), Tríona Ní Dhomhnaill (vocals and clavinet), MICHEÁL Ó DOMHNAILL (guitar), and DÓNAL LUNNY (bouzouki and BODHRÁN); Peoples was replaced by Kevin Burke in 1977. The group's much-imitated sound was characterised by a

Boucicault. *A sketch by Queen Victoria of the duel scene from Dion Boucicault's play* The Corsican Brothers, *the only sketch she ever made of a professional performance. She saw the play five times during its first season in 1852; the dates of her first three visits (28 February, 23 March, and 19 September) are noted in the bottom right. [Royal Archives © Her Majesty Queen Elizabeth II]*

strong melody line, accompanied by a driving rhythm section. Recordings include *The Bothy Band* (1975), *Old Hag, You Have Killed Me* (1976), and *Out of the Wind, Into the Sun* (1977). **Pat Ahern**

Boucicault, Dionysius (Dion) Lardner (1820–1890), dramatist. Born in Dublin, probably the son of DIONYSIUS LARDNER. In a career spanning fifty years and three continents he was to become one of the most successful and prolific dramatists of the nineteenth century. His first success on the London stage was the drawing-room comedy *London Assurance* (1841); but he is best remembered now as the author of the three Irish MELODRAMAS *The Colleen Bawn* (1860), *Arrah-na-Pogue* (1864), and *The Shaughraun* (1874), as a proponent of the spectacular 'sensation' scene, and for popularising the touring company. **Nicholas Daly**

Boundary Commission. During the Treaty negotiations of 1921 the idea of a boundary commission was dangled before GRIFFITH and COLLINS as an inducement to sign. Nationalist expectations were that such a body would transfer to the IRISH FREE STATE the counties of Fermanagh and Tyrone, other possibilities being the city of Derry, south Co. Down, and south Co. Armagh. The result would be to leave NORTHERN IRELAND unviable. LLOYD GEORGE's statement to the British Cabinet on 6 December that the Boundary Commission might add territory to Northern Ireland leaves doubts about his sincerity.

The commission began work at the end of 1924, and the evidence it heard in BORDER areas provides a rich source of information for attitudes at the time. Its chairman was the South African jurist Richard Feetham, while EOIN MACNEILL and J. R. Fisher represented the Free State and Northern Ireland governments, respectively. Feetham took the view that article 12 of the Treaty charged him with defining a border, not with reconstituting Northern Ireland *de novo*. On these grounds he rejected the Free State case for Cos. Fermanagh and Tyrone. Article 12 also provided that the wishes of the inhabitants had to be compatible with economic and geographical considerations, and he ruled that this precluded the transfer of Derry or Newry. When his decisions were leaked to the *Morning Post* in November 1925 they caused such a reaction in the Free State that MacNeill resigned, and the report was not published. **T. G. Fraser**

Bourke, Brian (1936–), artist. Born in Dublin; studied briefly at the NCAD and St Martin's, London, but his real education came in studying early Flemish and Italian masters at the National Gallery, London. He was also influenced by FRANCIS BACON; the discovery of the work of the Irish post-impressionist RODERIC O'CONOR made a profound impression on him. Returning to Dublin in 1957, he won prizes at the IRISH EXHIBITION OF LIVING ART, 1964, 1965, and 1967. Since 1965 he has had many one-man shows, latterly in the Taylor Galleries, Dublin. An independent figurative artist, he represents portrait, figure, and landscape in a vibrant, 'expressionist' style and with distinctive drawing skills. He has also produced a series on Don Quixote and the 'Sweeney' legend. He works in a variety of media: pencil, gouache, oil, etching, wood, and bronze. He is a member of AOSDÁNA (see p. 719). **Julian Campbell**

Bourke, Fergus (1934–), photographer. Born in Wicklow. He began photographing the Irish landscape in the 1960s, and later became official photographer in the ABBEY THEATRE, producing distinguished black and white portraiture later published in *Kindred: Collected Portraits 1984–1991*. One of the founding photographers of the Source Gallery in Mayo, his work has been exhibited widely. He is a member of AOSDÁNA. **Martin Clancy**

Bowden, John (c. 1780–1821/22), architect. He studied at the DUBLIN SOCIETY's School of Architectural Drawing from 1798 and served an apprenticeship to RICHARD MORRISON. He was one of the first Irish architects to visit Paris in the immediate aftermath of the defeat of Napoleon Bonaparte in 1815. By that time he was architect to the BOARD OF FIRST FRUITS. His best-known church is St Stephen's (the 'Peppercannister Church') in Upper Mount Street, Dublin, completed in 1824 by his assistant, Joseph Welland. His public buildings include the County Courthouse in Derry (1813); he also worked on the erection of Monaghan Jail and Dundalk Courthouse. **Frederick O'Dwyer**

Bowen, Elizabeth (1899–1973), novelist and short-story writer. Born in Dublin, the only child of Anglo-Irish parents; educated at Downe House School, Kent. The family wintered in Dublin but spent the summers at Bowen's Court, Kildorrery, Co. Cork, the 'BIG HOUSE' that she inherited on her father's death in 1930. Her memoir, *Seven Winters* (1942), records her early childhood before her father's mental breakdown in 1906; she and her mother, Florence, then went to live with successive relations on the English south coast—where several of her novels are set—until Florence's death in 1912. *Bowen's Court* (1942) analyses the history of Anglo-Irish Ireland through stories of ancestors and houses—a territory she returned to in several essays and in her best Irish novel, THE LAST SEPTEMBER (1929). In 1923 her first collection of short stories, *Encounters* (1923), was published; it was a genre that suited her talent for balancing understatement and fantasy. Her three major collections are *The Cat Jumps* (1934), *Look at All Those Roses* (1941), and *The Demon Lover* (1945). Her debut novel, *The Hotel* (1927), shows the influence of Henry James, as an older woman disabuses an alienated woman about love—a theme that recurs in *The House in Paris* (1935) and the highly regarded *The Death of the Heart* (1938). Emotional and physical distance also features in *Friends and Relations* (1931) and the uneven but interesting *To the North* (1932).

In 1940 she began reporting on Irish attitudes to the war for the British Ministry of Information. London in the Blitz is memorably described in her wartime stories and in her bestselling novel, *The Heat of the Day* (1949), which interlinks personal and political betrayal to brilliant effect. *A World of Love* (1955), her only other novel to be set in Ireland, was followed by *The Little Girls* (1964) and *Eva Trout* (1969). She moved to Hythe, Kent, after selling Bowen's Court in 1959 (demolished 1960) and in 1958 was made a commander of the Order of the British Empire. Her prose style was admired by contemporaries such as Virginia Woolf and Graham Greene. Her work is enjoying a critical revival that identifies her as a major figure in twentieth-century women's writing and a keen analyst of the ambivalences of Anglo-Irish identity. [see ANGLO-IRISH SOCIETY.] **Selina Guinness**

Bowen, Gretta (1880–1981), painter. Born in Dublin. In Belfast, she began to paint just before her seventieth birthday; her first show, in 1955, was at the CEMA (Council for the Encouragement of Music and Art) Gallery. In 1956 she exhibited at the Victor Waddington Galleries, Dublin; all thirty-six paintings were sold, the proceeds going to charity. She also showed at the OIREACHTAS, RHA, and Tom Caldwell Gallery, Dublin. In Belfast the Caldwell Gallery also hung her work, as well as the Ulster Society of Women Artists. In 1979 she was included in the International

Naïves Exhibition at the Hamiltons Galleries, London. The *Times* found that 'whatever she paints conveys a feeling of happiness, of brightness, of delight in life.' She is represented in the ULSTER MUSEUM. **Theo Snoddy**

Bowles, Michael (1909–1998), composer, arranger, and conductor. Born in Riverstown, Co. Sligo, he joined the Army School of Music in 1932 and graduated from UCD in 1936 and became the first full-time director of music at Radio Éireann in 1944. From 1941 he conducted the Radio Éireann Symphony Orchestra, establishing a series of public concerts. In 1948 he resigned due to policy disagreements, and became conductor of the National Orchestra of New Zealand and in 1954 he was appointed professor of music at the University of Indiana; he returned to Ireland in 1970. His compositions mainly include songs for voice and piano. His *Three Pieces for Orchestra* date from 1947. **Paul J. Kerr**

Bowles, William (1705–1780), scientist. Born near Cork; he gave up his career as a lawyer in 1740 and went to Paris, where he studied natural history, chemistry, and metallurgy. He travelled through France, investigating its natural history and mining. He was appointed by the Spanish government to superintend the state mines, to form a collection of natural history objects, and to set up a chemical laboratory. His *Introduction to the Natural History and Physical Geography of Spain* was published in Spanish in 1775 and translated into French and Italian. He spent the latter half of his life in Spain and died in Madrid. **Christopher Moriarty**

bowling, road, also called 'bullets' in Northern Ireland, a game played with a solid iron ball called a *bowl* (rhyming with 'owl'). It is most popular in Cos. Armagh and Cork but is also played elsewhere. The game is thought to have been introduced in the seventeenth century, either by immigrant English weavers or by WILLIAM OF ORANGE's Dutch soldiers. The ball weighs 0.79 kg ($1\frac{3}{4}$ lb) and is 18 cm (7 in.) in diameter. The courses are curving, undulating stretches of the public road, usually about 4 km ($2\frac{1}{2}$ miles) long. Two players compete in throwing the bowl with optimum speed and control, aiming to reach the finishing line in the smallest number of shots. Important matches attract thousands of spectators and substantial wagers. Some courses are used regularly for major championships, such as Knappagh, near Armagh, and Ballyshonin, near Blarney, Co. Cork. Each course has a recognised par for the distance, and almost every hill and bend is known to enthusiasts by name.

Heroes of the game go back to John McGrath of Cork, pre-eminent at the turn of the century, Tim Delaney of Fairhill, Co. Cork, famous in the 1930s, and the idolised Joe McVeigh of Armagh. A roadside stone marks the spot where, in August 1955, McVeigh completed the 4 km Knappagh course in twenty-two shots, his last shot travelling 160 m beyond the finishing line. Danny McParland (Armagh) won the men's senior championship four times between 1963 and 1976 and in 1964 achieved the longest shot ever recorded, of 466 m (509 yards), on the Moy Road, Armagh. McParland's principal rival was Mick Barry of Waterfall, Co. Cork, eight times senior champion and widely regarded as the greatest bowler of all time. One of his feats came in a famous all-Ireland final against McParland at Dublin Hill, near Cork, in August 1964. The two masters matched each other shot for shot until the three-quarters stage, when Mick Barry cut a corner with a gigantic throw over a public house, telephone wires and all, to land the bowl safely back on the road 18 m (20 yards) beyond the corner. This gave him the lead; but McParland, facing a double bend, rounded it with an astonishing 'pulled' shot, which won him the match.

Bourke, Brian. Knock-a-Lough *(1977) by Brian Bourke, one of the most distinguished of late twentieth-century interpreters of the landscape of the West of Ireland. [AIB Art Collection]*

More recent champions have included Denis Scully, Pat Butler, Bill Daly and James Buckley of Co. Cork and Michael Toal and Harry Toal Junior of Armagh. Notable among woman bowlers have been Gretta Hegarty-Cormican, Róisín Toal-Mackle, and later champions such as Sharon O'Driscoll, Geraldine McCluskey, Susan Cullen, and Kathleen Cooney.

Ból-Chumann na hÉireann was formed in 1954 to organise the game in the Republic; in 1963 it amalgamated with the northern association to administer the game nationally. There are national championships for men and women and for juniors and veterans—twelve grades in all—as well as international contests. **John Wakeman**

Bowyer, Brendan (1932–), singer. Born in Waterford. He was the lead vocalist with the Royal Showband, stars of Ireland's ballroom era from the late 1950s. A dynamic live act, Bowyer and his band had several hits, the most famous of which was 'Hucklebuck' (1965). In 1971 he left the Royal Showband and moved to Las Vegas, where he and his new band, the Big 8, became a cabaret attraction. **Mick Heaney**

boxing. The OLYMPIC sport of amateur boxing is controlled by the Irish Amateur Boxing Association, founded in 1911, whose objective is 'to develop and foster moral, social and physical education generally, and in particular to develop, foster and control amateur boxing in Ireland.' The association organises an extensive annual programme of national and international events; these have included the European championship (1939, 1947, 1978), the world championship (2001), the World Cup (1990), and the prestigious World Challenge Match (1993).

Boxing has been one of Ireland's sporting success stories. The 1939 championships, held at the newly built National Stadium, Dublin, produced two gold medal winners in Jimmy Ingle (flyweight) and Paddy Dowdall (featherweight), with Gearóid Ó Colmáin crowned European heavyweight champion in 1947. Maxie McCullagh claimed the lightweight crown and Best Boxer award two years later in Oslo. Other notable European medal winners (more than thirty since 1939) include Harry Perry (winner of nine national titles), Mick Dowling (eight titles), Terry Milligan (Commonwealth champion, 1958), John McNally (Olympic finalist, 1952), and Paul Griffin (European champion, 1991).

Among the outstanding boxers of the modern era are Fred Teidt, John Caldwell, Freddie Gilroy, Jim McCourt, Wayne McCullough, and Michael Carruth—all Olympic medallists. Caldwell and McCullough were among those who went on to become world champions in the professional ring. Others include Steve Collins, Dave McAuley, and the 'Clones Cyclone', Barry McGuigan, all of whom followed in the footsteps of Mike McTigue of Co. Clare, the first Irishman to win a world title on home soil—against Battling Siki on ST PATRICK'S DAY, 1923—and Rinty Monaghan from Belfast, the first Irish boxer to be crowned world champion (1947–8).

Professional boxing is regulated by the Boxing Union of Ireland, whose founding president, Mel Christle, is one of three remarkable brothers, all of whom won Irish senior titles in the 1970s (see p. 1073). **Breandán Ó Conaire**

boxing. *The featherweight champion Barry McGuigan, the 'Clones Cyclone', in the ring on 15 February 1986 in Dublin, where he successfully defended his title against Danilo Cabrera. [Ray McManus, Sportsfile]*

boycott, the social and economic ostracism of individuals who violated the 'unwritten law' of rural Ireland. The practice did not originate during the LAND WAR but was widely and effectively used during it. It derived its name from the famous 'boycotting' of Captain Charles Cunningham Boycott in the autumn of 1880. Boycott, agent on the Earl of Erne's estate at Lough Mask, Co. Mayo, was compelled to import labourers, recruited in Ulster and protected by 1,000 soldiers, to harvest his crops after his tenants and labourers refused to do so in a dispute over rent and wages. Father John O'Malley, parish priest of the Neale and a leader of the protest, is credited with coining the term. [see ACHILL.] **Donald Jordan**

Boycott. *Captain Charles Boycott (centre, front row) at Lough Mask, Co. Mayo, 1880, surrounded by Cavan Orangemen and some of the 1,000 soldiers used for their protection while they were engaged in harvesting Boycott's crops. [Irish Picture Library]*

Boyd, John (1912–), playwright. Born in Belfast; educated at RBAI, QUB, and TCD. He has been a teacher, a producer with the BBC, and literary adviser to the Lyric Theatre. His influence as an editor and a promoter of young talent has been expressed through his work with *Lagan* (1942–6) and *Threshold* (1971–), the magazine of the Lyric Theatre. In his own writing, a central concern of which has been to explore immediate experiences, he has produced five or six plays of regional importance, *The Flats* (1971) being the best-known. **Sam Burnside**

Boyd, John McNeill (1812–1861), naval officer. Born in Co. Donegal; he joined the British navy when still a youngster and was quickly noted as a hard worker, a man of extraordinary courage, and he became an officer who easily won the admiration and the affection of men serving under him. In 1857 he published *A Manual for Naval Cadets*, which formed the basis of an official manual of seamanship, published in the Netherlands in 1860. This was a period when the switch from sail to steam was causing many problems.

In February 1861 he was in command of the *Ajax*, operating as guard ship at Kingstown (Dún Laoghaire), as was customary in minor naval ports of the day. DUBLIN BAY, notorious for sudden destructive gales, was struck by the most ferocious of these ever recorded. Boyd saw two sailing colliers vainly attempting to enter the harbour, and he had one of the *Ajax's* boats launched. He went with it to where the colliers were being driven by the storm onto the outer wall of the East Pier; there he joined a rescue party assembled by the harbour master. When an exceptional wave knocked down the entire rescue party, Boyd jumped in, in an attempt to rescue the drowning seamen but was himself drowned. His funeral procession, six miles long, was said to be the longest seen in Dublin.

There are three public monuments to Boyd: one on the East Pier, Dún Laoghaire, just above the spot where his death occurred, and others in ST PATRICK'S CATHEDRAL, Dublin, and St Columb's Cathedral, Derry. **John de Courcy Ireland**

Boydell, Brian (1917–2000), composer, lecturer, broadcaster, conductor, and adjudicator. Born in Dublin; educated at Cambridge (receiving a First in natural sciences in 1938), the Royal College of Music, London, the RIAM, and TCD. A founder-member of the MUSIC ASSOCIATION OF IRELAND and the Dowland Consort, of which he was director, he conducted the DUBLIN ORCHESTRAL PLAYERS for over twenty years and guest conducted with the RTÉ SYMPHONY ORCHESTRA. A member of the ARTS COUNCIL and AOSDÁNA, he received an honorary DMus (NUI), Commendatore della Repubblica Italiana, and honorary fellowship of the RIAM. His compositions are for orchestral, chamber, and choral groups and include four string quartets, a violin concerto (1954), *In Memoriam Mahatma Gandhi* (1948), *Megalithic Ritual Dances* (1956), *Symphonic Inscapes* (1968), *Masai Mara* (1988), and *Viking Lip Music* (1996). His compositions are essentially tonal, crafted along conventional forms, and employ octotonicism. He was professor of music at Trinity College, Dublin, 1962–82, where he transformed the undergraduate music syllabus and examination system. **Paul J. Kerr**

Boylan, Clare (1948–), novelist and short-story writer. Born in Dublin. She became popular as an award-winning journalist with the *Irish Press* and then editor of the magazine *Image* before turning to full-time writing. Her fiction typically explores the dynamics of family relationships from a female viewpoint, concentrating on the painful yet liberating experiences connected with loss of innocence, coming of age, confronting ghosts from the past, and new beginnings. Her first novel, *Holy Pictures* (1983), containing a bizarre international domestic plot twist, attracted much attention and praise. Her short fiction, exemplified in such collections as *Concerning Virgins* (1989), has also been well received. **Rachel Sealy Lynch**

Boyle, Alicia (1908–1997), painter. Born in Bangkok; in 1909 she returned to the family home at Limavady, Co. Derry, and in 1920 moved to London. At the Byam Shaw School of Art she won two scholarships. She first exhibited at the Royal Academy in 1932, and became an art teacher in various institutions. Her first one-person show was held in London in 1945. In 1950 and 1952 CEMA organised exhibitions in Belfast. She studied lithography at the Central School of Arts and Crafts, London. She was the subject of an exhibition at Belfast Museum and Art Gallery in 1959 and won the CEMA open painting competition in 1962 for *The Red Weaver, Ardara*. She held exhibitions at Belfast, 1963, and Derry, 1967. In 1971 she moved to Co. Cork. Retrospectives were held by the ACNI, 1983, and Crawford Gallery, Cork, 1988. **Theo Snoddy**

Boyle, Henry (1684–1764), a leading UNDERTAKER and manager of British government business in the Irish Parliament. Born in Castlemartyr, Co. Cork. A long-serving Speaker of the House of Commons (1733–56), revenue commissioner, and lord justice, he opposed the government in the MONEY BILL DISPUTE (1753). He accepted a pension and the title Earl of Shannon in 1756 and remained a dominant force in Irish politics until his death. **Charles Ivar McGrath**

Boyle, Selina (Ina) (1889–1967), composer. Born in Co. Wicklow, she studied harmony, counterpoint, and composition with GEORGE HEWSON, Charles Kitson, her cousin CHARLES WOOD and, from 1928 until the late 1930s, Vaughan Williams. Her compositions include fifteen *Gaelic Hymns* (1921) for choir, *The Magic Harp* (1919) and *Wildgeese* (1942) for orchestra, the ballet *Virgilian Suite* (1930), a symphony *Glencree* (1924), and the opera *Maudlin of Paplewick* (1964), based on Ben Jonson's *The Sad Shepherd*. **Paul J. Kerr**

Boyle, Katherine Lady Ranelagh (1614–1695), intellectual. Born in Co. Cork, a daughter of RICHARD BOYLE. She married Arthur Jones, Viscount Ranelagh, when she was fifteen and moved to England, where she lived for the rest of her life. Following her husband's death in 1670 she shared her London home with her brother ROBERT BOYLE, the scientist. Lady Ranelagh was renowned in London and Dublin court circles for her intellectual ability. She corresponded with the group of scientists and natural philosophers who founded the Royal Society, including Samuel Hartlib, who frequently stayed with her. Two of her books of medical recipes and remedies have survived. **Mary O'Dowd**

Boyle, Mary (1625–1678), Puritan and diarist. Born in Co. Cork, a daughter of RICHARD BOYLE. Her mother died when she was six and she was raised in the Mallow home of Lady Anne Clayton. In 1638 the family moved to England, where Mary remained for the rest of her life. She refused her father's first choice of a marriage partner, preferring instead Charles Rich, later made Earl of Warwick. The marriage was not a happy one. The couple had two children, both of whom died young. Mary found comfort

Boydell. *Brian Boydell (1917–2000), composer. The landscape and wonders of natural phenomena were important inspirations for his music which is noted for its lyricism and powerful handling of form and structure. [Denis Mortell]*

in religion and became a strongly committed Puritan. She maintained Puritan ministers in her home and regularly discussed religious issues with them and with her sister, KATHERINE BOYLE. She is best known for the diary she kept for the last eleven years of her life, in which she recorded her daily religious practices as well as her disagreements with her husband, who did not share her Puritan zeal. She also wrote a memoir in which she recorded her regret at disobeying her father. **Mary O'Dowd**

Boyle, Patrick (1905–1982), short-story writer and novelist. Born in Ballymoney, Co. Antrim. He worked for the Ulster Bank in Cos. Derry, Donegal, Tyrone, and Wexford; he began to write stories in his forties, but his first collection, *At Night All Cats Are Grey*, remained unpublished until 1966. This was followed by his only novel, a rewriting of the myth of Samson, *Like Any Other Man* (1966). Subsequent collections of stories include *All Looks Yellow to the Jaundiced Eye* (1969) and *A View from Calvary* (1976). Boyle's reputation is mostly as a fine craftsman of moral tales, often colloquial in style. **John Brannigan**

Boyle, Richard, first Earl of Cork (1566–1643), entrepreneur and politician, known as the 'Great Earl' of Cork. Born in Canterbury, younger son of ROGER BOYLE; educated at the University of Cambridge and the Middle Temple, London. Unable for financial reasons to complete his legal studies, he came to Ireland in 1588 in search of advancement. He acquired a substantial fortune through exploiting the legal uncertainty of many land titles and through his first marriage in 1595 to an heiress, Joan Apsley (who died four years later). He was appointed clerk to the Council of Munster by the Lord President, Sir GEORGE CAREW, who suggested his name to WALTER RALEIGH as a potential purchaser of the lands Raleigh had acquired in the PLANTATION OF MUNSTER. Boyle thus acquired 4,900 ha (12,000 acres) in Munster for a bargain price. He was an energetic and improving landlord, building castles, towns, harbours, and bridges and establishing ironworks. As a reward for his initiative he was knighted on the occasion of his second marriage, to Catherine Fenton, in 1603. He was created Earl of Cork in 1620 and served as one of the Lords Justices of Ireland, 1629–32. He successfully resisted the attempt by THOMAS WENTWORTH in the later 1630s to undermine his power and was a leading figure in the defence of the Protestant interest in Munster following the outbreak of the 1641 rebellion. Four of his sons, including Roger Boyle, acquired titles, while the youngest, ROBERT BOYLE, became a notable scientist. His daughters KATHERINE BOYLE and MARY BOYLE also earned reputations as educated women. **Liam Irwin**

Boyle, Hon. Robert (1627–1691), scientist. Born at Lismore Castle, Co Waterford; educated at the University of Oxford. Robert Boyle is often called the 'father of CHEMISTRY', as he was influential in the subject at the time when it was emerging from the mysteries of alchemy as an empirical science. However, his genius contributed to the foundation of modern science over a much wider field, including physics and medicine. He was a prolific writer in these fields as well as on philosophy and theology, where he sought a reconciliation of Christianity and science. He was born the youngest son of RICHARD BOYLE, the Great Earl of Cork, an English adventurer who found royal favour and considerable fortune in Ireland. Rejoicing that in his case this privilege did not extend to the 'glittering kind of slavery' imposed on the principal heir to a noble family, he devoted his life to scholarship and experimental investigation. Sent to England for an education, he spent little time thereafter in his homeland, though he did visit his Irish estates in 1652–3. While there he lamented the lack of chemical equipment in Ireland but found a suitable occupation in anatomical dissection with Sir WILLIAM PETTY. His view of nature was empirical and mechanistic, in opposition to the prevailing dogma of Aristotle. Many of his books were written in English rather than Latin, which was preferred by most scholars at that time. They are mostly illustrative and discursive, so that few important generalisations were inferred. Nevertheless, they are a model of the scientific method and include significant discoveries, such as Boyle's Law for gases, and inventions, such as a vacuum pump. **Denis Weaire**

Boyle, Roger, first Earl of Orrery (1621–1679), politician, soldier, and dramatist. Fifth son of RICHARD BOYLE, the first Earl of Cork, created Baron Broghill in 1627; he entered TRINITY COLLEGE, Dublin, at the age of nine. He spent the years 1636–9 on an extended grand tour of Europe and on his return married Lady Margaret Howard, daughter of the Earl of Suffolk. He helped to rally the Munster Protestants after the 1641 REBELLION; though a royalist, he recognised the necessity for co-operation with the parliamentary forces to defend the Protestant interest in Ireland. This conviction led him to join CROMWELL in the reconquest of Ireland; as a reward he was made president of the Council in Scotland in 1655. As the Cromwellian regime collapsed he rediscovered his royalism and played an important role in the restoration of CHARLES II, for which he was created Earl of Orrery. He was a leading figure in ensuring that the Cromwellian planters retained their lands, and he became Lord President of Munster in 1662. He was an energetic administrator, striving to develop the economy of the province in which so much of his own land and wealth lay. His insensitive anti-Catholic policies led to his dismissal from office in 1672. A prolific author of pamphlets, poetry, and plays, he was noted for his series of dramatic tragedies and a military manual, *A Treatise on the Art of War* (1677). **Liam Irwin**

Boyle Medal, awarded by the ROYAL DUBLIN SOCIETY since 1899 for scientific work of exceptional merit. The medal commemorates the seventeenth-century scientist ROBERT BOYLE. During the twentieth century the Boyle Medallists formed a committee to agree on the next recipient; in 2000 a new system was established, whereby an international jury selects the recipients. The medal goes in alternate years to a scientist working in Ireland (in which case it is accompanied by funding for a research associate) and to an Irish scientist working abroad. **Christopher Moriarty**

Boyne, Battle of the (1 July, 1690), the first major battle in the war of 1689–91 between JACOBITES and Williamites. It actually took place on 11 July (new style) on the River Boyne at Oldbridge and Donore Hill, 3 km (2 miles) west of Drogheda. JAMES II commanded an Irish army of 25,000, including 7,000 French, in defensive positions on the south bank; WILLIAM III led an army of 36,000, including English, Dutch, French, German, Danish, and Ulster Protestant regiments, on the north bank. The engagement began at 6 a.m. with a westward flanking movement by a Williamite force of 10,000, which crossed the river at Rosnaree, 6 km (4 miles) south-west of Oldbridge. James overreacted, sending two-thirds of his army, including the French, towards Rosnaree. These two forces remained inactive, facing each other across a BOG, while the battle took place to the north-east. The main body of the Williamite army crossed the Boyne at Oldbridge, and to the east at Drybridge, in three waves between 10 a.m. and midday. Thereafter the battle continued for another hour. The outnumbered Jacobite forces fought bravely before being forced to retreat southwards towards Duleek. On learning of events at Oldbridge and Donore, the main Jacobite army also retreated, and ensuing panic led to uncontrolled flight. Losses were about 1,000 Jacobites and 500 Williamites. William's commander-in-chief, the Duke of Schomberg, was killed during the battle (see p. 966). In the wake of the defeat James fled to France, and the Williamite forces gained control of Dublin and south-eastern Ireland. The battle has become more famous than the truly decisive Williamite victory a year later at AUGHRIM, because of the presence of both kings at the Boyne. The focal point of ORANGE ORDER celebrations in the 1790s, it is celebrated annually by Ulster Protestants on 12 July (through an erroneous recalculation of the date following the change to the Gregorian calendar in 1752). **Charles Ivar McGrath**

Boyne, River, a river 110 km (68 miles) long with its source in the Bog of ALLEN north of Edenderry, Co. Kildare. It flows in a north-easterly direction over glacial deposits through Co. Meath, past Trim, to the IRISH SEA near Drogheda. East of Slane, Co. Meath, is the 'Bend of the Boyne', where the river abruptly changes direction to flow south and eastwards around a ridge of high ground before turning northwards to flow through a glacial gorge. On this high ground is the concentration of prehistoric monuments known as BRÚ NA BÓINNE (now a UNESCO world heritage site), including NEWGRANGE, KNOWTH, and DOWTH. Not far from Newgrange, about 6 km (4 miles) west of Drogheda, the BATTLE OF THE BOYNE was fought on 11 July (new style) 1690.

Lying in the BOYNE VALLEY below the south side of the ridge are gravel terraces formed by the river cutting into a former FLOODPLAIN, which had been built up by the deposition of large volumes of glacially derived sediment carried by the river at the end of the last Ice Age. The Boyne is canalised in its lower reaches, in a section extending approximately 32 km (20 miles) upstream from Drogheda. At Drogheda the river cuts a deep trench through glacial deposits, which overlay an irregular rock surface. In 1855 this trench was bridged for the first time when the BOYNE VIADUCT was built for the railway. The Boyne has a tidal estuary 6 km ($3\frac{3}{4}$ miles) long, which widens to a width of 1 km (0.6 mile) before narrowing to a series of dunes. At low tide, large areas of mudflats are exposed, which are frequented by migrant wading birds. **R. A. Charlton**

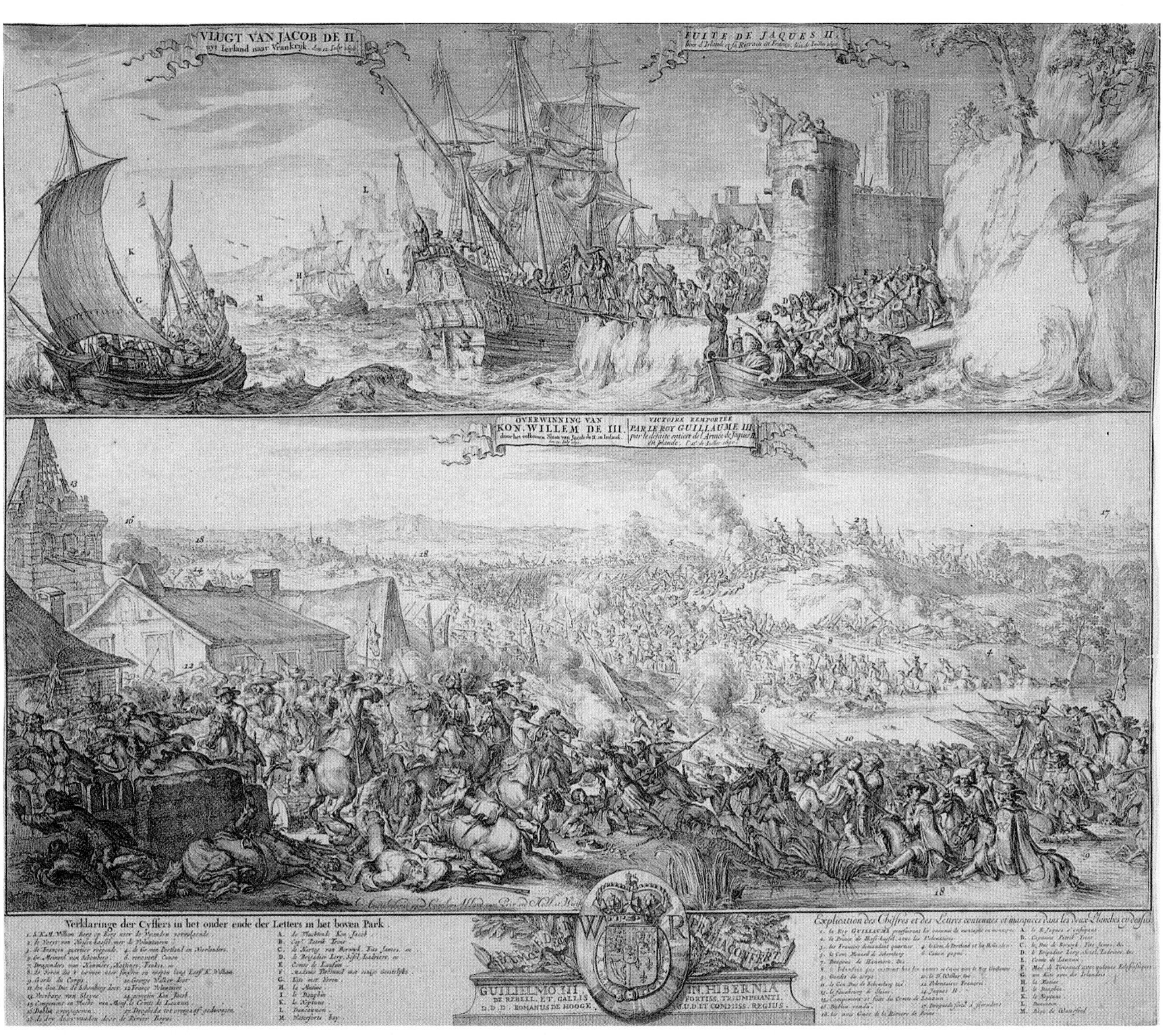

Boyne, Battle of. The Battle of the Boyne *by Romeyn de Hooghe, a two-section contemporary etching depicting (above) the departure of the defeated James II from Kinsale on 12 July 1690 and (below) William III's victory at the Boyne. [National Gallery of Ireland]*

Boyne Valley. *Kerbstone 52, one of ninety-seven large decorated stones surrounding the Passage Tomb of Newgrange in the Boyne Valley, Co. Meath, featuring spirals, diamond patterns, crescents, and cup marks. [Dúchas, The Heritage Service]*

Boyne Valley (Brú na Bóinne), part of the valley of the River BOYNE, Co. Meath, 12 km (7½ miles) from the mouth of the river at DROGHEDA. It is one of Ireland's most important archaeological landscapes, designated a world heritage site by UNESCO in 1993. It consists of a roughly U-shaped tongue of land measuring a little over 2 km (1¼ miles) in maximum width and close to 5 km (3 miles) in length, bordered on three sides by the river. It is a low-lying area, only three elevations within it reaching the 60 m (200-ft) contour. The base rock is mainly Carboniferous shale, formed about 3 million years ago; it was this rock that caused the river, during its formation about 10,000 years ago, to take its meandering course here. Today the area is rich agricultural land, with the river providing an artery of communication with the sea.

So far there is no definite evidence for human occupation during immediate post-glacial times, but a couple of late MESOLITHIC flakes of chert have been found beside NEWGRANGE. It is in the subsequent NEOLITHIC PERIOD that definite evidence for extensive settlement comes to light. About 4000 BC, farming families moved into the area. Land clearance was begun, and plots suitable for agriculture were established. From the start, mixed farming was practised, with the people living in rectangular wooden houses averaging 4 by 7 m (13 by 23 ft) in size. Their artefacts included stone AXES, flint scrapers (which could have been used in woodworking), and flint blades (which could have served as knives); pottery vessels were also widely used.

The Early Neolithic settlement was succeeded by a different cultural complex. This was on a grander scale, with parallels in the other Atlantic lands and in the West Baltic region. These PASSAGE-TOMB people lived in round wooden houses about 7 m (23 ft) in diameter and had a range of everyday artefacts, including stone tools and pottery vessels. Their striking legacy is the MEGALITHIC TOMBS they built, a cemetery of at least forty sites, with the three great tombs of Dowth, KNOWTH, and Newgrange constituting the largest and most lavish constructed in Ireland. Their building involved a huge expenditure of human resources, while their architectural sophistication reflects a prestigious society. Each tomb consists of a massive round mound, approximately 85 m (275 ft) in diameter and 10 m (33 ft) in height and covering close to 0.6 ha (1½ acres). They are delimited by substantial kerbstones, averaging 2 m (6½ ft) in length. Many structural stones and kerbstones are carved; there may have been up to a thousand decorated stones in the cemetery as a whole.

By 2500 BC further changes were under way, part of parallel developments in Britain and elsewhere, including major ritual innovations. The rituals of the enclosed chambers of the passage tombs gave way to open-air ceremonies in circular enclosures, sometimes called HENGE monuments. Four of these have been identified in the Boyne Valley, the most notable being a great earthwork at Dowth, 170 m (560 ft) in average external diameter, its bank averaging 20 m (65 ft) in width at the base and 3–5 m (10–16 ft) in height. The STONE CIRCLE at Newgrange also dates from this time. Economically there need not have been major change, but new pottery fashions, such as *grooved ware* and *beaker pottery*, emerge. The Beaker People (c. 2400 BC), with their characteristic pottery, played a major role in the introduction of early metallurgy.

Despite such significant developments at the end of the Neolithic Period and the dawn of the metal age, there is little archaeological evidence at present for activity for some 2,000 years thereafter, for most of the BRONZE AGE and the early IRON AGE. When activity resumed in the later Iron Age (in the early centuries AD) it was again entirely ritual in purpose. A series of burials in pit graves is known from Knowth, which, in the seventh century, had its passage-tomb mound transformed into a well-protected settlement. The wider changes of the twelfth century also affected the Boyne Valley. The old Breagha dynastic families came to an end, and a major change was the incorporation of the valley in the CISTERCIAN lands of MELLIFONT. Knowth became the site of a grange (a large farming establishment); as the name implies, this must also have happened at Newgrange. That situation continued down to the late sixteenth century, when the REFORMATION brought about the dissolution of Mellifont Abbey and its lands. This led to the emergence of new farming families in the area but also to a prominent position for the newly reformed church in the lives of the people. The changes that then took place continued, at least in part, up to modern times. In 1690 the valley was the scene of the decisive BATTLE OF THE BOYNE. **George Eogan**

Boyne Viaduct, the railway bridge carrying the main Dublin–Belfast line over the River BOYNE at Drogheda, Co. Louth. Conceived by Sir JOHN MACNEILL, the viaduct was completed in 1855 under James Barton, who designed much of the structure. The principles of multi-latticed girder construction in wrought iron were first applied on a large scale on the viaduct, leading to an increase in knowledge of the structural properties of wrought iron and encouraging more exact computation of the stresses in structural components. The original girders were replaced in 1932 with steel girders, the central span being given a curved top chord to improve its appearance. **Ronald Cox**

'Boyne Water, The', a celebratory song written soon after WILLIAM III's victory at the BATTLE OF THE BOYNE. Its distinctive tune afterwards served other songs—loyalist, nationalist, and non-political—and is played also as a reel; the best known is the song 'Rosc Catha na Mumhan'. The tune was in print by 1721, but the lyrics sung today, beginning 'July the first in Oldbridge town', are thought to have been written early in the nineteenth century by Colonel William Blacker. Orange songbooks frequently give an undoubtedly older but undatable version. **John Moulden**

Boys of the Lough, the, a long-running traditional band formed in 1967 by CATHAL MCCONNELL, Tommy Gunn, and Robin

Morton. Their first 'official' album (1972) included McConnell and Morton with the Shetland fiddle-player Aly Bain and the Leith guitarist Dick Gaughan. In the intervening years the membership has continually evolved and has included Dave Richardson (cittern), Christy O'Leary (UILLEANN PIPES), Chris Newman (guitar), Brendan Begley (ACCORDION), and Tich Richardson (guitar). **Pat Ahern**

Bracken, Brendan, Viscount Bracken (1901–1958), publisher and politician. Born in Templemore, Co. Tipperary, son of John K. Bracken, a founder-member of the GAA. He ran away from school and was sent to Australia but returned and moved to England in 1919, where by 1924 he was working in publishing in London. He founded the *Banker* and rapidly acquired various titles, including the *Financial News* and *Investor's Chronicle*. During his career he concealed his Irish nationalist background. He became an election worker for Winston Churchill and MP for Paddington, 1929–45, and Bournemouth, 1945–51, parliamentary private secretary to Churchill, 1939–41, and, during the SECOND WORLD WAR, Minister of Information, 1941–5, and First Lord of the Admiralty, 1945; appointed Viscount in 1952. **Brian Lalor**

Bradley, Michael (Mick) (1962–), rugby footballer. Born in Cork. He played forty matches between 1984 and 1995, is Ireland's most-capped scrum-half, and was captain fourteen times. He was first capped against Australia on their Grand Slam tour of 1984 in MICK DOYLE's first season as national coach, and after that narrow 9–16 defeat he was PAUL DEAN's half-back partner as Ireland went on to win the 1985 Triple Crown. He played in the 1987 inaugural Rugby World Cup, was passed over for the second in 1991, and played his last match against New Zealand at Ellis Park, Johannesburg, in the 1995 event. **Karl Johnston**

Brady, Liam (1956–), soccer player. Born in Dublin. He started out on his career in under-age football with St Kevin's. He signed for Arsenal in 1971 and, having walked out on the club because of homesickness, returned to play a leading role in some of their successes in the late 1970s. He signed for Juventus in 1980, winning two championship medals with them before playing with Inter Milan, Sampdoria and Ascoli during a seven-year stay in Italy—the longest by a British or Irish player up to that time. He had already slipped past his best before the good times dawned for the Republic of Ireland, but in seventy-three appearances for his country he demanded the admiration of friend and foe alike. **Peter Byrne**

Brady, Paul (1947–), singer and songwriter. Born in Strabane, Co. Tyrone; educated at TCD. He began his musical career in Dublin's R&B scene in the early 1960s, playing in highly regarded beat groups, the Kult and Rockhouse. His facility at interpreting TRADITIONAL MUSIC came to the fore in 1967 when he joined the Johnstons, the premier ballad group of the time. They released albums of both traditional material and contemporary songs, including *The Barleycorn* (1968) and *Give a Damn* (1968). They toured extensively in Ireland and Britain but split up in 1973. In 1974 Brady joined PLANXTY, the finest traditional group of the period. Following the band's split, Brady and ANDY IRVINE, a fellow-member of Planxty, worked together on two albums, their eponymous debut in 1976 and *Welcome Here, Kind Stranger* (1978). In the 1980s Brady released a series of rock albums, beginning with *Hard Station* (1981). He received much critical acclaim with albums such as *Back to the Centre* (1986), *Primitive Dance* (1987), *Trick or Treat* (1991), and *Spirits Colliding* (1995). His songs have been covered by artists such as Dave Edmunds, Roger Chapman, Santana, Tina Turner, and Bonnie Raitt. In 1999 his solo back catalogue became available. A 'Best of' collection, *Nobody Knows*, was also released in tandem. In 2000 a new studio album, *Oh, What a World*, was released, confirming the fact that Brady is among the best original singer-songwriters Ireland has produced. **Tony Clayton-Lea**

Brady. *Paul Brady has earned acclaim as one of Ireland's most highly regarded and original singer-songwriters. [Colm Henry]*

Branagh, Kenneth (1960–), stage and film actor, director, and producer. Born in Belfast; trained at the Royal Academy of Dramatic Art, London, and began his career with the Royal Shakespeare Company at the age of twenty-three. He came to wider attention in 1987 in the television series 'Fortunes of War' and in the same year jointly founded the Renaissance Theatre Company, earning comparisons with Laurence Olivier for his performances, notably in *Hamlet* and *Much Ado about Nothing*. His first film as both actor and director was *Henry V* (1989); he returned to Shakespeare as director and actor in *Much Ado about Nothing* (1993), *Hamlet* (1996), and *Love's Labour Lost* (2000). His first Hollywood film as director and actor was *Dead Again* (1992), a *film noir* thriller; he also directed *Peter's Friends* (1992), *Mary Shelley's Frankenstein* (1994), and *In the Bleak Midwinter* (1995), and acted in *High Season* (1987), *A Month in the Country* (1987), *Othello* (1995), *The Gingerbread Man* (1998), and *Wild Wild West* (1999). **Kevin Rockett**

Bransfield, Edward (1783–1846), seaman. Born in Cork. He went to sea in a coaster, from which he was pressed into the British navy by the frigate *Dryad* in 1803. He was brought to Plymouth naval base, from which he served for eleven years in various warships, not seeing Cork again until 1814. His remarkable aptitude as a seaman was noted and he was promoted to quartermaster and then—exceptionally for a man of his background—received from Trinity House, London, his certificate as master, with competence to act as navigator of ships of any kind. After the Napoleonic wars, in which he served in the Atlantic and Mediterranean, he was chosen before many masters with greater seniority to accompany a naval expedition to southern South America. There he was given command of a merchant ship and instructed to sail south and explore. He discovered and meticulously charted the South Shetland Islands and, late in 1819, became the first person ever to see the Antarctic continent. On his retirement from the navy he commanded merchant ships in European waters. **John de Courcy Ireland**

Brase, Fritz (1875–1940), musician and composer. Born at Egestorf, Germany, he trained at the Leipzig Conservatoire and the Royal Academy of Music, Berlin. Having served as bandmaster to the 1st Grenadier Guards, Berlin, 1911–18, he came to Ireland in 1923 as first director of the Army School of Music. He arranged Irish airs and wrote *Six Irish Fantasias for Band* (later orchestrated) for the Army No. 1 Band, which played regularly in the THEATRE ROYAL, DUBLIN. With Turner Huggard he founded the Dublin Philharmonic Society in 1927, which revived choral and orchestral concert performances in Dublin after the demise of the DUBLIN ORCHESTRAL SOCIETY. **Paul J. Kerr**

Brave Irishman, The, or *Captain O'Blunder* (1743), a comedy by THOMAS SHERIDAN, first performed at the SMOCK ALLEY THEATRE, Dublin. This popular afterpiece reverses the negative connotations of the stage Irishman as O'Blunder proves to his English hosts that his manner and speech are manifestations of natural nobility and eloquence. **Christopher Morash**

Bray (*Bré*), Co. Wicklow, a seaside town on the border with Co. Dublin; population (2002) 26,215. Though the manor of Bray dates from the early years of the ANGLO-NORMAN CONQUEST, it was still a village at the end of the eighteenth century when it became a popular destination for travellers because of its proximity to the WICKLOW MOUNTAINS, POWERSCOURT waterfall, and the coast. The completion of the RAILWAY from Dublin under the supervision of WILLIAM DARGAN spurred the creation of a 'new town', consciously planned as a seaside resort after the English model. New roads were laid out, houses and villas were built, the Esplanade was designed, and elaborate Turkish baths were constructed. The Carlisle Grounds (1862) are now home to Bray Wanderers Football Club. In the fifty years after the arrival of the railway the population more than doubled. By 1900 Bray's great period of expansion as a seaside town was at an end, despite a short revival in the 1950s; in the late 1960s its declining role as a seaside resort was replaced with a new function as a dormitory town, providing easy rail access to Dublin. The opening of the electrified DART rail service in 1986 gave a new impetus to commuter development. **Ruth McManus**

Bray Head, Co. Wicklow, a large rocky projection of hard quartzites extending beyond the softer glacial drifts that form most of the eastern coastlands. Withstanding marine erosion, it also features steep cliffs inhabited by seabirds, whose guano provides a nutrient-rich mineral source for the sea thrift and maritime grasses clinging to crevices. Heathers predominate on the steep, nutrient-poor soils, with some rhododendron cover, introduced in the eighteenth century. Like Howth, proximity to Dublin has caused it to come under much pressure for development. **Patrick Duffy**

Brazil, the Irish in. As in most of South America, Irish adventurers, soldiers and missionaries—many of them in the service of the Spanish and Portuguese colonising powers—can be found in Brazil from the earliest decades of Portuguese settlement. Brazil's first documented Irish visitor was Thomas Field, a Jesuit scholastic from Co. Limerick who spent a decade, 1577–87, at Piratininga (modern São Paulo) before leaving for the Jesuits' mission fields in Paraguay. The long-term failure of all Irish attempts at collective settlement in Brazil, however, stands in sharp contrast to Irish success in ARGENTINA. Between 1612 and 1629 Irish entrepreneurs established profitable tobacco plantations near the mouth of the Amazon River, a region then claimed by both Spain and Portugal. These tropical outposts, under the leadership of James and Philip Purcell, believed to be brothers from Dublin, and Bernard O'Brien from Co. Clare constitute the first documented Irish colonies in the New World. Despite attempts to win permanent settlement rights from the Portuguese consistent with their shared religious beliefs, the Irishmen's status as English subjects led to their expulsion.

Two centuries later Colonel William Cotter, an Irish officer in the Brazilian service, recruited settlers from Munster. In 1827, 2,400 Irish men, many with wives and children, reached Rio de Janeiro; but on arrival, promises of land and part-time militia duties were replaced by forced enlistment in the Brazilian army, then at war with Argentina. By 1828 the majority were repatriated to Ireland, destitute and disillusioned. An agricultural colony formed by 220 Irish people who remained quickly failed, with most abandoning Brazil for sheep farming in Argentina.

Between 1850 and 1892 hundreds of other Irish settlers, many from emigrant communities in New York and the English midlands, were lured to Brazil with spurious visions of free land or easy wealth. The isolated and poorly planned agricultural colonies that awaited them in the southern Brazilian states of Santa Catarina and Rio Grande do Sul were no more successful than the earlier attempt by Cotter's recruits to establish farms in Bahía in north-eastern Brazil. **Brian McGinn**

bread. Wheat and barley have been cultivated since the Neolithic Period (c. 4000 BC), and it is probable that bread, however rudimentary in form, was part of the diet. The introduction of oats, possibly from Roman Britain, and a greater emphasis on bread wheat in the pre-Christian period diversified the range of bread types. In the early Middle Ages flat breads of oats and barley baked over an open fire were standard. Wheat is a less successful crop, and consequently wheaten loaves were highly valued and associated with the diet of the wealthy, or reserved for days of celebration.

The ANGLO-NORMAN emphasis on the cultivation of wheat, combined with the introduction of the built-up oven, made leavened wheaten loaves a more prominent feature of the diet, particularly in the areas of Norman control. Maslin bread of mixed cereals (wheat and rye), and bread composed of meal and pulse meal, were also produced.

As MILLING techniques became more advanced throughout the seventeenth and eighteenth centuries the increased availability of finely bolted flour facilitated the production of refined white bread and cakes. However, flat cakes of oats and, to a lesser extent, barley remained popular, particularly in the west and north, where SOIL conditions were poor. Throughout the eighteenth century increased reliance on a POTATO-dominated diet displaced these former staples.

The nineteenth century was a formative period for bread-making. The introduction of reliable chemical leavens (notably bicarbonate of soda or 'bread soda', which reacts with buttermilk to aerate the dough), together with the importing of pot ovens from English foundries, made the production of a leaven loaf a possibility for those who operated an open hearth. From the second half of the nineteenth century soda bread was daily fare in rural households; for festive occasions it was enriched with dried FRUITS, eggs, BUTTER, and spices. The incorporation of maize meal in the soda bread mix, to produce 'yellowmeal' bread, also proved popular. With the upsurge in the number of bakeries, white factory-made bread also became increasingly prevalent in both town and country. In the former it became a staple in the DIET of the poor, while in rural areas its novelty made it the choice for special occasions. [see FOOD, TRADITIONAL; HEARTH, THE.] **Regina Sexton**

Breathnach, Breandán (1912–1985), piper, music collector, and publisher. Born in Dublin; he became one of the most significant and effective twentieth-century collectors of traditional dance music. He examined and indexed all previous collections of dance music, printed and manuscript; his index enabled him to identify unpublished tunes and variants, and this work gradually became a project to compile a comprehensive collection of the dance music of Ireland. The material he collected and the index he created made possible for the first time an assessment of the extent of the corpus of this music, which he estimated to consist of some 7,000 distinct items. A portion of his collection has been published as CEOL RINCE NA HÉIREANN in five volumes, containing 1,200 tunes. While carrying on this work he also founded NA PÍOBAIRÍ UILLEANN and jointly founded the Folk Music Society of Ireland, published *Ceol*, his own journal of Irish music, initiated the National Traditional Music Collection Scheme, with TOM MUNNELLY as the first collector, wrote *Folk Music and Dances of Ireland* (1993), taught, lectured, organised, and inspired many projects that were completed by his associates. **Terry Moylan**

Breathnach, Colm (1961–), poet. Born in Cork; educated at UCC. He has worked in the public service as a terminologist and translator. Among his poetry collections are *Caintic an Bhalbháin* (1991), *An Fearann Breac* (1992), *Scáthach* (1994), *Croí agus Carraig* (1995), and *An Fear Marbh* (1998), a work celebrating his father. **Seán Ó Cearnaigh**

Breathnach, Micheál (1881–1908), London GAELIC LEAGUE employee. Born in Indreabhán, Co. Galway. He translated KICKHAM's *Knocknagow* (1906) into Irish and pioneered the writing of Irish history in Irish (1909–11). From 1905 he was principal of Connacht Irish College. Contracting tuberculosis, he went to Switzerland, the subject of *Seilg i measc na nAlp* (1917). **Diarmuid Breathnach and Máire Ní Mhurchú**

Breathnach, Paddy (1964–), film director. Born in Dublin. He emerged as a director with a fresh sensibility following his feature film debut, *Ailsa* (1994), a European-style art film concerning a man's obsession with a woman tenant in his house, and *I Went Down* (1997), a comedy-crime hybrid featuring BRENDAN GLEESON and Peter McDonald, who also featured in his *Blow Dry* (2001), a big-budget British film. **Kevin Rockett**

Breathnach, Pádraic (1930–), writer. Born in Moycullen, Co. Galway. He is a prolific writer of well-wrought SHORT STORIES, published in eight collections, from *Bean Aonair agus Scéalta Eile* (1974) to *An Pincín agus Scéalta Eile* (1996). He has also published two less successful novels, *Gróga Cloch* (1991) and *As na Cúlacha* (1998), and an oral history of his home place, *Maigh Cuilinn: A Tásc agus a Tuairisc* (1986). **Gearóid Denvir**

Bredin, Hugh (1939–), philosopher. Born in Coleraine, Co. Derry; educated at Queen's University Belfast and the Universities of Turin, Bologna, and Rome. Senior lecturer in scholastic philosophy at Queen's University, Belfast. He has published translations of Umberto Eco's *Art and Beauty in the Middle Ages* (1986), *The Aesthetics of Thomas Aquinas* (1988), and (with Liberato Santoro-Brienza) *Philosophies of Art and Beauty* (2000). Widely recognised as an authority on structuralism and formalism, his research interests include the semantics of figurative language, aesthetics, and the philosophy of literature. **Fionola Meredith**

brehon law, the legal system of early medieval Ireland. Developed by a class of professional jurists, who produced detailed legal treatises, it was unusually advanced in many of its rules and principles.

The writing of these texts began in the seventh century, almost certainly on the initiative of the church, although some of the laws were clearly contrary to Christian teachings. By that time the church had the resources necessary to undertake the task; it also had considerable legal interests in landholdings, rights over tenants, and the recognition of the status of the clergy. These rights were advanced and protected by recording the law in an authoritative form. The greatest compilation of law texts from this time was the *Senchas Már* ('Great Collection of Ancient Learning'). It consists of approximately fifty separate texts, twenty-one of which survive more or less intact; the remainder exist in various stages of fragmentation. The compilation of this massive collection was completed between AD 650 and 750. Many other legal texts were also written during this period.

The law described in these texts is remarkably sophisticated. By the eighth century brehon contract law had already developed an implied warranty that goods would be fit for sale. Sellers who were aware of concealed defects in their goods had a duty to point these out, and there were also mandatory 'cooling-off periods', within which unwise bargains could be terminated. In the area of injuries to the person, brehon law developed the concepts of accident, self-defence, and negligence at a very early period. The remedies provided dealt chiefly with compensation. (If compensation was not paid, offenders might be enslaved or killed; however, brehon law is largely free of the terrible mutilations and cruel methods of execution that are found in other medieval systems.)

Most brehon law texts deal with a distinct topic. There are texts on legal procedures, such as distraint and the giving of pledges and appointment of sureties; on the proper methods of pleading in court and the seating arrangements; on the enforcement and dissolution of contracts and the regulation of loans; on theft, arson, and the compensation to be paid for deliberate and negligent injury. There are tracts that set out the rights of an injured person to be provided with medical care, and the fees due to doctors, and others that discuss damage caused by livestock (with separate tracts dealing with cows, cats, dogs, and bees), rights of access to water, and the trapping of wild animals. Other texts deal with various social relationships (MARRIAGE, fosterage, LORDSHIP, status, and the rights of FAMILY members). Brehon family law recognised DIVORCE as well as polygyny (concurrent marriage to multiple wives), although not permitted in early Christian society.

Once the great collections of law had been completed, later scholars added GLOSSES and commentaries, which sought to explain the earlier works or to expand on them, and this process continued into the sixteenth century. After the arrival of the ANGLO-NORMANS in

1169 brehon law was gradually ousted by English common law, and it finally disappeared as a living system in the early seventeenth century.

The term 'brehon law' (*breithiúna*, 'judges') accurately conveys the fact that the law was developed by skilled jurists rather than legislated by kings; this explains its sophistication but marked it out as 'abnormal' in the eyes of the medieval Anglo-Norman settlers. The term used by the Irish for their own law was *féineachas* ('ways of the Irish people'). **Neil McLeod**

Brendan. The fame of the younger Brendan (the older was Brendan of Birr) rests mainly on the NAVIGATIO SANCTI BRENDANI, arguably the most influential of all medieval Irish texts, which was written, probably on the Continent, at least as early as the ninth century. The saint's three main churches were ARDFERT, Co. Kerry, traditionally the place of his birth; Clonfert, where his *Life* (in Latin and Irish) seems to have been written; and Annaghdown, Co. Galway, where he is reputed to have died. His feast-day is 16 May (see p. 774). [see SEVERIN, TIM.] **Pádraig Ó Riain**

Brennan, Cecily (1955–), painter. Born in Athenry, Co. Galway; studied at the NCAD. Initially her subject matter was inspired by landscapes in Ireland and also in Iceland, where she lived for a time in the 1980s. Her more recent works, stainless-steel cast sculptures, are inspired by the human figure. Whether painting or sculpture, her works can be read as metaphors for psychological and emotional states of mind. A member of the board of the Project Arts Centre, Dublin, 1984–6, she is a member of Independent Artists and of AOSDÁNA. **Suzanne McNab**

Brennan, Maeve (1919–1996), journalist and short-story writer. Born in Dublin, she lived in the United States from 1934. She wrote for *Harper's Bazaar* and in 1949 joined the *New Yorker*, where she spent her entire career as a staff writer. She was an accomplished stylist; her short stories, set in Ranelagh, the Dublin suburb where she grew up, were first published in the *New Yorker* and later in two collections, *In and Out of Never-Never Land* (1969) and *Christmas Eve* (1974). Her wryly humorous observations of Manhattan life from the *New Yorker* were gathered in *The Long-Winded Lady* (1969). She ceased writing in 1973. **Brian Lalor**

Brennan, William (Willie), 'Brennan on the Moor' (died 1840), highwayman. While working as a labourer at Kilmurry House, near Fermoy, Co. Cork, he was caught trying to steal a guest's watch. Fleeing prosecution, he took to the nearby Kilworth Mountains and became an outlaw. He acquired a reputation as a benign thief, one who stole from the rich to give to the poor. The authorities finally caught up with him and he was hanged in Clonmel in 1840 and buried at the old parish church of Kilcrumper, near Fermoy. He should not be confused with the Brennan outlaws of Co. Kilkenny. **Ciarán Deane**

brewing, Ireland's most important food-processing industry in the eighteenth and nineteenth centuries. Like DISTILLING, its essential ingredient was malted barley, hops (imported from England), and clear water. Maltings, in which the barley was transformed into malt, were formerly very common throughout Ireland, with notable concentrations in Cos. Cork and Wexford; important maltings complexes at Castlebridge, Co. Wexford, Lee Maltings, Cork, and Muine Bheag, Co. Carlow, can still be seen. By the end of the eighteenth century, breweries in Dublin and Cork were already becoming important industrial concerns. Beamish and Crawford's Cork Porter Brewery (established 1792) was the largest Irish brewery until 1833, when its output was exceeded by GUINNESS'S BREWERY in Dublin. Large sections of the original eighteenth-century Beamish and Crawford complex survive. By the end of the nineteenth century, the Guinness brewery in James's Street, Dublin, was the largest in the world, and it remains the largest industrial complex in Dublin. In its day it was an engineering marvel and included Ireland's first recorded industrial use of electric lighting. [see GOSSETT, WILLIAM SEALY; HERON, JOHN.] **Colin Rynne**

Brian Bórú (c. 941–1014), originally Brian mac Cennétig, named 'Bórú' from Béal Bórú, Co. Clare; ruler of Dál gCais, Munster, and Ireland, one of the most significant figures of the eleventh century. He came to prominence following the murder of his brother, Mathgamain, in 976. Within two years Brian was King of Munster and by the turn of the century the most powerful Irish ruler. In 1002 he had MÁEL SECHNAILL mac Domnaill, the UÍ NÉILL King of TARA, deposed and was recognised as King of Ireland. In 1011 the Leinstermen rebelled and in 1014 they and their VIKING allies challenged Brian at the BATTLE OF CLONTARF, near Dublin. The Leinstermen were defeated, but Brian was killed. This was a severe blow to Munster; however, Brian's descendants, the O'Brien kings, staged a come-back and challenged for the KINGSHIP of Ireland. Undoubtedly one of his greatest achievements was breaking the monopoly of the Uí Néill kings of Tara. He made the overlordship of Ireland a prize worth the fight. [see COGADH GÁEDHEL RE GALLAIBH.] **Elva Johnston**

'Brian Bórú harp': see TRINITY COLLEGE HARP.

'Bricriu's Feast': see 'FLED BRICRENN'.

bridges. The earliest bridge remains in Ireland so far discovered are those of a timber bridge crossing the River SHANNON at Clonmacnoise, Co. Offaly, which has been dated to 809. Late medieval stone bridges survive at Trim and Slane, Co. Meath, and Ardee, Co. Louth. There was a spate of bridge-building between 1750 and 1850, when the influence of Palladio, Perronet, and the French engineering schools is evident, for example in some of the bridges over the River NORE and in SARSFIELD BRIDGE (1836), Limerick. Many important bridges were constructed or rebuilt by government agencies, such as Drainage and Navigation Commissions and the BOARD OF WORKS, during the eighteenth and nineteenth centuries. The earliest metal bridge, the cast-iron arch of the HA'PENNY BRIDGE, Dublin, dates from 1816. The wrought-iron latticed truss was introduced c. 1840. There has been a limited use of steel for rail bridges and VIADUCTS. Many bridges were rebuilt following damage sustained during the CIVIL WAR (1922–3). Reinforced concrete bridges were constructed from c. 1908 (MIZEN HEAD BRIDGE) and pre-stressed concrete from 1952. More recently there has been a return to the suspension principle with the construction of cable-stayed structures. **Ronald Cox**

bridges, cast-iron. A preference for working with locally available stone, the absence of large foundries and the high cost of importing ironwork all had the effect of limiting the use of iron for BRIDGES in Ireland. Of the seven surviving cast-iron arch bridges, the earliest to be erected was the HA'PENNY BRIDGE, Dublin (1816), cast at Coalbrookdale, Shropshire, with a relatively large span for the time of 42 m (138 ft). King's Bridge (Seán Heuston Bridge) (1828) and Victoria Bridge (Rory O'More Bridge) (1861) complete the trio of iron bridges spanning the River Liffey in Dublin. The

Albert Bridge, Belfast, with three 256 m (85-ft) spans, was completed only in 1890. **Ronald Cox**

bridges, masonry. There are some 25,000 masonry arch bridges in Ireland with at least one span of 1.8 m (6 ft) or greater. Until the coming of the ANGLO-NORMANS towards the end of the twelfth century no masonry bridges of any significance were erected, though it is likely that a native style of arch design was developing, possibly influenced by monastic architecture. Early bridges, such as King John's, Limerick city (1210) and Leighlinbridge, Co. Carlow (1320), had multiple arches that were either pointed or semicircular and of small span—rarely more than 9 m (30 ft)—and were narrow, sometimes with pedestrian refuges over the piers. The great majority of stone bridges from before 1750 were planned and built by stonemasons; but from that time onwards, most large bridges were designed, and their construction supervised, by engineers or architects. As theories of how arches act under imposed loads were developed, the designers were able to use other forms of arch, such as segmental, and to greatly increase the spans, the main arch at Lismore, Co. Waterford (1775), being the first to reach 30 m (100 ft). Many masonry bridges were constructed to convey roads over CANALS and RAILWAYS. The increased weight of commercial vehicles has prompted a structural evaluation of masonry bridges on some routes. **Ronald Cox**

Brigid. Though Leinster's chief saint, and second in order of importance of the Irish saints, Brigid probably originated as the Celtic divinity Brigantia. Her main church at Kildare vied with Armagh for supremacy over the Irish church in the seventh century. Regarded as 'Mary of the Irish' from a very early period, she became the subject of two early Latin Lives, the sequence of which is a subject of dispute. She was the first saint to have a Life written for her in Irish, at Kildare in the early ninth century. Her successor at Kildare had a status equivalent to that of a bishop. St Brigid's 'fire' was maintained at Kildare until the late medieval period. Brigid's cult continues to be vigorous, especially around the time of her feast on 1 February, when, among other practices, the 'ST BRIGID'S CROSS' is still fashioned in many parts of the country. Her feast-day coincides with one of the four principal days of the Celtic year. [see CALENDAR CUSTOMS; ST BRIGID'S DAY; ST BRIGID'S MANTLE.] **Pádraig Ó Riain**

Brinkley, John (1766–1835), astronomer and cleric. Born at Woodbridge, Suffolk; educated at the University of Cambridge, where he excelled in mathematics. After a short time at Greenwich Observatory he was appointed Andrews Professor of ASTRONOMY at TCD in 1790; from 1792 this post carried the title Royal Astronomer of Ireland. At DUNSINK OBSERVATORY he devoted himself at first to mathematical investigations. With the arrival of the great 8-ft meridian circle ordered from Ramsden in 1788 and completed by Berge, Brinkley started observational work on stellar parallaxes, for which he was awarded the Copley Medal of the Royal Society, 1824. Other distinctions included fellow of the Royal Society, 1803, president of the RIA, 1822–35, and president of the Royal Astronomical Society, 1831–4. He became CHURCH OF IRELAND Bishop of Cloyne in 1826 and devoted his remaining years exclusively to church matters. **Ian Elliott**

Briscoe, Robert (Bob) (1894–1969), politician. Born in Dublin. He was an envoy to Germany and the United States for MICHAEL COLLINS during the WAR OF INDEPENDENCE and was involved in gun-running. He opposed the Treaty and became a friend of DE VALERA. A member of Dáil Éireann from 1927 to 1965, he was also Lord Mayor of Dublin in 1956 and 1961. As a member of the Jewish community he was a strong supporter of Jewish settlement in Palestine from 1939. **Tom Garvin**

Britain, Irish writing in. Though distinct Irish enclaves existed in British towns and cities since Elizabethan times, literary representations of the Irish immigrant experience from within were slow to emerge. Few impoverished immigrants had the means, the opportunity, or the inclination to write about their lives, while the more privileged Anglo-Irish writers who were part of the literary milieu of Georgian and Victorian London rarely wrote explicitly about exile or dislocation. While some early nineteenth-century immigrant artisans published memoirs in working-class journals and craft periodicals, they were eclipsed by the autobiographies of such middle-class professionals as JUSTIN MCCARTHY, T. P. O'CONNOR, and William O'Malley, whose benign representations of Irish life in England provide a significant counterpoint to the heroic prison narratives of FENIAN autobiographers, such as JEREMIAH O'DONOVAN ROSSA and THOMAS CLARKE.

Valuable insights into the role of IMMIGRANT networks in the organisation and development of the Irish Party in late nineteenth-century Britain are found in John Denvir's *The Life Story of an Old Rebel* (1910) and James Mullin's *The Story of a Toiler's Life* (1921), which contain vivid accounts of their authors' crusading home-rule activities in Liverpool and Cardiff, respectively. Denvir, a pioneering chronicler of the historical achievements of the Irish in Britain, also wrote *The Brandons* (1903), the first novel about the LIVERPOOL IRISH, a community that subsequently featured in James Hanley's *The Furys* (1935), Joseph McKeown's *Back Crack Boy* (1978), and the short stories of Moy McCrory. PÁDRAIC Ó CONAIRE's *Deoraíocht* (1910) is one of the earliest novelistic representations of immigrant Irish life in London, a modernist text that, together with SAMUEL BECKETT's *Murphy* (1938), powerfully registers the alienated voice of the deracinated urban emigrant.

Contemporary evocations of the milieu and *mentalité* of the London Irish can be found in novels by JOHN BRODERICK, Ian Cochrane, and J. M. O'Neill, while the work of the Anglo-Irish writers ELIZABETH BOWEN, WILLIAM TREVOR, and Maurice Leitch shows a recurring preoccupation with the nature and effects of displacement, marginality, and difference.

The year 1914 may be said to be a landmark in the literary history of the Irish in Britain, as two seminal socialist novels appeared in that year: ROBERT TRESSELL's *The Ragged Trousered Philanthropists* and PATRICK MACGILL's *Children of the Dead End*. MacGill's harrowing portrayal of the lives of outcast, itinerant navvies became an instant bestseller and a highly influential text for later creative emigrants, including JOHN B. KEANE and DÓNALL MAC AMHLAIGH. Their autobiographical accounts of life in 1950s England reinforced the archetype developed by MacGill of the rural, poorly educated, unskilled, and unassimilated Irish immigrant struggling to reconcile the values of a traditional, Catholic society with those of a modern, industrialised one. This archetype has been heavily ironised in much contemporary Irish migrant fiction, including Robert McLiam Wilson's politically irreverent metafiction *Ripley Bogle* (1989) and Joseph O'Connor's iconoclastic *Cowboys and Indians* (1991), both of which feature bright, disaffected protagonists who gleefully subvert the deterministic claims of nation and tradition.

Novelistic and autobiographical accounts of second-generation Irishness constitute an important part of the literary tradition of the Irish in Britain. Whereas the memoirs of many Irish-born immigrants testify to a heightened awareness of their identity in exile, second-

British culture in Ireland. *Engraving after a drawing by T. Crofton Croker (c. 1824) of Kilcolman Castle, Co. Cork, Edmund Spenser's home on the 3,000-acre estate he was granted in 1586; Kilcolman was destroyed in the Rebellion of 1598. [Council of Trustees of the National Library of Ireland; IR 91414 c 5)*

generation writers tend to be preoccupied with the complex process of identity-formation, a theme that unites such works as Joseph Keating's *My Struggle for Life* (1916), Tom Barclay's *Memoirs and Medleys: The Autobiography of a Bottle Washer* (1934), and John Walsh's *The Falling Angels* (1999). **Liam Harte**

British army in Northern Ireland. British soldiers were deployed on the streets of Derry on 14 August 1969 and in Belfast a day later, following a few days of intense violence in Derry known as 'the BATTLE OF THE BOGSIDE', the culmination of several months of gradually increasing conflict.

From the beginning there was a tension between the army's perceived role as a guarantor of the reforms demanded by the CIVIL RIGHTS MOVEMENT and its function of supporting the RUC and re-establishing the authority of the STORMONT government. The 'honeymoon' period, during which British soldiers were welcomed and widely accepted within Catholic communities, gradually came to an end as the reform programme faltered and soldiers became involved in clashes with Catholic crowds. The British army had fought a series of colonial conflicts before 1969, such as those in Kenya and Cyprus, and in many respects it treated Northern Ireland as another such conflict, making it much easier for republicans to portray the conflict as an anti-colonial war. The first soldier to die was Gunner Robert Curtis, shot in Belfast in February 1971 by the PROVISIONAL IRA, the first of approximately 450 regular soldiers to be killed. In the course of the conflict about 300 people were killed by the army. On BLOODY SUNDAY in Derry in January 1972 thirteen civilians were shot dead by soldiers. The army suffered its greatest loss of life in the conflict at WARRENPOINT, Co. Down, in August 1979, when eighteen soldiers were killed in an IRA bomb attack.

Beginning in the mid-1970s, the British government began to scale back the army presence. Under a policy that came to be known as 'Ulsterisation' the size of the RUC and of the ULSTER DEFENCE REGIMENT was greatly increased and the number of regular British soldiers was significantly reduced. Nonetheless the army continued to play an important role; and when violence increased in the early 1980s and again in the early 1990s, extra soldiers were brought in from Britain and deployed on the streets. In the wake of the IRA ceasefire of 1994 (which subsequently broke down), and the renewal of that ceasefire in 1996, the British army presence was scaled back considerably, in tandem with the reform of the RUC. This process of 'demilitarisation' involved the withdrawal of soldiers and the physical dismantling of BORDER posts, watch-towers, and bases, many of which had been in place since the early stages of the conflict. This 'demilitarisation' was an integral component of the NORTHERN IRELAND PEACE PROCESS and represented a tacit official acknowledgment that the British army had been widely perceived by nationalists and republicans as a combatant force in the conflict rather than as a neutral, peace-keeping force. **Niall Ó Dochartaigh**

British culture in Ireland. Cultural influences from Britain exerted an increasingly powerful hold in parts of Ireland from the period of ANGLO-NORMAN conquest and colonisation in the late twelfth century. In the later Middle Ages such influences, notably in language and the legal system, were centred on the Pale, the group of eastern counties around Dublin. Significantly, Dublin became particularly associated with St George, the patron saint of England. In 1366 the STATUTE OF KILKENNY sought to defend the character of the colony around Dublin by insisting on the use of the English language, names, and legal processes.

The spread of English was to be the key to cultural penetration. A further impulse came with the Henrician REFORMATION, subsequently pursued under Edward VI, ELIZABETH, and JAMES I, though unsuccessfully. While the bulk of the population remained faithful to Catholicism, the fact that the CHURCH OF IRELAND was identified with the English Reformation had clear cultural implications, not least through the presence of large numbers of English clergy. As part of the attempt to spread Protestantism, the BOOK OF COMMON PRAYER was printed in Dublin in both English (1551) and Irish (1608). The complexity of British cultural interaction with Ireland in the late Tudor period can best be seen in EDMUND SPENSER's poem THE FAERIE QUEEN (1590–96) and his *A View of the Present State of Ireland* (1596, but printed in 1633), which both reflected contemporary attitudes to the colonisation of Ireland and helped shape the perceptions of its Protestant elite.

The Elizabethan conquest of Ireland, and the subsequent policy of PLANTATION in Ulster in the seventeenth century, opened up the possibility of further cultural influences from Britain, including those associated with Scottish PRESBYTERIANISM. A principal conduit for the transfer of cultural values came with the period of the eighteenth-century Anglican ASCENDANCY. The taste of the Dublin upper middle class for contemporary British 'high' culture may be seen in the fact that HANDEL's oratorio *Messiah* had its first performance in the city, in 1742. Further impetus came with the Union of 1800, which bound Ireland into the British political system, expanding capitalist economy, and global empire. The impact of this on the popular culture of Ireland may be seen by the increasing prevalence of British newspapers from the middle of the nineteenth century as well as by the establishment of RUGBY, SOCCER, GOLF, TENNIS, and HOCKEY and the popularity of MUSIC-HALLS with visiting artists from Britain. The British Empire, and its wars, were also reflected in the public architecture of the time, of which the NELSON and WELLINGTON monuments in Dublin were prime examples.

With independence and partition, British cultural influence inevitably took different paths in the two political jurisdictions. The new government in Belfast sought to assert 'British' cultural values in a variety of ways. Somewhat fortuitously, they were aided in this by the new medium of radio. The BBC's Belfast station, established in 1924, was instrumental in relaying contemporary British culture to the people of Northern Ireland. Radio Éireann, set up in 1926, had different priorities, but many people in independent Ireland could listen to BBC broadcasts. By the 1950s some 30 per cent of the Republic's inhabitants had access to the new medium of television through the BBC and Ulster Television. But while television and radio meant that Ireland was still open to British cultural influence, more significant in the long run was the late twentieth-century impact of a global culture dominated by the United States, not least through the new medium of the INTERNET. **T. G. Fraser**

British Empire, the Irish in. Contemporary Irish streetscapes often provide vivid clues to the competition for public recognition between Ireland's different heritages. The juxtaposition of memorials in a town such as Tralee, Co. Kerry, are an apt example. In the central thoroughfare of Denny Street is the statue of a pikeman commemorating republican martyrs since 1798, while in nearby Ashe Street are two fine cannon at the foot of the courthouse, commemorating Kerrymen who died in action during the CRIMEAN WAR and the Indian mutiny of the 1850s, serving as tangible reminders of the role of Ireland within the British Empire during its nineteenth-century zenith.

In many ways the most challenging aspect of teasing out these historical links between the Irish people and the British Empire is in ascribing a starting-point. It is clear, however, that Ireland came to play an increasingly significant part in English and then British overseas expansion during the seventeenth century. EMIGRATION reflected this developing role in the origins of empire. The British West Indies, in particular, grew significantly in the later seventeenth century as a destination for emigrants from Ireland. Many went as involuntary transports during the Commonwealth (1649–60); but Irish Catholics also made their way to the Caribbean as merchants and landowners. On islands such as Montserrat they proved no more benign than contemporary English or other European colonisers.

During the eighteenth century Ireland came to play a more central role in the emergence of the first British Empire. More than 100,000 emigrants left Ireland for colonial America, with Ulster Presbyterians disproportionately represented. Members of the CHURCH OF IRELAND were particularly drawn towards service in the emerging imperial infrastructure. Trinity College, Dublin, was training ministers for the Church of Ireland and administrators for DUBLIN CASTLE, but its graduates were already sprinkled around those areas conventionally coloured red as British territories on maps of the world. The eighteenth century also saw the establishment of a major strand of Irish involvement in the British Empire: recruitment into the British military. The flow of the 'WILD GEESE' into the armies of the Continental powers shifted towards the increasingly overstretched British forces. Irish Catholics were already clearly evident in the ranks of British regiments serving in America during the Seven Years' War (1756–63). During the Napoleonic wars (1793–1815) more than 100,000 Irishmen joined the British navy and army.

The nineteenth century marked the high point of the British Empire; and while Ireland may not have benefited as tangibly as Scotland from the fruits of empire, continuing imperial emigration guaranteed the persistence of a very visible Irish tinge. While the United States and Britain absorbed the mass of Irish emigrants, Canada, Australia, New Zealand and, to a more limited extent, South Africa all received their share of Irish settlers. Even where permanent settlement was less obvious the Irish contribution should not be underestimated. The army of the East India Company in particular, and the British Raj more generally, drew heavily on the support of the Anglo-Irish.

Precise measurement of the contribution that Irish people made to the British Empire, or, conversely, that the empire made to the Irish, is difficult. Ultimately it may be that Irish influence affected aspects of life that defy neat quantification, such as social attitudes, cultural expression, and the use of language. **Patrick Fitzgerald**

British in Ireland. The implementation of PARTITION in 1921 meant that the government of Northern Ireland would assert symbols that would help define the new political entity as an integral, but distinctive, part of the United Kingdom. That these symbols would differ from those being adopted by the IRISH FREE STATE in the 1920s was only to be expected. Fortuitously, the government in Belfast was aided by the new medium of radio. The BBC's Belfast station, 2BE, established in 1924, was instrumental in relaying contemporary British culture to the people of Northern Ireland. 2RN (later Radio Éireann), set up in 1926, had different priorities, but many people in independent Ireland had access to BBC broadcasts. British cultural inputs were strengthened in the 1950s with the introduction of television. In a political sense, the concept of Britishness was less straightforward. The country's name, the United Kingdom of Great Britain and Northern Ireland, was both inclusive and yet denoted Northern Ireland as different from England, Scotland, and Wales. While the flying of the Union Jack and the playing of 'God Save the King' were reminders of a British loyalty and identity, other aspects of Northern Ireland's political and cultural life were less obviously 'British'. No other part of the United Kingdom had the office of Governor. The distinctive nature of Northern Ireland's constitutional position was clearly marked by the inauguration of the Parliament building at STORMONT in 1932, which echoed state capitols in the United States or public buildings in parts of the empire.

Commemorations also reflected this ambiguity. The annual Armistice Day parades and services of the British Legion were important, and emotive, occasions for people for whom the Battle of the Somme held deep personal and symbolic importance. It was perhaps inevitable that the wearing of the poppy would become a political as well as a commemorative statement. But the main commemoration remained the annual celebration of the BATTLE OF THE BOYNE by the ORANGE Institution on 12 July. Its centrality was emphasised when in 1926 it was designated a public holiday, but in the rest of the United Kingdom only among the Orange lodges of Scotland and Merseyside would the Twelfth celebrations have been seen as a symbol of Britishness.

A sense of Britishness was enhanced by Northern Ireland's participation in the SECOND WORLD WAR, not least through the common experience of the Blitz, which Belfast shared with such cities as Coventry, Plymouth, and Clydebank, even though conscription was not adopted. With the Labour government of Clement Attlee in power between 1945 and 1951 the provisions of the British WELFARE STATE in areas such as HEALTH and EDUCATION were extended to Northern Ireland. When the southern state separated from the British Commonwealth in 1949, the Ireland Act confirmed Northern Ireland's position within the United Kingdom.

While Northern Ireland was moving more closely into the British system, its politics were not. Though ULSTER UNIONIST MPs took the Conservative whip at Westminster, and the NORTHERN IRELAND LABOUR PARTY enjoyed a brief success between 1958 and 1965, the Conservative-Labour divide in Britain was not reflected in Northern Ireland. Politics continued to be based on attitudes to the border, rooted in communal division. Ironically, the imposition of DIRECT RULE by Edward Heath's government in 1972, deeply resented by unionists, made the government of Northern Ireland more in tune with the rest of the United Kingdom. The office of Governor was abolished, devolved government was suspended, and the initiative passed to a Secretary of State for Northern Ireland in the British Cabinet. Integrationist unionists, such as Enoch Powell, sought to build on this. Their hopes were confounded when the ANGLO-IRISH AGREEMENT (1985) gave the Government of the Republic a say in the affairs of Northern Ireland.

Britain itself was undergoing substantial change, becoming a multi-cultural country. Loss of empire and membership of the European Union meant a different set of political and economic priorities. At the same time, concepts of Britishness were under challenge from Scottish and Welsh nationalists, and the need to acknowledge Scottish and Welsh aspirations led to the establishment of devolved administrations in Edinburgh and Cardiff. Just what Britishness implied in political or cultural terms was increasingly open to interpretation, not least among unionists in Northern Ireland. [see BELFAST BLITZ.] **T. G. Fraser**

broadcasting. The establishment of a radio service in Dublin in 1926 (for the Irish Free State) and a television service in 1961 was informed by two central ideas: that it was appropriate for the state to be centrally involved in broadcasting, and that broadcasting should contribute to nation-building by fostering Irish culture. Two further themes have subsequently influenced broadcasting policy since the 1980s: the willingness of the state to facilitate the development of commercial broadcasting to compete with the public service broadcaster, RTÉ, and a decreasing concern with building a unifying national culture, allied to a recognition of cultural differences in Ireland and increasing cultural and economic self-confidence.

The immediate post-colonial circumstances within which the state established the first radio station in 1926, 2RN (subsequently Radio Éireann), influenced its concern to retain direct control of the station. A parliamentary committee of the new state in 1923, inquiring into the establishment of a national radio service, recommended that it be a purely state service, financed by licence fees and advertising. When the service began, under the aegis of the Department of Posts and Telegraphs, both the range of programmes offered and the hours of transmission were severely limited. It was not until after the SECOND WORLD WAR that radio expanded to include a proper news service. There was no political comment or discussion of contentious domestic issues on Radio Éireann until the 1950s.

The recognition of the limitations that direct state control placed on the independence of the radio service, as well as the desire to develop a national television service, led to the passing of the Broadcasting Authority Act (1960), which established the RTÉ Authority to run both radio and television as a public service. For almost thirty years RTÉ ran a greatly expanded range of broadcasting services. Its monopoly was abolished with the passing of the Radio and Television Act (1988), which allowed for the licensing of private commercial broadcasting. Since then a dual system has existed, within which public-service and commercial broadcasting have competed.

While instituting structures that would give RTÉ, and subsequently commercial broadcasters, relative autonomy from the state, successive governments continued to be sensitive to the broadcasting coverage of contentious issues, particularly the conflict in Northern Ireland. From the early 1970s to 1994 governments instituted and maintained CENSORSHIP in broadcasting. This ensured that named organisations that in the view of the state were attempting to achieve their aims through violent means, including SINN FÉIN, were forbidden access to radio and television.

In its early days as a state service, the state defined Radio Éireann's programming remit primarily as the promotion of cultural nationalism and the development of the nation-state. However, its hours of broadcasting were limited to breakfast-time, midday, and evening transmissions, and its finances were equally limited. Nonetheless it provided a forum for TRADITIONAL MUSIC, the reporting of Gaelic games, and programmes in Irish, as well as radio drama, classical and light music, and talks. It competed for listeners with British and other stations. In this sense RTÉ broadcasters have never had a monopoly of the air waves. Competition for listeners, and subsequently for viewers when the expensive medium of television was introduced, is reinforced by RTÉ's dependence on advertising as well as the licence fee.

From the 1960s the competitive situation within which RTÉ operates, as well as its public-service remit, dictated its television programming policy. News and current affairs have been well served and have attracted large audiences. Broadcasters argue that home-produced drama, talk shows and other forms of light entertainment must be produced to as high a standard as foreign productions to attract audiences. Such programming has indeed proved to be highly popular. However, original television programmes are very expensive, while foreign programmes can be bought at a small fraction of the cost. Roughly half the RTÉ television schedule has consisted of imported programmes.

In 2000, as for some years previously, more than three-quarters of the population could receive some of the main British terrestrial channels (BBC 1 and 2, ITV—mainly Ulster Television—and Channel 4), while more than half could receive satellite stations. Distribution is mainly by cable. In 2000, RTÉ retained 50 per cent of audience share in the Republic.

The need to attract large audiences for advertising purposes had a particular impact on programmes in Irish, which did not attract substantial audiences. As a response to repeated criticism of the dearth of such programmes in both radio and television schedules, an Irish-language radio station, Raidió na Gaeltachta, was established in 1972 and a television station, Teilifís na Gaeilge (now TG4), in 1996.

A powerful group that might have been expected to influence the ethos of broadcasting is the Catholic Church. However, since the 1960s the previously strong ideological role of the church has been lessened. Some have argued that this is in part because of the fact that the Catholic Church no longer had control over how a range of subjects, such as SEXUALITY, were discussed: on the contrary they were now being openly discussed, debated, and laughed at in both home-produced and imported television. Despite daily and weekly broadcasting of some Catholic rituals, such as the midday and six o'clock ringing of the ANGELUS bell and Mass on Sundays, and some excellent documentary and discussion series on religious and related topics, the role of the Catholic Church in broadcasting has been peripheral, and indeed broadcasting may have contributed to the weakening of its ideological role.

In 1988 the state abolished RTÉ's monopoly of broadcasting. In this it was influenced by political and ideological trends in western Europe that favoured commercial broadcasting and were critical of public-service monopolies as 'anti-competitive' and by increasingly strident demands from business and financial interests, some closely associated with FIANNA FÁIL, then in Government, as well as by the need to regularise pirate radio. It established a new regulatory authority, the Independent Radio and Television Commission (now called the Broadcasting Commission), to allocate licences to independent commercial broadcasters. These included local and community radio stations, one national radio station, and one national television station. Local commercial radio has been, in the main, a success, and ownership remains predominantly in Irish hands, though this is beginning to change. However, there is considerable foreign investment in both commercial national radio (Today FM) and television (TV3). Programmes on TV3 are mainly imported, its recent programme policy, built around acquiring rights to popular sports coverage and transmitting popular British serials.

A further challenge in the formulation of broadcasting policy is the development of digital television. The main question being discussed by state and broadcasters is that of who will have control over gateways and relay mechanisms through which the projected 200 television channels will be distributed.

In the present broadcasting regime the state appears committed to supporting RTÉ's public service remit. It has also supported the expansion of services for particular minorities, for example Irish-speakers. At the same time commercial broadcasting has been introduced, and considerable foreign ownership of this has been accepted with little debate. A particular form of cultural nationalism has given way to broadcasting policies based on a number of themes, including continuing support for public-service broadcasting, a pragmatic acceptance of the international economic market, including the media market, an acknowledgment of the rights of some cultural minorities, and a cultural confidence—some might argue an unwarranted one—regarding the role of Ireland's cultural industries, both nationally and internationally. [see BROADCASTING IN NORTHERN IRELAND; BYRNE, GABRIEL; CLANDILLON, SÉAMUS; GORHAM, MAURICE; O'BRIEN, CONOR CRUISE.] **Mary Kelly**

broadcasting and the Catholic Church. In the early years of Irish radio there was a conscious attempt to construct a national identity for the IRISH FREE STATE that was explicitly Catholic. There was a similarity between the world view of Radio Éireann and that of the Catholic Church, which enjoyed considerable access to the air waves. It was keenly aware of the power of radio (and later television) and was concerned to influence broadcasting. Archbishop JOHN CHARLES MCQUAID was instrumental in

broadcasting. *Sean O'Faolain during the filming of the series 'We the Irish' in the 1970s, produced by Neil MacCarthy, with Godfrey Graham, lighting cameraman (left), and Denis O'Callaghan, sound recordist (right). [RTÉ Stills Library]* having the ANGELUS bell broadcast every day on radio from 1950 and also set up a production unit, Radharc, to ensure that programmes with a religious ethos were broadcast on RTÉ television.

This symbiotic relationship continued up to the 1960s. RTÉ continues to broadcast worship programmes (both Catholic and Protestant) and retains a religious programming division, and diverse religious programming is viewed as an intrinsic part of RTÉ's public service remit. However, there have been changes in the relationship between the two institutions since the 1960s, following the decline in the power of the church and the rupture of the alliance between church and state. RTÉ appointed a lay religious affairs correspondent in the 1960s, heralding a move towards a more critical approach to church issues and teaching. The church and the media now offer opposing interpretations of society and are often in direct competition as a result. RTÉ has developed an increasingly commercial orientation and is no longer concerned with contributing to the construction of a particular version of Irishness. One area in which this competition has been visible is that of sexual mores and practices. Originally it was imported television programmes and films that brought a more open treatment of sex into Irish homes. Radio and television programmes, such as 'The Late Late Show', began covering more adventurous topics. GAY BYRNE is argued to have played an important role in challenging conservative mores and values; he is now seen as the first Irish broadcaster to publicly discuss many previously taboo subjects and was denounced from the pulpit on occasion for doing so.

In the early 1990s the authority of the church was undermined by a series of scandals involving the clergy, which were covered extensively by RTÉ and changed the way in which many people viewed the church, reinforcing the tension between the church and the media. A consensus has emerged that the media played a pivotal role in the SECULARISATION process in Ireland. Some have welcomed the role played by RTÉ in challenging the power of the Catholic Church; others have drawn attention to the growing power of the media and have questioned the wisdom of replacing CATHOLICISM with a system of beliefs and values based on individualism and consumerism. **Sara O'Sullivan**

broadcasting, commercial, the broadcasting of programmes that will maximise the audience and therefore attract advertisers to pay for the placing of commercial messages around the programmes. Unlike public-service broadcasting, the profit made is not necessarily invested in additional broadcast programmes. Commercial broadcasters usually have to adhere to less onerous duties and regulations than public-service broadcasters. In the Republic there are twenty-three licensed independent radio stations, consisting of one national independent station, Today FM, and twenty-two independent local stations. Somewhat less commercial, in that they broadcast public-service type programmes for the community in which they operate, are the thirteen community or 'community of interest' stations and one special-interest radio station in Dublin; the remainder consist of hospital and college stations. Traditionally the ownership of local radio was indeed local, in that the owners were generally local businesspeople; this is beginning to change, with other media companies, especially non-Irish ones, buying into the independent radio sector.

The programming on independent radio stations tends to be quite similar, consisting largely of continuous music in some form, whether 'top forty' hits, 'middle of the road' or COUNTRY AND WESTERN MUSIC, interspersed with advertising, talk from disc jockeys, and cheaply produced current affairs programmes made to comply with the legal requirement that 20 per cent of broadcasting time consist of news and current affairs. There are some exceptions, in that some of the more rural local stations do provide talk programmes with information about the locality for the local community.

The Republic has one commercial television channel, TV3, primarily owned by the Canadian company Can-West Global and the British media group Granada Media. Its programming is very much entertainment-led; TV3 sees itself as an entertainment station, although under the Radio and Television Act (1988) it is required to provide a 'reasonable proportion of news and current affairs programming.' TV3 is committed to providing what the station calls 'bright, breezy, watchable news.' Most of its programmes consist of American, British, or Australian series and films, advertising, and a minimum of home-produced programmes. Commercial broadcasters have to adhere to the requirements of the Radio and Television Act (1988) and the Broadcasting Act (2001) as well as the rulings of the Broadcasting Commission (formerly the Independent Radio and Television Commission).

Other commercial broadcasting services available in Ireland include foreign—mainly British—radio and television channels, cable radio, local television, unlicensed or 'pirate' radio stations, and internet radio. Cable television and MMDS subscribers receive the standard analogue television services provided by cable operators, which include the four Irish television channels, the four British channels (BBC1, BBC2, ITV, and Channel 4), and seven satellite channels. The subscription to this service also provides for cable radio, which consists of the relaying of the principal Irish and British radio channels. In addition, cable and MMDS subscribers can opt to receive 'discretionary services', such as Sky Movies and Sky Sports, for an additional charge. Subscribers to the cable companies NTL and Chorus can also receive the local television channels run by these companies.

Unlicensed or 'pirate' radio stations have existed since the beginning of radio broadcasting in Ireland; in 2001 the listener or radio enthusiast could find on any day of the year fifty to sixty pirate stations operating in different parts of the country. Pirate radio seems to be run by disenchanted applicants for broadcasting licences and others who believe that radio offers no real choice other than popular music stations and one or two 'proper' radio stations, that is, stations like RTÉ Radio 1, catering for all groups in society. Furthermore, the state does not seem to be too concerned to shut down the pirate stations, unless their radio transmissions interfere with those of emergency services or of legal broadcasters.

Streaming audio over the INTERNET is provided by some of the legal radio stations as well as by some private individuals to well over a million people who have internet access. Web radio offers a way of broadcasting that is untouched by regulation, and a few disgruntled licence applicants are now broadcasting over the internet. **Wolfgang Truetzschler**

broadcasting in Irish. There have been regular but limited broadcasts in Irish since 2RN began broadcasting in 1926. At first there were few such broadcasts, and the transmission range was limited, but by the 1940s both the range and the number of broadcasts had increased; since then, however, there has been a gradual increase in the number of hours of IRISH-LANGUAGE broadcasting. Together with the many learners' programmes during those first few decades, a number of English-language programmes had their counterpart in Irish. Since then two Irish-language radio stations have been established: RAIDIÓ NA GAELTACHTA, which emerged from the Irish-language civil rights demonstrations of the late 1960s, established as part of RTÉ in 1972 and aimed primarily at Irish-speaking communities, and Raidió na Life, which has held a private community radio licence since 1993 and serves the Dublin region. Raidió na Gaeltachta has a policy of broadcasting nothing in English, even songs; Raidió na Life includes songs in English.

RTÉ broadcasts primarily in English, with a few programmes in Irish on Radio 1. A few of the many community stations also broadcast a small number of programmes in Irish. Since the Broadcasting Authority Act (1960) and its amendment in 1976, the RTÉ Authority has been expected to 'bear constantly in mind' and 'have special regard for' Irish.

From the time RTÉ television began broadcasting in 1961 the number and range of programmes in Irish has been limited. These limitations received criticism from a number of sources, including the Irish-language movement, an advisory committee reporting to RTÉ in 1977, and a working group reporting to the Taoiseach, CHARLES HAUGHEY, in 1987. The Irish-language television station Teilifís na Gaeilge (renamed TG4 in 1999) began broadcasting in 1996; it was established as part of RTÉ following the language movement's lobbying of the Government and the criticisms of RTÉ's minimal fulfilment of its obligations. As well as broadcasting in Irish, TG4 broadcasts many programmes in English, in order to appeal to a wider audience. With the addition of TG4 to RTÉ's other two television stations, the number and range of programmes in Irish has increased substantially. In 1998 the independent television station TV3 began broadcasting; it broadcasts no programmes in Irish.

BBC Northern Ireland broadcasts a range of radio programmes in Irish on Radio Ulster and Radio Foyle. A small number of television programmes in Irish are also broadcast by BBC Northern Ireland. RTÉ's broadcasts, but not those of TG4, are also available in Northern Ireland. **Iarfhlaith Watson**

broadcasting, Northern Ireland. Broadcasting arrived early in Northern Ireland. In 1924, a year after the formation of the BBC, that organisation's second regional station, 2BE, was established in Belfast. Eventually all the broadcasting developments of the twentieth century left their mark. A wide choice is now available, with local television and radio stations, channels from Britain and the Republic, and satellite and cable television. The BBC locally benefits from its links to a large centralised organisation; this is frequently obvious in news programming, where a dearth of local news can mean simply rerouting items from London. Some critics have argued that this close but subordinate relationship has led to a lack of initiative: there is much less local coverage of drama and the arts, for example, than might be expected. Ulster Television, which arrived in 1957, has sometimes shown more imagination, especially in relation to current affairs.

Both public and commercial broadcasting have been influenced by political divisions. The BBC in its early decades was openly pro-unionist. Commercial television at first appeared more open and non-sectarian, not least because of a desire not to alienate 40 per cent of the potential audience. Despite these differences, the BBC and ITV reacted in remarkably similar ways when political violence emerged in the late 1960s. A pattern was established that involved three main components. Firstly, both stations instituted a system of 'reference upwards', whereby all programmes on Northern Ireland had to be vetted; more than seventy programmes were directly censored between 1970 and 1988. Secondly, there was a requirement, especially in the first two decades of the conflict, that each programme be 'balanced': the result was the silencing of voices considered more extreme and the privileging of official voices as being 'moderate', no matter how non-inclusive the policies they were supporting. This dovetailed with an over-reliance on official sources, in particular press statements and briefings from the Northern Ireland Office, RUC, and British army. Thirdly, there were specific patterns regarding interviews with 'extremists'. Interviews with spokespersons for illegal organisations—in particular the IRA and INLA on the republican side and UVF and UDA on the LOYALIST side—while not banned outright, were rare: there were only six each on the BBC and ITV between 1969 and 1979, after which there have been none. The result was that, with some notable exceptions, self-censorship became (in the words of the journalist Mary Holland) an art form in the British broadcasting media.

State control reached new heights in 1988 with the introduction of a ban, unprecedented in peacetime, on the broadcasting of the voices of spokespersons for SINN FÉIN and a number of other organisations, including the ULSTER DEFENCE ASSOCIATION. This ban had two clear effects. Firstly, despite the claim that there was no intention of restricting coverage of the conflict, this is what occurred, with appearances of Sinn Féin spokespersons dropping by 60 per cent in the year after the ban. The second effect was that the ban in practice quickly expanded to ensnare a range of people who were not spokespersons for Sinn Féin: for example, the POGUES' song 'Streets of Sorrow/BIRMINGHAM SIX' was banned from BBC radio.

The broadcasting ban was lifted after the republican ceasefire of 1994. The NORTHERN IRELAND PEACE PROCESS that led to this and the subsequent loyalist ceasefire proved confusing at first for broadcasters. Accustomed to reporting war, they found reporting peace problematic and came to rely even more on government agenda-setting. All too often they concentrated on such questions as the decommissioning of arms, to the detriment of other important stories. Ulster Television has bought commercial radio stations in the Republic and commerce may accomplish what politics has not: making the border somewhat less relevant, at least as far as the media are concerned. **Bill Rolston**

Brocas family (eighteenth and nineteenth centuries). No fewer than six artists bearing this name flourished in Dublin from c. 1754 to c. 1873: James, his brother Henry (c. 1762–1837), and the latter's four sons: James Henry (c. 1790–1846), Samuel Frederick (c. 1792–1847), William (c. 1794–1868), and Henry Junior (c. 1798–1873). The family were descended from a Robert Brocas, a native of Derbyshire who arrived in Ireland in the time of Cromwell. Henry and James were the sons of Robert and Bridget Brocas, the latter being the daughter of Nicholas Taylor of Wexford.

Henry was appointed master of the School of Landscape and Ornament in the DUBLIN SOCIETY Schools in 1801. Self-taught, he practised as a landscape painter, chiefly in watercolour. A prolific engraver and caricaturist, he contributed to a wide variety of publications and exhibited publicly in Dublin. In 1838 he was succeeded as master by Henry Junior. Under the mastership of father and son the school produced many distinguished practitioners in the fields of landscape and portraiture, such as GEORGE PETRIE, JOHN HENRY CAMPBELL, FRANCIS DANBY, and Sir FREDERICK BURTON. A series of twelve well-known topographical views of Dublin drawn by Samuel Frederick and engraved by Henry Junior was published by J. Le Petit, Dublin, 1818–29. Their brother James Henry also trained in the society's school under his father. A particularly fine animal painter, he contributed portraits of cattle to the DUBLIN

SOCIETY's statistical surveys (1802). William, a landscape and portrait painter, was a member of the RHA and also a caricaturist, many of his hand-coloured etchings being based on the work of the English caricaturist James Gillray (1757–1815).

The NATIONAL LIBRARY OF IRELAND possesses an extensive collection (2,571 items) that confirms the family's close involvement with a wide range of interests, including publishing, portraiture, political and social caricature, anatomy, landscape, theatre, natural history, dress, and agriculture (see p. 841). [see PRINTS.] **Patricia Butler**

Broderick, John L. (1927–1989), writer. Born and educated in Athlone. Broderick wrote novels from 1961 onwards that offer dismal portraits of embittered lives in the midlands. *The Pilgrimage* (1961), his first novel, combines the themes of marital infidelity and religious devotion. Many of his novels contain misogynistic depictions of women alongside scathing attacks on mid-century Irish society, including *The Waking of Willie Ryan* (1965), *An Apology for Roses* (1973), and *London Irish* (1979). In later novels he reflected a more liberal Ireland, but the characteristic tone of much of his fiction is antagonism towards the bourgeois morality of Catholic Ireland. **John Brannigan**

Broighter Hoard, a hoard of seven gold objects unearthed by a ploughman at Broighter, Co. Derry, in 1896. After a sojourn in England, and a celebrated court case in which it was found to be treasure trove, the hoard was deposited on loan with the ROYAL IRISH ACADEMY; it is now in the NATIONAL MUSEUM. The individual objects are a tubular collar of Continental ('Celtic') form decorated with *repoussé* 'Celtic' art, two twisted collars of INSULAR origin, two necklaces of Graeco-Egyptian manufacture, and a model boat and model cauldron of unknown cultural designation but probably Irish. The datable items belong to the first century BC, and the deposition of the hoard was probably no later than the first century AD. The find-spot, now some distance from the shore of LOUGH FOYLE, was then salt marsh on the edge of the sea-lough. The hoard's cosmopolitan nature and the presence of the model boat have prompted the suggestion that it was deposited to appease a sea god, probably MANANNÁN MAC LIR, who is located in early Irish tradition under Lough Foyle. **Richard Warner**

Brontë, Patrick (1777–1861), clergyman and poet. Born Patrick Brunty near Loughbrickland, Co. Down; after working as a weaver and then a schoolmaster he was ordained in the Church of England at Cambridge in 1806. From 1820 he served as perpetual curate of Haworth, Yorkshire. He outlived his seven children, including Charlotte, Emily, and Anne Brontë, whose literary fame far outshone his own modest fictional and poetical successes. **Terence Brown**

Bronze Age burial. Bronze Age graves ranged from simple or stone-lined circular and oval pits to more substantial slab-lined rectangular and polygonal *cists*. Many people were inhumed in contracted or flexed positions in small pits or cists or, more rarely, in extended position in large pits. Some individuals were bound or tied before burial. Sometimes the remains were stored, allowing the flesh to decay, and the disarticulated bones interred. The body could be partially or completely cremated on a funeral pyre and, sometimes after further crushing or cleaning, placed in the grave. Some graves contained single individuals, but many people were buried in groups of up to seven in a single grave. The remains were buried with, or in, pottery containers or with food vessels and urns, and occasionally with stonework or beads, daggers, or battleaxes. The graves were frequently in cemeteries, which might be either flat or in stone cairns or in *barrows* (earthen mounds). In the later Bronze Age cists, pottery and inhumation went out of use and burial is characterised by cremation in simple pits.

Relatively small numbers of women and children are represented in the burials, suggesting that they did not have an automatic right to burial with men, and their remains were disposed of in a different manner. This variation in treatment probably indicates a range of social status, reflecting each person's particular occupation and role in society.

Analysis of the physical remains suggests that people lived a short life of hard work, in poor living conditions, and suffered from arthritis. Men ranged in height between 160 and 183 cm (5 ft 3 in. to 6 ft) and women between 152 and 168 cm (5 ft to 5 ft 6 in.). Child mortality was high; most people did not live much beyond their thirties, though some lucky individuals did live into their fifties. [see CIST BURIAL.] **Charles Mount**

Bronze Age copper-mining. The BRONZE AGE in Ireland has left a great volume of metal, consisting of several thousand copper, bronze, and gold objects. These bear witness to extensive mining operations in many areas, and to organised production and supply networks. Bronze Age copper mines are known or suspected from several regions, most notably Cos. Cork and Kerry. These include the mine at ROSS ISLAND, Killarney, which dates from the dawn of Irish metallurgy, and the workings of MOUNT GABRIEL type found scattered through the peninsulas of west Cork. These ancient mines provide a considerable insight into the approach to copper-mining during the Bronze Age. The discovery of work camps at these sites also reveals the domestic life of early miners, from the food they ate to the huts they sheltered in.

In prospecting for copper, the miners identified accessible deposits of surface mineralisation, carefully searching rock outcrops in geologically favourable areas for brightly coloured copper minerals. Bronze Age miners were able to extract this mineralisation to a depth of 12 m (40 ft) or more, depending on local circumstances. These mines generally took the form of open-cast pits, narrow trench workings, or inclined drifts, while underground tunnelling is also known. The mining strategy at different sites depended on the geological setting, as well as on manpower, technology, and the social context of different operations. Some Bronze Age mining took the form of surface extraction, the miners flitting from one mineralised outcrop to the next, with minimum effort at each site. This approach is best seen in the mines of Mount Gabriel type in west Cork, which were possibly seasonal operations adapted to a sporadic type of surface mineralisation. Other mines represent a long-term exploitation of an individual copper deposit, as seen at Ross Island, a particularly rich source, where some 600 years of Bronze Age mining are recorded.

Bronze Age copper mines are usually marked by an economy of effort, where only those rock types that actually contained ore minerals were extracted. This mining involved the use of fire in combination with stone hammers and bone and wooden tools. Fire-setting involved burning wood fires against the mine face, causing it to weaken, a fracturing effect that was sometimes increased by quenching with water. Rock was then removed by pounding the heat-shattered face with stone hammers, either hafted or hand-held. The miners also used pick-like implements and fingers to prise out rock along fracture planes. Pointed wooden sticks used for this purpose have been discovered on Mount Gabriel, while there is some evidence for the use of antler picks at Ross Island.

Metal mining tools do not appear to have been used in Bronze Age mining in Ireland. Broken rock extract and charcoal residues from these mines was generally removed to the surface for sorting, using shovels and containers of some kind. The use of wooden shovels has been confirmed on Mount Gabriel, while Ross Island has produced evidence for the use of cattle shoulder-blade bones as scoops. While many Bronze Age copper mines were surface operations, some deeper workings required the use of wooden ladders or ropes. Torches were also necessary in these mines, as seen by the discovery of numerous charred splints of pine at Mount Gabriel. To limit the seepage of water into open workings, the miners may have confined their operations to the summer months, though the seasonality of Bronze Age copper mining is poorly understood.

Once mineralised rock was extracted, the miners were faced with removing the barren rock matrix around these copper minerals. The aim here was to prepare an ore concentrate that could then be reduced to metal by smelting. There is evidence of a multi-stage approach, beginning with the crushing of rock extract that was already highly broken by fire-setting extraction. This rock was further broken using stone hammers and anvil stones, and possibly washed before the sorting by hand of visibly mineralised fragments. Today this activity is marked by the presence of low mounds of crushed rock spoil, rich in charcoal and broken stone hammers, near the mine entrances.

Once an ore concentrate was produced, the next stage was reducing these copper minerals to metal by smelting in furnaces. The identification of Bronze Age smelting sites is a particular problem, because of their low archaeological visibility and the fact that copper minerals may occasionally have been removed from the mine for smelting at another site. So far Ross Island is the only early copper mine that has produced evidence of smelting, in the form of simple pit furnaces fuelled with charcoal. **William O'Brien**

Bronze Age metalwork and metallurgy. The middle of the third millennium BC saw the spread of a new technology across Atlantic Europe, leading to the appearance and earliest production of copper objects in Ireland. This development coincided closely with the arrival of *beaker* pottery c. 2400 BC. The practice of metallurgy was successfully introduced to this culture, with copper objects widely distributed throughout Ireland by 2300 BC. By 2100 BC the widespread adoption of tin metallurgy and of expertise in sheet goldworking is evidence that metalworking in Ireland was on a technological par with most other parts of western Europe. The transition from use of metal to dependence on metal that followed in the early second millennium BC culminated in an 'industrial' scale of production, distribution and consumption in the later Bronze Age (c. 1200–600 BC).

The introduction of metallurgy had profound implications for many aspects of life in Ireland, including art, warfare, AGRICULTURE,

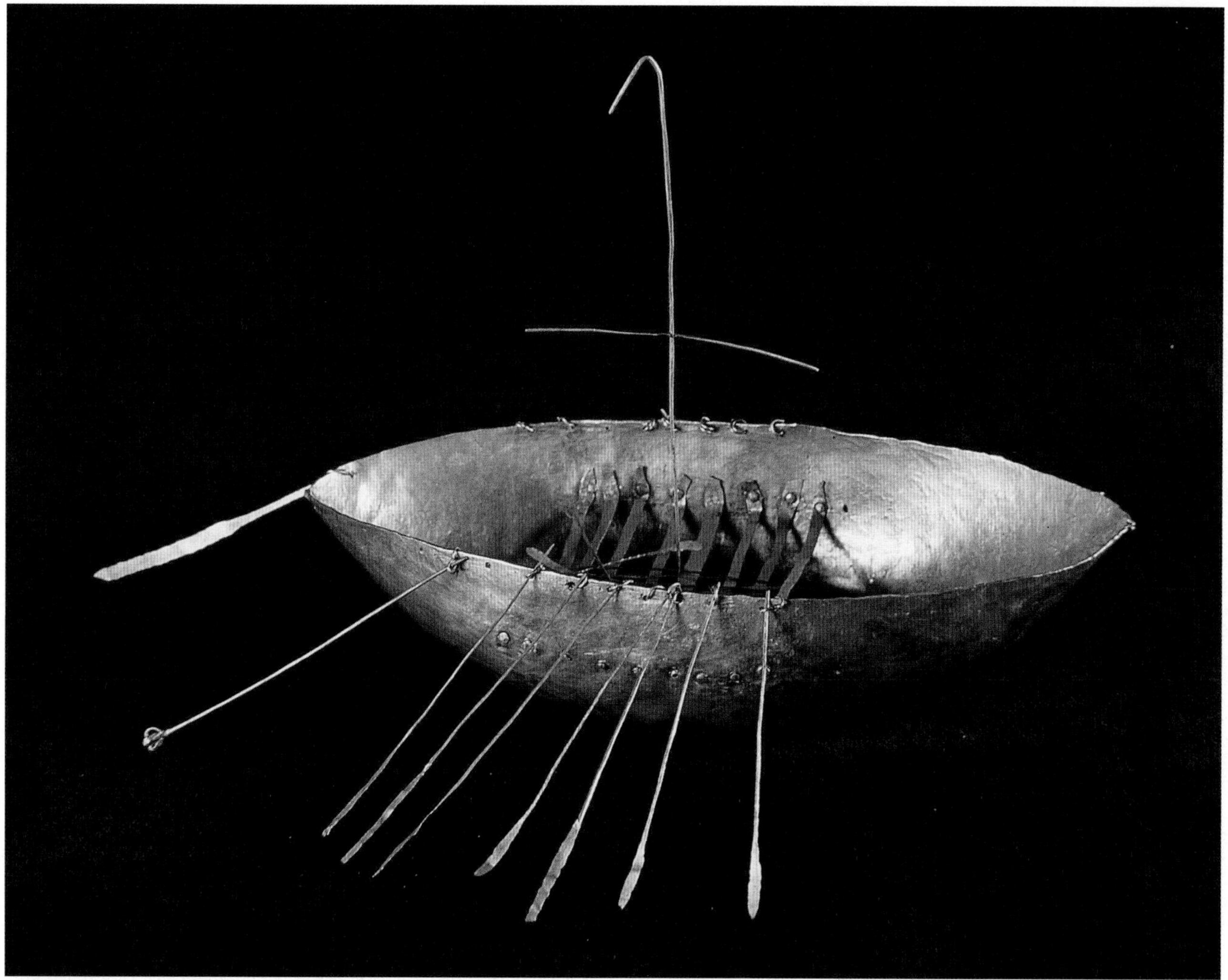

Broighter. *The Broighter Boat from a hoard of gold objects, including a La Tène style collar, a bowl with suspension rings, two chains, and two twisted collars, unearthed at Broighter, Co. Derry, in 1896. The boat is possibly a votive offering. [National Museum of Ireland]*

woodworking, and related crafts. The new technology opened up a range of new fabrication possibilities that Bronze Age craft workers were quick to exploit. The aesthetic potential of these metals was also exploited by individuals and groups as a new medium of social expression. The supply of metal to regions lacking local sources laid the basis for an enduring trade network in a range of commodities, both within Ireland and overseas; the control of this metal production and circulation had important repercussions within society and contributed to the social changes that mark the Bronze Age.

Central to the successful introduction of metallurgy was the discovery of accessible copper resources in many parts of Ireland. Bronze Age mines appeared in some regions, the earliest possibly being ROSS ISLAND, Co. Kerry, where there was large-scale production of copper between 2400 and 1800 BC. Another early development was the widespread adoption of tin-bronze from 2100 BC as the standard copper alloy of the Bronze Age. This led to a wider use of metal in society through the production of better tools and weapons. This innovation was all the more remarkable given the paucity of natural tin sources in Ireland, which led to exchange contacts with other regions, most notably Cornwall in the south of England.

The first thousand years of the use of metal in Ireland (c. 2400–1400 BC) was marked by a limited range of artefact types. These included copper and bronze axeheads, daggers, and halberds, as well as GOLD discs and LUNULAE. As the early Bronze Age progressed, the scale of production increased, linked to new mine

Bronze Age. *The Bishopsland Hoard, dating from 1200 to 1000 BC, a collection of tools found in 1942 outside Bishopsland, Co. Kildare. It consists of woodwork and metalwork equipment as well as a sickle for harvesting cereals. [National Museum of Ireland]*

sources, progressive recycling, and a spreading knowledge of metallurgy throughout Ireland. The use of these objects was rooted in their social context, with copper, bronze, and gold objects much prized as items for display and prestige. Metalwork continued to play an important role in social transactions throughout the Bronze Age; however, bronze axeheads and blades assumed a greater utilitarian role as this period progressed. Few were ever deposited with BRONZE AGE BURIALS.

By 1500 BC the transition from metal-using to fully metal-dependent societies was under way. The move to what might be termed an industrial scale of metal supply began with developments in the middle Bronze Age. With some 2,500 bronze artefacts dating approximately from 1600–1300 BC we see an increased scale of production, with metal now used for weapons and work implements as well ornaments and prestige items. The use of flat axeheads, daggers, and halberds gave way to flanged axeheads (including palstaves), dirks and rapiers, and looped spearheads. The appearance of these new forms reflects developments in production technology, such as the ability to cast hollow forms and the widespread use of bivalve stone moulds. The technical accomplishment of the bronzesmiths is illustrated by the production of long, elegant rapiers, most notably that from Lissane, Co. Derry.

The move to a new level of production, marked by a diverse range of products and a considerable volume of metal in circulation, occurred during the *Bishopsland phase*, c. 1300–1000 BC. With influences from Continental Europe channelled through southern Britain, new metalworking techniques were introduced and a novel range of bronze and gold artefacts. This Bishopsland metalworking in Ireland saw the development of specialised toolkits, the first appearance of bronze swords, and the appearance of novel types of gold ornament. The skill of the goldsmith is visible in the use of solid bar in addition to gold sheet and in the production of a range of twisted neck-rings, including bar TORCS, flange-twisted torcs, and ribbon torcs. Outstanding examples from this period, such as the TARA torcs, clearly indicate an emerging craft specialisation. An important innovation was the widespread adoption of clay moulds for casting, after which stone moulds were no longer used.

A renewed hoarding of metal in this period testifies to a marked increase in the amount of metal in circulation. From c. 1000 BC a further intensification of bronze and gold production occurred, culminating in the metal 'industry' of the *Dowris phase* (c. 900–600 BC). Metalworking reached new heights in this period—in the scale of production, in the great variety of metal products, and in the technical accomplishment of the craft workers. This was a time of conspicuous wealth, most visibly expressed through large-scale production and the use of prestige metalwork. The amount of metal in circulation is attested by the marked increase in hoard deposition and the size of individual finds, such as those from DOWRIS (Co. Offaly) and MOOGHAUN (Co. Clare). The proliferation of new object types shows diverse influences from southern and western Britain, northern and central Europe, Atlantic Europe, and the western Mediterranean. Irish metalwork was also widely exchanged abroad in this period. The Dowris phase saw important advances in fabrication, including the working of sheet bronze to make buckets, cauldrons, and shields. Joining techniques, such as riveting and soldering, were developed, as was the use of gold wire and foil. The use of leaded bronze and gold alloying is also known, as is the continued use of clay moulds. Evidence of specialist craft-workers in bronze, gold, and other materials, such as amber, is provided by the technical quality of the products and the use of specialised tool-kits. The discovery of scrap hoards points to carefully organised supply networks, with much metal obtained through recycling and foreign trade. Sources in Ireland were also probably exploited, although, curiously, no mines dating from this period have been discovered.

The Dowris phase is best known for the excellence of its goldworking, with a great variety of ornaments made from solid bar and sheet gold, gold wire, and foil. Included here is a range of arm, neck, and hair ornaments, as well as gold vessels. The best-known products of Dowris goldworking are gorgets, 'dress-fasteners', and lock-rings. The gorgets are magnificent crescent-shaped neck ornaments, with broad collars and circular terminals that are richly decorated with *repoussé*, stamping and chasing techniques. The bow-shaped, cup-ended ornaments called dress-fasteners are evidence of gold-casting, including the production of hollow forms. Finally, the soldering of fine gold wire onto face-plates to make hair ornaments called lock-rings represents some of the most advanced metal fabrication ever practised in prehistoric Europe.

There was a marked increase in the production of bronze weaponry during the Dowris phase. The flange-hilted leaf-shaped sword was developed under direct influence from southern Britain, while circular bronze shields appeared, and spearheads were produced in great quantities. The production of prestige weaponry and ornaments reveals a concern with ostentatious display in what was probably a highly politicised society of tribal chiefdoms. It is also indicative of cult practices involving the votive deposition of metalwork.

During the seventh century BC the first contacts with iron-using cultures on the Continent emerged. This began a slow process of technological change, marked first by the appearance of *Hallstatt C* material in Ireland and culminating in the widespread adoption of iron metallurgy during the *La Tène phase*, from c. 300 BC. The mechanisms by which iron was introduced to Ireland are much debated, as is the cultural context within which this innovation occurred. There is clear evidence from finds that Late Bronze Age metalworkers were experimenting with iron in the centuries between 600 and 300 BC, against a background of contact with southern and western Britain and with France.
William O'Brien

Bronze Age. *Pure gold gorget or dress-fastener found at Clones, Co. Monaghan, dating from the Dowris phase of the Late Bronze Age, c. 900–700 BC. It has a length of 21.27 cm and is decorated with small circular discs in a repetitive pattern. It was probably used for ceremonial occasions. [National Museum of Ireland]*

Bronze Age settlement and society. In the Later Bronze Age (c. 1300–600 BC), Ireland displayed the same type of centralised society, defensive architecture, and emergent military aristocracy seen elsewhere throughout Europe. By c. 1200 BC the traditional pattern of dispersed settlement was augmented by the appearance of large enclosures surrounded by one to three earthen banks and ditches (such as HAUGHEY'S FORT) or stone walls (such as RATHGALL, MOOGHAUN, and DÚN AONGHASA). The evidence of their interiors is varied and may range from the large round house, 15 m (50 ft) in diameter, at Rathgall to what may have been two large double-circle enclosures at Haughey's Fort. The purpose of the Haughey's Fort enclosures may have been ritual, and the nearby site of NAVAN FORT also revealed a Late Bronze Age timber-built enclosure surrounded by a wide and shallow ditch. Adjacent to Haughey's Fort was the 'King's Stables', an artificial pond contemporary with the HILL-FORT that contained the possible remains of sacrificed animals and portion of a human skull. These hill-forts presumably served as political and ritual centres (though the distinction may not have been important) and are generally associated with the emergence of tribal chiefdoms. Still larger enclosures, known as PROMONTORY FORTS, are largely undated, but one, Knockdu in Co. Antrim, has recently yielded a Late Bronze Age date.

Smaller enclosed settlements are found both in dryland and wetland locations. At Carrigillihy, Co. Cork, a stone wall surrounded an oval stone-built house, while a timber palisade surrounded at least half a dozen timber-built huts at Curraghatoor, Co. Tipperary. Lakeside or island dwellings have been well preserved and indicate the presence of wooden palisades surrounding timber-built circular huts at CLONFINLOUGH, Co. Offaly, and Cullyhanna, Co. Armagh, while rectangular timber platforms at Ballinderry, Co. Offaly, suggest that other architectural forms were possible. Lakeside settlements such as Lough Eskragh, Co. Fermanagh, have revealed dug-out boats, while paddles were recovered from Clonfinlough.

The subsistence economy of the Late Bronze Age combined the cultivation of cereals with stock-raising. Though wheat, generally the preferred crop of consumption, was found at Curraghatoor along with barley, the latter was found in very large quantities and to the exclusion of other crops at Haughey's Fort. Patterns of livestock exploitation generally suggest that cattle were the primary domestic species, followed by pigs (at LOUGH GUR the species were reversed), though the environmental conditions at Dún Aonghasa dictated the raising of sheep, a species only minimally present at other sites. The hunting of deer was practised to a small extent.

Late Bronze Age settlements reveal a limited range of material culture, which must be augmented by the large quantity of chance finds and hoards. A flat-bottomed, bucket-shaped coarse ware is typical of many sites and represents the terminal use of ceramics in Ireland, before the production of pottery ceased altogether by the Iron Age. Stone saddle-querns and rubbers were employed in processing the grain, while the finds of spindlewhorls suggest the manufacture of textiles. Workshops are poorly attested; other than some traces of metalworking at LOUGH GUR, Dún Aonghasa and Rathgall there is very little evidence for the type of specialised industries that might be found concentrated on Continental sites.

The production of metal artefacts can be divided broadly into four classes: weapons, tools, ornaments, and decorated metalwork.

Many objects attest to the existence of an aristocratic class engaged in the display of its status in society. Buckets and cauldrons, some holding up to 45 litres (12 gallons), suggest communal feasting. Bronze TRUMPETS, frequently found in pairs, were presumably associated with rituals.

Late Bronze Age society is generally described as consisting of chiefdoms, related through exchange networks and marriage and centred on hill-forts. Though this system of peer societies has been suggested throughout much of western Europe, it does not account for the wide variety of settlement types, and the flourishing of the hill-fort may have lasted for only a few centuries. The vertical relationships between the different classes of society during the Late Bronze Age is one of the principal challenges in modern Irish archaeology. [see GOLD, PREHISTORIC.] **J. P. Mallory**

brooches, penannular, high-status ornaments consisting of a long pin that swivels freely on a gapped ring. The pin passes through the gap in the ring, enabling the brooch to function as a cloak fastener. The cloth was skewered with the pin, and the ring was pressed down so that the pin passed through the gap. The ring was rotated *under* the pin, so that the cloth pulled the pin against it and locked it.

Irish penannular brooches originated in late Roman Britain, but the dating of the earliest examples is unclear. They were widespread in the fifth and sixth centuries, when workshops producing them are known. Made of bronze, they have ring terminals in the form of stylised beast heads. Gradually the terminals were enlarged to carry reserved ornament in fields of enamel, including spiral scrollwork in the Ultimate La Tène style. By about 600 AD imposing brooches—such as that from Ballinderry Crannóg, Co. Offaly—were decorated with millefiore glass and tinning, in addition to enamel. Penannular brooches seem to have been somewhat eclipsed with the emergence of the TARA BROOCH type, but in the later ninth century a variety of new silver penannular forms, the *thistle*, *ball*, and *bossed* varieties, appeared. They were especially fashionable in the areas of Viking influence. Examples cut up for use as small change have been found in tenth-century Viking silver hoards. **Michael Ryan**

Brooke, Alan (1883–1963), military leader. Born in the south of France, the ninth child of Sir Victor Brooke of Colebrooke, Co. Fermanagh. He served in an artillery regiment from 1902 and was awarded the Distinguished Service Order during the FIRST WORLD WAR, in which he was the first British officer to apply the French tactic of the creeping barrage. After helping to organise the retreat from Dunkirk in 1940 he was appointed commander of the home forces and then in 1941 Chief of the Imperial General Staff. A brilliant strategist, he did much to co-ordinate British and American operations. He was created Viscount Alanbrooke of Brookeborough in 1945. **Jonathan Bardon**

Brooke, Sir Basil, first Viscount Brookeborough (1888–1973), politician. A Co. Fermanagh landowner and distinguished veteran of the FIRST WORLD WAR, Brooke returned to his native county following the war to play a central organisational role in local militant LOYALISM, becoming head of the Special Constabulary in the county in November 1920. Elected to the Northern Ireland House of Commons in 1929, he held office as Minister of Agriculture, 1933–41, and Minister of Commerce and Production, 1939–45. His opposition to government laxity in its approach to the war effort made him in 1943 the obvious choice as Prime Minister in succession to the ousted JOHN ANDREWS. In the post-war era he oversaw the extension of the new British WELFARE STATE to Northern Ireland, securing parity of social services with Britain. He was created Viscount Brookeborough in 1952. His premiership saw rising standards of living and improved public access to EDUCATION, while on the constitutional front a pledge was secured from the British government that Northern Ireland's status as part of the United Kingdom would not be altered without the consent of the regional parliament. Known for his genial and easy-going rapport with supporters, he remained unsympathetic to the claims of the Catholic minority and, despite his lack of strong Protestant convictions, retained an emphatically traditionalist stance on the question of community relations. An increasing sense of torpor engendered by the government's inability to deal with economic difficulties in the later years of his premiership brought about his replacement as Prime Minister in 1963 by the more forward-looking TERENCE O'NEILL. Rare attendance at Parliament from 1963 to 1968, when his son John Brooke replaced him as MP for Lisnaskea, did not prevent his identification with opposition to O'Neill's liberalising policies, with traditionalist unionists unfavourably contrasting O'Neillite 'appeasement' of Catholics with the comparative political certainties of the Brookeborough years. [see A, B, C SPECIALS.] **Alan Scott**

Brooke, Charlotte (c. 1740–1793), poet and translator. Probably born at Rantavan, near Mullagh, Co. Cavan, the youngest child of Lettice Digby and HENRY BROOKE, author and polemicist. Her interest in Irish was sparked when she overheard a workman reading from a manuscript. JOSEPH COOPER WALKER fostered her interest in translation, which was further encouraged by the Ossian controversy. *Reliques of Irish Poetry* (1789) is a pioneering work, not least because of the bilingual text. She has been judged harshly on her perceived inadequacies as a translator, particularly of Irish metre, and the work itself has received little critical attention, but lately her reputation as a poet has risen. [see OSSIANIC POEMS AND TALES.] **Siobhán Kilfeather**

Brooke, Henry (c. 1703–1783), dramatist, novelist, poet, and pamphleteer. Born in Co. Cavan, son of a Protestant clergyman; educated at TCD. His play *Gustavus Vasa* (1739) was banned in London; renamed *The Patriot* and performed in Dublin, it was acclaimed by audiences sympathetic to its political sentiments. His pamphlet *Farmer's Letters* (1745) warns Protestants of possible Catholic rebellion, while *The Tryal of the Cause of the Roman Catholics* (1761) argues for a relaxation of the Penal Laws. His sentimental novel *The Fool of Quality* (1765–70) was admired by JOHN WESLEY, who published his own version of it. **Jacqueline Belanger**

Brooking, Charles (fl. 1728), cartographer. He was named as author on the earliest separately printed map of Dublin, issued by the London publisher John Bowles in 1728. Hardly any biographical information is available. His map, which appears to have been based on an original survey, shows streets, built-up street blocks, and public buildings from Kilmainham to Ringsend and from the Linen Hall (North King Street) to St Stephen's Green. It was accompanied by a panorama of the city seen from the north and twenty close-up views. A second, pirated edition was issued by Henry Overton and John Hoole of London in 1729 and a third by an anonymous publisher c. 1740. **J. H. Andrews**

Brosnan, Pierce (1953–), actor. Born in Drogheda, Co. Louth. He got his first large roles in the television drama-documentary 'Murphy's Stroke', the television series 'The Mannions of America', and the American series 'Remington Steele', 1982–7. Though his feature film debut was in *The Long Good Friday* (1979), most of his early roles are forgettable, as in *The Fourth Protocol* (1987) and *Taffin*

(1988), a pattern that continued in the 1990s in films as various as *Mister Johnson* (1991), *The Lawnmower Man* (1992), *Mrs Doubtfire* (1993), *The Nephew* (1997), and *The Thomas Crown Affair* (1999). It was his role as James Bond, the quintessential Englishman, in *Goldeneye* (1995), *Tomorrow Never Dies* (1997), and *The World Is Not Enough* (1999), that made him an international star. **Kevin Rockett**

Brown, Christy (1932–1981), writer. Born in Crumlin, Dublin. Brown's writing career began with his best-known work, *My Left Foot* (1954), an autobiographical account of his childhood in working-class Dublin. He suffered from cerebral paralysis, which led some to believe him mentally retarded, until he learnt to write with his toes. He wrote a novel based on the same experiences, *Down All the Days* (1970), but his later novels are generally regarded as less convincing. He also wrote poetry, collected as *Come Softly to My Wake* (1971) and *Of Snails and Skylarks* (1978). His early work is noteworthy for its vivid realism, particularly concerning sexuality. *My Left Foot* was filmed in 1989 by Jim Sheridan, starring Daniel Day-Lewis. **John Brannigan**

Brown, Deborah (1927–), sculptor. Born in Belfast; attended Belfast College of Art and subsequently studied at the NCAD, 1947–50, and Paris. She held solo exhibitions at the CEMA Gallery, Belfast, 1951, Belfast Museum and Art Gallery, 1956, and ARTS COUNCIL Gallery, Belfast, 1962 and 1969. She created a series of eight canvases for Ferranti Ltd, Manchester, in 1965. She later moved from papier-mâché to fibreglass. She won the Carroll's open award and was a prizewinner in the ACNI open painting competition, 1970. With THEO MCNAB she represented Ireland at Cagnes-sur-Mer International Festival in 1973. A retrospective was held in the ULSTER MUSEUM in 1982. She was represented at the 1984 Rosc exhibition in Dublin. Her *Sheep on the Road* (1990) was commissioned for the ACNI Sculpture Park but was later purchased for Waterfront. She is represented in the HUGH LANE MUNICIPAL GALLERY OF MODERN ART and the IRISH MUSEUM OF MODERN ART. **Theo Snoddy**

Brown, Terence (1944–), professor and CRITIC. Born in Loping, China; educated at Magee University College, Derry, and TCD. As a teacher at TCD, where he is professor of ANGLO-IRISH LITERATURE and a fellow, and as joint chairman of Encounter, he has been an important representative of the Northern Protestant mind in the Republic, exemplified in *Louis MacNeice: Sceptical Vision* (1975), *Ireland: A Social and Cultural History* (1981, 1985), and his essays *Ireland's Literature* (1988). His 'critical biography' of W. B. YEATS (1999) studies Yeats's literary, historical, and social contexts. **Richard Pine**

Brown, Admiral William (1777–1857), seaman. Born in Foxford, Co. Mayo, probably the illegitimate son of a local official with noble connections, through whom he was put into the British navy. After his period in the navy he became a merchant seaman and, in time, master of his own ship. When rumours came to Europe about the alleged millions to be made in Buenos Aires, recently captured by the British, he sailed there in command of a cargo ship, prospered, and became the owner of a number of cargo ships trading in the River Plate (Rio de la Plata). The Spanish authorities at Montevideo, at the mouth of the Plate, still claiming control of Buenos Aires, from which the British had been expelled by a popular revolt, interfered with his ships; and when the people of Buenos Aires rebelled against Spain, in the name of the whole population of what is now Argentina, he agreed to improvise and lead a fleet to ensure the expulsion of Spanish forces from the region. Great victories revealed in Brown a naval genius who remains to this day the hero-founder of the Argentine Republic, for which he later won a naval war against Brazil. **John de Courcy Ireland**

Browne, Frances (1816–1879), writer. Born in Stranorlar, Co. Donegal; blinded from smallpox when eighteen months old,

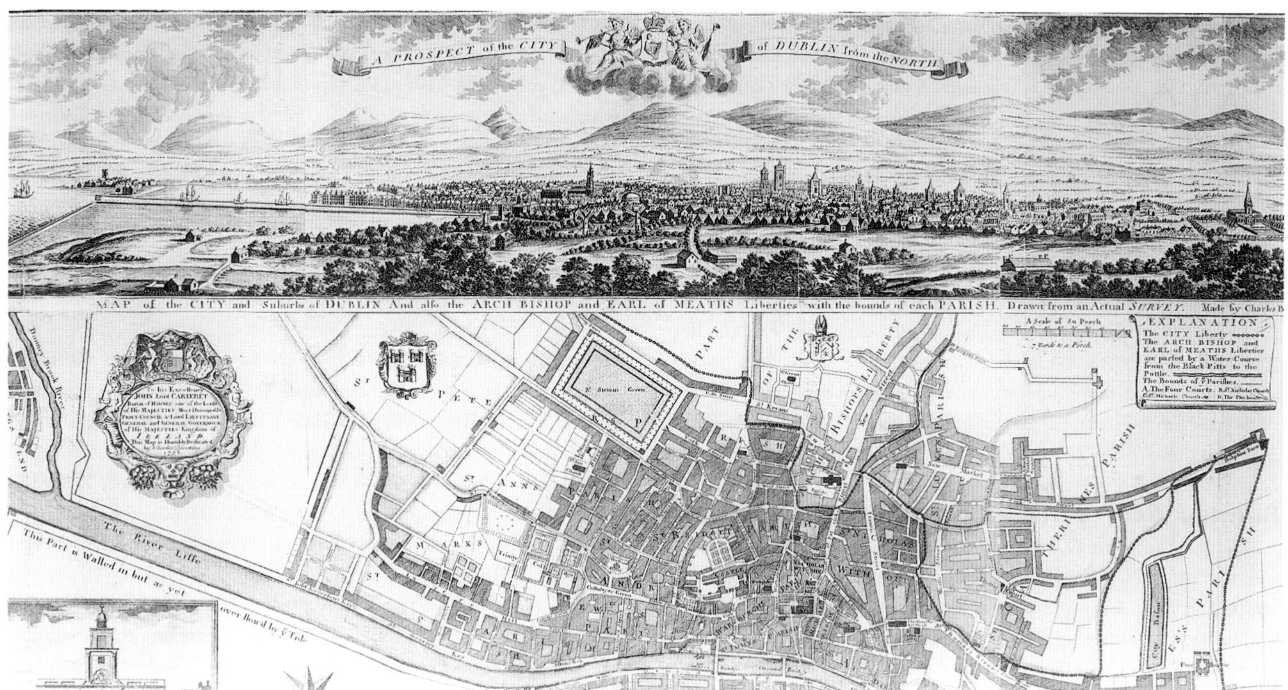

Brooking. *Charles Brooking's* Prospect of Dublin *(1728), showing the city from the north, with (left to right) Ringsend, Sir John Rogerson's Quay, the Trinity College Campanile, the Tholsel, St Patrick's Cathedral, St Werburgh's, Christ Church Cathedral, St John's (Thomas Street), and the Royal Hospital, Kilmainham. [National Gallery of Ireland]*

she educated herself by listening to other children recite their lessons. She moved to Edinburgh and London, where she made her living from her novels, poetry, and children's books. Her best-remembered work is *Granny's Wonderful Chair and its Tales of Fairy Times* (1856); a fairy-tale, it is peopled with such characters as Dame Frostyface, Buttertongue, Queen Wantall, and Fairyfoot. She also wrote 'improving' tales: *The Ericksons* (1852), *The Foundling of the Fens* (1852), and *The Clever Boy, or Consider Another* (1886). **Patricia Donlon**

Browne, Francis (Frank) (1880–1960), Jesuit priest and photographer. Born in Cork. He took up to 42,000 black-and-white photographs over his lifetime, providing an image of Ireland from the 1920s to the 1950s (see pp. 743, 929). He is best known for his pictures of the TITANIC on its maiden voyage from Southampton to New York in 1912. He disembarked at Cobh before the Atlantic crossing, and his images were printed all over the world following the loss of the vessel. He took many photographs of life during the FIRST WORLD WAR while serving as chaplain to the Irish Guards. He later travelled to Australia, documenting his travels as he went, and continued his passion for photography on his return to Ireland. He was also involved in the Salon movement to promote photography as an art form. His photographic archive was rediscovered in 1985, and more than a dozen collections of his work have been published by the Jesuit E. E. O'Donnell (their discoverer), including *Father Browne's Ireland* (1988) and *Father Browne's Titanic Album* (1997). [see PHOTOGRAPHY.] **Martin Clancy**

Browne (or de Browne), Count George (1698–1792), Russian general. Born in Camas, Co. Limerick, an uncle of Field-Marshal MAXIMILIAN ULYSSES BROWN; educated at Limerick Diocesan School. He left Ireland to soldier in the Palatinate and in Russia in 1730, where he served as a major under Peter de Lacy, whose daughter he married. He fought with valour in the Polish, French, and Turkish wars; during the last he was taken prisoner yet obtained state secrets, which earned him a major-generalship on his return to Russia. He rose to the rank of field-marshal and was later governor of Livonia (Latvia and Estonia), where he ruled until his death. **David Kiely**

Browne, Maximilian Ulysses, Count (1706–1757), Austrian general. Born in Basel, son of an exiled Irish JACOBITE officer in the emperor's service and nephew of the mercenary GEORGE BROWNE. He rose through the ranks of the Austrian army and in 1739 was made field-marshal by Charles VI. He led the Austrians against the Turks, French, and Prussians. The Archduchess Maria Theresa appointed him one of her privy councillors, and in 1752 he assumed supreme command of the armed forces. He had a distinguished military career, which ended when he received a mortal wound at the Battle of Prague. **David Kiely**

Browne, Nöel Christopher (1915–1997), physician and politician. Born in Waterford; educated at Beaumont College, London, and TCD. Browne, whose comfortable family background was ravaged by tuberculosis, was informally adopted by a wealthy Dublin family following the death of his parents and qualified as a doctor in 1940. In 1948 he was elected a TD for the new CLANN NA POBLACHTA and became Minister for Health on his first day in Dáil Éireann. Between then and his forced resignation in 1951, when the medical profession and the Catholic bishops opposed his plans for a free MOTHER-AND-CHILD medical service, he achieved a reputation as a forceful and visionary—if individualistic and unpredictable—minister, with a dedication to public health that was in advance of its time. He remained in active politics, with some breaks, until 1982, in five different parties (CLANN NA POBLACHTA, FIANNA FÁIL, National Progressive Democrats, LABOUR PARTY, and the Socialist Labour Party) and as an independent, but never again held office. Despite frequent changes of position—sometimes anti-communist, sometimes pro-Soviet—he became a lodestar for many on the left for whom the Labour Party (to which he belonged from 1963 to 1977) was an often unsatisfactory champion. **John Horgan**

Browne, Nöel. *Nöel Browne, physician and Minister for Health, 1948–51, who clashed with conservative elements in the Catholic Church and the medical profession over the Mother and Child Scheme. [Eamonn Farrell/Photocall Ireland]*

Browne, Peter (1664–1735), philosopher and theologian. Born in Co. Dublin; educated at TCD. He was appointed Anglican Bishop of Cork and Ross, 1709. His 'representationalism' was intended as an answer to TOLAND's pantheism: for Browne, what we know of God is not God *per se* but certain representations of him. The theological point was closely connected with Browne's radical empiricism: all our thoughts are derived from sensations, he argued, and so the mind can have no innate ideas (about, for example, God). His most important philosophical critic was BERKELEY; his so-called sensationalism influenced the aesthetic theory of BURKE. **Ian Leask**

Browne, Vincent (1944–), journalist and publisher. Born in Broadford, Co. Limerick; educated at UCD. He was already a respected journalist when he founded MAGILL in 1977. It was the livliest and most trenchant journal of the 1980s, with a stable of outstanding writers. He was editor of the *Sunday Tribune*, 1983–93, has written a weekly column for the IRISH TIMES since 1994, and has been a broadcaster since 1996 with RTÉ. He was called to the bar in 1997. In October 2001 he received an apology from the TAOISEACH, BERTIE AHERN, for improper state interference in his affairs in 1975 when the Special Detective Unit tapped his phone. Browne's published work includes *The Magill Book of Irish Politics* (1981). **Ciarán Deane**

Browne's Hill, Co. Carlow, a spectacular PORTAL TOMB in the townland of Kernanstown, famed for its massive granite roof-stone measuring some 6 m by 4.6 m (20 by 15 ft) and 2 m ($6\frac{1}{2}$ ft) thick. Reputed to weigh about 100 tonnes, it is supported by three upright blocks, averaging 1.9 m ($6\frac{1}{4}$ ft) high, at the front or eastern end, with a fourth standing beside them. **Paul Walsh**

Bruce, Robert (1274–1329), Earl of Carrick and King of the Scots as Robert I (1306–29). He was a grandson of Robert Bruce, competitor for the Scottish throne in 1291, and son of Robert Bruce and Marjory of Carrick. He first married Isabella of Mar (died 1296) and then Elizabeth de Burgh, daughter of the Red Earl of Ulster, in 1302, who produced his heir, David II, in 1324. Bruce was crowned at Scone in March 1306; after initial defeats that resulted in his probable refuge on RATHLIN ISLAND during the winter of 1306/7 he managed to secure his own position and independence for Scotland with his decisive victory at Bannockburn on 24 June 1314. In 1317 he led an army in support of his brother Edward's invasion of Ireland, marching as far as Castleknock, Co. Dublin, but failing to take Dublin. Scottish independence was finally recognised by England in the Treaty of Northampton (1328). Bruce died on 7 June 1329 at Cardross, Dunbartonshire, possibly of leprosy. His body is buried in Dunfermline; his heart is reputed to lie in Melrose Abbey. [see BRUCE INVASION.] **Susan Foran**

Bruce invasion. In May 1315 a Scottish invasion fleet landed in Co. Antrim, led by Edward Bruce, younger brother of ROBERT BRUCE, King of the Scots; a large, well-planned expedition, it lasted over three years. Edward Bruce called himself 'King of Ireland'; he was supported by some Irish kings, principally Dónall Ó Néill of Tír Eoghain. He set up his own administration to replace that of the English colony in Dublin, and sought to bring English rule in Ireland to an end. The invaders' aims were to exploit Irish unrest in forcing the weak English king, Edward II, to concede Robert's claim to Scotland, to create a diversion by opening up a second front, and to cripple Ireland as a source of supply to the English. It is not true that Robert simply sought to rid himself of a troublesome sibling: the brothers were close, and Robert spent the winter of 1316/17 in Ireland assisting Edward in what they hoped would be a permanent conquest.

The invasion failed, partly because it coincided with one of the worst FAMINES to afflict medieval Europe. Also, though the Bruces had Irish support and uprisings broke out all over the country, political divisions in Ireland meant that support was limited to those who acknowledged Dónall Ó Néill's supremacy. Some of the ANGLO-NORMAN colonists also joined the Scots, but most stayed loyal and suffered several defeats in battles against the Scots until an army of Anglo-Norman colonists killed Edward himself in the BATTLE OF FAUGHART, near Dundalk, on 14 October 1318, bringing the Scottish kingdom of Ireland to an end. The destruction wreaked by the invasion meant that the area of Ireland under the effective control of the Dublin government shrank, while the O'Neills re-emerged as the dominant force in Ulster. **Seán Duffy**

Brück, Hermann Alexander (1905–2000), astronomer. Born in Berlin; educated at Kiel, Bonn, and Munich. He worked at the Einstein Institute in Potsdam until Nazi aggression forced him to flee to the Vatican Observatory at Castel Gandolfo. On Eddington's invitation he moved to Cambridge, where he spent the war years. In 1947 ÉAMON DE VALERA invited him to Dublin as director of DUNSINK OBSERVATORY (which had been assimilated into the DUBLIN INSTITUTE FOR ADVANCED STUDIES). His research at Dunsink was concerned mainly with solar spectroscopy and stellar photometry. He was largely responsible for organising the ninth general assembly of the International Astronomical Union in Dublin in 1955. In 1957 he went to Edinburgh to become Astronomer Royal for Scotland and to direct the Royal Observatory. A member of the Pontifical Academy of Sciences, he was made a Knight Grand Cross of St Gregory the Great in 1995. **Ian Elliott**

Brugha, Cathal (1874–1922), revolutionary. Born Charles Burgess in Dublin; educated at Belvedere College, and worked as a chandler. He joined the GAELIC LEAGUE in 1899 and the IRISH VOLUNTEERS in 1913. He was severely wounded in 1916, was chief of staff of the IRA, 1917–19, Minister for Defence, 1919–22, and acting president, January 1919. As MP (1918) and subsequently TD for Waterford, 1919–22, he voted against the Treaty. Legendary for his republican intransigence and physical bravery, he was killed in Dublin fighting a rearguard action. **Tom Garvin**

Brú na Bóinne: see BOYNE VALLEY.

Brünnow, Franz Friedrich Ernst (1821–1891), astronomer. Born in Berlin; educated at Berlin University under Encke. He was present in Berlin Observatory when Neptune was discovered. Later, as director of Bilk Observatory near Düsseldorf, he published a textbook on spherical astronomy, which was widely used. In 1854 he became director of the new observatory at Ann Arbor, Michigan, where he commissioned a meridian telescope by Pistor and Martins and introduced German methods and rigour to the American curriculum. In 1865 he was appointed director of DUNSINK OBSERVATORY, where he reorganised the observational work by installing the James South 12-in. refractor and another Pistor and Martins meridian telescope. His research on stellar parallax was meticulous. **Ian Elliott**

Bruton, John (1947–), politician. Born in Dublin; educated at UCD and King's Inns. In 1969 he was elected to DÁIL ÉIREANN for FINE GAEL as TD for Meath; he was parliamentary secretary to several ministers, 1973–7, Minister for Finance, 1981–2, in a Government defeated by a Dáil vote against his budget. In 1986 he returned to

Browne's Hill. *Frontal view of the Browne's Hill portal tomb (2500 BC), Co. Carlow, which supports the largest capstone of any megalithic monument in Ireland. [Dúchas, The Heritage Service]*

the post of Minister for Finance, but his Government left office in 1987. Defeated for the leadership of Fine Gael by Alan Dukes in 1987, he replaced him as leader in 1990. The party lost ten seats in 1992, but Bruton survived, and with the disintegration of the coalition of FANNA FÁIL and the LABOUR PARTY in 1994 he formed what became known as the 'Rainbow' coalition of Fine Gael, the Labour Party, and DEMOCRATIC LEFT. His period in office was successful although there was a decline in party support; ECONOMIC GROWTH continued, the prohibition on DIVORCE was abolished, and relations with Britain continued to improve, to the extent that IRA supporters accused him of being pro-British. IRA murders did not destabilise his Government, however, nor did his stance against ORANGE ORDER marches in DRUMCREE. This Government was replaced after an election in 1997 by an alliance of Fianna Fáil and the PROGRESSIVE DEMOCRATS; Bruton was replaced as leader of Fine Gael by Michael Noonan in 2001. **Tom Garvin**

B Specials: see A, B, C SPECIALS.

Buchanan Report (1968). Colin Buchanan and Partners, the English architects and town planners, were commissioned by the United Nations on behalf of the Government of Ireland in 1966 to undertake studies of the nine PLANNING REGIONS in the Republic and to provide physical development policies for these regions. The consultants' final report, *Regional Studies in Ireland*, and the two accompanying technical volumes, *Regional Development in Ireland*, were published in 1968. Together these reports constitute one of the most comprehensive studies of Irish regions, covering a wide range of topics, such as POPULATION and population forecasts, EMPLOYMENT and employment forecasts, MIGRATION and migration forecasts, INDUSTRY, TOURISM, AGRICULTURE, TRANSPORT, utilities, power, HOUSING, and INFRASTRUCTURE. However, the report is most widely known for its policy recommendations and particularly the proposed policy of promoting growth centres. This concept derives from the assumption that growth will be self-sustaining only in centres above a critical size. If, through the promotion of growth in selected centres, these centres reach this critical size they will grow in a self-sustaining way. The Buchanan Report identified Dublin, Cork and Limerick-Shannon as main centres and Waterford, Dundalk, Drogheda, Galway, Sligo, and Athlone as part of a second tier of growth centres. Controversially, priority was to be given exclusively to these centres, with the possibility of some support for the development of a number of smaller centres. The subsequent debate about this policy was extensive, and the Government finally decided on a policy of more dispersed development in 1972. [see NEW TOWNS.] **Edgar Morgenroth**

Buck. Portrait of a Lady with an Artist's Portfolio *(1803) by Adam Buck. Portraitist and miniaturist, he was a master of delicate and decorative small neo-classical full-length portraits. [National Gallery of Ireland]*

Bucholz McEvoy, architects, Dublin, established 1996. Merritt Bucholz was born in 1966 in Chicago; educated at Cornell and Princeton Universities; worked with Emilio Ambasz in New York and Michel Kagan in Paris, and taught at DIT and UCD. Karen McEvoy was born in 1962 in Dublin; educated at UCD; worked with Michael Graves in New York, and teaches at the DIT. They won first prize for Fingal County Hall, Swords, Co. Dublin (1996), with a curving glass screen (engineered by RFR of Paris) to a tall public atrium. They designed the welcoming pavilions at Government Buildings, Dublin; and County Hall, Limerick (1999–2003). **Raymund Ryan**

Buck, Adam (1759–1833) and Frederick Buck (1771–c. 1840), portraitists, miniaturists. Born in Cork, sons of a silversmith; while Adam was apparently self-taught, Frederick attended the DUBLIN SOCIETY Schools, enrolling in 1783. Frederick practised primarily as a miniaturist in Cork, executing numerous portraits of military figures. Adam produced neo-classical portraits in watercolours and as miniatures. His sitters included the Edgeworth and Sawyer families. Adam moved to London in 1795, remaining until his death. He exhibited at the Parliament House in Dublin in 1802 and at the Royal Academy from 1795 to 1833; in 1811 he published *Paintings on Greek Vases*, which he illustrated and engraved himself. **Brendan Rooney**

Buckingham Palace Conference (1914), a conference called in response to the crisis over the third HOME RULE Bill. In July 1914 George V dramatically called a round-table conference at Buckingham Palace as part of an attempt to defuse the crisis over the third Home Rule Bill. Sir EDWARD CARSON and ANDREW BONAR LAW represented Irish and British UNIONISM; JOHN REDMOND and Herbert Asquith, the Prime Minister, represented Irish nationalism and British liberalism, respectively. The conference broke up after three days, the parties being unable to agree whether or how Ireland should be partitioned. **Thomas Hennessey**

Buckley, John (1951–), composer. Born at Templeglentan, Co. Limerick, he studied flute with Doris Keogh and composition with JAMES WILSON at the RIAM and later with Alun Hoddinott. He has represented Ireland at the International Rostrum of Composers on five occasions and at the 1990 Prix d'Italia. Awards include the Varming Prize (1976) and the Marten Toonder Award (1991). He is a member of AOSDÁNA. In addition to works for solo instruments, chamber ensembles, choirs, bands and orchestra he is also a successful film composer (*The Woman Who Married Clark Gable*). His opera *The Words Upon the Window-Pane* commissioned by OPERA THEATRE COMPANY was premiered at the 1991 DUBLIN THEATRE FESTIVAL. **David Mooney**

Buffoonery: see CROSÁNTACHT.

'Buile Shuibhne' ('Suibhne's frenzy'), one of the best-known medieval Irish tales. Composed probably in the twelfth or thirteenth century, it combines a prose account of Suibhne's adventures with his verse reflections on his surroundings and condition. Cursed by St Rónán for desecrating a sacred book, Suibhne wanders Ireland as a feathered madman until he is healed by St Moling, who writes down his poems. The tale is of particular interest in its treatment of conflicts between PAGANISM and CHRISTIANITY and between orality and literacy. It has been reworked by, among others, FLANN O'BRIEN in AT SWIM-TWO-BIRDS (1939) and SEAMUS HEANEY in *Sweeney Astray* (1983). **Philip O'Leary**

Bulfin, Michael (1939–), sculptor. Born in Birr, Co. Offaly; educated at UCD and Yale. He first showed in Dublin at the IRISH EXHIBITION OF LIVING ART, 1966, and Project Arts Centre, and at the OIREACHTAS, 1969. He won the Adjudicators' Special Award, Living Art Exhibition, 1969. Solo exhibitions have been held at the Project in 1970 and 1974, and he is a former chairman. He represented Ireland at the Paris Biennale in 1971 and was awarded an ARTS COUNCIL bursary in 1977. His painted steel sculpture *Reflections* (1975) is at the Bank of Ireland offices in Baggot Street, Dublin, and he has also used coloured Perspex for smaller work. He is a member of AOSDÁNA and was chairman of the Sculptors' Society of Ireland, 1983–91. He was an invited guest at the Skulptur Biennale, Copenhagen, in 1990. **Theo Snoddy**

Bulfin, William (c. 1864–1910), journalist and author. Born at Derrinlough, Co. Offaly. He spent much of his life in Argentina, where he worked on and eventually bought the *Southern Cross*, the newspaper of the Irish community. Visiting Ireland in 1902, he travelled the country, gaining impressions for his writing, returning to Argentina in 1904. He is best known for *Tales of the Pampas* (1900), and his travelogue, *Rambles in Eirinn* (1907). He retired to Ireland in 1909, settling at Derrinlough and becoming active in SINN FÉIN (see p. 43). [see ARGENTINA, THE IRISH IN.] **Peter Costello**

Bull, George Lucien (1876–1972), scientist and inventor. Born in Dublin; educated at the University of Paris. He researched phenomena of natural science and worked as an assistant to Étienne-Jules Marey at his cinematography laboratory in Paris. In 1902 he developed a form of ultra-rapid cinematography, which recorded 500 images per second. In 1908 he invented the electrocardiograph, and made pioneering discoveries in the fields of sound recording and optics. In 1952 he recorded a million images per second. He was an honorary director of the Marey Institute in Paris. **Ciarán Deane**

bullaun stones, boulders with between one and nine human-made concave depressions, widely found at old monastic sites (such as Glendalough). They are taken by some to have acted as mortars for grinding corn or ore; others believe they held water for blessing and curing. **Peter Harbison**

Bullock, Shan F. (1865–1935), civil servant and writer. Born in Crom, Co. Fermanagh; educated at Farra School, Co. Westmeath. He subsequently moved to London. His works include *By Thrasna River* (1895), *Irish Pastorals* (1901), *The Squireen* (1903), *The Red Leaguers* (1904), *Dan the Dollar* (1906), *Thomas Andrews, Shipbuilder* (1912), *Mors et Vita* (1923), *The Loughsiders* (1924), *Gleanings* (c. 1925), and his autobiography, *After Sixty Years* (1931). Bullock's plots sometimes strain towards the implausible; however, his characters excel in raillery, or what is called locally 'sconsing'. His poetry, as he modestly avowed, 'has no pretensions.' *Mors et Vita* is distinguished by its plangent melancholy. **Tess Maginess**

Bull Walls. The North and South Bull Walls are the arms that enclose the shipping channel in Dublin Bay. The name is taken from large sand bars on either side of the entrance to the River LIFFEY, traditionally named as the North and South Bulls. Poolbeg Lighthouse was completed in 1767, the South Bull Wall which connects the Poolbeg to the southern shore in 1796, and the North Bull Wall which enclosed the bay from the suburb of Clontarf (*Cluain Tarbh*, the meadow of the bull) in 1825. The latter caused the formation of the NORTH BULL ISLAND. The walls have provided effective scouring and deepening of the approach channel to DUBLIN PORT. **Ronald Cox**

Bunbury, Selina (1802–1882), writer. Born in Kilsaran, Co. Louth, daughter of the Church of Ireland rector, but moved to Dublin when she was fifteen, and worked as a teacher. As was the fashion of the time, her early books were published anonymously. She wrote travel books, novels, and many children's books. Many of her works are pious books, clearly intended for the instruction and edification of their young readers. The titles tell it all: *The Triumph of Truth, or Henry and His Sister* (1847), *Glory, Glory, Glory: A Story for Little Children* (1855), *Little Dora Playfair, or 'I won't go to school'*, and *The Indian Babes in the Wood*. **Patricia Donlon**

Bunratty Castle, Co. Clare, a TOWER-HOUSE classified as a larger CASTLE of the late Middle Ages, because of its size; other examples include BLARNEY CASTLE, Co. Cork and DUNSOGHLY CASTLE, Co. Dublin. It is basically a rectangular tower-house with a projecting square tower at each angle and is three storeys high. The original castle was built in 1425 by Maccon Mac Conmara but the present structure is mainly of the late fifteenth century and can be attributed to the O'Briens, Earls of Thomond. Some fine seventeenth-century stucco work can still be seen. **David Sweetman**

Bunting, Edward (1773–1843), music collector. Born in Co. Armagh. He was a church organist who, at the age of nineteen, acted as music scribe at the BELFAST HARP FESTIVAL of 1792. He continued to collect traditional music, and especially harp music, throughout his life, either personally or through agents and correspondents. As a professional musician he worked in various churches in Belfast and subsequently in Dublin, where he moved after his marriage in 1819. He was also well known as a pianist and a teacher and was involved also in music publishing and instrument sales. He published three volumes of Irish music, arranged for piano: *A General Collection of the Ancient Irish Music* (1796), *A General Collection of the Ancient Music of Ireland* (1809), and *The Ancient Music Ireland* (1840). After his death his manuscripts and papers disappeared until they were accidentally rediscovered by Charlotte Milligan Fox, secretary of the Irish Folk Song Society, in 1907. The Bunting Collection is now in the library of Queen's University, Belfast, and is a rich source of music, texts, and lore from the eighteenth and nineteenth centuries. [see SONG COLLECTORS; TRADITIONAL MUSIC COLLECTION.] **Colette Moloney**

Burdett, Sir Francis (1770–1844), English MP and radical. His Catholic Relief Bill (1825), drafted with the assistance of DANIEL O'CONNELL, featured two 'wings' to help it fly smoothly through Parliament: the disfranchisement of 'FORTY-SHILLING FREEHOLDERS' and state salaries for Catholic clergy. The House of Lords rejected the bill after it was passed by the House of Commons. **Gary Owens**

Burgh, Thomas (1670–1730), architect and military engineer. Educated at TCD. His early career was in the British army; he served in Ireland during the WILLIAMITE WARS and subsequently in campaigns on the Continent. In 1697 he became third engineer in the Irish establishment under Sir WILLIAM ROBINSON, Surveyor-General, whom he succeeded in 1700. In Dublin he continued Robinson's works at DUBLIN CASTLE and the ROYAL HOSPITAL, in addition to designing the Royal Barracks (Collins Barracks) (1701), Trinity College Library (1709) (see p. 39), St Werburgh's Church (1715)—and probably also St Anne's Church, Dawson Street (1720)—DR STEEVENS' HOSPITAL (1718), and the Linen Hall (1722, demolished). In 1713 he was elected member of Parliament for Naas, Co. Kildare, where he began building a country house, of which only the pavilions were ever constructed. In 1728 he competed unsuccessfully with the young EDWARD LOVETT PEARCE for the design of the new PARLIAMENT HOUSE in College Green, Dublin. Pearce, a more radical architect, succeeded him in office (see p. 39). **Frederick O'Dwyer**

Burgoyne, John Fox (1782–1871), military engineer and civil administrator. Born in London; educated at Woolwich Academy. He was chairman of the Board of Public Works in Ireland, 1831–45, and founder-president of the Institution of Civil Engineers of Ireland, 1835–44. He had a long and distinguished military career, attaining the rank of field-marshal. **Ronald Cox**

Burke, Edmund (1729–1797), philosopher and politician (see p. 60). Born at 12 Arran Quay, Dublin, to a Catholic mother and a Protestant father who was an attorney at the Court of Exchequer; educated at ABRAHAM SHACKLETON's Quaker school in Ballintore, Co. Kildare, and at TCD, 1743–8; he also received an honorary degree in December 1790. In April 1747 he enrolled in the Middle Temple, London, though he may not have moved to London until 1750. His introduction to letters was *A Vindication of Natural Society* (1756), which satirised Lord Bolingbroke's freethinking. He followed this with *A Philosophical Enquiry into the Origin of Our Ideas of the Sublime and Beautiful* (1757), an influential work that built on the empirical epistemology of John Locke to provide a theory of aesthetic response. Burke frequented Samuel Johnson's social circle and appears briefly in Boswell's *Life of Johnson* (1791). In 1758 he began an association with the *Annual Register*, acting as both editor and active contributor. He returned to Ireland briefly in 1761 as private secretary to William Gerard Hamilton, Chief Secretary in a pro-Catholic relief administration headed by Lord Halifax. In 1764 he broke with Hamilton, with some acrimony.

His election to Parliament in 1765 and his first speech in 1766, concerning the Stamp Act, led to his being associated with American colonial grievances and in 1771 to his appointment as an agent in England for the colony of New York. *Thoughts on the Causes of the Present Discontents* (1770) was a stringent critique of the court interest in Parliament. In 1773 he visited France, and in 1774 he moved his political base to the popular seat of Bristol. During the election campaign he theorised on the nature of parliamentary representation, arguing that the representative owed his constituents his free judgment and was not constrained by their demands.

He supported the American revolutionaries in a series of parliamentary interventions, published as *Speech on American Taxation* (1775) and *Conciliation with America* (1775). He argued that it was impracticable to enforce taxation on a colony so distant from the motherland and impolitic to refuse the liberties granted to British subjects to their colonial offspring. He also refused to support trade restrictions between Ireland and England, later arguing for FREE TRADE in *Thoughts and Details on Scarcity* (written 1795, published 1800). His opposition to Bristol's trading community in this matter led to his defeat at the polls in the spring of 1780. He returned to Parliament in December 1780 as member for the Marquis of Rockingham's pocket borough of Malton, Yorkshire, acting as Paymaster-General of the Forces under Rockingham as First Lord of the Treasury. Following Rockingham's death in July 1782 he resigned his post. He never gained a seat in the Cabinet. The general election of March 1784 saw the defeat of his political allies, though Burke retained his seat; in the same year he was made Lord Rector of the University of Glasgow. In 1786 he proposed the removal from office of Warren Hastings, Governor-General of Bengal, for his tyrannical treatment of the people. The case rumbled on until 3 April 1787, when Hastings was impeached; a trial followed in 1788. During the Regency Crisis of 1788 Burke sided with the opposition, led by Charles James Fox, though George III's remission in February 1789 dashed hopes of a return to office.

On 9 February 1790 he began his campaign against the FRENCH REVOLUTION with a speech in the House of Commons. On 6 May 1791 he dramatically split with Fox over the implications of the revolution, siding with WILLIAM PITT. His campaign was waged primarily outside Parliament, however, in a series of publications against French radicalism, notably REFLECTIONS ON THE REVOLUTION IN FRANCE (1790) and *Letters on a Regicide Peace* (1796). His anxieties about the situation in Ireland were articulated in his *Letter to Sir Henry Langrishe* (1792), and in the early 1790s he campaigned for Catholic relief, lambasting the Irish Ascendancy establishment for their recalcitrance and welcoming the extension of the franchise to Catholics in 1793. He resigned from Parliament in July 1794, being succeeded in his seat at Malton by his son, Richard, who died on 2 August 1794, leaving his father distraught. In April 1795 there was a further blow when Warren Hastings was acquitted.

Burke died on 9 July 1797 at his estate of Beaconsfield in Buckinghamshire, which he had bought in 1768. His writings were to be influential in the reformulation of Tory politics in the crisis of the 1790s, while he himself remained committed to Whig values. He has been read variously as an empiricist, a natural law theorist, a utilitarian, a constitutional theorist, and a Conservative, an array of views indicative of the polemical purpose of much of his writing. His legacy has been dominated, however, by his thoughts on France, with their rejection of ideological politics and *a priori* speculation in favour of a traditionalism grounded on the drawing of analogies from past experience to present circumstance. **Michael Brown**

Burke as social theorist. Combining hard-headed 'realism', an almost Romantic stress on community and an unprecedented appreciation of the role of history, Edmund Burke stands out as one of the most original of all Anglophone social theorists. Much of his specifically political thought was based on and informed by a deep suspicion of abstract principle: for Burke, the pernicious effects of such thinking stretched far beyond academic debate and could infect the body politic itself. Thus, against the indeterminate universalism of so-called natural rights he stressed the primacy of tradition; and against revolutionary upheaval in the name of freedom he urged the organic continuity of 'proven' practice. According to this provocative but never unthinking conservatism, political discourse had to be located in its wider practical context: principles that were not immanent and socially embedded were thoroughly dangerous; meanwhile, custom, and even prejudice, were positive factors in shaping collective identity. In general, Burke stressed that society should be understood as historical and developmental; that disembodied, transcendental concepts were hopelessly one-dimensional and failed to account for wider 'sentiments'; and that shared institutions provided stability and a sedimented wisdom without which barbarism could easily flourish. Unsurprisingly, his thought has attracted continuous critical attention, from Lessing to Lyotard and beyond. **Ian Leask**

Burke, Joe (1939–), traditional musician. Born in Loughrea, Co. Galway. An outstanding ACCORDION stylist, his B/C method was learnt from PADDY O'BRIEN, Kevin Keegan, and JOE COOLEY. An all-Ireland champion in 1959 and 1960, he was one of the first professional traditional musicians of modern times. **Fintan Vallely**

Burke, John (1946–), sculptor. Born in Clonmel, Co. Tipperary; studied at the Crawford School of Art, Cork. Awarded a McCauley Fellowship in 1970, Burke moved to London, where he studied sculpture at the Royal College of Art under Brian Kneale. His first exhibition, at Jury's Hotel, Cork, in 1973, included abstract welded and painted steel sculptures, that showed the influence of Phillip King and Anthony Caro. In 1976 he exhibited in New York and since then has had a number of one-man shows in Ireland and abroad. A well-known work in painted steel, *Red Cardinal* (1978), stands outside the head office of the Bank of Ireland in Baggot Street, Dublin. He is a member of AOSDÁNA. **Peter Murray**

Burke, Sir John Bernard (1814–1892), barrister and genealogist. Born in London, a son of JOHN EDWARD BURKE; educated in England and at the University of Caen. He succeeded Sir WILLIAM BETHAM as Ulster King of Arms in 1853 and continued with the latter's work on the classification of records; he also continued the work of his father on *Burke's Peerage* and produced a new edition every year between 1847 and his death. Among his other works were *A General Armory of England, Scotland, Ireland and Wales* (1842) and *A Genealogical and Heraldic History of the Colonial Gentry* (1891). The *General Armory* is a useful work but has to be read with caution: Burke ascribes the same coat of arms to different families of the same name; many are not described correctly, and some are without authority of any kind, for example the arms ascribed to different O'Neills of Ulster. Burke was Keeper of the State Papers from 1855 onwards; he was also a governor of the NATIONAL GALLERY OF IRELAND. He was knighted in 1854. [see FAMILY HISTORY; GENEALOGY; HERALDRY.] **Fergus Gillespie**

Burke, John Edward (1787–1848), genealogist and archivist. Born in Co. Tipperary. In 1826 he published *A Genealogical and Heraldic Dictionary of the Peerage and Baronetage of the United Kingdom* (commonly known as *Burke's Peerage*); by the time of his death nine

Burke, Edmund. *Edmund Burke, statesman, writer and philosopher and one of the foremost political thinkers of the eighteenth century, in an engraving by John Jones (1790) after a portrait by George Romney (1776). [Irish Picture Library]*

editions had been published. This work superseded John Lodge's *Peerage of Ireland* (1754), revised by Mervyn Archdall (1785). Among his other works were *A Genealogical History of the Commoners of Great Britain and Ireland*, whose title in later editions became *A Genealogical and Heraldic Dictionary of the Landed Gentry*. Editions for Ireland in the twentieth century were entitled *A Genealogical and Heraldic Dictionary of the Landed Gentry of Ireland* (such as those of 1912 and 1958) and *Burke's Irish Family Records* (1974). [see FAMILY HISTORY; GENEALOGY.] **Fergus Gillespie**

Burke, Robert O'Hara (1820–1861), explorer. Born in Craughwell, Co. Galway, to a well-known family with a British army background. His early career was inauspicious; he enrolled in Woolwich Military Academy but in 1840 was asked to leave, and his subsequent experience as a soldier in the Imperial Austrian army met with no better success. Forced to retire, he returned to Ireland and joined the Constabulary in 1849. Three years later he decided to emigrate to AUSTRALIA, where he secured a position in the Victoria police as a district inspector.

In 1860 he was appointed leader of the Great Northern Exploration Expedition, to explore Australia's interior and to find the continent's northern limits. The journey proceeded rapidly until the party reached Cooper's Creek on 11 November 1860. Here Burke decided to leave a depot with most of the expedition's men and supplies and make a dash for the coast, 800 km (500 miles)

Burke, Robert O'Hara. *Bronze memorial statue of Robert O'Hara Burke and William John Wills in City Square, Melbourne. Charles Summers was commissioned to produce the memorial in 1864, the first and the largest bronze casting undertaken in Australia. Burke led the first successful crossing of the Australian continent from south to north. [William Henry]*

to the north. Together with his deputy, William Wills, and his subordinates Charles Gray and John King (another Irishman), he reached the mangrove swamps on the Gulf of Carpentaria on 11 February 1861. On their return Grey died on 17 April 1861; when the three survivors reached Cooper's Creek on 22 they found that the camp had been abandoned that very day. Wills asked his companions to leave him to die; his last poignant note read: 'Nothing now but the greatest good luck can save us; and as for myself, I may live four or five days if the weather continues warm.' Burke and King struggled on. King was to be the only survivor of the four, being rescued and kept alive by aboriginals, while Burke died of starvation on 28 June 1861, within reach of salvation. If the support members of the expedition had stayed one day longer at Cooper's Creek, or if the rescue party had seen Burke's note left at camp number 65, they could have survived.

Burke has been criticised for his lack of experience and his impulsive judgments, in particular the decision to divide the party at Cooper's Creek. He has been described as 'a quick tempered, impulsive, dare-devil sort of Irishman, of untidy appearance, who tended to drop saliva over his beard.' But there was no doubt about his courage, and elements of his story have assumed the poignancy of legend: the bitter disappointment of finding the abandoned camp, and the struggle towards a lonely death. Sir John Longstaff's painting *The Arrival of Burke, Wills and King at the Deserted Camp* (1907), now in the National Gallery of Victoria, is an Australian icon, while Burke and Wills's bronze memorial in Melbourne has become a national monument. Burke was posthumously awarded the Founder's Medal of the Royal Geographical Society. His death, together with that of his companions, cannot diminish the huge achievement of the expedition he led—the first successful crossing of the Australian continent from south to north. **Peter Somerville-Large**

Burke, Ulick, first Marquis of Clanricarde (1604–1657), politician and soldier. Born in Co. Galway, son of an established family of ANGLO-NORMAN descent. He spent most of his life as a Catholic courtier in England; as a consequence he was able to thwart the attempt of WENTWORTH to claim his lands for the Crown in 1635. A committed royalist, he did not join his relatives in the Confederate rebellion; but their involvement and his close links with James Butler, first Duke of Ormond, made him a valuable facilitator in the lengthy and difficult negotiations with the king after the truce of 1643. He was made royalist military commander in Connacht in 1645, but a lack of resources prevented him from taking any effective action. He became Lord Deputy on Ormond's departure from Ireland in 1650 and fought valiantly against the Cromwellian reconquest up to his final surrender in 1652. He was treated with surprising leniency by the COMMONWEALTH, being allowed to keep his estates. His letter-books are an important source for the Confederate war. **Liam Irwin**

Burke and Hare, William Burke (1792–1829) and William Hare (fl. 1828), murderers. Born in Urney, Co. Tyrone, into a Catholic labouring family, Burke served in the Donegal militia as musician (which included playing the drum at events such as floggings and executions). He migrated to Scotland in 1818 for navvy work. Only 5 ft 6 in. in height, he was helped by his strength, geniality, industry, and camaraderie. Unusually (despite wife and family in Ulster) he chose as lover a Scots Presbyterian woman, Helen MacDougal, resisting religious and xenophobic pressures to discard her. Literate and multi-talented, he became a cobbler in Edinburgh, lodging with Margaret Hare, an Ulster Catholic who had inherited a flophouse from her late husband, Laird. A tenant died owing Margaret money. Her new husband, William Hare (born in Newry or Derry), was led by Burke to offer the corpse to Robert Knox (1791–1862), anatomist and racial theorist, whose extra-mural classes offered bodies to students. Knox and his associates refused to hear where the corpse came from but paid for it, promising comparable future co-operation. A month later, early in 1828, Hare and Burke, witnessing the slow death of a plague-ridden lodger, smothered him in fear of the public health authorities' intervention to close the lodging-house as pestiferous. Knox bought this and another premature victim for £10. Thenceforward Burke and Hare usually got victims drunk and stifled them, normally without leaving a sign of violence. They killed sixteen in this manner, some of them Irish IMMIGRANTS. Outside term-time Knox paid £8 (preserving bodies in whiskey); in term, he paid £10. One victim, the prostitute Mary Paterson, was recognised by Knox's assistant, William Fergusson (1808–1877), as anatomically familiar; Burke explained that she had drowned in her own vomit. On 1 November 1828 a body was discovered at the house Burke had bought. MacDougal, Burke, and the Hares were arrested. MacDougal (who was almost certainly ignorant of the murders until the last one, which she tried to stop) refused to inform against Burke. The Hares turned king's evidence.

Burke proved much more anxious to exonerate MacDougal than to escape and rejoiced when their trial on Christmas Eve won her a 'not proven' verdict, while he was found guilty. Burke was hanged on 28 January 1829 before an excited audience of 25,000, having first received Catholic sacraments, attended by Catholic and Presbyterian clergy ('I never was a bigot: I should like them all'). His body was dissected at the University of Edinburgh, where his skeleton is its oldest Irish inhabitant. Hare went to England, his wife to Ulster. **Owen Dudley Edwards**

Burncourt Castle, a fortified house at Clogheen, Co. Tipperary. The fortified house evolved towards the end of the sixteenth century. It was usually symmetrical, had no more than three storeys, and contained large windows above the ground floor and high gables with massive, tall lozenge-shaped chimney-stacks. Burncourt, built by Sir Richard Everard in 1641 and burned by Cromwellian forces in 1650, is a fine example, with twenty-six gables with chimney stacks, mullioned and transomed windows, and stone corbels to carry a wooden gallery around the outside wall-tops. The space within the walls was divided by wooden partitions, and there were numerous fireplaces. Such houses mark the end of castle-building in Ireland. **David Sweetman**

burnt mounds, also called *fulachta fia* ('deer roasts'), the most common of Irish prehistoric field monuments, with more than 6,000 examples recorded. They are widely thought to be cooking sites, though alternative explanations have been put forward, including such diverse uses as saunas, metalworking, the cloth-making process, and part of a cremation ritual. RADIOCARBON DATING has shown that they date mostly from the BRONZE AGE, c. 2000–500 BC. Recognisable as low horseshoe-shaped mounds in low-lying wet areas or as patches of blackened soil and burnt stone in ploughed fields, they range in diameter from 7 to 15 m (23 to 50 ft) and are usually 0.5 m ($1\frac{1}{2}$ ft) high, though examples 5 m ($16\frac{1}{2}$ ft) high have been found. Excavated examples consist of a central pit dug into the underlying clay, or a wooden trough built from planking or caulked branches, or occasionally of stones in barren areas. The troughs are usually about 2 m ($6\frac{1}{2}$ ft) long, 1 m (3 ft) wide and 1 m deep. Associated with these are areas of burning, interpreted as HEARTHS, and occasionally post-holes, suggesting transitory structures such as windbreaks or tents. Burnt stone and charcoal were deposited on three sides of the trough, creating the classic horseshoe or kidney shape.

During reconstructions a trough was filled with water and stones heated at the nearby hearth until red-hot. These stones were then cast into the trough and the water brought to the boil. Meat was wrapped in straw and lowered into the water, and more hot stones were added to keep the water boiling. Experiments have shown that by boiling meat in this manner it cooks at twenty minutes to the pound, with twenty minutes extra. The straw wrapping protects the meat from scorching and contamination. After the cooking process is completed and the water has cooled, the stones that filled the trough are extracted. Because of cracking during the firing and then cooling, they are no longer usable and would have been thrown up around the trough on three sides, other than the side closest to the water source. **Victor Buckley**

Burntollet Bridge, Co. Derry, scene of an ambush of a CIVIL RIGHTS march by militant loyalist sympathisers on Saturday 4 January 1969. The four-day march, over a 170 km (105-mile) route from Belfast to Derry, was organised by the student-dominated PEOPLE'S DEMOCRACY and explicitly modelled on Martin Luther King's famous march from Selma to Montgomery, Alabama, in 1965. Its aim was to re-energise the secular, radical spirit that, it was believed, had forced reform on TERENCE O'NEILL's unionist government. As it moved through Cos. Antrim and Derry, however, the march also provoked attacks from militant loyalist supporters, culminating in the carefully organised ambush at Burntollet, about 10 km (6 miles) from Derry. Here the marchers, originally about seventy strong but at this point joined by some 400 local supporters and escorted by eighty RUC men, were violently attacked by 200 loyalists led by Major Ronald Bunting, an associate of Rev. IAN PAISLEY. It emerged afterwards that a large proportion of the assailants were members of the B Specials, the exclusively Protestant reserve branch of the RUC. The apparent complicity of policemen in the attack, and the inability of their full-time colleagues to protect the marchers, undoubtedly contributed to the progressive alienation of the RUC from the Catholic community. The march itself, far from sustaining secular radicalism, powerfully boosted the unambiguously sectarian violence that accompanied its progress and followed it in Derry and other places. [see A, B, C SPECIALS.] **Keith Jeffery**

Burren, Co. Clare, an area of exposed Carboniferous limestone at the north of the Clare Plateau that continues on to the ARAN ISLANDS. Elsewhere this limestone is covered by the Namurian shales and flagstones seen in the CLIFFS OF MOHER, which were stripped from the Burren largely by southbound glaciers from Connemara, which also eroded the tiered limestone escarpments of the Burren's northern margin. Once the limestone was exposed, its constituent calcium carbonate began to be dissolved by glacial meltwater, rain, and groundwater, resulting in a gaunt glacio-karstic

Burren. *Limestone pavement and flora in the Burren, Co. Clare. The grikes (fissures) in the limestone plateau provide a habitat for rare flora. [Michael Diggin Photography]*

terrain characterised by subterranean drainage. The joints in the limestone were enlarged by solution, creating *grikes*, deep ruts separated by *clints* or bare rock slabs. The Burren's limestone pavement appears lifeless, but rare Alpine, Mediterranean, and Arctic plants grow in thin calcareous soils in the grikes. Many rivers, such as the Fergus, disappear through *sluggas* (swallow-holes in the limestone), to flow underground before re-emerging as springs. Entire cave systems, such as Pollnagollum and Pollelva, arose from the enlargement of small fissures by subterranean waters. Dry valleys, such as the Ballyvaghan, were formed when rivers cut through remaining Namurian strata only to be swallowed on reaching the underlying limestone. Closed surface depressions or *dolines* reflect the collapse of shallow underground caverns, becoming *poljes* when enlarged by solution and glacial erosion, such as the 3 km^2 (1 sq. mile) Carran depression. The Burren is also rich in archaeological remains, with MEGALITHIC TOMBS such as POULNABRONE from 3500 BC and RING-FORTS from the Iron Age to the Middle Ages, such as Caherballykinvarga. **Colman Gallagher**

Burton, Sir Frederic William (1816–1900), watercolour painter and antiquarian. Born in Corrofin, Co. Clare; moved to Dublin in 1826 and attended the DUBLIN SOCIETY schools under ROBERT WEST and Henry BROCAS Senior. His early years as a portrait miniaturist were influenced by SAMUEL LOVER, and he was a friend of GEORGE PETRIE. He exhibited at the RHA, 1832–61. His pictures set in the west of Ireland, 1838–41, include *The Aran Fisherman's Drowned Child* (1841) in the NATIONAL GALLERY OF IRELAND, engraved by the Royal Irish Art Union, 1843 (see p. 1117). He worked as curator for Maximilian II of Bavaria, 1851–7, and executed a series of German peasant subjects. He settled in London in 1858 and developed a pre-Raphaelite style, employing fine, detailed brush-strokes, exemplified in his masterpiece, *The Meeting on the Turret Stairs* (1864), now in the National Gallery of Ireland. He ceased painting after his appointment as director of the National Gallery, London, 1874–94. **Marie Bourke**

bus: see TRANSPORT.

Butcher, Eddie (1900–1980), traditional singer. Born in Magilligan, Co. Derry. His extensive repertoire is featured on five recordings: *Adam in Paradise* (1969), *Folk Ballads from Donegal and Derry* (1970), *I Once Was a Daysman* (1976), *Shamrock, Rose and Thistle* (1976), and *The Titanic* (1978). His life and songs (edited by HUGH SHIELDS) were published as *Shamrock, Rose and Thistle* (1981). He is buried in St Aidan's Churchyard, Magilligan. **Len Graham**

Butcher, Richard George Herbert (1819–1891), surgeon. Born in Killarney, Co. Kerry, a son of Admiral S. Butcher; educated at Cork School of Medicine, Peter Street School of Anatomy, Dublin, and Guy's Hospital, London. He became a fellow of the RCSI, 1844, and was surgeon to Mercer's Hospital and later Sir PATRICK DUN'S HOSPITAL, Dublin. He invented a surgical instrument, 'Butcher's saw', in 1851. Awarded an MD by the University of Dublin, 1863, he was president of the RCSI, 1866–7. In 1879 he set up a lifeboat station in Tralee Bay. **Pierce A. Grace**

Butler, Lady Eleanor (1745–1829), recluse and writer. Born in Dublin, a sister of the seventeenth Earl of Ormond. She formed an intense and enduring relationship with her cousin Sarah PONSONBY (1755–1831), and they set up home together in 1780 at Plas Newydd, their house outside Llangollen, Wales, with their maid Mary Carryll, where they sought to establish a rural idyll, adhering to the ideals of the romantic tradition. Their writings, inspired by a Rousseauan reverence for nature, attracted considerable attention, and as the celebrated 'Ladies of Llangollen' were visited by the Duke of Wellington, Walter Scott, EDMUND BURKE, Lady Caroline Lamb, and William Wordsworth. **Brian Galvin**

Butler, Elizabeth, née Poyntz, Duchess of Ormond (1615–1684), daughter and heiress (through her mother) of her grandfather, THOMAS BUTLER, tenth Earl of Ormond. In 1629 she married her cousin JAMES BUTLER, twelfth Earl and later first Duke of Ormond. The marriage was an attempt on the Butler side to prevent their inheritance from being fragmented. The couple had five children. In 1650 the family left Ireland and went to live in France as exiled royalist supporters of CHARLES II. In the early 1650s Elizabeth returned to Ireland with her children. She successfully petitioned members of the government, including OLIVER CROMWELL, for a portion of her grandfather's estate, which she argued was legally separate from her husband's property. She continued to live in Ireland while her husband remained on the Continent until 1660. Following the restoration of Charles II the couple were reunited and for the rest of their lives moved between England and Ireland, depending on Ormond's political career. As Duchess of Ormond, Elizabeth Butler was recognised as an influential figure in the Dublin and London courts of the RESTORATION period. **Mary O'Dowd**

Butler, Hubert (1900–1991), essayist and translator. Born at Bennetsbridge, Co. Kilkenny; educated at the University of Oxford. He travelled extensively in the 1920s and 30s, especially in the Balkans, about whose religious politics he wrote with an engaged acuity that aroused controversy in Ireland. Having settled in his family home at Kilkenny in 1941, he wrote for THE BELL and other journals; he also revived the Kilkenny Debates, reflecting his commitment to local affairs and to intellectual freedom. His was a voice for pluralism in independent Ireland, and he believed that the Protestant minority had a valuable role to play in national life. He published three collections of essays—*Escape from the Anthill* (1985), *The Children of Drancy* (1988), and *Grandmother and Wolfe Tone* (1990)—notable for the lucid elegance of their style and their intimate perspectives on national and international themes. **R. B. Tobin**

Butler, James, first Earl of Ormond (c. 1305–1388), son and heir of Edmund Butler and Joan, daughter of John fitz Thomas, first Earl of Kildare. He was a minor when his father died in September 1321, and he was summoned to England by Edward II. Though James was still under age, Edward, as a mark of special favour, took homage from him on 2 December 1326 for 2,000 marks. James returned to Ireland and in 1327 was granted custody of his inheritance and the prise of wines that his ancestors had held. (Theobald Walter, founder of the Butler family and butler in the household of Prince John, was granted a levy on all wines.) At the Salisbury Parliament in 1328 he was created first Earl of Ormond and afterwards was given the liberty of Tipperary, possibly in return for supporting the Mortimer regency. He married Eleanor de Bohun, daughter of Humphrey de Bohun, Earl of Hereford, and granddaughter of Edward I.

In 1330 he set out from a parliament at Kilkenny with other leading magnates to fight Brian Bán O'Brien and was later to boast that he maintained 500 horse and 1,000 foot against O'Brien in this campaign. He fell foul of Edward III for a period in 1331, when he lost Tipperary, the prise of wines, and smaller grants; these were returned to him in 1332, and he was one of the leaders of an Irish army to Scotland in support of Edward III in 1335. His titles were again revoked in 1335 but were restored in 1337. He was buried at Gowran, Co. Kilkenny, the chief seat of the family before the purchase of Kilkenny Castle. **Susan Foran**

Butler, James, fourth Earl of Ormond (c. 1390–1452), known as the 'White Earl', son of the third Earl of Ormond and Anne Welles, daughter of Lord John Welles. He was granted custody of his lands on 2 October 1405 and for the rest of his life was to dominate the political scene in Ireland, holding the post of Chief Governor eight times. He frequently visited England and served three times with English armies in France, 1412–13, 1418–19, and 1430. When his first wife, Joan Beauchamp, died in 1430 he married Elizabeth Fitzgerald, heiress of Gerald Fitzgerald, fifth Earl of Kildare, in 1432, thus greatly increasing his estates. The appointment of John Talbot as Chief Governor in 1414 restricted Ormond dominance and ignited a power struggle between the two men that was to last for years. Both used their control of the office of Chief Governor to exploit each other; each accused the other of misrule, peculation, oppression, and treason. Though an agreement was reached in 1444 and sealed with the marriage of Talbot's son to Butler's daughter, the feud continued.

Butler, Hubert. *Hubert Butler, the foremost Irish essayist of the twentieth century, in the garden of his family home, Maidenhall, in Co. Kilkenny, 1989. [Thomas Crampton]*

Butler initiated vigorous campaigns against the Irish but was also quick to enter into marriage alliances with his Irish neighbours to ensure peace within his lordship. He was a patron of Irish culture, probably the first of the ANGLO-NORMAN lords to appoint a BREHON to his service, and spoke Irish. He died at Ardee, Co. Louth, on 23 August 1452; his earldom was conferred on his absentee son, the Earl of Wiltshire. **Susan Foran**

Butler, James, twelfth Earl and first Duke of Ormond (1610–1688), soldier and politician. Born in London, the eldest son of Thomas Butler, Viscount Thurles, and ELIZABETH BUTLER (née Poyntz); received a Protestant education in England after his father's death in 1619. He faced continued financial difficulties, which were partly relieved by his marriage in 1629 to his cousin Elizabeth Preston, claimant to half the Butler inheritance. On his return to Ireland in 1633 he was advanced by WENTWORTH, whose administration he strongly supported. As commander of the army at the outbreak of the 1641 REBELLION, his military effectiveness was hampered both by the ambiguity of the King's reaction and by the mistrust of the Lords Justices who had replaced Wentworth. Entrusted with the delicate task of negotiating with the Confederates, he refused to countenance their demand for full toleration of Catholicism. After the failure of the treaty of 1646 with the CONFEDERATION he surrendered the garrisons under his command to the parliamentary commander, Colonel Michael Jones, in 1647. He subsequently formed a new royalist alliance, but, faced with a lack of confidence in his leadership following his defeat by Jones at the Battle of Rathmines, Dublin, in 1649 and the arrival of Cromwell two weeks later in 1649, he joined the future CHARLES II in exile. At the Restoration his loyalty was rewarded with a dukedom and his appointment as LORD LIEUTENANT. He ensured stability by supporting the Protestant interest against the claims of the dispossessed royalist Catholic landowners. He was dismissed in 1669, restored again in 1677, and finally lost office in 1685. He died in July 1688 and is buried in Westminster Abbey, London. **Liam Irwin**

Butler, Rudolph Maximilian (1872–1943), architect. Born in Dublin, son of a Carlow barrister and a German mother. After the death of his father in 1882 he spent six years in Germany; he returned to Dublin to enter the wine trade but c. 1891 was articled to the architect W. G. Doolin, joining him in a partnership in 1896. His first big commission was the Passionist church and monastery at Ardoyne, Belfast (1900). After Doolin's death in 1902 he was briefly in partnership with J. L. Donnelly. Though a member of the MORAVIAN faith, Butler was extensively patronised by the Catholic Church and religious orders; St Patrick's, Newport, Co. Mayo (1914), is perhaps his best church. In 1912 he won the competition for the buildings of UNIVERSITY COLLEGE in Earlsfort Terrace, Dublin. Among his other significant buildings are St Mary's College, Galway (1910–12), THOOR BALLYLEE, Co. Galway (1917–19), the restoration of a medieval tower-house for W. B. Yeats, and St Patrick's Basilica, LOUGH DERG, Co. Donegal (1919–31). In 1923 he was appointed examiner in architecture and the following year professor, a post he held until 1942. He also found time between 1899 and 1935 to edit the *Irish Builder.* **Frederick O'Dwyer**

Butler, Thomas, tenth Earl of Ormond (Black Tom) (1532–1614). Succeeding to the earldom as a minor because of the sudden death (perhaps by poisoning) of James Butler, ninth earl, in 1546, he determined on the rapid reconstruction of his family's failing fortunes on his return to Ireland in 1554. Through a shrewd development of a close personal bond he had formed with his distant relative ELIZABETH I during his long stay at court, the cultivation of the friendship of the Viceroy, THOMAS RADCLIFFE the Earl of Sussex, and the exploitation of internal weaknesses in the rival house of Desmond, by the mid-1560s he had more than recovered gains made in Munster by the Desmonds. But he had in a sense succeeded too well. His campaign against the Desmonds, which included provoking the unstable earl into a full-scale feudal battle at Affane (1565), precipitated the rapid decline of that house and its destruction in rebellion in 1583. At the same time his influence with Elizabeth aroused the hostility of English officers in Ireland, in particular the Lord Deputy, SIDNEY, and other courtiers, notably the Earl of Leicester. Sidney's hostility provoked Butler's brothers into rebellion in 1569–70, and though the earl managed quickly to secure their submission, his reputation suffered. Butler rendered invaluable service during the DESMOND REBELLION (1579–83), but fears of his potential influence in Munster, coupled with the promise of lucrative plantation lands in the province, intensified opposition to him both in Dublin and in London. Isolated in Munster and with no support from the followers of Desmond, his influence continued to wane during the 1590s, hastened by constant allegations against him and his failure to secure the submission of his one-time friend HUGH O'NEILL. Recognition by the turn of the century that he was to die without leaving a male heir heightened the determination of his enemies to set about the dismantling of his earldom on his death (see p. 843). **Ciaran Brady**

Butt, Isaac (1813–1879), politician. Born in Co. Donegal; educated at TCD. Editor of DUBLIN UNIVERSITY MAGAZINE, 1833–6, he was professor of political economy at TCD, 1836–40, and was called to the bar, 1838. An opponent of O'CONNELL in the Dublin Corporation Repeal debates, 1843, he defended WILLIAM SMITH O'BRIEN after the 1848 RISING and CHARLES KICKHAM and other FENIANS in 1867. He was MP for Youghal, 1852–65; president of the AMNESTY ASSOCIATION, 1869; founder of the HOME GOVERNMENT ASSOCIATION, 1870; and president of the HOME RULE Confederation of Great Britain, 1873–7. He lost leadership of the Home Rule Confederation to C. S. Parnell in 1877. Butt was the 'Father of Home Rule' and remained committed to achieving a constitutional settlement for Ireland within the British Empire. **Joseph Spence**

Butte, Montana, the Irish in. Butte, in south-western Montana, is now a city of about 35,000 people. It was built on what was called the 'richest hill on earth,' an area of abundant mineral deposits, particularly of silver and copper. By 1900 it was the world's greatest mining city, producing more than 25 per cent of the world's copper ore. It was also by that time the most Irish city in America. Irish immigrants travelled to the region in great numbers, drawn by the promise of high wages and the assurance that the leading mines, owned by the giant Anaconda Copper Mining Company, would not discriminate against them. The company was run by Marcus Daly, an Irish Catholic from Ballyjamesduff, Co. Cavan. He favoured Irish miners and sought them out; they would ultimately run the city, its mines, churches, and trade unions. Their political involvement extended also to the cause of Irish NATIONALISM. The second-largest CLAN NA GAEL camp (branch) in America, the ROBERT EMMET Literary Association, was in Butte; it was joined by three divisions of the ANCIENT ORDER OF HIBERNIANS. Both organisations sent hundreds of thousand of dollars to Ireland, most of it in the name of revolutionary REPUBLICANISM. [see THE UNITED STATES OF AMERICA, IRISH IN.] **David Emmons**

butter. From earliest times both climate and topography have favoured DAIRY FARMING in Ireland, as noted by the English historian BEDE in the eighth century. High annual rainfall created rich pastures, while extremes of climate were also rare. Such conditions were particularly advantageous for the making of butter, especially in MUNSTER. Butter-making is susceptible to wide variations in temperature; but in the south of Ireland the relative coolness of the summer months—the period in which milk was available in large quantities—facilitated the manufacture of high-quality butter.

Until the late seventeenth century butter was a staple component of the Irish DIET; but the introduction of the potato increasingly enabled farmers to manufacture it for the market. By the early decades of the eighteenth century the trade in butter from the port of Cork was of international significance, while Cork's Butter Exchange (established 1769) had become the largest of its type in the world by 1800.

Towards the end of the nineteenth century butter had to compete with stiff foreign competition, which included not only high-quality butter from Scandinavia but also newly developed butter substitutes, such as margarine. Butter-blending factories were beginning to be established in Ireland; but the most important structural change in the butter trade was the establishment of independent creameries, a development augmented by the spread of the co-operative movement. The butter trade stagnated in the inter-war years, and it continued to languish until the establishment of a central marketing board, An Bord Bainne (later renamed the Irish Dairy Board) in 1961, through which Irish butter has once again captured important international markets. [see FOOD.] **Colin Rynne**

Byerley Turk (c. 1680s–1690s), the original thoroughbred horse, one of the three stallions from which all present-day thoroughbreds are descended in the male line. When Buda was captured from the Turks in 1687, the horse was brought to Ireland by a Captain Byerley, when he came in 1689 to fight in the BATTLE OF THE BOYNE. He was later sent to stud in Durham and York in England. **Ciarán Deane**

Byers, David (1947–), composer, born Belfast. Chief executive of the ULSTER ORCHESTRA (2002–), formerly chief music producer with BBC Northern Ireland (1977–2002). He studied at the Royal Academy of Music in London and pursued postgraduate studies at Liège conservatoire. His compositions span most genres except opera and have been performed and broadcast throughout Europe and the United States. He has also edited much eighteenth and nineteenth-century music, primarily by English composers. He has served on many international competition juries, boards, and committees. He is a director of the National Chamber Choir and a governor of the RIAM. **David Mooney**

Byers, Margaret (1832–1912), educational pioneer. Born in Rathfriland, Co. Down; she lived with paternal uncles in England following her father's death in 1840. She attended a ladies' college in Nottingham, where she later taught, before returning to Ireland to marry Rev. John Byers in 1852. She accompanied her husband to Shanghai, where he became ill, dying on his journey home in 1853. In 1854 she worked as a teacher in Cookstown Ladies' Collegiate School, Co. Tyrone, but moved to Belfast to open her own school in 1859. Recognised as a vociferous campaigner for equal educational rights, she was appointed president of the Ulster Schoolmistresses' Association in 1903, awarded an honorary LLD by the University of Dublin in 1905, and appointed to the Senate of Queen's University, Belfast in 1908. She was a liberal UNIONIST in politics, supporting the Women's Liberal Unionist Association and serving on the committee of the North of Ireland Women's Suffrage Society. She was involved in numerous philanthropic endeavours in Belfast and was superintendent of the Ladies' Temperance Union in Belfast in 1862, secretary of Belfast Women's Temperance Association from its establishment in 1874 until 1895, when she became its president, and first president of the Irish Women's Temperance Union in 1894. By the time of her death she was acknowledged as an authority on education, and her school, now operating under the name Victoria College, was the largest of its type in Ireland. **Diane Urquhart**

Byrne, Anthony (1958–), pianist. Born in Dublin; studied at the Municipal College of Music (now DIT Conservatory of Music and Drama) and with JOHN O'CONOR at the RIAM, and with Adele Marcus (Juilliard) and Alexander Kelly (Royal College of Music). He teaches piano at the RIAM and has worked extensively as soloist and chamber musician, with important CD recordings of the solo piano music of RAYMOND DEANE and JOHN BUCKLEY. **David Mooney**

Byrne, Charles (1761–1783), giant. Born in Ireland to parents of normal stature. In 1780 he was 244 cm (8 ft) tall. He toured Britain for exhibition, and died at the age of twenty-two in London after a bout of heavy drinking, allegedly distraught at having lost £700. His skeleton is preserved at the Hunterian museum, Royal College of Surgeons, London, where there is also a portrait of him. The eponymous protagonist of Hilary Mantel's novel *The Giant O'Brien* (1998) is based on Byrne. **Ciarán Deane**

Byrne, Donn (1889–1928), SHORT-STORY writer and novelist. Born in New York, he returned with his parents to Co. Armagh just after birth; educated at the Sorbonne and Leipzig. He began by writing for New York magazines, such as *Red Book* and *Scribner's*; his first collection, *Stories Without Women*, appeared in 1915, and his first novel, *The Stranger's Banquet*, in 1919. Though never really beyond magazine entertainment, his novels are polished, and some—such as *Messer Marco Polo* (1921), *The Wind Bloweth* (1922), and *The Power of the Dog* (1929)—have retained some popularity. **Joley Wood**

Byrne, Francis Barry (1883–1967), architect. Born in Chicago; he was a student and later (1902–9) an assistant of Frank Lloyd Wright. In 1927 he was appointed by the Bishop of Cork, Dr Daniel Cohalan, to design a new church for the growing suburb of Turner's Cross. The CHURCH OF CHRIST THE KING, a striking modern design with a figure of Christ the King by the American sculptor John Storrs at the western portal, was completed in 1931 under the superintendence of J. R. Boyd Barrett. Probably owing more to Byrne's travels in Europe than to any American prototypes, it was built in concrete, with a wide-span concealed steel-truss roof. Admired for its economy, it proved a false dawn for Irish church architecture. **Frederick O'Dwyer**

Byrne, Gabriel (1950–), actor. Born in Dublin. He began his career at the Dublin Shakespeare Society in 1974 and thereafter worked at the FOCUS, Project, and ABBEY THEATRES. His first television appearances were in the rural serial 'The Riordans' and its successor, 'Bracken', while his early film roles were in the experimental feature *On a Paving Stone Mounted* (1978), *The Outsider* (1979), and *Excalibur* (1981). He subsequently appeared in more than twenty films, with memorable performances in *Defence of the Realm* (1985), *Miller's Crossing* (1990), *Into the West* (1992), *The Usual Suspects* (1995), *End of Days* (1999), and *Stigmata* (1999). He also produced and acted in *An Draíocht*, the first television drama broadcast on TG4. He starred opposite Ellen Barkin in *Siesta* (1987), and in 2000 he returned to the New York stage for a well-received role in *A Moon for the Misbegotten*. **Kevin Rockett**

Byers, Margaret. *Pioneers of women's education illustrated in* Lady of the House, *Christmas, 1903: Margaret Byers, principal of Victoria College, Belfast, is portrayed bottom left. [Council of Trustees of the National Library of Ireland]*

Byrne, Gabriel (Gay) (1934–), radio and television broadcaster. Born in Dublin; educated at Synge Street CBS. He joined Radio Éireann in 1958 and began presenting 'The Late Late Show' on RTÉ television in 1962; by the time he retired from the programme in 1999 it had become the longest-running popular television programme with the same broadcaster. He is also well known as the presenter of such top-rating programmes as 'THE ROSE OF TRALEE' and 'Housewife of the Year' and for his work on radio, including music programmes and the 'Gay Byrne Show'. His radio and television programmes are renowned for their reflection of the public changes in Ireland since the 1960s, contributing to national debate on social and cultural issues. [see BROADCASTING.] **Bernadette Grummell**

Byrne, Miles (1780–1862), UNITED IRISHMAN and French army officer. Born in Ballylusk, Co. Wexford. He led the rebels of the Monaseed district in the REBELLION OF 1798 at the battles of Tubberneering, Arklow, and VINEGAR HILL. As resistance crumbled in his home county he led a rump of Wexford rebels into the Wicklow mountains to wage a guerrilla struggle before hiding in Dublin in November 1798. On the collapse of ROBERT EMMET's conspiracy in July 1803 he fled to France, where, following a distinguished military career, he retired from the army in 1830 as *chef de bataillon* of the 56th Regiment. **Ruan O'Donnell**

Connolly, Sybil
(see page 231). Haute couture design by the couturière and designer Sybil Connolly, a blouse and skirt made from her signature pleated handkerchief linen. [National Museum of Ireland]

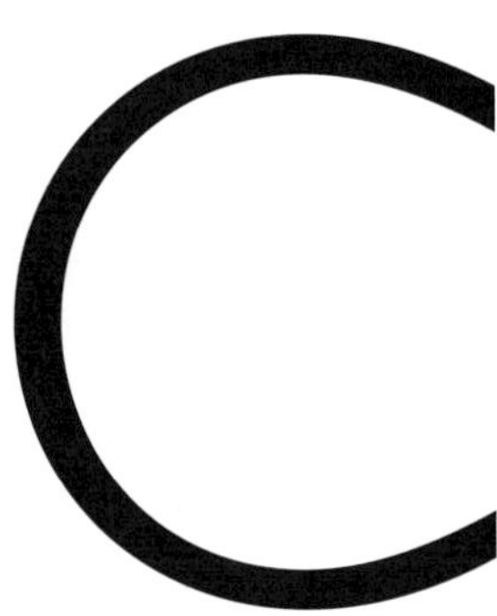

Caher Castle, Co. Tipperary, a multi-period fortress but with mainly post-1300 standing remains, sited on a rock island in the middle of the River SUIR. The castle was granted to Philip of Worcester in 1192, but the appearance of a well-preserved medieval CASTLE is due to nineteenth-century restoration. It has three wards (inner, middle, and outer), the outer dating from the seventeenth century. The earliest work, from the middle of the thirteenth century, consists of an almost square gate-house, the curtain-walls of the inner ward, the great tower in the north-west angle, and the remains of the hall. The gate-house was originally centrally pierced but was blocked in the fifteenth century and made into a keep. The gateway was moved at that time with its portcullis to the east of the old gate building (see p. 167). **David Sweetman**

Cahill, Martin (1949–1994), criminal. Born in Dublin to an impoverished family; he began a lifetime of crime by stealing food at the age of eight. Nicknamed 'the General' by journalists, he had, by the time of his death, stolen up to €50 million worth of property. Among his most notorious exploits were the bombing of the car being driven by the chief scientist of the State Laboratory, James Donovan, in January 1982; the theft of €25 million worth of paintings from the BEIT Collection at Russborough House, near Ballymore Eustace, Co. Wicklow, in 1986; and the attempted murder of Garda John Moore in January 1990. He was shot dead on a Dublin street on 18 August 1994, and the IRA claimed responsibility. His life was documented by the journalist Paul Williams in the best-selling book *The General: Godfather of Crime*; a film, *The General*, directed by John Boorman and based on the book was released in May 1998, while Kevin Spacey starred as Cahill in *Ordinary Decent Criminal* (2000), directed by Thaddeus O'Sullivan. **Ciarán Deane**

Cairbre, the MGM lion (1927–1944). Born in DUBLIN ZOO on 20 March 1927, the son of Selim Bey and Deirdre. He sired twenty-four cubs. He was filmed as the lion on the original introduction to Metro-Goldwyn-Mayer films. **Ciarán Deane**

Cairdeas na bhFidléirí, an organisation in Co. Donegal devoted to the promotion of the county's FIDDLE style through classes, workshops, and performance. Begun in the 1980s under the direction of Caomhín Mac Aoidh, it is run by a committee of fiddle-players. It organises an annual summer school at Glencolumbkille, Co. Donegal, and an autumn gathering at Glenties. [see DONEGAL FIDDLE TRADITION.] **Fintan Vallely**

Cairde na Cruite, founded 1960, a society dedicated to promoting interest in the Irish HARP through teaching, concerts, the publishing of music, and the commissioning of new works. The society organises courses, workshops, and master classes throughout Ireland and operates a harp hire scheme; at various times members have set up harp schools at Derry, Wexford, Mullingar, and Nobber, Co. Meath. A week-long residential summer school is held each June at Termonfeckin, Co. Louth. Publications include *The Irish Harp Book*, *My Gentle Harp*, and a large collection of graded music in *Sounding Harps*, volumes 1–4. **Gráinne Yeats**

Caithréim Chellacháin Chaisil ('The Triumphs of Cellachán'), a pseudo-historical account of the career of the tenth-century King Cellachán, written in the twelfth century—perhaps in emulation of 'COGADH GÁEDHEL RE GALLAIBH'—to glorify Cellachán's descendants, the Meic Carthaig. **Máire Ní Mhaonaigh**

Caithréim Chellaig ('The Triumphs of Callach'), a twelfth-century tale recounting the murder of St Cellach, sixth-century king and bishop, and of his avenger, his brother Muiredach. It reflects contemporary attitudes to church reform in Connacht. **Máire Ní Mhaonaigh**

Caithréim Thoirdhealbhaigh ('The Triumphs of Toirealach'), a text probably composed in the middle of the fourteenth century, attributed to Seán mac Ruaidhrí Mac Craith. A combination of prose and poetry, it describes a conflict in the Co. Clare area between two rival branches of the local ruling dynasty of Uí Briain and a group of would-be ANGLO-NORMAN colonisers led by THOMAS DE CLARE and his son, Richard, in the period 1276–1318. It is an important source for the history of warfare, politics, regnal succession, burial customs, and other aspects of medieval Irish life. It was edited and translated by STANDISH HAYES O'GRADY in 1929. **Aoife Goodman**

Caitilín Dubh (fl. c. 1624), author of five elegiac compositions preserved in a seventeenth-century collection of poems addressed to the O'Briens of Thomond. The absence of a surname points to her probable low social status; as the theme of wandering from place to place is found in some of the poems, it is possible that she was recognised as a semi-professional KEENING woman who went where her services were needed. She seems to have operated on the periphery of the literary culture of the early seventeenth century, and the poems ascribed to her provide an intriguing insight into the possibility of female authorship at a period in Irish literary history when the official practice of poetry was still a predominantly male preserve. In personality she seems to have been agreeable, but formidable. The first of her compositions in the manuscript is on the death of Donogh O'Brien, fourth Earl of Thomond (died 1624), one of the foremost Irish noblemen of his day. There is a sense of distance between poet and subject in this elegy that most probably reflects O'Brien's elevated status. But the other items ascribed to her—two elegies on Diarmaid, fifth Baron of Inchiquin (died c. 1624), one on Máire, daughter of the third Earl of Thomond, and one on Máire's husband, Toirdhealbhach Rua Mac Mathghamhna (died 1629)—contain sentiments of personal loss and, addressing the deceased in the first person, convey a sense of familiar acquaintance. It was this familiarity, combined with Caitilín Dubh's sureness of touch in the elegiac genre, that ensured the preservation of her poems in manuscript form. **Liam P. Ó Murchú**

Caledon, Co. Tyrone, a focus of attention in June 1968 when the Nationalist MP AUSTIN CURRIE, together with local nationalists, symbolically squatted in a house allocated to a nineteen-year-old single Protestant, Emily Beattie. The protest followed the eviction from the neighbouring house of the Catholic Goodfellow family, which included three young children. Its aim was to draw attention to perceived malpractices in housing allocation perpetrated by a number of Unionist-controlled local authorities. Needy Catholics, it was argued, were consistently denied adequate accommodation, while Protestants facing lesser hardship were provided with the houses they desired. Beattie's connection with a local Unionist politician (whose secretary she was) was seen to confirm Nationalist suspicions. The controversy arose out of growing Catholic frustration at Unionist unwillingness to introduce a compulsory points system for the allocation of houses. Local authorities were accused of apportioning houses in such a way as to sustain a finely balanced sectarian population distribution, thus enabling Unionists to preserve control of local councils, particularly those west of the River BANN. Currie's action is often seen in retrospect as having laid the groundwork for later CIVIL RIGHTS protests. [see CAMERON COMMISSION; GERRYMANDERING.] **Alan Scott**

calendar customs, the various verbal, artefactual or behavioural expressions that recur at certain times of the year. Calendar customs are linked to changes in the cosmic cycle that determine alternate periods of social or economic activity. The FESTIVALS, FAIRS, and PATTERNS of the yearly cycle have long been associated with 'FOLKLORE' when it is viewed as a colourful survival from a more ancient time. The many rites and rituals associated with these times of the year speak of a blending of past and present, Christian and PRE-CHRISTIAN, official and 'vernacular'.

Feasts and festivals are related to time and the changes that occur in the natural cycle, the feasts often being positioned at turning-points, such as the beginning of summer or winter (BEALTAINE, SAMHAIN) or the solstices (St John's Eve). The traditional year was marked by four main festivals: *Samhain* (HALLOWE'EN), ST BRIGID'S DAY (1 February), *Bealtaine* (MAY DAY), and LÚNASA (1 August). In a largely agricultural society, the festivals of Samhain and Bealtaine divided the year into a dark and relatively dormant half and a bright and busy half: this is evidenced by the popular saying 'STORYTELLING from November to May.' St Brigid's Day and Lúnasa further quartered the year. St Brigid's Day is the Christianised form of IMBOLC, the older festival of spring, lambing, and lactation. All four festivals show a remarkable variety of practices, including verbal and artefactual expressions. Many have featured a combination of storytelling, rhyming, bonfires, pageants, family meals, PILGRIMAGES, and fireworks. There is a marked carnival aspect to many of the celebrations, which invert the normal everyday world, ridicule authority and prevailing mores, and create an atmosphere of community based on a common humanity.

The richness of vernacular cultural life yesterday and today is evidenced by such calendar customs as the ST BRIGID'S CROSS and 'BIDDY BOYS' of Iveragh, Co. Cork, by VALENTINE cards, May altars and processions, jumping over bonfires at St John's Eve (Bonfire Night), pilgrimages to CROAGH PATRICK, or PATTERN days, such as that of St Declan at ARDMORE, Co. Waterford, on 24 July, as well as the pre-Lenten Shrove Tuesday or Pancake Night, barm bracks on Hallowe'en ('Snap-Apple Night'), and WOMEN'S CHRISTMAS.

Calendrical occasions have always been a core feature of popular culture and reflect the cultural process in general, constantly transforming or translating older elements, adding newer ones, and continuing to speak of contemporary social and historical circumstances in any given era: St Brigid's crosses being sold from supermarket trolleys, St John's Eve becoming a night of joyriding. Though the significance of New Year's Eve and other contemporary festivals is unexplored, there may have been a shift of emphasis over time from calendrical to life-cycle rites, such as birthdays and retirements. [see FOLK-LIFE; FOLKLORE.] **Stiofán Ó Cadhla**

calendar customs. *A 'Biddy boy', Kilgobnet, Co. Kerry, wearing an intricate headdress of woven straw for St Brigid's Day which falls on 1 February and marks the first day of spring. [Department of Irish Folklore, University College, Dublin H032.18.18]*

Callan, Nicholas (1799–1864), priest and inventor. Born in Darver, near Dundalk, Co. Louth; his initial education was at an academy in Dundalk run by a Presbyterian clergyman, William Nelson. He entered ST PATRICK'S COLLEGE, Maynooth, as a clerical student in 1816 and was to remain at this seminary for most of his life. In his third year there he studied natural and experimental philosophy under Dr Cornelius Denvir, who had an interest in electricity and magnetism and who introduced the experimental method into his teaching. After ordination in 1823 Callan went to Rome, where he studied at the Sapienza University, being awarded a doctorate in divinity in 1826. While there he became acquainted with work that had been carried out by Luigi Galvani (1737–1798) and Alessandro Volta (1745–1827), both pioneers in the study of electricity. On the resignation of Dr Denvir, Callan was appointed to the chair of natural philosophy at Maynooth in 1826, and he remained in that post until his death.

Callan's principal claim to fame is as the inventor of the CALLAN INDUCTION COIL. Much of Callan's original coils, batteries, and other apparatus, and his textbooks, are now housed in the National Science Museum, Maynooth. **Niall McKeith**

Callan induction coil (c. 1859–63), the first induction coil, was invented by NICHOLAS CALLAN. A cylindrical bundle of annealed iron wires forms the core, about which a *primary coil* of heavy copper wire, insulated with tape, is wound in three layers. The primary coil is insulated with several layers of thin-sheet gutta-percha (natural latex), cemented with a paste of gutta-percha, resin, and beeswax initially dissolved in boiling oil. The *secondary coil* consists of three separate coils of fine iron wire. The secondary coils are so arranged as to divide the primary into four equal parts, the planes of the coils being perpendicular to the axis. In each coil the ends of the windings are left projecting so that they can be joined in series or in parallel. Callan used about 45,000 m (150,000 ft) of wire in the secondary. The contact-breaker is an automatic mercury break of the type developed by Callan in 1858, but it is now incomplete. The coil is also fitted with a Rühmkorff-type commutator.

Callan reported that he made an induction coil 'of considerable power' in 1859–60, with the secondary in three parts. In early 1863 he improved it with a new primary coil and core and with better insulation between the primary and secondary. With these modifications he produced sparks 38 cm (15 in.) in length across a point-and-plate arrangement, using three cells of the Maynooth battery; to produce such a spark a potential difference of 600,000 volts is required. With this coil Callan carried out many experiments on sparking potentials and on the influence of the shape of the electrodes on the character of the spark produced. He discovered a method of rectifying high-tension alternating current, which was employed in suppressing the reverse current in early X-ray tubes. He also constructed two large condensers, which he used with the coil to reduce the spark at the break in the primary coil. **Niall McKeith**

Callanan, James (Jeremiah) Joseph (1795–1829), poet. Born in Ballinhassig, Co. Cork; studied for the priesthood at Maynooth but left, and attended TCD. He returned to Co. Cork, where he worked as a tutor and teacher. He travelled throughout south-west Ireland collecting songs and poems, some of which furnished material for his poems and translations. In 1829, suffering from ill health, he travelled to Lisbon, hoping to recover his health, but died there. Only a few poems appeared during his lifetime; his long poem *The Recluse of Inchydoney* was published post-humously. Callanan is remembered mainly for introducing the temper and rhythms of Irish poetry into English. **Peter Denman**

Callis, Charles A. (1865–1947), MORMON elder. Born in Dublin. His mother converted to the Church of Jesus Christ of Latter-Day Saints (Mormons), and in 1875 the family emigrated to the United States, where Callis pursued a career in law and politics in Utah. As a missionary he became president of the Irish Conference of the Latter-Day Saints, 1893–4, and for most of his life travelled extensively in the United States as preacher and missionary.

In 1933 Elder Callis was ordained a member of the Quorum of Twelve Apostles, the supreme body of the church. **Brian Lalor**

Cambridge, Alice (1762–1829), preacher. Born in Bandon, Co. Cork; she left school early and worked as a shop assistant. In 1780 she converted to Methodism and began to speak at public meetings, obtaining JOHN WESLEY's approval of her right to preach. She was excluded from the Methodist Society in 1802 when the Conference outlawed female preaching, but she was readmitted in 1811. From 1813 she made several tours throughout Ireland, enjoying particular success in Ulster. She retired in 1824. **Rosemary Raughter**

Cameron, Sir Charles Alexander (1830–1921), chemist, physician, and hygienist. Born in Dublin of Scottish parentage; educated in Dublin. Having held numerous posts in the Dublin MEDICAL SCHOOLS over the years, he was appointed Dublin's first public analyst in 1859, only the third such post in Ireland or Britain and one that he held for fifty-nine years. He published extensively, producing original work on agricultural chemistry, the analysis of FOODS, DIET and health, and on hygiene, in addition to textbooks on the same topics. He left detailed and amusing records of his life in *Reminiscences* (1913) and *Autobiography* (1921). He was a prominent freemason. **D. Thorburn Burns**

Cameron Commission (1969), a commission of inquiry established by the Northern Ireland government of TERENCE O'NEILL in January 1969 to investigate the causes of civil disturbances since 5 October 1968. It was chaired by Lord Cameron, a Scottish judge, assisted by two local academics, Sir John Biggart and J. J. Campbell. It had the right to call witnesses, and the Northern Ireland Attorney-General gave an assurance that no statement made to it would result in prosecution. BRIAN FAULKNER, Minister of Commerce, resigned in protest at the inquiry.

In its report, published in September 1969, the commission identified the main causes of disorder as (1) a rising sense of injustice and grievance among the Catholic population with the unfair allocation of houses by UNIONIST LOCAL AUTHORITIES, anti-Catholic DISCRIMINATION in LOCAL GOVERNMENT appointments, and 'the deliberate manipulation of local government boundaries' in order to perpetuate Unionist control, which complaints the commission found 'amply justified'; (2) a powerful sense of resentment and frustration among Catholics at the failure of the government to address these grievances; (3) Catholic resentment at the existence of the Special Constabulary and the use of the Special Powers Act; and (4) 'fears and apprehension among Protestants of a threat to Unionist domination and control by an increase of the Catholic population,' feelings that had been inflamed by loyalist organisations, which had provoked a hostile reaction to civil rights claims, resulting in violence against marchers. The report criticised the Northern Ireland government, the RUC, and REV. IAN PAISLEY, while also concluding that the CIVIL RIGHTS MOVEMENT had been infiltrated by subversive left-wing elements. [see A, B, C SPECIALS; CALEDON.] **Eamon Phoenix**

camogie, a form of HURLING played by women. Cumann Camógaíochta na nGael was formed in 1904 to regulate the game. The playing rules were quite different from those for hurling, the length and width of the pitch being considerably shorter; more recently these were altered to match those of hurling. In 1998 it was agreed that, for the first time, teams would also be of fifteen.

The first all-Ireland senior championship took place in 1932, with Dublin winning the first of its record twenty-six titles. The Dublin player Kathleen Mills, one of the legendary figures of camogie, won fifteen all-Ireland senior championships. In 1973 it was decided to abandon the provincial structure of the all-Ireland championship, and the open draw was introduced. Cork won the title that year; a year later Kilkenny made the breakthrough and went on to dominate the game until the early 1990s. The inspiration in the Kilkenny team was Angela Downey, regarded as possibly the most skilful camogie player ever. Her twin sister, Ann, shared in most of the triumphs.

The game continues to grow in strength, and the Tipperary team has emerged as a power, winning its first senior title in 1999 and retaining the title in 2000 and 2001. **Donal Keenan**

Callan. *The great induction coil first developed in 1836 by Nicholas Callan, priest, inventor, and scientist. [Callan Museum, Maynooth; photo: Denis Mortell]*

Campbell, Agnes (1540–1590), daughter of the fourth Earl of Argyll. In 1569 she married TURLOUGH LUINEACH, chief of the O'Neills; in the same year her daughter by a previous marriage, Fionnuala (Iníon Dubh) married Hugh O'Donnell, chief of the O'Donnells. Both marriages were political. Agnes brought as her dowry a contingent of Scottish mercenary soldiers and on several occasions returned to Scotland to secure more military help for her husband. Her skill as a negotiator also proved a valuable asset for Turlough Luineach. Before her marriage she had spent some time in the Scottish court, and she could speak English and French. More importantly, she knew, unlike her husband, how to speak to the Crown's representatives in Ireland. A number of Dublin officials praised her benign influence on her husband, the Earl of Essex describing her as 'a wise and civil woman, and an instrument of peace.' Apart from defending her husband's interests in Ulster she was also involved in protracted discussions in Scotland to secure her son's inheritance. **Mary O'Dowd**

Campbell, George (1917–1979), landscape, still life, figure, and subject painter. Born in Arklow, Co. Wicklow, a son of GRETTA BOWEN; brought to Belfast as a child. Mainly self-taught, he began to paint during the Second World War and, with his brother Arthur Campbell, GERARD DILLON, DAN O'NEILL, and Nevill Johnson, soon came to prominence in exhibitions in Belfast and Dublin. He visited Spain in 1951, returning regularly thereafter, his use of colour and manipulation of mood being much influenced by that country—as was his interest in flamenco music, of which he became a master. Technically he veered towards expressionism in his handling of paint. **S. B. Kennedy**

Campbell, John Henry (1757–1828), artist. Born in England, he came to Ireland with his parents as a child; trained at the DUBLIN SOCIETY Schools. He exhibited in Dublin from 1800. A water-colourist and landscape painter, he painted a few portraits and some oils. He is well known for numerous small pictures, very blue in tone; but his larger works are his best, especially those including little foliage, as in his views of DUBLIN BAY. **Anne Crookshank**

Campbell, John P., also known as Seaghan Mac Cathmhaoil (1883–1962), illustrator. Born in Belfast, brother of the poet JOSEPH CAMPBELL; he had little formal art training. He is thought to have attended the Feis of the Nine Glens in 1904 and provided the illustrations for the publication of lyrics by Joseph Campbell with MUSIC by Herbert Hughes under the title *Songs of Uladh*. He has given us some of the most powerful and imaginative black-and-white illustrations of the LITERARY REVIVAL period. His most imaginative and stylised suite of drawings was for the second edition of Mary Hutton's *The Táin*, which shows the influence of Japanese prints, much in vogue at the time. Both here and in his work for the journal *Uladh* he drew on his knowledge of local sites and Celtic ornamentation to produce works of real mood and enchantment. Working in a totally different style, he produced several halftone frontispieces for school stories by Angela Brazil, a popular author of the day. In 1911 he emigrated to the United States, where he died in straitened circumstances. **Patricia Donlon**

Campbell, Joseph (1879–1944), poet. Born in Belfast. He became editor of *Uladh*, the quarterly journal of the ULSTER LITERARY THEATRE, and a contributor to ARTHUR GRIFFITH's *United Irishman* and STANDISH O'GRADY's *All-Ireland Review*. He divided his later life between Dublin and New York and spent a brief period in London. He was interned during the CIVIL WAR in Mountjoy Jail, Dublin, and the Curragh. Most gifted as a poet, he also had a play, *Judgement*, produced at the ABBEY THEATRE in 1913. Campbell was fascinated by nature, and his romantic religious sensibility marks him as a vital practitioner of the modern Irish lyric. **Nicholas Allen**

Campbell, Peter (Pedro) (c. 1782–1832), Uruguayan naval commander. Born in Co. Tipperary. He joined the British army and saw service during the invasions of ARGENTINA, 1806–7, before deserting. He joined the Uruguayan freedom-fighter José Artigas and helped him achieve his country's independence from Brazil. Dubbed 'Don Pedro', he is regarded as the founder of the Uruguayan navy; he was appointed its supreme commander in 1817. He became embroiled in internal politics and was exiled to Paraguay, where he worked as a tanner until his death in Paraná. His remains were brought to Uruguay and interred with great ceremony. **David Kiely**

Campbell, Séamus Oliver (Ollie) (1954–), rugby footballer. Born in Dublin. He was one of Ireland's most influential out-halves of the modern era. Between his first appearance against Australia in Dublin in 1976 and his last, against Wales in 1984, he won twenty-two caps, three of them in the centre, and in that period he was a central figure in Ireland's Triple Crown win of 1982. He toured South Africa with the British Lions in 1980, playing in the third and fourth Tests; with the 1983 British Lions team in New Zealand he played in all four Tests and was top scorer, with 124 points. **Karl Johnston**

Campbell-Sharp, Nöelle (1943–), publisher and patron of the arts. Born in Co. Wexford. She worked for a number of years in advertising and public relations. Her career in publishing began with her purchase of the *Irish Tatler*, which she relaunched as *IT*. In 1989 she sold her interest in the company, though remained as chief executive, devoting her time mainly to her interest in the visual arts. She established an artists' retreat in the reconstructed pre-famine village of Cill Rialaigh, near Ballinskelligs, Co. Kerry, once home to the storyteller SEÁN Ó CONAILL. **Brian Galvin**

Canada, the Irish in. The patterns of Irish EMIGRATION to Canada are in many respects singular. Both in chronology and in composition, Irish settlement in British North America has differed from that in the United States, Australia, and New Zealand. The largest part of Irish emigration to British North America had substantially ended by the time of the GREAT FAMINE; and the denominational composition of the Irish-Canadian community, though varying widely by region, has been predominantly Protestant, especially Episcopalian and Methodist. Immigration was also characterised in many areas by predominantly rural settlement.

In the 1991 census some 3.8 million Canadians claimed partial or full Irish ancestry—a sizeable segment of the population, reflecting the lasting impact of Irish emigration on the demographic profile of English-speaking and (to an important if lesser extent) French-speaking Canada. New France had an Irish population of indeterminate size, the community establishing a presence in French-speaking North America that grew after the British conquest of the French colony in 1763. The British island colony of Newfoundland was the destination for thousands of Irish immigrants, primarily from Co. Waterford, accounting for half the island's population in the 1830s. There were significant levels of late eighteenth and early nineteenth-century immigration in Halifax, Nova Scotia, and the colonies of Prince Edward Island and New Brunswick in the early nineteenth century.

It was in the period after 1815 that large-scale Irish settlement in British North America got under way. Between 1825 and 1845 the area attracted some 450,000 Irish people—in contrast with 400,000 who arrived at American ports. In this period the Protestant element of Irish immigrants was the largest. Québec and St John were the principal points of entry, though the numbers arriving at these destinations dispersed widely, not only through the British colonies but also to the United States, which probably served as the final destination for a large majority of the immigrants. The structure of settlement in Canada varied widely, with patterns of immigration following traditional trading links between ports in Ireland and the colonies (such as those between St John and Derry) reinforcing strong patterns of chain MIGRATION. Most settlement was unassisted and was undertaken by emigrants of comfortable, if not substantial, means; the most notable assisted settlement scheme was undertaken by Peter Robinson, brother of the Attorney-General of Upper Canada (later Ontario), who settled some 2,500 immigrants from the Cork area between 1822 and 1825.

In Upper Canada generally the Irish were notable for their rural settlement, an aspect of the Irish-Canadian experience now emphasised as a corrective to the perceived urban bias of the history of the Irish community in North America. Nonetheless, cities such as Toronto and Montréal were also important destinations for immigrants, especially in the middle of the nineteenth century, and were centres of an associational culture for both Protestant and Catholic sections of the Irish immigrant community, with churches and affiliated societies serving as focal points for a wider institutional network. In some places the Irish Catholic Church developed into a microcosm within a wider church structure—notably in

Canada. *Memorial erected in 1909 on Grosse Île in the St Lawrence River near Québec. Irish immigrants perished in their thousands at Grosse Île as they were quarantined to check the spread of cholera into North America. [Photo: Jules-Ernest Livernois/National Archives of Canada, PA-136924]*

Montréal, where it carved out a significant measure of administrative autonomy within the French-speaking Catholic milieu. Similarly, the diocesan structure of the Catholic Church in Nova Scotia sought to accommodate the predominantly Irish Catholic community in Halifax and the colony's wider Scottish Catholic population. Areas of heavy Catholic settlement in the pre-famine era, including the Miramichi in New Brunswick and the port of Halifax, received few Famine emigrants, more than 100,000 of whom arrived during 1847, the year of the highest level of emigration to British North America; instead, these made their way to Upper and Lower Canada (later Québec). For the remainder of the century, however, numbers tapered off dramatically, and Ulster's numerical predominance reasserted itself. By 1871 less than half of Canada's Irish-born population was Catholic; the proportion had increased since the 1830s but even so had failed to significantly alter the complexion of the Irish-Canadian community in places such as Ontario, where the largest number lived and in which Protestants were numerically dominant. By contrast, Newfoundland's Irish community was almost exclusively Catholic, and Catholics were in the majority in Québec, Nova Scotia, and Prince Edward Island. The consequences of this pattern of migration included the development of a strong tradition of Orangeism in areas of mixed and heavy Protestant settlement, notably in regions of Upper Canada and New Brunswick, where the lodge structure served as a focus for communities and eventually included wider sections of the colonial Protestant population. Among these Protestants, Anglicans were the largest denomination, followed by Methodists; the remarkable contrast in the proportion of Methodists in British North America and in Ireland is due partly to the denomination's extraordinary success in gaining adherents through conversion throughout the colonies.

Settlement of the Canadian West, which occurred in the second half of the nineteenth century, comprised large numbers of second and third-generation Irish-Canadians. In contrast to the United States, twentieth-century Irish emigration to Canada was comparatively light, though the country continued to receive immigrants from Ireland, north and south. Throughout Canada's history, Irish-born figures have played a leading role in the country's political, social, and economic development, from early colonial political leaders such as Robert Baldwin and Francis Hincks, both Cork Protestants, to THOMAS D'ARCY MCGEE, a dynamic personality who played a central role in forging the colonial federation of 1867 and the most famous victim of political assassination in Canadian history.

The contemporary Irish-Canadian community, now overwhelmingly comprising Canadian-born people of Irish descent, has created institutions that nurture a sense of national identity and asserts its place within the framework of multi-cultural Canada. The deep roots of the Irish in Canada provide a foundation for strong contemporary links between Canada and Ireland, expressed through extensive cultural, political, and human interactions. **K. J. James**

Canada, Irish writing in. Irish writing in Canada began in the late eighteenth century, when the country was designated 'British North America'. The Irish cultural divide of the eighteenth century is represented by DONNCHADH RUA MAC CON MARA and Butler Lacy, who wrote poems about their experiences in Talamh an Éisc (Newfoundland), whose fishery was an important source of income for many generations. Mac Conmara's poems constitute the earliest body of verse in Irish written anywhere in North America. From later in the century there are accounts of Irish life in Newfoundland in the edited letters of the first Bishop of Newfoundland, Rev. James O'Donel, and his successors.

Sizeable immigration from Ireland began following the British conquest of Canada in 1759. Many of those who went in the early nineteenth century became engaged in journalism. John Sparrow Thompson from Waterford, Edward Whelan from Ballina, Co. Mayo, Timothy Anglin from Clonakilty, Co. Cork, Thomas Coffey from Castleconnell, Co. Limerick, and Patrick Boyle from Newport, Co. Mayo, founded newspapers in Nova Scotia, Prince Edward Island, New Brunswick, and Ontario that were strong advocates of Irish Catholic immigration and of Irish nationalism. The most famous voice in French-Canadian poetry in the nineteenth century was that of Émile Nelligan, born in Québec of Irish-French parents. William Henry Drummond of Mohill, Co. Leitrim, wrote popular droll verse employing French-Canadian characters' ungainly English. William Francis Butler of Suirville, Co. Tipperary, wrote the appropriately titled *Great Lone Land* (1870), an account of western Canada that went into seventeen editions.

The writer and politician THOMAS D'ARCY MCGEE, a prolific writer on both Ireland and Canada, promoted a distinctly Canadian literature. Nicholas Flood Davin from Kilfinnane, Co. Limerick, published *The Irishman in Canada* (1877), intended 'to raise the self respect of every Irish person in Canada.' Kit Coleman (born Catherine Ferguson in Castleblakeny, Co. Galway) was the best-known woman journalist in Canada at the end of the nineteenth century; her struggles for a place in a male-dominated profession led her to found the Canadian Women's Press Club in 1904.

The twentieth century saw many Canadians, Irish by birth or descent, such as Katherine Hughes of Prince Edward Island, support the ideals of Irish national independence in their writings. There are accounts of the Irish and of Irish life in Canada in works as diverse as James Reaney's dramatic trilogy *The Donnellys* (1975), Alden Nolan's *Various Persons Named Kevin O'Brien* (1973), Patrick Slater's *The Yellow Briar* (1941), and W. O. Mitchell's *Who Has Seen the Wind* (1947). *Home is the Stranger* (1950) by Edward McCourt from Mullingar, Co. Westmeath, deals with the struggles of an Irish war bride in western Canada. Brian Moore's *The Luck of Ginger Coffey* (1972), concerning an Irish immigrant in Montréal, won the Governor-General's award for fiction in 1960.

Recent Canadian writing has dealt with a variety of Irish themes. Charles Foran's *The Last House of Ulster* (1995) and *Kitchen Music* (1994) and John Brady's *Kaddish in Dublin* (1992), *All Souls* (1993), and *The Good Life* (1995) are set in Ireland. Jane Urquhart's award-winning *Away* (1993) deals with Irish influence on Canada, while a complex murder in nineteenth-century Ontario with Irish principals furnished the plot for Margaret Atwood's novel *Alias Grace* (1998). **Cyril Byrne**

canals. The canal age in Ireland began with the passing of an act of 1715, but little capital was available, and a second act was passed in 1729, setting up Commissioners of Inland Navigation for each province (dissolved 1787) and providing public funding. The NEWRY CANAL, begun in 1731 to provide access to the Co. Tyrone coalfields and completed in 1742, was the first summit-level canal in Ireland or Britain. Directors-General of Inland Navigation were appointed in 1800 and for thirty years controlled the development of waterways. Work on the GRAND CANAL, linking Dublin with the River SHANNON, began in 1756 and was completed to Shannon Harbour, Co. Offaly, by 1804. The considerable challenge of building the canal through deep bogs was overcome. The competing ROYAL CANAL, begun in 1789, was connected to the Shannon Navigation at Cloondara, Co. Longford, in 1817. Each canal has two major AQUEDUCTS. The Barrow Line of the Grand Canal connects with the Barrow Navigation, providing access to Waterford.

The Royal Canal is now undergoing restoration, and it is also proposed to restore the ULSTER CANAL and Lagan Navigation, thus linking Belfast with the inland waterways system. The canals are now under the control of an all-Ireland authority, Waterways Ireland. **Ronald Cox**

Canon tables, often illuminated, form part of the apparatus of manuscript GOSPEL books before the twelfth century. They are the index to a system of divisions given to the sacred text (indicated by marginal numbers) to show which portion of text is present in more than one Gospel. [see MANUSCRIPTS.] **Thomas O'Loughlin**

Cantwell, Noel (1934–), soccer player. Born in Cork. A fine athlete who anchored the Republic of Ireland team in a difficult period, he started in the League of Ireland with Cork Athletic before signing for West Ham in 1953. He joined Manchester United in 1961 and, as team captain, became one of Sir Matt Busby's most trusted players in the rebuilding process that followed the loss of eight Manchester United players in the Munich air crash of 1958. He led the team to victory in the 1963 FA Cup final before being appointed manager of Coventry City. As an Ireland player he alternated with marked success between defence and attack, scoring many important goals. One of the few to act as player-manager of the national team, he embodied the passion of Irish football more than most. As a cricketer he was good enough to represent Ireland before concentrating on football. **Peter Byrne**

***caoineadh* (literature),** a poetic and performance genre, with primordial origins, framed as a dirge in praise of the dead, composed in irregular stanzas using a stressed metre. Most surviving texts are from eighteenth and nineteenth-century Munster manuscripts. The term *rosc*, applied to the metre, has convincingly been challenged as a misnomer.

This poetry has been the source of intense scholarly fascination, beginning in the late nineteenth century. CAOINEADH AIRT UÍ LAOGHAIRE (edited by SEÁN Ó TUAMA, 1961) provided a fixed text and an analysis of the historical background of one poem. Coupled with its continuing fame in different translations, this text has been overemphasised by many, to the neglect of others. More recently, cross-cultural, oral formulaic performance and feminist theories have been employed to support a thesis of *caoineadh* as essentially a women's performance genre, often as much a protest

canals. The Opening of Ringsend Docks, Dublin *[1796], by William Ashford, depicting the celebrations on the completion of the Docks in 1796, which would by 1805 provide a link between the Liffey and the Shannon. The Lord Lieutenant, Lord Camden (under the flag, right), confers a knighthood on the kneeling John Macartney, chairman of the Grand Canal Company. Refreshment tents are on the right, the Lord Lieutenant's gondola is in the foreground, and a salute is being fired on the left. [National Gallery of Ireland]*

against colonial oppression and male domination as a eulogy for the dead. This has been challenged on the grounds that hard evidence of performance is lacking and that existing descriptions cannot be directly equated with manuscript sources. The Munster provenance of all the surviving poems has been invoked to assert that the genre was adopted and adapted by eighteenth-century literary poets there; in this view the naming of extemporising female mourners as the authors of poems was merely a literary device. This assessment does not consider distinct but metrically and thematically related Connacht and Ulster texts, such as 'Donnchadh Bán' and 'Fill, Fill, a Rún-ó', nor does it satisfactorily resolve the question of manuscript and oral variation. Consequently, many issues remain unsettled, and the complex interplay between history, politics, extempore composition and recitation, orally transmitted and literary texts, and their relevance to musical elements, will continue to engage scholars. **Lillis Ó Laoire**

***caoineadh* (traditional music),** a ritual lament publicly extemporised over a corpse, usually by specialist women singers. Though moribund, it covertly endures in some Irish-speaking communities. No electronic recording of such a ritual exists, though some tunes were recovered from oral tradition. One demonstrates a striking intensification of voice, gradually shifting from high-pitched chanted speech to a recognisably musical form. A descending melody, simply and loosely constructed, facilitated the composition of verse. The *caoineadh* may have had three distinct musical parts: the *gairm* or murmured preparation, the extemporised verse, and the *gol* or choral cry, taken up by the assembled mourners. [see WAKE.] **Lillis Ó Laoire**

Caoineadh Airt Uí Laoghaire 'The Lament for Art Ó Laoghaire'. The subject of this powerfully emotive lament was Art Ó Laoghaire (1747–1773) of Rathleigh, near Macroom, Co. Cork, a former officer in the Austrian army who was killed in 1773 by followers of a local magistrate, Abraham Morris. The circumstances that precipitated Ó Laoghaire's death involved his refusal to comply with a request to sell his horse to Morris (in accordance with a PENAL LAW designed to prevent Catholics from possessing horses or firearms fit for military use), but the tension between the two men was more deeply seated and had a sectarian and possibly also a personal aspect.

Though it was long considered an extempore oral composition composed largely by Ó Laoghaire's widow, Eibhlín Dhubh Ní Chonaill (c. 1743–c. 1800), a member of the O'Connell family, of Derrynane, Co. Kerry, modern scholarship has cast doubts on her authorship, arguing that the dramatic speaking voice employed in

Caoineadh Airt Uí Laoghaire. *A group of elegantly dressed nineteenth-century antiquarians standing among the ruins of Kilcrea Abbey, Co. Cork, 1858. Art Ó Laoghaire (of 'Caoineadh Airt Uí Laoghaire') is buried here, directly behind the foreground figure. [Getty Images/Hulton Archive]*

the text may be an example of a long-standing literary convention whereby the widow of the deceased is presented as narrator of the lament composed for him. While historians of eighteenth-century Ireland may consider its value in the context of its association with two propertied Catholic families, literary scholars have hailed it as the most outstanding example of the traditional lament to have survived. Drawing heavily on themes and motifs of earlier laments, the work is a poetic *tour de force* that has been lauded for its lyric beauty, its dramatic strength, and its passionate representation of the emotions of a bereaved young wife and mother.

The lament was recorded from oral sources in the early nineteenth century and survives in various versions, some of which give a less than favourable impression of the relationship between the deceased and his wife. It has been widely anthologised and translated (by FRANK O'CONNOR, 1962, SEÁN Ó TUAMA and THOMAS KINSELLA, 1981, and EILÍS DILLON, 1993) and is the subject of a play by TOM MCINTYRE and a film by BOB QUINN. **Máirín Nic Eoin**

Čap, Jan (1944–), pianist. Born Czechoslovakia; studied at Prague and Moscow Conservatoires. Since 1975 he has taught at the Cork School of Music, where he has been responsible for training many notable young Irish musicians. **Richard Pine**

Cape Clear Bird Observatory, established on CLÉIRE (Clear Island), Co. Cork, in 1959 for the study of bird migration. The island has become famous for its bird-life; its breeding population includes chough, black guillemot, and rock dove. Migrant birds include vagrants from America and Asia. Seabirds also pass the island in impressive numbers, as well as whales and dolphins, making Cléire one of the foremost sea-bird watching sites in Europe. The observatory is on the picturesque North Harbour (Cuas an Bháid), opposite the berthing-place of the mail boat. **Oran O'Sullivan**

Captain O'Blunder: see BRAVE IRISHMAN, THE.

Carbery, Ethna, pseudonym of Anna MacManus, née Johnston (1866–1902), writer. Born in Belfast, a daughter of Robert Johnston, a founder-member of the IRB. She contributed verse and short stories to a number of periodicals, then jointly founded and from 1896 to 1899 edited *Shan Van Vocht* with her friend ALICE MILLIGAN. She worked with Milligan and others to maintain a flourishing nationalist culture in Belfast, writing mainly patriotic verse and historical romances based on folk customs and myths. An early member of INGHINIDHE NA HÉIREANN, she died suddenly in Co. Donegal one year after her marriage. **Robbie Meredith**

Carew, Sir George (1555–1629), soldier and administrator. Son of George Carew, Dean of Windsor; he followed his father to the University of Oxford but eschewed the church for a military career. He was active in Ireland from 1574, chiefly around his brother's bailiwick at Leighlin, Co. Carlow. In 1588 he was made Master of the Queen's Ordnance in Ireland and in 1590 a privy councillor for Ireland. Two years later he became Lieutenant-General of the Ordnance in England. He joined Essex's expeditions to Cádiz, 1596, and the Azores, 1597. Following Essex's failure in the NINE YEARS' WAR, Carew was appointed President of Munster in 1600. With 3,000 soldiers, good communications by sea and the walled towns of Munster to operate from, he quickly restored English control of the province by a mixture of diplomacy and harsh measures. He ably assisted Mountjoy in blockading the Spanish force under Don Juan del Águila that landed at Kinsale, Co. Cork, in September 1601 and in routing the Irish Confederates led by HUGH O'NEILL as they tried to join their Spanish allies on Christmas Day. He retired from service in Ireland soon after the close of the Nine Years' War but returned briefly in 1610 to survey the PLANTATION OF ULSTER (see p. 877). He amassed a great collection of manuscripts relating to Ireland, now preserved in Lambeth Palace, London, which formed the basis of *Pacata Hibernia* (1633), an account by his son Thomas Stafford of the final stages of the Nine Years' War. [see KINSALE, BATTLE OF.] **Henry A. Jefferies**

Carey, D. J. (1970–), hurler. Born in Gowran, Co. Kilkenny. He is a technically brilliant player, a classical performer with flair, perception, pace, and creativity, and an outstanding artist of the modern game. He revealed his HURLING brilliance early in life, winning two all-Ireland colleges titles with St Kieran's College. At inter-county level he won all-Ireland minor hurling and under-21 hurling medals and four senior hurling, in 1992, 1993, 2000, and 2002. He also has two National Hurling League medals, one Oireachtas and two Railway Cup medals. A versatile forward, he can play in any position and is a prolific scorer from play or placed balls. He won nine All-Star awards, 1991–5, 1997, 1999, 2000, and 2002. He won the Texaco Hurler of the Year award in 1993 and 2000. At club level he captained Young Irelands-Gowran to their first county senior title in 1996. A master handballer, he achieved twenty-two major national successes in the game, as well as two world championships. He is also an accomplished golfer. **Séamus J. King**

Carey, Jackie (1919–1995), soccer player. Born in Dublin. Fifty years after his retirement he is still regarded as one of the finest defenders to play for Manchester United. His career straddled the Second World War, and in 1947 his standing in the game was high enough to warrant his appointment as captain of the Europe team that played Great Britain at Hampden Park. He captained his club to success in the 1948 FA Cup final, the year before leading the Republic of Ireland to a 2–0 success over England at Goodison Park—the first time England had been beaten by a foreign team on home terrain. He was honoured by the FAI as the first winner of their silver statuette for twenty-five international appearances. **Peter Byrne**

Carey, Patrick (1917–1999), documentary film-maker and cameraman. Born in London. In his early career he worked in Dublin theatres, but in 1945 he switched to films, making his first documentary in 1947. In 1953 he was part of the crew that filmed the ascent of Mount Everest; later he worked for the National Film Board of Canada, specialising in nature documentaries. He won an Academy Award for his photography on *Wild Wings* (1966). His most admired film, *Yeats Country* (1965), visualised W. B. YEATS's poetry using the landscape of Co. Sligo. **Kevin Rockett**

Caribbean, the Irish in the. It is likely that at least one Irishman—possibly Guillermo Ires, described in Spanish records as a native of Galway—was a crew member on a voyage of exploration to the West Indies before 1500. By the sixteenth century several Irishmen are documented in the Spanish Caribbean. In 1525 Achilles Holden, an Irish priest, was teaching at Santo Domingo. In 1587 Darby Glavin and Dennis Carroll, Irish sailors in WALTER RALEIGH's service, deserted in Puerto Rico from a colony bound for Roanoke Island; Glavin survived and served from 1595 as a soldier in Spanish Florida.

During subsequent centuries Irish adventurers, MISSIONARIES and soldiers played prominent roles in the Spanish, French, Dutch, and Danish West Indies. In 1764 Alejandro O'Reilly from Co. Meath, an officer in the service of Spain, recommended Irish emigration to Cuba as a tonic for that island's sluggish economy, and in 1765 he reorganised Puerto Rico's defences in collaboration with his compatriot Colonel Tomás O'Daly, chief engineer in San Juan. At the same time Nicholas Tuite, born into an Irish family in Montserrat, became a leading planter in St Croix, then a Danish colony, importing Irish overseers to manage his seven estates and Irish Dominicans to minister to his staff.

Whether arriving as voluntary or involuntary IMMIGRANTS, most Caribbean Irish settled in the English West Indies: the Leeward Islands, Barbados, and Jamaica. Both planters and indentured servants of Irish origin were involved from an early date in the mother colony of St Christopher, colonised by England, 1624–5, in uneasy partnership with the French. Religious tensions regularly boiled over as Irish Catholics encountered a hostile pre-Commonwealth diaspora of Puritan planters and merchants. Between 1628 and 1633 the other Leeward Islands—Antigua, Nevis, and Montserrat—were colonised from overcrowded St Christopher. A report by missionaries in 1637 estimated a total of 3,000 Irish people in the Leeward Islands.

On rugged and remote Montserrat, Anthony Briskett from Co. Wexford was the first of six Irish-born officials who ruled a predominantly Catholic population of Irish servants, traders, and tobacco planters. By 1678 seven out of ten resident Montserrat whites—1,869 men, women, and children—were Irish.

Barbados, colonised by England in 1627, is synonymous in Irish memory with TRANSPORTATION and the slave-like servitude endured by many Irish prisoners of war and their dependants after the REBELLION OF 1641. While transportation to the Americas did not begin or end with CROMWELL's rule, contemporary accounts from the peak years of COMMONWEALTH transportation, 1652–7, show that kidnapping was used to supply labour-hungry planters

Cape Clear. *Birdwatching at Cape Clear Bird Observatory, Cléire, Co. Cork. The island has become famous for its bird life, including chough, black guillemot, and rock dove. [Richard Coombes]*

with Irish servants. In the absence of reliable records, the Irish Jesuit historian Aubrey Gwynn estimated Commonwealth transportation at 50,000 Irish people sent to the Caribbean and North America. Servants who survived voluntary indentures—typically four to seven years—or ten-year terms of penal servitude were officially free; but opportunities for the unskilled were severely limited by the consolidation of fertile lands into large estates and an increasing reliance on African slave labour as planters switched from tobacco to sugar. This change, completed by the late seventeenth century, is reflected in Montserrat's census of 1729, which shows just ninety white servants and 5,855 black slaves, many of them owned by families with Irish surnames, such as Daly, Farrill, Hussey, Lynch, and Roach. The post-servitude fate of indentured Irish servants—of which Barbados had 8,000 in 1669—is largely undocumented. The popular belief that most migrated to Virginia and Carolina is not supported by the only surviving departure record, that for Barbados from 1679. Out of ninety with likely Irish surnames, a quarter left for North America; almost a third moved to other English islands in the Caribbean, while 45 per cent departed for ports in England and Wales. This suggests that, contrary to accepted belief, significant numbers made their way home.

Contemporary accounts confirm that Jamaica, captured by the English from the Spanish in 1655, attracted large numbers of Irish people with promises of generous land grants and religious toleration. Here, as in Antigua and Montserrat, a minority made a successful transition from servant to slave-owning planter. Their descendants, often intermarried with English families, gradually abandoned the Caribbean for lives of opulence as absentee landlords in London, Philadelphia, or (in Nicholas Tuite's case) Copenhagen. Others turned to subsistence agriculture, living quiet lives in isolated Caribbean back country. One poor white community, the 'Redlegs' of Barbados's windward coast, is believed to descend from English, Irish, and Scots servants. Untypically, these whites clung stubbornly to their racial identity even as the abolition of slavery, in 1834, transformed them into second-class citizens of the black-majority island. In Montserrat and Jamaica, in contrast, historians believe that many of the Irish people who remained were absorbed, through intermarriage, into dominant Afro-Caribbean populations. **Brian McGinn**

Carleton, William (1794–1869), novelist. Born in Prillisk, Co. Tyrone, of a farming family; educated at a HEDGE SCHOOL and intended by his family to join the priesthood. As a young man he moved to Dublin, where he worked first as a tutor. From 1828 his sketches of rural life appeared in CAESAR OTWAY's anti-Catholic *Christian Examiner*, he also contributed to the NATION, DUBLIN UNIVERSITY MAGAZINE, and other periodicals. The publication of TRAITS AND STORIES OF THE IRISH PEASANTRY (first series) in 1830 established his literary reputation. His first novel, *Fardorougha the Miser*, appeared serially in 1837–8; later novels include *The Black Prophet* (1847), a famine novel, *The Emigrants of Ahadarra* (1848), *The Tithe Proctor* (1848), and *The Squanders of Castle Squander* (1852). He died in Dublin in 1869; his unfinished autobiography was published in 1896.

While Carleton's religious and political loyalties remain a matter of debate, his life and career are a vivid reflection of the divisions and tensions in early nineteenth-century Ireland. His work was praised by MARIA EDGEWORTH, W. B. YEATS, and others for its authentic representations of Irish life. He was the first writer of fiction to publish principally in Ireland, and his work has played a defining role in the development of Irish fiction in English (see p. 1065). **Margaret Kelleher**

Carlingford Lough, a narrow fjord on the east coast between Co. Down and Co. Louth, flanked by the Mourne and Carlingford Mountains. It lies in a glacially deepened valley carved out by ice-sheets exploiting existing valleys on its way to the sea. The deepened valley became flooded when the sea level rose after the melting of the ice sheets to form the drowned fjord or lough. It is aligned along north-west to south-east faults associated with the Mourne-Carlingford complex of igneous rocks. It was named by the VIKINGS (the name meant 'bay of the hag'), though there is little evidence to suggest a permanent Viking settlement. The lough is narrower and shallower at its entrance, because of outcrops of limestone that obstruct the channel.

Carlingford, on the south-west shore, originated as an ANGLO-NORMAN settlement. The Newry ship canal, now disused, connects Newry with Carlingford Lough. [see NEWRY NAVIGATION.] **R. A. Charlton**

Carlow, County (*Contae Cheatharlach*)

Province:	LEINSTER
County town:	CARLOW
Area:	896 km^2 (347 sq. miles)
Population (2002):	45,845
Features:	Blackstairs Mountains
	River Barrow
	River Burren
Of historical interest:	BROWNE'S HILL portal tomb
	Carlow Castle
	Old Leighlin Cathedral
	Saint Mullins
Industry and products:	Barley, wheat, and sugarbeet
	Dairy farming
	Food-processing

Petula Martyn

County Carlow, a county in south Leinster between the River BARROW and the Blackstairs Mountains, is the second-smallest county (after LOUTH). It is one of the premier TILLAGE regions in Ireland, with wheat, barley, and sugarbeet the main crops. A wealthy agricultural past is reflected in a rich legacy of rural buildings dating from the Middle Ages to the nineteenth century. Co. Carlow, established in 1306, was part of the strategic corridor to Dublin following the ANGLO-NORMAN conquest, and throughout the Middle Ages it was a source of conflict. Castles were erected by the new settlers at Carlow, Tullow, and Leighlinbridge, which were frequently attacked by the neighbouring Irish. Eventually much of the county was taken over by MACMURROUGH KAVANAGH. **Patrick Duffy**

Carlow, population (2002) 13,188, the county town, was besieged by CROMWELL in 1650 and was the scene of the slaughter of hundreds of insurgents in the REBELLION OF 1798. It has the first Catholic cathedral built after CATHOLIC EMANCIPATION, erected by JAMES DOYLE, the formidable Bishop of Kildare and Leighlin. The courthouse, by Richard Morrison, is one of the finest neo-classical buildings in Ireland. LEIGHLINBRIDGE, with its ancient nine-arched bridge and castle, was the birthplace of JOHN TYNDALL, one of the greatest scientists of the nineteenth century. Bagnelstown (Muine Bheag) and SAINT MULLINS, with its Early Christian and later medieval remains, mark the course of the River BARROW, which is

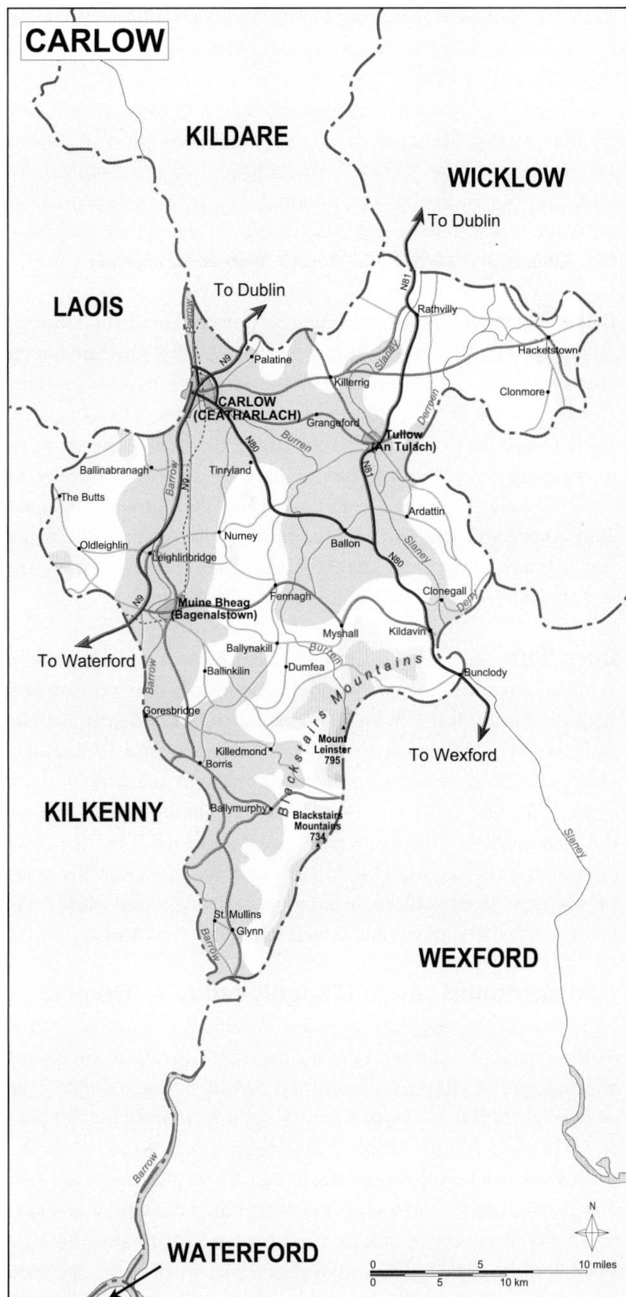

navigable from the Grand Canal southwards to Saint Mullins and northwards from Waterford harbour. **Patrick Duffy**

Carman, Fair of, a three-yearly fair reputedly held in Leinster in August, documented by EUGENE O'CURRY from manuscripts, supposedly begun c. 580 BC by TUATHA DÉ DANANN in memory of one Carmen of Athens. Here the province's laws were reviewed ('There aloud with boldness they proclaimed, the rights of every law, and the restraints') and provisions, precious metals, stock, and clothes offered for sale. The professors of verbal and visual arts, professional and amateur, demonstrated their prowess ('inscribed tablets, and books of trees, satires, and sharp edged runes') and music-makers played ('Pipes, fiddles, chainmen, bone-men, and tube players'). Failure, poverty, and baldness were among the penalties for neglecting the event. **Fintan Vallely**

Carnduff, Thomas (1886–1956), poet and playwright. Born in Belfast. He served in the British army during the FIRST WORLD WAR. His poetry and drama largely deal with the industrial life of his native city from a working-class and socialist viewpoint. **Terence Brown**

Carnfree, Co. Roscommon, inauguration place of the Ó Conchobhair dynasts of Síol Muireadhaigh, from whom the kings of Connacht were drawn as early as the ninth century. It is poetically cited in connection with CATHAL CROBHDHEARG in 1189, while the ANNALS record four inaugurations there between 1225 and 1407. Fráech (after whom the mound is named) appears as the central character in 'Táin Bó Fraích' and in an incident in the epic 'TÁIN BÓ CÚAILNGE'. JOHN O'DONOVAN identified the site as a small mound on Ard Cáin near Tulsk, claiming as supporting evidence a reference to its location in the Rennes DINNSEANCHAS. **Elizabeth FitzPatrick**

Carolan, Nicholas (1946–), TRADITIONAL MUSIC archivist, lecturer, and broadcaster. Born in Drogheda. He is director of the IRISH TRADITIONAL MUSIC ARCHIVE in Dublin and general editor of its publications, presenter and researcher of the radio series 'The Irish Phonograph' and the television series 'Come West Along the Road', and long-term secretary of the Folk Music Society of Ireland. He lectured in traditional music in TRINITY COLLEGE, Dublin, from 1985 to 1998. Among his published work is an edition of the first collection of Irish music, *A Collection of the Most Celebrated Irish Tunes of 1724* (1986), and *A Harvest Saved: Francis O'Neill and Irish Music in Chicago* (1997). **Maeve Ellen Gebruers**

Carolan, Turlough, Anglicised name of Toirealach Ó Cearúlláin (1670–1738), harper and composer. Born near Nobber, Co. Meath. When he was a child the family moved to Alderford, Co. Roscommon, to work for the MacDermott Roe family. Carolan was educated by them; and when he was blinded by smallpox at the age of eighteen Mrs MacDermott Roe had him taught the harp. When he was twenty-one she provided him with a horse, a servant, and money; thus began his life as an itinerant harper. As a professional player Carolan was welcomed in many of the 'big houses' of Connacht and Ulster, often providing his patrons with songs and airs dedicated to them. He was not a remarkable musician, but he quickly established a reputation as a composer, which gave him a status superior to that of his fellow-harpers. His music was published in his own lifetime; some of it by EDWARD BUNTING in his collections. This work reflects the influence of 'folk' music as well as that of the great Italian composers of his day. When Carolan became ill he returned to the MacDermott Roes at Alderford, where he died. **Maeve Ellen Gebruers**

Carpenter, G. H. [George Herbert] (1865–1939), scientist. Born in London; educated at the University of London. On the staff of the NATIONAL MUSEUM under R. F. SCHARFF, he worked on huge groups of insects and arachnids (spiders and mites), especially spiders and difficult insect groups such as springtails, bristletails, and warbles. One of the first editors and founders, with R. LLOYD PRAEGER, of the *Irish Naturalist*, he became professor of zoology in the Royal College of Science for Ireland, 1904, and secretary of the ROYAL ZOOLOGICAL SOCIETY OF IRELAND, 1911. He moved to Manchester in 1923, where he became keeper of the University Museum of Manchester until he retired in 1937. While still there he took Holy Orders.

Carpenter is responsible for beginning the resolution of the problem of warble fly in cattle. Warble flies lay eggs on cattle in summer, thereby causing them to run away to avoid infestation by 'gadding' (hence the term 'gad-fly'). Eventually the warbles migrate to the

Carolan, Turlough. *A plaque in St Patrick's Cathedral, Dublin, honouring Turlough Carolan, 'the last of the Irish bards,' with a relief portrait sculpted by John Hogan Junior (1824). [Mark Joyce]*

cattle's back, where they mature and emerge as larvae. They thereby cause distress to cattle and significant damage to cattle hides. With T. R. Hewitt, Carpenter showed that they could be eradicated by hand extraction from the backs of cattle in an identified and isolated area. This research eventually led to the eradication of warbles from cattle in Ireland, which has greatly benefited farming. **D. Patrick Sleeman**

carpets. The first textile floor coverings used in Ireland were *flat-weaves* or tapestry carpets. In the sixteenth century, Flemish artisans in Kilkenny brought in by the second Earl of Ormond made pile carpets. Throughout the eighteenth century the DUBLIN SOCIETY offered premiums for quality Turkey or Persian carpets; the most notable recipient was William Reed of the Royal Charter School, Clontarf, Co. Dublin.

Alexander Morton, supported by the CONGESTED DISTRICTS BOARD, founded the Donegal Carpet Factory (1899–1974), where carpets of Turkish, floral, and 'Celtic' designs were hand-knotted on vertical looms; by 1906 the factory had produced 25,000 m^2 (30,000 sq. yards) of carpet. Robert T. Flower set up the Durrow Carpet Factory (1902–4) at Durrow, Co. Laois, where he made Turkey-knot carpets with his patented latch-hook needle; two years later he sold the business, under licence, to Viscount de Vesci of Abbeyleix, Co. Laois, who in turn established the Abbeyleix Carpet Works. The Naas Home Industries Co-operative Society (1902–9) was established with aid from Brinton's of Kidderminster to make hand-tufted carpets on vertical looms. Abbeyleix amalgamated with Naas, making carpets for the ocean liners *Olympic* and TITANIC under the 'Kildare' label.

The DUN EMER GUILD produced carpets of floral, eastern, and 'Celtic' styles designed by Evelyn Gleeson and Katherine McCormack. In the 1960s Tintawn Carpets was established as a subsidiary of Irish Ropes Ltd. Among the centres of carpet-making today are Cos. Donegal and Galway, Newbridge (Droichead Nua), Co. Kildare, and Navan, Co. Meath. **Mairead M. Johnston**

Carr, Marina (1964–), playwright. Born in Dublin and brought up in Co. Offaly. Several of her plays have been presented at the ABBEY and Peacock Theatres, Dublin. Her early works, including *Low in the Dark* (1989), are non-naturalist in form. *The Mai* (1994), *Portia Coughlan* (1996), and *By the Bog of Cats* (1998) are set in the midlands and deal with events leading up to the suicide of the central female character. *On Raftery's Hill* (2000) presents an apparently respectable family that is hiding a history of abuse and incest; it was followed by *Ariel* (2002). Carr's plays are linguistically rich and characterised by black humour. **Anna McMullan**

Carr, Tom (1909–1999), landscape painter. Born in Belfast; studied at Slade School of Fine Art, London, and in Italy. He was associated with the Euston Road School and exhibited in London at Leicester Galleries, Redfern Gallery, Royal Academy, and Wildenstein Gallery. In Belfast he was represented in CEMA solo exhibitions in 1948, 1953, and 1960. He also exhibited in Dublin at the RHA and the OIREACHTAS. Retrospectives were organised by the ARTS COUNCILS in Belfast and Dublin in 1983 at the ULSTER MUSEUM and the Douglas Hyde Gallery. In London he is represented at the Tate Gallery and the Victoria and Albert Museum. **Theo Snoddy**

Carrauntoohil and Macgillycuddy's Reeks, the highest and most rugged mountains in Ireland, west of KILLARNEY in the IVERAGH PENINSULA. Macgillycuddy's Reeks form an east-west ridge of old red sandstone 10 km (6 miles) long, with six peaks of over 3,000 feet (914 m). Carrauntoohil is Ireland's highest peak, at 1,039 m (3,409 ft). Lying at the western end of the Reeks, it is usually approached from the north-east by way of the Hag's Glen and Devil's Ladder; on a clear day it affords panoramic views as far north as Galway Bay—though misty days are far more common. It overlooks the cirque of Coomloughra to the north-west, the circuit of which forms Ireland's finest horseshoe walk, with Beenkeragh (1,010 m, 3,314 ft), Carrauntoohil, and Caher (1,001 m, 3,284 ft). The Reeks extend eastwards from this group to the Gap of Dunloe. The main peaks are Cnoc an Chuillin (957 m, 3,141 ft), Bearna Rua (963 m, 3,159 ft), Knocknapeasta (973 m, 3,191 ft), and Cruach Mhór (933 m, 3,062 ft). In places the ridge is a knife-edged *arête*, with cliffs dropping precipitously to cirque lakes such as Coomeennapeasta and Lough Callee. A Reeks walk is organised annually around late May. **Kevin Hourihan**

Carrickfergus (*Carraig Fhearghais*), Co. Antrim, a town founded by JOHN DE COURCY in 1177; population (1991) 22,786. It prospered as the chief town and seat of the Earls of Ulster and outpost of English influence throughout the Middle Ages. Protected by CARRICKFERGUS CASTLE—itself begun by de Courcy as early as 1178—the town quickly acquired the trappings of medieval urban status: the parish church of St Nicholas was begun at much the same time, burgess plots and town walls were laid out, and two friaries were built. Carrickfergus survived repeated attacks by the Scots and

Irish between 1386 and 1575 and subsequently experienced radical improvement, particularly at the hands of Sir ARTHUR CHICHESTER, appointed governor of the castle shortly after 1600. He extended and completed the town wall, oversaw the construction of new courthouses and jails, and built his own mansion, Joymount, on the site of the FRANCISCAN friary. Thereafter, despite retaining its strategic importance as a heavily defended site at the mouth of Belfast Lough, Carrickfergus was gradually eclipsed economically by the growth of Belfast.

Modern Carrickfergus continues to experience similar problems. While retaining many historic traces of its medieval origins, the town also bears the scars of its more chequered recent history, arising from the failure of overseas investment, particularly in textiles, and the difficulty of attracting adequate substitute forms of employment. **Lindsay Proudfoot**

Carrickfergus Castle, Co. Antrim, built on Belfast Lough by JOHN DE COURCY c. 1178. It consisted of a great tower with a hall inside a simple curtain-wall. The early castle had no mural towers and only a simple gateway and depended on its natural defences, being surrounded by water on all but the north side, where it has a rock-cut fosse. There are several subsequent phases of building: period II, c. 1225, saw a middle curtain-wall added, and period III, c. 1226–42, an outer curtain-wall and great gate-house. Subsequent alterations were mainly to existing buildings, such as the gate-house. Carrickfergus's strength and strategic position as a fortress made it a significant location in numerous conflicts and it was besieged and captured a number of times, by Edward Bruce in 1315–16, by the Duke of Schomberg in 1689, and by the French Commander Thurot in 1760. **David Sweetman**

Carrickmacross lace, an embroidered net inspired by Italian LACE and introduced to the women of Carrickmacross, Co. Monaghan, by Mrs Grey Porter in the early 1820s. The industry was revived twice, first by the Bath and Shirley Lace Schools, founded in 1846, and later by the nuns of the St Louis Convent, Carrickmacross, who ensured its survival; it is still made today. Carrickmacross appliqué lace is made by applying cambric to net, cutting the cambric according to the design, and using point stitches to enhance the design. 'Guipure' lace is made when the cambric is cut away and needlepoint 'bars' or 'ties' are inserted to link the patterns. **Alex Ward**

Carrick-on-Suir (*Carraig na Siúire*), Co. Tipperary, a market town on the River SUIR, long associated with the BUTLER family, later Earls of Ormond; population (2002) 5,543. A priory was established at the end of the twelfth or beginning of the thirteenth century for the canons regular of St Augustine. Later the lands formed part of the possessions of Theobald Butler; his grandson Edmund Butler built the first castle in 1309. Edmund Mac Richard Butler rebuilt the castle in the fifteenth century and the first stone bridge (1447) across the suir. In the middle of the sixteenth century THOMAS DUFF BUTLER (Black Tom) built ORMOND MANOR HOUSE close by the earlier castle, and this is widely regarded as the finest Elizabethan manor-house in Ireland. Part of the surviving town wall can be seen at SEÁN KELLY Square (named after a local cycling hero). The Town Clock (1784) was a gift of the Galleway family. In 1670 the Butlers established a WOOLLEN industry in the town, which survived until the nineteenth century. There were strong links with Newfoundland through extensive local emigration to the cod fishery in the eighteenth and nineteenth centuries.

Carrauntoohil. *Rowan trees at Macgillycuddy's Reeks, Co. Kerry. In the background stands Carrauntoohil, the highest peak in the mountain range and the highest in Ireland, at 1,039 m (3,409 ft). [Gareth McCormack]*

Tipperary Crystal and Glanbia Food are the main industrial employers, but retail activity is constrained by the strong influences of nearby CLONMEL, WATERFORD, and KILKENNY. **Ruth McManus**

Carroll, Mella (1934–), judge. Born in Dublin; educated at UCD and the KING'S INNS. She was called to the bar in 1957 and became a senior counsel in 1976, specialising in conveyancing and commercial law. She was appointed a judge of the High Court in 1980, the first woman appointed to a superior court. She was also the Bar Council's first woman chairperson, 1979, and is chairperson of the Legal Aid Board. **Neville Cox**

Carroll, Paul Vincent (1900–1968), playwright. Born in Dundalk, Co. Louth; educated at St Patrick's College, Dublin. In 1921 he emigrated to Scotland, working as a teacher in Glasgow. His first play, *The Watched Pot* (1930), was produced at the Peacock Theatre, Dublin; *Things That Are Caesar's* (1932) followed at the ABBEY THEATRE. Ironic and satirical, his major work is *Shadow and Substance* (1937), produced at the Abbey and subsequently in New York, where it won the Drama Critics' Circle Award in 1938 for best foreign play; it also received the Casement Award from the IRISH ACADEMY OF LETTERS. An investigation into conflict between modernity and custom, it subtly suggests the complex possibilities that faced citizens of the Free State, among them religious orthodoxy and sexual liberation. *The White Steed*, a lyrical lament for a young innocent in a material world, was rejected by the Abbey on grounds of anti-clericalism but was produced in New York to win a second Circle Award in 1939.

Established as a successful writer, Carroll retired from teaching in 1937 and moved to America, before settling in England in 1941. Of his later plays, *The Strings, My Lord, Are False* (1942), set in Glasgow during the SECOND WORLD WAR and produced at the OLYMPIA THEATRE, Dublin, and *The Devil Came from Dublin* (1951) stand out. Carroll was also a capable prose writer, as his *Irish Stories and Plays* (1958) suggests. **Nicholas Allen**

Carrowkeel, Co. Sligo, one of two major PASSAGE-TOMB cemeteries in Co. Sligo which date from the late NEOLITHIC, 3000–2000 BC, with occupation up to c. 1500 BC. Sited towards the northern end of five limestone ridges in the Bricklieve Mountains, it consists of thirteen round cairns or mounds, a long cairn, and a megalithic cist. Investigation of nine sites in 1911 yielded cremated bone and typical PASSAGE-TOMB finds. Several were found to contain cruciform or related passage tombs. No megalithic art is known from this cemetery. On a plateau immediately below the cemetery at the north-east is a dense cluster of hut sites. [see CARROWMORE.] **Paul Walsh**

Carrowmore and Knocknarea, Co. Sligo, a PASSAGE-TOMB complex on the Cúil Iorra peninsula. Carrowmore, a NEOLITHIC cemetery 0.5 km^2 (0.2 sq. miles) in area, was the ritual centre in the region. It had originally about sixty-five boulder circles with central burial chambers (of which thirty remain), the largest cluster of megalithic monuments in Ireland. The mountain of Knocknarea, overlooking Carrowmore, is dominated by the huge passage-tomb cairn of Miusgan Meabha. Passage tombs, hut sites, and extensive enclosures show that Knocknarea was intensively used in the Neolithic Period. Dates of use from Carrowmore span the period 4500–3300 BC, while the Knocknarea monuments probably date from 3500 to 3000 BC. **Stefan Bergh**

Carson, Ciarán (1948–), writer, musician, and poet. Born in Belfast; educated at QUB. He has been described as the 'circus act of contemporary Irish letters—a double-jointed marvel who defies the narrow classifying imagination.' Though his work shuns categorisation, it could be said that it consistently shows the inter-connectedness of all things, fusing a directness of language with long, circular narratives on topics as diverse as growing up in Belfast, Vermeer's painting, and recipes for quince jelly. A noted traditional flute-player, he has written two books on TRADITIONAL MUSIC, including *Last Night's Fun* (1996). *The Irish for No* (1987), *Belfast Confetti* (1989), and *First Language* (1993) are his best-known works of poetry; *First Language* was awarded the T. S. Eliot Prize in 1993. His eclectic vision is particularly evident in his prose works, including *The Star Factory* (1997), *Fishing for Amber* (1999), and his first 'novel', *Shamrock Tea* (2001), which combine travelogue, memoir, and meditation on art and mythology to truly original effect. **Alison Walsh**

Carson, Sir Edward (1854–1935), politician. Born in Dublin; educated at TCD. One of the most accomplished lawyers of his day, he became successively Solicitor-General for Ireland and for England. His classic defence of the Marquess of Queensberry against OSCAR WILDE resulted in the latter's disgrace and subsequent conviction for acts of gross indecency. In 1910 he succeeded WALTER LONG as the leader of Irish UNIONISM; between 1912 and 1914 he led the Ulster unionist campaign against HOME RULE, using his considerable talents as a public speaker and his connections in British politics. He was willing to negotiate for some form of Ulster exclusion but really with a view to retaining the whole of Ireland within the Union. His period of leadership saw the signing of the ULSTER COVENANT, the raising of the ULSTER VOLUNTEER FORCE, the Provisional government of Ulster, the LARNE GUN-RUNNING, and the BUCKINGHAM PALACE CONFERENCE. In 1916 he negotiated with DAVID LLOYD GEORGE and JOHN REDMOND for the exclusion of six Ulster counties for the duration of the war, foreshadowing partition; he also played a notable part in British politics during the First World War. His post-war career was something of an anti-climax; disliking the Government of Ireland Act (1920) and the ANGLO-IRISH TREATY (1921) as betrayals of Southern loyalists, he increasingly withdrew from politics. **T. G. Fraser**

cartography. Until the sixteenth century Ireland was mapped either in a worldwide context or as part of Europe. Of outstanding interest among these pre-modern maps were the Italian and Catalan *portolan* charts of the fourteenth and fifteenth centuries, which record a large number of coastal names for Ireland and other parts of maritime Europe, though for Britain and Ireland their outlines were not very accurate. Progress in mapping the interior of Ireland began only c. 1540 with the arrival of a succession of surveyors in the wake of the English military forces. Few stayed long, but together they produced an impressive collection of regional maps, typically on scales from 1:250,000 to 1:450,000, as well as plans of towns, forts, and battles (see pp. 400, 877, 915). Among the most successful of these surveyors were ROBERT LYTHE (1567–71), Francis Jobson (1587–98), and Richard Bartlett (1600–2) (see p. 595). Despite their official origin, such surveys were sometimes copied for editing and printing by private publishers, both in England and on the Continent. Especially influential among these derivative maps were those of JOHN SPEED (1612), which provided a standard image of Ireland for several generations of European readers.

The best Irish maps of the seventeenth century, however, were large-scale manuscript surveys showing the names, boundaries, and acreage of lands confiscated from native owners for redistribution to loyal proprietors. They include the Strafford Survey of Connacht and adjoining areas (1636–40) and the DOWN SURVEY of other forfeited land (1654–9), conducted by WILLIAM PETTY. It was Petty's idea to reduce and combine these two surveys for publication as a set of county, provincial, and national maps of Ireland, the only national maps in seventeenth-century Europe to be based on direct admeasurement with chain and compass. His atlas, *Hiberniae Delineatio* (1685), though incomplete, was for its time remarkably accurate.

After Petty, the cartography of Ireland was dominated by an accelerating process of articulation and refinement in which maps became larger, more numerous, more informative, and more correct—and also more dependent on the talents of native Irish surveyors and cartographers. These efforts lacked co-ordination: the counties, surveyed at various times by direction of their GRAND JURIES, remained the largest units of civil mapping throughout the eighteenth century, and much of the best surveying of the time was devoted to individual towns, estates, farms, roads, and waterways. Commercial publishers copied and combined these sources as best they could. Early attempts at centralised direction were CHARLES VALLANCEY's unfinished military survey of Ireland (1776–96), followed more successfully by the mapping of the country's post roads in 1805–17 and its larger BOGS in 1809–14. This period ended in the 1830s when the whole country began to be surveyed afresh, the interior by the ORDNANCE SURVEY and the coasts by the British Admiralty. Henceforth almost every map of Ireland, whether scholarly, scientific, or commercial, would be based on the same official outline. [see BROOKING, CHARLES; GRIFFITH, SIR RICHARD; LARCOM, T. A.; LEWIS'S 'TOPOGRAPHICAL DICTIONARY'; MERCATOR, GÉRARD; PTOLEMY; ROGER, JOHN.] **J. H. Andrews**

Carton, Maynooth, Co. Kildare, seat of the Fitzgeralds, Dukes of Leinster (see p. 29). Carton went through a number of drastic transformations from the seventeenth to the nineteenth century, with the original house extended by RICHARD CASTLE for the nineteenth Earl of Kildare. He added a storey and transformed the house into a Palladian composition with projecting end-bays, and curved colonnades connecting to service wings. Sir RICHARD MORRISON altered and further enlarged Carton for the third Duke of Leinster, reversing the order of the façades, with the entrance front becoming the garden side of the house. The result is a vast, dignified, and complex exterior. The two-storey salon with elaborate LAFRANCHINI plasterwork (c. 1739) was maintained in the nineteenth-century alterations and is one of the most sumptuously decorated eighteenth-century interiors in Ireland. **Brian Lalor**

Carver, Robert (fl. 1750–1791), artist. The son of an artist, he trained at the DUBLIN SOCIETY Schools. He is best remembered as a scene-painter in the Dublin theatres and, after 1770, in London, where his 'Dublin drop' was a sensation as a drop curtain. Like his father, he painted landscapes that are classical in composition, warm in colour, and usually peopled. **Anne Crookshank**

Cary, Joyce, pen-name of Arthur Joyce Cary (1888–1957), novelist. Born in Derry, he spent his childhood holidays in Co. Donegal, brilliantly captured in *A House of Children* (1941). After studying art in Paris and Edinburgh he studied law at Oxford and joined the colonial service in 1913, leaving it to settle in Oxford in 1920. Much thought went into his novels. *Aissa Saved* (1932) was the first of four set in Africa, the best of them *Mister Johnson* (1939). He set two trilogies in England, the first portraying creative adults, notably in *The Horse's Mouth* (1944), filmed under the same title in 1958 with Alec Guinness, the second the destructiveness of power. Other novels and essays explored change and choice in the contemporary world. **A. Norman Jeffares**

Carson, Edward. *Bronze statue of Sir Edward Carson (unveiled 8 July 1933), the founding father of Ulster unionism, at the bottom of the mile-long Prince of Wales Drive outside Parliament Buildings at Stormont, Belfast. [Northern Ireland Tourist Board Photographic Library]*

Casadh an tSúgáin (1901), a one-act play by DOUGLAS HYDE, based on W. B. YEATS's scenario, staged by the Irish Literary Theatre in the GAIETY THEATRE, Dublin, on 21 October 1901, with a cast largely from the Keating Branch of the GAELIC LEAGUE. It was first published, with English translation by LADY GREGORY, in *Samhain*, October 1901. **Pádraig Ó Siadhail**

Casement, Sir Roger (1864–1916), civil servant and nationalist. Born in Sandycove, Co. Dublin. In 1892 he entered the British colonial service in Africa, earning international fame for reports exposing the atrocities committed against native workers in the Belgian Congo and later in Peru, as a result of which he was awarded a knighthood in 1911. He joined the IRISH VOLUNTEERS in 1913 and went to Berlin to enlist Irishmen among British army prisoners of war for service in a rising. In April 1916 he attempted to smuggle a shipment of arms from Germany in support of the rising, but he was arrested on Banna Strand in Tralee Bay, Co. Kerry, and conveyed to London where he was charged with treason. His private diaries were circulated by the British government during the trial with the intention of damaging his international reputation by revealing his HOMOSEXUALITY. His knighthood was withdrawn and he was hanged on 3 August 1916; in 1965 his remains were returned to Ireland and reinterred following a state funeral. **Seán Farrell Moran**

Casey, Eamonn (1927–), bishop. Born in Co. Kerry. As a young priest he served the Irish emigrant community in the London area with great energy. He was national director of the Catholic Housing Aid Society, 1963, and joint founder of Shelter, the organisation for the homeless. Returning to Ireland, he became Bishop of Kerry, 1969–76, and of Galway, 1976–92, and a charismatic and popular media performer. In 1992 it was revealed that while in Co. Kerry he had had a sexual liaison with an American woman, Annie Murphy, and that they had a son. Resigning, he emigrated to Ecuador to take up pastoral duties there. His resignation caused a crisis in the Irish Catholic Church and hastened the decline of its moral authority. **Fergal Tobin**

Casey family, noted oarsmen and women, tug-of-war champions, wrestlers, and boxers. Known as 'the toughest family on earth,' the Caseys were natives of Ballaugh, Sneem, Co. Kerry. Michael ('Big Mick') Casey had been a bare-knuckle sparring partner for John L. Sullivan in the United States. His wife, Brigid Sullivan, herself an oarswoman, was a member of a family of noted rowers. The Caseys worked at the Cornelius Vanderbilt summer home in Newport, Rhode Island, where Michael Casey supervised the Vanderbilt fleet of racing sculls.

Michael and Brigid Casey's family of seven boys—Steve (born 1908), Paddy (born 1910), Jack (born 1911), Jim (born 1912), Mick (born 1913), Tom (born 1914), and Dan (born 1917)—and three girls—Mary Margaret (born 1916), Josephine (born 1920), and Catherine (born 1922)—were reared on the family farm at Sneem. The brothers achieved fame in Ireland, England, and the United States.

Steve and his brother Paddy won all their competitions in British wrestling during the 1930s. With Tom and Mick, as members of the Ace Rowing Club, London, they won the All-England Rowing Championships in 1935 but were disqualified from the 1936 Olympic Games because they had wrestled professionally. Running out of competition in Britain and the Continent, Steve Casey moved to the United States, where he became NWA heavyweight wrestling champion of the world at Boston Garden on 11 February 1938 when he defeated the reigning champion, Lou Thesz. Popularly known as 'Crusher' Casey, a nickname he handed on to his brothers, noted for the 'Killarney flip', he held the world title until he retired undefeated in 1947, the only Irishman to retain a world title in any discipline for such an extended period. He began boxing in 1940 when he defeated the American champion, Tiger Warrentown. Joe Louis declined Casey's invitation to fight. For a time a rowing instructor and wrestling coach at Harvard University, he opened a bar, Crusher Casey's, with his brother Jim in Boston, 1947. His daughter Margaret was a distinguished oarswoman while a student at Harvard. The subject of a ballad by BRYAN MACMAHON, 'The Famous Steve Casey', and a song, 'Steve Casey of Sneem', he is commemorated by a life-size bronze statue in Sneem.

Steve, Jim, and Tom failed to find any challengers when they placed a notice in the *Boston Globe* challenging any four to a race on the Charles River. However, Russell Codman, recent winner of a silver medal in the American national singles championship, challenged them in single sculls, for which the Governor of Massachusetts, Leverett Saltonstall, put up a cup. On 10 November 1940 an estimated 250,000 spectators saw Tom, Jim, and Steve Casey finish first, second, and third.

Tom, at first a wrestler, took up boxing in 1937 and became British amateur heavyweight champion nine days later. Jim was Pacific Coast heavyweight wrestling champion in the 1940s. Jack, the only brother to stay at home, was thought by some to be the strongest of the family. Paddy was Irish heavyweight wrestling champion from 1936 to 1938, when he broke his back in a bout that he won in Manchester. A wrestling promoter after that, he also trained his brother Mick, who fought some 200 wrestling bouts over twenty years before retiring to run his pub in Sneem.

Jack's son, Michael Noel Casey, coached the England rowing team at the 1984 Olympic Games in Los Angeles, while his daughters Bernie and Caroline, all-Ireland champions, won the sculls and pairs at the Henley Regatta in the same year.

All seven brothers were inducted into the Irish Sports Hall of Fame in 1987, the only group so honoured. **James E. Doherty**

Casey, John (1820–1891), mathematician. Born near Mitchelstown, Co. Cork. He taught at schools in Kilkenny and Kingstown (Dún Laoghaire), Co. Dublin; his early independent researches in geometry led him to enter TRINITY COLLEGE, Dublin, in 1858 to study for a degree. He was appointed professor of mathematics at the CATHOLIC UNIVERSITY, Dublin, in 1873 and in 1879 became a fellow of the Royal University. His later studies were devoted to the modern geometry of the circle and triangle. The six popular geometry textbooks he wrote in the 1880s, including *A Sequel to Euclid* (1881), are the basis of his enduring reputation. **Rod Gow**

Casey, John Keegan, popularly known by his NATION pen-name 'Leo' (1846–1870), poet and FENIAN. Born in Mullingar, Co. Westmeath, son of a small farmer. He published his first poem in the *Nation* at sixteen and his first collection, *A Wreath of Shamrocks*, four years later. He was arrested in 1867 and jailed for seven months. Though his romantic poetry is unconvincing, his popular songs are more successful, and his militant ballad of 1798, 'The Rising of the Moon', is still popular. His health damaged from incarceration, Casey died aged twenty-four on 17 March 1870. [see REBELLION, 1798, IN SONG.] **Nicholas Allen**

Cashel, Rock of, Co. Tipperary, a dramatic limestone outcrop dominating the modern town of Cashel that served as the principal fortification of the kings of Munster from the fourth century. Throughout the early Middle Ages the dominant EOGHANACHT dynasty had a close relationship with the church. At least four kings of Cashel between the eighth and tenth centuries were also ecclesiastics. Archaeological investigation has revealed the existence of a ninth or tenth-century wooden church and several phases of burial earlier than the twelfth century, suggesting a dual temporal and ecclesiastical presence during this period. In 1101 the rock was formally granted to the church, and ten years later it became the centre of the diocese.

The skyline is dominated by a number of medieval buildings, comprising the ROUND TOWER, Cormac's Chapel, the gothic cathedral, the archbishop's TOWER-HOUSE, and the hall of the vicars choral. The round tower, the earliest surviving building on the site, is constructed from dressed sandstone laid in even courses, which suggests a construction date in the early twelfth century.

In 1127 Cormac Mac Carthaigh, King of Desmond, commissioned the building now known as Cormac's Chapel. The original function of the church is far from clear, but its small size, unusual form and lavish decoration suggest that it may have been intended as a royal chapel. The twin square towers flanking the junction between nave and chancel are unique in Ireland, but the steep-pitched stone roof, which accommodates a chamber above the chapel vault, harks back to native methods of church roof construction. The style of the architectural sculpture and the quality of surviving fresco decoration suggest that craftsmen were brought in from western England. Clergy and nobility from all over Ireland attended the consecration of the chapel in 1134.

The stone sarcophagus housed in the chapel also dates from the twelfth century. The front face is carved with Scandinavian interlace ornament of extremely high quality. Traditionally it was associated with Cormac, though scholars have recently suggested that this unique monument may have been intended for his brother Tadhg, who died in 1124.

The stone cross of St PATRICK follows the Irish tradition of erecting great stone HIGH CROSSES but relies on the Continent for its iconography. The full-length figure of Christ is ultimately based on the *Volto Santo*, a famous image of Christ kept at Lucca. The desire to copy a foreign model may account for the bizarre strut under the remaining arm, necessary to support the horizontal transom of the cross.

The gothic cathedral was begun in the middle of the thirteenth century. Stylistically it reflects the simplified form of gothic typical of many contemporary Irish buildings. During the fifteenth century a fortified tower-house was incorporated in the west end of the nave to serve as the archbishop's residence.

The cathedral was burned in 1495 and again in 1647. The rock was finally abandoned in the eighteenth century when a new church and archbishop's palace were built in the town. **Rachel Moss**

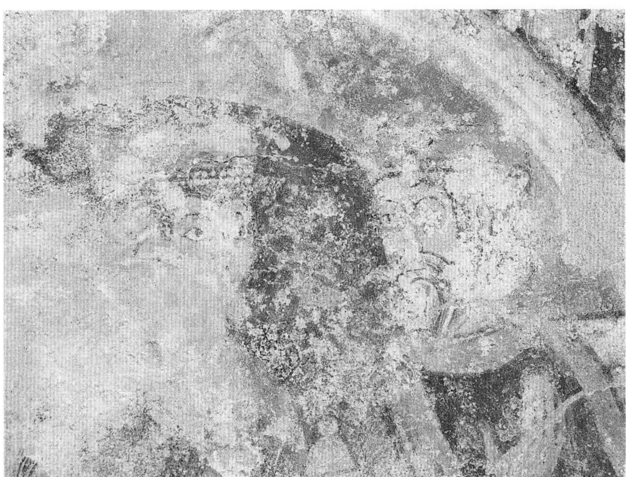

Cashel. *Fragment of fresco on the chancel-arch of Cormac's Chapel, Cashel, Co. Tipperary, a rare example of high-quality Romanesque fresco in Ireland (c. 1160–70). Two crowned figures are depicted against a rich blue background. [Dúchas, The Heritage Service]*

Casino, Marino, Dublin, a neo-classical Doric temple designed for an elevated site overlooking DUBLIN BAY in the demesne of JAMES CAULFIELD, first Earl of Charlemont, by Sir WILLIAM CHAMBERS, the architect of Somerset House in London. Charlemont's ambition was to create an Italianate landscape setting at Marino, with the Casino as its villa and ornamental focus. It was begun in 1759 and under construction for almost twenty years. Externally, the scale of the Casino suggests that it contains a single storey, whereas its spacially ingenious interior of jigsaw-like assemblage of rooms is of two storeys over basement, with a roof terrace. In plan a Greek cross, the four columned façades support a superbly carved entablature. Charlemont brought Simon Vierpyl from Rome to do the carving and supervise the construction; he may also have designed some of the interiors. Joseph Wilton created the benign lions at the angles of its base. The Casino is among the most remarkable and beautiful architectural achievements of late eighteenth-century enthusiasm for Roman classicism (see p. 183). **Brian Lalor**

Castle, Richard, also known as Cassell (c. 1690–1751), architect. A HUGUENOT from Hesse-Cassel, he began his career as an army engineer, travelling much in Europe studying fortifications and CANALS. He went to England in 1725, where he became interested in Palladian ideas. In 1728 he designed Castle Hume at Enniskillen, Co. Fermanagh, for Sir Gustavus Hume (who may have been responsible for bringing him to Ireland); the same year he was employed by Sir EDWARD LOVETT PEARCE on drawings for the PARLIAMENT HOUSE, Dublin. He was highly recommended by Pearce, whose practice he inherited. One of his first works after Pearce's death was the design for the Printing House in TRINITY COLLEGE, Dublin, a small building with a Doric temple-front. This free-standing portico contrasts with Castle's other work, in which this motif is transformed into engaged columns or pilasters onto the building.

Castle became the most prominent and probably the most prolific architect in Ireland. He was the first to build houses of cut stone in Dublin, where he built 85 St Stephen's Green (now Newman House), Tyrone House, Marlborough Street (now the Department of Education and Science), LEINSTER HOUSE (see p. 620) (now Dáil Éireann), and the ROTUNDA HOSPITAL. He built many of Ireland's most important country houses, including POWERSCOURT and Russborough, both in Co. Wicklow, CARTON, Co. Kildare, and Westport House, Co. Mayo. **Patricia McCarthy**

Castlebar (*Caisleán an Bharraigh*), Co. Mayo, a town on the Castlebar River, county town and second-largest town in Co. Mayo; population (2002) 6,581. It is on the Dublin–Westport railway line and at a main road junction; there is a small airport to the south-east. The town was founded in the early seventeenth century by John Bingham and developed by his descendants, the Earls of Lucan, during the eighteenth and nineteenth centuries. On 27 August 1798 French forces and local people under the command of General Jean Humbert advanced on the British garrison, who fled to Hollymount and Tuam in a rout known as the 'races of Castlebar'. MICHAEL DAVITT founded the LAND LEAGUE in the Imperial Hotel, Castlebar, on 16 August 1879. Castlebar is an important administrative and service centre and site of a college of the Galway-Mayo Institute of Technology and the county hospital. An industrial estate was established in the 1970s. **Mary E. Cawley**

Castle Coole, Co. Fermanagh (1789–95), a Portland stone neo-classical house with Ionic portico and pavilions connected by Doric arcades. It was built for Armar Lowry-Corry, first Earl of Belmore, by the English architect JAMES WYATT to plans originally submitted by Richard Johnston. The plasterwork is by Joseph Rose, and much of the Regency decoration and furniture was done for the second earl by Joseph Preston, the Dublin upholsterer. The Castle Coole estate on the banks of Lough Coole had been in the Corry family since 1656. **Brian Lalor**

Castledermot, Co. Kildare, site of a MONASTERY founded in 812 and plundered by VIKINGS in 842. Its oratory, burned in 1106, was replaced by a ROMANESQUE church, of which the portal survives. Its thirteenth-century enlargement, dedicated to St James, is partially incorporated in the present church, beside which stands a ROUND TOWER with (presumably secondary) crenellations. Nearby are two ninth-century granite HIGH CROSSES, sharing scenes of Adam and Eve, David the harp-player, the sacrifice of Isaac, the multiplication of loaves and fishes, the Crucifixion, the twelve apostles, and Sts Paul and Anthony. Spiral ornament on the base of the North Cross suggests copying from metalwork. The South Cross has only geometrical ornament on one face, a possible David cycle on one side, and a hunting scene on the base. Close by is a cross-decorated hog-back tomb-slab, suggesting northern English connections. The MEDIEVAL TOWN, venue for the first parliament held in Ireland (1264), was walled and had a thirteenth or fourteenth-century Franciscan friary and an Augustinian hospital. **Peter Harbison**

Castle Rackrent (1800), MARIA EDGEWORTH's first Irish fiction. It comprises a tale told by a servant, Thady Quirke, framed by a preface and glossary that explain many of his distinctive attitudes and turns of phrase. The narrator delivers a detailed chronicle of the downfall of the Rackrent family (by turns extravagant, mean, cruel, and foolish), even as he declares their great merits. His protestations of loyalty begin to sound hollow when his son, an attorney and representative of the new Catholic professional class, buys the estate from the last of the Rackrents. This ironic masterpiece had its beginnings in oral form, as tales told by Edgeworth to her siblings, in which she draws on local idiom, personalities, and scandal (see p. 340). **Claire Connolly**

Castlereagh, Viscount: see STEWART, ROBERT.

castles, medieval. The main period of building of ANGLO-NORMAN stone fortresses in Ireland was from 1175 to c. 1310 and is largely linked to historic figures and events. The earliest castles were built by a handful of powerful knights, in particular HUGH DE LACY in the east, JOHN DE COURCY in eastern Ulster, and, slightly later, William Marshal in the south-east. Hugh de Lacy, having established his authority in Meath with earth-and-timber castles, began to build more permanent and more spectacular stone structures; the earliest and most impressive of these is at TRIM, Co. Meath. John de Courcy's largest and best-known castle is that of CARRICKFERGUS.

A number of these early large stone fortresses were built on existing Anglo-Norman earth-and-timber castles, which were sited in strategic locations and in particular near large rivers. Recent excavations at Trim, Carlow, Kilkenny, and Limerick have shown that large fortresses were built on *ringworks*, a type of earth-and-timber castle. There are similar examples at Adare, Co. Limerick, and CLONMACNOISE, Co. Offaly. Other castles, such as those of DUNAMASE, Co. Laois, Carlingford and Castleroche, Co. Louth, and Ferns, Co. Wexford, are built on rock.

The castle is essentially feudal and was the fortified residence of a lord in a society dominated by the military. The earliest castles in Ireland, though they were the homes of the conquering knights, had to be well defended, because the territory in which they were being erected was hostile. All early stone castles in Ireland are fortresses and are built in strategic positions to control and dominate the newly acquired territories. The defensive emphasis in early stone structures was on the *keep* or great tower, which was the last place of refuge should the curtain-walls of the castle be breached; it also acted as the main residence of the lord and his knights. Often the keep was defended by outer and inner curtain-walls, as can be clearly seen at Carrickfergus and Trim (see p. 32). Some early castles, such as those of Dublin and Limerick, had no great tower, and accommodation was provided in the towers of the gateway and curtain-wall. The outer curtain-wall was always protected by a moat, usually filled with water, and was frequently cut out of the bedrock on which the castle was built. The digging of the moat also provided a ready source of stone for building. At Ferns the building line of the rock taken from the moat can be clearly seen.

Dunamase, built by William Marshal between 1190 and 1210, is high up on a rock outcrop and is visible for miles. The castle has outer defences that now consist of a wide, deep ditch but originally also had a wooden palisade. There is a curtain-wall enclosing a barbican, which protects the gate to the *bailey* (courtyard). The curtain-walls of the bailey have narrow, deep arrow-slits and are strongly defensive. Inside these walls at the top of the rock is a hall-keep. Dunamase was fairly typical of the system of defences employed in these early castles.

Towards the end of the thirteenth century and the beginning of the fourteenth century a small number of large fortresses were built without a great tower. The defence of the early fortress was passive and depended on the great tower and its strategic location, but later castles relied on well-fortified walls and towers. Gate-houses were large, as were many of the mural towers that contained accommodation instead of the great tower. Ballymote, Co. Sligo, Ballintober, Co. Roscommon, and Greencastle, Co. Donegal, are good examples of later castles, which are influenced by Welsh castles of this period. A particular feature is their large twin-towered gateways.

A number of later medieval fortresses, such as that of LISCARROLL, Co. Cork, can be termed *enclosure castles*. They date from the first half of the fourteenth century and consist essentially of an enclosing wall with a relatively simple gateway and mural towers. Clonmore and Ballymoon, Co. Carlow, are typical of this group. Other large castles, such as those of CAHER, Co. Tipperary, and ASKEATON, Co. Limerick, were first built in the thirteenth century but were much altered, so that they now appear mainly as later medieval fortresses.

In the later thirteenth and early fourteenth centuries a number of small castles called HALL-HOUSES were built. These consist of a rectangular building with a defended ground-floor and first-floor hall, with an entrance at the higher level. Later versions of the hall-house to be found in the eastern half of the country have many features in common with TOWER-HOUSES and appear to be their exemplars. In the late sixteenth and early seventeenth centuries strong houses and fortified houses, such as BURNCOURT, Co. Tipperary, and PORTUMNA and GLINSK, Co. Galway, were built, which mark the end of castle-building in Ireland. [see EARTHWORKS, MEDIEVAL.] **David Sweetman**

Castletown, Celbridge, Co. Kildare, the largest and most influential great house of the early eighteenth century. Its central block has been attributed to the Florentine architect of the façade of St John Lateran in Rome, Alessandro Galilei, and built (1722–5) for WILLIAM CONOLLY, Speaker of the Irish Parliament. Castletown has the severe and monumental grandeur of a Florentine palazzo, balanced by the curved screens that link it to the kitchen and stable wings, added by Sir EDWARD LOVETT PEARCE c. 1730, to whom the house has also been attributed. Lady Louisa Conolly, wife of Tom Conolly, was mistress of the house for over sixty years, from 1759, and during her lifetime its interior was transformed. The two-storey entrance and stair halls are decorated with plasterwork by the LAFRANCHINI BROTHERS and the great cantilevered staircase with its brass balusters was added by Simon Vierpyl in 1763. The Pompeian long gallery on the first floor was painted by Thomas Reilly with motifs derived from the mural decorations of first-century AD Roman art from Pompeii and Herculaneum. The Print Room c. 1786, papered with formal arrangements of eighteenth-century engravings by Chardin, Guido Reni, Metsu, and Poussin, is the sole Irish example of such an interior to survive. The south entrance façade faces the River LIFFEY, while the vista from the north is ended by 'Conolly's Folly' (42 m, 140 ft), built by RICHARD CASTLE for LADY LOUISA CONOLLY in order to provide employment during the 1741 famine winter. To the east of the house is the 'Wonderful Barn' (1743), a brick-built bottle-shaped granary, with an external spiral staircase.

Castletown remained in the Conolly family until 1967, when its demesne was sold for housing. The house, in danger of demolition, was purchased by DESMOND GUINNESS and was conserved and furnished by the IRISH GEORGIAN SOCIETY. It was taken into state care in 1994 by DÚCHAS, the Heritage Service. **Brian Lalor**

castles. *Caher Castle, on an island in the River Suir and now surrounded by the town of Caher, Co. Tipperary, is one of the best-preserved and largest surviving Irish castles. In Butler hands since 1375, the present castle was begun by them in the fifteenth century. [Dúchas, The Heritage Service]*

Castletown Cox, Co. Kilkenny (1767–71). Masterpiece of the Italian architect DAVIS DUCART and built for Michael Cox, Archbishop of Cashel, it is one of the most distinguished of the smaller stone-fronted Palladian houses. The seven-bay central block has a Corinthian pilastered break-front and balustraded cornice. Arcaded screens connect to pavilions with octagonal domes and delicate cupolas. The principal rooms have plasterwork by the stuccodore PATRICK OSBORNE. **Brian Lalor**

Castle Ward, Co. Down, a three-storey, seven-bay Palladian house with formal pedimented south-west entrance front, built for Bernard Ward, first Lord Bangor, in the 1760s. The garden front, which overlooks STRANGFORD LOUGH, is in the Gothick manner of the late eighteenth century, with ogee windows and Gothick glazing bars. Internally the suites of rooms to north and south reflect the stylistic variations of the exterior, allegedly representing Lord Bangor's Classicism and Lady Bangor's enthusiasm for Gothick. **Brian Lalor**

cath (battle). The medieval saga lists devote a section to *catha* (battles), tales in which a battle is the fulcrum of the narrative. The dates of the supposed occurrences range from the prehistoric period (Cath Maige Tuired, Cath Maige Mucrama, Cath Maige Léna) through the ULSTER CYCLE (Cath Bóinne, Cath Airtigh, Cath Ruis na Ríg) and the Fenian Cycle (Cath Fionntrágha, Cath Cnucha) to the EARLY HISTORICAL PERIOD (Cath Bealaigh Dúin Bholg, 598, Cath Maige Rath, 637, Cath Cairn Chonaill, 649, Cath Almaine, 721, and even CATH CLUANA TAIRBH, 1014). The dates of the composition of the tales lie between the eighth or ninth century (Cath Maige Mucrama, Cath Cairn Chonaill) and the seventeenth (Cath Cluana Tairbh). The battles of the prehistoric period may be regarded as unhistoric. 'Cath Maige Tuired' in particular, which tells of the rivalry between mythical peoples—TUATHA DÉ DANANN, Fomorians, and FIR BOLG—and of the great battle between the two last-named is an amalgam of traditions and motifs of diverse origin. The battles of the sixth century and later are authenticated by references in the ANNALS and other sources, though they have been largely fictionalised in the tales. The function of battle stories was not to tell of the violent encounters themselves—the fighting is seldom described and in many tales is only a minor part of the narrative—but to act as a setting for the narration of events relevant to the battle or of explanatory anecdotes about the characters or events in the story. In 'Cath Maige Rath', for example, the story of the feast at Dún na nGéd and the insult offered to Congal Claen is related as the alleged cause of the battle. In 'Cath Bealaigh Dúin Bholg' the account of the battle is adapted to provide an explanation of the place-name, which was taken to mean 'the fort of the bags', and the story tells how the Leinstermen drove a herd of wild horses with bags of stones tied to their tails through the Ulster camp to cause the utmost confusion before the attack. [see CLONTARF, BATTLE OF; FLED DÚIN NA NGÉD; MYTHOLOGICAL CYCLE OF EARLY IRISH TALES.] **Gearóid Mac Eoin**

Cathach, 'The Battler', a BOOK SHRINE, so called because the book it contained was carried into battle by the O'Donnells to bring victory. It enclosed a copy of the Latin Psalter long believed to have been written by COLM CILLE, founder of the monastery on IONA, who was remembered as a famous scribe and was said to have been transcribing a Psalter on the day of his death in 597. Generally accepted as the oldest surviving example of the newly invented *insular majuscule* script, the Psalter was written rapidly, suggesting an easy familiarity with an already established style. Each psalm opens with an elaborate penwork initial in revolutionary new designs. Certain elements of the decoration, such as the dolphin and the little cross on a stand, may indicate recent Continental contacts. The Emperor Tiberius II (578–82) used this type of cross on his coins. The eleventh-century shrine (now in the NATIONAL MUSEUM) was repaired and added to in the fourteenth and eighteenth centuries. [see BENTHAM, SIR WILLIAM.] **William O'Sullivan**

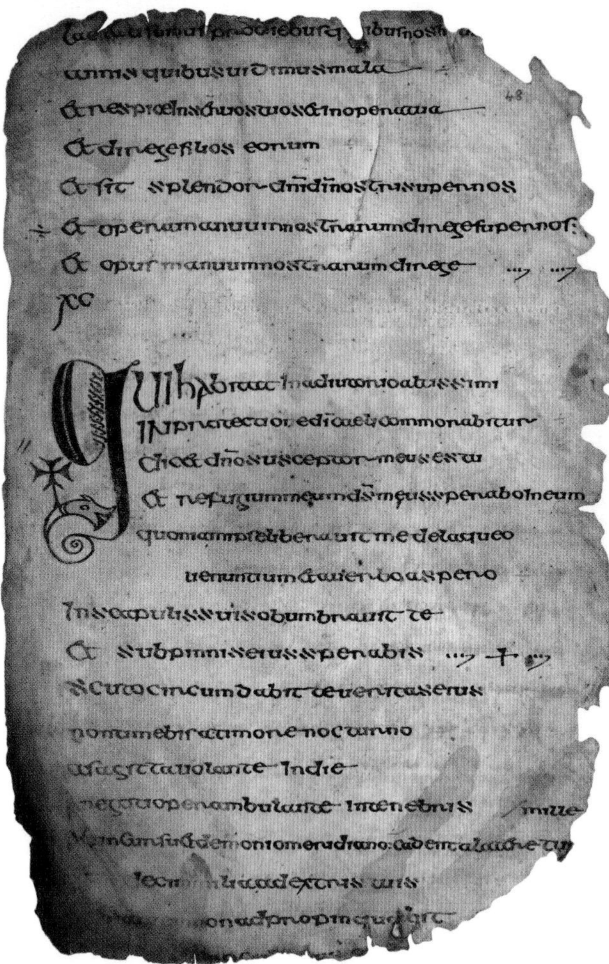

Cathach. *Folio 48r of a Latin Psalter, one of the oldest surviving Irish manuscripts, traditionally ascribed to St Colm Cille, who allegedly made this copy of the Psalter of his master, St Finnian. In the middle of the page, psalm 91 starts: 'Qui habitat in adiutorio Altissimi …' (He that dwelleth in the aid of the Most High …'). [Royal Irish Academy]*

Catholic Association. Established in Dublin in 1823 to promote CATHOLIC EMANCIPATION, it became the prototype of the modern mass political organisation. It was especially admired at the time by Continental liberal Catholics (Jean Baptiste Lacordaire and Charles Montalembert in France) for whom it showed the possibility of reconciling liberal theory with Catholic belief. The 'CATHOLIC RENT' gave membership in the association to tens of thousands. Suppressed in March 1825 under the Unlawful Societies Act, it re-formed a few months later as the New Catholic Association. In 1826 its members organised the victories of pro-emancipation parliamentary candidates, and in 1828 they helped DANIEL O'CONNELL to win his decisive election triumph in Co. Clare. **Gary Owens**

Catholic Committee, a body formed to advance the interests of Catholics. The formation of the Catholic Committee in 1760 marked an acceptance by Catholics of the need for reconciliation with the Hanoverian state. Moderate objectives, such as the breaking of the power of the Protestant trade guilds, were pursued in the early years. However, by the 1790s the Committee had become more militant and contributed to securing extensive political rights for Catholics in 1793. Thereafter it existed only for short periods, in 1795 and 1809–11. **C. D. A. Leighton**

Catholic Convention (1792), an assembly intended to advance Catholic political claims in Ireland. In an attempt to appear more representative in its campaign to gain political rights for Catholics, the CATHOLIC COMMITTEE brought delegates from throughout the country to the Tailors' Hall, Back Lane, in Dublin. The assembly, known as the 'Back Lane Parliament', proved surprisingly radical and unified in its demands and in its decision to bypass the Irish government and take its case directly to London. A large measure of success was achieved with the passing of the CATHOLIC RELIEF ACT (1793). **C. D. A. Leighton**

Catholic Emancipation, the campaign for the right of Catholics to sit in Parliament and to hold high office without having to take the Oath of Supremacy. This had been denied them in the Catholic Relief Acts of the late eighteenth century and became an issue that waxed and waned from the 1790s onwards. Numerous proposals to provide Catholic Emancipation failed to win parliamentary or royal approval during the first two decades of the nineteenth century, despite growing support in many political circles. Thanks in part to the establishment of the CATHOLIC ASSOCIATION in 1823, emancipation soon came to dominate politics in Ireland and Britain. The movement faltered in 1825 with the controversy over Sir FRANCIS BURDETT's Bill, but it revived the following year when pro-emancipation candidates won election victories in Waterford and elsewhere. The triumph of DANIEL O'CONNELL, a Catholic, in the Clare election in 1828 persuaded the Prime Minister, Wellington, and Home Secretary, PEEL, to concede the inevitability of emancipation and to act. After months of negotiations the final Catholic Relief Act became law on 13 April 1829. It granted emancipation but replaced the FORTY-SHILLING (£2) FREEHOLD franchise with a £10 voting qualification. **Gary Owens**

Catholicism (sixteenth to nineteenth centuries). There has been considerable scholarly debate over the survival of Catholicism in sixteenth-century Ireland. This used to be taken for granted as a reaction by the Irish and OLD ENGLISH to the identification of Protestantism with alien rule and the NEW ENGLISH; but it also had to do with the failure to endow the new reformed CHURCH OF IRELAND with the property to sustain an educated clergy or to find those who, like the remarkable WILLIAM BEDELL, would show a proper sympathy with the outlook and aspirations of the mass of the population. The Calvinism of the Church of Ireland also provided a useful explanation of its missionary failure: that Irish Catholics were not members of the elect.

The polarisation of Catholic and Protestant was an important aspect of the DESMOND REBELLIONS, Tyrone's Rebellion, and that of 1641, with its bloody outcome in the Cromwellian plantation, resulting in the dispossession of large numbers of Catholics. The

Irish were caught between the COUNTER-REFORMATION, as the only people in Europe to remain largely Catholic under a Protestant government, and the exigencies of English rule, secured by WILLIAM III at the battles of the BOYNE and AUGHRIM. William's re-conquest of Ireland resulted during the following half century in a large if haphazardly conceived and unevenly enforced body of PENAL LAWS, intended to limit Catholic and other non-Anglican religious practice, to prevent or discourage Catholic ownership of land, and to deny Catholics any part in official public life. The Penal Laws had the excuse that Catholics remained formally loyal to the JACOBITE cause until the death of the Old Pretender (James Stuart, son of James II) in 1766; but the resulting spasmodic and unequal persecution of Catholicism did little to wean the great majority of the rural population from their church, which combined the surviving medieval hierarchy of bishops and parochial system with the folkloric practice of WAKES, weddings, and PATTERNS, abolished or discouraged elsewhere in Catholic Europe. The clergy were trained at an extensive network of thirty IRISH COLLEGES in Continental Europe.

Catholic loyalism to the British Crown helped secure RELIEF ACTS in 1778, 1782, and 1793, the last following the outbreak of the FRENCH REVOLUTION, which resulted in the abolition of most of the Continental colleges and the foundation in 1795 of the national seminary of ST PATRICK'S COLLEGE, Maynooth, with funds provided by the British government. The clergy were generally opposed to the revolutionary movement in Ireland itself, which climaxed in the REBELLION OF 1798, and condemned those priests who took up arms against England, such as the leader in Co. Wexford, Father JOHN MURPHY. Again, the bishops welcomed the union of England and Ireland (if not the concomitant union of the established churches of England and Ireland) in 1801.

The alternative, constitutional path to reform was defined by DANIEL O'CONNELL. In 1824 he enlisted the parochial clergy to get their people to subscribe a penny a month to his CATHOLIC ASSOCIATION and in 1829 was instrumental in securing the passing of the Catholic Relief Act, which won Catholics the right to sit in the British Parliament. O'Connell so fused Catholicism and modern democratic NATIONALISM as to make them inseparable in the modern era, despite the failure of his subsequent campaign to secure the repeal of the UNION with England.

It was from a constitutional nationalist position that most of the clergy opposed the RISINGS OF 1848 AND 1867, the lead against the FENIANS being taken by Cardinal PAUL CULLEN, Archbishop of Armagh, 1849–52, and of Dublin, 1852–78, who also presided over a reform of the discipline and devotion of the Irish church. Cullen's programme may not have amounted to a 'devotional revolution', as there had been a great boom in church-building before 1850, and many of the Roman devotional practices of modern Irish Catholicism had already been introduced in religious houses and in churches in the better-off parts of eastern Ireland, especially Dublin. The religious changes, however, coincided with the church's promotion of LITERACY through its schools and with the GREAT FAMINE, with the subsequent EMIGRATION and fall in population, especially among the poorer classes and in the west, where religious practice was less strongly centred on priest and chapel. The resulting demographic pattern of decline turned a worsening ratio of priests to people into an improving one. Cullen dominated the Papal appointment of bishops to the new dioceses of the Irish diaspora in North America and Australasia, with some seventy bishops of Irish birth and 150 of Irish descent at the First Vatican Council (1869–70). **Sheridan Gilley**

Catholicism. *Cardinal Cahal Daly (centre) at the opening of the Cardinal Tomás Ó Fiaich Heritage Centre in Cullyhanna, Co. Armagh, 1996, with Archbishop of Armagh, Seán Brady (left) and Archbishop of Cashel and Emly, Dermot Clifford. [Belfast News]*

Catholicism (devotional revolution to twenty-first century). A besetting problem for institutional Catholicism in Ireland in the first quarter of the nineteenth century was its lack of political influence. Though the church had supported the ACT OF UNION (1800), WILLIAM PITT, the British Prime Minister, was unable to give Catholics full political rights, because of the opposition of George III. By the 1820s DANIEL O'CONNELL had emerged as a national and political saviour of Irish Catholicism, and his efforts, supported as they were by large sections of Catholic public opinion, secured through the Catholic Relief Act (1829) the much-sought political privileges that would enable institutional Catholicism, in principle, to wield the influence on Irish society that the bishops believed it ought to have.

Political change coincided with the beginnings of what has become known as the 'devotional revolution', a process whereby Irish Catholicism was transformed from an essentially pre-modern phenomenon into a bastion of TRIDENTINE ultra-orthodoxy. In the process of reconstruction it gained those features of high practice and absolute loyalty to Rome that arguably have marked it since the 1850s. Though historians are divided about the nature and scope of the devotional revolution, it is a useful conceptual tool for designating the transformation in Catholic ecclesiastical practice and outlook associated in particular with the arrival in Ireland in 1850 of PAUL CULLEN as Archbishop of Armagh. Cullen, subsequently Archbishop of Dublin from 1852 and Cardinal from 1866, gave to the Irish church a more defiantly Roman aura; his leadership represents a great contrast to that of less belligerent individuals, such as DANIEL MURRAY of Dublin and JAMES WARREN DOYLE ('JKL'), Bishop of Kildare and Leighlin. Cullen ultimately was also to encounter the opposition of more robustly political prelates, such as JOHN MACHALE, Archbishop of Tuam, the first Catholic bishop since the REFORMATION to be wholly educated in Ireland.

The role Cullen played in the metamorphosis of nineteenth-century Irish Catholicism was assisted by a range of social and religious factors. The activities of CATHERINE MCAULEY, founder of the SISTERS OF MERCY, and of EDMUND RICE, founder of the Irish CHRISTIAN BROTHERS, coincided with attempts by Cullen and his supporters to Catholicise every aspect of Irish life. Opposition to the national school system, set up in 1830, and the QUEEN'S COLLEGES, established in 1845, became the *leitmotif* of the church's opposition to everything it could not control. The university issue would not be settled to the satisfaction of the hierarchy until the Irish Universities Act (1908). In the political sphere, as was to be expected, the church resisted, with great determination, the radicalism that led to the YOUNG IRELAND RISING OF 1848 and the FENIAN rising OF 1867. Fenianism in particular posed an enormous challenge to the church, competing with it for influence over the mass of the Catholic population.

In the general trend towards greater episcopal control of Irish life, the epoch-making SYNOD OF THURLES (1850) cannot be overestimated. Though there was division among the bishops over the Queen's Colleges, Thurles marked the transition from the home to the church building as the focus for sacramental life. In some ways it merely extended to the country the customs that had been established by the Dublin diocesan synod of 1831. It was left to the First Synod of Maynooth (1875) to deal with that *bête noire* of Irish ecclesiastical practice, the WAKE. The 1875 synod also reiterated the condemnation of Fenianism that had been issued by Pope Pius IX in 1870.

The church's political manoeuvring is also seen in the attempts to resist 'independent opposition' in the British Parliament in the 1850s. Cullen in particular wanted Irish Catholic MPs to compete for government jobs and rejoiced when his policies bore fruit in the 1860s with the appointment of Thomas O'Hagan as the first Catholic Lord Chancellor in Ireland since the days of JAMES II. The degradation of the Anglican Church by GLADSTONE's Irish Church Act (1869) also gave a fillip to the fortunes of institutional Catholicism.

As with so many aspects of Irish life, the GREAT FAMINE (1845–9) was something of a watershed for the church. The enormous reduction in the population through death and EMIGRATION began a trend that improved the ratio of priests and religious to lay people and that, in principle, meant that the church's functionaries could be more effective in meeting the spiritual and catechetical needs of the people. In 1850 there were 5,000 priests, friars, and nuns for a Catholic population of 5 million; by 1900 the ratio was 14,000 to 3.3 million.

The increase in the number of clergy and the improvement in the quality of their education was made possible by generous subsidies from the British government to ST PATRICK'S COLLEGE, Maynooth. That institution, together with other seminaries, such as St Patrick's College, Carlow, enabled the church to provide for the needs of its adherents at home and abroad. Indeed the MISSIONARY spread of Irish Catholicism became a distinct feature of the church's *modus operandi* after mid-century. Ironically, this was in part further facilitated by the British government, as one aspect of the missionary expansion was serving the needs of Irish Catholic soldiers in the far-flung reaches of the British Empire.

Undoubtedly the religious and devotional life of Catholics improved as the nineteenth century wore on; but in addition to Continental ultramontane practices and devotions, more traditional aspects of Irish Catholicism continued to appeal, not least the annual PILGRIMAGES to St Patrick's Purgatory, LOUGH DERG, Co. Donegal, and, from 1879, to the purported site of an apparition of the Virgin MARY at Knock, Co. Mayo. The church also continued to produce leaders of high calibre, such as WILLIAM WALSH, Archbishop of Dublin, 1885–1921. Walsh's episcopate coincided with the difficulties posed for the church by its growing nationalist sympathies. Unlike his two predecessors, Walsh was not made a cardinal, because of the opposition of the British government to his all-too-obvious 'advanced nationalism'. The cardinal's hat went to Armagh in 1893, where its symbolic importance was underlined in the light of political partition in 1921. In an astounding *volte-face*, largely because of internal ecclesiastical dynamics, the cardinal's hat returned to Dublin in 2001. Walsh's nationalist penchant did not prevent him from playing a fateful role in the downfall of PARNELL over the O'Shea divorce scandal. Parnell's humiliation at the hands of the clergy was symptomatic of the church's need to control all social and political movements, such as the LAND LEAGUE and the Irish revival; when the IRISH PARTY was reunited under JOHN REDMOND the church would continue to exercise influence, not least by the fact that Patrick O'Donnell, Bishop of Raphoe, 1882–1922, and subsequently Cardinal Archbishop of Armagh, was treasurer of the parliamentary party fund.

The church's ability to consolidate its hold on society was not always finely honed. The rise of SINN FÉIN and an increasingly militant political climate served to alienate church officials from a more radicalised laity. This became especially clear after the early stages of the FIRST WORLD WAR and was made even more obvious by the 1916 RISING and its aftermath. By 1918 the church had placed itself, with Sinn Féin, at the head of the anti-conscription campaign, which helped it to regain its lost position of political significance as far as the mass of Irish Catholics was concerned.

The church in many respects acquiesced in the WAR OF INDEPENDENCE and was very guarded in the CIVIL WAR, though Daniel Cohalan, Bishop of Cork, took a more independent line than many of his colleagues and excommunicated members of the ANTI-TREATY IRA. PARTITION in 1921 placed Catholics in Ulster at a relative disadvantage, though in the end the Northern Ireland government was more generous with regard to provisions for Catholic EDUCATION than many bishops had feared it would be. The church was therefore content to wield its influence in the overwhelmingly Catholic Irish Free State and correspondingly to let it sit lightly on the affairs of Northern Ireland.

The establishment of diplomatic relations with the Vatican in 1929 was a milestone for the Free State in international diplomatic recognition, even if it did prove discommodious to some bishops. The EUCHARISTIC CONGRESS of 1932 was an enormous success and provided a rallying point for the assertion of Catholic identity in the state, even if it was regarded with ill-disguised contempt by Northern Protestants. Catholic triumphalism on such a scale would do little to enhance understanding between Catholics and Protestants.

The appointment of JOHN CHARLES MCQUAID as Archbishop of Dublin in 1940 brought to the centre of Irish life the last Catholic clergyman to exercise real influence at a national level. His combination of obvious talent, ultra-orthodoxy, and somewhat progressive social views made him a power to be reckoned with. He frustrated Government ambition, most notably over the MOTHER AND CHILD SCHEME of 1950. The years of economic deprivation in the 1930s, 40s, and 50s saw continued and sustained emigration, which the church could do little to counter. These were also decades of relative theological idleness on the part of the Irish church, so that when the SECOND VATICAN COUNCIL (1962–5) met, the Irish contribution was insignificant. Some Irish bishops took the view that the council indicated no real change in ecclesiastical life.

A similar lack of *realpolitik* was displayed in the church's attempts to come to terms with the thirty years of violence in Northern Ireland that erupted in 1968. Some priests, such as DENIS FAUL of Dungannon and Raymond Murray of Armagh, were attuned to the causes of violence and did much to press the case for human rights, as did TOMÁS Ó FIAICH in his tenure as Archbishop of Armagh; but by the time of his death in 1990 the church was beginning to be faced with the scandals of priestly child sexual abuse and the loss of credibility engendered by sexual activity among the clergy, drunken bishops, and the revelation that both a bishop and

Catholicism and the state. *John Charles McQuaid, newly consecrated Archbishop of Dublin and Primate of Ireland, gives his first blessing to a crowd of well-wishers on 27 December 1940. [Courtesy of Dublin Diocesan Archives]*

a prominent priest had fathered children. The visit of Pope John Paul II in 1979 had widespread if ephemeral appeal; within ten years the church's moral teaching and its general mores no longer seemed to have much of an impact. HOMOSEXUALITY and DIVORCE were legalised in the face of opposition by the church; ABORTION too was the subject of divisive REFERENDUMS.

Though Ireland still has one of the highest rates of religious practice in Europe, the lack of vocations to the priesthood and religious life and the inability of the church to appeal to the mass of younger people, coupled with increasing secularisation, means that Irish Catholicism must respond with greater *élan* than its contemporary complacency exhibits if it is to have any significant future. **Oliver P. Rafferty**

Catholicism and the Irish Constitution. There is no established church or other religious denomination in Ireland. English constitutional and legal principles concerning religion apply in Northern Ireland; in the Republic the core constitutional provisions are found in article 44 of the CONSTITUTION OF IRELAND (1937). Freedom of conscience and the free profession and practice of religion are guaranteed to every citizen, subject to public order and morality. The state also guarantees not to endow any religion, nor may it impose any disability or otherwise discriminate on the grounds of religious profession, belief, or status. Other significant provisions are that legislation providing state aid for schools may not discriminate between schools under the management of different religious denominations, or affect prejudicially the right of any child to attend a school receiving public money without attending religious instruction at that school. Every religious denomination has the right to manage its own affairs, to own, acquire and administer property, and to maintain institutions for religious or charitable purposes; and the property of any religious denomination or any educational institution cannot be diverted, save for necessary works of public utility and on payment of compensation.

Up to 1972 article 44 contained a recognition of the 'special position' of the Roman Catholic Church 'as the guardian of the Faith professed by the great majority of the citizens,' though it recognised also the other religious denominations existing in Ireland at the date of coming into operation of the Constitution. Opinion was divided on whether the 'special position' of the Catholic Church implied juridical privilege. The SUPREME COURT declared against this view in 1965, and in 1972 the section was abrogated by REFERENDUM.

The influence of Catholic teaching on the drafting of the Constitution—generally attributed to the role played by Father (later Archbishop) JOHN CHARLES MCQUAID in advising the Taoiseach, ÉAMON DE VALERA—is perceptible first in the preamble, which states that the people adopt the Constitution 'in the Name of the Most Holy Trinity, from Whom is all authority and to Whom, as our final end, all actions both of men and States must be referred,' and 'humbly acknowledging all our obligations to our Divine Lord, Jesus Christ, Who sustained our fathers through centuries of trial.' There is a distinct echo of a particular Catholic theological position in article 44.1, which provides that 'the State acknowledges that the homage of public worship is due to Almighty God. It shall hold His Name in reverence, and shall respect and honour religion.' The influence of Catholic doctrine can be noticed also in the prohibition of DIVORCE (removed by referendum in 1996), in an amendment of 1983 that guarantees the right to life of the unborn, and in some of the directives on social policy of article 45, not cognisable by the courts but intended for the guidance of the Oireachtas. It should also be remembered that belief in a trinitarian god, and moral objections to divorce and to abortion, are by no means confined to Roman Catholics. **Patrick Hannon**

Catholicism and the Irish diaspora. A new impetus was given to Catholicism by the spread of Irish Catholic emigrants throughout the English-speaking world, principally to the United States but also to Britain, AUSTRALIA, and NEW ZEALAND and, through the British army, to other parts of the British Empire, such as India and SOUTH AFRICA, and even beyond the Anglophone countries to South America, sometimes introducing the faith to places where it was unknown. The faith itself, however, changed over time. Before 1850 many of the Irish-speaking emigrants from the west and south of Ireland were devout but did not or could not attend Mass every Sunday, instead practising their religion in a sacred landscape of holy wells and holy sites according to a sacred calendar of PATTERNS—a setting very different from that of the chapel and priest-based Catholicism of the British or north American city. The older Irish Catholic culture was largely given its quietus by the GREAT FAMINE, and the progress of the 'devotional revolution' in an increasingly Anglophone Ireland in the nineteenth century diminished the shock of transition between Catholicism abroad and at home. Many of the demoralised and traumatised emigrants of the Famine years perished of destitution and disease in the squalor of their new surroundings; others clung to the church as the link between their old lives and their new ones and found in their faith a discipline for survival. The degree of attachment of the emigrants to their religion, and the extent to which it flourished in the New World, also differed from one place to another and over time, despite the common fact that British emigrant culture was overwhelmingly Protestant. In Britain itself sectarian antagonisms contributed to the higher degree of *émigré* Irish practice in Liverpool than in London. The perpetuation of a quantifiable Catholic religious behaviour was a communal matter, connected with the creation of an expatriate community; and in spite of variations the church was everywhere the chief agent in this creation.

The IRISH LANGUAGE did not survive the first generation, and a sense of Irish nationality, which was probably strongest among the refugees from the Great Famine, was weaker than the church's institutional structures of DIOCESES, parishes, schools, newspapers, and charities. Beyond a militant minority, sentimental nationalism became largely confined to the celebration of ST PATRICK'S DAY, despite a continuing ambivalence about the BRITISH EMPIRE, and the church generally encouraged integration in the host society while reserving to itself the control of religion and education. The church, however, was a multinational institution, especially in its leadership. In England and Scotland the bishops were natives, and largely remained so, though a number of modern English cardinals have had Irish mothers. There were French and Spanish bishops in North America, where the Irish also had to compete for influence over the church with large devout populations of immigrant Germans and Poles. The hierarchy in Australia was originally English. The first bishop in New Zealand was French. The European Catholic countries exported priests throughout the nineteenth century, many of whom ministered to the Irish faithful. The College of All Hallows, Dublin, for educating Irish priests to minister abroad, was founded only in 1842, by Father John Hand, though by 1900 it had trained some 1,500 clergy for the Irish diaspora. Many Irish priests served British parishes before returning to Ireland.

The creation of an international Irish Catholic hierarchy was largely the work of Cardinal PAUL CULLEN, Archbishop of Armagh, 1849–52, and of Dublin, 1852–78, who had the ear of Rome as Papal Legate in Ireland. Eighteen of Cullen's protégés were appointed bishops in Australia, while his nephew Patrick Francis Moran became the first Cardinal Archbishop of Sydney.

There were seventy bishops of Irish birth and 150 of Irish descent at the First Vatican Council (1869–70). These bishops, with their extensive family networks, imported Irish priests, nuns, and brothers, so that Irish orders such as the SISTERS OF MERCY and CHRISTIAN BROTHERS became great international institutions, closely tied to their mother communities in Ireland. The emergence of an international Irish church had secular consequences at home and abroad. Abroad the church became a political power; prelates like Moran in Sydney, Henry Edward Manning in London, and James Gibbons in Baltimore favoured the development of TRADE UNIONS and of alliances with parties of the moderate left, while others, such as Archbishop Michael Corrigan of New York, inclined to the political right.

Meanwhile in Ireland the DIASPORA church gave the Irish a pride in their international spiritual empire, an influence comparable to that of the British Empire of the world and the flesh. This imperialism of the spirit did much to sustain the Irish at home through the darker years of the early and middle twentieth century. [see CATHOLIC MISSIONS.] **Sheridan Gilley**

Catholicism and the state. The Irish state, from the beginning, was ostentatiously Catholic. Throughout the nineteenth century the power and influence of the Catholic Church increased considerably as older traditions and conservative attitudes became strongly associated with the identification of the nation with the rural population. The influence of the church was further secured when it became enmeshed with the national independence struggle and as Catholicism became an important element in the construction of Irish identity. In contrast to its position in other countries, in Ireland the Catholic Church was not a great landowner and did not cause much envy or discontent among the people—quite the reverse: parish clergy were often local community leaders who not only identified with the agrarian and nationalist aims of the people but often went out of their way to support them. As a consequence the CONSTITUTION OF IRELAND (1937), which replaced the negotiated Constitution of the Irish Free State (1922), was a deliberate attempt to integrate Catholic social teaching in the liberal-democratic tradition inherited from Britain.

Though DE VALERA resisted the more extreme demands for a constitutional expression of 'a Catholic state for a Catholic people,' his drafting of the Constitution did create a special, though symbolic, position for the Catholic Church. Moreover, in terms that were more than symbolic the new constitution made a clear-cut prohibition on DIVORCE and perhaps began the Irish preoccupation with prescribing standards of personal morality through constitutional provision. In 1983 the insertion of an anti-ABORTION clause in the Constitution led only to further controversy. The provision was amended in 1992, though pursuant legislation remains to be enacted, and demands for another REFERENDUM on the issue are never far away, a further one followed in 2002. More unusually, article 41 refers to the FAMILY as the 'natural, primary and fundamental unit group of Society' and further declares that WOMEN 'should not be obliged by economic necessity to engage in labour to the neglect of their duties in the home.' Feminists have argued that this provision gave in effect a constitutional blessing to state payments for women at home and could therefore have laid the basis for quite radical and progressive treatment of women. This, however, did not happen.

In government, the impact of Catholic social teaching was always evident in the content of public policy on marriage, divorce, CONTRACEPTION, the HEALTH SERVICES, and above all on EDUCATION, which continues to be organised and managed on religious lines. Catholic Church thinking strongly affected attitudes to women, the family, and home and was reflected in the civil service MARRIAGE BAR (requiring women to resign on marriage, widely copied throughout the public service), access to contraception (banned outright in 1935 and remaining largely unavailable until the late 1980s), the denial of WELFARE payments to unmarried mothers, deserted wives, and prisoners' wives, the absence of recourse to exclusion orders for women abused by their husband, and the denial of free legal aid to women.

Developments towards the end of the 1960s, however, marked the beginning of the separation of church and state. The process of modernisation begun by Pope John XXIII and the SECOND VATICAN COUNCIL (1962–5) broached issues that were previously 'beyond discussion' for many Irish people, such as the liturgy, relations between clergy and laity, MARRIAGE, divorce, contraception, attitudes to other religions, and the role of the state. Though it failed at first to produce the intellectual ferment that was caused in other Catholic countries, by the late 1960s increasing numbers of younger clergy and a few more senior ones began to acknowledge that some change was inevitable. These developments within the church coincided with a series of liberalising trends outside it that began to challenge traditional conceptions of Irish Catholicism.

Ireland's entry into the European Economic Community in 1973 incurred a series of legal obligations relating to non-DISCRIMINATION and EQUALITY of pay that began to challenge attitudes to women, the work-place, and the family. Foreign travel increased, and Irish people began to notice and take an interest in what was happening in Europe. This, combined with an influx of returned emigrants when the economy improved in the 1970s, led to changing social attitudes, a tendency even more marked with the influx of returned emigrants associated with the economic boom of the 1990s. Throughout the 1980s even those who did not leave Ireland were able to gain a wider view of the world: around 35 per cent of the Republic (mostly along the east coast) was able to gain access to British television stations, a figure that increased massively with the widespread availability of cable and digital television during the 1990s. Added to this is the fact that the population is getting younger and is moving to the towns. The 1996 census concluded that the average age of an Irish person in the Republic was 33.6 and that by 2001 four out of every ten people would be under the age of twenty-five. Well over half the state's population (58 per cent) now live in towns, compared with 28 per cent in the 1901 census. The Republic now has 132 towns with a population exceeding 1,500 and twenty-three with a populations exceeding 10,000. Social trends associated with DEMOGRAPHIC change and URBANISATION contributed both to the process of separation between church and state and also to a reinvention of Irish identity, one in which the influence of the church is important but no longer hegemonic. The introduction of legislation dealing with the availability of contraceptives and abortion information, the decriminalisation of HOMOSEXUALITY and the relinquishing of the constitutional ban on divorce all attest to this view.

The last census that asked for religious affiliation, that of 1991, showed that the Republic is still predominantly Catholic, with 91.7 per cent of the population professing to be Roman Catholics, with the main Protestant churches (CHURCH OF IRELAND, PRESBYTERIAN, and METHODIST) accounting for 2.8 per cent. Minority religions comprise 1.3 per cent of the population, and 4.2 per cent are of no religion or refuse to declare. The relative stability of Irish Catholicism is in fact remarkable. Even after joining the EC and developing a society broadly comparable with other EC states in life-style, sexual behaviour, and social problems, 82 per cent of the population still attend Mass at least once a week. The significance of the Catholic Church in Ireland should no longer, however, be confused with its influence. Irish Catholics have become more individualistic and diverse, while the younger and more educated, living in towns and cities, have become less willing to conform to traditional values. [see VATICAN II.] **Maura Adshead**

Catholicism. *The relics of St Thérèse at Knocklyon parish church, Co. Dublin. Touring Ireland from 15 April (Easter Sunday) to 28 June 2001, they were brought to all twenty-six diocesan cathedrals and all churches and chapels of St Thérèse's Carmelite Sisters and Brothers, as well as the principal shrines. [David Stephenson]*

Catholic missions (nineteenth and twentieth centuries). The history of Irish missions in the modern era is difficult to separate from the DIASPORA of Irish Catholics throughout the world and the resulting growth of an Irish Catholic Church overseas ministering primarily to Irish expatriates and their descendants. All Hallows College, Dublin, founded in 1842, was devoted to training priests for Catholics in the Anglophone countries rather than to the evangelisation of non-Catholics; but the new churches abroad in time developed their own missionary activity. The assignment of certain Indian sees to Irish bishops resulted in the Maynooth Mission to India and the involvement of the Irish Loreto Sisters in the conduct of schools and orphanages in Madras and of the Irish CHRISTIAN BROTHERS in schools centred on Calcutta. Various Irish missionary efforts in Africa, in Liberia, and elsewhere, chiefly through the Holy Ghost Fathers and the Society of African Missions (which was extended to Ireland in 1877 and founded a seminary in Ireland in 1909), were at first less well sustained and successful, not least because of the premature death of so many young missionaries.

The great growth of foreign Irish Catholic missions to non-Christians belongs to the twentieth century, the most famous institute being the Maynooth Mission to China, originally inspired by a visit to Maynooth in 1911 by Father John M. Fraser. The resulting St Columba's Foreign Mission Society (the Columban Fathers) extended their work to the Philippines in 1929, Korea in 1933, and Burma in 1936. The college for the mission was established at Dalgan Park, Shrule, Co. Galway, in 1918; the associated Missionary Sisters of St Columba were founded in 1922. The African missions assumed another institutional form with the foundation by Bishop Joseph Shanahan of southern Nigeria of the Missionary Sisters of Our Lady of the Rosary in Killashandra, Co. Cavan, in 1924. Also involved in the African mission were the Society of St PATRICK for Foreign Missions, with its centre at Kiltegan, Co. Wicklow, and the Medical Missionaries of Mary, founded by MOTHER MARY MARTIN at Anua, eastern Nigeria, in 1937. By 1964 there were more than 6,000 Irish Catholic missionaries abroad—priests, brothers, sisters, and lay people—associated with more than eighty congregations.

Criticism of Irish missionary enterprise has been directed against its Eurocentric and otherworldly character and has argued that it served chiefly to confirm the sense of spiritual superiority of the Irish themselves. Such one-sided critiques ignore both the underlying presumption of racial if not religious equality in the Irish missions and their heavily practical emphasis on doing good, through schools and hospitals. There was a marked decline in Irish missionary activity during the last years of the twentieth century, in contrast to the increasing vigour of the indigenous churches created by the Irish missionaries. [see CATHOLICISM AND THE IRISH DIASPORA.] **Sheridan Gilley**

Catholic Relief Acts, eighteenth-century legislation removing restrictions on Catholics. From the middle of the eighteenth century, Catholics had used unconvincing economic grounds to appeal to the Irish Parliament for mitigation of the laws against them. However, the decisions about granting relief in the last quarter of the century were taken mostly by British governments, which perceived military and political necessity. The legislation of 1778 and 1782 removed the most serious afflictions of the church, and most restrictions on landownership. An act of 1792 facilitated the practice of law by Catholics and removed checks on education.

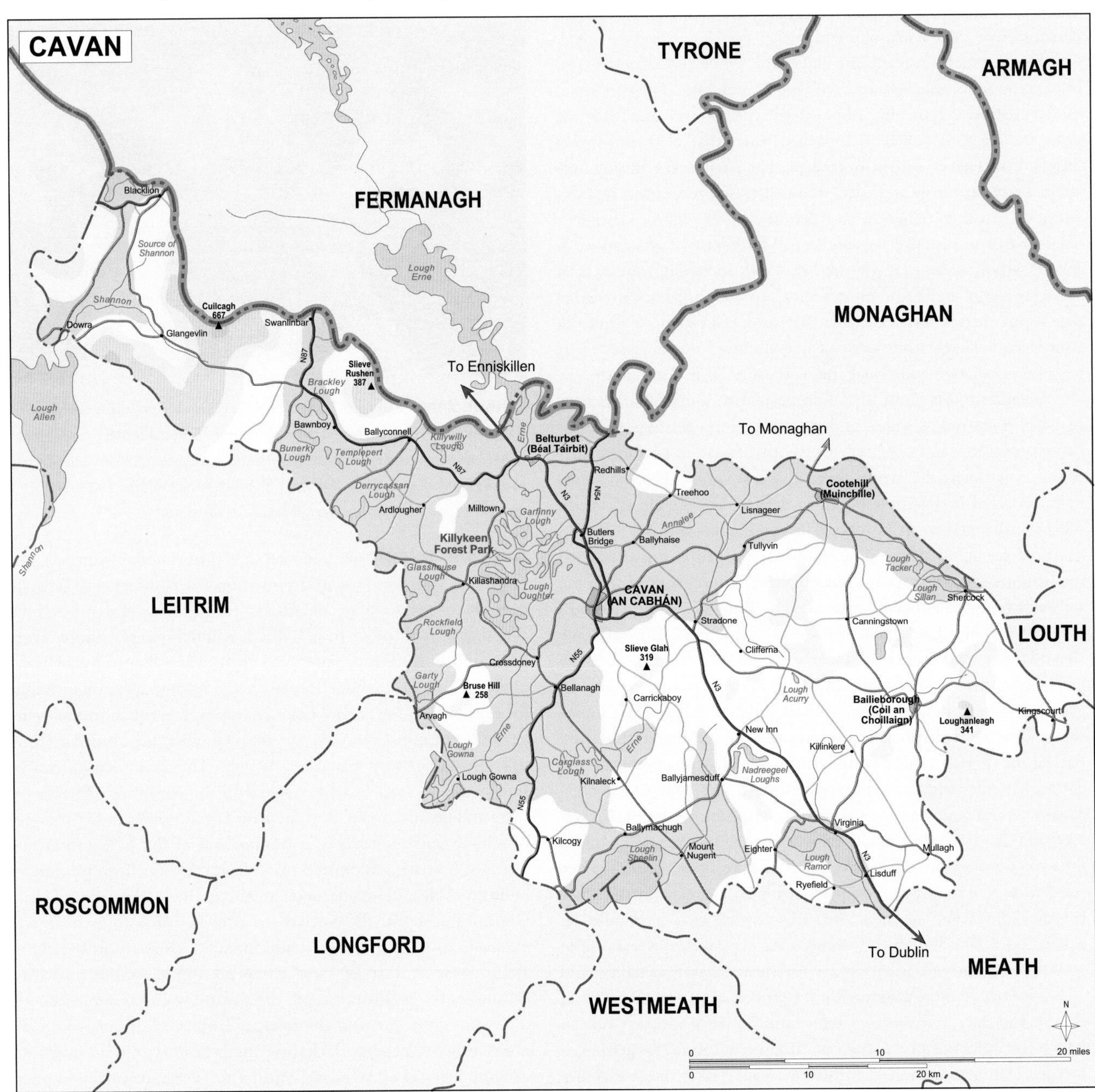

More important was the act of 1793, which gave Catholics their first substantial political rights. **C. D. A. Leighton**

Catholic rent, the name given to the subscription of 1 penny per month paid by associate members of the CATHOLIC ASSOCIATION. Besides giving tens of thousands a sense of participation in the movement for CATHOLIC EMANCIPATION, its collection created a network of committees and agents around the country as it filled the coffers of the association. The total raised by early 1829 was almost £52,000 (€66,000). As one contemporary noted, the rent amounted to 'an Irish revolution.' **Gary Owens**

Catholic University of Ireland. John Henry Newman (1801–1890), the famous convert from Anglicanism—ordained to the priesthood in 1847, founder of the English Oratorians, brilliant in intellect, eloquent in speech—was invited by the Irish hierarchy, on the advice of the Pope, to found a Catholic university in Dublin, as an alternative to the QUEEN'S COLLEGES established by Sir ROBERT PEEL in 1845. These colleges had been condemned by Rome and the Irish hierarchy, on the grounds that they were non-denominational and that religion was excluded from the syllabus. Newman accepted the invitation, seeing it as an opportunity for the education of a Catholic laity. As a preparatory step he delivered a series of lectures in 1852 in which he outlined his views on Catholic EDUCATION, with theology having a place within the whole circle of knowledge; these lectures formed the first part of his celebrated work *The Idea of a University*. In June 1852 he was formally installed as Rector, and the Catholic University of Ireland opened on 3 November 1854 at 86 St Stephen's Green, Dublin, now Newman House. There were faculties of theology, philosophy and letters, and science. The Catholic University Medical School was opened the following year in Cecilia Street. The University Church was opened in 1856.

Newman had a vision for education and a desire to involve the laity that came into conflict with the views of Archbishop PAUL CULLEN, the controlling influence on behalf of the bishops; as a result Newman experienced a great deal of frustration during his seven years as Rector. Having crossed the Irish Sea fifty-six times in the service of the university, he finally returned to take care of affairs at the Oratory in Birmingham and in 1858 formally resigned as Rector. Despite his difficulties, Newman said of his time in Ireland that he 'experienced nothing but kindness and attention.' **Consilio Rock**

Catholic worship. The appropriation by the CHURCH OF IRELAND of traditional places of worship and the persecution of Catholics, first in the Tudor and Stuart periods and later under the PENAL LAWS, left intact the traditional Catholic hierarchy of bishops and a remoulded parochial system, so that Catholics still had access to their clergy and sacraments, especially to the central and compulsory weekly rite of attendance at Mass and annual confession and communion. There was, however, also a body of extra-ecclesiastical devotion at holy wells and PATTERNS or PILGRIMAGES on the feasts of SAINTS, a tradition of prayer—especially the Rosary—in the home, and, in places where parishes were large and priests few, especially in the west and in Ulster, the custom of Masses not in churches but at large houses or 'stations' or even in the open air at a Mass rock. In the eighteenth century, however, chapels were public buildings. The nineteenth century saw a building boom in churches and convents, which became shrines for a whole new range of Continental devotions in the vernacular, especially shrines to the Blessed Sacrament and the Virgin and saints—the product of what has been described as a 'devotional revolution', owing much to the work of RELIGIOUS ORDERS, both male and female. The emphasis after the SECOND VATICAN COUNCIL on a simpler liturgy has resulted in a decline in these devotions and has meant a great deal of vandalism of church interiors to accommodate the modern vernacular rite; there has also been a considerable fall in Mass attendance itself. [see VATICAN II.] **Sheridan Gilley**

Catterson Smith, Stephen, the Elder (1806–1872), artist. Born in England; trained as a portrait painter and draughtsman in the Royal Academy school, London, and in Paris. He came to Ireland in 1839, first to Derry, moving in 1845 to Dublin, where he made his career, becoming a member of the ROYAL HIBERNIAN ACADEMY in 1845 and president in 1859. He painted an enormous number of portraits and a few subject pictures. His work is always competent, sometimes magisterial, and his portraits of women gave him the opportunity to show off his brilliant drapery painting. His son, Stephen Catterson Smith the Younger (1849–1912) continued his father's practice. **Anne Crookshank**

cattle raid: see TÁIN BÓ.

'Cattle Raid of Cooley': see 'TÁIN BÓ CUAILGNE'.

Caulfield, James, first Earl of Charlemont (1728–1799), landowner and politician. Born in Dublin; educated privately. Like many young aristocrats, he undertook the Grand Tour (1746–54) and remained a leading patron of the arts. In Dublin his support for scholarship, architecture, and literature had a profound influence—in the building of the CASINO at Marino (see p. 183), at his townhouse in Rutland Square (now Parnell Square) and in the founding of the Royal Irish Academy. He is also remembered for his opposition political activities, particularly in the VOLUNTEERS, which he commanded in Ulster. Though a critic of the government, he rallied to the establishment in 1796 and helped the northern YEOMANRY. A vehement opponent of legislative union, he did not live to see it pass in 1800. **Allan Blackstock**

Cavan, County (*Contae an Chabháin*)

Province:	ULSTER
County town:	CAVAN
Area:	1,890 km^2 (730 sq. miles)
Population (2002):	56,416
Features:	Annalee River
	Cuilcagh Mountains
	Lough Ramor
	Lough Sheelin
	River Erne
Of historical interest:	Blacklion cashel
	Clogh Oughter round castle
	Maigh Sleachta
Industry and products:	Glass-making
	Meat and dairy processing
	Pig and chicken farming
	Printing

Petula Martyn

County Cavan, the southernmost part of Ulster and a border county between NORTHERN IRELAND and the REPUBLIC. Modern

Co. Cavan was 'new formed' in 1579 out of east Bréifne, ancient lordship of the O'Reillys. It forms part of the south Ulster Drumlin Belt and displays its characteristically undulating and dissected topography. The waterlogged lowlands of the Upper Erne valley form a central feature, and the land rises steadily to the west and to the Carboniferous limestone and sandstone summits of the Cuilcagh Mountains on the Co. Fermanagh border. The seventeenth-century plantation of Cavan introduced significant numbers of English and Scots settlers, adding further complexity to the already complex human landscape of this ancient cultural frontier between Ulster and Leinster. With its high population density greatly reduced by the GREAT FAMINE, Co. Cavan experienced severe population decline and economic stagnation, which continued until the inter-war period. TOURISM is increasingly important, especially with the reopening of the BALLINAMORE AND BALLYCONNELL CANAL as the Shannon-Erne waterway in 1994. **Lindsay Proudfoot**

Cavan (*An Cabhán*), county town of Co. Cavan and cathedral town of the Catholic diocese of Kilmore; population (2002) 3,497. A Franciscan friary was built here c. 1300, and by the middle of the fifteenth century Cavan was a thriving market town, under the O'Reillys, Lords of Bréifne. Chosen as one of Co. Cavan's three boroughs in 1609–11, the town was incorporated in 1613. It grew slowly in the seventeenth century and was destroyed in 1690, but under Farnham and Maxwell patronage it was extended and rebuilt in the early nineteenth century, when Farnham Street and many of the existing architecturally significant buildings were erected. These include the Royal School (1819), CHURCH OF IRELAND parish church (1820), Courthouse (1824), and Farnham Hall. Thereafter the town had a prolonged period of stagnation, which lasted until the inter-war period. The modern Catholic cathedral of St Patrick (1941–7) is by Francis Byrne. **Lindsay Proudfoot**

'C' case. In August 1997 a thirteen-year-old girl was raped by a family friend while babysitting in north Co. Dublin. She became pregnant as a result and was taken into care by the Eastern Health Board. The girl and her foster-mother were permitted by the District Court to travel to England for an ABORTION, as psychiatric assessment had proved that she was suicidal. Her parents, who had at first supported her wish, changed their minds 'as the result of outside influence' (in the words of Mr Justice Geoghegan) and appealed the decision to the High Court.

The 'C' case was significant because of the High Court's interpretation of the constitutional amendments following the 'X' CASE. The 'travel amendment', in the court's view, was intended to prevent unreasonable injunctions against travelling abroad for an abortion but did not confer a right to termination outside Ireland. The court could not authorise travel to another jurisdiction for an abortion that was not lawful in Ireland under the CONSTITUTION. However, in striking down the motion of C's parents it followed the SUPREME COURT's judgment in the 'X' case: that where there was a risk to the life of the mother (in this case through SUICIDE), a termination of pregnancy was not unlawful according to the Constitution. Attempts by the Government in 2002 to amend the Constitution to remove the threat of suicide as grounds for abortion were narrowly defeated in a referendum. **Alison Walsh**

Ceannt, Éamonn (1881–1916), republican. Born in Glenamaddy, Co. Galway. He worked as a clerk in the Treasury Department of Dublin City Council. Joining the GAELIC LEAGUE in 1900, he served on its executive. He joined SINN FÉIN in 1908 and the IRB and IRISH VOLUNTEERS in 1913; from 1915 he served on the IRB's Supreme Council. He helped organise the HOWTH GUN-RUNNING of 1914 and in 1916 was one of the signatories of the PROCLAMATION OF THE IRISH REPUBLIC. In command of the South Dublin Union during the Rising, he was executed by firing squad in KILMAINHAM GAOL on 8 May 1916. **Seán Farrell Moran**

Cecilian movement: see CHURCH MUSIC, EIGHTEENTH AND NINETEENTH CENTURIES; LYRA ECCLESIASTICA.

Céide Fields, an extensive tract of enclosed NEOLITHIC farmland on the northern coast of Co. Mayo. Field boundaries of stone have been preserved intact for more than 5,000 years, because blanket BOG covered the main field boundaries before the end of the Neolithic Period. Modern turf-cutting of the shallower peats on the slopes has exposed the field boundaries in many areas. By pushing long iron rods into the peat to establish the depth to the pre-bog surface and the location of the stone walls under the bog, it has been possible to extend the known area of the fields to more than 10 km^2 (4 sq. miles). The Céide Fields comprise two contiguous blocks of co-axial fields, with the different axes aligned on the natural alignment of two spurs of hills. Within the rectangular fields are small oval and circular enclosures, which appear to be dispersed dwelling-places of individual families. **Seamas Caulfield**

céilí, originally meaning an informal social gathering, came to be used from 1934 for figure dances performed at public social evenings. The first céilí was organised in Bloomsbury Hall, London, in October 1897. Most of the figure dances were first published in 1902; only twenty or less of the hundred or more figure dances are referred to as céilí dances. Some dances, such as the *rince fada*, date from the seventeenth century; others were composed early in the twentieth century. 'The Walls of Limerick' was first recorded in 1902. The PUBLIC DANCE HALLS ACT (1935) boosted céilí dances by outlawing traditional private house dances, so gradually replacing the relatively simple house set-dances with the greater variety of more intricate céilí dances. **John P. Cullinane**

céilí bands. Traditional dance music was originally played by solo musicians. The ensemble was a late arrival, becoming popular only in the first quarter of the twentieth century, encouraged by dancing in larger public venues. Generally formed from musicians in one locality, bands varied considerably in their composition but almost always had a rhythm section of PIANO and drums, with FIDDLES and ACCORDIONS being popular melody instruments. The tunes were played in unison, with the piano giving a basic chord accompaniment. After the arrival of radio, some céilí bands became popular throughout the country, and the genre reached a peak of popularity in the 1950s. After the revival introduced other forms of ensemble playing the bands' popularity declined, but many still play regularly throughout the country, particularly at 'sets', events generated by the revival in SET-DANCING. [see AUGHRIM SLOPES; BALLINAKILL; BROADCASTING; MCCUSKER BROTHERS; RADIO; TULLA.] **Colin Hamilton**

céilí Dé ('companions of God'), later Anglicised as 'culdees', a monastic movement of the ninth century that presented its message as a CHURCH REFORM and whose myth of 'reform' most modern writers have uncritically accepted. The movement appeared first with MÁEL RUÁIN, founder of Tallaght (c. 770), and spread rapidly throughout Ireland, though its most famous products (rules, MARTYROLOGIES, and the STOWE MISSAL) come directly from

Tallaght. As a movement it was short-lived, but its memory survived in some places until the twelfth century. Its theme was that a rigorous penitential life was the route to monastic perfection. It legitimated this as a return to the purity of the desert, as presented in monastic hagiography, expressed in extreme fasting (far beyond Cassian's demands, so that they even ignored joyful feasts, such as Christmas), extended offices, and the rejection of 'luxuries' (such as music). In devotional tracts they also popularised their views on the Christian life, such as penalties for not observing Sunday. This rigour was not without opponents, and the NAVIGATIO SANCTI BRENDANI can be read as a satirical rejection of their extremism from the standpoint of ordinary MONASTICISM. **Thomas O'Loughlin**

Céitinn, Seathrún: see KEATING, GEOFFREY.

Celbridge (*Cill Droichid*), Co. Kildare, a town on the River LIFFEY west of Dublin; population (2002) 14,251. The town has grown rapidly in recent years—by 28 per cent between 1991 and 1996—in response to the establishment of high-technology industries nearby, such as Intel and Hewlett-Packard, and because its proximity to Dublin has facilitated its growth as a commuter town. Its earliest associations are with St Mochua, who is believed to have ministered in the area during the time of St PATRICK. The eighteenth-century character of the town was strongly influenced by the Conolly family, who lived at nearby CASTLETOWN house. Ireland's first grand Palladian house and the model for Leinster House, Castletown was built c. 1722 for William Conolly, Speaker of the Irish House of Commons, 1715–29, and the richest man in Ireland. Conolly's widow was responsible for a number of local buildings, including the Obelisk or Conolly's Folly, built to provide employment during the Great Frost of the 1740s, the Death House, and the Wonderful Barn (1743). Celbridge Abbey was the home of ESTHER VANHOMRIGH (1688–1723), the ill-starred lover of JONATHAN SWIFT, while Oakley Park was home to the Napier family. Both are now owned by the Order of St John of God, which provides a school and training centre for the mentally handicapped. **Ruth McManus**

Celtic art derives in essence from the plant and vegetal designs of the Greek and Etruscan worlds. Contacts in the sixth and fifth centuries BC between the Mediterranean region and central Europe gave rise to a distinctly Celtic adaptation of classical motifs, such as *palmettes*, *peltae*, and vine tendrils. From the middle of the fifth century BC craft centres in different parts of Europe were producing abstract designs of elegance and originality and of great technical sophistication, principally, but not solely, on METALWORK. In Ireland this art is first recognisable on an imported gold torc of the early third century BC from Knock, Co. Roscommon. Within a century or so, native craft centres were established, notably in the north-east (such as Lisnacrogher, Co. Antrim). These were producing high-status objects, principally swords and finely decorated BRONZE scabbards; the art on the latter, extending the full length of the scabbard, is freehand and consists of recognisably Irish combinations of designs such as spirals, running scrolls, and wave tendrils. Soon designs in *repoussé* (hammered sheet-bronze) were being produced (for example on a horn from LOUGHNASHADE) and in cast bronze, as on many of the bridle-bits.

About the first century BC there is a gradual change in Irish art. Freehand engraving gives way to organised, compass-drawn patterns, as is well illustrated on a gold collar from the BROIGHTER HOARD. After the turn of the millennium the use of the compass becomes virtually universal; this is exemplified by compass-drawn designs on a series of cattle rib-bones from LOUGHCREW. Precisely

Céide Fields. *Céide Fields, west of Downpatrick Head on the north coast of Co. Mayo, more than 10 km² (4 sq. miles) of Neolithic farmland comprising the oldest enclosed agricultural landscape in Europe, dating from c. 3,700 to 3,200 BC. [Dúchas, The Heritage Service]*

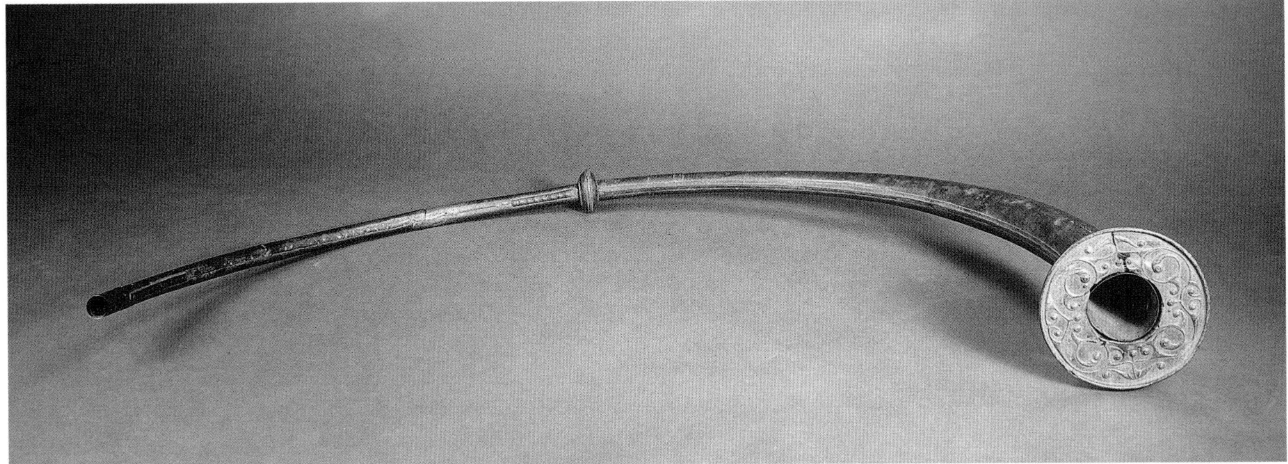

Celtic art. *The Loughnashade Trumpet, the finest surviving sheet-bronze trumpet of the Celtic Iron Age, one of four Iron Age musical instruments discovered at the edge of Loughnashade Lake, Co. Armagh, in 1798. [National Museum of Ireland]*

the same designs, though on a larger scale, occur on a low standing-stone from Derrykeighan, Co. Antrim, and this, as well as several other carved stones (such as the TUROE STONE), illustrates the versatility of the Irish craftsmen.

The art of the IRON AGE in Ireland is predominantly abstract, but bird heads (generally waterbirds) also occur, as is best illustrated by the cast bowl-handle from Keshcarrigan, Co. Leitrim. The human form is known only in stone (for example CORLECK, Co. Cavan), but it can be taken as certain that carvings in wood were widely known. **Barry Raftery**

Celtic languages. Now spoken in the western fringes of Ireland and Britain and in Brittany, Celtic languages were once spoken throughout most of Western Europe; traces survive in place-names as far east as Asia Minor (though that was probably due to eastward migration). Classical writers report encounters with Celtic-speakers throughout Western Europe, for example the Gauls (in present-day France), the Celtiberi in Spain, and the Celtic-speaking tribes of northern Italy; and PTOLEMY'S MAP (second century) contains a large number of identifiable Celtic names.

The Celtic languages form a branch of the Indo-European family of languages, which includes Italic (Latin and the Romance languages deriving from it), Greek, and Indo-Iranian (including Sanskrit, Avestan, etc.). They may be classified in different ways. One convenient classification, based largely on geographical considerations, divides them into the *Continental languages* (Celtiberian in Spain, Gaulish in Gaul, and Lepontic—and perhaps also Cisalpine Gaulish, if this is a separate language—in northern Italy) and the *insular languages* (the languages spoken, or formerly spoken, in Britain and Ireland, and Breton, spoken in Brittany—the outcome of a subsequent migration from south-west Britain). The insular languages can be subdivided into GOIDELIC or Gaelic and *Brittonic* or British, the former developing into Irish, Gaelic (Scotland), and Manx (no longer spoken), the latter into Cumbric (once spoken in present-day northern England and lowland Scotland), Welsh, Cornish (no longer spoken), and Breton. Pictish, once spoken in Scotland, may also have been a Brittonic language. Other analyses, however, would align the Brittonic group more closely with Gaulish to form a 'Gallo-Brittonic' group; there is good classical evidence for contacts between Gaul and Britain in the pre-ROMAN period.

The early evidence for Celtic is mostly inscriptional, the earliest being from northern Italy, perhaps as early as the sixth century BC; there is also a large collection written in Greek script from southern Gaul. The bulk of the Continental inscriptions date from the second and first centuries BC. The evidence of Ptolemy's map can be dated to the second half of the second century AD, though preserved in later MANUSCRIPTS: the earliest is from the thirteenth century. The earliest manuscript evidence for the insular languages (apart from stray vocabulary items in classical sources), and the beginning of the main bulk of material, dates from the seventh century for Irish and the eighth or ninth century for Brittonic. In both instances the earliest material frequently takes the form of GLOSSES on Latin texts.

There is no single feature that marks out a Celtic language; it is rather the combination of features that makes a language Celtic. With regard to the sound system, the loss of /p/ is distinctive: Irish *athair* 'father' < Indo-European **pater* (compare Latin *pater*); Old Irish *én*, Welsh *edn* 'bird' < **petn* (compare Latin *penna*); Old Irish *for*, Old Welsh *guor*, Gaulish *ver-* 'over' < **wer* < **uper* (compare Greek *hyper*, Latin *super*). Goidelic and Brittonic can be distinguished by their treatment of /kw/, which becomes Irish /k/ but Brittonic /p/ in most environments (hence the distinction sometimes made between 'Q Celtic' and 'P Celtic'): OLD IRISH *cethar*, Welsh *pedwar* 'four' < *k^w*etwores* (compare Latin *quattuor*); Old Irish *cía*, Welsh *pwy* 'who?' < *k^w*eis* (compare Latin *quis*). Other features regarded as distinctly Celtic are the system of initial mutations used to mark grammatical categories, the use of verbal nouns (which behave like nouns rather than infinitives), and the regular use of a word order with an initial verb. **Paul Russell**

Celtic Sea, a name invented in the 1970s as an alternative to St George's Channel, sometimes applied to portion of the Atlantic Ocean to the south of Ireland as well as to the southern part of St George's Channel. An important front occurs between its stratified waters and the mixed waters of the southern IRISH SEA. The Celtic Deep, at the entrance to the Irish Sea, is the main topographical sea-bed feature. The sea-bed consists of a glacial till deposited by the retreating ice in a series of moraines. **Chris Emblow**

'Celtic Tiger'. It has been argued that from 1987 the economy of the Republic of Ireland entered into a 'virtuous circle' of economic management whereby rapid growth, low INFLATION, declining UNEMPLOYMENT, and an external budgetary surplus led to sustained high-level growth. Throughout the 1990s Irish growth rates were the highest among the fifteen member-states of the

EUROPEAN UNION and twenty-nine member-states of the OECD and even surpassed those of the four Asian 'tiger' economies before their collapse in 1997–8. While critics argue that such high growth rates have come at the cost of increasing inequalities, some foreign commentators, analysts, and especially the Irish media have referred to Ireland as the 'Celtic Tiger' economy of Europe, leading the European Union in nearly every economic sphere. **Maura Adshead**

Celtic Twilight, The (1893), the title W. B. YEATS gave to his collection of stories of the supernatural, based on country beliefs, traditions, and FOLK TALES he had gathered. Such was the poetic power of its romantic imagery at a crucial moment in the Irish cultural revival that the epithet came to symbolise the mood of a national movement aspiring to evoke a mythical past and fast-disappearing imaginative tradition while establishing a meaningful identity. **Nicola Gordon Bowe**

Celts, a term used for one of the peoples of Europe, ancient and modern. It has been applied most frequently as a means of categorising other people and less frequently, until the modern period, as a means of self-identification. The term has had many different uses in different fields of discourse, especially linguistics, history, archaeology, and politics. The origin of the word is obscure; it is first recorded in the Greek form *Keltoi* in the works of writers of the sixth and fifth centuries BC to refer to people in southern France, on the Atlantic coast, and around the headwaters of the Danube. They attacked Rome in 387 BC and later became widely used as mercenaries in the Hellenistic armies of the Mediterranean. They were known and admired as soldiers, with a propensity for drunkenness.

The name 'Celts' was also used more generally to refer to the population of western Continental Europe to indicate geographical location rather than racial identity. In 279 BC Greece was invaded from the north by people known as Galatai, some of whom went on to settle in Asia Minor. These invaders may have been of very mixed origin, but some at least spoke a Celtic language, which survived well into the Roman period among the Galatians of Turkey. The Romans knew their northern neighbours under the Latin term *Galli*, or Gauls. In time the terms *Keltoi*, *Galatai*, and *Galli* came to be regarded as synonymous, denoting the people of or originating in Western Continental Europe, but not the islands of Britain or Ireland. Classical concepts of racial identity were weakly developed, however, and the degree to which this was understood as indicating a shared tradition of language, material culture, or social organisation, rather than a common geographical origin, is not clear.

Until the rise of ARCHAEOLOGY in the nineteenth century, the study of language offered the only basis for tracing the history of peoples before written records. In the Middle Ages the ancient Gaulish language was still referred to as 'Celtic', and an affinity between it and contemporary Welsh was recognised, though IRISH was not regarded as connected; the idea of a Celtic identity shared by Gaels, Scots, Welsh, Bretons, and possibly others scarcely existed. Some scholars in the sixteenth century recognised the affinity of Irish; but it was not until the early eighteenth century, through the work of Pezron and Edward Lhuyd, that the various surviving Celtic languages and ancient Gaulish were recognised as forming a coherent family. The choice of the name 'Celtic' for this family allowed its speakers to be called Celts, and the term was used generally for the pre-Roman population of Western Europe. They were thought to be the first inhabitants, and their origin was often placed in the east, especially among the Scythians. A romantic

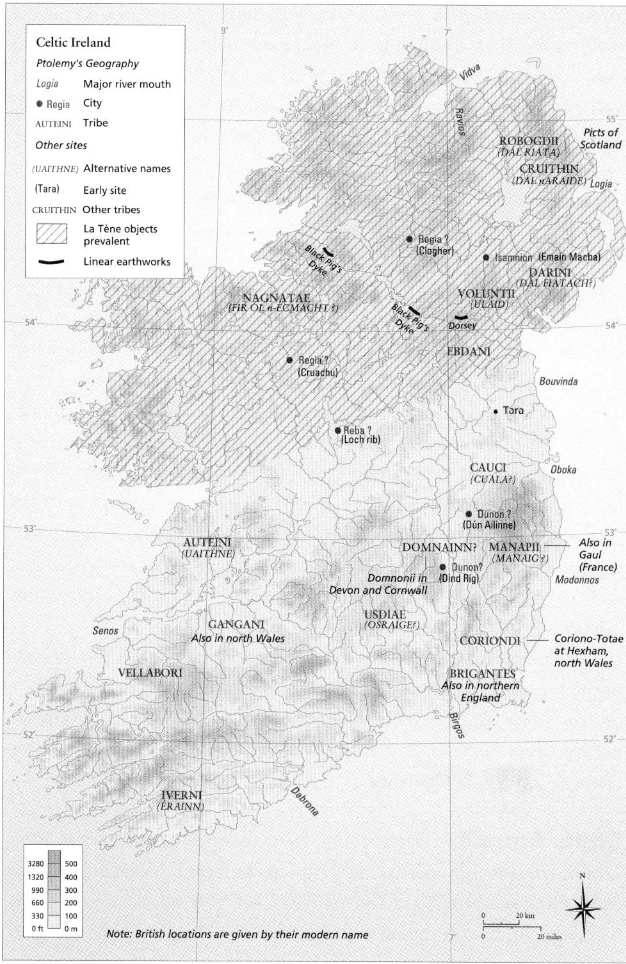

enthusiasm for ancient Celtic culture flourished, and its traces were avidly recorded; their literature was transcribed and published—or occasionally manufactured, as with James Macpherson's publication of the works of Ossian (OISÍN). Many types of prehistoric monument, especially megalithic and neolithic tombs, were associated with the druids, regarded as the priests of the ancient Celts. The distribution of these monuments and the evidence of surviving Celtic languages allowed the term 'Celts' to be used more widely than its classical meaning, especially in Britain and Ireland.

At the end of the eighteenth century the Indo-European family of languages was recognised, and it was subsequently demonstrated that the CELTIC LANGUAGES are part of that family. Since these were not the first languages spoken in Europe, it followed that the Celts could not be the original inhabitants, and they were increasingly identified with later phases of prehistory, especially the BRONZE AGE and the introduction of metallurgy. The rise of physical anthropology in the early nineteenth century provided an alternative avenue to the past through the analysis of human skeletal remains, especially skulls. It was expected that the history of the various races could be traced through the identification of characteristic human types, linking modern peoples with archaeologically recovered evidence. The Celts, however, resolutely refused to conform to this expectation. A multiplicity of modern human forms, and a wide variety of skull measurements, led some scholars to the view that the Celts were not a race at all.

The rapid development of archaeology in the nineteenth century provided yet another means of reconstructing the past. By the middle of the century the long antiquity of the human occupation of Europe was beginning to be accepted, and the Celts were more and more associated with only the later periods (particularly the IRON AGE), rather than the whole of prehistory. The material culture and burial practices of Western Europe in the later Iron Age, from the fifth to the first century BC, named after the Swiss site of La Tène, were thought to represent the Celts, and the striking La Tène art style has often been called CELTIC ART. In this way the term 'Celts' was used with yet another meaning, as the producers of a particular group of archaeological material, though such a simple equation would now be widely questioned. The recognition of a shared tradition of Celtic language and culture provided the basis for the contrasting of Celt and Saxon, a major theme of nineteenth-century thought in England. English critics such as Matthew Arnold, emphasising the antiquity of this tradition and of Celtic qualities such as artistic creativity, in contrast to Saxon practicality, used this difference to justify English political dominance over the peoples of the Celtic lands. They, however, though recognising a common origin in the remote past and a shared history of domination in more recent times, more often expressed their resistance through contemporary culture and politics, emphasising the unique historical experience of each of the separate nations; their own specifically Irish, Scottish, or Welsh past was often more important than any shared identity as Celts.

In recent times the Celts have been reinvented to suit yet other purposes, especially as a spiritual source for a brand of CHRISTIANITY or for 'New Age' mystics or as the prototypes for the contemporary utopia of a united Europe. [see ON THE STUDY OF CELTIC LITERATURE.] **T. C. Champion**

Cenél Conaill, a dynasty and, by extension, its territory in west Ulster, lying mainly within modern Co. Donegal. Claiming descent from Conall, allegedly a son of NIALL OF THE NINE HOSTAGES, it formed part of the dynastic federation of UÍ NÉILL. According to tradition the eponymous Conall helped to conquer the north-west from the ULAIDH. COLM CILLE belonged to the dynasty, which long retained close Columban connections. From an early date several Cenél Conaill rulers—notably Domhnall (died 642) son of Áed and Loingsech (sl. 704) son of Óengus—successfully contested the kingship of TARA with rival Uí Néill dynasties. However, having lost a power struggle with CENÉL NEOGHAIN in the 730s, few of its kings later held more than sub-provincial importance. Ruaidrí (sl. 950) ua Canannáin, who claimed supremacy over Uí Néill, was an exception. From the twelfth century the ruling line adopted the surname Ó Domhnaill. **Ailbhe Mac Shamhráin**

Cenél nEoghain, a dynasty and, by extension, its territory in mid-Ulster, which originally bridged INISHOWEN and modern Co. Derry, later extending into Co. Tyrone. Claiming descent from Éogan, an alleged son of NIALL OF THE NINE HOSTAGES, it ranked within the UÍ NÉILL federation. Tradition credited the eponymous Éogan and his brothers, including Conall (ancestor of CENÉL CONAILL), with having wrested the north-west from the ULAIDH. Regardless of claims that the early Muirchertach Mac Ercae (died c. 536) reigned as King of Tara, it seems that the dynasty's real advancement dates from the 630s, when the mid-Ulster CRUITHIN succumbed to an Uí Néill conquest which Cenél nEoghain was best-positioned to exploit. Several of its members attained the KINGSHIP OF TARA, including Áed Uaridnach (died 612) and Fergal (fl. 722), son of Máeldúin, ancestor in turn of many kings. Later rulers of the line adopted the surnames Ó Néill and Mac Lochlainn. **Ailbhe Mac Shamhráin**

Cenn Fáelad mac Ailella (died 679), scholar. He occupies a special place in the early literary tradition, being reputed to have brought about a merger between Latin learning, native law, and vernacular poetry. His interest in the church is reflected in compositions ascribed to him in legal tracts compiled about fifty years after his death. **Séamus Mac Mathúna**

Cennick, John (1718–1755), MORAVIAN evangelist. Born in Reading, Berkshire, to an Anglican family. He experienced a religious conversion in 1737. BAPTISTS visiting London heard him preach and invited him to Dublin in 1747. About this time Cennick was in the process of joining the Moravians, a quietist German sect; after quarrels with his Dublin hosts he concentrated his attention on Ulster, where he founded some 200 Moravian communities between 1747 and 1752 and helped to establish EVANGELICALISM in Ireland. **Kevin Herlihy**

censorship, broadcasting. Until 1960 BROADCASTING in the Republic was directly controlled by the state. Though Radio Éireann was established in 1926 in the Irish Free State (as 2RN), it was only in the 1950s that the discussion of contentious political issues began, tentatively, to be tolerated. Direct state control was particularly evident during the SECOND WORLD WAR, when the state was concerned that Ireland's NEUTRALITY should not be compromised by its news coverage, especially if heard by listeners outside the country, and interpreted as favouring one side rather than the other. This eventually led to broadcasters reading their news coverage in advance to the head of the Government Information Bureau.

The RTÉ Authority was established in 1960 as the body responsible for public service broadcasting and to act as a relatively independent buffer between the state and broadcasters. Despite this, successive Governments showed considerable concern over the increasing independence of broadcasters in raising contentious issues in news and current affairs programmes. While there was skirmishing between the Government and RTÉ in the 1960s, the most contentious issue, RTÉ's coverage of the 'TROUBLES' in NORTHERN IRELAND, came to a head in the early 1970s. In the Government's view, the RTÉ Authority did not adequately comply with a ministerial directive to refrain from broadcasting interviews, or journalists' reports of interviews, with those who advocated obtaining their objectives through violent means. In 1972 the minister consequently dismissed and replaced the RTÉ Authority, as permitted by the Broadcasting Act (1960), though this was subsequently amended in 1976. In 1976 Government censorship of the Northern conflict was clarified and specified, as permitted by section 31 of the act. The Minister for Posts and Telegraphs, CONOR CRUISE O'BRIEN, directed RTÉ to refrain from broadcasting interviews, or reports of interviews, with spokespersons of prohibited organisations. While loyalist organisations were included in this ban, the main target was SINN FÉIN. For the following eighteen years, until 1994, the Government renewed this ban annually. The consequence of this overt censorship, as well as the culture of more covert self-censorship that it bred among broadcasters, was that there was little serious investigation in broadcast news or current affairs of the causes of violence in Northern Ireland, little analysis of the motivation, organisation, or interests of any of the principal participants, and little exploration of the role of the British or Irish state in the conflict: the violence was represented instead as a procession of inexplicable events, unmotivated and irrational. The fact of the electoral success of Sinn Féin in Northern Ireland, for example, was left unexplained. One of the effects of the directive was to prevent candidates for Sinn Féin, a legal political party, having access to broadcasts in the period before an election. This was challenged in the courts in 1982; but the SUPREME COURT upheld the ban, equating Sinn Féin with the IRA and hence committed to the use of violent means to undermine the state. A further challenge in 1992, however, led to the High Court and Supreme Court ruling that RTÉ's interpretation of the section 31 directive was too broad and that it did not prohibit all access at all times by a person who was a member of Sinn Féin.

In 1994 the minister, MICHAEL D. HIGGINS, did not renew the ban, responding to continued criticism of it by journalists and human rights activists. It was also thought by some that the lapsing of the directive might be an added incentive to republicans to become further involved in the NORTHERN IRELAND PEACE PROCESS. Section 31 of the 1960 act was repealed by the Broadcasting Act (2001). [see BROADCASTING, NORTHERN IRELAND.] **Mary Kelly**

Censorship of Publications Act (1929). A reflection in the Irish Free State of a general international concern in the post-First World War period about the mass-production of pornography, the act was also the product of an Irish concern to protect a newly independent population from contamination by alien and sexually explicit literary influences. A central clause defined 'indecent' as 'suggestive of, or inciting to, sexual immorality or unnatural vice or likely in any other similar way to corrupt or deprave.' This broad definition—vigorously opposed by writers at the time—allowed the Censorship Board to ban numerous works by twentieth-century writers, including many by Irish authors (among them SEAN O'FAOLAIN, FRANK O'CONNOR, and AUSTIN CLARKE), until by the 1940s it came under increasing attack from writers and readers. An Appeal Board was legislated for in 1946, and in 1967 the Minister for Justice, Brian Lenihan, introduced legislation that permitted books to be re-examined by the board after the passage of twelve years. Literary censorship quickly ceased to be draconian, though the board remains in existence. **Terence Brown**

census. While a partial official census was conducted from 1813 to 1815, the first comprehensive census of Ireland's population was carried out in 1821, and subsequent censuses were conducted each decade until 1921, after which Northern Ireland and the Irish Free State began separate records. The 1841 census is widely regarded as the first thoroughly systematic enumeration of the country's population, having been conducted on a single day by members of the RIC. Only fragments of nineteenth-century census manuscripts now exist, while the 1901 and 1911 manuscript censuses are available for public consultation. **K. J. James**

Census Office for Northern Ireland (CONI), the agency responsible for conducting the census of POPULATION in Northern Ireland, which is held every ten years. From 1821 until 1911 a census of population was conducted for the whole of Ireland. The planned census of 1921 was postponed until 1926 because of the War of Independence and subsequent civil unrest. It was not until 1951 that the census in Northern Ireland was again held at the same time as the census in England, Scotland, and Wales. **Myra Dowling**

census of population. Probably the most fundamental data about a country concerns its POPULATION: number, location, age distribution, educational level, occupation, etc. When a census is undertaken, householders are legally bound to complete the census forms for a specified date, recording information about all those present on that night. Hotels and other institutions and even ships within territorial waters count as households for census purposes. The first systematic and complete census of Ireland was conducted as part of the census of the United Kingdom in 1841, and this was repeated at ten-year intervals. The first census in independent Ireland was undertaken in 1926 by the Statistics Branch of the Department of Industry and Commerce; this was extremely important, as the 1921 census had been abandoned in Ireland because of the WAR OF INDEPENDENCE. The census was repeated at ten-year intervals and then at five-year intervals by the Statistics Branch and its successor, the CENTRAL STATISTICS OFFICE, CSO; the only exception occurred in 1976, when the Government, in a foolish economy measure, cancelled it.

In Northern Ireland the census continued as a regional component of the United Kingdom census and is now conducted by the NORTHERN IRELAND STATISTICS & RESEARCH AGENCY, NISRA. Comparability of census data from North and South is desirable, and indeed the CSO and NISRA jointly publish a North-South Statistical Profile. There are minor differences in approach: for example, the NISRA seeks information on those normally resident in a household rather those present on the night. Perhaps more importantly, synchronisation can fail. The CSO's planned census for 2001 would have coincided with that conducted in Northern Ireland but was postponed to 2002 in a remarkably zealous measure to minimise risk to farm animals following the outbreak of foot-and-mouth disease in Britain. **Denis Conniffe**

Centlivre, Susanna (c. 1667–c. 1722), actor and dramatist. Born in Lincolnshire. In alternative versions of her biography, her father was a parliamentarian who lost his estates and in 1660 went to Ireland, where Susanna spent her first eleven years; or one of her husbands was an Irish cook, Joseph Centlivre, and they married in 1707. In *A Wife Well-Managed* (1715) there is notable use of HIBERNO-ENGLISH. Many of her comedies were produced anonymously; at least eighteen plays are attributed to her, and she may also be the writer of poetry, letters, periodical pieces, and anti-Catholic essays. **Siobhán Kilfeather**

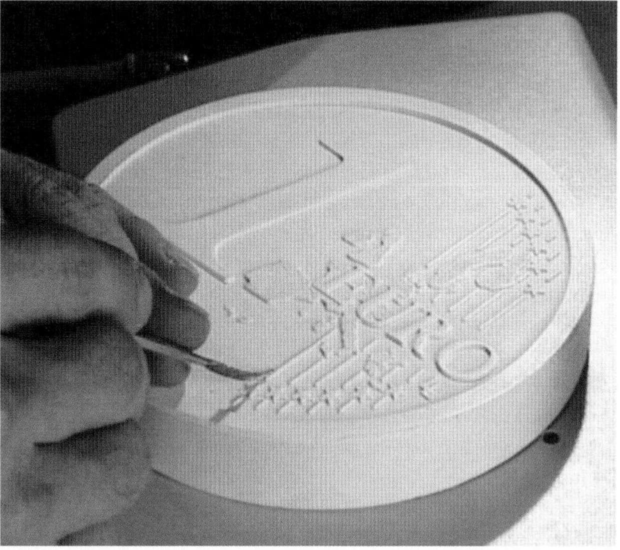

Central Bank. *The common EU face detail being engraved on to a model of the 1-euro coin. The euro became legal tender in Ireland and eleven other participating countries on 1 January 2002. [European Central Bank]*

Central Bank of Ireland, the institution regulating the banking and monetary system in the Republic. Although it assumed the title and legal status of a central bank in 1943, the Central Bank of Ireland for many years largely restricted its activities to those of a currency board, issuing IRISH POUNDS at par against sterling and investing the proceeds in foreign assets. Only during the late 1960s and 70s did it begin to act fully as the bankers' bank and the Government's bank, and only from 1979 was the value of the currency subject to fluctuation. This expanded role found a reflection in the imposing and controversial head office building in Dame Street, Dublin, completed in 1978 (to a height substantially exceeding that authorised). During the 1980s the Central Bank's response to fiscal and speculative pressures combined high interest rates and very restricted financing of the budget with a generally soft approach to currency depreciation. By the end of the century the Central Bank had once again lost its monetary independence, this time to its European counterpart, though it retained a role in the prudential supervision of financial institutions. **Patrick Honohan**

Central Statistics Office (CSO), the agency that collects, compiles, and publishes statistical data pertaining to the Republic's economy and society; it also co-ordinates official statistics produced by other state agencies. It has about 600 full-time employees, though it recruits temporary staff to tackle intermittent large surveys. The CSO, which evolved from the Statistics Branch of the Department of Industry and Commerce, was established in 1949 as an office within the Department of the Taoiseach. The Statistics Branch achieved much, conducting the first CENSUS OF POPULATION for the independent state in 1926 and the first census of industrial production the same year. By world standards the Republic was well to the fore in developing official statistics: when the Statistics Branch compiled the first official estimate of national accounts in 1946, only a handful of other countries had already done so. These achievements were due to the energy and talents of some remarkable staff, above all ROY GEARY, who became the first director of the CSO and whose publications on statistical methods won international recognition. In the 1950s the CSO was the Republic's reservoir of skills in the analysis and interpretation of data. This did not remain so: though staff numbers tripled between 1949 and 1999, demands for data rose faster still, especially as membership of the European Economic Community in 1973 meant substantial commitments to an EEC statistical system. The CSO became largely a producer of data, while technical research and analysis of the socio-economic implications of the statistics were ceded to academics and commentators outside the CSO. In 1984 the Government set up a Statistical Council to examine the state of official statistics, and its report eventually led to the Statistics Act (1993), which established the CSO as a statutory body, with a National Statistics Board to provide strategic direction. [see NORTHERN IRELAND STATISTICS AND RESEARCH AGENCY.] **Denis Conniffe**

Ceol Rince na hÉireann, a series of volumes containing traditional dance music collated from a large manuscript collection by the piper and scholar BREANDÁN BREATHNACH. Breathnach edited the first three volumes (1963, 1976, 1985); his work has been continued in two subsequent volumes edited by JACKIE SMALL (1996, 1999). Each volume has its own identity. Volume 1 contains tunes collected by Breathnach from musicians around Dublin; volume 2 continues with music from twenty-one other counties; volume 3 contains only music transcribed from commercial recordings but nonetheless from the living tradition. The fourth volume draws mainly on the manuscript collections gathered or copied by Breathnach up to the late 1960s and the fifth from recorded music transcribed by him. Of the TUNE TYPES represented, approximately 54 per cent are REELS and 24 per cent double JIGS, with HORNPIPES, slip jigs, slides, and POLKAS making up the rest. **Jimmy O'Brien Moran**

Ceoltóirí Chualann, a traditional music group, formed in 1961 by SEÁN Ó RIADA with Paddy Moloney to provide music for BRYAN MCMAHON's play *The Honey Spike* at the ABBEY THEATRE. The original musicians included Martin Kelly and John Kelly (fiddle), Sonny Brogan and Éamon de Buitléar (accordion), Michael Tubridy (flute), Paddy Moloney (pipes), Ronnie McShane (bones), Seán Ó Sé (vocals), and Seán Ó Riada (harpsichord and bodhrán); Seán Keane and Peadar Mercier joined soon after. One of their goals was to play Irish music in an innovative way and to revive the music of CAROLAN and other composers. Ceoltóirí Chualann disbanded in 1964 but reunited to record two acclaimed albums in 1969 and 1971. Many members of the group formed the CHIEFTAINS in 1963. **David Mooney**

Chaigneau, William (1709–1781), Irish-born army agent and novelist of HUGUENOT descent. He consciously placed his successful novel *The History of Jack Connor* (1752) in the European fictional tradition of Le Sage's *Gil Blas* (1715–47) and the work of Henry Fielding and Tobias Smollett. The novel follows the varied fortunes of its hero—son of a Protestant father and Catholic mother in Co. Limerick—through rural Ireland to Dublin, whence he departs for England and the Continent before his successful homecoming to Ireland. Chaigneau was also the author of *Harlequin Soldier,* a farce staged by the actor Tate Wilkinson in Edinburgh in 1765. **Ian Campbell Ross**

Challoner, Luke (1550–1613), cleric and university administrator. Born in Dublin; educated at the University of Cambridge. Together with HENRY USSHER he was one of the principal founders of TRINITY COLLEGE. The site for the new college, donated by Dublin Corporation, was held on a lease by a member of the Challoner family. He oversaw the raising of funds in Ireland and went on to be the most active man in the building and management of the college and a mainstay in its early years. One of the first fellows named in the charter of 1592, he was lecturer in divinity from 1600 to 1607, vice-provost of the college in 1601, and vice-chancellor of the university in 1612–13. He was a prebendary of ST PATRICK'S CATHEDRAL and preached more than a thousand sermons in churches round Dublin. **William J. Davis**

chamber music, music for performance by a small number of instrumentalists. The earliest initiative of importance in the promotion of chamber music in Ireland was the RDS's chamber music recital series, inaugurated in 1886 to 'enable Music as an Art to be systematically brought before the public as effectually as Painting and Sculpture are now in our public galleries.' The endeavour, in its early decades, was steered almost single-handedly by the then towering figure in Dublin musical life, MICHELE ESPOSITO. After 1901 the recital series featured outstanding international string quartets and other ensembles, including the Brodsky, Hans Wessely, and Smetana Quartets, the Pasquier String Trio, Beaux Arts Piano Trio, and Boccherini String Quintet.

In addition to the activities of the RDS and the Belfast Music Society, the Limerick Music Association, founded by the impresario JOHN RUDDOCK in 1967, has contributed notably to the appreciation of chamber music by Irish audiences, having brought more than 700 international instrumentalists and ensembles to Limerick, Dublin, and other parts of Ireland; these have included the Berlin Philharmonic Octet, Moscow Piano Trio, and Borodin String Quartet.

Two significant events in the Irish chamber music calendar are the annual course in Termonfeckin, Co. Louth, established in 1958 and organised by the Dublin Chamber Music Group, and the more recent West Cork Chamber Music Festival, founded by the members of the acclaimed VANBRUGH STRING QUARTET and held in Bantry House. The latter festival in particular, which features concerts and master classes, has become an important international chamber music event.

Recent decades have witnessed a proliferation of chamber ensembles covering the full spectrum from early to contemporary music. Such groups include the Douglas Gunn Ensemble, the Consort of St Sepulchre, the Dublin Viols, Trio Cervantes, the Belfast Wind Quintet, CONCORDE, and the Crash Ensemble. **Paul Collins**

Chambers. *The Casino at Marino, Dublin. Designed for Lord Charlemont by Sir William Chambers, it is the major architectural achievement of neo-classicism in Ireland. [Dúchas, The Heritage Service]*

Chambers, Sir William (1723–1796), architect. Born in Sweden, where his Scottish father was a merchant; he followed him into trade, making several trips to the Far East before moving to Italy in 1750, where he was to spend five years in the study of architecture and antiquities. He returned to set up as an architect in London and was to enjoy an extensive private practice while holding senior positions in the Office of Works. Among his patrons was JAMES CAULFIELD, FIRST EARL OF CHARLEMONT, whom he met in Rome and who commissioned the CASINO at Marino, Dublin (1758–76), one of the most significant buildings of the neo-classical age. He also designed Charlemont's town-house, Charlemont House, Rutland Square (Parnell Square), Dublin (1763–75), now the HUGH LANE Municipal Gallery of Modern Art. There is no evidence that Chambers visited Ireland: the supervision was entrusted to others, chiefly the sculptor and builder Simon Vierpyl, whom he had met in Rome; his Examination Hall and Chapel at Trinity College, Dublin (designed 1775), were executed by Christopher and Graham Myers. Chambers also provided designs for remodelling the Long Gallery at CASTLETOWN HOUSE (1759) and for internal alterations to RATHFARNHAM CASTLE (1770). **Frederick O'Dwyer**

changeling (Irish *iarlais* or *síofra*), in FOLK BELIEF, a substitute child (or occasionally young woman) left by the FAIRIES after they had abducted a human child (or woman) for their own purposes. FOLKLORE abounds in stories of the banishment of changelings and the restoration of the humans to their families. [see CLEARY, BRIDGET.] **Anne O'Connor**

charitable music societies. Especially prevalent in eighteenth-century Dublin, such societies provided an important motive for attending concerts (particularly oratorios) by supporting 'a grand and noble charity'; indeed they contributed greatly to the foundation and maintenance of at least eight Dublin hospitals. While they originally lacked formal constitutions, the titles used to describe them are very inconsistent, but of particular importance were the Charitable Musical Society (1723–c. 1755)—which hosted the premiere of HANDEL's *Messiah* in 1742—and the Musical Academy. Founded primarily by the Earl of Mornington in 1757, the Musical Academy was the first with a constitution, and in 1778, under statute, it became (confusingly) the Charitable Musical Society. Outside the capital, the Charitable Musical Society in Cork was active in the 1730s. Indeed significant numbers of musical societies were established in Dublin during the first half of the eighteenth century and in Belfast during the nineteenth century; though not nominally 'charitable', some did perform occasionally for the benefit of educational and orphan societies in particular. The most remarkable example was two performances of HANDEL's *Israel in Egypt*, given in the Rotunda in Dublin in early 1847 'for the relief of the Poor of the city,' under the auspices of some eleven societies and at least 250 performers. **Philip Graydon**

charity. Modern charity dates from an English statute of 1601. This was associated with the Elizabethan Poor Law and had thus a SECULAR, political purpose. It provided for the legal constitution of charities (bodies set up to dispense charity) and the scope of appropriate activities, including education, relief of poverty or distress, construction and repair projects (such as BRIDGES, churches, and roads) having 'public utility'. In 1634 a similar statute was introduced in Ireland. In the eighteenth century many lay (Protestant) philanthropic institutions, notably hospitals, emerged within this legal framework. With the decline and repeal of the PENAL LAWS, Catholic philanthropy became widespread in the nineteenth century, organised on religious and clerical lines (that is, run by religious congregations under diocesan control). For the nineteenth and much of the twentieth century, public welfare needs were met largely through a mix of charity and the POOR LAW (1838). The nineteenth-century concept of scientific charity anticipated the mentality behind the Poor Law, discriminating between the 'deserving' (incapacitated) and 'undeserving' (able-bodied) poor. With the rise of WELFARE STATES, the concept was questioned, though with a view to a redefinition of its role rather than its replacement. The purposes of charity have been questioned, as, for example, when used to finance health or education services for the better off, or through covenants, and increasingly by a more vigorous assertion of rights. Today's voluntary sector is also influenced by other traditions, including mutualism, co-operation, and modern self-help movements, and often casts off the paternalism and elitism of the past in favour of democratic organisational principles. **Joe Larragy**

Charles I (1600–1649), King of England, Scotland, and Ireland, married to Henrietta Maria, sister of Louis XIII of France. He repaid the sincere, if not unconditional, loyalty of the Catholic communities in Ireland with indecisiveness. The concessions he negotiated with the OLD ENGLISH in 1628 in return for substantial subsidies were not, as he had led them to believe, made into law;

charity. *The Sick and Indigent Roomkeepers' Society building, Palace Street, Dublin, with a monumental inscription on its façade. Dublin's oldest charity, the society had its offices here from 1851 until 1992.* [Dublin, Ninety Drawings, *1979, Brian Lalor.*]

the threat in the 1630s to confiscate their lands in Connacht as a method of increasing royal revenue intensified their sense of betrayal. His contacts with the rebels OF 1641 and the subsequent negotiations with the CONFEDERATION OF KILKENNY were characterised by ineptness and deception. He alienated Protestant opinion, resulting in their giving support to Parliament, through his apparent willingness to give concessions to Catholics; yet he failed to achieve a timely agreement with the Confederates that would have strengthened his position. His failure to capitalise on the potential help available to him in Ireland was an important factor in his defeat and execution in England (see p. 676). **Liam Irwin**

Charles II (1630–1685), King of England, Scotland, and Ireland. Charles's main aim as king was to avoid the mistakes of his father, CHARLES I. Having experienced exile in the 1650s, he was famously pragmatic; in Ireland this meant rewarding those who had benefited from his father's execution through maintaining the CROMWELLIAN LAND SETTLEMENT to ensure the loyalty of all Protestants, who united to prevent any significant return of land and political power to Catholics. JAMES BUTLER, the Duke of Ormond, whom he appointed LORD LIEUTENANT for two lengthy periods, strongly influenced this moderate but firmly Protestant Irish policy. Having restored Anglicanism, Charles II presided over an era of comparative religious toleration, applied equally to Dissenters and Catholics—though he was in no position to prevent the execution of Archbishop OLIVER PLUNKETT on patently trumped-up charges in 1681. The popular view that he had secret Catholic sympathies should be considered in the context of his sometimes pro-French foreign policy. **Liam Irwin**

Charles Fort, Kinsale, Co. Cork, the finest defensive military ARCHITECTURE in Ireland. It was designed by the architect and Surveyor General Sir WILLIAM ROBINSON. Begun in 1677 at Rincurran, overlooking the approach to Kinsale, and later named in honour of CHARLES II, it remained a military barracks and establishment until 1922, when its barrack buildings were burned by the Irregulars during the CIVIL WAR. Planned as an immense star-fort surrounded by a moat, Charles Fort is vulnerable only from the eastern landward side, where it is overlooked and from where its defences were breached during the siege of 1690. The principal entrance and some of the barrack buildings have fine pedimented doorcases, and the water is overlooked by cantilevered circular sentry boxes, perched on the points of the ramparts. **Brian Lalor**

Charlesworth, John Kaye (1889–1972), geologist. Born in Yorkshire; educated at the University of Leeds. From 1914 to 1919 he lectured in geology at Queen's University, Belfast. After two years at the University of Manchester he returned to Queen's University as professor of GEOLOGY, holding the post until his retirement in 1954. Until his death, he continued his research and writing. In addition to his papers on the geology of the Ice Age, and the publication in 1957 of a major international work, *The Quaternary Era*, he wrote two books on the geology of Ireland—the first aimed at a wide public, the second produced for specialists. **Christopher Moriarty**

Charlton, Jack (1935–), soccer player and manager. Born in Ashington, Northumberland. 'Big Jack' played his club football at Leeds United and won a world cup medal for England in 1966. He went on to manage Middlesborough and Sheffield Wednesday in the 1970s. In 1986 he was invited to become manager of the Republic of Ireland team. Fielding many players from the Irish DIASPORA, Charlton brought the team to the European Championships in 1988 and to the World Cup finals for the first time in 1990 (see p. 1001). Amid widespread euphoria at home, the team progressed to the quarter-finals, to be defeated by the hosts, Italy. The team qualified again for the 1994 World Cup in the United States, defeating the eventual runners-up, Italy, only to be knocked out by the Netherlands. Charlton bowed out after the competition, having brought unprecedented success to the Republic's football team and becoming a national celebrity in the process. **Martin Clancy**

Chartism, a British movement for parliamentary reform that emerged in the winter of 1837/8. It demanded the six points of the 'People's Charter', including universal manhood suffrage. Support came mainly from three groups of hard-pressed workers: traditional craftsmen, factory workers, and domestic outworkers. Irish immigrants were prominent in all three. The geography of Chartism reflected the dispersal of these trades as well as the settlement patterns of Irish immigrants. Its activities were greatest in Barnsley, Bradford, and Ashton-under-Lyne, where the Irish-born made up approximately 10 per cent of the population and TEXTILES were dominant; but it also enjoyed lesser support among northern miners, Scottish workers, in Wales, and the Midlands.

Chartism has been characterised as a potential point of schism between the immigrants who supported FEARGUS O'CONNOR, the Chartist leader, and those following DANIEL O'CONNELL, a sworn enemy of Chartism. However, some Irish activists maintained a dual allegiance. One such was the journalist John Cleave, a supporter of CATHOLIC EMANCIPATION and HOME RULE and a member of O'Connor's Great Radical Association. Numerous Chartism operators were Irish; but because many of them renounced Catholicism to pursue a radical political career, their Irishness is sometimes lost in the records. Peter Brophy of the Irish Universal Suffrage Union (castigated by both O'Connell and the Catholic Church), who was active in England during the great strikes of 1842 and imprisoned during the conspiracy trials of 1843, was known as a radical, not as an Irishman. Timothy Higgins of the Ashton Working Men's Association declared 'no sect or persuasion' when the police asked him his religion.

It is difficult to deduce levels of Irish support within grass-roots Chartism. No Irishman was arrested after John Frost's 'Newport Rising' in 1839; yet immigrants from Ireland numbered seventeen among those arrested for Chartist offences in other areas during the same winter. There was significant pressure on Irishmen not to join political movements, particularly after 1842, when O'Connell inaugurated the Loyal National Repeal Association, forbidding links with Chartism and returning subscriptions to those who joined both groups. The year 1848 saw Chartism and YOUNG IRELAND's newly formed Irish Confederates offering a twin programme of REPEAL and democratic reform linked with Chartism.

Chartism, Irish REPUBLICANISM, and the European revolutions led to the development by the state and the press of a vituperative anti-Irishness. Chartism was a bridge between immigrants and hosts, and it was fostered through immigrant networks and associational culture. August 1848 saw some clandestine co-operation between northern Chartists and Confederates but nothing to suggest a revolution, even if the press still made the connection. For *Punch* the conspirators were easily identified as Irish from their imaginary names, 'Mooney, Rooney, Hoolan, Doolan.'

The vitriol of the newspapers, the assiduity of the state and the inherently constitutional approach of Chartism made revolution unlikely. In the end there was no rising in Lancashire, though many were primed until the state unleashed its full powers against them, with wholesale arrests. The Irish of Bradford had been among the hundreds of men in the town armed with pikes, awaiting a signal to begin insurgency. In general, however, the expected support for WILLIAM SMITH O'BRIEN's ultimately failed effort in Ireland did not materialise. [see ENGLAND, IRISH IN.] **Donald MacRaild**

Chavelita Dunne, Mary: see EGERTON, GEORGE.

cheesemaking. Early monastic and secular records describe many different kinds of cheese, both soft and hard, notably in the eleventh-century 'AISLINGE MEIC CONGLINNE'. Legend credits Irish monks with bringing the secrets of cheesemaking to central Europe in the sixth century. But cheesemaking in Ireland died out in the seventeenth and eighteenth centuries, probably as a result of the transfer of lands to new owners and the rise of the BUTTER trade. There was sporadic production during the eighteenth and early nineteenth centuries, mainly in the midlands. Cream cheese was on sale in Cork in the 1920s and 30s. Pont l'Évêque was made by French nuns of the Order of the Franciscan Missions of Mary at Loughglinn, Co. Roscommon, in the 1940s.

The newly established Department of Agriculture, with the CO-OPERATIVE movement, established the industrial production of cheese, starting with trials in 1902 and rising steadily to an output of 100,000 tons in 2000. In the 1950s and 60s thirteen creameries, mainly in north Cork and west Limerick, made cheese. Peg Travers and her sister made an outstanding unpasteurised cheddar type in Milford Creamery; in the same period Maura Fennelly taught cheesemaking in the Munster Institute; but this was not taken up on farms, and Irish people seemed to have lost their taste for cheese. Farmhouse cheesemaking was successfully reintroduced by Veronica Steele at Milleens, Co. Cork, in 1978. Through her work and as a result of the imposition of milk quotas, the annual production of farmhouse cheeses has reached 1,000 tons. **Myrtle Allen**

cheesemaking. *Towling the rind of one of the maturing Kilshanny cheeses, a type of Gouda made by Janette and Peter Nibbering in Co. Clare. Irish farmhouse cheeses are an important element in the quality food industry. [Mike Bunn]*

chemical industry. The earliest records of the chemical industry in Ireland show that in 1823 there were two alkali plants, seventeen chemical manure plants, eleven sulphate and ammonia plants, and eleven salt-extraction plants. These industries, however, did not thrive, and by 1940 there were only two processing chemical plants, manufacturing fertilisers from sulphuric acid production. It was not until the late 1950s, with the Government's First PROGRAMME FOR ECONOMIC EXPANSION, that the extraordinary expansion of the chemical industry began, where, by 2000, some fifteen of the world's twenty leading pharmaceutical chemical companies had a production facility in the Republic. The construction of the Whitegate oil refinery in Co. Cork in 1957 signalled the beginning of this expansion, followed by the discovery of natural gas off the south coast in the Kinsale gas field. This discovery, together with the creation at Navan in Co. Meath of the largest lead-zinc mine in Europe, confounded the belief of centuries that Ireland had no natural resources. Natural gas, which is almost pure methane, was used for the manufacture of ammonia-based fertiliser, for the generation of ELECTRICITY, and for the establishment of the national gas grid. However, it was in the 1970s and 80s that the expansion of the pharmaceutical industry took place, largely as a result of the INDUSTRIAL DEVELOPMENT AGENCY's strategy for attracting FOREIGN INDUSTRY, mostly from the United States. By 2000 there were 220 pharmaceutical and chemical plants in the Republic, employing 18,600 people, with more than €6 billion in exports and contributing more than €350 million to the exchequer. **John Kelly**

chemistry. From earliest times, chemistry was closely allied to the study of MEDICINE. Irish chieftains had their own physicians; but with their demise at the end of the sixteenth century any movement towards the development of chemistry failed to materialise. In 1653, according to ROBERT BOYLE, Ireland was 'a barbarous country where chemical spirits are so misunderstood and chemical instruments so unprocurable, that it is hard to have any Hermetic thoughts in it.'

The following century saw a revival of interest in the subject with the establishment of the School of Physic (medicine) in Trinity College, Dublin in 1711 and the appointment of a lecturer in chemistry. Robert Perceval became the first professor of chemistry in 1785 but failed to fully establish the subject in its own right. WILLIAM HIGGINS—who anticipated some aspects of Dalton's atomic theory—established an effective school of chemistry at the DUBLIN SOCIETY, which was continued by others such as EDMUND DAVY and ROBERT KANE. Davy had previously been professor of chemistry at the ROYAL CORK INSTITUTION. In 1847 Kane became director of the MUSEUM OF IRISH INDUSTRY and president of Queen's College, Cork. Under his guidance the museum was to provide important training in chemistry as well as research into the exploitation of the country's natural resources. In 1867 its staff was transferred to the recently opened ROYAL COLLEGE OF SCIENCE FOR IRELAND. Chemistry formed a central part of the college's course, directed as it was to those sciences 'connected with and applied to all descriptions of industry including AGRICULTURE, MINING, and manufactures.' In 1908 the College of Science, together with the Catholic University, was incorporated in University College, Dublin, where HUGH RYAN, together with his former pupil Thomas J. Nolan, developed a thriving school of chemistry over the next thirty years.

The period after the SECOND WORLD WAR saw a burgeoning of institutions teaching chemistry and a growth in their research activities and in industries associated with chemistry. An important feature of this period was the establishment of annual Research Student Conferences, at which postgraduate students discussed their work in progress; the number attending these conferences has increased from fewer than fifty in the 1950s to more than 300 today. By the 1960s the seven university institutions had active chemistry departments, as had the newly founded regional technical colleges. Chemical research was also being carried on in An Foras Talúntais (now Teagasc) and the Institute for Industrial Research and Standards (successively renamed National Board of Science and Technology, Eolas, Forbairt, and Enterprise Ireland). Industries in which chemistry plays some part, such as the Irish Sugar Company and Bord na Móna, established by the state in the 1930s to exploit the country's natural resources, have been joined by the operations of transnational chemical companies specialising in the production of fine chemicals and pharmaceuticals, such as Loctite, Pfizer, Elan, Yamanouchi, and Wyeth. In the fifty years since 1947 employment in this industry has grown from 3,500 to 19,300. From 1973 to 1995 exports of chemical products grew by more than 6,000 per cent, from a value of €100 million to over €6,000 million. **William J. Davis**

Chenevix, Helen (1890–1963), trade unionist and pacifist. Born in Dublin, daughter of a CHURCH OF IRELAND bishop; educated at TCD. She organised women of the IRISH WOMEN WORKERS' UNION, and was also vice-chairwoman of the Irish pacifist movement. In 1951 she was president of the IRISH TRADES UNION CONGRESS; she was also a member of the LABOUR PARTY. She was noted for calm, logic, and courage. **Mary Jones**

Chenevix, Richard (1774–1830), chemist. Born at Ballycommon, Co. Laois; educated at the University of Glasgow: specialist in analytical CHEMISTRY and mineralogy. At first he went to France—inspired by the new chemistry under development there by Antoine Lavoisier—and later to England. His work attracted the attention of the Royal Society and he was elected a fellow in 1801 and awarded the Copley Medal in 1803. He left England for France following a mistaken attack on William Hyde Wollaston's claim concerning the nature of palladium. His career thereafter remarkably changed direction, as he started to write poems and plays. The mineral chenevixite, discovered in 1866, is named in his honour. **Susan McKenna-Lawlor**

Chesney, Francis Rawdon (1789–1872), EXPLORER. Born in Annalong, Co. Down. His career in the Royal Artillery was largely confined to garrison duty until he began his explorations in 1829. He explored Egypt, Syria and the Euphrates valley and proposed a route to India through Syria and the Persian Gulf. His report, which showed a canal at Suez to be a possible undertaking, encouraged the French engineer, Ferdinand de Lesseps, to take on the project and to describe Chesney as 'the father of the Suez Canal.' In 1835 he navigated the Euphrates to the Persian Gulf, explored the Tigris and Karu River, and journeyed overland to India. In 1851, having achieved the rank of general, he retired to the family estate at Kilkeel, Co. Down, where he died in 1872. **Peter Somerville-Large**

Chester Beatty Library, Dublin, a collection of more than 6,000 manuscripts on paper, vellum, and other media, together with about 4,000 fine and early printed books and some hundreds of items of decorative arts interest. The library was begun by ALFRED CHESTER BEATTY, an American mining engineer who established a mining consultancy in New York and later in London. A collector of minerals, Chinese snuff bottles, and stamps since childhood, as an adult he began to collect more widely, buying European and Persian manuscripts and fine and early printed books. In 1914, following a visit to Egypt, he bought some decorated copies of the Qur'an; a journey to Asia in 1917 added Japanese and Chinese painting to his interests. He was attracted to richly illustrated material, fine bindings, and calligraphy but was also concerned to preserve texts for their historical importance. Working with scholars, he rapidly built up important collections of papyri, Indian miniatures, Arabic scholarly texts, and a superb collection of Qur'an manuscripts. His Persian and Turkish manuscripts are exceptionally fine; he also acquired important Japanese, Chinese, south-east Asian, Armenian, Ethiopian, Byzantine, and Western European manuscripts. The quantity and quality of these holdings make the library one of the most important collections of its kind, and certainly the finest to have been brought together by one person during the twentieth century.

Having made a significant contribution to the supply of strategic raw materials for the Allies during the SECOND WORLD WAR, for which he was knighted in 1954, in 1950 Chester Beatty move to Ireland and built a library for his collection in Shrewsbury Road, Dublin, which opened to the public in 1954. In 1957 he became Ireland's first HONORARY CITIZEN. On his death in 1968 the collection was bequeathed to a trust for the benefit of the public. It is now supported by the Government of Ireland, and the library is one of the country's national cultural institutions. It was moved to the Clock Tower Building in DUBLIN CASTLE in 1999 and reopened to the public in 2000.

Among the most important treasures of the library are the Biblical and Manichaean papyri, the great collections of Islamic manuscripts (including more than 300 complete or fragmentary copies of the Qur'an), and many works of philosophy, liturgy, and

Chester Beatty Library. *'Sacred Traditions Gallery', one of the permanent displays at the Chester Beatty Library, Dublin, exhibiting sacred texts, illuminated manuscripts, and miniature paintings from the principal religions and systems of belief, with a particular emphasis on eastern cultures. [Courtesy of the Trustees of the Chester Beatty Library; photo: Barry Mason]*

spiritual belief from China, Japan, south-east Asia, and non-Islamic India. The Christian collections include illuminated manuscripts from Egypt, the Levant, Byzantium, Western Europe, Ethiopia, Russia, and Serbia and an interesting archive of documents relating to Christian missions to eastern Asia in the seventeenth and early eighteenth centuries. The Islamic collections include more than 2,700 manuscripts of scholarship, Islamic law, prayer, and commentary on the life of Muhammad, medicine, mathematics, science, and books of pilgrimage. In addition to these, which are illuminated with abstract ornament, there are finely illustrated codices from Persia, Turkey, and the Mughal Court of India. **Michael Ryan**

Chetwynd Viaduct (1851), south-west of Cork, erected for the Cork and Bandon Railway. Now disused, it has cast-iron arches, each having four ribs with transverse diagonal bracing and latticed spandrels. It was designed by Charles Nixon, a pupil of Isambard Kingdom Brunel. It is an important listed engineering structure. **Ronald Cox**

chevaux de Frise ('Friesian horses'), a dense barrier of stone uprights used as an anti-cavalry device at later prehistoric forts. This system of defence is found mainly in north-western Iberia but also at three Irish forts: Ballykinvarga, Co. Clare, and Dúchathair and DÚN AONGHASA, Inishmore, Aran Islands, Co. Galway. The band of stone pillars at Dún Aonghasa, approximately 35 m (115 ft) wide and over 1.75 m ($5\frac{3}{4}$ ft) high, is the most spectacular example known to exist. **Claire Cotter**

Cheyne, John (1777–1836), physician. Born in Leith, Scotland. He settled in Dublin, where he built up a large practice. Contributing to Dublin Hospitals Reports, 1818, he described a patient who for days before death displayed waxing and waning of breathing. His paper was recalled by WILLIAM STOKES, who presented a similar case in 1846. The 'ascending and descending respiration' was named the 'Cheyne-Stokes phenomenon' by Ludwig Traube of Berlin. **J. B. Lyons**

Chicago, the Irish in. Chicago, in Cook County, Illinois, is the largest city in the state: the census for 2000 reported a population of 2.9 million for the city, 5.4 million for Cook County, and 9.2 million for the greater tri-state metropolitan area.

The Irish have been intertwined with the history of Chicago since its beginning in the 1830s. Among the city's earliest inhabitants were Irish immigrants who came to the area to work on the Illinois and Michigan Canal and then settled in the city. By 1850 Irish immigrants made up about 20 per cent of the city's population. Though significant numbers of Irish arrived in the decades following, their share of the city's population declined. By 1900 Irish immigrants and their children accounted for 14 per cent of the population. In 1990 persons of Irish (including a small number of 'Scotch-Irish') ancestry made up 9 per cent of the population of Chicago and 13.7 per cent of the population of Cook County.

Most early Irish immigrants found themselves on the lowest rungs of the economic ladder; but gradually their economic status improved. After the SECOND WORLD WAR thousands of upwardly mobile Irish left the city and flocked to the suburbs.

The Irish have had a significant impact on the growth of Catholicism in the city. Until 1915 all but one of the city's bishops were Irish. Under the leadership of prelates such as Archbishop Patrick J. Feehan, 1880–1902, the church developed into a multi-ethnic institution, with an extensive network of schools, churches, and charitable institutions. The Irish have also played a prominent role in local politics. By the 1870s they were the most powerful national group in politics, holding important positions in the Democratic Party and on the city council. Since 1933 all but two of Chicago's mayors have been of Irish descent; these include Richard J. Daley, 1955–76, and his son, Richard M. Daley, 1989–. Irish Chicagoans have also made significant contributions to literature and the arts; these include Finley Peter Dunne, who wrote the 'Mr Dooley' columns, James T. Farrell, author of the Studs Lonigan trilogy and other novels, FRANCIS O'NEILL, who published collections of Irish TRADITIONAL MUSIC, and MICHAEL FLATLEY, the dancer.

The Chicago Irish have also given significant support to Irish nationalist movements. In the 1860s the Fenians were active in the city, while in the 1880s the land reform and HOME RULE MOVEMENTS received strong support. In the late nineteenth and early twentieth centuries the city also had several camps (branches) of CLAN NA GAEL. In 1889 the murder of a local Clan na Gael leader, Dr Patrick Cronin, by members of a rival faction had repercussions on the nationalist movement on both sides of the Atlantic. During the WAR OF INDEPENDENCE, support groups flourished in the city; this activity subsided after the creation of the Irish Free State but underwent something of a revival when the 'TROUBLES' broke out in the North of Ireland in the late 1960s. **Michael F. Funchion**

Chichester, Sir Arthur (1563–1625), Lord Deputy (see p. 486). An Elizabethan adventurer from Devon, Chichester served in Ireland during the NINE YEARS' WAR (1594–1603), when, as governor of Carrickfergus, his devastating raids were instrumental in subjugating the rebellion led by HUGH O'NEILL, Earl of Tyrone. A virtual bankrupt at the turn of the century, Chichester's highly effective military performance marked him out for rapid promotion and ultimately spectacular riches. Taking up office as Lord Deputy of Ireland in 1605, he served for the inordinately long period of eleven years, playing a leading role in consolidating the Elizabethan conquest. However, he was well rewarded for his labours, acquiring Irish estates of some 40,000 ha (100,000 acres). His period as Viceroy was eventful, marked by such well-known events as the FLIGHT OF THE EARLS (1607) and the PLANTATION OF ULSTER (1610). Other notable events included the rebellion of CAHIR O'DOHERTY (1608) and the fractious Irish Parliament of 1613–15. In general, his administration was marked by religious repression of Catholics, as he believed that religious affiliation was the key to political loyalty. While virulently anti-Catholic, he was far from anti-Irish, wishing to see an accommodation with the indigenous population in the country where he intended to spend his retirement. Therefore, at the time of the Plantation of Ulster, Chichester staunchly, if unsuccessfully, campaigned to ensure that the 'deserving' Irish in Ulster would be provided with a substantial stake in the new settlement. He ended his career as a senior member of the Privy Council in London. **John McCavitt**

Chichester-Clark, Major James, Lord Moyola (1923–2002), politician. Educated at Eton College, Windsor. Like his predecessor, TERENCE O'NEILL, Chichester-Clark was a member of Ulster's long-established landed class. He joined the British army in 1942, retiring in 1960 to succeed his grandmother, Dame DEHRA PARKER, at STORMONT as Unionist MP for South Londonderry. In 1963 O'Neill appointed him chief whip, and he served as Minister of Agriculture, 1967–9. Granite-faced, with a notable hesitancy of speech, he broadly endorsed O'Neill's reformist policies, providing him with vital support in the wake of the CIVIL RIGHTS march of 5 October 1968. In April 1969 he resigned abruptly from O'Neill's Cabinet, ostensibly over the timing of 'one man, one vote' but possibly to position himself for the leadership contest. He succeeded O'Neill on 1 May, defeating BRIAN FAULKNER by one vote in the ULSTER UNIONIST parliamentary party.

During his twenty-two-month premiership, 1969–71, he faced the invidious task of reconciling nationalist demands for reform with unionist fears and mounting violence on the streets. The breakdown of law and order in August 1969 forced him to request the introduction of British soldiers, and the resulting transfer of security responsibility to the officer commanding British forces and the disbanding of the B Specials weakened his authority. Faced with an increasing IRA offensive in 1970–71, and under withering attack from the Unionist right wing, he lost enthusiasm for a thankless job. He resigned on 20 March 1971 following the failure of the British government to sanction new security policies. He was given a life peerage in 1971. [see A, B, C SPECIALS.] **Eamon Phoenix**

Chichester family, Earls of Donegall. Sir ARTHUR CHICHESTER, made Lord Deputy of Ireland in 1605, was an able politician and administrator who had two years earlier been granted lands in Co. Antrim that included the castle of Belfast. In 1613 he was made Baron of Belfast, thus beginning a long and historic connection with the town. He died in 1625 without a surviving male heir, and the title transferred to his brother's family. His successor, also Arthur, saw service during the REBELLION OF 1641 and was made Earl of Donegall.

The charter of Belfast had given the family considerable power, enabling them to select the 'sovereign' or mayor, the burgesses, and in consequence the borough's two members of Parliament. In this way the Chichester family maintained a position of patronage in the town for well over two centuries. They profited greatly from the town's development as an industrial centre and built several fine houses at Doagh and Ormeau and in Belfast itself. In spite of its successes, however, the dynasty was almost destroyed by the activities of the second marquis, who ran up huge gambling debts, despite having an annual income of £30,000 in the early nineteenth century. His reputation as a debtor led to a stay in the debtors' prison in London and to the nickname 'Lord Done 'Em All'. **Roddy Hegarty**

Chief Secretary for Ireland, head of the Irish administration up to 1922. Originally chief secretary to the LORD LIEUTENANT, by the later eighteenth century the Chief Secretary had become the linchpin of the Irish administration, managing its business in Parliament and supervising the Chief Secretary's Office in Dublin. The responsibilities and work load expanded greatly in the nineteenth century, and the occupant frequently sat in the Cabinet. The post was widely regarded as a testing ground for talented younger politicians; prominent occupants included ROBERT PEEL (1812–18), Edward Stanley (1830–33), and ARTHUR BALFOUR (1887–91), all subsequently Prime Minister, and GEORGE WYNDHAM (1900–5). [see PHOENIX PARK MURDERS.] **Peter Gray**

'chiefs of the name'. The most senior known male descendant of an inaugurated or *de facto* Irish chief is regarded by the Chief Herald of Ireland as 'chief of his name.' This recognition is merely the acknowledgment of a genealogical fact and does not carry with it any rights or privileges. Among those so recognised are O'Conor Don, the O'Neill of Clanaboy, the O'Donovan, and the MacDermott of Coolavin. **Micheál Ó Comáin**

Chieftains, the, a traditional music ensemble following the model of CEOLTÓIRÍ CHUALANN, formed in 1963 by the uilleann-piper Paddy Moloney and included Seán Keane and Martin Fay (fiddlers), Matt Molloy (flute-player), Derek Bell (multi-instrumentalist and harper), and Kevin Conneff (bodhrán-player and singer). Noted for outstanding arrangements of dance music and airs, the group became professional in 1975, touring extensively to become ambassadors of Irish music around the world. In 1984 they visited China, then began a policy of engaging with other music forms while retaining a core Irish traditional repertoire. By 2000 they had produced thirty-five albums; their many awards include an OSCAR and six Grammys. **Fintan Vallely**

Child, A. E. [Alfred Ernest] (1875–1939), STAINED-GLASS artist and teacher. Born in London; he won a scholarship to the Goldsmiths' Institute c. 1891 before becoming an assistant to Christopher Whall, the stained-glass artist of the English ARTS AND CRAFTS MOVEMENT. In 1901 Whall recommended Child for the posts of instructor in stained glass at the reconstituted Metropolitan School of Art, Dublin, and manager of An Túr Gloine, the proposed stained-glass co-operative workshop. Child was thus responsible for training a new generation of the finest twentieth-century stained-glass artists in a strong idiom, both arts and crafts and specifically Irish. **Nicola Gordon Bowe**

childbirth. With dramatically falling fertility rates for Irish women during recent decades, childbirth remains an experience that, annually, more than 75,000 women throughout the country undergo. They do so within a system of MATERNITY CARE that has a heavy emphasis on medical intervention. In the Republic, a tiny fraction of births—0.4 per cent—are home births, assisted by a small number of independent MIDWIVES; all the rest take place in hospitals. In Northern Ireland, despite recent policies sanctioning home birth as a woman's choice, the rate remains at 0.2 per cent. The birth experience has been over-determined by an increasingly strong consultant OBSTETRIC profession, to the detriment of professional midwifery. In the Republic, over 50 per cent of women attend obstetricians for private antenatal care. HOSPITAL births now include a range of technological and medical interventions as a matter of course. The pre-eminent model is the approach known as active management of labour, strongly associated with the National Maternity Hospital, Dublin, since the 1970s but widely used throughout Ireland and also in Britain and the United States. Under active management, 50 to 70 per cent of first-time mothers in the Republic have their labour accelerated with artificial oxytocic drugs, while up to a further 25 per cent have their labour similarly induced. Caesarean section rates have increased to over 18 per cent in the Republic, while the present rate in Northern Ireland is 23.9 per cent, with spontaneous deliveries slipping to 64 per cent. The deep disaffection of Irish midwives with this system has led to a critical hospital shortage, as many have left the profession. As an attempted counterweight to this medical model of birth in the Republic, the 1998 Commission on Nursing recommended direct-entry midwifery training and pilot home-birth schemes. However, similar initiatives to support midwifery-led care in Northern Ireland have failed to stem the rising intervention rates and the outflow of midwives. **Jo Murphy-Lawless**

childbirth, home. Until the beginning of the twentieth century, birth was a female domain, unregulated by the state. Mothers were attended by women skilled in childbirth known as 'handy-women'. MIDWIFERY practice was a family tradition, and home was the place of birth.

Since 1976 the proportion of home births has remained static, at less than 0.5 per cent. The Health Act (1970) entitles all women, irrespective of income, to a home birth service from the state. Buttressed by a growing body of research testifying to its safety, and fuelled by spiralling hospital intervention rates, the demand for home birth is growing. As a movement stemming from 'natural childbirth', FEMINISM, and complementary HEALTH, home birth opposes what it sees as high-technology 'conveyor belt' obstetrics, rejecting routine hospital care as authoritarian, invasive, risky, and painful. Home birth is perceived as offering safe, autonomous care, continuous one-to-one attention from a chosen midwife, unrestricted paternal and FAMILY participation, privacy, a gentle environment for birth, and unlimited mother-baby contact. **Marie O'Connor**

child care, the term commonly used for the minding of children by paid child-minders, whether this takes place in the child's home, in the minder's home, or in a crèche. Child-minding by parents or other family members is often referred to as 'unpaid child care'. Paid child care has become common in recent decades with the growing participation in work outside the home by mothers of young children. A survey carried out for the Commission on the Family in 1996 and 1997 showed that about 30 per cent of two to three-year-old children in the Republic were cared for by paid minders for some portion of a typical working day. The subject attracted public attention in the 1990s because of the rising cost and insufficient availability of paid child care, in a situation of emerging labour shortage. Proposals in the late 1990s to provide public subsidy for paid child care led to claims by parents who provide all their child care themselves that they were being unfairly neglected. Subsequently, Government policy aimed to provide public subsidy for child care that took account of the needs of both paid and unpaid child care. **Tony Fahey**

Childers, (Robert) Erskine (1870–1922), politician and author. Born in England and raised in Ireland; educated at the University of Cambridge. He was Clerk of the House of Commons, 1894–1910, and author of the popular thriller *The Riddle of the Sands* (1903). A member of the British forces in the ANGLO-BOER WAR and the FIRST WORLD WAR, he was awarded the Distinguished Service Order in 1916. He became an Irish nationalist, first a HOME-RULER and subsequently an ardent REPUBLICAN. He used his yacht, *Asgard*, to import arms for the IRISH VOLUNTEERS in 1914. A republican propagandist, 1919–22, he was a member of Dáil Éireann, 1921–2, and secretary to the Irish Treaty delegation in 1921. He opposed the ANGLO-IRISH TREATY, was anti-Treaty publicity director during the CIVIL WAR, and was shot by firing squad on 24 November 1922. He was the father of ERSKINE HAMILTON CHILDERS. **Marie Coleman**

Childers, Erskine Hamilton (1905–1974), politician. Born in London, eldest son of (ROBERT) ERSKINE CHILDERS; educated at the University of Cambridge. He worked for the IRISH PRESS and in industrial development in the 1930s, became a FIANNA FÁIL TD in 1938, and held many Government posts. Elected fourth President of Ireland in 1973, he died suddenly while in office. **Marie Coleman**

child poverty is often seen as a particular problem because of the long-term impact it may have on their well-being. Figures produced by the EUROPEAN UNION showed Ireland to have one of the highest rates of child poverty among the member-states in the mid-1990s; this was on the grounds of the number of children living in households falling below relative INCOME poverty lines, such as half average income. One of the main factors producing these high rates was UNEMPLOYMENT, which affected a substantial number of families with children from the early 1980s. As unemployment fell sharply from 1994, these measures of child poverty also fell; however, by the end of the 1990s it was still seen as a significant problem, focusing attention on the support provided by the state to families. Income support is provided to all families with children through monthly child benefit, but the general level of support provided through the tax and SOCIAL WELFARE systems is less than in some other European countries. Trends in family formation and dissolution also influence the extent and nature of child poverty, with an increasing number of children living with only one parent and these generally facing a relatively high risk of poverty. [see NATIONAL ANTI-POVERTY STRATEGY.] **Brian Nolan**

child poverty. *Father Peter McVerry (right) and Barry Gannon on the high-rise local authority housing estate at Ballymun, Dublin, where McVerry runs a home for deprived teenage boys. [Eamonn Farrell/Photocall Ireland]*

Children of Lir. The FOLK-TALE 'Oidhe Chlainne Lir' (The Tragic Fate of the Children of Lir) dates approximately from the fifteenth century and is largely based on an earlier international legend. Following the death of his first wife, the mythical chieftain Lir remarries. His second wife, Aoife, jealous of her four step-children, turns them into swans. After 900 unhappy years they return and find their home deserted. They then go to Inis Gluaire (an island off Co. Mayo), where they are well treated by a holy man. Shortly afterwards they resume their human form as four very old people; the holy man then baptises them before they die. **Ríonach uí Ógáin**

children's and illustrated literature, nineteenth and twentieth centuries. MARIA EDGEWORTH was the first Irish novelist whose books for children were peopled with real children and not animated moral values. Her children's books had been translated into Irish by 1833. Irish children's literature paralleled its English counterpart, with the bluestocking writer ANNA MARIA HALL representing the Anglo-Irish Ascendancy and Cecily M. Caddell writing for Catholic children. Occasional works of originality emerged from such authors as FRANCES BROWNE and OSCAR WILDE, with girls' stories by L. T. MEADE, Clara and Rosa Mulholland, and boys' adventure tales by META MAYNE REID.

It was not until the twentieth century that a distinctive Irish literature emerged, which drew on both cultures. MYTHOLOGY, FOLKLORE, and magic emerged as themes and were the core of the writings of JAMES STEPHENS and PÁDRAIC COLUM, with fantasy and magic of a different kind from SOPHIA ROSAMOND PRAEGER. At the beginning of the twentieth century PATRICK PEARSE and DOUGLAS HYDE were writing tales in Irish. From time to time gems emerged from adult authors, such as JAMES JOYCE's *The Cat and the Devil*, WALTER MACKEN's *The Island of the Yellow Ox*, MARY LAVIN's *Second-Best Children in the World*, LOUIS MACNEICE's *The Sixpence That Rolled Away*, and EDNA O'BRIEN's *The Dazzle*. During the 1940s, 50s, and 60s children were well served by a handful of talented writers writing fantasies, fairy-tales, adventure, and realistic dramas—PATRICIA LYNCH, ÉILÍS DILLON, EILEEN O'FAOLAIN, and MARY FLYNN—together with the illustrators Eileen Coghlan, Austin Molloy, and Naomi Heather. The artists HARRY CLARKE, NANO REID, NORAH MCGUINNESS, ELIZABETH RIVERS, and HARRY KERNOFF illustrated a handful of diverse works for children. AN GÚM produced excellent picture books, including Liam Mac Uistin's DEIRDRE (1982), Marie Louise Fitzpatrick's delightful *An Chanáil* (1988), and Mary Arrigan's *Mamó* books. In 1981 the Children's Press was established, and other publishers moved into this field. Certain themes have emerged: an interest in wildlife, as exemplified by Tom McCaughren and Soinbhe Lally (*A Hive for the Honey Bee*, 1996); historical novels by Michael Mullen, Elizabeth O'Hara, and Gerard Whelan; time-slip fantasies by Maeve Friel, MARTIN WADDELL, Cormac Mac Raois, and John Quinn; and contemporary themes handled with freshness and openness by Margrit Cruickshank, Marilyn Taylor, and SIOBHÁN PARKINSON, with MARITA CONLON-MCKENNA by far the most popular contemporary writer. Mark O'Sullivan writes successfully in a range of themes: history, fantasy, and highly original work such as *Angels Without Wings* (1997). Non-fiction themes include biography, history, craft, and the ENVIRONMENT. G. O. SIMMS wrote on ST PATRICK and ST BRENDAN and, memorably, *Exploring the* BOOK OF KELLS. Irish illustrators have been making a name both at home and abroad, with P. J. LYNCH, Barry Castle, Niamh Sharkey, and Marie Louise Fitzpatrick producing timeless work. **Patricia Donlon**

children's literature. The complex world of Irish children's literature has a history of at least 300 years; beyond that its origins lie in Ireland's vast quantities of traditional story, myth, legend, and FOLK-TALE. These ancient narratives have served, and continue to serve, as the starting-point for numerous retellings, adaptations, and novelisations.

Particularly significant contributions to this area of children's literature have been made by such contemporary writers as Cormac Mac Raois and Michael Scott and by such earlier writers as FRANCES BROWNE (1816–1879), STANDISH JAMES O'GRADY, Ella Young (1867–1956), and PÁDRAIC COLUM. Other important early contributions to children's literature were made by JONATHAN SWIFT (if we allow GULLIVER'S TRAVELS, or parts of it, as a children's book), by MARIA EDGEWORTH in her moral tales, and by OSCAR WILDE in his fairy stories. The Narnia novels of C. S. LEWIS are among the most widely known works of twentieth-century children's literature, a period that also saw distinguished writing from PATRICIA LYNCH, META MAYNE REID, WALTER MACKEN, and ÉILÍS DILLON.

The years 1980–2000 saw a remarkable increase in the quantity and range of writing, illustration, and PUBLISHING for the young. The picture-book texts of MARTIN WADDELL, the nature stories of Tom McCaughren, the historical fiction of MARITA CONLON-MCKENNA, the poetry of MATTHEW SWEENEY, and the illustrations of P. J. LYNCH have already earned widespread acclaim. **Robert Dunbar**

Chinnery, George (1774–1852), artist. Born in England; in 1795 he came to Ireland and in 1802 left for a career in India and China. He spent a successful seven years in Ireland, painting portraits, landscapes, and miniatures in both oils and watercolours. Only two large oils are now known in Ireland: *Miss Vigne*, in the RDS, and *Mrs Eustace*, in the NATIONAL GALLERY OF IRELAND. Both are painted in strong chiaroscuro, while his watercolours have charming clarity. He taught in the DUBLIN SOCIETY Schools from 1796 and organised an exhibition in 1801. **Anne Crookshank**

choirs and choral music. The longest-established choirs in Ireland are those associated with St Patrick's Cathedral (1432) and Christ Church Cathedral (1480), Dublin, which not only provide music for worship but have also been associated with performances for charitable purposes, including the first performance of HANDEL's *Messiah* (1742).

The earliest and longest-running amateur society is the Hibernian Catch Club, founded in 1680 by the vicars-choral of St Patrick's and Christ Church Cathedrals. Many choirs in the eighteenth century were connected with CHARITABLE SOCIETIES, including the Charitable Musical Society, SONS OF HANDEL (1790), and Irish Musical Fund Society (1787). Choirs were also associated with the Anacreontic Society, Philharmonic Society, and Society of Antient Concerts, founded in 1834 by JOSEPH ROBINSON.

The earliest public choirs include the Sacred Harmonic Society (1841), Metropolitan Choral Society (1842), Amateur Melophonic (1844), Dublin Madrigal Society (1846), and Dublin Choral Society (1847), many of which combined in 1847 for performances of HANDEL's oratorio *Israel in Egypt*. The oldest university choir, Dublin University Choral Society, was founded in 1837. In the twentieth century many excellent chamber choirs and choral societies have been associated with universities and other educational and cultural institutions throughout the country.

Choirs also flourished at cathedral and monastic establishments in Cashel, Cork, and Belfast. The era following CATHOLIC EMANCIPATION (1829) saw the establishment of many choirs in Catholic churches, in particular the choir of St Mary's Church (now St Mary's Pro-Cathedral) in Marlborough Street, Dublin, where Haydn Corri was director, 1827–48, and which continued until EDWARD MARTYN founded the PALESTRINA CHOIR (1902).

Numerous choral societies flourished during the twentieth century. These include the CULWICK CHORAL SOCIETY (1898), VINCENT O'BRIEN's Dublin Oratorio Society (1906), OUR LADY'S CHORAL SOCIETY (1945), Guinness Choir (1951), St James's Choir (1965), Limerick Choral Union (1967), the Goethe Institut Choir, and Dublin County Choir (1975). Specialist early music groups include BRIAN BOYDELL's Dowland Consort (1958–69), Camerata (1973), Renaissance Singers (1976), and Galway Baroque Singers (1983). The ERIC SWEENEY Singers and Cantique were founded to perform contemporary music. In 1992, to celebrate the quatercentenary of TCD, Mahler's eighth symphony ('the Symphony of a Thousand') was performed by 1,000 singers from ten choirs with the NATIONAL SYMPHONY ORCHESTRA and RTÉ Concert Orchestra conducted by Owain Arwel Hughes—the largest such collaboration in Ireland since the 1847 concert for the relief of the poor.

Twentieth-century broadcasting led to the formation in 1943 of Cór Radio Éireann and in 1952 of the amateur Radio Éireann Choral Society. The ten members of the professional chamber choir

Children of Lir. *Oisín Kelly's* Children of Lir *(1966) in the Garden of Remembrance, Dublin. Based on the mythological legend of the children who were turned into swans, the sculpture commemorates those who died in the struggle for Irish freedom. [By permission of the Office of Public Works]*

the RÉ Singers (later RTÉ Singers), 1953–85, specialising in twentieth-century music, broadcast regularly, toured on the Continent, and made numerous recordings. In 1985 the choir was re-formed as the RTÉ Chamber Choir and later the National Chamber Choir, its student members financed by way of bursary from RTÉ. The National Chamber Choir is based in DCU, but continues to have access to the extensive library of the former RTÉ Singers. RTÉ established the Philharmonic Choir in 1985 and Cór na nÓg in 1987.

Specialist choral groups which have represented Ireland abroad include the Lindsay Singers, Cantairí Óga Átha Cliath, the Choir of St Mary's College, Arklow, and the Park Singers. The Irish Youth Choir was established in 1982 and the National Children's Choir in 1985. Other successful groups include Madrigal, Canzona, and the choirs of Dublin Choral Foundation, in particular the Lassus Scholars. [see CHURCH MUSIC.] **Ite O'Donovan, Geraldine Guiden and Richard Pine.**

Christ Church Cathedral, Dublin, the principal church of the OLD ENGLISH colony, played an important role in the civic life of Dublin. Though largely rebuilt during the 1870s, it incorporates late twelfth-century fabric in the crypt and parts of the transepts and a thirteenth-century north wall in the nave. The style of medieval ARCHITECTURE and SCULPTURE suggests that English masons constructed it. It was here the viceroys and LORDS LIEUTENANT took their OATH OF ALLEGIANCE until the sixteenth century and LAMBERT SIMNEL was crowned Edward VI of England in 1487. The building now serves as the cathedral church of the Church of Ireland united diocese of Dublin and Glendalough. **Rachel Moss**

Christian Brethren. In the early 1820s a group of mainly well-educated laity and clergy began meeting in Dublin in the manner of first-century Christians. The movement spread rapidly; by 1832 the largest of these congregations was in Plymouth, hence the popular name Plymouth Brethren (now little used). An early leading figure was John Nelson Darby of Co. Wicklow. The congregations are led by lay members and are independent of each other. A vigorous missionary spirit led to congregations being established in many countries; there are now about 170 in Ireland, twenty of them in the Republic. **Gabrielle Brocklesby**

Christian Brothers, a lay teaching order. The order was founded by EDMUND RICE, who established a school in Waterford in 1802 for the education of poor boys. Modelled on NANO NAGLE's Presentation Sisters, the Christian Brothers, who received a Papal brief from Pope Pius VII in 1820, played a leading role in the revitalisation of the Catholic Church in Ireland following the dislocation of the Penal Era. From the beginning, the Brothers' influence far exceeded their numbers, on account of the efficiency of their teaching methods and their textbooks. Their early curriculum was a hybrid—a pragmatic mixture of contemporary practice. The Brothers were uncompromising in their insistence on the Catholic nature of their teaching; accordingly, they were unwilling to co-operate with the NATIONAL SCHOOL SYSTEM, despite pressure from their patron, Archbishop DANIEL MURRAY. From the middle of the nineteenth century the Brothers became closely associated with NATIONALISM and the revival of the IRISH LANGUAGE. In recent years their reputation has suffered because of a rejection of these values, combined with allegations of child abuse in their industrial schools. By the beginning of the twenty-first century there were 2,000 Brothers working in twenty-five countries throughout the world. **Daire Keogh**

Christianity. The date of arrival of Christianity in Ireland is unknown, but there were Christian communities in Britain in the late second century. The first Irish contacts were probably through traders. We know that by the early fifth century there were Christian communities in Ireland, for in 431 Pope Celestine sent them a bishop, PALLADIUS. These communities were probably composed of captives. There is evidence from the middle of the fifth century that the care of these groups was still a matter of Papal concern. These Christians have left no record, but later traditions about 'pre-Patrician saints' (KEVIN, Declan, Ailbe, CIARÁN) may be a memory of this earliest Christianity.

Irish history begins with PATRICK's writings, but we cannot date his mission. He conveys the notion that he is the first MISSIONARY in a wholly PAGAN environment, and later traditions build on this myth of Patrick as the sole 'apostle of Ireland'. It seems likely that his mission was in the later fifth century, and we must assume that he worked in areas untouched until then by Christianity. He was familiar with the practice of MONASTICISM and must have left some organisation behind him, for his memory and writings were preserved (though against this, and arguing for the limited effect of his mission, there is no other mention of him before the early seventh century). Only in the later sixth century does Christianity become visible to us in records, and then we find a confident, complex organisation whose MONASTERIES (such as that of BANGOR) are important centres, which is theologically creative (for example the Penitentials), and exporting missionaries (such as COLM CILLE and COLUMBANUS). We do not know how widespread Christianity was, nor what its relationship with the larger community was, but our scant evidence points to its having connections with every level of society and to its having integrated some native legal thought within its practices. We have no evidence of a pagan resistance: when, a century later, Muirchú wished to imagine pagan opposition to Patrick his only images for what pagans were like came from the BIBLE.

From the seventh century onwards we have much better evidence, and in contemporary ANNALS we have accurate dates. At this period the monasteries began to grow, to become the great centres of learning and economic life, and we see Christianity emerging as the intellectual form of the society. For while the church took over several native features into its law, its canon law was taken over into secular law and became its pattern as a written corpus. At the same time we see Ireland emerging as one more region within Latin Christendom, with travel in both directions by monks, teachers, and administrators. By the early eighth century there was a vibrant theological community in Ireland, whose works were influencing the rest of the Latin church. The best examples are in the area of law. The SYNOD of Birr (697), where, under ADOMNÁN's influence, there was an attempt to limit the effects of warfare, shows how the church influenced Irish society. At the same period the first systematic canonical collection (the Collectio Canonum Hibernensis) was being compiled in Ireland and was soon copied and imitated abroad; this gave new direction to and affected all subsequent Western canon law. It is against this background that we should view the Irish clerics active in Charlemagne's kingdoms, and later writers such as AUGUSTINE ERIUGENA. [see BREHON LAWS; DIOCESAN SYSTEM; EPISCOPACY; HIBERNO LATIN; HIERARCHY, ECCLESIASTICAL; MISSIONARY ACTIVITY.] **Thomas O'Loughlin**

Christian Otherworld, conceived of in Irish FOLKLORE as Heaven or Paradise (*Párrthas na nGrást*), while Hell (*Ifreann*) was defined as the realm of Satan. Purgatory and Limbo are also widely discussed in the oral tradition: stories of souls 'doing their purgatory' in the most unlikely places abound. These places include between the bark and the wood of a tree, various rocks and promontories around the coast, and places in deserted houses, such as beside the hearth or on chimneystacks. Limbo, *limbus puerorum* (Irish *dorchadas gan phian*—'darkness without pain'), was believed to be the abode of the unbaptised and, according to Catholic teaching before the SECOND VATICAN COUNCIL, a 'place or state of rest' where souls were destined to remain until the Day of Judgment.

The OTHERWORLD features greatly in early Irish literature and MYTHOLOGY, with tales such as the IMMRAMA or voyages, in which the Otherworld is imagined as being on islands in the Western Ocean. There are accounts of cities beneath the sea and legendary Otherworld islands, such as TÍR NA NÓG (the Land of Youth, the Irish Elysium) and Í Bhreasail, a wondrous submerged land. These tales were Christianised by the ninth century. [see FOLKLORE; MYTHOLOGY.] **Anne O'Connor**

Christian Science Church, founded in 1879 by Mary Baker Eddy to reinstate primitive Christianity and its lost art of healing. Churches were established in Dublin and Belfast in the early 1900s. Membership was thought to number about 200 by the end of the twentieth century. **Gabrielle Brocklesby**

Christ the King Church, Cork (1927), by the Chicago architect Barry Byrne (1884–1967), who had been a student of Frank Lloyd Wright and worked on a number of his most important buildings, including Unity Temple, Illinois (1905). In his only

Irish building Byrne produced a pioneering work of European ARCHITECTURE and the most experimental church to be built in Ireland before the 1970s. Christ the King, constructed of concrete with serrated walls, is an Expressionist building of great power and places Byrne in the avant-garde of church design. The oval, column-less open plan anticipates by some thirty-five years the recommendations of the SECOND VATICAN COUNCIL on church design in the uninterrupted relationship between sanctuary and congregation: plan and elevation express a remarkable harmony of approach. A monumental figure of Christ by the American sculptor John Storrs spans the double entrance doors. The interior has an opus-sectile crucifixion by the stained-glass artist HUBERT MCGOLDRICK. The church was dedicated in 1931, but because of the collapse of his practice following the Wall Street Crash of 1929, Byrne never saw the building. **Brian Lalor**

Chronicum Scotorum, a collection of ANNALS belonging to the 'CLONMACNOISE group', covering the period from prehistoric times to 1150 but with some gaps, closely related to the 'Annals of Tigernach'. It survives in a paper copy made by DUBHALTACH MAC FHIRBHISIGH c. 1640 from an exemplar no longer extant. The manuscript later passed into the hands of Roderic O'Flaherty and moved to France for a time in the 1760s, before being bought by Trinity College, Dublin, in 1776. It is the source of some dozen eighteenth and nineteenth-century copies. The text was edited by William M. Hennessy and published in 1866. It contains valuable computistical data that has been obscured or distorted in other annalistic compilations. [see ANNALS.] **Nollaig Ó Muraíle**

chronology of Irish history. The principal resources for dating events in medieval Irish history are the ANNALS, which survive in seven major and five lesser collections and between them provide a continuous, year-by-year cryptic summary of Irish political and ecclesiastical events from c. 313 BC to AD 1590. The custom of keeping an annual summary of events began in IONA in the second half of the sixth century, where an early fifth-century Christian chronicle of Italian origin was interpolated with the reigns of the kings of EMAIN MACHA (Navan Fort, Co. Armagh) and TARA (Co. Meath) and then continued with a summary of Early Christian history and political affairs, predominantly those of the northern UÍ NÉILL. Since this material was retrospective, clearly the chronological and historical status of these PRE-CHRISTIAN and Early Christian entries is uncertain. However, from the later sixth century onwards the majority of the entries are contemporaneous, though some subsequently are interpolated. This compilation, known as the Iona Chronicle, was maintained in Iona until c. 740, when it was brought to Ireland, where it formed the basis for all the early medieval annals.

For modern students of Irish chronology, accustomed to referring to years by their AD dates, a serious obstacle is that until the eleventh century only one of these collections, the annals of Ulster, employs AD notation, and it, up to the middle of the seventh century, exhibits duplication and occasional triplication of records, thereby generating serious chronological ambiguity and uncertainty. Further problems arise from the fact that the modern editors of the various collections have in most instances inserted a marginal AD notation, and for events recorded in more than one collection these editorial AD dates repeatedly disagree with each other and with the Annals of Ulster.

However, in 1998 it was demonstrated that the best witnesses to the chronology of the Iona Chronicle are the Annals of

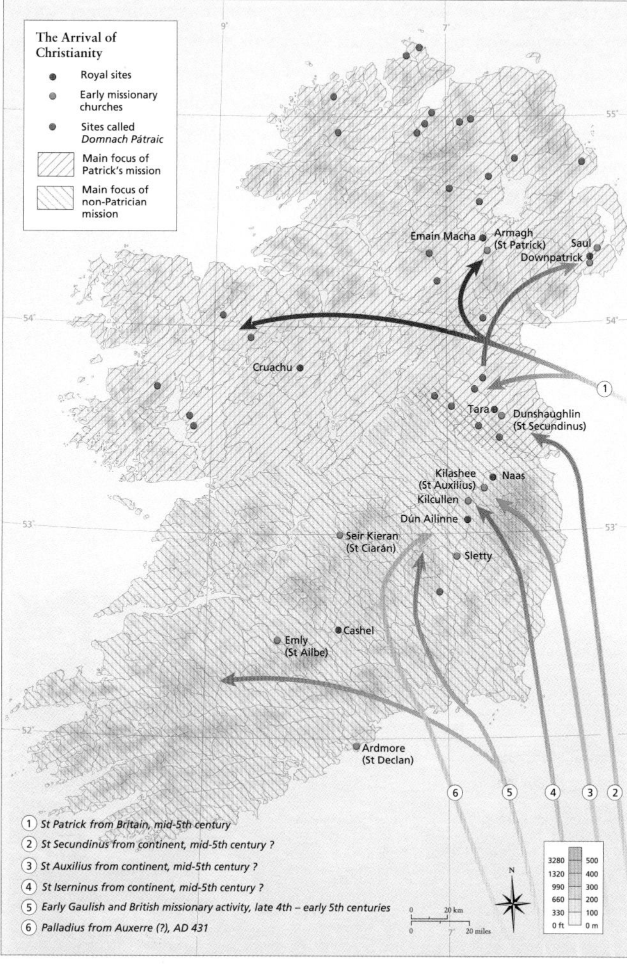

Tigernach and CHRONICUM SCOTORUM, which together provide a reliable chronology for the Iona Chronicle from AD 1 to 660 and resolve the problems of ambiguity inherent in the Annals of Ulster. After this date it has been demonstrated by continuous collation that these three collections preserve essentially the same chronology up to 1178, at which year the Annals of Tigernach conclude. In this way a consistent chronology spanning the years 1–1178 has been compiled, and most of the events recorded in the major and minor annals have been synchronised within these years. The resulting table, indexed by AD years, has been made available on the INTERNET. The absolute accuracy of this chronology to AD 660, when judged by references to prominent persons (such as emperors, popes, or saints for whom we have independent chronological information) or records of astronomical events (such as eclipses, which may be checked by computation) is typically better than ± 2 years; and all astronomical records from AD 773 onwards correspond exactly to the independently supplied date of the phenomena.

After 1178 the Annals of Ulster, collated with the closely related annals of Loch Cé and Annals of Connacht, together provide a satisfactory AD chronology up to 1590. This has a typical error of ± 1 year, because of some conflict between the collections regarding their placing of the year boundaries. It should be noted that the chronology of the annals of the FOUR MASTERS, the annals most widely known, is the result of a seventeenth-century recompilation and is chronologically untrustworthy. **Daniel McCarthy**

Church, Sir Richard (1784–1873), Greek army commander. Born in Cork, son of a QUAKER merchant. He ran away from school and joined the British army, serving as an ensign in Egypt in 1801 under Sir Ralph Abercromby, whose expeditionary force he accompanied to the Ionian Islands in 1809. He espoused the cause of an independent Greece and raised two Greek regiments, financed by London, to fight the Turks. Knighted in 1822, he entered the struggle against the Ottomans in 1827 and was quickly appointed supreme commander of the Hellenic forces. He resigned the post, but acquitted himself bravely in the revolution of 1843. **David Kiely**

churches. *Temple Benen, Killeany, Inishmore, Aran Islands, Co. Galway: a small steep-gabled stone oratory constructed of exceptionally large stones, with flat-topped doorway and east window. [Brian Lalor]*

churches, early. Ireland's earliest churches were built of wood, which remained the principal building material for several centuries. Wooden churches are known to have preceded stone buildings on the Continent and in Britain. None survives in Ireland, but something can be learnt about them from written sources, stone-carving, and archaeological excavation.

Cogitosus's seventh-century Life of BRIGID describes a large, probably wooden, church at Kildare, with dividing screens, painted pictures, and splendid tombs flanking the altar. Laws mention specialist builders of wooden churches, and other sources refer to churches of smooth oak planks and, less often, wattles and clay, roofed with wooden shingles or thatch. There were both large and small churches. The word *dairtheach* ('oak house', meaning wooden church) appears regularly in the ANNALS from 762 to 1000 but less frequently thereafter. Information from excavation is so far disappointing: a few post-hole structures merely and a larger wattle building on Inishcealtra, Co. Clare.

Damhliag ('stone church') appears first as a place-name (Duleek, Co. Meath) in the later seventh century, suggesting an early, exotic example, but a stone church first features in the annals at Armagh in 789. Though recent RADIOCARBON DATING of mortar may support claims that widespread building in stone began c. 800, the evidence still suggests that stone churches remained exceptional in the ninth and tenth centuries and into the eleventh century and were largely confined to important sites, such as KELLS and Dulane (both Co. Meath) in 920. A large church built at CLONMACNOISE in 909 partly survives, with boldly projecting *antae* (side walls extending beyond the gables). The nave at Tuamgraney, Co. Clare, has *antae* and a lintelled west door with a surrounding architrave, datable to before 966, when its builder died. Similar substantial churches survive at GLENDALOUGH, Co. Wicklow, Fore, Co. Westmeath, Lorrha, Co. Tipperary, Tullaherin, Co. Kilkenny, and elsewhere, probably dating from the tenth century. At important sites, such as Armagh and Clonmacnoise, there could be many churches.

Smaller stone churches also survive, with *antae*, with eave corbels, and without either feature. Windows are few and gables steep. Some may be specialist buildings associated with particular saints, such as Temple Diarmuid on Inchcleraun, Co. Longford. Some that now stand isolated were once part of a bigger, largely wooden, complex. The small corbelled churches in the south-west, such as GALLARUS ORATORY, are not in the architectural mainstream and their dating remains unclear, despite much debate. An eleventh-century church has been excavated in Co. Waterford, and by the later eleventh century stone churches were increasingly common, though the *dairtheach* still occasionally appeared.

The twelfth century brought great changes to the Irish church and to Irish churches. The main change in plan was the introduction of a structurally distinct chancel: Reefert at Glendalough is an early example, with a lintelled west door and a semi-circular chancel arch. ROMANESQUE work first occurs in the 1120s in Munster, where church reform was active, at Lismore, Co. Waterford, and Cormac's Chapel, CASHEL (1127–34). This remarkable building stands somewhat isolated, as most Irish Romanesque churches retained a simple one or two-celled plan, largely confining decoration to the west door and chancel arch. This decoration drew on French, English, and Scandinavian sources, but Irish craftsmen interpreted these in a distinctive way, carving in low relief and emphasising surface decoration rather than architectural forms. There are a few datable landmarks, such as the Nuns' Church at Clonmacnoise (1167) and Tuam Cathedral, Co. Galway (after 1184). The magnificent portal at CLONFERT must date from about 1180 (see p. 909) and the elaborate door in Killaloe Cathedral, Co. Clare, from about 1200. The new religious orders, especially the CISTERCIANS, provided a fresh architectural stimulus, and gothic elements were appearing before 1200. [see ROUND TOWERS.] **Ann Hamlin**

Church of Ireland, the reformed, established state church in Ireland until 1871, authorised by the Irish Parliament of 1534–7, under HENRY VIII. The eighteenth century was a period when the constitutional privileges of the established Church of Ireland were further secured by laws against Catholics and Dissenters, though the church, a minority throughout the country, was not immune to feelings of insecurity and well into the following century resisted government moves towards toleration as undermining the Protestant nature of the state. Even 'high church' clergy, deeply conscious of the need to preserve the prerogatives of church as against state, looked to the government to support the church's mission to promote morality and fight infidelity, Popery, and dissent. The changing intellectual climate of late eighteenth and early nineteenth-century Europe made the position of the minority Church of Ireland increasingly untenable, as did British political necessity. The government increasingly sought to appease Catholic opinion by major concessions, particularly in EDUCATION and the TITHE system, and by addressing by legislation the glaring anomalies presented by an established church that was slow to reform its own structures, in which wealth was inequitably distributed, and some of whose evangelising societies were engaged in proselytising activities. State-imposed reform culminated in DISESTABLISHMENT (1871), whereby the Church of Ireland became a totally voluntary body, governed by general synod and stripped of many of its financial assets, though it kept churches and schools and some endowments, and the life interest of clergy and other personnel was guaranteed. [see CHURCH TEMPORALITIES (IRELAND) ACT; DISESTABLISHMENT; REFORMATION; SECOND REFORMATION.] **Kenneth Milne**

church music. Church music in Ireland can be traced back to the early sixth or seventh century, such as *The Antiphonary of Bangor.* There followed, in time, the music of the Gregorian Renaissance, of Anglo-Norman times (twelfth century), and of the fourteenth century, when folk-influence was apparent, as for example in the *Red Book of Ossory*. In the seventeenth century texts were being set to secular songs. The main influence on music of the period 1500–1800 was the PENAL LAWS, which ensured that there was no high culture of sacred music in the Catholic tradition in this period. With reforms in the 1780s, a more elaborate style of music was performed, such as Giordani's *Te Deum*. Many foreign musicians were appointed to positions in Catholic churches, such as Haydn Corri to the Pro-Cathedral, Dublin. Towards the middle of the nineteenth century, under the direction of the Cecilian movement, there was a trend towards a return to music influenced by Gregorian chant. The PALESTRINA CHOIR was formed in 1902 to sing music of that style in the Pro-Cathedral. In the twentieth century the use of hymnals characterised church music, of which *Hosanna* is an example. This has continued to the present day. In recent years, however, a more popular style has emerged, with many masses being commissioned, such as King's *Mass of Christ the King*. Other Masses of note are those by SEOIRSE BODLEY (*Mass of Peace*, 1976, *Mass of Joy*, 1978, and *A Concert Mass*, 1984), SEÁN Ó RIADA (who composed two Mass settings and a requiem), and COLIN MAWBY (*Festival Mass*, 1978, and *Mass of the Holy City*, 1993).

Church music of the Protestant tradition was much more elaborate, being influenced by music performed in England. However, music in Irish cathedrals adhered more closely to the forms set out in the Book of Common Prayer than to others of the Anglican Communion. Much of the music used—anthems and services—was similar to that of British cathedrals, as were the composers, who included Purcell and Boyce. The exception was the use in the Dublin cathedrals of music by Anglo-Irish and Irish composers, such as STEVENSON and Woodward. Music performed in the parish churches was of the same style, only on a much smaller scale. [see SEÁN Ó RIADA MASSES.] **Éamonn O'Keeffe**

church music, eighteenth and nineteenth centuries. The repression of Catholicism during the eighteenth century under the PENAL LAWS resulted in Irish CHURCH MUSIC at this period being exclusively Protestant. Anglican cathedral music flourished particularly at CHRIST CHURCH and ST PATRICK'S CATHEDRALS, Dublin, whose organists and choirmen came largely from England. Prominent Irish cathedral composers of the eighteenth and nineteenth centuries include Ralph ROSEINGRAVE, Richard Woodward, JOHN STEVENSON, and ROBERT STEWART. From the late seventeenth century wealthier CHURCH OF IRELAND parishes, especially in Dublin, installed organs to accompany the congregational singing first of metrical psalms and later of hymns. Catholic church music began to develop in the nineteenth century, often on Italian operatic models, with the appointment of Continental organists being

Church of Ireland. *(Left to right) Dr Walton Empey, Archbishop of Dublin, Dr Robin Eames, Archbishop of Armagh, and Michael Davey at the 2001 General Synod of the Church of Ireland, the main decision-making body of the church, which meets anually. [Maxwells]*

widespread. HEINRICH BEWERUNGE, first professor of music at ST PATRICK'S COLLEGE, Maynooth, from 1886, was prominent in the Cecilian movement, which advocated a return to plain chant and the polyphonic style of Palestrina. The PALESTRINA CHOIR in the Pro-Cathedral, Dublin, was founded in 1902. **Barra Boydell**

church reform, a recurring historical myth within CHRISTIANITY, whereby organisational ideas that conflict with existing practice—which claim their justification as 'tradition'—are legitimised by arguing that an earlier ideal (ultimately the 'apostolic church') has decayed: changes, therefore, are not innovative but a return to that earlier state of purity and rigour. Reformers assume that innovations need an established lineage and so require that existing practices be found doctrinally or devotionally wanting.

The theme first becomes important in Ireland with the CÉILÍ DÉ, a rigorist monastic movement that presented itself as 'restoring' a primitive devotion. 'Reform' was again invoked in the twelfth century to legitimise the new diocesan arrangements, culminating in the Synod of Kells (1152), and also by LAURENCE O'TOOLE to promote his restructuring of clerical life (including CLERICAL CELIBACY). The theme was central to the justification of the ANGLO-NORMANS' intervention in LAUDABILITER and the writings of GIRALDUS CAMBRENSIS (who used it extensively in Wales also).

The theme's most famous use was with the sixteenth-century REFORMATION, which subsequently affected Ireland; the rhetoric of 'reformed' versus 'original' played a part both in denominational disputes and in claims of 'ownership' for the early Irish church until the middle of the twentieth century. Protestants have used the theme to justify various 'revivals'; among Catholics, both OLIVER PLUNKETT and PAUL CULLEN used it to justify their desire for ROMAN uniformity, while more recently it has 'explained' the innovations of the SECOND VATICAN COUNCIL. **Thomas O'Loughlin**

church-state relations. A wide variety of relationships between church and state is possible in the contemporary world, from full establishment, as in Scandinavia, where the church often seems to be an arm of the state, to legal separation, as in France or the United States. In the Republic of Ireland, for historical reasons connected with its role in cultural defence during the period of dominance by a Protestant British state, the Catholic Church has always been a central participant in state affairs. Its 'special position' enshrined in the CONSTITUTION OF IRELAND (1937) was only removed following a referendum in 1972. For decades the Catholic Church exercised a moral monopoly in the Republic; this was particularly apparent in the events surrounding the 'MOTHER AND CHILD SCHEME' in 1951, which led to the resignation of NÖEL BROWNE, Minister for Health. In the last decade of the twentieth century, in the wake of a series of sexual scandals involving clergy, it lost a great deal of its authority and legitimacy in the sight of many people, and it is clear that its influence on the state is very much on the wane. **Michael Hornsby-Smith**

Church Temporalities (Ireland) Act (1833), legislation intended to rationalise the finances of the Established CHURCH OF IRELAND. This rationalisation of finances was to be achieved by, among other measures, reducing the number of archbishops and bishops, taxing the wealthiest sees, and enabling the tenants of episcopal lands to apply to purchase their holdings. The funds thus made available were vested in ecclesiastical commissioners, to be used for church purposes. The act was a major state intervention in the governance of the church. It alarmed the Tractarians in England and paved the way for DISESTABLISHMENT in Ireland. **Kenneth Milne**

Ciarán of Clonmacnoise (c. 512–545). Of the more than thirty reputedly distinct saints named Ciarán, only those attached to CLONMACNOISE and Seirkieran (Saighir Chiaráin), both Co. Offaly, attained prominence. Of these, the Clonmacnoise saint was by far the best known, mainly because of the outstanding role of his church as a centre of cultural and politico-ecclesiastical activity at many levels. Lives, which have yet to be evaluated, were written for him in Latin and Irish. A legendary brown cow associated with him, *odhar Chiaráin*, is commemorated in the name of the earliest surviving vernacular manuscript, the Book of the DUN COW (Lebor na hUidre). His feast-day is 9 September. **Pádraig Ó Riain**

Ciarán of Saighir (c. 500–560). Though less well known in Ireland than his namesake of CLONMACNOISE, Ciarán of Saighir exercised wider influence abroad through his (groundless) assimilation to the cult of Peran of Perranzabuloe in Cornwall, which led to the adaptation of one version of his Life for use as a Life of Peran. Until superseded by Canice of Aghaboe, Ciarán is reputed to have been Ossory's chief saint; his monastery is at Seirkieran, near Birr, Co. Offaly. He is also said, spuriously, to have brought CHRISTIANITY to Ireland before PATRICK. His mother allegedly belonged to the Corca Laoighdhe of the Clonakilty area (Co. Cork), whence his church on Cape Clear (CLÉIRE). His feast-day is 5 March. **Pádraig Ó Riain**

Cillian (died 687/689). Anglicised name of Cillíne. His Irish background is unknown. He worked for a while as a missionary in eastern Franconia and is said to have baptised Duke Goszbert, resident at Würzburg, together with his people. He was murdered together with his companions Kolonat and Totnan in 687 or 689. The bishopric of Würzburg was established by Boniface in 742. Cillian's feast-day is 8 July. [see MISSIONARY ACTIVITY.] **Michael Richter**

Cináed ua hArtacáin (died 974), poet. He composed poems based on Irish history and myth, including 'Fianna bátar i nEmain' on the deaths of certain heroes, a poem on the sling-stone (Mess-Gegra's brain) cast by Cet mac Mágach into the brain of Conchobhar mac Nessa, the King of Ulster, and a number of poems in the metrical DINDSHENCHAS on TARA, BRÚ NA BÓINNE, Benn Étair, and other places. **Séamus Mac Mathúna**

cinema. Irish cinema—as distinct from the more numerous films made by the American and British film industries either about Ireland or about Irish immigrants in their new countries—has had an intermittent history. While the Irish-Canadian SIDNEY OLCOTT made the first fiction film in Ireland, *The Lad from Old Ireland* (1910), an EMIGRATION story, it was not until 1916 that the first film production company, the FILM COMPANY OF IRELAND, began to produce films. During the early decades of the IRISH FREE STATE the Government showed little interest in the cinema, beyond the cultural protectionist measures incorporated in the CENSORSHIP OF FILMS Act (1923). As a result it was left to independent film-makers to fill the breach, but in the 1920s only one film stands out: the WAR OF INDEPENDENCE drama *Irish Destiny* (1926), which follows the fortunes of a young couple, one of whom is an IRA volunteer captured by British forces. In the 1930s films about the War of Independence became increasingly popular, including BRIAN DESMOND HURST's *Ourselves Alone* (1935), JOHN FORD's *The Informer* (1935), and *The Plough and the Stars* (1936), while Tom Cooper's successful indigenous feature film *The Dawn* (1936), made by amateurs in Co. Kerry over a period of two years, featured people who had been active during the war, which gave an added frisson to the production. While *The Dawn* was enthusiastically endorsed by politicians and commentators alike, its low production values could not be disguised, nor could the subject matter be repeated *ad nauseam*. The film was poorly received abroad, a fact that puts into focus Ireland's relatively weak position in the global film economy.

With annual ticket sales of €15.8 million (1998), valued at €40.6 million (1996), the Irish figure of 3.2 admissions per capita is slightly above the average in the EUROPEAN UNION, with the value of video and DVD rental and sales estimated at twice this amount. These figures put into relief the inability of an Irish-produced film to generate a surplus in its own country. While the Irish record for a film with an Irish theme, *Michael Collins* (1996), earned €5 million in Ireland, out of a production budget of about €25 million, other Irish films have had much more modest revenues at home, with few going over €1.25 million and many making less than €25,000. As a result, until recently private investors rarely put money into films, while the state did not commit any significant resources to a cinema industry in the decades after independence.

The early years of the Irish state had seen an attempt to build Irish society behind economic and cultural protectionist barriers. By the 1950s these policies were being abandoned in favour of embracing foreign capital as the means of developing an industrial base. In this situation the cinema was seen as another industry that could generate employment and produce foreign earnings. As a result, state policy became firmly linked to INDUSTRIAL POLICY, with little or no concern with film culture. When this approach culminated in the establishment of ARDMORE STUDIOS in 1958, no provision was made for a policy of Irish employment, let alone a cultural policy, at the studios. The consequence of encouraging foreign investors to make films, and of providing state aid for the studios, was that support for indigenous production was minimal until the early 1980s. By then the struggle had shifted from concern with the direct and indirect subsidising of foreign productions to a debate within the film community between those who favoured a committed indigenous cinema and those who championed a commercial film 'industry'. The outcome of this debate is that all sides are relatively satisfied, at least at the level of subsidy: tax-based investments allow for large private and corporate investments, while the rejuvenated BORD SCANNÁN NA HÉIREANN, and increased sums from RTÉ for independent productions, resulted in a huge expansion in native and foreign productions from 1994 onwards. These changes put into sharp relief the struggle for an Irish cinema during the relatively barren decades from the 1930s to the 1970s, when film-makers were largely confined to servicing information campaigns for Government departments through documentaries and drama-documentaries on public HEALTH, farming, and TOURISM. While these films were part of the impulse that saw a shift from PROTECTIONISM to internationalisation in the 1960s, the film-makers themselves were not to benefit from the changes.

In the post-war period, excluding Ardmore productions, almost no indigenous fiction films were made until the 1970s, when a new generation of film-makers began to look with a critical eye at aspects of Irish culture and society previously unexplored. In this new cinema a more complex notion of the past and contemporary politics was explored by film-makers such as BOB QUINN, JOE COMERFORD, KIERON HICKEY, PAT MURPHY, and THADDEUS O'SULLIVAN, with the previous nationalist and unionist certainties being interrogated for the first time. Similarly, the bedrock of both Catholic and state ideology, the FAMILY, came under scrutiny, with the fragmented or incomplete family becoming a theme. Additionally, questions of repressed SEXUALITY began to be addressed, though even supposedly liberal and modern Irish cinema still finds it difficult to represent independent or liberal women, repeatedly favouring films in which men set out on a quest for money or power. Many of the films of the 1970s and 80s were informed by a realist aesthetic in their rejection of earlier romantic representations of the Irish people and their landscape. Some—such as Quinn's *Poitín* (1978), where greed, drunkenness, and attempted rape occur in a traditional lakeside cottage, and Comerford's *Reefer and the Model* (1988), in which two gay men dance at a CÉILÍ—suggest that a new cinema was challenging the powerful cinematic inheritance produced by foreign film-makers. The 1980s also saw the beginnings of an indigenous commercial cinema, which has since become strongly associated with NEIL JORDAN, JIM SHERIDAN, and PAT O'CONNOR, all of whom have successfully combined working in Ireland with commitments to British and American investors.

The huge expansion in the film industry in the 1990s and later saw the emergence not just of a new generation of film-makers and actors but of new thematic and formal concerns. The cinema of the 1990s was marked by high production values and a move away from the non-linear narratives and the themes of independent film-makers in the late 1970s and 80s and spoke, in the first instance, to the international rather than the national audience. On the other hand, these films—such as *The Commitments* (1991), *Spaghetti Slow* (1997), *This Is My Father* (1998), and *Angela's Ashes* (1999)—often celebrate their Irishness, but it is one that draws on and plays into

cinema. *Richard Harris as Bull McCabe in Jim Sheridan's film* The Field *(1990), based on John B. Keane's play about a tradition-bound man's greed for land. [©Ferndale Films/Irish Film Archive of the Film Institute of Ireland]*

cinema. *The Commitments performing on stage with their lead singer, Deco (Andrew Strong, centre) in Alan Parker's film* The Commitments *(1991) based on Roddy Doyle's novel. [Courtesy of Beacon Communications LLC/Irish Film Archive of the Film Institute of Ireland]*

an outsider's preconceived ideas about the nation and its people or, as in PADDY BREATHNACH's gangster film *I Went Down* (1997), filters the narrative through American comedy and gangster genres. In short, Irish cinema has become less obviously Irish and more self-consciously American or, less often, European (as in Breathnach's *Alisa*, 1994) and universal in appeal, a trend that is not unique to Ireland and can be seen throughout Europe. This shift can be seen in the work of Damien O'Donnell, whose short *35-Aside* (1995) opens up an underdeveloped area of indigenous cinema comedy; notwithstanding its difficult subject of school bullying, it is generally regarded as the funniest short of the decade. However, O'Donnell's feature debut, *East Is East* (1999), a Pakistani comedy set in Manchester, greeted with acclaim and winner of the *Evening Standard* Film of the Year award, bears no relation to Ireland other than at the level of the post-colonial experience. It is this pull of the international film industry that awaits all European film-makers as they try to balance the lure of the global film industry with the local issues with which they are most familiar. Even as experienced a film-maker as Neil Jordan has trouble reconciling his sensitivity to Irish stories—such as *The Butcher Boy* (1997)—with the complexities of the international arena, where unrealised ambitions are more the norm, as in *We're No Angels* (1989).

The rapid expansion of the film industry in the 1990s provided opportunities not only for a new generation of directors but also for producers, actors, writers, and technicians to make their mark. While there are many fine actors, unfortunately, given the nature of commercial film production, this generation, like its predecessors, has not always been offered the chance to play leading roles, even when the director is Irish. Examples include the use of Julia Roberts in MICHAEL COLLINS (1996) and Meryl Streep in *Dancing at Lughnasa* (1998), a film that also featured Bríd Brennan, who had played the title role in Pat Murphy's *Anne Devlin* (1984). The potential of such actors as Angeline Ball, Andrew Connolly, Tony Doyle, Tina Kellegher, Ruth McCabe, DÓNAL MCCANN, Emer McCourt, Seán McGinley, Gerald McSorely, and Ger Ryan has not really been tested in the cinema, with many doing most of their screen work on television. There are a few exceptions: BRENDAN GLEESON, Liam Cunningham, Lorraine Pilkington, Jonathan Rhys-Myers, Peter McDonald, Elaine Cassidy, Flora Montgomery, Cillian Murphy, and Colin Farrell have been able to display their talent on the cinema screen. New directors and producers include Vinny Murphy, Martin Duffy, Damien O'Donnell, Kieron J. Walsh, CONOR MCPHERSON, Ed Guiney, Johnny Gogan, John Carney and Tom Hall, Fintan Connolly, Stephen Bradley, Geraldine Creed, Joe O'Byrne, Frank Stapleton, Kevin Liddy, David Caffrey, and Kristen Sheridan (see pp. 389, 903). [see CINEMA, NORTHERN IRELAND.] **Kevin Rockett**

cinema architecture, art deco and modernist period. After the establishment of the IRISH FREE STATE in 1922 the language of modern ARCHITECTURE was employed in national campaigns, such as public HOSPITALS and the ESB. The increasing popularity of the CINEMA during the 1930s led to a substantial increase in the number of auditoriums constructed, affording architects the opportunity of experimenting with new styles. The Savoy Cinema in O'Connell Street, Dublin (1929), by F. R. Mitchell, its decoration inspired by Scarpagnino's Bridge of Sighs in Venice, was typical of the 'atmospheric' style of early cinema design. The THEATRE ROYAL in Hawkins Street, Dublin (1935), by Leslie Norton, was a glamorous hybrid: its façade was a streamlined art deco style with elegant decoration, while the auditorium adhered to the old-fashioned 'atmospheric' style. Built the same year, the Green Cinema in St Stephen's Green, Dublin, by Jones and Kelly, was radically different: in a pure modernist style throughout, it used opulent materials simply and elegantly. Two slightly later Dublin cinemas, the Carlton, O'Connell Street (1937), by ROBINSON KEEFE DEVANE, and the Adelphi, Middle Abbey Street (1938), by W. R. Glen and Robert Donnelly, displayed mixed adherence to modern principles of cinema design. The Carlton's façade, dominated by tall windows, demonstrated an understanding of the principle of 'night architecture', the style developed to reflect the function of the cinema, whereby the façade, radiant with light, comes to life after nightfall. The Adelphi's façade was more progressive, with an Egyptian flavour to its almost austere modernist style; however, the interior was very traditional.

Some of the finest cinemas in Ireland were designed by JOHN MCBRIDE NEILL. His masterpiece was the Tonic in Bangor, Co. Down (1934). This building, now destroyed, was stunning in conception: a complex massing of different forms yet with an overall visual simplicity redolent of the international style. MICHAEL SCOTT designed a fine modernist cinema, the Ritz in Athlone (1939), now demolished. Like McBride Neill, his design reflected the search for a new style of architecture to represent a building form new to the twentieth century. **Eve McAulay**

cinema, the Irish in international. The cinematic image of the Irish people is irrevocably bound up with their representation in American cinema, illustrated by the fact that more fiction films—at least 500—were produced about the Irish in the United States before 1930 than in the whole history of indigenous Irish cinema. Central to such Irish-American cinema has been the experience of the Irish immigrant. The first fiction film made in Ireland, *The Lad from Old Ireland* (1910), made by the American company Kalem, was an immigration story in which an impoverished labourer (played by the film's director, the Irish-Canadian SIDNEY OLCOTT) goes to New York, where he becomes wealthy, is elected to political office, and returns to Ireland just in time to save his sweetheart from EVICTION. While this established the template for EMIGRATION narratives, most films about the Irish were set in America rather than in Ireland and concerned the difficulties of cultural and social adjustment that emigrants faced in the new country. Though the Irish are often depicted in insular environments, most frequently they live in multi-cultural communities, while their cinematic representation reflected their mediating role between the dominant Anglo-Saxon culture of the establishment and the more recent eastern and southern European immigrants. These films explored inter-cultural and later inter-class relations, with tensions usually resolved through a mixed love affair, leading to marriage. Often these films involved Irish and Jewish relationships, as in *Abie's Irish Rose* (1929), or Irish women marrying into upper-class WASP families, as in *Irene* (1926).

Despite the comic format of many of these films, a serious assimilative message lay beneath the ribaldry: the need for the most dissimilar cultures to work together. The contrast between the two generations of women, the immigrant mother and the first-generation Irish-American daughter, whether within the working or middle classes, is often striking. The mother is represented well into the sound era as the matriarchal linchpin of the Irish FAMILY, while her daughter is often more interested in sexual desire and love than in traditional family security within her own community. The Irish male world of the cinema is populated by policemen, gangsters, sports heroes (especially boxers), and politicians (often corrupt). In validating the WASP view of the Irish, most fighting in the Irish-American cinema did not involve the English (though a number of 'political' films set during the period 1798–1803 were made before the 1916 RISING) but was among the Irish themselves; the 'donnybrook' sequence at the end of JOHN FORD's *The Quiet Man* (1952) remains the classic example. The representation of the Irish as professional fighters (and professionals in other professional sports) was a major element of these films. The professional fighters John L. Sullivan and 'Gentleman Jim' Corbett were both the subject of biographical films, while the returned emigrant Seán Thornton (John Wayne) in *The Quiet Man* is also a boxer, in this instance seeking solace in the Irish rural idyll after killing another boxer in the ring. Fighting was a means whereby a member of the Irish-American working class—a foundry worker in Thornton's case—could improve his lowly social status.

With the rise of the feature film in the late 1910s the racial specificity of American cinema began to dissipate as film producers sought to make a product with cross-cultural appeal. As a result, with the advent of the capital-intensive sound cinema in the early 1930s such stories were in decline, with often only the milieu, accents or characters signalling to the audience the national origin of the characters, as in James Cagney's Irish gangster world in *The Public Enemy* (1931). Also, with the numbers of Irish immigrants falling from the 1920s onwards, American cinema became more concerned with second and third-generation Irish-Americans, or in its reflections backwards, constructing a nostalgic or imagined history of the Irish in America.

In more recent years the basic motifs of diaspora cinema have remained: immigrants played by Tom Cruise and Nicole Kidman find solace and land in America's mid-west in *Far and Away* (1992), while coming in the other direction is an Irish-American teacher searching for his origins in *This Is My Father* (1999).

The two other countries whose cinema occasionally concerned itself with the Irish, Britain and Australia, produced entirely different types of films. While Australia dealt on a number of occasions with the infamous Irish-Australian outlaw NED KELLY, as in the country's first feature film, *The Story of the Kelly Gang* (1906), and in many other films explored the particularities of the Irish-Australian experience, British cinema, by contrast, influenced by historical and ideological amnesia, featured the Irish as having an insatiable appetite for mostly irrational violence. In films as varied as *Captain Boycott* (1947) and *Odd Man Out* (1947), dealing with the LAND WAR and with IRA activity in Northern Ireland during the SECOND WORLD WAR, respectively, what remained absent was any critical reflection on the British presence in Ireland. Another British cinematic and general cultural tradition, found predominantly in comedy and particularly biased from the 1910s onwards, was the depiction of the Irish as pre-modern buffoons who needed to be civilised by the English. Typical of this genre is *Alive and Kicking* (1958), which features three enterprising English women who bring modern manufacturing and marketing techniques to the 'innocents' of the west of Ireland. **Kevin Rockett**

cinema, Northern Ireland. Northern Ireland has been most prominently represented in the cinema in a negative light by film-makers (mainly British) concentrating on political violence, in films such as *Odd Man Out* (1947), *The Gentle Gunman* (1952), *Hennessey*

(1975), *Cal* (1984), and *A Prayer for the Dying* (1988). Independent film-making has developed since the 1970s, though the 1930s were a prolific period, during which a number of 'quota quickie' comedies were produced by Donovan Pedelty and Richard Hayward. During the 1970s and 80s a number of independent production companies were formed, such as those of the documentarist John T. Davis and David Hammond, a prolific independent television producer. Fiction film-makers have included the late Bill Miskelly, whose feature *The End of the World Man* (1985) won first prize at the Children's Festival in Berlin, 1985, while Margo Harkin's *Hush-a-Bye-Baby* (1989) is a story of teenage pregnancy set against the background of British occupation and of conservative moral attitudes towards SEXUALITY. More recently Enda Hughes set about demystifying the solemn representations of politics in the North in his action-packed feature *The Eliminator* (1996), while David Caffrey made an impact with *Divorcing Jack* (1998), a satire of contemporary politics from the novel by Colin Bateman. Institutionally, these developments are supported by the Northern Ireland Film Commission, an agency that receives state funding. **Kevin Rockett**

circus. Circuses in Ireland go back to 1775, when Duffy's Circus was formed, though performing animals were to be seen here from the middle of the seventeenth century, and troupes of acrobats and other entertainers even earlier. Duffy's Circus is still touring, as is Fossett's, established in 1888 by the sword-swallower, juggler, and ventriloquist 'Doc Powell' (Frank Lowe) and originally called Powell and Clarke's Circus. Edward Fossett, a member of an English circus family renowned for its horsemanship, married Lowe's daughter Mona in 1924 and took charge of the circus that later bore his name. It has remained a family business, with winter quarters in Lucan, Co. Dublin. The most famous of Edward Fossett's sons was Bobby (1925–2002), who as Bobo the Clown featured, with his trademark comedy car, in films and on television as well as in the ring.

The traditional travelling circus had its heyday in the nineteenth century, when spectacular British and Continental European circuses included Ireland in their itinerary. Since then the popularity of the circus has steadily declined in the face of competition from spectator sports, television, and Saturday evening Mass. The shortage of suitable sites has also contributed to the decline, as have high fuel costs and value-added tax. Even more telling is an increasing public disquiet over the plight of caged animals, subjected to endless travelling. Circus people vigorously deny cruelty, arguing that unhappy animals will not breed, whereas circus animals of many species do. However, serious damage was done to the standing of the industry in 1999 when the English animal-trainer Mary Chipperfield, a member of a famous circus family, was covertly filmed whipping and kicking a young chimpanzee. The Dublin Society for the Prevention of Cruelty to Animals responded with a nationwide campaign urging a boycott of circuses.

Small circuses using no animals have made their appearance, as have training courses in circus skills conceived of as an art form or as exercise. **John Wakeman**

cist burial. Cists are stone-lined graves, characteristic of the earlier BRONZE AGE, usually constructed in underground pits or, alternatively, covered by earthen mounds or stone cairns. The most common examples are rectangular and sub-rectangular, but few are strictly geometrical rectangles. Polygonal cists are generally circular or sub-circular and just large enough to contain an urn and a quantity of cremated bone. Rectangular cists were the most common type, polygonal examples less common. Most rectangular cists were constructed of four stone slabs, but the number ranges from two to eleven. Some were built with a combination of slabs and dry-stone walling, a few with dry-stone walls only. Many cists are paved; most were covered with a single capstone, but some had from two to three capstones. The cists range in length from 50 to 243 cm ($1\frac{1}{2}$–8 ft) and in width from 20 to 69 cm (8 in.–$2\frac{1}{4}$ ft). Most consisted of a single compartment, but a few had up to three. Polygonal cists were usually constructed of between five and nine smaller slabs.

The construction of a rectangular cist would have been a sizeable undertaking for a family group. The stones, and especially the capstones, can be of considerable size and if not locally available would have had to be transported to the desired site. The quarrying of the pit and the construction of the cist would have required the labour of a number of people. The work would have been greater where the cist was covered by a contemporary barrow or cairn. Polygonal cists are smaller in scale and required a significantly smaller investment of labour. [see BRONZE AGE BURIAL.] **Charles Mount**

Cistercians. The Cistercian order, a reform of Benedictine MONASTICISM that emerged at Citeaux in Burgundy in 1098, was introduced into Ireland as part of the twelfth-century reform of the Irish church promoted by ST MALACHY of Armagh. It experienced rapid and widespread expansion after the establishment of the first house at MELLIFONT in Co. Louth, 1142; by 1228 there were approximately thirty-four houses of either Irish or ANGLO-NORMAN foundation, and the order had reached the peak of its expansion. Though influential in promoting CHURCH REFORM, the order's own expansion rested on an insecure foundation, as there was no significant tradition of Benedictine monasticism in Ireland on which to draw. The Irish houses soon became isolated from the disciplinary structures of the order, and Irish abbots were often chastised for not attending the annual general chapter at Citeaux. Lax monastic observance and rivalry between Irish and Anglo-Norman foundations reached a crisis in the early thirteenth century, culminating in the 'Conspiracy of Mellifont', 1216–28, as a result of which Abbot Stephen of Lexington assigned Mellifont's daughter-houses to English, Welsh, and French houses for reformation. The Mellifont affiliation was restored in 1274.

The emergence of the mendicant orders and the disappearance of the lay brother in the thirteenth and fourteenth centuries deprived the Cistercians of much of their recruitment base and labour force. The BLACK DEATH (1348–9), endemic WARFARE in Ireland, unsuccessful speculation on the wool market and lay encroachments on monastic resources also contributed to the decline. By the late fifteenth century, despite attempts at reform by Abbot John Troy of Mellifont, regular monastic life had collapsed in many houses, with only Mellifont and St Mary's, Dublin, having a substantial community. A number of monasteries were changed into secular colleges at the REFORMATION, but most were dissolved between 1538 and 1540. [see RELIGIOUS ORDERS.] **Colmán N. Ó Clabaigh**

civil rights movement. The civil rights movement in Northern Ireland was inspired by the black civil rights campaigns in the United States. Unlike previous nationalist protests against the STORMONT regime, the campaign concentrated on the unfair treatment of Catholics as citizens, rather than on PARTITION. The movement got under way in DUNGANNON on 28 August 1963 when Catholic families, mobilised by the Homeless Citizens' League (formed earlier in the year by Patricia McCluskey and Dr Conn McCluskey) occupied prefabricated bungalows due for demolition.

Soon afterwards several organisations emerged to become part of the movement: the Campaign for SOCIAL JUSTICE in Northern Ireland (1964), the Campaign for Democracy in Ulster (launched in the House of Commons on 3 June 1965), the Derry Unemployed Action Committee (1965), the Northern Ireland Civil Rights Association (January 1967), and the Derry Housing Action Committee (September 1967). The main demands were the fair allocation of council houses and of jobs, universal suffrage in LOCAL GOVERNMENT elections, and the repeal of the Special Powers Act. Some 2,500 joined the first civil rights march, from COALISLAND TO DUNGANNON, on 24 August 1968. The situation was transformed by the assault by police on peaceful marchers at the banned civil rights march in Derry on 5 October. Three days later the PEOPLE'S DEMOCRACY at Queen's University and the Civil Rights Association organised a series of large marches, notably in Armagh and Derry. TERENCE O'NEILL conceded most of the movement's demands, and marches were called off in December 1968. The People's Democracy went ahead with its march on 1 January 1969, and there was another upsurge of protest after the loyalist attack on marchers at BURNTOLLET. Thereafter the movement broke up into a series of organisations with a wide range of aims and methods. [see CALEDON.] **Jonathan Bardon**

civil service. The structures and practices of the Republic's civil service have evolved considerably since independence, but its underlying ethos remains essentially unchanged. Independent Ireland's central bureaucracy was a deliberate replication of the British apolitical and meritocratic 'Whitehall' model. This was highly successful in preventing jobbery, ensuring probity, and securing impartiality of policy advice and of administration, but it was not always conducive to the generation of new ideas and solutions to Ireland's problems of economic and social underdevelopment or to the effective management of public services.

Since the 1960s there have been a number of initiatives intended to modernise the civil service, to cope with both domestic change and the challenge presented by European integration. Among the most important was that in 1984, when civil service numbers were halved overnight after the POSTAL and TELECOMMUNICATIONS SERVICES were hived off to state companies. In the same year a system of open competition for the most senior positions was introduced, facilitating the introduction of new blood into departments throughout the civil service. In recent years there has been some progress in reducing inequality between women and men. The Public Service Management Act (1997) and changes in the budgeting process have facilitated a greater emphasis on effective management, but ministers still retain control of and are answerable for policy. **Eunan O'Halpin**

Civil War (1922–3), a conflict stemming from deep divisions between pragmatists and republican irreconcilables over the ANGLO-IRISH TREATY of December 1921. The following six months saw unsuccessful efforts to reach compromise with an agreed election and REPUBLICAN constitution. Meanwhile about 80 per cent of the

civil rights. *Supporters of the civil rights campaign at the Diamond, inside Derry's city walls, on 16 November 1968. The First World War cenotaph to Irish casualties of the war is on the left. [Kelvin Boyes Photography]*

Civil War. *The events of the Civil War provide the subject for Jack B. Yeats's painting* Communicating with Prisoners, Dublin *(1924), depicting the crowds who gathered to exchange news with anti-Treaty prisoners in Kilmainham Gaol, Dublin, in 1923. [Model Art and Niland Gallery, Sligo; photo: John Searle]*

IRA declared their independence of political control and took over many evacuated barracks. Following the pro-Treaty election victory of June 1922 and the assassination by the IRA of Sir Henry Wilson in London, the British government demanded an end to the republican occupation of buildings in Dublin. Reluctantly, MICHAEL COLLINS ordered the night attack of 27/28 June on the FOUR COURTS, Dublin. The Public Record Office that housed an irreplaceable archive of state papers was destroyed during the burning of the Four Courts. The republicans evacuated. Whatever advantages the republicans had over the hastily recruited pro-Treaty army were nullified by confused military strategy. By the middle of August the forces of the PROVISIONAL GOVERNMENT controlled all centres of population. The IRA's guerrilla warfare thereafter proved only sporadically effective. The political assassinations of KEVIN O'HIGGINS and others provoked harsh measures, notably the shooting of more than seventy-seven republican prisoners by the government. By the time of the republican ceasefire, 24 May 1923, the conflict had almost petered out. The war made possible the establishment of stable civilian government but left, in addition to the fatalities and economic dislocation, a residue of bitterness that, ironically, reinforced PARTITION. **Michael A. Hopkinson**

clachans, a term originating in Scotland and now used to describe the small clusters of rural cottages that reached their maximum distribution in pre-FAMINE Ireland, found particularly in western counties and in agriculturally marginal upland areas generally. Mostly irregular in plan, they displayed complex variations in the design and layout of their buildings, which have been attributed to differences in regional styles of VERNACULAR ARCHITECTURE and to the topographical constraints imposed by individual sites. In contrast, a minority of clachans, for example Rushtown, Co. Galway, displayed regular linear plans; these may represent attempts by early nineteenth-century LANDLORDS to impose some form of planning. Functionally simple and typically lacking all services, in the early nineteenth century most clachans were associated with partnership or RUNDALE farming. Here they are held to have been the homesteads of extended families or kin groups, who undertook the joint tenancy of farms and worked them collectively on an infield-outfield basis, frequently under the direction of a 'headman'.

The origins of pre-famine clachans are obscure. Though there have been suggestions that they represent the continuity of a settlement tradition of medieval or earlier origin, there is no real evidence for this. Nineteenth-century clachans are as likely to have been simply a function of the regionally varied growth in pre-famine population and the consequent growth in demand for LAND, itself facilitated by the willingness of landlords to encourage the agricultural colonisation of marginal land; the rapid disappearance of clachans with the post-famine population collapse suggests that this was so. [see BOOLEYING.] **Lindsay Proudfoot**

Claddagh Records, a TRADITIONAL MUSIC label established in 1959 by Garech Browne and Ivor Browne. The poet and writer

JOHN MONTAGUE has also had a long association with the company. Paddy Moloney, a founder-member of the CHIEFTAINS, worked as label manager from the mid-1960s until the early 70s, helping oversee a pioneering series of traditional music recordings that included Denis Murphy and JULIA CLIFFORD, MÁIRE ÁINE NÍ DHONNCHADHA, SEÁN Ó RIADA, TOMMY POTTS, and the Chieftains. High design standards and reliable music quality typify a Claddagh release. The label has also issued an important series of spoken-word recordings that includes PATRICK KAVANAGH, AUSTIN CLARKE, DEREK MAHON, SEAMUS HEANEY, and John Montague. **Tom Sherlock**

Claddagh ring, traditionally associated with the Galway area and the ARAN ISLANDS, though they were also made elsewhere in the country from the early eighteenth century. Originally worn by men, and later by both sexes as a MARRIAGE token, the ring consists of a plain band with a hammered or cast bezel of two hands holding a crowned heart. The hands represent both parties, the heart the seat of affection, and the crown perfection. The name derives from the now vanished fishing village at the mouth of the River Corrib. Claddagh rings are still widely worn by men and women in the west of Ireland. **Brian Lalor**

Claidheamh Soluis, An (1899–1932), weekly bilingual newspaper published by Conradh na Gaeilge, the Gaelic League, originally edited by PATRICK PEARSE, to promote the language revival. It was widely read and made a significant contribution to emerging NATIONALISM and laid the basis of modern literature and JOURNALISM in Irish. **Caoilfhionn Nic Pháidín**

Clancy, Willie (1918–1973), uilleann-piper. Born in Milltown Malbay, Co. Clare. His mother played CONCERTINA, his father played concertina and FLUTE; both were singers. Willie also played flute, sang, and step-danced, taking up the pipes in his late teens after hearing JOHNNY DORAN play; he was also influenced by the legacy of the local piper Garret Barry, and he went on to win the OIREACHTAS award of 1947. A cheerful but serious musician, his settings are notated in Pat Mitchell's book *The Dance Music of Willie Clancy* (1993) and recorded on *The Minstrel from Clare* and *The Pipering of Willie Clancy.* His charisma as a mentor and teacher prompted the setting up of a summer school in his memory, SCOIL SAMHRAIDH WILLIE CLANCY at Milltown Malbay, in the year of his death. **Fintan Vallely**

Clancy Brothers and Tommy Makem, the, a seminal ballad group that originally comprised the brothers Tom, Pat, and Liam Clancy of Carrick-on-Suir, Co. Waterford, and Tommy Makem of Keady, Co. Armagh. All singers, Liam played the guitar, Pat the HARMONICA, and Makem the TIN WHISTLE and BANJO. They came together in the United States in 1959 after recording an album and adopted their hallmark white Aran sweaters for an appearance on the 'Ed Sullivan Show' on American television. This brought them instant fame in America for their unselfconscious, unsentimental, and unapologetic ballad delivery and repertoire. The largely unison style created a huge and eager audience in Ireland also, ultimately drawing many people into the playing of TRADITIONAL MUSIC. Liam Clancy went solo in 1969, but the Clancys continued sporadically as a family group until the death of Pat in 1998. **Fintan Vallely**

Clandillon, Séamus (1878–1944), teacher, singer, collector, and arranger of Irish songs. Born in Lough Cutra, Gort, Co. Galway; educated at UCD. He was the first director of 2RN, precursor of Radio Éireann; he engaged traditional musicians and early CÉILÍ BANDS to play live on radio, thus promoting TRADITIONAL MUSIC, a policy continued by Radio Éireann. With his wife, Margaret Hannagan, he sang frequently on 2RN to his own piano accompaniment; together they published *An Londubh* (1904) and *Londubh an Chairn: Songs of the Irish Gaels* (1927). He made eleven records of songs in Irish and English. [see BROADCASTING.] **Liam Mac Con Iomaire**

Clannad. *Máire, Pól, and Ciarán Ó Braonáin and their uncles Pádraig and Noel Duggan, the original members of the traditional music group Clannad, in Gweedore, Co. Donegal, 1970. [Bill Doyle]*

Clannad, a music group formed in 1970 in Gweedore, Co. Donegal, by three members of the Ó Braonáin family: Máire, Pól, and Ciarán, joined by their uncles Pádraig and Noel Duggan. Eithne Ní Bhraonáin joined in 1979 but left in 1982 to enjoy solo success as ENYA. Chart successes include *Harry's Game*, which won an Ivor Novello Award in 1982. Their soundtrack for *Robin of Sherwood* received a British Academy Award in 1984. **Pat Ahern**

Clan na Gael, nationalist organisation. Founded in New York in June 1867, the 'United Brotherhood' tried to end the factionalism of American Fenianism, which had fragmented in 1865 over the question of military tactics. In its early years the Clan's leading lights were Dr William Carroll (of Ulster Presbyterian stock) and JOHN DEVOY. The organisation was a rallying point for thousands of working-class Irish-Americans. Its most successful propaganda coup was the rescue of six FENIAN prisoners (Robert Cranston, Thomas Darragh, Michael Harrington, Thomas Hasset, Martin Hogan, James Wilson) from Fremantle, Western Australia, in 1876 on the Whaling vessel *Catalpa.* Attempts at negotiations with the Russian ambassador to Washington in the same year came to nothing. The Clan did, however, manage to gain control of the 'Skirmishing Fund', set up by JEREMIAH O'DONOVAN ROSSA for purposes of subversive acts against the BRITISH EMPIRE. Having split in the 1880s over the issue of support for the 'NEW DEPARTURE', the group re-emerged in the early twentieth century and in 1914 helped to equip the IRISH VOLUNTEERS with German armaments. **Oliver P. Rafferty**

Clann na Poblachta ('Party of the Republic'), founded in 1946 by Seán McBride, a former chief of staff of the IRA, with Neil Hartnett, Jack McQuillan, and Michael Kelly. It won ten seats in the 1948 General Election and was part of the first inter-party government, 1948–51, with FINE GAEL, CLANN NA TALMHAN, and the LABOUR PARTY. The party, with a platform of social reform, the most controversial of which proved to be the MOTHER AND CHILD Bill, was a vigorous opponent of FIANNA FÁIL at its inception but after early success it faded as a political force. The failure of McBride to support Nöel Browne's Mother and Child Scheme seriously damaged the party. The party was dissolved in 1965 by which time it had only one seat in DÁIL ÉIREANN. **Neil Collins**

Clann na Talmhan ('Party of the Land'). A farmers' party founded in 1938; it participated in the inter-party Governments of 1948–51 and 1954–7. Its main support was in the west of Ireland. After an initial electoral success, winning thirteen DÁIL seats in 1943, it faded steadily. Its last TD retired in 1965. **Neil Collins**

Clara Bog, the largest intact raised BOG in Ireland, covering 665 ha (1,600 acres) south of Clara, Co. Offaly, now a national nature reserve. Silt and clay beneath the bog record its development on the site of a lake formed during deglaciation. At the start of the present interglacial period, when plants and algae began to flourish, calcium carbonate precipitated out of the water to form a new lake floor of marl. The marl was quickly succeeded by fen peat, which accumulated between 10,000 and 6,300 years ago, with a phase of sphagnum peat growth between 8,400 and 8,000 years ago. From 6,300 to 2,000 years ago well-humified sphagnum peat expanded beyond the original lake margins in relatively warm, dry conditions; buried pine stumps testify to the extension of the bog over mineral soils.

Over the last 2,000 years, peat humification has diminished, reflecting cooler, wetter conditions. In modern times the cutting of turf and drainage have significantly lowered water levels in the bog, though remedial measures have been taken to stabilise the soak system, as elements of it are of great interest. Shanley's Lough, developed in a depression on the western side of the bog late in the nineteenth century, supports a birch woodland, unusual for growing in undrained, nutrient-deficient peat. Also, the sediments of Lough Roe and Lough Beag, which formerly existed in the sphagnum peat on the eastern side of the bog, provide a 4,000-year record of lake environments within the bog. [see ALLEN, BOG OF; BOG BODIES.] **Colman Gallagher**

Clare, County (*Contae an Chláir*)

Province:	MUNSTER
County town:	ENNIS
Area:	3,188 km^2 (1,231 sq. miles)
Population (2002):	103,333
Features:	BURREN
	CLIFFS OF MOHER
	LOUGH DERG
	River SHANNON
	Slieve Bernagh
Of historical interest:	BUNRATTY CASTLE
	Dysert O'Dea
	Ennis Friary
Industry and products:	Forestry
	Salmon fishery
	TOURISM

Petula Martyn

County Clare, bordered by the Atlantic Ocean to the west, the River Shannon to the south and east, and Galway Bay to the north. The county's maritime tradition derives from its expansive coastline.

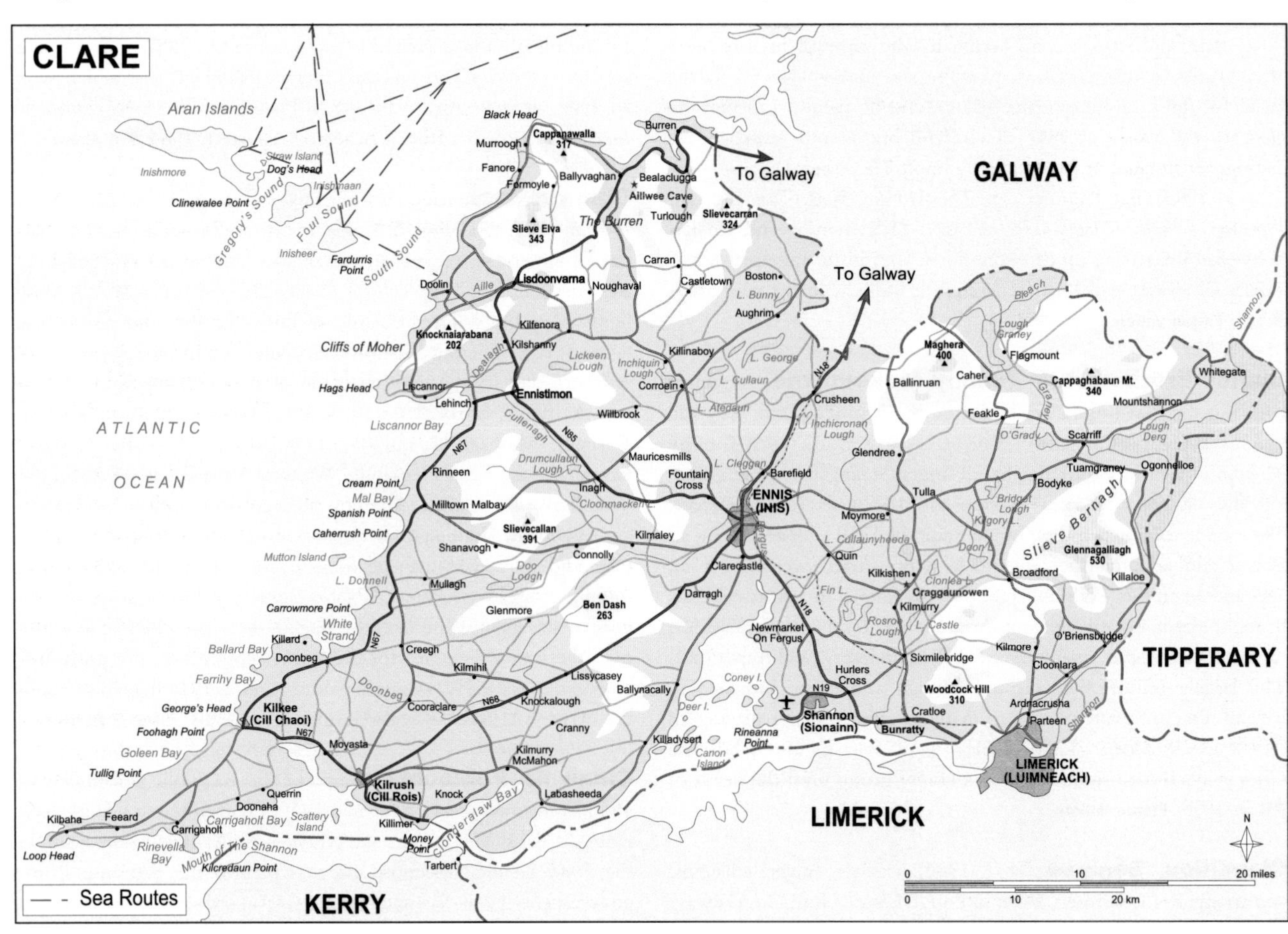

Clare Island. *Posed in front of Grace O'Malley's castle on Clare Island, Co. Mayo, are participants in the ninth party of the Clare Island Survey, June 1910: (back, left to right) N. H. Foster [insert], R. L. Praeger, Carl Lingner, A. D. Cotton, W. J. Lyons, R. J. Welch; (front, left to right) Thomas Greer, W. F. de V. Kane, R. J. Ussher, P. Kuckuck, H. Wallis Kow. [Royal Irish Academy]*

The landscape is marked by a drumlin belt in the east of the county, while the Burren region in the north-west contains a unique karst and limestone landscape. The CLIFFS OF MOHER have an enduring appeal for tourists, and tourism is one of the most important industries in the county. Other important tourist destinations include Bunratty Castle and the coastal resorts of Lahinch, Kilrush, and Kilkee. Cruising on the Shannon and ANGLING on LOUGH DERG are important activity-based tourist industries. Planning has become a controversial issue in the county, given the scale and intensity of development in coastal regions. The new town of Shannon was built in 1959 to house workers for the industries that developed at SHANNON AIRPORT, the first duty-free airport in the world. Ennis has expanded rapidly in recent years and in 1997 became Ireland's first 'Information Age town', with an investment of £15 million by Telecom Éireann in new technology. **Raymond O'Connor and John Crowley**

Clare embroidery, a style of needlework devised by Mrs Vere O'Brien in Ennis, Co. Clare, during the 1890s, inspired by the flowers and foliage of the surrounding countryside. Satin stitch and stem stitch in coloured threads on white linen and cotton characterised this embroidery, which was worked on children's clothing, aprons, and cushions. [see EMBROIDERY.] **Alex Ward**

Clare Island Surveys (1909–11; 1989–2000). Clare Island, Co. Mayo, was the site of a multidisciplinary scientific survey sponsored by the ROYAL IRISH ACADEMY, 1909–11, the first such systematic large-scale study carried out anywhere in the world. Clare Island was chosen as an example of the European periphery and also as an island, there being then much scientific interest in islands, following the work of Charles Darwin and Alfred Russel Wallace. The survey was led by ROBERT LLOYD PRAEGER, and more than a hundred researchers visited, in groups of between six and sixteen, most from Ireland but others from England, Scotland, Germany, Denmark, and Switzerland. (For decades thereafter, the islanders called large groups of visitors 'praegers'.) The survey concentrated on FLORA and FAUNA but also considered archaeology, history, and place-names. Sixty-seven reports were published in the *Proceedings of the Royal Irish Academy*, 1911–15. The survey was successful in its systematic cataloguing of the species of a small, bounded area; however, Clare Island proved not to be of particular interest in evolutionary BIOLOGY, as the island had become separated from the mainland relatively recently, and most of its flora and fauna are similar to mainland species.

From 1989 to 2000 the RIA, supported by the National HERITAGE COUNCIL, conducted the New Survey of Clare Island, which measured environmental changes since the first survey and brought modern methods of investigation to bear on the island's natural history. The new survey studied GEOLOGY, BOTANY, SOILS, marine BIOLOGY, zoology, ARCHAEOLOGY, FOLKLORE, and PLACE-NAMES. **Stephen A. Royle**

Clarke, Adam (1762–1832), Methodist scholar, preacher, and theologian. Born in Co. Derry. Having undergone a religious conversion in 1779, he became an itinerant Methodist preacher in 1782. An effective and inspiring preacher, he travelled throughout Ireland, Britain, and the Channel Islands. He established six Mission Day schools in Ulster in 1831. His reputation, however, is as a scholar. Among other academic honours he was elected a member of the ROYAL IRISH ACADEMY, and he was an accomplished linguist, proficient in about twenty languages. His major work was a multi-volume Bible Commentary, renowned for both its scholarship and its accessibility. In theology, his inability to believe in the eternal sonship of Christ was unorthodox. **Myrtle Hill**

Clarke, Austin (1896–1974), poet. Born in Dublin; educated at UCD. His flawed early epic poetry earned him comparison with YEATS. After a period as assistant lecturer in UCD and a brief marriage to the eccentric writer Lia Cummins he settled into literary JOURNALISM in London and, from 1937, in Dublin. The strong folk flavour and frank sensuality of *The Cattledrive in Connaught* (1925) gave way to the ascetic *Pilgrimage* (1929), set in the late Middle Ages, also the scene of his prose romances. With this and his experiments with Irish prosody he established a literary domain distinct from Yeats's. *Night and Morning* (1938) tortuously documents his scrupulous individualism and loss of faith. His career as a verse dramatist, begun with *The Son of Learning* (1927), blossomed in the 1940s, aided by the Dublin Verse-Speaking Society, which he and ROIBEARD Ó FARACHÁIN jointly founded; from this evolved the Lyric Theatre, which staged verse plays until 1951. The acerbity and hyperbole of his journalism is also evident in the poetry of *Ancient Lights* (1955) and after, its Swiftian indignation igniting his local complaints. In old age he returned to the long narrative poem, treating sexual topics light-heartedly, the exuberant amplitude of diction testifying to hard-won near-serenity. His intricate prosodic procedures testify to the anguished complexity of his subject matter and his protracted loyalty to literary revivalism. His twenty-one plays and his theatre's challenge to naturalism constitute a significant achievement, as does his early recognition of the potential of radio. **Mary Thompson**

Clarke, Henry (Harry) (1889–1931), STAINED-GLASS artist, graphic designer, and book illustrator. Born and educated in Dublin; brought up in his father's decorating and stained-glass firm. His exceptional skill and imagination, soon recognised at the Metropolitan School of Art, led to early commissions in stained

Clarke, Harry. *Detail from* The Eve of St Agnes *(1924), a stained-glass window in eight sections. Based on John Keats's poem of the same name, this detail illustrates the lines 'Awake, arise, my love and fearless be, | For o'er the southern moors I have a home for thee.' [Hugh Lane Municipal Gallery of Modern Art]*

glass, graphic design, and book illustration, to a seminal travelling scholarship in France and England, and to his first and greatest full-scale work, eleven windows for the Hiberno-Romanesque Revival HONAN CHAPEL (1915–17). His reputation thus established for windows full of medievalised detail and resonant of Ireland's spiritual past, he embarked on a series of unique miniature stained-glass panels for private collectors, using an inimitable virtuoso technique to illustrate scenes from literature (such as Flaubert's *S. Julien*, 1919). These are analogous to his published book illustrations, the most famous being those to Edgar Allan Poe's *Tales of Mystery and Imagination* (1919 and 1923) and Goethe's *Faust* (1925). A prolific and influential exhibitor with the ARTS AND CRAFTS SOCIETY OF IRELAND between 1910 and 1925, his work was admired nationally and internationally, helping to establish Ireland's enviable artistic reputation during the golden years of the Celtic Revival. The studios he took over on his father's death in 1921 perpetuated his name until their closure in 1973. **Nicola Gordon Bowe**

Clarke, Thomas James (1857–1916), revolutionary. Born on the Isle of Wight, England, of Irish parents. The family settled in Dungannon, Co. Tyrone, having spent time in South Africa. Clarke travelled to America at twenty-one, where he joined CLANN NA GAEL. He was arrested during a FENIAN bombing campaign in England and spent fifteen years in penal servitude. He returned to Ireland and was made a freeman of the city of Limerick. After another period in America he returned to reorganise the IRB and in 1910 published the journal *Irish Freedom*, with SEÁN MAC DIARMADA as manager. The following year he organised the first commemorative gathering at WOLFE TONE's grave in Bodenstown, Co. Kildare. In 1915 he joined the Military Council of the IRB, which planned the 1916 RISING. He was in the GPO during the rising and was the first to sign the PROCLAMATION OF THE IRISH REPUBLIC. He was shot by firing squad on 3 May 1916. **Martin Clancy**

class: see SOCIAL CLASS; UNDERCLASS.

classical Irish poetry, the formal verse of the FILÍ (professional poets) in Ireland and Scotland in the period of classical EARLY MODERN IRISH (1200–1650), also referred to as *filíocht na scol* or *bardic poetry*. The advent of the style, characterised by the use of a standardised idiom and metre, coincides with the reform of ecclesiastical government and the reordering of monastic life in twelfth-century Ireland. The revival of spiritual piety that followed the establishment of foundations by the reform-minded CISTERCIAN order led to the decline of the older monastic centres of learning, leaving the way open for the development of secular schools of poetry, history, and law, under the auspices of mainly old-established learned families. Many of these traditionally resided on monastic lands and held hereditary office as guardians of church property. POETIC FAMILIES, by far the most numerous among the learned groups, concerted to standardise the literary language at this time, basing the new norm on a comprehensive codification of twelfth-century speech forms, and also accommodating a copious stratum from the literary usage of MIDDLE IRISH (c. 850–c. 1200). The metrical system adopted, known as *dán díreach* (strict poetry), represents an adaptation of the syllabic system of Old and Middle Irish prosody to suit a twelfth-century phonology but with the application of stricter rules for ornamentation and a reduced repertoire of individual metres. A looser metrical form, known as *óglachas*, in which strict rules for ornamentation are waived, is seen as a formal continuation of the Middle Irish prosodic tradition and is common both in informal compositions of the classical period and in the compositions of some *seanchaidhe* (chroniclers).

The cultivation of classical poetry depended on the continuity of schools of learning conducted by the hereditary families. Branches of the more celebrated of these conducted such schools over several generations, often accommodating each of the three disciplines of poetry, history, and law. Among the most enduring are the poetic families of Uí Dhálaigh (O'Daly), with branches in Ulster, Leinster, and Munster, Clann Chon Midhe (Macnamee) and Clann an Bhaird (Ward) in Ulster, Uí Uiginn (O'Higgins) in Connacht, Uí Chobhthaigh (O'Coffey) in Leinster, Clann Chraith (McGrath) in Munster, and Clann Mhuireadhaigh (MacVurich) in Scotland; the chronicler families of Clann Uí Mhaoil Chonaire (O'Mulconry) in Connacht and Clann Bhruaideadha (Mac Brody) and Uí Dhuinnín (Dinneen) in Munster; and the several branches of the legal family Clann Aodhagáin (MacEgan) in Munster, Connacht, and Leinster. Schools were commonly directed by a single outstanding OLLAMH (master-poet), who often also maintained a house of general hospitality or guest-house. Students attended in the period November–May, being billeted on local farming households. The duration of training, while fixed in theory at seven years, with students achieving a grade at the end of each (the so-called *seacht ngrádha fileadh* or 'seven grades'), was variable in practice, just as the emphasis of the curriculum may have depended on the interests and discipline of the master. The content of the curriculum comprised a basic repertoire of STORYTELLING and GENEALOGY, language, style, metre, and possibly also figures of thought and speech. A particularly emphatic focus on the language and metre of *dán díreach* was applied in the case of the trainee poets and may have included some tuition in the arcane idiom known as *béarla na bhfileadh*.

Rich data concerning the linguistic and metrical sides of the curriculum is available not only in the poetry but also in the extant classical Irish grammatical and metrical tracts, of which the most important deal with issues of syntax, declension of the noun, forms of the irregular verbs, abstract nouns, and metrical faults. Our principal source concerning the extra-linguistic training of the poet is the content of the verse itself. Methods of teaching and composition are only occasionally adverted to, but the practice of composing while reclining in a dark cell is well documented. References to performance are likewise rare, but the delivery of poems may have been in the form of recitative and is known to have been accompanied by HARP music.

The subject matter of classical poetry is governed by the fact that poets were dependent for their livelihood on the patronage of local rulers. Accordingly their compositions are mainly encomiastic in content, and the bulk of the surviving verse from the twelfth to the sixteenth century comprises eulogies and elegies. But while the range of subject matter is narrow, and the metrical and linguistic techniques seem uniform and stereotyped, there is a high degree of variation in artistic skills, which is measurable in such aspects as stylistic elegance, the organisation of subject matter, the deployment of motifs, and the command of figurative language.

Every century produced one or two outstanding practitioners whose compositions were held in special esteem, including MUIREADHACH ALBANACH Ó DÁLAIGH and DONNCHADH MÓR Ó DÁLAIGH (thirteenth century), GOFRAIDH FIONN Ó DÁLAIGH (fourteenth century), Tadhg Óg Ó hUiginn (fifteenth century), and TADHG DALL Ó HUIGINN, EOCHAIDH Ó HEÓDHUSA, and FEARGHAL ÓG MAC AN BHAIRD (sixteenth and seventeenth centuries). In addition to secular panegyric a substantial body of classical religious poetry has survived also, much of it composed by professional authors for payment at the behest of ecclesiastical patrons. Personal poetry, including the poetry of love, tends to survive from the later centuries only. Rewards for compositions were determined in the first instance by the resources of the patron, but poets customarily demanded and obtained substantial payment and lived well. Gifts of cattle, horses, clothing, and plate were the commonest forms of such payment. Thus, to mention one example, a highly reputed Leinster poet of the sixteenth century, Tadhg Mór Ó Cobhthaigh, is known to have been awarded a brood mare for each of the quatrains of a poem he addressed to MAGHNUS Ó DOMHNAILL, as well as a silver gallon for the horses.

The surviving corpus of classical poetry comprises in all approximately 2,000 compositions. The majority of these are transmitted in a range of MANUSCRIPT sources, of which the largest proportion are miscellaneous collections belonging to the seventeenth and eighteenth centuries. A number of important contemporary family poem-books survive also, the earliest being that for the Magauran family (Leabhar Méig Shamhradháin) from the thirteenth and fourteenth century (see p. 73) and among the latest those for O'Hara (Leabhar Í Eaghra), Maguire (Duanaire Mhéig Uidhir) and O'Donnell (Leabhar Inghine Í Dhomhnaill) from the beginning of the seventeenth. While many family collections have been edited, others have not; of the entire extant corpus of classical verse up to one half still await the attention of editors. [see CROSÁNTACHT; BARDIC DUNAIRE; DÁNTA GRÁ; EARLY MODERN IRISH PROSE; IRISH GRAMMATICAL TRACTS; POETIC FAMILIES IN MEDIEVAL IRELAND.] **Pádraig A. Breatnach**

CLÉ (Cumann Leabharfhoilsitheoirí Éireann), the Irish book publishers' association, founded in 1970 following the establishment of a PUBLISHING presence at the Frankfurt Book Fair in the later 1960s. It adopted a constitution modelled on that of the Australian Publishers' Association; its first president, 1970–74, was Liam Miller of the DOLMEN PRESS. From small beginnings, with fourteen firms listed in its first promotional catalogue, *Books from Ireland, 1969–70*, its growth reflected the steady progress of the industry. With assistance from CÓRAS TRÁCHTÁLA and subsequently from the ARTS COUNCIL it participates in international book fairs and is a member of the International Publishers' Association and of the Federation of European Publishers, the presidency of which it held in 2000–2. The association campaigned actively against value-added tax on books (rescinded 1982), and immediately thereafter the Irish Books Marketing Group was formed jointly with the Irish Branch of the Booksellers' Association, the British representative body. This group was responsible for several national book promotions and sponsored the first statistical survey of the industry, the Fishwick Report (1987). A merger of the publishers' and booksellers' trade associations under the title Book House Ireland failed after a number of years. In 2000 CLÉ had forty-four member-companies, while full-time EMPLOYMENT in the industry was estimated to be more than 500. **Bernard Share**

Cleary, Bridget. *The cottage of Bridget Cleary, Cloneen, Co. Tipperary, where she was burned to death by her husband, in the presence of relatives and neighbours, who was convinced that the 'fairies' had taken his wife and left a changeling in her place. The porch on the left is a recent addition to the cottage. [Denis Mortell]*

Cleary, Bridget, née Boland (1869–1895), exorcism and murder victim. Born at Cloneen, near Fethard, Co. Tipperary. Raised on a small farm, she married Michael Cleary, a cooper, and they settled locally. When she was still childless at the age of twenty-six she went into rapid physical, and possibly mental, decline. Her husband became convinced that she was a CHANGELING. On 14 March 1895, with a herbalist, Bridget's father, and others of her relatives, he began an exorcism that culminated the following night in her death by burning. All involved were charged with murder, but the charge was eventually reduced to manslaughter, and varied sentences were handed down. [see FOLKLORE.] **Ciarán Deane**

Cleary, Shay (1951–), architect. Born in Cork; educated at UCD. He was a design tutor at UCD, 1977–96, and a visiting professor at Princeton University, 1989. He worked with Marcel Breuer in Paris and in 1987 set up practice in Dublin. His crisp renovations include the Point Depot, Dublin, an 1878 train terminus (which won the AAI Downes Medal, 1989), and the IRISH MUSEUM OF MODERN ART at the 1680 Royal Hospital and Deputy Master's House, Kilmainham, Dublin. A member of Group 91 (which produced the TEMPLE BAR FRAMEWORK PLAN, 1991), he designed the Arthouse, Curved Street, and the Project, East Essex Street, both in Dublin. **Raymund Ryan**

Cleburne, Patrick Ronayne (1828–1864), Confederate commander. Born in Co. Cork. He emigrated to the United States in 1849 and settled in Arkansas. On that state's secession he was appointed a colonel in the Confederate army and in 1862 promoted to brigadier-general. He distinguished himself at the Battles of Kentucky, Perryville, Richmond, and Shiloh and became a major-general. His division was the pride of the Army of Tennessee, recording many victories, and he served bravely in the Atlanta campaign. He strongly advocated the enlisting and freeing of slaves, which prevented his further promotion. He died in battle at Franklin, Tennessee. **David Kiely**

Cléire, Co. Cork (also known as Clear Island and CAPE CLEAR), the southernmost inhabited part of Ireland, 13 km (8 miles) from the mainland ferry port of Baltimore. The island has an area of 6.1 km^2 ($2\frac{1}{2}$ sq. miles) and a landscape of steep, rolling hills. Near the harbour is the twelfth-century St Ciarán's church, named for the early saint reputedly born on the island. The population of 1,052 in 1841 (before the GREAT FAMINE) had fallen to 601 by 1901 and was 145 in 1996. Cléire is Irish-speaking, and summer schools provide income in addition to the traditional activities of farming and fishing, now supported also by TOURISM. A CO-OPERATIVE founded in 1969 helps to manage the economy and provides some services. Conchúr

Ó Síocháin's *Seanchas Chléire* (1940), later issued as *The Man from Cape Clear* (1975), depicts traditional life. [see CIARÁN OF SAIGHIR.] **Stephen A. Royle**

Clements, Nathaniel (1705–1777), politician and amateur architect, a younger son of Robert Clements, Deputy Vice-Treasurer for Ireland. Member of Parliament for Duleek, Co. Louth, and a teller of the Exchequer, he was a protégé and associate of the property developer LUKE GARDINER, whom he succeeded as Deputy Vice-Treasurer and Deputy Paymaster-General of Ireland in 1755. He has been credited with the design of two houses he occupied, no. 7 Henrietta Street, Dublin (1733), and Phoenix Lodge (1751), the core of the present ÁRAS AN UACHTARÁIN, which he built after his appointment as park ranger, possibly with the assistance of the Bath architect John Wood. **Frederick O'Dwyer**

clerical celibacy, unknown in Ireland (ordained monks apart) until the twelfth century, when it was introduced as part of the Gregorian reformers' plans for a ROME-centred clergy. However, adherence to the new discipline was sporadic until the sixteenth century. The *Collectio Canonum Hibernensis* (early eighth century), and other legislation, assumed clerical MARRIAGE, as do accounts of actual clerics. Later the importance of the friars, especially FRANCISCANS, meant that celibacy was increasingly seen as the priestly ideal—an attitude promoted by church leaders. Its rejection by Protestants galvanised it for the COUNTER-REFORMATION as the distinctive caste mark of Catholic clergy. [see CHRISTIANITY.] **Thomas O'Loughlin**

Clerke, Agnes Mary (1842–1907), astronomer. Born in Skibbereen, Co. Cork; her father taught her how to make observations with a 100 mm (4-in.) telescope. She became an accomplished writer, linguist, and pianist (once playing for Franz Liszt). Her first book and masterpiece, *A Popular History of Astronomy during the Nineteenth Century* (1885), was followed by *Problems in Astrophysics* (1903) and *Modern Cosmogonies* (1905). She was awarded the Actonion Prize (1862) by the Royal Institution and Honorary Membership of the Royal Astronomical Society (1903). The special value of her books today lies in the very accurate picture they provide of the dynamic astronomical progress resulting from the development of spectrographic techniques. **Susan McKenna-Lawlor**

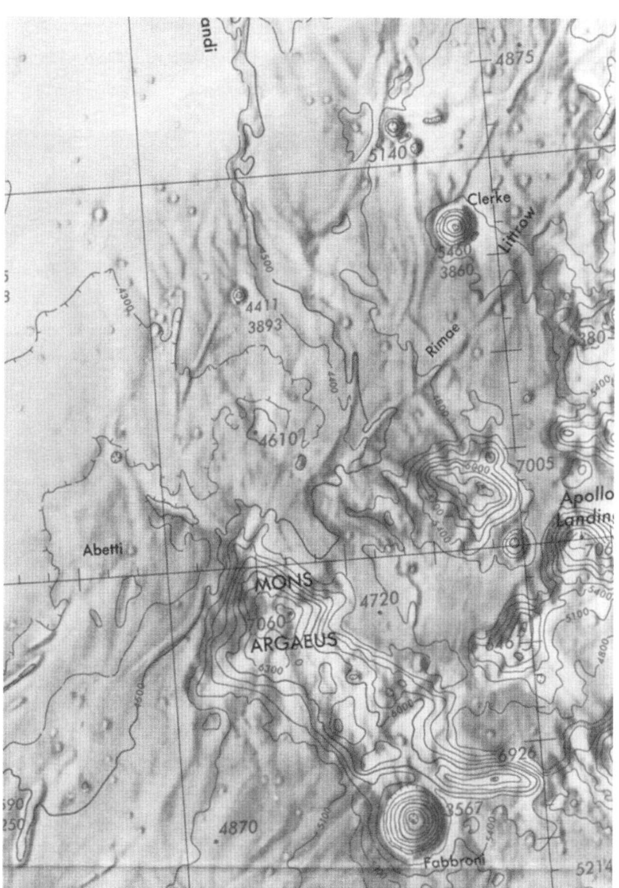

Clerke, Agnes. *Map of the Moon showing (top right) the Clerke Crater, named after the Cork astronomer. Also visible are the Sea of Serenity and (extreme right) the landing site of Apollo 17, launched on 7 December 1972. [Lunar and Planetary Institute, Texas]*

Clerke, Ellen (1840–1906), poet and journalist. Born in Skibbereen, Co. Cork, sister of AGNES CLERKE. She published *Judenthum in Der Musik* (1859), and *The Flying Dutchman and Other Poems* (1881). An article published in the *Observatory Magazine* (1892), based on her readings in Arabic, demonstrated that the variability of the star Algol had been noticed by Arabian astronomers. She also wrote poetry and published works in English, Italian, and German. **Susan McKenna-Lawlor**

Clew Bay, a down-warped and down-tilted trough bisecting the west coast of Co. Mayo, coinciding with the western extension of the Scottish Highlands Boundary Fault, which runs north-eastwards through Ulster and into Scotland. CLARE ISLAND, at the mouth of the bay, now linked by ferry to Roonagh Quay, has a history of habitation from at least 3500 BC; a ruined fifteenth or sixteenth-century island castle bears the name of the local seafaring leader GRACE O'MALLEY. The inner bay is dominated by many small islands (allegedly 365), which are drowned drumlins. The towns of Newport and Westport to the north and south, respectively, served as important regional ports in the nineteenth century. The development of the modern town of Westport (population 5,109), begun by a local landowner, John Browne, Earl of Altamont, in the middle of the eighteenth century, has many fine stone buildings. Lecanvey on the south coast is a seaside resort of note. To the north is the Nephin Beg range, trending north-east to south-west; to the south is CROAGH PATRICK. Several minor west-flowing rivers enter the bay from north to south: the Newport, Rossow, Owennabrockagh, Moyour, and Carrowbeg. **Mary E. Cawley**

clientelism in the Republic, a reciprocal relationship in which votes are exchanged for public goods between a patron and a client. This is not a feature of politics in the Republic, where *brokerage* is more common: this is where elected representatives act as intermediaries for individuals dealing with public bodies, normally for those unfamiliar with bureaucratic procedures. The politician anticipates support as a result, but this is not guaranteed. Academic opinion is divided on its importance in the political process; politicians believe it generates a high profile in the constituency; and constituents expect the service to be available. More generally, individual TDs are expected to provide benefits for the constituency, especially when their party is in government. **Brian Girvin**

Clifford, Julia (1914–1997) and Denis Murphy (1910–1974), a sister and brother from Lisheen, Gneeveguilla, Co. Kerry, highly regarded FIDDLE-players in the tradition of their home area, Sliabh Luachra on the Cork/Kerry border. Both spent long periods living and working abroad— Julia in London and Norfolk and Denis in

New York. Their duet playing was particularly noteworthy; their music can be heard on *The Star above the Garter* and *Denis Murphy: Music from Sliabh Luachra*. **Peter Browne**

Clifford. *Julia Clifford, fiddle player, seen here playing the horn fiddle at the Olympia Theatre, Dublin, 1988. [Derek Speirs/ Report]*

Clifton, Harry (1952–), poet. Born in Dublin; educated at UCD. He has worked as a teacher and aid administrator, living in Thailand, Italy, and France; exile and nomadism are persistent themes in his work. His collections are *The Walls of Carthage* (1977), *Office of the Salt Merchant* (1979), *Comparative Lives* (1982), *The Liberal Cage* (1989), and *Night Train through the Brenner* (1994). Selected poems were published as *The Desert Route* (1992). *On the Spine of Italy* (1999) is a memoir of a year in an Italian village. A volume of short stories, *Berkeley's Telephone*, appeared in 2000. **David Wheatley**

climate. The climate of a place includes its average weather and its regular variations over a stable period. The properties of climate will change over time, as they have in the past, because of natural fluctuations in the behaviour of the earth's atmosphere and perhaps increasingly because of human activity.

The chief controls on the Irish climate are its latitude and distinctive geography. Ireland is in the middle latitudes (between 52° and 55°N), which means that the amount of energy received from the Sun changes significantly during the year as the length of daylight and solar altitude change. At 53°N on 21 December daylight lasts for just eight hours, with the Sun at noon at an angle of 14° above the horizon; on 21 June these values are sixteen hours and 60°, respectively. As a consequence Ireland has distinct seasons, particularly with regard to air temperature.

Ireland's position in the middle latitudes also places it within a broad and deep band of westerly airflow. Within these winds a series of *cyclones* or *depressions* (low-pressure systems) move from west to east, drawing in air of differing origins. The distinctive attributes of large bodies of air are acquired by interaction with homogeneous surfaces of great extent. Air masses of polar origin are comparatively cold, while those of tropical origin are warm; the middle latitudes do not produce identifiable air masses and represent a zone of mixing. In addition, by comparison with air masses that form over land, those that form over oceans have a high moisture content and experience little variation in temperature during the year. Within a depression these differing air masses converge, and the lighter (warm and moist) air rises, producing cloud and precipitation. It is these storms that are responsible for exchanging energy received on Earth from the Sun, from areas of comparative excess (the tropics) to those of deficit (the poles). Throughout the year Ireland's climate is marked by the regular passage of depressions and their associated air masses.

Because of Ireland's position on the north-western edge of Europe, the air masses it receives are invariably of maritime origin, either tropical or polar. The air arriving at the Irish coast has travelled long distances over ocean and has been modified in its passage. In the final part of its journey it passes over a warm ocean current, the North Atlantic Drift, which originates in the Gulf of Mexico as the GULF STREAM and moves as a river of Caribbean water north-eastwards, surrounding the Irish coast. The extent of Ireland is sufficiently small for air masses to experience little change as they traverse the land area, so that Ireland may be described as having a marine, west-coast climate.

As a consequence of all these factors the Irish climate has few extremes. The average air temperature in July is between 17° and 18°C (62–64°F), in January between 1.5° and 4°C (35–39°F). The pattern of air temperatures is generally from north to south, but with a coastal pattern superimposed. By comparison with inland areas, coastal areas have comparatively warm winters and cooler summers, while the first and last occurrences of frost are in the midlands. In addition to these general patterns there are localised high and low temperatures associated with changing elevation.

The Irish atmosphere is generally humid throughout the year, with relative humidity values of between 70 and 90 per cent. Any spatial variations in relative humidity can be attributed to changes in air temperature rather than water-vapour content. Ireland's position close to the paths of cyclones, and the fact that the air has passed across a relatively smooth surface, means that the country has a windy climate, and that the windiest places are coastal, with an average wind speed along the north coast of 6.7 m/s (15 miles/h). With regard to wind energy, Ireland is considered to have the best resource in Western Europe.

Precipitation nearly always occurs as rainfall (snowfall is a rare event at low elevations) and is relatively evenly spread throughout the year, with February the driest month. On average there is measurable precipitation on 175 days a year, with an annual total of 1,000 mm (39 in.) However, there is considerable spatial variation. Generally, precipitation decreases from west to east and from north to south. The wettest parts of the country (parts of Cos. Kerry, Mayo, and Donegal) receive more than 1,500 mm (59 in.), spread over 200 days, while the driest areas (parts of Cos. Dublin, Meath, and Kildare) receive less than 800 mm (31 in.) over 150 days. Not surprisingly, total hours of sunshine show an opposite pattern to precipitation, with the south-east receiving more sunshine than any other area and the north-west the least.

In the past hundred years it is estimated that average global temperature has increased by more than 0.5°C. There is considerable debate about the significance of this value, given the uneven global distribution of weather stations; and even among those who accept that there has been an increase there is debate on its causes. For Ireland 1999 was the sixth consecutive year of above-average temperatures; of those years 1997 was the warmest year on record. There is now broad agreement that the warming trend is real and that it represents clear evidence of the effects of human activity, in particular the emission of certain gases, most notably carbon dioxide, associated with the burning of fossil fuels. Over the last 250 years the concentration of carbon dioxide in the atmosphere has increased from 270 parts per million in the pre-industrial period to 350 parts per million today. Global climate models suggest that increased levels of carbon dioxide will result in global warming, raised sea levels (and drowned coastlines), and changed precipitation and storm patterns. These models are imperfect, but all agree that warming will occur, and that it will be greatest at higher latitudes; the most recent estimates suggest an increase in average temperature of 1.5°C for Ireland. [see EXTREME WEATHER; THE NIGHT OF THE BIG WIND.] **Gerald Mills**

climate change. The emission of pollutants into the atmosphere is arguably one of the greatest pressures on the global environment. In Ireland, awareness of atmospheric pollution first arose as a result of the local effects of winter smog on human health, particularly in urban and heavily industrialised areas. Then came an appreciation of regional influences and of environmental damage caused by acid rain, the result of human-made emissions of sulphur and nitrogen. In addition there was widespread concern about the depletion of stratospheric (upper atmosphere) ozone caused by the presence of certain chemicals, particularly chlorofluorocarbons. An awareness of photochemical pollution has also developed, related to unprecedented growth in road traffic. More recently the importance of global impacts has been recognised; at this scale, the adverse effects of 'greenhouse gases', such as carbon dioxide, are now causing widespread concern. It became apparent that these would give rise to changes in the global climate, with impacts including a rise in sea level and more frequent storms and such consequences as the erosion and inundation of vulnerable coasts.

The UN Framework Convention on Climate Change (1992) had as its main objective the effective stabilisation of the concentrations of 'greenhouse gas' in the atmosphere. The three main gases are carbon dioxide, methane, and nitrous oxide; others include the halogenated gas groups, such as hydrofluorocarbons and perfluorocarbons, as well as sulphur hexafluoride. Increased quantities of these chemicals in the atmosphere exacerbate the natural greenhouse effect of the atmosphere. INDUSTRIALISATION has resulted in the emission of large quantities of human-made greenhouse gases into the atmosphere; activities responsible include the burning of fossil fuels, the release of carbon dioxide, and the increase in the number of cattle, releasing methane. AGRICULTURE is the dominant source of both methane and nitrous oxide emissions in the Republic, while ENERGY and TRANSPORT account for a large proportion of carbon dioxide emissions. In Northern Ireland the energy industry accounts for approximately 25 per cent of emissions, most of which come from power generation. The lack of a piped supply of natural gas has also until recently been an important factor; the increasing availability of gas for industrial and domestic use should be reflected in lower emissions in future.

The UN convention and other international agreements on stricter controls on the emission of greenhouse gases resulted in the adoption of the Kyoto Protocol (1997), under which industrialised countries would reduce their combined emission of six greenhouse gases by 5.2 per cent over 1990 levels by 2008–12. The target for the Republic is a limitation of growth of 13 per cent; this was negotiated as Ireland's contribution to the EUROPEAN UNION's agreement to reduce levels by 8 per cent. Northern Ireland is covered by the United Kingdom's commitment to a reduction of 12.5 per cent by 2008–10.

As the economy of the Republic developed, its energy requirements increased correspondingly. The total primary energy requirement—a measure of all energy consumed—has increased by 35 per cent since 1990. Ireland relies heavily on the use of fossil fuels: oil, coal, natural gas, and peat. There is also some use of renewable energy, such as that provided by wind. Northern Ireland is moving towards the British target of renewable energy providing 10 per cent of electricity supply by 2010. Northern Ireland Electricity is required, under the Non-Fossil Fuel Obligation Order, to contract for specified amounts of electricity from non-fossil sources; and other forms of renewable energy are being explored and introduced.

The over-reliance on the burning of fossil fuels continues to have a detrimental effect on the environment and contributes to climate change globally. The only noticeable decrease in the use of one traditional fossil fuel is that of peat harvested from raised BOGS; but its use has been replaced largely by oil and electricity. The use of natural gas is continuing to increase, as part of a strategy to reduce emissions of carbon dioxide and sulphur dioxide. Approximately half the supply of natural gas is imported through the pipeline between Ireland and Britain, from the North Sea gas field. More discoveries of gas off the west coast of Ireland should lead to a wider availability of cheaper natural gas, with its important low emission rate, and it is estimated that Ireland's reliance on this energy source will double by 2010.

Hydro-electricity production and the burning of wood in open fires were, until the early 1990s, the only noteworthy examples of renewable energy in the Republic. Since then the energy supply from renewable sources has increased, because of the contributions of independent producers of hydro-electric power, developers of wind energy, and wood-processing plants. Large-scale hydro-electric power and traditional and industrial bio-mass are the main sources of renewable energy but provide only 2 per cent of energy requirement in the Republic (compared with 5–6 per cent in the European Union). Ireland has some of the highest wind energy potential in Europe, both onshore and offshore (see p. 353). According to the Irish offshore wind energy report, Ireland's territorial waters provide a significant wind energy resource and could provide 32 per cent of predicted energy consumption by 2005.

The expansion of industry and the increase in energy requirements has had further consequences for air pollution. Acid rain—a

climate. *A view of Luggala in the Wicklow Mountains. Wicklow's climate, like that of most of Ireland, is dominated by the Atlantic Ocean, resulting in mild summers and cool wet winters. [Bord Fáilte]* result of increased emissions of sulphur and nitrogen—can lead to the acidification of soil and surface waters. The rapid growth in car ownership and the number of commercial vehicles has resulted in the appearance of a phenomenon known as summer smog. Transport is the most significant source of emission of nitrogen oxides, volatile organic carbons, and carbon monoxide. In the Republic, catalyst controls have been mandatory since 1993, but the benefits that may have resulted from this advance have been offset by the massive increase in the use of transport fuels. [see ENVIRONMENT AND HERITAGE SERVICE.] **Anne-Marie Cunningham**

Clinch, Phyllis E. M. (1901–1984), plant pathologist. Born in Dublin; graduated in chemistry and botany from UCD. She worked in London, Galway, and Paris on the biochemistry of conifers. In 1929, in the Department of Plant Pathology in UCD she embarked on her principal contribution to science, achieving world renown in pioneer studies to solve important problems concerning the transmission of POTATO viruses. Her work had an important economic impact, making it possible to develop stocks of virus-free potatoes. Subsequently she made a significant contribution to knowledge of viruses affecting tomatoes and sugarbeet. She was awarded the BOYLE MEDAL. **Christopher Moriarty**

Clogher, Co. Tyrone, site of a well-preserved group of EARTHWORKS that has been the subject of excavation. A 'timber-laced' stone enclosure of Late BRONZE AGE date was followed in the Early IRON AGE by a sub-rectangular hill-fort that incorporated an existing ring-barrow. In the fourth century AD a ring-ditch enclosure was dug within the hill-fort, and from that time until the ninth century the place was known as Clochar macc nDaimíni, the capital of the Airghialla kingdom of Uí Cremthainn. Late in the sixth century a strong single-banked ring-fort was constructed on the line of the ring-ditch. The excavation of the ring-ditch and ring-fort has provided a detailed archaeological picture of early medieval Irish royalty, with pottery imported from the Mediterranean and from Gaul and extensive evidence of industry, including the manufacture of bronze BROOCHES in the sixth century. A mound adjoining the ring-fort may be interpreted as both the inauguration mound of the kings living there and the ritual focus of the kingdom. The hill-fort, ring-fort, ring-barrow, and mound are still standing. The foundation of the nearby monastery of Clochar, where high crosses and a splendid early sun-dial can be seen, is traditionally ascribed to St PATRICK. **Richard Warner**

Clonard, Co. Meath, site of a monastery founded by St Finnian in the sixth century, though the original church site may have been at nearby Ard Relec. Famous for its MONASTIC SCHOOL, Clonard came under the control of various rival political dynasties from the eighth century onwards. It fell into decline during the twelfth century but was the seat of a bishopric from 1111 to 1202. **Paul Byrne**

Clonfert Cathedral, Co. Galway, the cathedral of ST BRENDAN, the only surviving structure at this important monastic site. Its nave, with western and eastern antae, may date from the tenth century. The building is most famous for its extravagant ROMANESQUE portal, comprising (now) six orders of lavishly sculpted ornament and a steep tangent gable (see p. 909). Its erection may have coincided with a SYNOD convened at Clonfert in 1179. In 1414 Papal indulgences were granted for repairs to the church, which probably resulted in the erection of the slender west tower, the inner order of the west doorway, and the quirkily decorated chancel arch. **Rachel Moss**

Clonfinlough, Co. Offaly, a Late BRONZE AGE SETTLEMENT site constructed at the edge of a lake c. 908 BC and occupied until c. 886 BC. An oval palisade of wooden posts enclosed the settlement, which consisted of at least three houses and some smaller structures. The circular houses, some with flagstone floors, were 9 m (30 ft) in diameter and built of wooden posts and wattle on complex wooden foundations. Artefacts found include coarse ware pottery, amber beads, a fish basket, and two large wooden paddles. The agricultural economy of the site is indicated by quern-stones and cattle, sheep, and pig bones. **Conor McDermott**

Clonmacnoise, Co. Offaly, one of the most important ecclesiastical sites in EARLY HISTORIC IRELAND, originally a MONASTERY founded by ST CIARÁN in the 540s. It is situated on the River Shannon in the centre of the country, and the long-deserted site is now a national monument. It benefited from its position on important routes and on the boundary between the provinces of Leinster and Connacht, whose kings patronised its churches. For the first few centuries its buildings were made of perishable materials, such as post-and-wattle and timber, but gradually, from c. 900, its churches were rebuilt in stone. From the early ninth century it became the target of raiders, both Irish and VIKING, and the ANNALS record many plunderings up to the early thirteenth century. By the eleventh century it appears to have grown into a populous settlement with a large dependent lay population, many of whom were engaged in trade and in metalworking and other crafts. As part of the reform of the Irish church in the twelfth century it became a diocesan centre, but soon after, as a result of the ANGLO-NORMAN incursion, it lost its wealthy royal patrons and its DIOCESE was reduced in size and marginalised. It was plundered and devastated by the English garrison from Athlone in 1552 and, apart from a short-lived restoration in the middle of the seventeenth century, never recovered.

The earliest buildings on the site are the smallest church, Temple Ciarán, regarded as the burial place of St Ciarán, and the largest, now called the Cathedral, which was built (according to the annals) in 909. Both were constructed of similar sandstone masonry with *putlog* (scaffolding) holes and *antae* (continuations of the side walls beyond the end walls for a roof that extended over the gables). The cathedral was partly rebuilt c. 1200, again c. 1300 (when the south wall was rebuilt to the north of its original line), and in the 1450s, when, together with other work, the ornate gothic north doorway was inserted. The last High King of Ireland, RUAIDHRÍ Ó CONCHOBHAIR, was buried in the cathedral in 1198. Other churches at the site include Temple Dowling (eleventh to seventeenth century), Temple Melaghlin (early thirteenth century), and the twelfth-century ROMANESQUE Temple Finghin with its attached ROUND TOWER. The large free-standing round tower, completed in 1124, is now missing most of its upper half. About 500 m (550 yards) to the east of the main site is the Nuns' Church, a ruined Romanesque nave-and-chancel church built in 1167.

Clonmacnoise has three HIGH CROSSES: the CROSS OF THE SCRIPTURES, dating from c. 900 and carved with figured scenes; the South Cross, with abstract ornament mainly; and the North Cross (shaft only). Also from the site are more than 600 complete or fragmentary cross-inscribed grave-slabs, many with inscriptions in Irish seeking a prayer for the deceased (see p. 455). Recent archaeological excavations have thrown light on the date, nature and extent of the settlement, and underwater survey and excavation in the river adjacent to the castle, which dates from the early thirteenth century, have uncovered the remains of a wooden bridge dating from 804.

Clonmacnoise. *On the near bank of the River Shannon are (left) the Anglo-Norman castle and earthworks; the remains of the monastic enclosure consist of six churches, the cathedral, and two round towers. Across the Shannon, which divides the provinces of Leinster and Connacht, can be seen mechanically harvested bogland. [Imagefile]*

Before the thirteenth century Clonmacnoise had a thriving scriptorium and school of learning. A number of surviving chronicles are associated with Clonmacnoise, and a surviving manuscript, the Book of the DUN COW (Lebor na hUidre), which contains secular literature, is known to have been at the site. There is also some fine associated metalwork, such as the CROZIER of the Abbots of Clonmacnoise and the shrine of the Stowe Missal (see p. 105). **Conleth Manning**

Clonmel (*Cluain Meala*), Co. Tipperary, a town on a bridging point of the River SUIR, which is tidal to this point, 48 km (30 miles) upriver from Waterford, and the county town of South Tipperary; population (2002) 15,721. According to local tradition the town was founded by Norsemen who travelled up the Suir from Waterford. The Norman town was probably founded in the early thirteenth century, with both Dominican and Franciscan friaries built at this time. It became a walled trading town, loyal to the English Crown, like Waterford to the east. It was besieged twice, first in 1516 and later in 1650 by CROMWELL. A new Protestant oligarchy was imposed on the town for the next two centuries. In the eighteenth century Clonmel became an important market town for local produce as well as a centre of BREWING and DISTILLING, a tradition that survives in the manufacture of cider. In 1815 it was the centre of a new public TRANSPORT system, set up by CHARLES BIANCONI. This was at first a horse-drawn coach service running between Clonmel and Caher but by 1843 had expanded to almost a hundred coaches, serving much of the country. Bianconi was elected mayor in 1844, the first Catholic to hold the post in more than 150 years. In 1841 the population was over 13,500; after the GREAT FAMINE it declined, to 10,200 in 1901, and it remained at about this level until the 1960s. The town's resurgence since then is based on both SERVICES and manufacturing, and TOURISM is also expanding. [see MAIN GUARD, THE.] **Kevin Hourihan**

Clontarf, Battle of (1014), fought near Dublin on Good Friday, 23 April 1014. It is widely regarded as one of the most important engagements of Irish history and has been represented as the turning-point in an attempted 'VIKING conquest' of Ireland. In reality, the battle postdated the Viking period proper; it arose from a revolt by the Leinstermen and Dublin Norsemen (with Manx and Hebridean support) against BRIAN BÓRÚ, the claimant to the HIGH-KINGSHIP. Brian fell in the battle, which was a pyrrhic victory for the Munster forces. Enshrined in Middle Irish and Old Norse literature, Clontarf had a major impact on the consciousness of both peoples. **Ailbhe Mac Shamhráin**

Close, M. H. [Maxwell Henry] (1822–1903), scholar. Born in Dublin; graduated from TCD in 1846, and ordained in the Church of England. He held several minor clerical posts in England before returning to Ireland in 1861 to live the life of a gentleman scholar possessed of private means. His life revolved around bodies such as the ROYAL DUBLIN SOCIETY, the ROYAL GEOLOGICAL SOCIETY OF IRELAND, and the ROYAL IRISH ACADEMY, where he was treasurer from 1878 until 1903. He contributed to astronomy, geology, mathematics, physics, and the study of Irish. Above all, he was a pioneering student of Ireland's Pleistocene glaciation, publishing—among other significant contributions—his influential 'Notes on the General Glaciation of Ireland', in 1867 in the *Journal of the Royal Geological Society of Ireland*. In his will he left £1,000 towards the cost of an Irish dictionary; the fund went towards the publication of the Royal Irish Academy's *Dictionary of the Irish Language* (1913–76). **Jean Archer**

Clossy, Samuel (1724–1786), physician. Born in Dublin; educated at TCD, graduating as BA in 1744, MB in 1751, and MD in 1755. Having studied pathology at Dr Steevens' and Mercer's

Hospitals, he published *Observations on Some of the Diseases of the Parts of the Human Body* (1763). He gave the first course on anatomy at the medical school of King's College, New York. **J. B. Lyons**

clothing as described by foreigners. The condemnatory judgment by a colonial official or foreign writer on the hair and clothing styles worn in Ireland should not be accepted at face value but evaluated according to the motives of the writer. The reference by GIRALDUS CAMBRENSIS to Irish dress as made 'in a barbarous fashion' meant to him that the styles were unsophisticated in his world. Similarly, throughout the centuries many poor Irish people were described as being 'naked', but during a period when layers of clothing were worn by fashionable people, this term meant 'wearing few clothes.' **Mairead Dunlevy**

clothing, traditional. Though eighteenth-century Ireland was characterised in its early years by famine, this was generally a relatively prosperous century. What had become standard dress for men and women in the later seventeenth century was now being adopted by all classes and was to remain as traditional clothing in some parts of the country until the opening decades of the twentieth century. For women the main components of this dress were a cloak, a heavy petticoat, usually red, a buttoned jacket, and an apron, while men wore knee-breeches, a waistcoat, and a coat with lapels and tails.

Nineteenth-century poverty among a huge section of the population saw thousands dressed in rags. In areas with a tradition of cloth-making from wool and LINEN, regional styles became strong and distinctive. In the middle of the nineteenth century a farmer's wife from a prosperous part of Co. Tipperary wore, under her hooded cloak, a WOOLLEN skirt made from 2–3 m (2–3 yards) of material gathered in to the waist and a quilted petticoat, which was red flannel on the inside and black serge on the outside; over the skirt and petticoat she wore a tight-fitting bodice.

In Inishkeel, Co. Donegal, later in the century an itemised list of typical women's clothes included a shift and inside petticoat of white flannel next to the skin and a second petticoat of red flannel, which was sometimes quilted and had trimming of two or three rows of blue or black braid near its bottom edge. In summer the second petticoat might have been replaced with one of cooler white linen. The bodice (*corpán*), also known colloquially as the 'polky', was also of wool and was worn over the skirt. It was worn buttoned up to the neck; for extra warmth, a small shoulder shawl was secured under the chin with a pin or brooch. White frilled cotton and lace caps remained popular until the end of the century, generally worn covered with a coloured handkerchief, placed in position on the head so as to keep the frill exposed. Shoes were only occasionally worn, but soleless stockings (*máirtíní*) were common.

For men in Inishkeel, underclothes were of white flannel, and the shirt was of cotton or calico. Knee-breeches were of corduroy or the local homespun, *báinín brocach* or *báinín glas caorach*, with white or grey (*glas caorach*) thick woollen socks worn up to the knee. The workday waistcoat (*bheist mhuinchilleach*) was a double-breasted sleeved garment of bleached moleskin or corduroy. A wrapper or coat of white flannel and also the swallowtail coat (*casóg sciortach*) were still worn by some of the older men at the beginning of the twentieth century. The thick, heavy homespun of men's outer garments rendered them almost rainproof, and there was generally no need for an outer coat. Overcoats of frieze, a thick and heavy woollen cloth, were worn by wealthier men, and a saying recorded in several areas summed up the situation: *Comhartha bodaigh bheith ag caitheamh cóta móir agus bútaisí* (A sign of wealth is for a man to wear an overcoat and top-boots).

The distinctive clothing of the ARAN ISLANDS, especially of the men, attracted a good deal of attention from visitors over the years; and an accurate picture of men's everyday dress throughout the nineteenth century is available. It included a light inner shirt (*léine ghlas*) of blue flannel, a heavy outer shirt (*léine ghorm*) of dark-blue flannel, a sleeved waistcoat (*bástchóta*) of white flannel with a v-shaped neck, a sleeveless waistcoat (*bheist*) of grey, brown, or blue frieze, and wide, loose-fitting trousers of grey or brown frieze. Men, women, and children wore rawhide shoes (*bróga úrleathair*) with distinctive dark-blue knee-length stockings, which had a white pattern at the toes and knee. Children, both boys and girls, wore clothes similar to their mothers until they were about fourteen. The main item of children's clothing was a one-piece dress (*cóta cabhlach*), essentially a red or white flannel skirt stitched to a cotton bodice. It was a mark of advancing manhood when a boy was given his first pair of trousers, while girls donned the two-piece bodice and skirt as a sign that they were no longer children (see pp. 483, 1117). [see ARAN CRIOS; ARAN KNITTING; DRESS STYLE; IRISH DANCE COSTUME; IRISH MANTLE; IRISH STITCH; NATIONAL COSTUME; PAMPOOTIES.] **Anne O'Dowd**

Cloyne, a townland and parish in the barony of Imokilly, Co. Cork, and the diocese so named. COLMÁN MAC LÉNÉNI, reputed founder of Cloyne's Early Christian MONASTERY, died on 24 November 606. According to medieval tradition he had won high esteem as a secular poet before taking clerical orders, at which point he bequeathed his art to Dálach, ancestor of the famous bardic family of Ó Dálaigh. All the early buildings were burnt in 1137, and the cathedral of the present CHURCH OF IRELAND diocese was begun c. 1250; remains of this can be traced under the later modernisations, and a ROUND TOWER, almost complete, also survives. **Máirín Ní Dhonnchadha**

Cloyne harp, the only example of a partly chromatically tuned Irish HARP, apparently made to help harpers to play complex music. It had forty-five main-row strings and seven further strings in a second row, midway in the range; how exactly it was tuned is a matter for conjecture. Made in 1621 for John Fitz-Edmond Fitzgerald and his wife, Ellen Barry of CLOYNE, Co. Cork, only two parts now survive. Every inch of these is exquisitely decorated with patterns of fruit and foliage and carvings of animals and reptiles, some mythological. A carving of a queen on the top of the harp has the Latin inscription 'I am queen of harps.' The names and positions of thirteen of the Fitzgerald servants are inscribed, including those of the harp-maker, Donnchadh Mac Taidhg (a carpenter), and two harpers. A recently constructed replica of this harp as well as the surviving fragments is displayed in the NATIONAL MUSEUM, Collins Barracks, Dublin. **Gráinne Yeats**

Coady, Michael (1939–), poet. Born in Carrick-on-Suir, Co. Tipperary, which has been his home and the principal focus of his work for most of his life. He has a gentle and lively sense of great and small history, of respect for the local tragedies and victories of unremarked lives, leavened by an occasional humorous wickedness, which adds savour to a restrained and dignified poetry. His occasional prose essays or meditations are as dense in meaning and reference as his lyric poems are elegant and sure. His publications are: *Two for a Woman, Three for a Man* (1980), *Oven Lane* (1987) *All Souls* (1997), and *Full Tide* (1999). He is a member of AOSDÁNA. **Theo Dorgan**

clothing, traditional. *Island funeral on Inisheer, Aran Islands, Co. Galway, 1965. The mourners are in traditional island dress: the women wear red petticoats with a black or paisley shawl draped over their head and shoulders, while the majority of the men are in homespun waistcoats, jackets, and trousers, with tweed caps. [Bill Doyle]*

Coalisland to Dungannon march (1968), the first CIVIL RIGHTS march in Northern Ireland and the culmination of nationalist frustration at the failure of the British and regional governments to deal with GERRYMANDERING and with discrimination in jobs and housing. Those agitating for change in the 1960s included a Dungannon doctor, Dr Conn McCluskey, his wife, Patricia McCluskey, and the Nationalist MP for East Tyrone, Austin Currie. The McCluskeys had formed the Homeless Citizens' League in Dungannon in 1963 to campaign for houses for poor Catholics before launching the influential Campaign for SOCIAL JUSTICE in 1964 to campaign against civil rights abuses. In 1967 the NORTHERN IRELAND CIVIL RIGHTS ASSOCIATION was formed.

Only two of the 204 houses built by Dungannon Rural District Council between 1944 and 1965 had been allocated to Catholic families. In June 1968 Currie led a protest 'squat' in a council house in CALEDON that had been allocated to a nineteen-year-old single Protestant. Two months later, on 24 August 1968, he joined the McCluskeys, GERRY FITT MP, and Labour and republican figures in a civil rights march from the nationalist village of Coalisland to Dungannon, sponsored by the NICRA. Some 2,500 people took part. The march was rerouted by the RUC from the town centre, where a Paisleyite counter-demonstration was held. The event passed without serious incident; yet it marked a new tactic by Catholics in their campaign for equal rights, leading to the pivotal march in Derry on 5 October 1968. TERENCE O'NEILL wrote in his autobiography: 'Had we all known it, that unreported civil rights march was to be the start of something which would shake Northern Ireland to its foundations, split the ruling Unionist Party and initiate more reform in two years than I had thought possible in ten.' [see CIVIL RIGHTS MOVEMENT.] **Eamon Phoenix**

coastal erosion, a function of the combined action of waves and storms, long-term rises in sea level, the strength of coastal rocks and sediments, the width of the intertidal zone, and human impacts. Ireland's coasts, approximately 7,800 km (4,800 miles) in total length, are exposed to high wave energy, with breaking swell waves on Atlantic coasts reaching heights of up to 3 m (10 ft).

The many types of coast vary in their susceptibility to erosion. Rock-dominated coasts—with a total length of approximately 3,000 km (1,800 miles)—are the least vulnerable, with erosion rates of approximately 10 mm (0.4 in.) per century; erosion may also occur, however, in the form of sudden rock-falls and landslides. Coastal features associated with rock-erosion include steep cliffs (such as Torr Head, Co. Antrim, and the CLIFFS OF MOHER, Co. Clare), headlands and bays (such as Galley Head, Co. Cork), sea-stacks, and arches and caves (as in Co. Waterford). Coasts most vulnerable to erosion are those composed of unconsolidated (soft) sediments, totalling approximately 3,500 km (2,200 miles) and comprising glaciated debris, sandy beaches—totalling approximately 1,000 km (600 miles)—sand and gravel barriers, dunes, and *machair* (a coastal grassland habitat formed when calcareous sand is blown inland from beaches and dunes). These coastal sediments are most common on eastern and southern coasts and occur as more isolated areas on western and northern coasts (such as Inch, CLEW BAY, and LOUGH FOYLE). Erosion rates for these 'soft' coasts average 0.2–0.5 m ($\frac{1}{2}$–$1\frac{1}{2}$ ft) per year but often reach values of 1–2 m (3–6 ft) per year. The effects of this erosion are visible as 'rapid' cliff retreat and inland movements of dunes and other barriers, at rates of 0.6–6 m (2–20 ft) per year and on beaches the lowering of levels with the loss of the finer sediments. Rock and sediments eroded generally move onshore, providing an essential source of materials for the development of beaches, dunes, and estuaries at other coastal sites.

Coastal erosion is often noticed most because of its impacts on people, as at DUBLIN BAY. This erosion, while part of a natural pattern of environmental changes, may have human causes. In the future, increased coastal erosion as a result of global warming will be one consequence of human impacts on the ENVIRONMENT. An approach to the treatment of such erosion needs careful management to ensure environmental sustainability. Assessments of global warming caused by increased emissions of greenhouse gases predict an increase in temperature of 1.4–5.8°C by 2100. An outcome of this change will be an accelerated increase in relative sea level and changing storm patterns. Ireland's increase in relative sea level at present is approximately 1 mm per year; with the present rate of climate warming this will accelerate to approximately 4–6 mm (0.15–0.25 in.) per year by 2100. It is predicted that Ireland will experience fewer but more powerful storms, with the north-west and south-east becoming more stormy. Approximately 1,700 km (1,100 miles) of the coastline is particularly vulnerable to change; at present approximately 350 km (220 miles) of coasts have some type of defence structures. [see CLIMATE CHANGE; CONTINENTAL SHELF.] **Robert J. N. Devoy**

Cobbe, Frances Power (1822–1904), feminist and anti-vivisectionist. Born in Dublin; educated at home and at Brighton. In 1858 she moved to Bristol, where she worked with street children and visited WORKHOUSES. She moved to London in 1864, with her female companion, and became involved in campaigns for women's rights. She spearheaded England's anti-vivisectionist movement by founding the Victoria Street Society (1875) and the British Union for the Abolition of Vivisection (1898). She moved to Wales in 1884. A conservative in politics, she opposed HOME RULE for Ireland, while protesting against power hierarchies and the exploitation of the powerless. **Lori Williamson**

Cobh (*An Cóbh*), Co. Cork, a port and town on Great Island in Cork Harbour, 24 km (15 miles) by road from Cork; population (2002) 6,771. Cobh was a fishing village until the late nineteenth century but became an important naval port and supply depot during the American and Napoleonic wars. It was named Queenstown in 1849 (to mark the visit of VICTORIA) and renamed in 1922. It remained a British naval station until 1937, with the harbour heavily fortified. In the nineteenth and twentieth centuries large numbers of emigrants departed from Cobh, a fact now commemorated in a HERITAGE CENTRE. Cobh was also a port of call for transatlantic liners, including the SIRIUS (the first steamship to cross the Atlantic Ocean) and the TITANIC, and the burial place for many of the victims of the sinking of the LUSITANIA, torpedoed in 1915. Its port activity has largely disappeared, and Cobh is now a tourist and industrial centre and a dormitory town for Cork. It is built along a steep south-facing slope, with its brightly painted terraced streets rising along the contours parallel to the quayside. ST COLMAN'S CATHEDRAL, a soaring neo-gothic structure designed by PUGIN AND ASHLIN in the 1860s, dominates the skyline. On a sunny day Cobh has one of the most attractive townscapes in Ireland, especially when viewed from a ship in the harbour (see p. 54). **Kevin Hourihan**

Cobh Cathedral: see ST COLMAN'S CATHEDRAL.

Codex Usserianus Primus, the earliest known Irish MANUSCRIPT, a Latin GOSPEL book with a pre-Vulgate text written in half-uncial SCRIPT and so probably dating from before the invention of insular script, which seems to have happened towards the end of the sixth century. It was the work of two scribes, and the damage it suffered shows that it was formerly enshrined as the relic of a saint; it is now in Trinity College Library. [see MANUSCRIPTS, EARLY.] **William O'Sullivan**

Coercion Acts, a generic term for legislation giving governments emergency powers to deal with breakdowns in law and order. Special legislation was a regular feature of the government of Ireland throughout the nineteenth century. The measures varied considerably in scope and severity, from restricting the carrying of arms to a dusk-to-dawn curfew on disturbed districts and the suspension of habeas corpus. Coercion Acts were traditionally temporary; but as the century continued, some special powers, such as the suppression of political organisations considered to be dangerous, were incorporated in the ordinary law. Coercive legislation was rarely passed in isolation and was usually followed by conciliatory measures intended to tackle the roots of popular discontent. In 1881, for example, the Protection Act, designed to contain agrarian violence by providing for detention without trial, preceded the Land Law (Ireland) Act. **Virginia Crossman**

Coffey, Aeneas (1780–1852), industrial chemist. Born either in Dublin or Calais to Irish parents, he spent his early years in France. On arriving in Ireland in 1800 he entered the Excise Department. Active in operations against illicit DISTILLING, he rose to the position of Inspector-General of Excise but resigned in 1828 to set up his own distillery in Dublin. In 1831 he invented a still incorporating some of the features of the modern fractionating column. Scottish distillers were quick to appreciate the advantages of this device, known both as the Patent Still and the Coffey Still. He moved his operations to London in 1835. His energy-saving heat exchanger continues to serve in many important commercial applications. **Susan McKenna-Lawlor**

Coffey, Brian (1905–1995), poet and diplomat. Born in Dublin; educated at UCD, where he met DENIS DEVLIN, with whom he published *Poems* (1930). He lived in London and Paris, where he came under the influence of modernism and became a lifelong friend of SAMUEL BECKETT; the poetry collection *Third Person* followed in 1937. In the late 1940s he taught philosophy in St Louis University, Missouri, USA, which inspired *Missouri Sequence* (1962). Following his return to England he continued his search for poetic expression. His highly acclaimed later work, *Advent* (1971) and *Death of Hektor* (1979), experimented with the visual effects of typographic treatment. Before his death in Southampton, *Poems and Versions, 1929–1990* (1991) was published. **Sandra O'Connell**

Coffey, Peter (1876–1943), theologian. Born near Innfield, Co. Meath; studied at the University of Louvain under Cardinal Mercier, whom he admired. From 1902 he was professor of general metaphysics at ST PATRICK'S COLLEGE, Maynooth. He published works on logic (1912) (WITTGENSTEIN's first published work is a hostile review of this book), ontology (1914), and epistemology (1917). An intelligent and compassionate idealist, he was for his time a radical social reformer, supporting trade unionism and, though qualifiedly, Christian socialism, and the ideas of JAMES CONNOLLY. He managed to publish his views on social questions despite certain difficulties with ecclesiastical censorship. **Thomas A. F. Kelly**

Cogadh Gáedhel re Gallaibh (the War of Gaedhil with the Gaill), a pseudo-historical account of VIKING activity in Ireland in the ninth and tenth centuries and in particular of the resistance to the invaders by BRIAN BÓRÚ and his brother Mathgamain, culminating in the victory of Brian's forces at the Battle of CLONTARF (1014). Though it is based in part on annalistic sources, the author deliberately reworked and considerably expanded the material at his disposal to create a heroic biography of Brian. The language and style of the text, as well as internal references, suggest that it was written at the behest of Brian's great-grandson MUIRCHERTACH (died 1119), who, by creating an illustrious past for his dynasty, sought to bolster his own claim to political power. In effect, therefore, it is a skilful piece of Uí Briain dynastic propaganda. **Máire Ní Mhaonaigh**

Cogan, Philip (c.1748–1833), composer. Born in Cork, he was organist of St Patrick's Cathedral, Dublin, 1780–1810. A noted pianist, he wrote twenty-one sonatas and two piano concertos, which progressively explore the resources of the piano and display both technical brilliance and an impressive sense of structure; the most notable Irish pianist before FIELD. **Richard Pine and Adrian Scahill**

Coigly, James (1761–1798), Catholic priest executed for high treason. Born in Kilmore, Co. Armagh; educated at the Lombard College, Paris. Returning to Ireland, following the outbreak of the FRENCH REVOLUTION in 1789, he quickly became involved in the political and sectarian strife, the so-called 'Armagh Troubles', that disturbed his native county. He was associated with the DEFENDERS, and there is evidence that he was involved in the UNITED IRISHMEN's attempts to forge an alliance between Catholics and Dissenters. He made several visits to England, attempting to secure the support of English radicals, and was finally arrested, along with ARTHUR O'CONNOR, as they were about to cross to France. He was convicted on incriminating evidence alleged to have been taken from his coat. Awaiting execution, he wrote a memoir exposing the tyranny suffered by his countrymen and the illegality of his sentence. He was hanged in Kent. **Daire Keogh**

Coimín, Mícheál (c. 1688–1760), poet. Born in Kilcorcoran, near Milltown Malbay, Co. Clare, a Protestant who supported JACOBITISM. He is best known for his poem 'Laoidh Oisín ar Thír na nÓg', first published for the OSSIANIC Society (1859); he also composed the prose romance 'Eachtra Thoroilbh mhic Stairn', numerous copies of which were written by GAELIC SCRIBES. **Meidhbhín Ní Úrdail**

Coimisiún Béaloideasa Éireann: see FOLKLORE COMMISSION, IRISH.

Coimisiún le Rincí Gaelacha (Commission for Irish Dances), set up by Conradh na Gaeilge (the Gaelic League) in 1929 to 'protect and promote Irish dancing.' It sought to establish a 'canon' of Irish dancing, which would provide the basis of a repertoire for the growing number of dancing schools under its auspices; it also published many of the old group dances, some of which are still danced at traditional céili. It continues to direct competitive dancing, both nationally and internationally, the high point of which is the annual World Irish Dancing Championship. [see IRISH DANCE COSTUME.] **Helen Brennan**

coinage. Coins were first minted in Ireland c. AD 995, under the authority of the Hiberno-NORSE King SITRIC III of Dublin. Silver pennies copied from Anglo-Saxon prototypes, they deteriorated in quality during the eleventh century. From c. 1100 they were replaced with even lighter, thinner coins, called *bracteates*, with a design on one side only. Under the ANGLO-NORMANS silver halfpennies and farthings were struck at several mints; and c. 1205 JOHN introduced a new issue of pennies, halfpennies, and farthings. The design featured a triangle on both sides, and this distinctive device remained a feature of Irish coins of the thirteenth century, after which production virtually ceased.

The production of coins began again in 1461 under Edward IV. During the following decades several designs and denominations were issued in Dublin, Limerick, Cork, Galway, Drogheda, and Trim. The groat and half-groat (4 pence and 2 pence, respectively) appeared, and copper halfpennies and farthings were issued for the first time. The harp first appeared on coins during the reign of HENRY VIII; it was also at this time that Irish coins were first dated. The silver content of the coins varied considerably during this period, and no official silver issues were struck after the reign of JAMES I (1603–25). The Great REBELLION (1641–53) caused the minting of several emergency issues of varying shape and design, in gold, silver, and copper, while the war between William III and James II (1689–92) saw the introduction of the infamous 'gun-money', emergency coins made from melted-down gun barrels, dated by month as well as by year. During the eighteenth century only copper halfpennies and farthings were issued.

In 1826 the Irish coinage came to an end, and for the next hundred years the only coins current in Ireland were the issues of the United Kingdom. In 1926, following independence, it was decided to produce a new coinage, and a committee under W. B. YEATS judged the suggested designs. The winning designs, those of the English sculptor Percy Metcalfe, were to remain essentially unaltered until decimalisation in 1971, when several denominations disappeared. The half-crown (2 shillings and 6 pence), sixpence, threepence and farthing went out of circulation, and two new denominations—50 pence and 2 pence—were struck. Later changes included the demise of the halfpenny, the issuing of a 20 pence coin in 1986, and the striking of a £1 coin in 1990. The Irish currency was replaced by the euro on 1 January 2002. [see BANKING; GABRIEL HAYES.] **Michael Kenny**

coinage. *A silver penny, one of the first Irish coins issued by Sitric Silkbeard, Norse King of Dublin and founder of Christ Church Cathedral. These pennies characteristically bore the head and name of Sitric as well as the word Dyflin (Dublin). [National Museum of Ireland]*

Colby, Thomas Frederick (1784–1852), surveyor. Born in Rochester, Kent; educated at the Royal Military Academy, Woolwich. In 1801 he was commissioned into the Royal Engineers, where, in 1846, he achieved the rank of major-general. In 1802 he joined the staff of the ORDNANCE SURVEY in England and proved to be a meticulous instrumental observer, despite serious injury and the loss of his left hand in a pistol explosion in 1803. He took charge of the Ordnance Survey in 1820 and, five years later, brought the Survey into Ireland. The resulting almost 2,000 sheets forming the 6-inch (1:10,560) county survey of Ireland are his crowning achievement. *Londonderry* (1833) was the first county to be published and *Kerry* (1846) the last, after which he retired. **Jean Archer**

Cole, Grenville Arthur James (1859–1924), geologist. Born in London; educated at the Royal School of Mines where, in 1880, he became demonstrator under Prof. John Wesley Judd, 1840–1916. In 1890 he was appointed professor of geology at the ROYAL COLLEGE OF SCIENCE FOR IRELAND. In 1904 he assumed the additional post of director of the GEOLOGICAL SURVEY OF IRELAND and in 1905 was in charge when its links with the Geological Survey of the United Kingdom were severed in the following year. He was a fine geologist whose eloquent writings did much to popularise both geology and geography. Though of stunted physique, he was an enthusiastic cyclist who travelled widely in Europe on two wheels. **Jean Archer**

Cole, William Willoughby, third Earl of Enniskillen (1807–1886), geologist. Born at FLORENCE COURT, Co. Fermanagh; educated at Harrow School (Middlesex) and the University of Oxford, where he studied geology under William Buckland. He formed a lifelong friendship with a fellow-student, Sir Philip Egerton of Oulton Park, Cheshire, with whom he collaborated in collecting fossil fish. Cole fitted out a room at Florence Court as a museum for his collection, which amounted to 10,000 fossil fish; leading geologists travelled to Florence Court to study the collection which, shortly before his death, he sold to the Natural History Museum, London, where it remains important to science. **Kenneth W. James**

Coleman, James (1941–), artist. Born in Ballaghadereen, Co. Roscommon; studied art at the NCAD and the history of art at UCD. After further periods of study in Paris, London, and Milan, he settled in Milan and remained there for twenty years. He works with light, sound, slides, video, and live performance. One of Ireland's foremost international artists, he has represented the country at various exhibitions since the Paris Biennale of 1973. Typical of his expressive use of rhythm and repetition is *Living and Presumed Dead* (1982–5), in the Musée Nationale d'Art Moderne, Paris, in which the imagery is visualised by way of an interaction of three carousel projectors. His work is not fixed in time, nor even necessarily finished when it leaves his studio as in *Strongbow* (1978), in the IRISH MUSEUM OF MODERN ART, Dublin: in 2001 he created a new installation of the work, in which he re-examines the context while projecting inherent continuity and 'non-finito.' **Paula Murphy**

Coleman, Michael (1891–1946), traditional fiddler. Born in Killavil, Co. Sligo; emigrated to America in 1914. His talent found expression among the Irish community in New York, leading to recordings on 78 r.p.m. records from 1921 to 1945. A step-dancer, he could accompany himself on stage; but it was his music on radio and gramophone that made his name, particularly when heard at home in Ireland. His playing became an incentive both to existing players and to learners, his phrasing, bowing, ornamentation, and repertoire establishing standards against which playing ability came to be judged. Though this contributed to the decline of regional styles of fiddling, it was not the only cause, and today the 'Coleman style' can be seen more as a strong, challenging playing fashion that itself owes much to the style of his home locality. Much of his music has been remastered on the recording *Michael Coleman*. **Fintan Vallely**

Coleraine (*Cúil Raithin*), Co. Derry, an administrative, market and university town on the River Bann; population (1991) 20,721. Despite evidence for ANGLO-NORMAN settlement in the immediate area between the twelfth and fourteenth centuries, the modern town dates from the Plantation of Derry. The streets radiating from the Diamond (central square) date from 1611, when the IRISH SOCIETY laid out a port on this site; but most of the surviving historical buildings are nineteenth-century and mark the town's modest prosperity as an agricultural market centre. Society Street, Beresford Place, and Waterford Place all mark the early influence of the Irish Society; but the most important focal buildings are the Town Hall (1859) and the Anglican parish church (rebuilt 1884). Badly damaged by an IRA bomb in the early 1990s, the town centre has been rebuilt and pedestrianised to provide a retail centre for much of east Derry and north Antrim. **Lindsay Proudfoot**

Colgan, Nathaniel (1851–1919), botanist. Born in Dublin; educated at the Incorporated School, Aungier Street. He wrote literary criticism and travel articles but his principal interest was in wildlife and led to his crowning achievement, *Flora of the County Dublin* (1904). This book not only catalogues the distribution of the wild plants but contributes to FOLKLORE studies by including a glossary of local names for the plants. He was also a major contributor to the all-Ireland flora *Cybele Hibernica* (1898) and to the CLARE ISLAND SURVEY (1911). He served as a clerk in the DUBLIN METROPOLITAN POLICE court until his retirement. **Christopher Moriarty**

collective bargaining, negotiations between an employer or group of employers and members or representatives of a TRADE UNION or group of unions. Typical issues include pay and non-pay benefits, terms and conditions of EMPLOYMENT, and procedural matters, including organisation of work and codes of conduct. Collective bargaining in the early twentieth century was limited in scope, localised in extent, and conflictive in character. In the Republic the Industrial Relations Act (1946), which established the Labour Court, helped establish collective bargaining on a firmer footing, though still wholly voluntary. Pay bargaining took the form of pay 'rounds' of varying degrees of formalisation from the late 1940s onwards. At the enterprise level, collective bargaining became more professionalised from the 1960s, when larger firms developed personnel management functions. The rise of national-level bargaining did not displace company-level collective bargaining, though it altered the context and substance of negotiations.

The growth of high-technology industry and of private-sector services resulted in an increase in the number of enterprises that do not recognise unions. It has been argued that enterprise-level collective bargaining since the 1980s was influenced by a 'new realism' in European industrial relations, involving a decline in adversarial collective bargaining and an acceptance that the success of the enterprise requires a co-operative stance. Some firms, both unionised and non-unionised, have adopted a 'human resources management' approach to the employment relationship. However, employee relations and pay negotiations in non-union firms are frequently individualised rather than subject to collective bargaining. [see NATIONAL PAY AGREEMENTS; SOCIAL PARTNERSHIP.] **Niamh Hardiman**

Colleen Bawn, The (1860), a melodrama by DION BOUCICAULT, based on GERALD GRIFFIN's novel THE COLLEGIANS (1829). A tale of doomed entanglement between a peasant girl and a young landowner, its Co. Kerry setting, rescue scene, and comic turns of Myles-na-Copaleen made the play a favourite up to the 1920s. [see HANLEY, ELLEN.] **Christopher Morash**

Collegians, The (1829), a novel by GERALD GRIFFIN. Based on the real murder of the sixteen-year-old Ellen Hanley by John Scanlan in 1818 in Co. Limerick, it is a tragic romance, in which the necessities of the rural class system frustrate the possibilities of love. Eily O'Connor, daughter of a ropemaker, has secretly married the volatile Hardress Cregan, of a marginal gentry background. But he is pressured into an engagement with his prosperous cousin, Anne Chute. Now an embarrassment, O'Connor is drowned by Cregan's servant, who, when apprehended, denounces Cregan as his provocateur. Cregan is sent into exile on a convict ship, while Chute marries the steadier Kyrle Daly, son of a middleman. BOUCICAULT's play THE COLLEEN BAWN (1860) and Sir Julius Benedict's opera *The Lily of Killarney* (1862) are both adaptations of the novel. **James H. Murphy**

Colleran, Enda (c. 1942–), Gaelic footballer. Born in Moylough, Co. Galway. He gained early prominence when he won an All-Ireland minor championship in 1960 on a team that would form the basis for one of the finest senior teams in history. He was corner-back on the Galway team that won three All-Ireland championships in a row between 1964 and 1966. He was also captain of the team for the second and third victories. He played for his province when Connacht won the Railway Cup in 1967. **Donal Keenan**

Colles, Abraham (1773–1843), surgeon. Born in Millmount, near Kilkenny; educated at TCD, RCSI, Edinburgh, and London. He became surgeon to DR STEEVENS' HOSPITAL. Skilled in anatomy and surgery, he held chairs in both subjects and was elected president of the RCSI. He described the details of a common fracture at the wrist—'Colles's fracture'. **J. B. Lyons**

Collins brothers, John and Cornelius (fl. 1916–20), seamen. Born in Carrigaline, Co. Cork. Twin sons of a poor tenant farmer, they joined the British navy at its nearby Haulbowline base in Cork and quickly drew the attention of their officers through their intelligence and initiative. When the Japanese emperor decided in 1873 that his country needed a large and modern navy, he obtained from Haulbowline a party of thirty-four instructors. After four years of exemplary effort the brothers were kept on in Japan at the request of the local naval command, and they remained there until 1888, by which time the Japanese empire had a well-equipped and well-trained navy. In Japan the extraordinary influence of the brothers is fully recognised, and the meticulous notes they drew up for the lectures given daily have survived as proof. They received from the emperor the unprecedented honour for commoners of the Order of the Rising Sun. In 1994 the Japanese ambassador to Ireland unveiled a plaque at Carrigaline to the memory of the brothers. **John de Courcy Ireland**

Collins, Finghin (1977–), pianist. Born in Dublin, he studied at the RIAM with JOHN O'CONOR, DCU, and at the Geneva Conservatoire with Dominique Merlet. He won the RTÉ MUSICIAN OF THE FUTURE competition. His international career was launched in 1999 when he won the Clara Haskil International Piano Competition, indicating his status as one of the most exceptional talents among young Irish musicians. **Richard Pine**

Collins, Michael (1890–1922), revolutionary. Born in Co. Cork; educated at Lisavaird National School. He emigrated to London at the age of fifteen and worked in the Post Office. Becoming involved in the GAA, GAELIC LEAGUE, and IRB, he fought in Dublin in the 1916 RISING and was afterwards interned in Wales. He became head of the IRB, a position of great influence and control, and Minister for Finance in the DÁIL Government in 1919, in which capacity he successfully raised Dáil loans in Ireland and the United States. When DE VALERA went to America, Collins became *de facto* leader of the entire revolutionary movement. His key role was that of director of organisation and intelligence for the IRISH VOLUNTEERS (soon to become known as the IRISH REPUBLICAN ARMY). He displayed an extraordinary ability to penetrate the British security apparatus in Ireland; he had many British agents killed and played a central role in convincing the British that the Irish leaders would have to be negotiated with.

Collins went to London as part of the delegation that negotiated and signed the ANGLO-IRISH TREATY in December 1921. The terms were immediately denounced by de Valera but were passed in the Dáil on 7 January 1922 after an impassioned debate. Collins became chairman of the Provisional Government formed to administer the twenty-six counties of 'Southern Ireland' until the formal establishment of the IRISH FREE STATE. Tensions over the Treaty split were heightened when anti-Treatyites occupied the FOUR COURTS in Dublin in April 1922. On 28 June, under severe pressure from London, Collins authorised the attack on the Four Courts that marked the beginning of the CIVIL WAR (see p. 533). He assumed the position of commander-in-chief of Government forces. While on a tour of duty in his native west Cork he was killed in an ambush at Bealnablagh, near Macroom.

Collins was perhaps the outstanding talent of the Irish revolution, combining formidable powers as administrator, soldier, negotiator, counter-intelligence chief, and ruthless terrorist. He has since become recognised as a founding father of Irish democratic independence. **Tom Garvin**

Collins, Patrick (1910–1994), painter. Born in Dromore West, Co. Sligo; self-taught. He worked in an insurance company for twenty-two years before devoting himself full time to painting. In 1958 he was selected for the Guggenheim Exhibition in New York. Considered one of the most interesting Irish landscapists, he has an individual vision of the land shrouded in grey mist. Towards the end of his life he lived in the south of France, where his palette became more colourful and his painting more abstract. He was a member of AOSDÁNA and a *saoi*. **Dorothy Walker**

Collis, (William) Robert Fitzgerald (1900–1975), physician. Born in Dublin; educated at the University of Cambridge, Yale University, Trinity College Hospital, London, and Johns Hopkins Hospital, Baltimore, Maryland. He became director of the Department of Paediatrics at the ROTUNDA HOSPITAL, Dublin, in 1932 and physician to the National Children's Hospital, 1932–57. He took up a position as head of paediatrics at the University of Ibadan, Nigeria, in 1957. He had an abiding interest in literature and wrote a successful play, *Marrowbone Lane* (1943), which dealt with the poverty of the Dublin slums; he was the first to recognise

Collins, Michael. *The body of Collins lying in state in Dublin City Hall. Collins was shot dead in an ambush at Bealnablagh, Co. Cork, on 22 August 1922 during the Civil War that followed the signing of the Anglo-Irish treaty. [Getty Images/Hulton Archive]*

the potential of the writer CHRISTY BROWN. He was a brother of the authors John Stewart Collis and Maurice Stewart Collis. **Davis Coakley**

'Colloquy of the Old Men': see 'ACALLAMH NA SEÁNÓRACH'.

Colmán mac Léníni (died c. 606), poet and cleric. Reputed founder of the monastery of CLOYNE, he was apparently a late entrant to monastic life. A small number of verses attributed to him survive, including a poem of gratitude for the receipt of a sword ('Luin oc elaib') from a certain Domnall and an elegy on the death of Aed Sláine (died 604). **Ruairí Ó hUiginn**

Colm Cille, also known by the Latinised name Columba/Columb (c. 521–597), monk, MISSIONARY, and founder and first abbot of IONA (see p. 1112). He was the great-great-grandson of NIALL OF THE NINE HOSTAGES. We have few details of the life of this saint, who was a figure of major importance in the development of CHRISTIANITY in Ireland; what we know of him derives almost entirely from ADOMNÁN's 'Vita Columbae', which, though it is based on solid traditions within his monastery and earlier written accounts, was written almost a century after Colm Cille's death and portrays him in idealised terms as the perfect disciple, specially chosen by God, and given 'prophetic revelations' and the power 'to work miracles' and receive 'angelic visitations' (second preface). Since the Vita is episodic, without a chronological frame (though Colm Cille's death is at its end), much of our information comes from this statement: 'From his youth he devoted himself to growing in the Christian life, with God's help studying wisdom and keeping his body chaste ... [and] he spent thirty-four years as an island soldier of Christ' (second preface). We know that he studied with Finnian of CLONARD and then founded several monasteries in Ireland before setting out in 563 for Iona, which became the centre for a large *familia* of monasteries in Ireland and Britain. Being on Iona made him 'a pilgrim for Christ' and allowed him to engage in missionary work among the Picts. He established many contacts, both with other monasteries (such as BANGOR) and with rulers such as the Pictish King Brude. By the time of his death Iona was an important monastic centre, forming a link between Ireland, Strathclyde, and Northumbria; and this importance grew during the following two centuries.

Many aspects of insular monastic spirituality—such as the special place of islands—can be traced to the inspiration of Colm Cille, and he may have inspired others (for example COLUMBANUS) to combine the notion of monastic exile with that of missionary work. Traditionally several Latin hymns, such as the 'Altus Prosator', have been attributed to him, and his authorship cannot be excluded; Adomnán presents him as both a scholar and a scribe. Legend, reaching back almost to his lifetime, revered him as a patron of poets. [see MISSIONARY ACTIVITY.] **Thomas O'Loughlin**

Colum, Pádraic (1881–1972), writer. Born in Longford; educated at Glasthule National School, Co. Dublin. He worked as a clerk in the Irish Railway Clearing House and was a founder-member of the National Theatre Society and editor of *Irish Review*, 1912–13. His early plays were produced in the ABBEY THEATRE. He emigrated to the United States in 1914, working as an editor, author, and lecturer. His stories in the children's column of the *New York Sunday Tribune* further established him as a writer, with Anne

Carroll Moore of the New York Public Library promoting his work. It ranges from retellings of traditional tales and myths, such as *The Girl Who Sat by the Ashes*, to autobiographical works, such as *A Boy in Éirinn* and *The Big Tree of Bunlahy*. In the latter works he both recaptures his own childhood and explains Ireland to young American readers. His writing is truthful, direct, and simple, with evocative description and dialogue that is lively and playful. *The Poet's Cicuits: Collected Poems of Ireland* (1960) contains his best-known poem, 'An Old Woman of the Roads'. **Patricia Donlon**

Columbanus, Latinised name of Colmán (c. 543–615), most famous of the medieval *peregrini* on the Continent. What we know of him comes from a *Vita* written by Jonas of Bobbio soon after his death, from later lives of his companion St GALL, and from what we can glean from his own writings. He was born in Leinster, and from Jonas we learn that he studied with Sinell (Vita 1:3) and later with Comhghall at BANGOR (Vita 1:4), becoming learned in Latin and in the Scriptures. The quality of this education is borne out in Columbanus's writings (he is the first Irish writer with a sizeable surviving corpus), which show him as a skilled theologian. About 590–91 (the dating is controversial) he arrived in Gaul, and King Guntram gave him land in the Vosges, where he established several monasteries and convents, Luxeuil being the most famous. These houses quickly developed a reputation for the rigour of their monastic observance, which is reflected in his *Regulae* and a Penitential that survive in later forms.

In 603 Columbanus came into conflict with the local bishops. They claimed that the problem was his Irish method of dating EASTER, but clearly this also involved his recognition of their authority and his attacks on what he saw as their degenerate morals. He refused to appear before them at a council and appealed directly to ROME for support. His letter to the Pope is interesting, as it reveals on the part of one born in the far west a perception of Europe (Vita 1:2) as a Christian cultural unit focused on Rome (Ep. 1:1). Seven years later Columbanus fell foul of the local ruler, King Theuderic, who, to secure the succession of his kingdom, recognised his illegitimate sons. Columbanus refused to bless these, and Theuderic in response expelled him—an action undoubtedly welcomed by the local clergy. Having left Luxeuil, Columbanus and a group of monks passed into Nuestria (southern Gaul) and the region of modern Switzerland; there is evidence to link him with Zürich, Bregenz, and Chur. Finally, c. 612, he arrived at Bobbio in northern Italy and established a monastery there, where he spent his last years. The authenticity of some writings attributed to him has been the subject of a long-running dispute. [see MISSIONARY ACTIVITY.] **Thomas O'Loughlin**

Colum Cille type, an Irish printing type. In the early 1930s Colm Ó Lochlainn began the production of an Irish type for use at his Three Candles Press, Dublin. He had his assistant, Karl Uhlemann, prepare the initial designs, based on half-uncial letter-forms and the earlier round PETRIE TYPE, working closely with Stanley Morison of the Monotype Corporation in England. The typeface, which he named after the scribe COLM CILLE, was finally made available towards the end of the decade, at a time when the need for printing types in the Irish character was being questioned. As a consequence it was not widely used outside the Three Candles Press. **Dermot McGuinne**

'come-all-ye', a term used to describe any old-fashioned song in English in popular currency. In North America the term referred to Irish songs, traditional or vaudeville. 'Come all ye' was a formulaic device commonly used by writers of narrative songs to gain the attention of their listeners: 'Come all ye Roman Catholics of high and low degree,' or 'Come all you loyal heroes and listen unto me.' The singer then let his audience know the subject of the song, the first verse acting as a prologue or overture:

> Come all ye young fellows who follow the gun,
> Beware of going shooting by the late-setting sun.
> It could happen to anyone, as it happened to me,
> To shoot your own true love in under a tree.

The form was much favoured by street singers to attract a passing audience to buy their broadsheets. **Tom Munnelly**

comedy. Irish people have long been celebrated for humour, on the one hand for their literary tradition and a reputation for cleverness and wit, on the other as the butt of jokes—the illogical, drunken, fighting Paddy. Some of the characteristics that inform Irish comedy are STORYTELLING and a love of words, a delight in the absurd or fantastic, a dark streak and sense of the macabre, a predilection for 'slagging' or teasing, and apparent obsessions with religion, alcohol, and politics.

The type of comedy that can be defined as 'front-cloth', 'sketch', or 'stand-up'—individual comedians or troupes connecting directly with the audience and often extemporising—began in the era of the music-halls, c. 1860, climaxing about the turn of the century in the golden years of that form of robust entertainment. Music-hall began in England as an elaboration of the amateur 'turns' previously offered in the back rooms of pubs; it soon crossed the sea to become hugely popular in Ireland, at the QUEEN'S ROYAL THEATRE, Dan Lowrey's (later the OLYMPIA), and THEATRE ROYAL in

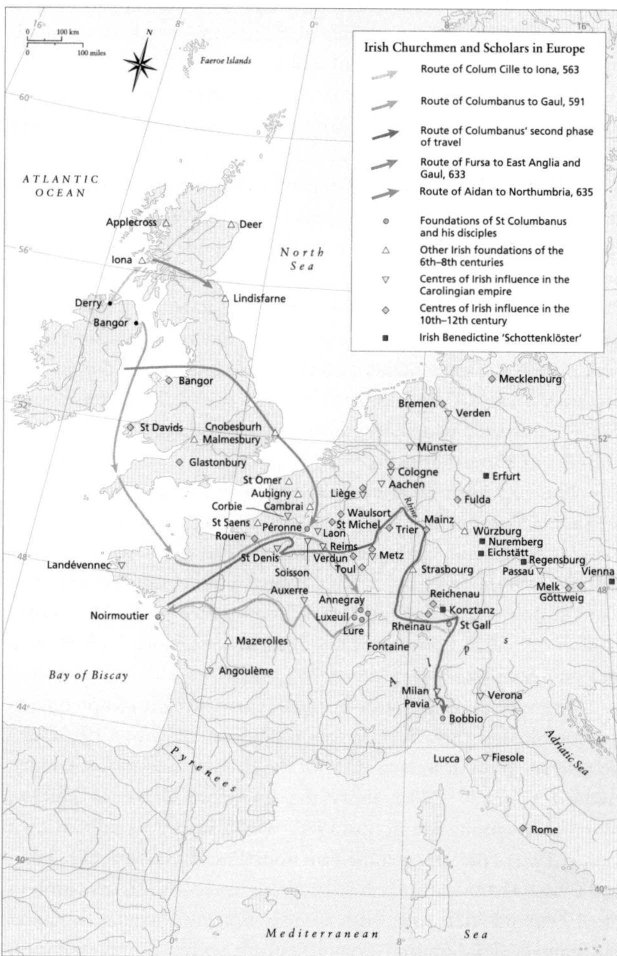

Dublin, CORK OPERA HOUSE, the Empire Theatre and Grand Opera House in Belfast, and many others. Ireland produced a number of music-hall comedians in this period—such as Johnny Patterson, the Clare bagpiper and clown—but the stars were visiting artists from England, some of whom were of Irish origin. The famous Dan Leno was born George Galvin in London of Irish parents and began his career billed as 'the Quintessence of Irish Comedians'.

Music-hall developed into twice-nightly variety around the end of the FIRST WORLD WAR. Partly because of the political situation, visiting British acts became less frequent in the 1920s and a more distinctly Irish trend in comedy developed; on the outbreak of the SECOND WORLD WAR, British touring acts dried up further, leading to the emergence of more local artists, mainly in Dublin. The greatest of the variety comedians was JIMMY O'DEA, who, especially in his 'Biddy Mulligan' character, captured the nuances and subtleties of working-class Dublin life. Through the 1930s, 40s and 50s more Irish comedians came to the fore in variety and PANTOMIME, among them Danny Cummins, Cecil Sheridan, Noel Purcell, Eddie Byrne, Jack Cruise, MAUREEN POTTER, and Harry Bailey. Some also became famous in England, either as variety artists or (especially Purcell and Byrne) as comic character actors in films.

When variety declined in the late 1950s and early 60s a new breed of Irish humour became popular: the club or cabaret comedian. Notable exponents include Hal Roach and, later, Brendan Grace, who has had a long dual career in Ireland and the United States. Irish comedians working in England at the time—Frank Carson, Jimmy Cricket, and others—tended to pander to 'Oirish' stereotypes; in this they were following in a tradition of 'stage-Irish' acts of the variety years, such as 'Old Mother Riley', who fostered a boisterous, sentimental, whimsical, aggressive, and hard-drinking image. The first Irish comedian in England to break this mould, and the first to work in more observational comedy, was the enormously successful DAVE ALLEN, who appeared in a number of television series in the 1970s, portraying a more realistic Irishman: an urbane, thoughtful, analytical character, though still preoccupied with sex and religion. In Ireland, gentle satire achieved great popularity with the television series 'Hall's Pictorial Weekly', which ran for twelve years, presented by Frank Hall and featuring sketches with Frank Kelly, Éamonn Morrissey, 'Cha and Miah', and others. On the stage the revues of ROSALEEN LINEHAN and Des Keogh, written by Fergus Linehan, were satirical and very popular. In the early 1990s the remarkable DERMOT MORGAN, with the writer-producer GERARD STEMBRIDGE, devised the satirical radio series 'Scrap Saturday', which was innovative and daring and achieved critical and popular acclaim.

The comedian most associated with Northern Ireland in the 1960s and 70s was Jimmy Young, whose range of characters—one being 'Orange Lil'—gave an insight into Protestant working-class attitudes. More recently, young comics at the Empire Comedy Club in Belfast have defiantly laughed in the face of danger, and the Hole in the Wall Gang have also challenged stereotypes, both live and on television.

The type of new, youth-oriented, alternative stand-up comedy that dominated comedy internationally from the early 1980s was slow to catch on in Ireland. One of the first successes was the long-running Comedy Cellar above the International Bar in Dublin, founded by young comics in 1988, which became a cult student venue. Two of the young comedians from those days, Ardal O'Hanlon and DYLAN MORAN, went on to become stars on British television in the 1990s and afterwards. Irish comedy became a regular fixture at the influential Edinburgh Fringe Festival, with a number of Irish comedians winning the prestigious Perrier Award, including Seán Hughes, Tommy Tiernan, and Dylan Moran. Further success came with 'Father Ted', a brilliantly surreal and influential situation comedy about three priests written by Arthur Mathews and Graham Linehan and broadcast first on Channel 4, featuring Dermot Morgan, Ardal O'Hanlon, and Frank Kelly, with Pauline McLynn as their housekeeper. Together or separately, Mathews and Linehan went on to write more comedy series for British television.

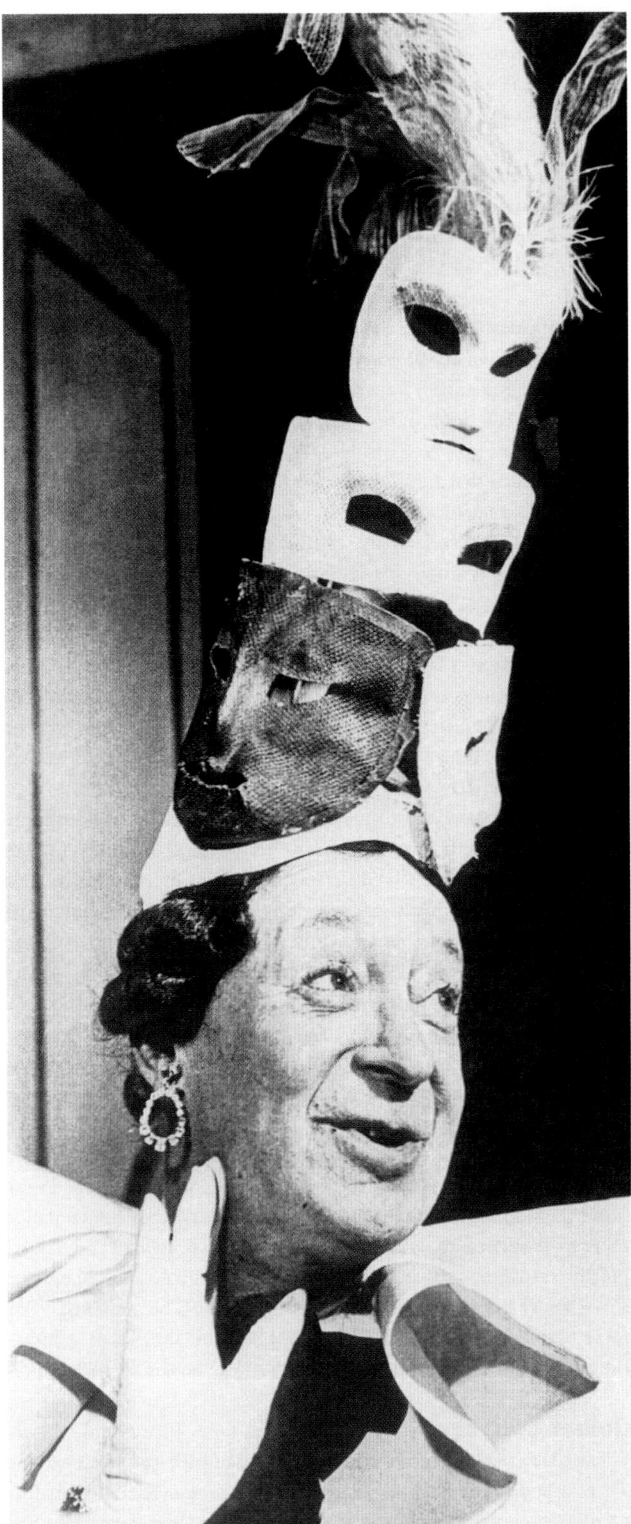

comedy. *Jimmy O'Dea as a pantomime dame in* Goody Two-Shoes *at the Gaiety Theatre, Dublin, 1962. [Dublin City Council/City Archives]*

On Irish television, comedy was notably less successful, with some exceptions, including 'Nighthawks' (1988–92), the spoof sports commentary of 'Apres Match' in the 1990s, and the mock documentary 'Paths to Freedom' (2000). The risqué gay former actor and stand-up comedian Graham Norton also won big television audiences in Britain as a camp chat-show host; Patrick Kielty moved from hard-hitting political satire in Belfast to mainstream television; Ed Byrne had stand-up and television success internationally; and the Derry comedian Jimeoin became a star of Australian stage and television.

One of the characteristics of Irish comedy in the late twentieth and early twenty-first centuries was its diversity, from the rural, character-based shows of D'Unbelievables (Jon Kenny and Pat Shortt) and the storytelling of Owen O'Neill, Tommy Tiernan, and Kevin McAleer to the blue-collar bravado of Brendan O'Carroll. **Stephen Dixon and Deirdre Falvey**

'comely maidens', used as a shorthand reference to the traditional view of women's place in Irish society, taken from ÉAMON DE VALERA's historic 'vision of Ireland' speech printed in the IRISH PRESS on 18 March 1943. In it he stated that 'the Ireland that we dreamed of would be a land whose countryside would be bright with cosy homesteads, whose fields and villages would be joyous with the sounds of industry, with the romping of sturdy children, the contests of athletic youths, the laughter of comely maidens, whose firesides would be the forums for the wisdom of serene old age.' This popular and romanticised view of Ireland, postulated by de Valera in the middle of the SECOND WORLD WAR, as a place that is simple and rural was an anachronism then and has been challenged by the processes of modernisation, URBANISATION, and SECULARISATION. **Maura Adshead**

Comerford, Joe (1949–), film director and writer. Born in Dublin. He was one of a group, including BOB QUINN, CATHAL BLACK, and PAT MURPHY, who made culturally and socially critical films in the 1970s and 80s. His dark and sombre style usually deals with marginalised people: the working class in *Down the Corner* (1977), drug addicts in *Withdrawal* (1982), the travelling people in *Traveller* (1981), social and political outcasts in *Reefer and the Model* (1987), and victims of the Northern 'TROUBLES' in *High Boot Benny* (1993). **Kevin Rockett**

Comhairle Ealaíon An: see ARTS COUNCIL.

Comhairle Mhic Clámha ó Achadh na Muileann, a seventeenth-century satirical text allegedly composed by Father Eoghan Ó Donghaile c. 1680. The work satirises the poor education and lack of learning among the Catholic clergy in Cos. Monaghan and Cavan in the late seventeenth century. **Ciarán Mac Murchaidh**

Comhaltas Ceoltóirí Éireann, the principal organisation for those involved in TRADITIONAL MUSIC. It was formed in June 1951 by musicians concerned about the rapid decline of the music, among them members of the DUBLIN PIPERS' CLUB: Jim Seery, Jack Naughton, and LEO ROWSOME. Their meeting with other interested people at Mullingar led to a gathering of musicians from all over Ireland and the establishment of a steering organisation; in 1952 the name Comhaltas Ceoltóirí Éireann was adopted. In the same year the first FLEADH CHEOIL was held, at Monaghan. In 1956 a constitution was adopted; in 1960 a provincial structure was instituted, with local and county branches, provincial councils, and an Ard-Chomhairle at national level. An annual congress elects the officers, though in practice the organisation is managed by an executive director, a post created in 1968 (though not provided for in its constitution) and occupied since then by LABHRÁS Ó MURCHÚ.

CCÉ publishes recordings as well as books and pamphlets relating to the music and its performers; it also has a quarterly magazine, TREOIR, edited by Ó Murchú. It is administered from the Cultúrlann at Monkstown, Co. Dublin, and also has eleven regional music centres. Its aims are the promotion of traditional music, song, and dancing, particularly the revival of the HARP and the UILLEANN PIPES. It addresses itself also to the broader field of national culture. It claims some 600 branches, some in areas of Irish EMIGRATION and cultural influence abroad, notably in the United States and Britain but also in Europe and Japan. These teach music and dancing and organise local fleadhanna ceoil and other music functions within a network that sustains group identity and social life. The fact that membership is open to non-musicians frees players from the burden of organisational chores but at the same time has created a structure that is largely run on their behalf. CCÉ in its constitution pledges itself to 'co-operate with all bodies working for the restoration of Irish culture.' In its fifty years it has contributed greatly to the revival of the music, the fleadh cheoil being its principal intervention, which is of significant cultural and economic value to the various regions in which it is held. In addition it functions as a galvaniser of national identity and social cohesion among people of Irish descent overseas, both through the regional fleadhanna ceoil and through touring cabaret shows. [see TRADITIONAL MUSIC IN NORTH AMERICA.] **Fintan Vallely**

Comhar (1942–), a monthly review for literature and current affairs, founded by the intervarsity organisation An Comhchaidreamh. It introduced a new generation of Irish writers and was directed at educated readers; it continues to encourage new writing in Irish. Its best-known editor was BREANDÁN Ó HEITHIR; illustrious contributors have included SEÁN Ó RÍORDÁIN, MÁIRTÍN Ó DIREÁIN, MÁIRTÍN Ó CADHAIN, ALAN TITLEY, and Seán Mac Mathúna. **Caoilfhionn Nic Pháidín**

Comhlámh, a voluntary organisation founded in 1975 by returned development workers to support aid workers returning to Ireland. It enables volunteers to readjust to life in Ireland by providing information on SOCIAL WELFARE and careers and offers a means to share experiences gathered overseas through its support groups and counselling. It also promotes solidarity with the developing world and with refugees in Ireland. Membership is open to anybody with an interest in development issues. **Martin Clancy**

Commissioners of Irish Lights, founded in 1867 to provide navigation aids around the coast of Ireland. The service is supported by 'light dues' paid by shipowners. In addition to lights and LIGHTHOUSES (see pp. 385, 597), all now automated, the Commissioners maintain aids such as buoys and light-floats, as well as the service craft required to maintain them. There are now eighty automated lighthouses (twenty-one with radar beacons), 132 buoys, fifty beacons and perches, seven helicopter shore bases, and the support vessel *Granuaile*. The last permanently manned lighthouse was the Baily Lighthouse at Howth, Co. Dublin, automated in 1997.

New technologies, such as satellite positioning systems and electronic charts, are revolutionising navigation. In recent years, obligations to a wider community have been increasingly recognised. Solar and other forms of renewable energy are now widely

Comhar. *Cover of the December 2001 issue of the literary journal* Comhar, *founded in 1942, featuring one of its prominent contributors, Máirtín Ó Cadhain. [Comhar]*

used, with innovative wind and solar technology used to power offshore buoys, and ways are sought to preserve lighthouses, machinery, and buildings where they contribute to the national heritage. [see KISH BANK LIGHTHOUSE.] **Fiacc OBrolchain**

Commission for Irish Dances: see COIMISIÚN LE RINCÍ GAELACHA.

Committee for Quaternary Research in Ireland, convened by ANTHONY FARRINGTON at the behest of ROBERT LLOYD PRAEGER and Adolf Mahr of the NATIONAL MUSEUM. It first met under the auspices of the ROYAL IRISH ACADEMY on 25 January 1933. The Committee numbered fourteen, its leading members being Praeger, chairman, Farrington, secretary, and Henry Joseph Seymour (1873–1954), treasurer. Its objective was the furtherance of an understanding of Ireland's Quaternary history (the most recent geological period, spanning the last 2 million years); to that end Knud Jessen (1884–1971) of Copenhagen was invited to visit Ireland during the summer of 1934 to study the stratigraphy of Irish BOGS and to train two young Irish geologists in the associated techniques involved, one of whom was G. FRANK MITCHELL. Jessen's visit laid the foundation for modern study of the Irish Quaternary. In 1940 the committee passed its responsibilities to the Royal Irish Academy. **Gordon L. Herries Davies**

commonages. There is a total of approximately 500,000 ha (1.2 million acres) of LAND in Ireland either owned in common or with common grazing rights; this is less than 12 per cent of all land farmed. It is estimated that 11,600 farms use commonage; their average size is 37 ha (91 acres). Commonage is to be found mainly in mountainous and marginal areas in the western counties of Donegal, Mayo, Galway, south and west Kerry, and west Cork; but most counties have some of their land area in commonage.

Present-day commonages arose from estates divided by the Land Commission during the 1890s and the early twentieth century. When land was being divided in lowland areas adjacent to a commonage, farmers were allocated a share of the common land, defined or undefined (as was previously exercised). Around a particular commonage there might be a division of twenty farms, each of which might be allocated one-twentieth. Over time some farms were sold, with the commonage share being part of the sale. In some instances farmers may have bought or inherited all the shares, which meant that the land was no longer a commonage.

Commonages are normally attached to the land folio of the farm. However, there are some farmers who farm land in common but do not own the land; they may simply have a right to graze a certain number of sheep. The Land Commission divided some commonages, but only by agreement among all the shareholders. Much of this land was subsequently reclaimed and became productive.

In recent times there has been much debate about overgrazing by sheep in some commonage areas. This problem is now being tackled through commonage framework plans, whereby each commonage is assessed on sustainable stocking levels. Most commonages are in areas of high amenity, and many are designated special areas of conservation under the EU Habitats Directive. **Gerry Gunning**

Common Agricultural Policy (CAP), established under the Treaty of Rome (1957), which was signed by the six original member-states of the European Economic Community. Ireland joined the EEC in 1973. It was the early 1960s before the principal decisions on the mechanisms of the CAP were taken. Article 39 of the Treaty of Rome laid down the underlying objectives, which can be summarised as increasing agricultural productivity, securing a fair standard of living for those employed in AGRICULTURE, and securing a food supply at stable and reasonable prices to consumers.

The CAP was designed to operate through two sets of policy instruments. Price and market policy incorporates such measures as guaranteed prices to producers, levies on imports and refunds on exports, an 'intervention' system under which the authorities buy up agricultural produce at guaranteed prices (which is then stored and subsequently sold), and direct payments to producers and supply controls. The second set of instruments relates to socio-structural policy, which is concerned with improving the structure of agriculture and the modernisation of farming. The costs are financed partly through the taxpayer, by means of national and EU budgets, and partly by the consumer, through higher food prices. Historically, price support was the dominant mechanism through which European farmers were assisted, and they responded enthusiastically with increased productivity. Even in the early years of its implementation in the 1960s the supply of many agricultural commodities was outstripping demand, and the budgetary costs of disposing of these surpluses was increasing rapidly. Consequently, the CAP was not long in operation before attempts were made to reform it, and this process is likely to continue for as long as the policy exists. Early attempts at reform of the policy in the 1970s were concerned with modest decreases in the guaranteed prices paid to producers, but these proved to be of little use in correcting growing imbalances between supply and demand for many commodities. In the mid-1980s the European Commission extended the use of supply control with the introduction of the milk quota system, which proved to be an effective method of curbing production. However, production in other sectors continued to expand. A more radical set of reforms was implemented under the MACSHARRY package of 1992. This consisted of substantial cuts in the support prices paid to farmers, which were offset by increases in direct payments, the extension of supply control to livestock and cereals, and a set of accompanying measures related to afforestation, farm retirement, and improving the rural environment.

The most recent round of reform, known as 'Agenda 2000', is to some extent a continuation of the 1992 reforms, in that it is based on further price cuts, accompanied by compensation in the form of direct payments and additional supply control but with an increased emphasis on environmental considerations and RURAL DEVELOPMENT.

Agricultural policy in the Republic and in Northern Ireland has been integrated in the CAP since Ireland and Britain joined the EEC in 1973. The agricultural industry in both jurisdictions is characterised by similar structural, CLIMATE, and market conditions and is subject to the same general agricultural policies, with some minor differences in implementation. Consequently it is not surprising that, for much of the period of its operation, the CAP has had a similar impact on the pattern of farm incomes in both the Republic and the North. However, throughout the 1990s farm incomes in Northern Ireland were considerably more variable, while those in the Republic have been almost static in real terms. The dramatic fall in agricultural incomes in the North since the mid-1990s can be accounted for by a combination of reasons, such as the outbreak of BSE and unfavourable movements in exchange rates. **Deirdre O'Connor**

Commonwealth government. OLIVER CROMWELL was nominally LORD LIEUTENANT as well as commander-in-chief of the army while in Ireland, and a civil administration was established in October 1650, with the appointment by the English Parliament of four commissioners. In reality, however, nothing was implemented until the military conquest was completed and CHARLES FLEETWOOD was appointed Principal Commissioner of Government in July 1652. Ireland was integrated with England in the Act of Union (1653), under which thirty Irish members sat in the three Cromwellian Parliaments, 1654, 1656, and 1659. Elections were held for these seats, but the government ensured that only safe men were returned. Though the Irish Parliament was abolished, a separate Irish executive was retained. A common economic policy was not operated, and Ireland was denied the benefits of free trade. In July 1654 Fleetwood, who favoured the radicals, was made Lord Deputy, and a Council of State of six members was established. HENRY CROMWELL was added to this council later in the year, and he exerted a moderating influence after Fleetwood was forced to return to England in September 1654. Henry Cromwell came to Ireland in 1655, though he was not formally made Lord Deputy until 1657 and was made Lord Lieutenant in 1658. Except for the crucial areas of LAND and RELIGION, only very general lines of policy were laid down in the instructions given to both Fleetwood and Cromwell, and as a consequence both men largely determined policy in Ireland. [see CROMWELLIAN LAND SETTLEMENT.] **Liam Irwin**

communal violence, 1920–24. Intercommunal violence became general throughout Ireland after 1919, the inevitable consequence of an increasing struggle not just between republicans, unionists, and the United Kingdom but also between and within communities. Communal violence was primarily directed against local minorities, with the aim of suppressing or uprooting perceived enemies within. Between 1920 and 1924 Catholics in the north-east and Protestants elsewhere became the object of threats, robbery, arson, and murder. The great majority were innocent of any hostile acts. Thousands of Northern Catholics, mostly in Belfast, were displaced from homes and work-places, as were thousands of Southern Protestants. However, while Catholics typically sought refuge within Northern Ireland, Protestants more often left the Free State for Britain or the British colonies. In this way the Southern minority lost a third of its population, while the North's fell by only 2 per cent. Nevertheless the events of 1920–24 did not constitute 'ethnic cleansing'; no state, party, church, or army attempted or considered such an all-out campaign or promulgated such an ideology. Violence fell far short of eliminationist levels, and very few minorities, if any, disappeared outright. FREE STATE soldiers defended Protestant households in Munster during the years after the CIVIL WAR ceasefire. After the revolution, both minorities were tolerated by the new states, so long as neither challenged their officially majoritarian identities. [see WAR OF INDEPENDENCE.] **Peter Hart**

communism. The first Communist Party of Ireland (CPI) was established in 1921 by JAMES CONNOLLY's son, Roddy. It supported the anti-Treaty IRA in the CIVIL WAR but remained minuscule and was disbanded by the Moscow-based Communist International in 1923 in favour of JIM LARKIN's Irish Worker League. When that languished, a second CPI was launched in 1933 by Larkin's son, Jim Larkin Junior. It attracted militant workers and left-wing republicans, but in 1941 it disbanded its Southern section, with former members joining the LABOUR PARTY to promote Ireland's entry to the SECOND WORLD WAR. The Northern rump supported Britain's war effort, adopted neo-unionist policies, and went on to promote a civil rights agenda. The Irish Workers' League (later Irish WORKERS' PARTY) was established in the Republic in 1947, merging with the Communist Party of Northern Ireland in 1970 to form the third CPI. It faded rapidly with the demise of Soviet-style communism in the 1990s. **Mike Milotte**

Communist Party of Ireland (CPI), a successor to JAMES CONNOLLY's Socialist Party of Ireland, formed in 1921 and dissolved in 1924. Re-established in 1933 on the basis of the Revolutionary Workers' Groups, it divided into two sections during the SECOND WORLD WAR, the Communist Party of Northern Ireland maintaining a separate existence. This merged with the Southern party in 1970 to re-establish the Communist Party of Ireland on an all-Ireland basis. It promotes an all-Ireland secular, socialist republic. Its electoral support is negligible. [see O'FLAHERTY, LIAM.] **Neil Collins**

community. 'Community' is one answer to the question 'How is social order or cohesion possible?' In complex societies there are other answers, such as coercion, a social contract, the state, and the invisible hand of the market. Community is nonetheless a compelling answer, in relation both to traditional, pre-market forms of social integration, and to aspects of contemporary ones. The idea of community is deceptively simple. At its heart, community entails the notion of shared beliefs, mutual interests, reciprocity, and co-operation, often associated with pre-capitalist or pre-industrial societies. Tönnies made the classic distinction between simpler forms of integration (*gemeinschaft*, or community) and more sophisticated social structures (*gesellschaft*, society). A study of Irish rural life carried out by Arensberg and Kimball in the 1930s centred on such a concept of community. Subsequent studies either recorded the breakdown of community, such as Brody's *Inishkillane*, or contested this account as too idyllic, particularly in masking the conflicts between individual, family, or class interests. Scheper-Hughes identified more negative aspects in her work on mental illness in rural Irish communities. Community nonetheless has contemporary appeal in Ireland, though the emphasis is on community development in response to increased marginalisation in rural and urban areas. Community development also has historical roots, such as Muintir na Tíre, established in the 1930s. Government today acknowledges the importance of the 'community and voluntary sector', and the European Community has assisted with community development in Ireland since the 1980s. As Ireland has become more urban and prosperous in the 1990s, and a country of immigration, new interest concentrates on community identities that have emerged based on national, religious, or other lines, such as SEXUALITY or DISABILITY. **Joe Larragy**

Community Support Framework, a structural plan for the distribution of EU funds. In 1988, following a significantly increased European Community budget, reforms were introduced in the distribution of structural (regional, social, and agricultural guidance) funds. These were designed to increase cohesion between more and less prosperous regions at the time of the single market programme. The Community Support Frameworks were intrinsic to the way such funds were to be distributed. Previously, the Commission had dealt with thousands of projects in the various member-states. Under a CSF the European Commission in effect contracted funds to member-states and regional and LOCAL AUTHORITIES, underpinning programmes of regionally and functionally concentrated development. The main emphasis was on regions where GDP per capita was less than 75 per cent of the average in the European Community. Known as objective 1 regions (which initially included all of Greece, Portugal, Ireland, much of Spain and southern Italy, and some other areas), these accounted for a fifth of the population. Each CSF covered approximately five years. Since 2000 only the Border, Midlands, and West region of the Republic remains an objective 1 region, but the remainder, the Southern and Eastern region, is designated objective 1 in transition and will continue to receive support until 2006. **Joe Larragy**

companions of God: see CÉILÍ DÉ.

Compendium of Knowledge about Ireland: see FORAS FEASA AR ÉIRINN.

compert ('conception'), an EARLY IRISH TALE TYPE relating the wondrous pregnancies of the mothers of kings and heroes. Related to the heroic biography genre, they incorporate international motifs: women becoming pregnant by ingesting insects, by sleeping with gods or birds, or through INCEST. The heroes conceived in these tales include mythical, heroic, Fenian, and semi-historical figures. In 'Compert Con Culainn' (The conception of Cú Chulainn), CÚ CHULAINN's mother, Deichtire, adopts an abandoned male child, son of the god Lugh, who soon dies. She later becomes pregnant after drinking water containing an insect. Lugh visits her, informs her that the child she is carrying is the same child she has just lost, and advises her to call him Sétanta. Rumours abound that she is pregnant by her father, and she is hurriedly married to Sualdam mac Roach. She aborts the foetus, becomes pregnant naturally, and gives birth to Sétanta, who is later renamed Cú Chulainn. **Muireann Ní Bhrolcháin**

competition policy. The purpose of competition policy is to promote effective competition and thereby further the economic interests of consumers and the efficiency of business. Competition law is designed to protect the competitive process. The Competition Act (1991) and the Competition (Amendment) Act (1996) are the two governing pieces of legislation in this area. Breaches of the act can result in fines of £3 million or 10 per cent of turnover; officials of the company may also be sent to prison for up to two years. The Competition Authority is the statutory body in the Republic charged with enforcing the Competition Acts. It has the power to bring civil and (summary) criminal proceedings but cannot impose fines, as only the courts can perform this function; the power to prosecute on indictment is reserved for the Director of Public Prosecutions. The Competition Acts contain two basic prohibitions, which are modelled on articles 81 and 82 of the Treaty of Rome. The first makes illegal any agreements between firms that restrict competition. Agreements between competitors, for example to fix prices or to divide markets, are generally considered to have the most harmful effect on competition and will generally be prosecuted criminally. Agreements between firms at different levels of the supply chain are generally treated under a 'rule of reason' approach. In some circumstances, potentially anti-competitive agreements may be granted a licence if it can be shown that there are compensating gains in efficiency. The second prohibition prevents firms that are dominant or have a monopoly in a market from abusing that position. The responsibility for mergers lies with the Department of Enterprise, Trade and Employment; however, the minister may refer a merger to the Competition Authority for consideration. The competition law of the EUROPEAN UNION also applies to Ireland, where it has an effect on trade between member-states.

Northern Ireland is covered by British legislation, namely the Competition Act (1998). The Office of Fair Trading is the main body with responsibility for enforcing the act. Firms can be fined up to 30 per cent of turnover for breach of the act. Unlike the situation in the Republic, the Office of Fair Trading can itself impose fines, without recourse to the courts. **John Fingleton**

'Comrac Líadaine ocus Chuirithir' ('The Union of Líadain and Cuirither') (c. 900), a verse-and-prose work of just under a thousand words with a vivid narrative and one exquisite love poem. It tells the tale of the lovers and poets Líadain and Cuirither, who forswear the joys of secular union for spiritual marriage, under the direction of the stern monastic disciplinarian St Cummaíne Fota. Ultimately unable to bear his celibate existence in close proximity to Líadain, Cuirither exiles himself to another MONASTERY, and Líadain dies of grief for him. All three characters belonged in reality to the seventh century and had associations with Munster. [see CUMMIAN FADA.] **Máirín Ní Dhonnchadha**

conacre, a form of land tenure under which owners, tenants, or agents for absentsee LANDLORDS sub-let portions of LAND seasonally in exchange for rent in money or labour. Plots varied from 0.13 ha ($\frac{1}{8}$ acre) to 0.8 ha (2 acres) and provided land for small dwellings, crops, and some livestock. The precarious system by which many of the increasing POPULATION survived was destabilised throughout the nineteenth century. Incidences of partial crop failures increased, leading to an intensification of EVICTIONS, with the incoming lessee being charged a higher rent. Estimates suggest that by 1831 the price had reached £10 per year, while labourers earned 5 pence daily. Conacre undermined the profitability of consolidated pasturelands, and increasingly the system was terminated, with attendant problems of homelessness and UNEMPLOYMENT. [see LAND OWNERSHIP AND TENURE.] **Margaret Morse**

Conall Gulban (fl fifth century), both a historical figure and one whom oral tradition makes its own. He lived in the middle of the fifth century and was therefore a contemporary of St PATRICK. His descendants, CENÉL CONAILL, later called Ó Domhnaill, promoted his memory and fame. The claim that Conall was the favourite son of NIALL OF THE NINE HOSTAGES can hardly be quite accurate, as Niall's successor was in fact called Laoghaire.

One narrative recounts that an uncle of Conall, FIACHRA, was his foster-father and sent him to be trained in Co. Sligo. He was forced to run an extra stretch each day until he was able to reach the top of Binn Ghulbain (BENBULBIN) without stopping—hence his name Conall Gulban. Conall was a victorious leader in numerous battles, in particular those against the ULAIDH or Ulstermen. Among these were two battles in Co. Donegal, one in Ballyshannon and the final battle, fought with the assistance of Conall's three brothers, near Lifford, after which the territories were divided between the four warriors. Conall's prowess and power are underlined in his subsequent conquests, which included the defeat of the King of Munster and the taking of Connacht. An important text associated with him is the sixteenth-century 'Eachtra Chonaill Gulban', which celebrates Conall's life in accordance with medieval romantic style. **Ríonach uí Ógáin**

conception, tale type: see COMPERT.

Concern, a development agency that directs resources and personnel to alleviating poverty in some of the world's poorest countries. It was founded as Africa Concern by a group of missionaries and their supporters to relieve famine distress during the Biafra war in Nigeria in 1968. By 1971 it had begun activities in the newly independent state of Bangladesh and soon changed its name to Concern. Since then it has worked in twenty-six of the poorest countries in Africa and Asia, in both emergency and long-term development projects. By the late 1990s it had more than 2,500 people—fewer than 5 per cent of them expatriates—working in nineteen of the world's poorest countries. It spent over £20 million on overseas projects in 1998. Concern adopts a threefold approach. The first is responding to emergencies, such as natural disasters or war. It devotes approximately half its budget to such work and at the end of the 1990s had emergency schemes in Sudan, Rwanda, Sierra Leone, Liberia, Somalia, Democratic Republic of the Congo and Burundi, as well as in Afghanistan, north Korea, and Honduras. Development programmes—helping people acquire the means to overcome poverty—constitute the second part of its approach; in the late 1990s it ran such schemes in Bangladesh, Ethiopia, Tanzania, Mozambique, Cambodia, Laos, Angola, Uganda, and Haïti. About 5 per cent of Concern's budget is devoted to development education and advocacy. Donations from the public make up almost half its income. [see COMHLÁMH.] **Peadar Kirby**

concertina in traditional music. A relative of the HARMONICA, ACCORDION, and melodeon, the concertina became popular during the romantic period that accompanied the Industrial Revolution in England and Germany. In 1852 the Dublin concertina manufacturer Joseph Scates advertised his concertinas in the FREEMAN'S JOURNAL. By the 1880s, *single-action* German concertinas (with two notes per button) enjoyed popularity among traditional players in many parts of Ireland. Cheap, fragile, and short-lived, they were adapted from Uhlig's diatonic *konzertina* made in Chemnitz in the 1830s and popularised by Manen's twenty-key concertinas, which reached the English market in 1847. German concertinas remained standard instruments until the 1930s, when higher-quality Anglo-German models, made by Jeffries, Wheatstone, Lachenal and Crabb in England, became popular among Irish players. The earliest Irish concertina recordings were made in the United States in the 1920s by William J. Mullally from Co. Westmeath.

For over a century the lower Shannon has been considered the heartland of Irish concertina music. Its initial courier was maritime traffic plying the river between Loop Head and Limerick, the last port of call for ships crossing the Atlantic. Women were its main patrons in Co. Clare, which has four internal 'dialects' of concertina music. The county has produced more concertina masters than any other part of Ireland, including Paddy Murphy, ELIZABETH CROTTY, Pakie Russell, Chris Droney, Mary McNamara, and Noel Hill. Concertina music has experienced a considerable renewal since the 1980s as a result of its promotion in the county at the WILLIE CLANCY Summer School and Éigse Mrs CROTTY, both held annually. **Gearóid Ó hAllmhuráin**

Concorde. *(Left to right) Alan Smale, Madeleine Staunton, David James, Richard O'Donnell, Jane O'Leary (the director), and Paul Roe, members of Ireland's leading contemporary music ensemble, Concorde, formed in 1976. [Amelia Stein]*

Concorde, a chamber music ensemble formed in 1976 specialising in the performance of new music, at venues throughout Ireland and abroad under the directorship of the composer JANE O'LEARY. It is an active participant in the European Conference of Promoters of New Music and regularly takes part in international exchanges. The group has developed the repertoire of Irish composition through the commissioning of new work and the encouragement of young composers. **David Mooney**

concrete structures. The patenting of Portland cement in 1824 marked the arrival of modern concrete. Early Irish structures included work at the NATIONAL GALLERY, Dublin (1850s), DUBLIN PORT (1860s), especially development by BINDON STONEY, who may be named the 'father of Irish concrete', and Clonalis, Co. Roscommon (1870s), by Pepys Cockrell, one of the earliest concrete country houses, home of the O'Connor Don.

Reinforced concrete, using iron or steel rods embedded in the concrete, primarily to increase its tensile strength, was introduced after 1880. Significant examples include the 52 m span MIZEN HEAD FOOTBRIDGE, Co. Cork (1909) by Ridley and Crammell, John's Bridge, Kilkenny (1910), and many public utility and industrial buildings throughout Ireland. Following 1916, reinforced concrete was used extensively in rebuilding O'Connell Street, Dublin. Irish concrete, mass and reinforced, 'came of age' during the 1920s in the construction of the SHANNON SCHEME at Ardnacrusha, where no other medium was practicable.

After 1945 new technology introduced pre-stressed concrete, using indigenous and transnational techniques, thin-shell roofs, including Donnybrook Garage, Dublin (1951), and Athy Dominican church (1965), and sophisticated pre-casting in many modes. The burgeoning elegance of Irish concrete design and construction is readily evident in many bridges and buildings erected during recent decades. Some examples are the Waterfront Hall, Belfast, and the Civic Offices at Wellington Quay, Dublin. Reinforced concrete and mass concrete, principally blockwork masonry, now constitute the predominant building medium in Ireland. [see HIGGINS, BRYAN; KISH BANK LIGHTHOUSE; WALLER, J. H.] **John W. de Courcy**

Confederation of Kilkenny: see KILKENNY.

***Confessio* of Patrick.** This, the longer of his two writings, together with the *Letter to Coroticus's Soldiers*, constitutes our only reliable evidence for Patrick's life and work. He recounts his Romano-British clerical background, his capture by slavers, his escape, and his subsequent return to Ireland. The title is later and is taken from its concluding paragraph ('This is my declaration before I die') and does not explain the document's nature. It is a statement made to justify Patrick's status as God's appointed minister in Ireland: so it is addressed to God, to those who would decry Patrick, and to his own followers. It is only incidentally autobiographical: events are related to show that his life is part of a providential plan, within a Pauline historical perspective, for he is the final apostle, bringing the Gospel to the final land before Christ's second coming. **Thomas O'Loughlin**

Cong, Cross of, a processional cross containing a relic of allegedly the True Cross, first recorded at Cong, Co. Mayo, in the seventeenth century (see p. 712). It is a composite object, with plates of gilt bronze fastened to a wooden core, the relic originally viewed through a polished rock crystal at its centre. It bears a lengthy inscription recording the names of Domnall Ua Dubtaigh, Bishop of Connacht, and Toirdhealbhach Ó Conchobhair, King of Connacht, among others. This makes it possible to identify it with an annalistic entry of c. 1123 recording the enshrinement of a piece of the True Cross at Roscommon. It is considered the finest expression in metalwork of the Irish *Urnes* style. [see MEDIEVAL METALWORK.] **Raghnall Ó Floinn**

Congested Districts Board, a body established by Arthur Balfour in 1891 to address problems of underdevelopment in the west of Ireland. It engaged in a wide range of development activities in the areas of farming, fishing, and domestic industry, and bought estates from landlords, which it reorganised and sold to tenants. It drew up the Base Line Reports, surveying conditions in the most impoverished counties. In 1909 the area defined as congested was expanded, and the board was given increased powers under the Irish Land Act (1909). In 1923 the Congested Districts Board was dissolved by the Free State Government and its functions transferred to the Land Commission. **Carla King**

Congreve, William (1670–1729), playwright. Born near Leeds to a British army family stationed in Ireland; educated at Kilkenny College and TCD. By 1691 he was back in England and began studying law in London. He published a novel, *Incognita* (1692), under the pseudonym Cleophil. He became a friend and protégé of Dryden and collaborated with him in translations of the satires of Juvenal and Persius (1693). His first play, *The Old Bachelour*, was produced early in 1693; *The Double Dealer* followed at the end of 1693 and *Love for Love* in 1695.

He began to write public occasional verse in 1695, but his reputation as a man of letters was already well established. His only tragedy, *The Mourning Bride* (1697), was considered by contemporaries his most successful play. His last play, *The Way of the World*, produced in 1700, was considered by contemporaries to be his least successful; conversely, it is perceived by modern audiences and readers as the pinnacle of his art. He subsequently wrote two OPERA librettos, a masque, and a collaborative translation of Molière's *Monsieur de Pourceaugnac* (1704). Poems and translations from Homer, Juvenal, Ovid, Horace and Pindarus followed.

He lived comfortably on his private income, royalties from plays, and several civil service sinecures; his friends included SWIFT, Gay, Pope, and STEELE. He was closely associated with the actor Anne Bracegirdle, who played all his heroines, but there is no proof that their relationship was more than close friendship. He most probably had a love affair with the Duchess of Marlborough, to whom he left the bulk of his fortune on his death, and was in all likelihood the father of her daughter, Lady Mary Godolphin.

Congreve is considered the outstanding writer of the English comedy of manners. Influenced by Jonson and Molière, he concerned himself with the behaviour of his largely upper-class audience. His main themes deal with sexual life, with its philosophy of freedom and hedonism, while casting a critical eye on the excesses and extravagant assumptions of the age. Where Molière exposes folly and wishes wherever possible to cure it, Congreve shows not the slightest interest in reform. He peoples his world with an artificial society consisting of good-natured fools and intelligent, sophisticated, and graceful gentlemen and ladies who play the social game with perfect wit in a world where good taste, rather than good sense, is the mark of right living. Congreve surpasses similar writers because of his delicacy of feeling and a perfection of phrasing in which characters are best revealed and where a way of life is recorded with vivacity, sparkle, and brilliance of language. **Carolyn Duggan**

Conlon, Evelyn (1952–), novelist and short-story writer. Born in Co. Monaghan; educated at ST PATRICK'S COLLEGE, Maynooth. Her collections of stories are *My Head Is Opening* (1987) and *Taking Scarlet as a Real Colour* (1993); her novels include *Stars in the Daytime* (1989) and *A Glassful of Letters* (1998). Her fiction, which deals with women's role in society, is marked by a gritty realism (see p. 321). **Terence Brown**

Conlon-McKenna, Marita (1956–), writer. Born in Dublin; educated at Mount Anville and Montessori College, Dublin. Her first book, *My First Holy Communion* (1990), was followed by the best-seller *Under the Hawthorn Tree* (see p. 1040). Despite its unlikely theme—the survival of three children during the GREAT FAMINE—

Congested Districts Board. *Lace class, Ardara, Co. Donegal, 1900. This workshop was set up by the Congested Districts Board to encourage home industry in the area. [Welch Collection, Ulster Museum; photograph reproduced with the kind permission of the Trustees of the National Museums and Galleries of Northern Ireland]*

young readers responded to the author's gentle wit and humanity. An exceptional storyteller, she recognises and portrays the innate courage and hopes of the young through a range of tough, believable characters in this and the sequels *The Wildflower Girl* and *Fields of Home*. *The Blue Horse* and *No Goodbye* are firmly rooted in twentieth-century urban Ireland, with its social problems of prejudice and marital breakdown. Conlon-McKenna's picture-books *Little Star, The Very Last Unicorn* and *Granny McGinty* are both lyrical and funny. She received awards from the Reading Association of Ireland, 1991, and the International Reading Association, 1991, the Bisto Book of the Year award, 1992/3, Österreichischen Kinder und Jugendbuchpreis, 1993, and Grand Prix Européen du Roman pour Enfants, 1994. **Patricia Donlon**

Connacht

Connacht	Cúige Chonnacht
Counties:	Galway, Leitrim, Mayo, Roscommon, Sligo
Major towns:	Galway, Sligo
Rivers:	Moy, Shannon and Suck
Highest Point:	Mweelrea 817m
Population 1991	423,071
Population 2002	464,050

Connacht (Connachta), one of the four provinces of modern Ireland. Its name derives from the mythological Conn of the Hundred Battles. Its ancient capital was at Cruacha (RATHCROGHAN, Co. Roscommon), and its early rulers were Uí Briúin; they later produced the O'Flaherty, O'Rourke, and especially the O'Connor line, who, under Ruairí, held the HIGH KINGSHIP at the ANGLO-NORMAN CONQUEST in 1169, their ecclesiastical capital at Tuam having become an archdiocese in 1152. Anglo-Norman settlement in the thirteenth century under the de Burghs (Burkes) deprived the O'Connors of all but part of Roscommon and pushed others into Sligo. Their power was smashed at Athenry (1316), and thereafter several branches (Donn, Roe, and Sligo) competed for power with now-Gaelicised Burkes and other settler families. The province's principal town, Galway, looking to SPAIN for its associations, became an important trading port, reaching its apogee in the sixteenth century (as the beauty of its merchants' town-houses still affirms) before going into a steep decline. Its most flamboyant leader at this point was GRACE O'MALLEY (c. 1530–1603) (see p. 875), the pirate-queen whose exploits rivalled those of Connacht's mythological MÉABH. The Presidency of Connacht was established in 1570 to spread English law and order, the most infamous of its presidents being Sir RICHARD BINGHAM, who made war on the Mayo Burkes, the O'Rourkes, and others to reduce the province to English rule. Piecemeal PLANTATION followed, but after the 1641 REBELLION surviving Catholic landholders throughout Ireland were transported there, OLIVER CROMWELL allegedly issuing the threat 'To Hell or to Connacht!' Connacht was the scene of perhaps the bloodiest battle in Irish history when 7,000 JACOBITES were slaughtered by Williamite forces at AUGHRIM (12 July 1691); it also played a significant part in the 1798 REBELLION when the landing at KILLALA of the French General Humbert inspired a briefly successful campaign. The devastation caused by the GREAT FAMINE (1845–9) was crucial to the establishment by MICHAEL DAVITT of the LAND LEAGUE in 1879, and Connacht was the scene of much of the agrarian unrest associated with the LAND WAR of the 1880s. [see AGRARIAN PROTEST.] **Seán Duffy**

Geography. The westernmost of the provinces, with an area of 1,712 km^2 (661 sq. miles), comprising Cos. Galway, Mayo, Sligo, Roscommon, and Leitrim, and with a population of 464,050 (2002). Only Co. Roscommon is landlocked. The population grew by 30,819 or 7.6 per cent between 1996 and 2002. All counties registered an increase, ranging from 14.9 per cent in the city of Galway to 3.0 per cent in Co. Leitrim. There was an inward migration of 23,742, greatest in Galway city and county. Much of the province is rural but with an extensive network of settlements. The largest urban centres are the city of Galway (population 65,774) and the borough of Sligo (population 18,429).

The name of the province derives from the former ruling Connachta tribes. In the early Middle Ages Co. Cavan was considered part of Connacht. Breffny (*Bréifne*) was an important territory in the north of the province from the seventh century up to the time of CROMWELL. The ANGLO-NORMAN de Burgos were granted the greater part of Connacht, becoming in time the Burkes. Despite the Anglo-Norman presence, the province remained remote from the centre of power in Ireland and was inaccurately portrayed on maps of Ireland even in the seventeenth century. Its present county structure is relatively recent. Shiring did not occur until the reign of ELIZABETH I, when Sir Philip Sydney, her Lord Deputy, undertook the process c. 1570. The effect of the GREAT FAMINE and subsequent EMIGRATION was particularly severe: by 1901 the population had fallen to 323,265, having been 711,017 in 1841.

The provincial structure has no administrative function. Regional authorities came into operation in 1994, with Cos. Galway, Mayo, and Roscommon comprising the West Region and Cos. Sligo and Leitrim forming part of the Border Region. **Joseph Brady**

Connaughton, Shane (1946–), novelist and screenwriter. Born and educated in Co. Cavan. His fiction, which includes *A Border Station* (1989), deals with the border country during the modern 'TROUBLES', with the local person's knowledge of neighbourhood politics. **Terence Brown**

Connell, Desmond (1926–), bishop and philosopher. Born in Dublin; educated at UCD and the University of LOUVAIN. He was a lecturer in UCD, 1953–72, and professor of general metaphysics, 1972–88. He published *The Vision in God: Malebranche's Scholastic Sources* (1967) and *Essays in Metaphysics* (1996). A Thomistic philosopher, he cultivated the study of scholastic metaphysics at University College, Dublin, and was involved in broadening and modernising philosophy there. Appointed Archbishop of Dublin in 1988, he was created a cardinal in 2001. He has held various offices in the Irish Episcopal Conference and has been a member of the Roman Congregation for the Doctrine of the Faith, the Congregation for Bishops, and the Pontifical Council for the Laity. **Thomas A. F. Kelly**

Connemara, the part of western Co. Galway north of the coastal district of Cois Fharraige, south of KILLARY HARBOUR, and west of Oughterard. The interior is dominated by the quartzite peaks and metamorphosed schists and gneisses of the Twelve Pins and their intervening valleys. Shallow blanket BOGS are the dominant land cover. Land use is limited to hill sheep-grazing throughout much of the uplands, where unenclosed commonage persists. State-owned coniferous plantations cover the floors and sides of the interior valleys. Connemara NATIONAL PARK lies south-east of Letterfrack, a mid-nineteenth-century QUAKER foundation, where the Connemara West development organisation occupies the former industrial school. Clifden, 10 km (6 miles) south, at the head of Clifden Bay, is the main town; it was founded in the 1820s by John D'Arcy, the ruins of whose residence, Clifden Castle, are west of the town. Nineteenth-century buildings of note are Ballynahinch House Hotel (former home of RICHARD MARTIN), Kylemore Abbey (built in the 1860s by a Manchester businessman, Mitchell Henry, now a Benedictine girls' boarding school), and Renvyle House Hotel (former home of OLIVER ST JOHN GOGARTY). INISHBOFIN is 10 km (6 miles) offshore from Cleggan. **Mary E. Cawley**

'Connerys, Na', three folk-songs concerning the escapades of Pádraig, Séamus, and Seán Ó Conaire, three brothers from Bohadoon, near Dungarvan, Co. Waterford. Their resistance against EVICTION from their smallholding, success at avoiding capture and dramatic jail-breaks earned them the status of popular heroes in pre-FAMINE Ireland. Seán was transported to Botany Bay in 1835; Pádraig and Séamus were apprehended for the third and last time in 1838 and transported to the penal colony in New South Wales. **Éamonn Ó Bróithe**

Connolly, James (1868–1916), socialist theorist and revolutionary. Born in Edinburgh, of Irish parents; he left school at the age of eleven to work at odd jobs, then enlisted in and later deserted from the British army. He joined the Scottish Socialist League in 1889 and in 1896 founded the Irish Socialist Republican Party in Dublin. He began to write articles and pamphlets arguing that the national question was also a social question. He emigrated to the United States in 1903, returning to Ireland in 1910, becoming acting general secretary of the IRISH TRANSPORT AND GENERAL WORKERS' UNION and Commandant of the IRISH CITIZEN ARMY from 1914. Denouncing partition and participation in the FIRST WORLD WAR, he joined the IRB in planning the 1916 RISING, in which he led the Citizen Army. Following the rising he was shot by firing squad on 12 May. Connolly is remembered chiefly as a 1916 martyr and for his writing on socialist republicanism and on syndicalism. **Emmet O'Connor**

Connolly as social theorist. Before New Left and 'post-Marxist' thinking, before even Gramsci's broadened notion of 'superstructure', James Connolly had understood that any approach to liberation needed to look beyond the confines of economic forces and relations. Accordingly, he developed a wholly original, 'dialectical' synthesis: rigorous Marxist analysis was injected into debate on the national question, and, in one and the same moment, Marxist theory was expanded beyond a purely class-based position. For Connolly, the struggles for socialism and for national freedom were in no sense mutually exclusive; instead, the one could—and should—inform the other.

The main intellectual outcome of this fusion was *Labour in Irish History* (1910), where clan ownership was invoked as an important non-capitalist social model and private property was denounced as an alien imposition upon communal, traditional Irish society. Connolly's guiding principle for this Celtic socialism was not so much CELTIC TWILIGHT sentimentality as a conscious effort to follow Marx's own schema (primitive COMMUNISM—class division—higher communism). His conclusion was that opposition to English rule could be equated with opposition to an 'English' socio-economic system. Hence Connolly's declaration that 'the struggle for Irish freedom has two aspects: it is national and it is social.'

Evaluations of the success or otherwise of Connolly's thinking have been mixed. Perhaps it is best seen, overall, as an appropriately variegated, uneven, and 'impure' response to a distinctly variegated, uneven, and 'impure' phenomenon: imperialism. **Ian Leask**

Connolly, Sybil (1921–1998), couturière and designer. Born in Wales; trained at Bradley's, London, until her return to Ireland in 1939. In 1940 she joined 'Richard Alan' and started a couture workroom for which she was the designer, 1952–7, under her own name. She showed collections in the United States from 1953, with great success, and became Ireland's most internationally known FASHION designer. In 1957 she established her own fashion house at 71 Merrion Square, Dublin. She was known for her innovative use of Irish fabrics, most notably her trademark pleated handkerchief LINEN. She continued to design clothes for her clientele but after the 1960s began to expand her design work. She produced fabric designs for Brunschwig et Fils, the most successful of which was based on the court dress of the eighteenth-century MRS MARY DELANY, whose famous floral paper mosaics were displayed in a New York exhibition that Connolly organised. As a design consultant for Tiffany of New York she was responsible for successful lines of Tipperary glass, Nicholas Mosse pottery, and parian porcelain by Tommy Daly. She was the author of *Irish Hands* (1995) and *In an Irish House* (1988) and joint editor of *In an Irish Garden* (1986) and was largely responsible for the restoration of the interior of the SWISS COTTAGE, near Cahir, Co. Tipperary. Awards she received included Woman of the Year in Britain, 1958, frequent appearances in the annual 'Best-Dressed Women of the World' list, an honorary doctorate from the National University of Ireland, 1991, and honorary associateship from the National College of Art and Design (see p. 148). **Elizabeth McCrum**

Connor, Jerome (1874–1943), sculptor. Born in Anascaul, Co. Kerry; his family emigrated to the United States in 1888, settling in Holyoke, Massachusetts. He trained as a stone-cutter in New York before going to the Arts and Craft Roycroft Institution, East Aurora, New York, in 1899. He began exhibiting at the Pennsylvania Academy of Fine Arts in 1900, then settled in Syracuse, New York, where he embarked on a successful career as a sculptor of portrait busts and public monuments, including those of Archbishop John Carroll, Washington (1912), ROBERT EMMET, unveiled first in Washington (1917), then San Francisco (1919) and Dublin (1968), and an American Civil War memorial, *The Angels of the Battlefield* (1924). Commissioned in 1925 to design a memorial in Cobh, Co. Cork, to those who died in the sinking of the LUSITANIA, he established a studio in Dublin and began a series of designs that were completed in 1936 in the form of two mourning fisherman standing before an elevated Angel of Peace. He cast the fishermen using the *cire perdue* (lost wax) process. This impressive monument was completed posthumously in 1968. His other Irish designs, all abortive, include *Éire* for the Kerry Poets Memorial (cast posthumously for Merrion Square, Dublin), *Pikeman* (1927–31 and c. 1941) for Tralee, and *The Patriot* (1929, posthumously cast for the NATIONAL GALLERY OF IRELAND). After his death there was a memorial section for Connor in the IRISH EXHIBITION OF LIVING ART. Influenced by AUGUSTUS SAINT-GAUDENS, Connor was a figurative sculptor who included ordinary figures on public monuments, where he imbued them, and his allegorical figures, with character and emotion. Always interested in the expressive effects of patination, by c. 1940 he was producing more expressionist bronzes. He is unique as an Irish-American sculptor, bringing the secular values and political aspirations of Irish America to both his American and Irish public monuments. **Judith Hill**

Connor, Jerome. The Patriot *(1929) by Jerome Connor, a posthumously cast low-relief bronze figure of a revolutionary, intended for an unrealised public monument. [National Gallery of Ireland]*

Conolly, Lady Louisa, née Lennox (1743–1821), a philanthropic landowner; third daughter of the second Duke of Richmond, a prominent WHIG. When her parents died she was sent to live at CARTON, Co. Kildare, with her elder sister EMILY LENNOX, whose husband became the first Duke of Leinster. In 1758 she married their neighbour, Thomas Conolly, who had inherited Speaker WILLIAM CONOLLY's CASTLETOWN. She became responsible for its interior decoration and the layout of the grounds. After her husband's death in 1803 she devoted herself to caring for her many tenants. She had the help of her niece, Emily Napier, whom she had adopted in 1783. She built a church and school of industry in nearby Celbridge. She had been very upset and confused by the 1798 REBELLION, but she managed to visit her nephew, Lord EDWARD FITZGERALD, in prison just before he died. **Eleanor Burgess**

Conolly, William (1662–1729), politician 'Speaker Conolly'. Of obscure, possibly Co. Donegal Catholic, descent, though of sufficient importance in the Protestant community to be attainted by the JACOBITE Parliament (1689). Considered the richest commoner in Ireland, with a fortune arising from shrewd land dealings following the Williamite confiscations, he built CASTLETOWN, Co. Kildare. He came to political prominence in the period 1703–14 as an associate of the Brodrician WHIGS. Chief Revenue Commissioner from 1714, in 1715 he became Speaker of the Irish House of Commons. A regular appointee as Lord Justice thereafter, he was the first great eighteenth-century parliamentary manager and UNDERTAKER. **Charles Ivar McGrath**

Conor, William (1881–1968), painter of portraits and genre scenes. Born in Belfast; trained at Belfast Government School of Art. He was an apprentice lithographer, 1904–10, lithography subsequently influencing his painting technique. He briefly visited Paris, working with André Lhôte, and London, where he frequented the celebrated Café Royal. He was an official war artist during the FIRST WORLD WAR, thereafter devoting himself to recording everyday life in his native city. His early work—*The Twelfth* (1918), *Washing Day* (c. 1930), *The Jaunting Car* (c. 1933)—is his most inventive and successful, capturing precisely the atmosphere of working-class Belfast. His portraits include one of DOUGLAS HYDE. **S. B. Kennedy**

Conradh na Gaeilge: see GAELIC LEAGUE.

Conscription Crisis. In March 1918 the British government decided to impose conscription on Ireland with the support of JOHN REDMOND, bringing it into line with the rest of the United Kingdom. Nationalists were outraged, and the Catholic Church helped organise the campaign of resistance. It became clear that any attempt at enforcement would provoke widespread violence, and ultimately the government backed down. The crisis helped radicalise nationalists, weakened the IRISH PARTY, strengthened SINN FÉIN, and accelerated a drift towards violence. **Michael Laffan**

constitutional nationalism, a movement of the nineteenth and early twentieth centuries that sought self-government for Ireland by way of legislation rather than revolution. It was mainly expressed through the REPEAL MOVEMENT of the 1830s and 40s and the HOME RULE campaigns from 1870 onwards. Despite the sporadic prominence of 'physical force' separatists, the great majority of rank-and-file nationalists consistently identified themselves with groups advocating change by constitutional means. [see O'CONNELL, DANIEL.] **Gary Owens**

Constitutions of Ireland. Though the first DÁIL ÉIREANN had adopted a constitution of sorts in 1919, the Constitution of the IRISH FREE STATE (1922) was the first constitution of the Irish state in any real sense. The 1922 constitution represented a hybrid of influences: British, American, and European. The British influence was the most obvious: the legislature and executive were largely organised along Westminster lines; and the British government had insisted on the retention of certain imperial symbols. The referendum procedure and extern ministers were borrowed from contemporary Continental European constitutions; but the most important legal change was the existence of a bill of rights and the vesting in the courts of the power of JUDICIAL REVIEW of legislation.

The 1922 constitution ultimately collapsed in failure. Article 50 allowed the constitution to be amended by ordinary legislation for a period of eight years, and this was extended for a further eight years in 1929. Following the accession of FIANNA FÁIL to power in 1932 the constitution was dismantled piecemeal; by 1936 the OATH OF ALLEGIANCE, the SENATE, appeal to the Privy Council, and the office of Governor-General had been abolished and all references to the Crown removed. Following the recommendations of the Constitution Review Committee of 1934, which were generally in favour of an entrenched bill of rights, judicial review, and a rigid constitution, ÉAMON DE VALERA entrusted the drafting of a new constitution to an elite group of civil servants headed by John Hearne, legal adviser to the Department of External Affairs. Though de Valera retained ultimate political control, Hearne was principally responsible for the drafting of the Constitution, and many of its innovative legal influences can be ascribed to him. The new constitution reinforced the powers of judicial review, strengthened the provisions for fundamental rights, and created the office of President of Ireland. It came into force in December 1937, following a referendum in July. Once the transitional period expired, in June 1941, the Constitution could be amended only by referendum.

After a slow start, judicial review of legislation has played a prominent role in vindicating personal rights and creating a 'rights' consciousness. Notable decisions include the SINN FÉIN *Funds* case, 1947 (judicial independence from legislative interference), *Byrne v. Ireland*, 1971 (the state no longer immune from suit), *McGee*, 1973 (the prohibition on the importing of contraceptives unconstitutional), and *Murphy*, 1980 (the right of married couples to a fair tax system).

Though the Constitution has been amended on nineteen occasions, the basic structure remains the same. The more obviously Catholic and nationalist features have been largely diluted by changes to the special position of the Catholic Church (1972), the introduction of DIVORCE (1995), and changes to articles 2 and 3 defining the national territory necessitated by the BELFAST AGREEMENT (1998). Though the Constitution Review Group (1996) recommended significant technical and other changes, it praised the 'sophistication' and 'elegant drafting' of the Constitution and concluded that the general impact of the Constitution and the case law it generated had been 'beneficial, rational, progressive and fair.' [see REFERENDA.] **Gerard Hogan**

construction workers in Britain. The excavators of the inland navigation CANALS built throughout Ireland and Britain from the middle of the eighteenth century were known as 'navigators' or 'navvies', who acquired skills that earned them elite status in construction during the Railway Age. The Newry Canal (1742) was the earliest summit-level canal in Ireland, and Irish labourers could therefore be considered the first navvies. In Britain only a small minority of railway labourers were Irish (seldom, except in Scotland, exceeding 10 per cent), but they were a major force in railway-building in North America, Australia, and New Zealand. Gradually the term 'navvy' came to be applied to all labourers employed on the earthworks of civil engineering, though it was officially dropped in Britain in 1960.

In the late nineteenth and early twentieth centuries unskilled Irishmen increasingly found employment on public works as the better-educated English workers moved away from unskilled manual labour. The SECOND WORLD WAR severely depleted British civilian manpower, and thousands of Irishmen obtained construction jobs in Britain, with established companies such as Wimpey and MacAlpine exploiting their pre-war labour networks to recruit in Ireland. After 1945 the urgency of the rebuilding of Britain gave Irish labourers unprecedented opportunities to bid for demolition, housing and utilities contracts. Between 1951 and 1961 400,000 Irish workers (almost equally men and women) emigrated to Britain, and the construction industry became the largest employer of Irish men. Employees of the main contractors benefited from national insurance contributions and pension schemes and could become plant operators and supervisors, though lack of education normally precluded advancement to management positions. However, the opportunity to sub-contract, coupled with access to a large pool of Irish labour, enabled ambitious Irishmen to build up substantial businesses, typified by the Murphy, McNicholas, Clancy and Kennedy groups. Direct labour was phased out in the 1970s, and thereafter numerous Irish 'subbies' hired day-labourers, known colloquially as 'skins', for cash in hand, without paying social insurance or deducting income tax. This encouraged a casual attitude that may have been exhilarating for young men but often left them destitute in later life. Many laboured in all weathers without protective clothing, drank excessively, and ate poorly, and their health declined rapidly after the age of forty.

Estimates of Irish construction workers as a proportion of the Irish-born population of Britain varied from 18 per cent in 1963 to 14 per cent in 1985. However, many worked under false names to evade income tax, while the unrepresented workers of Irish descent are an increasingly large proportion of the work force. Irish dominance of ground works is universally acknowledged throughout the industry. An estimated one-third of the 15,000 operatives on the Channel Tunnel were Irish, mostly from Co. Donegal; and such workers provide much of the manpower in hard-rock tunnelling around the world.

Irish-owned construction companies in Britain earned one-tenth of the industry's total turnover in the year 2000. There is also a significant Irish presence in construction on the Continent, in Australia, and in the United States. **Ultan Cowley**

'Contention of the Poets': see 'IOMARBHÁGH NA BHFILEADH'.

Continental shelf, a zone of low-angle sea floor approximately 10 m (30 ft) above the 200 m (656-ft) isobath. The steeper Continental slope (3–6°) and the ocean basins, more than 3,000 m (10,000 ft) deep, occur oceanwards. Ireland has a wide shelf area of approximately 110,500 km^2 (43,000 sq. miles), exclusive of the IRISH SEA, forming a portion of an even larger sea-bed territory of approximately 900,000 km^2 (350,000 sq. miles). Ireland's Continental shelf is part of the seismically quiet North-West European shelf. This results from the processes of ocean spreading, sediment accumulation, changes in relative sea level, and GLACIATION.

The formation of the shelf began approximately 100 million years ago with the development of the North Atlantic Ocean under the action of Continental drift. Over time the igneous crustal rocks underlying the shelf have been overlaid by thick sequences of sedimentary rocks, accumulating to form the low-angle 'bench' of the shelf. Structural troughs (*graben*) linked to the ocean spreading also underlie the shelf. These structures often coincide with palaeo-valley systems, which were formed at times of low sea level—sea levels periodically falling by more than 100 m (300 ft)—particularly during the Ice Age, cutting deep canyons across the shelf. Seismic surveys show that river channels (for example from Dingle Bay and the Rivers LEE, BLACKWATER, BARROW, and SUIR) probably connect into the palaeo-valleys. The Shamrock and Whittard canyons lie to the south of Ireland, with smaller canyons, channels and notches (such as the Gollum Channel and Porcupine Sea Bight) found northwards along the margin of the Irish shelf. Sediment fans, greater than 1–2 km ($\frac{1}{2}$–1$\frac{1}{2}$ miles) thick, accumulate at the ocean ends of these canyons, as well as independently along the shelf edge (such as the Donegal and Barra Fans). Surface sediments form a thin veneer, approximately 1–30 m (3–100 ft) deep, of mainly fine materials over the shelf. Large areas of bare rock also occur, swept clear by wind-wave and tidal current action. These water flows also produce sea-bed forms of sand sheets, waves, and ribbons. Some of these features may be inherited from times of lower sea levels and glaciation.

At the present time Atlantic wave action produces high-energy conditions on the Irish shelf, with maximum significant wave heights of 15–20 m, with a fifty-year return period. Thick sequences of glacigenic sediments also occur offshore from the northern and southern coasts of Ireland, with relict *moraines* (glacial ridges) present on the sea-bed, for example off Galway Bay and CLEW BAY. The shelf forms a zone of potentially rich resources: of minerals, hydrocarbons (the Porcupine Sea Bight), wave-energy, and fish and mariculture. [see CELTIC SEA; COASTAL EROSION.] **Robert J. N. Devoy**

Continental thought. Contemporary Ireland has witnessed an enormous change in its intellectual and moral self-image since 1990. One of the many reasons for this is a growing interest in certain currents of Continental thought. 'Continental thought' refers broadly to a host of intellectual movements that developed in France and Germany throughout the twentieth century. The most prominent of these movements include phenomenology, existentialism, critical theory, deconstruction, hermeneutics, feminist theory, and post-modernism. Through the work of the Irish philosophers PATRICK MASTERSON and RICHARD KEARNEY the insights of the French and German phenomenologists and existentialists (such as Martin Heidegger, Jean-Paul Sartre, and Paul Ricœur) became familiar to many in the Irish academic world and beyond. Kearney's *The Wake of Imagination* (1988) is considered by many in the world of Continental philosophy a work of major significance. More recently, academics such as LUKE GIBBONS, TONY O'CONNOR, Maeve Cooke, DERMOT MORAN, and Tom Inglis have served to popularise the writings of Edmund Husserl, Jürgen Habermas, Jacques Derrida, and Michel Foucault. It is not an exaggeration to say that the debate around what constitutes Irish identity was in many respects stimulated by these innovative Irish advocates of Continental thought. This is evidenced most dramatically in the ways in which such influential figures as the former President of Ireland MARY ROBINSON and the SDLP leader JOHN HUME developed and deepened their political understanding as a response to such intellectual innovation. Both politicians consistently appropriated quintessentially Continental themes and ideas, such as the notion that it is only in and through an affirmation of our differences that genuine identity can be celebrated and realised. Robinson's vision of Ireland as a place of openness and hospitality to the refugee and the stranger is one that is highly infused with the quasi-Biblical ethics of people like Ricœur, Levinas, and Derrida. Hume's belief that an antidote to the Northern Ireland conflict can be found in a recognition that the people of Northern Ireland, despite their manifest differences, have much more in common than they previously supposed also owes much to the ethical strains of Continental thought. It is no surprise that since her time as President of Ireland, Mary Robinson has taken up the position of UNITED NATIONS High Commissioner for Human Rights, a role that has allowed her to expand on her vision of 'ethical globalisation', formed in conjunction with the Swiss theologian Hans Küng. Moreover, Hume's commitment to the European project can be explained by his equally deep commitment to the view, again inspired by recent movements in Continental intellectual history, that traditional differences ultimately do not make too much of a difference. **Mark Dooley**

contraception. The legalisation of contraception was one of the aims of the WOMEN'S MOVEMENT in the Republic, as cited in its manifesto, *Chains or Changes?: The Civil Wrongs of Irish Women* (1971). As part of a publicity campaign it organised a 'contraception train' to Belfast on 22 May 1971 to bring back condoms and spermicides, in defiance of the law. Legalisation was strongly opposed by the Catholic Church, and contraception was not made legally available until 1979. From the late 1960s, however, Family Rights Planning Groups sought to subvert the law by distributing contraceptives free of charge, while clients made donations to the organisation. FAMILY PLANNING Centres were set up in a number of towns, prescribing the contraceptive pill and dispensing condoms and diaphragms. In 1973 the Supreme Court held that the constitutional right to marital privacy encompassed the right to obtain contraceptives for personal use. The Health (Family Planning) Act (1979) provided for contraceptives, including condoms, to be made available on prescription for medical reasons or for 'bona fide' family planning purposes. From 1985 a range of named outlets were permitted to sell condoms and spermicides to persons over the age of eighteen without a prescription. In 1992 the sale of condoms was deregulated, and the Health (Family Planning) (Amendment) Act legally obliges Health Boards to provide family planning services. **Evelyn Mahon**

contraception. *Contraception Action Programme campaign caravan active in Ballymun, Dublin (13 October 1979), one of the many temporary family planning centres offering free contraceptives and advice before contraception was made legally available. [Derek Speirs/Report]*

Conway, Arthur William (1875–1950), mathematical physicist. Born in Wexford; educated at UCD and the University of Oxford. In 1901 he was appointed professor of mathematical physics at University College, Dublin, holding this position until 1940, when he was elected president of the college. His research interests lay in electromagnetism, relativity, and the quantum theory of elementary particles, and he showed how quaternions may be used with advantage to study problems in these areas. He also edited two volumes of the collected papers of WILLIAM ROWAN HAMILTON, the discoverer of quaternions. **Rod Gow**

Conway, Edward Joseph (1894–1968), biochemist. Born in Nenagh, Co. Tipperary; educated at UCD, where he graduated in medicine and science. In 1921 he took up a lectureship in physiology at University College, Dublin, and in 1932 he was appointed first professor of BIOCHEMISTRY and pharmacology. He developed a method for analysing the constituents in tiny quantities of body fluids to work on cellular chemistry and the source of acid in the stomach, and discounted the notion that blood plasma and seawater are similar. Elected a fellow of the Royal Society, 1947, and member of the Pontifical Academy of Sciences, 1961, he was the first experimental biologist working in Ireland to carve out an international reputation. **C. S. Breathnach**

Cooke, Barrie (1931–), artist. Born in England, though most of his childhood was spent in the United States and Bermuda; he has lived and worked in Ireland since 1954. After studying marine biology and art history at Harvard University, he studied art at Skowhegan, Maine, where he was influenced by Abstract Expressionism. His Irish landscapes have been imbued with a feeling for boglands, LAKES, and the wild landscapes of the BURREN. A well-known series of paintings in the 1970s celebrated the extinct giant Irish ELK. A painting in the Crawford Gallery, Cork, *Portrait of the Lough Derg Pike, Life Size, with Relics* (1980) (see p. 416), combines elements such as an antique fishing reel with a painterly depiction of a legendary fish. **Peter Murray**

Cooke, Henry (1788–1868), religious controversialist. Born Henry Macook in south Co. Derry, youngest son of a small farmer; educated at the University of Glasgow and later TCD. He emerged in the 1820s as the leading theologian of his era, playing a central role in changing the character and direction of Ulster PRESBYTERIANISM. In the sphere of religion he became the most articulate opponent of 'New Light' theology in the SYNOD of Ulster and within the Belfast Institution. Though he was unpopular in his early years, in time his opinions gained prominence and acceptance, and he was pivotal in bringing about the split between Unitarian and orthodox Presbyterianism. He was elected Moderator of the Synod of Ulster in 1824 and was twice Moderator of the General Assembly, in 1841 and 1862. He was central also in the establishment of the Free Church of Scotland. Politically he was an early opponent of DANIEL O'CONNELL's REPEAL MOVEMENT, and the origins of UNIONISM in Ulster owe much to his skill as a travelling preacher and his ability to stir popular opinion. He challenged O'Connell to a public debate during the latter's only visit to Belfast, but the offer was declined. Later he was vociferous in his condemnation of the DISESTABLISHMENT of the CHURCH OF IRELAND. His followers built him a church in May Street, Belfast, where he preached until his death. **Roddy Hegarty**

Coole Park, near Gort, Co. Galway, the Gregory family estate. It was bought in 1768 by Robert Gregory, whose descendants had a history of political service, including Sir William Gregory, Governor of Ceylon (Sri Lanka) and husband of LADY GREGORY, who managed the property from his death until its sale in 1927 to the Government. From the late 1890s until her death in 1932 Lady Gregory made Coole Park a literary retreat for many writers of the day, most particularly W. B. YEATS. It also gave her a base for studying Irish and gathering the folklore so prominent in her own writing. The house was demolished in 1941. **Brian Cliff**

Coole. *Lady Gregory with George Bernard Shaw outside her house, Coole Park, Co. Galway (c. 1913). Her grandchildren look on from an upstairs window. [Bernard F. Burgunder Collection of George Bernard Shaw, Carl A. Kroch Library, Cornell University, Ithaca, New York]*

Cooley, Joe (1924–1973), ACCORDION-player. Born in Peterswell, Co. Galway; reared in an intensely musical home, which hosted regular house dances. Building work took him to Co. Clare, to London, and then to the United States in 1954. His intensely emotional MUSIC and charismatic personality made a lasting impact on the Irish music scene in America, where he played with his brother, the FLUTE-player Séamus Cooley. He returned to Ireland in 1972. A selection of his music was released as *Cooley.* **Fintan Vallely**

Cooley, Thomas (1740–1784), architect. Apparently English, he was a carpenter and joiner who studied architecture in his spare time. His draughtsmanship earned him several prizes, and in 1765 he joined the London practice of Robert Mylne as a clerk. In 1768 he won the competition for the Royal Exchange (now City Hall), Dublin, which he came to Ireland to build; from 1775 until his death he was clerk and inspector of civil buildings in Ireland. His other Dublin works include Newgate Prison (1773, demolished) and the earliest ranges of the FOUR COURTS (1776), completed by GANDON. Among his private patrons were the Archbishop of Armagh, Richard Robinson, and the Bishop of Killaloe, Robert Fowler. **Frederick O'Dwyer**

Cooney, Joe (1965–), hurler. Born in Co. Galway. He made his inter-county debut in 1983, winning an all-Ireland minor hurling medal with Galway. Since then his achievements have been impressive: under-21 in 1986 and senior medals in 1987 and 1988. He has four National League medals (1987, 1989, 1993, 2000), and five Oireachtas medals. At centre-forward, his displays of skill, positional sense, and sportsmanship have delighted followers of the game over twenty years. His honours include five All-Stars, Texaco Hurler of the Year, 1987, and selection at centre-forward on the GAA. Supreme All-Star team, 1971–2000. With his club, Sarsfields, he won under-16, under-21 and four county senior hurling titles, as well as two all-Ireland club titles in 1993 and 1994. **Séamus J. King**

Cooper, Edward Joshua (1798–1863), astronomer. Born in Dublin; educated at the University of Oxford. In 1830 he established a private observatory at his family seat MARKREE CASTLE, Collooney, Co. Sligo, described in 1851 at the annual meeting of the Royal Astronomical Society as 'the most richly furnished private observatory in existence.' Observations there resulted in the discovery by Andrew Graham in 1848 of a new minor planet, which was named Metis. Cooper, who was elected to the Royal Society (1853) was awarded the Cunningham Gold Medal (1858) for his *Markree Catalogue* of the positions of 60,066 stars, only 8,965 of which had previously been referenced. **Susan McKenna-Lawlor**

co-operative movement, a movement dedicated to the establishment of co-operative creameries, co-operative societies and credit societies in late nineteenth-century Ireland. Several efforts at co-operative organisation were attempted during the nineteenth century, but the co-operative movement emerged in 1889, when HORACE PLUNKETT began his campaign in the Irish countryside. In its early years it concentrated on three areas: co-operative creameries; co-operative societies, which jointly bought agricultural necessities and sold their produce; and credit societies, providing small loans to farmers. Other specialised societies were added. In 1895 the movement was brought together in the IRISH AGRICULTURAL ORGANISATION SOCIETY. The movement may be seen as a part of a range of associations aimed at regenerating social and cultural life in late nineteenth-century Ireland. By the end of the following century the movement had been transformed from one of local economic progress to the sphere of multinational corporations with their bases in Ireland but pursuing a worldwide market. [see AGRICULTURE.] **Carla King**

co-operative. *Farmers with horse and donkey carts queue with their daily delivery of milk outside Cooraclare Creamery, Co. Clare, 1944. Creameries such as this were widely established by the co-operative movement. [Irish Picture Library]*

Coote, Charles (died 1661), appointed parliamentary commander of Connacht in 1645. Operating from west Ulster, he temporarily overran the north-west of the province over the next two years. The execution of Charles I in 1649 brought local Protestant and Scottish forces in Ulster to join the Duke of Ormond's royalist coalition, thereby isolating Coote. He defended DERRY against a protracted siege (March–August 1649) and was again forced onto the defensive in 1650 by an Irish Catholic army. Reinforced, in June 1650 he advanced on the Irish at Scarrifhollis near Letterkenny, Co. Donegal, and routed them, killing at least 2,000 in the action and pursuit, followed by the execution of officer prisoners after the battle. In June 1651 he marched on Athlone from the north-west, bypassing a blocking force. This bold manoeuvre gained the town, the key to Connacht. He besieged Galway throughout the winter and spring of 1651/2 and ultimately secured its surrender in April 1652.

Coote inherited the extensive PLANTATION lands acquired by his father, Charles Coote (died 1642), in the midlands, together with his MINING and manufacturing enterprises. In December 1659 Coote (now Parliamentary Lord President of Connacht) participated in a coup against the Commonwealth government, seizing Dublin Castle and control of the army. By the spring of 1660 he was one of two interim resident commissioners for the government of Ireland. Subsequently, CHARLES II ennobled him as Earl of Mountrath. Coote was stridently anti-Catholic and suspicious of PRESBYTERIANISM, and his brief prominence during the interim period between Commonwealth and RESTORATION helped ensure that the 'Old Protestant' interest in Ireland would dominate the Restoration settlement. **Pádraig Lenihan**

Córas Iompair Éireann (CIÉ), the national rail and road TRANSPORT system of the Republic. Formed in 1945 by a merger between Great Southern Railways and Dublin United Transport Company (successor to Dublin United Tramway Company), CIÉ became a statutory company under the Transport Act (1950), with responsibility for road and rail transport and the obsolescent canal system. Given the formidable task of returning services to profitability, it began replacing steam with diesel traction and renewing rolling stock, but its fortunes continued to disimprove, and in a submission to the Beddy Committee (1956) it sought restrictions on private road freight transport as an alternative to ever-increasing subsidies. The Transport Act (1958) required CIÉ to break even by 1964; when it became clear that this was not achievable, another act recognised the distinction between commercial services and those socially desirable, which would in future be subsidised.

The RAILWAY system seemed to have little economic future, though the McKinsey Report (1970) concluded that it would cost more to close it down than to attempt to remedy the situation. The rail development plan of 1974 attempted to give reality to this assessment by changes in work practices and by further closures of little-used lines, while the introduction of a central traffic control system and the acquisition of powerful new LOCOMOTIVES in the mid-1970s greatly improved services on remaining trunk routes. By 1979 passenger-journeys were exceeding 17 million annually, while freight, concentrated on container and heavy bulk traffic, was buoyant. Deficits, however, were not contained, rising from £9.6 million in 1974 to £39.5 million five years later. Road services fared somewhat better. The introduction of the first Bus Éireann 'Expressway' services in 1961 was followed by an increase in the number of routes to fifty; in 1975 some 307 million people travelled by bus, as against 14 million by train.

In 1980 another McKinsey Report recommended dividing CIÉ into three operating companies—for rail, provincial road, and Dublin city bus services—but this was not acted on until 1987 with the establishment of Iarnród Éireann, Bus Éireann, and Bus Átha Cliath, respectively. In the meantime the electrification of Dublin suburban lines in 1984 demonstrated that rail still had a role to play, particularly with regard to commuter movements; but in 1987 long-standing plans to extend this system and to build an underground line between Heuston Station and Connolly Station were abandoned by the FIANNA FÁIL Government, which also abolished the Dublin Transport Authority, set up twelve months previously by the Coalition Government of FINE GAEL and the LABOUR PARTY. A Green Paper of 1985 had noted that, of ten railways in EEC countries, eight were receiving a higher subsidy than CIÉ; but no remedial action was taken, with the result that by the late 1980s the underfunded system was unable to replace obsolescent equipment or to maintain adequate safety standards without drastically reducing speeds, and several lines came under serious threat of closure.

The rapidly worsening traffic situation in Dublin and the extension of commuting to towns up to 80 km (50 miles) from the city finally forced a serious attempt to tackle the shortcomings of public transport in the 1990s. A start was made on the provision of dedicated bus lanes; but the three CIÉ companies continued to be seriously hampered not only by the legacy of bad INDUSTRIAL RELATIONS but by their inability to secure a clear mandate, supported by adequate funds. Transport in Dublin continued to lack any central planning authority, though an essentially advisory body, the Dublin Transport Initiative, came out strongly in favour of light rail transit. In April 2000 a strategic review of rail services for the greater Dublin area proposed an expenditure of £1.6 million, while funds made available under the National Development Plan, 2000–2006, and from the EUROPEAN UNION were enabling CIÉ to embark on a major upgrading and renewal scheme, principally of its rail infrastructure.

In April 2000 the Minister for Public Enterprise announced plans to remove the ownership of Iarnród Éireann, Bus Éireann, and Bus Átha Cliath from CIÉ, with the possible privatisation of one or more of them, opening transport services in general to private operators. **Bernard Share**

Córas Tráchtála, a Government agency established in the Republic in 1951 in the form of a limited company (also known as the Irish Export Board) for the promotion and development of exports, originally to the United States and, from 1958, throughout the world. In 1959 it became a statutory body as Córas Tráchtála and then in 1991 An Bord Tráchtála (the Irish Trade Board) on its merger with the Irish Goods Council. In 1998 it merged again, with Forbairt, to become Enterprise Ireland, the development agency for indigenous companies. **Rose Mary Craig**

Cór Chúil Aodha, founded in 1964 by SEÁN Ó RIADA as a church choir in Coolea, Co. Cork; subsequently developed a secular role, using the rich local song tradition as a foundation. The choir has been conducted since Ó Riada's death in 1971 by his son Peadar Ó Riada. [see Ó RIADA MASSES.] **Pat Ahern**

Corcomroe Abbey, Co. Clare, a CISTERCIAN monastery founded c. 1195. The remains consist of a cruciform church with a single chapel projecting eastwards from each transept from c. 1210–25. The east end of the building is distinguished by the high-quality carvings, several of which demonstrate precociously naturalistic renderings of plants. The church was altered in the fifteenth century by the shortening of the nave and the addition of a bell-turret. The tomb effigy in the presbytery is of King Conchúr na Siudaine Ó Briain (died 1267). [see ABBEYS.] **Rachel Moss**

Corcoran, Frank (1944–), composer. He studied in Dublin, Maynooth, Rome, and Berlin and was a music inspector for the Department of Education from 1971 to 1979. In 1980 he was awarded a composer fellowship in Berlin and subsequently professorships at Berlin and Stuttgart; since 1983 he has been professor of composition and theory at the Staatliche Hochschule für Musik und Darstellende Kunst, Hamburg. His output includes orchestral, chamber, vocal, choral, and electro-acoustic works. He was visiting professor and Fulbright scholar at the University of Wisconsin at Milwaukee 1989–1990, and is a member of AOSDÁNA. **David Mooney**

Corcoran, Seán (1946–), singer, researcher, and musician. Born in Drogheda. Greatly influenced by local singers such as Mary Ann Carolan, Corcoran began collecting songs while at school. During the 1970s he was assistant editor of BREANDÁN BREATHNACH's publication *Ceol*. Under the auspices of the ARTS COUNCIL OF NORTHERN IRELAND and the IRISH TRADITIONAL MUSIC ARCHIVE he has undertaken fieldwork throughout Ireland and is a recognised authority on traditional song. His published works include *Here's a Health* (1986). Highly regarded as a singer, he also plays the bouzouki and has recorded three CDs with the group Cran: *Crooked Stairs* (1992), *Black, Black, Black* (1998), and *Lover's Ghost* (2000). **Desi Wilkinson**

Corcoran, Timothy (1872–1943), JESUIT priest and educationalist. Born in Co. Tipperary, educated at Clongowes Wood and University College, Dublin. As professor of EDUCATION at UCD, 1909–42, he exerted considerable influence on educational policy-makers in the new FREE STATE and founded *Studies* in 1912. His advice to the First and Second National Programme Conferences, the reports of which were published in 1922 and 1926, respectively, contributed to the policy of immersion in Irish in infant classes and the teaching of all subjects through Irish in primary school classes, which underpinned the primary school curriculum for the first forty years after independence. He was also influential in the reform of the secondary school curriculum, especially the curriculum in English and history. Though not an Irish-speaker, he was convinced that schooling had a crucial role to play in the revival of Irish. **Áine Hyland**

Cork, County (*Contae Chorcaí*)

Province:	MUNSTER
County town:	CORK
Area:	7,459 km^2 (2,880 sq. miles)
Population (2002):	448,181
Features:	BANTRY BAY
	Boggeragh Mountains
	Nagle Mountains
	River BLACKWATER
	River LEE
Of historical interest:	BLARNEY CASTLE
	CHARLES FORT
	Kanturk Castle
	ST COLEMAN'S CATHEDRAL, COBH
	St Mary's Collegiate Church, Youghal
Industry and products:	BREWING
	Dairy farming
	DISTILLING
	Fishing
	Marble-quarrying
	Natural gas
	Pharmaceuticals
	TEXTILES

Petula Martyn

County Cork is the largest county in Ireland. Sandstone ridges and limestone valleys that are east–west in orientation dominate the landscape; in these valleys flow the River Blackwater, River Lee,

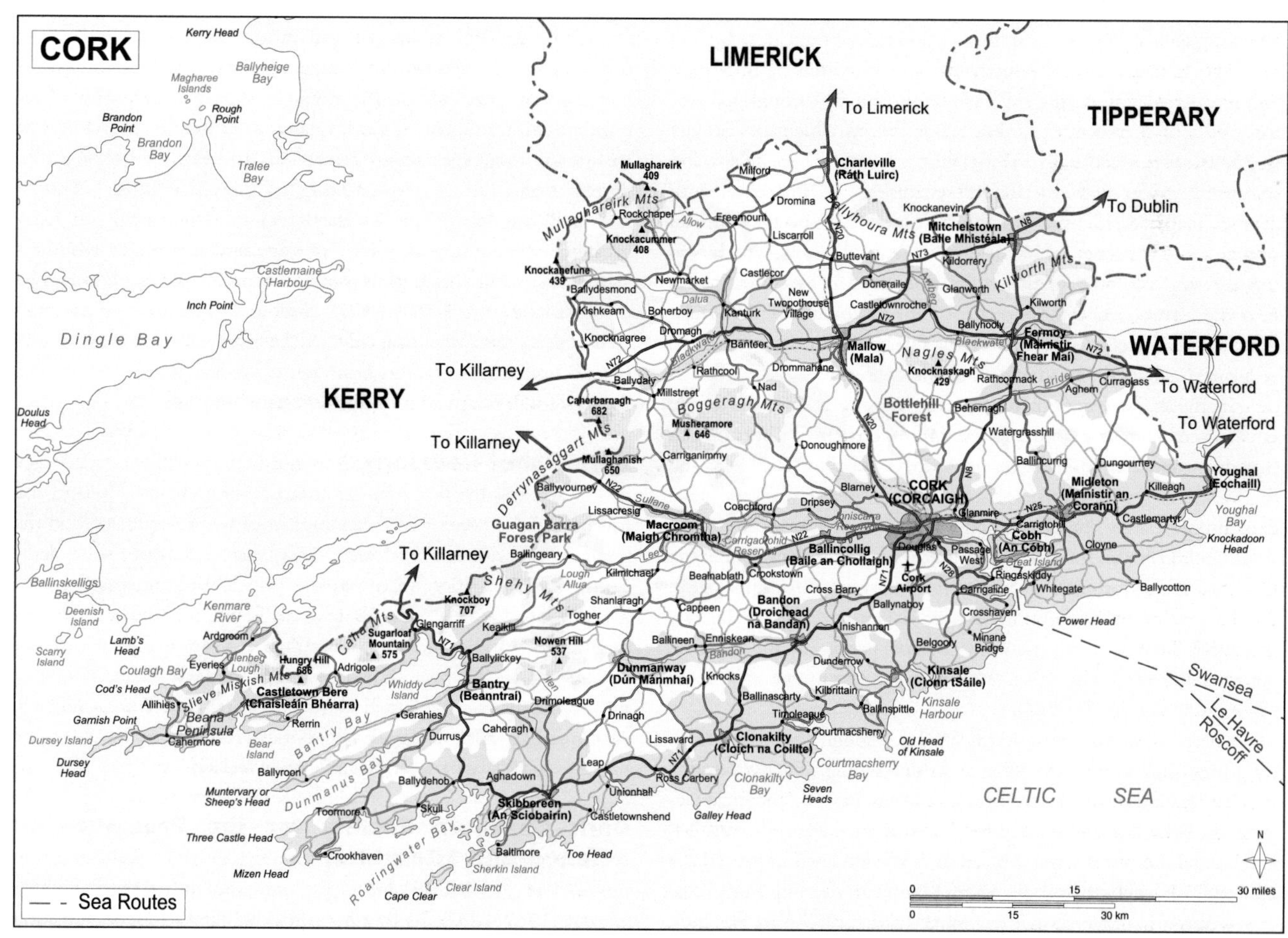

and River Bandon. AGRICULTURE is important, with dairying predominant, while arable production is significant to the east of the harbour area. According to legend, the city of Cork owes its origins to St FINBARR, who was formerly believed to have established a MONASTERY and school in the seventh century on dry land overlooking *Corcach Mhór na Mumhan* (the Great Marsh of Munster), the site today of St Finbarr's Cathedral. Cork is host to both a university and an institute of technology, which provide a skilled workforce for the greater Cork region. Cork's maritime tradition has played an important role in the development of both the city and its hinterland. The HARBOUR area is the principal site of the pharmaceutical and CHEMICAL INDUSTRIES in Ireland. Traditional industries include brewing (Murphy's and Beamish and Crawford's breweries) and distilling. There is a ferry terminal at Ringaskiddy, with links to Swansea and Cherbourg. The growth in importance of AVIATION has seen the expansion of Cork Airport and an associated industrial estate 8 km (5 miles) to the south-west of the city. Tourist attractions include the villages and towns of Blarney, Kinsale, Clonakilty, Cobh, and Youghal. **Raymond O'Connor and John Crowley**

Cork (*Corcaigh*), the third-biggest city in Ireland and second city of the Republic, at the mouth of the River LEE. The town was established by the VIKINGS in the tenth century on a low-lying marshy site on the valley floor. In the twelfth century the ANGLO-NORMANS built a fortified city between the two main river channels; the walled city measured approximately 640 by 220 m (2,000 by 720 ft), with SUBURBS later developing on the higher land to the north and south. The city wall was damaged in the siege in 1690 and was demolished when the marshes were reclaimed and the city expanded. The new developments were laid out in small gridiron patterns of commercial streets, with little of the elegance of the Georgian developments in Dublin and Limerick and none of the great squares or parks of that period. Nevertheless Cork became an important and prosperous city during the eighteenth century through its control of the market in BUTTER and pickled meat, which were vitally important when travel by sailing-ship was subject to delays and uncertainty. The introduction of steamships in the nineteenth century badly affected the provision business. Despite the erection of many fine churches, public and commercial buildings, trade was stagnant and the bulk of the population lived in wretched slums near the centre, while the merchant elite had built suburban villas in the more attractive areas outside the city. Its population remained at approximately 80,000 throughout the century.

In the early twentieth century the economy was boosted by new factories built by Ford and Dunlop on reclaimed slobland, and the civic survey of 1926 began the process of slum clearance and the building of new public HOUSING estates on the outskirts. Like that of other cities, the population of the inner city was in continuous decline for most of the twentieth century as new suburban developments, both public and private, spread into rural areas. At the end of the twentieth century the population of the city was over 127,000, with a further 53,000 people in the suburbs. Another 61,000 lived within 24 km (15 miles) of the city, in its commuting region.

Cork's economy has a healthy mix. Though the older heavy industries, such as Ford, Dunlop, and shipbuilding, all closed during the 1980s, Cork now has the largest concentration of chemical factories in Ireland, established in the harbour area. Many COMPUTER and related industries are also based in Cork, attracted in part by the National Microelectronics Research Centre in the university. The city is also a regional shopping centre. In the 1970s and 80s most new developments were in suburban sites, but more recently the city centre has been revived, with both purpose-built SHOPPING CENTRES and the conversion of obsolete buildings. So far Cork has resisted out-of-town superstores, though some have been proposed. Pubs, clubs, cinemas, and restaurants are also heavily concentrated in the centre, helping to maintain the city's vibrancy. University College is within walking distance, though Cork Institute of Technology is 6 km (4 miles) away from the centre in the western suburbs. The office and financial sector in Cork has only regional importance and is dominated by Dublin.

Cork has benefited since the 1970s from careful and sensitive planning. In 1968 a report proposed the building of a raised limited-access road around the city centre and the provision of large car parks; the public was outraged, though Cork City Council accepted the proposals. But they were never implemented and were succeeded by a more sensible plan (known as LUTS) in 1978; this encouraged public transport and restrained private cars. Some new roads were proposed, though along the line of former railways, with new BRIDGES to relieve congestion. Though the restraints on motorists were not imposed, most of the other proposals were implemented, culminating in the opening of the JACK LYNCH tunnel under the River Lee in 1999. Today Cork has more than two dozen bridges, both vehicular and pedestrian, and several multi-storey car parks; but traffic remains a serious problem. Since 1986 the city has benefited from URBAN RENEWAL, which has led to the first population increase in the central area in more than a century and an improved townscape. During the 1990s Cork participated in the Urban Pilot Project initiated by the EUROPEAN UNION and developed a Historic Centre Action Plan to enhance the medieval core. Cork City Council was awarded the Silver Jubilee Cup by the Royal Town Planning Institute in 2000 for these plans.

Cork remains a city of narrow streets and church spires, though its traditional building-stones, limestone and red sandstone, have given way to more modern materials. Despite these homogenising influences, Cork retains a distinctive character. The traditional food specialities, tripe and drisheen, are thought to derive from the meat-processing of the eighteenth century. Culturally the city is split by the River Lee: the north side has a greater concentration of public housing and a stronger working-class ethos, while the south is more affluent. Rivalries are expressed through HURLING and FOOTBALL clubs and even through the brass bands of the two opposing sides of the river. Cork also has a long literary and artistic tradition, though nowadays it is better known for its choral, jazz, and film festivals. **Kevin Hourihan**

Cork Ballet Company, founded by JOAN DENISE MORIARTY in 1947. It was the first amateur company of its kind in Ireland and for over forty years produced high-quality performances of the standard repertoire and of many Irish works, thanks to the dedication of its founder, who was the principal choreographer, and ALOYS FLEISCHMANN, who made available the services of the Cork Symphony Orchestra. The success of the company led to the creation of the first professional company, the Irish Ballet Company, in 1963, later renamed Irish National Ballet. The Cork company continued to produce works, to critical acclaim, until 1993. [see BALLET; DANCE, CONTEMPORARY.] **David Mooney**

Cork Cuvierian Society for the Promotion of Science and Literature, founded in 1835 and named in honour of the French anatomist and zoologist Baron George Cuvier (1769–1832). Its founders included James Roche, a banker

Cork. *Ireland's third city and the commercial, cultural, educational and industrial capital of the province of Munster. The River Lee runs west-to-east through the city in two main channels. [Imagefile]*

(the society's first president), and Richard Sainthill, a numismatist; other original members included the antiquarian T. CROFTON CROKER, Robert Day, John Windele, and Father Matt Horgan. Richard Caulfield, Denny Lane, and GEORGE BOOLE later became associated with it, as did Col. J. E. PORTLOCK, director of the ORDNANCE SURVEY. It was linked with the ROYAL CORK INSTITUTION, with which its membership overlapped, and it acquired the resources of the institution and supplanted it as a unifying body for the study in Cork of SCIENCE, literature, and antiquities.

The society's interests included statistics and political economy; its exclusively male members investigated such phenomena as rainfall and POTATO blight. Its monthly meetings were held in the library of the Royal Cork Institution (now the Crawford Gallery). Much of its intellectual power was supplied by members of the academic staff of Queen's College, Cork. It did not publish a journal. From the 1860s, as scientific studies became more specialised and interest in antiquities increased, the society became the Cork Cuvierian and Archaeological Society. When it eventually broke up in the early 1880s some of its surviving members, such as Robert Day, joined the Cork Historical and Archaeological Society (founded 1891), which still flourishes and whose Council continues to meet in the library of the Crawford Gallery. **John A. Murphy**

Corkery, Daniel (1878–1964), schoolteacher and GAELIC LEAGUE activist. Born in Cork; attended St Patrick's College, Dublin. Corkery jointly founded the Cork Dramatic Society with TERENCE MACSWINEY in 1908 and from 1916 achieved literary fame through his short stories. He supported SINN FÉIN after 1916 and supported the republicans in the CIVIL WAR. After 1923 he became more intransigent; his view of Irishness as Catholic, Gaelic, and rural, as in *Synge and Anglo-Irish Literature* (1931), alienated his protégés SEAN O'FAOLAIN and FRANK O'CONNOR. He is best remembered for his influential study of eighteenth-century Munster poets, *The Hidden Ireland* (1924), a flawed but devastating evocation of cultural loss. **Patrick Maume**

Cork Folk Festival, established in 1979, with Timmy McCarthy as director; other directors have included Jim Walsh and William Hammond. A TRADITIONAL MUSIC slant later gave way to a wider musical base. Those who have taken part include Mary Black, CHRISTY MOORE, the CHIEFTAINS, PAUL BRADY, ALTAN, Emmy Lou Harris, Billy Bragg, Flaco Jiminez, Michelle Shocked, DÉ DANANN, and Martin Carthy. **Pat Ahern**

Cork gunpowder explosion. On 3 November 1810 twenty-two people were killed and more than forty injured when gunpowder stored in a labourer's house in Brandy Lane (now St Finbarr's Road), Cork, exploded. An inquiry revealed that workers from the BALLINCOLLIG gunpowder factory had been selling stolen gunpowder to quarrymen; it also established that the method used for drying stolen gunpowder was to hold a lighted candle to it, and that one of the men implicated in the theft had been drinking heavily on the night of the explosion. **Ciarán Deane**

Cork International Choral and Dance Festival, an annual event founded in 1954. Over the years it has gained a reputation as one of the world's premier choral festivals, noted for its presentation of outstanding amateur national and international choirs. The national section presents competitions for both school and adult choirs. The festival organises a number of other activities around the competitions, including informal choral performances, church music, a 'composers in the classroom' scheme, and an acclaimed seminar on contemporary choral music, organised jointly with UCC. **David Mooney**

Cork Opera House, a multi-purpose theatre with a seating capacity of 2,000. Originally built as the Athenaeum in 1854, it was rebuilt in 1875 after the closure of the THEATRE ROYAL and renamed the Opera House. The building was destroyed by fire in 1955 and was replaced by the present building at Lavitt's Quay designed by MICHAEL SCOTT. The original opera house was an important centre in the musical and cultural life of Cork, providing a venue for amateur and professional opera companies and for the CORK BALLET COMPANY. **David Mooney**

Cork Port. Cork is the principal commercial port of the south of Ireland. A Ballast Board was established in 1785 and Harbour Commissioners in 1813. The main quays along the River LEE were built between 1864 and 1906 and the north and south deep-water quays in 1877–84. Retaining walls and a dredged channel to Blackrock lead to a natural deep-water harbour. Construction of the Marina Estate was begun in 1917, container terminals in 1970 and 1991, and Ringaskiddy deep-water terminal in 1992. **Ronald Cox**

Cork School of Music, founded in 1878, the first municipal school of music to be established in the British Isles. Under the City of Cork VEC (1930–92) staff and student numbers grew significantly; its third-level status was enhanced in 1993 when it became part of Cork Regional Technical College, now Cork Institute of Technology; it is now the largest conservatory in Ireland, with a staff of 120 and more than 3,600 students. In 1999 the Government approved major funding for the rebuilding of the school. The director of the school is DR GEOFFREY SPRATT. **David Mooney**

Corlea Bog, Co. Longford, site of the discovery in the 1980s of a number of wooden TRACKWAYS, most of NEOLITHIC and BRONZE AGE date. The most impressive, however, was an exceptionally large example of IRON AGE date, 1 km (0.6 miles) in length. This was made of split oak planks 15–50 cm ($\frac{1}{2}$–$1\frac{1}{2}$ ft) in width and up to 4 m (13 ft) long. These were placed edge to edge on parallel pairs of longitudinal roundwood stems on the original surface of the bog. Sharpened pegs had been hammered through rectangular mortices in the ends of the planks to prevent lateral movement of the main timbers. Tree-ring analysis has established a date of 148 BC for the felling of the oaks. The only finds found in association with it, however, were of wood. These included fragments of vessels, portion of an *ard* (an early form of plough), and what may be a very primitive anthropomorphic or zoomorphic carving. Most spectacular was a beautifully carved composite object of ash, of unknown function, which is one of the finest surviving examples of Iron Age carpentry in Europe.

It can be assumed that the construction of the Corlea road involved an organised and sizeable work force, directed and controlled by a central power. Similarly it may be assumed that it was part of a wider regional network of communication. In the absence of any contemporary settlement in the surrounding area, however, or of any other evidence of contemporary activity, we cannot be certain of its precise original purpose. Nonetheless there can be little doubt that it was intended for wheeled transport, though no unequivocal evidence of this was discovered. At any rate it is known that the wheel was already in use in Ireland at this time, as in the examples from the fourth or third century BC from Doogarrymore, Co. Roscommon. In northern Germany and in the eastern Netherlands similar roads of split oaks have been found that are not only of precisely similar construction but almost exactly contemporary with that from Corlea. [see BOGS; DENDOCHRONOLOGY; WETLAND ARCHAEOLOGY.] **Barry Raftery**

Corleck, Co. Cavan, site of a three-faced head, now in the NATIONAL MUSEUM, Dublin, representing a triple god or goddess, carved from a block of sandstone. The features are reduced to the simplest forms: round eyes, rudimentary nose, and narrow slit mouth. One face has a small hole cut in the middle of the mouth, a feature found on some Continental heads and suggesting a link with oracular practices. A small hole at the base was probably a mortise for attaching the head to a stand. [see IDOLS.] **Helen Lanigan Wood**

Cormac mac Airt, the most famous of the kings of Ireland. He probably had some historical basis and is said to have reigned during the third century. Regardless of his origin, he came to represent the sacred KINGSHIP OF TARA and, having assumed this vital role, to be associated with other groups and leaders. Peace, prosperity, and an abundance of crops and growth were synonymous with his reign, though he was occasionally forced to go into exile from Tara when his kingship came under threat.

Cormac was never reluctant to go into battle, and always emerged victorious. Numerous hero-tales were told about him; and the various accounts of his birth and infancy, including elements of prophecy, magic, and ritual, indicate his future greatness. One narrative recounts that after a druid had made signs around him to protect him from wounding, drowning, fire, sorcery, and wolves, a she-wolf came and took him away and thereafter nursed him—an immediate reminder of the classical story of Romulus and Remus. Cormac's judgments as king were recorded as being good and just. In some texts he is said to have married Eithne, daughter of the King of Leinster, Cathaoir Mór, and he is also said to have fallen in love with Cearnait, daughter of the Pictish king. They became lovers, but the jealous Eithne made a slave of Cearnait, and Cormac employed a tradesman who built a mill for Cearnait so that she was no longer obliged to work as a slave. Cormac lost his wife, daughter and son, whom he had to exchange for a magic branch that produced music that would heal every ill. Another magic possession was his exceptionally sharp sword of light; and, like other leaders and kings, he had his personal druid-adviser and seer, Ciothruadh. It would appear that Cormac became associated with FIONN MAC CUMHAILL in narratives from the eighth century onwards. [see CATH; MYTHOLOGY.] **Ríonach uí Ógáin**

Cormac mac Cuileannáin (died 908), Bishop and King of Cashel, 902–8, when he was killed at the battle of Bealach Mughna (Ballymoon, Co. Kildare). The fullest biography is preserved in the annals of the FOUR MASTERS, and his death is recorded in the Fragmentary Annals, where he is described as 'a scholar of Latin and Irish ... a pure chief bishop ... a sage in government.' Traditionally, a wide range of literary works has been attributed to him, including Leabhar na gCeart (the Book of Rights), Sanas Chormaic (Cormac's Glossary), and the manuscript collection known as the Psalter of Cashel, but recent scholarship has tended to play down his involvement in such literary projects. **Paul Russell**

'Cormac's Instructions': see 'TECOSCA CORMAIC'.

Corn Laws. The Corn Law (1815) was largely a response to the lobbying of Sir Henry Parnell and Irish landowners, who feared that the end of Napoleonic wartime conditions would lead to the collapse of grain prices and landed prosperity. The laws promoted TILLAGE FARMING by placing tariffs on imported corn but were abolished by ROBERT PEEL in 1846 in the wake of the GREAT FAMINE. **Peter Gray**

Cornwallis, Charles, first Marquis (1738–1805), soldier and administrator. Born in London; educated at Eton College, Windsor. After service as a commander in America (where he suffered defeat at Yorktown) and in India, he was appointed joint commander-in-chief of the forces in Ireland and LORD LIEUTENANT in June 1798. He directed the final suppression of the UNITED IRISHMEN and their French allies. Loyalists dubbed him 'Cornywallis' for his leniency towards defeated rebels. The main object of his viceroyalty was the passing of the ACT OF UNION. **Allan Blackstock**

Corrigan, Dominic John (1802–1880), physician. Born in Dublin; educated at the University of Edinburgh. He served as physician at various Dublin hospitals, including the Richmond, and also established a lucrative private practice. In 1832 he published his paper 'On permanent patency of the mouth of the aorta,' describing the condition now known as Corrigan's disease. He was elected MP for Dublin in 1870, but his advocacy in Parliament of non-denominational university education led him into conflict with the Catholic Church. He was the first Catholic to achieve prominence in the Irish medical establishment. **Rod Gow**

Corrigan, Douglas ('Wrong-Way Corrigan') (1907–1995), American aviator. Born in Texas. Having worked on Lindbergh's *Spirit of St Louis*, he attempted an Atlantic crossing from New York on 16 July 1938. Because his plane, a Curtiss 'Robin' monoplane, did not pass the requirements of the American authorities for the 4,800 km (300-mile) flight, he told them he would be flying to Los Angeles. Twenty-one hours later he arrived at Baldonnel, Co. Dublin, and enquired, tongue in cheek, whether it was California, earning him the nickname 'Wrong-Way Corrigan'. **Donal MacCarron**

Corrymeela Community, Co. Antrim, a project to promote reconciliation in Northern Ireland. One of its most striking features is that it dates from before the eruption of the violence that heralded the 'TROUBLES', having been formed in 1965 largely on the initiative of Rev. Ray Davey, Presbyterian chaplain at Queen's University, Belfast, to promote better relations by bringing together people of differing backgrounds. Rev. Trevor Williams succeeded Dr John Morrow as leader in 1993, and five years later an impressive complex of extensions was opened, sensitively set into the basalt escarpment near Ballycastle, Co. Antrim. The organisation involves an 'all-inclusive Christian community with members from all major denominations' (an indication that most 'conservative evangelicals' exclude themselves) and provides opportunities to individuals, groups and communities to meet, 'to dispel ignorance, prejudice and fear,' and to promote initiatives for social and political development. [see GLENCREE CENTRE FOR RECONCILIATION.] **Jonathan Bardon**

Corrymeela. *Students take part in a 'co-operation game' at the Corrymeela Community, Ballycastle, Co. Antrim. An inclusive Christian community, it aims to bring together both sides of the sectarian divide. [Corrymeela Community]*

Cosgrave, Liam (1920–), politician. Born in Dublin, a son of W. T. COSGRAVE; educated at KING'S INNS. He was called to the bar in 1943, served in the DEFENCE FORCES during the years of the SECOND WORLD WAR, and became a senior counsel in 1958. He was elected to DÁIL ÉIREANN for FINE GAEL in 1943, becoming Government secretary, chief whip and parliamentary secretary to the TAOISEACH and Minister for Industry and Commerce, 1948–51, and Minister for External Affairs, 1954–7. As leader of Fine Gael, 1965–77, he was Taoiseach in a Coalition Government, 1973–7, that introduced stringent measures against the IRA and played a controversial role in the resignation of President CEARBHALL Ó DÁLAIGH. His term of office saw the conclusion of the SUNNINGDALE AGREEMENT of Northern Ireland, the creation of the post of Director of Public Prosecutions and the successful first Irish presidency of the European Community. He resigned as leader of Fine Gael after its electoral defeat in 1977 and retired from politics in 1981. **Marie Coleman**

Cosgrave, William T. (1880–1965), revolutionary and politician. Born in Dublin; educated at Francis Street CBS and O'Brien Institute. Elected SINN FÉIN member of Dublin City Council 1909, he joined the IRISH VOLUNTEERS in 1913 and fought in the South Dublin Union during the 1916 RISING. He was elected for Sinn Féin in the Kilkenny by-election of August 1917 but did not take his seat in Westminster; re-elected in the 1918 general election, he remained a TD until 1944. He was Minister for LOCAL GOVERNMENT in DÁIL ÉIREANN, 1919–21, and in the PROVISIONAL GOVERNMENT, 1922, overseeing Sinn Féin's control of local government. After the deaths of ARTHUR GRIFFITH and MICHAEL COLLINS in August 1922 he became president of the Dáil Government and chairman of the Provisional Government. In 1923 he established and became first leader of CUMANN NA NGAEDHEAL (later Fine Gael). As first President of the Executive Council (head of government) of the IRISH FREE STATE, 1922–32, he oversaw the defeat of IRA resistance during the CIVIL WAR and presided over the establishment of the new state until his Government was defeated by FIANNA FÁIL in 1932. His policy of fiscal rectitude created an enduring stability for the state. His administration established the ESB, the first state-sponsored company, and in foreign affairs established Irish diplomatic representation abroad. He ceded the leadership of Fine Gael to EOIN O'DUFFY in 1933 but returned as leader in 1935, remaining until his retirement from politics in 1944. **Marie Coleman**

Costello, Elizabeth Mary (Betty) (1908–2001), pianist. Born in Co. Kildare. One of the last piano students of MICHELE ESPOSITO, she also studied with Jean du Chastain and Annie Lord at the RIAM. From 1950 she taught piano at the Municipal School of Music (now DIT Conservatory of Music and Drama) and was subsequently vice-principal, 1969–73. Her pupils included GERARD GILLEN and MÍCHEÁL O'ROURKE. **Ite O'Donovan**

Costello, John A. (1891–1976), politician. Born in Dublin, educated at O'Connell Schools and UCD. Costello was a barrister and a pro-Treaty nationalist. He served as a legal officer (Attorney-General, 1926–32) in the first governments of the IRISH FREE STATE until 1932. Elected a TD for CUMANN NA NGAEDHEAL in 1933, he was chosen as a compromise TAOISEACH for the first inter-party Government, 1948–51, in place of his party leader, RICHARD MULCAHY. He was a prime mover in 1949 in the decision to declare Ireland a republic but also in the rejection of NÖEL BROWNE'S

Cosgrave, W. T. *Election sticker or lapel badge in support of the Sinn Féin candidate W. T. Cosgrave in the 1918 general election, in a vaguely shamrock-like shape. [Stephen Lalor collection]*

public health plans. His Government brought about the near elimination of tuberculosis, the setting up of the Industrial Development Authority and the entry of the Republic into the UNITED NATIONS. He was again Taoiseach from 1954 to 1957. **John Horgan**

Costello, Michael J. (1904–1986), soldier and businessman. Born in Cloghjordan, Co. Tipperary. He fought in the WAR OF INDEPENDENCE, 1919–21, and joined the FREE STATE ARMY in 1922, becoming a colonel-commandant at the age of eighteen during the CIVIL WAR, 1922–3. In 1923 he was Director of Intelligence and in 1926–7 a member of the military mission to the United States that greatly influenced future planning. He was Assistant Chief of Staff, 1937–9, and during the years of the SECOND WORLD WAR was officer commanding Southern Command, 1939–41, and officer commanding the First Division, 1941–5. In 1945 he entered civilian life as general manager of the Irish Sugar Company, retiring in 1966 (see p. 350). **Patrick Long**

costume. *Costume plates by Lucas de Heere from* Beschrijving der Britische Eilander *illustrating different forms of dress in Ireland from c. 1575: (left to right) noblewoman, townswoman, kern or foot-soldier, and 'wild' Irishman, clothed only in an Irish mantle. [By permission of the British Library; Ms. 28300]*

costume plates. Unlike FASHION plates, which illustrated designs for CLOTHING, costume plates were records of the clothing worn. In the sixteenth century costume plates illustrated people of different nations at a time when, in a quickly expanding world, there was a need to understand the clothes and manners of strangers. In the seventeenth century this expanded into looking at class distinctions and the clothing that represented occupations. Those who recorded the dress of Irish people included Albrecht Dürer, c. 1521, Christoph Weiditz, 1529–32, Lucas de Heere, 1567–77, Caspar Rutz, 1588, John Speede, c. 1610, and Wenceslaus Hollar, c. 1640. [see CLOTHING, TRADITIONAL.] **Mairead Dunlevy**

Cotter, Maud (1954–), artist. Born in Wexford; studied at Crawford School of Art, Cork, 1972–8. Stained glass dominated her first solo show (Crawford Gallery, 1983). She was joint founder of the National Sculpture Factory in 1989. Major glass and sculptural pieces include *Tensile Myriads* (1983), in the AIB collection, the MICHAEL SCOTT memorial window in Kingston Lewes, Sussex (1994), and *Absolute Jellies Making Singing Sounds* (1994) in TEMPLE BAR. Solo shows—such as 'Mute Displacement' (1995), 'In Absence' (1998), and 'Shadow' (1999)—indicate the more conceptual direction of her work. *Four Clouds Approaching* (card and plaster, 2000) was commissioned by the Incorporated Law Society, Dublin. She is a member of AOSDÁNA. **Vera Ryan**

Cotter, Patrick (c. 1761–1806), giant. Born in Kinsale, Co. Cork. He worked as a bricklayer before he toured himself as an attraction, then retired to Clifton, Gloucestershire, in 1804. He is buried at the Jesuit chapel in Trenchard Street, Bristol, where a tablet states that he was 8 ft 3 in. (251 cm) tall; his coffin plate gives his height as 8 ft 1 in. (246 cm). **Ciarán Deane**

Coughlan, Mary (1957–), singer. Born in Galway. She was discovered at a talent contest, and her evocative renditions of old JAZZ and blues songs won her acclaim in the early 1980s. After she moved from Galway to Dublin in the mid-1980s her life quickly became as emotive as the material she covered. Her debut album, *Tired and Emotional* (1985), revealed an interpretative singer of depth. After a series of personal crises in the 1990s she has become one of Ireland's most instinctive and intuitive vocalists. **Tony Clayton-Lea**

Coughlin, Charles Edward, 'The Radio Priest' (1891–1979), priest, broadcaster, and demagogue. Born in Hamilton, Ontario, of Irish extraction; studied for the priesthood and was ordained in 1916, becoming a parish priest and popular preacher. In 1926 he began religious broadcasts from WJR, Detroit, gradually expanding his themes to include social issues, current affairs, and the perceived threat of international communism. Known as 'the Radio Priest', his increasingly right-wing views embraced anti-Semitism in his broadcasts and through his journal *Social Justice*. By the late 1930s his followers in the Christian Front were emulating the thuggery of Nazi Germany. From 1940 he was prevented by the National Association of Broadcasters from remaining on the air, and he was eventually silenced by his bishop in 1942. At the height of his popularity Coughlin broadcast to an audience of up to 40 million listeners. **Brian Lalor**

Coulter, Phil (1942–), performer, songwriter, producer, and entrepreneur. Born in Derry. During the 1960s he jointly wrote songs for Them, Sandie Shaw, and Cliff Richard. In the 1970s he became a pop Svengali, moulding the Bay City Rollers into British teeny-bop stars and writing such hits as 'Shang-a-Lang'. A respected producer of TRADITIONAL MUSIC, working with PLANXTY and the DUBLINERS, he wrote two of the most famous songs associated with Luke Kelly, 'The Town I Love So Well' (about Coulter's native city) and 'Scorn Not His Simplicity' (about disability). In the 1980s and 90s Coulter and his orchestra recorded the commercially successful 'Tranquillity' series of Celtic-flavoured easy-listening albums. **Mick Heaney**

Council for the Status of Women: see NATIONAL WOMEN'S COUNCIL OF IRELAND

Counter-Reformation, a movement for the revival of the Roman Catholic Church and countering the REFORMATION, formalised during the Council of Trent (1545–63). Though three bishops from the west of Ireland attended the closing session of the council, efforts to implement in their dioceses its decrees concerning the reformed practice of Catholicism and the disciplining of clergy and laity were frustrated by the outlawing of worship outside the Anglican state church. In the 1560s and 70s a Papal emissary, DAVID WOLFE, and other members of the newly established Society of Jesus who had been educated abroad laboured, without much success, to establish a mission to confirm the faith of their fellow-countrymen. The papally appointed Archbishop of Armagh, Richard Creagh (1523–1586), failed to gain a foothold in his diocese and spent most of his episcopal career in prisons in Dublin and London. Among the OLD ENGLISH community of the PALE and the towns, resistance to the state church took the form of a defence of traditional rites and institutions that provided a basis for more organised Roman Catholic reform in the early seventeenth century. Though most of these recusants preferred quietist opposition to PROTESTANTISM, a minority was attracted to protest in arms in REBELLIONS such as those of Viscount BALTINGLASS and JAMES FITZMAURICE. The formation of a Counter-REFORMATION ideology resulted from the execution in the 1580s of Catholic clergy and lay people who were perceived by their co-religionists as having died in defence of their RELIGION. Practical effect was given to this ideology by missioners who were trained abroad in Continental seminaries, some of which, such as those of LOUVAIN and SALAMANCA, were exclusively for Irish students.

By the early seventeenth century, under the aegis of a newly resident Catholic episcopate, an alternative system of parish worship, shadowing that of the state church, had come into being. Diocesan SYNODS supervised the regulation of parish life, the cultivation of the Catholic sacraments, and the provision of catechetical instruction. The pace of Catholic reform varied, as new ecclesiastical standards frequently came into conflict with social mores and traditions in relation, for example, to baptism, MARRIAGE, and funeral customs; but by 1640 the congregations of the state Protestant church were dwarfed by large Catholic communities, inspired and confirmed by the work of the Counter-Reformation ministers.

Despite internal divisions between regular and secular clergy over jurisdictional matters, and disagreements over relations with the state, the Counter-Reformation organisation proved strong enough to survive, with difficulty, the severe dislocation of the middle decades of the seventeenth century. Though hampered by bouts of state repression, most notably in the 1650s, the work of the Irish Counter-Reformation proved resilient enough to reorganise the Catholic Church, supported by the strong network of Irish educational institutions abroad, which produced a growing supply of diocesan and regular clergy, of the newer and older orders. Also significant was the activity of the Irish Franciscans at Louvain and elsewhere in making available devotional literature in Irish for dissemination in Ireland. [see BALTINGLASS REBELLION; IRISH COLLEGES IN CONTINENTAL EUROPE; PLUNKETT, OLIVER.] **Colm Lennon**

Counter-Reformation literature in Irish. Printing in Irish was introduced to the Gaelic world during the REFORMATION.

Coughlan. *One of Ireland's most instinctive jazz and blues singers, Mary Coughlan is celebrated for the rich and intimate quality of her vocals. [Rex Features Ltd, London]*

Given the Reformers' insistence on making the Scriptures available in the vernacular, it is not surprising that the first religious works to be printed in Gaelic came from the Protestant side, John Carswell's translation of the Book of Common Order, published in Edinburgh in 1567. Written in the literary dialect common to Ireland and Scotland, this Calvinistic work was intended for dissemination in both countries. Given that Carswell's patron was the Earl of Argyll, who was related to the most powerful Gaelic families in the north of Ireland, Calvinism seemed to pose a greater threat than Catholicism to the Anglican settlement. This fear spurred ELIZABETH I to urge the Dublin authorities into action. An Irish catechism was published in Dublin in 1571, followed by the New Testament (1602) and the BOOK OF COMMON PRAYER (1608).

The Catholic reaction was initiated in the Franciscan IRISH COLLEGE of LOUVAIN. FLAITHRÍ Ó MAOILCHONAIRE, the founder of the college and a member of a professional learned family, had already translated, but not published, Jeronimo de Ripalda's catechism into Irish in Spain in 1593. The fact that a number of literary scholars joined the Franciscan order at this time facilitated the Louvain enterprise, and the first work to emanate from this circle was *An Teagasg Críosdaidhe* (Antwerp, 1611), written by the former poet GIOLLA BRIGHDE Ó HEÓDHUSA. The friars subsequently acquired their own printing press, using a font of type based on Irish handwriting, and Ó hEódhusa's catechism reappeared in 1615. Other works soon followed: *Desiderius* by Ó Maolchonaire (1616), *Scáthán Shacramuinte na hAithridhe* by AODH MAC AINGIL (1618), *Riaghail an Treas Oird* by Brian Mac Giolla Choinne (1641), and

Parthas an Anama by Antaine Gearnon (1645). A spy reported that copies of Ó hEódhusa's catechism were circulating among Irish soldiers stationed in the Spanish Netherlands, and the English authorities tried in vain to get these works suppressed. We do not know how many copies were printed, or how they were sent back to Ireland. Evidence suggests that the influence of *An Teagasg Críosdaidhe* derives more from the MANUSCRIPT tradition than from the published versions.

These works are all written in a deliberately simple style, but the authors excuse themselves on the grounds that their primary aim is catechetical and not linguistic. Trained in Continental universities, they were well versed in the teachings of the Council of Trent. In the promotion of the tenets of Counter-Reformation Catholicism a polemical dimension is understandably present, which rises occasionally to an unacceptable level of abuse. This polemical dimension is not only religious but political, however, as the nature of the allegiance due by Catholic subjects to a Protestant sovereign was a burning contemporary issue for Irish Catholics. The Louvain enterprise came to an end when the necessary funds from Ireland were diverted to the military campaign during the 1640s. **Mícheál Mac Craith**

Countess Cathleen, The (1899), a play by W. B. YEATS. First performed on 8 May 1899 as the inaugural production of the Irish Literary Theatre (forerunner of the ABBEY THEATRE), it tells the story of a rural community who in time of FAMINE turn from God to the Devil for material gain (see p. 1045). They are saved by the heroine, Countess Cathleen, who pledges her soul to redeem her people. This depiction of rural Ireland was offensive to some nationalists, including Frank Hugh O'Donnell, who wrote a pamphlet, *Souls for Gold*, attacking it, and CARDINAL LOGUE, who condemned the play without having seen or read it. JAMES JOYCE recalled the controversy in a passage in A PORTRAIT OF THE ARTIST AS A YOUNG MAN. **P. J. Mathews**

country and western music, a musical hybrid that grew up largely in the 1960s. It is played by electrified bands on GUITARS, FIDDLES and drums and is similar in content to American country MUSIC, including in its repertoire many songs and instrumental pieces imported directly from the American music charts. The genre emanated from a much earlier affinity with rural American music. In the era of 78 r.p.m. records many American recordings were sent home by emigrants, and later they became available on the Irish market. There was a familiarity with and affection for the work of Jimmie Rodgers (died 1933) and Hank Williams (died 1953), and their records were very popular in Ireland. The music they played was not dissimilar to and in fact had some of its roots in traditional Irish music, and song themes were familiar to a public that had and still has a fondness for nineteenth-century sentimentality.

With the growth of the dance halls following the PUBLIC DANCE HALLS ACT (1935) there was a need for larger bands and for amplification. The form of a dance evening was similar to the older HOUSE DANCES, with frequent breaks for song. However, it is not possible to dance to the rhythms of traditional Irish song, whereas American country songs are often made for dancing. Many of the imported songs are ballads in dance tempo and so allow the dancing to continue without a break. Irish songs, not strictly traditional and in 3/4 time, are also used, and the WALTZ has long been traditional in Ireland.

A yearning for 'modernity', boosted by American films and later television, swept Ireland after the SECOND WORLD WAR, with imported music seen as 'modern'. There was also an efficiently run ballroom circuit, which had a commercial demand for performers, and country bands developed to serve that demand. The home of the best performers and the area in which the bands are most popular is a narrow strip on both sides of the BORDER, from Co. Louth to Co. Donegal; in other parts of Ireland dances are played by bands more in the style of mainstream American and British pop and cabaret music. Among the most popular practitioners were Brian Coll, 'Big Tom', Larry Cunningham, and Susan McCann; the undisputed queen and king of country music were Philomena Begley and Ray Lynam. The heyday of country and Irish music was the 1960s, but its popularity persists, despite the growth and success of rock music. It is an American-inspired music but one that has developed a legitimate and totally Irish accent. **Finbar Boyle**

country furniture. Traditional Irish country furniture reflects the needs and ingenuity of its rural makers and users. It also provides a window onto Irish rural culture: its study reveals how families slept, and how kitchen furniture was influenced by diet. Timber was scarce, so stone, turf, wicker, straw, driftwood, and recycled objects were used to create a primarily functional range of furniture, made by householders or miscellaneous woodworkers, coopers, wheelwrights, cartwrights, coffin-makers, thatchers, boat-builders, or house carpenters, their various specialisms influencing style. Items were often built in to save space and materials, and designs varied according to region.

The rural majority lived in poor and overcrowded conditions. Rough stone or beaten earth floors, and the absence of chimneys (to save fuel), gave rise to slab-seated 'creepy stools', with wedged legs. People crouched low on these, keeping their heads beneath the ubiquitous pall of smoke. Among numerous chair designs the most widespread 'hedge chairs' evolved from creepies, with wedged back-sticks supporting naturally bent 'knees' for back-rests. The *súgán* chair had an ash frame and a seat made of straw or hay rope, reflecting its name.

The poor slept communally, 'in stradogue', in improvised beds made up each night before the fire. In the north-west the 'outshot bed' was recessed into the back wall near the HEARTH. Canopy beds had arched or hipped roofs and curtained fronts. The settle bed was a high-backed bench that unfolded, creating a broad floor-level bed with high sides; its folding seat stored the bedding by day (see p. 768). Other dual-purpose settles were long enough to sleep on, or their backs were folded to create tables, or incorporated storage drawers. A 'press bed' folded up to look like a cupboard. Hanging cradles were cleverly suspended by ropes, away from animals; others were made entirely of straw, as were baskets, stools, and armchairs.

The kitchen dresser combined a functional base with decorative upper shelves, to show off the family's 'ware' or china. Positioned prominently opposite either the front door or the hearth, it invited admiration; the plates were tilted forward to reflect firelight and to avoid dust. Early dressers had an open base for pails of milk or water. Hen-coop dressers or separate straw-lined slatted coops encouraged fowl to continue laying eggs indoors during the winter. Flour and oatmeal were packed tightly into a tall rectangular meal chest, or bin, with a sloping lid.

The hearth was the focal point of the home (see p. 483). Boiled potatoes were strained through a *scib* or shallow basket, placed on a three-legged pot, around which people ate. Single-legged, hinged 'falling tables', which folded up flat against the kitchen wall, were widespread. A substantial, scrub-topped rectangular table with double or laddered stretchers was placed beneath the front window. Catholic kitchens had a 'holy shelf' for a votive light, or a wall-hung shrine housing plaster figures.

country furniture. *Built-in painted pine dresser, Co. Cork, made by the wheelwright and furniture-maker Paddy Crowly (1857–c. 1940s). The scooped and beaded decoration is especially ornate, as he made it for his own kitchen. [National Museum of Ireland; Claudia Kinmonth]*

Traditionally, furniture was grained to imitate fashionable mahogany or oak; striking combinations of dual colour schemes became popular later. The 'stripped and polished pine' look is an innovation imposed since the 1960s by antique-dealers. [see ARCHITECTURE, VERNACULAR.] **Claudia Kinmonth**

Country Girls, The (1960), a novel by EDNA O'BRIEN. This highly regarded first novel of a trilogy deals with Caithleen Brady and her alter ego, Baba. Caithleen, the first of many similar female O'Brien protagonists, lives in the country with her abusive, alcoholic father and her gentle but dysfunctional mother. After Caithleen's mother drowns, the girls board at a convent school. Baba engineers their expulsion, and they move to Dublin. Caithleen works in a grocer's, still yearning for her first love, the chilly, unattainable Mr Gentleman, while Baba attempts sophistication. Finally Baba is admitted to hospital with TUBERCULOSIS, and Mr Gentleman leaves Caithleen. **Rachel Sealy Lynch**

country house cooking. The seventeenth-century English settlers, especially at the upper levels of society, brought to Ireland new cooking styles and taste preferences and, to facilitate the preparation of these, introduced an array of new ingredients. Older medieval styles of cookery, which concentrated on a mix of spices with dried fruit and sugar to enliven meat and fish dishes, were still very much to the fore in seventeenth-century England, though increasingly subject to change under the influence of Continental fashions. This intense sweet and spice mode of flavouring, used in conjunction with an expansive array of ingredients, distinguished the diet of the wealthy newcomers as something rich, exotic, and sophisticated.

As promoters of gardening and horticulture and to support a varied diet, LANDLORDS and their agents undertook the importing of seed and fruit trees to stock their gardens, especially in the period of relative peace and stability after 1660. Different varieties of fruit trees, such as apple, cherry, pear, and plum, together with such delicacies as peaches, apricots, and nectarines, were obtained from England and grown successfully. Walled gardens, sited close to the house, made a gradual appearance. One of the earliest and best surviving was that constructed by the Earl of Cork at Lismore, Co. Waterford, in the 1630s. The fad for collecting, growing, and eating exotics such as grapes and melons was boosted by the introduction of the glasshouse at the end of the seventeenth century, though it would remain a rarity for some time. Furthermore, by the 1680s commercial seedmen were operating in Dublin, selling seed and seedling vegetables to supply the gardens of the upper and middle classes. The choice of vegetables and legumes on offer was impressive, and items such as garden cresses, lettuce, lamb's lettuce, winter cabbage, turnip, thyme, marjoram, beans, peas, cucumber, spinach, radish, cauliflower, artichoke, and curled endive were used in cooked dishes and the preparation of salads and preserved for winter use. Most significantly, the new settlers introduced the potato to Ireland, possibly in the late sixteenth century, as a New World exotic that was gown first in the gardens of the wealthy for its novelty.

The treatment of these new ingredients, imported or home-grown, is dealt with in a limited number of seventeenth-century manuscript 'receipt books'. One collection of recipes, dated 1666, calls for such exotic imported ingredients as rosewater, sugar, almonds, and spices. Garden produce is well represented by cherries, barberries, artichokes, and the potato. There are numerous recipes for preserving, pickling, and syrup-making; work in the dairy is represented; and there is a great emphasis on meat and game dishes. These recipes fit into the mainstream of English cookery of the seventeenth century; and the recipes emanating from the Irish country house, which survive from throughout the eighteenth century in the form of family manuscript receipt books, reveal a food culture that follows closely English styles and fashions, with a substantial body of recipes bearing a close resemblance to those in contemporary English published cookery books.

Within this limited social circle, tastes were modified during the eighteenth century, and a simpler approach to flavouring was adopted. Meat, fish, fowl, and vegetable fricassees and ragout dishes became more prevalent, while a growing taste for sweet cakes is also discernible, using eggs in place of yeast as the leavening agent. The fashion for cake was facilitated by improvements in MILLING technology, with the more effective production of finely bolted white flour. For the affluent and socially conscious, cakes, in particular plum cakes, went well with the emerging fashionable custom of taking afternoon tea, coffee, and chocolate. An array of baked or steamed puddings also became a prominent feature of the tables of the wealthy in the eighteenth century. Underpinning the rich and diverse tastes of the ANGLO-IRISH elite was the expansion and solidification of the estate system from the 1700s onwards. The demesne lands were not only carefully landscaped for their aesthetic appeal but were also planned with the table in mind. Ice-houses were constructed on estates close to rivers and streams to ensure a supply of ice for the house and kitchen and to act as a cold store in summertime, especially for fish, meat, poultry, and BUTTER.

The walled garden, now at a remove from the house and hidden from view, flourished from the middle of the eighteenth century onwards. Within the microclimate of these well-organised and carefully tended gardens, delicacies thrived that would not survive elsewhere. Specialised hothouses for the cultivation of oranges, lemons, and peaches became more apparent by the end of the eighteenth century, and by the 1840s glasshouses had gained in popularity, with the removal of glass tax and the availability of cheaper glass. The dairy offered a supply of CHEESES, creams, and syllabubs together with cream and curd for cooking. Some estates were sited near BOG or wetlands and were maintained and stocked to accommodate the taste for game, especially game birds, such as pheasant, woodcock, grouse, and snipe. Venison and rabbit were equally popular. Access to game and its consumption in winter months introduced a seasonal variation to the diet of the affluent, while the organising of HUNTING parties and post-shoot celebratory dinners affirmed the shared tastes of those of similar cultural outlook. [see BIG HOUSE, THE; DIET; FOOD.] **Regina Sexton**

Country Shop, the. Between 1930 and 1978 the basement of no. 23 St Stephen's Green, Dublin, was the premises of 'The Country Shop, Depot for Irish Country Industries', the outlet, café, showcase and centre of a web of handcraft organisations run by the indefatigable organiser MURIEL GAHAN, one of the most influential figures in the encouragement and preservation of Irish craft traditions; she was also a founder-member of the ARTS COUNCIL and the first woman vice-president of the RDS. The Irish Homespun Society, the IRISH COUNTRYWOMEN'S ASSOCIATION and the Country Markets (of which Gahan was a founder) all at some time had their head offices at the Country Shop, the essential principle of which was that it existed to serve the producer, not the purchaser. Basketry, weaving, ironwork, woodturning, woodcarving, leatherwork, patchwork, furniture-making, and ceramics were among the CRAFTS supported and displayed there. **Brian Lalor**

court cairns and tombs. Probably the earliest of the Irish MEGALITHIC TOMBS, these monuments were probably built between 4000 and 3500 BC. The 411 known examples are distributed almost exclusively north of a line from Galway to Dundalk. Court tombs take a number of forms, and many are quite complex structures. Essentially they comprise a long rectangular or trapezoidal cairn of stone, averaging between 25 and 30 m (80 to 100 ft) in length and varying from about 15 m ($4\frac{1}{2}$ ft) at the front to about half that at the rear. At the broader end of the monument there is usually an open forecourt area, which was unroofed. This gave access to the burial gallery, placed axially within the cairn and divided into two, three or four chambers by jambs or sill-stones, the two-chambered variety being the most common. A small number of galleries also possess *transepts* or side-chambers. The galleries were originally covered by a low corbelled roof, though few of these survive. The shape of the court varies from a shallow semi-circle to horseshoe-shaped or oval. Some possess a large enclosed or full court with a narrow entry (as at CREEVYKEEL, Co. Sligo, and CREGGANDEVESKY, Co. Tyrone), and there are a number of tombs where the galleries are positioned back to back, with the courts at each end of the cairn (as at AUDLEYSTOWN, Co. Down). The long straight sides of the cairn are usually marked by a retaining kerb of upright stones, though in some tombs both the court and the sides are faced with dry-stone walling. Besides the main galleries, small subsidiary burial chambers are sometimes found set in the sides of the long cairns, and some of these are morphologically similar to PORTAL TOMBS. In general, court tombs display a preference for an easterly orientation.

The evidence suggests that the galleries were used for repeated burial over a long period. Cremation is the predominant practice, though inhumation also occurs. The finds from the excavated examples present coherent evidence for a NEOLITHIC date and include leaf-shaped and lozenge-shaped arrowheads, javelin or lance heads, a variety of scrapers (especially concave scrapers) of flint and chert, and polished STONE AXES, together with round-bottomed shouldered pottery, either plain or decorated. There is an acknowledged relationship between the court tombs and similar monuments in England, Wales, and Scotland, and it would appear that they are all different manifestations of a tradition of burial in long mounds. **Paul Walsh**

court dress, worn at formal events in DUBLIN CASTLE up to the early twentieth century. Strict convention in the nineteenth century required that men not wearing military uniform wear a 'court uniform' of a single-breasted coat of black velvet or dark cloth with cut steel buttons, matching breeches, a waistcoat of black velvet or white satin, black hose, black patent-leather shoes with steel buckles, a cocked hat, a dress sword with cut-steel mountings, a white bow tie, and white gloves. Similarly, strict convention for women decreed short sleeves, a low neckline, and a long train, with unmarried women wearing white. Ostrich feathers and veils came to replace the lappets that were the required headdress during earlier times. **Alex Ward**

courts of poetry (*cúirteanna éigse*), assemblies held by poets in the eighteenth century in those areas of Munster where the Irish literary tradition was still strong. The meetings would be held at regular intervals and would, at least sometimes, be open to those members of the public interested in Irish poetry. The courts of poetry imitated the law courts in that the chief poet was known as the *uachtarán* ('president'), *giúistís* ('magistrate'), or *breitheamh* ('judge'); a BARÁNTAS ('warrant') was sometimes issued as a summons to the members to attend the court, and a *coiste* ('jury') would sometimes pass judgment on a perceived misdemeanour.

Among the objectives the poets hoped to achieve for the courts of poetry were to provide training for the poets and to improve the quality of their output; to examine the work of young poets before considering them fit to speak in their verse with the full authority of the court; to prevent, with the aid of sanctions, unqualified people from practising verse without the permission of the court; to foster the use of Irish and to cultivate the study of Irish poetry. But above all the courts of poetry were social gatherings, where poets and people of like mind met to enjoy themselves in convivial surroundings. Part of this enjoyment consisted of readings, followed by discussion, of recently composed verse. Extempore readings were sometimes demanded of the younger poets before they could be accepted as full members of the court. Among the better known of the courts of poetry were those held in Blarney and Carraig na bhFear, Co. Cork, in Croom, Co. Limerick, and in Ennis, Co. Clare. [see DÁMHSCOIL MHÚSCRAÍ UÍ FHLOINN.] **Breandán Ó Conchúir**

court system, Northern Ireland. Following the enactment of the Government of Ireland Act (1920), which provided for a separate court system for Northern Ireland, the region reverted to the system that operated under the Supreme Court of Judicature Act (1877), comprising a Supreme Court of Judicature for Northern Ireland (consisting of the High Court and Court of Appeal, with a Court of Criminal Appeal added in 1930), with ultimate appeal to the Appellate Committee of the House of Lords. Under the Judicature (Northern Ireland) Act (1978) the Family Division of the High Court was created, to operate alongside the Queen's Bench and Chancery Divisions, while the Court of Criminal Appeal merged with the Court of Appeal. Beneath these courts are the County Courts, dealing with less significant issues, and Magistrate's Courts, including Juvenile Courts. **Neville Cox**

court system, Republic of Ireland. The Irish court system is the successor to that established by the Courts of Justice Act (1924), itself based on the English model established by the Supreme Court of Judicature Act (1877). The CONSTITUTION OF IRELAND (1937) envisaged the establishment of a new court system, eventually completed through the Courts (Supplemental Provisions) Act (1961). It is a hierarchical system, comprising the District Court, Circuit Court, High Court (also known as the Central Criminal Court), and SUPREME COURT. The latter two (known jointly as the *superior courts*) sit in the FOUR COURTS in Dublin, save when the High Court goes on annual circuit. In addition there is the SPECIAL CRIMINAL COURT, created by statute to deal with terrorist offences and other issues with which the normal courts cannot deal. The Court of Criminal Appeal was abolished under the Courts and Court Officers Act (1995). Under article 34.1 of the Constitution the courts must in general sit in public, save in such special instances as may be prescribed by law. **Neville Cox**

Cousins, Margaret Elizabeth, née Gillespie (1878–1954), suffragist, theosophist, and philanthropist. Born in Boyle, Co. Roscommon; educated at the Royal University of Ireland, from where she graduated with a BMus degree. She was a joint founder of the Irish Women's FRANCHISE League and was jailed for suffrage militancy in London, 1910, and Tullamore, 1913. She went to India in 1915 and founded a girls' school there. The first woman magistrate in India, 1922, she was involved in the Indian suffragist and national independence movements. Imprisoned in India for political activism, 1933, she was later awarded 5,000 rupees by the Madras government, 1949. With her husband, James Cousins, she wrote the biographical *We Two Together* (1950). **Clíona Murphy**

court cairns. *Creevykeel Court Tomb, Co. Sligo, consisting of a wedge-shaped cairn, entrance passage, and double burial chamber, restored in 1935. [Dúchas, The Heritage Service]*

Cousser (Kusser), Johann Sigismund (1660–1727), composer. Born in Bratislava of Hungarian parentage; studied with Lully in Paris (1674–82), where he changed his name to Cousser. He held numerous posts as teacher and operatic conductor at Ansbach, 1683, Brunswick, 1690–94, Hamburg, 1694–5, and Stuttgart, 1700–4. Having formed his own travelling opera company, he travelled to London in 1704 and from there to Dublin, 1707. In 1711 he was Chapel Master of Trinity College, and in 1716 he succeeded William Viner as Master of State Musick in Ireland. His compositions include an opera, *Erindo* (1694), *Te Deum* (1713), and *Royal Birthday Odes.* **Ite O'Donovan**

crafts (after 1945). When the IRISH FOLKLORE COMMISSION was established in 1935 to systematically classify and record the oral and material customs of Ireland, many craft traditions had already been lost. In his book *Irish Heritage: The Landscape, the People and Their Work* (1942), E. ESTYN EVANS praised the simplicity of form, soundness of construction, and fitness for purpose of age-old country crafts but lamented that 'the Ireland I am writing about is one which is passing away.'

The early twentieth-century ARTS AND CRAFTS MOVEMENT had tried to revive the enlightened patronage that supported those craft skills that had thrived in the perceived 'golden ages' of early Christian monastic and eighteenth-century GEORGIAN Ireland. After his invaluable support for craft industries through the founding of the GAELIC LEAGUE in 1893, DOUGLAS HYDE's inaugural Presidency of Ireland, 1938–45, saw various attempts to chronicle and revive material culture through traditional practice. The survival of a pre-industrial civilisation, which relied on the indissoluble connection between people and the ENVIRONMENT, was unlikely without its necessary spiritual and economic ingredients. After Hyde's death the crafts, when not directly functional and an integral part of living memory, were increasingly absorbed into the propaganda of NATIONALISM. The folklorists Seán O'Sullivan, E. Estyn Evans, KEVIN DANAHER, and Alan Gailey, through their writings on vernacularism, the IRISH COUNTRYWOMEN'S ASSOCIATION, through constructive practice and marketing, and the ULSTER FOLK AND TRANSPORT MUSEUM, through example, sought to inform and preserve. The KILKENNY DESIGN WORKSHOPS were set up in 1963 to support craft industries as a result of the report *Design in Ireland* (1962), commissioned by the Government. The CRAFTS COUNCIL OF IRELAND, since its establishment in 1971, has encouraged, exhibited, and promoted craft initiative, supported by the ROYAL DUBLIN SOCIETY, while various crafts are integrated in the design curriculum at all levels of education.

David Shaw-Smith's films and his book *Ireland's Traditional Crafts* (1984) and Claudia Kinmonth's *Irish Country Furniture* (1993) have offered vital visual and technical documentation as rural skills disappear without the need for their ingenious inventiveness. Those crafts that have survived or have been re-invented—such as furniture, glass, musical instruments, fly-tying, basketwork, stone-carving, pottery, ceramics, and calligraphy—still have a home or export market, are appreciated for their unique quality as skilled and hand-made artefacts, but rarely spring spontaneously from need or within a tradition, or come from a long line of makers. [see COUNTRY SHOP, THE.] **Nicola Gordon Bowe**

crafts: basketwork. *Traditional basketwork techniques are used to create new forms in* Outside the Wild Wood, *a willow garden bower by Lynn Kirkham, part of a series called* Outside In *commissioned by Surrey Docks City Farm, London. [Greenmantle]*

Basketwork. Commercial and domestic demand for baskets during and after the SECOND WORLD WAR enabled established businesses to thrive through the 1950s, notably in the Suir valley and on the shores of LOUGH NEAGH. Basketwork survived in the 1960s largely because of promotional work by the Irish Countrywomen's Association and the COUNTRY SHOP, Dublin. From the late 1970s Joseph Shanahan (1928–1992), Thomas Quinlan (1916–1995), James Mulholland (1925–), and others taught skills to a new generation. An exhibition organised by the Crafts Council of Ireland and a symposium organised by Joe Hogan in 1994 led to the founding of the Irish Basketmakers' Association, generating new aesthetic values, applications, and professional standards for the contemporary craft. **Mairead McAnallen**

Calligraphy and lettering. The use of the edged rather than the pointed pen marked the renewal of Irish calligraphy pioneered by Myra Maguire in her work for the Irish Government, particularly on grants of arms for the Genealogical Office. Timothy O'Neill specialises in the adaptation of historical script and design and also teaches the craft. Sam Somerville of Belfast, an expert on vellum and gilding, has designed and written the RUC BOOK OF REMEMBRANCE since 1977. Frances Breen works mainly in Irish minuscule script in different media. Denis Brown, whose creative work pushes the craft to its limits, is the calligrapher of the GREAT BOOK OF IRELAND. Peannairí, a national society of calligraphers, fosters interest in the craft; and the ROYAL DUBLIN SOCIETY has a calligraphy category in its annual craft awards. Lettering is an important element in many of the intricately painted pages of LEABHAR NA HAISÉIRGHE, designed by Art O'Murnaghan (1872–1954). In Dublin, adaptations of classical Irish LETTER-FORMS may be seen in the carvings of Michael Biggs at Arbour Hill and the Garden of Remembrance. The Cork sculptor KEN THOMPSON and Gareth Colgan continue the tradition of designing and cutting inscriptions. **Timothy O'Neill**

Ceramics. Peter Brennan (1916–1995) established the first ceramic studio in Ireland in 1945 when he opened Ring Ceramic Studio in Kilkenny; he was also responsible for establishing and running a ceramics course in the National College of Art and Design, Dublin, from 1964. Victor Waddington, a Dublin gallery-owner, exhibited the ceramics of Brennan and of John ffrench (1919–), who was a director of Ring Ceramic Studio before establishing the Arklow Studio Pottery in 1962 within the Arklow Pottery (established 1934). Waddington also exhibited the work of Grattan Freyer (1915–1983), who had trained under the English potter Bernard Leach and established Terrybaun Pottery in Co. Mayo in 1949. Brennan produced wheel-thrown stoneware and porcelain ceramics; ffrench hand-builds colourful vessels and plates; and Freyer produced thrown and press-moulded pottery with, for example, strongly graphic pictorial references to animals. The arrival of the Dutch ceramist SONJA LANDWEER in Ireland in 1963 and her involvement in glaze and clay research and development for the Kilkenny Design Workshops was a pivotal point in the development of Irish ceramics. Later groups, such as the Craft Potters' Society of Ireland and Irish Contemporary Ceramics, represent contemporary ceramic practitioners, such as Cormac Boydell, Henry Pim, Neil Reid, Sonja Landweer, Deirdre McLoughlin, and Katharine West. Among thriving commercial potteries are the Shanagarry Pottery (established in Co. Cork in the 1950s by Philip Pearce), the Stephen Pearce Pottery, and Nicholas Mosse's spongeware production in Bennettsbridge, Co. Kilkenny. The NATIONAL MUSEUM at Collins Barracks, Dublin, houses a small collection of twentieth-century Irish ceramics, as does the ULSTER MUSEUM, Belfast. **Michael Moore**

Country furniture. During the second half of the twentieth century the development of the economy encouraged a dramatic shift towards more comfortable HOUSING and TRANSPORT. With the widespread abandonment of traditional thatched houses and the working horse, the associated range of trades that made country furniture (thatchers, wheelwrights, blacksmiths, and coopers) also declined. Competitively priced mass-produced furniture was imported, or provided by Irish factories in its place. There was an increasing demand for upholstered seating and for fitted kitchens and bedrooms in households that were focused on the television rather than the HEARTH. The apprenticeship system gradually gave way to college-trained designer-craftspeople, whose hand-made furniture, often inspired by functional vernacular design, aimed instead at the luxury market. **Claudia Kinmonth**

Fly-tying. After the Second World War the craft of fly-tying was in decline, but improved fishing opportunities in the 1960s regenerated interest. The ANGLING media in the 1970s made a significant educational contribution to its growth, and talented young professional tyers emerged, the most notable being Frankie McPhillips of Enniskillen. The craft flourishes today. **Peter O'Reilly**

Furniture. Traditional cabinet-making was dominated by Hicks, the leading Dublin firm, which supplied the market for mahogany furniture in a baroque-revival style that was hand-crafted and well constructed. Less expensive traditional domestic furniture was produced by Lawlor Briscoe. Modern furniture was manufactured by companies in Dublin, Cork, Monaghan, and Navan; the leading makers were the Court Cabinet Company of Dublin, producing furniture in modern designs, using wood veneers and moulded plywood. During the 1960s and 70s a number of state-sponsored reports and initiatives recommended Scandinavian design as a model for the production of functional, useful and economical furniture. The KILKENNY DESIGN WORKSHOPS and Crannac (supported by Gaeltarra Éireann) produced successful ranges of domestic and office furniture. Furniture-makers continue to work in the handcraft tradition, producing one-off pieces. During the 1990s a new style of design-led furniture manufacturing emerged, emanating from the Government school at Letterfrack, Co. Galway, and such individuals as Gearóid Ó Conchubhair at the National College of Art and Design, Tadhg O'Driscoll and others trained at Parnham in Dorset. This furniture was designed for small-scale batch production, using a mixture of traditional and modern forms, materials, and construction techniques. **Paul Caffrey**

Glass. As technology and new discoveries are embraced by glass communities around the world, this is slowly being reflected in glass work being produced in Ireland. Ireland already has a reputation for cut crystal, and in 1950 a glass-making factory in Waterford was re-established after an absence of a hundred years. Work reflecting the Bohemian tradition of cut crystal is the mainstay of factory production today. In recent years crystal firms have been reviewing their products by inviting fashion designers to create a contemporary look that reflects market trends. WATERFORD Crystal has also made links with the artist Dale Chihuly and now produces a Waterford-inspired Chihuly chandelier. The first small-scale glass studio was established in Kilkenny in 1972 by Simon Pearce, producing simple free-blown domestic ware. Jerpoint Glass was set up by Keith Leadbetter in 1977 and now produces functional glassware with simple lines and minimal use of colour.

During the 1970s John Murphy was head of the glass department in the National College of Art and Design, Dublin. The course had a strong tradition in STAINED GLASS. Inspired by advances in the glass movement in America and Britain, Murphy began to experiment with a hot-glass facility at the college. It now offers BA and MA courses in glass design, the only full-time glass courses in Ireland; more than fifty students have graduated since its foundation, many of them now active in the international glass scene, including Donna Coogan, Róisín de Buitléar, Robert Frazier, Elaine Griffin,

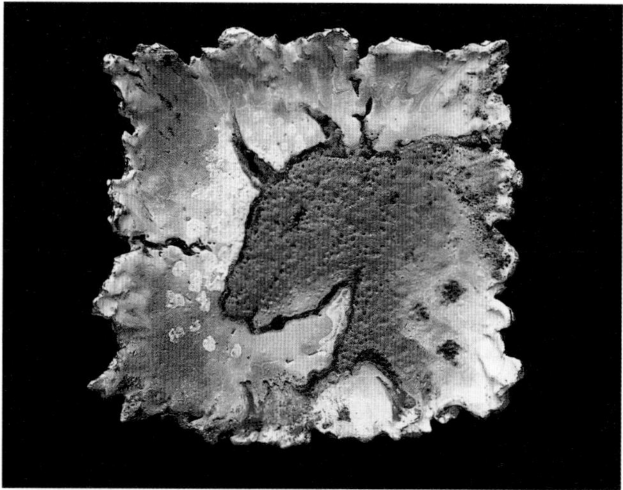

crafts: ceramics. Bull, *45 by 45 cm (18 by 18-in.) hand-formed dish with fretted edge in terracotta edged with gold, by the ceramic artist Cormac Boydell. The glazes used are recipes developed by the artist; the subject is inspired by prehistoric drawings in the Lascaux caves, Dordogne, France. [Cormac Boydell]*

Noelle Higgins, Peadar and Katherine Lamb, Niamh Lawlor, Viki Rothschild, Deirdre Rogers, Paula Stokes, Ruth Short, and Catherine Wilcoxson.

The majority of artists make work to commission and exhibit unique pieces in galleries. Many are benefiting also from the '1 per cent for art' Government scheme, which must be incorporated in each new building project. This has led to a series of well-financed projects that have allowed glass artists to make exciting architectural and installation work. Many have collaborated with commercial manufacturing companies in carrying out this work. Work by MAUD COTTER, Róisín de Buitléar, Salah Kawala, Katherine Lamb, Mary Mackey, Michelle O'Donnell, JAMES SCANLON, and Killian Schurman can be seen in public and private spaces. Artists have established their own workshops and make use of public access facilities, such as the Fire Station Studios in Dublin and the Sculpture Factory in Cork. They support artists by offering subsidised studio space and ancillary workshop facilities and equipment as well as running short courses given by Irish and foreign artists.

Galleries solely devoted to promoting glass are yet to emerge, though the number of galleries showing artists using glass is increasing. The Glass Society Contemporary Makers was established by Mary Mackey and Róisín de Buitléar in 1999 as a forum in which artists could exchange ideas and information. It aims to promote the awareness of contemporary Irish glass by hosting conferences, lectures, workshops, and exhibitions. **Róisín de Buitléar**

Glove-making. In the 1940s Thady Campbell and Company of Co. Donegal produced knitted WOOLLEN gloves, while Dublin manufacturers, such as Redgauntlet, produced fancy gloves from new duplex fabrics. In the 1950s manufacturers made fine stockinette gloves in every conceivable colour; brands included Glovewear, Lorrac, and Golden Gloves. The following decade saw the establishment of glove factories in Cos. Cork, Tipperary, Donegal, and Dublin. The formality of wearing gloves had ceased by the 1980s, and a decade later no fashion glove manufacturer survived. **Mairead M. Johnston**

Hat-making. With Dior's 'new look' in 1947 came 'off-the-face' hats and shorter haircuts. The millinery department at Atkinson's, Dublin, made hats of Irish poplin, while Cassidy's of South Great George's Street produced Easter bonnets in fine felt. Les

Modes Modernes Ltd of Bohermore, Co. Galway, manufactured fashion hats from the 1940s to the 60s, while Margaret Blythe of Kildare Street, Dublin, produced hats for fashion houses in the 1950s. In the 1960s and 70s the hat gave way to hairstyles; and Catholic women were no longer required to wear a head-covering in church. The millinery industry declined. The reintroduction of the hat as a fashion accessory in the 1990s saw the rise of young designers, notably the acclaimed Philip Treacy (see p. 369). **Mairead M. Johnston**

Interior design. Among the most notable long-established Dublin firms of manufacturers, furnishers, and designers were R. Strahan and Company of St Stephen's Green (established in 1776), H. Sibthorpe and Sons, Molesworth Street, Pim Brothers, South Great George's Street, and O'Dea and Company, Wolfe Tone Street. These practised a variety of conservative styles, ranging from outright reproduction to tentative attempts at modernism. RAYMOND MCGRATH (1903–1977) was the most significant architect practising interior design; as principal architect with the OFFICE OF PUBLIC WORKS he worked at Dublin Castle, Áras an Uachtaráin, and numerous Irish embassies, in both classical and modern styles. In the private sector Alan Hope (1909–1965) promoted a modernism influenced by Scandinavia. Contemporary architectural firms such as ARTHUR GIBNEY and Partners, SHEEHAN AND BARRY, and DE BLÁCAM AND MEAGHER, all of Dublin, carry out a limited decoration service as part of their restoration projects. Notable English decorators who worked on Irish projects were Felix Harbord (Luttrellstown Castle and Crom Castle), Oliver Messel (BIRR CASTLE), David Hicks (Baronscourt), and Colefax and Fowler (Kilboy). Perhaps the most talented amateur was Mariga GUINNESS (1932–1989), who influenced a wide circle of friends and admirers with her use of striking colours and dramatic furnishings and her promotion of 'faded grandeur' as a decorative concept. **Christopher Moore**

Jewellery. Mass-produced jewellery in both classical and native designs (such as the CLADDAGH RING, paraphrases of BRONZE AGE TORCS, and motifs from Early Christian ornaments) remain the mainstay of Irish jewellery sales. The precious-metals workshop at the Kilkenny Design Workshops, established in the mid-1960s, promoted hand-crafted Irish jewellery in original designs. The German silversmith Rudolf Heltzel headed the workshop, his modernist geometrical style influencing many Irish jewellers. Though the Kilkenny Design Workshops closed in 1988, the CRAFTS COUNCIL OF IRELAND still operates jewellery workshops in Kilkenny. The National College of Art and Design and the University of Ulster both award degrees in metalwork and jewellery design. Quality privately run craft shops opened around the country in the late 1980s and 90s, while Designyard, the first specialist jewellery exhibition space, opened in Dublin in 1993, giving Irish jewellers greater exposure. A wide variety of styles has emerged, from works evoking Irish heritage and mythology, such as those by Séamus Gill and Erica Marks, to satirical narrative work by Alan Ardiff. Abstract jewellers work in various materials, including precious metals (Breda Haugh and Michael Fitzgerald), glass (Killian Schurmann), and even recycled plastic (Brigitte Turba). Jewellers now also explore body sculpture and conceptual jewellery (SONJA LANDWEER, Slim Barrett, and Fiona Mulholland). **Catherine Bates**

Machine knitting. In the middle of the 1980s a group of enthusiasts came together to establish the Machine Knitters' Guild, in association with the ULSTER FOLK AND TRANSPORT MUSEUM. The guild helped promote a skill that had suffered from a poor image. Good design and experimentation were encouraged in a craft that had played an important part in domestic production of clothes for the family throughout the twentieth century. Knitting machines were available on the domestic market by the second half of the nineteenth century. These changes mirrored developments in commercial production. The emerging fashion knitwear industry, largely dependent on machine knitting, was a far cry from the mid-century mass-production of clothing in synthetic yarns. Today, for example, in Inishmaan in the ARAN ISLANDS computer technology is wedded to a noble knitting tradition to produce garments that are in high demand. **Linda Ballard**

Musical instruments. The making of musical instruments in Ireland declined from the eighteenth and early nineteenth centuries, when significant numbers of makers were active, especially in Dublin. The dramatic increase in musical activity during the later part of the twentieth century saw a resurgence of instrument-making, in particular catering for the growth in TRADITIONAL MUSIC from the 1970s. Joyce Pye's *Ireland's Musical Instrument Makers* (1990), though not comprehensive, lists some seventy makers, both full-time and part-time, mostly of instruments for traditional music, including BODHRÁN, wooden FLUTE, HARP, UILLEANN PIPES, and violin. A violin-making school in Limerick founded in 1975 and a short-lived school in Cork in the 1970s and 80s encouraged the craft. Notable among instrument-makers catering for classical music are William Hofmann, the doyen of Irish violin-makers and repairers, Cathal Gannon, active as a harpsichord-maker in the 1970s and 80s, and Kenneth Jones, who since 1973 has established an international reputation for his pipe organs. **Barra Boydell**

Patchwork. In the 1950s, as synthetic fabrics became popular and the effects of wartime rationing abated, patchwork fell into disfavour, and few practised the craft. In the 1970s there was a reassessment of the tradition, exhibitions encouraged the study of historical pieces, and many guilds and groups were established to foster interest. By the beginning of the twenty-first century Irish patchwork had emerged as a well-established craft, reflecting international influences, the pieces often being made as art rather than purely as functional items. **Linda Ballard**

Precious metals. Precious metals have played a significant role in crafts in Ireland, most notably in the production of sacred vessels, especially for the Catholic Church, in the manufacture of reproduction antique domestic items, and in the jewellery trade. The most commonly used metals are sterling silver, 9-carat and 18-carat gold, and, more recently, platinum. Though the work of silversmiths and goldsmiths was of a high standard, up to the end of the 1960s the individual workers were tradesmen rather than independent artist-craftspeople. During the early 1970s there was a great revival of interest in individually designed pieces made by artist-craftspeople. This was made possible by the KILKENNY DESIGN WORKSHOPS, set up in 1963 by the Government to increase the awareness of good design in crafts and industrial design. With increasing prosperity and the new awareness of good design it became possible for the artist-craftsperson to make a living designing and making pieces on commission; at the same time some independent silversmiths, and many independent jewellers, were setting up workshops, a process that continues at the present time. **Brian Clarke**

Shoemaking. The craft of the shoemaker has altered little over the centuries, with the same tools still in use—and now virtually impossible to replace. Since the late nineteenth century, however, the demand for hand-made shoes has steadily declined and with it the number of shoemakers. The lack of materials during the years of the Second World War severely affected the craft; and the boom of the 1950s in cheap, mass-produced footwear, combined with the vagaries of fashion, ensured that only a handful of craftsmen remained active. The prosperity of the 1960s lured struggling shoemakers into more secure jobs; those few that continued adapted by making orthopaedic as well as bespoke footwear. **Alex Ward**

Silver. During the post-war period the silver trade was in the grip of perennial depression, with a small number of craftspeople trying to compete with English imports. The export market was virtually unknown, apart from occasional ecclesiastical pieces commissioned by religious orders in America. In 1962 CÓRAS TRÁCHTÁLA published the report *Design in Ireland*, resulting in the setting up in 1963 of the KILKENNY DESIGN WORKSHOPS; these included workshops for silversmiths with expert designers from Sweden, England, and Germany, such as Rudolf Hetzel, who could convey new European taste to a trade with very few apprentices. Commemorative hallmarks for 1966, 1973, and 2000 were introduced by the Assay Office to try to boost sales. The booming economy and the efforts of the CRAFTS COUNCIL OF IRELAND, Designyard, the Metalwork Department of the National College of Art and Design (Derek McGarry, Kevin O'Dwyer, and Brian Clarke) and its former students, such as Erika Marks, helped to substantially improve production, which has to contend with competition from Continental imports. **Douglas Bennett**

Stained glass. By 1945, though the golden years of the early twentieth century arts-and-crafts revival were over, the HARRY CLARKE (see pp. 206, 498) and Earley Studios in Dublin continued to operate until the 1970s, and EVIE HONE was to produce a large number of windows and panels, introducing a new, loosely painted, resonantly coloured and sombrely religious treatment in the ten densely packed years before her death. Her most famous windows were for Tullabeg Jesuit College at Rahan, Co. Offaly (1946), Kingscourt, Co. Cavan (1947–8), and Eton College, Windsor (1949–52). An Túr Gloine, the Dublin co-operative where she had worked since 1935, was dissolved in 1944, though her influence was seminal in establishing Patrick Pollen and PATRICK PYE as the foremost ecclesiastical stained-glass practitioners of the next generation.

crafts: precious metals. *Sterling silver water pitcher, form folded and constructed, by Brian Clarke, one of Ireland's most successful contemporary precious-metal artists. [Brian Clarke]*

Other contemporaries included Helen Moloney and John Murphy, who taught the craft at the National College of Art and Design.

In the 1980s the craft was reinvigorated in Cork by two young sculpture graduates, MAUD COTTER and JAMES SCANLON (see p. 1014), whose lively, idiosyncratic treatment dealt with current international issues through inventive yet distinctly national expression. In the 1990s Peter Young's autonomous panels, painted on thick glass slabs, introduced a quizzical illustrative dimension, while Donna Coogan incorporated suspended kiln-formed elements into panels rich with autobiographical and textural allusions. **Nicola Gordon Bowe**

Stone-carving. The traditional stone trade in Ireland survived until the 1940s. With the increasing use of concrete, quarries closed, and the journeymen stone-carvers were without work. For many years stone-carving was confined to monumental work and the work of a very few artist-craftsmen, such as SEAMUS MURPHY (1907–1975), who, in *Stone Mad* (1950), vividly describes the traditional stone trade and its demise. These artist-craftsmen accept commissions from public bodies, churches, and private patrons; they make no distinction between fine and applied arts. Their work also involves good-quality lettering. Architects are again using cut stone in their buildings, and the limestone quarries in the Carlow-Kilkenny area are flourishing, with modern sculptors carving stone in fresh and interesting ways. **Ken Thompson**

Crafts Council of Ireland, an umbrella organisation for the craft industry of the Republic, formed in 1971 following the World Crafts Council Conference in Ireland in 1970. It includes the Irish Society for Design and Craftwork, the IRISH COUNTRYWOMEN'S ASSOCIATION, Country Markets, the ROYAL DUBLIN SOCIETY, BORD FÁILTE ÉIREANN, and others. It became a limited company in 1976 and was given a statutory function by the Minister for Industry and Commerce, financed by the Industrial Development Authority. Since 1983 the Minister for Enterprise and Employment has nominated five members of the Management Committee, while the council nominates ten; it is now financed by Enterprise Ireland. Its activities include an annual trade fair, information services, and courses in jewellery, pottery, blacksmithing, and business skills; it also maintains a register of craft enterprise and the National Crafts Gallery in Kilkenny. Contemporary Crafts on the Border, set up with Craftworks Northern Ireland in 1998 and financed by the EU Peace and Reconciliation Fund, supports craft development in Northern Ireland and the border counties. [see CORAS TRÁCHTÁLA.] **Mairead McAnallen**

'craic', a modern Irish loanword (from the English *crack*), meaning 'conversation', widely used in Ireland since the 1960s to mean 'lively entertainment', especially in connection with TRADITIONAL MUSIC events. In this context it is commonly spelt 'craic', being generally assumed by English-speakers to be of Irish origin. **Fintan Vallely**

Craig, James, Lord Craigavon (1871–1940), politician. Born in Belfast, son of a millionaire distiller. He began his career as a stockbroker in London and Belfast, then served in the ANGLO-BOER WAR (1900–1), attaining the rank of captain and displaying a flair for organisation. Assisted by a legacy of £100,000 from his father, he followed his brother Charles into politics and was elected Unionist MP for East Down in 1906. A Presbyterian, Orangeman, and typical representative of the unionist business class of east Ulster, he quickly emerged as one of the 'young Turks' within UNIONISM, wresting power from the remote, aristocratic leadership and reconstructing the party around the ULSTER UNIONIST COUNCIL, with its distinctly partitionist mentality. A lacklustre parliamentarian who came to personify Ulster intransigence, he helped secure the election of the charismatic CARSON as leader of the Irish Unionists in 1910. He was chief organiser of the ULSTER COVENANT (1912), ULSTER VOLUNTEER FORCE (1913), and LARNE GUN-RUNNING (1914) and endorsed the six-county PARTITION scheme in 1916.

During the period 1918–21 he eclipsed the ageing Carson, holding junior ministerial office in the LLOYD GEORGE coalition government as Parliamentary Secretary to the Minister of Pensions, 1919–20, and Financial Secretary to the Admiralty, 1920–21. He was thus well placed to press for permanent exclusion in 1920, securing his preferred six-county Northern Ireland and the reconstitution of the UVF as the Ulster Special Constabulary, 1920. He became Northern Ireland's first Prime Minister in 1921, successfully resisting both IRA attacks and pressure from Lloyd George to accept Irish unity. During his nineteen-year premiership he tended to ignore the Catholic community in favour of maintaining Unionist unity. His educational policy and the abolition of proportional representation in LOCAL GOVERNMENT elections in 1929 alienated nationalists (though it had a more damaging impact on a variety of labour and independent candidates), while his two pacts with MICHAEL COLLINS in 1922 were stillborn. The agreement of 1925 confirming the BORDER was a triumph for Craig. By the 1930s he had established, in his own words, 'a Protestant Parliament and a Protestant state.' He died secure in history as the architect of Northern Ireland. **Eamon Phoenix**

Craig, J. Humbert (1877–1944), landscape painter. Born in Belfast and brought up in Bangor, Co. Down; briefly employed in his father's tea business before turning to painting, at which he was largely self-taught. He worked mainly in Cos. Antrim, Donegal, and Galway. Elected an associate of the RHA, 1925, and full member, 1928, he was one of the most influential Irish landscapists of his generation. Adopting a *plein air*-cum-impressionist technique, he concerned himself with recording the visible scene and the topography of the landscape. He is well represented in the North Down Borough Council Collection, Bangor. **S. B. Kennedy**

Craig, Maurice James (1919–), architectural historian and writer. Born in Belfast; educated at TCD and the University of Cambridge. He worked as Inspector of Ancient Monuments for the Ministry of Works, London, 1952–70, and subsequently in Dublin for An Foras Forbartha and AN TAISCE. Many of his publications have become definitive in their separate fields; his architectural study *Dublin, 1660–1860* (1952) is regarded as the most significant twentieth-century work on Irish classical ARCHITECTURE, while his satirical 'Ballad to a Traditional Refrain' (1948) has passed into the colloquial tradition of Northern Ireland. His publications include *The Volunteer Earl* (1948), *Irish Bookbindings* (1954), *Architectural Drawings of Sir John Vanbrugh and Sir* EDWARD LOVETT PEARCE (with Howard Colvin, 1964), *Ireland Observed* (with the Knight of Glin, 1970), *Classic Irish Houses of the Middle Size* (1976), *The Architecture of Ireland from the Earliest Times to 1880* (1982), *W. S. Landor: One Hundred Poems* (1999), *Mausolea Hibernica* (with Michael Craig, 1999), and *Cats and their Poets* (2002). **Brian Lalor**

Craig, William (1924–), politician. Elected as Unionist MP for Larne in 1960, he served under LORD BROOKEBOROUGH as chief whip, 1962–3, and in a variety of posts in TERENCE O'NEILL's governments from 1963. As Minister of Development he co-ordinated the creation of the new city of CRAIGAVON. As Minister of Home Affairs he banned the DERRY CIVIL RIGHTS MARCH of 5 October 1968 and defended the police action there. He was sacked in December 1968 for criticising O'Neill's reform programme and led Ulster Vanguard when it was formed in 1972. He won the East Belfast seat in the Westminster Parliament in 1974 and played a leading role in the ULSTER WORKERS' COUNCIL STRIKE. **Jonathan Bardon**

Craigavon, Co. Armagh, a new town between Lurgan and Portadown, founded in 1965 under the provisions of the Mathew Report; population (1991) 9,201. Planned as a regional growth centre, Craigavon was designed to attract overspill population from Belfast (where further growth was to be checked) and rural and urban migrants from further west, employing them in new industries attracted to the town by relocation packages. It is typical of the ambitious TOWN PLANNING projects of the 1960s, and is generally regarded as a failure. Industry failed to arrive in sufficient quantity, and by 1983 important factories, such as Goodyear, were closing. In the late 1980s and early 90s the surplus public HOUSING was used to accommodate people displaced by sectarian violence in Belfast, which heightened existing tensions in the area. Many of the new housing estates became semi-derelict, and some have been demolished; others, for example in Brownlow, have been renovated in a continuing attempt to attract residents. **Lindsay Proudfoot**

Craig-Martin, Michael (1941–), conceptual artist. Born in Dublin; spent his childhood in Washington, and studied art at Yale University. He moved to England in 1966 to a teaching post at the Bath Academy of Art. An influential advocate of conceptual art, he taught at Goldsmiths College, London, from 1974 and was appointed professor of fine art in 1993. In early works, such as *Six-Foot Balance with Four Pounds of Paper* (1970), he often explored unexpected physical relationships between familiar objects, questioning the role of art and the nature of representation. His best-known works are large-scale mural outline drawings, made using black adhesive tape, representing domestic objects and furniture. In Dublin he exhibited at the Oliver Dowling Gallery in 1977; a retrospective exhibition was held at the Whitechapel Art Gallery, London, in 1989. **Peter Murray**

Cramillion, Bartholomew (fl. 1755–c. 1760s), stuccodore. Of probable French origin, he came to Ireland in 1755 to work as chief stuccodore on the ceiling and altarpiece of the chapel in the Lying-In Hospital (ROTUNDA), Dublin, for Dr BARTHOLOMEW MOSSE. He introduced the German rococo style to Ireland. The chapel is a curious mixture of exuberance and a certain constraint not found in the Continental rococo. He spent some six or seven years working on a variety of ceiling projects, and a number of pictorial ceilings have been attributed to him (formerly in Mespil House and La Touche Bank, Dublin). He left Dublin in the early 1760s, returning in 1773, but the nature of his later work has not yet been established. **Christopher Moore**

Cranberries, the, rock group. Formed in Limerick in 1990, the group consists of vocalist Dolores O'Riordan (1971–), Noel Hogan (1971–), Mike Hogan (1973–), and Feargal Lawlor (1971–). Their debut album, *Everybody Else Is Doing It, So Why Can't We?*, was released in 1993, and the band toured extensively in the USA, finding success there long before finding it at home. They built up a huge following through continual touring and the release of extraordinarily popular albums, such as *No Need to Argue* (1994) and *To the Faithful Departed* (1996). However, their later albums *Bury the Hatchet* (1999) and *Wake Up and Smell the Coffee* (2001) proved less popular. **Tony Clayton-Lea**

crannógs, essentially defended lake dwellings, established on artificial or semi-artificial islands in lakes (see p. 595). Approximately 1,200 crannógs can be seen throughout the Irish countryside today; they also occur in large numbers on Scottish lakes. They are mostly found on the many small lakes that occur throughout the drumlin belt, which stretches from Co. Mayo across north Connacht and Ulster to Co. Down, often surviving as small tree-covered islands. It is also clear, however, that lake levels have risen in places over the centuries, which means that many crannógs have been submerged. Sometimes they reappear above the waters of a lake after a hot summer or possibly as a result of drainage works. A large number of crannógs were uncovered during drainage operations on Lough Gara during the 1950s and 60s.

Crannógs were often constructed by dumping layers of timber, brushwood, rubbish, peat, and stones onto a shallow area of a lough out from the shore, so that the site was completely surrounded by water. This dumped material created a circular, dry occupation platform of between 20 and 30 m (65 to 100 ft) in diameter. Very often this platform was girdled by a ring of strong timber posts, which kept the crannóg-matrix firmly anchored in place. In rocky areas, crannógs were simply created by dumping a cairn of rocks into a lake, though girdling underwater timbers were also put in place at such sites to help keep the stones from shifting. Stone crannógs are common in many parts of the west of Ireland, such as Co. Donegal and Connemara. It might be added that even in such counties as Sligo and Roscommon, apparently well wooded up to the seventeenth century or so, stone appears to have been the main material used. Houses were built on the occupation platforms of these crannógs, often with oak-plank or post-and-wattle palisades around their edges to act as peripheral defences.

Crannógs were reached from the adjacent shore in two ways. BOATS—such as wooden dug-out canoes or small skin-covered craft—could obviously be used to ferry people and goods, and the remains of little stone or timber jetties can sometimes be seen around these sites. Underwater stone causeways were also built to connect the crannóg to dry land.

There is some debate about the origins of crannógs as a settlement form. Certainly undefended lakeside dwellings and island habitations were established from the MESOLITHIC PERIOD up to the Late BRONZE AGE, but it has been argued that large defended artificial crannógs, entirely surrounded by water, began to be built during the fifth and sixth centuries, at the same time that RING-FORTS began to appear. This theory sees the joint appearance of ring-forts and crannógs as a response to some form of little-understood political or social upheaval. However, RADIOCARBON DATES from crannógs on Lough Gara suggest that they began to be constructed during the Late Bronze Age and IRON AGE.

Whenever they began, it is clear from archaeological excavation that crannógs flourished spectacularly during the Early Historical Period, apparently functioning as the dwellings of the more powerful and wealthy members of society. Some crannógs, such as the excavated ones at LAGORE and Moynagh Lough, Co. Meath, appear to have been royal residences. Excavation has clearly shown the richness of these sites, with a wide range of activities being carried out on them, such as various forms of craftwork and metalwork. Farming activities took place on the adjacent land, with farm equipment and stock being stored in some form of enclosure opposite the crannóg. In general, crannógs were clearly important places in the landscape of Early Historic Ireland.

The available evidence also suggests that crannógs continued to be occupied throughout the Middle Ages and down to the seventeenth century. Some may have acted merely as a refuge from attack for local Irish lords during this whole period. Yet again the evidence suggests that many functioned as the residences of Irish kings and lords to beyond 1600. [see MEDIEVAL SETTLEMENTS.] **Kieran O'Conor**

Cranwill, Maria (Mia) (1880–1972), designer, enamellist, and metalworker. Born in Dublin; educated principally at home before moving to Manchester at the age of fifteen. She attended Manchester and Salford Schools of Art, then taught art and farmed before returning to Dublin in 1917, where she set up a one-room workshop. Her self-taught Celtic-inspired jewellery, often illustrating contemporary poetry, became artistically and ideologically fashionable among romantic nationalists. She is best known for her imposing altar furniture (1924–31) for St Patrick's Church, San Francisco, her casket for the first Irish Free State senate roll (1924), and her tabernacle door in St Michael's Church, Ballinasloe (1926). **Nicola Gordon Bowe**

Crawford, William Ernest (Ernie) (1891–1959), rugby footballer. Born in Belfast. Between his first appearance against England at Lansdowne Road in 1920 and his last at the same venue against Wales in 1927 he won thirty caps at full-back. He was regarded as an astute player who 'often outwitted opponents with acts of pure genius.' He captained Ireland fifteen times—then an Irish record—and was president of the IRFU, 1957–8. **Karl Johnston**

Crawford Observatory, established in 1878 in the grounds of University College, Cork, under the joint patronage of the brewer William Crawford and the Duke of Devonshire. The complete observatory was designed by HOWARD GRUBB. The largest TELESCOPE, an equatorial, won a gold medal for design at the Paris Exhibition, 1878. It was replaced with a Grubb astrograph sited on the same mounting, developed to provide photographs of sections of the northern sky for the Carte du Ciel Project (begun in Paris in 1887). Some of the trial plates made at the Crawford Observatory survive at University College, Cork. **Susan McKenna-Lawlor**

Crean, Thomas (1877–1938), explorer. Born in Anascaul, Co. Kerry, one of a family of ten of a poor small farmer; at the age of fifteen he ran away from home, forged his age as sixteen, and was accepted as a recruit in the British navy. He learnt all that could be known about seamanship and began to climb the promotion ladder when he was appointed to the torpedo school. Also studying this new weapon was Robert Falcon Scott, an English officer with ambitions to become a celebrated explorer in the Antarctic. Scott's determination impressed his superiors, and he became the leader of three Antarctic expeditions in the years just before the FIRST WORLD WAR, bringing with him Crean (1901 and 1910), whose skill, courage and initiative he had divined. Scott's expeditions can be described as heroic, poorly led, and unproductive; but Crean stands out as the most practical and understanding member. In 1912 he received the Albert Medal for Bravery. When ERNEST SHACKLETON, a former merchant seaman from Co. Kildare, took on the leadership of British Antarctic exploration he chose Crean as his main supporter in 1914. Crean's exploits were legendary, perhaps above all in Shackleton's fifteen-day voyage in an open boat, the *James Caird*, from Elephant Island to South Georgia. Crean finally settled down at Anascaul, building and running a pub called the South Pole Inn. **John de Courcy Ireland**

Creevykeel, Co. Sligo, a magnificent COURT TOMB consisting of a wedge-shaped cairn 55 m (180 ft) long and 25 m (80 ft) wide at the broader (eastern) end, where a short entrance passage leads to

Crean. *The 'indestructible' Thomas Crean, Antarctic explorer and a prominent figure on three major expeditions to Antarctica, on the* Discovery, *1901–4,* Terra Nova, *1910–13, and* Endurance, *1914–16, where he served as second officer to Ernest Shackleton. [Collins Press]*

a large oval court that gives access to a two-chambered burial gallery. Behind this are three further burial chambers opening off the sides of the cairn. Excavations in 1935 yielded cremated human remains and typical grave-goods, including NEOLITHIC pottery and flint implements. The small circular structure at the west end of the court dates from the early Middle Ages (see p. 247). **Paul Walsh**

Cregan, Éamon (1945–), hurler. Born in Limerick. His county career with Limerick spanned the period 1964–83. Noted for his skill level, ball control, and scoring ability, he had great mental strength and was an outstanding forward, winning two All-Star Awards in the full-forward line. He was also a distinguished centre-back. His achievements include one all-Ireland senior hurling medal (1973), four Munster senior HURLING medals, one National League (1971), one Oireachtas, and one Harty Cup medal. With his club, Claughaun, he won three county senior hurling medals and eight county senior FOOTBALL medals. Since retiring he has become a noted manager, coaching Limerick, Clare, and Offaly. His father, Ned Cregan, featured on the Limerick team during the MACKEY era. **Séamus J. King**

Creggandevesky, Co. Tyrone, a well-preserved COURT TOMB with many important surviving structural features. Trapezoidal in plan and 18 m (60 ft) long, it has a semi-circular court at the south-east end and three burial chambers, formerly roofed, decreasing in size and height from the entrance inwards. A dry-stone wall retained the sides of the cairn and may have been well over 2 m ($6\frac{1}{2}$ ft) high. When it was excavated between 1979 and 1982 the cremated remains of some twenty-one people were recovered, including five males, seven females, and one adolescent. Associated objects include flint tools and weapons, pottery, and stone beads. RADIOCARBON DATING suggests a use from 3700 to 3300 BC. **Claire Foley**

Crehan, Martin 'Junior' (1908–1998), FIDDLER, CONCERTINA-player, and storyteller. Born in Mullach, Co. Clare; he studied under the master Scully Casey and with him from an early age provided music for crossroads and HOUSE DANCES, WREN balls, and 'AMERICAN WAKES'. The composer of many tunes, he was almost unique among traditional musicians in not emigrating, becoming the solid reference-point in local music as his contemporaries left to work in Britain and the United States, which helped make his name synonymous with local music. President of SCOIL SAMHRAIDH WILLIE CLANCY, he taught there for twenty-five years. In 1989 he was honoured as Clareman of the Year; in 1988 and 1998 his lifetime in music was honoured by the ARTS COUNCIL. **Fintan Vallely**

Cré na Cille (1949), a novel by MÁIRTÍN Ó CADHAIN. His first novel, it offers a totally different view of GAELTACHT life from the rural idyll portrayed in IRISH-LANGUAGE writing of the previous fifty years. Though narrated as a series of conversations between dead bodies in a graveyard, the novel has no metaphysical dimension and deals with what the protagonists call 'life above the ground.' It recounts the life story of the recently buried Caitríona Pháidín and her lifelong, all-consuming jealous, though ultimately petty, conflict with her sister Neil. *Cré na Cille's* great strengths are its rich and colourful use of language, its raucous and sometimes acerbic humour, its hard-hitting social satire, and the unflinching honesty with which each character is portrayed. The book, while severely criticised on publication by conservative elements, was avidly read—sometimes aloud in homes in Irish-speaking Connemara—and remains one of the high points of literature in Modern Irish. **Gearóid Denvir**

cricket, a ball game brought to Ireland by the English. The gentry around Dublin played in the late eighteenth century, but the game was later popularised by soldiers in garrison towns, particularly Kilkenny and Ballinasloe, Co. Galway, and spread among Irish people. There was steady progress from 1820 to 1850; clubs were founded at Trinity College, Dublin, Phoenix, Dublin, Lisburn, Co. Antrim, and Cork.

As in England, the RAILWAYS brought a huge spread in towns and villages from 1860 to 1880. Then came a halt, from two sources: the social alienation of tenant from landlord caused by the LAND WARS, and the contemporaneous foundation of the GAELIC ATHLETIC ASSOCIATION in 1884. The GAA's ban on its members playing certain foreign games, including cricket, came into being in the 1890s and remained until 1971.

Provincial cricket unions began in the late 1880s, and local leagues were formed from that time. An embryo Irish Cricket Union was set up in 1890, though the present body dates from 1923. There are now 135 clubs affiliated, with approximately 10,000 players. Ireland is a member of the International Cricket Council. Ireland played its first match in 1855, long before any test-playing country. In Toronto in 2001 Ireland failed to qualify for the 2003 World Cup in South Africa. In two previous attempts it finished seventh in Kenya in 1994 and fourth in Malaysia in 1997—one place away from qualification. Ireland won the inaugural biennial European Cup in Copenhagen in 1996. The Irish women's team is ranked seventh in world cricket, the men's thirteenth. **Derek Scott**

crime. Crime in Ireland falls into distinct periods, defined by the extent to which it tends to be urban or rural, violent or non-violent, and directed at changing mass opinion or at a specific purpose, such as acquiring property. Faction fighting—mêlées involving hundreds of participants in local, essentially private conflicts—was commonplace in late seventeenth and early eighteenth-century rural Ireland. Factions at times augmented the ranks of secret societies; their combined efforts gave rural Ireland a partly deserved reputation for pervasive disorder. The earliest identifiable period, 1760–1882, began with the founding of the WHITEBOYS, the prototype for agrarian secret societies. 'AGRARIAN outrages' sought to intimidate an audience of LANDLORDS as well as smallholders who co-operated or might be tempted to co-operate with the landlord system.

From 1882 to 1921 the momentum driving crime became decisively urban and directed at acquiring property. Rural crime declined in numbers; violent crime nonetheless remained more prevalent in rural than in urban areas. By the end of the nineteenth century Dublin and Belfast had reputations as centres of crime. The DUBLIN METROPOLITAN POLICE recorded half of all Ireland's indictable (ostensibly serious) crime in the 1880s while policing one-fifteenth of the country's population. From the 1890s Belfast and other cities began to take a larger share of the crime statistics, while Dublin's contribution waned to between a fourth and a third of the total. Cities were noted for their high levels of public drunkenness and for prostitution, which flourished in Dublin up to 1920. The establishment of the Free State and the end of the CIVIL WAR opened a forty-year period of stable and relatively low crime rates. Crime, like the economy and society, was stagnant. Small numbers of not very proficient property crime offenders were responsible for much of the crime.

A comparable period of stable and low crime rates did not begin in Northern Ireland until sectarian violence subsided after 1935. The Republic and Northern Ireland had roughly similar rates of indictable crime until c. 1960; thereafter crime rose at a faster pace in the North than in the South, a differential influenced, but not governed, by the 'TROUBLES'. The rate of violent crime in Northern Ireland was particularly high relative to the Republic, in large measure because of crimes committed in order to influence a large audience of people not directly affected. From c. 1963 to c. 1980 the main feature in both jurisdictions was the rapid increase in the rate of property crime. Crime remained concentrated in the largest towns, but the share of smaller towns was increasing. Fear of crime rose, and politicians adopted the imagery and language of a 'war on crime'. Nevertheless, throughout this period violent crime, including homicide, remained rare.

The period after 1980 has been dominated by change in the nature of crime. Crime became more rational, more businesslike, involving specialisation and sophistication, the illegal drug trade providing the critical mass of profitability and networking to sustain organised criminal activity. Widespread use of marijuana and of barbiturates and amphetamines was evident by the mid-1970s; but it was the successful importing of heroin in large quantities into Dublin in late 1979 that sparked a rapid expansion in the numbers of drug-users. Another change during the 1980s was to the public image of crime in the Republic. A series of scandals involving EU subsidies, rezoning, tax evasion, and other matters revealed long-standing practices of fraud and bribery that linked the corporate and political worlds in networks of WHITE-COLLAR CRIME. [see ALCOHOL ABUSE; DRUG ABUSE; MONTO; TRIBUNALS.] **David Rottman**

Crimea Bob (died 1862), horse, a survivor of the CRIMEAN WAR. He served with the 11th Hussars in the Crimea and took part in the infamous Charge of the Light Brigade at Balaklava on 25 October 1854. He was buried with military honours at Wellington Barracks, CAHER, Co. Tipperary, in 1862 where he is commemorated by a plaque in the town square. **Ciarán Deane**

Crimean War (1853–56). Irishmen constituted up to two-fifths of the British army in the Crimea; Captain James Armar Butler of Kilkenny, who died in June 1854 during the siege of Silistria, was the war's first British fatality. Irish participants in the war included

Croagh Patrick. *Pilgrims making their way down Croagh Patrick, Co. Mayo. On Garland Sunday (the last Sunday in July), pilgrims attend Mass and Confession and pray at St Patrick's Bed on the summit. [John McElroy]*

the first sailor and first soldier to win the VICTORIA CROSS: Lieutenant Lucas of HMS *Hecla* (1857) and Sergeant O'Connor of the 23rd Foot. On the instructions of Lord Raglan at Balaklava, Lord Lucan (of Westport, Co. Mayo) ordered the Charge of the Light Brigade. **Brian Griffin**

Croagh Patrick, a distinctive quartzite cone and ridge formation with characteristic scree slopes immediately south of CLEW BAY in Co. Mayo, 764 m (2,507 ft) in height. Also known as the 'Reek', it is named after Ireland's patron saint, who is reputed to have spent forty days in prayer on its summit. For more than 1,500 years an annual PILGRIMAGE has been held, originally on the last Friday of July (*Aoine Chrom Dubh*, Crom Dubh's Friday) or, since the early nineteenth century, on the following Sunday, which involves the completion of penitentiary rites at 'stations' on the journey to the summit. Mass is celebrated in a small oratory, built in 1905. A statue of St PATRICK was erected in 1928 at Murrisk at the base of the mountain. Nearby a bronze *Famine Ship* (1997) by JOHN BEHAN commemorates the GREAT FAMINE. During the intense geological processes that produced the quartzite a rich seam of gold and other minerals was introduced into the rocks. The withdrawal of a mining licence by the Minister for Energy in 1990 prevented the mining of gold reserves in the environs of the mountain. **Mary E. Cawley**

crochet, a type of needlework linked to tambour LACE, in that it is built up of chain stitches with a hooked needle. Irish crochet tends to have complex designs, often three-dimensional in appearance.

"TELL ME WHERE THE MONEY IS?" HE HISSED

Crock of Gold, The. *Illustration by Thomas Mackenzie for James Stephens's classic allegory* The Crock of Gold *(1912). [Council of Trustees of the National Library of Ireland; LO 960]*

Manufacture began in the 1840s in Cork, where the nuns of the Ursuline convent, Blackrock, taught the technique to local girls. It proved a valuable economic resource during the years of the GREAT FAMINE, and manufacture rapidly spread throughout the south. The second area of importance was Clones, Co. Monaghan, where crochet was introduced in an effort to provide employment following the famine. Clones became noted for its 'guipure' crochet and for fine copies of Continental styles, known as *point d'Irlande*.

The industry as a whole suffered with the introduction of machine-made lace; but commercial and artistic interest during the late nineteenth century led to a boost in popularity. The first decade of the twentieth century saw the peak of the industry, with French couturiers incorporating Irish crochet in their designs. Changes in dress following the FIRST WORLD WAR greatly affected the industry, and the production of crochet subsequently continued on a far smaller scale. **Alex Ward**

Crock of Gold, The (1912), a novel by JAMES STEPHENS. In its weaving of myth and realism this semi-allegorical fantasy novel anticipates FLANN O'BRIEN, but critics differ on Stephens's success in fusing Blakean sensibilities with Irish FOLKLORE. He claimed that the book had in effect only one character, Man, with multiple natures (sensual, emotional, 'intellect at play,' 'intellect spiritualised,' logical, elemental, and innocent) represented by different personae (Pan, Caitilin, the Philosopher, Angus Óg, the policemen, the LEPRECHAUNS, and the children, respectively). The narrative concludes when the personae who have harmonised their divided natures return 'again, dancing and singing to the country of the gods ...' **Brian Cliff**

Croke, Thomas William (1823–1902), bishop. Born in Dromin, Castlecor, Co. Cork; educated at the Endowed School, Charleville, and the Irish College, Paris. Ordained a priest in ROME in 1847, he served in the diocese of Cloyne as curate, president of St Colman's, Fermoy, and parish priest of Doneraile. He was Bishop of Auckland, New Zealand, 1870–75, and Archbishop of Cashel, 1875–1902. An Irish nationalist and public figure, he was deeply involved in the LAND WAR, the HOME RULE struggle, and the founding of the GAA. Croke Park, the national GAA stadium in Dublin, is named in his honour. **Mark Tierney**

Croker, T. Crofton (1798–1854), folklorist. Born in Cork; worked in London as an Admiralty clerk. He appears to have known little Irish, and was accused of lacking in sympathy for the Catholic rural community whose traditions he sought to collect. Nevertheless his works are still valued, partly because of their early date, especially his *Researches in the South of Ireland* (1824) and *Fairy Legends and Traditions of the South of Ireland* (1825). **Mícheál Briody**

Crolly, William (1780–1849), archbishop. Born at Ballykilbeg, Co. Down; educated at ST PATRICK'S COLLEGE, Maynooth. He spent his early career as a professor in Maynooth but in 1812 was appointed parish priest of Belfast. After much success there he was consecrated Bishop of Down and Connor in 1825; ten years later he was made Archbishop of Armagh and Primate of All Ireland. As one of the Commissioners for Charitable Donations and Bequests he incurred much odium and was personally criticised by DANIEL O'CONNELL for his co-operation with DUBLIN CASTLE. **Thomas Kelley**

Crommelin, A. C. D. [Andrew Claude de la Cherois] (1865–1939), astronomer. Born in Cushendun, Co. Antrim, a descendant of LOUIS CROMMELIN; educated at the University of

Cambridge. Working at the Royal Greenwich Observatory, near London, he was famed for his computations of cometary orbits and in particular his work on Halley's Comet; he traced the appearance of the comet back to 240 BC and made the most accurate prediction of its return in 1910. This led to an honorary doctorate from the University of Oxford and to the award (with P. H. Cowell) of the Lindemann Prize of the Astronomische Gesellschaft. Nine years after his death Comet Coggia-Winneche-Forbes was renamed Comet Crommelin by the International Astronomical Union. **Rod Jenkins**

Crommelin, Louis (1652–1727), a promoter of LINEN. Though he was given credit in the past for the development of the fine linen industry, it is now generally accepted that he only promoted the production of fine cambric and 'Hollands' in the style of his own place of origin in France. The quest for improvements in weave and finish was championed as early as 1635 by THOMAS WENTWORTH and promoted c. 1660 by the introduction of colonies of Dutch linen-weavers. **Mairead Dunlevy**

Cromwell, Henry (1628–1674), Lord Deputy of Ireland during the COMMONWEALTH. Born at Huntingdon, Cambridgeshire, the fourth son of OLIVER CROMWELL. He fought in the English Civil War and accompanied his father in his Irish campaign; in the 1653 'Barebones Parliament' he sat as a representative for Ireland. In 1655 he was sent to Ireland, in effect to take charge of the government, though he did not formally become Lord Deputy until 1657. His appointment was designed to end the power of the ARMY officers in Ireland and their indulgence of BAPTISTS and QUAKERS. Civilian government was restored, and legal and administrative reforms were instituted. He ensured that the pre-Cromwellian Protestants were involved in his administration, and he came to rely on them in his struggle against the residual and resentful influence of the extremists on the Irish Council. While relatively moderate in his religious views, opposing, for instance, the OATH OF ABJURATION imposed on Catholics, he was vehemently anti-Irish and enthusiastically promoted the policy of sending Irish people (particularly women of childbearing age) to the English colonies of the West Indies. He also favoured the TRANSPLANTATION of all the native Irish to Connacht until persuaded by the Old Protestants of the undesirability and impracticality of the scheme. He surrendered his authority to Parliament in 1659, was pardoned, and was allowed by CHARLES II to retain the lands he had obtained in Ireland. He spent the remainder of his life in retirement. **Liam Irwin**

Cromwell, Oliver (1599–1658). While in Ireland (from 15 August 1649 to 29 May 1650), Cromwell 'like a lightning passed through the land,' in the words of a contemporary. The speed and decisiveness of his siege operations were indeed remarkable, compared with the plodding pace of reconquest after he returned to England. Apart from his botched storming of Clonmel, Ireland added to Cromwell's considerable reputation as a military leader. However, while his historical reputation in Britain has been broadly favourable, he earned a niche in the demonology of Irish popular history. The question whether this condemnation is merited usually concentrates on atrocities associated with the storming of DROGHEDA and WEXFORD.

Cromwell might better be judged on his personal responsibility for the prolongation of war in Ireland. The war could have been ended much more quickly if moderately acceptable terms concerning land ownership and RELIGION had been offered to the Irish. As *de facto* leader of the English republic, Cromwell's hands were not tied by the Adventurers Act (1642), which necessitated wholesale

Cromwell, Oliver. *Engraving of Oliver Cromwell against an imaginary depiction of Dublin; his tenure as Governor of Ireland began in August 1649. [National Library of Ireland]*

land confiscation. However, in contrast to his dealings with the Scots, Cromwell was motivated by religious and national bigotry; he was also driven by the conviction that Irish Catholics shared a collective blood guilt for atrocities against Protestant settlers in 1641. The desire for a punitive post-war settlement therefore accounts for the duration, intensity and high human cost that characterised the most destructive phase (1649–53) of the Wars of Religion (see p. 676). [see COMMONWEALTH.] **Pádraig Lenihan**

Cromwellian land settlement. The confiscation of most land owned by Catholics was partly intended to settle the enormous debts faced by the Cromwellian regime, though future security and retribution for past actions were also factors. The main provision of the scheme was the removal of all Catholic landowners to west of the SHANNON. Those innocent of any involvement in the war were to receive the full equivalent of their former lands; the guilty would receive an allocation appropriate to their degree of guilt, including, in extreme instances, no land at all. The vacated estates were granted principally to the government, ARMY, and 'adventurers', men who had lent money to Parliament in 1642. The majority of Catholic landowners did not transplant, many choosing instead to become tenants on their former estates. Those who moved to Connacht inevitably displaced existing owners there, leading to complex and confused reallocation, and few received their notional entitlement. Only a third of the adventurers became settlers, receiving more than 400,000 ha (a million acres); the rest, like the great majority of the soldiers, sold their shares, which were bought by army officers and the existing Old Protestant landowners. The result was a massive redistribution in land ownership but little change in land occupancy. Tenants and labourers who had been pardoned in 1652 were not required to transplant and were kept on by the new owners. The

Cronin, Elizabeth. *Elizabeth Cronin, traditional singer, with the American singer and song-collector Jean Ritchie, photographed by Ritchie's husband, the Smithsonian Institution photographer George Pickow. [Ritchie-Pickow Collection, James Hardiman Library, National University of Ireland, Galway]*

settlement generated a major shift of political power to Protestants, which was to be maintained in the RESTORATION period. **Liam Irwin**

Crone, Joni (1953–), writer and lesbian activist. Born in Dublin. She was joint organiser of the Women's Conference on Lesbianism at Trinity College, Dublin, 1978, and a founder-member of Dublin Lesbian Line Liberation for Irish Lesbians and Lesbian Disco, where she was DJ for thirteen years from 1977. She was elected to the steering committee of the Irish Gay Rights Movement and the National Gay Federation in the 1970s and 80s. A community arts worker, she has written fiction, plays, and television drama; her play *It's Not a Tragedy* was performed by the Raised Eyebrow Theatre Company (which she also jointly founded) in Dublin, Drogheda, and Cork in 1986. **Katherine O'Donnell**

Cronin, Anthony (1928–), poet, novelist, memoirist, biographer, cultural critic, and originator of AOSDÁNA. Born in Co. Wexford. His poetry is noted for its modernist rigour and wit, shot through with a perceptive understanding of emotional frailty. He has been both celebrant and critic of Ireland's growing pains—as gifted assistant editor on the BELL, as caustic and mordant commentator (notably in his IRISH TIMES columns, collected as *An Irish Eye* (1985)), in his memoirs of mid-century bohemia in *Dead as Doornails* (1976) and in his survey of Irish literature in English, *Heritage Now* (1982). His novels, *The Life of Reilly* (1964) and *Identity Papers* (1979), are characterised by a dry humane intelligence and scrupulously exact prose style, qualities that also inform his much-praised biographies of FLANN O'BRIEN and SAMUEL BECKETT. His poetry collection, *The End of the Modern World* (1989), shows him at his inventive, tough-minded and compassionate best. **Theo Dorgan**

Cronin, Elizabeth (Bess), née Ó hIarlaithe (1876–1955), traditional musician. Born in Réidh na nDoirí, Co. Cork. From a family steeped in song and poetry, she was a rich source for archivists, among whom were JEAN RITCHIE, Alan Lomax, Robin Roberts, Brian George (BBC), and SÉAMUS ENNIS. She married Seán Proinsias, son of Dónal Proinsias Ó Cróinín. In 2000 Dáibhí Ó Cróinín published *The Songs of Bess Cronin: Irish Traditional Singer.* **Peadar Ó Riada**

Crookshank, Anne (1927–), art historian. Born in Whiteabbey, Co. Antrim, but spent much of her early childhood in India, where her father was employed in the Indian Geographical Survey Office; educated at TCD and the Courtauld Institute of Art, London. After working as a publication assistant at the Tate Gallery, London, and later as assistant librarian in the Witt Photographic Library at the Courtauld Institute, in 1957 she was appointed Keeper of Art in the Belfast Museum and Art Gallery (now the ULSTER MUSEUM), where she instituted the policy of collecting contemporary international art. She also organised pioneering exhibitions of historical Irish art, such as 'Pictures from Ulster Houses', 1961, 'Irish Houses and Landscapes', 1963, and 'Great Irishmen', 1965. In 1965 she moved to TRINITY COLLEGE, Dublin, where she established the Department of the History of Art, subsequently being appointed professor. Her collaboration with the Knight of Glin began with the exhibition 'Irish Portraits, 1600–1860', shown in Dublin, Belfast, and London, 1969–70, which broke new ground in the study of Irish PAINTING and SCULPTURE. The Anne Crookshank Prize for Art History was inaugurated in 1985. She was elected a member of the ROYAL IRISH ACADEMY, 1985, and a fellow of Trinity College. She has been chairperson of the ARTS COUNCIL OF NORTHERN IRELAND, a member of the Irish Stamp Design Committee, and a member of the board of the National College of Art and Design. Her portrait by DEREK HILL is in the NATIONAL GALLERY OF IRELAND, that by Sir Lawrence Gowing in Trinity College. In 1994 the Ulster Museum commissioned a portrait of her from the American painter Larry Coulter. The culmination of a life's work *Ireland's Painters 1600–1940* (with the KNIGHT OF GLIN) was published in 2002. **Martyn Anglesea**

crosántacht (buffoonery), a comic literary genre in which formal praise poetry in *snéadhbhairdne* metre is interspersed with humorous and often nonsensical prose passages. The term derives from the word *crosán* (buffoon or jester), and the genre itself appears to have originated in the incorporation of elements of medieval entertainment and folk drama in the repertoire of the learned poets and the performance of literary compositions. The twelfth-century tale 'Séanadh Saighre' provides an imaginative account of such a process, in which two poets witness the performance of a group of crosáns and memorise and subsequently imitate it. It has been argued that this text served to authenticate a literary trend associated with the twelfth-century displacement of learned activity from the MONASTERIES to the lay schools of poetry. Of the thirty surviving examples of crosántacht, however, most date from the late classical or post-classical period, and it has been suggested that the function of the often bawdy prose interludes was to provide comic relief for the audience from the tedium of formal eulogy. Two of the most well-known examples of the genre are epithalamia by the seventeenth-century poet DÁIBHÍ Ó BRUADAIR, in one of which the poet presents himself as a crosán. **Máirín Nic Eoin**

Cross, Dorothy (1956–), artist. Born in Cork. One of the leading Irish artists of her generation, she has become synonymous with work that is challenging because of its innovative use of found objects, new media, and unusual materials, often installed in unorthodox sites. She has been deeply influenced by psychoanalytical writing, especially by the theories of Carl Gustav Jung. Through her art she explores areas of sex and SEXUALITY, notably in such work as *Powerhouse* (Philadelphia, 1991, Dublin, 1992, Bristol, 1992), where she used furniture and tools found in a disused power station to make objects that wittily undermine assumptions about sex roles. In another series of works, such as *Croquet*, she combined domestic and sporting objects with stretched cows' udders to parody attitudes to male and female identity. More recently she has begun to engage with the environment, especially the sea, and to work on an enormous scale in such works as *Chiasm*, a video projection in which imagery of a waterfall and the accompanying sound of a woman's voice singing an operatic aria fill a traditionally male preserve—a rural handball alley. In 1999 she was awarded the Nissan Public Art Award at the Irish Museum of Modern Art, for *Ghost Ship*. She represented Ireland at the Venice Biennale, 1993, and was included in the First Liverpool Biennial in 1999. **Catherine Marshall**

Cross, Eric (1905–1980), writer. Born in Newry, Co. Down. A man of polymathic interests, he was best known as a writer for *The Tailor and Ansty* (1942), a compilation of anecdotes, tales, and sketches based on the conversation of his friend Tim Buckley (the Tailor), who lived with his wife Anastasia (Ansty) in Gougane Barra, Co. Cork. Capturing the irreverence and earthiness of a traditional storyteller, Cross's work fell victim to the draconian literary censorship of the Free State in 1943, stimulating a four-day debate on the matter in SEANAD ÉIREANN. **Terence Brown**

cross-border co-operation. Throughout its history the Irish BORDER has been highly permeable by European standards. It has never functioned as a linguistic or racial border, nor has it ever been governed by passport controls. It did, however, serve as a customs border between 1923 and 1992 and as a boundary between two distinct administrative, legal, and POLICING systems. Until the mid-1970s it marked off a Northern Ireland regional economy that was noticeably more industrialised than that of the rest of Ireland. However, its symbolic function as a barrier was highly significant, in that it distinguished two areas, one dominated by Protestant UNIONISM, the other by Catholic NATIONALISM. For many of their adherents these two religious and political perspectives were antagonistic and mutually exclusive. Though there has been considerable

Cross, Dorothy. The Ghost Ship *by Dorothy Cross, an installation that won the Nissan Art Project for Temporary Public Work in Dublin, 1998. It involved the creation of a 'ghost ship' from a decommissioned lightship anchored in Scotsman's Bay, Dún Laoghaire, Co. Dublin.* [Irish Times]

cross-border interaction, particularly in the areas contiguous to the land boundary, underlying political and religious antagonisms ensured that there was a remarkable lack of formal cross-border co-operation until relatively recently.

Unionist concern to give priority to the maintenance of the Union and the Irish state's refusal to formally recognise the STORMONT administration ensured that the first formal meeting of the two prime ministers, LEMASS and O'NEILL, did not occur until 1965, more than forty years after the inception of the boundary. Negative unionist reaction to this meeting was one of the factors contributing to the conflicts that ended the Stormont regime in 1972.

For much of the 'TROUBLES', cross-border co-operation between the British and Irish governments concentrated on political and security matters. However, by the 1980s there was a growing constituency for practical North-South economic links and co-operation at local and regional levels. This co-operation was facilitated by the various initiatives financed by the International Fund for Ireland, in association with the ANGLO-IRISH AGREEMENT, and by successive Interreg funds from the EUROPEAN UNION, introduced to facilitate the single European market. Joint cross-border business initiatives sponsored by the IRISH BUSINESS AND EMPLOYERS' CONFEDERATION and by the Confederation of British Industry in Northern Ireland were geared to the establishing of an efficient all-Ireland economy capable of competing in the single European market and the wider international economy.

With the signing of the BELFAST AGREEMENT in 1998, formal cross-border co-operation was moved onto a new plane. Six cross-border implementation bodies have been established, to deal with inland waterways, food safety, trade and business development, special EU programmes, language (Irish and Ulster Scots), and AQUACULTURE and marine matters. Six further areas were identified for co-operation through existing bodies: transport, agriculture, education, health, environment, and tourism. Co-operation is overseen by a North-South Ministerial Council, which is accountable to DÁIL ÉIREANN and the NORTHERN IRELAND ASSEMBLY. Wider co-operation on matters not devolved to the Northern Ireland Assembly occurs within a British-Irish Council, convened by the British and Irish governments, which consists of representatives of both governments and the Northern Ireland Assembly, together with the devolved assemblies of Scotland and Wales.

These novel institutions are complemented by co-operative networks between local authorities in the border region and between a range of cross-border voluntary bodies promoting socio-economic and cultural development. The European Union's Special Programme on Peace and Reconciliation and its Interreg III funding will help finance cross-border co-operation until 2006. **Liam O'Dowd**

Crotty, Elizabeth, née Markham (1885–1960), CONCERTINA-player. Born in Cooraclare, Co. Clare. She developed a sweet, easy sound, with many delicate idiomatic nuances. Her playing became very popular through frequent radio broadcasts in the 1950s, and she was an influence on many concertina-players of later generations. Her music can be heard on *Elizabeth Crotty: Concertina Music from West Clare*. She was a publican in Kilrush, where an annual music festival, Éigse Mrs Crotty, is held in her honour. **Peter Browne**

'crown jewels, Irish', a name sometimes given to a jewelled star of the ORDER OF ST PATRICK, a jewelled badge and a partially jewelled gold and enamel badge for the use of the LORD LIEUTENANT of Ireland in his capacity as grand master of the order. At an unknown date between 11 June and 6 July 1907 these and five knights' collars were stolen from a safe in the Office of Arms in DUBLIN CASTLE. Police investigations and a Viceregal commission of inquiry failed to lead to an arrest or the recovery of the insignia. In January 1908 their official custodian, Sir Arthur Vicars, Ulster King of Arms and knight attendant upon the order, was dismissed for negligence. He remained convinced until his death that his subordinate, Francis Shackleton (brother of the explorer), was responsible, though Shackleton had satisfied both the police and the commission of his innocence. There is evidence that in 1927 a jeweller in Paris offered to sell the jewels to the state for £2,000 and that the offer was declined; in 1928 the box in which they had been stored was anonymously returned. **Micheál Ó Comáin**

Crozier, Francis (1796–1848), EXPLORER. Born in Banbridge, Co. Down; entered the Royal Navy as a midshipman in 1810. He served with Captain Parry on three voyages of Antarctic exploration, 1821–6, and accompanied Captain James Ross on a further Antarctic voyage, 1839–43. In 1845 he sailed as commander of the *Terror* with Sir John Franklin to discover the North-West Passage. Disaster struck the following year when the expedition's ships were crushed in ice. After Franklin's death, in June 1847, Crozier assumed command; together with the survivors he landed on an island named on charts as King William Land and journeyed towards Back's Great Fish River. He and his men all perished, and their fate remained a mystery for many years. Crozier is commemorated in Banbridge by a statue flanked by two polar bears. **Peter Somerville-Large**

Crozier, William (1930–), painter. Born in Troon, Ayrshire; studied at Glasgow School of Art. He lives and works in Ireland, England, and Spain, was head of painting at Winchester College of Art and is a member of AOSDÁNA. Crozier's semi-abstract landscapes are executed in broad brush-strokes and luxuriant primary colours, which combine to convey a raw, primal energy. He is represented in the Crawford Gallery, Cork. The film *Truth about a Painter* (1992) was made for RTÉ television. **Suzanne McNab**

croziers. The staff as a symbol of office has a long ancestry and appears in various forms according to association, time, and place. The crozier of CHRISTIANITY recalls the rods of Moses and Aaron and that of the Shepherd from the twenty-third Psalm. The crozier (Latin *baculus*; Irish *bachall*) is essentially a pastoral staff, typically shaped like a shepherd's crook, and has been used by both bishops and abbots. It was an attribute of bishops in fifth-century Gaul and was probably adopted in Ireland during the process of conversion. But the earliest references belong to the seventh century; the earliest fragments are from the eighth century; and the earliest complete croziers are no earlier than the ninth century. Invariably a wooden core is encased in sheet bronze and subdivided by cast *knops*. The core might be regarded as a relic, a simple staff enshrined, but is more likely to be a structural element contemporary with its mounts. One staff, from Lemanaghan, Co. Offaly, has no mounts (though a ferrule seems to have existed) and may represent a pre-enshrinement phase; but its profile is not that of croziers in the strict sense, and it is best classed separately, perhaps as a pilgrim's staff.

Irish croziers resemble their Continental counterparts, except that the end of the crook, the *drop*, is differentiated and sometimes designed to hold relics. It is to this extent that Irish croziers are shrines. Croziers vary in complexity: the Toome crozier is almost plain, whereas the 'Kells crozier' has multiple panels of ornament and is enriched with silver and *niello*. Two croziers made c. 1100, from LISMORE and CLONMACNOISE, are among the finest known and attest to the wealth and status of these churches (see p. 635).

The use of croziers was doubtless restricted to ceremonial occasions. When not in use the crozier might have been stored in a treasury or displayed at a saint's tomb. Indeed the fact that Irish croziers have been attributed to the saints might derive from a role as trophies, to be placed in the hands of statues or suspended over tombs. The thirteenth-century seal of Dunkeld Cathedral, Perthshire, shows a crozier inside the building above an architectural shrine; the shrine held relics of the Irish saint COLM CILLE—transported from IONA—and the crozier was linked with his name. After the twelfth century the distinctive Irish crozier was no longer made. The only later crozier of native workmanship, made in 1418 for the Bishop of Limerick, is in contemporary Continental style. [see MEDIEVAL METALWORK.] **Cormac Bourke**

Cruise, Sir Francis (1834–1912), physician. Born in Dublin; educated at TCD, graduating with MD in 1861; fellow of the Royal College of Physicians of Ireland, 1864, and physician in the Mater Hospital, 1861. He designed the first effective endoscope by improving the lighting system. He had an interest in psychiatry, hypnosis, music, and the works of Thomas à Kempis. President of the RCPI, 1881, he was knighted in 1896. **Pierce A. Grace**

Cruithin, a collective name for population groups and their dynasties, lying mainly within Ulster. At an early date these were subject to ULAIDH overkings, though a strong mesne-kingship emerged under the Uí Moccu Uais dynasty, whose sway extended into the midlands. From the sixth century, UÍ NÉILL advances into mid-Ulster precipitated a transfer of allegiances by Cruithin dynasties, several of which were ultimately forged into a new mesne-kingship of Airghialla ('hostage-givers'), whose rulers came increasingly under Uí Néill control. Other Cruithin kingdoms, under the Dál Riada and Uí Echdach Cobo dynasties in modern Cos. Antrim and Down, continued under Ulaidh LORDSHIP. **Ailbhe Mac Shamhráin**

Cuala Industries. In 1908 Susan Mary (Lily) and Elizabeth (Lolly) Yeats, sisters of W. B. YEATS, split their EMBROIDERY and handprinting Dun Emer Industries from Evelyn Gleeson's DUN EMER GUILD to form Cuala Industries, based until 1923 in the cottage they shared at Churchtown, Co. Dublin. Elizabeth, their brother JACK B. YEATS and other artist friends designed and Lily and her employees embroidered a wide range of domestic articles, hangings, and dress and furnishing details. They were later housed by George Yeats (W. B. Yeats's wife) at 82 Merrion Square, Dublin, 1923–4, at 133 Lower Baggot Street, 1925–41, and at 46 Palmerston Road, 1942–69. Their loosely worked, boldly coloured free-style images of flowers, fruit, butterflies, Celtic knots, and shamrocks were favoured by aesthetes and nationalists on both sides of the Atlantic. [see ARTS AND CRAFTS MOVEMENT.] **Nicola Gordon Bowe**

Cú Chulainn, the best known of the heroes of Irish MYTHOLOGY. In keeping with the classical heroic life pattern found in literature and oral tradition generally, his birth is sacred, involving procreation by a god and also incest. Following the heroic pattern, he proves himself to be exceptional at a young age. His name, meaning 'hound of Culann', derives from the story of his remarkable slaying of a savage hound owned by the smith Culann. When Culann lamented the loss of the hound, the young boy, then called Sétanta, said he would henceforth assume the role of the hound as Culann's protector.

Also at a very young age Cú Chulainn proves his amazing skill in arms. He succeeds in killing three infamous young men, thereby proving his warrior status, and receives further instruction and training from Scáthach, a supernatural female figure, whose teaching made him invincible. He meets Aoife at this time, and she gives birth to his son, Conlaí, who is killed by his own father when he later comes to Ulster. In a war or battle Cú Chulainn's body reacts in a dramatic manner by turning around inside his skin; his hair stands on end, his eyes and mouth change form, and a warrior's light appears at his head. His death was in keeping with the heroic pattern and quality of his short life. Despite the *geasa* (prohibitions) that dominated his life, circumstances forced him to break them, and he was mortally wounded. He tied himself to a pillar so that he could die while standing, and after his death he was eventually beheaded (see p. 1090).

Cú Chulainn typifies the brave, invincible warrior who also had powers of second sight associated with the supernatural and who died at a young age having achieved great deeds and status. Many of the events in his short life and his tragic end are predictable, given the nature of the heroic life pattern. Cú Chulainn was probably introduced into the story of the TÁIN BÓ CÚAILGNE at a later stage in the development of the tale. [see GENERAL POST OFFICE; SHEPPARD, OLIVER.] **Ríonach uí Ógáin**

cúirt éigse: see COURTS OF POETRY.

culdees: see CÉILÍ DE.

Cullen, Michael (1946–), painter. Born in Kilcoole, Co. Wicklow; studied at the NCAD and the Central School of Art and Design, London. He travelled in Africa and North America before returning to Dublin, where he was one of an influential group of new expressionist painters in the 1980s. He spent a year in Berlin on an exchange scholarship. In contrast to the work of many expressionists, his paintings are cheerful, often concerned with metaphors of human life in studies of the artist and model. He is a member of AOSDÁNA. **Dorothy Walker**

Cuala. The Four Seasons *(1920), a folding screen with embroidered landscape panels by Cuala Industries, run by the sisters Lily and Elizabeth Yeats, with Lily in charge of embroidery. [National Museum of Ireland]*

Cullen, Paul (1803–1878), cardinal. Born in Prospect, near Ballitore, Co. Kildare; educated at Shackleton QUAKER School, Ballitore, Carlow College, and PROPAGANDA FIDE University, Rome. Ordained to the priesthood in ROME in 1829, he became rector of the Irish College, Rome, in 1832 and acted as agent for members of the Irish hierarchy. He became rector of Propaganda Fide University in 1848 and was consecrated Archbishop of Armagh in 1850, serving as Archbishop and Apostolic Delegate; he summoned and presided over the SYNOD of Thurles in 1850. Following the death of Archbishop DANIEL MURRAY in 1852 he was transferred to Dublin as Archbishop. He promoted the use of constitutional means to promote an improvement in living conditions in Ireland, while banning active political involvement by clerics; he also promoted the foundation, in 1854, of the CATHOLIC UNIVERSITY, under the rectorship of John Henry Newman. He oversaw the structural and pastoral redevelopment of the archdiocese of Dublin and founded Holy Cross College, Clonliffe, the diocesan seminary, in 1859; he centralised clerical structures and promoted ULTRAMONTANISM; he also actively condemned Fenianism and republican revolutionary NATIONALISM. Appointed cardinal in 1866, he was influential in the drafting of the dogma on papal infallibility at the First Vatican Council (1870) and in the appointment of numerous bishops. **Ciarán O'Carroll**

Cullen, Shane (1957–), painter and sculptor. Born in Edgeworthstown, Co. Longford; awarded a diploma in fine art by Sligo RTC, 1976. He works in a variety of media, often basing PAINTINGS and sculptures closely on texts and legal and political documents as well as corporate images and logos. He exhibited *The Council for the Preservation of Monuments to Martyrdom and Resistance* at the City Arts Centre, Dublin, and Limerick City Art Gallery, 1992. He represented Ireland at the Venice Biennale, 1995, with a monumental painting composed entirely of texts, *Fragments sur les Institutions Républicaines IV*. This work, first shown at the Douglas Hyde Gallery, Dublin, is based on republican prisoners' messages during the HUNGER STRIKES of 1981; it was shown at the PS1 Institute for Contemporary Art, New York, 1998, before being acquired by the IRISH MUSEUM OF MODERN ART, Dublin. **Peter Murray**

Cullen, Shane. Fragments sur les Institutions Républicaines IV *(1993–7; 96 panels, 216 x 60 x 6 cm) by Shane Cullen records the messages smuggled out of prison by Republican activists during the H-block protests in Northern Ireland. The work was created in France in the 1990s. [Centre d'Art Contemporain de Vassivière en Limousin/ Jacques Hoepffner]*

Culliton Report (1992), a report to the Republic's Minister for Industry and Commerce by the Industrial Policy Review Group (chaired by Jim Culliton). Entitled *A Time for Change: Industrial Policy for the 1990s*, the report called for a broader approach to formulating policy for industry and made recommendations on a wide range of relevant public policy areas, including TAXATION, INFRASTRUCTURE, EDUCATION, training, SCIENCE, and technology. It also recommended reducing reliance on industrial grants, a greater emphasis on fostering clusters of related industries, greater commitment to developing Irish INDIGENOUS INDUSTRY, and reformed institutional structures for INDUSTRIAL POLICY. **Eoin O'Malley**

Culwick Choral Society, a mixed-voice choir founded in 1898 by James Culwick as the Orpheus Choral Society. After his death it was re-established in 1913 by his daughter, Florence, as Miss Culwick's Choral Society. Having been a prizewinner at the 1927 National Eisteddfod of Wales, it was renamed the Culwick Choral Society in 1929 and continues to flourish. Its early repertoire of part-songs has gradually expanded. Historic performances have included *Messiah*, 1942, and early collaborations with the Radio Éireann Symphony Orchestra for Bach's *B minor Mass*, 1950, and Brahms's *Requiem*, 1951. Its conductors have included Turner Huggard, 1929–44, Alice Yoakley, 1944–53, JOSEPH GROOCOCK, 1953–8, SEOIRSE BODLEY, 1961–70, ERIC SWEENEY, 1971–81, COLIN MAWBY, 1982–5, and Colin Block, 1986–. **Ite O'Donovan**

Cumann Chluain Ard, Belfast MUSIC and cultural society established c. 1935 as an Irish-speaking club, offering language classes at its premises in Hawthorn Street. At first no music instruction was offered, as singing classes supported language, whereas music did not. Weekly céilí were held that, from the early 1960s, featured the McPeake Céilí Band. This led to the establishment, under Francie McPeake's direction, of the very successful Clonard Music School. **John Moulden**

Cumann na mBan, women's auxiliary to the IRISH VOLUNTEERS formed on 5 April 1914. Its initial aims included 'to advance the cause of Irish liberty' and 'to assist in arming and equipping a body of Irish men for the defence of Ireland.' Members participated in the 1916 RISING. Thereafter, revised aims incorporated 'arming and equipping ... men and women.' By 1921 almost a thousand branches existed, reflecting women's participation in the WAR OF INDEPENDENCE. Members rejected the Treaty by a vote of 419 to sixty-three. During the CIVIL WAR more than 300 were imprisoned. It remained an adjunct to the IRA until the 1980s, when women gained direct entry to the IRA. **Margaret Ward**

Cumann na nGaedheal: see FINE GAEL.

Cummian Fada (the Tall) (589–661), bishop. Born in Co. Kerry; studied at Finnbarr's school, Cork. An influential scholar, versed in church history, scripture, theology, and computistics, he served as Bishop and Abbot of Clonfert, 621–61. His letter to Segienus, Abbot of Iona (c. 633), is an important document on the Irish EASTER CONTROVERSY. Works attributed to him are *De Ratione Computandi*, *Liber Hymnorum*, and *Liber de Mensura*. [see COMRAC LÍADAINE.] **Juan José Pérez-Camacho**

Cúndún, Pádraig Phiarais (1777–1857), poet. Born in Ballymacoda, Co. Cork. He earned his living on a small farm before emigrating with his family c. 1826 to the United States. As well as his verse, some of the letters he wrote from America to his friends survive. **Breandán Ó Conchúir**

Cunningham, Edward Patrick (1934–), geneticist. Brought up in Waterford; graduated from UCD in agricultural science. His master's degree was in animal nutrition, but having been awarded a W. K. Kellogg Fellowship at Cornell University he turned his attention to animal genetics. In this field, and in management roles in research and development, he has served in An Foras Talúntais, the World Bank, and the Food and Agriculture Organisation of the United Nations; in 1974 he was appointed to a personal chair in animal genetics in TRINITY COLLEGE, Dublin. His research in genetics has led to improvements in the breeding of cattle and horses and in evaluating genetic stocks. He was awarded the BOYLE MEDAL of the ROYAL DUBLIN SOCIETY in 1996. **Christopher Moriarty**

Curragh Camp, Co Kildare, used as a military campsite since the later decades of the seventeenth century. A temporary hutted encampment to accommodate 10,000 infantry was established during the CRIMEAN WAR, 1855. Post-war reforms included the establishment of camps of instruction for all arms, and the Curragh became a permanent training-ground. Gradually the wooden buildings were replaced with brick barracks, including married quarters, a church, and a hospital. With the withdrawal of the British army from Ireland the camp was handed over to the FREE STATE army in 1922. **Con Costello**

Curragh Mutiny at the Curragh military camp, Co. Kildare (1914), a series of blunders rather than a mutiny, which began in March 1914 when Lieutenant-General Sir Arthur Paget, commander-in-chief of British forces in Ireland, allowed his Irish officers the option of avoiding service in Ulster to enforce HOME RULE. Sixty officers, led by Brigadier-General Hubert Gough, resigned their commissions. The War Office compounded Paget's mistake by assuring them that the British army would not coerce Ulster unionists. The ensuing outcry forced the resignation of the Secretary of State for War, J. E. B. Seely, and the Chief of the Imperial General Staff, Field-Marshal Sir John French, destabilising the military command shortly before the FIRST WORLD WAR and undermining nationalist faith in the LIBERAL government's Irish policy. **Fearghal McGarry**

Curran, John Philpot (1750–1817), lawyer and politician. Born in Newmarket, Co. Cork; educated at TCD. A brilliant orator and lawyer, he defended many of the UNITED IRISHMEN in the 1790s, including WOLFE TONE. An opponent of the ACT OF UNION, he lost some of his prestige following EMMET'S REBELLION. He was furious at discovering a relationship between his daughter, Sarah Curran, and ROBERT EMMET, and refused to defend him. He was later made Master of the Rolls in Ireland. **Patrick Geoghegan**

Curran, Sarah (1782–1808), nationalist heroine. Born in Rathfarnham, Co. Dublin, daughter of JOHN PHILPOT CURRAN. She met ROBERT EMMET when she was sixteen; though her father disapproved, she and Emmet later became engaged. She left home following Emmet's execution and in 1805 married Captain R. H. Sturgeon. She died of TUBERCULOSIS three years later at Hythe, Kent. **Rosemary Raughter**

Currey, Fanny (died 1912), artist. Born in Lismore, Co. Waterford, daughter of the Duke of Devonshire's agent at Lismore

Cumann na mBan. *Annie Derham in an early version (before 1918) of the Cumann na mBan uniform. The militarism of the organisation is evidenced by the symbolism of its badge, a rifle intertwined with the initials of the organisation, above the breast pocket. [Courtesy of Kilmainham Gaol Museum]*

Castle. She became well known for her work as a nursery gardener, specialising in daffodils. As a watercolour artist she was one of the founders of the group of women that held the first Irish exhibition of watercolours in Lismore, 1871, and that eventually became the Watercolour Society of Ireland. Few of her works are known, but her *West Gate of Clonmel on Market Day*, painted in a loose, free style, shows her to be aware of modern trends. **Anne Crookshank**

Currie, Austin (1939–), politician. Born in Co. Tyrone; educated at QUB. Elected STORMONT MP for East Tyrone in 1964, he was involved in the housing protest at CALEDON, Co. Tyrone, in 1968, was a member of the Northern Ireland CIVIL RIGHTS Association, and became a founder-member of the SDLP in 1970. Successively a member of the NORTHERN IRELAND ASSEMBLY, Convention, and Executive, he gravitated from parliamentary representation in Northern Ireland to the Republic and in 1989 was elected to DÁIL ÉIREANN for Dublin West. He was the unsuccessful FINE GAEL candidate in the 1990 Presidential election. **Brian Lalor**

Curtin, Jeremiah (1836–1906), folklorist and ethnologist. Born in Detroit. He conducted fieldwork in Ireland in the 1880s, using interpreters, though he knew some Irish. Among his works on Ireland is *Hero Tales of Ireland* (1894). His recorded folk-tales, though presented in translation, are viewed as reliable, and valuable because of their early date. **Mícheál Briody**

Cusack, Cyril (1910–1993), stage and film actor. Born in Durban, South Africa; brought to Ireland as a child by his mother, Alice Violet Cole, and her companion, Breffni O'Rourke, both of whom were actors. He made his first stage appearance at the age of seven as Little Willie in *East Lynne* and as a film actor in the adaptation of Charles Kickham's *Knocknagow* (1918). He joined the ABBEY THEATRE in 1932 and between then and 1945 appeared in more than sixty productions, while also playing in London and at the GATE THEATRE, Dublin. In 1947 he formed his own production company and staged productions in Dublin, Paris, and New York. In 1947 he came to international prominence as a film actor in Carol Reed's *Odd Man Out*. In all he appeared in more than fifty film and television productions, but, like most Irish actors, he was rarely given the leading role, though interesting films include *Shake Hands with the Devil* (1959), *A Terrible Beauty* (1960), *Fahrenheit 451* (1966), *Poitín* (1978), and *My Left Foot* (1989). His theatrical career was more important artistically for Cusack, who joined the Royal Shakespeare Company in 1963. One of his final stage appearances was in Chekhov's *The Three Sisters*, in which three of his daughters played the sisters. He received honorary doctorates from the National University of Ireland, 1977, and the University of Dublin, 1980. He published three collections of poetry: *Time Pieces* (1970), *Poems* (1976), and *Between the Acts* (1981). [see ACTING AND PERFORMANCE.] **Kevin Rockett**

Cusack, Margaret Anna, known as the 'Nun of Kenmare' (1832–1899), religious activist and writer. Born in Dublin, the daughter of Episcopalian parents; educated in England. In 1861 she entered the Poor Clares' convent in Kenmare, Co. Kerry, taking the name Sister Mary Francis Clare, from where she campaigned for relief of the local poor. Following conflicts with the ecclesiastical authorities she founded St Joseph's Sisters of Peace in Nottingham in 1884, but she resigned her position as Mother-General in 1888. She was the author of more than fifty published works, including popular histories of Ireland, two novels, biographies of religious and political figures, two autobiographies, and educational manuals such as *Advice to Irish Girls in America* (1872) and *Woman's Work in Modern Society* (1874). She may have returned to Protestantism before her death at Leamington Spa in England (see p. 924). **Margaret Kelleher**

Custom House, Dublin. JAMES GANDON's masterpiece, its siting on the north quays of the River LIFFEY gives it an unrivalled status in the civic ARCHITECTURE of Dublin, which it has gracefully maintained despite the encroachment of nineteenth-century railway engineering and twentieth-century high-rise architecture. Begun in 1781 in the midst of controversy, the Custom House led the trend of Dublin's commercial expansion towards DUBLIN BAY and away from the medieval city around CHRIST CHURCH CATHEDRAL. The north and south are the main façades, with subsidiary ones to the east and west. A pedimented central block on the southern river front is capped by a columned drum with slender ovoid dome bearing a figure of *Commerce* by EDWARD SMYTH. Flanking the pediment are open arcades, terminated by pavilions that bear the royal arms with lion and unicorn on the parapet. Smyth also carved the Riverine Heads as keystones for the principal doors and windows of the ground floor; they represent personifications of the rivers of Ireland. The Custom House was destroyed when set on fire in 1919 by the IRA in order to destroy the administrative records that it housed. It has been twice restored, in 1932 and 1999. **Brian Lalor**

customs, excise, and tariff protection. A tariff is a tax levied specifically on imports. Individual countries may forgo the right to impose unilateral tariffs by joining a customs union, membership of which entails a common external tariff as well as FREE TRADE between participant countries. An excise duty is a tax levied on a specific commodity, regardless of where it is produced. Unlike tariffs, excise duties are not necessarily protectionist, though they may have protectionist consequences. The first FIANNA FÁIL Government in 1932 reversed the largely free-trade policies that had prevailed since independence leading to a six-year economic war. High tariff levels and new quotas (quantitative restrictions on imports) were imposed, and the economy became almost entirely self-sufficient in a range of goods, including sugar, clothing, and footwear. PROTECTIONISM produced a sharp rise in industrial employment in the 1930s. The adverse long-term effects of the policy were masked by the enforced near self-sufficiency of the SECOND WORLD WAR period and became apparent only when the Republic missed out on the post-war economic boom of the 1950s. The fundamental rethink that the dismal performance of the 1950s produced saw tariff levels reduced substantially with the negotiation of the ANGLO-IRISH FREE TRADE AREA AGREEMENT (1965). The European Common Market had developed a customs union for industrial goods by 1968. Ireland's membership of the EEC from 1973 heralded full integration in the customs union over the next four years. Since then external trade policies, which continue to protect the production of coal, steel, textiles, and agricultural goods, have been determined at supranational level. Member-states continue to maintain control over excise duties, however; the revenue from such duties comprises a higher proportion of Irish tax revenue than is the case for the OECD as a whole. **Frank Barry**

cycling, controlled in Ireland by Cycling Ireland (which is affiliated to the Union Cycliste Internationale), though a few clubs in Northern Ireland affiliate to the British Cycling Federation. The Irish organisation has four regional federations, but most racing is organised at club level. Many leisure events are organised regionally; the 'Wicklow 200', a tough 200 km (124-mile) ride, attracted 850 entries in 2001. From March to September there is a full calendar of road-racing events, the biggest being the 'FBD Milk Rás', an eight-day stage race held in May, with teams coming from all over the world. The Tour de France held three stages in Ireland in 1998.

In 1896 Harry Reynolds won the world championship in Copenhagen; he claimed the victory for Ireland by demanding that the Green Flag be raised, instead of that of Britain. In 1962 Shay Elliott took the silver medal in the world championship; the following year he became the first Irishman to wear the leader's yellow jersey in the Tour de France. In the 1980s SEÁN KELLY won the Paris–Nice race seven times, the Tour of Switzerland twice, the Tour of Lombardy three times, the Paris–Roubaix, Milan–San Remo and Liège–Bastogne–Liège twice, the Super Prestige Pernod trophy three times, and the World Cup once. He also won stages in the Tour de France and was third twice in the world championship. Also during the 1980s STEPHEN ROCHE scored many victories, his most successful year being 1987, when he won the Tour of Italy, the Tour de France, and the World Road Race championship. In 1998 Mark Scanlon won the World Junior Road Race championship at Valkenberg. **Séamus Shortall**

Docwra *(see page 303). Stained-glass window in the Guildhall, Derry, depicting the landing of Sir Henry Docwra at Culmore, 15 May 1600, as part of the English Campaign in the Nine Years' War. [Derry City Council]*

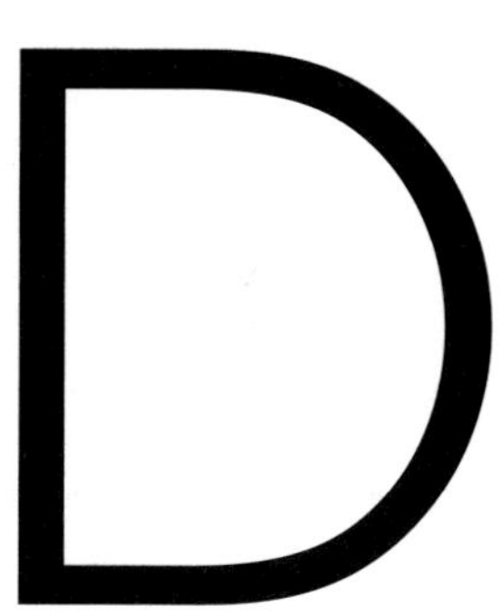

Da, a largely autobiographical play by HUGH LEONARD. It was produced at the Dublin Theatre Festival in 1973; its subsequent Broadway production earned the Tony Award for Best Play in 1978 and other prizes. Da, who has just died, returns as a ghost to take Charlie, his foster-son, back in time to revisit episodes of their life together. The play is theatrically clever and full of humour, managing to eschew the trap of sentimentality and convincingly portraying the strained, though loving, relationship between the two men. *Da* was filmed in 1987 and has enjoyed several revivals on the Dublin stage. **Martine Pelletier**

Dagda ('good god'), also known as Eochaid Ollathair (Great Father), a leader of TUATHA DÉ DANANN and one of the major gods of PAGAN Ireland. He is best known for his appearance in the saga 'Cath Maige Tuired' ('the Battle of Moytura'), where his adventures, gastronomic and sexual, are presented in a serio-comic light. Elsewhere, in 'TOCHMARC Étaíne' (the wooing of Étaín), he is the father of Óengus, Lord of Brú na Bóinne (the BOYNE VALLEY), through an adulterous liaison with Bóand. The Dagda was the possessor of a magical cauldron of inexhaustible bounty, one of the four treasures of Tuatha Dé Danann. **Elva Johnston**

Dáil courts. By a decree of 29 June 1920, Dáil Éireann authorised the creation of courts with civil and criminal jurisdiction, and a constitution was drawn up that established a SUPREME COURT of the Irish Republic, circuit and district courts in each parliamentary constituency, and parish courts with locally elected justices. The four professional judges of the superior courts were all barristers. The initiative received a widespread welcome; the 'British courts' were in effect boycotted in rural areas, while attendance for jury service was actively discouraged by the IRA. At the height of the 'TROUBLES', British forces broke up court sittings, officials were imprisoned, and some of those involved were shot. The courts went underground and could continue only in a sporadic manner, mostly in Munster.

The cessation of hostilities under the Truce in July 1921 made it possible for the Dáil Ministry of Home Affairs to organise a LEGAL SYSTEM under its central authority; and following the ANGLO-IRISH TREATY, criminal trials with juries were conducted in local courts, as were the bulk of civil cases. However, after the CIVIL WAR had broken out the PROVISIONAL GOVERNMENT moved against the Dáil courts, following a successful *habeas corpus* application to a Dáil judge on behalf of George Plunkett, a republican prisoner. It closed down the courts abruptly on 25 July 1922 and rescinded the decree of Dáil Éireann that had set them up. A Judicial Commission was established by statute in August 1923 to wind up more than 5,000 cases that were outstanding at the time of closure and to register judgments. Two years later, with the work still continuing, jurisdiction in Dáil court matters was transferred to the High Court of Justice of the Irish Free State. **Mary Kotsonouris**

Dáil courts and brehon law. BREHON LAW, Ireland's only indigenous LEGAL SYSTEM, developed by *breithiúna* or travelling judicial scholars, was the dominant system of law in Ireland before the ANGLO-NORMAN invasion in the twelfth century. The first law tracts in which the brehon system of law was recorded date from the seventh and eighth centuries, though it is known that the system is considerably older than this. In 1919, following the development of the first Irish constitution and the first Dáil Éireann, in which the revolutionary leaders rejected all previous English legislation, brehon law was again used in the Dáil courts for a brief period as a SOURCE OF LAW. **Neville Cox**

Dáil Éireann: see GOVERNMENT IN IRELAND.

dairy industry.

Table 1: Market Percentage

	Republic (2000)	Northern Ireland (1998)
Home	20	41
Britain	18	35
Other EU countries	38	12
Rest of world	24	6
Republic	—	6

Table 2: Milk Utilisation Percentage, 2000

	Republic	Northern Ireland
Liquid milks consumed	10%	13%
Liquid milk exports	—	17%
Butter, cream, yoghurt, etc.	39%	4%
Whole and skim powders	28%	49%
Cheese manufacture	23%	17%

Traditionally, most Irish farmers kept a small herd of dual-purpose shorthorn and Friesian cows, cattle, and pigs, fed on home-grown forage and cereals. Milk was produced for home consumption and the surplus sold for the manufacture of butter. The by-product, skim milk, was fed to calves and pigs. Since the 1980s dairy farming has become a highly specialised enterprise, operated on a minority of farms with large herds of high-yielding Holstein Friesian cows, fed on forage and compound feeds. The owners of these farms enjoy an above-average income, and milk is now processed into a variety of added-value products in high-technology plants.

Ireland accounts for 6 per cent of milk supplies in the European Union and approximately 30 per cent of all casein produced. Ireland also supplies 90 per cent of the world market for cream liqueurs. There are approximately 29,000 dairy farmers in the Republic, with an average herd size of thirty cows and gross output of €1,396 million, equivalent to approximately 35 per cent of agricultural output. The milk supply for 2000 was 5,011.5 million litres, the quota set by the European Union. However, 304.2 million litres was imported from Britain and Northern Ireland, helping Southern processors to reduce overhead costs. The production of milk is seasonal, mainly produced from grass from April to September.

Processing is carried out by more than thirty CO-OPERATIVES and public limited companies. The four leading processors in the Republic are Glanbia, Kerry PLC (which has acquired Golden Vale), Dairygold Co-op, and Lakeland Dairies; other co-operatives are Arrabawn, Connacht Gold, and Town of Monaghan Co-op. All have grown in recent years by means of amalgamations and acquisitions. Other sizeable operations include Carbery Milk Products (owned by four west Cork co-operatives, Tipperary Co-op, and Wexford Creameries). Abbotts Ltd, Nutricia and Wyeth Nutritionals manufacture baby formula; this market, including Nestlé, is worth an estimated €270 million per annum.

The biggest companies have their own marketing operations but also supply the Irish Dairy Board, which was established in 1961 by dairy co-operatives and has annual sales of €1,757 million (this includes sales of non-dairy products by its subsidiaries in the European Union and the United States). Most co-operatives use the IDB for export business. Exports from the Republic increased in value by 4.9 per cent to €1,650 million in 2000. Glanbia is the largest cheese-processor and the principal supplier of consumer dairy products; others include Golden Vale (now part of Kerry PLC), Carbery, Dairygold, and Tipperary Co-op.

Dairygold is the largest co-operative in the Republic, with a milk supply of 845 million litres, as well as the biggest supplier of dairy spreads. It employs approximately 3,000 people and has a turnover of €857 million. While Kerry PLC is a significant processor, most of its activities are no longer in Ireland, its emphasis being on transnational sales of food ingredients. Only 10.3 per cent of group sales (€1,339 million) are now in Europe.

In Northern Ireland the production of milk has grown from approximately 1,300 million litres in 1994 to 1,700 million litres in 2000, as an extra quota (the production permitted by the European Union) was acquired from Britain. There are approximately 5,000 active milk-producers, with an average herd size of sixty cows. Gross output in 2000 was €372 million, equivalent to 27 per cent of agricultural output. Between 1993 and 2000 the average yield increased by 2 per cent per annum, to 5,630 litres per cow (25 per cent higher than in the Republic). Northern farmers produce more milk from compound feed and rely less on forage.

Approximately ten co-operatives and public limited companies process milk in the North, while three processors in the Republic (Donegal PLC, Lakeland Dairies and Town of Monaghan Co-ops) purchase approximately 15 per cent of Northern production. The principal processors are United Dairy Farmers, Leckpatrick (Town of Monaghan Co-op), Fane Valley, Glanbia PLC, Express, Nestlé (Lakeland Dairies), and Pritchitt Foods. United has more than 3,000 members, a milk supply of 965 million litres and a turnover of €272 million and owns Dromona Quality Foods, the largest milk-processor in Northern Ireland. United also sells a significant volume of milk by means of a computerised auction system to other milk-processors.

Falling profits since the early 1990s, exacerbated by the strength of the English pound and high milk prices, allowed Southern firms to acquire Northern processing capacity and milk supplies. A report on the dairy industry published in 2001 by the Department of Agriculture and Rural Development showed that turnover increased from €551 million in 1989 to €731 million in 1998. However, added value fell by 23 per cent, while profits fell from €27.8 million to a loss of €3.17 million.

Despite a 29 per cent drop in employment, to 2,624 full-time jobs, the dairy industry is still the third-largest employer in the Northern FOOD and drinks industry. **Liam de Paor**

Dál gCais, a journal published irregularly in Milltown Malbay, Co. Clare, since 1972. It sets out to stimulate a positive appreciation of the past; contributions deal with local MUSIC, history, FOLKLORE, culture, politics, wildlife, archaeology, and biography, with occasional creative writing. It is illustrated heavily with photographs and graphic art. Later issues have more coverage of TRADITIONAL MUSIC, obtained primarily from the organisers of the annual Willie Clancy Summer School. [see SCOIL SAMHRADH WILLIE CLANCY.] **Glenn Cumiskey**

Dalkey (*Deilginis*), Co. Dublin, a fashionable suburb to the south of Dublin. The locality has a lengthy history. Its English name derives from a NORSE version of the Irish name; all referred originally to Dalkey Island off the coast. MESOLITHIC flints provide evidence for some of the earliest human settlement in Ireland. In Early Christian times St Beagnait was associated with the village. The shelter provided to ships from the dangers of DUBLIN BAY helped the settlement develop in the Middle Ages into a substantial town, where trade was an important activity. Seven 'strong CASTLES' were erected to protect traders and their merchandise; two of these survive, and the town retains much of its medieval street plan. It has recently been designated a heritage town. The quarrying of granite from Dalkey Hill provided materials for the construction of Dublin port's South Wall and the piers of DÚN LAOGHAIRE HARBOUR while giving work to labourers, whose cottages remain. From the 1840s the seaward slopes of Dalkey and neighbouring Killiney became dotted with the villas of the wealthy. The experimental ATMOSPHERIC RAILWAY designed by Robert Mallet ran from 1844 to 1854, after which the conventional line was laid, stimulating further residential development. Dalkey became a township in 1867 and was merged with the former borough of Dún Laoghaire in 1930. **Ruth McManus**

Dallán Forgaill (fl. 600), said to have been the author of AMRA COLM CILLE. Nothing is known with certainty about him, but according to legend he was the chief poet of Ireland and was defended by COLM CILLE when the poets were threatened with banishment from Ireland. The content of the Amra suggests that it is the work of a cleric; if Dallán was indeed the author, some at least of the traditional poets and the clerics must have been on good terms with each other by the end of the sixth century. This is consistent with some other evidence that points in the same direction. **Tomás Ó Cathasaigh**

Dallas, A. R. C. [Alexander] (1791–1869), EVANGELICAL clergyman. Born in Colchester, Essex; educated at the University of Oxford. In 1828 he was appointed rector of Wonston, Hampshire. He first visited Ireland in 1840; in 1843 he founded the Society for Irish Church Missions, taking advantage of what he saw as the God-given opportunity of the GREAT FAMINE to spread Protestantism throughout Connacht. [see SECOND REFORMATION.] **Thomas Kelley**

Dál Riada, a dynasty and, by extension, its territories, straddling north-east Ulster and Argyll in Scotland. Tracing its origin to the prehistoric Érainn, Dál Riada originally ruled a small realm in northern Co. Antrim subject to the ULAIDH overkings. Involved in colonisation movements across the North Channel, probably from the fifth century, the dynasty established itself in Argyll. Later tradition credited this achievement to one Fergus Mór. By the 560s, Dál Riada was sufficiently well established in Scotland for its king, Conall son of Comgall, to be able to grant IONA to COLM CILLE. For decades the dynasty pursued détente with the Columban community and with UÍ NÉILL; a political alignment with Cenél Conaill against ULAIDH pretensions was apparently one outcome of

dairy. *A rotary milking parlour on the farm of Tom Browne at Killeagh, Co. Cork. Such automated systems designed for smooth and continuous milking process are central to modern dairy farming.* [Irish Farmers Journal]

the Council of DRUIM CETT. Eventually the Dál Riada King Domnall Brecc rejected this arrangement, supporting the Ulaidh against Uí Néill and suffering a disastrous defeat at Mag Roth (Moira, Co. Down) in 637. After this the dynasty gradually distanced itself from political affairs in Ireland, concentrating instead on expanding its influence in Argyll at the expense of the Picts and the Strathclyde Britons. Over time its kings enhanced their reputation as rulers of the Scoti (Irish) of northern Britain and built marriage links with Pictish dynasties, which facilitated joint KINGSHIPS of the Scoti (ultimately meaning 'Scots') and Picts. In the middle of the ninth century Dál Riada, in the person of Cináed mac Ailpín, managed to permanently unite these kingships, laying the foundation for a Scottish monarchy. **Ailbhe Mac Shamhráin**

Dalton, Emmet (1898–1978), military officer and film-maker. Born in Dublin. An officer in the British army during the FIRST WORLD WAR, he was Director of Training for the IRA in 1921 and in June 1922 led the artillery attack on the FOUR COURTS, Dublin. As officer commanding the Cork Command of the Free State ARMY he was in the convoy when MICHAEL COLLINS was killed in August 1922. In September he resigned in protest at the execution of prisoners, later becoming Clerk of SEANAD ÉIREANN, a film-maker in Hollywood and London, encyclopaedia salesman, and professional gambler in Britain. **Michael A. Hopkinson**

Daly, Cahal (1917–), cardinal. Born in Loughguile, Co. Antrim. He taught scholastic philosophy at Queen's University, Belfast, before being appointed Bishop of Ardagh and CLONMACNOISE in 1967. Bishop of Down and Connor, 1982, and Archbishop of Armagh, 1990 and Primate of All Ireland. An ECUMENIST, he opposed paramilitary violence and encouraged inter-church dialogue. A liberal on economic issues, he was conservative on matters of doctrine. He opposed attempts to reform laws in the Republic touching on CONTRACEPTION, DIVORCE, and ABORTION. His tenure was blighted by a series of clerical sexual scandals that rocked Irish Catholicism to its foundations. He retired in 1996 (see p. 169). **Fergal Tobin**

Daly, Ita (1945–), novelist and SHORT STORY writer. Born in Drumshanbo, Co. Leitrim; educated at UCD. In *A Singular Attraction* (1987) and *All Fall Down* (1992) she deploys psychological realism to reflect on the bleak, emotionally fraught lives of independent women. **Terence Brown**

Daly, James (1937–), philosopher. Born in Wallasey, Cheshire; educated at ST PATRICK'S COLLEGE, Maynooth, and Queen's University Belfast. Senior lecturer in Scholastic Philosophy, Queen's University, Belfast, 1974–2001. Daly's work has produced a unique synthesis of Marxism, Scholastic philosophy and phenomenology. He has published *Marx: Justice and Dialectic* (1996) and *Deals and Ideals: Two Concepts of Enlightenment* (2000). **Fionola Meredith**

Dámhscoil Mhúscraí Uí Fhloinn, one of the last remaining survivors of the ancient BARDIC schools of poetry. Established in its present form in 1925 and meeting annually in Coolea, Co. Cork, it is a gathering of local poets, under the guidance of a 'president' and a 'clerk', to recite or sing their work. The president issues an invitation, the clerk a 'ceist' (a question or subject for debate). Singers and poets connected with the Dámhscoil have included Amhlaoibh Ó Loinsigh (1872–1947), Dómhnall Ó Mulláin (died 1965), Seán Eoin Ó Súilleabháin (died 1968), and Dónall Ó Liatháin (1935–). [see COURTS OF POETRY.] **Éilís Ní Shúilleabháin**

Dana: see SCALLON, ROSEMARY.

Danaher, Kevin (*Caoimhín Ó Danchair*) (1913–2002), ethnologist. Born in Athea, Co. Limerick; studied in UCD, Berlin, and Leipzig. He worked with the Irish FOLKLORE COMMISSION from the mid-1940s and subsequently as a lecturer in the Department of Irish Folklore, UCD. A versatile scholar with a deep understanding of oral and material tradition, he published numerous books and articles, both scholarly and popular. **Mícheál Briody**

Danby, Francis (1793–1861), landscape painter. Born at Killinick, Co. Wexford; educated at the Dublin Society Schools, where he showed early promise. He travelled to London in 1813 with the artists JAMES ARTHUR O'CONNOR and GEORGE PETRIE. En route home, he stopped in Bristol; he remained there until 1824, when he returned to London to evade creditors. Already a much acclaimed artist, he visited Norway in 1825. In 1829 he was defeated by John Constable in an election to full membership of the Royal Academy. He moved to Paris with his partner and was soon joined by his children. They spent the subsequent ten years living in penury in various European cities. He returned to London in 1839 and in 1846 retired to Devon, where he spent the rest of his life. **Brendan Rooney**

dance, contemporary, first brought to Ireland in 1939 by Erina Brady. Of Irish-German parentage, she studied with Dalcroze in Geneva, von Laban in Frankfurt and Mary Wigman in Dresden, fleeing Nazi Germany in 1938 to open a dance school in Dublin in 1939. After solo recitals and choreographing for AUSTIN CLARKE's Lyric Theatre Company, she founded the Dublin Dance Theatre Club in 1948 but retired soon afterwards to Switzerland, where she died in 1961. Her star pupil, Jacqueline Robinson, went to Paris on graduating in 1946; there she became well known as a dancer, choreographer, teacher, and writer of books on dance.

Contemporary dance was not seen again in Ireland until the arrival of the Irish-American Terez Nelson. A pupil of Martha Graham, she founded a company that performed in the ABBEY THEATRE and elsewhere, choreographing for Dublin City Ballet in 1979. Her student Joan Davis founded Dublin Contemporary Dance Studio in 1977 and Dublin Contemporary Dance Theatre in 1979. Its most notable production was *Lunar Parables* (1984) by the American choreographers Sara and Jerry Pearson, which was set to the music of CLANNAD, the BOTHY BAND, DÉ DANANN, and Stockton's Wing, with the verse and prose of W. B. YEATS spoken by the actor Niall Tóibín. Davis both taught in the studio and danced and choreographed for the company, from which many of today's companies evolved.

The American dancers Robert Connor and Loretta Yurick joined Dublin Contemporary Dance Theatre in 1980 and went on to direct Dance Theatre of Ireland, for which they have choreographed many pieces, including *Dances in Dreams* (1993) and *Soul Survivor* (1999). They have also brought other choreographers from abroad, such as the Portuguese Rui Horta from Germany and Blok and Steel from Amsterdam. Mary Nunan joined Dublin Contemporary Dance Theatre the same year and in 1988 founded Daghdha Dance Company in Limerick, a dance-in-education and, more recently, performance company. Since she left to become director of the MA course in contemporary dance at the University of Limerick the company has been directed by the Japanese-American Yoshiko Chuma.

In 1986 Paul Johnson joined Dublin Contemporary Dance Theatre after training at the Studio and the Laban Centre, London. In 1991 he founded and became sole choreographer for maNDaNCE, an all-male company designed to explore contemporary male culture. Working with the composer Eugene Murphy, he produced such work as *Sweat* (1994), *Beautiful Tomorrow* (1996), and *Without Hope or Fear* (2000). He was dancer in residence at the Project Arts Centre, Dublin, 1998–2000, and published his account of those years in *Fine Lines on Shifting Ground* (2000).

John Scott formed Irish Modern Dance Theatre in 1991, having danced with Dublin City Ballet after training at its Irish National College of Dance in Blackrock, Co. Dublin. He was much influenced by the American artist-musician Meredith Monk. His choreography has included *Macalla* (1995), *Slam* (1995), *Just Bodies* (1997), and *Intimate Gold* (1998). He also brought over unmistakeably contemporary choreographers from abroad, such as John Wisman from the Netherlands, Fabrice Dugied from France, and the Irish-American Seán Curran. Also from a ballet background are Fiona and Zelda Quilligan (subsequently known as Zelda Francesca), who formerly danced with Irish National Ballet. Founding Rubato Dance Company in 1987 to perform ballets for children, Fiona Quilligan found her choreographic strength in work such as *Cúchulainn a Chroí* (1974), which mingled Irish folk dance, ballet and contemporary dance with virile male dancing in its exploration of Irish mythology.

Adrienne Brown founded New Balance Dance Company in 1987, having been outreach worker and director of schools projects at the Dublin Dance Centre. She studied at the Martha Graham Centre in New York, and her choreography includes *Sculptura* (1996) and *Colmcille* (2000). Liz Roche, who trained with the College of Dance in Dublin and London Contemporary Dance School, formed Rex Levitates Dance Company with her sister Jenny in 1999. Working to original music by her brother Denis, she choreographed *Peeling Venus* (1999), *The Salt Cycle* (2000), and *To Time Taking Blush*, which was choreographed for the Peter Darrell Choreographic Award, 2000.

The two most successful choreographers in the field of contemporary dance have been DAVID BOLGER, founder of Coiscéim Dance Company, and MICHAEL KEEGAN DOLAN, founder of Fabulous Beast Dance Company. [see BALLET.] **Carolyn Swift**

dancers and choreographers overseas. Irish dancers working overseas include Gillian and Michael Revie from Bangor,

dance. *JJ Formento and Robert Connor in Dance Theatre of Ireland's* Soul Survivor *(1999), choreographed by Robert Connor and Loretta Yurick. The twenty-eight-minute piece incorporated abstract three-dimensional animated characters, time-lapse film, and web-gathered imagery. [Dance Theatre of Ireland/Tony Higgins]*

Co. Down, the former a soloist with the Royal Ballet, London, the latter principal dancer with the Zürich Ballet, and Killian O'Callaghan from Cork, who, after training at the Royal Ballet School, performed with Scottish Ballet before becoming principal dancer with the Royal New Zealand Ballet. Babil Gandara (Junior), born in Cork, works with the National Ballet of Cuba. Monica Loughman of Dublin works with the Russian State Ballet and Mick Dolan of Dublin with the Tanztheater, Vienna. Gavin de Paor toured internationally with Moscow City Ballet, and Andrew Wilson became a soloist with Birmingham Royal Ballet after training at the Royal Ballet School.

Choreographers include MICHAEL KEEGAN DOLAN and Marguerite Donlon, who trained at the Shawbrook School of Ballet in Legan, Co. Longford; she danced with London Festival Ballet before becoming a soloist with the Berlin Deutsche Oper and has choreographed many ballets, including *Celtic Touch* (1992) and *Different Directions* (2000). She became director and chief choreographer of the Saarbrücken Staatstheater in 2001, also choreographing for Nederlands Dans Theater and Stuttgart Ballet. The dancer and choreographer Finola Cronin toured internationally with the Pina Bausch Tanztheater of Wuppertal and in 1999 was appointed first dancer artist in residence at University College, Dublin. **Carolyn Swift**

dance training and studies. Full-time courses for the profession are taught only in Dublin, Cork, and Bangor, Co. Down. In Co. Dublin there is the College of Dance in Monkstown, directed by Joanna Banks, formerly of the Royal Ballet, Ballet Rambert, Royal Canadian Ballet, Bavarian State Ballet, and Irish National Ballet as well as Bat Dor, Israel. There is also the VEC college at Sallynoggin, Co. Dublin, directed by Deirdre O'Neill, formerly with Pact Ballet Company, Pretoria, and New Balance Dance Company. In Cork there is the Institute for Choreography and Dance at Firkin Crane Studios, Shandon, directed by Mary Brady, formerly director of Footwork Dance Company, Belfast; while in Bangor there is the Dance Studio, directed by Graham and Nicola Drake, both formerly with the Kiel Ballet Company. There is an MA degree course in contemporary dance at the University of Limerick, directed by Mary Nunan, former director of Daghdha Dance Company, and a course in contemporary dance at University College, Dublin, directed by Finola Cronin, formerly of Pina Bausch's Tanztheater of Wuppertal. **Carolyn Swift**

dánta grá, late medieval love poems. The term refers to a body of verse written in CLASSICAL IRISH metres but exhibiting the features of courtly love poetry found throughout Europe during the Middle Ages. Since the first known practitioner of this poetry in Irish, Gerald Fitzgerald, fourth Earl of Desmond (1338–1398), was of Norman extraction, it was long felt to have derived from French exemplars. The great majority of these poems, however, mainly anonymous, occur in seventeenth-century manuscripts, while the twenty or so named authors, Fitzgerald apart, belong to the sixteenth and seventeenth centuries. This suggests that the predominant foreign influence was English rather than French; and in fact a number of these poems exhibit familiarity not only with the contemporary English literary milieu but occasionally with particular poems in English. Though the craft of poetry in traditional Irish society was confined to professional hereditary families, with admittance to the profession granted only after long and rigorous training, aristocratic amateurs feature prominently among the known composers of the *dánta grá*: MAGHNUS Ó DOMHNAILL, Domhnall Mac Carthaigh, MUIRIS MAC DHÁIBHÍ DHUIBH MAC GEARAILT, Riocard de Búrc, PIARAS FEIRITÉIR, GEOFFREY KEATING, and the Scottish poet Isibeul Ní Mhic Cailín. This ability to compose light verse was considered a necessary accomplishment for the nobility in late medieval and Renaissance Europe, and in this regard the Irish evidence is in keeping with that of the Continent.

The professional poets did not take this invasion of their exclusive domain lightly, however, and by the end of the sixteenth century poets such as EOCHAIDH Ó HEÓDHUSA, Cúchonnacht Ó Cléirigh, Mac-con Ó Cléirigh, Anluan Mac Aodhagáin, and Niall Mór Mac Muireadhaigh were occasionally turning their hand to amatory verse. T. F. O'Rahilly's anthology *Dánta Grádha* (1926) contains 106 poems, but, allowing for the priority that MANUSCRIPTS accorded to formal eulogistic verse, it is likely that this is only a small fraction of the total number of amatory poems composed in the classical period. Furthermore, the fact that twenty-seven of these poems occur in a single manuscript, compiled in Ostend in 1631, shows how much we are depending on the fortuitous survival of manuscripts to make up this fraction.

The poems fall into two categories, serious and light-hearted. It is hardly coincidental that the majority of the serious poems were composed by amateurs, while the ironic poems were mainly composed by professional poets, more interested in the possibility offered by love poetry for word play than in the subject of love itself. A typical example is Eochaidh Ó hEódhusa taking the conceit of the dying lover to logical but absurd conclusions, finding himself simultaneously dead and alive. While the serious poems tend to be clichéd and conventional, there are at least two notable exceptions, both dramatic lyrics: 'A Bhean Lán de Stuaim' by Geoffrey Keating and 'Soraidh Slán don Oidhche Aréir' by Niall Mór Mac Muireadhaigh. [see COURTS OF POETRY.] **Mícheál Mac Craith**

Danu (modern *Dana*, genitive *Danann*), the goddess of TUATHA DÉ DANANN (People of the Goddess Danu), with whom the Sí

dánta grá. Kerry Poets' Memorial, *Killarney, Co. Kerry* (An Spéirbhean, *by Seamus Murphy), commemorating four local poets: Piaras Feirtéir, Séafraidh Ó Donnchadha, Aogán Ó Rathaille, and Eoghan Rua Ó Suilleabháin. [Bord Fáilte]*

(OTHERWORLD beings) are identified in medieval literature and who may also be associated with earlier CELTIC deities. Dánu was the name of a river goddess in Sanskrit literature; the name of the Continental river Danube also suggests worship of this GODDESS by the ancient Celts. The name may well have travelled with the Celts as they made their way through Western Europe. In legends about the invasions of Ireland, Danu features in matters related to druids and magic. She was the land-goddess of Munster, also known as Anu, later Áine, but not much narrative is available about Danu.

The myth of Tuatha Dé Danann dates from PRE-CHRISTIAN times and was adapted with the passing centuries. It is recounted that in a battle between the divine race, Tuatha Dé Danann, and the demonic race, the Fomhóire, Tuatha Dé Danann were victorious. They included highly talented craftsmen and beings associated with magic. The LEBOR GABÁLA ÉRENN tells of their arrival in the west of Ireland, where they eclipsed the Sun for three days, an indication of their power and their magic potential. They brought four items with them to Ireland: the Lia Fáil or stone of destiny, which screamed under the rule of the rightful king; the spear of LUGH, by which victory was certain; the sword of Nuadhu, from which no-one could escape; and the DAGDA's cauldron, which would satisfy everyone. They defeated the FIR BOLG at the first battle of Magh Tuireadh, at which the leader of Tuatha Dé Danann, Nuadhu, lost an arm and was therefore replaced by Bres, who proved unsatisfactory, so that Nuadhu—now with a replacement arm of silver—was re-instated. Then Lugh was accepted into Tuatha Dé Danann, and Nuadhu passed his royal role to him. Tuatha Dé Danann were eventually conquered by the sons of MÍL, and the battle resulted, according to one twelfth-century text, in their going underground to live. Numerous narratives associate them with archaeological sites and remains, and these in turn contributed to their close affinity with the deities. All these accounts and later developments regarding Tuatha Dé Danann ensured their identification with more recent FAIRY lore in oral tradition. **Ríonach uí Ógáin**

Daramona Observatory (1871–1908), established by WILLIAM E. WILSON at Street, Co. Westmeath. His first instrument was a 305 mm (12-in.) reflector by HOWARD GRUBB. A laboratory and workshop were installed in 1889, where the 610 mm (2-ft) reflector was fitted with electrical controls for astronomical photography in 1891. Photographic observations of stellar transits and photographs of clusters and nebulae made at Daramona were widely reproduced in astronomical journals. Before 1899 Wilson, sometimes in association with ARTHUR RAMBAUT of DUNSINK OBSERVATORY and GEORGE MINCHIN of Trinity College, Dublin, carried out research described in *Astronomical and Physical Researches Made at Mr. Wilson's Observatory, Daramona, Westmeath* (1900). Significant also was an accurate method developed to determine the effective temperature of the Sun. **Susan McKenna-Lawlor**

D'Arcy, Michael (1968–), violinist. Born in Belfast; studied at the Royal Northern College of Music, Manchester, and in Montréal. His teachers included Harry Cawood, Pavel Crisan, and Lydia Mordkovitch. He won many prizes, including RTÉ MUSICIAN OF THE FUTURE, 1987, and the Lombard and Ulster Foundation String Award, 1989–90. Since his London debut, 1990, he has performed and broadcast throughout Europe, North America, and Japan as soloist, orchestral leader, and recitalist. He has premiered many new works. He was leader of the RTÉ CONCERT ORCHESTRA between 1993 and 2000 and is a member of the Irish Piano Trio. **Ite O'Donovan**

Darcy, Patrick (1598–1668), lawyer and politician. Born in Galway; educated at the Middle Temple, London. Having established a formidable reputation as a barrister, he was elected to the Parliament of 1634 and became an implacable opponent of WENTWORTH after the failure to enact the Graces (concessions promised by Charles I to the OLD ENGLISH). He placed his legal and political skills at the disposal of the Galway Old English landowners when the Lord Deputy attempted to seize their lands through the revival of Crown claims. As a result he was prosecuted and prevented from practising LAW. In 1641 he argued for the independence of the Irish Parliament and took a leading role in the campaign to ensure that the government would act within the law. He was an influential member of the CONFEDERATION OF KILKENNY and one of the chief architects of the peace treaty agreed with the Marquis of Ormond in 1646, and resumed his legal career in the RESTORATION period. **Liam Irwin**

Dargan, William (1799–1867), civil engineering contractor. Born near Carlow. He worked for Thomas Telford at Holyhead, Anglesey, 1820, before becoming a road contractor in Ireland, 1821–30, his work including part of the Dublin–Howth road. He was the contractor for Ireland's first public railway, the DUBLIN AND KINGSTOWN RAILWAY, 1831–4, and became a major contractor for canal and railway projects, including the ULSTER CANAL and the Dublin–Cork railway. In 1853 he sponsored the Dublin Exhibition of Industry. There is a statue of Dargan by Sir THOMAS FARRELL outside the NATIONAL GALLERY OF IRELAND, an institution he helped financially to establish. **Ronald Cox**

'Dark Rosaleen' (1846), an English version by JAMES CLARENCE MANGAN of the anonymous Irish poem 'Róisín Dubh'. Mangan's version, which first appeared in the NATION on 30 May 1846, was based on a prose translation that SAMUEL FERGUSON published in the DUBLIN UNIVERSITY MAGAZINE in August 1834. JAMES HARDIMAN in *Irish Minstrelsy* (1831) claimed that the poem was a political allegory, Róisín representing Ireland, an interpretation disputed by Ferguson, who claimed that the poem was the love song of a priest, waiting for dispensation from Rome to marry. Mangan favoured a political reading of the poem; and the dramatic, highly rhythmic structure of the translation was to make it one of the most popular poems of the nineteenth century. **Michael Cronin**

Darley, Frederick (1798–1872), architect. Born in Dublin into a noted building family; his father, Alderman Frederick Darley, was head of the Dublin police, while his maternal grandfather was ARTHUR GUINNESS. Articled to FRANCIS JOHNSTON in the Board of Works, he entered private practice in 1822. His Dublin works include Merchants' Hall (1822), the library of the KING'S INNS (1825), and the north extension to the Inns (1847). He was at various times architect to Trinity College, secretary of the ROYAL INSTITUTE OF THE ARCHITECTS OF IRELAND, and architect to the Commissioners for National Education, for whom he designed a number of model schools. **Frederick O'Dwyer**

Darley, George (1795–1846), mathematician and poet. Born in Dublin; educated at TCD. He settled in London in 1822 and remained there until his death. An eccentric personality and a speech impediment made him a recluse. He is best remembered for *The Errors of Ecstacie* (1822), *Sylvia*, a fairy drama (1827), and *Nepenthe* (1839), all of which were written in a disembodied romantic style that eschewed local reference or specifically Irish subject matter; they won him cordial recognition from fellow-poets such as Browning and Tennyson (who offered to publish his verse) though little public acclaim. He also wrote several original works on science and mathematics, which ran through numerous editions. **Jason King**

Darwin, Elinor, née Monsell (1879–1954), illustrator. Born in Limerick, sister of J. R. MONSELL; educated at Slade School of Fine Art, London, where she later taught wood-engraving. In Ireland she is best remembered for the DUN EMER Press device, showing Emer and the tree, and the woodcut device of the ABBEY THEATRE, showing MÉABH with a wolfhound, still used today. She produced some of her finest work in collaboration with her husband, Bernard Darwin, for his children's books *The Tale of Mr Tootleoo* (1925), *Tootleoo Two* (1927), and *Oboli, Boboli and Little Joboli* (1928). These are illustrated with stylised, simplified, brightly coloured line drawings. **Patricia Donlon**

Daughters of Ireland: see INGHINIDHE NA HÉIREANN.

Davey, Shaun (1948–), art historian, record producer, and composer of 'cross-over' POPULAR MUSIC. Born in Belfast. Taking his titles mainly from characters and events in Irish history and legend, Davey has found particular success in the combination of orchestra and UILLEANN PIPES. His best-known works include 'The Brendan Voyage', 'The Pilgrim', 'Granuaile', and 'The Relief of Derry', which employ rhythmic and melodic motifs from TRADITIONAL MUSIC. He has also composed music for the THEATRE, television, and films, including a Broadway version of JAMES JOYCE's 'The Dead', the television series 'Ballykissangel', 'The Hanging Gale', and 'Waking Ned Devine'. His record production includes Sonny Condell, LIAM O'FLYNN, and Rita Connolly and the groups Midnight Well and Stockton's Wing. **Jimmy O'Brien Moran**

Davies, Christian (Kit), also known as Kit Cavanagh and Mother Ross (1667–1739), woman soldier. Born in Dublin to a prosperous BREWING family. She inherited an inn from her aunt, and at the age of twenty-one she married her aunt's manservant, Richard Welsh, who disappeared suddenly after their wedding. A year later she received a letter from him explaining that he had been pressed into the English army to fight in Flanders. She set out to find him, enlisting in Marlborough's army under the name Christopher Welsh. She fought with the Scots Greys in the campaign of 1702–3 and remained in Marlborough's army until the Battle of Ramillies (1706), when she was wounded and her sex was discovered. She earned celebrity with her regiment and, though discharged by the military authorities, was allowed a new marriage service with her husband. She continued to follow him as a butler and supplied food to the soldiers, who gave her the name Mother Ross. Richard Welsh was killed in action at Malplaquet in 1710, and she married a grenadier in her former regiment. He too was killed in action shortly afterwards, and she was awarded a pension and returned to Dublin. She married for a third time to an ex-soldier called Davies, whom she followed to London. She became impoverished in her later years and was given refuge in Chelsea Pensioners' Hospital. While nursing her third husband through a bout of fever she became ill herself, died, and was buried with military honours. Daniel Defoe wrote her biography, *The Life and Adventures of Mrs. Christian Davies, Commonly named Mother Ross* (1740). **Ciarán Deane**

Davies, Sir John (1569–1626), lawyer and colonial administrator. A man of considerable literary fame, Davies devoted his principal energies to advancing his legal career. As Solicitor-General of Ireland, 1603–6, he considered Ireland a stepping-stone in this respect, his expectations meeting with mixed success. Within a short time he was promoted to the position of ATTORNEY-GENERAL of Ireland, 1606–19, not least because he played a leading role in employing English law as a means of consolidating the Elizabethan military conquest. He was responsible for important legal decisions that asserted primogeniture in the matter of land inheritance, abolishing the traditional Irish practices of *tanistry* (succession by any male member of the chieftain's family circle) and *gavelkind* (partible inheritance). Accused by HUGH O'NEILL, Earl of Tyrone, of being instrumental in provoking the FLIGHT OF THE EARLS (1607), he was later to play a pivotal role in orchestrating the PLANTATION OF ULSTER. Arguing that it was critically important that Protestant settlers outnumber the local inhabitants, he was partly responsible for the fact that the settlement scheme was so resented by the indigenous population. He also played an important part in the Irish Parliament, 1613–15, where he assumed the position of Speaker. Prone to gaffes, despite his undoubted intellectual capabilities he found himself marooned in the Crown administration of Ireland while craving for advancement in England. Returning to England in 1619, he was later appointed Lord Chief Justice of England, only to die the night before he assumed his new position. His most important literary work is his poem '*Nosce Teipsum*' on the immortality of the soul, '*A Contention betwixt a Wife, a Widdow, and a Maide*', and his discourse on Ireland, *A Discovery of the True Causes Why Ireland*

Was Never Subdued Nor Brought under Obedience of the Crown of England (1612). **John McCavitt**

Davis, John T. (1947–), film-maker. Born in Belfast; studied at the Belfast College of Art before emerging in the 1980s as Ireland's most consistently innovative documentary director and cameraman. While his first major film, *Shell Shock Rock* (1978), dealt with the Northern punk MUSIC scene, many of his films, including *Route 66* (1985) and *Hobo* (1991), explore American culture during transcontinental trips. His experience in the American 'Bible Belt' found a ready echo when he dealt with fundamentalist religion in Northern Ireland in *Dust on the Bible* (1989) and *Power in the Blood* (1989). *The Uncle Jack* (1996) is a moving portrait of his uncle, the cinema architect JOHN MCBRIDE NEIL, who designed many of Ulster's most spectacular cinemas. **Kevin Rockett**

Davis, Thomas (1814–1845), poet and cultural nationalist. Born in Mallow, Co. Cork; educated at TCD and called to the bar 1838. He joined the Repeal Association in 1840 but split with O'CONNELL over the issue of non-denominational education. He became the unofficial leader of the YOUNG IRELAND movement and jointly founded the NATION (1842) with JOHN BLAKE DILLON and CHARLES GAVAN DUFFY. All their literary endeavours combined a romantic aesthetic with patriotic sentiment to inculcate a sense of cultural NATIONALISM. Never considered an accomplished poet, Davis was nevertheless a major literary and political influence on his contemporaries and is renowned for some of the most popular Irish ballads, including 'A Nation Once Again'. He died prematurely in Dublin from scarlet fever aged thirty-one; his funeral was a major public event. **Jason King**

Davitt, Michael (1846–1906), agrarian radical, journalist, and 'father of the LAND LEAGUE'. Born in Straide, Co. Mayo. He emigrated to England following his family's EVICTION in 1850 and lost his right arm in a mill accident in Lancashire in 1857. In 1865 he joined the FENIAN MOVEMENT; five years later he was convicted of arms trafficking and spent seven years in Dartmoor Prison before being released on parole. Within two years he had become instrumental in formulating the NEW DEPARTURE, organising the first public meetings of the LAND WAR and establishing the National Land League of Mayo and the Irish National Land League. In 1882 he was one of the founders of the Irish National League. He was MP for South Mayo from 1895 to 1899, when he resigned in protest against the ANGLO-BOER WAR. He published six books, including *The Fall of Feudalism in Ireland* (1904). **Donald Jordan**

Davy, Edmond William (1785–1857), chemist. Born at Penzance, Cornwall; educated locally. He moved to London in 1804 to work as an assistant in the laboratory of the Royal Institution. In 1813 he took over the joint posts of professor of chemistry and secretary to the ROYAL CORK INSTITUTION, thereby directly succeeding one of its founders, Rev. Thomas Dix Hincks. In 1825 he was appointed professor of chemistry at the ROYAL DUBLIN SOCIETY in succession to WILLIAM HIGGINS. Davy's greatest legacy to chemistry lies in his being the first to make acetylene gas (in 1836). As a public service he gave popular courses of lectures throughout Ireland on themes concerning the applications of chemistry to AGRICULTURE. **Susan McKenna-Lawlor**

Dawe, Gerald (1952–), poet and critic. Born in Belfast; educated at NUU. After twenty years as a lecturer at UCG he moved to TCD in 1994. His five books of poetry are *Sheltering Places* (1978), *The Lundys Letter* (1985), *Sunday School* (1991), *Heart of Hearts* (1995), and *The Morning Train* (1999). An influential CRITIC and editor, he edited *The Younger Irish Poets* (1982) and the review *Krino* (founded 1985) and has published important collections of essays: *Against Piety: Essays in Irish Poetry* (1995), *The Rest is History: A Critical Memoir* (1998), and *Stray Dogs and Dark Horses* (2000). Dawe is a searching realist whose work investigates cultural and personal identity in Ireland by means of the 'small change' of everyday experience. **Hugh Haughton**

Day-Lewis, Cecil (1904–1972), poet. Born in Ballintubbert, Co. Laois, and raised in England; educated at the University of Oxford. In the 1930s he became associated with the 'pylon' school of poets (among whom were W. H. Auden, Stephen Spender, and LOUIS MACNEICE), whose work struck left-wing attitudes and exploited industrial imagery. Essentially an English man of letters who valued an Irish patrimony, Day-Lewis wrote poetry throughout his life, but his reputation depends on the work of the 1930s and 40s. He was appointed Poet Laureate in 1968, and his *Collected Poems* appeared in 1992. He also published detective fiction under the pseudonym Nicholas Blake. **Terence Brown**

Dean, Paul (1960–), rugby footballer. Born in Dublin. A magnificent distributor, he made an immense contribution to the Triple Crown triumph of 1985, when arguably Ireland fielded one of their best back lines ever; he won thirty-two caps, twenty-seven at out-half and five at centre, between 1982 and 1989. In the defeat of Wales in Cardiff in 1989 he became the first Ireland out-half to score a try at Cardiff Arms Park since JACK KYLE in 1951. He was selected to tour Australia with the 1989 British Lions team, but a leg injury in the first match, against Western Australia at Perth, prematurely ended his playing career. **Karl Johnston**

Deane, John F. (1943–), poet and publisher. Born in ACHILL ISLAND, Co. Mayo; educated in Limerick and at UCD. He founded the Dedalus Press and POETRY IRELAND (the National Poetry Society). Following his first collection of verse, *Stalking After Time* (1977), he published steadily, achieving a reputation as a poet who deals courageously with the mystery of life and its suffering, from a distinctively religious viewpoint. He has also published fiction. **Terence Brown**

Deane, Raymond (1953–), composer. Born in ACHILL ISLAND, Co. Mayo. He studied piano at the College of Music, Dublin, and in 1969 attended a 'Ferienkurse für die Neue Musik' at Darmstadt; he graduated from UCD in 1974 and subsequently studied composition in Basel with Gerald Bennett and Earle Brown, with Stockhausen in Cologne, 1976–7, and with Isang Yun in Berlin, 1978–9. He made his debut as a composer at the 1969 DUBLIN FESTIVAL OF TWENTIETH CENTURY MUSIC, and his works have been represented at numerous international festivals. He was elected to AOSDÁNA in 1986. His compositions include *Ripieno* (1998–9), two chamber operas, concertos, and chamber music. **Ite O'Donovan**

Deane, Seamus (1940–), CRITIC, professor, and poet. Born in Derry; educated at QUB and the University of Cambridge. He was professor of modern English and American literature at UCD, 1980–93, and subsequently became Keough professor of Irish studies at the University of Notre Dame, Indiana. His writings comprise three related categories: poetry—*Gradual Wars* (1972), *Rumours* (1977), and *History Lessons* (1983)—criticism stemming from his interest in BURKE and ideas of polity, and cultural politics. *The French Revolution and the Enlightenment in England, 1789–1832* (1988) was complemented by *Strange Country: Modernity and Nationhood in Irish Writing since 1790* (1997); together they chart the history of ideas about collective society and the individual imagination and their constitution of a tradition of nationhood. The nature of dissent and of minority identity has been explored more explicitly by Deane as a joint founder of FIELD DAY as a theatre company and a publishing house; he was general editor of *The Field Day Anthology of Irish Writing* (1991), which was presaged by his essays *Celtic Revivals* (1985). The three threads of Deane's nationalism coalesce in his memoir of childhood and adolescence, *Reading in the Dark* (1996). **Richard Pine**

Deane, Sir Thomas (1792–1871), architect. Born in Cork. His father, Alexander Deane, a builder, died in 1806, leaving his wife, Elizabeth, to carry on the business. Thomas assisted her and in 1811 designed his first building, Cork Commercial Buildings (now the Imperial Hotel) in South Mall. They also engaged in speculative building and in contracting for public works. Deane was a Conservative member of Cork City Council, serving three terms as High Sheriff, 1815, 1830, 1851, and was knighted in 1830. He was also a patron of the arts, his protégés including the sculptor JOHN HOGAN. In 1851 he formed a partnership with his son Thomas Newenham DEANE and Benjamin WOODWARD, whom he had first employed in 1846 on the design of Queen's College, Cork (UCC). [see DEAN AND WOODWARD.] **Frederick O'Dwyer**

Deane and Woodward, architectural practice. In 1851 the practice of Sir THOMAS DEANE in Cork was reconstituted as a partnership with his son and pupil Thomas Newenham Deane (1828–1899) and Benjamin Woodward (1816–1861), a native of Tullamore, Co. Offaly. Woodward had trained as an engineer but had an exceptional architectural talent, as well as an interest in antiquities. He joined Deane as an assistant on Queen's College, Cork, in 1846, later working on Killarney Asylum (1847–52), both gothic revival buildings. The practice moved to Dublin in 1853 to superintend the erection of the Museum Building at Trinity College, won in competition. The elevations, in the Venetian Cinquecento style, and the naturalistic carved ornament were heavily influenced by the writings of John Ruskin, with whom Woodward became friendly after they won another competition, for the University Museum at Oxford, in 1854. This celebrated building consisted of three stone-faced ranges around a glass-and-iron central court, all in the gothic manner. Further English commissions followed, including the Crown Life office in Blackfriars, London (1856–8, since demolished), the Oxford Union (1856–7), decorated by the pre-Raphaelites William Morris, Dante Gabriel Rosetti, and Edward Burne-Jones, and a design for government offices in Whitehall, London (1857), which received a premium. Their last major commission, the Kildare Street Club, Dublin (1858–61), was almost complete when Woodward died in France of TUBERCULOSIS (see p. 39). **Frederick O'Dwyer**

Deasy, H. H. (c. 1867–c. 1938), EXPLORER and pioneer MOTORIST. Born in Waterford. He won a gold medal for his driving in the 1901 British Auto Tour, and manufactured cars under his own name at Coventry from 1906 to 1911. He also won a Royal Geographical Society Gold Medal for exploration in India, Tibet, and China. **Brendan Lynch**

'death tale' tale type: see AIDED.

Deane and Woodward. *One of the O'Shea brothers at work on the stone-carving of the windows of the University Museum, Oxford, designed by Deane and Woodward in 1854. [Irish Architectural Archive/© Oxford University Museum of Natural History]*

de Bhailís, Colm (1796–1906), oral poet in the Connemara tradition. Born in Ceantar na nOileán, Co. Galway. He worked as a stonemason and sawyer in Cos. Mayo, Clare, and Galway; on the death of his second wife, c. 1900, he entered the poorhouse at Oughterard, Co. Galway. His songs were transcribed there at the instigation of PATRICK PEARSE and SEOSAMH LAOIDE by nineteen-year-old Pádraic Ó Domhnalláin and were published by the GAELIC LEAGUE in 1904. Some of the songs—'Cúirt an tSrutháin Bhuí', 'Amhrán an Tae', and 'An Seanduine Cam'—are still sung in Connemara. His work, traditional in content and narrative technique, describes the ordinary life of his time through the critical yet sympathetic eye of the insider. There is a modern edition by Gearóid Denvir, *Amhráin Choilm de Bhailís* (1996). **Gearóid Denvir**

de Blacam and Meagher, architects. Shane de Blacam (1945–) was born in Dublin; studied at UCD and the University of Pennsylvania; worked in the office of Louis I. Kahn, Philadelphia, 1970–3; was a tutor and associate professor at UCD, 1973—94. John Meagher (1947–) was born in Dublin; studied at DIT and Helsinki; worked with Venturi and Rauch, Philadelphia; was a design tutor at UCD, 1975–83. De Blacam and Meagher was established in Dublin in 1976. They designed churches (through competition) at Rowlagh and Firhouse, Co. Dublin (1976–8), and carried out the restoration of the Dining Hall at TRINITY COLLEGE, Dublin, adding a new atrium in the spirit of Kahn and a reproduction of Adolf

Loos's Kärntner Bar in Vienna (RIAI Silver Medal for Architectural Conservation, 1984–6). They designed the Beckett Theatre at Trinity College, Dublin, including an oak-clad studio tower, which won the AAI Downes Medal, 1993. They won first prize in the competition for the Chapel of Reconciliation at Knock, Co. Mayo (1989–90), a tranquil area within a grass mound. They won first prize for the ceremonial entry of the University of Limerick. Other work includes the library of Cork Institute of Technology, Bishopstown (1991–6), a formal brick screen to triple-height galleries; the Wooden Building, a nine-storey teak-clad apartment tower at TEMPLE BAR, Dublin (1998–2000); and the Esat Digifone head office at GRAND CANAL Dock, Dublin (1999–2001). **Raymund Ryan**

de Blacam and Meagher. *Interior of the award-winning Library of Cork Institute of Technology (1991–6), showing the view down the east-west passage between reading rooms. [Courtesy of de Blacam and Meagher, Architects; photo: View Pictures (London), Peter Cook]*

de Breffny, Baron Brian O'Rorke (1929–1989), architectural historian and editor. Born in Cimiez, Alpes-Maritimes, France, to a family of Irish extraction ennobled by Empress Maria Theresa in the 1760s; studied at the Sorbonne and Harvard. He came to live permanently in Ireland in 1979 and began the restoration of DAVIS DUCART's masterpiece, CASTLETOWN COX, Co. Kilkenny, where he lived until his death. He was general editor of *The Irish World* (1977) and *Ireland: A Cultural Encyclopaedia* (1983), and founder and editor, 1984–9, of the visual arts journal *Irish Arts Review*, which remains his most significant achievement. His architectural publications include *The Houses of Ireland* (with Rosemary ffolliott, 1975), *The Churches and Abbeys of Ireland* (1976), *The Castles of Ireland* (1977), and *The Synagogue* (1978), all with photographs by George Mott. **Brian Lalor**

de Bromhead, Jerome (1945–), composer. Born in Waterford; studied at the RIAM (with A. J. POTTER, JAMES WILSON, and SEÓIRSE BODLEY), and with Franco Donatoni. In 1980 RTÉ (where he was senior music producer) presented his choral piece *Iomramh* at the International Rostrum of Composers, which led to requests to broadcast his works in thirteen countries. His harpsichord piece *Flux* was performed at the ISCM World Music Days in Germany (1987). He is a member of AOSDÁNA. His compositions, many of which were premiered with the RTÉ SYMPHONY ORCHESTRA, include two symphonies, *Concerto for Guitar and Strings* (1991), *Hy Brasil* (1980), *Abstract Variations* (1976), and CHAMBER MUSIC, and he has won many prizes for composition. **Ite O'Donovan**

de Brún, Monsignor Pádraig (1889–1960), priest, scholar, and writer. Born in Grangemockler, Co. Tipperary; educated at Holy Cross College, Dublin, NUI, and in Paris and Göttingen. Ordained in 1913, he was professor of mathematics at ST PATRICK'S COLLEGE, Maynooth, 1914–45. An accomplished translator from Greek, Latin, French, and Italian to Irish, he believed that a modern literature in Irish would benefit from European exemplars. Best known as a translator of classical authors such as Sophocles and Homer and of Dante's *Divine Comedy*, he also wrote poetry in Irish and English. **Ciarán Ó Coigligh**

de Burgh, Chris, stage name of Christopher Davison (1948–), singer. Born in Argentina. He began his singing career in Captain America's, a Dublin restaurant. After graduating from TCD in the early 1970s he moved to London. Despite many setbacks he eventually released his debut album, *Far Beyond These Castle Walls*, in 1974. Hugely successful in Europe, his best-known hit, 'Lady in Red', remains an immense international radio favourite. **Tony Clayton-Lea**

de Burgh, Richard (died 1243), conqueror of Connacht and Justiciar of Ireland, 1228–32. It was he who realised the grant of Connacht made c. 1195 by Lord John to his father, William de Burgh (died 1205). After 1215, when this grant was renewed, he exploited internecine rivalries within the leading dynasty of Connacht, the O'Connors (Uí Conchobhair); but it was not until after the death of CATHAL CROBHDHEARG Ó CONCHOBHAIR in 1224 that he launched his conquest, 1226–7, with the support of his uncle, Hubert de Burgh, Justiciar of England. He lost Connacht for a time in the early 1230s when his uncle fell from power in England; when he recovered his title in 1234 he embarked on another conquest to make it a reality. He died on an expedition with Henry III to Poitou, leaving only minors, and his lands were taken into the king's wardship. **Susan Foran**

de Burgh, Richard, Earl of Ulster and Lord of Connacht (c. 1250–1326), known as the Red Earl; eldest son of Walter de Burgh and Avelina, daughter of John fitz Geoffrey. His long-standing feud with John fitz Thomas Fitzgerald, head of the Geraldines and later first Earl of Kildare, was finally resolved in 1298 when a transfer of lands was agreed on. Richard led violent campaigns in Connacht and Ulster in 1286, 1288, 1291, and 1292, consistently dethroning Dónal O'Neill of CENÉL NEOGHAIN in favour of his own candidates for KINGSHIP. On 27 September 1286, at Turnberry Castle in Ayrshire, he and THOMAS DE CLARE of Thomond entered into a 'band' of mutual support with a group of Scottish nobles, including members of the Bruce and Stuart families. He captured the Isle of Man and gave it to Edward in 1290. He served in the Scottish campaigns of Edward I and Edward II, being appointed king's commissioner to treat for peace in 1309 with ROBERT BRUCE, who had married his daughter Elizabeth in 1302.

In May 1315 his earldom of Ulster was invaded by Robert's brother Edward Bruce, and Richard was defeated at the Battle of Connor in September 1315. In 1317 he was imprisoned for a time by the citizens of Dublin, suspected of complicity with the Scots. He died on 29 July 1326 in the priory of ATHASSEL, Co. Tipperary, and was succeeded by his grandson WILLIAM DE BURGH. **Susan Foran**

de Burgh, William, Earl of Ulster (1312–1333), called the 'Brown Earl' by the annalists; son of John de Burgh and Elizabeth de Clare, an heiress of the Earl of Gloucester, and grandson and heir of RICHARD DE BURGH, the 'Red Earl'. He was a minor when he succeeded to his grandfather's estates in 1326; he was raised in England and married Matilda of Lancaster, a cousin of Edward III, before coming to Ireland in 1328 to take possession of his inheritance at the age of sixteen. Arriving in Ireland, he found that his ANGLO-NORMAN tenants, who were used to their independence, greatly resented his interference. From 1329 he was engaged in conflict in Munster with Maurice fitz Thomas FitzGerald, the rebellious first Earl of Desmond, who he found to be acting in complicity with Henry de Mandeville (died 1337), Seneschal of Ulster, and his own kinsman, Walter de Burgh, who dominated Connacht. He used his position as king's lieutenant in Ireland, 1331–2, to imprison Walter de Burgh in the castle of Northburgh, where he died in 1332. A call for revenge from the relatives of Walter de Burgh led to William's assassination on 6 June 1333 by his own men. His wife and his baby daughter and heir, Elizabeth, fled to England for safety. Elizabeth later married Prince Lionel of Clarence, son of Edward III, and the vast LORDSHIPS of Ulster and Connacht passed by English LAW to a royal absentee, thus greatly accelerating their eventual disintegration. **Susan Foran**

decentralisation. There are strong centralisation tendencies in a market ECONOMY, and a policy of decentralising reflects the attempt by governments to counteract this tendency. The main policy measures to bring about more decentralisation relate to REGIONAL POLICY. The regional distribution of economic activity is partly dependent on the relative costs of siting businesses in particular locations. The costs of those locations, however, are affected by Government decisions in relation to such matters as TRANSPORT, HOUSING, and other INFRASTRUCTURE. It is clear that the Dublin region dominates the Republic in economic activity, with a similar situation applying to Belfast in Northern Ireland. It is easy to see why. Outward transport routes for exports are concentrated eastwards, towards Britain and the Continent, and sites convenient to the principal ports on the east are favoured by industrialists. Nonetheless, with a move to a more service-based economy, North and South, transport costs have become less important. Besides, very rapid growth, as happened in the Republic in the 1990s, imposes its own constraints on centralisation tendencies through increasing problems with infrastructure deficits and congestion. Not all opinion favours a policy of decentralising economic activity, especially in such small economic entities as the Republic and Northern Ireland. In the Republic the BUCHANAN REPORT (1968), recommending a policy of growth centres in the Republic, is still favoured by some; and the concentration of the electronics sector in small pockets in the 1990s lends support to this view. It is unlikely, though, that such reservations would apply to the decentralisation of services activities, such as Government departments. **John W. O'Hagan**

Declaratory Act (1719), a British act denying the Irish House of Lords any appellate jurisdiction and asserting the right of the British Parliament to enact legislation binding in Ireland. It was primarily a response to the long-running civil case of *Sherlock* v. *Annesley*, when one party appealed to the English House of Lords after his adversary had secured a verdict from the Irish Lords. The result was almost a constitutional crisis, defused by this act. **Neal Garnham**

de Clare, Thomas, Lord of Thomond (1276–1287), second son of Richard, Earl of Gloucester, and Maud, daughter of the Earl of Lincoln. He was a confidant of Edward I, whom he accompanied on the Crusade, 1270–2. In 1274 he sailed to Ireland and was employed in judicial activities. Through his marriage to Juliana, daughter and eventual heiress of Maurice fitz Maurice, he allied himself with the Geraldines. On 26 January 1276 he was granted the Uí Briain kingdom of Thomond by Edward I, with a view to pacifying it. From 1277 to 1287 he attempted to consolidate his position in Thomond, siding with Brian Rua Ó Briain, whom he later murdered, an atrocity condemned in the REMONSTRANCE OF THE IRISH PRINCES (1317) and CAITHRÉIM THOIRDHEALBHAIGH. He built castles at BUNRATTY and QUIN, Co. Clare, and was active as Edward's agent in Ireland; in 1277 he led two campaigns against the Irish of Co. Wicklow, and in 1282 he raised loans in Ireland for Edward's Welsh wars. On 27 September 1286 he and RICHARD DE BURGH, Earl of Ulster, entered into a 'band' of mutual support with a group of Scottish nobles, including members of the Bruce and Stuart families. He managed to protect his interests in his lordship until his death on 29 August 1287, but his attempts to colonise Thomond did not long outlast him; his son Richard was killed at the Battle of DYSART O'DEA in 1318, and his lands were partitioned among heiresses. **Susan Foran**

de Courcy, John (died c. 1219), conqueror of Ulster, styled 'Prince of Ulster' by contemporaries. Of uncertain parentage, he appears to have been a member of a family with lands in Somerset and connections in Cumbria, and came to Ireland in 1176 with HENRY II's deputy, William fitz Audelin. In 1177 he assembled an army of 300 men and marched north to invade the kingdom of ULAIDH (modern Cos. Down and Antrim); he seized Downpatrick and forced the King of Ulaidh to flee. About the year 1180 he married Affreca, daughter of the King of Man and the Isles. He was a renowned patron of churches and enthusiastic in promoting devotion to Irish SAINTS. From 1188 he intervened in Connacht and elsewhere with the de Lacys of Meath. He held the post of Chief Governor of Ireland from 1185 to c. 1192. When Lord JOHN rebelled against Richard in 1193–4, de Courcy remained loyal to the king, serving as one of his representatives in Ireland, 1194–5.

From 1201 HUGH DE LACY embarked on a series of challenges to de Courcy's lordship, eventually ousting him in 1204, and in 1205 he was made first Earl of Ulster by John. De Courcy launched an unsuccessful invasion of Ulster from the Isle of Man in 1205 with the support of his brother-in-law, the Manx King Reginald. Though assisting John in overthrowing de Lacy in 1210, he failed to recover his estates in Ulster and died without leaving an heir c. 1219. **Susan Foran**

de Courcy Ireland, John (1911–), maritime historian and campaigner. Born in India; educated in England and at TCD, then ran away to sea before taking up a teaching post in Dublin. His extensive historical knowledge of maritime affairs has been used to try to make the Irish people and politicians realise the importance of the seas around the coast. Forty years' service to the ROYAL NATIONAL LIFEBOAT INSTITUTION and the Maritime Institute and a life of scholarship and dedication resulted in many awards for a man who at ninety years of age was a daily campaigner on maritime issues, world peace, and socialism. He was a recipient of the Caird Medal (1996) as well as honours from the governments of Argentina, France, Spain, and many other countries. His publications include *Ireland and the Irish in Maritime History* (1986). **Fiacc OBrolchain**

Dé Danann, a music group that grew out of SESSIONS in Hughes's pub in Spiddle, Co. Galway, in 1974. The original quintet consisted of FRANKIE GAVIN (FIDDLE and FLUTE), Alec Finn (bouzouki), Charlie Piggott (BANJO and bouzouki), DOLORES KEANE (vocals), and Johnny 'Ringo' McDonagh (bodhrán). Singers have included ANDY IRVINE, Johnny Moynihan, Mary Black, MAURA O'CONNELL, Eleanor Shanley, JIMMY MCCARTHY, Tommy Fleming, and Andrew Murray. The accordion-players Jackie Daly, Máirtín O'Connor, Aidan Coffey, Tim Lyons, and Derek Hickey, together with the bodhrán-player Colm Murphy, have contributed to the band's distinctive sound. Recordings include *Dé Danann* (1975), *Mist-Covered Mountain* (1980), and *Half Set in Harlem* (1991). **Pat Ahern**

Deer Park Farms, Glenarm, Co. Antrim, site of a large earthen mound 5 m (16 ft) high, with a flat top some 25 m (80 ft) in diameter, examined in rescue excavations from 1984 to 1987. A detailed sequence of superimposed RING-FORT settlements of the eighth and ninth centuries was revealed. The monument began as a ring-ditch 25 m (80 ft) in diameter on the natural surface of the north-sloping hillside at a height of 150 m (500 ft) overlooking the Owencloghy Water. No buildings were associated with the early phase, but the site was soon transformed into a normal ring-fort by the construction of a surrounding bank and east-facing entrance. This probably took place before the end of the seventh century. The ring-fort was remodelled and added to on numerous occasions. The lowest levels were waterlogged, preserving the pushed-over walls of abandoned wickerwork houses and associated organic deposits, including MIDDEN layers and bedding material. Typically, the main circular-plan house stood at the centre of the ring-fort, with a smaller *backhouse* attached on the west, giving the whole structure a figure-of-eight plan. A kerbed path led from the rath entrance to north and south around the central structure to two other circular-plan wicker houses a little to the rear of the central house in the west half of the ring-fort. The houses had central, stone-kerbed HEARTHS and were double-walled, the cavity being packed with wisps of grass and other soft vegetation to provide a form of cavity-wall insulation. Eventually the lower levels of the ring-fort were covered over, and the living surface rose until the site became a platform mound in a later phase, revetted with a massive and impressive-looking wall of basalt boulders more than 3 m (10 ft) high. There were plentiful remains of buildings in upper levels, but they survived mainly as circles of stake-holes, the organic material in the upper levels having rotted away completely.

The site was very rich in finds, particularly glass beads and workaday iron tools. Most remarkable were the organic objects not seen elsewhere at dry-land sites: parts of stave-built wooden vessels, an oak door-frame, bed ends, and a shoe last, as well as parts of leather shoes and the hub and a paddle of a horizontal mill wheel. Detailed study of environmental samples is producing a very full picture of life on the site, comparable with urban contexts of the same period but with clear evidence for agricultural and domestic craft work.

The excavations at Deer Park Farms provide rich data for comparison with many other excavated sites of the same period. The well-preserved remains accord well with the picture of life at the time independently developed from contemporary literary sources, such as the BREHON LAWS. [see EARTHWORKS, MEDIEVAL.] **Christopher J. Lynn**

Deevy, Teresa (1903–1963), playwright. Born in Waterford; educated at UCD and UCC. She developed Ménière's disease, which caused her to become totally deaf in her twenties. Her first play, *The Reapers*, was produced at the ABBEY THEATRE in 1930, followed by *The King of Spain's Daughter* (1935), *Katie Roche* (1936), and *The Wild Goose* (1936). Following the rejection of *Wife to James Whelan* by the Abbey in 1937 she wrote a number of plays for radio. Her last Abbey production was *Light Falling* (1948). Deevy was the only woman playwright of note in the period following the death of LADY GREGORY. **Riana O'Dwyer**

Defence Forces. The origins of the Defence Forces of the Republic may be traced to the foundation of the IRISH VOLUNTEERS in November 1913, formed to counter the threat posed by the newly formed ULSTER VOLUNTEER FORCE to the passing of a HOME RULE Bill. Following the 1916 RISING the Volunteers reorganised, and the subsequent WAR OF INDEPENDENCE lasted until the Truce (11 July 1921), during which time the Volunteers had become popularly known as the IRISH REPUBLICAN ARMY. The army split over the terms of the ANGLO-IRISH TREATY (1921), and a bitter CIVIL WAR was fought (1922–3).

The formal structures of the new army established by MICHAEL COLLINS in 1922 reflected a desire to eschew the irregular formations and tactics of the War of Independence in favour of a conventional land force, supported by a small air arm. With ships used to move forces around the coast, the main cities and towns were quickly brought under Government control. There followed a dispiriting guerrilla war, with atrocities on both sides. The army administered draconian public order measures, including the execution of more than seventy republican prisoners following cursory trials. By May 1923, when the war ended, the army had more than 50,000 men under arms. A short-sighted decision was taken to scrap the planned coastal patrol service, leaving the state with no means of policing its territorial waters. Numbers were quickly run down, causing unrest among officers, which culminated in the abortive Curragh Mutiny of March 1924; this was defused without violence but left an enduring mark on civil-military relations. The fact that soldiers were widely dispersed throughout the country, occupying the many installations vacated by the British, made intensive training impossible; however, it did have the effect of keeping the army in contact with local communities and so increased its public acceptability. Despite its military deficiencies, the army came to command public affection and respect through its bands, its SHOW-JUMPING team, and its ceremonial role.

Fears in 1932 that FIANNA FÁIL in government would take its revenge for Civil War defeat proved unfounded. In fact matters improved a little for the emaciated force, particularly through the establishment of a new reserve, the VOLUNTEER FORCE, in 1934. While this proved a short-term burden on the army, it provided the nucleus of rapid expansion in the crisis of 1940. As war in Europe became more likely in the late 1930s, furthermore, a certain amount of valuable staff work was done in matters including plans for coastal security and for CENSORSHIP; these bore fruit with the Government's declaration of NEUTRALITY in September 1939. With regard to capacity, the Defence Forces were then in a pitiable state. There were only 6,000 men in full-time service, distributed in small groups around the country on garrison and coastal security duties.

Defence Forces. *The* LE Niamh *off the south coast, commissioned in September 2001 as one of the Naval Service's fleet of eight ships that patrol the territorial waters of the Republic. [Public Relations Section, Defence Forces, Ireland]*

There were virtually no modern weapons or equipment, and most deficiencies could not be remedied by purchases abroad, as other states were also rearming. After the unexpected fall of France in May 1940 there appeared a strong likelihood of a German airborne assault as a prelude to or as part of an attack on Britain. This led to secret Anglo-Irish military plans for joint action, and to a dramatic enlargement: within a year full-time numbers stood at 41,000. While this rush to the colours proved important in demonstrating public willingness to defend neutrality, it took two years of intensive effort to bring the army to a reasonable state of military efficiency. It remained gravely short of equipment and heavy weapons and had almost no air defence capability.

The army's other main contribution to neutrality was in the secret world of INTELLIGENCE and security. Directed by officers of great experience and judgment, Military Intelligence proved remarkably efficient both in detecting and in monitoring the clandestine activities of foreign states, including both the Allied and the Axis powers, and the links between Irish REPUBLICANISM and Germany. Liaison with British security and code-breaking organisations became close, and this played a major part in convincing British policy-makers that the Irish could counteract German espionage and so safeguard effectively British strategic secrecy.

In the post-war world the Defence Forces suffered as a result of Ireland's international isolation. In 1949 the state declined to join NATO, because of PARTITION, but, unlike the other European military neutrals, took no steps to provide for more than symbolic independent defence (though it did pursue a bilateral defence understanding with the United States). The following decade was probably the army's bleakest, with only border security duties after 1956 providing any variety. In 1958, however, fifty officers were attached to the UN observer mission in Egypt's Sinai desert. This was followed by the sudden commitment of a full battalion to the UN peace-keeping operation in the Congo in 1960. Despite some fatalities in combat, this and other international service proved enormously important for the morale, training, and effectiveness of the Defence Forces; it provided professional purpose for a force whose only other military role was an internal security one. Coming from one of the few European states without a colonial past, the Defence Forces became an important arm of Irish foreign policy at the United Nations. International engagements also brought some modernisation of equipment and, despite many problems, reinvigorated the Defence Forces from top to bottom.

International service did not directly benefit the Defence Forces' subordinate air and naval arms. At the nadir of its fortunes in 1970, the Naval Service found itself without any sea-going ships, though the expansion of Ireland's territorial waters and the needs of the EU Common Fisheries Policy resulted in the development of a modern though still small fleet. The AIR CORPS found new life with the purchase of helicopters in the 1960s. Helicopter operations, together with maritime observation and a limited ground support role, have since emerged as its main military tasks.

From 1969 the Northern Ireland crisis brought new challenges. For a time in 1969–70 some politicians expected that the Defence Forces might be used to stage at least local cross-border interventions; in the event, their main tasks arising from the crisis have been BORDER security duties, to deter both republican cross-border activities and loyalist paramilitary attacks, escort duties for the movement of cash and prisoners, and security for prisons housing paramilitaries. The Naval Service performed anti-gun-running duties, including two notable captures of weapons shipments in 1973 and 1984.

The Northern crisis had a serious impact on the army's international role. Between 1974 and 1978 large-scale UN commitments were abandoned because of domestic security needs. In 1978, however, the pattern of having one battalion serving abroad resumed with Irish engagement in Lebanon. The late 1990s saw a change in the pattern of commitment, with Irish involvement in a number of UN-mandated missions controlled by regional alliances, including the NATO-led forces in Sarajevo and Kosovo of former Yugoslavia and the Australian-led intervention in East Timor, as well as in military observer missions mounted by other regional blocs.

The defence white paper of 2000—the first such document Ireland produced—envisages revamped Defence Forces with a clearer domestic role and a more focused approach to international service. By 2003 the army is to have a fully equipped infantry battalion in readiness at all times to participate in UN-mandated peace operations mounted by the EU Rapid Reaction Force. This poses a challenge for the Defence Forces and requires a massive effort in unit training as well as a re-equipment drive. This is to be financed largely by the selling of surplus barracks and lands, measures that should also facilitate the concentration of forces and resources necessary for effective training.

The role of the Defence Forces remains a sensitive one in Irish political culture. The Government has always taken the view that Ireland needs an army primarily to counter the internal security threat and for symbolic ceremonial and external purposes. There is a strong if vague attachment to military neutrality; on the other hand, there has never been political willingness to face up to the logic of that stance, which is to ensure that Ireland has the military means to act as a credible deterrent to aggression, as do other European neutral states. Geography ensured that Ireland would enjoy the benefits of British and later of NATO protection; this fact of life has allowed the perpetuation of the illusion that a neutral state can protect itself from external aggression by fine words and declarations alone, and that military neutrality equates with military defencelessness. **Eunan O'Halpin**

Defence Forces, command. The CONSTITUTION of the Republic vests supreme command of the DEFENCE FORCES in the PRESIDENT, the exercise of which is to be regulated by LAW. This is done by the Defence Act (1954), which specifies that military command of the Defence Forces is exercisable by the Government. This is normally done, on behalf of the Government, by the Minister for Defence. The Chief of Staff, who is appointed by the President, is directly responsible to the minister for the performance of certain duties that have been delegated to him by the minister. The actual chain of command passes from the Minister for Defence to the general officers commanding brigades, the Defence Forces Training Centre, the AIR CORPS, and the flag officer commanding the Naval Service, who directly command the personnel who make up the Defence Forces. **Paul Connors**

Defence Forces School of Music, established in 1923 as the Army School of Music, with professional direction from two distinguished German musicians, COLONEL WILHELM FRITZ BRASE and Captain Friedrich Sauerzweig. The name reflects the vocationalist intention of RICHARD MULCAHY, who was the driving influence behind the initiative. By 1936 it comprised a headquarters in Cathal Brugha Barracks, Dublin, and bands in each of the four command areas of the time, Southern, Eastern, Western, and Curragh. The School supports the bands of the 1st (Southern) Brigade and 4th (Western) Brigade. The Band of the Defence Forces Training Centre was disbanded in 1995. The school also supports the various pipe bands and buglers within the Defence Forces. **Paul Connors**

Defence of the Realm Act (1914), a wartime statute giving extensive powers to the British government for security within the United Kingdom, in effect placing the whole state under military law. The 1916 insurgents were court-martialled and shot under powers created by the act, as was the banning of SINN FÉIN and the prohibition of political meetings. The act was extended after the war until it was replaced by the equally wide-ranging Restoration of Order in Ireland Act (1920). **Keith Jeffery**

Defenders, a secret society that began among the rural Catholics of Co. Armagh during the 1780s in response to clashes with the PEEP O' DAY BOYS. Originally, as their title suggests, the Defenders were a local vigilante movement; by 1798, however, they had spread into Cos. Down, Louth, and Monaghan, and by 1791 Defenderism had reached Dublin and parts of Connacht. By this time also they had developed an organisational structure of affiliated lodges, drawn from the example of FREEMASONRY, and had also developed a crude political awareness. These ideas saw the combination of old notions of the loss of Catholic lands and the exile of the Stuart monarchy with new revolutionary ideas from republican France.

Defender violence, particularly arms raids against Protestants, increased during the early 1790s and was further stimulated during the riots against the raising of the Irish MILITIA in 1793. In September 1795 a large Defender force from several Ulster counties attacked Protestants near Loughgall, Co. Armagh, but were defeated at the BATTLE OF THE DIAMOND, after which the first Orange lodges were formed as a counterweight. Also in 1795 a military alliance began between the Defenders and the UNITED IRISHMEN, and there was some co-operation during the 1798 REBELLION, though its extent remains unclear. Groups calling themselves Defenders emerged in Co. Antrim after the rebellion; but generally the old Defenderism was absorbed in the RIBBON movement in the early nineteenth century. [see AGRARIAN PROTEST.] **Allan Blackstock**

deforestation. The increase and decline in the abundance of different tree species since the last Ice Age, approximately 10,000 years ago, is revealed by analysing the stratified POLLEN deposits from trees and plants in peat and water-laid sediments. Three main factors contributed to the decline of the vast forested area that had developed in Ireland by approximately 8,000 years ago: disease, CLIMATE change, and human activities.

The effects of disease can be inferred from a sharp decline in the pollen record of elm about 5,900 years ago, which may indicate the effects of an early outbreak of a recurring cycle of 'Dutch elm' disease. Climate change may have altered the balance between species as increased rainfall caused waterlogging of SOILS and the spread of peat BOGS. Undoubtedly human activities have had the greatest and most lasting effect on forests. MESOLITHIC people, being hunter-gatherers, would have lived on the products of the forest, causing little destruction; NEOLITHIC people, using both fire and tools, made clearings in the forest to provide forage for their animals. While at first STONE AXES were used, the advent of bronze and later iron tools increased the speed of forest clearance, as shown by a decrease in tree pollen and a rapid increase in grass pollen.

Deforestation continued gradually during the IRON AGE and EARLY HISTORIC period; but the greater portion of Ireland's forests was removed during the last millennium. It has been estimated that by 1600 woodland cover was 12.5 per cent, primarily in river valleys and more isolated mountain regions. Exploitation continued during the Tudor and later periods, and by 1900 only 1 per cent of the land was under trees. [see FORESTRY; POLLEN ANALYSIS.] **Michael Bulfin**

Deirdre, one of the most tragic figures of the ULSTER CYCLE. The druid Cathbhadh prophesied before her birth that, despite her beautiful appearance, she would cause strife and bloodshed. She was chosen nonetheless by King Conchobhar to become his wife. Having seen a raven in the snow, drinking the blood of a slaughtered animal, Deirdre says she will marry a man with a white body, red cheeks, and black hair. Her nurse, Leabharcham, tells her that the handsome young Naoise fits this description, and so Deirdre falls in love with him. Despite the prophecy and the planned marriage to Conchobhar, they elope to Scotland. Conchobhar is persuaded by the ULAIDH to invite the pair back to Ireland, and he sends Fearghus mac Róigh to them with this message; but on their return to EMAIN MACHA, the sovereign centre for the Ulaidh, Naoise and his brothers are slain through treachery, and Conchobhar then takes Deirdre. Rather than acquiesce in Conchobhar's command and spend a year with the man who had killed her beloved Naoise, Deirdre throws herself from a chariot, and her head is shattered. [see MYTHOLOGY.] **Ríonach uí Ógáin**

'Deirdre story', a designation frequently used for the different versions of the narrative relating to Deirdre and the sons of Uisneach. Versions include 'Longes Mac nUislenn', possibly as old as the eighth century, and 'Oidheadh Chloinne hUisneach', probably composed in the fourteenth or fifteenth century. Anglo-Irish literary adaptations include JAMES STEPHENS's *Deirdre* and J. M. SYNGE's *Deirdre of the Sorrows*. Such titles reflect the importance attached to Deirdre in most treatments of this narrative. It has been argued, however, that the emphasis placed on Deirdre may have obscured somewhat the purpose of composition of 'Oidheadh Chloinne hUisneach'. A striking feature in this narrative is the omission of many of the biographical details pertaining to Deirdre found in the earlier 'Longes Mac nUislenn'. It has also been argued that 'Oidheadh Chloinne hUisneach' may originally have formed part of a longer narrative, the purpose of which was to focus attention on another character in the tale, Fearghus mac Róigh. The later manuscript tradition was greatly influenced by GEOFFREY KEATING's version of the narrative in FORAS FEASA AR ÉIRINN, which, based mainly on 'Longes Mac nUislenn', restored the prominent role of Deirdre. **Caoimhín Breatnach**

Déise, a tribal group that dominated what is now Co. Waterford during the early Middle Ages. They were a powerful people, though their name literally identifies them as vassals. According to the saga 'The Expulsion of the Déise' they were expelled from the midlands and after many adventures settled in Munster; but this is pure fiction. More credible is the link of the Déise with Irish colonial activities in Wales in the pre-Christian and Early Christian period, particularly with Dyfed in the south-west. These links became a distant memory; nevertheless the Déise retained a sense of their importance and claimed that their own saint, Declan, was Christian before the coming of ST PATRICK. **Elva Johnston**

Déise, Na. The Déise is a former principality once encompassing Co. Waterford and south Co. Tipperary. The distinctive singing style and repertoire of songs indigenous to the area is now largely confined to the Irish-speaking district of Ring and Ballymacart south of Dungarvan and a handful of enthusiasts elsewhere. Apart from its great beauty, this folk-singing tradition is of great cultural and historical importance, representing a tangible link with the pre-FAMINE world of east Munster. Great exponents such as LABHRÁS Ó CADHLA (1889–1961) and Nioclás Tóibín (1928–1994) profoundly influenced the singers of today. **Éamonn Ó Bróithe**

de Lacy, Hugh, first Earl of Ulster (died 1242), second son of Hugh de Lacy (died 1186) and his first wife, Rose of Monmouth. His elder brother, Walter (died 1241), succeeded to his father's estates in Meath. From 1195 Hugh, in alliance with JOHN DE COURCY of Ulster, intervened in the politics of Connacht. With JOHN's connivance, from 1201 he launched a series of attacks on de Courcy in Ulster, finally ousting him in 1204, and was made Earl of Ulster by John in 1205. Hugh and his brother fell foul of John, who forfeited their estates in 1210, forcing them to flee to Scotland and from there to France, where Hugh took part in the Albigensian Crusade until 1219. In 1220 Hugh was fighting in Wales in alliance with Llywelyn ap Iorwerth of Gwynedd against William Marshal II. After Llywelyn was defeated, Hugh returned to Ireland in 1223 to win back his earldom, allying himself with Aodh Méith O'Neill, King of CENÉL NEOGHAIN. He surrendered to the Justiciar, William Marshall II, in October 1224; but in April 1227 Ulster was restored to him as earl, which he ruled until his death, remaining loyal to the king. In 1235 he was involved in the conquest of Connacht by RICHARD DE BURGH, receiving lands in Sligo. He died at CARRICKFERGUS before February 1243, leaving no surviving sons; his lands escheated directly to the Crown and remained in royal hands until 1254. **Susan Foran**

Delaney, Edward (1930–), sculptor. Born in Claremorris, Co. Mayo; in 1954 he won an ARTS COUNCIL fellowship to study bronze casting in Munich and in 1959 studied in Rome, later working with Giacomo Manzù. In 1961 he settled in Dún Laoghaire, Co. Dublin, where he established an art foundry, at which JOHN BEHAN, among others, was trained. For the next twenty years his bronzes, loosely figurative in the 1950s style of Henry Moore and F. E. MCWILLIAMS and inspired by Irish mythological and literary themes, brought him recognition as one of Ireland's most progressive sculptors. He represented Ireland in Paris, Buenos Aires, Tokyo, and New York, and his work entered major Irish and American collections. With the *Thomas Davis Memorial* (1966) in College Green and *Wolfe Tone*

'Deirdre story'. *Folio from* O'Farrell's Pocket Companion for the Irish or Union Pipes *(c. 1810), with a transcription 'Deirdre's Lament for the Sons of Useach' (top) one of the oldest extant pieces of Irish music. [Antique Prints, Dublin; photo: Denis Mortell]*

Memorial and Famine Group (1967) in St Stephen's Green he introduced a modernist approach to monuments in Dublin. In the 1980s he moved to Carraroe, Co. Galway, to make abstract, kinetic stainless-steel constructions inspired by natural forms, now exhibited in Connemara Sculpture Park. His many public commissions include *Family Group* (1992) in Fitzgerald Park, Cork, in loosely figurative bronze, and an abstract stainless-steel structure (1992) at Mount Street Bridge, Dublin. He is a member of the RHA and AOSDÁNA. **Judith Hill**

Delany, Mary, née Granville (1700–1788), artist and social commentator. Born at Coulston, Wiltshire; between 1731 and 1733 in Ireland, she frequented the circle of JONATHAN SWIFT. In June 1743 she married Dr Patrick Delany. They divided their time between Downpatrick and Delville, their house at Glasnevin. Her husband encouraged her to draw landscape wherever they travelled. These records, with her thousands of letters, provide one of the richest sources on eighteenth-century Irish and English society. When over seventy she completed the Hortus Siccus, a collection of nearly a thousand botanical collages (now in the British Library). [see CONNOLLY, SYBIL.] **Martyn Anglesea**

Delap, Maude Jane (1866–1953), marine biologist. Born in Templemore, Co. Donegal; the family moved to Valentia Island, Co. Kerry, where she was educated by her father, the rector. As well as helping run the island hospital she became a keen NATURALIST, concentrating on collecting and studying marine invertebrates, especially plankton. She discovered several rare species of jellyfish, and in 1835 a sea anemone, *Edwardsia delapiae*, which was named after her. She maintained marine aquaria for studying and monitoring the growth and metamorphosis of relatively unknown species. In recognition of her scientific contributions the Linnean Society of London made her an Associate Member in 1936. **Helena C. G. Chesney**

Delap. *The* Edwardsia delapiae*, a burrowing sea anemone first identified by Maud Delap in Valentia Harbour, Co. Kerry, in 1835. This species has not yet been found anywhere else in the world. [Bernard Picton]*

Delargy, James: see Ó DUILEARGA, SÉAMUS.

Democratic Dialogue, an organisation established in 1995 as the first new-style think tank in Ireland. Based in Belfast, it has sought to address the deadlocking political issues that militated against a resolution of Northern Ireland's conflict, as well as the underlying economic and social issues neglected over three decades of violence. These topics include policing and parades, victims of the 'TROUBLES', social inclusion, women in public life, and public expenditure priorities. A flagship project has been work on the Programme for Government of the Northern Ireland Executive.

Democratic Dialogue also maintains an interest in issues of North-South policy co-ordination; it has also taken an interest in questions of British devolution, European integration, and globalisation. Its modus operandi is to generate reports and discussion papers, arising from round-table discussions, citizens' juries, focus groups, and other participatory forms of research. It has attempted to strengthen policy networks linking government, non-governmental organisations, and the academic world. It is a partner with Queen's University, Belfast, in the Institute of Governance, Public Policy, and Social Research. **Robin Wilson**

Democratic Left, a political party established in 1992 by former members of the WORKERS' PARTY. It contested elections in Northern Ireland and the Republic; in December 1994 it joined the Government formed by FINE GAEL and the LABOUR PARTY. With four members of Dáil Éireann, the party merged with the Labour Party in 1999. **Neil Collins**

Democratic Unionist Party (DUP), founded in 1971 by REV. IAN PAISLEY to consolidate his earlier Protestant Unionist Party. It combines uncompromising traditional UNIONISM with populist social policies. With 11 per cent of the poll in the STORMONT ASSEMBLY elections of 1973, the DUP vigorously repudiated the SUNNINGDALE AGREEMENT and supported the ULSTER WORKERS' COUNCIL STRIKE of May 1974, which overthrew the power-sharing Executive. In the Northern Ireland Convention of 1975–6 it insisted on Unionist majority rule, rejecting WILLIAM CRAIG's plan for a 'voluntary coalition' with the SDLP. In the 1979 elections to the European Parliament it scored its greatest success, when Paisley topped the poll with almost 30 per cent of first-preference votes, though this did not translate into seats in the British House of Commons. Despite its hopes of overtaking the ULSTER UNIONIST PARTY in the crisis following the 1981 HUNGER STRIKES, the DUP co-operated with its rivals against the ANGLO-IRISH AGREEMENT (1985), refusing for a period to meet British ministers.

Bitterly hostile to the NORTHERN IRELAND PEACE PROCESS, the DUP boycotted the multi-party talks of 1998 because of the presence of SINN FÉIN but failed in its REFERENDUM campaign against the BELFAST AGREEMENT. Since then it has adopted a more pragmatic approach, accepting its two seats in the new Executive while attacking DAVID TRIMBLE's policies and demanding the renegotiation of the Belfast Agreement. **Eamon Phoenix**

demographic patterns. The population of Ireland has been increasing steadily in recent decades, following a lengthy period of either decline or stagnation. According to the most recent CENSUS, the population of the Republic was 3.917 million (2002), while that of Northern Ireland was 1.573 million (1991). Population figures from before 1841 are unreliable, but there appears to have been a rapid increase in the last few decades of the eighteenth century; this trend continued until the 1840s. The highest recorded population was 8.175 million, in 1841; this was followed by a marked decrease triggered by the GREAT FAMINE of the 1840s. High mortality during the Famine was followed by high rates of EMIGRATION. The population in what became the Republic declined continuously until the 1960s. The decline in what became Northern Ireland ceased in the 1890s, but numbers remained fairly static until after the SECOND WORLD WAR; since then there has been a fairly steady increase, though the rate of increase has declined since the outbreak of the 'TROUBLES'. The population in the Republic began to increase in the 1960s and has generally tended to increase ever since, apart from a slight decline in the late 1980s. The rate of increase, however, has been irregular, being sluggish at times and quite dramatic at other times.

Changes in total population are determined by only three factors: births, deaths, and net MIGRATION. Population increases occur if the number of births exceeds the number of deaths or if the number of immigrants exceeds the number of emigrants.

The annual number of births in the Republic was in the range 60,000–65,000 for most years between 1940 and 1970. This began to increase throughout the 1970s, reaching a peak of 74,064 in 1980. This was followed by a continuous decline until 1994, when there were only 48,255 births, though this downward trend has been reversed since the mid-1990s. The number of births appears to be related to the state of the ECONOMY. The increase in the 1970s corresponds to a period of favourable economic conditions, which encouraged an increase in the number of MARRIAGES and also the return of emigrants. The FERTILITY rate consequently increased—despite a decline in the average size of families—because of an increase in the number of new households. The fertility rate declined following the economic downturn in the 1980s but began to increase again in the mid-1990s with the advent of the economic boom.

One other striking feature of recent decades has been the increase in the number of children born outside marriage. In the 1980s approximately 5 per cent of children were born out of wedlock; the figure in the 2000s is about 25 per cent, and since 1993 the majority of children born to mothers under the age of twenty-five have been born to SINGLE MOTHERS. While this might be regarded by some as an indication of declining moral standards, it should be noted that the total number of children born to young mothers (married or single) has declined markedly, suggesting that in the past one of the reasons why many young women may have married was that they were already pregnant.

The death rate in Ireland, as in most industrialised countries, declined substantially throughout the twentieth century, resulting in increased life expectancy. Massive reductions in infant mortality were especially significant, but adult life expectancy was improved by a reduction in deaths from infectious diseases (such as TUBERCULOSIS). Deaths from some major degenerative diseases, such as stroke and heart disease (though this remains the principal cause of death), have also been declining over recent decades.

The main influence on total population is migration. The number of births has always exceeded the number of deaths, resulting in a net natural increase. However, this was offset in the past by a very high rate of emigration. Since the 1960s the excess of births over deaths has been enough to compensate for the loss of population due to emigration (except for a brief period in the late 1980s), while in the late 1970s and again in the late 1990s the net flow of population was into the country, which, reinforcing a net natural increase, resulted in a rapid increase in population.

Migration is also the main determinant of the distribution of population within the country. The greater range of economic opportunities in towns, especially Dublin and other cities, has stimulated a flow of people, typically in their late teens or early twenties, from rural to URBAN areas. Less than a third of the population in the Republic lived in urban areas on the creation of the state in 1922; this had increased to more than half in the late 1960s and has continued to increase, because of the influx of predominantly young migrants. Migration flows also have regional implications, with predominantly rural areas in the north-west being among those worst affected by migration and emigration, and areas within commuting distance of cities, especially Dublin, experiencing rapid rates of growth.

Migration creates serious problems for both source and destination areas. Source areas suffer from the depletion of their younger and often more able population, while the destination areas suffer from problems associated with congestion and rapid growth, such as traffic congestion and rapidly increasing house prices. Migrants and their families may also experience family, psychological, or social traumas arising from dislocation.

The decline in birth and death rates is generating changes in the AGE STRUCTURE of the population. People are now on average living longer than previously and are not being replaced by as many new-born babies as previously. There is therefore a tendency towards an increase in the average age of the population, with a growing proportion of people in the post-retirement age group. This will create additional demands for certain types of medical and other services. However, the problem should be less acute than in many other industrialised countries, because of the fact that the birth rate remained high in Ireland long after it had declined elsewhere. Ireland should consequently retain a relatively high proportion of people in the economically active age groups, especially if the curtailment of emigration generated by the economic boom continues. [see DEPOPULATION; POPULATION, STATISTICAL PROFILE.] **D. G. Pringle**

demography

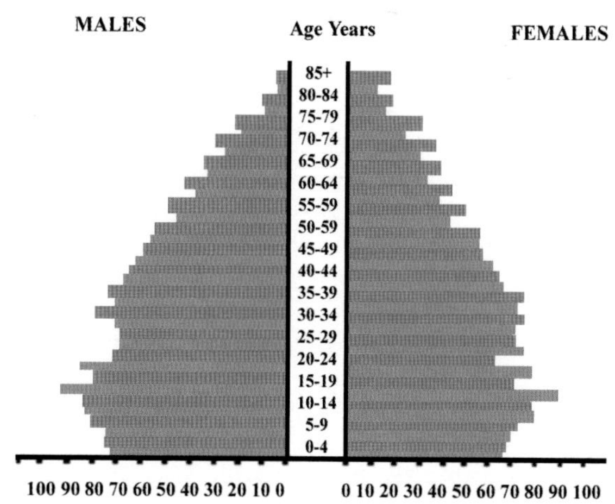

demography. *Populations of the Republic of Ireland and Northern Ireland, classified by sex and by age group, in 1999.*

Demography is the statistical description of human populations, their structure and change. The English political economist Thomas Malthus, in his *Essay on the Principle of Population* (1798), provided a theory based on the balance between population and subsistence. Nowadays the demographic and socio-economic development of modern societies is usually explained through the theory of demographic transition.

The principal source of population statistics is the CENSUS. (The last census in the REPUBLIC was held in 2002, having been postponed from 2001 because of the outbreak of foot and mouth disease; the last census in NORTHERN IRELAND was that of 2001.) The census is complemented by the registration of births, marriages, and deaths, which, together with quarterly LABOUR FORCE and HOUSEHOLD SURVEYS, make possible an annual estimate of the population. These are published by the CENTRAL STATISTICS OFFICE and, in Northern Ireland, by the NORTHERN IRELAND STATISTICS & RESEARCH AGENCY.

The population of the Republic in 2002 was 3.917 million and that of Northern Ireland 1.692 million, compared with 2.818 million and 1.425 million, respectively, in 1961. The composition by sex and age affects society culturally, socially, economically, and politically. AGE DEPENDENCY—the number of dependants in the population—was higher in Northern Ireland, at 55.7 per cent, than in the Republic, at 50.2 per cent. This was reflected in young and old dependency too.

The number who marry and the age at marriage are of great social significance, especially in Ireland, where the traditional relatively high permanent celibacy and late age at marriage provided the classic example of the Malthusian preventive check through 'moral restraint'. Since the early 1970s Ireland, like other Western European countries, has experienced a decline in marriages with an increasing incidence of extramarital cohabitation and marital breakdown.

Fertility has fallen significantly; in Northern Ireland it has been consistently lower than in the Republic, though higher than most Western European countries, including Britain, with Catholic and Protestant fertility broadly similar to the former and the latter, respectively. In 1999 the total period fertility rate—the number of children a woman would have if present fertility patterns persisted throughout her childbearing years—was 1.89 in the Republic and 1.70 in Northern Ireland. Nevertheless, extramarital births rose significantly between 1980 and 1999, from 5 to 30.9 per cent in the Republic and from 6 to 30.1 per cent in Northern Ireland.

In 1995–7, life expectancy at birth was seventy-three years in the Republic and seventy-four in Northern Ireland for males and seventy-nine for females. Life expectancy for sixty-five-year-old males and females was fourteen and seventeen years, respectively, in the Republic and fifteen and eighteen years, respectively, in Northern Ireland. In 1998 approximately two-fifths of deaths were caused by circulatory diseases and about a quarter by cancer.

In the Republic, MIGRATION has been a greater determinant of population change than natural increase (the difference between births and deaths). There were an estimated 47,500 immigrants and 29,000 emigrants in 1999, compared with 26,700 and 70,600, respectively, in 1989. In Northern Ireland there were about 18,900 immigrants and 21,800 emigrants in 1999. **Damien Courtney**

dendrochronology, prehistoric. Since 1984, with the completion of a year-by-year record of Irish oak growth for every calendar year from 5289 BC, it has been possible to date precisely the ring patterns of oak timbers. This is achieved routinely by comparing the patterns of timbers retrieved from archaeological sites, BOGS, river-beds, and LAKE margins with the master chronology. This dendrochronological or tree-ring dating of oak timbers is widespread throughout northern Europe, and dates obtained can be directly compared between Ireland and other regions. Archaeologists now have access to two important reservoirs of chronological information. On the one hand there is the year-by-year quasi-environmental record provided by the master chronology itself: this is a detailed record of the response of Irish oaks to their growth conditions over time. Because this record is precisely dated it is the yardstick against which all human history for the last seven millennia must be viewed. It can best be thought of as the chronological 'backbone' on which all the archaeological 'ribs'—all archaeological and environmental information obtained by archaeologists and palaeo-ecologists—must be hung. This record contains numerous hints of powerful environmental events and changes that must have had effects on human populations, particularly those dependent on AGRICULTURE. On the other hand there is the ability to date archaeological sites and artefacts to a previously unimaginable precision.

Some of the first sites dated, where the oak samples were complete to the under-bark surface—that is, to the last year of growth—include Cullyhanna hunting lodge, Co. Armagh, dated to 1526 BC, and the 40 m (130-ft) structure at NAVAN FORT, Co. Armagh, dated to 95 BC. These dates set the scene for the present situation, which is that some fifty prehistoric sites have provided datable oak timbers. The dates are not randomly distributed but occur in clusters, in the following time ranges: 1600–1380 BC (fifteen sites), 1050–850 BC (nineteen sites), 500–400 BC (four sites), and 200–95 BC (six sites). It is strongly suspected that these clusters reflect relatively dry episodes, when oak timbers were deposited in wet sites, such as exposed lake margins or accessible bog surfaces. Oak trees, and some pines, from natural settings, such as bogs, lake edges, and river-beds, can also be dated to provide environmental information on changes in bog wetness and lake levels over time. **M. G. L. Baillie**

Denham, Sir John (1615–1669), poet. Born in Dublin, son of the Lord Chief Justice of the King's Bench, but spent most of his life in England; he was a close associate of Queen Henrietta Maria. He translated Virgil's *Aeneid* and wrote many occasional poems but is remembered now for 'Cooper's Hill', a reflective poem describing the countryside around his English estate. His ability to combine the strong line of Jacobean verse with the elegance of neo-classicism was much admired, and 'Cooper's Hill' was often quoted and imitated, most famously by Alexander Pope in his early poem 'Windsor Forest'. **Andrew Carpenter**

Denham, Susan, née Gageby (1945–), lawyer and judge. Born in Dublin; educated at TCD, the KING'S INNS, and Columbia University, New York. She was called to the bar in 1971 and became a senior counsel in 1977. Appointed a judge of the High Court in 1991, she made history in 1996 as the first woman appointed to the SUPREME COURT of the Republic. An expert in JUDICIAL REVIEW and extradition matters, in 1995 she became the first chairperson of the Working Group on the Courts Commission, appointed by the Government to make recommendations on how the Courts Service should be managed. **Neville Cox**

Denny, Lady Arbella (1707–1792), philanthropist. Born in Lixnaw, Co Kerry. Interested in various charitable causes, she was best known for the reforms she initiated at the Dublin Foundling Hospital, 1759–78. Thanked by the Irish House of Commons in 1764, she was awarded the Freedom of the City of Dublin the following year and elected an honorary member of the Dublin Society in 1766. She founded the first MAGDALEN asylum in Ireland in Leeson Street, Dublin, in 1767. **Rosemary Raughter**

Deoraíocht (1910), the only novel by PÁDRAIC Ó CONAIRE, the first modernist novel in Irish. The short first-person narrative recounts a year in the life of Micil Ó Maoláin, a young Galwayman living in London. Maimed following an accident, the destitute Ó Maoláin is involved in a series of tenuously linked events involving several grotesque characters and culminating in his death (either by SUICIDE or murder). The death is related in the third person, and the source of the narrative is then revealed to be papers discovered on the dead man. Though textually flawed because of poor editing, this powerful study of alienation exemplifies the avant-garde quality of Ó Conaire's writing. **Pádraigín Riggs**

de Paor, Liam (1926–1998), archaeologist and historian. Born in Dublin; educated at UCD. He had a distinguished academic career in the United States and Canada as well as in University College, Dublin, where he lectured in history from 1965. He collaborated with his wife, Máire de Paor, on a number of archaeological projects; they jointly wrote *Early Christian Ireland* (1958). In 1964 they travelled to Nepal, where de Paor worked as UNESCO adviser on the conservation of national monuments. He was a frequent commentator on political issues and national identity and wrote a regular column for the IRISH TIMES. His later publications include *The Peoples of Ireland: From Prehistory to Modern Times* (1986) and *Saint Patrick's World* (1993). **Brian Galvin**

de Paor, Louis (1961–), poet, anthologist, and critic. Born in Cork; educated at UCC. He emigrated to Australia in 1987 but returned and now lives in Galway. Among his collections of poetry are *Próca Solais is Luatha* (1988) and *Corcach agus Dánta Eile* (1999). *Faoin mBlaoisc Bheag Sin* (1991) is a psychological study of MÁIRTÍN Ó CADHAIN's SHORT STORIES. **Seán Ó Cearnaigh**

de Paor, Tomás (1967–), architect. Born in London; educated at DIT and UCD. He has been a studio tutor at UCD since 1992. He won first prize for the visitors' building at Ballincollig Gunpowder Mills, Co. Cork (1991–2, with Emma O'Neill). Many inventive small projects include the Van, a lead-wrapped office module at the National Sculpture Factory, Cork. Interested in both contemporary art practice and industrial and furniture design, he is responsible for continuing works on the A13 motorway in Essex. He designed N3, a temporary Irish pavilion made of turf briquettes for the Venice Biennale, 2000, subsequently exhibited at Tokyo, Porto, and Rotterdam, 2001. **Raymund Ryan**

Department of Finance. Nothing better demonstrates the conservative character of the final stages of the Irish revolution than the pre-eminence of the Department of Finance in the independent Irish Government. Much of the personnel was inherited from DUBLIN CASTLE, and, as in the British system, the department's officials dominated other ranks of the CIVIL SERVICE in the making of economic policy. The economist PATRICK LYNCH commented that it was 'Whitehall writ small in Merrion Street.' From the birth of the Free State up to 1959 the Department adhered to classical economics: balanced budgets; a cheeseparing attitude to PUBLIC EXPENDITURE; opposition to borrowing and to state intervention; and priority given to TAX cuts and concern about the balance of payments. Despite a change of attitude towards PROTECTIONISM following the FIANNA FÁIL victory in 1932, politicians of all main parties accepted these nostrums. The terms of office of Joseph Brennan (1922–7) and J. J. MCELLIGOTT (1927–53) as Secretary of the department show this conservatism and continuity. On the positive side, the policies helped to establish the solvency and stability of the new state and ensured a civil service free of the spoils system. On the negative side, the department discouraged policies aimed at achieving ECONOMIC GROWTH and SOCIAL WELFARE. In 1959 the department's fourth Secretary, T. K. WHITAKER, in his report *Economic Development*, revolutionised attitudes to public policy, recommending an end to protection, the encouragement of FOREIGN INVESTMENT, and increased public spending. Broadly speaking, these policies were followed by Governments up to the oil crisis of the 1970s, and Whitaker has a valid claim to being regarded as the founding father of a more prosperous, outward-looking country. The department's pre-eminence remained; the establishment of the Department of the Public Service in 1973 made explicit Finance's control of other civil service departments.

The economic slump of the 1970s coincided with a slide in the department's control. This can be attributed in part to inflationary policies driven by electoral considerations, notably the Haughey administration of 1979–81, and by the challenge from state-sponsored bodies. The failure in the late 1970s of the Department of Economic Planning and Development, together with a return to stricter Government controls over the economy, led to a recovery in the department's authority. **Michael A. Hopkinson**

depopulation, a constant phenomenon in Ireland from 1841 to 1946. During this period the population fell from 8.175 million to 4.3 million. There have been large differences between the counties, both in the persistence and the severity of the decline. The population of Co. Dublin declined for only a short period, from 1861 to 1871, but increased steadily thereafter, so that in 2001 it was almost three times that of 1841. In contrast, the population of Co. Leitrim declined throughout the period 1841–1996, from more than 155,000 to just over 25,000. For many counties the population declined from 1841 to 1961 or 1966, in many declining to less than 40 per cent of the 1841 figure. Since then the population has increased in most counties, although, with the exception of Cos. Dublin and Kildare, all had a smaller population in 1996 than in 1841. For Northern Ireland the trends are somewhat different, in that the population declined from 1841 until 1891 and has increased since that time, with the exception of the 1971–81 intercensal period.

Together with depopulation there has also been increased URBANISATION. The proportion of the population living in aggregate town areas, 16.8 per cent in 1841, had increased to 41.5 per cent by 1951 and to 58.1 per cent by 1996. [see DEMOGRAPHIC PATTERNS; DEMOGRAPHY.] **Edgar Morgenroth**

depositions, collected in the aftermath of the 1641 REBELLION, a major historical source for the period. The collection, now in TRINITY COLLEGE, Dublin, was compiled from a number of sources. To establish the validity of claims for compensation arising from property destroyed or stolen in the rebellion, a special commission took evidence to 1647; the English Parliament independently obtained evidence on atrocities from Munster in 1642–3. The collection also contains material gathered for intelligence during the war, which has information from Confederate prisoners as well as displaced Protestants. Judicial depositions used in 1652 by the Cromwellian High Court of Justice also form part of this material.

The collection has always been controversial, with regard to both its accuracy and the use to which it has been put. Carefully selected extracts were used to support the argument that the rebels planned a general massacre of Protestants in 1641, an interpretation subsequently used to justify the brutality of CROMWELL's Irish campaign, the penal legislation of the eighteenth century, and sectarian attitudes in the nineteenth and even twentieth centuries. Much of the detail in the individual depositions, often lurid and almost certainly exaggerated, has long been used to inflame anti-Catholic feelings and activity. Modern scholars are agreed that the documents do not support the case that there had been a deliberate Catholic policy of extermination of Protestants and emphasise instead the important evidence the collection provides for the wider social and economic history of the period. **Liam Irwin**

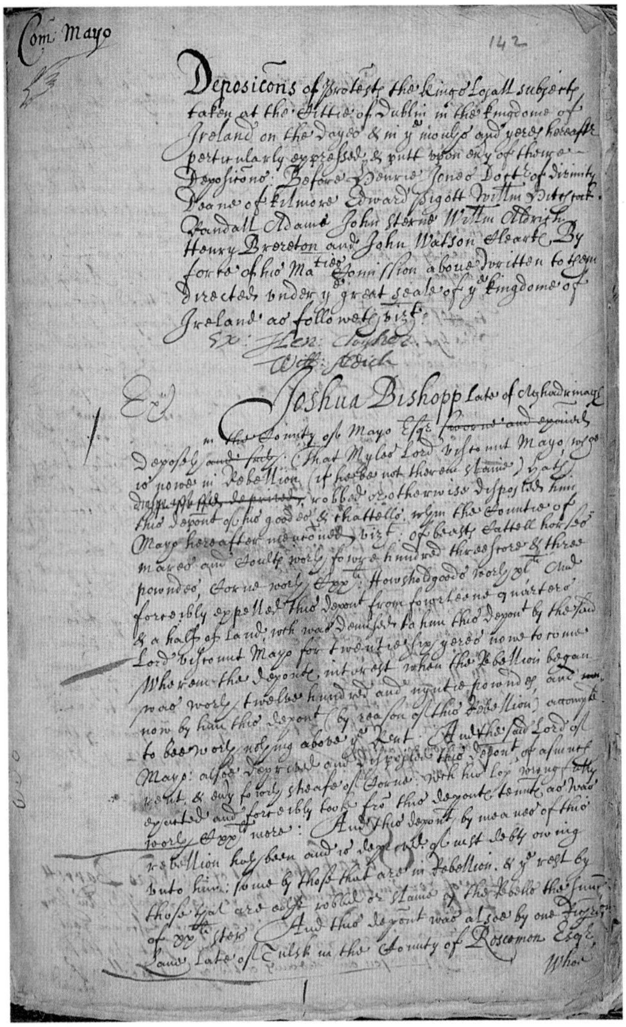

depositions. *The first page of the Mayo set of Waring copies, certified by Henry Jones and William Aldrich, part of the collection of depositions recorded in the aftermath of the 1641 rebellion. [Board of Trinity College, Dublin]*

de Rossa, Proinsias (1940–), rebel and politician. Born in Dublin; educated at Kevin Street College of Technology. He worked in his parents' greengrocery business. Joining the IRA in the mid-1950s, he was interned. A Dáil deputy from 1982, member of the European Parliament, 1989–92, and Minister for SOCIAL WELFARE, from 1999, he migrated politically from SINN FÉIN to Sinn Féin the Workers' Party, to DEMOCRATIC LEFT, to LABOUR. **Tom Garvin**

'Derry Air, The', the popular name for a song published (without a title) by GEORGE PETRIE in 1855, soon becoming known as 'The Londonderry Air'. Petrie's version had come to him from notation supplied by Jane Ross of Limavady and appears to bear a close relation to BUNTING's 'Aisling an Ógfhir', published some sixty years earlier. Bunting's version had been collected by him in the same area from the harper Denis Hempson, and it seems probable that Ross adapted a local variant. The air became established in the repertoire of trained singers, with the unrelated words of 'Danny Boy' (1913), by the English songwriter Fred Weatherly, later becoming the accepted text. **Glenn Cumiskey**

Derry/Londonderry, County (*Contae Dhoire*)

Province:	ULSTER
County town:	DERRY/Londonderry
Area:	2,108 km^2 (799 sq. miles)
Population, including city (1991)*:	187,000
Features:	LOUGH FOYLE River BANN River Foyle Sperrin Mountains
Of historical interest:	Derry city walls Dungiven Priory
Industry and products:	BREWING Chemicals LINEN Tanning TEXTILES

Petula Martyn

* last year of census by county, [see NORTHERN IRELAND.]

County Derry, called Co. Londonderry (from 1613), a maritime county in north-west Ulster, created during the seventeenth century PLANTATIONS by the amalgamation of the county of Coleraine with adjacent parts of Cos. Antrim, Donegal, and Tyrone and originally administered by the London livery companies. Of considerable scenic beauty, the landscape varies from the fertile lowlands of the Myroe flats and the Bann, Roe, and Foyle valleys to the high moorlands of the majestic basaltic outcrop of Binevenagh overlooking Magilligan in the north and the ancient Pre-Cambrian rocks of the Sperrin Mountains in the south. Part of 'inner Ulster', Co. Derry enjoyed higher and earlier rates of URBANISATION and INDUSTRIALISATION (based on LINEN and SHIRT-making) than areas further west and relatively less disruption during and after the GREAT FAMINE. The modern ECONOMY relies heavily on AGRICULTURE and TOURISM and is influenced by the presence of Derry as Northern Ireland's second city. **Lindsay Proudfoot**

Derry/Londonderry, a city on the north bank of the River Foyle, 8 km (5 miles) upstream from the estuary, cathedral city of the CHURCH OF IRELAND diocese of Derry and second city of Northern Ireland; population (1991) 72,334. Derry's history dates from at least 546, with the founding of a monastery in an oakwood by COLM CILLE; this acted as a nucleus for proto-urban growth. In 1164 eighty houses were destroyed to enlarge the enclosure surrounding Colm Cille's church, and in 1254 Derry was declared a diocese. Under Mac Lochlainn patronage a Dominican abbey and Franciscan friary were built in the fourteenth century; but during the later Middle Ages, Derry appears to have declined. Partially destroyed during English occupation in 1566, it was temporarily abandoned until 1599, when it was reoccupied by Sir HENRY DOCWRA. In 1608 it was overrun by Sir CAHIR O'DOHERTY. Derry is famous in Protestant tradition for the action of the APPRENTICES, who, on shutting the city gates in the face of the Earl of Antrim's French and Irish JACOBITE forces in December 1688, initiated the events leading to JAMES II's unsuccessful siege and his eventual defeat by WILLIAM III.

The history of modern Derry began with its grant to the London livery companies (guilds of craftsmen, merchants, and artisans) under a charter of JAMES I in 1613, which established the HONOURABLE IRISH SOCIETY as the corporation of the city. The present walls were built by 1618 and the town laid out on Renaissance planning principles as a simple grid with a Diamond (central square). St Columb's Church was built in 1618–19. Thereafter growth was slow until the 1790s, when the Foyle was bridged and the city's trade opened up to a wider hinterland. Suburban expansion began both beyond the walls and on the Waterside, and the city entered a period of considerable trade and prosperity, based on TEXTILES, which lasted for much of the nineteenth century. SHIPPING links were established with North America, and specialist SHIRT manufacture became a mainstay of the ECONOMY. During this time Derry developed its modern character. The Bogside grew as an area of INDUSTRY and industrial housing; the northern City side suburbs and parts of the Waterside developed as professional or merchant housing, while the commercial, civic, and institutional core expanded beyond the city walls. Among the notable buildings constructed during this time are the former jail (1791–1824), Foyle College (1814), Courthouse (1817), Magee College (1856–65), St Eugene's (Catholic) Cathedral (1873), and the Guildhall (1908–12).

The BORDER has separated the city from its natural hinterland to the west and limited its growth as a regional centre. During the recent 'TROUBLES' Derry suffered extensive bomb damage, which destroyed much of its fine eighteenth and nineteenth-century architectural heritage. It has also witnessed significant population segregation, whereby the City side is now almost exclusively Catholic and the eastern suburb of the Waterside (across the Foyle) predominantly Protestant. Modern suburban development has enveloped the PLANTATION core, and much of the historic fabric has been lost, but enough survives to guarantee Derry's unique importance in Ireland as the last Renaissance walled city to be built in Europe. **Lindsay Proudfoot**

Derry civil rights march (5 October 1968). Organised by the Northern Ireland CIVIL RIGHTS Association (NICRA) in conjunction with the Derry Housing Action Committee to publicise

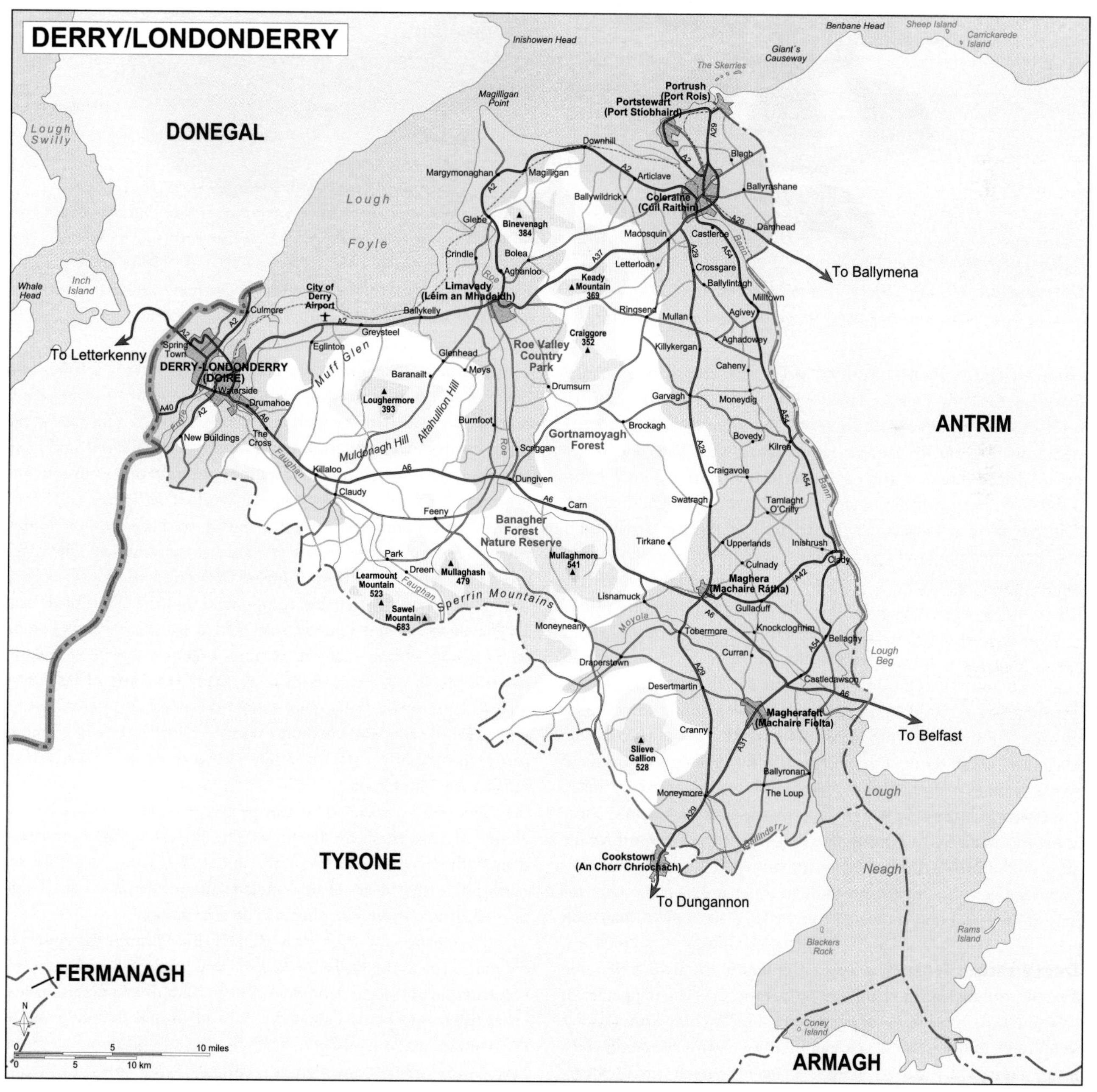

Derrynaflan. *Unearthed in 1980 at the monastic site of Derrynaflan, Co. Tipperary, the Derrynaflan Hoard (eighth and ninth centuries) consists of a chalice (left), patten (right), patten stand (behind chalice), strainer (in front), and large bowl. [National Museum of Ireland]*

claims of anti-Catholic DISCRIMINATION, the march was banned following the announcement by the APPRENTICE BOYS OF DERRY of a procession over the same route on the same date. The route's significance lay in its sectarian associations: the Waterside was a traditionally Protestant area, and the mainly Catholic civil rights activists wished to begin their protest there as a sign that their demands were non-sectarian. In defiance of the ban, civil rights marchers attempted to bypass an RUC cordon, but a heavy-handed police response following a number of scuffles resulted in the batoning of protesters and the use of water-cannon against bystanders. The events were witnessed by three British Labour Party MPs and captured graphically on film by a cameraman employed by RTÉ. The images brought Northern Ireland to the attention of the world, and the British Prime Minister came under growing pressure to bring about reform. The assessment by the STORMONT Minister of Home Affairs that the civil rights movement was a republican front, while inaccurate, was accepted by many Protestants, who saw the marchers as trouble-makers. Catholic anger at the treatment of the campaigners heightened their support for the aims of the NICRA and like organisations. The Derry march is now seen as an important psychological departure in the chronology of the civil rights campaign and the later 'TROUBLES'. **Alan Scott**

Derrynaflan Hoard, a hoard of liturgical metalwork found in 1980 on the ancient monastic site of Derrynaflan, Co. Tipperary. It contained five objects: a large silver chalice, a composite paten, a hoop (which may have been a stand for the paten), a strainer, and a basin. The objects had been placed in a pit and covered with the basin.

The *paten* or communion plate is complex. It is a large, thin silver plate, with a diameter of 370 mm ($14\frac{1}{2}$ in.), seated on a decorated rim that raises it about 30 mm ($1\frac{1}{4}$ in.). The top of the paten carries twenty-four bronze frames with filigree and glass ornaments. Its polychrome decorations are imitation gemstones of glass, familiar on the very best insular work. The filigree consists of animal, anthropomorphic motifs and abstract designs, including patterns and miniature scenes of Christian symbolism. The edge-mouldings of the paten are formed of knitted silver and copper wire. The paten's detachable components and the silver plate bear a code of letters and symbols that guided its assembly, suggesting that a literate person—almost certainly a cleric—was concerned in its creation. It was made from more than 200 components, using such techniques as casting, engraving, lathe-polishing, die-stamping, wiremaking, fire-gilding, riveting, and soldering. Its closest counterpart is the ARDAGH CHALICE. Large patens were once widely used in the early church.

The stand for the paten was probably made necessary by the choice of wire mesh for the rims. The fingers would easily have dented these when the paten was lifted, and some structure for raising it so that it could be handled without damage was clearly needed. It may have been made as an afterthought.

The chalice is a large two-handled silver ministerial vessel, of the same type as the well-known Ardagh Chalice, whose composite construction and form it mirrors closely. Like the Ardagh Chalice, it has filigree decoration applied to a band around the bowl and to the handles; it also has filigree on the stem and upper surface of the foot. Instead of glass ornament it is enriched with amber. Its filigree animal style is technically simpler than that of the paten and Ardagh Chalice. It is dominated by fragmentary motifs—including wingless griffins—of Christian, mainly Christological significance. Its style suggests it was manufactured during the ninth century.

The strainer was made by adding a pierced metal plate to the bowl of an insular bronze ladle. It has a long handle with a decorative terminal in which is set a hemispherical rock crystal. Its style is fairly simple, and its decoration of coloured glass suggests that it belongs to the polychrome style of the eighth century. The basin is of a familiar insular type and was probably used for the ritual ablutions of the Mass.

The Derrynaflan treasure represents an accumulation of altar vessels of different dates and styles, made probably in the eighth and ninth centuries and, at a guess, concealed in the tenth century. The monastery of Derrynaflan (Doire na bhFlann, 'oakwood of the Flanns') was a prominent foundation near the royal seat of Cashel, which enjoyed kingly patronage in the ninth century. [see MEDIEVAL METALWORK.] **Michael Ryan**

Derry, Siege of (16 April–1 August 1689). Preliminaries began in December 1688 with the closing of the city gates by thirteen Apprentices against a JACOBITE force, against the wishes of the corporation and the Anglican bishop. The action was advised by Colonel George Philips, who served as governor until a compromise was reached whereby a small Protestant force under ROBERT LUNDY was accepted as JAMES II's garrison. Derry soon became the focus for Protestant resistance in Ireland, and the news in March of a Williamite relief fleet being sent from England forced the Jacobites to go on the offensive. Lundy lost the nerve to resist after defeat by the Jacobites at Clady and Lifford in mid-April, and the siege proper was overseen by the joint governors, Rev. GEORGE WALKER and Major Henry Baker (succeeded on his death by Colonel John Mitchelburne). In Williamite accounts the inhabitants were reduced to eating mice, rats, and dogs fattened on human corpses. The population, normally about 2,000, was supposedly increased to 30,000 refugees and 7,000 soldiers, while 15,000 were said to have died of starvation and disease. The siege continued until a Williamite relief force broke through the Jacobite boom on the River Foyle. The Jacobite failure was due as much to the fact that they were ill-equipped to expedite a siege, and lacked the necessary manpower, as it was to the resistance within Derry. The siege is still a central part of Ulster Protestant mythology and is commemorated twice a year: on 12 August, for the relief of the city, and in December, with the closing of the city gates by the APPRENTICE BOYS' Clubs, the first of which is said to have been formed in 1714, when the siege was supposedly commemorated for the first time (see p. 1121). **Charles Ivar McGrath**

Dervorgilla, Latinised name of Derborgaill (1108–1193), daughter of Murchad Ua Máelsechlainn, King of Meath, and wife of Tígernán Ua Ruairc, King of Bréifne. Abducted by the Leinster King DERMOT MACMURROUGH for likely political motives, she is sometimes called the 'Irish Helen of Troy'. The enmity between Dermot and Tígernán, which the kidnapping considerably increased, helped bring about Dermot's expulsion from Leinster and subsequent invitation of the ANGLO-NORMANS to Ireland. Though sometimes depicted as complicit in her seizure, Dervorgilla returned to Tígernán within the year. A patron of churches associated with both her own family and Tígernán's, she died at one of them, that of Mellifont, in 1193. **Anne Connon**

Deserted Village, The (1770), an extended poem in heroic couplets by OLIVER GOLDSMITH, his most popular non-dramatic work. Its theme is the disintegration of rural communities in eighteenth-century England and Ireland, when LANDLORDS enclosed common land for their own use, often so that they could purchase luxuries. Goldsmith contrasts the idyllic appearance of 'Auburn' (a romanticised version of the Co. Westmeath villages of his youth) before the ENCLOSURES with its desolate and abandoned state afterwards. The poem contains famous portraits of the village parson and schoolmaster, and memorable couplets:

> Ill fares the land, to hastening ills a prey,
> Where wealth accumulates, and men decay.

Andrew Carpenter

Desmond, Dermot (1950–), financier and entrepreneur. Born in Cork; educated at Good Counsel College, New Ross, Co. Wexford. He joined Citibank as a clerk in the 1970s and some years later left the company as a credit analyst. He worked for the Investment Bank of Ireland, then moved to the World Bank project in Afghanistan. In 1981 he established the hugely successful NCB Stockbrokers, which he disposed of in 1994. He has interests in a range of companies, including London City Airport and Glasgow Celtic Football Club, and was a key figure in the establishment of the INTERNATIONAL FINANCIAL SERVICES CENTRE, Dublin. **Martin Clancy**

Desmond, William (1951–), philosopher. Born in Cork; educated at UCC and Pennsylvania State University. Since 1994 he has

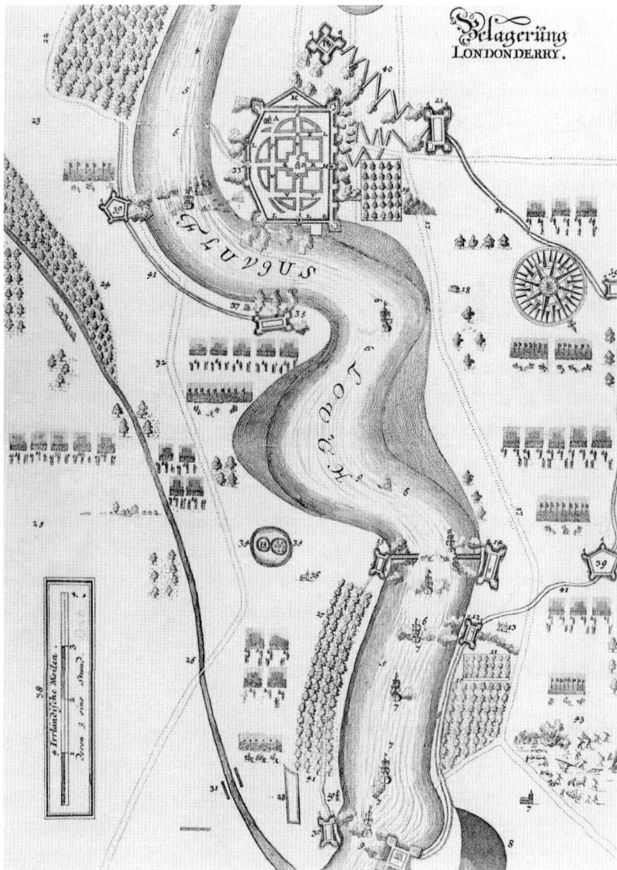

Derry. Belägerung Londonderry, *a map from* Theatrum Europaeum, *1698, detailing the Siege of Derry, which lasted for 107 days. The city (top centre) is on the west bank of the River Foyle; lines of encirclement are shown with forts and the boom blocking passage on the river (right centre). [National Gallery of Ireland]*

been professor of philosophy at the Institute of Philosophy, Catholic University of Louvain, and since 1997 has held the John N. Findlay chair of philosophy at Boston University. He is a former president of the Metaphysical Society of America and general editor of the SUNY (State University of New York) Series in Hegelian Studies. He has published *Art and the Absolute* (1986), *Beyond Hegel and Dialectic: Speculation, Cult and Comedy* (1992), *Being and the Between* (1995), *Perplexity and Ultimacy: Metaphysical Thoughts from the Middle* (1995), and *Ethics and the Between* (2001). His philosophical interests include developing a metaphysics that rethinks perplexity, in contrast to the closed system of Hegel. He is also concerned with establishing a genuine dialogue between philosophy and other areas, such as art and religion. **James McGuirk**

Desmond Rebellions (1569–73, 1579–83), related uprisings against Tudor centralisation, demilitarisation, and landgrabbing in the patrimony of Gerald Fitzgerald, fourteenth Earl of Desmond. In 1569, backed by dissident BUTLERS, JAMES FITZMAURICE FITZGERALD, cousin and captain-general of the earl and champion of the COUNTER-REFORMATION, led a revolt. Sir Humphrey Gilbert and Sir JOHN PERROT, Governor and President of Munster, respectively, ruthlessly suppressed disturbances. In February 1573 Fitzmaurice submitted and subsequently went into exile to solicit aid in France, Spain, and Rome. Pope Gregory XIII obstructed Fitzmaurice's designs by assigning a thousand swordsmen for an expedition to Ireland under the command of the English adventurer Thomas Stukeley. However, this army was largely commandeered by King Sebastian of Portugal for a crusade to Morocco. In July 1579 Fitzmaurice returned to Ireland with a small force and proclaimed a holy war. He was killed in a skirmish on the Connacht border in August. Desmond was proclaimed a rebel in October. In 1580 Lord GREY DE WILTON, Lord Deputy, annihilated a Papal force at SMERWICK, Co. Kerry, and instituted a scorched earth policy, which quenched residual resistance. Hostilities ended with the murder of Desmond in November 1583. The way was cleared for the PLANTATION OF MUNSTER (see p. 915). **Mary Ann Lyons**

Despard, Charlotte, née French (1844–1939), suffragist, nationalist, and novelist. Born in Edinburgh. She was radicalised by her experience of the conditions in the London slums, and after the death of her husband, Max Despard, she devoted herself to politics. She became a member of the Independent Labour Party and the Women's Social and Political Union, which she later left to form the Women's Freedom League. She moved to Ireland in 1910, becoming active in labour politics and joining SINN FÉIN during the WAR OF INDEPENDENCE, despite the fact that her brother, Lord French, was LORD LIEUTENANT for a time. She was later a member of the COMMUNIST PARTY. **Brian Galvin**

destruction, tale type: see TOGAIL.

de Valera, Éamon (1882–1975), revolutionary and politician. Born in New York, a son of Vivion de Valera, of Spanish extraction, and Kate Coll from Co. Clare. Sent home by his mother as an infant and reared by his uncle in Bruree, Co. Limerick, he was educated at Bruree National School, Charleville, Co. Cork, Blackrock College, Dublin, and UCD. A conservative young man, he was financed through his secondary education at Blackrock by scholarships and, reportedly, by donations from a local landowner. He claimed afterwards that his Bruree parish priest taught him his *tírghrá* (patriotism). He showed a flair for mathematics and taught in several Dublin schools and later at Carysfort College, Blackrock, the teacher training college for women. He applied for a National University professorship but was unsuccessful. Joining the GAELIC LEAGUE in 1908, he learnt IRISH from his future wife, Sinéad (de Valera) Flanagan, whom he married in 1910.

In 1913 he joined the newly founded IRISH VOLUNTEERS; he also, reluctantly, joined the secret IRB, contrary to his religious principles. During the 1916 RISING he was commandant at Boland's Mills and was sentenced to death by the British MARTIAL LAW authorities, but the sentence was commuted to life imprisonment because of a revulsion in public opinion. De Valera was imprisoned in Dartmoor, England, but was released in June 1917; shortly afterwards he won a by-election in Co. Clare and became president of SINN FÉIN, in succession to ARTHUR GRIFFITH. When the British government introduced CONSCRIPTION for Ireland in March 1918, public opinion, already aroused by the events of 1916, became more separatist. Sinn Féin won seventy-three seats in the general election of 1918; in January 1919 the elected members assembled as DÁIL ÉIREANN, a separatist parliament, and in April de Valera became prime minister of an underground republic. Between June 1919 and December 1920 he was in the United States, drumming up political and financial support for Sinn Féin. On his return he found a guerrilla war raging and his rival MICHAEL COLLINS in control. Following the Truce of 11 July 1921 de Valera began discussions with the British, but he refused to go to London for the final negotiations, the Irish team being led by Griffith and Collins. He rejected the final dominion settlement without seeing it and aggravated the bitterness of the subsequent split, and he permitted himself to be appointed president of a shadow 'Government of the Republic' in opposition to WILLIAM COSGRAVE's Free State Government.

de Valera. *Wearing the uniform of the Irish Volunteers, Éamon de Valera speaks from the plinth of the O'Connell Monument in Ennis, Co. Clare, at a Sinn Féin meeting during the East Clare by-election of 10 July 1917. [Irish Press PLC]*

After the CIVIL WAR he was imprisoned by the Free State Government, being released in July 1924. While in jail he was re-elected TD for Clare. Between 1923 and 1926 he was in the political wilderness, adhering to an extremist refusal to recognise the legitimacy of the Free State Dáil or the new Irish regime. In 1926 he and his supporters seceded from Sinn Féin and founded FIANNA FÁIL; in 1927 he took the hated Oath of Fidelity and Allegiance and entered DÁIL ÉIREANN. In 1932 he became President of the Executive Council (head of Government) of the IRISH FREE STATE and proceeded to dismantle the 1922 settlement, introducing a new constitution in 1937. In 1936 he turned on his old IRA allies, declaring the organisation illegal.

His economic policies were PROTECTIONIST, his cultural policies mainly consisting of linguistic revivalism and conservation of rural and Catholic values. He declared the country NEUTRAL during the SECOND WORLD WAR and in 1945, in a characteristic piece of logical foolishness, expressed official condolences on the death of Hitler. He lost power in 1948, regaining it briefly in 1951 and 1957. He retired as Taoiseach in 1959, becoming President of Ireland afterwards, an office he retained till 1973.

De Valera was a charismatic and enigmatic figure. His followers revered him and loved his ability to stand up to the British, his self-respect, and his air of mystery. A man of great personal charm, many of his opponents could never forgive him for his behaviour in 1921–2. His legacy is a mixed one: his constitutional framework has endured and is his greatest legacy; he supplied the Irish people with a refounded state more to their liking than that of 1922. His protectionist ideas, though making some sense between 1932 and 1945, arguably deprived Ireland of half a generation of growth after the war; significantly, his successors immediately set to dismantling both his economic edifice and, later, his programme of cultural transformation through the educational system. Like many other leaders of his time, he had no answer to the problem of Northern Ireland, and never quite admitted it. [see COMELY MAIDENS; DUBLIN INSTITUTE FOR ADVANCED STUDIES; IRISH, RESTORATION OF.] **Tom Garvin**

de Valera, Sinéad, née Flanagan (1879–1975), writer. Born in Balbriggan, Co. Dublin; worked as a national teacher, and taught Irish for the GAELIC LEAGUE, where she met her husband, ÉAMON DE VALERA. She devoted herself to her family and began writing only when her children were grown. She published some thirty titles—plays in Irish and English for children and collections of fairy-tales. Her passions were children's drama competitions and the IRISH LANGUAGE, and these are shown by her first book, *Cluichidhe na Gaedhilge* (1935). Her fairy-tale collections include *The Emerald Ring and Other Irish Fairy Tales* (1976), *The Four-Leaved Shamrock* (1964), and *The Miser's Gold* (1970). **Patricia Donlon**

de Valois, Ninette (1898–2001), dancer, choreographer, and dance director. Born Edris Stannus in Blessington, Co. Wicklow; trained at Lila Field's Academy, having moved with her family to Walmer, Kent, in 1905. She made her West End debut as a leading dancer in *Jack and the Beanstalk* at the Lyceum Theatre in 1914. Training with Espinosa and Cecchetti, she danced with Diaghilev's Ballets Russes, 1923–5. In 1926 she founded the London Academy of Choreographic Art and in 1927 the Abbey BALLET School, Dublin, choreographing and dancing in YEATS's plays for dancers until 1934, most notably *At the Hawk's Well* and *The King of the Great Clock Tower.* In 1931 she became founder-director with Lillian Baylis of the Vic-Wells Ballet, London; this became the Sadler's Wells Ballet and, in 1964, the Royal Ballet, based at the Royal Opera House, Covent Garden. She also directed the Royal Ballet School. She retired from directorship of the Royal Ballet in 1963 but continued directing the Royal Ballet School until 1972, becoming patron of the Irish National Ballet in 1973. Her many honours include commander of the Order of the British Empire, 1947, chevalier of the Legion of Honour, 1950, dame commander of the Order of the British Empire, 1951, and the Dutch Erasmus Prize, 1961, the money from which she donated to the struggling Irish Theatre Ballet. She also received the Albert Medal of the Royal Society, 1964, the Irish Community Award, 1980, and Companion of Honour, 1981. Her choreography includes *Job* (1931), *The Rake's Progress* (1935), and *Checkmate* (1937). Her publications include *Invitation to the Ballet* (1937) and *Come Dance with Me* (1957). She is known as 'the mother of British ballet'. [see ABBEY THEATRE; BALLET.] **Carolyn Swift**

de Valois. *Ninette de Valois, a central figure in twentieth-century ballet, seen here in her 1927 solo performance,* Pride. *[Victoria and Albert Museum Picture Library; JD 249]*

Devane, Andrew (1916–2000), architect. Born in Limerick; studied at UCD. He worked in the office of Frank Lloyd Wright in Wisconsin, 1946–8; subsequent projects, including Devane's home, 'Journey's End', at Howth, Co. Dublin (1962), maintain Wright's characteristic interest in horizontal planes and an organic modernism. He became a partner in ROBINSON KEEFE DEVANE on its establishment in 1958, where his work includes St Patrick's Training College, Dublin; St Fintan's Church, Sutton, Dublin (1973); Irish Life Centre, Abbey Street, Dublin (1977); and the well-landscaped AIB Bank Centre, Ballsbridge, Dublin (1979) (see p. 69). In later life he worked among disadvantaged people in India. **Raymund Ryan**

development aid, aid given for development programmes in the developing world. It is sometimes distinguished from emergency aid, given for the short-term relief of distress caused by natural disaster or war. Development aid from Ireland is provided by a large number of organisations, including TRÓCAIRE, CONCERN, GOAL, Oxfam, and Gorta, and by the Republic's official aid programme, Ireland Aid. Established in 1974, the Republic's Official

Development Assistance (ODA) gives aid through two principal channels: multilateral assistance (consisting of grants to the EUROPEAN UNION and various UN agencies, many of which are mandatory and some of which predate the ODA programme), and bilateral assistance (the Government's own development programme). Total ODA in 1974 was €1.9 million, of which only 13 per cent was in the form of bilateral aid; in 1999 total ODA came to €226 million, of which 55 per cent was bilateral aid. As a proportion of GNP, the Republic's aid rose from 0.05 per cent in 1974 to 0.31 per cent in 1998, that is, from one of the lowest in the OECD to above the average. About half the bilateral aid fund is spent on schemes in a number of priority countries: Lesotho, Tanzania, Zambia, Mozambique, Uganda, and Ethiopia; Sudan was also a priority country from 1975 to 1998. Irish aid concentrates on health, education, local infrastructure, and building institutional capacity. Aid is given in the form of grants rather than loans. In 1998, 15 per cent of bilateral aid (€25.3 million) was spent on the joint financing of NGO projects.

Northern Ireland, as it is not a sovereign state, has no official development aid programme. However, most of the large development organisations operate on an all-Ireland basis. **Peadar Kirby**

Devenish, Co. Fermanagh, an island and monastery in Lower LOUGH ERNE founded by St Molaise in the sixth century. It has two ROUND TOWERS, one surviving only as foundations; the other, with a twelfth-century frieze, can be climbed to the top. The ruined St Molaise's House, with ROMANESQUE corner decoration, had a stone roof, and the island museum contains fine fragments of another twelfth-century church (disappeared). Teampall Mór (thirteenth century) stands near the foot of a hill dominated by the fifteenth-century Augustinian priory, outside which there is a rare fifteenth-century cross. **Peter Harbison**

de Vere, Aubrey (1814–1902), poet. Born at Currahchase, Co. Limerick; educated at TCD. He succeeded Sir Aubrey de Vere to become proprietor of the estate in 1846, and he remained at Currahchase until his death. In 1851 he converted from the CHURCH OF IRELAND to Catholicism. He was active in nineteenth-century literary circles and was befriended by Wordsworth, Tennyson, and Newman. He was a prolific writer, whose *Poetical Works* have been published in six volumes (1884), though he is best known for *Inisfail: A Lyrical Chronicle of Ireland* (1862) and for his pro-emigration famine relief tract *English Misrule and Irish Misdeeds* (1848). His combination of an Ascendancy ethos of progressive landlordism, Catholic devotional writing, British imperial fervour, and Irish patriotic (rather than nationalist) sentiment informs much of his work. **Jason King**

Devereux, Robert, second Earl of Essex (1566–1601), LORD LIEUTENANT of Ireland. He succeeded his father WALTER DEVEREUX as Earl of Essex in 1576, and from 1587 he enjoyed the affections of ELIZABETH I. His audacious raid on Cádiz in Spain in 1596 made him a national hero, but it failed to achieve its objectives, as did his expedition against the Azores in 1597. These setbacks cost him much of the queen's favour. To restore his credit he took the office of Lord Lieutenant of Ireland in March 1599, with a huge army of 17,300 against the Irish confederates led by HUGH O'NEILL. However, his army was decimated by disease and desertion. Ordered to Ulster by Elizabeth, he parleyed with O'Neill in private at Bellaclinthe, on the province's border, and agreed to a truce. He left for England without licence on 29 September to justify himself but was arrested for deserting his post. He never regained Elizabeth's favour and in February 1601 was beheaded following an abortive *coup d'état*. **Henry A. Jefferies**

Devereux, Walter, first Earl of Essex (c. 1541–1576), colonial adventurer. He won the favour of ELIZABETH I for his support against the northern English earls in 1569, and in 1572 she made him Earl of Essex. To win fame and fortune commensurate with his new status he undertook to colonise Clandeboye in east Ulster, and the queen lent him £10,000 for the project. However, his ambitions were thwarted by unexpectedly effective Irish opposition. Faced with imminent failure and financial ruin, he took desperate measures, including the killing of Sir Brian mac Phelim O'Neill and his wife and brother after the murder of their attendants in Belfast Castle in October 1574. In July 1575 Essex's men massacred all the people on RATHLIN ISLAND. Elizabeth made him earl-marshal of her army in Ireland and granted him Farney, Co. Monaghan. He returned to Ireland in July 1576 but died of dysentery in September. **Henry A. Jefferies**

de Vere White, Terence (1912–1994), novelist. Born in Dublin; educated at Trinity College. He was a Dublin solicitor who became literary editor of the IRISH TIMES (1963–78) and wrote twelve novels, mostly entertaining social comedies—the best probably *Prenez Garde* (1961) and *The Distance and the Dark* (1973)—as well as three volumes of short stories. His biographies of ISAAC BUTT (1946), KEVIN O'HIGGINS (1948), and THOMAS MOORE (1977), like *The Parents of Oscar Wilde* (1967), are elegantly written. He also edited the correspondence of GEORGE EGERTON (1958). His sharp wit and shrewd observation informed *The Anglo-Irish* (1972), while his autobiography, *A Fretful Midge* (1950), skilfully illuminates social nuances in a changing Ireland. **A. Norman Jeffares**

Devlin, Bernadette: see MCALISKEY, BERNADETTE.

Devlin, Denis (1908–1959), diplomat and poet. Born in Greenock, Scotland, of Irish parents; studied for the priesthood but transferred to UCD in 1927; he also studied in Munich and Paris. He published *Poems* in 1930, with BRIAN COFFEY; SAMUEL BECKETT regarded him as 'without question the most interesting of the youngest generation of Irish poets.' His poetry is marked by sensibility, intelligence, and religious quality; collections include *Intercessions* (1937) and *Lough Derg and Other Poems* (1946). Throughout his diplomatic career his poetry remained deeply affected by the places he visited (Italy, New York, Washington, and London). His *Collected Poems* (1964) was published posthumously with an introduction by Brian Coffey. **Sandra O'Connell**

Devlin, Joseph (1871–1934), politician. Born in west Belfast into a working-class family; he left school at twelve to become a pot-boy in a public house, later becoming a journalist with the IRISH NEWS. A small man with a resonant voice, 'Wee Joe' was a compelling orator and superb organiser. After the PARNELL split he became Belfast leader of the Dillonite Irish National Federation, crushing an attempt by the local Catholic bishop to establish a clericalist machine. Elected for North Kilkenny in 1902, he saw his ability rewarded in his appointment as general secretary of the UNITED IRISH LEAGUE, 1903. In 1906 he was elected for West Belfast, which remained his electoral base until 1922. He opposed William O'Brien's conciliation policy and in 1905 revived the ANCIENT ORDER OF HIBERNIANS, a sectarian and politically active society, as

development aid. *Miriam Nyathi (left), her sister Clara, and her mother, Edna (centre), at the Kapane Community Development Project in Matabeleland North, Zimbabwe, 1998. The project is assisted by APSO, part of the Irish Government aid programme. [Derek Speirs/Report]*

the main nationalist organisation in Ulster; this damaged his reputation as a non-sectarian populist, though his exposure of sweat-shop practices in the LINEN mills resulted in much-needed reforms. He dismissed the UVF threat as 'bluff' but reluctantly advocated the six-county exclusion scheme of 1916. A supporter of recruitment to the British army and a member of the IRISH CONVENTION (1917–18), he was the leading survivor of the rout of the IRISH PARTY in 1918, defeating ÉAMON DE VALERA in Falls. In the British House of Commons, 1919–21, he opposed partition and LLOYD GEORGE's reprisals policy. Elected to the Northern Ireland Parliament in 1921, he led the Nationalist opposition, 1925–32, helping to reunite Northern nationalists in the National League, 1928.

Devlin championed the rights of Catholics but disliked leading 'a Catholic party'. Elected to the British Parliament for Fermanagh-Tyrone in 1929, he died in 1934, mourned by Protestant and Catholic alike as a genuine social reformer. **Eamon Phoenix**

Devlin, Paddy (1925–1999), politician. Born in Belfast to a working-class family and raised amid the poverty of 1930s west Belfast. He joined FIANNA ÉIREANN and was interned as a member of the IRA, 1942–5. After the SECOND WORLD WAR, on returning to Belfast from a brief spell of employment in England, he involved himself in the TRADE UNION movement, severing links with the IRA as his socialist thinking began to crystallise. Elected to Belfast City Council in 1956 for the Irish LABOUR PARTY, he became a member of the Northern Ireland Labour Party in 1958 and was returned to STORMONT as MP for Falls in 1969. Disillusioned by the NILP's approach to the CIVIL RIGHTS campaign, he was a founder-member in August 1970 of the SOCIAL DEMOCRATIC AND LABOUR PARTY, becoming responsible for health and social services in the 1974 power-sharing Executive. His continued trade union involvement brought about his appointment as Northern organiser of the ITGWU in 1975. By 1977 differences with colleagues regarding the priority given to nationalist over socialist policies led to his expulsion from the SDLP. In 1979 he stood unsuccessfully for the European Parliament as an independent socialist. **Alan Scott**

Devon Commission (1843). Under pressure for land reform, Sir ROBERT PEEL instigated a royal commission of inquiry into the Irish agrarian system under the chairmanship of Lord Devon, an Irish landowner. In 1845 the commissioners published three large volumes of evidence and made some weak recommendations, few of which were adopted. **Peter Gray**

Devotional Revolution: see CATHOLICISM, DEVOTIONAL REVOLUTION TO TWENTY-FIRST CENTURY.

Devoy, John (1842–1928), nationalist and journalist. Born in Kill, Co. Kildare, and brought up in Dublin. He joined the IRB in 1861 and spent a year in the French Foreign Legion. He successfully recruited many Irish members of the British army into the ranks of the FENIAN MOVEMENT. Imprisoned for his activities in 1866, he benefited from an amnesty in 1871 and spent the rest of his life in New York, where he worked as a journalist. Determined and ruthless, he expended his considerable energies in the cause of militant Irish NATIONALISM. On his death he was accorded, in effect, a state funeral in Dublin. [see CLANN NA GAEL.] **Oliver P. Rafferty**

Dexter, John (1954–), organist and choir director. Born in Surrey; he received his first musical education as a chorister in Guildford Cathedral and graduated from Oxford. He was appointed organ-scholar at St Paul's Cathedral, London. His teachers included Barry Rose, John Birch, Edwin Roxburgh, and Norman del Mar. He was organist and master of the choristers at St Patrick's Cathedral, Dublin, 1977–2001, and conductor of the Guinness Choir, 1984–91. He is chorus master with Dublin South County Choir and director of the Goethe Institut Choir. He broadcasts regularly and has made numerous recordings as organist and with the choir of St Patrick's Cathedral. **Ite O'Donovan**

DGOS: see DUBLIN GRAND OPERA SOCIETY.

dialects of Modern Irish. Until the decline of the bardic schools in the early seventeenth century, Irish scribes wrote in a standard literary language that ignored dialect differences; by the time dialects came to be studied scientifically, at the end of the nineteenth century, spoken IRISH had disappeared from much of the country. Of all dialect studies, Heinrich Wagner's *Linguistic Atlas and Survey of the Irish Dialects* (1958–69) is the most important, giving a comprehensive account of the speech of Cos. Donegal, Mayo, Galway, Kerry, Cork, and Waterford and less detailed evidence for the Irish of Cos. Antrim, Cavan, Derry, Monaghan, Tyrone, Louth, Leitrim, Sligo, Roscommon, Clare, and Kilkenny.

There were three main dialect groupings. The Ulster dialects, spoken north and west of a line from Co. Leitrim to the BOYNE VALLEY, were distinguished by their shortening of unstressed syllables, for example *scadan*, 'herring'. A southern dialect, spoken in Munster and Ossory, had a strong tendency in disyllables to move the accent from a short first syllable to a second long one, for example *scudán*. A third group of dialects ('Galeonic Irish') was spoken in Connacht, across the midlands to Cos. Kildare and Dublin and south to Cos. Wicklow, Carlow, and Wexford; only the Connacht forms of this varied group survive into recent times. Like Munster Irish, the Galeonic dialects first moved the stress forward to unstressed long syllables; thereafter the stress shifted back to the reduced first syllable, for example *scudán*. A variety of Munster 'forward stress' was also found sporadically in the Shannon basin as far north as Cos. Roscommon, Leitrim, and Longford.

Features of Ulster Irish include the raising of long *a* to [æ:] in words like *bán*, 'white', and *tá*, 'is'; two varieties of long *o*, for example in *leor* (open), 'enough', and *leabhar* (closed), 'book'; the weakening or loss of *ch* internally and finally; *cha*, 'not', instead of *ní*, often used with the present to render the future, for example *cha dtig*, 'won't come'; the presence of *ch* [h] in the future stem of second-conjugation verbs, for example *imeachaidh*, 'will go'; the pronunciation of final *–(e)amh* and *–(e)adh* as *ú*, for example *déanú*, 'to do,' *rinniú*, 'was done', *cogú*, 'war'; and the universal use of lenition instead of eclipsis after preposition + article, for example *leis an fhear*, 'with the man', *ar an chnoc*, 'on the hill.' The south-eastern variety of Ulster Irish was a distinct sub-dialect, with its own particular lexicon, for example *gearrán*, 'horse' (*beathach* elsewhere in Ulster < *beithíoch*, 'animal'), *arsaím*, 'I tell', and *cealaím*, 'I eat.'

The Irish of Connacht can be sub-divided into a northern and eastern dialect spoken in Co. Mayo and north and east Galway and a southern variety in Connemara and the Aran Islands. Like the Irish of Ulster, Connacht almost everywhere pronounces historic *cn–*, *gn–* and *mn–* as *cr–*, *gr–* and *mr–* (for example *croc* for *cnoc*, 'a hill'). Connacht Irish has simplified its verbal system, generalising dependent forms in the pairs *gheibhim/ní fhaighim* and *chím/ní fheicim*. North and east Connacht Irish, like Ulster Irish, maintains historic short vowels before *nn*, *ll*, and *m*, for example *crann*, 'tree', *mall*, 'slow', *im*, 'butter', *fonn*, 'tune', while south Connacht lengthens: *cránn*, *máll*, *ím*, *fúnn*. In north and east Connacht final *–(e)amh*, *–(a)imh*, *–(a)idh*, *–(a)igh* and *–(e)adh* are variously treated; in south Connacht, apart from inflected verbal forms in *–(e)adh*, all are reduced to *–e* or *–a*. The Irish of Menlo, just north of Galway, is an east Connacht dialect of special interest, since it may be a continuation of the Irish of the city itself.

All Munster dialects diphthongise *a* and *o* before *ll*, *nn*, and *m*, for example *thall*, 'over' > *thaul*, *ann*, 'there' > *aun*, *donn* 'brown' > *daun*, and *cam*, 'bent' > *caum*, while in the Decies and Co. Clare (and presumably in the intermediate areas) *i* was diphthongised to *ai* in such environments, for example *tainn*, 'sick' (for *tinn*) and *aim*, 'butter' (for *im*). Munster further diphthongises historic *é* before a broad consonant > *ia*, for example *ian*, 'bird', *dianav*, 'to do', though the ensuing diphthong remains separate from the historic *ia* in words like *siad*, 'they', and *iasc*, 'fish'. In Munster *bh* is lost internally, for example *barr an tslé*, 'the top of the mountain'; *–idh* and *–igh* are de-lenited, for example *tig*, 'house', *cruaig*, 'hard'; and *g* in *chugam*, 'to me', *chugat*, 'to you', etc. is lost, giving *chúm*, *chút*, etc. Unlike Ulster and Connacht, Munster Irish has also abandoned separate relative forms of the verb, replacing *a bhíos*, 'who is (usually)', *a thiocfas*, 'who will come', for example, with *a bhíonn* and *a thiocfaidh*, respectively. On the other hand, Munster retains historic synthetic forms, for example *thánag*, 'I came', *chuamar*, 'we went', and *ní rabhais*, 'you were not', where Ulster and Connacht prefer *tháinig mé*, *chuaigh muid*, and *ní raibh tú*. In Munster alone one finds the fossilised deponent *ní fheadar*, 'I don't know.' [see EARLY MODERN IRISH; HIBERNO-ENGLISH; OLD IRISH.] **Nicholas J. A. Williams**

Diamond, Battle of the. Political and economic rivalries in Ulster, in north Co. Armagh in particular, gave rise to the formation of a number of offensive and defensive movements during the late eighteenth century. Some Protestants, who had seen their economic and religious rivals experience a measured degree of progress with the dilution of the PENAL LAWS, formed companies of vigilantes that were to become known as PEEP O' DAY BOYS. These clandestine groups would search the homes of their Catholic neighbours in the early hours of the morning, ostensibly looking for arms but often damaging looms in the process. In opposition, Catholics formed their own secret society, the DEFENDERS.

In an abortive attempt to establish Catholic control of the area and to acquire arms, on 21 September 1795 a group of Defenders attacked and wrecked the inn of a Protestant man, Dan Winters, at a crossroads near Loughgall known as the Diamond. They were met by stern resistance from local Protestants, including some well-armed former VOLUNTEERS, who shot and killed as many as forty of their attackers. The incident marked a great psychological victory for the Protestants of north Armagh and led directly to the establishment of the Orange Society, later to become the ORANGE ORDER. [see AGRARIAN PROTEST.] **Roddy Hegarty**

diaries and journals. In Ireland, as elsewhere, the best-known diaries and journals have generally been thought of as sources of useful, if essentially supplementary, information on the already well-documented lives and times of their illustrious authors. Regarded more as data-bases than as distinctive pieces of writing with their own rhetorical and formal features, journals and diaries tend to be assigned a subsidiary role in the production of the public record and the life story. Yet it is clear that even if it occupies a comparatively minor place in the canon of his works, JONATHAN SWIFT's *Journal to Stella* (1779; edited by Harold Williams, 1948) is of more than biographical interest. The same may be said of THEOBALD WOLFE TONE's *Journals* (edited by William Theobald Wolfe Tone, 1826; edited by Thomas Bartlett, 1998) or the *Journals of Thomas Moore* (edited by Lord John Russell, 1853–56; edited by Wilfred S. Dowden, 1983–91), of JOHN MITCHEL's *Jail Journal* (1854) or LADY GREGORY's *Journals* (edited by Daniel J. Murphy, 1978, 1987) and *Diaries, 1892–1902* (edited by James Pethica, 1996), or the various adaptations of the diary and journal forms to be found in W. B. YEATS's *Autobiographies* (1955; edited by William H. O'Donnell and Douglas N. Archibald, 1999).

In all these works, though in different ways and to varying degrees, factual data of historical interest vies for significance with material of a more personal character. This material typically concerns matters of identity and self-representation, status and prospects, sides taken and positions evaluated, thought evolving and circumstances in flux. The private and relaxed tone typical of diaries and journals not only releases authors from the custody of their public image but also conveys their experiences of the common human lot of pains and pleasures, thereby giving the works an exemplary dimension. As well as their obvious and invaluable chronicling role, therefore, the diaries and journals of notable personalities, in their inconclusiveness, their informality, and even their lacunae, are the formal and stylistic converse of the completeness and finality to which the official record subscribes, and suggest by their openness the improvisatory rhythm of life in process.

In addition to their value as records of the intimate thoughts and personal details of eminent persons, diaries and journals are arguably of even greater value in the hands of the less prominent, whose typically more limited perspective and range of public experiences is of great importance in particularising the life of a particular locality, era, or generation. An understanding of the nineteenth century in Ireland, for example, is greatly enhanced by the details of domestic life contained in *The Leadbeater Papers* (1862; edited by Maria Luddy, 1998), the picture of small-town Ireland preserved in AMHLAOIBH Ó SÚILEABHÁIN's *Cín Lae Amhlaoibh* (edited by Tomás de Bhaldraithe, 1970), and the view of estate life in Mary Carbery's *West Cork Journal, 1898–1901* (edited by Jeremy Sandford, 1998). These works complement the narrative of public events by recapitulating certain typical strands within it, but they also add valuable nuances to that narrative by recording distinctive local practices and attitudes, giving a more variegated and less commonplace view of social relations and communal values of the day. Such a view receives particularly noteworthy expression in *The Leadbeater Papers* by virtue of the author, MARY LEADBEATER, being a member of the Society of Friends, and is substantiated by not only the content of Ó Súileabháin's diary but also its linguistic interest.

On the other hand, diaries and journals have also provided unique views on events of national significance. An early example is a diary of the journey into exile of HUGH O'NEILL, kept by a member of his entourage, TADHG Ó CIANÁIN, and published in English as *The Flight of the Earls* (1916). A distinctive view on the 1798 REBELLION is contained in *The Diary of Elizabeth Richards (1798–1825): From the Wexford Rebellion in Ireland to Family Life in the Netherlands* (edited by Marie de Jong-Ijsselstein, 1999). W. J. O'Neill Daunt's *A Life Spent in Ireland* (1896) records the author's involvement with DANIEL O'CONNELL in his efforts to secure repeal of the ACT OF UNION. Important eye-witness accounts of the GREAT FAMINE and of pre-famine conditions are provided in the various journals of ASENATH NICHOLSON, notably her *Annals of the Famine in Ireland* (1851; edited by Maureen Murphy, 1998), with which *The Irish Journals of Elizabeth Smith, 1840–1850* (edited by Thomson and McGusty, 1980) may be mentioned.

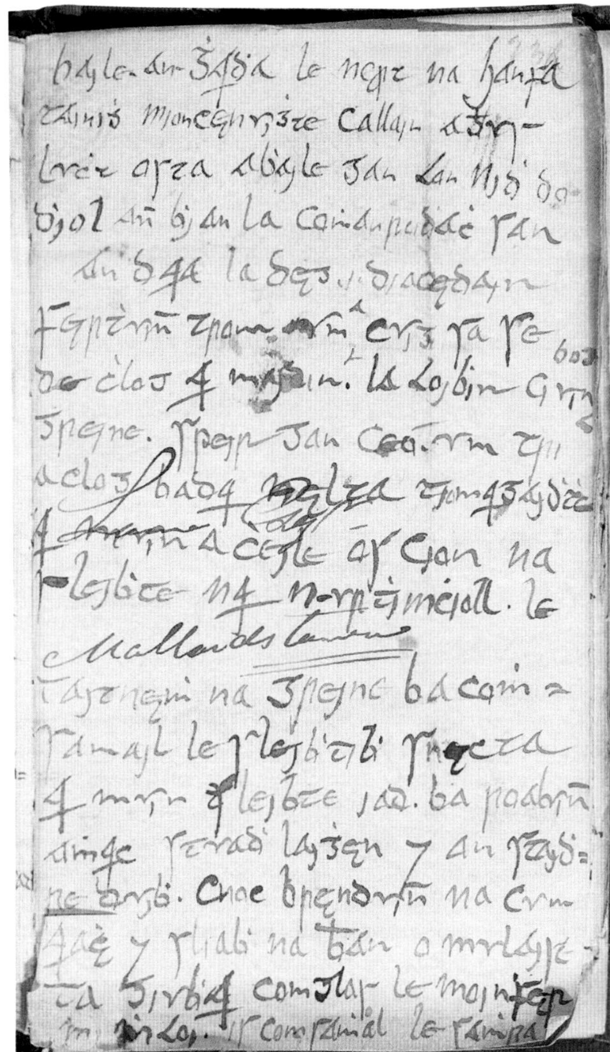

diaries. *A page from the diary or 'cín lae' of Amhlaoibh Ó Súilleabháin, which he kept during 1827–35; it gives a unique insight into the life of a cultured and educated Irish speaker in early nineteenth-century Ireland. [Royal Irish Academy]*

One of the most frequently cited accounts of the 1916 RISING, though by no means the only one in diary or journal form, is *The Insurrection in Dublin* (1916) by the novelist JAMES STEPHENS. Also related, but not confined, to that period are *The Diaries of Roger Casement* (the Black Diaries prepared by Singleton-Gates and Girodias, 1959, the Black and White Diaries edited by Roger Sawyer, 1997), works that are, among their other claims to significance, a case study in the complicated public usages of diaries. A decisive event in cultural history is documented in the voluminous diary of JOSEPH HOLLOWAY, published in part as *Joseph Holloway's Abbey Theatre* (edited by Robert Hogan and Michael O'Neill, 1967). An author who is also remembered largely for his personal writings, where he touches on some of the same ground as Holloway, is STEPHEN MACKENNA; his *Journal and Letters* (edited by E. R. Dodds, 1936) is a minor classic of this type of writing. Personal accounts of more recent public events by those who participated in them remain few and far between, with Gemma Hussey's ministerial diary, *At the Cutting Edge* (1990), a rare exception.

TRAVEL diaries and journals constitute a distinct sub-set of the two genres. Dating from at least as early as WILLIAM PENN's *My Irish Journal, 1669–1670* (edited by Isabel Grubb, 1952), this body of work not only provides views of the country as a whole, which distinguishes it from that produced by resident diarists and journal-keepers, but also reveals the variety of surprising perspectives and preconceptions that travellers to Ireland brought with them. Since temporary residents tend to perceive their stay in Ireland with a traveller's eye, the works in question range from John Stevens's *A Journal of My Travels since the Revolution, Containing a Brief Account of All the War in Ireland* ... (1691; edited by Robert H. Murray, 1912) to Alexis de Tocqueville's *Journey in Ireland, July–August 1835* (edited by Emmet Larkin, 1990), and from Florence Arnold-Foster's *Irish Journal, 1880–1882* (edited by T. W. Moody and Richard Hawkins with Margaret Moody, 1988) to HEINRICH BÖLL's *Irisches Tagebuch* (1957; translated as *Irish Journal*, 1967).

Of equal interest are the travel diaries and journals of the Irish abroad. Covering a large amount of ground, these works help to preserve a valuable sense of the diversity of Irish experience. One such work is Thomas Campbell's *Doctor Thomas Campbell's Diary of a Visit to England in 1775* (edited by James L. Clifford, 1947); while Catherine Wilmot's *An Irish Peer on the Continent, 1801–1803* (edited by Thomas U. Sadleir, 1920; edited by Elizabeth Mavor, 1992, with her *Russian Journals, 1805–1807*) is not only replete with the sights and logistics of the Grand Tour but is keenly perceptive regarding the taste and manners of the ASCENDANCY aristocrats whom she is accompanying. Other examples of writing of this kind notable for their aesthetic, cultural, or linguistic significance are MÍCHEÁL MAC LIAMMÓIR's *Put Money in Thy Purse* (1952), which combines travel experiences with those of filming an Orson Welles production of *Othello*; DÓNALL MAC AMHLAIGH's *Dialann Deoraí* (1960); and AIDAN HIGGINS's *Images of Africa: Diary (1956–60)* (1971). And an oblique connection may be suggested between such works and WILLIAM ALLINGHAM's experiences of nineteenth-century literary London as recorded in *A Diary, 1824–1889* (1907).

The nature of what has come to be known as life-writing is such that each instance of it is assured of being idiosyncratic and surprising and in the Irish context of conjuring up images of national life contrary to the standard ones. In view of such writing's diversity, therefore, it is all the more regrettable that, as may be gathered from *Diaries of Ireland: An Anthology, 1590–1987* (edited by Melosina Lennox Conyngham, 1998), many of the potentially most informative and colourful examples of Irish diaries and journals remain unedited and unpublished. [see TOKSVIG, SIGNE.] **George O'Brien**

DIAS: see DUBLIN INSTITUTE FOR ADVANCED STUDIES.

diaspora. Since 1700 more than 10 million men and women have left Ireland, with the numbers who departed reaching a peak during the GREAT FAMINE and its immediate aftermath—an enormous exodus of people relative to the size of the population. Those destined for the United States account for approximately half the total number who emigrated, with Britain being the next most important destination, followed by Canada, Australia, and New Zealand; smaller numbers travelled to South Africa and to other parts of the British Empire, such as India, and to Central and South America. Though the majority emigrated between 1815 and 1914, the twentieth century also saw large-scale movement out of Ireland. The scale of this outflow over the past three centuries is reflected in the estimated 70 million people throughout the world who today declare some element of Irish ancestry. In the United States alone a sixth of the total population in 1990 identified their national background as being Irish, and significant Irish communities also exist in ENGLAND and WALES, SCOTLAND, AUSTRALIA, CANADA, and NEW ZEALAND.

Since the early 1990s the concept of 'diaspora' has been widely employed to describe this process of emigration and settlement of people born in Ireland and the existence of subsequent generations of Irish descent. Until recently this term was associated with collective trauma and exile, most notably with regard to the Jewish, African, Armenian, and Palestinian diasporas. The growth in the use of the term in relation to Ireland was a consequence of the presidency of MARY ROBINSON, 1990–97, who sought to place the diaspora at the centre of Irish consciousness and chose the theme of 'Cherishing the Diaspora' for her address to the joint houses of the Oireachtas in February 1995. Her frequent visits to centres of Irish settlement around the world demonstrated that living in Ireland was not necessarily a prerequisite for expressing Irish identity. This emphasis on a worldwide Irish community has been continued by her successor, President MARY MCALEESE, who took office in 1997.

Whereas previously the emphasis was on emigration from Ireland and its effects on the development of Irish society, the concept of diaspora shifts the exclusive focus away from the homeland to include the countries and regions that Irish people settled in. Diaspora also invokes a sense of identity that caters for subsequent generations with Irish origins but born outside Ireland. By the early years of the twenty-first century the Irish diaspora was truly a global phenomenon. What this means for the Irish at home is a heightened sense of belonging to a worldwide community. For those of Irish descent living in other countries this explicit acknowledgment of the existence of an Irish diaspora allows for legitimate expressions of national identity.

The Irish diaspora, however, never was and is not now a homogeneous unit. Significant differences exist within the diaspora in background, RELIGION, political outlook, and degree of attachment to some form of Irish identity. Protestant emigrants from Ulster who left for North America in the eighteenth century perceived that they had little in common with the poor Catholic FAMINE REFUGEES who arrived in the 1840s and 50s seeking to escape the ravages of the GREAT FAMINE; the development of the 'SCOTCH-IRISH' identity in North America in the nineteenth and twentieth centuries was an endeavour to distinguish Ulster Presbyterians from their Catholic Irish counterparts. The competing political identities of NATIONALISM and UNIONISM also served to distinguish Irish immigrants from one another, especially in North America and Britain, where such differences were often the cause of tension, as in the 'Orange and Green' riots that occurred in Liverpool in July 1849 and New York in 1870 and 1871.

Older, celebratory accounts of the Irish around the world tend to stress adversity in the face of hostility. In reality, however, the experiences of the millions of people who left Ireland is a far more complicated story, as recent scholarship has demonstrated. How the Irish fared in their new environments has been the subject of extensive research since the 1960s, and the findings of numerous studies emphasise the fact that there was no single experience of emigration and settlement. To a large extent the process of adjustment and adaptation was shaped by the wider environment and could occur over successive generations of immigrants. In North America, for instance, the Irish were one of a number of national groups that arrived in large numbers during the nineteenth century. In the United States and Canada scholars disagree about such controversial issues as economic success or failure, levels of upward SOCIAL MOBILITY, and the degree of assimilation in dominant cultures. These often apparently contradictory findings are a reflection of the considerable regional variations in the nature of the Irish experience in North America. For Britain, large-scale Irish immigration coincided with intense bouts of anti-Catholic prejudice and political tensions in the nineteenth century; yet the reaction to successive waves of Irish immigrants was by no means exclusively hostile.

Interaction between the diaspora and Ireland took many forms, though the continuous flow of emigrants to a variety of destinations served to reinforce established links, as did emigrant letters and repeated visits home. By the end of the nineteenth century, advances in transport ensured that emigrants were able to return home without having to endure a long and arduous journey. The advent of inexpensive air travel in the 1960s enabled emigrants to maintain even closer contact with family and friends; while developments in information technology, such as electronic mail and the worldwide web, facilitate virtually instantaneous contact today between emigrants and home.

The complex relationship between the diaspora and the homeland can be seen most clearly in relation to nationalism. The revolutionary FENIAN MOVEMENT of the 1850s and 60s originated in the United States and also involved activities in Britain. IRISH-AMERICAN NATIONALISM in the nineteenth century was a central element of the campaign to achieve independence for Ireland in the 1880s, especially in the form of fund-raising. Equally in the early twentieth century political organisations such as the UNITED IRISH LEAGUE and SINN FÉIN sought support from the large Irish communities in the United States and Britain. The outbreak of conflict in Northern Ireland from 1969 also saw significant Irish-American involvement, especially intense in the period before the signing of the BELFAST AGREEMENT in May 1998.

The diaspora therefore occupied an important role in Irish politics in the nineteenth and twentieth centuries, not simply in the provision of funds but also in emphasising on the international stage the political issues that were at stake. In this way the diaspora has served to raise consciousness about Ireland and its politics far in excess of the levels of public awareness achieved by other small nations. The collective memory of harsh and ill-judged British government policy that was cultivated in the United States, particularly in the wake of the Great Famine, ensured that even though Ireland seemed a faraway place, its politics were firmly etched in the minds of many of the Irish throughout the world.

The links between Ireland and its diaspora were not solely political in character. The dispersal of the population ensured that identifiable forms of Irish culture, such as literature, drama, dancing, films, theatre, and music, were also evident in the countries that the Irish settled in. Around the world the Irish abroad enhanced, modified and transformed cultural practices that were part and parcel of popular culture at home. The most obvious example was Gaelic sports and games, an integral element of what was perceived as being distinctive about being Irish or of Irish descent. These cultural activities also served to lessen the dislocation for first-generation emigrants and to rekindle a sense of what it was to be Irish or Scotch-Irish. Expressions of political identity could be directly associated with festive celebrations, such as annual events held outside Ireland on ST PATRICK'S DAY or the Twelfth of July. Both were celebrated as the Irish abroad strove to assert distinctive and competing expressions of Irish identity.

RELIGION was also a distinguishing feature of the Irish diaspora. Since the middle of the nineteenth century the number of

diaspora. *Andrew Jackson (1767–1845), seventh President of the United States of America (1829–37), third son of immigrant parents from Ireland. Dated 1845, this daguerrotype is the first photograph taken of an American President. [Courtesy of George Eastman House; GEH 5654]*

Protestants leaving Ireland has been dwarfed by the exodus of Catholics, though Protestants were heavily represented in the emigrant flow to Canada, Scotland, New Zealand, and other parts of the British Empire. Missionaries and RELIGIOUS ORDERS were the most obvious evidence of this element of the diaspora. Irish Catholics played important roles in the development of the church in North America, Britain, and Australia, and not solely in personnel for pastoral work and education: the influx of Irish Catholics significantly boosted the total Catholic population of Britain in the nineteenth and twentieth centuries. Religion, however, was associated with other aspects of the diaspora than the growth in numbers of a particular denomination. For Catholics and Protestants religion was a central element of identity and what it meant to be Irish in Boston, Glasgow, Sydney, or Auckland.

To view the diaspora as a monolithic movement of people out of Ireland fails to capture the complex reasons why people left in the first place, the stark differences between the experiences of the Irish around the world, and the uncoordinated nature of the exodus over three centuries. The diaspora should therefore be seen as the outcome of a sustained process of large-scale emigration to a number of countries throughout the world. On occasions this movement took place during a period of crisis, such as the Great Famine, but in general this was not an exodus that occurred within the context of traumatic dislocation or forced exile. That exile emerged as such a poignant motif of the Irish abroad serves to remind us that only in recent times could Ireland begin to acknowledge the centrality of the diaspora to Irish consciousness and allow for expressions of identity that were not restricted to the geographical boundaries of Ireland. In this sense the use of the term 'diaspora' to describe the worldwide dispersal of people born in Ireland provides for an inclusive understanding of the emigration and settlement of the millions of people who left and the relationship with subsequent generations of Irish descent. [see ARGENTINA, IRISH IN; AUSTRALIA, IRISH IN; BOSTON, IRISH IN; BRITISH EMPIRE, IRISH IN; CANADA, IRISH IN; ENGLAND, LONDON, IRISH IN; NEW ZEALAND, IRISH IN; SCOTLAND, IRISH IN; UNITED STATES, IRISH IN.] **Enda Delaney**

diaspora, archaeology of the. Unlike the more defined archaeology of the African diaspora, the archaeology of the Irish diaspora is in its infancy. Most of the Irish-related excavations have been in the United States and, to a lesser extent, in Canada and Australia; future excavations may take place in other parts of the world as the research expands. Excavations have been carried out in most historical periods, extending from the plantation era (exemplified by Ivor Nöel Hume's comparison of remains excavated at Martin's Hundred, Williamsburg, Virginia, with sites in Ulster) to the early twentieth century (characterised by Sonoma State University's detailed examination of Irish immigrant consumer patterns in San Francisco). Archaeologists in the United States and in Australia have excavated individual home sites of Irish immigrants, such as that of WILLIAM SMITH O'BRIEN in Port Arthur, Tasmania.

Perhaps the most extensive excavation of Irish materials in the United States was that carried out in the 1990s at Five Points, the infamous slum in lower Manhattan, New York, described vividly by Charles Dickens in 1842. Archaeologists there excavated the remains of a five-storey tenement built by Peter McLoughlin (a member of the executive committee of the Irish Emigrant Society), unearthing thousands of objects owned and used by the Irish working-class families that lived there. As in most other projects, however, the archaeologists at Five Points just happened to discover Irish materials, rather than having a research design specifically intended for Irish immigrant sites. One of the few projects planned around Irish immigrant sites was Illinois State University's survey and limited excavation along the Illinois and Michigan Canal, south of Chicago, designed to discover the remains of the Irish shanty towns built during the construction of the canal in the early nineteenth century.

A central topic of interest to archaeologists working with Irish immigrant artefacts is determining what makes the Irish collections unique. Towards this end, archaeologists work to discover whether the objects used by Irish men and women are substantially different from those used by other immigrant groups. By the early 1990s most archaeologists had abandoned the facile association of specific objects with certain national groups, such as linking smoking-pipes embossed with HARPS and shamrocks with the Irish and opium pipes with the Chinese. After several studies dealing with the material culture of ethnicity, archaeologists had come to realise the complexities inherent in associating a group of artefacts with specific living populations. Archaeological research on the Irish diaspora will certainly continue as the catalogue of excavated sites grows and as archaeologists develop more sophisticated perspectives for recognising immigrant affiliation in unearthed material culture. **Charles E. Orser Jr.**

Diceman, the: see MCGINTY, THOM.

Dicuil the Geographer (c. 770–c. 825), geographer, astronomer, computist, and grammarian. Educated at CLONMACNOISE, he lived in the Scottish islands. Arrived at the Frankish court before 810; he taught at the palace school c. 816. He wrote *Liber de Astronomia* (814–818) and *De Mensura Orbis Terrae* (825), employing classical sources, including Aethicus Ister's *Cosmographia*. Some grammatical works are also attributed to him. **Juan José Pérez-Camacho**

dietary patterns, late twentieth to early twenty-first century. Increasing affluence and wider contact with other cultures were the main influences on patterns in Irish food during the second half of the twentieth century. As people became better off they tended to eat MEAT on more days of the week. Side by side with this was a long-term shift away from red meat and particularly towards poultry. Paralleling each other were two contrary trends: on the one hand a growing interest in healthy eating and nutrition, on the other hand an explosion in 'fast food', which arrived in Ireland in the mid-1970s. This drove a move towards eating away from home, which, together with the growth of individual snacking at the expense of the traditional family meal, changed the fabric of Irish home life. Partly driven by the faster pace of the working day, the increased number of women in the work force, and the growth in television viewing, there was a falling off in the home preparation of meals, even for those eaten there, as take-away and prepared meals increased in popularity.

On the other hand, home entertaining in the form of dinner parties grew rapidly, as did the market for gourmet restaurants. Outside influences radically changed what Irish people ate: previously unknown products, such as pizzas and yoghurts, became fixtures on the national menu, as did a wide range of exotic fruits and vegetables from all parts of the world—a far cry from the generation of young people at the end of the SECOND WORLD WAR who had to be taught how to open a banana. [see FOOD.] **Feargal Quinn**

diet, Northern Ireland. Since 1922, food in Northern Ireland has developed from local farm produce to a familiar contemporary pattern of largely urbanised eating habits. By the 1950s the population was mostly urbanised. Today there is a ready acceptance of new foodstuffs and customs from Continental Europe and elsewhere. Ulster farms were small and mixed. Produce for both home and export markets included 'Ulster' cured bacon and sweet-cured 'Belfast' hams, liquid milk, condensed milk, creamery BUTTER, eggs, and POTATOES. Northern farmers slaughtered their pigs on the farm and sold them in local markets; after 1932 this practice declined as a result of the introduction of the factory-based 'Wiltshire cure'. Later, wartime food rationing restricted choice but improved standards, as with the pasteurisation of milk. Older concerns include flour-MILLING, WHISKEY-DISTILLING, and the distinctive eel and pollan fisheries of Lough Neagh. During the 1980s new and revived enterprises included select cheesemaking, salmon and oyster fisheries, and bottled water. Immigrant groups have made their own contributions to local food habits. From the 1890s Italian families opened ice-cream parlours and seaside cafés; in the 1960s Chinese and Indian immigrants opened restaurants that provide cheap exotic meals. Popular food culture accommodates American-style 'fast food' outlets and 'pub grub'. Independent restaurants and hotels provide quality cuisine, often using fresh, locally supplied foods. **Fionnuala Carragher**

diet, present-day. The second half of the twentieth century was a period of sustained dietary change in Ireland, manifesting a slow erosion of a long-lived conservative approach to FOOD and cookery. Increased economic prosperity during the 1960s fuelled demand for a greater variety of foodstuffs and for cooking equipment, refrigerators, and kitchen gadgets. In addition, the possibilities offered by the availability of air travel during the 1950s and 60s, together with the liberating effects of television from the 1960s onwards, encouraged dietary experimentation. Furthermore, easier access to and an increased uptake in higher education produced a

Dillon, Gerard. Cut Out, Drop Out *(1968), by the Belfast painter Gerard Dillon. A dreamlike work in which the artist reflects on the fleeting nature of existence as 'cut-out' visions of himself float overhead. [AIB Art Collection]*

younger generation who were amenable to sampling the merits of different ethnic foods. At the same time an emerging youth culture, with reasonable purchasing power, eagerly strove after all that was considered modern in global tastes. A number of influential cookery writers supported and directed these trends, and accordingly recipes for foreign dishes, in particular those of Mediterranean origin, became a feature of Irish cookery books, though these developments were largely on the back of the huge strides made in this area by the English food writer Elizabeth David during the 1950s.

Central to making these developments and aspirations a reality was the emergence and rise of the supermarkets. These offered the working woman and mother an array of convenience, often highly processed foods, which made manageable the demands of work within and outside the home.

In the social sphere, Indian and Chinese restaurants became increasingly prevalent, with their appeal resting on the comparative difference between their highly spiced and flavoursome dishes and the bland nature of the Irish plate. Food cooked in French styles, and establishments that offered French cuisine, were taken to be the epitome of fine dining, in part because of the high reputation of French food culture and also the influence of Irish chefs trained in France.

The mid-1970s saw the beginnings of a movement that would redirect critical and popular attention back to home-produced quality foods. In 1976, on a smallholding in Co. Cork, Veronica and Norman Steele began producing cheese with their surplus milk stocks, heralding the emergence of the hugely successful farmhouse CHEESE industry. In a near-contemporary development Myrtle Allen, proprietor and chef at Ballymaloe House, near Midleton, Co. Cork, began a vocal and persuasive campaign to promote the taste and nutritional merits of quality Irish foods. In time, carefully hand-made foods found a following, especially among those who found the production of cheap industrial-style foods objectionable.

The unprecedented economic boom of the 1990s provided another launching pad for further dietary diversification. For the economically buoyant, knowledge and appreciation of food and an adherence to a regular pattern of restaurant dining became a life-style choice, if not a hobby. In the home, life-style changes also encouraged a more fluid and unconventional approach to eating and meal-time rituals, while at the same time the link between good diet and sound health encouraged many people to adopt specialised dietary regimes. The fear of fat has seen an upsurge in low-fat food products, an increased consumption of chicken, and an unrealistic demand for fat-free red MEATS. The continuing BSE (bovine spongiform encephalopathy) crisis and the epidemic of foot-and-mouth disease in 2001 made food safety front-page news. Both have also shaken people's confidence in the produce of large-scale specialised farming; and as the consumer becomes increasingly distanced from the source of food products, the issue of traceability has become an important concern.

In more recent times the movement of non-European food products into a global market has heightened the issues of traceability and the demand for effective and honest labelling. On the one hand a high price is now commanded for ORGANIC, locally produced foods in season that have been ethically produced, with attention to animal welfare where applicable; on the other hand a thriving transnational food industry finds a ready market among those whose food purchases are dictated by price alone. In addition, a fast-food industry is booming, providing a steady stream of high-fat, high-sugar, salty, low-fibre food to an insatiable youth population. If older dietary survivals are detectable they are in the continued taste for BUTTER, pig meats, POTATOES, and to a lesser extent oatmeal. But at the beginning of the twenty-first century the arrival and settlement of various national groups in Ireland provides the potential for even further and interesting dietary expansion. **Regina Sexton**

Dillon, Eilís (1920–1994), writer. Born in Galway; educated at the Ursuline Convent, Sligo. As a writer for adults she is known principally for her historical fiction, especially the novel *Across the Bitter Sea* (1973). She achieved national and international recognition with her writing for children, which comprises some thirty-eight books; many of them, such as *The Lost Island* (1952), *The Island of Horses* (1956), *The Singing Cave* (1969), and *The Island of Ghosts* (1989), are exciting adventure stories set in the west of Ireland. **Robert Dunbar**

Dillon, Gerard (1916–1971), artist. Born in Belfast. Leaving school at the age of fourteen, Dillon trained as a housepainter, but a keen interest in art led to his becoming a full-time artist. During the war years he worked in Belfast and Dublin; in 1944 he went to London to work on building sites. In 1958 he represented Ireland at the Guggenheim International and represented Britain at the Pittsburgh International Exhibition. He travelled on the Continent and taught for brief periods in London. In 1968 he was in Dublin, designing sets and costumes for SEAN O'CASEY's play *Juno and the Paycock*. His style of painting is personal and idiosyncratic, inspired by Gauguin, Chagall, and van Gogh, a type of magic realism, with dreamlike landscapes and interiors, peopled by farmers and fishermen but also by pierrots and strange hallucinatory figures. *The Yellow Bungalow* (1954), his painting of a domestic interior with figures seated around a stove, is in the ULSTER MUSEUM. **Peter Murray**

Dillon, James (1902–1986), politician. Born in Dublin, a son of JOHN DILLON; educated at UCG and KING'S INNS and studied business in London and Chicago. He was manager of his family's business in Ballaghaderreen, Co. Roscommon, before being elected to Dáil Éireann for West Donegal, 1932–7, and Monaghan, 1937–69. He was deputy leader of FINE GAEL in the 1930s, resigning from the party in 1942 after making a pro-Allies speech. He was Minister for Agriculture, 1948–51 and 1954–7, and leader of Fine Gael, 1959–65; he retired in 1969. A rare representative of the pre-revolutionary nationalist and Hibernian tradition, Dillon was a brilliant orator who outshone other parliamentarians in debate. **Tom Garvin**

Dillon, John (1851–1927), politician. Born in Blackrock, Co. Dublin, the son of JOHN BLAKE DILLON; he trained as a physician but devoted nearly his entire life to politics. He was instrumental in the LAND WAR (1879–82) and the PLAN OF CAMPAIGN (1886–91), serving terms of imprisonment during both. He sat in the British House of Commons, 1880–83, 1885–1918, and was chairman of the Anti-Parnellites, 1896–99, and of the IRISH PARTY, 1918. An earnest Catholic, he always opposed clerical interference in politics. His youthful radicalism was supplanted by a growing social conservatism. During the FIRST WORLD WAR he became increasingly disillusioned by British policy. At the general election in December 1918 the Irish Party was overwhelmed; he was defeated in East Mayo by ÉAMON DE VALERA. Afterwards he played little active part in Irish affairs. His reputation was scarred by the long years of parliamentary manoeuvres after PARNELL's fall. **Alan O'Day**

Dillon, John (1939–), philosopher. Born in Madison, Wisconsin, USA; educated at the University of Oxford and University of California, Berkeley. Since 1980 he has been Regius professor of Greek at Trinity College Dublin. One of the world's foremost scholars of Platonism, he has published *The Middle Platonists: A Study of Platonism, 80 BC–220 AD* (1977), *The Golden Chain: Studies in the Development of Platonism and Christianity* (1991), and *The Great Tradition: Further Studies in the Development of Platonism and Christianity* (1997). **Fionola Meredith**

Dillon, John Blake (1814–1866), Young Irelander. Born at Ballaghaderreen, Co. Mayo, son of Luke Dillon, a UNITED IRISHMAN; educated briefly at ST PATRICK'S COLLEGE, Maynooth, and then TCD. He helped to establish the NATION in 1843. After the RISING OF 1848 he escaped to America, disguised as a priest; there he practised law until 1855, when he returned under amnesty to the Irish bar. A moderate nationalist, he opposed FENIANISM. He was elected to Dublin Corporation and in 1865 was elected MP for Tipperary. He died suddenly of cholera on 15 September 1866. **Richard P. Davis**

Dillon, Myles (1900–1972), Celtic scholar and Indo-European philologist. Born in Dublin, a son of JOHN DILLON; educated at UCD. After postgraduate study in Germany and France, 1922–6, he lectured in TRINITY COLLEGE, Dublin, 1927–30, and University College, Dublin, 1930–37, before becoming professor of Irish at the University of Madison, Wisconsin, 1937–45. He returned to Ireland in 1949 as senior professor at the DUBLIN INSTITUTE FOR ADVANCED STUDIES, subsequently becoming its director, 1960–68. His principal publications are *The Cycles of the Kings* (1948), *Early Irish Literature* (1948), and *The Celtic Realms* (1967). **John Dillon**

Dillon, Wentworth, fourth Earl of Roscommon (c. 1633–1685), poet. Born in Ireland; educated at the Protestant University, Caen. He travelled the Continent, moved to England after the RESTORATION, and became a poet at the court of CHARLES II. He was noted for his great learning and technical ability; his best-known work, *Essay on Translated Verse*, displays his ability with heroic couplets. His desire to standardise English attracted some interest from Dryden; he was dismissed by Johnson and Pope as polished yet unoriginal. He remains an occasionally anthologised minor poet. **Joley Wood**

Dimma, Book of, an enshrined illuminated Latin 'pocket' GOSPEL, now in TRINITY COLLEGE Library, Dublin. It is dated by its decoration to the end of the eighth century and is the work of at least two scribes, whose names have been erased and Dimma's substituted. Dimma mac Nathí was a legendary scribe who wrote a Gospel book for St Crónán, the founder of a monastery at Roscrea. The book's shrine dates from the twelfth and fifteenth centuries. [see BOOK SHRINES.] **William O'Sullivan**

Dingle (*An Daingean*), a town on the south coast of the Dingle peninsula, Co. Kerry, 15 km (9 miles) east of Blasket Sound. After the ANGLO-NORMAN CONQUEST it became an important port and the only walled town in Co. Kerry apart from Tralee. In 1841 the population was almost 3,400; by 1986 it had fallen to 1,253. Since then it has recovered to 1,629 (2002), and Dingle is now an important tourist town with a reputation for good restaurants and numerous pubs. **Kevin Hourihan**

Dingle Peninsula, Co. Kerry, the northernmost of the five peninsulas on the south-west coast. It measures 51 km (32 miles) long and a maximum of 19 km (12 miles) wide, bounded by Dingle Bay to the south and Tralee Bay and Brandon Bay to the north. Like IVERAGH, it is mountainous, with the Slieve Mish Mountains on its east side and BRANDON MOUNTAIN near its western tip. The BLASKET ISLANDS extend a further 13 km (8 miles) into the Atlantic. The peninsula is particularly scenic and varied, with rugged, glaciated mountains and lakes, fine beaches, and high sea-cliffs. The use of the peninsula in the filming of *Ryan's Daughter* (1969) began a TOURISM boom in the area.

The Dingle Peninsula has a particularly rich heritage. It has been suggested that Irish monasticism began here. The monuments include GALLARUS ORATORY and the twelfth-century Hiberno-ROMANESQUE complex at Kilmalkedar (both near the western tip). Huts, especially the corbelled BEEHIVE HUTS known as clochāns, are also widespread, with more than 500 sites. The peninsula is one of the strongest IRISH-speaking districts in the country, and the literature of the area, especially that of the Blaskets, is particularly significant. **Kevin Hourihan**

Dinneen, Patrick (1860–1934), editor and lexicographer. Born near Rathmore, Co. Kerry; educated at UCD, he was a member of the Society of Jesus, 1880–1900. He played an energetic and independent role in the affairs of the GAELIC LEAGUE, 1900–9. *Cormac Ó Conaill* (1901) was the first Irish novel published in book form. He produced some thirty creative works as well as editions of KEATING and Munster poets of the seventeenth and eighteenth centuries but is best remembered as the compiler of *Foclóir Gaedhilge agus Béarla* (1927), the Irish–English dictionary with its famously individualistic entries. He is fortunate to have been the subject of an enlightened biography by PROINSIAS Ó CONLUAIN and Donncha Ó Céileachair, *An Duinníneach* (1958), itself a classic (see p. 556). **Liam Mac Mathúna**

dinnseanchas ('place-name lore'), established as a dominant literary genre in the MIDDLE IRISH period (c. 900–1200). The term is applied to a corpus of several hundred accounts and reflects a preoccupation with organising formerly disparate elements into an aesthetically more satisfying compilation. The relationship between the various versions—metrical, prose, and combined metrical and prose—is complex, and the subject is one of continuing debate. Closely related thematically is 'ACALLAMH NA SENÓRACH' ('The Colloquy of the Old Men'), a loosely constructed Middle Irish tale in which ST PATRICK travels the country accompanied by OISÍN and Caoilte of the Fianna, who recount the lore attached to the various places visited.

The *dinnseanchas* genre evolved from the broader, more general interest in people and landscape that permeates early Irish literature. In the pivotal saga 'TÁIN BÓ CUAILNGE' ('The Cattle Raid of Cooley') the young CÚ CHULAINN is taught the names of places by his charioteer; extended lists celebrate heroes and the places associated with them, and the climax of the tale deals with the origins of PLACE-NAMES, rather than the contests of bulls and men.

Based largely on Isidore of Seville's etymological method, the origin tales of the *dinnseanchas* regularly derive a place-name from a

Dingle Peninsula. *Panoramic view of Clogher Bay on the Dingle Peninsula, a striking coastline carved by the Atlantic Ocean. [Gareth McCormack]*

word for a physical feature and the name of a person. Alternative explanations are frequently advanced and accorded equal validity, emphasising the fact that medieval analysis differed from the modern linguistic approach to onomastics. Its *modus operandi* was to interpret the component elements of a name and the traditional lore associated with it in order to access, understand, and proclaim the essence of a specific feature of the environment. It is this perception of intertwined landscape, reality, and being that underlies much of the continuing significance and appeal of *dinnseanchas*. [see PLACE-NAMES; PLACE-NAME LORE.] **Liam Mac Mathúna**

diocesan system, the organisation of the Irish church according to provinces and dioceses under episcopal authority, often reflecting political boundaries. The system was planned by the reforming SYNODS OF RÁTH BHREASAIL (1111) and Kells-Mellifont (1152). At the latter, the Papal legate conferred pallia on the four metropolitans of Armagh, Dublin, Cashel, and Tuam, recognising the primacy of Armagh. Although it took some time to implement, the pattern has remained largely unchanged, even by the Tudor REFORMATION. However, the CHURCH TEMPORALITIES (IRELAND) ACT (1833) reduced the number of provinces of the established CHURCH OF IRELAND to Armagh and Dublin, and reduced the number of its sees by uniting bishoprics. [see ADMINISTRATIVE DIVISIONS; HIERARCHY, ECCLESIASTICAL.] **Kenneth Milne**

'Diplock courts', the name given to the special non-jury courts in Northern Ireland in which 'scheduled' (terrorist) offences were tried from 1973. Following the imposition of DIRECT RULE in 1972, the British government appointed a British judge, Lord Diplock, to head an inquiry into legal aspects of the government's response to political violence. Concerned with the intimidation of witnesses and jurors, Diplock proposed the temporary establishment of non-jury courts for the duration of the 'TROUBLES', and his recommendations were incorporated in the Northern Ireland (Emergency Provisions) Act (1973). In the first instance suspects were tried before a judge sitting alone, while all appeals were heard before three judges. Other changes initiated by Diplock included extended police powers of arrest and detention and the relaxation of the legal test for the admissibility of confessions. Under the new system a series of dramatic trials based on the uncorroborated testimony of both republican and loyalist informers was held, which led to a widespread disenchantment—particularly in nationalist circles—with the probity of the Northern Ireland legal process. The Diplock courts were accused of sustaining 'conveyor-belt justice', where the function of the courts was less to administer justice than to defeat terrorism. [see SPECIAL CRIMINAL COURT.] **Keith Jeffery**

direct rule (1972–99). The deployment of the BRITISH ARMY IN NORTHERN IRELAND in August 1969 meant that the British government was directly involved in the affairs of Northern Ireland. The governments of JAMES CHICHESTER-CLARK (1969–71) and BRIAN FAULKNER (1971–2) found their authority diminished, especially once the campaigns of the Official and PROVISIONAL IRA began in 1970 and security primacy increasingly fell to the British army. Faulkner's introduction of INTERNMENT on 9 August 1971, which notably failed in its purpose of quashing the IRA, further undermined the credibility of his government. The events of 'BLOODY SUNDAY' in Derry on 30 January 1972, when thirteen unarmed civilians were killed by members of the Parachute Regiment, seem to have convinced Edward Heath's government that the Northern Ireland government could no longer be sustained. Sensing that this was so, Ulster VANGUARD, led by the former Minister of Home Affairs, WILLIAM CRAIG, held a series of mass rallies designed to sustain the existing constitutional position; but the British government was not deflected. On 22 March, Faulkner flew to London, where he was asked to surrender security powers, end internment, accept the appointment of a Secretary of State for Northern Ireland, and begin moves for a community government. When his Cabinet refused to agree, on 24 March the Northern Ireland Parliament was suspended. After the final meeting of the Cabinet, on 28 March, Faulkner was joined by Craig in addressing a mass rally at STORMONT. Responsibility for the government of Northern Ireland now passed to the Secretary of State, a member of the British Cabinet, the first holder of which was William Whitelaw. As successive attempts at a political settlement failed in the face of communal division, successive Secretaries of State, their junior ministers and civil servants assumed a pivotal role in Northern Ireland's affairs, with a consequent diminishing of the role of local politicians. Direct rule ended in December 1999 with the inauguration of the Northern Ireland Executive. [see SECRETARIES OF STATE.] **T. G. Fraser**

disability. The definition of disability in the Republic's Employment Equality Act (1998) reflects a medical model: it includes total or partial absence of bodily or mental functions, chronic illness, disease, and conditions that affect thought processes, emotions, judgments, or behaviour. Many see this as insufficient. The Commission on the Status of People with Disabilities in its *Strategy for Equality* (1996) defined such people as those whose capacity to participate in economic, social, or cultural life is restricted because of a physical, sensory, learning, MENTAL HEALTH, or emotional impairment; attitudes, services and facilities are therefore seen as critical. Disability is now recognised as one of the bases on which DISCRIMINATION may exist.

No comprehensive statistics are available, but it has been estimated that 10 per cent of the population have a disability (roughly half of these being over the age of sixty). The National Rehabilitation Board, a lobbying, information, advice, and EMPLOYMENT organisation, was the public service body most concerned with disability; it is to be disbanded and its functions reallocated to a statutory body, the National Disability Authority: these will include assisting the minister in the co-ordination and development of policy, undertaking research, devising codes of practice, and strategic planning. 'Comhairle', an information, advice, and advocacy service, is also to be set up, while training and employment will be allocated to FÁS. **Pat O'Connor**

disadvantaged farming areas. Under the EU COMMON AGRICULTURAL POLICY, each member-state can designate areas as 'disadvantaged' for special help. In Ireland the designation of such areas began in 1975; following five reviews, up to 75 per cent of the land of both the Republic and Northern Ireland is so designated. To qualify, areas had to meet objective criteria based on low population density, dependence on AGRICULTURE, low farm incomes, and the proportion of land suitable for tillage. Areas are designated according to the degree of handicap, from 'more severely handicapped' and 'less severely handicapped' to areas with specific handicaps, such as those subject to COASTAL EROSION, representing about 4 per cent of the area. From 1975, among the supports to farmers in disadvantaged areas were payments of livestock headage, increased investment grants, special integrated rural development schemes, and preferential treatment under EU policies, such as the 'top-up' rural world ewe premium. Payments under the disadvantaged areas scheme are in the main partly financed by the EUROPEAN UNION. Under recent changes in the common agricultural policy the livestock headage payment system has now changed to an area-based payment. This change has been brought about to ensure that the payments are not a factor of production but a social payment, as was the original intention of the measure. **Gerry Gunning**

Discovery Programme, established on the initiative of the Taoiseach, CHARLES HAUGHEY, in 1991 to enhance understanding of Ireland's past through integrated archaeological and related research. The work is carried out through research projects (six long-term projects had been established by 2002) and the publication of academic monographs and reports, as well as popular and educational literature. The organisation is financed by the HERITAGE COUNCIL. Research so far has included studies of TARA and excavations at DÚN AONGHASA and MOOGHAUN, Co. Clare. [see AXES.] **Brian Lacey**

discrimination. Under the Republic's Employment Equality Act (1998) discrimination is defined as the treatment of one person in a less favourable way than another on grounds of age, sex, race, marital status, FAMILY status, sexual orientation, RELIGION, DISABILITY, or membership of the travelling community. The emphasis of this act is on EMPLOYMENT, but discrimination can also occur in the provision of goods and services, in EDUCATION, with regard to property, etc., and this was reflected in the Equal Status Act (2002). Indirect discrimination arises where practices or terms and conditions that are unnecessary are applied and have a perhaps unintended but disproportionate impact on the outcome. It is sufficient to show that a practice bears more heavily on one sex than another to constitute indirect discrimination. Indirect discrimination may be so embedded in state practices that it is not even perceived. In the implementation of the 1979 EC directive on equal treatment of men and women in social welfare, compensatory payments were paid, 1986–92, solely to married men; this was found to be discriminatory by the European Court of Justice in 1995. It also found that the CIVIL SERVICE had discriminated against job-sharers. The emphasis of the majority of FÁS schemes on the live register of unemployed, thereby excluding many married women, may constitute indirect discrimination, as may various practices affecting the promotion of women in occupational structures. Under the Employment Equality Act (1998) employers in religious, educational, and medical institutions run by religious bodies may, in making decisions about recruitment or promotion, discriminate in favour of those with similar religious beliefs. [see TRAINING; TRAVELLERS.] **Pat O'Connor**

discrimination legislation. The main emphasis in the Republic has been on the elimination of discrimination in paid EMPLOYMENT. At first this was done through the Anti-Discrimination (Pay) Act (1974) and the Employment Equality Act (1977), in compliance with EC directives; such legislation now includes the Employment Equality Act (1998)—replacing the two previous acts—the Pensions Act (1990), the Maternity Protection Act (1994), the Adoptive Leave Act (1995), and the Parental Leave Act (1998). Under the Employment Equality Act (1998) positive action is allowed, but is not mandatory, with regard to the promotion, training or work experience of women and to facilitate the integration into employment of those over the age of fifty, those with a DISABILITY, and members of the travelling community. The Equal Status Act (2002) allows for positive action outside the area of employment and on all nine grounds of DISCRIMINATION. The efficacy of the Parental Leave Act is limited, since the leave is unpaid. The inadequacies of legislation as a way of promoting equality have been widely noted. **Pat O'Connor**

disestablishment, the removal of the minority CHURCH OF IRELAND's privileged position as state church and its partial disendowment. GLADSTONE regarded this as contributing to the pacification of Ireland. The Irish Church Act (1869) placed the formerly established church on the same voluntary basis as other churches; while all its property was for a time vested in commissioners, church buildings and some other assets were subsequently restored. Elaborate schemes were introduced to secure the life interest of clergy and other church officials through the setting up by charter of the Representative Church Body, and provision was made for the creation of a General Synod and its enactment of a written constitution for the church. **Kenneth Milne**

distilling. For the most part, Irish WHISKEY was distilled in *pot stills*—enormous copper vessels in which *wash* (raw beer) was evaporated and condensed into a raw spirit. In the Irish process three successive distillations were undertaken to purify the spirit and give it a smooth taste; and almost all Irish whiskey continues to be manufactured in this way. Nonetheless Irish distillers played a pioneering role in the development of the patent still. In 1830 AENEAS COFFEY (1780–1852), a former Inspector-General of Excise in Ireland, patented a continuous or patent still, which was widely adopted in Irish and Scottish distilleries.

Significant archaeological remains of whiskey distilleries survive throughout Ireland, but only a handful continue to manufacture it. The best example of a rural distillery is Locke's Distillery at Kilbeggan, Co. Westmeath (established 1757, the oldest recorded in Ireland), which retains a significant proportion of its original machinery. The Midleton distillery, Co. Cork (established 1825), is the best surviving example of a large distillery; as at Kilbeggan, most of its early plant is intact, including the world's largest pot still, with a capacity of 976,790 m^3 (31,648 gallons), installed in 1826. [see ALCOHOL CONSUMPTION.] **Colin Rynne**

distilling industry. Bushmills Distillery, at Bushmills, Co. Antrim, claims to be the oldest distillery in Ireland. However, while a licence to distil was granted in the area in 1608, there is no evidence that a distillery was established then. The first definite evidence of the distillery comes from the early 1780s. At that time distilling was centred in Ulster and the midlands; but large commercial distilleries were established in Dublin in the late eighteenth century, including those of JAMESON (see p. 1135), Power, and Roe. In the early nineteenth century Murphy's distillery was set up in Cork, and in 1867 it and several smaller distilleries amalgamated to form Cork Distilleries Company. From the early twentieth century this company produced the well-known Paddy whiskey, in addition to Cork Dry Gin. In Belfast from the 1870s to the 1930s the Royal Irish Distilleries was noted for its popular Dunville's whiskey. Many smaller distilleries were forced to close during the early twentieth century, and in 1966 most of the remaining companies amalgamated with the Irish Distillers Group, which in 1976 moved to a new distilling centre at Midleton, Co. Cork. Today all the best-known brands of Irish whiskey are produced by Irish Distillers, mainly in Co. Cork. **Elizabeth Malcolm**

district partnerships, established in Northern Ireland under the European Union Special Support Programme for Peace and

Reconciliation ('Peace II') in 1995 with a view to maintaining peace and reconciliation following the paramilitary ceasefires of the previous year. There are twenty-six district partnerships, corresponding to the administrative areas of LOCAL GOVERNMENT, which are responsible for distributing funds in four areas of priority: EMPLOYMENT, urban and rural regeneration, social inclusion, and productive investment and INDUSTRIAL DEVELOPMENT. The partnerships are an innovative form of local governance, with each board comprising elected representatives from the relevant district council and nominees from community and VOLUNTARY ORGANISATIONS, public bodies, TRADE UNIONS, and business. In each instance, therefore, the hallmark is diversity and inclusiveness of membership, as the partnerships mirror the political and organisational diversity of Northern Ireland. The primary aim of the partnerships is to harness the energy and talent of local groups in formulating and implementing local action plans. The programme is administered by the Northern Ireland Partnership Board, which oversees the district partnerships and approves their strategies and action plans. 'Peace II' (2000–2004), however, aims to devolve more autonomy in decision-making to the new local strategy partnerships that will replace the district partnerships. **Jonathan Greer**

Divine Comedy. *Neil Hannon, original member and lead vocalist of the band Divine Comedy formed in 1989.* [Hot Press]

Divine Comedy, the, rock group. Primarily consisting of Neil Hannon (1970–), a native of Derry, the group was formed in Enniskillen in 1989 with John McCullagh and Kevin Traynor. Their debut album, *Fanfare for the Common Muse* (1990), introduced Hannon's quaint Eurocentric world view to a small public. Future albums saw Hannon go it alone, eventually teaming up in 1996 with Joby Talbot (BBC Young Composer of the Year). Subsequent albums—*Casanova* (1996), *A Short Album about Love* (1997), and *Fin de Siècle* (1998)—have shown Hannon to be a master-craftsman of clever, amusing but emotional and classic pop music. In late 2001, following the *Regeneration* album, Hannon dissolved the band's regular touring line-up, returning to the status of solo artist. **Tony Clayton-Lea**

divorce. Under British rule, the divorce courts established in England in 1857 were not extended to Ireland, and divorce was possible only through private acts of Parliament. Legal separation (divorce *a mensa et thoro*) could be obtained through the courts, but this did not confer the right to remarry. This remained the position in the IRISH FREE STATE until 1937, when article 41.3.2 of the CONSTITUTION OF IRELAND imposed an absolute ban on divorce ('No law shall be enacted providing for a grant of the dissolution of marriage'). The system of legal separation was unaffected by the Constitution, though the low rate of marital breakdown meant that it was not widely used.

From the 1960s onwards the incidence of legal separation began to rise. On 26 June 1986 a Government-sponsored proposal to alter article 41 to allow for divorce was rejected in a REFERENDUM (see p. 33). The Judicial Separation and Family Law Reform Act (1989) extensively reformed and liberalised the law on judicial separation but did not provide for remarriage. In November 1995, in a second referendum on divorce, the electorate voted to abolish article 41.3.2, though by a very narrow margin (50.25 per cent in favour, 49.75 per cent against). The ensuing Family Law Act (1996), which came into force in February 1997, provided for 'no-fault' divorce after five years of separation. The number of applications for divorce during 1997 was relatively low but rose somewhat over the years 1998–2000. In Northern Ireland, divorce has been available under British Legislation since 1937. **Tony Fahey**

Divorce Action Group, founded in the Republic in 1980 to lobby for the introduction of DIVORCE. It was the main pro-divorce campaigning group in both the 1986 and 1995 REFERENDUMS on divorce. It was headed by Jean Tansey and drew its main active support from separated men and women. Based largely in Dublin, it also had branches around the country. Though it had a high public profile, it had limited campaigning ability and did not have the door-to-door canvassing capacity possessed by anti-divorce groups such as the ANTI-DIVORCE CAMPAIGN and FAMILY SOLIDARITY. **Tony Fahey**

divorce, medieval. Medieval Irish customary BREHON LAW regarded MARRIAGE as a contract. It could be annulled by mutual consent or if either partner failed in his or her duty as a spouse; in the latter case the contribution of the guilty party to the household was declared forfeit. The rules on divorce and remarriage were to the advantage of noblemen, who often ignored clerical opinion on the subject. About 1100 the Archbishop of Canterbury complained that Irish men 'exchange wives freely and publicly, just as one exchanges one HORSE for another.' The relatively tolerant attitude towards divorce finally changed with English rule and the REFORMATION. [see BREHON LAW; MARRIAGE, EARLY IRISH.] **Bart Jaski**

Dixon, Henry Horatio (1869–1953), botanist. Educated at TCD, transferring from classics to natural science in 1891. He joined the staff at Trinity College in 1892 and became professor of botany in 1904. Meanwhile he had spent a year at Bonn, where Strasburger was working out the details of meiosis in cell division and studying the transport of sap in trees. With the help of his friend JOHN JOLY he demonstrated the cohesive strength of water, helping to explain how water is transported from the roots to the tips of the tallest trees. He received many honours, including the BOYLE MEDAL of the ROYAL DUBLIN SOCIETY in 1917. **Donal Synnott**

Dr Steevens' Hospital, Dublin, built following a bequest from Dr Richard Steevens, professor of medicine at Trinity College, Dublin, who died in 1710. The hospital, designed by THOMAS BURGH, opened its doors in 1733; JONATHAN SWIFT was among the first governors. Another governor was Edward Worth, who died in 1733 and bequeathed his library to the hospital; a room that also served as the Board Room was specially designed by EDWARD LOVETT PEARCE to house the books. It was a busy general hospital. Several famous physicians and surgeons served on the staff, including SAMUEL CLOSSY, ABRAHAM COLLES, and Walter Clegg Stevenson. WILLIAM WILDE and CHARLES LEVER were students there, and NÖEL BROWNE was a house surgeon. A special Burns Unit was constructed in 1980, which did heroic work following the STARDUST TRAGEDY a year later.

The hospital closed in 1987 and its services were moved to St James's Hospital, the Meath Hospital, and the Adelaide Hospital. In 1988 the building was bought by the Eastern Health Board and became the head office of the board. **Davis Coakley**

Docwra, Henry (died 1631), English soldier, most notably associated with the amphibious landing of an English army at Derry during the NINE YEARS' WAR (1594–1603). Orchestrated as a flanking movement on the Irish insurgents led by HUGH O'NEILL, Earl of Tyrone, Docwra's performance at Derry came in for much contemporary criticism; ELIZABETH I was unhappy that the expensive operation did not make a decisive contribution to the English war effort. Historians are now more disposed to appreciate the difficulties Docwra faced, his army being blighted by sickness, and to credit him with relative success. In particular, by winning round to the royal cause such important Irish lords as Niall Garbh O'Donnell, CAHIR O'DOHERTY, and Dónall Ó Catháin, he greatly undermined the rebel alliance in the north. Despite this, Docwra was poorly rewarded for his endeavours when the war ended, the governorship of the tiny settlement at Derry being his only tangible material reward. Appalled at the slight, he sold his position and returned to England, where he wrote a lengthy justification of his role at Derry. Belatedly, in 1616, benefiting from important changes in the Crown administration in Ireland, Docwra was appointed to the important position of Treasurer-at-War (see p. 265). **John McCavitt**

Doherty, Jim (1939–), jazz musician. Born in Dublin. A self-taught musician, he has had a varied career as pianist, arranger, musical director, and composer. A member of the Viscounts, he later led a resident organ-saxophones-drums trio in the Inter-continental (Jury's) Doyle Hotel, Dublin, for seven years. In 1968 he led the quartet sent by RTÉ to the Montreux Jazz Festival. His compositions include several musicals written with the librettist Fergus Linehan, among them *Innish* (staged in the ABBEY THEATRE in 1976). He has been musical director for several shows produced by Noel Pearson, including *Side by Side by Sondheim* and *Hunky Dory.* He composed *Spondance* as a jazz ballet, first performed at the Cork Jazz Festival in 1986. Much given to musical quotations and jokes, Doherty plays jazz with a light touch and a strong melodic sense. **Brian Trench**

Doherty, John (1900–1980) and family, FIDDLERS. John Doherty was the best known of a family of travelling craftsmen who are widely recognised as master fiddlers in the DONEGAL FIDDLE TRADITION. The family has its origins in the dispossessed Mac Suibhne

Doherty, John. *Doherty, master fiddler, outside McIntyre's bar in Ballyshannon, Co. Donegal, August 1979. [Courtesy of the Department of Irish Folklore, University College, Dublin; N102.14/photo: Christine Bond]*

family of Doe Castle, including the piper and fiddler TOIREALACH MAC SUIBHNE. Recordings and FOLKLORE suggest that John's style deviated somewhat from that of his father and brothers through the development of vigorous, attacking staccato bowing. Through their travels and contact with local fiddlers the family dispersed a rich repertoire, which continues to strongly influence the tradition. **Caoimhín Mac Aoidh**

Doherty, Kenneth (Ken) (1969–), snooker player. Born in Dublin. In 1989 he won the world amateur snooker championship, the first player from the Republic to do so. He turned professional in 1992 and beat Stephen Hendry to become world champion in 1995. **Myra Dowling**

Doherty, Peter (1913–1990), soccer player. Born in Magherafelt, Co. Derry. He played with Raich Carter in Derby County's victorious FA Cup team in 1946, forming what is considered to have been one of the finest inside-forward partnerships of any era. One of the first advocates of total football, he ranged the length of the pitch with bottomless energy. He attempted to bring the same qualities to the Northern Ireland team, which he managed from 1951 to 1963. **Peter Byrne**

Doherty, Willie (1959–), photographer and video artist. Born in Derry; studied at Belfast School of Art. He works exclusively in PHOTOGRAPHY and video, a pioneer of large-scale black-and-white photography works, initially with one line of text or single words superimposed on the image; he subsequently moved to colour photography and then to video, but his work remains based on the political realities of living in Northern Ireland. His work is subtle, powerful, and, while often dealing with issues of violence, is itself in no way violent. He teaches at the National College of Art and Design and is a member of AOSDÁNA. **Dorothy Walker**

Dolan, Michael Keegan (1969–), dancer, choreographer, and dance director. Born in Dublin; trained with JOHN REGAN and at the Central Ballet School, London. He founded Cartoon Dance Company, London, in 1991 and Fabulous Beast Dance Company in 1997. His choreography includes *Sunday Lunch* (1997), *Fragile* (1999), and *The Flower Bed* (2000). He has also choreographed for Sir Peter Hall's *Oedipus Plays* and for numerous OPERA companies in Britain, the United States, Belgium, and Germany. He won the Hamlyn Choreographic Award in 1995 and choreographed for the Peter Darrell Choreographic Award in 1998. **Carolyn Swift**

Dolin, Anton (Patrick Healey Kay) (1904–1983), dancer, choreographer, and dance director. Born at Slinfold, Sussex, second son of Henry George Kay and Helen Maude Healey of Dublin. In his early autobiography, *Divertissement* (1931), he attributed his love of dance to his mother's delight in watching Irish dancing. Training with Astafieva and Legat, he was listed as 'Patrikieff' in Diaghilev's 1921 Stoll production of *The Sleeping Princess*, becoming Dolin on joining Ballets Russes as soloist in 1923. He founded the Nemchinova-Dolin Company in 1927 and helped establish the Carmago Society in 1930, creating the role of Satan in DE VALOIS's *Job*. He led the Vic-Wells Ballet, 1931–5, before founding and directing the Markova-Dolin company, which in 1950 became London Festival Ballet. He was premier danseur and choreographer with American Ballet Theatre, 1940–46, played the role of Cecchetti in the film *Nijinsky* (1980), and was joint chairperson of the University of Indiana ballet department. His choreography included *Pas de Quatre* (1941), mounted by Irish National Ballet, 1975, and Dublin City Ballet, 1984. He received the Queen Elizabeth Coronation Award, 1954, the Peruvian Order of the Sun, 1959, and a knighthood, 1981. His publications include *Markova* (1953) and *Last Words* (1985). **Carolyn Swift**

Dolly's Brae (1849). Orangeism and Ribbonism emerged in the early 1800s as the most obvious manifestation of sectarian rivalries in rural Ulster and contributed as much to conflict as any social or economic deprivation. On 12 July 1849 local Orangemen made their way to the Earl of Roden's estate at Tollymore, Co. Down. They had been confronted en route by groups of RIBBONMEN and their supporters. On their return journey they were again met by local opposition at Dolly's Brae, near Castlewellan. A firework was hurled into their ranks by one of their opponents; the Orangemen responded by firing into the crowd. Reports of what happened next vary; but in the exchange of fire that took place about thirty Catholics were killed.

The underlying tensions are believed to have been fuelled by the anti-Catholicism that pervaded the popular evangelical Protestantism of the period and the resultant resurgence of Ribbonism. The Orangemen, however, saw the incident as evidence both of anti-Protestant aggression and of their ability to deal with such matters in an effective manner. The clashes at Dolly's Brae led directly to the introduction of the Party Processions Act the following year. **Roddy Hegarty**

Dolmen Press, founded as a small private press in 1951 by Liam Miller (1924–1987), an architect by training with an interest in literature and the theatre. He taught himself the craft of printing, aided by a disciplined sense of design and clear objectives: to make a positive and distinctive contribution to the revival of literary publishing. He began with modest chapbooks and volumes of verse, which drew both on established writers and on newcomers, such as THOMAS KINSELLA, RICHARD MURPHY, and JOHN MONTAGUE. In the 1960s he broadened his field to include prose works and those of non-Irish writers, his sights being set from the beginning on an international audience. He also commissioned distinguished artists, such as Ruth Brandt, Michael Biggs, and LOUIS LE BROCQUY, as illustrators, with Le Brocquy's design for Thomas Kinsella's translation of the *Táin* (1969) being perhaps Dolmen's outstanding achievement (see p. 1032). The limited edition was subsequently reissued in paperback and jointly published with Oxford University Press, with which Dolmen established a distribution relationship. His fascination with W. B. YEATS generated a distinguished series of *Yeats Papers*, with contributions by international scholars.

Miller took great pains with every aspect of book production—paper, binding, design, and imposition—with a particular concern for fine typography. In all these facets of publication he set standards that greatly influenced his publishing contemporaries. His books won many design awards, including a medal for his edition of *Holinshed's Irish Chronicle, 1577* (1979) at the Leipzig International Design Exhibition. The closure of the Dolmen printing works in Dublin in the 1970s had an unfavourable impact on the press's high standards, and all publication ceased on Miller's death in 1987. **Bernard Share**

Domhnach Airgid, a silver gilt shrine (NATIONAL MUSEUM OF IRELAND) composed of decorative elements dating from the seventh, fourteenth and fifteenth centuries. It originally contained relics of various SAINTS, but when these were lost, probably in the sixteenth century, a folded-up fragmentary ninth-century illuminated GOSPEL book in very poor condition (ROYAL IRISH ACADEMY) was substituted. [see BOOK SHRINES.] **William O'Sullivan**

Domhnach Airgid. *The Domhnach Airgid, an eighth or early ninth-century silver-gilt shrine; it was remodelled in the mid-fourteenth century. The lower left panel shows St Patrick delivering a book to St MacCairithinn, patron saint of Clones. [National Museum of Ireland]*

dominion status, a vague term attempting to reconcile British insistence that Ireland remain under the Crown and a member of the COMMONWEALTH with Irish demands for a fully independent state. During 1919–20 it was regarded by much liberal opinion as a possible means of settlement but seen by the British government as too near independence and by SINN FÉIN as a contradiction of the PROCLAMATION OF THE IRISH REPUBLIC (1916) and Declaration of Independence (1919). The military stalemate of the WAR OF INDEPENDENCE, the establishment of the Northern Ireland government and the intervention of dominion leaders raised the concept during the Anglo-Irish negotiations of July–December 1921. The ANGLO-IRISH TREATY explicitly granted independence largely on the same terms as that given to Canada. Many held, however, that Ireland's proximity to Britain and the legacy of Anglo-Irish relations made the idea impractical. The pro-Treaty party, notably KEVIN O'HIGGINS, regarded Commonwealth membership as reconciling British and Irish interests: Ireland played a constructive role in strengthening the powers of individual dominions as in the Statute of Westminster (1932). When DE VALERA's FIANNA FÁIL came to power in 1932 all but the most tenuous Commonwealth links were progressively severed; nominal membership ended with the declaration of the Republic in 1949. **Michael A. Hopkinson**

Don, Kaye (1893–1982), racing driver. Born in Dublin; he lived mostly in England. A former trials MOTORCYCLIST, he set lap records at the banked Brooklands track and won the 1928 Tourist Trophy at the Ards circuit near Belfast. He was British champion in 1928 and 1929 and also broke the world water speed record in 1930 before retiring from sport after a road accident in 1934. **Brendan Lynch**

Donaghadee Harbour, Co. Down, built between 1821 and 1836 under the direction of JOHN RENNIE. The harbour is formed by a south pier with four arms and a north pier separated by a channel from the shore. Mail packet vessels called at Donaghadee until 1867, when the service was transferred to Larne. **Ronald Cox**

Donaghy, John Lyle (1902–1949), poet and teacher. Born in Larne, Co. Antrim; educated at TCD. He published eight volumes of poetry, including *At Dawn above Aherlow* (1926), *Into the Light* (1934), and *Wilderness Sings* (1942), and verse drama. His poetry appeared in magazines in Ireland, England (*Criterion*), and France (*Transition*). He regarded his verse as 'integrally classical and aristocratic' and rejected the 'insincerities of the CELTIC TWILIGHT.' SAMUEL BECKETT praised his poem 'The Fort' as 'admirable objectless'. A poem dedicated to Donaghy by George Buchanan describes him as 'filled with Whitman energy.' He lived in Rathfarnham, Co. Dublin, and later near Glendalough, Co. Wicklow. **Sandra O'Connell**

Donegal, County (*Contae Dhún na nGall*)

Province:	ULSTER
County town:	Lifford
Area:	4,830 km^2 (1,864 sq. miles)
Population (2002):	137,383
Features:	Bluestack Mountains
	Derryveagh Mountains
	Lough Derg
	LOUGH SWILLY
	River Finn
	River Foyle
Of historical interest:	Doe Castle
	DONEGAL CASTLE
	Grianán of Aileach
Industry and products:	Cattle and sheep
	Fishery
	Hand-made tweed
	Knitwear
	Linen
	Tourism

Petula Martyn

County Donegal, the most north-westerly county in Ireland, for the most part separated from the rest of the Republic by its border with Northern Ireland. The modern county boundaries were established during the seventeenth century but follow the ancient division between Tír Chonaill (to the west) and UÍ NÉILL hegemony to the east. Co. Donegal combines great natural beauty with limited natural resources. Much of the mountainous interior consists of ancient Pre-Cambrian quartzites, granites, and sedimentary rocks, together with the more recent intrusive volcanics of the Derryveagh and Bluestack Mountains; younger, Carboniferous rocks occur around Donegal Bay. The topography hampers communications, especially in an east-west direction, and is a barrier to ECONOMIC DEVELOPMENT. Agricultural land is relatively limited; the best is on the Fanad peninsula and Inishowen and in the Finn and Foyle valleys. Social conditions led to unrestricted pre-famine population growth and consequently high famine EMIGRATION and mortality rates and pronounced population decline, social disruption, and economic stagnation thereafter.

By the 1960s the county was one of the most depressed in Ireland. Since then, TOURISM, regional grants from the EUROPEAN UNION and, more recently, the advent of footloose high-technology industries have combined to alleviate the decline, while Government GAELTACHT policies have helped maintain traditional cultural values. Aran Island (population 602 in 1996; 543 in 2002) is one of the most populous of Ireland's islands. **Lindsay Proudfoot**

Donegal (*Dún na nGall*), a town on the Eske estuary in Donegal Bay; population (2002) 3,723. Used by the VIKINGS as a sheltered anchorage, in the Middle Ages it was a stronghold of the O'Donnells, chiefs of Tír Chonaill. The first Red Hugh O'Donnell started the present castle and built the Franciscan friary in 1474; it was here that the writing of the ANNALS OF THE FOUR MASTERS was begun in 1632. The castle was subsequently remodelled c. 1563 and burnt by RED HUGH O'DONNELL (1571–1602) in 1595 to prevent its capture by the English. There are extensive remains of both buildings, and they are among the most important of their type in Ireland. In 1609–11 Donegal was listed for incorporation as a borough and was granted to Sir Basil Brooke, who laid out the Diamond (central square) and rebuilt and extended the CASTLE, 1616. Thereafter Donegal grew little. Intended improvements in the early nineteenth century by its then proprietor, the Earl of Arran, never materialised, and in 1846 it was described as 'a mere village', an assessment that is not inappropriate today. **Lindsay Proudfoot**

Donegal Castle, a sixteenth-century TOWER-HOUSE built by the O'Donnells that was much altered in the seventeenth century by Sir Basil Brooke, with an early seventeenth-century gable-fronted fortified house attached. It is enclosed by a fifteenth-century bawn wall rebuilt in the seventeenth century. Mullioned and transomed windows have been inserted in the tower-house to match the three-storey house. There is finely carved stonework in the doorway of the house and a magnificent ornate Jacobean fireplace in the tower-house. **David Sweetman**

Donegal fiddle tradition, one of a limited number of local traditional music styles that have survived intact through aural transmission between generations of performers. Though it is commonly thought of as the style of Co. Donegal, it is really an amalgamation of more localised styles that developed within rural communities defined by natural watersheds and market centres. The common features among these local styles are an attacking sound based on staccato bowing, with some Scottish influences: these include the use of *double stops* (the simultaneous bowing of two strings, one for the melody, the other a drone) to imitate pipe drones, and playing in octaves in group performances. It is true that each local style demonstrates exceptions to these characteristics. The use of a sharpened seventh and to a lesser extent fourths, a technique once more common in Irish FIDDLE music, remains strong, particularly in the Teileann area and is a feature of the playing of the late Con Cassidy, Frank Cassidy, and Jimmy Lyons (see p. 559). The music originated as music for dancing, though performance is now almost entirely for listening, because of the decline in traditional dancing. The REEL is the most common metre, with double JIGS, single jigs, HORNPIPES, WALTZES, and MAZURKAS also common; less common are POLKAS and MARCHES. The prevalence of strathspeys and highlands—a local variant of strathspeys, most of which derive from the Scottish tradition—are almost unique to the Donegal tradition. [see DOHERTY, JOHN.] **Caoimhín Mac Aoidh**

Donegal tweed. Clothing in Ireland has traditionally been made from LINEN and wool. There were primarily two types of wool: flannel, which has a tabby weave and was fine enough for underwear and SHIRTS, and a rougher and coarser material, formerly called frieze but now known to us as tweed. This was used to produce an array of garments, including skirts, trousers, jackets, and coats. Until the end of the nineteenth century, lengths of woollen cloth woven by local weavers were produced for domestic markets. The quality of the material varied greatly; and though Irish tweed had become a fashionable fabric by the middle of the nineteenth century, it was not until the end of the century that any effort was made to introduce quality control in its manufacture.

The Donegal Industrial Fund, together with the CONGESTED DISTRICTS BOARD, helped to improve both the technical teaching and the production quality of Donegal tweed in the last two decades of the nineteenth century. By the 1930s, with the aid of markets provided by the Irish Homespun Society and the COUNTRY SHOP in Dublin, Donegal tweed was a very saleable commodity. Local business people, such as James Molloy of Ardara and the Magee family of Donegal, established the identity of the industry. The labels of Studio Donegal and (somewhat controversially for a Co. Donegal product) Connemara Fabrics were available for national and export markets. Donegal tweed, which had begun as a so-called cottage industry in the nineteenth century, was almost completely operated by power looms by the 1970s. [see CLOTHING, TRADITIONAL.] **Anne O'Dowd**

Doneraile conspiracy (1829). In response to WHITEBOY activity in the area around Doneraile, Co. Cork, twenty-one men were arrested and charged with conspiracy to murder local LANDLORDS. After four defendants were found guilty and sentenced to death, friends of the others summoned DANIEL O'CONNELL to act as counsel on their behalf. His courtroom performance became one of the most celebrated of his career: he won acquittal or dismissal for his clients, gained commuted sentences for those already convicted, and earned public plaudits from the judges. PATRICK SHEEHAN immortalised the case in his novel *Glenanaar* (1905). **Gary Owens**

Donleavy, J. P. [James Patrick] (1926–), novelist. Born in New York; educated at TCD. After the SECOND WORLD WAR he frequented many of the same bohemian establishments as BRENDAN BEHAN and ANTHONY CRONIN. He is best known for his clever Dublin comedy *The Ginger Man* (1955); his other works include *A Singular Man* (1964), *The Beastly Beatitudes of Balthazar B* (1968), *The Destinies of Darcy Dancer, Gentleman* (1977), *Schultz* (1980), *Leila* (1983), and *Are You Listening Rabbi Löw* (1987), as well as the play *Fairy Tales of New York* (1960) and his autobiography, *A History of the Ginger Man* (1994). He became an Irish citizen in 1967. **Joley Wood**

Donn, the dark or brown one, god of the dead in Irish MYTHOLOGY. He is said to dwell in Teach Doinn (the house of Donn), off the south-west coast. Not much material is available about him in the early literature, in which he appears to be a solitary, somewhat distant god, but he has survived and is well documented in oral tradition. In the earlier literature he is associated with the darker side of the OTHERWORLD, but in later tradition he assumes a more benevolent role and is seen to be a kind god, though one still to be feared. Legends and traditions associated with Donn have a close affinity with those of the Norse god Odin. **Ríonach uí Ógáin**

Donnellan, Luke (1878–1952), priest and music collector. Born in Creggan, Co. Armagh; ordained in 1902. While ministering in Drumintee, Co. Armagh, 1903–10, and in Crossmaglen, Co. Armagh, 1910–37, he recorded some of the last local Irish-speakers on Ediphone cylinders; the recordings amount to some 150 songs. Some fragmentary sound recordings have survived and are now in the Donnellan Collection in the Department of Irish Folklore, UCD. All the cylinder recordings have been transcribed by SÉAMUS ENNIS in staff notation. Also in staff notation, in Donnellan's own hand,

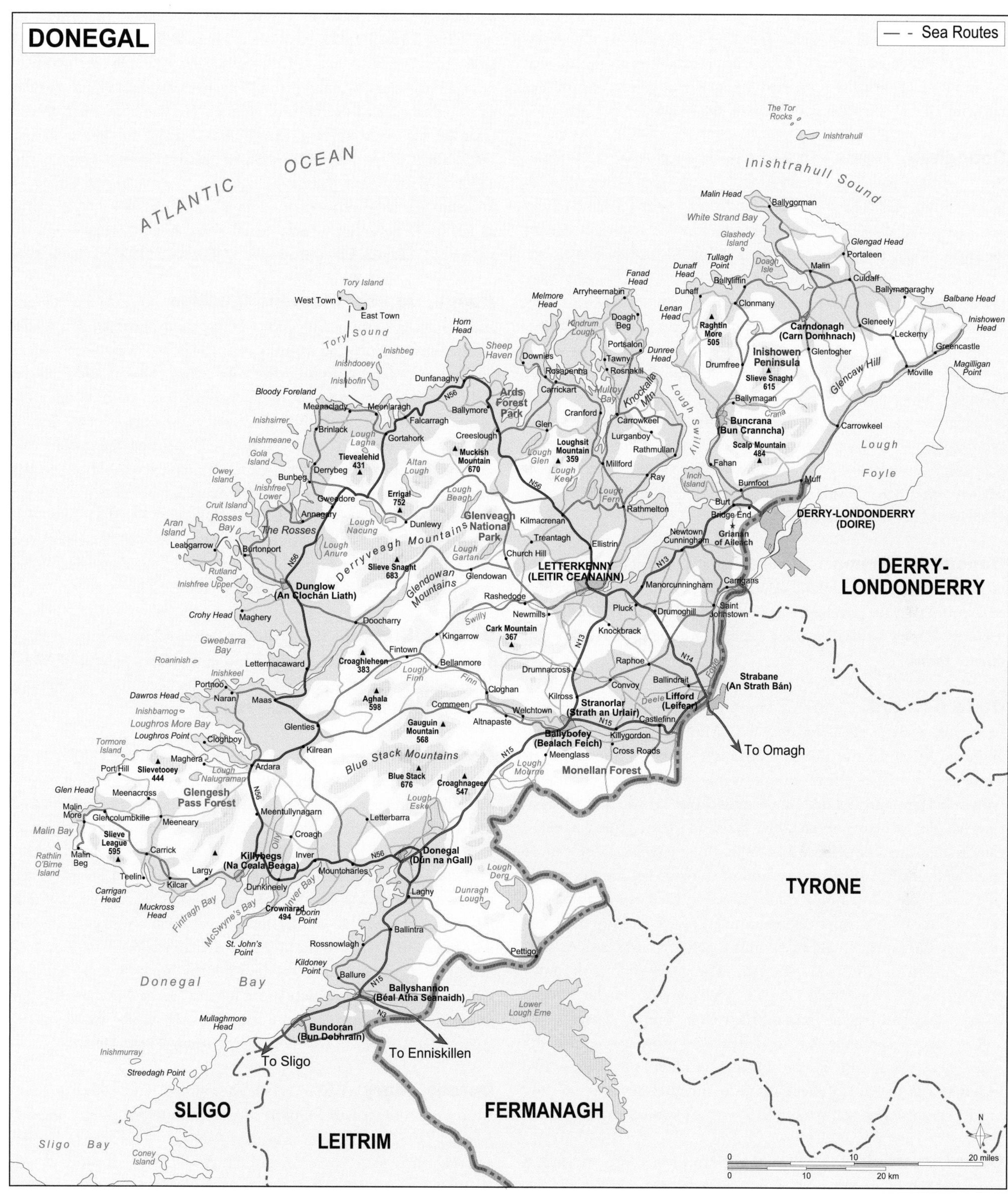

are more than 300 dance tunes, mainly REELS, HORNPIPES, and MARCHES, collected in south Armagh, demonstrating a strong connection with Scottish dance music. Much of Donnellan's collected song material was published in 2002; most of his other manuscript collection of local poetry and folklore is in ST PATRICK'S COLLEGE, Maynooth. **Pádraigín Ní Uallacháin**

Donnelly, Charles (1914–1937), poet and political activist. Born near Dungannon, Co. Tyrone; educated by the CHRISTIAN BROTHERS and, briefly, at UCD. A life of left-wing agitation in Dublin and London was ended, aged twenty-three, in battle with the republican forces in Spain, where he wrote his best poems, 'The Tolerance of Crows' and 'Heroic Heart'. [see SPANISH CIVIL WAR.] **Terence Brown**

Donnelly, Dan (died 1820), pugilist. Born in Dublin. His open-air bare-knuckle prize-fights attracted crowds of up to 40,000 in Ireland and Britain. 'Dan Donnelly's Hollow' at the CURRAGH, Co. Kildare, was the scene of his 1814 victory against Tom Hall and again in 1815 his bout with the English prize-fighter George Cooper, which he won in eleven rounds. The site is marked by an obelisk. In 1819 outside London he fought thirty-two rounds against another English pugilist, Tom Oliver. A prodigious appetite for ALCOHOL and a disregard for his health undermined his superb constitution. Donnelly's petrified right arm is preserved in the Hideout Bar in Kilcullen, Co. Kildare. **Brian Lalor**

Donoghue, Denis (1928–), university professor and critic. Born in Tullow, Co. Carlow, but spent his early years at Warrenpoint, Co. Down, where his father was a sergeant in the RUC; educated at UCD, where, after a brief period as music critic of the IRISH TIMES, he became a lecturer in English and then professor of Modern English and American literature, 1967–80, and later Henry James professor of English and American letters at New York University in 1980. Donoghue's reputation as a critic rests on his ability to place Irish literature in a non-parochial relation to world literature. He reads Irish subjects not because they are Irish but because they evoke his response to his principal interest, the nature and exercise of the poetic imagination. His most significant publications are *The Ordinary Universe* (1968), *Thieves of Fire* (1974), *The Sovereign Ghost* (1976), *Ferocious Alphabets* (1981), *The Arts Without Mystery* (the BBC Reith Lectures, 1983), *We Irish* (1986), and *Warrenpoint* (1990). **Richard Pine**

Donoghue, Emma (1969–), novelist, playwright, and short-story writer. Born in Dublin; educated at UCD and the University of Cambridge. Her novels *Stir Fry* (1994) and *Hood* (1995) broke new ground in Irish writing in their explicit treatment of LESBIANISM. **Terence Brown**

Donore Hoard, a hoard of door furniture found (1985) on the banks of a river at Moynalty, Co. Meath, consisting of two engraved metal discs of tinned bronze just over 130 mm (5 in.) in diameter, a similar square plaque, some portions of decorative frames, a large and elaborately decorated cast bronze animal-head ring-handle, and parts of what may be two further, plainer handles. One frame, the animal-head handle and one engraved disc can be assembled to form an insular version of the lion-headed door-pulls of classical antiquity, a type reinterpreted in medieval Europe and used commonly on church doors. The art of the Donore objects is of a very high quality, and in its animal patterns and trumpet-and-spiral combinations it stands especially close to the style of the TARA BROOCH and LINDISFARNE Gospels. The patterns on the tinned-bronze discs and plaque are constructed on compass-drawn grids, and in layout and approach to design they closely resemble the work of MANUSCRIPT illuminators. It is likely on comparative grounds that the pieces were made in the later seventh or early eighth century. [see MEDIEVAL METALWORK.] **Michael Ryan**

Donovan, Jack (1934–), painter. Born in Limerick; studied at Limerick School of Art and Design. He works in two distinct styles. As a portrait painter he works in a loose, realist style, which expresses the psychology of the sitter; he has also done many self-portraits. He also paints high-keyed, rather darkly humorous, and surreal figurative subjects, which usually include doll-like, sometimes dismembered female nudes, of which there is a collection in Limerick City Art Gallery. **Suzanne McNab**

Donovan, Katie (1962–), poet. Born in Dublin; educated at TCD and the University of California. She has published *Watermelon Man* (1993) and *Entering the Mare* (1997), which engage with erotic and mythic themes in warmly celebratory terms. **Terence Brown**

Donovan, William J. 'Wild Bill' (1883–1959), founder of the Central Intelligence Agency. Born in Buffalo, New York, of Irish extraction; educated at Columbia University. He practised LAW until 1916, when he joined the National Guard, later the regular army, advancing to the rank of colonel. He was appointed district attorney for western New York, 1922, and held office in the Department of Justice, 1924–9. He resumed his legal practice in the 1930s. On President Roosevelt's urging he created the Office of Strategic Services, a covert-operations arm of the War Department; in 1947 it became the Central Intelligence Agency, with Donovan at its head. He was US ambassador to Thailand, 1953–4. **David Kiely**

Dooge, James Clement Ignatius (1922–), hydrologist and politician. Born in England to Irish parents; graduated in mathematics and engineering from UCD in 1942. His early employment was in hydrometry with the OFFICE OF PUBLIC WORKS and then the ESB. After two years at the University of Iowa he held appointments as professor and head of engineering departments, first in UCC and, from 1970 to 1984, in UCD. During these years and subsequently in retirement he made immense contributions to the study of hydrology. He had a distinguished political career as a senator and was Minister for Foreign Affairs, 1981–2. He served as president of the ROYAL IRISH ACADEMY, 1987–90, and received many international awards for his work in hydrology and global CLIMATE studies. **Christopher Moriarty**

Doolan, Bridget (1932–1997), pianist and administrator. Born Waterford; studied UCC; taught piano at the Cork School of Music 1956–92 (director 1973–80) where she influenced many generations of young Irish musicians. **Richard Pine**

Doran, Johnny and Felix Doran, pipers. Johnny (1908–1950), born in Rathnew, Co. Wicklow, into a family of travelling pipers, made his living playing at FAIRS, races , and sports gatherings around the country as well as from horse-trading. His very fluid style, with variation of melody and regulator rhythm, influenced WILLIE CLANCY and PADDY KEENAN. A recording made in 1947 by KEVIN DANAHER of the IRISH FOLKLORE COMMISSION was later released as *The Bunch of Keys*. He was fatally injured when a wall collapsed on his caravan in 1948. His brother Felix Doran (c. 1915–1972), a successful businessman, had a less fluid but rhythmically more exciting style, with staccato ornamentation; his son Michael Doran and son-in-law John Rooney continue the style. He can be heard on the record *The Last of the Travelling Pipers*. **Jimmy O'Brien Moran**

Dorcey, Mary (1950–), poet, short-story writer, and novelist. Born and educated in Dublin. Her collections of poetry include *Kindling* (1982), *Moving into the Space Cleared by Our Mothers* (1991), and *The River that Carries Me* (1995). A collection of short stories, *A Noise from the Woodshed*, was published in 1989 and her novel *Biography of Desire* in 1997. **Terence Brown**

Dorgan, Theo (1953–), poet and broadcaster. Born in Cork; educated at UCC. He served as director of POETRY IRELAND (1989–2000). His poetry, marked by assured yet moving cerebration, especially on personal themes, has been collected in *The Ordinary House of Love* (1991), *Rosa Mundi* (1995), and *Sappho's Daughter* (1998). He is a member of AOSDÁNA. **Terence Brown**

Douai, a town in northern France, originally part of the Low Countries and an English recusant colony. The Irish connection came with the establishment of an IRISH COLLEGE in 1594 by Father Christopher Cusack of Co. Meath. As numbers grew, Douai became the mother house of a group of Jesuit colleges, including Antwerp, Tournai, and Lille. The object of the college was to produce an educated Catholic clergy who would prevent the spread of the REFORMATION in Ireland. It was predominantly OLD ENGLISH and, regarded as a model seminary, had a strong formative influence on the COUNTER-REFORMATION, particularly in Munster and Leinster. Partly financed by Spain, the college mainly depended on donations from the Irish military and merchant communities in the Spanish Netherlands and later France. It also took in lay students. Douai came under French rule in 1667, and this cluster of IRISH COLLEGES did not survive the FRENCH REVOLUTION. **Gráinne Henry**

Douglas, Barry (1960–), pianist. Born in Belfast; educated in Belfast and at the Royal College of Music, London, where he studied with Maria Curcio. He has won many international prizes, including Silver Medal in the 1983 Arthur Rubinstein Competition (Israel) and first prize in the Moscow Tchaikovsky Competition in 1986. He has enjoyed a major international career, touring extensively throughout Europe, the United States, and Japan, appearing as soloist with the world's most renowned orchestras. His recordings include the complete works of Tchaikovsky for piano and orchestra. **Ite O'Donovan**

Douglas, Sholto, Lord Douglas of Kirtleside (1893–1969), aviator. In 1917 he was detailed to survey possible aerodrome sites for training. He selected sites at the Curragh, Co. Kildare, Baldonnel, Co. Dublin, Tallaght, Co. Dublin, Collinstown (later Dublin Airport), Gormanston, Co. Meath, Fermoy, Co. Cork, Aldergrove (later Belfast International Airport), Oranmore, Co. Galway, and other minor landing strips. Training aerodromes at these sites became operational, but the Armistice of November 1918 caused them to be little used thereafter until the WAR OF INDEPENDENCE. **Donal MacCarron**

Douglas Hyde Summer School of Traditional Irish Music and Dance, established in 1996 at Ballaghaderreen,

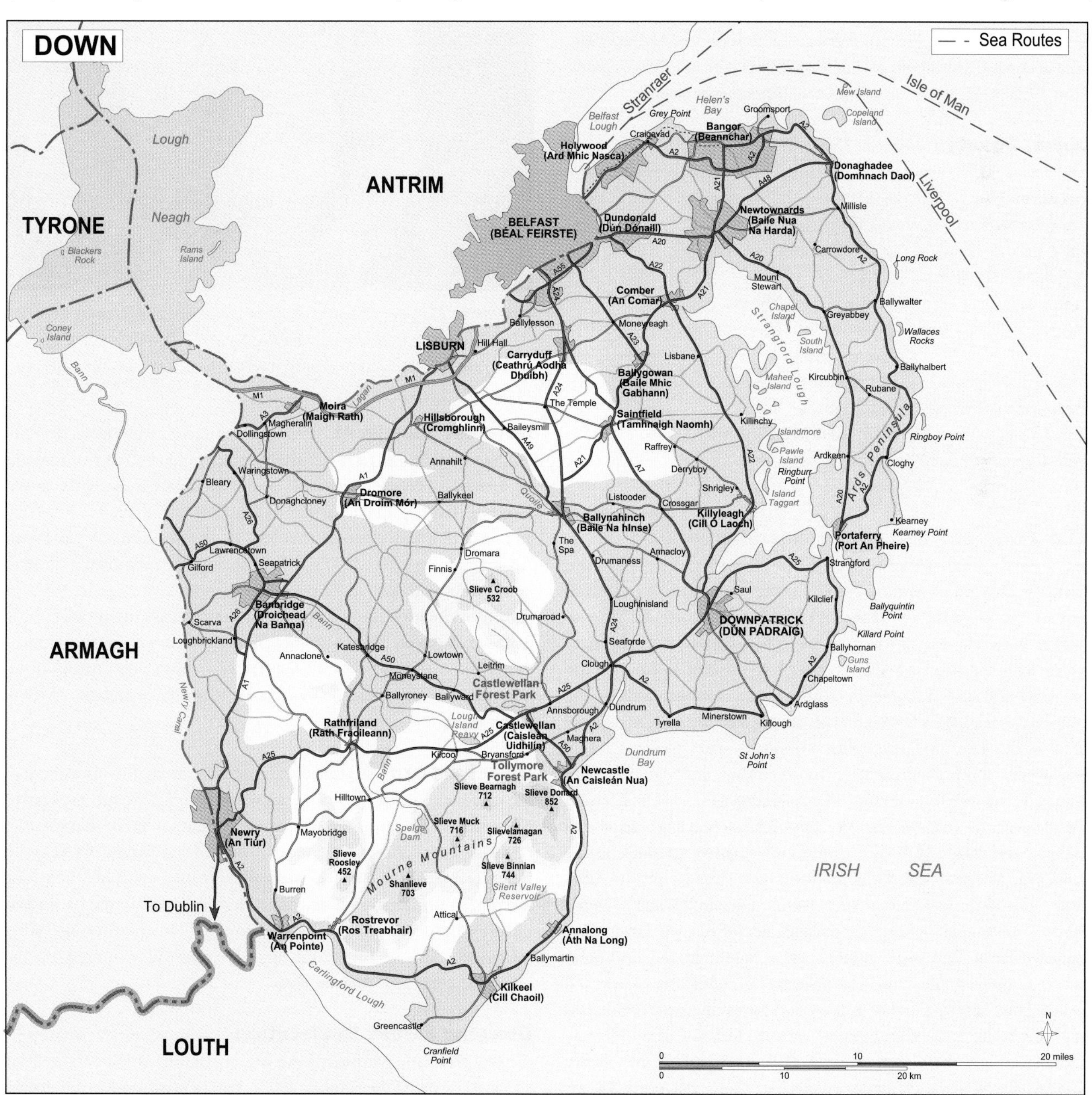

Co. Roscommon, to pass on musical skills using largely local, but nationally known, expertise. The object is to stem EMIGRATION by reinvesting the area with a sense of its strong musical legacy and its place in the continuity of culture, as defined by HYDE and the GAELIC LEAGUE. **Fintan Vallely**

Dowden, Edward (1843–1913), poet and literary scholar. Born in Cork. He is best known for his editions of Shakespeare's plays and his critical study *Shakespere: His Mind and Art* (1875). In 1867 he was appointed to the chair of English literature in TCD, where he pursued the characteristic life of the Irish Victorian man of letters. His critical essays included studies of Shelley and George Eliot. His political leanings were towards UNIONISM and opposition to HOME RULE; he was nonetheless insistently cosmopolitan in his literary outlook, championing Walt Whitman and criticising what he saw as the provincialism of YEATS and the early LITERARY REVIVAL. **Eve Patten**

Dowling, Joe (1948–), theatre manager, director, and actor. Born in Dublin; educated at UCD. He began acting at the ABBEY THEATRE, where he rose rapidly through the ranks to become its youngest artistic director, 1978–85. He founded the Gaiety School of Acting, 1986, later becoming artistic director of the Guthrie Theatre, Minneapolis, from 1993. [see GUTHRIE, SIR TYRONE.] **Christopher Morash**

Down, County (*Contae an Dúin*)

Province:	ULSTER
County town:	DOWNPATRICK
Area:	2,466 km^2 (953 sq. miles)
Population (1991)*:	63,828
Features:	MOURNE MOUNTAINS
	River BANN
	Slieve Croob
	STRANGFORD LOUGH
Of historical interest:	Grey Abbey
	Nendrum Monastic Site
Industry and products:	Dairy farming
	LINEN

Petula Martyn

* last year of census by county, [see NORTHERN IRELAND.]

County Down, a maritime county in the north-east of Ireland, is part of the province of Ulster and of modern Northern Ireland. Archaeologically and historically its cultural links have been as much with south-west Scotland as with the rest of Ireland. In the late sixteenth and seventeenth centuries the northern half of the county was settled by lowland Scots in advance of the PLANTATION OF ULSTER. The modern county boundaries date from the 1570s but in the south incorporate a much earlier political boundary between the twelfth-century CELTIC kingdoms of Uí Eachach Cobha and the Ind Airthir. The physical landscape is varied and includes the 760 m (2,500-ft) granitic MOURNE MOUNTAINS in the south, the Slieve Croob Hills, STRANGFORD LOUGH and the ARDS PENINSULA in the east and the DRUMLIN country in the north. Much of south and mid-Down remains a landscape of pastoral agriculture, scattered farms, and small towns, such as Saintfield and Dromore, but it is increasingly closely connected to Belfast for work and leisure. The fishing ports of Kilkeel and Annalong, and the resorts of Newcastle and Warrenpoint at the foot of the Mourne Mountains, add their own sense of place to a part of the county that has always been culturally distinctive. Along the north Down coast from Bangor to Holywood, and in the Lagan valley as far as Lisburn and beyond, extensive suburbanisation has occurred, making these districts in effect part of the greater Belfast urban area. **Lindsay Proudfoot**

Downes. *Margaret Downes, chartered accountant and business woman. The first woman to be appointed a director of the Bank of Ireland in 1986, she held the post of deputy governor from 1993 to 1995. [Bank of Ireland]*

Downes, Margaret (1934–), chartered accountant. Born in Dublin; educated at UCD and the Institute of Chartered Accountants in Ireland. Having practised as an accountant in Dublin and London, she became a partner in Coopers and Lybrand, 1964–84, and in 1983 was elected president of the Institute of Chartered Accountants in Ireland. The first woman to be appointed a director of the Bank of Ireland, she became deputy governor in 1993. A patron of the arts, she is a trustee of the CHESTER BEATTY LIBRARY and the Douglas Hyde Gallery and chairwoman of the DUBLIN INTERNATIONAL PIANO COMPETITION. She was awarded an honorary doctorate by the National University of Ireland in 1988. **Alison Walsh**

Downhill harp (also called the GUINNESS harp), the instrument of the celebrated harper Denis Hempson (1695–1807), the last known player to use the traditional fingernail technique. It has thirty strings of brass wire and was made in 1702 by Cormac O'Kelly of Ballinscreen, Co. Derry. It is simply ornamented and has a long inscription on the soundbox. After Hempson's death the harp came into the possession of the Bruce family of Downhill House; after several changes of ownership it was eventually acquired by the Guinness company. **Gráinne Yeats**

Downing Street Declaration (1993), a joint declaration by the British Prime Minister, John Major, and the Taoiseach, ALBERT REYNOLDS, on 15 December 1993. An essential prerequisite to the achievement of the IRA and loyalist ceasefires of 1994, it owed much to the rapport between the two prime ministers, who had been in contact on a peace strategy since February 1992, and was intended as a response to the Hume-Adams initiative and what appeared to be a significant shift by SINN FÉIN towards a peace policy. The two prime ministers pledged themselves 'to foster agreement and reconciliation, leading to a new political framework founded on consent' and encompassing arrangements within Northern Ireland, for the whole of Ireland, and between Britain and Ireland. The British government affirmed that it had 'no selfish strategic or economic interest in Northern Ireland', declaring that self-determination—a central issue for republicans—was 'for the people of the island of Ireland alone, by agreement between the two parts ...' The Irish Government reiterated its commitment to the principle of consent and undertook to seek to amend the definition of the national territory in the CONSTITUTION OF IRELAND as part of a general settlement. Finally, the governments declared that if Sinn Féin accepted its terms and violence ended permanently, it could enter political dialogue on the way ahead.

The declaration was broadly welcomed by the SDLP and ULSTER UNIONIST PARTY (which was consulted by Major), but Sinn Féin, while acknowledging its significance, never endorsed it. **Eamon Phoenix**

Downpatrick (*Dún Pádraig*), Co. Down, a town occupying a DRUMLIN site to the south of the (now-drained) Quoile marshes, 10 km (6 miles) from STRANGFORD LOUGH and 40 km (25 miles) south of Belfast; population (1991) 10,113. Tradition has it that St PATRICK founded a church here and that he is buried in Downpatrick. The town's origins lie in the foundation of a MONASTERY on the site of the present cathedral some time before the eighth century and the construction of a defensive enclosure a little to the north soon after, probably by the local Dál Fiatach. JOHN DE COURCY annexed the site in 1177 and founded a Benedictine abbey on Cathedral Hill. During the Middle Ages the town prospered as a local market centre for Lecale but went into decline during the wars of the sixteenth century, beginning to recover only under the patronage of the Cromwell family after 1603 and, more particularly, under the Southwells between 1703 and 1823. During this period many of the town's finest surviving buildings were constructed, including the Southwell Charity (1733), the old jail (1796), and the CHURCH OF IRELAND cathedral, reopened in 1818, having lain derelict since it was burnt in 1538. The later nineteenth century saw further decline as the town's marketing role was lost to Belfast, connected by rail in 1858. The population fell to 2,993 in 1901, recovering only slowly until the late 1960s, when the town became an overspill centre for Belfast and extensive public housing was built. The creation of jobs did not keep pace, however, and the town remains reliant for EMPLOYMENT on a limited range of public services. **Lindsay Proudfoot**

Down Survey, begun as an apportioning of several million acres of Irish land by the English government to soldiers who had been

Downing Street Declaration. *In a public house in the Shankill Road, Belfast, December 1993, surrounded by loyalist symbols—the Union Jack, Queen Elizabeth II, and a banner of Linfield Football Club—customers watch the British Prime Minister, John Major, addressing the House of Commons on the Downing Street Declaration. [Pacemaker]*

employed in suppressing the 1641 REBELLION. With the coming of peace this task was assigned to the Surveyor-General of Ireland, Benjamin Worsley, but in December 1654 it was transferred to an outsider, WILLIAM PETTY, who had undertaken to survey all the estates in question by piecework within thirteen months. The distinctive epithet 'down' is generally thought to indicate that Petty's surveys were laid down on large-scale maps instead of being expressed entirely in verbal and numerical form, like the previous 'Civil Survey'. Technically, his method of boundary traversing with chain and compass was not new; its originality lay in dividing the work among a large and relatively unskilled labour force. The success of Petty's system led to his appointment in 1656 to survey the lands due to 'adventurers' who had helped to finance the English army, and this operation, completed in 1659, is usually classed as part of the Down Survey.

Thanks to Petty, the Cromwellian and RESTORATION land settlements proceeded with remarkable efficiency. His surveys also influenced methods of private estate mapping throughout the country for more than a century and on a smaller scale provided much of the basis for a famous county atlas, Petty's *Hiberniae Delineatio* (1685), in which the map of Ireland appears for the first time as recognisably modern. [see CARTOGRAPHY.] **J. H. Andrews**

Dowris Hoard, the largest collection of prehistoric bronzes ever discovered in Ireland, comprising some 200 objects found in the 1820s in reclaimed bogland near Birr, Co. Offaly. Among the artefacts represented are spearheads, swords, chapes, horns, hollow-cast pendants, socketed axeheads, gouges and hammers, knives, razors, TRUMPETS, buckets, and cauldrons. Though labelled a 'hoard', this large collection of bronzes may have accumulated over time, possibly through votive deposition at a sacred pool or lake. The find is clear evidence of the wealth of Late BRONZE AGE societies between 1000 and 600 BC and the technical accomplishment of their metal workshops. **William O'Brien**

Doyle, Colman (1932–), photographer. Born in Dalkey, Co. Dublin; trained with Norman Ashe. He worked with the IRISH PRESS from 1951–95, during which time he won numerous photographic awards, including the silver and bronze medals at the New York World's Fair, and he was a regular contributor at the Hague World Press photo exhibition. The 'TROUBLES' in Northern Ireland helped to establish his name; his work could also be seen in *Paris Match*. His first book was *The People of Ireland* (1971). His pictures are a record of an Ireland before the era of the CELTIC TIGER. His imagery recognised the vitality of people and made a major contribution towards a greater appreciation of photo-journalism in Ireland (see p. 1097). **John Minihan**

Doyle, James (Jimmy) (1939–), hurler. Born in Thurles, Co. Tipperary. He came to prominence as a precocious fifteen-year-old with the Tipperary minors and won three All-Ireland championships in that grade before graduating to senior ranks. He won six All-Ireland senior championships with Tipperary between 1958 and 1971. He played for the seniors for the first time as a goalkeeper and ended his career in that position, but his scoring feats over a decade and a half made him a legend in the game. His range of skills, wrist work, and unerring accuracy made him one of the most celebrated players of his time. **Donal Keenan**

Doyle, João Milly (fl. nineteenth century), pioneer of steamship power. Having settled in Portugal in the years immediately following the Napoleonic wars, he became the pioneer of steamship navigation in Portugal. He successfully accomplished the first voyage in a steamship from north to south of the Bay of Biscay. His vision of the great possibilities of steamships was far ahead of his time and was presented in detail in 1824 to João VI of Portugal. His proposal to establish a steam navigation company in Lisbon that would provide a regular mail and passenger service connecting the main ports of northern Europe with those of the Mediterranean was considered too ambitious for the Portuguese government, which was on the verge of civil war. However, his idea inspired far-seeing steamship-owners in various parts of Europe and was eventually put largely into operation by one of the biggest British steamship companies, the Peninsular and Oriental Steamship Company (P&O Line). He ran Portugal's first steamship passenger service between Lisbon and Porto. **John de Courcy Ireland**

Doyle, James Warren 'JKL' (1786–1834), bishop. Born in New Ross, Co. Wexford, into a prosperous farming family; educated at the Augustinian seminary, New Ross, and University of Coimbra, Portugal. Bishop of Kildare and Leighlin, 1819, he was a supporter of DANIEL O'CONNELL and a skilled controversialist. He signed his pamphlets JKL (James of Kildare and Leighlin). Widely respected for his intellect and personality, he testified before parliamentary committees in London on three occasions and was one of the leading Gallican bishops in the pre-famine church. **Fergal Tobin**

Doyle, John (1930–), hurler. Born in Holycross, Co. Tipperary. Along with another legend of the game, CHRISTY RING, he holds the record of eight all-Ireland senior HURLING medals; he was just nineteen when he won the first in 1949. One of the game's early stars, he was part of a full-back line known as 'Hell's Kitchen'; he was a tough defender who was also blessed with wonderful skills. In his nineteen years playing for Tipperary he never missed a championship game. **Donal Keenan**

Doyle, Joseph (1891–1974), botanist. Born in Glasgow; educated at UCD. He joined the staff of the biology department at University College, Dublin, in 1913, becoming professor of botany in 1924. He established a separate botany department and developed his research on embryology and on the reproductive biology of the conifers and related plants. His survey of how pollination occurs in conifers, published in 1945, is still the definitive text on the subject. He was a recipient of the BOYLE MEDAL of the RDS in 1942. He was a lifelong member of the RDS, serving on many committees and as vice-president, 1968–74. **Donal Synnott**

Doyle, Lynn C., pseudonym of Leslie Montgomery (1873–1961), humorous writer. Born in Co. Down; earned his livelihood as a banker. As a writer he was a humorist to the core, among the best of Ireland's humorous writers; his pseudonym—'linseed oil'—is a pun on what humour can do to ease life's frictions. In a writing career that spanned thirty-nine years he produced a substantial body of comic prose (essays and stories) as well as poetry and drama, together with the autobiographical *An Ulster Childhood* (1921). His work is fresh, gentle, and rooted in its place and time. **Sam Burnside**

Doyle, Michael (Mick) (1940–), rugby footballer. Born in Castleisland, Co. Kerry. He scored a try on his debut against France at Lansdowne Road, and between 1965 and 1968 he won twenty caps. He played in the first Test, at Pretoria in South Africa, for the 1968 British Lions team. After a successful period as Leinster coach, he was national coach from 1984/5 to 1986/7, guiding the team to a Triple Crown triumph in 1985. His autobiography, *Doyler* (1991) was a bestseller. **Karl Johnston**

Doyle, Peter and Mary, architects. Peter Doyle (1936–1995) was born in Dublin; educated at UCD and Illinois Institute of Technology. He worked in the office of Ludwig Mies van der Rohe, Chicago, 1964–6, and taught at DIT and UCD. Mary Doyle (1936–) was born in Cork; educated at UCD. She worked in Boston, 1959–62. Both subsequently worked with MICHAEL SCOTT and Partners, Dublin; they established their joint practice in Dublin, 1973. The Community School, Birr, Co. Offaly, with its concrete portal frame, was awarded the Triennial Gold Medal of the RIAI, 1989. They designed houses in Cos. Dublin and Wicklow, community schools in Firhouse, Co. Dublin, and Cashel, Co. Tipperary, the National College of Art and Design, Thomas Street, Dublin (1986–98, a converted distillery), the Women's Aid hostel, Rathmines, Dublin, and the visitors' centre at Valentia Island, Co. Kerry. **Raymund Ryan**

Doyle, Richard (Dicky) (1824–1883), artist. Born in London, son of the caricaturist John Doyle (known as HB), and lived there, having little contact with Ireland; taught by his father, a product of the DUBLIN SOCIETY Schools. He was a fine watercolourist, famous for his FAIRY subjects, including *The Triumphal Entry* and *The Fairy Pageant* (now in the NATIONAL GALLERY OF IRELAND). He is best remembered for his cover for *Punch*, which was used for more than a hundred years. **Anne Crookshank**

Doyle, Roddy (1958–), writer. He worked as a teacher in Dublin before becoming a full-time writer in 1993. His first novel, *The Commitments* (1989), follows the fortunes of working-class musicians who interpret their social marginality through black soul music (see p. 198). *The Snapper* (1990) and *The Van* (1991) continued to explore the humour and tragedies of working-class life. *Paddy Clarke Ha Ha Ha* (1993), for which he won the Booker Prize, shifted Doyle's focus to childhood impressions of social breakdown, while *The Woman Who Walked into Doors* (1997) dealt with domestic violence. *A Star Called Henry* (1999) broke new ground for Doyle in featuring a historical setting, the WAR OF INDEPENDENCE. **John Brannigan**

Doyle, Roger (1949–), composer. Born in Dublin, studied at the RIAM, Utrecht, Salzburg, and Helsinki. He specialises in electro-acoustic works, his most extensive and ambitious work to date being the *Babel Project*, a multi-CD integration of live and electronic music and dance, and the scores for BOB QUINN's television drama 'Budawanny' and Steven Berkoff's production of *Salome* at the Dublin GATE THEATRE. **Richard Pine**

Dracula (1897), a novel by BRAM STOKER. Part of a more general late nineteenth-century vogue for invasion stories, Stoker's supernatural thriller is written in the form of a series of diary entries, letters and newspaper articles that describe the ultimately unsuccessful efforts of the Transylvanian vampire Count Dracula to establish his dominion in England. Its eroticised vampirism helped to make it a modern myth, the basis of countless stage, screen, and television adaptations, including the first, F. W. Murnau's *Nosferatu* (1922). The novel itself has become the object of critical attention in recent years, largely as a compendium of *fin-de-siècle* fears and anxieties. **Nicholas Daly**

Drama League of Ireland. Formerly the Amateur Drama League of Ireland, the league co-ordinates the activities of approximately 500 AMATEUR AND COMMUNITY THEATRE companies, centred on the competitive All-Ireland Drama Festival, held annually in Athlone since 1953. Every year amateur drama companies play to combined audiences of half a million. **Christopher Morash**

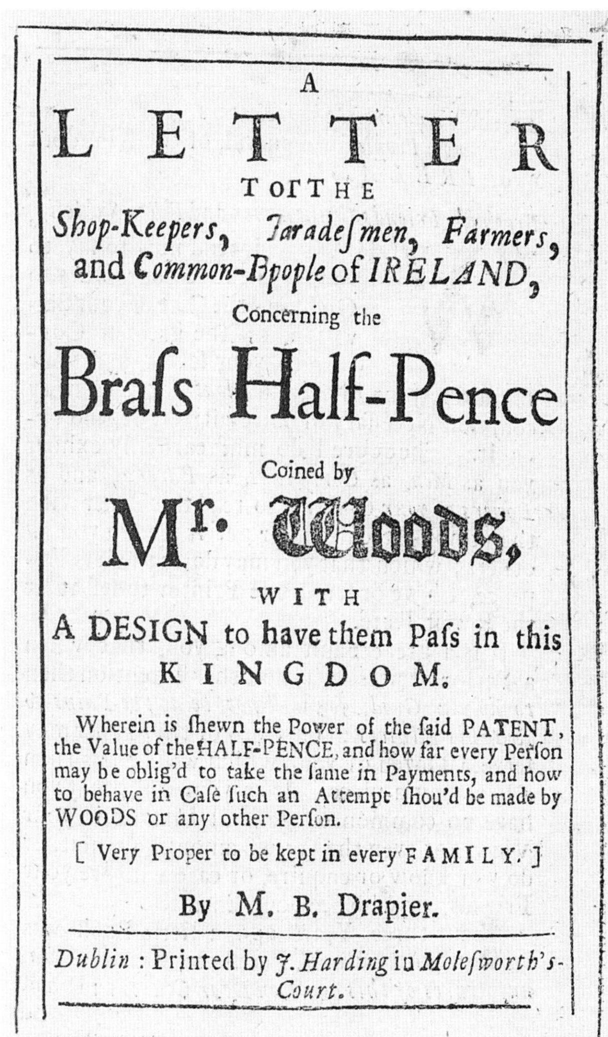

A LETTER TO THE Shop-Keepers, Tradesmen, Farmers, and Common-People of IRELAND, Concerning the Brass Half-Pence Coined by Mr. Woods, WITH A DESIGN to have them Pass in this KINGDOM.

Wherein is shewn the Power of the said PATENT, the Value of the HALF-PENCE, and how far every Person may be oblig'd to take the same in Payments, and how to behave in Case such an Attempt shou'd be made by WOODS or any other Person.

[Very Proper to be kept in every FAMILY.]

By M. B. Drapier.

Dublin : Printed by *J. Harding* in *Molesworth's-Court*.

Drapier. *Title page of* The Drapier's Letters *(1724–5), six pamphlets written anonymously by Jonathan Swift against the monopoly granted by the English government to William Wood to provide Ireland with copper coinage. [Board of Trinity College, Dublin]*

Drapier's Letters, The, six pamphlets written in 1724–5 by JONATHAN SWIFT in the guise of a Dublin linen-draper, attacking the grant of a patent for minting copper coinage for Ireland to the Englishman William Wood. While the WOOD'S HA'PENCE controversy was ostensibly restricted to economic affairs, *The Drapier's Letters* were (rightly) understood to attack the subordinate position accorded the Irish Parliament in relation to Great Britain's by the DECLARATORY ACT (1719). Though Swift was shielded by his anonymity, the printer was tried for seditious libel. Wood's patent was eventually withdrawn, but the constitutional issue remained unchanged, to Swift's increasing despair. **Ian Campbell Ross**

Drennan, William (1754–1820), physician, poet, and radical. Born in Belfast, son of a 'New Light' Presbyterian minister; educated at Glasgow and Edinburgh (MD, 1778) and practised in

Newry, 1783–9, and Dublin, 1790–1807. He wrote *Letters of Orellana* (1784) in an attempt to revitalise the VOLUNTEER movement. He was a founder-member of the Society of UNITED IRISHMEN in Dublin and wrote many of their addresses. In 1794 he was tried for sedition but was acquitted. He withdrew from the movement as it became a revolutionary force, but he remained committed to radical reform and CATHOLIC EMANCIPATION and wrote a number of pamphlets on reform topics. In his poem 'Erin' (1795) he introduced the term 'EMERALD ISLE' as a name for Ireland. His influential poem 'The Wake of William Orr' was written in 1797 on the execution of a United Irishman; his other poetry ranged from election squibs and light verse to hymns. On inheriting a fortune from a cousin in 1807 he moved with his family to Belfast, where he published a literary magazine and was a founder of the Royal Belfast Academical Institution. His correspondence with his elder sister, MARTHA MCTIER, is an invaluable source for the political, social, literary, and medical history of this period. [see VOLUNTEERS.] **Jean Agnew**

dress style. The term 'traditional' is generally regarded as describing a dress style worn by particular social groups that relates to their sex, class, type of work, or domicile. Such clothes also aspire to an appearance of permanence, group feeling, self-sufficiency, and modesty. This contrasts with fashionable CLOTHING, which changes constantly in an attempt to attract the opposite sex and to present a display of contemporary taste, wealth, and status. Traditional costume, however, often follows FASHION at a distance. The Kinsale cloak, for example, is descended from the eighteenth-century 'cardinal' cloaks; the Irish shawl evolved because of the fashion for Kashmir, Paisley, and similar shawls c. 1800, while the swallowtail coat and knee breeches followed eighteenth-century fashionable wear. **Mairead Dunlevy**

Drew, Sir Thomas (1838–1910), architect and writer on ARCHITECTURE. Born in Belfast, son of a clergyman; apprenticed to CHARLES LANYON. In 1862 he moved to Dublin, where he was W. G. Murray's chief assistant for five years. A dynamic person, he had an extensive practice with much church, cathedral, and commercial work. He was president of the ROYAL INSTITUTE OF THE ARCHITECTS OF IRELAND, 1892–1901, and of the ROYAL HIBERNIAN ACADEMY, 1900–10. His best-known buildings in Dublin are the Ulster Bank, College Green (1888), Rathmines Town Hall (1894), and the Graduates' Memorial Building, Trinity College (1897). His magnum opus, St Anne's Cathedral, Belfast, was begun in 1898, but only the nave (consecrated in 1904) was completed in his lifetime. He was knighted in 1900. **Frederick O'Dwyer**

Dreyer, John Louis Emil (1852–1926), astronomer. Born in Copenhagen; educated at the University of Copenhagen. He began astronomical research at BIRR CASTLE OBSERVATORY in 1874. He moved to DUNSINK OBSERVATORY in 1878 and, four years later, to ARMAGH OBSERVATORY. He published the *New General Catalogue of Nebulae and Clusters of Stars* (1888) from Armagh. He wrote the standard historical ASTRONOMY texts, *History of the Planetary Systems from Thales to Kepler* (1906) and *Tycho Brahe: A Picture of Scientific Life and Work in the Sixteenth Century* (1890). In 1912 he edited the works of Sir William Herschel. He also edited the works of Tycho Brahe, resigning his post in Armagh in 1916 to continue this work in Oxford. To mark the centenary of the Royal Astronomical Society he edited, jointly with Herbert Hall Turner, the *History of the Royal Astronomical Society* (1923). **John McFarland**

Drogheda (*Droichead Átha*), Co. Louth, a town on the narrowest tidal point of the River BOYNE; population (2002) 28,308. The town is based on an ANGLO-NORMAN foundation, established where the river has cut a deep trench through glacial deposits. In the late twelfth century a *motte* was built on the south side of the river at Millmount, protecting the Norman bridge, and a substantial town grew on both sides of the river. The street pattern, with its narrow lanes and steeply rising steps, retains a medieval quality, while excavations have yielded important finds. Among the remains of this period are St Mary's Abbey, Magdalene Tower, and St Laurence's Gate, a thirteenth-century barbican. Drogheda was one of the largest and most important medieval walled towns, enclosing 46 ha (114 acres). It fell to CROMWELL following a short siege in 1649, and a massacre followed. The embalmed head of St OLIVER PLUNKETT, Archbishop of Armagh, who was hanged, drawn, and quartered in London in 1681, is preserved in St Peter's Church.

By the nineteenth century Drogheda was a centre for the linen industry, while flour-MILLING and BREWING also provided EMPLOYMENT. Some of the mill buildings are now converted into apartments. The RAILWAY from Dublin to Drogheda was opened in 1844, and Sir JOHN MACNEIL's Boyne VIADUCT (1855) made possible uninterrupted rail travel from Dublin to Belfast. Drogheda remains a busy port. Its population is growing rapidly, partly because commuters can travel to work in Dublin by road or high-speed rail link. **Ruth McManus**

Drogheda, Siege of (3–11 September 1649). After landing in Dublin, OLIVER CROMWELL first marched on Drogheda. His capacity to ship and deploy heavy siege artillery meant that the medieval curtain walls of Drogheda were soon breached. The crucial mistake of the royalist defenders lay in not raising the drawbridge over the River Boyne after Cromwell's troops stormed the southern part of the town. Most of the garrison, some 2,000–3,000 men, were killed in the attack. The killing of a garrison that had declined the offer to surrender was considered permissible, if severe, by the standards of contemporary siege WARFARE. However, it is likely that the 250–500 defenders of the Millmount, a strong position in the southern part of the town, were promised their lives but, once disarmed, were killed outright. Moreover, Anthony Wood's vivid eyewitness account of the killing of women and children congregated in St Peter's Church suggests that civilians were also massacred. **Pádraig Lenihan**

Drombeg, Co. Cork, one of the best-preserved of a distinctive type of STONE CIRCLE known as an *axial stone circle*, found only in Cos. Cork and Kerry. Its axis is roughly aligned on sunset at the winter solstice; but the fact that this is not repeated at any of the other several dozen axial stone circles makes it unlikely that this was intentional. **Clive Ruggles**

Dromore, Break of (1689), the first significant open engagement in the war of 1689–91 in Ireland. At Dromore, Co. Down, on 12 March 1689 a force of about 500 Ulster Protestants from Hillsborough, led by Sir Arthur Rawdon, encountered a force of about 3,000 men advancing northwards from Dublin, under the command of Richard Hamilton. Rawdon's men were part of the Protestant forces, commanded by Lord Mount Alexander, that had come out in active resistance to the Irish government of the Catholic JAMES II following the king's flight from England in the wake of the arrival of the Protestant WILLIAM III. The military encounter lasted only a few minutes. Rawdon's failure to wait at

Hillsborough for Protestant reinforcements, and his decision to seek an open action with Hamilton's superior force, resulted in the rout of the Ulstermen. Rawdon's infantry, in danger of being surrounded by Hamilton's cavalry, took flight almost immediately. More than 100 of Rawdon's men were killed as Hamilton's soldiers pursued them to Hillsborough. The defeat resulted in the collapse of organised Protestant resistance in east Ulster and Mount Alexander's flight from the country. Hamilton's advance into the north was not checked thereafter until he reached Coleraine. **Charles Ivar McGrath**

Dromore Castle, Pallaskenry, Co. Limerick. Designed by the English aesthetic architect E. W. Godwin in 1867 for the third Earl of Limerick, it is simultaneously the most scholarly and the most romantic of all nineteenth-century attempts to re-create the spirit of Irish medieval ARCHITECTURE. Most of the buildings are arranged in an L around two sides of a courtyard, and the massive keep and lower domestic buildings are offset by a ROUND TOWER. The silhouette very convincingly pays homage to the ROCK OF CASHEL, as well as to closer examples such as ASKEATON CASTLE, and the massing of the building on a rocky height is an excess of Gothic Revival splendour. The detailing of the architecture shows Godwin's antiquarian skill and diligent study of late medieval examples. The building is now a ruin. **Brian Lalor**

drug abuse, normally understood to mean the use of illegal substances, such as opiates, cannabis, and ecstasy (methylenedioxymethamphetamine). In the Republic there was a dramatic increase in the use of illegal drugs in the 1970s with the increased availability of heroin, leading to a virtual heroin epidemic. What appeared to be a lull occurred in the late 1980s and 90s; this was succeeded, however, by a renewed and growing problem, particularly of heroin abuse in Dublin but also of a nationwide abuse of cannabis and ecstasy. In addition there is emerging evidence that heroin abuse is now spreading outside Dublin and evidence also of the use of cocaine in Dublin and elsewhere. While the profile of the typical drug-user has been that of a young unemployed man in Dublin, either smoking or injecting heroin, with the change in patterns of abuse in recent times this profile is likely to alter.

The main Government anti-drug strategy combines the 'supply reduction' approach of the Department of Justice and the 'harm reduction' approach of the Department of Health. For the former, a range of new initiatives have been introduced, particularly the establishment of the Criminal Assets Bureau of the GARDA SÍOCHÁNA, put on a statutory footing by the Criminal Assets Bureau Act (1996), and the setting up of the National Drugs Strategy Team, with local task forces operating in areas with the most serious problems. From the point of view of the Department of Health, while a drugs-free society is regarded as the ideal, the 'harm reduction' model of treatment has been adopted to counteract the health risks to injecting drug-users posed by HIV and AIDS. The greatest problems have arisen in the Eastern Health Board area; this board took the lead in the harm reduction or minimisation movement, providing a wide range of services.

Parallel to official initiatives has been the development of a community anti-drug movement. Residents, notably in some working-class communities in Dublin, became disillusioned with official initiatives and formed local voluntary organisations such as Concerned Parents Against Drugs. The more radical of these groups occasionally acted in violent ways; however, more recently community action groups have been formed and partnerships established, now supported by the authorities, with general approval and some financial assistance. [see ALCOHOL ABUSE; ALCOHOL CONSUMPTION.] **Kathleen O'Higgins**

drug abuse. *A protest rally in Dublin, 27 September 1996, organised by the Coalition of Communities against Drugs (COCAD). [Derek Speirs/Report]*

drug abuse, Northern Ireland. Research for the most part began in the early 1990s, and little is known about the extent and nature of drug abuse before that time. Most research so far has concentrated on self-report surveys of youths or young adults. The first such study examined drug-taking and the associated life-style of users of ecstasy. Publications based on that study have dealt with patterns of use, positive and negative drug experiences, and users' perceptions about the long-term effects of the drug, as well as accounts of relationships between Catholics and Protestants who share venues where drugs are consumed. Considerably less is known about the use of other drugs, such as cocaine, amphetamines, heroin, and cannabis.

No cross-border research into drug abuse has so far been conducted. Some research has suggested that the extent of illicit drug use is considerably lower in the North than in the Republic or in Scotland, England, and Wales; other research, however, has disputed this claim. Research has shown that interest by the media in illicit drug use surfaced shortly after the 1994 ceasefires, but not much data is available that would allow researchers to examine trends in drug-taking before and after the ceasefires. Various public health indicators suggest that the extent of heroin use is considerably lower than that reported for Dublin, Glasgow, Edinburgh, and various places in England and Wales. However, a considerable social stigma attaches to the use of heroin and drug injection in the North, so that the accuracy of this data is questionable. Nevertheless, some data shows that the use of heroin may be increasing in various places in the North. In contrast to neighbouring regions, very little is known about the prevalence of HIV infection and AIDS among injecting drug-users. Some research has shown that such users in the North engage in behaviour that poses a great risk of HIV and other infectious disease. Moreover, some injecting drug-users have very little knowledge of types of behaviour that reduce the risk of infectious disease.

In general, treatment and other interventions for heroin users are quite limited. Methadone is generally not available, therapeutic communities have not been implemented, needle exchange was not offered until 2001, and formal street work with injecting drug-users has not been developed. This situation could improve considerably, however, as several drug policy decisions now rest with the Department of Health, Social Services and Public Safety, having previously been under the authority of the Northern Ireland Office. This important change suggests that HEALTH issues are likely to be given priority in the development of future interventions that will be available to drug-users, such as prevention, education, and treatment. **Karen McElrath**

Druid Theatre Company, Galway, founded in 1975 by the director GARRY HYNES and actors Mick Lally and Máire Mullen. At first it produced plays by a range of American and European writers, but it achieved most acclaim for productions of SYNGE'S PLAYBOY OF THE WESTERN WORLD in the early 1980s. This led to an association with the playwright TOM MURPHY, whose BAILEGANGAIRE the company staged in 1985. In the 1990s Druid was associated with a number of innovative new writers, notably MARTIN MCDONAGH, whose Leenane Trilogy brought the company international acclaim. Though they tour widely, they usually premiere their work in the Town Hall Theatre, Galway. **Christopher Morash**

Druim Cett, site of a meeting between the kings Áedán mac Gabráin of DÁL RIADA and Áed mac Ainmirech of the northern UÍ NÉILL, which took place near present-day Limavady, Co. Derry, c. AD 590. Also present was COLM CILLE of IONA, who had links with both kingdoms and is thought to have organised the conference, which addressed relations between the two kingdoms. ADOMNÁN's Life of Colm Cille also refers to the presence of Scandlán, son of Colmán, King of Osraige, who was being held hostage by Áed mac Ainmirech, and Áed's son Domnall. Later accounts hold that Colm Cille secured Scandlán's freedom and saved Ireland's poets from banishment at the meeting. While the Annals of Ulster record the year of the meeting as AD 575, a later date may be more consistent with the historical evidence. **Martin Clancy**

Drumcolliher Cinema Disaster (1926), a fire that claimed the lives of forty-eight people. On 5 September 1926 the cinema in Drumcolliher, Co. Limerick, was showing *The Ten Commandments* when a reel of film was set alight by an overturned candle. A number of other reels quickly caught fire; the sudden blaze caused the crowd to panic and rush towards the only exit, a narrow doorway leading to wooden stairs. The victims were buried in a communal grave; a memorial library was built on the site of the destroyed cinema. [see STARDUST TRAGEDY.] **Brian Galvin**

Drumcree, Co. Armagh, site of a confrontation between members of the ORANGE ORDER and local nationalists since 1995. The traditional Orange march from Drumcree CHURCH OF IRELAND church to the centre of Portadown on the Sunday preceding 12 July was a contentious one from the late 1970s onwards, with the route passing through a Catholic housing estate on the Garvaghy Road. The first confrontation took place in 1995 when the RUC blocked the march; the Orangemen refused to disperse, and after intense rioting for three days they were allowed through. A similar confrontation in 1996 led to widespread disorder and destruction throughout Northern Ireland, and the RUC had to be reinforced by 1,000 British soldiers. As in 1996, the Orangemen were allowed down the Garvaghy Road in 1997, and the damage inflicted in the ensuing violence was estimated at £10 million. The Parades Commission rerouted the march in 1998, and soldiers and police

Drumcree. *Journalists covering the confrontation outside Drumcree Church, Co. Armagh, 12 July 1998; members of the Orange Order protest against being prevented from marching down the Garvaghy Road. [Leon Farrell/Photocall Ireland]*

erected a massive steel shield at the entrance to the Garvaghy Road. Some Orangemen maintained a year-round vigil at Drumcree in protest. Because members of the Orange Order would not negotiate directly with representatives of the residents, the Parades Commission also continued to ban the Garvaghy route. The result was more confrontations and violent incidents. **Jonathan Bardon**

Drumm, James (1896–1974), chemist and industrial technologist. Born in Dundrum, Co. Down. He invented an alkaline battery capable of being charged at very high rates and thus suitable for traction purposes. The positive plates were nickel oxide mixed with graphite, the negative very pure nickel and the electrolyte a composite of potassium and lithium hydroxide and zinc oxide. A Drumm battery was mounted in a demonstration rail coach built by the Great Southern Railway Company in 1930; the second entered service on the Bray–Dublin line; by mid-1945, four trains equipped with Drumm batteries had covered 1.2 million km. These units were withdrawn in 1949 at the end of the batteries' useful life. **D. Thorburn Burns**

Drummond, Thomas (1797–1840), engineer and administrator. Born in Scotland, he worked on the Irish ORDNANCE SURVEY before serving as Under-Secretary for Ireland, 1835–40. He was an efficient and popular reformer, implementing WHIG policy on law and police reforms, LOCAL GOVERNMENT, and the dissolution of the ORANGE ORDER. He coined the significant and in Ireland too frequently ignored phrase that property has its duties as well as its rights. His funeral in Dublin drew large crowds. **Peter Gray**

Drummond, William Hamilton (1778–1865), poet. Born in Larne, Co. Antrim; educated in Belfast and at the University of Glasgow, and served as an ordained minister of Unitarian conviction in Belfast and Dublin. His major work is the long poem *The Giant's Causeway* (1811), which mingles topographical, historical and geological material in an eighteenth-century manner that admits moments of romantic Celticism. He contributed verse translations from Irish to JAMES HARDIMAN's *Irish Minstrelsy* (1831); his own *Ancient Irish Minstrelsy* was published in 1852. **Terence Brown**

Drury, Susanna (fl. 1733–1776), topographical painter. Probably born in Dublin to a well-established Anglo-Irish family. She produced a series of gouache drawings on vellum, including views of the GIANT'S CAUSEWAY, for which she was awarded a premium by the DUBLIN SOCIETY Drawing Schools in 1740. Engravings after the Giant's Causeway drawings were produced by François Vivares (1777). Further works include other views of the Causeway and a London scene entitled *One Tree Hill, Greenwich Park*. Her brother Franklin was a painter of MINIATURES. **Brendan Rooney**

Drury Byrne, Aisling (1945–), cellist. Born in Dublin; studied at the RIAM with Coral Bognuda and with Paul Tortelier at the Paris Conservatoire, where she was awarded the premier Prix. Before being appointed principal cellist of the RTÉ Symphony Orchestra (later NATIONAL SYMPHONY ORCHESTRA), 1978–2001, she was principal cello teacher at the RIAM. She has performed at the Wexford Festival, the Festival in Great Irish Houses and the DUBLIN FESTIVAL OF TWENTIETH CENTURY MUSIC and has premiered many works. A regular soloist with the NSO, she has also performed with the Testore Quartet and the Dublin Piano Trio. **Ite O'Donovan**

Duanáire: see BARDIC DUANAIRE.

'Duanaire Finn' ('The Poem-Book of Fionn'), the most important anthology of OSSIANIC lays. The sixty-nine poems date from the twelfth to the sixteenth centuries. The manuscript in which it is found also contains a copy of 'ACALLAMH NA SENÓRACH' and other material from the FIONN CYCLE. It was written in Ostend and Louvain between 1626 and 1627 by two scribes, one of whom, Aodh Ó Dochartaigh, collected and transcribed the lays. The work was commissioned by Somhairle Mac Domhnaill, a captain in the Irish Regiment of the Spanish Army based in the Spanish Netherlands. **Máirtín Ó Briain**

Dublin, County (*Contae Bhaile Átha Cliath*)

Province:	LEINSTER
County town:	DUBLIN
Area:	922 km^2 (355 sq. miles)
Population, including city (2002):	1,122,600
Features:	DUBLIN BAY
	Dublin Mountains
	River LIFFEY
Of historical interest:	CASINO, Marino
	CHRIST CHURCH CATHEDRAL
	DUBLIN CASTLE
	KILMAINHAM GAOL
	Malahide Castle
	ST PATRICK'S CATHEDRAL
	TRINITY COLLEGE
Industry and products:	BREWING
	DISTILLING
	Electronic goods
	Manufacturing
	Pharmaceuticals
	TEXTILES

Petula Martyn

County Dublin, one of the smallest counties in Ireland, with an area of 922 km^2 (356 sq. miles): only Cos. Carlow and Louth have a smaller area. In population, however, it is by far the largest, with 1,122,600 people (2002), or 28.7 per cent of the population of the Republic. Historically, the Dublin region was a buffer zone between the Laighin to the south and the southern Uí Néill to the north. With the establishment of the Hiberno-Norse overlordship in the tenth century the modern county began to take shape, and it was consolidated with the arrival of the ANGLO-NORMANS. It remained solidly under English control, 'within the PALE,' even at the height of Irish power, except at the edge of the Dublin Mountains.

North Co. Dublin is characterised by gentle hills that merge into the central lowlands. It is only to the south that the land rises to any height, in the Dublin Mountains. FINGAL, to the north, was seen as a distinctive area, having experienced more than 250 years of Viking rule, with distinctive speech patterns up to the seventeenth century. It was crucial to the survival of the more urbanised area to the south, producing much of the food for the city.

There are four administrative units within the present-day county, and the contrast remains between the built-up area—comprising the city of DUBLIN, the administrative county of Dún Laoghaire and Rathdown, and most of South Dublin—and the less built-up, more rural landscape of modern-day Fingal. Economically and socially, however, Fingal is becoming more and more integrated into the city.

The population of Co. Dublin increased by 6.1 per cent between 1996 and 2002, with the greatest increase in Fingal (17 per cent), compared with the city (2.7 per cent), Dún Laoghaire and Rathdown (0.7 per cent), and South Dublin (9.7 per cent). Much of the growth in Fingal reflects the expansion of the city along its northern edge (the Ward +63 per cent, Dubber +44 per cent) and into the towns and countryside of north Co. Dublin. Swords has a population of 30,989 (+19.5 per cent), while Rush and Donabate grew by 24.6 per cent and 42.3 per cent, respectively. Previously rural areas are also experiencing increased urbanisation, especially those near the city: Clonmethan and Ballyboghil each grew by more than 22 per cent. Only in this region of Co. Dublin is there a substantial agricultural population, market gardening being particularly important. In the north-west of the county this accounted for more than 14 per cent of the labour force (1996 figures); and over most of the region, with the exception of Blanchardstown, Swords, and the coastal towns, more than 5 per cent work in this industry. Fingal is also an important cultural and recreational resource for the county. The coastline offers many beaches, and the cultural landscape is rich in Early Christian monuments. LAMBAY ISLAND, with an area of 241 ha (596 acres), is the largest island on the east coast. The Vikings landed here in 795, but the presence of a stone-axe production site indicates occupancy in the Neolithic Period. **Joseph Brady**

Dublin (*Baile Átha Cliath*), largest city in Ireland and capital city of the Republic; population, including greater Dublin suburbs (1996) 952,692. The origins of Dublin may be complex, though the VIKINGS were central to its early development. In 841, according to the Annals of Ulster, they set up a permanent raiding-camp at the mouth of the River Liffey, which remained until they were expelled by the Irish in 902. They returned in the early tenth century but this time more to trade than to raid and established a settlement on high ground on the south bank of the Liffey near *Dubhlinn* (the black pool), where they berthed their boats. There is also evidence for a monastic enclosure on the southern bank, close to *Áth Cliath* (the ford of hurdles), an important crossing-point for four trade routes. In addition, there may have been a small settlement.

The medieval town was small but vibrant, with a culturally diverse population, speaking Norse, English, and Irish, which maintained a strong export trade in WOOLLENS, pelts, and combs. The earliest surviving map of Dublin is that of JOHN SPEED (1610), which shows a walled town with substantial suburbs on both sides of the river, where the religious houses were important landowners. The most impressive buildings are DUBLIN CASTLE, symbol of royal power and of the city's subject status; CHRIST CHURCH CATHEDRAL, rebuilt in stone c. 1186; and the suburban ST PATRICK'S CATHEDRAL (c. 1220). The domestic architecture of the town changed from the post-and-wattle houses of the Viking Age to heavier timber-framed houses with an increased use of stone in building. Very little survives from this period except in elements of the street plan.

Dublin grew dramatically from the late seventeenth century in a climate of greater political and economic stability. The Corporation sought to develop Dublin in a manner befitting its importance as a capital city. Early successes included the laying out of St Stephen's Green and its environs; but congestion in the narrow streets was an intractable problem. The solution was found in the appointment by the Parliament in 1757 of the WIDE STREETS COMMISSIONERS, who were given executive powers. For almost a hundred years they attempted to solve the city's problems by creating long, straight and wide streets with a unified ARCHITECTURE in keeping with the best European ideas of the time. Private individuals, such as LUKE GARDINER, Humphrey Jervis, and Lord Fitzwilliam, were important in developing large tracts of land, and the four GEORGIAN-style squares—Rutland Square (Parnell Square), Mountjoy Square, Merrion Square, and Fitzwilliam Square—are part of their legacy.

Dublin was at its grandest at the end of the eighteenth century, and its wealthy citizens enjoyed a leisured life-style. They favoured the new housing areas to the east of the old city, and an east-west social gradient developed. The south-east, containing St Stephen's Green, Merrion Square, and Fitzwilliam Square, was dominated by the nobility, gentry, and professions; the north-east, including Mountjoy Square and Rutland Square, was inhabited by the business community; the rest, particularly the south-western city outside the old walls, was left to the great mass of the poor, who lived in squalor.

With regard to the nineteenth century a distinction must be drawn between the city proper, governed by Dublin Corporation,

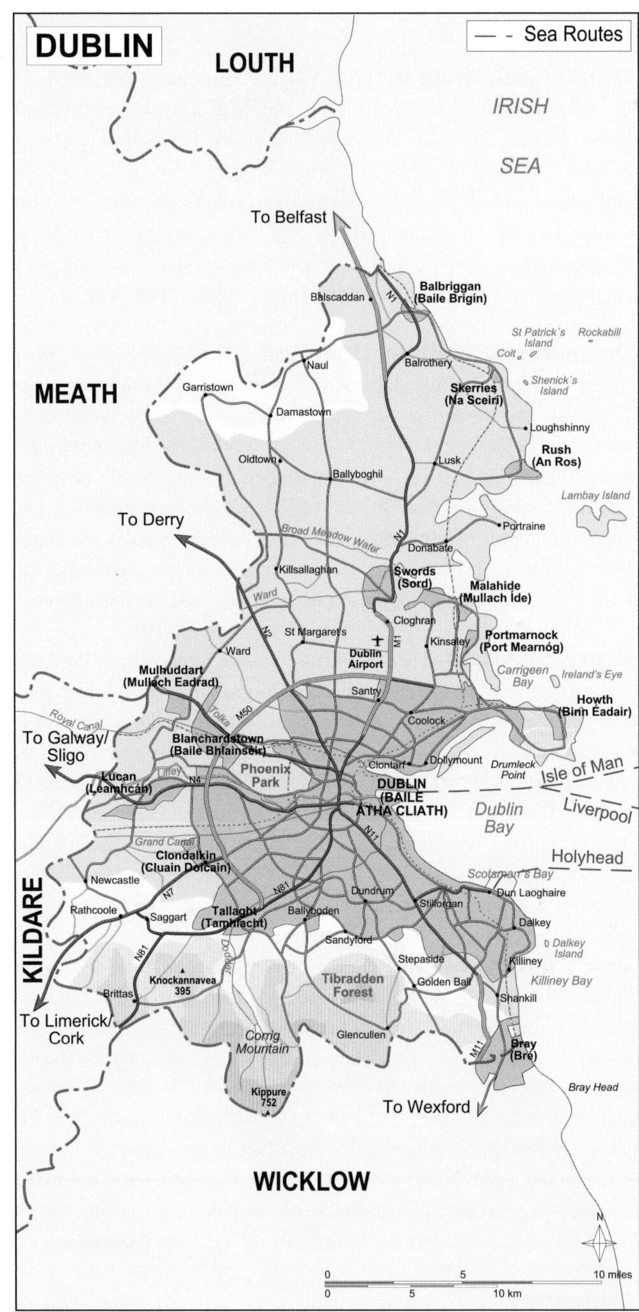

Dublin. *The thirteenth-century great seal of Dublin, showing (right) the original coat of arms of the city, with three watchtowers surrounding a gate in the medieval city wall, and (left) a ship at sea representing trade. [Dublin City Council/City Archives]*

and the independent suburban townships. The ACT OF UNION (1800) resulted in the upper stratum of society leaving for London, while the townships attracted the better-off professional classes in large numbers. The inner city became associated with poverty and slums as its population grew from 182,000 in 1800 to 285,000 in 1851, mainly by MIGRATION, and it failed to develop labour-intensive industry. The problem of poor housing was not tackled with any seriousness until towards the end of the century.

Townships developed beyond the CANALS—in effect the borders of the city. But the northern townships of Drumcondra and Clontarf failed to prosper, in contrast to the southern townships of Pembroke and Rathmines-Rathgar, which retained their independence until 1930. Pembroke, under the Pembroke family, attracted an upper-middle-class population, while Rathmines-Rathgar was developed along speculative lines and appealed to the wider middle class. After 1832 the RAILWAY facilitated the growth of the townships of Kingstown (DÚN LAOGHAIRE), DALKEY, and Killiney, but these remained small. The townships created a middle-class sector in the south city, not replicated north of the Liffey, and set the pattern for the city's social geography in the twentieth century.

By 1901 the population was 290,000, and the city, while still spatially compact, was about to experience massive suburban expansion. The middle class already enjoyed a suburban life-style, but it was realised that the housing crisis among the poorer classes could be solved only by large-scale suburban housing projects. Marino was completed in the late 1920s, followed by Cabra and the massive Crumlin scheme after 1935, containing almost 5,400 houses. Private development continued in the south-east and, in a more fragmented way, on the north side. The development process was haphazard, and for most of the century the city lacked a coherent PLANNING strategy. This was not helped by the existence of three local authorities: Dublin City Council, Dún Laoghaire Borough Council, and Dublin County Council. In 1967, as recommended in the Wright Report, it was decided to concentrate the development of the city in three western 'new towns': Tallaght, Clondalkin, and Blanchardstown. In the late 1970s and 80s Malahide and Portmarnock became favoured middle-class locations. Suburban appeal was enhanced by SHOPPING CENTRES from 1967, while much industry also deserted the increasingly congested central areas for cheaper and more accessible sites. In consequence the population in the city proper declined, from 567,866 in 1971 to 478,389 in 1991; the inner city's population was less than a third of that of fifty years previously. Growth was concentrated on the edge of the city, where imbalanced AGE STRUCTURES created problems in the allocation of resources.

By the 1960s much of the central city's physical fabric was decayed, especially along the quays, while the once-elegant Georgian houses of the north city especially were in terminal decline as tenements. Renewal rather than renovation was favoured, with a drive to replace the old with modern, and often unsympathetic, buildings. The demolition of Georgian houses in Fitzwilliam Street to build the head office of the ESB (1964) saw the first of many struggles between developers and conservationists, while the failure to conserve Viking remains at Wood Quay in the 1970s was one of many losses. Street-widening schemes proved equally controversial, especially in the environs of St Patrick's Cathedral.

Though the urban fabric remains relatively unprotected in law, there is a greater acceptance of the need for conservation. Since 1986 the state has financed urban renewal schemes that have helped regenerate city areas such as the docklands, TEMPLE BAR, and Smithfield. These initiatives have attracted apartment-dwelling young professionals into these areas, changing their social composition and helping to reverse long-term population decline.

Dublin experienced rapid growth again in the 1990s, fuelled by a booming economy. Despite the absence of a formal strategic plan for the metropolitan area, it is seen as desirable to contain as much growth as possible within the built-up area, where services are already provided, and often underused, and to limit the city's spatial growth. This has coincided with a renewed interest by house-buyers in older residential areas as commuting becomes increasingly difficult. The result has been many in-fill developments, facilitated in part by the sale of building land by religious orders and by the renewal of vacant industrial sites. Nonetheless, growth will continue in the greater Dublin area, especially in such towns as MAYNOOTH, Celbridge, Skerries, BRAY, and Greystones, and it can be expected that even longer-distance commuting will become a reality for many. In an era that emphasises 'sustainable' urban development, Dublin urgently needs to find solutions to its problems of TRANSPORT, air quality, and waste management. **Joseph Brady**

Dublin Baroque Players, an amateur orchestra founded in 1966 by Michael Clifton, Kieran Egar, and Liam Fitzgerald, who has been conductor since 1969. In its early years the group concentrated on music from the baroque period, aiming for the highest standard in playing; its repertoire has now expanded to include classical, romantic and contemporary music. With a reputation for technical excellence, the orchestra gives two provincial tours each year and performs regularly on the Continent and in the United States. It also performs regularly with CHORAL SOCIETIES. It has a policy of providing Irish composers and soloists with a platform for performance, through an extended concert series. **Ite O'Donovan**

Dublin Bay, a semi-circular sandy bay, somewhat modified by the eighteenth-century harbour walls and the subsequent emergence of NORTH BULL ISLAND. There is an extensive inter-tidal area of 10 km^2 (3.9 sq. miles), dominated by the cockle *Cerastoderma edule*, though at rather low densities. The bay shows signs of eutrophication (rich in nutrients) in the growth of macro-algal mats in the lagoons, which, however, support very high numbers of over-wintering waders. In general the bay copes well with the human inputs because of the high flushing and the low level of persistent contaminants. **James G. Wilson**

Dublin Castle, the seat of British power in Ireland until 1922. The building of the castle began in 1204 on the orders of JOHN. By the early seventeenth century it included courts of law, council chambers, and the Parliament chamber; it was also the residence of the LORD LIEUTENANT until the building of the Viceregal Lodge in the PHOENIX PARK in the late eighteenth century. The castle was greatly damaged by fire in 1684, and extensive rebuilding was undertaken, which continued throughout the eighteenth century. As a symbol of English authority in Ireland the castle was attacked by SILKEN THOMAS FITZGERALD in 1534, by ROBERT EMMET in 1803, and during the 1916 RISING. After the WAR OF INDEPENDENCE it was handed over to the IRISH FREE STATE on 16 January 1922 (see p. 529). **Martin Clancy**

Dubliners (1914), a collection of short stories by JAMES JOYCE. The fifteen stories, which constitute Joyce's first published volume of prose fiction, were published in London by Grant Richards, who had been primarily responsible for the postponement of the work's appearance since 1905, for fear that it would attract legal action for obscenity. *Dubliners* offers a series of vignettes of Dublin life notable for their realism and disenchanted atmosphere. All but one of the stories present a central persona whose aspirations for other modes of life and experience are shown to be hopeless in the conditions of urban and national atrophy that the stories make manifest. Joyce indeed reckoned that his representative distresses of his characters amounted to a chapter of the 'moral history' of his country.

The collection exhibited signs of the radically experimental writer Joyce would become. A volume of discrete stories was given broad general structure through Joyce's decision to deal with his theme 'under four of its aspects: childhood, adolescence, maturity and public life', while one story, 'Grace', followed for parodic purposes the Dantean structure of Inferno, Purgatorio, and Paradiso. *Dubliners* also offered, without disturbing its ostensible realism and in the absence of an omniscient narrator, a structural and thematic symbolism in which colour effects, geography, weather, and aspects of the settings, including their historical associations, served to intensify the individual and collective significance of the stories. [see GORDON BENNETT CUP.] **Terence Brown**

Dubliners, the, a ballad group originating in 1962 from sessions held in O'Donoghue's pub, Merrion Row, Dublin. The group was unique in blending tenor BANJO (Barney McKenna), TIN WHISTLE (Ciarán Bourke), and FIDDLE (John Sheehan) with the voices of Ronnie Drew (also guitar) and LUKE KELLY (also five-string banjo). Their marriage of traditional instrumentation with lively and sometimes irreverent songs, combined with an image that portrayed them as bearded, hard-drinking troubadours, led to increasing popularity with audiences; for many people they provided the first point of contact with the Irish song and instrumental tradition. Together with the CLANCY BROTHERS AND TOMMY MAKEM they were leaders in Ireland's ballad boom of the 1960s. Over the years the group has also included the singers Bobby Lynch, Jim McCann, Seán Cannon, and Paddy Reilly and the guitar-player Éamon Campbell. **Tom Sherlock**

Dublin Festival of Twentieth-Century Music, established to present a broad spectrum of solo, chamber, and orchestral music of the twentieth century. Founded in 1969 by Gerard Schürmann, BRIAN BOYDELL, and GERARD VICTORY, it was organised by the MUSIC ASSOCIATION OF IRELAND, and works of renowned international composers were performed. Special attention was given to works of Irish composers, and a concert of new works by young Irish composers was presented at each festival. With support from RTÉ and the ARTS COUNCIL, the festival continued until 1986. Distinguished visitors to the festival included Messiaen, Stockhausen, Elliott Carter, Kagel, and Lutoslawski. **Ite O'Donovan**

Dublin Grand Opera Society (DGOS), founded in 1941 by Captain (later Lt. Col) William O'Kelly, with Captain J. M. Doyle as first musical director and with support from the RÉ (later RTÉ) orchestras and the Army No. 1 Band, the DGOS presented two seasons annually at the GAIETY THEATRE, encouraging national talent (including VERONICA DUNNE, William Young, and ANNE MURRAY) and presenting international companies to Dublin including those of Munich and Hamburg. From 1955 to 1967 the Spring Festival of Italian Opera received funding from the Italian government, with the young Luciano Pavarotti appearing in 1963–4. Reconstructed into a company limited by guarantee in 1985, it now receives assistance from the ARTS COUNCIL. In 1996 the society was renamed Opera Ireland. **Ite O'Donovan**

Dublin Institute for Advanced Studies—Scientific Schools (DIAS), established in 1940 as a result of the vision of ÉAMON DE VALERA, who, inspired by his love both of Ireland's

Celtic heritage and of advanced mathematics and theoretical physics (particularly astrophysics), sought, when TAOISEACH, to enhance significantly the cultural life of the country through providing the means of pursuing these activities at the highest scholarly level. On 5 July 1939, introducing in DÁIL ÉIREANN the bill to establish the institute on a statutory basis, he remarked:

> This is the country of Hamilton, a country of great mathematicians. We have the opportunity now of establishing a School of Theoretical Physics which could be specialised in the same way as the School of Celtic Studies and which I think will again enable us to achieve a reputation in that direction comparable to the reputation which Dublin and Ireland had in the middle of the last century.

The first director of the School of Theoretical Physics, chosen by de Valera, was the Austrian Nobel laureate ERWIN SCHRÖDINGER. For sentimental reasons and because of its association with WILLIAM ROWAN HAMILTON, de Valera always contemplated the inclusion of DUNSINK OBSERVATORY in the DIAS but at first forbore to acquire this property—then derelict—because of the limited number of observing nights at the site. Later ERIC LINDSAY, director of Armagh Observatory, raised the possibility of an observatory jointly operated by personnel from Armagh, Dunsink, and Harvard being established at Bloemfontein, South Africa, to acquire high-quality astronomical measurements for scientific analysis. This suggestion was accepted with the inauguration of the Armagh-Dunsink-Harvard (ADH) observatory, and in March 1947, when the DIAS was expanded with the establishment of a School of Cosmic Physics, it had three sections—Astrophysical, Cosmic Ray, and Meteorological—with the Astrophysics Section accommodated at Dunsink. The three sections were led by individual senior professors: HERMANN BRÜCK, LAJOS JÁNOSSY, and L. W. POLLAK.

Schrödinger invited the German physicist WALTER HEITLER to take up a permanent position at the DIAS. His most important scientific contribution while at Dublin was a theory of radiation damping, which he later applied, together with quantum electrodynamics, to the study of cosmic ray physics. While at Dublin he collaborated with E. T. S. WALTON, Lajos Jánossy, Cormac Ó Ceallaigh, and THOMAS NEVIN and provided inspiration for a generation of young theoreticians. The next senior professor appointed, in 1948, was JOHN LIGHTON SYNGE, who had an international reputation in a wide range of fields but particularly in that of Einstein's theory of relativity. Another luminary was CORNELIUS LANCZOS, a Hungarian physicist and mathematician whose research in a wide array of disciplines is now recognised as having had a profound impact on twentieth-century science.

When the DIAS was expanded in 1947, Hermann Brück, a Prussian scientist, was appointed director at Dunsink, where he worked vigorously to restore the derelict building. Lajos Jánossy was born in Hungary and instituted the experimental and theoretical investigations of extensive air showers. Jánossy was succeeded in 1953 by Cormac Ó Ceallaigh, the first Irish scientist to be appointed senior professor at the school. Ó Ceallaigh already had an international reputation in particle track detection, involving nuclear emission techniques. Through his personal influence, facilities at CERN (Conseil Européen pour la Recherche Nucleaire) in Geneva were made available to the DIAS as part of the European K-Meson Collaboration (a co-operative study with UCD and laboratories in five other countries).

A joint research scheme organised by Ó Ceallaigh between the DIAS and the General Electric Research Laboratories in Schenectady, New York, led to the development of a new technique of charged-particle identification in solid-state nuclear track detectors. This technique was used when Berkeley-DIAS detectors were flown on *Apollo 16* and *17* in the 1970s, resulting in the first detection of heavy cosmic ray nuclei outside the Earth's magnetosphere.

Following his retirement in 1984 Ó Ceallaigh was succeeded by the theoretician Luke O'Connor Drury, who shifted the emphasis to plasma astrophysics. Leo Wencelas Pollak arrived in Ireland in 1938 from Czechoslovakia to take up a senior post in the Meteorological Service and was thereafter appointed senior professor of the School of Cosmic Physics and in 1947 director of the DIAS. He took meteorological records in Merrion Square over the next sixteen years and used his data to predict the average yield per acre of the national sugarbeet crop. In 1949 he appointed Thomas Murphy, who instituted gravity and magnetic surveys of Ireland. In 1978 Murphy appointed Brian Jacob to expand the seismological work at the DIAS, and he became senior professor when Murphy retired. Through his efforts the institute in 2002 had six short-period seismic stations and one very broad-band station. In 1999 the Cosmic Ray Commission of the International Union of Pure and Applied Physics established a commemorative award, the Ó Ceallaigh Medal for Distinguished Contributions to Cosmic Ray Research.

The School of Theoretical Physics consists of two research groups, the Theoretical Particle Physics Group and the Applied Probability Group. The former was led from 1958 to 2000 by

Dubliners. *Luke Kelly, folk singer and founder-member of the Dubliners. He suggested the name of the group, having read James Joyce's short-story collection* Dubliners. *[RTÉ Stills Library; 5H/93]*

LOCHLAINN Ó RAIFEARTAIGH. Of fundamental importance to theoretical physics were his mechanisms in super-symmetry theory. His book *The Dawning of Gauge Theory* (1979) follows a historical approach. The Applied Probability Group owes its origin to fundamental research developed from 1985 at the DIAS by J. Lewis, who applied large deviation theory to problems in statistical thermodynamics. This led to work on the foundations of large deviation theory that was found to have a practical application in tele-traffic engineering. Ensuing collaboration with engineers in Cambridge and Stockholm involved developing techniques for resource allocation for multimedia communications and processing using on-line measurements. **Susan McKenna-Lawlor**

Dublin International Organ and Choral Festival, founded by GERARD GILLEN in 1980 as the Dublin International Organ Festival. Since its inception it has attracted competitors from all over the world. Supported by the MUSIC ASSOCIATION OF IRELAND, this biennial or triennial festival seeks to give a public presentation of a series of concerts and recitals of the highest standard. Members of the distinguished international jury have also been recitalists. A strong choral element, with concerts by internationally renowned choirs, the combined forces of Dublin's three cathedral choirs and Irish chamber choirs, was reflected in the change of title in 1992. **Ite O'Donovan**

Dublin International Piano Competition, inaugurated in 1988 as a triennial event. It was first sponsored by GPA and from 1996 by the Guardian Group, subsequently AXA. Chaired by JOHN O'CONOR and adjudicated by a distinguished international jury, the competition attracts entries from around the world. Engagements for prizewinners include debut recitals in London and New York, appearances at international festivals, and concertos with leading world orchestras. Previous winners now engaged in professional careers include Philippe Cassard (France), Pavel Nersessian and Alexei Nabioulin (Russia), Max Levinson (United States), and Davide Francheschetti (Italy). **Ite O'Donovan**

Dublin Lock-Out, 1913, an epic struggle for its scale, the raw issues involved, and a personalised clash between WILLIAM MARTIN MURPHY, prominent magnate and leader of the business community, and JAMES LARKIN, radical labour leader and founder in 1909 of the IRISH TRANSPORT AND GENERAL WORKERS' UNION. On 15 August 1913 Murphy dismissed members of the ITGWU working in the Dublin United Tramway Company and INDEPENDENT NEWSPAPERS. The union responded by declaring a general strike on 26 August. Violent conflict ensued, notably on 'Bloody Sunday', 31 August. In September 400 employers supported Murphy in locking out more than 20,000 workers. Larkin raised a 'fiery cross' in Britain to appeal for help, but despite substantial aid the ITGWU was forced to admit defeat on 18 January 1914 (see p. 558). **Emmet O'Connor**

Dublin and Kingstown Railway, Ireland's first railway. Following an earlier attempt that failed financially, a group of Dublin bankers, supported by British interests, subscribed £100,000 for a line to convey both passengers and goods; a loan from the Board of Public Works was also secured. The coastal strip between Dublin and Kingstown (DÚN LAOGHAIRE) was attracting a steadily increasing suburban population, while the port of Dublin, developed in the era of sail, was subject to silting and inadequate berthing for large iron vessels. Kingstown harbour suffered from neither of these disadvantages, while the proposed railway would also facilitate the rapid troop movements considered necessary to deal with political and agrarian agitation.

CHARLES VIGNOLES was appointed engineer for the line, and the contractor was WILLIAM DARGAN. Work began on 11 April 1833; and, following delays caused by construction difficulties, the first train left the Dublin terminus, Westland Row (now Pearse Station), at 9 a.m. on 17 December 1834. The line was built to the gauge of 1.44 m (4 ft $8\frac{1}{2}$ in.), later converted to the Irish standard of 1.6 m (5 ft 3 in.). In 1844 the line was extended to DALKEY using the principle of the ATMOSPHERIC RAILWAY. **Bernard Share**

Dublin Metropolitan Police (DMP) (1838–1925), a force closely modelled on the London Metropolitan Police. The intelligence-gathering of its G Division was central to the defeat of the FENIANS in the 1860s. After decades of uneasy relations with working-class Dubliners the force's unpopularity increased as a result of its brutality during the 1913 DUBLIN LOCK-OUT, and in 1925 it was absorbed into the GARDA SÍOCHÁNA. **Brian Griffin**

Dublin and Monaghan bombings (1974). On 17 May 1974 twenty-two people were killed and more than a hundred injured when three car bombs exploded during the evening rush hour in Talbot Street and South Leinster Street, Dublin (see p. 651); five more people were killed and twenty injured when a car bomb exploded in Monaghan the same day. All four cars used in the bombings had Northern Ireland registrations; two of the three used in Dublin had been stolen in Protestant areas of Belfast. Though the UDA and UVF both at first denied involvement, in 1993 the UVF finally admitted responsibility for the bombings. The final total of thirty-three deaths (twenty-eight in Dublin and five in Monaghan) was the largest number of fatalities to result from the events of a single day of the 'TROUBLES'. Claims have been made that British intelligence or British military personnel were involved in the planning of these attacks, though this has never been proved. [see LOYALIST BOMBINGS IN THE REPUBLIC; OMAGH BOMBING.] **Gordon Gillespie**

Dublin Orchestral Players, established to train young players in the art of orchestral playing and to give public performances of works of educational merit. Founded in 1939 by HAVELOCK NELSON and Constance Hardinge, the orchestra, in providing a training ground for future professionals, also provides a platform for young conductors and soloists. Since its formation it has introduced to the public many new and unusual works, including many new Irish compositions and gave the first European performance outside Russia of Prokofiev's *Peter and the Wolf.* **Ite O'Donovan**

Dublin Orchestral Society, 1899–1914. Founded by MICHELE ESPOSITO as a professional co-operative orchestra, it received the support of Margaret O'Hea, Leopold Dix, W. P. Geoghegan, and EDWARD MARTYN. The inaugural concert of this first Irish resident orchestra took place in March 1899 at the Royal University, Earlsfort Terrace. Players included staff and former students of the RIAM and the Municipal School of Music. Over the next fifteen years the orchestra gave more than 200 concerts of symphonies, concertos, and overtures. Venues included the Royal University, the GAIETY THEATRE and, from 1905, the ANTIENT CONCERT ROOMS, where Sunday afternoon concerts were held. An attempt to revive it in 1926 was halted by Esposito's ill-health and led to the formation of the Dublin Philharmonic Society. **Ite O'Donovan**

Dublin Pipers' Club. Founded towards the end of the nineteenth century, it had an intermittent existence until it was revived by LEO ROWSOME in 1936. It was instrumental in the setting up of Cumann (later COMHALTAS) CEOLTÓIRÍ ÉIREANN in 1951, into which it was later subsumed as Craobh Leo Rowsome. Its most famous secretary was ÉAMONN CEANNT, one of the executed leaders of the 1916 RISING; the papers of another secretary, Séamas Ó Casaide, survive in the NATIONAL LIBRARY. In the early years it organised competitions and contracted Nicholas Markey, a master piper, to give tuition to its members. Through its activities it provided an important link with the piping of the nineteenth century. **Jimmy O'Brien Moran**

Dublin Port. In 1708 the Corporation of Dublin was empowered to establish a Ballast Office, to be responsible for the maintenance and development of the port. The building of the South Wall in stone began in 1748 and was substantially completed by 1786, when the powers of the Ballast Office were transferred to a Ballast Board, in turn replaced in 1867 by the Dublin Port and Docks Board. During this time the South and North BULL WALLS, north and south quays and a graving dock were completed. Alexandra Basin, a deep-water tidal basin, was begun in 1871 and completed in 1937. Bulk cargo handling facilities, passenger and vehicle, roll-on/roll-off and container terminals were built later by the Port Company. [see GRIFFITH, JOHN PURSER; STONEY, BINDON BLOOD.] **Ronald Cox**

Dublin Society: see ROYAL DUBLIN SOCIETY.

Dublin Society Drawing Schools: see ROYAL DUBLIN SOCIETY.

Dublin tramways. The Tramways (Ireland) Act became law in 1867, but it was not until 1 February 1872 that the Dublin Tramway Company opened the first route, laid to the standard gauge of 1.6 m (5 ft 3 in.) from College Green to Rathgar, shortly afterwards extended in both directions to O'Connell Street and Terenure. The stock of draught HORSES soon proved inadequate to the task, and the company was obliged to undertake a breeding programme. New routes were introduced progressively, and in 1875, when six cars were acquired from the defunct Cork tramways, it was operating with some seventy-six tramcars and 480 horses.

From 1873 two rival companies had also laid lines, and in 1881 all three pooled their resources to form the Dublin United Tramway Company, with a combined route of 51 km (32 miles). Under the directorship of WILLIAM MARTIN MURPHY the DUTC prospered. Electrification, originally involving another small enterprise, the Dublin and Southern Districts Tramways Company, which had opened a line to Dún Laoghaire and Dalkey, took place from 1896, the first service operating from Ballsbridge to Dalkey on 16 May. The DUTC, sensing serious competition, was quick to follow suit, and the last Dublin horse tram travelled on the Sandymount line on 13 January 1901.

Dublin Lock-Out. *The Dublin Metropolitan Police clash with strikers in Sackville Street (O'Connell Street), Dublin, on 31 August 1913, during the conflict between transport workers and big-business interests. Four hundred were injured during the incident. [RTÉ Stills Library; Cashman Collection 0510/033]*

By 1914 some 330 trams were serving the city over some 97 km (60 route-miles); but the 1920s saw the beginning of serious competition from BUS transport, and the DUTC introduced its own buses from 1925, subsequently buying out the other operators under the terms of the Road Transport Act (1933). In 1938 it announced its intention of replacing the entire tram network over four years, but the war years of 1939–45 led to a reprieve for the five routes then remaining. On 1 January 1945 the DUTC became part of CIÉ, and on 9 July 1949 the last tram ran from NELSON PILLAR to Blackrock, stripped to its ironwork by souvenir-hunters. **Bernard Share**

Dublin University Choral Society, the oldest choral society in Ireland. Founded in 1837 by Hercules MacDonnell, its objective was stated to be the cultivation of choral music in general. Membership, at first limited to eighteen men (occasionally joined by boys from the cathedral choirs), was opened to women in the 1870s and now reaches 200. The society presented the first performance in Ireland of some thirty-five choral works, including Mahler's *Eighth Symphony* (1992), with combined Dublin choirs. Conductors have included Charles Graves, JOSEPH ROBINSON, SIR ROBERT PRESCOTT STEWART, Charles Marchant, GEORGE HEWSON, JOSEPH GROOCOCK, David Milne, Martin Adams, Gráinne Gormley, and Bernie Sherlock. **Ite O'Donovan**

Dublin University Magazine (1833–77), an independent literary, cultural and political monthly. It was founded by a group of young men associated with TRINITY COLLEGE, Dublin, to represent a radical Tory position in Irish politics in opposition to the university's Board, then noted for its liberalism of outlook. Its unionism, however, did not preclude a keen interest in Irish life and letters, often considered from a Protestant point of view. Consciously modelled on the great Edinburgh reviews, it sought to achieve an intellectual leadership in the country. Among its editors were ISAAC BUTT, CHARLES LEVER, and SHERIDAN LE FANU. Many of the best-known Irish writers of the nineteenth century contributed work throughout its life, making it the most distinguished of periodical publications in the period. **Terence Brown**

Dublin University Press. A printing house in the form of a small Doric temple designed by Richard Castle was built in TRINITY COLLEGE in 1734–6 and served thus until 1976. Though much of its output was associated directly or indirectly with the college, it was leased throughout its existence to a succession of printers, several of whom owned printing or PUBLISHING undertakings elsewhere in the city. Trinity College therefore had no direct control over or interest in the press, a factor that contributed to its consistent failure to fully develop the publishing side of the business and earned the college the nickname of the 'Silent Sister' in the eighteenth century. The press printed and published its first book, 780 copies of an edition of *Plato's Dialogues*, in 1738, followed by a modest output of classical texts, few of more than local student significance.

Under the nineteenth-century management of M. H. GILL, 1842–75, a more positive policy was pursued, resulting in the publication of *James Usher's Works* in seventeen volumes (1847–64) and the seminal Annals of the FOUR MASTERS (1851). As printer, publisher, wholesale and retail bookseller Gill came tantalisingly close to establishing an effective university press, but continuing academic reluctance to become involved in 'trade' frustrated his ambitions. A 'Dublin University Press Series' of scholarly works, the majority printed at the press, was in fact inaugurated in 1878, continuing intermittently until 1943.

In 1944 Ireland's oldest printing and publishing business was sold to the Allman family, who incorporated Dublin University Press Ltd as a limited company, with college representation on the board. In 1976 it merged with Brunswick Press, also owned by the Allmans, in new premises in a Dublin suburb. **Bernard Share**

Ducart, Davis (Daviso de Arcort) (fl. c. 1760–before 1786), architect. Possibly born in Piedmont. He is first recorded in Ireland in the early 1760s; by 1764 he was in Cork. Not unusually, he served as a CANAL engineer as well as as an architect, and he worked on the canal between Coalisland, Co. Tyrone, and Drumglass collieries. As part of the project he designed the aqueduct near Newmills. The Custom House, Limerick, begun in 1765, was his earliest known building. He worked in a very mannered Palladian style. Other works include Mayoralty House, Cork, and villas in Kilshanning, Co. Cork, and CASTLETOWN COX, Co. Kilkenny. **Brendan Rooney**

Dúchas, The Heritage Service of the OPW became part of the then Department of Arts, Heritage, Gaeltacht and the Islands in 1996–7. It is responsible for the protection and conservation of the natural and built heritage; the management of national parks and nature reserves; the conservation of ARCHAEOLOGY and ARCHITECTURE, including prehistoric burial sites, monastic settlements, and historic houses; and the maintenance and development of inland waterways. [see OFFICE OF PUBLIC WORKS.] **Ruth McManus**

Du Cros, Harvey (1846–1918), sportsman and businessman. Born in Dublin. He won Irish BOXING and fencing championships and founded Bective Rangers Football Club. He saw the potential of the pneumatic tyre in 1889 when a Dunlop rider beat his sons (who dominated Irish cycle racing in the 1880s and 1890s), and later that year he jointly founded the world's first pneumatic tyre company with JOHN BOYD DUNLOP and partners. He was awarded membership of the Légion d'Honneur by the French government for his contribution to transport. His son Arthur du Cros, who was Conservative MP for Hastings from 1908 to 1918, succeeded him as head of the Dunlop Corporation on his death in 1918. **Brendan Lynch**

duelling. Duelling emerged in Ireland in the sixteenth and seventeenth centuries as part of the socio-cultural identity of the newly emerging landed aristocracy, reaching a peak in the confrontational environment of the second half of the eighteenth century. Because it was the most identifiable index of a man's honourable reputation, virtually every major political name 'smelled powder', as JONAH BARRINGTON memorably observed. Changes in social attitudes associated with the decline in the aristocratic mores that sustained the code of honour, and the example of leaders like DANIEL O'CONNELL, hastened its eclipse in the nineteenth century. [see GILLESPIE, ROBERT ROLLO; MAGINN, WILLIAM.] **James Kelly**

Duff, Arthur (1899–1956), composer. Born in Dublin; studied piano and organ at the RIAM. He was appointed assistant organist at CHRIST CHURCH CATHEDRAL at the age of fifteen and entered TCD in 1917. He completed his BMus degree in 1922 and was awarded a DMus in 1942. He was the first Irish-born bandmaster in the Army School of Music (now DEFENCE FORCES SCHOOL OF MUSIC) and joined Radio Éireann in 1937, becoming assistant music director in 1945. His works are much influenced by Vaughan Williams and Delius. His output consists primarily of orchestral works. **David Mooney**

Duff, Frank (1889–1980), founder of the Legion of Mary. Born in Dublin. He was a civil servant until 1933. In 1921 he founded the Legion of Mary, a Catholic lay organisation that concentrated on social work among the derelict poor and the reform of prostitutes, particularly in the MONTO area of Dublin, while promoting Marian devotion. It is the largest such organisation in the Catholic world, claiming more than 3 million active members in 2001. **Fergal Tobin**

Duffin, Emma (fl. twentieth century), nurse and diarist. Born in Belfast to a middle-class liberal-unionist merchant family. She served with the Voluntary Aid Detachment during the FIRST WORLD WAR, first as an untrained auxiliary nurse, in front-line military hospitals in northern France and Egypt and recorded her wartime experiences in five diaries dating from 1915 to 1917. She was later involved in numerous Belfast charities, serving as honorary secretary of the Council of Social Welfare, 1927–43, and secretary of the School Pictures Committee, c. 1925–54. During the SECOND WORLD WAR, because of her age, she did not nurse at the front line but instead remained in Belfast, registering for nursing service at a first aid post. She assisted the wounded and the bereaved during the BELFAST BLITZ of 1941, when the German air force bombed the city. She was deeply affected by this experience, as she recorded in her diary: 'It was a hideous nightmare ... Death should be dignified, peaceful, Hitler had made even death grotesque ... I came away drawing deep breaths of fresh air. So this was the result of a Blitz.' [see DIARIES AND JOURNALS.] **Diane Urquhart**

Duffy, Sir Charles Gavan (1816–1903), Young Irelander. Born in Co. Monaghan. A journalist, he edited the *Belfast Vindicator* and, after 1842, the NATION. Seceding from the Repeal Association in 1846, he dominated the YOUNG IRELAND Confederation. Several juries failed to convict him for his insurrectionary plans in 1848. He was MP for New Ross before emigrating to AUSTRALIA in 1855, where he became premier of Victoria and later speaker of its parliament. Knighted, he returned to Ireland and wrote the history of Young Ireland. **Richard P. Davis**

Duffy, James (1809–1871), printer, publisher, and bookseller. Born in Co. Monaghan; educated in HEDGE SCHOOLS. He began his career as a pedlar of cheap Catholic literature, becoming a bookseller's assistant in Dublin and setting up his own business c. 1830. He exploited the new invention of stereotyping, producing cheap popular books and pamphlets. In co-operation with the YOUNG IRELAND movement and in particular CHARLES GAVAN DUFFY he published the shilling 'Library of Ireland', in which each of the prominent Young Irelanders was allocated a historical volume. He became publisher to the CATHOLIC UNIVERSITY OF IRELAND on its foundation, 1854. During his long and active life he is reputed never to have taken a holiday—nor allowed one to his employees, whom he otherwise treated well. **Bernard Share**

Duggan, William (Willie) (1950–), rugby footballer. Born in Kilkenny. He made his debut against England at Lansdowne Road in 1975 and made his last international appearance at the same venue in 1984. Ireland's most-capped number eight, he won forty-one caps, two of them on the flank, and was a superb player, hard and all but indestructible. He captained Ireland in his last two matches for the team, when CIARÁN FITZGERALD was ruled out by injury. He toured New Zealand with the British Lions in 1977, one of four Irish players in a team that was largely drawn from Wales. He was the only Irish player to be chosen in all four Test matches and was the tourists' sole try-scorer in the third Test at Dunedin. **Karl Johnston**

Duley, Mark (1960–) , musician. Born in New Zealand; studied at the University of Auckland and pursued postgraduate studies in Germany and the Netherlands. In 1992 he was appointed organist and director of music at CHRIST CHURCH CATHEDRAL, Dublin. His work at the cathedral has led him to reinstitute the lay vicars choral and to found the girls' choir and most recently Christ Church Baroque, the cathedral's own orchestra, used principally for the performance of early music. In addition to his work at the cathedral he is chorus master of the RTÉ Philharmonic Choir. **David Mooney**

Dun, Sir Patrick (1642–1713), physician. Born in Aberdeen. He was president of the Irish College of Physicians on thirteen occasions, and was knighted in 1696. He bequeathed his lands to the college for the establishment of professorships of medicine; the income was later used to establish SIR PATRICK DUN'S HOSPITAL, Dublin. **Robert Mills**

Dunamase Castle, Co. Laois, a large early ANGLO-NORMAN CASTLE. It is sited in an elevated position on a rock outcrop and is mainly the work of William Marshal in the first decade of the thirteenth century. There are remains of earth-and-timber defences (outer barbican), an outer gate, and outer curtain-walls defending the inner barbican. The main gate-house leads into the main bailey, which has a thirteenth-century hall-keep. **David Sweetman**

Dún Aonghasa ('the fort of Aengus'), a prehistoric stone fort dramatically sited at the edge of steep cliffs on the northern coast of Arainn (Inis Mór), Aran Islands, Co. Galway. The fort covers an area of 5.7 ha (14 acres) and commands a spectacular view down the west coast of Ireland. It belongs to the HILL-FORT class, a monument type that first appeared in Ireland towards the beginning of the first millennium BC.

Three main enclosing walls divide the interior into inner, middle and outer enclosures; a fragment of a fourth wall survives along the north-west. A broad band of CHEVAUX DE FRISE, which runs outside the middle enclosure, was probably added at a later date. The walls are constructed of limestone blocks with a rubble core; the weathered limestone pavement in the immediate area would have provided ample building material. The fort was excavated in 1992–5 under the auspices of the DISCOVERY PROGRAMME. The remains of approximately ten houses were found in the inner and middle enclosures; the accompanying domestic assemblage included coarse cooking pottery, bone pins and needles, and a range of stone tools. Evidence for bronze casting, and a small hoard of buffered bronze rings found near the cliff edge, testify to the prestigious role of the site during the Late BRONZE AGE.

The RADIOCARBON evidence points to a marked falling off in activity after c. 700 BC, and thereafter the fort may have been occupied only intermittently. The present ground plan results from a major rebuilding carried out probably some time during the first millennium AD. During this phase the inner and middle enclosure walls were substantially strengthened, the former being raised to a height of approximately 6 m (20 ft) and terraced on the interior. In the early Middle Ages, Dún Aonghasa may have been a royal seat associated with a branch of the EOGHANACHTA dynasty. The fort was extensively repaired shortly after it was taken into state care at the end of the nineteenth century. [see STAIGUE.] **Claire Cotter**

Dunbar, Adrian (1958–), stage and screen actor. Born in Portadown, Co. Armagh; studied at the Guildhall School of Music and Drama, London. He came to prominence for his role in *Hear My Song* (1991), which he jointly wrote; other films include *My Left Foot* (1989), *The Playboys* (1992), *The Crying Game* (1992), *Force of Duty* (1992), *Widow's Peak* (1994), and *The General* (1998). He also featured in 'Tough Love' (2000), a police series for Granada Television, RTÉ Television's 'Relative Strangers', and one of the episodes of George Lucas's *Star Wars* cycle. **Kevin Rockett**

Dunbar-Harrison incident. In 1930 the Local Appointments Commission of the Civil Service nominated Letitia Dunbar-Harrison for the post of County Librarian in Co. Mayo. The Library Committee of Mayo County Council and the council itself refused to endorse the appointment, arguing that the nominee's Irish was inadequate; but the fact that she was a Protestant and a graduate of TRINITY COLLEGE, Dublin, was widely believed to be the real prohibiting factor. The Government dissolved the county council, replacing it with a commissioner, who appointed Dunbar-Harrison. A BOYCOTT of the library services ensued, and in 1931 Dunbar-Harrison was transferred to the Military Library in Dublin. The headline in the *Catholic Bulletin* of February of that year—'Well done, Mayo!'—shows clearly the sectarian interpretation of the incident. **Myra Dowling**

Duncannon Fort, Co. Wexford, a late sixteenth-century star-shaped fort, so called because of the shape of the outer defences. It is built on a promontory jutting into the estuary and was originally defended with a TOWER-HOUSE. It had an 8 m (26-ft) rampart, a ditch 2.4 m (8 ft) deep, and stone towers, with four gun platforms at the west end. It was further fortified in 1611 and was besieged by Confederates in 1641 and 1645 and by CROMWELL in 1649. It was garrisoned until 1857 and was burnt by the IRA in 1921. **David Sweetman**

Dun Cow, Book of the, the oldest surviving MANUSCRIPT written wholly in Irish. It takes its name (Lebor na hUidre in Old Irish) from the tradition that it was written on the hide of a dun cow belonging to St CIARÁN of CLONMACNOISE. It was probably written towards the end of the eleventh century, perhaps in Clonmacnoise but possibly in the monastery of Louth. In the fragment now surviving, three main hands may be discerned. One of the three scribes was MAEL MUIRE MAC CÉILECHAIR, who was killed in Clonmacnoise in 1106. The work contains—usually in fragmentary form—some of the most important works of early Irish literature, most notably part of the earliest version of TÁIN BÓ CUAILNGE. It was in Co. Donegal for some time before 1359 and in Co. Sligo until 1470, after which it returned to Co. Donegal. It turned up in Dublin in 1837 and was bought by the ROYAL IRISH ACADEMY in 1844. **Nollaig Ó Muraíle**

Dundalk (*Dún Dealgan*), county town of Co. Louth, half way between Dublin and Belfast on the Castletown River; population, including environs (2002), 27,399. The lands of Dundalk were granted to Bertram de Verdon in 1185 by HENRY II, and the walled royal borough remained an important northern frontier town of the PALE throughout the Middle Ages. Among the medieval remnants are the fifteenth-century tower of the FRANCISCAN friary at Seatown. The introduction of the linen trade by the Earl of Clanbrassil in the eighteenth century was the start of Dundalk's INDUSTRIAL DEVELOPMENT. BREWING has been important for more than 300 years, while P. J. Carroll's tobacco works has operated since 1824 (see p. 41). Dundalk's industrial core was the locomotive works of the Great Northern RAILWAY (1881–1958), which at one time employed more than 1,300 people.

Industrial decline in the 1960s was accentuated by the town's uneasy BORDER location. Recent renewal has seen the development of a new SHOPPING CENTRE and a HOUSING boom. Dundalk Institute of Technology has provided third-level EDUCATION since 1970, training a local work force for employment in new industries, including Rank Xerox. **Ruth McManus**

Dun Emer Guild (1902–c. 1960), a philanthropic educational, nationalist and William Morris-inspired enterprise, named after the needleworking wife of the legendary CÚ CHULAINN. With the collaboration of Elizabeth and Lily Yeats, sisters of W. B. Yeats, it was founded in a large house in Dundrum, Co. Dublin, by Evelyn Gleeson, newly returned to Ireland to do something for her country by setting up a craft settlement that would train workers and create jobs using local labour and natural materials. Elizabeth Yeats mastered an old Albion hand press to produce hand-coloured prints, bookplates, broadsides, and the only true ARTS AND CRAFTS books published in Ireland; Lily Yeats ran an EMBROIDERY workshop. Both availed of their brothers' and their artistic friends' advice and designs. In 1908 the Yeatses seceded and established CUALA INDUSTRIES at Churchtown, Co. Dublin; in 1912 Gleeson moved her workers to Hardwicke Street, Dublin, later to Harcourt Street, continuing to weave rugs and tapestries, embroider, bind books, and print ephemera. **Nicola Gordon Bowe**

Dungal (died c. 834), theologian, astronomer, and poet. From the school of BANGOR, he arrived at the Carolingian court and taught in Pavia. He wrote a remarkable letter to Charlemagne on the nature of eclipses, c. 810, and a treatise against Claudius, Bishop of Turin, defending Catholic doctrine during the western iconoclastic controversy. He bequeathed his books (now in the Ambrosian Library, Milan) to the monastery of Bobbio, where he died. **Juan José Pérez-Camacho**

Dungannon (*Dún Geanainn*), Co. Tyrone, a town and regional market centre; population (1991) 9,190. The site's medieval history is obscure until the O'Neills moved their political capital here from Grianán in the thirteenth century and built a fort on Castle Hill (still in the town centre). Dungannon remained an O'Neill stronghold until the defeat of HUGH O'NEILL (first Earl of Tyrone) in the 1608 Rebellion. The site and lands were granted to Sir ARTHUR CHICHESTER, who revived O'Neill's market patent of 1578 and established a flourishing town on the south slope of Castle Hill, between the newly rebuilt castle and the River Rhone. Destroyed in the 1641 Rebellion, the town recovered slowly until its sale to the Scottish Knox family (later Earls of Ranfurly) in 1698. Under their patronage it developed as a LINEN and brickmaking town in the eighteenth century, undergoing extensive improvement c. 1800.

Despite continuing suburban development of varying aesthetic quality, the varied, hilly and irregular skyline retains its nineteenth-century flavour, and the town includes a number of individually excellent late eighteenth and nineteenth-century buildings, including the Royal School, Tyrone Printing Works (1798), the Courthouse (1830), Northumberland Row (early nineteenth century), and St Anne's CHURCH OF IRELAND and Catholic churches (1869, 1876). **Lindsay Proudfoot**

Dungannon Clubs, an organisation of Ulster nationalists formed in March 1905 by Bulmer Hobson and Denis McCullough, both members of the IRB, named to evoke memories of the DUNGANNON CONVENTION of 1782 and the winning of legislative independence. Its newspaper, the *Republic*, declared that it belonged to 'the SINN FÉIN movement', but the group's separatism went further than that of ARTHUR GRIFFITH, for it declared: 'An Irish Republic is our aim. We do not ask it as a concession—we will take it as our right.' All young members were obliged 'to attend the GAELIC LEAGUE and to be absolute teetotallers' (it was expected of those over twenty-five merely that they 'must never be seen drunk'). In 1907 the group became part of Cumann na nGaedheal, the forerunner of SINN FÉIN. **Jonathan Bardon**

Dungannon Convention (1782). During the crisis brought on by England's poor performance in the American War, 'Patriot' politicians, led by HENRY GRATTAN, saw an opportunity to free the Irish Parliament from what they saw as the excessive interference of that of London in matters of legislation. As relatively few people then could vote in parliamentary elections, Grattan and his supporters needed to devise other means of raising sufficient public support for pushing the British government into concessions. Accordingly, on 15 February 1782 a convention of delegates from VOLUNTEER corps throughout Ulster was held in the Presbyterian church in Dungannon. A variety of political proposals was debated and a series of demands drawn up, now known as the Dungannon Resolutions. As the Volunteers were mostly Protestant, the most famous was the thirteenth resolution, which 'rejoiced in the relaxation of the Penal Laws', implying that Grattan also had Catholic support.

Following the convention the Dungannon Resolutions were published in the newspapers and were adopted at meetings throughout Ireland. This apparent growing wave of public opinion gave Grattan the moral support to force the British government to grant legislative independence to the Irish Parliament in April 1782. The fact that the Volunteers were a military body has led some historians to call this episode the first introduction of the gun into Irish politics. There were other Dungannon Volunteer conventions—in June 1782, September 1783, and February 1793—but they lacked the impact of the original. **Allan Blackstock**

Dungarvan (*Dún Garbhán*), Co. Waterford, a market and tourist town and county town of Co. Waterford; population (2002) 7,218. According to tradition, Dungarvan was the site of an Augustinian monastery founded by St Garbhán in the seventh century, where the Colligan River enters a wide, shallow bay. After 1175 the ANGLO-NORMANS built a series of CASTLES in the area, and the town developed alongside one of these. Dungarvan was granted borough status c. 1200, with additional privileges over the next half century. Walls were built enclosing the town, and these survived until the early nineteenth century. In the Middle Ages, Dungarvan's harbour, its initial attraction, began to silt up, and the town was overshadowed by Youghal to the west and by WATERFORD to the east. In 1582 the town was largely burnt down during the DESMOND REBELLION and in the early seventeenth century again suffered. Its economy was dependent on the export of fish, but it became progressively poorer and more decayed throughout the eighteenth century. The Duke of Devonshire owned some of the poorest properties in the town, and in the early nineteenth century he began a major improvement by building new houses, streets, and churches, in effect creating the townscape of today. Dungarvan's population was 8,600 in 1841, but, as with other towns, the GREAT FAMINE began a century-long decline in its fortunes. In 1961 the population was less than 5,200; since then Dungarvan has become an attractive service and manufacturing town with an expanding TOURISM role. **Kevin Hourihan**

Dunguaire, Co. Galway, a rectangular TOWER-HOUSE of four storeys on a small promontory in Kinvara Bay, restored and much altered. The original doorway is obscured by a modern addition, but the finely decorated original jambs can still be seen. Spiral stairs give access to the upper levels. There is a six-sided bawn wall with a mural tower and gateway. **David Sweetman**

Dunkin, William (c. 1709–1765), clergyman and poet. Born in Dublin; educated at TCD. A brilliant classical scholar who involved himself in the literary skirmishes of the time, he joined the circle of poets around SWIFT, who thought highly of him. He wrote poetry in Latin, English, and Greek. His best poems are 'The Parson's Revels', a burlesque containing fine comic portraits, and 'The Murphæid', a translation of a comic poem about student escapades at TCD. He became headmaster of Portora Royal School, ENNISKILLEN, in 1746; his poems were published posthumously. Dunkin is the most underrated Irish poet of his age. **Andrew Carpenter**

Dún Laoghaire, Co. Dublin, a port and town that forms the core of the administrative county of Dún Laoghaire and Rathdown; population (2002) 24,395. In 1821 it was named Kingstown to mark a visit by George IV, but the Irish name was restored (with altered spelling) a century later. The modern town dates from the establishment of an 'asylum harbour' for the port of Dublin after 1817, and a new town gradually developed to the east of the original fishing village of Dunleary. Growth was encouraged by the transfer of the mail packet ships to the port (from Howth) after 1826 and by the opening of the Dublin and Kingstown RAILWAY from Dublin in 1834—the first suburban railway in the world. From the 1840s there was a building boom as many people chose to live in new stucco houses with a sea view, commuting by train to Dublin. The town's personality as a centre of leisure and FASHION was enhanced by yachting activity. In 1834 the Kingstown Town Commission was established to control the town's development; it erected the Venetian-style Town Hall (1880), designed by J. L. Robinson, now incorporated in the county council offices. Dún Laoghaire remains one of the Republic's principal ports of entry, catering for car traffic and a high-speed catamaran service. [see ANEMOMETER; BOYD, JOHN MCNEILL.] **Ruth McManus**

Dún Laoghaire Harbour. Following a number of calamitous shipwrecks in DUBLIN BAY, an 'asylum harbour' was planned, and work began in 1815. JOHN RENNIE was appointed consultant in 1817 and proposed the East and West Piers. The granite to form the piers was quarried at nearby DALKEY and transported to the harbour by funicular railway. Sir John Rennie took over from his father in 1821, and the work was substantially completed by the BOARD OF WORKS by 1860. Carlisle Pier, with its rail link, was opened in 1859. A car ferry terminal was built in 1970 and the earlier rail link abandoned. A terminal for a high-speed ferry was completed in 1995. [see ATMOSPHERIC RAILWAY; DUBLIN AND KINGSTOWN RAILWAY.] **Ronald Cox**

Dunlap, John (1747–1812), printer and American revolutionary. Born in Strabane, Co. Tyrone, where he served his apprenticeship at Gray's printing works. When a boy he joined his uncle William Dunlap, a printer and publisher, in Philadelphia and in 1771 was apprenticed to him. He founded what became the first American daily newspaper, the *Pennsylvania Packet*, later the *North American and United States Gazette*. Appointed printer to the Congress, he printed the Declaration of Independence (1777). He was an officer in the Philadelphia cavalry, which became George Washington's bodyguard. In 1780 he gave £4,000 to supply provisions to the Revolutionary army. [see UNITED STATES, IRISH IN.] **David Kiely**

The Pennſylvania Packet, *and Daily Advertiſer.*

[Price Four-Pence.] WEDNESDAY, SEPTEMBER 19, 1787. [No. 2690.]

WE, the People of the United States, in order to form a more perfect Union, eſtabliſh Juſtice, inſure domeſtic Tranquility, provide for the common Defence, promote the General Welfare, and ſecure the Bleſſings of Liberty to Ourſelves and our Poſterity, do ordain and eſtabliſh this Conſtitution for the United States of America.

ARTICLE I.

Dunlap, John. *The* Pennsylvania Packet, *19 September 1787, with the Constitution of the United States of America. Printed in Philadelphia by John Dunlap of Strabane, Co. Tyrone, it was America's first daily newspaper. [Prints and Photographs Division, Library of Congress, Washington; LC-USZ62-58266]*

Dunlop, John Boyd (1840–1921), veterinary surgeon and inventor. Born in Ayrshire. He made the first pneumatic tyre in Belfast in 1889 to provide his son with a more comfortable ride on his bicycle. The racing cyclist Willie Hume used Dunlop tyres to beat the champion du Cros brothers at the 1889 Belfast Easter Sports; the entrepreneur HARVEY DU CROS quickly appreciated the tyre's potential and he, Dunlop and partners established the world's first pneumatic tyre company later that year in Stephen Street, Dublin. **Brendan Lynch**

Dunlop, William Joseph (Joey) (1952–2000), motorcyclist. Born in Ballymoney, Co. Antrim. He started local road racing in 1969, expanding his activities to the Isle of Man TT in 1976. He joined Honda for 1982, remaining with them until the end of his career. His achievements were immense, including five formula 1 titles, twenty-six TT races, and twenty-four Ulster grands prix. He was made a member of the Order of the British Empire for charity work—driving relief supplies to Romania—and for services to MOTORCYCLING. He died while competing in Estonia; his funeral was virtually a state affair, attended by an estimated 50,000 people. **Don McClenahan**

Dunluce, Co. Antrim, one of the most picturesque settings for an Irish castle, on a precipitous rock outcrop overlooking the sea. It is one of the few large castles of the late fourteenth century, though most of it dates from the sixteenth century during the ownership of the McDonnells. The original castle consisted of a rectangular courtyard with strong walls and angle-towers. The rectangular gate-house and extensive remains of domestic buildings that now dominate the castle are attributed to its restoration at the end of the sixteenth century. The kitchen, with some of the servants, collapsed into the sea in 1639. Nearby terraces and raised beds are the remains of a seventeenth-century formal garden. **David Sweetman**

Dunmore Cave, a stream passage linking several chambers, lying within a limestone ridge 11 km (7 miles) north of Kilkenny. The chambers, which predate the last Ice Age, were dissolved out of the limestone by water occupying joints in the rock. The stream passage was created later by swift glacial meltwaters that were forced underground, with flowstone floors formed at least 35,000 years ago. However, between 15,000 and 2,500 years ago the cave began to decay and became choked by boulder collapses, between which water was impounded. Despite having only 300 m (990 ft) of passages, Dunmore is the only significant cave in the central midlands and has been well documented throughout history as a result. The most important reference comes from the Annals of the FOUR MASTERS, which record a massacre here by the VIKINGS of Dublin in 928. RADIOCARBON DATING of human bones found in the cave confirms that many people, mainly women and children, died in the cave early in the tenth century; the bones show no evidence of violence, but plentiful charcoal implies that the victims died by suffocation induced by fire. COINS found in the cave mostly originated in Viking England in the 920s. In 1999 a hoard of unique Viking silver was found in the cave, dating, intriguingly, from forty years after the massacre. The cave has been a national monument since 1940. **Colman Gallagher**

Dunmore East Harbour, Co. Waterford. The original pier and lighthouse at Dunmore East were completed by ALEXANDER NIMMO in 1825 to accommodate the mail packet steamers from Milford Haven in Wales. Partial rebuilding of the pier and additions culminated in the development of the harbour between 1963 and 1972 as a major fishery port. **Ronald Cox**

Dunne, Ben (1949–), businessman. Born in Cork; educated at Presentation College, Cork. He became managing director of Dunnes Stores, his family's retail business, founded by his father, Ben Dunne senior. In 1992 he was arrested in Florida on drugs charges following a cocaine binge, which precipitated a bitter power struggle among his siblings. The dispute became litigious, and details emerged of irregular payments made to senior politicians during Ben Dunne's tenure as managing director of Dunnes Stores. A series of TRIBUNALS followed to investigate political corruption.

He left Dunnes Stores in 1993 following a buy-out and now runs a leisure centre. **Martin Clancy**

Dunne, Joseph (1948–), philosopher. Born in Dublin; educated at UCD. He is senior lecturer in education and co-ordinator of human development at Dublin City University, and is widely recognised as an important philosopher of education. He has published *Back to the Rough Ground: Phronesis and Techne in Modern Philosophy and in Aristotle* (1993) and was joint-editor of *Questioning Ireland: Debates in Political Philosophy and Public Policy* (2000). **Fionola Meredith**

Dunne, Seán (1956–1995), poet. Born in Waterford; educated at UCC. He became a JOURNALIST with the *Cork Examiner*, where he was the paper's brilliant literary editor. His collection *Against the Storm* (1985) was followed by *The Sheltered Nest* (1992); *Time and the Island* was published posthumously in 1996. He edited *Poets of Munster* (1985), *The Cork Anthology* (1993), and *The Ireland Anthology* (published posthumously, 1997). *In My Father's House*, a memoir, was published in 1991; *The Road to Silence* (1994) is his spiritual autobiography. One of the best Munster writers, he was a unique poet of solitude. **Thomas McCarthy**

Dunne, Veronica, (1927–), singer and teacher. She began her vocal studies in Dublin with Herbert Rooney, who quickly realised her talent for bel canto singing. From 1946 she studied in Rome and two years later made her operatic debut in Dublin. She won first place in the Concorso Lirico Milano, following which her operatic career flourished, and in 1952 she joined the Royal Opera House, London, where she performed with the world's leading singers and conductors. She has also made several recordings. In 1961 she took up a teaching post at the Municipal College of Music in Dublin. She has taught many of Ireland's leading singers and continues to teach at the Leinster School of Music Opera Studio and the RIAM of which she is an honorary fellow. Her place in Irish musical life has been commemorated by the international Veronica Dunne Singing Competition established in 1995. In 2002 she came out of retirement to sing the role of the Countess in Tchaikovsky's *Queen of Spades* for OPERA IRELAND. **David Mooney and Richard Pine.**

du Noyer, George Victor (1817–1869), geologist, artist, and antiquarian. Born in Dublin, of Huguenot descent; he studied art under GEORGE PETRIE and from 1834 to 1842 worked with the ORDNANCE SURVEY as an artist, geologist, and archaeologist. In 1844–5 he was drawing master at the newly established College of St Columba at STACKALLAN House, Co. Meath; and in June 1847 he joined the GEOLOGICAL SURVEY OF IRELAND 'on special service.' It was his task to map the geological features exposed during the construction of the RAILWAY lines radiating from Dublin. He became assistant geologist in 1848 and a district surveyor in 1867. He was one of the Geological Survey's most skilled field geologists, and his field-sheets are veritable works of art. In 1852 he was responsible for the geological lines on a published geological version of *Fraser's Travelling Map of Ireland*. In the field his pencil, pen and brushes were in constant use; many books, together with the survey's memoirs, contain examples of his artistry, and numerous other specimens of his work are in the Geological Survey, ROYAL IRISH ACADEMY, ROYAL SOCIETY OF ANTIQUARIES OF IRELAND, and elsewhere. In 1995 the NATIONAL GALLERY OF IRELAND mounted an exhibition of his work. **Gordon L. Herries Davies**

Dunphy, Eamon (1945–), soccer player, journalist, and broadcaster. Born in Dublin; educated at Sandymount High School. He was apprenticed to Manchester United in 1960, played English league football for York City, Millwall, Charlton, and Reading, and in 1978 won an FAI Cup medal as player-coach with Shamrock Rovers. He was capped twenty-three times for the Republic of Ireland, 1966–77. He was soccer correspondent of the *Sunday Tribune*, a contributor to *Magill*, 1978–84, and a controversial columnist with the SUNDAY INDEPENDENT, 1984–97. He presented his own radio programme, 'The Last Word', on Today FM from 1997 to 2002. His publications include *Only a Game* (1976), an account of his professional football career, *Unforgettable Fire* (1985), the story of U2, and *A Strange Kind of Glory* (1992), a biography of Matt Busby and *Keane: the Autobiography* (2002). **Ciarán Deane**

Dunsany, Lord: see PLUNKETT, EDWARD.

Dunsink Observatory, the principal astronomical observatory in Ireland, part of the DUBLIN INSTITUTE FOR ADVANCED STUDIES. It is situated on a low hill 7 km ($4\frac{1}{2}$ miles) north-west of the centre of Dublin, with fine views of the city and surroundings. Founded by TRINITY COLLEGE in 1783, it was under the direction of nine successive Andrews professors of ASTRONOMY until 1921. As well as being a centre for observational astronomy, theoretical studies were pursued, most notably by Sir WILLIAM ROWAN HAMILTON and Sir EDMUND T. WHITTAKER. The observatory became part of the School of Cosmic Physics of the Dublin Institute for Advanced Studies in 1947. **Ian Elliott**

Dunsoghly Castle, near St Margaret's, Co. Dublin, a very large TOWER-HOUSE built by one of the Plunketts c. early sixteenth

Durcan. *Paul Durcan is one of Ireland's foremost contemporary poets, noted for readings of his own work. [Harvill Press; photo: Caroline Forbes]*

century, classified as a larger castle of the late Middle Ages but little different in design from tower-houses. It is square in plan, with a square tower at each angle, and retains its original roof timbers. There are substantial portions of its bawn wall. Castletown Castle, Co. Louth, BUNRATTY CASTLE and BLARNEY CASTLE are similar. A sixteenth-century chapel is close to the tower-house and within the remains of a bawn wall. **David Sweetman**

Durcan, Paul (1944–), poet. Born in Dublin. He has evolved a poetic strategy that uses hyper-real attention to detail and an incantatory style to confront the enemies of common human decency. He has been called an iconoclast but in Durcan's poetry both well-known and unknown heroes of the heart are held up for veneration. 'Durcan', the figure in many of his poems, holds the world in care, a self-imposed duty which frees the poet to vent his fury and to expend his heart in a self-feminising poetry of praise. Among his many books since *O Westport in the Light of Asia Minor* (1975) are *Teresa's Bar* (1976), *Jesus, Break his Fall* (1980), *Jumping the Train Tracks with Angela* (1983), *The Berlin Wall Café* (1985), *Going Home to Russia* (1987), and *Daddy, Daddy* (1990). His most recent works, *A Snail in my Prime* (1993), *Christmas Day* (1996) and *Greetings to Our Friends in Brazil* (1999), are triumphs of poetic maturity. He is a member of AOSDÁNA. **Theo Dorgan**

Durkan, Mark (1960–), politician. He worked as a full-time assistant to JOHN HUME and was chairman of the SOCIAL DEMOCRATIC AND LABOUR PARTY, 1984–98. He was elected for the Foyle constituency to the Northern Ireland Forum in 1996 and was a leading negotiator for his party at the talks that led to the BELFAST AGREEMENT (1998). He was elected to the Northern Ireland Assembly and was appointed Minister of Finance. In November 2001 he became leader of the SDLP and Deputy First Minister after Hume and SÉAMUS MALLON, respectively, stepped down from these positions. **Jonathan Bardon**

Durrow, Book of, a late seventh-century Latin MANUSCRIPT of 248 vellum leaves, approximately 245 by 145 mm, now in TRINITY COLLEGE Library, Dublin. The earliest of the surviving fully illuminated insular GOSPEL books, it contains, in addition to the four Gospels, St Jerome's prefaces, interpretations of Hebrew names, and CANON TABLES. The text of the Gospels is essentially St Jerome's fourth-century Vulgate translation, but the arrangement of the text and the illustrative pages displaying the four Evangelists' symbols, as well as occasional variants in the text, stem from the earlier 'Old Latin' version. The deserved fame of the book rests on the expert calligraphy of the text, executed in *insular half-uncial* SCRIPT, and the exceptional quality and great variety of its decoration, surpassed in very few comparable Gospel books. Eleven fully decorated pages, for which red, yellow, green, and occasionally brown paint have been used, include the symbols of the four EVANGELISTS but also several 'carpet pages', filled with biting animals and abstract designs, such as trumpets, spirals, roundels, and interlace. In addition the manuscript contains magnificent initial letters for the opening of each Gospel.

The presence of the manuscript in the monastery of Durrow, near Tullamore, Co. Offaly (founded in the sixth century by COLM CILLE), is attested from the tenth century onwards, though it was not written there. Although absolute certainty cannot be attained, because of the limited number of comparable manuscripts, it seems likely, on the strength of several elements in the decoration and of a number of readings in the Gospel texts, that it was executed in Northumbria in a MONASTERY founded by Colm Cille and his successors and therefore under Irish influence. A subscription at the end of the manuscript, possibly at least in part the work of a devout forger, seems to indicate that the book was copied from a manuscript written by Colm Cille himself, which led to additional reverence for it in the Middle Ages. After the suppression of the monastery of Durrow the book remained in the area; later in the sixteenth century a local farmer was using it to cure sick cattle by dipping it in water that was then offered to the cattle to drink. Henry Jones, Protestant Bishop of Meath, obtained possession of it in the seventeenth century and in 1652 presented it to Trinity College. **Rijcklof Hofman**

Dursey Island, Co. Cork, a sandstone island of 5.7 km^2 ($2\frac{1}{4}$ sq. miles) at the end of the Beara Peninsula, 200 m (650 ft) from the mainland across Dursey Sound. The island has been inhabited since the BRONZE AGE. In 1602 most of its population were slaughtered by English forces as a consequence of the involvement of the O'Sullivans in the Munster Rebellion. The island recovered to support, through farming and fishing, 358 people in 1841. This fell to 201 in 1901 and to nine in 1996. By 1997 there were six islanders left, all elderly, forming five households. The post office and school closed in the 1970s, and Dursey seems destined to join the list of depopulated islands. A few houses have become holiday homes. Dursey's decline continued despite accessibility being improved in 1969, when a cable-car service connected it to the mainland; those exploiting island farmland now commute by cable-car. Dursey has many archaeological ruins, including a church, as well as a lighthouse and signal tower. **Stephen A. Royle**

Dyer, Reginald Edward Harry (1864–1927), colonial soldier. Born in Murree in the Punjab to an Irish father; educated at Midleton College, Co. Cork and the Royal Military Academy, Sandhurst, Berkshire. He gained notoriety as the general who ordered the Amritsar massacre in 1919, when British soldiers fired on a demonstration, killing 379 people and wounding a further 1,200. The Governor of the Punjab at the time was the Irish-born Sir Michael O'Dwyer (1864–1940), who was later assassinated by Undahn Singh, a survivor of the massacre. **Ciarán Deane**

Dysert O'Dea, Co. Clare, site of a monastery of St Tóla in the eighth century, where the stump of a ROUND TOWER stands close to a church with a jumbled ROMANESQUE south doorway (seventeenth-century reconstruction). The chancel with arch and lancet windows (also reconstructed) is from c. 1200; a seventeenth-century west gable incorporates further Romanesque fragments. In an adjoining field stands a twelfth-century HIGH CROSS of two separate parts, with Christ and an ecclesiastic in high relief (east face), animal and geometrical decoration (west face and sides), and Adam and Eve, a possible Daniel and possible reliquary procession on the base, which stands on transposed church fragments. Further finds are in the archaeological Heritage Centre in the castle nearby. **Peter Harbison**

Eriugena *(see page 361). A depiction by Honorius Augustodunensis in his* Clavis Physicae *of John Scotus Eriugena's four divisions of nature as argued in his most important work* De Divisione Naturae. *These divisions are (from bottom) God, the uncreated creator; creation; non-creating species; and God as the goal. [Bibliothèque Nationale de France; Latin 6734 fol. 3v]*

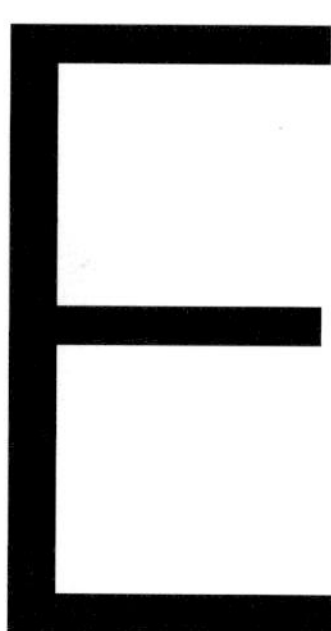

'Eachtra Bhodaigh an Chóta Lachtna' ('Adventure of the Churl of the Grey Coat'), a late literary tale of the FIONN CYCLE. Ireland is spared from invasion when Caol an Iarainn, a handsome foreigner, is defeated in a race by the ungainly Churl. The victor is an OTHERWORLD being in disguise. **Máirtín Ó Briain**

Eager, Edward (1787–1866), lawyer, Methodist pioneer, and convict. Born near Killarney, Co. Kerry. He was appointed a solicitor in Dublin in 1804 but in 1809 was convicted of forgery and sentenced to TRANSPORTATION for life. He arrived in Sydney in 1811. Following a pardon, he began lobbying for the legal recognition of ex-convicts' rights. He travelled to London to argue his case and was rewarded for his efforts by the passing of the Transportation Act (1824). He contributed significantly to the constitutional reform of New South Wales, was foremost in establishing the Methodist church in the colony, and was joint-founder of the Bank of New South Wales. **Ciarán Deane**

'Éamann an Chnoic', a song about the eighteenth-century outlaw Éamann Ó Riain from Cnoc Maothail in the parish of Templebeg, Co. Tipperary. In the song he seeks shelter at the house of his love, but she, fearing the consequences of harbouring an outlaw, turns him away, and he resolves to escape to the Continent. This was not to be, however, as he was treacherously slain in 1724. **Éamonn Ó Bróithe**

Eamhain Mhacha: see NAVAN FORT.

'Eanach Dhúin', a song by RAIFTEARAÍ which commemorates the drowning of nineteen people in a boating accident on LOUGH CORRIB in 1828. Thirty people boarded the boat at Annaghdown (Eanach Dhúin), together with sheep and other goods, to travel the 13 km (8 miles) to the fair of Galway. When they were only 2 miles from the shore the boat sank. The tune is said to be a version of the English folk song 'Dives and Lazarus'. A number of versions of the poem exist. **Maeve Ellen Gebruers**

Earhart, Amelia (1897–1937), aviator. Born Kansas, USA. She was the first woman to complete a west-to-east Atlantic solo flight. She landed her single-engined Lockheed Vega in a field at Culmore, Derry, some thirteen hours after taking off from Harbour Grace, Newfoundland. From 1932 to 1936 she broke several other records, but on 2 July 1937, in the course of a Pacific crossing, she and her navigator vanished without trace. A small museum has been opened close to her Derry landing site. **Bernard Share**

Early, Biddy, née O'Connor or Connors (c. 1798–1874), seer and *bean feasa* (healer). Born in Faha, Co. Clare. For more than sixty years she was credited with healing thousands of people through herbal medicines and through her mystical powers. It was widely believed that she was in league with the FAIRIES. She was famous for her 'dark bottle', which she used as other clairvoyants use a crystal ball. She died in poverty at her home in Kilbarron, Co. Clare. **Ciarán Deane**

Early Historic Period, generally dated from the introduction of CHRISTIANITY to the arrival of the ANGLO-NORMANS (fifth to twelfth centuries AD). Archaeological evidence points to the establishment of the Christian church in Ireland by the sixth century, when monastic sites were founded throughout the country. These places also formed an important element of contemporary settlement and played a major role in the economy; they acted as storehouses for local produce and valuables, hosted fairs and markets, were centres of learning and craft, and provided access to foreign trade.

Many of the most well-known 'treasures' of Early Historic Ireland are ecclesiastical in nature, manufactured within a monastic enclosure or under the patronage of the church. The most famous of these are the artefacts of the ARDAGH HOARD (Co. Limerick) and DERRYNAFLAN HOARD (Co. Tipperary). Scholarship and prayer obviously played an integral role in the church, requiring the use of books containing the GOSPELS, Psalms, and other ecclesiastical texts. A small number of these MANUSCRIPTS survive, some illustrated in great detail. The earliest ILLUMINATED MANUSCRIPT, the CATHACH, dates from the sixth century, the style reaching its zenith in the eighth-century Book of KELLS, a lavishly illustrated Gospel-book (see p. 523).

Early Irish society was strictly hierarchical, consisting of several classes connected by a system of tribute and fiefdom. This was not, however, a caste system: individuals could move from one class to another, in both directions. Essentially, society was divided into three groups: the nobility, the free, and the unfree. The system of clientship that operated consisted of a series of contractual agreements between a lord or king and a number of socially inferior clients. In return for a grant of land or livestock, and legal and military protection, the client paid an annual 'rent' or tribute of foodstuffs and also provided the lord with hospitality, labour, and military service. The hierarchical society portrayed in the laws is reflected in both the economic evidence recovered from excavated sites and the differing types of settlement from the period.

Much of the population of early historic Ireland lived in RING-FORTS (enclosed homesteads, the most common type of settlement site from this period) or on CRANNÓGS (wholly or partially artificial islands). The picture presented of the basic economy is one of mixed AGRICULTURE, with an emphasis on dairying, while a range of different crafts was undertaken. Any surplus produced was used for barter and trade.

The ninth and tenth centuries saw the introduction of yet another influence on Irish society: the VIKINGS. Initial contact consisted of raids, followed by temporary settlements to facilitate further raiding. Permanent settlements were established in the tenth century with the founding of the towns of DUBLIN, WATERFORD, LIMERICK, WEXFORD, and CORK. Mostly from Norway, the Vikings introduced the first true towns into Ireland, which proceeded to interact with the native Irish and gradually became Hiberno-Norse.

The end of the Early Historic Period was heralded by the introduction of new architectural styles, an influx of new monastic orders from the Continent, and the arrival of the Anglo-Normans from Wales and England. [see CHURCHES, EARLY; KINGDOMS OF IRELAND; KINGSHIP; MONASTICISM; ROMAN WORLD.] **Michelle Comber**

Early Irish lyrics. The early Irish did not use poetry for epic narrative but retained it for lyrical expression. The term 'early Irish lyrics' is primarily used of short poems that convey impressionistic and emotionally charged responses to the phenomenal world, often as an aspect of divine creation, but it may be extended also to poems of eulogy or love, ranging from single quatrains to lengthier compositions. There are lyrics that show no evidence of Christian influence, but in many of these praise of nature blends into praise of the god of CHRISTIANITY, and appreciation of a minutely observed world hinges on the idealisation of ascetic life. The Irish love of enumeration and categorisation is prominent in such lyrics, as is a sensuous enjoyment of the visual and tactile world. Some of the greatest lyrics concern human love, or the conflict between it and divine love. The relationship between lyric praise-poems for SAINTS and church figures, on the one hand, and secular lords on the other has yet to be clarified. The great majority of medieval lyrics are written in syllabic metres, rather than the accentual ones that they eclipsed.

While there is no syllabic verse in existence that may be dated to earlier than AD 600, such metres (*'núachrutha'*) predominate throughout the next millennium. With few exceptions, the names of the authors have not survived. Some of the longer lyrics on secular themes have prose introductions in later MANUSCRIPTS, suggesting how readers may have interpreted them. Many of the shorter secular lyrics, particularly those of a humorous or satirical kind, were preserved by virtue of their inclusion in Middle and Modern Irish metrical tracts as illustrations of particular metres. [see IRISH METRICS.] **Máirín Ní Dhonnchadha**

Early Irish tale types. It is now customary to group early Irish tales according to the characters who appear in them. Accordingly, four cycles of tales are distinguished: the MYTHOLOGICAL CYCLE, which recounts the various prehistoric conquests and inhabitants of Ireland; the ULSTER CYCLE, recounting the exploits of CÚ CHULAINN, Fearghus mac Róich, and the other heroes of ancient Ulster who are supposed to have lived at the time of Christ; the Fenian or FIONN CYCLE, which tells of the adventures of FIONN MAC CUMHAILL, a contemporary of CORMAC MAC AIRT, who is reputed to have lived in the third century; and the KING CYCLE, a collection of tales about certain kings, some of whom may have been historical, who lived in the early centuries of the Christian period. A different system of classification is found in early Irish tradition, which arranged tales according to theme rather than characters. Tales may therefore be grouped under headings such as *tána* ('cattle raids'), *catha* ('battles'), *fisi* ('visions'), and IMMRAMA ('sea voyages'). Given the heroic nature of much of the literature, many of the tales centre on important stages in the lives of various heroes, such as COMPERTA ('births'), TOCHMARCA ('wooings'), *aitheda* ('elopements'), and AIDEDA ('violent deaths'). Under this system, tales from several of the cycles listed above may be grouped under the same heading. **Ruairí Ó hUiginn**

Early Modern Irish prose. The great majority of tales written in the Early Modern Irish period (c. 1200–1500) survive only in later MANUSCRIPT copies written, for the most part, between 1400 and 1900, the bulk of them between 1700 and 1900. It is the norm that no information is given in later copies about the original authors or the place, time and cause of composition. Many of these tales are later versions of narratives written before 1200. It is important, however, to realise that Early Modern Irish versions of earlier tales are not simply modernisations of their earlier counterparts. Whereas they generally retain the basic plot of the earlier narratives, they invariably include important modifications to the original texts.

Opinions vary about the purpose of composition of Early Modern Irish prose tales, especially of later versions of earlier narratives. Some argue that these tales were written for entertainment only, mainly for the benefit of members of the nobility in general. One serious counter-argument is that there is no manuscript evidence for widespread distribution of any of these tales before the beginning of the seventeenth century, a fact that can hardly be attributed solely to the loss of many of the manuscript sources. It has been alternatively argued that, as with the surviving poetry from the same period, Early Modern Irish prose tales were written for the benefit of individual patrons and reflect matters directly relevant to these patrons.

Early Modern Irish prose includes those tales that are popularly known as the 'Three Sorrows of STORYTELLING': 'Oidheadh Chloinne hUisneach', 'Oidheadh Chloinne Lir', and 'Oidheadh Chloinne Tuireann'. There is much evidence to suggest, however, that this designation pertains only to the later manuscript tradition. Whereas there are some similarities between the three tales, there are also crucial differences between them. 'Oidheadh Chloinne Lir' (possibly written in the fifteenth century) stands apart from the other two tales in its strong religious content. Particularly noteworthy is the fact that it was apparently written by an author who subscribed to the belief that the purpose of temporal life was to prepare the soul for the afterlife, and that temporal suffering could aid the soul to this end. Though it is easy to see how this tale could have subsequently been regarded as a tale with a tragic ending, it would appear that its author's intention was to emphasise the Christian virtue of patient endurance. **Caoimhín Breatnach**

Early Music Organisation of Ireland, an organisation committed to providing performance and educational opportunities in all areas of early music, as well as a forum and information service for those interested in early music. The organisation's definition of early music is broad and includes music from the medieval, renaissance and baroque periods, with an emphasis on historically informed performance practice. It publishes a quarterly newsletter and regularly hosts workshops and master classes, given by both Irish and international early music specialists. **Paul Collins**

Earthwatch, one of Ireland's principal environmental organisations, founded in 1986, and a member of Friends of the Earth International, one of the largest networks of environmental groups in the world. It seeks to achieve its aims through education, research, advocacy, and solution-based projects. It has conducted independent research and campaigned on a variety of environmental and social issues, including sustainable development, resource and waste management, CLIMATE change, nuclear power, and alternative sources of ENERGY. **Anne-Marie Cunningham**

earthworks, linear, a term applied to an eclectic range of linear monuments comprising various combinations of banks and ditches. FOLKLORE and MYTHOLOGY attribute some of them to the rootings of a giant magical pig, a tradition reflected in names such as the BLACK PIG'S DYKE, the Cliath Dubh, and the Mucklaghs. Some, such as those occurring on Knockainey, Co. Limerick, and at NEWGRANGE and Loughcrew, Co. Meath, bear quite close comparison with British *cursus* monuments, which are dated generally to the fourth and third millennia BC. These Irish specimens appear as low-profile, widely spaced, largely straight parallel banks (or possibly ditches only in the case of NEWGRANGE), with or without internal or external ditches. The rounded terminus of the Newgrange cursus is also a feature of British specimens. Their siting among ritual complexes is a further point of comparison. The 203 m (666-ft) long Teach Midhchuarta (Banquet Hall) at TARA may also fall into this group, though its comparatively high, curved banks and hollowed-out interior set it apart. Tall, curving banks are also a feature of the Mucklaghs at RATHCROGHAN, Co. Roscommon, and the Knockauns, Teltown, Co. Meath.

Early Historic Period. *Detail of the helmet-like hilts of three Viking swords, among the artefacts found during excavations at the Viking cemeteries at Islandbridge and Kilmainham, Dublin. [National Museum of Ireland]*

There is a consensus that these types of monuments fulfilled religious purposes. A more practical explanation is suggested in the case of strategically situated linear earthworks, such as the Black Pig's Dyke, the Riverstown linear earthwork, near Tara, and the Doon of Drumsna, Co. Roscommon. These appear to demarcate genuine political boundaries: the Black Pig's Dyke may mark part of the traditional border of ancient Ulster. Unlike cursus monuments, these latter comprise close-set banks or single, imposing banks, often with associated ditches. The available evidence suggests that such earthworks date from about the end of the first millennium BC. **Conor Newman**

earthworks, medieval. The first CASTLES built by the ANGLO-NORMANS in Ireland after the invasion of 1169–70 were constructed of earth and timber in the south and east of the country. There is also evidence from Britain that motte castles could be constructed in a few weeks to provide defensive strongholds for the numerically inferior Norman forces, and the same is arguably true for the ringwork castles. The limited archaeological evidence at present suggests that the two main types of earthwork castle, mottes and ringworks, were probably built contemporaneously. But the archaeological and historical evidence that survives for the approximately 350 motte castles is much more substantial than that for the 100 or so ringwork castles. Nevertheless it is probable that both types of earthwork castle were being built in Ireland from the late twelfth century until as late as the fourteenth century.

Mottes can easily be identified in the landscape as large flat-topped mounds with a surrounding ditch. On average they are under 5 m (16 ft) in height, though there are a few examples up to 10 m (32 ft) in height or more. Originally they had a wooden palisade around the perimeter of the summit and a *bretasche* or wooden tower in its centre. Traces of palisades and tower-like structures have been found as a result of archaeological excavations at a small number of sites, such as Lurgankeel, Co. Louth. Some

earthworks, medieval. *The motte and bailey at Clonard, Co. Meath, known as the 'cup and saucer'. [Dúchas, The Heritage Service]*

examples also had an attached *bailey*, a larger earthwork enclosure again with a fosse around it, often rectangular, which was originally connected to the motte by a *flying bridge* or raised walkway.

There are far fewer surviving motte-and-baileys in Ireland than elsewhere in Europe, for reasons that are still largely unclear. The motte acted as the final citadel, where the inhabitants of the bailey would have retreated if the castle came under attack. It also provided the defenders with a useful height advantage over any attacking force, and it was resistant to the two main forms of siege WARFARE of the period, mining and fire.

Mainly because their morphology is so similar to that of the RING-FORT, medieval ringwork castles have been identified in Ireland only over the last thirty years. They are annular or penannular earthworks with an internal palisaded bank and external ditch, as well as a fortified gate-tower. In comparison with the motte, where the major defensive element was the height of the mound, ringwork castles depended on the strength of their perimeter defences. They are easily distinguished from the indigenous ring-forts, as they are often sited at strategically defensive locations, such as on promontories overlooking rivers, and their ditches are often very wide in comparison with the small size of their internal areas. If a particular site had such naturally defensive characteristics, the Anglo-Normans often constructed one of these ringwork castles there, rather than a motte. Both archaeological and contemporary historical evidence suggests that the first Anglo-Norman fortification at TRIM CASTLE was such a ringwork.

Moated sites are generally associated with the period of secondary colonisation, from the middle of the thirteenth century, after the eastern two-thirds of the country had been conquered. In the field they can be identified as rectangular platforms usually only slightly raised above the level of the surrounding countryside, surrounded by a U-shaped moat and an internal earthen bank. They are on average 30 m (100 ft) across, with the banks at each of the four corners usually raised. The surviving 1,000 examples are distributed all over the Anglo-Norman lordship but are especially concentrated on its periphery, where the colonists felt most threatened by their Irish or indeed their Anglo-Norman neighbours. Archaeological evidence from the six excavated sites suggests that they were all occupied from the second half of the thirteenth century up to the middle of the fourteenth century.

We are fortunate in possessing a contemporary surviving manorial account, which gives unparalleled details of the construction of a moated site in south Co. Wexford in 1282–4. These constructions were mainly built by middle-ranking members of the Anglo-Norman aristocracy, and perhaps even by prosperous freemen, to function as defensive farmsteads. However, some smaller examples may only have been cattle pens or other subsidiary agricultural enclosures. Generally these sites have no military or strategic importance, unlike the mottes or ringwork castles. **Terry Barry**

Easter controversy. Easter is linked to the day of Jesus' crucifixion, which occurred at the Jewish Passover; and the Jews calculated the date of Passover according to a lunar calendar. To determine the date of Easter, Christians needed to harmonise lunar data (to establish the Passover full moon) and solar data (as Easter must fall after the spring equinox, and on a Sunday). Not surprisingly, different churches adopted differing solutions to the complications that arose. COLUMBANUS's 'pilgrimage' to the Continent in 591 revealed that the Irish (and Britons) calculated Easter according to different rules from those of Victorius, whose Easter table was followed in Frankia. Controversy ensued, in which opponents were sometimes accused of being heretics. Columbanus refused to conform, but his Continental foundations did so in 626–8. Pope Honorius wrote to the Irish, prompting debate and then the conformity of southern Ireland in 632. Northumbria conformed in 664 and northern Ireland by 700; meanwhile the Papacy had abandoned Victorius's tables in favour of the superior Alexandrian system. The last Irish churches (IONA and the Columban federation) conformed in 716, the last British churches (the Welsh) in 768.

The Easter controversy was important in that it stimulated closer links between Ireland and the Continent and debate within Ireland, and raised the issue of Irish conformity to Continental practices and of where authority in the church lay. Meanwhile Armagh used the controversy to assert its headship, beneath the Papacy, of the Irish church; though not accepted at the time, this bore fruit later. **Clare Stancliffe**

Easter rising: see RISING 1916.

Ebling, Francis John Grovier (John) (1918–1992), endocrinologist and marine biologist. Born in Bristol; educated at the University of Bristol. As professor of zoology at the University of Sheffield, 1968–83, he became an authority on the hormonal control of skin glands, and edited the definitive *Textbook of Dermatology*. Having visited LOUGH HYNE, Co. Cork, on a student trip in 1937, he returned almost every summer for forty years. His collaboration there with J. A. KITCHING transformed marine ecology and made Lough Hyne the best-studied patch of sea water in the world. **Trevor Norton**

echtrae ('expedition, adventure'), an early IRISH TALE TYPE that tells of the hero's journey to another world. In 'Echtrae Chonnlai' ('Connlae's expedition') the hero is son of Conn Cétchathach. He is approached by an unnamed woman, who declares herself to have come from 'the land of the living, where there is neither death nor sin.' She invites Connlae to go with her; and despite the efforts of his father and his father's druid to detain him, he departs with her, and is never seen again. In 'Echtrae Chormaic' ('Cormac's expedition') CORMAC MAC AIRT rescues his wife and family from the OTHERWORLD. He also brings back some treasures, notably a cup that enables him to distinguish truth from falsehood. In 'Echtrae Nerai' ('Nerae's expedition') the hero secretly takes a bride in a *síd* (Otherworld dwelling). On foot of a warning from her the Connachta warriors destroy the *síd*, and Nerae returns to live in it. 'SERGLIGE CON CULAINN' ('Cú Chulainn's wasting-sickness') also belongs in this category, as it recounts the hero's journey to the Otherworld, where he performs heroic deeds and enjoys the love of an Otherworld woman, Fann. Cú Chulainn finally returns to his wife, Emer, and Fann to her husband, the God MANANNÁN MAC LIR. **Tomás Ó Cathasaigh**

'Echtrae mac n-Echach Muigmedóin' ('the expedition of the sons of Echu Muigmedón'), a tale in MIDDLE IRISH that shows how NIALL OF THE NINE HOSTAGES acquired the kingship of TARA for himself and his descendants, the UÍ NÉILL. The crucial episode in the tale is a hunting expedition undertaken by Niall and his four half-brothers. Having lost their way, they cook and eat their quarry, then each of the brothers in turn sets out in search of drinking-water. They find a well, but it is guarded by a hideous *cailleach* (hag), who demands a kiss in return for water. Niall is the only one who is prepared to make love to the *cailleach*. She is immediately transformed into a beautiful young woman; she identifies herself as the 'Sovereignty of Ireland' and decrees that Niall and his descendants will be kings of Ireland for ever. **Tomás Ó Cathasaigh**

economic development, viewed until quite recently as largely synonymous with ECONOMIC GROWTH. The concept embraces a number of other concerns, however, including congestion, environmental degradation, and INCOME DISTRIBUTION. It is clear, for example, that economic growth will not necessarily translate into increased welfare if it is associated with congestion and increased pollution. A related problem in Ireland is that the extent of the domain accorded to private property rights leaves little room for the notion of communal property, so that scenic views and the historical built ENVIRONMENT can disappear as private property expands. An increasing disparity in income distribution also brings problems broader than those associated with a possible increase in the crime rate. One is that those at the lower end of the income scale can suffer greater exclusion from resources that are in relatively fixed supply, such as housing. Perhaps more fundamental is that it becomes more difficult to bridge the class divide, as richer groups are able to maintain their advantage over time through access to better EDUCATION. The UN Human Development Index for Ireland in the late 1990s and early 2000s is, however, over-pessimistic in its view of how well the Republic managed the economic boom of the period. For example, most of the other peripheral countries in the EUROPEAN UNION with which Ireland should arguably be compared are not included in the data. Secondly, the report uses out-of-date statistics, which exaggerate Ireland's rate of long-term UNEMPLOYMENT. Thirdly, the low literacy scores ascribed to Ireland have been shown to be due to the high proportion of older people who left full-time education with only the most basic education, as the expansion in second-level education occurred later than in most other industrialised countries; the Republic's educational system appears in fact to be more efficient than those of Northern Ireland or Britain in transforming years of schooling into high literacy scores. **Frank Barry**

economic growth, a narrower concept than that of ECONOMIC DEVELOPMENT, referring to growth in national income (*extensive growth*) or in income per head (*intensive growth*); given traditional concerns about EMIGRATION, Irish policy-makers have typically been interested in both. Between groups of relatively similar countries, convergence is the norm, with poorer countries tending to grow more rapidly than rich ones. By this measure Ireland performed poorly, both extensively and intensively, until the late 1980s; since then, however, this experience has been strongly reversed. Northern Ireland has done poorly in converging on average UK income per head and has actually diverged in private consumption per head in recent decades. **Frank Barry**

Economic and Social Research Institute (ESRI), an independent research institute founded in Dublin in 1960, with the help of the Ford Foundation, as the Economic Research Institute. Although for many years it was largely dependent for its existence on state grants, it quickly won and has maintained a reputation for impartial and unvarnished commentary on economic and social affairs. This is reflected in the importance attached by the public and private sectors to its quarterly commentary on the Republic's ECONOMY, which is particularly valued for its analysis of performance and its occasional strictures about national and EU policy failings. [see NORTHERN IRELAND ECONOMIC COUNCIL.] **Eunan O'Halpin**

Economic War (1932–8), a name given to a series of tariff, financial, and other disputes between the IRISH FREE STATE and Britain. The trigger was the refusal of the new Fianna Fáil Government to permit the paying of LAND ANNUITIES due under the LAND ACTS to the British government, and the abolition of the OATH OF ALLEGIANCE. The British imposed tariffs on Irish agricultural imports; the Irish side retaliated with duties on British industrial and fuel imports. The 'war' was intimately entangled with FIANNA FÁIL's resentment of large cattle farmers and also with the protectionist drive that was central to Fianna Fáil policy at the time. It was also associated with the party's near-obsession with dismantling the Treaty settlement of 1922, in particular its symbolic and constitutional aspects: the oath of allegiance to the Constitution of the Irish Free State and fidelity to the British monarch in his capacity as head of the Commonwealth, the undemocratic character of the Senate and of university representation in Dáil Éireann, and the links to the Commonwealth.

The damage to Irish trade was considerable; but the looming crisis in Europe impelled the British to come to terms in 1938. The return of the TREATY PORTS was part of the package. The economic damage done was severe, but the psychological boost was considered by many Irish people to have been almost worth it. In the short term the cattle-grazier was defeated by a democracy driven by the smaller arable and mixed farmer; but in the long run the wealthier farmers triumphed. **Tom Garvin**

economy, 1200–1700. The economy of Ireland continued to be based on AGRICULTURE throughout this period. Oats and, to a lesser degree, wheat and barley were grown. 'BOOLEYING' (*buailteachas*) or transhumance (transferring livestock to summer upland pasture) was commonly practised. By the end of the fourteenth century the Irish ploughed with HORSES (the plough being attached to the horse's tail), and crop rotation was followed. Undoubtedly pastoralism was the mainstay of agriculture. Chiefs and notables possessed enormous herds of cattle. Sheep, pigs, horses and, by the early sixteenth century, goats were also reared. Settlement in native Irish areas tended to be scattered or in small clusters, with the principal towns and a higher instance of nucleated settlement occurring in districts of more intensive Norman settlement. Down to the end of the thirteenth century, wool, grain, and hides produced by the manorial economy were marketed widely through ports stretching from the Baltic to the Bay of Biscay and the Mediterranean. Wool was the most important export item. Flemish and Italian merchants dominated the Irish wool trade, which prospered during the thirteenth

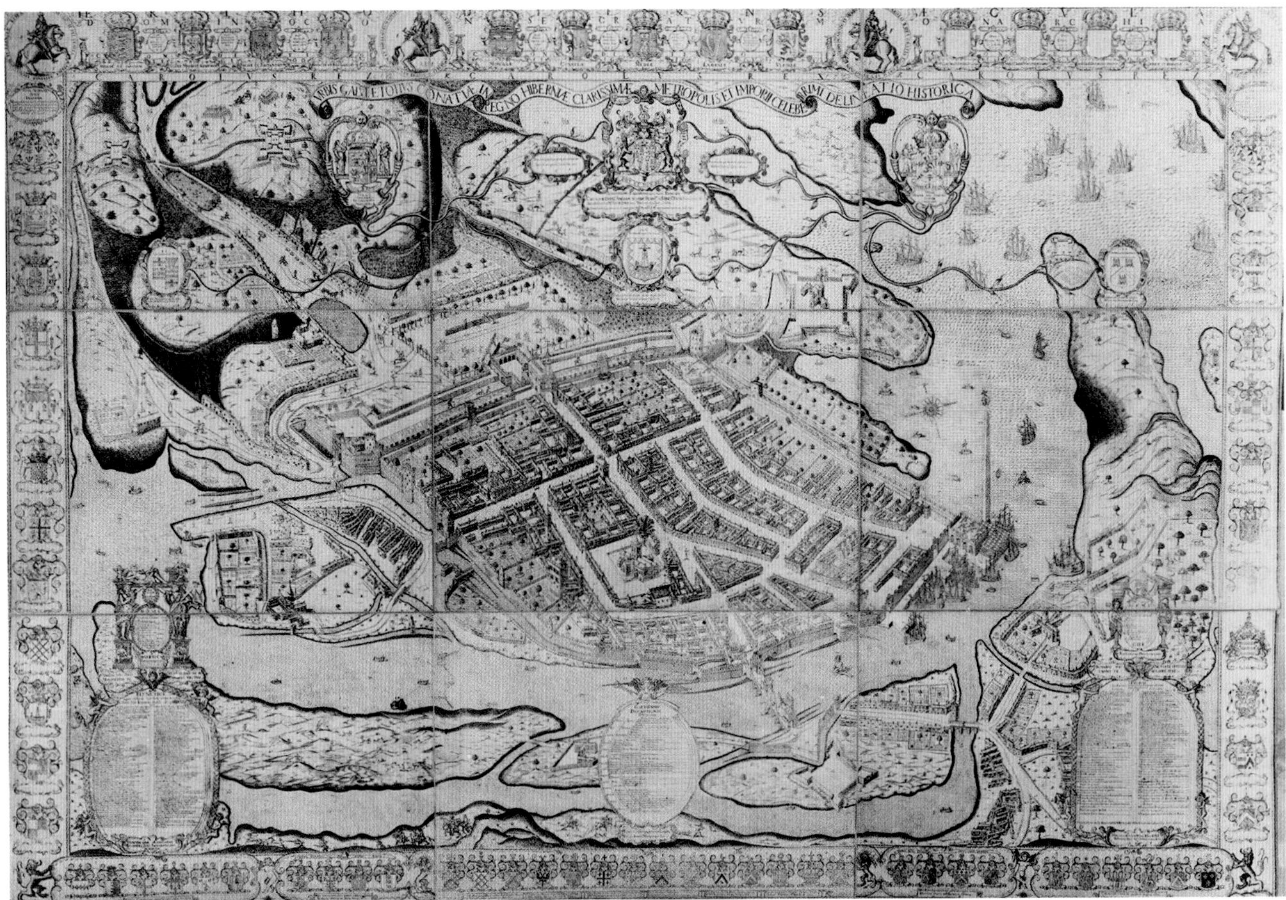

economy, 1200–1700. *An engraved map of Galway, 1652, showing the town at the zenith of its prosperity and development, with the River Corrib (bottom), St Nicholas's Church (centre), the Spanish Arch (right), and the Penrice and Shoemaker's Towers in the upper corner of the city walls. Only two copies are known to survive. [Board of Trinity College, Dublin]*

and fourteenth centuries. The export of worsted, serge, frieze, and ready-made cloaks in the later Middle Ages probably caused a decline in wool exports. Hides were also an important export commodity, with the Continent being the main market. Other exports included LINEN, rugs, skins, furs, MEAT, hawks, horses, timber, lard, tallow, wax, some cereals, and a limited range of manufactured articles. Throughout the late Middle Ages, Ireland's main imports remained unchanged, with salt, iron, wine, fine cloth, and some manufactured goods being the staple commodities.

Though foreign trading vessels anchored in Irish ports, trade was almost entirely in the hands of merchants of the corporate towns, and down to the late sixteenth century Irish merchants preferred to charter ships from English or Continental owners. Port towns such as Galway in the fifteenth century manifested physical evidence of wealth and a demand for luxury goods that was met with regular consignments of spices, silk, jewels, precious ornaments, and rich cloths. By the late fifteenth century Ireland's exports were products associated with fish, cattle, and sheep, while imports remained unchanged. Though many southern and western ports retained their links with the Continent, considerable traffic in goods into and out of Ireland was by way of England and Wales. The port towns of the Pale—Dublin and Drogheda—traded with ports such as Chester and Liverpool as well as with Brittany, Spain and Scotland and other Irish littoral towns to the north and south. The fisheries of the IRISH SEA contributed to the prosperity of the merchant communities in ports and harbours of the Pale and north-east Ulster, attracting fleets of foreign fishing vessels, mostly from Spain. The fisheries off HOOK HEAD in the south-east, at Baltimore in the south-west and the herring fishery off Aran Island in Co. Donegal were especially lucrative. It was through Bristol that Ireland's fish exports, especially salmon, reached the English market. After fish, hides were the most important export, the main Continental market being Flanders, from which the hides were channelled into the main European trading routes. Irish frieze, mantles and linen TEXTILES remained the most popular cloth exports.

By 1500 Ireland also had a flourishing internal and coastal trade, and agrarian manor and town were inextricably linked, as most commerce was based on agriculture. The sixteenth-century economy remained uncommercialised, partly owing to political turmoil and a lack of requisite regional specialisation, diversification and native skills to process raw materials. Lucrative fishing and mining enterprises were monopolised by foreigners. The native Irish economy remained dominated by livestock, though grain production was significant. However, in the late sixteenth century the trade in timber, wool, grain, fish and, in Ulster, linen yarn increased dramatically.

The seventeenth century saw the introduction in part or *en bloc* of many elements of English commercial organisation and landholding. Through plantation and informal colonisation, English styles of agriculture were introduced, and a shift from arable farming to pasture occurred. The early years of the century brought a trade boom, especially in the export of live cattle and cattle products, which constituted approximately half the total value of trade, followed by fish, sheep, wool, and grain exports. The timber trade grew rapidly, only to collapse in the 1630s. The population increased. Port towns expanded dramatically to cope with the new volume of trade, and Dublin in particular but also Belfast, Derry, Cork, Youghal, Kinsale, Limerick, and Waterford grew dramatically. The country's market system became more developed; yet the structures of the pre-1641 economy remained essentially unaltered, as a lack of skills and capital and a poor marketing structure continued to impede economic development. The late 1630s saw a decline in the economy, mainly owing to political disturbances that eventually erupted in REBELLION IN 1641. The trade of the ports of the south-east, south, and west was badly hit, and the 1650s proved extremely difficult. From the mid-1650s good harvests resulted in a surge of exports, property prices rose, and rents increased; but the early 1660s brought another slump in trade, and in 1665–7 Ireland experienced a financial crisis. The English Cattle Acts (1663 and 1667), prohibiting the import of live cattle, undermined the mainstay of Irish trade. Late seventeenth-century price movements favoured BUTTER and wool over cattle and beef, and exports moved away from live cattle to processed goods. From the 1650s transatlantic trade to the West Indies and the American colonies absorbed an increasing proportion of Ireland's export trade in barrel beef, pork, CHEESE, and butter. This trade expanded rapidly and was interrupted only by the WILLIAMITE WARS. The 1690s saw the rapid recovery of the economy. By the end of the seventeenth century the beginnings of a nationally integrated economy were emerging, with evidence of regional specialisation, standardisation of weights and measures necessitated by increasing inter-regional and overseas trade, a dramatic increase in output, and involvement in large-scale international commerce. [see FOOD, LATE MEDIEVAL.] **Mary Ann Lyons**

economy, 1700–1922. Ireland was the only country in Europe with fewer people at the end of the nineteenth century than at its beginning. The population reached a peak at 8.17 million in 1841; thereafter the combination of FAMINE, EMIGRATION and the decline in marriages reduced it to little more than half by 1921. Before the Great Famine it was Ireland's poverty and headlong population growth that most struck outside commentators. The half-century before the Famine was almost certainly an era of impoverishment for the mass of the people, dependent as they were on the POTATO. Disastrous failures of the potato crop were relatively uncommon. Ireland's 3 million or so 'potato people' consumed quantities (the equivalent of 4–5 kg daily per adult male) that seem incredible today. On the eve of the Famine the area under potatoes had reached a peak at about 800,000 ha (2 million acres), or one-third of all tilled land. Supplemented with cabbage, milk, and fish, potatoes made a monotonous but nutritious diet. Coupled with a plentiful supply of turf for fuel, this offered some compensation for poor HOUSING and tattered CLOTHING; as a result, the Irish poor were healthier and lived longer than people on similar incomes elsewhere in Europe.

Cheap labour and the tariff protection given by the CORN LAWS ensured that Irish farming was more TILLAGE-oriented before 1845 than ever before or since. Tillage accounted for two-thirds or so of agricultural output (compared with a fifth in the 1920s and about an eighth today). Crop yields per acre were not much lower than those in Britain; but output per worker was only about half. Farming made some modest progress between the Union and the Famine. Improving communications, both by land and by sea, helped. The improvement was reflected in higher exports, improved livestock strains, and higher crop yields. A rise in both the wage-rental ratio and the relative price of livestock products reinforced the shift to livestock-oriented farming after 1845.

Ireland's land tenure system, a variant of the British, was a product of colonialism: the bulk of the land was in the hands of the descendants of those who had fought against the native Irish or professed the Protestant religion. Irish LANDED ESTATES were bigger than British, but Irish farms were much smaller. Partly for that reason, LANDLORDS tended to be less involved in the running of their estates, and were more likely to be absentees. Before the Famine they were also much more likely to be broke than their British counterparts. The ENCUMBERED ESTATES Act (1849) helped free the market in encumbered land.

The 1850s and 60s were decades of relative harmony and progress on the land, but the agricultural downturn of the late 1870s sparked off a 'LAND WAR' between a tenantry represented by the LAND LEAGUE and their landlords. The 'war', which began in 1879 with demands for rent reductions and fixity of tenure, culminated in peasant proprietorship. The verdict of recent historiography is that the change to owner-occupancy made little difference to output or productivity. The outcome showed that landlords were dispensable, but also implied that the Land War was largely about rent-seeking. The victory of the farmers both reflected and contributed to democratisation.

The era of the Land War was one of new challenges and opportunities for farmers. The more pastoral orientation of post-famine AGRICULTURE shielded them from the impact of the 'grain invasion'. New opportunities were represented by the centrifugal separator and its institutional concomitant, the CO-OPERATIVE creamery. These innovations failed to have the same impact in Ireland that they had in Denmark, though lower cow densities and the earlier presence of a strong BUTTER merchant interest partly account for Irish 'failure'. Milk production was constrained by farmers' resistance to winter dairying, which had less to do with laziness than with climatic conditions. The shift to owner-occupancy occluded the more serious problem of too many small farms.

Industrial output and EMPLOYMENT in the country as a whole continued to grow until the 1840s, though relatively speaking Ireland was losing out to Britain. LINEN, which in turn became increasingly localised in east Ulster, offered some compensation for the decline of the cotton industry. Ireland remained competitive in a range of products linked to agriculture. Dwelling on 'deindustrialisation' ignores the fact that east Ulster went through an industrial revolution after 1800. Belfast's population quintupled between 1800 and 1850 and doubled again by 1880; by 1900 it was higher than that of Dublin. The combined population share of Cos. Antrim and Down, the two counties most transformed, doubled (from 8.8 to 16.8 per cent) between 1821 and 1901. The North's INDUSTRIAL REVOLUTION was founded mainly on LINEN, ENGINEERING, and SHIPBUILDING, areas in which it became a world leader. Just as Lancashire increasingly monopolised cotton, Belfast and its hinterland came to be Linenopolis. Before the FIRST WORLD WAR, linen provided employment for 100,000 people, mainly women, while Belfast's shipyards were producing some of the biggest and most advanced ships in the world. The North's success was not due to its endowment with natural resources: flax could grow as well in Munster as in Ulster, and Queen's Island, where HARLAND AND WOLFF began building ships in 1861, was an artificial creation of Belfast's harbour commissioners. Ulster's literacy and culture helped, however.

The nineteenth century was one of dramatic advances in communications and in BANKING. Belfast–Greenock was the world's first scheduled steamship route in 1818; the first RAILWAY between Dublin and Kingstown (DÚN LAOGHAIRE) was opened in 1834, and by the early 1850s the main-line network had been established, with Dublin as its node. Before the railways, travel by coach had extended to all main roads. The rail network continued to expand into the new century, though traffic was always light compared with Britain. The evolution of the BANKING SYSTEM was modelled closely on that of England, and legislation permitting joint-stock banking (1825) and restricting note issue (1845) mimicked that governing English banking. The banking system that emerged in the 1820s and 30s proved enduring. It offered stability, with the Bank of Ireland, established by charter in 1783, operating as a quasi-CENTRAL BANK; it exercised competently its function of lender of last resort, helping out most banks at one time or another but allowing rogue banks to go under.

The Famine gave a big impetus to the mass emigration and low marriage rate that would characterise Ireland for more than a century. Irish emigration was distinctive for its size, its mainly permanent character, and its large proportion of women. Most emigrants headed for the United States, but destinations shifted in response to relative prospects. The outflow brought higher living standards to those who remained; the era between the Famine and the First World War was one of considerable convergence in this limited sense. By 1900 there was still much poverty, but now the disease-infested slums of Dublin attracted almost as much attention as the remote west.

The nineteenth century was one of increasing intervention in the economy. In the pre-famine era the introduction of free schooling and the WORKHOUSE system followed public inquiries into elementary education and poverty in the 1830s. Similar inquiries into the possibilities of creating a national rail network and land reform were less productive. The late nineteenth century brought a further cluster of reforms, the most radical being the shift from landlordism to peasant proprietorship. Meanwhile, public expenditure on Ireland continued to grow, with the result that the fledgling Irish Free State was faced with the challenge of financing a relatively large public sector. [see FOOD, POST-FAMINE.] **Cormac Ó Gráda**

economy, late twentieth-century. The economy of the Republic has an extremely positive profile, being ranked highly in international income and competitiveness tables; UNEMPLOYMENT is low; and there has been a high level of IMMIGRATION in recent years. Another recent development is that the Republic has bypassed Northern Ireland in income per person, reversing a decades-old pattern.

However, much of this ECONOMIC GROWTH has occurred since the 1980s, with growth taking off in 1987 and accelerating after 1994. The previous record of the Irish ECONOMY was much less positive. Though there had been some periods of strong economic performance (the 1960s and a brief period in the late 1970s), the general experience was poor relative to other OECD countries. The 1950s were perhaps the bleakest decade, but 1981–6 was also a sustained period of economic stagnation.

After independence in 1922 the first Free State Government pursued a conservative economic policy. Ireland was allowed to develop as a predominantly agricultural economy, with limited state intervention. In the 1930s, under the new FIANNA FÁIL Government, an 'ECONOMIC WAR' with Britain was pursued, with trade tariffs imposed and a suspension of LAND ANNUITY payments. This had the effect of stimulating the growth of indigenous manufacturing industry, serving the domestic market under the cover of protection. The Control of Manufactures Acts (1932 and 1934) restricted foreign ownership of domestic firms, though this legislation was not rigidly enforced. In general the new manufacturing firms were not efficient by international standards, producing low-quality products or acting as a final assembler of imported parts. In the world in general the 1930s were a time of inward-looking economic policies, and the Republic was not unusual in its orientation at this time. Successive governments were slow to liberalise the economy after the SECOND WORLD WAR. Restrictions on imports and foreign ownership were gradually lifted during the 1950s, and the Republic missed out on the 'golden age' of European economic growth during that period. Heavy EMIGRATION meant that the population fell by about 5 per cent during the 1950s, reaching its lowest point of 2.82 million in 1961.

With policy-makers recognising the failure of the isolationist model, the 1960s saw a much greater integration of Ireland into international markets. The ANGLO-IRISH FREE TRADE AREA AGREEMENT (1966) eliminated trade barriers between the Republic and Britain, and tariffs against other European countries were lowered as part of the accession process leading to full membership of the European Economic Community in 1973. Incentives for transnational investment were also actively promoted during this decade. The economy grew at a healthy 4 per cent per annum during the period 1960–73.

The oil shocks of the 1970s posed policy challenges for Ireland, as for other industrialised countries. Though INFLATION rates and budget deficits rose almost everywhere in the mid-1970s, it is now recognised that a crucial strategic mistake was not reversing more quickly the expansionary fiscal policy introduced by the Fianna Fáil Government after its 1977 landslide election victory. As international interest rates rose at the turn of the decade and the American and British economies went into recession, the Irish public finances sharply deteriorated, and unemployment began to climb. The main task of the coalition Government of FINE GAEL and the LABOUR PARTY during the period 1982–6 was to stabilise the public finances. Some progress was made on this front by means of TAX increases, but economic conditions continued to deteriorate, with large-scale emigration resuming, unemployment continuing to climb, and the public debt burden rising quickly. By the end of 1986 there was a pervasive sense of crisis concerning future economic prospects.

The year 1987 is acknowledged to have been a clear turning-point. With support from Fine Gael, the new Fianna Fáil minority Government implemented a significant fiscal reform that concentrated on cutting Government spending. A tripartite agreement between the Government, employers, and unions ensured industrial peace and moderation in wage increases. A fortuitous improvement in external conditions, with rapid growth in the United States and Britain and the further integration of the European internal market, also contributed to the economic turn-around.

Despite a temporary halt during the European currency crisis of 1992–3, the economy has performed strongly ever since. Output grew by a world-leading 52 per cent during the period 1995–2000, while the expansion of employment was even more remarkable, rising from 1.13 million in 1991 to 1.77 million in 2000. By 2001 output per person was 127 per cent of the EU average, placing IRELAND firmly in the club of rich countries and among the potential net contributors to the EU budget. Net immigration has resulted in an increase in the population from 3.53 million in 1991 to 3.92 million in 2002.

A specially notable feature of this boom was the high share of total American investment in Europe that accrued to Ireland, enabling the country to disproportionately benefit from the high-technology boom that defined global innovation in the 1990s. This economic boom transformed the country, with a rising female participation rate in the LABOUR FORCE, urban congestion, and a sharp rise in house prices.

The defining characteristic of the economy is now its extreme level of integration in the global economy, anchored by its long-standing membership of the EUROPEAN UNION. Transnational companies account for the majority of domestic industrial activity (especially in the electronics and pharmaceutical sectors); in the other direction, Irish-owned firms are increasingly global, with affiliates and subsidiaries around the world. In 1999 the Republic was a founder-member of the EUROPEAN MONETARY UNION, giving up the option to run a national monetary policy in exchange for potential gains from the deeper integration of goods and capital markets. Increasingly, the regulation of markets is constrained by EU rules, while privatisation has sharply reduced the role of the state in the commercial sphere. The links between the domestic and international labour markets are strong, not only with Irish-born workers moving in both directions but with the Republic also proving attractive to workers from other countries, both inside and outside the European Union.

The new economic environment has also meant a re-design of the role of the government. Setting low corporate taxes has been successful in helping to attract transnational enterprises; and reductions in income tax have also improved the dynamism of the economy. However, the government must also ensure the provision (either directly or by providing incentives to the private sector) of the high-level INFRASTRUCTURE required by a leading-edge economy and the social services and amenities demanded by an increasingly affluent population. A priority is overcoming the accumulated infrastructural deficit that is a legacy of the sustained decline in public investment during the 1980s and early 90s. Comparatively high income inequality has also intensified the pressure on the government to improve economic opportunities for people in disadvantaged areas.

economy, late twentieth-century. *T. K. Whitaker, Secretary of the Department of Finance, 1956–69, implemented the First Programme for Economic Expansion in 1959 with the Taoiseach, Seán Lemass. [Joe Dunne/Photocall Ireland]*

Looking forward, with the convergence process nearing completion, it is clear that the recent extraordinary growth rates cannot persist; the hope is rather that incomes will grow in line with productivity growth in leading-edge countries. If Ireland proves to be an attractive location for production, the population may continue to rise quite significantly, as immigration more than compensates for a decline in the FERTILITY RATE.

Northern Ireland. At the time of PARTITION, Northern Ireland was much more heavily industrialised than the Free State, with its SHIPBUILDING, ENGINEERING and LINEN industries being especially prominent. Moreover, unlike the Free State during its isolationist episode from the 1930s, Northern Ireland has been integrated with the British economy throughout its history. Though the Great Depression hurt shipbuilding, all the traditional industries benefited from a sharp increase in demand during the SECOND WORLD WAR. Beset by technical change and increased international competition, its traditional industries began to shrink during the 1950s. Though the 1960s did see an inflow of transnational investment to replace the jobs lost in declining industries, security fears meant that it was unable to attract much private transnational investment once the 'TROUBLES' began in 1969.

More generally, the Troubles substantially distorted the evolution of the economy. The social unrest and military presence led to a large net flow of funds from the British exchequer: up to a quarter of output was accounted for by these subsidies. This expansion in the relative size of the public sector skewed the structure of the economy, with a diminished role for the private exporting sector. In particular, the high-technology sector is tiny relative to its counterpart in the Republic. Another negative effect of the Troubles was the persistent emigration of graduates. By 1998 output per person was only 65 per cent of that of the Republic.

The NORTHERN IRELAND PEACE PROCESS offers much brighter prospects for the economy. CROSS-BORDER CO-OPERATION would also be helpful, especially in the provision of infrastructure and the promotion of TOURISM. However, the restructuring of the economy and the development of thriving export industries are likely to involve a prolonged transition process. **Philip R. Lane**

ecumenism, the worldwide movement to promote Christian unity, begun at the International Missionary Conference, Edinburgh, in 1910. In Ireland the movement began officially in 1923 when the various churches, other than the Roman Catholic Church, met for the first time in the United Council of Christian Churches and Religious Communions in Ireland. Five years later Pope Pius XI condemned such initiatives; but in 1973 the hierarchy and other official representatives of the Catholic Church in Ireland met their Protestant counterparts for the first time at Ballymascanlan, Co. Louth. Such meetings continue under the name Irish Inter-Church Meeting.

Before the Second VATICAN COUNCIL (1962–5) unofficial pioneering work was done by the Irish Christian Fellowship, in which Kathleen Huggard of the CHURCH OF IRELAND was a leading figure, and by the Mercier Society, a Dublin initiative of FRANK DUFF, founder of the Legion of Mary. Since the Second Vatican Council a prominent role has been played by the Benedictine ABBEY of Glenstal, Co. Limerick, which began to host an annual ecumenical conference in 1964; by the CORRYMEELA Centre for Reconciliation in Co. Antrim, which the PRESBYTERIAN minister Rev. Ray Davey founded in 1965; by the Irish School of Ecumenics, which began in Dublin in 1970; and by the Charismatic Renewal movement as a whole, notably the Rostrevor Centre, Co. Down, established by Rev. Cecil Kerr (Church of Ireland) in 1974.

The outbreak of sectarian violence in Northern Ireland in 1968 finally spurred the churches into initiating official contact in 1973 at Ballymascanlan. Leading roles in this initiative were played by Bishop (later Cardinal) CAHAL DALY and the METHODIST minister Dr Eric Gallagher. More inter-church contact and co-operation, less ignorance and bigotry, and more relaxed attitudes to mixed MARRIAGE and eucharistic sharing can be counted among the achievements of Irish ecumenism; and because the Northern Ireland problem is politico-religious, the contribution of ecumenism to the NORTHERN IRELAND PEACE PROCESS has been significant.

Ecumenism is also understood more broadly to include the movement to improve relations between Christianity and other RELIGIONS, especially Islam and Judaism. Ecumenism in Ireland in that sense is making some small beginnings. **Michael Hurley**

Edgeworth, Francis (1845–1926), mathematician. Born in Edgeworthstown, Co. Longford, a grandson of RICHARD LOVELL EDGEWORTH and nephew of MARIA EDGEWORTH and of FRANCIS BEAUFORT; educated at TCD and the University of Oxford. He was called to the bar in 1877 and in 1891 became professor of political economy at the University of Oxford. He was the first editor of the *Economic Journal*, 1891, and remained as editor until his death. President of the Royal Statistical Society, 1912–14, and a leader in the development of mathematical ECONOMICS, he applied probability and statistics to the analysis of economic and social data. **Fiacre Ó Cairbre**

Edgeworth, Henry Essex, Abbé de Firmont (1745–1807), confessor to Madame Elizabeth of France. Born in Edgeworthstown, Co. Longford, a cousin of RICHARD LOVELL EDGEWORTH; educated at Jesuit College and the University of Paris. He worked tirelessly for the Parisian poor until his health failed, then ministered to the expatriate Irish and English. In 1791 he became spiritual adviser to Elizabeth, sister of Louis XVI; he accompanied the king to the guillotine but had to flee France during the Revolution. In 1796 he settled in Lower Saxony and was appointed chaplain to the exiled Louis XVII. He accompanied the court to Russia in 1798 and died of a fever when ministering to French prisoners of war. **David Kiely**

Edgeworth, Maria (1768–1849), writer. Born in Oxfordshire, daughter of RICHARD LOVELL EDGEWORTH; the family moved to Edgeworthstown, Co. Longford, in 1782. Apart from a brief period in an English boarding-school, her education and professional training as a writer were accomplished in the family home. The Edgeworths maintained contact with the nearby Pakenham family and with the BEAUFORTS (relatives by marriage), as well as with members of the Lunar Society of the English midlands, Scottish Enlightenment philosophers, and Continental educators. Maria also grew up an active participant in the new world of print culture, reading not only the latest works of history, political economy, and fiction but also literary reviews, such as the *Edinburgh* and the *Quarterly*.

Her writing career began with the publication of *Letters for Literary Ladies* (1795), CASTLE RACKRENT (1800), and *Belinda* (1801). At first sight these do not appear to have much in common, dealing as they do with education, Irish history, and courtship, respectively; yet Edgeworth's fiction continued to embrace this diverse and ultimately interrelated set of concerns. With her father she published *Practical Education* (1798), which, together with *The Parent's Assistant* (1796), *Moral Tales for Young People* (1801), and *Popular Tales* (1804), made an important contribution to the theory and practice of education in the early nineteenth century.

Edgeworth wrote within a network of family, friends, and regular correspondents, and her literary output was read and commented on by a wide circle of readers. By far the most productive of these writing relationships was that with her father: they published jointly on education and worked together on a number of essays and pamphlets. Her tales for children and young adults—*The Parent's Assistant*, *Moral Tales for Young People*, and *Popular Tales*—were written to illustrate the educational principles she and her father developed.

All her fiction is informed by the complexity of Ireland's status under the Union. Her Irish tales—*Castle Rackrent*, *Ennui* (1809), *The Absentee* (1812), and *Ormond* (1817)—draw equally on English and French literary culture, Scottish Enlightenment thought, and Irish allusions, combining these disparate elements in work that examines attitudes to the Irish past, legitimacy, and property. Even the novels with an English setting—*Belinda*, *Leonora* (1806), many of the *Tales of Fashionable Life* (1809 and 1812), and *Helen* (1834)—

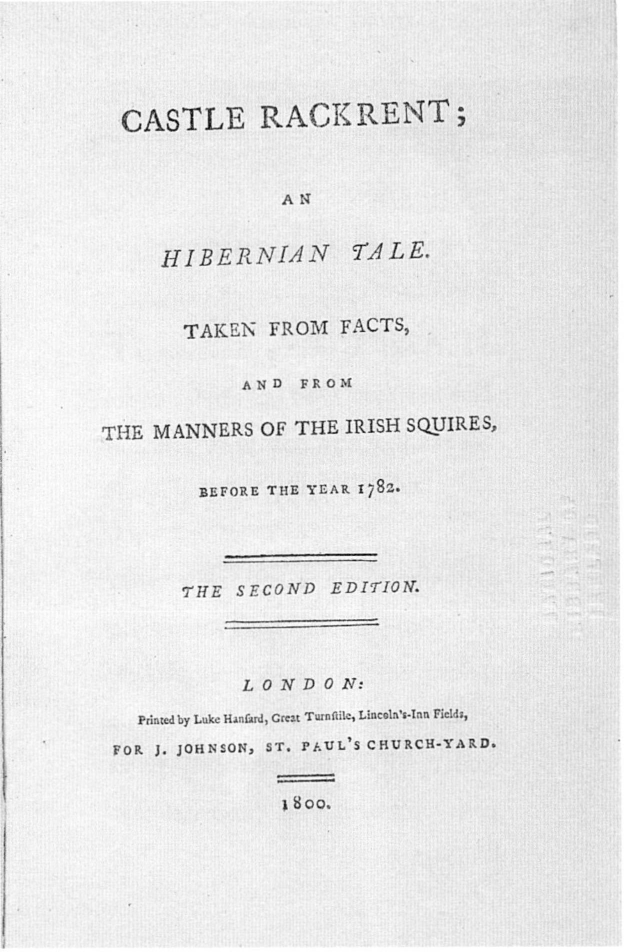
CASTLE RACKRENT;

AN

HIBERNIAN TALE.

TAKEN FROM FACTS,

AND FROM

THE MANNERS OF THE IRISH SQUIRES,

BEFORE THE YEAR 1782.

THE SECOND EDITION.

LONDON:

Printed by Luke Hanfard, Great Turnftile, Lincoln's-Inn Fields,

FOR J. JOHNSON, ST. PAUL'S CHURCH-YARD.

1800.

Edgeworth, Maria. *The title page of Maria Edgeworth's first Irish novel,* Castle Rackrent *(1800). Sir Walter Scott would later say that his aim in his novel* Waverley *was 'in some distant degree to emulate the admirable Irish Portraits drawn by Miss Edgeworth.' [Council of Trustees of the National Library of Ireland; LO 3446]*

Educate Together. *Pupils of the Dalkey School Project making Islamic prayer mats. Opened in September 1978, the school was the first multi-denominational school in the Republic; there are now twenty-seven such schools under the umbrella body Educate Together. [Mark Joyce]*

do not attempt to disguise English values as universal ones; and a prominent feature of all Edgeworth's fiction is the testing of national norms, often by placing what are assumed to be shared values in antagonistic relation to other cultures. In this she provided a model for Walter Scott, as he acknowledges in his postscript to *Waverley* (1814).

Edgeworth's most significant sustained fictional achievement is her series *Tales of Fashionable Life*, two separately published sets of fiction set in Ireland, France, and England that scrutinise national and sexual character and find them to be inter-related. Written from within an increasingly sectarian society, it is not surprising that Edgeworth's novels were preoccupied with the possibilities of religious tolerance, and in 1817 she published together *Harrington* and *Ormond*, the first an exploration of anti-Semitism and the second an attack on the evangelical established church. On her death she left sketches for literary projects she wished members of her family to execute, including notes based on her correspondence with David Ricardo on the desirability of POTATOES as a crop in Ireland. **Claire Connolly**

Edgeworth, Richard Lovell (1744–1817), improving landlord, inventor, and educationalist. Born in Bath; educated at TCD and the University of Oxford. He was member of the Irish Parliament for Edgeworthstown, Co. Longford. Having lived in England, where he was a member of the circle of Erasmus Darwin, and in France, where he was engaged in mechanical and land engineering projects, he returned to Ireland in 1782 to live on his estates. Married four times, he was the father of twenty-two children, the second of whom was the writer MARIA EDGEWORTH, who collaborated with him on a number of publications, including *Practical Education* (1798), very advanced for its time in anticipating Montessori and Froebel, and *Essays on Irish Bulls* (1802). Among his inventions was a telegraph system between Dublin and Galway, a velocipede (pedal-less bicycle), a pedometer for land measurement, for which he was awarded a silver medal by the Society of Arts, and advanced methods of road engineering. Aide-de-camp to the Earl of Charlemont in the VOLUNTEERS, he was a founder-member with him of the ROYAL IRISH ACADEMY. Other publications were *Professional Education* (1809) and *Memoirs* (1820, completed by Maria Edgeworth). **Brian Lalor**

Educate Together, the co-ordinating body for multi-denominational schools. In the 1970s an impetus developed both north and south of the BORDER for the setting up of multi-denominational or religiously integrated schools, where children of all RELIGIONS and none could be educated together. In the South the first multi-denominational primary school, the Dalkey School Project, opened in south Co. Dublin in 1978. This was followed by others in the 1980s and 90s; by 2001 there were twenty-seven multi-denominational primary schools in the Republic. The first integrated school in Northern Ireland, Lagan College, Belfast, opened in the early 1980s under the auspices of All Children Together. There are now forty-six integrated schools in Northern Ireland—twenty-nine primary and seventeen second-level—with an enrolment of 14,000 pupils, co-ordinated by the Northern Ireland Council for Integrated Education. **Áine Hyland**

education. Ireland enjoys a long tradition of education and of schooling, dating from pre-Christian times. The BREHON LAW laid down what children in fosterage were to be taught. Sons of noblemen should be taught 'horsemanship, and horn-playing, and shooting, and chess-playing and swimming.' Their sisters were to be taught 'sewing and cutting out and embroidering.' Boys from less exalted families should be taught 'the herding of lambs and calves and kids and young pigs, and kiln-drying, and combing, and wood-cutting.' According to *The Ancient Laws of Ireland*, girls from such families should be taught 'the use of the quern and the kneading trough and the use of the sieve.'

Before the introduction of Christianity, OGHAM was the only form of writing practised in Ireland. From Early Christian times, education became synonymous with the written word and scholarly learning, and MONASTIC SCHOOLS developed in parallel with bardic schools. In the monastic schools boys were taught in a Latin, ecclesiastical tradition; they learnt Latin and read the Latin Psalter. The bardic schools or 'poetical seminaries' were open only to 'such as were descended of poets.' The qualifications required for entry to these schools were 'reading well, writing the mother-tongue and a strong memory.' During the later centuries of the first millennium Ireland had come to be known as *Insula Sanctorum* (the Island of Saints), and large numbers of monks and scholars travelled to other European countries to spread Christianity and to extend scholarship.

The VIKING invasions of Ireland from the tenth to the twelfth centuries caused considerable disruption to the MONASTERIES. These invasions were followed by the ANGLO-NORMAN CONQUEST, which was to have significant implications for education and learning. From the fourteenth century onwards a series of statutes and ordinances attempted, at first without any great success, to suppress the IRISH LANGUAGE and customs, and it was not until the reign of ELIZABETH I that the influence of English rule began to be felt in education. In 1570 an act for the erection of free (diocesan) schools was passed, and this was followed in 1592 by the granting of a charter for the setting up of the University of Dublin (TCD). The reign of JAMES I in the following century saw the setting up of the Royal Schools, followed later in the seventeenth century by the setting up of the King's Hospital School in Dublin by CHARLES II.

The introduction of the PENAL LAWS at the end of the seventeenth century was intended to restrict the education of Catholics. Earlier legislation had been successfully circumvented by many students, who travelled abroad to seek higher education in Spain, France, Italy, and elsewhere. The Penal Laws sought to restrict such travel as well as to forbid Catholics to teach in public or private schools in Ireland. These laws led to a considerable growth in the number of illicit schools, and during the eighteenth century a widespread and unofficial educational system had come into being in the form of 'HEDGE SCHOOLS' or 'pay schools'. Contrary to popular belief, these schools were not universally conducted in hedgerows: more often than not they assembled in the house or hut of the schoolmaster or of a local family. The Penal Laws were repealed at the end of the eighteenth century, but by this time schooling was widely available to children through the hedge schools or pay schools.

Schools were set up by various Protestant religious societies in the seventeenth and eighteenth centuries. These included the Incorporated Society for Promoting English Protestant Schools in Ireland—the Charter Schools—founded in the early years of the eighteenth century by Archbishop Boulter of Dublin; the Sunday School Society (originally known as the Hibernian Sunday Society when it was set up in 1809); the Bible Society; and the Society for Discountenancing Vice. Some of these received considerable royal and parliamentary support. In 1811 the British government agreed to give financial support to the Society for Promoting the Education of the Poor in Ireland (otherwise known as the Kildare Place Society) to promote mixed-religion schools throughout the country. This society set out to bring organisation and structure to schooling. It produced a series of graded readers, employed inspectors to inspect its schools, and provided training for teachers. During the first decade of its existence the Kildare Place Society was supported by all the Christian churches, but by 1820 the Catholic Church had lost confidence in the society and accused it of supporting proselytism. Grants were withdrawn from the society when the national school system was set up in 1831.

After the repeal of the Penal Laws at the end of the eighteenth century, schools were set up, especially in towns, by RELIGIOUS ORDERS and congregations. One of the first of these was the Presentation Congregation (originally known as the Sisters of Charitable Instruction of the Sacred Heart of Jesus), founded by NANO NAGLE in Cork in 1776. The first school and monastery of the Irish CHRISTIAN BROTHERS were built by EDMUND RICE in Waterford in 1802. The Sisters of Mercy, founded by CATHERINE MCAULEY in Dublin, were formally recognised by the Catholic Church as a religious congregation in 1830. The schools of these religious orders and congregations, which catered largely for poor children, were not at first supported financially by the government.

By 1824 there were more than 11,000 schools in Ireland, the great majority of them small hedge or pay schools, and most of them catering exclusively for either Catholic or Protestant children. Very few schools received financial aid from the government, and there was increasing pressure on the government to provide such support. In 1831 it set up a national system of education under the supervision of a Board of Commissioners of National Education. The government's plan for education was set out in a letter from the CHIEF SECRETARY, Lord Stanley, to the Duke of Leinster, who was to be the first chairman of the board. The board would provide financial aid (capital and current grants) and support in the form of textbooks and school requisites for schools that catered for children of all Christian denominations. The children would be taught together for moral and literary instruction but would be separated into their various religious groups for religious instruction.

The national school system grew rapidly following its foundation in 1831. By 1850 there were 4,500 schools, catering for about 250,000 pupils; by 1900 this had grown to 8,700 schools with an enrolment of 1,250,000 pupils. However, the government's intention of supporting only mixed-religion schools was quickly thwarted by the churches. By the middle of the nineteenth century, the three main churches—CATHOLIC, CHURCH OF IRELAND, and PRESBYTERIAN—had each gained concessions, and the system rapidly became denominational, with individual schools owned by different churches. This situation remains largely unchanged to the present day in the Republic, where 99 per cent of national schools are under the control of either the Catholic or Protestant churches.

It was not until 1878, from funds that became available following the DISESTABLISHMENT of the Church of Ireland in 1869, that intermediate (secondary) education was supported to any significant extent by the state. The Intermediate Education (Ireland) Act (1878) made available a fund of £1 million to finance an examination system for secondary-school pupils. The interest from the fund was used each year to pay grants to schools according to the results of their pupils in the annual examinations and to pay gratuities and prizes to the highest-achieving pupils. Under the terms of the act, secondary schools remained private institutions. They were predominantly religious schools; the Catholic schools were almost all controlled and managed by nuns, brothers, or priests. The payment-by-results system provided the basis for the state examination system that still dominates Irish education. While payment to schools in accordance with their pupils' results ended in 1922, the dominance of public examinations in the education of second-level pupils continues to the present day. It should be noted, however, that in the nineteenth and early twentieth centuries secondary education was the preserve of the few: less than 10 per cent of the population attended a secondary school, and only about 1 per cent successfully completed the Senior Grade examination.

Education after 1921. Following PARTITION in 1921, the systems of education developed separately. That of Northern Ireland began to gravitate towards the British system, while the system in the South remained largely unchanged, at least at first. The Education Act (Northern Ireland) (1923) sought to establish a new educational framework that would be both decentralised in its administration and non-denominational in application and ethos. The churches regarded this act as usurping their traditional role in education, especially in relation to curricular issues and to the appointment of teachers. The Education Act (Northern Ireland) (1930) reversed many of the provisions of the 1923 act that the churches had regarded as unacceptable; it also laid down a new basis for the administration and management of the majority of schools, characteristics of which are still to be found in the present system. Schools that before partition had been under Protestant control accepted the local authority framework and were subsumed into that framework: in effect they became non-denominational schools, while retaining a voice on the school's governing authority. Schools that had been under Catholic control refused to submit to the locally elected authorities and remained autonomous; they continued to receive state support but not at the same level as the local authority schools. This would subsequently give rise to accusations of discrimination against Catholic schools.

Free secondary education was introduced earlier in the North than in the South. The Education Act (Northern Ireland) (1947) provided for a three-stage system for all: primary education, secondary education, and further education. Local education authorities were charged with 'securing that efficient education throughout those stages shall be available to meet the needs of the population of their area.' While the 1947 act brought second-level education within the reach of all young people, it also introduced a selection system based on an examination at the age of eleven. This examination, the ELEVEN-PLUS, selected only a minority of eleven-year-olds for 'grammar school' (academic) education and relegated the others to a less highly regarded 'intermediate' school. The Eleven-Plus continued to be a feature of the Northern Ireland system of education until 2002. A report by the Post-Primary Review Body, published in October 2001, which involved widespread consultation with parents, schools, and the wider community, had recommended that the Eleven-Plus examination be abolished.

In the South there was little change in the control and management of education in the first decades of the new state. However, the curriculum in both primary and secondary schools was revised to emphasise Irish language, history, and culture. In 1924 the Intermediate Education Act was amended and a two-level examination system was introduced: the Intermediate Certificate after two or three years and the Leaving Certificate after a further two years. The School Attendance Act (1926) introduced compulsory school attendance for all children between six and fourteen. The Vocational Education Act (1930) introduced a system of continuation education for pupils aged from fourteen to sixteen, and this was followed in 1947 by the introduction of the Day Group Certificate examination to provide national certification for pupils in vocational schools.

It was not until the 1960s that substantial changes occurred in the structure of the Republic's education. Comprehensive education at post-primary level became Government policy in the mid-1960s, and in 1966 the first of the comprehensive schools were opened. Later that year the Minister for Education, DONOGH O'MALLEY, announced the introduction of free post-primary education. From September 1967 all children would be entitled to free post-primary schooling. Transport would be provided for those living 3 miles or more from their nearest school. School catchment areas were delineated, and a scheme of expansion of post-primary facilities was undertaken. The Primary Certificate examination, which had been introduced as an option in 1929 and had been compulsory since the early 1940s, was abolished and replaced by a school record card. In the mid-1970s boards of management, comprising nominees of the patrons (school owners), of parents and of teachers were set up in all primary schools; in this way a degree of democratisation was introduced into the management of schools, but this did not interfere with the ownership rights of the churches. The move towards democratisation and a greater recognition of the rights of parents in education was also reflected in the growing demand in the 1970s, 80s and 90s for IRISH-MEDIUM SCHOOLS and for multi-denominational (EDUCATE TOGETHER) schools at primary level. During the same period the curriculums at primary and post-primary levels were revised to take account of the growth of knowledge and new developments in teaching and learning, as well as the opportunities provided by information and communication technologies. At the same time a network of regional technical colleges (since renamed institutes of technology) was created, and from the late 1960s onwards enrolments in post-primary, further, and higher education grew dramatically.

At second level the proportion of an age group taking the Leaving Certificate increased from less than 20 per cent in the mid-1960s to more than 80 per cent in the mid-1990s. The numbers attending second-level and third-level education continued to grow until the late 1990s; but, as a result of demographic trends, enrolments at second level began to fall in the late 1990s. While the numbers of school-leavers going on to third-level education is beginning to level out, the Republic has a relatively low rate of participation by mature students in third-level education, but this is expected to grow in the decade to 2010 in line with the experience in other industrialised countries. **Áine Hyland**

education: co-education. Compared with other countries, Ireland has a relatively high proportion of pupils in single-sex education. Over two-thirds of pupils at primary level attend co-educational schools, with an additional number in mixed junior classes within otherwise single-sex schools. In total, 62 per cent of second-level schools are co-educational, with 59 per cent of all pupils attending these schools. Almost all vocational and community or comprehensive schools are co-educational, with 64 per cent of voluntary schools remaining single-sex. Single-sex schooling remains somewhat more prevalent for girls, with 46 per cent attending single-sex schools in 1997/8, compared with 35 per cent of boys. Co-educational education has become more prevalent over time, partly as a result of the amalgamation of smaller single-sex schools in rural areas into co-educational schools.

The effects of co-educational schooling, particularly on academic performance, have been the subject of much debate internationally. Initial research suggested that girls tended to do better academically in single-sex than in co-educational schools, while the effects for boys were somewhat positive or neutral. However, such studies rarely took account of the fact that single-sex schools tended to be more selective in their intake (in socio-economic background or in ability levels). More recent studies have tended to take account of differences between single-sex and co-educational schools in their intake; however, research findings have continued to differ, with some American research indicating an advantage to girls in single-sex schools, while British and Australian studies suggest little or no performance difference between the two systems.

The first systematic study of co-education in the Republic suggested that girls in single-sex schools tended to outperform their counterparts in co-educational schools. However, this study was limited to one area and did not adequately take into account differences in intake between schools. A larger-scale study of co-education at second level showed no significant differences between co-educational and single-sex schools in average performance or in aspects of personal and social development (such as self-image and stress levels). However, girls in co-educational schools were found to have lower grades in mathematics than those in single-sex schools. **Emer Smyth**

education and the sciences. Modern science began in Europe during the late Renaissance. TRINITY COLLEGE, Dublin, founded in 1592, offered lectures in logic, moral philosophy, natural philosophy, astronomy, and mathematics. It initiated a Baconian philosophy of science education, which advocated that scientific knowledge should be sought and applied for practical advantage. A Jesuit college flourished in Dublin in the early seventeenth century associated with Father CHRISTOPHER HOLYWOOD (1562–1626), who produced the first printed scientific book by an Irishman, *De Meteoris* (1613).

The Dublin Philosophical Society, founded in 1683, helped to create an Irish scientific tradition in science, engineering, and technical education. The writings of WILLIAM PETTY, its first president, prefigured all the facilities that subsequently developed out of Trinity College and the Dublin Society (later the ROYAL DUBLIN SOCIETY), including the ROYAL IRISH ACADEMY (1785), the School of Chemistry and Mineralogy (1786), DUNSINK OBSERVATORY (1787), the NATIONAL BOTANIC GARDENS (1790), the ROYAL CORK INSTITUTION (1805), BELFAST NATURAL HISTORY AND PHILOSOPHICAL SOCIETY (1821), the NATURAL HISTORY MUSEUM (1857), and the Royal College of Veterinary Surgeons (1895). The Dublin Society set out to improve Ireland's AGRICULTURE and industry by educating farmers and tradesmen. The chemist WILLIAM HIGGINS became an officer of the society in 1795 and established a laboratory to teach experimental CHEMISTRY. In 1812 the society founded professorships in mineralogy, geology, and mining engineering. The chemist ROBERT KANE, who succeeded Higgins, wrote the world-famous textbook *Elements of Chemistry* (1841).

Three Queen's Colleges were established in 1845, in Belfast, Cork, and Galway. Magee College opened in Derry in 1865. The Catholic population began to appreciate Baconian education. This eventually led to the formation of a new educational establishment with the incorporation in 1908 of the CATHOLIC UNIVERSITY OF IRELAND (which had opened in 1854) and the Queen's Colleges of Cork and Galway in the National University of Ireland, with three constituent colleges (Dublin, Cork, Galway) and several 'recognised' colleges. Queen's College, Belfast, subsequently became Queen's University. The three constituent NUI colleges and ST PATRICK'S COLLEGE, Maynooth, were reconstituted in 1997 as constituent universities of the NUI. The University of Ulster opened in 1984 with colleges at Belfast, Jordanstown, Coleraine, and Magee College. The University of Limerick and Dublin City University were established in 1989 (entering from NIHE).

All the universities offer degrees in science and engineering. Natural science subjects were increasingly taught in secondary schools in the second half of the nineteenth century. Science was introduced to primary schools in 1900. It was dropped in 1934 but by 2001 was being phased in again. In 1997, some 96 per cent of secondary schools offered BIOLOGY, 80 per cent offered physics and 71 per cent offered chemistry at Leaving Certificate level. Little higher-level technical education was available during most of the nineteenth century. Kevin Street Technical College was established in Dublin in 1887 and Bolton Street College in 1911; these were federated into the Dublin Institute of Technology in 1978.

As Ireland's industrial economy developed in the 1960s, the demand for technicians rose, leading to the foundation of regional technical colleges in the 1970s, later redesignated Institutes of Technology. **William Reville**

education: statistics. Between 1987/88 and 1997/98 the number of pupils in the Republic decreased by more than 8 per cent, reflecting a sharp fall in the numbers attending primary education, which itself followed a large drop in the number of births, from a peak reached in 1980. In Northern Ireland the number of pupils increased by 3 per cent over the same period, mainly because of an increase of 9,000 in the numbers at second level.

Table 1: Schools, pupils, and teachers, 1987/88–97/98

	1987/88	1992/93	1997/98	1987/88	1992/93	1997/98
	Republic			Northern Ireland		
Schools						
First level	3,562	3,530	3,674	1,097	1,071	1,036
Second level	817	785	762	295	280	285
Total	4,379	4,315	4,436	1,392	1,351	1,321
Pupils						
First level	565,487	521,531	460,845	191,161	195,594	193,377
Second level	339,556	358,347	368,168	148,811	149,725	157,775
Total	905,043	879,878	829,013	339,972	345,319	351,152
Teachers						
First level	21,217	20,791	21,100	8,052	8,698	9,721
Second level	19,314	21,193	23,310	10,347	10,194	11,247
Total	40,531	41,954	44,410	18,399	18,892	20,968

In 1997/98 there were approximately 19 pupils per teacher in the Republic and 17 pupils per teacher in Northern Ireland; at primary level the figures were 22 in the Republic and 20 in Northern Ireland, down substantially from 1987/88 in both cases. The corresponding figures at second level were 17.5 and 14, respectively, largely unchanged from the ratios of ten years earlier.

education and the sciences. *Science students at the National University of Ireland, Galway which has a Science Faculty of ninety professors and lecturers and approximately 2,300 students. [National University of Ireland, Galway]*

Table 2: Pupil-teacher ratio, 1987/88–97/98

	1987/88	1992/93	1997/98	1987/88	1992/93	1997/98
		Republic			Northern Ireland	
First level	26.7	25.1	21.8	23.7	22.6	19.7
Second level	17.6	18.1	17.5	14.4	14.5	14.0
All schools	22.3	21.0	18.7	18.5	18.2	16.7

Between 1987/88 and 1997/98 the number of students from the Republic enrolled in full-time or part-time undergraduate courses increased by 72 per cent, while the number of postgraduate students more than doubled. Over the same period the numbers of both undergraduate and postgraduate students from Northern Ireland more than doubled. **Central Statistics Office/Northern Ireland Statistics & Research Agency**

Edwards, Hilton (1903–1982), THEATRE manager, actor, director, and designer. Born in London; educated at St Aloysius' College, Highgate. In 1927 he met MÍCHEÁL MAC LIAMMÓIR, with whom he founded both the TAIBHDHEARC in Galway and the GATE THEATRE in Dublin, 1928, where they acted together until the 1970s. He was awarded an honorary doctorate by the NUI in 1974. His acting can be seen in Orson Welles's film *Othello* (1951) (see p. 497). **Christopher Morash**

Egan, Desmond (1936–), poet. Born in Athlone, Co. Westmeath; educated at ST PATRICK'S COLLEGE, Maynooth, and UCD. His volumes of poetry include *Midland* (1972), *Siege!* (1976), *Athlone* (1980), *A Song for My Father* (1989), *Famine* (1997), and *Music* (2000). His collected PROSE was published as *The Death of Metaphor* (1990); he has also published translations of Euripides' *Medea* (1991) and Sophocles' *Philoctetes* (1998). He is a recipient of the National Poetry Foundation of USA Award, 1983, the Bologna Literature Award, 1998, and an honorary doctorate from Washburn University, Kansas, 1997. Employing a highly concentrated and defamiliarising style (including an experimental technique of multi-voicing), Egan has produced compelling poetry on many topics, including landscape, politics, love, and death. He has been translated into many languages. **Brian Arkins**

Egan, Felim (1952–), painter. Born in Strabane, Co. Tyrone; studied at the Slade School of Fine Art, London. His paintings are abstract; like harmonies in music, forms are echoed in rhythmic layers. The images, often large-scale, project a cool, fragile beauty. He represented Ireland in the Rosc exhibition, 1984, and is a member of AOSDÁNA. He is an accomplished printmaker and has collaborated with SEAMUS HEANEY on the publications *Squarings* (1991) and *Sandymount Strand* (1993). A retrospective exhibition was held at the IRISH MUSEUM OF MODERN ART, Dublin, 1995. **Suzanne McNab**

Egerton, George, pen-name of Mary Chavelita Dunne (1860–1945), writer. Born into an army family in Australia; the family returned to Dublin in 1868. In 1887 she eloped with Henry Higginson, a bigamist, to Norway, where she read Ibsen, Hansson, and Hamsun, whose novel *Sult* she translated. Following her husband's death she returned to Ireland, where she remarried, living and writing in Millstreet, Co. Cork, 1891–4. Her short-story collection *Keynotes* (1893), which 'told the truth about sexuality', created a sensation in the 1890s. Subsequent collections include

Discords (1894), *Symphonies* (1897), and *Fantasias* (1898). Her experimental feminist writing was overshadowed by the conservative reaction following the OSCAR WILDE trials in 1898. **Tina O'Toole**

Eglinton, John, pseudonym of William Kirkpatrick Magee (1868–1961), writer. He was assistant librarian at the NATIONAL LIBRARY OF IRELAND, 1895–1921. He made crucial interventions in the cultural debate during the LITERARY REVIVAL. His most famous essay, 'What should be the subjects of national drama?', drew W. B. YEATS into debate in advance of the opening productions of the Irish Literary Theatre. He argued that a preoccupation with the 'ancient legends of Ireland' could produce only a form of *belles-lettres*, rather than a genuinely national drama; these exchanges were reprinted as *Literary Ideals in Ireland* (1899). He was joint-editor of the journal *Dana* (1904) and author of *Irish Literary Portraits* (1935). He appears as the librarian in JAMES JOYCE'S ULYSSES. **P. J. Mathews**

'Eibhlín, a Rún', a celebrated love song, traditionally attributed to the seventeenth-century bard CEARBHALL Ó DÁLAIGH of Pallice, Co. Wexford. He was said to have fallen in love with Eleanor, daughter of Murcha Caomhánach of Clonmulen, Co. Carlow. It is more likely, however, that the song was composed before Ó Dálaigh's time. **Éamonn Ó Bróithe**

Éire. The Modern Irish name (officially the name of the state (1937–1949) *Éirinn* (earlier *Éire*) derives from Old Irish *Ériu*, the commonest name for Ireland, possibly meaning 'good land'. Other names included *Banba, Elg, Fál, Fótla,* and *Inis Fáil*. These names were associated with sovereignty and kingship, often in the guise of a woman, though in reality some simply denoted topographical features. **Edel Bhreathnach**

elderly, the. The elderly in Ireland entered the twentieth century with one of the highest average life expectancies in Europe yet by 1990 ranked lowest among twenty-three OECD countries for both men and women. Combined with a higher than average FERTILITY rate and high emigration, this means that Ireland enters the twenty-first century with a lower proportion of older people than any other European country. Unfortunately this section of the community carries a considerable burden of ill HEALTH, with 44 per cent having a chronic physical or MENTAL HEALTH problem. Such illness often requires care from others; because of the poorly developed care services in the Republic, the carer tends to be someone in the household, usually female, often aged over fifty-five themselves.

In the two decades after 1970 the living standards and incomes of older people improved considerably relative to the general population, helped by the increased availability of non-cash benefits after 1967. However, growth in PENSION incomes has not matched that of workers in the economic boom of the mid-1990s, driving up relative income poverty among the elderly. Nonetheless real living standards continue to improve. **Richard Layte**

electricity. *Seán Keating's* Building Site with Luffelbagger and Wagon Train, *illustrating the excavation work for the headrace at Ardnacrusha power station. Keating was commissioned to record the construction of the Shannon Scheme in the 1920s. [ESB Art Collection]*

electoral system. The electoral system of the Republic, enshrined in the CONSTITUTION OF IRELAND, is proportional representation with a single transferable vote and multi-seat constituencies.

The voter has a single vote but can use this sequentially according to his or her preferences by marking *1, 2, 3* and so on against the various names on the ballot paper. The counting of votes begins with the calculation of the *quota* for each constituency, which is arrived at by dividing the total valid poll by the number of seats + 1, and adding 1 to the result (ignoring any fractions). Candidates who reach the quota are deemed to be elected. An elected candidate's *surplus* (votes in excess of the quota) are redistributed to the remaining candidates in proportion to the distribution of the next available preferences on the ballot papers received by the candidate in the count on which he or she was elected. When all available surpluses have been distributed, the candidate with the smallest number of votes is eliminated, and his or her votes are redistributed. This process of redistributing surplus votes and the votes of eliminated candidates continues until all the seats are filled, or until a seat remains to be filled and there are no more votes to be redistributed, in which case the candidate with the largest number of votes is deemed to be elected without reaching the quota.

The quota can be thought of as an extension of the majority-rule principle to multi-seat constituencies. If there were only one seat the quota would be 50 per cent plus 1; in a two-seat constituency it would be 33 per cent plus 1; and so on. This varying threshold is the mechanism by which the system achieves the objective of a reasonable degree of proportionality between share of votes and share of seats and the related objective of facilitating the representation of minorities. Debate about the merits of the system is concerned mainly with its alleged role in encouraging politicians to concentrate on their constituency service function, at the expense of their legislative function. **Richard Sinnott**

electoral turn-out. Over the last three decades of the twentieth century the turn-out of voters in general elections in the Republic averaged 72 per cent; this puts Ireland at the bottom of a ranking of the eleven members-states of the EUROPEAN UNION that do not have compulsory voting. (The average turn-out in the other ten states for the same period was 80 per cent.) Moreover, turn-out in Ireland is declining, having gone from 77 per cent in the general elections of the 1970s to 73 per cent in the 80s, 67 per cent in the 90s, and 63 per cent in the general election of 2002.

Turn-out also varies by type of election. In the same period it was 60 per cent in local elections, 58 per cent in presidential elections, and 46 per cent in European Parliament elections that were not held on the same day as other elections. Turn-out varies even more in REFERENDUMS, depending on the issue. However, even within the category of EU referendums, all of which could be regarded as dealing with important issues, turn-out has ranged from a maximum of 71 per cent (in the referendum on membership of the EEC in 1972) to a minimum of 35 per cent (in the referendum on the Treaty of Nice in 2001). Turn-out tends to be lower among young people, among those in lower socio-economic groups, and in urban areas.

In trying to make sense of these and other correlations one must distinguish between circumstantial and voluntary abstention. The former is undoubtedly augmented by the time pressures that characterise contemporary life; the latter is a function of perceptions of and attitudes to politics and politicians. **Richard Sinnott**

electricity supply. Until 2000 the supply of electricity in the Republic was vested in the Electricity Supply Board (ESB), which by an act of 1927 was responsible for the generation, transmission, and distribution of electricity. The ESB took over the SHANNON SCHEME, an 80 MW hydro station, together with a 110 kV grid and 38 kV and 10 kV distribution network. By 2000 this had built to a generating capacity of more than 4,000 MW from twenty stations, using a strategic mixture of energy: hydro, turf, oil, gas, and coal. The transmission network was enlarged, with 400 kV and 220 kV grids. Rural electrification brought a single-phase or three-phase 400 or 230 V 50 Hz supply to practically all the country. By 2000 the ESB was supplying 17 billion kWh per year to 1.7 million customers.

In the same period Northern Ireland reached a total generation capacity of 2,250 MW from four stations, using gas, coal, and oil. Northern Ireland is connected to Scotland by an undersea high-voltage direct-current 500 MW cable, which in turn is connected to the ESB network by a 600 MW interconnector. With deregulation required by EU directives, private generators can now supply and sell electricity to consumers up to an agreed amount. **Joseph McEvoy**

Eleven-Plus, an examination taken by children in Northern Ireland between the ages of ten and eleven. The result has a fundamental effect on post-primary school choices and subsequent life chances: almost all the seventy grammar schools use the results to decide whom to admit. This selection test has been abandoned in Britain in the 1960s but remained at the core of Northern Ireland's education system until 2002. Performance in the examination appears to be linked to SOCIAL CLASS rather than to any other variable: middle-class children disproportionately attend grammar schools, while working-class children are over-represented in secondary schools. Grammar schools have more resources than secondary schools and guarantee higher rates of examination performance than secondary schools. The Gallagher Report (2000) found that the test scored poorly in its power to predict which children have the ability to benefit from a grammar school education; interviews with children found that they labelled themselves as 'smart' or 'stupid' according to their performance in the test. **Madeleine Leonard**

Elizabeth I (1533–1603), Queen of England, 1558–1603. The daughter of HENRY VIII and Anne Boleyn, his second wife, Elizabeth was considered illegitimate by the Catholic Church. She imposed a Protestant settlement on the church in England and, gradually but persistently, sought to do the same in Ireland. She was drawn into increasing involvement in Ireland by 'programmatic' governors who promised to extend English rule within specific periods at minimal cost. However, the expansion of her authority provoked a series of rebellions from Irish lords anxious to preserve local liberties

elk. *Full skeletal remains of* Megaloceros giganteus, *the giant deer known as the 'Irish elk', which became extinct about 10,000 years ago. Their remains are commonly found in bogs and lakelands. [Geological Museum, Trinity College, Dublin]*

or Catholicism. HUGH O'NEILL, Earl of Tyrone, leading modernised military forces, presented Elizabeth with the greatest challenge of her reign. However, the Spanish expedition sent to support O'Neill in 1601 was inadequate and drew him into the disastrous BATTLE OF KINSALE. With O'Neill's surrender at MELLIFONT a week after her death in March 1603, Elizabeth's conquest of Ireland was complete, though her REFORMATION had largely failed. **Henry A. Jefferies**

Elizabeth I type, an Irish printing type. In 1570—about twenty years after the introduction to Ireland of printing from cast metal type—John Kearney and Nicholas Walsh, both of ST PATRICK'S CATHEDRAL, Dublin, arranged to have a font of Irish type made available at the behest of ELIZABETH I for the purpose of printing the New Testament and other religious texts of the Reformed Church in Irish. This hybrid font consisted mainly of existing roman letters to which an italic capital and lower-case letter *a* and some distinctive Irish forms were added. It was used in 1571 to print the poem 'Tuar Ferge Foighide Dhé' and the catechism, AIBIDIL GAOIDHEILGE AGUS CAITICIOSMA. Later, in 1602 and 1608, it was used for the printing of the *Tiomna Nuadh* (New Testament) and *Leabhar na nUrnaightheadh gComhchoidchiond* (BOOK OF COMMON PRAYER) and, to a lesser extent, by a succession of Dublin printers up to 1652. [see BIBLE IN IRISH; PRINTING IN IRISH.] **Dermot McGuinne**

elk, Irish, an extinct giant deer. This animal was not exclusively Irish, nor yet an elk, but rather the largest-antlered deer that ever lived, with a height of 2.1 m (7 ft) to the shoulders and an antler span of up to 3.6 m (12 ft). It was found principally in Ireland but also in Britain, the Isle of Man, France, Italy, Switzerland, Germany, Austria, Russia, and Siberia; there are cave drawings of the elk in France, showing that it was contemporary with early humans. It was once common on Irish lowland sites with good grazing, where it ate grass; its bones have never been found in the mountains but are often found with those of reindeer. Skeletons can be seen in the NATURAL HISTORY MUSEUM and the GEOLOGY Museum in TRINITY COLLEGE, Dublin; the antlers are often displayed in aristocratic houses. It became extinct 10,000 years ago in Ireland, Britain, and the Continent but survived for a further 1,000 years in the Isle of Man. The reasons for its extinction are still not understood. **D. Patrick Sleeman**

Ellis Island, New York, the first federal IMMIGRATION facility established by the United States. From 1892 to 1954 more than 12 million people passed through the complex in New York harbour, the majority before 1924. 'Ellis Island' subsequently became a shorthand term for the entire American immigration experience, but the facility was most relevant to southern and eastern European emigrants. Before 1855, immigrants (including Irish FAMINE REFUGEES) had disembarked directly on the New York quays, without any official protection. Ellis Island superseded Castle Garden, a state immigration depot on the southern tip of Manhattan island that received 8.2 million people between 1855 and 1890. Approximately a quarter of these were Irish, compared with just over 4 per cent of all those who landed at Ellis Island.

By the 1890s concerns over the volume of immigration led to restrictive legislation requiring the medical inspections, LITERACY tests, and other types of processing encountered there. Irish people who travelled on second-class tickets underwent a cursory examination on board ship, while 'steerage' (third-class) passengers were required to go to Ellis Island. The first immigrant processed was Annie Moore, a fifteen-year-old from Co. Cork; in 1993 President MARY ROBINSON unveiled a statue of Moore at the Ellis Island Immigration Museum. **Marion R. Casey**

Ellison, Mervyn Archdall (1909–1963), astronomer. Born in Fethard, Co. Wexford, son of REV. W. F. A. ELLISON; educated at TCD. His father owned a private observatory, and he was introduced at an early age to the making of astronomical observations; his first paper (on double stars) was published while he was still at school. During the SECOND WORLD WAR he served as a scientific adviser to the British Admiralty. After working as deputy director of the Royal Observatory, Edinburgh, he was appointed director of DUNSINK OBSERVATORY and senior professor at the School of Cosmic Physics of the DUBLIN INSTITUTE FOR ADVANCED STUDIES. **Susan McKenna-Lawlor**

Ellison, W. F. A [William Frederick Archdall] (1864–1936), astronomer. Born in Kilkenny; educated at TCD, graduating in classics and experimental science in 1887. In 1894 he was awarded the Elrington Theological Prize; he was ordained for the diocese of Durham in England, becoming curate of Tudhoe and Wearmouth, Co. Durham. In 1902 he returned to Ireland as rector of Fethard, Co. Wexford. He developed an interest in ASTRONOMY, producing lenses and mirrors of outstanding quality for TELESCOPES of all sizes, and published *The Amateur's Telescope* (1920) and contributions to scientific publications. In 1919 he was appointed director of ARMAGH OBSERVATORY, where he used an 18-in. Calver equatorial reflector and a 10-in. GRUBB refractor for the measurements of double stars. He carried out important work on Mars, on Saturn's rings and moons, and on eclipses of the Sun. In 1934 he was appointed canon of Armagh Cathedral. He was a Hebrew scholar and an accomplished organist at the cathedral, a member of the ROYAL IRISH ACADEMY, and a fellow of the Royal Astronomical Society and Royal Meteorological Society. **William Ellison**

Ellmann, Richard (1918–1987), critic and writer. Born in Michigan; studied at Yale University, and served in the US forces that took part in the liberation of Germany. At TRINITY COLLEGE, Dublin, he wrote a doctoral thesis on W. B. YEATS; with the co-operation of George Yeats, the poet's widow, and this appeared as *The Man and the Masks* (1948). A closer study of the poetry, *The Identity of Yeats*, followed in 1954. While a professor at Northwestern University, Evanston, Illinois, Chicago, he wrote his masterpiece, *James Joyce* (1959), arguably the greatest literary biography in English of its era, combining original interpretation with a detailed but coherent biographical portrait. *Eminent Domain* (1965) and *The Modern Tradition* (edited with Charles Feidelson, Junior, 1965) confirmed his credentials as his generation's leading analyst of literary modernism; his Joycean reputation was consolidated by *Ulysses on the Liffey* (1972) and *Selected Letters* (1975). Though dying of motor neurone disease he completed *Oscar Wilde*, the last of his great biographies, published posthumously in 1988. The foremost authority on the principal Irish modernists, he was Goldsmith's professor of modern literature at the University of Oxford from 1970 to his death. **Declan Kiberd**

Ellman. *Richard Ellman, university professor, critic, and noted Joyce scholar, at a book-signing in Kenny's Bookshop, Galway. [Courtesy of Kenny's Bookshop and Art Gallery, Galway]*

emblems and symbols. Illustrators have employed many images to symbolise Ireland. 'Erin' or 'Hibernia', a female representation of Ireland, is the most recognised, often portrayed in sorrowful repose; she exhibits other emotions when confronting instances of injustice. The colours green and yellow and images of the HARP, wolfhound, HIGH CROSS, and ROUND TOWER combine with Celtic motifs to signify Ireland's past. Another symbol, the RED HAND OF ULSTER, derived from the O'Neill family seal, contributed to the coat of arms of Ulster, a form of which was the flag of Northern Ireland until 1973. Politicised variations of the red hand appear in nationalist and loyalist communities' political murals. [see POLITICAL STREET ART.] **Lawrence W. McBride**

embroidered textiles. EMBROIDERY was central to the magnificence of ancient Irish dress. The legendary CÚ CHULAINN, whose wife, Emer, was a famous embroiderer, went into battle dressed in LINEN embroidered with gold. But no ancient embroidery survives, or even any from the sixteenth century, when HENRY VIII prohibited gowns embroidered 'after the Irish fashion.' As a consequence, in the Celtic Revival bright embroideries based on traditional devices became central to the assertion of Irishness, and remain so, as for example in Irish dancing costumes. From the seventeenth century, embroidery in Ireland conformed largely to European fashions and was done by professionals, though women at home gained a particular reputation for 'SPRIGGING' and 'flowering' on household linen in the late nineteenth century. Embroidery was taught in national schools from the nineteenth century but, challenged by FEMINISM as well as by new art practices, not since the 1970s. Both new and traditional can be seen in the work of the DUN EMER GUILD and the Embroiderers' Guild (established 1975). **Hilary O'Kelly**

embroidery, used in Ireland to decorate costume since before the tenth century. The *léine* (shirt or shift) of the wealthy often included heavy bands of appliqué and embroidery worked in silver and gold wire threads; such threads were originally imported from the Continent but were later manufactured in Dublin by skilled craftsmen. Traditional metal embroidery survives today, through the skilled outworkers employed by the Ulster Bullion Company in Annalong, Co. Down, to produce vestments and badges for the local and export market. One of the most elaborate examples of Irish embroidery is the magnificent floral bed-cover made in 1712 by Martha Lennox (1686–1729), daughter of the first Mayor of Belfast, now in the Ulster Museum.

The mass-production of LINEN in the eighteenth century provided the basis for much white embroidery. The 'sewed muslin' industry, in particular, provided employment for tens of thousands of women throughout Ireland in the nineteenth century. The skills of Irish embroiderers were highly regarded and recognised with awards at exhibitions of arts and industry at home and abroad during the period 1880–1910. Large shops, such as that of Robinson and Cleaver in Belfast, maintained their own workroom of stitchers to cater for the demand for the decorated bed linens and handkerchiefs of late Victorian and Edwardian times. In the ARTS AND CRAFTS MOVEMENT, Evelyn Gleeson and Lily Yeats in the DUN EMER GUILD and CUALA INDUSTRIES produced hand-embroidered banners and furnishings that achieved critical and commercial success at the beginning of the twentieth century. Nowadays the skills of hand embroidery are fostered through craft guilds and the textile degree courses of the colleges of art throughout Ireland. **Valerie Wilson**

embroidery, ecclesiastical. The splendour of the mitre made by Thomas O'Carryd in 1418 for Conor O'Dea, Bishop of Limerick, and the vestments of northern Italian cloth of gold, with Flemish embroidery, acquired by the Bishop of Waterford in the late fifteenth and early sixteenth centuries indicate the wealth of the late medieval church, as well as of the citizens of those cities. The vestments and altar embroideries that survive, particularly in Kilkenny, Clonfert, Mullingar, Galway, Kylemore, Drogheda, and Maynooth, show that this applied in various parts of the country. The increase in demand after CATHOLIC EMANCIPATION (1829) meant that commercial suppliers of vestments and church embroideries evolved. Later, elaborate ecclesiastical embroideries were produced by the ROYAL IRISH SCHOOL OF ART NEEDLEWORK, including hand-embroidered altar falls for ST PATRICK'S CATHEDRAL, Dublin, and Kildare Cathedral, 1897–1902. Equally, William Egan and Sons of Cork, the DUN EMER GUILD and convent schools, such as the Convent of the Poor Clares, Kenmare, embroidered vestments, frontals, dossals, and banners for churches in Ireland and the United States, particularly in the Celtic Revival style. **Mairead Dunlevy**

embroidery, ecclesiastical. *Detail of an embroidered silk cope, the panel illustrating the Annunciation. Dating to the fifteenth century it is part of a set of medieval vestments from Waterford. The splendour of such garments reflects the wealth of the church in late medieval Ireland. [National Museum of Ireland]*

embroidery, machine, a controversial process among those concerned with embroidery. Purists eschew machines, insisting that only hand-produced goods may be called embroidery; but at present machines are used to produce TEXTILE art by both the professional and the amateur. Since the end of the nineteenth century Irish embroidery has also been produced by machine. Seeking to stay competitive, northern LINEN-producers turned to Switzerland, where machine embroidery was well established. Some brought designers and engineers to Ireland to develop the industry; others entered partnerships with Swiss firms. The Swiss embroidery machine could produce dozens of items at a time, and the technique can be difficult to distinguish from hand-done work. Various types of embroidery machine were used in Ireland throughout the twentieth century, commercial production ranging from handkerchiefs to badges. Ironically, as computerisation took increasing control, it became permissible to sell 'Swiss' embroidery as hand work, the old and reliable machine being entirely manual. **Linda Ballard**

embroidery, sprigging, a traditional style of embroidery. In the nineteenth century, Ireland vied with France in producing the most beautiful hand EMBROIDERY. French influences on Irish work were strong, if not always direct. Ayrshire work, developed in western Scotland and widely produced in Ireland by the 1820s, was based on a French original. This exquisite embroidery was usually worked in white on white, and as LINEN manufacturing came into the ascendant in Ireland this quickly became the base for beautiful embellishment. Commercial production went hand in hand with domestic work, with some women producing goods for their own use, others for the market. In the twentieth century, organisations including the Women's Institute, the IRISH COUNTRYWOMEN'S ASSOCIATION and guilds of enthusiasts have helped maintain the tradition of fine embroidery.

Purists identify 'sprigging' as a distinctive style, but in the past the term seems to have had broad connotations. For out-workers employed through various agencies, and for women working in factories, 'sprigging' was, like 'flowering' and 'parcelling', one of the terms used to describe their work. In some instances this was so specialised that up to seven women might contribute to decorating a single handkerchief, while in other instances a needlewoman adapted her skills to suit contemporary fashion. **Linda Ballard**

Emerald Isle, the, an epithet that has become synonymous with a romantic image of Ireland and had wide literary and popular currency during the nineteenth century. It was first used in the ballad 'When Erin First Rose' (1795) by the Belfast UNITED IRISHMAN and poet WILLIAM DRENNAN (1754–1820).

Arm of Erin! prove strong; but be gentle as brave,
And, uplifted to strike, still be ready to save;
Nor one feeling of vengeance presume to defile
The cause, or the men, of the Emerald Isle.

Brian Lalor

Emergency. *General Michael J. Costello (left) and staff officers in a map exercise, 1944, during the Second World War; they are following the progress of the war in eastern Europe. [© Stephen Lalor]*

Emergency, the, a name sometimes given to the years of the SECOND WORLD WAR (1939–45), during which the Southern state Éire (later—1949—the Republic of Ireland) remained neutral. NEUTRALITY had almost universal support, though many from the South volunteered for the British war effort and neutrality was pro-Allied in practice; on the other hand it meant that the TREATY PORTS were denied to Britain. Nazi adventurers and their allies in the IRA were dealt with brusquely. The Emergency Powers Act (1939) allowed for military courts; INTERNMENT was introduced; rationing and censorship were widespread. DE VALERA observed the outward formalities by offering condolences at the German embassy on the death of Hitler (see p. 725). **Fergal Tobin**

emergency legislation, a marked feature of twentieth-century Irish history. The FIRST WORLD WAR saw the introduction of the DEFENCE OF THE REALM ACT (1914), a catch-all measure that conferred draconian powers on the British government, not only in security and defence matters but also in areas affecting daily life, such as public health, food production and distribution, and even controls on the sale of alcohol.

The violent years of the WAR OF INDEPENDENCE and CIVIL WAR (1919–23) and the establishment of Northern Ireland in 1920 saw the widespread use of emergency laws in both parts of Ireland, first by the British government and after 1921 by the newly founded Northern and Southern states, to quell political violence. Though the IRISH FREE STATE adopted a markedly liberal written constitution in 1922, this allowed for exceptional laws in exceptional circumstances. Severe measures, such as the use of non-jury courts, trial before military courts, and internment without trial, were accommodated and were justified by reference to the armed republican threat to the state's existence. In Northern Ireland, emergency powers also allowed the widespread use of internment without trial to quell nationalist agitation against the state, as well as summary courts for political offences. In both states such measures were used in a stop-start way; those incarcerated could usually expect early release once the political climate calmed down. Though FIANNA FÁIL came to office in 1932 committed to dismantling repressive legislation, it soon found it very useful against both the crypto-fascist BLUESHIRT movement and the IRA. The CONSTITUTION OF IRELAND (1937), like its predecessor, provided for the introduction of emergency laws that bypassed normal safeguards. Of these, the most far-reaching was the Offences Against the State Act (1939), which remains the cornerstone of the state's anti-terrorism legislation.

After 1969 the Northern Ireland 'TROUBLES' saw the revival in both Ireland and Britain of some emergency measures and the introduction of new ones under controversial laws such as the PREVENTION OF TERRORISM ACT. Both states also used emergency legislation to ban the publication of broadcast interviews with advocates of political violence. Since 1995 the NORTHERN IRELAND PEACE PROCESS has seen some explicit bargaining between the states and loyalist and republican organisations, whereby the phasing out of emergency laws and measures forms part of the general package designed to put an end to political violence. **Eunan O'Halpin**

emigrant letters. The stream of EMIGRATION from Ireland during the eighteenth and nineteenth centuries saw the establishment of significant Irish communities abroad, in North America and Britain and throughout the British Empire. Wherever emigrants travelled and settled, they generally endeavoured to keep in touch with home through correspondence, producing a written legacy that collectively represents an unparalleled window for historians on the historical experience of Irish emigrants.

Those who crossed the Atlantic in the century before 1815 often wrote home with news of their progress in the New World. Many, especially Presbyterians, were literate, but they usually had to rely on someone returning across the ocean to deliver their letter by hand. Lyrical testimony to the value of emigrant correspondence was paid by one emigrant in 1810 who wrote home from Philadelphia to Co. Tyrone with the lines:

What fine things letters are now prithee say
That can make friends converse though far away
Can make a distant husband straight appear
Unto a faithful wife and children dear.

Even at this early time in the nineteenth century letters can be seen as an important component in the mechanism of chain MIGRATION that was so characteristic of Irish patterns of emigration. The letter home frequently provided the practical information necessary for friends or relatives in Ireland to follow the path of the pioneer correspondent. As the nineteenth century progressed, the 'American letter' increasingly carried the remittance that either paved the way for further emigration or supplemented the household income, often allowing otherwise uneconomic smallholdings to survive.

Critical to sustaining the flow of letters was the fact that increasing numbers of the younger generation who departed had learnt to read and write in the local national schools, established throughout the country from 1831. Emigrants were increasingly able to compose rather than dictate letters; but transatlantic post remained slow, expensive, and inconsistent in the middle of the nineteenth century—a point often made by an errant son or daughter excusing the infrequency of correspondence. The rapid transition from sail to steam during the 1860s, and the signing by the American and British governments of the international postal money order convention in 1871, resulted in a more efficient and more popular mail service.

The analysis of emigrant letters as a historical source has advanced in recent years from a reading of the bare facts contained in the documents to a greater emphasis on their form and function and the context within which they were composed. [see DIARIES AND JOURNALS.] **Patrick Fitzgerald**

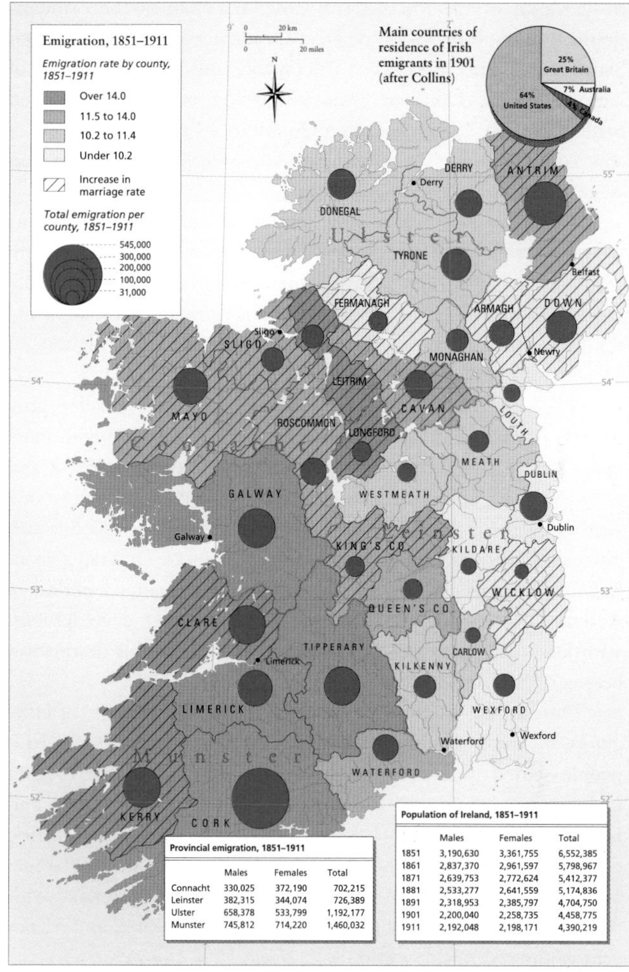

Provincial emigration, 1851–1911

	Males	Females	Total
Connacht	330,025	372,190	702,215
Leinster	382,315	344,074	726,389
Ulster	658,378	533,799	1,192,177
Munster	745,812	714,220	1,460,032

Population of Ireland, 1851–1911

	Males	Females	Total
1851	3,190,630	3,361,755	6,552,385
1861	2,837,370	2,961,597	5,798,967
1871	2,639,753	2,772,624	5,412,377
1881	2,533,277	2,641,559	5,174,836
1891	2,318,953	2,385,797	4,704,750
1901	2,200,040	2,258,735	4,458,775
1911	2,192,048	2,198,171	4,390,219

Emigration, Commission on. The Commission on Emigration and Other Population Problems (1948–54) was the Republic's most ambitious attempt to investigate the causes of emigration. Chaired by James Beddy, an economist and later head of the IDA, the commission of twenty-two men and two women included statisticians, economists, doctors, sociologists, trade unionists, Government officials, writers, and clergymen. It met 115 times and received submissions from numerous individuals and organisations. Intending emigrants were interviewed, and surveys of conditions in rural areas were undertaken. A strong thread of pragmatism ran through the proceedings.

The reasons for emigration cited by emigrants included poverty, restlessness, absence of freedoms, difficulty in getting farmers to marry, and the attractions of life in cities and towns abroad. The remedies offered included DECENTRALISATION and the supply of running WATER and lavatories. The late age of marriage and high rate of female emigration attracted attention. The IRISH HOUSEWIVES' ASSOCIATION attributed the latter to the inferior status of women in Irish society, conditions on small farms, and the 'MARRIAGE BAR'; this was rejected by Bishop Cornelius Lucey, whose minority report argued that urban society was corrupt and advocated a back-to-the-land alternative.

The majority report concluded that while the fundamental cause of emigration was economic, it arose from an interplay of social, political, economic, and psychological factors and was affected by conditions in Ireland and elsewhere. The commission did not produce any miracle cure for emigration but it did contribute to a more realistic understanding of its causes. **Pauric Travers**

emigration patterns. Geographical patterns of EMIGRATION from Ireland have changed over time and involve people with a varying mix of sex, RELIGION, and SOCIAL CLASS settling in different destinations. These include a wide range of continents and countries, though the Irish have overwhelmingly settled in certain English-speaking places. Within these national boundaries there has been further regional clustering and distinctive patterns of urban and rural location. Though the general picture can be traced, precise statistical data is much harder to provide. Emigration destinations from Northern Ireland have not been recorded separately from totals for the United Kingdom.

Numbers leaving for Britain are especially elusive, because of the ease of movement between the two countries and its treatment as internal migration between 1800 and 1921. But Britain has the longest history as a destination for Irish emigrants, stretching back to the period before transatlantic travel. Even when CENSUS statistics appear to provide a more accurate picture in the nineteenth century, it has been estimated that they missed at least a million Irish-born people, giving Britain closer to 25 per cent of the total rather than the 10 per cent of official figures. This proportion rose sharply in the second half of the twentieth century to more than 80 per cent of the total but declined again after the mid-1980s, when Continental destinations became popular.

In the nineteenth century the majority of emigrants went to North America. Before the GREAT FAMINE the highest proportion went first to CANADA (60 per cent of the recorded flow between 1825 and 1840); thereafter the UNITED STATES became by far the largest destination, receiving 990,000 people in the decade 1851–60,

81 per cent of the international flow. It remained the principal destination until the 1920s, when economic recession in the United States led to strict IMMIGRATION controls and the introduction of national quotas. The proportion of the flow entering the United States fell from 71 per cent in 1926–30 to 47 per cent in 1931–5 and continued to fall in the post-war period as the direction switched even more strongly to Britain.

A smaller but nevertheless substantial number of emigrants went to AUSTRALIA. Records for this destination are fuller and more accurate, as most nineteenth-century emigration was officially assisted. Estimates show that the peak years were in the 1850s, while the proportion of the total outflow from Ireland was highest (at 11 per cent) between 1871 and 1880.

The remaining destinations make up a much smaller proportion of the total. Estimates suggest that 2,000–3,000 Irish emigrants per year settled in NEW ZEALAND during the nineteenth and early twentieth centuries. However, the numbers travelling to New Zealand were more uncertain, as most left English and Scottish ports and were therefore not counted as direct emigrants from Ireland. Moreover, many arrived indirectly, often after a period in Australia. Settlement in SOUTH AFRICA was a later development, with just over 2,000 people leaving Irish ports for this destination between 1905 and 1920.

Outside the English-speaking world, smaller pockets of emigrants are found at different periods. Approximately 30,000 Irish people settled in ARGENTINA between 1825 and 1875, working mainly as shepherds on the pampas. More recently, young and highly qualified emigrants have been moving to other EU countries, especially Germany, France, and the Netherlands. In 1999 these accounted for 16 per cent of the recorded outflow, compared with 35 per cent to Britain, 19 per cent to the United States, and 31 per cent to the rest of the world.

The characteristics of emigrants entering different destinations have varied markedly. Whereas women were over-represented among emigrants to the United States in the later nineteenth century, the Australian stream was much more strongly male. Social class is also an important source of difference. Those settling in the United States have been identified as the least skilled (in the sense of industrial experience); emigrants to South Africa, on the other hand, came predominantly from the professional, commercial, and skilled classes. The balance of Catholic and Protestant emigrants altered over time. In earlier periods Protestants were generally wealthier and could afford the costs involved, but after the Great Famine, Catholics predominated. After PARTITION the proportion of Protestants emigrating from the South again rose sharply, because of fears of discrimination in a strongly Catholic state. In Northern Ireland, however, emigration by the Catholic community has exceeded that of Protestants. [see DIASPORA.] **Bronwen Walter**

Emmet, Robert (1778–1803), revolutionary. Born in Dublin, younger brother of THOMAS ADDIS EMMET; educated at TCD, where he was a leading debater in the College Historical Society. Expelled from university for radical activity in 1798, on the eve of the rebellion, he helped reorganise the UNITED IRISHMEN. In 1800 he visited the Continent but quickly became disillusioned with the French. After his return to Ireland he became embroiled in a conspiracy for a new rebellion. This took place on 23 July 1803 and was an abject failure. Arrested soon after, he was charged with treason and found guilty. His speech from the dock is considered one of the greatest courtroom orations in Irish history. He was hanged and beheaded on 20 September 1803 in Thomas Street, Dublin. His youthful romance with SARAH CURRAN, the daughter of JOHN PHILPOT CURRAN, his idealistic nature, and his heroic sacrifice all combined to make him a nationalist icon. **Patrick Geoghegan**

Emmet, Thomas Addis (1764–1827), United Irishman and lawyer; elder brother of ROBERT EMMET. Born in Cork; educated at TCD, the University of Edinburgh, and the Inns of Court, London, qualifying in medicine and law by 1791. He practised on the Munster circuit and in Dublin, where his services were in demand from the United Irishmen, an organisation of which he had been an early adherent. A skilled propagandist and planner, his arrest in 1798 was a coup for the authorities. After internment in Fort George, Inverness-shire, 1799–1802, he lived in Amsterdam and Paris before emigrating to the United States in 1804. He became the first Attorney-General of New York State. **Ruan O'Donnell**

Emmet's Rebellion (1803), a failed insurrection in Dublin. The UNITED IRISHMEN conspired to overthrow the British administration in Ireland, aided by the French, and made ROBERT EMMET, younger brother of THOMAS ADDIS EMMET, the leader of the rebellion in Dublin. The plan was attempted on 23 July 1803 but failed, for many reasons: the rebels were drunk and disorganised, they were not well armed, and they proved incapable of following orders. Lord Kilwarden, the Lord Chief Justice, was the only notable casualty. Nevertheless the rebellion was a daring effort and succeeded in catching DUBLIN CASTLE by surprise. Emmet fled but was soon captured and indicted for treason. His stirring oration at his trial, his youthful idealism, and his romance with SARAH CURRAN combined to make him a nationalist icon. He was hanged and beheaded at Thomas Street, Dublin, on 20 September 1803. **Patrick Geoghegan**

employment. Employment trends were quite erratic during the last two decades of the twentieth century. During the deep recession of the 1980s total employment fell by about 65,000—nearly 6 per cent—between 1981 and 1986. Stronger growth in the ECONOMY generated employment growth between 1989 and 1991, but this was followed by adverse international conditions and sluggish growth in the domestic economy. From 1993, however, the booming economy generated unprecedented growth in employment: the number of those at work increased by over 400,000 between 1993 and 1999, an annual growth rate of 6 per cent. During the 1990s women's employment was far more buoyant than men's: the total employment of males increased by 2.5 per cent per annum, while the rate of increase among women was 7 per cent; this meant that women's share of employment increased from 33 per cent of the total in 1988 to over 40 per cent in 1999. Employment in AGRICULTURE continued its decline during the last two decades of the twentieth century, down from 17 per cent of total employment in 1981 to 10 per cent in 1997. The largest growth took place in the SERVICES SECTOR, up from 51 per cent of total employment in 1981 to 61 per cent in 1997. Employment in manufacturing also increased during the 1990s, and in this respect Ireland deviates from the European trend of declining manufacturing employment. This was mainly due to continued success in attracting FOREIGN DIRECT INVESTMENT.

In the 1990s there was a general tendency in industrialised countries to move from passive measures that provide financial support for unemployed workers to active measures that provide training and temporary work experience designed to enhance employment prospects. Ireland has participated in this trend and is a comparatively big spender on such schemes: expenditure on such schemes accounted for over 1.5 per cent of GDP in 1997, considerably higher than the average of about 1 per cent for the OECD group of industrial countries, though lower than in a number of Scandinavian countries, where active policies play a particularly large role. There is a continuing debate about whether such schemes are successful in their main objective of enhancing the employment prospects of those who participate in them: research in Ireland shows that schemes with strong links to the labour market—training in specific employable skills, and temporary employment subsidies for real jobs—do improve the employment prospects of participants and enhance their earnings in subsequent employment, even when account is taken of other relevant factors, such as age, sex, education, and previous labour market experience. The research also suggests that schemes with weak links to the market, including general training schemes as well as direct employment schemes in the public or voluntary sectors, are of limited effectiveness, if any, in improving the participants' employment prospects. However, in the last years of the twentieth century the largest active labour market schemes, and those experiencing the highest rate of expansion, have been direct employment schemes, the impact of which on the employment prospects of their participants is highly dubious. **Philip O'Connell**

enclosure, the practice whereby land formerly held in common by a community was consolidated into individually owned units with secure boundaries. It was particularly associated with modernising or 'improving' LANDLORDS who wished to run their estates on commercial lines. It was resented by the landless poor, now denied customary access to COMMONAGE. Most enclosure in Ireland took place between 1760 and 1850, setting the modern rural pattern of dispersed individual holdings, a process continued after the Great Famine. **Fergal Tobin**

encumbered estates, estates burdened with debt. The GREAT FAMINE resulted in the financial collapse of a significant number of Irish estates, through the fall in rental income, the rise in the level of poor rates, and the closure of credit facilities. The Encumbered Estates Act (1849) was designed to alleviate the plight of indebted landowners by simplifying the legal procedure involved in the sale of land. Under the auspices of the Encumbered Estates Court, an estimated 25 per cent of Irish land was sold over the next thirty years or so. **Terence Dooley**

energy sources. As the ECONOMY of Ireland has grown, so too has its total primary energy requirement (TPER). The consumption of energy increased by 58 per cent between 1980 and 1998 and will increase by a further 37 per cent by 2010. The oil crises of the 1970s made the supply of indigenous energy a prime concern, and the exploitation of the offshore Kinsale gas field and increased turf-fired electricity generation brought this to a peak in 1985, at 40 per cent of TPER. However, while indigenous supply remained constant throughout the 1990s, during a period of unprecedented ECONOMIC GROWTH TPER accelerated, with most of the increased demand—dominated by transport—being met by oil. The depleted Kinsale field may be replaced by the newly discovered Corrib field. At the same time imported natural gas will satisfy 30 per cent of TPER by 2010 through electricity production, with gas-fired generation growing by 150 per cent.

Coal-fired electricity generation increased from 1 per cent to 39 per cent of TPER between 1985 and 1987, together with greater industrial and domestic use. However, by 1998 coal contributed only 16 per cent to TPER, and this will fall to 11 per cent by 2010. Similarly, peat declined from 15 per cent of TPER in 1980 to 8 per cent in 1998 and will fall to 4 per cent by 2010.

Renewable energy remains a minor contributor, with hydro-electricity, wood, and wind satisfying only 2 per cent of TPER. Consequently, oil and gas are now prime energy sources and by 2010 will together account for 83 per cent of TPER. This combination, together with the increasing use of energy, will see Ireland's target for reduced emissions of 'greenhouse gases' under the Kyoto Protocol for the period 2008–12 reached by 2000. **Colman Gallagher**

energy. *Tursillagh wind farm, Co. Kerry. Construction of the 23-turbine farm was completed in 2000. The turbines supply 50 million units of electricity per year to the ESB network. [Michael Diggin Photography]*

ENFO, a Dublin-based public information service established in 1990 by the Department of the Environment and LOCAL GOVERNMENT to provide public access to wide-ranging and authoritative information on the environment. **Anne-Marie Cunningham**

engineering schools. A School of Civil Engineering was established in 1841 at the University of Dublin (TRINITY COLLEGE), and in 1842 John Benjamin Macneill was appointed first professor of the practice of civil engineering; the first diplomas were awarded in 1843. The Queen's Colleges, founded in 1845 at Belfast, Cork, and Galway, began engineering courses the same year, diplomas being awarded by the Queen's University of Ireland. Mechanical and electrical engineering were introduced into the curriculum c. 1900. The ROYAL COLLEGE OF SCIENCE offered a course in mechanical sciences. UNIVERSITY COLLEGE, Dublin, founded in 1909, developed a large Engineering School. Queen's University, Belfast, which developed independently, also has a large engineering faculty. Developments in technical education in the 1970s led to the establishment of several new engineering schools at regional institutes of technology in Dublin, Cork, and other centres. The new universities—University of Limerick, Dublin City University, and University of Ulster—have each developed a distinctive engineering school. **Ronald Cox**

England, the Irish in.

The Irish-born population of England and Wales, 1841–1931

1841	289,404	(1.8%)
1851	519,959	(2.9%)
1861	601,634	(3.0%)
1871	566,540	(2.5%)
1881	562,374	(2.2%)
1891	458,315	(1.6%)
1901	426,565	(1.3%)
1911	375,325	(1.0%)
1921	364,747	(0.9%)
1931	381,081	(1.4%)

Irish immigrants in England have been noticed, sometimes unfavourably, since the Middle Ages. Only in the eighteenth century, however, did large, permanent communities begin to emerge outside London.

Problems in the Irish ECONOMY allied to opportunities in England created a classic push-pull model of EMIGRATION. Irish people in England tended to be poorer than those emigrating to the UNITED STATES. Some were simply following family and friends along well-beaten paths; others, such as harvesters, maintained an itinerant life-style in search of work; still others, such as Ulster weavers, sought out the mill towns of Lancashire, where their skills would be well received. By the 1820s there were noticeable Irish settlements in many towns outside the capital and the principal ports of entry. These communities grew considerably in the 1830s and were swollen by the emigration of the GREAT FAMINE and continued to be augmented for a long time after the mass exodus. The Irish went overwhelmingly to larger towns: there were virtually no Irish people in rural shires such as Dorset, while more than half of England's Irish-born were found in three places: LONDON, LIVERPOOL, and MANCHESTER. Regions such as Cumbria and the midlands also had important Irish centres. Distinct Irish communities were still noticeable in the inter-war period in the cities.

The Great Famine enhanced migratory patterns that were already in train. However, if Irish settlement was geographically concentrated beforehand, famine emigration made it more so. If Irish workers were generally found at the lower end of the jobs market, the Famine enforced this. If Irish immigrants had been drawing negative comment in the 1830s because of their perceived backwardness and poverty, the Famine apparently confirmed such prejudices. The association of the Irish with urban crisis in England grew as the Irish-born population of England increased.

Religious prejudice featured in Irish immigrants' lives. Even though up to a quarter of the Irish-born were Protestants, the Catholicism of the majority became a kind of badge for the whole community. What the *Times* called the 'Papal Aggression' of 1850, when Pope Pius IX restored the Catholic hierarchy to England and Wales, increased the hostility towards Irish people. Anti-Catholicism was often exacerbated by the ORANGE ORDER, which was strongly supported by Protestant Irish immigrants. No-Popery lecturers such as WILLIAM MURPHY encouraged party violence, while Irish immigrants' support for Fenianism, real or alleged, added to tensions. Later in the century the HOME RULE movement and religious education added ingredients to the sectarian tension.

Irish immigrant life in England was nevertheless richly varied. As time went on, a greater proportion of the children of first-generation immigrants achieved higher social status, though mostly in the ranks of the working class. A metropolitan Irish middle class existed in the eighteenth century, as politics, law, and journalism attracted many wealthier immigrants. Traders, merchants, and clerks in west-coast port towns, such as Whitehaven, were often Irish. Skilled jobs in shipyards were open to Protestant Irish immigrants, but not to Catholics. Some Irish workers progressed through the building trades, did well in transport, and went on to own their own business.

Women probably had greater opportunities for self-improvement in England than in Ireland, if only because of the new jobs open to them. This was true of Lancashire and Yorkshire, where TEXTILES dominated. Irish women found teaching attractive; and most nuns running Catholic organisations in England were Irish. This was less so in centres of heavy industry, where high male wages led to working women being denigrated. Particularly after 1900, opportunities for employment and education grew. The Irish role in organised labour was probably slow to develop, but by the 1920s, with home rule agitation past, early Irish potential for trade union activity and CHARTISM paved the way for their central role in the Labour Party.

It has been common to characterise post-famine emigration from Ireland as a traffic primarily to the United States. While America remained the most popular destination between 1850 and 1914, the flow to Britain never dried up entirely. Moreover, during the 1930s this movement grew again, and after 1945 Britain was once again the preferred destination. As late as 1971 people born in the Republic, numbering 957,830, constituted the largest immigrant group in the United Kingdom, despite the 'New Commonwealth' immigrations.

In the period after the creation of the Irish Free State, emigration to Britain did change. Northern industrial centres attracted fewer emigrants, and new economic development in the midlands and the south of England encouraged alterations to the flow. Irish immigration throughout the twentieth century was both typical and unique: typical in that it consisted mostly of rural-to-urban migration, unique because, while the migrants were leaving Irish rural parishes, they were headed almost entirely for British, not Irish, towns. In both the nineteenth and twentieth centuries British capitalism continued to rely on Irish muscle-power; from RAILWAY navvying to motorway building, the Irish played an integral part in the laying of infrastructure and in the erection of buildings. The National Health Service and the school system relied heavily on Irish nurses and teachers. British cultural institutions—churches, clubs, pubs, and sports—were enriched by the large-scale arrival of young Irish people. As in the earlier period, however, political issues continued to make life uneasy for Irish people in Britain. The reactions against immigrants during the FENIAN bombing campaigns of the 1860s were not unlike the attacks made on Irish residents during later events, for example the IRA bombs in Warrington, Manchester, and Canary Wharf, London.

There remains a tendency to view Irish people in Britain as part of a homogeneous community, yet many new arrivals came from Ulster and were Protestants. Women too were much more numerous among twentieth-century immigrants than before 1900. Though Ireland today receives more people as immigrants than it sends as emigrants, strong associations, built on centuries of interaction, still exist between the two countries. [see BOMBING CAMPAIGNS IN BRITAIN; CONSTRUCTION WORKERS IN BRITAIN; SCOTLAND; WALES.] **Donald MacRaild**

English dialects of Ireland. *Anglo-Irish* is the preferred term of some scholars for describing a characteristically rural variety of English, compounded of Irish and English or Irish and Scots.

England, Irish in. *Anti-Catholic hand-coloured engraving c. 1850, commenting on the appointment by Pius IX of Catholic bishops to English sees and expressing fear of the influence of Catholicism in England. [Irish Picture Library]*

This developed since the beginning of the eighteenth century. The second strand of English spoken in Ireland is a more urban, regional, and standard variety; the proponents of the term *Anglo-Irish* call this second strand HIBERNO-ENGLISH. It is essentially the language first brought to Ireland by the English who settled in the seventeenth century. The third strand of English spoken in Ireland is ULSTER SCOTS, and its germinal period was also the seventeenth century.

This categorisation does not win universal approval (some scholars prefer *Hiberno-English* as an inclusive term for all three varieties mentioned), but it points to three separate and distinct strands in the English of Ireland. **Diarmaid Ó Muirithe**

English government and administration, eighteenth and nineteenth centuries. English royal authority in Ireland was represented by the LORD LIEUTENANT and in his absence by the Lords Justices. The relationship between the executive and the legislature followed English precedent, though POYNINGS' LAW restricted the activities of the Irish Parliament. During the eighteenth century and, more particularly, the nineteenth the scope and scale of government expanded, both at the centre and in the localities, and this was reflected in the growing number of people employed by the state. Intended to integrate Ireland more closely in the United Kingdom, the ACT OF UNION (1800) had relatively little impact on the way Ireland was governed, which owed more to a colonial than a metropolitan model. The office of Lord Lieutenant was retained; but it was the CHIEF SECRETARY's Office in Dublin Castle, under the management of the UNDER-SECRETARY FOR IRELAND, that became the real centre of government. Public appointments increasingly came to depend more on qualifications than on influence, and in 1871 competitive examinations were introduced for CIVIL SERVICE applicants. While the cabinet system of government, together with a dual legislature, was retained in independent Ireland, the adoption of a written constitution and proportional representation gave Irish government its own character. Levels of public sector employment have remained high in both parts of Ireland. **Virginia Crossman**

English settlement. This began with the Anglo-Normans in the later twelfth century, following directly from the military conquest, as the new owners encouraged tenants and labourers from England and Wales to settle in Ireland. It would appear that the majority came from the same areas as their overlords, though little is known of the operation of this process, because of the scarcity of surviving source materials. Existing territorial divisions appear to have been used; and the south and east were more extensively settled than the north and west. These French-speaking lords created manors on their lands based on the French feudal model, though modified to take account of local conditions. Motte-and-bailey castles were erected by the earliest settler lords, while the substantial freeholders appear to have constructed the moated sites that are found in large numbers in the south-east. The transition to the building of stone CASTLES was a gradual process. The development of new towns was an important feature of this settlement, though Ireland still remained overwhelmingly rural. There was an important immigration of merchants, artisans, and tradesmen into these urban centres. This process expanded until the later thirteenth century, when the BLACK DEATH decimated the colonial population and opened the way for an Irish revival, which halted and then reduced the extent of English settlement. From the fourteenth to the early sixteenth centuries the areas under Norman control shrank until only the area of the PALE, the larger towns and the territories of important magnates such as the Earls of Kildare, Desmond, and Ormond retained any significant English influence.

The defeat of the KILDARE REBELLION and the expropriation of monastic land in the 1530s began the process of renewed English settlement. A small number of soldiers and other NEW ENGLISH settlers obtained some of these lands; this was followed by the first official plantation scheme, in Cos. Laois and Offaly in the 1560s. Though it failed to attract the planned number of English settlers it did establish a permanent colony in the area. The most important of the TUDOR PLANTATIONS was in Munster, where in the aftermath of the DESMOND REBELLION 200,000 ha (500,000 acres) were offered to English settlers. It was intended to create a mixed colony of gentry and YEOMANRY who would live apart from and create a bulwark against the native occupiers. A limit was placed on the amount of land any one person could own, together with a requirement that each undertaker introduce a designated number of tenants, who would be allocated varying amounts of land to be held on differing leases.

The scheme first failed to attract enough settlers and was then virtually destroyed in 1598 during the rebellion. On its re-establishment in the early seventeenth century, ownership was concentrated in fewer hands, with RICHARD BOYLE acquiring a preponderant share. The PLANTATION did invigorate the economy of the area, leading to an increase in exports of cattle and wool, while the port towns expanded and drew further immigrants from England. English adventurers and racketeers used another method of obtaining land for settlement in this period, through searches for defective titles and concealed estates. On such discovery and a reversion to the Crown of the title, a grant of the estate or leases at low rents might be obtained; in extreme instances a plantation might result, such as those in Co. Westmeath in 1606 and in Co. Wicklow in 1609. The plantation of six counties in Ulster, facilitated by the abandonment of their lands and tenants by O'NEILL, O'DONNELL and MAGUIRE in 1607, introduced a vigorous settlement of English and Scottish settlers in the period 1610–30. At first many native Irish were kept on as tenants, but eventually the arrival of further settlers, with whom they could not compete, forced them onto marginal land; in this way separate English, Scottish, and Irish areas emerged more clearly than elsewhere in Ireland. The strong Scottish Presbyterian colonisation of Cos. Antrim and Down, which occurred without government involvement, further changed the character, economy and politics of this region.

The CROMWELLIAN land confiscation in the 1650s was intended to implement social engineering through the transplantation of Catholic landowners to Connacht. In reality it merely changed the ownership of vast areas of land in the other three provinces, without introducing any significant permanent wave of immigration or settlement. The confiscation of JACOBITE estates after the WILLIAMITE WARS did not lead to increased English settlement either, as the bulk of the land was bought by existing Protestant landlords. [see ADMINISTRATIVE DIVISIONS.] **Liam Irwin**

Enlightenment thought. The Enlightenment was a rational philosophical and political movement in Western Europe stretching from the seventeenth to the beginning of the nineteenth century. At the core of Enlightenment thinking on the Continent and in Ireland was the idea that by the use of reason, human beings could grow up, ceasing to be as children ruled by the authority of kings and priests.

The great Enlightenment event in Ireland was the publication of JOHN TOLAND's *Christianity Not Mysterious* (1696). Born a Catholic in Co. Donegal, Toland forcefully questioned one of the bases of clerical authority: religious mysteries. In Dublin in 1697 he soon raised against himself 'the clamour of all parties.' His book was ordered to be burnt by the hangman, and it was moved in the Irish Parliament that 'Mr Toland himself should be burnt.' He fled from Ireland, never to return. Others, such as Thomas Emlyn, were to follow Toland's brave attempt to bring Enlightenment to Ireland. Emlyn, a Dissenting minister in Dublin, in his *Humble Inquiry* (1702), questioned the orthodox view of the Trinity; for this he was imprisoned, 1702–5. A more diffuse light can be seen in the Molesworth circle, those who in the 1720s gathered around ROBERT MOLESWORTH, author of the anti-clerical *Account of Denmark* (1694) and a patron of Toland. The views of the circle were partly expressed in ARBUCKLE's *Dublin Letters* (collected in two volumes, 1729) and, more influentially, by the circle's leading figure, FRANCIS HUTCHESON, who, in his *Inquiry* (1724), argued for a this-worldly morality based on his theory of moral sense (see p. 150). A more dramatic Enlightenment thinker was Robert Clayton, Bishop of Clogher. Like Toland and Emlyn, he took up the cause against mysteries, most provocatively in his *Essay on Spirit* (1750). In 1756 he argued in a speech in the Irish House of Lords for the repeal of the orthodox Athanasian articles relating to the Trinity, according to which the first and second persons of the Holy Trinity are co-eternal and co-equal. Heresy proceedings were begun, but Clayton died before charges were formally brought against him.

One conclusion that might be drawn from these events is that Ireland was not a hospitable place for Enlightenment thinking. There is evidence, however, that moderate Enlightenment thinking was increasingly infiltrating itself into Irish culture in the later eighteenth century, as can be seen in the writings of the United Irishmen, most notably TONE's *Argument on Behalf of the Catholics of Ireland* (1791). Probably the last interesting Enlightenment figure was George Ensor, whose political works were influential, though it is not clear that his radical *Principles* (1801) and *Janus on Sion* (1816) had much impact in Ireland. Enlightenment thinking was important in an indirect way, however, in helping to provoke some of the most creative Counter-Enlightenment productions in eighteenth-century Ireland, most notably BERKELEY's immaterialism (the rejection of the existence of matter) and emotivism (the doctrine that words can be meaningful even if they do not stand for ideas or have descriptive meaning, provided they evoke emotions) and BURKE's conservative political philosophy but also the pragmatism of WILLIAM KING, the sensationalism of PETER BROWNE, and some of SWIFT's liveliest satires. To paraphrase Wilde, Ireland put its talent into Enlightenment but its genius into Counter-Enlightenment. **Patricia O'Riordan**

Ennis (*Inis*), county town of Co. Clare, 32 km (20 miles) north-west of Limerick; population (2002) 18,977. Ennis is on the River Fergus, which loops around to create an island. It was the site of a Franciscan monastery founded c. 1247; this became an important seat of learning and today is an impressive ruin. Though Ennis became the most important town in medieval Clare, it was not granted borough status until 1612. Co. Clare was badly affected by the wars of the 1640s, but Ennis recovered its market in hides and BUTTER, which were transported by river to Limerick. By the early nineteenth century it was an important market town, with a population of 9,300 in 1841. It became famous for electing DANIEL O'CONNELL as member of the British Parliament in 1828, a fact commemorated by the O'Connell Monument in the town centre. This was the first time an Irish Catholic was elected to the House of Commons, and it earned for Clare the nickname 'Banner County'.

Like most country towns, Ennis began a long decline after the GREAT FAMINE, its population falling to 5,100 in 1901. Its resurgence began with the building of Shannon International Airport in 1936–9 which was designated as the world's first customs-free airport in 1947. The Shannon industrial estate and TOURISM associated with BUNRATTY CASTLE also contributed to Ennis's rapid growth, with the town becoming an important manufacturing centre.

Despite this prosperity, Ennis's past survives in the celebrated horse fair held every summer at nearby Spancel Hill. Ennis became the country's first Information Age Town in 1997, with each household in the town being offered a personal computer. **Kevin Hourihan**

Ennis, John (1944–), poet. Born in Correllstown, Co. Westmeath; studied for the priesthood but left before ordination. A rigorous and mature spirituality informs his verse. His ten volumes include *Night on Hibernia* (1976), *Selected Poems* (1996), and *Tráithníní* (2000). Family elegy, rapt observation of the natural world, homage to poets he admires, and Biblical analogy are important strands in a prolific tapestry that marks Ennis as a serious and dedicated poet of considerable accomplishment. In 1996 he received the Irish-American Cultural Award. **Rory Brennan**

Ennis, Séamus (1919–1982), uilleann piper, singer, music collector, broadcaster, storyteller, and translator. Born in Jamestown, Finglas, Co. Dublin. He started to learn the UILLEANN PIPES at the age of twelve and quickly progressed to become a player of immense ability. He was one of the most important collectors of TRADITIONAL MUSIC and song, working for the Irish FOLKLORE COMMISSION, 1942–7, Radio Éireann, 1947–51, and the BBC, 1951–c. 1960. From 1960 until his death he gave recitals, concerts, and lectures in Ireland and abroad; he spent the last seven years of his life in Naul, Co. Dublin. A selection of his recordings spanning over forty years can be heard on *Séamus Ennis: The Return from Fingal*. **Peter Browne**

Enniscorthy (*Inis Córthaidh*), Co. Wexford, a market town occupying a strategic site on the River SLANEY, 19 km (12 miles) north of Wexford; population (2002) 3,742. The river is tidal and was a busy trade route in the past, exporting agricultural produce and facilitating emigration to CANADA, especially NEWFOUNDLAND, in the early nineteenth century. The castle, now a museum, was constructed in the early thirteenth century. As part of the Plantation of Wexford, Henry Wallop was granted lands here in 1618; for several centuries the Wallops, Earls of Portsmouth, were patrons of the town. The site of the battle of VINEGAR HILL (1798), a decisive defeat for the United Irishmen, overlooks the town, which now houses the National 1798 Visitor Centre. Enniscorthy is the cathedral town of the Catholic diocese of Ferns; its Gothic Revival St Aidan's Cathedral (1843–8) was designed by PUGIN. Following economic stagnation in the 1960s with the closure of smaller industries, including bacon-curing, cutlery, and flour-milling, the town has recently undergone considerable renewal. **Ruth McManus**

Enniskillen (*Inis Ceithleann*), Co. Fermanagh, a diocesan county town and regional market and service centre, occupying a historically strategic island site at the narrows between Upper and Lower Lough Erne; population (1991) 11,436. During the later Middle Ages it was a Maguire stronghold, and Hugh Maguire built the first castle here in the fifteenth century. This was repeatedly besieged during the Elizabethan wars and was rebuilt by William Cole to form the nucleus of his new town. This was laid out after 1611 as a single curving main street, linking bridges or fords at each end of the island, by way of the market-place and Protestant church, which occupied the summits of the island's twin hills. The town quickly prospered; it survived the 1641 REBELLION and 1690 war as the sole Protestant refuge in Co. Fermanagh. It grew slowly until the late eighteenth century, being described in 1739 as a collection of 'thatched cabbins', but much more quickly thereafter, when it acquired the numerous public and commercial buildings that give it its character today. Notable among these are the infantry barracks (now PSNI depot) (1790), the Redoubt (originally a military hospital) (1796), the Courthouse (1821), St Macartan's (Protestant) Cathedral (1842), and St Michael's (Catholic) Church (1875). Recent arterial roads and suburban development have combined to isolate the town centre from its lakeside environs, but it nevertheless continues to prosper as a centre for heritage and 'lakeland' TOURISM. **Lindsay Proudfoot**

Ennis, Séamus. *Séamus Ennis, uilleann piper, broadcaster, folklore and music collector, pictured in the Phoenix Park, Dublin, 1952/3, with the American singer Jean Ritchie. [Ritchie-Pickow Collection, James Hardiman Library, National University of Ireland, Galway]*

Enniskillen bombing: see REMEMBRANCE DAY BOMBING.

Enright, Anne (1962–), novelist and short-story writer. Born in Dublin; educated at TCD and the University of East Anglia. Her collection of inventive short stories, *Portable Virgins*, appeared in 1991. It was followed by two lively novels: *The Wig My Father Wore* (1995) and *What Are You Like?* (2000). **Terence Brown**

ensembles. Ensemble music activity in Dublin can be traced back to sixteenth-century records of the Dublin City Musicians. It is likely that groups of various sizes provided music for civic processions and ceremonies, as well as in cathedrals, theatres, and gardens during the seventeenth and eighteenth centuries.

In 1886 the ROYAL DUBLIN SOCIETY inaugurated CHAMBER-MUSIC recitals, many of which were given by international artists. Numerous recitals also took place at this time in the Rotunda and the ANTIENT CONCERT rooms. Because of the arrival of many foreign instrumentalists in Ireland in the late 1940s, many new chamber groups were formed. These included the Cirulli String Quartet (1949), comprising two Italians, a Frenchman, and an Irish viola player; Dublin String Quartet (1949–50), with a Hungarian leader, German cellist, and two Irish players; the Prieur Ensemble, a flute, harp and string quartet founded in 1950 by André Prieur; and Les Amis de la Musique, an ensemble of wind players formed in 1949. Several other ensembles were formed, predominantly from the members of the RTÉ orchestras, including the RTÉ Wind Quintet, directed by Gilbert Berg, and the RTÉ Brass Ensemble.

The concept of a RTÉ STRING QUARTET was established in 1958. The Academica String Quartet, formed in Romania in 1969, was its resident group in Cork, 1978–85, and won prizes at the International String Quartet competitions in Liège (1972), and Munich (1973). It was succeeded in 1985 by the VANBRUGH STRING QUARTET. Other successful groups include the Georgian Brass Ensemble (1964), Hesketh Piano Trio (1975), Testore String Quartet (1976), Ulster Brass (1980), and Ulysses Ensemble (1976). The Irish Youth Wind Ensemble was formed in 1985. Since the 1990s numerous high-quality ensembles have been formed, including the Irish Piano Trio and Dublin Piano Trio.

Specialist ensembles in early music have played an important role since the 1970s. These include the Consort of St Sepulchre, Prelude Brass, Douglas Gunn Ensemble, Musica Sacra, and Christ Church Baroque. The DUBLIN FESTIVAL OF TWENTIETH-CENTURY MUSIC encouraged the formation of many new ensembles, including the Pulcinella Ensemble, CONCORDE is Ireland's premier contemporary music ensemble, while Crash Ensemble (1997) is the leading electro-acoustic ensemble. **Ite O'Donovan**

Ensor, John (fl. 1734–87), architect and builder. An associate of RICHARD CASTLE from 1734, he came to Ireland from Coventry with his younger brother, George Ensor (died 1803). After Castle's death in 1751 Ensor completed his work on the Dublin Lying-In Hospital (ROTUNDA HOSPITAL) (1757). In its grounds he built an orchestra (circular performance space) (1763) and the Rotunda Assembly Room (begun 1764). He was also involved in laying out the surrounding square (now Parnell Square), where he built a number of houses. He planned Merrion Square (1762) and later developed sites in Hume Street. George Ensor, who was clerk of works in the Surveyor-General's office, 1744–51, subsequently pursued a career as architect and builder. **Frederick O'Dwyer**

entomology, the scientific study of insects. For an island off Continental Europe, Ireland boasts a rich insect FAUNA, featuring some 16,000 species. Most colonised Ireland by natural means after the last Ice Age, 10,000 years ago. A few are pests, causing human health problems or damage to goods, crops, or livestock. One, the plague flea, killed thousands of people during the Middle Ages; malaria-transmitting mosquitoes were also once present. In modern times bark-beetles destroyed elm trees by spreading Dutch elm disease. The majority of insects, however, are harmless, and there are many beautiful species. The caddis fly (*Apatania auricula*), which survives from the Ice Age, thrives today in the south-west. Though there are no native species, sub-species have evolved in Ireland, especially among butterflies and moths; attractive immigrants, like the red admiral and painted lady butterflies, regularly visit our shores.

Alexander Henry Haliday (1806–1870) was the most famous Irish entomologist. He described many new species and invented the scientific term for thrips (Thysanoptera). There are major scientific collections in the NATIONAL MUSEUM OF IRELAND (Natural History), Dublin, and the ULSTER MUSEUM, Belfast, whose entomologists are co-operating in the production of check-lists of the Irish fauna. **James P. O'Connor**

environment. Ireland's environment has always been governed by natural cycles. This is especially evident along the coast, where natural processes of erosion and accretion have operated down the ages, with human influence apparent only in comparatively recent times. The influence of human society is most apparent on the LAND, where the felling of trees over the centuries left only 1 per cent of the country covered in forests by the year 1900.

In recent decades population growth, URBANISATION, and the intensification of AGRICULTURE have given rise to increasing environmental pressures. During the 1990s, together with ECONOMIC DEVELOPMENT, a number of strong trends were noticeable. New HOUSING development increased dramatically, as did the personal consumption of goods and services. Energy requirements have increased considerably, and there has been a substantial expansion in FORESTRY, TOURISM, and trade. An additional pressure on the environment is the number of vehicles on the road: in the Republic, the total increased by more than half over this period.

Emissions to all elements of the environment have increased. Of particular importance with regard to emissions into the air are 'greenhouse gases', because of their implication in the enhanced 'greenhouse effect', which gives rise to CLIMATE change. The main threat to WATER quality is an increase in the level of nutrients entering inland waters from agricultural and other sources. The increasing production of waste, and the high reliance on landfill as the main mechanism for disposing of it, is another area of concern.

As awareness of the importance of environmental issues has grown, so too has the number of non-governmental organisations and other community groups concerned with the environment. The need for a body that would be a source of information on the quality of the environment and that could provide advice and assistance to public authorities led to the establishment in the Republic of the Environmental Protection Agency; a similar role is performed in Northern Ireland by the ENVIRONMENT AND HERITAGE SERVICE, though its spread of functions is wider, as it also covers nature conservation and heritage.

A range of environmental legislation has been enacted in recent years, some of which arises from the steady output of directives from the EUROPEAN UNION, as well as from international agreements and obligations. The development of EU legislation has had a substantial influence on Irish policy. The Environmental Impact Assessment Directive requires the preparation of detailed assessment and proposed amelioration measures for a wide range of developments. The European Union is also committed to meeting the limits for emissions of greenhouse gases agreed under the Kyoto Protocol. As a result of the UN Conference on Environment and Development (1992), sustainable development was identified as an important goal for the twenty-first century. This essentially means development that meets the needs of the present generation without compromising the ability of future generations to meet their needs: requiring present populations to live within their ecological means. 'Agenda 21' was developed as an action plan for the twenty-first century to facilitate the move towards sustainable development. Governments are required to develop plans for their own countries, at national and LOCAL GOVERNMENT level. In the Republic the Government produced the document *Sustainable Development: A Strategy for Ireland* and subsequently established a National Environment Partnership Forum. Northern Ireland was included in the United Kingdom's sustainable development strategy, which dates from 1994, but there is a commitment in the Executive's Programme for Government to publish proposals for a specific Northern Ireland strategy during 2001.

However, absolute pressures on the environment have continued to increase, and Ireland continues to face many environmental challenges, in particular controlling emissions into the air from TRANSPORT and energy production, reducing pollution in water from agricultural

environment. *Panoramic view of the 200-ft peaks of the Sperrin Mountains and the rich grazing land of Co. Tyrone, one of the many unspoilt landscapes of Ulster. [Michael Diggin Photography]*

and municipal sources, and improving waste management and nature protection. [see LAND.] **Anne-Marie Cunningham**

environmental protection. Mechanisation and the adoption of scientific methods and management systems revolutionised farming in Ireland from the 1960s. In the 1960s and 70s there was large-scale development of farmyards to accommodate the growing numbers of livestock made possible by an increased use of fertiliser and the change to silage for winter feeding. In 1973 Ireland joined the EEC, and agricultural policy in Western Europe further boosted stock numbers and agricultural output. In the Republic the number of cattle increased from 7.5 million in 1978 to 7.9 million in 1998; in the same period the number of sheep increased from 3.3 million to 8.4 million. During the period 1981–8 sales of nitrogen fertiliser increased from 275,000 tonnes to 432,000 tonnes, while phosphate levels increased to the point where 20 per cent of farms have levels above their needs. The excessive use of nitrogen and phosphate causes problems for water quality.

This rapid increase in stock numbers and intensification has had significant environmental impacts. 'Point source' pollution, which caused large fish kills, has largely been rectified but has given way to diffuse pollution. There continues to be pressure on the environment from agricultural waste, eutrophication, overgrazing (especially on the blanket peat soils on the western seaboard), and emissions of 'greenhouse gases'. During this period of increased productivity, consequential effects on landscape, habitats and wildlife were not adequately considered. Reforms in the EU common agricultural policy set about limiting agricultural output in member-states. These measures were also to encourage farming practices that were compatible with environmental protection and the upkeep of the landscape and the countryside. In response to this regulation the Department of Agriculture and Food launched the Rural Environmental Protection Scheme in 1994. This was open to all farmers with more than 3 ha ($7\frac{1}{2}$ acres) of land who were prepared to farm within given nutrient limits and to carry out environmental protection work and habitat enhancement. During the first period, 1994–9, up to 46,000 farmers participated. Under EU regulations a new scheme, modelled closely on the first one, was launched in November 2000, and it is hoped to have 70,000 farmers participating in this scheme.

Prompted by EEC regulations, the Department of Agriculture for Northern Ireland developed and implemented agri-environmental measures, beginning in 1988. Two areas of national importance for their landscape, habitat and heritage value, were originally identified; within these areas farmers were offered the opportunity of entering into voluntary five-year management agreements. With the introduction of further regulations these areas were expanded to the point where 20 per cent of Northern Ireland was designated. In May 1999 the Countryside Management Scheme was launched, and this continues to operate.

The schemes in both jurisdictions have as their objective the appropriate compensation of farmers for taking action towards farming in an environmentally sustainable manner, to compensate them for the cost incurred or loss of income, and to familiarise them with methods of environmentally responsible farming. The quality of the schemes is high, and the amount of checking involved has contributed to the maintenance of a high degree of compliance with the schemes outlined for each farm. These will form the blueprint for future schemes aimed at requiring all farming activities to be compatible with the requirements of environmental protection and renewal. **Eugene Ryan**

Environment and Heritage Service (Northern Ireland), an executive agency of the Department of the Environment, its aim being to protect and conserve Northern Ireland's natural heritage and built ENVIRONMENT, to control and regulate pollution, and to promote a wider appreciation of the environment and best environmental practices. The agency carries out a range of activities to promote policies of sustainable development, bio-diversity, and CLIMATE change. **Anne-Marie Cunningham**

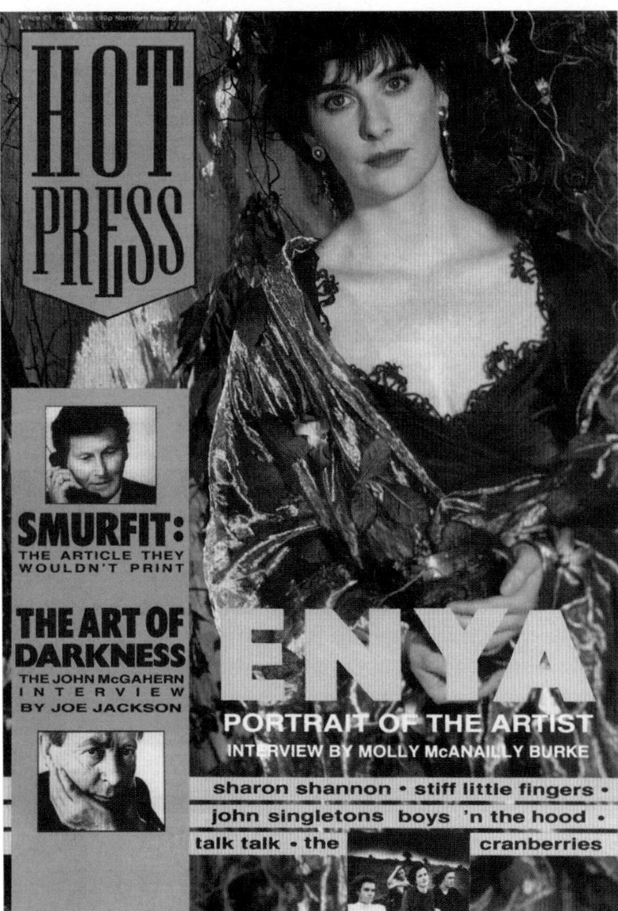

Enya. *Eithne Ní Bhraonáin, known as Enya. While briefly a member of the family band Clannad, she has since earned acclaim as a solo artist without giving live performances.* [Hot Press]

Enya, stage name of Eithne Ní Bhraonáin (1961–), singer. Born in Co. Donegal. Briefly a member of CLANNAD, her family's band. In the mid-1980s she began a solo career. She is unique in Irish popular and rock music in that she has sold millions of records without ever playing live: she assiduously creates studio-born music that deploys layer upon layer of vocals and keyboards, collaborating with Nicky and Roma Ryan, the former her producer and engineer, the latter her lyricist. Her albums include *Shepherd Moons* (1991), *The Memory of Trees* (1995), and *A Day Without Rain* (2000). **Tony Clayton-Lea**

Eochaid ua Flannacáin (Eochaid grandson of Flannacán), also known as Eochaidh Ó Floinn (936–1004), author of quasi-historical, genealogical, and topographical poems. More than twenty of these survive, mostly incorporated in LEBOR GABÁLA ÉRENN. A member of the Armagh ecclesiastical family Clann Sínaich, he is described in his annalistic obituary as superior of Lios Aoigheadh (an unidentified place) and of Clonfeacle. A son and several other descendants were abbots of Armagh. **Nollaig Ó Muraíle**

Eoghanachta, a dynastic federation that, from the sixth century, provided overkings of Munster. Its leading dynasties, including the Eoghanacht of CASHEL (Co. Tipperary), Glendamain, Áine, and Loch Léin (Co. Kerry), claimed descent from Conall Corc, in turn traced to the eponymous Éogan Már. Eoghanachta overkingship, closely associated with Cashel, was at times powerful enough to contest UÍ NÉILL claims of political supremacy, especially under Cathal mac Finguine (died 742) and Fedelmid mac Crimthainn (died 847). In the tenth century a divided federation yielded dominance to the rising DÁL GCAIS. Reduced to suzerainty of Desmuman (south Munster), the principal Eoghanachta ruling line ultimately adopted the surname Mac Carthaigh. **Ailbhe Mac Shamhráin**

episcopacy. Scholars long believed that, after the period of conversion, the episcopal office (enjoyed by PALLADIUS and claimed by PATRICK) lost its importance in Ireland. Instead, an unusual church structure developed, dominated by abbots and monastic communities, in response to the supposedly exotic milieu of the 'Celtic fringe'. According to this view, episcopacy was restored to an orthodox governing role in the Irish church by the twelfth-century reformers. Evidence has been adduced more recently, however, that, while abbots and non-clerical 'resource-managers' were important in pre-twelfth-century churches, bishops also continued to be so. The bishop, not the abbot, conferred the highest status on a church, was the archetypal ecclesiastical judge, and regulated pastoral ministry. Episcopacy apparently functioned within defined if unstable territorial spheres, by the tenth century if not before, notwithstanding the commonly held belief that dioceses in Ireland can be traced only to the twelfth century. **Colmán Etchingham**

EPONA instrument, the first Irish experiment selected to fly on a mission of the European Space Agency. EPONA is an acronym of *energetic particle onset admonitor*—the measurement function of the instrument; it was also the name of a Celtic goddess associated with the beginning of the solar year. This experiment was selected to be one of ten flown in 1985–6 aboard the European Space Agency's *Giotto* mission to Halley's Comet. EPONA is installed on the 'experimenter's platform' of the spacecraft. Prominent are its three solid-state telescopes, which were configured to build up a three-dimensional picture, with respect to energy, species, and directionality, of the energetic particle regime through which the spacecraft was flying. *Giotto* traversed comet P/Halley in March 1986. **Susan McKenna-Lawlor**

equality. Public discussion about equality typically assumes that substantial inequalities of income and power will always exist in society, differences in status being ignored in a context where standards of normality are implicitly set by the dominant group. This is the underlying liberal model of equality in the the Republic's Employment Equality Act (1998). Attempts to tackle inequalities generally concentrate on equal access to opportunities (for example providing working-class children with equal access to EDUCATION, or women with equal access to promotion). Such access is no guarantee of equal participation, since it ignores the effect of past DISCRIMINATION and the continuing impact of structures, organisational cultures, and attitudes that in effect maintain the status quo. Even with positive action, less privileged groups—such as working-class children, women, and the disabled—are unlikely to succeed at the same rate and in the same situations as more privileged groups. Yet such action, which is essentially remedial and limited in impact, often fuels a backlash. A radical model, with an emphasis on transformative action, challenges the idea that inequalities in income, power and status are inevitable. [see DISCRIMINATION LEGISLATION; SOCIAL CLASS; UNDERCLASS.] **Pat O'Connor**

Equality Authority, established in the Republic in 1999 under the Employment Equality Act (1998). It replaced the Employment Equality Agency, established under the Employment Equality Act (1977), which, with skeletal staff and minimal funds, worked to eliminate discrimination in EMPLOYMENT based on sex or marital status, to promote equal treatment of men and women, to keep employment equality legislation under review, to advise the Government, to initiate legal proceedings, represent individuals, and take cases to court, to provide a free, individual, confidential advisory and information service, and to raise awareness. The functions of the new structure are broadly similar but reflect an increasing awareness of the extensive nature of DISCRIMINATION. The Equality Authority retains the responsibility for actively promoting equality of opportunity and combating discrimination; it has the power to provide information, advice and, where possible, legal representation, to prepare codes of practice, to conduct research, to prepare equality reviews and action plans, to establish advisory committees, and to monitor and review relevant legislation. Its statutory basis reflects the structural reality of inequality in Irish society. [see DISCRIMINATION LEGISLATION.] **Pat O'Connor**

Equal Opportunities Commission for Northern Ireland. Northern Ireland is regarded as having the most wide-ranging, well-developed EQUALITY framework in Europe, though this has developed unevenly within the various social dimensions of inequality. The Equal Opportunities Commission was established in 1976 to administer and implement the Sex Discrimination Act (1975) and Equal Pay Act (1976). It could conduct investigations, undertake research, and support individual complainants but had no powers in relation to affirmative action, contract compliance, or grant denial nor powers equivalent to those of the FAIR EMPLOYMENT COMMISSION in obtaining regular information from employers. Its research function was especially important, given the skewing of resources, political attention, and administrative statistics towards issues of fair EMPLOYMENT and community relations after 1969 and away from other social divisions, such as those of sex and race. The commission's survey and book, *Women's Working Lives* (1993), and its Money Matters series remain primary sources on women's economic circumstances in Northern Ireland. Its responsibilities were taken over in 1998 by the Equality Commission. **Eithne McLaughlin**

Erck, Wentworth (1827–1890), astronomer. Born in Dublin; educated at TCD. He was called to the bar in 1850. Interested from childhood in ASTRONOMY, he erected an observatory at Sherrington, his home near Wicklow. He was an enthusiastic and proficient observer of double stars and of sunspots which he recorded for twenty years, even when away from home. His voluminous observations remained largely unpublished, his love of astronomy being its own reward. **M. T. Brück**

Eriugena, John Scotus (c. 810–c. 877), philosopher, theologian, translator, exegete, poet, and polymath. Born in Ireland (Eriugena means 'Irish-born'). He was probably CHRISTIANITY's greatest systematic thinker between the times of Augustine and Aquinas. Though biographical details are hazy, it is known that he eventually established himself at the court of Charles the Bald in France. There he produced translations of and commentaries on Greek texts hitherto ignored in the Latin west: works by Dionysius the Areopagite, Gregory of Nyssa, and Maximus Confessor. In turn, this immersion in Greek thought gave a highly particular bent to his own theological and philosophical speculation, particularly in the *Periphyseon* (or *De Divisione Naturae*).

Stressing that all of being is the manifestation of God, the *Periphyseon* attempts a dialectical comprehension of theophany. For Eriugena, all creation 'is' God: Natura, as genus, has four species, which show the Deity as beginning, middle and end of the universe. The first of these species is God as uncreated creator; the second is the group of primary, created causes, which themselves create a non-creating third species; lastly there is God as the goal of the previous stages. Eriugena's schema is thus circular and yet hierarchical. Despite the description of God becoming more 'visible' via his effects, Eriugena also maintains an emphasis on God's hiddenness. Strongly influenced by the Greek Fathers, this negative theology stresses that, while God is immanent in creation, he is also utterly transcendent: beyond definition, conception, even being, God is the no-thing from which all emerges; the deity is both within and beyond all that is. Accordingly, any over-hasty charge of pantheism is undermined—as is any suggestion that human understanding is somehow 'total' or absolute.

Though his work as a whole undoubtedly did much to re-inject specifically Greek Christian Platonism into the more Latinised, Augustinian west, the *Periphyseon* itself remained a source of controversy; condemned in the thirteenth century because of alleged pantheism, it was eventually placed on the Index of banned writings in 1684. Nonetheless, and despite long periods in philosophical obscurity, it has exerted a continuing fascination—upon Meister Eckhart and Nicholas of Cusa, upon German idealism (which it prefigures remarkably), and, more recently, upon the dedicated scholars, in Ireland and abroad, who have done much to illuminate its significance and stature (see p. 331). **Ian Leask**

Ervine, St John (1883–1971), playwright, novelist, critic, and biographer. Born in Belfast, but moved to London while in his teens. For a brief period in 1915 he managed the ABBEY THEATRE, Dublin. In a writing career that lasted more than forty years, distinguished by strong emotions often expressed forthrightly, he explored and presented a view of the collective Ulster personality as complex and often gnarled but almost always enduring when underpinned by the ethics of hard work, tenacity, and endurance. Of his Ulster plays, *Mixed Marriage* (1911) and *Boyd's Shop* (1936) met with significant popular success in amateur drama circles. **Sam Burnside**

Esler, Erminda Rentoul (c. 1860–1924), novelist and SHORT-STORY writer. Born in Manorcunningham, Co. Donegal; educated privately and at QUB. She settled in London after her marriage. Her works include *Almost a Pauper* (1888), *The Way of Transgressors* (1890), *The Way They Loved at Grimpat* (1894), *A Maid of the Manse* (1895), *'Mid Green Pastures* (1895), *The Wardlaws* (1896), and *Youth at the Prow* (1898). A contemporary reviewer hailed her work as 'strong, winsome, breezy, sane and altogether delightful.' Her short stories are especially impressive in their portraits of courageous and stoical women. **Tess Maginess**

Esmonde, Eugene (died 1942), naval officer and pioneer of commercial aviation. Born in Borrisokane, Co. Tipperary, son of Dr John Esmonde, home rule MP for North Tipperary. He was an early airline pilot on the large flying-boats carrying mail between Britain and Australia. He resigned his airline captaincy to join the Fleet Air Arm on the outbreak of the SECOND WORLD WAR and was in the aircraft-carrier *Courageous* when it was sunk by a German submarine in September 1939; later he was in the aircraft-carrier *Victorious* in May 1941 when the German battleship *Bismarck* headed out into the Atlantic, sank the battleship *Hood*, the pride of the British navy, and threatened all shipping between Britain and North America. At night and in appalling weather he flew 195 km (120 miles) in search of the *Bismarck*, which he found and damaged with a bomb that greatly assisted its final destruction by a squadron of warships. In February 1942 the German warships *Scharnhorst Gneisnenau* and *Prinz Eugen* made a daring dash up the English Channel from occupied France to German bases in the North Sea. They had successfully driven off all attacks and were approaching the Dover Strait when the last effort to stop them was made by Esmonde, in charge of six obsolete aircraft that had no hope of success, as he well knew. All were shot down, and all their crews lost. A German officer in the *Scharnhorst* said of the attack: 'Such bravery was incredible. One was privileged to witness it.' **John de Courcy Ireland**

'Esnada Tige Buched' ('the melodies of Buched's house'), a tale that belongs to the cycle of early tales concerned with King CORMAC MAC AIRT and forms an important part of his biography. Buched, a Leinster hospitaller of great generosity, is impoverished through the insatiable demands of the sons of Cathaír Már, King of Leinster. The elderly Cathaír is unable to check his sons; together with his foster-daughter Eithne Thoebfota, daughter of Cathaír, Buched is forced to flee his home and live a humble existence. Observing Eithne early one morning, Cormac seizes her and forces her to lie with him. From this violent union his son, Cairbre Liphechar, is born. Eithne eventually agrees to marry Cormac, and Buched's wealth is restored to him. The allegorical significance of this tale has been discussed by several scholars. **Ruairí Ó hUiginn**

Esposito, Michele (1855–1929), pianist, composer, teacher, conductor, and music publisher. Born in Castellamare di Stabia, Italy; studied piano and composition at the Conservatory San Pietro a Majella, Naples, graduating in 1873. After a four-year period in Paris he moved to Dublin in 1882 to teach piano at the RIAM, beginning a long and distinguished association with musical life in Ireland that was to last forty-seven years. He founded the Dublin Orchestra Society in 1899, which he conducted until 1914, and also established a music recital series at the RDS in 1886. He was active in the FEIS CEOIL Association from 1897; in 1905 he was awarded an honorary MusD by TRINITY COLLEGE, Dublin. He returned to Italy in 1928. His works include the opera *The Tinker and the Fairy* (1910), two string quartets (1899, 1914), a cello sonata (1899), *My Irish Sketch Book* (c. 1920) for solo piano, an Irish symphony, a piano concerto, and many works for solo piano. **Paul Collins**

ESRI: see ECONOMIC AND SOCIAL RESEARCH INSTITUTE.

estates, the predominantly rural but also urban property owned by the LANDLORD class and generally leased by them to various tenant groups. The 'estate system' was not unique to Ireland but acquired colonial overtones as a result of the land confiscations and PLANTATIONS of the sixteenth and seventeenth centuries, which were unique in Europe (see p. 915). By 1703 the great majority of estates were owned by the descendants of the 'NEW' ENGLISH and Scots planters, adventurers, government servants, and soldiers who had been the beneficiaries of these schemes. The pattern of estate ownership did not remain stable, however: the sale and inheritance of estates ensured that recruitment to the ranks of landownership was a constant process.

Estates were very varied in size and value. By the middle of the nineteenth century a small minority of 'magnate' landlords, such as Earl Fitzwilliam and the Duke of Devonshire, owned estates of more than 36,500 ha (90,000 acres), worth more than £45,000 in rents; but the majority were much smaller, averaging less than a tenth of this in size and value. Most rural estates possessed a BIG HOUSE and demesne, and many estates were highly fragmented and widely dispersed (see p. 29).

The end of the estate system was marked by the sale of land to tenants under the LAND ACTS (1881–1909), but in its traditional form the system had already been weakened by the compulsory FAMINE-induced estate sales between 1848 and 1860 under the ENCUMBERED ESTATES and landed estates courts, when more than 2 million ha (5 million acres), worth more than £21 million, were sold. [see ANGLO-IRISH SOCIETY.] **Lindsay Proudfoot**

ether-drinking, introduced to Ireland in the 1840s, when it was believed to have medicinal benefits. Its recreational use, confined almost entirely to Cos. Derry and Tyrone, became popular in the 1870s, thanks to a shortage of cheap ALCOHOL. By the 1880s some 50,000 people were consuming about 17,000 gallons (77,000 litres) annually. Some SHEBEENS sold nothing else, and the streets of Cookstown and Moneymore, Co. Tyrone, stank of ether.

Liquid ether turns to gas at body temperature, irritating the stomach lining and inducing violent wind and vomiting. To avoid such waste, the 'etheromaniac' would 'rench his gums' with cold water, hold his nose, swallow the ether, then drink more water. In this way users could consume anything between an occasional spoonful and a daily half-pint or more. Seasoned drinkers could even dispense with 'renching' and gulp their ether straight.

The effects of ether-drinking are almost immediate. The pulse quickens, the face flushes, and a wave of excitement is followed by visions, perhaps of dancing on clouds to heavenly music; it was said that Continental imbibers were more prone than the Irish to erotic dreams. The user might shout, dance, or be convulsed. The symptoms pass within minutes, leaving slight depression and a desire for another dose, but no hangover. Less is known about the long-term consequences. Reformers warned of blindness and insanity, but medical observers charged it only with digestive problems, attributing more serious effects to concomitant alcoholism. From December 1890 ether was scheduled as a poison, and in 1923 ether-drinking became a criminal offence in Northern Ireland. [see ALCOHOL ABUSE.] **John Wakeman**

ethnography, the scientific study of races and cultures. Research by Conrad Arensberg and Solon Kimball in north-west Co. Clare in the 1930s was the first and the most influential extended ethnographic study in Ireland, an attempt at a holistic description of the community structure of a few rural localities, centred on tradition, FAMILY dynamics, labour exchange, and land tenure. It was conceived as an illustration of functionalist theory, for which local society consists of a system of related sociocultural institutions that act in concert to maintain social equilibrium. This work was later criticised for its treatment of local communities as isolated social systems, exaggerating their 'traditional' stability and equilibrium while neglecting processes that transcend the local. Likewise, their synchronic approach to social research made for a lack of historical depth and failed to deal with the realities of long-term change and decline in rural Ireland.

Subsequent ethnographic work pursued similar themes and methods for several decades, concentrating on kinship and family dynamics in rural communities. A series of studies analysed processes of decline, social breakdown, and psychological malaise in the rural west. Implicitly taking Arensberg and Kimball's work as a baseline, and accepting its rose-tinted view of 1930s rural Ireland, these studies traced an apparently catastrophic social breakdown, which they tended to attribute to recent causes, neglecting to consider the long-standing presence of social change and instability in post-FAMINE rural society.

Ethnographic research in Northern Ireland has tended to emphasise the fact that Catholic and Protestant communities inhabit quite similar sociocultural worlds in spite of segregation, sectarian division, and social conflict. Henry Glassie's study of rural Fermanagh in the 1970s was an impressive attempt to document the entire narrative and expressive culture of a local community, concentrating on the construction of social history in local ritual and memory. More recent work has dealt with political violence in urban localities, principally in Belfast, or has compared sectarian social formations in urban and rural localities.

Recent ethnographic work in rural Ireland has taken a more seriously dynamic and historical approach, examining contrasting practices and ideologies within Irish Catholicism, or developing a social history that combines the analysis of documents with ethnographic fieldwork.

Present-day ethnographic research is narrower in focus and more varied in theoretical outlook, pursuing a bewildering array of topics, ranging from the university system to the asylum system. Fieldwork has been undertaken by ethnomusicologists, folklorists, and linguistic anthropologists, studying topics such as traditional dancing, IRISH-LANGUAGE discourse, and the use of sign language among the deaf. **Steve Coleman**

Eucharistic Congress (1932), a mass rally of Catholics intended to deepen spiritual awareness through a greater understanding of the Eucharist. The first Eucharistic Congress was held in Lille in 1881, the thirty-first in Dublin in June 1932. Only ten years after independence, it was an emphatic public assertion of Irish Catholicism as well as an organisational triumph. More than a million people attended an open-air Mass in the PHOENIX PARK celebrated by the Papal Legate, Cardinal Lauri, at which JOHN MCCORMACK sang 'Panis Angelicus'. **Fergal Tobin**

European Convention on Human Rights, created by the Council of Europe in 1950 and ratified by the Republic in 1953. It serves as a model human rights document, protecting classic civil

Esposito. Michele Esposito *(1926) by Sarah Cecilia Harrison, Italian composer and pianist who held a central position in Irish music in the late nineteenth and early twentieth centuries. [National Gallery of Ireland]*

and political rights, such as the right to life, to privacy, and to expression. It is enforced by the European Court of Human Rights in Strasbourg. Individual victims of human rights abuses can take an action against their state, provided they have exhausted all national remedies; a state can take an action against another state for abuses within the latter's territory. Before the incorporation of the convention, decisions of the court were not directly binding in the Republic, though it was obliged to bring its laws into line with such decisions. Decisions of the court have led to the amendment of Irish and Northern Ireland law in areas such as HOMOSEXUALITY, legal aid, the treatment of prisoners, and the rights of natural fathers in ADOPTION cases. Ireland is required under the BELFAST AGREEMENT to incorporate the convention into domestic law. **Neville Cox**

European Monetary System (EMS) **and European Monetary Union** (EMU), the system used in the European Union for stabilising exchange rates between member-states. The Republic's membership in EMS from 1979 was a political decision designed to cement the national commitment to European integration, but, despite the subsidised loans received in return for joining, the economic consequences for Ireland were generally unfavourable. It meant an end to the one-for-one peg of the Irish pound to sterling, and marked the start of a lengthy period of financial turbulence and uncertainty. Against sterling, currency of the major trading partner, the Irish pound fluctuated sharply between a low of less than 74p and a high of £1.10; against the German mark, anchor of the system, repeated devaluations totalled 37 per cent by 1993. Faced with this uncertainty, financial markets drove Irish interest rates to a significant premium—averaging 2.5 per cent per annum on an exchange-rate adjusted basis. However, it is not clear whether the old peg could have remained politically sustainable in the early 1980s, faced with the contemporary strength of sterling and high UNEMPLOYMENT at home and abroad.

The advent of EMU from 1999 offered Ireland the prospect of lower interest rates, and of restoring nominal exchange-rate stability, though not with the major trading partner. Once again the entry decision was taken on largely political grounds. Though various campaigners foretold huge economic benefits or costs, in reality the economic arguments were finely balanced. The risk that sterling might depreciate sharply, exposing Irish exporters to price competition, had to be a consideration. In the first years of EMU the opposite was the case, with sterling remaining strong and the Irish economy in danger of overheating.

While critics rightly pointed to the need for budgetary action to dampen domestic demand, given that national monetary policy was no longer available to do so, it has to be said that, even when it was available, monetary policy had rarely been used as an effective counter-cyclical policy tool. **Patrick Honohan**

European Union (EU), the formal title of what was known as the European Community in the Treaty of Maastricht (1992). It consists of fifteen member-states; a further ten states will gain membership in May 2004. The European Union will become Continental in range as the countries of eastern and central Europe join. The new title for the European Community codified a number of EC activities into a single constitutional framework. The union consists of three 'pillars': the European Communities (pillar 1), the common foreign and security policy (pillar 2), and co-operation in justice and home affairs (pillar 3). Pillar 1 constituted the original treaties that founded the common market and the SINGLE EUROPEAN ACT, whereas the other two pillars represented additional areas of EU activity. Pillar 1 encompasses the main body of the union's economic policies and the federal system of EC law. All the treaty provisions for the euro are in pillar 1. Pillars 2 and 3 are more intergovernmental in nature; this means that the member-states have more control over decision-making in these spheres. The official anthem of the European Union is Schiller's 'Ode to Joy' set to the final movement of Beethoven's Ninth Symphony. [see NATIONAL ANTHEMS.] **Brigid Laffan**

European Union politics and Ireland. Ireland joined the European Economic Community in January 1973, the Republic as a full member and Northern Ireland as a region of the United Kingdom. For Northern Ireland, the fact that the region has not got full-member status and that most negotiations with the EUROPEAN UNION are carried out on its behalf by the British government, which has generally been ambiguous in its response to European integration, has meant that Northern politicians are not as firmly embedded in the EU system as their Southern counterparts. For the Republic, integration with the European Union has occurred to such an extent that on all principal European issues there is a virtual consensus among parties represented in DÁIL ÉIREANN with the exception of SINN FÉIN, the GREEN PARTY, and the Socialist Party. From the outset, successive governments have been in favour of further European integration and have been actively involved in all major EU policy initiatives, in order to maintain Ireland's position as a core member of the European Union. Consequently, considering its small population, Ireland has enjoyed disproportionate influence in the European Union: as well as supplying a number of noted Europeanists (such as DOOGE, MACSHARRY, and SUTHERLAND) it helped to develop a number of EU pilot schemes that were subsequently successfully adopted. These include the Leader rural development scheme and various Community Initiatives run by the European Commission. This, together with good use of sizeable aid transfers from EU Structural Funds and the successful adoption of Western-European styles of economic management and policy-making, led the Irish population to be generally 'pro-European'.

As well as significant economic benefits, membership offered the Republic a chance to move out from 'Britain's shadow' in international relations. In 1972, when the question of membership was put to the people in a REFERENDUM, 82 per cent voted in favour in a poll of 71 per cent of the population. This remains the highest 'yes' vote in any member-state. For Northern Ireland, however, the issue of membership coincided with the extreme political unrest that marked the beginning of the 'TROUBLES'. Membership of the European Union was not the most pressing political issue, and even if it were, the parties of Northern Ireland remain divided on the issue. Most Unionist parties tend to be opposed, with only the SDLP and the ALLIANCE PARTY maintaining their pro-European position. Sinn Féin continues to oppose membership, both North and South, seeing it as a further diminution of Irish SOVEREIGNTY.

Until the mid-1990s the poor economic situation in Ireland, both North and South, was the primary determinant of Irish approaches to the European Union. As a country with a small, open and peripheral economy, average incomes were well below the EU average, and as a result, successive governments argued for solidarity and cohesion among EU members. During the negotiations on the Single European Act, which facilitated the creation of the European 'single market', the Republic joined with other less well-off member-states to press for a commitment to economic and social cohesion. This was achieved through the addition of a protocol to the act and through a renegotiation of the EU budget, giving increased financial and administrative commitments to structural funds for disadvantaged regions. Both the Republic and Northern Ireland were designated 'objective 1' or high-priority regions for aid from EU structural funds for the period 1988–99.

Similar pressures were brought to bear in the negotiation of the Treaty of Maastricht and resulted in the creation of an EU Cohesion Fund, providing financial assistance for projects in the fields of environment and trans-European networks to member-states whose GNP per capita is less than 90 per cent of the EU average. In this case, however, Northern Ireland was excluded from a share of the fund, as its provisions related to member-states, not regions.

Though the Irish have traditionally been regarded in Brussels as 'good Europeans', this status was challenged in the 1990s when the Republic's economic boom led the Government into conflict with the European Union over its management of the economy. As the European Union entered the final preparations for economic and MONETARY UNION, requiring all member-states to develop broadly convergent economic policies, the Government was criticised for its refusal to damp down the extremely successful 'CELTIC TIGER' economy. The Minister for Finance, Charlie McCreevy, in particular, was publicly rebuked for his tax concessions to foreign investors, which were regarded by the European Commission as breaking the spirit, if not the law, of the single market.

In May 2001 the Republic's rejection of the Government's proposed constitutional amendment required for the ratification of the Treaty of Nice heralded a new popular scepticism concerning Irish interests and deeper European integration. The Treaty of Nice was the outcome of a complex set of negotiations over the institutional changes necessary to facilitate the proposed eastward enlargement of the European Union. The treaty, which runs to some hundred pages, did not need to be ratified until the end of 2002; the Irish 'no' vote probably represented not so much an outright rejection of the treaty as a public trouncing of the political parties and Government officials who thought they could rely on the electorate to endorse a series of political changes that had been given a summarily short explanation and scant public discussion. In the absence of a strong pro-treaty endorsement, anti-treaty campaigners were able to promote the idea that a vote for the Treaty of Nice would lead to a diminution of the Republic's NEUTRALITY: in fact it would not, and the idea that the Republic's foreign policy has ever been really neutral is a misnomer; but most voters who were unsure about the treaty decided not to vote. Compared with other referendums on the European Union, the actual number of 'no' votes decreased, but with a turn-out of only 35 per cent these were sufficient to reject the treaty. A second referendum in 2002 reversed this decision and approved the treaty. **Maura Adshead**

Eurovision. *Dana (Rosemary Scallon) returning to Dublin Airport following her winning of the 1970 Eurovision Song Contest with the song 'All Kinds of Everything'. [Michael O'Reilly]*

Eurovision Song Contest. Ireland first entered the European Broadcasting Union's televised song contest in 1965 and subsequently won it a record seven times. The first victory came in 1970 with 'All Kinds of Everything', sung by Dana (ROSEMARY SCALLON). Johnny Logan triumphed in 1980 with 'What's Another Year?', written by Shay Healy, and again in 1987 with his own composition, 'Hold Me'—the only artist to win the contest twice. Logan also wrote Ireland's next winner, in 1992, 'Why Me?', performed by Linda Martin. Ireland dominated the contest in the mid-1990s, winning in 1993 with 'In Your Eyes', sung by Niamh Kavanagh, in 1994 with 'Rock and Roll Kids', sung by Paul Harrington and Charlie McGettigan, and again in 1996 with 'The Voice', performed by Eimear Quinn. The frequent success became a national joke as well as a drain on the resources of RTÉ, which was obliged to host the contest following each victory. **Mick Heaney**

evangelicalism, loosely, the practice of spreading the Christian GOSPEL. Historically, this term has been subject to many changes. In the eighteenth century a synonym for 'Protestant' or 'Lutheran', it was later used to describe the revival connected with Methodism. In the following century, defined as stressing the importance of the literal truth of the Bible, personal conversion, and justification by faith, evangelicalism permeated the major Protestant denominations. Formerly characterised by anti-Catholicism, evangelicals cannot today be seen as a coherent group. Ranging from liberal to conservative, they are present within many denominations and embrace considerable theological flexibility. However, the authority of Scripture, the work of the Holy Spirit and the need to be 'born again' in Christ remain common themes. **Myrtle Hill**

evangelicalism in Northern Ireland. In one sense all Christians are evangelicals, as Scripture enjoins Jesus's followers to preach the GOSPEL. The name is derived from the Greek for 'good news', the early Christian term for the four Gospels; to share the 'good news' is therefore to evangelise. With the Protestant REFORMATION the term developed a narrower meaning, becoming associated with a critique of Catholicism; evangelicalism in this sense means belief in Biblical literalism, in Jesus as the sole mediator with God, salvation through faith alone, and an emphasis on being 'born again'. Very conservative evangelical positions merge with Christian fundamentalism.

Historically, Ulster Protestantism was dominated by conservative evangelicalism and is only slightly less so today. Protestant unity in the 1830s, largely the result of the theology and politics of REV. HENRY COOKE, had evangelicalism as its sacred canopy, and the religious revivals common in the nineteenth century took on progressively conservative positions. Religious revivals tended to coincide with threats to Protestants' constitutional position; and conservative evangelicalism became associated with strong defence of the Union. This is not a necessary link: the modern charismatic tradition of neo-Pentecostalism is conservative in its evangelical theology but tends to be politically liberal in attitudes towards the Union. [see SECOND REFORMATION.] **John Brewer**

Evans, E. Estyn (1905–1989), geographer, archaeologist, and student of FOLK LIFE. Born in Shrewsbury; educated in Welshpool and then at University College, Aberystwyth, where he studied geography and anthropology. In 1928 he was appointed first lecturer in geography at Queen's University, Belfast, where he passed the remainder of his career as lecturer, 1928–44, reader, 1944–5, and foundation professor of geography, 1945–68. Possessed of great charisma, he became one of the principal ornaments of his university, and he and his former students made an enormous impact on the life of Northern Ireland. He was chairman of the Historic Monuments Council, the Ulster Folk Life Society, and the Ulster Archaeological Society. He played a leading role in the establishment of the ULSTER FOLK AND TRANSPORT MUSEUM and was chairman of the museum's trustees. He was elected to membership of the ROYAL IRISH ACADEMY in 1938, and received many academic honours. In 1968 he resigned his chair to become the first director of the INSTITUTE OF IRISH STUDIES, an office he held until his final retirement in 1970; in the same year he was made a commander of the Order of the British Empire. The author of numerous scholarly papers, he reached a wide international audience through such books as *Irish Heritage* (1942), *Mourne Country* (1951), *Irish Folk Ways* (1957), and *The Personality of Ireland* (1973). **Gordon L. Herries Davies**

Evans, John David Gemmill (1942–), philosopher. Born in London; educated at the University of Cambridge. He was a fellow and lecturer at Sidney Sussex College, Cambridge, 1964–78, and visiting professor at Duke University, 1972–3; appointed professor of logic and metaphysics at Queen's University, Belfast, 1978, and elected to the ROYAL IRISH ACADEMY, 1983. As well as serving on a multitude of Irish, British, and international academic committees, he has produced well-respected publications, such as *Aristotle's*

Evans, E. Estyn. *Evans (on far left wearing beret) with students at the entrance to Newgrange passage tomb before it was reconstructed: (left to right, standing) Evans, Don Clerk, Gwyneth Evans, Darby Reid, the caretaker (unidentified), Mrs McCrae, Joe Frey, Billy Kelly, Ernie McCrae; (left to right, seated) Harold McCourt, Margaret Buchanan, Sheelagh Wallace. [Noel Mitchel]*

Concept of Dialectic (1977) and *Aristotle* (1987). He has also written on moral philosophy and on the philosophy of education. **Ian Leask**

Everyman Palace, Cork, built in 1897 by H. Brunton, part of a string of theatres, including the GRAND OPERA HOUSE, Belfast, and GAIETY THEATRE, Dublin, that made up the backbone of the Irish touring circuit. Following extensive renovations in the early 1990s the theatre still hosts theatre, music, and an annual Christmas pantomime. **Christopher Morash**

eviction, the enforced dispossession of tenant-farmers who lacked security of tenure, most notably tenants-at-will and yearly tenants. Evictions occurred from time to time during the second half of the eighteenth century, but from 1820 reports of evictions by ESTATE-owners became more frequent. In the wake of the GREAT FAMINE, evictions became widespread throughout the western counties. Estate-owners dispossessed countless small tenant-farmers between 1849 and 1855 in what were termed the 'clearances', in an effort to create more commercially viable estates, with large cattle and sheep farmers often replacing the evicted tenants. Thereafter the incidence of evictions declined sharply, but it rose again during the LAND WAR of the 1880s, when tenant-farmers were unable to pay rents as a result of poor harvests, or withheld rents as a protest against the LANDLORD system.

The LAND ACTS of 1881 and 1887 gave tenant-farmers a certain amount of protection from arbitrary dispossession, but full security of tenure was achieved only with later legislation that enabled them to become owners of their holdings. Evictions led to hardship and suffering and were an important influence in sparking land agitation during the Land War and in mobilising support for the home rule movement. [see ENCLOSURE.] **David S. Jones**

executions, 1916. Under martial law, and in the aftermath of the 1916 RISING, British authorities court-martialled the leaders of the rising. Between 3 and 12 May 1916 fourteen men were executed in Dublin (PATRICK PEARSE, WILLIE PEARSE, THOMAS CLARKE, THOMAS MACDONAGH, JOSEPH PLUNKETT, Edward Daly, Michael O'Hanrahan, JOHN MACBRIDE, ÉAMONN CEANNT, Michael Mallin, Con Colbert, SEÁN HEUSTON, JAMES CONNOLLY, and SEÁN MACDIARMADA) and one in Cork (Thomas Kent). ÉAMON DE VALERA and CONSTANCE MARKIEVICZ were both sentenced to death but had their sentences commuted to life imprisonment. It is widely believed that the executions stirred much public sympathy and played a role in SINN FÉIN's electoral triumph in 1918. [see CASEMENT.] **Seán Farrell Moran**

Exhibition of Subjective Art (January 1944), an art exhibition in Dublin organised by members of the WHITE STAG GROUP and Margot Moffett. Thirteen artists participated, and fifty-six works were shown. The exhibition was conceived in response to a lack of public awareness of contemporary art and a need for informed criticism; artists were invited to submit work that was selected by Kenneth Hall and Basil Rakoczi in conjunction with the artist. Funds were raised through subscription, and an illustrated catalogue was published, with an introduction by Herbert Read. He was invited to open the exhibition and to lecture on 'The subjective in art' but was prevented from travelling from London and sent an essay, 'Art and crisis', which was read in his absence at the COUNTRY SHOP, St Stephen's Green, Dublin; the text of 'The subjective in art' appeared in the BELL in February 1944.

The work in the exhibition ranged from a semi-abstract to surrealist style and reflected the White Stag Group's emphasis on personal expression. It received mixed reviews, and succeeded in causing some controversy. The participating artists, in addition to Rakoczi and Hall, were Jocelyn Chewett, Paul Egestorff, PATRICK SCOTT, Doreen Vanston, Ralph Cusack, Thurloe Conolly, Phyllis Hayward, Nick Nicholls, BRIAN BOYDELL, Bobby Dawson, and Stephen Gilbert. **Róisín Kennedy**

Expedition of the Sons of Echau Muigmedón: see ECHTRAE MAC NECHACH MUIGMEDÓIN.

Expedition, tale type: see ECHTRAE.

explorers. A useful definition of an explorer is a traveller who is the first person from a particular culture to see new lands and describe them. Such a person's efforts are usually associated with qualities of curiosity, bravery, and endurance. Occasionally, like Columbus and Cortez, he may be rewarded with outstanding moments of discovery; an Irishman, ROBERT M'CLURE, knew one of these when he came upon the North-West Passage.

Travel and exploration date from the beginning of human endeavour, as people migrated all over the globe from their unknown places of origin. Ireland's first explorers, the invaders who settled beside the River BANN, made their discoveries of the unknown less than 10,000 years ago. The difference between travelling and exploring is a fine one, particularly since so much exploration is accompanied by other purposes, such as commerce and conquest. The goal of missionaries also took them into unknown territories. In the course of his work ROGER CASEMENT penetrated parts of the Congo previously unknown to European travellers. SCIENCE and BOTANY have always provided important inducements to travel; men like James King, the astronomer on Captain Cook's third voyage of discovery, who took command of the *Resolution* after Cook's death, or the doctor James Patton, who sailed on Cook's second voyage and collected items that make up the core of the ethnographic collection in the NATIONAL MUSEUM OF IRELAND, must be considered travellers rather than explorers. So should botanists such as HANS SLOANE (born in Killyleagh, Co. Down), personal physician to the Governor of Jamaica, whose collection of natural history formed the nucleus of the British Museum after he died in 1753. A more recent botanist, AUGUSTINE HENRY, explored unfamiliar parts of China, but it is for his significant contribution to horticulture that he is remembered.

The question of nationality bedevils any consideration of Irish explorers. Though ERNEST SHACKLETON, one of the greatest explorers of all time and an unsurpassed leader of men, belonged to an Irish family of quaker origin, he lived in Ireland only for the first ten years of his life. The majority of Irish explorers came from an Anglo-Irish background, and at a time before Ireland became independent there was no conflict in the idea of their loyalty to Britain. For most of them the British army and navy gave many openings into exploration. Soldiers such as FRANCIS RAWDON CHESNEY were involved in the discovery of new territory in the course of their

eviction. *A hand-tinted postcard, c. 1900, from an original photograph of 1888 by Francis Guy, Cork, featuring an evicted tenant and his family outside their demolished cottage at Glenbeigh, Co Kerry. [Mary Evans Picture Library]* military duties. HENRY BLOSSE LYNCH, who mapped the great rivers of the Middle East, began his career in the Indian navy. THOMAS PARKE, an army doctor, was recruited for Stanley's expedition after his army service. The former policeman ROBERT O'HARA BURKE began as an unsuccessful British army cadet, while his failed military career involved service in the Austrian army.

A remarkable number of Irishmen made their reputation in the steely waters and frozen wastes of the Poles, enduring terrible hardships. In nearly every case, including that of the redoubtable THOMAS CREAN, the opportunity for exploration was opened up by their career in one of the British services. The secrets of the world were revealed to Europeans slowly throughout the nineteenth century as the interior of Africa was encountered, the interior of the South American continent was mapped, and the North and South Poles were conquered. In the twenty-first century, since there is little left on this earth to discover and the old spirit of exploration has inevitably dwindled with knowledge, the definition of 'exploration' will have to evolve. Viewing the world with a fresh vision has resulted in a doctrine of discovery that permits a traveller like DERVLA MURPHY to take her place among the ranks of explorers. One aspect of modern exploration is repetition: the work of Thor Heyerdahl on *Kon-Tiki* has encouraged other sailors, such as TIM SEVERIN, to imitate the skills and methods of earlier travellers into the unknown.

Meanwhile, while our world has become restricted and all too well known, there is the challenge of space. Will the exploration of the Moon prove to be a start, or will the aspiration of acquiring knowledge of the unknown continue to be pursued solely with unmanned craft, such as *Galileo*, still on its mission to discover distant mysteries? It may be optimistic to assume that humans will be more directly involved; but we have time. **Peter Somerville-Large**

Expugnatio. *Extract from* Expugnatio Hibernica, *a narrative of the Anglo-Norman Conquest (1169–85) by Giraldus Cambrensis. The manuscript is enlivened by marginal illustrations: (from top) mouse, wolf, hound, spider, leech, and lizard. [Council of Trustees of the National Library of Ireland; Ms. 700]*

Expugnatio Hibernica (The Taking of Ireland) (1189), the most detailed contemporary account of the ANGLO-NORMAN CONQUEST, covering the years 1169–86. The author, GIRALDUS CAMBRENSIS, was related to several of the first invaders and wrote from their standpoint. His education as a churchman at the University of Paris, his familiarity with the English court and his interest in natural history raise *Expugnatio Hibernica* above the level of a mere chronicle. However, his family is given undue prominence in the conquest, he is dismissive of royal officials sent to Ireland, and he portrays the Irish as barbarians. The work was attacked by Irish writers of the Renaissance period for its anti-Irish bias. [see KEATING, GEOFFREY.] **A. B. Scott**

extreme weather. Extremes in any meteorological characteristic cannot be objectively defined but must be considered in relation to the average. Ireland's present CLIMATE is extraordinarily moderate by comparison with other places at the same latitude; the rare meteorological occurrences that are extreme in Irish conditions would not be considered extremes globally.

In the instrumental record the lowest recorded temperature is −2°F (−19°C) (January 1881, Omagh, Co. Tyrone); the highest is 91°F (33°C) (June 1887, Kilkenny). For precipitation, the heaviest annual recorded rainfall was 3,965 mm (Kerry Mountains, 1960), while the most intense recorded over a twenty-four-hour period was 184 mm (Dublin, June 1963). At sea level the greatest wind speed recorded was 54 m/s (120 miles/h) at Kilkeel, Co. Down, in 1974. Such weather-related events as floods and droughts are relatively rare. The longest dry spell on record was during 1975 and 1976 and had the greatest effect on the south and east. FLOODING usually occurs after a period of above-normal precipitation during the winter months and can be attributed to the gentle gradient of Irish rivers (such as the River SHANNON) over much of their course.

There are some records of extremes from the period before instrumental records. Two events of particular note are the NIGHT OF THE BIG WIND in 1839 and the Great Frost of the winter of 1740/41. However, in the absence of quantitative measurements it is difficult to compare these events with those of the past 150 years. **Gerald Mills**

Fashion *(see page 377). Hat from Philip Treacy's spring–summer 2000 collection, shown in January 2000 at the Paris haute couture shows, the first time a show had been dedicated purely to millinery. [Courtesy of Philip Treacy Ltd]*

F

Faerie Queene, The (1596), an epic poem by EDMUND SPENSER. It was written in Co. Cork during Spenser's residence as a Munster planter and administrative official (see p. 124). Ostensibly set in 'faerieland' and influenced by classical literature, medieval romance, and Italian Renaissance epic, it is also an assertion of English power and self-confidence in the period. It traces the 'fashioning' of a noble character by way of the knightly adventures of six heroes, representing the virtues. Permeated with Irish material (landscapes, violent conflict, and fantasy images of the 'salvage' Irish), the poem vividly reveals its colonist-author's interior struggles, fears, and desires during the attempt to reduce Ireland to compliance with English government. **Patricia Coughlan**

Fagan, Robert (1761–1816), portraitist, art dealer, archaeologist, and diplomat. Born in London into an Irish Catholic family; educated at Royal Academy Schools. He visited Flanders, Paris, and Rome and in 1784 settled in Rome, where he worked in the neo-classical style; his sitters included Sarah and Geoffrey Amherst and Sir George Wright. He also worked as a dealer in antiquities and paintings and an agent for British collectors. He excavated in Rome and the Papal States. Ejected from Rome in 1807 for political activities, he moved to Palermo. He was involved in an unsuccessful attempt to rescue Pope Pius VII in 1808. Appointed British Consul-General for Sicily and Malta in 1809, he visited England in 1815. In financial straits, he committed suicide in Rome the following year. **Brendan Rooney**

Fahan Mura, Co. Donegal, a sixth-century ecclesiastical foundation of COLM CILLE, with a cross-slab decorated on both sides with an INTERLACE cross and stem. On the west face are two figures, possibly ecclesiastics, on whose garments there may be very eroded inscriptions. Above the cross on the east face are two opposed birds with interlocking beaks. Along one edge is inscribed a Greek version of the *Gloria Patri* ('Glory and honour to God the Father, and the Son, and the Holy Ghost'), known in Ireland from as early as the seventh century but thereafter declining in popularity. One authority has proposed a seventh-century date, suggesting that the 'vestigial' arms anticipate developed, free-standing crosses; another has suggested a ninth-century date for this and the related sculpture at Carndonagh. [see HIGH CROSSES.] **Conor Newman**

Fahy, Paddy (1926–), traditional musician. Born in Kilconnell, Co. Galway. His family operated a venue famous for traditional music and dancing, and he was a founder of the AUGHRIM SLOPES CÉILÍ BAND. One of the most influential, though often uncredited, composers of traditional FIDDLE music in the twentieth century, he

Fagan. *Robert Fagan and his wife, Maria Ludovica Flajani, titled* Self-Portrait with His Second Wife à la Grecque *(1803). Fagan, who was involved in the excavation of classical sculpture in Rome, depicts his wife in the manner of an antique marble figure. [The Hunt Museum, Limerick]*

was also endowed with a distinctive fiddling technique, marked by a temperate pace, a sparing use of syncopation, and a special lyricism. **Martin Dowling**

fáinne ('ring'), a gold or silver lapel badge in the form of a ring worn by some Irish-speakers. Instituted in 1915 under the auspices of the GAELIC LEAGUE (Conradh na Gaeilge) by PIARAS BÉASLAÍ, its object was to encourage the use of Irish by identifying the wearer as an Irish-speaker. **Martin Clancy**

Fair Employment Commission, established by the Fair Employment Act (1989) to promote equality of opportunity, affirmative action, and fair EMPLOYMENT and to work for the elimination of DISCRIMINATION on religious and political grounds in Northern Ireland. It replaced the Fair Employment Agency, established in 1976. The commission could conduct investigations and provide support and advice to those who believed they had been discriminated against. However, it was also expected to promote and direct affirmative action and contract compliance and to operate the grant denial and monitoring provisions of the 1989 act. The commission was subsumed within the NORTHERN IRELAND EQUALITY COMMISSION in 1998, following a review of fair employment legislation and policy in the mid to late 1990s by the Standing Advisory Commission on Human Rights (percursor of the NI Human Rights Commission). [see EQUAL OPPORTUNITIES COMMISSION.] **Eithne McLaughlin**

fairies. From the earliest period of Irish tradition to the present day, FOLKLORE speaks of a community of spirits or supernatural beings who are living beside human beings but are normally concealed from them. These supernatural beings, known in Irish as *sióga* and in English as fairies, are also given other names, such as *na daoine maithe* ('the good people'). The *Sí* originally meant a hill or mound in which these spirits were traditionally believed to dwell. Folk legend ascribes the origin of the fairies to the story of the fall of Lucifer and his angels from Heaven; while falling earthwards they were halted by God, and thereafter those who had already fallen to earth became the fairies. Another legend explores their prospects of salvation on the Day of Judgment, usually concluding on a pessimistic note. Occupying this parallel OTHERWORLD, the fairies were said to interact with humans, for both good and ill. In folklore they are often confused with the spirits of the dead, and much overlapping occurs in the tradition. **Anne O'Connor**

Fairley, J. S. [James Saintfield] (1940–), scientist. Born in Belfast; educated at QUB. He was professor of zoology at the National University of Ireland, Galway, until 2000. He worked on wild Irish MAMMALS, previously a somewhat neglected area; his four books—*Irish Wild Mammals: A Guide to the Literature* (1972), *An Irish Beast Book* (1975), *Irish Whales and Whaling* (1981), and *A Basket of Weasels* (2001)—form the basis for our knowledge of the subject today. **D. Patrick Sleeman**

fairs. The network of fairs and markets after 1600 built on an INFRASTRUCTURE of trading centres that dated back centuries, but the numbers, geographical range, functions, and relative integration of commercial institutions varied markedly in the modern period. In the first half of the seventeenth century more than 500 new sites received a market patent. Typically, outside large towns, the smaller sites of exchange that predominated in Ireland served populations ranging up to 130 adults, providing a mechanism for the distribution of local produce and livestock. In the second half of the seventeenth century, as towns grew and export trade and regional transport infrastructure developed, growth was most marked in the large commercial centres, such as Dublin and Belfast, at the expense of minor ports. This trend continued through a process of consolidation in the eighteenth century, during which the commercial functions of smaller markets were subsumed by those of larger, often neighbouring centres. The market was still an important site of exchange: that of Cork was famous for its BUTTER; and throughout Ulster a few LINEN markets, such as Ballymena, remained important throughout the nineteenth century. But fixed-shop retailing removed some of the traditional market functions. Fairs, by contrast, which specialised in particular in livestock, grew rapidly with the increase in commercial AGRICULTURE in the later eighteenth century, numbering more than 5,000 by 1845. They declined in number in the later nineteenth century, though a number of specialist fairs retained and expanded their original functions as sites of exchange. [see ECONOMY 1700–2000.] **K. J. James**

fairs and livestock markets. *Aonaigh* (fairs) were the traditional means of selling livestock in Ireland and were great festive and religious events, undoubtedly with pagan origins. An important event in the calendar of ancient Ireland was the Tailteann fair, held at TARA in August to celebrate the festival of LÚNASA. Similar events were the week-long fair held on the CURRAGH of Kildare and the Old LAMMAS FAIR in Ballycastle, Co. Antrim.

Cattle and milk underpinned the ECONOMY and social fabric of Ireland, with cattle representing the wealth of a farming family in a period when LAND was owned in common and grazing rights were paramount. Up to the 1950s and the emergence of livestock auction marts, approximately 500 local fairs operated, with the greatest concentration in the west. They were generally held monthly in areas convenient to a RAILWAY—essential in the days before road haulage for moving cattle to the ports and on to England. The fairs usually started at or before daybreak, and the animals were sold on a headage basis, with no means of weighing the stock. Prices were arrived at after considerable bargaining, with payments in cash. Cattle were walked to the fairs, and home again if unsold. By contrast, in modern cattle marts the stock is publicly weighed and sold publicly by auctioneers. Sellers of stock are guaranteed payment, and holding facilities for stock are standard. With the advent of such organised livestock auction marts in the 1960s and 70s the fair system went into terminal decline.

Marts were already firmly established in Ulster much earlier than in the South. In the Republic, farmer-owned CO-OPERATIVE marts count for a large proportion of mart business (70 per cent) and predominate in Munster, south Leinster, and Connacht, the traditional strongholds of farmer co-operatives. By 2002, livestock marts handled 1.5 million head of cattle and more than 2.5 million sheep, with combined turnover approaching €1 billion per annum in 2000. [see HIRING FAIRS; LIVESTOCK INDUSTRY.] **Maurice Colbert**

Fallon, Brian (1933–), critic. Born in Cootehill, Co. Cavan; educated at TCD. He spent his working life, 1953–98, at the *Irish Times*, where he was literary editor and art critic. His columns were the main site of discussion of international art matters for three decades, while his monographs on EDWARD MCGUIRE (1991), TONY O'MALLEY (1984), and IMOGEN STUART (2002) have been important benchmarks for the appreciation of contemporary artists. He was a member of the board of the IRISH MUSEUM OF MODERN ART, 1990–95. **Richard Pine**

Fallon, Conor (1939–), sculptor. Born in Co. Wexford; studied at TCD. A self-taught artist, he lived among the artists of St Ives, Cornwall, in the 1960s. He works mainly in welded or painted stainless steel, his sculptures spare and sleek in form and derived from the animal world; the forms are full of a contained energy and echo belief in the animal and bird deities of the IRON AGE CELTS. He is a member of the RHA and of AOSDÁNA. *Conor Fallon, Sculptor*, with essays by Vera Ryan, HILARY PYLE, and SEAMUS HEANEY, was published in 1996. **Suzanne McNab**

Fallon, Pádraic (1905–1974), poet. Born in Athenry, Co. Galway. For forty years he worked as a customs official, mainly in Wexford. One of the most gifted poets of his generation, he published poems, stories, and reviews in many periodicals, but the first collection of his work, *Poems* (1974), appeared only in the year of his death, which partly explains his neglect. His poetry is notable for its intelligence and formal skill. *Poems and Versions*, edited by his son, BRIAN FALLON, appeared in 1983; *Collected Poems*, with an introduction by SEAMUS HEANEY, was published in 1990. He also wrote a series of remarkable radio plays derived from Irish myths and legends, including *Diarmuid and Grania* (1950) and *The Vision of Mac Conglinne* (1953). **Peter Sirr**

Fallon, Peter (1951–), poet and publisher. Born in Osnabrück, Germany; educated at TCD. In 1970 he founded the Gallery Press, which published a number of his early collections in quick succession: *Among the Walls* (1971), *Co-incidence of Flesh* (1973), and *The First Affair* (1974). Later collections show the influence of life on a sheep farm in Co. Meath and the work of American poets, especially Wendell Berry. *The Speaking Stones* 1978), *Winter Work* (1983), *The News and Weather* (1987), and *Eye to Eye* (1992) were followed by *News of the World: Selected and New Poems* (1998). **David Wheatley**

family. Article 41 of the CONSTITUTION OF IRELAND (1937) refers to the family as 'the natural primary and fundamental unit group of Society' and identifies MARRIAGE as the institution on which the family is founded. Public policy in the first half of the twentieth century did much to promote a model of the family based on Catholic moral teaching and on a large role for the family production unit (particularly the family farm) in the ECONOMY. It was a model of family life based on limited emotional expressiveness, a strict division of roles between men and women, a subordinate role for children, and limited restriction of FERTILITY. Marital separation was rare, though marriage break-up through the death of a spouse was relatively common (partly because spouses were often widely separated by age). This model was gradually transformed from the 1960s onwards as Catholic moral teaching lost its hold, the family production unit ceased to have central economic significance, and new thinking on love, sex, and the nature of childhood emerged. Today's dominant model of family life idealises love, open communication and EQUALITY between spouses, an independent economic role for women, small family size, and relative freedom for children. Marital breakdown has replaced widowhood as the principal cause of premature family disruption. **Tony Fahey**

family history. With EMIGRATION a feature of Irish life for several centuries, there are now an estimated 70 million people throughout the world who claim Irish descent; some 40 million of these are citizens of the UNITED STATES. The descendants of the Irish emigrants of the eighteenth and nineteenth centuries have been in the vanguard of interest in Irish family history in recent decades. Events such as the election of JOHN F. KENNEDY to the Presidency of the United States have heightened interest in re-establishing and reasserting old links. This interest is increasingly mirrored by the descendants of more recent emigrants, including those who left during the 1940s and 50s, when emigration to England was at a particularly high level. In recent years, growing URBANISATION in Ireland itself, together with a heightened consciousness of the pace of change in many rural communities, has contributed to a growth in the number of those studying family and community history. A number of libraries and archives, including the NATIONAL LIBRARY OF IRELAND, find that the largest group of users are those conducting family history research.

The National Library, the NATIONAL ARCHIVES, the GENERAL REGISTER OFFICE, the Public Record Office of Northern Ireland and the General Register House (Belfast) are the focus of much of the family history research conducted in Ireland; between them these institutions hold the principal materials for family history research. The four main resources are (*a*) civil or state records of birth, MARRIAGE, and death (held in the General Register Office, Dublin, and General Register House, Belfast), (*b*) surviving CENSUS records (held in the National Archives), (*c*) parish and church registers (copies—and some originals—of which are held in the National Library, National Archives, Public Record Office of Northern Ireland, and Representative Church Body and other denominational repositories), and (*d*) nineteenth-century land valuations (copies of which are held in the National Library, National Archives, and Public Record Office of Northern Ireland). In addition, these institutions hold the archives of many of the former LANDED ESTATES, testamentary material, and other manuscript collections that constitute important—if less widely applicable—resources for researchers. The archives of the Registry of Deeds and the Valuation Office are also much used, as are the National Library's holdings of trade and social directories, published family histories, voters' lists, the archives of the Office of Arms, and a multitude of important local history publications. In the 1980s the work of local indexing projects led to the establishment of a network of research centres. Technological advances, which have led to the development of new ways of making research material accessible and of sharing information, have proved a boon to family history research;

family history. *Clonalis House, Co. Roscommon, home of the O'Conor Don family, descendants of the last high kings of Ireland; they have lived on their ancestral lands since the sixth century. The house contains the O'Conor archives and the library of the eighteenth-century antiquarian Charles O'Conor. [Bord Fáilte]*

GENEALOGY is believed to be the second-largest subject for which the INTERNET is used. [see CHIEFS OF THE NAME; GENEALOGY.] **Colette O'Flaherty**

family planning. Statistical patterns of births indicate that some degree of deliberate FERTILITY limitation within MARRIAGE had begun to emerge in urban areas in Ireland by the early decades of the twentieth century and had become widespread by the 1960s. However, there was only limited access to 'artificial' CONTRACEPTION. The Republic's CENSORSHIP OF PUBLICATIONS ACT (1929) outlawed as 'obscene' any literature that advocated contraception, while the Criminal Law (Amendment) Act (1935) banned the importing and sale of contraceptives. Pressure to liberalise the law began to emerge from women's groups, principally the Women's Liberation Movement, in the late 1960s; the most famous event in their campaign was the 'contraceptive train', a day-return trip to Belfast on 21 May 1971 on which consignments of condoms and spermicides were brought back to Dublin in defiance of the law (contraceptives were freely available in Northern Ireland). In 1973, in the landmark McGee case, the Supreme Court ruled that the legal prohibition on the importing and sale of contraceptives was unconstitutional, on the grounds that it unjustifiably interfered with the right to marital privacy. In June 1979 the Health (Family Planning) Act (1979) legalised the provision of contraceptives to married couples on a doctor's prescription 'for bona fide family planning purposes.' This legislation attracted much criticism and derision. Over three subsequent amendments to the act (1985, 1992, and 1993) the law moved in a steadily liberalising direction, to the point where virtually all restrictions were removed by 1993. [see FEMINISM.] **Tony Fahey**

Family Solidarity, a group formed after the 1983 ABORTION REFERENDUM. The Tenth Amendment of the Constitution Bill (1986) proposed that article 41.3.2 would no longer ban DIVORCE. Family Solidarity led the campaign against the removal by supporting the formation of the ANTI-DIVORCE CAMPAIGN, launched in April 1986. William Binchy, its legal spokesperson, argued cogently against the legalisation of divorce on social and economic grounds. The Catholic bishops supported the anti-divorce campaign and in 1986 issued a detailed statement on MARRIAGE, the FAMILY, and divorce. The campaign was successful, and 63 per cent of the electorate rejected the introduction of divorce. Family Solidarity is protective of a traditional form of family life: it supports mothers in the home and seeks CHILD CARE payments for women in the home, and it opposed the sale of condoms and the decriminalisation of HOMOSEXUALITY. In a second divorce referendum in 1995 a slim majority voted in favour of divorce legislation, resulting in the Family Law (Divorce) Act (1996). **Evelyn Mahon**

Famine, the: see GREAT FAMINE.

Famine of 1739–41, the most severe subsistence crisis of the eighteenth century, caused by the failure of the POTATO crop. The potato had only recently replaced DAIRY products as the staple food of the poor. Famines had been a regular feature of Irish history, caused by poor harvests in times of harsh weather; but the potato famine of 1739–41 brought a degree of suffering for which there was no precedent. Contemporary accounts claimed that one in three of the rural poor died. Exceptionally cold conditions in the winter of 1739/40 were followed by a short, wet summer and an early return to harsh conditions in the autumn. Because of the shortage of supply, potato prices increased to up to six times their normal value. Cereal production was also affected, and there were BREAD riots in Dublin in the summer of 1740. Typhus and dysentery followed in 1741. In all, it is estimated that as many as 400,000 people may have died, out of a total population of about 2 million. **Fergal Tobin**

famine refugees in Canada. In the seventeenth and eighteenth centuries, Irish emigrants to what would later become Canada were most numerous in the fishing villages of NEWFOUNDLAND. Between 1817 and 1847, however, successive Irish famines stimulated more EMIGRATION to North America, mainly through passage to Québec. In the 1830s Irish IMMIGRANTS were the largest national group in regions of Nova Scotia, New Brunswick, Prince Edward Island, Lower Canada (Québec), and Upper Canada (Ontario), particularly in port towns, such as Halifax and St John. Though CENSUS statistics after the GREAT FAMINE show that many Irish people continued west to Upper Canada and south to the United States, there may have been more permanent Irish settlement in Québec than the figures suggest, as records involving Irish women married to French-Canadians often obscured the national background of women and their children.

Though Irish settlements became sizeable in Winnipeg and parts of Manitoba, the largest influence was in eastern Canada. Irish Catholics participated in earlier emigrations to Canada, though in smaller numbers than Protestants; however, Catholics dominated the massive 'Famine Irish' immigration in the late 1840s. Typhus spread among already weakened passengers overcrowded on poorly provisioned ships, and thousands of Irish people died in many Canadian towns in 1847–8, the peak years of Irish emigration to Canada.

Groups of Irish immigrants developed diverse institutions to deal with the health and social needs of the new arrivals, but divisions along religious lines grew between Catholics, who maintained an Irish identity, and Protestants, more inclined towards strengthening their British connections. Protestant settlement was often facilitated not only by more substantial personal resources but also by support from such Canadian organisations as the ORANGE ORDER. By contrast, Catholicism had long been institutionalised in French-speaking Québec and provided an initial sub-structure for Irish community-building; however, as clerical divisions grew along linguistic lines and economic struggles widened among established and incoming immigrants, further Irish MIGRATION ensued. The Irish poor supplied much of the labour for Canadian economic growth from 1850 to the 1860s, with many workers moving with canal and railway expansion. On both sides of the religious divide, Irish-born doctors, writers, entrepreneurs, and politicians were also influential, including THOMAS D'ARCY MCGEE, a powerful voice in the Canadian Confederation, many mayors and colonial assembly members, and the Eaton and McCord family business ventures. By 1871 the Irish were the largest national group in most Canadian towns, particularly in Upper Canada east of Toronto; in the city of Québec and Montréal the Irish were second only to French-Canadians.

While vibrant communities still exist among their descendants and later Irish immigrants, most Canadian communities associated with Irish culture today were established before the arrival of the famine refugees. In the 1990s, commemorative monuments to Irish famine immigrants were erected or expanded in the Maritime provinces and along the St Lawrence River, most notably at the GROSSE ÎLE quarantine station but also at Partridge Island, Cap-des-Rosiers, Québec, Montréal, St John's, St Andrews, and Kingston, places where thousands buried in mass graves were victims of famine, disease, or shipwreck (see p. 153). **Kathleen O'Brien**

famine refugees in England and Wales. One consequence of the GREAT FAMINE was the influx of poor Irish IMMIGRANTS into ENGLAND and Wales from the spring of 1846 onwards. Cheap passage and regular crossings enabled hundreds of thousands of famine-stricken emigrants to make the sometimes perilous journey across the Irish Sea. Because of the incomplete nature of contemporary records it is impossible to estimate the exact number who travelled to England and Wales during the crisis; however, an indication of the scale of the exodus is provided by the fact that the Irish-born population of England and Wales almost doubled between 1841 and 1851. Many sailed to Liverpool with a view to making the transatlantic voyage to North America, though lack of funds ensured that a substantial number never completed the journey.

From 1846 until the mid-1850s a constant stream of famine refugees arrived at LIVERPOOL, Newport, Cardiff, Swansea, Whitehaven, and LONDON. The famine Irish were conspicuous by their poverty and ill health; their way of life was considered alien, reinforcing widely held negative stereotypes. The great majority of those who made the journey were poor, and many were in need of immediate relief from the POOR LAW authorities in the ports of entry. Between 1847 and 1850 an estimated 368,423 Irish paupers were recorded as having landed in Liverpool; other ports, such as Newport and Cardiff, experienced similar large inflows.

The response of the Poor Law authorities was to provide short-term relief to prevent deaths by starvation. The arrival of the famine Irish coincided with an economic recession in 1847 and unemployment and poverty among the indigenous population, resulting in an enormous strain on the capacity of the Poor Law to assist those in need. In these exceptional circumstances the Poor Law authorities sought to cope rationally, even though deaths still occurred, the circumstances surrounding which received extensive coverage in the press. But it was not solely the ports of entry that experienced the influx of famine refugees as Irish immigrants travelled on foot inland. A process of dispersal was evident from Liverpool, radiating outwards to other parts of Lancashire, Yorkshire, Cheshire, and the midlands and even reaching as far as the industrial centres of north-east England, such as Newcastle and Sunderland. The famine Irish posed a problem for municipal authorities throughout England and Wales, as many were suffering from various forms of disease, particularly typhus, referred to by contemporaries as 'Irish fever'. The typhus epidemic of 1847 was at the time attributed to the influx of famine refugees, fuelling alarm in many cities and towns.

The principal long-term effect of the famine influx was the large growth in the already established Irish-born population of England and Wales throughout the second half of the nineteenth century. **Enda Delaney**

famine refugees in Scotland. Refugees from the GREAT FAMINE first arrived in Scotland in late 1846, and over the next few years tens of thousands more flooded into the country. Most of them landed at Glasgow; in 1847 alone more than 50,000 Irish paupers entered the city. The total number of destitute Irish people who came to Scotland between 1846 and 1853, the main period of famine IMMIGRATION, is not known.

The authorities in Glasgow, for economic and social reasons, were alarmed at the Irish influx. In 1847 the immigration coincided with high levels of unemployment in the city and with the arrival of refugees from the famine in the Western Highlands and Islands of Scotland. The poverty-stricken Irish immigrants were therefore an additional burden on the poor rates. In January 1847 more than 7,000 Irish immigrants received assistance from the parochial boards of Glasgow and its SUBURBS, an increase of almost 6,000 on the previous year's total. The famine Irish were mostly responsible for the massive increase in begging and overcrowding in Glasgow, and thousands of the immigrants died of typhus; indeed the authorities were convinced that the Irish famine refugees were responsible for the typhus epidemic that engulfed the city, and other parts of the western lowlands, during that year. Newly arrived Irish immigrants were likewise blamed for the outbreaks of cholera in Glasgow and Edinburgh in 1848.

Many of the Irish people who landed at Glasgow during the famine years eventually found employment either in the city or in the industrial areas of the western lowlands. A considerable number returned to Ireland; between 1846 and 1853 the Scottish authorities shipped back almost 47,000 Irish immigrants. The famine refugees attracted considerable hostility from sections of Scottish society, and this was one of the reasons behind the rise of the No-Popery agitation in Scotland in the 1850s. **Martin Mitchell**

famine refugees in the United States. In the decade 1846–55 an estimated 2.1 million people fled Ireland as a result of the GREAT FAMINE. Of these, 1.8 million went to North America, all but 300,000 of them to the United States (and many who landed in Canada quickly made their way south). Not surprisingly, the Irish during the famine crisis accounted for a higher proportion of American immigrants than ever before or since: 45.6 per cent in the 1840s and 35.2 per cent in the 1850s.

The Irish famine refugees in America have aptly been described as 'urban pioneers'. It is estimated that three-quarters of them settled in cities, towns, and mining and industrial areas. The American cities with the largest Irish-born populations in the middle of the nineteenth century were NEW YORK, PHILADELPHIA, BOSTON, CHICAGO, and SAN FRANCISCO, followed by St Louis, Jersey City, Pittsburgh, Providence, and Cleveland. New York was the principal port of arrival; in 1860 a quarter of the population of both New York city and Boston were Irish-born, as was 16 per cent of the population of Philadelphia. The poorest of the refugees, especially in New York city, lived in shanty towns on the outermost rim of the city's development. In the 1850s as many as 30,000 Irish men, women, and children could be found living in cellars in New York city, without light or drainage. Living in poverty and squalor wherever they settled, the famine refugees fell victim to a variety of infectious diseases, the most destructive being TUBERCULOSIS, pleurisy, pneumonia, yellow fever, and cholera, as well as malnutrition. About 4,000 of the 12,000 people who died during the yellow fever epidemic of 1853 in New Orleans were Irish-born. While natives of Ireland made up 54 per cent of New York city's immigrants in 1855, they accounted for 85 per cent of all foreign-born admissions to the city's public hospital. The Irish-born accounted for an estimated 70 per cent of the recipients of charity in New York city in the 1850s and more than 60 per cent of the population of almshouses (where the indigent poor were housed). In Buffalo the Irish-born constituted 63 per cent of the poorhouse population at the height of the Famine in 1849 and an average of 51 per cent in the 1850s.

Ravaged by illness, disease, and psychological trauma, Irish famine refugees also suffered from alarmingly high rates of mental illness. In the period 1849–59 three-quarters of admissions to Bellevue asylum in New York were foreign-born, and two-thirds of these were Irish. Rates of arrest and incarceration for famine refugees all over the United States were correspondingly high, easily exceeding those of all other groups. By 1870 the American Irish were the most socially disadvantaged of all Americans of European origin by several measures. The wonder is not that this was so, given the catastrophe of the 1840s, but that their situation would be so thoroughly transformed over the next two generations. **Kevin Kenny**

famines. Large-scale famines have been exceptional in Irish history, though population pressure, bad weather, war and adverse market conditions sometimes produced concentrations of food crisis years. Ireland shared in the northern European crisis of the 1270s to 1320s, which included three serious famines. The first half of the seventeenth century also witnessed harvest failures, exacerbated by military devastation. In 1727–9 and again in 1739–41 large-scale famine caused mass mortality: up to 10 per cent of the population perished in the latter. Localised and limited crises affected the west in 1799–1801, 1816–17, 1822, and 1831; but nothing prepared Ireland for the shock of the GREAT FAMINE of 1845–50. The danger of famine retreated thereafter, but parts of the west were again threatened in the 1860s, 1880s, and 1890s. **Peter Gray**

famine and subsistence crises, medieval and early modern Ireland. Arguably no event in Irish history has cast a longer shadow than the GREAT FAMINE of 1845–50; one consequence has been the relative lack of awareness of the considerable impact of food crises in the centuries before the catastrophe of the nineteenth century. It is largely to the annalists and chroniclers, both native Irish and ANGLO-NORMAN, that we are obliged for our knowledge of such crises in the Middle Ages. With the exception of the years 1224–7, the period 900–1270 appears to have been marked by crises that extended for one season only, limiting the wider economic and demographic impact. The frequency and the effect of subsistence crises increased sharply after 1270. The mid-1290s and the first decades of the fourteenth century in particular were periods of intense famine throughout the country.

Following the outbreak of the BLACK DEATH in 1348 it becomes more difficult to measure the impact of subsistence crises, but in general the preceding half-century was a period of demographic erosion. The fifteenth century, while experiencing crisis years, can be portrayed broadly as one of recovery. The sixteenth and seventeenth centuries were marked also by periodic food crises, often exacerbated by the impact of warfare. The later 1580s, the early 1600s and early 1650s were periods when crop failure and livestock disease coincided with the ravages of war, often consciously exacted as an extension of military strategy. The failure of harvests and the death of livestock, besides leading to excess mortality, could also affect patterns of MIGRATION. The 1620s, for example, witnessed food crises at the beginning and end of the decade and also a reduction in the inward flow of British settlers and a movement of subsistence emigrants to Britain and the near Continent. **Patrick Fitzgerald**

fan-makers. Eighteenth-century Dublin fan-makers supplied the nobility with elegantly painted silk and paper fans. In 1719 fans were being sold at the Sign of the Golden Fan in Dame Street. By the 1750s Mrs Banks of Ormond Quay was making fans; her daughter, Elinor Dixon, continued business at the Fan and Masque in Castle Street. In 1800 an Irish fan was produced to mark the ACT OF UNION. By the 1850s Dublin fan manufacturers included Mansfield and the award-winning Paris House. Bog-wood fans, with gold and lace adornments, are found from the 1860s to the

famine. The Irish Famine *(c. 1849–50) by George Frederick Watts, one of the few contemporary responses by a major artist either in or outside Ireland to the catastrophe. [Trustees of the Watts Gallery, Crompton, Surrey/Bridgeman Art Library; TWG114701]*

1890s. The Hungarian government bought work by Alice Jacobs, exhibited in Budapest. In 1900 the DUN EMER GUILD decorated fans. The Dublin International Exhibition, 1907, encouraged a fan-making industry, but silk and lace fans had become unfashionable by the 1920s (see p. 602). **Mairead M. Johnston**

farmhouse types. Ireland possesses a strong and regionally varied tradition of vernacular rural ARCHITECTURE, which survives to the present day despite the widespread use of simplified 'polite' GEORGIAN styles for many FARMHOUSES during the nineteenth century. All vernacular farmhouse styles share the same basic characteristics of single-storey construction using commonly (and cheaply) available field materials: mud, straw, and stone; they therefore symbolise both the relative poverty and the local skills and knowledge of the tenant-farmer and smallholder classes who built them.

Three broad vernacular traditions may be identified: hip-roofed mud houses with a central HEARTH in Leinster; stone-built, gable-ended long-houses in Connacht, Munster, and west Ulster; and stone-built, two-roomed, twin-hearthed gable houses in north-east Ulster. Each tradition overlapped with numerous local variations, and the origin of each is obscure. It has been suggested that the Leinster and east Ulster styles reflect ANGLO-NORMAN and Scottish plantation cultural influence, respectively, while the western long-houses may reflect a more ancient tradition of 'byre-houses', housing livestock and people together. The widespread use of mud and stone is thought to reflect the early DEFORESTATION of the Irish landscape. **Lindsay Proudfoot**

farm mechanisation. Irish farmers were slow in adapting to the use of machinery on the LAND, but by 1869 horse-drawn mowing machines were being promoted by Goodbody of Tullamore, and these gradually replaced the traditional teams of men using scythes. By 1917 there were just seventy tractors in the whole of Ireland; by the end of the century the number had reached more than 200,000. In 1919 the Ford Motor Company began production of the Fordson model F tractor in Cork, and this proved popular. However, in 1940 there were still more than 500,000 men and 300,000 horses engaged in agricultural work.

The later introduction of the Ferguson hydraulic three-point linkage mounting system revolutionised the way in which tractors could be used for operations such as ploughing and harrowing. In 1919 at the RDS Spring Show in Dublin there were eight different tractors on display; by the late 1930s there were tractor-drawn ploughs, harrows, mowers, POTATO-diggers, and reapers and binders. By the mid-1950s the reaper and binder and the threshing machine were being slowly replaced by the combine harvester. The number of tractors in Northern Ireland was double that in the Republic in 1947, but by 1960 this position had more than reversed, with 22,000 in the Republic and 9,000 in the North.

The widespread use of the milking machine began in the late 1950s, and this, together with the availability of mechanised harvesters for gathering and storing winter fodder, resulted in the virtual disappearance of permanent hired labour from farms. The start of the twenty-first century saw many farms being run by only one man, who relied heavily on contractors, often using huge machinery, with some tractors costing more than €110,000 and capable of ploughing 6 ha (15 acres) per hour. [see AGRICULTURE.] **Joe Barry**

farm mechanisation. *The combine harvester is a multi-purpose grain-harvesting and threshing machine. Harvesting was once an arduous community task; now the grain is cut, threshed, and cleaned in one operation. [Derek Speirs/Report]*

farm organisations. The National Farmers' Association was formed in the Republic in January 1955. Under its first president, Juan Greene, it sought the right of direct negotiations with the Government, merchants, and processors, reform of the rates on land, and an improvement in farming methods. Led by Rickard Deasy, the farmers' rights march on Dublin in 1966 demanded the right to negotiate with the Government. A rally of 30,000 farmers was followed by a twenty-day sit-in on the steps of Government Buildings. After merging with beet, horticulture, and dairy organisations in 1971 the NFA became the Irish Farmers' Association, which by 2002 had a membership of 80,000.

The Irish Creamery Milk Suppliers' Association was founded in 1950, primarily for dairy farmers, and represents 36,000 farmers of all types. In the 1980s it fought the introduction of the milk quota system.

Macra na Feirme was founded in 1944 by Stephen Cullinan to provide young farmers with essential training and social opportunities. More than a quarter of a million young people have passed through its ranks, including future farming and political leaders. It took part in the development of the *Irish Farmers Journal*, Foróige, the NFA, and the ICMSA.

The Irish Cattle and Sheep Farmers' Association (formerly the Irish Cattle Traders' and Stock Owners' Association) was re-formed in 1992 to represent and to provide services to livestock farmers; by 2002 it had a membership of 8,000. It drew attention to the cross-border smuggling of lambs for processing plants before the outbreak of foot-and-mouth disease in 2001. **Pat O'Toole**

Farquhar, George (1677–1707), playwright. Born in Derry, where his father was a CHURCH OF IRELAND clergyman whose home was burnt by JAMES II's army during the siege; from 1694 he attended TCD as a sizar (paying reduced fees in exchange for performing certain menial duties), but his university career was cut short when he wrote of Christ walking on water that 'the man cannot be drowned who was born to be hanged.' He began writing poetry, including a solemn Pindaric ode 'The Death of General Schomberg, Kill'd at the Boyne' (1697). He also acted in SMOCK ALLEY THEATRE but quit after accidentally wounding a fellow-actor on stage. At the prompting of the Smock Alley actor Robert Wilks he took the text of his first play, *Love and a Bottle* (1698), to London, where it opened at Drury Lane Theatre. His first success was *The Constant Couple* (1699), which ran for an unprecedented fifty-three nights, with Wilks in the leading role, and led to a sequel, *Sir Harry Wildair* (1701). In the interim he wrote *The Inconstant* (1699) and a collection of prose and verse, *Love and Business* (1702), containing the influential 'Discourse on Comedy', in which he wrote: 'The rules of English comedy don't lie in the compass of Aristotle, or his followers, but in the pit, box, and galleries.'

Continually short of money, Farquhar wrote with desperate fluency in the next few years, producing *The Twin Rivals* (1702) for Drury Lane and *The Stage Coach* (1704). In 1704 he returned to Ireland as a British army recruiter, an experience he reworked in *The Recruiting Officer* (1706). While in Ireland he made an appearance at the Smock Alley Theatre, playing Sir Harry Wildair in a benefit production of *The Constant Couple*. Impoverished, he died of tuberculosis, just as his final play, *The Beaux' Stratagem* (1707), was achieving success.

Farquhar's reputation grew after his death; by the end of the eighteenth century only Shakespeare and Colley Cibber would be more frequently performed on the Irish stage, and a succession of Irish actors, from Wilks to PEG WOFFINGTON, would achieve success as Wildair. Farquhar was an admirer of WILLIAM III, to whom he dedicated *Sir Harry Wildair*, his heroes show little respect for archaic traditions of honour or decorum and are, at points, strongly anti-Catholic. However, Wildair and Roebuck, the 'Irish gentleman of wild, roving temper' in *Love and a Bottle*, are not the conventional libertines of earlier Restoration comedy but libertarians bound together by economic self-interest. **Christopher Morash**

Farran, George Philip (1876–1949), marine scientist. Born in Dublin; educated at TCD, where he won the gold medal for natural SCIENCE, 1898. He served in the ROYAL DUBLIN SOCIETY marine laboratory under E. W. L. HOLT, 1899, and was appointed assistant naturalist in 1900 when the laboratory was transferred to the government fisheries branch. He was chief inspector of fisheries from 1938 until his retirement in 1946. He specialised in marine plankton and in herring, becoming a world authority on the taxonomy of copepods. He also published local history and a comprehensive list of Irish names of fishes (1946). **Christopher Moriarty**

Farrell, Bernard (1939–), playwright and screenwriter. Born in Sandycove, Co. Dublin. He has written eighteen plays, as well as children's plays, a number of screenplays, and television series. The best of his work includes *I Do Not Like Thee, Dr Fell* (1979), *Last Apache Reunion* (1993), *Stella by Starlight* (1996), and *Kevin's Bed* (1998). Farrell's work is very different from that of most of his Irish peers: it deals primarily with the plight, failures, anomalies, and victories of the bourgeoisie, with little overt emphasis on history or on issues of national identity. **Eamonn Jordan**

Farrell, Brian (1929–), political scientist and broadcaster. Born in Dublin; educated at UCD and Harvard University. He worked as a lecturer and department head for UCD extramural studies and politics departments and has published numerous books on Irish political life. He joined RTÉ in 1957 as a radio presenter and commentator on current affairs and RTÉ television in 1961, working on 'Newsbeat', 'Seven Days', 'Today Tonight', and 'Primetime'. He is well known for his incisive interviews with politicians and his election coverage. **Bernadette Grummell**

Farrell, David (1961–), photographer. Born in Dublin; educated at UCD, where he was awarded a doctorate in chemistry. He began working as a freelance photographer in 1990. His first solo exhibition, *Innocent Landscapes*—a beautiful but haunting series of photographs taken during the search for the remains of people killed and secretly buried by the IRA—won him the prestigious European Publishers' Award for PHOTOGRAPHY, 2001. **Myra Dowling**

Farrell, Eibhlis (1953–), composer. Born in Rostrevor, Co. Down; educated at QUB and the University of Bristol, studied composition with RAYMOND WARREN, Charles Wuorinen, and Robert Moevs, and awarded a doctorate in composition by Rutgers University, New Jersey. She has written orchestral, band, chamber, organ, choral, and vocal works, including *Popcorn Overture* (1977), *Play* for organ (1985), *Quintalogue* for brass (1989), *Soundshock* for concert band (1992), and *O Rubor Sanguinis* for unaccompanied choir (1998). A former head of the DIT Conservatory of Music and Drama, she is a fellow of the Royal Society for Arts and a member of AOSDÁNA. **Paul Collins**

Farrell, M. J.: see KEANE, MOLLY.

Farrell, Terence (1798–1876), sculptor. Born in Creve, Co. Longford; trained in Dublin at the studio of THOMAS KIRK. He established a reputation as a portrait sculptor and regularly exhibited commissioned busts at the ROYAL HIBERNIAN ACADEMY, of which he was elected a member in 1859. He became the head of a family sculpture-yard that included his six sons. In the 1840s the LORD LIEUTENANT, Earl de Grey, commissioned work from him, notably his wife's monument for the family mausoleum at Flitton, Bedfordshire. Farrell's academic style, careful compositional arrangement, and diligent craftsmanship can be seen in his relief monuments in ST PATRICK'S CATHEDRAL, Dublin, commemorating the dead of the wars in China, 1842, and Burma, 1852. **Paula Murphy**

Farrell, Sir Thomas (1827–1900), sculptor. Born in Dublin, son of the sculptor Terence Farrell; won awards in the 1840s at the Dublin Society Modelling Schools and the Royal Irish Art Union. Elected a member of the ROYAL HIBERNIAN ACADEMY in 1860, in 1893 he became the first sculptor to be president. He was the leading sculptor in Ireland in the second half of the nineteenth century; he had an established and prolific practice in portrait SCULPTURE and commemorative work, with many public monuments in Dublin. St Mary's Pro-Cathedral houses two fine statues representing Archbishop MURRAY (c. 1855) and Cardinal CULLEN (1882), which reveal Farrell's neo-classical leanings. Somewhat more vigorous modelling can be seen in his Waterloo relief panel (1861) on the Wellington Testimonial in the PHOENIX PARK. He was knighted in 1894. **Paula Murphy**

Farrington, Anthony (1893–1973), geologist. Born in Cork; he entered UCC to study engineering but his studies were interrupted by ill health, and he passed the years 1915–19 in the warmer climate of Portugal. After attending a course at Camborne School of Mining in Cornwall during the summer of 1919 he returned to UCC, where he graduated in engineering in 1920. In December the following year he was appointed to the GEOLOGICAL SURVEY OF IRELAND as an assistant geologist. He investigated deposits in many parts of Ireland, but his chief task was a mapping of the drifts in western Co. Wicklow. Frustrated by the Geological Survey's inability to publish his work, in March 1928 he resigned to join the staff of the ROYAL IRISH ACADEMY, where he served as resident secretary from 1928 until his retirement in 1961. He was much involved with bodies such as AN TAISCE, the Bibliographical Society of Ireland, the COMMITTEE FOR QUATERNARY RESEARCH in Ireland, the Geographical Society of Ireland, and the ROYAL ZOOLOGICAL SOCIETY OF IRELAND. His interest in geomorphology and in the Irish Pleistocene Epoch never wavered, and from 1927 onwards he published numerous papers that helped to place our understanding of Ireland's history during the Ice Age on new foundations. Ever receptive to fresh interpretations of the evidence, he was a superb field geologist. **Gordon L. Herries Davies**

fashion. Until the middle of the twentieth century Ireland followed the lead of the established centres of Western European fashion, essentially Paris and London. Edward Molyneux

fashion. *'Jezebel', a black Connemara shawl, usually worn over the heads of countrywomen, draped to make an elegant wrap-around evening skirt, from the Irene Gilbert boutique collection of many seasons. [National Museum of Ireland]*

(1894–1974) was the only Irish figure of note; he opened his successful couture house in Paris in 1919, then moved to London in the 1930s, where he was a founder-member of the Incorporated Society of London Fashion Designers. He was responsible for dressing some of the most stylish figures of the time in his elegant, understated outfits.

Since c. 1950 Ireland's fashion designers have periodically had an impact on the international course of fashion. Despite the country's small size and relative poverty, in the 1950s buyers travelled every season to Dublin as well as to the more established centres. Several factors worked together to produce this situation. There was an energetic export board, CÓRAS TRÁCHTÁLA, which effectively promoted exports, especially to the United States. Distinctive Irish fabrics and trimmings were a direct source of inspiration to designers, who then encouraged the fabric industries to renew and refine the quality of their products until they could satisfy international standards. The third and vital factor was the creative and entrepreneurial skills of a new generation of Irish designers. Of these the person who did most to give Irish fashion an international profile was SYBIL CONNOLLY (1921–1998) (see p. 148). In the 1940s she worked at Richard Alan, the retail outlet of the coat and suit manufacturing firm of Jack Clarke (1908–1974), first as manager then as designer, and in 1952 she began a couture section, using her own name. Her first collection established the pattern of strongly tailored day wear of predominantly Irish tweeds and highly romantic evening wear, again often using Irish fabrics and embellishments. From 1953, when her trip to the United States with her collection generated a huge amount of interest, she enjoyed a strong international profile, thanks to her design and marketing skills, and in 1957 she set up her own fashion house in Merrion Square, Dublin. The fabrics she used appealed greatly to the American market, with its nostalgic love of things Irish. These included red flannel, specially commissioned wool and tweeds, dyed CROCHET and LACE, Dublin poplins, and her best-known material, her trademark pleated handkerchief LINEN.

Irene Gilbert (c. 1910–1985), a traditional couturière of impeccable standards, was an influential figure in Irish fashion from the late 1940s, when she opened her first shop, until her retirement in 1968. Her salon opened in 1950, and her collections attracted an enthusiastic clientele, which included Princess Grace of Monaco. She showed her collections in England and in the United States as well as in Dublin. Irish fabrics were a dominant feature in her designs, though she also worked with English, Continental and even some new synthetic fabrics. She worked closely with mills to produce richly coloured tweeds light enough for dress use, being particularly associated with Avoca Handweavers. Her tailoring ability was seen to best advantage in her day wear, but her evening wear, especially her hand-made lace dresses and her draped dresses, was also much admired.

Neilí Mulcahy (1925–) trained at the Grafton Academy of Dress Design, Dublin, the training-ground of many Irish designers, and in Paris with Jacques Heim (1899–1967), then set up her own couture house in 1952. She made effective use of Irish fabrics, such as wools, poplins, and linen, and used them as a selling point. The vibrant colour she often used was a strong feature of her work, as was, in the 1960s, printed woven or knitted wool.

In the 1960s Clodagh O'Kennedy was influential not only as a designer of garments, often of Irish inspiration or fabrics, but also as a journalist, boutique owner, and creator of innovative fashion shows. Mary O'Donnell, whose work often has reference to Ireland's literary and artistic heritage, trained in the United States with Mainbocher (1890–1976) before returning to Ireland, where she set up her own house in 1963.

One of the most successful exporters was Donald Davies, whose SHIRTS, in strong, rich colours, typically of fine 'Crock of Gold' wool, were international best-sellers; his shirt dress became a design classic.

Irish fashion designers who worked outside Ireland in the 1950s, mostly in London, included such well-known names as Digby Morton (1906–1983), John Cavanagh (1914–), and 'Michael' (Michael Donnelly, 1915–1985). In the 1960s international fashion became increasingly oriented towards youth, using cheap synthetic materials, which militated against the traditional strengths of Irish fashion. A new generation of designers appeared in the late 1960s and early 70s: Ib Jorgensen (1935–), whose impeccably finished garments often used Patricia Jorgensen's fabric designs; Pat Crowley (1933–), originally a knitwear designer, now probably best known for her grand evening dresses; Thomas Wolfangel (1935–), from Stuttgart, known for his day-wear tailoring; Richard Lewis (1945–), renowned for his mastery in working with jersey; and the knitwear designer Michelina Stacpoole (1942–), originally from Italy. Most of these designers owed less to Irish and more to international influences.

At the end of the 1970s international fashion's move back to natural fibres and towards a new high-fashion profile for knitwear was advantageous for Irish products. Two designers who were to win an international reputation for Irish fashion, this time primarily with ready-to-wear, started their businesses at this time. Paul Costelloe (1945–) had his breakthrough collection in 1984, when his use of Irish tweeds, knitwear and linen conformed perfectly to the contemporary taste for natural fabrics and finishes, and he remains one of the best-known Irish designers. His soft tailoring is now a distinctive feature. The Chinese-Portuguese designer John Rocha began his association with Ireland in the late 1970s. Inspired originally by Irish fabrics, his work, which has continued to evolve, is simple in shape, its dominant feature being the quality and treatment of the fabric. He was named British Designer of the Year in 1993 and a year later showed in Paris for the first time. Other strong designers in this period include Mariad Whisker (1954–), well known for her beautifully cut linen and viscose garments. Quin and Donnelly began to work together in 1979 and now design for the A-Wear chain; their designs often feature interesting fabric and texture mixes. Michael Mortell's designs were international and eclectic in inspiration, and in the 1980s he was one of the best-regarded designers in Ireland; he now concentrates on coat design.

Ireland's knitwear industry enjoys a strong, distinctive, and adaptable tradition, design talent, well-organised production (which takes advantage of both old and very new production skills), and good marketing. The continuous development by Lainey Keogh (1957–) of new stitches, shapes, and fabrics has kept her work featured in the world fashion press. Hers is probably the dominant international name in knitwear, though the work of many other knitwear designers has thriving home and export markets. In the 1990s a new group of designers emerged. Louise Kennedy (1960–) has built up a successful business in Ireland and Britain based on her unstructured, easy suits and separates; she has now opened a 'lifestyle' shop and showroom. Mary Gregory, whose work has a romantic feel, Marc O'Neill (1970–), whose sharp styling is urban and international, and Jen Kelly (1960–), whose designs keep the couture tradition alive, illustrate the various types of current Irish fashion. Miriam Mone (1965–) and Michelle O'Doherty both make tailored styles. Pat McCarthy and Cuan Hanley both design for men. Outside Ireland, particularly successful designers include Daryl Kerrigan's company in New York with its Daryl K label; Peter

O'Brien (1951–), house designer for 'Rochas' in Paris, who has just begun a couture line; and Sharon Wauchob (1971–), who also works in Paris, now with her own label. Lorcan Mullany (1953–) works in London; many other Irish designers work for their own or other labels in Britain, on the Continent and in the United States as well as in Ireland.

Probably the best-known Irish fashion designer is Philip Treacy (1967–) from Ahascragh, Co. Galway, now one of the most renowned milliners in the world. His imaginative creations, often using feathers in innovative ways, appear every season in the fashion press (see p. 369).

Ireland and its culture have a positive and distinctive international profile and have also given the world textiles such as tweeds, fine linen, ARAN KNITWEAR, lace, and crochet. These distinctive advantages have helped and in some instances directly inspired Irish designers and have played a part in Irish fashion's international success. The creative and business skills of the designers, however, are the vital factors that have given Irish fashion its creative and economic success in a competitive and demanding world market. [see CLOTHING, TRADITIONAL; CRAFTS AFTER 1945.] **Elizabeth McCrum**

Fastnet. *The Fastnet Rock and lighthouse, 7 km ($4\frac{1}{2}$ miles) off the south-west coast. The present 44.5 m (146-ft) lighthouse (1898) replaced a lighthouse of 1848. [Imagefile]*

Fastnet Rock (*Carraig Aonair*), a rock 7 km ($4\frac{1}{2}$ miles) off Cléire, Co. Cork, and Ireland's most southerly point. It first came to prominence for the Fastnet Rock Lighthouse (1854), designed by George Halpin and constructed of cast iron. Work began in 1848, with workers and materials being ferried by steamer. The first light, amounting to 38,000 cd, came in 1854 after a period of arduous construction that saw no fatalities. During the GREAT FAMINE and the subsequent period of high EMIGRATION to the New World the rock became known to those departing from Cobh as 'Ireland's Tear', as it was the last sight of Ireland that most would have. By 1865 the power of the Atlantic waves had removed part of the rock foundation on which the tower was built, and a new lighthouse was commissioned. The present light, designed by William Douglas, 44.5 m (146 ft) high, was begun in 1898 and began operation in 1906 with a lamp of 750,000 cd. The tower is constructed from 5-tonne blocks of Cornish granite and rises 60 m (200 ft) from its base. The light was automated in 1989 and produces 1,300,000 cd. Today the rock is also known as the turning-point in the FASTNET YACHT RACE, which came to the world's attention in 1979 when the flotilla sailed into a severe storm and seventeen competitors were drowned. **Colman Gallagher**

Fastnet Yacht Race, the finale of a week-long series of races in the Admiral's Cup competition, the most prestigious yacht series staged in English or Irish waters. The race, which has taken place every second August since 1957, is organised by the Royal Ocean Racing Club and the Royal Western Yacht Club of Plymouth. Beginning in Cowes, Isle of Wight, it takes a fleet of more than 200 yachts around FASTNET ROCK before returning to Cowes, a round trip of 990 km (615 miles).

The original Fastnet race, first held in 1925, was won by the 17 m (56-ft) former pilot boat *Jolie Brise* in a time of 6 days, 1 hour, and 45 minutes; the winner of the 2000 race, the 18 m (60-ft) trimaran *Eure et Loire*, completed the course in 1 day, 18 hours, and 19 minutes. One of the most dangerous and extreme tests of seamanship, the race saw the death of seventeen participants in 1979, when the fleet of 303 boats was caught in force 11 winds. In 1985 storms forced 100 yachts to retire. **Fiacc OBrolchain**

'Father O'Flynn', a popular song written by A. P. GRAVES, first published in the *Spectator* in 1874 and set to the air of the Kerry jig 'The Top of the Road'. The song refers to a Father Michael Walsh from Buttevant, Co. Cork, parish priest of Sneem for almost four decades and a collector of traditional music. **Maeve Ellen Gebruers**

Faughart, Battle of (14 October 1318). Edward Bruce, self-proclaimed King of Ireland, was defeated and killed on the hill of Faughart, outside Dundalk, marking the end of the BRUCE INVASION of Ireland. The imposing force under the command of John de Bermingham and the Archbishop of Armagh was mainly composed of the gentry of Cos. Louth and Meath. Deciding against waiting for the arrival of the reinforcements promised by his brother ROBERT BRUCE, Edward Bruce marched his army of 3,000 Scots and Irish allies against the much greater ANGLO-NORMAN force. Two-thirds of the Scottish army fell in the battle. Bruce was killed by John Maupas, a burgess of Drogheda, whose body was found on Bruce's after the fight. His head was delivered by de Bermingham to Edward II, who rewarded him with a grant of the new Earldom of Louth for competently disposing of the greatest threat faced by the English lordship in medieval Ireland. **Susan Foran**

Faul, Denis (1932–), priest and CIVIL RIGHTS campaigner. Born in Co. Louth. For several years he was president of St Patrick's Academy, Dungannon, but he is better known for his opposition to political violence in Northern Ireland and for his criticism of the North's judicial system and the actions of the police and British army. He was Catholic chaplain in the Maze prison during the HUNGER STRIKES of 1980–81 (which he strongly opposed). In the late 1990s his support for the reformed police service earned him the enmity of republicans, some of whom campaigned unsuccessfully to have him removed as parish priest of Carrickmore, Co. Tyrone. **Brian Galvin**

Faulkner, Brian (1921–1977), politician. Born in Co. Down, the son of a shirt manufacturer; educated at St Columba's College in Dublin. He was elected to the Northern Ireland Parliament for East Down in 1949; he first achieved prominence by leading controversial Orange marches in south Co. Down. Always an exceptionally able speaker and a fluent broadcaster, he was appointed Chief Whip in 1956 and Minister of Home Affairs in 1959, and it was he who had responsibility for dealing with the IRA border campaign (1956–62). As Minister of Commerce in TERENCE O'NEILL's Government formed in 1963 he directed the largely successful drive to attract transnational firms to set up in Northern Ireland. Despite protestations to the contrary made in later life, he doggedly opposed O'Neill's programme of reforms, as the Cabinet records of 1968 and 1969 show. He resigned in January 1969 in protest at the setting up of the CAMERON COMMISSION. Appointed Minister of Development in April 1969, he oversaw reforms in LOCAL GOVERNMENT and HOUSING. He became Prime Minister in 1971 and the same year introduced INTERNMENT, which was followed by an intensification of violence. He joined in the massive protest against DIRECT RULE at Stormont; nevertheless he helped to formulate the SUNNINGDALE AGREEMENT, and he became Chief Executive in the power-sharing Executive. After the collapse of the Executive and hostile votes in the ULSTER UNIONIST PARTY he formed his own Unionist Party of Northern Ireland, but it fared badly, and he retired from politics in 1976. He was killed in a hunting accident in February 1977. **Jonathan Bardon**

Faulkner, George (c. 1699–1775), printer and bookseller. Born in Dublin; apprenticed to a printer. He emigrated to London to follow his trade before returning in 1724 to open his own printing, PUBLISHING and bookselling business, in which he was for some time in partnership with a Catholic printer, James Hoey. In 1729 they were operating from 'The Pamphlet Shop' in Skinners' Row (now Christ Church Place). When the partnership dissolved, his new premises in Essex Street became a focus of Dublin literary life. He acquired the title of two newspapers, the *Dublin Post Boy* and *Dublin Journal*, the latter earning him both fame and fortune, as did his many reprints of books published in London. He was the first to issue a collected edition of the works of JONATHAN SWIFT (1735), who dubbed him the 'prince of Dublin printers'. On a visit to England he lost a leg in equivocal circumstances; Dublin wits thereafter nicknamed him 'oaken-footed Elzevir', with reference to his preferred typeface. A confidant of Lord Chesterfield, he refused the offer of a knighthood. **Bernard Share**

fauna. The first list of the animal species of Ireland was compiled by AUGUSTINE ERIUGENA in the seventh century, the next by GIRALDUS CAMBRENSIS in the thirteenth century (see p. 368). Both are of particular interest, because the authors were aware of the problem of explaining how land animals could have reached Ireland. The greater part of the Irish fauna was brought to extinction during the last Ice Age; many of the land and freshwater animals, however, recolonised Ireland before its connection with the Continent was finally severed as the ice receded and sea level rose. In the nineteenth century, WILLIAM THOMPSON published his *Natural History of Ireland*, which remains the most comprehensive work on the fauna.

Its position at the extreme edge of the Eurasian landmass, in addition to its island status, explains why Ireland has far fewer species of animals than neighbouring countries. There are overall sixty-five species of MAMMALS, reptiles, amphibians and freshwater fish, whereas Britain has 123 and the European Continent has 512.

The native land mammals are very few and include red deer, HARE, fox, badger, pine-marten, STOAT, and pygmy shrew. Some species, such as wild boar, bear, reindeer, and IRISH ELK, are extinct. Others, including rabbit, bank vole, rats, and house mouse, have been introduced by humans in historical times. The origins of a few, such as red squirrel and field mouse, are uncertain. Ireland has two species of amphibians and one land reptile: natterjack toad, frog, and viviparous lizard. The frog was a seventeenth-century introduction; the other two may be natives. The only native freshwater fishes are those that can survive in salt water, such as salmon, trout, char, and pollan. The others—including pike, perch, bream, rudd, and roach—have been introduced since the sixteenth century.

The situation with regard to birds and marine mammals, reptiles and fishes is very different. As an oceanic island, close to the Continent, Ireland has a rich variety of all these forms. Both oceanic and Continental species are present. Migratory birds and fishes add greatly to the numbers of resident species.

The invertebrates, insects, shellfish, spiders, worms, and many others are much more numerous, both in species and individuals, than are the vertebrates. However, the same pattern of a smaller number of species than in neighbouring countries is apparent. **Christopher Moriarty**

Fay, Frank (1871–1931), actor and critic. Born in Dublin. With his brother W. G. Fay (1872–1947) he was a founder of the incipient ABBEY THEATRE in the 1890s but in 1908 broke with the directors and worked in the United States and England. His criticism, collected by ROBERT HOGAN as *Towards a National Theatre* (1970), was seminal in establishing a sense of identity and purpose for the fledgling Irish dramatic movement. **Richard Pine**

fear dána ('man of art or skill'), a stereotyped term associated with the art of poetry, especially of the learned register of syllabic poetry, so that *fear dána* came to denote a poet. The plural, *fir dhána* or AES DÁNA, referred to 'poets' or 'artists'. [see AOSDÁNA.] **Michelle O Riordan**

Feast of Dun na Géd: see FLED DÚIN NA NGÉD.

Fegen, Edward Stephen (Fogarty) (1891–1940), merchant marine officer. Born in Ballinlonty, Co. Tipperary, the son and grandson of officers in the British navy. He was in the *Amphian* when it was sunk by a mine on the second day of the FIRST WORLD WAR but survived and rose steadily through the ranks. On the outbreak of the SECOND WORLD WAR he was made captain of the liner *Jervis Bay*, which was turned into an auxiliary cruiser with seven rather aged 6-in. guns. In November 1940 he was in charge of an important convoy of thirty-seven merchant ships nearing Britain from Canada in nine columns. A ship was seen to the north, which turned out to be the German pocket-battleship *Admiral Scheer*, with six 11-in. and eight 5.9-in. guns. He ordered the convoy to disperse and head individually for Britain, and ordered his warship to steam full speed ahead for the German battleship, with all guns firing. The result was inevitable, and the *Jervis Bay* was sunk after a fight of two-and-a-half hours. Meanwhile all but five ships of the thirty-seven in the convoy were able to get safely away, while the German battleship was kept in action by Fegen, who lost his life along with 189 of his crew of 254. **John de Courcy Ireland**

Feiritéir, Piaras (died 1652), poet. Of Norman aristocratic stock, he was imprisoned for his part in the 1641 REBELLION and hanged in Killarney in 1652. He was described in a contemporary document as an eminent poet in both Irish and English, but none of his English works has survived. Most of his Irish poems are in the late courtly love tradition, similar to those composed by the Cavalier poets. He also composed a number of remarkable poems on male friendship, which convey a strong sense of emotion and show a keen awareness of the Renaissance concept of the dignity of the human person (see p. 270). **Mícheál Mac Craith**

feis, literally meaning 'assembly', now generally refers to any of the competitive MUSIC and DANCING events inspired by the first FEIS CEOIL (1897). The first dancing feis was held at Macroom, Co. Cork, in 1899. Non-dance feiseanna, now rare, were usually organised by Conradh na Gaeilge, the GAELIC LEAGUE, branches as a basis for promoting Irish culture and could include music, song in Irish and English, elocution, and instrumental music. Dance feiseanna remain popular, organised nationally and internationally by the Irish Dancing Commission and An Cumann Rince Náisiúnta. [see FLEADH CHEOIL.] **Fintan Vallely**

Feis Ceoil, an association founded in Dublin in 1894-6 'to promote the general cultivation of music in Ireland, with particular reference to Irish music.' First competitions, totalling thirty-two, took place over one week in Dublin in 1897 and included choral, solo and composition sections. Apart from 1898 and 1900, when the festival's competitions were held in Belfast, the Feis has been held at various venues in Dublin. Since 1983 the RDS grounds in Ballsbridge have been the principal venue for the competitions, which now take place over a two-week period during March, featuring approximately 168 sections. [see MARTYN, EDWARD.] **Paul Collins**

feminism. Feminism in Ireland has had a long and complex history, and the struggle for women's EQUALITY has gone through many different stages. The first wave of the WOMEN'S MOVEMENT, originating in the second half of the nineteenth century and lasting until 1921, was dominated by the question of suffrage and links with the national independence movement. The legislation of 1922 giving women the vote, following the creation of the Irish Free State, has been described as the last progressive law concerning women to be passed until a new generation of Irish feminists began to emerge fifty years later.

During the years 1922–70 the collective voice of the women's movement in the Free State and Republic was publicly silent. It would occasionally revive, as with the laundry workers' strike organised by the IRISH WOMEN WORKERS' UNION; but for most of the time it remained deeply buried. Those women's organisations active during this period, such as the IRISH COUNTRYWOMEN'S ASSOCIATION and IRISH HOUSEWIVES' ASSOCIATION, sought to develop women's role within the FAMILY in order to influence society as a whole. They took on a campaigning role at times, the IHA, for example, actively supporting the proposed MOTHER AND CHILD SCHEME in 1951. However, the accepted social function of women remained firmly within the home, expressed through the teaching of the Catholic Church and the LAW, most notably through the CONSTITUTION OF IRELAND (1937). Article 41.2 of the Constitution recognises woman's 'life within the home' and requires the state to endeavour to ensure that mothers will not be obliged by economic necessity to engage in labour 'to the neglect of their duties in the home.'

Change began to occur with a second-wave feminist movement emerging in the 1970s and 80s. Ailbhe Smyth has documented the movement's four phases between 1970 and 1990. Firstly, there was a growing mobilisation and politicisation between 1970 and 1974, with the founding of the Irish Women's Liberation Movement

feminism. *Members of the Anti Amendment Campaign march in Dublin on 13 November 1982 in support of a no vote in the first Abortion referendum which if passed would have seen an amendment to the constitution keeping abortion illegal. Among those marching are Mary Holland [2nd from left] with Ann Marie Hourihan and Evelyn Conlon [centre] and Inez McCormick [far right]. [Derek Speirs/Report]* in 1970, the 'contraceptive train' event in 1971, the establishment of the Council for the Status of Women in 1972, and the passing of the Anti-Discrimination (Pay) Act (1974). Ireland's membership of the EEC in 1972 may also be seen as a significant catalyst for change, obliging the state to enact EMPLOYMENT equality and maternity protection legislation.

The years 1974–7 were a period of high energy and radical action, with the emergence of the radical feminist organisation Irish Women United in 1975 and the passing of the Employment Equality Act (1977). The movement was consolidated between 1977 and 1983 with the call for legal ABORTION by the Women's Right to Choose Campaign in 1979 and the establishment of the RAPE CRISIS CENTRES and such groups as WOMEN'S AID to support women suffering violence in the home. The academic discipline of women's studies began to develop, and women became more sexually liberated, with a distinctive lesbian voice emerging within Irish feminism during the 1970s.

The years 1983–90, however, saw a succession of political defeats and personal tragedies. A defeat with significant lasting effect was the passing of the Eighth Amendment to the Constitution in 1983, giving the foetus an equal right to life with the pregnant woman. This provision was used for many years by anti-abortion campaigners in taking legal action against those women's clinics and students' unions that were providing information on how to obtain abortion in England, in effect silencing many organisations.

Other setbacks included the defeat of the DIVORCE REFERENDUM in 1986 and the Eileen Flynn case, in which a teacher was dismissed from her job in a convent school after becoming pregnant. Most tragically, there were the deaths of ANNE LOVETT, dying in childbirth at a grotto in Granard, Co. Longford, and of Sheila Hodgers, a pregnant woman denied certain medical treatment, who died in hospital in Drogheda in 1983.

These were often bleak years for feminism; but change was to come. A political turning point in 1990 was the election of MARY ROBINSON as President of Ireland after a lively political campaign. In 1992 the SUPREME COURT ruled in the 'X' CASE that where a woman's life is threatened by the continuance of her pregnancy she is entitled to have the pregnancy terminated. Following this decision, in November 1992 referendums guaranteeing the freedom to obtain information on abortion and the right to travel abroad for abortion were passed. In the same month a record number of women were elected to Dáil Éireann, and the new Government established for the first time a Department of Equality and Law Reform.

In 1995 a referendum to permit divorce was finally passed, enabling no-fault DIVORCE legislation to be enacted. Other progressive legislation passed in the 1990s included laws liberalising the sale of contraceptives and the Employment Equality Act (1998), which provides greater protection against discrimination on grounds of sex as well as a range of other grounds. This was followed by the Equal Status Act (2000), prohibiting sexual and other forms of discrimination in the provision of goods and services. In 2002 a referendum that would have restricted the application of the judgment in the 'X' case by ruling out the risk of suicide as grounds for abortion was defeated. There was a successful opposition campaign by a combination of pro-choice groups under the Alliance for a No Vote, together with other organisations, including the Irish FAMILY PLANNING Association.

The years since 1990 can be seen as a fifth stage in the development of feminism, with a great move forward in the liberation of women economically, socially, and sexually and the mainstreaming of the concept of equality through legislative and policy developments. Feminism has made many advances in a very short time. Ireland has had two women presidents; two out of eight Supreme Court judges are women. But mainstreaming has not achieved substantive change for the majority of women, who remain infinitely less powerful than men, economically, politically, and socially. The largest proportion of low-paid workers are women, and there are continuing problems with OCCUPATIONAL SEGREGATION. The victims of domestic violence are overwhelmingly female; after nearly thirty years of equal pay legislation a huge pay differential remains; and proper child care remains unaffordable for most, and abortion unavailable. **Ivana Bacik**

Fenian invasions of Canada. The Fenian Brotherhood was founded in New York in 1858 by JOHN O'MAHONY, a veteran of the RISING OF 1848, as a sister organisation of the IRISH REVOLUTIONARY BROTHERHOOD, organised in Dublin by JAMES STEPHENS in the same year. Its aim was to rid Ireland of English rule by providing American money and manpower to encourage insurrection. By 1865 it had attracted at least 50,000 followers, many of them Civil War veterans (from both the Union and the Confederate sides). An Irish Republican government in exile, based on the American model of executive and legislature, was set up at Philadelphia. While Fenianism in both America and Ireland had as its primary goal the fomenting of rebellion in Ireland, an American faction led by William V. Roberts, an Irish-born merchant in New York, favoured an indirect method for achieving this aim. A Fenian invasion of Canada, they believed, might provoke an Anglo-American conflict, perhaps even a war, allowing Ireland to strike for its independence as Britain's attention was deflected elsewhere.

Thus began one of the more outlandish episodes not only in Irish nationalist and Irish-American history but in American history as a whole. On 12 April 1866 the Fenians attempted to seize the Canadian island of Campobello in the Bay of Fundy, only to be thwarted by the British and American navies at Eastport, Maine. The US navy intercepted a shipment of arms, and American soldiers under Major-General George Meade forced the Fenians gathered at Eastport to disperse. Then, on 1 June, a force of 600 Fenians, led by Colonel John O'Neill, entered Canada by land, defeating a Canadian militia company before retreating to Buffalo.

In the meantime James Stephens had arrived in New York on 10 May 1866, fleeing from the threat of arrest in Ireland. Denouncing the attacks on Canada, he ousted O'Mahony from the leadership of the movement and reasserted the goal of insurrection on Irish soil alone. A final foray into Canada on 25 May 1870, led once again by O'Neill, was easily repelled. Fenianism collapsed in both Ireland and America, to be replaced in the United States by the sterner and more secretive CLAN NA GAEL, under the leadership of the redoubtable JOHN DEVOY. Partly as a result of the Fenians' efforts, Irish NATIONALISM had taken on an irrevocable American dimension. **Kevin Kenny**

Fenian movement, the most important Irish revolutionary organisation of the nineteenth century. Fenianism grew out of the failed attempts of the YOUNG IRELAND 1848 RISING. The Fenians were founded simultaneously in Ireland and the United States, by JAMES STEPHENS and JOHN O'MAHONY, in March 1858. Strictly speaking, the name Fenian belonged to the American branch of the movement but it quickly became the indispensable term for the organisation in both countries. It attracted to its ranks such diverse individuals as Michael Doheny, John Deniffe, JOHN O'LEARY (see p. 1159), and JEREMIAH O'DONOVAN ROSSA. Its first successful operation was the orchestration, under its cover organisation, the National Brotherhood of St Patrick, of the funeral in Dublin in November 1861 of TERENCE BELLEW MACMANUS, one of the minor figures of the Young Ireland rising. Propagating its views through its newspaper, the *Irish People* (which was suppressed in 1865), the movement caught the imagination of revolutionaries and romantics alike in Ireland, Britain, and North America in the 1860s and 70s. Following the failure of the 1867 RISING, the movement by the 1880s was split between those who argued for a constitutional approach to Irish political reforms and those who maintained that violent revolution was the only means of gaining independence. Sporadic acts of violence in the 1880s helped to underline the feelings of hopelessness and alienation of the movement's more ardent members. The legacy left by Fenianism was long to influence militant nationalist thinking, as exemplified by PEARSE's oration at the funeral of O'Donovan Rossa at Glasnevin, Dublin, in 1915. [see IRISH REPUBLICAN BROTHERHOOD.] **Oliver P. Rafferty**

Ferdomnach, described by the ANNALS on his death in 846 as a scholar and scribe. He was one of the finest scribes in the long history of the Irish minuscule or pointed script and an elegant draughtsman; he is responsible for the illuminated copy of the GOSPELS in the Book of ARMAGH, written for Abbot Torbach (807–8). **William O'Sullivan**

Ferguson, Godfrey (c. 1855–1939), architect. Apprenticed to CHARLES LANYON, he subsequently worked for seven years on the London board schools, whose Queen Anne style, promoted by his first employers, Stevenson and Robson, was extremely influential. By 1882 he was back in private practice in Belfast. Before 1914 his work was mostly commercial, including more than twenty branches of the Northern Bank in a variety of styles; one of the earliest and best was that in Dunglow, Co. Donegal, in the art nouveau style (1896, demolished). After 1920 his work was mostly domestic, including groups of houses and individual villas around Belfast. Dublin University Boat Club at Islandbridge, Dublin (1897), is also his. He was High Sheriff for Co. Antrim in 1935. **Frederick O'Dwyer**

Ferguson, Henry (Harry) (1884–1960), mechanic and inventor. Born in Growell, Co. Down; educated locally. In 1909 he built his first aeroplane, achieving a flight of 1.6 km (1 mile) at Magilligan Strand, LOUGH FOYLE, the following June. Turning to improvements in agricultural machinery, he designed a lightweight plough, 1917, and developed the prototype of the Ferguson tractor. With a wide range of attachments, it was introduced in 1936 as the Brown-Ferguson and in 1939, under an agreement with Henry Ford, was marketed internationally as the Fordson tractor. In 1947, when Ford's grandson refused to honour the agreement, Ferguson opened his own factory in Detroit. **Bernard Share**

Ferguson, Sir Samuel (1810–1886), poet. Born in Belfast; educated at the RBAI and TCD. During the 1830s he contributed poems and articles to leading periodicals. Called to the bar in 1838, he practised law until 1867, when he became Deputy Keeper of the Public Records. He was active in the ROYAL IRISH ACADEMY, principally as an antiquarian. In later life he produced a series of verse narratives drawing on Irish history and legend; this made little impact during his own life but assumed significance retrospectively as a precedent for YEATS. **Peter Denman**

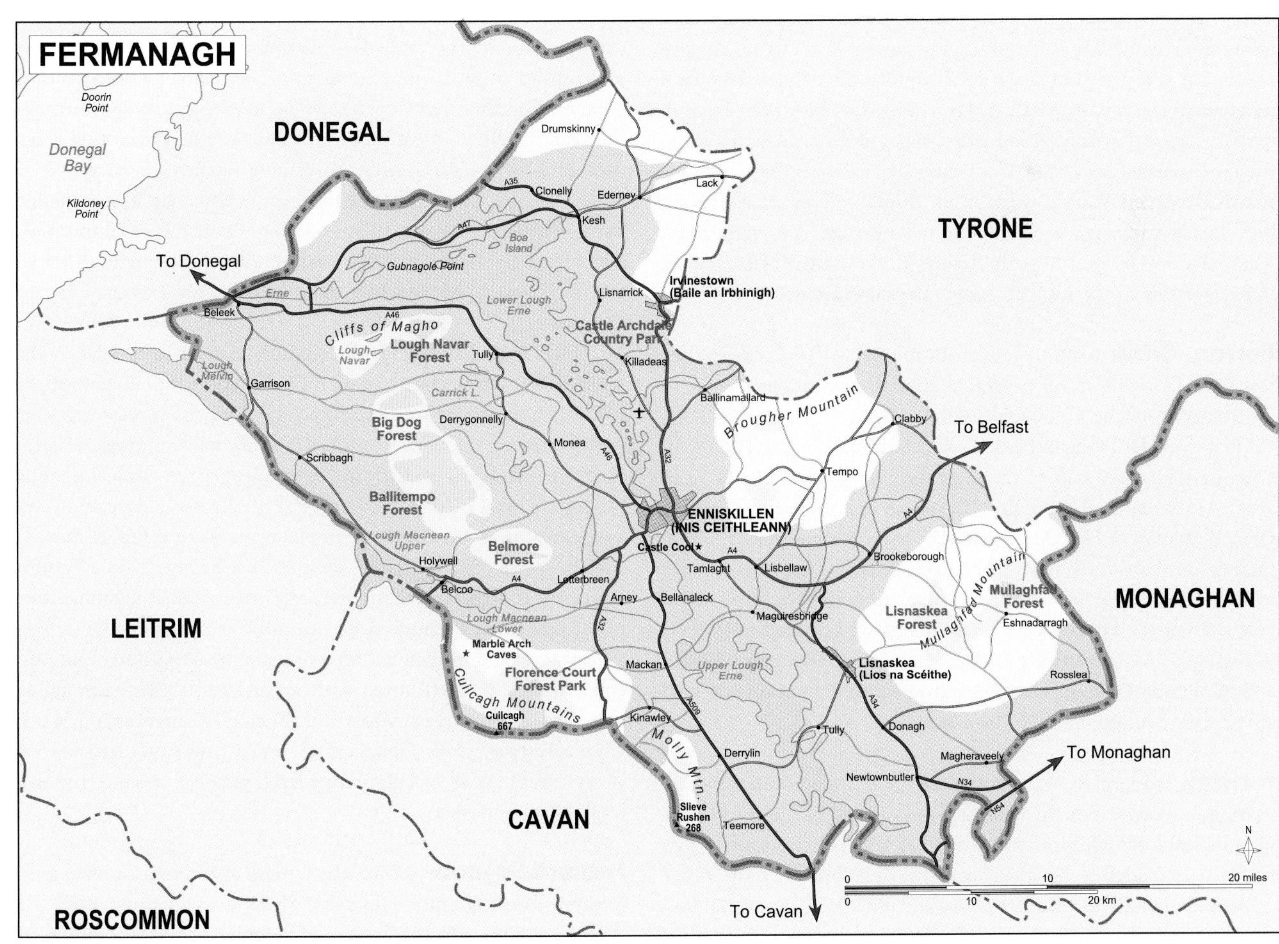

Fermanagh, County (*Contae Fhear Manach*)

Province:	ULSTER
County town:	ENNISKILLEN
Area:	1,852 km^2 (648 sq. miles)
Population (1991)*:	52,000
Features:	Cuilcagh Mountains
	LOUGH ERNE
	River Erne
Of historical interest:	DEVENISH
	Enniskillen Castle
	Tully plantation castle
Industry and products:	CLOTHING
	Fishing
	Livestock
	Porcelain
	Tweed

Petula Martyn

* last year of census by county, [see NORTHERN IRELAND.]

County Fermanagh comprises virtually all of the Erne catchment basin, including Upper and Lower Lough Erne, together with the spectacular limestone tableland of Mount Belmore of 366 m (1,200 ft) along the Cavan-Leitrim border to the south and the lower old red sandstone plateau extending into Co. Tyrone to the north-east. Historically part of the kingdom of the Maguires between the thirteenth and fifteenth centuries, Co. Fermanagh was planted by English Anglicans rather than Scots Presbyterians during the early seventeenth century. Notoriously waterlogged and prone to FLOODING before the construction of modern drainage schemes, the Erne lowlands traditionally supported pastoral beef and dairy farming. The county suffered badly during the GREAT FAMINE (1845–50) and shared in the general population decline of the later nineteenth century. In 1921 it was included in Northern Ireland, despite opposition from local nationalists. Both then and during the more recent 'TROUBLES' Co. Fermanagh experienced significant sectarian violence and population displacement, exacerbating the already extensive problems created by rural deprivation and depopulation. In recent years 'lakeland' TOURISM has played an important role in the local economy. **Lindsay Proudfoot**

Ferran, Brian (1940–), painter. Born in Derry; trained as an art teacher at St Joseph's College of Education, Belfast, and graduated in art history from the Courtauld Institute, London. His OIREACHTAS exhibit won the Douglas Hyde Gold Medal in 1965 and 1978. In 1966 he joined the staff of the ACNI, retiring as chief executive in 2000. He won the Leverhulme European Scholarship in 1969 to Brera Academy of Fine Art, Milan, 1970–71. His enduring painting themes are the carved heads in Fermanagh Basin, the stone figures on BOA ISLAND. He participated in nine exhibitions in the United States, 1975–83. His work includes STAINED-GLASS windows (1989) in the chapel of St Patrick's College, Maghera, and a mural (1990) at St Columb's College, Derry. A retrospective exhibition was held at the RHA, Dublin, in 1996. **Theo Snoddy**

fertility, as a term in DEMOGRAPHY refers to levels of reproduction in the population. For the century from c. 1880 to 1980 Irish fertility patterns differed from those in other Western countries in that family sizes tended to be larger than elsewhere but the proportions of the population who did not marry and did not have any children also tended to be larger. In consequence, marital fertility was for long unusually high, but overall fertility (the birth rate averaged over the whole adult female population) was usually much less so. In the early 1960s approximately a third of births were to mothers who already had four or more children. From the late 1960s to the early 1980s, though average family size declined steadily, Ireland experienced a surge in fertility (a 'baby boom'), arising from a large increase in the number of marriages. Fertility declined sharply in the 1980s as the number of marriages decreased and the average family size also continued to decline. In 1989 the total fertility rate (a measure of the number of children women on average are likely to have) fell for the first time below replacement level (conventionally defined as 210 children per 100 women). A small recovery in fertility occurred in the mid-1990s, and the rate has since stabilised at just below replacement level. At this level Irish fertility is considerably higher than the average for Europe and slightly below that of the United States. **Tony Fahey**

festivals. Festivals have always been part of the Irish way of life. Puck Fair in Killorglin, Co. Kerry, and the old LAMMAS FAIR in Ballycastle, Co. Antrim, have their origins in antiquity. ST PATRICK'S DAY is celebrated throughout the world; in the 1990s the Dublin event was reinvented as a four-day St Patrick's Festival, to include fireworks, concerts, and street theatre. The modern tradition of a festival as an inclusive event with a party-like atmosphere, characterised by free entertainment (usually provided by a corporate sponsor—often a brewery) and in which visitors and local people mingle in the streets and bars, can be traced to the spring festival of AN TÓSTAL in the 1950s, designed to bring some cheer to a population demoralised by economic stagnation.

Modern festivals are often held at dates that extend the tourist season and in towns that tourists might otherwise bypass. Festivals can be placed in two categories: those primarily designed to attract visitors and show them a good time, and those with a cultural content. Together they offer a calendar of events spread throughout the year. The Rose of TRALEE Festival in August is one of the most successful in the first category. Young women from the Irish DIASPORA compete for the title in a personality contest, surrounded by much merrymaking. The GALWAY Oyster Festival in mid-September, the Roaring 1920s Festival in KILLARNEY in mid-March and the BANTRY Mussel Fair in May are other examples in this category.

The most famous Irish cultural festival is probably the WEXFORD FESTIVAL OPERA, which celebrated its fiftieth anniversary in 2001. Every year three lesser-known operas are given a full-scale professional production, to packed houses, while a programme of fringe events ensures that the townspeople are included. The BELFAST Festival held in November is the largest and most diverse arts festival in Ireland with an emphasis on classical music, theatre, and the visual arts, while the West Cork Chamber Music Festival in Bantry is a classical music event of international standing. The CORK Jazz Festival brings more than 40,000 visitors to the city on the last weekend in October for a programme of both free and paid concerts (see p. 564). Both Galway and KILKENNY have highly successful Arts Festivals, while the DUBLIN Theatre Festival, Cork Choral Festival, Cork Film Festival, and WATERFORD FESTIVAL OF LIGHT OPERA are all successful on a local, national, and international level. **Alannah Hopkin**

Fethard Boycott (1957). The boycott at Fethard, Co. Wexford, can be traced to the refusal by Sheila Cloney (née Kelly), a Protestant, wife of Seán Cloney of Dungulph Castle, a Catholic, to

Fethard Boycott. *The Cloney family, focus of the Fethard Boycott—(left to right) Seán, Eileen, Sheila, and Mary—on their return from Scotland in 1958. [Private collection]*

send their daughters to the local Catholic school and the persistent pressures she faced from the Catholic curate, William Stafford. She left home on 27 April 1957, taking her daughters with her to Northern Ireland and then Scotland. From 13 May local Catholics refused to buy in Protestant-owned shops, the Protestant music-teacher lost all but one of her twelve pupils, the Catholic teacher withdrew from the CHURCH OF IRELAND school, and the Catholic bell-ringer and cleaner gave up her job at the Church of Ireland church. The boycott was supported by Bishop Michael Browne and other members of the Catholic hierarchy. It was condemned by the Taoiseach, ÉAMON DE VALERA, in Dáil Éireann on 4 July as 'ill-conceived, ill-considered and futile.' It was also the subject of debate at STORMONT. De Valera urged the hierarchy to use their influence to end the boycott. A truce was called in August, and the boycott ended with the parish priest buying cigarettes in a Protestant-owned shop. Sheila Cloney returned home briefly on New Year's Eve, 1957, and permanently the following April. The family continued to live in the Fethard area, educating their three daughters at home. Despite paralysing injuries in a car accident in 1995, Seán Cloney was an inspiring influence on the REBELLION OF 1798 commemorations in 1998, during which Bishop Brendan Comiskey apologised publicly for the hurt caused by the Catholic Church during the episode. The boycott inspired the film *A Love Divided* (1999); Seán Cloney died later that year, on 19 October 1999. **Patrick Comerford**

Fethard Observatory (1908–18), established at the rectory in Fethard, Co. Wexford, by REV. W. F. A. ELLISON. He installed an 470 mm (18.5-in.) equatorial reflector by George Calver within a dome of his own making. This instrument had a 610 mm (24-in.) diameter declination circle, (read using vernier scale to a precision of ten seconds), and an 457 mm (18-in.) hour circle. The driving clock for its polar axis could be set for solar, lunar or sidereal time. When Ellison was appointed director of ARMAGH OBSERVATORY in 1918 he transported the telescope there and employed it for marking planetary observations, and also for observing eclipses. **Susan McKenna-Lawlor**

feudalism, a term applied to the political, economic, and social organisation of society that defined the relationship of lord to vassal in north-western Europe during the Middle Ages. This relationship was made recognisable through specific institutions, such as primogeniture, CASTLES, knighthood, and chivalry. Obligations of homage, fealty, and protection were made between lord and vassal; a vassal could hold his fief from his lord for payment or for military service.

Not coined until the nineteenth century, the term 'feudalism' covers a series of wide-ranging characteristics labelled by successive generations of historians with conflicting perceptions of the past. It is often confused with the manorial or seigniorial system of relations between vassals and sub-vassals and their tenants. It is an established (but highly contested) view that the Anglo-Normans brought feudalism to England and in turn transferred the institution to Ireland, thus defining feudalism as a set of innovations peculiar to post-Norman society.

By the early twelfth century, Irish society was exhibiting features in its social relations and land tenure that resembled the 'feudal' system on a small and localised scale. With the conquest of Ireland by ANGLO-NORMAN adventurers in the late twelfth century, Ireland was brought more into line with the European order of society and its associated Anglo-Norman concept of feudalism. Lands were divided into *manors* and ultimately held of the Lord of Ireland through the process of sub-infeudation. *Scutage*, a money payment commonly accepted in place of military service, and the associated idea that a knight's *fief* or fee should be a certain size and value were readily applied to Irish society, with varying degrees of success. The feudal system consolidated the power of the barons on their estates, but the native Irish were for the most part excluded from this set of tenurial relations and continued to use their own dynastic system of succession. **Susan Foran**

Fiacail Phádraig ('St Patrick's Tooth'), a purse-shaped shrine (and a lost relic) associated with the west of Ireland, now in the NATIONAL MUSEUM, Dublin. The wooden core bears a bronze cross in a distinctive Connacht style of the twelfth century. Additions were commissioned, according to a Latin inscription, by Thomas de Bermingham (died 1376), Lord of Athenry. **Cormac Bourke**

Fiacc, Padraic (1924–), poet. Born Patrick Joseph O'Connor in Belfast; he spent his formative years in New York, returning to Belfast in 1946. He is the last poet of the 'CELTIC TWILIGHT', reflecting the conservative influence of his early mentors, PADRAIC COLUM and MICHAEL MCLAVERTY. He is best known for his raw and powerful response to the sectarian violence of the Northern 'TROUBLES'. His deceptively traditional first collection was *By the Black Stream* (1969). He suppressed the modernist urban idiom of much of his work until the controversial *Odour of Blood* (1973). He received the Æ Memorial Award, 1957, and Poetry Ireland Award, 1981, and was elected to AOSDÁNA in 1981. **Aodán Mac Póilin**

Fiachra/Fiacre (c. 590–670), herbalist and patron SAINT of gardeners, taxi-drivers, and sufferers from sexually transmitted diseases; known in France as *Fiacre*. He was a hermit by disposition and a skilled horticulturist; his reputation as a herbalist brought people to his hermitage now represented by a twelfth-century church at Ullard, near Graiguenamanagh, Co. Kilkenny. In sailing to France in 626 he sought the solitude to devote himself to God, unknown to the world. He settled at Meaux, near Paris, on the old Gallo-Roman route south. His fame, however, was quickly re-established as a result of his generosity and his supposed ability to cure a wide range of diseases. In the seventeenth century the Bishop of Meaux granted indulgences to pilgrims visiting his shrine. An enterprising innkeeper in Paris organised a cab service to Meaux and renamed his inn the Hôtel Saint-Fiacre; carriages thus came to be called *fiacres*, which remains a French name for taxi-cabs. His feast day is 1 September. **John Joe Costin**

Fianna Éireann, a Nationalist 'boy scout' movement formed in 1909 by Bulmer Hobson and CONSTANCE MARKIEVICZ. Members received arms training, participated in the HOWTH GUN-RUNNING, and played an important role in the 1916 Rising. The Belfast branch, prior to 1916, admitted female members. Fianna membership evolved into a conduit for the IRA. **Margaret Ward**

Fianna Fáil (FF), the largest political party in the Republic. The ANGLO-IRISH TREATY (1921) divided SINN FÉIN, the party that led the struggle for independence. At the general election of 1922 opponents of the Treaty won only thirty-six out of 128 seats. Twelve days after the election CIVIL WAR broke out between the opposing sides; it ended in May 1923 when the anti-Treaty forces laid down their arms but refused to accept the legitimacy of the Government or the state. The anti-Treatyites—reorganised by ÉAMON DE VALERA to fight the election as Sinn Féin—won 27 per cent of the vote and forty-four seats at the subsequent general election. Their electoral programme consisted of an outright refusal to sit in Dáil Éireann or to accept the Free State. In 1926 de Valera, SEÁN LEMASS and others who had taken the anti-Treaty side in the Civil War founded Fianna Fáil as a constitutional Republican party.

Fianna Fáil has approximately 2,500 *cumainn* or branches. The party's average first-preference vote at all elections is 43 per cent, and it has been in government for most of the state's existence. On first taking office in 1932 Fianna Fáil tried to sever all constitutional links between the state and Britain. It also established a broad social and economic appeal. The development of Fianna Fáil into a catch-all party made the formation of alternative governments exceedingly difficult, and it was not until 1948 that a coalition opposed to Fianna Fáil became practicable.

Fianna Fáil's predominance owes much to its record of advancing the economic prosperity of the Republic. It did this from 1932 to 1948 with its policy of economic self-sufficiency. Changing direction, the Fianna Fáil Government of 1957 developed a new economic strategy, based on INDUSTRIALISATION by foreign direct investment; the economic prosperity that resulted enabled it to win a further three general elections. The election of 1973 ended Fianna Fáil's second run of sixteen years in office. In 1989, though it retained its share of the vote, it was forced into a coalition for the first time, having been denied a clear majority. Today coalition governments are the norm, and Fianna Fáil has shared power with both the LABOUR PARTY and the PROGRESSIVE DEMOCRATS. In 1997 it gained 39.3 per cent of the votes and elected seventy-seven members of DÁIL ÉIREANN; in the 1999 local elections its support was 38.9 per cent; and in the 1999 election for the European Parliament it won 37.4 per cent of the vote and six seats. **Neil Collins**

Fiannaíocht: see FIONN CYCLE.

Fiche Bliain ag Fás (Twenty Years a-Growing) (1933), a memoir of a Blasket Islands childhood by MUIRIS Ó SÚILEABHÁIN (see p. 847). Inspired by TOMÁS Ó CRIOMHTHAINN's autobiographical AN TOILEÁNACH, and written with the assistance of the classical scholar George Thomson, it is widely acclaimed as a classic in the genre and as a valuable social and cultural document. **Stephen Newman**

fiddle, the, the most widely used instrument in Irish TRADITIONAL MUSIC. The instrument is a standard violin; and though it is not indigenous and is found in many other cultures and types of music, notably art music, the way it is played for traditional music is distinctively Irish. Traditional music is based primarily on a single melodic line, and therefore ornamentation or decoration of the melody is an intrinsic element of playing. On the fiddle, different types of ornamentation can be achieved by the left hand (the fingering hand) and the right hand (the bow hand). In the 'roll', a sequence of five notes is played, with one bow-stroke, in place of the note to be decorated. 'Trebling' involves the bow being used to play three notes, with very short bow-strokes, in place of a crotchet. Depending on how they are played, these decorations can impart rhythmic and percussive nuances to the music. It is also with the bow that the characteristic rhythm, or 'swing', is created; this is particularly so in dance music.

The fiddle has had a significant influence on the shape of many tunes, as traditional music is composed primarily on the instrument itself. As with other instruments, there are different styles of playing, either in the way in which one musician plays compared with another or in the features of playing that distinguish musicians of a particular region. Before the era of mass communication, styles of playing were confined largely to their own geographical areas. Since music in all styles has now become available to everyone, regional styles are no longer confined to their own areas and the boundaries between them are less obvious. The main regional fiddle styles are generally considered to be those of Co. Donegal, Co. Sligo, Co. Clare, and SLIABH LUACHRA, Cos. Cork and Kerry. The Donegal style features single-note bowing, with short bow-strokes, and the tempo is generally fast. Trebling is used to a much greater extent than rolls, creating a general staccato-like sound. One of the principal exponents of this music was JOHN DOHERTY (1894–1977). In the Sligo style the playing is rhythmic, with smoother bowing, and the pace is fast. Rolls as well as trebles are features of the ornamentation. The fiddle music of this region is probably more widely known than any other, mainly from the playing of MICHAEL COLEMAN (1891–1945) and JAMES MORRISON (1893–1947). The slower tempo of the Clare style allows the player to concentrate on the melodic aspects of the music. The bowing is fluid, and extensive use is made of left-hand ornamentation, such as the roll. The west Clare style is well represented by the playing of Bobby Casey (1926–2000) and the east Clare style by Paddy Canny (1919–). Sliabh Luachra, on the Cork-Kerry border, is renowned for slides and POLKAS. The inherent rhythm of these tunes has influenced the playing of the other dance tunes. Ornamentation is achieved mainly with the left hand, while the bow hand provides the characteristic rhythm. The recordings of PÁDRAIG O'KEEFFE (1887–1963), Denis Murphy (1910–1974), and JULIA CLIFFORD (1915–1997) feature this music.

There are other players whose music does not fall readily into any of these regional styles. The music of SEÁN MAGUIRE (1924–) has many of the Sligo characteristics and much of its repertoire yet at the same time is unique. The Dublin fiddler TOMMY POTTS (1912–1988) played in a highly personal way, with unusual versions of tunes combined with extraordinary interpretation. During the final quarter of the twentieth century, through the increased availability of commercially recorded music on CD as well as on radio and television, many fiddle-players developed an individual way of playing that includes elements from various regional styles, including (among many others) Kevin Burke, Liz Carroll, John Carty, Séamus Connolly, Séamus Creagh, FRANKIE GAVIN, PADDY GLACKIN, MARTIN HAYES, Seán Keane, James Kelly, Brendan McGlinchey, Connie O'Connell, and Tommy Peoples. The sound and repertoire of the local accent can be heard to varying degrees in their music (see pp. 404, 567). [see ACCORDION; BANJO; BODHRÁN; FLUTE; HARMONICA/MOUTH ORGAN; HARP; INSTRUMENT MAKERS; IRISH PIPE MAKERS; LAMBEG DRUM; PIANO; PÍOBAIRÍ.] **Matt Cranitch**

Field, John (1782–1837), composer and pianist. Born in Dublin. He was taught by his father (a violinist in Dublin theatres), his grandfather, and the composer TOMMASO GIORDANI. He made his debut as a pianist at the age of nine and his first London appearance in 1793. He worked as a piano salesman and demonstrator for Muzio Clementi in London, who took him on a European tour in 1802, visiting Paris, Vienna, and St Petersburg. Settling in Russia in 1803, he divided his time between St Petersburg and Moscow in the years that followed, while continuing his concert appearances throughout Europe. He initiated an important school of romantic pianism, exemplified in the famous 'nocturnes' for solo piano which found their ultimate expression in the music of Chopin. His works include seven piano concertos (1799–1832) and a piano quintet (c. 1815). The Irish pianists VERONICA MCSWINEY, JOHN O'CONOR, and MÍCHÉAL O'ROURKE have recorded his work extensively. **Paul Collins**

Field Day (1980–1992), a THEATRE company founded in Derry by the playwright BRIAN FRIEL and the actor STEPHEN REA. After the success of its production and all-Ireland tour of Friel's *Translations*, it set up a board including SEAMUS DEANE, SEAMUS HEANEY, TOM PAULIN, David Hammond, and (later) THOMAS KILROY. Through its publications and plays (by Friel, Heaney, Kilroy, Parker, and Paulin), Field Day played a major and often controversial role in the critical debates of the 1980s over the redefinition of Ireland's cultural identity. Its impressive three-volume *The Field Day Anthology of Irish Writing*, edited by Deane, was published in 1991, followed by vols. iv/v in 2002. **Martine Pelletier**

field patterns. There are considerable differences in the size, shape and regularity of traditional field patterns, reflecting Ireland's regionally varied agrarian history. In marginal areas in west Connacht and Munster, small irregular fields remain common and may result from the intense pre-FAMINE population pressure on LAND in these districts. Elsewhere, particularly in north Connacht and west Ulster, pre-famine LANDLORDS rationalised the numerous highly sub-divided smallholdings into fewer but larger and more efficient 'ladder' farms (so called because of their characteristic linear regularity). In more environmentally favoured central and eastern districts, where farming had a long tradition of responding to changing demands from overseas markets, fields tended to be larger and more regular and were frequently created by the ENCLOSURE of medieval 'open' fields. Much of this enclosure was completed during the seventeenth century, and therefore, unlike England, few parishes were enclosed by nineteenth-century act of Parliament. Since 1973 many traditional field patterns have been modernised and enlarged with the aid of grants from the EUROPEAN UNION (see pp. 359, 605). **Lindsay Proudfoot**

fiddle. *Oona MacFarland plays traditional music on the fiddle. Though it is not an indigenous instrument, when played by traditional musicians it is uniquely Irish. [Imagefile]*

Figgis, Darrell (1882–1925), nationalist, politician, and writer. Born in Rathmines, Dublin. He became involved in the revolutionary separatist movement while working in London as a freelance journalist, and he accompanied ERSKINE CHILDERS on his arms-buying expedition to Germany in 1914. He became secretary of SINN FÉIN in 1917 and represented Co. Dublin in the first Dáil Éireann. He supported the Treaty and played an important role in drafting the CONSTITUTION of the IRISH FREE STATE (1922). His writings include a study of GEORGE RUSSELL (1916), *The Economic Case for Irish Independence* (1920), and a novel, *The House of Success* (1921). He committed suicide in London. **Brian Galvin**

filí, the early medieval professional poets, who frequently had strong ecclesiastical ties; they also fulfilled the functions of storyteller, historian, and genealogist. Ideally the *file* came from a family of *filí*. The *filí* were subdivided into grades that reflected their general competence, literacy, and learning; the most exalted grade, that of OLLAMH, had the status of a petty king or bishop. Not every poet was a *file*, for a distinction was made between the *file* and the less scholarly *bard*. Following the traumas of the ANGLO-NORMAN

CONQUEST the *filí* became secularised and merged with the bards; yet they remained important and were certainly loathed by English colonists as potent representatives of Irish culture. Ultimately the fate of the *filí* was closely associated with the fortunes of the Irish elites, whom they followed into ruin with the destruction of their society in the seventeenth century. [see CLASSICAL IRISH POETRY; EARLY MODERN IRISH.] **Elva Johnston**

film: see CINEMA.

film censorship. National film censorship was introduced into the IRISH FREE STATE and later the Republic with the Censorship of Films Act (1923), which made it an offence for a film to be shown in public without a certificate from the Film Censor, a government appointee operating under the aegis of the Department of Justice; a voluntary Films Appeal Board, which has included Protestant and Catholic clergy since its inception, adjudicates on appeals by distributors. The censors are obliged to ban or cut a film if it is considered indecent, obscene, or blasphemous or is contrary to public morality. The first censor, James Montgomery, who held the post for seventeen years, applied these moral precepts with gusto, banning approximately 1,700 films and cutting many more, while also ensuring that all films were suitable for children, a policy that was continued largely unchanged by his successors, Richard Hayes, Martin Brennan, Liam Ó Hóra, and Dermot Breen. In 1965 the Appeal Board was revamped and a more liberal policy was introduced when the provisions of the act allowing for limited certificates were activated, allowing adults to see over-18 films for the first time, though still often cut. Since then the gradual liberalisation has continued: the last censor, Sheamus Smith, banned only ten films from his appointment in 1986 to 2002, rarely cut a film, and reduced the over-18 limitation mostly to an over-16 certificate. In 2001 he introduced the categories 12PG and 15PG, which allow those under these ages to see such films if accompanied by an adult. The Film Censor's office also oversees the implementation of the Video Recordings Act (1989), which requires that a video or DVD be certified by the censors before it can be released. [see CINEMA.] **Kevin Rockett**

Film Company of Ireland, the most important Irish film production company in the era of silent films. During the period 1916–20 it made more than twenty fiction films, including three features, the most interesting of which were the adaptations of CHARLES KICKHAM's *Knocknagow* (1918), a drama of landlord and tenant set during the GREAT FAMINE, and WILLIAM CARLETON's *Willy Reilly and his Dear Colleen Bawn* (1920), which takes place in the 1740s and 50s and concerns the relationship between a Catholic gentleman and a Protestant woman; the director was the playwright John MacDonagh. J. M. Kerrigan of the ABBEY THEATRE, who directed eight of the first year's nine shorts, later became a Hollywood actor. **Kevin Rockett**

Film Institute of Ireland, an independent organisation that runs the Irish Film Centre, Dublin. The National Film Institute of Ireland, established in 1945 as a Catholic body engaged in film production and distribution as well as in issuing moral ratings of films, was left behind by the secularising tide of the 1960s and 70s. A new generation of film activists took over in the early 1980s, renamed it the Irish Film Institute, and removed the Catholic ethos from its constitution. Following the establishment of the Irish Film Centre in 1992, a project initiated by the Film Institute, it was renamed the Film Institute of Ireland. Its activities include the Irish Film Archive, which houses the largest collection of Irish film material held anywhere, two art cinemas, the promotion of media education, occasional publications, a bookshop, a library, and bar and restaurant areas that are the meeting-places for the Irish film community. The building also houses the Access Cinema, which organises the distribution of non-mainstream films; Filmbase, a co-operative training body that also publishes the bimonthly *Film Ireland*; and the European Union's Media Desk Ireland. **Kevin Rockett**

Finbarr (Fionnbharr). The patron saint of the church and diocese of Cork originated as a localisation of the widespread cult of Finbarr, alias Finnian, patron and probable founder of the church of MOVILLA, Co. Down. Among other achievements, this man wrote a penitential, corresponded with Gildas, and taught COLM CILLE. Following its adoption in Cork, Finbarr's cult achieved considerable prominence and is still vigorous. A Life was written in Latin c. 1200, and a vernacular version was produced shortly afterwards; an office Life was composed c. 1300. These texts perpetuated the erroneous belief that the saint was born near Cork and founded many local churches, as well as famous schools at Cork and Gougane Barra; it was the cult, not the saint, that travelled to Cork. The saint's Cork feast-day is 25 September. **Pádraig Ó Riain**

Fine Gael (FG), the second-largest party in the Republic, formed in 1933 by the merger of Cumann na nGaedheal, the National Centre Party, and the 'BLUESHIRTS' (National Guard). The ANGLO-IRISH TREATY (1921) divided SINN FÉIN, the party that led the struggle for independence. In April 1923 the pro-Treaty deputies in DÁIL ÉIREANN organised themselves into the first new post-independence party, Cumann na nGaedheal. Membership was open to anyone who supported the Treaty and the Constitution of the IRISH FREE STATE (1922). At the general election of August 1923 Cumann na nGaedheal won 39 per cent of the vote, giving it sixty-three seats in a Dáil of 153, and thereupon formed a minority Government. In 1932, following an election defeat and the transfer of power to FIANNA FÁIL, Cumann na nGaedheal entered opposition for the first time.

The National Centre Party had been formed in 1923. In a 'snap' election Cumann na nGaedheal held forty-eight seats and the Centre Party eleven seats. These parties, together with the National Guard, subsequently merged to form Fine Gael. W. T. COSGRAVE became its Dáil leader and, in 1935, at its second ard-fheis, was elected president of the party.

After a protracted period of declining support, Fine Gael's fortunes improved in the late 1940s. It secured thirty-one of a total of 144 Dáil seats and in 1948 headed the first inter-party Government. It has since held office on five occasions. Its best election results were in 1982, when it won more than 39 per cent of the vote and seventy seats. In 1982 the Coalition Government of Fine Gael and the Labour Party was led by GARRET FITZGERALD and enjoyed a five-year term (see p. 394). With the support of the Labour Party and DEMOCRATIC LEFT, Fine Gael was in office again from 1994 to 1997, with JOHN BRUTON as head of the first Government to be formed by the opposition without a general election taking place. In 1997 it gained 28 per cent of the votes and fifty-four seats; in the 1999 local elections its support was 28.1 per cent, and in the 1999 election to the European Parliament 23.8 per cent of the vote gave Fine Gael four seats. **Neil Collins**

'Fingal Rónáin' (Rónán's kin-killing), one of the most coherent medieval Irish narratives. The earliest surviving text is in the Book of Leinster, but the tale can be dated to the tenth century. Tempted by his stepmother, Rónán's son Mael Fhothartaigh rejects her. She then accuses him of seduction, as proof reciting half a quatrain, to which he responds. Seeing guilt in this poetic compatibility, Rónán orders his death; thereupon Mael Fothartaigh's foster-brother attacks and kills the wife's family. On seeing their heads she commits suicide. Rónán dies thereafter. SÉAMUS Ó NÉILL based his play *Iníon Rí Dhún Sobhairce* on this tale. **Philip O'Leary**

Finlay, Thomas (1922–), lawyer and judge. Born in Dublin; educated at UCD and the KING'S INNS. He was called to the bar in 1944 and became a senior counsel in 1961. He was a FINE GAEL member of DÁIL ÉIREANN, 1954–67, and became a judge of the High Court in 1972, becoming president of the High Court, 1974–85, and Chief Justice, 1985–92. As a barrister he represented Captain James Kelly in the ARMS CRISIS (1970) and in 1972 represented Ireland at the European Court of Human Rights when Britain was accused of torturing prisoners in Northern Ireland. He was Chief Justice at the time of the 'X' CASE (1992), delivering the majority judgment. **Neville Cox**

Finnegans Wake (1939), a novel by JAMES JOYCE, written and revised in Paris between 1923 and 1939, published in instalments in small literary magazines under the title 'Work in Progress', and released in book form in 1939. His final and most demanding work, *Finnegans Wake* is Joyce's last courageous attempt to rewrite the genre of the novel and to encourage readers to read differently. It is written in an allusive and elusive language of portmanteau words loosely based on English syntax and includes often irreverent references to as much history, language, and culture (both 'high' and 'low') as Joyce could manage. For this reason it is often thought of as an attempt to express a universal story through particular instances. Nonetheless it carries many allusions to stories and interests of the 1920s, when it was mostly written. Its main theme is the rise and fall of HCE (Humphrey Chimpden Earwicker) ('here comes everybody'), his wife, ALP (Anna Livia Plurabelle) (also the River Liffey), their twin sons, Shem (a partial self-portrait) and Shaun, and their daughter, Issy, who suffers from a split personality. The fall of HCE appears to be occasioned by his anxiety at a sexual indiscretion or crime that he may or may not have committed and the exact nature of which remains unclear. This apparently simple narrative is enmeshed in a rich and complex textual fabric of multiple allusions. Sometimes regarded as 'unreadable', the work has been increasingly recognised as a masterpiece of linguistic exuberance that is at once both deeply comic and deeply frustrating. **John Nash**

Fintona horse tram. The short branch of the Great Northern Railway from Fintona, Co. Tyrone, to Fintona Junction was worked for 104 years by a horse-drawn tramcar catering for first-class and second-class passengers in the saloon and third class on the open top. Drawn by Dick, it was much visited by enthusiasts in the latter years, until the closure of the service on 1 October 1957. The tram has been preserved. **Bernard Share**

Fionn Cycle, also known as the *Fiannaíocht* or Fianna Cycle, a tale cycle originally more popular among the lower social orders than the rúraíocht. Despite its early origin and pre-Christian associations, it did not emerge as a highly esteemed form of literature until the twelfth century, though it has been established that the first of the associated tales appeared in eighth-century texts.

A great deal of the narrative of the Fionn Cycle describes the hunting adventures of the heroes and warriors, and the tales present a close association with nature and with rural scenes. These elements are among those that give it a different flavour from the other cycles and also bring the corpus closer to the reality of the period of its creation. The word *fianna* is the plural of *fiann*, denoting a band of young male warriors. Their leader, and the main character, is FIONN MAC CUMHAILL. Because of his prowess in hunting, the tales contain numerous references to hunting and related escapades, and Fionn and his hunting companions are also said to have made several conquests of an amorous nature. Though the hunting scenes are much to the fore, the themes and descriptions have become more warlike with the passing of time and retelling of the tales. In more recent oral tradition this is the most popular of the cycles, and even today storytellers recount the adventures of Fionn and the Fianna. The Fiannaíocht also appeared in the form of *lays* that were chanted or sung in verse form, and these could be heard in Irish-speaking districts until comparatively recently. Among the principal heroic characters in the Fiann are the warriors Oscar, who is Fionn's grandson and perceived as the strongest of all the Fianna, and Goll mac Morna, who fought against Fionn himself on several occasions. Diarmaid Ó Duibhne, who had a love-spot that rendered him irresistible to women, was a handsome warrior of the Fiann who eloped with Fionn's betrothed, Gráinne. Caoilte mac Rónáin, an athlete renowned for his speedy running, was Fionn's faithful companion, while OISÍN (whose name means 'little fawn') was Fionn's son, who followed in his father's footsteps as hunter, seer, and poet. He is depicted in the text 'ACALLAMH NA SENÓRACH' (Colloquy of the Old Men) as having spent some time in his mother's Otherworld dwelling following the last defeat of the Fianna.

'Acallamh na Senórach' is probably the best-known composition of the Fionn Cycle. In it, contrasting images of the warrior-hunter life and of the saintly, monastic life are portrayed, with each supporting his own. Ecclesiastical influence is evident in some texts, in which Christianity has the final word through St PATRICK's contribution; but other texts, compiled doubtless by lay people, underline the narrowness of Patrick's moral stance and also the positive attributes of the Fianna.

The Fionn Cycle underwent many changes and developments, especially between the thirteenth and eighteenth centuries, when the argumentative verses in the 'Acallamh' were developed and

Film Company. *A scene from the Film Company of Ireland's* Willy Reilly and His Colleen Bawn *(1920), directed by John MacDonagh: four men carrying torches make their way to burn down Willy Reilly's manor-house. [Irish Film Archive of the Film Institute of Ireland]*

added to. A story that has become famous in more recent times tells of Oisín, in the company of a beautiful woman, visiting TÍR NA NÓG, the Land of Youth. **Ríonach uí Ógáin**

Fionn mac Cumhaill, a name synonymous with a mythical warrior-seer figure whose origins are in Leinster. Tales of Fionn appear in literary texts from the eighth century onwards. In accordance with his heroic stature, Fionn's birth, frequently associated with water, and his feats in infancy and childhood all bear signs of his future greatness. His exploits as a young man are described in the medieval text 'Macgnímartha Find' (The Boyhood Deeds of Fionn).

While serving Conn Cétchathach, the High King of Ireland, Fionn's father, Cumhall, is killed at the battle of Cnucha by Goll mac Morna. To protect Fionn from his father's enemies he is cared for by two women on Sliabh Bladhma (Slieve Bloom) in Co. Laois, where he becomes proficient in athletic skills, such as HURLING and SWIMMING. The young Fionn travels to briefly visit his father's brother Criomhall in Connacht and then proceeds to the valley of the BOYNE to study the art of poetry.

The descriptive tale of how he acquires the power of knowledge, dating from the eighth century, tells of the young Fionn meeting a wise man, Finnéigeas, on the banks of the Boyne. Finnéigeas has spent seven years trying to catch the salmon of knowledge and has eventually caught it. When it is cooked, he warns Fionn not to eat it; but Fionn, burning his thumb on the roasted salmon, puts it in his mouth to cool it and thus receives the gift of knowledge. This tale occurs frequently in Irish and Scottish FOLKLORE, and the gift itself is testimony to the essential, sacred importance of second sight and of wisdom. The theme of Fionn putting his thumb in his mouth to gain knowledge is well attested in the FIONN CYCLE, as are two other significant themes, that of his competence in obscure rhetoric and the fact that the head of a dead person is capable of speaking in his presence. Humour is also a trait associated with Fionn: in a story of the giant who is attempting to entice Fionn to fight with him, Fionn pretends he is a baby in a cradle and manages to bite the giant's finger as he amuses the 'baby'.

Fionn's ability to attract women is well attested in the Fionn Cycle. At one point a strange OTHERWORLD woman appears to Fionn and the Fiann, claiming to be the daughter of the mythical, somewhat sinister personage Dearg and that she was once Fionn's lover. 'TÓRAÍOCHT DHIARMADA AGUS GHRÁINNE' (The Pursuit of Diarmaid and Gráinne), which can be dated to at least the tenth century, portrays Fionn as an older man, jealous of Diarmaid's youth but nevertheless successful in getting Gráinne back.

The character of Fionn has attracted motifs and traits from other personages and Otherworld beings, and some narratives describe his involvement in Otherworld battles in the company of his band of warriors, the Fiann. As leader of the Fiann on their expeditions, Fionn hunted deer and wild pigs, and numerous references are also made to his special hounds. Countless natural features and place-names throughout Ireland are identified with Fionn, who has left his mark on hills, mountains, standing stones, and islands. [see FOLK TALES.] **Ríonach uí Ógáin**

Fir Bolg, former inhabitants of Ireland, according to medieval history. They are sometimes said to have been of Greek origin. According to the LEBOR GABÁLA ÉRENN (Book of Invasions), on arrival in Ireland their five leaders divided the country among them, and this is the reputed origin of the five provinces. The Fir Bolg are said to have ruled Ireland for thirty-seven years, until conquered by TUATHA DÉ DANANN near Lough Arrow, Co. Sligo. Certain medieval accounts state that the Fir Bolg then went to islands off the Scottish coast, and that they were driven away and then returned to Ireland, where they were protected by MÉABH before being conquered and slain by the ULAIDH. **Ríonach uí Ógáin**

'fireside magazines', apparently the invention of JAMES DUFFY, a publisher of popular historical and other works for Catholics. He turned his attention to the mass periodical market with the *Irish Catholic Magazine* (1847–8), *Fireside Magazine* (1850–54), and *Hibernian Magazine* (1860–64). All provided 'healthy fireside reading' in the form of pious and patriotic stories, poems, and news items, and this successful formula was much emulated during the nineteenth century. In 1902, conscious that the market had become dominated by British magazines, Michael J. Walsh of the People newspaper group in Wexford launched the illustrated weekly *Ireland's Own*, which still commands a circulation of 50,000. It largely eschews politics but continues the 'fireside' genre with a comfortable mixture of stories, poems, letters, features on nature and popular history, children's pages, puzzles, jokes, novenas, and 'lonely hearts' advertisements. **John Wakeman**

First World War (1914–18). Known at the time as the Great War, the First World War (1914–18) was fought mainly in Europe and the Middle East and saw the Allies (France, Russia, Britain, Italy, and the United States) defeat the Central Powers (Germany, Austria-Hungary, and Turkey). Over 200,000 Irishmen served in the war, with casualties in the region of 30,000, which included the poet FRANCIS LEDWIDGE, and the MPs WILLIAM REDMOND and T. M. KETTLE. The war transformed the Irish question. The HOME RULE Act was passed in September 1914 but its operation was suspended until the end of hostilities. JOHN REDMOND's appeal to nationalists to join the British army alienated a minority of radical nationalists, leading to the 1916 RISING. Redmond saw the war as an opportunity to build a new, inclusive sense of Irishness by proving to unionists that home rule was compatible with imperial loyalty. His position was undermined by the formation of a coalition government of Liberals and Unionists in 1915. Many nationalists now thought that home rule would never be implemented. The British response to the rising further undermined his support and saw a revamped SINN FÉIN challenge and supplant the Irish Party. The 36th (Ulster) Division's heavy casualties at the Battle of the Somme in July 1916 emphasised the psychological division that the war was producing between nationalists and Ulster unionists. The latter's sacrifice for king and empire was contrasted with advanced nationalism's rebellion and intrigue with the German enemy.

The IRISH CONVENTION of 1917–18 was a final attempt to seek a compromise between moderate nationalists and unionists. Southern unionist representatives agreed to home rule on the evidence of nationalist support and sacrifice in the war; Ulster unionists vetoed the proposals, insisting on PARTITION instead. The failed British attempt to implement conscription in 1918, because of the serious military situation on the Western Front, reinforced divisions in Ireland. To nationalists it re-emphasised the intentions of British militarism to conscript a subject nation, while to unionists it proved once more the inherent disloyalty of nationalists. **Thomas Hennessey**

Irish regiments. When Britain declared war on Germany, the British Expeditionary Force moved immediately to France. In 1914 and 1915 seventeen Irish infantry battalions and four cavalry regiments of the British regular army took part in all the opening battles in France and the Gallipoli landings. At the encounter

First World War. *John Redmond, leader of the Irish Parliamentary Party, addressing a rally. Following the outbreak of war, Redmond called for support of the British war effort and an estimated 200,000 Irishmen signed up to the British army. [Courtesy Kilmainham Gaol Museum/Independent Newspapers]*

battles of Mons, Le Cateau, the Marne and the Aisne, and the holding battles of La Bassée and Ypres, Irish regiments played a notable part in halting massed German assaults. At Cape Helles in Gallipoli the sea was red with blood.

Ireland raised three New Army divisions—the 10th, 16th, and 36th. The first two were predominantly Catholic and nationalist, the last completely Protestant and unionist. The 10th Division saw action in Gallipoli, Serbia, Macedonia, and Palestine, and most units were brought back to the Western Front in 1918 to take part in the final 'advance to victory'. The 16th Division took the field in December 1915 and in April 1916 in the Loos salient was subjected to the heaviest gas attacks of that year. The 36th Division arrived in France in December 1915, and on the first day of the Battle of the Somme its gains were the bright point of a dismal day, but at grievous cost. Half way through the Battle of the Somme the 16th Division captured Guillemont and Ginchy, creating a hiatus in the German defences. At Messines in 1917 the 16th and 36th Divisions constituted an Irish assault corps that captured the fortress village of Wytschaete. However, during the Third Battle of Ypres both divisions suffered two weeks in swamps around Frezenberg before being repulsed with heavy loss at Langemark. Later that year Cambrai saw each division reach its objective: the 16th captured Tunnel Trench and the 36th got into Mœuvres. During the great German offensives of March–May 1918 the 16th and 36th Divisions in the Fifth Army suffered severe casualties. Their defence lines, though repeatedly driven back, were never broken. Losses of approximately 13,250 inevitably changed the character of both divisions. However, the arrival in France of the 10th Division infantry and support units rejuvenated the regular Irish regiments. Twenty-seven battalions still largely Irish in character took part in the final offensive, which broke German resistance and led to an armistice on 11 November 1918.

Events in Ireland during the war years, notably the 1916 Rising, the resistance to conscription, and the ineffectual debate at the Irish Convention, were known and spoken about by troops at the front. However painful they may have been to the soldiers, these events never affected either the morale or the operational capabilities of Irish formations. **Tom Johnstone**

First World War, songs of the. Like their contemporaries, Irishmen in the British army sang 'Hanging on the Old Barbed Wire', 'TIPPERARY', and bitter parodies of popular songs. Irishmen were separated into Ulster and Irish Divisions, and their songs were traditional, some of them sectarian. Song-makers gave local views of the war, its casualties and heroes, condemned 'slackers', and praised particular regiments. Few of the songs are still sung, though 'Neuve-Chapelle' and 'Bonny Woodgreen' survive in the North and 'Salonika' in the South. Anti-recruiting songs of the period express uncompromising REPUBLICANISM. The popularity in the 1970s of Eric Bogle's 'Green Fields of France' and 'The Band Played Waltzing Matilda' implies a modern revulsion at the wastefulness of this war. **John Moulden**

'Fís Adomnáin' ('The Vision of Adomnán'), an anonymous work that purports to describe the vision of Heaven and Hell beheld by St ADOMNÁN of IONA (died 704), written in the tenth or eleventh century. A minor medieval masterpiece that has been described as 'an Irish precursor of Dante,' it combines apocryphal material with themes and motifs from Irish secular literature. **Máirín Ní Dhonnchadha**

fiscal crisis, a momentum of debt accumulation in the Republic in the 1980s, the result of expansionist policies. The fiscal crisis of 1981–8 is the defining event of recent Irish economic history. Its origins lie in the expansionism of the FIANNA FÁIL government elected in 1977, which sought to achieve full EMPLOYMENT by tax cuts and the expansion of public-sector employment. Though the policy of tax cuts was short-lived, the spending spree resulted in an apparently unstoppable momentum of debt accumulation, fuelled by the global downturn and interest-rate increases of 1979–82. With domestic and foreign demand both depressed, and the safety-valve of EMIGRATION to Britain closed by the Thatcher recession, UNEMPLOYMENT soared to over 17 per cent, aggregate economic activity was almost at a standstill, and public debt approached 130 per cent of GNP.

From 1981 to 1985, governments attempted to balance the books, largely through tax increases, but this scramble for revenue damaged confidence and was ultimately politically unsustainable. Only when a bipartisan political consensus for spending cuts emerged in 1987 could a decisive correction be achieved. The tough measures then adopted by the Minister for Finance, RAY MACSHARRY, succeeded beyond expectation, helped by the strong recovery of the British economy, by favourable exchange-rate movements (notably the devaluation of 1986), by pay moderation centrally negotiated, and by lower world interest rates.

The fiscal crisis has had a lasting legacy in dissolving some of the institutional sclerosis that had seen Ireland's economy under-perform for generations. Apparently faced with the alternative of continued steep economic decline, a new TRADE UNION leadership and a new generation of job-market entrants successfully adopted a pragmatic approach to pay negotiations and work-place flexibility, which saw total employment rise by almost 50 per cent in a decade, unemployment fall well below 5 per cent, and living standards converge on the European average. **Patrick Honohan**

Fisher, Jonathan (fl. 1763–1809), artist. Though he does not seem to have trained in the DUBLIN SOCIETY Schools, he won premiums for landscape paintings in 1763 and 1768. He painted series of pictures, such as six of Killarney and six of Carlingford Lough, which he had engraved. He intended, beginning c. 1795, to issue a set of sixty views of Ireland, though the work was not completed. His oils are of high quality; he used chiaroscuro to establish the changing light of Ireland, where the sun breaks through and illuminates features in an otherwise dark and broadly painted scene. He painted both in Ulster and the South, and painted several versions of his more popular works. **Anne Crookshank**

Fitt, Gerry, Lord (1926–), politician. Born in Belfast into a working-class family; worked as a merchant seaman, 1941–53, before being elected to Belfast City Council in 1958 and STORMONT in 1962 as representative for Dock. He attained political prominence as Westminster MP for West Belfast from 1966. A publicist in Britain of Catholic grievances, he was accompanied by three British Labour Party MPs during the DERRY CIVIL RIGHTS MARCH of October 1968. Influential in bringing together civil rights and nationalist interests to form the SOCIAL DEMOCRATIC AND LABOUR PARTY in August 1970, he served as its first leader and as Deputy Chief Executive in the 'Sunningdale' power-sharing Executive of 1974. He was driven from his home in 1976 by intimidation as a result of his opposition to paramilitary activity. In 1979 his abstention from a critical Westminster vote led to the Labour government's downfall, while later in the year his disenchantment with the prominence accorded by the SDLP to nationalist issues led to his replacement as its leader by JOHN HUME. Having opposed REPUBLICAN HUNGER STRIKES, he was defeated in West Belfast by GERRY ADAMS of SINN FÉIN; a month later, in July 1983, he was awarded a British life peerage as Lord Fitt. **Alan Scott**

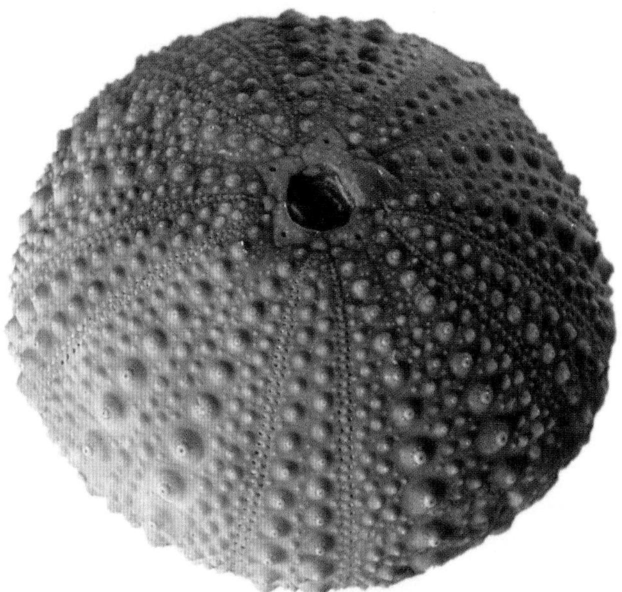

Fitton. Pseudodiadema fittoni, *a fossil echinoid (sea urchin) from the chalk of England named after the geologist William Henry Fitton. [Geological Museum, Trinity College, Dublin]*

Fitton, William Henry (1780–1861), geologist. Born in Co. Dublin, the son of a solicitor; educated at TCD. While an undergraduate he developed an interest in GEOLOGY, though it was to medicine that he eventually turned as his profession. He practised in Northampton until 1820, when his marriage to a woman of ample fortune allowed him to abandon medicine in favour of the life of a gentleman geologist. He became a leading authority on the English Mesozoic strata and was president of the Geological Society of London, 1827–9; he received the society's Wollaston Medal in 1852 for his outstanding contributions to geology. **Jean Archer**

Fitzgerald, Barry, stage name of William Joseph Shields (1888–1961), stage and film actor. Born in Dublin. Playing occasionally at the ABBEY THEATRE from 1916, he had his first film role in *Land of Her Fathers* (1925); he later appeared in Alfred Hitchcock's version of SEAN O'CASEY's *Juno and the Paycock* (1930) (see p. 2). After playing one of his most famous stage roles, that of Fluther Good in JOHN FORD's film version of O'Casey's *The Plough and the Stars* (1936), he settled in Hollywood, where he won an Academy Award for *Going My Way* (1944) and went on to play his most memorable role as the impish matchmaker in Ford's *The Quiet Man* (1952). **Kevin Rockett**

Fitzgerald, Ciarán (1952–), rugby footballer. Born in Galway. One of the most successful Ireland captains of the twentieth century, he led Ireland to Triple Crown triumphs in 1982 and 1985. He won his first two caps in both Tests during Ireland's Australian tour of 1979, when Ireland won the series 2–0. He played twenty-five times for Ireland between 1979 and 1986, when he made his last appearance against England. He commanded the respect of his senior players and led by example on the field. He captained the 1983 British Lions team in New Zealand, playing in all four Tests. He was a national selector and coach from 1990/91 to 1992/3. **Karl Johnston**

FitzGerald, Desmond, twenty-ninth Knight of Glin (1937–), art and architectural historian. Educated at the University of British Columbia and Harvard University. In 1965 he joined the staff of the Victoria and Albert Museum, London, becoming deputy keeper of FURNITURE and woodwork, 1972–5. He has published widely on topography, architecture, and landscape gardening, sometimes in collaboration with MAURICE CRAIG and Edward Malins. The first of several collaborations with ANNE CROOKSHANK was the exhibition 'Irish Portraits, 1600–1860', shown in Dublin, Belfast and London, 1969–70, a milestone in modern research into Irish art. He has been president of the IRISH GEORGIAN SOCIETY since 1991. Among his publications are *Ireland Observed* with Maurice Craig (1975); *Lost Demesnes* with Edward Malins (1976); *The Painters of Ireland, 1660–1920* with Anne Crookshank (1978); *The Watercolours of Ireland, 1600–1914* with Anne Crookshank (1994); *Ireland's Painters 1600–1940* with Anne Crookshank (2002). **Martyn Anglesea**

Fitzgerald, Lord Edward (1763–1798), United Irishman. Born at Carton House, Co. Kildare, into Ireland's premier aristocratic family. (His father was the twentieth Earl of Kildare and first Duke of Leinster.) He served as an officer in the 19th Regiment during the American war of independence. Travels in North America and revolutionary France coincided with his membership of the Irish Parliament from 1783, representing the Co. Kildare borough of Athy. His radicalism increased during the 1790s, and in May 1796 he accompanied the Cork radical ARTHUR O'CONNOR to Paris to invite the French army to invade Ireland on behalf of the UNITED IRISHMEN. On renouncing his title (as a younger son of a duke he had the courtesy title of Lord Edward, by which he was always remembered) and his parliamentary seat in July 1797, he became the primary military strategist of the proscribed republican organisation. He narrowly escaped arrest on 12 March 1798 and attained joint control of the United Irishmen in the advent of the rebellion that began on 23 May. His seizure in Thomas Street, Dublin, on 19 May contributed to the failure of the national uprising. He died in Newgate Prison, Dublin, on 4 June, from wounds sustained while violently resisting arrest. **Ruan O'Donnell**

Fitzgerald, Eleanor (fl. sixteenth century), daughter of GERALD FITZGERALD, eighth Earl of Kildare, and Alison Eustace. Her first husband was Dónall McCarthy, Lord of Carbery, Co. Cork. The marriage formed part of the dynastic network that her father established throughout Ireland in the early sixteenth century. In the marriage agreement Eleanor was granted considerable control within the lordship. Dónall died in 1531. Following the rebellion of the ninth Earl of Kildare in 1534, Eleanor offered protection to the surviving Geraldine heir, Gerald Fitzgerald. She was involved in organising the GERALDINE LEAGUE and married Manus O'Donnell in order to strengthen the alliance between the supporters of the Fitzgeralds and the northern chief. Within a year of the marriage Eleanor suspected that Manus intended to surrender the boy to the English administration, and she arranged for him to be smuggled aboard a ship bound for France. She also abandoned her marriage and returned to Munster. She was pardoned by the Crown in 1545, being described as 'but a woman.' **Mary O'Dowd**

Fitzgerald, Eleanor, née Butler, Countess of Desmond (1554–1638), daughter of Edmund Butler, Baron of Dunboyne, and Síle MacCarthy, daughter of Cormac MacCarthy, Lord of Muskerry. She married GERALD FITZGERALD, fifteenth Earl of Desmond, in the early 1560s. After her husband's arrest and detention in London in 1567 she endeavoured to preserve his control over the Desmond territories in Munster. She joined her husband in London in 1570, and their son, James, was born in 1571. In 1573 the couple returned to Ireland. In the subsequent conflict between Fitzgerald and the English administration her main aim was to preserve her husband's estate intact for her son. She acted as an intermediary between her husband and the government and wrote many times to the Dublin administration requesting permission to travel to London to plead for mercy for him and to negotiate an end to the war. English officials in Ireland suspected her of duplicity and refused her permission to leave Ireland. Following the Earl of Desmond's death in rebellion in 1583 the Desmond lands were forfeited to the Crown and became the basis for the PLANTATION OF MUNSTER. Eleanor was deprived of her widow's claim to the estate and given instead an annual pension of £100. She subsequently married Sir Donogh O'Connor Sligo and lived in Co. Sligo for the rest of her life, from where she continued to petition the Crown concerning her second husband's property and for arrears of her pension. Her will is dated 1638; she is buried in Sligo Abbey, where she had erected a large monument in honour of her second husband in 1624. **Mary O'Dowd**

Fitzgerald, Elizabeth (c. 1537–1589), youngest daughter of GERALD FITZGERALD, ninth Earl of Kildare. She was brought to England by her mother in 1533; following the rebellion and execution of her half-brother Thomas Fitzgerald, tenth Earl of Kildare (Silken Thomas), in 1537, she remained there for the rest of her life. She served in the household of Princess Mary, a kinswoman of her mother, and was later a maid of honour to Queen Catherine Howard. The Earl of Surrey dedicated a number of poems to her, in which he extolled her beauty. Her portrait in the NATIONAL GALLERY OF IRELAND is the best-known portrait of a sixteenth-century Irish woman; it was painted c. 1560, after Elizabeth had become Countess of Lincoln through her second marriage. **Mary O'Dowd**

FitzGerald, Garret (1926–), politician and economic commentator. Born Dublin, educated at Belvedere and UCD. He began his career in 1947 working for AER LINGUS. There he developed his interest in economics, and over the following twenty-five years, through regular contributions to newspapers in Ireland and abroad, he gained a reputation as an economic commentator. In 1965 he entered politics as a senator, taking the FINE GAEL whip. He became a TD in 1969 and Minister for Foreign Affairs in the Coalition

FitzGerald, Garret. *Garret FitzGerald, leader of Fine Gael and Taoiseach. A professor of political economy and an* Irish Times *columnist, he helped frame Ireland's policy on European integration in 1973 and was an architect of the Anglo-Irish Agreement of 1985. [Camera Press Ireland]*

Government formed following the 1973 general election. An ardent supporter of Ireland's participation in the EUROPEAN UNION (then the EEC), his intellect and enthusiasm gained much influence for Ireland in Europe. Regarded as the natural leader of the liberal, social democratic wing of Fine Gael, he succeeded the more conservative LIAM COSGRAVE as party leader following defeat in the 1977 general election. He was Taoiseach in a Fine Gael-Labour coalition from June 1981 until February 1982 and again from November 1982 until 1987. His period in office was dominated by the economy and Northern Ireland. His Government struggled with the disastrous state in which it found the national finances: it was caught between the need for severe budgetary restraint and the instinct for high public spending shared by some in Fine Gael and all in the Labour Party. Nonetheless, it began the process of recovery that continued under later Governments and that prepared the way for the economic boom of the late 1990s. In 1983, FitzGerald established the NEW IRELAND FORUM. Although its conclusions were unremarkable, it concentrated the minds of nationalist Ireland and prepared the ground for the ANGLO-IRISH AGREEMENT of 1985, FitzGerald's finest achievement. He retired from politics following defeat in the general election of 1987, published his autobiography, *All in a Life* (1991) and *Reflections on the Irish State* (2002) (see p. 27). **Jim Power**

Fitzgerald, George Francis (1851–1901), physicist. Born in Monkstown, Co. Dublin; educated at TCD. Erasmus Smith professor of natural and experimental philosophy at Trinity College, Dublin, he was also a fellow of the Royal Society and winner of its Royal Medal, 1899. He was a widely admired leader of the Maxwellians (including Larmor, Lodge, Heaviside, and Hertz), who perfected James Clerk Maxwell's theory of the electromagnetic field, applying it to light, telegraphy, etc. He was admired as a source of ideas and criticism for others and as a passionate advocate of scientific research and technical education. He was the first person in Ireland to fly the Lilienthal glider (in the grounds of Trinity College, 1895). Stimulated by the Michelson-Morley experiment (1881), Fitzgerald suggested that a body travelling through the ether must be shortened by virtue of its motion. This effect eventually found its place in the theory of special relativity. **Denis Weaire**

Fitzgerald, Gerald, fifteenth Earl of Desmond (died 1583). Son of James Fitzgerald, fourteenth Earl of Desmond, whom he succeeded in 1558. He married ELEANOR FITZGERLAD, née Butler. His disputes with THOMAS BUTLER, tenth Earl of Ormond—a cousin of ELIZABETH I—intensified into open warfare in 1560 and again in 1564–5. In February 1565 he was wounded and captured in a skirmish with Butler's men at Affane, Co. Waterford. The two were summoned to Elizabeth's court, and recognisances for £20,000 were imposed on them for their future peaceable conduct; but in 1567 a judgment by Lord Deputy SIDNEY to Fitzgerald's disadvantage so disgruntled him that Sidney arrested him to preclude rebellion. Together with his brother John he was sent to the Tower of London, and though released in 1570 he was detained in England until he signed articles promising conformity in March 1573. He was re-arrested on his return to Ireland; he escaped and was proclaimed a traitor, but soon submitted. He did not join JAMES FITZMAURICE FITZGERALD's crusade for 'faith and fatherland' in 1579; however, after Fitzmaurice's death, and under pressure from his kinsmen, he temporised and on 1 November 1579 was proclaimed a traitor. His castles were quickly captured by Crown forces, and his estates were devastated, creating a FAMINE that killed an estimated 30,000 people. By 1583 he was an isolated fugitive. On 11 November he was taken by surprise and killed near Castlemaine, Co. Kerry. His estates were subsequently confiscated and formed the basis for the PLANTATION OF MUNSTER. **Henry A. Jefferies**

Fitzgerald, Gerald (Gearóid Mór), eighth Earl of Kildare (1456–1513), the most authoritative figure in the English LORDSHIP OF IRELAND from his accession as earl in 1478 to his death. He served as Governor of Ireland under five kings, 1478, 1479–92, and 1496–1513. HENRY VII endured the most consequential resistance from the Yorkist Fitzgerald, who crowned the pretender LAMBERT SIMNEL as Edward VI in 1487 and probably covertly supported another, PERKIN WARBECK, in the 1490s. In 1496, however, their relations stabilised. Fitzgerald was reappointed Deputy Lieutenant and married the king's cousin, Elizabeth St John. He entered into an agreement with Henry that ensured that during the remainder of Fitzgerald's career the Crown's interests were assiduously protected; he remained on peaceable terms with his old rival Thomas Butler, Earl of Ormond; the PALE was relatively peaceful and prosperous, and effective royal government was extended in the lordship. Fitzgerald's readiness to use his unrivalled strategic position and *manred* (his network of alliances and his tenants for military service) in defending the Pale provided the Crown with a cheap and effective form of provincial government. His success as governor stemmed largely from his unique capacity to reconcile the divergent interests of successive English monarchs, the Englishry, and the Irishry. His authority and the efficacy of his alliances with both English and Irish parties was most manifest in his victory at the BATTLE OF KNOCKDOE (1504), for which he was made a knight of the Garter, 1505. He was shot while on campaign, died on 3 September 1513, and was succeeded as Earl of Kildare and as Deputy by his son, Gerald. **Mary Ann Lyons**

Fitzgerald, Gerald (Gearóid Óg), ninth Earl of Kildare (1487–1534). He succeeded his father, GEARÓID MÓR, as Earl of Kildare and Governor of Ireland in 1513. Until 1519 he fulfilled both roles, as his father had done: he extended his dynastic landholdings, improved the farming of his estates, added to his inherited pool of tributaries, and dominated the Dublin government. His terms as Governor, 1513–20, 1524–8, and 1532–4, were interspersed with detentions in England. From 1515 he was embroiled in a feud with Piers Butler, eighth Earl of Ormond, and Palesmen increasingly criticised his imposition of *coign and livery* (a system by which a lord's military supporters and their animals were quartered on the tenantry who were obliged to house and feed them). Responding to Fitzgerald's critics, in 1519 HENRY VIII removed him from the Deputyship and throughout the 1520s and early 1530s endeavoured unsuccessfully to rule Ireland independently of Fitzgerald's involvement. However, Fitzgerald obstructed the Earl of Surrey's Lieutenancy, 1520–22, and Butler's Governorship, 1522–4, and had the Vice-Deputy, Delvin, kidnapped in 1528. In 1530 he returned to Ireland with the newly appointed Governor, Sir WILLIAM SKEFFINGTON; within a year he had undermined Skeffington, leaving Henry VIII no alternative but to reappoint him as Governor in 1532.

Disturbed by Thomas Cromwell's projected reforms for the Irish administration and by Butler's connivance against him, Fitzgerald pre-emptively transferred ordnance from DUBLIN CASTLE to his fortress at Maynooth in August 1533. He reluctantly responded to a summons to England in early 1534, appointing his son, THOMAS FITZGERALD, Lord Offaly (Silken Thomas), as his deputy during his absence. It was on his instructions that Thomas resigned and renounced allegiance to Henry in June 1534. Gerald was imprisoned in the Tower of London on 29 June, died on 3 September, and was succeeded by Thomas, then in outright rebellion. **Mary Ann Lyons**

Fitzgerald, James Fitzmaurice (died 1579), Catholic leader; son of Maurice Fitzgerald of Kerrycurrihy, Co. Cork, and cousin of GERALD FITZGERALD, FIFTEENTH EARL OF DESMOND. While the earl and his brother were detained in England, 1567–73, he became Captain of Desmond, in effect the ruler of the earldom. However, the earl granted Fitzgerald's lands in Kerrycurrihy to Sir Warham St Leger, an Englishman, partly to secure St Leger's good services and partly to undermine Fitzgerald's pretensions. He responded by trying to seize the earldom in 1569 while claiming to fight for 'faith and fatherland'. His rebellion gained widespread support, but the rebels stood little chance against superior English forces supported by the Earl of Ormonde. Nonetheless the English authorities encountered enormous difficulties in apprehending Fitzgerald, and in February 1573 JOHN PERROT, President of Munster, reluctantly accepted his submission and his promise of good conduct.

In March 1575 Fitzgerald left Ireland for France. Having failed to secure a French army for service in Ireland, he went to Spain early in 1577 but found Philip II too preoccupied to become involved in Irish affairs. Pope Gregory XIII, however, sponsored a military expedition. Fitzgerald landed near Dingle, Co. Kerry, on 17 July 1579. His small army of Spanish and Italian troops constructed a fort at SMERWICK and waited in vain for the main body of the Papal force. Fitzgerald was killed in a skirmish. His ill-fated crusade was taken up by the Earl of Desmond, but its defeat was virtually inevitable and was followed by the PLANTATION OF MUNSTER. **Henry A. Jefferies**

Fitzgerald, Mary (1956–), artist. Born in Dublin; trained at the National College of Art and Design and Tama University of Fine Art, Tokyo. Her studies in Japan heavily influenced her painting and drawing, particularly with regard to the oriental art of calligraphy. Her large-scale abstract painting makes free use of fluid calligraphic forms with great delicacy. She also relates her compositions to the architectural space or features of a room. In recent years she has incorporated relief elements, such as sheet glass, nails, and steel wire, in the painted background. She represented Ireland at the São Paulo Bienal in 1985 and is a member of AOSDÁNA. **Dorothy Walker**

Fitzgerald, Thomas, tenth Earl of Kildare, known as Silken Thomas (1513–1537), son of GERALD FITZGERALD, NINTH EARL OF KILDARE, and his first wife, Elizabeth Zouche. In February 1534, when Gerald Fitzgerald, then Lord Deputy, answered a summons to the court of HENRY VIII, he appointed his son Vice-Deputy during his absence. Acting in compliance with his father's instructions, on 11 June Fitzgerald dramatically resigned at a Council meeting in St Mary's Abbey, Dublin, repudiating his allegiance to the king. He proclaimed a Catholic crusade and established contacts with English and Welsh Catholics, and from December 1534 his envoys solicited aid from the Papacy, the Emperor Charles V, and James V of Scotland. He unsuccessfully besieged Dublin from late July to 4 October, by which time his imprisoned father had died in London, and Thomas became Earl of Kildare. Publicly proclaimed a traitor in October by Sir WILLIAM SKEFFINGTON, he was attainted by the English Parliament c. 18 December. Fitzgerald observed a truce from 19 December to 6 January; however, his principal fortress, Maynooth Castle, surrendered to Skeffington in March. Thereafter he sought refuge in Thomond. Having failed to secure Continental support, he surrendered on promise of his life on 24 August 1535 to his uncle-in-law, Lord LEONARD GREY, who took him to England, where he was imprisoned in the Tower. The attainder and subsequent beheading of Thomas and his five uncles in London on 3 February 1537 and their attainder by the Irish Parliament the following May precipitated the confiscation of the Kildare estates and left the Kildare Geraldines leaderless. **Mary Ann Lyons**

Fitzgibbon, John, Earl of Clare (1749–1802), politician. Born in Donnybrook, Co. Dublin; educated at TCD and the University of Oxford. He was well disposed towards the demand for legislative independence on entering the House of Commons in 1778, but his appointment as ATTORNEY-GENERAL in 1783 hastened his emergence as one of the most resolute defenders of the political status quo. He was appointed to the Lord Chancellorship following his impressive stand during the REGENCY CRISIS (1788–9), and his skill as a judge and his assertive opposition to the empowerment of Catholics and the revolutionary aspirations of the United Irishmen consolidated his reputation during the 1790s. A long-time advocate of an Anglo-Irish union, he was prominently involved in its elaboration, though he did not prosper at Westminster. He died, widely loathed, in January 1802. **James Kelly**

Fitz Gilbert, Richard (Strongbow), also known as Richard de Clare, Earl of Pembroke and Lord of Strigoil (died 1176). A disaffected subject of HENRY II, he was recruited by DIARMAID MAC MURCHÚ to help recover his kingdom of Leinster. He landed at Waterford in August 1170, where he married Aoife, Diarmaid's daughter, Diarmaid supposedly having promised him the succession to the kingdom of Leinster. Strongbow's father had been Earl of Pembroke, but Henry had refused to recognise Strongbow's claim to that title. His intervention in Ireland, and his greatly augmented resources, obliged Henry to come to terms with him and to acknowledge him as Earl of Strigoil, though not of Pembroke. He died from an injury to his foot in April 1176 and was buried in CHRIST CHURCH CATHEDRAL, Dublin. In 1189 his daughter, Isabella, married William Marshal, who became Lord of Leinster in right of his wife. In 1199 William persuaded King John to restore to him the title Earl of Pembroke. **Marie Therese Flanagan**

Fitzhenry, Mrs, née Flannigan (died c. 1790), actor. Born in Dublin, the daughter of a man who owned a tavern in Abbey Street. She moved to London in 1753 following the death of both her father and her husband. She took to the stage, but her Irish accent was at first an impediment to her success. She returned to Dublin to work at SMOCK ALLEY THEATRE. In January 1757 she reappeared at Covent Garden, London, and about this time also she married a lawyer named Fitzhenry. As Mrs Fitzhenry she played in Dublin and London theatres up to 1773 or 1774 before retiring, but she may have returned to the stage briefly in the period 1782–3. It is believed that she died in Ireland or in Bath, England, in 1790. The *European Magazine* described her as a 'celebrated actress ... excellent, but lacked great beauty, acting original, character blameless, sharp in pecuniary affairs.' **Ciarán Deane**

FitzJames, James, Duke of Berwick (1670–1734), soldier. Born and raised in France as a Catholic, a son of James, Duke of York (later JAMES II) and Arabella Churchill (sister of the Duke of Marlborough). In 1686–7 he gained his first military experience in Hungary. Created duke in 1687, he joined his exiled father in France in 1689 and accompanied him to Ireland. He commanded a force at Clady and the SIEGE OF DERRY, where he was wounded. Having recovered, he was entrusted with taking Enniskillen, though he was ordered back to Derry after capturing Trillick. That autumn around Newry he initiated a scorched-earth policy, which he repeated in Munster a year later. Having suffered defeat at Cavan, he led several cavalry charges at the BATTLE OF THE BOYNE. Later he foiled a coup against the EARL OF TYRCONNELL, in whose absence he commanded the army, overseeing a siege at Birr and the loss of Cork, after which illness and JACOBITE intrigues ensured that he was only nominally in command. In early 1691 he returned to France. Commended for bravery at Steenkirk and captured at Landen, he became a marshal of France, commanded the victory over the Anglo-Portuguese army at Almanza, and was killed by a stray cannon-ball at Philipsburg. **Charles Ivar McGrath**

Fitzmaurice, George (1877–1963), playwright and civil servant. His experiments with the ABBEY THEATRE peasant play—*The Country Dressmaker* (1907), *The Pie Dish* (1908), and *The Magic Glasses* (1913)—might have made him the successor of JOHN MILLINGTON SYNGE, but YEATS's rejection of *The Dandy Dolls* (1913) and his disparagement of *'Twixt the Giltinans and the Carmodys* (1923) alienated him. He continued writing, however, and enjoyed a brief post-war vogue with productions of *The Dandy Dolls* (1945), *The Moonlighter* (1948), *The Linnaun Shee* (1949), *One Evening Gleam* (1952), and *There Are Tragedies and Tragedies* (1953). Despite writing seventeen plays and some fiction, Fitzmaurice never quite found his audience and now excites literary rather than theatrical interest. **Ger Fitzgibbon**

Fitzmaurice, James Christopher (Fitz) (1898–1965), aviation pioneer. Born in Dublin. Though under age, he joined the British army during the First World War but was subsequently discharged. He rejoined and eventually became a pilot in the Royal Flying Corps (later the Royal Air Force). After the war he was given a permanent commission, which he resigned in 1922 to become one of the first members of the Irish Air Service (later the AIR CORPS). He commanded Fermoy Aerodrome and operated against the anti-Treaty forces. In 1926 he became officer commanding the Air Corps. In 1927, in company with R. H. MacIntosh ('All-Weather Mac') he made an attempt at the east-to-west North Atlantic flight in a Fokker aircraft called *Princess Xenia*; foul weather forced a landing on a Co. Kerry beach. He succeeded the following year when he co-piloted, with Captain Herman Köhl, the Junkers aircraft *Bremen*. Their passenger was Baron Günther von Hünefeld, owner of the aircraft, which landed on Greenly Island, Labrador, after $36\frac{1}{2}$ hours in the air. In 1934, sponsored by Irish Hospital Sweepstakes, he entered the London–Melbourne Air Race in a Bellanca aircraft named *The Irish Swoop*. He was the favourite to win, but because of a technicality concerning his aircraft's fuel system he was disqualified from entering. [see ALDRITT.] **Donal MacCarron**

FitzRalph, Richard (died 1360), scholar and Archbishop of Armagh. Born in Dundalk, Co. Louth. A popular preacher, he became chancellor of the University of Oxford. Archbishop of Armagh from 1347, he wrote on philosophy and theology. Having written his controversial *Nine Conclusions against the Mendicant Orders*, he was called to Avignon by Pope Innocent VI, who reprimanded him and condemned his opinions. He retired to Belgium. **Juan José Pérez-Camacho**

fitz Stephen, Robert, (died c. 1192) ANGLO-NORMAN adventurer. He was recruited in south Wales by DERMOT MACMURROUGH to help recover the kingdom of Leinster, which Dermot lost in 1166. He landed in Wexford in May 1169 and died before 1192, leaving no direct heirs. His nephew GIRALDUS CAMBRENSIS, who wrote as an apologist for the Anglo-Norman settlers, extolled his uncle's military prowess and attributed a leading role to him in establishing the English colony in Ireland. **Marie Therese Flanagan**

Fitzwilliam, Sir William (1526–1599), Lord Deputy of Ireland, 1571–5, 1588–94. One of the longest-serving English administrators in Ireland, he first headed the commission of inquiry that discredited Sir ANTHONY ST LEGER in 1556, and between 1559 and 1569 he acted as treasurer of the royal finances in Ireland. An audit of his period in that office revealed a deficit of almost £10,000, for half of which he was held responsible. This massive debt profoundly influenced his conduct as Lord Deputy thereafter, as he used the office to sell appointments, issue military commissions, and generally dispense patronage as a means of making good his debt. Despite a propensity to alarmism, intended perhaps to keep the garrison at strength, Fitzwilliam eschewed all political initiatives, preferring to react to circumstances in a manner that in his last term of office was to prove disastrous. His refusal then to continue the 'composition' policy (whereby traditional duties of supporting private armies were commuted to conventional taxes) begun by his predecessor, Sir JOHN PERROT, his tolerance of the steady political aggrandisement of HUGH O'NEILL in Tyrone and of the actions of HUGH O'DONNELL following his escape from DUBLIN CASTLE, his arbitrary resettlement of Co. Monaghan, and his failure to curb the freebooting activities of English captains along the southern borders of Ulster all contributed to the rapid destabilisation of the province in the early 1590s and the emergence of an unprecedented alliance of O'Neill, O'Donnell, and Maguire in rebellion against the Crown. **Ciaran Brady**

Fitzmaurice, James. *Colonel James Fitzmaurice (in military uniform, with hand raised), with Captain Herman Köhl (left) and Baron Günther von Hünefeld (right), receiving cheers and a confetti-storm greeting on their triumphant ride through New York, 8 May 1928, following the first east-west transatlantic flight. [Associated Press]*

Fitzwilliam episode, an event early in 1795 that raised and then dashed the hopes of Irish Catholics, that the agitation of the CATHOLIC COMMITTEE during the first half of the 1790s would result in their emancipation from the few remaining Penal Laws. It takes its name from William Wentworth Fitzwilliam, second Earl Fitzwilliam (1748–1833), a high-minded English Whig grandee who had Irish ancestry, an Irish estate, and an Irish wife. Having arrived in Ireland as LORD LIEUTENANT on 3 January, he quickly dismissed hostile officials at DUBLIN CASTLE. The Irish Whig leader in the Irish House of Commons, HENRY GRATTAN, brought in a Catholic Relief Bill. Irish Tories used their influence against Fitzwilliam and the British Cabinet considered he had acted precipitately. Fitzwilliam was recalled and left Ireland on 25 March. Catholics demonstrated and protested but the dismissed officials were reinstated. Grattan's bill was defeated and the Irish Tories' self-confidence increased. Catholic and liberal disillusionment at the event was a factor in the radicalisation and militarisation of the UNITED IRISH movement. **C. J. Woods**

Flags and Emblems Act (1954), an act passed by the Northern Ireland Parliament seeking to protect the flying of the Union Jack while specifically preventing the display of the TRICOLOUR. It made it illegal to interfere with the display of the British flag except on one's own property; the second clause empowered the RUC to remove any flag or EMBLEM considered likely to cause a breach of the peace. That the act was directed at the Tricolour was implied by the Minister of Home Affairs, George Hanna, who described its display as 'close to an act of treason.' The act led to the Divis Street riots in Belfast during the 1964 British general election campaign, when Rev. IAN PAISLEY threatened to march to SINN FÉIN election headquarters to remove a Tricolour. On 1 October 1964 the RUC, invoking their powers under the act, forcibly removed the flag; the resulting riots between nationalists and the RUC were the worst since 1935. The act was repealed under the terms of the ANGLO-IRISH AGREEMENT (1985). **Eamon Phoenix**

Flanagan, Father Edward (1886–1948), founder of Boys' Town. Born in Ballymoe, Co. Roscommon; emigrated to the United States in 1904. Having graduated from Mount St Mary's College, Emmetsburg, Maryland, he was drawn to the priesthood and was ordained in 1912. He witnessed great poverty in Nebraska and Omaha and vowed to assist destitute men and homeless boys. He began a small shelter and in 1922 established Boys' Town, a 4 ha (10-acre) farm in Omaha, which gained a worldwide reputation and inspired similar projects elsewhere. **David Kiely**

Flanagan, Seán (1922–1993) Gaelic footballer and politician. Born in Ballyhaunis, Co. Mayo; educated at St Jarlath's College, Tuam (a famous football nursery) and UCD, from where he graduated with a law degree. Regarded as revolutionary in his thinking on how to prepare for and play GAELIC FOOTBALL, he was a charismatic figure who inspired team-mates and supporters by his presence on and off the field. He was Mayo's captain for the all-Ireland victories of 1950 and 1951. When his footballing career ended he entered politics and served as a minister in two FIANNA FÁIL governments. **Donal Keenan**

Flanagan, T. P. (1929–), painter. Born in Enniskillen, Co. Fermanagh; attended Belfast College of Art and became an art teacher. In 1965 he was appointed head of the art department of St Mary's College of Education, Belfast, and was the president of the Royal Ulster Academy, 1977–83. He has also lectured in the United States. Having retired from teaching, he became a full-time painter. CEMA and the ACNI arranged one-person shows. Commissions have included a 1971 postage stamp and a Co. Fermanagh mural and portraits of John D. Stewart and Sadie Patterson for the ACNI. His first retrospective exhibition was held at the ULSTER MUSEUM in 1995. In 1999 BBC television presented 'The Irish Landscape, a personal approach' by Flanagan. He is represented in several public collections, including the Hugh Lane Municipal Gallery of Modern Art, Dublin, and the Ulster Museum. **Theo Snoddy**

Flann mac Lonáin (died 891, 896, or 918), poet. His death and murder are variously recorded in the ANNALS under various dates. He is described in the Annals of the FOUR MASTERS as 'Firgil Gáedel' ('the Virgil of the Irish') and is linked with the poets MUIRCHEARTACH MAC LÍACC and Urard mac Coisse (died 990) in the tale 'Trí hOllamain Chondacht' ('Three poets of the Connachta'). While many works have been erroneously attributed to him, he appears to have been the author of a small number of poems, including one on Eochu Mugmedón's five sons, 'Maiccni Echach ard a nglé.' **Séamus Mac Mathúna**

Flann Mainistrech (died 1056), scholar and poet. He is described in the ANNALS of Ulster as 'chief Latin scholar and professor of Irish history'. Head of the Latin school at MONASTERBOICE, Co. Louth, he was a 'synthetic historian', combining Irish historical lore with Christian world history. Poems on the Christian and pre-Christian kings of Ireland and on the dynasties of Aileach, Meath, and Brega are attributed to him. **Séamus Mac Mathúna**

Flann Sinna, King of TARA, 879–916. Son of MÁEL SECHNAILL of Clann Cholmáin, he married Gormlaith of Brega and succeeded ÁED FINDLIATH of CENÉL NEOGHAIN. In 908 he defeated CORMAC MAC CUILEANNÁIN, Bishop-King of Cashel, at Bealach Mughna. He erected the 'CROSS OF THE SCRIPTURES' at CLONMACNOISE. Followed by NIALL GLÚNDUB; his son Donnchad later reigned. **Ailbhe Mac Shamhráin**

Flatley, Michael (1958–), Irish-American dancer and flute-player. Born in Michigan; the family later moved to Chicago, where his parents, Michael and Eilish Flatley, were important figures in the Irish music and dance world. His formal training in Irish dancing began in the Dennis Dennehy school in Chicago in 1969; in 1975 he became the first American to win the World Irish Dancing Championship; and in 1982 he joined the CHIEFTAINS as their featured dancer. In 1994 he and his dancing partner, Jean Butler, achieved fame through their interval act during the 1994 EUROVISION SONG CONTEST and subsequently in the 'RIVERDANCE' spectacular. Flatley later went on to star in his own shows, 'Lord of the Dance' (1997) and 'Feet of Flames' (2000). **Helen Brennan**

fleadh cheoil, a festival of TRADITIONAL MUSIC, usually organised by COMHALTAS CEOLTÓIRÍ ÉIREANN, built around formal instrumental, singing, and dancing competitions. First held in Monaghan in 1952, the fleadh spreads out through an entire small town, creating an environment exclusive to the music's ethos. Impromptu sessions in pubs and on the street are its strong feature, with night-time occupied by sets and CÉILÍ DANCING. Organised outdoor stage shows with music, costumes, and choreographed STEP-DANCING are also common. The fleadhanna are the key to the competitive system of CCÉ: winners at county events progress to four provincial events, these producing 'firsts' and 'seconds' to contest the All-Ireland Fleadh Cheoil, held each August in a larger town. 'Provincials' are also held in Britain (London, the Midlands, Northern and Scottish regions) and the United States (Mid-West and Mid-Atlantic), which also send winners to the All-Ireland.

The All-Ireland Fleadh Cheoil is a popular weekend entertainment, promoted by CCÉ as a family affair but involving mostly younger people. It attracts large crowds—up to 100,000, some 40 per cent of these from abroad. Many, however, get to hear comparatively little music, attending for the holiday spirit and sociability (though briefly in the late 1960s there were riotous disturbances). The competition structure has been the dominant standard-setter in traditional music since the 1950s but today is challenged by modern commercial recording, rendering the fleadh awards important only to those under twenty. [see FEIS.] **Fintan Vallely**

'Fled Bricrenn' ('Bricriu's feast'), a tale concerned with the contest between the three Ulster warriors CÚ CHULAINN, Laoghaire Buadhach and Conall Cearnach to establish which should be given the *curadhmhír* ('hero's portion'), the choicest part of a magnificent pig that is to be awarded to the bravest warrior. The occasion is a feast arranged by Bricriu Neimhtheanga ('poison-tongue'), who foments rivalry and strife between the Ulster warriors and between their wives. Cú Chulainn's triumph in a series of heroic trials is disregarded by his two competitors until they submit to the will of Cú Roí mac Dáire, who arranges a beheading contest. Triumphant also in this, Cú Chulainn is finally acknowledged as the pre-eminent of the Ulstermen. **Ruairí Ó hUiginn**

'Fled Dúin na nGéd' (feast at Dun na Géd), a Middle Irish tale, dating probably from the twelfth century. It tells how good, represented by the High King Domnall mac Aeda, prevails over evil. The King of the Ulaid, Congal Cláen, attends a feast prepared by Domnall at which goose-eggs are served, some of which were stolen from Bishop Erc Sláine and others provided by two monstrous giants. Congal is the victim of curses put on the feast by Bishop Erc and the giants; conflict with Domnall, in which the latter is victorious, is unavoidable. The story is closely related to BUILE SHUIBHNE ('Suibhne's frenzy') and Cath Maige Rath ('The Battle of Moira'). **Uáitéar Mac Gearailt**

Fleetwood, Charles (died 1692), soldier and politician. Son of a Northamptonshire landowner, he entered the legal profession in 1638 and took the parliamentary side in the English Civil War, becoming commander of a cavalry regiment in CROMWELL's New Model Army. Elected to Parliament in May 1646, he played an important role in ensuring that the army accepted political decisions and was rewarded by Cromwell with military and political office. In 1652 he was appointed commander-in-chief of the army in Ireland and one of the Commissioners for the Civil Government of Ireland; in 1654 he became Lord Deputy. He strongly advocated the TRANSPLANTATION of the Irish to Connacht and bitterly resented the opposition to this policy from the Old English in Ireland, such as Vincent Gookin, who wrote a treatise against it. Vehemently anti-Catholic, he favoured the Baptists and Quakers among the army and as a consequence was disliked by Anglicans and Presbyterians. This led to his recall to England in 1655 and his replacement by HENRY CROMWELL, who reversed some of his policies; however, he retained the title of Lord Deputy until 1657. He escaped execution at the RESTORATION but was debarred from holding public office and lived in obscurity until his death. He married three times; his second wife was Cromwell's daughter Bridget, widow of HENRY IRETON. **Liam Irwin**

Fleischmann, Aloys (1910–1992), composer, writer, teacher, and conductor. Born in Munich; educated at UCC and studied composition and conducting at the Staatliche Akademie für Tonkunst, Munich, and musicology at the University of Munich. Professor of music at University College, Cork, 1934–80, he founded the Cork Symphony Orchestra, 1934, and CORK INTERNATIONAL CHORAL AND FOLK DANCE FESTIVAL, 1954. He collaborated with JOAN DENISE MORIARTY and CORK BALLET COMPANY, Irish Theatre Ballet, and Irish National Ballet, 1947–92. His output comprises works for chorus and orchestra, five ballets, a symphony, song cycles, and many chamber and solo works, including *Sreath do Phianó* (1933), *Clare's Dragoons* for baritone, chorus, warpipes, and orchestra (1945), *Sinfonia Votiva* (1977), *The Táin*, a ballet in three acts (1981), and *Games* for mixed choir, harp, and percussion (1990). His most important publication was the posthumous *Sources of Irish Traditional Music, c. 1600–1855* (1998), jointly edited with MÍCHEÁL Ó SÚILLEABHÁIN, the fruit of a thirty-year research project; he also edited *Music in Ireland* (1952). In 1963 he was awarded a doctorate by the National University of Ireland; other honours included an honorary doctorate from the University of Dublin, 1964, membership of the Order of Merit of the Federal Republic of Germany, 1966, and the Silver Medallion of the Irish-American Cultural Institute, 1976. **Paul Collins**

Flight of the Earls, a popular name for the hurried departure from Ireland of HUGH O'NEILL, Earl of Tyrone, and RORY O'DONNELL, Earl of Tyrconnell, in September 1607. With its tragic and romantic connotations, it is considered one of the most enigmatic events in Irish history. Historians have attempted to offer an explanation. The earls have been accused by some of abandoning their people to English rule; at the very least the flight is perceived as the inevitable consequence of the defeat of Hugh O'Neill's forces during the NINE YEARS' WAR (1594–1603). In this view it is considered to mark the final recognition that Ireland had succumbed to English hegemony. Why the earls fled in such hurried circumstances is addressed in alternative explanations. Alleged to have become involved in renewed conspiratorial machinations, they are depicted as fleeing in fear that their treasonable activities were about to be exposed. For others, by contrast, the sudden nature of the flight is viewed as proceeding from the unwarrantable treatment of the earls by the Protestant English authorities, the earls being goaded into taking flight in fear for their lives. If the debate about the causes of the flight will continue to rage, there is little disagreement about the enormous consequences of the event, paving the way, as it did, for the PLANTATION OF ULSTER and the concomitant impact of the concentrated settlement of so many Protestants in the north on the future course of Irish history. **John McCavitt**

Flood, Henry (1732–1791), politician. Born in Donnybrook, Co. Dublin; educated at TCD and the University of Oxford. He studied but never practised law. Elected to the Irish Parliament for Co. Kilkenny in 1759, he soon attracted notice as an exceptional debater and as an independent patriot. Persuaded that he could best advance his reforming political agenda from a position of power, he concluded a labyrinthine negotiation with the Irish administration by accepting the office of Vice-Treasurer in 1775; it proved the biggest mistake of his career. Unable to work closely with the administration, and treated with suspicion by his erstwhile allies, he was not welcomed back into the Patriot fold following his dismissal from office in 1781. However, his brand of radical patriotism struck a chord with the public, and his objection in 1782–3 to the 'simple repeal' of the DECLARATORY ACT enabled him to eclipse HENRY GRATTAN as the most popular politician of the day. He consolidated his appeal by taking an active part in the parliamentary reform movement in 1783–4; but his election to the British Parliament meant he spent less and less time in Ireland. He never registered the impact he desired at Westminster, and he retired from politics when he failed to be re-elected in 1790. **James Kelly**

Flood, William Henry Grattan (1857–1928), church organist, music teacher, and historian. Born in Lismore, Co. Waterford. Though he published widely in other fields, including European music and local history, he is best known for his writing on Irish music. His principal works are *A History of Irish Music* (1905), *The Story of the Harp* (1905), and *The Story of the Bagpipe* (1911). He was also the contributor on Irish music to Grove's *Dictionary of Music and Musicians*. Though he was one of the few

Fleischmann. *Aloys Fleischmann, an active and influential figure in musical life as composer, writer, and conductor. He undertook the cataloguing of traditional Irish tunes dating from c. 1600 to 1855.* [Irish Examiner]

Flight of the Earls. *Map of Ireland (1567) by John Goghe. The 'Flight of the Earls' is the popular term for the departure of Hugh O'Neill, Earl of Tyrone, Rory O'Donnell, Earl of Tyrconnell, and their followers from Ireland in 1607. Lough Swilly, from which they sailed, is shown centre right. The size of Lough Erne reflects the cartographers' lack of knowledge of the interior. [Public Record Office, London; MPFI/68]*

writers of the time publishing on TRADITIONAL MUSIC, his contribution is weakened by the poor scholarship evident in many of his works, notably *A History of Irish Music*. He was largely instrumental in introducing the term *uilleann pipes* for the Irish pipes, generally known previously as the 'union pipes'. **Colin Hamilton**

flooding, caused by a combination of meteorological, topographical, geological, and other factors. Seasonal flooding affects many parts of Ireland, though floods can occur at any time of year. Extreme falls of rain centred over the WICKLOW MOUNTAINS associated with 'Hurricane Charlie' caused widespread damage to parts of south Co. Dublin in August 1986. Seasonal flooding is a serious problem, the rivers most prone to flooding being those that drain the central lowlands. Many of these flow sluggishly for much of their course, which can lead to a backing up of water. The RIVER SHANNON has a long history of serious yearly flooding; the worst floods in the twentieth century were in 1915 and 1925, and severe disruption was caused to Athlone by the floods of 1954. River flooding can be exacerbated in coastal areas by interactions between high tides and high flows; this has long been a problem in Cos. Waterford and Cork. Seasonal flooding can also be caused by turloughs, a feature of the limestone lowlands of Cos. Galway and Mayo. They drain slowly by way of underground routes, which can result in a backing up of water during the winter, causing the lakes to expand. Extensive areas can become inundated if the accumulation of rainfall is greater than average over the autumn and winter months. In the winter of 1994/5 there was severe flooding in the Gort and Ardrahan area of Co. Galway, causing about £10 million worth of damage. [see CLIMATE; COASTAL EROSION; WATER.] **R. A. Charlton**

floodplains, areas of relatively flat land found on each side of river channels that are periodically inundated during high flows. They are formed from *alluvium* (fluvial deposits) left by migrating river channels and by finer deposits that build up over time, veiling the floodplain when flood waters spread out across it. The finer deposits are rich in nutrients, and floodplain soils are typically fertile but can also be prone to waterlogging. Most natural river channels can be expected to flow over their banks once a year on average, though this varies according to circumstances. Farmland and settlements on floodplains are therefore at risk, though these areas do provide good agricultural land and are in close proximity to a WATER supply as well as a means of TRANSPORT; for these reasons many settlements are sited on floodplains, including Dublin, Belfast, and Cork. These cities, as well as many towns (for example

Clonmel), villages and farmland all have a long history of FLOODING. This can be controlled to some extent through engineering works, such as widening, deepening, and straightening river channels to increase capacity, and building flood walls and embankments to prevent encroachment. Engineering works are being completed at Clonmel and Carrick-on-Suir, Co. Tipperary, though for economic reasons such schemes can provide protection only for floods up to a certain magnitude, the largest floods being comparatively rare. Floodplain zoning can also be used to identify the areas most at risk and to restrict development in those areas. **R. A. Charlton**

flora. The flora of Ireland is relatively well known and includes just over a thousand species of flowering plants and ferns. Most of the species are found also in Britain and in adjacent parts of Western Europe. A small number are not found in Irish latitudes elsewhere in Europe. About twenty Irish plants have their centre of distribution around the Mediterranean or in the warmer areas of Western Europe. These Lusitanian or Mediterranean elements in the Irish flora, which include maidenhair fern, strawberry tree, St Dabeoc's heath, St Patrick's cabbage, Irish orchid, and Kerry butterwort, are commonest in the milder areas of western and southern Ireland. A smaller group of American plants have gained a European foothold in Ireland and have scarcely spread outside the country on this side of the Atlantic. These include the undoubtedly native pipewort, an aquatic found in bog pools in the west, the American lady's tresses orchid, the doubtfully native blue-eyed grass, and the recently arrived slender St John's wort.

Other groups of plants, such as the mosses, liverworts, and lichens (the cryptogams), also show similar reduced numbers when compared with Britain and the Continent; but there is also a selection of species that do not occur in the adjacent parts of Europe. The mild and moist areas of the west of Ireland are particularly rich in these cryptogamic plants.

Areas of floral richness in Ireland include the Burren, Co. Clare (see p. 143), Connemara, and south Mayo, the limestones of the BENBULBIN range, the Kerry and Donegal Mountains, the Galty Mountains, the Antrim coast and Garran plateau, Co. Antrim, the sand dunes of the east and south, and the bogs, fens, and lakes of the Central Plain. [see ARBORETA; BOTANIC GARDENS; FAUNA.] **Donal Synnott**

Florence Court, Enniskillen, Co. Fermanagh. In the demesne of the Earls of Enniskillen on the banks of LOUGH ERNE, the house was built in the middle to late eighteenth century for John Cole, later first Lord Mount Florence. Its heavily enriched main façade has a three-storey break-fronted seven-bay central block, to which DAVIS DUCART added arcaded wings and pavilions c. 1768. Florence Court is noted for the fine PLASTERWORK of the interior, possibly by ROBERT WEST, with the dining-room and first-floor Venetian Room ceiling decorated with characteristic Rococo swirling foliage and birds in relief. The Florence Court yew, from which all Irish upright yews have been propagated, is in the park. Florence Court was taken over by the National Trust in 1953. **Brian Lalor**

Flower, Robin (1881–1946), Irish scholar. Born in Leeds; educated at the University of Oxford. He worked at the British Museum, London, where he was involved in the cataloguing of Irish MANUSCRIPTS. He devoted much of his life to studying the culture of the BLASKET ISLANDS, Co. Kerry, and encouraged the Irish-speaking islanders to record their memoirs. He translated TOMÁS Ó CRIOMHTHAINN's *An tOileánach* as *The Islandman* (1929), and also his *Seanchas ón Oileán Tiar* as *Lore from the Western Island* (1956), and published PEIG SAYERS' stories in *Béaloideas*. Among Flower's other publications are *The Great Blasket* (1924) and *The Western Island or The Great Blasket* (1945). **Brian Lalor**

flute. The flute played in traditional music is essentially the pre-Boehm nineteenth-century orchestral instrument, the eight-keyed or simple system flute in the key of D. It is often called the *concert flute*, with reference to the common pitch, or the *wooden or timber flute*, with reference to its construction. Though probably present in Ireland from the late seventeenth or early eighteenth century in the hands of amateurs among the Anglo-Irish community, it probably became a common instrument in the hands of traditional players only during the nineteenth century. Its subsequent popularity was influenced by the ubiquitous fife-and-drum bands and temperance bands, which used higher-pitched flutes in F and B flat. It was also reinforced by the availability of mass-produced flutes, mostly made in Germany, from the last quarter of the nineteenth century. Flutes sent home by emigrant workers in England from the 1930s onwards were also an important source in more modern times.

Though the flute is found in every county, the majority of players, especially before the revival period altered traditional demographic patterns, were to be found in the mid-western counties of Sligo, Leitrim, Roscommon, east Mayo, and east Galway, with significant numbers in the bordering counties of Fermanagh and Clare. In common with other instruments two broad styles, which can be characterised as *legato* and *staccato*, can be observed (see p. 1064). [see FIDDLE.] **Colin Hamilton**

flute bands, an important cultural element in Northern Ireland, associated with a variety of political processions though especially with the ORANGE ORDER. They arose in the middle or late nineteenth century in imitation of those of the British army, displacing the LAMBEG DRUM and fife in most areas. The total membership of such bands at the end of the twentieth century may have been as high as 7,000. *First flute bands* play two-piece simple-system B flat flutes, with one or more keys, together with snare drums and a bass drum. The repertoire is eclectic though with the emphasis likely to be on political tunes, with simple musical arrangements and the accent on drums. These bands are locally organised, and their religio-political associations are important. *Part bands*, which developed from first flute bands, are perceived as more respectable, with the political aspect much less obvious. They play various sizes of flute (usually of the Boehm system), from B flat bass to B flat first flute, with a small corps of drums. They employ complex musical arrangements, their repertoire including much classical material, and they are highly competent musically. **Gary Hastings**

flute styles. There are as many styles as there are players of the wooden concert flute. Taste may be informed by conceptions of regional style that have taken root over the last century. The flute is played all over Ireland, yet players will often single out a particular region as being important, such as Cos. Leitrim, Sligo, Roscommon, Fermanagh, Clare, and east Galway. The Leitrim style is breathy and percussive; the Sligo style is robust, with flowery ornamentation; the east Galway style is lyrical and smooth. The socio-historical reasons for this classification may be complex, but it remains a useful guide to the aesthetics of Irish-style flute-playing. **Desi Wilkinson**

Foley, Dónal (1922–1981), journalist. Born in Ring, Co. Waterford; educated at St Patrick's College, Waterford. He began his career in JOURNALISM in London with the Irish News Agency and later as London editor of the IRISH PRESS. While still in London he joined the IRISH TIMES, becoming news editor in 1963 and deputy editor in 1977. He had a significant influence on its development as a more critical and socially aware newspaper during the 1960s and 70s. While he wrote on a variety of topics, he was most closely associated with his satirical 'Man Bites Dog' column. **Brian Galvin**

Foley, John Henry (1818–1874), sculptor. Born in Dublin; he was a prizewinner at the RDS Modelling Schools. In 1835 he went to study in London and subsequently established his studio there. Talented in the modelling of ideal statuary and portrait images, combining classical restraint and natural ease, he became the leading sculptor of his day and was elected to membership of the ROYAL HIBERNIAN ACADEMY, the Royal Academy (London), and the Belgian Academy of Fine Art. He received many commissions for public monuments in Ireland and Britain, among them the O'Connell Monument (1865) for O'Connell Street, Dublin, and the statue of Prince Albert (1868) for the Albert Memorial in London, for which he also carved the Asia group. **Paula Murphy**

Foley, John Henry. The O'Connell Monument *(1864–82), O'Connell Street, Dublin, by John Henry Foley, composed of three elements: a monumental figure of O'Connell, a frieze of figures on the drum, representing commerce and the professions, with Hibernia holding the scroll of emancipation (centre); and below the drum four winged victories, representing O'Connell's qualities of patriotism, fidelity, courage, and eloquence. Bullet holes from the 1916 Rising scar the figures. [Denis Mortell]*

folk belief, central to the concept of FOLKLORE and affecting almost all aspects of human life and experience. Folk beliefs are seen more in the way people behave than in what they say and are particularly visible in aspects of CALENDAR CUSTOM, such as traditions surrounding MAY DAY and HALLOWE'EN (*Oíche Shamhna*) and in folk medicine practices, such as the blending of particular herbs or performing ritual actions.

Potent examples of folk belief relate to the rites of passage, when a person moves from one human status to another, such as birth, MARRIAGE, and death. CHILDBIRTH in folk tradition involved many beliefs and practices, observed from conception through pregnancy to birth: for example, various activities were engaged in by women seeking to conceive or seeking to know if they were able to conceive. In addition, the pregnant woman had to take great care, as it was believed that she was especially vulnerable during this time and that actions she might take could harm the unborn child. The birth itself, its timing, the way the child came into the world, the actions of the midwife, and the subsequent care of the new mother were all surrounded by folk belief. Tongs might be placed over the cradle to protect the newborn child from abduction by the FAIRIES. The same obtained for marriage and death customs, with prescriptive rules governing proper and improper practice. Marriage customs include the wearing of 'something old, something new, something borrowed, and something blue', and the tradition that it is unlucky for the bride and groom to see each other on the wedding day before the wedding ceremony. In death customs, traditional belief and practice surrounded the laying out of the body, the prayers for the deceased, the WAKE, and the funeral.

Much folklore treats of the consequences of not doing the right thing at the right time, in the right place, and such tradition serves as an admonition to people who would transgress the inherited wisdom. In this way powerful social and communal controls and mores were established and maintained, with belief and practice woven into the fabric of daily life.

Continuity and change are inherent in folk belief and practice, and the nature of folklore as ever-changing provides insights into the value systems, at particular times and in particular places, of groups and communities. Tracing the development of folk belief is complex, as folklorists can often only situate beliefs in a relational way, with practices that become obsolete being remembered but not necessarily believed. An example of this is the belief in fairies, which was widespread for numerous generations but had noticeably declined by the 1950s. [see CLEARY, BRIGID.] **Anne O'Connor**

folk festivals. In the early 1950s the first FLEADH CHEOIL was held. These gatherings of musicians were organised by the fledgling COMHALTAS CEOLTÓIRÍ ÉIREANN; and while informal music-making was important, a competition structure was central. By the mid-1960s large crowds attended. At the same time the commercial and artistic success of gatherings such as the Newport Folk and Blues Festival and later the Woodstock festival in America were to inspire similar events around the world. The emergence of weekend events, such as the Lisdoonvarna Festival, Co. Clare, 1979–83, organised by Paddy Doherty and Jim Shannon, and the Ballysadare Festival, Co. Sligo, 1977–82, were notable in that they were professionally staged events that presented well-known folk and traditional performers to large audiences. Ballysadare's programme remained essentially based on folk music; Lisdoonvarna, having had the CHIEFTAINS as its first leading act, broadened its policy to feature international rock artists but continued to present traditional musicians also. A notable aspect of these events was the number of music followers who camped in tents, creating a festive atmosphere. The Carnsore Point Festival (1978), organised to protest against plans by the ESB to develop a nuclear power plant in south Co. Wexford, featured a range of folk performers. Folk club organisers and enthusiasts in Dublin, Cork, Belfast, Ballyshannon, Drogheda, Kenmare, and Killarney developed their own, usually weekend-long, events. **Tom Sherlock**

folk life. The notion of the 'folk' became widespread during the nineteenth century as a useful way in which to categorise rural people, whom scholars increasingly saw as somehow separate from the large-scale urbanised national societies in which they lived. For some early scholars, remote rural societies seemed more deeply rooted and more harmonious than the cosmopolitan world. In important respects, rural life seemed to preserve unchanging remnants of ancient societies and beliefs.

The intellectual and political impulses that led to the development of both FOLKLORE and folk life as distinct subjects were similar: a negative reaction to international modernisation, and an engagement with the values of romantic nationalism. Many nationalist thinkers of the period postulated an organic relationship between the traditional way of life of a region and its physical environment. Buildings and techniques can often be shown to be products of long-term sensitive adjustments to local conditions: for example, cultivation ridges and some types of dry-stone wall found under bog at prehistoric sites such as the CÉIDE FIELDS in Co. Mayo are still sometimes constructed today. Early folk-life research uncovered a mass of techniques and objects that were unique not only to Ireland but to the locality in which they were used. For romantic nationalists in Ireland and throughout Europe, the synthesis between culture and nature that they believed had been discovered in the world of the folk revealed the essential, timeless qualities of their landscape and society—a pure, unsullied peasant life, which was increasingly under threat from outside forces.

The academic study of folklore and folk life became established in Europe during the late nineteenth century. In Ireland, folklore studies became organised at institutional level in 1927 with the foundation of the Folklore of Ireland Society. Though there is a large overlap between the two disciplines, folklore tends to centre on the expressive worlds of popular belief, language, and music, while folk life concentrates on the distinctive physical manifestations of local culture, including housing, crafts, agriculture, and domestic life. The seminal Irish text used by folklore collectors in classifying material, SEÁN Ó SÚILLEABHÁIN's *Handbook of Irish Folklore* (1942), was also used in developing a classification index for folk-life artefacts when collections of these began in Northern Ireland in the 1950s. The largest Irish collection of folk-life artefacts is in the NATIONAL MUSEUM OF IRELAND, and part of this internationally important collection is on display in the Museum of Country Life at Turlough Park, Co. Mayo. However, the main intellectual impulse to the development of folk-life studies in Ireland came from the North, with the work of E. ESTYN EVANS, whose vision from the 1920s to the 50s led to the development of several new departments in Queen's University, Belfast, and of the ULSTER FOLK AND TRANSPORT MUSEUM.

The achievements of folk-life studies have been considerable. Researchers in the field were some of the first to draw attention to the importance of the lives of ordinary people; their fieldwork methods, including oral history, have significantly changed the study of history. In a number of specialist research fields, such as archaeology and the history of technology, the discoveries of folk life have a continuing relevance. Such specialist research will not ensure the development of the subject, or create widespread public interest; however, once the subject moves beyond the notion of a harmonious relationship between the folk and their environment, new fields of study become relevant. The problems of pollution, overproduction, and the destruction of resources by farming can be shown to have ancient parallels, and modern studies tend to examine both the ingenuity of local responses in situations of scarcity and the social and economic forces that produced disastrous environmental imbalances. By examining these issues, folk-life research becomes relevant for ecologists interested in biodiversity, and how it was maintained, or reduced, in the past.

For urban people interested in rural issues, the main concern now is not to celebrate unchanging balance between country people and their world but to understand how things have gone so badly wrong. The appearance of BSE ('mad cow disease') in the 1990s and the epidemic of foot-and-mouth disease in Britain in 2001 have significantly transformed popular notions about rural life. The emphasis in folk-life studies on examining past organisation and techniques means that it can make important contributions to understanding the historical basis for these issues. The established approach—of viewing artefacts and processes within a wider social and economic totality—has contributed to the breaking down of reified analytical boundaries, while the ideological quest for cultural essences, which were believed to reside in the world of the 'folk', has become increasingly hard to justify. Even in remote areas, where untainted tradition was seen as most easily found, the international connections revealed by artefacts and techniques can be shown to be deep and long-lasting. Cultures are an accumulation of historical developments, and their distinctiveness arises from this, rather than from the ageless qualities that some early folk experts believed they could uncover. The early emphasis on identifying uniquely local cultural patterns, with deep historical antecedents, made the subject a useful tool for polemicists committed to developing anti-historical mythologies of racial and national identity. At a less sinister level, the concern to identify local links between the ancient past and the present meant that the subject could not deal easily with urban ways of life, where an examination of international mass society is obviously necessary in understanding local history. However, the techniques of fieldwork recording developed by folk-life scholars have provided tools for local histories and popular culture that are of immense value. The best way forward for the subject will be to develop interdisciplinary links with historians and social scientists, and to develop intellectually challenging research projects that link socio-economic issues with popular culture, in order to deepen understanding of the impact of global forces on local society. [see ARCHITECTURE, VERNACULAR.] **Jonathan Bell**

folklore. The notion of folklore can be seen as part of an attempt to value cultural difference. The development of society from the eighteenth century led to the gradual extinction of popular agrarian traditions in Western Europe, though less so in Ireland. A pre-romantic sensibility, and romanticism itself—which opposed the inheritance of the ENLIGHTENMENT and of the Industrial Revolution—helped to transform the negative attitude of the educated classes to popular culture by seeing it as a source of artistic inspiration. The German folklorist Johann Gottfried von Herder (1744–1803) insisted that each nation was different, its *volksgeist* ('soul') expressed in its folk songs. The 'people' was the means of renewing the nation, the German word *volk* having connotations both of common people and of nation. The culture of the peasantry came to be identified as a resource for the retrieval of an 'authentic' national culture.

folklore. The Harvest Dance at Rossana, *Co. Wicklow (c. 1815) by Maria Spilsbury. Outside the windows of an eighteenth-century house in Ashford, strawboys dance to the music of uilleann pipe, fiddle, and whistle. [Christies Images Ltd]*

Herder, directly or indirectly, was a major influence everywhere on the development of cultural NATIONALISM and of the notion of folklore. THOMAS DAVIS was strongly influenced by German romantic thought—linking, for example, IRISH LANGUAGE and nation—and his YOUNG IRELAND movement established in Ireland the idea of the peasantry as the most authentic part of the nation, to be reflected in turn in the cultural nationalism of the GAELIC LEAGUE and the LITERARY REVIVAL, in twentieth-century politics (particularly that of ÉAMON DE VALERA), in literature, THEATRE, and CINEMA, and in the tourist representations of Ireland today.

The brothers Jacob Grimm (1785–1863) and Wilhelm Grimm (1786–1859) helped to lay the foundations of international folklore, and particularly folk-tale, scholarship, inspiring vast collections of folklore. T. CROFTON CROKER's pioneering collection of oral tales, *Fairy Legends and Traditions of the South of Ireland* (1825), was inspired by and in turn translated by the Grimm brothers. The English antiquarian W. J. Thoms coined the word 'folklore' in 1846, as an alternative to the existing notion of 'popular antiquities'. The first folklore society was founded in England in 1878 and was widely imitated. It had Irish members, and Irish contributions to its journal.

From the middle of the nineteenth century, Darwinian concepts of evolution were a strong influence on folklore studies in England and France. It was less so in Ireland and other countries—the prototype was Germany—where national movements rejected the existing models of high culture. A distinct notion of the culture of the 'folk' (a sort of ahistorical peasant society) arose. It was authentic because of its supposed isolation and lack of contamination from modern high culture and social dynamics. The 'folk' were simply reproducers of the high culture of the past. This understanding is often explicit in the writings of SÉAMUS Ó DUILEARGA and other Irish folklorists. The 'folk' was often contrasted in the nineteenth century with the urban proletariat, so threatening to traditional values, as in DOUGLAS HYDE's disparaging references to the emerging urban popular culture in *The Necessity for De-Anglicising Ireland* (1892).

Romanticism validated non-elite forms of culture and so provided a broader repertoire of national symbols; but it disdained the 'inauthentic' city; this lack of interest in urban life was to remain in folklore studies until the 1960s. The study of folk culture, known as 'folkloristics' or as 'ethnology', became well established in German-speaking, Nordic, and central and eastern European universities from the end of the nineteenth century, usually through the influence of cultural revival and nation-building movements, whereas anthropology was associated with the outward ethnographic gaze of countries establishing colonial empires. Today folklorists and ethnologists study both residual peasant culture and everyday life in urban and rural settings and are strongly influenced by the social sciences.

T. Crofton Croker, Patrick Kennedy (1801–1873), and the American JEREMIAH CURTIN are pioneering figures for folklore studies in Ireland, consciously part of international folklore studies and publishing important collections of oral narratives. Earlier, CHARLOTTE BROOKE and the music-collector EDWARD BUNTING had included popular and learned Irish traditions in their work. The founding of the Gaelic League in 1893, with the aim of reviving and creating a modern literature in Irish, maintained the popular-learned connection. Folklore became a source for accessible texts in Modern Irish as well as the model for an Irish literature and an ideal of cultural authenticity.

DOUGLAS HYDE was an important folklorist and an important link between the projects of reviving Irish and of creating a national literature in English. Engagement with folklore was one of the defining characteristics of Irish literature in English, exemplified in the work of W. B. YEATS, LADY AUGUSTA GREGORY, and J. M. SYNGE—all well versed in contemporary folklore studies. Spurred by the Irish Literary Revival, the work in Irish of the Blasket islanders TOMÁS Ó CRIOMHTHAINN, PEIG SAYERS—both important oral narrators—and MUIRIS Ó SÚILEABHÁIN depicts traditional life from the inside.

The IRISH FREE STATE helped to institutionalise the collection and archiving of folklore, carried out under the leadership of Séamus Ó Duilearga. The founding of the Folklore of Ireland Society and its journal BÉALOIDEAS in 1927 and of the Irish Folklore Institute in 1930 and its successor, the IRISH FOLKLORE COMMISSION, in 1935 were other important developments. The commission's extensive archival holdings were transferred to the newly established Department of Irish Folklore in UNIVERSITY COLLEGE, Dublin, in 1970. The NATIONAL MUSEUM began to assemble a FOLK-LIFE collection from the late 1920s, with A. T. LUCAS taking charge of the Folklife Collection in 1947, the first such full-time appointment. The Museum of Country Life at Turlough Park, Castlebar, Co. Mayo, opened in 2001.

In Northern Ireland the pioneer in folk life (material culture being emphasised more than oral narrative traditions) was the geographer E. ESTYN EVANS. Important developments were the publication of the journal *Ulster Folklife* (1955–), the passing of the Ulster Folk Museum Act (1958), and the merging of the Ulster Folk Museum and Belfast Transport Museum to form the ULSTER FOLK AND TRANSPORT MUSEUM at Cultra, Co. Antrim, in 1967. From 1971 folklore and folk life have been taught in English in the Department of Irish Folklore in UCD and from 1977 in English and from 1989 in Irish in what is now the Department of Folklore and Ethnology, UCC. **Diarmuid Ó Giolláin**

Folklore Commission, Irish (Coimisiún Béaloideasa Éireann), established in 1935 to collect and preserve the oral tradition and to disseminate a knowledge of it. Its honorary director, SÉAMUS Ó DUILEARGA, a founder-member, was first professor of Irish FOLKLORE at UCD. Full-time, part-time, and special collectors were employed throughout Ireland, and other collecting methods, such as a questionnaire system and the 'schools scheme' (1937–8), were used to document all aspects of folklore. In 1971 the commission, its staff and its holdings were transferred to UCD to become the newly created Department of Irish Folklore (Roinn Bhéaloideas Éireann). The collections have been indexed in accordance with *A Handbook of Irish Folklore* (1942) by SEÁN Ó SÚILLEABHÁIN. The material is mostly in manuscript, audio, video, and photographic form. In addition to offering undergraduate and postgraduate courses, the department is open to the public. **Ríonach uí Ógáin**

folklore, urban. The discipline of ethnology aims to understand the processes whereby FOLKLORE and traditional and popular culture contribute to the definition of identity in a particular society or group. The use of ethnography as a method of investigation has relevance for cultural research in urban settings, where it seeks to identify and elucidate significant cultural practices specific to city life. Such research aims at examining urban generic categories and the dynamics of the relationship between residents and their environment—the street, the housing estate, and the town in general. Urban ethnology is concerned with the customary practices, verbal genres, and other aspects of the cognitive and vernacular culture that emerge from the relationship of city people to their environment. It looks at the value systems and the negotiated identities that people develop from navigating within and experiencing complex social networks.

Urban culture is a relatively new academic field in Ireland, as scholarly attention in folklore and anthropology had until recently concentrated on the rural environment; the distribution of the population also contributed to this discrepancy. Historians, geographers, and sociologists preceded anthropologists and ethnologists in their interest in the urban field, dealing with such aspects of URBANISATION as MIGRATION patterns, DEMOGRAPHY, and economic activities. The first collection of Irish urban ethnographies, Curtin, Donnan and Wilson's *Irish Urban Cultures* (1993), illustrates how the use of ethnography as a common approach allows scholars from different academic backgrounds to communicate views that would otherwise be restricted by the boundaries of their individual fields.

An urban folklore project sponsored by the Department of Education and organised by the Department of Irish Folklore, UCD, was carried out in Dublin, 1980–81. The Northside Folklore Project began in September 1996 as a joint venture between the Folklore and Ethnology Department of UCC and Northside Community Enterprises, which, in co-operation with FÁS, uses training schemes to combat unemployment in Cork. Members of the community are trained in a variety of ethnographic research techniques, and the material produced is available on location, through the project's annual journal, and electronically through its web site. **Marie-Annick Desplanques**

folk-tales. Ireland is renowned for the number of folk-tales recorded, mainly during the second quarter of the twentieth century. These tales can be divided into two broad categories: (*a*) native hero-tales, many of them about FIONN MAC CUMHAILL and his warriors, mostly deriving from late medieval romances that circulated in manuscript form during the eighteenth and nineteenth centuries, and (*b*) international folk-tales also found elsewhere in Europe, in parts of Asia, and in North America. Some of these arrived in Ireland during the Middle Ages, but it appears that many of them are relative latecomers. International folk-tales have been allocated numbers in a classification devised by Antti Aarne and perfected by Stith Thompson. Irish versions are recorded in Ó SÚILLEABHÁIN and Christiansen's *The Types of the Irish Folktale* (1963).

Folklore Commission. *Séamus Ó Duilearga (sitting on the ground), folklorist and Celtic scholar, taking a break from recording by the roadside in Co. Waterford, 1948. [Courtesy of the Department of Irish Folklore, University College, Dublin]*

These two categories of tale share many stylistic and thematic features, particularly native hero-tales and wonder-tales (generically known as the FIONN CYCLE), a sub-category of the international tales. Many of these tales took more than an hour to tell, some many hours and occasionally a number of nights. Though also told to children, they were mainly adult entertainment. **Mícheál Briody**

food of the Blasket Islands, 1850–1950. Life on the BLASKET ISLANDS was sustained by the sea, and in this respect the food-supply systems of other islands off the west coast were probably not very different from that of the Blaskets. To feed themselves the Blasket Islanders had to spend a great deal of their time fishing. But it would be inaccurate to describe the islanders as simply 'fishermen', as this term does not convey adequately how they got their food. Hunting for seals, porpoises, rabbits and seabirds was extremely important to the islanders, as this was the way in which they supplemented their basic diet of fish, and so they were as much hunters as fishermen. Women looked after domestic animals and fowl and foraged along the islands' shores for limpets, periwinkles, edible seaweed, and mosses. Fishing for crabs was left to the men and boys.

Apart from POTATOES, the produce of the land was incidental to the islanders' food-supply system. Beef was only rarely eaten, and cows were valued for their milk. BUTTER was a luxury. Traditionally, sheep were killed for Christmas, and most of the meat was salted down. In the nineteenth century the meat of six-month-old seal pups was thought to be as good as pork. Fledgling gannets and puffins were a delicacy; the latter were called *sicíní mara* ('chickens of the sea'). Seabirds' eggs were eaten frequently, though they gave the eater bad breath. Flour, tea, and sugar were luxuries and were bought on the mainland. **Malachy McKenna**

food, post-famine. The second half of the nineteenth century was a period of intense and rapid commercialisation, a process that was propelled and sustained by a general improvement in living standards, especially among the poor. Accordingly, dietary patterns at the lower end of the spectrum diversified, with a notable increase in the consumption of shop-bought foods. At the same time the continuing spread of a RAILWAY network, together with improvements to the road system, facilitated the distribution of goods and the growing demand for commercial products in rural areas. The increased number of grocers' shops offered an alternative to foods born of self-sufficiency. In this period white yeast-leavened baker's BREAD, traditionally the prerogative of the wealthy, became increasingly popular as a result of the importing of cheaper American wheat. This development, coupled with further improvements in milling technology, directed quantities of refined flour to the baking trade. The white loaf was held in high esteem above the home-made and was the choice for special occasions.

Nevertheless, domestically a wider variety of HEARTH-baked breads became prevalent from the late nineteenth century. A triad of developments merged to facilitate the establishment of a strong home-baking tradition. The availability of gluten-rich American wheat, together with the increased use of chemical leavens, in particular bread soda (bicarbonate of soda), in conjunction with the wider use of a pot-oven or bastible, made possible the successful production of a raised wheaten soda bread. The pot-oven, suspended over the fire and with embers placed on its lid, was a multi-functional baking tool. Wheaten meal or flour, bread soda and buttermilk, together with the pot-oven, were the basic requirements for home baking, and with additional farm-produced ingredients—eggs, milk, and BUTTER—enriched special-occasion cakes were prepared.

Maize meal (Indian or yellow meal), first introduced in 1799 in an attempt to prevent or alleviate localised famine and used extensively as a relief food during the GREAT FAMINE, retained a foothold. It was used in the production of maize bread, maize porridge, and maize dumplings, and these remained a feature of the rural diet in some areas until well into the twentieth century.

By the close of the nineteenth century the food ECONOMY of the rural populace, especially those of very poor to moderate means, was balanced by a system that saw a proportion of home-produced goods hived off to supply the market, with the income from sales subsidising further food purchases, rent, household necessities, stock, and seed. The sale of a pig or two, butter, POTATOES, eggs, and fowl allowed for the purchase of wheat flour, white 'shop' bread, yellow meal, tea, sugar, salt fish, and fatty American bacon. In a curious response to market forces, relatively high-quality home-produced bacon was sent to the market, where it earned a good return, while cheaper, inferior American bacon was bought for home use. In the poorest households, notably those of the impoverished west coast, bacon was only an occasional indulgence, and good use was made of every scrap: the fat was rendered and poured over cabbage, or boiled with milk and flour to season a white sauce for potatoes.

Late nineteenth-century rural dietary change was also promoted by the work of the CONGESTED DISTRICTS BOARD (established in 1891) and by institutionalised intervention by the Department of Agriculture and Technical Instruction (founded in 1899). Both bodies sought to improve agricultural output and the quality of food for sale through education and practical instruction. On a domestic level the food economy was also identified for betterment, and even the smallest holdings were encouraged to produce a broader diversity of nutrient-rich plant foods for the table. Travelling cookery instructors advised on practical cooking and the most beneficial means of exploiting the produce of the cottage garden. The fowl yard was also identified for improvement, with attempts to introduce more productive stock and to augment the quality and freshness of eggs destined for both the table and the market.

Throughout the first half of the twentieth century the rural diet, though increasingly susceptible to the influence of commercial forces, was one that depended largely on home-produced goods and local produce. Potatoes, oatmeal, imported Indian meal, buttermilk, sour milk, and butter were staples, along with home-cured meats, and in particular pig meat remained standard. The days following the slaughter of the pig brought a feast of fresh MEAT, and, not surprisingly, Irish foodways were at their most creative in dealing with these products.

The diet followed seasonal changes, with wild foods when accessible—berries, mushrooms, watercress, and rabbits—making an occasional presence, while the coastal diet was differentiated by its leanings towards fish, shellfish, and seaweeds and at times seabirds and their eggs. Festive occasions were upheld with the desire to bring fresh meat or fresh fowl, especially a goose and shop-bought luxuries, into the pattern, while fast days were strictly adhered to, with a concentration on salted fish taken with potatoes and a simple white sauce. Open-hearth cooking remained a feature of a sizeable proportion of rural households until the second half of the twentieth century, thereby promoting a sense of continuity with past procedures, while at the same time fostering a sense of distance and isolation from modern innovations.

In the towns, the increased commercialisation and industrialisation of food production brought easier access to a variety of goods, many highly processed and of questionable quality. In line with rural patterns, the urban poor became increasingly reliant on refined white bread, spread or fried with lard or taken with cheap factory-made jams. In time bread and tea became a constant among the mass of the urban poor; it is believed that this highly refined but nutritionally poor simple carbohydrate diet would compound the levels of ill health and endemic disease of urban Ireland in the twentieth century. The establishment and growth of substantial bacon-curing factory-based industry throughout the nineteenth century, supplying both the home and foreign market, saw an increase in the availability of pig offal and inferior meat cuts in the cities strongly engaged in the trade. Shops specialised in the sale of fresh and salted offals and offcuts. At home these were simply boiled or stewed with potatoes and available root vegetables.

Even for those of better means in the towns, cooking styles and taste preferences remained largely conservative and highly repetitive. Beef, mutton, pigmeats, and fowl, with the occasional rabbit, were boiled, stewed or baked and served with a limited range of root vegetables or cabbage and the indispensable potato. Cakes and tarts of apple and rhubarb reigned supreme. However, dietary diversification was seen in the increased availability and use of a variety of processed, packaged, and tinned foods. A wide range of commercially produced confectionary was enjoyed, while grain products such as macaroni, sago, cornflour, semolina, and tapioca made strong inroads into the diet as thickening agents and the base ingredients for milk puddings. In time a realisation of their blandness and ubiquity, together with the fact that they were

food, post-famine. *Fire (below), crane, bastible pot, kettle, and griddle (right), the essential elements for cooking (nineteenth and early twentieth centuries); clothes dry on the 'clevy' above the fire. [Courtesy of the Department of Irish Folklore, University College, Dublin]* promoted as 'invalid foods', saw them reviled and eventually rejected. **Regina Sexton**

food, thirteenth to seventeenth centuries. By the later Middle Ages, Ireland was home to a number of dietary systems, which differed in accordance with social rank, region, and access to market. The older Irish diet, based on dairy produce, salted meats, and fat, in addition to oats, co-existed with the wheat-dominated, plant-rich spicy MEAT, fish, and fowl diet of the Norman regions, notably around Cos. Dublin and Meath and stretching through the south-east. Whatever the extent and consequences of any interaction and fusion between these two dietary traditions, the evolution of Irish foodways was interrupted by the period of general unrest, political insecurity, and economic deterioration that characterised the fourteenth and early fifteenth centuries. Subsequent economic recovery throughout the fifteenth century and the resurgence of the native Irish saw a growing political and economic dependence between those of consequence at the upper levels of society. If literary references and descriptions of Irish feasts and banquets are to be believed, some degree of dietary blending is detectable in their adoption and use of spices in cookery. However, for the majority the staple foods were cereals and dairy produce, supplemented with salted meats and cured fish. The proportion of DAIRY food to cereals that entered the diet varied from region to region, as did the choice and availability of cereal types. Extensive tracts of woodland still untouched by large-scale clearance were also exploited for animal, bird, and plant foods, notably in times of FAMINE and want.

Continued political turmoil and violent disturbances throughout the sixteenth century disrupted the normal patterns and practice of husbandry. In a climate of continuing unrest, cereal crops were particularly vulnerable, whether in the field or in store, leading to an unbalanced emphasis and reliance on the pastoral economy among the native Irish. As mobile units of wealth and food, milch cows brought the best sense of food security in troubled times. In addition, in death their hides brought additional profit as export goods, with the bonus of meat for consumption or for sale to local markets. The inflated importance of pastoralism must therefore be seen as a sound and calculated reaction to war and political instability; and the polemic, promoted by later writers, that the native Irish were wandering pastoralists, reluctant to toil and ignorant of the ways of arable agriculture, are misrepresentations or misunderstandings of the economic realities of the time.

Nonetheless, pastoralism was of immense significance, effecting important consequences for the make-up of the diet. Whitemeats in the form of milk and thickened milks, whey products and curd and soft CHEESE dominated the summer and autumn diet, with BUTTER and hard cheese serving winter needs. In addition we should acknowledge that this was a society with an ingrained and expansive knowledge of working with the dairy to produce an array of foods and drinks of differing tastes and textures. One product that seems to have enjoyed widespread popularity was *bainne clabair*, often Anglicised bonnyclabber. This dish has been interpreted as a thickened sour milk, but a mid-seventeenth-century source advises leaving renneted milk to stand for two days to produce a thick cream curd. This preparation was held in high esteem as a 'dainty' dish, and its reputation spread to England, where it joined a litany of similar curd-type junkets and creams.

Oats continued to be used in pot preparations and in the production of flat oaten cakes. For the latter, oatmeal was simply mixed to a stiff paste with water, milk or buttermilk and fat or butter. The flat cake was baked on a griddle over an open fire and subsequently transferred to a wooden (later a metal) tripod-like stand to dry out before the fire. Oatcakes were notoriously dry, and an array of whitemeats was an ideal accompaniment in rendering them more palatable, while such was their dry quality that they served as a storable food item and made the ideal choice as travelling fare. They also functioned as thickening agents when crumbled into broths and pottages.

On occasion cattle were bled for food (a practice that continued intermittently into the nineteenth century in times of hardship). The fresh or coagulated blood was variously mixed with butter or meal and often sprinkled with salt to make rudimentary pudding-type mixtures. In more affluent circles whitemeats and oatcakes were eaten with large quantities of boiled and roasted meats, often served at once to the table, along with a surfeit of wine and fruit-and-spice-flavoured whiskey.

To the incoming Tudor and Stuart settlers, Irish foodways were seen as objectionable and at times unacceptable. The practice of burning an entire sheaf to free the grain from the straw and chaff, for example, was forbidden by statute in the seventeenth century. (This practice, while eliminating the need for more laborious threshing and drying, was carried out to impart a certain desirable smoky flavour to the grain.) In addition, the practice of blood-letting, the taste for offal foods and the slovenliness of the cooking were identified as examples of Irish barbarity. It was not so much the choice of ingredients that offended as the carelessness of the cooking and the lack of attention to dressing; 'ill-cooked and without sauce' is a phrase cited in condemnation of Irish cookery. The unconventional nature of Irish table manners was also isolated to emphasise the waywardness of the 'wild Irish.' In line with the general colonial mentality of the rapidly expanding English state, the Irish were identified and defined in accordance with the peculiarity of their social mores. The food of the native Irish, its preparation and the means of consumption were an easily identified expression of difference, and with a divergent food culture that lay outside acceptable conventional practice the native Irish were seen as uncivilised, open to betterment, and therefore deserving of colonial subjugation. **Regina Sexton**

food, traditional. The most celebrated Irish traditional food is the POTATO. Preparation varies according to region; fadge, a triangular potato cake common to northern counties, is an essential part of the 'Ulster fry'. Colcannon (*cál ceannann*), made with potato and kale, cabbage or scallions, is eaten everywhere on HALLOWE'EN. Boxty (*bacstaí*), bread made with raw grated potato, is common to the west and north, while the Armagh region, famed for apples, is home to a cake made with potato pastry, apples, sugar, and BUTTER.

Potatoes also combine with apples as a stuffing for goose or pork steaks (fillets). Black pudding, a sausage of pork and pig's blood, is popular throughout the country, though beef blood is often used in commercial puddings. Drisheen (*drisín*), a sausage-shaped preparation unique to the Cork area, uses a mixture of beef and sheep's blood. A variation called packet is made in the Limerick region.

Bacon, to a greater extent than the once-popular corned (pickled) beef, remains a staple food. Spiced beef, pickled and marinated in spices, is now a Christmas speciality. Mutton (now lamb) was the basis for the Dingle pie, which is first baked, then served in mutton broth, and is now enjoying a revival. Lamb is also used for stew, though this was often made with whatever meat was available. Salmon is prepared in numerous ways, including smoking, popular since the 1920s and 30s. Mackerel, trout, eels, and mussels are also smoked. The native oyster, *Ostrea edulis*, once widely available, is now concentrated around the west coast, where Galway holds an oyster festival each September.

Ireland's BREAD traditions are rich and varied, with brown and white soda bread, currant and oatmeal breads. Maize (called yellow meal), introduced in the early nineteenth century, was made into bread and porridge. Oatcakes, part of the diet from ancient times, are associated with northern counties and are now made commercially there. Barm brack (*bairín breac*), a spicy yeast fruit bread, is made at Hallowe'en, when charms baked in the bread foretell the future. [see DIET.] **Nuala Cullen**

food engineering. Food engineers design and apply engineering technologies to the processing, manufacture, packaging, storage, and handling of foods, food products, food ingredients, and beverages. Food engineering in Ireland was pioneered by University College, Cork, which introduced a dairy engineering course in the 1920s. More recently, in the 1980s and 90s, food engineering courses were introduced by University College, Dublin, Queen's University, Belfast, and University College, Cork. Graduates in these and related disciplines have revolutionised the Irish food industry by introducing the latest technologies, including process automation, process and manufacturing innovations, information technologies, and food quality and safety engineering. **Paul McNulty**

Foras Feasa ar Éirinn ('compendium of knowledge about Ireland'), a history of Ireland from the creation of the world to the coming of the Anglo-Normans, written by GEOFFREY KEATING. It first went into circulation in manuscript c. 1634. It was translated into English by Michael Kearney in 1635 and into Latin by John Lynch, probably in the 1650s; it was a 'best-seller' by the late seventeenth century, when numerous versions of the text, as well as a number of English translations, were in circulation through a system of scribal publication. It was first issued in print in 1723 in an unreliable English translation by Dermod O'Connor. The full Irish text was published for the first time, with English translation, by the IRISH TEXTS SOCIETY, 1902–14.

Keating adapted the framework for his history from LEBOR GABÁLA ÉRENN ('Book of Invasions') and the *Réim Ríoghraidhe* ('Succession of Kings'), versions of which he found in medieval manuscript sources. He combined this material with traditional place lore, bardic poetry, genealogies, and stories of the exploits of early Irish kings to construct an elegant prose narrative of early Irish history that had lasting appeal. Printed sources in Latin and English were also extensively used as a means of rebutting the writings of authors who had portrayed the Irish people in a negative light. The polemical preface criticising hostile commentators set the context within which *Foras Feasa* was intended to be read.

The main narrative is divided into two books, the first of which tells the story of Ireland down to the coming of Christianity, the second beginning with the coming of St PATRICK and concluding with the establishment of HENRY II as King of Ireland in succession to Rory O'Connor in the late twelfth century. The story of the Irish church is narrated in tandem with the story of king-heroes, so that the history formed a coherent origin myth for the Irish nation that was taking shape in the early seventeenth century. The work includes genealogical appendixes recording the purported succession of many Irish families from the beginning of time. This emphasis on GENEALOGY and on the ancient history of Ireland was designed to convey to readers a sense of the antiquity of the Irish kingdom and the illustrious origins of the Irish people. Keating emphasised that Ireland had never been conquered by the Romans or by any other power; rather, he asserted, the Irish represented a civilisation older than that of Rome or Egypt.

food. *Jack Bennett, baker at the Courtyard in Schull, Co. Cork, displays a range of traditional loaves. [Mike Bunn]*

Though written with Catholic readers in mind, *Foras Feasa ar Éirinn* appealed to readers who regarded themselves as Irish, irrespective of their national origin and religious allegiance, because it gave them a sense of pride in their country and in themselves. **Bernadette Cunningham**

Forbairt: see INDUSTRIAL DEVELOPMENT AGENCY.

Ford, Henry (1863–1949), car manufacturer. Born in Michigan, son of an Irish emigrant from Ballinascarty, Co. Cork. He was a farmer before he made his first experimental vehicle in 1896. Publicity from two racing cars brought the financial backing to set up the Ford Motor Company at Dearborn, Michigan, in 1901. The breaking of the land speed record in a Ford Arrow at 147 km/h (91.37 miles per hour) in 1904 attracted further publicity; it was the only time a manufacturer set a world record in a petrol-fuelled car of his own construction. Ford saw the potential of a mass-produced cheap car, and in October 1908 he launched the first Model T. It was an immediate success and hastened the worldwide transport revolution. From 1913 the Model T was produced on an assembly line, which lowered the cost even further. Ford also introduced an eight-hour working day and a relatively high basic wage. He opened a factory in Cork in 1917 to produce the Fordson tractor, after which a car assembly plant was established there, which closed in 1984. He resigned the presidency of the Ford Motor Company in 1947, two years before his death. [see FERGUSON, HARRY.] **Brendan Lynch**

Ford, John (1894–1973), film director. Born John Feeney in Cape Elizabeth, Maine, the youngest of thirteen children of Irish immigrants. In 1913 he joined his brother Francis Ford (who was already an established film director, writer, and actor) in Hollywood, where he worked as a stuntman and film extra, as in Griffith's *The Birth of a Nation* (1915). While his career is marked by a series of ground-breaking westerns—his directorial debut in *Straight Shooting* (1917), *The Iron Horse* (1924), *Stagecoach* (1939), *Fort Apache* (1948), *She Wore a Yellow Ribbon* (1949), *Rio Grande* (1950), and *The Searchers* (1956)—in many of these, as in his non-westerns, it was his Irish roots that often showed most clearly. His first non-western, *The Prisoner of Avenue A* (1919), featured the Irish-American boxer 'Gentleman Jim' Corbett, while all through his career his interest in Irish subjects never waned, from *Shamrock Handicap* and *Hangman's House* in the 1920s to his adaptations of O'CASEY's *The Plough and the Stars* and O'Flaherty's *The Informer* in the 1930s and especially in his first Irish-made film, *The Quiet Man* (1952), which features the familiar theme of the returned emigrant. The most enduring of all films made about Ireland, its Technicolor gives a richness to 1950s Ireland otherwise absent from the period, while the playful engagement with such themes as the church, community, political violence, status of women, tradition, and modernity, even its subversion of the representation of the 'idyllic' west of Ireland, allows present-day critics to claim it as post-modern. **Kevin Rockett**

Forde, Samuel (1805–1828), artist. Born in Cork; at thirteen he enrolled in the new School of Art, studying under Chalmers. He was friendly with DANIEL MACLISE, a fellow-student, and while a student worked for the architect GEORGE RICHARD PAIN. In 1826 he completed a large painting inspired by Milton, *The Vision of Tragedy*, now lost (a drawing is in the Victoria and Albert Museum, London). His ceiling paintings at James Morgan's house at Tivoli, Cork, were lost in a fire. In 1827 he painted a Crucifixion triptych for Castlehaven church, near Skibbereen, Co. Cork. Early the following year, ill with TUBERCULOSIS, he began *The Fall of the Rebel Angels*, bought unfinished by Edward Penrose of Woodhill (now in the Crawford Gallery, Cork); the young artist died shortly afterwards. **Peter Murray**

Forde, William (1795–1850), musician and collector. Born in Cork. A much-travelled prolific writer about many musical genres, he dedicated the last ten years of his life mainly to Irish music. His papers are today housed in the ROYAL IRISH ACADEMY, Dublin, and include his extensive collection of tunes, his writings and lectures. Researched by Caitlín Ní Éigeartaigh, the Forde Collection of Music comprises approximately 1,900 melodies, primarily songs but also including some JIGS, REELS, CAROLAN tunes, and country dances. It also includes some English, Scottish, Manx, and Shetland melodies. Compiled methodically, the collection brought together all the available settings of each melody. Forde was unable to procure funds for publication, and the work remains unpublished except for a small portion published by P. W. JOYCE in *Old Irish Music and Song* (1909). **Siobhán Ní Chonaráin**

foreign direct investment. To most analysts, the principal factor behind the Republic's dramatic ECONOMIC GROWTH during the 1990s was the success achieved in attracting foreign direct investment, primarily by American TRANSNATIONAL CORPORATIONS. Ireland's share of American investment in manufacturing industry in the EUROPEAN UNION, for example, quadrupled between the mid-1980s and the mid-1990s; this increase is ascribed to a combination of the improved cost-competitiveness and industrial relations environments of the period, the development of agglomerations of companies, and an apparent increase in the importance of an English-speaking population. Even before this, the Republic had been successful as a 'green field' site (where foreign companies set up new operations rather than purchasing existing Irish companies), because of low corporate profits tax, together with membership of the European Union. **Frank Barry**

Northern Ireland. Foreign direct investment is a crucial component of the Northern Ireland economy. It is estimated that there are more than 200 externally owned manufacturing plants, providing more than 45,000 jobs and accounting for approximately 40 per cent of manufacturing EMPLOYMENT. Much of this investment is in British-owned companies, with American companies and those owned from other parts of the European Union also important. The majority of foreign investment is in traditional industries, such as TEXTILES, clothing, food-processing, and engineering. Compared with the Republic and with Britain, Northern Ireland has a relatively low proportion of foreign direct investment in high-technology industries, such as computers, electronics, and chemicals. Despite extremely generous levels of public assistance to attract foreign investment compared with the rest of the European Union, especially with regard to rates of capital grants (approximately 25 per cent and on occasion much higher), the level of investment has been badly affected by the continuation of violent conflict and political instability over many decades. **Douglas Hamilton**

foreign policy. Three linked themes are visible in the Republic's foreign policy: (a) Anglo-Irish relations, at the core of concerns since 1922; (b) the continual effort to demonstrate Irish SOVEREIGNTY in the international system through involvement in the LEAGUE OF NATIONS (up to 1946), adherence to military NEUTRALITY, and participation in the UNITED NATIONS (from 1956); and (c) engagement in the process of European integration, involving a radical reorientation of economic as well as foreign policy during the 1950s.

Anglo-Irish relations remain of crucial concern, both because of the Northern Ireland issue and because of close economic and human links. Early hopes that PARTITION would be dealt a fatal blow by the BOUNDARY COMMISSION were dashed in 1925, and thereafter partition was grudgingly accepted as something about which independent Ireland could do nothing except complain. Anglo-Irish relations were difficult for some years after DE VALERA came to power in 1932: the substantive issues were ones of finance and trade and were addressed in the Anglo-Irish agreement of 1938. This also saw Britain relinquish its defence rights under the ANGLO-IRISH TREATY (1921), which in turn made the maintenance of neutrality possible during the SECOND WORLD WAR. Neutrality severely worsened Anglo-Irish relations, though it caused greater long-term damage in the United States. In 1946 Ireland's application to join the United Nations was blocked; in 1948 the Taoiseach, JOHN A. COSTELLO, unexpectedly announced that Ireland would shortly declare itself a republic and leave the British Commonwealth; while in 1949 the Minister for External Affairs, SEÁN MACBRIDE, adduced partition as the sole reason for Ireland refusing to join NATO. He did oversee the state's first step away from isolation—Irish accession to the Council of Europe—and he unsuccessfully sought a defence treaty with the United States. When the Republic was finally admitted to the United Nations in 1956 it adopted a firm anti-communist and pro-Western stance. From 1957 to 1961, however, its UN policy under the direction of the Minister, FRANK AIKEN, was characterised by sympathy for decolonisation and by action to reduce the threat of nuclear weapons. From 1958 the Republic became a military contributor to UN peace-keeping operations. Economic and social stagnation in the 1950s saw gradual acceptance of the need for abandoning industrial protection, for foreign investment, and for eventual participation in the European Common Market.

Under SEÁN LEMASS as Taoiseach the drive for growth through internationalisation produced a new emphasis on pragmatism in foreign policy. Relations with Britain were strengthened and a conciliatory approach towards Northern Ireland was adopted, involving some infrastructural co-operation, marked in 1965 by Lemass's visit to Belfast to meet the Prime Minister of Northern Ireland, TERENCE O'NEILL. These tentative steps towards a long-term redefinition of relations were thwarted by the gradual eruption of the Northern Ireland 'TROUBLES' in 1968. In the 1970s and 80s the foreign policy agenda adapted by the Minister, and later Taoiseach, GARRET FITZGERALD was dominated by the need to maximise the benefits of European integration, while in the era following the Cold War there has been a sustained effort to increase engagement with the problems of the developing world. In 1973 and again in 1985 sustained Anglo-Irish negotiations produced ground-breaking agreements on Northern Ireland. In the 1990s the development of the NORTHERN IRELAND PEACE PROCESS, with American help, brought ceasefires and relative though uneasy peace. As a result of a referendum in 1998 the constitutional definition of the national territory as the whole of Ireland was replaced with an aspirational statement about agreed unity. At the start of the third millennium, both continuity and change are visible in the fundamentals of Irish foreign policy. **Eunan O'Halpin**

forestry. Ireland is the least-forested country in Europe apart from Iceland. By the beginning of the twentieth century the country had become almost totally deforested; the 8 per cent of forest cover achieved by the end of the twentieth century was due almost entirely to state-supported planting schemes. The average area under forest in countries of the EUROPEAN UNION is 33 per cent. Yet c. 8000 BC Ireland was almost entirely covered by forest. Its geographical isolation meant that there was far less diversity of species in these forests than in those of Britain or the Continent. While oak and other broadleaves dominated the sheltered valleys, and pines, birch, alder, and willows colonised the poorer sites, there is no evidence of the beech, hornbeam, or limes that thrived in Britain at this time, nor of the spruces and firs of northern Europe. Climate change c. 3000 BC began the destruction of these great forests shortly before the start of systematic clearances by human settlers.

Steady increases in population and the development of agriculture gradually opened up vast tracts of the previously densely forested country. By the eighth century one native species, Scots pine (*Pinus syslvestris*), had disappeared, as a direct result of human activity. The twelfth-century ANGLO-NORMAN CONQUEST and the introduction of new grazing practices halted the regeneration of much of the broadleaf forest, and by 1600 the extent of land covered by trees had been reduced to about 12 per cent. The commercial exploitation of the oak forests for shipbuilding, leather-tanning, and charcoal in the seventeenth century almost completed the destruction of the deciduous woodlands; and by the early eighteenth century Ireland had become a timber-importing country. However, this was also the beginning of a long period of political stability, which saw the gradual extension of the amount of land under trees through private planting, often with conifers. These private plantations reached a peak of about 140,000 ha (350,000 acres) by the middle of the nineteenth century; but afforestation projects came to an abrupt halt as the landlords' estates were dismantled through tenant purchase.

By the time state forestry began with the establishment in 1904 of the Avondale Forestry School at Rathdrum, Co. Wicklow, the total area of forest was 122,000 ha (300,000 acres), or 1.4 per cent of the land area. A central figure in this new phase in Irish forestry was AUGUSTINE HENRY, professor of forestry at the Royal College of Science for Ireland and joint author of the seminal *Trees of Great Britain and Ireland* (1913). He advocated the planting of species from the western coast of North America, which he was convinced were more suited to Irish conditions than European species. In 1920 the state afforestation scheme was begun on land acquired by the Forestry Commission in Co. Tyrone.

The newly independent Irish state continued to support the planting of trees but was determined that forestry should not be allowed to compete with agriculture for available land. The Forestry Act (1946) and subsequent legislation helped to ease restrictions on the purchase of land; however, the process of land acquisition continued to be a politically sensitive element in the state forestry scheme. Despite the extreme fragmentation of the forest estate as a result of official land use policy, and the consequent problems with management and harvesting, the yield of timber from Irish forests is higher than in any other European country.

From the 1970s the state has adopted a policy of strongly supporting private and farm forestry; and this industry now accounts for 22 per cent of all forests and receives large subsidies through EU grants. Coillte, a commercial state body, has had responsibility for

forestry. *Plantation forests in the Slieve Bloom region, Co. Offaly. Foreign species—Sitka spruce* (Picea sitchensis) *and lodgepole pine* (Pinus contorta)*—dominate most of the coniferous woodlands of Slieve Bloom, the largest cover of forestry in Ireland. [Coillte]* the state forestry scheme since 1989, when it took over from the Forest and Wildlife Service. The target of this scheme, to be achieved through both state and private planting, is a total forest estate of 1,000,000 ha (2,470,000 acres) by 2015, representing a landscape cover of 14.7 per cent, with a sustainable production of 10,000,000 m^3 of timber a year.

From the beginning of the state-supported forestry schemes, exotic species from western North America were used for commercial planting, and these have dominated the state forestry scheme. Sitka spruce (*Picea sitchensis*) is very suited to Ireland's moist climate and thrives on the type of wet mineral soils that have typically been chosen for afforestation; by 1960 it accounted for about 50 per cent of the trees being planted. In the 1960s particular varieties of lodgepole pine (*Pinus contorta*), with a similar native distribution to Sitka spruce, were shown to be suitable for planting in poorer soils; this species now accounts for more than a quarter of state planting in the Republic. Other commercially important conifer species include Norway spruce, Douglas fir, and Japanese larch, which is particularly useful as a nurse tree (used to shelter other trees in the early stages of growth) for Sitka spruce on very poor soils.

The concentration on non-native species and the fragmented nature of the forest estate has had unfortunate consequences in both habitat destruction—as a result of concentrating plantations on upland and lowland blanket bog—and landscape aesthetics. Furthermore, the planting of large monoculture stands of trees has done little to replace the bio-diversity lost through the destruction of native woodlands. Recent surveys of relict woodlands have provided evidence of the rich variety of wildlife they sustain and have helped to encourage a more flexible approach to afforestation policy. While broadleaves still account for only 3–4 per cent of the forest estate, the numbers planted have been increasing slowly, and there is far greater diversity of species among the conifers being planted and a considerable increase in mixed planting. An innovative scheme aimed at redressing this imbalance is the Republic's Millennium Tree Project, begun in 2000. The target is 1.2 million trees, which will cover a total of 600 ha (1,500 acres). This will involve extending existing forests and protecting native woodlands that are under threat. The species being planted include oak, ash, birch, alder, hazel, yew, and Scots pine. The increasing availability of better land to both state and private forestry will help the industry adhere to the principles of sustainable forest management as the extent of the country's forests rapidly increases (see p. 771). [see HAYES, SAMUEL.] **Brian Galvin**

forestry engineering, a branch of the forest sciences dealing with all engineering aspects of forestry, including the construction of forest roads, the design and modification of forest machinery, harvest planning and control systems, machine-soil interactions, saw-mill layout, environmental engineering, and timber construction. The site of many forests in Ireland on difficult soils causes problems in the construction of high-standard forest roads. The use of imported forest harvesting machinery has meant that modifications have been necessary to make them suitable for Irish conditions. The rapidly increasing harvest volumes—from 2.2 million m^3 in 1995 to 2.8 million m^3 in 2000, projected to rise to 5 million m^3 by 2035—added to the complex logistical requirements for the supply chains of the timber-processing industry, have necessitated the development of integrated timber harvest planning and control systems. **Maarten Nieuwenhuis and John J. Gardiner**

Fórsa Cosanta Áitiúil, An (FCA), the second-line reserve of the DEFENCE FORCES. It evolved from the LOCAL DEFENCE FORCE and was established on 1 January 1947. The FCA has units throughout urban and rural Ireland and consequently has strong links with local communities and makes a contribution to many local events. FCA membership is voluntary and part-time. The majority of FCA training consists of weekday evenings, weekends, and one-week or two-week summer training camps. In addition, full-time courses are available through the PDF system. Until 1991 membership was restricted to males but ten years after this restriction was lifted, females accounted for 25 per cent of FCA strength. The FCA is organised similarly to the PDF and is administered by a full-time PDF staff. **Paul Connors**

forty-shilling freeholders, those qualified to vote by virtue of holding an annual lease worth 40 shillings (£2). The electorate in county constituencies and some boroughs was qualified to vote by owning or holding by lease for life land worth 40 shillings yearly after rent and charges. The numbers of such tenancies increased rapidly, especially after 1793 when Catholics were enfranchised, as landowners sought to increase the numbers of poor, dependent electors on their estates. The county franchise was raised to £10 in 1829 in the aftermath of O'CONNELL's successful mobilisation of FORTY-SHILLING FREEHOLDERS in the campaign for CATHOLIC EMANCIPATION. **Peter Gray**

Foster, John, Baron Oriel (1740–1828), politician. Born in Collon, Co. Louth; educated at TCD. He represented Co. Louth in the Irish and, later, the British Parliament between 1769 and 1821, when he was elevated to the peerage. A man of great administrative capability as well as profoundly conservative instincts, his abilities resulted in his being appointed Chancellor of the Irish Exchequer in 1784. The following year he was elected Speaker of the Irish House of Commons; this gave him a degree of political independence, which he availed of to oppose Catholic enfranchisement in 1792–3 and the ACT OF UNION in 1799–1800. His reputation and abilities ensured his reappointment to the Irish Exchequer in 1804, a position he held, with one interruption, until his retirement from politics in 1811. [see FOSTER'S CORN LAW.] **James Kelly**

Foster, R. F. [Robert Fitzroy] (1949–), historian and writer. Born in Waterford; educated at TCD. He taught history in Birkbeck College, University of London, until his appointment in 1991 as Carroll professor of Irish history at the University of Oxford. His principal works are *Charles Stewart Parnell: The Man and His Family* (1976), *Randolph Churchill: A Political Life* (1982), *Modern Ireland, 1600–1972* (1988), and the first volume of the authorised biography *W. B. Yeats: A Life, I: The Apprentice Mage*, which appeared to acclaim in 1998. **Terence Brown**

Foster, Vere Henry Lewis (1819–1900), philanthropist. Born in Copenhagen; educated at Eton College and the University of Oxford. He joined the British diplomatic service, but after visiting Ireland in 1847 he was so affected by what he witnessed of the GREAT FAMINE that he decided to devote his time and personal fortune to the betterment of the Irish people. He subsidised fares for 25,000 emigrants to America and gave grants towards the building of several hundred parish schools. In 1868 he founded the Irish National Teachers' Association, and he devised and published a series of widely used instructional copybooks. He died in Belfast, unmarried and in virtual poverty. **Michael Gill**

fosterage. The institution of fosterage is frequently mentioned in the BREHON LAW texts of the seventh to ninth centuries and in literary sources of the same period. It is clear, therefore, that children were commonly sent away to be reared by foster-parents. According to the law texts, fosterage was undertaken for a fee or out of affection. Foster-parents were obliged to maintain their foster-children in accordance with their parents' rank, and to provide appropriate training. The son of a king or noble was taught board games, horsemanship, swimming, and marksmanship; a daughter was taught sewing, cloth-cutting, and embroidery. Lower down the social scale, the son of a tenant-farmer was taught how to care for animals, comb wool, and chop wood, while a daughter was taught the use of the QUERN and kneading-trough. Foster-children sometimes received specialised training in poetry, MEDICINE, or other arts. By law, foster-parents had to pay any fines incurred by the child; but for a serious misdemeanour the child was sent home. If the child was maltreated the fosterage agreement was annulled and the fee returned to the parents. Fosterage ended between the ages of fourteen and seventeen, but the foster-child retained strong bonds with the fostering family. The practice of fosterage survived for hundreds of years and was a potent force in the determination of political alliances. **Fergus Kelly**

Foster's Corn Law, the Corn Act (1784), which in effect subsidised Irish grain exports from provincial ports, and restricted imports under normal conditions. It allegedly promoted an expansion in tillage, with a subsequent increase in prosperity, and also encouraged a growth in MILLING. However, grain supplies to Dublin suffered as a result, and the scheme was substantially modified in 1797. **Neal Garnham**

Fota House, Carrigtohill, Co. Cork, a Regency mansion created in the 1820s by Sir RICHARD MORRISON and his son WILLIAM VITRUVIUS MORRISON around an earlier eighteenth-century house. The distinction of the house is its opulent interiors. Wings added to the eighteenth-century block, which contain the library and dining room, are linked through the entrance hall, which runs the full length of the original building. The principal rooms, entrance, and staircase hall have highly enriched PLASTERWORK. Columned screens of yellow scagliola marble introduce a sense of splendour to the entrance hall. **Brian Lalor**

Fota Wildlife Park was opened in 1983 on 28 ha (70 acres) of land on the west end of Fota Island, Co. Cork, the fruit of a joint project between University College, Cork, and the ROYAL ZOOLOGICAL SOCIETY OF IRELAND. The university provided the land, while the Society provided the animals and husbandry advice. The park has adopted an extensive approach to animal husbandry, with many species being able to roam freely. It has also excelled in the captive breeding of cheetahs, with more than 150 cubs born in the park since its opening. **Peter Wilson**

Four Courts, Dublin. Following the building of JAMES GANDON's Custom House by only five years, the Four Courts, begun in 1786, is the most monumental example of GEORGIAN civic ARCHITECTURE in Ireland. Similar to the CUSTOM HOUSE in its siting, with a river front on the north quays of the LIFFEY, the Four Courts is otherwise a more variegated structure, with only a single significant front. The central block, with Corinthian portico, supports a heavy drum surrounded by columns, over the internal rotunda from which the four courts radiate. The drum is capped by a shallow dish-shaped copper dome. Statuary by EDWARD SMYTH—of Justice, Moses, and Mercy—decorates the pediment, with Wisdom and Authority on the corners of the balustrade. Flanking the central block are courtyards separated from the street by pierced screens with central triumphal arches capped by trophies representing Justice and Law, linked to flanking wings. The wing to the west (the Public Records Office) was built in 1776 by THOMAS COOLEY and incorporated seamlessly by Gandon into his own conception. The Four Courts was severely damaged during the CIVIL WAR in 1922, and the irreplaceable medieval and later archives of the Public Records Office, housed in the building, were incinerated. Restored in 1932, modifications were made to the wings and the arc of the dome (see p. 533). **Brian Lalor**

Fourknocks, Co. Meath, a PASSAGE TOMB excavated in 1950–52 consisting of a round mound 19 m (62 ft) in diameter, delimited by a dry-stone revetment. A short passage gives access to an exceptionally large pear-shaped chamber 7.5 m (25 ft) across, off which open three small recesses in cruciform fashion. Eleven stones bear

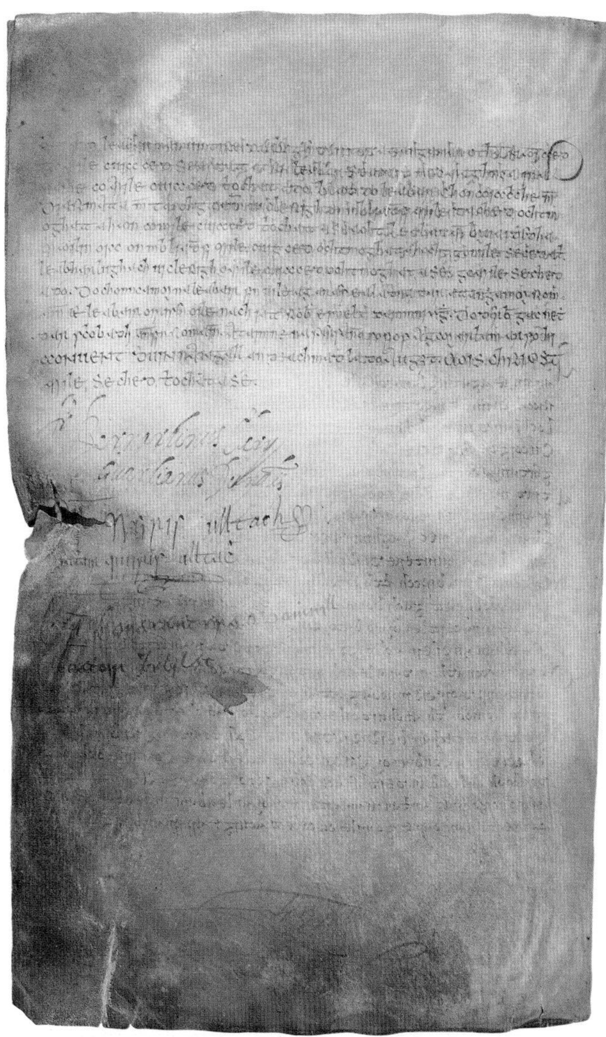

Four Masters. *The testimonial page from Annals of the Kingdom of Ireland (Annals of the Four Masters). Dated 10 August 1636, it bears four signatures: Brother Bernardine O'Clery (Guardian of Donegal), and two signatories named Brother Maurice Ulltach and Brother Bonaventura O'Donnell (Jubilate Lector) as witnesses to the work of Micheál Ó Cléirigh and the team of scribes. Behind the signatures, text from the reverse side of the vellum page is visible. [Royal Irish Academy]*

megalithic art. Burials were found principally in the passage and recesses, accompanied by typical passage-tomb artefacts. A second mound, 150 m (500 ft) to the east, was shown on excavation to be a complicated ritual and burial monument erected by passage-tomb builders. Both mounds were reused for burial in the earlier BRONZE AGE. **Paul Walsh**

Four Masters, the, a team of scribes led by the Franciscan scholar Brother MÍCHEÁL Ó CLÉIRIGH of Co. Donegal (c. 1590–c. 1643), which produced copies or compilations of some significant Irish texts, most notably the collection of ANNALS variously known as 'Annals of Donegal', 'Annals of the Kingdom of Ireland', and, more popularly, Annals of the Four Masters. Sent back to Ireland from Louvain in 1626, Ó Cléirigh was instructed to collect or copy materials on the lives of early Irish SAINTS. Having done this for four years, he then began to cast his net wider. In the late 1630s at Killinure, Co. Westmeath, he and his three assistants—Fearfeasa Ó Maolchonaire from Co. Roscommon, Cúchoigcríche Ó Cléirigh from Co. Donegal (a kinsman of Mícheál), and Cúchoigcríche Ó Duibhgeannáin from Co. Leitrim—compiled, under the patronage of a local gentleman, Toirealach Mac Cochláin, a collection of genealogies of the kings and saints of Ireland. A year later, at Lisgoole, Co. Fermanagh, Brother Mícheál and four assistants—the previous three and Giollaphádraig Ó Luinín—compiled for Brian Rua Mag Uidhir, Baron of Enniskillen, a new recension of LEBOR GABÁLA ÉRENN (The Book of the Taking of Ireland). In 1632, on the banks of the River Drowes in Co. Donegal, work began on a fourth project, a great collection of Irish annals. Working with the original three assistants, Ó Cléirigh also obtained some help from two others, Muiris mac Torna Uí Mhaolchonaire (for a month) and (for a slightly longer period) Conaire Ó Cléirigh, an older brother of Mícheál's. Under the patronage of Fergal O'Gara, MP for Co. Sligo, the first half of the annals was complete by the end of 1632; after a hiatus, the remainder was written in 1635. In 1645 Ó Cléirigh and his colleagues were memorably, if slightly inaccurately, dubbed the 'Four Masters' by Brother Mícheál's fellow-Franciscan hagiographer John Colgan. **Nollaig Ó Muraíle**

Fournier d'Albe, Edmund Edward (1868–1933), scientist, writer, and promoter of the pan-Celtic movement. Born in London; educated at the Royal Gymnasium, Düsseldorf, and the Royal College of Science, London. He served as assistant to GEORGE FRANCIS FITZGERALD. Author of the biography of Sir William Crookes (1913) and the first popular work arising out of the discovery of the electron (*The Electron Theory*, 1906), he was an early user of the concept of fractal structure in physics. Other books include an English–Irish dictionary (1903) and *The Moon-Element* (1924). In the latter, his invention of the optophone (a device to enable the blind to substitute hearing for sight) and an early form of television are described. He was honorary secretary of the Pan-Celtic Congress and the Celtic Association, and editor of *Celtia*. **Denis Weaire**

Fox, Rock, stage name of Charles Meredith (1933–), jazz musician. Born in Dublin; trained and practised as a solicitor. He adopted a stage name in 1952 because, as a solicitor's apprentice, he was prohibited from taking a second job. He featured as trumpeter in the pioneering Jazz Heralds of the early 1960s and in the Butler-Fox Band, 1967–74. He continued to straddle the styles for several decades, appearing in 'trad' line-ups as well as leading his own 'little big band', Rock Fox and his Famous Orchestra. He played with visiting musicians such as Gerry Mulligan, Pepper Adams, Danny Moss, Teddy Wilson, and Sarah Vaughan. In the 1970s he wrote *Civil Rights Suite*, inspired by the death of Martin Luther King, which has been performed several times by groups under his leadership. A lifelong devotee of Duke Ellington's music, he was leader and arranger of the band that performed an Ellington Centenary Concert in Dublin in 1999. Fox is an accomplished, versatile and always stylish musician on three saxophones, clarinet, and trumpet. He presented jazz programmes on RTÉ Radio for more than a decade. **Brian Trench**

Foynes, Co. Limerick, a small port on the south bank of the Shannon Estuary. Following trial flights in 1937–9, regular trans-atlantic flying-boat services by Pan-American, Imperial Airways (subsequently BOAC), and American Export Airlines operated from 1939 throughout the SECOND WORLD WAR. Foynes was designed as a temporary base pending the development of a joint facility for land-planes and sea-planes at Rineanna (now SHANNON AIRPORT), but this was never commissioned. The Foynes service was of vital strategic importance to the Allies during the war, and a shuttle land-plane connection operated to and from Britain. Scheduled flying-boat services ended in early 1946, and the former terminal building now houses the Foynes Flying-Boat Museum. **Bernard Share**

France and Ireland. After Spain, France was historically the Continental country with which the Catholic part of Ireland had the closest links. While France first enlisted Irish troops in 1635, the Williamite defeat over half a century later saw an exodus of Irish soldiers to France and the creation of an Irish Brigade that fought with distinction in a number of battles in the eighteenth century, notably at Fontenoy (1745). IRISH COLLEGES were also established in Douai (1577), Paris (1578 and 1776), Bordeaux (1603), Lille (1610), Toulouse (early 1600s), Poitiers (1674), and Nantes (1680). Apart from training for the Catholic priesthood, Irish expatriates were also enabled to pursue such professions as medicine and the law, supported in part by an established Irish merchant class in a number of French cities and ports.

The period before the FRENCH REVOLUTION marked both the high point and the beginning of the end of a significant Irish presence in France for nearly two centuries. Irish interests in France, which would have been mainly loyal to the *ancien régime*, lost ground. WOLFE TONE was an able and influential politician who managed to secure the support of revolutionary France for a rebellion in Ireland; but after the failure of Hoche's expedition in 1796 and of the subsequent rebellion in Ireland two years later, French interest in Ireland declined. The Irish presence in France did not disappear, however, as evidenced by such well-known names as the Hennessy cognac family, originally from Cork, and Maréchal Patrice de Mac Mahon, who became President of France, 1873–9.

In the nineteenth and twentieth centuries many Irish writers and artists, including RODERIC O'CONOR, J. M. SYNGE, JAMES JOYCE, and SAMUEL BECKETT, lived in France. But apart from those who fought on French soil during two world wars, the Irish presence in France was modest in numbers. After Ireland joined the European Economic Community in 1973 a new relationship developed, with an estimated 16,000 Irish people living in France by the late 1990s. The recently restored Irish College is now a cultural centre, symbolising the renewed links between the two countries (see p. 539). **Piaras Mac Éinrí**

franchise. Before 1800 the Irish parliamentary franchise was highly varied. FORTY-SHILLING FREEHOLDERS had the vote in the counties, and the two MPs for TRINITY COLLEGE, Dublin, were elected by the fellows and scholars. The BOROUGH electorate ranged from close corporations, freemen and 'potwallopers' (whose right to vote depended on the possession of a fireplace) to forty-shilling freeholders in the larger 'open' boroughs. In 1829 the county franchise was raised to a £10 freehold, thus reducing the electorate by 83 per cent. The Irish Reform Act (1832) admitted some leaseholders in the counties and standardised the borough franchise at a £10 occupancy rate. A further reform in 1850 introduced a £12 occupancy franchise in the counties and lowered the borough rate to £8, greatly increasing the electorate. The Reform Act (1867) had little impact, but the 1884 act enfranchised most male heads of households, increasing the electorate to 738,000. In 1918 the vote was extended to all men over twenty-one and to women over thirty. **Peter Gray**

Francis, Mark (1962–), painter. Born in Newtownards, Co. Down. Now living in London, since the late 1980s he has exhibited throughout Europe, the United States, and Japan. His paintings, which begin with a loosening and elaboration of the quintessential modernist grid, reflect the expansion of vocabulary of abstraction through the influence of the photographic image. A characteristic painting laces a slightly blurred mesh of lines, irregularly threaded with ovoid forms, over a monochrome ground. Yet his blurred and beaded lines also relate to a range of imagery only recently available to the human eye through advances in electron-microscopic PHOTOGRAPHY. **Caoimhín Mac Giolla Léith**

Franciscans, an order of friars who first established themselves in Ireland in the thirteenth century. Principally attached to the Hiberno-Norman colony until the middle of the fifteenth century, thereafter their influence was greatest among the Gaelic Irish. They opposed the REFORMATION and provided spiritual leadership in resisting alike the advance of PROTESTANTISM and the Tudor state. The Annals of the FOUR MASTERS is probably the greatest intellectual legacy of the early modern Franciscans. Following the defeat of the Gaelic Irish in 1603 and the FLIGHT OF THE EARLS, most houses of the Irish Franciscans were suppressed. The order established IRISH COLLEGES on the European Continent, of which those at LOUVAIN (1617) and Rome (1625) were the most celebrated. Their fortunes in Ireland continued to decline throughout the seventeenth and eighteenth centuries: the closure of the Irish novitiate by Rome in 1751 was the nadir. In the post-FAMINE years the Franciscans, along with other orders, revived as part of the Renaissance of institutional Catholicism. **Fergal Tobin**

freedom of the city of Dublin. The honorary freedom of Dublin is the highest award in the city's gift and has been conferred on seventy people since it was initiated in 1876. Recipients are chosen by Dublin City Council for their contribution to the life and work of the city, and they sign the Freedom Roll at a formal ceremony presided over by the Lord Mayor of Dublin. Those honoured include politicians, such as CHARLES STEWART PARNELL, ÉAMON DE VALERA, and JOHN A. COSTELLO, theatrical performers, such as MÍCHEÁL MAC LIAMMÓIR, HILTON EDWARDS, Noel Purcell, and MAUREEN POTTER, the artist Sir JOHN LAVERY, the playwright GEORGE BERNARD SHAW, the tenor JOHN MCCORMACK, the sports stars JACK CHARLTON and STEPHEN ROCHE, and the broadcaster GAY BYRNE. The honorary freedom has also been presented to distinguished visitors, such as Nelson Mandela, Pope John Paul II, and Presidents JOHN KENNEDY and Bill Clinton of the United States.

Fournier d'Albe. *Mary Jameson at the optophone, an instrument invented by Fournier d'Albe in 1912 as a reading device for the blind. An expert student of the device, she attained a reading speed of sixty words per minute. [Council of Trustees of the National Library of Ireland]*

Recent recipients include the Burmese politician Aung San Suu Ky and the four members of the Dublin rock band U2—Bono (PAUL HEWSON), Adam Clayton, Larry Mullen, and the Edge (David Evans)—and their manager, PAUL MCGUINNESS. **Mary Clark**

Freeman, Alexander (1878–1959), musician. Born in London; educated at the University of Oxford. He compiled one of the most significant collections of Irish songs. His wife, the Donegal fiddler Harriet Eda Peoples, was active in IRISH-LANGUAGE organisations in London. Like her, Freeman joined the Irish Folk Song Society, an organisation dedicated to the preservation of Irish songs. The society published its material in its *Journal of the Irish Folksong Society*. During 1913 and 1914 the Freemans visited the Irish-speaking region of Ballyvourney, Co. Cork, and while there he notated approximately 100 songs from the singers he met. These songs, taken as they were from the oral tradition and including words, music, translations and notes, were then published in the Folksong Society's *Journal*. **Siobhán Ní Chonaráin**

***Freeman's Journal*,** a Dublin newspaper founded in 1762–3 to support CHARLES LUCAS. In the 1790s it was owned by the government spymaster Francis Higgins, the 'Sham Squire'; later it supported O'CONNELL. Its heyday as the daily journalistic voice of middle-class Catholic NATIONALISM was the mid-Victorian era under the proprietorship of Sir John Dwyer Gray (1816–1875) and his son, Edmund (1845–1888). During the PARNELL split it was taken over by the Dillonite wing of the Irish Party. Underinvestment left it vulnerable to the revitalised *Irish Independent* after 1905, and it shared the downfall of the Irish Party. Despite new ownership from 1919, it ceased publication in 1924. **Patrick Maume**

freemasonry, a fraternal organisation open to men who profess a belief in a divine being and based, according to its own writers, on 'a system of morality, veiled in allegory and illustrated by symbols.' The Grand Lodge of Freemasons of Ireland, established c. 1725, is the autonomous governing body of the organisation in Ireland. During the eighteenth century the growth of the society was rapid, and hundreds of lodges were established throughout

Ireland, meeting in local taverns or coffee-houses. Nowadays lodges meet about eight times a year. **Barry Lyons**

Free Presbyterian Church, a Protestant denomination founded in 1951 by REV. IAN PAISLEY. Then an independent evangelist, Paisley was highly critical of the mainstream Protestant churches for the alleged dilution of reformed theological principles. Founded on separatist and highly conservative evangelical principles, the church has about a hundred congregations around the world, fifty-nine of them in Northern Ireland and a few in the Republic. It is well known for its antipathy towards Roman Catholicism on theological grounds, which includes naming the Papacy as the Anti-Christ, though leaders and ordinary members alike contend that they are opposed only to the institution of Catholicism rather than individual Catholics. Often considered the 'religious wing' of the DEMOCRATIC UNIONIST PARTY (though this match is not absolute), the church's influence in Northern Ireland has been significant. This, however, has had more to do with the elision between cultural conservatism in Northern Ireland at large and the values of conservative Protestantism, along with the dual role of Paisley as popular politician and church leader, than any widespread sympathy for Free Presbyterianism itself. The church's defining characteristic, conservative separatism, was exemplified when it made headlines in May 2001 for its contention that line dancing was sinful, as it 'incites the lust of the flesh.' **Gareth Higgins**

Free State: see IRELAND, REPUBLIC OF.

free trade. After several decades of PROTECTIONISM, the Republic moved towards free trade with the adoption of the ANGLO-IRISH FREE TRADE AREA AGREEMENT (1966) and accession to the European Economic Community in 1973. Since then, trade policy has been determined by the EUROPEAN UNION, which has adopted a largely free-trade stance towards manufactured goods together with a heavily protectionist agricultural policy. The general principle that protectionism advances the interests of a politically powerful lobby group to the detriment of society at large can be seen here, since agricultural protectionism feeds into a higher cost of living, making it more difficult for the European Union to compete in international markets as a producer of manufactured goods. The benefits of trade liberalisation for Ireland have been enhanced by its success in attracting FOREIGN DIRECT INVESTMENT, which is crucially dependent on membership of the European Union. [see SINGLE EUROPEAN MARKET.] **Frank Barry**

French, William Percy (1854–1920), 'parlour' songwriter and performer. Born into a 'BIG HOUSE' family in Co. Roscommon, he was educated with his siblings at home and from an early age showed imaginative creativity. He began singing to his own BANJO accompaniment in a 'minstrel' act while studying at TCD, his first song, 'Abdullah Bulbul Ameer', becoming hugely popular. Incidents experienced while employed with the BOARD OF WORKS in Co. Cavan inspired many of his songs, notably 'Phil the Fluther's Ball', 'Slattery's Mounted Fut', and 'Inspector of Drains'. Editing the *Jarvey* (1888), a short-lived satirical journal, led to his jointly writing Ireland's first musical comedy, *The Knight of the Road* (1891), with William Collisson, then to a solo career that involved caricature sketching, recitation, and songs. He laughed with his subjects, not at them, such pieces as 'The West Clare Railway' ('Are ye right, there, Michael, are ye right?')—which arose from one of his gruelling tours—achieving immortality as much for universal as for parochial application. His lyrics played on the poetry of PLACE-NAMES, anecdote and parody and, though sung as light classical song in the twentieth century, remain symbolic and interesting to traditional singers. One hundred and thirty of his songs are published in Brendan O'Dowda's biography, *The World of Percy French* (1981). **Fintan Vallely**

French Revolution. Beginning in 1789, the French Revolution raised political consciousness in Ireland, inspiring the formation of two radical clubs—the Societies of UNITED IRISHMEN of Belfast and Dublin—and emboldening the CATHOLIC COMMITTEE to seek more vehemently equality of treatment for Catholics. After the outbreak of war between France and England in February 1793, support in Ireland for French revolutionary principles increased fears in DUBLIN CASTLE, which tried to appease the Catholics with two relief acts (1792 and 1793) and to emasculate the radicals by suppressing the Volunteer Corps, 1793. However, the FITZWILLIAM EPISODE and the prospect of a French invasion made dissidents resort, disastrously, to armed REBELLION IN 1798. [see BANTRY BAY EXPEDITION; EMMET'S REBELLION; KILLALA EXPEDITION; NAPOLEON IN SONG; REBELLION OF 1798 IN SONG; WOLFE TONE, THEOBALD.] **C. J. Woods**

freshwater species. Ireland's extensive river network and multitude of LAKES, as well as its CANALS, host a variety of native and non-native freshwater species. Bream (*Abramis brama*) is widely distributed throughout lowland rivers, canals, and lakes, with major populations found in the Rivers SHANNON, Suck, and Erne as well as in Lough Allen, Lough Ree, Lough Oughter, and Lough Gowna. Brown trout (*Salmo trutta*) are to be found in almost all Irish lakes and rivers, with the large and deep limestone lakes of the west, north-west, and south-west particularly noted for the size and number of their brown trout populations (see p. 25). Carp (*Cyprinus carpio*) have been stocked in Irish waters since, it is believed, the seventeenth century and can be found in a small number of lakes and canals throughout Ireland, most notably the GRAND and ROYAL CANALS, Galmoylestown Lake, Ballinafid Lake, the Lough in Cork, and the Lakelands Fishery in Roosky, Co. Roscommon. Char (*Salvelinus alpinus*) are to be found in a handful of the cold and deep lakes of the west, north-west, and south-west, with notable populations in Lough Inagh on the Ballynahinch River, Lough Mask, Lough Melvin, and Lough Eske. Dace (*Leuciscus leuciscus*) were introduced to Ireland in the late nineteenth century and are to be

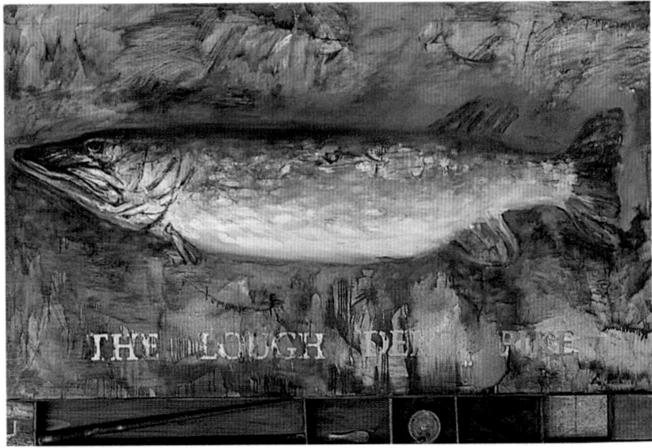

freshwater species. The Lough Derg Pike: Life-Size with Relics *by Barrie Cooke, (1980), portrait of a 1.52 m (5-ft) pike caught in Lough Derg in 1862, preserved in a pub in Co. Clare. A predella panel below the painting contains a nineteenth-century rod and reel. [Courtesy of Crawford Municipal Art Gallery, Cork]* found only in the River BLACKWATER in Munster and the River BARROW and Doon Lake, Co Clare. Eels (*Anguilla anguilla*) are widely distributed throughout almost all Irish waters, with the River Shannon, LOUGH CORRIB, and LOUGH NEAGH noted for their substantial eel populations. Perch (*Perca fluviatilis*) are widely distributed throughout almost all lowland waters, with Lough Neagh particularly noted for its large perch population. Pollan (*Coregonus autumnalis*) are found in just four Irish waters: Lough Erne, Lough Neagh, Lough Ree, and LOUGH DERG. Pike (*Esox lucius*) are to be found in most lowland waters; a noted predatory fish, they inhabit rivers, canals and lakes alike but grow to over 13 kg (29 lb) in the larger midland lakes and river systems. Roach (*Rutilus rutilus*) were introduced to Ireland in the late nineteenth century and have since spread from the Munster Blackwater throughout most of the major river, lake, and canal systems. Roach-bream hybrids and rudd-bream hybrids, as their names imply, are present in most of those waters where roach, bream, and rudd proliferate. Rudd (*Scardinius erythrophthalmus*) are widely distributed throughout lowland lakes and canals and are present in small numbers in some slow-moving rivers.

Salmon (*Salmo salar*) are to found in many sea-going rivers, where they migrate to spawn, as well as in some lakes. A number of rivers along the west coast are particularly noted for their runs of migratory salmon, including the Rivers Drowes, Moy, Erriff, Corrib, Shannon, and Laune. Sea trout (*Salmo trutta*) are a migratory fish also to be found in many sea-going rivers, with noted runs in a number of rivers in Connemara and along the eastern seaboard. Twaite shad (*Alosa fallax*) and allis shad (*Alosa allis*) are found in the Rivers Barrow, Blackwater (Munster), NORE, SLANEY, and SUIR, where they migrate to spawn, as well as in Lough Leane in Killarney. Tench (*Tinca tinca*) are present in many lowland lakes and canals as well as in some slow-moving stretches of river, with the greatest concentrations found in the Royal and Grand Canals. [see ANGLING, COARSE; GAME, SEA; WATER.] **Colm O'Gaora**

Fricker, Brenda (1944–), stage and screen actor. Born in Dublin. She appeared in 'Tolka Row', the first urban serial on Irish television, in the 1960s, in the British television hospital series 'Casualty', 1986–90, and in the Australian television series 'Brides of Christ'. Her television films have included PAT O'CONNOR's *The Ballroom of Romance* (1982), in which she played an unmarried woman in search of a husband in 1950s rural Ireland (see p. 903), and *Utz* (1991). She came to international prominence after winning an Academy Award for her role as CHRISTY BROWN's mother in *My Left Foot* (1989), directed by JIM SHERIDAN, with whom she worked again on *The Field* (1990). **Kevin Rockett**

Friday, Gavin (1960–), singer. A former member of the VIRGIN PRUNES, he discovered his niche as a latter-day crooner of European-influenced rock music. Despite his excellent albums—including *Each Man Kills the Thing He Loves* (1989), *Adam 'n' Eve* (1992), and *Shag Tobacco* (1996)—and his superlative film soundtrack work—*In the Name of the Father* (1993) and *The Boxer* (1997)—he has not crossed over into the mainstream market. In 2000 he jointly composed (with Maurice Seezer) music for the radio series 'Emerald Germs of Ireland', written by PATRICK MCCABE. **Tony Clayton-Lea**

Friel, Brian (1929–), short-story writer and playwright. Born in Omagh, Co. Tyrone, he moved to Derry in 1939; educated at ST PATRICK'S COLLEGE, Maynooth, and St Joseph's Training College, Belfast. He worked as a primary school teacher until 1960, writing short stories for various magazines, including the *New Yorker*; his first collection, *The Saucer of Larks* (1962), was followed by *The Gold in the Sea* (1966). In the mid-1960s he decided to devote himself entirely to drama. *The Enemy Within* (1962), his first major work for the stage, had already attracted some critical attention; fame came with the Dublin Theatre Festival production of *Philadelphia, Here I Come!* (1964), a theatrically daring work in which two actors play two aspects of the same character. In 1967 he moved across the border to live in Co. Donegal. With the outbreak of violence in Northern Ireland his drama took on a darker and more political tone as both the controversial *The Freedom of the City* (1973), loosely based on the events of BLOODY SUNDAY, and the more distanced *Volunteers* (1975) demonstrate. In 1980 he jointly founded FIELD DAY, the theatre company that premiered and toured *Translations* (1980), which has now become a national classic, and, later, *Making History* (1988). *Dancing at Lughnasa* (1990) proved immensely popular with audiences around the world; a film version directed by PAT O'CONNOR came out in 1998.

Friel has written more than twenty plays, including adaptations of Chekhov and Turgenev, and is widely regarded as among the best Irish playwright of the twentieth century. Many of his plays deal with the erratic workings of memory, and with the family, using Ballybeg, the archetypal small town, as a backdrop. In formal terms he has shown himself to be consistently capable of experimenting, challenging the limits and conventions of the genre—intrusive narrators and disruption of chronology in *Lovers* (1967) and *Living Quarters* (1977) or, most memorably, use of the monologue form in the superb *Faith Healer* (1980)—while never losing his ear for dialogue, his sense of humour and irony, and his ability to create deeply affecting characters that appeal to Irish and non-Irish audiences alike. **Martine Pelletier**

friendly societies, societies typically established to provide income and medical assistance to subscribers in sickness, or burial funds to families on the death of a member. Some societies' long history dated back more than a century when the Friendly Society Act was passed in 1797, outlining the requirements of qualifying societies to which certain privileges were granted. Subsequent legislation developed a more precise relationship between the LAW and these voluntary associations, which in 1841 totalled some 281 societies and branches. Friendly societies performed important social, economic, and cultural functions during the nineteenth century; they tended towards federated structures, with single-branch societies, organised as 'tontines', persisting most notably in Dublin. By 1911, 341 were recorded in Ireland, with 71,923 members. **K. J. James**

Fromel, Gerda (1931–1975), sculptor. Born in Czechoslovakia; educated at Stuttgart, Darmstadt, and Munich. She came to Ireland with her husband, the sculptor and opera-singer Werner Schurmann, in 1956 and quickly established a reputation as an artist of the highest quality, working both in figurative bronze and in abstract steel and alabaster. She received many public commissions, of which the most renowned is the high, three-part stainless steel sculpture at Carroll's factory in Dundalk; standing in a large rectangular pool, the three poetic elements turn in the wind and are reflected in the water. She died in a drowning accident in Co. Mayo (see p. 41). **Dorothy Walker**

fruits. PLACE-NAMES and ancient poetry show the early existence of apples in Ireland. The BREHON LAW included the protection of apple trees, and ANGLO-NORMAN leases specified the planting of orchards. No mention of indigenous varieties of apple appeared until the seventeenth century. No names of these earliest apples have been traced, but in the opening years of the nineteenth century Irish varieties were described by John Robertson of Kilkenny. Dessert varieties and cider apples were grown extensively in several counties. At this time the importing of British varieties began, but the native apples were still grown and appreciated, many of them specific to particular counties.

The establishment of the Department of Agriculture and Technical Instruction in 1900 marked the beginning of the standardisation of fruit production. The demands of commerce meant that the planting only of internationally known kinds was encouraged. A survey in 1951 showed that the distinctly Irish apples survived in old non-commercial orchards and gardens. Fifty years later, most of these were rescued from extinction by the Irish Seed Savers' Association.

Efforts to encourage the planting of approved standard varieties concentrated on dessert apples on suitable soils in the south and on culinary varieties (especially Bramley's seedling) in the north. The war years and official protectionist policy encouraged production, but the coming of the European Union and trade liberalisation led to the dying out of all but a few specialised commercial orchards. The production of soft fruits was also encouraged during those years. The largest fruit farms were those of the jam and fruit-juice manufacturers, who also had contracts with private growers and organised the collection of wild blackberries. This industry too has contracted, though Co. Wexford is still noted for strawberries, sold throughout the country, and Co. Armagh for its apples. [see DIET; FOOD.] **Keith Lamb**

Frye, Thomas (1710–1762), portraitist and engraver. Born in Edenderry, Co. Offaly; he may have been trained by JAMES LATHAM. As a youth he travelled to England, possibly with Herbert Stoppelaer. In 1736 he received a commission for a portrait of Frederick, Prince of Wales. Other sitters included Mrs Wardle, the Duchess of Chandos, and John Allen of Bridgewater. He founded the Bow porcelain factory in 1744, which he managed while continuing to paint. He also produced MINIATURES and mezzotints (see p. 895). He exhibited at the Society of Artists in 1760 and 1761. **Brendan Rooney**

fulachta fia: see BURNT MOUNDS.

Fuller, James Franklin (1835–1924), architect. Born in Co. Kerry; trained in England, where he worked for several practices before returning in 1862 to take up a post in the west of Ireland with the Ecclesiastical Commissioners. He entered private practice after the DISESTABLISHMENT of the CHURCH OF IRELAND seven years later. He was employed by a number of wealthy proprietors, including the Guinnesses (Ashford Castle, Co. Galway, St Anne's, Iveagh House, and Farmleigh, all in Dublin), Mitchell Henry MP (Kylemore Abbey, Co. Galway), and the Knoxes of Co. Mayo. Arguably his most successful designs were his Hiberno-Romanesque churches: Clane, Co. Kildare (1881), Carnalway, Co. Kildare (1889), and Rathdaire, Co. Laois (1890). He published several novels and a volume of memoirs, *Omniana* (1916). **Frederick O'Dwyer**

Fungie (born c. 1975), a male bottlenose dolphin that has lived in Dingle Bay, Co. Kerry, since 1984. Many dolphins live off the coast of Ireland; but Fungie's friendly behaviour has won him a nationwide reputation. He is also a significant tourist attraction. **Ciarán Deane**

Fureys, the, a ballad and traditional group consisting of the brothers Eddie (1944–), Finbar (1946–), Paul (1948–2002), and George Furey (1951–), sons of the fiddle-player Ted Furey, together with Davey Arthur (1954–). Between them they play a wide range of instruments, including UILLEANN PIPES, ACCORDION, BANJO, GUITAR, and mandolin. Their music is a sometimes incongruous mix of ballads, sentimental popular songs, and traditional tunes, led by Finbar's piping. **Pat Ahern**

Furniss, Harry (1854–1925), illustrator. Born in Wexford, and moved to Dublin in 1864; educated at Wesleyan School and the ROYAL HIBERNIAN ACADEMY. He became a commercial artist with the engraver George Hanon. He provided sketches for ZOZIMUS when only sixteen and later for the *Illustrated London News*. He moved to London in 1873 and continued his contributions to that magazine, together with political caricatures for *Punch* and most of the principal periodicals and newspapers. He stands out from the

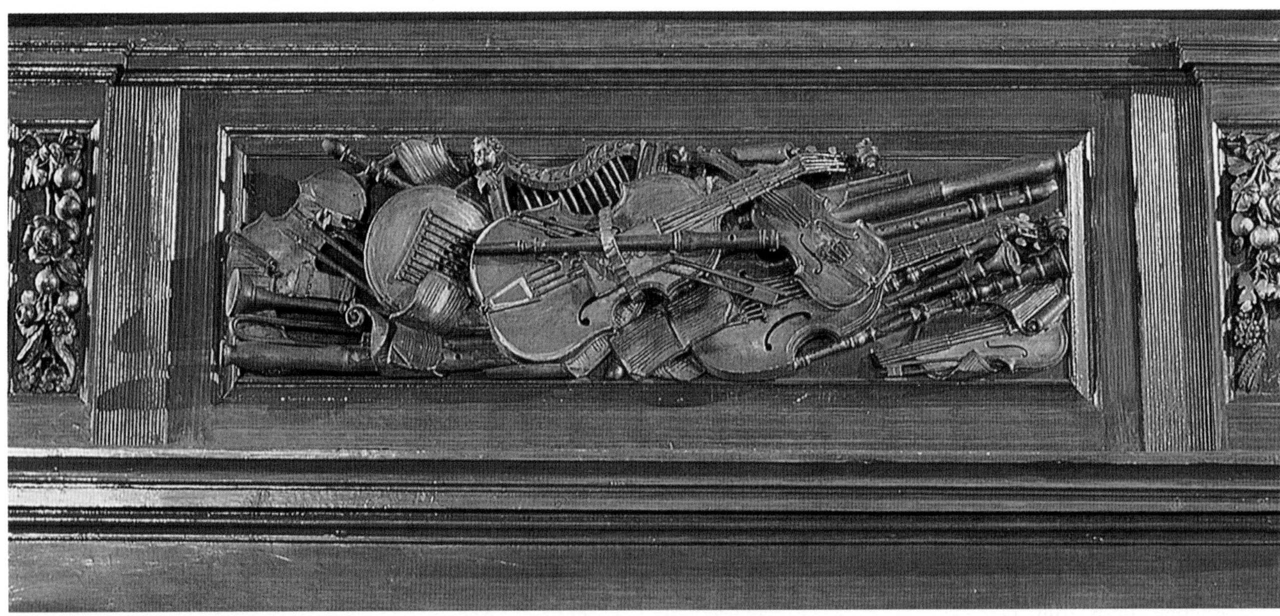

furniture. *Wood carving on the balcony of the organ loft at St Michan's Church, Dublin, thought to be the work of Henry Houghton (died 1727); sheet music, wind and stringed instruments are carved in high relief. [Bord Fáilte]*

mass of illustrators of the period by his almost impressionistic line, different from the careful modelling of Tenniel, his predecessor at *Punch*. There is great energy and movement in his work, with elements of fantasy. Following an argument with *Punch* he set up his own short-lived periodical, *Lika Joko*, inviting contributions from JACK B. YEATS and GEORGE MORROW. From 1885 he worked on illustrations for Lewis Carroll's last book, *Sylvie and Bruno* (1889), the adventures of two fairy children. He also provided illustrations for Dickens and Thackeray; but his preferred work was children's books of nonsense and fantasy, such as G. E. Farrow's *The Wallypug of Why* (1895) and *The Missing Prince* (1896). **Patricia Donlon**

furniture. Ireland's furniture history really begins only in the middle to late seventeenth century, though a few medieval pieces remain in churches and cathedrals; of these, the fifteenth-century misericords in Limerick Cathedral are the most important survivors. The so-called Armada table (dated to the 1580s), with its O'Brien provenance, now at Bunratty Castle, Co. Clare, is a piece of considerable elaboration, though it was possibly made up of carvings from a wrecked Spanish galleon.

By far the most important surviving examples of seventeenth-century woodwork are the magnificent carved baroque altar-table from the ROYAL HOSPITAL, Kilmainham (now in the NATIONAL MUSEUM, Collins Barracks, Dublin), and the elaborate oak chapel panelling still in the Royal Hospital, which dates from 1683–7, which were executed by the Huguenot Jacques Tabary. His patron was the enlightened JAMES BUTLER, First Duke of Ormond, LORD LIEUTENANT during the RESTORATION period. Butler's extraordinarily elaborate furnishings and decoration at Kilkenny Castle survive only in the pages of the detailed inventories (now in the NATIONAL LIBRARY OF IRELAND). Tabary must have been responsible for the stone and wooden overdoors and armorials on the exterior of the Royal Hospital; and he and his school clearly influenced the wooden trophies in the great hall at Beaulieu, Co. Louth, which date from c. 1710. Similarly, the exquisite decoration and musical trophy on the organ-case and gallery of St Michan's Church, Dublin (1724–5), show echoes of Tabary's decorative style.

Another influential craftsman of this time was the English statuary William Kidwell, who had been trained by the sculptor and wood-carver Edward Pierce (who, like most carvers of the period, worked in both wood and stone). Kidwell was in Ireland between 1711 and 1726. It seems highly likely that the author of the woodwork at St Michan's was Henry Houghton (died 1727), and that he was the father of John Houghton (died 1774). John Houghton, with the younger John Kelly (fl. 1739–59), are documented as working together on stonework, and Houghton carved chimney-pieces and picture-frames, while Kelly made BARTHOLOMEW MOSSE's state bed for the ROTUNDA HOSPITAL, Dublin, in 1739. These two craftsmen, with Richard Cranfield (1739–1809), were the finest carvers and furniture-makers in Ireland at this period.

Houghton and Kelly seem to have created much of the woodwork and probably furniture for the great new Palladian buildings that were being built in Dublin and elsewhere. It was the influence of Ireland's first Palladian architect, Sir EDWARD LOVETT PEARCE, and his assistant and successor, RICHARD CASTLE, that brought the baroque furniture style of William Kent to Ireland. This style created the taste for elaborate carved mahogany sideboards and tables, often decorated with lion masks and with their aprons groaning with acanthus, birds, fruit, flowers, and oak leaves. Though this style emulated English George II fashion it was imbued with an Irish individuality and fantasy. The table's cabriole legs were often composed with a break, terminating in square lion's-paw feet with acanthus-decorated hocks. Other legs have the plain panelled club foot, the trifid foot composed with scrolled volutes, or the webbed claw-and-ball foot, with the claw sometimes pierced.

This heavily carved furniture has a concurrent line of plain, simply drawn pieces with a minimum of decoration, conceived with considerable elegance. Chairs with serpentine stretchers, compass seats, carved knuckled arms and splat backs echo the Hogarthian line of beauty (published 1725), and their contours are carefully controlled. Scalloped skirts on chests, tables, and desks composed with a curve of the cabriole leg demonstrate a new concern for the balanced disposition of mass and void, swell and restraint, which lends this GEORGIAN style its characteristic power, simplicity, and grace.

The development of Irish furniture in the 1730s was much encouraged by the philosophy of self-sufficiency promoted by such patriots as BERKELEY, SWIFT, SAMUEL MADDEN, and THOMAS PRIOR that led to the founding of the Dublin Society (later the ROYAL DUBLIN SOCIETY). Later that century neo-classicism and the Adam style overwhelmed the baroque and rococo, with its urbane Roman motifs and filigree detail. Much fine inlaid furniture, such as the products of William Moore (fl. 1782–1815), was produced in Dublin in the late eighteenth century.

By the early nineteenth century Ireland's furniture, though sometimes continuing with its robust animal style, was influenced by Regency pattern-books, such as those published between 1808 and 1828 by the London designer George Smith. This style became universal all over Europe, and soon it is difficult to differentiate Ireland's craftsmanship from that of London and other workshops. Luckily, the labelling of mirrors by Dublin makers, such as the Booker brothers and the firm of Jackson, both of Essex Bridge, allows for easy identification of their Dublin origins.

Noble mahogany furniture was made by such firms as the early nineteenth-century Mack Williams and Gibton, Gillington, and James del Vecchio (who specialised in elaborate carved and gilt wood products). By the middle of the nineteenth century the importing of machine-made furniture and the imported material, often labelled by Irish firms, for display at the great exhibitions in Dublin from 1854 onwards sounded the death knell of Ireland's highly individual and distinguished craftsmanship, which saw its high point in the eighteenth century. [see GEORGIAN PERIOD; PLASTERWORK.] **Knight of Glin**

Fursa, patron saint of Péronne in Picardy and of Lagny near Paris. A native of south-east Ulster, he travelled through England with his brothers Ultán and Fáelán and founded the church of Lagny in the 640s. His relics were brought to the newly founded Péronne after his death c. 650. Péronne's Irish ties lasted for upwards of 150 years after Fursa's death. A Life composed for him there is quoted extensively in BEDE's Ecclesiastical History. A second Life, composed at Lagny c. 1100, established for him a close association with south Connacht, where a church, Killursa (Cill Fhursa), near LOUGH CORRIB, commemorates him. His feast-day is 16 January. **Pádraig Ó Riain**

Fürst, Janos (1935–), violinist and conductor. Born in Budapest; studied there at the Liszt Academy and the Paris Conservatoire (premier prix). Came to Ireland in 1958 as a rank-and-file violinist with the RTÉ Symphony Orchestra (acting leader, 1965-6) founding the IRISH CHAMBER ORCHESTRA and becoming inaugural leader of the ULSTER ORCHESTRA in 1966. He returned to Dublin as Principal Conductor of the RTÉSO 1988-9 and has also held positions at the Helsinki Philharmonic and Marseilles Opera, and is professor of conducting at the Paris Conservatoire. **Richard Pine**

Galway hookers
(see page 428). Traditional sailing boats in Bertraghboy Bay, Co. Galway. The large hookers were used for carrying turf to the Aran Islands and Co. Clare, while smaller boats, the gleoiteog *and* púcán, *were used for fishing. [Bord Fáilte]*

Gaelic Athletic Association (GAA). Michael Cusack, generally credited with being the founder of the Gaelic Athletic Association, described its function as being 'for the preservation and cultivation of the national pastimes of Ireland.' Cusack, a schoolteacher, and P. W. Nally, a renowned athlete from Co. Mayo, set in motion events that would lead to the formation of the GAA at a meeting in Thurles on 1 November 1884. Though formed to promote the national sports of HURLING and football, as well as ATHLETICS, the new association had a strong political aspect. Nally was subsequently imprisoned for his political activities. Another influential figure in the early years was Maurice Davin, an international athlete who held the world hammer-throwing record and was highly respected in political and ecclesiastical circles.

While Cusack was a tireless worker, he had a short temper and made enemies easily, and he was removed as secretary of the GAA after twenty months in office. Davin was the first president, and his diplomacy steered the association through many difficulties. As a political as well as a sports association the GAA was dominated for a period by the IRB; but Davin's leadership, with the support of MICHAEL DAVITT, founder of the LAND LEAGUE, and Archbishop CROKE of Cashel, who became the GAA's patron, brought the association through the turbulence.

Davin completed an early draft of the rules of hurling and football, and the first recorded game of football was played at Feagh, near Tynagh, Co. Galway. In 1887 the first entries for the all-Ireland football and hurling championships were sought. It was agreed that the winner of the local championship in each county would represent the county in the championship. Twelve counties entered, though only five contested the hurling championship. The finals were delayed until 1888 because of administrative difficulties; the hurling final took place on 1 April in Birr, between Meelick (Galway) and Thurles (Tipperary). The football final was played in Clonskeagh, Dublin, between Commercials (Limerick) and Dundalk Young Irelands (Louth); Commercials won by 1–4 to 0–3. Though no attendance figures are available, there are records that show gate receipts of £200, which suggests a very large attendance at the final on 29 April 1888.

By 1902 a provincial structure, such as exists today, had been established. James Nowlan of Co. Kilkenny would serve as president for twenty years and, with Luke O'Toole of Co. Wicklow as secretary, would guide the GAA into calmer times. The WAR OF INDEPENDENCE and the CIVIL WAR had a severe effect on the GAA, but the foundations remained secure. When the political situation became more settled by 1925 the GAA began to move away from politics, and the development of the games and facilities continued.

The election of William P. Clifford as president in 1926 was important, as he pioneered the development of grounds: 'a field in every parish' is how he described his dream.

Another significant event was the appointment of Pádraig Ó Caoimh as general secretary in 1929. Born in Co. Roscommon, he grew up in Cork and had been active in the GAA from an early age. He was also politically active and in 1920 was arrested for his activities, at a time when he was secretary of the Cork GAA Board. Though sentenced to ten years' imprisonment, he was released after a year under a general amnesty. Ó Caoimh oversaw the development of Croke Park, Dublin, put the GAA on a sound financial footing, and ensured that the policy of providing facilities in every parish and town was implemented.

By the 1960s the GAA had become a less political organisation. It continued to promote Irish culture and music, but the emphasis had shifted towards football and hurling. A rule from the early days known as 'the ban', banning members from playing foreign games began to arouse controversy, and in 1971 it was rescinded. The acceptance of sponsorship and the live televising of games brought the GAA into a new era. The completion of the new, architecturally distinguished 80,000-seater Croke Park (see p. 440), the fourth largest stadium in Europe, at a cost of €250 million, is a monument to the GAA of modern times (see pp. 440, 509). [see BOWLING, ROAD; CAMOGIE; GAMES, MEDIEVAL; GREYHOUND RACING; HANDBALL; HOCKEY.] **Donal Keenan**

Gaelic football. It is popularly believed that Gaelic football is a modern game, but there are references to a game as far back as 1537 in the Statutes of Galway; these laws banned hurling but allowed the playing of football. Other early references include the poem 'Iomáin na Bóinne' (1670). While the term *iomáin* suggests that the poem refers to hurling, it was used at that period to describe football. The poem describes a game at Fennor, Co. Meath, in which wrestling was allowed. Other texts suggest that Cos. Meath, Louth, and north Dublin were football strongholds during the sixteenth and seventeenth centuries. The poem 'Iomáin Léana an Bhábhdhúin' by Réamann Ó Murchadha describes an eight-a-side football game in Omeath in 1750 that lasted from midday until sunset.

Different versions of football were played in various parts of the country. Games were played between parishes or between baronies and would sometimes last for hours. However, there was no organised form of the game, and little interaction between the various regions. The rules also varied according to region, some games being more disciplined than others. The number of players varied from place to place, though the basic principle of moving the ball from one end of the field to the other was the same. The ball

GAA. *The 1903 Hibernian London Team, captained by Sam Maguire (1879–1927), after whom the present-day All-Ireland football trophy is named. [Irish Picture Library]*

was generally round, but that depended on the materials used: sometimes it was oval, but by accident rather than design. The first known rules were drawn up by the Commercials club in Limerick, but these were not widely used. With the formation of the GAELIC ATHLETIC ASSOCIATION, however, football became more organised. While the founders were more concerned about the preservation of hurling, it became clear from the early days of the association that Gaelic football had a stronger foundation throughout the country. The first all-Ireland championship was played in 1887. Limerick, represented by Commercials, were the first winners, beating Louth, represented by the Young Ireland club of Dundalk. Co. Kerry is the most successful football county, having won thirty-two championships. The county also produced the most famous team, which won eight championships in eleven years, 1975–86, managed by Mick O'Dwyer. Dublin comes next, with twenty-two all-Ireland senior titles, while Galway lies third, with nine titles. Modern Gaelic football is played by teams of fifteen players, on a pitch approximately 137 m (450 ft) long and 82 m (270 ft) wide. The ball used is round, and slightly smaller than a soccer ball. The goalposts consist of a crossbar between two upright posts. Three points are awarded for a goal, which is scored by kicking or by punching the ball under the crossbar; a point is scored by kicking or punching the ball over the crossbar. Most games comprise two halves of thirty minutes each, or thirty-five minutes in senior inter-county championship football. **Donal Keenan**

Gaelic League (Conradh na Gaeilge), founded in 1893 to preserve and revive Irish as a popular vernacular. Its founder-president was DOUGLAS HYDE. A key organisation in the LITERARY REVIVAL, its newspaper, AN CLAIDHEAMH SOLUIS ('the sword of light'), provided a forum for writers and poets in Irish (see p. 553). It established the OIREACHTAS festival in 1897, campaigned successfully to have Irish accepted as a compulsory matriculation subject for the National University of Ireland, 1908, and ran language training colleges for teachers. It was formally non-political until 1915, when IRB radicals carried a motion asserting Irish independence as a central ambition of the league. Hyde resigned. Since independence, Conradh na Gaeilge has continued to promote Irish language and culture. **Fergal Tobin**

Gaelic lordship (1200–1600). In sixteenth-century English parlance a 'country' was a lordship more of men than of land, a complex of rights, tributes, and authority rather than a closed and defined territorial unit. *Tuath*, the early Irish term for a lordship, became obsolete in this sense soon after the arrival of the Anglo-Normans. By 1300 the term *oidhreacht* was used, interpreted by contemporaries as meaning both the people and the territory ruled by a lord; the term *pobal* similarly emphasised the primacy of the people. *Dúthaigh* was occasionally used to denote the territory ruled by a lord, as distinct from its inhabitants, though it could also refer to landed property. The Latin term *patria* was used in early sixteenth-century deeds to denote landed territory. TAOISEACH, the pre-Norman title for the leader of a lordship, remained in use in the sixteenth century, though the term *tiarna* (lord) had become more common. Theoretically the chief and the TÁNAISTE, his second in command and successor-designate, were elected by the *oireachtas* (assembly of the lordship's potentates) from the *deirbhfhine*, an extended four-generation kin group, the choice falling upon 'the eldest and worthiest' candidate; in practice, bloody conflicts for the succession often ended in the accession of the strongest or most unscrupulous. Contests between evenly matched candidates frequently led to the temporary or permanent division of lordships. Most had a demesne land inhabited by the hereditary lineages (*lucht tí*), though it was often indistinguishable from the private inheritance estate of the *sept* (extended family group) in which the chieftancy was vested. The chief was entitled to claim custody of the land of any absentee owner within the lordship. Land could be alienated with the consent of other members of the sept but in practice tended to be conveyed by pledge or 'mortgage', the owner surrendering the land in return for payment while retaining the option of recovering it on repayment.

In the thirteenth century the O'Connor kings of Connacht had a rudimentary 'household', employing a chancellor and seneschal (steward), but there is no evidence of a central administrative structure in even the largest lordships in the late Middle Ages. A lord's power depended on his ability to levy 'coign and livery', a system of arbitrary exactions that obliged vassals to provide him and his retinue with food and lodgings, and by customs of *cuide oíche*, *cóisireacht*, and *bunnacht*. A substantial part of a vassal's obligations was service in risings-out (*gairm slua*), in which affluent landowners had hereditary obligations to serve as horsemen and to provide soldiers.

In the sixteenth century most ambitious lords employed mercenary soldiers to supplement the rising-out of horsemen and KERN. By then a drive towards provincial overlordship by certain magnates led to more demanding lord-vassal relations, which entailed the heavy deployment of force and the exaction of military support from lesser lords in return for an overlord's protection (*slánaíocht*). This practice of buying protection created a network of supporters on a non-territorial basis, cutting across the existing system of lordships and greatly restricting the power of local lords over their vassals. [see GAELIC SOCIETY; GENEALOGY; GENEALOGY AND POLITICS; GRAVELKIND; INAUGURATION SITES; KINGDOMS OF IRELAND.] **Mary Ann Lyons**

Gaelic scribes and scribal traditions (eighteenth and nineteenth centuries). Important scribal networks were being formed during the eighteenth century, and poets assembled as a CÚIRT ÉIGSE (court of poetry). Mobility, the exchanging of MANUSCRIPTS by scribes and reciprocal messages in verse were an integral part of literary activity, continuing into the nineteenth century. Literary 'schools' or centres flourished, mainly in Munster, south-east Ulster, and Meath.

Dublin also attracted numerous migrant scholars and poets from the early eighteenth century onwards, offering important sources for scribal work. The city's vibrant literary activity was celebrated in a poem composed in 1728 by TADHG Ó NEACHTAIN, in which he refers, for example, to AODH BUÍ MAC CRUITÍN of Co. Clare, whose *Elements of the Irish Language* (Louvain 1728) was the first printed grammar of Irish in English. Ó Neachtain also mentions the renowned manuscript collectors CHARLES O'CONOR Don (1710–1791) of Belanagare, Co. Roscommon, and Dr John Fergus (c. 1700–1761) of Dublin. In his library at Clonalis House O'Conor possessed Leabhar Méig Shamhradháin (Book of Magauran, fourteenth century) and the Book of O'Conor Don (seventeenth century) (see pp. 73, 372), two extensive sources for bardic poetry, while Liber Flavus Fergusiorum (fifteenth century) formed part of the Fergus Collection. Fergus also commissioned prolific scribes, such as MUIRIS Ó GORMÁIN (c. 1720–1794) of south Ulster and Mícheál (mac Peadair) Ó Longáin of Co. Limerick (c. 1693–1770), father of MÍCHEÁL ÓG Ó LONGÁIN.

The eighteenth and nineteenth centuries were a period of considerable scribal activity, ample testimony of which is given by the surviving corpus of Gaelic manuscripts. Loose collections of leaves and jottings make up much of this corpus; these were bound when deposited in public institutions or by subsequent private owners. Because of the widespread destruction and loss of manuscripts from earlier periods these later copies are often the only source of a lost original. Their content is extensive, encompassing material from the Middle and EARLY MODERN IRISH periods (such as annalistic compilations, bardic poetry, hagiography, historiography, medical and grammatical tracts, and prose tales) and contemporary material (including religious works, herbals, *orthaí* or charm-prayers, prose tales, poetry, and occasional verse).

By the nineteenth century, numerous translations of religious material, which ultimately derive from Latin, French, Spanish, and English sources, had entered the Gaelic world. Later scholars and scribes were motivated mainly by a keen sense of retrieval and conservation of native Irish sources, thereby ensuring that manuscripts would remain the principal mode of vernacular literary transmission until c. 1850.

Though an exhaustive account of scribal activity would entail recording numerous scribes (particularly as 'Gaelic' in the area of manuscript studies refers to the shared cultures of Ireland and Scotland), a notable contribution is that of the Ó Longáin scribes of Munster, which spans the entire eighteenth and nineteenth centuries. Scribes in general supplemented their income by working as labourers, teachers, innkeepers, or farmers. Clergymen also contributed significantly to literary scholarship, working as scribes, offering scribal patronage, or publishing religious reading matter in Irish. Examples include ANTHONY RAYMOND (1675–1726), a Protestant minister, and Edmund Byrne, Catholic Archbishop of Dublin, 1707–24, each closely associated with scholars in Dublin; John O'Brien, Catholic Bishop of Cloyne and Ross, 1748–69, who published an Irish–English dictionary in Paris (1768) and compiled annalistic material; and John Murphy, Catholic Bishop of Cork, 1815–47, generous patron of Cork scribes and founder-member of the Gaelic Society in Cork. Notable contributions by Presbyterian clergymen in Ulster include *Introduction to the Irish Language* (1808) by William Neilson (1774–1821) and *Ancient Irish Minstrelsy* (1852) by WILLIAM DRUMMOND (1778–1865).

In considering eighteenth and nineteenth-century scribal activity it is necessary to examine the context (geographical, economic, and socio-cultural) in which the scribes worked. A striking feature is a marked urban-rural divide in the eighteenth century, which had diminished considerably by the early decades of the nineteenth century; a rural, Catholic scribal network became a context in which class and religion were not decisive factors. Mícheál Óg Ó Longáin and his sons established close contact from the early nineteenth century with scholars, both Protestant and Catholic. Manuscript evidence also suggests a growing Anglicised patronage, particularly in the nineteenth century. Heightened interest by antiquarians in native Irish sources influenced in turn scribal production; a new patronage, of English-speaking background yet attracted to such sources, indicates a new duality in the milieu of the later scribes.

The scribe's concern in the eighteenth century was generally with a more select reading public of fellow-scribes and poets already literate in Irish. By the nineteenth century, however, while scribes were commissioned to produce manuscripts, the influence of a print culture was well established. The effects of printing on form and style also become evident in nineteenth-century manuscripts; matters of layout and presentation to a new literate readership, for example, and the question of language and typography became increasingly important. By the nineteenth century also a substantial number of printed exemplars were being copied. Significant in all of this is the changing role of the scribal practitioners themselves, who worked not only as lexicographers but also as translators, abridgers, and indexers of their material. The Gaelic Society was one of a number of Irish-language societies that were aware of the necessity to have material from manuscripts printed, and copyists were of prime importance in the early stages of this work. By the second half of the century the ROYAL IRISH ACADEMY sought the expertise of Seosamh Ó Longáin (1817–1880), one of the finest of the later scribes, to provide transcripts for lithographic reproductions of medieval codices. The script component, therefore, was a necessary part of the printing process. This no doubt had further implications also for Gaelic sources, as an individual-oriented manuscript culture came to be replaced by a collectivised one of print culture. [see BARDIC DUNAIRE; IRISH GRAMMATICAL TRACTS; IRISH PRINTING TYPES; SCRIPT.] **Meidhbhín Ní Úrdail**

Gaelic society (1200–1600), a complex and organised system of institutions with its own principles and rules of arrangement. Though rooted in tradition, it was not static but capable of changing internally and adapting to outside influences. Entire native Irish social systems survived down to the sixteenth century, even in those regions populated by ANGLO-NORMAN settlers. The native population tended to be defined by an adherence to stock-raising, to non-village communities, and to mobility associated with pastoralism. Though native Ireland had a proliferation of ruling dynasties, society was not rigidly divided into two classes, landowners and cultivators. Each lordship's chief and his TÁNAISTE or second in command and successor-designate were elected by the *oireachtas*

(assembly of the lordship's potentates) from the *deirbhfhine*, an extended four-generation family group. The chief's power rested on his ability to levy on his vassal exactions collectively termed 'coign and livery'.

In traditional Irish society, large herds of cattle were the true symbol of wealth. Noble families enhanced their prestige through patronage of the church and learning. Chiefs conferred upon the officially recognised head of a hereditary learned family the title of OLLAMH or master of his discipline, typically poetry, law, history, medicine, genealogy, music, or smithcraft. Poets—the *aes dána* or FILÍ—were especially important, being believed to have quasi-sacred powers, which they could use for inflicting harm on their enemies. They also eulogised the attributes and achievements of chieftains. Professional genealogists compiled pedigrees of lords to endow their patrons with an ancient and hallowed ancestry, while historians recounted the past glories of the ruling sept. Brehons administered the traditional legal system, which punished offences such as theft, murder, or arson by forcing the criminal to pay damages to the injured party or their family.

Among the peasantry there were gradations of influence and wealth. There were no serfs or unfree bondsmen in a feudal sense; yet most of the cultivators were economically depressed, subject to an array of exactions from their landlords, having few rights and no recourse to local estate courts. Secular marriage was standard. Divorce was readily permitted, and it was usual for men and women of the aristocracy to have had several spouses. The Irish usually married their kinsfolk, and their promiscuity created innumerable ties of 'affinity'; most marriages were therefore invalid according to canon law. Many of the aristocracy entered trial marriages and had children with new partners before obtaining Papal dispensations for previous marriages considered invalid under canon law. Brehon law drew no distinction between 'legitimate' and 'illegitimate' successors and entitled women to 'name' their offspring as sons to men with whom they had a liaison, thus securing for their sons a share in the paternal estate. FOSTERAGE was common, cementing alliances among septs and creating associations with Anglo-Norman and English families. Partible inheritance was the norm.

During the sixteenth century the advance of Anglicisation and orthodox Christianity (occasioned by SURRENDER AND REGRANT agreements, PLANTATION schemes, and the introduction of the Protestant and Catholic Reformations) led to the demise or mutation of many of these practices and mores. [see GAELIC LORDSHIP.] **Mary Ann Lyons**

Gael-Linn, a promotion agency for Irish, founded in 1953 by Dónal Ó Móráin. Until the advent of the national lottery its principal fund-raisers were football pools and bingo, which financed grants for attendance by school-goers at GAELTACHT summer schools. From 1959 it began making cinema newsreel films in Irish as well as feature films, such as MISE ÉIRE and SAOIRSE?, directed by GEORGE MORRISON and with music by SEÁN Ó RIADA. Gael-Linn's first recording was of the *sean-nós* singer SEÁN 'AC DHONNCHA in 1957; its first LP featured the Radio Éireann Light Orchestra in arrangements of Irish airs by Ó Riada and SEOIRSE BODLEY. The catalogue of *sean-nós* singers includes SEOSAMH Ó HÉANAÍ, DARACH Ó CATHÁIN, and CAITLÍN MAUDE; its traditional music has the seminal *Playboy of the Western World* (1962) by Ó Riada and much material by leading performers released regularly until the late 1990s, totalling almost 200 albums. **Fintan Vallely**

Gaeltacht. The terms *Gaeltacht* (now used to mean Irish-speaking district) and its inverse, *Galltacht* (district where Irish is not spoken), have a long history, both in Ireland and Scotland. One of the earliest examples of the use of *Galltacht* in an Irish context comes from the fourteenth century, where it clearly refers to people rather than place. The first use of *Gaeltacht* in a geographical sense comes from Scotland c. 1700, where it describes an area in which Gaelic is spoken. It appears that such a definition was then imported into Ireland from Scotland, but not until the end of the nineteenth century.

The language revival movement came to associate *Gaeltacht* with an ill-defined region in the west of the country. One of the first tasks of the IRISH FREE STATE Government was to define the precise boundaries of areas where Irish was spoken as a community language. In 1925 a commission was established to investigate two categories of district: *'fíor-Ghaeltacht'* (fully Irish-speaking district), where 80 per cent or more of the population could speak Irish, and *'Breac-Ghaeltacht'* (partially Irish-speaking district), where between 25 and 79 per cent could speak Irish. The commission's evidence indicated that there were Irish-speaking communities in twelve of the twenty-six counties of the Free State. Successive governments failed to implement most of the recommendations.

The official Gaeltacht remained unchanged until 1956, when the Government decided to review the boundaries. The result was a drastic shrinkage of each Gaeltacht district. At the same time a Government department to co-ordinate Gaeltacht affairs, Roinn na Gaeltachta, was set up. This was followed in 1957 by the establishment of the first state development agency for the Gaeltacht, Gaeltarra Éireann, which took responsibility for Gaeltacht industry. A Gaeltacht Civil Rights Movement (Cearta Sibhialta na Gaeltachta) in the 1960s, the emergence of Gaeltacht co-operatives in the 1970s and the establishment in 1972 of the radio station Raidió na Gaeltachta culminated in a campaign for a more democratic Gaeltacht agency. This led to the establishment in 1980 of Údarás na Gaeltachta (the Gaeltacht Authority), part of whose board was to be elected directly by Gaeltacht residents. In developmental terms, a significant growth area in recent years has been the audiovisual sector, particularly since the establishment in 1996 of Teilifís na Gaeilge (now TG4) in Connemara.

The socio-economic development of the Gaeltacht has, however, been accompanied by declining proportions of Irish-speakers. An analysis of the CENSUS of 1996 revealed that of the official Gaeltacht population of 86,039, only about 20,813 adults speak Irish every day, and these proportions are declining steadily. In 2000 the Government established another Gaeltacht Commission to investigate the causes of decline and to make recommendations. In 2002 the commission reported that of the 154 district electoral divisions in the Gaeltacht there are only eighteen that have 75 per cent or more who are daily speakers of Irish. Twelve of these are in Co. Galway, four in Co. Donegal, and two in Co. Kerry. Gaeltacht community and voluntary organisations are endeavouring to reverse the trend. [see BROADCASTING IN IRISH; GAEL-LINN; GALL; IRISH LANGUAGE; IRISH, RESTORATION OF.] **John Walsh**

Gahan, Muriel (1897–1995), rural organiser and campaigner. Born in Co. Donegal. In 1900 her family moved to Castlebar, Co. Mayo, where she spent crucial years in her development before moving to Dublin in 1926. She joined the Society of United Irishwomen in 1929; by 1930 she had founded Country Workers Ltd and the COUNTRY SHOP, St Stephen's Green, Dublin. The motivation behind the opening of the Country Shop, which remained in business until 1975, was twofold: her realisation of the lack of respect for craft workers, and their need for a retail outlet for their products. In 1935 she launched the Irish Homespun Society as her contribution to saving Ireland's homespun tradition. In association with the ROYAL DUBLIN SOCIETY, rural craft workers were invited to exhibit at the annual Spring Show. Country Markets, an organisation set up in the market conditions following the SECOND WORLD WAR, led to the establishment of An Grianán, a permanent centre for craft training, in association with the IRISH COUNTRYWOMEN'S ASSOCIATION, at Termonfeckin, Co. Louth.

Muriel Gahan was a founder-member of the ARTS COUNCIL in 1952, vice-president of the Royal Dublin Society, 1976, awarded an honorary doctorate by the University of Dublin, 1978, Rehab Institute Person of the Year, 1978, and was awarded the Plunkett Award for Co-Operative Endeavour, 1984. The Muriel Gahan Scholarship of £1,000 is awarded annually at the RDS National Craft Competition. **Anne O'Dowd**

Gaiety Theatre, Dublin, designed by C. J. Phipps and built for John and Michael Gunn in 1871 as a touring venue. It is an ornate Victorian theatre, with boxes, stalls, and a dress circle, now with seating for 1,124 patrons. In its early years the Gaiety hosted such actors as Beerbohm Tree, Sarah Bernhardt, and Coquelin. As young men, SHAW, WILDE, and O'CASEY had their first exposure to the theatre in the Gaiety, as did the actors who made up the original Abbey company. From the beginning the Gaiety regularly played host to visiting opera companies, and in the 1920s opera and musical recitals dominated its stage, with the DUBLIN GRAND OPERA SOCIETY (called 'Opera Ireland' from 1996) being based in the theatre since 1941. From 1940 to 1968 the GATE THEATRE company of HILTON EDWARDS and MÍCHEÁL MAC LIAMMÓIR frequently played in the Gaiety. The annual Christmas pantomime has been an unbroken Dublin tradition from 1871 (see p. 222). **Christopher Morash**

Gall (derived from 'Gaul'), translated 'foreigner' and an antonym (opposite in meaning) of Gael (from the Old Irish 'Goídel'). Since the defining characteristic of the latter was use of the IRISH LANGUAGE, to the early Irish the world was composed of those who spoke Irish, Goídil, and those who did not, Gaill. The name became attached to the VIKINGS who settled in Ireland in the ninth century, hence the title of the early twelfth-century tract celebrating BRIAN BÓRÚ's victories over them, COGADH GÁEDHEL RE GALLAIBH ('The War of the Gaeil against the Gaill'). It transferred to the ANGLO-NORMANS after their invasion in 1169, and the rest of the Middle Ages saw another relentless war of Gaeil and Gaill, though to distinguish between the newcomers of the Tudor age and the descendants of the Anglo-Normans, now heavily Gaelicised and still largely Catholic, were termed Sean-Ghaill ('Old Foreigners'). [see GALLOGLASS; OLD ENGLISH.] **Seán Duffy**

Gallagher, James (c. 1684–1751), bishop. Most probably born near Ballyshannon, Co. Donegal; educated at the University of Paris and at Rome. Ordained Bishop of Raphoe in 1725, he was translated to the diocese of Kildare and Leighlin in 1737. His *Sixteen Irish Sermons in an Easy and Familiar Stile* were published in Dublin in 1736; the latest edition appeared in 1911. Details of his early life are vague, but he was an active pastor from his appointment in 1725 until his death. He issued diocesan regulations banning merriment and lewd games at wakes in 1748. **Ciarán Mac Murchaidh**

Gallagher, Rory (1948–1995), singer. Born in Ballyshannon, Co. Donegal, he moved to Cork at an early age. He served his musical apprenticeship from the age of fifteen in a series of showbands, notably the Fontana and Impact. In 1965 he formed Taste, which was eventually to become one of the best rock trios of the decade. They released two albums: *Taste* (1969) and *On the Boards* (1970). When the band split up in late 1970 Gallagher was well on the way to becoming an international guitar legend. His early influences were Woody Guthrie, Chuck Berry, Muddy Waters, and Lonnie Donegan, and he rarely strayed from these throughout his career. He recorded three albums—*Rory Gallagher* (1971), *Deuce* (1971), and *Rory Gallagher Live in Europe* (1972)—that confirmed his burgeoning reputation as an accomplished guitarist. The 1980s proved to be less successful, with Gallagher releasing only two studio albums, *Jinx* (1982) and *Defender* (1987). Only one album was released in the next decade—*Fresh Evidence* (1990). In the late 1990s his entire back catalogue was reissued, reminding a new generation of the power and simplicity of his love for the blues—electric and acoustic. He remains a towering presence in Irish rock music, having influenced the Edge of U2, among many others. In 2000 Rory Gallagher Square in Paul Street, Cork, was named in his honour. **Tony Clayton-Lea**

Gallagher, Rory. *The blues guitarist and singer Rory Gallagher at Macroom, Co. Cork, in the 1970s. He bought a Sunburst Fender Stratocaster guitar in 1963; the 'battered Strat' was to be his trademark. [Bill Cooper, Bilcop Photography]*

Gallarus Oratory, Dingle Peninsula, Co. Kerry, resembles an upturned boat in shape, having stone side walls and roof merging in a continuous curve. Built in the corbel technique without mortar by a highly skilled mason, it stands on the Saints' Road to Brandon Mountain and was probably connected with pilgrimage. Its entrance, with inclining jambs, had a wooden flap-door opening inwards. The date is uncertain, probably between the seventh and twelfth centuries. Nearby is a *leacht* (low altar platform) with an inscribed cross-decorated stone. **Peter Harbison**

Gallicanism, a complex combination of political and theological theories of French origin. It seeks to curtail Papal power and claims the authority of the national church at the expense of the authority and autonomy of the Pope. This teaching was first condemned by Pope Alexander VIII in 1690. The assertion of Papal supremacy by the First Vatican Council in 1870 effectively repudiated Gallicanism. In nineteenth-century Ireland, Gallicanism was championed by the nationalist archbishop JOHN MACHALE, who opposed the centralising ULTRAMONTANIST policies advocated by Cardinal PAUL CULLEN. **Ciarán O'Carroll**

galloglass (Irish *gallóglach*, 'foreign warrior'). From the thirteenth to the sixteenth century 'galloglass' meant a mercenary from the Western Isles of Scotland and Argyll. They were much employed by Ulster and north Connacht chiefs in their resistance to English rule and settlement, as their frequent mention in the Annals of Ulster, Annals of Inisfallen and those of Connacht attest. Hebridean Scots are first mentioned as plunderers and later as seekers of Irish wives before they are noticed as mercenary soldiers in the fifteenth and sixteenth centuries. They then became a common feature of Irish warfare, much mentioned by contemporary writers, such as SPENSER, Dymock, STANIHURST, Rich, and indeed Shakespeare. Visual evidence of them and their ferocity survives on tomb carvings, such as on the O'Connor tomb in Roscommon, the Burke effigy at Glenisk, and on Goghe's map of 1567 (see p. 400) and in the celebrated engravings of Derricke. Outstanding galloglass families included the MacDonalds, MacCabes, MacSheehys, MacDowells, MacRorys, MacDougals, MacLeods, and MacSweeneys. The MacSheehys were exclusively settled in the Munster lands of the Earls of Desmond.

The galloglass are best described as foot-soldiers, armed with long-handled and short-handled battleaxes, their characteristic weapon until the sixteenth century, when some are portrayed with the two-handed sword. In battle they were adept at diverting cavalry charges by forming a defensive wall across the field of battle in front of the more lightly accoutred Irish horsemen. In return for their services they often received grants of land from the MacDonalds and the MacSorleys, for example, in north Antrim, but these grants were not tenured on the same basis as those of freemen; yet in time, especially through intermarriage, many became indistinguishable from the Irish nobility.

The traditional system of hiring galloglass fighters continued into the sixteenth century, but by then they were simply known as 'new Scots' mercenaries. In the fifteenth century Scottish galloglass can be found as bodyguards or in policing services for the OLD ENGLISH lords, such as the Fitzgeralds, Butlers and O'Briens in Munster and Leinster. In Ulster in the reign of Elizabeth I it was policy to keep the Scots out; but HUGH O'NEILL, second Earl of Tyrone, and HUGH O'DONNELL, Earl of Tyrconnell, frequently employed them in the skirmishes, sieges, and battles of the NINE YEARS' WAR. In the denouement of that war at KINSALE at least 300 Scots mercenaries were slain. Thereafter the change of dynasty and the demise of the old Irish order heralded the end of Scottish military help to the Irish. [see GAELIC LORDSHIP; GALL.] **John J. N. McGurk**

Gallus, Latinised name of Ceallach. According to Jonas of Bobbio, who wrote a Life of Columbanus c. 643, Gallus was one of COLUMBANUS's brethren at Luxeuil; but in the Lives written for Gallus himself in the eighth century he is presented as Columbanus's associate already at Bangor. They are said to have travelled together to the Continent, as far as the area about Lake Constance, where, falling ill, Gallus remained behind on his own. The famous church named St Gall (Sankt Gallen), Switzerland, grew up after his death; through its influence Gallus's cult spread into many parts of Switzerland and southern Germany. However, despite a continuing Irish connection with the Swiss church, whose library holds many important MANUSCRIPTS of Irish provenance, the saint was little known in Ireland. His feast-day, which is unnoticed in the Irish martyrologies, is 16 October. **Pádraig Ó Riain**

Galvin, Patrick (1927–), poet, playwright, and autobiographer. Born in Cork. He has been called 'our balladeering Lorca', a reference to his radical social vision as well as to his immersion in the oral and ballad traditions that framed his childhood in the poorer quarters of Cork. In two highly unreliable but immensely readable volumes of autobiography, *Song of a Poor Boy* (1989) and *Song for a Raggy Boy* (1991), he gives us the sources for the vivid, highly coloured, and sometimes savage imagination that informs his work. *Heart of Grace* (1957) and *Christ in London* (1960), his first books, signalled a unique talent, modified and matured in his next collection, *The Wood-Burners* (1973), which appeared at the time when he was appointed playwright in residence at the Lyric Theatre, Belfast. Among the plays he produced there are *The Last Burning* (1974) and *We Do It for Love* (1976). Later collections of poems include *Man on a Porch* (1980) and *New and Selected Poems* (1995). **Theo Dorgan**

Galway, County (*Contae na Gaillimhe*)

Province:	CONNACHT
County town:	GALWAY
Area:	5,939 km^2 (2,293 sq. miles)
Population, including city (2002):	208,826
Features:	Lough Corrib
	LOUGH DERG
	Maumturk Mountains
	River SHANNON
	River Suck
	Slieve Aughty Mountains
	Twelve Pins
Of historical interest:	ARAN ISLANDS, forts and churches
	Church of St Nicholas, Galway
	Clonfert Cathedral
	Kilmacduagh
	PORTUMNA CASTLE
Industry and products:	Chemicals
	Clothing and food products
	Electronic and engineering equipment
	Textiles
	Tourism

Petula Martyn

County Galway is the second-largest county in Ireland and the largest in Connacht, in both area and population. It is bounded by Cos. Mayo, Roscommon, Offaly, Tipperary, and Clare and on the west by the Atlantic Ocean. The ARAN ISLANDS lie across the entrance to Galway Bay. LOUGH CORRIB forms a divide between the east and west of the county. The west is dominated by highly metamorphosed geological structures: rolling granite hills on the north coast of Galway Bay and schists, gneisses, and quartzite peaks in the Twelve Pins and Maumturk Mountains further north. Lower Carboniferous limestone extends eastwards from Lough Corrib and provides fertile grassland but also presents problems of seasonal

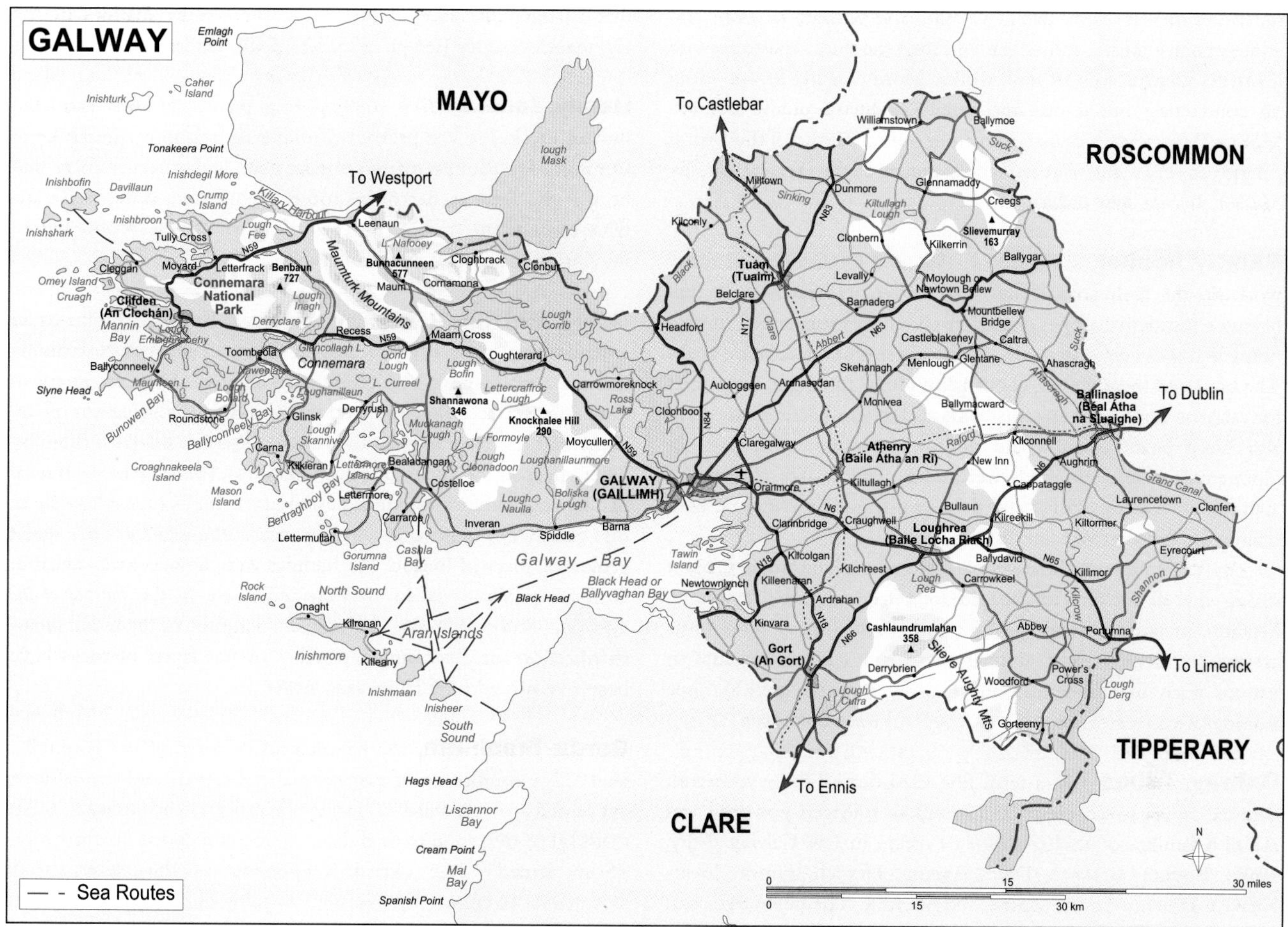

flooding in TURLOUGHS. The Slieve Aughty Mountains in the south-east are formed of old red sandstone. Mountain and lowland sheep-grazing dominate in the west and east, respectively, and dairying is of some importance in the vicinity of Galway and Headford. Average farm size in 1991 was 19.7 ha (48 acres). The county contains the largest Irish-speaking district; ÚDARÁS NA GAELTACHTA, RAIDIÓ NA GAELTACHTA, and the television station TG4 are based in Connemara, west of Galway. [see GAELTACHT.]
Mary E. Cawley

Galway (*Gaillimh*), a city (since 1985) and the county town of Co. Galway, situated on the inner north coast of Galway Bay where the short Galway River enters the Atlantic Ocean from Lough Corrib. It is the fourth-largest and most rapidly growing city in the Republic; population (2002) 65,774. It is the cathedral town of the Catholic diocese of Galway and the site of the National University of Ireland, Galway (quadrangle by Joseph B. Keane, 1846–50), Galway-Mayo Institute of Technology, and three hospitals. It is also a railway terminus and road junction, with a regional airport 6 km (4 miles) to the east.

Galway's urban origins date from the seizure in the thirteenth century of O'Flaherty-O'Halloran territory and the building of a castle by the river by Richard de Burgo. Letters patent were granted in 1396 and mayoral and borough status in 1484. From the fifteenth century a number of primarily ANGLO-NORMAN merchant families, including fourteen named 'TRIBES OF GALWAY', ruled the town. Lynch's Castle (now occupied by Allied Irish Bank) at the corner of Shop Street and Upper Abbeygate Street is a much-altered early sixteenth-century tower-house. The Collegiate CHURCH OF IRELAND in Market Street, dedicated to St Nicholas of Myra, dates from the fifteenth century. SPEED (1610) provides a map of the city as an insert to his Connacht sheet, but there is a large-scale detailed map, *Galway: The Capital of Connaught*, for 1651 (see p. 336). Some house-fronts preserve medieval doorways, windows, and coats of arms, and part of the town wall survives in the Eyre Square Shopping Centre. During the 1840s and 50s waterways were extended to provide navigation to Lough Corrib (the Eglinton Canal) and to power mills and distilleries.

Following the GREAT FAMINE, Galway experienced a period of decline. Growth since the late 1960s may be traced to industrial development (notably to the east, between Mervue and Ballybrit), the expansion of SERVICES, and the development of TOURISM. Out-of-town shopping centres are at Terryland to the east and Séamus Quirke Road and Knocknacarra to the west. Retail development and residential reoccupation have accompanied inner-city renovation under the provisions of the Urban Renewal Act (1986) and subsequent initiatives. The Galway Arts Festival takes place in early July, with the Galway Races during the last week of July. The CLADDAGH is a former fishing village in the west of the city. Salthill, which developed as an early nineteenth-century seaside resort, 3 km (2 miles) west of the city, is a residential and recreational area. Since the 1970s suburban development has been marked, and in 1985 the city boundary was extended to enclose an area twice that of the existing borough (see pp. 336, 534, 575). **Mary E. Cawley**

Galway, James (1939–), flautist, teacher, and conductor. Born in Belfast; studied at the Royal College of Music, London, the Guildhall School, Paris Conservatoire, and privately with Marcel Moyse. After fifteen years playing in British orchestras and the Berlin Philharmonic he established a solo career. His broad repertoire ranges from Bach, Vivaldi, and Mozart to JAZZ and contemporary music, and he has enriched the flute repertoire with his many commissions of new works. More recently he has taken up conducting and is principal guest conductor of the London Mozart Players. He was made a member of the Order of the British Empire in 1979 and was named Musician of the Year, 1997, by *Musical America*. **Paul Collins**

Galway hooker, a traditional craft used for fishing and cargo work on the west coast. It is a gaff cutter, its heavily built hull having a distinctive shape, characterised by the exaggerated tumble home that is designed to throw off the big seas of the Atlantic coast. The bigger of these vessels, about 12 m (40 ft) in length, were used for carrying turf to the ARAN ISLANDS and to Co. Clare; many were also 'shop boats', owned and run by shop-owners in parts of Connemara where the roads were poor. The smaller *gleoiteog*, of approximately 8 m (25 ft), and the lugsail-rigged *púcán* were used mainly for drift-net and line fishing.

By 1970 most of these vessels were ashore and unused, but a strong revival movement, headed to a large degree by Johnny Healion, means that there are now more than fifty of these boats around the coast. Every summer there is a series of regattas in various ports in Connemara and Galway Bay (see p. 420). [see BOATS, TRADITIONAL; MURPHY, RICHARD.] **Fiacc OBrolchain**

Galway, Tribes of, a term first used during the seventeenth century to negatively describe a group of fourteen powerful and clannish families of ANGLO-NORMAN origin in Co. Galway: Athy, Blake, Bodkin, Browne, Darcy, Deane, Ffrench, Ffront, Joyce, Kirwan, Lynch, Martin, Morris, and Skerrett. The pejorative term was later adopted by the families themselves as a badge of honour. **Brian Lalor**

Gandon, James (1742–1823), architect. Born in London to a HUGUENOT family; he joined WILLIAM CHAMBERS' office as an apprentice when he was fifteen and remained there until c. 1763. The design for the CASINO at Marino, Dublin, for Lord Charlemont was initiated in Chambers' office during Gandon's apprenticeship, and its influence can be seen in Gandon's CUSTOM HOUSE in Dublin. On leaving Chambers, Gandon set up his own practice; subsequently, with the Irishman John Woolfe, he published volumes 4 and 5 of *Vitruvius Britannicus* (1767 and 1771). In the latter volume Gandon included his own design for the County Hall at Nottingham, a commission he received in 1768 and his first major work. Also in 1768 he entered a design in the competition for the Royal Exchange in Dublin and was placed second to THOMAS COOLEY. He won the first gold medal in ARCHITECTURE to be offered by the Royal Academy in 1769.

John Beresford, whom he had met through Charlemont's circle in London, persuaded Gandon to come to Dublin in 1781 to build the Custom House. His other great works in Dublin include the FOUR COURTS, the KING'S INNS (see p. 618), the eastern extension to the PARLIAMENT HOUSE, and Carlisle Bridge (O'Connell Bridge). His houses include Emsworth and Abbeville, Co. Dublin, and Emo Court, Co. Laois, where he also designed Coolbanagher Church. It was with Chambers that Gandon's style and approach to architecture was formed, a style noted for its economy and its leaning towards French neo-classicism but later refined and adapted to include influences from other sources, particularly Wren. He remained for the rest of his life in Dublin, where, as Ireland's greatest neo-classical architect, he consolidated that tradition in Ireland, creating buildings that changed the face of Dublin in the closing decades of the eighteenth century (see pp. 525, 533, 729). **Patricia McCarthy**

Gandy, James (1619–1689), portrait painter. He was instructed by Van Dyck. He was probably brought to Ireland by the Duke of Ormond. He painted many portraits here, and it seems likely that he was the first teacher of his more famous son, William Gandy, who early in his career also painted portraits in Ireland before moving to the Exeter area. **Jane Fenlon**

Ganly, Patrick (1809–1899), geologist. Born in Dublin to an artisan family; probably educated in Cork; in his mature years he became a graduate of TCD (1849). His known career was spent in the public service, 1827–60, and principally in the valuation office. Some 600 letters (mostly in the ROYAL IRISH ACADEMY) written by him to the commissioner for valuation, Sir RICHARD GRIFFITH, reveal that he engaged for prolonged periods from 1837–46, exclusively in the geological fieldwork, thereby underpinning Griffith's great geological maps of Ireland. His findings were however subsumed in Griffith's publications. In 1857 he published, in the *Journal of the Geological Society of Dublin*, an original description of the use of cross-stratification for determining whether or not layers of rocks have been overturned by folding. **Jean Archer**

Garda Síochána, the national police force of the Republic. In 1922 a committee of professional policemen and IRA officers appointed to organise a force to replace the ROYAL IRISH CONSTABULARY, soon to be disbanded, recommended the formation of an armed Civic Guard. Opponents of the PROVISIONAL GOVERNMENT among the recruits, rebelling at the appointment of RIC officers to senior rank, challenged the authority of Commissioner Michael Staines. The seizure of the armoury by the mutineers had a positive outcome in the emergence of the new police as an unarmed force, now named An Garda Síochána (Guard of the Peace), and Staines defined a philosophy of moral authority for policing independent Ireland.

His successor, EOIN O'DUFFY, took command in 1922 of a body of young men ready to respond to his call for discipline. His proposal to rearm the force led to the confirmation of an unarmed police as government policy. After the CIVIL WAR the detective division of the DUBLIN METROPOLITAN POLICE was transferred to Garda Headquarters to form the Special Branch; but the absorption of the general body of the disparate DMP was to undermine morale in the national force. The turmoil that accompanied the change of Government in the 1930s tested the loyalty of the Garda Síochána. Accused of political favouritism and obliged to accept overnight into its ranks supporters of the new ruling party, the force with difficulty restored order at election meetings and contained the riots resulting from the ECONOMIC WAR. Its role in the formation of the Local Security Force in 1940 contributed to the healing of political wounds.

In the following decade an interdepartmental committee recommended reorganisation in rural areas to increase strengths in Dublin. Against the advice of successive Commissioners, stations were closed, and the local garda on a bicycle was replaced by motorised patrols, with a consequent dissipation of local knowledge. In Dublin in 1961 a new generation of gardaí, revolting at delays in addressing grievances, forced the Government to negotiate directly with rank-and-file representatives.

During the years of civil disturbance in Northern Ireland the response to subversive activities was robust; the resulting deaths of fourteen gardaí brought to thirty the number murdered on duty since 1922. Much progress was made in modernising headquarters management. An advanced command and control system and new information technology revolutionised communications. A National Forensic Science Laboratory, Bureaux of Criminal and Fraud Investigation, and a Criminal Assets Bureau, together with older specialist units, strengthened and re-equipped, contributed to a new attack on criminal activity. The training centre at Templemore, Co. Tipperary, evolved into a modern, well-equipped Garda College. A helicopter wing was commissioned, mounted police reappeared on the streets of Dublin, and overseas duty with the UNITED NATIONS became a feature of Garda service. **Gregory Allen**

garden design. The development of garden design in Ireland parallels that in the rest of Europe, though it boasts a number of distinctive features. Early Irish MONASTERIES had small orchards as well as herb and kitchen gardens in simple enclosures; late medieval monasteries and manors possessed substantial walled gardens. The Renaissance pleasure garden was introduced c. 1600; a painting of that for TRINITY COLLEGE, Dublin, and the remains of that at Lismore Castle, Co. Waterford, survive. The French baroque garden style was current from c. 1660, the best surviving example being at Killruddery House, near Bray, Co. Wicklow. From c. 1740 the informal English landscape garden style was practised by professional landscape gardeners, such as John Sutherland (died 1826) and James Frazer (1793–1863). The chief garden designer in nineteenth-century Ireland was Ninian Niven (1799–1879), whose work combined elements from many different European traditions. WILLIAM ROBINSON (1838–1935) was the most influential gardener in the early twentieth century. His naturalistic approach to gardening can be seen at Mount Usher, Co. Wicklow, and Mount Congreve, Co. Waterford. A parallel influence on the Irish twentieth-century garden was the modern English style, in which formality of planning is combined with informality of planting; great gardens in this mode include Ilnacullin (GARINISH), Co. Cork, and Mount Stewart, Co. Down. Important twentieth-century gardens that attempt to synthesise a comprehensive range of different gardening traditions include those of BIRR CASTLE, Co. Offaly, and Glenveagh Castle, Co. Donegal.

The distinctiveness of Irish garden design arises from the mild climate, which allows plants from sub-tropical as well as temperate climes to be grown, particularly in coastal gardens. Noteworthy are the many plants native to the southern hemisphere that thrive. Also distinctive is the way in which a deliberate attempt is made to incorporate views of the natural landscape beyond the garden. Finally, a studied informality characterises Irish gardens of every period and style. [see BOTANIC GARDENS AND ARBORETA; FLORA; NATURALISTS ABROAD.] **Patrick Bowe**

Gardiner, John Joe (1882–1979), FIDDLE and FLUTE-player. Born in Ballymote, Co. Sligo. A talented teacher and performer from a musical background (and a political activist in the 1920s), he lived in Dundalk, Co. Louth, from 1929 onwards. His influence on musical life there was seminal. **Desi Wilkinson**

Gardiner, Luke. Much of the north-east of Dublin, within the arc of the ROYAL CANAL, was developed by the Gardiner family

Garda. *Night shift at Store Street Garda Station, Dublin, 1992. In 1922 the Garda Síochána was formed as the national police force of the Irish Free State. Today there are more than 11,230 gardaí. [Leo Regan]*

Garinish. *View of the Italian Gardens at Garinish Island, Glengarriff, Co. Cork. Over the period of a century the barren island has been transformed into an exotic Italianate landscape. [Michael Diggin Photography]*

between c. 1720 and c. 1820. There were two Luke Gardiners. The first (died 1755) was a banker and property developer who married into the Mountjoy family; his developments at Henrietta Street, Gardiner's Mall (later Sackville Street, now O'Connell Street) and Rutland Square (Parnell Square) created a high-status area on the north side. His grandson, the second Luke Gardiner (1745–1798), Lord Mountjoy, built eastwards from Marlborough Street along Gloucester Street on the axis of St Thomas's Church; Gloucester Diamond and Buckingham Street followed. The fragmented nature of their estate limited their plans somewhat: Dominick Street, Temple Street, and Eccles Street commemorate other developers. Mountjoy Square and its environs, begun in the 1790s, was their last large-scale project. Unified palatial façades on all four sides were planned, with entrances at regular intervals to separate the dwellings. A new church for the parish of St George was envisaged for the centre of the square, but this plan was too expensive, and uniform four-storey brick houses were built instead, and the square remained open. It was linked by Gardiner Street to GANDON's semicircular Beresford Place, focusing on the centre of the rear façade of the CUSTOM HOUSE in the approved classical manner and as befitted a WIDE STREETS COMMISSIONER. Though it appeared on maps into the nineteenth century, a plan for a Royal Circus at the top of Eccles Street, with radial streets joining the Gardiners' three principal holdings at Rutland Square, Mountjoy Square, and Hardwicke Place, remained unrealised. **Joseph Brady**

Garinish (Ilnacullin), Co. Cork, a small island in Bantry Bay, with an area of 15 ha (37 acres). It was the home of Annan Bryce MP, who bought it from the British War Office in 1910. With the garden-designer Harold Peto he planned (but never built) a mansion and laid out much of the island in gardens. The Italian-style gardens are notable for magnolias, camellias, and rhododendrons. There is also a MARTELLO TOWER. The island has been state property since 1953. Garinish is a ten-minute boat journey from the immediate shoreline. [see GARDEN DESIGN.] **Stephen A. Royle**

Garranes, Co. Cork, a large *trivallate* (triple-banked) earthen RING-FORT between the Rivers LEE and Bandon. It comprises a roughly circular interior surrounded by three concentric banks, each accompanied by a flat-bottomed external *fosse*. The ring-fort measures 110 m (360 ft) in external diameter and is tentatively identified as Ráth Rathleann, the seat of a branch of the ruling EOGHANACHTA dynasty of Munster. Garranes was partially excavated in the 1940s by Seán P. Ó Ríordáin and is dated to the late fifth or early sixth century. The wealth of artefactual evidence and morphology of Garranes reflects a high-status settlement. **Michelle Comber**

Garrett, James Ramsey (1817–1855), ornithologist. Born in Belfast to Thomas Garrett, a solicitor, and Ann Garrett, daughter of Samuel Nielson; he practised in the family firm. A dedicated naturalist, like his great friend WILLIAM THOMPSON, he specialised in ornithology and contributed many observations and records to volumes 1–3 of Thompson's landmark publication, *The Natural History of Ireland* (1849, 1850, 1851). From 1852, under the terms of Thompson's will, from 1852 he undertook with Robert Patterson the editing of the final volume, covering MAMMALS and invertebrates. His untimely death occurred before its completion in 1856. **Helena C. G. Chesney**

Garstin, Norman (1847–1926), painter. Born in Co. Limerick. He worked as a journalist and as a diamond-miner before becoming an artist. Studying first in Antwerp, 1878–80, and later in Paris under Charles Verlat and Carolus Duran, he met a number of English artists who would later be part of the Newlyn School in Cornwall. In 1886 he settled in Cornwall, initially in Newlyn, afterwards in Penzance. His best-known painting, *The Rain It Raineth Every Day*, is in Penlee House Art Gallery, Penzance. An autumnal scene, *Sunshine in the Beguinage*, is in the Crawford Gallery, Cork. **Peter Murray**

gas, natural, a hydrocarbon, mainly methane but including ethane and nitrogen, formed by the long-term burial, bacterial decomposition and heating of organic debris washed into ancient sedimentary basins. Ireland's natural gas fields are offshore in Cretaceous and Triassic sedimentary rocks. The Kinsale field, discovered in 1971, lies 50 km (31 miles) off Co. Cork in 90 m (300 ft) of water and was Ireland's first commercial field. The gas reservoir 1,000 m (0.6 miles) below the sea-bed had an initial reserve of 48 billion m^3 (1.7 trillion cu. ft), enough to last until 2004. Production began in 1978 following the completion of a terminal at Inch, Co. Cork, and a transmission pipeline. In 1995–6 Kinsale's two platforms produced 83 per cent of Ireland's gas requirement, but this fell to 18 per cent by 2001, a shortfall met by imports piped from Britain. Recently smaller gas fields, including the Ballycotton, South-West Kinsale, and Seven Heads fields, have augmented Kinsale, using existing infrastructure. Exploration in the Atlantic led to the discovery in 1996 of the Corrib field, 70 km (45 miles) off Co. Mayo in 335 m (1,000 ft) of water. Its gas reserves of 28 billion m^3 (1 trillion cu. ft), 3,500 m (2 miles) below the sea-bed, are enough for fifteen years of production, with transmission by way of a pipeline from Bellanaboy Bridge, Co. Mayo. Gas exploration continues off Ireland, and despite challenges of great water depths and

EXTREME WEATHER, improvements in technology and geological modelling have raised hopes that new domestic fields can contribute to the increasing demand for natural gas. **Colman Gallagher**

Gate Theatre, Dublin, founded in 1928 by HILTON EDWARDS and MÍCHEÁL MAC LIAMMÓIR (see p. 497). Their first production, *Peer Gynt* (staged in the ABBEY's Peacock Theatre), established their distinctive aesthetic, which used innovative visual design and a traditional regard for showmanship to make challenging modernist theatre accessible to a wide audience. In 1929 they performed DENIS JOHNSTON's *The Old Lady Says 'No!'* (also in the Peacock) before moving in 1930 to a theatre in the ROTUNDA HOSPITAL complex, which subsequently became the Gate Theatre. In spite of its limitations (it has no fly system, limited backstage space, and a cramped lobby), Edwards and Mac Liammóir made the Gate into a director's theatre, continuing to perform there (with occasional forays to the GAIETY THEATRE) until the middle of the 1970s. After Edwards's death in 1982 (Mac Liammóir had died in 1978) Michael Colgan became artistic director of the Gate, which he runs as a producing theatre, with no permanent company. The Gate continues to uphold its reputation for innovative design and a commitment to modernist work, staging critically acclaimed festivals of the plays of SAMUEL BECKETT (1991) and Harold Pinter (1994 and 1997). **Christopher Morash**

gavelkind, the English term denoting the custom of partible (divisible) inheritance practised in Wales and by Irish and Hibernicised ANGLO-NORMAN families in Ireland. The Irish practice was distinct from its English equivalent, as communal land tenures, abolished in 1606, resulted in collective partible inheritance. The principle involved sub-division between male heirs only, including both illegitimate and 'named' males. Partition procedures varied greatly between families and patrimonies. In some regions division only followed the death of a co-heir, while in others it occurred annually, often on MAY DAY. In certain areas all eligible males were allocated an equal share. Elsewhere the chief divided anew all the sept's land, distributing shares according to seniority. Occasionally the most junior of the co-heirs devised the partition, or sons of a deceased elder brother were given preference over their seniors. Gavelkind led to the fragmentation of landholdings. A penal law passed in 1704 made partible inheritance mandatory for Catholic landholders who refused to convert to PROTESTANTISM. [see GAELIC LORDSHIP; LAND OWNERSHIP AND TENURE.] **Mary Ann Lyons**

Gavin, Frankie (1956–), virtuoso traditional fiddler and flute-player. Born in Corrandulla, Co. Galway. He won several all-Ireland whistle and fiddle titles before forming the seminal group DÉ DANANN with the bouzouki-player Alec Finn in 1974. In this he created and maintains a unique dynamic style while exploring cross-over to gospel, blues, and jazz. He has recorded six personal albums, one of them with Stéphane Grappelli. **Fintan Vallely**

gay icons. Despite the poverty of historical record which itself was the function of cultural repression, there are a number of Irish gay icons, though about several of them there still hangs an element of ambiguity. The most famous is OSCAR WILDE, about whom there is no ambiguity at all: Wilde in fact is not just an Irish but a global icon for gay people. In the political sphere, prominent figures have been careful to hide their sexuality. It is probable that PATRICK PEARSE had homosexual inclinations, as evidenced in his writing; but his entire nature was so ambiguous that he may not have been consciously aware of this. ROGER CASEMENT was also homosexual, though the cynical use by the British government of the infamous 'Black Diaries', in which Casement detailed his homosexual encounters, in order to turn world opinion against him has confused the issue. Many nationalists have used the British government's treatment of Casement to suggest that he was not homosexual and that the diaries are a forgery, but textual scholarship suggests that this would have been virtually impossible.

One should also remember the distinguished short-story writers SOMERVILLE AND ROSS: their relationship was undoubtedly Sapphic in emotional if not in physical content, and (following Martin's death) Somerville went on to engage in a passionate emotional relationship with the avowedly lesbian composer Dame Ethel Smyth. The novelist KATE O'BRIEN, one of whose books, *The Land of Spices*, was banned in the 1940s because of a glancing reference to male homosexuality, was also lesbian.

MÍCHEÁL MAC LIAMMÓIR and HILTON EDWARDS, the famous theatrical couple, are also held in high regard, though after his death it emerged that Mac Liammóir had succeeded in inventing a personality for himself and that he was not even Irish, having been born in London of English parents. The bisexuality of the playwright BRENDAN BEHAN is now also widely accepted (see p. 497).

In the present generation the poets CATHAL Ó SEARCAIGH and MARY DORCEY, and Stephen Gately of Boyzone, as well as TV personality Graham Norton, have not found it necessary to conceal their sexuality and are consequently held in high esteem by the gay community. [see HOMOSEXUALITY; LESBIANISM.] **David Norris**

Geary, Robert (Roy) (1896–1983), economist and statistician. Born in Dublin; educated at UCD. He served as a statistician in the Department of Trade and Industry, 1923–49, and as director of the CENTRAL STATISTICS OFFICE, 1949–57. His contributions to economic theory include the determination of the utility function attached to certain linear expenditure systems (the Stone-Geary function) and a method of comparing data relating to real income and purchasing power in different countries. He also wrote influential statistical papers on the analysis of ratios and on tests for normality. **Rod Gow**

Gébler, Carlo (1954–), novelist. Born in Dublin; educated at the University of York. He published *The Eleventh Summer* (1955) and *The Cure* (1994). His historical novel *How to Murder a Man* (1998) is a disturbing study of rural society with implications for twentieth-century Ulster, which the author studied in the documentary *The Glass Curtain: Inside an Ulster Community* (1991). **Terence Brown**

Geddes, Wilhelmina (1887–1955), STAINED-GLASS and graphic artist. Born at Drumreilly, Co. Leitrim; educated at Methodist College and the School of Art, Belfast, then the Metropolitan School of Art, Dublin. In 1910 her strongly characterised book illustrations attracted the attention of SARAH PURSER, who invited Geddes to join her Dublin stained-glass co-operative, AN TÚR GLOINE. From 1912 until 1925, when she left Ireland to continue making stained glass at a rented studio in London, she designed and made powerfully figurative masterpieces. Her best-known windows are those in St Bartholomew's Church, Ottawa (1919), commemorating Irish officers killed in the FIRST WORLD WAR, and St Martin's Cathedral, Ypres (1938), commemorating the King of the Belgians. **Nicola Gordon Bowe**

Geldof, Robert (Bob) (1954–), rock musician. Born in Dublin; educated at Blackrock College. He formed the Boomtown Rats in

Geddes. *The Wheeler Memorial Window,* The Leaves of the Trees Were for the Healing of the Nations *(1920), by Wilhelmina Geddes in St John's (Church of Ireland) Church, Malone Road, Belfast. [Irish Picture Library]*

1975, which was very successful in the late 1970s and early 80s with singles that topped the British charts, such as 'Rat Trap' (1978) and 'I Don't Like Mondays' (1979). In 1985 he masterminded the charity concert 'Live Aid', which raised millions for famine-stricken Ethiopia. The Boomtown Rats split up soon afterwards and Geldof launched his solo career. His second solo album, *The Vegetarians of Love* (1990), is widely considered to be the highlight of his later musical career. He was knighted in 1986 for his humanitarian work.
Tony Clayton-Lea

Geminiani, Francesco (1687–1762), violinist, composer, and music theorist. Born in Lucca, Italy; studied with Corelli. He was one of the greatest violin virtuosos of his day, his best-known treatise being *The Art of Playing on the Violin* (1751). He owned a residence at Spring Gardens (off Dame Street) in Dublin, 1733–40, where he had his own 'Great Music Room'. He made his Irish debut at Crow Street Concert Hall, Dublin, in 1733. After almost twenty years spent mainly in England and France he returned to Ireland in 1759 as music teacher to the family of Charles Coote (later Earl of Bellamont) of Cootehill, Co. Cavan. His compositional output consisted mainly of violin sonatas and concerti grossi. He died in Dublin and was buried in the grounds of St. Andrew's Church.
Paul Collins

genealogy. The earliest Irish genealogies—poems on the kings of Leinster—can be dated linguistically to the early seventh century. These have survived in a twelfth-century manuscript (now in the Bodleian Library, Oxford), probably written in a Leinster monastery, which also includes early genealogies of leading dynasties of Munster. The Book of LEINSTER, another monastic compilation of the twelfth century, lays great emphasis on Leinster dynastic families, but the leading families of the other provinces are also represented. Included too are the genealogies of Irish SAINTS.

Until the twelfth century the writing of manuscripts was done in monastic scriptoria, but by the fourteenth century a new class of scholars had emerged, literary men in the service of ruling families. Among the most distinguished of these was the family of Mac Fir Bhisigh, historians to the Ó Dubhda family, rulers of the kingdom of Tirearagh (Co. Sligo), with whom they shared a supposed common ancestry. From this family we have the Book of Lecan, which contains comprehensive genealogies of leading families throughout Ireland. As well as the genealogies, the manuscript contains a copy of LEBOR GABÁLA ÉRENN (the Book of Invasions), which purports to tell the history of the Irish people from pre-Christian times to the twelfth century. The last great scholar of this family was DUBHALTACH MAC FIR BHISIGH, who compiled Leabhar na nGenealach (The Book of Genealogies), which he began to write c. 1650; the autograph manuscript is now in University College, Dublin. Another such family was that of Ó Duibhgheannáin, who kept schools under the Mac Donnchadha Lords of Corran and Tirerrill (Co. Sligo) and the Ó Fearghail Lords of Annaly (Co. Longford). From them comes the Book of BALLYMOTE, which used as sources the genealogies in the Book of Leinster and the Bodleian Library manuscript. The family continued to be scholar-scribes down to the seventeenth century, and one of them, Cúchoigríche, worked with MICHEÁL Ó CLÉIRIGH in compiling the Annals of the FOUR MASTERS. The Ó Cléirigh family had been historians to the Ó Domhnaill rulers of Tír Chonaill since the middle of the fourteenth century; apart from the annals the greatest achievement from their hands known to us is the late seventeenth-century Book of Genealogies, most probably compiled by

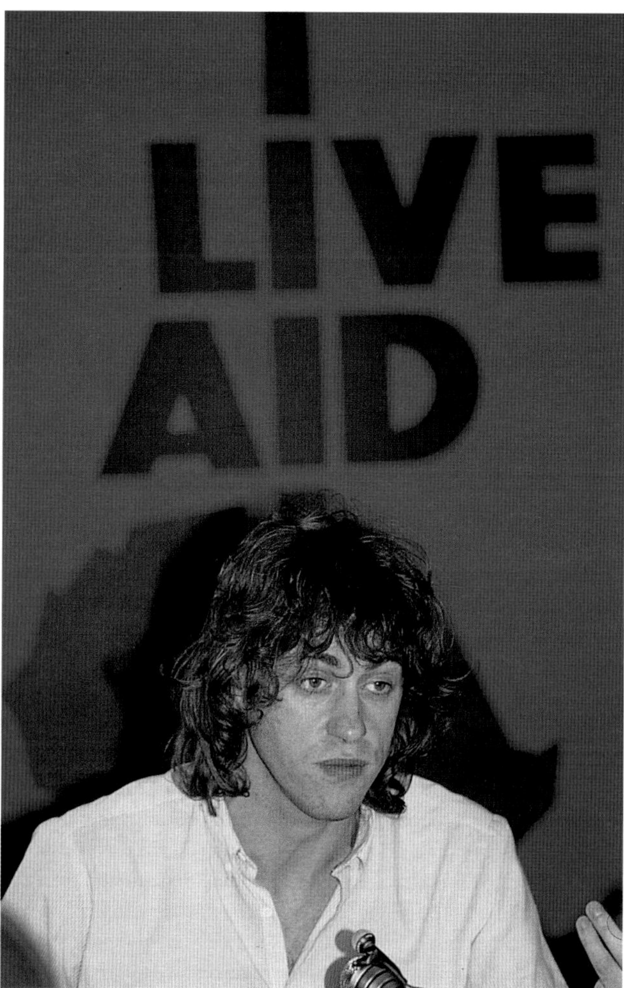

Geldof. *Bob Geldof, lead singer of the 1980s rock group Boomtown Rats, making an appeal in Dublin on 20 September 1985 for 'Live Aid'. He used his contacts in the music business to co-ordinate the 'Live Aid' concerts, which raised Stg£123 million in 1985 to help the victims of famine in Ethiopia. [Derek Speirs/Report]*

Cúchoigríche Ó Cléirigh. The work begins with the genealogies of the Hapsburg kings, which shows the political bias of the author, followed by the genealogy of Ó Domhnaill and those of the major (and often the minor) Irish dynasties of Ulster, Munster, Leinster, and Connacht. Like Dubhaltach Mac Firbhisigh, the compiler also included the genealogies of the Norman families of Ireland.

From the eighteenth century comes the Leabhar Muimhneach, which is mainly concerned with Munster families, and from the early nineteenth century Geinealaighe Fearmanach, which was transcribed by Pól Ó Longáin from an early eighteenth-century compilation, done most likely by a member of the Ó Luinnín family, former historians to Mag Uidhir of Fermanagh. This corpus is concerned only with Fermanagh families. These learned families and their monastic predecessors transmitted in their writings the *seanchas coiteann* or 'accepted doctrine' regarding Irish history and genealogy, according to which the genealogical lines of Irish families converged long before the Christian era into a line that descended from a common ancestor, Míl Espáine or Milesius of Spain, and from him to Japheth, son of Noah. This tradition is best known from Lebor Gabála, found in the Book of Leinster and later manuscripts. The narrative is a mixture of genuine history, mythology, the Bible, and gleanings from early Spanish writers such as Isidore of Seville and is the subject of a poem by Máel Mura of Fahan, who died in 887. Míl Espáine had already been accepted as the remote ancestor in the seventh-century Leinster poems mentioned above. The doctrine sought to legitimise the hegemony of dynasties such as UÍ NÉILL of the north and the EOGHANACHTA of Munster, who had subdued earlier population groups. As time passed, the older subject peoples, such as the DÉISE and the Airghialla, were also given Milesian genealogies, thus assimilating them into a genealogical scheme that provided a racial and cultural homogeneity for all prominent pre-Norman and non-Viking peoples of Ireland.

After the establishment of the office of Ulster King of Arms (now the Genealogical Office) in 1552, brief pedigrees of the native Irish, but mostly the Old English, are found, for instance, in the visitations of Dublin and Wexford and in the funeral entry volumes. Most of the extensive registered pedigrees in the following centuries are of English and Scottish planter stock, but the Old English and Irish families also feature, most notably in registers containing copies of coats of arms and pedigrees issued in the eighteenth century to Irishmen entering the service of France, Spain, and Austria. It is known that James Terry, Athlone Pursuivant of Arms in Dublin and after 1690 at the Stuart court at Saint-Germain-en-Laye, kept pedigrees of émigrés, collections of which are now housed in the Archives Nationales in Paris and elsewhere. The most notable genealogical collection for native Irish families in the Genealogical Office is Roger O'Ferral's *Linea Antiqua* (1709), copied by Sir WILLIAM BETHAM. The Genealogical Office also houses collections of unregistered pedigrees. [see CHIEFS OF THE NAME; FAMILY HISTORY; GENERAL REGISTER OFFICE; HERALDRY.] **Fergus Gillespie**

genealogy and politics played a crucial role in the secular and ecclesiastical politics of early and medieval Ireland. The two main collections of pre-Norman secular genealogies are in the Book of LEINSTER and in the compilation Rawlinson B502; there are also the genealogies of the SAINTS. The importance of genealogy owed much to the system of inheritance, whereby rights were vested not in the nuclear family but in the *deirbhfhine* or four-generation extended kin group; serial marriage, not uncommon among the aristocracy, could render succession to KINGSHIP even more complex. In this way royal genealogies, maintained by official historians, certified the king's right to rule—establishing his lineage and dynastic affiliations and indicating his kingly predecessors. Manipulation of genealogies to justify dynastic change can, in some instances, be detected. Similarly, a tendency may be noted for genealogies of saintly founders to coincide with those of families that later enjoyed succession rights in ecclesiastical foundations. **Ailbhe Mac Shamhráin**

General, the: see CAHILL, MARTIN.

General Post Office (GPO), Dublin (1814–18). Designed by FRANCIS JOHNSTON, it was from its completion the architectural focus of Sackville (O'Connell) Street, though NELSON PILLAR (1808) was the eye-catcher (see p. 804). The dominance of the GPO would originally have appeared even more formidable than today, as the entire street was composed of brick-fronted houses of uniform rooflines. Built of granite, the massive sixteen-bay façade has a rusticated ground floor with a six-column Portland stone Greek Revival Ionic portico. A heavy cornice with balustrade unites the extended façade. THOMAS KIRK's sculptures of Hibernia flanked by Fidelity and Mercury (appropriate deities for the national post office) decorate the pediment.

In 1916 the GPO became the headquarters of the Rising, and the PROCLAMATION OF THE IRISH REPUBLIC was read from its steps by PATRICK PEARSE. The building (and much of the street) was gutted by the ensuing fires when it was shelled by the British gunboat *Helga*, moored in the River Liffey. OLIVER SHEPPARD's sculpture *The Death of Cuchulainn* (1911) was installed in the GPO in 1935 as a memorial to the dead of 1916 (see p. 1090). The GPO occupies a symbolic role in nationalist mythology as birthplace of the Republic. The ruins were not restored until 1929. [see GARDINER, LUKE.] **Brian Lalor**

General Register Office. The office of Registrar-General was established in 1845, with responsibility for the registration of civil marriages and the regulation of all non-Catholic marriages. These responsibilities were widened from 1864 as a result of new legislation that provided for a comprehensive registration system, with the inclusion of Catholic marriages, together with all births and deaths. The records held by the General Register Office form a continuous source of information, its archives constituting one of the principal sources for family history research. The modernisation of the registration system has been a concern of the office in recent years, with electronic records systems being established, in tandem with a comprehensive review of registration law. In Northern Ireland since 1922 the registration of births, marriages, and deaths has been the responsibility of the Registrar-General for Northern Ireland. **Colette O'Flaherty**

geographical information systems (GIS). Geographical information is of increasing importance in planning and decision-making; and since the early 1960s computer-based technologies have been developed that give faster and better access to the geographical component of data. These technologies combine tools for creating and displaying maps with databases for storing and retrieving information and also provide statistical, modelling, and analytical tools that allow the geographical relationships between phenomena to be studied. In this way GIS makes it possible to rapidly find out what occurs at a particular place, where something we are interested in may be found, why certain things occur together, and how they interact.

Typical applications of GIS include natural and human resource management, route PLANNING and navigation, agriculture, FORESTRY, ENVIRONMENT, heritage, fisheries and related activities, town and country planning, policy-making, market analysis, PUBLISHING, and scientific research. The use of GIS in Ireland is growing rapidly, extending to national and local government and state-sponsored bodies, regional health authorities, the GARDA SÍOCHÁNA and DEFENCE FORCES, telecommunications, gas, electricity and other utilities, universities and schools, business and retail trade, and sales and marketing organisations, as well as data-providers and publishers, mapping organisations, consultancy firms, and a growing number of private companies.

By the beginning of the twenty-first century there was an increasing tendency for GIS techniques and methods to merge with or be embedded in related technologies, such as satellite remote sensing, television and video production, multimedia computing, virtual reality, the internet and worldwide web, mobile telephony, and other developments in modern telecommunications. **Darius Bartlett**

geological landscape. At least 1,700 million years of Irish history is recorded in its rocks. The diverse Irish landscape, with mountain ranges near coasts and within the Central Plain, is partly the result of an exceptional richness in different types and ages of rocks of varied hardness. During the last 60 million years the opening of the North Atlantic Ocean and the collision of Africa and Europe, lifting the Alps, created a vice-like compression of Ireland that lifted up mountain ranges. This landscape was slightly modified by ice movements during the last 1 million years. Sixty-five million years ago a plume of partly molten rock rose under Iceland from a depth of 2,900 km (1,800 miles), triggering the opening of the north-east Atlantic and the eruption of basalt lava flows in north-eastern Ireland, including the famous GIANT'S CAUSEWAY, Co. Antrim. From 65 to 180 million years ago Ireland was occasionally covered by thin layers of marine sediments, such as the chalk and Jurassic clays still preserved in the north-east. About 240 million years ago the island was a hot, dry desert, which created the deposits of red sandstones and salt also preserved in the north-east. Between 360 and 330 million years ago Ireland was south of the equator, and up to 3 km (2 miles) of limestones rich in fossils such as corals were deposited across the country on a broad CONTINENTAL SHELF north of the major Rheic Ocean. During the closure of that ocean, earth movements raised land areas, and sheets of sand with local coal seams covered the limestones. About 280 million years ago the final closure of the Rheic Ocean brought southern and central Europe together, causing the folding of rocks of Cos. Cork and Kerry. Beneath the limestones lie red sandstones that thicken southwards, representing floodplain sediments from rivers draining mountains to the north.

Between c. 550 and 400 million years ago the Iapetus Ocean, with a width like the North Atlantic Ocean, separated north-western Ireland and North America from south-eastern Ireland and central Europe. About 400 million years ago this ocean closed along a suture zone stretching from Dundalk Bay to the Shannon Estuary, bringing Ireland together from two separate Continental masses and creating a range of mountains. The oldest rocks of north-western Ireland, the gneisses of north Mayo and Inishtrahull, record sediment deposition and injection of igneous rocks adjacent to a closing ocean c. 1700 million years ago. The 1,000-million-year-old granite gneisses of north Mayo record the closure of a younger ocean. Between c. 750 and 480 million years ago the metamorphic rocks (Dalradian Supergroup) of Co. Tyrone, Co. Donegal, north Mayo and Connemara were sediments deposited on a Continental shelf during the initial opening of the Iapetus Ocean. The collision of this northern continent with a major continental block within the Iapetus Ocean 470 million years ago caused these sediments to be overridden by about 20 km (12 miles) of rock, heating them up to approximately 700°C and converting them to metamorphic schists, marbles, and quartzites. The Dalradian rocks of Connemara were also moved from eastern North America to their present position. A chain of volcanoes from south Mayo to Tyrone formed just before this collision event. Between c. 480 and 400 million years ago a great thickness of mud and sand was deposited in a deep submarine trench along the northern edge of the Iapetus Ocean. It was scraped up onto the north-west continental margin, while the denser oceanic crust sank below it. This process formed the Ordovician and Silurian sedimentary rocks, which extend through Cos. Down, Longford, and Clare.

South of the Iapetus Suture Zone, the oldest rocks are the gneisses of south Wexford. They include basic igneous rocks formed during the closure of an ocean c. 600 million years ago. Between c. 550 and 400 million years ago there was a continuous deposition of marine sands and muds on the south-east continental shelf to the Iapetus Ocean. About 480 million years ago the dense oceanic crust subsided beneath south-eastern Ireland. Parts that melted created a chain of volcanic rocks stretching from Louth through Waterford to the Dingle Peninsula. The closure of the

Iapetus Ocean with the collision of the bounding continents 400 million years ago caused major compression and uplift of low mountains. Molten rock rose up along major fractures in both south-eastern and north-western Ireland and crystallised as granite. [see GLACIATION.] **Adrian Phillips**

Geological Survey of Ireland (Suirbhéireacht Gheolaíochta Éireann), the national earth science agency, responsible for acquiring data relating to the rocks of Ireland and for providing such data to all those needing information about Ireland's geological environment. The ORDNANCE SURVEY pioneered the mapping of Ireland's rocks during the years following 1826. The Geological Survey of Ireland came into being on 1 April 1845; originally part of the Geological Survey of the United Kingdom, the Irish section passed into the control of the Department of Agricultural and Technical Instruction for Ireland on 1 April 1905. Since then the Geological Survey has been under the aegis of several departments. The PARTITION of Ireland in 1922 left the six northern counties bereft of a geological survey, and it was not until 1947 that an office of the Geological Survey of Great Britain was established in Belfast.

Until 1890 the prime task of the Geological Survey was the construction of a 1-inch (1:63,360) map of the solid GEOLOGY of Ireland in 205 sheets, each sheet accompanied by a descriptive memoir. That map being completed, the Geological Survey embarked on the revision of maps and, between 1901 and 1913, the publication of maps depicting the superficial geology of Ireland around some of the main towns.

Some distinguished geologists have directed the Geological Survey, the principal ones being Thomas Oldham (1846–50), Joseph Beete Jukes (1850–69), EDWARD HULL (1869–90), and GRENVILLE ARTHUR JAMES COLE (1905–24). With national independence the Geological Survey lost much of its former vigour, and from 1924 to 1963 a financially starved institution achieved little that was innovative. After 1963 the scene was revolutionised by the discovery of a wealth of minerals. The Geological Survey shared in this revolution, and its establishment, budget and field of operation were enormously increased. In 1992 the Geological Survey published the first sheet (with memoir) of a new 1:100,000 bedrock map of Ireland, scheduled for completion during 2000. The Geological Survey has now embarked on a seven-year sea-bed survey of the entire Irish offshore territory, employing the latest geophysical techniques. **Gordon L. Herries Davies**

geology, the study of the Earth and its history. Ireland, though small in area, displays a wide range of rock types of various ages. The oldest are Precambrian, which date from 1,500 million years ago and are found in Cos. Donegal and Mayo. In the Cambrian Period, when shelly marine animals first appeared, deep-water sediments were widely distributed; they are now seen at BRAY HEAD, Co. Wicklow, and contain the unusual trace fossil Oldhamia. Later, during the Ordovician and Silurian Periods (500–400 million years ago), a wide ocean that separated North America from Europe closed, causing widespread volcanism and the development of granitic bodies, such as those that formed the Dublin and Wicklow Mountains. Highly fossiliferous sediments were deposited in Cos. Kerry and Waterford and in the Longford–Down region.

During the Devonian Period, hot desert conditions prevailed, with dune systems and ephemeral river channels. These produced the old red sandstone characteristic of much of Munster. Later, in the Carboniferous Period (360–280 million years ago), a shallow, warm tropical sea invaded the land from the south, and limestones were deposited in the midlands. Overlying these are thin coal measures. In north-east Ireland younger rocks, including chalk, are preserved beneath the basalt flows formed during the Tertiary Period (65–2 million years ago), when the North Atlantic Ocean opened.

Much of Ireland's present topography was shaped during several glacial advances over the last 300,000 years, when ice covered a large area of the country. This ice eroded mountainsides and deepened valleys; the melting of the ice left eskers, moraines, drumlins, and a covering of glacial *till*. Sedimentary basins off the coast contain exploitable reserves of gas.

Many of Ireland's industries rely on geological raw materials; among the most valuable are building materials, including dimension stone, from Cos. Wicklow and Kilkenny, limestone for cement, gypsum from Kingscourt, Co. Cavan, and lead and zinc from Navan, Co. Meath. **Patrick N. Wyse Jackson**

geophysical survey, a non-invasive, non-destructive means of investigating features that may be hidden beneath ground, wetland, or water. Surveys can be used to identify potential excavation sites in urban and rural areas. Techniques such as magnetic gradiometry and electrical resistance, in conjunction with high-resolution topographic surveys, can map walls, ditches and ferrous metal buried up to 1.5 m (5 ft) beneath the ground. Magnetic susceptibility can map areas of occupation debris, such as burnt ground, ash and MIDDEN spreads resulting from anthropogenic activity. Techniques such as electrical tomography and ground-penetrating radar can produce sections across mounds, walls, and ditches, showing their internal structure. Water-borne techniques, used in marine and freshwater environments, can identify features lying on or below sea-bed, lake or river sediments. High-resolution surveys can be used to map large areas to indicate potential archaeological importance, which is then investigated by divers. Acoustic techniques such as multi-beam bathymetry and side-scan sonar can find features such as wreck sites, fish traps, landing points, and submerged CRANNÓGS. An acoustic sub-bottom profiler can be used to investigate features buried in sediments. A total-field magnetometer survey can find ferrous metals such as hulls, cannons, and anchors from modern and ancient wreck sites.

Possibly the earliest geophysical survey carried out in Ireland was in 1952, when a resistance survey was conducted on the Hill of TARA. The first published survey dates from 1968, when a magnetic gradiometer survey was carried out at Burrishoole Castle, Co. Mayo. During the 1980s magnetic gradiometer surveys were conducted on ring-forts at Cunningburn, Co. Down, and Ballykelly, Co. Antrim, and along the Cork–Dublin gas pipeline. Resistance surveys identified a SOUTERRAIN at Lisnagun, Co. Cork, and mapped structures in the deserted medieval town of Clonmines, Co. Wexford. The large-scale surveys at Tara and RATHCROGHAN carried out in the 1990s have revealed much about the role and function of these sites.

The first water-borne survey in Ireland, integrating geophysical and diver surveys, was carried out in 1998 in BANTRY BAY, Co. Cork; it successfully mapped the French frigate *La Surveillante*, which had been scuttled off Whiddy Island in 1797. On the River SHANNON at CLONMACNOISE, multi-sensor surveys have mapped archaeological and river-bed features associated with a newly discovered early ninth-century wooden bridge. [see AERIAL PHOTOGRAPHY; DENDROCHRONOLOGY.] **Kevin Barton**

geophysics, the study of the physical and internal characteristics, properties and processes of the Earth. It includes seismology (the study of earthquakes and the shock waves they produce), the Earth's gravitational and magnetic fields, and temperature gradients in the Earth.

Robert Mallet (1810–81) produced the first artificial seismic waves through making controlled explosions on Killiney beach, Co. Dublin, in 1849. Richard Dixon Oldham, working in India, determined the presence and nature of the Earth's core through his study of seismic waves produced by earthquakes. Different rocks in the Earth's crust display different properties with regard to their density, elasticity, and magnetic susceptibility. Various geophysical techniques developed to study such properties have been extensively used to determine sub-surface geological features or to find commercially important resources, for example during the discovery of the lead-zinc deposits at Navan, Co. Meath, and Lisheen, Co. Tipperary, and in determining the structure of offshore sedimentary basins, in which considerable GAS reserves were found.

Several institutions and universities carry out research in geophysics. The School of Theoretical Physics at the DUBLIN INSTITUTE OF ADVANCED STUDIES was established by the Government in 1940; its geophysical section has been predominantly engaged in mapping the country. The institute has produced a series of magnetic and gravity anomaly maps and continues collaborative research into the structure of Ireland's CONTINENTAL SHELF. The Applied Geophysics Unit at the National University of Ireland, Galway, is engaged in offshore research and has developed geophysical techniques used in archaeological, hydrological, and environmental surveys. Similar research groups operate from University College, Dublin, and the University of Ulster. The Geophysical Association of Ireland was established in 1999. **Patrick N. Wyse Jackson**

George IV's footprints. On 12 August 1821, George IV, somewhat the worse for drink, disembarked from the steam packet *Lightning* at the West Pier of HOWTH HARBOUR, to the north of DUBLIN BAY, the first British monarch to visit Ireland since the arrival of the warring JAMES II and WILLIAM III in 1689 and 1690, and the first one to do so peacefully. To the cheers of a small group of bemused onlookers, the king planted his neat if unsteady feet on Irish soil. A local artist, Robert Campbell, traced the outline of his feet onto the granite boulder on which he was standing and subsequently carved their imprint into the rock, where they can still be seen at the end of the pier. Meanwhile the LORD LIEUTENANT, Dublin Corporation and a crowd estimated at 20,000 were in vain awaiting the king at Dunleary on the southern shore of the bay. When George IV departed on 3 September he bestowed on the latter village the honour of its being called Kingstown, which it remained until the establishment of the IRISH FREE STATE in 1922, when it reverted to its former name but with revised spelling as Dún Laoghaire. **Brian Lalor**

Georgian period (1714–1830), so called from the reigns of the four successive Hanoverian English kings: George I (1714–27), George II (1727–60), George III (1760–1820), and George IV (1820–30). This most formative period of civic and social development began during the hundred years of peace and prosperity between the BATTLE OF THE BOYNE (1690) and the 1798 REBELLION, and its influence lasted well into the middle of the nineteenth century. During the Georgian era, ARCHITECTURE and town planning, the fine arts, the applied and decorative arts, and manufacture reached levels of excellence and coherence only sporadically achieved in the following centuries. The period also saw the establishment of the majority of those philanthropic societies that promoted scholarly activity, medicine, agricultural improvements, scientific inquiry, and the appreciation of objects of antiquarian significance. The Dublin Society for Improving Husbandry, Manufactures and Other Useful Arts (1731) (later the ROYAL DUBLIN SOCIETY), the ROTUNDA HOSPITAL (1751), the WIDE STREETS COMMISSIONERS (1757), the ROYAL IRISH ACADEMY (1785), the Corporation for Preserving and Improving the Port of Dublin (1786), and the ROYAL HIBERNIAN ACADEMY OF ARTS (1823) are among the most influential of those founded in Dublin, while related or similarly philanthropic bodies were established in Cork, Limerick and Belfast. Palladianism dominated architectural taste for much of the century, with neo-classicism and Gothic Revival becoming popular in the 1790s. Dublin, and to a lesser degree other cities, acquired their grid plans and major public buildings during this period, and the production of fine PLASTERWORK, FURNITURE, glass, silverware, fabrics, BOOKBINDING, and printing all contributed to creating the characteristic of an Irish Georgian style. MUSIC and THEATRE flourished during the Georgian period, producing playwrights and musicians of international reputation. Political progress was also achieved in the emergence of a measure of LEGISLATIVE INDEPENDENCE from London with 'GRATTAN'S PARLIAMENT' in 1782, and although this freedom lasted a mere eighteen years, to the ACT OF UNION in 1800, it made visible the concept of a national Dublin-based government. The Catholic Relief Bill followed at the end of the era in 1829, by which act Catholics were freed from the restrictions that had previously prevented them from sitting in Parliament, holding senior government office, or being a judge or privy councillor. The term 'Georgian' has become synonymous with fine craftsmanship, with the principles of the Enlightenment, and with the life on great LANDED ESTATES; yet the fact that the eighteenth century ended in rebellion, and the following century began with a further one, emphasises the absence of civil liberties and the political unrest that paralleled an era of artistic and intellectual achievement. [see ANGLO-IRISH SOCIETY; BIG HOUSE; DUELLING; FURNITURE; GANDON, JAMES; GARDINER, LUKE; IRISH GEORGIAN SOCIETY; LANDLORDS AND LANDLORD VILLAGES; PEARCE, EDWARD LOVETT; PLASTERWORK.] **Brian Lalor**

Geragh, Sandycove, Co. Dublin, a private house built for himself in 1937 by the the architect MICHAEL SCOTT. It displays many of the maritime stylistic features based on the great passenger liners of the day that are characteristic of Modern Movement houses of the early twentieth century: porthole windows, deck-like terraces, and sheer white-painted façades. Sited next to the MARTELLO TOWER (1804) made famous by JAMES JOYCE as the location of the opening scene of ULYSSES, the curved façade of the house also reflects the form of the tower. **Brian Lalor**

Geraldine League, a somewhat misleading term for a predominantly native Irish alliance formed in the late 1530s and led by MANUS O'DONNELL, husband of ELEANOR FITZGERALD, aunt and guardian of GERALD FITZGERALD, the fugitive Geraldine heir. Though Fitzgerald's restoration and the recall of Lord Deputy Grey were the league's nominal aims, it strongly opposed the REFORMATION. The leaders strove to be party to Cardinal Reginald Pole's pan-European Catholic alliance against HENRY VIII, solicited support from the Papacy, François I of France, and Charles V, Holy Roman Emperor, and offered the sovereignty of Ireland to James V of Scotland. The league represented an unprecedented departure from traditional dynastic Irish politics in aligning O'Neill, O'Connor Sligo, O'Donnell, O'Brien of Thomond, the thirteenth Earl of Desmond, O'Connor Faly, and lesser Irish lords, almost becoming a national movement. In August 1539 its forces were defeated by

Georgian period. The Dublin Volunteers on College Green, 4 November 1779 *(1779–80) by Francis Wheatley recording the regiments gathering at Grinling Gibbons' statue of William III in celebrations of the king's birthday. The ceremony takes place against a background of two key examples of early Georgian architecture, the west front of Trinity College (right) and the Parliament House (centre). The houses on the left show the Dutch gables which predate horizontal Georgian rooflines. [National Gallery of Ireland]*

Grey at Bellahoe. After Gerald Fitzgerald's flight to France and Desmond's withdrawal early in 1540, the league became purely Irish in composition. By 1541 it was defunct. **Mary Ann Lyons**

Gerald of Wales: see GIRALDUS CAMBRENSIS.

'German Plot'. In May 1918 widespread opposition, and the threat of a mass rebellion, forced the British government to abandon its plans for imposing CONSCRIPTION on Ireland. SINN FÉIN was singled out for retribution, and many of its leading figures were arrested on the pretext that they had conspired with Germany. Few people were convinced, and Sinn Féin's 'martyrdom' won the party much sympathy and support. Most of the prisoners remained in jail until March 1919. [see FIRST WORLD WAR.] **Michael Laffan**

gerrymandering. Proportional representation, both for LOCAL GOVERNMENT and Northern Ireland Parliament elections, had been provided for in the Government of Ireland Act (1920). The Unionist government abolished PR for local government elections in 1922, and this necessitated the re-drawing of council and ward boundaries. The following year Judge John Leech, Deputy Recorder of Belfast, headed a commission established to make the new arrangements. Except in Irvinestown and Ballycastle, nationalists and republicans refused to meet this body; the result was that local Unionist parties, with the enthusiastic co-operation of members of the Northern Ireland government, were able to dictate the positioning of boundaries with meticulous care to their own satisfaction. The British government made no attempt to intervene in what was a blatant exercise in gerrymandering. The results spoke for themselves: in 1920 opposition parties won control of twenty-four local councils out of twenty-seven; by 1927 this was reduced to twelve. Further boundary refinements were made, to Unionist advantage, in 1935, 1936, 1946, and 1967. The worst examples were west of the River BANN, notably in Derry, where in 1966 14,429 Catholic ratepayers and 8,781 Protestant ratepayers returned eight Nationalist and twelve Unionist councillors. [see CIVIL RIGHTS MOVEMENTS.] **Jonathan Bardon**

Giall, An (1958), a play by BRENDAN BEHAN. Commissioned by GAEL-LINN for the Damer Theatre, Dublin, and first produced in June 1958, it concerns a young British soldier held as a hostage in a Dublin boarding-house for an IRA prisoner who is to be hanged in Belfast. A moving tragedy in the original Irish, it became a music-hall variety show in the process of being rendered into English as *The Hostage* for Joan Littlewood's Theatre Workshop in London. **Máirín Nic Eoin**

Giant's Causeway, a volcanic formation near Portrush, Co. Antrim, associated with the opening of the Atlantic Ocean in the Tertiary Period, about 60 million years ago; it is Ireland's most distinctive geological formation. As the Earth's crust was faulted and fractured, waves of volcanic outpourings inundated the existing chalk landscape with basaltic lava. The lower basalt columns of the causeway represent the cooling of lava lakes at the Earth's surface during the earliest stages of this extrusive volcanism. Like desiccation cracks on exposed lake-beds, the honeycomb structure of the columns reflects the cooling and contraction of the lava from the surface of the LAKES downwards. During a gap in volcanism the lower basalts were exposed to the elements, leading to weathering and the development of SOIL. The resulting red soils, rich in iron and aluminium hydroxides, and the abundant fossilised plants in contemporaneous lignite deposits, imply that tropical conditions prevailed at the time. In the centre of columns not fully penetrated by weathering, pristine black basalt is visible, forming the distinctive 'Giant's Eyes'.

Following this quiescence, the extrusion of lava resumed, but the tropical soil, which was cooked and buried by the new lava, is still visible as the red *interbasaltic horizon*. This igneous phase produced the upper basalt and the most spectacularly architectural columns, with downward gradations in form and texture reflecting increasingly slow cooling of the parent lava with depth. [see DRURY, SUSANNA; GEOLOGICAL LANDSCAPE; GEOLOGY.] **Colman Gallagher**

Giant's Causeway Tramway. Linking Portrush with Bushmills and the Giant's Causeway, Co. Antrim, this was the first in the world to be operated by hydro-electric power, which it drew from the River Bush. The service between Portrush and Bushmills opened on 29 January 1883, using a steam-operated generator, with electric traction introduced the following September. The Causeway extension opened in 1887. The whole system closed in 1949, at which time it was the longest-running electric tramway in existence. A partial reopening is in progress. **Bernard Share**

Gibbings, Robert (1889–1958), writer, wood-engraver, and illustrator. Born in Cork, son of a rector; he studied MEDICINE for two years at UCC before going to London in 1911 to study at the Slade School of Fine Art and etching at the Central School. Commissioned in the British army in 1914, he fought at Gallipoli; invalided out in 1918, he resumed his work as an engraver and was a founder-member of the Society of Wood-Engravers (London). He bought Eric Gill's Golden Cockerel Press and was its director from 1924 to 1933; his work there did much to raise the standard of book production and influenced the direction of the book arts in the 1920s and 30s. He wrote and illustrated a series of travel books, the best known of these being the river books *Sweet Thames Run Softly* (1940), *Lovely Is the Lee* (1945), and *Coming down the Seine* (1953). These later productions were perfect vehicles for his talents as author, illustrator, and book designer. His style is precise, crisp, and distinctive and shows acute observation and sensitivity to the relationship of art on the page. Elected to the ROYAL HIBERNIAN ACADEMY in 1952, he published his last work, *Till I End My Song*, in 1957. [see PRINTS.] **Patricia Donlon**

Gibbon, William (Monk) (1896–1987), poet and man of letters. Born in Dublin; educated at the University of Oxford. He served in the British army during the FIRST WORLD WAR. His verse is based on traditional forms and employs conventional diction in a way that has been compared to that of the English Georgians. Among his various prose works, which included travel writing and criticism, his autobiographical *Mount Ida* (1948) and his memoir of W. B. YEATS, *The Masterpiece and the Man: Yeats as I Knew Him* (1959), retain their interest. **Terence Brown**

Gibbons, Luke (1951–). Born in Dublin and raised in Roscommon; educated at UCG and at TCD. Professor of film, television and theatre at the Keough Centre for Irish Studies, Notre Dame University and DCU, he is joint-author (with KEVIN ROCKETT and John Hill) of *Cinema and Ireland* (1987). His collected essays, *Transformations in Irish Culture* (1996), published as a FIELD DAY monograph, indicate his significant contribution to cultural studies in Ireland. **Emilie Pine**

Gibney, Arthur (1931–), architect. Born in Dublin; studied at DIT and National College of Art. He worked for MICHAEL SCOTT. He established Stephenson Gibney Associates (with SAM STEPHENSON), Dublin, in 1960, which designed the ESB head office, Fitzwilliam Street, Dublin, and later formed Arthur Gibney and Partners, Dublin, 1975. His work includes the IRISH MANAGEMENT INSTITUTE, Sandyford, Co. Dublin (1974–6), awarded the RIAI Gold Medal. He carried out the restoration of the early eighteenth-century DR STEEVENS' HOSPITAL, Dublin, for the Eastern Health Board (1991), which won the Europa Nostra award; Dublin City University master plan (1990), with subsequent buildings (with Deirdre O'Connor); the Irish pavilion at the World Exposition, Seville (1992) (with James O'Connor); and Bookend Building, apartments at Essex Quay, Dublin. A distinguished watercolourist, he is a past president of the ROYAL INSTITUTE OF THE ARCHITECTS OF IRELAND and the ROYAL HIBERNIAN ACADEMY. **Raymund Ryan**

Gibson, John (1951–), pianist and composer. Born in Dublin; studied at the Municipal College of Music, RIAM (composition with A. J. POTTER) and Staatliche Hochschule für Musik, Munich, and with Prof. Valentyna Schubinskaya in Moscow. Active as a concerto soloist, recitalist, accompanist, and chamber musician, he has also lectured in piano at CORK SCHOOL OF MUSIC since 1982. He is a founder-member of the Association of Irish Composers and was awarded the Nijinsky Medal by the Polish Ministry of Arts and Culture in 1997 for his piano piece *Nijinsky*. He has written orchestral, chamber, keyboard, choral, and vocal works, including *Siollabadh* for mixed choir (1976), *Sounds* for strings (1981), *Four Emily Dickinson Songs* for voice and piano (1991–2), and *Toccata* for piano (1995). **Paul Collins**

Gibson, Cameron Michael (Mike) (1942–), rugby footballer. With sixty-nine appearances between 1964 and 1979, he is Ireland's most-capped player. He won forty caps at centre, twenty-five at out-half, and four on the wing. He won his first cap against England at Twickenham when he succeeded Mick English at out-half in 1964 as Ireland won by 18–5, and he played his final match on Ireland's 1979 tour to Australia in the second Test, at Sydney, when Ireland won by 9–3. During his Ireland career he scored nine tries and kicked sixteen penalty goals, six dropped goals, and six conversions, and he also captained the team on two occasions. He toured with the British Lions three times: to New Zealand in 1966, South Africa in 1968, and New Zealand again in 1971, when the British Lions won their first Test series. He played in twelve Tests, four of them at out-half, and is also the British Lions' most-capped centre, with eight midfield appearances. **Karl Johnston**

Gibson, Violet (born 1876), would-be assassin of Benito Mussolini. Born in Dalkey, Co. Dublin, daughter of Edward Gibson, first Baron Ashbourne, Irish Lord Chancellor in two Conservative governments. On 7 April 1926 at the Campodoglio in Rome she shot Mussolini at point-blank range as he passed through a cheering crowd; the bullet perforated his nostrils, causing only minor injury. The crowd tried to lynch her, but Mussolini intervened to ensure her arrest. Interrogation soon established that she was of unsound mind and suffering from religious mania. She was carrying a vial of poison around her neck at the time of her arrest. It also emerged that she had been arrested in London in 1923 while roaming the streets wielding a knife; she had also attempted suicide in Rome in February 1925. Though she had converted to Catholicism in 1900, she apparently spoke of her desire to kill the Pope. **Ciarán Deane**

Giesecke, Sir (Karl Ludwig) Charles Lewis, born Johann Georg Metzler (1761–1833), mineralogist. Born in Augsburg,

Bavaria, Germany; educated in Gottingen, Germany, 1781–3. He changed his name in 1781. As a student he became interested in mineralogy, but he also had theatrical interests. He reputedly co-operated with Emmanuel Johann Schikaneder (1751–1812) in writing the libretto for Mozart's *Die Zauberflöte* (*The Magic Flute*). From 1806 until 1813 he collected minerals in Greenland, and in 1814 he was appointed professor of mineralogy at the DUBLIN SOCIETY, despite his then inability to lecture in English. He conducted mineralogical surveys in seven Irish counties, 1825–29. **Jean Archer**

Gifford, Grace (1888–1955), cartoonist (as Grace Plunkett). Born in Dublin; studied under William Orpen at the Metropolitan School of Art and at the Slade School of Fine Art, London. She is principally remembered for her marriage to the 1916 leader Joseph Mary Plunkett on the day before his execution and for her work as a cartoonist of politicians and figures of the LITERARY REVIVAL in a witty, stylised manner influenced by the black-and-white work of Aubrey Beardsley. She was an active republican and opposed the ANGLO-IRISH TREATY, subsequently being imprisoned in KILMAINHAM GAOL. She published three books of cartoons: *To Hold as 'Twere* (1919), *Twelve Nights at the Abbey Theatre* (1929), and *Doctors Recommend It!* (1930) (see pp. 879, 918). **Brian Lalor**

Giles, John (1940–), soccer player. Born in Dublin, a member of a successful footballing family; he joined Manchester United as a boy. Having helped Manchester United to victory over Leicester City in the 1963 FA Cup final, he fell out with Sir Matt Busby and moved to Leeds United; in a different role as a midfielder, he was largely responsible for establishing the club at the pinnacle of English football. Few players have made a more telling impact on their international debut, for it was his goal that gave the Republic of Ireland a 3–2 win over Sweden in 1959, just a year after the Swedes had reached the World Cup final against Brazil. He made fifty-nine appearances in an international career that lasted twenty years and he is the man frequently credited with laying the foundation for the fruitful years of the Republic of Ireland team during his seven years in charge of the team, 1973–80. **Peter Byrne**

Gill, M. H. (1794–1879), printer and publisher. Born in Dublin, son of a woollen-draper; apprenticed at the DUBLIN UNIVERSITY PRESS in 1813, becoming its sole lessee in 1842, a position he held until 1875. Under his aegis the press produced and published work of high technical and literary quality, including the Annals of the FOUR MASTERS. In 1855 he acquired the extensive business interests of James McGlashan, a Scottish immigrant bookseller and publisher, together with his premises at 50 Upper Sackville Street (O'Connell Street), Dublin, and founded the publishing firm of McGlashan and Gill, which became M. H. Gill and Son in 1875. The firm specialised in religious, educational, and popular nationalist titles; following association with Macmillan of London in 1968, under which it became Gill and Macmillan, it greatly broadened its scope, while retaining the family connection with the founder. Since 1995 it has been associated internationally with the Verlagsgruppe Georg von Holtzbrinck, following the acquisition of Macmillan by Holtzbrinck. **Bernard Share**

Gilla na Náem úa Duinn (died 1160), poet and man of learning. Of Leinster origin, he worked in the monastery of Inisclearaun on Lough Ree, Co. Longford. The author of regnal poems probably composed in the 1150s on the Christian kings of Connacht and Leinster, he was also a reviser of the topographical tracts known as DINNSEANCHAS Éireann ('The place-lore of Ireland'). **Edel Bhreathnach**

Gillen, Gerard (1942–), musician. Born in Dublin; studied at UCD, Oxford, and the Royal Conservatoire of Music, Antwerp (where he gained the Prix d'Excellence). Titular organist of the Pro-Cathedral, Dublin, since 1976 and professor of music at the National University of Ireland, Maynooth, since 1985, he was founder-chairman of the DUBLIN INTERNATIONAL ORGAN AND CHORAL FESTIVAL. An organ recitalist of international repute, he has sat on organ-playing competition juries in Oxford, Ann Arbor, London, and Dublin. He was awarded a knighthood of St Gregory by the Vatican in 1984 and was nominated classical-section winner in Ireland's National Entertainment Awards in 1996. **Paul Collins**

Gillespie, Robert Rollo (1766–1814), soldier of fortune. Born in Comber, Co. Down; he was bought a commission in the 45th Regiment of Foot. By 1783 he was a cornet in the 3rd Horse, garrisoned at Clogher, Co. Tyrone. He shot and killed 'Mad' Will Barrington in a duel and was forced to flee to the West Indies. There he was involved in plots to destabilise the French colonies. He was captured by the French but saved himself with a Masonic handshake. He returned to Ireland but was soon forced to flee again following a brawl in a Cork theatre. He returned to the West Indies, where he killed six settlers who had accused him of cheating them. He fought in India and Java, and died in action in Nepal. **Ciarán Deane**

Gilroy McMahon, architects. Desmond McMahon (1940–) was born in Beragh, Co. Tyrone; educated at DIT and later taught there. With Frank Gilroy (1945–1975) he established Gilroy McMahon in Dublin, 1971. They won the RIAI Triennial Gold Medal, 1986–8, for the extension to DIT College of Technology, Bolton Street, Dublin, inspired by Nordic modernism. They designed south Co. Dublin civic offices, Tallaght (1992–4). Croke Park (GAA stadium), Dublin (1995), employs dramatic concrete

Giant's Causeway. *The 'Small Causeway' part of the Giant's Causeway near Portrush, Co. Antrim, formed from a mass of basalt columns caused by volcanic activity in the region more than 6 million years ago. [Topham Picturepoint]*

engineering to create stands with a capacity of 80,000. They demonstrate a robust engagement with existing buildings and context in the conversion of the early eighteenth-century Collins Barracks, Dublin, for the Museum of Decorative Arts and History of the National Museum of Ireland (1993–); and the Viking Interpretative Centre and Isolde's Tower (apartments), West Essex Street, Dublin. An exhibition of their work was held at the Architecture Centre, Dublin, 1997. **Raymund Ryan**

Gilsenan, Alan (1964–), film-maker. His controversial documentary *The Road to God Knows Where* (1988) angrily satirised the Republic's response to the social and economic crises of the 1980s and brought him to national prominence. He has made a wide variety of films, including one of SAMUEL BECKETT's play *Eh Joe!* (1986); *Stories from the Silence* (1990), about AIDS; *Prophet Songs* (1991), about laicised priests; *God Bless America* (1996), which featured American literary figures; *Home Movie Nights* (1996–8), in which he drew on amateur film from well-known Irish families; *The Green Fields of France* (1999), about Irishmen in the British army in the FIRST WORLD WAR; and two episodes of the history of the Irish diaspora, *The Irish Empire* (1999). Other films include the fictional avant-garde *All Souls Day* (1997). In 2001 he was appointed to BORD SCANNÁN NA HÉIREANN. **Kevin Rockett**

Ginkel, Godard van Reede, Baron, first Earl of Athlone (1630–1703), leader of WILLIAM III's army in Ireland, 1690–1. He arrived in England with William's expeditionary force in 1688 and in 1690 accompanied him to Ireland, where he distinguished himself at the BATTLE OF THE BOYNE. As a result, when William returned to England in August 1690 Ginkel was appointed general-in-chief of the forces in Ireland. His first important victory was at Athlone on 30 June 1691, followed by that of the BATTLE OF AUGHRIM on 12 July 1691. Ginkel also commanded the Williamite army during the SIEGE OF LIMERICK, which ended the JACOBITE wars on 3 October 1691 with the TREATY OF LIMERICK. Soon afterwards he returned to England, where he was created Baron of Aughrim and Earl of Athlone. He died of a short illness on 11 February 1703 while serving with William's forces on the Continent. **Rosemary Richey**

Giordani, Tommaso (c.1730–1806), composer. Born in Naples, he was in Dublin 1764–7, working at the SMOCK ALLEY THEATRE where three of his operas were premiered in 1765. *L'eroe cinese* (1766)) was the first *opera seria* to be staged in Ireland. He returned to Dublin in 1783 for concerts at the ROTUNDA, becoming music director at CROW STREET in 1787. With FRANCESCO GEMINIANI he was the most notable of Italian musicians working in Ireland in the eighteenth century. **Richard Pine**

Giraldus Cambrensis (Gerald de Barry) (c. 1146–c. 1223), ecclesiastic, scholar, and author. Born at Manorbier, near Pembroke, of mixed Norman and Welsh descent; educated at the University of Paris. He served both church and state in Wales and England, without achieving his ambition to be bishop of St David's. Between 1183 and 1186 he visited several parts of Ireland, mainly in Leinster and east Munster, and collected material for two of his seventeen books. *Topographia Hiberniae* (1187) deals with the physical and biological geography of Ireland, especially its FAUNA, and also with the country's many natural wonders, its experience of foreign invasion from earliest times to the ANGLO-NORMANS, and the manners and customs of the people. EXPUGNATIO HIBERNICA (c. 1188) (see p. 368) is a detailed history of the first twenty years of the Norman conquest. Some early copies of these books are illustrated with pictures and maps, including a unique map of Europe, but it is not certain that the author was responsible for these.

Giraldus's merits are his keen intelligence and powers of observation, his command of both oral and written sources, and his literary skill. His weaknesses are credulity (of which he was unashamed) and a prejudice against the native Irish. Most foreign writers on Ireland until the late sixteenth century were strongly influenced by his books. **J. H. Andrews**

glaciation. The Swiss geologist Louis Agassiz, who visited Ireland in 1841, established that the sand, gravel, and boulder 'drift' covering the surface was similar to Alpine glacial sediments. In the Irish mountains he noted many amphitheatre-like corries from which extended deep U-shaped valleys; in form these were identical to the cirques and glacial valleys of the Alps. In Co. Wicklow an excellent example of such a landform assemblage can be seen extending down GLENCREE from Upper and Lower Lough Bray. This evidence convinced Agassiz that Ireland had been glaciated in the geologically recent past. The glacial sediments were later assigned to the Quaternary Period, because they overlay rocks of at least Tertiary age.

Ireland's Quaternary geomorphology indicates that ice caps covered most of the uplands. In the lowlands an ice dome radiated across the midlands and the Atlantic CONTINENTAL SHELF from south Co. Galway; another radiated from a snowfield extending from present-day Co. Longford to central Ulster. These two ice domes met along a line running from west to east across south-east Galway and Offaly. The eastern seaboard and the IRISH SEA basin lay beneath an enormous ice sheet originating in south-eastern Scotland that merged with the eastern margin of ice spreading southwards from central Ulster. A narrow strip of the south coast was affected by glaciers from east Cork and north Waterford. The uplands of Cos. Cork, Kerry, Galway, Mayo, Donegal, Down, and Wicklow lay beneath ice caps that radiated outwards and coalesced with lowland ice pushing up into the mountains. Isolated parts of south Kilkenny and Wexford had no glacial cover but experienced permafrost conditions, with mean annual temperatures below –6°C (21°F).

Detailed reconstructions of glacial configuration and processes have emerged from the analysis of particular Quaternary landforms. The sedimentology of Ireland's eskers shows that they are the remnants of debris-choked tunnels that formerly ran through the ice domes that merged across the midlands. As the ice domes separated, as at Ballyduff, near Tullamore, Co. Offaly, a meltwater lake was impounded in the west–east ice-free corridor between the diverging ice domes. Sediment-rich meltwaters from the ice to the south entered the lake and covered the coarse tunnel deposits with sand and silt. Near Trim, Co. Meath, the eskers consist of numerous short *beads*, each representing an annual discharge of sediment-laden meltwater into ice-marginal lakes. Running at right angles to the Trim eskers, the Galtrim moraine trends north-east to south-west and represents the south-eastern margin of the northern ice dome.

Drumlins—low, streamlined hills—are Ireland's most distinctive glacial landform, but their morphological simplicity belies a complicated origin. The most spectacular drumlin 'swarm' lies at the eastern end of Clew Bay, Co. Mayo. Here some drumlins have a bedrock core that was faulted and shunted by overriding ice, for example at Pigeon Point. Others consist of layers of sediment plastered into position beneath the moving ice, for example at Thornhill Quay. Near Kingscourt, Co. Cavan, a recently excavated drumlin contains

Gilroy McMahon. *Exterior of Croke Park GAA stadium, Dublin, the fourth-largest sports stadium in Europe. A major reconstruction of the stadium was undertaken by Gilroy McMahon, 1997–2002, involving the rebuilding of the Cusack Stand, Canal End and Hogan Stand into one massive structure with a capacity of 80,000 spectators. [Inpho Photography]*

the remains of trees that grew before the last glaciation, vividly representing the way glaciers erode and reprocess older landscapes. At Meath Hill, Co. Meath, drumlins consist of glacially overridden and streamlined meltwater deposits. Drumlins therefore represent a range of sub-glacial transport processes intermediate between erosion and deposition.

Meltwater channels are common throughout Ireland, reflecting powerful discharges of water both beneath and beyond the ice itself. The GLEN OF THE DOWNS, Co. Wicklow, is a classic example of a sub-glacial meltwater channel. The Liffey Valley between Lucan, Co. Dublin, and the PHOENIX PARK operated originally as a sub-glacial conduit but later functioned as an exposed meltwater river. Both the Shannon and the Barrow valleys were major conduits through which meltwaters from the midland ice domes flowed to the sea.

In the Quaternary Period, sea level has responded to the fluctuations of the ice sheets, and this can be detected in relict (raised) beaches. During glaciation, Ireland's continental shelf was exposed, and both glaciers and meltwaters passed across it. By contrast, the raised beaches found around the coast indicate interglacial periods, with sea levels higher than today's. Along the north and east coast, for example at MALIN HEAD, Co. Donegal, and Howth, Co. Dublin, *tills* (glacial sediments) from the last glaciation underlie the raised beaches, which represent the global rise in sea level during the last deglaciation 15,000 to 7,500 years ago. Conversely, around the southern coastline, for example near Fethard, Co. Wexford, and Fenit, Co. Kerry, the raised beaches underlie either permafrost sediments or till, showing that these beaches were deposited before the last glaciation. Luminescence-dating of the raised beach at Fethard confirms this, suggesting that it was last active 130,000 years ago, at the beginning of the last interglacial period. In Ballybunnion, Co. Kerry, the raised beach overlies the remains of an earlier till, representing glacial conditions some time before the last interglacial period.

Many people have observed that the glacial geomorphology of lowland Munster is less varied and more subdued than that of the midlands. Limestone weathering in the Munster tills is also more advanced than in midland tills. These observations may mean that the 'Munsterian' geomorphology reflects earlier glacial conditions, before the 'Midlandian' glacial advances that began 30,000 years ago; whether this represents two separate glaciations or two cold stages within the last glaciation is a matter of debate. Complementing these observations, the discovery in Gort, Co. Galway, of tree pollen in a peaty deposit beneath till proved that Ireland experienced a warm interglacial period before the last glaciation. Uranium-thorium disequilibrium dating of the interglacial sediments at Gort showed that they are up to 400,000 years old. This is much older than the overlying till and shows that the sedimentary record is incomplete, probably because of an intervening period of glacial erosion. Though evidence exists for at least two Quaternary glaciations in Ireland, therefore, with associated changes in sea level, much more evidence has been lost because of glacial erosion. Future research will deal with the offshore area, where many of the sediments eroded from the Irish landmass by the glaciers may be found (see p. 443). [see CLIMATE; COASTAL EROSION; GEOLOGICAL LANDSCAPE; GEOLOGY; WATER.] **Colman Gallagher**

Glackin, Paddy (1954–), FIDDLE-player. One of Ireland's leading fiddle stylists, he was influenced by family associations with Co. Donegal and the musicianship of the DOHERTY brothers. An all-Ireland award-winner in the 1960s, he played with the early BOTHY BAND in 1975, produced and presented traditional music radio and television programmes for RTÉ, and was the ARTS COUNCIL's first TRADITIONAL MUSIC officer, 1985–90. His six albums include *Rabharta Ceoil* (with DÓNAL LUNNY) and work with the pipers PADDY KEENAN and Robbie Hannan. [see DONEGAL FIDDLE TRADITION.] **Fintan Vallely**

Gladstone, William Ewart (1809–1898), British politician. Born in Liverpool into a prosperous merchant family; educated at the University of Oxford. He had assembled a formidable career before becoming 'as fast bound to Ireland as ULYSSES was to his mast.' Ireland was not his sole political concern, but it became his main preoccupation in the later 1860s, and as Prime Minister he personally took charge of the major Irish legislation—DISESTABLISHMENT of the CHURCH OF IRELAND and the Land Acts of 1870 and 1881—together with the abortive University Bill of 1873 and HOME RULE measures in 1886 and 1893, the first of which precipitated a split in the Liberal policy, leading to the formation of the Liberal Unionists under Joseph Chamberlain. From 1886 his purpose for remaining in political life was to make a further effort at securing home rule for Ireland. In March 1894 he retired from public life, and the Liberal Party thereafter was less enthusiastic about the home rule crusade. **Alan O'Day**

Glasgow, the Irish in. Many of the Irish people who emigrated to SCOTLAND in the nineteenth century settled in Glasgow, then one of the great industrial cities of the world. In 1841 there were approximately 44,000 people of Irish birth in Glasgow, or 16.2 per cent of its population; ten years later the number had risen to approximately 59,000 (18 per cent). In 1901 Irish immigrants numbered about 68,000 (8.9 per cent).

Between 1800 and 1850 Irish men in the city were employed chiefly as handloom weavers or as labourers, while Irish women worked mainly in the cotton factories. From the 1840s onwards many Irish immigrants in Glasgow were employed in heavy industry. While the majority of these workers were in unskilled or semi-skilled occupations, a significant minority—mostly Protestants—were tradesmen. Throughout the nineteenth century the Irish constituted the majority of the unskilled labour force in the city.

Irish IMMIGRATION had a significant impact on the Catholic Church in Glasgow. In the early 1790s there were 500–600 Catholics in the city, of whom most were recent migrants from the Highlands; forty years later there were approximately 44,000 Catholics, the bulk of whom were Irish. At first the church struggled to cope with the influx. However, by 1878 there were twenty chapels or missions and more than fifty priests in the city and its suburbs, at a time when the Catholic population numbered about 100,000. Furthermore, in the second half of the nineteenth century the Catholic Irish community in Glasgow supported its own schools, welfare, social and cultural organisations, sports clubs (such as Celtic Football Club), and newspapers (see p. 1012). The Catholic Irish had a strong sense of national identity and gave considerable support to the campaigns for Repeal and HOME RULE.

The Catholic Irish community, however, was not isolated or divorced from the rest of Glasgow society. Irish Catholics participated, often in significant numbers, in strikes, TRADE UNIONS, temperance activities, and political and labour campaigns alongside Scottish workers, who both welcomed and sought their involvement. Moreover, though the Catholic Irish in Glasgow encountered opposition from sections of the middle class and from Protestant Irish immigrants, there was little open popular hostility towards them during the nineteenth century. However, in the inter-war years there was significant working-class opposition in Glasgow to the Catholic Irish community, and until recent times SECTARIANISM and anti-Catholic discrimination in employment were serious problems in the city. [see ENGLAND, IRISH IN; WALES, IRISH IN.] **Martin Mitchell**

Gleeson, Brendan (1955–), film actor. Formerly a schoolteacher, he emerged as the most versatile Irish film actor of the 1990s. His screen inarticulateness has become a trade mark, especially in his award-winning performance as the Dublin criminal MARTIN CAHILL in *The General* (1998) and as a small-time crook in *I Went Down* (1997). While he had only a minor part in *Michael Collins* (1996), he had already played COLLINS in 'The Treaty' (1992), a television series. In demand internationally, his distinctive style can be seen in films as various as *The Butcher Boy* (1998), *This Is My Father* (1998), *Lake Placid* (1999), and *Gangs of New York* (2002). **Kevin Rockett**

Glenavy, Beatrice, née Moss Elvery (1883–1970), painter, sculptor, designer, decorator, and illustrator. Born in Dublin; she won early acclaim for her modelling at the Metropolitan School of Art and then for her stained glass made at AN TÚR GLOINE and narrative prints for the CUALA INDUSTRIES. From 1910 she concentrated on painting at the Slade School of Fine Art in London before marrying Gordon Campbell (who subsequently became Lord Glenavy) in 1912. On their return to Ireland in 1918 she resumed decorative PAINTING on a range of surfaces and became a prolific and popular annual exhibitor with the ROYAL HIBERNIAN ACADEMY. Her later paintings are characterised by muted tones and surreal settings. **Nicola Gordon Bowe**

Glencar, Co. Sligo, a deep, cliff-lined glacial valley incised into the Dartry and Glencar limestones between Knocknarea and the Castlegall Hills. Once through the limestones, glacial scour formed the trough in the underlying, softer Benbulbin shale, now occupied by Glencar Lough. On deglaciation the sides of the valley lost their glacial support and collapsed along slippage planes between the shale and the overlying limestone. The narrow rocky ridges and valleys below the cliffs, such as Swiss Valley on the north side of the glen, are formed by the listing surfaces of these slumped blocks lying against the valley walls. Fissures north of the cliffs indicate future landslips. Rivulets, springs and waterfalls, including Glencar Waterfall and Sruth in aghaidh an Aird (which appears to flow uphill during gales), now line the cliffs.

Though Glencar's landscape principally reflects natural processes, the region has a rich human heritage. Before blanket bog formed four thousand years ago, when the climate became wetter and cooler, Neolithic farmers had worked the land and constructed the many MEGALITHIC TOMBS for which Glencar is named (*Gleann an Chairthe*, 'valley of the standing stone'). The Annals of the FOUR MASTERS record that in 1029 three local chieftains and their entourage died in a fire that swept through one of the CRANNÓGS in Glencar Lough. The untamed landscape and its ancient human imprint attracted W. B. YEATS to Glencar; in 'The Stolen Child' he portrays the glen's wilderness of rock and water as a sanctuary where childhood might be preserved among dancing fairies. **Colman Gallagher**

Glencree, one of Co. Wicklow's spectacular glacial valleys. During the last glaciation the Glencree glacier extended from corries in Upper and Lower Lough Bray to Knockree, a glacially moulded hill that marks the confluence of the Glencree glacier and the enormous ice-sheet that occupied the Irish Sea basin. Importantly, the moraines of Upper Lough Bray record the final presence of glaciers in Ireland 11,500 years ago. In the climatic amelioration that followed, Glencree became mantled in dense forests, parts of which survived into historical times. By the eighth century Glencree was controlled by the sept of Uí Briúin, but it came under Crown dominion following the ANGLO-NORMAN CONQUEST, when the Royal Forest of Glencree was enclosed by a deep fosse and bank. In 1290 Queen Eleanor established a timber works in the glen that supplied wood for construction projects in Dublin and in England. POWERSCOURT Estate, at the foot of the glen on the site of a thirteenth-century motte, was given to Sir Richard Wingfield for his role in the Spanish surrender at KINSALE in 1601.

Glencree's importance as a strategic military route, particularly during the 1798 REBELLION, prompted the construction of a barracks at the head of the glen along the newly constructed Military Road. Today the barracks houses the GLENCREE CENTRE FOR RECONCILIATION, run by a charity that aims to unite groups sundered by religious intolerance. Opposite the Reconciliation Centre is a cemetery for German airmen who died in Ireland during the SECOND WORLD WAR. **Colman Gallagher**

Glencree Centre for Reconciliation, near Enniskerry, Co. Wicklow, conceived in 1972 in reaction to the violence in Northern Ireland and established in 1974. Its main aim is to encourage respect and understanding between groups or individuals in conflict, with the goal of creating peace and reconciliation. One of the courses offered is 'Let's Involve the Victim's Experience (LIVE)', directed towards victims of violence, both North and South. [see CORRYMEELA COMMUNITY.] **Suzanne Mulligan**

Glendalough, Co. Wicklow, a valley and ecclesiastical site associated with St KEVIN and St LAURENCE O'TOOLE. The former is said to have died here as a hermit in 618; his tomb-shrine is probably the small 'Priest's House', and around his grave grew a monastery that survived until about 1400. Access to the inner sanctuary was through a unique two-storey double-arched tower, with cross-inscribed boulder beyond. The ruined multi-period cathedral is, after CLONMACNOISE, the second-largest surviving pre-Cistercian church in Ireland, its chancel being a twelfth-century addition. Nearby is a possibly tenth or eleventh-century ROUND TOWER, over 30 m (98 ft) high, its conical cap restored in 1876; St Kevin's Church or 'Kitchen' with a round tower added to its stone roof (probably twelfth century); and a stone cross (possibly later medieval).

A path beside the foundations of St Ciarán's church leads to a BULLAUN STONE—one of many in the area—traditionally linked with St Kevin's childhood and, further down the valley, to St Saviour's Priory, an ill-reconstructed Augustinian monastic church probably founded by Laurence O'Toole, abbot from 1153 to 1162, who may also have been responsible for much of the twelfth-century building and carving activity elsewhere in the valley. The eastern approach passes Trinity Church, which had a round tower at its western end that fell in 1818.

The area around the Upper Lake had at least two further churches, Reefert and Temple na Skellig, and a rock-cut chamber (St Kevin's Bed), as well as a number of 'stations' and a circular enclosure. These were probably associated with PILGRIMAGE, known here from the eighth century onwards and closed down in 1862 because of 'drink and debauchery'. Stone crosses dotted around the valley are also connected with pilgrimage, and a pilgrims' path, the 'St Kevin's Road', led to the valley across the Wicklow Gap from the Central Plain; a section is exposed beside the roadway leading to the Turlough Hill power station. An interpretative centre near the lower car park houses the twelfth-century market cross, decorated stones and gravestones, and a model of the monastery. The churchyard near the cathedral also has some fine eighteenth and nineteenth-century carved tombstones (see p. 944). **Peter Harbison**

Glendalough. *Glendalough, Co. Wicklow. In the centre of the U-shaped valley are the upper and lower lakes and the ecclesiastical remains of the monastic settlement, St Kevin's Church with belfry (left), and the round tower (right). [Dúchas, The Heritage Service]*

Geology of Glendalough (*Gleann dá Loch*), Co. Wicklow, one of the county's most striking glacially overdeepened valleys, and named for its two lakes. The glen straddles the geological boundary between domed, adamellite granite uplands and lower-lying schist and slate. These latter rocks originated as Ordovician sea-floor sediments but were metamorphosed by contact with rising magma that formed the Wicklow granites 405 million years ago. In this geological setting lead and zinc mineralisation took place, providing Glendalough with rich reserves of base metals. During the Quaternary Period ice-caps radiated outwards from the granite uplands, and Glendalough, an existing river valley, was overdeepened by glacial erosion. This is best seen where the present river plummets off the granite boundary into a glacial trough incised particularly deeply in the lower-lying metamorphic rocks. Though coincident with the geological boundary, this morphology is due to the focusing of glacial accumulation and incision in a reach of the lower valley already deeply fluvially incised following uplift in the Tertiary Period. During deglaciation, short-lived meltwater lakes formed between recessional moraines and the retreating glacier. The lower of the present lakes is impounded by a delta that formed in the last of these glacial lakes, the delta top reflecting the vanished meltwater lake's surface elevation. Glendalough's monastic settlement was built on this delta. In turn, the present upper lake is separated from the lower by an alluvial fan formed by the Pollanas River, tumbling into Glendalough from a hanging valley overlooking the glen's south wall. **Colman Gallagher**

Glendalough, Book of. Cited as a valuable and venerable source in several MANUSCRIPTS of the period beginning c. 1400, the Book of Glendalough, which was until recently thought to be lost, has been shown to be identical with the main part of Bodleian Library manuscript Rawlinson B502. This most beautiful of twelfth-century Irish codices was written by a single scribe c. 1120–30. It contains, among other texts, the earliest copy of Saltair na Rann as well as a large corpus of secular and saints' genealogies and some Leinster origin legends. Up to 1600 the manuscript was kept mainly in Connacht; soon after 1600 it formed part of Sir JAMES WARE's library. **Pádraig Ó Riain**

Glengarriff, Co. Cork, a village on the shores of Bantry Bay, 18 km (11 miles) north of BANTRY. During the nineteenth century it became one of the most popular tourist resorts in Ireland, partly for its mild CLIMATE but especially for the 'singular variety and indescribable beauty of its scenery', as noted in LEWIS'S TOPOGRAPHICAL DICTIONARY (1837) and reiterated by many visitors' accounts. Glengarriff is a striking combination of coast, mountain, and woodland, with a luxuriant, almost sub-tropical vegetation, which is encouraged by the warm waters of the North Atlantic Drift. After improvements in TRANSPORT in the nineteenth century, several hotels and guesthouses were built in the village, and it still has a thriving tourist business. Glengarriff is also noted for the gardens of GARINISH ISLAND. **Kevin Hourihan**

Gleninsheen gold collar, a prehistoric gold collar found in 1932 in a rock crevice at Gleninsheen, Co. Clare. It is one of eight similar collars of the Late BRONZE AGE found in Cos. Clare, Limerick, and Tipperary. The superbly crafted collar is made of sheet gold decorated with raised ribs alternating with bands of rope-like patterns. The front discs of the composite terminals are decorated with an elaborate pattern of conical bosses set in concentric circles. The back discs are stitched to the collar with gold wire, the edges of which fold over, holding the front discs in place. [see GOLD, PREHISTORIC.] **Mary Cahill**

Glenmalur, Battle of (25 August 1580), the only notable engagement during the BALTINGLASS REVOLT. Acting against the advice of experienced soldiers, the Lord Deputy, Lord GREY DE WILTON, sent half his army under the command of George Moore into Glenmalur, Co. Wicklow, to engage the rebel force of James FitzEustace, Viscount Baltinglass, and his accomplice FIACH MAC HUGH O'BYRNE, who had retreated to that rocky, thickly wooded district. Mostly inexperienced and readily distinguishable by their red-and-blue doublets and white hose, the Crown forces were easy targets for the rebels, who lay in waiting armed with guns, bows, and axes. The disoriented pikemen endeavoured to escape the ambush by climbing the other side of the glen. Sir William Stanley, whose rearguard company sustained several casualties, described the battle as 'the hottest piece of service for the time that ever I saw in any place.' At least thirty Englishmen were killed, including Moore. **Mary Ann Lyons**

Glen of Imail, a valley running west from Lugnaquilla Mountain, Co. Wicklow's highest peak, towards the Leinster Plain. During the last GLACIATION it marked the zone where ice spreading from the mountains met ice covering the surrounding lowlands. The glen takes its name from the sept of Uí Máil, which controlled both Cuala, the fertile lands of western Wicklow, and the ancient trackway of Slí Chualann, which led through Wicklow to the Leinster lowlands. Following the ANGLO-NORMAN CONQUEST in the twelfth century the glen was a centre of resistance, and west Wicklow became a 'marchland' or 'place of war'. In the 1798 REBELLION, Co. Wicklow was known for its militancy and was one of the first counties to experience fighting; Michael Dwyer, born in the glen in 1772, was a prominent leader in Co. Wicklow and raised significant numbers of men in the glen. He and a core of his men held out in the WICKLOW MOUNTAINS until 1803, when they negotiated a surrender; they were finally transported to New South Wales. The Dwyer-Macallister Cottage in Derrynamuck, a vernacular thatched house of the eighteenth century, is now a national monument. Today, echoing its martial history, a large part of the Glen of Imail is used as a military firing range. **Colman Gallagher**

Glen of the Downs, a valley in the Wicklow Mountains incised by meltwaters beneath the ice sheet that once covered the eastern seaboard. Meltwater deposits flanking the glen at progressively lower altitudes reflect the gradual thinning and retreat of the ice towards the north. The channel cut by the sub-glacial meltwaters provided an important pass linking Wicklow and Dublin. The glen became singularly important from the Late BRONZE AGE and is the only site in east Wicklow where HILL-FORTS are found from this time. This strategic importance continued through the ANGLO-NORMAN CONQUEST, with tower-houses constructed nearby in Fassaroe and POWERSCOURT. The territory came firmly under the control of the new establishment, and by the late eighteenth century the area around the glen from Enniskerry to Bray and Delgany had become the 'Garden of Ireland', the hillsides displaying elegant villas with landscaped grounds. In the eighteenth century the Dublin Society awarded grants to landowners for the planting of native trees, and so the afforestation of the glen began; by 1853 it was reported to be covered in 'luxuriant foliage', and this significant, though managed, NATIVE WOODLAND survives today. The decision in 1997 to widen the road through the glen prompted the occupation of the woodland by ecological activists, provoking a heated public debate on the glen's importance as part of the principal route linking Dublin with the port of Rosslare and as a site of environmental significance. **Colman Gallagher**

Glens of Antrim: see ANTRIM, GLENS OF.

Glinsk, Co. Galway, site of a fortified house probably built by the Burkes c. 1630, very similar to those of Monkstown and Mountlong, Co. Cork. Such houses are rectangular in plan and three storeys high. Features include numerous gables surmounted by chimney-stacks, towers at each angle, and mullioned windows. Sections of the bawn and foundations of a mural tower remain. **David Sweetman**

glosses, comments and annotations elucidating the main text in medieval MANUSCRIPTS, written between the lines of the main text (usually Latin), on which they form a commentary, or in the margins, and most often in smaller script. Main texts written in Irish are elucidated in a similar fashion. Glosses in Irish manuscripts can be formulated in either Latin or Irish, or in both languages within the same gloss. They perform a variety of functions. Some explain morphological or syntactic features of the main text; others provide synonyms or translations of difficult words (*lexical glosses*) or phrases (*paraphrase glosses*). More ambitious and often longer glosses consist of comments on the main text. The number of glosses in different manuscripts varies from sporadic entries to continuous commentaries in gloss form.

Three important early Irish gloss commentaries survive: on the Pauline Epistles in a manuscript dating from c. 750 and now in Würzburg, on a commentary on the Psalms in a manuscript dating from c. 800 and now in Milan, and on the Latin grammar written by Priscian in 526 in a manuscript dated c. 845 and now in Sankt Gallen. **Rijcklof Hofman**

GOAL, an international humanitarian organisation dedicated to alleviating the suffering of the poorest people of the developing world. Founded in 1977 by the sports journalist John O'Shea (in response to a television programme about an Irish priest sending aid to the poor in developing countries), it has responded to many humanitarian crises since then. Now working in twenty countries, it has a budget of €30 million and a staff of almost 3,000, the majority of whom are recruited locally. There is a heavy emphasis on assisting street children and those affected by HIV and AIDS. The organisation also finances the work of indigenous groups that share its philosophy. Many sports stars around the world support its work, and a number of its aid programmes incorporate sports activities to develop the participants' self-esteem. [see DEVELOPMENT AID.] **Gabrielle Brocklesby**

Goban Saor (Gobbán the wright), a legendary, possibly pagan figure who appears in some of the earliest literature written in Ireland; he also had a long life in oral culture. He is imagined as a master-craftsman as well as a prodigious, and prodigiously fast, builder of CHURCHES for the SAINTS. **Elva Johnston**

Gobnait. Best known for her connection with the church of Ballyvourney, Co. Cork, Gobnait is said to have been a native of the ARAN ISLANDS, whence she journeyed, via several other churches still named after her, to her Cork church. This lay on the boundary between the territories of Uí Eachach Mumhan and Múscraí Midíne, which explains her genealogical attachment to the Múscraighe. The saint's name derives from *gobba*, a pet form based on *gobha* or *gabha*, 'smith'. That Gobnait was originally a (pre-Christian) patron of iron-workers is indicated not only by her name but also by excavations at her church in Ballyvourney, which yielded considerable evidence of iron-working on the site. The saint's feast-day, still the focus of much devotion, is 11 February (see p. 498). **Pádraig Ó Riain**

gods and goddesses. Irish PAGANISM was polytheistic. Some of the pagan gods and goddesses worshipped in Ireland were known also throughout Europe; others remained strictly local. Unfortunately we have no direct evidence concerning the pagan Irish divinities or indeed Irish paganism. However, the Christian and medieval Irish sagas concerning the shape-shifting, immortal, and sorcerous TUATHA DÉ DANANN offer a tempting glimpse of pagan gods stripped of their divine status but still in possession of Otherworldly powers. The identification of many personalities of Tuatha Dé Danann with pagan divinities is strengthened by what is known concerning the gods of the Continental Celts—though it should be remembered that this knowledge comes through the biased eyes of classical commentators. Nevertheless the Irish LUGH is clearly the same as the powerful Celtic god Lugus. Certain divinities seem to have had adherents on both sides of the IRISH SEA; these arguably included Nuadu, MANANNÁN MAC LIR, Goibniu, and DANU, who may roughly correspond to the British Nodens and the Welsh Manawydan fab Llŷr, Gofannon, and Dôn, respectively. Others, particularly goddesses, were native to Ireland and are associated with the natural landscape. The River BOYNE commemorates Bóand, while Ireland was supposedly named for three women of Tuatha Dé Danann: Fódla, Banba, and Ériu. 'Cath Maige Tuired' (the Battle of Moytura), the saga that tells of the conflict between Tuatha Dé Danann and their rivals, the Fomhóire, has often been read as a type of Irish *theomachy* (a war between the gods) and has been compared to the battles between Titans and Olympians known from classical MYTHOLOGY. Care must be taken, however, for 'Cath Maige Tuired' is a Christian text.

Tuatha Dé Danann are not the only remnants of Irish pagan deities. Many commentators have seen the shadowy figures of gods and goddesses behind heroes such as FIONN MAC CUMHAILL and saints such as BRIGID. Ultimately, however, our records are the products of Christians, for whom Tuatha Dé Danann were fabulous immortals, the heroes great men, and the SAINTS divinely inspired; there was no room here for gods and goddesses. [see BOA ISLAND; IRELAND, NAMES FOR; PAGANISM; PRE-CHRISTIAN RELIGIONS.] **Elva Johnston**

Gogarty, Oliver St John (1878–1957), surgeon and writer. His fifteen volumes of verse (*Collected Poems*, 1951) prove him an accomplished lyricist akin to Herrick; he also wrote classic love poems with insouciant ease and struck dignified, stoic attitudes to death. His unpublished parodies and bawdy poems date from student days, when he rented the Sandycove MARTELLO TOWER (where JOYCE stayed briefly); these can be seen in *The Poems and Plays* (2001). A senator of the IRISH FREE STATE, he was kidnapped by the IRA in the CIVIL WAR and escaped being shot by plunging into the River LIFFEY (in mid-January) and swimming downstream to safety. He attacked urban poverty in plays and in speeches in the Seanad. A conversationalist and wit whose friends included GEORGE MOORE, GEORGE RUSSELL, and W. B. YEATS, he wrote entertaining autobiographies, notably *As I Was Going Down Sackville Street* (1937). **A. Norman Jeffares**

Goidelic in Ireland, Scotland, Wales and the Isle of Man, a term used for the group of CELTIC LANGUAGES containing Irish, Gaelic (Scotland), and Manx (spoken in the Isle of Man until the 1970s). It has been claimed that the latter two may not have separated from Irish until the Middle Irish period (c. twelfth century) and so share a common past in Old Irish. However, Scotland was settled from Ireland from the fifth century onwards, and evidence of early Irish settlement, in the form of OGHAM inscriptions, is also found in western Britain, notably in south-west Wales; the geographical spread of speakers of Goidelic languages would probably have encouraged dialectal distinctions from an early period (though there is no evidence for dialectal variation in OLD IRISH). Another approach to the separation of these languages is to suggest a dialect continuum running from Co. Kerry to Lewis; this would perhaps better explain the close similarities between southern dialects of Gaelic and northern dialects of Irish. **Paul Russell**

Goidelic or Primitive Irish. Irish is a CELTIC LANGUAGE, a language of the ancient Celtae or 'Celts' and a member of the branch of the Indo-European family of languages that includes Gaelic (Scotland), Manx, Welsh, Breton, and Cornish. Being Indo-European in origin, the Celtic languages are related to Gothic, Hittite, Latin, Old Slavonic and Sanskrit and to such modern languages as Hindi, English, Russian, and the Romance languages.

Caesar restricted the name *Celtae* to the people of Gallia Celtica or Middle Gaul—roughly modern France—but most other writers used it of all the Gauls, including the peoples of Spain and Upper

Italy believed to be of the same language and race; it was never, it would appear, extended to the Britons. It is generally accepted that the Celts emerged as a culturally distinct people in Western Europe towards the end of the second millennium BC and that by 300 BC, when their territories spread from Asia Minor to Western Europe, they held sway in Ireland. The earliest form of Irish known to us is that which we find in the OGHAM inscriptions on stone monuments, in which the alphabet is rendered in strokes cut along the monument's edges; this is called Primitive Irish. **Diarmaid Ó Muirithe**

gold, prehistoric. Over a thousand gold objects from prehistoric Ireland are known to survive. Though gold has been found in Ireland, particularly in Cos. Wicklow and Tyrone, it has not been possible yet to identify where the ore was found. The sources most likely to have been exploited by prehistoric people are alluvial deposits from rivers and streams, using simple washing techniques such as panning, though gold from hard rock sources cannot be excluded. The earliest evidence for goldworking in Europe dates from the fifth millennium BC; by the end of the third millennium the working of copper, bronze, and gold had become well established in Ireland. We do not know precisely how the late NEOLITHIC people of Ireland became familiar with metalworking; however, it is clear that essential metalworking skills were introduced by people experienced at every level of production, including the recovery of ores and all manufacturing stages.

During the early BRONZE AGE, between 2400 and 1500 BC, Irish goldsmiths produced a limited range of ornaments. The principal products were discs, usually found in pairs (for example those from Tedavnet, Co. Monaghan), plain and decorated bands, and crescent-shaped collars, called LUNULAE, all made from sheet gold. Decoration consists mainly of geometrical motifs such as triangles, lozenges, and groups of lines arranged in patterns. Incision with a sharp tool and *repoussé* (working from behind to produce a raised pattern) were the principal techniques. The lunula from Rossmore, Co. Monaghan, is particularly fine.

At the beginning of the Late BRONZE AGE, c. 1200 BC, there was a remarkable change in the types of ornaments made. New goldworking techniques were developed, and new styles began to appear. Twisting bars or strips of gold became the most commonly used method. Twisted ear-rings and TORCS varying greatly in size are represented. Many, such as the exceptional pair from TARA, required large amounts of gold, suggesting that a new source had been discovered.

Between 1000 and 850 BC there seems to have been a lull in goldworking. However, the succeeding phase (850–600 BC) was an extremely productive one. The goldwork of this period can be divided into two main types. Solid objects, such as bracelets and dress-fasteners, were cast or hammered from bars and ingots; these contrast dramatically with delicate collars and ear-spools made of sheet gold. Bracelets are the most numerous type, made from bars of different thicknesses with simple terminals. Occasionally a bracelet may be decorated with incised patterns using motifs such as hatched triangles, zigzags, and lozenges. Dress-fasteners are thought to have been used to close a garment by using double buttonholes or loops. They were made in a range of sizes, including some very heavy ones weighing over 1 kg (2.2 lb), for example from Clones, Co. Monaghan (see p. 133). Sleeve-fasteners are smaller versions of dress-fasteners but differ from them in that the bows are deeply grooved.

Gold wire was also used in a number of ways but especially to produce the ornaments called *lock-rings*, such as the pair from Gorteenreagh, Co. Clare. Thin gold foil, sometimes highly decorated, was used to cover objects made of other metals, such as copper, bronze, or lead. This technique can be well observed in the *bulla* from the Bog of ALLEN, a heart-shaped lead core covered with a highly decorated gold foil. The purpose of this and similar objects is not fully understood, but they may have been used as amulets or charms.

Decoration is an important feature of Late Bronze Age goldwork. A limited range of motifs was used to achieve complex patterns, which often cover the entire surface of the object. Among the most popular designs are arrangements of geometrical patterns, concentric circles, raised bosses—domed or conical—and rope and herringbone patterns. The goldsmiths used a variety of techniques to produce these motifs, including combinations of repoussé and chasing, stamping with specially made punches, and incising the surface of the gold. These features can be seen on the gold collars from GLENINSHEEN, Co. Clare, and Ardcrony, Co. Tipperary, and the gold ear-spools from Ballinesker, Co. Wexford.

Our knowledge of Bronze Age goldwork is largely dependent on the discovery of groups of objects in hoards. During the Late Bronze Age many hoards were deliberately deposited as ritual or votive offerings, with no intention—and in many instances no possibility—of recovery. A large hoard of gold ornaments discovered accidentally in 1854 by workmen building a railway at MOOGHAUN North, near Newmarket-on-Fergus, Co. Clare, contained over 150 objects, mostly bracelets but also at least six gold collars and two neck-rings. This discovery close to a lake in what may once have been marshy ground suggests a ritual deposit. Today only thirty original pieces can be identified from Mooghaun, the rest having been melted down by jewellers and recycled as nineteenth-century jewellery.

During the Bronze Age, Irish goldsmiths did not function in isolation but maintained links with Britain and the Continent, drawing some of their inspiration from trends abroad but always imparting a characteristically Irish style to each product. They also expressed their individuality by producing gold ornaments that are unparalleled elsewhere.

Gold ornaments occur in small numbers in the IRON AGE. [see BRONZE AGE COPPER MINING; BRONZE AGE METALWORK; MEDIEVAL METALWORK.] **Mary Cahill**

Goldsmith, Oliver (1728–1774), poet, playwright, essayist, and novelist. Born in Pallas, Co. Longford, son of a clergyman; educated locally and at TCD, and studied medicine in Edinburgh and Leyden. He frequented the theatres while in Dublin, and travelled widely on the Continent before settling in London in 1756. He earned his living there partly as a physician but principally as a hack writer, contributing to many of the encyclopaedias and magazines of the day. His hack work includes *A History of Earth and Animated Nature* and the introduction to *A General History of the World*. He also wrote *An Enquiry into the Present State of Polite Learning in Europe* and two periodicals, the *Bee* and the *Citizen of the World*. He did not despise his role as a populariser but maintained that 'true learning and true morality are closely connected: to improve the head will insensibly influence the heart.'

In 1760 he became acquainted with Samuel Johnson and other members of Johnson's literary 'Club', to which he was elected. His poem 'The Traveller' was well received; even more successful was his novel THE VICAR OF WAKEFIELD (1766), which endures as a masterpiece of irony and the most attractive example of eighteenth-century sentimental fiction. His most famous poem, 'THE DESERTED VILLAGE', appeared in 1770.

golf. *The fairway of the Royal County Down Golf Club, Newcastle, Co. Down, with the Mourne Mountains in the background. Considered one of the best in the world, the eighteen-hole championship course is one of the oldest clubs in Ireland. [Northern Ireland Tourist Board Photographic Library]*

Meanwhile Goldsmith turned his attention to drama, and his first play, *The Good-Natured Man*, was staged in 1768. His greatest dramatic success, *She Stoops to Conquer*—one of the most enduring comedies of the eighteenth century—followed in 1773. Just before his death at the age of forty-six he had been involved in a disagreement at Johnson's Club, which led to his last poem, 'Retaliation'. He died in April 1774 after treating himself for a kidney complaint.

Goldsmith wrote with elegance and confidence in prose, verse, and drama. Though he paid less attention to Ireland than most eighteenth-century expatriates, he left interesting essays on 'The Manners and Customs of the Ancient Irish' and on CAROLAN, whom he described as 'the last Irish bard'. Goldsmith was an important figure in the literary London of his day; his reputation can be summed up in the words of the Latin epitaph written for his monument in Westminster Abbey by his friend Johnson: 'There was almost no subject he did not write about, and he wrote about nothing without enhancing it.' **Andrew Carpenter**

golf. The popular notion of golf's origins in Ireland was described in the March 1933 issue of the magazine *Inisfail*. Lionel Hewson, the sport's leading writer at that time, noted how CÚ CHULAINN was reputed to have hit a ball from one hole to another, 300 yards apart, with his trusty camán. However, Hewson acknowledged that the birth and early spread of the game in Ireland was attributable directly to the Scots. He wrote that 'the Scots of Ulster began to play golf, the first club being what is now known as the Royal Belfast Golf Club, which dates from 1891.'

The first known reference to golf in Ireland is to be found in the 'Montgomery Manuscripts', which describe the activities of the first Viscount Montgomery, an early seventeenth-century Scottish planter in the ARDS PENINSULA, Co. Down. The chronicler tells us: 'His Lordship also built the quay or harbour at Donaghadee ... and built a great school at Newtown, endowing it, as I am credibly told, with twenty pounds yearly salary for a Master of Arts to teach Latin, Greek and Logyks, allowing the scholars a green for recreation at goff, football and archery ...' In *Early Irish Golf* (1988) William H. Gibson reported having discovered that the game was played on the CURRAGH, Co. Kildare, in 1852. He also established direct links between Scottish military regiments and the rapid spread of golf in Ireland during the second half of the nineteenth century.

Ireland played a significant role in the regularising of the sport. In 1891 the Golf Union of Ireland became the first such organisation in the world; it was followed in 1893 by the Irish Ladies' Golf Union, which filled a similarly pioneering role. The two bodies now control the golfing activities in almost 400 clubs throughout the country, of which thirty-nine have premier links courses—26 per cent of the world's total. Proper organisation increased playing activities. In the light of later controversies over inequality it is interesting that the outstanding early players were women. May Hezlett and Rhona Adair of Ulster became known as the game's golden girls, because of their success in the British women's championship from 1899 to 1907. Ireland's first outstanding male golfer was Michael Moran, who was born on NORTH BULL ISLAND, Dublin, in 1886 and died in 1918 in the First World War. In his short career he dominated Irish professional golf, winning successive national championships from 1909 to 1913, when he also finished third in the British Open at Hoylake. Another milestone was the establishment of the Irish Open professional championship at Portmarnock, Co. Dublin, in 1927. Though discontinued after the 1953 event, it was revived in 1975 and has since been won by Severiano Ballesteros (1983, 1985, 1986), Bernhard Langer (1984, 1987, 1994), and Nick Faldo (1991, 1992, 1993). Ireland played host to such international events as the British amateur championship (1949), Canada Cup (1960), and Walker Cup (1991), all at Portmarnock, and the Curtis Cup at Royal County Down in 1968 and at Killarney in 1996.

Irish-born players have contributed to the game internationally. Fred Daly, a native of Portrush, Co. Antrim, became the only Irish winner of the British Open (1947); successes by Christy O'Connor senior, born in Galway, included the 1970 John Player Classic. Harry Bradshaw, another outstanding professional, combined with O'Connor to capture the Canada Cup at Mexico City in 1958. In 2000, Darren Clarke of Dungannon, Co. Tyrone, beat Tiger Woods for the World Matchplay crown. Outstanding male amateurs were Joe Carr, who won three British amateur titles, Jimmy Bruen, a Walker Cup player as an eighteen-year-old in 1938, and Garth McGimpsey, British amateur winner in 1985. Mary McKenna became Ireland's leading woman player with eight national titles, 1969–89, and a record nine successive Curtis Cup appearances, 1970–86. **Dermot Gilleece**

gombeen man (from the Irish *fear gaimbín*, 'usurer'), a pejorative term for a small-time moneylender in nineteenth-century rural Ireland. Most gombeen men were shopkeepers, and they charged high rates of interest on their credit. Those dependent on them were, in the main, small tenant-farmers who needed the credit to support their subsistence and pay the rent due to the landlord; this was especially so in years of poor harvest or when livestock prices fell. Gombeen men were highly unpopular, not only because of the high rates of interest they charged but also because of the means they used to recover their debt, sometimes taking the stock or produce of the indebted farmer. [see FOLK-LIFE; FOLKLORE.] **David S. Jones**

Gonne MacBride, Maud (1866–1953), nationalist. Born in Aldershot, Hampshire, daughter of a British army officer of Irish background. She inherited wealth and became the lover of the French Boulangist politician Lucien Millevoye, by whom she had a daughter, Iseult. She campaigned for evicted Irish families and Fenian prisoners, and was prominent in the Irish Transvaal Committee. The muse and friend of W. B. YEATS, she founded INGHINIDHE NA HÉIREANN in 1900 and linked nationalism with women's interests. Her influence declined after her separation from her husband, JOHN MACBRIDE, whom she had married in 1903, and exile in Paris with their son, SEÁN MACBRIDE. She returned to Ireland after John MacBrides's execution in 1916 and worked for the Irish White Cross. During the CIVIL WAR she formed the Women's Prisoners' Defence League, opposing the policies of the PROVISIONAL GOVERNMENT, by whom she was imprisoned. She remained strongly republican, an iconic figure in nationalist mythology (see p. 521). **Margaret Ward**

Good Friday Agreement: see BELFAST AGREEMENT.

Goodman, Canon James (1828–1896), Church of Ireland priest, professor of Irish in TCD, uilleann piper, and folk music collector. Born in Dingle, Co. Kerry; he worked in Ardgroom on the Beara peninsula, Co. Cork, 1858–67, and later as rector of Abbeystrewery, Skibbereen, Co. Cork, 1867–96. While in Ardgroom he completed a copy of his collection (1866), which includes music transcribed from the oral tradition, with many tunes attributed to the piper Thomas Kennedy as well as music copied from secondary and printed sources. The melodies of the complete collection number some 2,200. Goodman fares well in comparison with his fellow-collectors of the nineteenth century; his personal background and musical accomplishments facilitated his understanding of TRADITIONAL MUSIC and culture. Part of his collection, in particular 'Tunes of the Munster Pipers', has been edited by HUGH SHIELDS and published under the same title. This selection contains vocal and instrumental airs (approximately 40 per cent) as well as double JIGS (34 per cent), REELS (13 per cent), tunes in 9/8 time (4 per cent), and a number of other types, including HORNPIPES, SET DANCES, and MARCHES. A second volume is being prepared for publication. Goodman's music MANUSCRIPTS are in TRINITY COLLEGE Library, Dublin. **Jimmy O'Brien Moran**

Gordon Bennett Cup. The 1903 Gordon Bennett Cup motor race, which took place on 2 July 1903 around a circuit based on Athy, Co. Kildare, was the first international motor event to be held in Ireland. It was won by Camille Jenatzy of Belgium, the 'Red Devil', whose Mercedes completed the 526 km (327-mile) marathon in 6 hours and 39 minutes, an average of 79.25 km/h ($49\frac{1}{4}$ miles per hour). The pioneer French driver René de Knyff was second, ahead of his compatriot Henri Farman, both driving Panhards; also taking part was the first American team to race in Europe. The event attracted thousands of automobilists from England and the Continent, and huge crowds welcomed the racers and the visitors back to Dublin, as recalled later by JAMES JOYCE in one of his DUBLINERS stories, 'After the Race'. Two days later speed trials were held in the PHOENIX PARK, where Baron de Forest of Belgium exceeded the world record with a speed of 134 km/h ($83\frac{1}{2}$ miles per hour). **Brendan Lynch**

Gore-Booth, Eva (1870–1926) poet, feminist, social reformer, and Christian mystic. Born in Lissadell, Co. Sligo, younger sister of CONSTANCE MARKIEVICZ. In 1897 she moved to Manchester with

Gonne. *Photograph of Maud Gonne, inscribed '... Onward always till liberty is won,' dated 19 November 1897, the year in which she launched her nationalist news-sheet* L'Irlande Libre. *[Courtesy of Kilmainham Gaol Museum/Anna MacBride White]*

her companion, Esther Roper, where she campaigned among textile workers for women's emancipation; she became editor of *Women's Labour News* and in 1914 joined the Women's Peace Crusade. Included by GEORGE RUSSELL in *New Songs* (1904), she published nine volumes of poetry and five mythological plays, notably *The Triumph of Maeve*, a pacifist revision of Irish myth. *Broken Glory* (1918) commemorates the 1916 RISING. She also edited the *Prison Letters of Countess Markievicz* (posthumously published, 1934). **Selina Guinness**

Gore's Observatory (1879–1910), a small observatory at Ballysadare, Co. Sligo, established by John Ellard Gore after he retired from the Public Works Department in India in his early thirties. From 1879 he made observations from no. 3 Northumberland Road, Dublin, where he had lodgings. Possessing only a 76 mm (3-in.) refractor and binoculars, he discovered the variability of several stars, including U. Orionis, S. Sagitae, W. Cygni, and X. Herculis. His up-to-date list of binary stars for which orbits had already been determined, accompanied by a tabulation of their elements, was published in *Transactions of the Royal Irish Academy*, 1890. He wrote, and translated from French, several books on astronomy and contributed numerous articles to the *Monthly Notices* of the Royal Astronomical Society, London. A founder-member of the British Astronomical Association, he acted as director of its Variable Star Section for many years. **Susan McKenna-Lawlor**

Gorey (*Guaire*), Co. Wexford, a market town 42 km (26 miles) north of Wexford; population, (2002), 3,093. Though a town may have existed here in the late thirteenth century, it was not until 1619 that the town of Newborough was granted a charter by JAMES I as part of the plantation of Wexford. The Ram family played a powerful role in this plantation and was to determine Gorey's affairs for three centuries. Gorey was the scene of many battles during the 1798 REBELLION and changed hands several times. Its site on the mail-coach road and its agricultural hinterland, producing poultry and BUTTER, were important to its economy. The Courthouse (1819) also houses the town library. Other notable buildings are the old Erasmus Smith School House (1834), St Michael's (Catholic) Church (1839), built to designs by PUGIN, and CHRIST CHURCH (Church of Ireland) (1861), with magnificent STAINED-GLASS windows, especially by HARRY CLARKE and CATHERINE O'BRIEN. **Ruth McManus**

Gorham, Maurice (1902–1975), journalist and broadcaster. Born in London, his father came from Clifden, Co. Galway. He was educated at the University of Oxford. From 1926 until 1947 he worked in many different capacities with the BBC in London, as editor of the *Radio Times* (1933), founder of the BBC Light Programme (1945), and director of television (1946). He also directed the service's broadcasts to North America and, during the Second World War, established the Allied Expeditionary Force broadcasting programme. From 1953 to 1959 was involved in Irish radio, as Chief Executive of Radio Éireann and director of broadcasting. Under his leadership the service expanded greatly in hours of broadcasting, in programming, and in its music personnel, and during this period outside broadcasts and transmissions from abroad were introduced. Gorham's books on broadcasting include *Sound and Fury* (1949) on the BBC and *Forty Years of Irish Broadcasting* (1967). *Dublin Old and New* (1975) is a photo-album on change in the city, comparing historic and 1970s' images. **Brian Lalor**

Gorman, Richard (1946–), painter. Born in Dublin; studied at TCD and Dún Laoghaire College of Art. He lives and works in Milan and exhibits regularly there as well as in many venues in Ireland and around the world. His painting has developed over the years in a sombre, serious and handsome form of abstraction, occasionally using shaped canvases, which convey a sense of architecture, as if painted for a particular doorway or archway. He is a member of AOSDÁNA and recipient of the Pollock-Krasner Prize. **Dorothy Walker**

Gormfhlaith (died 947), daughter of FLANN SINNA, King of TARA. She became the wife of his successor, NIALL GLÚNDUB, and is credited with two earlier marriages also, the first to the Munster King CORMAC MAC CUILEANNÁIN, the second to the Leinster King Cerball mac Muirecáin (died 909); but the first at least of these is a literary fiction. The surviving texts concerning Gormfhlaith constitute the largest dossier on any historical Irishwoman from the period before the twelfth century. These are various in genre, and mainly of a non-historical kind, but agree in representing Gormfhlaith as an exemplar of the serially married royal consort. In the course of a long life she is depicted as experiencing extremes of happiness and sadness in marriage, divorce, remarriage, and extended widowhood, when she is sequestered in a monastery. The traditions that represent her as a poet are probably founded on fact, but all the surviving poems in her voice are written in EARLY MODERN IRISH. These are mainly concerned with celebrating her first husband, Niall Glúndubh, and lamenting his death and her own reduced circumstances thereafter. [see DIVORCE, MEDIEVAL; GAELIC LORDSHIP.] **Máirín Ní Dhonnchadha**

Gospel manuscripts, the most numerous class of surviving Latin MANUSCRIPTS from early medieval Ireland. They vary in size and content. Ten examples of one recognisably conservative Irish 'pocket GOSPELS' type have survived from the late eighth to the twelfth centuries. Small in size, written often in a minute cursive script, sometimes heavily abbreviated, they can be regarded as personal portable copies of their sponsors (MacDurnan, DIMMA) or as relics of the saint to whom they were attributed (Mulling). Two of them place each Gospel on a single quire or a pair of large quires, a practice of great antiquity, found as early as the fifth century in the East; the diminutive format of some of these Irish books has precursors in early Coptic Egypt. The opening of each Gospel was announced by a large decorated initial, which extended sometimes over a full page, and also occasionally by an evangelist or evangelist symbol page. Nearly all of them confined their contents to the Gospel text and did not have the textual accessories of prefaces, chapter lists and concordance or CANON TABLES so often found in contemporary Gospel books in England or on the Continent. This restrictive feature is found in eight other late eighth and early ninth-century Irish books of much larger format (MacRegol Gospels or 'Garland of Howth'), and with elaborately decorated full initial and facing evangelist pages. Different from them in having textual accessories, and illustrated sumptuously and with dazzling virtuosity, is the Book of KELLS, the chief glory of Irish illumination (see p. 523). Before each Gospel it had full initial, evangelist, four-symbols pages; it also has illuminations of the Virgin and Child, of Christ and of the Temptation and Arrest of Christ and a set of exuberantly decorated canon tables, and on each page inventively embellished initials and space-fillers. Made within the *paruchia* of COLM CILLE, probably at IONA in the later eighth century, it represents the final development of a distinctive insular method of illustrating Gospel books, of which the earlier Book of DURROW, made probably in the later seventh century at Iona or its offshoot, LINDISFARNE, is the first surviving example. The many surviving illuminated Anglo-Saxon Gospel books from the eighth and early ninth centuries were an important part of this peculiarly insular development, and in them Irish influence may have persisted. The Gospel text of the Irish manuscripts was generally mixed Old Latin and Vulgate, though purer Old Latin (CODEX USSERIANUS PRIMUS) and Vulgate (Durrow) examples also occur. [see CATHATH; GLOSSES; MANUSCRIPTS, EARLY IRISH.] **Patrick McGurk**

Gosset, William Sealy ('Student') (1876–1937), brewer and statistician. Born in Canterbury, Kent; educated at the University of Oxford. He was appointed at Guinness, Dublin, in 1899. Not primarily a statistician, he needed statistical tools to indicate the reliability of tests involving small sample sizes. With assistance from Ronald Aylmer Fisher, he developed his t-test. Because Guinness forbade staff to publish under their own names, he used the pseudonym 'Student' in his twenty-two papers. He also worked on correlation coefficients, randomisation of field trials (such as in barley) and genetics. He supervised the start-up of the new London Guinness brewery from 1935. **Adrian Somerfield**

gothic fiction. Driven by the spirit of transgression, gothic fiction escapes from the categories and periods within which critics attempt to contain it. Less a genre or tradition than a distinct (if discontinuous) mode, it reworks forms and themes like those identified by Chris Baldick: 'a fearful sense of inheritance in time [combined] with a claustrophobic sense of enclosure in space ... [produces] a sickening descent into disintegration.' In Irish examples, such as CHARLES MATURIN's *Melmoth the Wanderer* (1820) and SOMERVILLE AND ROSS's *The Big House of Inver* (1925), the inherited crime involves colonial dispossession, and an ANGLO-IRISH mansion is a central incarcerating location. These examples of so-called 'Protestant gothic' also dwell on the historical, political and aesthetic implications of Catholicism or Irish FOLKLORE, a tendency also visible (though often with a different ideological inflection) in 'Catholic gothic' fiction, such as JOHN BANIM's 'The Fetches' (1825) and 'The Ace of Clubs' (1838), MICHAEL BANIM's 'Crohoore of the Bill-Hook' (1825) and *The Ghost Hunter and His Family* (1833), GERALD GRIFFIN's *The Rivals* (1830) and 'The Barber of Bantry' (1835), and JAMES CLARENCE MANGAN's *Autobiography* (first published 1968). Though lacking Irish characters or settings, SHERIDAN LE FANU's 'Carmilla' (1872), OSCAR WILDE's *The Picture of Dorian Gray* (1891) and BRAM STOKER's *Dracula* (1897) also deal with folklore, Catholicism, BIG HOUSES, and buried secrets. Renovations of the mode include FLANN O'BRIEN's *The Third Policeman* (written 1939–40, published 1967), BRIAN MOORE's *The Mangan Inheritance* (1979) and *Cold Heaven* (1983), JOHN BANVILLE's *Birchwood* (1973) and *Mefisto* (1986), and SEAMUS DEANE's *Reading in the Dark* (1996). **Richard Haslam**

governance of the Republic of Ireland. The highly centralised nature of the Irish state is a legacy of its colonial past. Firstly, the majority of the Republic's political institutions and the administrative bureaucracy were inherited from Britain—an unequivocally unitary state; secondly, the manner in which they were placed under Irish control was the ultimate act of political consolidation. After a long struggle for independence and a bitter CIVIL WAR, the state established in 1922 was consciously and deliberately a centralised one. The revolutionary Government that took over was determined to show itself fully in control and to establish its capacity to rule. The desire for centralised power, however, was less concerned with political principle and more with finding immediate and pragmatic solutions to the problems of government in the aftermath of war. The strong preference for functional efficiency, even at the expense of clear democratic accountability, is a trait that has characterised governance in the Republic since its foundation. It is reflected in the *ad hoc* establishment of a plethora of public institutions and STATE-SPONSORED BODIES operating at regional and local levels.

On the one hand, a number of authorities responsible for the administration of some service have a governing body consisting both of members of the local authority and of interested associations or groups in the region, such as the eight area Health Boards and the eight regional tourism organisations. On the other hand, some central authorities have themselves decentralised their business regionally for administrative, managerial, or customer convenience; these include such state-sponsored bodies as the Electricity Supply Board and FÁS, as well as certain Government departments, such as the office of the REVENUE COMMISSIONERS in Limerick and the Department of Education in Athlone. The authorities with devolved powers and those with decentralised administrations all operate boundaries to suit themselves. As a consequence, their areas of responsibility do not coincide, creating what one political commentator referred to as an 'administrative jungle'.

Even when, in November 1998, the Government created two new regional authorities—the Border, Midlands and West (BMW) Regional Authority and the Southern and Eastern Authority—this was widely recognised as a 'quick fix' designed to facilitate continued access to EU regional aid by maintaining objective 1 status for the less well-off BMW region. It did not represent any attempt to reform existing regional structures or to introduce devolved government in any shape or form. Despite this, membership of the EUROPEAN UNION did introduce new approaches to public administration. In 1988, when the reform of EU regional aid policies required the completion of comprehensive development plans, Irish governments responded with the introduction of five-year 'national development plans', outlining the strategic integration of a variety of policy initiatives and public agencies operating at sub-national level. While the institutional mosaic at ground level remained complex, if not chaotic, the design and direction of their activities began to change. Even without any major institutional overhaul, a renewed emphasis on negotiation, partnership and subsidiarity in the organisation of public policy pointed to a change in governing style.

The influence of the European Union might not have been so extensive were it not combined with the experience of severe economic recession. Large-scale external shocks to the economy throughout the 1970s and 80s—such as the oil crisis, the emergence of stagflation, and worldwide recession—illustrated serious flaws in long-standing approaches to state development. In the years after independence it had been assumed that successful national policies designed to attract foreign investment and increase industrial activity would benefit the whole country through a 'trickle-down' effect, whereby the less well-off regions would be lifted by a rising tide of development. When it was clear that this approach was not working, the emphasis of policy changed to reflect a keener interest in new technologies and product innovation. Governments began to concentrate more on the development of INDIGENOUS INDUSTRIES and the promotion of small and medium-sized enterprises. A particular emphasis was given to improving the research, development and marketing capacities of industry. Throughout this period, however, attempts at further INDUSTRIALISATION and the generation of export-led growth led to Ireland's total participation in, and inextricable ties

government in Ireland. *President Mary McAleese (on dais) addressing a joint session of Dáil Éireann and Seanad Éireann on 16 December 1999, the first time she exercised her right to do so. [Michael Quinn]*

to, the international economy. As a country with a SMALL OPEN ECONOMY, Ireland was particularly vulnerable to the international recession and, arguably, not in a good position to deal with its consequences.

In seeking both to reform the economy and to respond to the demands of the international market, governments attempted to introduce greater flexibility in product development, production processes, and the organisation of labour. To achieve this they introduced a system of national concordat with the representatives of business and labour. The 'national understandings' of 1979 and 1980 marked a subtle shift in the nature of decision-making, beginning the integration of management and TRADE UNIONS in the formulation of public policy. This trend was inhibited by the turnover of governments and the recession of the early 1980s but was later re-established in a yet more developed form towards the end of the decade. The Programme for National Recovery (1987–90), the Programme for Economic and Social Progress (1991–3), the Programme for Competitiveness and Work (1994–6) and the most recent Partnership 2000 illustrate successive governments' commitment to reaching a consensus regarding the appropriate levels of growth and agreed measures to achieve them. The making and implementing of these agreements shows how closely employers' associations and unions have become involved not only in the making of policy but also in its administration. The willingness of governments to relinquish their exclusive responsibility for public policy for the inclusion of agreed 'social partners' is illustrative of a changing attitude towards governance. This change, which has come to be known in Ireland as 'government by partnership', has been characterised by some as a move towards a corporatist style of government. **Maura Adshead**

government in Ireland. The CONSTITUTION of the REPUBLIC OF IRELAND provides that the Government shall consist of a PRESIDENT and a two-chamber national parliament (Oireachtas Éireann) consisting of a house of representatives (Dáil Éireann) and a senate (Seanad Éireann).

The President is elected by universal adult suffrage for a seven-year term (and a maximum of two terms). Every citizen over the age of thirty-five is eligible to be nominated for the office, provided they are nominated either by at least twenty members of the houses of the Oireachtas or at least four county or city councils. Where only one candidate is nominated there is no need to proceed to a ballot; this happened with the presidencies of DOUGLAS HYDE in 1938, the re-election of SEÁN T. O'KELLY in 1952, CEARBHALL Ó DÁLAIGH in 1974, and PATRICK HILLERY, who was elected in 1976 and re-elected in 1983. The office and functions of the President are dealt with in articles 12 and 13 of the Constitution.

Though the President has no executive powers and acts mainly on the advice of the Government, he or she does exercise a limited number of significant functions. The President appoints the TAOISEACH (head of Government) on the nomination of Dáil Éireann, and the members of the Government, on the advice of the Taoiseach. The Taoiseach also advises the President on the acceptance or otherwise of ministerial resignations and on the summoning and dismissing of Dáil Éireann. The President reserves the right both to dissolve the Dáil on foot of a successful no-confidence vote and to refuse dissolution. Subject to the Defence Act (1954), the President is vested with supreme command of the DEFENCE FORCES. He or she receives and accredits all ambassadors and may, acting on the authority and advice of the Government, exercise limited executive functions in connection with international affairs. All bills passed by the Oireachtas are promulgated by the President, who may refer any bill (other than a money bill) to the SUPREME COURT to test its constitutionality. This action is carried out in consultation with the Council of State, which comprises the Taoiseach, TÁNAISTE (deputy head of Government), Ceann Comhairle (chairperson of Dáil Éireann), Cathaoirleach (chairperson of Seanad Éireann), ATTORNEY-GENERAL, president of the High Court, and Chief Justice. Other members may include previous Taoisigh, Presidents or Chief Justices who are willing to serve and up to seven nominees of the President. In the event of the President becoming incapacitated, the Council of State may carry out the functions of the Presidency.

By LAW, a general election to Dáil Éireann must be held at least once every five years. There are 166 *teachtaí Dála* (Dáil deputies, TDs), representing forty-one electoral constituencies, each constituency returning three, four or five deputies, depending on population.

The single transferable vote system of proportional representation used in all elections is intended to create as close a relationship as possible between the proportion of votes and the number of seats won by each party, in order to produce a parliament that is truly representative of the division of political opinion. Candidates' names are printed on the ballot paper in alphabetical order, followed by their party affiliation. The voter places a '1' beside the name of their first preference, a '2' beside their second preference, and so on. To be elected, a candidate must reach a quota, calculated as

$$\frac{\textit{number of valid votes cast}}{\textit{number of seats in constituency} + 1} + 1$$

A candidate who reaches this quota is automatically elected. Where a candidate obtains more than the quota, the surplus vote is reallocated to the other candidates in order of voters' preferences. If no candidate reaches the quota on the first count, the candidate with least votes is eliminated, and their second-preference votes are transferred to the remaining candidates for a second count. Counts continue until enough candidates achieve the quota. If, after all transfers have been allocated, there are still seats to be filled, then the candidates remaining with most votes are elected.

Seanad Éireann has sixty members: eleven are nominated by the Taoiseach, forty-three are elected from five 'panels' of candidates (cultural and educational, agricultural, labour, industrial and commercial, and administrative), and the remaining six are elected by a selection of universities (three by the National University of Ireland and three by the University of Dublin). Under the Seventh Amendment of the Constitution Act (1979) provision may be made to alter the selection of these six senators to incorporate the new universities and other third-level institutions.

Under the Constitution the authority to legislate is exclusively vested in the Oireachtas, on the understanding—provided by the Third Amendment of the Constitution Act (1972)—that no constitutional provision or law deriving from it may invalidate a law or action required as a consequence of membership obligations to the EUROPEAN UNION. Government policy and administration may be examined and criticised in both houses of the Oireachtas, but under the Constitution the Government is responsible to the Dáil alone. The primacy of the Dáil vis-à-vis the Seanad is most clearly illustrated in relation to Government budgets, where the Seanad has no authority to amend bills but is empowered only to make recommendations, and then within a time limit of twenty-one days.

The Constitution provides for a Government of between seven and fifteen members. At present there are fourteen departments, each headed by a Government minister: Agriculture and Food; Arts, Sport and Tourism; Communications and Natural Resources; Community, Rural and Gaeltacht Affairs; Defence; Education and Science; Enterprise, Trade and Employment; Environment and Local Government; Finance; Foreign Affairs; Health and Children; Justice, Equality and Law Reform; Social and Family Affairs; and Transport. The Government is headed by the Taoiseach, in practice the leader of the largest party (or coalition arrangement) in the Dáil. The Tánaiste is appointed by the Taoiseach and is most usually leader of the smaller coalition party in the Government.

Political Parties. In 2002 there were nine registered political parties in a position to nominate candidates in national and European Parliament elections. Historically the two principal parties, FIANNA FÁIL and FINE GAEL, are distinguished according to the side they took in the CIVIL WAR. Those in favour of the ANGLO-IRISH TREATY (giving independence from Britain and dominion status within the British Commonwealth for twenty-six of the thirty-two counties) joined together in Cumann na nGaedheal. Under the leadership of WILLIAM T.COSGRAVE this party merged with other parties to form Fine Gael, broadly Christian Democrat in orientation. Opponents of the Treaty formed the rival Fianna Fáil, led by ÉAMON DE VALERA. De Valera's iconic status, first as party leader and later as President of Ireland, did much to cement Fianna Fáil's self-image as a unifying and nationalist 'catch-all' party. This view was not seriously challenged until 1985, when a split in the party led to the formation of the PROGRESSIVE DEMOCRATS, a small, broadly liberal party that is now generally relied on to provide support for coalition governments led by Fianna Fáil.

In 1999 the LABOUR PARTY (founded in 1912 as the political wing of the Irish Trades Union Congress) merged with DEMOCRATIC LEFT (a small left-wing party created by a split in the WORKERS' PARTY in 1992). It is joined on the left by the GREEN PARTY and SINN FÉIN, both small parties with limited electoral support but becoming of increasing significance. The Green Party was founded in 1981 as the Ecology Party of Ireland, re-formed in 1986 as the Green Party. Sinn Féin was founded in 1905 as an umbrella group for small nationalist organisations. In 1922 it rejected parliamentary politics in the Republic with its withdrawal from Dáil Éireann, when it refused to recognise the Anglo-Irish Treaty and the subsequent political organisation of the Republic. It suffered a further split in 1970 when two factions emerged: 'Official Sinn Féin', later to become the Workers' Party, and 'Provisional Sinn Féin', now sharing government in the NORTHERN IRELAND ASSEMBLY. The Christian Solidarity Party, COMMUNIST PARTY OF IRELAND, Natural Law Party, and Workers' Party are the other parties registered to contest general elections, while the Cork City Ratepayers' Party and Donegal Progressive Party are registered to contest local elections.

Northern Ireland. The most recent constitutional initiative in Northern Ireland is provided by the BELFAST AGREEMENT of 10 April 1998. This provides for three interlocking and interdependent strands of governance. The first strand creates an Executive comprising up to twelve ministers from the 108-member Northern Ireland Assembly, allocated in proportion to party strengths. The Assembly takes charge of the internal affairs of Northern Ireland, including health, education, and agriculture; other areas, such as security, taxation, and justice, remain the responsibility of the British government through the Secretary of State for Northern Ireland. Decisions taken by the Executive must be ratified by a majority in the Assembly of both nationalists and unionists. The second strand of the agreement provides for a North-South Ministerial Council, with members from the Executive and the Irish Government; its membership will participate in consultation, co-operation, and action in areas of mutual interest. The third strand is a British-Irish Council, comprising representatives of the British Parliament, Dáil Éireann, the Northern Ireland Assembly, and any elected parliaments and assemblies in Scotland, Wales, the Isle of Man, and the Channel Islands. It is envisaged that this council will meet twice a year to discuss matters of mutual interest. Despite considerable highs and lows, discussions over the implementation of these arrangements are continuing and, though still far from a conclusion, represent the potential for stable government in Northern Ireland (see p. 791). [see ELECTORAL SYSTEM.] **Maura Adshead**

Governor-General of the Irish Free State, official representative of the British Crown in the Irish Free State under the provisions of the ANGLO-IRISH TREATY (1921). The three people to hold the office were T. M. HEALY, 1922–8, James MacNeill, 1928–32, and Domhnall Ó Buachalla, 1932–7. A symbolic office offensive to republicans, it was abolished by ÉAMON DE VALERA's FIANNA FÁIL Government under the terms of the Executive Authority (External Relations) Act (1936). **Fergal Tobin**

Grafton Architects, Dublin, established in 1978 by Yvonne Farrell (1952–) and Shelley McNamara (1952–); both educated at UCD. Both have been studio lecturers at UCC since 1978. They have designed schools at Oughterard, Co. Galway, Castleblayney, Co. Monaghan, and Celbridge, Co. Kildare, and the Department of Mechanical and Manufacturing Engineering at TRINITY COLLEGE, Dublin. Their reinterpretation of the modern movement in the context of Irish towns and countryside can be seen in Boland and Kane Mews, Clyde Lane, Dublin, Gray O'Connell House, Doolin, Co. Clare, and Mara House, Kinvara, Co. Galway. Members of Group 91 (which produced the TEMPLE BAR FRAMEWORK PLAN, 1991), they designed Temple Bar Square (see p. 1039). They won first prize for apartments at North King Street, Dublin, 1997, and auditorium library and offices for Bocconi University, Milan, 2002. **Raymund Ryan**

Graham, Len (1944–), singer and song-collector. Born in Glenarm, Co. Antrim; he learnt his early repertoire from his parents and at gatherings of the ANTRIM AND DERRY FIDDLERS' ASSOCIATION. He developed this in partnership with the singer JOE HOLMES, later performing with the group Skylark. His principal collection is *The Harvest Home* (1993); he has also produced three solo albums: *Wind and Water, Do Me Justice*, and *Ye Lovers All*. **Fintan Vallely**

Graham, Patrick (1943–), painter. Born in Mullingar, Co. Westmeath; studied art at the National College of Art. He worked first for an advertising agency before becoming a full-time painter. He exhibited at the Emmet Gallery, Dublin, 1974, at the Lincoln Gallery, 1982, and the Jack Rutberg Gallery in Los Angeles in 1987. A retrospective exhibition was held at the Douglas Hyde Gallery, Dublin, and at the Crawford Gallery, Cork, in 1994. Graham's expressionist paintings are frequently inspired by memories of his childhood in Co. Westmeath. He is a member of AOSDÁNA. **Peter Murray**

Gráinne, daughter of CORMAC MAC AIRT in Irish MYTHOLOGY. Having agreed to marry FIONN MAC CUMHAILL, she falls in love with Diarmaid and by means of a *geis* (taboo) persuades him to elope with her. Pursued by Fionn and his warriors, they flee from place to place and have many dramatic, often violent adventures along the way. Eventually, through treachery, Diarmaid is wounded by a boar and dies without the curative water that Fionn lets pass through his hands. Oral tradition today still calls many places, such as portal tombs, the 'bed of Diarmaid and Gráinne', in the belief that the fugitive lovers slept there. Their adventures are recounted in the tale 'TÓRAÍOCHT DHIARMADA AGUS GHRÁINNE' (the Pursuit of Diarmaid and Gráinne). **Ríonach uí Ógáin**

Grand Canal. Two rival schemes to link Dublin with the River SHANNON were laid before a committee of the Irish Parliament in February 1756. That advocating a southern route through the Bog of ALLEN was accepted, and the first section, to Sallins, Co. Kildare, was opened for freight in 1779, acquiring a passenger service the following year. The passage boats, generally 16 m (52-ft) wooden vessels with an average beam of 2.75 m (9 ft), normally carried forty-five first-class and thirty-two second-class passengers, smoking being prohibited in both cabins. After numerous delays caused by staunching problems, the canal was finally opened for traffic through the thirty-sixth lock at Shannon Harbour in 1805. In 1791 a branch giving access to the River BARROW at Athy was completed; further branches were opened to Naas, 1789, Ballinasloe, 1828, Mountmellick, 1831, and Kilbeggan, 1835.

In the face of competition from the RAILWAYS, the last of the passage boats was withdrawn in 1852. In 1950 the Grand Canal Company, which had operated the waterway since 1772, was merged with CIE, which withdrew the remaining trade boats in 1960. The minor branches were closed to all traffic the same year, followed in 1954 by the Dublin terminus at James's Street harbour, which catered for the once-substantial traffic from the adjacent GUINNESS BREWERY. Plans to fill in the Dublin city circular line to Ringsend were successfully opposed by conservation groups in the 1960s, since when the canal, latterly the responsibility of the Heritage Service, has seen restoration and increasing use by pleasure craft (see p. 155). [see CANALS; NEWRY CANAL; ROYAL CANAL.] **Bernard Share**

grand juries, the main organ of local government until 1898. Selected by the high sheriff from the leading male property-owners in each county, the grand jury ruled on the validity of indictments at assizes and was responsible for approving the expenditure of local taxes in matters such as the maintenance of roads and jails. Having lost their administrative role under the LOCAL GOVERNMENT ACT (1898), grand juries were abolished in independent Ireland in 1948 and in Northern Ireland in 1969 (see p. 641). **Virginia Crossman**

Grand Opera House, Belfast. Designed by leading British theatre architect, Frank Matcham (1854–1920) and opened during Christmas, 1895. The lavish interior is a unique and glorious amalgam of the work of architects, painters, and craftsmen. Although converted to a cinema between 1949 and 1972 and subsequently almost demolished, it reopened in 1980. The opera house, which was badly damaged by two bomb blasts, in 1991 and 1993, presents a varied programme that includes drama, musicals, opera, ballet, and pantomime, and plays host to companies from around the world, including The Royal Ballet (London), Royal Ballet of Flanders, Welsh National Opera, and Royal National Theatre (London). **Paul Collins**

Grand Prix, Irish, a series of motor races in the PHOENIX PARK, Dublin, from 1929 to 1931. The first event was won by the Russian Boris Ivanovski at a speed of 122 km/h (76 miles/h), while the German Mercedes ace Rudolf Caracciola took the 1930 race and Norman Black of MG the final event in 1931. Competitors also included the famous Bentley racers and Le Mans winners Sammy

Davis and Tim Birkin, the leading Italians Giuseppe Campari and Achille Varzi, and the record-breakers Malcolm Campbell, George Eyston, and KAYE DON. The British championship contender Raymond Mays and Prince Bira of Thailand were regular competitors at subsequent events in the Phoenix Park, which became Europe's fastest road circuit when Bira lapped at over 164 km/h (102 miles/h) in 1936. Motor races take place each year in the Phoenix Park, which is now the world's longest continuously used circuit. [see GORDON BENNETT CUP.] **Brendan Lynch**

Grattan, Henry (1746–1820), politician. Born in Dublin; educated at TCD. His poor relationship with his father meant that he did not inherit the family seat at Belcamp, Co. Dublin. Obliged as a result to enter the Middle Temple, London, to study law, he became attracted to a life in politics. He contributed to the 'Baratariana letters' against Lord TOWNSHEND in the early 1770s; but it was not until Charlemont nominated him in 1775 that he became an MP. Within a few years he had established a reputation as one of the most powerful and outspoken Patriot orators of the day. His successful advocacy of LEGISLATIVE INDEPENDENCE in the early 1780s consolidated his reputation, and a grant of £50,000 by a grateful Irish Parliament freed him from money worries. His career thereafter was something of an anti-climax; but his advocacy of tithe reform in the mid-1780s, of CATHOLIC RELIEF in the early 1790s and of a middle way between the forces of conservatism and revolution in the late 1790s ensured that he remained prominent. He also made a last-ditch effort to resist a legislative union, though his election to the British Parliament, where his energies were devoted to the pursuit of CATHOLIC EMANCIPATION, gave his later years direction as well as purpose. His burial in Westminster Abbey in 1820 epitomised the respect in which he was generally held by the time of his death. **James Kelly**

'Grattan's parliament', a name given to the Irish Parliament in relation to the eighteen years (1782–1800) during which it possessed the unrestricted power to make law, though not used at the time. HENRY GRATTAN, who proposed the motion that hastened the achievement of LEGISLATIVE INDEPENDENCE, was an MP for most of those years. In the 1830s and 40s, as repeal of the ACT OF UNION rose to the top of the political agenda, figures such as DANIEL O'CONNELL and Henry Grattan Junior, looking back to the late eighteenth century for validation of their cause, coined and popularised the term; it has remained current ever since. **James Kelly**

Graves, Alfred Perceval (1846–1931), poet and anthologist. Born in Dublin; educated in England and at TCD. He spent his working life as an educationalist and civil servant in London. He wrote popular light verses, among them the well-known ballad

Grattan's parliament. The Irish House of Commons: Henry Grattan urging the Claim of Irish Right *by Francis Wheatley* (1780). *Henry Grattan (standing right, in red) addresses the assembly, during the debate on the repeal of Poynings' Law (19 April 1780), in the rotunda of the Parliament House; the mace of the Commons lies on the baize-covered table; the Lord Chancellor sits under the canopy (left). [Leeds Museums and Galleries (Lotherton Hall)/Bridgman Art Library; LMG100389]*

'FATHER O'FLYNN', and assembled pioneering anthologies of ANGLO-IRISH LITERATURE. He was the father of the English poet and novelist Robert Graves. **Terence Brown**

Graves, Robert James (1796–1853), physician. Born in Dublin; educated at TCD. He worked at the Meath Hospital, where he introduced the use of the stethoscope in 1821; he is responsible for describing exophthalmic goitre ('Graves' disease'). A lecturer at Park Street Medical School, he was also king's professor of the institutes of medicine at Trinity College, Dublin, and president of the College of Physicians. He is credited with descriptions of peripheral neuritis and angioneurotic oedema. **J. B. Lyons**

grave-slabs, flat stones usually inscribed or decorated with crosses, and frequently both, dating from the EARLY HISTORIC period. More than 800 are known, at least half of them (many fragmentary) from CLONMACNOISE. Important collections also come from other sites in Co. Offaly, such as Gallen and Durrow, but Inishcealtra, Co. Clare, GLENDALOUGH, Co. Wicklow, NENDRUM, Co. Down, INNISHMURRAY and Carrowntemple, Co. Sligo, Tullylease, Co. Cork, and Church Island, Co. Kerry, have produced further interesting specimens. Not surprisingly, the greatest variety is found at Clonmacnoise, where equal-armed crosses of various forms are placed in roughly square (or occasionally round) frames, though Latin crosses with long stems predominate, their forms—usually with a ring around the junction of arms and shaft—probably copied from wooden or metal models. One of the commonest variations in Clonmacnoise (though also found elsewhere) has expanded terminals, which, together with the central circle, are decorated with spirals or interlace.

The equal-armed square-framed type may be the earliest, as the inscription *Ailill aue Dunchatho* found on one with Greek meander decoration from Athlone county may be equated with Ailill ó Dúnchaidh, a Connacht king who died in 764. The group with Latin crosses having decorated expanding terminals probably flourished during the ninth and tenth centuries, as witnessed by the lost example bearing the name *Suibine mac Mailae Humai*, probably identifiable with Suibhne son of Maolumha, a Clonmacnoise scribe who died in 887; but equating names on slabs with historically recorded persons is now considered less reliable than previously thought.

The inscriptions are usually in Irish, starting with the words *Ōr do*, asking a prayer for the person whose name follows. One on Innishmurray uses the Latin formula *Hic dormit*, 'Here sleeps', one of the few proofs that such slabs were in fact gravestones. While they were probably placed flat in the ground, few have been recorded in their original position. The style of such slabs continued into the later Middle Ages. [see CHURCHES, EARLY; HIGH CROSSES.] **Peter Harbison**

grave-slabs. *Grave-slab, Clonmacnoise, Co. Offaly, with cross with D-shaped terminals and the inscription Ōr do Thuathal Saer ('a prayer for Thuathal the Wright'). [Dúchas, The Heritage Service]*

Gray, Eileen (1878–1976), designer, architect, and artist. Born in Enniscorthy, Co. Wexford; attended Slade School of Fine Art, London. She moved permanently to Paris in 1907. Initiated into Japanese lacquerwork by the Japanese artist Sugawara, she became famous for her exquisite lacquer screens, furniture, and interior designs. After the FIRST WORLD WAR, however, she became disillusioned with the extravagant luxury of the Parisian beau monde and became deeply interested in the new architectural ideas coming out of the Netherlands with the De Stijl movement. She formed a liaison with a young Romanian architect, Jean Badovici, who encouraged her interest in ARCHITECTURE and introduced her to Le Corbusier and other avant-garde architects of the time. She designed a house at Roquebrune in the south of France called 'E1027' (the first letters and last digit represent EG, the middle three digits, JB) (completed 1929) that is considered a seminal work of twentieth-century architecture; she also designed all the furniture for the house as prototypes for mass production. From the 1920s on she designed only in the modernist vein, and she is considered a central figure of the modern movement. The NATIONAL MUSEUM OF IRELAND has acquired the contents of her apartment in Paris, including some original prototypes, her portfolio, and archives. **Dorothy Walker**

Gray, Elizabeth (Betsy) (c. 1780–1798), a heroine in popular accounts of the BATTLE OF BALLYNAHINCH (1798). Historians cannot agree about her origins, with rival claims from Killinchy, Dromara, and Gransha, near Bangor, Co. Down. Tradition holds that she was a beautiful young woman who encouraged the rebels while mounted on a white horse and carrying a green flag. Betsy, her brother George and sweetheart Willie Boal were brutally slain after the battle by yeomen, and all three were buried near where they fell at Ballycreen, near Ballynahinch. Her memory was used ambiguously in the nineteenth century. Home-rule nationalists used the story to illustrate the brutal repression of Ireland's bid for independence, while unionists, including many Presbyterian descendants of the United Irishmen, used her to remember the heroism of 1798 but to forget the politics. Ugly tensions surfaced in 1898 when unionists destroyed her gravestone to prevent home-rulers appropriating her memory. **Allan Blackstock**

Gray, Eileen. *Adjustable chrome table designed by Eileen Gray in 1927 for* E1027, *the house she designed and furnished in association with Jean Badovici at Roquebrune on the French Riviera. [National Museum of Ireland]*

Greacen, Robert (1920–), poet and literary journalist. Born in Derry; educated at Methodist College in Belfast, which remains the city most associated with him. His father failed at farming and other pursuits, and Greacen's poem on their painful relationship, 'Father and Son', is one of the finest on this theme in modern Irish writing. After moving to Dublin during the war years, when he shared lodgings with PATRICK KAVANAGH, he made an auspicious start as a poet and as anthologist with *Northern Harvest* (1944), *Irish Harvest* (1946), and *Contemporary Irish Poetry* (1949). His romantic and earnest early verse succumbed to leaner, more astringent tones, frequently expressed through the persona of Captain Fox, a furtive and powerful figure of cosmopolitan interests. However, in the final version of his memoirs, *The Sash My Father Wore* (1997), it is to the Protestant lower middle-class Belfast of his youth that he ruefully returns. His election to membership of Aosdána in the 1980s brought a return to Dublin and a warm recognition of his place in Irish letters. **Rory Brennan**

Great Book of Ireland, The, a gallery and anthology of contemporary Irish art and poetry. A huge volume of 250 pages (510 by 360 by 110 mm), it brings together the work of 121 artists, 143 poets, and nine composers, who painted, drew and wrote directly on the vellum leaves. The response of the calligrapher Denis Brown to each opening serves to unify the book, which was bound in elm by A. G. Cains. Éamonn Martin and Gene Lambert of Mills Trust (which caters for people with disabilities) and THEO DORGAN of *Poetry Ireland* initiated the project in 1989. [see CALLIGRAPHY; CRAFTS AFTER 1945.] **Timothy O'Neill**

Great Eastern, steamship. When completed in London in June 1859 it was 211 m (692 ft) long and more than 18,000 tons burden, four times longer than any other ship afloat; no bigger ship was completed for another forty years. The tourist industry and transatlantic commercial exchanges were not developed enough for its numerous cabins and large holds to be nearly filled; but it was a triumphant success both in proving that much larger ships than previously existed were safe and capable of better speed and in its laying from Valentia Island, Co. Kerry, of the first North Atlantic and later the first South ATLANTIC TELEGRAPH CABLES, under the command of ROBERT HALPIN. This cable-laying exercise followed a paper presented to the ROYAL DUBLIN SOCIETY by Matthew Fontaine Maury, a Virginian of Irish Huguenot origin. The *Great Eastern* visited Dublin once in 1886 with a trade fair, where its size greatly perturbed the port authority (see p. 469). **John de Courcy Ireland**

Great Famine, the. Between 1845 and 1850 some 1.1 million people in Ireland—about an eighth of the population—died from famine-related causes and a further 1 million emigrated in what was the greatest social catastrophe of modern Irish history. The trigger was the appearance in 1845 of POTATO blight, a fungal disease that devastated the potato crop for four of the next five seasons.

Ireland suffered more than neighbouring countries for two reasons. The country was highly vulnerable because of rapid POPULATION growth, agricultural and industrial stagnation after 1815, chronic underinvestment, a highly inequitable agrarian system, and increasing exposure to British and international markets; and by the 1840s large sections of the rural population were wholly dependent on the subsistence potato harvest, while much of the grain and animal production was exported, often by Catholic farmers and merchants, who might have been expected to be more sensitive to the plight of their co-religionists. The second reason was the failure of the British government to alleviate the crisis. Though small amounts of food were procured by the PEEL government in 1845–6, in the wake of the repeal of the CORN LAWS imports were left to private enterprise, and price regulation was abandoned. Large quantities of INDIAN MEAL arrived from the summer of 1847 but only after a six-month 'starvation gap' produced massive mortality. Lord JOHN RUSSELL's government continued the provision of relief works under the BOARD OF WORKS in 1846–7 but was forced to abandon

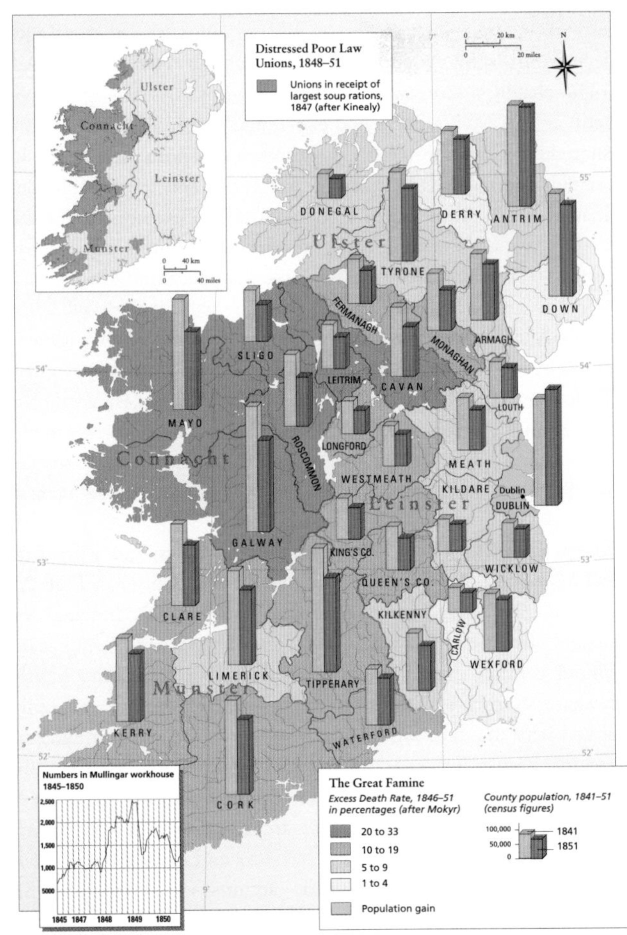

Great Famine. The Discovery of the Potato Blight in Ireland *(1847) by Daniel McDonald. Painted at the height of the Famine, it depicts a farmer and his family discovering that their potato store is destroyed by the disease. [Courtesy of the Department of Irish Folklore, University College, Dublin]*

this as an expensive failure. Only the provision of 'stirabout' (a thin porridge made from maize, rice and oats) to 3 million people at soup kitchens in the summer of 1847 reduced the death rate from starvation and related diseases. Relief was subsequently restricted to what was available under the Poor Law at the overcrowded and pestilential WORKHOUSES and their outdoor yards. Further government expenditure was vetoed by Sir CHARLES TREVELYAN at the Treasury, who believed the Famine was divinely ordained to force the Irish into self-reliance. Famine conditions continued in much of the west until 1850 and in some places beyond.

The Famine was exacerbated by widespread clearances by landlords, assisted by the GREGORY CLAUSE of the Poor Law. Private charity, especially by the QUAKERS, provided some assistance in 1846–7 but fell away afterwards. The Great Famine transformed Irish society and the ECONOMY and left a legacy of bitterness in Ireland and its DIASPORA (see pp. 153, 375). [see FAMINES; FAMINE OF 1739–41; FAMINE REFUGEES IN CANADA; IN ENGLAND AND WALES; IN SCOTLAND; IN THE UNITED STATES; FAMINE AND SUBSISTENCE CRISES; FOOD, POST-FAMINE; FOOD, TRADITIONAL; MOORE, DAVID.] **Peter Gray**

Great Famine, diseases of the, Between 1845 and 1852, marasmus (starvation) and opportunistic diseases accounted for more than a million excess deaths in Ireland. The prevalent infections were typhus fever, relapsing fever, enteric fever, dysentery, diarrhoea, influenza, measles, pneumonia, smallpox, TUBERCULOSIS, and Asiatic cholera in 1848–9. Scurvy and dropsy, two non-infectious conditions arising from food deficiencies, were also rife. [see PEASANT SOCIETY.] **Laurence M. Geary**

Great Hunger, The (1942), a poem by PATRICK KAVANAGH. It is one of the most powerful, moving and visionary of twentieth-century Irish poems; in it Kavanagh debunks the myth of the happy peasant and idyllic rural life. Through his protagonist, Patrick Maguire, a middle-aged farmer living with his aged mother, he explores the harsh world of the small farmer. Maguire is poor, sexually frustrated, angry, and deadened by privation; his farm is a spiritual desert on which he has wasted his life. A landmark long poem, *The Great Hunger* has had a wide influence on Kavanagh's successors. [see PEASANT SOCIETY.] **Eamonn Wall**

Greatrakes, Valentine (the 'Irish Stroker' or faith healer) (1628–1683), healer. Born in Affane, Co. Waterford. A farmer who served in CROMWELL's army, he was also registrar for transplantation. In 1662 he claimed that he could cure the king's evil (scrofula) by 'stroking' or touching but failed in a demonstration before CHARLES II. He resumed farming in 1668 on £1,000 a year. **C. S. Breathnach**

Green, Rev. William Spotswood (1847–1919), marine scientist. Born in Youghal, Co. Cork; graduated from the University of Dublin in 1871 and ordained in the Church of Ireland in 1872.

Always interested in the sea, he became an expert in marine science. He was commissioned by the Royal Irish Academy and the Royal Dublin Society to organise marine expeditions and to write reports on the fishing industry. In 1890 he became an inspector of Irish fisheries and in 1900 the chief inspector. He made an immense contribution to the expansion, modernisation, and scientific management of Ireland's fisheries. **Charles Mollan**

Green Party, formed in the Republic by the ecology movement and the Green Alliance of the 1970s. A meeting to form a party was held in Dublin in 1981, and the Ecology Party of Ireland emerged. In the general election of November 1982 this party put up seven candidates and won 0.2 per cent of the first-preference vote, an average of 1.3 per cent in the constituencies contested. It changed its name in 1983 to the Green Alliance (Comhaontas Glas) and to the Green Party (Comhaontas Glas) in 1987. The party's first significant electoral success was in 1989, when Roger Garland became the party's first member of Dáil Éireann, representing Dublin South. This breakthrough was reflected in LOCAL GOVERNMENT elections in 1991. In June 1994 the Green Party won a significant achievement with the election of two members (out of fifteen) to the European Parliament; it has improved on this level of electoral support at subsequent EU, national, and local elections. In 1997 it gained 2.8 per cent of the first-preference vote and elected two members to DÁIL ÉIREANN; in the 1999 local elections its support was 2.5 per cent; and in the 1999 election 6.5 per cent of the vote gave the party two members of the European Parliament. **Neil Collins**

Greatrakes. *Valentine Greatrakes, the 'Irish Stroker', in an engraving by William Faithorne the Elder, 'curing' his first patient, William Maher of Salterbridge, Cappoquin, Co. Waterford. Greatrakes claimed he could heal by the stroke of his hand alone. [Council of Trustees of the National Library of Ireland]*

Greevy, Bernadette (1940–), singer. Born in Dublin; studied with Jean Nolan in Dublin, at the Guildhall School of Music in London, and with Helen Isepp. She has performed on all five continents and is acclaimed as one of today's finest mezzo-sopranos. While principally a recitalist and concert singer, she has also embraced opera in her career; she made her operatic debut in 1962 at the WEXFORD FESTIVAL OPERA and her Covent Garden debut in 1982. A holder of honorary doctorates of music from the National University of Ireland and Trinity College, Dublin, she was appointed the first artist in residence at the DIT Conservatory of Music and Drama in 1996. She has also given master classes in Ireland and abroad and is founder and artistic director of the Anna Livia International Opera Festival. **Paul Collins**

Gregg, John Robert (1867–1948), educationist. Born in Rockorry, Co. Monaghan. He first formulated his new system of shorthand in *Light Line Phonography and Gregg Shorthand Manual* in Liverpool in 1888. He moved to the United States in 1893, where he established the Gregg Publishing Company to promote the system of stenography he had invented, based on a study of the natural movements of the hand. *Gregg Speed Studies* followed in 1917 and the journal *American Shorthand Teacher* in 1920, which later became *American Business World*. The Gregg system became the most widely used system of shorthand in the United States. **Brian Lalor**

Gregory, Lady Isabella (Augusta), née Persse (1852–1932), dramatist, folklorist, and translator. Born in Roxborough, Co. Galway, she became mistress of COOLE PARK, near Gort, on marrying Sir William Gregory in 1880. Here she entertained many writers and provided a summer retreat for W. B. YEATS from 1897. He encouraged her to collect FOLKLORE and to write plays, while she became his enduring patron, collaborator, and colleague. In 1898 she began a lifelong association with the theatre when she obtained a patent and guarantors for the new Irish Literary Theatre, established with Yeats and EDWARD MARTYN. She was posthumously credited as joint author with Yeats of *Cathleen Ni Houlihan* (1902); her own debut as a playwright for the Irish Literary Theatre came the following year with *Twenty-Five*, a one-act comedy, the genre for which she is chiefly renowned.

As well as theatre work she used her newly acquired Irish to translate two collections of epic literature, *Cuchulain of Muirthemne* (1902) and *Gods and Fighting Men* (1904). In 1904 she became a director of the ABBEY THEATRE with Yeats and SYNGE; she proved an able administrator and wily negotiator in her dealings with the theatre's English benefactor, Annie Horniman. She was the author of more than forty plays and translations, several collections of folklore, and 'A Woman's Sonnets', inspired by an early love affair with Wilfrid Scawen Blunt. Her main literary achievements were realising the domestic politics of rural Ireland with comic vivacity for the stage and the development of 'Kiltartanese', a stage mixture of local dialect and Irish syntax that became a standard marker of Abbey speech (see p. 235). **Selina Guinness**

'Gregory clause', an amendment to the POOR RELIEF (IRELAND) ACT (1847) introduced by the Conservative MP and Irish landowner Sir William Gregory (1817–92) of Coole Park, Co. Galway. It excluded from relief all tenants holding more than a quarter of an acre (0.1 ha) of land, and their dependants, and was widely used by landowners to facilitate clearances during the GREAT FAMINE. **Peter Gray**

Grennan, Eamon (1941–), poet. Born in Dublin; educated at UCD and Harvard University. He lives in the United States, where

Greevy. *Bernadette Greevy, one of Ireland's finest mezzo-sopranos. She made her operatic debut at the Wexford Festival Opera in 1962 as Beppe in Mascagni's* L'Amico Fritz. *[RTÉ Stills Library]*

he teaches at Vassar College. His collections include *Wildly for Days* (1983), *What Light There Is* (1987), *As If It Matters* (1991), *So It Goes* (1995), and *Still Life with Waterfall* (2000). His poetry engages warmly with domestic and personal life in richly realised natural settings. **Terence Brown**

Grey, Lord Leonard (died 1541), Lord Deputy of Ireland, 1536–40. The first English Viceroy to take office after the destruction of the FITZGERALDS of Kildare, Grey was faced with a formidable list of problems. Required to pacify the remaining allies of the Fitzgeralds without encouraging the rival BUTLERS of Ormond, Grey was instructed to reduce his garrison and expenditures to a minimum while overseeing the establishment by Parliament of the Reformation of Henry VIII. He moved to ameliorate his position by extending favour to the leaderless but influential GERALDINE LEAGUE in a manner that reduced the threat of disorder and increased his room for manoeuvre; but it also aroused the hostility of the Ormondists and of disappointed English officials in Dublin. Similarly, his refusal to antagonise local opinion by an aggressive enforcement of the REFORMATION lost him the support of the Archbishop of Dublin, George Browne. Serious complaints against him from a variety of sources prompted the establishment of a royal commission of inquiry in 1538; but despite the serious nature of the charges against him, the commission's findings were shelved through the protection of Henry VIII's secretary, Thomas Cromwell, who valued Grey's service in keeping Ireland at peace at minimum cost. In 1540, however, Grey's friendship with Cromwell proved fatal when he fell victim to a palace coup launched against the too-powerful secretary. Mistakenly, Grey pleaded guilty to false charges of treason in the hope of pardon but was executed as a traitor in July 1541. [see FITZGERALD, THOMAS; GERALDINE CONSPIRACY.] **Ciaran Brady**

Grey de Wilton, Arthur (1536–1593), Lord Deputy of Ireland, 1580–82. A professional soldier, appointed Viceroy without any previous experience of Ireland at the height of the second DESMOND REBELLION (1579–83), Grey was determined to re-establish English authority by force. A hasty and poorly planned expedition against the O'Byrnes in Co. Wicklow resulted in disaster at GLENMALUR and heavy loss of life. The landing of a small Papal force in support of the Desmond rebels at Dún an Óir, SMERWICK, Co. Kerry, offered him the opportunity to restore his reputation, which he did by the slaughter of the surrendered garrison and of the civilian population who had sought protection in the fort. His reputation for ferocity was heightened by a purge of suspect elements in the English PALE, during which several leading figures were arrested and charged with treason and several, including a Chief Justice, summarily put to death. Grey, however, failed to end the Desmond Rebellion or even to stifle disorders in Leinster, and his lack of progress, together with rising protests from the Pale, led to his early recall. A sincerely religious man of some literary talent who employed the poet EDMUND SPENSER as his private secretary while in office, Grey's conduct contributed greatly to the alienation of hitherto sympathetic OLD ENGLISH groups in Ireland from the Tudor monarchy. **Ciaran Brady**

greyhound racing. Racing after a mechanical lure was introduced in America in 1921. Celtic Park, Belfast, staged the first such race in Ireland on 18 April 1927, followed some weeks later by the opening of Shelbourne Park, Dublin, on 14 May. The Irish Coursing Club had been the governing body until the state-sponsored Bord na gCon assumed control of racing in 1958. Racing in Northern Ireland remains the responsibility of the Irish Coursing Club.

The sport suffered badly during the recession of the 1990s but under the chairmanship of Paschal Taggart has been one of the great success stories of recent years. Attendances have soared, in line with a redevelopment programme that has seen the building of multi-million-pound stadiums. There are now fifteen tracks in the Republic and three in Northern Ireland. The greatest greyhound was Spanish Battleship, trained by Tom Lynch to win the Irish

Derby in 1953, 1954, and 1955. The Irish Derby, the richest greyhound event in the world, is run at Shelbourne Park. It was run over 480 m (525 yards) up to 1985, with Bashful Man the fastest winner, in 28.83 seconds, while the winner in 2000, Judicial Pride, was the fastest over 502 m (550 yards), in 29.68 seconds.

Coursing a live hare is one of the oldest sports in the world. The first official meeting was held in 1858 on Lord Lurgan's estate in Co. Armagh. The principal events today are the National Coursing Meeting at Clonmel, Co. Tipperary, each February, first staged in 1925, and the Irish Cup, first run on the Earl of Dunraven's estate in Clounanna, outside Adare, Co. Limerick, in 1906 and held annually there between 1913 and 1999; Tralee, Co. Kerry, became its new venue in 2000. MASTER MCGRATH is regarded as the greatest coursing dog of modern times. **Michael Fortune**

Greystones (*Na Clocha Liatha*), Co. Wicklow, a seaside town 8 km (5 miles) south of Bray; population (2002) 7,369. The town owes its name to a local outcrop of Cambrian rock and slate. Recent growth is associated with its proximity to Dublin, for which it now functions as a dormitory suburb, while the extension of the DART electric rail service is likely to lead to a further increase in population. The RAILWAY has been of great significance in the evolution of the town. Originally a fishing village, with the extension of the Dublin–Bray line in 1855 it began to develop as a seaside resort. Thirty years later the harbour was built (1885–97) to encourage the fishing industry, to allow for the importing of coal and Bangor slates, and to provide amenities for visitors. During the nineteenth century the La Touche family, local landowners, developed their lands for summer visitors, while at the beginning of the twentieth century the Burnaby estate was developed to cater for permanent residents. A notable feature of the local population was the high proportion of Protestant residents, at more than 70 per cent in 1861. **Ruth McManus**

Grier, Stephen (1824–1894), collector of TRADITIONAL MUSIC. Born in Abbeylara, Co. Longford, he lived at Gortletteragh, Co. Leitrim. A farmer by occupation, he was a noted piper and FIDDLE-player, collecting and transcribing almost a thousand tunes during his lifetime. His manuscript, completed in 1883, was passed on to his protégé William Mulvey and remains unpublished. Sixty-four tunes from the manuscript appear in BRENDÁN BREATHNACH's *Ceol Rince na hÉireann, 4* (1996); almost thirty tunes taken from the manuscript are featured on the recordings *Leitrim's Hidden Treasure* (1998) and *A Piper's Dream* (2000). **Brian McNamara**

Griffin, Gerald (1803–1840), writer. Born in Limerick into a middle-class Catholic family. He had a scrappy education but an idyllic childhood, brought to an end in 1820 by his parents' emigration to America. Inspired by his friendship with JOHN BANIM, he decided to be a writer and went to London to work as a playwright. Failing at this, he turned to journalism and in 1826 published a collection of regional stories, *Holland-Tide*, before returning to Ireland the following year. THE COLLEGIANS was his most successful novel, published in 1829, the year in which he met Lydia Fisher, with whom he fell in love. Growing restive with writing, he burnt most of his manuscripts and entered the CHRISTIAN BROTHERS in 1838. He died of typhus in Cork. [see GOTHIC FICTION.] **James H. Murphy**

Griffith, Arthur (1871–1922), journalist and politician. Born in Dublin; educated at Mary's Place CBS and Strand Street. He left school at twelve and became a compositor, and worked in South Africa, 1897–8. He edited a series of newspapers: *United Irishman*, *Sinn Féin*, *Scissors and Paste*, and *Nationality*. In 1905 he founded SINN FÉIN, which aimed to achieve a 'dual monarchy' between Britain and Ireland, based on the Austro-Hungarian model, and advocated a non-violent struggle for independence. Imprisoned many times between 1916 and 1921, he led the Dáil Éireann delegation that negotiated the ANGLO-IRISH TREATY (1921). He was President of Dáil Éireann from January 1922 until his death on 12 August (see p. 43). **Brian Maye**

Griffith, John Purser (1848–1938), civil engineer. Born in Holyhead, Wales; educated at TCD. He was Assistant Engineer of DUBLIN PORT, 1871–98, and Chief Engineer, 1899–1913, responsible for dredging the port, rebuilding the north quays, and installing ELECTRICITY. He was chairman of the Water Power Resources Committee, 1918, and established a machine-won peat operation in 1920. **Ronald Cox**

Griffith, Sir Richard John (1784–1878), geologist, engineer, valuator, and surveyor. Born in Dublin; educated at schools in Portarlington, Rathangan, and Dublin. One of the most talented Irishmen of the nineteenth century, he served briefly in the Royal Irish Regiment of Artillery before resigning in 1801 to devote himself to scientific studies. In 1809 the DUBLIN SOCIETY commissioned him to undertake a geological investigation of the Leinster coal district, and he soon began to display his remarkable ability in the simultaneous performance of the duties of several offices. He worked as an engineer with the Bog Commissioners, 1809–13, and was mining engineer with the Dublin Society, 1812–29. For many years following 1822 he was responsible for the construction of roads over much of Munster. From 1825 to the 1840s he had close involvement with the ORDNANCE SURVEY as director of the Boundary Survey. He was Commissioner of the General Survey and Valuation of Rateable Property, 1827–68, in which capacity he devised what is still known as the GRIFFITH VALUATION.

In 1811 he began the construction of a pioneering geological map of Ireland, and later he conducted an unofficial geological survey of Ireland from within the Valuation Office. As one of the four railway Commissioners appointed in 1836 he secured the publication of his geological map, first on a small scale in 1838 and then on the quarter-inch (1:253,440) scale in 1839. A superb map, it has led to Griffith being acclaimed the 'father of Irish geology'. He was deputy chairman of the BOARD OF WORKS, 1846–50, and chairman, 1850–64. He was made a baronet in 1858. **Gordon L. Herries Davies**

Griffith valuation. The Primary Valuation of Tenements, 1848–64, was initiated under acts of the British Parliament of 1846 and 1852. It was undertaken by RICHARD J. GRIFFITH to provide a basis for assessing local taxes through an equitable and uniform system; the valuation is most commonly referred to as the Griffith valuation, commemorating his influential role in its realisation.

A survey of the entire country was undertaken by 150 surveyors, with detailed instructions from Griffith on how the values were to be calculated. Land was valued in respect of its productive capacity. The assumed potential value of yearly agricultural produce was based on an assessment of the fertility of the SOIL; what were termed 'peculiar local circumstances,' such as CLIMATE and proximity to markets, modified this value either up or down. Building valuations were calculated in respect of net annual letting value. With the publication of the Armagh valuation in 1865 the project was completed. Details are recorded in tabular form, with townlands arranged alphabetically within their civil parishes, baronies, and POOR LAW unions. The information at tenement scale includes reference numbers to the position in the Griffith valuation maps, 6 in. to 1 statute mile (1:10,560), the name of each occupier and immediate lessor, a description of the tenement, its acreage (if relevant), and individual annual valuations for both land and buildings. The final column provides the total annual valuation of the property.

The production of the valuation as a national survey of land value, uniform in both content and form, acted as a reliable guide to the relative value of land in the country. It was employed as an assessment of land value until 1977 in the calculation of RATES, which were paid by owners of agricultural land. The detail recorded at townland level provides the genealogist, historian, and historical geographer with a unique source with which to analyse the changing ownership and occupation of land in Ireland from the middle of the nineteenth century. **Jonathan Cherry**

Grimes, Karl (1955–), photographer. Born in Dublin; educated at UCD and New York University. His work, which explores the aesthetics of science and nature, is represented in a number of public collections in Europe and the United States. His exhibitions include 'Still Life' (1998), 'Stuffed Histories' (2000), and 'Future Nature' (2002). He lectures on photography at DUBLIN CITY INIVERSITY. **Martin Clancy**

Grimes, Philly (1929–1989), hurler. Born in Waterford. His county hurling career spanned the period 1947–65. A fine athlete and a hurler with all the skills, he moved 'like poetry in motion' around centrefield. Playing first as a county minor in 1947, he made his senior county debut in the 1948 Munster championship but was not available for the all-Ireland, as he had emigrated to the United States. After his return he won many honours with his club, Mount Sion, and county. He was the holder of Munster senior hurling titles of 1948, 1957 (when he was captain), 1959, and 1963. He won an all-Ireland in 1959, an Oireachtas title in 1962, a National League in 1963, and Railway Cup medals in 1958 and 1960. He won thirteen senior hurling and four senior football medals with Mount Sion. **Séamus J. King**

Grogan, Nathaniel (c. 1740–1807), landscape and genre painter. Born in Cork, son of a wood-turner; taught painting by John Butts. He enlisted in the British army, serving in the West Indies and also in Philadelphia during the American War of Independence. Returning to Ireland, by way of London, c. 1781, he settled again in Cork, where he painted views of the city and its environs and genre scenes in watercolour and oil. He decorated ceilings in Vernon Mount, Cork, c. 1784, and produced a set of aquatints of Cork in the 1790s. His *Boats on the River Lee below Tivoli* is in the NATIONAL GALLERY OF IRELAND. **Peter Murray**

Groocock, Joseph (1913–1997), composer, organist, adjudicator, accompanist, and broadcaster. Born in Croydon, Surrey; attended St Michael's, Tenbury, as a choral scholar and studied classics and music at Oxford. Living in Ireland from 1937, he was director of music at St Columba's College, Rathfarnham, Co. Dublin, and lectured at the music department, TCD, conducting the University of Dublin Choral Society for more than forty years. He made the works of J. S. Bach his lifelong study and excelled in fugal writing, many of his works being fugues and canons. **Paul Collins**

Grose, Francis (1731–1791), antiquarian and topographical draughtsman. Born in Greenford, Middlesex, son of a Swiss jeweller; studied drawing at Shipley's Drawing School and was a member of the Society of Artists. He exhibited drawings at the Royal Academy,

Griffith, Arthur. *Bronze portrait of Arthur Griffith (1922) by Albert Power. Griffith was the founder of Sinn Féin, chief negotiator of the Anglo-Irish Treaty, and President of Dáil Éireann. [National Gallery of Ireland]*

London, 1769–77, mostly of architectural remains. Of independent means, he was able to follow his interest in antiquarian pursuits; he published many works, including *Antiquities of England and Wales* (1773–6) and *Antiquities of Scotland* (1789–91), and was preparing a similar work on Ireland when he died suddenly at the house of Horace Hone in Dublin. *Antiquities of Ireland* (two volumes, 1791–5) was completed after his death, with engravings by other artists, including his nephew, Daniel Grose. **Eve McAulay**

gross domestic product (GDP) **and gross national product** (GNP), measures of national income. The two measures are distinguished in that GNP is the value of all goods and services produced in a country plus the value of net income from abroad, while GDP is not adjusted for net foreign income. For Ireland, net income flows from abroad are negative, and therefore the value of GDP exceeds that of GNP; in 1999 this difference was just over 15 per cent. This significant difference is to a large extent the result of the activities of subsidiaries of transnational businesses established in Ireland. The total GNP of Ireland in 1999 amounted to €75,975 million. In comparison with the EU average, Irish GNP per capita for 1999 was just below the EU average, at 96.2 per cent, while GDP per capita exceeded the EU average, at 110.6 per cent. These figures, which show that Ireland has almost reached or exceeded the EU average national income levels per capita, are the result of a rapid convergence process. This process occurred largely during the 1990s, since Irish GDP per capita grew only modestly relative to that of the European Union, from 60.8 per cent in 1960 to 63.7 per cent in 1986. **Edgar Morgenroth**

Grosse Île, Canada, now officially Grosse Île and the Irish Memorial National Historic Site, a 3 km^2 (1 sq. mile) island in the

St Lawrence River 46 km (29 miles) north-east of the city of Québec. A quarantine station was opened on the island in May 1832 to check the spread of cholera into North America. More than 60,000 people passed through the station that year; of these, some 50,000 were Irish or British. Despite quarantine efforts, an estimated 6,000 died in Québec and Montréal in 1832–4. Records of the station's 105 years of operation show the most dramatic increase in immigration in 1847, a year of typhus epidemics and extreme famine conditions in Ireland. Numerical accounts from this period vary considerably, because of massive overcrowding and poorly regulated passage conditions. In 1847 Grosse Île's medical superintendent, George Douglas, reported that more than 90,000 people were examined at Grosse Île. He listed 441 ship arrivals during six months of operation; these ships reported approximately 5,000 deaths at sea. Though it has long been contested as an under-estimate of the death toll, the list of 5,424 recorded burials on the island shows mostly Irish names.

After the quarantine station closed in 1937, biological research was conducted under restricted access. The island has since been opened as a national heritage site (see p. 153). [see COFFIN SHIPS; ELLIS ISLAND; FAMINE REFUGEES IN CANADA; FAMINE REFUGEES IN THE UNITED STATES; GREAT FAMINE, DISEASES OF THE.] **Kathleen O'Brien**

Grubb, Sir Howard (1844–1931), instrument-maker. Born in Dublin, son of THOMAS GRUBB; he studied engineering at TCD but in 1865 abandoned this course to enter his father's instrument factory. In 1868 he transferred the factory from Charlemont Bridge on the Grand Canal to its new premises in Rathmines (where Observatory Lane today commemorates its presence), and there he built astronomical TELESCOPES for observatories the world over (see p. 53). He also constructed gun-sights, range-finders, and submarine periscopes; during the FIRST WORLD WAR the Ministry of Munitions transferred the factory to St Albans in Hertfordshire. In 1925 this business became part of a new firm of Sir Howard Grubb, Parsons and Company of Walker Gate, Newcastle-upon-Tyne; he retired in the following year (see p. 53). **Gordon L. Herries Davies**

Grubb, Thomas (1800–78), instrument-maker. Born in Kilkenny; he was a self-taught mechanic of brilliance. By the 1830s he had established in Dublin a firm—soon to become internationally famed—for the construction of astronomical telescopes. Initially his factory was on the Grand Canal near Charlemont Bridge, but in 1868 it was moved to new premises in Rathmines. He built instruments for ARMAGH OBSERVATORY; MARKREE CASTLE, Co. Sligo; Greenwich Observatory, Melbourne; and many other establishments. He also built some microscopes, as well as machines for the printing of bank notes; from 1853 he was engineer to the Bank of Ireland. He retired in 1868, to be succeeded in the business by his son Sir HOWARD GRUBB. **Gordon L. Herries Davies**

Guaire Aidni, overking of Connacht, 656–63. A son of Colmán of Uí Fiachrach Aidni, he married Deog, daughter of Fíngin, King of Cashel, then Órnait of Éoganacht Áine—connections that doubtless reflect his pursuit of ambition in Munster. Defeated near Gort (649) by Diarmait, son of Aed Sláine, King of TARA, he continued to promote Uí Fiachrach against the rival dynasty of Uí Briúin. His successors included his son Muirchertach Nár and grandson Fergal Aidni. Guaire features prominently in HAGIOGRAPHY and king-tales associated with Caimmín of Inishcealtra, Co. Clare, and Ceallach of Killala, Co. Mayo. Portrayed as a paragon of generosity, his daughter Créide features as lover of CANO MAC GARTNÁIN. [see KINGSHIP.] **Ailbhe Mac Shamhráin**

'GUBU'. Public scandals involving politicians are part and parcel of the Republic's politics, and it is ironic that perhaps the most infamous of all comprised no more than a curious set of coincidences that were so badly handled by the Government that they achieved iconic status. In July 1982 Malcolm Macarthur bludgeoned a nurse, Bridie Gargan, to death in the back seat of her car, which was parked in the PHOENIX PARK, Dublin. He was escorted from the scene of the crime by an ambulance, whose driver, seeing the hospital sticker on the car windscreen, mistook him for a doctor with a patient. In August, Macarthur was arrested at the home of the ATTORNEY-GENERAL, Patrick Connolly, where he had been staying as a house guest for some weeks. The Attorney-General continued with his holiday plans and left the country for New York without making a statement to the Gardaí, thus adding to the immense damage to the Government. The TAOISEACH, CHARLES HAUGHEY, subsequently described the affair as 'grotesque, unbelievable, bizarre, and unprecedented,' leading to the invention of the acronym 'GUBU', coined by CONOR CRUISE O'BRIEN and widely used to describe some of the strange incidents that continue to dog Irish governments. **Maura Adshead**

Guerin, Veronica (1959–96), journalist. Following periods in accountancy and public relations she became a journalist with the *Sunday Business Post* and later the *Sunday Tribune*. After moving to the *Sunday Independent* in 1994 she zealously investigated Ireland's gangland. In 1996 she was shot dead in her car while stopped at traffic lights on the Naas Road outside Dublin. Her murder—the only one of a journalist in the Republic—was planned and carried out by a drugs-importing gang; it led to more than 150 arrests and a crackdown on organised CRIME. **Eddie Holt**

Guevara, Ernesto 'Che' (1928–1967), Marxist revolutionary. Born in Rosario, Argentina, son of Ernesto Guevara Lynch, descendant of a Galway woman, Ana Lynch y Oritz, who settled in Argentina in the eighteenth century; educated at the University of Buenos Aires. He abandoned his medical practice to become a Marxist revolutionary, ranging over Central and South America. He joined Fidel Castro in Mexico in 1955 and helped plan and execute the overthrow of the right-wing Batista regime in Cuba, 1954–9. From 1965 he attempted to export revolution to other Latin American countries and the rest of the world. In Bolivia he was captured and shot by state forces. **David Kiely**

'Guildford Four', a name given to the victims of the first in a series of miscarriages of justice concerning convictions for IRA bombings in England. Patrick Armstrong, Gerard Conlon, and Paul Hill, all from Belfast, and Carole Richardson, an Englishwoman, were convicted of the bombing of two pubs in Guildford, Surrey, in 1974 in which five people died. Despite a confession by the real perpetrators a short time later, they spent fifteen years in prison on the strength of forced confessions. Their convictions were found to be unsafe in 1989. **Martin Clancy**

guilds, associations of craftsmen or merchants formed to provide for their mutual aid and protection in the cities and towns of medieval Europe. The system was introduced to Ireland with the Anglo-Normans and was nowhere more developed than in Dublin, where it remained in operation for more than 600 years. In 1192

Lord John granted the city the right to have guilds. This, known as the *guild merchant*, is probably the earliest establishment of a Dublin guild and included merchants and craftsmen. Members had an exclusive right to trade in their locality or within a particular branch of industry or commerce. The native Irish were excluded from membership. By the fifteenth century the population of craftsmen had grown to warrant the establishment of separate craft guilds.

Guilds came to dominate the economy and social life of towns and cities. Guild halls were constructed for meetings, and in the fifteenth century guilds were established under the patronage of a saint and maintain a local chapel in the parish church to be used by its members. In 1451 Henry VI permitted the foundation of a guild under the patronage of the Holy Trinity, with an associated chapel for members.

From the eighteenth century the economic power of the guilds began to decline as their monopoly over commerce and industry faltered. This led to a concentration on politics instead, which later created a political hegemony that ceased only with the Municipal Corporations (Ireland) Act (1840). **Susan Foran**

Guilfoyle, Ronan (1958–), jazz musician. Born in Dublin. Self-taught, he has been a central figure in the development of JAZZ in Ireland. He has been the main influence in developing formal jazz tuition at Newpark Music Centre, Blackrock, Co. Dublin, where he is director of jazz studies. His first musical experiences as a bass guitarist were in jazz-rock, but soon afterwards he began playing jazz professionally. At the age of twenty-one he became one of Ireland's very few full-time jazz musicians. He formed early associations with the bassist Dave Holland and the saxophonist Dave Liebman through attending a jazz summer school in Banff, Alberta, and has since developed a wide international network of jazz connections. Four in One, formed with his brother, the drummer Conor Guilfoyle, the guitarist Mike Nielsen and the American saxophonist Mike McMullen, set new standards for ensemble playing in the late 1980s. He has been a tireless organiser of jazz events, including concerts based on the music of composers such as Ornette Coleman, Kenny Wheeler, Thelonius Monk, Charlie Haden, and Charlie Parker. One of his several CDs, *Bird* (2000), features Parker's music played by Lingua Franca, which includes the New York musicians Rick Peckham (guitar) and Tom Rainey (drums). Long interested in expanding the rhythmic range of jazz, Guilfoyle has published *Creative Rhythmic Concepts for Jazz Improvisation* (1999) and has worked with Irish and Indian traditional musicians. He has also written material for theatre and television. **Brian Trench**

Guinness, Hon. Desmond (1931–), writer and architectural preservationist. A member of the Guinness brewing family, he is a son of the poet and novelist Lord Moyne and Diana Mosley, one of the famous Mitford sisters; educated at the University of Oxford. With his wife, Mariga Guinness (1932–1989), he founded the IRISH GEORGIAN SOCIETY in 1958, with a view to preserving the eighteenth-century architectural heritage of Ireland; he was acting president of the society, 1958–91. He has published many books on Irish architectural history, including *Irish Houses and Castles* (1971), *Georgian Dublin* (1979), and, with Jacqueline O'Brien, *Great Irish Houses and Castles* (1992) and *Dublin: A Grand Tour* (1994). **Ciarán Deane**

Guinness, Mary Catherine (May) (1863–1955), artist. Born in Dublin; studied in Paris at the Académie de la Grande Chaumière, c. 1907–10, as a pupil of Kees van Dongen, 1912, and at the Académie Lhôte, 1922–5. She was in her forties before she began her professional career. She exhibited in Dublin, London, and Paris, showing work regularly at the progressive Salon des Indépendants. Despite her studies with the cubist André Lhôte, her work more generally reflects the influence of Fauvism, especially her use of strong colour. Her subject matter was frequently drawn from her travels in France, Belgium, Italy, and Palestine. She was awarded the Croix de Guerre for her work as a military nurse, 1914–18. She collected modern European paintings, including work by Bonnard, Dufy, Picasso, and Rouault. **Daire O'Connell**

Guinness Brewery. In 1759 Arthur Guinness acquired a brewery in James's Street, Dublin. Restructuring of the beer taxation regime in 1795 and a wartime boom contributed to the brewery's dramatic growth in the early nineteenth century. The firm became Ireland's premier brewery in the 1830s, specialising in 'single' and 'double' stouts. The growth of the brewery was fuelled by an expanded British export trade and by the penetration of Irish provincial markets. Guinness became a public company in 1886; it is now part of the drinks giant Diageo. **K. J. James**

Guinness family, philanthropists and politicians, one of the world's greatest brewing dynasties. Arthur Guinness (1725–1803) took possession of a small brewery in James's Street, Dublin, in 1759. Later he began brewing a dark-coloured beer that became known as 'stout' in the 1820s. In 1893 his son, Arthur (1768–1855), became head of the firm and other family interests, building the brewery into a large-scale enterprise before surrendering effective

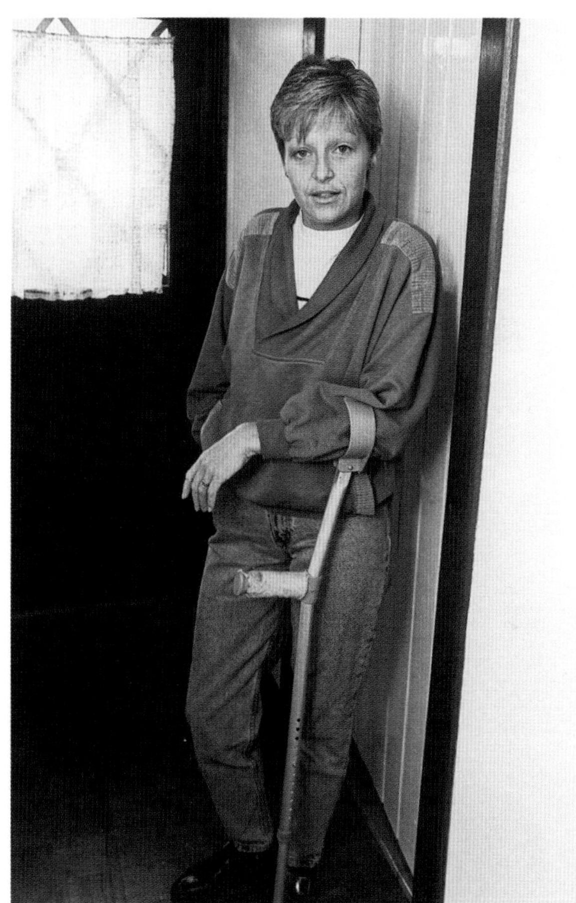

Guerin. *Veronica Guerin, investigative journalist, in the hallway of her home (20 February 1995), where three weeks previously an unidentified assailant shot her in the thigh. She was murdered in 1996 in retaliation for her extensive reporting on organised crime. [Derek Speirs/Report]*

control in 1839–40 to his son, Richard Samuel. Arthur was a director of the Bank of Ireland from 1808, deputy governor from 1818, and governor from 1820. A moderate Liberal, he supported CATHOLIC EMANCIPATION in the 1820s and the Reform Bill (1832). Richard Samuel Guinness (1797–1857) and his brother, Benjamin Lee Guinness (1798–1868), ushered in a period of dynamic expansion while also being involved in politics and philanthropic work. Richard Samuel served as an MP, while Benjamin Lee (knighted in 1867) was Lord Mayor of Dublin in 1851 and Conservative MP for Dublin from 1865 until his death. He contributed large sums for the restoration of ST PATRICK'S CATHEDRAL, Dublin. His two sons, Arthur (1840–1915) and Edward Cecil (1847–1927), took over the business in 1868. Arthur was Conservative MP for Dublin, 1874–80. Withdrawing from the business in 1878, he was created Baron Ardilaun in 1880 and is remembered for contributing substantial sums for the restoration of MARSH'S LIBRARY, for the Coombe Hospital, for the construction of artisans' dwellings, and for the donation of St Stephen's Green, Dublin, as a public park in 1880.

Under Edward Cecil Grimes, Guinness was converted into a public company in 1886. He contributed large sums for slum clearance, housing projects, and medical causes; he was created Baron Iveagh in 1891. Created first Earl Iveagh in 1919, he headed the firm and also served as Chancellor of the University of Dublin. His son, Rupert Edward Cecil Lee Guinness (1874–1967), was chairman from 1927 to 1962 and an MP, 1908–10, 1912–27. Thereafter the family remained prominent in the company until the 1980s, and continued its philanthropic tradition. **Alan O'Day**

Gúm, An. *Cover of* Buntús Cainte, *published by An Gúm. A Government initiative, An Gúm was founded in 1926 to provide reading material in Irish for schools and the general public. [An Gúm]*

Guinness Jazz Festival, established in 1978 and held annually in Cork. Ireland's foremost jazz event, the festival is held annually during the last weekend of October, attracting upwards of 35,000 visitors to Cork. The festival has featured many of the world's leading jazz performers, including LOUIS STEWART, Ella Fitzgerald, Dizzy Gillespie, Sonny Rollins, Oscar Peterson, Dave Brubeck, and George Shearing. Originally sponsored by John Player and Sons, the principal sponsor of the festival since 1981 has been Guinness (see p. 564). **Paul Collins**

Gulf Stream and North Atlantic Drift, part of the main *gyre* or circulation cycle of surface water in the North Atlantic Ocean, moving heat from the Equator to the Arctic. Solar-heated WATER from equatorial areas collects around the Caribbean and the Gulf of Mexico; this is forced northwards as *geostrophic current* by wind action and the Earth's rotation (Coriolis and horizontal pressure gradient forces) off the coast of eastern North America. It moves as a fast 'river' of warm water, reaching depths of more than 600 m (2,000 ft), at a maximum speed of approximately 2 m/s ($4\frac{1}{2}$ miles/h) and with a surface temperature off Florida of more than 24°C (75°F). Peak values of water transport of approximately 150,000 m^3 per second occur at approximately 65° W.

Under the influence of dominant westerly winds the Gulf Stream fans out progressively and diffuses heat eastwards. In this process the changing warmer water mass becomes the North Atlantic Drift. At approximately 30° W this splits. Cooled water returns southwards (as the Canaries Current); the remaining relatively warm water continues on to European coasts. Further dividing of the North Atlantic Drift takes place, moving this water around Ireland and Britain, northwards to Scandinavia, and north-westwards to Iceland and south-west Greenland.

The effect of the North Atlantic Drift on Ireland's shelf waters and atmosphere is to maintain much warmer conditions than would be expected for its northerly position—approximately the same latitude as southern arctic Canada. It increases the biological productivity and biodiversity of marine environments and helps reduce extremes of atmospheric temperature and climate over land, with a difference between winter and summer temperatures of only approximately 10°C (50°F). A possible result of increased global warming would be a reduction in ocean circulation, in effect shutting down the warming effects of the North Atlantic Drift on Ireland, Britain, and Continental Europe and allowing cold polar water to move southwards, as happened during earlier glacial times. [see CLIMATE; COASTAL EROSION.] **Robert J. N. Devoy**

Gulliver's Travels (1726), a satirical novel by JONATHAN SWIFT. It is one of the most famous satires in English, with a strong moral purpose; Swift told Alexander Pope that he wrote it to prove that man was not a rational being but merely an animal capable of reason. The narrator, Lemuel Gulliver, travels to lands where the humans are minute (Lilliput), where they are gigantic (Brobdingnag), where they lack common sense (Balnibarbi), and where they are bestial creatures ruled over by rational horses (Houyhnhnmland). On each voyage we see human behaviour through the eyes of creatures not equipped to judge it sympathetically—and see its irrationality. The Lilliputians appear not as entertaining miniature people but as vain, envious hypocrites. When Gulliver tries to explain normal human behaviour—wars, religious controversies, politics, and social conventions—to the giant King of Brobdingnag, the king dismisses humans as 'little odious vermin'. Swift satirises contemporary science in Gulliver's third voyage, while in the last book he brings Gulliver to a land where horses behave rationally and creatures with the appearance of humans (the Yahoos) behave like brutes. Gulliver tries desperately to copy the horses and to appear rational, but they recognise him as a Yahoo with clothes on and expel him.

Swift's message is clear: humans are a mixture of the rational and the animal; we should recognise our limitations and strive to reform ourselves. Ever since the book's appearance readers have recognised the validity of Swift's criticism of humankind as well as enjoying the lucid prose style and the humour of this fantastic tale. [see ENLIGHTENMENT IN IRELAND.] **Andrew Carpenter**

Gúm, An, publishing branch of the Department of Education. An Gúm ('the scheme') was established in 1926 to provide textbooks and reading material in Irish for schoolchildren and for the public. Scholars and writers, such as DOUGLAS HYDE, sat on the committee that advised on the suitability of works chosen for publication. The scheme succeeded in providing a substantial body of material in Irish, both through original works and translations. By 1935, however, translations accounted for more than half of the 200 general books published, giving rise to complaints that original writers were being stifled, and indeed insulted, by the demands of the translation scheme. Not only classics but books by such authors as Freeman Wills Crofts and E. C. Bentley were translated under the scheme before it began to peter out in the late 1930s. Among those translating for An Gúm in the early years were SEOSAMH MAC GRIANNA and NIALL Ó DÓNAILL.

At the same time An Gúm was responsible in this period for the publication of fine original works by SÉAMUS Ó GRIANNA and MÁIRTÍN Ó CADHAIN; but its principal importance has for long been in the area of educational publishing, providing high-quality textbooks for post-primary schools in particular, a range of general and specialist dictionaries, music scores, and a large selection of first-class children's books. **Gearóidín Uí Laighléis**

Gunning sisters, celebrated beauties. Maria, Countess of Coventry (1733–1760), and Elizabeth, Duchess of Hamilton and Argyll (1734–1790), were daughters of John Gunning of Castlecoote, Co. Roscommon. They went to London in 1751, gaining instant celebrity. In 1752 they were both married—Elizabeth to the Duke of Hamilton and Maria to the Earl of Coventry. The Duke of Hamilton died in 1758 whereupon Elizabeth married the Marquis of Lorne, later Duke of Argyll within the year. Such was their fame that hundreds of people waited up all night to see Elizabeth at her presentation, while Maria had to be provided with an armed guard to protect her from being mobbed. Maria died, aged twenty-seven, from cosmetic poisoning. **Ciarán Deane**

Guthrie, Sir Tyrone (1900–1971), actor, director, and theatre manager. Born in Tunbridge Wells, Kent, a great-grandson of the actor TYRONE POWER (1797–1841); educated at the University of Oxford, where he began acting. He was associated with the Old Vic Theatre, London, 1937–52, and later with the Guthrie Theatre in Minneapolis, USA. He was knighted in 1961. After his death his home at Annaghmakerrig, Co. Monaghan, was left by him to the state as a retreat centre for writers and artists as the Tyrone Guthrie Centre; it is funded jointly by the Northern and Southern Arts Councils. **Christopher Morash**

Gunning. Maria Gunning, Countess of Coventry *(1751) by Francis Cotes. Maria was eighteen when this portrait was painted during her first year in London. She and her sister Elizabeth were celebrated beauties who married into the British aristocracy. [National Gallery of Ireland]*

Gypsies. The earliest historical evidence of Romani presence in Ireland dates from 1541, for which year *The Irish Fiants of the Tudor Sovereigns* has two entries for 'Egyptians'—the usual contemporary term, subsequently corrupted to 'Gypsies'. The earliest references for Scotland, England, and Wales are 1505, 1515, and 1579, respectively. Records from all these countries refer to this group under a variety of names, and it is impossible to know the proportion of Romanies to indigenous TRAVELLERS who were the target of legislation dealing with 'Egyptians and counterfeyte Egyptians'. However, the fact that newcomers and local Travellers were classed collectively indicates that non-Travellers saw them as such. It was not until the late nineteenth century that, fuelled by a combination of Orientalism, 'scientific' RACISM, and an upsurge in anti-Irish feeling, British scholars began to divide the Traveller population of Britain and Ireland into essentially Indian 'Gypsies', speaking the remnants of a language closely related to Sanskrit and whose exotic 'blood' was deemed to confer cultural legitimacy, and mere 'tinkers' of indigenous origin, purportedly speaking an artificial backslang.

This model was quickly refined to its present form which regards Travellers in or of Britain as 'genuine Romanies', whereas Travellers in or of Ireland are bogus copies. In both jurisdictions lip-service is paid to respecting the cultural rights of Romanies; in practice, flesh-and-blood Travellers are deemed to be 'tinkers' with no claim to such rights. As a result, Irish Traveller presence in Britain is overstated, while Romani presence in Ireland is systematically denied. In fact both groups have been crisscrossing the IRISH SEA for centuries, and a number of Romani families—including Prices, Grays, and Reillys—are firmly established in Ireland. Irish Gypsies are not strikingly distinct from Irish Travellers in appearance, speech, or life-style but maintain a separate identity, speaking a form of Romani as their ethnic language and preferring to marry among themselves. In the past few years there has been a substantial influx of eastern European Romani immigrants, whose appearance and language make them conspicuous; it is too early to predict what *modus vivendi* these new arrivals and more established Traveller groups will evolve. **Sinéad ní Shúinéar**

Hamilton, Hugh Douglas *(see page 468). Frederick Augustus Hervey, Bishop of Derry and fourth Earl of Bristol, with his granddaughter Lady Caroline Crichton in a double portrait by Hugh Douglas Hamilton, set in the gardens of the Villa Borghese, Rome, c. 1790. The Roman Altar of the Twelve Gods (Ara Borghese) with a relief of the Three Horai (left) is now in the Louvre. [National Gallery of Ireland]*

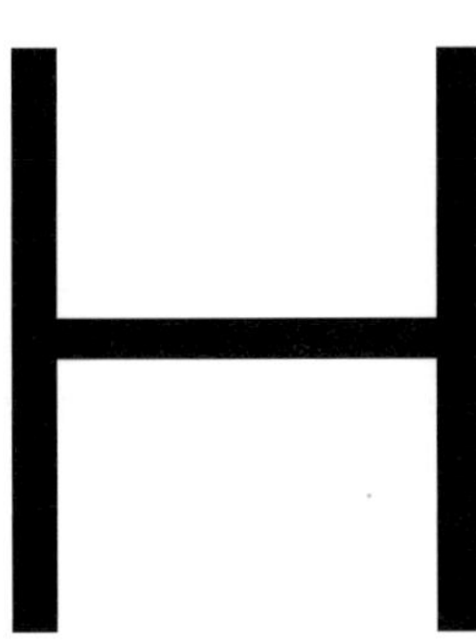

Hackett, Francis (1883–1962), biographer, novelist, and critic. Born in Kilkenny of a Parnellite family; educated at Clongowes Wood College, which features in his 'novel of youth', *The Green Lion* (1936). At eighteen he emigrated to the United States, where he worked as a literary journalist and critic. He is now remembered as a popular historian, author of *Henry the Eighth* (1929), a companion piece, *Francis the First* (1934), and a novel, *Queen Anne Boleyn* (1939). After a period in Ireland, in 1937 he moved to Denmark with his wife, the diarist, novelist, and psychic SIGNE TOKSVIG. Visiting New York in 1939, they were unable to leave the United States for the duration of the war. They returned to Denmark, but there Hackett ceased to write. **Peter Costello**

Hackett, Rosie (1892–1976), trade unionist. As a messenger at Jacob's biscuit factory, Dublin, in 1909 she joined the IRISH TRANSPORT AND GENERAL WORKERS' UNION. She took part in the general labour unrest of 1913 and assisted in relief efforts during the lock-out. She trained as a printer while employed by the Irish Women Workers' Co-operative Society, and as an associate of JAMES CONNOLLY she helped to print the PROCLAMATION OF THE IRISH REPUBLIC (1916) and participated in the Rising as a member of the IRISH CITIZEN ARMY. She was subsequently clerk to the IRISH WOMEN WORKERS' UNION. In 1970 she received a gold medal for sixty years' service to TRADE UNIONISM. [see DUBLIN LOCK-OUT, 1913.] **Rosemary Raughter**

hagiography, a genre of Christian religious writing that sets out in a *'vita'* (life) the deeds of someone considered to be a saint because his or her cult is ritually celebrated. The genre's archetype was the fourth-century *Vita Antonii* by Athanasius (c. 296–373), which, together with other accounts of early Egyptian monks in Greek and Latin, established it as an important part of the Christian imagination for the whole medieval period. While perceived as a species of biography, because most 'lives' of SAINTS follow the structure of birth and early life, then career centred around his or her miracles, then death and *post mortem* events (such as miracles at the tomb), the real purpose of the lives is edification through setting out an ideal of holiness (such as VITA SANCTI COLUMBAE) (see p. 1112) or a demonstration of the power of Christian faith (such as Muirchú's *Vita Patricii*). Often hagiographers had only meagre historical details, but these merely added specifics to their understanding of the saint's significance, derived from his or her cult and of the essential character of what a saint must be. Early Irish 'lives' should therefore be viewed primarily as theological, not historical, works.

The early monastic 'lives' set the form and tone for those composed in Ireland, first in Latin and subsequently in Irish. We know that lives of monastic founders were being written in the first half of the seventh century, but our earliest examples come from its later half: Cogitosus's *Vita Brigidae*, the lost *Liber de Virtutibus Sancti Columbae* ('Book of Miraculous Deeds of St COLM CILLE') by Cummenaus (Abbot of IONA, 657–69), and then the lives by Muirchú and ADOMNÁN—sophisticated examples of the genre. The popularity of hagiography can be observed in many ways: in Irish monastic customs, many of which have their origin in Palladius's *Historia Lausiaca*; in the MARTYROLOGIES; and in the multiplication of 'lives' for major saints, which steadily adapted each cult to new circumstances.

The study of hagiography has been important in Irish studies since the time of the seventeenth-century Franciscan 'masters', especially John Colgan. Until recently many people have read the 'lives' as direct evidence (omitting miraculous elements) for early history or chronology, rather than as evidence for the world-view of their time of composition (where miraculous elements are revealing). [see MONASTICISM; MONASTIC SCHOOLS.] **Thomas O'Loughlin**

Haicéad, Pádraigín (c. 1600–1654), priest and poet. Born in the vicinity of CASHEL, Co. Tipperary; joined the Dominican order and spent some time studying in LOUVAIN. An ardent supporter of RINUCCINI during the 1641 REBELLION, he was uncompromising in denouncing those who took a conciliatory line after the split in the CONFEDERATION OF KILKENNY in 1646. Following the expulsion of religious from Ireland he returned to Louvain, being embroiled in his final years in controversy over internal Dominican matters. A prolific author of fifty-two poems, Haicéad composed in both *dán díreach* and *amhrán* metres. He is a fine example of a new kind of amateur poet that emerged in the seventeenth century, not belonging to a professional POETIC FAMILY. He seems to have received patronage from the BUTLERS of Cashel, the Catholic branch of the house of Ormond. His political poetry provided stirring rallying calls for the Rinuccini side during the split in the Confederation, and he is scathing about those who sided with Ormond. Despite his truculent nature, Haicéad was capable of composing warm and witty occasional verses to his friends. He also composed in the courtly love tradition; one such poem, on the death of a Máire Tóibín, is particularly moving. **Mícheál Mac Craith**

Haire, John Wilson (1932–), playwright. Born in Belfast, son of a Protestant father and Catholic mother, and grew up in Carryduff, Co. Down. His plays (which have been produced in Belfast, Dublin, and London) take Northern Ireland's divided society for their subject; they display an even-handed sense of the terrible effects on individuals of the 'TROUBLES' of the last three decades of the twentieth century. *Within Two Shadows* (1972) is his best-known work. **Terence Brown**

Halferty, Tommy (1945–), JAZZ musician. Born in Derry. He turned to jazz after moving to Dublin, where he became a pupil of LOUIS STEWART on jazz guitar. Starting relatively late—already in his thirties—he quickly became an original voice on the Irish jazz scene. A teacher of English and music by day, he led a trio with RONAN GUILFOYLE (bass guitar) and JOHN WADHAM (drums) that broke from the more usual reliance on standard tunes and predictable, straight-four rhythms and developed intense interplay between the individual musicians. Irish-French Connection, comprising Halferty and the Lavergne brothers on organ and drums, has been together since 1992. Halferty also features in a trio with the American drummer Keith Copeland and Ronan Guilfoyle that has released two albums, *The Irish Connection* (1996) and *Round Trip* (1997). He has played with the guitarists John Abercrombie and John Etheridge as well as many other leading international figures, including Lee Konitz and Art Themen, and several times with the English singer Norma Winstone. He performs regularly with Khanda, which blends Irish traditional, Indian, and jazz influences, and has recorded a duo album with the guitarist Mike Nielsen, *In Two* (1997). **Brian Trench**

Hall, Anna Maria, née Fielding (1800–1881), writer. Born in Dublin but moved to England as a teenager, where she married the journalist Samuel Carter Hall. Her first book was *Sketches of Irish Character* (1829), which was followed by nine novels, beginning with *The Buccaneer* (1831) and including *Marian, or A Young Maid's Fortunes* (1840). She contributed tales of rural Ireland to several magazines and jointly wrote travel books with her husband, including *Ireland, Its Scenery, Characters, etc.* (1842) (see p. 1152). Her later life was devoted to charitable causes (she helped to found the Nightingale Fund), and she received a civil list pension in 1868. **David Latané**

Hall as a children's writer. Hall wrote many children's books of an edifying and didactic nature. Some of her children's books were written specifically for Thomas Hood's young daughter Fanny. A contemporary reviewer described her children's fiction as 'a pleasing combination of fancy and instruction.' It includes *Animal Sagacity* (1868), *Grandmamma's Pockets* (1880), *The Boy's Birthday Book* (1885), and *Uncle Sam's Money Box* (1890). **Patricia Donlon**

Hall, Patrick (1935–), painter. Born in Roscrea, Co. Tipperary; studied at Chelsea College of Art and the Central School of Art and Design, London. He was one of the small group of painters who came to prominence in the general wave of new expressionism in Western Europe in the 1980s, though many, including Hall, had been painting seriously for many years before that. His most powerful paintings were the series *The Flaying of Marsyas* (1984), transposing the Apollonian myth to the lynching of a black musician in New York. He is a member of AOSDÁNA. **Dorothy Walker**

hall-houses, small two-storey rectangular CASTLES. They have a first-floor entrance and a defensive ground floor with slit *opes*; the wooden first-floor level contained a hall with more open windows.

Hackett. *The veteran trade unionist Rosie Hackett (third left) on the steps of the original Liberty Hall, head office of the ITGWU before its demolition in 1958. [Courtesy of University College, Dublin, Archives Department]*

Hall-houses are similar to the hall-keeps of large stone fortresses, such as those at Athenry, Co. Galway. The earliest examples, from the early thirteenth century, are in the western half of the country, found in limited areas of Cos. Mayo, Limerick, Galway, Sligo, and North Tipperary: typical examples are Shrule, Co. Mayo, and Dunmore, Co. Galway. Many hall-houses later had their wooden floors replaced with stone vaults and had a third storey added, with defensive features such as bartisans. A few examples are found in the eastern half of the country and are dated to the fourteenth century. Examples at Dunmoe, Co. Meath, Delvin, Co. Westmeath, and Kindlestown, Co. Wicklow, have much in common with TOWER-HOUSES. Late hall-houses with service towers are also found, especially in Co. Wexford. **David Sweetman**

Hallowe'en, a traditional festival falling on 31 October (coinciding with the ancient Irish festival of SAMHAIN), known in Irish as *Oíche Shamhna* and also as *Oíche na hAimléise* or the night of misery. *Samhain* is thought to mean simply 'feast'; this was anciently considered the beginning of the new year and popularly perceived as a resumption of primordial time. On this night the boundary between the natural and the supernatural worlds is open, allowing for free transgress. Popularly known as Hallowe'en or Snap-Apple Night, it features a palpably otherworldly pageant marked by costumes, bonfires, divination, fireworks, and devilment. **Stiofán Ó Cadhla**

Halpin, Captain Robert (1836–1894), merchant seaman. Born in Co. Wicklow; at the age of ten he went to sea and joined a collier, the *Briton*, where he learnt seamanship in what was one of the hardest schools of the time, the coal trade in the IRISH SEA and English Channel. When in 1851 the *Briton* was wrecked off Bude, Cornwall, with considerable loss of life, he managed to scramble ashore with the ship's canary. He joined a London-registered barque, the *Henry Tanner*, and in it reached the rank of third mate at the remarkable age of seventeen. After a short period on regular voyages in the North Atlantic he joined as second mate the *Boomerang*, a ship engaged in the arduous Australian wool trade. In 1855 he became convinced that the future of the shipping industry lay with the steam engine. After a period in his first steamship and his first ship of over 1,000 tons, at twenty-two he got his first command. Meanwhile the first experiments with under-sea cables were taking place; not yet thirty, he took over command of the world's largest ship, the GREAT EASTERN (over 18,000 tons). He triumphantly laid cables from Valentia Island to Newfoundland (1866) and from France to the same destination (1869). Henceforward, in various ships, including the first custom-built cable-layer, *Hooper* (the world's second-biggest ship), he laid 6,569 km (4,082 miles) of cables, equivalent to the world's circumference. He was the only person to command the *Great Eastern* without accident or damage. [see ATLANTIC TELEGRAPH CABLE.] **John de Courcy Ireland**

Hamilton, Anthony (1645–1720), soldier and writer. Born in Roscrea, Co. Tipperary. In France from 1651 at the court of CHARLES II and later in the army of Louis XIV, he returned to Ireland to become JACOBITE Military Governor of Limerick, 1685–7. His anonymously published *Mémoires du Comte de Grammont* (1713), a scandalous memoir of life in the court of Charles II (the count was his brother-in-law), is a classic of French literature. His *Oeuvres Complètes* were issued posthumously (1749–76). **Brian Lalor**

Hamilton, Elizabeth ('La Belle Hamilton') (1641–1708), courtier. Born in Ulster, probably Co. Tyrone. One of the most brilliant and beautiful women in the court of Charles II, her portrait was painted by Lely. The sister of ANTHONY HAMILTON, she married Philibert, Comte de Grammont, and moved to France in 1663. **Ciarán Deane**

Hamilton, Hugh (1905–1934), racing driver. Born in Omagh, Co. Tyrone. A fearless and accomplished driver, he finished third in his debut race at Brooklands in 1930. He won his class for MG in the 1932 German Grand Prix before crashing in his home Tourist Trophy race at Ards, Co. Down. He was second in his class in the 1933 Italian Mille Miglia, and repeated his German Grand Prix success at Avus. Runner-up to the great Tazio Nuvolari in the 1933 TT, he was lucky to escape from another serious accident in the Czech Grand Prix. Invited to drive for Whitney Straight's 1934 Maserati team, he was fifth at Montreux, fourth in the Marne Grand Prix, and second at Albi. He died of a heart attack during the subsequent Swiss Grand Prix, and hundreds of fans and Grand Prix drivers attended his funeral in Bern. [see MOTOR SPORT.] **Brendan Lynch**

Hamilton, Hugh Douglas (1740–1808), painter. Born in Dublin; trained at the DUBLIN SOCIETY Schools. He set up practice producing small pastel portraits. Having moved to London with his wife, he exhibited at the Society of Arts from 1765. His patrons included George III, George, Prince of Wales, and Lady Caroline Stuart. He began to paint in oils and travelled to Italy with his family in the early 1780s; he spent the next nine years in Rome and Florence, where he earned an enviable reputation among the Grand Tourists. He was back in Dublin by early 1792 and from 1794 worked predominantly in oil, producing portraits of a number of Irish public figures. Later he directed his energies to the study of pigments (see pp. 466, 623). **Brendan Rooney**

Hamilton, Hugo (1953–), novelist and SHORT-STORY writer. Born in Dún Laoghaire, Co. Dublin; educated in Dublin. His novels include *Surrogate City* (1990), *Last Shot* (1991), *Headbanger* (1997), and *Sad Bastard* (1998). He has also published a collection of short stories, *Dublin Where the Palm Trees Grow* (1996). His work encompasses Irish and European perspectives. **Terence Brown**

Hamilton, James Archibald (1748–1815), astronomer. Born near Athlone, Co. Westmeath; educated at TCD, where he developed an interest in ASTRONOMY. He took holy orders and became rector of Kildress in 1776. During the 1780s he operated a private observatory near Cookstown, Co. Tyrone, and corresponded with Nevil Maskelyne, the Astronomer-Royal, on such topics as meteors and the 1782 transit of Mercury. His publications include details of a portable barometer, the determination of longitude, and thoughts regarding the distances to the stars. He began regular daily meteorological observations in 1795, instigating a series that continues to this day. Instruments acquired by Hamilton for ARMAGH OBSERVATORY included an equatorial TELESCOPE by John and Edward Troughton and two Astronomical Regulators by Thomas Earnshaw. His correspondence regarding Earnshaw's astronomical regulators was reproduced in the latter's *Appeal to the Public* (1808). **John McFarland**

Hamilton, Letitia Mary (1878–1964), painter. Born in Dunboyne, Co. Meath, sister of the portrait painter Eva Hamilton (1876–1960) and cousin of the watercolourist ROSE BARTON. She attended Alexandra College, then the Metropolitan School of Art, Dublin, studying under ORPEN, followed by further studies at London Polytechnic and in Belgium under Frank Brangwyn.

Awarded the Board of Education silver medal in 1912 for an enamelled panel, she exhibited *Bog of Allen* at the Irish Exhibition in Paris, 1922. She moved from Co. Sligo to Co. Dublin, and travelled on the Continent, particularly in France, Italy, and Yugoslavia, painting local scenes. A founder-member of the Dublin Painters, 1920, she exhibited regularly at the ROYAL HIBERNIAN ACADEMY, being elected a member in 1944. She specialised in Irish landscapes and fox-hunting scenes, her painting style characterised by thick impasto. Her painting *Snow in Co. Down* is in the Hugh Lane Municipal Gallery of Modern Art, Dublin. **Peter Murray**

Hamilton, Liam (1928–2000), lawyer and judge. Born in Mitchelstown, Co. Cork; educated at UCD and the KING'S INNS. He was called to the bar in 1956. In 1958 he contested a local election on behalf of the LABOUR PARTY. As a barrister he specialised in trade union law; he also represented Neil Blaney in the ARMS CRISIS (1970). He passed judgment in the Geraldine Kennedy case (1987), holding that the state-authorised tapping of journalists' telephones violated their constitutional right to privacy. Regarded as a very humane judge, he was president of the High Court, 1985–92, and Chief Justice, 1992–2000. He conducted the beef tribunal (1991–4) and in 1999 an inquiry into the conduct of two judges involved in the early release of a man convicted of driving while under the influence of drink. In January 2000 he was appointed to chair an inquiry into the DUBLIN AND MONAGHAN BOMBINGS of 1974. **Neville Cox**

Hamilton, Rev. William (1755–1797), geologist. Born in Derry; educated at TCD, where he was elected a fellow. He helped found the 'palaeosophers' society' in 1785, which constituted the nucleus of the ROYAL IRISH ACADEMY. His *Letters Concerning the Northern Coast of the County of Antrim* dealt with the origin of the Antrim basalts—whether they had been caused by fire or water was still a matter of controversy. His observations and reasoning advanced the belief in the igneous origin of these stratified rocks. Also a magistrate, he was murdered as a result of civil unrest in Co. Donegal. [see GIANT'S CAUSEWAY.] **Geoff Warke**

Hamilton, Sir William Rowan (1805–1865), mathematician. Born in Dublin; educated in Trim, Co. Meath, by his uncle, the Rev. JAMES HAMILTON, and at TCD, where he excelled in classics and mathematics. An infant prodigy in languages, he later made outstanding contributions to mathematics, especially the theory of optics and dynamics. He was appointed Andrews professor of Astronomy in 1827, while still an undergraduate, and spent the rest of his life at DUNSINK OBSERVATORY. His prediction of conical refraction in 1832 and the discovery of quaternions in 1843 brought him international fame. His personal life was unhappy, but he found solace in poetry and counted Wordsworth and Coleridge among his friends. He was knighted in 1835, was twice honoured with the gold medal of the Royal Society, and was president of the RIA, from 1837–46. Shortly before his death he was appointed the first foreign associate of the (American) National Academy of Sciences. **Ian Elliott**

Hanbury-Tenison, Robin (1936–), explorer. Born at Lough Bawn, Co. Monaghan. He made the first land crossing of South America at its widest point in 1958. From 1962 to 1966 he explored the Tassili, N'Ajjer, Tibesti and Air mountains in the southern Sahara. He crossed South America in a small boat from the Orinoco

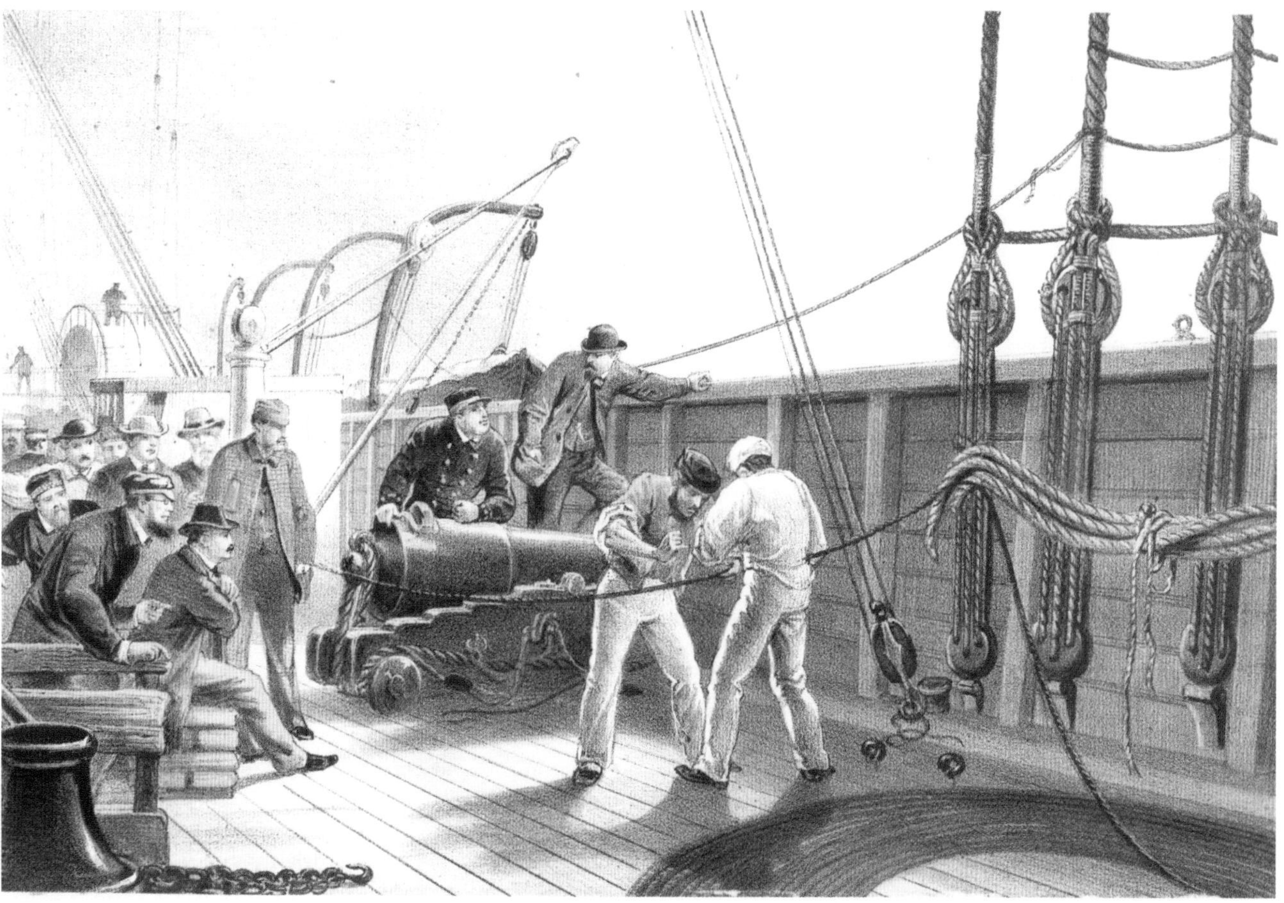

Halpin. Splicing the Cable (after the first accident), July 25th, *a lithograph by R. Dudley, illustrating the repair to a section of faulty cable on board the* Great Eastern *on its successful attempt to lay the first transatlantic telegraph cable in 1866. [National Maritime Museum]*

Hamilton, William Rowan. *Unattributed portrait of Sir William Rowan Hamilton, donated in 1894 to the Royal Irish Academy. Hamilton's discovery of the theory of the quaternions is commemorated in a plaque on Broombridge, Glasnevin, at the spot where he inscribed his formula on 16 October 1843. [Royal Irish Academy]*

to Buenos Aires in 1964–5. Two expeditions by hovercraft in 1968 and 1969 took him up the Amazon and across Africa. He explored the outer islands of Indonesia in 1977. More recently he has used the horse for transport, riding through New Zealand in 1988 and along the Great Wall of China in 1987. Since 1969 he has been associated with Survival International, an organisation that tries to preserve endangered peoples in Brazil. He is a fellow of the Royal Geographical Society and was made a member of the Order of the British Empire in 1981. **Peter Somerville-Large**

handball, a traditional Irish ball game, played by bouncing a ball against a wall, with the open palm. As the game developed and the Irish Handball Council came to regulate it in the mid-1920s, the court was standardised at 18 by 9 m (60 ft by 30 ft), and four-wall handball alleys were built throughout Ireland. Widely played in the eighteenth and nineteenth centuries, the game was brought by Irish emigrants to the United States, Canada, Mexico, Australia, and Spain. The modern game—unique among the sports administered by the GAELIC ATHLETIC ASSOCIATION—now thrives at an international level. By the end of the 1960s a move indoors was beginning. New courts measuring 12 by 6 m (40 ft by 20 ft), which had become the norm in the United States, were developed and are now in general use. Such players as Paddy Perry, Pat Kirby and the present-day player Michael 'Ducksie' Walsh have become national sporting heroes. **Donal Keenan**

Handel in Ireland. Dublin audiences were no strangers to the music of George Frederick Handel (1685–1759) when, in 1741, the composer arrived in Ireland at the invitation of the Duke of Devonshire, LORD LIEUTENANT. Handel's opera *Acis and Galatea*, for example, had received the first of many Dublin performances on 1 May 1734, in Crow Street Music Hall. The composer arrived in Dublin from London via Chester on 18 November 1741 and took lodgings in Abbey Street. He had just completed what was to become his most famous work, the oratorio *Messiah*, composed between 22 August and 14 September. Handel's librettist, Charles Jennens (1700–1773), had also collaborated with him in the writing of *Saul, L'Allegro, il Penseroso ed il Moderato,* and *Belshazzar.* The first performance of *Messiah* took place in the New Musick Hall in Fishamble Street on 13 April 1742 and was the culmination of two series of subscription concerts undertaken by Handel, beginning on 23 December 1741. Unlike its subsequent reception in London over the next eight years, the work was received enthusiastically at its Dublin premiere. On 25 May, Handel conducted *Saul*, while the second performance of *Messiah* on 3 June was the composer's final Dublin performance before he returned to England on 13 August. **Paul Collins**

Hanley, Ellen (c. 1804–1819), murder victim, known as the 'COLLEEN BAWN'. Born in Ballingarry, Co. Limerick. On 29 June 1819 she disappeared from her home, taking with her £112 of her uncle's money. On 6 September her body, bound with a rope, was washed ashore near Moneypoint, Co. Clare. Evidence pointed to a local squire, John Scanlan, and his manservant, Stephen Sullivan. It emerged that Scanlan had eloped with Hanley and had married her. Though well defended at his trial by DANIEL O'CONNELL, Scanlan was convicted and hanged; Sullivan was also hanged for his part in the crime. The story of the murder acquired the status of myth, providing the plot for GERALD GRIFFIN's novel THE COLLEGIANS (1829), DION BOUCICAULT's play *The Colleen Bawn* (1860), and Julius Benedict's opera *The Lily of Killarney* (1862). **Ciarán Deane**

Hanlon, Jack (1913–1968), priest and painter. Born in Dublin; studied with MAINIE JELLETT at the Ablett Studio, London, and later ordained a Catholic priest. One of the founder-members of the IRISH EXHIBITION OF LIVING ART, he painted many religious subjects but also still lifes in a pale, delicate style reminiscent of the French painter Marie Laurencin. He exhibited annually at the Irish Exhibition of Living Art and in many solo and group shows and at the New York World's Fair in 1939; his first solo exhibition was at the Victor Waddington Galleries, Dublin, 1941. Murals and stations of the cross include *The Virgin of the Seas* at the naval base, Haulbowline, Co. Cork. **Dorothy Walker**

Hanna, Geordie (1915–1987), traditional singer. Born in Derrytresk, Co. Tyrone. He was an original interpreter in a style that was both familial and local, described by JOHN MOULDEN as 'a breaking up of the tune and words into short phrases delivered with great force,' which earned him a considerable reputation throughout Ireland and inspired an annual song festival in his name. [see SONG STYLES.] **Fintan Vallely**

Hanna, Hugh (1824–1892), 'Roaring Hanna', Presbyterian clergyman. Born in Dromara, Co. Down; ordained in 1852. He completed the building of St Enoch's, Belfast's largest Presbyterian church, in 1872. He was a well-known street preacher and sectarian controversialist whose forceful delivery earned him the sobriquet 'Roaring Hanna' and who incited violence against Catholics, especially during the disturbances of 1857. He was a commissioner of national education, 1880. **Fergal Tobin**

Hannay, James Owen: see BIRMINGHAM, GEORGE.

Hapaska, Siobhán (1963–), sculptor and installation artist. Born in Belfast; studied at Middlesex Polytechnic and Goldsmiths College, London. She now lives in London. In 1997 she participated in the exhibition 'Documenta X' at Kassel, Germany, and the following year was awarded an IMMA Glen Dimplex Artists' Award. She participated in the exhibition '0044' shown at PS1 Institute for Contemporary Art, New York, Albright-Knox Art Gallery, Buffalo, New York, and Crawford Gallery, Cork, 1999–2000. She represented Ireland at the Venice Biennale, 2001, with the video installation *Mayday*. Hapaska's work often explores boundaries separating human-made systems and structures from the natural and organic. **Peter Murray**

Ha'penny Bridge, popular name of the Liffey Bridge, Dublin (from the toll formerly charged until 1916) (originally called Wellington Bridge). Erected in 1816 and renovated in 2001, it is the earliest known metal bridge in Ireland. A cast-iron arch footbridge with a span of 42 m (138 ft) and three arched ribs, it has become a symbol of Dublin. The sections of the bridge were cast in Coalbrookdale, Shropshire. **Ronald Cox**

Harbison, Janet (1955–), harpist. Born into a Dublin music family that had associations with Ó RIADA. Visiting the Irish-speaking district of Ring, Co. Waterford, inspired her to supplement her piano studies with learning the harp under Máirín Ní Shé. She formed Cláirseoirí na hÉireann in 1984 (later renamed the HARP FOUNDATION) and initiated a harp summer school at Ballycastle, Co. Antrim, and a harp festival at Glencolumbcille, Co. Donegal. She was curator of music at the ULSTER FOLK AND TRANSPORT MUSEUM, Cultra, Co. Down, 1986–94, in that period organising a bicentennial of the Belfast Harp Festival and setting up the BELFAST HARP ORCHESTRA. **Fintan Vallely**

harbours. Ireland possesses several natural harbours that provide deep-water anchorage, including Cork Harbour, Bantry Bay, Galway Bay, and the Shannon Estuary. During the first half of the nineteenth century a number of state-owned 'asylum' harbours were built to accommodate vessels carrying passengers and mail from British ports; these are at Dunmore East, Co. Waterford, Howth, Co. Dublin, Donaghadee, Co. Down, and Dún Laoghaire, Co. Dublin. ALEXANDER NIMMO was the engineer for Dunmore East, while JOHN RENNIE (and later his son Sir John Rennie) was responsible for the design of the others. The early years of the nineteenth century also saw an extensive scheme of harbour improvement and pier-building to stimulate the fishing industry, particularly on the west coast. Many of these piers were designed, and their construction directed, by Alexander Nimmo in his capacity as Government engineer.

In the 1960s and 70s a number of harbours were designated centres for the fishing industry and were considerably redeveloped and extended, including those of Dunmore East, Co. Waterford, Killybegs, Co. Donegal, Kilmore Quay, Co. Wexford, and Howth, Co. Dublin. The harbours at Rosslare, Co. Wexford, Kilkee, Co. Down, and Larne, Co. Antrim, have been developed to handle much of the container traffic in addition to passenger and vehicle ferries. **Ronald Cox**

Handel. *Excerpts from George Frederick Handel's oratorio* Messiah *have been performed on 13 April each year since 1989 by Our Lady's Choral Society at the site of the New Musick Hall in Fishamble Street, Dublin, where it had its first performance in 1742. In 1999 it snowed on the day.* [Irish Times*/photo: Pat Langan*]

Hardebeck, Carl Gilbert (1869–1945), organist, arranger, teacher, and collector. Born in London. Blind from birth, he was an early prodigy in music, studying at the Royal National School for the Blind and qualifying as a teacher. The failure of a music business he opened in Belfast led him to teaching and to a position as organist at St Peter's Church. Influenced by FERGUSON, MANGAN, and O'GRADY, he learnt Irish and collected songs in Co. Donegal, using Braille notation. His 'Gaelic Choir' won a composition prize at the FEIS CEOIL of 1897, and his *Gems of Melody* (1908) led to his appointment as head of the CORK MUNICIPAL SCHOOL OF MUSIC and to the chair of music at UCC in 1918. Shunned there for his nationalist beliefs, he returned to Belfast in 1923, later moved to Dublin, and was rescued from poverty by a pension organised by friends at the *Capuchin Annual*. **Fintan Vallely**

Hardie, Kerry (1951–), writer and poet. Born in Singapore and brought up in Co. Down. Her collection of verse, *A Furious Place* (1995), is marked by a sense of suffering transcended in intensity of vision. Her works of fiction include *Cry for the Hot Belly* (2000). **Terence Brown**

Hardiman, James (1782–1855), solicitor, librarian, and historian. Born in Westport, Co. Mayo. His vocation for the priesthood having been thwarted by blindness in one eye, he went on to study law. He worked in the Public Record Office, Dublin, c. 1811–30, then moved to Galway. Refusing the chair of Irish, he was appointed librarian at Queen's College (now NUIG) in 1848. He collected many old MANUSCRIPTS and conducted fieldwork with Myles John O'Reilly in 1827, concentrating on the literary remains of CAROLAN. His publications include a history of Galway (1820) and an edition of RODERICK O'FLAHERTY's *Chorographical Description of West or h-Iar Connaught* (1846); but his principal work is his *Irish Minstrelsy* (two volumes, 1831), a compilation of poetry from several periods, with an emphasis on the work of Carolan. Hardiman's political commentary prompted SAMUEL FERGUSON's famous retaliations in the DUBLIN UNIVERSITY MAGAZINE. **Jimmy O'Brien Moran**

Harding, Michael (1953–), novelist and playwright. Born in Co. Cavan; educated at ST PATRICK'S COLLEGE, Maynooth, and ordained a priest in 1981. Among his plays are *Misogynist* (1990) and *Annoying Grace* (1998). His novel *Priest* (1986) is a study of the stresses involved in that calling. His work is marked by a powerful mythic awareness. **Terence Brown**

Hardman, Edward Townley (1845–1887), geologist. Born in Drogheda, Co. Louth; educated at the ROYAL COLLEGE OF SCIENCE FOR IRELAND. In 1870 he joined the GEOLOGICAL SURVEY OF IRELAND as a temporary assistant geologist. He mapped the rocks in various parts of Ireland, contributed to many of the Survey's published *Memoirs*, and took a keen interest in Ireland's archaeology. In February 1883 he was seconded 'on colonial service' to Western Australia where he played a major role in the discovery of the Kimberly Goldfield. He returned to Ireland in 1885. **Jean Archer**

hare, Irish, an endemic sub-species of the arctic hare. It is found all over Ireland, which is the only temperate country where such hares are present from the mountains to the sea. It lives at a density of one per square kilometre on BOGS, feeding on grasses and sedges. It is redder and larger than the same species of hare in Scotland, and was introduced to the Isle of Mull and to south-western Scotland. For centuries it has been hunted with greyhounds, a practice that is today closely regulated. **D. Patrick Sleeman**

hare. *The 3-pence coin, with an Irish hare on the reverse, one of the coinage series designed by Percy Metcalfe in 1928 for the Irish Free State, which continued in circulation until the introducion of decimal currency in 1971. [Courtesy of Department of Finance]*

Hare coursing: see GREYHOUND RACING.

Harland, Sir Edward (1831–1895), shipbuilder. Born in Scarborough, Yorkshire, the sixth child of William Harland, a medical doctor and amateur engineer. He received a classical education at Edinburgh Academy before beginning a five-year apprenticeship with the firm of Robert Stephenson and Company, Newcastle-upon-Tyne, at the age of fifteen. As an engineer he had an interest in the design of sea-going vessels. He moved to Belfast in 1854, at the age of twenty-three, as manager of Robert Hickson's shipyard; four years later he bought the yard for £5,000, and in 1861 he entered into partnership with GUSTAV WILHELM WOLFF, who had been employed as his personal assistant since 1857. Harland's engineering genius kept the firm in the forefront of shipbuilding design. The early vessels were narrow-beamed 'ocean greyhounds', stabilised with square bilges and flat bottoms; the *Oceanic*, launched in 1870, was arguably the world's first modern passenger liner. From 1874 Harland began passing control to WILLIAM PIRRIE, increasingly withdrawing from the activities of the firm until Pirrie became in effect managing director in 1888; this was mainly to allow Harland time to engage in a political career as a Conservative-Unionist. He became Mayor of Belfast in 1885 and was created a baronet for his services in that office. He was elected Unionist member for North Belfast in 1889, retaining his seat in the election of 1892, and again in 1895, serving until his death. **John Patrick Lynch**

Harland and Wolff, shipbuilders. Ship repairing on the Co. Antrim shore of the River Lagan at Belfast was begun by William Ritchie in 1791, when the first dry dock was built. Clarendon No. 1 dock followed in 1800. Though a small-scale operation, it led to the formation of the shipbuilding firm of Workman Clark, which ceased business in 1935.

An approach channel was dredged in 1841–7, the spoil forming Dargan's Island (later named Queen's Island) on the Co. Down side of the river. Robert Hickson built ships here from 1853; in 1858 he sold the yard to his manager, EDWARD HARLAND, who in 1861 joined with GUSTAV WOLFF, and shipbuilding prospered. The White Star liners built after 1870 established the company's reputation with such vessels as the *Oceanic*, *Olympic*, TITANIC, and *Britannic*. Output reached a peak between 1914 and 1918, halved in 1931, rose again between 1939 and 1945, was at a high level until 1961, then declined sharply. The *Canberra* was the last liner to employ the company's finishing trades with their high labour content. The company then concentrated on simple, large vessels, such as oil tankers and bulk carriers, and specialised vessels for the oil industry. Less labour was needed for these simpler ships, especially after 1970, when the Building Dock permitted the construction under cover of large sections, with computer-controlled cutting and welding. In 1977 two ships, with a tonnage of 226,272, were launched; in 1912 there had been eighteen, with a tonnage of 214,121. There has been a marked decline in the work force over recent years. **Michael Gould**

Harmon, Maurice (1930–), professor and critic. Born in Dublin; educated at UCD, Harvard University, and NUI. He first taught in the United States and was lecturer and associate professor of English, UCD, 1965–90. *Sean O'Faolain: A Critical Introduction* (1967) provided an informed insider's view; his biography of O'FAOLAIN followed in 1994. He also published studies of AUSTIN CLARKE (1989) and THOMAS KINSELLA (1974) and edited the *Irish University Review*, 1970–86. **Anthony Roche**

harmonica or mouth organ, a simple mouth-blown free-reed instrument tuned in the same way as the ACCORDION. It was first manufactured in Germany in 1825, the clockmaker Matthias Hohner coming to dominate its production after 1857; today it is made principally in China. In its *diatonic* and *chromatic* versions (of a fixed key and with all semitones, respectively) it came to be the most popular musical instrument in Ireland up to the 1950s. Today it is most widely played in blues music, but in TRADITIONAL MUSIC it has many exponents, such as John and Pip Murphy, Eddie Clarke, Mick Kinsella, and Brendan Power. **Fintan Vallely**

Harney. *Mary Harney, elected Tánaiste in 1997 and 2002. Leader of the Progressive Democrats since 1993, she was one of the party's founder-members in 1985. [Joe Dunne/Photocall Ireland]*

Harmsworth, Alfred, Viscount Northcliffe (1865–1922), newspaper proprietor. Born at Chapelizod, Co. Dublin. In 1867 he moved with his family to London; there he founded *Answers*, a popular weekly, in 1888. In 1894 he bought the ailing *London Evening News* for £25,000; in 1896 he founded the *Daily Mail*. News, leaders and features were kept short, and the *Mail* became a huge success. In 1903 Harmsworth launched the *Daily Mirror* as a paper for women. With his brother Harold, Lord Rothermere (1868–1940), he undertook many other publishing ventures. In 1908 he secured control of the *Times*. He was a leading British propagandist during the FIRST WORLD WAR and was used as a megaphone by people more politically astute than himself. Success made him megalomaniac and autocratic. **Eddie Holt**

Harney, Mary (1953–), politician. Born in Galway; educated at TCD. She became a FIANNA FÁIL senator in 1977 and a TD in 1981; in 1985 she left Fianna Fáil to help found the PROGRESSIVE DEMOCRATS. She became Minister of State at the Department of the Environment, 1989, leader of the Progressive Democrats in 1993, and TÁNAISTE in 1997. **Tom Garvin**

harp. It is not known how or when the harp came to Ireland, or even what shape it may have been before the twelfth century. The instrument mentioned in early Irish manuscripts as the *cruit* was, technically, almost certainly a lyre, though in later years the word came to mean a true harp. Stone crosses from the ninth and tenth centuries show stringed instruments of various shapes and sizes, some of them clearly lyres; others may reflect the imagination of the stone-cutter. The earliest Irish depiction of the familiar triangular frame harp is on Breac Mhaodhóg (the late eleventh-century shrine of St Maodhóg). The appearance of a harp on such a shrine suggests that by then it was established as an important instrument. Two later depictions in stone show triangular frame harps. One is on the outside west wall of the twelfth-century Ardmore Cathedral; the other is on a fifteenth-century tomb in JERPOINT ABBEY, Co. Kilkenny—though this may represent a harp of greater antiquity then the tomb itself.

The general design of the harp remained much the same until the nineteenth century, though the instruments varied in size from small knee-harps to those over 1.5 m (5 ft) tall. The number of strings, of brass and steel wire, could be as high as forty-five, though typically it was between thirty and thirty-six. The harps were made of hard wood and featured a one-piece hollowed soundbox. They were solid, heavy instruments, often intricately carved and painted, sometimes inset with precious stones. The harpers were probably trained in schools similar to the poets' bardic schools. They plucked the strings with long fingernails, and the harp's long-lasting resonance required a complex damping technique in order to produce a clear tone.

Over the centuries many visitors to Ireland described the harp and its music, from GIRALDUS CAMBRENSIS in the late twelfth century to the German traveller J. G. Kohl in the nineteenth. Nearly all these accounts emphasise the same traits: the sweet and bell-like tone, the skill, speed and liveliness of the playing, and the 'sporting of the grace-notes' above the heavier sound.

In early Irish society the *cruitire* (harper) was always an important figure, the instrumentalist of the aristocracy and second in stature

A General
Collection of the Ancient
MUSIC OF IRELAND,
Arranged for the
Piano Forte,
some of the most admired
MELODIES are adapted for the VOICE,
To Poetry chiefly translated from the
Original Irish Songs,
BY
Thomas Campbell Esq.
AND
OTHER Eminent POETS:
To which is prefixed
A
Historical & CRITICAL Dissertation
ON
The Egyptian, British and
Irish Harp
BY
EDWARD BUNTING.
Vol: 1st.
LONDON. Printed & Sold for the Editor by Clementi & Compy. No. 26 Cheapside,
and all other Music Sellers in the United Kingdom.

harp. *Title page of Edward Bunting's* Collection of the Ancient Music of Ireland *(1796), a major collection of Irish traditional music, compiled by Bunting during the Belfast Harp Festival, 1792, and on his subsequent tour of Ireland. [Antique Prints, Dublin; photo: Denis Mortell]*

only to the poet. Both were maintained as members of the chief's household, and their business was to provide poetry and music as required. This could be a recitation of heroic lyrics, of a chief's pedigree or great deeds, or the ritual mourning of the dead (an important function of poet and harper); on occasion a performance would be part of a dinner entertainment. Poet and harper were joined by the *reacaire* (reciter), who chanted the poems to harp accompaniment. It is not known what kind of music was played, as the tradition was wholly oral. Two descriptions of performances are of particular interest. In 1599 the performance of a lament by a solo harper was described as 'a sort of singing which was yet hardly singing, but rather a chant or crooning noise ... which swelled to the rafters and again sank to a whisper; the harp more a thing of separate life joining in at its own pleasure ...' On that occasion the harper was performing by himself, but it seems that as late as the early seventeenth century the old style of performance was still current, though relatively rare. In the *Memoirs* of the Earl of Clanricarde (1722) there is a description of the formal chanting of a poem by reciter and harper that had taken place some hundred years earlier.

The coming of the ANGLO-NORMANS made little difference to Irish society, as the Normans soon adopted IRISH LANGUAGE and culture, including the arts of poetry and music. This secure position of poets and harpers continued until the destruction of the old order by the TUDOR PLANTATIONS, as a result of which by 1600 the formal poets and reciters began to disappear. Some harpers gained positions with the new landed gentry, while others became itinerant musicians, moving from house to house, playing, teaching, and composing. They had to face the chromatic changes taking place in European art music, which became the main interest of many of their new patrons. Their instrument was ill suited to such music, unlike the piano, which became a popular domestic instrument in the eighteenth century.

The harpers continued to decline, both in numbers and in standards, until by the end of the eighteenth century only a few players—most of them old—were left, and the greater part of the old harp music had disappeared. Three festivals were held in Granard, Co. Longford, during the 1780s to encourage interest, and a final and most important one took place in Belfast in 1792. On this last occasion the work of EDWARD BUNTING ensured that the surviving harp music and lore did not disappear for ever. He wrote down the music as it was played, and the 'Memoirs' he noted from the great harper Arthur O'Neill are the main source of information about the harpers of former times. Among the many harper-composers mentioned by O'Neill are John and Harry Scott, famous for their 'Lamentations', Ruaidhrí Dall Ó Catháin, composer of the well-known 'Tabhair dom do lámh', and William and Thomas Connellan, who between them wrote at least 700 airs. Best known of all was TURLOUGH CAROLAN, famous for his compositions in the Italian style, the only harper whose melodies and poems have survived in any quantity. Prominent harpers mentioned in the 'Memoirs' include Charles Fanning, Rose Mooney, and Daniel Black (harper and singer). Strangely enough, there is no mention of Denis Hempson (1695–1807), the last known player to use the fingernail technique.

After the 1792 festival some Harp Societies were formed in Belfast, Dublin, Drogheda, and (surprisingly) India. These did not last long; and by the end of the nineteenth century the traditional harp was gone, to be gradually replaced by the light gut-strung harp of today. The professional players were largely replaced by amateurs. It is not until comparatively recently that professional players of the Irish harp are travelling once more, though their new patrons are agents and concert promoters. The wire-strung harp is now enjoying a modest revival, but it is still little heard in its own country (see pp. 160, 739). [see BELFAST HARP FESTIVAL; MUSICAL INSTRUMENTS; TRINITY COLLEGE HARP; YEATS, GRÁINNE.] **Gráinne Yeats**

harp emblem. The harp has been recognised as an emblem of Ireland since at least the thirteenth century. It first appeared on Anglo-Irish coinage in 1534, was described as 'the special emblem of the realm' by the Italian Vincenzo Galilei in 1581, and was incorporated in the British royal coat of arms in 1603. A crowned 'winged maiden' harp, bearing little relationship to the Irish harp, represented Ireland under British rule from the later seventeenth century. This harp occurs, for example, on eighteenth-century coins and public buildings. Nineteenth-century NATIONALISM adopted the harp as one of its most popular symbols, now (often loosely) modelled on early Irish harps, including the TRINITY COLLEGE or 'Brian Bórú' harp. It was officially adopted as Ireland's national symbol following the foundation of the Irish Free State in 1922. Since then it has appeared on coins and government publications and in other official contexts. **Barra Boydell**

Harper, Charles (1943–), painter. Born in Co. Kerry; trained at the NCAD and then in Germany, studying film-making and animation in Bonn. He has been an influential figure in the visual arts of the Limerick area, as head of fine art in Limerick School of Art and as a working artist. He was one of those who established the yearly EV+A exhibition, with a curator selected each year from outside Ireland. His painting in oils and watercolours and his prints often feature a distinctive series of multiple head or figure images. He is a member of AOSDÁNA. **Dorothy Walker**

Harper, Heather (1930–), singer. Born in Belfast; studied singing and piano at Trinity College of Music, London. A soprano, she made her stage debut in 1954 as Lady Macbeth with Oxford University Opera Club. Subsequently she sang operatic roles at Glyndebourne, Covent Garden, Bayreuth, and Buenos Aires. A versatile performer, she has been particularly associated with the music of Benjamin Britten (1913–76) and Michael Tippett (1905–98). Appointed CBE in 1965, she has been professor of singing at the Royal College of Music since 1985 and director of vocal studies at the Britten-Pears School since 1986. **Paul Collins**

Harp Foundation (formerly Cláirseoirí na hÉireann), an association established in the 1980s by JANET HARBISON to promote the Irish HARP, with a particular emphasis on learning the harp 'by ear'. Originally based in Dublin, it subsequently moved to Belfast, where in 1993 it became the Harp Foundation. It organises the Belfast Harp Orchestra (a national harp ensemble) and the Glencolumbkille Harp Festival in Co. Donegal, as well as festivals in the Mourne Mountains in Co. Down and in Co. Antrim. It also provides a 'harp bank' to facilitate beginners and visiting harpers. [see BELFAST HARP FESTIVAL.] **Maeve Ellen Gebruers**

Harrington, Timothy C. (1851–1910), nationalist politician and barrister. Born in Castletown Bearhaven, Co. Cork. He first came to public attention as founding editor of the *Kerry Sentinel* in 1877. He was appointed secretary of the IRISH NATIONAL LEAGUE in 1882 and became an MP the following year. One of the leaders of the PLAN OF CAMPAIGN, as a barrister he also defended many political cases. Taking the Parnellite side when the party split, he served on the Recess Committee (1895–6) and helped to found the UNITED IRISH LEAGUE, 1898. Lord Mayor of Dublin, 1901–4, he represented the tenant side at the Dunraven Land Conference. **Carla King**

Harris, James (Frank) (1856–1931), journalist, editor, and writer. Born in Galway, of Welsh parents; emigrated as an adolescent to the United States, where, amid many adventures, he received some university education in Lawrence, Kansas. On his return to Europe he attended universities in Germany before embarking on his spectacular London and American career as successful journalist and editor, failed businessman, and indefatigable seducer. He wrote biographies of OSCAR WILDE and GEORGE BERNARD SHAW. His sexually explicit *My Life and Loves* appeared in four volumes in the 1920s. **Terence Brown**

Harris, Richard (1933–2002), actor. Born in Limerick. After studying acting in London he appeared in minor film roles, with his international breakthrough coming as a North of England Rugby League player in *This Sporting Life* (1963), for which he received the Best Actor award at the Cannes Film Festival, while his most commercially successful role was in *A Man Called Horse* (1970). His career was marred by personal vicissitudes, but he made a comeback with his performance as Bull McCabe in *The Field* (1990), while his role in *Unforgiven* (1992) was also well received. He also appeared in two *Harry Potter* films (2001 and 2002) (see p. 197). **Kevin Rockett**

Harrison, Frank Llewellyn (1905–1987), musicologist. Born in Dublin; he was a boy chorister at ST PATRICK'S CATHEDRAL, studied music at the RIAM and TCD. He was assistant professor of music at Queen's University, Kingston, Ontario, 1935–46, professor at Colgate University, 1946–7, and Washington University, St Louis, until 1952, senior lecturer at the University of Oxford until 1970, and professor of ethnomusicology at the University of Amsterdam; he was also a visiting professor at Yale, Princeton, and Utrecht and was elected a fellow of the British Academy in 1965. His *Music in Medieval Britain* (1958) became a standard reference text, and he also edited much early music. **Paul Collins**

Hart, Henry Chichester (1847–1908), botanist and walker. Born in Dublin, son of Sir Andrew Hart, vice-provost of TRINITY COLLEGE. A brilliant botanist, he served in the British Polar Expedition to the Arctic of 1875; he was also a knowledgeable geologist and in 1883 took part in the Palestine Exploration Fund's important geological expedition to Palestine. STANDISH O'GRADY described him as 'the handsomest, noblest looking, most superbly formed Irishman of modern times.' His great physical fitness and mountaineering skills often allowed him to be the first botanist to obtain access to wilderness mountain areas. Enlisted by A. G. MORE in the preparation of the second edition of *Cybele Hibernica*, he found and identified many new species; laconic descriptions of his treks appear in his botanical papers. His strength and stamina as a walker were legendary; on one occasion, for a bet, he walked from the suburbs of Dublin across the WICKLOW MOUNTAINS to their highest peak, the summit of Lugnaquilla Mountain (924 m), and back in less than twenty-four hours (a round trip of over 90 km). He edited the Arden edition of Shakespeare's plays (1903). **Michael Fewer**

harp. *A poignant detail of the harper in* The Marriage of Strongbow and Aoife *(1854) by Daniel Maclise. The old harper, a symbol of ancient Ireland, is silent in the wake of the victory by Strongbow (Richard de Clare) over the Irish. The interlace decoration of the harp reflects the artist's antiquarian interests. [National Gallery of Ireland]*

Harte, Frank (1933–), architect, singer, and lecturer. Born in Dublin; educated at Blackrock College and DIT. An authority and source singer of the Irish song tradition, he has also received international recognition as a lecturer and SONG-COLLECTOR. His albums include *Through Dublin City* and *Daybreak and a Candle End*, and he has also published the book *Songs of Dublin* (1993). **Anthony McCann**

Hartley, Walter Noel (1846–1913), chemist. Born in Staffordshire; his early studies were at the Universities of Edinburgh and Marburg. He left King's College, London, for Dublin in 1879 to take up the professorship of chemistry at the ROYAL COLLEGE OF SCIENCE and married the writer MARY LAVIN. Absorption bands between 200 and 300 nm in the stratosphere and mesosphere are called *Hartley bands* in recognition of his observations. He made significant contributions to a wide variety of studies in chemistry. He received many honours for his work in spectroscopy, including fellowship of the Royal Society, 1884. **Susan McKenna-Lawlor**

Hartnett, Michael (1941–1999), poet. Born in Newcastle West, Co. Limerick; educated at local schools and UCD. In 1963 he jointly edited the literary journal *Arena* and thereafter lived for periods in Spain and London. His experience of translating and reworking poetry in Irish powerfully informed *Anatomy of a Cliché* (1968). He followed this with a major version of the *Hag of Beare* (1969) and *Gypsy Ballads* (1973), versions of Lorca. For him all poetry was a form of translation, a moment when the author without liberates the artist within. Nonetheless, in *A Farewell to English* (1975) he announced that henceforth he would write only in Irish. In the same year he produced *Cúlú Íde* and *The Retreat of Ita Cagney*, which, though seeming like versions of one another, may well be distinct poems. He returned with his family to a frugal life in Co. Limerick. Work that followed included *Adharca Broic* (1978), *An Phurgóid* (1983), and *Do Nuala: Foighne Crann* (1984). In 1985 he resumed publishing in English with *Inchicore Haiku* but also produced *An Lia Nocht* as well as versions of DÁIBHÍ Ó BRUADAIR. *Selected and New Poems* appeared in 1994. He was arguably the most underrated Irish poet of his generation. Since his death an annual Éigse Michael Hartnett has been held at Newcastle West, with an accompanying prize for poetry. **Declan Kiberd**

Hartnett. The poet Michael Hartnett *by Edward McGuire (1971). Hartnett announced his intention of writing only in Irish in his poem 'A farewell to English' (1975). [Sally McGuire]*

Harty, Sir (Herbert) Hamilton (1879–1941), musician, composer, and conductor. Born in Hillsborough, Co. Down. He became conductor of the London Symphony Orchestra and the Hallé Orchestra, 1920–30, introducing works of Sibelius, Berlioz, Strauss, and Shostakovich and giving the first English performance of works such as Mahler's 4th Symphony (1927). Knighted in 1925, he was awarded honorary doctorates in Dublin, Manchester, and Belfast and the Gold Medal of the Royal Philharmonic Society, 1934. His orchestral works include *Comedy Overture (1907)*, *Violin Concerto* (1909), and *Irish Symphony* (1910); chamber works include *Trio* (1901) and *Piano Quintet* (1904). He also composed the tone poem *With the Wild Geese* (1910) and *Cantata: The Mystic Trumpeter* (1913). He was a lifelong friend of MICHELE ESPOSITO, whom he regarded as his mentor in composition. **Éamonn O'Keeffe**

Harvey, (Beauchamp) Bagenal (1762–1798), United Irishman. Born at Bargy Castle, Co. Wexford. A landowner and lawyer, he was commander-in-chief of the Wexford rebel army from 31 May to 7 June 1798 and led its failed attack on New Ross on 6 June. He was captured after the rebellion and hanged on Wexford Bridge. **Daniel Gahan**

Harvey, William Henry (1811–1866), botanist. Born in Limerick; educated at TCD. He botanised in South Africa during his service as Colonial Treasurer in the Cape Colony, 1836–42, before being appointed professor of botany to the RDS and later at TCD. Specialising in marine algae, he published the compendious *Phycologica Britannica* (1846–51). In the mid-1850s he undertook a collecting trip to Sri Lanka, Australia, Tasmania, and the Pacific Islands and published *Phycologica Australica* (1853–63). Considered the foremost botanist of his day, he was elected a fellow of the Royal Society in 1858. [see SHACKELTON, ABRAHAM.] **Helena C. G. Chesney**

Haslam, Anna, née Fisher (1829–1922), suffragist and philanthropist. Born in Youghal, Co. Cork. A QUAKER, she devoted most of her life to the promotion of women in education and local and national government. A campaigner for married women's property rights and against the Contagious Diseases Acts (1869–86), she founded the Dublin Women's Suffrage Association, 1876, which later became the Irish Women's Suffrage and Local Government Association. While the IWSLGA had about 500 members by 1914, its anti-militancy deterred younger women, who joined the more strident Irish Women's Franchise League. [see WOMEN'S SUFFRAGE MOVEMENT.] **Clíona Murphy**

Haughey, Anthony (1963–), photographer. Born in Keady, Co Armagh; studied film, photography and video at West Surrey Institute of Art and Design and fine art media at the NCAD. He is director of the photography degree course at the Dublin Institute of Technology. His major exhibitions include 'Home' (1992), 'The Edge of Europe' (1996), also published as a book, and 'Monitor'

Harty. *Sir Herbert Hamilton Harty, a composer but probably best known for his work as a conductor of the Hallé and London Symphony Orchestras. He made well-known arrangements of Handel's* Fireworks *and* Water Music *suites. [Getty Images/Hulton Archive]*

(2001). His work has appeared in numerous publications, including the *British Journal of Photography* and *Source Magazine* and is held in collections in the Victoria and Albert Museum, London, and the University of Salamanca. He won the prestigious Mosaique Programme international art award in 2000. **Myra Dowling**

Haughey, Charles (1926–), politician. Born in Castlebar, Co. Mayo; educated at UCD, where he studied commerce. In 1949 he was called to the bar, and he also qualified as a chartered accountant. The most controversial leader of FIANNA FÁIL, he led the party for twelve years, 1979–92, and was elected TAOISEACH four times (1979–81, 1982, 1987–9, and 1989–92). The son-in-law of SEÁN LEMASS, he quickly rose through the ministerial ranks following his election to Dáil Éireann on his fourth attempt in 1957. He was Minister for Justice, 1961–4, and Minister for Agriculture, 1964–6, before attaining the pivotal role of Minister for Finance in 1966, following the accession of JACK LYNCH to the leadership.

Haughey moved to undermine Lynch's tenure when the conflict in Northern Ireland broke out in August 1969. Delegated authority to oversee the provision of aid to refugees from the North, Haughey and his ministerial colleague Neil Blaney used the conflict to foment insurrection in Belfast, hoping thereby to destabilise Lynch's Government. When the ministers authorised a shipment of arms to be provided to Northern nationalists who in reality were representing the PROVISIONAL IRA, the divisions within the Government over Northern policy were brutally exposed. Haughey and Blaney were dismissed and faced conspiracy charges. Haughey was acquitted but lost the power to direct Fianna Fáil for a decade. After five years in the political wilderness he returned to the front bench as spokesman on health, a portfolio he retained when Lynch was returned to power in 1977. He distanced himself from the economic policies adopted by the Government as internal dissatisfaction with Lynch forced his resignation amid economic recession in 1979. He also capitalised on the unease in the parliamentary party about the Government's response to the deteriorating security situation in Northern Ireland, gaining the leader's mantle in disputed circumstances.

Widely regarded as the most brilliant politician of his generation, Haughey never lived up to the potential he showed as a minister, in part because the internecine feuding within Fianna Fáil demanded the use of his undoubted tactical skills. He was forced to resign in 1992 because of allegations that he lied about his knowledge of a telephone bugging scandal ten years earlier. His removal was the price demanded of Fianna Fáil by its coalition partner, the PROGRESSIVE DEMOCRATS, led by DESMOND O'MALLEY, who had been a rival for the leadership of Fianna Fáil at the time of the original scandal. Throughout his career Haughey had political charisma in abundance—a quality that generates respect and hatred in equal measure. His association with violent REPUBLICANISM, stemming from the position he took during the ARMS CRISIS, gave the political boss a dangerous political edge. He self-consciously adopted the sobriquet of vindicated patriot. His ambition, drive, and charm, combined with a messianic ruthlessness, were instrumental in creating a political culture based on unquestioning loyalty; but by 1992 he had run out of loyal friends.

In retirement Haughey has been the subject of two judicial TRIBUNALS of inquiry into allegations of political corruption. The tribunals established that, while in office, he received more than £8 million in payments from a cartel of prominent businessmen. [see AOSDÁNA; ARMS CRISIS; 'GUBU'.] **Justin O'Brien**

Haughey's Fort, a Late BRONZE AGE HILL-FORT within the NAVAN complex near Armagh. The site, dated to c. 1100–900 BC, was surrounded by three ditches, with a maximum diameter of approximately 340 m (370 yards). Two double-ringed enclosures and the remains of many smaller structures occupied the interior and revealed traces of gold, bronze, glass beads, and ceramics. The waterlogged ditches preserved wooden handles, stakes, fragments of a wooden bowl, and a wide variety of environmental evidence. Closely associated with the site was the artificial pool of the 'King's Stables'. Haughey's Fort appears to have served as a tribal centre before the rise of NAVAN FORT. **J. P. Mallory**

Haughton, Samuel (1821–1897), polymath. Born in Carlow; graduated from the University of Dublin in 1843 and ordained in the CHURCH OF IRELAND in 1846. He was professor of geology in TCD, 1851, a fellow of the Royal Society, 1858, and president of the ROYAL IRISH ACADEMY, 1886–91; while still professor he took a medical degree in 1862. He made contributions in mathematics (on elasticity), in geology (on tidal motion), in climate change, and in medicine (on the action of joints). As Council member, secretary and president of the ROYAL ZOOLOGICAL SOCIETY OF IRELAND over many years he is credited with saving Dublin Zoo from closure. He is remembered particularly for 'Haughton's drop'—the distance a person being hanged should fall in order to ensure immediate death and so prevent further suffering. **Charles Mollan**

Haverty, Anne (1959–), novelist, poet, and biographer. Born in Holycross, Co. Tipperary. Her first novel, *One Day as a Tiger*, was published in 1997; a second novel, *The Far Side of a Kiss*, appeared in 2000. A collection of her poems, *The Beauty of the Moon* (1999), was a Poetry Book Society recommendation. Her biography of CONSTANCE MARKIEVICZ was published in 1988. **Terence Brown**

Haverty, Joseph Patrick (1794–1854), artist. Born in Galway; he was exhibiting in Dublin by 1814 and in 1829 became a member of the ROYAL HIBERNIAN ACADEMY. He painted portraits and portrait groups, such as O'CONNELL at the Clare election of 1828, and domestic groups, at which he was more successful. He was also a painter of religious subjects, such as Father Mathew receiving a pledge-breaker, now in the NATIONAL GALLERY OF IRELAND, and altarpieces, of which one survives in ST PATRICK'S COLLEGE, Maynooth. His most famous work is *The Limerick Piper*, a patriotic theme of a blind piper playing for a lost Ireland, of which numerous lithographs were made. **Anne Crookshank**

Hayes, Joanne: see KERRY BABIES CASE.

Hayes, Catherine (1825–1861), singer, known as 'the Swan of Erin'. Born in Limerick; studied singing in Dublin, Paris, and Milan. Following her appearance in Bellini's *I puritani* she made her debut at La Scala, Milan, in 1845. She became established in France and Italy as a prima donna, interpreting the works of Donizetti, Rossini, and Verdi, and toured extensively in North and South America, where her concerts were enormously successful, earning her international acclaim and substantial fees. From 1856 she lived in England but performed less frequently. **Brian Lalor**

Hayes, Edward (1797–1864), artist. Born in Co. Tipperary; studied at the DUBLIN SOCIETY schools. He was a watercolourist doing small portraits, then in vogue, but these became more dramatic in

Haughey. *Charles Haughey, one of Ireland's most controversial twentieth-century political leaders, in front of Leinster House after his election as Taoiseach in 1987, surrounded by supporters. [Photocall Ireland]*

style and very romantic. His landscapes often use a vortex-like composition, and their delicate detail is very fine. He taught and also painted MINIATURES and the occasional oil. **Anne Crookshank**

Hayes, Edwin (1820–1904), marine painter. Born in Bristol; in 1833 he moved with his family to Dublin, where he attended the DUBLIN SOCIETY's Drawing Schools. A keen yachtsman, he specialised in marine views of the Irish coast. Though elected an associate member of the ROYAL HIBERNIAN ACADEMY in 1853, he had by then moved to London, where he exhibited at the Royal Academy in 1855. Working in both oils and watercolours, he produced marine views of Britain, France, Spain, and Italy, exhibiting mainly in London. He maintained his connection with Ireland and was elected a member of the RHA in 1871. **Peter Murray**

Hayes, Gabriel (1909–1978), sculptor. Born in Monasterevin, Co. Kildare; attended the Metropolitan School of Art, Dublin, won the RDS Taylor Scholarship, and subsequently studied in France and Italy. She was an assured draughtswoman as well as a sculptor of distinction; her most accomplished works are the boldly carved socialist-realist bas-relief limestone panels on the Department of Industry and Commerce, Kildare Street, Dublin (1942), cut *in situ*. Other major public commissions include *The Three Graces* (1941) on the College of Catering, Cathal Brugha Street, Dublin, *Stations of the Cross* (1957–69), Galway Cathedral, and a monumental bronze figure of Luke Wadding (1958) in Waterford. She also designed the $\frac{1}{2}$p, 1p and 2p decimal coins introduced in 1971. **Brian Lalor**

Hayes, Sir Henry Brown (1762–1832), convict and founder of Australian freemasonry. Probably born in Cork, he was the son of a wealthy merchant. He became sheriff of the city in the 1780s and was knighted in 1790. In 1797 he kidnapped a QUAKER heiress, Mary Pike, and forced her into a spurious marriage; he was immediately outlawed. In 1800 he was sentenced to TRANSPORTATION for life. In Australia, on 14 May 1803, he founded the colony's first masonic lodge. He succeeded in business and lived in great style at Vaucluse House, near South Head. He was pardoned in 1809, and in December 1812 he left Australia to return to Cork. [see ABDUCTION OF HEIRESSES.] **Ciarán Deane**

Hayes, Martin (1962–), FIDDLE-player. Born in Feakle, Co. Clare, a son of P. Joe Hayes, founder-member of TULLA CÉILÍ BAND. Living in Seattle, he formed a successful partnership with the Chicago guitarist Dennis Cahill. He continues to teach at the WILLIE CLANCY SUMMER SCHOOL in Milltown Malbay, Co. Clare, each July. Recordings include *Martin Hayes* (1993), *Under the Moon* (1995), *The Lonesome Touch* (1997), and *Live in Seattle* (1999). **Pat Ahern**

Hayes, Michaelangelo (1820–1877), artist. Born in Waterford, son of EDWARD HAYES; trained at the ROYAL HIBERNIAN ACADEMY. He was a horse painter but is best remembered for his six engravings of *Car Driving in the South of Ireland* (1836), depicting Bianconi's coach service. He was an oil painter as well as a watercolourist, many of his large battle scenes being in the latter medium. He exhibited at the RHA, becoming a member, and at the Royal Academy, London. His study of horses in motion led him to reject the 'flying gallop' he used in his early works, and he gave a lecture on this topic in 1876 in the Dublin Society (see pp. 529, 1068). **Anne Crookshank**

Hayes, Samuel (died 1795), forester and politician. Probably born in Co. Wicklow. A barrister by profession, he was MP for Wicklow, 1783–90, and a colonel in the VOLUNTEERS. In Parliament he introduced various pieces of legislation to improve agriculture and industry; he is best remembered as one of the most influential figures in the development of modern FORESTRY in Ireland. On his country estate near Rathdrum, now known as Avondale, he had a large oak forest and introduced many exotic trees; a few of which still survive. The year before his death he published a *Practical Treatise on Planting and the Management of Woods and Coppices*. **Christopher Moriarty**

Heads of Government (Irish Free State, Éire/Ireland, Republic of Ireland

1922	Michael Collins (pro-Treaty Sinn Féin)
1922–32	William T. Cosgrave (pro-Treaty Sinn Féin/Cumann na nGaedheal)
1932–7	Éamon de Valera (Fianna Fáil)
1937–48	Éamon de Valera (Fianna Fáil)
1948–51	John A. Costello (Fine Gael/Labour Party/National Labour/Clann na Poblachta/Clann na Talmhan)
1951–4	Éamon de Valera (Fianna Fáil)
1954–7	John A. Costello (Fine Gael/Labour Party/Clann na Talmhan)
1957–9	Éamon de Valera (Fianna Fáil)
1959–66	Seán Lemass (Fianna Fáil)
1966–73	Jack Lynch (Fianna Fáil)
1973–7	Liam Cosgrave (Fine Gael/Labour Party)
1977–9	Jack Lynch (Fianna Fáil)
1979–81	Charles Haughey (Fianna Fáil)
1981–2	Garret FitzGerald (Fine Gael/Labour Party)
1982	Charles Haughey (Fianna Fáil)
1982–7	Garret FitzGerald (Fine Gael/Labour Party)
1987–9	Charles Haughey (Fianna Fáil)
1989–92	Charles Haughey (Fianna Fáil/Progressive Democrats)
1992	Albert Reynolds (Fianna Fáil/Progressive Democrats)
1993–4	Albert Reynolds (Fianna Fáil/Labour Party)
1994–7	John Bruton (Fine Gael/Labour Party/Democratic Left)
1997–2002	Bertie Ahern (Fianna Fáil/Progressive Democrats)

health. As measured by life expectancy at birth and mortality rates, Irish people's health compares favourably with the best international standards. In the Republic, life expectancy in 1996 for men was 73.3 years (compared with an average for EU countries of 74 years). In Northern Ireland the figure for men was slightly higher, at 74; for women the situation is somewhat less favourable, at 78.7 (compared with an EU average of 80.5). The crude death rate in 1996 in the Republic was 8.7 deaths per 1,000 POPULATION (compared with an EU average of 10).

The Republic has by far the most youthful population in the EUROPEAN UNION, with 88.6 per cent of the population in 1997 under 65, compared with the EU average of 84.2. The population of Northern Ireland is only slightly less youthful. In 1997 infant mortality in the Republic was 6.2 deaths per 1,000 live births (compared with an EU average of 5.3).

When asked about their health status, Irish people tend to report lower levels of ill health than nationals of other EU countries. In 1994 less than 2 per cent reported their health as 'very bad' and less than 4 per cent as 'bad'; the corresponding averages for EU countries were 3 per cent 'very bad' and 7 per cent 'bad'.

The main causes of death are cardiovascular disease and cancer. The Republic has one of the highest death rates from cardiovascular disease among EU countries; the rate in Northern Ireland is slightly higher. About 30 per cent of the population smoke, a proportion that has remained stubbornly high over recent decades. There is a growing problem with obesity: on average, people in the Republic gained 6 kg (13 lb) in weight during the 1990s. ALCOHOL consumption has also risen dramatically; consumption per capita is among the highest among EU countries. Road traffic accidents claimed 12.4 deaths per 100,000 population in 1998 in the Republic, compared with 9.5 such deaths in Northern Ireland.

The number of SUICIDES in the Republic has increased, particularly among young males. In 1998 there were 12.4 deaths from suicide per 100,000 population, compared with a rate of 9.5 in Northern Ireland. Inequalities in health between those in different socio-economic groups is attracting increasing public attention, North and South. **Ruth Barrington**

health, economics of. The Irish health care system is complex, composed of both private and public sectors that are inter-mixed. Just over a third of the population is entitled to free means-tested medical care financed by the state, with the remainder entitled to free public out-patient and in-patient services but not to primary care services nor to prescription medicines. Significantly, despite full entitlement to public HOSPITAL care, a large and increasing section of the population—approximately 43 per cent—holds PRIVATE HEALTH INSURANCE. The reasons for this include the sense of security engendered, as well as speed of access and perceived quality of care. Ireland spends approximately 8.5 per cent of GNP on HEALTH SERVICES (public and private), slightly above OECD and EU averages; PUBLIC EXPENDITURE on health, at approximately 6.9 per cent of GNP, is well above OECD and EU averages.

Expenditure on public health has increased dramatically in recent years as the Government tries to overcome serious deficiencies in the public health system, such as long waiting lists and delays for consultant referral and surgical procedures. This follows years of underinvestment and significant cutbacks during the fiscal retrenchment of the late 1980s. About 10 per cent of total health expenditure is financed through private health insurance. Until recently there was a monopoly provider of private health insurance services, the Voluntary Health Insurance (VHI) Board, a STATE-SPONSORED enterprise. The health insurance market was opened to competition in 1996, but so far only one other insurance provider, the British United Provident Association (BUPA), has entered the market. The Irish system of private health insurance is based on the principle of solidarity between insured generations through community rating, open enrolment, lifetime cover, and risk equalisation.

A significant policy issue that is emerging is the potential for greater co-operation in health services between the Republic and Northern Ireland. While there are notable differences (such as the existence of universal coverage and the purchaser-provider split in Northern Ireland), the two systems have common core principles and face similar health care problems. The two jurisdictions share the same leading causes of premature death—cardiovascular disease, cancer, and car accidents—suggesting considerable scope for co-operation in public health promotion campaigns. Equally, the health care system as a whole could improve through enhanced collaboration in such areas as training and peer review and in certain specialist hospital services, such as transplantation and kidney dialysis. **Orla Lane**

health services. The health services of the Republic and Northern Ireland share common roots in developments in medical care and public health in the nineteenth century. After 1920 the two systems began slowly to diverge. In 1948 a national health service was established in Northern Ireland on the same principles as in the United Kingdom. The organisation of the service is similar to that in Britain, except that the span of responsibility includes welfare and child protection services.

An attempt in the late 1940s to establish a similar service in the Republic was thwarted by the combined opposition of the medical profession and the Catholic Church. What was achieved was the provision of hospital and specialist services at little or no charge to the whole population; but the majority of people still have to pay for the services of general practitioners. As in Northern Ireland, the main source of finance for the health services is central government. Expenditure per capita on health services has been more generous in Northern Ireland than in the Republic, where public expenditure on health has been falling as a proportion of GNP and in 1999 was less than 6 per cent. There has been criticism of the relatively small number of hospital beds and medical specialists, exacerbated by the problem of finding and keeping suitably qualified staff. About 40 per cent of the population is covered by insurance for private care, most of which is provided in public hospitals. Insurance premiums are subsidised by income tax relief and by subsidised charges in public hospitals. There is concern at the inequities that have arisen from what has been described as a two-tier health service. Reconciling local access to services with the need to provide specialist services centrally is proving a continuing political issue in both jurisdictions. [see MOTHER AND CHILD SCHEME.] **Ruth Barrington**

health, statistics. Between 1970 and 1998 the birth rate in the Republic decreased from 21.9 births per 1,000 population to 14.5. Over the same period the corresponding rate in Northern Ireland declined from 21.1 births per 1,000 to 14. The marriage rate also fell significantly in both jurisdictions. In the Republic the number of marriages per 1,000 fell from 7.1 to 4.5; in Northern Ireland it fell from 8.1 to 4.6.

Table 1: Marriages, births, and deaths, 1950–98

	Republic			Northern Ireland		
	Marriages	Births	Deaths	Marriages	Births	Deaths
1950	16,018	63,565	37,700	9,084	28,794	15,939
1960	15,465	60,735	32,700	9,881	31,989	15,296
1970	20,778	64,382	33,686	12,297	32,086	16,551
1980	21,792	74,064	33,472	9,923	28,582	16,835
1990	17,838	53,044	31,370	9,588	26,251	15,426
1995	15,604	48,787	32,259	8,576	23,693	15,310
1998	16,783	53,551	31,683	7,826	23,668	14,993
Rate per 1,000 population						
1950	5.4	21.4	12.7	6.6	21.0	11.6
1960	5.5	21.5	11.5	7.0	22.5	10.8
1970	7.1	21.9	11.4	8.1	21.1	10.9
1980	6.4	21.9	9.7	6.5	18.6	11.0
1990	5.1	15.1	9.1	6.0	16.5	9.7
1995	4.3	13.5	8.8	5.2	14.3	9.3
1998	4.5	14.5	8.5	4.6	14.0	8.9

Between 1980 and 1998 the proportion of births outside marriage increased from 5 per cent to 28.3 per cent in the Republic and from 6.1 per cent to 28.5 per cent in Northern Ireland.

Table 2: Births outside marriage, 1940–98

	Republic			Northern Ireland		
	Total births	Births outside marriage	Proportion of total	Total births	Births outside marriage	Proportion of total
1940	56,594	1,824	3.2	25,363	1,169	4.6
1950	63,565	1,627	2.6	28,794	986	3.4
1960	60,735	968	1.6	31,989	815	2.5
1970	64,382	1,709	2.7	32,086	1,214	3.8
1980	74,064	3,723	5.0	28,453	1,736	6.1
1990	53,044	7,767	14.6	26,251	4,946	18.8
1995	48,787	10,862	22.3	23,693	5,487	23.2
1998	53,551	15,133	28.3	23,668	6,743	28.5

Life expectancy in the two jurisdictions is broadly comparable. Female life expectancy at birth is 79 in both jurisdictions; male life expectancy at birth is 73 in the Republic and 74 in Northern Ireland. Deaths from circulatory diseases accounted for approximately two-fifths of both male and female deaths in 1998; deaths from cancer accounted for approximately a quarter. **Central Statistics Office/Northern Ireland Statistics & Research Agency**

Healy, Dermot (1947–), novelist, poet, and short-story writer. Born in Finea, Co. Westmeath. His second novel, *A Goat's Song* (1994), a powerful, almost mythical study of Catholic-Protestant relationships, established his reputation as a writer of fiction. This was followed by the mesmeric autobiographical work *The Bend for Home* (1996). He has also published two collections of poetry. **Terence Brown**

Healy, John (1930–1991), journalist. Born in Charlestown, Co. Mayo; educated at St Nathy's College, Ballaghaderreen. He started work in the *Western People* in 1948, worked in the IRISH NEWS AGENCY and the IRISH PRESS GROUP, and edited the *Sunday Review*, 1959–63, where, with Ted Nealon, he introduced the influential 'Backbencher' column, which he transferred to the IRISH TIMES. The column mixed comment and innovative 'behind the scenes' reporting. A champion of the people of rural and small-town Ireland, Healy was also an award-winning television broadcaster. He returned to his Connacht roots in 1975 to jointly found and edit the weekly *Western Journal*. Selected articles were published as *The Death of an Irish Town* (1968), which became a journalism classic. **David Quin**

Healy, Michael (1873–1941), STAINED-GLASS artist. Born and raised in a Dublin tenement; he worked from the age of fourteen, attending evening classes at the Metropolitan School of Art and subsequently studied art in Florence. In 1903 he joined SARAH PURSER's studio, AN TÚR GLOINE, where he remained until his death. The most representative collection of his work can be found in St Brendan's Cathedral, Loughrea, Co. Galway. More influenced by Renaissance painting than by the major art movements of his day, his windows are characterised by the excellent draughtsmanship of the figures, fondness for detail, and superb craftsmanship. **David Caron**

Healy (or Haly), Robert (died 1771), portraitist. He entered the DUBLIN SOCIETY Schools c. 1766, where he became a friend of John O'Keefe, later an actor. He excelled in drawing portraits in pastels and chalk grisaille; sitters included Miss Cunningham, Mrs Gardiner, the Countess of Mornington, and members of the Conolly family of Castletown, whom he painted in situations of varying formality in 1768–9. He also drew horses expertly, and *Tom Conolly and the Castletown Hunt* is one of his finest works. His father, Robert, and brother, William, were also artists. He exhibited just once, at the Society of Artists in Dublin. **Brendan Rooney**

Healy, T. M. [Timothy] (1855–1931), lawyer and politician. Born at Bantry, Co. Cork. He emigrated to England at sixteen, living in Newcastle-upon-Tyne. Active in émigré politics, he became a publicist for and secretary to PARNELL, and was elected to Parliament in October 1880. His private disenchantment with Parnell festered, and in the crisis surrounding the O'SHEA DIVORCE CASE of 1890–91 he rallied the outmanoeuvred opposition to Parnell, whom he derided with inspired ferocity. Shamelessly sycophantic towards the Catholic hierarchy, he set a record in attacking each successive leader of the IRISH PARTY. He was GOVERNOR-GENERAL OF THE IRISH FREE STATE, 1922–8. **Frank Callanan**

Heaney, Seamus (1939–), poet and scholar. Born near Castledawson, Co. Derry; educated at QUB and St Joseph's College of Education, Belfast. He taught at St Thomas's Intermediate School, Ballymurphy, Belfast, 1962–3, and St Joseph's College, 1963–6. He joined the staff at Queen's in 1966 and was guest lecturer at the University of California, Berkeley, 1970–71. In 1972 he moved to Glanmore, Co. Wicklow, to write full-time. He taught at Carysfort College, Blackrock, Co. Dublin, 1975–81, and began teaching at Harvard University in 1982, becoming Boylston professor of rhetoric and oratory in 1984, resigning in 1996 to become Emerson poet in residence and concurrently professor of poetry at the University of Oxford, 1989–94. He is the recipient of numerous prizes, including the Somerset Maugham Award (1967), Cholmondeley Award (1968), Duff Cooper Prize (1975), Whitbread Award (1987, 2000), and NOBEL PRIZE for Literature (1995). His poetry collections include *Death of a Naturalist* (1966), *North* (1975), *Station Island* (1984), *Seeing Things* (1991), *The Spirit Level* (1996), and *Electric Light* (2001). He has also translated the medieval Irish tale 'BUILE SHUIBHNE' as *Sweeney Astray* (1984) and the Old English epic *Beowulf* (1999). He jointly edited the *Rattle Bag* anthology of poetry (with the English poet Ted Hughes) in 1982; his own *Opened Ground: Poems, 1966–1996* appeared in 1998. His adaptation of Sophocles' *Philoctetes* was published as *The Cure at Troy* in 1990 and was performed in Derry by FIELD DAY (of which he is a founding director) in the same year. He is also the author of collections of critical essays: *Preoccupations* (1980), *The Government of the Tongue* (1988), and *The Redress of Poetry* (1995), this last volume offering a collection of lectures delivered during his tenure at Oxford, and *Finders Keepers* (2002). Early in his career Heaney was much influenced by the aesthetic of PATRICK KAVANAGH, whom Heaney characterised as seeking to register in his poetry 'the unregarded data of the usual life.' Like Kavanagh, Heaney in his early work often seeks to create a poetic image of the habitual routines of rural life, finding deeper resonances at play within these quotidian rituals.

Heaney had just begun his publishing career when the political situation in Northern Ireland began to deteriorate. As the Northern state spiralled into crisis, increasing demands were made on Heaney to produce poetry that would engage directly with the situation, and he felt impelled to write in a way that was supportive of his own community. He resisted this pressure, preferring to engage with politics in a more oblique manner and endeavouring to address contemporary political concerns through the medium of MYTHOLOGY and IRON AGE history. He has been variously criticised for this, some commentators accusing him of producing poetry that is evasive and empty of real meaning, others claiming that he cleaves too much to the concerns of his own community. Heaney's most intense engagement with the Ulster situation came in *North*, of which CONOR CRUISE O'BRIEN observed: 'I have read many pessimistic analyses of "Northern Ireland", but none that has the bleak conclusiveness of these poems.' In *Station Island* Heaney appeared to register something of a break with his past and drew the figure of JAMES JOYCE in to the final poem of the title sequence to provide him with a new aesthetic, in which 'The main thing is to write for the joy of it.'

Heaney's later work operates at a greater distance from specifically Irish concerns, and in *The Haw Lantern* (1987) and, especially, *Seeing Things* he seems to be moving towards a poetry more densely considered and elusive than his earlier work. This later material was also informed by Heaney's developing interest in the work of poets from eastern Europe, such as Zbigniew Herbert, Miroslav Holub, and Czeslaw Milosz. The unfolding NORTHERN IRELAND PEACE PROCESS did, however, bring Heaney back to native concerns in *The Spirit Level*, a volume tinged with a sense of hopefulness for the passing of conflict. Heaney has achieved in his career the rare feat of being both critically respected and genuinely popular. **Andrew Murphy**

Heaney. *Seamus Heaney, poet and scholar; he was awarded the Nobel Prize for Literature in 1995. [Camera Press Ireland]*

Hearn, Lafcadio (Koizumi Yakumo) (1850–1904), writer and orientalist. Born in Lefkas in the Ionian Islands to a Dublin-born naval surgeon and a Greek mother. He spent his childhood in Rathmines, Dublin, before, aged fifteen, he embarked on his itinerant career in the United States, where he became in 1869 a controversial crime reporter with the *Cincinnati Enquirer*. Following sojourns in New Orleans and Martinique, he moved to Japan in 1890, later adopting a Japanese name, Koizumi Yakumo. He devoted the remainder of his life to the study of Japanese culture and philosophy, which he sought to present to Western readers in a succession of pioneering publications. Among his books are *Two Years in the French West Indies* (1890), *Glimpses of Unfamiliar Japan* (1894), and *Japan: An Attempt at Interpretation* (1904). **Brian Lalor**

hearth, the, traditionally the core and heart of the Irish home (up to the beginning of the twentieth century), with a host of beliefs and portents gathered around it. The turf fire, burning day and night, winter and summer, symbolised both FAMILY continuity and hospitality to the stranger; it served to prepare and to cure food, to dry clothes, to warm the family and sick animals, to keep the thatch dry, and to preserve the timbers. It was around the hearth that family and friends gathered in the evening for games, STORYTELLING, and singing. The cooking was most commonly done in a heavy iron cauldron, round-bottomed, with three short legs, which hung over the fire from an iron or wooden crane. An alternative was the flat-bottomed oven-pot, with a dished lid on which hot turf sods could be placed. BREAD was baked either on the griddle or in the oven-pot (generally called a bastable or bastible, from Barnstable in Devon, where it was first made). Around the hob were the griddle, kettle, tongs, shovel, and fire machine (bellows).

The fire was in the care of the woman of the house, whose last duty at night was to 'smoor' it, burying a live turf in the ashes, to be fanned to life in the morning. If the fire went out, it was said, the soul of the family went out with it. Many fires remained alight for centuries, with the help of prayers like this one:

> Coiglim an tine seo mar a choigleann Críost cáidh;
> Muire ar mhullach an tí, agus Bríd ina lár;
> An t-ochtar ainglí is tréine i gCathair na nGrás
> Ag cumhdach an tí seo is a mhuintir a thabhairt slán.
> (I save this fire, as noble Christ saves;
> Mary on the top of the house and Brigid in its centre;
> The eight strongest angels in Heaven
> Preserving this house and keeping its people safe.)

Some of these practices and beliefs survived at least into the 1970s (see pp. 407, 568). [see FOLK-LIFE; FOLKLORE.] **John Wakeman**

Hearts of Steel, or Steelboys, a Protestant secret society that came into existence during the later eighteenth century to protest against EVICTIONS, high taxes in the form of the local 'cess', and excessive rents. Following in the tradition of local vigilante groups, the organisation emerged in 1767 among the Protestant tenants of the Donegall (Chichester) estate in Co. Antrim; from there it spread during the early 1770s to the neighbouring counties of Armagh, Derry, and Down.

On 23 December 1770 some 1,200 Steelboys marched from the meeting-house in Templepatrick, Co. Antrim, to Belfast Barracks, determined to free by force David Douglas, a local farmer who was being held on a false charge of cattle-maiming. The attempt was repulsed by the military; five of the raiding party were killed and nine injured in the clashes that ensued. Some reports claim that the vanquished revolutionaries then fled *en masse* to the American colonies, where they were to form the backbone of the anti-English revolutionary movement; other sources describe the movement as the precursor of the ORANGE ORDER and even of the UNITED IRISHMEN. **Roddy Hegarty**

Heath, Lady Mary, née Sophie Pierce (1896–1939), aviator and athlete. Born in Newcastlewest, Co. Limerick. In 1928, she was the first person to fly solo from Cape Town to London. Just over a year later, after moving to the United States, she barely survived a serious crash while practising for the National Air Races in Cleveland. As a pioneering athlete, Heath set world records for the high jump and javelin and was a founding member of the Women's Amateur Athletic Association. She never fully recovered from her horrific crash and died in 1939 after a fall from a London tram car. **Lindie Naughton**

Hebrides, the. The Hebrides and Argyll in Scotland were settled by the DÁL RIADA by the middle of the first millennium AD, IONA being chosen by COLM CILLE as the site of his principal monastery. Subject to VIKING colonisation from the ninth century, they thus became known to the Irish as Innse Gall ('Isles of the Foreigners'), developing a hybrid Gaelo-Scandinavian society, though the Gaelic element remained paramount. Viking Dublin and the Isles frequently shared rulers, and by the middle of the eleventh century Dublin's Irish masters exerted considerable influence in the Isles. The descendants of the twelfth-century Hebridean ruler Somerled, notably the MacDonalds and MacDougalls, played an active part in Irish affairs as suppliers of galley fleets for use in war and a type of heavily armed warrior, known as GALLOGLASS (Gallóglach, 'warrior from Innse Gall'); these and other Hebridean lords, such as MacSweeneys and MacCabes, later settled extensively in Ireland. **Seán Duffy**

hedge schools. Privately owned schools were a significant source of literacy and numeracy before the development of large-scale state-financed schooling. They were known by various terms, including 'pay schools', 'cabin schools', and 'petty schools', but from 1780 onwards 'hedge schools'—widely used to describe a humble, and sometimes clandestine, enterprise—became general. Some accounts gave them a heroic role; others emphasised low standards or subversive teachers. A single model is of little use: curriculum and pupils were a response to social and economic conditions, while the profile of the teachers reflected market forces rather than a specific pathology. They increased rapidly in the half century to 1831, after which most became national schools. **John Logan**

Heffernan, Honor (1953–), jazz musician. Born in Dublin. She has had a diverse career as singer and actor since 1971. After some years performing mainly pop and folk music, she took up singing JAZZ in 1981. She has performed regularly with NOEL KELEHAN, MIKE NIELSEN, and, most frequently, LOUIS STEWART. She performed in 1995 in Norway with the Knut Mikalsen Trio and the Sandvika Big Band, has recorded two broadcast concerts with the BBC Big Band, and performed Duke Ellington's music in Ireland with the National Concert Orchestra. She has released two solo albums, *Stormy Waters* (1986) and *Chasing the Moon* (1991), on which she is accompanied by Noel Kelehan, Richie Buckley, and other leading jazz musicians. Her most notable acting credit is as the female lead in NEIL JORDAN's film *Angel* (1982). **Brian Trench**

Heffernan, Kevin, Gaelic footballer. Born in Dublin. As a player in the 1950s he was regarded as one of the most dangerous forwards in the game and a man before his time with regard to preparation. He won one all-Ireland championship in 1958 and also won seven inter-provincial titles with Leinster between 1952 and 1962. He went on to achieve even greater fame when he master-minded the rise of the Dublin team of the 1970s, which became known as Heffo's Heroes and changed for ever the image of GAELIC FOOTBALL. **Donal Keenan**

hearth. *A couple by an Aran fireside, Co. Galway, c. 1907, seated on home-made furniture. The hearth has traditionally been the centre of household activity. [Courtesy of the Department of Irish Folklore, University College, Dublin]*

Hegarty, Frances (1946–), artist. Born in Teelin, Co. Donegal; educated at Leeds College of Art and Manchester Polytechnic. Professor of fine art at Sheffield Hallam University since 1970, she was central to establishing its performance, film and video course. In 1994 she was awarded a professorship of fine art. Works such as *Turas* (1985), *Marital Orders* (1989), *Gold* (1993), *Voice Over* (1995), and *Auto Portrait Trilogy* (1999–2001), shown in European and American exhibitions, demonstrate a concern with cultural and sexual politics, performance, technology, and installation. Public art commissions include *Point of View* (1996) at Heathrow Airport, London, and, with Andrew Stones, *For Dublin* (1997) at Dublin, *Seemingly So Evidently Not Apparently Then* (1998) at Sheffield, *Orienteer* (2000) at Birmingham, and *Overnight Sensation* (2001) at Belfast. **Shirley MacWilliam**

Heitler, Walter Heinrich (1904–1981), physicist. Born in Karlsruhe, Germany; studied in Karlsruhe, Berlin, and Munich. Having worked in Copenhagen, Zürich, Göttingen, and Bristol, he was appointed professor at the DUBLIN INSTITUTE FOR ADVANCED STUDIES, a post he held from 1941 to 1949. He left Dublin in 1949 and was professor of theoretical physics at the University of Zürich from 1949 to 1974. His main contributions were to theoretical chemistry, quantum electrodynamics, and meson theory. During his period at the Dublin Institute for Advanced Studies he carried out pioneering work on radiation damping in scattering theory and applied it to cosmic ray physics; he was the first to derive the consequences of isospin-invariance for scattering processes. A member of the ROYAL IRISH ACADEMY, he was awarded many honorary degrees, as well as the Planck medal. **Gunther Rasche and Armin Thellung**

Hellawell, Piers (1956–), composer. Born in Derbyshire, England; he studied with James Wood and Nicholas Maw. He is composer-in-residence and lecturer at Queen's University, Belfast; his works have been commissioned for, performed and broadcast at, the 1989 and 1993 ISCM World Music Days, the 1997 Helsinki Biennale, and the 1993 Antwerp European City of Culture. He has also had commissions from the Hilliard Ensemble, Holst Foundation, and London Symphony Orchestra. His orchestral works include *Drum of the Náid* (1997) and *Sound Carvings from the Water's Edge* (1996). Chamber works include *Second Curves from the Ice Wall*

(1994) and *The Building of Curves* (1998). Vocal works include *Do Not Disturb* (1997), *The Hilliard Song Book, Volumes 1 and 2* (1995), and *Quem Quaritis* (1995, revised 1998). **Éamonn O'Keeffe**

Helsham, Richard (1682–1731), scientist. Born in Kilkenny; educated at Kilkenny College and TCD. Originally a physician, he lectured on natural philosophy and became the first Erasmus Smith professor of natural and experimental philosophy at Trinity College, Dublin. His lectures were published posthumously by Bryan Robinson in 1739 and may be considered to provide the first student textbook on Newtonian physics. A genial man-about-town, he was a member of JONATHAN SWIFT's circle. **Denis Weaire**

Hely-Hutchinson, John (1724–1794), politician. Born John Hely in Cork; he acquired the name Hutchinson as a result of marriage to Christina Hutchinson, heiress of Richard Hutchinson of Knocklofty, Co. Tipperary. An adept if acquisitive politician, his success in acquiring patronage for himself and his family meant that his political skills and his achievements as provost of TRINITY COLLEGE have not received the attention they deserve. **James Kelly**

Henchy, Séamus (1917–), lawyer and judge. Born in Co. Clare; educated at UCG, UCD, and the KING'S INNS. Called to the bar in 1942, he became a senior counsel in 1959. He was a judge of the High Court, 1962–72, and of the SUPREME COURT, 1972–88, and has been chairman of the Radio and Television Commission since 1988. Arguably the greatest intellectual force to sit on the Supreme Court, he gave judgment in a number of important cases, including the de Búrca case (dealing with the exclusion of women from juries); he also gave a memorable dissenting judgment in the NORRIS case, finding that legislation that criminalised homosexual behaviour was unconstitutional. He is regarded, with Mr Justice BRIAN WALSH, as the central figure in the development of the Republic's jurisprudence. **Neville Cox**

Henderson, Brian (1950–), sculptor. Born in Co. Wicklow. He won the Carroll Award at the IRISH EXHIBITION OF LIVING ART in 1969 and 1970. His first one-person exhibition was in 1971 at the Project Arts Centre, Dublin. He moved to New York in 1971. His first solo show in the United States was at Rutgers University, New Jersey, in 1975. He also participated in OIREACHTAS exhibitions in Dublin in the 1970s and held exhibitions at the Tompkins Square Gallery, New York, in 1987 and 1988. He was represented for the second time at the International Festival of Painting at Cagnes-sur-Mer, France, in 1989. Four solo shows were held at the Taylor Galleries, Dublin, and from 1999 he produced sculptural relief forms in painted plywood, bondo, and steel; paper collages are also in his œuvre. He is represented in the ARTS COUNCIL, Dublin, and ULSTER MUSEUM collections. **Theo Snoddy**

Henebry, Rev. Richard (1863–1916), scholar. Born in Co. Waterford; studied at the University of Freiburg and Greifswald; ordained 1892; professor of Irish, UCC, 1909–16. Henebry was an amateur musicologist, one of the first who attempted to analyse the structure of Irish music. His work was published posthumously as *A Handbook of Irish Music* (1926), an idiosyncratic work that appears very dated today. In other areas he was innovative: he made the earliest field collection of Irish music on wax cylinder, some time after 1911. Most of this is now inaudible, but surviving cylinders given to him by FRANCIS O'NEILL in 1907 are a unique window into Irish music in America in the early years of the twentieth century, with recordings of Patsy Touhey, James Early, and James McFadden. **Colin Hamilton**

henge monuments, widely distributed Late Neolithic earthen enclosures 30–275 m (100–900 ft) in diameter and commonly defined by a bank up to 4 m (13 ft) high, with one or more entrances. The bank material was scraped from the interior or quarried from a shallow internal ditch. There is some evidence for an internal revetment of the flat-topped bank, which may have functioned as a stand from which public ceremonies were watched. They are often found in groups, with passage grave association (as at BALLYNAHATTY, Co. Down, and in the BOYNE VALLEY), in ceremonial complexes on gentle slopes or valley bottoms. Less common variants include embanked STONE CIRCLES, circle henges, and timber enclosures associated with grooved ware. **Barrie Hartwell**

Hennessy, Patrick (1915–1980), still life, portrait, and landscape painter. Born in Cork; he went to Scotland as a child, returning to Ireland in 1939, having studied at Dundee, Paris, and Rome. From 1968 he lived in Tangier and Morocco; his long-time companion was the painter Harry Robertson-Craig. Hennessy exhibited successfully in Ireland, England and America and was a member of the RHA in 1949. His highly realist paintings are very distinctive, sometimes fusing the genres. A steely elegance, meticulous brushwork, deliberate composition and a feeling of stillness characterise many of his paintings. A sense of disquiet is often conveyed, partly through the separateness of the elements in the paintings. Hennessy's work is in all major Irish public collections. **Vera Ryan**

Henry II (1154–1189), King of England. The constitutional link between Ireland and the English Crown dates from the personal intervention of Henry II of England in 1171–2. He led an expedition to Ireland in the wake of his subjects' involvement there since 1167 as mercenaries in the pay of DERMOT MACMURROUGH, King of Leinster. Henry confirmed the kingdom of Leinster to STRONGBOW, granted the kingdom of Meath to HUGH DE LACY, and retained for his own use the towns of Dublin, Waterford, and Wexford. A substantial number of Irish kings submitted to him, though not Ruaidhrí Ó Conchobhair, King of Connacht, who claimed to be High King of Ireland. However, Ruaidhrí subsequently negotiated the Treaty of Windsor with Henry in September 1175, which partitioned Ireland into an Irish sphere under Ruaidhrí and an English sphere under Henry. In 1177 Henry designated his youngest son, JOHN, as Lord of Ireland. The fact that John became King of England in 1199 ensured the permanence of the link between the English Crown and Ireland. [see ANGLO-NORMANS.] **Marie Therese Flanagan**

Henry VII (1447–1509), King of England. Son of Edmund Tudor, Earl of Richmond, he secured the Crown from the Yorkist Richard III at the Battle of Bosworth (1485) and established the Tudor dynasty. He overcame repeated Yorkist challenges, including that of LAMBERT SIMNEL, whom Yorkists in Ireland crowned as Edward VI. Henry VII allowed the Yorkist GERALD FITZGERALD, EIGHTH EARL OF KILDARE, to remain as his deputy in Ireland until 1494, when he replaced him with Sir Edward POYNINGS. However, once Poynings had strengthened royal control of the English administration in Ireland, Fitzgerald was restored to the deputyship. For the remainder of Henry VII's reign Fitzgerald governed the English lordship in Ireland effectively and economically on behalf of the Crown. It has been argued that Henry VII, by resisting the temptation of expansionist ambitions, was the most successful of the Tudor monarchs in his dealings with Ireland. **Henry A. Jefferies**

Henry VIII (1491–1547), King of England. Son of HENRY VII and Elizabeth of York, from 1519 he tried to rule Ireland without GERALD FITZGERALD, NINTH EARL OF KILDARE, but generated considerable political instability, which culminated in the KILDARE REBELLION (1534–5). That rebellion coincided with Henry's breach with Rome on account of his first divorce and took on the character of a Catholic crusade. Having crushed the rebellion, he had the Irish PARLIAMENT of 1536–7 authorise the establishment of the CHURCH OF IRELAND, with himself as supreme head. The Irish Parliament of 1541–2 recognised Henry as King of Ireland as part of a constitutional revolution that aimed to peacefully assimilate the entire country into the Tudor state. Though the revolution lost momentum before his death in 1547, Henry's kingship was widely acknowledged in Ireland although his ecclesiastical supremacy tended more towards lip service. **Henry A. Jefferies**

Henry, Augustine (1857–1930), botanist. Born in Dundee, Scotland, soon moving to Cookstown, Co. Tyrone. He joined the Chinese Imperial Maritime Customs in 1882 and sent large numbers of plant specimens to Kew Gardens, London, many of them new to science and some named in his honour. From 1900 he studied forestry in Nancy, France, and travelled widely, collecting and studying trees. He became professor of forestry at the ROYAL COLLEGE OF SCIENCE, Dublin, in 1913 and was influential in the establishment of a national forest service. He wrote *The Trees of Great Britain and Ireland* with H. J. Elwes and is celebrated in *The Wood and the Trees* by Sheila Pim. **Donal Synnott**

Henry, Grace. Sails at Cioggia *by Grace Henry, showing the vibrant colours of her late work. [Hugh Lane Municipal Gallery of Modern Art]*

Henry, Emily (Grace), née Mitchell (1868–1953), painter of landscapes, still lifes, and portraits. Born in Peterhead, Aberdeenshire; educated privately and in Paris at the Delecluse Academy, where she came under the influence of Whistler. She lived in London and Surrey, 1900–10, producing occasional MINIATURES. With her husband, PAUL HENRY, she went to ACHILL ISLAND in 1910 and, apart from occasional visits elsewhere, remained there until 1919, when she settled in Dublin. Of her Achill work *The Top of the Hill* (1910–12) is the most important and best known. Throughout her career, whatever her subject matter, a sense of experiment characterises her work. Temperamentally vivacious, she grew introspective after her separation from her husband in 1929. Her earliest surviving work, such as *Girl in White* (1900–10), is Whistlerian; but later, for example in *The Black Shawl* (c. 1915) and *The Country of Amethyst* (c. 1920–21), she adopted a more illustrative style. In the later 1920s, in pictures like *Spring in Winter, No. 9* she adopted an expressionist manner. She lived in Paris, 1924–5, working with André Lhôte though little influenced by him. She spent most of the 1930s on the Continent, painting in a loose Fauvist manner, with strong light and bright colours; in 1939 she returned permanently to Ireland. Her work is represented in the NATIONAL GALLERY OF IRELAND and the Hugh Lane Municipal Gallery of Modern Art, Dublin. **S. B. Kennedy**

Henry, Paul (1876–1958), landscape and figure painter. Born in Belfast; trained at Belfast Government School of Art, the Académie Julian and Whistler's Académie Carmen, Paris. He settled in London in 1900 to work as an illustrator, meanwhile making charcoal drawings of landscapes, which he exhibited at the Goupil Gallery. In 1903 he married the painter GRACE HENRY. In 1910 he went on holiday to ACHILL ISLAND and was so captivated by the people, their way of life, and the landscape that he decided to stay there. Between then and 1919, when he moved to Dublin, he created a powerfully evocative view of the landscape of the west of Ireland and of the life it sustained. Figures predominate in his early works, but from the 1920s he devoted his interests more or less entirely to the landscape, capturing its moods and rugged terrain, which at his best he set down with a post-impressionist rigour and economy of means that was new to Irish painting. In 1920 he was one of the founders of the SOCIETY OF DUBLIN PAINTERS. In popular acclaim he was at his most influential in the 1930s; thereafter his work became repetitive. **S. B. Kennedy**

Henry, Sam (1878–1952), song-collector. He was principal editor of a weekly column in the *Northern Constitution* (Coleraine), 1923–39, presenting approximately 900 songs with music in tonic sol-fa. Most were collected near Coleraine, 600 by Henry, sixty by James Moore, and 150 by Willie Devine. Moore's collection was made partly in north Donegal; apart from a few, Devine took his from books. Henry's published songs are presented as *Sam Henry's 'Songs of the People'* (1990); his important personal collection and those of Moore and Devine are not yet generally available. **John Moulden**

Henry the Navigator (1394–1460), pioneer of European oceanic exploration. Born in Portugal, the fifth son of King João of Portugal. He is universally associated with the burgeoning in the fifteenth century of European maritime exploration, which revolutionised the history of the known world. He was the pioneer of trans-oceanic navigation guided by the scientific method. Understanding the importance of Ireland's geographical situation, he kept a permanent agent in the port of GALWAY and was responsible for the despatch to Galway of the first lion ever seen there. He was largely able to meet the huge expenses of the great expeditions he sent into the Atlantic and down the coast of west Africa from the profits of the fifteenth-century triangular Lisbon–Bristol–Galway trade. The intensive research of the Portuguese historian Magalhaes Godinho has revealed the extreme importance of Galway cloth to fifteenth-century Portuguese noble households, the first imports into Ireland of sugar (from Madeira), and the venerable age of the Portuguese wine trade with Ireland. **John de Courcy Ireland**

heraldry. The introduction to Ireland of heritable personal emblems on shields and banners can be dated precisely to the ANGLO-NORMAN CONQUEST of 1169–72, during the period when this relatively new practice was taking root throughout Europe. The heraldry of Norman-Irish families is typical of early military heraldry: simple in design to facilitate recognition on the battlefield or at the tournament, such as the white shield with red saltire (diagonal cross) of the FITZGERALDS and the yellow shield with red cross of the BURKES. The known use of banners by the Irish before the invasion is slight and should not be understood as an indigenous form of heraldry; they did not carry heraldic shields in battle or engage in the tournaments that promoted the use of heraldry elsewhere in Europe. Though its adoption by the Irish was not immediate, nor ever universal, heraldry may have been in use by the early thirteenth century, when certain Irishmen on the Continent were recorded as bearing arms, though these may have been assumed once there.

heraldry. *The heraldic achievement of Sir Arthur Chichester, Lord Deputy between 1605–15, from* Knights Dubbed in Ireland. *The manuscript is a contemporary register listing the names, dates, places of creation and coats of arms of knights dubbed in Ireland in the period 1565–1615. [Council of Trustees of the National Library of Ireland]*

Our knowledge of medieval Irish heraldry derives almost entirely from seals of a later period. The oldest surviving Irish heraldic artefact is a seal of Rotherick (Ruairí) O'Kennedy, 'chief of his nation,' attached to a treaty made with the Earl of Ormonde in 1356. Aodh Reamhar O'Neill, King of Ulster (died 1364), used a seal from which later coats of arms of O'Neill apparently evolved. The use of heraldry by certain Irish families appears to be linked to the adoption by some of them of inheritance by primogeniture, which Aodh Reamhar O'Neill introduced into his family. The coat of arms of Domhnall Riabhach MacMurrough Kavanagh, which appears on a fifteenth-century seal, was still in use by his grandson Murrough MacMurrough Kavanagh in 1515, confirming the use of the same coat of arms through successive generations. The use of heraldry by the native Irish developed with little reference to the rigid conventions that had evolved elsewhere. Such arms are usually quite distinctive, lacking the geometrical symmetry of military heraldry and incorporating peculiarly Irish references derived from pre-Norman and even pre-Christian traditions. Widely used devices include the salmon, boar, deer, and oak tree, all familiar from Irish mythology.

While the Irish chiefs at first assumed coats of arms without reference to any authority, voluntary registration of those arms in Dublin from the sixteenth century was related to acceptance of English rule. Some of the settlers of the Tudor and Cromwellian periods already possessed coats of arms before coming to Ireland; others either claimed this status without provable right or sought grants from the heraldic authority in Dublin. Their heraldry is in the English style of the time. Though a succession of heralds with the territorial designation 'Ireland King of Arms' existed from 1382, they were apparently members of the English College of Arms after its incorporation. It is not known whether the post continued after the time of Edward IV. In 1552 the Office of 'Ulster King of Arms' was created by Edward VI; this title was probably chosen to reflect the fact that the Anglo-Norman Earldom of Ulster had long been vested in the Crown. The first appointee, Bartholomew Butler, appears to have enjoyed some relationship with the College of Arms, though Ulster King of Arms was always independent of the college. In 1649 one of his officers, Albon Leveret, Athlone Pursuivant, prepared a register of the coats of arms of the Parliamentary officers almost immediately on their arrival in Ireland and probably avoided for the office the abolition that had befallen the College of Arms in London. Leveret's action apart, the fact that the post continued through every change of dynasty is testament to the herald's neutral status. It was filled by several notable officers, sometimes members of the same families of professional heralds: the names Hawkins, Carney and St George recur in the history of the Office of Arms, as it came to be called.

In the nineteenth century the Office of Arms grew in significance through the efforts of Sir WILLIAM BETHAM, whose enthusiasm for the ordering of records and the creation of new ones was of huge service. He was followed by the equally industrious Sir JOHN BERNARD BURKE, who compiled numerous volumes of pedigrees, which—despite his being (at his own suggestion) a salaried civil servant—he regarded as his personal property. In 1898 Irish members of the British Parliament defeated an attempt to absorb the office into the English College.

On the establishment of the Irish Free State in 1922 the serving Ulster King of Arms, Sir Neville Wilkinson, remained in office. On his death in 1940 Thomas Sadlier, his deputy, continued to operate the office until 1943, when the Irish and British governments agreed that the office and its records should pass to the Irish state, which renamed it the Genealogical Office and incorporated it in the NATIONAL LIBRARY. EDWARD MACLYSAGHT, who came to be styled Chief Herald of Ireland, succeeded to the functions of Ulster King of Arms, except those relating to the moribund ORDER OF ST PATRICK. Today the functions and practices of the office in relation to heraldry remain the same, altered only in the consideration given to the equality of men and women. The old title of 'Ulster' was subsequently attached to the existing one of 'Norroy King of Arms', a member of the English College of Arms, creating the new post of 'Norroy and Ulster King of Arms'.

The practice of granting coats of arms to people of Irish descent who are resident abroad was established following the SIEGE OF LIMERICK in 1691, when thousands of Irishmen followed JAMES II to France and others took service in Spain, Portugal, and Austria. James Terry, Athlone Pursuivant, a member of Ulster's Office, took his seal of office and heraldic records to the court at Saint-Germain, where he was appointed 'Athlone Herald' and granted and confirmed coats of arms to the Irish throughout Europe. In this he was assisted by the Dublin heralds as well as those of England and Scotland, in the tradition of officers of arms communicating and co-operating with one another. An attested pedigree and the right to a coat of arms were necessary proofs of gentility for those seeking a commission in European armies. Many had to search for coats of arms that had been used at some earlier date, while others sought a new grant, either from James Terry or, after his death in 1725, from Ulster King of Arms. An unestablished herald of the eighteenth century was Charles Linegar, hereditary genealogist to the Maguires of Fermanagh. Documents issued by him, and those of James Terry, are among the records in the Genealogical Office, begun in 1552. The tradition of the Irish abroad and their descendants seeking grants of coats of arms from home continues to the present. Responding to this demand is seen as an expression of the nation's 'special affinity with people of Irish ancestry living abroad who share its cultural identity and heritage' (Constitution of Ireland, article 2). [see FAMILY HISTORY; GENEALOGY.] **Micheál Ó Comáin**

Herbert, Dorothea (c. 1768–1829), writer. Born in Kilkenny; educated at Carrick-on-Suir. She wrote plays, poetry, and a diary and suffered the worst possible fate for a writer, in that almost all her work has been lost, including the manuscript of her only published work. She developed a passion for a neighbour, John Roe, who married another woman, which contributed to Herbert's mental breakdown. Her diary, a mixture of realism and heightened gothic melodrama, recounts her conviction that she and the intended were 'spiritually wed'; it was published as *Retrospection of Dorothea Herbert, 1760–1806* (1929). **Brian Lalor**

Herbert, Victor (1859–1924), musician and composer. Born in Dublin; studied cello with Cossmann, 1874–6, and composition with Seiferitz at the Stuttgart Conservatory. He taught at the University of Stuttgart, 1885, and the National Conservatory of Music, New York, 1889. A member of the court orchestra of Stuttgart, 1885, the Metropolitan Opera, New York, 1886, and the Band of the 2nd Regiment of the New York National Guard, 1893, he was conductor of the Pittsburgh Symphony Orchestra, 1898–1903. He founded the Victor Herbert Orchestra and the American Society of Composers, Authors and Publishers, 1913. His orchestral works include two cello concertos (1884 and 1894) and *Irish Rhapsody* (1892). He also composed more than forty operettas, such as *Babes in Toyland* (1903). **Éamonn O'Keeffe**

heritage and interpretative centres. From the late 1980s, heritage and interpretative centres have become increasingly common throughout Ireland. Arguments in favour of interpretative centres suggest that they are important in monitoring and controlling the impact of visitors, particularly at sensitive sites; opponents argue that by offering improved facilities the centres lead to even greater concentrations of visitors, with a serious long-term negative impact. Also at issue is the question of objectivity in the interpretation that is offered.

Both the public sector and the private sector have been involved in their establishment. The early 1990s saw a surge of provision linked to the availability of funds under the OPERATIONAL PROGRAMME FOR TOURISM (1989–93); interpretative centres and museums now account for more than 42 per cent of all fee-paying visitor attractions. The BOYNE VALLEY centre, managed by the Heritage Service, was designed both to inform visitors and to protect the site. It is some distance from the monuments, access to the site is by way of the centre only, and the number of visitors is strictly controlled. In Northern Ireland, Moyle District Council developed the visitor centre at the GIANT'S CAUSEWAY, a National Trust property; at NAVAN FORT the visitor and interpretative centre have been privately developed.

The siting of centres in environmentally sensitive areas—for example in the BURREN and at Luggala, Co. Wicklow—was a contentious issue in the 1990s. In a controversy spanning almost a decade the case of the Burren National Park interpretative centre at Mullaghmore, Co. Clare, drew attention to issues relating to heritage management; the final decision not to proceed with the centre may mark the beginning of more careful consideration of their role. **Ruth McManus**

Heritage Council, the. The Heritage Act (1995) established the Heritage Council as an independent statutory body in the Republic with responsibility for proposing policies and priorities for the identification, protection, preservation, and enhancement of the national heritage. The act defines heritage as including monuments, archaeological objects, heritage objects, architectural heritage, FLORA, FAUNA, wildlife habitats, landscapes, seascapes, wrecks, GEOLOGY, heritage gardens and parks, and inland waterways.

The Heritage Council's functions include promoting interest, education and pride in, and facilitating the appreciation and enjoyment of, the national heritage and promoting the co-ordination of activities relating to these functions. The council may make recommendations to the Minister for Arts, Heritage, GAELTACHT and the Islands on any matter relating to the council's functions, and the minister must respond within six months.

The members of the Heritage Council are appointed by the minister. Four standing committees—on archaeology, architecture, wildlife, and inland waterways—are required by the Heritage Act. These are made up of members of the Heritage Council, three members appointed by the Minister, and co-opted members. Two additional committees have been established, a Museums and Archives Committee and an Education and Communication Committee. Working groups carry out specific tasks, with time limits, for the council or committees. The professional and support

heritage and interpretative centres. *The Céide Fields Interpretative Centre, Co. Mayo, 1993, designed to inform and manage visitors while preserving the site. The steps on the exterior of the building enable visitors to view the ancient landscape from outside the centre. [Dúchas, The Heritage Service]* staff, headed by a chief executive, implement policy, conduct day-to-day business, provide policy advice, and undertake development and representational work as required. **Charles Mount**

Heron, John (1850–1913), chemist. Born in Bandon, Co. Cork; graduated from Queen's College, Cork, as an engineer in 1871 and then entered the Royal School of Chemistry, London. In 1877 he was appointed assistant chemist at Worthington's Brewery, Burton, where he carried out classical research on the transformation products of starch, as well as studies on enzyme action. Subsequently he worked in other breweries and in the sugar industry. His use of the polarimeter in BREWING was an important innovation, and his work on sugar and sugar analysis, malt analysis, hops, the influence of mineral salts in the extraction of hops and the determination of brewer's extract contributed substantially to the science of brewing. **Susan McKenna-Lawlor**

Hervey, Frederick Augustus, fourth Earl of Bristol (1730–1830), bishop and patriot. Educated at the University of Cambridge. His brother was LORD LIEUTENANT of Ireland when Hervey was appointed Bishop of Cloyne in 1767 and later Bishop of Derry in 1768. He succeeded another brother as Earl of Bristol in 1779. He opposed TITHES and argued for an end to the PENAL LAWS. During his time in Ireland he became one of the leaders of the Irish Patriots, who supported the American colonists' campaign for independence, and a member of the Convention of Delegates from the VOLUNTEERS, held in Dublin in 1782. He spent most of the later part of his life travelling, especially in Italy (see p. 466). **Brian Galvin**

Hertzog, Chaim (1918–1997), Israeli politician. Born in Belfast and spent his youth in Dublin where his father, Isaac Halevy Hertzog, became Chief Rabbi in 1919; educated at the Universities of Cambridge and London. He lived in Palestine with his family, 1935–8, after the appointment of his father as Chief Rabbi. He served as a tank commander in the British army during the Second World War and after the war joined the Zionist paramilitary movement Hagannah. He held a number of senior posts in the Israeli armed forces, then pursued a career in business and in writing. He was appointed Israeli ambassador to the UNITED NATIONS in 1975, was elected to the Knesset in 1981, and served two terms as president of Israel, 1983–95. **Brian Galvin**

Heuston, Seán (1891–1916), republican. Born in Dublin. He helped to organise FIANNA ÉIREANN and in 1913 joined the IRISH VOLUNTEERS. With some of the Fianna he unloaded rifles from the ASGARD in the HOWTH GUN-RUNNING of July 1915. During the 1916 RISING he led republicans in the Mendicity Institute; aged twenty-three, he was shot by firing squad on 8 May 1916. **Seán Farrell Moran**

Hewetson, Christopher (1737–1798), sculptor. Born in Kilkenny; in the late 1750s he became a pupil of JOHN VAN NOST THE YOUNGER, then working on the ROTUNDA HOSPITAL. He was in Rome by 1765 and remained there for the rest of his life. He was very successful sculpting portrait busts of *'milordi'* from many European countries; he made several of Pope Clement XIV and sculpted the funerary monument of Cardinal Rezzonico. His most important work in Ireland is the memorial to Provost Baldwin in the Examination Hall in TRINITY COLLEGE, Dublin. **Anne Crookshank**

Hewitt, John (1907–1987), poet, art historian, and socialist. Born in Belfast; educated at Methodist College and QUB. He was employed by the ULSTER MUSEUM and subsequently by the Herbert Art Gallery, Coventry. His best-known poems, 'Once Alien Here' (*No Rebel Word*, 1948) and 'The Colony' (*Collected Poems*, 1968) represent his long-term preoccupation with the complex relationship between planter and Gael in north-east Ulster. During the 1940s his response to the dilemma of a bifurcated identity was to promote a regionalist ideology, giving priority to local association and place above the problematic affiliations of nation. As a result he is frequently cited as an important influence on the young SEAMUS HEANEY and the poets of the Ulster Renaissance. **Eve Patten**

Hewson, George Henry Phillips (1881–1972), musician and composer. Born in Dublin; educated at the Cathedral Grammar School and TCD. He was organist at Armagh Cathedral, 1916–20, ST PATRICK'S CATHEDRAL (where he was also choirmaster) 1920–60, Trinity College, Dublin, 1927–72, and the Chapel Royal, Dublin. An honorary fellow of the Royal College of Organists, London, he was professor of music at Trinity College, Dublin, 1936–62, and professor of organ at the RIAM. He composed church music, including anthems and four services. **Éamonn O'Keeffe**

Hewson, Paul, known as Bono (1960–), rock musician and political activist. Born in Dublin; educated at Mount Temple Comprehensive School, where he met future fellow-members of the rock group U2, with whom a band was formed called 'Feedback', later 'The Hype'. As the singer with U2, Bono has always displayed a strong social consciousness in his lyrics and engagement with social issues. He has used his fame to support various causes, including the Drop the Debt Campaign, which promotes the waiving of Third World debt. **Martin Clancy**

Hibernian Bible Society types, Irish printing types. After the implementation of the ACT OF UNION in 1801 there was a renewed enthusiasm for the promotion of the Reformed Church in Ireland. Consequently, reaching the Irish-speaking population was of prime importance to the Hibernian Bible Society. With the support of the British and Foreign Bible Society, two fonts of type were prepared: the Watts type in 1818 and the Fry type in 1819, named after the foundries involved in their production. They were used to great effect to print various religious publications and were widely available and popular with many printers. [see SECOND REFORMATION.] **Dermot McGuinne**

Hiberno-English. Great as the influence of the plantations was from the point of view of the English language, greater still was the influence of the Cromwellian settlement of the 1650s. By the end of the 1650s the transfer of the native population to Connacht was complete; and a new English, the English of Cromwell's planters, took root in Ireland. Their great houses became the focal point of linguistic change. Tenants and servants had to learn English to speak to the Cromwellians; and they in turn picked up the Gaelicised English of the native Irish. Today's Hiberno-English is a fusion of these two strands.

In his burlesque writings *A Dialogue in Hibernian Stile* and *Irish Elegance*, SWIFT castigates the kind of English he found spoken by the planters just two generations after the Cromwellian confiscations. The language of these pieces is strongly influenced by Irish; some of the sentences quoted are direct translations: 'Pray, how does he get his health?' (What sort of health has he?); 'It is kind father to you' (You have inherited that trait from your father); 'I wonder what is gone with them?' (I wonder what has happened to them). Hibernicisms such as these and the modern-sounding 'Pray lend me a lone of your news paper till I read it over' are the result of the planters' daily intercourse with their Irish-speaking servants. For their part, the Irish, to survive, had to learn English. They had to rely on Irish teachers, men whose own English was very different from standard English. These men were often self-taught, relying on books for guidance on grammar and syntax and often guessing the pronunciation of difficult words. As the system in the illegal 'HEDGE SCHOOLS' was self-perpetuating—the master training his brightest pupil as an assistant, and he in turn becoming a master some day and training his own assistant—mistakes in pronunciation were passed on from generation to generation. This led to two noteworthy features of Anglo-Irish dialect. The first is a tendency to stress a different syllable from the one stressed in standard English. The Irishman says discípline, laméntable, architécture, where the Englishman says díscipline, lámentable, árchitecture. Another feature of Anglo-Irish speech is a tendency towards malapropism, the use of the wrong word or the use of a word in a meaning it does not have in standard English. This tendency is common all over Ireland; recently an educated Government minister asked in Dáil Éireann what could be deducted from a statement issued by the opposition, when he clearly meant deduced. O'CASEY made extensive use of this tendency in his plays: he has 'formularies' for 'formalities' and 'declivity' for 'proclivity', for instance.

But the greatest influence of Irish on the English of Ireland is the extensive Gaelicisation of the vocabulary. Thousands of words and phrases have filtered into the speech of the people from Irish and seem to have a permanent place in it. Sadly, this new language, Hiberno-English, was not allowed develop as a national speech norm. Like Irish, it was considered to be somewhat unsophisticated and unsuited to educational, social, and political use—though Lady Gregory, Synge, Hyde, and others vehemently disagreed.

Irish was under siege in the eighteenth century; the emergence of a strong Catholic middle class in the towns—a class engaged in trade and commerce and whose language was, of necessity, English—led to the weakening of Irish. But the policy of replacing it outright with English really got under way with the introduction of the national schools, under clerical management, in 1831. The GREAT FAMINE marked a crucial point in the fate of Irish. A million people died; another million emigrated. It left as legacy the fear of a recurrence; and English came to be looked on as the key to America. By 1900 English had become the sole language of 85 per cent of the population, and of the remaining 15 per cent only 21,000, residing in the poorest areas of the country, were monoglot Irish-speakers. The transformation was complete. **Diarmaid Ó Muirithe**

Hiberno-Latin. Ireland was never part of the Roman Empire, and the first surviving Latin writings to be composed there (two letters sent by ST PATRICK) date from the fifth century, after Rome had fallen. Within a few generations, however, Hiberno-Latin, with its distinctive Celtic pronunciation, was firmly established as an ecclesiastical and literary language, as influential Irishmen such as COLUMBANUS (died 615) spearheaded a monastic movement throughout Europe that did much to keep Latin learning alive during troubled times.

Irish writers in MONASTERIES at home and abroad continued to produce a rich literature of their own in Latin, with about 500 separate surviving works by the year 1200, totalling some 3 million words. In the early period Hiberno-Latin compositions included poetry and hymns, theology, history, and numerous lives of Irish SAINTS, as well as works dealing with penitential regulations (a genre pioneered by Celtic churchmen). Some authors, such as the self-styled Virgilius Maro Grammaticus (seventh century), used the language with Joycean inventiveness. Much later, Latin was

Hewetson. *Commemorative cenotaph to Provost Richard Baldwin at the Examination Hall, Trinity College, Dublin, completed by Hewetson in 1781. Depicting Baldwin on his deathbed with an angel and Science, the figures are in white Carrara marble on a black marble sarcophagus with gilt bronze ornaments. [Board of Trinity College, Dublin]*

employed in Ireland, as elsewhere, in debates about the Reformation. Most pre-Norman Hiberno-Latin texts are anonymous; writers whose names we know include ADOMNÁN (died 704) and, on the Continent, ERIUGENA, a philosophical genius active in the 870s. The post-Norman period is dominated by such influential authors as PETER OF IRELAND (teacher to Aquinas) and the controversialist RICHARD STANIHURST. **Anthony Harvey**

Hiberno-Latin prose rhythms. Greek writers from the fifth century BC and classical Latin writers from the first century BC composed prose in *clausulae*, in which clauses and phrases sometimes—and sentences always—ended in quantitative rhythms of alternating long and short syllables, later in mixed quantitative and stressed rhythms, and later still in rhythms of the *cursus*, alternating stressed and unstressed syllables. From the very beginnings of Latin literacy in Ireland, Hiberno-Latin writers composed both clausular and cursus rhythms systematically and comprehensively.

Quantitative clausulae		*Cursus rhythms*	
1. cretic + trochee or spondee	– ˘ – – ×	1. planus	| × × | ×
2. double cretic	– ˘ – – ˘ ×	2. tardus	| × × | × ×
3. cretic + double trochee or trochee + spondee	– ˘ – – ˘ – ×	3. uelox	| × × | × | ×
4. cretic + iambus	– ˘ – ˘ ×	4. medius	| × | × ×
5. resolved cretic + trochee or spondee	– ˘ ˘ ˘ – ×	5. trispondiacus	| × × × | ×
6. resolved cretic + cretic	– ˘ ˘ ˘ – ˘ ×	6. dispondeus dactylicus	| × × × | × ×

In all clausular forms the first cretic (¯ ˘ ¯) may be strengthened to a molossus (¯ ¯ ¯), and the last syllable is common, either long or short. The third form appears sometimes only as a trochaic metron (¯ ˘ ¯ ×) without the cretic. The cursus rhythms may be understood as reflexes of the quantitative forms. [see IRISH METRICS.] **David Howlett**

Hickey, Kieran (1936–1993), film director and writer. Born in Dublin; he was one of only a few film-makers of his generation to formally study film. He began his career as a director of documentaries with the cameraman Seán Corcoran and editor J. Patrick Duffner, who made sponsored documentaries for state agencies while also producing films on JONATHAN SWIFT and JAMES JOYCE. In the 1970s Hickey was one of the first, with BOB QUINN, to make fiction films with an Irish theme. *Exposure* (1978), which concerned the sexual repression of Irish men when they meet a foreign woman, identified an interest in middle-class mores, pursued in *Criminal Conversation* (1981). **Kevin Rockett**

Hickey, Patrick (1927–1998), artist and print-maker. Born in India; attended the School of Architecture, UCD, and Scuola del Libro, Urbino, Italy. He worked as an architect in the practice of MICHAEL SCOTT, then went to Italy to study print-making. On his return he founded the Graphic Studio in Dublin (with Liam Miller, ANNE YEATS, and ELIZABETH RIVERS), which remains the most significant centre for print-making in Ireland. He continued painting but also taught in the School of Architecture at UCD; subsequently he was professor of painting in the National College of Art and Design, 1986–90. He won many international prizes for print-making and was included in the leading print biennales and specialist exhibitions. **Dorothy Walker**

hierarchy, ecclesiastical. In a sense, Ireland owes its ecclesiastical hierarchy to twelfth-century reformers and Papal endorsement. At that time, diocesan and provincial boundaries were established that have substantially endured until today. By the seventh century, however, Irish ecclesiastical legislation already recognised archbishops as well as bishops. Then and thereafter, powerful churches, such as those of Armagh, Kildare, and IONA (in Scotland), promoted their rival claims to primacy over the Irish church; Armagh was most successful in making this a reality. Moreover, these and many other churches established local and regional hegemonies over lesser churches. These hegemonies may be seen as the practical genesis of an ecclesiastical hierarchy that was, however, not fixed but subject to fluctuation in the political fortunes of the churches concerned. While rival pretensions gave rise to disputes and even violence between churches, those who constituted the pre-twelfth-century hierarchy were also capable of reaching consensus at SYNODS or councils. [see CHRISTIANITY; DIOCESAN SYSTEM; EPISCOPACY.] **Colmán Etchingham**

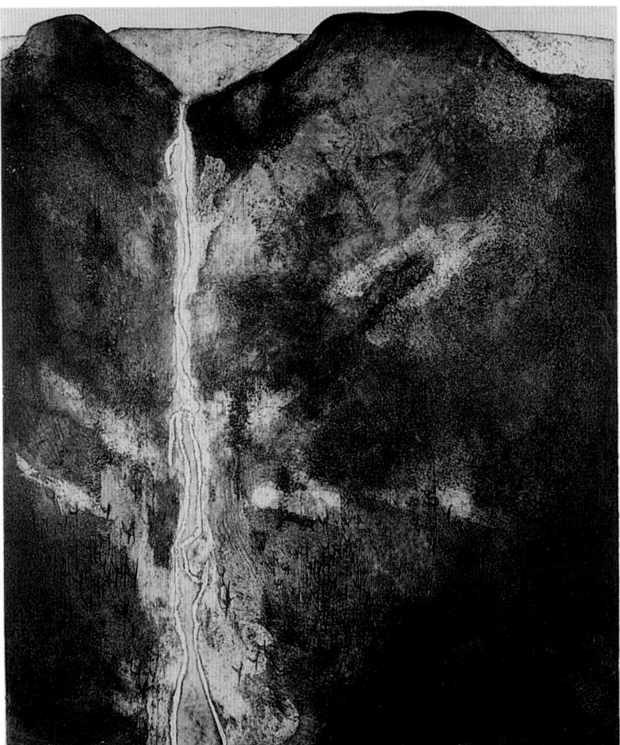

Hickey, Patrick. Waterfall *(etching, 1974) by Patrick Hickey, the founding figure of modern fine art print-making in Ireland. [By permission of the Office of Public Works]*

Higgins, Aidan (1927–), novelist and short-story writer. Born near Celbridge, Co. Kildare; educated at Clongowes Wood College. His first and best novel, *Langrishe, Go Down* (1966), is a magnificent metaphysical meditation on life and relationships that breathed new life into the well-worn genre of the 'BIG HOUSE' NOVEL. Other novels include *Balcony of Europe* (1972) and *Lions of the Grünewald* (1995); but it has been argued that none has been able to match the coherence and brilliance of his first novel. He has also published three volumes of autobiography, *Donkey's Years* (1996), *Dog Days* (1998), and *The Whole Hog* (2000). **Derek Hand**

Higgins, Alexander ('Hurricane') (1949–), snooker player. Born in Belfast. A controversial but hugely popular player, he turned professional in 1971 and won the Irish snooker championship four times. He became world champion twice, in 1972 (against John Spencer) and in 1982 (against Ray Reardon). **Myra Dowling**

Higgins, Bryan (1737–1818), physician and chemist. Born in Collooney, Co. Sligo; educated at the University of Leyden, where he was awarded a doctorate. He practised as a physician in London and, assisted by his nephew WILLIAM HIGGINS, opened a school of practical CHEMISTRY (1774), where he carried out research until 1796. His course *Syllabus* contained much of practical and theoretical interest and was published many times. He made early contributions to theories of chemical affinity and structures of molecules, which in some ways approached Dalton's concepts of atomic weights. He studied and published a book on cement manufacture (1780). Between 1797 and 1802 he investigated sugar and rum production in the West Indies. **D. Thorburn Burns**

Higgins, F. R. (1896–1941), poet. Born in Foxford, Co. Mayo. He founded a Clerical Workers' Union and edited TRADE UNION journals. In the 1920s he edited several short-lived literary publications and contributed poetry and reviews to more established journals. In 1938 W. B. YEATS was instrumental in having him appointed managing director of the ABBEY THEATRE, a post he held until his death. His poetry collections include *Island Blood* (1925), *The Dark Breed* (1927), *Arable Holdings* (1933), and *The Gap of Brightness* (1940), his most critically acclaimed collection. **Michael McAteer**

Higgins, Joseph (1885–1925), sculptor. Born in Cork; studied at night at Crawford School of Art. Sculptures of his nephews, such as *Liam* and *Boy with a Boat* (1913) (Fitzgerald Park, Cork), have particular ease and freshness. His modelled heads of his friend DANIEL CORKERY (1909) and Prof. W. F. P. Stockley (1924) were later cast through the efforts of his son-in-law SEAMUS MURPHY. He did not travel outside Ireland, despite winning many prizes. Settling in Youghal, Co. Cork, to teach, he modelled fishermen, such as *An Stracaire Fir* (1916, Crawford Gallery). Carvings of PEARSE and COLLINS (1922) survive. His sculpture is Rodinesque, his craftwork Celtic revival in style. **Vera Ryan**

Higgins, Michael D. (1941–), poet, politician, sociologist, and political scientist. Born in Limerick; educated at UCG and the Universities of Indiana and Manchester. Formerly a lecturer in sociology and politics at University College, Galway, he has been a LABOUR PARTY TD for Galway West since 1987, having first been elected in 1981–2; he was the first Minister for Arts, Culture, Gaeltacht, and the Islands, 1993–7 and was instrumental in setting up the Irish-language TV station TG4 (TnaG). He also allowed a ministerial order under Section 31 of the Broadcasting Act to lapse. Amongst his poetry collections are *The Betrayal* (1990) and *The Season of Fire* (1993). [see BROADCASTING; BROADCASTING IN IRISH; CENSORSHIP, BROADCASTING.] **Brian Galvin**

Higgins, Rita Ann (1955–), poet and playwright. Born in Galway; left school early and worked at various jobs until her marriage. She read widely while recovering from TUBERCULOSIS and joined the Salmon Writers' Workshop in 1982. Her principal poetry collections are *Goddess on the Mervue Bus* (1986), *Witch in the Bushes* (1988), *Philomena's Revenge* (1992), *Higher Purchase* (1996), and *An Awful Racket* (2001). *Sunny Side Plucked: New and Selected Poems* (1966) was a Poetry Book Society recommendation. She has written four plays, including *Down All the Roundabouts* (1999). Higgins's writing expresses the life of working-class Ireland, relying on paradox, humour, and witty inversion to create an ironic, yet sympathetic, poetic commentary. She is a member of AOSDÁNA. **Riana O'Dwyer**

Higgins, William (1763–1825), chemist. Born in Collooney, Co. Sligo; educated at the University of Oxford, he left without a degree, perhaps because he espoused the new CHEMISTRY then emerging from France, while his teachers did not. At twenty-six he published his most famous work, *A Comparative View of the Phlogistic and Antiphlogistic Theories*. This was a near approach to the atomic theory (his 'ultimate particle' is the same as Dalton's 'atom') that John Dalton was to present in a more detailed and quantitative way fifteen years later. He returned to Ireland in 1791 and was chemist to the Apothecaries' Hall, with a concurrent appointment to the Linen Board of Ireland. He then moved to the DUBLIN SOCIETY. Though he spent much of his subsequent career attempting to establish his prior claim to the atomic theory, his real success was twofold: he popularised the study of chemistry through his RDS lecture courses and he can be credited with being the first to bring the new chemical philosophy to Ireland. **William J. Davis**

high crosses, though found also in Britain, one of Ireland's most monumental contributions to the art of medieval Europe and the most extensive corpus of stone SCULPTURE during the Carolingian era. Their epithet 'high' comes from references in the ANNALS; the tallest (at MONASTERBOICE) is over 7 m (23 ft). The earlier and most numerous group flourished in the ninth and tenth centuries. Animal and other symbolism dominates early pillars and crosses at places such as CLONMACNOISE and MOONE. The practice of applying panels of Biblical sculpture spread among MONASTERIES in the east and midlands by the middle third of the ninth century and continued probably into the tenth. In contrast with much of

high crosses. *One of two sandstone crosses at Ahenny, Co. Tipperary, the North Cross (east face) stands over 3 m (10 ft) high. Detail on the base depicts a chariot procession, possibly David bringing the defeated Goliath to Jerusalem. [Dúchas, The Heritage Service]*

early medieval Irish art, the figures are naturalistically represented (if often squat), suggesting an origin in central or southern Europe, where the tradition of classical sculpture in relief was preserved; but how it was transmitted to Ireland remains uncertain. Old Testament subjects illustrated include, among other things, events from the Books of Genesis and Exodus, the life of David, and examples from the Book of Daniel showing how the Lord saves the good and faithful in time of danger—a favourite theme. The New Testament is represented by a Childhood of Christ cycle, events from his public life, and a detailed coverage of his passion, death, resurrection, and ascension. The importance of the sacrament of baptism is emphasised by extracts from a John the Baptist cycle. Non-Biblical figures include the model desert fathers Paul and Anthony.

The broadest selection of such scriptural material is found on the great sandstone crosses of the east and midlands, as at KELLS, Monasterboice, Clonmacnoise, and Durrow. The selection of Bible scenes, different on each cross, was intended to illustrate scriptural stories for the faithful and to induce piety among them. In this they are Ireland's answer to the frescoes of Continental and particularly Roman churches, which they emulate in function and composition. That people knelt in front of the crosses is suggested not only by the placing of significant panels low down on the shaft but also by the presence beneath them of inscriptions, some of which have recently been deciphered. These show that high kings of the Clann Cholmáin branch of UÍ NÉILL—MÁEL SECHNAILL (846–62) and his son FLANN SINNA (879–916)—were involved in commissioning such crosses, demonstrating co-operation between political and church authorities at the time.

Related crosses were found in Ulster, where Old Testament and New Testament material is rigidly separated. The cross at ARBOE may be the only northern cross still in its original position and shape, others consisting of separate fragments mounted on top of one another. Moone and CASTLEDERMOT are the main representatives of a group of granite crosses in the Barrow valley that feature apostles shown in pairs, threes, or fours. Another important group, concentrated in the old kingdom of Osraí (Ossory) further to the south, includes Killamery and Kilkieran, Co. Kilkenny, and AHENNY, Co. Tipperary. The two crosses at Ahenny, now being more frequently ascribed to the middle of the ninth century than to the eighth, are copied from complicated wooden models that were covered in geometrically decorated bronze sheeting, with figure sculpture (Adam, a possible David and Goliath, and the 'Raised Christ' on the North Cross) being confined to the base. A small Co. Donegal group of crosses at FAHAN, Carndonagh and elsewhere suggests Scottish links, but opinions about their date vary widely.

The ring around many of the crosses may have a structural function in preventing the indented arms from snapping off but may also have played a role as a symbol of the cosmos, at the centre of which is the Crucifixion of Christ. Historical records do not tell us whether the stone-carvers were monks or laymen (perhaps in travelling workshops), though one Clonmacnoise grave-slab tersely asks a prayer for Turcán, 'by whom this cross was made.' While no trace of paint has ever been found, the crosses were probably coloured.

Munster and Connacht possess few crosses of the earlier group but preserve the greatest number of examples of the later group, which dates from the twelfth century. Two crosses at Tuam bear inscriptions naming TOIRDHEALBHACH Ó CONCHOBHAIR (1119–56) and an abbot Aodh Ó hOisín, showing how king and church were again co-operating in erecting crosses, and one names a carver, Giollachríost Ó Tuathail—possibly a Wicklow man. The market cross of Glendalough, along with the DYSERT O'DEA cross, shows a high-relief figure of Christ above an ecclesiastic or bishop, whereas Tuam, Cashel, Roscrea, and Kilfenora reproduce them back to back, perhaps symbolising the twelfth-century church reform movement, of which these late crosses may be a product. Many are decorated with Scandinavian-inspired animal INTERLACE. Aran Island examples illustrate the Crucifixion, while many of the Co. Clare crosses may have been associated with PILGRIMAGE (see pp. 735, 737). [see GRAVE SLABS.] **Peter Harbison**

high-kingship. The title 'high king' is a translation of the Irish *ard-rí*, which in early medieval sources usually refers to God. In the tenth century it came into vogue to denote a distinguished king who had enforced his power over external territories. It was often used in flattery, like the titles 'high poet' and 'high lector'. After 1022, when the KINGSHIP of TARA had fallen into decline, historians began to regard Tara as the seat of the high-kingship of Ireland. An unbroken succession of high kings was traced back to the legendary sons of Míl of Spain, who allegedly came to Ireland many centuries before Christ. From Míl's three sons—Éremón, Éber, and Ír—all the royal dynasties descended, which continuously contended for the high-kingship. The reigns of the high kings then formed the chronological and genealogical framework of Irish history.

This eleventh-century view of the Irish past created unity and order in the distant past. It drew on earlier constructions in which the possibility of winning the kingship of Tara was open to all Irish kings, until the UÍ NÉILL monopolised it in the Christian period. Two of the kings of Tara, Domnall (died 642) and Loingsech (died 704), are called *rex Scotorum* or *rex Hiberniae* in contemporary records, but later traditions hold that certain kings of Ulster and Munster had been kings of Ireland around that period also. When Uí Néill lost their domination over Ireland the Munster King BRIAN BÓRÚ (died 1014) made himself King of Ireland, but he never called himself King of Tara and was regarded as high king only after his death.

The idea of a high-kingship of Ireland is mainly an invention, and its usage is, strictly speaking, misleading and anachronistic. Yet for long it was regarded as a national doctrine, and in the nineteenth and twentieth centuries its nature became an issue in ideological debates about Ireland's past (see p. 1035). [see GAELIC LORDSHIP; KINGDOMS OF IRELAND; KINGSHIP.] **Bart Jaski**

highland, a dance and tune type from Co. Donegal, derived from the 'highland Schottische'. Its original accompanying dance is no longer common, and most of its melodies derive from existing Scottish or Irish tunes or have been newly composed. It is characterised by 4/4 time, dotted rhythms, and a relaxed tempo. **Liz Doherty**

Hill, Arthur (1846–1921), architect and antiquarian. Born in Cork, son of the architect Henry Hill (1806–87); studied at Cork School of Art and later at Queen's College, where he obtained a diploma in civil engineering in 1865. He next worked with T. H. Wyatt in London, where his draughtsmanship won him awards from the Royal Academy, Royal Institute of British Architects, and other institutions. In 1869 he joined his father in practice, working until 1917, when a stroke forced early retirement. His elder son, Henry Houghton Hill, joined him in 1909. His work in Cork includes the magnificent extensions to the Crawford School of Art (1884), buildings for the International Exhibition of 1902, the Crawford Technical School (1909), the Munster and Leinster Bank, South Mall (a competition winner, 1909), and the Metropole Hotel (1910). **Frederick O'Dwyer**

Hill, Derek (1916–2000), painter. Born in Southampton; educated at Marlborough college, Wiltshire. He became interested in painting and drawing and in 1933 studied stage design at Munich. He visited Vienna, Russia, China, and Japan and lived and painted on Bernard Berenson's Italian estate, I Tatti. He became a celebrated portrait painter of royalty and also painted James Dixon, first of the TORY ISLAND painters. Hill painted the landscape of Tory from a primitive hut; one superb example is *Tory Island from Tor Mór*, now in the ULSTER MUSEUM. In 1981 he gave his Co. Donegal home, St Columb's (now Glebe House and Gallery), and its contents to the state; in 1999 he was made an HONORARY IRISH CITIZEN. **Brian Ferran**

Hillen, Seán (c. 1961–), photographer. Born in Newry, Co. Down. At first he specialised in documentary PHOTOGRAPHY, concentrating on the 'TROUBLES' in Northern Ireland. In 1982 he moved to London, studying at the London College of Printing and then at the Slade School of Fine Art. In 1993 he moved to Dublin, where he embarked on a series of works titled *Irelantis*, an imaginary juxta-position, using found imagery, of the landscape and people of Ireland with the mythical island state of Atlantis. His photo-montages, or more correctly photo-collages, often combine Irish scenes with unlikely and 'exotic' elements, such as Egyptian pyramids set by the banks of Lough Neagh. His works are a wry, sophisticated and often humorous commentary on the construction of identity through imagery. **Peter Murray**

Hillery, Patrick (1923–), doctor, politician, European Commissioner, President of Ireland. Born in Milltown Malbay, Co. Clare; educated at UCD. A FIANNA FÁIL TD for Clare, 1951–73, he was Minister for Education, 1959–65, Minister for Industry and Commerce, 1965–6, Minister for Labour, 1966–9, and Minister for Foreign Affairs, 1969–73. As Minister for Education he oversaw significant developments in third-level education, and as Minister for

Foreign Affairs he co-ordinated the negotiations for Irish entry into the EEC in 1973. Later that year he was appointed vice-president of the Commission of the European Communities, with special responsibility for Social Affairs. He held this position until 1976 when, after CEARBHALL Ó DÁLAIGH's resignation, he accepted the all-party nomination to serve as his replacement. His renomination in 1983 was unopposed and he served a full second term. **Brian Galvin**

hill-forts. The term implies defence; but not all such sites were necessarily defensive. Some hill-forts could have been central places in a tribal landscape, constructed for purposes of prestige and ostentation; but in Ireland (which possesses approximately sixty to eighty examples) very few have been excavated, and some are likely to have been defended settlements. Most have ramparts of stone. Their greatest concentration is in southern and eastern Ireland. A handful of sites, such as Knockadigeen, Co. Tipperary, and Hughstown Hill, Co. Kildare, are more than 10 ha (24 acres) in area, though most have an area of less than 5 ha (12 acres).

Hill-forts are of three principal types: those consisting of a single enclosure, those with two or three widely spaced enclosures, and a small number on inland promontories. DÚN AONGHASA, Co. Galway, is a cliff-top fort overlooking the Atlantic. An enormous enclosure of 132 ha (325 acres) enclosing two summits at Spinans Hill, Co. Wicklow, remains enigmatic; dating evidence is poor. RATHGALL, Co. Wicklow, HAUGHEY'S FORT, Co. Armagh, MOOGHAUN, Co. Clare, and Dún Aonghasa were certainly occupied c. 1000 BC, or shortly afterwards, and this is undoubtedly the main period of hill-fort construction and use. There is slight evidence of occupation in the BRONZE AGE (RATHGALL, and Freestone Hill, Co. Kilkenny), and in the IRON AGE (Haughey's Fort) and even into the Middle Ages (Rathgall).

Our knowledge of the internal organisation of hill-forts is scant. Scattered circular huts seem to have been the norm, and there is evidence of agriculture and animal-rearing, as well as bronze-working and, in one instance, IRONWORKING. All sites have produced fragments of bucket-shaped pots; and weapons, personal items and domestic equipment have also come to light. Haughey's Fort yielded the skull of a very large dog. While the origins of the hill-fort in Ireland are obscure, it is now clear that they are an indigenous development; earlier views regarding them as bridge-heads of invading groups are unsustainable. [see EARTHWORKS; PROMONTARY FORTS; RING-FORTS.] **Barry Raftery**

Hillsborough Agreement: see ANGLO-IRISH AGREEMENT.

Hincks, Edward (1792–1866), scholar and minister. Born in Cork; educated at TCD. His father, Thomas Dix Hincks, was Unitarian minister of the Prince's Street Dissenting congregation in Cork and founder of the ROYAL CORK INSTITUTION. In 1819 Edward Hincks was appointed Anglican rector of Ardtrea, Co. Armagh, and in 1825 he moved to the parish of Killyleagh, Co. Down. His work on ancient Near Eastern languages forms the basis of his reputation as a scholar, and he made many significant contributions to the *Proceedings of the Royal Irish Academy*, which awarded him the Cunningham Medal in 1848. His discovery in 1846 of the vowel system of Babylonian cuneiform script was made simultaneously with Henry Rawlinson's discoveries at Baghdad. Hincks's studies of Egyptian hieroglyphics and Assyrian and Persian scripts were also important. He has been honoured by the erection of a bust at the Cairo Museum in commemoration of his work on hieroglyphics. **Brian Lalor**

Hinde, John (1916–1997), photographer and postcard producer. Born in Somerset, England. Having had an interest in PHOTOGRAPHY from childhood, he moved to Ireland in 1955 and founded John Hinde Ltd a year later. The company printed and published colour

hill-forts. *Dún Ailinne (Knockaulin), Co. Kildare, an Iron Age hill-fort on a dome-shaped hill overlooking the surrounding landscape, with a ring of banked fortification half way up the hill. [Dúchas, The Heritage Service]* postcards for the burgeoning tourist industry. His Ireland was an intensely colourful place, with blue skies, dramatic landscapes, and smiling people. Though often criticised for depicting a clichéd view of Ireland and the Irish, the postcards were hugely popular and by 1972 (when he sold his interest) the company's sales were over 50,000 per annum. In 1993 the IRISH MUSEUM OF MODERN ART hosted a major exhibition of the Hinde collection. **Myra Dowling**

Hinkson, Pamela, née Tynan (1900–1982), novelist and children's writer. Born in London, daughter of KATHARINE TYNAN; educated privately. Some of her fiction—*End of All Dreams* (1923), *Deeply Rooted* (1935), and *The Lonely Bride* (1951)—chronicles the decline of the BIG HOUSE, while she collaborated with Lady Fingall to produce an aristocrat's memoir of Ascendancy life, *Seventy Years Young* (1937). **Terence Brown**

hiring fairs, fairs held in order to organise the employment of the agricultural work force. They were usually held twice a year, in May and November, when farmers negotiated the terms of employment with prospective agricultural workers, usually for a period of six months. The fairs betokened both increasing wage dependence in the contract of rural labour and the persistence of long-term contracts (eventually supplanted by day-labour contracts). In the later nineteenth century Ulster was the centre of hiring fairs, but the practice of contracting labour through fairs declined markedly from the beginning of the twentieth century. [see MIGRATORY LABOUR.] **K. J. James**

Hitler, William Patrick (born 1911), nephew of Adolf Hitler. Born in Liverpool to Bridget Hitler, née Dowling (born in Dublin in 1892), and Aloïs Hitler, half-brother of the German chancellor. His parents met at the Dublin Horse Show in 1909, eloped to London and married in September 1910. His mother claims in her memoirs that Adolf Hitler spent some months in her home in Liverpool in 1912, which would partly account for the 'missing year' in Hitler's life. His father disappeared during the FIRST WORLD WAR, feigning his own death, remarried but was discovered and prosecuted for bigamy. William corresponded with Adolf Hitler following the Munich Putsch, hoping for financial support. From 1929 the British press often sought him out to make comment on his uncle's political moves. He joined the US Navy in 1944 and after the war worked in an American hospital. **Ciarán Deane**

Hoban, James (1758–1831), architect. Born in Kilkenny; studied under THOMAS IVORY at the DUBLIN SOCIETY Schools. Having emigrated to the United States in 1785, he settled first in Philadelphia and then Charleston, South Carolina. A meeting with George Washington in 1787 prompted him to take part in a competition to design the President's House (now the White House); he won, though Washington subsequently made significant changes to the house. He moved to Washington and supervised the building of the President's House (completed 1820), and the rebuilding of State and War Department blocks. He served on Washington City Council and designed several other civic buildings. **Brendan Rooney**

hockey, almost certainly a derivative of the ancient Irish game of *camánacht*; HURLING as played at present and hurley as played in the second half of the nineteenth century, as well as shinty, the Scottish variant, all came from the same source. The divergence of hockey came with the adoption of the regulation ball, which was harder and much heavier than a hurley ball and was smooth, to allow it to travel truly along the ground.

Ireland has the world's oldest women's hockey union, established on 22 October 1894 by members of Old Alexandra Hockey Club. Junior and senior competitions were begun, and the first international match was played against England in 1896. Ireland won 2–0. The centenary was celebrated in 1994 by hosting the eighth Women's World Cup. Members of the High School, King's Hospital, and Palmerston Hockey Clubs (all Dublin) established the men's union in 1892. Canon Gibson of King's Hospital was the first president; but the credit for introducing the game to Ireland goes to W. E. Paterson of High School. The first men's international was against Wales in February 1895. Ireland won 3–0.

In both the men's and the women's game the regional expansion from Dublin was rapid, and by 1903 all provinces had their own branch affiliated to the women's union, with more than a hundred teams affiliated to the men's game by 1908. Irish hockey has enjoyed many successes, including the Triple Crown in 1977 and the Intercontinental Cup in Kuala Lumpur in 1983 for the women, while the men won five Triple Crowns in six seasons between 1937 and 1944. In 2000 a single Irish Hockey Union was formed, encompassing the men's and the women's game. **Daphne Hosford**

Hogan, Desmond (1950–), novelist, short-story writer, and playwright. Born in Ballinasloe, Co. Galway; educated at UCD. Among his novels are *The Ikon Maker* (1976), which was adapted as a play, *The Leaves on Grey* (1980), *A Curious Street* (1984), and *A New Shirt* (1986); his collections of short stories include *The Morning Thief* (1987) and *Lebanon Lodge* (1988). He also published a collection of travel and reflective pieces, *The Edge of the City* (1993). His work is marked by a keen appreciation of social atmospherics. **Terence Brown**

Hogan, John (1800–1858), sculptor. Born in Tallow, Co. Waterford, the son of a builder, and grew up in Cork. In 1818 he became an apprentice carver with the architectural firm of THOMAS DEANE; he also drew from the Vatican plaster cast collection newly arrived in Cork. Commissioned by Bishop J. Murphy, he carved twenty-seven statues of saints for the North Chapel, Cork, in 1820–23. W. P. Carey helped to raise a subscription that enabled him to travel, by way of London, to Rome, where he settled from 1825 to 1849. He studied at the English Academy and the Capitoline Museum and was deeply influenced by Thorwaldsen's neo-classical style. He established his reputation in Ireland with the exhibition of *The Drunken Faun* (1826) and *The Dead Christ* at the Royal Irish Institution in 1829, and he returned regularly to Ireland to deal with clients. The Pietà was one of his favourite subjects, as in St Nicholas of Myra (1831) and the Loreto Convent, Rathfarnham (both Dublin) (1843). In 1837 he won the competition for the memorial to Bishop JAMES WARREN DOYLE (completed 1839), for which he was made a member of the Virtuosi of the Pantheon. He received many Irish commissions during the 1840s, the zenith of his career, notably funerary reliefs, such as those of Jeanette Farrell (1842) in Westland Row Church, Dublin, William Beamish (1844) in Cork, and Bishop Brinkley (1845) in TCD. He created heroic full-length figures of William Crawford (1843) for Cork, THOMAS DRUMMOND (1843) and THOMAS DAVIS (1853), both for Dublin, and two of DANIEL O'CONNELL, one for the City Hall, Dublin (1846), and the other for the Crescent, Limerick (1857). He also made a large number of portrait busts, such as those of FATHER THEOBALD MATHEW (1841) and Archbishop DANIEL MURRAY (1844). He had a close relationship with the art patron Lord Cloncurry, for whom he carved *Hibernia with a Bust of Lord Cloncurry*, his masterpiece, now in the NATIONAL GALLERY OF IRELAND. He provided a *Dead Christ* and two episcopal funerary reliefs for St John's Cathedral, NEWFOUNDLAND. Following the Roman Revolution he returned to Ireland in 1849, but his career did not thrive. He exhibited in the Dublin International Exhibition of 1853 and the Paris International Exhibition of 1855. One of his late works was *Hibernia and Brian Boroimhe* [Bórú] (1855); at the time of his death he was working on a large relief of *Civil and Religious Liberty* for the Wellington Testimonial, Dublin, which was completed by his son, John Valentine Hogan, and his Italian colleague Giovanni Benzoni. **John Turpin**

Hogan, Robert (1930–1999), literary historian and critic. His essays *After the Irish Renaissance* (1967) and *After O'Casey* (1983) are valuably succinct. As editor of the *Dictionary of Irish Literature* (1979, 1996) and (with several joint editors) the six-volume series *The Modern Irish Drama* he is invaluable for the breadth and depth of his knowledge and critical judgment of Irish literature. **Richard Pine**

Holland, John Philip (1841–1914), inventor of the submarine. Born at Liscannor, Co. Clare; joined the CHRISTIAN BROTHERS in 1858 to train as a schoolteacher but left in 1873 for America. Over a period of thirty years he perfected his ideas for a submarine, at first with funds from the IRISH REPUBLICAN BROTHERHOOD. Like the Wright brothers, he mastered the safe piloting of a vehicle in three-dimensional space. In 1900 the United States Navy bought his vessel, the *Holland*, now acknowledged as the true ancestor of modern submarines. **W. Garrett Scaife**

Holloway, Joseph (1861–1944), Dublin architect and theatre enthusiast. His diaries and journals from the 1880s to the 1940s document significant moments of theatre history, including controversial plays by YEATS, SYNGE, and O'CASEY. He notes the performances of such actors as WILLIE FAY, FRANK FAY, Arthur Sinclair, Máire O'Neill, SARAH ALLGOOD, BARRY FITZGERALD, and F. J. MCCORMICK. The diaries also record audience reactions, the attendance of various luminaries, and Holloway's personal reflections. He redesigned the ABBEY THEATRE for its opening in 1904. **P. J. Mathews**

Holmes, Sir Gordon Morgan (1876–1965), neurologist. Born in Dromiskin, Co. Louth; educated at TCD, the Richmond Asylum, Dublin, in Frankfurt and at the National Hospital for Nervous Diseases, London. Remaining in London, he became the leading neurologist at the National Hospital for Nervous Diseases and made major contributions to the physiology and pathology of the nervous system. A brilliant and formidable teacher, he developed a pattern of neurological examination that was accepted throughout the world. **Edward Martin**

Holmes, Joe (1906–1978), traditional singer and fiddler. Born in Killyramer, near Ballymoney, Co. Antrim, to a rich TRADITIONAL MUSIC background. His singing partnership with LEN GRAHAM resulted in two recordings: *Chaste Muses, Bards and Sages* (1975) and *After Dawning* (1978). **Len Graham**

Holt, Edward William Lyons (1864–1922), marine scientist. Born in London; educated at the Royal Military Academy, Sandhurst. Having served in the British army, 1884–7, he became assistant naturalist on the ROYAL DUBLIN SOCIETY fishing survey, 1890–91. He returned to Ireland in 1898 to take charge of the marine laboratory of the Royal Dublin Society until its transfer to the government in 1900, when he was appointed scientific adviser, succeeding W. S. GREEN, in 1914, as chief inspector of fisheries. He was noted for the excellence of his scientific work and the humanity of his official reports. **Christopher Moriarty**

Holt, General Joseph (c. 1758–1826), UNITED IRISHMAN. Born in Castlemacadam, Avoca, Co. Wicklow. After the Battle of the Midlands in July 1798 he was undisputed military leader of the remaining United Irish forces in the field. Only after his surrender on 10 November could it be said that the 1798 REBELLION was over. In 1799 he was transported to New South Wales as a political prisoner. In 1814 he returned to Ireland and lived in Dublin and later at Dunleary. The New South Wales section of his memoirs was published for the first time in 1988, the Irish section in 1998. Although he conceals the truth about the circumstances of his enlistment as a United Irishman and writes in a self-serving spirit, the memoirs are historiographically indispensable as a first-hand account of the events of the Rebellion of 1798 and of life in the foundation days of the colony of New South Wales. **Peter O'Shaughnessy**

Holywood, Christopher (John Geraldine) (1559–1626), philosopher, theologian, and priest. Born in Artane, Dublin; he studied at Padua, and joined the Jesuit order in 1584. A professor of philosophy, theology, and scripture, he was leader of the Irish COUNTER-REFORMATION. Following imprisonment in England he was exiled. He returned to Ireland in 1604 as superior of the Irish mission. He was admired for his virtue and learning. He published in Latin *The Defence of the Council of Trent* and *Treatise on the True Church of Christ* in 1604. His *De Meteoris* in 1613 (as John Geraldine) is probably the first scientific book by an Irish author. His letters are preserved in the Jesuit Archives. **Juan José Pérez-Camacho**

Holycross Abbey, Co. Tipperary, a CISTERCIAN abbey founded c. 1180 by Dónall Mór O'Brien, King of Munster. Surviving remains include a large church of typical Cistercian plan, extensively renovated during the fifteenth century. Of particular interest are the richly carved *sedilia* (altar seats) bearing the coats of arms of England and the BUTLERS, Earls of Ormond, and the fragmentary wall painting in the north transept. In the south transept is a unique shrine, probably constructed to display the alleged relic of the True Cross from which the abbey took its name. The church was restored during the 1970s and now serves as a Catholic parish church. **Rachel Moss**

Home Arts and Industries Association (fl. 1886 to early 1900s), founded in England in 1884 as the Cottage Arts Association, part of the ARTS AND CRAFTS MOVEMENT. It changed

Holland. *John Philip Holland, Irish-American inventor, looking out of his diving torpedo-boat, the* Holland. *[Mary Evans Picture Library]*

its name the same year and extended its activities to Ireland in 1886, when it established a number of woodcarving classes, mainly in rural areas. Its aim was to foster simple arts and crafts by organising classes and providing sales outlets. The woodcarving output ranged from small picture-frames to substantial items of furniture, much of it decorated in a 'Celtic' style. Two of the most prolific groups were the Ahane and Clonkeen classes in Co. Limerick, set up by Charlotte and Maria Barrington; some of their work survives at Glenstal Castle. Other particularly accomplished groups were those at Stradbally, Co. Laois, Bray, Co. Wicklow, Terenure, Dublin, and Killarney, Co. Kerry. In addition to the annual sales of the association held in London, the Irish groups also sent their work to the annual exhibitions of the ROYAL DUBLIN SOCIETY. **Paul Larmour**

Home Government Association (1870–73), established by ISAAC BUTT, who wrote its manifesto, *Irish Federalism* (1870). It sought a modification of the Union, with the establishment of an Irish Parliament responsible for domestic affairs under a federal constitution. The association was non-sectarian, and notable support came from some middle-class Protestants, liberal and conservative. It was also supported by a few Fenians, who trusted Butt because of his work for the AMNESTY ASSOCIATION. The association was succeeded by the HOME RULE League in 1873. **Joseph Spence**

home rule movement. The home rule movement originated from an informal meeting in May 1870 and was given shape in the HOME GOVERNMENT ASSOCIATION, which in November 1873 became the Irish Home Rule League. At the general election of 1874 sixty constituencies elected home-rulers, and in March of that year most of these formed themselves into the Home Rule Party, with ISAAC BUTT as its chairman.

The early movement lacked funds, organisation, and cohesion. After Butt's death in 1879, more militant figures, headed by CHARLES STEWART PARNELL, took over the movement. In the general election of 1885 the IRISH PARTY captured eighty-five Irish constituencies, giving it a total of eighty-six seats (including one in Liverpool). This electoral success was capped by WILLIAM GLADSTONE's abortive Home Rule Bill (1886), which failed to gain a majority in the House of Commons. Further Home Rule Bills were presented in 1893, 1912, and 1920; the first three were produced by Liberal governments and the last by a Conservative-dominated coalition. These schemes sought to transfer Irish business (but not imperial, foreign affairs, and certain other matters) to an executive responsible to an elected assembly in Ireland (under the 1920 bill to two bodies, one in Dublin and another in Belfast with jurisdiction over six counties in the North).

At the close of 1890, in the face of the Parnell divorce crisis, the national movement split into two factions, weakening Gladstone's second attempt in 1893 to implement home rule, which, though it passed in the House of Commons, was rejected by the House of Lords. In 1900 the Irish Party was reunited under the chairmanship of JOHN REDMOND, with the UNITED IRISH LEAGUE serving as the public arm, though it did not command the respect and unanimity of Parnell's movement. At the third attempt, following pruning of the powers of the House of Lords in 1911, home rule was enacted in September 1914 but was suspended for the duration of the FIRST WORLD WAR. By then Redmond was dead and the Irish Party supplanted by SINN FÉIN. Home rule was implemented in 1921, though it came into effect only in Northern Ireland; in the South it was superseded by the ANGLO-IRISH TREATY (6 December 1921).

Throughout its existence the over-arching purpose of the movement was the attainment of autonomy for Ireland in internal affairs, though in practice numerous other issues were promoted as well. By the mid-1880s the movement contained few Protestants, essentially acting as a vehicle for Catholic aspirations and responsive to the expectations of the Catholic Church. From 1886 it was confronted by a powerful unionist force, especially by 1912 in Ulster. **Alan O'Day**

homosexuality, traditionally an unmentionable topic in Irish society. Only within the last quarter of the twentieth century has the subject been broached at all in general conversation. There has been no credible survey of the incidence of homosexual behaviour or orientation in Ireland; but the most accessible interpretation of the authoritative Kinsey statistics suggests an incidence of about 10 per cent of the adult male population and slightly less in the female population.

The conspiracy of silence resulting from these attitudes makes it difficult to reconstruct a history of homosexual experience in Ireland. We have some indicators, however. In the BREHON LAW, though there was no punishment for sexual acts between members of the same sex, if a husband was found in bed with a serving youth this provided grounds for divorce by the wife. We also find traces of homosexual activity incidentally through the early medieval Catholic penitentials, such as those of CUMMEAN FADA. These manuals, compiled for the assistance of priests hearing confession, listed sins in one column while specifying appropriate penances in the other; the listing of such acts as mutual masturbation and intercrural and anal intercourse occurs with sufficient frequency to suggest that these activities were indulged in by a similar proportion of the community then as now. However, there is little trace of a specifically homosexual (gay) life-style or sensibility.

Until the reign of HENRY VIII homosexual behaviour was subject to ecclesiastical rather than civil law. In tandem with the sequestration of the material goods of the monasteries Henry also, perhaps unwittingly, acquired jurisdiction over the ecclesiastical courts. It was thus that homosexual behaviour made the transition in sixteenth-century English law from sin to crime. An Acte for Punysshement of the Vice of Buggerie was passed in 1534; this was continued and strengthened by the advisers of Henry's successor, Edward VI, in 1548. Curiously, Mary repealed virtually everything enacted by her Protestant predecessors, including the prohibition on buggery. She was succeeded by ELIZABETH I, in whose reign in 1562 was passed an Act for the Punishment of the Vyce of Sodomye, showing that as far as the Elizabethans were concerned, buggery and sodomy amounted to the same thing.

For technical reasons this legislation did not extend to Ireland. Nevertheless, in 1631 an Anglo-Irish peer, the Earl of Castlehaven, was found guilty of the crime of sodomy and put to death. The man with whom the offence was committed was a servant named Fitzpatrick. Perhaps it was in the wake of this sensational case that an Act for the Punishment of the Vice of Buggery was passed by the Irish House of Commons on 11 November 1634. It is widely believed that the principal promoter of this act, though he did so for political reasons, was John Atherton, Anglican Bishop of Waterford and Lismore. Bishop Atherton was subsequently arrested for the same offence, convicted, and hanged outside Christ Church Cathedral in Dublin on 5 December 1640, the first victim of the legislation he had helped introduce.

Our knowledge of homosexual behaviour until modern times continues to be tragically dependent on such scandals, upheavals, and court cases. In July 1822 another Irish ecclesiastic, the fifty-seven-year-old Percy Jocelyn, Bishop of Clogher, was caught while engaged in sexual activity with a soldier in the back room of a public house, the White Lion, in St Alban's Place, London. Convicted in both ecclesiastical and civil courts, he fled the jurisdiction with the aid of relatives and disappeared into obscurity. The fate of the soldier is unknown.

Throughout the nineteenth century there were sporadic eruptions of scandal involving DUBLIN CASTLE and society figures. There is little evidence of homosexual people leading a successful private life, with the exception of some odd couples such as LADY ELEANOR BUTLER and her cousin Sarah Ponsonby, who eloped together and lived in a cottage in Wales, where they were visited as a curiosity by literary enthusiasts and sightseers. There is a twentieth-century parallel to this in the tacit acceptance of the lifelong relationship of the Dublin theatrical duo MÍCHEÁL MAC LIAMMÓIR and HILTON EDWARDS.

There were, however, some alterations to the law in the nineteenth century. Section 11 of the Offences Against the Person Act (1861) removed the death penalty for sodomy and replaced it with a maximum sentence of ten years' imprisonment with hard labour. In 1885 the infamous Labouchère Amendment, which became known as the 'blackmailer's charter', was passed, which criminalised all forms of 'indecency' between males without defining such behaviour. This was the section of the law under which OSCAR WILDE was sentenced to two years' imprisonment.

The laws of 1861 and 1885 continued to operate in Ireland after the creation of the FREE STATE and subsequently the Republic. In the 1980s they were challenged in both the High Court and the SUPREME COURT, on constitutional grounds. The failure of these two actions opened the way to the European Court of Human Rights, where a continuation of the action was ultimately successful in 1988.

By the beginning of the 1970s, in response to the Northern 'TROUBLES', a group was launched in Dublin to support the struggle for civil rights for Catholics in Northern Ireland, calling itself the South of Ireland Civil Rights Association. Like its Northern counterpart, this movement was inspired by the civil rights struggles of women and blacks in America. As a result it was comparatively easy to persuade those responsible to adopt as one part of its programme the need for change in the repressive laws against male homosexuals. Discussion groups also began to form in the universities. The student welfare officer in TRINITY COLLEGE, Dublin, helped to establish a group called the Sexual Liberation Movement. Because so many of the universities had similar discussion groups, an umbrella body, the Union for Sexual Freedoms in Ireland, was established.

The Irish Gay Rights Movement was founded in 1974. This was the first movement to make it clear in its title that it was unashamedly Irish and gay, regarded gay rights as human rights, and was prepared to fight for them. It catered for the social needs of the small but growing number of relatively confident gay people while using the money generated by social activities to finance the political side of the movement. In the North a sister organisation, the Northern Ireland Gay Rights Association, was established.

In time the more politically motivated minority moved on to create a new organisation, the Campaign for Homosexual Law Reform, in 1977, which would campaign specifically on the issue of changing the discriminatory legislation.

On St Patrick's Day, 1979, the first real community centre in Dublin for gay people was established, in Fownes Street, containing a disco, a library, counselling rooms, an outreach group, a cinema, and a theatre. Named the Hirschfeld Centre, its discotheque (Flickers) became one of the most popular discos in Dublin, drawing in at its peak 1,500 people over the weekend. It was as a direct result of the imaginative cultural and social contribution of the gay community that the TEMPLE BAR area was born as a bohemian district. The Hirschfeld Centre, however, was the target of a number of attacks with both concrete blocks and crude bombs, and eventually, in 1988, it was burnt to the ground.

homosexuality. *Mícheál Mac Liammóir (at the piano) and his partner, Hilton Edwards (left), joint-founders of the Gate Theatre, Dublin, with (right) the playwright Brendan Behan at Mac Liammóir and Edwards' home in Harcourt Terrace, Dublin, 1952. [Getty Images/Hulton Archive]*

Within the ambit of the Hirschfeld Centre many new groups sprang up, some dealing with isolated gay individuals, as well as Alcoholics Anonymous for Gay People, Gay Men's Health Action (which played a crucial role in fighting the onset of the AIDS virus), and the Gay and Lesbian Equality Movement (which was subsequently to prove an effective lobbying group). Women were represented on the committee of the National Gay Federation, though both on the committee and at social functions women remained in a minority. A separate lesbian organisation, Liberation for Irish Lesbians, was also initiated. [see LESBIANISM.] **David Norris**

homosexuality and language. Since the 1960s there has been a remarkable shift in the way in which the public perceives the subject of homosexuality, from abhorrence to acceptance. This process is reflected clearly in linguistic developments.

Historically, great efforts had been made by both church and state to suppress any discussion of the topic; the early ecclesiastical courts in fact described sexual activity between males as 'that crime which is so horrible that it must not be mentioned among Christians.' The two most frequently used words in legal and religious texts, 'sodomy' and 'buggery', display clear signs of ecclesiastical origins. Both essentially describe merely the geographical place of origin of a particular population group, Sodom being the ancient city in Old Testament Israel and 'buggery' coming from the Middle French term *Boulgre*, meaning Bulgarian.

The campaign to silence the discussion of homosexuality was so successful that at the beginning of the twentieth century E. M. Forster's character Maurice in the novel of the same name could find no words in which to express his condition other than by describing himself as 'an unspeakable of the OSCAR WILDE sort.' By the middle of the twentieth century, however, the word 'homosexual' had achieved acceptance in scientific and sociological circles; even so it rarely made its appearance in respectable literature until the beginning of the Wolfenden debates in Britain in the 1960s. There was also at this period some timid and muted discussion of the topic in Irish newspapers.

The word 'gay' came into use by way of American slang of the 1920s and was unknown in Ireland until the 1960s. However, it soon became part of international currency and made its way into usage in Ireland, despite protests from some who complained of the colonisation and corruption of this erstwhile innocent word by the gay movement. That this acceptance took some time is clear from the manner in which the word appears in Irish newspapers throughout the 1960s, 70s and 80s. On its first appearance it invariably appeared between inverted commas, usually capitalised, and followed by a question mark. Nowadays the word appears as a matter of course. [see IMPORTANCE OF BEING EARNEST, THE.] **David Norris**

homosexuality legislation. Despite the growth of what became known as the 'gay scene' in Dublin in the 1960s and 70s, sexual activity of any kind between males, regardless of age or circumstance, remained a criminal offence. This was seen as psychologically damaging, politically insulting, and a negative factor in the self-image of gay people. It was decided then to attempt by various means, including political campaigning and legal action, to overturn this unjust law. In November 1977 proceedings were formally initiated by DAVID NORRIS, represented by MARY ROBINSON, and papers were served seeking a declaration that sections 61 and 62 of the Offences Against the Person Act (1861) and section 11 of the Criminal Law (Amendment) Act (1885) had lapsed with the adoption of the CONSTITUTION OF IRELAND in 1937. This was as a result of the conflict between those sections and the provisions of article 40.1 and 40.3 of the Constitution, which guarantee the rights of the individual. A wide range of expert evidence from all over the world was introduced, and for the first time the unvarnished facts about homosexuality, its incidence, possible cause, effect on psychological balance, and relationship to mental illness and criminal behaviour, were all addressed.

All the witnesses appeared for the plaintiff: the Government failed to introduce any evidence on its own behalf. This was a public relations victory for the gay movement. On 10 October 1980 Mr Justice McWilliams delivered his judgment, which is notable for its favourable findings of fact regarding homosexuality as a condition. He accepted the evidence presented that there was a surprisingly large number of homosexual people living undetected in Ireland, that they were not more prone to criminal activity than any other section of society, that they were not less intellectually gifted, and that they were not child-molesters. Nevertheless he made it clear that he could not find on behalf of the plaintiff, because of the Christian and democratic nature of the state established in 1937.

In 1981 a parallel case taken in Northern Ireland in the name of Jeffrey Dudgeon had gone to the European Court of Human Rights in Strasbourg and had been successful. In the Republic the High Court decision was unsuccessfully appealed, and the case was rejected by a majority decision of the SUPREME COURT, leaving the way open to the European Court of Human Rights, where a judgment in favour of the plaintiff was delivered in 1988.

Though this judgment placed an onus on the Government to change the law, it showed no enthusiasm for change. The Taoiseach, ALBERT REYNOLDS, indicated clearly in an interview that this would not be a priority for his Government. However, the delay proved useful and allowed for a period of negotiation and information

Honan. St Gobnait *(1916), one of the eleven stained-glass windows by Harry Clarke in the Honan Chapel, University College, Cork. Gobnait, patron saint of beekeepers, is shown holding a model of her monastery at Ballyvourney, Co. Cork, the leading of her gown in honeycomb pattern; at bottom (right) she uses her bees to protect her sanctuary from thieves. [University College, Cork]*

exchange. For the first time sexual orientation clauses were successfully inserted in legislation protecting the human rights of Irish citizens. This was certainly ironic in the light of the continuing existence of the criminal law, but this contradiction was nothing new for Ireland.

In 1980 the Irish Federation of University Teachers adopted a resolution favouring decriminalisation and securing the rights of gay workers against DISCRIMINATION on the grounds of sexual orientation. In 1988 the Gay and Lesbian Equality Network, in co-operation with other groups, successfully lobbied from within the CIVIL SERVICE to achieve a remarkable advance, under which discrimination on the grounds of either HIV status or sexual orientation was outlawed.

By 1993 the Minister for Justice, Máire Geoghegan-Quinn, opened negotiations with gay political leaders and as a result the Criminal Law (Sexual Offences) Act (1993) was passed, granting parity before the law to homosexual citizens and introducing a common age of consent of seventeen years for both heterosexual and homosexual relations. There have subsequently been some small changes in the area of inheritance legislation; but a comprehensive examination of the status of gay people under the law, with regard to such areas as hospital visiting rights, inheritance rights, and joint mortgages, has still not been undertaken.

Among recent changes in legislation are the following:

Prohibition of Incitement to Hatred Act (1989): protection under several categories, including that of 'sexual orientation'.

Unfair Dismissals Act (1993): protection for all workers from dismissal because of 'sexual orientation'.

Powers of Attorney Act (1995) and Domestic Violence Act (1995): both laws use definitions that implicitly recognise lesbian and gay relationships.

Refugee Act (1996): the definition of 'refugee' includes persecution on the grounds of 'sexual orientation'.

Employment Equality Act (1997) and Equal Status Act (1997): full anti-discrimination protection at work and in society, to be enforced by a new Equality Authority. Protection covers nine categories, including HIV status and sexual orientation, and guarantees access to housing, services, education, etc. After constitutional difficulties were resolved, both acts and the Equality Authority were reintroduced in 1999. The Equality Authority, and the Director of Equality Investigations, have been operational since 2000. **David Norris**

Honan Chapel, Cork. The Honan Chapel at University College, Cork, represents one of the best examples of work of the Celtic Revival. Conceived as a unit in architecture, furnishings, plate, vestments, and fittings, it was designed and built by the leading designers, artists, and craftworkers of the day, who used the finest materials available. Among the works that decorate the chapel are STAINED GLASS by HARRY CLARKE and the artists of AN TÚR GLOINE, altar plate by W. A. SCOTT, sculpture by OLIVER SHEPPARD, embroidery by the DUN EMER GUILD, and metalwork by PERCY OSWALD REEVES. Consecrated in November 1916, the building was designed by a local architect, James F. McMullan, in the Celtic ROMANESQUE revival style. Every detail of design and manufacture was carefully considered; the plainness of the architecture is complemented by the richness of the interior furnishings and finishings. The significance of the chapel can be understood only when it is considered as an artistic and symbolic entity. Although the chapel contains the work of different artists and craftworkers, the result is harmonious, each piece having a unique intrinsic quality. Their work is a remarkable record of the Irish ARTS AND CRAFTS MOVEMENT. **Virginia Teehan**

Hone, Evie (1894–1955), painter and stained-glass artist. Born in Co. Dublin; privately educated at home and through trips to the Continent after a crippling childhood accident. Art classes in London with the painters Byam Shaw, Walter Sickert, and Bernard Meninsky led in 1920 to extended studies in Paris with her lifelong friend MAINIE JELLETT, under the semi-abstract cubist André Lhôte and the more formal Albert Gleizes. Her profound sense of devotion led to her temporary withdrawal into an Anglican community of nuns in 1925 (and her later conversion to Catholicism in 1937) and to her decision in 1932 to synthesise faith and art through stained glass. Instructed in the craft by WILHELMINA GEDDES in London, in 1935 she became a member of AN TÚR GLOINE, the stained-glass co-operative, where she worked until 1943, designing and painting mostly figurative windows using a powerfully innovative vocabulary of deep, smouldering colour and loose expressionist brushwork. From 1944 she worked in a converted studio at Marlay Grange, Rathfarnham, Dublin, making increasingly monumental windows and small, painterly panels, while exhibiting internationally. In ten densely packed years she introduced a new, loosely painted, resonantly coloured, and sombrely religious treatment; her most famous works were for Tullabeg, Co. Offaly (1946), Kingscourt, Co. Cavan (1947–8), and Eton College, Windsor (1949–52). **Nicola Gordon Bowe**

Hone, Nathaniel the elder (1718–1784), artist, founder of the Hone dynasty of painters. Born in Dublin; nothing is known of his education, but his earliest works were mostly enamel miniatures. He was in England by 1742, where he remained for the rest of his life, except for brief visits to Ireland. He never went to Italy but was much influenced by Dutch painting, including that of Rembrandt, which affected his fine series of self-portraits. By 1760 he had achieved a large, fashionable clientele and turned entirely to life-size oil portraits; he is noted for his fine portraits of children and theatre personalities. He became a founder of the Royal Academy, London; but his jealousy of Reynolds led to difficulties, culminating in the refusal of the academy to hang his *Conjuror* (of which there are two versions, one in the NATIONAL GALLERY OF IRELAND and one in the Tate Gallery, London), which was a satire on Reynolds's use of Old Masters for his compositions and thought to be an attack on Angelica Kaufmann. In 1775 he held the first one-man show in England, which was, in modern terminology, a retrospective. **Anne Crookshank**

Hone, Nathaniel the younger (1831–1917), artist. Born in Dublin; great-grand-nephew of NATHANIEL HONE THE ELDER; studied engineering at TCD, then left for Paris to study art with the French painter Couture. Residing in the Forest of Fontainebleau, 1856–70, he painted landscapes profoundly influenced by the naturalistic landscape of Corot and the Barbizon School. Returning to Ireland

Hone, Nathaniel the elder. *Self-portrait of Nathaniel Hone, seen in an Italianate landscape with classical temple. His arm rests on a sculpted pedestal, a classicised relief portrait of his wife, Mary. [National Gallery of Ireland]*

in 1872, he devoted himself to Irish subjects: meadows, beaches and cliffs, sailing vessels on choppy seas. Hone was the first Irish artist to introduce the influences of French naturalistic landscape painting into Ireland; yet early critical reaction to his work was bemused, even hostile. His work is characterised by its sensitivity to subdued Irish tones and cloudy skies, his early 'French' style giving way to a freedom of manner and breadth of vision. Painting visits to the south of France, the Netherlands, Greece, and Egypt provided stimulus to his work. He exhibited at the RHA almost continuously, 1876–1917. By the turn of the century he was regarded as the leading Irish landscapist of his generation, numbering among his admirers GEORGE MOORE, SARAH PURSER, GEORGE RUSSELL, and THOMAS BODKIN. His widow bequeathed hundreds of his oils and watercolours to the NATIONAL GALLERY OF IRELAND. **Julian Campbell**

Hone, Nathaniel the younger. The Sphinx *(1862) by Nathaniel Hone. Regarded as the leading Irish plein-air landscapist of his generation, he became professor of painting at the Royal Hibernian Academy in 1894, a position he retained until his death in 1917. [National Gallery of Ireland]*

honorary citizenship. The Republic's Irish Nationality and Citizenship Act (1956) makes provision for the granting of honorary citizenship to individuals who have made an outstanding contribution to public life. The first recipient, in 1963, was Sir ALFRED CHESTER BEATTY (1875–1968). An American-born mining engineer, art collector, and philanthropist, he moved to Dublin in 1953. He left his library of Eastern and Western books and manuscripts—one of the finest of its type in the world—in trust to the Irish nation, and they form the core of the CHESTER BEATTY LIBRARY, Dublin Castle.

Dr Tiede Herrema (1921–), a native of the Netherlands, was granted honorary citizenship in 1975 in recognition of his ordeal at the hands of IRA kidnappers who held him to ransom between 3 October and 7 November 1975. He was managing director of the Ferenka factory in Limerick when he was kidnapped. His wife, Elizabeth, was also awarded honorary citizenship.

Thomas Phillip 'Tip' O'Neill (1912–1994), Speaker of the US House of Representatives, born in Cambridge, Massachusetts, was granted honorary citizenship by the Taoiseach, GARRET FITZGERALD, at a ST PATRICK'S DAY celebration in Washington on 17 March 1986. FitzGerald praised O'Neill for his lifelong commitment to a peaceful solution to the Northern Ireland crisis and for winning American financial and political support for the ANGLO-IRISH AGREEMENT. O'Neill's wife, Mildred, was also awarded honorary citizenship.

Sir ALFRED BEIT (1903–1994) was granted honorary citizenship with his wife, Lady Clementine Beit, in 1993. In 1976 they transferred their home, Russborough House, near Blessington, Co. Wicklow, and its contents to the Alfred Beit Foundation for the benefit of the Irish public and later donated important paintings by Vermeer, Goya, and others to the NATIONAL GALLERY OF IRELAND.

JACK CHARLTON (1935–), a native of Ashington, Northumberland, was granted honorary citizenship in 1995 in recognition of his contribution to the Republic of Ireland SOCCER team, of which he was manager, 1986–95. The team qualified for the final stages of the European Championships in 1988 and the World Cup in 1990 and 1994.

Jean Kennedy Smith (1928–), a native of Massachusetts, was granted honorary citizenship in July 1998 in recognition of her services as US ambassador to Ireland, 1993–8, during which time she was credited with contributing to the development of the NORTHERN IRELAND PEACE PROCESS.

The English artist DEREK HILL (1916–2000) became an honorary citizen in January 1999. Born in Southampton, he moved to Co. Donegal in 1954, from where he introduced the public to the TORY ISLAND school of naïve painters. He donated his home (now Glebe House and Gallery, Churchill, Co. Donegal) and its substantial art collection to the Irish nation in 1981. **Ciarán Deane**

Hook Head Lighthouse, on the eastern side of Waterford Harbour, first erected by the ANGLO-NORMANS in 1172 to serve as a defensive and look-out tower. The present lantern and supporting turret were erected in 1864; the light is now operated automatically. A visitor centre was opened in 2000. **Ronald Cox**

Hopkins, Gerard Manley (1844–1889), priest and poet. Born in London and brought up in Hampstead; educated at the University of Oxford. He converted from Anglicanism to Catholicism and then became a Jesuit priest. A compulsive writer, he constantly experimented with poetic vocabulary to define his hidden life. After years of comparative silence he wrote the long poem 'The Wreck of the Deutschland' and several sonnets, including 'The Windhover'. Failing a theology examination, he left the comparative happiness of Wales and filled many posts unhappily, disgusted at industrial Britain and increasingly alienated and eccentric. He spent his final years in Ireland, teaching at the Catholic University in St Stephen's Green, Dublin (now Newman House), unsympathetic to Irish patriotism and culture but writing remarkable poems of psychological anguish. His unmarked grave in the Jesuit plot at Glasnevin, Dublin, is symbolic of his sense of lonely duty. **Norman White**

Hopkirk, Paddy (1933–), rally and racing driver. Born in Belfast. He won the 1964 Monte Carlo Rally as well as the 1964 and 1966 Austrian Alpine Rallies and the 1967 Acropolis. [see MOTOR SPORT.] **Brendan Lynch**

Horan, Monsignor James (1911–1986), priest and entrepreneur. Born in Partry, Co. Mayo. Appointed parish priest at the Marian shrine of Knock, Co. Mayo, 1967, he revolutionised facilities for pilgrims. In the 1980s he led the controversial and successful campaign for the building of Knock Airport; he was lionised in the west but regarded with suspicion by many in the Dublin establishment. **Fergal Tobin**

hornpipe, a tune type and dance originating in eighteenth-century England. A version in common time was adopted by Irish

Horan. *Monsignor James Horan watching the arrival of the first plane at Knock Airport, Co. Mayo, May 1986. [Frank Dolan]*

dancing-masters as an exhibition piece, and it exists today as a solo dance, featuring intricate footwork, and as part of certain set dances. The tune type features a slow, deliberate tempo, accents on beats 1 and 3 in a bar, and three crotchets to mark the end of a part. [see SET DANCING.] **Liz Doherty**

horse, Irish, a descendent of the native Connemara pony and draught horse that can be traced back to prehistoric times. The first horses raced at ancient FESTIVALS and pulled chariots into battle; the BREHON LAW described them as 'big, sound, noble, load-carrying, lively, and easy-bearing.' At the Battle of Waterloo (1815) the Duke of Wellington rode an Irish black horse called 'Copenhagen', while Napoleon Bonaparte's horse, 'Marengo', came from Co. Wexford.

From these beginnings came the present-day Irish sport horse. Traditional breeding crossed the Irish draught mare, which was developed to suit the small farm, with the thoroughbred stallion. The strength and placid temperament of the draught combined with the speed and athleticism of the thoroughbred are the basic ingredients of the famous Irish chargers of warfare, the hunter, and more recently the competition horse. The Irish thoroughbred is one of the best racehorses in the world. It has won all the principal races on numerous occasions, including the Derby, Grand National, and Cheltenham Gold Cup. The breeding of sport horses produced many international show-jumpers, such as 'Boomerang' and 'Goodbye', during the middle of the twentieth century. Since 1980 jumping horses are three-quarters to seven-eighths thoroughbred, as more speed and athleticism are required. Recently, Continental breeds have been introduced to improve jumping ability. The Irish event horse is at least three-quarters thoroughbred. From 1994 to 2000 Irish-bred event horses have been ranked the best in the world. The Irish horse is ideally suited to the leisure rider because of its quiet nature. It is an excellent hunter, often HUNTING up to three days a week. It is used in riding schools and is very suited to beginners.

The typical Irish horse is 1.6–1.75 m high, with 230 mm of bone; the main colours are brown, bay, chestnut, and grey. The majority are registered with the Irish Horse Board, and each has its own identification passport. The modern Irish horse is noble, correct, sound, athletic, has good paces, is pleasant to ride, and has a good temperament. [see BALLINASLOE FAIR; BYERLEY TURK; SHERGAR.] **Norman Storey**

horse-racing. *A steeplechase: horses clear the fence during a steeplechase at Punchestown, Co. Kildare, one of the most demanding courses for horse and jockey. [Colman Doyle]*

horse-racing. There are twenty-five racecourses in the Republic and two in Northern Ireland. There are approximately 270 meetings each year and an average of seven races at a meeting. There are 5,000 horses in training, the biggest concentration (nearly 1,500) being on the CURRAGH, Co. Kildare, where owners and trainers have to pay a twice-yearly fee to the Curragh Racecourse for the use of the extensive gallops. The horses are distributed among 370 licensed trainers, with a further 320 permit-holders who are restricted to training horses belonging to themselves or their immediate family.

Racing is split between flat racing and national hunt racing, where the horses race over fences or hurdles or in bumper races confined to amateur riders. There are sixty licensed flat jockeys and a further eighty-five apprentices who also ride on the flat, while 130 riders have a national hunt jockey's licence. The most successful modern-day flat jockeys are Mick Kinane, Johnny Murtagh, and Pat Smullen; and Paul Carberry, Ruby Walsh, Charlie Swan, and Barry Geraghty over jumps. Aidan O'Brien has the top flat stable; his Ballydoyle training centre, near Cashel, Co. Tipperary, is widely acknowledged to be among the best in the world. He trains principally for John Magnier, the owner of Coolmore stud, and Michael Tabor and has won big races all over the world. Dermot Weld, who has won the biggest races in America and Australia as well as in Europe, has a similar worldwide reputation, while John Oxx and Jim Bolger invariably finish in the top four. The best jumping horses tend to be spread over a greater number of stables, but Willie Mullins, Noel Meade, Frances Crowley, Edward O'Grady, Arthur Moore, Jessica Harrington, Michael O'Brien, Ted Walsh, Mouse Morris, Pat Hughes, Dessie Hughes, and Christy Roche all have powerful teams.

Racing is administered by Horse Racing Ireland, a state-backed body set up in 2001, and the Turf Club. The industry is heavily subsidised by the Government, which contributes nearly €47 million a year. Betting is a significant component of horse-racing, and annual on-course turnover amounts to some €200 million, with the bookmakers handling the bulk of this. Racing is supported by a massive breeding industry, which has an annual turnover at bloodstock sales of €120 million. Some 9,000 foals are born each year, while mares come from all over the world to be mated with stallions at Irish studs, notably Magnier's Coolmore Stud in Co. Tipperary. **Michael Clower**

horse-racing, history. There was racing on the Curragh, Co. Kildare, from prehistoric times. Written records survive from the early Norman period testifying to the presence of the sport. In 1634 Lord Digby and the Earl of Ormond ran their horses in a 4-mile race there (Ormond's horse won). The first properly organised race was the King's Plate, whose origins go back to the 1670s but whose formal articles date from 1717. In 1752 there occurred the most celebrated race ever run in Ireland. Horses owned by Edmund Blake and Mr O'Callaghan raced over open country in Co. Cork from Buttevant church to the steeple of the St Leger church at Doneraile, 7.25 km ($4\frac{1}{2}$ miles) distant: this was the world's first steeplechase. From that time flat racing and racing over fences co-existed in Ireland. The latter form quickly spread to Britain. The Turf Club, the governing body for flat racing, dates from 1790 and the Irish National Hunt Steeplechase Committee from 1869. The Irish Derby, renewed annually at the Curragh, was first run in 1866. The four other Irish flat classics came later and, like the Derby, are based on English models.

The railways greatly expanded the scope of racing as a spectator sport: popular venues such as Fairyhouse, Co. Dublin, Listowel, Co. Kerry, and Ballybrit, Co. Galway, date from the 1850s and 60s, though Bellewstown, Co. Meath, still the site of a popular four-day meeting each July, can trace its origins to the middle of the seventeenth century. Punchestown, Co. Kildare, the most celebrated of the National Hunt festivals, dates from 1861. The Irish Grand National, run at Fairyhouse over a course of 5.8 km ($3\frac{5}{8}$ miles), was first contested in 1870.

In 1907, Orby, owned by Richard 'Boss' Croker and trained by F. F. MacCabe, became the first Irish-owned and Irish-trained horse to win the Epsom Derby. It was a feat not repeated until 1958, though increasingly frequent since then. On the National Hunt side, the Cheltenham festival in England was inaugurated in the early twentieth century and has always been a major attraction

horse-racing. *Engraving of the royal visit to Punchestown, Co. Kildare, in 1868, after a painting by Henry Barraud (1811–1874). The royal party can be seen at the back left of the lower range of the two-tier stand: the Princess of Wales, the Duke and Duchess of Abercorn, and the Viceregal party. Directly below the royal box, and to the fore on a white horse, is the Prince of Wales. [Thomas Lethbridge, Sporting Pictures]* for Irish race-goers. The greatest of all Irish horses, ARKLE, won its blue riband event, the Cheltenham Gold Cup, successively in 1964, 1965 and 1966, a feat matched by the remarkable Istabraq in the Champion Hurdle in 1998, 1999, and 2000. At the close of the twentieth century, Irish racing and the bloodstock industry generally had never been stronger. **Fergal Tobin**

Horslips, a 'Celtic rock' or folk-rock band formed in 1971 that combined elements of TRADITIONAL MUSIC—FIDDLE, mandolin, concertina, and UILLEANN PIPES—with electric guitar, keyboards, bass, and drums. The group based many of their songs on traditional airs: their hit single 'Dearg Doom' presented the traditional air 'Máirseáil Uí Néill' ('O'Neill's March')—popularised by SEÁN Ó RIADA and CEOLTÓIRÍ CHUALANN—in a rock setting. With a background in advertising and graphic design, members of the band brought a visual awareness and strong stage presentation to their work and were pioneers in bringing what was identified as an Irish form of popular music to a young audience not previously exposed to rock culture, as in their album *The Táin*. **Tom Sherlock**

hospitals. The earliest hospitals were medieval monastic foundations. During the Tudor period most of those in Ireland were destroyed. In the eighteenth century various medical and charitable institutions were established by Protestant philanthropists. Unfortunately, many had notorious mortality rates and were frequented only by the impoverished. Until the twentieth century and the development of sophisticated medical techniques, the well-off did not use hospitals. In 1765, legislation was passed in order to establish public infirmaries. By the 1780s there were twenty local hospitals of varying quality throughout Ireland. The nineteenth century saw the establishment of large voluntary hospitals under Catholic management. As the medical profession expanded, smaller hospitals multiplied. In the twentieth century, the state attempted to amalgamate hospitals. The Hospitals Sweepstakes of the 1930s provided much-needed funds for hospitals in the Free State and Republic. In the 1940s and 50s, a large-scale building programme was begun in order to provide regional hospitals. By the 1970s, regional Health Boards, which included medical and political representatives, aided the development of hospital care. In the 1980s and 90s there was an increase in the provision of private health care, as an increasingly hard-pressed public hospital system tried to cater for the medical needs of the nation. [see DR STEEVENS' HOSPITAL; ROTUNDA HOSPITAL; ROYAL HOSPITAL KILMAINHAM; Sir PATRICK DUN'S HOSPITAL.] **Margaret Ó hÓgartaigh**

Hothouse Flowers, rock group. Formed in Dublin in the mid-1980s, they achieved tremendous success early in their career with two notable singles, 'Love Don't Work This Way' (1987) and 'Don't Go' (1988). The folk-tinged band, of which the nucleus is Liam Ó Maonlaí (1964–), Peter O'Toole (1964–), and Fiachna Ó Braonáin (1965–), achieved moderate success thereafter, the critics' main bone of contention being the lack of progression from one album to the next. They disbanded in the mid-1990s but re-formed in 1998 with the disappointing album *Born*. Ó Maonlaí is highly regarded in traditional music circles as an accomplished singer in the SEAN-NÓS style. A *Best of …* collection was released in 2000. **Tony Clayton-Lea**

houghers, an AGRARIAN PROTEST movement named for the action of *houghing* (cutting the hamstring of an animal). This short-lived movement, led by the mythical 'Ever Joyce' and concentrated first on west Galway and then spreading into Cos. Mayo, Sligo,

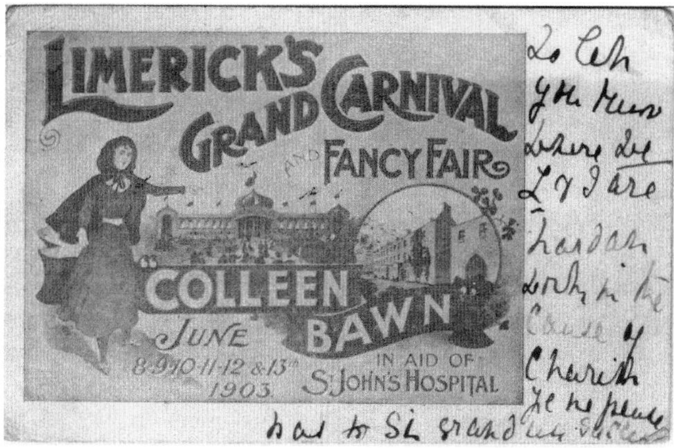

hospitals. *A postcard issued for the week-long civic Grand Carnival and Fancy Fair held in June 1903 to raise funds for St John's Hospital in Limerick City. [Collection: Limerick Museum]*

Leitrim, and Clare, lasted through the winter of 1711/12. Its aims are unclear, but the maiming of cattle and sheep suggests that the houghers wanted to stop landlords clearing their estates for grazing. [see ENCLOSURE.] **Eoin Magennis**

Houlihan, Robert (1952–), conductor. Born in Co. Kerry; trained at the Army School of Music and the Municipal College of Music. He taught at Westland Row CBS, 1971–80, and was instructor at the Army School of Music, 1976–80. He has been guest conductor and conductor with various European orchestras, his most recent post being as principal conductor and artistic director of the Savaria Symphony Orchestra, Hungary (1992). He works regularly with the NATIONAL SYMPHONY ORCHESTRA as guest conductor. He was a prizewinner at the International Competition for Young Conductors, Besançon (1980) and in Hungarian Television's International Conducting Competition (1983). **Éamonn O'Keeffe**

house churches, Christian groups characterised by a less traditional form of worship and the use of house or cell groups. Though the concept of the house church can be traced back to early CHRISTIANITY, less formal house meetings have provided a form of community that may have been lacking in larger church services for some believers during the final decades of the twentieth century. Their development in Ireland has reflected the wider growth of new religious movements offering spiritual change to the individual. Many developed from the 1960s onwards and were often interdenominational. They are more prevalent in Northern Ireland than in the Republic, where they have often struggled to survive. In Northern Ireland they have been more explicitly involved in reconciliation, because of the timing of their development, the early stages of the 'TROUBLES'.

Institutionalisation began as many house churches moved on to rent or buy buildings in which to meet and a full-time pastorate emerged. The resurgence of cell groups, house groups, and Alpha courses (Christian discussion groups) has since re-emphasised the more intimate nature of Christianity for these 'new churches'. They have remained small and middle-class in membership but may have effected change, as other traditional churches begin to employ similar methods. These changes seem to be a response from the Christian church as a whole, and from Protestantism in particular, to the sweeping social changes that are affecting church membership. [see CORRYMEELA COMMUNITY; GLENCREE RECONCILIATION CENTRE.] **Linda Thompson**

household budget survey, a sample survey of household spending on goods and services in the Republic conducted by the CENTRAL STATISTICS OFFICE at seven-year intervals (to be reduced). Eight thousand households are surveyed; participation is voluntary. The prime purpose of the survey is to make possible the calculation of the *consumer price index*, the key measure of the cost of living and INFLATION. Retail prices can be monitored frequently, but to deduce the effect of one price increase on the cost of living requires knowing how important that commodity is to households; the survey therefore provides weights for the prices. The data is also used in a range of studies, from household poverty to expenditure on luxuries. There are imperfections—respondents greatly understate expenditure on ALCOHOL, for example—but the survey is an important source of information. **Denis Conniffe**

housing. The most striking feature of the Irish housing system is the dominance of home ownership, in comparison with other tenure types. Home ownership now accounts for approximately 80 per cent of all housing stock, with private renting and social housing accounting for 11 per cent and 9 per cent, respectively. Home owners normally acquire their homes through mortgage borrowings from banks and building societies, usually over terms ranging from twenty to thirty years. In recent years, house price INFLATION, caused by a combination of low interest rates, demographic pressures, IMMIGRATION, and sustained ECONOMIC GROWTH, has led some observers to suggest that home ownership has reached its upper limit. Until recently, private renting has been viewed as a transitional tenure for students and young workers and has been characterised by wide variations in conditions, low levels of regulation, and poor security of tenure. Recent URBAN-RENEWAL measures have seen an expansion of this sector, especially in cities and towns; and a Commission on the Private Rental Sector has been established to examine all aspects of the tenure. Social housing (comprising local authority and voluntary providers) caters for less-well-off households and thus has a strongly residual profile, indicated by high levels of welfare dependence and socio-economic disadvantage. As a result of increasing house prices and a scarcity of affordable private rental accommodation, more than 45,000 households were on waiting lists by late 1999. While social housing has suffered from a poor, if largely undeserved, public image, recent innovations—such as participation by tenants in running estates, and improvements in management—have enhanced the housing service offered to households. **Cathal O'Connell**

housing. *New suburban housing at Lucan, Co. Dublin, with detached and semi-detached dwellings, typical of developments around all Irish towns. [Peter Barrow]*

housing in towns and cities. Residential housing dominates the urban landscape; especially in cities and towns, most housing dates from the twentieth century. Recent data (1991) shows that less than 15 per cent of urban housing in the Republic predates 1919, while more than 55 per cent was built after 1960. In Cork pre-1919 housing comprised 19 per cent, but it was slightly under-represented in Dublin, at 13 per cent. There is great variety in the older housing stock. Few examples survive from the Middle Ages, though much predates 1850, especially in smaller towns. Early twentieth-century working-class housing is best seen in Belfast and the north-east. Most twentieth-century housing in the Republic is of single dwellings (more than 90 per cent), mainly terraced or, in the suburbs, semi-detached, with only 8 per cent comprising apartments (12 per cent in Dublin), generally rented from the local authority. Apartments in cities have now become popular with young professionals, mainly those without children.

Home ownership is an important goal. In 1946 only 23 per cent of homes in the Republic were owner-occupied; this rose to over 52 per cent by 1971 and was over 73 per cent in 1991. This trend paralleled a decline in the rented sector, both local authority and private; but there has been a recent resurgence in the latter, particularly in cities. In Northern Ireland owner-occupancy was 68 per cent in 1993, with 38 per cent provided by the public rented sector. The figure for Belfast was lower (approximately 52 per cent in 1991), but this is a significant increase on 1961 (approximately 29 per cent). The public rented sector provides about 31 per cent, and its importance has also risen, paralleling a decline in the private rented sector. [see VERNACULAR ARCHITECTURE.] **Joseph Brady**

housing market. Long-term influences on the housing market include (1) a historical pattern of dispersed housing near agricultural holdings, as opposed to residence in towns (a tendency that has diminished with rural DEPOPULATION, though rural areas continue to be characterised by home-building on family-owned land), (2) poorly maintained rental housing stock in older urban areas and a private rental market impeded by legal restrictions, (3) sluggish ECONOMIC GROWTH and declining population for much of the post-independence era, resulting in little pressure for large-scale provision of housing, and (4) the provision of public housing by local authorities according to a rationed system.

The Republic has an extremely high owner-occupier rate (about 80 per cent in 2000), facilitated by the sale of public rented housing to tenants. Mortgage finance is of the British type, with intermediaries tending towards variable-rate loans financed by deposits, and housing being the principal component of household collateral. With development centralised in the Dublin region, haphazard PLANNING, and tax-induced and cultural preferences for single-family homes, there has been a proliferation of low-density housing developments in the suburbs. The boom of the 1990s saw the emergence of some high-density urban projects; but improvements in road TRANSPORT and pricing distortions (such as the absence of economic pricing for WATER and sewerage, almost non-existent property taxes, and the perceived malleability of the land zoning process) have enhanced the appeal of long-distance commuting for many people.

The 1990s saw an extended property boom in the Republic and a more modest boom in Northern Ireland with the improved

Howth gun-running. *Bullet-holes from gunfire by soldiers of the King's Own Scottish Borderers during the Bachelor's Walk incident in Dublin, 1914. Four people were killed and thirty-seven injured when the soldiers fired on a jeering crowd. [Getty Images/Hulton Archive]*

security situation, one result being that housing in the North is now substantially more affordable than in the South. The public sector plays a larger role in the provision of housing in Northern Ireland (more than one in four households rent public housing); noteworthy is the weaker role of local authorities relative to a centralised housing authority, reflecting concerns about discrimination. **Kevin Carey**

Houston, John (1802–1845), surgeon-anatomist. The son of a Presbyterian minister; educated at the Royal College of Surgeons in Ireland and the University of Edinburgh, where he was awarded a doctorate in 1826. He was curator of the Museum of the Royal College of Surgeons in Ireland, 1824–43. He described the valves of the rectum, known as Houston's valves, and introduced the use of the microscope and cellular pathology to Irish MEDICINE. A founder surgeon of the Royal City of Dublin Hospital in 1832, he performed the second post-mortem examination of JONATHAN SWIFT, following the flooding of ST PATRICK'S CATHEDRAL in 1835, when Swift's body was exhumed. **Dorothy Benson**

Howard-Bury, Charles (1881–1963), explorer. Born at Charleville Castle, Tullamore, Co. Offaly. Early travels included journeys in India, Tibet, Nepal, and Indo-China and big-game shooting and botanical collecting in the mountains of Baltistan and Amarkantak. In 1913 he explored the Tianshan mountains in China. In the FIRST WORLD WAR he fought with the British army before being captured and imprisoned. In 1921 he was invited to lead the first Everest expedition from Simla, with the aim of prospecting the mountain; until then no European had been within 65 km (40 miles) of it. During his leadership of this pioneering expedition, which established a practical way of reaching the summit, Howard-Bury became responsible for spreading the legend of the 'abominable snowman', which originated in his account for the *Times* (London) of the strange footprints the expedition came upon in the high Himalayas. He was awarded the gold medal of the Royal Geographical Society and of the Société Géographique de France. He died in Hammamet, Tunisia. **Peter Somerville-Large**

Howth gun-running (1914). On 26 July 1914 the IRISH VOLUNTEERS landed a consignment of arms and ammunition brought from Germany by ERSKINE CHILDERS on the ASGARD at Howth, Co. Dublin. This, together with an earlier shipment landed at Kilcoole, Co. Wicklow, consisted of 1,500 rifles. The arms landed at Howth were distributed to waiting Volunteers. Soldiers from the King's Own Scottish Borderers were despatched to intercept; as they returned to barracks a confrontation with a hostile crowd at Bachelor's Walk, Dublin, saw the soldiers open fire, killing four people and wounding thirty-seven others. [see HEUSTON, SEAN; LARNE GUN RUNNING.] **Thomas Hennessey**

Howth Harbour, Co. Dublin. Delays to the mails led to the construction of Howth Harbour, the East Pier begun in 1807 and the West Pier in 1810; the engineer in charge was JOHN RENNIE. The lighthouse at the end of the East Pier was added in 1818. The mail service was transferred to Kingstown (Dún Laoghaire) in 1826. Howth is now a fishery harbour and yachting centre. **Ronald Cox**

Howth Head, Co. Dublin, a large rocky projection of hard quartzites extending beyond the softer glacial drifts that form most of the eastern coastlands, connected to the mainland by a tombolo of gravel and sand. Like BRAY HEAD, proximity to Dublin has caused it to come under much pressure for development. **Patrick Duffy**

Huban, Mary Elizabeth (Lily) (1898–1976), pianist and teacher. Born in Gort, Co. Galway; educated at UCD, from where she graduated in 1918. She studied piano and cello at the École Normale in Paris. In Dublin she taught at the READ PIANOFORTE SCHOOL and the Leinster School of Music. She revisited Paris regularly to attend the Cours given by Cortot. Her pupils—including GERALD BARRY and MALCOM PROUD—benefited from her inspired teaching, unfailing encouragement, and understanding of all the arts. **Éamonn O'Keeffe**

Hudson, Henry (1798–1889), music-collector. Born in Rathfarnham, Co. Dublin, a member of a professional family who lived at Fields of Odin (the house later acquired by PATRICK PEARSE for his school and renamed St Enda's); educated at TCD. A dentist by profession and a member of the ROYAL IRISH ACADEMY, he collected folk music as a hobby. Beginning at the age of fourteen, he copied the music collection of the lexicographer Edward O'Reilly. O'Reilly's manuscript is now lost; Hudson's collection, which comprises 870 items, includes melodies copied from rare publications and manuscripts as well as tunes collected by him from informants in various parts of the country. Also included are 113 melodies composed by Hudson in a traditional style. With his brother, William Elliot Hudson—composer of the music for 'The Memory of the Dead' (1843) by JOHN KELLS INGRAM—he published melodies from his collection in the *Dublin Monthly Magazine*, including some of his own compositions that he passed off as folk tunes. **Jimmy O'Brien Moran**

Huguenots. *Plaque at the Huguenot cemetery in Merrion Row, Dublin, a memorial to the 239 families interred there. [Mark Joyce]*

Hughes, Anthony (1928–), pianist and teacher. Born in Dublin; trained at the RIAM and UCD. Also a graduate of the Staats Akademie für Musik und der Kunst, he was professor of music at University College, Dublin, 1958–91, and professor of piano at the RIAM, 1948–58. Having made his debut with the RTÉ Symphony Orchestra in 1947, he gave recitals in Europe, England, and Ireland, and lectured extensively. He received the ARNOLD BAX Medal, 1956. **Éamonn O'Keeffe**

Hughes, John (1865–1941), sculptor. Born in Dublin into an artisan family; studied at the Dublin Metropolitan School of Art from 1878 to 1890, where his fellow-students included W. B. YEATS, GEORGE RUSSELL, and OLIVER SHEPPARD. In 1890–91 he was at the Royal College of Art, London, a student of Edouard Lanteri, and in 1891–92 he went to Paris on a scholarship and also visited Italy. He taught at Plymouth School of Art, 1893–4, before returning to teach modelling at the Dublin school. From 1895 he exhibited at the RHA, of which he became a full member in 1900 and also professor of SCULPTURE. He introduced a vitality to Irish sculpture inspired by French and Italian Renaissance modelling, evident in his memorial to Charles Kickham (1895), *Orpheus and Eurydice* (1899), his relief *The Man of Sorrows*, and his statue of the Madonna for Loughrea Cathedral. He resigned his teaching post in 1901 to concentrate on commissions, notably the Queen VICTORIA memorial, Dublin (1901–6), moved (1987) to Sydney, New South Wales, and the memorial to W. E. GLADSTONE intended for Dublin but placed in Wales in 1925. From 1903 he spent the remainder of his life in Paris, to which he was greatly attached, and he participated in the Irish exhibitions in Paris and Brussels in 1922 and 1930. **John Turpin**

Huguenots, French Protestants who adopted the Calvinist form of the Reformed faith in the sixteenth century. The Edict of Fontainebleau (1685) issued by Louis XIV revoked the toleration they had enjoyed under the Edict of Nantes (1598) for the previous century and obliged them to abandon their religious beliefs. About a third of them chose to leave France and settle elsewhere in Europe, in North America, or South Africa. While there were individual Huguenots in Ireland from the late sixteenth century, the first permanent, organised settlement was due to the patronage of the Duke of Ormond, Lord Lieutenant of Ireland in the 1660s, who provided employment for them as weavers in Dublin. These and subsequent small immigrant groups came from the western provinces of France, particularly Poitou and Charente; the more numerous settlers in the 1690s tended to be from Languedoc. While some came directly from France, the majority were directed to Ireland from England or were brought from Switzerland as part of a formal resettlement scheme. In all, twenty-one settlements were established in Ireland, with a population of 5,000–10,000. The majority lived in towns and were involved in banking or trade; in Ulster, Huguenot settlers helped to develop the LINEN trade. Many also bought land and became prominent in eighteenth-century politics. While some separate Nonconformist congregations were formed, the majority found it possible to worship within the established church. Apart from Dublin, the most successful and enduring colony was that established at Portarlington, which had been created for the retired officers of the Huguenot regiments that had fought in the Williamite army in the war of 1689–91.

The Huguenot settlement in Ireland does not appear to have created any significant resentment, and the folk memory suggests acceptance of a hard-working and gentle community. [see BEWLEY; CROMWELLIN, LONG; LA TOUCHÉ, LE FANU; MORAVIAN CHURCH; PALATINES; ROCQUE.] **Liam Irwin**

Hull, Edward (1829–1917), geologist. Born in Antrim; educated at TCD. He became an officer in the Geological Survey of England and Wales and in 1867 was promoted to the rank of district surveyor with the geological survey of Scotland; throughout his years in Britain he specialised in the geology of coalfields. The first edition of his book *The Coal-fields of Great Britain* appeared in 1861. In 1869 he returned to Dublin as director of the Geological Survey of Ireland. The primary geological mapping of Ireland was completed under his control, before he retired in 1890. **Jean Archer**

Humanity Dick: see MARTIN, RICHARD.

Hume, John (1937–), politician. Born in Derry; an early beneficiary of the Education Act (1947), he was educated at St Columb's College, Derry, and ST PATRICK'S COLLEGE, Maynooth. As a young teacher in Derry he was drawn into the credit union and voluntary housing movements and was critical of the old Nationalist Party for its lack of a coherent strategy and failure to recognise constitutional realities. Following the CIVIL RIGHTS march of 5 October 1968 he became chairman of the Derry Citizens' Action Committee, earning the praise of the CAMERON COMMISSION for his resolute pursuit of non-violent protest.

In the 1969 Northern Ireland general election he unseated the Nationalist leader, Eddie McAteer, in Foyle, signalling the shift in nationalist thinking. Hume now became one of the most prominent and articulate representatives of the nationalist community, and in August 1970 he helped found the moderate nationalist SOCIAL DEMOCRATIC AND LABOUR PARTY (SDLP). He served briefly as Minister of Commerce in the 1974 power-sharing Executive and on its collapse forged links with influential American congressmen and EU leaders. His election to the European Parliament in 1979, coinciding with his leadership of the SDLP, enhanced his international status; his efforts led to the establishment of the New Ireland Forum (1984), which in turn contributed to the ANGLO-IRISH AGREEMENT (1985). In the early 1990s his joint peace initiative with the president of SINN FÉIN, GERRY ADAMS, led directly to the IRA ceasefire and the BELFAST AGREEMENT (1998). Declining the post of Deputy First Minister in the NORTHERN IRELAND ASSEMBLY, he shared the NOBEL PEACE PRIZE with DAVID TRIMBLE in December 1998. He resigned as leader of the SDLP in 2001. **Eamon Phoenix**

Humphreys, David (1971–), rugby footballer. His debut was in 1996 against France in Paris, when Ireland was going through difficult times in rugby's first full professional season. He won thirty-one caps, mostly at out-half, in the next five years. A great moment of triumph was when he captained Ulster to win the 1999 European Cup, defeating Colomiers before a capacity crowd at Lansdowne Road, Dublin. **Karl Johnston**

hunger strike, a tactic used by political prisoners, first used by THOMAS ASHE, who died after forced feeding in Mountjoy Jail, Dublin, in September 1917. TERENCE MACSWINEY, Lord Mayor of Cork, died on the seventy-fourth day of a hunger strike at Brixton Prison, London, in 1920. By the end of 1923 four more republicans had starved themselves to death; between 1940 and 1946 three hunger strikers died in a vain attempt to be granted political status by DE VALERA's Government.

Hume. *SDLP supporters outside the Guildhall in Derry celebrate John Hume's election to the British House of Commons as MP for Foyle, 9 June 1983. [Belfast Telegraph Newspapers Ltd]*

In Northern Ireland on 27 October 1980 PROVISIONAL IRA and INLA prisoners in the Maze Prison began a hunger strike in a campaign for the restoration of 'special category' status, to be excused prison work, and to be allowed to wear their own clothes. This was called off on 18 December; but on 1 March 1981 BOBBY SANDS, the commanding officer of the Provisional IRA prisoners, began his own fast. On the fortieth day he was elected to the British Parliament for the constituency of Fermanagh-South Tyrone. Meanwhile other republican prisoners had been selected to join the hunger strike. Sands died on Tuesday 5 May 1981, the sixty-sixth day of his hunger strike. On the day of the funeral at least 100,000 people crowded the route to Milltown Cemetery, Belfast. Francis Hughes died on 12 May; Raymond McCreesh and Patsy O'Hara on 21 May; Joe McDonnell on 8 July; Martin Hurson on 13 July; Kevin Lynch on 1 August; Kieran Doherty on 2 August; Tom McElwee on 8 August; and Mickey Devine on 20 August. The intervention of Father DENIS FAUL, and the replacement of Humphrey Atkins by James Prior as Secretary of State for Northern Ireland, helped to break the deadlock between the prisoners and the government. During the crisis sixty-four people died in violent incidents in Northern Ireland. **Jonathan Bardon**

Hunt Committee (1969). The actions of the ROYAL ULSTER CONSTABULARY and its reserve force, the Ulster Special Constabulary, came under considerable public scrutiny during the winter of 1969/70 as civil disturbances spread. The riots of August 1969 resulted in the deployment of the BRITISH ARMY in a peace-keeping role and the increasing involvement of Harold Wilson's government, which pressed for reform. On 26 August 1969 the Northern Ireland Minister of Home Affairs announced the establishment of an Advisory Committee on the Police in Northern Ireland, to be chaired by Lord Hunt, with the assistance of Robert Mark and Sir James Robertson. When the committee reported, in early October, it recommended that the RUC become an unarmed police service. It also dealt with the future of the Special Constabulary, which it advised should be replaced with a part-time reserve and a locally recruited force under the command of the

hunger strike. *H-block rally on O'Connell Bridge, Dublin, during the 1981 hunger strikes, during which Bobby Sands and nine other republican prisoners died. [Photocall Ireland]*

British army; this became the ULSTER DEFENCE REGIMENT. The abolition of the Special Constabulary was welcomed by nationalists, but the Hunt proposals aroused violent opposition in the unionist community. In the course of disturbances in the Shankill Road area of Belfast following the publication of the report Constable Victor Arbuckle was shot dead, the first policeman to be killed in the 'TROUBLES'. Sir Arthur Young of the City of London Police assumed the new rank of Chief Constable to implement the reforms, but by March 1971 the deteriorating security situation saw the rearming of the RUC. [see A, B, C SPECIALS.] **T. G. Fraser**

Hunter, Robert (died c. 1803), artist. Said to have been born in Ulster; taught by Justin Pope. He became the principal resident Irish portrait-painter of the second half of the eighteenth century. A series of portraits of the King family must date from c. 1748; by 1753 he was commissioned to paint the Lord Mayor of Dublin, Sir Charles Burton (now known only in mezzotint). He used pictures by English masters, such as Hudson and Reynolds, as the basis for his compositions, which were competently and at times very well painted. His works include portraits of the Earl and Countess of Belmore, Lord Newbottle, Christopher O'Brien, John Wesley, and Peter La Touche of Bellevue (now in the NATIONAL GALLERY OF IRELAND). He held an exhibition and sale of his paintings in 1792 and died in or shortly after 1803. **Anne Crookshank**

Hunt, Fionnuala (1957–), musician. Born in Belfast; studied at the Ulster College of Music with JAROSLAV VANĚČEK, the Royal College of Music, and Vienna Hochschule für Musik with Wolfgang Schneiderhan. She has been leader and soloist with the Vienna Chamber Orchestra and a member of the Bavarian State Opera Orchestra, Munich. Formerly co-leader of the RTÉ Symphony Orchestra, she was artistic leader and leader of the IRISH CHAMBER ORCHESTRA 1995–2002. With her sister, UNA HUNT, she has performed duo recitals in Ireland, Austria, Germany, Czechoslovakia, Italy, and Britain. **Éamonn O'Keeffe**

hunting. Ireland's hunting history dates from the early eighteenth century, and it is estimated that more than 90,000 people now hunt with registered packs. The Hunting Association of Ireland, formed in 1996, represents thirty-nine packs of foxhounds, forty-six harrier packs, twenty-six packs of beagles, four packs of minkhounds, two staghound packs, and approximately 150 foot harrier packs. Between the registered and unregistered packs there is a total of 300 packs of hounds in Ireland. The oldest of these is the Duhallow Hunt Club, Co. Cork, founded possibly as early as 1724, though records date only from 1745.

Though the Duhallow Hunt Club may lay claim to the longest history of hunting in Ireland, the Scarteen Foxhounds in Co. Limerick are the most famous. Known as the Black and Tans, because of the hounds' unique coloration, the pack is made up of pure-bred Kerry beagles that have been in the ownership of the Ryan family for more than 600 years.

The Irish Masters of Foxhounds' Association, founded in 1859, is one of the oldest field sports bodies in the world. Originally formed to govern the sport of fox-hunting, it has become one of the leading political lobbying bodies in Ireland for the defence of field sports. A founder-member of the umbrella organisation FACE, it was also the catalyst for forming the Hunting Association of Ireland. A survey conducted by University College, Dublin, estimated that hunting generated more than €79 million to the economy in 1995. Sales of sport horses produced in the hunting field were estimated to be worth €33 million in the same year. [see HORSE, IRISH; HORSE RACING.] **Grania Willis**

Hunt Museum, Limerick. Between 1930 and 1950 the antique and antiquities dealers John and Gertrude Hunt amassed in London an important collection of medieval ecclesiastical art, later donated to the Irish Government by their family. Having originally been housed at the University of Limerick, it was transferred to a permanent home in DAVIS DUCART's former Custom House (1765) as the Hunt Museum. Though the collection ranges from the NEOLITHIC to the nineteenth century, its focus is on the applied and decorative arts of the Middle Ages, ceramics, crystal, panel-painting, ivories, metalwork, jewellery, enamels, and fabrics. The collection is particularly rich in examples of the medieval crucifix and includes individual items of great importance, such as the eighth-century Antrim Cross, the Shrine of St PATRICK, and the Beverly Crozier. Among Renaissance works is a small bronze horse cast from a maquette attributed to Leonardo da Vinci. **Brian Lalor**

Hunt, Una (1953–), musician. Born in Belfast; educated at QUB. From an early age she toured with her sister, FIONNUALA HUNT, performing chamber music. She has performed in England, Germany, Austria, Switzerland, and Italy, has made numerous television and radio appearances and broadcasts, and has performed as a soloist with the NATIONAL SYMPHONY ORCHESTRA. She has an interest in Irish music and composers of the past two centuries. She has also produced documentaries on Irish composers and their music for RTÉ. **Éamonn O'Keeffe**

Hurley, Charles (Charlie) (1940–), soccer player. Born in Cork and brought up in London. It was for his adopted city that he won his first representative honour, in an inter-city game against Rome in 1957. On the strength of some outstanding performances for Millwall, he was chosen for his first appearance for the Republic of Ireland in a vital World Cup qualifying game against England at Dalymount Park later that year. He went on to become one of the pillars of the team over the next twelve years when, nicknamed 'King Charlie', he ranked with the best in Britain. He acted as joint manager of the national team, with Noel Cantwell, on several occasions in the 1960s. **Peter Byrne**

hurling, one of the oldest field sports, and also one of the fastest. The earliest mythological date given for hurling is 1272 BC, when two teams of twenty-seven a side contested a game before the Battle

hurling. *D. J. Carey, playing for Kilkenny (yellow and black) in action against Diarmuid O'Sullivan of Cork in the 1999 all-Ireland hurling final at Croke Park, Dublin. Cork won with a score of 13 points to 12. [Ray McManus/Sportsfile]* of Moytura. The source for this claim is the Book of LEINSTER, composed in the twelfth century AD.

In historical times the English authorities had a fraught relationship with the game and the people who played it. The STATUTES OF KILKENNY (1366) banned the playing of the game; but the ban had little effect, and 200 years later, in the Statute of Galway (1537), the playing of hurling was again banned. Hurling was commonly played in Dublin, in the rest of Leinster, and in Munster. There is some evidence of the game in the north of the country, while there are also references to games between parishes in Co. Galway. A number of newspaper reports from the middle of the eighteenth century mention games between Leinster and Munster, as well as games between counties.

The first rules of hurling were drawn up by Pat Larkin of Killimor, Co. Galway, and were printed in 1885. A new and very different set of rules was drawn up by Dublin University Hurling Club; when modified in the 1860s and 70s these rules made such fundamental changes to the game that the form of hurling played resembled HOCKEY. The native form of the game struggled to survive. Significantly, it was in the 1870s and 80s that Michael Cusack began to take an active interest in the game; he would soon lead the movement that would form the GAELIC ATHLETIC ASSOCIATION.

The modern game of hurling, as codified by the GAA, is played by teams of fifteen players. The pitch is approximately 137 m (450 ft) long and 82 m (270 ft) wide. The ball (*sliotar*) is similar in size and shape to a hockey ball and is struck using a wooden stick (*camán* or 'hurley'), generally made from ash, that is curved outwards at the end. The goalposts and scoring system are the same as those used for GAELIC FOOTBALL, with points and goals scored either by kicking the ball or striking it with the hurley. The duration of games is also similar to Gaelic football.

Top-class hurling is to be found principally in the southern half of Ireland: no county from the northern half has ever won the all-Ireland senior championship. The heartland of the game is in an arc from Co. Wexford in the south-east to Co. Galway in the west. However, there are pockets throughout the country where hurling is still the most popular sport. The GLENS OF ANTRIM are a hotbed of the game, while the ARDS PENINSULA in Co. Down has a strong hurling population. Cork, Tipperary, and Kilkenny are the most successful counties in championships won. However, the modern era has seen the emergence of new counties, such as Offaly, and the revival of others, such as Galway, Wexford, and Clare, which have provided some of the most exciting and skilful teams.

At its best, hurling is astonishingly skilful, a combination of speed, physicality, and grace. Best seen in dry summer conditions, it is one of the world's fastest and most dramatic field games. It is unique to Ireland, though distantly related to the Scottish *shinty* (see p. 711). **Donal Keenan**

AN
INQUIRY
INTO THE
ORIGINAL of our IDEAS
OF
BEAUTY and *VIRTUE*;
In Two TREATISES.

I. Concerning BEAUTY, ORDER, HARMONY, DESIGN.

II. Concerning MORAL GOOD and EVIL.

The Third Edition, Corrected.

Itaque eorum ipſorum quæ aſpectu ſentiuntur, nullum aliud animal pulchritudinem, venuſtatem, convenientiam partium ſentit. Quam ſimilitudinem natura ratioque ab oculis ad animum transferens, multo etiam magis pulchritudinem, conſtantiam, ordinem in conſiliis, factiſque conſervandum putat. Quibus ex rebus conflatur & efficitur id quod quærimus honeſtum: Quod etiamſi nobilitatum non ſit, tamen honeſtum ſit; quodque etiamſi à nullo laudetur, naturâ eſt laudabile. Formam quidem ipſam & tanquam faciem honeſti vides, quæ ſi oculis cerneretur, mirabiles amores excitaret ſapientiæ. *Cic. de Off. lib.* 1. *c.* 4.

LONDON:

Printed for J. and J. KNAPTON, J. DARBY, A. BETTESWORTH, F. FAYRAM, J. PEMBERTON, J. OSBORN and T. LONGMAN, C. RIVINGTON, F. CLAY, J. BATLEY, and A. WARD. M.DCC.XXIX.

Hutcheson. *Title page of* An Inquiry into the Original of our Ideas of Beauty and Virtue *(3rd edition, 1729) by Francis Hutcheson, philosopher and leader of the Scottish Enlightenment. [Board of Trinity College, Dublin]*

Hurst, Brian Desmond (1900–1986), film director. Born in Castlereagh, Co. Down. He went to Hollywood in 1925 but in 1934 moved to England, where he began directing films, one of the first of which was *Irish Hearts* (1934). Other films with an Irish subject include *Riders to the Sea* (1935), *Ourselves Alone* (1936), *Hungry Hill* (1946), and *The Playboy of the Western World* (1962); he also made crime, musical, war, comedy, historical romance, and horror films. **Kevin Rockett**

Hussey, Philip (1713–1783), portraitist. Born in Cloyne, Co. Cork. As a young man he went to sea and was involved in five SHIPWRECKS; he attracted attention painting the figureheads of ships on which he sailed. On his second visit to England he was introduced to the Prince of Wales and encouraged to stay there. He studied and copied Old Master paintings and began painting portraits in 1746; sitters included DAVID LA TOUCHE of Marlay and St George Caulfield. In Ireland he befriended some prominent figures, including the EDGEWORTH family and John Bowes, the Lord Chancellor. He was also keenly interested in botany and music. **Brendan Rooney**

Hussey, Thomas (1746–1803), bishop, politician, and first president of ST PATRICK'S COLLEGE, Maynooth. Born in Harristown, Co. Meath; educated at the English College in Seville. While serving as chaplain to the Spanish ambassador in London he was, at the request of George III, part of a secret embassy sent to Spain during the American war in an unsuccessful attempt to break the Franco-Spanish Alliance. A prominent activist in the campaign to establish a seminary at Maynooth, he became its first president in

1795. Appointed Catholic chaplain-general to the army in Ireland, 1796, and subsequently Bishop of Waterford and Lismore, 1796–1803, he was forced to leave Ireland in 1797 following the publication of a controversial pastoral and agitation regarding abuse of Catholic soldiers. A keen politician, he was among EDMUND BURKE's principal Irish correspondents and was rumoured to have negotiated the Napoleonic Concordat (1802). **Daire Keogh**

Hutcheson, Francis (1694–1746), philosopher. Born in Drumalig, Co. Down; educated at the Dissenting Academy, Killyleagh, and the University of Glasgow. From 1721–2 until 1729 he ran a Dissenting academy in Dublin. His major philosophical works originated from this time in Dublin: *An Inquiry into the Original of Our Ideas of Beauty and Virtue* (1725) and *An Essay on the Nature and Conduct of the Passions and Affections with Illustrations on the Moral Sense* (1728). In 1729 he was appointed professor of moral philosophy at the University of Glasgow, holding the post until his death. His later writings include *A Short Introduction to Moral Philosophy* (1747) and the posthumously published *A System of Moral Philosophy* (1755). Although these add little to his earlier discussions on beauty and morality, they do contain seminal contributions to legal theory, political rights, and economics. His importance as a philosopher rests primarily on his defence of two claims: (1) we possess a sense of beauty and a moral sense; (2) we are motivated to act by benevolent as well as self-interested affections. When our moral sense alerts us to virtuous actions, our benevolent affections cause us to desire so to act ourselves; our reason then identifies the best means to obtain the virtuous ends; and, finally, our achieving these ends gives us the most perfect happiness. This theory explains morality on principles that are neither self-interested nor exclusively rational, while at the same time assigning a significant role to reason and satisfying our own desire for happiness. Adopted by Hume and opposed by Kant, it is among the most influential of modern moral systems. Often called the father of the Scottish Enlightenment, Hutcheson was undoubtedly one of Ireland's greatest philosophers. **Andrew Ward**

Hutchins, Ellen (1785–1815), botanist. Born at Ballylickey, Co. Cork; educated in Dublin. During frequent childhood illnesses she was attended by a family friend, WHITLEY STOKES, professor of medicine at the Royal College of Physicians and founder of TRINITY COLLEGE Botanical Garden. In Dublin she met eminent botanists, including James Townsend Mackay, curator of the Garden, who encouraged her botanical studies. Returning to Cork, she collected, studied, and illustrated south coast mosses, lichens, and seaweeds. Her contributions to Mackay's *Muscologiae Hibernicae Specilegium* (1804) and to Dawson Turner's *British Confervae* (1807), one of the earliest and best works on seaweeds, confirm her as a talented botanist. **Helena C. G. Chesney**

Hutchinson, Pearse (1927–), poet and translator. Born in Glasgow but raised in Dublin from the age of five. He is a translator from the Catalan and the Galaico-Portuguese and an editor of the magazine *Cyphers*. Doubleness is a feature of his life and work: his first collection proper, *Tongue Without Hands* (1963), was preceded by translations of the Catalan Josep Carner, *Poems* (1962). *Faoistin Bhacach* (1968) was followed by *Expansions* (1969), while his translations from the medieval Galaico-Portuguese, *Friend Songs* (1970), were succeeded by *Watching the Morning Grow* (1972). His is a lyric sensibility, modified and inflected by an astute political awareness and sense of human compassion, qualities demonstrated in his *Selected Poems* (1982), *Climbing the Light* (1985), and *Le Cead na Gréine* (1989). *The Soul that Kissed the Body* (1990) gives the poet's own English translations from his work in Irish; his *Collected Poems* was published in 2001. He is a member of AOSDÁNA. **Theo Dorgan**

Hyde. *Pencil drawing by John B. Yeats (1895) of Douglas Hyde, founder and president of the Gaelic League and first professor of Modern Irish in UCD. [National Gallery of Ireland]*

Hyde, Douglas (1860–1949), scholar, cultural leader, and President of Ireland. Born in Castlerea, Co. Roscommon, son of the rector of Tibohine; educated at TCD. A brilliant linguist, he knew Latin, Greek, Hebrew, French, and German. He was awarded a doctorate of laws in 1888 and spent a year at the University of New Brunswick, after which he settled in Co. Roscommon and collected local FOLKLORE and poetry in Irish. In 1893 he founded the GAELIC LEAGUE, in conjunction with EOIN MACNEILL. The league expanded and became politicised in the first decade of the twentieth century, being taken over by the IRB and becoming a vehicle for separatism. Hyde disliked this development and was pushed out by the extremists in 1911. He was appointed professor of Modern Irish in UCD in 1909, retiring in 1932. He was a senator, 1925–6. In 1938 he became first President of Ireland by a bipartisan agreement, serving a full term until 1945. He was the author of many books and articles, including *Beside the Fire* (1889) and *Love Songs of Connacht* (1893). His play CASADH AN TSÚGÁIN (1901) was the first play in Irish to appear on a professional stage. **Tom Garvin**

Hynes, Garry (1953–), theatre director. Born in Galway; educated at UCG. In 1975 she jointly founded the DRUID THEATRE COMPANY, Galway, for which she continues to direct. She served a term as artistic director of the ABBEY THEATRE, Dublin, 1991–4. She was awarded an honorary doctorate by UCG and a Tony Award for directing MARTIN MCDONAGH's *The Beauty Queen of Leenane*, 1998. **Christopher Morash**

Importance of Being Earnest, The *(see page 513). Rosaleen Linehan as Lady Bracknell in an Abbey Theatre production of Oscar Wilde's play* The Importance of Being Earnest. *[Abbey Theatre; photo: Amelia Stein]*

ICA: see IRISH COUNTRYWOMEN'S ASSOCIATION.

IDA: see INDUSTRIAL DEVELOPMENT AGENCY.

idols. All but a few of the surviving stone idols come from the northern part of Ireland, and they were probably carved in the IRON AGE. Similar carvings found throughout the Celtic world provide evidence of the worship of numerous GODS AND GODDESSES. Apart from three animal deities representing dogs or bears in Armagh Cathedral, the Irish idols are all in human form. Sometimes in the shape of figures with enlarged heads, more often in the form of skull-like heads, they reflect the Celtic belief that the human head is the seat of the soul. The only surviving examples of two-faced and three-faced idols, from BOA ISLAND, Co. Fermanagh, and CORLECK, Co. Cavan, are remarkable carvings that still retain an aura of power and awesomeness. Two-faced and three-faced gods were worshipped among the Continental Celts, and hints of such cults survive in Irish MYTHOLOGY in the power attributed to twins and in the numerous references to deities in triple form, to semi-divine heroes with triple epithets, and to the magico-religious significance of the number three. One crudely carved wooden idol from Ralaghan, Co. Cavan, has been dated to c. 1000 BC. [see PRE-CHRISTIAN RELIGIONS.] **Helen Lanigan Wood**

Iglesias-Rozas, Teresa, philosopher. Born in Salamanca, Spain; educated at the University of Oxford. Ireland's foremost expert in biomedical ethics, she is senior lecturer in philosophy at UNIVERSITY COLLEGE, DUBLIN, lecturing in both the Faculty of Arts and the Faculty of Medicine. She has published *Russell's Theory of Knowledge and Wittgenstein's Earliest Writings* (1984), *Study on Euthanasia and Clinical Practice* (1984), *In Vitro Fertilisation and Justice* (1990), and *The Dignity of the Individual: Issues of Bioethics and Law* (2001). She has held visiting professorships at New Hall, Cambridge (where she worked with Elizabeth Anscombe), and the University of Chicago. **Thomas A. F. Kelly**

Ilnacullin: see GARINISH.

illegitimacy, a term formerly used in connection with children born outside marriage, now widely regarded as unacceptably pejorative. The Status of Children Act (1987), which aimed to eliminate discrimination against such children, provided that the term be abandoned in official usage in favour of terms such as 'NON-MARITAL BIRTHS' or 'births outside marriage'. **Tony Fahey**

Imbolc (1 February), one of the four principal feasts of the medieval Irish agricultural year, the others being BEALTAINE (1 May),

LÚNASA (1 August), and SAMHAIN (1 November). It shares the date of ST BRIGID'S DAY, which is probably not coincidental, as that saint is associated with agricultural miracles. **Elva Johnston**

IMMA: see IRISH MUSEUM OF MODERN ART.

immigration. Ireland has long been a country of emigration and experienced very limited immigration between the eighteenth and late twentieth centuries. The dominant trend after the GREAT FAMINE was a level of net emigration so high that it more than offset the natural increase in the population until the end of the 1950s. Membership of the European Economic Community in 1973 led to a brief phase of net immigration as returning emigrants and their families came back to fill specific skill shortages in the labour economy. But this was followed by a further surge in emigration in the 1980s as the baby-boom generation of the 1960s experienced a shrinking labour market and left the country in large numbers—70,600 in 1988/89 alone.

The 1990s saw the arrival of the so-called 'CELTIC TIGER' economy, with a substantial increase in the number of people at work. Labour demand was met in the first place by a fall in domestic unemployment and an increase in the number of women in the paid labour force; but this was followed from the mid-1990s onwards by a sharp increase in inward labour migration. Most immigrants were from other EU member-states, but there was also a strong growth in the number of workers from outside the European Union, from less than 4,000 in 1976 to more than 36,000 by 2001. The late 1990s also saw the arrival of asylum-seekers in numbers that were modest by international standards but new for Ireland, reaching a peak of just under 11,000 in 2001. Fewer than 10 per cent have been granted full refugee status.

A falling FERTILITY rate and continuing labour demand suggest that Ireland, in common with other former countries of emigration in Europe, will experience net immigration for some years to come. This poses new challenges for a country that largely lacks the infrastructure, policies, and experience of coping with multi-ethnicity. **Piaras Mac Éinrí**

immrama, early voyage tales. *Immram* literally means a 'rowing about', and this is a good structural guide. Starting from Ireland, the voyagers 'row about' several OTHERWORLD islands before, usually, returning to Ireland. The tales abound with the marvellous and are influenced by many sources, including the *Odyssey*, *Aeneid*, Biblical apocrypha, medieval bestiaries, other Irish tales, and traditions of real voyages. The majority are in Irish, but there are exceptions, such as the Latin 'NAVIGATIO SANCTI BRENDANI ABBATIS' (voyage of St BRENDAN the Abbot), which may date from the eighth century. Another noteworthy early narrative is 'Immram Brain maic Febail' (Voyage of Bran son of Feabhal), which combines the *immram* voyage with elements from other Irish tale types. The 'Navigatio' seems to be the more important as a direct influence on later tales, especially the late ninth-century 'Immram Maíle Dúin' (Voyage of Maoldúin). The son of a nun and a nobleman, he is a social hero whose exploits complement the spiritual heroism of Brendan. The decision to cast the two heroes of 'Immram Snédgusa ocus Maic Riagla' (Voyage of Snédgus and Mac Riagla) as clerics may also have taken its cue from the 'Navigatio'.

The *immram* always remained open to literary cross-currents. An example is 'Immram Ua Corra' (Voyage of Ua Corra), a tale of three repentant brothers that possibly found its extant form in the eleventh century. Its author's imaginative response to Continental literature includes a memorable vision of Heaven and Hell. The tale concludes, unusually, with the brothers founding a religious community on the Continent rather than returning to Ireland. The *immram* genre eventually went into decline; it could be argued that its last great example is SWIFT's *Gulliver's Travels*. **Elva Johnston**

Importance of Being Earnest, The (1895), a play by OSCAR WILDE, marking the apogee of his career. First produced on 14 February 1895, immediately before Wilde's downfall, it is a cynical comedy of manners circling around the central character's search for identity. The character of Lady Bracknell, a scheming matriarch, exposes the hypocrisy of the English upper classes, while the name 'Earnest', which gives the play its ambiguity, was a covert term for 'homosexual' in London during the 1890s. The play's instant success has been sustained by subsequent productions and several film versions. [see HOMOSEXUALITY AND LANGUAGE.] **Richard Pine**

imports, geography of. The Republic's imports have risen to provide raw materials for many of the new industries. Materials for further production accounted for 60–64 per cent of imports; in 1998 electronic equipment and components alone accounted for almost 20 per cent; chemical imports added another 11 per cent. Food imports form a relatively small proportion (5 per cent in 1998), with a concentration on cereals, fruit, and vegetables. More is spent on road vehicles (7 per cent). Britain is the principal (but declining) source of imports, supplying 31–33 per cent, with a further 3 per cent from Northern Ireland. In 1998 other EU countries supplied 20 per cent—similar to the previous five years. The main suppliers were Germany, France, and the Netherlands, also the main export markets. The relative importance of the EUROPEAN UNION has declined (72 per cent in 1973), reflecting the global nature of new industry and the importance of Ireland as a gateway to EU markets. Imports from the United States were 16 per cent of the total in 1998, compared with less than 7 per cent on Ireland's accession to membership of the European Union, and were dominated by chemical and electrical and electronic products. Similarly, Japan, at 7 per cent, was far more important than any single EU country with the exception of Britain. Only Britain and Germany exceeded Singapore.

Statistics on Northern Ireland, available only since 1999, do not provide the same level of detail. In 1999 almost 56 per cent of imports to Northern Ireland were from outside the European Union; these represented 1.5 per cent of the total for the United Kingdom. **Joseph Brady**

inauguration sites. Leaders of medieval Irish dynasties were ritually inaugurated at specially appointed assembly places on the open landscape. Frequently within the estate of the 'king-maker', inauguration sites were invariably situated on low but far-seeing hills, combining ease of access with panoramic views over the royal territory. Some early medieval tribal groups claimed their king-making sites from rival septs as a result of expansion, while others adopted and modified existing monuments that had associations, legendary or otherwise, with the progenitor of the sept. Mounds, hilltop enclosures, natural knolls and, very occasionally, church sites and RING-FORTS constitute most of the inauguration sites so far identified. Preferred venues were enclosed and unenclosed earthen mounds, the majority of which were prehistoric and sepulchral in origin, but others may have been purpose-built for medieval royal assembly and added to antique landscapes. The small summit diameter of some of these suggest that they were 'throne mounds', accommodating the royal candidate, who sat in a canopied 'chair' or stood placing his foot on a *leac* (stone). The only surviving inauguration chair is that attributed to the Clann Aodha Buidhe Uí Néill (now in the ULSTER MUSEUM). It may have been made in imitation of *Leac na Ríogh*, the chair of the main branch of Uí Néill at Tulach Óg, which was destroyed by Mountjoy in 1602 (see pp. 595, 1035). [see GAELIC LORDSHIP; KINGDOMS OF IRELAND; KINGSHIP.] **Elizabeth FitzPatrick**

incest. Incest is both an ancient and a modern phenomenon. It was the ANGLO-NORMANS, under HENRY II, who introduced laws in relation to incestuous marriages in Ireland. These were primarily to prevent the maintaining of power and wealth within certain families that might threaten not only the king but also the Roman church, which was trying to curb the power of the Celtic church.

In the thirteenth century St Dympna, a victim of her father's desires, escaped to Gheel in Belgium. Pursued there by her father, she was killed. After her death many cures of mental illness were attributed to her, and a hospital for the insane was founded in her name in Gheel, which survives to the present time. Since then many psychiatric hospitals in Ireland and elsewhere have been dedicated to this Irish patron saint of the mentally ill.

The Punishment of Incest Act (1908) was until recently the primary protection for children; previously incest did not constitute a specific criminal offence. Today, with child abuse in all its forms appearing almost endemic, a child's right to protection is principally guaranteed under the Child Care Act (1991), which was drafted in line with the UN Convention on the Rights of the Child. While there is no mandatory reporting of child abuse, there is an expectation that professionals will report suspected cases to the authorities. There is now a Government minister responsible for the welfare of children, who in 2000 launched the National Children's Strategy to cover the interests of all children for the first ten years of the new century; there are also plans for the appointment of an ombudsman for children. **Imelda McCarthy**

Inch Abbey, Co. Down, a CISTERCIAN abbey that supplanted an early Irish monastic foundation in the 1180s. It was founded by JOHN DE COURCY and colonised from Furness in Cumbria. The east end of the church is well preserved and shows the influence of northern English Cistercian architecture. **Rachel Moss**

income distribution. The way in which income is distributed in society is widely regarded as an important indicator of inequality. Whereas wealth is a stock of purchasing power, income is a flow: it is the amount a person could have spent in a given period while maintaining his or her wealth intact. The distribution of income among households is usually measured from surveys or tax records; measures of 'income inequality' can then refer simply to the fact that income is distributed unevenly, or seek to express a judgment that the distribution is more or less inequitable or unfair. The general shape of income distribution in Ireland is similar to that of other economically developed societies, where income is much more equally distributed than in many non-industrialised countries. Compared with other countries in the EUROPEAN UNION, Ireland appears to be similar to Britain, Spain, and Greece, with income distribution less unequal than in Portugal but rather more unequal than in other member-states. The top 10 per cent of households receive about 25 per cent of total income, while the bottom 20 per cent receive about 5 per cent of total income. The income tax and SOCIAL WELFARE systems each have a significant impact on the shape of income distribution, with those towards the bottom relying for the most part on cash transfers from the state. Income inequality appears to have increased in some large countries—notably the United States and Britain—in the last quarter of a century, having been on a downward trend since the SECOND WORLD WAR. Evidence for Ireland suggests that inequality was, if anything, decreasing up to the late 1980s but has subsequently been stable or rising. **Brian Nolan**

Independent News and Media (formerly Independent Newspapers Ltd), the largest newspaper group in Ireland. The *Irish Daily Independent*, launched in 1891 to counteract the influence of the *Freeman's Journal*, became the *Irish Independent* under WILLIAM MARTIN MURPHY in 1905. The first halfpenny popular paper in Ireland, the new-look *Independent* employed the populist style of ALFRED HARMSWORTH's *Daily Mail* and made innovative use of photographs. With sales of 25,000 a day at the outset, the new paper reached 40,000 in three years. As the *Irish Independent* prospered, the *Freeman's Journal* declined, and its title was bought by the Independent Group in 1924. Aimed at the Catholic middle class and farming community, the *Irish Independent*, later joined by the *Sunday Independent* and *Evening Herald*, was conservative during the decades of Catholic hegemony. During the 1920s it was pro-Commonwealth; during the 1930s it supported FINE GAEL. By 2000 its circulation had reached approximately 160,000.

Under Dr ANTHONY O'REILLY, who took it over in 1973, the Independent Group became an international media conglomerate, with newspaper and other interests in Ireland, Britain, South Africa, Australia, New Zealand, and Portugal. It added the *Sunday World* and 50 per cent of the *Star* (published jointly with Express Newspapers) to its titles; it has a 29.9 per cent share in the *Sunday Tribune*, controls the *Independent* (London), and in 2000 acquired the BELFAST TELEGRAPH. Independent-controlled newspapers account for almost 80 per cent of national newspaper circulation in the Republic, or almost 60 per cent of total newspaper circulation, including imported titles; in addition the group is the largest publisher of provincial newspapers. Such domination has given rise to fears of undue power, especially on the part of those opposed to its right-of-centre economics and, in the *Sunday Independent* in particular, its perceived anti-nationalist stance on the Northern conflict. **Eddie Holt**

Independent Opposition Party. In February 1852 forty-eight Irish members of the British Parliament pledged to remain independent of any party that failed to satisfy Irish demands for religious equality and land tenure rights. The group soon divided over the importance of tenantry, with some members joining the government, others remaining in opposition; most had left politics by 1860. **David Mock**

Independent Orange Order, founded in June 1903 by T. H. Sloan, an evangelical preacher, TEMPERANCE crusader and vociferous critic of the landed gentry, who had won the South Belfast parliamentary seat left vacant by the death of William Johnston of Ballykilbeg in 1902. However, soon afterwards he quarrelled with the ORANGE ORDER for being 'soft on Catholicism' and was expelled, whereupon he formed his own independent organisation. He was joined by the able Dublin journalist Robert Lindsay Crawford, editor of the *Irish Protestant*.

Sloan was keen to move the new organisation out of the sphere of sectarian politics and into coalition with labour groups and those in favour of radical agrarian change. These notes he first sounded with his 'Magheramorne Manifesto' of 13 July 1905, in which he urged all Irishmen to reach out in friendship to their fellow-countrymen,

Independent News. *Independent House designed by Robinson Keefe Devane (2001), the state-of-the-art headquarters of Independent News and Media at Citywest Business Campus, Dublin. Visible through the glass façade are the printing press and rolls of newsprint. [Courtesy of Independent Newspapers; Liam Mulcahy, group photographic manager]*

irrespective of faith. This ideal experienced some early electoral success in Ulster; but when Crawford took up a new journalistic post in Belfast and openly called for support for HOME RULE he found himself isolated from his Independent colleagues and was expelled. Sloan, who had remained staunchly unionist throughout, reverted to a more militant Protestant position. **Roddy Hegarty**

independent politicians. Independent parliamentary deputies are an unusual phenomenon in contemporary Western societies. The typical European electoral system, based on a mathematical allocation of seats to party lists, precludes their existence (though would-be independents may seek to bypass the logic of the system by endowing themselves with the trappings of a political party and recruiting colleagues or friends to a formal list). The older plurality system, still in operation in Britain, the United States, Canada, and elsewhere, permits independent candidates to contest elections, though few such candidates are ever elected: the system is entirely dominated by the large political parties.

The unusual form of proportional representation adopted in the Republic—based on the single transferable vote, rather than on choice between party lists—permits non-party candidates not only to contest elections but also to enjoy a reasonable prospect of success. They are not required, as in plurality systems, to outpoll all other candidates: they need only reach an electoral quota, a target that becomes less demanding as the number of members to be elected from a constituency increases. These provisions have permitted an unusual flourishing of independent Dáil deputies since 1922. On average their numbers have exceeded seven in a typical Dáil, dropping from a peak of about seventeen in 1923 to seven in 1938, then enjoying a revival to peak at about fifteen in 1951 before again declining to reach their lowest point (with a single independent deputy) in 1969. The Electoral Act (1963), which permitted the inclusion of party names on the ballot paper, was instrumental in reducing the number of independent and quasi-independent deputies by giving a slight electoral advantage to formally recognised parties. Nevertheless by the 1990s a small block of independent deputies was once again in a pivotal position.

Classifying deputies as independents is not always easy. In the 1920s the Cork Progressive Association and in Dublin the Business Party were little more than loose alignments of independent conservative deputies; Monetary Reform in the 1940s and 50s was a label used by Oliver J. Flanagan before he joined FINE GAEL; and SEÁN LOFTUS operated under a number of labels, including 'Christian Democrat'. On the other hand, the two 'H-Block' deputies elected in 1981 were technically non-party but in reality formed part of a well-organised political movement.

Independent deputies since 1922—numbering more than eighty in total—may be placed in one of four categories. First in importance, and concentrated in the early years of the state, was a set of independents linked to two political traditions that disappeared in organised form after 1922: the old Unionist and Nationalist parties.

The second group is that of dissidents from established parties, whether originating in expulsions or in voluntary secession. Historically, the LABOUR PARTY has been most vulnerable to defections of this kind, sometimes ideological in nature.

The third category comprises individuals defending a particular interest but not subjecting themselves to party discipline. These are not always distinguishable from the other groups: 'independent' farmer and business deputies in the 1920s and 30s functioned on the margins of party organisation, and these two sectors were also frequently places of refuge for ex-Unionist and ex-Nationalist activists.

The last category is a catch-all or residual one, comprising pure independents, standing in the name of personal or local considerations. This may include deputies who have embraced a single issue (such as a demand for regional access to British television); but deputies in this category tend to have in common a strong commitment to regional interests.

Of the twenty elections that have taken place since 1933, eight produced a government that was dependent for support on independent or minor party deputies. The period after the 1997 election illustrates the important role that independents who hold the balance of power can play in the political process; but the most visible display of independent power was arguably in 1948, when independents ended sixteen years of FIANNA FÁIL rule and themselves participated in the new inter-party government. **John Coakley**

Indian meal, maize or 'Indian corn', grown in North America and the Mediterranean, imported in small amounts into Ireland as a famine relief food from 1799. During the GREAT FAMINE it was promoted as a permanent replacement for the POTATO, and large quantities were imported by the British government and private enterprise. Dubbed 'Peel's brimstone', the roughly ground meal was found difficult to digest but later gained wider acceptance and became a lasting component of the labouring DIET. **Peter Gray**

indigenous industry. From the introduction of FREE TRADE in the 1960s up to the mid-1980s, Irish-owned industry lost market share at home and failed to increase market share abroad. EMPLOYMENT remained static in the face of this in the 1960s as both domestic and international markets were relatively buoyant. The weak international economy of the 1970s, however, and the particularly weak Irish domestic market of the 1980s saw a sharp fall in employment in indigenous industry. Since the late 1980s all these trends have been reversed. A number of competing explanations have been put forward, including the fact that the domestic crisis of the 1980s left stronger the more export-oriented firms predominant in the remaining pool, that the industrial development authorities began to pay more attention to the needs of indigenous industry in the 1980s, that particularly strong gains in cost-competitiveness were made against Britain, whose firms are the main rivals of Irish indigenous firms, and that the influx of TRANSNATIONAL CORPORATIONS into Ireland may have stimulated productivity gains among indigenous sub-suppliers, allowing them to branch out into export markets. Indigenous industry in Northern Ireland remains less export-oriented than in the South and has tended to shed jobs at the same rate as the rest of the United Kingdom, though without the parallel strong growth in private services that occurred in the more prosperous core UK regions. **Frank Barry**

industrial archaeology. Despite its immediate proximity to the cradle of European industrialisation, most of Ireland never became industrialised, in either an English or a European sense. Nonetheless industrialisation did occur, but it was extremely localised, and Ireland never experienced the changes it brought about in such countries as England, Germany, or France. However, industries of both national and international significance were established. The progress of truly large-scale industrialisation in the nineteenth century exhibits a pronounced regional bias, and the area around the Lagan Valley in Ulster is the only Irish region to experience it. By the beginning of the twentieth century Ulster had the largest shipyards in the world and the most extensive LINEN industry of any industrialised region in Europe. Belfast was in reality the only nineteenth-century industrial city in Ireland: the economic fabric of both Dublin and Cork was essentially commercial rather than industrial. Small pockets of dispersed INDUSTRIAL REVOLUTION activity became established near the ports and larger towns, such as Limerick, Dundalk, Waterford, and Galway, with varying degrees of success, but in general this patchwork of industry can in no way be compared to developments elsewhere in Europe.

The components of industrialisation that form the basis of the study of industrial archaeology in Ireland can be divided into four main categories, two embracing a broad spectrum of industrial activities and two being largely concerned with the INFRASTRUCTURE for industry: *extractive* or *primary industries*, such as MINING and quarrying; *manufacturing* or *secondary industries*, such as TEXTILES and IRONWORKING; *transport and communications*, such as roads, CANALS, RAILWAYS, ports, and harbours; and *utility industries*, such as water supply, GAS, and ELECTRICITY. For the most part the chronological span of industrial archaeology in Ireland is considered to cover the period 1750–1930. In the late 1950s and early 60s some of the earliest government-financed industrial archaeology surveys in the world were undertaken in Co. Down by Rodney Green, the publication of which in 1963 was the first of its type for any part of Ireland. Further survey work by Alan McCutcheon, who conducted a systematic industrial archaeological study in Northern Ireland between 1962 and 1968, became the first comprehensive, large-scale survey of its type in Ireland when published in 1980. Between 1990 and 1993 the ROYAL IRISH ACADEMY conducted a detailed survey of Cork, the first of any Irish city; the only counties in the Republic to have been covered in any detail are Cos. Kilkenny and Cork.

Ireland occupies a unique position in Europe in the extent of preservation of its industrial sites and monuments. About 100,000 sites of industrial archaeological interest are now believed to survive, a surprising number of which are of international significance. Individual sites vary in size from 1.75 km^2 (431 acres), as at BALLINCOLLIG gunpowder mills (1794–1903) in Co. Cork, to small agricultural limekilns (by far the most common type). Apart from Ireland's former pre-eminence in SHIPBUILDING and linen manufacture, the industrial archaeology of water power is also exceptional. The Manchester millwright Thomas C. Hewes (1768–1832) erected the first suspension water-wheel in a cotton mill at Overton, near Bandon, Co. Cork, in 1802. Irish ironfounders and millwrights made significant contributions to the development of water turbines, and the earliest known example built on the Fourneyron model, by MacAdam of Belfast, survives in its original site in Green's Mill, Cavan. **Colin Rynne**

industrial development (nineteenth century). The high proportion of the POPULATION engaged outside AGRICULTURE from the first decades of the nineteenth century belies the widespread assumption that Ireland was overwhelmingly agricultural. At the same time, the nineteenth century saw relative decline in traditional non-agricultural activity in some areas and increasing regional concentration in industries such as TEXTILES and SHIPBUILDING. Indeed Cork was the premier shipbuilding centre in Ireland as late as the 1840s, but it was soon displaced by Belfast, where the famous partnership of HARLAND AND WOLFF was established in 1861 (see p. 1145). Similarly, though the north-east, and Belfast especially, became the centre of Irish industrial enterprise, significant activity continued to take place in other regions and towns, including widespread DISTILLING and wool production in the south of Ireland. In the first decades of the century the production of cotton was centred on several areas, including Kildare, the Liberties of Dublin, Cork, and Belfast. Though there are a few examples of cotton production flourishing after the 1820s, there was a decisive shift in textile production to LINEN cloth, and regional concentration in the north-east. Patterns of industrial development varied: the hand-loom production of linen cloth persisted in areas of Ulster throughout the century, and industrial development also gave rise to growth in ancillary homework and outwork activity, particularly in shirt-making in the west of Ulster. [see INDUSTRIAL ARCHAEOLOGY.] **K. J. James**

Industrial Development Agency (IDA), the industrial promotion body in the Republic that encourages foreign firms to establish or to expand operations in manufacturing and international services. It also seeks to establish a wide distribution of firms around the country, particularly in less-developed areas. The original IDA (Industrial Development Authority) was established in 1949 to review tariffs and quotas; later it promoted industrial development. After an industrial review group in the early 1990s recommended that its emphasis be changed, the agency was divided into IDA Ireland, which concentrated on foreign firms, and Forbairt, which sought to develop indigenous industry. Forbairt, composed of Eolas and part of the IDA and, later, the Irish Trade Board, was to become Enterprise Ireland. The IDA seeks to encourage foreign investment, particularly outside Dublin, and to gain higher skilled EMPLOYMENT. By 2001 it had sponsored 1,300 companies, of which 500 were from the United States, with a total employment of 125,000. It gives grants to firms of approximately €132 million a year (2001 figures). The average cost per job declined from €41,000 in 1987 to just over €12,500 in 1999. There were 41,700 people employed in international and financial services in 2000, with 69,000 in electronics and engineering. **Paul Sweeney**

industrialisation, the process whereby industry is developed with the spread of manufacturing. In the nineteenth century there was extensive INDUSTRIAL DEVELOPMENT in the north-east of Ireland but de-industrialisation elsewhere. By the early twentieth century the high level of industrialisation in the north-east and the fear of tariffs were important reasons for seeking to maintain the union with Britain. What became Northern Ireland was highly industrialised by international standards. In the new state in the rest of the country there was little industry—mainly BREWING, food-processing, CLOTHING, and TEXTILES. Industrial employment grew behind the protectionism of the 1930s but was to stagnate in the 1950s because of lack of competition and innovation. In the late 1950s the Republic opened up to FOREIGN DIRECT INVESTMENT, and industry grew substantially in the 1960s. By this time many industries—SHIPBUILDING, clothing, textiles, and textile machinery—were affected by low-cost competition, and the state agencies sought foreign investment; both parts of the island competed for such investment, though there is now a degree of co-operation. The 1980s saw a high level of job losses, particularly in INDIGENOUS INDUSTRY, but from the late 1980s both economies picked up. After 1994 there was extraordinary job creation in the Republic; while this was mainly in services, industrial employment also grew, in contrast to the international trend. **Paul Sweeney**

industrial performance. Industrial policies and statistics in the Republic commonly distinguish between indigenous or Irish-owned industry and foreign-owned industry. Indigenous industry accounted for 52 per cent of industrial EMPLOYMENT and 31 per cent of industrial output in the late 1990s. Compared with foreign-owned industry, indigenous industry tends to be smaller in scale, more involved in traditional sectors, and less export-oriented. Since the 1960s, indigenous industry has generally grown more slowly than foreign-owned industry, though the performance of indigenous industry was relatively good by international standards after the late 1980s. In Northern Ireland, a distinction between indigenous and externally owned industry is not maintained to the same extent as in the Republic. **Eoin O'Malley**

industrial policy. Both the Republic and Northern Ireland pursue active industrial policies and are seen as competitive locations within the EUROPEAN UNION by companies with internationally mobile investment projects. In practice, and especially since the BELFAST AGREEMENT (1998), the two jurisdictions avoid competing directly with each other while adopting rather similar policy approaches, such as having well-financed promotional agencies: the Industrial Development Board in Northern Ireland and the INDUSTRIAL DEVELOPMENT AGENCY in the Republic. In both jurisdictions policies are discretionary, with the level of assistance linked to the characteristics of individual projects, including their location. The essential differences are the Republic's use as its principal policy instruments of a low corporate tax rate (10 per cent) for manufacturing and internationally traded services, together with employment-linked grants, whereas the North has no preferential tax policy and provides most assistance to projects in the form of grants for plant and machinery.

Industrial policy in the Republic dates from the 1950s, and its origins are linked to the ending of protectionism and membership of the EC. The North's industrial policies are part of the regional policy of the United Kingdom, which developed during the 1960s. In both jurisdictions, fostering FOREIGN DIRECT INVESTMENT especially in high-technology industries, is now a central objective, with increasing emphasis on the development of the knowledge economy. In the Republic the approach to indigenous industry has been to promote new projects to replace those that cannot compete in EU markets, while in the North more effort has been expended in modernising plants to assist them in becoming competitive. **Frances Ruane**

industrial relations. Industrial relations changed radically in the Republic with the development of SOCIAL PARTNERSHIP from the end of the 1980s. Previously the adversarial system, similar to that of Britain, was predominant, though that system still exists in parallel. Between 1987 and 2000 there were five national agreements involving social partnership, where moderate wage increases were traded for tax concessions and improvements in the social wage (for example welfare and pensions). Partnership at enterprise level is less developed than at national level, though it is more pervasive in non-union high-technology industries. The IRISH CONGRESS OF TRADE UNIONS represents unions in both the Republic and Northern Ireland and had 215,000 members in Northern Ireland in 2000. Most unions there are British, and partnership is developing slowly. The number of TRADE UNIONS has also fallen with amalgamations. Trade union membership had grown to 544,000 in the Republic in 2000, but union density declined with the rapid growth in EMPLOYMENT in the 1990s, standing at around 40 per cent of employees. In the Republic the state provides industrial relations arbitration through the Labour Court and the Labour Relations

Commission. Different areas of the public service have their own negotiating and arbitration systems, with those in Northern Ireland being similar to the systems in Britain. **Paul Sweeney**

industrial research and development. Like many Western countries, Ireland, both North and South, is seeking to expand the range of economic activities that can be described as 'knowledge-based'. For such development to take place it is essential both that companies engage in research and development, in order to improve existing products and processes and develop new products, and that the country has a capability (in third-level education) to support these activities. The Republic has espoused this policy for several decades, seeing the inflow of high-technology firms as an important way to do this. However, there is an inconsistency in this policy, as the low corporate tax rates that attract transnational companies in the first instance also reduce the incentives of such companies to undertake R&D in Ireland (as their R&D expenditure is set off against a low tax rate). A consequence of this is that business expenditure on research and development in Ireland as a proportion of gross sales in manufacturing, at 1.2 per cent, is still very low by OECD standards (an average of 2.4 per cent), despite having increased significantly in recent years. The low scale of such expenditure undertaken by indigenous industry is a cause for concern to policy-makers; and where such expenditure is undertaken it is primarily at the development rather than the research stage of the process. Only in very recent times have concerted efforts been made to build up the R&D capability in third-level education to support indigenous companies. **Frances Ruane**

Industrial Revolution, the term normally used to describe the quantum advance in economic activity from c. 1780 onwards. Its salient characteristics were the harnessing of steam power, the replacement of traditional cottage industry by centrally directed mechanised factory production, and the consequent rise of industrial cities and consumer markets. It first developed in the midlands and north of England, where abundant reserves of iron and coal provided the ideal basis for exploiting the new technological possibilities. By contrast, Ireland's lack of these resources meant that it was a less promising locale for INDUSTRIAL DEVELOPMENT. The ECONOMY of the three southern and western provinces remained largely agricultural during the nineteenth century, with cities and towns concentrating on professional and commercial activities. The principal exceptions here were Dublin and Cork, with significant BREWING and DISTILLING concerns, of which Guinness was the best known.

In eastern Ulster, however, the industrial revolution established itself, despite that province's similar absence of natural resources. Ulster had a thriving LINEN industry in the eighteenth century. The centralisation and mechanisation of linen-bleaching in Belfast during the 1820s and 30s began Ulster's industrial revolution, symbolised by the opening of the vast York Street linen mill in 1828. By 1850 there were sixty-two such mills in Belfast. The industry soon outran local supplies of flax, and the need to import flax—and coal—meant the development of Belfast port and the consequent rise of SHIPBUILDING. The yards of HARLAND AND WOLFF and Workman Clark date from 1861 and 1880, respectively. The former became one of the giants of shipbuilding; its most famous ship was the TITANIC. The industrial economy of Ulster also embraced brewing, processed foodstuffs, TEXTILES, and tobacco. Unlike the rest of Ireland, it was geared for exports and by the end of the century was in effect part of the larger economy of north-west Britain, with which it had many cultural similarities. The effect of the industrial revolution on Ulster can best be summarised by the statistics for Belfast, which was estimated to have a population of 25,000 in 1808; by 1901 this was almost 350,000. **Fergal Tobin**

industrial schools, schools established to inculcate in children under the age of fourteen habits of 'industry, regularity, self-denial, self-reliance and self-control.' In Ireland they were legislated for in 1868, based on the models already in operation in England and Scotland. Although the schools contained a small number of children who had committed minor acts of delinquency, the majority were placed in them because of the poverty of their parents. The first industrial school was certified in 1869, and by 1871 there were fifty-one, which grew to seventy by 1900, with a capacity for nearly 8,000 children. The schools were under religious auspices, either Catholic or Protestant. In 1917 the last non-Catholic school closed, and from then on all such schools were operated by Catholic religious congregations but financed by the state in the Republic. The publication of the Reformatory and Industrial Schools Systems Report in 1970 (better known as the Kennedy Report) gradually brought about the demise of the system, and the Children Act (2001) formally abolished the term 'industrial school'. Since the mid-1980s increasing numbers of allegations of sexual and physical abuse in industrial schools have emerged, culminating in several television documentaries. In 1999 the Government formally apologised to those who had been abused in industrial schools and established a Commission to Inquire into Child Abuse. A scheme for financially compensating those who were victims of abuse in the schools has also been promised. [see UNDERCLASS.] **Eoin O'Sullivan**

industry. For historical reasons, INDUSTRIALISATION began much later in Ireland than in most of North-Western Europe. Throughout the nineteenth century a specialised and export-oriented region developed in the north-east, centred on Belfast; the main industries were linen-based textiles, engineering, and shipbuilding. In the remainder of the country industrialisation was severely curtailed following the ACT OF UNION (1800), which resulted in the economy being mainly oriented towards the supply of agricultural products and labour to industrial Britain. By the time political independence was attained in 1922 for the twenty-six counties that were to form the Republic, less than 10 per cent of the work force was engaged in manufacturing, compared with more than a third in Northern Ireland.

Two distinct phases can be identified in the history of industrialisation in the post-independence era. The first, from 1932 to the late 1950s, has been described as the protectionist era. A vigorous policy of promoting and protecting Irish industry was pursued, especially in the 1930s, which led to an increase of 58,000 (50 per cent) in the number of people employed in manufacturing over the period 1926–51. This pattern of expansion slowed down considerably in the 1950s, however, when there were also significant job losses, so that the net increase in manufacturing EMPLOYMENT over the decade to 1961 was only 3,000. An important geographical outcome of the protectionist phase was an increase in the concentration of manufacturing employment in Dublin and the surrounding counties, from 43 to 57 per cent, with more than 90 per cent of the net gain in manufacturing employment between 1926 and 1961 occurring in these counties, together with the cities of Cork, Limerick, and Waterford.

In response to the trends that emerged under this policy, the Government in the late 1950s undertook a fundamental reappraisal of ECONOMIC POLICY, which led to the introduction of incentives

industry. *The East Park, Shannon Free Zone, Co. Clare, part of the Shannon development scheme, created to attract foreign investment to the region by providing a package of support for industry, including sophisticated industrial infrastructure and reduced taxes for investors. [Shannon Development Photo Library]*

to attract investment to Ireland and to the adoption of policies aimed at creating an export-oriented industrial base. Since then a comprehensive package of incentives has been vigorously promoted by the INDUSTRIAL DEVELOPMENT AGENCY, with considerable success. The impact of this policy has been dramatic, making Ireland in the 1990s a role-model economy that has achieved the highest rates of economic growth among OECD member-countries and a remarkable convergence in GDP per capita towards the level of those of the core regions of the EUROPEAN UNION.

The adoption of an industrialisation model that is heavily reliant on the ability to attract and retain foreign investment, coupled with membership of the EEC from 1973, has contributed to a surge in industrialisation, leading to an increase in the share of industrial output in GDP (measured in constant prices) from 25 per cent in 1960 to 30 per cent in 1973 and 47 per cent in 1998. Over this period employment in industry increased from 23 per cent of the total at work in 1960 to 31 per cent in 1973; since then the share has fluctuated around 30 per cent. However, within manufacturing there has been significant growth in the actual number employed throughout the 1990s (24 per cent between 1989 and 1998), in marked contrast to the experience of most other industrialised countries.

The geography of contemporary manufacturing industry is the outcome of a complex set of factors that have influenced in different ways the location decisions of firms at different times. The siting of many Irish-owned firms is heavily influenced by the place of birth or residence of the founding entrepreneurs, while others are guided by the distribution of raw materials (especially in the food-processing industry), while in some other instances proximity to domestic markets is an important consideration. There are also examples of clusters of Irish-owned small firms in some counties, such as furniture-making in Cos. Meath and Monaghan. Irish-owned manufacturing firms account for 52 per cent of total employment in this industry, but their contribution to total net output is much less, at 22 per cent, as net output per worker in these firms is only a quarter of that of workers in foreign-owned firms. These differences are mainly due to the much greater reliance on traditional sectors and a small proportion of high-technology firms.

Two-thirds of employment in Irish-owned industries is concentrated in such industries as food and drink, TEXTILES and CLOTHING, paper, publishing and printing, basic and fabricated metals, and timber-based industries. Productivity is generally lower in these firms, and fewer are trading in export markets. In 1998 only half of Irish-owned industrial units exported some of their output, with 41 per cent of the total exports going to the British market. The competitive pressures associated with a less restrictive trading climate have contributed to a significant restructuring in traditional industries since the early 1980s and has resulted in large reductions in employment. Many of the surviving firms have adapted by enhancing the quality of their products, improving management practices, concentrating on niche markets, and in some instances entering into an alliance with others in order to strengthen their position in the market. **James Walsh**

Industry, foreign-owned. The foreign-owned component of industry accounts for almost 80 per cent of net manufacturing output and almost 88 per cent of the value of industrial EXPORTS. These firms also accounted for 62 per cent of the growth in manufacturing EMPLOYMENT between 1989 and 1998. They are mostly concentrated in a small number of industries that have been identified by the IDA, including office and computing equipment, electrical machinery, optical and precision equipment, and pharmaceuticals, together with a number of internationally traded services in such areas as computer software, data-processing, financial services, and direct sales and customer services. The attraction of world leaders in these sectors—such as Intel, IBM, Dell, Gateway, Motorola, Hewlett-Packard, Siemens, Microsoft, and Rank Xerox—was a contributory factor in the exceptional growth of the economy in the 1990s.

These industries have been attracted to Ireland for many reasons, the most important being a favourable tax regime, the availability of educated, English-speaking workers, membership of the EUROPEAN UNION, good telecommunications INFRASTRUCTURE, and a strong commitment by the Government to SOCIAL PARTNERSHIP, which has contributed to moderation in wage increases and relatively few industrial disputes. The implementation of the strategy for attracting investment has been much more focused since the late 1980s than previously. The first phase of foreign investment was generally associated with low-skill assembly and packaging operations in a wide range of industries and with limited local linkages. A significant source of comparative advantage for Ireland at that time was relatively low labour costs, especially outside Dublin. The location strategy for foreign investment up to the late 1970s strongly favoured the dispersal of firms. While much of the dispersal was to small towns, a significant concentration emerged at the industrial zone established near Shannon Airport. However, following a highly critical review of industrial policy published in 1982 it became necessary to devise a more strategically focused long-term approach that placed more emphasis on creating additional added value and on supporting activities in industries that were likely to remain competitive.

This shift, which seeks to promote a knowledge-based industry rather than one drawing comparative advantage from low labour costs, has resulted in a more concentrated pattern of new industrial development. The highest growth rates in employment have been around the cities: Dublin, Cork, Limerick, and Galway. The tendency towards high concentration is most evident in internationally traded and financial services, with 77 per cent of the increase in employment between 1989 and 1998 being in Dublin. This concentration of foreign investment in and around Dublin has contributed to significant problems of traffic congestion, INFLATION in house prices, and a high demand for LAND to be used for infrastructure, new industrial and business estates, and HOUSING; it has also led to increased concerns about imbalances between and within regions. In response the Government and industrial agencies have produced strategies to encourage a greater dispersal of industrial activity while maintaining international competitiveness. A National Spatial Strategy has identified a number of 'gateways' and the requisite supporting infrastructures to achieve a more balanced distribution of industrial activity. Important considerations in selecting gateways will be the availability of third-level educational institutions, a high level of accessibility, and the infrastructure to support modern industries, as well as conditions that will contribute to a high quality of life. **James Walsh**

inflation, a progressive increase in the general level of prices. In the year 2000, average consumer prices in the Republic were sixty-eight times their level at the outbreak of the FIRST WORLD WAR. The general trend in Irish inflation has been strongly influenced by the exchange-rate policy pursued. When the IRISH POUND was linked to sterling (before 1979) price inflation in Ireland—North and South—closely tracked that in Britain, a result attributable to the considerable, though declining, dependence on Britain for IMPORTS and on other trading and institutional links. Accordingly, there were three great inflationary surges, the first two corresponding to the world wars and the third with a double peak in the period 1973–83. After joining the EMS—which allowed periodic devaluations—the Republic was slower than Britain and Northern Ireland in getting annual inflation permanently back to single digits but, with UNEMPLOYMENT rising, inflation dipped below 5 per cent in 1985, and wage-push pressure was thereafter limited by a series of moderate wage settlements centrally negotiated as part of tripartite agreements that also included Government commitment to tax reductions. From 1999, the adoption of the euro ensured that long-term average inflation in the Republic would remain close to EMU average, though booming demand conditions promised to keep general price inflation a few percentage points above that average for some years, with wages and property prices again rising faster. **Patrick Honohan**

Informer, The (1925), a novel by LIAM O'FLAHERTY. It recounts the last hours in Dublin of a former member of a revolutionary group sentenced to death for informing on an erstwhile colleague. The informer, Gypo Nolan, is represented as a crude force of nature, in conflict with the implacable will of the commandant of the conspirators. O'Flaherty combines a naturalistic vision of animal energy at work in human affairs with a Dostoevskian intensity of feeling to produce a fevered account of the political lower depths in the CIVIL WAR years. JOHN FORD directed a film version (1935). **Terence Brown**

infrastructure. Infrastructure is fundamentally characterised by external effects; the value of a network is greater than the sum of its parts. For this reason the state plays a central role in the planning, design and very often provision of networks in TRANSPORT, utilities, HOUSING, and urban development. Serious infrastructural deficits, especially with regard to roads, housing, and WATER systems, were evident in the Republic by the late 1990s. The National Development Plan, 2000–2006, was published in late 1999, its remit being to address these infrastructural deficits. An estimated €28.5 billion is to be spent on physical infrastructure over the period covered by the plan. Investment in social and affordable housing is the largest infrastructure component, with an allocation of €7.6 billion. Roads and public transport were also identified as a priority, with €5.9 billion going to national roads, a further €2 billion to non-national roads, and €2.7 billion to be invested in public transport.

In Northern Ireland the report *Shaping Our Future* (1998) was published by the Department of the Environment. It offers a strategic and long-term view on the future development of Northern Ireland up to 2025 and covers such areas as social disadvantage and infrastructural needs. **John W. O'Hagan**

Inghinidhe na hÉireann, the first women's nationalist organisation. Formed by MAUD GONNE in October 1900, following the success of the 'Patriotic Children's Treat' protest against the visit of Queen VICTORIA to Ireland, it organised cultural events for children and provided actors for plays, including *Cathleen Ni Houlihan*. Its paper, *Bean na hÉireann* (1908–11), edited by HELENA MOLONY, publicised the views of nationalist women. Members participated in the early SINN FÉIN and Socialist Party of Ireland. Moribund by 1914, it merged with CUMANN NA mBAN. **Margaret Ward**

Inglis, Liam (1708/15–1778), priest and poet. Born in Newcastle, Co. Limerick, or in Co. Tipperary; as a young man he moved to Co. Cork and lived in the east and north of the county, where he became active in literary circles. Tradition records that he served as tutor to the young EDMUND BURKE. He entered the Augustinian order and was ordained in Rome in 1749; returning to Cork, he spent periods as prior of the Augustinian community there. More than thirty poetic compositions are ascribed to him in manuscript sources. These include a body of political verse in which contemporary European power struggles are discussed from an Irish JACOBITE viewpoint; his comic poem 'Cré agus Cill go bhFaighidh Gach Bráthair', popularly known as 'Leastar an Bhráthar' (the friar's firkin), parodies events of the Seven Years' War. **Diarmaid Ó Catháin**

Ingram, John Kells (1823–1907), economist and fellow of TRINITY COLLEGE, Dublin. Born in Templecarne, on the Donegal–Fermanagh border; educated at TCD. He had scholarly publications in archaeology, etymology, medieval MANUSCRIPTS, English literature and economics and was the author of the patriotic ballad 'The Memory of the Dead' ('Who fears to speak of Ninety-Eight?'). His *History of Political Economy* (1888) was translated into nine languages and earned him honorary membership of the American Economics Association in 1891. He was founder of the school of English at Trinity College, Dublin, of the classics journal *Hermethena*, and of the STATISTICAL AND SOCIAL INQUIRY SOCIETY OF IRELAND. He was vice-provost of Trinity College and president of the ROYAL IRISH ACADEMY. **Sean Barrett**

Ingram, Rex (1893–1950), film director. Born Reginald Ingram Hitchcock in Dublin, son of a CHURCH OF IRELAND clergyman; at eighteen he left Ireland for the United States, never to return. He studied sculpture at Yale University before starting work in 1913 at Edison Film Studios, New York, where he acted, wrote scripts, and in 1916 directed his first film. Following the popular and critical success of the feature films *The Four Horsemen of the Apocalypse* (1921), which made Rudolph Valentino a star, *The Prisoner of Zenda*

Inghinidhe na hÉireann. *Members of the revolutionary women's association Inghinidhe na hÉireann, c. 1905–6; seated centre is the founder of the association, Maud Gonne MacBride. The members wear replica gapped-ring brooches, based on seventh-century originals, as a symbol of Irish heritage and identity. [Courtesy of Kilmainham Gaol Museum]*

(1922), *Scaramouche* (1923), and *Mare Nostrum* (1926)—made in Nice at a studio purchased by Ingram—he was hailed as one of America's leading directors. Not willing to provide the happy ending demanded by American film studios, and not comfortable with sound cinema, he continued to work in Europe, making two of his last films there, *The Garden of Allah* (1927) and *Baroud* (1932), his only sound film, which were shot in Nice and North Africa. **Kevin Rockett**

Inishbofin, Co. Galway (not to be confused with the Co. Donegal island of the same name), an island of 9.4 km^2 ($3\frac{1}{2}$ sq. miles), 8 km (5 miles) from the mainland and accessible by ferry from Cleggan. St Colmán built a monastery here in the seventh century, the site of which was reused for a thirteenth-century church, St Colman's Abbey. A Spanish pirate fortified the island, and his castle, rebuilt, became part of a British military base in the turbulent seventeenth century. Isolation, however, brought its usual problems for the farmers and fishermen of Inishbofin: like that of other islands, its population has fallen dramatically. In 1841 (before the GREAT FAMINE) it was 1,404, falling to 762 in 1901 and to 200 in 1996. Recently TOURISM has helped to supplement farming and lobster-fishing, and there are two hotels. A generating station, shops, post office, restaurant, school and church are other services. **Stephen A. Royle**

Inishowen, Co. Donegal, a triangular peninsula bounded to the west by LOUGH SWILLY, to the east by LOUGH FOYLE, and to the north by the Atlantic Ocean, occupying an area of approximately 810 km^2 (313 sq. miles). At its apex is MALIN HEAD, the most northerly point of Ireland. The landscape is rugged, the result of alternating bands of hard quartzite and granite with less resistant schist. This has produced spectacular scenery and sandy beaches but has made farming difficult; most farms are small, with an emphasis on sheep.

There is a long history of settlement. The Grianán of Aileach, near Muff, is thought to date from the Late Bronze Age, while near Culdaff are the remains of a horned cairn and a STONE CIRCLE. There are many relics of early Christianity, such as the Donagh and Carrowmore HIGH CROSSES. The area was long associated with the O'Dohertys, who held sway until the rebellion of CAHIR O'DOHERTY in 1608 resulted in the confiscation of their lands. The present population is approximately 28,000; and while there are three medium-sized towns—Buncrana (population 3,433), Carndonagh (population 1,758), and Moville (population 2,253)—the greater part of the population is rural. Though Buncrana is a popular seaside resort, the peripheral location of the peninsula has hindered ECONOMIC DEVELOPMENT, resulting in higher rates of UNEMPLOYMENT. The traditional TEXTILE industry has declined recently, and it has proved difficult to attract alternatives. The presence of the border with Northern Ireland along its eastern edge has had a negative effect on the local ECONOMY, preventing until now its integration into the hinterland of Derry, the regional capital. **Joseph Brady**

INLA: see IRISH NATIONAL LIBERATION ARMY.

Innishmurray, Co. Sligo, an island 6 km (4 miles) off the coast, best known for its *cashel* (stone enclosure) containing the house-shrine of St MOLAISE of (possibly) the ninth century and later (with a wooden statue of the saint, now in the NATIONAL MUSEUM), two later medieval churches, BEEHIVE HUTS, cross-decorated slabs, and cursing-stones. The Women's Church stands outside, and there are PILGRIMAGE stations around the perimeter of the island. **Peter Harbison**

Innti (1970–), an IRISH-LANGUAGE poetry magazine, published irregularly, mostly under the stewardship of the poet MICHAEL DAVITT. It provided an early forum for an emerging generation of poets, including Davitt, NUALA NÍ DHOMHNAILL, LIAM Ó MUIRTHILE, and GABRIEL ROSENSTOCK, all students at UCC at the time. **Caoimhín Mac Giolla Léith**

Institute of Irish Studies, Belfast, established at Queen's University in 1965 to foster interdisciplinary research and scholarship. Visiting fellows and distinguished scholars have ready access to the university's extensive collection of Irish material, the LINEN HALL LIBRARY (established in the late eighteenth century), and the Public Record Office of Northern Ireland. In addition to providing a base for research on topics within the humanities and social sciences, the institute has a long history of supporting new work on environmental sciences and archaeology. It publishes books of Irish academic interest; recent works include the forty-volume series of the Memoirs that accompanied the nineteenth-century ORDNANCE SURVEY OF IRELAND. Courses in interdisciplinary study are available to undergraduate students, with further opportunities for advanced study through the institute's courses leading to the degree of master of arts, a course that is popular with foreign students. [see EVANS, E. ESTYN.] **Valerie Hall**

Institute of Public Administration (IPA), a source of management training and consultancy services for the higher public service and the public sector. Set up in 1957 as a voluntary body on the initiative of a small group of public servants, under its dynamic founding director T. J. Barrington, the IPA quickly won an influential place in Irish public affairs. Barrington was very conscious of the requirements of local as well as of central administration, and he ensured that the IPA was accessible to all parts of the public service. The IPA became an important source of management training for the higher public service, and it developed innovative and successful diploma and degree courses aimed at the broader public sector throughout Ireland. It also became an important provider of public-sector management consultancy services both in Ireland and internationally. In addition to its educational, training, and consultancy roles the IPA is now the leading Irish publisher of works on public-sector affairs, and through its quarterly journal, *Administration*, it provides a forum where officials and academics can discuss problems of public policy, politics, and administration. **Eunan O'Halpin**

Institution of Engineers of Ireland. Founded in 1835, The Institution of Civil Engineers of Ireland took its lead from the founding of the Institution of Civil Engineers in London in 1828. In his opening address the founding president of The Institution, JOHN FOX BURGOYNE, spoke of the elimination of low standards in engineering works as a principal objective of the new institution. It attracted many eminent engineers, and its members were significantly involved in the great infrastructural works of the nineteenth century, particularly RAILWAYS, BRIDGES and harbours, roads, water supply, and sanitation. The Institution received a royal charter in 1877.

The twentieth century saw the construction of the SHANNON POWER SCHEME, marking the beginning of Ireland's industrialisation, with new disciplines of engineering—particularly mechanical and electrical—working side by side with civil engineering, which had been the dominant discipline up to that time.

The charter of The Institution was amended by DÁIL ÉIREANN in 1960 to extend its objects by reason of the growth of other disciplines of engineering, which were not allowed for specifically in the 1877 charter. Coincident with the construction of the Shannon Scheme, Cumann na nInnealtóirí (the Engineers' Association) was founded in 1928, one of its main objects being the furthering of the interests of the profession, with particular emphasis on salaries and conditions of employment. Under The Institution of Civil Engineers of Ireland (Charter Amendment) Act (1969) the two organisations were merged under the name The Institution of Engineers of Ireland, emphasising its multidisciplinary nature. The Institution is the accreditation body for engineering courses and has agreements with similar national bodies throughout the world on the mutual recognition of qualifications. It is an examining body and has the authority within the State to confer the title 'chartered engineer'. **Finbar Callanan**

insular art, a term conventionally restricted to the distinctive and rich art style that reached a peak of outstanding artistic and technical achievement in Ireland in the eighth century. It developed in the later seventh century from the fluid, compass-based art of the Celtic IRON AGE, absorbing both the INTERLACE and abstract animal patterns seen in the fine metalwork of neighbouring Germanic peoples and the motifs of the late ROMAN world and in particular its Christian imagery. Craftsmen working in metal, stone and precious pigments were commissioned by the clergy and rulers of the kingdoms of Ireland and also of those areas of northern Britain linked to Ireland by proximity and Irish missionary activity, thus making the emerging art 'insular' with regard to both Ireland and Britain.

One of the most celebrated examples of Irish insular art style is the TARA BROOCH, in which a brooch type unique to Ireland bears panels decorated in a variety of ornamental styles and techniques; these blend into unified and distinctive decorative schemes on both front and back. The primary ingredient that gives a uniquely insular flavour is the use of abstract ornament in elaborate patterns, with a repertoire of curves, triskeles, and spirals, often infilled with linking pointed ovals that gave rise to the description 'trumpet pattern'. These motifs were derived from, but often are not identical with, the Celtic art of the pre-Roman and Roman Iron Age and were common to the peoples of northern and western Britain as well as those of Ireland, where they remained a unique European heritage. In contrast, the interlace in relief and the panels of very stylised animals in filigree wire on the Tara Brooch, together with areas of cast ornament heavily faceted to give depth and brilliance, show ideas taken from Germanic art of the MIGRATION period. The minute and complex gold filigree work is typical of the technical and artistic brilliance of insular art at its best in the first half of the eighth century.

Irish craftsmen came into contact with new influences through the kingdom of DÁL RIADA in western Scotland and the ensuing military, ecclesiastical, diplomatic and trade contacts with the new Anglo-Saxon states of eastern Britain. At the same time contacts were made from eastern and southern Ireland with the heavily Germanicised kingdoms of the Franks and beyond. These foreign traits were not only adopted but were adapted to make the insular art style. Secular patronage was important, both in the form of commissions and in the influence of the exchange of gifts, tribute, and dowries between kings and overlords. Workshop evidence from the royal stronghold of Dunadd, Argyll, shows that the Irish kingdom of Dál Riada in western Scotland was one of the places where smiths were working in the new style and were familiar with new technology and artefact types, from goldwork to cast

insular art. The Book of Kells, *folio 27v, illustrating symbols of the four Evangelists: (top left) Mark as a lion, (top right) Matthew as an angel, (bottom left) John as an eagle, and (bottom right) Luke as an ox. [Board of Trinity College, Dublin]*

silver buckles and elaborate PENANNULAR BROOCHES. Irish smiths learnt new goldworking techniques and took these skills to new heights on the great silver ARDAGH CHALICE and the paten from DERRYNAFLAN (see pp. 42, 286).

The third ingredient in insular art, and the great stimulus to its development, was the influence of the established imagery of the Christian world, married to the need to supply vessels and books for every Christian church. Images associated with the texts of the Bible, both Old and New Testament, were presented in a semi-natural way, with models drawn from the world of late antiquity and its successor. The central image was that of the Crucifixion, as can be seen on a late eighth-century plaque from Rinnagan, Co. Roscommon, unmistakable both in its universal theme and its Irish insular style.

Insular art was to find its main area of expression and its most enduring monuments in the presentation of God's word as found in the Gospels: the three contributory sources inspired discrete painted panels in the Book of DURROW, all bound together by knotwork frames. Bright colours are a feature of both manuscript art and contemporary enamelled metalwork. The spread of Christianity from Ireland and the diaspora of monks to Continental churches, however, were the main agencies through which this new hybrid style was created, spread, and developed. The best example of this is the Columban conversion of the newly united Anglo-Saxon kingdom of Northumbria from Holy Island (formerly Lindisfarne), where one of the great masterpieces of insular art, the LINDISFARNE Gospels, was made c. 700, precursor to the unique riches of the Book of KELLS. The new style was readily exported in books and portable objects and also by the exchange of scribes and other craftsmen. Insular art was thus carried to ecclesiastical centres in Continental Europe and central and southern England, where its influence can be widely recognised in manuscript decoration and fine metalwork.

In Ireland and western Scotland in the ninth century this style was also expressed in remarkable stone sculpture, where the finished works, both HIGH CROSSES and slabs, often remain in their original settings. This allows us to recognise regional schools of carving, such as the Barrow group associated with the AHENNY crosses (see p. 491), and to gain further insights into the patrons and craftsmen who created these unique monuments in the established tradition of insular art but who also remained receptive to the latest developments in Carolingian Europe. [see BOOK SHRINES; GRAVE-SLABS; MEDIEVAL METALWORK.] **Susan Youngs**

Insurrection Act (1796), legislation that provided the death penalty for those administering oaths. It also allowed the administration to proclaim areas as 'disturbed', and thereby to suspend trial by jury and impose curfews, and it gave special powers to magistrates. The act was in force until 1802, then reintroduced in modified form in 1807. Lapsing in 1810, it was re-enacted in 1814–18 and 1822–25. Later, less severe COERCION ACTS were clearly based on the 1796 act. **Neal Garnham**

Intelligence, Military. An intelligence section is an integral component of a military staff. In active operations the mission of an intelligence organisation is to collect and analyse information about the enemy and the area of operations on behalf of the commander. In many armies, including the Irish, the intelligence section of the staff is designated G2. At Defence Forces Headquarters the intelligence function is performed by the Intelligence Directorate, headed by its director. Perhaps the best known occupant of this post was Colonel Dan Bryan, who ran a very successful operation during the SECOND WORLD WAR, particularly in the field of counter-espionage. During this time Military Intelligence was given responsibility for this work inside the state. It still co-operates with the GARDA SÍOCHÁNA in internal security matters. Today Military Intelligence maintains up-to-date information on military activities and developments abroad, particularly those that might adversely affect Irish security. Regions in which Irish soldiers are serving, or are likely to serve, receive special attention. The implementation and monitoring of Ireland's responsibilities under the Vienna Document are also intelligence functions. This involves international exchanges of military information and verification inspections abroad. The director is a member of the National Security Authority. **Patrick Purcell**

intelligence services. The intelligence requirements of the Irish state have been met by special units within the GARDA SÍOCHÁNA and the DEFENCE FORCES. The army played a leading role in studying the domestic threat posed by republicanism within the state and abroad during and after the CIVIL WAR, but in 1926 responsibility for this work was given to the Garda Síochána, which has since been the state's main intelligence arm, save for the period 1939–45, when counter-espionage and defence security became crucial matters because of the threat to NEUTRALITY posed by the clandestine activities of both German and Allied organisations. Military Intelligence played a decisive role in counteracting such intrigues; it also provided much information on foreign diplomats, and developed close links with British and American security agencies, a co-operation that demonstrated that neutral Ireland was not a mortal threat to Allied security interests.

These links were retained in the post-war world with regard to Cold War security matters of concern to the Western powers, while a certain amount of military information is exchanged with other states involved in UN and other international peace-keeping operations. Through participation in the European Union Military Staff, established in 2000, the state's access to intelligence affecting the European security environment is likely to grow.

The Special Detective Unit (formerly the Special Branch) of the Garda Síochána and the headquarters section to which it reports are now the state's main source of political and criminal intelligence. Since the early 1970s there has been deepening contact with Northern Ireland and British police forces concerning terrorist threats arising from the Northern crisis, as well as with the Federal Bureau of Investigation in the United States, while European integration has brought about increased exchanges on terrorism, DRUGS, and the illegal arms trade with police and security agencies within and beyond the EUROPEAN UNION. This is done both bilaterally and through Europol. **Eunan O'Halpin**

interlace, a geometrical pattern formed by one or more bands repeatedly crossing each other. The principles of construction are those of woven interlace and are usually based on a square grid, often using four strands, which can vary in width and be either rounded or pointed at the corners. Ideally suited to fill spaces and form frames in MANUSCRIPTS, interlace may have been introduced to Britain and Ireland through that medium from some area of the Mediterranean c. AD 600. The illuminators of manuscripts were quick to exploit the possibilities it offered for endless variation in designs, and for centuries interlace was an integral part of the decoration of manuscripts and metalwork. By the eighth century the range of motifs was expanded with the introduction of animals of Germanic origin whose bodies and limbs interlaced with one another. [see INSULAR ART.] **Peter Harbison**

Intermediate Education (Ireland) Act (1878), legislation passed in order to provide national examinations and, by extension, a curriculum for pupils at second level. There were three grades: Junior, Intermediate, and Senior. Prizes were awarded to pupils who distinguished themselves, and the act stimulated the growth of secondary education. The three grades were replaced in the 1920s by the Intermediate and Leaving Certificate examinations. However, an enduring tradition of nationwide examinations for second-level pupils was established. **Margaret Ó hÓgartaigh**

International Financial Services Centre (IFSC), a designated area of Dublin's former docklands at Custom House Quay where firms benefit from reduced taxes. Since 1987, firms that have set up in this area benefit from a greatly reduced rate of corporation tax on profits derived from international financial services (there are also other reliefs, including reliefs from property taxes). The IFSC is now a thriving zone of new office blocks, occupied by dozens of mostly foreign-owned banks, insurance companies, fund management firms, and other financial services companies. Even at the low rate, tax revenue from the centre has been very buoyant. Job creation was much slower than forecast, though by the end of the twentieth century about 11,000 jobs had been created. Maintenance of the special tax regime, which is exploited by foreign firms to avoid their national taxes, has required

International Financial Services Centre. *The buildings of the International Financial Services Centre, Dublin, established in 1987, are gathered around the basins of the Custom House Docks, with James Gandon's Custom House (bottom right), Michael Scott's Busáras (bottom middle), and Stack A, scene of the banquet in 1856 for the 3,600 veterans of the Crimean War (above foreground basin). [Dublin Docklands Developments Authority]*

from EUROPEAN UNION partner governments a tolerance that has often seemed to be wearing thin. **Patrick Honohan**

internet. As in other industrialised countries, the internet has had a considerable impact on the social, educational and economic life of Ireland. The extent of this impact during recent years can partly be gauged from estimates of the level of its use and access in state-sponsored and in private research. Much detailed information in this area is provided in reports published by the Information Society Commission, a body set up by the Government to advise it on policy relating to information and communications technology. In December 2000 the Commission published its third report on the development of the 'information society' in Ireland. It estimated that 40 per cent of the population had access to the internet, an eight-fold increase over the previous four years. A report in September 2000 found that only 16 per cent of the population in Northern Ireland had such access, by far the lowest level of access for regions in the United Kingdom. The report of the Information Society Commission in December 2000 showed that levels of access to and use of the internet by Irish companies was as high as in any industrialised country, with 96 per cent of firms having internet access, an increase of 59 per cent above the level pertaining in 1996.

While knowledge and use of the internet is obviously high among companies, a very small number of them use it for sales or to conduct other business on line. Seventy-seven per cent of businesses have their own web sites, but these are used mainly for marketing and advertising purposes, rather than for commercial transactions. Smaller, more localised studies in Northern Ireland report much less awareness and use of the internet by businesses. Generally, the most successful organisations in this new business environment have been those that have used the internet primarily as a means of presenting information, rather than for selling products.

In 1994 the IRISH TIMES became the first newspaper in Ireland, and among the first thirty in the world, to publish on the internet. A number of other information services were added over the following years, with the ireland.com web site developing from its original function as the on-line edition of the *Irish Times* to being a portal (a web site that acts as a point of departure for on-line sources of information on a particular subject) for internet users around the world with an interest in things Irish. An important factor in the site's success has been its ability to attract a great deal of attention from the North American market, which accounts for a large proportion of the several million visits to the site each month. A number of Irish software companies have made a significant contribution to the technology that has made possible the internet's spectacular growth. The innovative work of Iona Technologies in the area of networking has rapidly increased the rate at which computer systems can be integrated. Baltimore Technologies was one of the world's leading companies in the area of encryption software, a vital component of any electronic commerce system. In 2000 Sarah Flanagan, a secondary school pupil from Blarney, Co. Cork, won the Irish YOUNG SCIENTIST OF THE YEAR COMPETITION and the EU Young Scientist Competition, and international recognition, for her work on encryption.

Despite the importance to the economy of information and communications technology, Ireland lags significantly behind other European countries in the integration of these technologies in primary and second-level education. Other indicators, such as the country's relatively low position on the IDC World Times Information Society Index (a complex measurement of technology use in selected countries), belie Ireland's image as a leader in the 'information age'. The Government, however, has often been innovative in its attempts to encourage the adoption of new technologies. In 1997 the then state-owned telecommunications company Eircom sponsored the 'Information Age Town' project, which selected the residents of ENNIS, Co. Clare, to participate in a unique experiment. Each household in the town was offered a personal computer, and during 2000 nearly half the town's citizens used the internet regularly. **Brian Galvin**

internment, or detention without trial, a power available to the Northern Ireland government under the Special Powers Act (1922). It was used in the 1920s, during the SECOND WORLD WAR, and notably, and successfully, during the IRA's BORDER CAMPAIGN of 1956–62, when similar action occurred in the Republic. Following the outbreak of serious violence in Northern Ireland in 1969, the Belfast government pressed London strongly for its introduction. As the situation worsened in 1970–71, the government in London was persuaded (though against the advice of the army commander, General Sir Harry Tuzo) that internment might work. When the measure was eventually applied, on 9 August 1971, the results were disastrous. The RUC Special Branch intelligence on which the initial sweep ('Operation Demetrius') was based was seriously out of date. Comparatively little was known about the recently formed PROVISIONAL IRA, and the majority of the 340 people arrested on the first day were 'old-style' republicans known for their involvement in the political side of the movement, members of the Official IRA, and some CIVIL RIGHTS activists. More than a hundred of the original internees were quickly released; the Provisionals were hardly touched.

The summary arrests, and the well-founded allegations of ill-treatment of the detainees that followed, caused grave resentment in the nationalist community and stimulated a sharp upsurge in violence. Within forty-eight hours twenty-three people had been killed or fatally injured in some of the worst rioting of the TROUBLES. Those imprisoned were themselves radicalised by the experience, and the internment camps became 'universities of terrorism'. Despite the immediately damaging consequences of the policy, internment continued to be used until December 1975, when the remaining seventy-five detainees were released by the Secretary of State for Northern Ireland, Merlyn Rees. **Keith Jeffery**

Invasions, Book of: see LEBOR GABÁLA ÉRENN.

investigative journalism. Irish newspapers, hugely inhibited by the defamation laws, have little tradition of sustained investigative journalism. Most exposure of corruption has relied on individual journalists, such as Joe MacAnthony of the Independent Group (who published an investigation of the Hospital Sweepstakes in 1971), the IRISH TIMES journalist Frank McDonald (who published *The Destruction of Dublin* in 1985) and VINCENT BROWNE on many issues in MAGILL. In the 1970s and 80s *Phoenix* led the field in examining security matters. Allegations in the 1980s and early 90s by Sam Smyth, Des Crowley, Vincent Browne, and others, reinforced by acute analysis by columnists such as Gene Kerrigan and FINTAN O'TOOLE, were confirmed beyond expectations by the series of official TRIBUNALS that began in the late 1990s. **David Quin**

Investment in Education. In 1962 a review of second-level education in the Republic was initiated by the Department of Education, in co-operation with the OECD, culminating in the publication of the report *Investment in Education* (1966). This report had significant consequences for the development of educational policy. It dealt with two main themes: the capacity of the educational system to meet skill requirements for ECONOMIC GROWTH, and inequalities in levels of participation. It found that the numbers of those giving up school, together with a restricted curriculum in many secondary schools, would result in a shortage in the qualified labour (particularly in relation to technical qualifications) necessary for economic development. In addition, the report dealt with considerable socio-economic and regional disparities in participation rates. *Investment in Education* provided the impetus for the introduction of the free education scheme in 1967. This scheme removed fees for participating secondary schools (to reduce socio-economic inequalities) and introduced a school transport scheme (to reduce regional inequalities). The scheme led to a significant increase in the number of enrolments in second-level schools; however, socio-economic and regional inequalities persist. **Emer Smyth**

Invincibles. The Irish National Invincibles was a secret society founded in 1881 'to remove all the principal tyrants of the country.' The society would probably not have acquired such a prominent place in history but for the assassination of Lord Frederick Cavendish, CHIEF SECRETARY, and Thomas H. Burke, UNDER-SECRETARY, in the PHOENIX PARK on 6 May 1882. The killings shocked the general populace as they introduced a policy of political assassination rather than agrarian killing or armed insurrection. The incident has been known ever since as the PHOENIX PARK MURDERS. The political opponents of CHARLES STEWART PARNELL sought without success to implicate both him and the LAND LEAGUE in the killings.

Five men were convicted of the murders, mainly on the evidence of the informer James Carey, and were hanged in KILMAINHAM GAOL. They were Daniel Curley, Joseph Brady, Thomas Caffrey, Michael Fagan, and Timothy Kelly, who was nineteen years old. There were many ballads written about the men who were executed: 'Tim Kelly Is No More' and 'Lamentable Lines on Joe Brady and Dan Curley'; there were also songs dispraising the informer James Carey.

He was a traitor from the first, says the Shan Van Vocht,
The ground he walks upon is cursed, says the Shan Van Vocht,
He's as treacherous as a cat, or a pig that's reared a pet,
Sure his equal you can't get, says the Shan Van Vocht.

A new identity was created for the informer James Carey, and under the name of Power both he and his family were given passage to South Africa. However, during the voyage, while on board the ship *Melrose* going from Cape Town to Durban, he was recognised by another passenger, Pat O'Donnell, an argument ensued, and O'Donnell shot him dead. O'Donnell was later tried and hanged in Newgate Prison, but his actions are loudly praised in the song that bears his name, 'Pat O'Donnell'. The song is still widely sung today.

My name is Pat O'Donnell and I come from Donegal,
I am you know a dangerous foe to traitors one and all.
For the shooting of James Carey I was tried in London Town,
And now upon the gallows tree my life I must lay down.

Frank Harte

'Iomarbhágh na bhFileadh' ('contention of the poets'), a seventeenth-century literary *jeu d'esprit* with political overtones, involving some fifteen poets and thirty separate compositions in syllabic metre (twenty-eight in two varieties of *deibhí* and two in *rannaíocht mhór*). Dating from c. 1617–26, it is among the best-known of such literary flourishes from the seventeenth century; others include one concerning claims about the origin of the RED HAND OF ULSTER and one about the status of the River SHANNON as a northern or southern river.

The 'contention' concerns the relative merits of Leath Chuinn (the northern half of Ireland) and Leath Mhogha (the southern half), whose mythical chiefs were Mugh Nuadhat (south) and Conn Cétchathach (north), from whom were descended the leading families of Ireland. The reputed instigator of the debate was the Co. Clare poet and chronicler TADHG MAC DÁIRE MAC BRUAIDEADHA, who disputed the claims made by the poet 'Torna' for the northern half. He was opposed by the poet and chronicler Lughaidh Ó Cléirigh (died c. 1620, author of 'BEATHA AODHA RUAIDH UÍ DHOMHNAILL'), Seán Ó Cléirigh, 'Roibeárd Mac Artúir' (possibly Dr Robert Chamberlain, a professor in Louvain), Hugh O'Donnell (a kinsman of RED HUGH O'DONNELL and also of the Earl of Thomond), and Brian Óg Mac Diarmada (died c. 1632, son-in-law of the Earl of Clanricarde); members of the Mac Aodhagáin family, Baothghalach and Anluan, associated with schools of law, also supported the northern claims. Tadhg Mac Dáire was supported by Toirdhealbhach Ó Briain (of whom no other known poem exists) and Art Óg Ó Caoimh, while the poets MATHGHAMHAIN Ó HIFEARNÁIN, FEARFEASA Ó'N CHÁINTE, and Eoghan Mac Craith, each of whom is also known for other work, contributed their support to the southern claims. **Michelle O Riordan**

Iona, a small Scottish island in the Inner Hebrides off the Ross of Mull. Its original name was probably Í or Io, which was rendered by ADOMNÁN in VITA SANCTAE COLUMBAE as *Ioua insula* and by Bede as *Hii insula*. 'Iona' derives from a late medieval misreading of *Ioua*.

In the early sixth century the Irish from DÁL RIADA began to settle this part of Britain, beginning an expansion that eventually led to a single kingship over Scotland. In this process Iona occupied a strategic position half way between the two Irish groups in the south-west of Scotland and the north-west of Ireland. Because of this central location, during its period of eminence (between 563, when COLM CILLE founded his monastery, and 794, when VIKING raids began) it was a force not only in Irish history but in the history of Britain—a link point between Ireland and the Picts (the Celtic-speaking people north of Hadrian's Wall) and with the Anglo-Saxons.

Adomnán presents COLM CILLE choosing Iona as a place for a life of penitential retreat; however, from other incidents in the *Vita*, and subsequent events, it is clear that he chose Iona as being suited for a monastic community and an ideal base for missionary work among the Picts. Islands had many of the apparently contradictory qualities monastic founders sought, including a clear distinction of monastic and secular worlds while still being close to the larger society, and isolation but with easy access by boat, linking the monks and the surrounding region. The monastery grew rapidly, becoming the leading house of a monastic *familia* and a centre of HIBERNO-LATIN scholarship. It played an important role in the ecclesiastical life of Britain and Ireland and the general life of Dál Riada and beyond, as can be seen in Colm Cille's links with other monasteries, such as that of BANGOR, and Adomnán's trips to Ireland for the Synod of Birr (697) and to Northumbria on behalf of hostages. As a missionary base it was equally successful, not only among the Picts but among the Anglo-Saxons; AIDAN OF LINDISFARNE, for example, came from Iona.

Iona's importance declined during the Viking period, when it was raided repeatedly, and it also became more clearly a part of Scotland rather than of Ireland. A monastic foundation continued until its suppression in 1561. **Thomas O'Loughlin**

Iona National Airways, Ireland's first airline, named by its founder, Hugh Cahill, after his motor works in Glasnevin, Dublin. In 1930 he acquired a Desoutter mark II, registration EI-ADD, and Iona National Air Taxis and Flying School began operations in August 1930 from the military airfield at Baldonnel, Co. Dublin; in 1931 it moved to Kildonan, near Finglas, Dublin, which became Ireland's first commercial airport. Cahill abandoned his interest in 1933, but the airline was revived by his son, Pearse Cahill, in 1952. It acquired the Cessna agency and in 1958 moved to a site on the west side of Dublin Airport, where it maintained a fleet of light aircraft until it ceased operations in the 1990s. **Bernard Share**

Íosagán agus Sgéalta Eile (1907), first collection of short stories by PATRICK PEARSE. There are four stories, written in a poetic style, presenting a sympathetic portrayal of an Irish-speaking rural community, particularly children. While slight in content and sentimental in tone, the collection played a significant role in the early development of the short story in Irish. **Aisling Ní Dhonnchadha**

Iota, pen-name of Kathleen Mannington Caffyn, née Hunt (1855–1926), writer. Born in Co. Tipperary; trained as a nurse. After her marriage she emigrated to Australia because of her husband's health. In 1893 she moved to London, where she was a frequent contributor to magazines and published *A Yellow Aster* (1894), her best-known work, an important feminist novel of the period and central to the New Woman fiction of the 1890s. Her

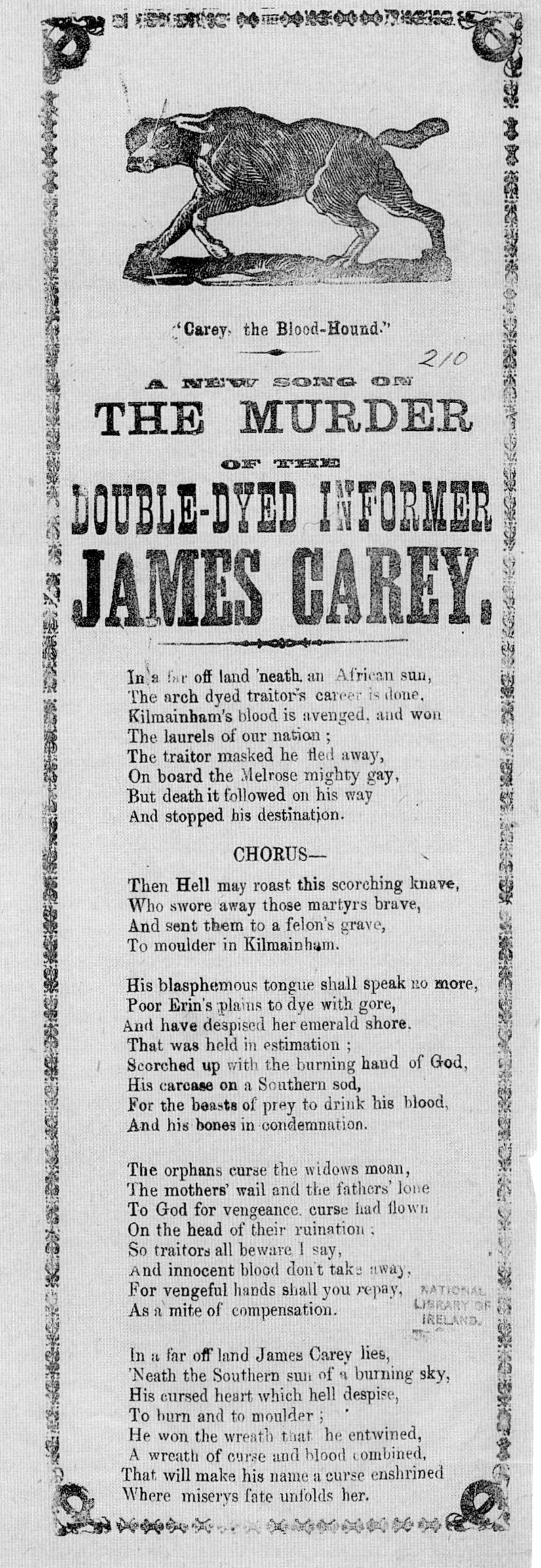

"Carey, the Blood-Hound."

2/10

A NEW SONG ON

THE MURDER

OF THE

DOUBLE-DYED INFORMER

JAMES CAREY.

In a far off land 'neath an African sun,
The arch dyed traitor's career is done,
Kilmainham's blood is avenged, and won
The laurels of our nation ;
The traitor masked he fled away,
On board the Melrose mighty gay,
But death it followed on his way
And stopped his destination.

CHORUS—

Then Hell may roast this scorching knave,
Who swore away those martyrs brave,
And sent them to a felon's grave,
To moulder in Kilmainham.

His blasphemous tongue shall speak no more,
Poor Erin's plains to dye with gore,
And have despised her emerald shore,
That was held in estimation ;
Scorched up with the burning hand of God,
His carcase on a Southern sod,
For the beasts of prey to drink his blood,
And his bones in condemnation.

The orphans curse the widows moan,
The mothers' wail and the fathers' lone
To God for vengeance, curse had flown
On the head of their ruination ;
So traitors all beware I say,
And innocent blood don't take away,
For vengeful hands shall you repay,
As a mite of compensation.

In a far off land James Carey lies,
'Neath the Southern sun of a burning sky,
His cursed heart which hell despise,
To burn and to moulder ;
He won the wreath that he entwined,
A wreath of curse and blood combined,
That will make his name a curse enshrined
Where miserys fate unfolds her.

Invincibles. *Ballad sheet recounting the murder of James Carey on 29 July 1883, for giving evidence against members of the Invincibles, hanged for the Phoenix Park Murders. [Council of Trustees of the National Library of Ireland]*

other novels include *Children of Circumstances* (1894), *A Comedy in Spasms* (1895), and *The Minx* (1899). **Tina O'Toole**

IRA: see IRISH REPUBLICAN ARMY.

IRB: see IRISH REPUBLICAN BROTHERHOOD.

Ireland

Area: 84,433 km² (32,595 sq. miles)
Jurisdictions: Ireland, Republic of; United Kingdom of Great Britain and Northern Ireland
Population: 5.602 million (Republic of Ireland 3.917 million (2002); Northern Ireland 1.685 million (2001))
Capitals: Dublin (Republic of Ireland), Belfast (Northern Ireland)
Counties: Antrim, Armagh, Carlow, Cavan, Clare, Cork, Derry/Londonderry, Donegal, Down, Dublin, Fermanagh, Galway, Kerry, Kildare, Kilkenny, Laois, Leitrim, Limerick, Longford, Louth, Mayo, Meath, Monaghan, Offaly, Roscommon, Sligo, Tipperary, Tyrone, Waterford, Westmeath, Wexford, Wicklow
Provinces: Connacht, Leinster, Munster, Ulster
Geographical features: Bantry Bay, Belfast Lough, Carlingford Lough, Clew Bay, Dingle Bay, Galway Bay, Kilalla Bay, Killary Harbour; Lakes of Killarney; Lough Allen, Lough Conn, Lough Corrib, Lough Derg, Lough Erne, Lough Foyle, Lough Measc, Lough Neagh, Lough Ree, Lough Swilly, Strangford Lough; Blackstairs Mountains, Blue Stack Mountains, Caha Mountains, Comeragh Mountains, Derrynasagart Mountains, Derryveagh Mountains, Galtee Mountains, Glens of Antrim, Knockmealdown Mountains, Maamturk Mountains, Macgillycuddy's Reeks, Mweelrea Mountains / Sheeffry Hills, Mourne Mountains, Nephin Mountains, Ox Mountains, Partry Mountains, Slieve Aughty Mountains, Slieve Bloom Mountains, Slieve Mish Mountains, Sperrin Mountains, Twelve Pins, Wicklow Mountains; River Bann, River Barrow, River Blackwater, River Boyne, River Erne, River Foyle, River Lagan; River Lee, River Liffey, River Moy, River Nore, River Shannon, River Slaney, River Suir; Bog of Allen, Burren, Cliffs of Moher, Giant's Causeway; Achill Island, Aran Islands, Blasket Islands, Rathlin Island
Historical interest: Brú na Bóinne (Newgrange), Boyne Valley, Céide Fields, Clonmacnoise, Croagh Patrick, Dún Aengus, Glendalough, Hill of Tara, Lough Derg, Navan Fort (Eamhain Macha), Skellig Michael, Rock of Cashel
Industry and products: Agriculture and Food, Clothing and Textiles, Chemicals and Pharmaceuticals, Computer and Information Technology, Distilling and Brewing, Tourism

Joseph Brady

Ireland became an island perhaps as recently as 6500 BC, when rising waters in the wake of the Great Ice Age wore down the land bridges linking it to that part of the European continent that would later break away as the island of Britain. The newly created Ireland differed little in size and shape from what it is today: area, 84,433 km² (32,595 sq. miles); length, 486 km (302 miles); width, 275 km (171 miles). It was, as it remains, saucer-like, with mountains around the coast and the centre mainly low and flat. The highest peak (Carrauntoohil, Co. Kerry: 1,041 m (3,415 ft)); the longest river (the Shannon: 257 km (160 miles)). Forests of oak, birch and hazel covered the central plain, with stretches of boggy lakeland.

Severance from the Continent would define some of the country's basic characteristics. Its immediate effect was to limit the variety of native FAUNA. Bears and wolves, foxes and HARES proliferated but not any species that had failed to find its way to Ireland before the sea separated it from the European land mass: hence the absence of snakes. Phenomena common to most island societies would show themselves in time; these included a delayed acknowledgment of developments elsewhere. In Ireland the plough was still attached to the horse's tail long after the harness had become the Continental norm, and people continued to construct BEEHIVE HUTS in an age when more comfortable housing had evolved abroad.

Concomitantly, novel ideas often met stubborn resistance. When the ANGLO-NORMANS' feudal system clashed with Irish custom outside the PALE, the Normans had to yield by adopting Irish legal and literary formulas. The REFORMATION settlement imposed after the NINE YEARS' WAR turned a blind eye to ecclesiastical as distinct from political Catholicism, a toleration of majority dissent that, though honoured as often in the breach as in the observance, had few parallels in the Europe of the day. The English language as spoken in Ireland (HIBERNO ENGLISH) incorporated medieval, Elizabethan, and Cromwellian features for centuries after these had been abandoned in England. This insular caution over abandoning the familiar can be traced to the country's physical separation from neighbouring countries. Had these countries been contiguous to Ireland, the nature and consequence of innovations might have been more readily apparent.

A human presence cannot be dated with certainty to earlier than 6000 BC, when hunter-gatherers established themselves. About 3500 BC, farmers were growing crops. They were possibly also cutting into the forest to clear more fields. Then came the builders of the NEOLITHIC PASSAGE TOMBS. Ore was extracted for metalworking in the BRONZE and IRON AGES (after 2000 BC), when tools, weapons, body ornaments, musical instruments, and other artefacts were skilfully fashioned.

Celtic peoples began to infiltrate from c. 500 BC. Only by the seventh century AD, long after St PATRICK's mission, can it be confidently asserted that they had fully established a social system of clans under their chieftains, provincial kings, and a (rarely unchallenged) High King. Monastic settlements had begun to spring up throughout the country in which the churches and dwellings, like those of the general population, were of timber, wicker, and thatch or sometimes of stone. Tillage, cattle-rearing, and barter constituted the economy. Woodland was further encroached upon. The more zealous of the monks went to Britain or the Continent in search of 'wildernesses' suited to their penitential instincts—sure evidence that Ireland was becoming too ordered for their liking. There was order in the BREHON LAW texts then being compiled, order in the division of the country into the provinces of Munster, Leinster, Ulster, Connacht, and Meath (later absorbed into Leinster). Craftsmanship of a high order underlay the personal ornaments and church vessels being worked in bronze, enamel, silver, and gold, as well as in the glorious illuminated Gospel-books.

Seaborne VIKINGS descended on Ireland, ripe for looting, and wreaked havoc throughout the ninth century yet in time became civilised themselves and, as Hiberno-Norse, added their own contribution by building the country's first towns, the seaports of Dublin, Cork, Limerick, Waterford and Wexford. The Anglo-

Ireland. St Patrick's Day, Military Parade at Dublin Castle *(1844), watercolour by Michaelangelo Hayes. The last day of the court season was celebrated with a military parade. The 11th Hussars are in the foreground, with trumpeters of the 3rd Dragoon Guards and infantry of the 16th Regiment. From the thirteenth to the twentieth centuries the Castle was the seat of British rule in Ireland. [By permission of the Office of Public Works]*

Normans followed in the late twelfth century, introducing English rule and the feudal social system. They built defensive EARTHWORKS, inland towns along the major rivers, and, later, TOWER-HOUSES. They sub-divided the provinces into counties.

The Normans were vassals of the English king, but unruly vassals who often sided with the native Irish against royal pretensions. Armies were eventually sent to put down rebellion—and rebellion in the later 1500s came to mean resisting not only the Crown but the Protestant Reformation, which had been adopted in England. Through intricate politics, much campaigning and widespread devastation—the remaining forests being largely destroyed—Ireland was finally pacified by the close of the seventeenth century. There had meanwhile been an addition to the melange of its peoples. The sixteenth and seventeenth-century PLANTATIONS were an English colonising policy. After each campaign, English and Scots settlers, often disbanded soldiers, received tracts of confiscated land. The planters farmed more methodically than the Irish, introduced regular markets, and built planned towns. It could be said that they tidied the country and rationalised its economy.

The Irish, whether of Celtic or Norman stock, were for the most part Roman Catholic—and Catholics, the majority of the population, were held suspect by the Protestant planters. The degree of persecution under the anti-Catholic PENAL LAWS can be exaggerated; the reduction of Catholics to second-class citizenship cannot. All political and most economic power devolved on the ASCENDANCY, the leading families of English planter descent and a few of native background who had converted to the Anglican CHURCH OF IRELAND. The capital, Dublin, was made elegant by the Ascendancy's taste for classical ARCHITECTURE and GEORGIAN townscapes, which maintained a commercial, craft and artisan population. But in the midlands, the west, and the south of the country vast numbers of Catholics became a rent-paying cottier class, lacking any hope of advancement. The ANGLO-IRISH, presiding over destitution, too often lived beyond their rents and declined into profligacy. Both planter and native population were trapped in a rigidly re-inforced order. Exceptions existed: landlords who strove after better husbandry, Catholics who prospered as merchants and farmers; the bigger provincial towns reflected the influence of Dublin. The overall picture, however, grew steadily worse until too much of the country consisted of grazing for cattle, with potato patches around mud cabins, and parkland around the mansions of a debt-laden Ascendancy. Thus was a fertile island put to fruitless use and its people propelled to the disaster of the GREAT FAMINE (1845–50).

Sundry relief measures and ultimately emancipation in 1829 improved the legal status of Catholics but not the fatally skewed economic circumstances of the country. With the abolition of the Ascendancy parliament under the ACT OF UNION, which in 1801 had merged Ireland into a United Kingdom with Great Britain, Dublin itself fell into decline: the encroachment of the slums on the splendour slowly began and was not arrested by the emergent industries of BREWING and DISTILLING or the RAILWAY works opened

Ireland. *A life-size crucifixion at the Franciscan Abbey, Collinstown, Co. Westmeath, an image of the public piety of twentieth-century Catholicism. [Mark Joyce]*

to service a new mode of transport. The GREAT FAMINE came, lingered, and abated, leaving a million dead, another million emigrated, and Ireland infected with the virus of emigration for a century and a half to come, its pre-famine population of around 8 million destined to dwindle to less than 5 million before redress set in.

Betterment came sooner in other ways. Except in the north-east, livestock exports continued to be the bedrock of the economy, while during the sixty years after the Great Famine successive British governments (largely but not entirely under nationalist pressure) introduced reforming measures that transferred the ownership of the land to those who lived and worked on it. Further benefits followed from the CO-OPERATIVE MOVEMENT, founded at the turn of the nineteenth century, whereby farmers in a district could combine to set up creameries to process and sell their products.

Another aspect of Ireland's potential was also being drawn upon: its intellectual and artistic potential. The IRISH LANGUAGE, replete with poetic imagery and the life-philosophy of an ancient people, was dying under the influence of English as the medium of economic and social progress. But at the same time the former Ascendancy were becoming more conscious of their recent roots in Ireland than of their distant roots in Britain. They evolved forms of literary and aesthetic expression in painting, in writing, and in theatre that, with their Anglican faith, marked them as a cultural class in their own right. With their compatriots of other traditions also producing English-language playwrights, poets and artists of distinction, nineteenth and twentieth-century Ireland could claim many whose genius redounded to the credit of the multi-layered Irish identity. Within that identity would be found during the twentieth century no fewer than four winners of the NOBEL PRIZE for literature (as well as one for physics and five for peace).

The Act of Union had been followed by a century of nationalist protest directed at obtaining Irish control over Irish affairs. Concessions stopped short of the autonomy sought. Proposals for HOME RULE made painfully slow progress. Frustration had occasionally erupted in minor insurrections, which achieved little, but in the years from 1916 to 1921 popular support retrospectively swung behind another revolt in arms, combined with the election of a majority of Irish MPs who formed their own parliament, Dáil Éireann, and proclaimed the separation of Ireland from the United Kingdom. A Treaty concluded with the British government in 1921 established the IRISH FREE STATE as a Commonwealth dominion. The Union was broken. But the six north-eastern counties opted to remain within the United Kingdom.

The Scots settlers in the north-east were Presbyterians, not Anglicans. For a time in the seventeenth and eighteenth centuries their descendants, like the Catholics, suffered political discrimination, but economic activity remained open to them. Their strength lay in what would later be called industrial development and business acumen. In the LINEN industry they created the country's first major manufacturing enterprise. Related cloth-based industries followed and in the nineteenth century the manufacture of machinery for mass-production. The resulting availability of engineering skills made Belfast a natural centre for shipbuilding, which from the 1860s lifted Ulster to the fore of the INDUSTRIAL REVOLUTION—the only part of Ireland to earn that distinction. Awareness of their difference from the rest of Ireland, combined with a race-memory of battles to defend their planter heritage, underlay the Ulster Protestants' assertion of Britishness, epitomised in the ORANGE ORDER, political unionism, and suspicion of the Catholic nationalist minority in their midst. The outcome (in 1920) was NORTHERN IRELAND, a self-governing unit within the United Kingdom with a local parliament subordinate to the United Kingdom parliament in London.

The two parts of Ireland, thus politically and economically sundered, developed in radically different ways. The North began with the advantage of its successful industrial base, but this was not to last. Foreign TEXTILES undermined the linen trade. The post-war slump reduced demand for shipping. Unemployment crept upwards. The Northern government could do little about it. London in effect controlled what revenue was available for Northern Ireland and how it was to be spent, notwithstanding the Northern government's limited power to levy taxes within its jurisdiction. Financial decisions for the United Kingdom as a whole often ran counter to the requirments of Northern Ireland. The Great Depression of the 1930s worsened these problems. Realistic planning became impossible, and schemes for better HEALTH, HOUSING and EDUCATION had to be left in abeyance.

These difficult economic circumstances exacerbated the mutual antipathy between the Protestant-unionist majority and the large Catholic-nationalist minority. Nationalists denounced DISCRIMINATION against them by the Unionist government, local councils and business firms in housing and employment. Unionists saw nationalists as disloyal subversives, bent on forcing Northern Ireland into unity with the Catholic Free State. GERRYMANDERING and the maintenance of the Special Constabulary were judged in a security context by unionists; to nationalists, these features of the regime were plainly sectarian. The SECOND WORLD WAR brought an industrial revival and much-needed employment; it also brought common suffering to both communities in the air attacks of the BELFAST BLITZ. The introduction of the United Kingdom welfare state brought a considerable improvement in living standards, but discrimination continued: the new town of Craigavon, Co. Armagh, and the new University of Ulster at COLERAINE, Co. Derry, were each assigned to staunchly Protestant-unionist regions rather than the more impoverished Catholic-nationalist areas.

Discrimination in housing precipitated the crisis that ultimately destabilised the 1920 settlement. It led to the formation of a nationalist CIVIL RIGHTS MOVEMENT, the Northern Ireland Civil Rights Association, in the late 1960s, which achieved notable measures of reform in housing administration and the municipal franchise but was followed by inter-communal strife. Organisations on the nationalist and unionist extremes resorted to lethal violence. More than 3,000 people died in the subsequent 'TROUBLES'. Successive governments in London and Dublin acted in unison to resolve the crisis in co-operation with moderate groups on both sides of the Northern divide, including elements from the once seemingly intransigent extremes. The opening years of the new millennium saw novel power-sharing arrangements in train, inspiring desperate hope as a challenge to the nagging uncertainty about the future of Northern Ireland.

The Irish Free State began in poverty. Its ethos of modest self-sufficiency behind tariff walls was vindicated when basic needs in food and fuel were met from home sources during the Second World War. A modicum of social progress was also initiated. City slums were replaced by suburban housing; in the countryside drainage schemes, piped water and electricity, when they eventually arrived, were much-appreciated amenities. Greater change was on the way. The Republic (as the Free State and later (1937) Éire, became in 1949 on leaving the Commonwealth) adopted a policy in the 1960s of inviting foreign investment. Tax incentives, prepared sites and other attractions were devised to lure transnational corporations to set up factories in the Republic.

From 1973, when both the Republic and the United Kingdom became members of the European Economic Community (now the EUROPEAN UNION), this development was accelerated. While bringing immense benefit to Irish agriculture, the outstanding contribution of the EEC to the economy was the diversification of markets in which produce could be sold, including the produce of the American and Asian manufacturers now established in the Republic and enjoying access from within to the Common Market of which Ireland was part. By the end of the twentieth century the Republic had become less the agricultural country it had been for so long than, remarkably, Europe's largest manufacturer and exporter of electronic components and similar advanced technological products. Former market towns had become industrial centres, and economic growth was proceeding at the fastest rate in Europe: more people were coming to work in Ireland than were leaving. Many, though not all, were manifestly more prosperous. How long such progress could be sustained, given the extent to which it left the Republic dependent on buoyant economic circumstances abroad, remained a question at the outset of the new millennium. **Louis McRedmond**

Ireland, names of. The early native form of the name was *Ériu*, from putative Old Celtic *Iveriu*; in the modern period *Ériu* became ÉIRE and later *Éirinn*. Outside its boundaries, however, Ireland was from the earliest times identified by other names, many of them nevertheless deriving directly or indirectly from *Ériu*; hence Greek *Ierne*, employed by the first-century geographer Strabo, and Latin *Ivernia*, by the cartographer PTOLEMY in the second century (the form *Hibernia* arose from confusion with the Latin *hibernus*, 'wintry'). Other names of varying origins included *Banbha*, *Britannia Parva*, *Ogygia*, and (confusingly) *Scotia*, from Late Latin *Scotus*, by which name the Irish were known when they settled what is now Scotland, in the sixth century.

Though the name *Ireland* became generally adopted following the ANGLO-NORMAN CONQUEST and therefore abroad (*Irland*, *Irlanda*, *Irsko*, etc.), the Irish name *Éirinn* was Anglicised as *'Erin'* by the nineteenth-century romantic movement, which also popularised such appellations as the *Four Green Fields* (i.e. the four provinces) and the EMERALD ISLE and female personifications such as 'Cathleen Ni Houlihan' (*Caitlín Ní Uallacháin*) and the *'Shan Van Vocht'* (*Seanbhean Bhocht*, poor old woman), which remain in demotic—if largely ironic—use.

From 1922 to 1937 the twenty-six-county state was officially known as the *Irish Free State* or *Saorstát Éireann*; this usage in English, abbreviated to 'the Free State', persists in popular parlance in Northern Ireland. *Éire* and *Ireland* were adopted jointly as the name of the state under the Constitution of 1937: 'The name of the State is Éire, or in the English language, *Ireland*.' The two parallel forms have led to some confusion, *Éire* being little used within Ireland though favoured externally, particularly in Britain, to distinguish that jurisdiction from the geographical entity. This is further complicated by the fact that *Ireland* may refer both to the Republic and the geographical entity, depending on context and circumstance. The 'description' *Republic of Ireland*, formally adopted in 1949, is principally employed as a means of distinction between that jurisdiction and Northern Ireland, as in the case of sports teams and for commercial reasons. Britain, for political reasons, tends to favour *'Irish Republic'*; but internationally the official name *Ireland* is generally accepted as the name of the twenty-six-county state. **Bernard Share**

Ireland, Patrick: see O'DOHERTY, BRIAN.

Ireland: place-names abroad. There are approximately forty-five known places in the world that carry the name 'Ireland'. While most of these are in the United States, others are to be found in such widely separated places as Bermuda in the Caribbean and Papua New Guinea.

Towns, villages and communities, mountain peaks, streams, islands, mines, and reservoirs that carry the name 'Ireland' do so for a variety of reasons. The most obvious, though possibly not the most common, is that the settlers who established the community or site were emigrants from Ireland, as in New Ireland, Mississippi, where Irish immigrants established a community in 1844. Another New Ireland, a group of 149 islands in the north-eastern part of Papua New Guinea, was called New Mecklenberg from 1884 until 1975, when Papua New Guinea declared its independence and changed the name of the islands. In West Virginia the village post office (and hence officially the name) of another New Ireland was so named in 1847 in honour of 114-year-old Andrew Wilson, born in Ireland in 1729, who was known in the community as 'Old Ireland' (no doubt from constantly talking about his homeland).

These examples typically belong to the middle to late nineteenth century, the period of mass Irish emigration to the United States. More numerous than Irelands overseas are place-names of more undoubtedly Irish origin, which appear all over the Irish-inhabited world, especially in the United States and Australia; typical examples are Dublin, Bantry, and Erin. The English surname Ireland has also contributed to the spread of new 'Ireland' names. The original bearers of this surname may have come from, traded with or owned land in Ireland.

Place-names are not always permanent and may become altered over time. Some Irelands that existed in the past now have other names, such as New Ireland, New York, a settlement in what is now Allegany State Park. This was established by a group of Irish emigrants who left Ireland at about the time of the GREAT FAMINE. Names can also be changed into something that they sound like, as with the Ireland Mine in California, named after 'Uncle' Billy Irelan (*sic.*) (a name of ambiguous origin), who discovered the quartz-bearing deposits of the region. An example of similar ambiguity within Ireland is the name IRELAND'S EYE, given to the uninhabited rocky island off Howth, Co. Dublin, an Anglicisation of a former name, *Inis Ereann* (Erc's island). [see SOUTH AFRICA, IRISH IN.] **Allegra D. Lalor**

Ireland, Republic of (Irish Free State; Éire/Ireland)

Area: 70,273 km^2 (27,136 sq. miles)
Population: 3.917 million (2002)
Capital: Dublin
Counties: Carlow, Cavan, Clare, Cork, Donegal, Dublin, Galway, Kerry, Kildare, Kilkenny, Laois, Leitrim, Limerick, Longford, Louth, Mayo, Meath, Monaghan, Offaly, Roscommon, Sligo, Tipperary, Waterford, Westmeath, Wexford, Wicklow
Provinces: Connacht, Leinster, Munster, Ulster (part of)
Geographical features: Bantry Bay, Carlingford Lough, Clew Bay, Dingle Bay, Galway Bay, Kilalla Bay, Killary Harbour; Lakes of Killarney; Lough Allen, Lough Conn, Lough Corrib, Lough Derg, Lough Measc, Lough Ree, Lough Swilly; Blackstairs Mountains, Blue Stack Mountains, Caha Mountains, Comeragh Mountains, Derrynasagart Mountains, Derryveagh Mountains, Galtee Mountains, Knockmealdown Mountains, Maamturk Mountains, Macgillycuddy's Reeks, Mweelrea Mountains/Sheeffry Hills, Nephin Mountains, Ox Mountains, Partry Mountains, Slieve Aughty Mountains, Slieve Bloom Mountains, Slieve Mish Mountains, Twelve Pins, Wicklow Mountains; River Barrow, River Blackwater, River Boyne, River Lee, River Liffey, River Moy, River Nore, River Shannon, River Slaney, River Suir; Bog of Allen, Burren, Cliffs of Moher; Achill Island, Aran Islands, Blasket Islands
Historical interest: Brú na Bóinne (Newgrange), Boyne Valley, Céide Fields, Clonmacnoise, Croagh Patrick, Dún Aengus, Glendalough, Hill of Tara, Lough Derg, Skellig Michael, Rock of Cashel
Industry and products: Agriculture and Food, Chemicals and Pharmaceuticals, Computer and Information Technology, Distilling and Brewing, Tourism.

Joseph Brady

The Irish Free State was established under the terms of the ANGLO-IRISH TREATY, agreed between the British and Irish delegations on 6 December 1921; Dáil Éireann ratified the Treaty settlement after an acrimonious debate on 7 January 1922. MICHAEL COLLINS believed that the Irish Free State was the first step towards greater independence and sovereignty; however, the Treaty divided the national independence movement and was followed by a short but vicious CIVIL WAR. The new Free State army defeated the Republican irregulars, and a ceasefire was declared on 30 April 1923.

The Republican opposition, including SINN FÉIN and the IRA, refused to accept the authority of the new state or the legitimacy of the Constitution of the Irish Free State (1922). At the general election of August 1923, parties in favour of the Treaty won approximately 70 per cent of the vote. The dominant party among the pro-Treaty groups was CUMANN NA NGAEDHEAL, led by W. T. COSGRAVE, who had become President of the Executive Council of the Irish Free State (head of government). Cosgrave and his colleagues were committed to stabilising the new state and securing its democratic foundations. The Free State was one of the few European successor states to maintain democracy throughout the inter-war period. Civilian control was exercised over the military, despite the abortive army mutiny of 1924. The GARDA SÍOCHÁNA was established as an unarmed police force and quickly received widespread public support. Cumann na nGaedheal's tough law-and-order policy contributed to the Free State's stability by the end of the 1920s.

The new government quickly demonstrated its freedom of action by joining the LEAGUE OF NATIONS and appointing a Minister to the United States to represent Free State interests, independently of the United Kingdom. The Statute of Westminster (1930) extended Irish sovereignty further, as it provided that a DOMINION parliament could repeal or amend any law enacted by the British Parliament. Cumann na nGaedheal also regularised relations with the government of Northern Ireland, though no progress was made in ending PARTITION. Disagreements over the BOUNDARY COMMISSION led to the Ireland (Confirmation of Agreement) Act (1925), which confirmed the existing BORDER between North and South. Cumann na nGaedheal also pursued an active economic development policy. New departments were established, most importantly those of Finance and Industry and Commerce. Policy-making concentrated on maximising the country's economic opportunities in the free-trade environment of the day. The principal concentration was on agricultural exports, in the belief that this was where the advantage lay. After recovering from the devastation of the CIVIL WAR, the agricultural economy grew rapidly until the early 1930s. Industry fared less well, but a Tariff Commission was established in 1927 to consider applications for protection by industry.

The most ambitious developmental project was the SHANNON SCHEME, a large-scale hydro-electric project and a sizeable undertaking for the new state. This led in turn to the emergence of STATE-SPONSORED BODIES as one of the central features of economic development: these were commercial entities, financed publicly but not controlled by civil servants. Among the most important were the Electricity Supply Board, the Agricultural Credit Corporation, and AER LINGUS. In 1930 the Vocational Education Act was introduced to provide education and training of relevance for agriculture and industry.

By the early 1930s the Irish Free State had established itself as an independent entity in world affairs, despite the constraints imposed by the Treaty. In domestic politics it had achieved a considerable amount in state-building and stability. ÉAMON DE VALERA established FIANNA FÁIL in 1926 to provide a republican alternative to the more conservative NATIONALISM of Cumann na nGaedheal. The new party, which continued to reject the Treaty settlement, won 26 per cent of the vote in the general election of June 1927, while still pursuing a policy of abstention. This policy was undermined when, after the murder of KEVIN O'HIGGINS by republicans in July 1927, the Government introduced the Electoral Amendment Act, which forced elected deputies to take the OATH OF ALLEGIANCE or lose their seats: in effect Cosgrave forced Fianna Fáil into DÁIL ÉIREANN, though the party remained, in the words of SEÁN LEMASS, a 'slightly constitutional party,' as it sought to transform the constitutional arrangements agreed in 1922.

Between 1927 and 1932 Fianna Fáil attracted those voters who were dissatisfied with the Government and those who wanted a more active nationalist policy; its success was also helped by the organisational effectiveness of Lemass. In September 1927 Fianna Fáil won 35 per cent of the vote; this increased to 44.5 per cent in February 1932 and to 49.7 per cent in January 1933. De Valera formed his first (minority) Government in 1932, with the support of the LABOUR PARTY; and Fianna Fáil remained in power for the next sixteen years.

In contrast to the previous Government, Fianna Fáil wanted to transform Ireland, undermine the Treaty settlement, and establish an independent republic. The new Government quickly down-graded the post of GOVERNOR-GENERAL and engaged in an 'ECONOMIC WAR' with Britain over LAND ANNUITY payments.

Ireland. *A huge plume of smoke rises over the Four Courts, Dublin, in 1922 (the dome of which can be seen behind the tower of St Paul's Church), the second of James Gandon's great buildings (after the Custom House) to be destroyed within four years. The Four Courts was rebuilt and functional again by 1932. [Irish Architectural Archive]*

De Valera introduced the Irish Nationality and Citizenship Act (1935) and the Aliens Act (1935) to clarify identity and citizenship. The Executive Authority (External Relations) Act (1936) redefined the relationship between the Irish Free State and the outside world.

In 1937 the Constitution of the Irish Free State was replaced by the Constitution of Ireland, written under de Valera's supervision and adopted by referendum on 1 July 1937. Ireland was declared to be a 'sovereign, independent democratic state.' Ireland remained a member of the British Commonwealth, and this permitted the British government to ignore what was a radical departure. The name Éire was adopted as the name of the state in Irish, received wide currency as the accepted name for the country, and still appears on postage stamps of the Republic. The Anglo-Irish Agreements (1938) further enhanced Ireland's sovereignty and resolved outstanding conflicts. Ireland agreed to pay £10 million to settle the outstanding claims under the land annuities, and Britain agreed to give Irish agricultural exports privileged access to its markets. The two governments also agreed that the TREATY PORTS retained by Britain under the Treaty should be returned, in effect ending any outside military involvement in the Irish state. This change allowed the Government to declare its NEUTRALITY when the SECOND WORLD WAR broke out in September 1939, and to maintain it throughout the war.

Important changes also occurred in the ECONOMY and in society. Lemass introduced an ambitious programme of industrial development, and agricultural policy was reorganised to make the country self-sufficient. Between 1932 and 1938 the number of Irish-owned industrial companies increased appreciably, and industrial employment also increased. However, agriculture was badly affected by both governments' insistence on tillage and the decline in cattle exports to Britain. These difficulties were only partially resolved by the 1938 Trade Agreements, and agriculture continued to suffer difficulties well into the post-war period. The Government proved to be especially sensitive to Catholic influence during this period, underlined in the Constitution of Ireland but also in the close relations established between the Catholic hierarchy and the Government. Irish society took on a more denominational character by the end of the 1930s, and was also more isolationist. The Second World War reinforced most of these features. De Valera was determined to remain outside the conflict; and in 1940 he rejected a British offer to promote Irish unity in return for entry to the war. The LOCAL DEFENCE FORCE was established in 1940 to resist an invasion by either Britain or Germany; its membership quickly rose to 100,000. Lemass became Minister for Supplies and reorganised the economy to provide the necessities for a people cut off from the rest of the world.

There was considerable hardship in cities and towns during the war, leading to mass EMIGRATION. Approximately 200,000 people emigrated to Britain, despite the imposition of severe labour controls. The majority were attracted by the high wages available in the British war industries and the absence of work in Ireland, but a significant minority, perhaps as many as 80,000, joined the British armed forces.

There was also some policy innovation during this time. Labour law was reformed by the Trade Union Act (1941) and the Industrial Relations Act (1946), while the Transport Act (1944) laid the basis

Ireland. *Crowds throng Shop Street, Galway, the most rapidly growing city in the Republic, with Lynch's Castle, a sixteenth-century merchant's town-house, on the right. [Denis Mortell]*

for CÓRAS IOMPAIR ÉIREANN. BORD NA MÓNA was established in an effort to process natural resources and to maintain energy during the war, while the CENTRAL BANK of Ireland began operation in 1943.

Continuity was the main characteristic of Irish life during the immediate post-war years. Fianna Fáil was replaced after the general election of 1948 by an inter-party Government led by JOHN A. COSTELLO of Fine Gael. The most innovative action of the new Government was the Republic of Ireland Act (1948), which declared Ireland a republic and formally recognised its withdrawal from the British Commonwealth. This final break prompted the British government to introduce the Ireland Act (1949), which guaranteed the status of Northern Ireland. This in turn led to the formation of the All-Party Anti-Partition Committee, representing all the main political parties, to protest against the British legislation.

Ireland participated in few of the major developments in Europe between 1945 and 1961. It received a loan under the Marshall Aid plan but was disappointed not to receive a grant, as Britain did. One of the conditions of American aid was membership of the Organisation of European Economic Development (later the OECD), but Ireland did not play an active role in its proceedings, continuing to protect its position in the British market secured by the Anglo-Irish Trade Agreement of 1948. Ireland did join the UNITED NATIONS in 1955 but did not join the International Monetary fund, GATT, the European Coal and Steel Community, or the Common Market.

Mass emigration, economic stagnation and political uncertainty were the main features of the 1950s. Approximately half a million people emigrated, and by 1961 the population was at its lowest level since the GREAT FAMINE. No Government between 1948 and 1957 had the confidence to question traditional policy. The Government published *Economic Development* (1958), written by T. K. WHITAKER, as a response to the crisis, and argued for a new approach. When Fianna Fáil returned to office in 1957 Lemass co-ordinated economic policy and drew on Whitaker's expertise to develop the First PROGRAMME FOR ECONOMIC EXPANSION (1958). When de Valera retired as TAOISEACH in 1959, Lemass succeeded him and began a programme of modernisation in economy and society. The Government played an important role in economic planning, introducing three programmes for economic expansion between 1958 and 1972. Ireland applied to join the European Economic Community in 1961, forcing the Government to change its priorities regarding FREE TRADE and the global economic system. Though Ireland's application to join the EEC lapsed with de Gaulle's veto in 1963, membership remained a central plank in Ireland's modernisation. The commitment to change was demonstrated by the decision to negotiate the ANGLO-IRISH FREE TRADE AREA AGREEMENT, which came into effect in 1966. This was complemented by a policy of attracting foreign capital to Ireland. The Industrial Development Authority was the principal instrument in this strategy; it was reorganised in 1969 to co-ordinate policy in respect of foreign investment. As a consequence, industry and industrial exports grew rapidly during the 1960s and 70s. The 1960s were also a period of reform and innovation in many areas, including education, the civil service, and social policy.

One of the most significant breakthroughs was Lemass's decision to meet his counterpart in Northern Ireland, TERENCE O'NEILL, in 1965. Though this closer relationship did not prevent the resumption of violence in Northern Ireland, it was an indication of the new mood in the Republic.

The electorate voted overwhelmingly to join the EEC (later the EUROPEAN UNION) in May 1972, and Ireland became a member in January 1973. The COMMON AGRICULTURAL POLICY provided substantial subsidies for farming, while EU regional policy transferred considerable resources to Ireland. Membership also provided the opportunity for Ireland to break its historic link with sterling when it joined the EUROPEAN MONETARY SYSTEM in 1979. The economy, education, law and culture have been progressively Europeanised. The European Union has been generally well received by the public, as demonstrated by the support given to the Single European Act (1987), the Treaty of Maastricht (1992), and the Treaty of Amsterdam (1992); more recently sentiment has been more divided, leading to the rejection of the Treaty of Nice in 2001 (although the treaty was endorsed in a subsequent vote in 2002). The Constitution of Ireland has also been changed in other ways, most significantly in the REFERENDUMS on DIVORCE (1986 and 1995), ABORTION (1983, 1992, and 2002), and the definition of the national territory (1998) (articles 2 and 3). Gradual constitutional change continues to be the main characteristic of modernisation in this area.

The breakdown of political order in Northern Ireland had important consequences for the Republic, especially in the area of security and law and order. The ARMS TRIAL emphasised strains within the political elite, while the SUNNINGDALE AGREEMENT failed to establish a cross-community basis for political co-operation. The ANGLO-IRISH AGREEMENT (1985) was an important breakthrough and was followed by the DOWNING STREET DECLARATION (1993) and Frameworks for the Future (1995); these established the diplomatic and political basis for the BELFAST AGREEMENT (1998), which provided the opportunity for a power-sharing administration in Northern Ireland and the end of IRA violence. The electorate in the Republic endorsed the agreement, which also amended articles 2 and 3 of the Constitution of Ireland, in May 1998.

Despite economic change and modernisation, Ireland's economic performance after 1973 had not been impressive. UNEMPLOYMENT, emigration and INFLATION were central features of society until the late 1980s. Economic reforms undertaken after 1982 secured the economy on a more stable basis and facilitated rapid economic growth during the 1990s. Ireland's economy became the fastest-growing economy in the European Union, increasingly wealthy and with low unemployment. This outcome was generally attributed to successful Government action, SOCIAL PARTNERSHIP, foreign investment, and European integration.

The Republic has changed in many ways since the 1980s. The economy is now predominantly industrial and the society urban. Dublin has mushroomed in size, reflected in its prosperity, house prices, and traffic congestion. Living standards have improved as the society has become more prosperous. In 1987 Irish GDP was 63 per cent of the EU average; by 1996 it had grown to 96 per cent. There has also been significant improvement in the HEALTH of the population and in the quality of HOUSING available. The position of women has also changed; in 1971 only 26 per cent worked, whereas by 2000 this had increased to 47 per cent. The population is also better educated, as can be seen in the expansion of third-level education opportunities. The population is largely urban, well educated, and affluent, though the elderly, unskilled and those living in rural areas do not always benefit from these changes. Agriculture has declined in significance, and rural Ireland has experienced serious DEPOPULATION. Ireland has also become more secular: church attendance has declined, the number of single-parent families has increased considerably, and the number of women travelling to Britain for ABORTIONS continues to rise, while the Catholic Church has suffered from a collapse in vocations and a growing indifference to its influence.

The population has increased rapidly over the past two decades, because of the absence of emigration, the return of former emigrants, and IMMIGRATION from the Continent and elsewhere. The cycle of emigration established after the Great Famine seems to have been broken. Ireland has become an attractive destination for refugees and economic migrants, though their arrival has also led to a rise in racist attitudes in society. **Brian Girvin**

Ireland Act (1949). The period 1948–9 saw a considerable change in the constitutional position of independent Ireland, with a consequent effect in Northern Ireland. In September 1948 the Taoiseach, JOHN A. COSTELLO, announced that he was going to declare Ireland a republic. This was done the following year, marking Ireland's formal break with the British Commonwealth. These events led the Prime Minister of Northern Ireland, BASIL BROOKE, to lobby the Labour Party government of Clement Attlee for a public guarantee of Northern Ireland's position. The Ireland Act, passed in June 1949, gave Brooke most of what he wanted. The Republic was acknowledged to have ceased to be part of the King's dominions, but the act made continuing provision for its nationals with regard to citizenship. It confirmed Northern Ireland as part of the United Kingdom and affirmed that 'in no event will Northern Ireland or any part thereof cease to be part of His Majesty's Dominions and of the United Kingdom without the consent of the Parliament of Northern Ireland.' The act also responded to Brooke's fears of voters from the Republic affecting elections in Northern Ireland. By introducing a residence qualification, it represented a considerable achievement for Brooke, especially as the British Labour Party had not been thought sympathetic to UNIONISM. **T. G. Fraser**

Ireland's Eye, Co. Dublin, a tiny island about 1 km ($\frac{1}{2}$ mile) from Howth harbour. There are remains of an early church and a MARTELLO TOWER. The island was plundered by VIKINGS in 798. It was the scene of one of the most notorious crimes of the nineteenth century, the 'Ireland's Eye murder', in June 1852 when William Kirwan, an artist, murdered his wife Maria, for which he served twenty-seven years' hard labour. DENIS JOHNSTON's play *Strange Occurrence on Ireland's Eye* (1956) is based on the incident. **Stephen A. Royle**

Ireland's War Memorial Records, 1914–1918, a privately printed book produced by Maunsel and Roberts Ltd, Dublin, in 1923, giving the names of the c. 35,000 Irishmen who died in the FIRST WORLD WAR. It was compiled by the Committee of the Irish National War Memorial and printed in a limited edition of a hundred copies on hand-made paper. HARRY CLARKE designed a title page and a series of seven decorative borders, which are used throughout the eight volumes. The granite book-rooms of the IRISH NATIONAL WAR MEMORIAL GARDENS designed by Sir EDWIN LUTYENS at Islandbridge, Dublin, were made to house the records, and a set is available there for consultation. **Timothy O'Neill**

Iremonger, Valentin (1918–1991), poet. Born in Dublin; educated at Synge Street CBS and Coláiste Mhuire. He entered the diplomatic service, serving as Irish ambassador to Sweden, Norway, Finland, and India. Awarded the Æ Memorial Prize in 1945, he was poetry editor of *Envoy*, 1949–51, and edited the Faber anthology *Contemporary Irish Poetry* (1949) with ROBERT GREACEN. *Reservations* (1950), a poetry collection, was republished in expanded form as *Horan's Field and Other Reservations* (1972). He wrote little poetry in later years but has kept his place in anthologies with poems such as 'This Hour Her Vigil', 'Shadows', 'Underworld', and 'Icarus'. **David Wheatley**

Ireton, Henry (1611–1651), soldier and politician. He first came to Ireland in June 1649 as second in command to OLIVER CROMWELL, his father-in-law. Apart from his service in Cromwell's campaign he undertook independent military activity in November 1649 in Cos. Kilkenny and Tipperary and in February 1650 captured Ardfinnan Castle. In May 1650 he assumed command of the army on Cromwell's return to England. In July he obtained the surrender of Carlow and followed this in August with the capture of Waterford and Duncannon; he had partial success at Athlone in September but achieved little else before retiring to winter quarters at Kilkenny in November 1650. He laid siege to Limerick from June to October 1651, but just after its surrender he caught the plague and died there on 26 November 1651. Legend has it that his final words were regret for having ordered the hanging of the Bishop of Emly, Terence Albert O'Brien, whom he blamed for his own imminent death, though there is no reliable basis for this story. Ireton was vehemently anti-Catholic and opposed any form of toleration, on the grounds that Catholics represented a permanent threat to the security of the state. A dedicated republican, he cared little for material possessions but was driven by a single-minded determination to achieve his aims. He married Oliver Cromwell's eldest daughter, Bridget; his widow subsequently married CHARLES FLEETWOOD (see p. 676). [see LIMERICK, SIEGE OF.] **Liam Irwin**

Irish abroad, the (1860–2000). Most Irish-born men in America and in Britain (if fewer elsewhere) were blue-collar or urban working people from the 1860s to the 1960s, if with a gradual broadening of callings and increasing skill levels. In 1950, 54.5 per cent of them in the United States were craftsmen, operatives, and labourers, as were over 50 per cent in Britain still in the 1990s. Immigrant women shifted in both societies from domestic service to other service tasks. The second generation was always better placed, with higher artisanal and clerical proportions, respectively.

Yet the immediate post-famine MIGRATION coincides with the origin of real changes in the fortunes of the Irish overseas in almost every receiving country. The upward mobility of tens of thousands of immigrants in the UNITED STATES, CANADA, AUSTRALIA, and even Britain by the Napoleonic or Jeffersonian period was now replicated from the late 1850s to 1914 in a vast social improvement within these countries, which paralleled the continuing EMIGRATION from Ireland itself. This era of long-cycle business growth saw a movement from slums to apartments to terrace housing, from hardship, labouring and domestic service to artisan skills and real savings, and thence to home-ownership and privately funded education at primary and secondary level. Acculturation and social integration variously accompanied these changes. The reality (or the real prospect) of all this moderated the militancy of organised Irish labour and the alienation of Irish NATIONALISM overseas. Both the beginnings and the degree of such change varied by locality. Earliest and therefore most striking in south-eastern Australia and California, improvement came last and was most limited in the industrial districts of Lancashire, south Wales, central Scotland, and New England. Even there, progress was real.

The most numerous cases of change were among the very large blue-collar and white-collar Irish-born and Irish-parented populations of NEW YORK, New Jersey, and Pennsylvania. Already by 1855 about a half of Irish-born males in New York city were artisans, many self-employed, while almost one in ten had white-collar employment or businesses. In 1900 New York state and city had 95,000 immigrant and second-generation Irishmen in the professions, in service and white-collar employment or in business management or ownership. Altogether one in five of all male New Yorkers were thus occupied. They made up both the largest Irish middle and lower middle-class group in the United States.

Smaller in numbers but larger as proportions of their Irish communities were those in such situations in the American Mid-West and the Canadian towns along the St Lawrence and Great Lakes, throughout eastern Australia, and (less well charted) in the English midlands and greater LONDON. All this was obscured by the arrival and initial (sometimes permanent) impoverishment of new generations of Irish from the western parts of Ireland, who dominated emigration after 1880. But newer migrants from other parts of Ireland (long literate and market-oriented) tended to benefit somewhat from the existing social gains of overseas cousins. Associations, churches and institutions built by 'their own kind' enhanced family esteem and prompted vital networks of job referral and local knowledge (as did saloons and schools).

An Irish farm population emerged that was collectively and visibly often the equal of its indigenous counterpart, most numerously so in America's upper Mid-West but proportionately strongest in New South Wales, Victoria, Ontario, and New Brunswick. Elsewhere the sheer scale of Irish social ascent was often hidden by the pell-mell growth and ethnic diversity of the larger late Victorian cities, if often clearer (and more organised) in towns of 50,000 to 100,000.

Most such ascent stemmed from calculated emigration from Ireland, and little enough from those who fled the Famine. Of approximately 8,000,000 emigrants from Ireland, 1815–1921, at most 2,500,000 left between 1846 and 1855, a third of whom would have left anyway at pre-famine emigration rates. 'Missing friends' and unsought 'disappeared ones' loom large among identified Famine emigrants. Upward mobility was low, but some did rise, if more simply survived high morbidity rates.

The existence of Irish born elites in all these countries encouraged general if more modest social ascent. Famous Irish-born (or Irish-parented) Americans, Canadians and Australians acted as both spur and model, regardless of their religious sub-group. The 480 Irish-born entries in the *Dictionary of Canadian Biography* for 1771–1920 account for one-twelfth of its entries, and the 326 Irish-born in the old *Dictionary of American Biography* are one-fortieth of its biographies, but both suggest open patterns in society. If in Canada the tilt to Protestant representation was marked, in Ontario this reflected Protestant preponderance among its Irish, as a similar tilt in all America before 1830 likewise did. Less representative, the Irish-born elites in Britain were said to be the reason that Ireland itself might accept its place in the United Kingdom, but their example was undercut by their usually ANGLO-IRISH background, by continuing mass emigration from Ireland, and by the then poorer prospects for the Irish in Britain.

By contrast, the working of democracy in the United States, and its gradual increase in Canada and Australia, made their Irish-born elites exemplars of decisive possibilities there. Careers fostered by political openness and public patronage, and those resulting from economic opportunity, also confirmed the progressive conservatism of most Irish immigrants, demonstrating the then conventional tie between representative politics, free exchange of information, and commercial prosperity. Lives as soldiers and religious had been early perceived as 'typical' avenues to Irish salience by others (as by themselves, whether Anglican or Catholic).

But from 1870 or so, businessmen, lawyers and politicians became more characteristic, reflecting the nature of liberal society. The pattern had been long dominant among Irish Presbyterians overseas (as in PHILADELPHIA, Baltimore and Albany from the 1780s to the 1820s). It was anticipated too by the small knots of Leinster and Munster families that had come to North America via trade skills in those years. Now it became a general thrust. Among the second generation, from 1870, the business-law-politics connections became overwhelming in both the United States and Canada. Businesses were inherited or transmitted in commerce and manufacturing. Breakthroughs to high-level banking and finance were not proportionately sustained except in Montréal, Toronto, Baltimore, and SAN FRANCISCO, whereas the second generation significantly increased its showing as factory-owners, independent wholesalers, transport and construction magnates, company officials, and industrial and commercial executives. Everywhere, lawyer-politicians, doctors, and teachers (the last almost all women) acted as constant links between both Irish and wider communities and between more stable, even stagnant immigrants and their upwardly bound fellows and offspring. In the past, religious leaders had been less able to do so because they were often confined to their roles among the Irish, and military and naval officers because they were clients in their own sub-culture.

Journalism was then the nervous system of democracy. Marked Irish entry to its metropolitan and communal outlets speeded social ascent by emphasising Irish concerns, setting them in the real, new contexts, and translating overseas cities into manageable human terms. All such elites owed much to the social and educational changes constant, if incomplete, in Ireland from the 1830s.

The convergence of large-scale industrialism and bigger businesses from c. 1900, with the passing of a workable farm frontier in the Americas and Australasia, together with rapid gains in overseas educational standards and their stagnation in Ireland, saw complex readjustment in Irish-born opportunity patterns. This was so even in skilled trades and led to a re-concentration in the larger cities abroad by the 1930s. Expanding white-collar and managerial posts in commerce, transport, construction, insurance, and government, and outlets for enterprise in services, education and consumer industries, were balanced by 'glass ceiling' restrictions in higher finance, banking and brokerage from c. 1920 until c. 1960, both for second-generation and for immigrant Irish. Newcomers from Ireland, often from unskilled, rural backgrounds, gained little in this, though those with secondary schooling, before the 1960s, were everywhere advantaged. Overseas, the general commitment from c. 1900 to secondary and increasingly tertiary education in the diaspora, with church support, reflected community recognition of the drag of its lack on many Irish emigrants. From 1924, and especially from 1965, immigration restrictions and quotas in America, and the shift to a more knowledge-based economy, redirected the flow of the unskilled to Britain and of the educated to America, Canada, and Australia. If in Britain livelihood was now less hard than before 1914, and cushioned by growing welfare state provisions, social ascent more usually came to the immigrants' children. In an encouraging final coda their children in turn enjoyed even greater ascent and integration, but this is scarcely 'Irish', taking place against backgrounds of full acculturation, multi-ethnic descent, and the intermarriage of 70 per cent and more of these emigrants' grandchildren.

So protean a history, European integration, rising prosperity and two decades of net immigration into Ireland (1966–76 and 1992–2002) have left it unclear whether general Irish emigration will resume, and, if so, towards what futures and destinations. **David Doyle**

Irish Academy of Letters, established in 1932 by GEORGE BERNARD SHAW and W. B. YEATS to promote creative literature and to combat censorship. Shaw and Yeats were elected president and vice-president, respectively. The original membership included AUSTIN CLARKE, PADRAIC COLUM, OLIVER ST JOHN GOGARTY, LENNOX ROBINSON, GEORGE WILLIAM RUSSEL (AE), JAMES STEPHENS, FRANK O'CONNOR, SEAN O'FAOLAIN, LIAM O'FLAHERTY, and SEAMUS O'SULLIVAN. Of the twenty-five academicians and ten associates invited to participate, JAMES JOYCE, DOUGLAS HYDE, DANIEL CORKERY, SEAN O'CASEY, and GEORGE MOORE refused. **Ciarán Deane**

Irish Agricultural Museum, established in 1975 and housed in the early nineteenth-century estate farmyard of Johnstown Castle, Co. Wexford. The extensive permanent displays include rural transport, farming equipment and COUNTRY FURNITURE from all over Ireland; the impressive study collection of more than 130 pieces of country furniture, reflecting regional variation, is second only to that of the NATIONAL MUSEUM OF IRELAND. There are three traditional farm kitchens, dating from 1800, 1900, and 1950. Large-scale reproductions of craft workshops include those of the blacksmith, wheelwright, cooper, harness-maker, and basket-maker. **Claudia Kinmonth**

Irish Agricultural Organisation Society (IAOS), founded to co-ordinate and promote the CO-OPERATIVE MOVEMENT. Now called the Irish Co-operative Organisation Society, the IAOS was founded by HORACE PLUNKETT in 1894. By 1904 there were 778 societies affiliated. Initially the IAOS maintained a staff of instructors in agriculture and co-operative organisation. In 1895 the weekly *Irish Homestead* was established to publicise the movement and its ideas. In the early twentieth century the IAOS head office was visited by agricultural reformers from many countries. **Carla King**

Irish-American nationalism. Wherever they settled, the American Irish founded organisations dedicated to the freedom of their country. As in Ireland, these organisations favoured one of two main approaches: constitutional NATIONALISM, which sought greater autonomy for Ireland within the BRITISH EMPIRE through gradual, peaceful change, and physical-force REPUBLICANISM, which insisted on outright independence by whatever means necessary.

The origins of Irish nationalism, on both sides of the Atlantic, can be traced to the republican movements of the 1790s. Branches of the Society of UNITED IRISHMEN, which demanded an independent republic, were formed in the United States in the 1790s, supporting Thomas Jefferson against his Federalist opponents. When the United Irishmen's rebellion of 1798 was crushed, many prominent Irish republicans came to the United States as political exiles, among them THOMAS ADDIS EMMET (1764–1827), W. J. MacNeven (1763–1841), and William Sampson (1764–1836). During the first half of the nineteenth century the primary aim of Irish nationalism was to repeal the ACT OF UNION (1800), which had abolished the Irish Parliament (though the Irish Executive continued to administer the country from DUBLIN CASTLE) (see p. 529). Led by DANIEL O'CONNELL, this 'REPEAL' MOVEMENT attracted followers throughout the United States—but O'Connell's outspoken support for the abolition of slavery eventually alienated most of his American supporters. Disaffected radicals in Ireland, meanwhile, launched the abortive 'YOUNG IRELAND' RISING OF 1848. Many of its leaders subsequently settled in America, the most influential being THOMAS FRANCIS MEAGHER and JOHN MITCHEL. The chief importance of the Young Irelanders in Irish-American history lies in their legacy to the FENIAN MOVEMENT of the 1860s. The Fenians were superseded in the 1870s by a new organisation, CLAN NA GAEL, under the leadership of JOHN DEVOY, the most formidable exponent of physical-force nationalism on either side of the Atlantic in the late nineteenth century.

Throughout this period, however, constitutional nationalism remained much more popular than hard-line republicanism in both the United States and Ireland. Its pre-eminent leader was CHARLES STEWART PARNELL, who led a mass movement for HOME RULE in the 1880s. Parnell entered into a strategic alliance with the land reformer and nationalist MICHAEL DAVITT and the hard-liner Devoy. Known as the 'NEW DEPARTURE,' this powerful but volatile alliance won the temporary support of such radical American and Irish-American social reformers as Henry George (1839–1897) and Patrick Ford (1837–1913). The New Departure soon crumbled, however, with moderate constitutional nationalists winning out over republican extremists and social radicals on both sides of the Atlantic. The home rule movement, in turn, fell apart in 1891 with the disgrace and early death of Parnell; and nationalism of all sorts went into temporary decline.

Irish-American nationalists reorganised themselves at the turn of the century. JOHN REDMOND, who reunited the various factions within the IRISH PARTY, visited the United States in 1901, where he helped found the United Irish League of America. Physical-force republicans also reunited at the turn of the century, with the ANCIENT ORDER OF HIBERNIANS and a rejuvenated Clan na Gael to the forefront. Under the leadership of John Devoy and Daniel Cohalan in New York and Joseph McGarrity in Philadelphia, the Clan continued to call for an independent republic in Ireland, to be achieved by force if necessary. It maintained close connections with the IRB in Dublin, provided the main link between the republican movement and the German government, and financed the visit to Germany by ROGER CASEMENT.

Irish-American hard-liners played an active role in planning the 1916 RISING. In the wake of 1916 Irish-Americans united almost unanimously behind the physical-force tradition, organising a new group, the Friends of Irish Freedom, to raise money for the cause of Irish independence; this group claimed more than 275,000 members at its peak in 1919. When the post-war settlement in Europe failed to recognise Ireland's right to self-determination, Irish-American nationalists lobbied strenuously against the ratification of the Treaty of Versailles. But when ÉAMON DE VALERA came to the United States in 1919–20 he broke with Devoy and Cohalan on this question, setting up his own organisation, the American Association for the Recognition of the Irish Republic, to ensure single-minded attention to the affairs of Ireland, rather than to American or international politics. The association quickly eclipsed the Friends of Irish Freedom, claiming some 800,000 members at its height in 1921.

After a forty-year hiatus Irish-American nationalism came alive once more with the outbreak of the 'TROUBLES' in Northern Ireland. The dominant figure in reviving the physical-force tradition in the United States was Michael Flannery, a veteran of the CIVIL WAR who had close ties with the newly founded PROVISIONAL IRA in Belfast. In 1970 he founded the Northern Ireland Aid Committee (Noraid), ostensibly for humanitarian relief in Northern Ireland but in reality to finance the purchase of arms and ammunition. Concerned with the growing appeal of physical-force nationalism, prominent Irish-American business and civic leaders created the Ireland Fund in 1976 to raise money for peaceful projects in Northern Ireland. Senator Edward Kennedy, Representative Tip O'Neill, Senator Daniel Patrick Moynihan, and Governor Hugh Carey of New York—known as the 'Four Horsemen'—came out in support of moderate constitutional nationalism, aligning themselves with JOHN HUME of the SDLP and issuing a joint condemnation of the IRA in 1977. Physical-force republicanism underwent a revival in the United States in the early 1980s with the posthumous election of the hunger-striker BOBBY SANDS as grand marshal of the New York ST PATRICK'S DAY parade in 1982 and the election of Michael Flannery the following year; but changes were already under way that would soon transform the political structure of Northern Ireland.

A combination of strategic reorientation within the republican movement and high-level political negotiations between Dublin and London paved the way for the transformation of the 1990s. From the early 1980s GERRY ADAMS, president of Sinn Féin, called increasingly for political as well as armed struggle. At the same time the ANGLO-IRISH AGREEMENT (1985) recognised for the first time some role for the Irish Government in the affairs of Northern Ireland. The resulting IRA ceasefire of 1994, followed by the historic BELFAST AGREEMENT (1998), fractured the republican movement in the United States as well as Ireland; but by the beginning of the twenty-first century, 200 years after the United Irishmen's insurrection, the mood among Irish nationalists on both sides of the Atlantic was one of cautious optimism. [see CANADA, IRISH IN; DIASPORA; UNITED STATES, IRISH IN.] **Kevin Kenny**

Irish Aviation Authority, originally the Air Navigation Services Office, established as a state company on 1 January 1994. It is responsible for the control of the 260,000 km^2 (100,000 sq. miles) of Irish air space up to 20,000 m (66,000 ft) through the Aeronautical Communications Station at Ballygireen, Co. Clare. It oversees safety standards in respect of the operation, maintenance and airworthiness of Irish-registered aircraft and the competence of Irish-licensed flight crew and aircraft maintenance engineers. It also provides an international consultancy service. **Bernard Share**

Irish aviators. A considerable number of Irish flyers joined the Royal Flying Corps (later the Royal Air Force) during the FIRST WORLD WAR. Typical of these was George McElroy, born in Donnybrook, Dublin, who served first in the trenches, where he was badly gassed. He transferred to the RFC at the beginning of 1917 and was posted to a fighter squadron; during seven months' service he scored forty-one victories, earning the Distinguished Flying Cross and bar. He was a comrade of another outstanding pilot of Irish extraction, 'Mick' Mannock, whose score reached sixty-one. These two pilots were lost within days of each other. Another ace was Oscar Heron from Armagh, who, during the last six months of the war, shot down ten aircraft, earning the Distinguished Flying Cross and other awards. He was an early member of the Air Corps and died in an air display accident in the Phoenix Park, Dublin, in 1933.

During the SECOND WORLD WAR flying Irishmen were prominent. Don Garland from Co. Wicklow won the VICTORIA CROSS during the battle for France in 1940; EUGENE ESMONDE from Co. Tipperary was later awarded this decoration for his gallantry during the 'Channel Dash' by German warships. Brendan 'Paddy' Finucane from Dublin was a top-scoring fighter-pilot active in the Battle of Britain; he was awarded the Distinguished Service Order and Distinguished Flying Cross with two bars in the autumn of 1941. All three lost their lives in action. **Donal MacCarron**

'Irish bars', or 'Irish pubs'. Public houses or 'pubs' fulfil a variety of social needs in Ireland: drink, conversation, and (since the 1960s) music and entertainment, though these priorities have changed with the introduction of television and bar food and the commercialisation of sports. The term 'Irish bar' is used only in relation to such establishments outside Ireland. Originating in the United States, they were renowned for a certain attitude to conversation and sociability, linked to the drinking of local brands of ALCOHOL. In Continental Europe after the 1960s 'Irish bars' specialised first in Irish beer and by the 1980s might include Irish music. In the 1990s 'Irish bars' became a profitable marketing concept, typified by wood decor, tourist iconography, Irish staff and Irish beer, and an aural smokescreen of traditional music. They are now to be found throughout the world, including Asia. Some are constructed according to off-the-peg designs, supplied ready-made in containers and sponsored by the GUINNESS BREWERY. While their 'difference' appeals to Europeans, their ubiquitousness also makes them convenient landmarks and meeting-places for Irish people abroad, particularly for travelling musicians, many of whom simultaneously regard them as merely pretentious kitsch. **Fintan Vallely**

Irish Brigades in Europe. Irish regiments became a feature of the armies of Spain and France in the seventeenth and eighteenth centuries. The earliest specifically Irish unit was formed in 1605 in the Spanish army, largely from men who had fought in the NINE YEARS' WAR (1593–1603). Five further Irish regiments were created between 1632 and 1646, the Thirty Years' War in central Europe (1618–48) providing a keen demand for new recruits. These regiments, which had been reduced to two in 1659, were disbanded in the 1680s. However, the War of the Spanish Succession (1701–13) saw the reintroduction of Irish regiments in the early eighteenth century, and these served with distinction until 1818, when they were finally disbanded.

The presence of specifically Irish units in the French army began in 1635 and was increased with the influx of the defeated Confederates in the 1650s. War with Spain ensured employment in the armies of both countries for the 30,000 soldiers who left Ireland after the Cromwellian conquest. In 1690 three Irish regiments were formed from the 5,000 Irish who were essentially swapped for the French force sent to Ireland by Louis XIV. The TREATY OF LIMERICK (1691) allowed the defeated JACOBITE army to go to France, where at first it served the exiled JAMES II and in 1697 became part of the French military establishment. The Irish Brigades in the French army retained their distinctive character until the Revolution, finally losing their names and separate identity in 1791.

While the Irish were both numerous and prominent in the Habsburg and Russian imperial armies, no specifically Irish units were created. **Liam Irwin**

Irish Business and Employers' Confederation (IBEC), the national organisation of employers, providing economic, commercial, employee relations and social affairs services to some 4,000 companies and organisations in the Republic in all areas of economic and commercial activity; its total membership (including indirect members) is approximately 6,000. It began as the Federated Union of Employers, the first national organisation of employers, established in 1942 in response to the requirement in the Industrial Relations Act (1941) that employers' organisations as well as TRADE UNIONS should hold a negotiating licence; it was renamed the Federation of Irish Employers in 1990. IBEC was established in 1993 as a result of a merger between the FIE and the Confederation of Irish Industries, combining employment and industrial interests in a single organisation. IBEC also represents the interests of business in other institutions, including the NATIONAL ECONOMIC AND SOCIAL COUNCIL, and is also represented in UNICE, the umbrella federation of employers' and business organisations in the EUROPEAN UNION. **Niamh Hardiman**

Irish Chamber Orchestra, originally founded in 1963 by JANOS FÜRST, disbanded 1966. Reformed in 1970 by André Prieur as the New Irish Chamber Orchestra and disbanded in 1994. This ensemble toured internationally, including Russia and China. In 1995 a completely new ensemble, the Irish Chamber Orchestra, was established and is based at the University of Limerick, under the artistic direction of the violinist FIONNUALA HUNT until 2002, when she was succeeded by Katherine Hunka. In addition to its concert schedule, the orchestra's activities include commissioning and performing new works, recording classical and contemporary works, organising the Killaloe International Music Festival, and managing a schools and community outreach scheme. **John Page and Richard Pine**

Irish Christian Brothers: see CHRISTIAN BROTHERS.

Irish Church Music Association, founded to implement the recommendations of the SECOND VATICAN COUNCIL on music and the liturgy, and to promote Irish music within that objective. The association was founded in 1969 under the direction of Cardinal William Conway. Its main activity is the annual summer school that meets in the first week of July; there is also a reunion 'Cecilian Date' meeting in November. The association is administered by a council of twelve members chosen through annual elections for a term of three years. **John Page**

Irish Brigades. *French engraving of soldiers in Irish regiments of the French army, where many were 'Wild Geese', emigrants who fled from English persecution at home to find employment with Catholic armies on the Continent. [Council of Trustees of the National Library of Ireland]*

Irish Citizen, newspaper of the Irish Women's Franchise League. It first appeared on 25 May 1912 as a weekly but later became a monthly and then began to appear less frequently. HANNA SHEEHY SKEFFINGTON was its editor for some of this time. Its slogan was 'For Men and Women Equality, the Rights of Citizenship'. Articles covered the suffrage movement around the world, court cases involving women, and news of visiting suffragists. In 1920 its presses were smashed by the BLACK AND TANS and it ceased publication. **Clíona Murphy**

Irish Citizen Army, founded on 13 November 1913 by JAMES CONNOLLY, on the suggestion of Captain James (Jack) White. Its original role was to protect labour rallies and to oppose EVICTIONS during the DUBLIN LOCK-OUT. Drawn largely from members of the IRISH TRANSPORT AND GENERAL WORKERS' UNION, its early membership fluctuated between 100 and 400. In 1914 JIM LARKIN transformed it into a uniformed military force and associated it with the IRISH VOLUNTEERS. After Larkin emigrated in October 1914 Connolly urged republicans to revolt while England was at war, and he led 210 (out of a total 340) Citizen Army men and women into the 1916 RISING. They were positioned mainly in St Stephen's Green and the College of Surgeons. Eleven were killed in action, and Connolly and MICHAEL MALLIN were subsequently shot by firing squad. The Citizen Army was reconstituted in 1917 under James O'Neill, but it remained virtually inactive. O'Neill was replaced in January 1922 by John Hanratty, who resisted efforts by the ITGWU to incorporate the force into a workers' army that

Irish Citizen Army. *Born out of the struggle between workers and employers during the Dublin 1913 Lock-Out, the Irish Citizen Army was formed to defend the men and women on strike from attacks by the Dublin Metropolitan Police. They are pictured here outside the old Liberty Hall under the banner We serve neither King nor Kaiser, but Ireland. [Council of Trustees of the National Library of Ireland; KE198]*

would be neutral in the event of civil war. On the outbreak of the CIVIL WAR the Citizen Army was in practice assimilated into the IRA; 143 members fought with republican units (see p. 3). **Emmet O'Connor**

Irish cloak, a full, sleeveless cloak stretching to the ankles and with one fastening of ribbons and a hook and eye in front under the chin, the standard outer garment for women throughout Ireland during most of the nineteenth century. The body of the cloak had tight rucking or pleating across the back and on the shoulders; attached to the back and sides was a large, tightly pleated rectangular hood. The heyday of the hooded cloak was in the closing decades of the nineteenth century, when the wives of wealthier farmers wore it as a status symbol. Previously, in the earlier and poorer decades of the nineteenth century, the cloak was a necessary garment for hiding rags and for providing night-time warmth for as many family members as could lie under it.

Red had been a fashionable colour for the hooded cloak in the eighteenth century. Blue became the prevailing colour in the early nineteenth century, replaced by navy blue and black during the years of Victorian respectability. In its heyday the cloak was made from finely woven broadcloth, a material that replaced the traditional frieze or heavy WOOLLEN cloth of earlier years. During this time also the cloak was predominantly worn by married women, and it became a prized possession, to be handed down from a woman to her eldest daughter. In many areas a cloak was bought by a bride's father as a wedding present.

The hooded cloak was still worn in parts of Munster in the 1940s and 50s as an item of everyday dress; it was last worn in Co. Cork in and around Bantry, Ballingeary, Clonakilty, Macroom, Kinsale, Ballyvourney, and Dunmanway. In Carbery, Co. Cork, the following materials and costs incurred in the making of a hooded cloak were recorded in 1940:

4 yards of 54″ black cloak cloth at 24 shillings per yard
3 yards 36″ black sateen at 3 shillings per yard
1 yard black satin 30 shillings per yard
6–7 yards black cord
3–4 yards black silk ribbon

[see IRISH MANTLE.] **Anne O'Dowd**

Irish coffee, a drink whose creation is attributed to the barman Joe Sheridan at Foynes flying-boat restaurant in 1943. It is served in most pubs and restaurants in Ireland and many abroad. Hot strong coffee is poured into a warmed whiskey glass, sugar is added to taste, and half an inch of Irish WHISKEY. A teaspoon is held across the glass, bowl side down, and a tablespoonful of double cream is poured over it so that it floats on the surface. **John Wakeman**

Irish colleges in Europe. Following the Council of Trent, colleges were established in various European cities to provide a

Catholic clerical elite who would spearhead the COUNTER-REFORMATION in Ireland. The first Irish college was founded under Philip II's patronage at SALAMANCA in 1592. In 1611 there were twelve Irish colleges in Spain, France, and the Low Countries; by 1690 there were thirty colleges throughout Europe. Recent research shows that many lay students attended these colleges, while a substantial number of Irish clerics who trained in these colleges remained on the Continent. However, there is no doubt that the work of those who did return to Ireland was decisive in checking the REFORMATION in the seventeenth and the eighteenth centuries.

Most colleges were run by religious orders, including the Dominicans, Capuchins, Augustinians, and Carmelites, though the most influential were the FRANCISCANS and the JESUITS. Prevailing regional and national rivalries in Ireland were reflected in the colleges. There were bitter disputes between 'OLD ENGLISH' and native Irish students in the seventeenth century, with the Jesuits regarded as being biased towards Old English applicants. Salamanca was accused of favouring Munster students, while Alcalá was founded exclusively for Ulstermen. Regional biases were accentuated by endowments that specified the sponsorship of students from particular parishes or dioceses.

Competition between colleges for funds was fierce. Colleges in Spanish realms received grants from the crown, local universities, or municipalities; otherwise money came from local alms or contributions made by the local Irish merchant and military community.

With the demise of Spanish power in Europe, many Irish colleges in Spain and the Low Countries got into serious financial difficulty. The growing Irish merchant community in France and the presence of the IRISH BRIGADE there ensured that after 1691 the Irish colleges in France became more influential. With the suppression of these colleges in 1793, ST PATRICK'S COLLEGE, Maynooth, became the leading Irish seminary. **Gráinne Henry**

Irish Congress of Trade Unions (ICTU), the national umbrella organisation for trade unions, representing members in the Republic and Northern Ireland. It was established in 1894 as the Irish Trades Union Congress. In 1912 the ITUC helped to establish the Irish LABOUR PARTY; they became separate in 1930. In 1945 the ITUC suffered a split when a number of unions formed an alternative Congress of Irish Unions; the two federations reunited in 1959. From the 1960s the ICTU has developed a range of advisory functions for its affiliates, including assisting with the rationalisation of trade union structures and activities. It became involved in a variety of consultative and policy-making bodies, most notably, since 1987, in processes of SOCIAL PARTNERSHIP. It is also affiliated to the European Trade Union Confederation. Total membership in 2000 was estimated at 726,000, in sixty-three unions, forty-eight of which organise 521,000 members in the Republic and thirty-three of which organise 204,900 members in Northern Ireland. Through its Northern Ireland Committee the ICTU has striven to maintain a politically neutral stance throughout the period of the TROUBLES. [see TRADE UNIONS.] **Niamh Hardiman**

Irish Convention (1917–18), constituted in July 1917 by LLOYD GEORGE to frame a scheme of self-government for Ireland 'within the Empire.' Chaired by Sir HORACE PLUNKETT, the Convention was attended by more than a hundred delegates representing NATIONALISM and UNIONISM. Crucially, SINN FÉIN boycotted it. Moderate nationalists and southern unionists agreed a scheme for self-government, but Ulster unionists rejected the proposals and instead proposed that Ireland be partitioned. **Thomas Hennessey**

Irish Countrywomen's Association (ICA), founded in 1910 at Bree, Co. Wexford, by ANITA LETTS as the Society of United Irishwomen, renamed Irish Countrywomen's Association in 1934. By the 1940s it had become a significant presence in Irish life, providing rural women with a social outlet and educational opportunities. Its summer schools, first held in 1929, found permanent expression from 1954 in its residential college, An Grianán, at Termonfeckin, Co. Louth. Despite its determinedly non-political stance it gave countrywomen a public voice, playing a vital part in the piped water and rural electrification campaigns of the early 1960s, and continues to articulate the concerns of large numbers of Irishwomen within a traditional framework. [see GAHAN, MURIEL; IRISH HOUSEWIVES' ASSOCIATION.] **Rosemary Raughter**

Irish Countrywomen's Association. *ICA guild members, surrounded by examples of embroidered and woven cushion covers, leatherwork, and knitting, examine a child's sweater made by a member [Irish Countrywomen's Association]*

Irish dance. Traditional dancing in Ireland has long included both solo and group forms. Solo dancing is seen as an expression of individual artistic creativity. It is essentially individualistic: its purpose is to entertain, to intrigue and to amaze the onlooker. The solo dance repertoire includes the JIG, REEL, and HORNPIPE tempos, as well as a number of specialised dances set to a particular tune, such as the 'Job of Journeywork'. Group dancing is fundamentally social dancing. Its forms include couple dances, such as the *barn dance*, the *Schottische*, and the old-time waltz, and two, four, six, eight, and sixteen-hand formations, danced mainly to jig and reel tempos and their variants. Before the nineteenth century the two, four, and sixteen-hand reels and jigs held sway; towards the end of the century the newer sets were grafted on to the older forms (see pp. 568, 934). **Helen Brennan**

Irish dance abroad. Emigrant ships are where the records of Irish dancing among the DIASPORA probably began. Musicians and dancing-masters were evident among ships' crews involved in long sea crossings; and this idea is supported by such well-known dances as the sailor's hornpipe. Little detail is available about the specific nature of the dances and footwork, but some evidence can be found in areas where the emigrants eventually settled, such as the Appalachian Mountains of the UNITED STATES.

The tradition of Irish dancing was practised by settlers around the world; and while many of the original forms were maintained, gradual evolution occurred as immigrants integrated their dances with, and were influenced by, existing cultures, for example the Kerry four-hand in Florida, American tap dancing, and popular minstrel dances. In more recent years voluntary emigrants and their descendants, seeking to re-create the culture they left behind, or perhaps their nostalgic recall of the 'old country', supported the emergence of modern dancing-masters through classes, competitions, festivals, feiseanna, and céilithe. Research shows that these events have acted as important social gatherings for Irish communities outside Ireland and have continued to attract those of Irish descent. Not surprisingly, Irish dancing has also provided the diaspora with a passageway through which to make regular visits to the homeland to compete in the dancing championships and attend other dance festivals. Many dancers in England and the United States attend festivals in Ireland.

Irish dancing has always been inextricably linked with the political status of Ireland. The emergence of the 'CELTIC TIGER' phenomenon resulted in a positive image and created interest from other cultures. This is particularly evident in SET-DANCING communities in Britain, where the attendance is made up, almost equally, of those of Irish origin and those who are not. Set-dancing communities also exist in areas not noted for Irish immigrant communities, including Tokyo. Perhaps the most powerful illustration of the new-found confidence of Irish dancing internationally was the 'RIVERDANCE' phenomenon of the late 1990s, as well as other Irish dance stage shows. Not only do troupes made up of dancers from the diaspora perform at all the leading Western cultural venues and beyond, but the dance demonstrates continual evolution. Choreographers and dancers such as Colin Dunne, MICHAEL FLATLEY, and Jean Butler have extended the influence of Irish dancing in a way that increasingly transcends its national origins and boundaries.

Academic interest has not developed at a rate equivalent to that of Irish music. However, in 1995 the Irish World Music Centre at the University of Limerick introduced Irish dance as a subject for academic and practical study at master's degree level. The resulting research included detailed records of practices outside Ireland, with a specific theoretical emphasis on such elements as identity, culture, and revival. [see IRISH MUSIC IN NORTH AMERICA.] **Bernadette A. Twomey**

Irish dance costumes, originally based on 'national costumes' introduced after the foundation of the GAELIC LEAGUE in 1893. They consisted of a *brat* (CLOAK) attached to one or both shoulders by replica TARA BROOCHES, with limited embroidery on the dress and cloak. During the later decades of the twentieth century women's costumes became highly adorned with interlace EMBROIDERY, appliqué, rhinestones, and sequins, together with ornate tiaras and other head-dress. For men, a kilt, jacket, and cloak replaced shirt and knee-breeches in the 1920s, but they in turn have been replaced recently by shirt and trousers, so that while women's costumes have become more elaborate, the men's costumes have become simpler. **John P. Cullinane**

Irish dance. *Set dancing on the pier, Clougher Head, Co. Louth, 1935; the dance and music session providing sociable community gathering. [Courtesy of the Department of Irish Folklore, University College, Dublin. N110.1500014; photo: Maurice Curtin]*

Irish Examiner, a daily newspaper published in Cork. It was founded as the *Cork Examiner* in 1841 by John Francis Maguire; when he died, in 1872, Thomas Crosbie became sole owner, and it has been controlled by the Crosbie family since. In 1996 it dropped 'Cork' from the title and in 2000 added 'Irish' to raise its national appeal among mid-market titles, but it made few gains against the Dublin nationals. The circulation is approximately 64,000. Since 1894 the Examiner Group has published the *Evening Echo* in Cork; it also has interests in provincial weeklies. **Eddie Holt**

Irish Exhibition of Living Art, 1943–87, an annual exhibition of visual art, founded on the suggestion of Sybil Le Brocquy after the rejection of work by her son, LOUIS LE BROCQUY, and other artists for the 1942 and 1943 annual exhibitions of the ROYAL HIBERNIAN ACADEMY. The inaugural committee comprised Louis Le Brocquy, NORAH MCGUINNESS, JACK HANLON, and MAINIE JELLETT, who was elected chairwoman; co-opted members were Lawrence Campbell, Margaret Clarke, Ralph Cusack, EVIE HONE, and Elizabeth Curran. The stated aim of the exhibition was 'to give a comprehensive survey of significant work, irrespective of school, or manner, by living Irish artists,' and to this end it incorporated a broad spectrum of artists and styles. Any resident Irish artist could submit work for selection by the committee, so that—like the RHA—it was an open-submission show.

The first exhibition opened on 16 September 1943 at the National College of Art, Dublin, and received a generally positive critical response, with about 5,000 visitors attending. There were 168 works in the exhibition, together with a retrospective of the work of JEROME CONNOR. From 1944 work by non-Irish artists was included, and a number of leading Continental artists exhibited. The practice of featuring a particular nationality began in 1944 with a selection of works by progressive English artists, such as Henry Moore, Ben Nicholson, and John Piper; the following year the French Provisional Government lent work; in 1964 paintings by Robert Motherwell, Willem de Kooning, and Robert Rauschenberg were featured.

Lectures and occasionally films on contemporary art accompanied later shows. The exhibition quickly established itself as the foremost showcase of Irish art in the late 1940s and 50s. From 1964 P. J. Carroll and Company, cigarette manufacturers, sponsored annual prizes, with a category for artists under the age of forty. These were adjudicated by curators of international standing.

The importance of the IELA in providing a forum for non-academic art lessened in the 1960s with the growth in commercial galleries, such as the Hendricks, the setting up of the Independent Artists, and the establishment of Rosc. In 1972 McGuinness, who had become chairwoman after the death of Jellett in 1944, resigned, and a new committee, chaired by BRIAN KING, took over. The 1972 exhibition, held at the Project Arts Centre, was distinguished by overtly political art by ROBERT BALLAGH and PATRICK IRELAND. The following year a new section, for work executed in experimental multimedia, was initiated; and installation and conceptual art became dominant in the exhibitions of the 1970s.

In 1982, because of the lack of a suitable venue, the show took the form of a book; and the following year no exhibition was held. With the proliferation of alternative shows, and the increasing number of gallery spaces, the IELA was losing its identity as an avant-garde event. The last exhibition was held in 1987. **Róisín Kennedy**

Irish Export Board: see CORAS TRÁCHTÁLA.

Irish Georgian Society. *Restoration work being carried out on stucco plasterwork at No. 20 Dominic Street, Dublin. The conservation of distinguished examples of architecture and the applied arts is central to the Society's work. [Irish Georgian Society]*

Irish Film Centre: see FILM INSTITUTE OF IRELAND.

Irish Free State: see IRELAND, REPUBLIC OF; IRELAND, NAMES OF.

Irish Georgian Society (IGS), founded in 1958 by DESMOND GUINNESS and his wife, Mariga Guinness, for the protection of buildings of architectural merit. Today the society has a worldwide membership and promotes the awareness and conservation of architecture and the allied arts of all periods in Ireland. It achieves this through education, grants, participation in planning, and fund-raising. It has succeeded in saving many fine buildings under threat, including CASTLETOWN, Co. Kildare, Doneraile Court, Co. Cork, and the Tailors' Hall, Dublin. From 1958 the society published a *Bulletin* of original research on Ireland's architectural and artistic heritage; since 1998 it has published the annual journal *Irish Architectural and Decorative Studies*. **Eve McAulay**

Irish grammatical tracts. The grammatical and syntactical tracts are found for the most part in MANUSCRIPTS of the sixteenth and seventeenth centuries and probably took their present shape about the beginning of the sixteenth century. They represent the distillation of bardic teaching and training in Classical Modern Irish over a period of some 400 years, and they are our most important source of information on the classical language of early modern verse. Never before in the history of the IRISH LANGUAGE had such detailed and painstaking analysis of its morphology, particularly the morphology of the noun and the verb, been undertaken, and nowhere else will there be found more copious illustration of the correct use of language than in the 4,000 citations from bardic verse that these tracts contain. These bear witness not only to the care with which the language was studied but also to the fact that so much of the literary output of the period has been lost. Of the 4,000 citations only a tenth have been identified so far from the surviving corpus, and these show that the thirteenth to the fifteenth centuries were regarded by the bardic grammarians as the golden era of classical verse. [see BARDIC DUNAIRE; CLASSICAL IRISH POETRY; EARLY MODERN IRISH PROSE; IRISH LANGUAGE; IRISH LANGUAGE, EARLY MODERN; IRISH LANGUAGE, MIDDLE; IRISH LANGUAGE, OLD.] **Damian McManus**

Irish Housewives' Association, founded in 1942 by HILDA TWEEDY, Andrée Sheehy Skeffington and others as a non-party, non-sectarian women's organisation, maintaining a voice on women's issues and consumers' rights from the 1940s to the 1980s. As an affiliate of the International Alliance of Women it provided a link with the international WOMEN'S MOVEMENT of the 1960s; in 1968 it was instrumental in creating an *ad hoc* committee seeking the establishment of a National Commission on the STATUS OF WOMEN. A largely middle-class and urban organisation, it failed to attract younger members, and it dissolved in 1992. **Rosemary Raughter**

Irish Hudibras, The (1689), a coarse verse travesty of the sixth book of Virgil's *Aeneid*, ingeniously adapted to the political and social scene in Fingall (north Co. Dublin) in the 1680s, when it was written. It tells, in crude but energetic HIBERNO-ENGLISH, of the descent of the hero, Nees, into the Netherworld and of his dead father's prophecy that the JACOBITE cause would be lost. The poem is important for the insight it gives into Irish life and because several passages are in the FINGALLIAN dialect. Learned footnotes show that its anonymous anti-Catholic author was familiar with histories of Ireland written in both Latin and Irish. **Andrew Carpenter**

Irish Independent: see INDEPENDENT NEWS AND MEDIA.

Irish-language films. The first sound film in Irish was a short, *Oidhche Sheanchais* (1935), made by the American-born Robert Flaherty shortly after his *Man of Aran* (1934). It was not until the late 1940s that film-making in Irish became more frequent, when Government-sponsored information films on health and safety began to be produced in both Irish and English. In the mid-1950s GAEL-LINN pioneered a cinema newsreel, *Amharc Éireann* (A View of Ireland), which ran from 1956 to 1964. Gael-Linn also made a number of documentaries, most notably two directed by GEORGE MORRISON, MISE ÉIRE (1959) and SAOIRSE? (1961), which traced the struggle for independence up to the outbreak of the CIVIL WAR in 1922. Gael-Linn continued producing documentaries until the early 1970s, mostly directed by LOUIS MARCUS. By then RTÉ had taken on this role through its news, current affairs, and occasional drama productions. Following a long campaign by language activists, including BOB QUINN, a pioneer of Irish-language fiction films with CAOINEADH AIRT UÍ LAOGHAIRE (1975), the Irish-language television station Teilifís na Gaeilge (now TG4) began broadcasting in 1995. **Kevin Rockett**

Irish-language journalism. AN CLAIDHEAMH SOLUIS, founded in 1899 as the newspaper of the GAELIC LEAGUE, was the first Irish-language paper to achieve wide circulation. Edited by EOIN MACNEILL and PATRICK PEARSE, it had several changes of title, including *Fáinne an Lae* (1918–19, 1922–30) and *Misneach* (1919–22), briefly reverting to the original title in 1930–31. During the first quarter of the twentieth century many other publications followed, most published by Irish-revival organisations or political groups. The longest-surviving Irish-language paper, *Inniu*, was published for more than forty years before it closed in 1984; *Amárach* and *Anois* have since come and gone. During the Gaeltacht revolution (1969–73) *Tuairisc* and *Iris Iarchonnacht* were published in south Connemara. The current Irish-language weeklies are *Lá* (1984–), published in Belfast, and *Foinse* (1996–), published in Connemara. The *Irish Press* published Irish-language journalism, and the IRISH TIMES publishes 'Tuarascáil', a weekly half page in Irish.

Periodicals and academic journals include CONRADH NA GAEILGE's *Feasta* (1948–), the left-wing republican *An tÉireannach* (1935–7), *An tUltach* (1924–), and *Comhar* (1942–), a political and literary journal, whose early contributors included FRANK O'CONNOR, CONOR CRUISE O'BRIEN, BRENDAN BEHAN, and MYLES NA GCOPALEEN. [see IRISH LANGUAGE; IRISH, RESTORATION OF.] **Eddie Holt**

Irish-language theatre. Theatre in Irish is either very ancient or relatively recent, depending on the definition of 'theatre'. An account of the banqueting hall at TARA in the seventh century, the Teach Míochuarta, found in the twelfth-century BOOK OF LEINSTER identifies sharply defined classes of performers, ranging from the OLLAMH (professor of poetry), through the *cleasamhnach* (juggler or trickster) and *seanchaí* (reciter of lore) down to the *braighideoir*, who entertained his master by breaking wind. What is missing from these early records, however, is any conclusive evidence of performances based on personification, in which a performer takes on the identity of another person.

If we define theatre as performance involving personification, there is no theatre in Irish until the beginning of the twentieth century. At the very least we can say that Irish-language drama came into being with DOUGLAS HYDE's CASADH AN TSÚGÁIN, first performed on 21 October 1901. In the early years of the Irish LITERARY REVIVAL there were strong arguments for the development of an Irish-language theatre tradition. PIARAS BÉASLAÍ, for instance, formed a company to tour Irish-speaking regions in 1913, for which he wrote thirteen plays. However, with theatre culture concentrated on the east coast and the principal Irish-speaking communities clustered along the west coast, theatre in Irish struggled for existence. It was not until 1928 that the first professional theatre, TAIBHDHEARC NA GAILLIMHE, opened in Galway with MÍCHEÁL MAC LIAMMÓIR's *Diarmuid agus Gráinne*.

The Taibhdhearc developed an extensive repertoire, performing both translations and original works and introducing writers such as MÁIRÉAD NÍ GHRÁDA. From 1923 to 1942 it was joined by An Comhar Drámaíochta of Dublin, which made use of the ABBEY THEATRE's second stage, the Peacock, and from 1955 to 1970 by An Club Drámaíochta, working from the Damer Theatre, Dublin, where it premiered BRENDAN BEHAN's AN GIALL (1958). Meanwhile, under the stewardship of ERNEST BLYTHE, the Abbey made strenuous (but often misguided) efforts at staging Irish-language theatre in the 1940s and 50s, performing short plays as after-pieces to English-language productions and presenting an annual Christmas pantomime in Irish. When the new Abbey building opened in 1966 the Peacock was intended as the home of productions in Irish, and the Abbey had an Irish-language touring company; however, within a decade the amount of Irish-language theatre at the Abbey was minimal.

Nonetheless, theatre in Irish at the beginning of the twenty-first century continues to have a strong institutional base. In addition to the Taibhdhearc there are two professional Irish-language companies—Aisling Ghéar (Belfast) and Amharclann de hÍde (Dublin)—as well as a support organisation for AMATEUR AND COMMUNITY THEATRE, An Comhlachas Náisiúnta Drámaíochta. **Christopher Morash**

Irish language, a member of the Gaelic or GOIDELIC branch of the Celtic languages, along with (Scottish) Gaelic and Manx. By the fifth century AD Irish was established as the predominant language. Irish-speaking settlements were established in Britain, and, following a period of expansion, the language was spoken throughout what is modern Scotland by the eleventh century. In Ireland a decline set in following the ANGLO-NORMAN CONQUEST from 1169, but by the fourteenth century Irish was once again the predominant vernacular. This time, however, the language was absent from legal and administrative affairs in cities and towns, a factor that weakened its status in important areas of life. In the sixteenth and seventeenth centuries the structures of traditional Irish society were destroyed as English rule was consolidated through the Elizabethan and Cromwellian settlements, the Williamite campaign, and the PENAL LAWS.

By the end of the eighteenth century almost half the population were still monoglot Irish-speakers, consisting primarily of the rural poor. This class was decimated by the GREAT FAMINE of 1845–50 and by subsequent emigration: by 1851 the number of Irish-speakers had declined to a quarter of the population. Forty years later, monoglot Irish-speakers amounted to only 1 per cent.

The first significant organisation dedicated to language revival, rather than mere preservation, the Society for the Preservation of the Irish Language (Cumann Buan-Choimeádta na Gaeilge), was established in 1876. One of its main aims was that the language be taught in the national schools, from which it had been absent since the Education Act (1831). IRISH-LANGUAGE JOURNALISM emerged during the same period with the publication of newspapers such as *Fáinne an Lae* (1898–1900, 1918–19) and AN CLAIDHEAMH SOLUIS (1899–1932) (see p. 553). The development of print media was important for a language that had all but ceased to be a vehicle of written communication.

The GAELIC LEAGUE (Conradh na Gaeilge), established in 1893, played a leading role both in securing native government and in consolidating policies for Irish in the new state. Though some historians have accused it of romanticising the poverty of the Irish-speaking west, leading figures in the movement repeatedly called for the economic development of Irish-speaking districts to be linked to that of the country as a whole. The League was highly successful in its early years: there were forty-three branches in 1897 but by 1904 there were 600, with an estimated membership of 50,000. While the organisation failed to arrest the decline of the traditional Irish-speaking districts, its influence on the new state's educational policy was considerable.

When the IRISH FREE STATE was established, the Government began a process of attempting to reverse the dramatic language shift. Irish was designated the national language in the Constitution; it became a core subject of the school curriculum; and competence in it was necessary for employment in the public service. In 1937 the CONSTITUTION OF IRELAND (Article 8) designated Irish the 'first official language' as it was the 'national language', while English was

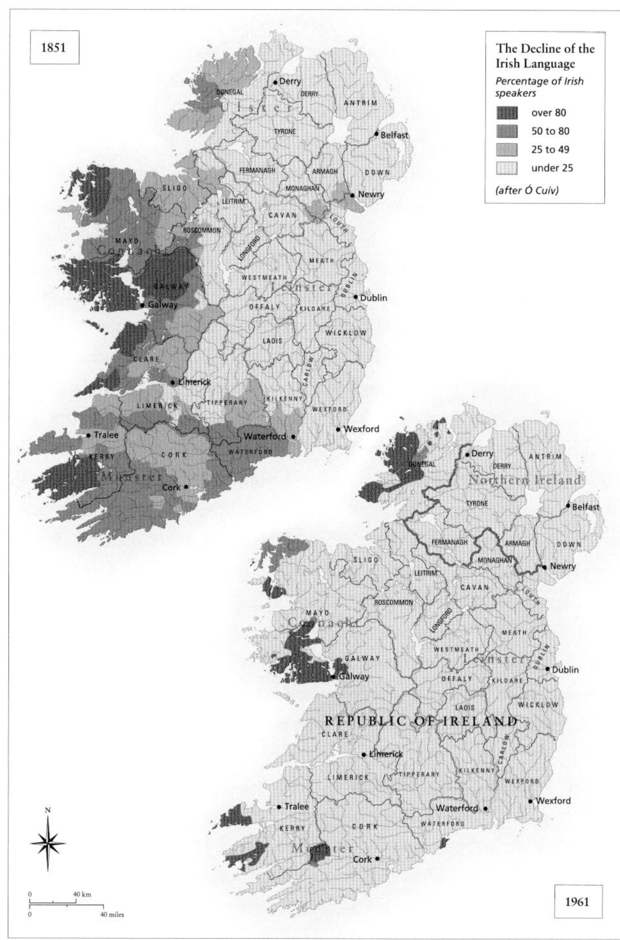

recognised as 'a second official language'. As no legislation exists to underpin the constitutional protection for Irish, citizens have frequently taken the state to court to achieve their rights. However, in 2002 the Government published the Official Languages (Equality) Bill, which, if passed, would oblige certain state agencies to provide a bilingual service.

Irish is spoken as a minority language throughout Ireland. The 1996 census indicates that 1.43 million people (43.5 per cent) in the Republic over the age of three are Irish-speakers. This includes a high number of second-language learners and those who have chosen Irish as their primary language as well as 86,039 residents of Irish-speaking districts. The apparently high figure masks variable levels of competence and frequency of use: based on an analysis of adults only, it has been estimated that 70,950 people speak Irish every day, 20,813 of them in the GAELTACHT. Taking the population of the state as a whole, it is thought that about 5 per cent have a high active competence in Irish, a further 10 per cent have a good competence, while a further 20–30 per cent have a lower passive ability in the language. Surveys reveal a high level of support for Irish as a symbol of identity, for the competent teaching of Irish in schools, and for policies supporting the Gaeltacht.

One of the most notable aspects of language revival in recent years has been the steady growth of Irish-medium schools. In the Republic in 2001 there were 174 such schools, both primary and secondary, compared with sixteen in 1972. Between 1990 and 2001 alone the number of pupils in Irish-medium education increased from 15,990 to 28,501. A limited number of degree courses through the medium of Irish are available.

In Northern Ireland the government supports Irish-medium education at pre-school, primary, and secondary level. The 1991 census in Northern Ireland revealed that 142,003 people (about 10 per cent of the population) were able to speak Irish. This figure includes a higher proportion of nationalists than unionists and is also thought to reflect varying degrees of competence. Legally, Irish in Northern Ireland is granted protection under the Belfast Agreement (1998), whereby the British government agrees to promote the language. The agreement also paved the way for the establishment of an all-Ireland body for the promotion of Irish and ULSTER SCOTS. The Irish-language section of this body, Foras na Gaeilge, has offices in Dublin and Belfast. Irish in Northern Ireland was given an additional boost in 2001 when the British government ratified the European Charter for Regional or Minority Languages.

There have been significant developments in Irish-language media in recent years. The radio station Raidió na Gaeltachta was established in 1972 and now broadcasts twenty-four hours a day. In 1996 a bilingual television station, Teilifís na Gaeilge (now TG4), began broadcasting. It received €22.89 million from the exchequer in 2001 and approximately €9.5 million from other sources. There are two weekly newspapers: *Foinse*, published in Connemara (circulation of up to 10,000), and *Lá*, published in Belfast (circulation of 3,500). English-language media, broadcast and print, carry smaller amounts of material in Irish. Excluding school textbooks, approximately 100 titles were published in Irish in 2001. [see IRISH LANGUAGE, RESTORATION OF.] **John Walsh**

Irish language abroad. Irish is a member of the Celtic branch of the Indo-European family of languages, which includes the other GOIDELIC languages (Gaelic and Manx) as well as the Brythonic group (Welsh, Breton, and Cornish). It was first used outside Ireland during the Goidelic expansion from DÁL RIADA c. AD 500, becoming dominant as a first language in Scotland until the introduction of the feudal system.

Among the DIASPORA of the modern era (seventeenth century onwards), monolingual Irish-speakers have always been a minority, and the language rarely had the function of a first language in the new territories, though it often survived as an ancillary language, functioning as a national identifier. Moreover, certain emigrant destinations were more critical than others for the survival or revival of Irish among subsequent generations, who were encouraged to maintain the language as a symbol of their bond with Ireland.

The EMIGRATION of Irish-speakers to towns in Britain began during the Plantation period and reached a climax, especially among the poor, during the GREAT FAMINE. Montague Gore in 1851 described this influx as 'squalid children, haggard men … many speaking Irish.' While it is difficult to ascertain the extent to which the language was maintained into the second and third generations, by the end of the nineteenth century a number of societies had been established for the maintenance of Irish. The most powerful and effective of these was a branch of the GAELIC LEAGUE established in London in 1881. As an example of its achievement, the *Capuchin Annual* for 1944 reports that in 1899–1900 Irish classes were held in Bermondsey, Clapham, Chelsea, and Dulwich, in addition to the central classes.

The existence of bilingual Latin-Irish phrase-books prepared for missionaries in the seventeenth century is testament to the survival of Irish elsewhere in Europe, as is the reported use of Irish as a language of command among Irish regiments in France. The war-cry *Fág an bealach!* ('Clear the way') used by Irish recruits during the Peninsular Wars subsequently gave the Royal Irish Fusiliers regiment of the British army its nickname of the 'Faughs'. There is also onomastic and anecdotal evidence of Irish being maintained by felons transported to the Americas. Irish-speakers settled in both North and South America in this period, their numbers being augmented in the eighteenth century following the 1798 REBELLION and in the nineteenth century by the GREAT FAMINE. After the famine, estimates derived from the *Irish World*, 1898–9, suggest that there were approximately 400,000 Irish-speakers in North America in the 1890s. The fact that these were concentrated in certain cities, such as Boston, New York, Philadelphia, and Chicago, augured well for ethnolinguistic vitality; so that while the great majority of speakers would have been bilingual, there was sufficient demand for their mother tongue as a cultural bond for it to be retained. Indeed North America has a higher rate of Irish survival than any other emigrant destination of the modern era. Likewise, it has been pivotal in the revival movement, as witnessed by the amount of institutional support Irish has received, despite the fact that it remains peripheral in general studies of the languages and literatures of America. As early as 1857 the first in a series of columns in Irish was printed in the *Irish-American*; this was followed in 1860 by the establishment of the Ossianic Society in New York and in 1873 by the founding of the Philo-Celtic Society of Boston.

The vitality of Irish among emigrants to the United States is not matched by their peers in Canada or in South America. The transfer of Irish to Atlantic Canada appears to have been largely inconsequential, apart from the marginal impact of the language in NEWFOUNDLAND, which supported seasonal MIGRATION from south-eastern Ireland since the seventeenth century. There is evidence of the need for Irish-speaking priests in the late eighteenth century in the Avalon Peninsula, where Irish immigrants were most concentrated, as shown by a letter written in 1784 to the Vicar Apostolic in London, which says, 'Without a perfect knowledge of the Irish tongue no priest can be of profit.' There are no such reports for Latin America, where Irish never gained a foothold, though it survives in certain phrases in the Irish-English of ARGENTINA. Evidence suggests that the Catholic Church in South America was always keen to stress the survival of English rather than Irish as an Irish cultural marker, which may well explain the rapid linguistic assimilation of its speakers.

The impact of Irish in NEW ZEALAND appears to have been similarly peripheral; here it may be because there was no TRANSPORTATION strategy for New Zealand, as there had been for both the Americas and AUSTRALIA. Moreover, Irish emigration to New Zealand did not begin in earnest until relatively late (after 1850), by which time the language had begun to retreat in Ireland. Irish emigrants to New Zealand came largely from Ulster, which had begun to show the effects of language loss as far back as the 1170s.

Irish fared better among emigrants to Australia, though it was not usually maintained beyond the second generation. There are reports that it may have been the second most widely understood language in Australia in the middle of the nineteenth century but that it was overtaken by German in the 1880s. There appear to have been two reasons for its subsequent decline. Firstly, as in Latin America, the Catholic Church openly discouraged the use of Irish; secondly, unlike the situation in North America, the Irish diaspora in Australia were not nearly so concentrated geographically, and this has been demonstrated to be an important factor contributing to language loss in other contact situations throughout the world. **Karen Corrigan**

Irish language, Early Modern (Classical Modern Irish). From c. 1200 to c. 1600 Irish was governed by a caste of professional scholars, the FILÍ, collectively called the *aos dána*. There are three broad stylistic tendencies. The first is a literary usage sometimes referred to as *ceart na bhfilí*, 'the poets' standard'; the second is called *canúin*, 'speech' or 'speaking', in the poets' grammatical treatises; this may have been quite close to the speech of the educated class, but from the evidence of the grammarians it was not the speech of the common people. Thirdly, especially in historical or pseudo-historical writings, it displayed an archaic style, as if this were a mark of the scholar, a stamp of authority and learning. Indeed in the thirteenth-century satire 'Tromdhámh Ghuaire' the king replies to his chief poet's recital of a poem of ludicrous pomposity with the opinion *'Is maith an duan gibé do thuigfeadh í.'* ('The poem is a good one, whoever might understand it.') Edmund Campion, as late as 1571, noticed that 'the true Irishe indeede differeth so much from that they commonly speake, that scarce one among five score, can either write, read, or understande it. Therefore it is prescribed among certaine of their Poets, and other Students of Antiquitie.' For all the constraints under which the professional poets worked, it should be noted that many of them achieved a literature of a high quality. [see IRISH, MIDDLE; IRISH METRICS; IRISH, OLD.] **Diarmaid Ó Muirithe**

Irish language, Middle (c. 1,000–c. 1,300). Before the tenth century dawned, the period of Classical OLD IRISH began to give way to that of Middle Irish, which lasted for about 250 years. It was a period of linguistic confusion, in which the archaic was mingled with new grammatical forms. Surviving texts from the period show no hint of the regional diversity that must have existed in the spoken language. The scholars still held sway, however; their pedantry and conservatism dictated the rules until, towards the end of the twelfth century, the variety of Irish known both as Early Modern Irish and Classical Modern Irish began to emerge. [see IRISH METRICS.] **Diarmaid Ó Muirithe**

Irish language, Old (c. 600–c. 1,000). It seems that Irish changed rapidly in the period of approximately three hundred years that separates Primitive Irish from the Old Irish of the GLOSSES, the most important of which are the eighth-century annotations in a text of the Pauline Epistles in the Codex Paulinus at Würzburg and those on a commentary on the Psalms in the ninth-century Codex Ambrosianus of Milan. It would appear that the first Christian scholars, who inherited a mature literary tradition, used a more colloquial form of language for the new literature they established. This, it has been pointed out, was consistent with their revisionary attitude to all aspects of the old PAGAN tradition.

Scholars make a distinction between Early Old Irish (late sixth century and seventh century) and Classical Old Irish (eighth and ninth centuries), the language of most of the Glosses, of the beautiful corpus of early lyric poetry, and of the earliest version of the epic TÁIN BÓ CUAILGNE. No definitive account of the characteristics of Early Old Irish exists, nor is there a comprehensive catalogue of its literature; the grammar of Classical Old Irish, on the other hand, has been adequately described. [see IRISH LANGUAGE, EARLY; IRISH METRICS; OGHAM.] **Diarmaid Ó Muirithe**

Irish language, restoration of. Even as the population of Irish-speaking Ireland was being drastically reduced by the cataclysms of the nineteenth century, Irish was gaining a new status among the Ascendancy and the literati. This was in great part due to the romantic movement, and its beginning can be traced to the publication of the first anthology of secular literature in Irish, CHARLOTTE BROOKE's *Reliques of Irish Poetry* (1789). One of Brooke's friends, Theophilus O'Flanagan, founded the short-lived Gaelic Society in 1807; it, however, was followed by similar societies that drew the interest of amateur archaeologists and historians. These organisations also published literature in Irish and restored Irish in the public mind as a language fit to be treated in a serious and scholarly manner. The Iberno-Celtic Society did useful work, as did the OSSIANIC Society, founded in 1853, which published important work by STANDISH O'GRADY and John O'Daly.

As the century passed and the Irish-speaking population was tragically reduced by famine and emigration, the emphasis began to be placed on the spoken language. In 1876 the Society for the Preservation of the Irish Language was formed. Its policies were thought by some to be less than radical, and so the Gaelic Union was formed, along with its journal, IRISLEABHAR NA GAEILGE, which was to prove a major influence in formulating revival policy for many years. The founding of the GAELIC LEAGUE (Conradh na Gaeilge) in 1893 by DOUGLAS HYDE, EOIN MAC NEILL, Eugene O'Growney and others was the culmination of the revivalists' efforts. Thanks almost entirely to the Gaelic League, Irish was declared to be the national language when the IRISH FREE STATE was established in 1922. It took its place in the curriculum of the primary schools, bolstering its position in the secondary schools, where it had been taught since 1913 as a compulsory subject for matriculation to the National University. The state also considered Irish necessary for entrance to various CIVIL SERVICE positions. In 1937 the CONSTITUTION OF IRELAND confirmed the official position of Irish: article 8 states, 'The Irish language as the national language is the first official language.'

The Irish state has helped to maintain the position of Irish in other ways. In 1943 it established Comhdháil Náisiúnta na Gaeilge to co-ordinate the work of various revival organisations. In 1952 Bord na Leabhar Gaeilge came into being to supervise the Government's funding of books published in Irish. The Department of the GAELTACHT was established in 1956. Irish-language radio and television stations have since been established, as has a state-sponsored industrial development authority for the Irish-speaking districts.

For all the work that has been done, recent surveys have shown that the language has gone into a new decline. One such survey carried out by John Harris in the 1980s showed that in the officially Irish-speaking districts, many Irish-speaking parents have been using English only in the home. Children in Gaeltacht schools reported that 46.1 per cent spoke English only at home; 33.7 per cent spoke both English and Irish; only 20 per cent spoke Irish only. Outside the Irish-speaking districts the figures reported in the 1971 census reveal that 789,429 people, or 28 per cent of the population, thought of themselves as Irish-speakers; these figures may be taken with a grain of salt, as they make no distinction between degrees of competence, nor degrees of use. The number of children between the ages of three and nine who were returned as Irish-speakers was 94,481, about 21 per cent of the age group. However, this figure includes many who were regarded as knowing Irish simply because they were studying it at school. In the three to four age group, the proportion of Irish-speakers was 5.5 per cent.

The same caveats may be entered when one studies the figures revealed in the 1981 CENSUS. The total number returned as Irish-speakers was over 1 million, representing approximately 32 per cent of the population; yet the number of speakers in the three to four age group had declined to 4.9 per cent. This may be linked to the recent deterioration of the position of Irish in the Gaeltacht areas.

Actual use is a different variable. According to a survey published by Institiúid Teangeolaíochta Éireann (Language Institute of Ireland) in 1984 and published by Ó Murchú, respondents reported the extent of their use of Irish as follows:

1. In conversation since leaving school	18%
2. In writing since leaving school	5%
3. Frequently or normally in the home	5%
4. Sometimes in the home	25%
5. Watching television programme in Irish	72%

The discrepancy between 1 and 4, Ó Murchú points out, is presumably because 4 does not necessarily involve the respondent personally. The response to 3 accords well with the census figure for the three to four age group. 5 is a passive activity and suggests a high level of passive competence in the language. Many people, however, would regard this assertion of passive knowledge as bogus. It may well echo the fervour that came to the surface in the institute's survey of the support for the use of Irish in public life. 76 per cent favoured its use on television, 75 per cent in the civil service, 66 per cent in DÁIL ÉIREANN, 70 per cent in public notices and forms, 71 per cent in tests for public servants. According to the same survey, 66 per cent of respondents thought that Ireland would certainly lose its identity as a separate culture should Irish die; 66 per cent thought it important that children should grow up knowing Irish; 73 per cent thought that no Irish person can be against the revival of Irish.

Modern Ireland has a complex linguistic profile. While the traditional Irish-speaking districts may be forsaking the language, many towns can now boast of schools that teach all subjects through Irish. These schools are known for their competence; their mushroom-like growth is a testimony to this fact. This is a new development in Irish education: it is too early to judge what the eventual influence will be in an Ireland where historical continuity is becoming increasingly vulnerable to the political and social stresses of modern times. [see IRISH LANGUAGE; IRISH-MEDIUM SCHOOLS.] **Diarmaid Ó Muirithe**

Irish Literary Theatre: see ABBEY THEATRE.

Irish Management Institute (IMI), an independent body that aims to promote best international practice in the management of Irish private and public-sector business and administration in the Republic. Set up in 1952 as an independent body, financed by its corporate members, it provides education and training services both for individuals and for companies and other organisations, catering primarily for senior and middle management. Its annual conference in Killarney is an important event in the business year. Sometimes criticised as focusing too much on the 'old reliables' of corporate Ireland—such as the banks and state enterprises—in recent years the IMI has made a determined effort to identify and address the development needs of the new breeds of companies and managers in the changing Irish economy. **Eunan O'Halpin**

Irish language, restoration of. *Achill Island, Co. Mayo, c. 1900, By the late nineteenth century, Irish-speaking Ireland was in retreat on Achill, with separate Irish or English-speaking areas. [National Library of Ireland]*

Irish Manuscripts Commission, established by the Government of the Irish Free State in 1928 to report on manuscripts relating to Irish history and literature and to publish editions of important MANUSCRIPTS; it subsequently operated under the auspices of the then Department of Arts, Culture, Gaeltacht, and the Islands. Its publications have ranged from facsimile reproductions of medieval Irish and Latin manuscripts to multi-volume printed editions, including *Proceedings of the Dublin Society of United Irishmen*, edited by R. B. McDowell (reprint, 1998), *Irish Exchequer Payments*, edited by Philomena Connolly (1998), and *The Irish Cartularies of Llanthony Prima and Secunda*, edited by St John Brookes (1955). The commission also publishes the journal *Analecta Hibernica* (1930–), in which documents unsuitable for publication in separate volumes are made available, together with reports on manuscript collections, descriptive catalogues, lists, and indexes. **Ciarán Deane**

Irish-medium schools, schools (outside the Irish-speaking districts) in which Irish is the language of the school community and in which all subjects are taught through Irish. Such a school may be under the patronage (ownership) of a church (usually the Catholic Church) or of An Foras Pátrúnachta—a limited company that supports Irish-medium schools; they are also supported by two voluntary organisations, Gaelscoileanna in the Republic and Gaeloiliúint in Northern Ireland. Parents are actively encouraged to participate in the management and running of the schools; in most instances the impetus for setting up such schools comes from parents. The movement to set up Irish-medium schools developed in the early 1970s; from fewer than ten in 1970 there are now 141 primary and thirty-five post-primary Irish-medium schools throughout Ireland (excluding Irish-speaking areas), catering for more than 25,000 pupils. [see IRISH LANGUAGE; IRISH LANGUAGE, RESTORATION OF.] **Áine Hyland**

Irish metrics. The oldest Irish verse, dating from the sixth and seventh centuries, is loosely accentual in structure. The smallest metrical unit consists of a line (or *colon*) of unfixed length, usually having two or three stresses. Alliteration within and between lines is optional. The metre is traditionally referred to by the term *rosc*, and its origins may be presumed to predate the earliest surviving examples by a considerable margin.

The influence of Latin hymn measures on the older accentual forms gave rise to the development in the seventh and eighth centuries of a new species of Irish metre alongside the old. This is distinguished by a four-line stanzaic structure in which corresponding lines have a fixed number of syllables, and certain corresponding endwords rhyme. These so-called syllabic verse forms are referred to in early contemporary commentaries as *núachrutha* (new measures), and their introduction is attributed to *núalitride* (new authors). Following their introduction, a large diversity of stanza structures grew up, providing the vehicle for the greater part of OLD and MIDDLE IRISH verse, 700–1100.

In the twelfth century, as part of the standardisation of the literary language that culminated in the advent of classical EARLY MODERN IRISH (1200–1600), the syllabic metres were adapted to suit contemporary phonology, stricter rules for ornamentation (rhyme, consonance, and alliteration) were applied, and the repertoire of individual metres was reduced. The resulting development is the species of syllabic versification known as *dán díreach* (strict poetry), which dominated the teaching of the poetic schools and literary activity generally, both in Ireland and Scotland during subsequent centuries, up to the destruction of the Gaelic policy during the seventeenth century.

A new and wholly different metrical system emerged in written sources during the sixteenth century, called *amhrán* (song poetry). This term, which is much older than the earliest attestation of the actual metre, signifies a stave sung to a tune. The defining metrical features are strophic structure and a regular rhythm based on the interplay of accented and unaccented syllables within the line and from one line to the next. Lines of between four and six stresses arranged in four-line stanzas are commonest in the earliest surviving examples. Identical rhythmical forms occur in the metrical tradition of all the main Western European vernaculars, indicating that the original prosody probably arose in the context of a migration of popular musical prototypes. Irish *amhrán* metre differs from its European congeners in exhibiting a systematic use of ornamental assonance, both line-internally and also vertically between vowels falling under the accent from one line to the next. Later *amhrán* poetry, in the eighteenth and nineteenth centuries, is marked by the development of a multiplicity of line and strophe forms. Corresponding air types are represented in the repertoire of Irish TRADITIONAL MUSIC, and manuscript sources frequently indicate the name of the particular tune to which individual poems were composed.

The twentieth century saw the abandonment of the regular rhythms of traditional accentual metre as versification adapted to the freer forms current in English and other European languages. **Pádraig A. Breatnach**

Irish Museum of Modern Art (IMMA), Dublin. The museum, devoted to contemporary international art practice, occupies the late seventeenth-century ROYAL HOSPITAL, Kilmainham, designed by Sir WILLIAM ROBINSON as a hospice for retired soldiers. Following virtual abandonment from 1922, the building was restored in 1998 as the National Centre for Culture and the Arts and, in 1991, as the Irish Museum of Modern Art, popularly known as IMMA. It holds a number of important collections of twentieth-century Irish and international art, the Sidney Nolan, Gordon Lambert, and McClelland Collections, as well as the Madden-Arnholz Print Collection (seventeenth to nineteenth-century Old Master prints, bequeathed to its previous manifestation). **Brian Lalor**

Irish music in North America. Music is one of the most portable items in the emigrant's cultural baggage. Irish emigrants brought their music with them to North America, where its fate depended on geographical patterns of settlement.

Irish immigrants in eastern Canada settled among English, French, Scots, and native Americans, each with their own musical traditions. Patchwork settlement patterns, especially in the maritime provinces, produced culturally distinct communities that preserved the music of their homelands; it is possible, therefore, to find areas where Irish fiddling styles and repertoires remain close to those of Ireland. At the same time, musical influences spread across national and cultural boundaries, with Irish music as part of an evolutionary mixture that has produced musical hybrids, such as the French-Canadian fiddling style and the driving sound of Prince Edwards Island. The results may be less uniquely 'American' than what one hears in the Appalachians, but there is greater musical variety.

Below the Canadian border the Appalachian mountain region drew most of its immigrants from Britain and from Ulster; they settled along with smaller numbers of Germans, African-Americans, and native Americans. National enclaves were generally not as distinct as those in Canada. As a result, Irish music was less often preserved in its original form; instead it became an important factor in the development of a distinctive American traditional music that eventually became the basis for country and bluegrass music. At the same time Irish musical influences contributed to the evolution of new, distinctly American types of popular music that first appeared in the minstrel shows and in early vaudeville. Yet while Irish music was being absorbed into American popular music it also retained its own identity. Irish JIGS and REELS were an important part of American dance music through much of the nineteenth century. In the cities, Irish music supported and was supported by the great post-famine immigration. Unlike rural areas, where the FIDDLE was the predominant instrument, urban Irish communities also nurtured pipers, FLUTE players, and box players.

Sustained by continued immigration and by the concentration of the immigrants in cities, Irish music by the end of the nineteenth century existed as much in urban North America as it did in rural Ireland. It was so strong, in fact, that it twice reversed the flow of musical influences across the Atlantic. In 1907 FRANCIS O'NEILL published *O'Neill's Dance Music of Ireland*. Until then, Irish tunes had been published as part of the mix of popular dance music. O'Neill set out to document and preserve the music he had collected among the Irish musicians of Chicago, where he was superintendent of police. Decorated with harps and shamrocks and with tune titles in Irish, O'Neill's collections were self-conscious products of an immigrant community that had proudly retained its identity in urban America. O'Neill himself was a flute-player from west Cork, and his tune collections had considerable influence in Ireland.

After the FIRST WORLD WAR a new generation of Irish immigrant musicians arrived in New York, where recording companies were already turning out records for Irish immigrant districts. The virtuoso performances of such fiddlers as MICHAEL COLEMAN, JAMES MORRISON, and Paddy Killoran found their way back to rural Ireland, where they were enthusiastically received. These recordings, together with O'Neill's collections, helped sustain interest among traditional musicians, expanding repertoires and no doubt adding to the level of performance. At the same time they helped weaken local playing styles and crowded out some local tune variations. In America, O'Neill's principal collection became known as the 'Bible', and the Sligo style of Coleman, Morrison, and Killoran came to define Irish-American fiddling.

The 1920s were the 'golden age' of Irish music in the United States. While the numerous Irish dance bands that proliferated in some American cities came to mix foxtrots with the jigs and reels, the hundreds of recordings of traditional Irish dance music testify to its extraordinary survival in the urban environment. However, the health of this urban tradition depended on continued immigration from Ireland. With the Depression and then the Second World War, Irish emigration to the United States dwindled. After the war, many of the old Irish urban districts disappeared as second and third-generation Irish scattered to the suburbs, where there were no Irish dance bands and where the old 78 r.p.m. recordings were strange relics of a half-forgotten immigrant past. But the urban tradition had survived long enough in cities such as NEW YORK, CHICAGO, and PHILADELPHIA to train a post-war generation of talented young musicians. The folk revival of the 1960s and jet-age travel to and from Ireland created renewed interest in Irish music, while

COMHALTAS CEOLTÓIRI ÉIREANN established branches throughout North America. Today there is hardly a city that does not have several 'Irish' bands, most of which, however, do not depend on an Irish community for support. In the meantime, Irish musicians journey to Nashville and Hollywood to add whistles and pipes to recordings and sound tracks. Irish music continues to be absorbed into American music while it retains its separate identity and its connection with Ireland. [see POPULAR MUSIC; POPULAR MUSIC AND THE DIASPORA.] **William H. A. Williams**

Irish Music Rights Organisation (IMRO), an organisation that administers the performing rights of publishers, songwriters, and composers by granting licences on behalf of its members and collecting and distributing royalties. It also represents foreign composers, authors, and music publishers through reciprocal agreements with societies in other countries. Musical performing rights entitle the owner of the copyright in a work to receive a royalty whenever the work is performed in public or is broadcast. Because of the inefficiency of large-scale self-administration of these rights, especially internationally, most creators exercise their rights collectively through administrative societies such as IMRO. These societies also lobby on behalf of their members and often provide advocacy in the event of legal disputes. IMRO was created in 1989 as a response to a growing need for a national society to administer performing rights on behalf of Irish publishers, songwriters, and composers, previously members of a British organisation, the PERFORMING RIGHTS SOCIETY. IMRO is a member of the International Confederation of Societies of Authors and Composers. **Anthony McCann**

Irish National League, established in Dublin on 17 October 1882 to provide popular support for the HOME RULE party, led by CHARLES STEWART PARNELL. In addition to the goal of national self-government, its programme included land reform aimed at introducing peasant proprietorship, local self-government, extension of the franchise, encouragement of industrial development, and better conditions for agricultural labourers. Splitting into pro- and anti-Parnellite factions in 1891, it was subsumed into the UNITED IRISH LEAGUE following reunification of the party in 1900. **Carla King**

Irish National Liberation Army (INLA), emerged in 1975 as the military wing of the Irish Republican Socialist Party and mainly composed of Official IRA dissidents, angry at the Officials' 1972 ceasefire. Other recruits came from the PROVISIONAL IRA during their 1974 ceasefire. Though always considerably smaller than the Provisionals (active numbers never seem to have exceeded 100), the INLA quickly gained a reputation for ruthlessness and unpredictability and developed into perhaps the most uncompromising of the terrorist organisations, adopting a strict anti-British, anti-Protestant, and apparently socialist revolutionary strategy. It is thought to have planted the bomb that killed Airey Neave MP at the House of Commons in London in 1979. An especially brutal attack in November 1983, when gunmen burst into a PENTECOSTALIST church in Co. Armagh during a service, killing three people and wounding seven, confirmed their reputation, even among republicans, as 'wild men'. In the 1980s a bloody internal feud severely weakened the organisation, but it recovered to launch a series of sporadic attacks during the 1990s, especially on loyalist paramilitaries, including the dissident terrorist Billy Wright, killed by INLA prisoners inside the Maze Prison. In August 1998 it announced a 'complete ceasefire'. **Keith Jeffery**

Irish National Organisation of the Unemployed (INOU), a federation of local UNEMPLOYMENT organisations and centres for unemployed people. Founded at a time of mass unemployment in the Republic, it proved effective in representing the interests of the unemployed to national policy-makers and in raising public awareness of the problems confronting unemployed people. The INOU co-ordinates research and the dissemination of information as well as lobbying on issues related to job creation, training, and education, and SOCIAL WELFARE. In the last years of the twentieth century it took its place in representing the interests of the unemployed in the institutions of SOCIAL PARTNERSHIP, including the NATIONAL ECONOMIC AND SOCIAL FORUM and NATIONAL ECONOMIC AND SOCIAL COUNCIL, and in the negotiation of the national wage agreements, Partnership 2000 and the Programme for Prosperity and Fairness, as well as on a range of other public consultative bodies concerned with employment and the LABOUR MARKET. **Philip O'Connell**

Irish National War Memorial, Islandbridge, Dublin. The c. 35,000 Irish soldiers who were killed during the FIRST WORLD WAR while serving in regiments of the British army are commemorated in a reflective and dignified memorial garden created on the south bank of the River LIFFEY in the late classical style of Sir EDWIN LUTYENS. The scheme, which was to be linked by a bridge across the Liffey connecting it to the PHOENIX PARK, was never completed. Terraces descend towards the river, screened from the roadway by plantations of holm oaks. A formal axis, centred on the stone of remembrance, is flanked by fountains, sunken rose gardens and pavilions linked by pergolas in which are kept memorial volumes inscribed with the names of the dead. [see GARDEN DESIGN; IRELAND'S WAR MEMORIAL RECORDS.] **Brian Lalor**

Irish News, a daily newspaper published in Belfast. Established by clerical elements in 1891 on an anti-PARNELL platform, it rapidly took over from and incorporated its rival, the pro-Parnell *Morning News* (1855–92). After the 1916 RISING it supported HOME RULE; after partition it became the voice of mainstream Northern nationalism. In 1966 a new editor, Terence O'Keeffe, diluted its Catholic content. Independently owned, it has a circulation of approximately 52,000. **David Quin**

Irish News Agency (1949–57), a Government agency, staffed by journalists, set up by SEÁN MACBRIDE to distribute Irish news throughout the world and to campaign against PARTITION. In 1952 it claimed that pictures of RUC men beating unarmed protesters in Derry had reached an audience of more than 8 million. Under its managing director, CONOR CRUISE O'BRIEN, it sold news stories abroad, particularly to the United States. Opposed by competing interests in Irish journalism, particularly Independent Newspapers, it closed in 1957. **David Quin**

Irish Party, HOME-RULE party, also called Nationalist Party and Irish Parliamentary Party. The Irish Party can be considered to have come into existence at the election of February 1874, or rather at the conference the following month at which it was resolved that those returned who favoured home rule ought to form a 'separate and distinct party in the House of Commons.' The emollient parliamentary manner of its first leader, ISAAC BUTT, was too mild for the more aggressive faction of 'obstructionists', among whom CHARLES STEWART PARNELL came to the fore. From 1880, Parnell created a formidable nationalist phalanx in the House of Commons

Irish National Liberation Army. *Members of the INLA stand beside the coffin of their leader, Gino Gallagher, shot dead by feuding INLA members in the Falls Road, Belfast, 30 January 1996. The coffin, with Gallagher's gloves and beret, is draped with the Tricolour; mass cards line the floor and mantelpiece. [Kelvin Boyes Photography]*

and the first recognisably modern political party in Britain or Ireland. The Liberal-Nationalist alliance ('the union of hearts') survived the crisis of the O'Shea divorce case, but in weakened form. The sundered Irish Party was reunited under JOHN REDMOND in 1900. A measure of home rule, originally introduced in 1912, was enacted in 1914 but suspended until the end of the FIRST WORLD WAR. Nationalist exasperation at the course of events in Ireland throughout the war crystallised around the prospect of PARTITION. The election of 1918 marked the end of the Irish Party as an effective force, though its actual vote was much more respectable than its humiliating tally of seats (six, compared with SINN FÉIN's seventy-three) might suggest. **Frank Callanan**

Irish Peatland Conservation Council (Comhairle Chaomhnaithe Phortaigh na hÉireann), an independent conservation charity established in 1982. Its purpose is to campaign for the conservation of a representative sample of living intact BOGS and peatlands for the benefit of the people of Ireland and to safeguard their diversity of wildlife. Its conservation campaigns include purchasing bogland nature reserves, providing resources and training on bogs for teachers and others, repairing damaged bogs, fostering a positive attitude towards peatlands, and encouraging ecologically sustainable life-styles that are in harmony with the environment. **Anne-Marie Cunningham**

Irish pound. Ireland joined the exchange rate mechanism of the EUROPEAN MONETARY SYSTEM on its inception on 13 March 1979, bringing to an end a formal one-to-one link between the Irish and the British pound that had persisted for more than 150 years. This link had occasionally created serious problems for the Irish ECONOMY, as a result of erratic management of the British economy. This was particularly so in the 1970s, as the British economy became embroiled in an economic crisis, and Ireland was compelled to import the worst excesses of British economic mismanagement, including high INFLATION and interest rates and a very unstable currency. It was hoped that by linking to a strong currency, such as the German mark, Ireland would enjoy German interest and inflation rates and a stable currency.

Britain decided not to join the exchange rate mechanism, and by the end of March 1979 the Irish pound had formally broken its link with the British currency as the latter appreciated following the discovery of North Sea oil. As Britain accounted for almost half of Irish trade, the instability of the British pound continued to create problems for the Irish economy and the Irish pound, now allowed to fluctuate by just 2.25 per cent around a central rate against the other ERM currencies. Successive Governments also failed to adhere to the disciplines inherent in membership of a semi-fixed exchange rate mechanism. Fiscal deficits widened sharply, and the balance of payments went into serious deficit. As a result there was little international confidence in the Irish pound, and it remained vulnerable to devaluation within the ERM. Irish interest rates and inflation therefore remained higher than in the other ERM member-countries. A unilateral downward adjustment in the value of the Irish pound against the other ERM currencies was forced on two occasions during the first decade of membership. The currency was unilaterally devalued by 3.5 per cent in March 1983 and by 8 per cent in August 1986.

A more prudent approach to economic and fiscal management was adopted after 1987. This resulted in an improvement in economic growth, a sharp reduction in the fiscal deficit, and increased confidence by international investors in the Irish economy and Irish financial markets. Interest rates fell sharply as a consequence, and for the first time since Ireland joined the ERM the benefits started to accrue. This period of low interest rates and currency stability lasted until 1992 but was damaged by the European currency crisis that traced its origins to German unification but was sparked by the Danish people's rejection of the Treaty of Maastricht in 1992. The British pound had joined the exchange rate mechanism in October 1990 but was forced to leave on 16 September 1992. Immediately, the British pound fell sharply in value against the ERM currencies, and Irish export competitiveness in the important British market was severely damaged. International speculation mounted against the Irish pound, and after enduring three-digit interest rates as the CENTRAL BANK sought to fight off devaluation, the currency was eventually devalued by 10 per cent at the end of January 1993. Pressure on the exchange rate mechanism continued, however, until eventually in August 1993 all currencies, except the Dutch guilder and German mark, adopted 15 per cent bands of fluctuation within the system.

These wider bands of fluctuation persisted until the launch of the single European currency on 1 January 1999. The Irish economy benefited enormously in the more flexible exchange rate mechanism. The wide bands allowed it enough flexibility to maintain comfortable exchange rate levels against the British pound outside the ERM and the bloc of currencies within the system. In March 1998, just before the launch of European monetary union, the Irish pound's central parity within the ERM was adjusted upwards by 3 per cent, from 2.4110 to 2.4833 against the German mark.

The Irish pound (known as the punt) became a member of the single currency on its inception on 1 January 1999, its value against the new currency set at 0.787564 euro. At the same time Irish interest rates converged to the EMU average, and control over interest rates was thereafter vested in the European Central Bank. Since the launch of the single currency it has fallen sharply in value against the American dollar and the British pound, which in effect means that the Irish pound as part of the euro has fallen against those currencies. Britain is still an important market for Ireland, and the weakness of the euro, combined with interest rates that were too low for a fast-growing economy, resulted in a sharp increase in Irish inflation. For the future one of the big issues for Ireland remains the question whether the British pound will become part of European monetary union. Its volatility against the euro prevented Irish business from gaining full advantage of the new exchange rate regime. The Irish pound ceased circulation as a currency with the adoption of the euro on 1 January 2002 (see p. 181). [see BANKING.] **Jim Power**

Irish Press Group (1931–95). The daily *Irish Press* was founded by ÉAMON DE VALERA as the voice of FIANNA FÁIL and mainstream REPUBLICANISM. Shares were bought by investors throughout Ireland, and de Valera raised an estimated half a million dollars in the United States. An early edition editorialised: 'Our ideal, culturally, is an Irish Ireland.' The *Irish Press* became a huge success, mainly with rural readers; in 1949 the *Sunday Press* was launched, and the *Evening Press* followed in 1954. All three titles prospered but failed to adapt as de Valera's 'Irish Ireland' began disintegrating. In 1987 the trenchantly nationalist Tim Pat Coogan, who had edited the paper for almost two decades, was replaced. In 1989 the American publisher Ralph Ingersoll took a 50 per cent share in the company; this arrangement soon soured, and lengthy legal battles over control and financing ensued. Dr ANTHONY O'REILLY of Independent Newspapers, the Press Group's historical rival, bought a 24.9 per cent interest, but the Competition Authority ruled that this was an abuse of a dominant position. The titles ceased publishing in 1995. **Eddie Holt**

Irish printing types. Up to the early 1960s, when ordinary roman type was officially adopted to replace the Irish character for printing in Irish, the alphabet consisted of just eighteen letters; in addition, the vowels carried a diacritical mark indicating length and some consonants a point indicating lenition. The Irish character developed from the roman, which was introduced into Ireland during the fifth-century conversion to Christianity through the various liturgical manuscript books that came into use then. Two distinct styles of lettering evolved, each in its own way destined to have an influence on the shape of Irish printing types. The first, the half-uncial majuscule style, had full, well-rounded forms with short, blunt ascenders and descenders normally contained within the height of the other letters. This style was more frequently used for writing Latin, as in the earliest known Irish manuscript, the CATHACH, and later to such great effect in the Book of KELLS. The second script, usually referred to as Irish minuscule, was more angular, with a pronounced vertical emphasis. This style was used more often for smaller books, where space was of greater concern, and frequently for writing Irish text, as distinct from Latin.

Shortly after the introduction of printing to Ireland, efforts to print in the Irish character for the Reformed Church used a type in 1571 that was made up from existing roman and italic type with some specially prepared Irish letters. Partly as a counter-measure, the Irish Franciscans, working in exile in Antwerp and later in Louvain and Rome, had a number of fonts made that were modelled on the current angular minuscule style; these were to become the predominant influence on Irish printing types for more than two centuries.

In 1835 GEORGE PETRIE, using for reference half-uncial manuscripts, together with Early Christian stone and metal inscriptions, designed a rounder type for the planned publication of *The Annals of the Kingdom of Ireland*, which elevated this very specialised design activity to new heights. About twenty years later, at the request of Cardinal Newman, he prepared the drawings for another typeface for use by the Catholic University Press; this NEWMAN TYPE in turn had a profound influence on a number of typefaces produced towards the end of the nineteenth century and in the early twentieth century that were available for the emerging mechanical typesetting systems. Despite the popularity of these typefaces, the publisher Colm Ó Lochlainn of the Three Candles Press was responsible in the late 1930s for the production of another face based on the round half-uncial style, COLUM CILLE. Despite its qualities, this type was not widely used, as the debate regarding the use of the Irish character took on a heightened significance at this time. Economic and pragmatic considerations eventually won out, and the change to the exclusive use of roman type was implemented officially in the early 1960s, putting an end to the vacillation that surrounded this fascinating typographic dilemma. [see BEDEL, WILLIAM; BIBLE IN IRISH; DUBLIN UNIVERSITY PRESS; FOUR MASTERS, THE; GILL, M. H.; MOXTON TYPE; PRINTING IN IRISH.] **Dermot McGuinne**

Irish Radium Institute (1914–30), established at the Royal Dublin Society at the instigation of John Joly. His initiative was based on an experience he had when, in his capacity of governor of Dr Steevens' Hospital, he successfully treated, by means of radiation from a sample of radium bromide sealed within glass, a facial ulcer first drawn to his attention by Dr Walter Stevenson. It was Joly's idea that the Irish Radium Institute would purchase a supply of radium salts so that the radon gas produced during the radioactive decay of the radium could be collected in fine glass needles for implantation in cancerous tumours. This form of treatment pioneered in Dublin hospitals by Joly and Stevenson was globally copied. **Susan McKenna-Lawlor**

Irish Republican Army (IRA). The IRA had its origins in the Irish Volunteers, a militia founded in 1913 under the influence of the Irish Republican Brotherhood, a small, conspiratorial revolutionary group committed to the belief that only armed struggle could establish an independent Ireland. The Volunteers split when, on the outbreak of the First World War, John Redmond, leader of the Irish Party, called on his followers to support the British war effort. The bulk of the Volunteers followed Redmond, creating the National Volunteers, while 2,000–3,000 radical nationalists remained to be the core of the Irish Volunteers who, under IRB leadership, launched the Rising of 1916 (see p. 918).

The execution by the British of the leaders of the rising unleashed a wave of emotional nationalism, which together with the threat of conscription allowed the Irish Volunteers to re-emerge with growing popular support. Arming, training, and open drilling sessions soon brought them into conflict with the authorities, and during 1918 the organisation went underground. Sinn Féin's sweeping victory in the 1918 general election led to the foundation of Dáil Éireann in January 1919, and the Volunteer organisation became increasingly known as the Irish Republican Army.

Sinn Féin's political success created tensions with some of the more militaristic local leaders of the IRA, who feared that the 'politicians' would compromise with Britain. As a result, they initiated violent action against the police, without the sanction either of their own leadership or the Dáil government, which developed during 1919 into the Anglo-Irish War. The IRA's guerrilla war, combined with its alliance with a politically sophisticated Sinn Féin, achieved substantial success, in that it extracted from the British more than they had been prepared to offer in 1918. At the same time, however, as Michael Collins pointed out, it had still been incapable of 'beating the British out of Ireland militarily.' The Anglo-Irish Treaty (1921), providing for a twenty-six-county Free State that enjoyed 'dominion status' within the British Empire, split both the political and the military wings of the republican movement and led to the Civil War.

Though the balance of combat experience probably lay with the anti-Treatyite section of the IRA, the pro-Treaty forces controlled the levers of governmental power and had the assurance of British support and popular legitimacy as a result of the 1922 'Pact' election, in which the pro-Treatyites had won a clear majority. Though it lost the Civil War, the IRA did not accept the legitimacy of either of the two states that had emerged from the Treaty settlement. Its arms had been hidden in dumps, not surrendered to the Free State, and it was determined to maintain and expand its organisation in preparation for a future assault on both states.

Tensions within the republican movement soon developed. Some in Sinn Féin began to doubt the wisdom of its policy of abstention, whereby the party contested Dáil elections but refused

An Claiḋeaṁ Soluis

(THE GAELIC LEAGUE WEEKLY)

Leaḃar I. Uiṁir 2. Áṫ-Cliaṫ, Márta 25, 1899. Pingin.
Vol. I. No. 2. DUBLIN, MARCH 25, 1899. One Penny.

Cúrsaiḋe an tSaoġail

Irish printing types. *Figgins type, modelled on the Newman type, attributed to Pádraig Ó Briain, was used to print* An Claidheamh Solúis, *the bilingual weekly. [Council of Trustees of the National Library of Ireland; IBL 05]*

to take seats won, as a means of indicating the illegitimacy of the twenty-six-county state. In 1925 the link with Sinn Féin was broken in protest at these reformist tendencies, and in 1926 the IRA was struck a blow when a large section of the party, led by Éamon de Valera, seceded and founded Fianna Fáil.

The formation of Fianna Fáil, its accession to power in 1932, and its increasing hegemony in the politics of the Free State drained the reservoir of nationalist and populist discontent in which the IRA could hope to swim. De Valera peacefully dismantled the Treaty settlement and used state patronage to absorb many IRA men into constitutional politics. The IRA itself was split between republican idealists, militarists, and a strong left-wing element led by Peadar O'Donnell. An attempt to create a left-wing party, Saor Éire, in 1931 failed, and in 1934 the left-wing element seceded to form the short-lived Republican Congress.

Having won over many IRA men with blandishments, de Valera used coercion against the irreconcilable rump, and in 1936 the organisation was banned. In a desperate attempt to reassert its role, the IRA, under its militaristic chief of staff Seán Russell, launched a futile bombing campaign in Britain in 1939. An attempt to start a campaign in the North in 1941 also failed, and by the end of the war, internment, special powers, and deaths by execution and on hunger strike had all but wiped out the IRA in both states.

The rebirth of the organisation after the war was assisted by the upsurge of Irredentism associated with the launch of the All-Party

Anti-Partition Campaign in the South in 1949. The BORDER CAMPAIGN against the Northern state launched in 1956 failed for lack of support and was called off in 1962. Subsequently the leadership launched an opening to the left, seeking to develop a 'national liberation front' type of strategy, including the COMMUNIST PARTY OF IRELAND, and promoting involvement in social agitations and in the movement for CIVIL RIGHTS in Northern Ireland. Traditionalists, particularly strong in the North, saw the new approach as a betrayal of the IRA's military vocation; and when the leadership's policy of dropping abstention in the South was accepted, the traditionalists seceded to form what became known as the 'PROVISIONAL IRA' in 1969.

The competition for support between the 'Officials' (as those supporting the shift to the left were called) and the Provisionals was heavily determined by the descent of the North into bitter sectarian conflict after 1969. The Officials suspended their military operations in 1972, on the grounds that republican armed struggle was leading to sectarian civil war. The Provisionals had no such qualms. In 1974 an ultra-left faction seceded from the Officials to form the IRISH NATIONAL LIBERATION ARMY, which ineffectively tried to compete with the Provisionals.

In the quarter of a century after their formation the Provisionals would be the agency responsible for most deaths from violence. In the early 1970s they believed that an intense campaign of bombings and shootings, particularly of British soldiers, would bring the British government to the conference table. From the mid-1970s a new policy of the 'long war' was adopted. This was based on a twenty-year strategy of attrition, whereby a smaller, cellular military organisation would maintain pressure, to be complemented by developing Sinn Féin as a political party in both states.

The HUNGER STRIKES by IRA prisoners for political status, which led to ten deaths in 1981, launched Sinn Féin into the political arena, and until the end of the 1980s the leaders of the movement supported the 'Armalite and ballot box' strategy. However, increasing evidence that the RUC and BRITISH ARMY had been able to contain the armed struggle, if not eliminate it, and the evidence that IRA violence was restricting the political appeal of Sinn Féin, led to the development of a republican 'peace strategy'. This produced tensions in the organisation, with a secession of more fundamentalist elements in 1986 who created Republican Sinn Féin and the Continuity IRA.

In August 1994 the IRA declared a 'complete cessation of military operations.' At this time GERRY ADAMS, MARTIN MCGUINNESS and other republican leaders told the rank and file that this was a tactic to divide the unionists and extract concessions—in particular joint authority—from the British. The IRA went back to war in February 1997 but declared a new ceasefire in July (see p. 901). This led to some leading members breaking away to found the 32-County Sovereignty Movement and the 'Real IRA', which was responsible for the second-largest atrocity of the TROUBLES when it bombed OMAGH in August 1998, killing twenty-nine people (see p. 827).

Sinn Féin's electoral fortunes improved significantly, and Adams and McGuinness became internationally fêted for their 'conflict resolution' skills. However, despite the BELFAST AGREEMENT of 1998, which guaranteed Sinn Féin a place in government, the release of all their imprisoned members, and the promise of radical reforms of the policing and criminal justice systems, there was little evidence that the IRA was planning to go out of business. Three years after the agreement was signed, and with Sinn Féin ministers in government and most of the reforms introduced, the IRA had still decommissioned little of its weapons or explosives. It appeared to see a continued role for itself, at least until the British government had made more radical constitutional concessions to Sinn Féin. **Henry Patterson**

Irish Republican Brotherhood (IRB), a covert revolutionary organisation. Founded in 1858, in part to perpetuate the more militant ideals of the YOUNG IRELAND movement, it derived some of its inspiration from the United Irishmen of the 1790s. Known to some of its members as the Irish Revolutionary Brotherhood, and more popularly as the FENIANS, it arose in the context of the failure of the Independent Opposition movement by Irish members in the British Parliament in the 1850s. Some of the most intriguing characters of the Irish social scene were among its members, including JAMES STEPHENS, THOMAS CLARKE LUBY, JOHN O'LEARY, and CHARLES KICKHAM. The suppression of its newspaper the *Irish People* in 1865 represented a great blow to the movement, and the failure of the 1867 RISING caused the movement to fracture into constitutional and pro-violence parties in the 1870s. Although it attracted widespread support, it lacked a single coherent doctrine of NATIONALISM and has been accused of naïvety with regard to its social programme. It was a non-sectarian organisation, but most of its members were, none the less, practising Catholics. The IRB was roundly opposed by the Catholic Church and attracted a Papal condemnation in 1870.

The movement was overshadowed by the success of HOME RULE under CHARLES STEWART PARNELL in the 1880s. Under the influence of MICHAEL DAVITT and JOHN DEVOY, the IRB joined with the LAND LEAGUE to form the NEW DEPARTURE of 1879, pursuing incremental and agrarian, rather than strictly revolutionary, goals. A minority of American Fenians, principally associated with JEREMIAH O'DONOVAN ROSSA, conducted a campaign of dynamite attacks on three British cities from 1880 to 1887, including one successful attack on the chamber of the House of Commons, 1885. The IRB was dormant for most of the succeeding generation but revived following the arrival in Dublin in 1907 of Thomas J. Clarke. Clarke gathered a new generation of revolutionary conspirators around him. It was this secret IRB group that infiltrated the leadership of the IRISH VOLUNTEERS and precipitated the 1916 RISING. Thereafter, IRB influence was maintained by its president, MICHAEL COLLINS, although its penchant for conspiracy created tensions in the wider nationalist movement. With the Anglo-Irish settlement of 1921–2 and the failure of the army mutiny of 1924, the IRB in effect disbanded. [see FENIAN MOVEMENT.] **Oliver P. Rafferty**

Irish R.M. and His Experiences, The (1928), a collected edition of the 'Irish RM' stories by SOMERVILLE AND ROSS. It includes three groups of stories about the English resident magistrate Major Yeates of Co. Cork: 'Some Experiences of an Irish R.M.', 'Further Experiences of an Irish R.M.', and 'In Mr. Knox's Country'. The first series appeared in *Badminton Magazine*, 1898–9, while the second and third appeared in the illustrated magazines *Strand* and *Graphic*, 1904–8, as well as in such periodicals as *Blackwood's*, 1913–15. They were subsequently published in book form in 1899, 1908, and 1915 and ensured the writers' popular success. Although originally perceived as comic Irish sketches, more recent scholarship investigates the socio-political satire of the series. **Julie Anne Stevens**

Irish Sea, a semi-enclosed shelf sea separating Ireland and Britain, between latitude 51° 40′ and 55° N and longitude 3° and 6° 15′ W, approximately 360 km (225 miles) in length from north to south and with a surface area of 47,000 km^2 (18,000 sq. miles).

Irish Republican Army. Men of the South *(1921) by Seán Keating is remarkable for being a contemporary image of revolution. It depicts a flying column of the North Cork Battalion of the IRA preparing to ambush a passing military vehicle. Following the Anglo-Irish Truce of 1921, members of the battalion (including Mick O'Sullivan) travelled to Dublin, where Keating sketched and photographed them in his studio at the Metropolitan School of Art. [Courtesy of Crawford Municipal Art Gallery, Cork]*

Ocean water and waves from the North Atlantic enter through the North Channel, approximately 40 km (25 miles) wide, and southwards via St George's Channel, approximately 80 km (50 miles) wide. Because of Ireland's protecting effect, wave energy in the Irish Sea is only about 20 per cent of that on Atlantic coasts. Deep-water significant wave heights decrease from south to north, with a median height of 1.6–2 m (5–6$\frac{1}{2}$ ft), though maximum storm waves can be more than 9 m (30 ft) in height.

The depth of the sea increases along a trend from north-east to south-west, reaching more than 100 m (330 ft) in St George's Channel. This channel forms part of a series of semi-connected deeps or hollows, some reaching to a depth of 200 m (650 ft), aligned north to south in a trough-like feature along the eastern side of the sea. This trough is probably of multiple origins and ages, incorporating deep geological structures (*graben*), palaeo-valleys, and glacifluvial scouring from the last 100,000 years. Most of the sea is shallow, at less than 60 m (200 ft); the eastern margin of Cardigan Bay and the Cumbrian-Lancashire embayments—approximately 40 per cent of the area—are less than 40 m (130 ft) deep.

Geologically, rocks of the Devonian and Carboniferous Periods form a basement to the region. Six main depositional basins further structure the sea; these contain variable thicknesses of sedimentary rocks, 3–6 km (2–4 miles) thick, dating from the Upper Palaeozoic Era to the present. Igneous rocks of a wide age range also occur extensively. A former cover of thick ice over the sea has led to a continuing land uplift in northern areas, at a rate of 0.1–0.3 mm per year. Southwards there is marginal subsidence of the crust, for example 0.1 mm per year at Cardigan Bay and 0.21 mm per year in the Severn Estuary, though the accuracy of these trends is disputed.

Sea-floor sediments comprise a relatively thin (3–60 m, 10–200 ft) and very varied cover of former glacial and also marine sands, gravels, and muds. The sea has a patchy 'rim' of fine-muddy sediments, with sands and gravel areas developed in deeper water, especially south of the Isle of Man. Concentrations of sands and gravels can also occur closer inshore, such as the KISH BANK, off the Co. Dublin coast. These deposits are of significant resource value as building aggregates.

Because of the complexity of coastal shape and sea depth, tidal patterns and current directions in the sea are equally complex. The height of tides along the coasts varies widely, from microtidal (less than 2 m) to macrotidal (more than 4 m): the spring tide range at south-east Ireland is 0.8 m (2$\frac{1}{2}$ ft), at Dundalk Bay 4.9 m (16 ft), and at Morecambe Bay, Lancashire, more than 8.3 m (27 ft).

The effect of the sea on regional climates is significant, its existence leading to increased precipitation in autumn and winter over the neighbouring land areas. In summer the relatively cool sea-water (July average 9–12°C) encourages stratification of the overlying air. This may intensify the effects of air pollution from surrounding industrial regions.

In the middle to late twentieth century, economic, resource, and political questions concerning the use of the Irish Sea assumed an increasing importance, including marine animal and fish conservation (such as the depletion of herring and cod stocks), emissions of radionuclides and other chemical pollutants, sea-bed resources, wetland conservation, and coastal protection. [see CELTIC SEA; CLIMATE; COASTAL EROSION; GEOLOGICAL LANDSCAPE; GEOLOGY.] **Robert J. N. Devoy**

Irish Society, the Honourable, an umbrella organisation created in 1609 to supervise the plantation obligations of the London companies in what was to become known as Co. Londonderry. Unable to finance the PLANTATION OF ULSTER from royal coffers, the authorities enlisted private capital to underwrite the scheme. The twelve primary London companies (Goldsmiths, Grocers, Fishmongers, Haberdashers, Clothworkers, Merchant Tailors, Ironmongers, Mercers, Vintners, Salters, Drapers, and Skinners) having been convinced to take part in the scheme, the Derry plantation was to be the central achievement of the Plantation of Ulster. In the short term, however, the experience of the Irish Society was far from trouble-free. While early progress was made in building the town of COLERAINE, the London companies were to find themselves accused of failing to fulfil their plantation commitments, such as removing the native Irish. So acute was Crown displeasure that by 1635 a huge fine of £70,000 was levied on the London companies, and the charter of the Irish Society was suspended. Having had its charter renewed in 1662, the society was largely to achieve its goals in the long run, ultimately being responsible for erecting the splendid walled city of Derry. The Irish Society, as a principally charitable organisation, remains in existence. **John McCavitt**

Irish spelling. When, in the fifth century, British missionaries taught Latin to the Irish, their pronunciation reflected Brythonic (i.e. early Welsh) phonology. The Irish applied this British Latin orthography to their own language. Accordingly, in Early Irish *p, t,* and *c* meant *p, t,* or *c* at the beginning of a word but *b, d,* or *g* in the middle or at the end of a word, while *b, d,* and *g* represented *b, d,* or *g* also but medially and finally indicated the *lenited* (softened) consonants *bh, dh,* or *gh.* From the twelfth century onwards the orthography developed in such a way that *b, d,* and *g* were written everywhere as *b, d,* and *g,* with the lenition of consonants regularly shown either by a following *h* or by a point (originally the *punctum delens*) above the letter. Eclipse of initial consonants was also indicated in the spelling, as in *a ttaoiseach* or *a dtaoiseach,* 'their leader'. The quality of a consonant ('broad' or 'slender') also came to be regularly conveyed by the vowels flanking it, for example *éaradh,* 'refuse', but *Éire,* 'Ireland'.

When, from the late sixteenth century onwards, Irish was printed in both Scotland and Ireland, the Scots used roman type, whereas the Irish used Gaelic letters almost exclusively, which were not finally abandoned until the 1960s.

By the seventeenth century the gap between spelling and pronunciation had become wide, and sporadic attempts at reform were made, among others by Theobald Stapleton in 1639. He used roman type, and removed many quiescent letters—a practice not universally adopted until the twentieth century. In the eighteenth and nineteenth centuries those who could not write Irish in traditional orthography spelt the language as though it were English; many of RAIFTEARAÍ's songs, for example, were transmitted in this way. A phonetic orthography for the Munster dialect promoted in the early twentieth century by Shán Ó Cuív was never generally accepted; the spelling of the surname Ó Cuív by one family is the only survival. After 1922 Irish became one of the languages of the state, and the Dáil translation staff were given the necessary task of devising a simplified official orthography. Their final version, the Caighdeán Oifigiúil (official standard), published in 1958, dispensed with many silent letters: for example, *i gcomhnaidhe, athchuinghe,* and *dearbhráithreacha* became *i gcónaí, achainí,* and *deartháireacha.* The Caighdeán Oifigiúil is not without ambiguity, however: the word *cuireadh,* for example, can be pronounced *cuire, cuireach,* or *cuiriú* according to sense ('invitation,' 'let him put,' or 'was buried', respectively). [see IRISH METRICS.] **Nicholas J. A. Williams**

Irish Texts Society. *Father Patrick Dinneen who compiled the Irish–English dictionary* Foclóir Gaedhilge agus Béarla. *He claimed that in the early twentieth century he was the only person making his living from writing in Irish. [Courtesy of Feasta/Conradh na Gaeilge]*

Irish State, titles of (1916–2001). The name of the state proclaimed by the 1916 insurgents and declared independent by DÁIL ÉIREANN in 1919 has varied and has been contentious. The 1916 PROCLAMATION referred to the Irish Republic or Poblacht na hÉireann, the 1919 declaration to the Republic of Ireland or Saorstát Éireann (literally, IRISH FREE STATE). The treaty of 1921 stipulated Irish Free State or Saorstát Éireann. The CONSTITUTION OF IRELAND (1937) swept away these titles of putative subordination in favour of the names Éire or Ireland (using both titles in the Irish and English-language texts). In 1949 the Government declared that the 'description' of the state was Republic of Ireland or Poblacht na hÉireann. [see IRELAND, NAMES OF.] **Tom Garvin**

Irish stitch, a long stitch worked with woollen or worsted thread on a loosely woven linen or canvas backing, generally in a flame design. It is known as such from the seventeenth century and was used particularly by home embroiderers for cushions and seat covers. **Mairead Dunlevy**

Irish Texts Society (Cumann na Scríbheann nGaedhilge), established in London in 1898 'to advance public education by promoting the study of Irish Literature, and as ancillary thereto to publish texts in the IRISH LANGUAGE ...' Texts were edited by a distinguished succession of scholars, including MYLES DILLON, DOUGLAS HYDE, EOIN MACNEILL, and STANDISH HAYES O'GRADY. In

1904 it published the landmark *Foclóir Gaedhilge agus Béarla* (Irish-English Dictionary) compiled by REV. PATRICK DINNEEN. The stereotype plates were destroyed in Dublin during the 1916 RISING; a revised edition, published for the society by the Educational Company of Ireland, appeared in 1927. In the 1970s some of the society's publications were reissued in photolithographic reproductions by the IRISH UNIVERSITY PRESS. **Bernard Share**

Irish Times, a daily newspaper published in Dublin. It was founded in 1859 by Major Lawrence Knox as Ireland's first daily penny newspaper. Conservative and unionist, it soon outstripped like-minded rivals at a time when the principles of the ANGLO-IRISH Ascendancy were threatened. On Knox's death in 1873 it was sold to the industrialist John Arnott, owner of the *Northern Whig* (Belfast). At the beginning of the twentieth century it had the highest circulation in Ireland, but it was quickly overtaken by the populist *Irish Independent.* A public company was established in 1900 but it continued to be controlled by the Arnott family for a further fifty years. In 1974 a trust was formed to secure and maintain the *Irish Times* as an independent newspaper. Following PARTITION, the paper's middle-class Protestant readership had declined in numbers and influence. As editor from 1934 to 1954, ROBERT SMYLLIE maintained its support for the British Empire; he was succeeded by Alan Montgomery. From the 1960s the paper increasingly attracted the growing Catholic bourgeoisie, to add to the liberal, left, and intellectual readers who gravitated towards it since the early 1950s; it now has a circulation of 120,000. Douglas Gageby as editor and DÓNAL FOLEY (1922–1981) as news editor and later deputy editor played leading roles in this transformation, which included the recruitment of women journalists such as Nell McCafferty, Mary Cummins, Mary Maher, and MAEVE BINCHY. Conor Brady, who became the first Catholic editor in 1985, presided over increasing expansion. Of the paper's readership, 86 per cent fit the advertising classification ABC1. It is the only Irish news medium to have maintained a permanent editorial presence in Brussels, London, New York, Washington, Berlin, Paris, and Beijing. However, despite the advertising bonanza of the 1990s economic boom, the management revealed in the autumn of 2001 that the paper faced a financial crisis. Since then its staff of 720 has been reduced by one third as the paper's period of greatest expansion—arguably excessive expansion—halted abruptly. Geraldine Kennedy became the first woman to edit the paper in 2002. **Eddie Holt**

Irish Tourist Board: see BORD FÁILTE ÉIREANN.

Irish Trades Union Congress (ICTU), founded in Dublin in 1894, modelled on its British namesake. From 1914 it was known as the Irish Trades Union Congress and LABOUR PARTY and from 1918 as the Irish Labour Party and Trades Union Congress. It separated from the Labour Party in 1930. Many private-sector unions decamped in 1945 to form the Congress of Irish Unions; the two federations reunited as the Irish Congress of Trade Unions in 1959. **Emmet O'Connor**

Irish Traditional Music Archive (ITMA), a reference archive and resource centre for the traditional song, music and dancing of Ireland, established in 1987 and based in Merrion Square, Dublin. It is a non-profit public facility, which also promotes public education through its own activities and its support for the activities of others. The archive is the first body to be concerned exclusively with the making of a comprehensive collection of materials—including sound recordings, books, and photographs—for the appreciation and study of traditional music. It now holds the largest such collection, with coverage of Ireland, areas of Irish settlement abroad, and non-Irish performers of Irish traditional music. A representative collection of the traditional music of other countries is also being made. **Glenn Cumiskey**

Irish Times. *Alec Newman, leader-writer for the* Irish Times, *making a point to the editor, Robert Smyllie (centre), in the Palace Bar, Fleet Street, Dublin. W. J. MacManus of the* Irish Press *is on Smyllie's left. [Getty Images/Hulton Archive]*

Irish Transport and General Workers' Union (ITGWU), founded in Dublin on 28 December 1908 by JAMES LARKIN from Irish branches of the National Union of Dock Labourers. Nationalist, and notably radical up to 1923, it led the revival of Irish trade unionism during these years. The DUBLIN LOCK-OUT (September 1913 to January 1914) was caused by the determination of employers to compel their employees not to join the ITGWU. Under William O'Brien, and as the biggest and most professional union, it was involved in largely unsuccessful efforts to reform organised labour from 1919 to the 1940s. After 1970 it supported centralised bargaining and SOCIAL PARTNERSHIP; in 1990 it merged with the Federated Workers' Union of Ireland to form the SERVICES, INDUSTRIAL, PROFESSIONAL AND TECHNICAL UNION (SIPTU) (see p. 601). **Emmet O'Connor**

Irish University Press, Shannon, Co. Clare, founded in 1966 by Tadhg MacGlinchey. It was by far the largest publishing operation in Ireland until its closure in 1974, employing some sixty people. It concentrated on high-quality photolithographic reproductions of scholarly and historical works of Irish interest long out of print; but

Irish Transport and General Workers' Union. *Marching banner of Cavan ITGWU which incorporates Celtic interlace panels and a historic image of the Dublin 1913 Lock-Out strike, on which are superimposed the stars of the Irish Citizen Army's Plough constellation symbol. [Francis Devine]*

its *pièce de résistance* was the reprint of *British Parliamentary Papers* (1968–72), which earned a place in the record books as the largest publication in the world, with 1,112 volumes, each set weighing 3.3 tonnes. The print run was 500 sets, each selling (in 1984) at £42,000. Following an unsuccessful takeover the IUP went into liquidation, its stock being acquired by Irish Academic Press, set up by one of its former employees, Michael Adams. Several others displaced by the closure established their own publishing ventures as well as the trade magazine *Books Ireland* (1976–). **Bernard Share**

Irish Volunteers (eighteenth century): see VOLUNTEERS.

Irish Volunteers (twentieth century), founded in November 1913 after EOIN MACNEILL published his article 'The North began' in *An Claidheamh Soluis*, in which he argued that nationalists should organise a volunteer militia much like the newly formed ULSTER VOLUNTEER FORCE. With the support of the IRISH REPUBLICAN BROTHERHOOD, the Volunteers attracted members from a wide spectrum of nationalist opinion. By August 1914 the organisation numbered nearly 200,000, constituting enough of a political force for JOHN REDMOND to seek to seize control of its leadership two months earlier. With the success of the Home Rule Act and then its suspension for the duration of the FIRST WORLD WAR, Redmond called on the Volunteers to support the British war effort. This split the organisation, a majority going with Redmond, calling themselves the National Volunteers, and a minority, some 11,000, remaining as the Irish Volunteers. This minority reorganised under MacNeill's leadership; leading posts on its executive were held by PATRICK PEARSE, JOSEPH PLUNKETT, and THOMAS MACDONAGH, all to become members of the secret Military Council of the IRB. It was they who successfully manipulated the Volunteers and brought out its members in the 1916 RISING. After the rising the Volunteers were reorganised, gradually transforming themselves into the IRISH REPUBLICAN ARMY. **Seán Farrell Moran**

Irish Wildlife Trust, established in 1979 as the Irish Wildlife Federation, a non-governmental conservation organisation and registered charity. Its aim is to conserve Ireland's wildlife and habitats by lobbying, campaigning, education, and practical conservation. Before the establishment of the trust no body existed specifically for the conservation of Ireland's terrestrial and marine wildlife. During the 1970s and 80s the main emphasis of the trust's work was on providing information to the public; subsequently it began examining habitat issues, including the loss of habitats and European designations. The trust has been working to ensure that legislation is adequate for the conservation of wildlife; integral to this is the examination of legislation and legal frameworks, such as the Wildlife Amendment Bill (1976 and 2000), the Planning and Development Bill (1999), and EU directives. The enforcement of these laws and regulations is also a principal concern of the trust. **Anne-Marie Cunningham**

Irish Women's Suffrage Federation, formed in 1911, under the leadership of LOUIE BENNETT and HELEN CHENEVIX, through the merger of a number of suffrage organisations, including the Irish Women's Suffrage Society. Bennet, who was secretary, collaborated with FRANCIS SHEEHY-SKEFFINGTON on the IRISH CITIZEN, the organ of the movement. The scholar Mary Hayden served as president for a time, and GEORGE RUSSELL was vice-president. After the passing of the Representation of the People Act (1918) women over the age of thirty were permitted to vote in parliamentary elections. [see WOMEN'S SUFFRAGE MOVEMENT.] **Brian Galvin**

Irish Women United (1975–7), a radical feminist organisation based in Dublin. In June 1975 it adopted a Charter of Women's Rights, demanding an end to legal DISCRIMINATION and calling for free legal CONTRACEPTION, equal pay, recognition for women, and the right to a self-determined SEXUALITY. Through its weekly meetings, its magazine, *Banshee*, and radical direct action, including occupying the offices of the Federated Union of Employers and invading male-only sports clubs, pubs, and bathing and other facilities, it drew attention to the daily discrimination experienced by women. It also provided a focal point for young feminists, lesbian activists, and left-wing women for debating issues in a radical and transformative way. [see FORTY FOOT.] **Ursula Barry**

Irish Women Workers' Union (1911–84). At its peak it organised more than 7,000 women, including laundresses, boxmakers, printing workers, contract cleaners, and electronics workers. Members came with social problems arising from high rents and poor working conditions, and also for help with First Holy Communions, the seeking of marriage partners, and provision of decent housing. Accepting the social life of its single-bedsitter membership to be an aspect of its brief, the union organised concerts and dances, and served as guardian to its younger members. **Mary Jones**

Irish World Music Centre, a centre for the promotion of research into Irish music. Created in 1994 by Prof. MÍCHEÁL Ó SÚILLEABHÁIN at the University of Limerick, the centre promotes research into Irish music throughout the world. Through the University of Limerick it provides postgraduate MA degrees in classical string performance, dance performance, ethnomusicology, music therapy, chant performance, traditional music performance and community music, and a postgraduate diploma in music education. **John Page**

Irisleabhar na Gaedhilge (1882–1909), bilingual monthly journal published by the Gaelic Union; its founding editor was

Dáithí Ó Coimín. It is recognised as the starting-point of the language revival and the forerunner of journalism in Irish. EOIN MACNEILL was appointed editor in 1894, and publication was continued by CONRADH NA GAEILGE from 1898. **Caoilfhionn Nic Pháidín**

Irisleabhar Mhá Nuad (1898–), a student journal in ST PATRICK'S COLLEGE, Maynooth, its chief areas of interest being Irish culture and spirituality. During the period 1966–78 it was devoted entirely to literary CRITICISM. Under the influence of BREANDÁN Ó DOIBHLIN it published a ground-breaking series of essays on modern literature which has been the inspiration of modern LITERARY CRITICISM IN IRISH. **Antain Mag Shamhráin**

Iron Age (c. 600 BC to AD 400). Ironworking developed in Europe from c. 750 BC; the associated archaeological culture is termed *Hallstatt* (after the village in Austria where typical remains were found). By c. 600 BC bronze swords of Hallstatt character appear in Ireland, mainly removed from rivers. These are not proof, however, of incoming groups, nor are they necessarily evidence of ironworking, for they are of insular character and exclusively made of bronze. A blade fragment of iron from the River SHANNON at Athlone has been regarded by some as a Hallstatt sword, but this remains unproved. The matter is especially problematic as those centuries that saw the development and spread of ironworking across Europe are the very centuries that in Ireland have often been termed a 'Dark Age'.

The nature of cultural developments c. 600 BC and immediately afterwards is obscure. A number of scattered artefacts of iron, such as two looped and socketed axeheads from Co. Antrim, have been seen as BRONZE AGE forms rendered—with some difficulty—in the new metal, thus constituting the first steps in an ironworking industry. Even if this widely held interpretation is accepted (and it is by no means certain that it is correct) the number of such items is tiny, suggesting at best a limited, piecemeal introduction of the new skills to isolated pockets of the country. There is no evidence that the art of ironworking spread widely until after the third century BC, when well-forged iron swords, which may with some confidence be accepted as of native manufacture, begin to appear in the archaeological record.

The introduction of ironworking does not necessarily indicate the influx of sizeable population groups. Such skills could have been acquired from a few immigrant blacksmiths or by native bronzesmiths returning from abroad with the new technology. The advantages of iron over bronze would soon have become apparent; and once the technique was mastered, the ready presence of iron ores in the country, especially bog ores, would have facilitated the development and spread of the new technology. [see BRONZE-AGE COPPER MINING; METAL TECHNOLOGY IN PREHISTORIC IRELAND.] **Barry Raftery**

ironfoundries. Charcoal-fired blast furnaces established in Ireland during the seventeenth and eighteenth centuries by English settlers lasted only as long as the forests. By the end of the eighteenth century, however, foundry work no longer necessitated the smelting of iron directly from its ores, as the development of new types of furnace enabled both pig and bar iron to be remelted and cast into increasingly complicated forms, such as machine parts. This processed iron could now be imported from Britain, where both iron ore and the coal used to smelt it were much cheaper, to be remelted in Irish foundries with locally acquired scrap iron and used to manufacture a wide range of implements and machines.

Irish Traditional Music Archive. *Con Cassidy, Co. Donegal fiddler, a photograph by Eamonn O'Doherty from* The Northern Fiddler, *the drawings, photographs, and recordings of which are preserved at the Archive. [Irish Traditional Music Archive]*

The spread of ironfoundries to the principal ports and county towns in the period 1799–1840 was a direct response to the rapidly changing technological climate of the late eighteenth century. Technological changes in the iron industry had made cast iron a much cheaper commodity, and it was beginning to replace wood in the basic components of water-powered wheels, power transmission systems, and machinery. The increased use of cast-iron framing and beams in building design and the emergence of steam-driven prime movers also encouraged the creation of new foundries. **Colin Rynne**

ironworking. Though iron technology probably came to Ireland by way of the CELTS about the middle of the first millennium BC, direct evidence for the production of iron is scarce before the middle of the first millennium AD. An enlarged range of improved tools and wedges was one of the legacies of the VIKINGS. HORSE equipment in iron (stirrups, spurs, and horseshoes) dates from the eleventh century onwards. Post-medieval blacksmithing in the form of tools, products, and practices seems to betray English influences, particularly in terminology and the compiling of ledgers. The decline since the Second World War in the number of working and hunting horses and ponies led to the closure of forges all over the country, a trend offset to a slight extent by increased ornamental ironwork. Horses are now cold-shod with prefabricated shoes. **Patrick Wallace**

Irvine, Alexander (1863–1941), evangelist, writer, and social reformer. Born in Co. Antrim; had little formal education because of poverty, and learnt to read in the Royal Marines. In an extraordinarily adventurous life he worked among the destitute and served as an army chaplain. His works include *My Lady of the Chimney Corner* (1913), *From the Bottom Up* (1914), *The Souls of Poor Folk* (1921), *The Carpenter and His Kingdom* (1922), *A Fighting Parson* (1930), and *Anna's Wishing Chair and Other Chimney Corner Stories*

(1937). His accounts of the poor are marked by a vigorous compassion anchored in a respect for social justice. **Tess Maginess**

Irvine, Andy (1942–), musician, singer, and songwriter. Born in London. An introduction to the work of Woody Guthrie diverted him from the theatre to folk music. He formed SWEENEY'S MEN in 1966 with Johnny Moynihan and Joe Dolan. He left for eastern Europe in 1968, and developed an interest in Balkan music. He was a founder-member of Planxty (with CHRISTY MOORE, DÓNAL LUNNY, and LIAM O'FLYNN) in 1972. He played with PAUL BRADY from 1976 to 1978; since 1986 he has been a member of 'Patrick Street'. **Pat Ahern**

Irvine, Edward (Eddie) (1965–), racing driver. Born in Newtownards, Co. Down. An extrovert driver who became the first Irishman to drive for Ferrari, he was fourth in 1998 and second in the 1999 Drivers' World Championship. He won four grands prix up to 2000, when he was signed for the Jaguar formula 1 team. [see MOTOR SPORT.] **Brendan Lynch**

Irvine, Jaki (1966–), artist. Born in Dublin; studied at the NCAD and Goldsmiths College, London. She now lives and works in Italy. Her super-8 and 16 mm films, exhibited in installation form, explore the 'psychographic' relationships between reality, fiction, memory, intimacy, and nostalgia, played out through the interweaving of moving images, music, and narration, blurring distinctions between the ordinary and the extraordinary. In 1997 she represented Ireland at the Venice Biennale; in 2000 her work was included in 'New British Art, 2000: Intelligence' at the Tate Gallery, London, and in 'Shifting Ground: Fifty Years of Irish Art' at the IRISH MUSEUM OF MODERN ART, Dublin. **Liam Kelly**

Irwin, Thomas Caulfield (1823–1892), poet and essayist. Born in Warrenpoint, Co. Down. Intended for the medical profession until the family fortune collapsed in 1848, he subsequently became a prolific writer and frequent contributor to both the NATION and DUBLIN UNIVERSITY MAGAZINE; in the 1860s he was recruited by JOHN O'LEARY to write for the *Irish People*, a Fenian publication. Among his many publications only *Irish Poems and Legends* (1869) has an exclusively Irish subject matter. Celebrated hyperbolically as the 'Irish Keats' and 'the only Irish Tennysonian', Irwin also became noted for his increasing eccentricity and ensuing dementia before his death in Dublin. **Jason King**

Islandman: see OILEÁNACH, AN T-.

islands. Ireland is surrounded by a fringe of islands, particularly numerous off the west coast, ranging in size from ACHILL ISLAND, Co. Mayo, to mere rocks. It has been suggested that Ireland has 365 islands; and there being no accepted definition of the size at which a rock becomes an island, this is as good a figure as any. The islands were formed by a variety of processes, many by a rise in sea level after the last Ice Age.

In 1841 (before the GREAT FAMINE), 211 islands were occupied by more than 38,000 people; in 1996 only sixty-one remained inhabited, with a combined population of approximately 9,300. Most of them are Irish-speaking. People left the islands because their resources, usually farming and fishing, could not offer them a sufficiently high standard of living; the small scale of the islands' society and their isolation were also factors. Islands with better connections to the mainland, particularly bridges or causeways, such as Achill Island and Valentia Island, Co. Kerry, retained more of their population. Sometimes, as on INNISHMURRAY, Co. Sligo, and Great Blasket Island, Co. Kerry, the abandonment was organised; but usually DEPOPULATION takes the form of a slow drift of people until, one winter, no one stays. The process is still taking place: DURSEY ISLAND, Co. Cork, has probably reached the point of no return. Many islands have limited services, though a post office, church and primary school are often found; the larger islands, such as Aran Island, Co. Donegal, Achill Island and Inishmore, Co. Galway, have a fuller range of services. Many islands retain aspects of traditional culture; some market these traditions, with TOURISM an important component of their economy. In the 1980s islanders in the Republic began to press collectively for the support they all needed, and a Department of the Arts, Heritage, Gaeltacht, and the Islands was established. Rathlin, Co. Antrim, which is inhabited, is the only significant island in Northern Ireland. [see ARAN ISLANDS; CLÉIRE, COASTAL EROSION; DALKEY; IRELAND'S EYE; RATHLIN.] **Stephen A. Royle**

Iveragh Peninsula, Co. Kerry, the largest peninsula in Ireland, measuring a maximum of 65 km (40 miles) in length and 32 km (20 miles) in width. It is also the most mountainous part of the country, with Macgillycuddy's Reeks at its eastern end and other east-west ranges covering most of the surface. Forty peaks exceed 600 m (2,000 ft) in height, with eight over 900 m (3,000 ft). There are numerous lakes, ranging from tiny mountain pools to the large lowland Lough Currane and Lough Caragh. The coastline is varied also, with sandspits on the north shore, high cliffs on the west, and small coves scattered throughout. Valentia Island lies off the north-west tip of the peninsula, and the Skelligs are 8 miles into the Atlantic.

There is evidence of settlement in Iveragh from the Neolithic Period, and the peninsula has a rich archaeological heritage. Of particular interest are the ROCK ART often found near the heads of river valleys, and the oratories and churches of the early and late medieval periods. The most spectacular site is SCEILG MHICHÍL, near the summit of the Great Skellig rock, 180 m (600 ft) above the sea. According to tradition this was founded by St Finan in the sixth century, but it was linked to St Michael by the time the Annals of the FOUR MASTERS were compiled in the sixteenth century. After the monks left the rock in the twelfth century it became an important PILGRIMAGE centre, and it was recognised by UNESCO as a World Heritage Site in 1996.

Iveragh is marketed for TOURISM as the 'Ring of Kerry'. This route follows the coast and passes through the main towns and villages of the peninsula: Kenmare, Sneem, Waterville, Cahersiveen, and Killorglin. A circuit of the Ring, about 160 km (100 miles), can begin and finish at KILLARNEY. **Kevin Hourihan**

Ivory, Thomas (c. 1732–1786), architect. Born in Cork; trained as a carpenter and gunsmith before studying draughtsmanship, apparently under the Dublin surveyor Jonas Blaymire. From 1764 until his death he was master of the DUBLIN SOCIETY's Drawing School. He had mixed success in architectural competitions in the city: he produced a winning though unexecuted design for a market house in Oxmantown Green (1768), was the leading Irish entrant in the competition for the Royal Exchange (1769), and received the premium and commission for the King's Hospital School ('Bluecoat School') in 1773. His other great work was the neo-classical Newcomen's Bank in Castle Street, Dublin (c. 1781). He designed bridges for CARTON (1772, unexecuted) and Lismore (1773). **Frederick O'Dwyer**

Joly, John *(see* *page 569)**. One of John Joly's colour slides, c. 1890, illustrating his successful experiments with colour photography. Joly's system involved taking a photograph on a monochrome negative through a screen of fine red, green and blue lines. A print was then made on a glass plate with a colour screen and the result projected. [Council of Trustees of the National Library of Ireland]*

J

Jackson, Walker (Piper) (died 1798), musician. Born in Ballingarry, Co. Limerick, into a family of minor gentry. He played UILLEANN PIPES and FIDDLE. He published a collection of dance music, *Jackson's Celebrated Irish Tunes* (1774), half a dozen of which are still popular with musicians. In the oral tradition many other tunes are associated with his name. **Siobhán Ní Chonaráin**

Jacob, Arthur (1790–1874), surgeon. Born in Knockfin, Co. Laois; trained at the Royal College of Surgeons in Ireland and in Edinburgh. A pioneering ophthalmologist, he discovered the light-sensitive layer of the retina now called Jacob's membrane and also identified the rodent ulcer originally called Jacob's ulcer. **Robert Mills**

Jacob, George Newsom (1854–1942), biscuit manufacturer. Born in Dublin, third son of William Jacob, joint-founder of the Jacob biscuit company; educated at the Rathmines School. In 1883 the firm became a limited company as W. and R. Jacob Ltd, with George Jacob and W. F. BEWLEY as its first managing directors. Jacob invented the cream cracker in 1885; it quickly became the company's best-selling product, and remains so today. He oversaw the expansion of the company into England; during the 1913 DUBLIN LOCK-OUT he earned a reputation as a hard-liner, and he was elected president of Dublin Chamber of Commerce in 1926 and of the Associated Chambers of Commerce of the Irish Free State in 1928. He campaigned against the hydro-electric SHANNON SCHEME and the founding of the Electricity Supply Board. A representative of the conservative business interests of the day, he lacked faith in the political and economic future of the Irish Free State. He was a keen amateur photographer, a traveller of the world, and a pioneer of motoring, owning a car as early as 1905. He was killed in a traffic accident in St Stephen's Green, Dublin. **Ciarán Deane**

Jacob, Joshua (1805–1877), founder of the White Quakers. Born in Clonmel, Co. Tipperary; he was a grocer by trade. Following a dispute with the Society of Friends he founded the White Quakers, so called because they revived the early QUAKER practice of wearing undyed garments. He established a community at Clondalkin, near Dublin; others formed at Clonmel, Co. Tipperary, Waterford, and Mountmellick, Co. Laois. Members lived communally, were vegetarians, and eschewed such manifestations of modernity as timepieces. Jacob published tracts and *The Truth As It Is in Jesus* (1843) before renouncing the sect on the death of his wife, marrying a Catholic, and returning to the grocery trade. **Fergal Tobin**

Jacob, Rosamund (1888–1960), feminist and nationalist. Born in Waterford. She became an early member of SINN FÉIN and a militant suffragist. Opposed to the ANGLO-IRISH TREATY, she later joined FIANNA FÁIL but was disappointed by the disregard for women's issues in independent Ireland. She maintained her feminist commitment through membership of such organisations as the Women's League for Peace and Freedom, the Women's Social and Progressive League, and the IRISH HOUSEWIVES' ASSOCIATION, while her ideological concerns were reflected in her historical account *The Rise of the United Irishmen* (1937) and novels such as *The Rebel's Wife* (1957). **Rosemary Raughter**

Jacobites. *Engraving of Charles Chalmont, Marquis de Saint-Ruth, Jacobite commander at the Battle of Aughrim, July 1691, at which he was killed by cannon fire. [Council of Trustees of the National Library of Ireland. R.15360]*

Jacobite poetry. The most substantial body of political poetry in Irish is undoubtedly the corpus of eighteenth-century Jacobite poetry, most of which was produced in Munster in the period after 1690 and preserved in manuscripts of the eighteenth and nineteenth centuries.

Literary Jacobitism has its origins in the acceptance by the Irish intelligentsia of the legitimacy of JAMES I as King of Ireland on his accession to the crown of England, Scotland, and Ireland in 1603, an event that was greeted with poems of welcome by both EOCHAIDH Ó HEÓDHUSA and FEARGHAL ÓG MAC AN BHAIRD. Tolerance of James's PROTESTANTISM was achieved in Irish COUNTER-REFORMATION texts by a judicious separation of the religious and political spheres; and support for the Stuarts among Irish Catholics persisted despite the displacements associated with seventeenth-century PLANTATION policies and religious conflict. A departure from the traditional Irish ideology of kingship was necessary in the acceptance of primogeniture, and Irish Jacobite allegiance continued under the reign of CHARLES I and CHARLES II, gaining momentum with the accession of the Catholic JAMES II in 1685. It was believed that Irish Catholics could now look forward with greater confidence to a future in which their legal position and religious rights were more secure.

Jacobitism as a political ideology is associated most dramatically with the century following the overthrow of James II by the Protestant WILLIAM III in 1688. After James's defeat at the BATTLE OF THE BOYNE (1690) and his subsequent exile in France, the AISLING became the main literary form in which Jacobite ideology was expressed. The Irish poetic tradition was eminently equipped to incorporate the messianic and millenarian dimensions of that ideology, and for several generations the prophetic message of hope was attached to different exiled members of the Stuart family. The early eighteenth-century 'Mac an Cheannaí' by AOGÁN Ó RATHAILLE expresses hopes for the reinstatement of the Old Pretender, James Stuart (son of the deposed James II), the 'Merchant's Son' of the title, while the mid-century 'Bímse buan ar buairt gach ló' (better known as 'Mo Ghille Mear') by SEÁN CLÁRACH MAC DOMHNAILL was one of the most popular songs associated in Ireland with the Young Pretender, James Stuart's son Charles, 'Bonny Prince Charlie'.

Jacobite poetry also had an important musical aspect, as certain tunes, such as 'Gráinne Mhaol' and 'Móirín Ní Chuileannáin', developed popular Jacobite associations. The use of vernacular names in place of the more classical sovereignty figure 'Éire' has been interpreted as a form of code to shroud or disguise the songs' treasonable political message, comparable to the other forms of disguise employed in Jacobite literature. The name of the particular Stuart claimant being referred to is often cloaked in pseudonyms, such as 'Cormac Óg' (linking him to heroic kings of Irish tradition) or in epithets such as 'Mac an Cheannaí', 'An Craoibhín Aoibhinn', or 'Mo Ghille Mear'. It has been argued, however, that the main function of vernacular names was as an aid to popular mobilisation and as signifiers of economic and religious injustice comparable to the use of female effigy in Jacobite popular culture or the allegorical use of female names, such as Sadhbh Ultach by the WHITEBOYS in the 1760s. Bonny Prince Charlie is himself described as a 'Buachaill Bán' (white-headed boy or Whiteboy) in a poem by the Co. Cork poet SEÁN Ó COILEÁIN, and the Jacobite tune 'The White Cockade' was frequently sung by the Whiteboys.

While one could argue that the royalism associated with Jacobite ideology was anathema to revolutionary thinking on the French model, Jacobitism did provide an idiom of protest adaptable to a wide range of social, economic, religious and cultural issues. While the death of James Stuart in 1766 and the subsequent refusal of European Catholic powers to recognise Bonny Prince Charlie as Charles III should have dealt a final blow to Irish Jacobite aspirations, the literary aspects of Irish Jacobitism persisted up to the nineteenth century as an actual Stuart claimant was replaced in poetry and song by other figures of liberation. The publication by John O'Daly of *Reliques of Irish Jacobite Poetry* (1845) and *Poets and Poetry of Munster* (1850) brought Jacobite poetry to the attention of several generations of readers. For long considered an empty formula devoid of political realism, the corpus of *aisling* poetry that was such an important medium for the expression of Jacobite political sentiment has been comprehensively and meticulously contextualised by Breandán Ó Buachalla in his path-breaking study *Aisling Ghéar: Na Stíobhartaigh agus an tAos Léinn, 1603–1788* (1996), which refutes the idea that Irish poets were engaging in escapist 'Charlie-over-the-waterism'. Instead, eighteenth-century political poetry can now be seen in the context of Jacobitism as an international political phenomenon. It is no coincidence that the periods of greatest Jacobite literary activity in Ireland coincided with periods of Jacobite rebellion in Britain; that both the content and the idiom of Irish Jacobite poetry mirrors that of popular Jacobite culture in England and Scotland; and that Irish authors such as LIAM INGLIS, Seán Clárach Mac Domhnaill, and TADHG Ó NEACHTAIN display a detailed knowledge and understanding of European political alliances, intrigues, and conflicts relevant to the Stuart cause, much of which they gleaned from contemporary newspaper accounts. In the wake of Ó Buachalla's study, specific aspects of Irish Jacobitism and Irish Jacobite literature have been illuminated by other scholars, including Mícheál Mac Craith, Neil Buttimer, Vincent Morley, and Éamon Ó Ciardha. Meanwhile most of the huge corpus of Irish poetry that is the central primary source for this work awaits scholarly editing. [see POLITICAL POETRY IN IRISH.] **Máirín Nic Eoin**

Jacobites, a term applied to the supporters of KING JAMES II and his heirs following the expulsion of the Stuart dynasty from their three kingdoms of England, Scotland, and Ireland and particularly to those who fought for the king in Ireland, 1689–91. The Lord Deputy, RICHARD TALBOT, Earl of Tyrconnell, persuaded James to use Ireland as a stepping-stone to regaining his throne, rather than directly invading England. The Irish Jacobites were soon disappointed in James, both by his military ineptitude and by his reluctance to agree fully to their political demands. In particular, his refusal to allow the Parliament he held in Dublin in 1689 to establish Catholicism as the state church, his insistence that the Protestant bishops sit in the House of Lords, and his clear lack of enthusiasm for the repeal of the RESTORATION land settlement severely tested the patience of his Irish allies. But the debacle of the BATTLE OF THE BOYNE and the cowardly and graceless flight of the king created a deep and permanent split among Irish Jacobites. They divided into the peace party, led by Talbot, anxious to reach a settlement with WILLIAM III, and the war party, led by SARSFIELD, determined to fight to secure better terms. The war ended with the unsatisfactory TREATY OF LIMERICK (1691) and the departure of the Jacobite army for France. While a popular Jacobite nostalgia, especially in literature and song, lingered on, it had lost its political teeth, as evidenced by the lack of any Irish response to the 1745 rebellion in Scotland. **Liam Irwin**

Jacobitism, adherence to JAMES II or to his descendants in their efforts to regain the throne. It produced no military activity in Ireland after the defeat of the Stuart cause in the WILLIAMITE WARS (1689–91). However, it was able to retain the allegiance of Irish Catholics until about the time of the Seven Years' War (1756–63), as it provided the only hope of a restoration of the Catholic Church and a reversal of the seventeenth-century land settlements. This loyalty supplied a pressing motive for enacting anti-Catholic legislation during the period. **C. D. A. Leighton**

Jail Journal (1854), an autobiographical work by the revolutionary JOHN MITCHEL. Beginning in May 1848, when Mitchel was transported from Ireland, and ending in November 1853, when he arrived in New York, *Jail Journal* circumnavigates the British Empire and the globe, from Bermuda's hulks to Tasmanian parole (by way of Brazil and South Africa), including an escape to Australia and a stop-over in Cuba. First published in Mitchel's New York newspaper, the *Citizen*, and astutely aimed at a politically influential Irish-American audience, the *Journal* is marked by Carlylean rhetoric and Swiftian irony. Mitchel excoriates England's treatment of Ireland from Elizabethan times to the GREAT FAMINE and the 1848 RISING. He prefaces 'the personal memoranda of a solitary captive' with the 'general history of a nation', because 'it was strictly and logically a consequence of the dreary story here epitomised, that I became a prisoner.' [see JOURNALISTS AS POLITICIANS.] **Richard Haslam**

James I (1566–1625), King of England. Son of Mary Queen of Scots, James was crowned King of England in 1603. Although he was a Protestant, Irish Catholics believed that his family background disposed him towards toleration of Catholicism. Though personally inclined to permit freedom of worship, he had to battle with his image as an interloping Scot in England. In an attempt to conform to expectations in his new kingdom he became persuaded of the need to pursue policies consistent with English interests. Consequently, he disappointed Irish Catholics when he sanctioned penal measures against them, though he managed to temper the more extreme inclinations of his officials. James I is principally associated with PLANTATIONS in Ireland, the most notable of which occurred in Ulster. Often considered an indolent monarch, he approached the task of planting Ulster with missionary zeal. His Scottish background resulted in large numbers of his fellow-countrymen being granted lands in Ulster. **John McCavitt**

James II (1633–1701), King of England, Scotland and Ireland. A convert to Catholicism, his promotion of Catholics in the political and military establishment from his accession in 1685 alarmed Protestants both in Ireland and England. This was a contributory factor to his loss of power, but it ensured the full and enthusiastic support of Irish Catholics when he landed at Kinsale in 1689 to attempt to regain control of his three kingdoms. His refusal to make Catholicism the established church, and his reluctance to sanction in the Jacobite Parliament the restoration of all land confiscated since 1641, was an unexpected contrast with his former policy. However, his awareness of the effect on English opinion of a pro-Catholic policy in Ireland had come too late to allow him to recover support there, while it disillusioned his Irish allies. The disastrous military campaign, culminating in the debacle at the Boyne in July 1690 and his hasty return to France, left the Irish JACOBITES demoralised and divided. [see JACOBITE POETRY.] **Liam Irwin**

Jameson, Andrew (1885–1941), businessman and politician. Scion of the family that established the Bow Street Distillery, Dublin, in 1780, he served as chairman of John Jameson and Sons Ltd but was also engaged in the politics of Dublin's powerful unionist business community. A vocal proponent of the Union in debates over HOME RULE, he later became a member of the Senate of the Irish Free State and leader of its independent group (see p. 1135). **K. J. James**

Jansenism, a movement named after Cornelius Otto Jansen (1585–1638), Bishop of Ypres. He asserted that human nature is thoroughly flawed by original sin and denied the ability to resist temptation without God-given irresistible grace, rejecting the teaching that Christ died for all. Jansenism was repeatedly condemned by several popes. It affected Irish Catholicism through the influence of Irish clergy who had trained on the Continent. It

jazz. *Frank Morgan plays the saxophone at the Cork Jazz Festival, 1999. The festival attracts leading international jazz musicians during the October holiday weekend. [Guinness Ireland Group]*

advocated rigorous austerity and moral living and maintained that only those with perfect contrition could receive the sacraments of Eucharist and Penance. The term Jansenism is also inaccurately used to refer to Puritan traits that infiltrated Irish Catholicism during the Victorian era. **Ciarán O'Carroll**

Jarlath, an Anglicised form of Iarlaith. Of the two SAINTS of this name, the patron of the church and diocese of Tuam is now the more important. However, his namesake Iarlaith of Dál Fiatach in east Ulster is reputed to have succeeded PATRICK as abbot of Armagh. Jarlath of Tuam figures in the Life of BRENDAN of Clonfert, which describes how his church at Tuam came to be founded. His feast-day is 26 December. **Pádraig Ó Riain**

jazz. Widely acknowledged as one of the most important expressions of twentieth-century culture, jazz has struggled to win a standing in Ireland as an art form and has had little influence on other forms of POPULAR MUSIC. From the 1990s, however, with more stable grants from state bodies, greater commercial sponsorship, more formal education, and more recordings, jazz might be said to have 'arrived'. It has won a wider, more diverse, and noticeably younger audience, and some formal recognition. Among the musicians chosen to represent contemporary Ireland at Expo 2000 in Hannover was Khanda, a band consisting mainly of jazz musicians playing a jazz-folk amalgam.

The jazz age, which intoxicated America in the inter-war years and had ripple effects on much of Europe, did not pass Ireland by but rather was actively resisted. The moral guardians who held sway determined that jive, jitterbug and other dance crazes associated with jazz, as they understood it, should not take root in Ireland. The Catholic bishops warned against the evils of indecent dancing, and CONRADH NA GAEILGE ran an 'anti-jazz campaign'.

In the Republic the PUBLIC DANCE HALLS ACT (1935) gave the courts extensive powers to control 'jazz-hall' dancing. As FLANN O'BRIEN pointed out in the BELL in 1941, the district justices who exercised their authority so generously in respect of 'jazz' dancing applied quite different standards to Irish dancing. According to the IRISH TIMES of 12 May 1943, a ban was placed on dance music in Radio Éireann; swing, jive, 'hot' music, 'or music with a vocal chorus sung by a crooner' were all covered by the ban. Still, dancing was to become a nationwide industry, and dance bands enjoyed great success in the 1950s and 60s, paving the way for the showbands. Despite the historical connection with jazz, the well-mannered music of the dance bands was almost entirely based on written scores, involving little or no improvisation.

In less censorious times, and as an effect of the jazz revival in Britain in the 1950s, Irish musicians—in small numbers—became interested in jazz. Some of these had their training and employment in the dance bands, but others came to jazz from a classical background. The British 'trad jazz' movement had its most immediate effect in Northern Ireland, where Dixieland and New Orleans-style bands have had a continuing presence for fifty years. They include the still-active Apex Jazz Band, formed in 1966. Belfast has also been home to a significant blues and R&B movement since the 1960s.

As Dublin grew in sophistication it became the main centre for jazz in Ireland, and specifically modern jazz. The Jazz Society in TRINITY COLLEGE was an important conduit for the newer sounds, bringing in British bands and soloists. A showcase of Irish jazz in the OLYMPIA THEATRE in 1962 included the Eblana Jazz Band (New Orleans style), the pianist Ian Henry's modern quartet, a Chicago-style group led by the trumpeter Bryan Hopper (with Ian Henry on piano), the bop-based Jazz Heralds (led by NOEL KELEHAN), and Jack Flahive and his Orchestra (Bryan Hopper on trumpet, Noel Kelehan on piano). ROCK FOX played clarinet in one band, trumpet in another; JOHN WADHAM also featured in two, as did his fellow-drummer Jack Daly. The many overlaps and frequent turnover of personnel continued to characterise the Dublin jazz scene for three decades. Venues turned over almost as rapidly; in contrast to most European cities, Dublin never acquired a dedicated jazz venue.

The pioneering Jazz Heralds lasted about three years, as did Noel Kelehan's later quintet and TOMMY HALFERTY's trio. Some larger ENSEMBLES lasted longer but played much less frequently; these included JIM DOHERTY's fusion band Spon, Noel Kelehan's Big Band, and Rock Fox's Famous Orchestra. Trad bands, such as the Jubilee Jazz Band, East Coast Jazz Band, Odyssey Jazz Band, and the Jazz Coasters, have also survived for many years, also with shifting line-ups. For a brief period in the 1980s Dublin also had several jazz-fusion bands, among them Metropolis, Fast Breeder, Supply Demand and Curve, and Stubbs. They helped to widen the audience and the recruitment of musicians for jazz.

Some aspirant jazz musicians left Ireland to work elsewhere. Joe McIntyre, a trumpeter from Derry, and BOBBY LAMB, a trombonist from Cork, worked with British big bands from the 1960s. Ian Henry, a modern jazz pianist as well as a doctor, moved to England in the 1960s and later to Spain, from where he toured with American and European musicians. The guitarist and designer

Norman Mongan went to Paris in the 1960s, where he won recognition as a musician and writer. The flautist Brian Dunning studied in Berklee College, Boston, in the 1980s and based himself in the United States, playing a cross-over between jazz and Irish folk music. The guitarist Dave O'Rourke and the pianist Fintan O'Neill have established themselves more recently in New York, while the vibraphonist Anthony Kerr lives in Britain. The drummer Stephen Keogh (son of the flautist and flute teacher Doris Keogh and himself a former percussionist with the NATIONAL SYMPHONY ORCHESTRA) has been living in Spain for several years.

After many years during which only the guitarist LOUIS STEWART was consistently connected with the international jazz world, many Irish jazz musicians have developed relationships with counterparts elsewhere, notably through involvement with jazz education. Opportunities for Irish audiences to hear, and for Irish musicians to play with, leading international jazz figures have also been increasing steadily. Individual enthusiasts have played an important role in this movement: the architect Allen Smith established Jazz on the Terrace as a vehicle for the promotion of jazz concerts from 1982 and has been associated with the Improvised Music Company from 1991.

From the 1970s the painter and gallery-owner Gerald Davis released recordings by Louis Stewart, Brian Dunning, and John Wadham. Writers and broadcasters about jazz have also been champions of the music, or of individual musicians; in some instances they have been musicians themselves. Rock Fox and John Wadham presented jazz programmes on RTÉ Radio at different times; the singer HONOR HEFFERNAN continues to do so on LYRIC FM. Jazz programmes on several community and pirate stations, and a strong jazz element in John Kelly's mixed-music programmes on RTÉ Radio 1, have increased the jazz exposure on radio. The *Irish Times* has maintained coverage of jazz since the 1970s, notably by George Hodnett.

Other supports for jazz and jazz musicians strengthened in the 1980s and 90s. Jazz tuition was established at Newpark Music Centre in Blackrock, Co. Dublin, from 1985, later in summer schools at the Jordanstown college of the University of Ulster and, since 1999, at a summer school under Louis Stewart's direction in Carrigaholt, Co. Clare. The bass guitarist and composer RONAN GUILFOYLE, who pioneered these efforts through Newpark Music Centre, has at the same time been prominently advocating the inclusion of jazz education in the planned Irish Academy of Performing Arts. **Brian Trench**

Jeffares, A. Norman (1920–), critic and teacher. Born in Dublin; educated at TCD and Oxford. After lecturing at TCD, Groningen, Edinburgh, and Adelaide, he was professor of English at Leeds, 1957–74 (subsequently at Stirling, 1974–86), a position in which he developed a legendary reputation as a teacher principally encouraging postgraduate study of ANGLO-IRISH LITERATURE. While his own original work is limited to a biography of W. B. YEATS (1988) and his essays on Irish literature *Images of Imagination* (1996), his role as an editor, in particular of Yeats's poetry, on which he is a perceptive commentator, has been a feature of critical work in Irish literature during the past five decades. While at Stirling he was a member of both the Scottish Arts Council and the Arts Council of Great Britain; he was also director of the Yeats International Summer School, Sligo, 1969–71. **Richard Pine**

Jehovah's Witnesses. There are 115 congregations of Jehovah's Witnesses in Ireland, comprising approximately 4,600 members. They consider the Bible the true word of God; Christ is God's son but is inferior to him. A clergy class and religious titles are considered improper, and the taking of blood into the body through the mouth or veins is believed to violate God's laws. **Suzanne Mulligan**

Jeffares. *A. Norman Jeffares, critic and teacher, acclaimed for his critical work in Anglo-Irish literature, most notably as an editor of W. B. Yeats's poetry. [© Douglas Robertson/courtesy of Colin Smythe]*

Jellett, John Hewitt (1817–1888), mathematician and educator. Born in Cashel, Co. Tipperary; educated at TCD, before being elected to a fellowship in 1840. He was admitted to holy orders in 1846 and appointed professor of natural philosophy at Trinity College, Dublin, in 1848, where he was principally concerned with mathematical research. He was, however, inspired during the GREAT FAMINE to conduct researches into POTATO blight, and he invented a split-field endpoint device saccharimeter; this null-balance principle, introduced in Ireland for the first time, was first used in Wheatstone's electronic bridge and became of fundamental importance to many later visual optical instruments. He produced two important mathematical publications, *The Calculus of Variation* (1850) and *The Theory of Friction* (1872), and was awarded the Royal Medal of the Royal Society in 1881, the year in which he became provost of Trinity College, Dublin. Of a conservative liberal mind, he published theological essays, sermons, and religious treatises, including *An Examination of Some of the Moral Difficulties in the Old Testament* (1867) and *The Efficacy of Prayer* (1878). **Norman McMillan**

Jellett, Mary Harriet (Mainie) (1897–1944), artist. Born in Dublin; she studied at the Metropolitan School of Art, Dublin, and with Walter Sickert at the Westminster Technical Institute, London. In 1920 she, with her fellow Irish artist EVIE HONE, travelled to Paris to study with André Lhôte, who taught a highly formalised form of cubism. From 1921 they began to work closely with Albert Gleizes, who had developed a severe form of non-representational art based on geometrical principles. In later years she returned to figuration but in a non-academic manner much influenced by Chinese art. Religious subject matter formed a large body of this work. She and Hone were the first Irish artists to exhibit abstract paintings in Ireland (Dublin Painters' Society, 1923). She also applied her principles of abstraction to the design of rugs and theatre sets. She produced murals for the British Empire Exhibition, Glasgow (1938) and exhibited work in the Irish

Pavilion at the New York World Fair (1939). She played a prominent role in the promotion of modernism in Ireland and regularly lectured and broadcast on aspects of modern art. She was the chairwoman of the founding committee of the IRISH EXHIBITION OF LIVING ART but died some months before the first exhibition in 1944. **Daire O'Connell**

Jellett. Decoration *(1923), by Mainie Jellett, shown at the Dublin Painters' Society group show in 1923 and one of the first purely abstract works by an Irish artist to be exhibited in Ireland. [National Gallery of Ireland]*

Jellicoe, Anne (1823–1880), educationist. Born in Mountmellick, Co. Laois, the daughter of a QUAKER schoolmaster. She was, unusually, both a visionary and a woman of action. She was joint founder of the first society for the employment of women in Ireland, the Queen's Institute, Dublin (1861–82), and in 1866 founded Alexandra College, Dublin, the first college for women in Ireland to offer a university-type education. Eschewing the suffrage cause, she concentrated on education as the foundation stone for women's advancement. **Anne V. O'Connor**

Jenkinson, Biddy (1949–), poet. The work of this pseudonymous poet illustrates her concern with biology, sexuality and ecology as well as a sense of historical continuity as manifested in landscape and literature. Her collections *Baisteadh Gintlí* (1987), *Uiscí Beatha* (1988), *Dán na hUidhre* (1991), and *Amhras Neimhe* (1997) display the sensibility of one well versed in the Irish literary tradition, the tone often exhibiting a playful irony. A selection of her poems, *Rogha Dánta* (2000), provides a useful introduction to her work. She has also written plays and has published a collection of short stories, *An Grá Riabhach* (2000). She prefers not to have her work appear in English TRANSLATION in Ireland. **Seán Ó Cearnaigh**

Jennings, Pat (1945–), soccer player. Born in Newry, Co. Down. A Gaelic footballer in his early years, he signed for Watford in 1964 and soon afterwards was summoned for his first cap against Wales. The most capped player in Irish football, with 119 appearances for Northern Ireland, he has enjoyed continuing success in an outstanding club career, with Tottenham and later with Arsenal, whom he joined in 1977. A pivotal figure in Northern Ireland's qualification for the 1982 World Cup finals, he held out against England in a memorable performance at Wembley, to enable them to qualify for Mexico four years later. **Peter Byrne**

Jerpoint Abbey, Co. Kilkenny, founded as a Benedictine abbey c. 1160, then colonised by the CISTERCIAN abbey of BALTINGLASS c. 1180. Early ornamental details and architectural similarities suggest that the same masons worked at both sites. Of particular interest is the late fourteenth or early fifteenth-century cloister arcade, which incorporates the most varied and lively collection of late medieval sculpture in Ireland. A number of sculpted monuments survive, including an effigy of Bishop Felix O'Dullany (died 1202), a thirteenth-century stone slab engraved with two knights in mail, and the tomb of Robert Walsh (died 1501) and Katherine Power signed by the sculptor, Rory O'Tunney. **Rachel Moss**

Jervas, Charles (c. 1675–1739), portraitist. Born in Shinrone, Co. Offaly; he studied under Kneller, having travelled to London in 1690. In 1698 he copied Raphael's cartoons at Hampton Court. Jervas acted as agent for English collectors and painted portraits in Paris and Rome. He returned to London c. 1708, where he established himself professionally, and infiltrated elevated circles. Patrons included the Duke of Marlborough and the Duke of Kent. He translated *Don Quixote* (published 1742). He made visits to Ireland between 1715 and 1734; Irish sitters included Speaker CONOLLY and Lord BOYLE. Jervas served as principal painter to George I and George II, and visited Italy again in 1738 to improve his health and to acquire pictures for the royal collection (see p. 593). **Brendan Rooney**

Jesuits. The first members of the Society of Jesus in Ireland were Paschase Broet and Alfonso Salmeron (close companion of Ignatius of Loyola), who landed in 1542. Their mission was principally one of information-gathering. It was not until 1561, with the arrival of Father DAVID WOLFE, a native of Limerick, that Jesuit involvement in Ireland began in earnest. In effect, Wolfe and the other early Jesuits were agents of the COUNTER-REFORMATION in Ireland. Their mission concentrated on the Old English, rather than the Gaelic Irish, among whom the FRANCISCANS were more influential. This division was particularly noticeable during the years of the CONFEDERATION OF KILKENNY in the 1640s. The Jesuits opened schools, provided pastoral care, and were a bulwark against the spread of PROTESTANTISM. In addition, many Irish Jesuits participated in the order's missions to the Far East and South America.

Jews. *The last wedding to take place in the Adelaide Road Synagogue, Dublin. Consecrated on 4 December 1892 by the Chief Rabbi of Britain and Ireland, Rabbi Hermann, it was closed after 107 years in 1999. [Gerry O'Dea]*

With the defeat of the Old English interest in 1691 and the subsequent enactment of the PENAL LAWS, Jesuit influence declined, without ever totally disappearing. Even the suppression of the order by the Pope in 1774 did not extinguish the Jesuit presence in Ireland. On the restoration of the order in 1814, Father Peter Kenney established Clongowes Wood College, Co. Kildare, the first of a distinguished series of Jesuit boys' schools in Ireland. Aimed at the wealthier Catholic classes, the Jesuit schools played an important role in the formation of the emerging nationalist middle class. In 1883 the order assumed control of Newman's CATHOLIC UNIVERSITY in Dublin, which they renamed University College, the precursor of the University College, Dublin. Since the 1960s the order has continued its principal work as educators while also placing a growing emphasis on questions of social justice. **Fergal Tobin**

Jews. The 1861 census records 341 Jews in Ireland. Many Ashkenazi Jews came to Ireland from Lithuania in the 1880s and 90s fleeing the pogroms of Tsar Alexander II. They settled in Dublin, Belfast, Cork, and Limerick and integrated without serious incidents of anti-Semitism being recorded, Limerick in 1904 proving to be the exception. The number of Jews rose to 1,506 in 1901 and 3,805 in 1911, yet by 1946 the number was 3,907. The Constitutions of 1922 and 1937 guaranteed religious freedom. Jews have played a prominent role in the professional, cultural, academic, and political life of Ireland. ROBERT BRISCOE was twice lord mayor of Dublin (1956, 1961), as was his son BEN BRISCOE (1988–9). Gerald Goldberg was lord mayor of Cork (1977) and there has also been a Jewish lord mayor of Belfast, Sir Otto Jaffe, in 1899 and 1904.

By the end of the twentieth century the Irish Jewish community was in radical decline due to emigration to the larger Jewish communities in Britain, the United States, and Israel, with 4,000 in Belfast, fewer than a thousand in Dublin, a diminutive community in Cork, and no community left in Limerick. [see HERTZOG, CHAIM; KERNOFF, HARRY; LIMERICK POGROM; RACISM; SOLOMONS, ESTELLA.] **Dermot Keogh**

jew's harp, also known as the *trump* or the *jaw harp*, a folk instrument combining a *lamella* or flexible tongue with a metal frame that is easily cupped in the hand. Manual oscillation of the lamella as the instrument is held to the mouth produces a sound of constant pitch, rich in overtones that can be varied by movement of the tongue, larynx, and mouth cavity. Once the most popular folk instrument, particularly in Co. Donegal, it is now almost obsolete, a considerable decline since its first presence in Ireland in the late sixteenth or early seventeenth century. **Anthony McCann**

jig, a traditional dance type. Four variants exist: the double jig, single jig, slip or hop jig, and slide. The double jig (generally referred to simply as *jig*) is the most common dance tune in Irish TRADITIONAL MUSIC after the REEL. In six-eight time, it is characterised by a motor rhythm of groups of three quavers. It is popular as a solo competitive dance, lively for soft-shoe dances and at a greatly reduced tempo for the more complex hard-shoe variant; it is also played for certain set (group) dances. The *single jig*, in 12/8 time, is associated with a soft-shoe competitive dance for women and girls only; it differs from the double jig in that the predominant rhythmic pattern is a crotchet followed by a quaver. A fast version of the tune is known as the *slide*, a type particularly

jig. The Irish Jig *(1845), a grisaille watercolour by Samuel Watson. Customers at an inn dance to the music of a fiddler seated by the open fire, while others drink, smoke clay pipes, or look on; the benches, straw-seated chairs and other furnishings are typical of country furniture. [Private collection; photo: Denis Mortell]*

associated with SLIABH LUACHRA, where it is played for SET-DANCING. The *slip jig* or *hop jig* is in 9/8 time and is also a competitive dance popular with women and girls. **Liz Doherty**

Jinks Affair. In August 1927 FIANNA FÁIL, the National League Party, and the LABOUR PARTY agreed to join forces with the aim of ousting the CUMANN NA NGAEDHEAL government. On 16 August a vote of no confidence was called in DÁIL ÉIREANN; but because Alderman John Jinks (1872–1934) of Sligo, a member of the National League Party, was not present, the result was a tie, and the Government was saved by the casting vote of the Ceann Comhairle, Michael Hayes. Jinks's absence is generally attributed to the scheming of two COSGRAVE supporters, the independent deputy and former Unionist MP Major Bryan Cooper and the journalist R. M. SMYLLIE (later editor of the IRISH TIMES). Cooper is suspected of having supplied large quantities of alcohol to Jinks the previous evening, and of persuading him that the ex-servicemen of his Sligo-Leitrim constituency would not want him to vote for Fianna Fáil. On 25 August, Cosgrave dissolved the Dáil and called an election, in which he won a comfortable majority. Jinks lost his seat; Cooper was re-elected on the Cumann na nGaedheal ticket. **Ciarán Deane**

John (1167–1216), King of England, youngest son of HENRY II and Eleanor of Aquitaine. In 1177 Henry granted John the LORDSHIP OF IRELAND, with the intention of making him King of Ireland. He arrived in Ireland in 1185 but failed to assert his authority over the principal ANGLO-NORMAN landholder, HUGH DE LACY, and managed to alienate the Irish kings. During the reign of Richard I, 1189–99, John retained control of his lordship, except for a brief period in 1194 when he rebelled against his brother. In 1199 he became King of England, thus attaching Anglo-Norman Ireland to the royal government. He launched a more successful second expedition to Ireland in 1210, when he forfeited the estates of dissident barons and enhanced the area of royal control. From 1212 he was consumed with pressures in England. He was succeeded by his young son as Henry III. **Susan Foran**

John Bull's Other Island (1904), a play by GEORGE BERNARD SHAW, his only major work set in Ireland. Though rejected by the ABBEY THEATRE it was outstandingly successful when produced by the Court Theatre, London. Designed to invert traditional stereotypes of national character, it shows the rational Irishman Larry Doyle and the romantic Englishman Tom Broadbent on a visit from London to Larry's provincial Irish home town, Rosscullen. There Broadbent's sentimental preconceptions and Doyle's political analysis are used to expose what Shaw regarded as the realities of Ireland. While Doyle and Broadbent move to take over and develop Rosscullen commercially, the third most significant character, Peter Keegan, an unfrocked priest, voices a utopian vision of Ireland beyond such neo-colonial exploitation. **Nicholas Grene**

John Scotus Eriugena: see ERIUGENA.

Johnson, Esther (1681–1728), known as 'Stella', JONATHAN SWIFT's friend. Born in Surrey, daughter of the housekeeper of Sir William Temple of Moor Park, Farnham, Surrey; Temple was possibly her father. Swift was Temple's secretary, 1689–99. In 1695 he undertook Esther's education; 'Stella' was his nickname for her. In 1700 or 1701, with her companion Rebecca Dingley, she followed him to Ireland, but there is no proof for the belief that Swift was secretly married to, or had a sexual relationship, with her. She is buried in St Patrick's Cathedral beside Swift. **Ciarán Deane**

Johnson, Thomas (1863–1954), botanist. Born in Lincolnshire; educated at the Royal College of Science, London. He was professor of Botany at the Royal College of Science, Dublin, 1890–1928. During his tenure he also held government positions as director of the Seed Testing and Plant Diseases Station, 1906–10, and keeper of botanical collections at the NATIONAL MUSEUM OF IRELAND. He made important contributions to industrial botany through his studies on a wide variety of plant pathogens, and to palaeontology in descriptions of fossil ferns and other plants from the KILTORCAN OLD QUARRIES in Co. Kilkenny. **Christopher Moriarty**

Johnston, (William) Denis (1901–1984), playwright. Born in Dublin; educated at the University of Cambridge. As a young barrister he wrote *The Old Lady Says 'No!'* (1929), an inventively expressionist attack on the condition of the IRISH FREE STATE, which, following its rejection by the Abbey, was a brilliant controversial success at the GATE THEATRE. The satirical edge to his Shavian comedy *The Moon in the Yellow River* (1931) discomfited ABBEY THEATRE audiences but gave him a wider reputation. Restlessness drove him from 1930s Dublin and into radio, television and war reporting with the BBC. He wrote ten more stage plays, while *Nine Rivers from Jordan* (1953) is a philosophical war memoir of abiding interest. He was also an obsessive diarist and an incorrigible reviser of his own work. **Bernard Adams**

Johnston, Francis (1760–1839), architect. Born in Armagh; the early part of his career was fostered by Archbishop Robinson, who sent him to Dublin in 1778 to be articled for four years to THOMAS COOLEY. From there he joined the practice of his cousin Samuel Sproule in the city. After Cooley's death in 1784 Johnston took over his projects for Robinson (including the building of Rokeby Hall), practising from a house in Co. Louth for the next ten years. He ran a private practice from Dublin, 1794–1805, designing such country houses as Townley Hall, near Drogheda (1794), Charleville Forest, Co. Offaly (1800), and MARKREE CASTLE, Co. Sligo (1802). He also won competitions for St George's

Church, Dublin (1800), and for the conversion of the Parliament House to the Bank of Ireland (1803). He worked for the BOARD OF WORKS, 1805–26, during which time he designed the Chapel Royal, DUBLIN CASTLE (1807), and the GENERAL POST OFFICE (1814). He also designed a number of asylums, including the Richmond in Dublin (1810) and, from 1820, with his cousin and assistant William Murray, four district asylums (Armagh, Limerick, Belfast, and Derry). Equally adept in gothic and classical styles, Johnston was also a patron of the arts, being one of the founders in 1821 of the ROYAL HIBERNIAN ACADEMY, whose house in Abbey Street, Dublin, he both designed and paid for. **Frederick O'Dwyer**

Johnston, Jennifer (1930–), novelist and playwright. Born in Dublin, daughter of DENIS JOHNSTON and SHELAH RICHARDS; educated in Dublin. Since the 1970s she has lived in Derry. She learnt much about the arts through the vigorous social life enjoyed by her family. Her acclaimed fiction deals primarily with women struggling towards individual identity across boundaries imposed by nationality, class, sex, and religion. Her first novel was *The Captains and the Kings* (1972). *The Old Jest* (1979) won the Whitbread Prize. *The Railway Station Man* (1984) was made into a film (1991). *Two Moons* (1998) continues her interest in both border crossings and female relationships in multi-generational Protestant families. Her plays include pieces collected in *The Nightingale, Not the Lark* (1988). **Rachel Sealy Lynch**

Joly, Charles Jasper (1864–1906), astronomer. Born in Tullamore, second cousin of JOHN JOLY; educated at TCD, where he came first in his year in mathematics. After studying experimental physics for a year with Helmholtz in Berlin he returned to Trinity and gained a fellowship in 1894. He went to DUNSINK OBSERVATORY in 1897 as Andrews professor of Astronomy and prepared a new edition of ROWAN HAMILTON's *Elements of Quaternions*. As well as directing observational work at Dunsink he took part in the successful RIA-RDS eclipse expedition to Plasencia, Spain, in 1900. He was elected a fellow of the Royal Society in 1904. **Ian Elliott**

Joly, John (1857–1933), polymath and inventor. Born in Hollywood, Co. Offaly, of French-German-Italian parentage; educated at TCD. In 1897 he was appointed professor of geology and mineralogy at Trinity College, Dublin, in part in recognition of his various inventions. These feature in particular a photometer, a meldometer, a differential steam calorimeter, and a constant-volume gas thermometer, all of which bear his name, together with other lesser-known contrivances, such as a radio method of signalling at sea. In the 1890s he developed a process for colour photography and went to the United States to defend his patents (unsuccessfully) against Kodak. He was a pioneer and enthusiast of motion pictures, making and showing them in TCD. His geological work was principally in geochronology. In 1898 his estimate of the age of the Earth based on Edmond Halley's method of measuring the salinity

Jones, Mary. *'Mother Jones', leader and spokesperson of the American labour movement, shown at the age of seventy-three heading a march from Philadelphia to New York, seeking the President's support for ending harsh labour conditions for children. [UMWA Archives]*

of the sea, was 80–90 million years (later revised to 100 million years). He subsequently correctly ascribed the discovery by Samuel Haughton of spherical pleochroic haloes as being caused by radioactive alpha emissions in certain rocks. In 1903 he drew attention to the importance to geochronology of this new phenomenon in that its appropriate exploitation could greatly extend Kelvin's estimate of the age of the Earth. He rapidly established an international reputation in pioneering the use of radioactive dating methods in geology. In 1913, in collaboration with Rutherford, he estimated the age of Devonian rocks as 400 million years—a value in good agreement with modern estimates. He was elected a fellow of the Royal Society in 1892. Eventually his published papers numbered 270. His books include the seminal *Radioactivity and Geology* (1909) and the influential *Surface History of the Earth* (1925). He pioneered microscopic examination procedures for rock-forming minerals to determine their suitability as road metal. With Walter Stevenson of DR STEEVENS' HOSPITAL, Dublin, he devised new methods of radiotherapy, which led to the establishment by the RDS of the IRISH RADIUM INSTITUTE, where they pioneered the 'Dublin method' of using a hollow needle for use in deep-seated radio-therapy, a technique that was to come into worldwide use. He won the Boyle Medal of the Royal Dublin Society in 1911 and the Murchison Medal of the Geological Society of London in 1923. He collaborated with H. H. Dixon in important work on the rise of sap in plants. A staunch unionist, he defended Trinity College in 1916 (see p. 561). **Norman McMillan**

Jones, Henry (1721–1770), poet and playwright. Born in Drogheda, Co. Louth. He was employed as a bricklayer until a poem he wrote on the occasion of the Lord Lieutenant, Lord Chesterfield's arrival in Ireland gained him Chesterfield's recognition. He left for London with Chesterfield in 1748, there publishing *Poems on Several Occasions* (1749) and the play *The Earl of Essex* (1753). His play gained him some fame and money, but he developed a reputation for drunkenness and a crude manner and eventually squandered his money. In 1770 he was run over in the street, and he died in the parish WORKHOUSE. **Joley Wood**

Jones, Mary Harris, 'Mother Jones' (1830–1930), American labour leader. Born in Cork. The daughter of poor Irish emigrants, she was reared in Canada, where she worked as a teacher, later as a dressmaker. In 1861 she married George Jones, an organiser with the Ironmoulders' Union, and moved to Memphis, Tennessee. Following the death of her husband and four children during an epidemic of yellow fever in 1867 she became active in the TRADE UNION movement, earning the honorific 'Mother Jones'. She was highly active, notably in the rail strike of 1877; in 1905 she founded the radical Industrial Workers of the World ('Wobblies'), with the participation of JAMES CONNOLLY. [see MOLLY MAGUIRES, THE.] **David Kiely**

Jordan, Edward (Eddie) (1949–), racing driver. Born in Dublin. He won the Irish karting championships and led the 1975 British Formula Ford Championship until a bad crash forced his premature retirement. He resumed racing to win the 1977 Irish formula Atlantic title, but after breaking his leg in a formula 3 race he embarked on a successful career as a team owner. An ambitious driver with an eye for talent and shrewd entrepreneurial skills, he quickly achieved success. His driver Johnny Herbert won the 1987 British formula 3 championship and his French protégé Jean Alesi the 1989 international formula 3000 series. He entered formula 1 with the Jordan Grand Prix team in 1991. [see MOTOR SPORT.] **Brendan Lynch**

Jordan, John (1930–1988), poet, short-story writer, editor, and critic. Born in Dublin. Editor of *Poetry Ireland*, 1962–8, and a lecturer in UCD, 1955–69, he published four volumes of poetry between 1971 and 1980 and a posthumous *Collected Poems* (1991) with an appreciation by MACDARA WOODS. *Yarns* (1977), short fiction, was followed by *Collected Short Stories* (1991). **David Wheatley**

Jordan, Neil (1950–), film director and writer. Born in Sligo but raised in Dublin; educated at St Paul's, Raheny, and UCD. He was a short-story writer (*Night in Tunisia and Other Stories*, 1978) and novelist (*The Past*, 1980) before he made his first film, a documentary on the making of John Boorman's *Excalibur* (1981). His first feature film, *Angel* (1982), set in Northern Ireland, featured STEPHEN REA, who has appeared in many of his films. His interest in Irish history and politics—seen in *The Crying Game* (1992) and *Michael Collins* (1996)—has been an important strand in his work, but equally significant has been his interest in the supernatural and the non-rational, as in *The Company of Wolves* (1984), *High Spirits* (1988), *Interview with the Vampire* (1994), *The End of the Affair* (1998), his acclaimed adaptation of PAT MCCABE's novel *The Butcher Boy* (1997), and *In Dreams* (2000). His other films include *Mona Lisa* (1986), a crime thriller, *The Miracle* (1991), an intense Oedipal story often cited as the director's favourite, and *The Honest Thief* (2002). [see CINEMA.] **Kevin Rockett**

journalism. Early Irish history was recorded in ANNALS, culminating in the Annals of the FOUR MASTERS, begun in 1632 and completed four years later. In combining fact, fiction and fable, the annals foreshadow the journalism that has followed all the way to today's satellite technology.

The forerunners of printed journalism included spoken news disseminated by messengers and balladeers. OLIVER CROMWELL's armies published the first newspaper produced in Ireland, the *Irish Monthly Mercury* (1649). The *Irish Intelligencer* (1662) was the first attempt at a commercial newspaper; others soon followed. Characterised by irregular publication, short survival periods, and circulations measured in the hundreds, such papers liaised in varying degrees of intimacy with DUBLIN CASTLE, the seat of British power in Ireland.

By the beginning of the eighteenth century the instability of the earliest titles was overcome by the thrice-weekly *Pue's Impartial Occurrences* (1703–73), which recorded the public opinion of Ascendancy Ireland. *Faulkner's Dublin Journal* (1725–1825) was published by GEORGE FAULKNER, printer to JONATHAN SWIFT. The *Freeman's Journal* (1763–1924), in the pocket of Dublin Castle, gradually developed into the organ of the IRISH PARTY of the middle of the nineteenth century. Such early Dublin papers recognised the importance of advertising and are valuable sources of commercial history. Outside Dublin, the *Cork Idler* (1715), *Limerick Newsletter* (1716), and *Waterford Flying Post* (1729) were published. In 1737 the NEWS LETTER appeared in Belfast; still published, it is the oldest Irish newspaper in continuous production. The *Northern Star* (1792) scorned Ireland's link with Britain. Reflecting the attitudes of the UNITED IRISHMEN, it was unapologetically republican, supporting, for instance, the beheading of Louis XVI. Inevitably, it was prosecuted, as the British rulers feared its influence.

At the beginning of the nineteenth century, with the United Irishmen defeated and the ACT OF UNION (1800) passed, Irish journalism remained controlled by interests favourable to Britain. However, by the time the century was over Catholic political agitation, technological innovation, and the rise of literacy in English, boosted by the founding of the national schools in 1831, had combined to produce a vigorous new press espousing the nationalist cause. DANIEL O'CONNELL made a 'cheap and enlightened press' one of the aims of the CATHOLIC ASSOCIATION, and in general, press support for Dublin Castle waned. Founded by the culturally separatist Young Irelanders CHARLES GAVAN DUFFY, THOMAS DAVIS, and JOHN DILLON, the NATION (1842) is generally accepted as the first truly popular Irish paper. Its readership, with multiple readers per copy, may have been as high as 250,000 by 1843. In creating a sympathetic climate of thought for nationalist ideals, the paper had a historic impact. Two leading dailies still in existence, the *Cork Examiner* (1841–), now the IRISH EXAMINER, and the IRISH TIMES (1859–), also date from this period.

JAMES STEPHENS founded the *Irish People* in 1863 as the official Fenian paper, but it was suppressed within two years. During the LAND WAR, which began in 1879, Richard Pigott used his *Irishman* (1858–81) to attack CHARLES STEWART PARNELL, leader of the IRISH PARTY and president of the LAND LEAGUE. The Irish Party bought the *Irishman* and another Pigott paper, the *Flag of Ireland*; this was renamed *United Ireland* (1881–98) and became Parnell's main press support. Following Parnell's love affair with KATHARINE O'SHEA, the nationalist press split, and even the hitherto hero-worshipping *Freeman's Journal* abandoned him. The bitterness of the conflict resulted in a retreat by the disillusioned from party politics into culture, principally literature. IRISH LANGUAGE JOURNALISM such as that in AN CLAIDHEAMH SOLUIS, founded in 1899 as the paper of the GAELIC LEAGUE, played an influential role within this refocused aim. However, there has never been a successful mass-circulation Irish-language newspaper.

As this revitalised urban press was developing, a dynamic provincial press began to emerge also. Many such papers were founded to advocate land reform and later to endorse nationalist policies. Ulster papers, apart from the liberal *Northern Whig* (1824–1963), reflected the sectarian divide even more acutely. The BELFAST TELEGRAPH was founded in 1870 to further the interests of the ORANGE ORDER. The unionist *News Letter* and nationalist *Irish News* (1891–) maintain the divide up to the present.

The launch by WILLIAM MARTIN MURPHY of the *Irish Independent* (1905–) provided a populist paper that is still the daily flagship of Independent Newspapers, by far the largest newspaper group in Ireland. Following the treaty that ended the Anglo-Irish war of 1919–21 and partitioned Ireland, the print media gradually adapted to new realities, including the establishment of radio broadcasting in 1926 and television in 1961. In the eight decades since partition, Irish journalism has divided along traditional and new fault lines. REPUBLICANISM, defeated in the CIVIL WAR, regrouped to form FIANNA FÁIL in 1926. Five years later ÉAMON DE VALERA established the IRISH PRESS, which flourished for half a century before floundering to a protracted demise by 1995. During the SECOND WORLD WAR, in which the Free State was neutral and Northern Ireland a combatant, journalism was severely censored.

In the 1960s television undermined Catholic cultural hegemony in the Republic and Protestant political hegemony in Northern Ireland. In the Republic, television beamed in the outside world to a state that had until then been isolationist. Film of America's black civil rights campaign and the fiftieth anniversary celebrations of the 1916 RISING helped to provoke the nationalist challenge to STORMONT rule. During the violent conflict in Northern Ireland, broadcasting in both parts of Ireland was censored, though print journalism was not. Since the 1960s, women have been employed in journalism in increasing numbers.

Jordan, Neil. *The film director and writer Neil Jordan. He won his first Academy Award for the film* The Crying Game *(1992), which he wrote and directed; since then he has had worldwide success with such films as* Michael Collins *(1996), and* The End of the Affair *(2000). [Photocall Ireland]*

Meanwhile print has had to face the fact that, even employing the latest technology, it cannot compete for immediacy with electronic news. As a result, 'hard news', though still the mainstay of the press, has been greatly augmented by features, reviews, supplements, and—like television—expanded sports coverage. Independent Newspapers, controlled since 1973 by Dr ANTHONY O'REILLY, has become the print industry's giant, dominating ownership of national and provincial titles in the Republic. The group has media interests in Britain, South Africa, Australia, New Zealand, and Portugal and has also crossed the border to buy the *Belfast Telegraph*. The formerly unionist, now liberal-bourgeois IRISH TIMES is the Republic's newspaper of record. The tabloid *Sunday World* (1973–) and the broadsheet *Sunday Independent* (1906–) are the biggest-selling titles. Sales of evening newspapers have declined. Since the mid-1960s, with the rise of air transport, English titles, most notably daily and Sunday tabloids, have strenuously competed in the Irish market and have gained an increasing share; British titles now account for a third of all daily and Sunday newspapers sold in the Republic. The spread of British-style 'tabloidisation' has raised public concern about journalism's ethical standards.

Following the collapse of the *Irish Press*, the Commission on the Newspaper Industry (1996) examined the consequent lessening of diversity of opinion, the dominance of the Independent Group, the threat posed by British titles, the tax burden on newspapers, and the libel laws. It recommended tax relief and libel reform but no protective measures against British competition. This took a new form in 1997 when the British group Trinity Holdings bought the *Sunday Business Post* (1989–) and in 2000 when Scottish Radio Holdings took over *Ireland on Sunday* (1997–).

While some journalists have taken advantage of the freedom of information laws introduced in 1996, press freedom remains shackled by financially fearsome libel suits. However, newspaper profits have risen substantially through advertising resulting from the Republic's economic boom. [see CENSORSHIP; NEWSPAPERS, NORTHERN IRELAND.] **Eddie Holt**

journalists as politicians and writers. There is a strong tradition, particularly from the nineteenth century, of Irish politicians' involvement with newspapers. James Bronterre O'Brien (1805–1864) on moving to London in 1829 became a leader of CHARTISM and edited *Poor Man's Guardian*, 1831–5. Another Chartist leader, FEARGUS O'CONNOR, advocated physical force in his paper, the *Northern Star*. CHARLES GAVAN DUFFY jointly founded the NATION in 1842, of which JOHN MITCHEL became assistant editor in 1845. Mitchel founded and edited the *United Irishman* in 1848. As a result of his 'seditious' exhortations he was transported to Australia; later, in the United States, he published a series of short-lived pro-slavery newspapers. The journalist THOMAS D'ARCY MCGEE fled to the United States after the 1848 Rising. The Fenian JOHN BOYLE O'REILLY, who escaped to the United States following deportation, was on the editorial staff of the *Pilot* (Boston) from 1870 and later proprietor and editor, 1876–90. CHARLES STEWART PARNELL appointed WILLIAM O'BRIEN editor of *United Ireland* in 1881; he was arrested when the paper was suppressed. ARTHUR GRIFFITH founded the weekly *United Irishman* in 1899, promoting self-government in his eloquent editorials. PATRICK PEARSE edited *An Claidheamh Soluis*, while in 1917 the future government minister ERNEST BLYTHE briefly edited the *Southern Star*. The scholar DOUGLAS HYDE, who in 1938 became first President of Ireland, made significant contributions to cultural nationalism through his journalism. Another future president, Seán T. O'Kelly, contributed to Irish and American newspapers and founded and edited the *Nation*, while three future presidents were involved with the IRISH PRESS: it was founded by ÉAMON DE VALERA, ERSKINE CHILDERS helped to establish it commercially, and CEARBHALL Ó DÁLAIGH was its first Irish-language editor.

Prominent Irish journalists who worked abroad include Emile Joseph Dillon (1854–1933), a foreign correspondent for the *Daily Telegraph* (London) between 1887 and 1914; FRANK HARRIS, who edited *Pearson's Magazine* in the United States and the *Evening News* and *Fortnightly Review* in London and acquired control of the *Saturday Review*; and MICHAEL MORRIS (Lord Killanin), who began his career in London as a war correspondent for the *Daily Express*, *Daily Mail*, and *Sunday Dispatch*.

Of Irish writers who worked in journalism the best known are BRAM STOKER, who reviewed theatre; SEAN O'FAOLAIN, who edited the BELL; FRANK O'CONNOR, broadcaster for the British Ministry of Information during the SECOND WORLD WAR; SÉAMUS O'KELLY (1881–1918), who edited several papers, including the Sinn Féin paper *Nationality* (1918); BRIAN O'NOLAN, who as Myles na gCopaleen wrote the 'Cruiskeen Lawn' column for the IRISH TIMES for twenty-six years; BRENDAN BEHAN, who wrote for the *Irish Press*; BRINSLEY MACNAMARA, *Irish Times* drama critic; BENEDICT KIELY, *Irish Press* literary editor; and the novelist COLM TÓIBÍN. **David Quin**

Journal to Stella (1766), a collection of letters by JONATHAN SWIFT. From 1710 to 1713 Swift, who was in London, kept a daily record of his thoughts and activities, which he sent in the form of letters to his close friend ESTHER JOHNSON and her companion Rebecca Dingley in Dublin. The letters show Swift's involvement in public affairs and are valuable for their commentary on people and events, but they also reveal the more intimate, affectionate, and eventually melancholy aspects of his character. Published some twenty years after his death, they constitute one of the finest private memoirs of their era. **Siobhán Kilfeather**

Joyce, James Augustine Aloysius (1882–1941), writer. Born in Rathgar, Dublin, into a middle-class family that suffered increasing hardship as a consequence of the father's alcoholism. After a brief spell with the Christian Brothers he was educated by the Jesuits at Clongowes Wood College, Belvedere College, and UCD. In 1904, accompanied by NORA BARNACLE, who was to remain his lifelong partner (and wife in 1931), he fled what he saw as the intellectual and political paralysis of Dublin and thereafter lived on the Continent, settling first in Trieste, then from 1920 in Paris, and eventually in Zürich.

Joyce published two volumes of poetry, *Chamber Music* (1907) and *Pomes Penyeach* (1927), but is primarily known as a prose writer. He portrayed the Dublin he had left behind in his collection of short stories, DUBLINERS (1914). His stultifying home life, religious education, and sense of social oppression are described in his first novel, A PORTRAIT OF THE ARTIST AS A YOUNG MAN (1916). Though he never returned to Dublin after a brief visit in 1912, he retained a lifelong interest in his native city and in the political fortunes of Ireland. To support his writing—and his partner, son, and daughter—he worked as an English-teacher in Trieste. Despite occasional grants, it was not until his late thirties that he lived somewhat comfortably, from which time he enjoyed the secure patronage of Harriet Shaw Weaver. In 1918 he published his only play, *Exiles*, whose autobiographical leading character explains that he cannot return to Ireland because he feels rejected and deceived by his country. Joyce carried with him a paradoxical love for his country and sense of persecution and betrayal by it.

It was the publication of ULYSSES, in 1922, that assured Joyce's immense literary reputation. It was banned for obscenity while still in serialisation, and Joyce's sense of rejection was increased in the following years as he began writing FINNEGANS WAKE, which faced strong objections from former supporters. Though he underwent numerous eye operations (which left him almost blind), and experienced the death of his father and the mental illness of his daughter Lucia, Joyce's characteristic stubbornness and single-minded dedication to his work made possible the completion of the book in 1939. He died from a duodenal ulcer in Zürich in 1941. With these two works, Joyce radically altered the history of prose fiction.

A number of thematic concerns consistently recur in Joyce's writing. Perhaps predominant among these is a self-conscious experimentation with language and narrative technique, from the careful symbolic resonances amid the realism of *Dubliners* to the stylistic variety of *Ulysses*, and the richly allusive portmanteau language of *Finnegans Wake*. Joyce was also deeply engaged with representations of Dublin and the politics of Ireland. Though he left the Catholic Church as a young man and never returned, the rituals and the historical and intellectual foundations of Catholicism continued to intrigue him. His politics are complex. Like his father, he was a confirmed Parnellite (he famously blamed the bishops for PARNELL's fall), and as a young man he rejected the LITERARY REVIVAL as sentimental folklorism aligned with an imperial image of Irish culture. He had espoused socialist principles and had some sympathies with Griffith's SINN FÉIN, yet he also disavowed stringent nationalism, which he saw as duplicating imperial values. He remained opposed to all forms of imperialism and was a committed pacifist.

Joyce, James. *The thirty-three-year-old James Joyce playing a guitar in Zürich, 1915. The guitar is now on display in the James Joyce Museum, Sandycove, Co. Dublin. [Photograph by Ottocaro Weiss; published with the permission of the Poetry and Rare Books Collection of the University Libraries, State University of New York at Buffalo]*

Joyce's achievement was immense: he was the leading prose writer in English in the twentieth century, a pre-eminent figure in European modernism, and one of the primary commentators on Ireland in the early decades of the century. His work revolutionised the novel, taking it from the realistic traditions of the nineteenth century towards the post-modern form of the post-war period. *Ulysses* is critically regarded as one of the greatest novels ever written and the most important literary work of the twentieth century. Joyce's writing has inspired countless writers and thinkers, and his work has been important to a range of social and intellectual movements, from feminism to deconstruction. There exists a large and productive industry of critical commentary; and because of the perception that he is a 'difficult' writer, he is still perhaps more notorious than read. **John Nash**

Joyce's aesthetics. The main source for Joyce's aesthetics is *A Portrait of the Artist as a Young Man*, where it is expounded by Stephen Dedalus towards the end of the novel. The theory consists of two parts: an account of aesthetic experience, and an account of what can loosely be called the metaphysics of art. The account of aesthetic experience makes use of three terms taken from Thomas Aquinas: *integritas*, *proportio*, and *claritas*. But Joyce employs them in quite a distinctive manner. For Aquinas, the three terms referred to properties by virtue of which objects are (or fail to be) beautiful; for Joyce, they referred instead to three stages in our experience of art. To apprehend an object as one thing (Stephen explains) is to apprehend its *integritas* (wholeness); to apprehend it as a thing is to apprehend its *proportio* (harmony); and to apprehend it as 'that thing which it is and no other thing' is to apprehend its *claritas* (radiance). These terms connoted for Aquinas properties of the aesthetic object; for Joyce they connoted successive phases of aesthetic experience. Joyce's account of the aesthetic object exploits the traditional genre terms *lyric*, *epic*, and *drama*. Lyric is filled completely with the artist's personality; epic achieves a partial degree of detachment from the artist; drama, the most perfect form of art, eliminates the artist's personality altogether. Drama (here used as a technical term; *Ulysses* is a drama in this sense) is therefore a perfect exemplar of a work of art—a new reality wrought by the artist and now made available for aesthetic experience. [see BECKETT, SAMUEL; BLOOMSDAY; CRITICS AND CRITICISMS; JAMES JOYCE CULTURAL CENTRE; JAMES JOYCE TOWER MUSEUM; PROSE FICTION IN ENGLISH; VOLTA PICTURE THEATRE.] **Hugh Bredin**

Joyce, P. W. [Patrick Weston] (1827–1914), antiquarian. His interest in TRADITIONAL MUSIC was stimulated by that of his native Ballyhoura mountains in Co. Limerick. Through the Society for the Preservation and Publication of the Melodies of Ireland he met GEORGE PETRIE, who encouraged him to begin noting down tunes. At first he passed these on to Petrie, who used many of them in his collections. After Petrie's death Joyce published several of his own collections, including *Ancient Irish Music* (1873) and the more important *Old Irish Folk Music and Songs* (1909), which also included material from the manuscripts of other collectors. His *Irish Music and Song* (1888) was a seminal work in matching Irish words to their airs. Joyce also published in the areas of FOLKLORE and history. **Colin Hamilton**

Joyce, Stanislaus (1884–1955), younger brother and confidant of JAMES JOYCE. He followed Joyce from Dublin to Trieste in 1905, where he worked as an English-teacher and offered crucial literary and financial support to his brother. The character of Maurice in Joyce's *Stephen Hero* is an early portrait of him. In the 1920s his support for Joyce's work waned and a rift developed between the brothers; during this period he was used as a model for Shaun in *Work in Progress*. He wrote *Recollections of James Joyce* (1950), *My Brother's Keeper* (1957), and *Dublin Diary* (1962). **John Nash**

Joyce, William Brooke, 'Lord Haw-Haw' (1906–1946), Nazi propagandist. Born in New York to an Irish father and an English mother; educated at St Ignatius' College, Galway, and the University of London. In 1933 he joined the British Union of Fascists; in 1937 he founded his own party, the National Socialist League. He moved to Germany in 1939 and worked for Radio Hamburg as a broadcaster of propaganda until April 1945. The nickname 'Lord Haw-Haw' arose from his rather exaggerated upper-class English accent. After the war he was captured in possession of an expired British passport, probably false, and it was on foot of this that he was condemned as a traitor and hanged in London on 3 January 1946. His plea of American citizenship based on his place of birth failed to save him, as it should have done. Although a man of odious views, he was the victim of an injustice. [see STUART, FRANCIS.] **Ciarán Deane**

judicial review, a legal procedure vested in the High Court whereby decisions of public bodies (generally those whose powers derive from public law or, by their nature, are operative in the public domain) can be reviewed for legality by the courts, with the ultimate objective of upholding the rule of law. The substance of the decision is not generally a matter for review: the emphasis is on the decision-making process and on whether the body acted within its powers and in accordance with fair procedures and natural and constitutional justice and, in certain circumstances, whether it gave sufficient reasons for its decisions. The CONSTITUTION OF IRELAND provides for a right of judicial review to consider the constitutionality of legislation, both with regard to a case and, under article 26, in abstract form before its enactment into law. **Neville Cox**

judiciary and judicial appointments. The judiciary comprises the Chief Justice and seven other SUPREME COURT judges, the President of the High Court and nineteen other High Court judges, the President of the Circuit Court and twenty-seven other Circuit Court judges, and the President of the District Court and fifty other District Court judges. A District Court or Circuit Court judge must be a barrister or solicitor of ten years' standing; a High Court or Supreme Court judge must be either a barrister of at least twelve years' standing (with service as a judge of the European Court of Justice or EC Court of First Instance counting as the equivalent) or a Circuit Court judge of four years' standing. Traditionally, only senior counsel (senior barristers) are appointed to the superior courts.

The judicial appointment system is occasionally criticised for being too politically motivated, though there is little if any suggestion that judicial decisions are politically influenced. This appeared to be borne out by the controversy in 1994 surrounding the appointment of the then ATTORNEY-GENERAL, Harry Whelehan, to the Presidency of the High Court by the TAOISEACH, ALBERT REYNOLDS (FIANNA FÁIL), without the approval of DICK SPRING, the leader of the LABOUR PARTY, with which Fianna Fáil was then in coalition—an appointment that resulted in the fall of the Government. As a result of this controversy the Judicial Appointments Advisory Board was set up in 1995 to identify and inform the Government of persons suitable for appointment to judicial office and generally to provide greater transparency in such appointment procedures. Management of the court system is now the responsibility of the courts service set up under the Courts Service Act (1998).

Northern Ireland. Judges in Northern Ireland are appointed by the Queen on the advice of the Lord Chancellor of Great Britain, though judges of the House of Lords (known as the Law Lords) are appointed on the advice of the Prime Minister, acting in consultation with the Lord Chancellor, while justices of the peace are appointed directly by the Lord Chancellor. At present there are eleven Law Lords. Such judges must either have fifteen years' experience as a barrister or have spent two years in high judicial office. There are also three Court of Appeal judges (having fifteen years' service as a barrister or having served as a High Court judge) and seven High Court judges (having ten years' experience as a barrister).

At the top of this system is the Lord Chief Justice of Northern Ireland, who is President of the Court of Appeal, the High Court, and the Crown Court. High Court judges are assisted by High Court masters, who deal with procedural matters relating to cases before they come to the High Court; they are generally former practitioners with at least ten years' experience. In the lower courts there are fourteen County Court judges, assisted by forty-one deputies (with ten years' experience as a practitioner), and four district judges, assisted by ten deputies (with seven years' practice as a solicitor). Below this are fifteen resident magistrates (assisted by seventeen deputies, with seven years' standing as a practitioner), who deal with minor criminal offences and civil disputes. Finally there are approximately 970 justices of the peace or lay magistrates, who deal with minor procedural issues. **Neville Cox**

juries. The law regarding juries is governed by the Juries Act (1976), under which every citizen in the Republic aged between eighteen and sixty-nine (inclusive) who is on the register of Dáil Éireann electors (unless he or she is at the time ineligible or disqualified) is liable to be called to serve as a juror. A panel of jurors is drawn from the electoral register using a method of random selection. The act lists the categories of people who are ineligible for or exempt from service; individuals may also be excused from jury service under certain conditions.

In Northern Ireland, under the Juries (Northern Ireland) Order (1974), juries are selected by the juries officer from area jurors' lists in each county court division, based on lists drawn up annually from the registers of the Chief Electoral Officer for Northern Ireland. The juries officer selects a jury to serve for all the hearings in a particular court or place over a specified period, not just for a particular trial.

In both jurisdictions there are rules whereby either side in a case may object to the empanelling of particular jurors. The jury deliberates in secret on all issues of fact pertinent to the case before them and, pursuant to the direction of the trial judge, may return either a unanimous or a majority verdict (11:1 or 10:2). **Neville Cox**

justices of the peace, an unpaid office introduced into Ireland in the fifteenth century to help maintain law and order. Appointments were made by the Lord Chancellor, generally on the recommendation of a leading local magnate. Justices were responsible for issuing warrants and hearing minor civil and criminal cases; they were also involved in local administration, acting at presentment sessions and as *ex officio* members of Poor Law boards. The office was abolished in independent Ireland after partition but survived in Northern Ireland. **Virginia Crossman**

Kennedy, John F. (Jack) *(see page 582). President John F. Kennedy smiles at the cheering crowds on his motorcade through Williamsgate Street, Galway, 29 June 1963, six months before his assassination in Dallas, Texas, in a similar motorcade. [White House/John F. Kennedy Archive; KN-C29430]*

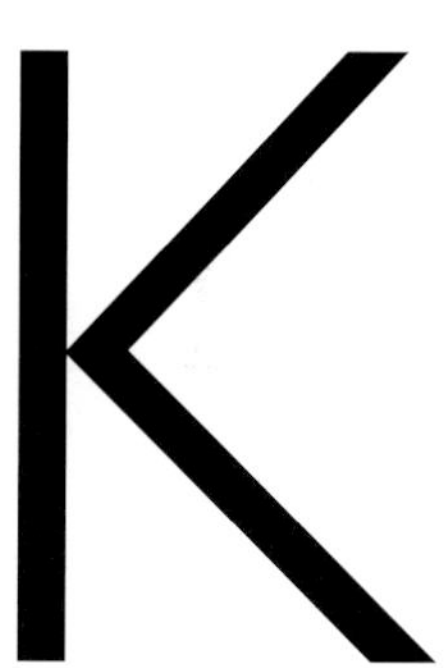

Kane, Michael (1935–), artist. Born in Dublin; studied at the NCAD. He exhibited with the Independent Artists and was a member of Group 65 and a joint-founder of the Project Arts Centre, 1967. He founded and edited the magazine *Structure* (1972–8). The subjects of his expressionist paintings and prints are rooted in everyday experiences, such as life in Dublin. There is frequent reference to classical MYTHOLOGY and modern Irish poetry in the work. Committed to democratic approaches to the production and display of art, Kane has been an outspoken critic of elitism in the Irish art world. He is a member of AOSDÁNA. **Róisín Kennedy**

Kane, Sir Robert John (1809–1890), scientist. Born in Dublin; studied medicine at TCD and chemistry in Paris. A child prodigy, he was appointed professor of chemistry to the Apothecaries' Hall, Dublin, at the age of twenty-two. His book *Elements of Chemistry* (1841–4) gained him an international reputation, while *The Natural Resources of Ireland* (1844, second edition 1845) was important in demonstrating the industrial potential of Ireland. He was made a fellow of the Royal Society, 1844; knighted 1846; president of the ROYAL IRISH ACADEMY, 1877; founder and director of the MUSEUM OF IRISH INDUSTRY; and president of Queen's College, Cork, 1845–73. **Patrick N. Wyse Jackson**

Kavanagh, Arthur MacMorrough (1831–1889), politician. Born on the family estate at Borris, Co. Carlow. Disabled from birth, having rudimentary arms and legs, he nonetheless learnt to hunt, shoot, fish, and sail. He became landlord of Borris in 1853 and in 1855 married his cousin Frances Mary Leathley. He earned the title 'landlord of landlords' from his energetic rebuilding of the villages of Borris and Ballyragget, his chairmanship of New Ross poorhouse, and his subsidising of the railway between Borris and Bagenalstown (Muine Bheag). He represented Co. Wexford, 1866–8, and his native Co. Carlow, 1868–80, in the Westminster Parliament. A keen traveller, he visited Egypt and Asia, where he excelled in tiger-hunting. **Alison Walsh**

Kavanagh, Joseph Malachy (1856–1918), artist. Born in Dublin; studied at the Metropolitan School of Art, 1877–78, and the RHA Schools. Winner of the Albert Scholarship, he studied at the Académie Royale, Antwerp, 1881–3. He painted village and street scenes in Antwerp, Normandy and Brittany in sober Realist style, influenced by seventeenth-century Dutch and contemporary Flemish genre painting. He showed skill at representing street scenes and architectural subjects and was one of the few Irish artists of his generation who was a skilful practitioner of etching. He painted woodland and farmland scenes in Co. Dublin; his most individual

Kane, Michael. The Diver *(1988), by Michael Kane, a colourful and vigorous image of a swimmer diving off Baggot Street Bridge, Dublin, one of many works relating to Kane's espousal of urban themes. [By permission of the Office of Public Works; courtesy of the artist and Rubicon Gallery, Dublin]*

body of work is a series portraying cockle-pickers on Sandymount Strand from the early 1890s. A member of the Royal Hibernian Academy from 1889, he exhibited regularly and was elected keeper in 1910. He was deeply shaken by the burning of the RHA premises in Lower Abbey Street in 1916, from which he escaped alive, though many of his paintings were destroyed. He saved the Royal Charters of the Academy and the President's chain of office when escaping from the burning building. **Julian Campbell**

Kavanagh, Patrick. Portrait of Patrick Kavanagh *(charcoal on paper) by Seán O'Sullivan, a sensitive and perceptive image of the young Kavanagh during the years in Dublin when he was establishing his reputation as a writer. [National Gallery of Ireland]*

Kavanagh, Patricia (1963–), musician and adjudicator. Born in Dublin, educated Dublin and Germany. International prizewinner in piano and classical accordion. Director, Irish Institute of Accordion Studies. Associate Professor of Piano at National Academy of Liberal Arts and Soochow University, Taiwan, 1988–92; Professor RIAM (1993), Head of Keyboard faculty (1999). **Richard Pine**

Kavanagh, Patrick (1904–1967), poet. Born in Inniskeen, Co. Monaghan, where his family owned a nine-acre farm. When his formal education ended at the age of thirteen, Kavanagh, like his father, worked as a small farmer and cobbler, continuing his education by reading from schoolbooks. In 1925 he found a copy of the *Irish Statesman* in a Dundalk newsagent's shop, and this served as his first introduction to Irish writing of the period. In 1929 GEORGE RUSSELL published three poems in the *Irish Statesman*, and this provided Kavanagh with the impetus to complete the poems that would comprise his first collection, *Ploughman and Other Poems* (1936). Following its appearance Kavanagh left Inniskeen to seek his literary fortune in London. After he published *The Green Fool* (1938), an autobiography about farm life that was greeted with critical acclaim, he settled in Dublin to become a writer and literary journalist. His long poem THE GREAT HUNGER (1942) is his masterpiece: in contrast to the romantic view of the peasant promulgated by the LITERARY REVIVAL, Kavanagh, through Patrick Maguire, represents the peasant as poor, dispirited, sexually frustrated, and at odds with the rural world. Another significant poem of the period is 'Lough Derg', a further exploration of rural poverty and religious hypocrisy. In 1948 his novel *Tarry Flynn*, also set in Co. Monaghan, was published. The final, important phase of his career as a poet followed his operation for lung cancer in 1955. As he recovered in Dublin he found there, where he had often felt embattled and unaccepted, a renewed sense of nature and the transcendence available from everyday life, and these themes are explored in *Come Dance with Kitty Stobling* (1960).

Though his work is uneven, Kavanagh is one of the giants of Irish poetry. Writing in a sophisticated yet vernacular style, he rendered everyday life remarkable and forced readers to consider ordinary citizens as imperfect humans and not as romantic symbols. With regard to his considerable influence on poets as various as SEAMUS HEANEY, EAVAN BOLAND, and others, it would not be an exaggeration to say that Kavanagh, more than YEATS, was the principal influence on Irish poets of the late twentieth century. **Eamonn Wall**

Kavanagh's Weekly (April–July 1952), edited by the poet and novelist PATRICK KAVANAGH. He wrote most of the articles and some of the poems himself under various pseudonyms, with some contribution by his brother Peter. His criticism of his fellow-writers was often scathing, and he was equally vitriolic in his attacks on the FIANNA FÁIL government and every trend towards a cult of Irishness. Literature, he believed, should use contemporary language and should originate in the love of the commonplace. Too extreme to attract advertising, the journal folded after thirteen issues. **John Wakeman**

Keadue Harp Festival, an annual FESTIVAL held since 1978 in Co. Roscommon to commemorate TURLOUGH CAROLAN, who is buried nearby. The festival, which includes concerts, lectures, master classes in a number of disciplines, and a HARP competition, has developed into an international celebration of the harp and TRADITIONAL MUSIC. **Maeve Ellen Gebruers**

Kealkil, Co. Cork, a STONE CIRCLE comprising five stones occupying a commanding position overlooking the valley of the Owvane River, in close association with a pair of STANDING STONES, one of which was originally 6 m (20 ft) in height, together with a radially kerbed cairn. **Clive Ruggles**

Keane, Dolores (1953–), traditional and contemporary singer. Born in Caherlistrane, Co. Galway, the fourth generation to be involved in music; her brother Seán Keane is also a distinguished professional singer. Her mother played the fiddle and her father and his siblings played as the Keane Céilí Band in the 1940s and 50s; her aunts Sarah and Rita Keane were highly regarded also as singers, and made several recordings. She established her reputation in the 1960s with all-Ireland awards for singing and in 1974 joined the group DÉ DANANN. In London in 1975 she appeared regularly at Ewan McColl's Singers' Club, and she toured and played with her own band, Reel Union, until 1981. She has recorded several albums but is best known for the iconic song 'Ramblin' Irishman', which she obtained from LEN GRAHAM. **Fintan Vallely**

Keane, Dolores. *One of Ireland's favourite traditional singers and original vocalist with De Dannan, Dolores Keane is best known for the song 'Ramblin' Irishman'. [Colm Henry]*

Keane, John B. (1928–2002), playwright, novelist, and journalist. Born in Listowel, Co. Kerry. His work reflects the local landscape, detailing the tensions between urban and rural, religion and paganism, emigration and exile, freedom and repression, ownership and dispossession—tensions much in evidence at the time of Ireland's shifting consciousness from the late 1950s onwards, when struggles for change and a resistance to domination took various forms. His best plays are SIVE (1959), *Sharon's Grave* (1960), *The Field* (1965)—filmed as *The Field* (1990) by JIM SHERIDAN (see p. 197)—and *Big Maggie* (1969), all of which contain characters that are engaging, verbally dexterous, and destructively defiant. **Eamonn Jordan**

Keane, Maurice (Moss) (1948–), rugby footballer. Born in Currow, Co. Kerry. Having made his debut against France, he won thirty-nine consecutive caps before missing the two matches against South Africa and one against Australia in 1981. However, he returned to share in the 1982 Triple Crown win and in Ireland's championship success the following year. He toured New Zealand in 1976 and Australia with Ireland in 1979, and also toured New Zealand with the 1977 British Lions team, playing in the first Test at Wellington. Between 1974 and 1984 he won fifty-one caps as a powerful lock. **Karl Johnston**

Keane, Molly (c. 1904–1996), writer. Born in Co. Kildare, daughter of MOIRA O'NEILL. She enjoyed two successful writing careers. In the first, spanning the years 1926–56, she published eleven novels under the pseudonym M. J. Farrell and four popular plays produced in London. Her black comedy *Good Behaviour* was published to acclaim in 1981. Like all her novels, its setting is the decaying 'BIG HOUSE' world of hunting and leisure, where children and other dependants are neglected and mistreated. Keane's heavily ironic view of dysfunctional ANGLO-IRISH families masquerading under a civilised veneer, a recurring theme, is a metaphor for the collapse of the Ascendancy. [see O'NEILL, MOIRA.] **Denise Laing**

Keane, Robert (Robbie) (1980–), soccer player. Born in Dublin. At the age of eighteen he scored two goals in the 5–0 win over Malta in October 1998, to become the youngest to score for the Republic. After a spectacular apprenticeship with Wolverhampton, he signed for Coventry in the FA Premiership; he also played with Inter Milan and Leeds United. He was one of Ireland's successes at the 2002 World Cup, scoring a dramatic extra-time equaliser against Germany, the eventual runners-up. He moved to Tottenham Hotspur in 2002 for €8 million. **Peter Byrne**

Keane, Ronan (1932–), lawyer and judge. Born in Dublin; educated at UCD and the KING'S INNS, winning the John Brooke Scholarship in 1954. He was a judge of the High Court, 1979–86, and of the SUPREME COURT from 1986, and was appointed Chief Justice in January 2000. He presided over the STARDUST inquiry in 1981 and was president of the Law Reform Commission, 1987–92. A specialist in a number of areas of law, including planning, commercial, equity, and constitutional law, he has published a number of legal textbooks and is regarded as intellectually distinguished. **Neville Cox**

Keane, Roy (1971–), soccer player. Born in Cork. Introduced to the game by the Cork junior club Rockmount, he played with Cobh Ramblers in the League of Ireland before being signed by Brian Clough for Nottingham Forest. He moved to Manchester United in September 1993 and later emerged as one of the most significant contributors to that club's sequence of successes. He captained the club to its unprecedented treble of the European Champions League, Premiership and FA Cup title. He missed the European final win over Bayern Munich through suspension but was later given a new contract. A member of the Republic of Ireland team that reached the 1994 World Cup finals, he was appointed team captain by MICK MCCARTHY in September 1998. However, a dispute with McCarthy over what Keane regarded as inadequate training facilities became embittered and resulted in his being sent home before the first match of the tournament. His memoir, *Keane: the Autobiography* (with EAMONN DUNPHY), was a controversial best-seller when it appeared some months later. **Peter Byrne**

Kearney, Peadar (Peadar Ó Cearnaigh) (1883–1942). Born in Dublin, he attended Marino CHRISTIAN BROTHERS' School until the age of thirteen, when he was apprenticed as a house painter. He developed an interest in all things Irish, and in the cause of Irish freedom in particular. He was a member of the IRISH REPUBLICAN BROTHERHOOD and the IRISH VOLUNTEERS. He was involved in the Howth gun-running, and he took part in the 1916 RISING in the Jacob's garrison under THOMAS MACDONAGH and JOHN MCBRIDE. He is perhaps best known as the author of 'AMHRÁN NA BHFIANN' or 'The Soldier's Song', which was first published in *Irish Freedom* in 1912 and later became the NATIONAL ANTHEM of the Republic. He wrote numerous political songs, both serious and sarcastic, throughout the period from the 1916 Rising right through the CIVIL WAR, including 'Whack Fol De Diddle', 'Erin go Bragh', 'Down by the Liffey Side', and 'Glory O to the Bold Fenian Men'.

> Some died by the glenside, some died 'midst the stranger,
> And the wise men have told us their cause was a failure,
> But they loved dear old Ireland and they never feared danger,
> Glory O, glory O, to the bold Fenian men.

He was the uncle of both BRENDAN BEHAN and Dominic Behan, who would inherit his talent for writing ballads. He is buried in the old Republican Plot in Glasnevin Cemetery. **Frank Harte**

Kearney, Richard Marius (1954–), philosopher, novelist, and cultural critic. Born in Cork; educated at UCD, McGill University (Montréal), and Paris. On completion of his doctorate in 1981 under the direction of the French philosopher Paul Ricœur he returned to Dublin, where he took up a post in the Department of Philosophy, UCD. Having received acclaim for his period as joint-editor of the *Crane Bag Book of Irish Studies*, a liberal journal, he went on to publish *Poetique du Possible* (1984) and *Dialogues with Contemporary Continental Thinkers* (1984). In 1986 he produced a major synthesis of CONTINENTAL THOUGHT, *Modern Movements in European Philosophy*, followed by a philosophical reflection on Irish literary culture, *Transitions: Narratives in Modern Irish Culture* (1987). In 1988 he won a number of awards for his magnum opus, *The Wake of Imagination*, which traced the history of the image from Ancient Greece to the present. Since then he has published a further ten works in philosophy, as well as two novels, *Sam's Fall* (1995) and *Walking at Sea Level* (1997), and a collection of poetry. His fiction and poetry are heavily autobiographical, mixing themes central to his philosophical endeavour and experiences. **Mark Dooley**

Keating, Geoffrey, Anglicised name of Seathrún Céitinn (c. 1580–c. 1644), theologian and historian. Born in the vicinity of Caher, Co. Tipperary, into a family of ANGLO-NORMAN origin; his early education may have been at the Mac Craith school of SEANCHAS conducted at Burges, not far from his probable home at Moorstown Castle in the parish of Inishlounaght. He chose a career as a secular Catholic priest and pursued his theological education in France, where he had links with the Universities of Reims and Bordeaux. He had returned to the diocese of Lismore and Waterford by c. 1610 and built a reputation as a fearless preacher. A commemorative plaque erected in 1644 over the west doorway of a chapel known as Cillín Chiaráin in the parish of Tubbrid records the esteem in which he was held in that locality.

Keating is now remembered for both his theological and his historical writings. His earliest significant prose work, *Eochair-Sgiath an Aifrinn* ('explanatory defence of the Mass'), is a theological tract written from a COUNTER-REFORMATION viewpoint and may have been written originally in Latin, perhaps for a university degree. Later, following a number of years' experience preaching in Ireland, he compiled a lengthy devotional tract entitled *Trí Bior-ghaoithe an Bháis* ('the three sharp shafts of death'). This meditation on sin and death derives in part from the work of a contemporary French preacher, Pierre de Besse; to judge by the surviving copies that had been owned by clergy it probably provided the raw material for many Catholic sermons in seventeenth and eighteenth-century Ireland.

FORAS FEASA AR ÉIRINN (c. 1634), a narrative history of Ireland from earliest times to the coming of the Anglo-Normans, is Keating's best-known work. It combines the view of a continentally educated COUNTER-REFORMATION secular priest with that of a scholar immersed in the Irish historical and bardic tradition. Written in elegant Irish prose, interspersed with occasional extracts from poetic sources, its style earned Keating a reputation as the outstanding exemplar of Classical Modern Irish. It had a profound influence on perceptions of Ireland and of Irishness and shaped the way the history of Ireland was written in the following centuries.

Keating also wrote poetry, and some of the compositions attributed to him suggest that he enjoyed the patronage of the Butlers of Dunboyne and of Caher. Much of the folklore surrounding his life—including the highly improbable tale that he wrote his great historical work while hiding in a cave in the Glen of Aherlow—derives from eighteenth-century printed sources whose accuracy must be doubted. The internal evidence of his writings provides ample testimony that in the writing of his history he had access to a considerable library of recently published books in Latin and English; he also consulted a range of manuscripts to which he would have had access through continuing contact with the learned families of Mac Craith, Ó Duibhgheannáin, Mac Eochagáin, and Ó Maolchonaire. **Bernadette Cunningham**

Keating, Seán. The Key Men, *by Seán Keating, c. 1928–9. One of a series of paintings charting the development of the Shannon hydro-electric scheme, it is a historical quasi-allegorical image showing Ireland independent and progressive. [Institution of Engineers of Ireland]*

Keating, Seán (1889–1977), artist. Born John Keating in Limerick; studied drawing at Limerick Technical School. Recognising his talent, WILLIAM ORPEN arranged a scholarship for him to the Metropolitan School of Art, Dublin, in 1911. Keating visited the ARAN ISLANDS in 1914 and the following year worked in Orpen's London studio, where he tried, unsuccessfully, to convince him to return to Ireland. Keating himself moved back to teach at the Metropolitan School. Through the ensuing years, in a series of ambitious academic realist canvases, he documented the struggle for independence. The unspoilt Aran Islands provided subject matter for many paintings, while he also celebrated the INDUSTRIALISATION of the newly emergent republic in a cycle of semi-allegorical paintings documenting the building of the SHANNON SCHEME hydro-electric plant at Ardnacrusha, Co. Clare, 1926–9 (see p. 346). His interest in progress was further revealed in a mural commissioned for the Irish Pavilion at the New York World's Fair (1939); however, the public on both sides of the Atlantic preferred his more traditional subject matter. *The Race of the Gael* (1939), showing a group of Irishmen in profile, a prizewinner at an exhibition organised by IBM in New York, has something of the feeling of a Norman Rockwell set piece. Keating was president of the RHA, 1949–62. In retrospect, his artistic output, though prolific, is uneven. While some of his paintings have deservedly achieved iconic status (see pp. 346, 555), he also produced theatrical and unconvincing works that betray an over-reliance on photographic sources. **Peter Murray**

Keegan, John (1809–1849), poet. Born in Co. Laois; educated in HEDGE SCHOOLS. He was a regular contributor to the NATION and the DUBLIN UNIVERSITY MAGAZINE. *Legends and Poems* was published in 1907. **Terence Brown**

Keenan, Brian (1950–), writer and hostage. Born in Belfast; trained as a heating engineer before studying English literature at the New University of Ulster, then worked in a number of countries before taking up a teaching position in Beirut, Lebanon. In 1986 he was kidnapped by a Shi'ah militia group and was held captive for four-and-a-half years, often in dreadful conditions. His ordeal was graphically described in his book *An Evil Cradling* (1992). His first novel, *Turlough*, was published in 2000. FRANK MCGUINNESS's play *Someone Who'll Watch Over Me* (1992) was largely based on Keenan's hostage experiences. [see CAROLAN, TURLOUGH.] **Brian Galvin**

Keenan, Paddy (1950–), piper. Born in Trim, Co. Meath, into a settled TRAVELLER family, and grew up in Ballyfermot, Dublin. He learnt the pipes from his father, John Keenan, a protégé of JOHNNY DORAN. He came to prominence as a member of the BOTHY BAND and recorded four albums with them. A duet album called *Doublin*, with PADDY GLACKIN, followed; he has also released a number of solo albums. Though his style is based on that of Doran, Keenan was also influenced by recordings of PATSY TOUHEY and others. His piping takes the form of flawless chanter technique overlaid with well-thought-out regulator accompaniment. His rhythm is a flow of even note values, with a noticeable absence of swing phrasing. Keenan is probably the most influential of today's pipers, his style attracting the greatest number of imitators and followers. A professional piper, he divides his time between Ireland and America. **Jimmy O'Brien Moran**

keening (*caoineadh*), an aspect of death customs that entailed lamenting the person's death and crying loudly over the body (see p. 1117). Professional keeners were sometimes employed; these women attended at the WAKE, standing beside the body and wailing and then following the funeral procession from the house to the church or graveyard, keening all the while. Keening could often be

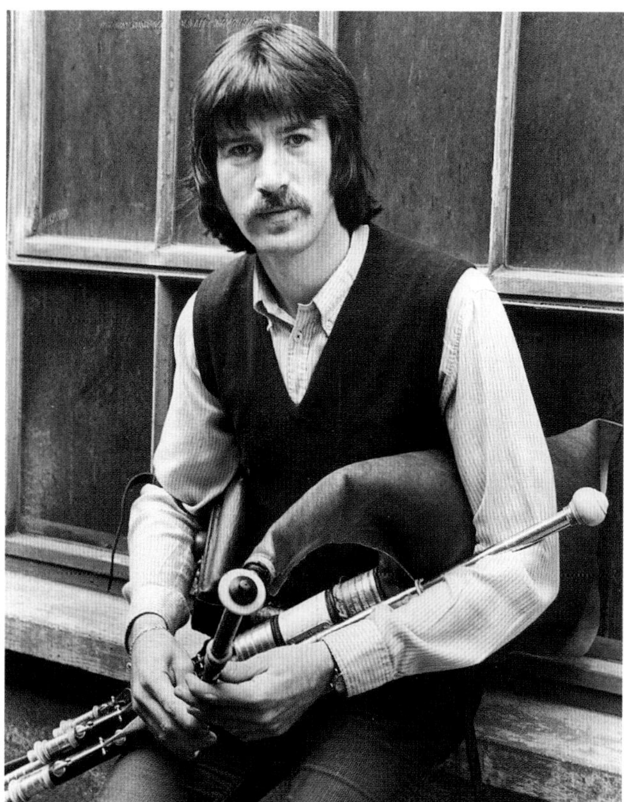

Keenan, Paddy. *Paddy Keenan, uilleann piper, was taught to play at the age of ten by his father. A member of the traditional group Bothy Band in the 1970s, he has since established a solo career as one of the most influential of today's pipers. [Bill Doyle]*

cathartic in nature, and sometimes those close to the dead person remembered their life and character in this fashion also. Church authorities denounced the practice, and yet it continued well into the twentieth century. **Anne O'Connor**

Kelburn, Alexander (fl. c. 1768–1789), bookbinder. Son of James Kelburn (1700–1766), bookbinder, stationer, bookseller, and publisher, he worked in George's Lane (South Great George's Street), Dublin, and seems to have inherited his father's business. He is recorded as being set free of the City and Guild on 5 July 1768. A considerable amount of Kelburn's business consisted of the binding of manuscript estate maps and plans; some of this was carried out for the surveyor Bernard Scalé, pupil of JOHN ROCQUE. Kelburn also bound architectural plans as well as general printed volumes. Worked in both large and small scale, his calf or goatskin bindings are elaborately decorated with rococo motifs in gold tooling. **Christopher Moore**

Kelehan, Noel (1935–), JAZZ musician. Born in Dublin; studied PIANO at the Municipal College of Music. As pianist with the Jazz Heralds in the early 1960s he was a leading influence in the establishment of modern jazz in Ireland. His quintet with Mike Nolan (trumpet), Keith Donald (saxophone), Frank Hess (bass), and JOHN WADHAM (drums) was for several years the only regularly performing modern jazz band in Dublin. The band recorded an album, *Ozone* (1980), and appeared at Ronnie Scott's Club in London as part of the Sense of Ireland festival, 1980. An arranger, conductor, and producer of jazz radio programmes, he has written scores for a dozen television dramas and for two runs of the serial 'Bracken'. He composed 'Episodes' on commission from Gorey Arts Festival for LOUIS STEWART and string quartet and 'Three Pieces for Percussion and Symphony Orchestra'. He has been involved with the EUROVISION SONG CONTEST as conductor for thirty years, appearing more often than any other person in any capacity. **Brian Trench**

Kellett, Sir Henry (1806–1875), explorer. Born in Clonaclody, Co. Tipperary. In 1845 he surveyed the Pacific coast in the *Herald*, at the same time taking three summer voyages between 1848 and 1850 in search of the missing Arctic explorer Sir John Franklin. In 1852, on another expedition seeking Franklin, he captained the *Resolute*, sailing through Baffin Bay to Melville Island, where he spent two winters in the ice-pack. After rescuing ROBERT M'CLURE and his crew he himself reluctantly abandoned ship on the orders of Sir Edward Belcher. The empty *Resolute* drifted down Baffin Bay and was picked up unharmed by an American whaler. Commander-in-chief of the China station 1868–71, he was made a knight commander of the Order of Bath, 1869. **Peter Somerville-Large**

Kells (*Ceanannas*), Co. Meath, a market town on the River BLACKWATER, 13 km (8 miles) from Navan and 50 km (31 miles) north-west of Dublin; population (2002), 2,619. Kells has a long history, having been a *dún* settlement in prehistoric times. From the Middle Ages it has been an important nodal point on routes west from Drogheda and north from Dublin. A Columban monastery was built after 807, which by the middle of the tenth century had replaced IONA as the head of Columban foundations in Ireland. The monastery's treasures included the shrine of the CATHACH and the BOOK OF KELLS, a masterpiece of medieval illumination (see p. 523). Because of its wealth, Kells suffered devastating VIKING raids during the tenth century; a ROUND TOWER, several elaborately carved HIGH CROSSES, and St Columb's House survive. HUGH DE LACY chose Kells as a manorial site, and it constituted a principal strongpoint of the PALE. It suffered during the Cromwellian era and finally fell into the hands of Richard Stephens in 1654, who later sold his interest to Thomas Taylor. In 1760 the head of the Taylor family was created Baron Headfort, and in 1770 Headfort House, 1.5 km (1 mile) north-east of the town, was completed. Kells was developed as an estate town in the late eighteenth century, with GEORGIAN houses at Headfort Place and a fine classical-style courthouse (now a heritage centre). Industrial development was hindered by a defective water supply and a lack of water transport in the nineteenth century.

The town still performs a market function and is a regional centre and seat of the District Court and Circuit Court. It suffers from heavy through traffic, though a bypass is planned. The population has grown from the 1990s as Kells has taken on a new role as a dormitory town for Dublin. **Ruth McManus**

Kells, Book of, an ILLUMINATED MANUSCRIPT containing the Latin text of the four Gospels, now in TRINITY COLLEGE Library, Dublin, to which it was brought in the 1660s. Its date and place of origin remain controversial, with IONA c. 800 being the most widely accepted attribution. The manuscript was certainly in Kells by the eleventh century, as attested by church transactions copied into it, and may have been taken there in the early ninth century by the Iona community, seeking refuge from VIKING raids.

The book now consists of 340 vellum (calfskin) folios (680 pages), written in insular majuscule script by at least three scribes. Its Gospel text is based on the Vulgate with an admixture of Old Latin elements. The Gospels are accompanied by preliminary texts, which comprise a list of Hebrew names, the *breves causae* (headings of the Gospel sections), the *argumenta* (brief lives of the Evangelists), and CANON TABLES (Gospel concordances), set within elaborate arcaded structures. The book's decoration, probably created by three artists, fuses a variety of influences—Celtic, Germanic, Pictish, and Mediterranean—with a Carolingian impact being disputed. The decorative scheme contains standard insular components: a carpet page, decorated initials on each Gospel and on Matthew's nativity story (the *chi-rho* initial), and the Evangelist symbols and two Evangelist portraits (see p. 523); however, it surpasses other manuscripts in variety, colour, and scale. The manuscript features full-page images of Christ and the Virgin and Child, as well as miniatures of the Temptation and the Arrest, which refer to the Gospel stories, but, like many Kells images, they evoke liturgical, eucharistic and exegetical meanings, while the book's minor embellishments introduce elements of humour. The Book of Kells shares many textual and decorative features with the earlier Book of DURROW, both manuscripts being associated with COLM CILLE. **Małgorzata Krasnodębska-D'Aughton**

Kells embroidery, devised by Alice Hart in the late nineteenth century to encourage women to organise EMBROIDERY classes for the rural poor by using naturally dyed and polished flax threads worked on Irish LINEN, using designs fundamentally based on Early Christian MANUSCRIPTS, such as the BOOK OF KELLS. An enlightened philanthropic entrepreneur, Hart had founded the Donegal Industrial Fund in 1883 to encourage a revival of cottage textile industries in post-famine rural Ireland. This popular and distinctive embroidery, in a variety of stitches, was used to embellish a wide range of fashionable items, having been introduced as a prize-winning novelty venture at the London Inventions Exhibition of 1885. **Nicola Gordon Bowe**

Kells lace, an embroidered net, principally in LIMERICK LACE style but with some also in CARRICKMACROSS LACE style. The industry was established in 1825 by Emma Hubbert at Kells, Co. Meath, to supply her brother's lace-manufacturing business in Nottingham. Kells lace won royal patronage and RDS awards. The industry closed c. 1850, unable to compete with the improvements in machine lace. **Mairead Dunlevy**

Kelly, Hugh (1739–1777), writer and dramatist. Born near Killarney, Co. Kerry, he later moved to Dublin, where he was educated, and took an interest in the theatre. In 1760 he left for London, working as an attorney's copying clerk and then writing and editing for various publications. He later wrote the theatrical commentary *Thespis* and the novel *Memoirs of a Magdalen* (1766–7). His first play, *False Delicacy* (1768), ran successfully against GOLDSMITH's *The Good-Natured Man*; other works include *A Word to the Wise* (1770), *The School for Wives* (1773), *The Romance of an Hour* (1774), and *The Man of Reason* (1776). **Joley Wood**

Kelly, John (1912–1987), fiddler, concertina-player, and raconteur. Born at Loop Head, Co. Clare; he learnt concertina from his mother and uncle and was influenced by the presence locally of the outstanding stylist Ellen Galvin of Moyasta, a friend of the travelling piper Garret Barry. He learnt also from the fiddler Patsy Geary, with whom he played for HOUSE DANCES before moving to Co. Kildare, then to Dublin in 1945, where his shop, the 'Horseshoe' in Capel Street, became a meeting-place and academic sparring-ring for the best-known musicians of the revival years, including TOMMY POTTS, Tom Mulligan, WILLIE CLANCY, JOHNNY DORAN, and SEÁN MAGUIRE. He collected on tape, was a founder-member of COMHALTAS CEOLTÓIRÍ ÉIREANN, and adjudicated competitions. In 1960, making music for a play for SEÁN Ó RIADA brought him, together with Michael Tubridy and PADDY MOLONEY, into CEOLTÓIRÍ CHUALANN and also into the influential Castle Céilí Band. For many years he was an institution at O'Donoghue's of Merrion Row, Dublin, then at the Four Seasons in Capel Street. **Fintan Vallely**

Kelly, Luke (1940–1984), singer and musician. Born in Dublin. A founder-member of the DUBLINERS, in 1963 he left for England, where he met Ewan McColl, from whom he learnt much of his repertoire, including 'The Travelling People', 'Shoals of Herring', and 'The Net-Hauling Song'. He rejoined the Dubliners in 1964, playing with them until his death (see p. 321). **Pat Ahern**

Kelly, Maeve (1930–), novelist and short-story writer. Born and educated in Dundalk, Co. Louth. Among her works, which deal with the lives of women, are *A Life of Her Own and Other Stories* (1976) and *Orange Horses* (1991). **Terence Brown**

Kelly, Mary Eva, known as 'Eva of the *Nation*' (c. 1825–1910), poet. Born in Headford, Co. Galway; educated privately. Under the pen-name 'Eva' she was a contributor of patriotic prose and poetry to the NATION and other nationalist periodicals. In 1854 she married KEVIN IZOD O'DOHERTY following his release from Van Diemen's Land (Tasmania); in 1857 the couple emigrated to Australia, where she continued to write. Her *Poems* (1877) were published in San Francisco; a revised and enlarged edition was published in Dublin in 1909. She died in poverty in Brisbane. **Margaret Kelleher**

Kelly, Michael (1762–1826), musician and singer. Born in Dublin into a musical family; he studied keyboard and singing, and made his first stage appearance in 1777 at the age of fifteen. His success was immediate, and he travelled to Italy to continue his studies. He undertook a tour of Italy, culminating in Vienna, where he befriended Mozart and met Haydn, Dittersdorf, Martini, and Gluck. He moved to London in 1787 and became a renowned tenor; he gave his last stage appearance in Dublin in 1811. He also composed more than sixty dramatic pieces (see p. 755). **John Page**

Kelly, Ned (1854–1880), Irish-Australian bushranger and popular hero. Born near Melbourne of Irish parents. In 1867 the family moved to north-eastern Victoria, a mountainous district where poor, mostly Irish settlers were regularly suspected by the police of cattle theft and other crimes. With a developing reputation for criminality, the Kelly family was under constant police harassment. In 1871 Ned Kelly was jailed for three years for a crime he did not commit. Some years later he was again suspected of criminal activity, and his mother and brother were accused of shooting a policeman. Kelly, his brother Dan and others took to the nearby mountain ranges, where on 25 October 1878, at Stringybark Creek, they surprised several policemen, three of whom (Sergeant Michael Kennedy, Constable Thomas Lonigan, and Constable Michael Scanlan) were killed. Subsequently Kelly and his gang were regarded by the state as outlaws. They robbed banks and spent the proceeds in the communities that protected them. Despite a considerable price on their heads they evaded capture for nearly two years, thanks mainly to the protection of sympathisers. In June 1880 a planned attack on a police train at Glenrowan was foiled, and Kelly was captured. He was taken to Melbourne, tried for the murder of Lonigan, and hanged in November 1880, aged twenty-five. In popular culture he has long been acclaimed as a defender of the underdog. The State Library of Victoria has the home-made body armour worn by Kelly at Glenrowan. From 1946, the Australian painter Sidney Nolan (1917–1992) painted a major series of works on the Ned Kelly theme. **Frank Molloy**

Kelly, Ned. *Ned Kelly, Australia's most notorious bushranger, photographed the day before his execution in November 1880. [Victoria Police Historical Unit (Aust.)]*

Kelly, Oisín (1915–1981), sculptor. Born Austin Kelly in Dublin, son of a schoolmaster; he likewise became a teacher, having studied Irish and French at TCD. He attended night classes at the NCAD and subsequently at the Frankfurt School of Art. He experimented with a wide variety of media but was particularly successful with small wooden pieces. Much of his work was based on traditional themes, and he had a special interest in portraying Irish dancers. Most of his early commissions were for the Catholic Church; perhaps the most dramatic of these is the large copper Crucifixion on top of the Church of the Redeemer, Dundalk. Later he received a number of important public commissions, including *The Children of Lir* (1964) in the Garden of Remembrance, Dublin (see p. 191), *Two Working Men* (1969) at the County Hall, Cork, *Roger Casement* (1971) at Banna Strand, Co. Kerry, and *Jim Larkin* (1977) in O'Connell Street, Dublin. In 1964 he resigned his teaching post at St Columba's College, Rathfarnham, Co. Dublin, and was appointed part-time artist in residence at KILKENNY DESIGN WORKSHOPs. There he designed a wide range of pieces in various materials, including a particularly successful series of ceramic birds. His last years were dogged by ill health, but he completed *The Chariot of Life* (1978) for the Irish Life Centre, Lower Abbey Street, Dublin, before his death in 1981. A retrospective exhibition of his work was arranged by the ARTS COUNCIL in 1978, the sole one-person showing in his lifetime. **Fergus Kelly**

Kelly, Seán (1956–), cyclist. Born in Carrick-on-Suir, Co. Tipperary. He became a national sports hero during the 1980s. He won the prestigious Paris–Nice race for the first time in 1982; in 1988 he won his first major race, the Vuelta de España. He was three times winner of the Pernod Super Prestige Trophy (world champion on points). An exceptional athlete, he achieved a total of 179 major race wins in his career. **Séamus Shortall**

Kelly, T. C. (1917–1985), composer. Born in Wexford; educated at UCD where he studied composition with JOHN F. LARCHET. He composed many works, including a song cycle, piano concerto, orchestral suites, two fantasies for harp and orchestra, and several arrangements of traditional music. His interest in folk music arrangement remains his most enduring legacy. As a teacher he held the position of professor of music at Clongowes Wood College, Co. Kildare, from 1952 until his death. **John Page**

Kelly, Thomas A. F. (1956–), philosopher. Born in Dublin; educated at UCD, TCD, and the University of Fribourg, Switzerland. A lecturer in the National University of Ireland, Maynooth, his areas of research include ontology, metaphysics, and anthropology. His work is systematic but dialogues with Aquinas, Anselm, Heidegger, WITTGENSTEIN, and others. He has published *Language and Transcendence* (1994) and *Language, World, and God* (1996). He is president of the Irish Philosophical Society and founder-editor of its Yearbook. **Éamonn Gaines**

Kelly, Thomas J. (1833–1908), Fenian. Born in Mount Bellew, Co. Galway. He emigrated to the United States in 1851 and fought on the union side in the American Civil War, attaining the rank of captain. Having served as an assistant to both JOHN O'MAHONY and JAMES STEPHENS, he temporarily headed the Fenian organisation in both Ireland and the United States and was given the rank of colonel in the 'army of the Irish Republic'. Following his arrest in Manchester, his dramatic rescue from a police van in Salford in September 1867 precipitated the MANCHESTER MARTYRS' affair. He ended his days in a less sensational role as an inspector at the Customs House in New York. **Oliver P. Rafferty**

Kelly-Rogers, J. C. (Jack) (1905–1981), pilot and airline administrator. Born in Dún Laoghaire, Co. Dublin; he joined the Royal Air Force in 1927. Transferring to civil aviation, he piloted transatlantic flying-boats throughout the SECOND WORLD WAR, with Winston Churchill one of his frequent passengers. He joined Aer Lingus in 1947 as technical manager, rising to the position of deputy manager before retiring in 1965. In 1975 he inaugurated the Irish Aviation Museum (now defunct) at Dublin Airport. [see FOYNES.] **Bernard Share**

Kendrick, Matthew (c. 1797–1874), marine painter. Born in Dublin; he spent much of his youth working on fishing vessels off NEWFOUNDLAND. Returning to Dublin, he found employment as a professional yachtsman. In 1825 he entered the DUBLIN SOCIETY'S Drawing Schools. He exhibited at the ROYAL HIBERNIAN ACADEMY, 1827–72, was elected a member, 1850, and Keeper, 1850–66. He specialised in marine views and ship portraits, exhibiting in both Dublin and London, where he lived between 1840 and 1848. **Peter Murray**

Kennedy, Brian (1966–), singer. Born in Belfast. He began his music career as part of Energy Orchard, the band formed by his brother Bap Kennedy, a respected roots and folk singer-songwriter. Living in London from the mid-1980s, Kennedy forged his own velvet-voiced solo career. Assisted along the way by VAN MORRISON, he has left his soft-folk past behind him and achieved international success. He interrupted this career in 2000 to take part in the Broadway run of RIVERDANCE. **Tony Clayton-Lea**

Kennedy, Jimmy (1902–1984), songwriter. Born in Omagh, Co. Tyrone; educated at TCD. He worked as a teacher and as a civil servant before concentrating on full-time songwriting from the mid-1930s. For more than twenty-five years he wrote, either separately or with George Grosz or Michael Carr, some of the most enduring songs of the day, including 'The Teddy Bears' Picnic' (1933) (which sold 4 million records), 'Isle of Capri' (1934), 'Red Sails in the Sunset' (1935), 'We're Going to Hang Out Our Washing on the Siegfried Line' (1939) (one of the most popular songs during the SECOND WORLD WAR), and 'The Hokey Cokey' (1942). As the early 1960s paved the way for rock and roll, Kennedy began to write songs for plays. His honours included two ASCAP (American Society of Composers, Authors and Publishers) Awards and two Ivor Novello Awards (Outstanding Services to British Music, 1971, and Life Achievement, 1980). In 1983 he was made an officer of the Order of the British Empire, and in 1997 he was admitted to the American Songwriters' Hall of Fame. **Tony Clayton-Lea**

Kennedy, John (1928–), traditional singer, flute, fife and whistle-player, band and music teacher. Born in Cullybackey, Co. Antrim. An award-winning singer, he is self-taught, influenced by considerable local talent, which found expression in marching bands and country hall recreational music. Some of his unique local repertoire of MARCHES and quicksteps was released in 1999 as *The Girls Along the Road*. **Fintan Vallely**

Kennedy, John F. (Jack) (1917–1963), politician. Born in Brookline, Massachusetts, son of a wealthy and ambitious father, Joseph P. Kennedy, and grandson of two of Boston's most powerful turn-of-the-century Irish-American political chieftains, Patrick J. Kennedy and John 'Honey Fitz' Fitzgerald. After graduating from Harvard University in 1940 he joined the US Navy and fought in the SECOND WORLD WAR. When the eldest Kennedy son, Joseph, died in action during that war, Joseph P. Kennedy concentrated his ambitions on his next son, John. Elected US senator for Massachusetts in 1953, John F. Kennedy was narrowly defeated for the Democratic vice-presidential nomination in 1956. He was elected President of the United States four years later, the first Catholic to have held this office. His Catholicism was a central issue in the campaign of 1960, but he skilfully persuaded the American public that there would be no conflict between his religion and his presidential duties: the real issue before the voters, he declared, was 'not what kind of church I believe in, for that should be important only to me, but what kind of America I believe in.' In his inaugural address he offered the memorable injunction: 'Ask not what your country can do for you; ask what you can do for your country.'

Kennedy's domestic policy concentrated on issues of poverty and civil rights. After facing down the Cuban government and its Soviet backers in the missile crisis of October 1962, he consolidated his Cold War foreign policy by stepping up American involvement in Vietnam. He was greeted with a rapturous welcome when he visited Ireland in June 1963, visiting distant relatives and addressing a joint session of the Oireachtas (see p. 575). He was assassinated in Dallas, Texas, on 22 November 1963. [see ULSTER AMERICAN FOLK PARK; UNITED STATES PRESIDENTS OF IRISH DESCENT.] **Kevin Kenny**

Kennedy, Kenneth (Ken) (1941–), rugby footballer. Born in Kent, England. He made his debut against France at Lansdowne Road in 1965 on a team that included four other new caps: Roger Young, Seán McHale, MICK DOYLE, and Ronnie Lamont. He won his first seven caps in succession, and remarkably his last twenty-eight appearances were also consecutive. He toured Australia and New Zealand with the 1966 British Lions team, playing in four Tests, and South Africa in 1974, when he failed to make the Test team. Ireland's most-capped hooker, he won forty-five caps between 1965 and 1975. **Karl Johnston**

Kennedy, Patrick Brendan (1929–1966), mathematician. Born in Clarecastle, Co. Clare; educated at UCC and the University of Exeter, where he studied with W. K. Hayman; he was awarded a doctorate by the NUI in 1954. In 1956 he was appointed professor of mathematics at University College, Cork, and in 1963 became professor of mathematics at the University of York. He specialised in the asymptotics of functions and was noted for the clarity and precision of his teaching. His unfinished book, *Subharmonic Functions* (1976), was completed and published by Hayman. **Rod Gow**

Kennedy, S. B. (1942–), art critic and curator. Born in Belfast; educated at Belfast and TCD. He is curator of the ULSTER MUSEUM and author of *Frank McKelvey* (1993), *Paul Henry* (2000), and the comprehensive *Irish Art and Modernism, 1880–1950* (1991). **Richard Pine**

Kennedy, Stanislaus (1940–), social justice campaigner. Born in Lispole, Co. Kerry; she joined the Sisters of Charity in Dublin on finishing school and completed a social studies degree at UCD and a postgraduate diploma at Manchester University. Appointed to the Kilkenny Social Services Centre, she was an outspoken critic of what she perceived as the Catholic Church's distance from the poor. In 1985 she set up Focus Point (later Focus Ireland), a centre for homeless people. She was the first chairwoman of the Combat Poverty Committee, precursor of the Combat Poverty Agency, established as a state agency in 1986. She is widely admired for her campaigning on behalf of Ireland's disadvantaged people. **Myra Dowling**

Kennelly, (Timothy) Brendan (1936–), poet, critic, and teacher. Born in Ballylongford, Co. Kerry; educated at TCD and at Leeds. Since 1973 he has been professor of modern literature at Trinity College, where he is also a senior fellow. He edited *The Penguin Book of Irish Verse* (1970, 1981). His early poetry was published in collaboration with Rudi Holzapfel. His first solo collection, *My Dark Fathers* (1964), celebrates the ancestral voices of his native Co. Kerry, the intimacy and immediacy of which inform much of his later work (collected in *Breathing Spaces* and *A Time for Voices*), which is also closely entwined with his personal life. The failure of his marriage and his subsequent treatment for alcoholism provoked his adaptations of *Antigone* (1986), *Medea* (1988), and *The Trojan Women* (1993), with their searing insights into the female psyche. Cardiac surgery influenced *The Man Made of Rain* (1998). In the 1980s he embarked on two major poetry sequences, *Cromwell* (1983) and *The Book of Judas* (1991), the former causing controversy with its examination of the mind of OLIVER CROMWELL, in dialogue with a stereotypical Irishman, Buffún; the latter, similarly probing the mind of Judas Iscariot, questions the black-versus-white of faith and morality. Some of his most sympathetic verse celebrates the privacies of the marginalised, the defeated and the misunderstood, while a strong strand of irreverence and anarchy is evident in *Poetry My Arse* (1995). His considerable critical output was collected in *Journey into Joy* (1994). **Richard Pine**

Kenner, Hugh (1923–), professor and critic. Born in Peterborough, Ontario. He has held professorships of English at the University of California, 1958–73, Johns Hopkins University (Maryland), 1975–91, and the University of Georgia, from 1991. A major critic of JOYCE and BECKETT, scrupulously attentive to the nuances of prose style and the quirks of the local, he has published *Dublin's Joyce* (1956), *Samuel Beckett: A Critical Study* (1961), *Joyce's Voices* (1978), and *A Colder Eye: The Modern Irish Writers* (1982). **Anthony Roche**

Keogh, John (1740–1817), Catholic political activist. Born in Dublin. A wealthy, self-made Dublin silk-mercer, he joined the CATHOLIC COMMITTEE in 1782. Real ability as well as self-regard brought him to challenge the established, cautious leadership early in 1791. His more aggressive tactics led to the CATHOLIC CONVENTION of 1792, which in turn was largely instrumental in securing the Relief Act (1793); among other concessions, the act enabled Catholics to vote in the election of MPs. However, tainted by his membership of the UNITED IRISHMEN, and growing old, he was active in public affairs for only a short period during the last two decades of his life. **C. D. A. Leighton**

Keohane, Joe (1919–), Gaelic footballer. Born in Co. Kerry. At the age of eighteen he first broke into the Kerry senior ranks and won an all-Ireland championship in 1937. It was the first of five all-Ireland titles in a remarkable career, adding to his titles in 1939, 1940, 1941, and 1946. He also won ten Munster championships. Although remembered in GAA folklore as one of the toughest footballers ever, he was also one of the most gifted players, with great fielding ability and accurate kicking. **Donal Keenan**

kern. *A kern (left) handing a spear to his chieftain, whose horse is held by an attendant; woodcut by an anonymous Dutch artist, from John Derrick's* Image of Ireland *(1581). [Council of Trustees of the National Library of Ireland; R4060 TX 1)*

kern (*ceithearn*, warrior band or individual trooper). In English the word stands for both the troop of lightly armoured native mercenaries and an individual member. From the late twelfth century the kern were freelance mercenaries, normally twenty in a troop, who roamed the country in search of employment but when idle intimidated the people into providing them with food and lodging. In warfare they often fought without armour, their only warlike equipment being a sword and a handful of small spears and their celebrated agility, a nuisance to the enemy and their own best defence.

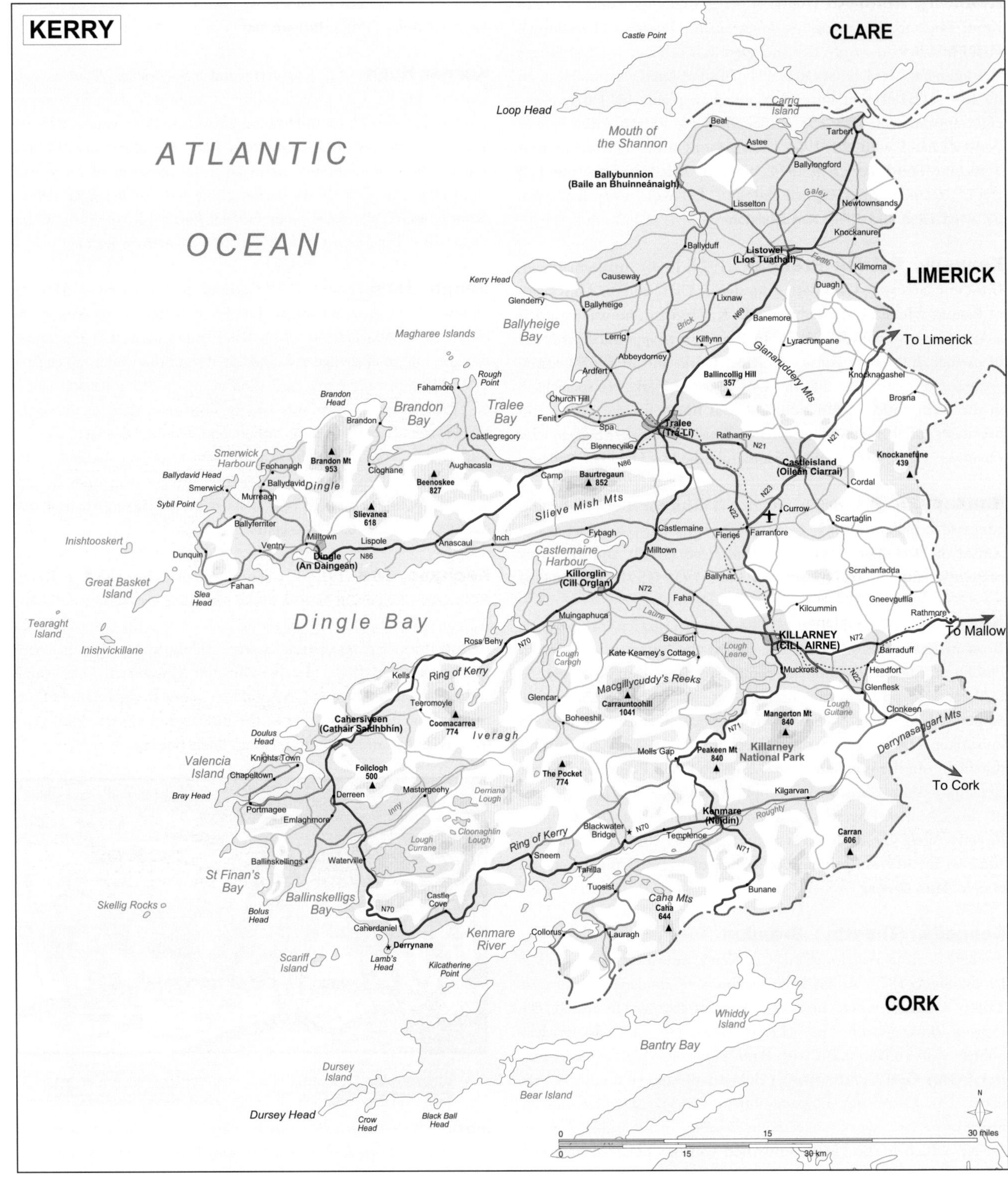

In the wake of armies they harassed the civilian population, often burning them out and stealing their cattle. Fourteenth-century accounts relate that they were paid a penny a day, but by the 1570s they were commanding eight pence a day—the normal rate for the foot-soldier. In English sources, such as the *fiants* (authorisations for letters patent), noteworthy GALLOGLASS families, such as the MacDonalds and MacSweeneys, are sometimes confusingly described as kern. As a distinct category, kern were not numerous until the second half of the sixteenth century, when HUGH O'NEILL and other Ulster chiefs used them in characteristic guerrilla tactics, and evidence suggests that they were then trained in firearms; indeed by then they had become indistinguishable from the Irish warlord's normal levy or 'rising out'. **John J. N. McGurk**

Kernoff, Aaron (Harry) (1900–1974), portrait, landscape and decorative painter. Born in London; the family moved to Dublin in 1914. He was apprenticed to his father, a cabinet-maker, and attended night classes at the Metropolitan School of Art. Loyal to the academic tradition, his portraits are full of characterisation, while his landscapes are concerned with the details of a scene rather than mood. Kernoff also did drawings for theatre sets and costumes and produced innumerable woodcuts and illustrations (see p. 896). He travelled widely in Ireland and visited the Soviet Union c. 1930. A regular exhibitor with the RHA, he was made a full member in 1936. **Síghle Bhreathnach-Lynch**

Kerr, Alfred E. (1901–1980), illustrator and writer. Born in Wollston, Hertfordshire; he moved to Belfast as a child, where he worked as a draughtsman for an engineering firm before becoming a commercial artist. Several books published by Quota Press in Belfast in the 1930s established him as an illustrator. He worked in a great variety of styles, from the striking linocuts of Florence Davidson's *Loan-Ends* (1934) to his delicate filigree pen-and-ink drawing in Kit Cavanagh's *A Dunleary Legend* (1934) and Avril Andersen's *Whist! Listen a While* (1935); these illustrations earned him the epithet of the 'Ulster Beardsley'. A limited edition of Claude Houghton's *The Beast* followed, and during the Second World War he wrote and illustrated some military handbooks for the Home Guard. Later he wrote and illustrated a number of children's books in the style of Disney under the pseudonym Patrick Sinclair—books so different as to appear not to be from the same pen. In 1959 he moved to the Isle of Wight, where he died. **Patricia Donlon**

Kerr, Virginia (1964–), singer. Born in Dublin, trained at the RIAM and the Guildhall School of Music and Drama, London. Her career as an operatic soprano includes roles as Lelia and Liu in *Turandot*; Musetta, Micaela, and Elvira in *L'italiana in Algeri* with the DUBLIN GRAND OPERA SOCIETY; Jenufa, Salomé, Julia in Dvořak's *Jakobin*; and the soprano lead in Judith Weir's *The Vanishing Bridegroom* with Scottish Opera, and Ortlinde in *Die Walküre* and Jenifer in *The Midsummer Marriage* at Covent Garden. Concert performances include Stravinsky's *Pulcinella*, Schreker's *Von Ewigen Leben*, and *Carmina Burana* at the Festival Hall, London. **John Page**

Kerry, County (*Contae Chiarraí*)

Province:	MUNSTER
County town:	Tralee
Area:	4,701 km^2 (1,814 sq. miles)
Population (2002):	132,424
Features:	LAKES OF KILLARNEY
	Lough Caragh
	Macgillycuddy's Reeks
	MOUNT BRANDON
	River Inny
	River Laune
	Slieve Mish
Of historical interest:	Ardfert Cathedral
	GALLARUS ORATORY
	Rattoo round tower
	SCEILG MHICHÍL
	Staigue fort
Industry and products:	AGRICULTURE
	Engineering
	Fishing
	Tourism

Petula Martyn

County Kerry, in the south-west of Ireland, is bordered to the north by the Shannon estuary and to the east by Co. Cork, with its extensive western coastline fronting the Atlantic Ocean. The principal towns are **Tralee**, **Killarney**, **Cahersiveen**, **Listowel**, and **Kenmare**. The northern part of the county is low-lying, while the south and west consist of two peninsulas, DINGLE PENINSULA the more northerly and IVERAGH PENINSULA to the south. The western parts of the county are mountainous and sparsely populated. It is a rural county, with one of the lowest aggregate urban populations in Ireland. While the traditional industries of fishing and agriculture are in decline, this has been ameliorated by industries sponsored by the IDA and Údarás na Gaeltachta and an expanding heritage tourism industry. The scenic landscape has always attracted visitors, making tourism the county's most important industry, employing more than 8,000 people (see p. 1057). The number of tourists has risen dramatically since the 1960s, when Co. Kerry attracted more than 100,000 visitors annually; that figure has since increased to a million visitors per year, resulting in great pressures on the landscape. The importance of the landscape and the environment has been recognised in recent discussion documents on the future of tourism. **Raymond O'Connor and John Crowley**

Kerry Babies. *Joanne Hayes, carrying flowers presented by well-wishers, leaving the public tribunal of inquiry in Tralee, Co. Kerry. Known as the 'Kerry Babies Tribunal', it inquired into the conduct of the Gardaí during their investigation of the deaths of two newborn babies in Co. Kerry in 1984. [Derek Speirs/Report]*

Kerry Babies Case (1984). Towards the end of 1984, following the 1983 ABORTION amendment to the CONSTITUTION, the 'Kerry Babies' brought infanticide to the attention of the Irish public. A baby with multiple stab wounds had been washed up on a beach at Cahersiveen, Co. Kerry. A Garda investigation to trace the mother led to a confession by Joanne Hayes, a single mother, to its murder; but the discovery of the body of a second baby on the farm in which she lived raised questions about this confession. The gardaí claimed that Joanne Hayes was the mother of both babies, until scientific tests showed that she was not the mother of the Cahersiveen baby. The mother of that baby has never been identified. An inconclusive internal Garda inquiry led to a public TRIBUNAL of inquiry into the affair, in which there was considerable public interest. It involved perjury, Garda intimidation, and infanticide; but by revealing a relationship between a lone mother and a married man in a small town it exposed the sexual mores of a hidden Ireland. The wrongful accusation of murder of the Cahersiveen baby generated considerable public support for Joanne Hayes, and the attendant news coverage made her a symbolic victim of patriarchal control over female SEXUALITY. The public empathised strongly with the plight of a woman forced to conceal the birth of her second child. **Evelyn Mahon**

Kettle, T. M. [Thomas] (1880–1916), poet and essayist. Born in Co. Dublin, son of a founder-member of the LAND LEAGUE; educated at UCD. He was IRISH PARTY MP for East Tyrone, 1906–10, and professor of national economics at UCD from 1909. He was in Belgium purchasing arms for the IRISH VOLUNTEERS when the FIRST WORLD WAR began. He enlisted in the British army in November 1914, and encouraged recruitment in Ireland. After the 1916 RISING he requested service overseas and was killed in action on the Somme in September 1916. His work challenges the aesthetic and political principles underlying the Rising. *Poems and Parodies* was published in 1912. **Fran Brearton**

Kevin, Anglicised name of Caoimhín (died 618), founder of Glendalough (see p. 443). Tradition names his parents as Cóemlug and Cóemell (Dál Messin Corb dynasty). Medieval 'Lives' associate him with Kilnamanagh, Co. Dublin, and Hollywood, Co. Wicklow, and make him fosterer of Fáelán mac Colmáin, later King of Leinster. His earliest successors at Glendalough supposedly included Mochonnóc of Kilmacanoge. [see SAINTS.] **Ailbhe Mac Shamhráin**

Kiberd, Declan (1951–), professor and critic. Born in Dublin; educated at TCD and the University of Oxford. He was a lecturer in UCD from 1979; appointed professor of Anglo-Irish Literature and Drama 1997. *Synge and the Irish Language* (1979) revealed the scholarship as well as knowledge of spoken Irish informing SYNGE's HIBERNO-ENGLISH dramatic speech. *Inventing Ireland* (1995) is a major work of post-colonial criticism, emphasising the centrality of YEATS; it won the IRISH TIMES Literature Prize in 1997. *Irish Classics* (2000) finds meaningful connection between works in the native Irish and Anglo-Irish traditions. **Anthony Roche**

Kickham, Charles (1828–1882), writer and revolutionary. Born in Mullinahone, Co. Tipperary, into a Catholic farming family. Despite severe eyesight and hearing problems he was active in the YOUNG IRELAND movement and became a leading FENIAN. Imprisonment with hard labour, 1865–9, further affected his health, but he remained active in the IRB until his death, distrusting the LAND LEAGUE as a sectional movement. He is best remembered for ballads such as 'Slievenamon' and 'Patrick Sheehan' and for his novel *Knocknagow* (1873), immensely popular for its rural nostalgia. Kickham's admirers tended to overlook his criticisms of farmers' exploitation of labourers and the misuse of clerical influence. **Patrick Maume**

Kiely, Benedict (1919–), novelist, short-story writer, broadcaster and critic. Born near Dromore, Co. Tyrone; educated at UCD. From 1945 to 1964 he was a journalist with the *Standard*, the *Irish Independent*, and the IRISH PRESS. Between 1946 and 1955 he published six novels on various topics, including *Honey Seems Bitter* (1952) and *The Cards of the Gambler* (1953). His reputation is strongest as a short-story writer. In collections such as *A Journey to the Seven Streams* (1963) and *A Ball of Malt and Madame Butterfly* (1973) he employs caricature to comic and ironic effect in a manner reminiscent of FLANN O'BRIEN. His *Collected Stories* appeared in 2001. **Michael McAteer**

Kiernan, Michael (Mick) (1961–), rugby footballer. Born in Cork. He won his first cap when he replaced the injured David Irwin against Wales at Lansdowne Road, when Ireland won by 20–12, en route to the first Triple Crown in thirty-three years. He became Ireland's first-choice goal-kicker in the season 1984/5, when his late dropped goal gave Ireland a 13–10 victory over England in the decider at Lansdowne Road, and Ireland won the Triple Crown again. He won forty-three caps between 1982 and 1991 and was Ireland's top international scorer, with 308 points, until overtaken by DAVID HUMPHREYS. He also toured New Zealand with the 1983 British Lions team, playing in three of the four Tests. **Karl Johnston**

Kiernan, Thomas (Tom) (1939–), rugby footballer. Born in Cork. He made his international debut against England in 1960 and then went on to win ten more caps in succession, including the only Test on Ireland's short four-match tour of South Africa in 1961. In that match, which Ireland lost by 24–8, he became the first Irish full-back to score an international try; he converted it himself and also kicked a penalty goal, thereby scoring all his team's points. He toured South Africa with the 1962 British Lions team, playing in the third Test, was captain of the British Lions on their South African tour of 1968, and played in all four Tests. He then coached Munster to victory over the All Blacks at Thomond Park in 1978 and was national coach from 1980/81 to 1982/83, during which time he steered Ireland to the Triple Crown victory of 1982. His last international match was against Scotland at Murrayfield, and at the time he was Ireland's most-capped player and top points-scorer, with 158 points. He is Ireland's most-capped full-back, with fifty-four appearances. He also captained Ireland on twenty-four occasions, which is another Irish record. He was president of the IRFU, 1988/89, and also served as Ireland's representative on the International Rugby Board and was a director of European Rugby Cup. **Karl Johnston**

Kildare, County (*Contae Chill Dara*)

Province:	LEINSTER
County town:	Naas
Area:	1,694 km^2 (652 sq. miles)
Population (2002):	163,995
Features:	Bog of ALLEN
	River BARROW
	River LIFFEY
	The CURRAGH
Of historical interest:	CASTLEDERMOT MONASTIC SITE
	CASTLETOWN HOUSE
	Kildare Cathedral
	MOONE HIGH CROSS
Industry and products:	Carpets
	Cattle
	Cutlery
	Horse-breeding
	Oats, barley, potatoes
	Quarrying
	Rope manufacturing
	Turf-cutting

Petula Martyn

County Kildare is part of the glacial drift-covered east midlands, its rich pastures in the north dotted with estates and stud farms,

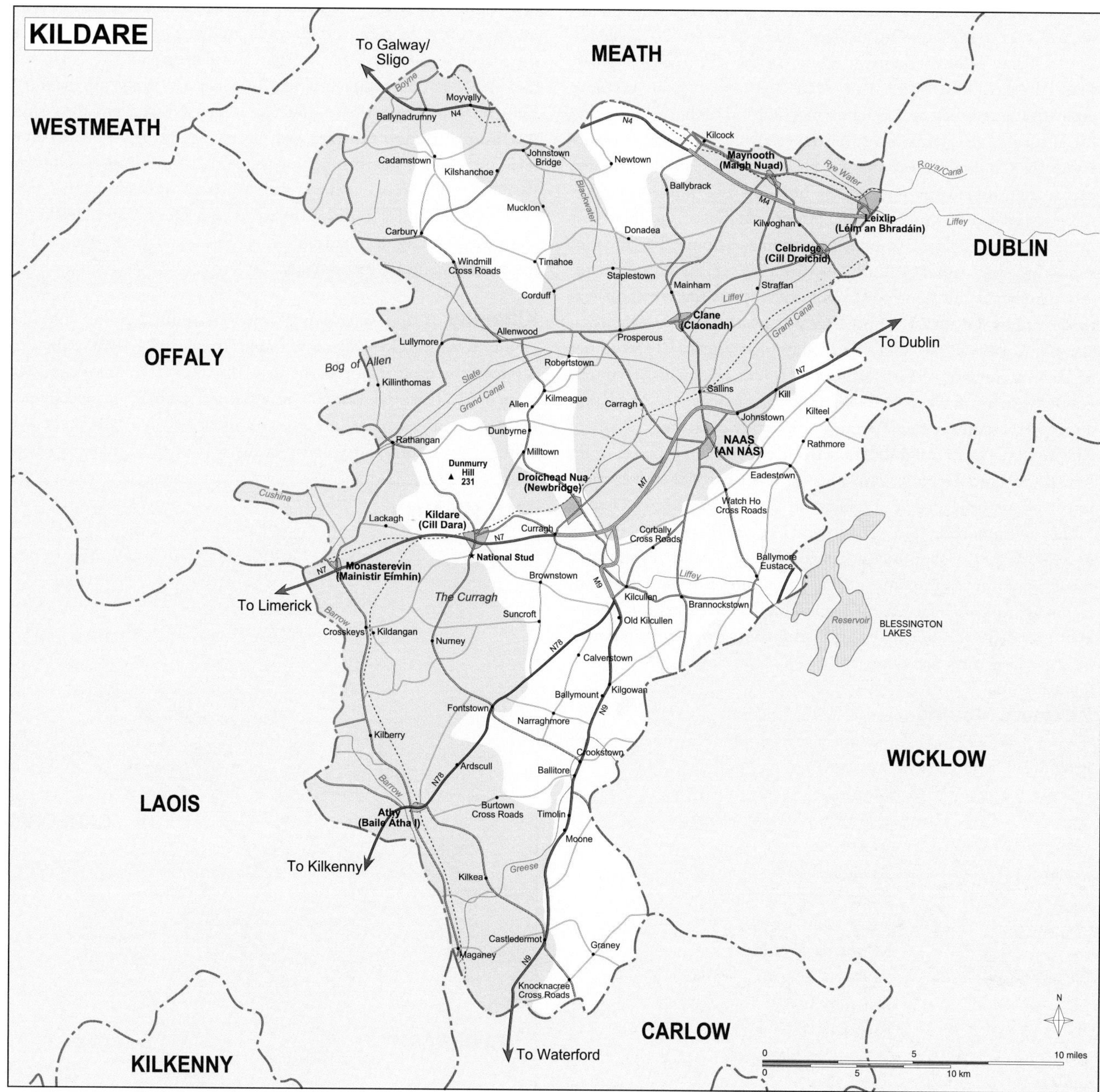

giving way to loamy tillage farms in the south and to great stretches of raised bog in the west. This landscape was occupied from early history, with Knockaulin (Dún Ailinne), near Kilcullen, an ancient hill-fort with ramparts of 450 m (1,500-ft) diameter, being the ancient seat of the kings of Leinster. ST BRIGID established a monastery at Kildare in the fifth century, where an incomplete ROUND TOWER stands near the cathedral. Castledermot has medieval monastic remains of round tower and HIGH CROSSES. Under the ANGLO-NORMAN Fitzgeralds, Kildare was established as a county in 1297; it became an important frontier zone in the English PALE, guarding it from incursions by the Irish of Wicklow and the south midlands. Defensive towers and castles were built, such as those at Kilkea, Maynooth, and Barberstown. The Fitzgeralds, the most powerful magnates in the late Middle Ages, survived with enormous estates into the nineteenth century, building a lavish mansion at CARTON, near their town of Maynooth, as well as a splendid town-house, LEINSTER HOUSE, in Kildare Street, Dublin, now the seat of DÁIL ÉIREANN (see pp. 29, 620). The county is the centre of the Irish bloodstock industry. The heath of the Curragh hosted horse-racing for hundreds of years, and today's racecourse is famous, as is Punchestown in the north of the county (see pp. 501, 502). **Patrick Duffy**

Kildare (population 6,893) is the site of the National Stud. CASTLETOWN House at Celbridge, now managed by the state, is the most distinguished Palladian stately home in Ireland. **Maynooth** (population 10,845) on the Royal Canal was selected in 1795 as the site of a Catholic seminary, ST PATRICK'S COLLEGE, now part of the National University of Ireland. NUI Maynooth was established in 1997. The countryside and towns of north Kildare are now part of Dublin's commuter belt, with such towns as **Leixlip** (population 15,143), **Celbridge** (population 14,251) and Maynooth having rapidly expanding populations. **Patrick Duffy**

Kildare Rebellion (1534–5). The rebellion has been interpreted either as a conscious show of Geraldine resistance to the general Tudor policy of increased government centralisation or as an error of judgment by the Fitzgeralds, when HENRY VIII was particularly vulnerable, grappling with the divorce issue and the introduction of the REFORMATION. On 11 June 1534 THOMAS FITZGERALD, Lord Offaly ('Silken Thomas'), acting on the advice of his father, GERALD FITZGERALD, NINTH EARL OF KILDARE, then in London, dramatically resigned at a Council meeting in Dublin, denouncing his allegiance to Henry. Angered especially by Thomas's solicitations for Continental support for his self-styled Catholic crusade, Henry imprisoned the earl on 29 June. In late July Fitzgerald's forces assassinated John Alen, Archbishop of Dublin, and thereafter unsuccessfully besieged Dublin. Meanwhile, Thomas became earl following his father's death in the Tower of London on 2 September. Henry's determination to suppress the rebellion was evidenced by the arrival of Sir WILLIAM SKEFFINGTON's 2,300-strong army at Dublin in late October. Following a truce (19 December 1534 to 6 January 1535), Fitzgerald's forces occupied Maynooth Castle, which was taken by Skeffington after a siege (18–23 March) and the garrison's summary execution, known as the 'pardon of Maynooth'. On 24 August, Thomas surrendered on promise of his life to the Lord Deputy, GREY, his uncle-in-law. He and his five uncles were beheaded in London on 3 February 1537. Despite Henry's unprecedented investment of soldiers and money (£23,000) in the suppression campaign, only about seventy-five rebel supporters were put to death. The removal of the Fitzgeralds facilitated fundamental reform of the Dublin administration, thereafter presided over directly by an English-born governor supported by a garrison. **Mary Ann Lyons**

Kilkenny, County (*Contae Chill Chainnigh*)

Province:	LEINSTER
County town:	KILKENNY
Area:	2,062 km^2 (795 sq. miles)
Population (2002):	80,421
Features:	River BARROW
	River NORE
	River SUIR
	Slieveardagh Hills
Of historical interest:	JERPOINT ABBEY
	Kilkenny Castle
	Kells Priory
	St Canice's Cathedral
Industry and products:	AGRICULTURE
	BREWING
	CRAFTS and design
	Printing
	Quarrying

Petula Martyn

County Kilkenny is a prosperous farming county in south Leinster whose geography and rich historical tradition are shaped largely by the presence of the Rivers BARROW, NORE, and SUIR (see p. 25). Much of the county is river lowland, separated by important Upper Carboniferous uplands, which form the basis for coal deposits in the Slieveardagh Hills and Castlecomer plateau and are also the source of the famed black Kilkenny 'marble'—in fact a polished limestone. The Castlecomer anthracite coalfields are now disused, but the district represents one of the few examples of an industrial landscape in the south of Ireland. The charming river valleys and rich farmland of the county resulted in the area becoming the core of the ANGLO-NORMAN Butler lordship in the thirteenth century; and its early political stability and wealth are reflected in the architecture of town and countryside. Farms today average 38 ha (100 acres), with up to a third of farmland devoted to tillage crops. Dairying is significant in the south of the county. **Inistioge** on the Nore was the site of an Augustinian abbey in the early thirteenth century. Kells on the King's River contains impressive remains of a large Augustinian priory. **Gowran** was an important pre-Norman strategic site, which became a principal castle of the Butlers; Gowran Park today has frequent horse race meetings throughout the year. JERPOINT, ten miles south of the town of Kilkenny, and Duiske, in picturesque Graiguenamanagh, are CISTERCIAN abbeys founded in the twelfth century. **Patrick Duffy**

Kilkenny (*Cill Chainnigh*), a town in south Leinster and the county town of Co. Kilkenny; population 8,594 (2002). Kilkenny is one of the most important heritage towns in Ireland. It originated as an Early Christian settlement associated with St Canice (hence the name *Cill Chainnigh*, St Canice's chapel). It is a cathedral town of the diocese of Ossory and was the seat of the Butlers, Earls of

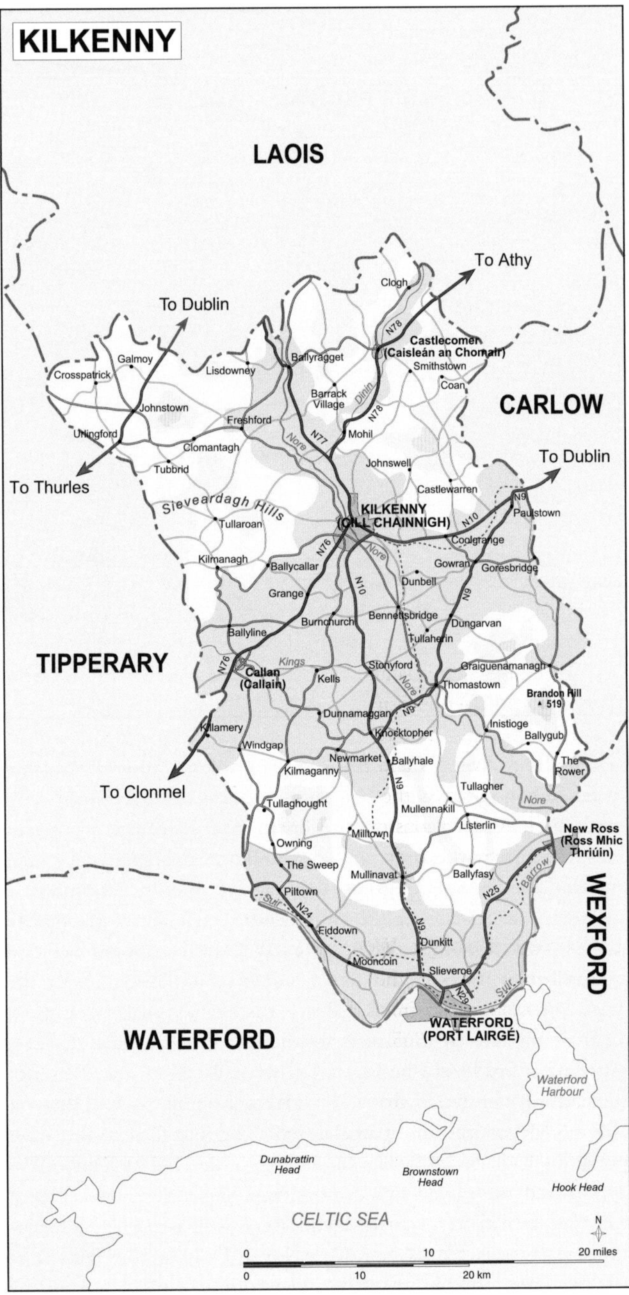

Ormond. The burning at the stake of Petronilla, maid to ALICE KYTELER, for witchcraft in 1324 links the town with the wider world of medieval Europe. During the Middle Ages, Kilkenny was frequently the seat of Irish parliaments in the PALE. The STATUTES OF KILKENNY were enacted in 1366 to prevent the Norman colonists from adopting Irish cultural manners. Kilkenny Castle, which overlooks the River NORE and the town, was the main residence of the Butlers from 1391. Granted city status in 1609 by JAMES I, the town became the headquarters of the Catholic Confederation during the uprising of the 1640s; it was captured by OLIVER CROMWELL in 1650.

Apart from the castle and gardens, Kilkenny has an extensive architectural legacy from the Middle Ages to the nineteenth century, notably St Canice's Cathedral (1111) and Round Tower (1100), St Mary's Church (1205), St John's Abbey (1211), Black Abbey (1225), the Shee Almshouse (1582), Rothe House (1594), the Tholsel (1760), the Castle Stables, now Kilkenny Design Centre (1790), and St Mary's Cathedral (1843). **Patrick Duffy**

Kilkenny, Confederation of (August 1642 to January 1649). Following the failure of the 1641 Rising, the Irish Catholic insurgents created a government in the summer of 1642 embracing the two-thirds of the country within their control. The Confederation comprised individuals taking an oath of association; it took its title from the fact that the Supreme Council most commonly convened in Kilkenny. The General Assembly, the other main organ of government, met on nine occasions.

The Confederation was established to provide effective national government, to counter the immediate military threats posed by the government (later royalist and Parliamentary) forces and by the covenanting Scots in Ulster, and to negotiate a settlement with the king. By January 1649 it had achieved these goals and voluntarily disbanded. In that sense the Confederation was a success; but subsequent unfavourable assessments have been inevitably influenced by OLIVER CROMWELL's destruction of Irish Catholic political and military power in the 1650s. The Catholic Confederates might have been able to avert this by securing an earlier definitive agreement with the king and sending timely military aid to avert a Parliamentary victory in the English civil wars. Alternatively, they might have secured control over the whole country, thereby making Parliamentary reconquest more problematic. They did neither.

Traditionally this failure has been blamed on 'Gaelic Irish' and 'OLD ENGLISH' factionalism and on Old English dominance of the Supreme Council. More recent research tends to play down national and cultural divisions and to emphasise the inherent difficulty of building consensus on the religious terms of a definitive peace deal with the king. Divisions on this complex issue were not clear-cut, as evidenced by the large grouping of pragmatic moderates in the General Assembly. [see RINUCCINI, GIOVANNI.] **Pádraig Lenihan**

Kilkenny Design Workshops (KDW), craft workshops established in 1963 in the former stables of Kilkenny Castle, the most important design initiative by an Irish Government. They were formally opened in 1965, with William Walsh as director; as head of CORAS TRÁCHTÁLA he had instigated the report *Design in Ireland* (1962), commissioned from Scandinavian experts, which recommended major reforms in design policy. He took inspiration from the Plus Craft Workshops in Frederikstad, Norway. The earliest workshops were for silversmithing, candle-making, wood-turning, and poplin weaving; later came ceramics and textiles. Outstanding designers included the Dutch ceramist SONJA LANDWEER, the German goldsmith Rudolf Heltzel, and the Irish sculptor OISÍN KELLY.

Kilkenny. *Rothe House (1594), Kilkenny, traditionally linked with the National Ecclesiastical Assembly convened by Bishop Rothe in May 1642. The meeting, attended by all the Catholic bishops of Ireland, led to the formation of the Parliament of the Confederation in October 1642. [Bord Fáilte]*

In the 1970s its activities were extended to include FURNITURE, graphics, FASHION, and packaging; but there was a tension between this and the parallel aim of developing prototypes for industrial design, which came to be overlooked. The workshops were staffed by designers from Britain, Denmark, Sweden, and Germany. An expansion into retail trade followed, very successfully in Dublin with the Kilkenny Design Shop in Nassau Street, unsuccessfully in Bond Street, London. It became a state-sponsored commercial company in 1982; but with accumulated debts and the decline of the economy and of state funding it was unable to continue trading, and it ceased to operate in 1988. [see CRAFTS AFTER 1945; CRAFTS COUNCIL OF IRELAND; DESIGN YARD.] **John Turpin**

Kilkenny, Statutes of (1366), legislation passed by a parliament at Kilkenny in 1366 presided over by Lionel, Duke of Clarence and Justiciar of Ireland. There are thirty-six clauses, dealing with administrative, legal, social, and military problems faced by the English colony in Ireland, but the statutes are remembered chiefly for their attempt to preserve the Englishness of the ANGLO-NORMANS by excluding all Irish influence that appeared to threaten their separateness. The colonists were required to use the English language, English names and English law rather than *march* or native Irish law; marriage, fosterage, and concubinage between the Anglo-Norman community and the native Irish was prohibited, as was the appointment of the Irish to certain ecclesiastical posts within the lordship. The colonists were forbidden to sell horses or armour to the Irish and were to prepare for war; they were not to engage in the Irish fashion of riding without a saddle, or to follow the Irish style of dress. The practice of patronising Irish poets and musicians was now strictly taboo.

Many of the problems addressed were the same as those dealt with in previous parliaments throughout the century; much of the legislation passed at Kilkenny built on these existing enactments, but the preamble set the tone of the statutes as a conscious programme of protecting a society and culture that was being eclipsed. The statutes did not have a lasting effect but were confirmed in future parliaments, further fuelling the reputation of their importance, until they were eventually repealed in the parliament of 1613–15. [see ANGLO-NORMAN AND ENGLISH ADMINISTRATION; ENGLISH SETTLEMENT.] **Susan Foran**

Killala expedition (1798), the last military invasion of Ireland. The expedition left La Rochelle on the west coast of France on 6 August 1798, led by an intrepid, reckless general, Jean-Joseph Humbert (1767–1823). It landed at Killala Bay on the north coast of Co. Mayo on 23 August and was joined by some local Irish insurgents; the main force, consisting of 800 French and some 600 Irish recruits, moved south to achieve an astonishing victory over a larger British force on 27 August at Castlebar, a British defeat known as 'The Races of Castlebar'. It then headed east until forced to surrender at Ballinamuck, Co. Longford, on 8 September. Perhaps as many as 2,000 Irish caught in arms were afterwards put to death. Humbert expressed great contempt for the Irish on both sides. [see FRENCH REVOLUTION; REBELLION OF 1798.] **C. J. Woods**

Killala. *General Jean-Joseph Humbert (1767–1823), who landed in Killala Bay, Co. Mayo, on 23 August 1798 with a French force of about 800 men to provide military assistance to the Rising of 1798. [Musée de l'Armée, Paris]*

Killarney (*Cill Airne*), Co. Kerry, the most famous tourist centre in Ireland; population (2002) 9,470. The town's main claim to fame is its spectacular mountain and lake scenery and the richness and variety of its FLORA. There is a long history of settlement in Killarney. In the sixth century a monastery was founded on Inisfallen in Lough Leane. A Franciscan monastery was founded at Muckross in 1448, and there are several ruined castles from the Middle Ages. Mining for iron, lead, and copper was carried out in the area; but for the past three centuries TOURISM and Killarney have been inextricably linked. By the early eighteenth century the town was attracting travellers; but it was the nineteenth-century travel writers who really publicised its beauty. Though the roads to Killarney were better than most by the eighteenth century, the opening of the railway from Mallow in 1853 was a huge boost, and the Great Southern Hotel opened the following year. In 1887 the town was lit by electricity from a turbine on the River Flesk. St Mary's (Catholic) Cathedral, designed by PUGIN in 1842, is regarded as one of the finest gothic revival churches in the country. Muckross House, completed in 1843, is a national property on the 4,000 ha (10,000-acre) Muckross Demesne, now the Bourn-Vincent Memorial Park (after its presentation to the state in 1932). Though tourism increased in Killarney after the GREAT FAMINE, the town began to decline. Its population fell from over 7,100 in 1841 to 5,700 in 1901. Killarney began to grow again with the tourism boom of the twentieth century. The town contains a huge concentration of hotels, guesthouses, pubs, restaurants, and souvenir shops. The area has many amenities and sights, including world-famous GOLF courses. [see HORSE-DRAWN TRANSPORT; TOURISM.] **Kevin Hourihan**

Killarney, Lakes of, a group of lakes at the foot of Macgillycuddy's Reeks near Killarney, Co. Kerry. They lie along the boundary between the high old red sandstones and the low-lying Carboniferous limestones of Co. Kerry, the geologically controlled relief having been accentuated by glaciers flowing north from the mountains. The solution of the limestone by glacial meltwaters and the depositing of moraines on the limestone piedmont impounded drainage from the mountains, resulting in the formation of numerous lakes. Lough Leane, the largest, is shallow and dotted with islands, such as Inisfallen, the site of a monastery founded by St Finian. Muckross Abbey, built in 1448 on the eastern shore, was destroyed in 1652 by CROMWELL; Ross Island, site of a fourteenth-century Anglo-Norman tower-house, was the last stronghold against Cromwell's forces. Along the shore are the remains of Bronze Age copper mines, swamp woodlands called *carrs*, and intricately shaped limestone formations. Lying beneath Torc Mountain, Muckross Lake is the deepest, with few islands, though the caves of Cailín Bán Island testify to the erosive powers of glacial meltwaters that coursed through the lakes. The northern shore is cloaked in ancient yew-woods and native arbutus trees, normally a Mediterranean species. The eastern shore is dominated by Muckross House and Gardens, built in 1843 and left to the state by Senator Arthur Vincent in 1932. The Upper Lake, smallest of the three main lakes, lies in a steep-sided glacial glen; for many it is the most beautiful of the lakes, with its myriad small islands and inlets set amid mountains covered by native oakwoods (see pp. 161, 1057). **Colman Gallagher**

Killary Harbour, Cos. Mayo and Galway, the most impressive fjord in Ireland, forming a spectacular natural barrier between

Mweelrea and the Sheeffry Hills of south Co. Mayo and the wild Maumturk Mountains of Connemara. From the village of Leenane at the head of the fjord to the Atlantic Ocean is a distance of 17 km ($10\frac{1}{2}$ miles), enough to make any link between the waters of Killary and the open sea seem unlikely. Killary is the product of deep glacial erosion that acted along the Killary Harbour fault system at the eastern end of the fjord and also exploited the relative weakness of the Lower Palaeozoic slates outcropping further to the west. The waters are generally about 24 m (80 ft) deep but become shallower towards the sea, typical of a fjord. This pattern of overdeepening is a classic indicator of glacial, as opposed to fluvial, erosion and shows that the zone of maximum erosion beneath a glacier occurs where melting and the accumulation of ice are exactly balanced. As if the mere existence of a fjord and all this implies about the evolution of the Irish landscape were not enough, the drama of Killary is enhanced by the great ridge of Mweelrea, rising 815 m (2,674 ft) straight out of the waters of the fjord. [see GEOLOGY; GLACIATION.] **Colman Gallagher**

Killary. *Twilight descends on Killary Harbour, between Cos. Galway and Mayo. Ireland's only true fjord, it extends 17 km ($10\frac{1}{2}$ miles) from the Atlantic Ocean to its easternmost point at Leenane. [Bord Fáilte]*

Killeshin, Co. Laois, site of a church with two patron saints, Diarmaid and Comhghán. Mid-Leinster dynasties controlled Killeshin up to the twelfth century. Dubhlitir Ua Uathghaile of Killeshin (fl. 1080–1120) is the reputed author of an exegetical text. The remains of the church consist of a ROMANESQUE doorway; a fragmentary inscription possibly commemorates DERMOT MACMURROUGH, King of Leinster. **Edel Bhreathnach**

Kilmainham Gaol, Dublin, is mostly remembered in relation to the struggles for political independence and is said to have been founded two years before the 1798 United Irishmen rebellion, in direct response to nationalist political agitation inspired by and following the FRENCH REVOLUTION. This history of the prison ends with its closure in 1924, two years after the founding of the Free State. The other history of Kilmainham Gaol is framed not by the politics of collective memory but by the history of common punishment in Ireland. In this story, the new building that opened in 1796 marks just one moment in the history of the prison and is most interesting when juxtaposed with the opening of the new east wing in 1863. Apart from Mountjoy Model Prison (1850), the east wing of Kilmainham Gaol is one of the earliest and best preserved examples of the surveillance-based 'panoptic' architecture most famously associated with Jeremy Bentham. This new design transformed part of the prison from a pre-modern dungeon-style jail into a modern 'penitentiary'. The origin of the prison is most probably connected to the presence of the courthouse. In the eighteenth century, law courts travelled throughout the country on 'circuits'. Because cases might be heard only every six months, persons were often held in 'bridewells' attached to the courthouse. These bridewells, as in the case of Kilmainham, often developed into 'county jails'. Within cities they were often called 'Marshalsea' (meaning marshal's seat) prisons. Before the late eighteenth century, prisons were not meant to be places of punishment. The circuit courts 'delivered' the jails, emptying rather than filling them. Punishment consisted of fines, public humiliations, floggings, torture, death, or transportation.

Throughout the eighteenth century, however, as the economy became increasingly commercialised, a new class of prisoners, known as 'debtors', were detained in prison. Because people unable to pay their debts were punished by fines and confinement, and because they were required to pay fees for their keep to the 'turnkeys', sheriff, and anyone else who incurred costs in their detainment, many languished in prison for years. John Howard, the famous prison reformer, visited Kilmainham Gaol in the 1770s and 80s. He described a scene common to prisons throughout Europe at the time: overcrowding, hunger, filth, and a general cruelty towards the prisoners. Women, men, and children were confined together. Extortion, brutality, and drunkenness were the norm. A prisoner who was moneyed could pay for the necessities and even luxuries of life. An impoverished one might endure the nightmare of the dungeon and, after a flogging for the crime, be detained indefinitely for non-payment of fees.

There was a general expansion of 'county' and 'city' jails in late eighteenth-century Ireland. Like the 'new' Newgate Prison opened in 1780, the Kilmainham bridewell was replaced in 1796 by a major prison, Newgate, serving all of Co. Dublin. The designs of Kilmainham and Newgate were very similar and represent a prison architecture already out of date in the designs of the new disciplinary penitentiaries. Howard was highly critical of the new prison at Newgate in this respect, and no doubt would have had the same criticism of Kilmainham. Both prisons were merely bigger and more elaborate dungeon houses. The new Kilmainham Gaol, and the courthouse to which it was attached, immediately served the detention, prosecution, and punishment of those who rebelled by force of arms against Ireland's political subordination to England. HENRY JOY MCCRACKEN was amongst Kilmainham's first political prisoners in 1796, to be followed by THOMAS ADDIS EMMET in 1798. ROBERT EMMET was detained and tried at Kilmainham in 1803 and was put to death for high treason, beginning a long historical connection between Irish nationalist rebellion and the police, court, and prison complex of Kilmainham. In the nineteenth century, JEREMIAH O'DONOVAN ROSSA, CHARLES STEWART PARNELL, and MICHAEL DAVITT were among the famous rebels detained there (see p. 705). In the twentieth century, the leaders of the 1916 RISING, including PATRICK PEARSE, THOMAS CLARKE, JOHN MACBRIDE, and JAMES CONNOLLY, were executed at the prison. The last prisoners to die there, including ERSKINE CHILDERS, were put to death by the Free State Government in 1922 because of their opposition to the treaty with Britain.

With regard to common punishment, however, the east wing opened in 1863 is of most interest. Chosen by competition, John McCurdy's design embodied the 'separate system' of corrective discipline, each of the 101 cells intended to hold just one prisoner. The entire wing, on three levels, could be viewed from a single position on the west side. As the purpose of the design was to correct deviant behaviour, prisoners charged with capital crimes were not ususally detained there. While it is the most interesting Irish monument to nineteenth-century 'therapeutic punishment', the east wing has the least connection of any part of the jail with the history of political prisoners (see pp. 202, 705). **Patrick Carroll**

'Kilmainham treaty' (May 1882), a name given to the informal bargain that brought an end to the LAND WAR (1879–82). CHARLES STEWART PARNELL and other land agitators were released from detention at KILMAINHAM GAOL, Dublin, and further legislation enabling tenants in arrears to come within the bounds of the Land Law (Ireland) Act (1881) was enacted. This agreement implied that special or coercive measures were to be phased out and that the IRISH PARTY would co-operate with the Liberal Party in promoting reforms. **Alan O'Day**

Kilmore carols (also known as the Wexford carols), a set of eleven Christmas songs published in Ghent in 1684 by the Anglo-Norman bishop Luke Wadding of Ferns. Popular elsewhere, they were reprinted for a Drogheda bookseller, and in 1728 three of them were included in a manuscript by Father William Devereux, parish priest of Drinagh; they have been under the guardianship of the Devereux family since the eighteenth century. They became the basis of a tradition of local carol-singing at Kilmore, Co. Wexford, still carried on by choristers today. Formerly sung also at Piercestown, Ballymore, Mayglass, Lady's Island, Tacumshane, and Rathangan, all in the county, the carols are performed by two groups of three men singing alternate verses. **Fintan Vallely**

Kilroe, James Robinson (1848–1927), geologist. Following study at the ROYAL COLLEGE OF SCIENCE FOR IRELAND he became a science teacher. In 1874 he joined the GEOLOGICAL SURVEY OF IRELAND as an assistant geologist, being promoted to the rank of geologist in 1890. He participated in the completion of the first 6-inch scale (1:10,560) geological mapping of Ireland in 1887. Thereafter he engaged in revision mapping; in drift mapping around Dublin, Belfast, Cork, Limerick, and Derry, and in the preparation of his *Soil-Geology of Ireland* (1907). **Jean Archer**

Kilroy, Thomas (1934–), dramatist, novelist, and critic. Born in Callan, Co. Kilkenny; educated at UCD, where he also lectured, 1965–73. He was professor of Modern English at NUIG, 1978–88, and a director of the FIELD DAY THEATRE COMPANY. His plays combine a strong literary sensibility with a theatrically experimental approach. His FIELD DAY play *Double Cross* (1986) examined the intertwined fates of two reinvented Irishmen, BRENDAN BRACKEN (Churchill's Minister for Information, who concealed his Irish nationalist background) and WILLIAM JOYCE (a broadcaster for the Nazis). Versions of European classics by Ibsen and Pirandello include *The Seagull* transposed to the west of Ireland. His novel *The Big Chapel* (1971) was short-listed for the Booker Prize and won the Guardian Fiction Prize. **Anthony Roche**

Kiltorcan Old Quarries, near Ballyhale, Co. Kilkenny, site of an assemblage of fossil plants and animals of international importance. Discovered in 1851 by James Flanagan of the Geological Survey, the greenish shale and yellow sandstone beds were deposited 345 million years ago at the end of the Old Red Sandstone Period. Species discovered include plants such as the fern-like *Archaeopteris hibernica*, the freshwater mussel *Archanodon jukesi*, and a number of species of fish and invertebrates. Most of them were described early in the 1860s, and their study made an important contribution to the understanding of the evolution of plants. **Christopher Moriarty**

Kinahan, George Henry (1829–1908), naturalist and geologist. Born in Dublin; educated at TCD, where he received a diploma in engineering. In 1854 he began his thirty-six-year career in the GEOLOGICAL SURVEY OF IRELAND. He was promoted to senior geologist in 1861 and district surveyor in 1869, though the Geological Survey archives suggest that a difficult temperament restricted his further advancement. His geological mapping covered most of Ireland and led to his jointly writing twenty-six memoirs. He was held in high regard as a pioneering geologist. His numerous publications covered diverse geological and archaeological topics; of these his *Manual of the Geology of Ireland* (1878) and a journal series on the economic geology of Ireland are the most noteworthy. **Matthew Parkes**

Kindness, John (1951–), artist. Born in Belfast; studied at Belfast College of Art. He draws on popular culture for his artistic expression, including sectarian icons from both communities in Northern Ireland. Working in multi-media, he creates unique imagery in ceramic and bronze sculpture, paintings, drawings, and prints. Keen observation and a wry sense of humour inform all his work. He has appeared in several group shows as well as solo exhibitions in Ireland, England, France, and the United States, and his work is included in several public collections, including the Hugh Lane Municipal Gallery of Modern Art, Dublin, and the Imperial War Museum, London. **Barbara Dawson**

Kindness. Scraping the Surface *(1990) by John Kindness. During his residence in New York he used the doors of yellow taxis as the support on which he etched images of urban life, in which he parodies Greek vase painting. [Irish Museum of Modern Art; courtesy of the artist]*

King, Brian (1942–), sculptor. Born in Dublin; studied at the NCAD. He was one of the first Irish artists to be influenced by International Modernist styles, such as Minimalism and Land Art, and has employed conceptual art ideas in an Irish cultural context to produce works in a distinct idiom. He has lived and worked in New York and London, was president of the IRISH EXHIBITION OF LIVING ART, 1972, and is now head of the Department of Sculpture, NCAD. He is a member of Aosdána. **Suzanne McNab**

King, Cecil (1921–1986), painter and printmaker. Born at Rathdrum, Co. Wicklow; self-taught, but attended life classes with Margaret Irwin. He gave up a career in business to become a full-time painter, developing from an early romantic, cloudy style to an elegant, hard-edged minimalist abstraction in the late 1960s. He also developed a successful series of abstract silkscreen prints for Editions Alecto, London. He was active in the Irish art world, commissioner for the Paris Biennale des Jeuns, and was a founder-member of the Rosc exhibitions. **Dorothy Walker**

King, Edward, Viscount Kingsborough (1795–1837), writer. Born in Cork; educated at the University of Oxford. He was MP for Cork, 1818 and 1820–26. His sumptuously illustrated nine-volume *Antiquities of Mexico* (1830–48) cost the then enormous sum of £32,000 to publish, leaving him heavily in debt, for which he was imprisoned, dying of typhus in the Debtors' Prison, Dublin. **Brian Lalor**

King, Kathleen, (1894–1978), botanist. Born in Dublin; educated at Dublin and Berlin. An early interest in amenity planting led her to join the Society of Irish Foresters and the Dublin Naturalists' Field Club. Against the background of a wide knowledge of flowering plants, her botanical interests concentrated on bryophytes. Through extensive fieldwork and study she developed an expertise in this area, and came to be recognised in her generation as Ireland's leading field bryologist. Her herbarium of some 4,000 specimens, including her many new Irish contributions, was donated to the NATIONAL BOTANIC GARDENS, Dublin. [see WOMEN NATURALISTS.] **Helena C. G. Chesney**

King, Philip (1952–), singer. Born in Cork. He has been a stalwart of Irish music from the early 1970s. A member of the respected folk-rock band Scullion, he has been involved in films, television, album production and radio broadcasting from the late 1980s. His ambitious television, album and book project *Bringing It All Back Home* in the early 1990s successfully traced the journey of Irish music to America and back. His subsequent television documentaries on the Canadian producer-singer Daniel Lanois, U2, Elvis Costello, CHRISTY MOORE, and LIAM O'FLYNN have demonstrated a sustained enthusiasm for music. **Tony Clayton-Lea**

King, William (1650–1729), archbishop and politician. Born in Co. Antrim, son of Scottish Presbyterian immigrants; educated at TCD, where he was awarded an MA in 1673, and ordained in the CHURCH OF IRELAND in 1674. He served in the diocese of Tuam until 1679, when he moved to Dublin, where he obtained the chancellorship of ST PATRICK'S CATHEDRAL. He soon became a controversial figure, engaging in disputes within the Church of Ireland and with PRESBYTERIAN ministers and, particularly, with Catholics, whose beliefs he vehemently attacked. He was among the earliest supporters of WILLIAM III and was appointed Bishop of Derry in January 1691. Later that year he published his most famous work, *State of the Protestants of Ireland under the Late King James's Government*. Though purporting to be a work of history it was a strongly political defence of the revolution and the legitimacy of William's position. In 1702 he published an important work on the nature of evil and how its existence can be reconciled with the notion of a loving and all-powerful God. In March 1703 he became Archbishop of Dublin, where he strove to promote internal reform and opposed the appointment of Englishmen to important Irish church positions. He was a Lord Justice on four occasions in the period 1714–22, strongly defending the independence of the Irish Parliament and promoting the economic interests of Ireland. He died unmarried, leaving his large fortune to charity. **Liam Irwin**

King, William (1809–1886), geologist. Born in Bishopwearmouth, Sunderland; he was apprenticed to a local ironmonger, but his real interests were scholarly, and he shortly moved into the book trade. Already GEOLOGY was his passion. He dealt in geological

WILLIAM KING

King, William. *William King, Bishop of Derry, 1691, and Archbishop of Dublin, 1703; mezzotint by Richard Purcell (fl. 1746–c. 1766), after a painting by Charles Jervas (c. 1675–1739). He encouraged the teaching of Irish in Trinity College so that clergymen could preach in Irish. [National Gallery of Ireland]*

specimens, and in 1841 he became the curator of the Hancock Museum in Newcastle-upon-Tyne. In 1849 he was appointed as the first professor of geology and mineralogy in the newly founded Queen's College, Galway. To Galway he brought his personal geological collection, which today forms a substantial part of the James Mitchell Museum. He was an authority on Permian fossils, but his writings also reveal an interest in Darwinian evolution, Neanderthal man, and the supposed 'dawn fossil', *Eozoon canadense*. **Jean Archer**

King Cycle of early Irish tales, a body of prose narratives, usually with verse passages, purporting to tell of events connected with the reign of various kings between the sixth and eighth centuries. Many of these tales appear to have been composed no earlier than the tenth century. The earliest of these kings was Diarmaid mac Cearrbhaill, King of TARA, 544–65, whose dispute with the clerics led to the cursing of Tara and the abolition of Feis Temro, the Feast of Tara, the royal inauguration rite. Mongán mac Fiachna (died 625) of Dál Fiatach (east Down) is the subject of some short anecdotes that illustrate his cleverness. A complex of tales relates to GUAIRE (died 663), King of Aidni (south Galway), who in later literature is seen as a model of generosity but appears cruel and cowardly in the earliest source. Many of the Guaire stories have a Connacht-Munster axis and include descendants of Aodh Bennán of west Munster. The story of Cano mac Gartnáin, a Scottish prince who came to Ireland in 668, also involves a love affair with Créd, daughter of Guaire. The longest tale in this cycle, entitled 'Bóramha Laighean', is a series of episodes strung together around the central theme of the *bóramha* (tax) said to have been owed by the Leinstermen to the kings of Tara and the efforts of these to collect it. The latest event narrated in the cycle is the attack on Leinster in 722 by Fearghal mac Maoile Dúin of Ulster and his death at the hands of the Leinster king at the Battle of Allen (Cath Almaine). Another famous battle was that of Magh Rath (Moira, Co. Down) in 637, which has its own set of tales, including that of 'BUILE SHUIBHNE' ('Suibhne's frenzy'). The tragic tale 'FINGAL RÓNÁIN', which tells how Rónán, King of Leinster, killed his own son out of jealousy, has no historical basis but is particularly well told. The early tales of this cycle are short and couched in an economic prose style, which later yields to a more prolix, alliterative prose. [see EARLY HISTORIC IRELAND; EARLY IRISH TALE TYPES; INAUGURATION SITES; KINGSHIP.] **Gearóid Mac Eoin**

kingdoms of Ireland. Pre-Norman Ireland consisted of a network of kingdoms defined by geopolitical and dynastic titles. The number of kingdoms in existence at any period is unknown; it is likely that the situation was fluid, given the constant rivalry among dynasties. In the eleventh and twelfth centuries a smaller number of dynasties dominated larger territories, which reduced the number of actual kingdoms. A hierarchy of kings was envisaged in early law tracts, defined by their relative honour-price. The essential territorial unit was a *tuath*, meaning a community or people; the leader of the tuath was the *rí tuaithe*. The size of the *tuatha* differed throughout the country. The King of a number of tuatha was a *rí tuatha*, 'King of tuath', or *ruirí*, 'great king'. A provincial king, variously described as *rí cóicid*, *rí ruirech*, or *ollam ríg*, was regarded by the laws as pre-eminent.

Sources other than the law tracts offer another view of the kingdoms of pre-Norman Ireland. A kingdom could be defined in geopolitical terms, such as *rí Muman*, 'King of Munster'. The practice of using a population group in a kingdom's title was also prevalent, such as *rí Uí Fidgeinti*, 'King of Uí Fidgeinte'. Specific dynasties could define a kingdom, for example *rí Ceniuil Conaill*, 'King of CENÉL CONAILL'. Royal titles that reflected political prestige rather than territorial extent were associated with important prehistoric sites, such as Temair (TARA, Co. Meath) and Crúachu (Rathcroghan, Co. Roscommon).

The provincial kingdoms ruled by a *rí cóicid* consisted of the kingdoms of Munster, Leinster, Connacht, Meath and Brega, and the northern part of Ireland. The kingdom of Munster was sub-divided into geographically oriented kingdoms: Desmumu (south Munster), Iarmumu (west Munster), Tuadmumu (north Munster), and Aurmumu (east Munster). The core of the province was at Imlech Iubair (Emly, Co. Tipperary) and at its capital, Caisil (Cashel, Co. Tipperary). Both sites were important ecclesiastical and royal centres in the early Middle Ages. Kings of Munster were accorded the title 'King of CASHEL'. The dominant dynasties were the branches of the EOGHANACHTA (descendants of Éogan) and, from the tenth century, the DÁL GCAIS, who became Uí Briain (descendants of BRIAN BÓRÚ). Leinster was divided between north and south along the division created by the Wicklow and Blackstairs Mountains. A king who succeeded in dominating the two parts of the province was sometimes accorded the title *rí diabul-Laigen*, 'King of double Laigin'. This division was reflected in dynastic control of the province, with Uí Cennselaig (descendants of Énna Cennselach) dominating the south and Uí Dúnlainge (descendants of Dúnlaing) the north. The north-west was controlled by Uí Failge, while the kingdom of the Osraige acted as a buffer between Munster and Leinster. Kildare, Ferns, and Dublin were important royal centres of Leinster.

The centre of authority in Connacht lay in Mag nAí (the Roscommon plain) and specifically at Crúachu (Rathcroghan, Co. Roscommon). Whereas a geographical division existed between fertile east Connacht, which extended as far as the River Shannon (and sometimes beyond) and west Connacht (Iar-Chonnacht), the royal titles of Connacht usually consisted of dynastic affiliations, Uí Briúin Aí, Uí Briúin Bréifne, Uí Maine, Uí Fiachrach, and Uí Ailello (descendants of Conn Cétchathach and Eochaid Mugmedón). The kingship of Connacht from the tenth century onwards was dominated by Uí Ruairc and Uí Conchobair, the latter ultimately gaining the upper hand. The midlands consisted of two kingdoms, Mide (later West Mide), which extended approximately from the River SHANNON to the River BLACKWATER, and Brega (later East Mide), which extended from the Blackwater to the coast. These kingdoms were controlled by two dynasties of the southern UÍ NÉILL, Clann Cholmáin (descendants of Colmán) and Síl nÁedo Sláine (descendants of Áed Sláine). From the eleventh century onwards, however, both kingdoms were under constant pressure from ambitious kings of other provinces, who regarded them as the ultimate prize in gaining recognition as kings of Ireland. Royal centres in Mide and Brega included LAGORE and KNOWTH, Co. Meath, Cró Inis on Lough Ennell, Co. Westmeath, and Rathconnell, Co. Westmeath.

The northern part of Ireland was a patchwork of kingdoms originally dominated by the east and mid-Ulster dynasties of the Ulaidh, who were replaced by the two northern Uí Néill dynasties of Cenél Conaill (descendants of Conall) and CENÉL EOGHAIN (descendants of Éogan). A federation of dynasties known as the Airgíalla ('hostage-givers'), who were clients of Uí Néill, were also ruled by a king. While Emain was the historical capital of the Ulaidh, the functioning royal centres of the north included Aileach (Grianán of Aileach, Co. Donegal), CLOGHER, Co. Tyrone, and DOWNPATRICK, Co. Down.

Ireland was later divided into two spheres of political influence, Leth Moga (south) and Leth Cuinn (north), to reflect the interests of the Eoghanachta and Uí Néill. With regard to the kingdom of all Ireland, the concept existed at least among the learned classes from the earliest historical period, echoed in the titles *rex Temro*, 'King of Tara', and *rex Hiberniae*, 'King of Ireland'. Whether any king actually succeeded in controlling the whole of Ireland and in gaining tribute from all its kingdoms is a matter for debate. [see EARLY HISTORIC IRELAND.] **Edel Bhreathnach**

kingship. In early medieval Ireland there were about a hundred people at any given time who could claim to be a *rí tuaithe* or King of a people or territory. The *tuath* was regarded as the basic socio-political unit in early Ireland, with an average size of 15–25 km (10–15 miles) across and perhaps a few thousand inhabitants. The king acted as its leader and representative in external affairs and was responsible for internal order and welfare. He had a small number of officials, including a poet, and hosted a yearly assembly and other meetings to conduct political and legal business. A king had the highest status of the lay population, from which he derived his prerogatives and authority. If he did not fulfil his obligations properly he risked a reduction in status and even deposition. The pre-Christian king was probably regarded as a sacral figure, who acted as a mediator between society and the supernatural. He concluded a sacred marriage with the goddess of the territory, which was thus rejuvenated and fertilised. If he upset this relationship by breaking the 'ruler's truth' or his taboos, or by sustaining a blemish, his own well-being and that of the kingdom suffered. In the Christian period, aspects of sacral kingship were continued as traditions in inauguration ceremonies and as themes in saga literature and poetry, and integrated with Christian principles about rulership.

The many petty kings were in effect ruled by about a dozen overkings, who held the rest in clientship by keeping their hostages. A subject king who refused to perform his services and pay tribute risked punitive CATTLE-RAIDS by the overking. Overkingships were created by ambitious kings. The equal distribution of the inheritance among legitimate brothers resulted in fragmentation of the family holdings and number of clients, heralding loss of status for one's descendants. Succession to the lordship or kingship was the best way to stay in power. Usually the succession devolved from brother to brother in order of seniority, and then alternated between the leaders of their descendants. However, an unsuitable candidate who lacked prominent ancestors or enough clients, experience, or personal qualities would be passed over in favour of a better-qualified junior candidate. To forestall fragmentation and rivalry, powerful kings set up brothers or sons as new lords over weakened neighbouring relatives or peoples. Powerful dynasties could expand beyond the confines of their own *tuath*, but the cadet branches remained nominally subject to the overking of the main lineage. Dynasties such as the UÍ NÉILL (kings of TARA) and EOGHANACHTA (kings of Cashel) consisted of a number of lordships and kingships whose rulers shared a common legendary or historical ancestor. A period of expansion was normally followed by succession struggles and disintegration. Often one lineage forced the others into obedience, and the whole cycle would start anew.

The overkingships reduced the importance of the *tuatha*. The eighth-century law tracts recognise the provincial king as the highest grade of overking, though some also refer to a (theoretical) kingship of Ireland. With the collapse of the kingship of Tara in the tenth century the titles of high king and King of Ireland with or without opposition came into vogue.

Dynastic kingship remained essentially untouched by the coming of the ANGLO-NORMANS, though rulership became more confined to one lineage and was more centralised. The relationship between kings and nobility became more 'feudal'. In time the title of 'king' fell into disuse, and it disappeared completely in the sixteenth century, when the Irish lordships were turned into earldoms and baronies. [see GAELIC LORDSHIP.] **Bart Jaski**

kingship. *Richard Bartelett's bird's eye view (1602) of the inauguration site of the McLaughlins and O'Neills at Tullahogue, Co. Tyrone, featuring the 'O'Neill Chair'. Within a moated enclosure are thatched cottages and a ruined castle (centre), while a crannóg (top) is being attacked from land by artillery. [Council of Trustees of the National Library of Ireland]*

King's Inns, Honourable Society of the, Dublin, the training college for barristers in the Republic, established under a royal charter of 1792 but now operated as a voluntary society managed by a group of senior barristers and judges known as the Benchers. Students wishing to become barristers must study in the King's Inns for four years (two years on a diploma course and two years on a degree course), unless they have a recognised law degree, in which case they need study only the two-year degree course. Entry to the King's Inns is highly competitive and is based on a mandatory entrance examination. As well as sitting annual examinations in a range of subjects, students must attend court, complete an examination in Irish, and dine at the King's Inns on ten occasions in each of the final two years. A student who successfully completes their studies is 'called to the bar' by the Chief Justice (see p. 618). **Neville Cox**

King's Printer in Ireland, an office modelled on a similar one in England, conferring a nominal monopoly on all printing, PUBLISHING, and bookselling until 1732. The first King's Printer was Humphrey Powell, who came to Dublin from London in 1551 and was responsible for the first book printed in Ireland. He was succeeded by William Kearney, the first known native printer, who undertook the printing of the BIBLE IN IRISH for proselytising purposes; in 1595 he was described in a proclamation as 'Queen's Printer'. There followed a succession of non-native office-holders, including several London stationers. George Grierson, first appointed in 1727, appears after 1730 to have held the office in conjunction with his wife, Constantia, a woman of formidable learning. The office remained in the Grierson family until awarded in 1876 to the Scotsman Alexander Thom, the last practising printer to occupy it; there followed a succession of civil servants until the office was extinguished in 1922. [see BEDELL, WILLIAM; PRINTING IN IRISH.] **Bernard Share**

Kinsale (*Cionn tSáile*), Co. Cork, a historic coastal town 26 km (16 miles) south-west of Cork; population (2002) 2,237. Kinsale was founded by the ANGLO-NORMANS, though the Old Head of Kinsale, 10 km (6 miles) away, was reputed to have been a residence of the kings of Ireland. The town received a royal charter in 1334 and later privileges in 1381 and 1482. The BATTLE OF KINSALE (1601) was a resounding defeat for the Irish and Spanish forces under O'NEILL and O'DONNELL. The harbour was fortified with the building of James's Fort (1601–3) near the town and CHARLES'S FORT (c. 1677) a mile downriver, both fine examples of European 'star-shaped' fortifications. Kinsale was then an important English naval base; it was also a stronghold of English PROTESTANTISM, from which Irish Catholics were excluded until the end of the eighteenth century. In the nineteenth century Kinsale was an important fishing port, with a population of 6,900 in 1841. Like many other towns, it began a long decline after the GREAT FAMINE, its population falling to less than

1,800 in 1961; in the 1960s it was typically described as 'decayed'. Since then it has experienced a remarkable revival and is now one of the most dynamic and fashionable tourist resorts in the country. It is often described as the 'gourmet capital' of Ireland, is twinned with Antibes in the French Riviera, and is popular with the international 'jet set'. Apart from astute marketing, there are deserved reasons for Kinsale's popularity. It is scenically located on the slopes of Compass Hill, overlooking a sinuous, sheltered harbour, and has an attractive townscape of narrow medieval streets, colourful shop fronts, and Georgian terraces. Historic buildings include the Church of St Multose (begun in the thirteenth century), the French Prison (a sixteenth-century tower-house), and the New Tholsel of 1706. Kinsale won the Tidy Towns competition in 1986. **Kevin Hourihan**

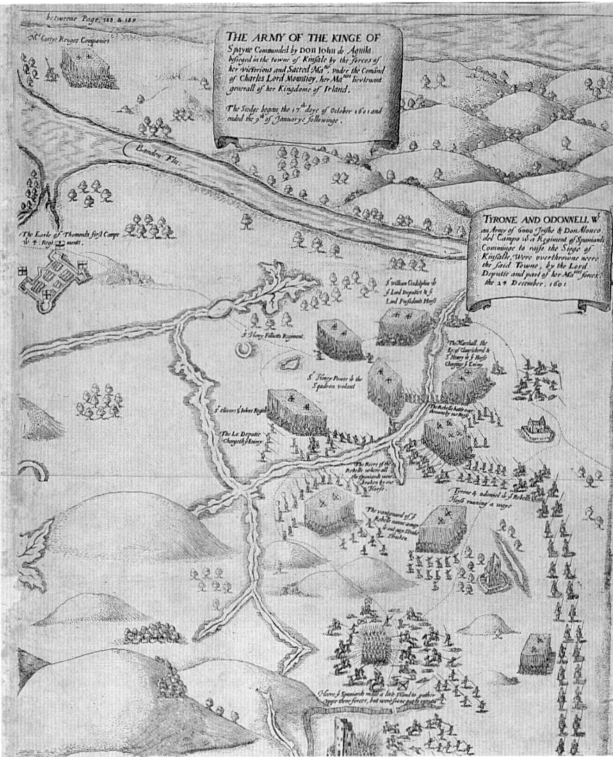

Kinsale, Battle of. *An engraving of the Battle of Kinsale from* Pacata Hibernica *(1633). The armies of O'Neill and O'Donnell flee (bottom right) from the victorious troops of Lord Mountjoy. [Council of Trustees of the National Library of Ireland]*

Kinsale, Battle of (1601), the decisive battle of the NINE YEARS' WAR (1593–1602). Having previously inflicted a series of heavy defeats on English forces, HUGH O'NEILL, Earl of Tyrone, and his allies finally succeeded in securing the assistance of Spanish forces. Unfortunately for the Irish leaders, the Spaniards landed in Kinsale, Co. Cork. O'Neill's failure to negotiate a liaison with the Spaniards, who were besieged at Kinsale, proved decisive in determining the outcome of the war. O'Neill and RED HUGH O'DONNELL marched with their troops from Ulster to Kinsale in the depths of winter. Exhaustion may well have played a part in the events that unfolded. A poorly co-ordinated attempt to combine a Spanish outbreak with an Irish assault on the English lines resulted in the forces of O'Neill and O'Donnell being isolated and subjected to a cavalry charge: a rout ensued, in which the Irish forces offered uncharacteristically poor resistance. O'Donnell and O'Neill's army suffered large-scale casualties, with the English suffering minimal losses. **John McCavitt**

Kinsella, John (1932–), composer. Born in Dublin, self-taught as a composer, he wrote predominantly small-scale, introspective works while working at RTÉ where he was head of music 1983–88. After early retirement he has written more dynamic and large-scale works, including eight symphonies, two cello concertos, and two violin concertos. Works have been commissioned by CONCORDE and the DUBLIN INTERNATIONAL PIANO COMPETITION. He has won the Marten Toonder award, and is a member of AOSDÁNA. **Richard Pine**

Kinsella, Thomas (1928–), poet. Born in Dublin; educated at UCD. Joining the CIVIL SERVICE, he worked in the DEPARTMENT OF FINANCE. In 1965 he became writer in residence at the University of Southern Illinois before taking up the position of professor of English at Temple University, Philadelphia. He returned to live in Co. Wicklow. His first collections of poetry include *Poems* (1956) and *Another September* (1958); but it was probably with *Downstream* (1962) that he struck a distinctive tone of poetic address, in poems such as 'Cover Her Face', 'A Country Walk', and 'Downstream'. These are highly controlled, austere poems that are ominously aware of loss and of life's struggles. In the title poem of *Nightwalker and Other Poems* (1968) he wrote one of the most significant Irish works of the second half of the twentieth century. It ostensibly records the journey of the narrator as he moves through familiar south Co. Dublin suburbs; in effect the poem charts the substantial religious, cultural, and political changes that have taken place in post-independence Ireland from the 1920s to the mid-1960s. The landscape of the mythological past and the lunar light of the poem combine to make 'Nightwalker' a haunting and complex meditation on the artistic imagination itself.

With *Notes from the Land of the Dead* (1972) Kinsella seemed to make a technical shift towards a more fragmentary and introspective poetry. The publication of *Butcher's Dozen* (1972), Kinsella's response to the Widgery Report into the shooting dead of thirteen unarmed civilians in Derry on 'BLOODY SUNDAY' (30 January 1972), heralded a series of further elegies, such as those on SEÁN Ó RIADA and the assassinated American President JOHN F. KENNEDY. These poems were published under Kinsella's own imprint, Peppercanister, and subsequently collected in *Fifteen Dead* (1976) and *Song of the Night* (1978). Since the mid-1970s Kinsella's Peppercanister poems have appeared regularly in single-volume editions; these have also been gathered into *Thomas Kinsella: Collected Poems, 1956–2001* (2001).

Kinsella is well known also as a translator of poems from Irish into English. His version of TÁIN BÓ CUAILNGE, *The Táin* (1969), with illustations by Louis Le Brocquy, was a landmark publication (see p. 1032); it was followed by *An Duanaire: Poems of the Dispossessed, 1600–1900* (1981), an anthology of Irish poetry edited and translated by Kinsella in collaboration with SEÁN Ó TUAMA. He edited *The New Oxford Book of Irish Verse* (1986), many of the translations from Irish being his own. He has also published an important critical view, *The Dual Tradition: An Essay on Poetry and Politics in Ireland* (1995). Though Kinsella is often seen as a remote and isolated figure in contemporary Irish writing, his international reputation is as a poet who takes up the legacy of JAMES JOYCE's urban vision. **Gerald Dawe**

Kirk, Thomas (1781–1845), sculptor. Born in Cork; trained at the DUBLIN SOCIETY Schools. After a period as a decorative carver he received the commission to carve the figure of Horatio Nelson for the NELSON PILLAR in Sackville Street (O'Connell Street), Dublin, 1809 (destroyed in 1966; the head is now in Dublin Civic Museum) (see p. 805). This launched a prolific career as a sculptor of busts and of funerary and public monuments. The Nathaniel

Kish Bank. *The telescopic Kish Lighthouse being towed from Dún Laoghaire Harbour, Co. Dublin, to its position on the Kish Bank, where the telescope sections were extended to their full height. [Commissioners of Irish Lights; photo by Rex Roberts Studios]*

Sneyd monument in CHRIST CHURCH CATHEDRAL, Dublin, is his masterpiece; he also carved the skyline statuary on the GENERAL POST OFFICE, O'Connell Street, Dublin. He was a founder-member of the ROYAL HIBERNIAN ACADEMY. Kirk pioneered the Victorian style in Ireland, counterbalancing classical pose and costume with realistic features and emotion. **Judith Hill**

Kirwan, Richard (1733–1812), scientist. Born at Cloghballymore, Co. Galway, the second son of Martin Kirwan of Cregg Castle; he was sent to the University of Poitiers to study for the priesthood, but on the death of his elder brother he inherited the family wealth and turned to his first love, the study of CHEMISTRY. At first most of his work was carried out in London, where he mixed with distinguished scientists of the day and became a fellow of the Royal Society; he received its Copley Medal for his work on the way chemicals combine. He was the fiercest defender of the long-established theory of phlogiston; his debate with the French chemists, led by Antoine Lavoisier, generated enough international research to prove that the new theory was better than the old in explaining the experimental facts, and he graciously accepted defeat. His book *Elements of Mineralogy* (1784) was the first systematic treatment of that subject. In his study of METEOROLOGY he conceived the idea of weather pattern recognition. In 1799 he returned to Dublin and became the second president of the ROYAL IRISH ACADEMY, a post he held until his death. **William J. Davis**

Kish Bank Lighthouse, Dublin. The eastern approach to Dublin Bay was marked by a light-vessel until a LIGHTHOUSE was erected in 1965. Designed by Christiani and Nielsen, it is a telescopic reinforced-concrete structure sitting on the sea-bed, the only one of its kind in Ireland. **Ronald Cox**

Kitchener, Horatio Herbert, first Earl Kitchener of Khartoum (1850–1916), British field-marshal. Born in Ballylongford, Co. Kerry; educated in Switzerland and at the Royal Military Academy, Woolwich. In 1871 he was commissioned in the Royal Engineers. He served as Governor-General of East Sudan and in 1892 was appointed sirdar of the Egyptian army. In 1896 he embarked on a campaign to quell the Sudan and on 2 September 1898 led the combined British and Egyptian forces that routed the Dervishes at Omdurman. Khartoum was recaptured two days later; this victory made him a national hero in Britain. He was posted to South Africa as chief of staff to Lord Roberts, whom he succeeded as commander-in-chief in 1900. During the ANGLO-BOER WAR he ordered the destruction of Boer homesteads and the internment of Boer families in specially constructed camps—the first concentration camps of the twentieth century. Following the defeat of the Boers in 1902 he was posted to India as commander-in-chief. In 1911 he was appointed Consul-General of Egypt. At the outbreak of the FIRST WORLD WAR he was appointed Secretary of State for War. His commanding image appeared on the now famous recruiting posters declaring, 'Your country needs you!' He was relieved of his responsibility for military strategy in 1915 following disagreement with Cabinet colleagues. On 5 June 1916 he was killed when the *Hampshire* struck a German mine off the Orkney Isles. **Ciarán Deane**

Kitching, John Alwyne (Jack) (1908–1996), physiologist and marine biologist. Born in York; educated at the Universities of Cambridge and London, he was also awarded an honorary doctorate of science by the NUI, 1983. He left the University of Bristol to become founding professor of Biology at the University of East Anglia in 1963. Already a leading cell physiologist, he explored the ecology of LOUGH HYNE, Co. Cork. Spending almost every summer there, 1938–86, at his private laboratories, he invented modern experimental marine ecology. Lough Hyne became the first statutory marine reserve in Europe. **Trevor Norton**

knitting, hand. Until the arrival of the Aran jumper in the early twentieth century, which became the focus of the Irish hand-knitting industry for many decades, the knitting industry was centred on the

Knowles, Matilda. *Matilda Knowles, botanist, pictured at her desk (centre) in the Dublin Science and Art Museum (now the National Museum of Ireland), 1910, where she managed the Botany Section from 1923. [National Museum of Ireland]*

provision of socks and stockings. Hand-knitting was probably introduced to Ireland at the end of the sixteenth century, primarily to provide stockings for soldiers in the English army; previously stockings had been fashioned from frieze, a coarse woollen material. J. G. Kohl in his *Travels in Ireland* (1844) noted: 'These people have a strange clothing for their feet; it is a kind of stocking without a sole, which covers only the upper part of the foot; and there is a hole in the fore part of the stocking, through which the great toe protrudes and thus the stocking is secured to the foot.' Because of the widespread practice of going barefoot, the soleless stocking—known in different parts of the country as *troithín, lópa, máirtín*, and *miotán*—was of more practical use.

Throughout the eighteenth and nineteenth centuries the knitting industry was encouraged, at first by philanthropists, who set up knitting schools in various places, and later by bodies such as the CONGESTED DISTRICTS BOARD at the end of the nineteenth century and the COUNTRY SHOP, Dublin, from the 1940s. [see CLOTHING, TRADITIONAL.] **Anne O'Dowd**

Knockdoe, Battle of (19 August 1504), a victory for the Lord Deputy, GERALD FITZGERALD, EIGHTH EARL OF KILDARE, over Ulick Finn Burke, Lord of the Burkes of Clanricarde, and Connor More O'Brien during a punitive expedition into Connacht following Burke's seizure of Galway. Ten thousand men participated in the battle, which took place 13 km (8 miles) north-east of Galway. The two sides comprised 'the greatest power of Irishmen that had been seen together since the conquest,' including several battalions of GALLOGLASS under the command of men descended from ANGLO-NORMAN families. The battle, the largest set-piece battle fought by these professional axemen down to that time, featured the first recorded use of a hand-gun. Approximately 2,000 deaths resulted. HENRY VII acknowledged Fitzgerald's victory by making him a knight of the Garter in 1505. The Fitzgerald ANNALS characterised the battle as the apogee of the earl's career. **Mary Ann Lyons**

Knockmany, Co. Tyrone, a hilltop PASSAGE TOMB commanding the Clogher Valley. It contains a single oval chamber set near the centre of a circular mound 25 m (80 ft) in diameter. Excavations in 1951 and 1958 yielded no evidence of an access passage. Nine stones are decorated with megalithic art. **Paul Walsh**

Knock Shrine, site of a silent apparition experienced by fifteen people at Knock, Co. Mayo, in 1879. The villagers reported seeing the Virgin Mary, St Joseph, and St John the Evangelist appear on the gable wall of the parish church during a storm; the figures were said to have been bathed in light and accompanied by a host of angels hovering over a lamb on a plain altar in front of a large cross. Two church commissions of inquiry, in 1879 and 1936, accepted the testimony of the witnesses and the verity of their story. Knock is a major Catholic PILGRIMAGE site, with more than a million visitors a year. **Martin Clancy**

Knowles, James Sheridan (1784–1862), playwright, actor, and clergyman. Born in Cork. A second cousin of RICHARD BRINSLEY SHERIDAN; studied medicine at the University of Aberdeen. He was a precocious playwright and actor, writing his first play at the age of sixteen and acting with Edmund Kean in Crow Street from 1808. His historical play *Brian Boroimhe* [*Bórú*] (1811) was not at first a success; however, his tragedy *Virginius* (1820) consolidated his reputation. By 1834 two of the leading actors of the age, William Charles Macready and Edwin Forrest, were touring in competing productions of this tale of dying for liberty, making Knowles a hero in America. Meanwhile, even as his *Brian Boroimhe* developed a following with nationalist audiences, Knowles renounced the theatre, becoming a Baptist pastor in 1844 and publishing *The 'Rock of Rome', or The Arch-Heresy* (1849). **Christopher Morash**

Knowles, Matilda (1864–1933), botanist. Born in Ballymena, Co. Antrim; studied at the ROYAL COLLEGE OF SCIENCE, Dublin. She was employed in the Botany Section of the Dublin Museum of Science and Art (now the NATIONAL MUSEUM). With Prof. THOMAS JOHNSON, head of botany, she greatly expanded the herbarium's national and international collections. Her expertise encompassed flowering and non-flowering plants, including lichens, which became her speciality. With Johnson she compiled a *Hand List of Flowering Plants and Ferns* (1910), and following his retirement in 1923 she managed the Botany Section. Her taxonomic and biogeographical knowledge of lichens culminated in her magnum opus, *The Lichens of Ireland* (1929). **Helena C. G. Chesney**

Knowth, Co. Meath, site of a MEGALITHIC PASSAGE TOMB in the BOYNE VALLEY, possibly completed towards the end of the fourth millennium BC. Excavations at the great mound at Knowth have revealed eighteen small passage tombs clustered around a huge mound that contains two passage tombs. The large mound is approximately circular and about 85 m (280 ft) in diameter, about 10 m (32 ft) in height, and surrounded by a series of 127 kerbstones. The tombs are placed almost back to back, the entrance to one facing west, the other east.

The western tomb was originally about 34 m (111 ft) in length and has an almost square chamber, divided in two by a low sill-stone and separated from the passage by a higher one. Both the chamber and the passage are constructed of orthostats and roofed with capstones that rested on the side stones; several of these are decorated, notably in the area of the chamber.

The eastern tomb is slightly longer, over 40 m (131 ft) in length, with a more or less straight passage and a fine corbel-vaulted cruciform chamber almost 6 m (20 ft) high, as in NEWGRANGE; within is a richly decorated basin-stone. The burial deposits consisted mainly of burnt bone, representing more than a hundred people. Grave goods included stone beads and pendants, antler pins, and a remarkable decorated flint macehead. Again the majority of decorated stones occur in or near the chamber. The eastern tomb may have been oriented towards the rising sun of the spring and autumn equinoxes; the setting sun could also have shone into the western tomb at the same times.

Like the midwinter solstice, so important at Newgrange, the spring and autumn equinoxes, when day and night are of equal length, would have been significant points in the calendar of a farming community. It is possible that burial or other rituals may have been timed to coincide with these events (see p. 860). **George Eogan**

Knox, Henry (1750–1806), US army commander. Born in Derry; he left school on his father's death. He became an assistant in a Boston bookshop and eventually opened one himself. In 1772 he joined the Boston Grenadier Corps and later developed a lifelong friendship with George Washington; they captured Boston together in 1776. Promoted to brigadier-general, Knox took part in much of the revolutionary war. He became a major-general in 1781 and was Secretary of War, 1785–94, the first under the US Constitution. **David Kiely**

Koizumi, Yakumo: see HEARN, LAFCADIO.

Kyan, John Howard (1774–1850), chemist and engineer. Born in Dublin, son of a Wicklow copper-mine owner; educated for management of the family mines. These mines failed, and after his father's death (1804) he worked in vinegar breweries in Newcastle-upon-Tyne, and later in London. He developed and patented in 1832 a process to preserve wood from rot, based on its impregnation with mercury (II) chloride. Timbers used in many famous London buildings were 'Kyanised'; Faraday's inaugural address at the Royal Institution, 1833, was on the topic of 'Kyanisation'. He sold the process to the Anti-Dry-Rot Company, 1833. He also patented ship propulsion by water jet, and ammonium salt production from gas liquor. He died in New York, while working on a plan for the filtration of water. **D. Thorburn Burns**

Kyle, John (Jack) (1926–), rugby footballer. Born in Belfast. Widely regarded as Ireland's greatest player and a true world-class footballer in his halcyon years, he won his first cap against France at Lansdowne Road in 1947, having earlier played in two of the unofficial matches against the British army in 1945 and in two of the unofficial internationals in 1946. Ireland's most-capped out-half, with forty-six international appearances between 1947 and 1958, he was the star of the 1948 team that won the Triple Crown for the first time since 1899 and that also achieved Ireland's only Grand Slam, scoring tries against England at Twickenham and against Scotland at Lansdowne Road. With Kyle again the anchor man, Ireland retained the Triple Crown in 1949, and he won thirty-two consecutive caps until his career was interrupted briefly by injury. He scored seven international tries, as well as one remarkable dropped goal, in Ireland's shock 11–3 defeat of Wales at Lansdowne Road in 1956. He toured Australia and New Zealand with the British Lions in 1950 and played in all six Tests, scoring tries in the first against New Zealand in Dunedin and in the second against Australia in Sydney. **Karl Johnston**

Kylesalia (*Caol Sáile*), Co. Galway, a shallow marine inlet opening into the north-west of Cill Chiaráin Bay. It is approximately 1.2 km ($\frac{3}{4}$ mile) long and varies between 100 and 200 m (330–660 ft) wide, with a maximum depth of approximately 5 m (16 ft). It is the site of several marine biological investigations and the only known site in Ireland of the marine algae *Apoglossocolax pusilla*. The creek was first spanned by Flannery Bridge in 1856; since then two replacement bridges have been built. **Chris Emblow**

Kyteler, Alice (fl. 1324), reputed witch. Of Flemish descent, she lived in Kilkenny and was the subject of the most famous of Irish witchcraft trials. Though known by her maiden name, she was four times married. In 1324 she and two accomplices were accused by Richard Ledrede, the English Franciscan Bishop of Ossory, of heresy, idolatry, and sorcery. It was alleged that she had cast spells to advance the career of William Outlaw, her son by her first marriage. Outlaw was a wealthy merchant and moneylender, related to Roger Outlaw, prior of the Hospitallers and Chancellor of Ireland. Ledrede had been educated in France and was a zealous advocate of the Papacy's stance against heresy and sorcery; he was also an English outsider in a closely knit ANGLO-NORMAN world, and his accusations brought him into conflict with Arnold le Poer, Seneschal of Kilkenny. Le Poer was related to Alice by her fourth marriage and was a close friend of William. The case appears to have had its origins in a property dispute between Alice and her son and the relatives of her later husbands, who initiated the accusations of sorcery.

What was a local dispute soon became a national case. Her maid, Petronilla was scourged into confession and burnt at the stake in the market square in Kilkenny—the first case of its kind in Ireland. Alice, aided by friends from the nobility, managed to escape to England and was not heard of again. **Susan Foran**

Knox. *Engraving of Henry Knox, soldier in the American Revolution. A close friend and adviser to President George Washington, he was the first Secretary of War, 1785–94. [Library of Congress, Prints and Photographs Division; LC-USZ62-12273]*

linen *(see page 633). An example of copperplate printed linen created by Francis Nixon (c. 1752–7). Nixon, of Drumcondra, Co. Dublin, developed and advertised a new technique of printing linen from engraved metal plates in 1752 making Ireland one of the first centres for this technique. [Private collection]*

L

Labbacallee, Glanworth, Co. Cork, one of the largest WEDGE TOMBS in Ireland. A long rectangular western chamber precedes a smaller one, the whole covered by three roof-stones sloping towards the rear. Excavations in 1934 yielded inhumations, burnt animal bones, pottery, and a bone pin. RADIOCARBON DATING places the earliest burials towards the end of the third millennium BC. **Paul Walsh**

labour force, female participation. Participation by women in the work force has risen dramatically in Ireland, particularly in the 1990s; in fact 90 per cent of the increase in the numbers at work between 1971 and 1996 was due to increases in women's participation. Women constituted 28 per cent of the labour force in 1971, 33 per cent in 1991, and 44 per cent in 1998 (when the participation of women was only slightly below the EU average, at 44 per cent, compared with 46 per cent). This was mainly due to increases in married women's participation. In the early 1970s, 7.5 per cent of married women were in the labour force, rising to almost 45 per cent by 1999 (third quarter). Married women's participation is highest in the peak childbearing and rearing years, with 66 per cent of married women aged twenty-five to thirty-four being in paid employment, compared with 46 per cent of those aged forty-five to fifty-four. This reflects the impact of the *marriage bar* (removed in 1973), whereby women were obliged or 'encouraged' to withdraw from the labour force on marriage, and the limited attempts to facilitate their re-entry. Women's participation in the labour force is likely to continue to increase, given the demand for labour in service activities. [see TRAINING.] **Pat O'Connor**

labour force survey, a representative sample survey of households in the Republic conducted by the CENTRAL STATISTICS OFFICE from 1975 (annually from 1983), designed to collect a range of indicators on labour market activity. The last survey, conducted in April 1997, had a sample of 47,665 private households, incorporating 147,933 individuals. The survey was an invaluable source of annual data on EMPLOYMENT, UNEMPLOYMENT and labour force participation among the adult population, as well as hours of work, participation in EDUCATION and training, and the sectoral and occupational distribution of employment. In 1998 the labour force survey was replaced by the quarterly national household survey, which collects labour market information from 3,000 households each week, giving a total sample of 39,000 households reported in each quarter. While this provides more frequent labour market information, it does not yet provide a detailed statistical breakdown similar to that previously available from the labour force survey. [see HOUSEHOLD BUDGET SURVEY.] **Philip O'Connell**

labour market. In 1995, 54 per cent of the population of the Republic aged fifteen and over was economically active—that is, in EMPLOYMENT or unemployed; this compares with 59 per cent of the population in Northern Ireland aged sixteen and over who were economically active. By 2000, economic activity in the Republic had increased to 59 per cent, with 1.746 million people in the labour force, compared with 1.459 million in 1995. The broadly corresponding proportion for Northern Ireland had fallen slightly, to 58 per cent, representing a labour force of 0.731 million, up from 0.707 million in 1995.

Between 1995 and 2000 participation by women in the labour force in the Republic increased from 40 per cent of all females aged fifteen and above to 47 per cent. In contrast, the broadly corresponding proportion for Northern Ireland remained stable, at 48 per cent.

Table 1: Labour force participation, 1995 and 2000

	Republic		Northern Ireland	
	1995	2000	1995	2000
Male	68.0%	71.0%	70.1%	68.6%
Female	39.7%	47.2%	48.1%	47.8%
Total	53.6%	58.9%	58.7%	57.8%

From 1995 to 1998 the Republic's UNEMPLOYMENT rate was higher than the corresponding figure for Northern Ireland. Over the period 1995–2000 the rate declined in both the Republic and Northern Ireland. However, between 1998 and 2000 the unemployment rate in the Republic declined substantially, and in both 1999 and 2000 it had a lower unemployment rate than Northern Ireland.

Table 2: ILO unemployment rates, 1995–2000

	Republic	Northern Ireland
1995	12.2%	11%
1996	11.9%	9.5%
1997	10.3%	7.5%
1998	7.8%	7.2%
1999	5.7%	7.2%
2000	4.3%	7%

Central Statistics Office/Northern Ireland Statistics & Research Agency

Labour Party, founded in 1912 as the party of the Irish Trades Union Congress. The Labour Party's claim to be the leading left-wing force in the Republic was enhanced by its much-increased vote in both 1989 and 1992. On average, the party's electoral base has stood at approximately 10 per cent; its high point was in November 1992, when it gained 19 per cent of the vote in the general election. It has served in five governments since 1973.

The Labour Party's long-term strategy has been to increase its distinctive left-wing appeal, but this is hard to do following coalitions with both FINE GAEL and FIANNA FÁIL. Many Labour deputies fear losing votes in working-class and urban areas to parties on the left. In 1999 the Labour Party absorbed DEMOCRATIC LEFT, once a competitor and coalition partner.

Ideologically the Labour Party belongs to the European social-democratic family. Unlike its Continental counterparts, however, it has never enjoyed periods of electoral hegemony. Spatially, parliamentary representation is not confined to cities and towns; some of its safest seats have been in rural constituencies, such as Kerry North. It is likely to remain a significant participant in the formation of governments for as long as Fine Gael and Fianna Fáil refuse to coalesce with each other. In 1997 the Labour Party gained 10.4 per cent of the votes and won seventeen seats in DÁIL ÉIREANN; in the 1999 local elections its support was 10.8 per cent; in the 1999 election 8.5 per cent of the vote gave the Labour Party one member of the European Parliament. **Neil Collins**

lace. White LINEN lace, evolving from sixteenth-century Italian cut-and-drawn linen work, became an important and valuable product in Western Europe in the seventeenth century. A luxury fabric, fine lace of good design indicated wealth. The two techniques of lace-making were *needlepoint* (built up stitch by stitch, the thread being looped with the point of a needle) and *pillow lace*, also called *bobbin lace* (made by the twisting and plaiting of weighted threads supported on a pillow).

Linen lace was introduced to Ireland during the seventeenth century and was soon more fashionable than gold lace. Pillow lace was made in Ireland from at least 1636, when, as a philanthropic gesture, RICHARD BOYLE the first Earl of Cork paid for it to be taught to a beggar girl; lacis (darned netting) was made from 1644 and needlepoint from about 1662. In the middle of the eighteenth century the DUBLIN SOCIETY encouraged high standards by giving grants and prizes; but it was in the nineteenth century that Irish lace-making became economically important. The invention of machine-made net in 1809 led to the development of embroidered net laces at Limerick, Kells, Co. Meath, and Carrickmacross, Co. Monaghan. During the GREAT FAMINE lace-making was promoted as a means of relieving the hardship of unemployment, and to this end the nuns of the Presentation convent, Youghal (Co. Cork), reintroduced needlepoint lace, based on an early Italian sample. The technique spread throughout the south, with the convent of the Poor Clares, Kenmare (Co. Kerry), becoming another centre.

Despite a serious decline, the later decades of the nineteenth century saw a revival of the lace industry, with strong commercial involvement, the promotion of good design by the colleges of art, and the establishment of lace schools by convents and patrons. Much of the lace produced between 1880 and 1910 was exported, securing the international reputation of Irish lace. **Alex Ward**

lace and embroidery (Congested Districts Board). The CONGESTED DISTRICTS BOARD organised cottage industry centres for

labour. *ITGWU members picket outside University College Dublin, 29 August 1985. The picket which continued into September began on 31 July when twenty-one cleaners were declared redundant after the firm they worked for lost the contract to clean the Arts and Library buildings at UCD, Belfield. [Derek Speirs/Report]* needlework in Cos. Donegal, Sligo, Leitrim, Mayo, Galway, Kerry, and Cork (see p. 229). Each specialised in SPRIGGING, drawn-thread work, knitting, weaving, or embroidered net lace (CARRICKMACROSS or LIMERICK). The initiative was important, as traditional centres for this work had been adversely affected by the McKinley tariff act (1891) in the United States. Each centre was organised by a teacher, who was frequently also the manager and salesperson. The normal outlets were the Irish Lace Depot in Dublin and in Paris. Originally pupils were paid 3 pence a day as encouragement; when trained, the workers were not paid for work until the item was sold, and so there was a preference for sewing to order. Though it was acknowledged that the remuneration was low, and many experienced workers were expected to pay for their own thread, the work gave some training for housework while also providing an income that was useful on the farm or for emigration. **Mairead Dunlevy**

lace, nineteenth-century. The earliest known piece of Irish lace dates from 1647; but the lace industry began only in the 1820s. By 1888 seven varieties of Irish lacework were being made.

Flat needlepoint is made with a needle and thread and no background. It was produced at convents in Youghal, Co. Cork, Kenmare, Co. Kerry, New Ross, Co. Wexford, and Killarney, Co. Kerry, and at Cappoquin, Co. Waterford, Tynan, Co. Armagh, and Inishmacsaint, Co. Fermanagh. *Raised needlepoint*, which is similar but with padding, was made at most of the same places.

Carrickmacross lace is cut cambric appliqué on net, sometimes guipure, with all the background cut away. This was a cottage industry begun in 1823 by Mrs Grey Porter in Carrickmacross, Co. Monaghan, that later spread to other areas.

Limerick lace, consisting of embroidery of net, with either darn stitch or chain stitch, was a substantial factory industry begun in Limerick in 1829 by an Englishman, Charles Walker. By the middle of the nineteenth century almost 3,000 women were employed in the Limerick area; by 1900 the craft had spread all over the country, mainly in convents.

Drawn-thread work was produced mainly in Ulster but also at Mrs Hall Dare's school at Bunclody, Co. Wexford. *Pillow or bobbin lace* was made in small quantities in Dublin, Headford, Co. Galway, Birr, Co. Offaly, Cong, Co. Mayo, and elsewhere.

Crochet is made with thread and a hooked needle. The first recorded sales were at the Ursuline Convent in Cork during the Great Famine, but the craft spread all over Ireland, especially when the CONGESTED DISTRICTS BOARD set up lace classes after 1891. Work of the best quality was produced in Clones, Co. Monaghan, and Cork (see p. 1005). [see CLOTHING, TRADITIONAL.] **Nellie O'Cleirigh**

Lacy, Count Peter (1678–1751), Russian field-marshal. Born in Killeedy, Co. Limerick; at the age of thirteen he served as a JACOBITE officer in the defence of Limerick. He joined SARSFIELD's brigade in France, and later fought in Italy and the Rhine, 1692–7. He trained troops of Peter the Great and led them against the Danes, Swedes, and Turks. By 1728 he was a general and governor of Livonia (Latvia and Estonia). He was promoted to field-marshal in 1736, saw further service against the Turks and Swedes, and received many honours. He retired to his estates in Livonia in 1743. **David Kiely**

Ladies' Land League. The Ladies' Irish National Land League in Ireland was formed in January 1881 by MICHAEL DAVITT to keep the land agitation alive in the event that he and the other leaders of the Land League were imprisoned for their activities. He invited ANNA PARNELL to administer the new organisation—a move supported only reluctantly by her brother, CHARLES STEWART PARNELL. The first meeting was held on 31 January, and immediately the task was begun of encouraging the formation of branches throughout Ireland, in London, and in the large cities of the industrial north of England. The leaders and executive of the Ladies' Land League came from the middle classes and included many young women, such as KATHARINE TYNAN, Jennie O'Toole (later Wyse Power), and Hannah Lynch, who would later make their mark in political and

lace. *A Youghal needlepoint fan cover (c. 1902), based on flat point de France lace, made for Queen Alexandra. The Irish inscription 'Uraighim Fionfhuaraighim agus is féidir liom Rún do chongdháil air nidh' translates as 'I cool, I freshen and I can keep a secret from everyone'. [National Museum of Ireland]* literary life. In country branches most of the members were farmers' wives and daughters and sometimes farmers in their own right, many of whom had been involved in land agitation from the beginning. Anna Parnell took on the task of speaking at public meetings when local women wished to start a league. By July 1881 the Ladies' Land League had 420 branches throughout the country and was providing relief for more than 3,000 evicted people, organising public meetings and prisoners' support and setting up a Children's Land League to educate children on the land issue.

By October 1881, Charles Stewart Parnell and most of the leadership of the Land League were in jail. Their response was to issue the No-Rent Manifesto—a purely propagandist strategy—exhorting farmers to pay no rent until the Land League leaders had been released. Immediately after the publication of the manifesto the Land League was proclaimed an illegal organisation. The Ladies' Land League was not named in the proclamation and so, taking the No-Rent Manifesto at face value, attempted to enforce it as best it could—mainly by the expedient of building huts for evicted tenants (14,600 over a period of four years), whose numbers were steadily increasing. Members were harassed by the ROYAL IRISH CONSTABULARY, and some of the leading members were jailed; but they managed to continue the publication of the Land League newspaper, *United Ireland* (founded in August 1881). Despite their best efforts it was an uphill battle, as it became clear that the men's league was not really intent on revolution and did not want the women to be either. In April 1882 GLADSTONE, anxious to see an end to the continuing crisis, struck an informal bargain with Parnell, known as the KILMAINHAM TREATY, signalling the end of the revolutionary dimension of the Land League.

The story of Anna Parnell's disillusionment with her brother's alleged sell-out of the goals of the Land League is contained in her 1907 historical memoir, *The Tale of a Great Sham* (published 1986). This is a searing critique of Land League politics as well as an indictment of the apparent inability of the men on the Land League executive to work on an equal footing with women. The memoir makes it clear that when the women of the Ladies' Land League executive came to realise how profoundly the two leagues differed in their aims, they were determined 'not to have any more to do with the men.' On 10 August 1882, after much wrangling and underhand treatment by the executive of the Land League, the Ladies' Land League disbanded, and Anna Parnell never again spoke to her brother. All her efforts to have her memoir published were in vain; but the experiences of the women of the Ladies' Land League lived on in the minds of politically active women in the new century as a reminder of the difficulties women were likely to face when they stepped into the public sphere. **Dana Hearne**

Ladies of Llangollen: see BUTLER, LADY ELEANOR.

Lafranchini brothers, stuccodores. Born in Ticino, Switzerland. Paulo (1695–1770) and Filippo (1702–1779) Lafranchini were stuccodores (plaster-modellers) of seminal importance who brought the seventeenth-century Italian baroque figurative and ornamental style to Ireland in 1739. Their early work is closely associated with that of Giovanni Bugatti and Giuseppe Artari (also from the same area), who worked in England a decade or so earlier, often on houses associated with James Gibbs. The Lafranchini, working in some fifteen Irish houses, were often associated with buildings designed by RICHARD CASTLE. Their figural ceilings were strikingly new to Irish interior decoration. At CARTON, Co. Kildare (1730), and in Newman House, 85 St Stephen's Green, Dublin

Lafranchini. *Apollo Room, 85 St Stephen's Green, Dublin, 1738–c. 1740. A theme from classical mythology forms the basis of the Lafranchinis' stucco decoration, with a figure of Apollo (god of light, beauty and reason) on the overmantel, surrounded by the nine muses, three of whom can be seen (from left): Urania (astronomy), Thalia (comedy), and Erato (hymns). [Courtesy of Newman House, University College, Dublin]*

(1738–c. 1740), the vigorously modelled deities were derived from Italian and French seventeenth-century baroque engraved sources. These figures were elaborately framed by swirling acanthus cartouches and swags, through which clambered *putti*. Though executing figural ceilings (at Kilshannig, Co. Cork) as late as 1766, they seem in the 1740s to have generally adopted a lighter, more rococo style, which depended on rhythmic acanthus foliage adorned with occasional putti (such as the saloons in Russborough House, Co. Wicklow, and Tyrone House, Dublin). When decorating the walls of the stair-hall at CASTLETOWN, Co. Kildare, in 1760, Filippo made a full transition to lively asymmetrical delicately rococo foliate stucco. Though both exerted a major influence on Irish stuccodores (such as ROBERT WEST), Paulo worked in England for at least part of the 1750s, Filippo remaining in Ireland, where he is recorded as having a room at Castletown as late as 1774. **Christopher Moore**

Lagore, Co. Meath, site of the Loch Gabair CRANNÓG, north-east of Dunshaughlin, originally at the eastern edge of a shallow marshy lake. It was excavated in the 1930s by the Harvard Archaeological Expedition, led by Hugh Hencken, and dates from the seventh to the eleventh century. The history of Lagore is inextricably bound up with that of the southern UÍ NÉILL, the powerful 'royal' dynasty of Meath. The archaeological record from the site also reflects a high status, containing evidence of a variety of craftworking, a rich food economy, and a range of luxury items. **Michelle Comber**

Lake, Gerard (1744–1808), English soldier and politician. Member of Parliament for Aylesbury, Buckinghamshire, he saw military service in the American War and various Continental campaigns before coming to Ireland, where, in December 1796, he took over the military command of Ulster from General Dalrymple. Lake was a courageous soldier who had distinguished himself in his previous campaigns. However, he was very much a man of action and found that the situation in Ulster, that of an underground terror campaign waged by the UNITED IRISHMEN, was less to his liking. He advocated a stringent counter-terror policy, which aimed to terrorise the insurgents and their supporters. Naturally hot-tempered, he once threatened to burn Belfast. Though his campaigns in 1797, known as the 'dragooning of Ulster', seriously weakened the United Irishmen, his brutal methods alarmed some members of the government, who thought he had gone too far. In April 1798 he was promoted to commander-in-chief of the army in Ireland, a position he held during the rebellion until replaced by Lord Cornwallis in June. He returned to England in 1799 and the following year was given a command in India, where he again distinguished himself in action and was made a viscount for his services. **Allan Blackstock**

lakes and lakelands. Roughly 2 per cent of the area of Ireland is covered by freshwater lakes and ponds, a much higher proportion than in many European countries. Ireland's numerous lakes (more than 4,000) owe their origin to various sequences of events in the recent and more distant geological past. Many lakes reflect glacial scouring or are associated with glacial deposition; but some of the larger ones, such as LOUGH NEAGH, may well date from before the onset of GLACIATION. Glacial erosion has allowed lakes to form on mountainsides as well as in over-deepened valleys, as for example the KILLARNEY LAKES (see p. 590). A large number of lakes are found on the Central Plain; the two main river systems draining this area, the Rivers SHANNON and Erne, widen out into a series of lakes along their course. In early post-glacial times high water-tables led to widespread flooding, particularly in these broad, shallow basins. Numerous smaller lakes occupied depressions in the glacial till deposits or were dammed by irregular glacial deposits. Though some of these still exist—the lakes of Co. Westmeath, for example—most have been transformed into large areas of raised bog. Many lakes lie on Carboniferous limestone and are often connected to underground drainage systems, such as LOUGH CORRIB AND LOUGH MASK, and LOUGH DERG AND LOUGH CONN. Ireland is famous for its numerous *turloughs*, ephemeral lakes that hold water in the winter and dry out during the summer. They drain slowly by way of underground routes, and a backing up of water causes them to expand over the winter months. [see CRANNÓGS; FLOODING.] **R. A. Charlton**

Lambeg. *William Hewitt of Charles Street, Belfast, maker of Lambeg drums, in his workshop with a selection of drums. [JFA Studio, London]*

Lalor, James Fintan (1807–1849), Young Irelander. Born in Tonakill, Co. Laois; educated at Carlow College, he became an apprentice chemist. He suffered lifelong ill health as a result of a spinal injury. He joined the Repeal Association, became involved in YOUNG IRELAND, and advocated land nationalisation, believing that the entire soil of a country belongs of right to the entire people and is the rightful property not of any one class but of the nation at large; he probably influenced Marx, who asserted that monopoly in land is the basis of monopoly in capital. He established the Tipperary Tenant League, 1845, jointly founded the Irish Confederation, 1846, and wrote for the NATION and the *Irish Tribune*. In 1848 with JOHN MITCHEL he co-founded the *Irish Felon* and was arrested for his part in the Tipperary rising. Released because of ill health, he led another rising in 1849, was arrested, and died in prison. **Marjorie Bloy**

Lalor, Peter (1823–1889), Australian politician. Born at Tinnakill, Co. Laois, younger brother of JAMES FINTAN LALOR; educated at TCD. He emigrated to Australia in 1852 and, as engineer and claim owner, became involved in mining at Ballarat, where he came into conflict with the police as the leader of the miners' revolt. In December 1854 he led the striking miners at Eureka in an incident known as the Eureka Stockade, during which twenty-two miners were killed and Lalor, among twenty-one others, was seriously wounded. He represented Ballarat in the legislative council of Victoria in 1855 and South Grant in the parliament, 1856–71 and 1875–7. He was subsequently Postmaster-General and, finally, parliamentary Speaker, 1880–88. **Brian Lalor**

Lamb, Bobby (1931–), JAZZ musician. Born in Cork, he has lived in Britain since the 1950s. He was lead trombonist with the outstanding big bands of their time, among them those of Stan Kenton, Louie Bellson, and Woody Herman; he also featured in the popular British bands of Ted Heath and Jack Parnell. A prolific composer, with more than 200 works to his name, he has written for symphony orchestra, for jazz quartet and orchestra, and for big bands. Several of his earlier compositions drew on Irish influences including the CHILDREN OF LIR. He is an established conductor of jazz and symphony orchestras and has worked with radio bands in Denmark, Germany, Norway, Britain, and Ireland. He has taught jazz at Leeds College of Music and since the 1980s has been director of jazz studies at Trinity College of Music, London. **Brian Trench**

Lamb, Charles (1893–1964) landscape, portrait and figure painter, and illustrator. Born in Portadown, Co. Armagh; apprenticed to his father's decorating firm and attended Belfast School of Art. He won a scholarship to the Metropolitan School of Art, Dublin, 1917–22, where he was a student-teacher in 1920; SEÁN KEATING was the dominant influence. In 1919 he began visiting the west of Ireland, which provided inspiration for his masterpiece, *Dancing at a Northern Crossroads* (1920); he also made regular painting trips to the north of Ireland from 1940 to the 1950s. He moved to Carraroe, Co. Galway, before visiting Brittany, 1926–7. In 1936 he launched an annual exhibition and summer school. He visited Germany, 1938–9. An academic realist with a strong, painterly style, his work has been shown in England, the United States, and Belgium. **Marie Bourke**

Lambay Island, Co. Dublin, a volcanic island of 2.5 km^2 (1 sq. mile). Lambay has produced BRONZE AGE artefacts and contains one of COLM CILLE's monasteries. In 795 it was the site of the first VIKING raid on Ireland. Lambay was bought by the Hon. Cecil Baring (later Lord Revelstoke), who in 1904 commissioned Sir EDWIN LUTYENS to design a house incorporating the medieval remains on the island. The gardens were designed by Gertrude Jekyll. The island is now a nature reserve, notable for shearwaters, falcons, and ravens. **Stephen A. Royle**

Lambeg drum, an instrument unique to the north of Ireland, having developed in the nineteenth century from the eighteenth-century *long drum*. Made from oak and goatskin, it is typically 0.9 m (3 ft) in diameter and 0.7 m ($2\frac{1}{4}$ ft wide, weighs 13.5 kg (30 lb), and is capable of producing a volume of 120 decibels. Associated chiefly with the ORANGE ORDER and the ANCIENT ORDER OF HIBERNIANS, the Lambeg drum is played as an accompaniment to the fife in ritual processions and in drum competitions and matches. It is played with canes, and the rhythms are fast and complex. Originally the drums were smaller and quieter, but through competitions, where drum is judged against drum, the size, tension, and volume increased dramatically from the 1850s to the 1920s. Playing styles also changed, from slow, syncopated single beats as accompaniment to the fife (single time) to fast, constant rolling (double or competition time). Set drumming tunes, common to different localities, were played without fifes, with the drum seen as an instrument in its own right. The old styles of drumming, and its use within the AOH tradition, are now moribund. By the middle of the twentieth century the Lambeg drum had been superseded in processions by flute and other bands, though there has been a slight comeback in recent years. **Gary Hastings**

Lament: see CAOINEACH.

Lament for Art O'Laoghaire: see CAOINEACH ART UÍ LAOGHAIRE.

Lament for Colm Cille: see AMRA CHOLUIM CHILLA.

Lament of Cailleach Bhéarra: see AITHBE DAMSA BES MARAÍ.

Lammas Fair, Old, held at Ballycastle, Co. Antrim, on the last Monday and Tuesday of August. Only this and Puck Fair, Killorglin, Co. Kerry, survive of such formerly common events, at which sheep and horses were disposed of before winter. The fair is traditionally associated with *dulse* (a seaweed), *yella man* (toffee), and the song 'At the Oul' Lammas Fair' written by John Henry MacAuley, but little music is now heard. **John Moulden**

La Mon House bombing (17 February 1978), one of the more grotesque atrocities of the 1970s. The attack was part of a continuing PROVISIONAL IRA strategy of undermining the economy of Northern Ireland and disrupting 'normal life' by attacking hotels, pubs, and other commercial targets. The site of the La Mon House restaurant in a part of north Co. Down that had remained relatively unaffected by the TROUBLES further added to its attractiveness as a target. The attackers used blast incendiary bombs, consisting of a small explosive charge attached to a petrol can, which could be hung on the wire window-grilles used for security; when the bomb exploded a ball of fire blew through the shattered glass. Very little warning was given, and the crowded restaurant (it was a busy Friday night) was consumed with fire. Twelve people were burnt to death and twenty-three injured, prompting such widespread revulsion that the Provisional IRA temporarily suspended its fire-bombing campaign. **Keith Jeffery**

Lamplugh, George William (1859–1926), geologist. Born in Great Driffield, Yorkshire, but grew up in Bridlington. There he embarked on a career in commerce, but the local rocks had captured his interest and he began to publish on geological research. In 1892 he joined the Geological Survey of the United Kingdom, and in 1901 he was sent to Dublin to take charge of the Survey's Irish office. Under his leadership, between 1901 and 1904, drift surveys of the regions around Dublin, Belfast, Cork, and Limerick were conducted. During 1904 he returned to England, where in 1914 he became an assistant to the Survey's director. Between 1918 and 1920 he was president of the Geological Society of London. He retired from the Survey in 1920. **Jean Archer**

Lanczos, Cornelius (1893–1974), theoretical physicist. Born in Hungary; he graduated in 1915 and was awarded a doctorate. From 1921 to 1931 he worked in various German universities on basic aspects of quantum mechanics and field theory; from 1931 to 1952 he worked in the United States on mathematical physics, numerical methods, and industrial applications. In 1952 he returned to Europe and carried out research in theoretical physics at the DUBLIN INSTITUTE FOR ADVANCED STUDIES where about half of his more than 120 papers and books were published. He made important contributions to quantum mechanics, relativity theory, matrix methods in numerical analysis, and presented the first formulation of the fast Fourier transform. In his honour an International Centenary Conference was held at North Carolina State University in 1993; a collection of his published work in six volumes, including English translations and his correspondence with Albert Einstein, was then published. **Péter Király**

land. Natural landscapes—the product of geological, climatic and biological processes with no human influences—are rare in today's

land. *The Beara Peninsula, between Cos. Cork and Kerry, showing a typical landscape of small fields, isolated farmhouses, and stone-walled boundaries. [Bord Fáilte]* world. Yet Ireland's landscape heritage includes a wealth of natural and cultural resources. Cultural elements of the landscape include field and settlement patterns, hedgerows, buildings, archaeological and historical monuments, woodlands, BOGS, and mines.

Ireland owes its rich and diverse landscape and natural distinctiveness principally to its unique GEOLOGY. The foundation rocks are crystalline metamorphic and igneous, lying beneath the sedimentary rocks of the midlands and south and exposed in the west and north. A great variety of metamorphic rocks occupy large areas in the north and west. Old red sandstone dominates the geology of the south and south-west, while Carboniferous limestone, which covers more than half the country, is the dominant rock formation in Ireland. Most of the higher ground is close to the coast, while the midlands are largely flat, lying above limestone, the landscape here mostly rich farmland or raised bogs. Towards the west the soil becomes poorer and the fields smaller.

AGRICULTURE has had a significant impact on the formation of the landscape throughout the centuries. Changes include the loss of natural habitats and altered scenery; more recently the intensification of agriculture, the abandonment of farms, the expansion of towns, the standardisation of building designs, INFRASTRUCTURE development, TOURISM, and recreation have resulted in some replacement of natural and regional diversity with homogeneity. In some instances this is accompanied by more environmental degradation. The landscape has also been affected by commercial afforestation policies.

The landscape is a natural resource that provides habitats for wild species of plants and animals, and the protection of the landscape and its diversity is closely linked to the preservation of natural habitats and endangered species. To aid conservation efforts, certain areas have been designated for protection, including national parks, nature reserves, special protection areas (SPAs), special areas of conservation (SACs), and natural heritage areas (NHAs). Despite Ireland's uniqueness, only one natural feature has been declared a world heritage site: the GIANT'S CAUSEWAY in Co. Antrim.

Apart from seals, which breed around the coast, and whales, which occasionally visit coastal waters, Ireland has twenty-seven species of MAMMALS, including the red deer, pine-marten, badger, OTTER, HARE, and stoat, which are native to the country, as well as introduced species such as the fallow deer, rabbit, and other rodents. Ireland's only reptile is a small lizard, while there are three amphibia: the newt, frog, and toad. The rivers and LAKES contain salmon, trout, char, pollan, perch, pike, and eels. Of the 380 species of wild bird recorded in Ireland only about a third breed in the country.

Ireland contains habitat types that are scarce or absent in much of Europe, including turloughs, shingle beaches, coastal lagoons, maërl beds, machir, and a complete range of peatlands. The peatlands are of particular importance; there is a considerable variety, including fens, raised bogs, Atlantic or western blanket bogs, and mountain blanket bogs, comprising an important resource that originally accounted for 1.3 million ha (3.2 million acres) or 17 per cent of the land surface. However, today less than 20 per cent of this remains in a relatively untouched condition. Since the fifteenth century, *turbary* (ancient turf-cutting rights) has been responsible for the loss of 233,830 ha (577,800 acres) of raised bog and 85,590 ha (211,500 acres) of blanket bog, or 73 per cent of the original area of raised bog and 11 per cent of the original area of blanket bog. The mechanisation of turf-cutting meant a considerable increase in the quantities of turf being harvested semi-commercially and over a wider area; in the recent past, exploitation for fuel, afforestation schemes, the intensification of agriculture, overgrazing by sheep and land reclamation have also taken their toll. The draining of bogs also results in the release of stored carbon in the form of carbon dioxide and methane, both potent greenhouse gases, with their deleterious effects on the CLIMATE. Tourism has also had an effect on peatlands, as the delicate balance of life in the bogs is negatively affected by trampling damage.

The importance of conserving peatlands derives from the fact that they are fragile, non-replaceable ecosystems that have developed over a long time. They are an essential part of the biosphere, each type having its own particular ecology and vegetation, with a unique FLORA and FAUNA that have adapted to these environments. As bogs are among the most ancient of habitats, they are also of considerable archaeological interest and have produced significant finds. Of the blanket bog habitats that cover more than 100,000 km^2 of the Earth's surface, 8 per cent are in Ireland. Peatlands also have a cultural importance as some of the last true wilderness areas in Europe. In both jurisdictions in Ireland the importance of peatlands has been recognised in the nomination of many sites as special areas of conservation.

Agriculture has had the biggest influence on land surfaces, and Ireland has one of the highest proportions of land devoted to agriculture in Europe, the principal use being pasture; other pressures include road-building, INDUSTRIAL DEVELOPMENT, HOUSING, afforestation, quarrying, and the exploitation of minerals. In the Republic the consumption of *aggregates* (sand, gravel, and crushed rock) is now estimated to be approaching 50 million tonnes a year (equivalent to approximately 14 tonnes per head of population). As extraction processes are damaging to the landscape, recent planning permissions for this activity include conditions relating to the visual impact and other potential environmental consequences. The recycling of construction and demolition waste can mitigate such environmental impacts, and Government policy is that 85 per cent of these materials will be recycled by 2013.

Ireland is the sixth-largest producer of lead-zinc in the world. Unless it is properly controlled, the extraction of minerals can have localised effects through air pollution, the generation of traffic, noise, and leaching from spoil heaps and tailing ponds. In the Republic most existing and new mining operations are required to apply to the Environmental Protection Agency for an integrated pollution control (IPC) licence. **Anne-Marie Cunningham**

Land Acts, passed by the British Parliament to address the discrepancy between conflicting perceptions by landlords and tenants of agricultural land tenure in Ireland. Cardwell's and Deasy's Acts (1860) tried to bring Irish practice into line with that of Britain but failed to meet the concerns of tenants. Later legislation dealt, in varying degrees, with two different purposes: to enshrine the rights of tenants, establishing a dual ownership between landlord and tenant, and to facilitate the purchase by tenants of their farms, thereby eliminating by consent the institution of landlordism. The former approach was favoured by Liberal governments, embodied principally in the Landlord and Tenant (Ireland) Act (1870) and the Land Law (Ireland) Act (1881), the latter by Conservative ones, the major measures being the Purchase of Land (Ireland) Act (1885), the Land Act (1887), the Purchase of Land (Ireland) Act ('Balfour Act') (1891), and the Land Act (1896), and—most effectively—the Irish Land Act (1903) 'Wyndham Act'. **Philip J. Bull**

land annuities. From 1870 onwards, British governments passed a series of LAND ACTS that gradually transferred ownership of Irish land from the Ascendancy landlord class to their former tenants. To finance the purchases the British exchequer extended long-term low-interest loans to the tenants. After the establishment of the Irish Free State in 1922 the repayments were collected by the Department of Finance in Dublin and forwarded to London. When FIANNA FÁIL came to power in 1932 the Government withheld the annuity payments in redemption of an election pledge. The British retaliated by levying duties on Irish agricultural exports to Britain, the so-called 'ECONOMIC WAR'. Under the terms of the Anglo-Irish Agreements of 1938 de Valera agreed to a single final payment of £10 million in full settlement of the issue. **Fergal Tobin**

landed estates, property owned by landlords (individuals or institutions such as Trinity College, Dublin) who rented some or all of it out to others. Estates ranged in size from around 500 acres to tens of thousands of acres. Small estates were usually concentrated in adjoining townlands, while large estates could be distributed throughout different counties and even provinces. Part of the estate was held in demesne land that surrounded the 'BIG HOUSE' (see p. 29). [see ANGLO-IRISH SOCIETY.] **Terence Dooley**

Land League. The National Land League of Mayo was founded on 16 August 1879 in Castlebar by MICHAEL DAVITT following four months of agrarian agitation in the county. It was soon incorporated in the Irish National Land League, founded on 21 October 1879 by Davitt and PARNELL. At Parnell's insistence, the programme of the league was to be one that could be defended in Parliament. Its two stated objectives were the reduction of rents and the establishment of peasant proprietary, whereby tenants would secure ownership of the land they tilled.

The league achieved a significant success with the passing of the Land Law (Ireland) Act (1881). It was proclaimed in October 1881 following the arrest of its leaders as a consequence of growing tension with the government over the workings of the LAND ACT and the persistence of boycotting. Despite efforts by the LADIES' LAND LEAGUE to keep the organisation alive, it did not long survive the arrest of its leadership and the internal disarray that plagued it. A year after its proclamation it was replaced by the IRISH NATIONAL LEAGUE. [see BOYCOTT, LADIES' LAND LEAGUE.] **Donald Jordan**

landlord villages. Landlords constituted the minority property-owning class that had been reconstituted on the basis of modern agrarian capitalism by the land confiscations and PLANTATIONS of the sixteenth and seventeenth centuries. During these events the bulk of Ireland's agricultural land passed into English or Scottish ownership and was subsequently held by the landlord minority in the form of tenanted agricultural and urban ESTATES. By the late 1770s, when Ireland's population was approximately 4 million, it is estimated that some 5,000 landed families owned more than three-quarters of all agricultural land; by the 1840s, when the population had grown to over 8 million, the total had risen to 10,000. Once represented as a predatory stereotype, derived largely from their colonial origins, Ireland's landlords have been rehabilitated by modern research to the extent that their economic behaviour is not seen as unique to Ireland nor uniquely exploitative: their typically limited investment in AGRICULTURE, conspicuous expenditure on houses and ornamental parks and maintenance of a metropolitan 'social season' were entirely typical of landed elites in *ancien régime* Europe. What was unique to Ireland was the colonial edge given by the recent character of most landlords' foreign origins, the national and religious differences that arose from this, and the significance of all these factors in contemporary European politics.

Ireland's landlords derived their economic authority, and the social status and political influence that arose from this, from their monopoly of landownership in what remained an essentially agrarian country. Central to this, arguably, was their control of the rural marketing network through which this agricultural wealth was generated. More than 600 villages and 150 provincial towns were either founded, refounded or otherwise 'improved' with the aid of their landlords between c. 1600 and 1850. The extent of the landlord's involvement varied. In many instances, such as at Edenderry, Co. Offaly, and Manorhamilton, Co. Leitrim, it was limited to providing institutional buildings, such as market houses or courthouses, and the offer to tenants of favourable building leases. In others, such as Cookstown, Co. Tyrone, Castlewellan, Co. Down, and LISMORE, Co. Waterford, the landlord either laid out an entirely new town or personally financed the construction of extensive new housing. The motivations for this were complex. By enhancing market facilities and offering favourable leaseholds, landlords sought to ensure both the success of the markets under their control and the alignment of their tenants' economic interests with their own. In other places landlords constructed elaborate and architecturally sophisticated buildings, such as the market house built by the Tynte family at Dunlavin, Co. Wicklow, in the 1730s, or devised plans that demonstrate a familiarity with Renaissance planning, as at Strokestown, Co. Roscommon. Here their motivation may have had at least as much to do with creating a status-enhancing 'polite' and formal environment, frequently as a backdrop for the BIG HOUSE. By the middle of the nineteenth century economic depression, combined with the post-FAMINE fall in population, rendered further market foundation redundant. [see ANGLO-IRISH SOCIETY; BIG-HOUSE NOVEL.] **Lindsay Proudfoot**

landlords and the land system, nineteenth and early twentieth century. Throughout the nineteenth century, landownership was the preserve of a privileged minority, predominantly Protestant. In 1804 there were 8,000 to 10,000 landlords in a population of 5.4 million. As many as 33 per cent of these were absentees. As the century progressed, more and more landlords found themselves becoming increasingly indebted for a variety of reasons, including their own extravagance and the existence of a middleman system that prevented them from raising their rents. From the 1850s, landlords who had survived the GREAT FAMINE largely intact (as well as those who had purchased the estates of insolvent landlords under the Encumbered Estates Acts) established more stringent management policies on their estates. Middlemen were ousted, sub-division and sub-letting were actively opposed, and the many small scattered holdings of evicted tenants were consolidated into larger, more compact units. Furthermore, landlords retained to themselves large tracts of untenanted land for their own farming purposes. The period from the mid-1850s to the late 1870s was one of sustained ECONOMIC GROWTH (with a temporary interruption in the early 1860s). However, landlords failed to exploit the full commercial capacity of their ESTATES by raising their rents in accordance with the increase in agricultural incomes. Instead they continued to borrow heavily, believing that the economic boom would last well into the future. The period from 1879 to 1903 was crucial in the economic decline of Irish landlords. Because of agricultural depression, the LAND WAR, the fixing of fair rents and the extinction of arrears, landlords found their disposable income greatly diminished. By the late 1880s they could no longer extricate themselves from indebtedness by recourse to borrowing, as Irish land was no longer regarded as safe collateral. Most began to see the sale of at least part of their estates as the only viable commercial option. However, land legislation up to 1903 did little to entice landlords to sell. The terms of the Irish LAND ACT (1903) were much more progressive and promoted the sale of landed estates on a revolutionary scale. However, neither this act nor the one that followed in 1909 ended landlordism in Ireland. By the early 1920s up to 3 million acres of land remained in landlord ownership. The Free State Land Acts from 1923 and the Northern Ireland Land Act (1925) provided for the compulsory completion of tenant purchase in both jurisdictions. [see MIDDLEMEN.] **Terence Dooley**

Land of Spices, The (1941), a novel by KATE O'BRIEN. It is set in an Irish convent school, run by a French order, in the period 1904–14. Its double narrative describes the career of the Reverend Mother, Helen Archer, offered headship of her order at the end of the novel, and the schooldays of the pupil Anna Murphy, enabled to proceed to university because of Reverend Mother's support. The book was banned by the Censorship Board because of a brief passage that refers to HOMOSEXUALITY. A feminist novel, concerned with women's right to EDUCATION and independence, it also considers the European dimensions of Catholicism and the limitations of NATIONALISM. **Riana O'Dwyer**

Land of Youth: see TIR NA NÓG.

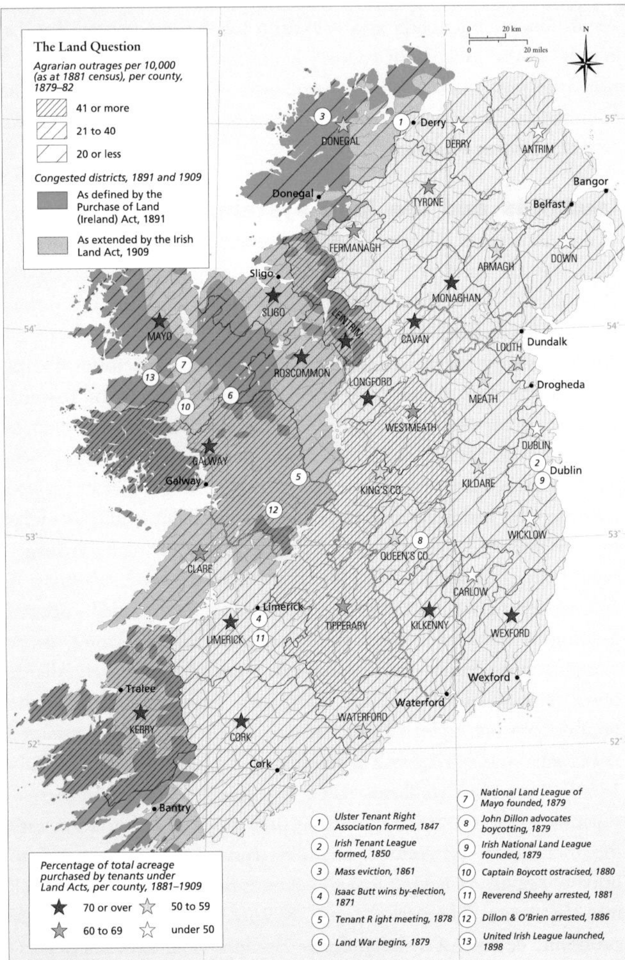

land war, a period of agrarian agitation from 1879 to 1903. The land war began in April 1879 with a meeting in Irishtown, Co. Mayo, and ended with the passing of the Irish LAND ACT (1903)—the 'Wyndham Act'. This was the culmination of a series of Land acts designed to bring about the transfer of ownership of tenanted land from landlord to tenant—the principal goal of the agitation. The land war went through three periods, each associated with a national organisation that mobilised the discontent in the Irish countryside: 1879–81, Irish National LAND LEAGUE; 1882–91, IRISH NATIONAL LEAGUE; and 1898–1903, UNITED IRISH LEAGUE. Its fortunes were closely tied to those of the IRISH PARTY. **Donald Jordan**

Landweer, Sonja (1933–), potter, jeweller, and sculptor. She arrived from her native Netherlands at the KILKENNY DESIGN WORKSHOPS in 1965 as a successful designer who had evolved a unique batiked ceramic technique. As well as pioneering into Irish glazes, she refined this technique to produce wheel-thrown vessels of symbolic and technical complexity, which she exhibited at the avant-garde Hendricks Gallery in Dublin. Extensive experimentation with materials and seminal forms led to her body SCULPTURE, where she incorporates clay, slate, feathers, felt, beads, wire, paper, or bone into exquisitely crafted wearable formations. Her sculpturally conceived, tactile *Seed Forms and Tokens*, hand-built, painted, polished, and sometimes gold-leafed or bronze-cast, reflect her continuing fascination with GEOLOGY, metamorphosis, and inter-related forms. A unique figure in her adopted country, she has exhibited widely internationally and is represented in major collections in Ireland, the Netherlands, and America. [see CRAFTS AFTER 1945.] **Nicola Gordon Bowe**

Lane, Sir Hugh (1875–1915), art dealer, collector, and founder of the Municipal Gallery of Modern Art, Dublin. Born in Douglas, Cork, and brought up in Redruth, Cornwall. While still in his early twenties he established a successful fine art business in London. Following a visit to Ireland in 1901 his aunt, Lady AUGUSTA GREGORY, introduced him to the other founders of the LITERARY REVIVAL movement: W. B. YEATS, DOUGLAS HYDE, and EDWARD MARTYN. Lane set about encouraging a complementary movement in the visual arts, and in 1908 he established the Municipal Gallery of Modern Art (now the HUGH LANE MUNICIPAL GALLERY OF MODERN ART) in Dublin. In 1909 Lane was knighted.

In 1913 he removed to the National Gallery, London, his conditional gift of thirty-nine French paintings, as Dublin had failed to build a gallery to house the collection. In 1914 he was appointed director of the NATIONAL GALLERY OF IRELAND. The following year, while returning from New York, he was drowned on board the LUSITANIA, torpedoed by a German submarine off the coast of Co. Cork. Before leaving for New York he had written a codicil to his will of 1913, returning his French collection to the Dublin gallery; but this codicil had not been witnessed, and it was subsequently contested by London. In a unique agreement, the paintings are now shared between two institutions, the Hugh Lane Gallery, Dublin, and the National Gallery, London, on a five-year rotation. **Barbara Dawson**

Langan, Tom (c. 1932–), Gaelic footballer. Born in Co. Mayo. He had an athleticism that made him one of the most difficult players to oppose. A goal scorer of the highest calibre, he was renowned for his fielding skills and a 'dummy' that perplexed defenders. While he enjoyed a long career with Mayo, it was during the early 1950s that he gained a national reputation when the county won the all-Ireland championships of 1950 and 1951. **Donal Keenan**

Langton, Jim (1919–), hurler. Born in Co. Kilkenny. One of the great stylists of the game, he first came to prominence on the

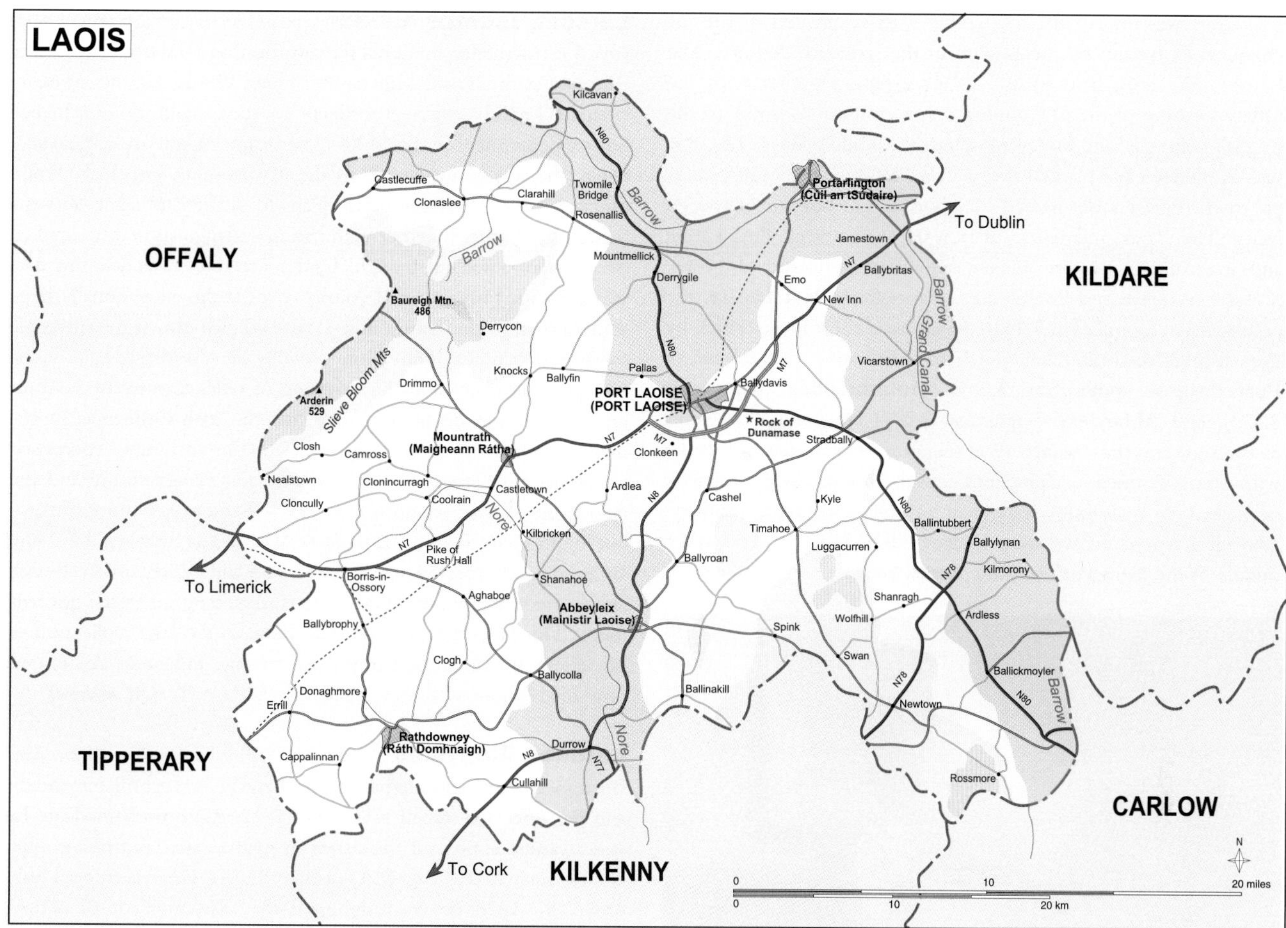

Kilkenny minor (under-18) teams that won the all-Ireland title in 1935 and 1936. Promoted to the senior team, he won the first of two all-Ireland senior medals in 1939, the second coming in 1947 when Kilkenny beat Cork in the final. **Donal Keenan**

Lanyon, Sir Charles (1813–1889), architect and engineer. Born in Eastbourne, Sussex; apprenticed to Jacob Owen, at first in Portsmouth and then in Dublin, following Owen's appointment to the BOARD OF WORKS. He was appointed county surveyor of Co. Kildare in 1834, transferring to Co. Antrim in 1836. He also established an extensive private practice in Belfast, being joined in partnership by W. H. LYNN in 1854 and by his own son John in 1860. Among his most important buildings in Belfast are the Palm House at Queen's College, the County Courthouse, the Prison, the Presbyterian College, and the Custom House and in Dublin the Campanile at Trinity College. He was president of the ROYAL INSTITUTE OF THE ARCHITECTS OF IRELAND and vice-president of the Royal Institute of British Architects, became Mayor of Belfast in 1862 and Conservative MP for Belfast in 1868, and was knighted in 1868. He ranks as one of the most important architects of his generation in Ireland. **Paul Larmour**

Laoide, Seosamh (1865–1939), scholar. Born in Dublin; educated at TCD. One of the founders of the GAELIC LEAGUE in 1893, he became joint treasurer. He was editor of *Irisleabhar na Gaedhilge*, 1899–1902, and general editor of Gaelic League publications, 1903–15, overseeing the production of some three hundred volumes. His pioneering *Post-Sheanchas* (1905, 1911) continues to underlie much of Ireland's bilingual administrative nomenclature. **Liam Mac Mathúna**

Laois, County (*Contae Laoise*)

Province:	LEINSTER
County town:	Port Laoise
Area:	1,719 km^2 (664 sq. miles)
Population (2002):	58,732
Features:	River BARROW
	River NORE
	Slieve Bloom Mountains
Of historical interest:	Aghaboe churches
	Emo Court
	ROCK OF DUNAMASE
	TIMAHOE round tower
Industry and products:	Agricultural machinery
	Coal-mining
	Dairy products
	FORESTRY
	MEAT
	Peat production
	Stone-cutting
	Sugarbeet
	WOOLLENS

Petula Martyn

County Laois is a county in the midlands, the only county in Ireland that does not touch a county that touches the sea. A comparatively wealthy agricultural landscape, apart from the Slieve Bloom Mountains, which straddle the Laois-Offaly border to the west, it specialises in grazing, with a considerable amount of cereal cultivation in the eastern parts extending into Co. Kildare.

Laois was one of the first counties to be created in the re-conquest of Ireland by the English in the sixteenth century. The lordship of Laois, held by the O'More sept, together with the Offaly lordship of the O'Connors, was a continuous threat to the English colony of the PALE throughout the Middle Ages. The area was confiscated and planted as Queen's County in 1556, its principal town (Port Laoise) named Maryborough in honour of Queen Mary. The Rock and Castle of DUNAMASE, between Port Laoise and Stradbally, is a historic ancient settlement site fortified by Gael, ANGLO-NORMAN, and English alike. Apart from **Port Laoise**, the county town (population 3,482), which has a courthouse (1812) by the distinguished architect Richard Morrison, the towns of **Portarlington** (population 3,263), **Mountmellick** (population 2,523), and **Abbeyleix** (population 2,374) are among the most picturesque in the county. Portarlington is a Huguenot town with some distinctive eighteenth-century houses; Mountmellick originated as a QUAKER settlement in the seventeenth century; Abbeyleix is an attractive estate village built by Lord de Vesci in the middle of the eighteenth century. **Patrick Duffy**

Larchet. *John F. Larchet, musician and composer. Traditional music was a source for many of his works, and as a teacher he was influential in developing a school of Irish composers'. [G. A. Duncan]*

Larchet, John F. (1884–1967), composer and teacher. Born in Dublin; educated at the CATHOLIC UNIVERSITY OF IRELAND and TCD. He also studied at the RIAM under MICHELE ESPOSITO and was appointed senior professor there in 1920. He was professor of music at University College, Dublin, 1921–58, and also held the position of director of music at the ABBEY THEATRE, 1907–34. Despite his influential position as the teacher of many of the twentieth-century Irish composers, his own works (which include compositions for orchestra, choir, and solo voice) are very slight. **John Page and Richard Pine**

Larcom, Thomas Aiskew (1801–1879), military officer, surveyor, cartographer, and civil servant. Born in Gosport, Hampshire; educated at the Royal Military Academy, Woolwich, one of many talented English engineer officers to serve with the Ordnance Survey department in the 1820s. After some experience of field surveying he was given charge of the department's principal Dublin office in 1828, receiving parish plans from the Ordnance Survey's field survey parties together with national triangulation data supplied by its trigonometrical branch. Under Larcom's direction this data was combined into printed county maps at the exceptionally large scale of 6 in. to the statute mile (1:10,560). He was also responsible for several technical innovations, notably the electrotyping of duplicate printing plates and the mapping of relief features by contour lines; and it was on his initiative that the Irish Ordnance Survey maps contributed to a number of important public purposes, including the CENSUS OF POPULATION and of agriculture and the delimiting of new administrative areas. Larcom left the Ordnance Survey in 1846 to join the BOARD OF WORKS. Between 1853 and 1868 he was Under-Secretary for Ireland and closely involved with almost every major issue that came to the attention of the government. This gives unique historical value to the large collection of his letters, memoranda, pamphlets, cuttings and other documents now held by the NATIONAL LIBRARY OF IRELAND. **J. H. Andrews**

Lardner, Dionysius (1793–1859), physicist and encylopaedist. Born in Dublin; educated at TCD, where he was a brilliant student and remained for fifteen years from 1812. As an undergraduate he was awarded almost all the prizes in mathematics and philosophy, and he graduated as BA, MA, LLB, and LLD. He also entered holy orders. In 1828 he was appointed the first professor of natural philosophy and astronomy at the newly founded University (College) of London. There he gave brilliant demonstration lectures but, after five years, he resigned to give himself over full time to the publication of his 133-volume *Cabinet Cyclopaedia*. While he wrote some of these himself, he persuaded many authors to contribute, including Sir Walter Scott and John Herschel. A flamboyant character and womaniser, he had an illegitimate son, the playwright DION BOUCICAULT. **William J. Davis**

Larkin, Delia (1878–1949), trade union activist. Born in Liverpool. She moved to Dublin, where by 1911 she was working in the labour movement alongside her brother, JAMES LARKIN. Editor of the 'Women Workers' column of the *Irish Worker*, in 1911 she became first general secretary of the IRISH WOMEN WORKERS' UNION. Elected to the Irish Trade Board in 1912, she was vigilant in opposition to sweated industries but capable of castigating women for their own failure to organise. Her relations with the trade union hierarchy were contentious. **Mary Jones**

Larkin, James (Jim) (1876–1947), labour leader. Born in Liverpool, of Irish parents; left school at the age of eleven to work at odd jobs and on the docks. In 1907 he came to Ireland as an agent of the National Union of Dock Labourers and in 1908 founded the IRISH TRANSPORT AND GENERAL WORKERS' UNION, enjoying spectacular success until the DUBLIN 1913 LOCK-OUT. He went to the United States in 1914, where he was involved in 1919 in founding the Communist Party of the United States, and was imprisoned for 'criminal anarchy' in 1920. Pardoned in 1923, he returned to Dublin and split the ITGWU in attempting to re-establish his dictatorial rule. He was leader of the breakaway Workers' Union of Ireland until his death and of the Irish Worker League (affiliated to the Communist

International), 1924–9. In 1932 he abandoned revolutionism and from 1936 was partially rehabilitated in the labour movement. He was a member of Dublin City Council, 1912, 1930–33, and from 1936, and was elected to Dáil Éireann in 1927, 1937, and 1943. He died following a fall on 30 January 1947. **Emmet O'Connor**

Larminie, William (c. 1849–1900), poet and folklorist. Born in Castlebar, Co. Mayo; educated at TCD. He worked for many years in the India Office. His English-language verse drew on the assonance-based prosody of Irish poetry, as in *Fand and Other Poems* (1892). In 1893 he published a volume of stories including material recorded in Donegal, Mayo and Galway, *West Irish Folk-Tales and Romances*. **Terence Brown**

Larmor, Joseph (1857–1942), mathematical physicist. Born in Magheragall, Co. Antrim; educated at QUB and the University of Cambridge. Successor to George Gabriel Stokes as Lucasian professor at the University of Cambridge, his book *Aether and Matter* (1900) represented the culmination of nineteenth-century classical physics, applied to the electron and the electro-magnetic field. Original contributions included the Larmor precession and the formula for power radiated by an accelerated charge. Knighted, he was also a fellow of the Royal Society. **Denis Weaire**

Larne (*Latharna*), Co. Antrim, an industrial town and ferry port offering roll-on/roll-off services to Scotland in competition with Belfast; population (1991) 17,575. The modern town dates from Scots settlement of the area in the late sixteenth and early seventeenth centuries, but a much earlier Norse town flourished here in the twelfth century. Though recorded as a borough in 1334, medieval Larne was little more than a village. During the PLANTATIONS the town was a point of entry for Scots settlers but, uniquely among Ulster's larger towns, was not incorporated as a borough at that time. Shipping continued to provide the town's *raison d'être*, and in the eighteenth century Larne became an important coal and cattle port. In the 1760s one of Ireland's earliest cotton mills was founded here. With the introduction of steamships in the 1820s Larne's import and export trade flourished; it was worth £77,000 a year by 1837. Its role as a ferry port was further enhanced by the construction of a rail link to Carrickfergus and Belfast in 1862. In 1914 the port was used by the UVF to land guns from the *Clyde Valley*. The modern town is architecturally undistinguished, and its visual amenity suffers considerably from the arterial roads linking the port. **Lindsay Proudfoot**

Larne gun-running (1914). At the end of March 1914, during the crisis surrounding the third HOME RULE Bill, Major Frederick Crawford loaded 216 tons of German, Italian, and Austrian rifles and ammunition on a steamer in Danish waters. Acting on behalf of the ULSTER UNIONIST COUNCIL, he transferred the weapons to a steamer, the *Clyde Valley*, off the Co. Wexford coast. Only twelve people knew for certain of the elaborate plan for landing and distributing the arms. On the night of 24/25 April, during a test mobilisation of the UVF, the arms were brought in at Larne, Co. Antrim, without interference, while the authorities searched a decoy vessel in Belfast Lough. Smaller consignments were landed at Bangor and Donaghadee. The guns were loaded onto cars, which sped throughout the night distributing them to prepared dumps all over Ulster—probably the first time that motor vehicles were used on a large scale for a military purpose. The CURRAGH MUTINY the previous month had made it clear that the British government could no longer depend on the regular army to quell rebellion in Ulster; this importing of German rifles now made such a rebellion a distinct possibility. [see HOWTH GUN-RUNNING.] **Jonathan Bardon**

Larne gun-running. *An Italian-made Vetterli bolt-action rifle, one of the 35,000 rifles landed at Larne for the UVF, 24/25 April 1914. [Courtesy Kilmainham Gaol Museum; photo: Denis Mortell]*

'Larnian', a name formerly given to the Irish MESOLITHIC PERIOD, from LARNE, Co. Antrim, site of an extensive area of post-glacial raised beach gravel containing battered and rolled remains of stone tools. From the 1860s onwards these gravels were the source for much of the research into what is now recognised as the Irish Mesolithic Period. **Peter Woodman**

La Rue, Danny, stage name of Daniel Carroll (1928–), female impersonator. Born in Cork, he moved to England as a child. A former chorus boy, after serving in the British navy he became a female impersonator in amateur 'drag shows', to become Britain's highest-paid entertainer in the 1960s. In 1966 he starred in *Come Spy With Me* in London; two years later, *Queen Passionella* at the Saville Theatre ran for six months, a record for a pantomime. He was voted Show Business Personality of 1969 by the Variety Club of Great Britain. His women were completely glamorous, but he always made a point of reminding audiences that it was a man under all the finery. **Stephen Dixon and Deirdre Falvey**

Last September, The (1929), a novel by ELIZABETH BOWEN. Bowen's second novel, it examines the personal and political transitions at Danielstown, the Naylors' BIG HOUSE, as garrison and Anglo-Irish society entertain each other uneasily during the WAR OF INDEPENDENCE. Lois Farquhar, the Naylors' nineteen-year-old niece, is a typical Bowen protagonist, orphaned and struggling against a code of manners to find her own emotional and sexual identity. The climax unites this struggle with the wider political crisis in the burning of Danielstown. One of only two Bowen novels set in Ireland, the author described it as being 'of all my books … nearest my heart.' It was made into a film, directed by Deborah Warner, in 2000. **Selina Guinness**

Latham, James (1696–1747), painter. Almost certainly a member of a Co. Tipperary landed family, though nothing is known of his immediate family or his education. His earliest known works, painted in the early years of the eighteenth century, are of Thomas Butler of Ballyricken and his brother, Archbishop Butler of Cashel. In 1724 Latham was in Antwerp, where he attended the art school for one term, travelling by way of Paris or London, as his work shows influences from both these cities. His style changed little after his return, when his manner was fully developed. He never signed his works, but enough were engraved for his distinctive style to be easily recognised. The finest Irish portrait painter of the first half of the eighteenth century, he had a solid, realistic manner, exquisite painting of lace and embroidery, and a fine appreciation of the character of his sitters. Among his best works are portraits of several members of the Cosby family of Stradbally, Co. Laois, Bishop BERKELEY, and Bishop Clayton and his wife, now in the NATIONAL GALLERY OF IRELAND. **Anne Crookshank**

La Tocnaye, Jacques-Louis de Bougrenet, Chevalier de (born c. 1763), soldier, traveller, and writer. Born an aristocrat in Brittany, he fled to England during the FRENCH REVOLUTION in 1792. Armed with letters of introduction, he embarked on a walking tour of England and Scotland and published a successful description of his travels in 1795. He began an Irish tour in May 1796, travelling light and frequently walking up to 30 miles (48 km) a day, his mode of travel ensuring that he had as much contact with the local people as he had with the nobility. The story of his extensive travels, published in 1797 in French and later in English as *Rambles through Ireland by a French Emigrant*, is a readable, witty and perceptive view of late-eighteenth-century Ireland. After a further tour in Norway and Sweden he returned to a more peaceful France to live on his estate in Brittany. **Michael Fewer**

La Touche, David Digges (1671–1745), textile manufacturer and banker. Born near Blois in Orléans; he joined the Huguenot cavalry in the Netherlands and fought in the army of WILLIAM III in Ireland. For long he was credited with introducing the weaving of poplin to Dublin; it is more likely that he introduced the manufacturing system. In this system men with capital owned a number of looms, which they rented to weavers; they then bought the woven fabric. **Mairead Dunlevy**

La Touche, William (1746–1802), banker. Born in London, son of DAVID DIGGES LA TOUCHE. His family was of Huguenot descent and its members had established themselves as cloth dealers and then bankers. After a period abroad he founded the Irish branch of the family bank and also built the family mansion in St Stephen's Green, Dublin. **Alan O'Day**

Laudabiliter, a Papal privilege issued by Pope Adrian IV (the Englishman Nicholas Breakspear) in 1155. It authorised HENRY II of England to undertake a conquest of Ireland to promote CHURCH REFORM. Henry took no action until the autumn of 1171, when he led a military expedition in the wake of his subjects' involvement in Ireland. *Laudabiliter* was then used to justify English intervention. [see ANGLO-NORMAN CONQUEST.] **Marie Therese Flanagan**

Lavelle, Patrick (1825–1886), priest and political agitator. Born in Mullagh, near Croagh Patrick, Co. Mayo; educated at ST PATRICK'S COLLEGE, Maynooth, and ordained to the priesthood in 1851. He spent four years in France before being forcibly ejected from the IRISH COLLEGE in Paris to become parish priest of Partry, Co. Mayo. There he championed the tenant cause by launching a well-publicised campaign against Dr Thomas Plunket for the better treatment of tenants on the estate. He preached at the funeral of the Young Irelander TERENCE BELLEW MCMANUS and acted as vice-president of the Brotherhood of Saint Patrick. In 1862 he lectured on 'the Catholic Doctrine of the Right of Revolution'. Following the Fenian rising he supported the HOME RULE MOVEMENT. He was appointed to Cong in 1869, where he continued his political agitation. **Ciarán O'Carroll**

Laverty, Maura, née Kelly (1907–1966), writer. Born in Co. Kildare; educated at Tullow, Co. Carlow. She worked as a governess in Madrid until 1928. *Never No More* (1942), highly praised by SEAN O'FAOLAIN, and *No More than Human* (1944) recount personal experiences in novel form. The television series *Tolka Row*, set in working-class Dublin, was based on her play *Liffey Lane*, itself based on her novel *Lift Up Your Gates* (1946). Her novels contain determined female characters but are often marred by unrealistic plot resolutions. Her distinctive narrative style and the use of local produce ensured the success of her cookery books. **Mary Thompson**

Lavery, Hazel, Lady, née Martyn (1880–1935), society hostess. Born in Chicago. In 1909 she became the second wife of the artist JOHN LAVERY. A noted beauty, she was active in London's political, artistic, and literary social scene and was an innovator of fashion. During negotiations for the ANGLO-IRISH TREATY (1921) her home was a centre for informal talks. She was a confidante of many, including MICHAEL COLLINS and KEVIN O'HIGGINS. She is best remembered as the model for the image of Hibernia on Irish Free State banknotes, which remained in use in the form of a watermark until 2001. **Sinéad McCoole**

Lavery, Sir John (1856–1941), painter. Born in Belfast; he began his career in Glasgow. During the 1880s he visited Paris and the artists' colony at Grez-sur-Loing, where he was influenced by the *plein-air* painter Bastien-Lepage. In 1888 he was commissioned to record the visit of VICTORIA to the Glasgow International Exhibition; the resulting studies launched his career as a society portraitist (see p. 664). He perfected the oil sketch as a means of planning his compositions, and during his frequent travels to north Africa, Switzerland, and France he evolved subtle colour harmonies that show the influence of Whistler. In 1909 he married Hazel Martyn of Chicago (LADY LAVERY); famous for her beauty and poise, she became Lavery's muse, and her social ease and popularity further enhanced his career. The Laverys closely followed political events in Ireland, and during the Treaty negotiations their friendship with both Winston Churchill and MICHAEL COLLINS played an important role. After Collins's death Lavery painted *Michael Collins, Love of Ireland*, showing the dead Collins (now in the Hugh Lane Municipal Gallery of Modern Art, Dublin). In 1927 he was commissioned to paint an idealised image of his wife as 'Cathleen Ni Houlihan', which appeared on banknotes from 1928 to 1975. **Anne Millar Stewart**

Lavin, Mary (1912–1996), novelist and short-story writer. Born in Walpole, Massachusetts, of Irish parents, moving to Ireland when she was a child, when she spent time in Athenry, Co. Galway; educated at UCD. Her first collection of stories, *Tales from Bective Bridge* (1942), was critically acclaimed; it was followed by many collections that established her as a skilled practitioner in a form that the Irish exploited with great panache in the twentieth century. Her use of the form was less obviously Irish than that of such writers as FRANK O'CONNOR, SEAN O'FAOLAIN, and LIAM O'FLAHERTY, being marked by the absence of colourful incident, characters, and dramatic dialogue. Her stories focus on the provincial lives of men and women in painfully difficult relationships. Her fundamental theme is endurance, with widowhood as one of its principal modes; moments of sweetness reward her character for an unconscious stoicism. Her prose style is unforced and achieves its effects by quiet, though studied, accumulation.

As well as collections of short stories she published two novels, *The House in Clewe Street* (1945) and *Mary O'Grady* (1950). Her *Collected Stories* appeared in three volumes in 1971. **Terence Brown**

law, branches of. Irish law is divided into a number of categories, based on three fundamental distinctions. The first distinction is between *public law*, involving the state and public bodies (including administrative law, criminal law, and constitutional law), and *private law*, involving private parties. The second distinction is between *criminal law*, where the law considers some action to be a CRIME (generally because the *mens rea* or mental state of the actor, combined with the *actus reus* or nature of the offending action, offends against society to the extent that the state feels obliged to intervene), and *civil law*, where the dispute remains in the domain of private parties. The third distinction is between *substantive law* (the law applied in a case) and *procedural law* (the law governing how cases operate, such as what evidence may be used and when).

Other branches of the law include jurisprudence (the study of law), administrative law, constitutional law, the law of evidence, criminal law and criminology, environmental and planning law, contract law, tort law, land law (including the ownership, leasing and disposition of property), family law (including ADOPTION law, separation law, divorce law, annulment law, succession law, and the law pertaining to children, as well as rules regarding the safety of parties, such as barring orders), business law (including company law, tax law, commercial law, partnership law, agency law, competition law, the law of restitution, and intellectual property law, comprising rules relating to patents, trade marks, commercial property, copyright, and related areas), employment law (including labour law and TRADE UNION law), and international law (including human rights law, EU law, conflicts of law or determination of jurisdictional rules, comparative law, the law of the sea, and the law of nations).

Common law. Also known as *case law* or 'judge-made law', common law is based on the doctrine of precedent, in that judgments made in one case by judges of the superior courts will create binding law for subsequent cases with materially similar facts. This system was introduced by the Normans in England, when travelling judges were permitted to resolve issues as they arose and in so doing to make law under royal seal. Systems of common law now operate in most countries where England has had some degree of domination, in contrast to countries in which a *civil code* operates, where the law is based on a written code and judges have no power to make law.

Constitutional law. Deriving from the CONSTITUTION OF IRELAND (1937) and previously the Constitution of the Irish Free State (1922), constitutional law is the primary law of the state. The Constitution of Ireland has three component parts. Firstly, the institutions of the state are set up in a tripartite separation of powers. Secondly, certain fundamental rights are listed, including a general rights clause in article 40.3, which has been interpreted as including unenumerated rights (including, among others, the right to marital privacy, bodily integrity, freedom from torture, fair procedures, and access to the courts), to be given form by the interpreting judge, and strong protection for the institution of the FAMILY. Finally, there are certain miscellaneous provisions notable in article 50 (the equivalent of article 77 of the Constitution of the Irish Free State), whereby specific provision is made that any law that was in force at the time

Lavery, John. Hazel in Black and Gold *(1916) by Sir John Lavery. Hazel, Lady Lavery was the subject of some of Lavery's greatest portraits. [Laing Art Gallery, Tyne and Wear Museums, by courtesy of Felix Rosentiel's Widow and Son Ltd, London, on behalf of the estate of Sir John Lavery]*

of the enactment of the Constitution will be carried over into Irish law, save to the extent that it is unconstitutional. As the Constitution is the supreme law of the state, any statute that is in violation of it may be reviewed and if found to be unconstitutional will be struck down. In 1996 the Constitution Review Group, appointed by the Government, produced a detailed report proposing what it felt were necessary changes to the Constitution.

Law of defamation. Defamation is the offence committed by publishing a false and damaging statement concerning another person without lawful justification, either in permanent form (*libel*) or transient form (*slander*). Defamation is a tort and on occasion also a crime. Defamation law seeks to balance the competing constitutional claims to freedom of expression and the right of a person to their good name. Well-known defamation actions in recent times include those taken by PROINSIAS DE ROSSA TD against the *Sunday Independent*, by Denis O'Brien against the *Daily Mirror*, and by Beverly Cooper-Flynn TD against RTÉ.

Law of equity. Historically a legal entity distinct from the COMMON LAW, the law of equity arose in the seventeenth century to deal with the increasing rigidity of the common law system, with the King of England affording authority to the Lord Chancellor to decide certain cases 'according to the justice and equity of the matter.' The number of such appeals was so great that the Chancellor's department developed into a separate court of law, known as the Court of Chancery. By the nineteenth century equity had developed into a separate body of rules, dealing with specific areas of law and specific forms of relief. Under the SUPREME COURT of Judicature Act (1875) and the Supreme Court of Judicature (Ireland) Act (1877) the common law and equity systems were merged, so that any court could apply either common law or equity, depending on which was more appropriate in the light of the facts of the case. At the present time equity, which is still more flexible and affords more discretion to judges than common law, covers such areas as trusts and wills and such reliefs as injunctions and specific performance.

European Union law. EU law is the law contained in the treaties establishing and regulating the EUROPEAN UNION, the regulations and directives of the Commission, Council, and European Parliament, and decisions of the European Court of Justice and Court of First Instance. All these forms of law are directly effective and binding in the legal system of member-states and are considered to be superior to national laws, including national constitutions. EU institutions can also create non-binding resolutions, opinions, and recommendations. **Neville Cox**

Lawless, Emily (1845–1913), writer. Born in Co. Kildare, a daughter of Lord Cloncurry and cousin of Sir HORACE PLUNKETT. She published novels, verse, history and biography, most notably *Hurrish* (1886), a novel that GLADSTONE felt explained the causes of Irish resistance to English law, and *Grania* (1892), her finest work, the tale of a young woman living on the ARAN ISLANDS. A unionist, she lamented and celebrated aspects of Ireland's historical struggle. She was a noted novelist and poet, though detached from the revival movement. She suffered ill health in later years and died in Gomshall, Surrey. **Robbie Meredith**

Lawless, Matthew (1837–1864), painter. Born in Dublin, son of a wealthy solicitor. The family moved to London in 1854, and he attended school near Bath. He began training under Francis Stephen Cary and James Matthew Leith and after attending Langham School completed his training with the Irish artist Henry O'Neill. An active career as an illustrator of periodicals and books followed. He exhibited narrative scenes at the Royal Academy, London, 1858–63. In Paris in 1860 he met the French artist Meissonier and was influenced by the detailed quality of his painting. *The Sick Call* (c. 1863), a finely executed painting with sad undertones, exhibited at the Royal Academy in 1863 and now in the NATIONAL GALLERY OF IRELAND, is the only known painting by Lawless. **Marie Bourke**

Lawless, William (1772–1824), French general. Born in Dublin; qualified as a surgeon and professor of anatomy at the RCSI. He entered the French service as a *chef de bataillon* in 1799 and served in a light infantry legion. In 1800 he was subjected to a mandatory retirement but in 1803 returned to the army and was appointed captain in the Irish Legion. He was decorated for bravery by Napoleon Bonaparte and eventually rose to regimental commander in 1812. During the Battle of Lowenberg (1813) he was wounded and lost a leg. He was retired for a second time in 1814. **David Kiely**

Law Library. Barristers in the Republic practise from a single chambers, known as the Law Library, in Church Street, Dublin. The requirement that barristers be members of the Law Library in order to practise was severely criticised by the report of the Fair Trade Commission in 1990 as being restrictive and anti-competitive.

In Northern Ireland barristers traditionally work out of the Bar Library in the Royal Courts of Justice, Chichester Street, Belfast. **Neville Cox**

Lawlor, John (c. 1820–1901), sculptor. Born in Dublin; trained at the Dublin Society Schools, and first exhibited at the RHA in 1844. Commissions followed his move to London in 1845, including statues for the new Houses of Parliament (1836–68) and the engineering group and plaques for the Albert Memorial (1863–72), and he exhibited regularly at the Royal Academy, 1848–79. A friend of JOHN HOGAN, he worked periodically in Ireland on public statues, including those of SARSFIELD in Limerick (1881) and Bishop Delany in Cork (1889). Lawlor's work has the Victorian mix of classicism and realism in costume, feature, and gesture. **Judith Hill**

Lawlor, Tom (1947–), photographer. In the early years of his career he travelled the world as a photo-journalist for the IRISH TIMES. His book *At the Gate* (1997), is a masterly collection of more than a hundred black-and-white photographs selected from productions at the GATE THEATRE, Dublin. He is known not just for his publications and exhibitions but as a commentator on photography for RTÉ Radio, and has an uncanny genius for capturing on film a theatrical scene that reveals a telling moment in a play. In *At the Gate* he immortalised some of the best-known actors from stage and screen. **John Minihan**

lay, medieval heroic verse composed in syllabic metres in four-line stanzas. Mostly they concern the exploits of FIONN MAC CUMHAILL and the Fianna, though one recounts DEIRDRE's lament for the Children of Uisneach. They were recited in Irish-speaking communities and, more frequently, in Gaelic Scotland into the twentieth century. In Ireland some eighteen examples of music survive, with only four recorded from modern oral performance. Generalisations about musical characteristics are consequently difficult, but a rhythmically free style of singing is implied, within a relatively narrow compass, quite different from the melodically based *amhrán*, resembling what is understood by 'chant'. [see AMHRÁIN SAOTHAIR.] **Lillis Ó Laoire**

Leabhar na hAiséirghe (The Book of Resurrection), a manuscript volume of twenty-five highly ornamented vellum pages, the life work of Art O'Murnaghan (1872–1954), who won a competition in 1922 to design an illustrated book commemorating the 1916 RISING and WAR OF INDEPENDENCE. Each page is unique, blending Celtic-revival motifs with art nouveau and oriental elements. In addition to allegorical and symbolic portrayals of aspects of the fight for freedom there are pages dedicated to saints, artists, clergy, patriots, and the provinces. Nine pages were produced by 1928 and a further sixteen between 1943 and 1951. Unfinished and unbound, the manuscript is now in the NATIONAL MUSEUM, Dublin. **Timothy O'Neill**

Leadbeater, Mary, née Shackleton (1758–1826), writer. Born in Ballitore, Co. Kildare. The only female student of Ballitore School, she married William Leadbeater in 1791. She was the mother of four children, worked as the village's first postmistress, directed a bonnet-making enterprise, and wrote for publication and reflection. She was an advocate of improvements in the condition of the poor and an opponent of slavery. Her publications include *Cottage Dialogues* (1811), *Cottage Biography* (c. 1816), and *The Leadbeater Papers* (1862), which contains the 'Annals of Ballitore'. [see SHACKLETON, ABRAHAM.] **Kevin O'Neill**

Leader, The (1900–71), a weekly newspaper first published by D. P. MORAN. Its most influential years were from its foundation to 1916. Its success was due to Moran's assertive writing style, its unapologetic and aggressive Catholicism, and its promotion of cultural and economic NATIONALISM. Its views, though strongly nationalist, were trenchantly critical of many national movements. SINN FÉIN (the 'green Hungarian band'), the LITERARY REVIVAL (GEORGE RUSSELL was dismissed as the 'hairy fairy'), the GAELIC LEAGUE, and the IRISH PARTY all felt the lash of the *Leader's* pen, and it produced one of the most negative reviews of SYNGE'S PLAYBOY OF THE WESTERN WORLD. It routinely exposed anti-Catholic discrimination practised by Protestant employers. Its association of Catholicism with nationalism was total, reflecting many of the prejudices and resentments of the nationalist lower middle class, its primary audience. **Fergal Tobin**

League of Nations, a precursor of the United Nations, established in Geneva in 1920 under the terms of the Treaty of Versailles to help prevent and resolve international disputes. Ireland joined in 1923—despite British opposition—and was elected to the Council of the League in 1930. ÉAMON DE VALERA was president of the Council, 1932, and president of the League's Assembly, 1938–9; the last Secretary-General, 1940–46, was the Irish diplomat SEÁN LESTER. The League, never robust, suffered significant defections in the 1930s—the United States had never been a member—and finally collapsed in 1946 following the cataclysm of the SECOND WORLD WAR. **Fergal Tobin**

Leamaneh Castle, Co. Clare, a very fine seventeenth-century fortified house attached to a narrow five-storey fifteenth-century tower at the east gable. It is a rectangular, three-storey gable-fronted house with attic, with a central doorway at ground level, very fine mullioned and transomed windows, and a bartisan on the south-west angle. The tower contains chambers and stairs. Leamaneh was the home of MAIRE RUA O'BRIEN in the seventeenth century, the subject of one of the earliest surviving Irish portraits. **David Sweetman**

Leap Castle, Co. Offaly, a modernised sixteenth-century three-storey TOWER-HOUSE with later Jacobean house and GEORGIAN wings, principal seat of the O'Carrolls of Ely. It was destroyed by fire in 1558 and rebuilt. A wood sample from the fine fireplace of the Jacobean house has been dated to c. 1571. **David Sweetman**

Learned families: see POETIC FAMILIES.

Lebor Gabála Érenn ('The Book of the Conquest of Ireland'; also called the Book of Invasions), an elaborate legendary account in prose and verse of the origins of Ireland and the Irish people, first written perhaps in the eleventh century. Its author drew on earlier material, much of it of Biblical inspiration; chief among his sources were a number of tenth and eleventh-century poetic compositions, some of which he incorporates unaltered in his complex origin-legend. Beginning with the creation of the world, he discusses the pedigrees and wanderings of the Gaídil, before describing the various settlers of Ireland down to the arrival of the Gaídil (including Cesair, granddaughter of Noah, Partholón, Nemed, the FIR BOLG, and TUATHA DÉ DANANN). The remainder of the work concerns itself with kings ruling in Ireland after its settlement by the Gaídil, descendants of Míl of Spain. Pre-Christian rulers are traced from Éremón, son of Míl, to Nath Í, while Christian monarchs from Láegaire mac Néill to the author's own time are listed. It was remarkably popular from the outset, as the existence of various medieval recensions of the narrative indicates. Moreover, its influence proved long-lived. While its traditions cannot be taken at face value, it provides a valuable insight into the intellectual and cultural milieu of its author and audience, as well as into the making of a national myth. [see GALL.] **Máire Ní Mhaonaigh**

Lebor na hUidre: see DUN COW, BOOK OF.

Le Brocquy, Louis (1916–) artist. Self-taught. Founder-member Irish Exhibition of Living Art, Dublin, 1940. Moved to London 1947. Represented Ireland, Venice Biennale 1956. Awarded Premio Acquisto Internationale. Included in historic exhibition Fifty Years of Modern Art, Brussels World Fair, 1958. Married artist ANNE MADDEN same year and moved to France. Important developments in the work comprise: Early works (1939–45) included *Girl in White* (Ulster Museum); Tinker series (1946–50) included *Tinkers Resting* (Tate Britain); Grey Period (1950–56) included *A Family* (National Gallery of Ireland); White Period (1956–64) included *Woman* (Tate Modern). Le Brocquy's painting underwent a profound change in 1964 when he encountered painted Polynesian human skulls in the Musée de l'Homme, Paris, kindling his interest in the Celtic head culture. He commenced a series of Ancestral Heads, including *Head of an Irish Martyr* (Smithsonian Institution, Washington) which, in due course, developed into images of great writers, JOYCE, YEATS, BECKETT, including *Image of Shakespeare* (Guggenheim, New York) whom the artist perceived as avatars of consciousness. In recent years, he has undertaken a major series entitled *Processions* and in 1996 has embarked on a large body of work entitled *Human Images*. The artist has designed notable series of tapestries, mostly woven at Aubusson, France, including *The Triumph of Cúchulainn* (National Gallery of Ireland, Millennium Wing). He has illustrated Beckett's valedictory book, *Stirrings Still* (1988); James Joyce's *Dubliners* (1986), and Thomas Kinsella's renowned translation of the *Táin* (1969), held to be the great Irish Livre d'Artiste of the twentieth century (see p. 1032). The artist has been honoured with retrospectives in Ireland, France, Japan, Belgium and the USA. He is represented in Public Collections worldwide. Conferred by President MARY ROBINSON with the title of Saoi, AOSDÁNA. Awarded

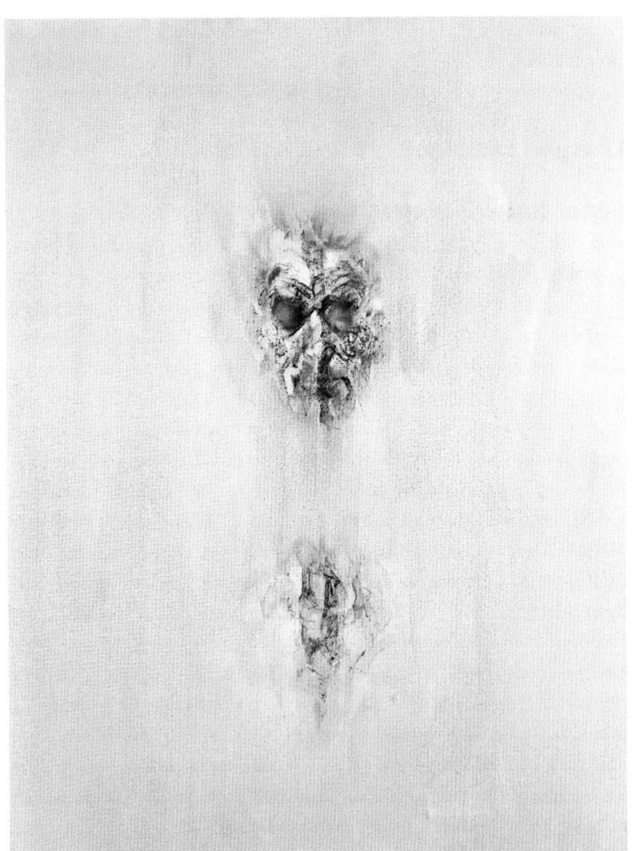

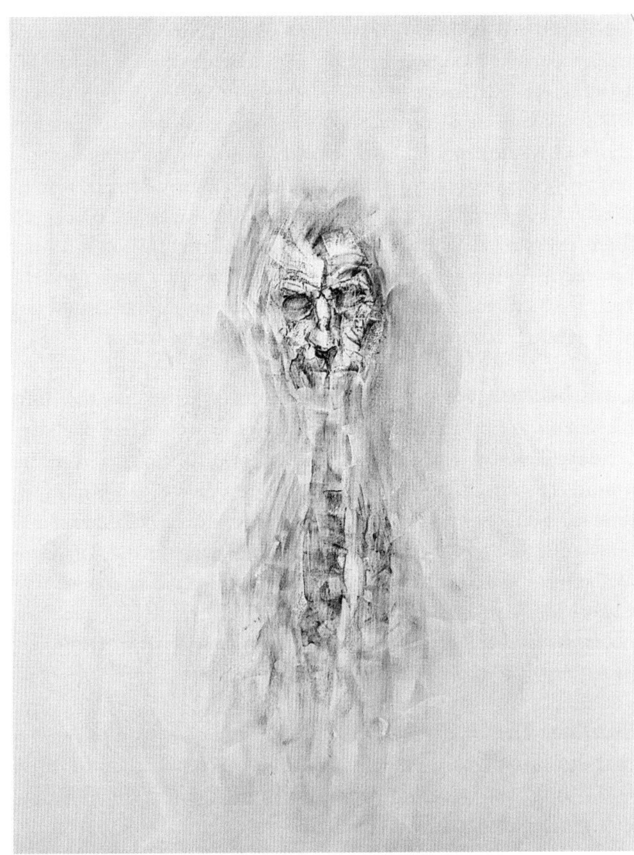

Le Brocquy. *Image of Samuel Beckett by Louis Le Brocquy (1994 (left) and 1995 (right)), two of a series of portraits by the artist featuring prominent writers, with a contemporary manipulation of the Celtic head image. [Louis Le Brocquy]*

honorary degrees by University of Dublin 1962, University College, Dublin 1988, Dublin City University 1999. Made Chevalier de la Légion d'Honneur, France 1975 and Officier des Arts et des Lettres, France 1999. Received first IMMA/Glen Dimplex award for a sustained contribution to the arts, Dublin 1998. Made Officier de l'Ordre de la Couronne Belge, 2001. **Dorothy Walker**

Lecky, W. E. H. [William Edward Hartpole] (1838–1903), historian. Born in Blackrock, Co. Dublin; educated at TCD. His major works include *Leaders of Public Opinion in Ireland* (1861, 1871, 1903), *The History of the Rise and Influence of the Spirit of Rationalism in Europe* (1865), *The History of European Morals from Augustus to Charlemagne* (1869), *History of England in the Eighteenth Century* (eight volumes, 1878–90), *History of Ireland in the Eighteenth Century* (five volumes, 1892), and *Democracy and Liberty* (1896). Though a unionist, his books on Irish history were seen as promoting the cause of Irish independence. **Dónal McCartney**

Ledwidge, Francis (1887–1917), poet. Born in Slane, Co. Meath; left school at thirteen to work as a farm labourer and later a road worker and union secretary. He began writing poetry in his youth and in 1912 sent some poems to LORD DUNSANY, who became his friend, adviser, and patron. Ledwidge's poetry approached the nation through the region, focusing on the myth, landscape, and history of Co. Meath. An early member of the IRISH VOLUNTEERS, he enlisted in the British army in October 1914 and was killed near Ypres on 31 July 1917. He saw one volume of poems, *Songs of the Fields* (1915), published before his death. **Robbie Meredith**

Leech, William John (1881–1968), painter. Born in Dublin, son of Henry Brougham Leech, regius professor in TRINITY COLLEGE and Registrar of Deeds; educated at St Columba's College, Rathfarnham, Co. Dublin, followed by a year in Switzerland. He entered the Metropolitan School of Art, Dublin, in 1899, the first year one of his paintings was exhibited at the ROYAL HIBERNIAN ACADEMY. In 1900 he transferred to the Academy Schools, where WALTER OSBORNE was his teacher. In 1901 he studied under Laurens at the Académie Julian, Paris, and in 1903 went to Concarneau, Brittany, with the New Zealand painter S. L. Thompson.

Leech painted genre paintings and harbour scenes in dark tones, employing calm horizontals and strong verticals; c. 1908 light and colour permeated his compositions of dramatic diagonals. In 1910 he left Dublin; he seldom returned to Ireland but exhibited annually at the RHA. He had successful exhibitions in England, and spent his time between London and the south of France. He became a virtual recluse after the break-up of his marriage; his wife is the subject of *The Convent Garden* and *The Sunshade*, now in the NATIONAL GALLERY OF IRELAND. The SECOND WORLD WAR ended his visits to France, and his subject matter and paint-handling reflected this change. He exhibited at the Dawson Gallery, Dublin, 1945, 1947, 1951, and 1953. **Denise Ferran**

Lee Guinness brothers, Sir Algernon (Algy) (1883–1954), and Kenelm (Bill) (1888–1937), racing drivers. Born in England, descendants of the Dublin brewery owner Sir Benjamin Lee Guinness. They were among the most successful early British racing drivers. Algy Guinness won many British sprints and international hill-climbs between 1904 and 1914. He finished second in the 1908 Isle of Man Tourist Trophy and returned to win it in 1922. Bill Guinness drove for the Sunbeam Grand Prix team and also won the 1914 Tourist Trophy race. A renowned engine-tuner, he founded the KLG spark plug company. He won the 1922 Grand Prix du

Voiturettes at Le Mans and set up a new land speed record of 215.25 km/h ($133\frac{3}{4}$ miles/h) in 1922 at Brooklands circuit. He won the 1924 Swiss Voiturette Grand Prix before retiring because of injuries suffered in the San Sebastián Grand Prix crash, which also killed his mechanic, Jack Barrett. This accident led to the banning of riding mechanics in Grand Prix racing. **Brendan Lynch**

Lee, River, together with the River BLACKWATER, the natural drainage for most of Co. Cork. The source is near Inchigeela, Co. Cork. Close to the source is Lough Allua, a large freshwater lake. The river flows eastwards in a limestone valley, with parallel sandstone ridges lying between the valleys of the Blackwater to the north and Bandon to the south, finally passing through Cork to its mouth in Cork Harbour. Near Macroom the Lee expands into the Gearagh, a crisscrossing network of streams and wooded islets, where there are hundreds of species of ferns, plants, and insects, many rare. The Gearagh was once more extensive, but much of it was flooded by the Carrigadrohid reservoir. The Lee hydro-electric scheme consists of two impoundments, the second one further downstream at Inishcarra. The creation of the reservoirs has changed the regime of the river and, in addition to generating electricity, has helped to control FLOODING in Cork. The city has a long history of floods, with serious damage caused in 1789, 1853, and 1916. Though the level of run-off for the 1916 flood has been exceeded in recent years, the reservoirs are used to store water and so reduce flows further downstream. **R. A. Charlton**

Lee Road Waterworks, Cork, first established in the 1760s, supplying the bulk of the city's water supply from the River Lee. The works used successively a water-wheel, water turbines, and STEAM ENGINES to provide the power to drive pumps that raised the water to elevated reservoirs. Large-scale improvements in the 1850s were designed by Sir JOHN BENSON. **Ronald Cox**

Leeson, Margaret, née Plunkett (1727–1797), brothel-keeper. Born in Co. Westmeath to a wealthy landed family. One of twenty children, she was abused by a brother and abandoned by several lovers before she turned to prostitution in Dublin. She took the name Leeson to gain some respectability after numerous liaisons with a Dublin merchant of that name. She became the most fashionable and wealthiest brothel-keeper in Ireland, winning the seal of social approval when the Duke of Rutland became a client; but after her retirement her collection of IOUs became worthless, and she was impoverished. Having written her memoirs to raise money, she later converted to Catholicism and repented. At the age of seventy, she was raped and contracted the sexually transmitted disease that killed her. **Ciarán Deane**

Le Fanu, J. Sheridan (1814–1873), writer. Born in Dublin but in 1826 moved to Abington, Co. Limerick, where his father had become rector; educated at TCD. Called to the bar, he was drawn instead to literature and journalism, eventually becoming editor and owner of various newspapers and periodicals. After the death of his wife in 1858 he secluded himself in his Dublin home at Merrion Square. He wrote reviews, political essays, ballads, poems, and historical novels but is remembered today for *Uncle Silas* (1864), a gothic suspense novel, and *In a Glass Darkly* (1872), a disturbing collection of supernaturally charged and psychologically credible short stories. **Richard Haslam**

legal profession. The legal profession in Ireland is divided into *barristers* and *solicitors*. Essentially, solicitors are involved in pre-trial work (though legislative developments have made it increasingly possible for solicitors to appear in court), while barristers work both in the preparation of documents for trial and also as advocates in front of the court. In most instances a person seeking legal assistance must consult a solicitor and is not allowed to directly consult a barrister. Barristers wear the traditional black gown; since 1995 the wearing of the traditional horsehair wig is optional.

Barristers train at the KING'S INNS, whereas solicitors train at the Law Society; in Northern Ireland both solicitors and barristers train at the Institute of Professional Legal Studies at Queen's University, Belfast. In both jurisdictions the period of training is accompanied by some degree of practical apprenticeship; for student barristers this apprenticeship, known as 'devilling', takes place after qualification. The Bar Council (in Northern Ireland the Bar Executive Council) is responsible for discipline within the bar, while the Law Society is responsible for discipline in the solicitors' profession. The ranks of the bar are divided into *junior counsel* and *senior counsel*. Appointment to the level of senior counsel (or the inner bar) is also known as 'taking silk' (as senior counsel barristers wear a silk gown). In Northern Ireland applications to take silk are made to the Lord Chancellor of Great Britain; if successful, the barrister is appointed as Queen's counsel. In 1990 the report of the Fair Trade Commission stopped short of recommending the fusion of the professions but did recommend substantial procedural reforms, many of which were brought into force by the Courts and Court Officers Act (1995).

The state is represented at solicitor level by the Chief State Solicitor (in Northern Ireland the Crown Solicitor, appointed by the

Le Fanu. Sheridan Le Fanu *(1916) by his son Brinsley Le Fanu; he excelled as a writer of mysterious and spine-chilling tales. [National Gallery of Ireland]*

Attorney-General) and at barrister level by the ATTORNEY-GENERAL. In Northern Ireland the two most powerful legal offices are those of the Lord Chancellor of Great Britain, a government minister and speaker of the House of Lords in its legislative capacity and its senior judge in its judicial capacity, who, acting through the Northern Ireland Courts Service, ensures the general efficiency and functioning of the legal order, and the Secretary of State for Northern Ireland, who is responsible for the content of the law. **Neville Cox**

legal system. The development of the Irish legal system has been inextricably linked with that of its English counterpart. From the middle of the twelfth century the English common law system replaced the existing system of BREHON LAW, though it was not until the time of the plantations in the early seventeenth century that such rules had practical application outside the PALE. The adoption of the common law system means that Ireland, unlike most countries, does not operate under a *civil code* but allows for law to be created by the judiciary. Equally, Ireland has a multi-sourced legal order and accepts the notion of parliamentary supremacy, prevalent in England since the sixteenth century.

In 1494 the passing of POYNINGS' LAW ensured that no parliament could be established in Ireland without the consent of the king's lieutenant in Ireland and hence that English law was supreme. The Irish Appeals Act (1783) repealed Poynings' Law and allowed for the creation of an independent Irish Parliament (often called GRATTAN'S PARLIAMENT). In 1800, as a response to the REBELLION OF 1798, the ACT OF UNION was enacted in 1801, making Ireland part of the United Kingdom, where it would remain until 1922, with legislation governing Ireland enacted by the British Parliament in London. Legal disputes were resolved by resident magistrates, with appeals to the English courts system.

The 1916 RISING led to the creation of the first DÁIL ÉIREANN in 1919 and the enactment of an embryonic constitution. The first Dáil rejected English law and reverted to the use of brehon law; as a result two legal systems—official and revolutionary—operated within the one jurisdiction. In 1921 the ANGLO-IRISH TREATY was signed, and the Government of Ireland Act (1920) came into force for Northern Ireland, providing for a devolved parliament and an independent court system, with an appeal to the English Court of Appeal and House of Lords. In 1922 the Constitution of the IRISH FREE STATE was enacted, and a court system very similar to the English model was created by the Courts of Justice Act (1924). Other influences on the modern legal system include membership of the United Nations, the Council of Europe, the EUROPEAN UNION, and the World Trade Organisation, as well as Roman Catholic teaching.

In Northern Ireland the Government of Ireland Act provided that, whereas the British Parliament in London would continue to exercise DIRECT RULE over the six counties, a local parliament would also exist with the right to enact legislation 'for the peace, order and good government of the province.' This parliament was suspended in 1972, with direct rule being imposed from London, because of what was perceived to be an emergency situation.

legal profession. *The Honourable Society of King's Inns, Henrietta Street, Dublin, the training school for barristers, founded in 1541. The central pedimental block with cupola (c. 1800) is by James Gandon, the wings (c. 1840) by Jacob Owen. [Irish Picture Library]*

Attempts were made in 1974 and 1982–6 to reform the Northern Ireland Parliament, with limited powers, but such attempts proved unsuccessful. Since 1998 and the coming into force of the BELFAST AGREEMENT a new NORTHERN IRELAND ASSEMBLY and Executive have been established, with democratically elected members representing all sections of society. Northern Ireland continues to elect seventeen members to the British Parliament and, as a single constituency, elects three members of the European Parliament. The British Parliament controls Northern Ireland through the Northern Ireland Office, headed by the Secretary of State for Northern Ireland. [see LAW, BRANCHES OF.] **Neville Cox**

legends can be described as localised narratives set in the recent, historical, or mythological past, such as the legend of Knockfierna which tells of the misfortune suffered by Carroll O'Daly, a Connacht man travelling through County Limerick, when he disbelieved and interfered with the fairies living in a castle on the mountain of Knockfierna.

Legends are based in reality and told and received as expressions of positive or negative beliefs. Legends are not identifiable by conventional linguistic markers, yet clues such as 'one time' or 'they used to say that …' situate the genre. These stories intend to educate rather than entertain people, arming them against dangers within their own cultural environments; they inform about important facts, extraordinary phenomena, or memorable events. Contemporary forms, known as modern legends, contain motifs linked to new technologies. As a narrative genre, legends function as an integral part of the folklore process. They cannot be totally dissociated from their earlier relatives, the fable, the folktale, and the myth while they also emerge from simpler narrative genres such as rumour and gossip. A continuum illustrated by the varsity of the modes of transmission and media representations of legends spans from the specifically oral and informal to the written, audio, and combined visual media. The work of Gearoid Ó Crualaoich on the legends of Cailleach Bhéarra, published in BÉALOIDEAS 1988 and 1995 may be referred to as illustrations of the Irish scholarly tradition on the subject. **Marie-Annick Desplanques**

legislative independence, the term used to define the constitutional changes approved in 1782 that empowered the Irish Parliament to make law for Ireland unconfined by legal restriction. It was brought into being by the repeal of the 1720 DECLARATORY ACT, which empowered the British Parliament to make law for Ireland and deemed the British House of Lords the final court of appeal in Irish law cases, and by the amendment of POYNINGS' LAW, which deprived both the British and Irish Privy Councils of the right to amend and to respite legislation emanating from the Irish Parliament; it was terminated by the ACT OF UNION. **James Kelly**

Leinster

Leinster	Cúige Laighean
Area:	1,963 km^2 (758 sq. miles)
Counties:	Carlow, Dublin, Kildare, Kilkenny, Laois, Longford, Louth, Meath, Offaly, Westmeath, Wexford, Wicklow
Major towns:	Bray, Drogheda, Dublin, Dundalk, Dún Laoghaire, Kilkenny
Rivers:	Barrow, Boyne, Liffey, Shannon
Highest point:	Lugnaquilla 924 m
Population 1991:	1,860,949
Population 2002:	2,105,449

Leinster (*Laighin*), a province encompassing the midlands and south-east. The name 'Leinster' consists of *Laighin* and Old Norse *stadir* (possibly meaning farm or homestead). The Laighin, with the Féni and the ULAIDH, were classified as the free races of Ireland in early law tracts. The territories of the Laighin and the Ulaidh met at the River Boyne, but both contracted by the seventh century under pressure from UÍ NÉILL. The derivation of the name Laighin itself is uncertain, despite its association with the word *láigen*, 'spear'; this etymology is more likely to explain the alternative name, Gaileoin, attributed to the Laighin in early texts. Traditions of the Laighin, including their origin legend, Orgain Denna Ríg, 'the destruction of Dind Ríg,' emphasise their racial difference from the rest of the people of Ireland. This belief may reflect the importance of tribes of British origin, including the Dumnonii (Domhnainn)—though the Laighin did not have a monopoly on such connections, which were common throughout prehistoric Ireland.

The province was divided into two parts, Laighean Tuathghabhair (north) and Laighean Deasghabhair (south), the determining geographical features for this division being the Wicklow and Blackstairs Mountains. The pass at Baltinglass, Co. Wicklow, marked a strategic corridor between north and south, which may explain the remarkable concentration of prehistoric HILL-FORTS in that region. Kings of Leinster occasionally used the title *rí diabul-Laigen*, 'King of double Leinster'. The primary prehistoric and medieval ceremonial sites in the province included Dún Ailinne (Knockaulin, Co. Kildare), Maistiu (Mullaghmast, Co. Kildare), Liamain (Newcastlelyons, Co. Dublin), Óenach Carmain (unidentified), Dind Ríg (unidentified, on the River BARROW), and Cnoc an Bhoga (Knockavoka, Co. Wexford). Its main churches included those of KILDARE, GLENDALOUGH, Ferns, and St Mullins. The kingship of Leinster up to the eighth century was held by the dynasties of Uí Garrchon, Uí Bairrche, Uí Máil, and Uí Failge. From the eighth to the twelfth centuries it was dominated by Uí Dúnlainge and Uí Cennselaig, both of whom claimed descent from a common ancestor, Cathaír Már. Among the most notable kings of Leinster during that period were Cerball mac Muirecáin (died 909), Diarmaid mac Máel na mBó (died 1072), and DERMOT MACMURROUGH (died 1171).

The Norse towns of Dublin and Wexford played an ever-increasing role in the province's economy, politics, and ecclesiastical affairs from the eleventh century, to the extent that the kings of Leinster probably ruled from Dublin. Dublin gained the archbishopric of the province in the twelfth century from the traditionally dominant churches of Glendalough and Kildare. On the death of Dermot MacMurrough the lordship of Leinster passed to Richard de Clare, alias Strongbow; on the latter's death in 1176 the Anglo-Norman lordship of Leinster fell to the Marshal family, Earls of Pembroke, who ruled the province up to the middle of the thirteenth century. During the later Middle Ages, Leinster was divided between the region around Dublin (the 'English PALE') and the territories dominated by powerful Irish and Anglo-Norman families. The present borders were drawn in the seventeenth century. **Edel Bhreathnach**

Geography. The easternmost of the provinces, with an area of 1,963 km^2 (758 sq. miles), comprising Cos. CARLOW, DUBLIN, KILDARE, KILKENNY, LAOIS, LONGFORD, LOUTH, MEATH, OFFALY, WESTMEATH, WEXFORD, and WICKLOW and with a population of 2,105,449 (2002), an increase of 180,747 (9.4 per cent) over the previous census (1996), equal to 53.7 per cent of the population of the Republic. The increase was greatest in Co. Kildare (21.5 per cent) and Co. Meath (22.1 per cent), reflecting the expansion of the Dublin metropolitan area, and least in Co. Longford (3.2 per cent).

Migration accounted for 87,406 of the increase, greatest in Cos. Kildare (17,932), Meath (17,802), and Dublin (13,257).

The present-day province incorporates the ancient territories of Midhe and Breagha, which roughly equate to Cos. Meath and Westmeath, respectively. Leinster came quickly under the control of the ANGLO-NORMANS following their landing in Co. Wexford in 1169. Dublin, taken by 1171, became the centre of the Lordship of Ireland, but by the middle of the fifteenth century the area of effective control had shrunk to that of the PALE, a region 50 km (30 miles) long by 30 km (20 miles) wide in Cos. Dublin, Meath, Louth, and Kildare, fortified by a double ditch of earth at the end of the fifteenth century. The present-day county structure took shape soon after the ANGLO-NORMAN CONQUEST, but the boundaries were not fixed until English rule was restored under ELIZABETH I. Co. Wicklow was the last county to be shired, in 1606.

Today the counties are grouped into four regional authorities, established in 1994, which sometimes cross provincial boundaries: Dublin, Mid-East (Kildare, Meath, Wicklow), Midland (Laois, Longford, Offaly, Westmeath), South-East (Carlow, Kilkenny, South Tipperary, Waterford, Wexford). **Joseph Brady**

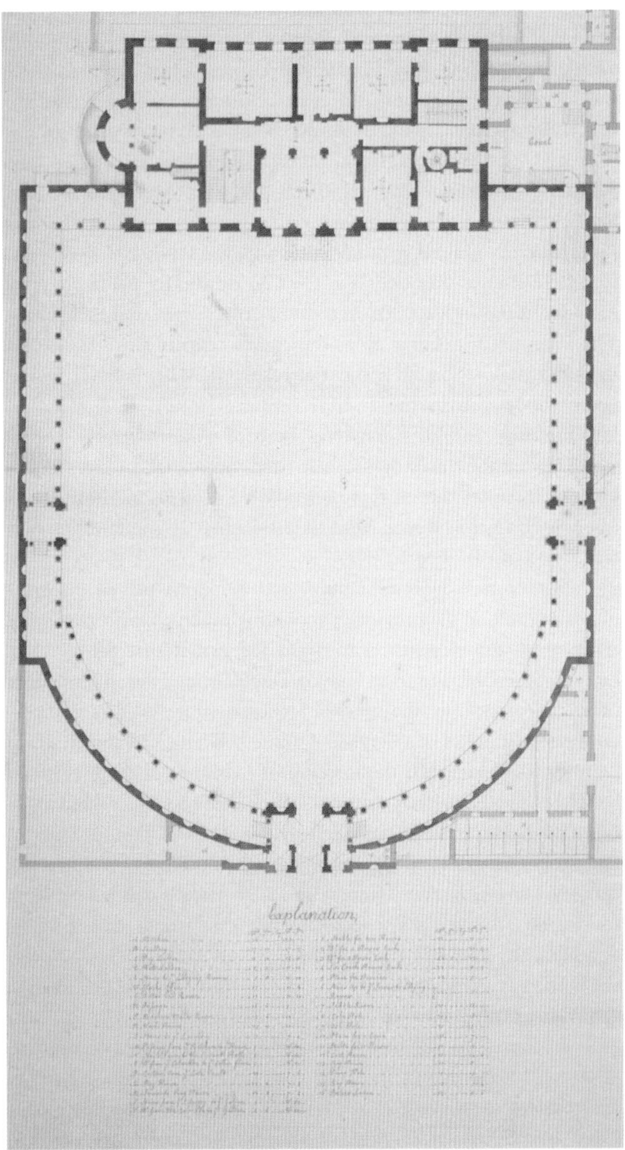

Leinster House. *A ground-floor plan of Kildare House (now Leinster House), Kildare Street, Dublin (1745), by the architect Richard Castle, built for the Earl of Kildare, showing his first, unexecuted, proposal for a colonnade forecourt. [Irish Architectural Archive]*

Leinster, the, a ship of the City of Dublin Steam Packet Company. Completed at Birkenhead dockyard in 1896, it was probably the most celebrated ship of this outstanding passenger and mail line. The first group of 'Provinces' steamers—paddlers in their first years—dated from 1860. Already this group of ships could claim to be the fastest short-sea passenger packets in the world. The 1896 group, with the same names, could make the same claim, and indeed at least one of this group claimed to be the fastest steamship in existence. The average crossing now took a few minutes less than three hours between Holyhead and Kingstown (Dún Laoghaire).

The *Leinster* was involved in the only serious accident that any of the 1896 'Provinces' group experienced before the FIRST WORLD WAR, but it had no serious casualties. In September 1902, in thick fog, it struck and sank the lightship maintained in those days on the KISH BANK, but it succeeded in rescuing all the crew. The war, with German submarines active before long in the IRISH SEA, greatly changed the situation. After many alarms, in October 1918, four weeks before the war ended, the submarine *U123* torpedoed and sank the *Leinster*, with the loss of at least 500 lives, including that of the master, Captain Birch. The *U123* was itself sunk, with all hands, on its way home. **John de Courcy Ireland**

Leinster, Book of. Known in the later Middle Ages as Lebor na Nuachongbála, this book takes its name from the church of Oughavall, near the castle of DUNAMASE, Co. Laois. When the ANGLO-NORMANS came to control the area the church was given by Meiler Fitz Henry to the priory of Great Connell near Naas, which would account for the addition of a copy of the Papal privilege LAUDABILITER granting Ireland to HENRY II of England. Similarly, the O'Mores' recovery of Dunamase is reflected in the fourteenth-century praise poems in English orthography by a cleric with only an oral knowledge of Irish. The manuscript, now in TRINITY COLLEGE Library, is the largest and latest of the three surviving compendia of Middle Irish learning dating from before the Anglo-Norman conquest. Today 197 leaves remain, but in the fourteenth century there were 250. The book begins with the LEBOR GABÁLA ÉRENN, the pseudo-history constructed under Biblical inspiration from Irish myths and legends, followed by king lists for Leinster, Ulster and Connacht, the story of TÁIN BÓ CÚAILGNE and other tales, DINNSEANCHAS or place-name lore, genealogies both secular and ecclesiastical, and the MARTYROLOGY OF TALLAGHT. The original compiler and scribe was Áed Ua Crimthainn, coarb or abbot of Terryglass, Co. Tipperary, working in the middle of the twelfth century with the help of other scribes. His monastery was destroyed by fire in 1164. Later in the century, when the manuscript had already fallen into disarray, another scholar-scribe completed it. In the seventeenth century it was in the hands of the O'Mores; it was then acquired by the Welsh scholar Edward Lhuyd in 1700 and returned to Ireland in 1786 by Sir John Sebright at the urging of his friend EDMUND BURKE. **William O'Sullivan**

Leinster House, Dublin. The largest of the eighteenth-century aristocratic town houses in the city, it was designed as Kildare House by RICHARD CASTLE in 1745 for the twenty-two-year-old James Fitzgerald, twentieth Earl of Kildare; after his elevation as first Duke of Leinster in 1766 it became known as Leinster House. The entrance façade, which influenced the design of the ROTUNDA HOSPITAL and other buildings (including, allegedly, the White

House, Washington DC, by the Dublin-born JAMES HOBAN), has a three-bay breakfront with pediment and was approached through a triumphal arch and forecourt, on the axis of Molesworth Street. The plainer garden front, which faces Leinster Lawn, has projecting end bays. The third duke sold Leinster House to the ROYAL DUBLIN SOCIETY in 1815, and around it was created the remarkable concentration of national cultural institutions: the NATURAL HISTORY MUSEUM (1856), NATIONAL GALLERY (1859), NATIONAL LIBRARY, and NATIONAL MUSEUM (1883) (see p. 947).

The Government of the Irish Free State bought Leinster House in 1924 as the seat of the Oireachtas; Seanad Éireann sits in the former picture gallery of Leinster House, and Dáil Éireann sits in what was the lecture theatre of the RDS, added in 1897. Despite such radical changes of ownership and use, Castle's interiors, with ceilings by the LAFRANCHINI, are substantially intact. Following Castle's death in 1751 work on the house was continued by Isaac Ware, JAMES WYATT, and Thomas Owen, and much of their contributions also survive. **Brian Lalor**

Leitch, Maurice (1933–), novelist. Born in Muckamore, Co. Antrim; educated in Belfast, where he trained as a teacher. He was employed by the BBC as a producer in Belfast and in London, where he now lives. *The Liberty Lad* (1965) inaugurated a career in which he has cast an acerbic eye on the sectarian social order of Northern Ireland. *Silver's City* (1981), which won the Whitbread Prize for Fiction, deals with paramilitary activity in Belfast, while *Gilchrist* (1994) addresses evangelical religion as a force in the Ulster Protestant psyche. *The Smoke King* (1998), set during the SECOND WORLD WAR, mixes anti-black racism with the customary sectarian brew in a typically dark imagining. **Terence Brown**

Leitrim, County (*Contae Liatroma*)

Province:	CONNACHT
County town:	Carrick-on-Shannon
Area:	1,525 km^2 (591 sq. miles)
Population (2002):	25,815
Features:	Lough Gill
	Lough Melvin
	RIVER SHANNON
	Slieve Anierin
	Truskmore Hills
Of historical interest:	Creevelea Abbey
	Parke's Castle
Industry and products:	Clothing, electrical and metal goods, food and timber products
	Coal
	Iron
	Lead
	POTATOES
	Pottery

Petula Martyn

County Leitrim, bordered by Cos. Sligo, Donegal, Fermanagh, Cavan, Roscommon, and Longford, is unique in having experienced a continuous decline in population since 1841; it has the smallest population of any county. Limestone plateaus dominate in the north and poorly drained rolling DRUMLIN topography in the south. Farms are small—on average 18.8 ha (46 acres) in 1991—and livestock production consists in the main of suckler cows and sheep in the north and beef cattle in the south. In the south, Lough Allen and a network of smaller lakes are linked to LOUGH ERNE by the

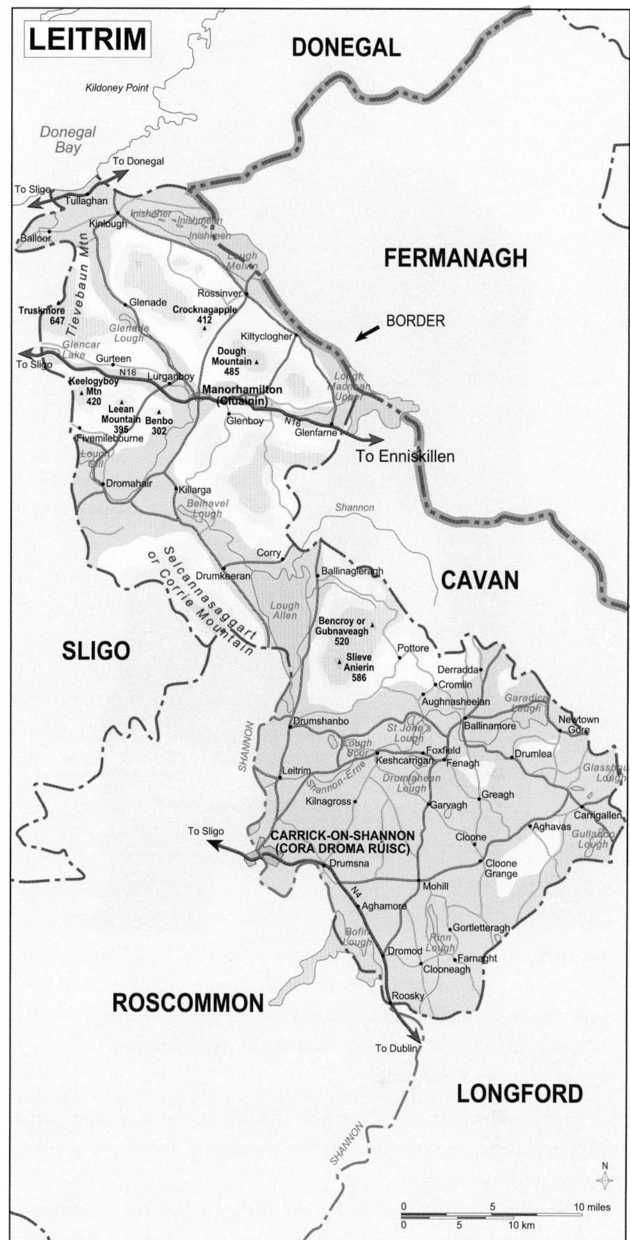

BALLINAMORE AND BALLYCONNELL CANAL. Carrick-on-Shannon, the county town, has a number of small and medium-sized industries and is an important centre for boat hire. There is a wood-processing plant on the River Shannon near Jamestown. **Mary E. Cawley**

Leixlip (*Léim an Bhradáin*), Co. Kildare, a town on the banks of the River LIFFEY 16 km (10 miles) from Dublin; population (2002) 15,143. It has one of the few NORSE PLACE-NAMES to be found inland in Ireland (*Lax-Hlaup*, 'salmon leap'). In the tenth century Leixlip was on the western boundary of the Scandinavian kingdom of Dublin; in the late twelfth century the lands were granted to Adam de Hereford, one of STRONGBOW's knights, whose castle was a stronghold of the PALE. Above the castle was the Salmon Leap, where the river cascaded down a limestone ledge to form an attractive waterfall. This area of the river was transformed by a hydro-electric power scheme (1946–9), the dam forming a reservoir of 600 million litres (160 million gallons). The river powered early industries, including an iron mill (from 1732), Dixon's LINEN and cotton-printing factory, and the brewery founded in 1752 by

Lemass. *Seán Lemass (left) and Commandant Patrick O'Brien during the occupation of the Four Courts in 1922. Lemass played a crucial role in the establishment of Fianna Fáil and succeeded Éamon de Valera as Taoiseach in 1959. [Courtesy of Kilmainham Gaol Museum; O'Brien/Cooney Collection]*

Richard Guinness, father of Arthur GUINNESS. An aqueduct carries the Royal Canal over the Rye Water, while the town is now served by two railway stations.

Now part of the greater Dublin area, Leixlip has experienced rapid growth both from its role as a dormitory suburb and from the employment offered locally by information technology companies. **Ruth McManus**

Lemass, John Francis (Seán) (1899–1971), revolutionary and politician. Born in Killiney, Co. Dublin; educated at O'Connell Schools and Ross's College. Lemass, who participated in the 1916 RISING as a schoolboy, was one of the youngest of the revolutionary generation and later served to bridge the gap between that generation and modern Ireland. Anti-Treaty in the CIVIL WAR, he later played a crucial role in the establishment and organising of FIANNA FÁIL, acting as one of its joint secretaries for many years, particularly when the party was in opposition. First elected to Dáil Éireann in 1927, he served as a formidable member of all DE VALERA's Governments, particularly as Minister for Industry and Commerce. During the Second World War his skills were employed to particular effect in his role as Minister for Supplies. Though at first he supported Fianna Fáil's somewhat isolationist ECONOMIC POLICY, he came to the conclusion soon after the war that Ireland's economic future lay in a closer alignment with the economies of neighbouring countries and gradually brought his party around to a more outward-looking stance. He was TÁNAISTE in all Fianna Fáil Governments after 1945. His period as TAOISEACH (1959–66), though delayed by de Valera's reluctance to retire, was marked by an orientation towards business, an enthusiastic endorsement of Keynesian economic planning, economic growth, social liberalisation, and a decisive option for membership of the EEC. He also pioneered a new openness to Northern Ireland, in contrast to the somewhat sterile irredentism of his predecessors. This was marked most significantly by his agreement to meet the Northern Prime Minister, TERENCE O'NEILL, in January 1965. After his retirement he played a modest but influential role in the all-party committee on the Constitution, whose discussions presaged many of the constitutional changes of the 1970s, 80s, and 90s. **John Horgan**

Lenihan, Dónal (1959–), rugby footballer. Born in Cork. He won fifty-two caps at lock between 1981 and 1992. He toured with the British Lions in New Zealand in 1983 and Australia in 1989, when he captained the undefeated mid-week team, and earlier captained the British Lions in the match marking the Irish Rugby Board centenary in 1986. Later he was manager of the Ireland A team, a national selector from 1995/6 to 1998/9, and national team manager until 2000; he was appointed manager of the British Lions team in Australia in 2001. **Karl Johnston**

Lenihan, Tom (1905–1990), traditional singer. Born in Milltown Malbay, Co. Clare. His home was a focus from the nineteenth century for musicians, such as the blind piper Garret Barry; his neighbours MARTIN CREHAN and WILLIE CLANCY frequently played under his thatch. His large repertoire of songs in English was recorded by many, including the BBC, the Department of Irish Folklore (UCD), and Topic Records. His biography and much of his repertoire were published by TOM MUNNELLY as *The Mount Callan Garland* (1994). **Tom Munnelly**

Lennon, Charlie (1938–), traditional musician. Born in Kiltyclogher, Co. Leitrim. A renowned fiddler, PIANO accompanist, and composer of TRADITIONAL MUSIC, he achieved early fame as a fiddle-player with the Liverpool CÉILÍ BAND in the 1960s. He has been in constant demand as an accompanist, with more than twenty-five piano recordings to his credit; but his widest influence has been through his compositions, published as *Musical Memories*. He is a master of the fiddling repertoire of the north Connacht region, his tunes being especially suited to the bowing and phrasing styles of that district. His fiddle music has been extensively recorded; he also founded a recording studio at Spiddle, Co. Galway. **Martin Dowling**

Lennon, Ciarán (1947–), painter. Born in Dublin; trained at the National College of Art and Design, graduated as a teacher and later graduated from the Painting School. He worked as a graphic artist in RTÉ, 1968–76. He developed a particularly rigorous form of abstract painting from the early 1970s, evolving from folded canvas, folded pencil drawings, and folded lithographs, and is especially gifted in the graphic skills of drawing, etching, and lithography. His large-scale paintings have been shown throughout Ireland, including the National Gallery of Ireland, and in London and Copenhagen and are included in the collections of the principal Irish galleries. He is a member of AOSDÁNA. **Dorothy Walker**

Lennox, Emily, Duchess of Leinster (1731–1814). Born in London, the second of five daughters of the Duke of Richmond, one of whom, Louisa, married Tom Conolly of CASTLETOWN, Co. Kildare.

Following the death in 1773 of her first husband, James Fitzgerald, Duke of Leinster, she married William Ogilvie, her children's tutor. She was charming, extravagant, and an admirer of Rousseau, and her Francophilia and radical political views were inherited by her favourite son, LORD EDWARD FITZGERALD. **Rosemary Raughter**

Leonard, Hugh, pseudonym of John Keyes Byrne (1926–), dramatist and writer. Born in Dublin, brought up in Dalkey by adoptive parents, and worked as a clerk in the Land Commission for fourteen years. He moved to Manchester to join Granada Television after the success of his comedy *Madigan's Lock* at the ABBEY THEATRE in 1958. His long association with the Dublin Theatre Festival—where seventeen of his plays were performed and of which he became programme director in 1978—dates from 1962, when *Stephen D*, his acclaimed adaptation of JOYCE's A PORTRAIT OF THE ARTIST AS A YOUNG MAN, earned him a London production. A skilled adapter of literary works for television and a prolific dramatist with a talent for comedy, he is often underrated by critics who suspect him of yielding to facility, writing well-crafted, entertaining but ultimately superficial plays. He is well known for his satirical pieces on contemporary Ireland, such as *The Patrick Pearse Motel* (1971); but his reputation and popularity rest chiefly on the largely autobiographical and compassionate DA (1973). *A Life* (1980) was a slightly less successful attempt at mining the same vein. He served as literary editor of the Abbey Theatre, 1977–8, and has also published two engaging autobiographical volumes, *Home Before Night* (1979) and *Out After Dark* (1989). He came back to the Abbey in 1992 with *Moving*, a comedy about the new affluent Ireland, and again in 1999 with the more lyrical *Love in the Title*. **Martine Pelletier**

leprechaun (*leipreachán*). While known in medieval Irish literature, the leprechaun of recent oral tradition is a male supernatural being, usually a shoemaker and the possessor of great wealth. Despite popularising representations, the leprechaun was an empirical being, believed in and sometimes the subject of first-hand experiences. A number of such narratives are known, in addition to more stereotyped legends, usually hinging on the leprechaun's escape from his captor through trickery. The leprechaun is linked to wider traditions both of household guardian spirits and of underworld spirits, whose abode in the earth connects them with agricultural fertility and mineral wealth (see p. 256). **Diarmuid Ó Giolláin**

lesbianism. Early Irish writing provides many temptations for lesbian-spotting according to how we might characterise a contemporary lesbian: there are many female characters who might fit into our modern mould of the lesbian if we understand the lesbian to be resistant to MARRIAGE or sex with men, to subvert gender roles, and to have intense passionate relationships with women. The hagiographies of St BRIGID recount that her resistance to marriage was so strong that she plucked out her eye rather than marry her betrothed. She was a bishop rather than a mere abbess and is traditionally depicted in male dress with a CROZIER. She had a beloved bed-warmer, Darlughdacha, whom she forced to walk in shoes filled with hot coals when she saw her look admiringly at a passing soldier. Enjoyable though this vision of a lesbian St Brigid might be, the scribes who recounted these stories understood them to reflect her closeness to God, the male honour of a bishopric underlining the fact that she had attained the masculine virtues necessary for salvation.

The early Irish custom and elevated status of same-sex 'bed-warmers' underlines the differences between the sexual mores of that age and today. It is difficult for us to discuss homosexuality without a context of homophobia; and early Ireland is remarkably free of homophobia. The BREHON LAWS were not concerned with homosexual relations unless they contravened the strict hierarchies of class boundaries: for example, an aristocrat having sex with a servant could be grounds for divorce.

Lennox. Emily Lennox, Duchess of Leinster, *pastel by Hugh Douglas Hamilton. Her son, Lord Edward Fitzgerald, one of the leaders of the United Irishmen, inherited his radical political views from his mother. [National Gallery of Ireland]*

From pre-modern to early modern. The Church Penitentials of Ireland, compiled in the early Middle Ages, do condemn sex between women, though the penance prescribed is less severe than that for men who have sex with men. However, the penance is increased if a phallic substitute is used. The condemnation of special friendships between nuns and the ensuing lusts these friendships engender came to Ireland from medieval Europe but does not seem to have been cause for concern to Irish churchmen as it was for their colleagues on the Continent. Witch-hunts and witch-burning had a devastating toll throughout Europe in the Middle Ages. Most of the victims were unmarried or widows, and many of the women accused of being witches were also accused of promiscuity and of having sex with women.

The mania for witch-hunts was remarkably absent in Ireland, with only two cases known: one, ALICE KYTELER and her maid Petronilla, in Kilkenny in 1324 and the second in Youghal in 1661. Central to the latter, at the trial of Florence Newton was the accusation that she had 'violently' kissed a woman called Mary at a well and bewitched her. The records end with the torture of Florence Newton.

Women who dressed and passed as men were an ever-present phenomenon throughout European history, and perhaps still are where the sexes are severely segregated. A number of Irish women passed as men and had sexual relationships with women. Most notable perhaps is ANNE BONNY, born in seventeenth-century Kinsale: she disguised herself as a man to become a pirate and met another passing woman, Mary Read; together they were notorious not only as pirates but as lovers.

Modern age. William King's mock-epic poem *The Toast* (1736) was a revenge on the widowed Duchess of Newburgh, Lady Frances Brudenell, written after he had lost a court case that argued that she owed him thousands of pounds. Throughout four books he depicts the Duchess as a promiscuous bisexual witch, in passionate love with Lady Allen and ruling over a circle of 'Tribades or Lesbians' in Dublin. The poem went into four editions, remaining popular for decades. King made a particular point of deriding what he saw as Brudenell's pretence of a chaste romantic friendship with Lady Allen as a cover for the 'practice [of] Lesbian Loves.'

Lady ELEANOR BUTLER and her kinswoman Sarah Ponsonby fell in love in eighteenth-century Kilkenny. They defied family pressure to marry and on their second attempt, and with the valiant assistance of their maid, Mary Carryll, they eloped to Wales in 1778.

Nineteenth-century Anglo-Ireland was fascinated with the literary depictions of lesbians. MARIA EDGEWORTH's *Belinda* introduces the redoubtable Harriet Freake, who favoured dressing in men's clothes, leading Lady Delacour astray with night-time adventures. SHERIDAN LE FANU's Carmilla is one of the first literary depictions of a vampire; here she is a typical nineteenth-century literary creation of monstrous women, in that she is a lesbian. GEORGE MOORE's *A Drama in Muslin* gives us another creepy lesbian in the character of Cecilia, a hunchback.

Biographical studies of actual nineteenth-century Irish lesbians remain insubstantial, though there are a number of likely candidates, such as the philanthropist and feminist FRANCES POWER COBBE. Studies of the writers EDITH SOMERVILLE and VIOLET MARTIN do make varying attempts to come to terms with their avowed devotion.

Twentieth century to the present day. Twentieth-century Ireland owes much to lesbians, particularly to a network of lesbians living in Dublin, many of whom met through their involvement with the suffrage movement and many of whom later became actively involved in the national independence movement, in TRADE UNIONS, LOCAL GOVERNMENT, and issues such as health care and social housing. Notable among these were DR KATHLEEN LYNN and her partner Madeleine ffrench-Mullen, founders of St Ultan's Children's Hospital; the nurse Elizabeth O'Farell and her partner Julia Grenan, buried together in the Republican plot in Glasnevin Cemetery, Dublin; the bisexual Abbey actor HELENA MOLONEY; LOUIE BENNETT, twice president of the IRISH TRADES UNION CONGRESS, and her inspiring partner, HELEN CHENEVIX. EVA GORE-BOOTH, a poet and sister of CONSTANCE MARKIEVICZ, did not live in Ireland, though she did visit and was in close contact through her sister with a number of the Dublin lesbians. She lived in Manchester with her partner Esther Roper.

Paris in the early twentieth century was a mecca for wealthy lesbians and bisexual women, especially those interested in art; indeed European modernism is indebted to the money and talents of such women, including Sylvia Beach, the publisher of ULYSSES. OSCAR WILDE's niece, Dolly Wilde, was part of this set, as was the decorative artist, designer, and architect EILEEN GRAY, one of modernism's most innovative and original artists.

Ireland after independence was not an easy place for women who did not conform to the narrowly defined role of wife and mother. However, the actor Marie Conmee and her partner Marie Brady were a notorious couple in Dublin in those decades, while the writer KATE O'BRIEN also kept the scandalmongers active.

According to oral histories, by the 1960s there were certain bars in Dublin and Belfast where lesbians met, generally on Saturday afternoons; but lesbian activism in Ireland had no visible presence until the 1970s, and even this was limited to Dublin and Belfast. The main influences on lesbian activism are still FEMINISM, socialism, and gay liberation and CIVIL RIGHTS MOVEMENTS. Though thousands walk in annual Lesbian and Gay Pride parades, and there are now hard-won social spaces, community services (largely supplied by volunteers), and annual cultural events to be found throughout Ireland, most lesbians find it necessary to be discreet, and many find it necessary to be secretive, about their love lives. [see BARRY, JAMES MIRANDA STEWART; HOMOSEXUALITY.] **Katherine O'Donnell**

Leslie, Sir Shane (1885–1971), writer. A member of a prominent Co. Monaghan landed family, he converted to Catholicism in 1908 and stood for Parliament as a nationalist in 1910. He wrote extensively on Irish and Catholic matters, mostly for English audiences, including a history of the Lough Derg pilgrimage site (which his family owned for several generations) and a study of SWIFT. His novel *Doomsland* (1926), a story of aristocratic decay loosely based on his own family, shows a morbid streak, also expressed in his fondness for ghost stories. He wrote several volumes of recollections. **Patrick Maume**

Lester, Seán (1888–1959), diplomat. Born in Carrickfergus, Co. Antrim; educated at Methodist College, Belfast. He joined the new Department of External Affairs on the formation of the Irish Free State in 1922. He was Irish representative at Geneva, 1929, and League of Nations high commissioner at Danzig (now Gdańsk, Poland), 1936, where he protested vigorously against the Nazis' persecution of Jews. He was the last Secretary-General of the League, 1940–46; isolated and overwhelmed by the war, he oversaw the winding up of the League following the international adoption of the United Nations charter. **Fergal Tobin**

Lett, Anita, née Studdy (1872–1940), founder of the Association of United Irishwomen, which later became the IRISH COUNTRY-WOMEN'S ASSOCIATION. Born in Devon, she moved to Co. Wexford in 1890 as a nurse to Captain David Beatty, whom she later married. Widowed in 1904, she married Harold Lett, a farmer of Enniscorthy. With the support of HORACE PLUNKETT, and inspired by the thoughts of GEORGE RUSSELL when he advocated grass-roots social development by rural communities, she founded the association in 1910 at Ballindara, Co. Wexford. Its aims were to aid the 'evolution of a healthy and progressive community life,' by providing education to rural women in matters of health care, child-rearing, horticulture, and craft skills. She resigned as president in 1912, ostensibly because a broken leg prevented her attending meetings, but it is thought that the organisation had outgrown her. She continued to be active in rural life, forming the Slaney Weavers in 1928. [see COUNTRY SHOP, THE; GAHAN, MURIEL.] **Alison Walsh**

letter-forms and handwriting. The scripts available in the Roman world in St PATRICK's time were *uncial* (a formal rounded script) and *half-uncial* (less formal, with some different letter-forms), both used for books, and the new Roman *cursive*, an informal script for everyday purposes. There is no evidence for the use of uncial in Ireland, but half-uncial of the pre-sixth-century canonical type appears in the CODEX USSERIANUS PRIMUS and in the wax tablets from Springmount, Co. Antrim. At some point in the later sixth century the Irish invented a new script, now called *insular majuscule* or *insular half-uncial*. It includes features from both uncial and half-uncial but is closer to the latter and was clearly intended primarily for formal liturgical books. Like uncial, it is rounded and ribbon-like, with reduced verticals and with some uncial letter-forms as alternatives. The most striking and abiding feature, however, is the use of strong triangular serifs on the verticals. The oldest surviving book in the new style is probably the CATHACH, and the script can be seen to develop through such manuscripts as the Bobbio Drosius, the Book of DURROW, the Durham GOSPELS, and the Book of KELLS.

When written rapidly, as in the Isidore fragment from Sankt Gallen, one can see how this bred out of itself another new script, the *insular minuscule*. Less rounded, this could be written rapidly, and it became the everyday Irish script, still in use in the twentieth century. The explosion of learning in seventh-century Ireland rendered such a script necessary for the production of multiple copies of books. However, even in its earliest days it was already being adapted for formal purposes, to produce such a splendid monument as the Echternach Gospels. While at first there was a considerable variety of minuscule in use in Ireland, by the eleventh century a standard, probably based on Armagh's dominance in learning, had been established. After the ANGLO-NORMAN CONQUEST, varieties of English script were adopted for writing Latin and at first also for Irish; but as vernacular writing passed from the clergy to the learned families, Irish script came back into use. From the fourteenth century, however, scribes modelled their script so closely on the old manuscripts they were copying that there is an absence of the development by which such hands might be dated. **William O'Sullivan**

Letterkenny (*Leitir Ceanainn*), Co. Donegal, a town on a straggling hillside site on the north bank of the River Swilly at the head of LOUGH SWILLY; population (2002) 8,109. Of seventeenth-century Plantation origin, Letterkenny is the cathedral town of the Catholic diocese of Raphoe and a regional market and service centre. In the 1980s and 90s it attracted significant foreign investment, though by 1999 this was in some difficulty. Earlier problems in developing adequate harbour facilities inhibited the full exploitation of the advantages of the town's site during the later nineteenth century; but—unlike many border towns—after partition it benefited from local and regional trading adjustment. Many of Letterkenny's predominantly nineteenth-century buildings have been insensitively modernised, and the town is architecturally undistinguished. The most important and most visually dominant building is St Eunan's (Catholic) Cathedral (1891–1901). **Lindsay Proudfoot**

letters. Emigrant Letter Series: Emigrant's Bag *(1988, collage, gouache and acrylic on paper) by Geraldine O'Reilly; an evocation of both the distance and the immediacy communicated by letters from those who have left. [Courtesy of the artist]*

letters. While the character and significance of the epistolary in the annals of Irish culture and Irish life generally have still to receive comprehensive attention, not only editorially but generically and contextually, the letter's distinctive and valuable contribution to these annals may be readily perceived. The range of its tonalities and usages, from the political to the documentary and from the ethnographic to the artistic, indicates the letter's discursive diversity and its flexibility of form and diction. An appreciation of such versatility, however, and the grounds for such eminence as the Irish letter possesses come from its importance as a public artefact. It is works such as SWIFT'S DRAPIER'S LETTERS (1724; edited by Herbert Davis, 1935), BURKE's *Letter to Sir Hercules Langrishe* (1792), YEATS's *Letters to the New Island* (1934; edited by Bornstein and Witemeyer, 1989) and *Devoy's Postbag* (edited by O'Brien and Ryan, 1948)—to take a representative sampling—on which the status of the letter rests, rather than on works belonging to the more conventional category of correspondence.

Each of these works, in varying degrees, not only invokes a specific and potentially influential body of readers but in doing so enacts complex formal and rhetorical questions concerning the nature of the addressees and the persona of the writer. Even though they were availing of a practice that was widespread in Ireland and elsewhere, both Swift and Burke, in presenting as letters what are in effect pamphlets, were adapting some of the private features of the epistolary for public ends. In this way their letters drew attention to matters of distance and intimacy, leadership and loyalty, and how common ground might evolve into common cause. Combining with certain tonal and stylistic elements, these letters are vital interpretative acts articulating by their form as much as by their content Anglo-Irish isolation, assertiveness, and vulnerability. They may also be regarded as crucial contributions to the initiation and consolidation of the Anglo-Irish as a distinctive linguistic, print-oriented cultural entity.

Yet recognition of the power of the public letter as a call for attention was not at all confined to the Anglo-Irish, as is exemplified by such heterogeneous works as WILLIAM HAMILTON'S *Letters Concerning the North Coast of Antrim ...* (1786), WILLIAM DRENNAN'S *The Drennan Letters* (edited by D. A. Chart, 1931), and *The Drennan-McTier Letters*, 1794–1801 (edited by Jean Agnew, 1998)—to mention the letters of just one member of the UNITED IRISHMEN; the *Letters on the State of Ireland* (1824) by JKL (Bishop JAMES DOYLE); and the letter by WILLIAM CARLETON to Lord John Russell that prefaces his novel *The Black Prophet* (1847). The public appeal of the epistolary form extends to *Letters to the New Island*, a work in which there are no letters but where the configuration of common interests and the evocation of an audience remain a primary concern—as they are also in *Letters from the New Island* (edited by Dermot Bolger, 1991). Of particular cultural interest in both *Letters to the New Island* and *Devoy's Postbag* is the manner in which, notwithstanding their vastly different viewpoints, they both attempt to align the interests of Irish America with those of Ireland, using news content to project and interpret visions of newness and change.

Not least for being a pendant to their public letters, the private correspondence of Swift and Burke is also of obvious historical interest. But correspondence may act not only as an illuminating supplement to the historical record but also as an essential component of it. Letters in such compilations as *The Wadding Papers, 1614–1638* (edited by Brendan Jennings, 1953), *Letters and Papers Relating to the Irish Rebellion between 1642 and 1646* (edited by James Hogan, 1936), the three-volume *Franco-Irish Correspondence* (edited by Sheila Mulloy, 1983–4), and *The Letters of St Oliver Plunkett, 1625–1681* (edited by John Hanly, 1979) are clearly indispensable to the establishment of a comprehensive view of exemplary personalities and complex historical developments. As well as their historical value, such materials contain invaluable evidence of the *mentalités* of the times. Their linguistic value is also significant, as they are a primary means of preserving English, Irish, and Latin styles and usages.

In addition to its biographical and archival value, private correspondence is important as a record of texture, milieu, context, and social activity. The depiction of eighteenth-century Ireland in MRS DELANY's *Autobiography and Correspondence* (1861–2) is a case in point. Correspondence of this documentary variety is all the more worthwhile because it not only adds a sense of the quotidian to a past frequently characterised by events of exclusively national relevance but also represents groups whose existence the public record may overshadow.

Foremost among such groups are emigrants. The recovery of their experiences of transit and resettlement through scholarly editions of their correspondence—for example *Oceans of Consolation: Personal Accounts of Migration to Australia* (edited by David Fitzpatrick, 1994)—draws attention to another distinctive expression of how letters help negotiate distance and intimacy. In addition it brings, among other cultural benefits, an end to an era in which the acknowledgment of emigrant experience seemed limited to sentimental ballads. At the other end of the social spectrum, notable ANGLO-IRISH families also constitute a marginal, loosely knit group of whose Irish experiences the general nature may be most readily appreciated from their correspondence, as illustrated by various editions of Edgeworth family letters and *The Synge Letters ... 1746–1752* (edited by Mary-Louise Legg, 1996). A correspondence that may be suggestively associated with these is *The Letters of Charles O'Conor of Belanagare: A Catholic Voice in Eighteenth-Century Ireland* (edited by Ward, Wrynne and Coogan Ward, 1988). Also illustrative of how correspondence can function as a means of representing the concerns and characteristics peculiar to a group is the compilation *Irish Women's Letters* (edited by Laurence Flanagan, 1997).

The most important personal correspondence, in content, cultural significance, and editorial expertise, is the editions published over the last half century of the letters of major Irish writers. JAMES JOYCE, OSCAR WILDE, GEORGE BERNARD SHAW, SEAN O'CASEY, JOHN MILLINGTON SYNGE, W. B. YEATS and, rather less systematically, GEORGE MOORE are the most prominent names in an incomplete list; the multi-volume editions of their letters, complete with editorial apparatus, are acknowledged landmarks in contemporary scholarship. In addition to the access these works provide to their subjects—an access that can take the form of controversial revelations, as in the publication of Joyce's intimate letters to his wife in *Selected Letters of James Joyce* (edited by RICHARD ELLMANN, 1975)—these editions also confirm the complicated significance of the letter for attempts to delineate the nature and status of the artist in modern culture. Related to these artists' correspondence, by virtue of temperament, style, and interest, is JOHN B. YEATS's *Letters to his Son W. B. Yeats and Others, 1869–1922* (edited by Joseph Hone, 1944; selected by JOHN MCGAHERN, 1999). The same may be said of MÁIRTÍN Ó CADHAIN's *As an nGéibheann: Litreacha chuig Tomás Bairéad* (1973), another case of a selection being greatly preferable to nothing at all. The existence of these works contrasts revealingly with the absence of any comparable edition of the letters of other public figures, notably politicians and clergymen; the multi-volume *Correspondence of Daniel O'Connell* (edited by Maurice R. O'Connell, 1973) is an exception. The value of correspondence for glimpses of the hearts and minds of public figures is suggested by *In Great Haste: The Letters of Michael Collins and Kitty Kiernan* (edited by León Ó Broin, 1983; revised and extended by Cian Ó hÉigeartaigh, 1996) and *The Prison Letters of Constance Markievicz* (1934).

The letter has also been intermittently adapted for artistic purposes. This formal strategy can be seen in some poems by Swift. But eighteenth-century literature's vogue for the epistolary did not translate to Irish literature; Maria Edgeworth's minor and belated *Letters for Literary Ladies* (1795) hardly counts. But works as diverse as Oscar Wilde's *De Profundis* (1897), LOUIS MACNEICE's *Letters from Iceland* (1937, with W. H. Auden), and SEAMUS HEANEY's 'An Open Letter' (1983) explore anew the expressive resources and cultural resilience of this most elementary and ostensibly most ephemeral of written forms. [see DIARIES AND JOURNALS.] **George O'Brien**

Letts, Edmund Albert (1852–1918), chemist. Born in Sydenham, Kent; studied in England, Austria, and Germany, obtaining a PhD at the University of Göttingen. In 1876 he was appointed professor of CHEMISTRY and three years later professor of chemistry and sanitation at Queen's College, Belfast. In 1906 he identified dissolved nutrients from sewage as a major cause of the observed excessive growth of green algae in the marine environment close to Belfast, and he recommended that a sewage treatment plant be provided for the city to combat this pollution. His final related report, *The Scheme of Sewage Purification for Belfast and Its Probable Effects on Lough Baird*, was produced in 1908. **Susan McKenna-Lawlor**

Letts, Winifred (1882–1972), writer, playwright, and poet. Born in Manchester, daughter of a clergyman; educated at St Anne's Abbots, Bromley, Kent, and Alexandra College, Dublin. She wrote poetry, children's stories, hagiography and fiction but is best remembered for her reminiscence *Knockmaroon* (1953) and her plays—two for the ABBEY THEATRE, *The Eyes of the Blind* (1907) and *The Challenge* (1909), and the three-act *Hamilton and Jones* (1941) for the GATE THEATRE. In her later years she lived in Faversham, Kent. **Joley Wood**

Lever, Charles James (1806–1872), novelist and essayist. Educated at TCD and RCSI; he was appointed dispensary doctor at Portstewart, Co. Derry, in 1832 but in 1842 abandoned medicine in favour of novel-writing and gained overnight success with roistering comic-military tales such as *Charles O'Malley* (1841). He also edited the DUBLIN UNIVERSITY MAGAZINE (1842–5). His later novels are more serious, but this change of tone, his sometimes hand-to-mouth serial method of composition and his unpopularity with nationalists cost him his fame. He was appointed British vice-consul at La Spezia, 1858, and consul at Trieste, 1867, where he died and is buried. **Tony Bareham**

Lewis, C. S. [Clive Staples] (1898–1963), scholar, children's writer, and Christian apologist. Born in Belfast; educated there and in England, where, following service in the British army during the FIRST WORLD WAR, he took degrees in the University of Oxford. He held a fellowship in Magdalen College, Oxford, until his appointment in 1954 to the chair of medieval and Renaissance English in the University of Cambridge. His reputation as a scholar was established by *The Allegory of Love* (1936), but his posthumous reputation rests on his genre fiction, in which orthodox Christianity is defended and promoted in fantasy and science-fiction works that retain a wide appeal. The landscape of his 'Narnia' chronicles for children (1950–56) owes something to the topography of his native Co. Down. **Terence Brown**

Lewis as a children's writer. He achieved recognition in the realm of children's literature with the publication of seven children's books written as a sequence, 1950–56, known collectively as the Chronicles of Narnia. The first and best known of these is *The Lion, the Witch and the Wardrobe* (1950). The children in the story find their way to an enchanted land through the back of an old wardrobe. Though more than half a century has elapsed since their publication, these books have retained their popularity while also attracting large numbers of adults. These are well-crafted children's fantasies and have given inspiration to a generation of time-fantasy writers for both children and young adults. Lewis's relatively small number of books for children have established themselves as timeless classics. [see CHILDREN'S AND ILLUSTRATED LITERATURE; CHILDREN'S LITERATURE.] **Patricia Donlon**

Lewis's *Topographical Dictionary* (1837). In the nineteenth century, topographical descriptions began to be structured alphabetically by place-name rather than as a series of itineraries. Besides making for quick and easy reference, a dictionary arrangement allowed the inclusion not just of towns, parishes and villages but also of larger areas, such as counties and dioceses. The most successful work of this kind produced for Ireland was *A Topographical Dictionary of Ireland* (1837), compiled and published by Samuel Lewis of London in two volumes, accompanied by a county atlas. Its contents are impressively wide-ranging, covering geography, history, ADMINISTRATIVE DIVISIONS, and public services, land use, fuel supply, GEOLOGY and minerals, manufactures and fisheries, communications, ancient monuments, and social conditions—including some rare glimpses of FOLK LIFE and FOLKLORE. For individual towns and parishes there is more emphasis on particular buildings, ESTATES, and institutions.

Lewis had already published topographical dictionaries of England and Wales, but he was not prepared for the shortage of topographical literature in Ireland, and much of his information came from original sources, which, he claimed, included 'nearly all the most intelligent resident gentlemen' in the country. By recruiting so many informants the dictionary secured for itself a correspondingly large readership: the first edition attracted more than 4,000 subscribers, and it has remained a major topographical source, the only successful example in Irish history of a comprehensive reference-book derived from local contributions. [see CARTOGRAPHY.] **J. H. Andrews**

Leydon, John (1895–1979), civil servant. Born in Co. Roscommon; educated at ST PATRICK'S COLLEGE, Maynooth. He joined the British CIVIL SERVICE in London in 1915, transferring to Dublin in 1923, where he shortly showed ability in the DEPARTMENT OF FINANCE. He became Secretary of the Department of Industry and Commerce in 1932 and a close colleague of SEÁN LEMASS, heavily involved in setting up AER LINGUS and BORD NA MÓNA. He and Lemass were in charge of supplies during the years of the SECOND WORLD WAR, founding Irish Shipping and the Insurance Corporation of Ireland. A leading administrator of his time, he retired in 1955. **Tom Garvin**

Liberals. The Liberal Party was formed in the 1860s from an amalgamation of WHIGS and radicals who had tended to be the more favourable than Conservatives to Irish reform. Between the 1830s and 1870, Irish constituencies with large majorities of Catholic electors had tended to send Liberals to Parliament. GLADSTONE personified the new party, which under him became identified with advocacy of HOME RULE. Following his retirement in 1894, party enthusiasm for home rule cooled, but it remained formally committed to the national agenda. Nationalists and Liberals were normally allied. After the two general elections of 1910 the Liberal government under Herbert Asquith attempted a further home-rule measure. The party was seriously undermined during the FIRST WORLD WAR and never formed a single-party government again. **Alan O'Day**

libraries. The earliest libraries in Ireland were established in the schools and MONASTERIES of the sixth to the ninth centuries. Besides Holy Scripture, each monastery library contained Irish literature and books on canon law and scientific subjects. Monks produced their own books in each school's *scriptorium*. The seventh-century poem 'Hisperica Famina' ('Western Sayings') describes how books were stored in satchels hung on pegs or racks on the walls of the library.

libraries. *Andrew Carnegie (left, in top hat) laying the foundation stone of the new Waterford Free Library at Lady Lane, 19 October 1903, with the librarian, John J. Morrin, the Lord Mayor (left, wearing chain of office), the town clerk, and members of the borough staff. [Council of Trustees of the National Library of Ireland; Poole WP 1313]*

The best indication of the type of material held by these libraries is provided by libraries in other countries, such as that in the monasteries of Sankt Gallen in Switzerland and Bobbio in Italy, which contained many volumes donated or written by Irish monks (see p. 1113). The monasteries of the middle to late Middle Ages also accumulated great collections of books; the Franciscans were particularly adept at acquiring valuable and useful volumes. An inventory of the books in the Franciscan library at Youghal, Co. Cork, held in the University of Tübingen gives some idea of the collections maintained by the monasteries before their dissolution and the dispersal of their libraries in the sixteenth century. There were 145 items in the collection, including works by Nicholas of Lyra, a renowned Biblical scholar, and by Jerome, Bonaventure, and Aquinas. All the books in the collection were in Latin.

Ireland's first academic library was established in TRINITY COLLEGE, Dublin, in 1592 and by 1604 held nearly 5,000 volumes. A new library was built in the 1730s, and under the direction of GEORGE BERKELEY the collection expanded greatly in the following decades. The opening of the Berkeley Library in 1967 and the Lecky Library in 1978 ended an acute shortage of space for the college's enormous collection of books, much of which it had received through its status as a copyright deposit library for all British publications since 1801. Trinity College Library has benefited from a number of bequests of very valuable material over the years and holds several extremely important MANUSCRIPTS, including the Book of KELLS, the eleventh-century Book of LEINSTER, and the annals of Ulster, compiled in the fifteenth century (see p. 39).

MARSH'S LIBRARY in Dublin was the first public library in Ireland. Archbishop NARCISSUS MARSH, when provost of Trinity College, was dissatisfied with the restrictions placed on scholars and students by the college library, and in 1701 he established a new library on a site adjacent to ST PATRICK'S CATHEDRAL (see p. 502). An act of Parliament of 1701 exempted the new library from taxes, and the collection grew rapidly through donations, such as those of John Stearne, Bishop of Clogher, and the first librarian, Elias Bouhéreau. Marsh himself bought a remarkable collection of 10,000 books belonging to Edward Stillingfleet, Bishop of Worcester, for £2,500.

The early eighteenth century saw the beginning of thriving PUBLISHING and bookselling industries and the creation of the first great private book collections. In 1734 a library was established in DR STEEVENS' HOSPITAL, Dublin, to hold the collection of Edward Worth, a physician. A larger collection was bequeathed to the library of the Royal College of Physicians by Sir PATRICK DUN, its first president, in 1713. Another great private collection, bequeathed to the library of Trinity College, was that of JAMES USSHER, Archbishop of Armagh, 1625–41. Several great diocesan libraries were established during the eighteenth century, the most prominent of which was that of Archbishop Bolton of Cashel. This library, which Bolton brought with him to Cashel in 1734, contained a large collection of textbooks of ecclesiastical law.

The establishment of circulating libraries as a tool of education in Ireland owes its origin to the work of the Sunday School Society, which was particularly strong in Ulster in the early nineteenth century, and of the Society for Promoting the Education of the Poor in Ireland (better known as the Kildare Place Society), which by 1831 had made more than 11,000 donations to schools throughout Ireland, enabling them to develop libraries of their own. The society itself published the bulk of the collections in these libraries, and it became one of the most prominent publishers of educational literature in Ireland. Despite accusations of proselytism, the society's influential *Hints on the Formation of Lending Libraries* (1824) emphasised the importance of making a diverse range of reading matter available to the users of libraries.

The first private circulating library was established by James Hoey in Dublin in 1737. By the end of the eighteenth century twenty-four such libraries were operating in Ireland.

While most of the eighteenth-century libraries were attached to ecclesiastical or educational institutions, the nineteenth century saw the development of a number of important collections by organisations dedicated to the advancement of knowledge in the natural sciences, philosophy, and the arts. In 1815 more than 10,000 volumes belonging to the Dublin Society for Improving Husbandry, Manufactures and Other Useful Arts (later the ROYAL DUBLIN SOCIETY) were transferred to the society's new library in LEINSTER HOUSE, Kildare Street. The society's library holdings, apart from its excellent collection of scientific material, were transferred to the new NATIONAL LIBRARY OF IRELAND, established under the Dublin Science and Art Museum Act (1877). In 1925 the RDS and its library moved to new premises in Ballsbridge, Dublin. Its superb collection of botanical literature is now housed in the new library of the NATIONAL BOTANIC GARDENS, Glasnevin, Dublin. Shortly after its foundation in 1785 the ROYAL IRISH ACADEMY established its own library, containing material relating to pure science, history, literature, and antiquities. Throughout the nineteenth century the RIA also acquired a large collection of early Irish literature.

A more modest but still socially and intellectually significant feature of late eighteenth-century Ireland was the establishment of small libraries providing opportunities for working-class and rural readers. This development was particularly successful in Cos. Antrim and Down. The Belfast Reading Society was founded in 1788, and in 1801 it established the Belfast Library and Society for Promoting Knowledge in the city's Linen Hall, now known as the LINEN HALL LIBRARY. Its second librarian was THOMAS RUSSELL, a prominent member of the UNITED IRISHMEN. By the 1990s the library had accumulated 200,000 volumes, including important collections on local studies, family history, early printed books, and a unique collection of ephemeral political material. Similar ventures were supported by the local intelligentsia in a number of other towns: the ROYAL CORK INSTITUTION, the Cork Subscription Library and the Kilkenny Library Society flourished for a time, but their collections were eventually dispersed or absorbed by the local public libraries. In the 1840s the Repeal Association used its reading-rooms and its newspaper, the NATION, to further the twin aims of encouraging agitation against the ACT OF UNION and educating the mass of the people, a role later taken up by the Mechanics' Institutes in the 1860s.

The National Library building in Kildare Street, Dublin, opened in 1890, was the first library in Europe to adopt the Dewey decimal classification, which was to become the most commonly used book classification in English-speaking countries (see p. 767). The RDS collection of 70,000 volumes and the Jasper Robert Joly donation of 25,000 books formed the basis on which the National Library's collection of printed books was established. The library was given the role of collecting all material relating to Ireland and works by Irish authors, and in 1927 it became a legal deposit library for all items published in Ireland. By the end of the twentieth century the collection of printed books consisted of almost a million titles, while the Department of Manuscripts holds more than a thousand Irish manuscripts.

The country's most remarkable special library is the CHESTER

BEATTY LIBRARY and Gallery of Oriental Art, which was moved from London to Dublin in 1953. A new home for the collection, which contains 7,000 books and some 10,000 manuscripts, including many superb copies of the Qur'an, was opened in the Clock Tower Building in DUBLIN CASTLE in February 2000 (see p. 187).

Legislative support for public libraries began with the Public Libraries Act (1855), and in 1858 Dundalk was the first town to open a municipal library. Other towns and cities were slow to follow, but publicly financed libraries were finally opened in Dublin in 1884 and in Belfast in 1888. The Public Libraries (Ireland) Act (1902) allowed rural districts and small towns to open public libraries. Financial support for the provision of eighty library buildings by local authorities came from the American philanthropist Andrew Carnegie in 1913, when the Carnegie United Kingdom Trust was created. In 1998 the sixty-two surviving Irish Carnegie libraries formed an important part of the existing library system.

The county library system developed rapidly, and by the early 1930s the responsibility for administering almost all public libraries lay with county councils. However, it was not until the passing of the Public Libraries Act (1947) that the Government adopted the principle of state aid for public libraries. The public library system in the Republic is now operated at three levels: library authorities, the independent library system in each local authority area; the Department of the Environment and Local Government; and An Chomhairle Leabharlanna, which was established under the Public Libraries Act (1947) to assist local authorities in providing a library service and to advise the Government on public library policy. [see MONASTIC SCHOOLS.] **Brian Galvin**

Lichfield House compact (1835), an understanding reached between DANIEL O'CONNELL and WHIG leaders whereby Repeal MPs and radicals would help the Whigs to attain power in return for social reform legislation concerning Ireland. The arrangement produced a number of important measures, such as administrative reform and a new POOR LAW, before the Whig government fell in 1841. **Gary Owens**

Liddy, James (1934–), poet, critic, editor, and novelist. Born in Dublin and raised in Kilkee, Co. Clare, and Coolgreany, Co. Wexford; educated at Glenstal Abbey, NUI, and KING'S INNS, Dublin. From the late 1960s he has divided his time between Coolgreany and the United States, where he is professor of English at the University of Wisconsin-Milwaukee. *Collected Poems* (1994) includes work from his eleven books of poems and a generous selection of new work; it is the volume that best displays his remarkable and original poetic talent. **Eamonn Wall**

Life of Colm Cille: see BETHA COLAIM CHILLE and VITA SANCTAE COLUMBAE.

Life of John Buncle, Esq., The (1756–66), a sprawling, quasi-autobiographical novel by THOMAS AMORY. It relates the uncommon adventures of an enthusiastic scholar, anti-Trinitarian and lover (husband to eight short-lived anti-Trinitarian wives) in Dublin, among the native aristocracy of the west of Ireland, and in the English Lake and Peak Districts. Claiming acquaintance with contemporaries from JONATHAN SWIFT and JOHN TOLAND to the White Knight and the Knight of Glin, Buncle encounters a remarkable array of Irish friends from his youth during his rambles. Popular in its day, *John Buncle* was later admired by Hazlitt and Leigh Hunt, among others. **Ian Campbell Ross**

Life of Red Hugh O'Donnell: see BEATHA AODHA RUAIDH UI DHOMHNAILL.

Liffey, River. The Liffey rises a short distance from the SALLY GAP on the slopes of Kippure in the WICKLOW MOUNTAINS and takes a 130 km (81-mile) course involving several changes in direction to DUBLIN BAY. The upper Liffey flows north-west before curving to the south-west to flow into POLLAPHUCA RESERVOIR. Downstream from the reservoir the river rapidly descends to Ballymore Eustace, through a small reservoir at Golden Falls. There is a third reservoir at Leixlip another 55 km (34 miles) downstream. Today the Liffey reservoirs are used primarily to regulate the supply of water to Dublin, with ELECTRICITY generation as a secondary role. Before the reservoirs were constructed, floods were often a problem, with river levels rising rapidly from the Wicklow Mountains. The middle and lower reaches of the river are cut in glacial drift deposits and occasionally solid rock. From Ballymore Eustace the Liffey meanders in a westerly direction until it reaches Kilcullen, where it swings to the north-west before taking a predominantly north-easterly route between Newbridge and Leixlip. From here it flows past Lucan, Palmerston, and Chapelizod, then through Dublin to Dublin Bay. The tidal stretch starts below the weir at Longmeadows Park, downstream from Chapelizod; the lower 11 km (7 miles) are channelised. **R. A. Charlton**

Lifford (*Leifear*), county town of Co. Donegal. It has a picturesque setting on the west bank of the River Foyle, joined by a bridge to STRABANE, Co. Tyrone, with which it is strongly linked economically. Lifford developed as a stronghold of the O'Donnells, who built a castle there, but the present town grew up around an English garrison that was established c. 1600. It was given a charter of incorporation under JAMES I and became a market and assize town, while retaining its garrison function into the twentieth century. The eighteenth-century courthouse, together with the county jail, have recently been restored and now house a heritage centre. Despite its relatively small population, Lifford retains its administrative importance as the seat of Donegal County Council. **Joseph Brady**

lighthouses. The oldest operational lighthouse in Ireland is that at HOOK HEAD, Co. Wexford (1172). In 1810 the Corporation for Preserving and Improving the Port of Dublin, set up in 1786, was given responsibility for Irish lights. During the period 1810–50 George Halpin Senior designed and constructed many lighthouses. In 1867 the COMMISSIONERS OF IRISH LIGHTS were established. Perhaps the best known of Irish lighthouses is the FASTNET ROCK LIGHTHOUSE off MIZEN HEAD, Co. Cork, the present tower being completed in 1903. Other types of structure include the Pile Light in Dundalk Bay and the KISH BANK LIGHTHOUSE off DUBLIN BAY. Since 1997 all lighthouses are operated automatically. **Ronald Cox**

'Lilliburlero', a song with an Irish chorus ridiculing JAMES II and his deputy, the Earl of Tyrconnell, credibly attributed to Sir Thomas Wharton. The air, which predates the text (and cannot, despite claims, have been written by Henry Purcell), has served many ORANGE SONGS (such as 'Protestant Boys') and English songs and is also the call tune of the BBC World Service. **John Moulden**

lilting, one of the terms used in Ireland for a musical style known as vocalisation, found in various forms throughout the world. Non-lexical syllables are used to communicate a melody with a strong, regular rhythm, primarily dance tunes in the Irish tradition. Lilting can be identified in four main forms: (*a*) as a memory aid when talking about or teaching a new tune; (*b*) as a method of supplying music for dancing (historically, lilting was used to provide music at HOUSE DANCES as an alternative to instruments); (*c*) as a novelty item, that is, as a chorus or refrain for songs, in Irish and English; and (*d*) as a refined recital form: lilting is a separate category in the various competitions organised by COMHALTAS CEOLTÓIRÍ ÉIREANN. **Angela Madden**

Limerick, County (*Contae Luimnigh*)

Province:	MUNSTER
County town:	LIMERICK
Area:	2,686 km² (1,038 sq. miles)
Population, including city (2002):	175,529
Features:	Galty Mountains Lough Gur River Maigue River SHANNON
Of historical interest:	ASKEATON CASTLE and Friary Kilmallock churches Limerick Castle and Cathedral LOUGH GUR
Industry and products:	Dairy farming Manufacturing

Petula Martyn

County Limerick is an agricultural county in the fertile plains of north Munster, specialising in dairy farming. The east of the county forms part of the Golden Vale, which extends through Co. Tipperary and north Cork and contains some of the most fertile farmland in Ireland. Farming practices in the county date from the NEOLITHIC PERIOD. Early cultivation took place in the limestone-rich soils of Lough Gur and its environs, about 3 km (2 miles) north-east of **Bruff**. The city of **Limerick** is at the lowest bridging point on the Shannon. Historically the city's port function has been important to its development, while the establishment of SHANNON AIRPORT at Rineanna, Co. Clare, has had a profound impact on the ECONOMIC DEVELOPMENT of the mid-west region. The regional development authority, Shannon Development (formerly SFADCo), has also played a critical role in the development of industrial employment in the county and the wider mid-west region (see p. 519). The principal towns in the county include **Patrickswell**, **Kilmallock**, **Newcastle**, and **Rathkeale**, while the scenic village of **Adare** has developed into an important tourist attraction. **Raymond O'Connor and John Crowley**

Limerick (*Luimneach*), a city at the head of the Shannon Estuary; population (2002) 54,058. It is a cathedral city and a road and rail terminus. The older city consisted of three parts: Englishtown, on King's Island in the River Shannon; Irishtown, to the south-east on the mainland; and the eighteenth-century red-brick Newtown Pery, laid out on a grid plan south-west of Irishtown. Originally a NORSE settlement established on King's Island in 922, Limerick became the seat of the O'Briens of Thomond in the late twelfth century and received a charter from Prince John in 1197. In 1691 the Jacobite-occupied town capitulated to WILLIAM OF ORANGE; on 3 October terms were agreed and signed (the TREATY OF LIMERICK), but these were breached by the Williamites almost immediately. There are several medieval remains in Englishtown, notably parts of St Mary's (Protestant) Cathedral, the thirteenth-century King John's Castle at Thomond Bridge, and the Dominican Priory of St Saviour (1227). Buildings of note in Irishtown are St John's (Catholic) Cathedral and the Custom House (1769) by DAVIS DUCART. O'Connell Street is the main axis of Newtown Pery, laid out by Ducart for Edmund Sexton Pery, Speaker of the Irish Parliament, 1771–85, and is dominated by a statue of DANIEL O'CONNELL by JOHN HOGAN (1857). Pery Square, south-west of O'Connell Street, contains the People's Park with the Rice Memorial Column by ALEXANDER NIMMO, which commemorates Thomas Spring Rice, first Baron Mount Eagle, Chancellor of the Exchequer, 1835–9, and champion of rights for Catholics.

Substantial renovation of the quays has taken place under the provisions of the Urban Renewal Act (1986) and subsequent initiatives. There is an Institute of Technology, a College of Education, and the University of Limerick at Plassey, 3 km (2 miles) to the south-east, site of the National Technological Park. The regional general hospital is at Dooradoyle to the south-west, and there is a large industrial estate at Raheen. The deep-water Shannon Estuary is capable of accommodating heavy bulk-carriers; on the estuary are cement and alumina manufacture and Moneypoint ELECTRICITY generating station. Shannon Airport and its industrial zone, site of the first customs-free manufacturing zone in the world, are 11 km (7 miles) to the north-west in Co. Clare. The first hydro-electric scheme (the SHANNON SCHEME) in Ireland (1925) is at Ardnacrusha, 5 km (3 miles) to the north. There are several museums, including the HUNT MUSEUM in the eighteenth-century Custom House, a collection of 2,000 works of medieval ecclesiastical art donated by the Hunt family. Limerick authors of note are KATE O'BRIEN and FRANK MCCOURT. **Mary E. Cawley**

limerick, a rhyming five-line humorous verse form, first common in Britain during the early nineteenth century and made famous by Edward Lear, among the most inventive practitioners of the genre. The first printed limericks appeared in the anonymous *The History of Sixteen Wonderful Old Women* (1820). The origin of the limerick is disputed, as is any relation it may have with Limerick city and county; the similarity in content and verse form between conventional limericks and the early nineteenth century Irish-language satirical verses of the Poets of the Maigue from Co. Limerick may be more than coincidence. **Brian Lalor**

Limerick Docks. The development of Limerick as a port included quays along the south bank of the River SHANNON and the west bank of the Abbey River. The wet dock was completed in 1853 and a graving dock provided in 1873. The dock was extended in 1932 and a new entrance provided in 1950. **Ronald Cox**

Limerick lace, an embroidered net worked with *tambour* (chain stitch) or *run* (darn stitch). At times used together on the one piece, the former is often used for outlining, while the latter is a darning stitch frequently used for filling. A commercial lace industry was founded in Limerick in 1829, but despite early success it went into decline in the middle of the nineteenth century. Successfully revived in the 1880s by the nuns of the Convent of the Good Shepherd and also by the founding of Mrs Vere O'Brien's lace school, it became an economically important local industry, boosted by exposure in the Industrial Exhibitions and philanthropic patronage. **Alex Ward**

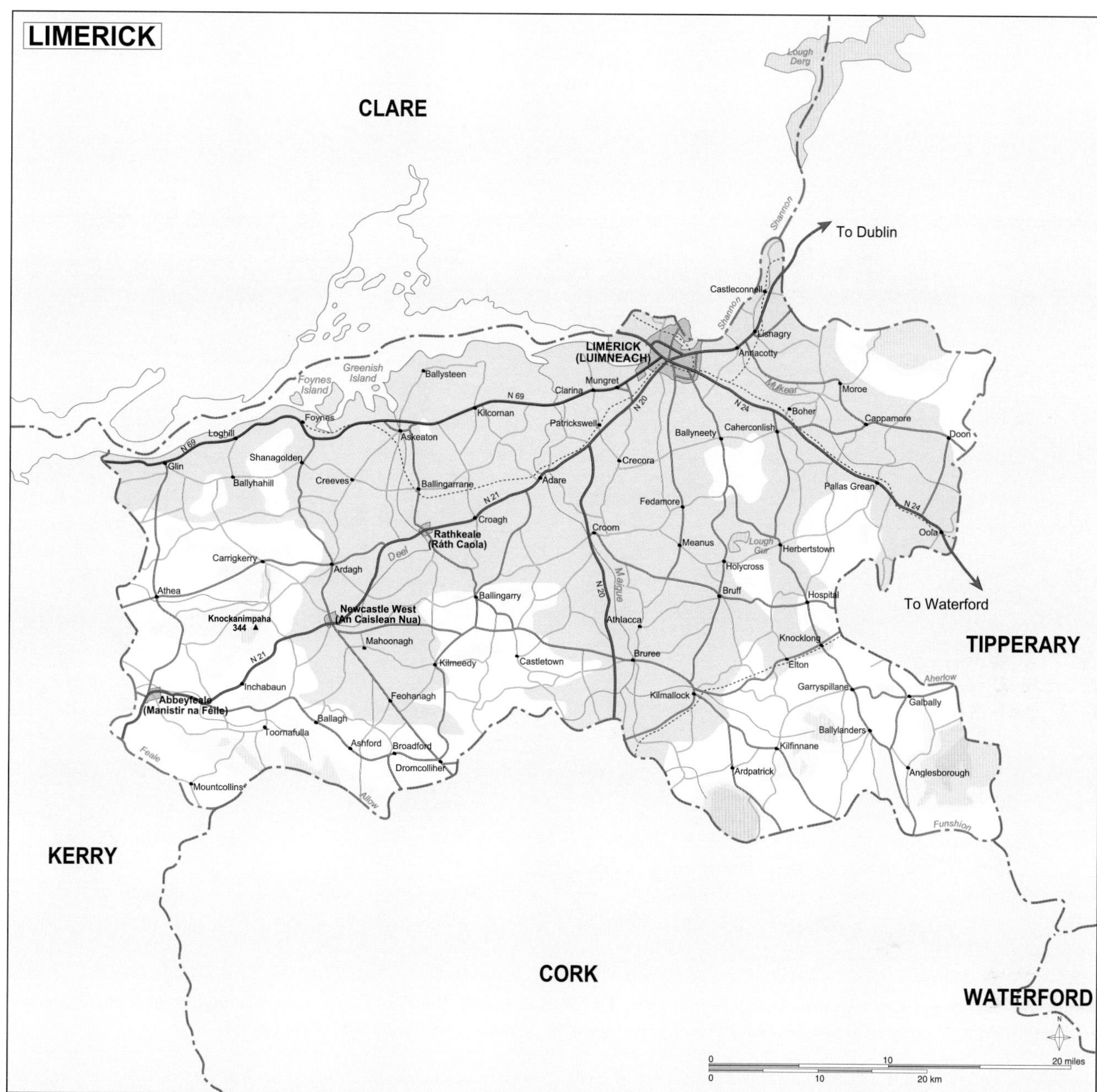

'Limerick Pogrom', a name given to two weeks of violence against the small Jewish community of Limerick that began on 11 January 1904. Sparked by an anti-Semitic sermon by the Redemptorist director of the Arch-Confraternity of Limerick, Father John Creagh, a mob made up of elements from the all-male congregation attacked the Jewish quarter in nearby Collooney Street. The ostensible reason was the alleged involvement of JEWS in money-lending. The houses faced onto the street, and the community was defenceless. Local police restored order.

Creagh returned to the attack on 18 January, when he told his congregation that 'the Jews have proved themselves to be the enemies of every country in Europe, and every nation has to defend itself against them.' The disturbances lasted for more than two weeks, during which time the fear of being assaulted prevented Jews from conducting their business. The episode divided public opinion: ARTHUR GRIFFITH supported Creagh's critique of the Limerick Jews; MICHAEL DAVITT was outspoken in their defence. Creagh helped organise an economic boycott of Jewish businesses in the city that lasted for months. Unable to earn a living, a number of families were ultimately forced to leave the city. A shameful episode, it is unique in the history of twentieth-century Ireland. **Dermot Keogh**

Limerick School of Music. The Municipal School of Music in Limerick was founded by the City of Limerick VEC in January 1961 under the direction of John MacKenzie. The school now occupies the site of what was the old County Hospital in Mulgrave Street. It has grown from an initial enrolment of thirty-five students to its present level of 1,500 students. Under its present principal, David A. O'Connell, the school caters for classical musicians of all abilities and provides performance opportunities in the form of a choir, brass, wind, and early music ensembles, and three orchestras. **John Page**

Limerick, Siege of (1690 and 1691). During the JACOBITE wars in Ireland (1689–91), Limerick was besieged on two occasions: following the BATTLE OF THE BOYNE (August 1690) and after the BATTLE OF AUGHRIM (August and September 1691). In July 1690 the Jacobite soldiers retreated to Limerick after their failure to hold

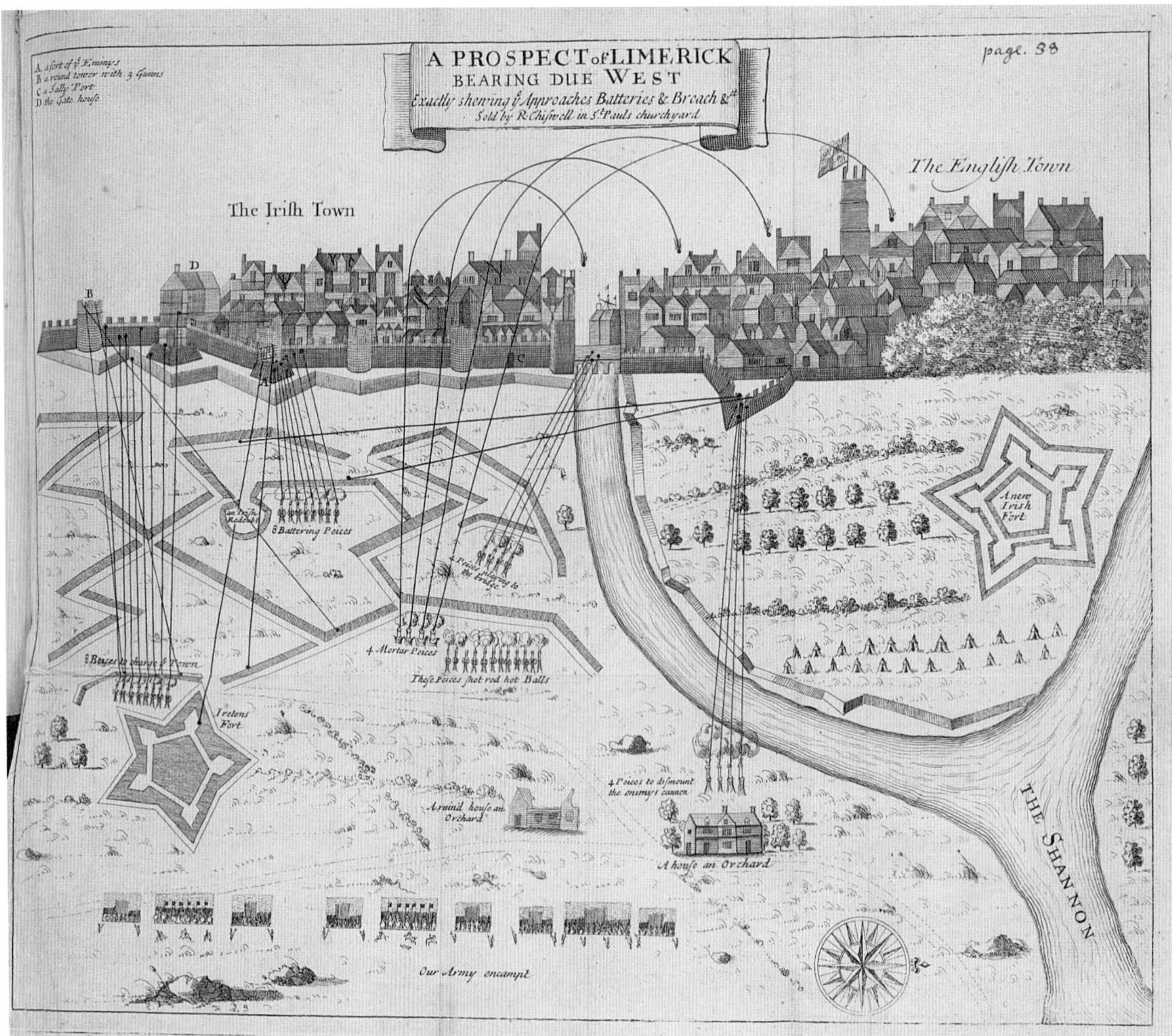

Limerick. *Engraving of Limerick during the siege of 1690, from* The Wars of Ireland *(1695) by Canon Story. The artillery attack was concentrated on Irishtown (left), where the walls were breached. [Council of Trustees of the National Library of Ireland; IR 94106 s 5]*

the Boyne. On 27 August WILLIAM III stormed the town but made little progress, save for a small hole in the wall near St John's Gate; this was because Limerick, though hampered by old-fashioned fortifications, had the natural defence of being an island connected to the mainland only by a bridge at the point of William's initial attack. His forces of 25,000 men had also been weakened when SARSFIELD raided his camp at Ballyneety while they were on the way to storm Limerick. Furthermore, the city's inhabitants, together with 14,000 soldiers, were determined to hold the town. The city's governor, the Marquis de Boisseleau, had led the defence in person, while the women of the city had taken part by hurling stones and broken bottles at their attackers.

After four hours, and faced with 2,000 casualties, William decided to call off the attack and instead to place the city under siege. However, bad weather forced him to lift the siege at the end of August, and he returned to England, disappointed at having failed to bring the war to a conclusion. This was a severe setback for William and an encouragement to the Irish resistance party.

Limerick became the centre of resistance to William's rule once again in August 1691, when it became the last Jacobite stronghold following their military disaster at Aughrim. However, this siege was on a much smaller scale than that of 1690: despite some artillery bombardment, GINKEL made no attempt to storm the city, preferring to persuade the Irish to negotiate. At first, buoyed up by promises of support from France, the Irish resolved to hold on, but as no supply ship materialised, the officers, mindful of the fact that they could have their estates forfeited, began to consider seeking terms. The Battle of Thomond Bridge (22 September), during which Ginkel extended the city's investment to the west and cut off the Irish cavalry, confirmed the Jacobites in this view, and on 23 September they asked for terms. These were finally resolved and the siege brought to an end by the TREATY OF LIMERICK (3 October 1691). **Rosemary Richey**

'Limerick Soviet'. On 9 April 1919 the British government invoked martial law in Limerick in anticipation of a large attendance at the funeral of Robert Byrne, a republican prisoner and trade union activist who was killed in a rescue attempt on 6 April. In response, on 14 April the Limerick Trades and Labour Council called a general strike. An estimated 14–15,000 workers took control of the city, organising the distribution of daily essentials and issuing a temporary currency. Press coverage was enhanced by the presence of foreign reporters who had been stationed in the city to cover the proposed transatlantic flight by Major Woods; it was they who nicknamed the general strike a soviet. There was no outside support for the workers, and the strike ended on 24 April following negotiations between the Catholic Bishop, Dr Hallinan, and the mayor, Alphonsus O'Mara of SINN FÉIN. **Ciarán Deane**

Limerick, Treaty of (3 October 1691), the official ending of the JACOBITE wars in Ireland. The treaty consisted of military and civil articles. The military articles allowed anyone serving in the Jacobite forces to leave Ireland for France; the civil articles promised Irish Catholics the same privileges they enjoyed under CHARLES II, a pardon and restoration of confiscated property for certain individuals, a bar on law suits arising from wartime incidents, and exemption from all oaths except the OATH OF ALLEGIANCE. However, Protestants felt that the terms were too lenient; and though 1,200 cases were heard between 1692 and 1699, the treaty was not ratified by the Irish Parliament until 1697, when several important issues were negated or ignored. This cleared the way for the PENAL LAWS of the eighteenth century and created considerable anger and controversy between the defeated community and Ireland's new rulers. **Rosemary Richey**

Lindisfarne, Book of (Lindisfarne Gospels), a Vulgate GOSPEL book with CANON TABLES, prefaces, Gospels (preceded by *argumentum*, *capitula*, and material on saints' feasts of Italian use). Each Gospel opens with an evangelist portrait, accompanied by their symbol: Matthew's includes a man holding a book who peeps from behind a curtain (interpreted variously as God the Father, Moses, the muse, and reconciliation of the Old and New Testaments through Christ), followed by a decorated *Incipit* facing a cross carpet-page (as is Jerome's *Novum Opus*). Unusually, it was made by one artist-scribe—an incredible act of *'opus Dei'* and input of resource.

The book was probably made at Lindisfarne, Northumbria, c. 710–720 in honour of St Cuthbert, whose cult was being promoted as a rallying point for a new sense of reconciliation and Christian identity, celebrating the fusion of Celtic, Germanic and Mediterranean cultures. Lindisfarne had been founded in 635 by AIDAN from the Columban community at IONA and retained active links with the Irish church, reflected in the decoration of the book and its stylistic relationship to Columban books such as the earlier Book of DURROW and the later Book of KELLS (see p. 523). About the year 950 Aldred, later Provost of Chester-le-Street, added a gloss in English—the earliest surviving translation into English of the Gospels—and a colophon naming Bishop Eadfrith of Lindisfarne (698–721) as maker, his successor, Bishop Aethilwald, as binder, and Billfrith the anchorite as fabricator of metalwork adornment. It is traditionally believed to have been made at Lindisfarne c. 698, when Cuthbert's relics were translated, associated with the Durham Gospels (which show the same correcting hand) and the Echternach Gospels, while an origin at Ráth Máelsigi or at Monkwearmouth-Jarrow (which probably lent an Italian Gospel book as textual model) has also been suggested; Lindisfarne nonetheless remains its probable birthplace. It was owned by Robert Bowyer in 1605 and by Sir Robert Cotton c. 1613; it has been in the British Museum (now British Library), London, since 1753. **Michelle P. Brown**

Lindsay, Eric Mervyn (1907–1974), astronomer. Born near Portadown, Co. Armagh; educated at QUB and Harvard University. He was appointed director of ARMAGH OBSERVATORY in 1937. Realising early the need for a large telescope far south of the equator, he expended much effort in setting up the Armagh-Dunsink-Harvard Telescope at the Boyden Observatory, Bloemfontein, South Africa. He acted as director of the Boyden Observatory on a number of occasions during the 1950s. He was one of the first to realise the need for international co-operation in the development and running of a large astronomical facility. He was responsible for establishing the Armagh Planetarium, which was officially opened in 1968, with Patrick Moore as its first director. His scientific research included studies of emission-line stars; the structure of our Galaxy and of its neighbours in the southern sky, the Magellanic Clouds. He died at Armagh Observatory. **John McFarland**

Linehan, Rosaleen, née McMenamin (1937–), comedian and actor. Born in Dublin; studied economics at UCD. Vivacious and mobile-faced, she appeared with Des Keogh in satirical revues in the 1970s written by her husband, Fergus Linehan. In the 1980s she moved successfully to serious stage and film roles (see p. 512), including Bessie Burgess in *The Plough and the Stars* (1989) and Kate in *Dancing at Lughnasa* (1990–92), as well as a solo show, *Mother of All the Behans* (1987–93). Her films include *The Butcher Boy* (1997) and *About Adam* (2000). **Stephen Dixon and Deirdre Falvey**

linen. Linen has been woven in Ireland from the Late BRONZE AGE or Early IRON AGE. It was worn throughout the first millennium AD and subsequently, particularly for underwear, SHIRTS, and accessories. Much was woven in traditional narrow lengths; various weights were also achieved, according to the intended use. In the sixteenth century fine linen was so valued that it was referred to regularly as a part payment in land transactions.

In the change from the medieval to the Renaissance way of life there was a drive to improve the quality of linen. In 1635 the LORD LIEUTENANT, THOMAS WENTWORTH, bought flax seeds from the Netherlands. In an attempt to improve weaving and finishing standards the administration introduced a colony of Dutch linen-weavers to Limerick in 1660–61 and French HUGUENOT weavers to Lisburn in 1707 and Dundalk in 1736. Throughout much of its history linen was woven by farmer-weavers, who involved family members in different stages of production. The weavers sold their webs of 'brown' (unbleached) linen at specialist local markets. Bought by linen-drapers or bleachers, the brown linen then went through a process of bleaching and finishing. Seal-masters appointed by the Linen Board stamped the completed linen as a guarantee of the correct length and quality. From the late seventeenth century Irish linen was highly regarded by the London and North American markets.

The introduction of water-powered bleach mills increased productivity in the eighteenth century; but INDUSTRIALISATION really began in the 1820s with the wet-spinning process for the production of fine linen yarns. Though a parliamentary inquiry in 1822 estimated that 60,000 people were employed in west Cork in spinning or weaving linen, by this time the Ulster linen industry was dominant, with its fine cambrics, damasks, and diapers and various weights of linen, from handkerchief weight to household TEXTILES. From 1851 Ulster weavers won prestigious awards at international industrial exhibitions, increasing their reputation. Factories were built to accommodate the new power looms for fine linens; by 1870 there were 15,000 such looms in use, and fine Ulster linen was sold in all the centres of the BRITISH EMPIRE and America.

From the 1950s the linen industry suffered through competition with synthetic fabrics. With the introduction of a new generation of wet-spinning machinery and new computer technologies, however, fine linens are again woven for international couturiers, while new uses have been developed in geo-textiles and the building industry (see pp. 148, 600). [see CLOTHING, TRADITIONAL; CONNOLLY, SYBIL; FASHION; INDUSTRIAL ARCHAEOLOGY; INDUSTRIAL DEVELOPMENT.] **Mairead Dunlevy**

linen and cotton, printed. Chintz—Indian cotton stained in designs with fast colours—was fashionable from the seventeenth century, used for DRESS fabrics and, in a heavier weight, for furnishing. To compete with such imports the Linen Board, from its appointment in 1711, encouraged the 'staining and printing' of linen in chintz style. Much of the work was done by block printing, though superior copperplate printing was developed at Drumcondra, Dublin, c. 1752 (see p. 600).

Cotton, a cheaper fabric, was printed in factories that were opened throughout Ireland from the 1770s. Their potential was so appreciated that ARCHIBALD HAMILTON ROWAN opened the first cotton-printing factory in the United States in 1797. Much was printed in simple designs, which were interchangeable between dress, furnishing fabrics, and wallpapers. There were also more splendid designs, such as those of William Kilburn of Capel Street, Dublin; though those of his designs that survive were drawn when he worked in England, they show the high standard that could be achieved in the 1790s.

By the 1820s competition with the heavily industrialised Manchester centres was difficult for Irish factories. Though some Irish producers continued to design and engrave up to five hundred new patterns a year, the copyright law did not give them real protection, and their trained designers moved to better-paid employment in Lancashire. They competed by working only on the cheaper, light-coloured and lightweight fabrics, which they sold in Ireland, the West Indies, and Mexico. The death knell for the Irish printed cotton industry came when cheap and fine cottons were imported regularly from India from c. 1850. **Mairead Dunlevy**

Linen Hall Library, Belfast, founded in 1788 as the Belfast Reading Society, the oldest library in Belfast and the last surviving subscription library in Ireland. The creation of 'intelligent artisans', it was soon colonised by the town's rising merchant class, becoming the Belfast Society for Promoting Knowledge. Their ENLIGHTENMENT vision included the collection of materials relating to 'their own country'.

The tensions of the time and the arrest in 1796 of the second librarian, the leading UNITED IRISHMAN THOMAS RUSSELL, threatened the very existence of the society. It was not until 1802 that it secured permanent premises in the White Linen Hall (hence the library's popular name). The move to the present city-centre building in Donegall Street, North, in 1892 coincided with a second flowering, which saw the creation of a separate Irish collection and major cultural programmes. The library was to remain the city's principal library at least until the end of the 1940s.

Though it remained an important centre for much of the creative talent of the city, the expansion of the public library service as well as the impact of the 'TROUBLES' threatened its viability. In 1981 it came close to closure, but a new emphasis on free public reference access and on areas of unique strength, and a widening of its role as a cultural centre, sparked a revival. In 2000 the library opened a large extension. Its main collections, principally in Irish and local studies, comprise some 250,000 volumes. Notable strengths include early Ulster printing and the Northern Ireland Political Collection; other active specialisms are in the languages of Ulster, and theatre and performing arts.

The Northern Ireland Political Collection at the Linen Hall Library owes its origins to the initiative of the then librarian, Jimmy Vitty, who, it is said, was handed a CIVIL RIGHTS leaflet in 1968, collected it, and sought other ephemeral items then appearing. The liberal and independent tradition of the library made collection possible and has also facilitated collection from all parties to the conflict. In addition to explicitly political material the collection covers the wider economic, legal and social dimensions of the conflict. It includes 11,500 books and pamphlets, approximately 100,000 issues of 2,000 periodical titles, 1,500 volumes of newspaper cuttings, 55,000 photographs, 5,000 posters, and 3,650 videos. It also includes some 75,000 other ephemeral printed items and a variety of other artefacts as well as significant archive holdings, including that of the Northern Ireland Civil Rights Association. [see LIBRARIES; POLITICAL STREET ART IN NORTHERN IRELAND.] **John Gray**

linen halls, official centres for the sale of finished linens. The Dublin White Linen Hall, which opened in Coleraine Street in 1728, was administered by the Linen Board. It guaranteed the quality and yardage of all linens sold there, which were bought principally by Irish and English buyers. The Dublin factors facilitated the sale of linen financially and so ensured the development of the industry at home. A dispute arose in 1782 between northern suppliers and the Linen Board; as the Ulster drapers were then able to finance their own exports, they established white linen halls in both Belfast and Newry. **Mairead Dunlevy**

Lionel of Clarence (1338–1368), third son of Edward III and Philippa of Hainault. Through his marriage to Elizabeth de Burgh (died 1363), daughter and heiress of the last resident Earl of Ulster, he received vast estates in Ireland. In July 1361 Edward III appointed him Justiciar of Ireland (to 1366), initiating a period of military intervention in Ireland financed by the English exchequer with a view to recovering the territories lost by the colony to the Irish and rebuilding the economy of what had once been a profitable lordship.

On his arrival in Dublin in September 1361 with an army of landholders, Lionel embarked on a campaign against the Irish of Wicklow. For the next five years he led armies against the Irish, receiving submissions from a number of kings. He began an elaborate reform of the administration; the exchequer was moved from Dublin to Carlow, in an attempt to exercise greater control over the Irish of the Leinster mountains. In February 1366 he held a parliament in Kilkenny that produced the infamous STATUTES OF KILKENNY, which sought to increase the social and political stability of the ANGLO-NORMAN community. Lionel's achievements proved transitory: the Irish were quick to renounce their oaths, and the financial recovery did not last. He was recalled from Ireland in 1366 to marry the wealthy niece of the Visconti ruler of Milan and fell ill at Alba, where he died on 7 October 1368. **Susan Foran**

Lisburn (*Lios na gCearrbhach*), Co. Antrim, a manufacturing and commercial town, since the late nineteenth century a dormitory suburb of Belfast and in recent years part of the greater Belfast urban area, despite being administered as a separate borough; population (1991) 42,110. The town is of PLANTATION origin; the site was granted to Sir Fulke (later Viscount) Conway in 1609, and in 1627 a castle was built and the settlement incorporated in 1662. Subsequently Lisburn has been associated with the growth of the linen industry, particularly after LOUIS CROMMELIN settled a colony of HUGUENOT refugees here in 1698. By the later nineteenth century the town's industries included the world's largest manufacturer of linen thread, Thomas Barbour. Destroyed by accidental fire in 1707, the town was quickly rebuilt on early GEORGIAN principles. The castle site, adjacent to Christ Church (Church of Ireland) Cathedral (1708), together with the Assembly Rooms (1707) and market square, still provide the town's visual focus. Elsewhere, continuing and frequently insensitive redevelopment and neglect have destroyed much of Lisburn's originally rich Georgian heritage. Today the town acts as a shopping centre for greater Belfast's southern periphery, only slightly affected by the recent development of out-of-town SHOPPING CENTRES, such as Sprucefield. **Lindsay Proudfoot**

Liscarroll Castle, Co. Cork, a large enclosure castle of the later Middle Ages, consisting of a rectangular enclosure with a three-quarter ROUND TOWER at each angle and a gate-tower in the middle of the south wall. There is a rectangular gate-tower with barrel-vaulted passage and portcullis in the centre, protected by a gate at each end. It was originally three storeys high and contained enough rooms to have been the principal accommodation. The fortress would have had wooden buildings inside the curtain-walls. A tower in the north curtain-wall was used mainly as a latrine. The angle-towers were originally three storeys high, with spiral stairs giving access to the upper chambers. **David Sweetman**

Lismore crozier, one of the finest and best-preserved Irish CROZIERS, discovered in 1814 in a blocked doorway at Lismore Castle, Co. Waterford, together with the late medieval Book of Lismore; both had perhaps been hidden for safekeeping in the seventeenth century. It is now in the NATIONAL MUSEUM, Dublin. The crozier is decorated in a native version of the Scandinavian *Urnes* style. An inscription records its manufacture by the craftsman Neachtan for Niall mac Mhic Aodhagáin, Bishop of Lismore from 1090 to 1113. **Cormac Bourke**

Listowel (*Lios Tuathail*), Co. Kerry, a market town on the River Feale, 25 km (16 miles) north-east of Tralee; population (2002) 3,569. Listowel was the site of a medieval castle, captured after a siege by Elizabethan forces in 1600; its ruins survive in the town centre as a town gate. The town is in a fertile agricultural area; it became a prosperous market and MILLING town in the nineteenth century, with a population of 2,600 in 1841. Unlike most similar towns, it continued to expand after the GREAT FAMINE. Its population declined in the twentieth century, from 3,400 in 1901 to 2,900 in 1961, but has since recovered. It is now a prosperous service and industrial town but is better renowned for its Listowel Writers' Weekend and its contributions to literature: the writer BRYAN MACMAHON was a schoolteacher here, and JOHN B. KEANE, the most popular Irish playwright of the late twentieth century, owned and ran a pub in the town. **Kevin Hourihan**

Listowel and Ballybunion Railway, Co. Kerry, a monorail RAILWAY operating from 5 March 1888, constructed to the innovative design of the French engineer Charles Lartigue. The single rail, 1–1.5 m (3–5 ft) above ground level, was supported on A-shaped trestles, with the two-boiler engine and the carriages hanging down on each side; this necessitated balancing the passengers, freight, and livestock, a cumbrous and often hilarious process. The line consistently failed to cover its expenses, and on 14 October 1924 it was closed by order of the courts. A partial reconstruction for tourist purposes has been undertaken. **Bernard Share**

Lismore Crozier. *A processional crozier (c. 1100) found in 1814 at Lismore Castle, Co Waterford. The drop of the crook (left) originally contained a reliquary. Two lines of text at the base of the crook record the name of the craftsman and of the client. [National Museum of Ireland]*

literacy. The issue of literacy in Ireland has recently been a controversial one, with the Republic achieving a low ranking in the International Adult Literacy Survey conducted by the OECD in 1997. The survey assessed three aspects of literacy: prose literacy (the knowledge and skill necessary to derive information from texts), document literacy (the knowledge and skill necessary to derive information from a range of document types), and quantitative literacy (the ability to carry out arithmetic operations). Adults were allocated to five levels of literacy, ranging from level 1 (the lowest) to level 5. A relatively high proportion of adults was found to have level 1 skills compared with other countries. However, the approach to literacy measurement taken in the survey has been subject to some criticism, in particular for its failure to reflect the common-sense notion of 'illiteracy' and for the difficulties in making valid comparisons among cultures. The survey also drew attention to a gap between literacy provision and local needs. Literacy services are co-ordinated by the National Adult Literacy Agency, mostly using local volunteers. The green paper on adult education emphasised the importance of literacy and stressed the need for the development of a comprehensive national literacy service. **Emer Smyth**

literary criticism in English. The emergence in Ireland of criticism as a discipline separate and distinct from the production of creative work dates from the middle of the nineteenth century. While there is a critical dimension in EDMUND BURKE's work on aesthetics, *The Sublime and the Beautiful* (1757), and that of such writers as JAMES CLARENCE MANGAN and MARIA EDGEWORTH, criticism as a genre was stimulated by such figures as MATTHEW ARNOLD and ERNEST RENAN and is demonstrated in the cross-cultural and inter-disciplinary writings of SAMUEL FERGUSON, W. E. H. LECKY, W. K. MAGEE, and, perhaps most significantly, EDWARD DOWDEN, first professor of English at TRINITY COLLEGE, Dublin. DUBLIN UNIVERSITY MAGAZINE (1833–77) was the principal voice of 'liberal unionism' in the middle of the nineteenth century, setting an establishment tone that was later reflected in *Dana* (1904–5) and was challenged, during the period of cultural mobilisation following the fall of PARNELL, by the *United Irishman* (1899–1906), *All-Ireland Review* (1900–6), and *Irish Review* (1911–14).

Ferguson's influence as a representative of 'middle Ireland' is reflected in the ambivalence of W. B. YEATS's cultural ambitions and critical writings as he commuted between the 'CELTIC TWILIGHT' and the LITERARY REVIVAL, of which he became the leading figure.

Criticism in Ireland, therefore, has never escaped from the claims of cultural politics. The imperatives of self-assertion during the struggle for independence, and more importantly of post-independence self-definition, have prevented critics from autonomously pursuing critical theory *per se* without engaging at the same time with the issues of nationalism and self-determination. Post-colonial experience has only recently been explicitly addressed—Gerry Smyth has written extensively on the subject, as in *Decolonisation and Criticism: The Construction of Irish Literature* (1998)—but it has subliminally affected almost every area of critical and artistic debate, including that of whether English is the appropriate medium for the expression of Irish experience and, if so, what relations the forms of English spoken and written in Ireland have with the English elsewhere.

One of the most specific instances of cultural mobilisation with a critical dimension was the formation in 1980 by BRIAN FRIEL and STEPHEN REA of the FIELD DAY COMPANY, originally to produce plays but later to publish a series of pamphlets. The momentum of this initiative, involving SEAMUS DEANE, SEAMUS HEANEY, TOM PAULIN, DAVID HAMMOND, and THOMAS KILROY, culminated in the publication under Deane's general editorship of the *Field Day Anthology of Irish Writing* (1991), a provocative manifesto of literary, political and cultural identity intended to focus debate, within a divided Ireland and between Britain and Ireland, on Irish achievements in a variety of literary milieus.

The generation of critics in the cultural resurgence that permeated the War of Independence and its unstable aftermath included DANIEL CORKERY, THOMAS MACDONAGH, SEAN O'FAOLAIN, FRANK O'CONNOR, and PEADAR O'DONNELL. Cultural ambivalence became more definitive as a polarisation emerged between 'Irish Ireland' (of which D. P. MORAN's *Leader* was the mouthpiece) and more cosmopolitan ENLIGHTENMENT principles. One can detect a palpable sense of irony, confusion, and antagonism between writers (for example Corkery and his erstwhile pupil O'Faolain) anxious to explore 'Irishness' yet divided among themselves and within themselves as to what Irishness might mean and how it might be expressed. This found its outlet largely in the medium of such magazines as *Studies* (1912–), the *Dublin Magazine* (1923–58), *Ireland Today* (1936–8), the BELL (1940–54), *Envoy* (1949–51), *Kavanagh's Weekly* (1952), and *Arena* (1963–5). These media were succeeded in the later 1960s, 70s and 80s by HIBERNIA (1937–80), *Atlantis* (1970–73), the *Crane Bag* (1977–85), *Fortnight* 1976–), *Krino* (1985–), and a fresh epiphany of the *Irish Review* (1986–).

Until the 1970s the intellectual, artistic and academic strands of Irish life were strongly entwined, pulling critical and creative talents together rather than allowing them to become separate and distinct pursuits. A significant example of this concatenation is the career of CONOR CRUISE O'BRIEN as critic, playwright, academic, journalist, diplomat, and government minister. The critic as a judge of, and commentator on, forms of cultural expression rather than as a producer has therefore been difficult to identify with any clarity: very few have been able to maintain an autonomous critical function, and even TERRY EAGLETON, one of the few to engage with critical theory, has written plays, while one of the most influential, Seamus Deane, is also a poet and novelist.

JOHN JORDAN, Seamus Heaney and DEREK MAHON have all been distinguished for their critical acumen besides their artistic achievements. The parallel emergence of cultural politics—an awareness of the political dimension of culture as a whole, and of a cultural dimension to political life—has identified many of these writers as products of, and influenced by, various strands of the cultural traditions of Ireland. DENIS DONOGHUE and VIVIAN MERCIER were perhaps the only Irishmen to establish an international reputation exclusively as critics of the first class. However, more recently critical voices have emerged independent of, and capable of more objective commentary upon, literature, visual arts, and music.

Criticism as a function of magazines and newspapers occupied a plateau of cosiness for many years, from which there were very few exceptions. While such criticism might have been 'intelligent', it has only since the 1970s been driven by trenchant examination of subject matter as distinct from style. In this sense the 'critic' as a commentator on Irish society and its behaviour in the modern world can now be recognised in writers such as Eoghan Harris, Mary Holland, Nell McCafferty, Kevin Myers, Nuala O'Faolain, and FINTAN O'TOOLE.

The universities have been the chief locus of critical transmission with respect to literature, with teachers of the calibre of Roger McHugh, AUGUSTINE MARTIN, Christopher Murray, J. C. C. Mays, Andrew Carpenter, Ailbhe Smyth, DECLAN KIBERD and ANTHONY ROCHE (at UCD), TERENCE BROWN, Nicholas Grene, KEVIN ROCKETT and GERALD DAWE (at TCD), Seán Lucy (UCC), Barbara Hayley and Peter Denman (Maynooth), THOMAS KILROY (NUIG), Robert Welch and Desmond Bell (University of Ulster), LUKE GIBBONS (DCU and Notre Dame), T. R. Henn (Cambridge), and ROY FOSTER (Oxford) inculcating a sense of the importance of analysis and of responsible commentary. The universities have also been a focus for critical debate and exchange, the most notable examples being in Anglo-Irish literature through the medium of the International Association for the Study of Irish Literatures and, at UCD, the *Irish University Review*. However, it has been largely resisted in Irish universities, chiefly because of what continues to be seen as the prior claim of considering Irish questions before engaging in disinterested or detached analysis of cultural production as a result, for example, of social or economic conditions.

Apart from literature, Irish critics have been slow to develop in either numbers or quality in other art disciplines, though since the 1970s there has been an exponential growth in the appreciation of the visual arts, mainly in monographs on individual artists, both historical and modern, the latter including LOUIS LE BROCQUY, JACK B. YEATS, HARRY CLARKE, RODERIC O'CONOR, and MAINIE JELLETT. In the IRISH TIMES BRIAN FALLON's and Aidan Dunne's columns have brought a view of both Irish and international art to a wide readership. An important annual publication is the *Irish Arts Review* (1984–). In film, pioneering work by KEVIN ROCKETT has led to a significant number of publications, supported by conferences and seminars largely stimulated by the IRISH FILM CENTRE, while Michael Dwyer has proved a stimulating and authoritative commentator in the *Irish Times*.

Music criticism has suffered from the same impoverishment as music itself, as a lack of both appropriate music education and an adequate musical infrastructure has inhibited the appreciation of classical music and the development of Irish musicology, while conversely the growing success of traditional music has resulted in a stimulating literature, among which the radio series 'Our Musical Heritage' (1962) by SEÁN Ó RIADA was seminal. Two exceptional figures in classical music criticism were Harold White (Dermot McMurrough) and CHARLES ACTON.

In all these disciplines the main thrust of inquiry has been directed towards Irish studies, which embraces a multi-disciplinary approach to the question of what it means to be Irish in the twentieth and twenty-first centuries. The acknowledgment of diversities of Irishness, and of ways of discussing Ireland, has facilitated a recognition of Ireland as a source of energies for a diaspora that is not only geographical but also notional. People of Irish descent or affinity in varying parts of the world have been enabled, by new historical and sociological discourse, to modify their perspectives on Irishness according to historical circumstance, gender, and class. Literature, films, and drama have been central in this critical revaluation of Irish mores, beliefs, and attitudes to both the imagined and the real worlds. In North America this new generation of critics has been led by such figures as Robert Tracy, David Krause, Harold Bloom, ROBERT HOGAN, Robert O'Driscoll, D. E. S. Maxwell, James Flannery, John Wilson Foster, and Ann Saddlemyer, who have been followed by younger writers such as David Lloyd and Elizabeth Butler Cullingford, with the *Irish Literary Supplement* and *Éire-Ireland* providing valuable platforms in the United States and the *Canadian Journal of Irish Studies* in Canada. In Britain the pioneers were David Cairns and Shaun Richards with their *Writing Ireland: Colonialism, Nationalism and Culture* (1988), which has contributed to the reorientation of the critical relationship of English literature and history with Irish literature and history, as evident in the appearance of *Irish Studies Review* (1991–).

Other cultural interests have come from the Germanic and Scandinavian areas, with Wolfgang Zach, Joep Leerssen, Birgit Bramsbäck, Rüdiger Imhof, Heinz Kosok, and, in Hungary, the partnership of Donald Morse and Csilla Bertha, while in France a parallel school of criticism has emerged under the tutelage of Patrick Rafroidi, Jacqueline Genet, and Maurice Goldring, with *Études Irlandaises* as a valuable medium. Finally, a strong interest in Irish culture has been demonstrated in Japan, where Masaru Sekine has been a leading figure and *Harp* a lively journal. **Richard Pine**

literary criticism in Irish. Literary criticism of works in Irish from the twentieth century onwards is underdeveloped. From the language revival period in the late nineteenth century it has been the fate of literature in Irish—as of other minority or endangered languages—to have had its literature judged chiefly on its linguistic richness and on how well it elucidated the cultural differences between the distinct culture from which it evolved and that of the majority language.

That the various modern approaches to criticism have begun to be applied to some degree to modern literature in Irish can be seen in *Faoin mBlaoisc Bheag Sin* (1991), LOUIS DE PAOR's psychological examination of MÁIRTÍN Ó CADHAIN's work, *B'Ait Leo Bean* (1998), Máirín Nic Eoin's feminist study of gender ideology in the literary tradition, and DECLAN KIBERD's post-colonial critiques in *Inventing Ireland* (1995) and *Irish Classics* (2000). In addition there is an eclectic critical tradition as espoused by critics such as ALAN TITLEY in his study of the novel in Irish, *An tÚrscéal Gaeilge* (1991), and Gearóid Denvir in his study of Ó Cadhain, *Cadhan Aonair* (1987), which is wary of the danger of individual methodologies being afforded more importance than the texts they should elucidate.

The astonishingly creative body of literature that has been produced since the language revival, however, has not evinced a commensurately rich critical response. Despite occasionally fruitful periods of interest in various universities—notably in the 1970s in Cork under the influence of SEÁN Ó TUAMA and particularly in Maynooth under the influence of BREANDÁN Ó DOIBHLIN, as documented by Antain Mag Shamhráin in *Litríocht, Léitheoireacht, Critic* (1986)—no journal devoted specifically to literary criticism has emerged, though individual critical articles appear in periodicals such as COMHAR and *Feasta* and annuals such as *Oghma*, *Bliainiris*, and *An Aimsir Óg*. The study of language and literature in Irish from before the twentieth century certainly makes demands of time and attention, but this cannot account for the low status afforded to the study and criticism of modern literature within the academic system. The official journals of the universities' Irish Departments and third-level bodies are mainly devoted to editions of pre-nineteenth-century texts and dialect study; as a consequence, younger scholars interested in criticism of contemporary literature are dependent on the support and enthusiasm of individual academics and in the continued interest in their work of academic publishers, such as An Clóchomhar, which has regularly included works of literary criticism in its prestigious 'Imleabhair Thaighde' series.

Such progress as has been made in recent years has been a result of publication initiatives involving inter-institution collaboration. Originally presented as Cumann Merriman lectures, the collection of essays *Nua-Léamha* (edited by Máirín Ní Dhonnchadha, 1996) offers fresh critical views on various aspects of the Irish literary tradition, while the theoretically focused essays in *Téacs agus Comhthéacs* (edited by Máire Ní Annracháin and Bríona Nic Dhiarmada, 1999) explore the use and usefulness of various critical paradigms in the study of literature in Irish. Series of critical monographs have also been commissioned by some publishers, such as *Aistí Léirmheasa* (Cló Iar-Chonnachta) and *Meas* (Cois Life); but the long-term success of these initiatives will depend on the active involvement and support of third-level institutions. **Seán Ó Cearnaigh**

literary magazines, 1900–2001. Published with little regard for profit and less for fashion, such journals provide a forum for writers and movements unrecognised by the literary establishment of their time. The Irish Literary Theatre had its own magazine, *Samhain* (1901–8), edited by W. B. YEATS, which published dramatic and other writings by himself and his companions in the LITERARY REVIVAL. *Uladh* (1904–5), published in Belfast, was similarly associated with the ULSTER LITERARY THEATRE, though not subordinated to it.

The first truly independent literary magazine in Ireland was *Dana* (1904–5), edited by Frederick Ryan and JOHN EGLINTON. It published poetry, essays, and controversial editorials, the latter often critical of Irish Catholicism and the cultural exclusivity of the GAELIC LEAGUE. The *Irish Homestead* (1895–1923) was a weekly magazine founded by Sir HORACE PLUNKETT as the organ of his agricultural co-operative movement. GEORGE RUSSELL became its editor in 1905; it advanced his visionary and liberal ideals and also published short works by new writers, including the first three of JAMES JOYCE's *Dubliners* stories. In 1923 Russell merged the magazine with a new one, the *Irish Statesman*, which continued the same policies, publishing work by most of the leading writers of the period. Writers from Ulster as well as the new Irish Free State contributed to SEUMAS O'SULLIVAN's *Dublin Magazine* (1923–5, 1926–58), among them PATRICK KAVANAGH, AUSTIN CLARKE, JOSEPH CAMPBELL, and MARY LAVIN. Considered staid by more avant-garde spirits, it was Ireland's leading literary magazine until SEAN O'FAOLAIN founded the BELL (1940–46, 1950–54). It published many of the same writers, as well as newcomers, such as BRENDAN BEHAN and FLANN O'BRIEN; LOUIS MACNEICE was poetry editor, 1946–7. O'Faolain also commissioned studies of social and political issues and in his trenchant and influential editorials attacked isolationism, literary censorship, and other nay-saying tendencies in the DE VALERA state. John Ryan's *Envoy* (1949–51) provided a link between Irish and Continental writing. The fortnightly journal *An Glór* (1941–8) carried essays on a wide variety of subjects as well as purely literary contributions; it was superseded by the monthly *Feasta* (1948–). Another monthly, *Comhar* (1942–), similarly mixes reviews and essays on public affairs with work by SEÁN Ó RÍORDÁIN, NUALA NÍ DHOMHNAILL, and others (see p. 224).

Thereafter, literary magazines tended to be less social in their concerns and more purely literary. The Cork novelist DAVID MARCUS founded *Poetry Ireland* in 1948, publishing poems by SAMUEL BECKETT, CECIL DAY-LEWIS, ANTHONY CRONIN, and others. It folded in 1954 but was resurrected under the editorship of JOHN JORDAN for a second series, 1962–8, which included work by younger poets, such as SEAMUS HEANEY, MICHAEL HARTNETT, and PAUL DURCAN. In 1981 JOHN F. DEANE revived the magazine once more, now calling it *Poetry Ireland Review* and with John Jordan again as its first editor. In the 1990s it became the organ of POETRY IRELAND/Éigse Éireann, the national poetry society; it is now generally regarded as the journal of record in Irish poetry, reviewing all books by Irish poets and, with a different editor each year, reflecting their diverse tastes in the poetry and essays it publishes.

In 1968 the *Honest Ulsterman* was founded in Co. Antrim by the poet JAMES SIMMONS. Impatient at the pretensions of the Dublin literary establishment, it welcomed work by non-conforming Dublin writers, such as BRENDAN KENNELLY and JOHN MCGAHERN, as well as Heaney, MICHAEL LONGLEY, DEREK MAHON, and other Ulster poets. Simmons was not much disposed to editorialise, but his magazine let light into some dark corners of a repressed society. Other influential journals emerging in the 1960s were JAMES LIDDY and Michael Hartnett's *Arena* (1963–5) and the internationalist *Lace Curtain* (1969–71), associated with the New Writers' Press. In 1970 Michael Davitt and other students at University College, Cork, launched INNTI and embarked on a series of Irish-language poetry readings that attracted audiences of hundreds. Originally a broadsheet, it was revived by Davitt in 1980 as an increasingly elegant and influential journal of poetry, reviews, and interviews. The *Innti* group, which included Nuala Ní Dhomhnaill, LIAM Ó MUIRTHILE, GABRIEL ROSENSTOCK, and Davitt himself, sought a renewal of Irish-language poetry from sources as diverse as American beat poetry, popular culture, and the Irish-language tradition. The magazine survived until 1996.

Of the many other magazines emerging in the 1970s and 80s mention must be made of *The Crane Bag* (1977–85), an influential journal of ideas about all aspects of Irish life and, importantly, the role of myth; *Cyphers* (1975–), which remains as open to foreign translations as to Irish-language poetry; and GERALD DAWE's *Krino* (1986–96). New journals continue to crowd forward: *Metre*, *Incognito*, and the *Stinging Fly* in Dublin, *Flaming Arrows* and *Force 10* in Sligo, and the *Shop*, *Cork Literary Review*, *Southword*, and *Brobdingnagian Times* in and around Cork. **John Wakeman**

Literary Revival (also known as the Irish Literary Renaissance), a term in literary history that refers to the period from the 1880s to the 1920s, when writers in both Irish and English turned to the Irish past for inspiration. STANDISH JAMES O'GRADY's English-language versions of bardic tales, especially those in which CÚ CHULAINN figures as hero (such as *History of Ireland: Cuculain and his Contemporaries*, 1880), were enormously influential, particularly on W. B. YEATS, who in poetry and drama made the mythical IRON AGE warrior represent the spirit of the nation in his pursuit of honour and glory, whatever the personal cost. Writers of this period, among them Yeats, LADY AUGUSTA GREGORY, JOHN MILLINGTON SYNGE, GEORGE RUSSELL, and JAMES STEPHENS, wrote works that took Irish MYTHOLOGY and FOLKLORE as inspiration and treated Irish experience from a viewpoint of romantic primitivism and spiritual idealism. The mythical achievements of the past served as a summons to future magnificence in a period when, after the fall of PARNELL and the defeats of the HOME RULE Bill in 1886 and 1893, many felt that Irish fortunes were at a low ebb. The revival also took considerable energy from an awareness of the country's bilingualism, as English-language writers sought to characterise their writings by a distinctive dialect that reflected the influence of Irish on the English spoken in Ireland. Lady Augusta Gregory's *Cuchulain of Muirthemne* (1902) and the plays of Synge are representative, as is DOUGLAS HYDE's dual-language text *The Love Songs of Connacht* (1893).

Revivalism, with its interest in translations, redactions and versions and its romantic vision of the past—which in lesser writers than Yeats and Synge was, arguably, indulged at the expense of personal expression—in time came to be an object of satirical and humorous treatment in the writings of JAMES JOYCE (in the 'Cyclops' chapter of ULYSSES) and FLANN O'BRIEN (in AT SWIM-TWO-BIRDS). In historical terms, the period is reckoned as one in which literary endeavour played a role in the national awakening that bore fruit in the 1916 RISING and in the quest for independence that was partially achieved in 1922. **Terence Brown**

Literary warrant: see BARANTAS.

Little Ice Age. During the period 1550–1700 Western Europe appears to have had its coldest temperatures since the Ice Age, 10,000 years previously. Since that time temperatures have generally increased, resulting in those 150 years being termed the Little Ice Age. As few instrumental records are available, the evidence consists of descriptions of activities (fishing and agricultural records) and events (occurrences of frost or snowfall and bird migrations). In addition, the thickness of the annual growth rings of trees may be related to changes in precipitation and temperature. The evidence suggests that during this period Europe experienced cold, wet winters, increased frequency of snowfalls, and the advance of mountain glaciers. The suggested causes of this cooling are an increased easterly airflow (off the cold European continent) and a substantial drop in the ocean temperature of the North Atlantic. The margin of ice around the North Pole in winter extended around Iceland—about 100 km (60 miles) further south than today—and cod, a species that requires relatively warm water, disappeared from the surrounding seas.

livestock industry. *Dungarvan Mart, Co. Waterford; as the farming industry became more specialised through modernisation, the 1960s saw purpose-built cattle marts replacing traditional open-air markets and fairs.* [Irish Farmers Journal]

In Ireland reports are sketchy, given the political state of the country during much of the period; but the winters of the 1680s are regarded in folklore as being the worst. Certainly in London the Great Frost of 1683/4 was the longest on record, with the Thames completely frozen and the ice reported to be some 280 mm (11 in.) thick. Ireland was revisited by these conditions during the Great Frost of 1740/41. In January 1741 the Rivers LIFFEY, SLANEY, and BOYNE, as well as LOUGH NEAGH and LOUGH CONN, froze. People walked across Lough Neagh from the Co. Tyrone shore to Antrim market. The cold played havoc with POTATO stocks, which froze and rotted. Tillage crops sown the previous autumn were destroyed in the non-existent spring, and animals died in the absence of fodder. FAMINE followed, resulting in between 310,000 and 450,000 deaths. There were disturbances in Belfast and food riots in Dublin as prices soared. Private relief included the building of the huge obelisk in the grounds of CASTLETOWN. [see BIG WIND, NIGHT OF THE; CLIMATE; EXTREME WEATHER.] **Gerald Mills**

Liverpool, the Irish in. A major port of entry for Irish emigrants, Liverpool was generally perceived as a temporary or transitional location rather than as a destination. However, many Irish people were to remain in this 'black spot on the Mersey.' Before the GREAT FAMINE influx, the 1841 census already recorded 49,639 Irish-born people in Liverpool, some 17 per cent of the population, living for the most part at the bottom of the residential and socio-economic hierarchy. According to Father James Nugent, a Liverpool-Irish priest, the Irish who remained in Liverpool were the 'dregs', unable or unwilling to take advantage of opportunities elsewhere in Britain or in the New World. Confronted by the immovable Irish presence, the Catholic Church was compelled to redefine its local mission, undergoing a distinct Hibernicisation in its philanthropic, associational, and pastoral provision.

Dialectical developments in other denominations completed the process by which 'Irish' and 'Catholic' became synonymous in nineteenth-century Liverpool. Irish Protestant immigrants merged, even to the point of anonymity, into the host mainstream. The Ulster-Scots, and their distinct Irish presbyteries, disappeared quietly from view, denied any equivalent to the 'SCOTCH-IRISH' identity of their compatriots in America, while Anglo-Irish migrants were enthusiastic advocates of Britishness, the populist Protestant identity that secured Tory hegemony in Liverpool until the SECOND WORLD WAR. Proudly apart, the Catholic parish became a focus for charity and 'cradle-to-grave' collective mutuality, adding to the informal infrastructure of solidarity and social security—based on the pub, court, and core street—that made the Irish reluctant to move on from Liverpool.

By the last decades of the nineteenth century this extensive parish and pub-based infrastructure facilitated an effective challenge to the traditional Liberal alignment. Elected for the Scotland ward in 1875, Lawrence Connolly was the first of forty-eight Irish Nationalists to sit on the city council between 1875 and 1922. Furthermore, the Scotland division became T. P. O'CONNOR's parliamentary fiefdom from 1885 to 1929, secured by the same Liverpool-Irish electoral machinery. As the local leadership of the IRISH PARTY passed steadily into the hands of second-generation Irish, with the Irish-born—some 66,000 people—constituting only 12.5 per cent of the city's population by 1891, it displayed less interest in the fate of Ireland than in the immediate needs of the local Catholic community in housing and employment. Even so the leadership remained distinctly middle-class, notably those who identified their niche as servicing the Irish enclave. It was not until the turmoils of the 1920s that the Liverpool-Irish eventually turned to the class politics of Labour. Thereafter, continuing economic depression and adversity made Liverpool less attractive as a destination for Irish emigrants, while new transport links diminished its role as port of entry. However, the 'CELTIC TIGER' economy rejuvenated the Dublin–Liverpool axis, symbolised by the twinning of the two cities. **John Belchem**

livestock industry

Cattle. Cattle have always been of central importance in Ireland's ECONOMY. About the eighth century cattle were the main form of currency, the cow being the standard unit. Cattle became the main component of EXPORT earnings; English parliamentary records show that c. 1620 annual exports of live cattle to England were about 100,000 head. Early in the nineteenth century large landowners began the importing of newly developed breeds, especially dual-purpose (milk and beef) Shorthorns, and these constituted the bulk of the cattle herd of 5 million head until the 1960s. Cattle for beef originated either as surplus male calves in milk-producing herds or in specialist beef (suckler) herds. The increase in profitability of milk production accelerated by membership of the EUROPEAN UNION from 1973 resulted in an increased emphasis on milk and the replacement of dual-purpose Shorthorn cows in milking herds with the single-purpose Holstein Friesian milking strain. The poor beefing qualities of this type forced beef-producers to increasingly breed their own requirements; and the suckler herd grew from being less than half the size of the milking herd to a position of near-equality in numbers. Approximate total figures for 2000 are 1.7 million dairy cows, 1.6 million beef cows, and a total of 9 million cattle. Farmers in cattle production number over 100,000. EU premiums account for substantial proportions of beef farmers' income; beef production is regulated by quotas on numbers of premiums paid.

Until the 1980s the main breeds for beef production were Angus and Hereford crosses on Friesian and Shorthorn-type cows. To cater for developing Continental markets and a demand for leaner beef, Continental beef breeds were increasingly used. The dominance of Hereford and Angus beef bulls gave way to principally Charollais, Limousin, Simmental, and Belgian Blue. Intervention buying financed by the European Union also favoured Continental breeds; but the demand for traditional types producing marbled beef also remains firm.

Grass is the main feed, grazed in summer and fed as silage in winter. Beef exports, adversely affected by the incidence of bovine spongiform encephalopathy (BSE) and foot-and-mouth disease, is now recovering. An Bord Bia and the Livestock and Meat Commission in Northern Ireland actively promote the trade in beef and live cattle; the export value in 2000 was approximately €1.8 billion, with a ratio of beef to live cattle of 14:1. Schemes of genetic improvement are also operated. **Austin Mescal**

Pigs. Pigs were reared on most farms in Ireland up to the 1950s, fed on home-produced feed and used as a source of protein for all the family. The situation has changed dramatically since that time: the Republic now exports more than 55 per cent of its production, with farm-gate value estimated at £275 million for 2001. There are 550 commercial pig producers (i.e. those with more than twenty sows) in the Republic, comprising 98 per cent of the national herd; there are a further 100 farmers with fewer than twenty sows. In Northern Ireland 60 per cent of production takes place on farms with fewer than twenty sows; the structure of production is, therefore, vastly different in the South and the North.

From the 1950s to the 1990s the pig herd was static, at approximately 1.1 million head, but a dramatic increase occurred in the 1990s, when the herd rose to 1.75 million, an increase of 50 per cent. In Northern Ireland the total herd is just 0.4 million, including 42,600 breeding sows, a 50 per cent reduction from 1996. The primary sites of pig farming in the South are Cos. Cavan, Cork, and Tipperary, which account for 46 per cent of production. In the North production is fairly evenly spread throughout five counties, the exception being Co. Fermanagh, which has very few pigs. **Ned Walsh**

Sheep. Ireland is the second-largest exporter of lamb in the European Union, exporting about 4.5 million fresh lambs annually, mainly to France, at a typical carcase weight of 18–20 kg. In value, sheep production contributes some 5 per cent to gross agricultural output, or 8 per cent including support payments. The breeding ewe flock consists of 5.5 million, including 1.3 million in Northern Ireland. Altogether there are 48,000 producers, with an average breeding ewe flock of 115 ewes, which is slightly larger in Northern Ireland than in the Republic. 70 per cent of sheep are farmed in the disadvantaged areas of the country. There are very few sheep-only farms (less than 3 per cent); and though the flock size is not very large, more than 70 per cent of flocks have more than 100 ewes. Suffolk crossbreds make up 50 per cent of the lowland flocks, with Leicester crosses being more commonly found in Northern Ireland. Cheviot and Scottish blackface ewes account for about a third of the population and predominate in the poorer hill and mountainous areas. The Suffolk is the predominant sire breed on the lowlands, though the Texel and the Charollais have become popular in recent years, while the majority of Scottish blackface and Cheviot ewes are bred pure. Lambing takes place in March and April; the lamb output per ewe is 1.31 on the lowlands, down to about 0.6 for the Scottish blackface in the poorer land area. Sheep dairying is not an important enterprise, with only about 3,000 milking ewes in total. **Frank Crosby**

Lloyd, Rev. Humphrey (1800–1881), physicist. Born in Dublin; educated at TCD and ordained into the CHURCH OF IRELAND. Professor of natural and experimental philosophy at Trinity College, Dublin, he was provost from 1867 to 1881. He was made a fellow of the Royal Society in 1836 and was president of the ROYAL IRISH ACADEMY from 1846 to 1851. He received international acclaim when he experimentally confirmed the theoretical prediction by WILLIAM ROWAN HAMILTON concerning the behaviour of light waves in biaxial crystals. He played a leading role in the development of international studies into terrestrial magnetism and participated in the foundation of the Trinity College engineering school. **Charles Mollan**

Lloyd, Richard (Dicky) (1891–1950), rugby footballer. Born in Dungannon, Co. Tyrone. He won nineteen caps at out-half in a career spanning the FIRST WORLD WAR. He and his Trinity scrum-half partner Harry Read were said to be Ireland's first specialist half-backs. He scored seventy-five international points, then an Irish record, and his seven international dropped goals are still an Irish record. **Karl Johnston**

Lloyd, Seón (died c. 1786), poet. Born in Limerick; moved to Co. Clare and taught school in the parish of Doonaha. He advertised a school in Limerick, 1773. There are two autograph manuscripts written in Cork in July and October 1775. He published *A Short Tour in the County of Clare* (1780). More than twenty surviving poems in Irish are ascribed to him; six autograph manuscripts survive. He died at Tureen, near Ennis. **Éilís Ní Dheá**

Lloyd George, David (1863–1945), British politician. Born in Manchester; educated in Gwynedd. Despite his Welsh origins, Lloyd George was unsympathetic to Irish nationalism. He supported concessions to Ulster before the third HOME RULE Bill (1912). In charge of an aborted attempt at settlement in 1916, as British Prime Minister he was responsible for the IRISH CONVENTION, 1917–18. He left Irish affairs to the inept Lord French, 1918–19, then followed a mixed policy of coercion and conciliation; he is forever associated in Ireland with the introduction of the BLACK AND TANS. The Anglo-Irish Conference and Treaty are a supreme example of his political skills. His methods, however, intensified bitterness in Anglo-Irish relations; his insistence on the strict application of the Treaty made CIVIL WAR in the twenty-six counties more likely. **Michael A. Hopkinson**

local authorities. The contemporary structure of Irish LOCAL GOVERNMENT is recognisably that established under the LOCAL GOVERNMENT (IRELAND) ACT (1898), with four tiers of authority up to county and city council level, each responsible to a local electorate and designed to manage a broad range of local services. In practice, however, the decades since independence have seen the progressive removal of responsibility from local authorities for important policy areas, such as HEALTH and EDUCATION services and environmental protection, and the reduction in their discretionary powers in other matters, such as roads, PLANNING, and infrastructural development. The introduction of city and county management between 1929 and 1942 produced a shift of power within authorities, giving full-time officials defined decision-making powers and curtailing the right of elected councils to interfere in matters of detail. The result is that, in theory if not always in practice, elected local politicians have very little real power. Despite this, for most aspiring politicians election to a local authority remains the necessary first step on their way to DÁIL ÉIREANN. The historic county, city or town, as delineated in 1898, also remains a natural and popular focus of identity. Finally, the centralised nature of Irish government means that the national administration can often be blamed for local problems. For these reasons local authorities continue to enjoy a high degree of legitimacy even though their powers have been sharply reduced. **Eunan O'Halpin**

Northern Ireland. Northern Ireland has a single-tier system of local authorities. Twenty-six district councils replaced the previous system of seventy-two local authorities in 1972–3 as part of a series of political and administrative reforms. These councils exercise three roles: direct provision of services, a consultative role, and a representative role. The main directly provided services are now limited to environmental health, building regulations, community service, refuse collection and disposal, street cleaning, parks, cemeteries, leisure and recreation facilities, and aspects of TOURISM and economic development. Local authorities carry out their representative role through the nomination of councillors to a range of statutory bodies. Government agencies are also obliged to consult district councils in relation to planning permission, HOUSING policies, strategic development, and POLICING.

A significant development in the 1990s was the growth of partnerships involving local authorities, voluntary and community bodies, statutory agencies, and the private sector. These initiatives relate mainly to economic and community development and are often financed by the EUROPEAN UNION. The 582 councillors, elected by proportional representation, make up an important form of political representation; with no single party dominating, there has been a growth in power-sharing arrangements between the political parties in almost all councils. **Derek Birrell**

local authorities. *A sitting of the last Grand Jury of Co. Cork, c. 1880. Dating from the seventeenth century, the Grand Jury system dealt with local judicial and administrative business, its members drawn from the land-owning classes. [Courtesy of Cork County Council]*

Local Defence Force (LDF). In June 1940, during the SECOND WORLD WAR, the Local Security Force was formed to assist the GARDA SÍOCHÁNA. Each Garda district was required to train six groups of volunteers to assist in the performance of police duties and one armed group to protect Garda stations, vital installations, and patrols. A large proportion of the 180,000 recruits enrolled by September 1940 opted for the armed groups. These were first designated LSF Group A but from 1 January 1941 were renamed the Local Defence Force, placed under military control, and given responsibility for local defence in the event of hostilities. From February 1942 the LDF in Dublin, Cork, Limerick, and Galway was formed into rifle battalions, so that they could take over garrison duties and release the regular ARMY for operational tasks. The force was lightly armed, at first with sporting weapons, later with Springfield .300 rifles; the rifle battalions had Lee Enfield .303 rifles. Artillery, cavalry, engineer, signals, transport, and medical units began to be formed in 1942, and in 1943 the strength of the force exceeded 103,000. It became AN FÓRSA COSANTA ÁITIÚIL (FCA) in 1947. **James Dukes**

local government, eighteenth century. During the eighteenth century, responsibility for the administration of counties increasingly passed from county courts to GRAND JURIES, which acquired powers to maintain public roads and buildings and to provide for the sick, the mad, and the poor. These powers were only intermittently applied, and from 1838 the provision of health and welfare services was taken over by partially elected Poor Law Boards, charged with an increasing array of statutory responsibilities. Under the LOCAL GOVERNMENT (IRELAND) ACT (1898) the administrative functions of grand juries were transferred to county and rural district councils, with rural district councillors also acting as Poor Law guardians. **Virginia Crossman**

Local Government (Ireland) Act (1898), established a democratically elected system of local government. County and rural district councils took over the administrative responsibilities of GRAND JURIES and Poor Law Boards, while in urban areas, municipal corporations and town commissions were reconstituted as borough and urban district councils, acting alongside separate Poor Law Boards. Councillors were elected on a parliamentary franchise that was extended to include peers and women, the latter also being able to serve as district councillors and, from 1911, county councillors. **Virginia Crossman**

local government. Local government in the Republic consists of 114 elected local authorities: twenty-nine county councils, five city councils, five borough councils, and seventy-five town councils. Most of these originate from the Local Government (Ireland) Act (1898). Some towns with town commissioners became urban districts after 1898; others were created later. Other changes since the 1898 act include the abolition of rural district councils in 1925; the elevation of the borough of Galway to city status in 1985; the creation of three new county councils (Fingal, South Dublin, and Dún Laoghaire and Rathdown) in Co. Dublin in 1994; and the renaming of urban districts and towns with town commissioners as towns under the Local Government Act (2001).

From 1 January 1994 eight regional authorities were established, nominated by city and county authorities, with functions mostly relating to EU structural funds. It is unlikely that these would exist but for intervention by the European Union, as there is little local enthusiasm for regionalism.

The 1898 act was an important development, though it was feared at the time as a substitute for HOME RULE. However, local authorities played a prominent part in recognising Dáil Éireann in 1920. After independence the new Government quickly acted to restore order. The Local Government (Temporary Provisions) Act (1923) gave power to the Minister for Local Government to suspend authorities not properly discharging their functions and to replace them with a Government-appointed Commissioner. This led to the introduction of city management structures in Cork in 1929, later in the remaining cities, and finally to counties in 1942. The 1923 act extended state control to all local authorities, and this remains, despite some relaxation since the repeal in 1991 of the doctrine of *ultra vires* and its replacement by general competence. Following independence, the main emphasis after reform of the POOR LAW related to repairing damage caused during the WAR OF INDEPENDENCE and CIVIL WAR and establishing a legislative basis for the proper functioning of local authorities. This included the introduction of city and county management. The years 1931 and 1932 saw the introduction of HOUSING legislation, dealing with the backlog of slum clearance. A significant occurrence in 1935 was the extension of the local government franchise to all qualified citizens aged twenty-one and over. Following the establishment of separate Departments of Health and Social Welfare in 1947 a new emphasis on health emerged. White papers (1947, 1951, and 1952), together with acts (1947, 1952, and 1970) laid the foundation for the removal of the service from local government and the establishment of eight regional health boards.

The white paper *Economic Development* (1958) led to the recognition of physical planning and the enactment of the Local Government (Planning and Development) Act (1963). Thereafter the local development plan became an instrument in INDUSTRIAL DEVELOPMENT and promotion and close involvement with the INDUSTRIAL DEVELOPMENT AUTHORITY and Shannon Free Airport Development Company. Though aspects of the planning system have been controversial, its contribution to national progress cannot be denied. Finance has been a persistent problem. Opposition to local authority rates—the original primary source of income—is almost as old as the system itself. Increased state grants to relieve rates have led to the weakening of local autonomy and the introduction of a political dimension. Rates relief became a major issue in general elections (1973 and 1977), leading eventually to the exemption of all domestic properties and success in general elections for parties advocating such measures. The search for a viable alternative has proved fruitless. An effort to supplement local income with domestic charges for water and sewerage services has met with sustained hostility, despite waiver schemes and tax relief. In 1996 an initiative included a new system of funding that provided for the abolition of these charges and making the full motor tax yield available to local authorities. A change of government in July 1997 established an independent Local Government Fund of £590 million in 1999, to be guaranteed against future inflation. This arrangement alleviated the immediate financial problems of local authorities but not without the perils of greater central control.

Some inroads into local autonomy have been effected by the creation of new state agencies, such as the National Roads Authority in 1991 and the Environmental Protection Agency in 1992. The programme entitled 'Better Local Government', introduced in 2000, provided for enhancement of the role of elected members by the establishment of Strategic Policy Committees and Corporate Policy Groups. An encouragement has been the 1999 constitutional REFERENDUM formally recognising the role of local government by the state.

Northern Ireland. As in the Republic, local government in Northern Ireland is the product of the 1898 LOCAL GOVERNMENT (IRELAND) ACT, with originally two county boroughs (cities), six counties, twenty-nine urban districts, and thirty-one rural districts. The establishment of Northern Ireland as a separate entity in 1920 did not affect local government structures; however, proportional representation was replaced in 1922 by simple majority voting, together with the introduction of property ownership as a qualification for voting. After extensive consultations, white papers, and the report of the CAMERON COMMISSION, the report of a review body (MacRory Report) formed the basis of an act in 1972 that divided the territory among twenty-six district councils, with limited functions, such as community, leisure, refuse collection, and street cleaning; other services were administered by area boards, including education and library boards (five) and health and social services boards (four), nominated with 30 to 40 per cent membership from district councils. Planning, water, and sewerage became a central responsibility. Rates have survived as part of local government finance, but the system is unusual. A district rate is set by each district council for a limited range of functions, which accounts for about 60 per cent of receipts, with variations between individual authorities, while a regional rate fixed by central government for regionalised services applies uniformly; curiously, this is not related to the cost of running the services but is equated with a comparable area in England.

Local government does not exist in isolation: progress is determined by the myriad of political, social and economic forces in which it operates. [see GRAND JURIES.] **R. B. Haslam**

Locke, Josef, stage name of Joseph McLaughlin (1917–1999), singer. Born in Derry. Locke was one of the most popular ballad singers in Ireland and Britain from the 1940s to the 1960s. His signature song was 'Hear My Song' (1947). Other successful recordings of the 1940s and 50s include 'I'll Take You Home Again, Kathleen', 'The Old Bog Road', and 'Blaze Away'. He was also well known for his mixture of Irish ballads, excerpts from operettas, and Italian standards. Retreating from public view for tax reasons, he returned to fame in the early 1990s when a fictionalised film of his life, *Hear My Song* (1991), was released. He died in October 1999, as well known as he was in his heyday. **Tony Clayton-Lea**

Lock-Out: see DUBLIN 1913 LOCK-OUT.

locomotives. The first RAILWAY locomotives in Ireland were built for the DUBLIN AND KINGSTOWN RAILWAY (opened 1834). At first railway companies had distinctive designs, to the Irish gauge of 1.6 m (5 ft 3 in.), but consolidations, amalgamations, and closures brought about some standardisation. In the 1860s the first of a fleet of more than a hundred standard three-axle general-purpose locomotives were introduced, many seeing service to the end of the steam era in 1963. Locomotive designers who worked in Ireland include Alexander McDonnell, Harold Ivatt, John Aspinall, Edgar Bredin, and Oliver Bulleid.

As improved materials facilitated higher steam pressures and improved efficiencies, larger and more powerful locomotives followed, culminating in 1939 in the building of the three Queen class 4-6-0 locomotives for the Dublin–Cork expresses. The high operating costs of steam locomotives led in 1950 to the introduction of diesel engines, with a greater operating range, reduced servicing requirements, and one-person operation. Experimental turf-burning locomotives and battery-driven units were also developed. [see DRUMM BATTERY TRAIN; RAILWAY ENGINEERING.] **Richard P. Grainger**

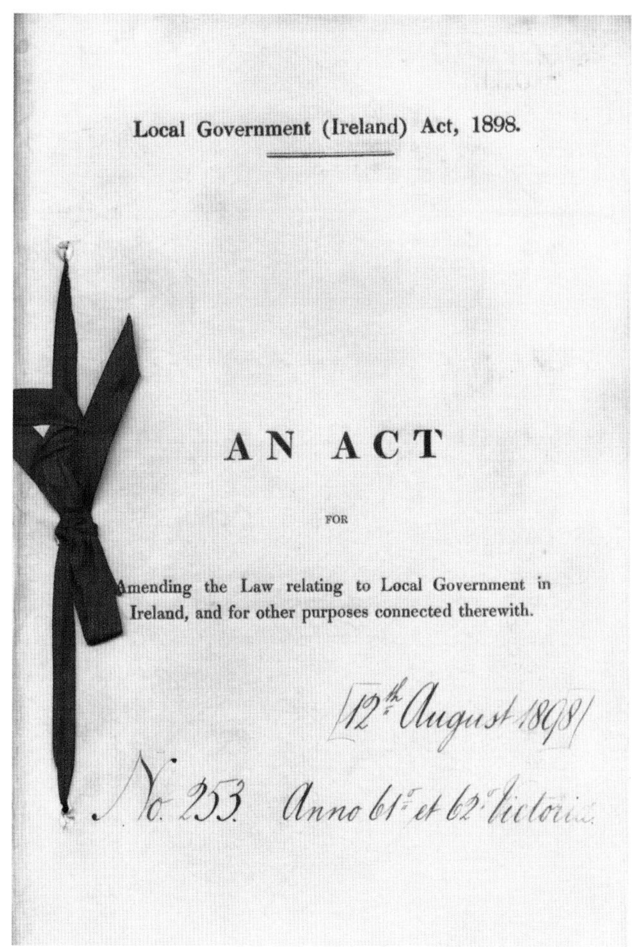

Local Government (Ireland) Act, 1898.

AN ACT

FOR

Amending the Law relating to Local Government in Ireland, and for other purposes connected therewith.

[12th August 1898]

No. 253 Anno 61° et 62° Victoriæ

local government. *The Local Government (Ireland) Act (1898), which transferred the administrative functions of grand juries to county and rural district councils. The first local authority elections were held on 6 April 1899. [House of Lords Records Office]*

Loftus, Adam (c. 1533–1605), CHURCH OF IRELAND Archbishop of Armagh, 1563–7, Archbishop of Dublin, 1567–1605, and Lord Chancellor of Ireland, 1581–1605. Born c. 1533 in Yorkshire; educated at the University of Cambridge and ordained a Catholic priest. He embraced the Elizabethan religious settlement, though with a pronounced Calvinist strain. He numbered John Knox and Thomas Cartwright, leading Calvinists, among his correspondents. He came to Ireland in 1560 as chaplain to the LORD LIEUTENANT of Ireland, the Earl of Sussex. He was consecrated Archbishop of Armagh in 1563 but petitioned ELIZABETH I, successfully, for the lucrative deanery of ST PATRICK'S, Dublin, to supplement his income. In 1567 he was translated from the see of Armagh to Dublin. He was a zealous preacher and in 1565 joined a royal commission to enforce the Reformation in Ireland but enjoyed limited success in propagating PROTESTANTISM. He played a leading role in the foundation of TRINITY COLLEGE, Dublin, in 1592 and became its first provost. As Lord Chancellor, and oftentimes as Lord Keeper and Lord Justice, he played an important part in the Elizabethan administration in Ireland. **Henry A. Jefferies**

Loftus, Seán Dublin Bay Rockall (1927–), lecturer, politician, and environmental campaigner. Born in Dublin; educated at UCD and KING'S INNS. A member of Dublin City Council for a number of years, he served as an independent member of DÁIL ÉIREANN for Dublin North-East, 1981–2, and as Lord Mayor of

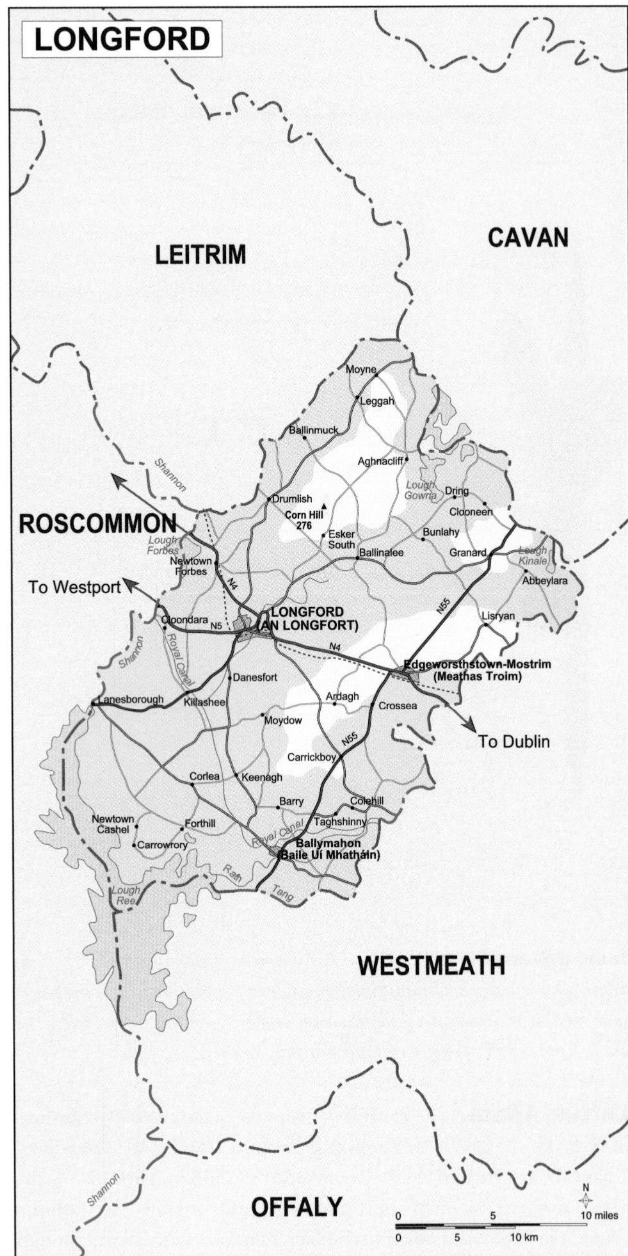

Dublin, 1995–6. He came to national prominence through the campaign to prevent an oil refinery being built in DUBLIN BAY. His commitment to the area's environmental integrity and to the campaign to assert Irish ownership of Rockall, on account of its potential oil and gas reserves, was reflected in his campaigning under the name Seán Dublin Bay Rockall Loftus to which he had legally changed it by deed poll. **Brian Galvin**

log-boats, the most common form of ancient boat, used throughout the world and still in use in parts of the tropics. Over 400 examples, almost all of oak, have been recorded in Ireland, where they were made since at least the middle of the fourth millennium BC and probably earlier. They fell out of use in the eighteenth century. Made by hollowing out a straight trunk (hence 'dug-out canoe'), they can be of any length, depending only on access to suitable timber. They are propelled by rowing, paddling, or punting or with the help of small sails. [see BOATS, ANCIENT; LURGAN LOG-BOAT.] **A. L. Brindley**

Logue, Michael (1840–1924), cardinal. Born in Carrigart, Co. Donegal; educated at ST PATRICK'S COLLEGE, Maynooth. Professor of dogmatic theology at the IRISH COLLEGE, Paris, 1866, he was appointed Bishop of Raphoe, 1879, Archbishop of Armagh, 1887, and cardinal, 1893. He completed the building of Armagh Cathedral. A trenchant anti-Parnellite, he was a supporter of the GAELIC LEAGUE. During the FIRST WORLD WAR he supported the anti-conscription movement. Though a strong nationalist, he opposed physical force. He also denounced PARTITION. **Fergal Tobin**

Lohan, Brian (1971–) hurler. Born at Shannon, Co. Clare. He made his inter-county debut in 1992 with Clare in the Munster under-21 championship, losing to Waterford in the final. He graduated to senior rank the following year and has been a permanent member of the team since then. A player of great skill, he is a majestic performer as full-back and has brought a new dimension to full-back play. His achievements include two senior hurling all-Irelands (1995 and 1997), three Munster senior hurling medals, and five Railway Cups with Munster. He has three All-Star Awards and won the Players' and Sports Writers' Player of the Year Award in 1995. At club level he won county senior hurling and Munster Club senior hurling medals in 1996. He won a Fitzgibbon Medal with University of Limerick in 1994. His father, Gus Lohan, won a variety of county hurling titles over a period of four decades. **Séamus J. King**

Lombard, Peter (c. 1555–1625), Catholic Archbishop. Born in Co. Waterford; educated at Westminster school, Oxford and LOUVAIN. He was appointed Catholic Archbishop of Armagh in 1601 at the request of HUGH O'NEILL, Earl of Tyrone. He was at first an enthusiastic supporter of O'Neill's Catholic crusade during the NINE YEARS' WAR (1594–1603); he later tempered his position in relation to the Crown in the wake of the completion of the English conquest of Ireland in 1603. The execution for treason of Cornelius O'Devany, Catholic Bishop of Down and Connor, in 1612 played an important role in convincing Lombard that the Catholic Church should play a less confrontational role in Irish politics, in a bid to defuse royal hostility. Central to this strategy was his contention that episcopal appointees should not be associated with the Earl of Tyrone. He impressed on the royal authorities that Irish Catholics recognised JAMES I as their lawful king, thus beginning a strategy whereby the Catholic hierarchy attempted to seek a *modus vivendi* with the English Crown. He was the author of *De Hibernia Insula Commentarius Stromaticus* (1600), an account of the war of the 1590s. **John McCavitt**

Lombard, Walter (c. 1565–c. 1620), mathematician and adventurer. Born in Waterford into a prominent mercantile and ecclesiastical family; educated at Westminster school and the University of Oxford. His cousin Anastasia was the mother of LUKE WADDING and Ambrose Wadding, an influential teacher of philosophy at Dillingen in Bavaria. A friend of the great astronomer Tycho Brahe, he was part of the brilliant circle of intellectuals associated with the court of Rudolf II of Bohemia, among them the mathematician Kepler and the mystic scholar Rabbi Judah Loew ben Bezalel. He is thought to have contributed to Kepler's early work on logarithms, which Kepler published in 1624 but which had circulated in manuscript some years before. With the catastrophic defeat of the Bohemian Protestants by the Habsburgs at the Battle of the White Mountain (1620) he disappears from history—whether through execution by imperial forces or flight is uncertain. **Friedrich-Maria Taaffe**

Londonderry: see DERRY.

London, the Irish in. A distinct Irish population existed in London by the late sixteenth century. Numbers rose in the late eighteenth century, while a dramatic increase took place during the FAMINE exodus. By 1851 at least 107,000 of London's inhabitants had been born in Ireland. In 1991 Ireland was the place of birth of the largest non-English-born group in Greater London, with 256,000 people (the second-largest, India, claimed 152,000), of whom some 42,000 were born in Northern Ireland and 214,000 in the Republic.

Irish people have been associated with poorer areas of the city. Once found within such inner-city districts as St Giles and Southwark, Irish populations have spread to outer districts, such as Kilburn and Camberwell. However, Irish people have been and still are distributed throughout London. Their association with less affluent areas has had a negative impact on perceptions of Irish people in the city and requires qualification. London is unique in the diaspora in that it has attracted a complete cross-section of Irish society. While historically the majority of immigrants have been the poor, there have also been members of the ANGLO-IRISH aristocracy, members of Parliament, professionals, merchants, writers, actors, artisans, and shop-owners. This diversity has been shaped by a multitude of factors. London's size has offered anonymity for those requiring separation from Irish society; on the other hand, proximity has provided relative ease in travelling and returning. This has not only benefited personal relationships but has also fostered cultural links through the exchange of fashions, styles, and ideas. London's status as a 'world city' has also attracted those in search of cosmopolitan exposure, while prospects in education and professional training have drawn others. The concentration of wealth in London has also been a central factor in shaping emigration choices. As a dynamic financial, commercial and manufacturing centre the city has offered diverse employment and investment opportunities. Its place in the political power structure has been equally influential. The ACT OF UNION brought the seasonal emigration of the Anglo-Irish political elite, while Irish radicals recognised the importance of being in the city if they were to influence the outcome of such important issues as CATHOLIC EMANCIPATION.

Such connections remain with Northern Ireland, while terrorist activity serves to remind us of London's importance for political pressure and as a place of anonymity. **Craig Bailey**

Lonely Passion of Judith Hearne, The (1955), a novel by BRIAN MOORE (originally published as *Judith Hearne*). Moore's first literary novel, relating the fall of a lonely Catholic woman into alcoholism and mental breakdown, is widely regarded as the definitive statement of his alienation from Belfast and his perception of its moribund colonial heart. However, the Catholic hierarchy, represented by Father Quigley and the affluent O'Neill family, is also castigated for neglecting Miss Hearne. Typically for Moore, seemingly straightforward realism is undercut by moments of the fantastic, here by a symbolic and specifically Catholic imagination mapping Belfast itself and Judith's descent into hell. **Aaron Kelly**

lone parents, the term now generally used to refer to parents with dependent children who are not living with a spouse or cohabiting partner. In the late 1990s lone-parent families accounted for approximately 14 per cent of families in the Republic with at least one child aged under fifteen; more than 90 per cent of such families were headed by a woman. Non-marital child-bearing and marital breakdown are now the two most common routes to lone-parenthood. Widowhood, formerly the dominant route, now accounts for approximately one in ten lone-parent families; CENSUS data from the 1920s shows that the lone-parenthood caused by widowhood was approximately as common as all forms of lone-parenthood today. Social provision for lone parents dates from the Widow's and Orphan's Pensions Act (1935) and was significantly expanded in the early 1970s with the introduction of SOCIAL WELFARE payments for deserted wives (1970), unmarried mothers (1973), and prisoners' wives (1974). Since 1997 these schemes have been consolidated into the one-parent family payment scheme. **Tony Fahey**

Long, Walter (1854–1924), politician. A dull but decent Anglo-Irishman of limited political intelligence, Long was a Unionist MP, 1880–1921, and CHIEF SECRETARY FOR IRELAND, 1905. He held a succession of ministerial posts between 1915 and 1921; between December 1916 and May 1918 he had considerable influence in Cabinet deliberations on Ireland. **Eunan O'Halpin**

Longfield, Cynthia (1896–1991), entomologist. She lived at Cloyne, Co. Cork, and was privately educated. Passionately interested in natural history, in 1924 she joined the St George Scientific Expedition to the Pacific, assisting the entomologists; she returned to an assistant's post at the Natural History Museum, London. Between 1927 and 1937 she travelled widely in Africa and Latin America and began to specialise in dragonflies (Odonata). A recognised authority on these insects in Europe and Africa, she published *The Dragonflies of the British Isles* (1937), long considered the standard work. A knowledgeable ornithologist, she became patron of Cork Ornithological Society in 1967. **Helena C. G. Chesney**

Longford, County (*Contae an Longfoirt*)

Province:	LEINSTER
County town:	Longford
Area:	1,034 km^2 (401 sq. miles)
Population (2002):	31,127
Features:	Camlin River
	Lough Gowna
	Lough Ree
	River Inny
	River SHANNON
Of historical interest:	Abbeyshrule Abbey
	Granard Motte
	Inchcleraun monastic site
Industry and products:	Peat production
	TEXTILES and CLOTHING

Petula Martyn

County Longford, a county on the borders of the north midlands, the southern two-thirds containing the rich grasslands of the Central Plain, the northern lands poorer and hillier as they blend into the drumlins of south Ulster. It is bounded on the west by the River SHANNON and Lough Ree; Lough Gowna and Lough Kinale lie on its north-eastern boundary. The ROYAL CANAL runs through the southern part of the county to join the River Shannon. The county was created out of the O'Farrell territory of Annaly in the sixteenth century, and parts of it were planted with English settlers in the 1620s. **Granard** was established on the northern frontier of the ANGLO-NORMAN colony by the Tuites, who built its large motte-and-bailey in 1199; the settlement was taken over by the O'Farrells in the fifteenth century. **Edgeworthstown** (population 737), to the south-east of the town of Longford, is named after the Edgeworth family, who were the landlords in the area in the eighteenth century and whose most famous member was the writer MARIA EDGEWORTH. The village of **Ardagh** is the site of an Early Christian church, in the vicinity of which OLIVER GOLDSMITH was born. **Patrick Duffy**

Longford (population 6,899), the county town, is a bustling market town. Its most significant building is St Mel's (Catholic) Cathedral, designed in the classical manner by Joseph B. Keane (1840). **Patrick Duffy**

Longford, Lord: see PAKENHAM.

Longford Productions. In 1931 Edward PAKENHAM, Lord Longford (1902–1961), offered to buy all the shares in the GATE THEATRE, Dublin, to save it from bankruptcy. Following disagreements with other directors of the Gate (HILTON EDWARDS and MÍCHEÁL MAC LIAMMÓIR) he formed his own company, Longford Productions, in 1936. Based at the Gate but also touring extensively throughout Ireland in the 1940s and 50s, the company produced original plays, translations by Longford and his wife, Christine Longford (1900–1980), classical Greek tragedy, and modernist works by Pirandello and Chekhov. **Christopher Morash**

Longley, Edna (1940–), academic and critic. Born in Dublin; educated at TCD. Though a Southern Catholic by upbringing, she has become an outspoken critic of cultural nationalism and a promulgator of the Protestant imagination, publishing *The Living Stream: Literature and Revisionism in Ireland* (1994) and *Poetry and Posterity* (2000) and editing, with GERALD DAWE, *Across the Roaring Hill: The Protestant Imagination in Modern Ireland* (1985). She is professor of English at Queen's University, Belfast. **Richard Pine**

Longley, Michael (1939–), poet. Born in Belfast, of English parents; he studied classics at TCD. On his return to Belfast he was associated with Philip Hobsbaum's influential group workshops at Queen's University. *No Continuing City* appeared in 1969, followed by *An Exploded View* (1973), *Man Lying on a Wall* (1976), and *The Echo Gate* (1979). The war poets Edward Thomas, Isaac Rosenberg, and Keith Douglas have been a constant presence in his work. He worked for the ARTS COUNCIL OF NORTHERN IRELAND from 1970, before taking early retirement in 1991, writing little in the 1980s but re-emerging with *Gorse Fires* (1991) and *The Ghost Orchid* (1995). A feature of these books is his increasing use of the classics, especially Homer, whose depictions of conflict offer powerful but never opportunistic analogies for events in Northern Ireland. The poem 'Ceasefire', appearing in the IRISH TIMES in the week of the IRA ceasefire of 1994, was one of the most memorable intersections of poetry and politics of the 1990s. *Selected Poems* was published in 1998; a further collection, *The Weather in Japan*, which won the Whitbread Prize, followed in 2000. *Tuppenny Stung* (1994) is a short prose memoir. Longley was awarded the Queen's Medal for Poetry in 2001. **David Wheatley**

Lonsdale, Kathleen, née Yardley (1903–1971), physicist and crystallographer. Born in Newbridge (Droichead Nua), Co. Kildare; educated at Bedford College, University of London, where she joined Sir William Bragg's crystallography research team. She married Thomas Lonsdale, a fellow-student, who later went to work for the British Silk Research Association in Leeds. While at Leeds she used X-ray diffraction to explore hexa-methylbenzene and published a paper explaining the planarity of the crystal. On returning to London she studied at the Royal Institution. In 1945 she was made a fellow of the Royal Society, and in 1946 Sir Christopher Ingold invited her to take the chair of CHEMISTRY at University College, London, the first woman incumbent. There she established a crystallography unit. In one of her last publications she detailed the transformation of single crystals of graphite into diamond, and this substance was named lonsdaleite in her honour. In 1956 she was made a dame commander of the Order of the British Empire. In 1968 she became the first woman president of the British Association for the Advancement of Science. **Dervilla Donnelly**

Lord Lieutenant, the title given from 1696 to the representative of the British Crown and chief governor of Ireland; the term 'Viceroy' was also used. Lords Lieutenant were usually senior ministers, directly responsible to the Cabinet in London; most were drawn from the English aristocracy, though several Irish peers held the position in the nineteenth century. Before 1767 they were mostly absentee but subsequently were permanently resident and active executive officers, managing the Irish Parliament on behalf of the British government. Following the Union (1801) the office appeared anomalous; administrative responsibility tended to shift to the CHIEF SECRETARY, and it came close to abolition in 1850. However, it survived as a centre of viceregal ceremony and executive authority until 1922. **Peter Gray**

Lordship of Ireland. Unlike the 'Kingdom of England' or the 'Kingdom of Scotland', the 'Lordship of Ireland' did not feature in the vocabulary of the Middle Ages. Ireland was a lordship only in the sense that its ultimate ruler, the King of England, used the title 'Lord of Ireland' to describe his authority there. 'The land of Ireland' rather than 'the lordship of Ireland' was the contemporary designation of the country's status within the King of England's dominions. The first English king to rule Ireland, HENRY II, did not include his new territory in his royal title after its acquisition in 1171–2; but the fact that in 1177 he sought a crown from the Pope for the son he wished to see rule there, JOHN, suggests that he considered Ireland to be a kingdom. For reasons that are unclear, nothing came of this scheme, and it was as 'Lord of Ireland' that John exercised his authority both before and after becoming King of England in 1199. Any ambiguity about the constitutional relationship between king and lord was removed in 1254, when Henry III declared that Ireland should never be separated from the English Crown; in other words, the King of England and Lord of Ireland would henceforth be the same person. Between 1385 and 1388 Robert de Vere held the title 'Earl of Ireland' and became direct overlord of the subjects of the Crown there, but this experiment was unique, and the constitutional position of Ireland in the dominions of the English king did not change until 1541, when HENRY VIII accepted the wishes of the colonial Irish Parliament and assumed the title 'King of Ireland'. [see ANGLO-NORMAN AND ENGLISH ADMINISTRATION IN IRELAND.] **Brendan Smith**

Lore of Women: see BANSHENCHAS.

Lough Boora, Co. Offaly, site of a MESOLITHIC hunting encampment discovered in 1977 at Broughal, near Ferbane, consisting of a number of hearths and areas for working *chert* (a siliceous stone) into tools. The site lay on the bed of Lough Boora (which was drained in the 1940s) on the fossil shore of an ancient post-glacial lake—a larger

Lonsdale. *The transformation of single crystals of meteoric graphite into carbon allotrope diamond, was first described by the crystallographer Kathleen Lonsdale; the substance was named lonsdaleite in her honour. [Dublin Institute for Advanced Studies]*

forerunner of the modern Lough Boora. The inhabitants exploited eel-runs, hunted wild pigs, and collected hazelnuts. Their tools consisted of chert flakes and blades, and *microliths* (diminutive stone points and rods used to arm the shafts of composite weapons) and axeheads ground from elongated pebbles. RADIOCARBON DATING showed that the site was occupied in the seventh millennium BC. The material culture of the site was very similar to that of MOUNT SANDEL, Co. Derry. The presence of human settlement in the middle of the country at such an early date suggests that the earliest settlement of Ireland was much more widespread than previously believed. **Michael Ryan**

Lough Corrib and Lough Mask, Cos. Galway and Mayo, the second-largest and fourth-largest lake, respectively, in Ireland. Both are very deep in places, extending well below sea level (45 m). Extensive areas of the shorelines are bordered by Carboniferous limestone, which displays some remarkable solutional features. Enlarged fissures in the rock allow a considerable volume of water to flow underground. There is no natural surface connection between the two lakes: water leaves Lough Mask by way of many sinks on the south and south-west shores and emerges as large springs at or near Cong. Galway is linked to Lough Corrib by a channel.

The Cong Canal was begun as a FAMINE relief project in 1848 to connect Loch Corrib to Lough Mask and thus make it possible to sail from Ballinrobe to Galway. By 1858 all activities associated with this construction came to an end because of a design flaw: the canal is not watertight. It is cut into the fissured limestone, allowing water to drain underground along its entire length. No attempt was made to line the canal, as it was evident by this time that competition from the railways would lead to a decline in the importance of waterways. Today surface flow occurs in the canal when the water level in Lough Mask is more than 17 m (56 ft) above sea level. The canal is dry for ninety days a year. **R. A. Charlton**

Loughcrew, Co. Meath, a PASSAGE-TOMB cemetery comprising at least twenty-five tombs clustered on three hilltops. Investigations in the mid-1860s and the later nineteenth century yielded typical passage-tomb finds. The Carnbane West group comprises eleven sites, dominated by cairns D and L; the latter contains a multi-celled chamber. Cairn H, re-examined in 1943, yielded both passage-tomb and later prehistoric material. The seven sites on the central hill, Sliabh na Caillí or Carnbane East, are grouped around cairn T, a classic cruciform passage tomb. There are remains of four sites on Patrickstown Hill to the east. Many stones bear MEGALITHIC art. **Paul Walsh**

Lough Derg. Lough Derg, with a surface area of 118 km^2 (46 sq. miles), is the largest lake on the River SHANNON, extending from Portumna in the north to Killaloe in the south (see p. 416). It lies at the southern limit of the Central Plain, bordered by Co. Clare and south Co. Galway to the north and west and by Co. Tipperary to the east. Most of the lake lies on limestone, where it is shallow. At the southern end there is a ridge of older rocks. There are a large number of islands in the shallower parts of the lake, and on many of these are the remains of early churches. Inishcealtra has an early medieval ecclesiastical settlement.

The level of Lough Derg, as well as the lakes upstream, is partly affected by groundwater levels beneath the lake-bed. Since the construction of the Ardnacrusha hydro-electric power station, THE SHANNON SCHEME, downstream from Lough Derg, WATER levels have been subject to more abrupt changes associated with ELECTRICITY demands. **R. A. Charlton**

Lough Erne, Lower, Co. Fermanagh, the largest of several lakes within the catchment of the River Erne, covering an area of 111 km^2 (43 sq. miles). The lake is fed from upstream by Upper Lough Erne and lies on non-calcareous rocks. It has an irregular floor, which reaches a depth of 60 m (200 ft) in some places, 15 m (50 ft) lower than sea level. There are a number of islands on the lake, and on many of them are remains dating from Early Christian and earlier times. These include DEVENISH, with a twelfth-century round tower and a ruined abbey, WHITE ISLAND, with its collection of Christian statues, and BOA ISLAND, with its two IRON AGE stone 'Janus' figures.

The Erne catchment is the fourth-largest river catchment in Ireland and crosses the border between the Republic and Northern Ireland. Flooding has long been a problem around the lakes. In the Republic the Erne Drainage and Development Act (1950) was introduced, with a twofold purpose: to improve drainage and to permit the Electricity Supply Board to employ storage in Lough Erne for the purpose of electricity generation. Two hydro-electric power stations, at Cliff and Cathleen's Falls (Ballyshannon), are situated downstream from Lower Lough Erne. The level of the lake is controlled by sluices at Cliff power station; the level of Upper Lough Erne is also regulated within certain limits, as the levels in the two lakes are interdependent. **R. A. Charlton**

Lough Foyle, a large, shallow, almost enclosed sea lough between INISHOWEN, Co. Donegal and Co. Derry, covering an area of 187 km^2 (72 sq. miles) and with a mean depth of about 5 m (16 ft). It overlies metamorphic rocks that have been extensively folded and faulted to give the north-east to south-west structural 'grain' that the lough follows. Derry, traditionally the regional centre and marine port of north-west Ireland, is on the River Foyle, which joins Lough Foyle from the south-west. The port of Derry was moved in 1993 from its traditional site at Meadowbank in the city centre to a purpose-built deep-water terminal at Lisahally, 5 km (3 miles) downstream. Since the closure of the Strabane Canal there have been no designated navigable inland waterways in the Foyle catchment. The combined catchment of the River Foyle and Lough Foyle is one of the largest in Ireland, covering an area of 3,700 km^2 (1,400 sq. miles); about 75 per cent of this catchment is in Northern Ireland. The Foyle system has a number of tributaries, the largest of which are the Mourne and the Finn. The River Foyle itself is tidal throughout its length. Apart from the Foyle, a number of rivers drain directly into the lough, the largest of which are the Faughan and the Roe, which drain the eastern side of the catchment. **R. A. Charlton**

Lough Gur. *A small C-shaped lake, the site of Neolithic settlement, inhabited c. 3000 BC; standing stones, burial mounds and megalithic tombs surround the lough. [Dúchas, The Heritage Service]*

Lough Gur, Co. Limerick. The small, C-shaped lake at Lough Gur is set in hilly terrain at the interface between volcanic and limestone terrain in north-east Co. Limerick. The limestone area, with its thin, easily worked soils, was attractive to early farmers, and pollen studies show that much of the area has been in continuous pasture since the early NEOLITHIC PERIOD. The Knockadoon peninsula juts out into the lake and was a focus for settlement from this time. Excavations by Seán P. Ó Ríordáin, 1939–54, recovered evidence for several separate occupation sites, including some with the remains of circular timber houses. This indicates continuous settlement during the Neolithic Period into the early BRONZE AGE.

From earliest times Lough Gur was the centre of a thriving society, with settlements concentrated in an area within 3 km (2 miles) of the lake. These people were mainly stock farmers, raising cattle, with some sheep and pigs; but they also grew wheat and barley. There is some evidence for funerary activity, including a COURT TOMB on the west edge of the lake; while the remains of mainly children and adolescents have been found buried on the habitation sites. In the Late Neolithic Period (2700–2300 cal. BC), WEDGE TOMBS were built on the southern lake edge. More recent research has shown that the peninsula was intensively occupied in the Middle to Late Bronze Age (1700–800 cal. BC). In this period the settlement sites were lightly defended by enclosing walls. There is evidence also for high-status bronzeworking; an important collection of artefacts includes bronze weapons and tools, and glass beads.

Two large ceremonial enclosures, the Grange Stone Circle on the western side and Circle O on the eastern side, were constructed as arenas for public ritual. It is probable that the two STONE CIRCLES near Grange also belong to this period. Towards the end of the Bronze Age, Lough Gur became a regional focus, and a widening hinterland extending to 10 km (6 miles) from the core at Knockadoon has extensive settlement as well as evidence of funerary and ceremonial practice. Throughout the prehistoric period the lake was also used for the votive deposition of high-quality artefacts. These include stone and bronze axes, halberds, swords, spearheads, a bronze shield, and a pair of IRON AGE chariot mounts. **Eoin Grogan**

Lough Hyne, south-west of Skibbereen, Co. Cork, a square-shaped salt-water marine lough with sides approximately 1 km (0.6 mile) long. The average depth is 40 m (130 ft), though this increases to 65 m (213 ft) in some places, with the land rising steeply above the lough on the west side. It is connected to the sea by a narrow channel known as the Rapids, which is approximately 1 m (3 ft) deep at low tide. It has a unique distribution of FLORA and FAUNA, with seventy-three species of sea-slug and more than a hundred species of sponge, and was designated Ireland's first marine nature reserve. [see EBLING, JOHN; KITCHING, J. A.; RENOUF, L. P. W.] **R. A. Charlton**

Loughnashade, Co. Armagh, a small lake, once much larger, immediately east of the great ritual enclosure of NAVAN FORT (Eamhain Mhacha), from which it is now separated by a quarry. In 1798 four 2 m (6 ft)-long curved bronze horns of Iron Age date

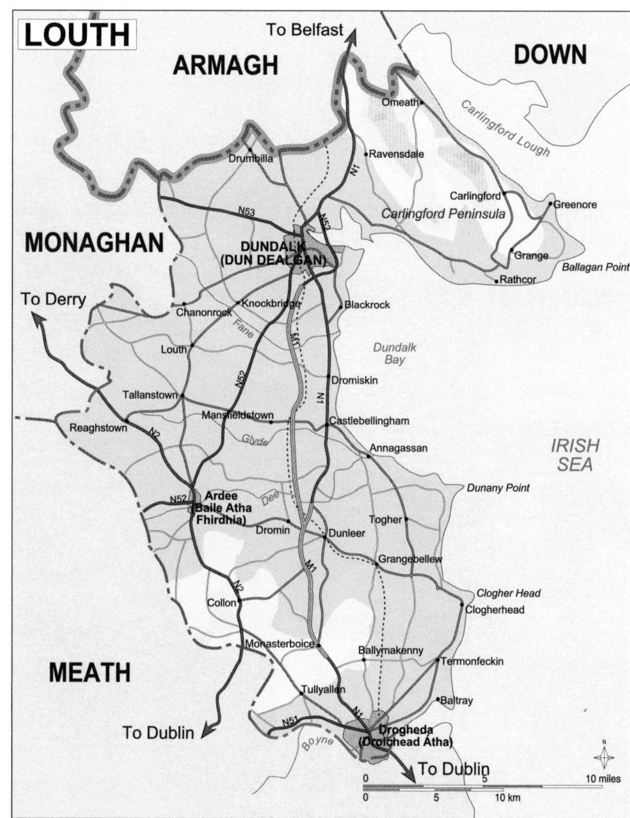

were discovered, with human bones and skulls. The only surviving horn (NATIONAL MUSEUM), is a work of remarkable technical achievement with an attached disc decorated in early 'Celtic' style (see pp. 178, 757). The lake was apparently used for human sacrifice as late as the Early Historical Period, and its name (Loch na Séad, 'lake of the treasures') hints at past discoveries. **Richard Warner**

Lough Neagh, Ireland's largest and oldest lake, covering an area of 383 km^2 (148 sq. miles). Several towns lie on the gentle slopes surrounding the lake, including ANTRIM, LURGAN, PORTADOWN, and DUNGANNON. The first lake here occupied the basin as early as 35 million years ago. The basin was formed as a result of Tertiary volcanic upheavals, which took place throughout North-Western Europe between 50 and 65 million years ago; this outflow of molten rock was compensated for by movements of the Earth's crust, such as the subsidence that formed the Lough Neagh depression. Over time, rivers flowing into the lake deposited vast amounts of sediment and plant debris, which built up to a thickness of 350 m (1,150 ft) and caused further subsidence. The pressure on the plant debris caused by the accumulation of sediment gradually turned it into *lignite* (brown coal). For a long time these lignite deposits were thought to be too deep to be profitable, but recent drilling has revealed extensive deposits at shallow depths around much of the lake. The surface of the lake today is 12.6 m (41 ft) above sea level, though several attempts at artificial drainage have been made. The first of these was in 1846, with subsequent drainage works carried out during the 1940s and 50s; these have lowered the level by at least 2 m ($6\frac{1}{2}$ ft).

Lough Neagh is a freshwater lake and contains some interesting fauna. Several species, such as the Irish pollan, a relative of the trout, are more usually found in sea water. It is not known how such species came to be in the present-day lake. Today the pollan is much in decline because of organic pollution from the surrounding area. Eels have played an important part in the local economy since the Middle Ages. **R. A. Charlton**

Lough Swilly, a sea lough in north Co. Donegal, formed in a similar way to CARLINGFORD LOUGH. It lies in a former river valley, over-deepened by glacial erosion and subsequently drowned by rising sea levels at the end of the last Ice Age. The south end of the lough is aligned along north-east to south-west faults (showing a similar trend to Belfast Lough and LOUGH FOYLE) but then swings abruptly to the north-west, cutting through the geological 'grain' at right angles. The lough is bounded on its eastern side by INISHOWEN (see p. 400). **R. A. Charlton**

Louth, County (*Contae Lú*)

Province:	LEINSTER
County town:	DUNDALK
Area:	821 km^2 (317 sq. miles)
Population (2002):	101,802
Features:	CARLINGFORD LOUGH
	Carlingford Mountain
	Dee River
	Fane River
	Glyde River
Of historical interest:	Carlingford Castle and Priory
	MELLIFONT Abbey
	MONASTERBOICE monastic site
	PROLEEK dolmen
Industry and products:	BREWING
	CLOTHING
	Engineering
	Footwear
	MEAT
	Tobacco

Petula Martyn

County Louth, the smallest county in Ireland, abuts onto the Ulster counties of Down, Armagh, and Monaghan. The region has historically been seen as guarding the gateway to Ulster: the 'gap of the north' was a historic pass into Ulster through the hills and mountains of south Armagh. The town of **Ardee** (population 3,568) also commemorates this historic frontier as the meeting-place of CÚ CHULAINN, the hero of Ulster, and Ferdia, MÉABH's champion in the epic tale 'TÁIN BÓ CUAILGNE' (see p. 1090). The landscape of Co. Louth represents part of the rich glacial drift-covered midlands, which extends north as far as Dundalk. North of the town are the mountains of the Cooley Peninsula. The Ulster borderlands are also marked by extensive drumlin landscapes of small hills. Following the ANGLO-NORMAN settlement, native Irish territories in the region were consolidated into Co. Louth in 1233.

The town of **Louth** was an important medieval borough in the thirteenth century, containing an Augustinian abbey from 1148; it is now a village, long superseded by **Dundalk** (population 27,399), which became the county town and secured the northern edge of the English PALE during the Middle Ages. With Ardee it was frequently attacked by the Irish of south Ulster. The countryside was part of a fortified marchland, where society and economy were quite unstable, reflected today in the remains of medieval motttes, CASTLES, and TOWER-HOUSES. The rich agricultural landscape in the southern half of the county is marked by an impressive legacy of rural buildings from the eighteenth and nineteenth centuries.

loyalism. *Residents of Brown Street, Belfast, celebrate the twelfth of July (c. 1930/40s), with an array of festive banners that attest to their loyalist pride and allegiance. [Topham Picturepoint]*

Co. Louth is an important tillage county, producing significant quantities of barley, oats, and oilseed rape. Today the county occupies an important strategic position in the eastern economic corridor between Belfast and Dublin, containing two of the most important road connections, the M1 and N2. **Patrick Duffy**

Louvain, Flanders, site of an Irish Franciscan house, St Anthony's, founded in 1606–7 by FLAITHRÍ Ó MAOLCHONAIRE. It generally housed between thirty and forty friars and sent MISSIONARIES to Ireland and Scotland. The college acquired a wide reputation for scholastic learning and became the centre of PRINTING IN IRISH; the press produced a steady stream of devotional, historical, and other works, 1616–50, which were strongly anti-Protestant and had a profound influence on the political and religious life of Ireland, particularly Ulster. The friars acted as advisers to the Ulster leaders in the Spanish Netherlands, while AODH MAC AINGIL's dual appointment as chief chaplain to the Irish regiment and guardian of St Anthony's strengthened the links between the two groups. The college was closely involved in a number of plans for a Spanish-financed invasion of Ireland spearheaded by Irish regiments on the Continent. Recruitment to the Franciscans declined after the Cromwellian period. [see IRISH COLLEGES IN CONTINENTAL EUROPE; SALAMANCA.] **Gráinne Henry**

Louvain type, an Irish printing type. Partly in response to the publishing efforts of the Reformed Church in Dublin, the Irish Franciscans working on the Continent had an Irish printing type prepared that was used first in Antwerp in 1611 for the printing of *An Teagasg Criosdaidhe*, a catechism by GIOLLA BRIGHDE Ó HEÓDHUSA. It was later used for a number of religious books issued from the printing press at the Irish College in LOUVAIN. The type, which may have been based on the writing style of Ó hEódhusa, was used as a model for a second font prepared in 1641. These were to influence the shape of IRISH PRINTING TYPES for many years. **Dermot McGuinne**

love poems: see DÁNTA GRÁ.

Lover, Samuel (1797–1868), writer. He left his Dublin family's stockbroking firm for the careers of artist, author, and songwriter. Already known for his miniatures and marine scenes, he moved to London in 1833, becoming a successful society painter and writer of more than three hundred songs. His 'Rory O'Moore' was transformed into both a novel and a play in 1837; he also wrote many librettos and musicals. Lover was a joint-founder of the DUBLIN UNIVERSITY MAGAZINE and of *Bentley's Magazine*, in which his *Handy Andy: A Tale of Irish Life* first appeared. When his sight weakened he toured America and England with 'Irish Evenings', one-man shows that pleased his audience, for he was by nature a popular entertainer. Often unduly attacked for stage-Irishism, he was a very gifted man. **A. Norman Jeffares**

Lovett, Anne (1969–1984), schoolgirl. She died, aged fifteen, while giving birth at the foot of a grotto in a churchyard in Granard, Co. Longford: the child also died. The event generated much public debate, as it occurred after the successful ANTI-ABORTION amendment campaign. The media were criticised for publishing her name and for drawing links between her tragedy and issues such as CONTRACEPTION, the Catholic Church, the PRO-LIFE CAMPAIGN, and sex education. Those in the school she attended said they did not know she was pregnant; others said it was a private matter for the girl and her family and that even if they knew she was pregnant they would not have interfered. While the COUNCIL FOR THE STATUS OF WOMEN called for a public inquiry, the people of Granard objected, and a private inquiry ensued. When it was reported on the 'GAY BYRNE Show' it sparked a flood of letters from women who had gone through pregnancy and given birth in secret. Anne Lovett had become a *cause célèbre* and Granard a scapegoat for the evils of a hypocritical society. **Evelyn Mahon**

low pay. When the earnings of some employees are regarded as 'low', the benchmark is generally the earnings of other employees in the same society. Commonly used benchmarks include half or two-thirds of the average or the median earnings of all employees (the median being the level above and below which half the employees fall). In the late 1990s more than one in five Irish employees earned less than two-thirds of median hourly earnings. Compared with many other industrialised countries this was a relatively high figure, though lower than that for the United States. Low pay may be a concern from two distinct aspects: it may be seen as unfair treatment of the individual employee, and as a cause of poverty. Most low-paid employees are not in fact living in households conventionally considered poor, because they are often not the only earner. For many years, minimum wages were set only for specific occupations or industries, by tripartite joint labour committees. A national minimum wage was introduced in April 2000; it is specified in terms of hourly earnings, the rate set on its introduction being €5.59 per hour, with lower minimums for young workers and trainees. **Brian Nolan**

loyalism, once loosely used as a synonym for UNIONISM but from the early 1970s increasingly identified with the rise of grass-roots sentiment in Protestant working-class areas, often associated with sympathy for the ULSTER DEFENCE ASSOCIATION or ULSTER VOLUNTEER FORCE. Feeling that the traditional power structures of the Unionist Party and ORANGE ORDER had let them down, many working-class Protestants were attracted to alternative forms of political mobilisation. The ULSTER WORKERS' COUNCIL, which organised the strike that overthrew the Sunningdale settlement in May 1974, also reflected working-class loyalist views, but its existence was not sustained. Loyalism found an increasing focus in the emergence of BLOOD-AND-THUNDER BANDS, composed of young working-class Protestant males. Often confrontational in tone, these bands developed a distinctive parading culture, organising their own band parades. For a time the UDA seemed interested in negotiated independence for Northern Ireland, but in 1987 it launched a policy document that advocated a power-sharing government. In 1993–4 the Combined Loyalist Military Command, representing the UVF and the UDA, set out a political programme that envisaged power-sharing structures and North–South bodies within the framework

loyalist bombings. *Aftermath of a loyalist bomb explosion in South Leinster Street, Dublin, 17 May 1974. Twenty-two people were killed when three car bombs exploded during the evening rush hour in South Leinster Street and Talbot Street.* [Irish Times] of the United Kingdom. These ideas were pursued by the Progressive Unionist Party and the Ulster Democratic Party in the negotiations leading to the BELFAST AGREEMENT of 10 April 1998. Their acceptance of the agreement was of crucial importance in securing support in Protestant working-class areas in the subsequent referendum. In the Assembly elections of 25 June 1998 the UDP failed to secure representation, but two leading members of the PUP were elected from Belfast constituencies. **T. G. Fraser**

loyalist bombings in the Republic. As with republican bomb attacks in Britain, two objectives of loyalist attacks in the Republic have been to draw attention to their existence and to bring the 'war' home to the 'enemy', in this case the Republic and its people. Unlike republicans, however, loyalists have had only a limited degree of success in planting explosive devices. For logistical reasons, loyalist paramilitary attacks have generally been restricted to Dublin and areas along the border. There have, however, been at least three significant loyalist bombing attacks in the Republic.

On 1 December 1972 two UVF car bombs exploded in Dublin, the first near Liberty Hall and the second at Sackville Place, killing two bus-drivers and injuring more than a hundred people. The explosions may have been intended to strengthen support for the Offences Against the State Bill, which was being debated in Dáil Éireann at that time. On 20 January 1973 another bus-driver was killed and seventeen people injured when a car, again parked in Sackville Place, exploded. The bomb had been planted by the UVF on the day of an international RUGBY match, which probably helped provide cover for the bombers. In the most devastating attack, the DUBLIN AND MONAGHAN BOMBINGS of 17 May 1974, twenty-two people were killed and more than a hundred injured.

Loyalist bomb attacks have continued intermittently since then, though never on the same scale as in the early 1970s. Bombs have often been aimed at identifiable republican targets: in May 1994 the UVF shot dead an IRA member during an abortive attempt to bomb a republican social function in a pub in Pearse Street, Dublin, and in March 1997 a loyalist bomb was discovered outside a SINN FÉIN office in Monaghan. Loyalists have also been prepared to bomb or threaten the wider community when they believed it might further their cause. As late as November 1997 there was a spate of loyalist bomb scares in the Republic. These attacks were clearly motivated by internal loyalist tensions and by concerns over the NORTHERN IRELAND PEACE PROCESS. Many loyalists believed that the British and Irish governments were pandering to nationalist concerns, and this campaign was a 'reminder' that loyalists' views could not be ignored. **Gordon Gillespie**

Luby, Thomas Clarke (1822–1901), nationalist. Born in Dublin; educated at TCD. He was involved in the risings of 1848 and 1849 and helped JAMES STEPHENS found the IRISH REPUBLICAN BROTHERHOOD in 1858. He edited the *Irish People*, 1863–5. Jailed for treason-felony in 1865, he went to the United States when amnestied in 1871, where he died. **Brian Griffin**

Lucan (*Leamhcán*), Co. Dublin, a town on the River LIFFEY on the western edge of Dublin. In 1204 Lucan was granted to Warris de Peche, who built a castle to guard this important river crossing. The lands later came into the possession of the Fitzgeralds of Kildare, who held them until 1537. PATRICK SARSFIELD was born at Lucan Castle in 1650; the castle was demolished c. 1771 by Agmondisham Vesey to build Lucan House (now the home of the Italian ambassador). In the eighteenth century Lucan became a popular health resort when an iron spa was discovered at Chapel Hill. This was gradually abandoned for a more modern sulphurous spring, discovered in 1758 near the present Spa Hotel. In 1795 the old hotel (now the County Bar) was built, while the Crescent was also built to house the holidaymakers who came to the spa. The arrival of a regular TRAM service in the late nineteenth century brought renewed but short-lived interest in the spa. In 1805 JAMES GANDON bought Cannonbrook and lived there from 1808 until his death in 1823.

Lucan-Clondalkin was promoted by Dublin County Council as one of three new towns to be developed on the western periphery of Dublin from the late 1960s. In 1972 the population of Lucan was 800; by early 2000 it was estimated to be more than 30,000 (see p. 504). **Ruth McManus**

Lucan and McShane, Arthur Lucan (1887–1954), and Kitty McShane (1897–1964), comedians. Lucan (born Arthur Towle in Boston, Lincolnshire) and his wife (born in Dublin) had a noisy slapstick 'Irish' comedy act, 'Old Mother Riley and Her Daughter Kitty', that was very popular from 1912 in variety and in a long series of cheap films, from *Stars on Parade* (1935) to *Mother Riley Meets the Vampire* (1952). Lucan's energetic and acrobatic impersonation of the vociferous, battling old Irish washerwoman is a wonderful creation, and the couple's films are still watchable today. **Stephen Dixon and Deirdre Falvey**

Lucan Bridge, the largest single-span masonry arch bridge in Ireland, erected over the River Liffey at Lucan, Co. Dublin, in 1814. The architect and builder, George Knowles, was probably inspired by the work of Alexander Stevens downstream at Islandbridge and created here an aesthetically pleasing arch bridge with a span of 33.5 m (110 ft). **Ronald Cox**

Lucas, A. T. (Tony) (1911–1986), ethnologist. Born in Clonsilla, Co. Dublin; educated at UCD, where he came under the influence of the archaeologist Seán P. Ó Ríordáin. He joined the Irish Antiquities Division of the NATIONAL MUSEUM in 1947 and became the first full-time curator of its Folklife Collection. He added systematically and significantly to the collection and its resources. In 1954 he was appointed director of the National Museum. With CAOIMHÍN Ó DANACHAIR, E. ESTYN EVANS, and Alan Gailey he was a pioneer of the study of FOLK LIFE in Ireland, writing on such subjects as furze and its uses, bog wood in the rural economy, cattle in ancient Ireland, sacred trees, turf as fuel, and ploughing practices. He organised the filming of several almost extinct practices, such as the making of mud-turf and of straw donkey-harness. He was president of the ROYAL SOCIETY OF ANTIQUARIES of Ireland, 1969–73, and president of the Society for Folklife Studies, 1967–72. **Séamas Mac Philib**

Lucas, Charles (1713–1771), politician. Born in Co. Clare. An apothecary in Dublin, he entered city politics in 1742 by campaigning for corporation reform. As a pamphleteer he was noted for supposedly vehement anti-Catholicism, and the Protestant 'Patriot' nationalism in his writings as a Dublin by-election candidate, 1748–9, resulted in temporary exile. He qualified as a doctor at Leiden in 1752, was elected MP for Dublin in 1761, and thereafter was a leading figure in the Patriot opposition, helping to establish the FREEMAN'S JOURNAL, supporting the corporations in the quarterage dispute, and instrumental in the OCTENNIAL ACT (1768). **Charles Ivar McGrath**

Luce, Arthur Aston (1882–1977), Anglican clergyman and philosopher. Born in Gloucester; educated at TCD, where he spent his academic career as a fellow, 1912–77. In 1915 he joined the British army, became a captain, and was awarded the Military Cross. In 1918 he returned to Trinity College, where he was professor of moral philosophy, 1934–49, vice-provost, 1946–51, and Berkeley professor of metaphysics, 1953–77. He was ordained in 1907, becoming a canon in 1930 and chancellor, then precentor, of ST PATRICK'S CATHEDRAL, Dublin. He established his reputation as a BERKELEY scholar, particularly through his pioneering *Berkeley and Malebranche* (1934), which established Malebranche as an important formative influence on Berkeley. Important too were *Berkeley's Philosophical Commentaries* (1944) and *Berkeley's Immaterialism* (1945). The edition of Berkeley's Works he edited with T. E. Jessop (1948–57) became the standard edition, and his *Life of George Berkeley, Bishop of Cloyne* (1949) is still valued as a biography. He defended a modernised version of Berkeley's philosophy in his *Sense without Matter* (1954), holding that such an idealistic position is consistent with common sense. He combined his enthusiasm as an angler with his philosophical preoccupations in *Fishing and Thinking* (1959). **Stuart Brown**

Ludlow, Edmund (c. 1617–1692), soldier. Born in Wiltshire; educated at the University of Oxford and the Inner Temple, London. He took a prominent part in the English Civil War, supporting the extreme Leveller and Anabaptist viewpoints and signing the death warrant for the king. CROMWELL appointed him second in command to IRETON in 1650, and Parliament named him one of the Commissioners for the Civil Government of Ireland. He took a prominent role in the SIEGE OF LIMERICK in 1651 but failed to gain the command on Ireton's death. He obtained the surrender of Galway in April 1652 and ensured that other pockets of resistance were gradually eliminated. By his own testimony he used a maximum of brutality to bring this about; he favoured the punishment of the Irish and was an enthusiastic advocate of the policy of TRANSPLANTATION TO CONNACHT. He retained his military command until 1655, when, following accusations of plotting against the government, he was recalled to England. At the Restoration he was forced to go into exile on the Continent; he died in Switzerland. Ludlow's *Memoirs*, written during his exile and first published in 1698–9, are an important source for the war in Ireland in the early 1650s and contain the famous remark about the Burren area of Co. Clare that it had not wood enough to hang a man, water enough to drown him, or earth enough to bury him. **Liam Irwin**

Lugh (Modern Irish Lú), the 'shining one', originally a GOD associated with the Continental Celts. It is generally accepted that the Gaulish parallel of Mercury and the Irish god Lugh are one and the same. Evidence about Lugh's status is to be found in Continental Europe; the place-names Lyon and Laon in France and Leiden in the Netherlands, derived from the Latinised form of his name, Lugudunum, are testimony to his importance. He is said to have killed his grandfather, who had a single, dreadful eye capable of destroying everything it saw. Among his many other talents Lugh is said to have invented the board-game *ficheall*, frequently mentioned in Irish literature and associated with heroes. He was an exceptional craftsman and harp-player and is also associated with bounty and appears to have been youthful, handsome, athletic, and skilled in fighting; he was known also as Lugh Lámhfhada (of the long arm). It has been documented that he arrived at a feast in the royal seat of TARA and that TUATHA DÉ DANANN refused him admission. When he asked if any among them could claim to possess his combination of skills and qualifications and it was discovered that they could not, he was admitted and became one of them.

The feast of LÚNASA (Lugh-assembly) was one of the QUARTER-DAYS in Irish tradition, celebrating the harvest. Some of the sites associated with the festival were burial places of female deities identified with the earth and with fertility. In some sources Lugh is also recorded as father to the hero CÚ CHULAINN.

It has been suggested that Lugh was introduced into the world of Celtic gods at a comparatively late stage, but there appears to be no definite evidence for this. **Ríonach uí Ógáin**

lúibíní, a song genre consisting of newly composed or extempore light-hearted verse in dialogue form, usually poking fun at people in the public eye, sung to a rollicking air such as 'Óra Mhíle Grá' or 'Ím Bím Babaró'. Associated mostly with the Cúil Aodha district in Co. Cork, from the latter half of the twentieth century it has been brought to a fine art at the annual OIREACHTAS festival. **Liam Mac Con Iomaire**

Luke, John (1906–1975), figure and subject painter. Born in Belfast; apprenticed to the LINEN trade and to SHIPBUILDING before attending Belfast College of Art, 1923–7, and the Slade School, London, 1927–30, where, under Henry Tonks, he developed a high regard for draughtsmanship. This led to an eccentric manner that placed great (some say obsessive) emphasis on severely stylised forms. He settled in Belfast in 1931 and remained there for most of his career. He worked in a slow, meticulous manner, often favouring tempera over oil paint; his output was therefore small. He also carved a number of stone sculptures, represented in the Ulster Museum. **S. B. Kennedy**

Lúnasa, a traditional festival falling on the Sunday closest to 1 August; the name is derived from that of the god LUGH and *násad* (game or assembly). Many PATTERNS and fairs are held in late July or early August, including Puck Fair in Killorglin, Co. Kerry, the OLD LAMMAS FAIR at Ballycastle, Co. Antrim, the CROAGH PATRICK

Lucan and McShane. *The comedians Arthur Lucan (right) as Mother Riley and Kitty McShane as Kitty in the film* Mother Riley's New Adventure *(1949), in which Old Mother Riley, a dishwasher, becomes the manager of a luxury hotel. [Courtesy of Stephen Dixon]*

pilgrimage, and Pattern Day in ARDMORE, Co. Waterford. Lúnasa was a festival of plenitude and described as the day on which 'all fruits ripen.' Picking bilberries or fraughans was common. In ancient times it was a time of assembly on heights and at wells and continued as an occasion for pilgrimage, sports, dancing, courting, and competition. [see BEALTAINE; IMBOLC; SAMHAIN.] **Stiofán Ó Cadhla**

Lundy, Robert (died c. 1717), governor of Derry during the siege of 1689. He was a Scottish Protestant who saw military service in Tangiers before serving in Ireland as lieutenant-colonel in Lord Mountjoy's regiment. In late 1688, as a compromise with the inhabitants of Derry following the closing of the gates, the Protestants in Mountjoy's regiment were installed as JAMES II's garrison under Lundy's command. However, Lundy made use of his military knowledge to prepare Derry for withstanding a siege by the Jacobite army. In early 1689 he accepted a commission from William III. In mid-April he attempted to shift the battle to Clady and Lifford, where defeat caused him to advocate the surrender of Derry. He sent away two Williamite relief regiments, while his refusal to participate in preparations for the siege led to his replacement. He left Derry disguised as a private soldier and was arrested in Scotland. He was rehabilitated and resumed his military career in later years as adjutant-general, in English pay, in the Portuguese service; he died some time before July 1717. Described in modern accounts as a defeatist rather than a traitor, he is still burnt in effigy during the annual celebrations of the closing of the Derry gates, and his name remains synonymous with 'traitor' in Ulster Unionist rhetoric. [see APPRENTICE BOYS.] **Charles Ivar McGrath**

Lunny, Dónal (1947–), musician, arranger, composer, and producer. Born in Newbridge, Co. Kildare. A founder-member of PLANXTY (with CHRISTY MOORE, ANDY IRVINE, and LIAM O'FLYNN) in 1972, in 1975 he joined the BOTHY BAND. He played with the re-formed Planxty from 1978; in 1981 he joined Moving Hearts. He has produced more than a hundred albums and has played on countless more. Television projects include 'Bringing It All Back Home', 'A River of Sound', and the 'Sult' series. He is credited with the development of the 'Irish bouzouki', which differs from the Greek original in that the back is flat rather than bowl-shaped. He has also experimented with large ten-string bouzoukis and with electric versions. He is noted for his attempts to mix and reconcile TRADITIONAL MUSIC with rock and international music influences. Recent projects include the band Coolfin and 'Dúiseacht', a commissioned work that formed part of the Irish contribution to Expo 2000 in Hannover. **Pat Ahern**

lunulae, crescent-shaped collars of thinly beaten sheet gold, of which over a hundred are known from Ireland. They are usually found singly, but occasionally three or four have been found together. Lunulae are the most common gold object of the Irish early BRONZE AGE. The finest are superbly decorated, with identical patterns of incised geometrical ornament arranged in panels along the narrowest areas of the crescent. The inner and outer edges are also decorated. Similar collars in jet and amber also occur. Irish lunulae have been found in Britain and on the Continent as copies made by foreign goldsmiths. [see GOLD, PREHISTORIC.] **Mary Cahill**

Lurgan (*An Lorgain*), Co. Armagh, one of the historic LINEN towns of Ulster; population (1991) 21,905. Lurgan was founded in 1610 by an English planter, John Brownlow, as the chief town of the estate he had acquired from the English Crown. The town's subsequent history was closely bound up with both linen and the Protestant interest. It was besieged and partly burnt in the 1641 REBELLION but was repaired by Sir William Brownlow, the founder's son, who set leases to 'British tradesmen' only. By the late seventeenth century Lurgan was renowned as a centre of linen manufacture and dairy marketing, and it retained this role throughout the eighteenth and nineteenth centuries, specialising increasingly in hand-produced fine linens and handkerchiefs. Since the 1940s the linen trade has suffered from the effects of increasing foreign competition; an attempt was made to secure the town's long-term prosperity by its inclusion in the new town of CRAIGAVON, designated in 1963 and begun two years later. Despite this, Lurgan retains its individual identity. **Lindsay Proudfoot**

Lurgan log-boat, a LOG-BOAT 15.2 m (50 ft) long found in a small peat-filled lake in Co. Galway, one of the largest surviving European log-boats; now in the NATIONAL MUSEUM, Dublin. Made from a large oak trunk with integral carved foot-rests and perforations in the side walls, it is probably unfinished. RADIOCARBON DATING shows it to be 4,500 years old. **A. L. Brindley**

Lusitania, a Cunard passenger liner torpedoed in May 1915 by the German submarine *U20* off the Irish coast at the Old Head of Kinsale, Co. Cork, while en route from New York to Liverpool during the hostilities of the FIRST WORLD WAR. Of the 1,906 passengers and crew, 1,198 were lost, including the director of the National Gallery of Ireland, Sir HUGH LANE. The sinking of the *Lusitania* influenced the decision by the United States in 1917 to enter the war. Controversy still attaches to the German allegation that the *Lusitania* was a legitimate target because it was claimed to be carrying arms. [see SHIPWRECKS.] **Brian Lalor**

Lutyens, Sir Edwin Landseer (1869–1944), architect. Born in London, son of an officer-turned-painter; his formal training consisted of two years in an art college and a year with the firm of Ernest George and Peto. His talents in planning and picturesque composition brought many large house commissions and, later, public works. In Ireland he designed two bridges over the Liffey, neither constructed: one for the LANE Gallery (1912), the other as an adjunct to the IRISH NATIONAL WAR MEMORIAL at Islandbridge (1931–7). His private work included the garden at Heywood, Co. Laois (1906), LAMBAY Castle, Co. Dublin (1905), and alterations to HOWTH Castle, Co. Dublin (1910). He was knighted in 1918. [see IRELAND'S WAR MEMORIAL RECORDS.] **Frederick O'Dwyer**

Lyle, Thomas Ranken (1860–1944), physicist. Born in Coleraine, Co. Derry; educated at TCD. Distinguished as an undergraduate by both academic and sporting prowess (sprint champion and international RUGBY player), he went on to be knighted and to become a fellow of the Royal Society. Professor of natural philosophy at the University of Melbourne, 1889–1914, he set up the first physical laboratory south of the equator and became an influential government adviser in Australia, particularly in relation to electrical power generation and supply. He is commemorated by the Lyle Medal, which recognises outstanding achievement in mathematics and physics by scientists in Australia. **Denis Weaire**

Lynam, Joss (1924–), mountaineer and engineer. Born in London. As an engineer he worked on harbour projects and on the restoration of monuments such as SCEILG MHICHÍL. A joint-founder of the Irish Mountaineering Club, 1948, he took part in and led many expeditions to Greenland, the Alps, the Himalayas, and the Andes; he was also joint-founder of the Association for Adventure Sports, 1969, and a member of the Long-Distance Walking Routes Committee, 1978–83, of which he became chairman in 1984. Despite triple-bypass heart surgery in 1986 he led an expedition to the Changtse (7,500 m, 25,000 ft) the following year. He edited and wrote many guidebooks and was founder and editor (until 1999) of *Mountain Log*. He was awarded an honorary doctorate by the University of Dublin in 2001, and he continues to devote much of his time and organisational skills to voluntary work. **Michael Fewer**

Lynch, Charles. *Charles Lynch, concert pianist. He worked with Stravinsky and Rachmaninov and assisted in the foundation of the Radio Éireann Symphony Orchestra, with which he was a frequent soloist.* [Irish Examiner]

Lynch, Charles (1906–1984), pianist. Born in Cork; studied at the Royal Academy of Music, where his principal teacher was Egon Petri (a favourite pupil of Busoni) and Benno Moiseiwitsch. He became a renowned concert pianist in London during the 1930s and worked with the cellist Beatrice Harrison, Stravinsky, and Rachmaninov, giving the first British performance of the latter's *First Piano Sonata in D minor*. In 1940 he returned to Dublin where he conducted many operas for the DGOS and performed extensively with the Radio Éireann orchestra. In 1971 he became the first pianist ever to perform the complete Beethoven symphonies in the Liszt transcription. His career declined severely in later years, during which he held a temporary lectureship in music at UCC. **John Page and Richard Pine.**

Lynch, Eliza (1835–1886), courtesan and consort of the dictator of Paraguay. Born in Co. Cork; the family left Ireland during the onset of the GREAT FAMINE. After a short stay in London, Eliza was in Paris by 1845. Before her sixteenth birthday she had married Xavier Quatrefages, an army officer; but the marriage lasted only a few years. Following a series of love affairs with wealthy 'protectors' she became permanently attached to Francisco Solano Lopéz, son and heir of the ruler of Paraguay. He was physically unattractive but extremely wealthy, while she was exceptionally beautiful and strong-willed. When Lopéz returned to Paraguay in 1855 she accompanied him, and they remained together until his death, though they did not marry. They had seven children. Lopéz became dictator of Paraguay on his father's death in 1862. Two years later he embroiled his impoverished country in a war against the triple alliance of Brazil, Argentina, and Uruguay, the three richest countries in South America. Paraguay was shattered by the five-year war, losing almost half its adult male population. Lopéz himself was killed in the final battle of that war, at Cerro Cora in 1870. Lynch fled to Paris, successfully smuggling more than $500,000 in jewels, gold, and cash. She returned briefly to Paraguay in 1875 before finally settling in Paris, at first in comfortable circumstances; later her spendthrift ways appear to have reduced her to penury. **Kenneth Neill**

Lynch, Henry Blosse (1807–1873), explorer. Born in Ballinrobe, Co. Mayo, the third of eleven brothers. He joined the Indian navy in 1823. In 1832, after being shipwrecked in the Red Sea, he crossed the Nubian Desert and descended the Nile to Egypt. In 1834 he accompanied FRANCIS RAWDON CHESNEY on his exploration of the Euphrates. A year later he partly surveyed the Euphrates, but the steamer *Tigris*, which he commanded, sank in a storm; among those who drowned was his brother Richard. In 1837 his most famous expedition followed, when he mapped the course of the Tigris from its source in Armenia. His subsequent career included charge of the postal service across Syria between Baghdad and Damascus, command of a flotilla off the mouth of the Indus, and service in the Indian navy during the Second Burmese War, 1851. He is remembered for his gifts as explorer, scholar, linguist, and diplomat. He died in Paris. **Peter Somerville-Large**

Lynch, John (Jack) (1917–1999), politician. Born in Cork; educated at UCC, and the KING'S INNS. Qualifying as a barrister, he worked as a civil servant. An outstanding GAA athlete, he excelled at both HURLING and GAELIC FOOTBALL. As a hurling midfielder, he played a pivotal role in the revival of Cork's fortunes from the late 1930s. He won four All-Ireland hurling medals in succession from 1941 to 1944 (captaining the side in 1942), a football medal in 1945, and another hurling title in 1946. His six consecutive championship wins are a record. Elected to DÁIL ÉIREANN for FIANNA FÁIL in 1948 in Cork, he became a parliamentary secretary in 1951, Minister for Education 1957–9, Minister for Industry and Commerce 1959–65, and Minister for Finance 1965–6, then becoming TAOISEACH following the retirement of SEÁN LEMASS. CHARLES HAUGHEY and George Colley were the other contenders, and Lynch was seen as a compromise candidate, with no deep republican ancestral roots. He won the 1969 general election handily, just in time to face the Northern Ireland crisis. He was conciliatory and cautious, but in 1970 he fired Neil Blaney and Haughey, suspecting them of gun-running and favouring an aggressive line on the North. Kevin Boland resigned his ministry in sympathy. Lynch's government undertook major educational initiatives and successfully negotiated Irish entry to the European Economic Community. Lynch narrowly lost the 1973 election but won that of 1977 by an extraordinary landslide, ironically ensuring that his opponents in the party were strengthened. In 1979 he resigned and was replaced by his opponent, Haughey, who defeated Colley. An extraordinarily popular and trusted figure, Lynch steered Fianna Fáil and the Republic through a dangerous period. **Tom Garvin**

Lynch, Patricia (1894–1972), writer. Born in Cork; educated in Ireland, England, Scotland, and Belgium. She began her career as a journalist for the *Christian Commonwealth* in London; there she met Sylvia Pankhurst, who sent her to Dublin to cover the events of 1916, her eye-witness account being published in the *Worker's Dreadnought*. Between 1925 and 1967 she published some forty-nine books and countless short stories of fantasy, realism, fairy-tales and legends, and the autobiographical *A Storyteller's Childhood* (1947). *The Cobbler's Apprentice* (1931) won the Silver Medal in the Tailteann Awards of 1931. With *The Turf Cutter's Donkey* (1934) came a general recognition of her talent; it was selected by the Junior Book Club in England, published in America, and translated into twelve languages. Lynch's favourite leitmotifs—fair days and races, Travellers' encampments, quests, and journeys—are all there; it is a heady mix of reality and fantasy and time travel that ends with the children back in their cottage on the edge of the Bog of ALLEN. *The Mad O'Haras* (1948) and *Delia Daly of Galloping Green* (1953) depict children on a different quest: towards emotional security against a setting of small rural communities. **Patricia Donlon**

Lynch, P. J. *Illustration by P. J. Lynch from* The King of Ireland's Son *by Brendan Behan. [Courtesy of Andersen Press, London © P. J. Lynch 1995]*

Lynch, Patrick (1917–2001), economist. Born in Dublin; educated at UCD and the University of Cambridge. He worked in the CIVIL SERVICE before entering academic life in 1952 at University College, Dublin, where he became professor of political ECONOMY. At various stages in his career he was chairman of AER LINGUS and deputy chairman of Allied Irish Banks, and a consultant to the Department of Finance, the OECD, the Council of Europe, and other national and international bodies. He was the director of the survey team that published the report *Investment in Education* (1965), which drew attention to deficiencies in the education system in the Republic and provided a blueprint for subsequent educational development. **Áine Hyland**

Lynch, P. J. (1962–), illustrator. Born in Belfast; educated at St Malachy's College and Brighton College of Fine Art. His first illustrated book, *A Bag of Moonshine* (1986) by Alan Garner, won the prestigious Mother Goose Award for the most promising newcomer in Britain, and he was twice winner of the principal prize for children's illustrated books, the Kate Greenaway Medal, for *The Christmas Miracle of Jonathan Toomey* (1995) and *When Jessie Came Across the Sea* (1997). *The Christmas Miracle of Jonathan Toomey* (1995) was also Bisto Book of the Year, 1995. His early work was varied in style, with painterly pastel for *Raggy Taggy Toys* (1988) and strong Rackham-influenced line drawings and silhouettes in black and white. His later work—such as *The Name upon the Harp* and *Ignis*—is a mixture of fantasy and realism, with stories and scenes meticulously researched for accuracy and mood. **Patricia Donlon**

Lynch, Susan (1971–), actor. Born in Newry, Co. Down; studied at the Ulster Youth Theatre, Belfast, and Central School of Speech and Drama, London, thereafter appearing at the Royal Court, Old Vic, and National Theatres, London. She came to wider prominence in the BBC television production of *Ivanhoe* and as Rosalind in *As You Like It*, while her main Irish television appearance was in the series *Amongst Women*. She played small roles in *Interview with a Vampire* (1994) and *The Secret of Roan Inish* (1994) and as Maggie in *Waking Ned* (1998) and was JAMES JOYCE's wife in PAT MURPHY's *Nora* (2000). **Kevin Rockett**

Lynch, Thomas Kerr Blosse (1818–1891), explorer. Born in Ballinrobe, Co. Mayo. After leaving TRINITY COLLEGE, Dublin, he joined his older brother HENRY BLOSSE LYNCH and accompanied him on his second Euphrates expedition, 1837–42, with the intention of investigating the possibility of steam navigation on the Tigris and Euphrates; he later financed and controlled this enterprise. During his long residence in the Middle East he travelled extensively in Mesopotamia (Iraq) and Persia (Iran); on his return he became consul-general for Persia in London and was awarded the decoration of the Lion and Sun on the Shah's visit to England. **Peter Somerville-Large**

Lynd, Robert, pen-name of Robert Wilson (1879–1949), journalist, essayist, and critic. Born in Belfast; educated at the RBAI and Queen's College. He was literary editor of the *Daily News*, London (subsequently the *News Chronicle*) from 1913 until the 1940s. As 'Y.Y.' he was a very popular contributor of essays to the *New Statesman*. His published literary criticism and general writings in essay and book form were urbanely thoughtful and, on Irish matters, informed by a strongly nationalist outlook. **Terence Brown**

Lynn, Kathleen (1874–1955), doctor and political activist. Born in Mullafarry, near Ballina, Co. Mayo, daughter of a Church of Ireland rector she was accredited with medical degrees by the RUI. She was active in the suffrage movement, vice-president of the IRISH WOMEN WORKERS' UNION, medical officer during the

DUBLIN 1913 LOCK-OUT, and medical director of the IRISH CITIZEN ARMY. During the 1916 Rising she took command of City Hall, Dublin, when she drove her car there with medical supplies and found the Citizen Army commander mortally wounded. She was elected to the executive of SINN FÉIN in 1917, becoming Surgeon-General. With Madeleine ffrench-Mullan she founded St Ultan's Hospital for Children, Dublin, in 1919, which was to be staffed entirely by women for many years. Opposed to the ANGLO-IRISH TREATY, in 1923 she became an abstentionist TD, refusing to enter DÁIL ÉIREANN with DE VALERA'S FIANNA FÁIL.

Committed to holistic pediatrics, she pioneered TB research with Dr Dorothy Stopford-Price, and St Ultan's became one of the world's first hospitals to vaccinate with BCG and to open a Montessori unit. From the time they met in suffrage activism she shared her political work and personal life with ffrench-Mullan; they lived together in Rathmines, Dublin, until ffrench-Mullan's death in 1944. [see LESBIANISM.] **Katherine O'Donnell**

Lynn, William Henry (1829–1915), architect. Born in Co. Down and brought up in Wexford; apprenticed to CHARLES LANYON in Belfast in 1846, working on Queen's College (now University). He was made a partner in 1854; the practice was both commercially and artistically successful but broke up in 1872. Lynn continued to practise into his eighties, his later works including extensions to Queen's University and in Dublin the Belfast Bank (later AIB), College Green (1893), and the Northern Bank, Grafton Street (1902). He entered many civic competitions in England, but only one of his designs—Chester Town Hall (1864)—was built. **Frederick O'Dwyer**

Lyons, William Edward (1939–), philosopher. Born in Melbourne, Australia; educated at the Australian National University, University of Calgary, and University of Dundee. He taught at the University of Glasgow, 1973–85, and was appointed professor of moral philosophy at TRINITY COLLEGE, Dublin, 1985; elected a TCD fellow, 1988, and a member of the Royal Irish Academy, 1994. Though best known for his analysis of emotion, he is internationally regarded for his general achievement in the philosophy of mind. His publications include *Gilbert Ryle* (1980), *Emotion* (1980), *The Disappearance of Introspection* (1986), *Approaches to Intentionality* (1995), and *Matters of the Mind* (2001). **Ian Leask**

Lyra Ecclesiastica (1879–93), journal of the Irish Society of St Cecilia. The founding of *Lyra Ecclesiastica* was an attempt to define the position and activities of the Cecilian movement in Ireland; it also gave accounts of the activities of parallel societies elsewhere, including a regular feature entitled 'Cecilian Intelligence' as well as a 'Monthly List of Sacred Music'. From 1891 to 1893 it was edited by HEINRICH BEWERUNGE. **John Page**

Lyric FM, national classical music radio station. Directed by Séamus Crimmins, Lyric FM was established by RTÉ in Limerick in 1999, having evolved from the previous FM3. From the beginning it has created an interesting middle-ground approach, bridging the gap between an uncompromising BBC 3 model and the populist, commercial Classic FM. **John Page**

Lyric Players, Belfast, founded in 1951 by Mary and Pearse O'Malley. The Lyric Players began in a small auditorium attached to the O'Malleys' home in Derryvolgie Avenue. They began with—and have continued—a commitment to the verse plays of W. B. YEATS and AUSTIN CLARKE (from whose Lyric Theatre Company in Dublin they took their name). However, responding to the lack of a permanent professional company in Belfast in the late 1950s, they expanded their repertoire, staging early work by BRIAN FRIEL and other Ulster writers. By 1968 they were able to move to their present site in Ridgeway Street. The Lyric has consistently encouraged an open cultural debate through its journal, *Threshold* (1957–), and attempting to present challenging theatrical responses to the situation in Northern Ireland. Its position since the early 1970s as Northern Ireland's major subsidised repertory company has enabled it to nurture Ulster playwrights, including JOHN BOYD (who also served as artistic director for a number of years), PATRICK GALVIN (the Cork playwright), CHRISTINA REID, and Gary Mitchell. [see MAYNE, RUTHERFORD.] **Christopher Morash**

Lynn, Kathleen. *Portrait of Dr Kathleen Lynn, physician and political activist, by Lily Williams. As one of the City Hall garrison during the 1916 Rising she tended the fatally wounded actor, Seán Connolly. [Irish Labour History Museum]*

Lythe, Robert (fl. 1556–74), English surveyor, cartographer, and military engineer. He surveyed the English pale at Calais in 1556. Appointed by the English government to make a map of Ulster in 1567, he was compelled by adverse local conditions to turn his attention southwards, and by the time illness forced him back to England in 1571 he had covered most of the country south of a line from STRANGFORD LOUGH to KILLARY HARBOUR, producing a more accurate and comprehensive map of coasts, rivers, lakes, mountains, woods, towns, and villages than had previously been available for any large part of Ireland. Besides a number of regional and local maps he made a general map of Ireland, based where possible on his own surveys and otherwise on second-hand information of lower quality. His work was never published under his own name but can be seen to have influenced the maps of subsequent compilers, including Jodocus Hondius, GERARD MERCATOR, Baptista Boazio, and JOHN SPEED. **J. H. Andrews**

McGarry Ní Éanaigh *(see page 670). Smithfield Public Space, Dublin (1997), designed by the architects McGarry Ní Éanaigh. Twelve monumental 26 m (87-ft) light reflectors and braziers define the 335 m (1,100-ft) length of Smithfield, a seventeenth-century cobbled market square. [Courtesy of McGarry Ní Éanaigh Architects; photo: Barry Mason]*

MacAdam, Robert Shipbuoy (Mac Ádhaimh, Róibeard) (1808–1895), industrialist, antiquarian, and Irish-language activist. Born in Belfast; educated at RBAI. With his brother James he founded the Soho Foundry, 1835. A prolific collector of MANUSCRIPTS, FOLKLORE, and songs, he employed scribes to collect, copy and compile material in Irish. He was active in Cuideacht Gaedhilge Uladh (the Ulster Irish-Language Society) and the BELFAST NATURAL HISTORY AND PHILOSOPHICAL SOCIETY; he founded the *Ulster Journal of Archaeology* in 1852 and was its editor until 1862. The foundry declined, and he died impoverished. **Joe Ó Labhraí**

Mac Aingil, Aodh, the name by which Aodh Mac Cathmhaoil (1571–1626) is popularly known. He was born in Downpatrick and studied in the Isle of Man. Tutor to the sons of HUGH O'NEILL, he accompanied Henry O'Neill to Spain in 1600 and joined the Franciscan order in SALAMANCA c. 1601. He taught in the university soon after his ordination. With FLAITHRI Ó MAOLCHONAIRE he was one of the founders of the Franciscan Irish College at LOUVAIN in 1606 and was appointed Guardian in 1609. A theologian of international repute, he published a catechetical work in Louvain in 1618, *Scáthán Shacramuinte na hAithridhe* ('Mirror of the sacrament of penance'), based on the Council of Trent's teaching on penance. The most important features of this work are the author's deliberate choice of simple language for catechetical reasons and his tendency to illustrate doctrinal points with exemplary tales and with anecdotes based on personal experience. The final section deals with indulgences and is remarkable for its attempt to present JAMES I as the legitimate sovereign of Irish Catholics. Mac Aingil was also an accomplished poet. Nominated Archbishop of Armagh in succession to PETER LOMBARD, he died of a fever in Rome in 1626 while preparing to return to Ireland. [see IRISH COLLEGES IN CONTINTENTAL EUROPE.] **Mícheál Mac Craith**

McAleese, Mary, née Leneghan (1951–), barrister, legal scientist, journalist, and President of Ireland. Born in Belfast; educated at QUB. She was called to the Northern Ireland bar after graduation and appointed Reid professor of criminal law at TRINITY COLLEGE, Dublin, in 1975. She worked as a journalist and presenter in RTÉ, 1979–81. In 1984 she was a member of the Catholic Church episcopal delegation to the NEW IRELAND FORUM. Ten years later she was appointed a pro-vice-chancellor of Queen's University, Belfast. As FIANNA FÁIL nominee, she won the 1997 presidential election (see p. 451). **Brian Galvin**

Mac a Liondain, Pádraig (c. 1665–1733), south Armagh farmer and poet, perhaps also a harper. Some nineteen poems survive, mainly concerned with poets and others for whom his home is said to have been a cultural centre. His work shows wide learning and stylistic variety but little depth of personal feeling. **Colm Ó Baoill**

McAliskey, Bernadette, née Devlin (1947–), politician. Born in Cookstown, Co. Tyrone, she rose to prominence while a student at Queen's University, Belfast, through involvement in PEOPLE'S DEMOCRACY. Her commitment to a republican-socialist philosophy assured her a leading role in the organisation, and she took part in the principal CIVIL RIGHTS marches of the period, including that from Belfast to Derry, about which she had at first expressed some reservations. She was selected as a compromise 'unity' candidate in the Mid-Ulster constituency for a Westminster by-election, and her vigorous campaigning ensured her election in 1969, at the age of twenty-one, as the youngest woman MP. Though she held the seat until 1974, she quickly lost faith in parliamentary methods and was active behind the barricades in the BOGSIDE, Derry, during August 1969, which led to six months' imprisonment on a charge of riotous behaviour. Always outspoken in her criticism of the British government's handling of Northern Ireland, she was seriously injured in a loyalist gun attack on her home in February 1981. Despite her injury she played a prominent role in the National H-Block Committee, which acted on behalf of republican prisoners engaged in the HUNGER STRIKE of the same year. **Alan Scott**

Mac Amhlaigh, Dónall (1926–1989), novelist, SHORT-STORY writer, and journalist. Born near Galway, where he lived until his family moved to Kilkenny in 1940. He joined the DEFENCE FORCES in 1947, then emigrated to England in 1951 and settled in Northampton, where he was to spend the rest of his life, working as a labourer and writing mainly in Irish. His description of navvy life in *Dialann Deoraí* (1960) was followed by an account of his army years in *Saol Saighdiúra* (1962). The novels *Diarmaid Ó Dónaill* (1965) and *Deoraithe* (1986) and the short-story collections *Sweeney agus Scéalta Eile* (1970) and *Beoir Bhaile* (1981) draw heavily on autobiographical material and on the experiences of Irish emigrants of his generation in Britain. A socialist, he contributed regularly to newspapers and journals in Ireland and England throughout the 1970s and 80s. [see CONSTRUCTION WORKERS IN BRITAIN.] **Máirín Nic Eoin**

Mac an Bhaird, Diarmaid (mac Laoisigh) (fl. 1670), participant in the 'Contention of the Red Hand', a poetic debate on whether the RED HAND OF ULSTER originated with UÍ NÉILL, Ulaidh or Airghialla. He was probably the same person as Diarmaid Mac an Bhaird, poet to Brian (mac Colla) Mac Mathghamhna of Farney. **Katharine Simms**

Mac an Bhaird, Eoghan Rua (c. 1570–c. 1630), POET. A prominent member of a Donegal bardic family; his earliest known poem, 'Rob Soraidh th'Eachtra, a Aodh Ruaidh', blessed RED HUGH O'DONNELL, leaving for Spain in January 1602 after the defeat of KINSALE. Thereafter he became *ollamh* to Hugh's successor, RORY O'DONNELL, commenting on that chief's journey to negotiate terms in Dublin ('Dána an turas trialltar sonn'), reproaching him for his coldness after becoming an earl, hailing the birth of his son Aodh c. 1606, and lamenting the FLIGHT OF THE EARLS in 1607 and Ruairí's death in Rome in 1608. Eoghan Rua himself crossed to the Continent, composing poems under the patronage of the earl's sister, Nuala, preserved in 'The Book of O'Donnell's Daughter' (now in the Bibliothèque Royale, Brussels). Eventually he seems to have become a Franciscan, and the author of several religious poems. **Katharine Simms**

Mac an Bhaird, Fearghal Óg (fl. 1600), poet. From a Donegal family of bardic poets, he received part of his education in Munster and excelled his kinsmen in artistry. He began composing for Mag Uidhir and Mag Aonghusa patrons in the 1580s and went on to address most of the leaders of the NINE YEARS' WAR; yet he never became *ollamh* in his homeland. At one time he attempted to ply his trade in Scotland but was deterred by its Protestantism. After the PLANTATION OF ULSTER he crossed to LOUVAIN and composed religious poetry for the exiled Archbishop of Tuam, FLAITHRÍ Ó MAOLCHONAIRE. **Katharine Simms**

Mac an Leagha, Uilliam (fl. 1450), scribe. A member of a well-known learned family, he is best known as the scribe of several important MANUSCRIPTS containing literature translated from Continental sources, including the stories of Hercules and Charlemagne, the Life of Mary of Egypt, and the Harrowing of Hell. It has been suggested that he was also the translator of some or all of these. **William Gillies**

Mac Anna, Tomás (1926–), theatre director. Born in Dundalk; educated at Dundalk CBS. He joined the ABBEY THEATRE, Dublin, in the 1940s, directing an influential production of Berthold Brecht's *Galileo* (1965). He was a central figure in the theatre's modernisation after 1966, serving as artistic director at two difficult transitional periods, 1972–8 and 1984–5. **Christopher Morash**

Mac Aingil, Aodh. *Fresco of Aodh Mac Aingil in the Aula Maxima, Collegio Sant' Isidoro, Rome, by Fra Emanuele of Como. He is depicted as the man of learning, with his bishop's mitre on the table. [Collegio Sant' Isidoro, Rome]*

McAliskey. *The civil rights activist Bernadette Devlin (McAliskey) with campaign worker during the 1969 British by-election in the Mid-Ulster constituency. She was elected, the youngest woman MP ever, at the age of twenty-one. [Camera Press Ireland]*

Mac Annaidh, Séamas (1961–), writer. Born in Dublin but largely associated with Enniskillen, because of his writing. He is best known for his trilogy *Cuaifeach Mo Lon Dubh Buí* (1983), *Mo Dhá Mhicí* (1986), and *Rubble na Mickies* (1990), in which he creates an anarchic and comic world that is playful and provocative. The first book was the most successful and was translated into Russian in 1989. For it he created a style that jumbled together the best of GAELTACHT speech with quotations from every period of literature and the demotic Irish and English of youth. He has written another novel, *Féirin, Scéalta agus Eile* (1992), a collection of short stories, and film scripts. **Alan Titley**

McAteer, Eddie (1914–1986), politician. Born in Coatbridge, Lanarkshire; his father, a native of Co. Donegal, brought the family to Derry, where McAteer was educated. Employed first as a tax officer and later as an accountant, his early political stance was strikingly encapsulated in a controversial pamphlet, *Irish Action*, in which he advocated a policy of civil disobedience. Elected as MP for mid-Londonderry in 1949 and for Foyle in 1953, he became leader of the Nationalist Party in 1964. The following year, as a result of the unprecedented meeting between TERENCE O'NEILL and SEÁN LEMASS, he led the party to adopt for the first time the role of official opposition at STORMONT. Representing by now a traditionalist, conservative brand of nationalism, McAteer and some of his colleagues were compared unfavourably with the younger, more dynamic Catholic leaders emerging during the 1960s with their civil rights orientation, one of whom, JOHN HUME, replaced McAteer as MP for Foyle in 1969. **Alan Scott**

McAuley, Catherine (1778–1841), Catholic activist and founder of the SISTERS OF MERCY. Born in Dublin. In 1831 she founded the Sisters of Mercy. The congregation developed from the House of Mercy, which she had established in Dublin in 1827. Her flexible approach allowed the sisters to respond to a range of public needs. Most communities had poor schools and refuges for vulnerable young women, and the sisters visited the sick. The congregation expanded rapidly and there were convents in Ireland and England by the time of her death. [see RELIGIOUS ORDERS, FEMALE.] **Séamus Enright**

Mac Bionaid, Art (1793–1879), poet and scribe. Born in Baile Caol, Forkill, Co. Armagh; he worked as a stonemason at Belleeks, Co. Armagh, 1846–9. One of his children died because of FAMINE. Some twenty of his manuscripts and thirty poems survive, many on local people. **Colm Ó Baoill**

McBratney, Sam (1943–), writer. Born in Belfast; educated at TCD. The author of more than seventy books, McBratney is one of the most accomplished writers for children of the twentieth century. He wrote his first novel, *Mark Time* (1976), in the late 1960s, though it was not published until 1976; alone of all his books, it deals with the reality of the 'TROUBLES' for teenagers. Another memorable book for young adults is *The Chieftain's Daughter*, set in the Ireland of fifteen centuries ago. He is acutely aware of his audiences and is adept at writing for the whole spectrum, from very young children to young adults. His characters are convincing and familiar, and he writes with clarity, humour, and pace. *Put a Saddle on the Pig* is a *tour de force*, with a double-sided narrative told from both mother's and teenage daughter's viewpoints. McBratney had been a relatively successful author for more than twenty years when his picture-book *Guess How Much I Love You?* (1994) brought him international fame and sales. He is skilled at evoking mood and sensations that are both universal and timeless, as in *The Dark at the Top of the Stairs* and *Just You and Me*. He won the Bisto Book of the Year award, 1992/3, the Silveren Griffel, 1995, and American Bookseller Book of the Year award, 1996. **Patricia Donlon**

McBreen, Joan (1946–), poet. Born in Sligo; educated at UCD. Her first book of verse, *The Wind Beyond the Wall* (1990), was followed by *A Walled Garden in Moylough* (1995) and *Poems Selected and New* (1998). She also edited *The White Page/An Bhileog Bhán: Twentieth-Century Irish Women Poets* (1999). Her poetry is marked by lyricism and a nice wit as she engages with the joys and pains of womanhood. **Terence Brown**

MacBride, John (died 1800), seaman and naval officer. Born in Co. Antrim. As a young man he joined the merchant service as an ordinary seaman. In 1784, when his ship was in the West Indies and he had advanced to able seaman, he seems to have been pressed into the British navy, as his name appears on the crew list of the *Garland*. In a period when promotion to officer rank depended almost exclusively on the influence of local nobility, he must have shown a special ability to get himself promoted to midshipman and then master's mate on the *Norfolk*, stationed in the Downs in south-east England. From then on his career was meteoric. By 1761 he was captain of a cutter that captured a French privateer; by 1767 he was captain of the frigate *Jason*, supervising the transfer of the ownership of the Falkland Islands from France to England and publishing a classic memorandum on the weather of the islands. During the American War of Independence he carried out remarkable exploits. In 1798 he became rear-admiral and in 1799 admiral and commander of the naval base at Plymouth, where the most popular pub is the Admiral MacBride. **John de Courcy Ireland**

MacBride, John (1865–1916), revolutionary. Born in Westport, Co. Mayo. He became involved in separatist politics with the IRB in the 1880s, then left the movement and emigrated to South Africa, where he developed strong pro-Boer sympathies, fighting on the Boer side in the Anglo-Boer war against the British. He rejoined the IRB shortly after his return to Ireland and was also a member of SINN FÉIN. He married MAUD GONNE in 1903, and they had one son, SEÁN MACBRIDE. Though not directly involved in planning the 1916 RISING he took part in it and on 5 May 1916 was shot by firing squad. **Brian Galvin**

McBride Neill, John (1905–1974), architect. Born in Belfast; studied at Belfast School of Art and apprenticed to Robert Lynn. In private practice from 1928, he specialised in CINEMA design and during the 1930s produced some of the definitive examples of cinema architecture. The names of his buildings—Apollo, Curzon, Forum, Majestic, Regal, Strand, Tivoli, Tonic, and Troxy—are as evocative of the era as the cinemas themselves, few of which have survived. The Tonic, Bangor (1934), Majestic, Belfast (1935), and Curzon, Belfast (1935), are assured modernist essays, white-walled and cubist in inspiration, in what was then an entirely new building type, the cinema palace. **Brian Lalor**

MacBride, Maud Gonne: see GONNE MACBRIDE, MAUD.

MacBride, Seán (1904–1988), lawyer, revolutionary, and politician. Born in Paris; educated at St Louis de Gonzaga College, Paris, Mount St Benedict's, Gorey, UCD, and KING'S INNS. He inherited his revolutionary politics from his mother, MAUD GONNE. He became an anti-Treaty Republican and as a lawyer specialised in political cases. In the 1930s and 40s, for part of which time he was chief of staff of the IRA, he argued for greater participation by republicans in constitutional politics, and in 1946 he jointly founded CLANN NA POBLACHTA, which critically drew support from former FIANNA FÁIL voters in the 1948 election and formed an important component of the inter-party Government of 1948–51. A bitter falling out with his former protégé NÖEL BROWNE, Minister for Health, ensued, leading to the collapse of the Government and the virtual extinction of his party. He lost his own seat in 1957. Thereafter—his long-standing ambition of reconciling traditional Catholicism and militant REPUBLICANISM frustrated—he expended his energies in a number of other organisations, notably as a founder-member of Amnesty International (chairman, 1973–6) and UNESCO. These activities won him the NOBEL PEACE PRIZE (1974) and the Lenin Peace Prize (1977). He also served on the International Commission of Jurists. **John Horgan**

MacBride, Seán. *Seán MacBride established an international reputation as a humanitarian as a founder-member of Amnesty International, being awarded the Nobel Peace Prize in 1974 and the Lenin Peace Prize in 1977. [Colman Doyle]*

McBride, William James (Willie John) (1940–), rugby footballer. A powerful forward, he was one of nine newly capped players when he made his international debut against England at Twickenham in 1962. His first eleven appearances were consecutive, before he was dropped for the game against Wales in 1964, an error of selection that was instantly rectified. He captained the national team on twelve occasions, starting with the match against Wales in Cardiff in 1973 and ending in 1975, also in Cardiff, which was his last Ireland appearance. Ireland's most-capped lock, with sixty-three matches between 1962 and 1975, he is also the most-capped British Lions player ever, with seventeen Test appearances on the tours to South Africa in 1962, 1968, and 1974, Australia and New Zealand in 1966, and New Zealand in 1971. In 1974 he was captain of the record-breaking team that was unbeaten but drew the fourth Test. He was manager of the British Lions on the 1983 tour of New Zealand. **Karl Johnston**

Mac Bruaideadha, Tadhg Mac Dáire (c. 1570–c. 1652), poet and chronicler. Clann Bhruaideadha were chroniclers to the O'Briens of Thomond. Tadhg Mac Dáire, born in Co. Clare, was associated with Donnchadh Ó Briain, fourth Earl of Thomond (died 1624), for whom and his family he composed praise poems. He is now best known for his role as instigator of IOMARBHÁGH NA BHFILEADH (some nine of the poems being attributed to him). His other works include religious compositions and an elegy for the Earl, 'Eascar Gaoidheal Éag Aoinfhir'. He was involved in the compiling of An Leabhar Muimhneach and is also recorded as a teacher of Irish to the immigrant Sir Matthew de Renzy. **Michelle O Riordan**

McCabe, Edward (1816–1885), cardinal. Born in Dublin; educated at ST PATRICK'S COLLEGE, Maynooth, and ordained in 1839. Having been assistant to Cardinal PAUL CULLEN, he succeeded him as Archbishop of Dublin in 1879 and was made a cardinal in 1882, the second Irishman to be so honoured. Intellectually capable but doctrinally rigorous, he continued Cullen's ULTRAMONTANISM. He was hostile to the land agitation and to popular political movements generally, and was denounced by nationalists as a 'Castle bishop'. **Fergal Tobin**

McCabe, Eugene (1930–), writer. Born in Glasgow, he returned with his family to Clones, Co. Monaghan, in 1940. He first came to prominence as a playwright; the controversial *King of the Castle* (1964) won the Irish Life Award. His compelling Northern Ireland trilogy *Victims: Cancer, Heritage, Siege*, was produced by RTÉ television in 1976. He has published a variety of prose works, including a historical novel, *Death and Nightingales* (1992), a children's story, *Cyril: The Quest of an Orphan Squirrel* (1998), and four FAMINE monologues, commissioned and jointly produced by RTÉ and TG4, entitled *Tales from the Poorhouse* (2000). **Des O'Rawe**

McCabe, Patrick (1955–), writer. Born in Clones, Co. Monaghan. He began his literary career as a writer of short stories and a book for children, *The Adventures of Shay Mouse* (1985). His first novel, *Music on Clinton Street* (1986), was followed by *Carn* (1989), *The Butcher Boy* (1992), *The Dead School* (1995), and *Breakfast on Pluto* (1999). *Mondo Desperado*, a collection of short stories, was published in 2000. He jointly wrote the screenplay for a critically acclaimed film version of *The Butcher Boy* (1997), directed by NEIL JORDAN. **Des O'Rawe**

McCann, Colum (1965–), novelist and short-story writer. Born in Dublin; educated at Rathmines College. A collection of short stories, *Fishing the Sloe-Black River*, appeared in 1994. He has also published the novels *Songdogs* (1995), *This Side of Brightness* (1998), and *Dancer* (2003). **Terence Brown**

McCann, Donal (1943–1999), actor. Born in Dublin; educated at Terenure College. He began acting at the ABBEY THEATRE. He was an intense, emotionally courageous actor, whose performances include *Tarry Flynn* (1966), *Faith Healer* (1980), and SEBASTIAN BARRY's *The Steward of Christendom* (1995). His film work includes John Huston's *The Dead* (1987), Thaddeus O'Sullivan's *December Bride* (1990) and Bernard Bertolucci's *Stealing Beauty* (1966). **Christopher Morash**

McCarthy, B. G. (1904–1993), critic. Born in Cork; educated at UCC and the University of Cambridge. She was professor of English at UCC (1948–1966). Her highly original study of women's contribution to writing in English, *The Female Pen*, published in two volumes (1944, 1947), is an important early work of feminist literary criticism. She also wrote plays and essays. **Brian Lalor**

MacCarthy, Denis Florence (1817–1882), POET. Born in Dublin; trained in law and for the priesthood but abandoned both for a literary vocation in the service of cultural NATIONALISM. He participated in the YOUNG IRELAND movement, was a frequent contributor to the *Nation* (from 1843) as well as DUBLIN UNIVERSITY MAGAZINE, and edited two anthologies of ballads and verse (1846). His original works include *Ballads, Poems, and Lyrics* (1850), *Under-Glimpses and Other Poems* (1857), *The Bell-Founder and Other Poems* (1857), and *Shelley's Early Life from Original Sources* (1872). He was appointed professor of English literature in the CATHOLIC UNIVERSITY, Dublin, in 1854. **Jason King**

MacCarthy, Jimmy (1953–), songwriter. Born in Cork. Regarded as one of Ireland's best songwriters, he wrote material for CHRISTY MOORE ('Ride On'), Mary Black ('No Frontiers'), and MARY COUGHLAN ('Ancient Rain'), among others. The release of his debut album, *The Song of the Singing Horseman* (1991), saw the beginning of a singing career, and McCarthy is now revered as much for his live performances as for his authorship. **Tony Clayton-Lea**

McCarthy, Joseph (Joe) (1908–1957), United States politician. Born in Grand Chute, Wisconsin; his mother, Bridget Tierney, was born in Ireland; his father, Timothy McCarthy, had one Irish-born parent. Educated at Marquette University, he became senator for Wisconsin, 1946–57, and came to prominence in 1950 during the Cold War when he made unsubstantiated claims of widespread communist infiltration of the State Department, the Truman administration, and the army; some 2 million federal employees were investigated. By 1954 McCarthy's accusations had been discredited, but not before he had managed to blacklist and seriously damage the careers of many people prominent in the arts, film industry, and public life. **Brian Lalor**

McCarthy, Justin (1830–1912), politician, journalist, and author. Born in Cork. He moved to England in 1853, wrote for the liberal press, and established a reputation as a novelist and historian. Elected to Parliament for Co. Longford, 1879, he was vice-chairman of the IRISH PARTY, 1880–90, and chairman, 1890–96, following the PARNELL split. He maintained unity among the majority of the party, facilitating the passing of the second HOME RULE Bill by the House of Commons in 1893. **Eugene J. Doyle**

MacCarthy, Justin, Viscount Mount Cashell (c. 1643–1694), soldier. Third son of Donogh MacCarthy, first Earl of Clancarty, he began his military career in France and from 1678 served in England. On the accession of JAMES II he was made lieutenant-general of a foot regiment, became a member of the Irish Privy Council, was appointed LORD LIEUTENANT of Co. Cork, and was given the title Viscount Mount Cashell. He assisted the Earl of Tyrconnell in the promotion of Catholics in the army and the civil administration. In February 1689 he recaptured Bandon, whose citizens had declared for WILLIAM III, and disarmed the Protestants in the entire Cork region following the arrival in Ireland of James II. He was a member for Co. Cork in the JACOBITE Parliament, where he introduced the bill for repeal of the Act of Settlement to the House of Lords. His regiment was decisively defeated by the Irish Williamites at the BATTLE OF NEWTOWN BUTLER in July 1689, following which he seems to have lost all hope of a Jacobite victory. He was put in command of the Irish regiments sent to France in April 1690 that formed the nucleus of the IRISH BRIGADES on the Continent and took a prominent part in campaigns in Italy, Catalonia, and the Rhineland. He died in July 1694 at Barages, in the Pyrenees, where he had gone to recuperate from the effects of old injuries. **Liam Irwin**

McCarthy, Michael (Mick) (1959–), soccer player. Born in Barnsley, Yorkshire. He was almost twenty-five when he made his first appearance for the Republic of Ireland, but he emerged as a highly effective international player, leading by example when he captained the team in the World Cup finals in 1990. After leaving Barnsley he enjoyed a successful club career with Manchester City, Celtic, Olympic Lyon, and Millwall. His most gratifying achievement, perhaps, was to make an almost seamless transition when succeeding JACK CHARLTON as manager of the national team, 1996–2002. He managed the team that qualified for the 2002 World Cup Finals but resigned later that year. **Peter Byrne**

McCarthy, Thomas (1954–), poet and novelist. Born in Cappoquin, Co. Waterford; educated at UCC. A librarian with Cork City Library, he has published two novels with a political theme as well as poetry. His reflectively lyrical verse is highly personal in content yet manages to suggest the public dimension in which the private life must find its place. His collections include *The Sorrow Garden* (1981), *Seven Winters in Paris* (1989), and *Mr Dineen's Careful Parade: New and Selected Poems* (1999). **Terence Brown**

McClintock, Sir Francis Leopold (1819–1907), explorer. Born in Dundalk; entered the Royal Navy in 1831. He led two expeditions to the Arctic, 1848 and 1852. In 1857 he was commissioned by Lady Jane Franklin, the widow of the missing explorer Sir John Franklin, to discover what had happened to her husband, though there had been many previous indications that he and his crew had perished. McClintock sailed in the *Fox* to King William Island, where he obtained confirmation from the Inuit of the fate of the expedition and numerous pathetic relics: silver plate with coats of arms of the missing men, spoons, forks, buttons, and bows and arrows made of English wood. He was knighted in 1860, became vice-admiral of the fleet in 1877, and knight commander of the Order of the Bath in 1891. **Peter Somerville-Large**

M'Clure, Sir Robert John Le Mesurier (1807–1873), discoverer of the North-West Passage. Born in Wexford. After entering the Royal Navy in 1824 he took part in an early Arctic exploration in 1836. In 1848 he served as first lieutenant to Sir John Ross on the first of many expeditions in search of the missing Sir John Franklin. In 1850 he went with another search party, during which his ship, the *Investigator*, became ice-bound. After it was released M'Clure discovered Baring's Island and sailed Barrow Strait into the Atlantic Ocean. On journeying overland along the coast of Bank's Land on 26 October 1850 he climbed a hill and saw clear water to Melville Island: the North-West Passage was discovered. When the *Investigator* again became ice-bound for two years, M'Clure and his crew set off on foot and were eventually rescued by Captain HENRY KELLETT. On his return to England, M'Clure was knighted and voted £10,000 by Parliament. **Peter Somerville-Large**

Mac Cóil, Liam (1952–), novelist and critic. Born in Dublin; educated at UCD and TCD. His first novel, *An Dochtúir Áthas* (1994), deals with Freudian psychology. His second novel, *An Claíomh Solais* (1998), is set around the television channel TG4 and also revisits some of the themes of the first. Mac Cóil's finely tuned critical faculties inform his fiction, bringing an added sophistication to the self-conscious post-modernity of his writing. **Seán Ó Cearnaigh**

Mac Con Mara, Donnchadh Rua (1715–1810), poet. Born probably in Cratloe, Co. Clare. In the early 1740s he began working as a teacher in Cos. Waterford and Cork where he spent much of his life. He also worked for a period c. 1764 as a clerk for the Church of Ireland. Mac Con Mara may have lived for a period in Newfoundland between 1745 and 1755, where his exile-poem 'Bánchnuic Éireann Óighe' was probably composed. 'Eachtra Ghiolla an Amaráin', possibly his most famous poem, humorously describes a journey overseas; separate sections describe an AISLING by the poet and his dramatic escape from a pursuing French frigate. Though he is generally regarded as a comical writer, 'Aoir do na Sagartaibh' is a caustic attack on the Catholic clergy of his day who, in promoting social injustice, proved to be 'without moral teaching, without principle, without decree.' The poem reflects an opposition to an oppressive Catholic clergy which became a common theme in Irish political poetry in the second half of the eighteenth century. Mac Con Mara is also known for an elegy, composed in Latin, on his friend TADHG GAEDHEALACH Ó SÚILLEABHÁIN. He composed a poem of penitence, 'An Aithrighe', towards the end of his life. **Meidhbhín Ní Úrdail**

Mac Con Midhe, Giolla Brighde (c. 1210–c. 1272), poet. Born in or near Ardstraw, Co. Tyrone; he is sometimes confused with an earlier poet, Giolla Brighde Albanach. Giolla Brighde Mac Con Midhe was hereditary poet to the O'Gormleys but composed poems for O'Donnell, O'Connor, and other chieftains. He is perhaps best known for his lament for Brian O'Neill and the many leaders slain at the disastrous Battle of Downpatrick in 1260. He also composed religious poetry, most notably the poem 'Déan Oram Trócaire, a Thríonnóid' ('Have mercy on me, O Trinity'), in which he begs God to grant him children in place of those who have died. **Nicholas J. A. Williams**

McConnell, Cathal (1944–), flute-player and singer. Born in Ballinaleck, Co. Fermanagh. He is an influential musician from a musical household in a county strong in tradition. His lyrical flute-playing and singing are highly regarded. Together with the singer Robin Morton and FIDDLE-player Tommy Gunn he founded the internationally known group BOYS OF THE LOUGH in 1967. He has recorded extensively both with the Boys of the Lough and as a soloist. *Long Expectant Comes at Last* (2001) is his most recent solo work. **Desi Wilkinson**

McConnell, Mickey (1947–), journalist, singer, and songwriter. Born in Ballinaleck, Co. Fermanagh, brother of CATHAL MCCONNELL. His most famous composition is 'Only Our Rivers Run Free', popularised by Planxty and by James Last. Many other artists have recorded his work. His one solo album is *Peter Pan and Me* (1991). **Desi Wilkinson**

Mac Consaidín, Séamas (fl. 1780), poet. Born and lived near Milltown Malbay, Co. Clare. Though not qualified as a doctor, he practised medicine as a livelihood. He composed poems and songs on conventional themes; sixteen of these have survived in manuscript. **Eoghan Ó hAnluain**

McCormack, Inez (1946–), trade unionist. Born in Belfast; educated at TCD and QUB. She became active in the CIVIL RIGHTS MOVEMENT in the late 1960s, taking part in the 1969 Belfast–Derry peace march. Appointed the first woman official of the National Union of Public Employees in 1976, she developed union organisation in 'forgotten' areas of the public sector, such as among hospital cleaners and home helps. In 1999 she was elected president of the IRISH CONGRESS OF TRADE UNIONS, the first woman to hold the office, and in 1976 she was a founder-member of the EQUAL OPPORTUNITIES COMMISSION and the Fair Employment Commission. Awarded an honorary doctorate by Queen's University, Belfast, in 2000, she writes, broadcasts and campaigns extensively on human rights, EQUALITY and TRADE UNION issues (see p. 381). **Alison Walsh**

McCormack, John. Count John McCormack and his Family *(c. 1925) by John Lavery. McCormack's singing and recording career made him one of the most successful lyric tenors of his era. [Hugh Lane Municipal Gallery of Modern Art; by courtesy of Felix Rosentiel's Widow and Son Ltd, London, on behalf of the estate of Sir John Lavery]*

McCormack, John (1884–1945), singer. Born in Athlone, Co. Westmeath; educated at the Marist Brothers, Athlone, and Summerhill College, Sligo. He won a FEIS CEOIL gold medal in 1902. He made his debut on the Dublin stage in 1906, followed by debuts in London, 1907, and New York, 1909. A member of the Boston Opera Company, 1910–11, and Chicago Opera Company, 1912–14, he also made guest appearances at the Metropolitan Opera. In later years he devoted himself to concert work, performing works by Mozart, lieder, and Irish songs. Having become an American citizen in 1917, he was made a Papal count in 1928. He made his farewell appearances in 1938. He received honorary doctorates from Holy Cross, Massachusetts, and NUI. His main roles were in *Rigoletto*, *Tosca*, *Don Giovanni*, and *La Bohème*. He was acclaimed as the greatest lyric tenor of his time. **Éamonn O'Keeffe**

McCormack, W. J. [William John] (1947–), literary historian. Born in Dublin; educated at TCD and NUU. Following teaching at Leeds and Clemson University (South Carolina) he became professor of literary history at Goldsmiths College, London. His particular interest in the Protestant imagination in the nineteenth century has resulted in *Sheridan Le Fanu and Victorian Ireland* (1980), *From Burke to Beckett: Ascendancy, Tradition and Betrayal in Literary History* (1985, 1994), and *Fool of the Family: A life of* J. M. SYNGE (2000), which is deeply imbued with its author's personal hinterland of Co. Wicklow, which also permeates his autobiography, *Waking* (1997). He also writes poetry under the pseudonym Hugh Maxton. **Richard Pine**

McCormick, F. J., stage name of Peter Judge (1891–1947), actor. Born in Dublin. He began acting in MELODRAMAS at the QUEEN'S ROYAL THEATRE. He joined the ABBEY THEATRE in 1918, becoming a versatile member of the company that premiered O'CASEY's Dublin Trilogy in the 1920s, playing the original Joxer Daly in *Juno and the Paycock* (1924). He can be seen in the film *Odd Man Out* (1947). **Christopher Morash**

McCormick, Liam (1916–1996), architect. Born in Derry; educated at the University of Liverpool, a leading school of ARCHITECTURE between the wars. He worked first in local government. He established Corr and McCormick, Derry, 1948–68, then McCormick Tracey Mullarkey, 1968–82. He designed many Catholic churches, especially in Co. Donegal (such as Milford, Murlag); Co. Derry (Maghera, Steelestown), and later near Dublin (Artane, Balally, Bettystown, Julianstown). He designed three iconic churches in Co. Donegal: Burt (1964–5), Creeslough (1970–71), and Glenties (1974–5). The church of St Aongus at Burt is formed from a circular outer wall of rough stone (a reference to the GRIANÁN OF AILEACH) and an asymmetrical inner band of white-painted concrete, topped by a sweeping conical copper roof sitting on a contiguous clerestorey of glass. Here and at Creeslough there are suggestions—in the plasticity and light—of Le Corbusier's pilgrimage church at Ronchamp (1954–7). He was awarded the RIAI Gold Medal, 1964–7. Other buildings include the Meteorological Office, Glasnevin, Dublin (1977–9), a truncated pyramidal block allowing light to neighbouring streets, and a shelter for TIM SEVERIN's boat St Brendan, Co. Clare. **Raymund Ryan**

McCosh, James (1811–1894), philosopher and Presbyterian minister. Born in Ayrshire; educated at the Universities of Glasgow and Edinburgh. He was appointed professor of logic and metaphysics at the newly founded Queen's College, Belfast, in 1850. During his sixteen years in Ireland he produced a series of celebrated texts—including *The Intuitions of the Mind Inductively Investigated* (1860), *The Supernatural in Relation to the Natural* (1862), and *An Examination of Mr. J. S. Mill's Philosophy* (1866)—which explored the relationship between reason and Christian revelation, promoted the role of intuitions in ethics, and attacked Mill's System of Logic (for alleged impiety). His reputation grew to such an extent that he was invited, in 1868, to become professor of philosophy and the eleventh president of Princeton University. His twenty-year presidency saw the college expand in status and size. **Ian Leask**

McCourt, Frank (1931–), writer. Born in New York to immigrant Irish parents and grew up in Limerick. In 1949 he emigrated to the United States, where he qualified as a teacher. *Angela's Ashes* (1996), his memoir of a Limerick childhood, was an immediate international success and won many prizes, including a Pulitzer Prize in 1997, and was the basis of Alan Parker's film of the same name (2000). A sequel, *'Tis: A Memoir*, appeared in 1999. **Terence Brown**

McCoy, Frederick (1823–1899), geologist and palaeontologist. Born in Dublin; studied medicine at TCD and the University of Cambridge but was attracted to the pursuit of natural science. He worked under Sir RICHARD GRIFFITH on palaeontological investigations required for the latter's geological map of Ireland. He was appointed professor of geology at Queen's College, Belfast, in 1852 but left two years later to assume the chair of natural history at the new University of Melbourne. He became a fellow of the Royal Society and was awarded an honorary doctorate by the University of Cambridge. In 1891 he was knighted. He published zoological and palaeontological works and was recognised in his day as the leading scientist in Australia. **Geoff Warke**

McCracken, Henry Joy (1767–1798), revolutionary. Born in Belfast, son of a wealthy Presbyterian merchant; educated at David Manson's experimental school. He was enthusiastic for radical reform and became a member of the UNITED IRISHMEN, using his travels on his family's cotton manufacturing business to conceal his political activities. He emerged as a leader of the movement in the north in 1795 and was confined in KILMAINHAM GAOL, Dublin, 1796–7. When the rising broke out in 1798 Robert Simms, the United Irish commander for Co. Antrim, refused to act, as the leaders of the movement were already in custody and there was no immediate prospect of help from the French. McCracken took his place, and on 7 June he led the insurgents in the battle for the key town of Antrim, where they were defeated. He went into hiding while his sister, MARY ANN MCCRACKEN, made plans for his escape. On his way to embark for America he was recognised and arrested; he was sentenced to death, refused the offer of a reprieve if he would name Simms, and was hanged in Belfast on 17 July 1798. He left an illegitimate daughter, who was brought up by his sisters. **Jean Agnew**

McCracken, Mary Ann (1770–1866), revolutionary and philanthropist. Born in Belfast; educated at David Manson's experimental school. She shared the radical ideals of her brother, HENRY JOY MCCRACKEN, and argued that liberty and equality should also be extended to women. Following the 1798 REBELLION she visited her brother in hiding and arranged for his escape. When this failed she attended his trial and, on the same day, walked with him to the place where he was hanged, after which she had strenuous efforts made to revive him. She remained committed to the revolutionary cause and helped THOMAS RUSSELL in 1803, organising his escape to Dublin and paying for his defence and for his gravestone. She and her elder sister ran a small muslin business, which closed c. 1815. She was a member and secretary (1832) of the Ladies' Committee of the Belfast Charitable Society and campaigned for the welfare of the women and children in the Belfast Poorhouse, winning approval for improvements by a combination of unflagging tenacity and

McCormick, Liam. *St Aengus's Church, Burt, Co. Donegal, designed by Liam McCormick (1964–5). The copper roof sweeps upwards, while the exterior walls are built with a squared stonewall finish, and a continuous window below the roof runs the whole way around the building. [Gandon Archive; photo: John Searle]*

trenchant common sense. She campaigned for the abolition of slavery and other causes and remained intellectually and physically active in old age. **Jean Agnew**

Mac Craith, Aindrias ('An Mangaire Súgach') (c. 1709–c. 1794), poet. Born at Fantstown, Kilmallock, Co. Limerick; he attended a HEDGE SCHOOL, and moved to Croom. With Seán Ó Tuama he was the best of the 'Maigue Poets'. An early poem welcomes SEÁN CLÁRACH MAC DOMHNAILL to the Croom court of poetry, held in Ó Tuama's alehouse. Living dissolutely, Mac Craith was banished to Ballineety, where he wrote his great song of exile, 'Slán le Máigh'. Growing alcoholism and Ó Tuama's refusal of help in opening a school ended their friendship. He later taught in various places before returning to Fantstown. His poems were collected by Bruen and Ó hÓgáin in *An Mangaire Súgach ... Beatha agus Saothar* (1996). **Diarmuid Breathnach and Máire Ní Mhurchú**

McCrann, Maighréad (1963–), violinist. Born in Dublin; educated at TCD. She won the 1982 RTÉ MUSICIAN OF THE FUTURE and made her solo debut at the Musikverein, Vienna, in 1986. In 1993 she became concertmaster of the Austrian Radio Symphony Orchestra. She has been a soloist and chamber musician performer in all major European cities. A member of the Chamber Orchestra of Europe and Concentus Musicus, she is a founder-member of the chamber music ensemble Contrasts Vienna. **Éamonn O'Keeffe**

McCrea, Sir William Hunter (1904–1999), astrophysicist, relativist, and cosmologist. Born in Dublin; educated at the University of Cambridge. Having held posts at the Universities of Edinburgh and London and at Queen's University, Belfast, he became research professor of theoretical astronomy at the University of Sussex, 1966–72. He was an adviser to the TAOISEACH, ÉAMON DE VALERA, in setting up the DUBLIN INSTITUTE FOR ADVANCED STUDIES in the late 1930s and a member of its first governing board. He was a member of the ROYAL IRISH ACADEMY, a fellow of the Royal Society, London, and president of the Royal Astronomical Society, 1961–3. Knighted in 1985, he was made a freeman of the City of London, 1988, and awarded the gold medal of the Royal Astronomical Society, 1976, and honorary doctorates from the Universities of Argentina and Sussex as well as from all three universities in Ireland. He published more than 280 scientific papers and six books. Some of his significant contributions are his pioneering work on star formation, the formulation of Newtonian cosmology (with E. A. Milne), observable relations in relativistic cosmology, and the contentious exchanges with Prof. Herbert Dingle on the so-called 'twin paradox' in the special theory of relativity. **Petros Florides**

Mac Cruitín, Aindrias (died 1738), poet, scribe, and teacher. Born in Moyglas in the parish of Kilmurry, Ibrickan, Co. Clare. Approximately forty surviving poems in Irish are ascribed to him and approximately twenty manuscripts. His patrons included O'Loughlins of the Burren, MacDonnells of Kilkee, O'Briens of Ennistimon, and MacNamaras of Rannagh. He is buried at Kilfarboy, near Milltown Malbay. **Éilís Ní Dheá**

Mac Cruitín, Aodh 'Buí' (c. 1680–1755), poet and antiquarian. Born near Liscannor, Co. Clare. His fifty surviving poems include praise poems on members of the local gentry and Jacobite verse composed for a popular audience. His *Brief Discourse in Vindication of the Antiquity of Ireland* appeared in Dublin in 1717. Leaving Ireland c. 1727, he published an Irish grammar (1728) at LOUVAIN; crossed into France, where he briefly served in Clare's Regiment; and proceeded to Paris, where he helped prepare Ó Beaglaoich's *English-Irish Dictionary* (1731) for the press. He returned to Ireland in 1739 and taught in his native district. **Vincent Morley**

Mac Cuarta, Séamas Dall (c. 1650–1733), poet. Born probably in Omeath, Co. Louth; lived between there and the Boyne. He lost his sight through illness. An accomplished poet, he used syllabic metres and perfected the *trí rainn agus amhrán* form, most notably in 'Fáilte don Éan'. **Joe Ó Labhraí**

MacCullagh, James (1809–1847), mathematical physicist. Born in Landahussy, Co. Tyrone; graduated from TCD in 1829 and was elected a fellow in 1831. In 1835 he was appointed professor of mathematics at TRINITY COLLEGE and in 1843 professor of natural philosophy. He applied geometrical methods to elaborate the theory of light waves begun by Augustin Fresnel and proposed a mechanical model of the aether, the medium in which light was supposedly propagated. His papers on a dynamical theory of reflexion and refraction were influential in nineteenth-century physics. He committed suicide ten weeks after failing to be elected MP for the college. **Rod Gow**

McCullough, Henry (1944–), guitarist. Born in Portstewart, Co. Derry. He joined the Skyrockets showband from Enniskillen at seventeen. He then joined the People, a Belfast psychedelic outfit, later renamed Eire Apparent. McCullough left the band in 1968 and joined Johnny Moynihan and Terry Woods in SWEENEY'S MEN, mixing blues and Irish folk. After a lengthy period touring with Joe Cocker's Grease Band he did session work on the show *Jesus Christ, Superstar.* There he met Denny Laine, who was setting up Wings with Paul McCartney; he joined the band, playing with it for two years. He returned to Ireland in the early 1980s, where he had a serious accident that severed the tendons in three fingers, almost ending his career. A gifted guitarist, he still performs his folk and blues sound around Ireland and the Continent. **Mick Heaney**

McCullough Mulvin, architects. Established in Dublin in 1985, a partnership of Niall McCullough (1958–) and Valerie Mulvin (1956–); both educated at UCD, Mulvin also at TCD. Both were studio lecturers at DIT, McCullough 1985–94, Mulvin 1986–95. They have undertaken many renovation and extension projects, including the Free Church, Dublin (which won the Ford Conservation Award, 1989), Institution of Engineers, Clyde Lane, Dublin, and new portico and foyers of the ABBEY THEATRE, Dublin. Members of the City Architecture Studio, 1984, and Group 91 (which produced the TEMPLE BAR FRAMEWORK PLAN, 1991), they designed the Music Centre, Curved Street, Temple Bar Gallery and Studios, and the Black Church Print Studio (which won the AAI Downes Medal, 1996), all in Dublin. They were awarded first prize (with ROBINSON KEEFE DEVANE) in the competition for Dún Laoghaire and Rathdown County Hall (1994–6) and also (with Keane Murphy Duff) for the Ussher Library, TRINITY COLLEGE (1997–2001). Other projects include the Model Arts and Niland Gallery, Sligo, JEROME CONNOR Sculpture Centre, Co. Kerry, and Waterford City Library (2000–). McCullough Mulvin are joint authors of *A Lost Tradition: The Nature of Architecture in Ireland* (1987), a prescient survey of Irish building types; McCullough has also published *Dublin: An Urban History* (1989) and *Palimpsest: Change in the Irish Building Tradition* (1994). **Raymund Ryan**

Mac Cumhaigh, Art (1738–1773), poet. Born near Creggan, Co. Armagh. His poems were popular among the songs of the people, especially 'Úrchill an Chreagáin'. Many of the song-poems that are still sung mourn the downfall of the Ulster O'Neill chieftains of Creggan. His poems were edited by TOMÁS Ó FIAICH, and all the songs that have survived were published in 2001. He is buried in Creggan. **Pádraigín Ní Uallacháin**

MacCurtain, Margaret (1929–), historian and feminist. Born in Cork; educated at UCC and UCD. She joined the Dominican congregation in 1950 and taught in Sion Hill Secondary School, Dublin, 1953–63, and in UCD, 1963–94. She has published widely on early modern and religious history. A pioneer in the field of Irish women's history, she has been prominent in the WOMEN'S MOVEMENT since the 1970s. She has held visiting professorships in Kansas, Boston, and Baltimore, is a recipient of numerous honorary doctorates and awards, and was appointed chairwoman of the National Archives Advisory Council, 1997–2002. **Rosemary Raughter**

MacCurtain, Tomás (1884–1920), politician. Born in Ballknockane, Co. Cork; educated at North Monastery CBS. He worked as a clerk and as a GAELIC LEAGUE teacher and in 1907 joined SINN FÉIN and the IRB. He became commandant of the Cork City Battalion of the IRISH VOLUNTEERS, and strongly opposed REDMOND's call to support the British war effort. He was elected Lord Mayor of Cork on 30 January 1920. During the WAR OF INDEPENDENCE he was responsible for communications between county and city brigades of the Volunteers. On 20 March 1920 members of the RIC shot him dead in his home. **Brian Galvin**

McCusker Brothers' Céilí Band, a family CÉILÍ BAND with nationwide popularity from the 1930s to the 1960s. Born to musical parents, eight boys played instruments, and two girls sang. The band started with HOUSE-DANCES and local hall performance around Kilcreevy, Co. Armagh; they later broadcast on the Radio Éireann programme 'Céilí House' and toured Britain and America. They were broadcast live from the Gresham Hotel, Dublin, for the launch of RTÉ television in 1961, and made several 78 r.p.m. and LP recordings. **Fintan Vallely**

McCusker, (James) Harold (1940–1990), politician. Born in Lurgan, Co. Armagh. A member of the ORANGE ORDER from an early age, he taught in his native town before moving into industry. Critical of the government in the early 1970s, he was elected Westminster MP for Armagh in 1974 and represented Upper Bann from 1983. Whip and secretary to the United ULSTER UNIONIST COUNCIL, 1975–6, in 1982 he topped the poll in being elected to the NORTHERN IRELAND ASSEMBLY, where he became deputy leader of the Unionist Party. An advocate of heightened security measures, he opposed the policies of Margaret Thatcher. He felt betrayed by the ANGLO-IRISH AGREEMENT (1985) and served a brief prison sentence in 1986 for withholding a motor tax payment in protest. His suggested alternatives to the agreement included tripartite arrangements and, later, as part of a unionist 'task-force', 'talks about talks'. He was party spokesman on education, commerce, and industry. **Alan Scott**

McDermott, Peter (born 1918), Gaelic footballer. Born in Co. Meath. He served his county team as a minor in 1937 and graduated to the senior team in 1940, winning six Leinster and two all-Ireland senior medals (1949 and 1954), and captained Meath to success over Kerry in 1954. In his early days he played at midfield but he is best remembered as a corner-forward of great scoring ability. He was an outstanding sportsman and also served the GAA in many capacities: as county secretary, Leinster and Central Council delegate, referee, and coach. He was at the forefront of the development of the Compromise Rules series between Australia and Ireland. He is perhaps the best-known and most popular of all Meath footballers. **Jack Mahon**

Mac Diarmada, Seán (1884–1916), revolutionary. Born in Kiltyclogher, Co. Leitrim. He emigrated at the age of sixteen and held various jobs in Glasgow and Belfast, where he joined the IRB; he was later appointed treasurer of the Supreme Council. In 1907 he became an organiser for SINN FÉIN and set up branches all over the country. He was manager of the journal *Irish Freedom* and a member of the Military Council of the IRB, which planned the 1916 RISING. He was in the GPO during the rising and was a signatory of the PROCLAMATION OF THE IRISH REPUBLIC. He was shot by firing squad on 12 May 1916. **Martin Clancy**

Mac Domhnaill, Aodh (1802–1867), poet and scribe. Born in the Drumcondra area of Co. Meath. A Bible teacher in the Protestant Irish Society and London Hibernian Society schools in Co. Antrim, he remained a Catholic. He collected manuscripts, songs, and lore for ROBERT MACADAM, 1842–56. His thesis on natural philosophy, *Fealsúnacht Aodha Mhic Dhomhnaill* (edited by Colm Beckett), was published in 1967, and his collected poems, *Aodh Mac Domhnaill: Dánta*, in 1987. He died in Cootehill poorhouse. **Diarmuid Breathnach and Máire Ní Mhurchú**

Mac Domhnaill, Seán Clárach (1691–1754), Jacobite poet, scribe, and teacher. Born near Charleville, Co. Cork. He became a prominent member of the poetic fraternity associated with the eighteenth-century Munster COURTS OF POETRY. He was celebrated by the Maigue poets at their court in Croom, Co. Limerick, in 1735 and again in a special commemorative gathering held in his honour in October 1754. He is best known for his JACOBITE POETRY, which is informed by a detailed knowledge of national and international affairs, gleaned from contemporary newspapers, and for his bitter satire on the infamous Co. Tipperary landlord Colonel James Dawson (died 1737). His Jacobite AISLING 'Mo Ghille Mear' is one of the most popular and widely anthologised of eighteenth-century Irish political songs. His poems were edited by Risteárd Ó Foghludha in *Seán Clárach* (1934) and analysed and contextualised by Breandán Ó Buachalla in *Aisling Ghéar: Na Stíobhartaigh agus an tAos Léinn, 1603–1788* (1996). **Máirín Nic Eoin**

MacDonagh, Donagh (1912–1968), poet, playwright, and broadcaster. Born in Dublin, son of THOMAS MACDONAGH; educated at UCD. He practised as a barrister for some years before becoming a district justice. His plays include *Happy as Larry* (1946) and *Step-in-the-Hollow* (1957). *God's Gentry*, a ballad opera, was performed in Belfast in 1951. A verse treatment of the DEIRDRE story, *Lady Spider*, appeared posthumously. As a poet he is best known for 'The Hungry Grass' and 'Dublin Made Me'. **Peter Sirr**

McDonagh, Martin (1971–), playwright. Born in London of Irish parents. His work includes the 'Leenane trilogy', comprising *The Beauty Queen of Leenane* (1996), *A Skull in Connemara* (1997), and *The Lonesome West* (1997). *The Cripple of Inishmaan* was first performed in 1997. Some champion the work for its harsh, tragicomic vision, while others see it as merely an indulgent reworking of old stereotypes that satisfy metropolitan audiences. **Eamonn Jordan**

Mac Diarmada. *Executed in May 1916, Seán Mac Diarmada fought at the GPO during the Easter Rising; postcard from a contemporary series commemorating the executed leaders. [Stephen Lalor collection]*

MacDonagh, Thomas (1878–1916), poet and revolutionary. Born in Cloughjordan, Co. Tipperary; educated at Rockwell College. His first collection, *The Ivory Gate*, was published in 1902. He came to Dublin in 1908 to teach with PEARSE at St Enda's School; his play *When the Dawn Is Come* was produced at the ABBEY THEATRE in October the same year. He worked in the English Department at UCD. His most important critical work, *Literature in Ireland*, was published posthumously. He commanded the garrison at Jacob's factory in Dublin during the 1916 RISING; a signatory of the PROCLAMATION OF THE IRISH REPUBLIC, he was shot by firing squad on 3 May 1916. **Nicholas Allen**

MacDonald, Daniel (1821–1853), painter. Born in Cork, son of the artist James MacDonald. He followed his father's footsteps as a painter of portraits, genre scenes, and caricatures (see p. 457). At the age of thirteen his etchings were published in the *Tribute*. He exhibited at the ROYAL HIBERNIAN ACADEMY, 1842–4, then moved to London c. 1845, where he exhibited at the British Institution, 1847–51. As well as oil paintings he produced many pen-and-ink drawings, a number of which are in the British Museum. His oil painting *Bowling Match at Castlemary Cloyne* is in the Crawford Gallery, Cork. **Peter Murray**

McDonald, Mary Frances, 'Mamo', neé Bowen (1929–), feminist. Born in Tuam, Co. Galway; educated at Sion Hill Dominican Convent. She began her working life in the Hibernian Bank, Cavan, before moving to Clones, Co. Monaghan, where she joined the IRISH COUNTRYWOMEN'S ASSOCIATION, forming a new guild. She became president of the association in 1982 and was instrumental in achieving its acceptance as part of the wider WOMEN'S MOVEMENT as well as communicating her interest in family issues, consumer affairs, and the education of rural women. In 1989 she formed Age and Opportunity, of which she is honorary president. In 1999 she received a People of the Year award in recognition of her work on behalf of women and of older people. **Alison Walsh**

McDonald, Peter (1962–), poet and critic. Born in Belfast; educated at Methodist College, Belfast, and the University of Oxford. Having taught at Cambridge and Bristol, he is Christopher Tower Student in Poetry and tutor at Christ Church, Oxford. He won the Newdigate Prize, 1983 (as did OSCAR WILDE and CHARLES BEWLEY before him), and the Gregory Award, 1987. His books of poetry include *Biting the Wax* (1989) and *Adam's Dream* (1996); critical works include LOUIS MACNEICE: *The Poet in His Contexts* (1991) and *Mistaken Identities: Poetry and Northern Ireland* (1997). He edited MacNeice's *Selected Plays* (1993) and gave the 1996 Chatterton Lecture. As a critic he is opposed to using modish 'identity politics' to interpret literary work; as a poet he is an urbane, highly accomplished formalist. **Jonathan Allison**

McDonnell, Alexander (1798–1835), chess master. Born in Belfast; he was taught to play chess by the English master William Lewis. From the foundation of the Westminster Chess Club, London, in 1833, he was recognised as the best player in England. In June 1834 the secretary of the Paris Chess Club, Louis-Charles Mahé de Labourdonnais, challenged him. A marathon competition ensued; gradually de Labourdonnais gained the upper hand, winning forty-four of eighty-eight games, with fourteen drawn. **Ciarán Deane**

MacDonnell, Sir Antony (1844–1925), administrator. Born in Shragh, Co. Mayo; educated at Queen's College, Galway. A celebrated imperial administrator in India, 1865–1901 (known as 'the Tiger of Bengal'), and UNDER-SECRETARY FOR IRELAND, 1902–8, he was heavily involved in the passing of the Irish (Wyndham) LAND ACT (1903) but failed subsequently to effect his proposals for legislative devolution. He resigned after the adoption of the Irish Universities Act (1908), with which he disagreed. A member of the IRISH CONVENTION, 1917–18, he refused a place in the SENATE, 1922. **Gary Peatling**

MacDonnell, Enrique (fl. eighteenth century), naval officer. Born in Spain, the son of an Irish emigrant from Co. Antrim. He joined the Spanish army as a young man and was stationed at Ceuta, the Spanish-owned city on the African side of the Strait of Gibraltar (now in Morocco). There he won permission to exchange into the navy. He redeemed Spain two days after the Battle of Trafalgar, 1805, with a daring sortie from Cádiz, in which four of Nelson's vaunted prizes were recovered. This action recalled in Spanish minds a previous extraordinary deed when he had been lent by Spain to Sweden to help in its war of 1788–90 with the Tsar of Russia; off Kymmene, Finland, he had held up a whole Russian squadron for twenty-four hours. Outspoken, he was disgraced by the tyrannical King Ferdinand VII and buried in a pauper's grave. **John de Courcy Ireland**

MacDonnell, John (1796–1892), surgeon. Born in Belfast, son of Dr James MacDonnell 'of the Glens'. He was variously surgeon at the RICHMOND HOSPITAL, professor of descriptive anatomy at the Royal College of Surgeons in Ireland, and POOR LAW medical commissioner. In 1847 he performed Ireland's first operation under general anaesthesia. He was the father of ROBERT MACDONNELL. **Peter Froggatt**

MacDonnell, Sir Randal, first Earl of Antrim (died 1636). Scion of the MacDonald/MacDonnell clan of the Scottish Isles and north Antrim, and son of SORLEY BOY MACDONNELL, he consolidated his family's hitherto vulnerable position in Ireland. During the NINE YEARS' WAR (1594–1603) they allied themselves with the northern insurgents led by HUGH O'NEILL, Earl of Tyrone. As the rebellion waned, MacDonnell deftly switched to the royal cause. His intervention in Scottish Isles politics at the same time in a manner that furthered the interests of the Scottish king, James VI, was to prove instrumental in securing MacDonnell's future at such a volatile time. When James VI of Scotland succeeded ELIZABETH I as JAMES I of England in 1603, royal favour was to insulate MacDonnell from the bitter hostility of Sir ARTHUR CHICHESTER, Lord Deputy of Ireland, whose brother had been killed by the MacDonnells during the rebellion. Agreeing to accept settlement conditions on his lands, including the building of fortifications, MacDonnell was considered a model subject by James I, who showered him with favours, despite the fact that he was a Catholic (at a time of relatively sustained persecution). Raised to the peerage by James I as Lord of Dunluce in 1618, he was created first Earl of Antrim in 1620. **John McCavitt**

MacDonnell, Robert (1828–1889), surgeon and scientist. Born in Dublin, son of JOHN MACDONNELL. In 1865 he performed the first human blood transfusion in Ireland. He was variously a civil surgeon in the CRIMEAN WAR, medical superintendent of Mountjoy Jail, and surgeon at Jervis Street and DR STEEVENS' HOSPITALS. A fellow of the Royal Society, he was president of the Royal College of Surgeons in Ireland (1877). **Peter Froggatt**

MacDonnell, Sorley Boy, Anglicised name of Somhairle Buí Mac Dónaill (c. 1505–1590), Lord of the Route and Constable of

DUNLUCE CASTLE. The sixth son of Alexander MacDonnell of Isla and Kintyre, Scotland; from 1558 he established himself as Lord of the Route, north Antrim, in place of the MacQuillans. The English Crown was keen to expel the Scots, but despite a number of campaigns, most infamously that of the Earl of Essex in 1575, in which many Scottish women and children on RATHLIN ISLAND were massacred, it proved impossible to keep MacDonnell and his followers out of Ireland. Eventually, having himself expelled the MacDonnells to Scotland, only to have them return shortly afterwards, Lord Deputy PERROT agreed to a settlement in 1586. After MacDonnell's solemn submission to ELIZABETH I he was made a denizen or subject of the English Crown and officially recognised as owner of most of the Route and Constable of Dunluce Castle. **Henry A. Jefferies**

MacDonogh, Patrick (1902–1961), poet. Born in Dublin; educated at TCD. He was employed in GUINNESS'S BREWERY in Dublin. He published five collections of verse between 1927 and 1958. 'No Mean City' is a much-anthologised satirical squib. **Terence Brown**

Macdonough, Thomas (1783–1825), American naval officer. Born in Trap (now Macdonough), Delaware, son of a physician and grandson of an emigrant from Co. Kildare. He worked as a shop assistant but requested an appointment to the US Navy, which he entered at sixteen. He served in the war with Tripoli, accompanying Stephen Decatur's raid to burn the *Philadelphia* in 1804. During the War of 1812 he commanded the American fleet on Lake Champlain. On 11 September 1814, in a naval battle in Cumberland Bay, near Plattsburgh, he defeated and captured a British squadron, causing the British to abandon the invasion of New York state. **David Kiely**

MacDowell, Patrick (1799–1870), sculptor. Born in Belfast; his father died when he was young, and his mother returned to England. In 1813 he was apprenticed to a London coach-maker. His talent was noted by the sculptor Peter Chenu, with whom he lodged; by 1822 he had begun to exhibit at the Royal Academy, London, and he continued to do so until his death. He also exhibited at the RHA, Dublin, between 1843 and 1847. In 1830 he attended the Royal Academy schools, where he made rapid progress, and in 1846 he became a full member. T. W. Beaumont, an early patron, sent him to Rome and commissioned *A Girl Reading* (1837). MacDowell came to greater public notice with his *Girl at Prayer* (1844), exhibited at Westminster Hall, and *Early Summer* (1851), at the Great Exhibition of that year. Two of his finest works are the memorial to the Earl of Donegall (1855) in Belfast and the group *Europe* for the Albert Memorial, London, completed after his death. He made a great many portrait busts and a smaller number of ideal subjects and public memorials, such as *The Earl of Eglinton and Wilton* (1866) for St Stephen's Green, Dublin, *Viscount Fitzgibbon* (1858) for SARSFIELD BRIDGE, Limerick, and four figures for the FOUR COURTS, Dublin (all destroyed). **John Turpin**

McElligott, James J. (1893–1974), civil servant. Born in Co. Kerry; educated at UCD, studying classics and economics. He joined the Local Government Board as a civil servant in 1913 and also the IRISH VOLUNTEERS. He took part in the 1916 RISING and was deported to England. On his release he became a journalist, then joined the new DEPARTMENT OF FINANCE in 1923. He was Secretary 1927–53, and Governor of the CENTRAL BANK (an institution he helped set up), 1953–60. He served on all important economic policy commissions, including those on tariffs and BANKING. McElligott was famous for his conservative attitudes towards government expenditure, which sometimes reached surreal levels. However, he was an able administrator and had a considerable grasp of economic principles. **Tom Garvin**

Mac Eoin, Seán (1894–1973), soldier and politician. Born near Ballinalee, Co Longford. He joined the IRISH VOLUNTEERS in 1914 and commanded North Longford IRA in the WAR OF INDEPENDENCE, 1919–21. He was captured in March 1921. Elected to DÁIL ÉIREANN and released after the July truce, he supported the ANGLO-IRISH TREATY (1921) and became a major-general in the FREE STATE army. During the CIVIL WAR he was officer commanding Western Command, becoming officer commanding the Curragh Camp, 1925–7, Quartermaster-General, 1927–9, and Chief of Staff, 1929. He resigned the same year because of friction with the Department of Defence and became CUMANN NA NGAEDHEAL (later FINE GAEL) TD for Sligo-Leitrim, 1929–32, and Longford-Westmeath, 1932–65, including periods as Minister for Justice and Minister for Defence. He unsuccessfully contested two presidential elections, 1945 and 1959. **Patrick Long**

McFadden, Roy (1921–1999), poet. Born in Belfast; educated at QUB. He began publishing poetry in the 1940s. In 1948 he was a joint founder of *Rann*, a literary periodical for a time associated with Northern Ireland cultural regionalism. He published eight collections of urbanely intelligent, occasionally astringent verse; his *Collected Poems* appeared in 1996. **Terence Brown**

Mac Fhirbhisigh, Dubhaltach (c. 1600–1671), genealogist, translator, and scribe. Born in Lackan, Co. Sligo, a member of a hereditary learned family; he may have been educated in part in Galway and at the Mac Aodhagáin school at Ballymacegan, Co. Tipperary. His principal works include compilations (such as the glossary Dúil Laithne, 1643, and accounts of ancient Irish authors, 1656–66, and of Irish bishops and bishoprics, 1666); transcripts (annalistic collections, CHRONICUM SCOTORUM, c. 1640, Fragmentary ANNALS of Ireland, 1643, and the law tract Bretha Nemed Déidinach, c. 1643); and translations (documents pertaining to the rule of St Clare, 1647, Annals of Lecan, 1443–68, 1666). Most important is his great genealogical compilation, Leabhar Genealach, written in Galway, 1645 and 1649–50 (with additions 1653, 1657, and 1664), and an abridged version, the Cuimre, 1666. Associated with the historians John Lynch and RODERIC O'FLAHERTY, he worked in Dublin, 1665–6, for the Anglo-Irish antiquarian Sir JAMES WARE. He was killed near his home in Sligo by one Thomas Crofton. **Nollaig Ó Muraíle**

Mac Fir Bhisigh, Giolla Íosa Mór (fl. 14–15 century), scholar, scribe, and poet. A member of a hereditary learned family at Lackan, Co. Sligo, he compiled c. 1392 an important collection of medieval literary texts (later included in a composite manuscript, the Yellow Book of Lecan) and later, c. 1397–1418, the Great Book of Lecan. He composed a long inauguration poem for his lord, Tadhg Riabhach Ó Dubhda, in 1417. **Nollaig Ó Muraíle**

Mac Gabhann, Micí (1865–1948), writer. He is best known for his autobiography, *Rotha Mór an tSaoil* (1959), which he dictated to his son-in-law, the FOLKLORE-collector Seán Ó hEochaidh. In it he gives a spirited and fascinating account of his youth in Cloghaneely, Co. Donegal, his experiences at the HIRING FAIR in Letterkenny, farm labouring in Scotland, and his adventures in America, where he worked on boats, in iron and steel works in Pennsylvania and silver and copper mines in Montana, and in particular his travels up the Yukon in the Klondyke gold rush. **Breandán Ó Conaire**

Mac Gabhráin, Aodh (fl. 1715), poet. Born in Glangevlin, Co. Cavan. His most famous composition is 'Pléaráca na Ruarcach', set to music by CAROLAN, translated into English as 'The Description of an Irish-Feast' (1720) by SWIFT. **Joe Ó Labhraí**

McGahern, John (1935–), novelist and short-story writer. Born in Dublin, brought up in Cootehall, Co. Roscommon; educated at St Patrick's College, Dublin, and UCD. His first novel, *The Barracks* (1963), takes its setting from his own childhood as son of a GARDA sergeant. It was published while he worked as a national school teacher in Clontarf, Dublin, a post from which he was dismissed after his second novel, *The Dark* (1965), was banned under the CENSORSHIP OF PUBLICATIONS ACTS. He moved to London and then lived in the United States before settling in Mohill, Co. Leitrim, in 1974. These experiences are reflected in the semi-autobiographical novel *The Leavetaking* (1975). In this novel and in his next, *The Pornographer* (1979), he experiments with the order and narration of the story to reflect the ways in which the imagination responds to sex, exile, and death. A revised version of *The Leavetaking* (1984) testifies to his talent for self-scrutiny—a talent reflected throughout his work in the bare exactitude of his prose, which plainly records the emotional tensions of domesticity. AMONGST WOMEN (1990) secured his place as the chief novelist of the topic of rural Ireland in the post-independence period. It was followed by the stories in *Nightlines* (1970), *Getting Through* (1978), and *High Ground* (1978), which were reissued in his *Collected Stories* (1992). A futher novel, *That They May Face the Rising Sun*, was published in 2002. **Selina Guinness**

McGarry Ní Éanaigh, architects, a partnership of Michael McGarry (1955–) and Siobhán Ní Éanaigh (1955–). Both born in Dublin, they were educated at UCD and the University of Virginia. They worked in Germany for Josef Paul Kleihues and the IBA, then established a practice in Drogheda, 1984. Members of Group 91 (which produced the TEMPLE BAR FRAMEWORK PLAN, 1991) and Urban Projects (which designed dockland housing at Clarion Quay, Dublin, 1998–2000), they designed the Scarlet Row apartment building in Temple Bar and the Liffey Boardwalk. They won first prize in the Smithfield Competition, 1997 (twelve 26 m high brazier-masts in a seventeenth-century market square), and the European Prize for Urban Public Space, 2000. McGarry Ní Éanaigh exhibitions have been held at the Architecture Centre, Dublin, and the RSUA in Belfast (see p. 658). **Raymund Ryan**

Mac Gearailt, Muiris mac Dháibhí Dhuibh (died c. 1630), Munster poet, son of the 'David Duff' extolled by RICHARD STANIHURST. The Fitzgeralds lost their land near Dingle after 1581 and moved to Pallice, near Killarney, where Muiris was living in 1601. He appears in PAIRLEMENT CHLOINNE TOMÁIS, being called '*marcach gallda*' (a horseman dressed in the English fashion). He is chiefly remembered for his poem of exile 'Beannaigh an Longsa' ('Bless this Ship'), published with translation by CHARLOTTE BROOKE in her *Reliques of Irish Poetry* (1789), and for his rather tedious estates satire 'Mór Idir na hAimsearaibh' ('Great the difference between the times'). **Nicholas J. A. Williams**

Mac Gearailt, Piaras (1702–1795), poet. Born in Ballykinealy, Imokilly, Co. Cork. Of a well-to-do family, he inherited some of the family's estate in Ballykinealy. According to tradition he spent some of his youth in Spain, where an uncle worked as a wine merchant in Cádiz. He spent the latter years of his life in Co. Waterford. Frequently signing himself *Árd-Sirriam Leithe Mogha* ('High Sheriff of the South of Ireland'), he was held in high regard by his fellow-poets. His surviving compositions, including the well-known 'Rosc Catha na Mumhan', were edited by Risteárd Ó Foghludha in *Amhráin Phiarais Mhic Gearailt* (1905). **Breandán Ó Conchúir**

McGee, Thomas D'Arcy (1825–1868) journalist and politician. Born in Carlingford, Co. Louth. He contributed to the NATION and in 1848 joined the YOUNG IRELAND rising. He escaped to America, where he worked as a journalist, continued to write poetry and popular history, and clashed with Archbishop Hughes of New York. From the late 1850s he became more conservative. He moved to CANADA, became active in Ontario politics, and was one of the 'Fathers' who negotiated the confederation of the Canadian provinces (1867). His denunciations of separatism were unpopular among Irish nationalists, and in 1868 he was assassinated in Ottawa, close to the Parliament Buildings. **Patrick Maume**

MacGill, Patrick (1891–1963), writer and journalist. Born in the Glenties, Co. Donegal; he left school at twelve and became a navvy in Scotland at fourteen. A self-taught writer, he wrote poems and prose based on his experiences; his reputation rests on two novels, *Children of the Dead End* (1914) and *The Rat Pit* (1915), based on migrant labour in Scotland, in parts romantic but also realistic and bitter. He later joined the British army and fought in the FIRST WORLD WAR and wrote accounts of the conflict. His novels were very popular and still maintain a readership. He died in New York. **Robbie Meredith**

McGinty, Thom 'the Diceman' (1953–1995), street mime and actor. Born in Strathclyde, Scotland. In 1976 he moved to Dublin, birthplace of his mother, and worked as the 'Dandelion Clown' at the Dandelion Market, St Stephen's Green. During the 1980s he developed a reputation as a motionless mime in Grafton Street, advertising The Diceman, a games shop; the persona outlived the shop. He was employed by other shops in Grafton Street and also took part in festivals in Paris, Seville, Berlin, and Moscow. He tested positive for the HIV virus in December 1990, and in November 1994 he appeared on the 'Late Late Show' to talk about his life and illness. Following his death three months later, his funeral procession passed down Grafton Street to sustained applause. **Ciarán Deane**

Mac Giolla Gunna, Cathal Buí (c. 1680–1756), poet. Allegedly born in Co. Fermanagh; he spent most of his life in Bréifne (Cos. Cavan and Leitrim), though he frequented various parts of Ulster in his later years. He studied for the priesthood as a young man but was not ordained; he was renowned as a rake and for his fondness for alcohol. He is known to have composed at least fifteen poems, of which 'An Bonnán Buí' and 'Aithreachas Chathail Bhuí' are among the more famous. He is buried in Donaghmoyne, Co. Monaghan. **Ciarán Mac Murchaidh**

Mac Giolla Phádraig, Brian (c. 1580–c. 1652), poet and priest. His works include compositions in syllabic and song metres on religious and other topics. He made a copy of the Leabhar Branach in 1622. Ordained c. 1610, he was made Vicar-General of Ossory in 1651. A tradition exists that he was murdered in 1652 by Cromwellians. **Michelle O Riordan**

McGirl, John Joe (1921–1988), revolutionary and politician. Born in Co. Leitrim. A lifelong republican activist, he joined the IRA in the 1940s and played a central role in its reorganisation during the post-war period. He was arrested and imprisoned in 1946. During the BORDER CAMPAIGN of the late 1950s he was a member of the Army Council of the IRA and for a short time was chief of staff. He was SINN FÉIN TD for South Leitrim, 1957–61. He continued to hold prominent positions in the party and became a central figure in (Provisional) Sinn Féin after the split in 1970. **Brian Galvin**

McGladdery, Robert (1935–1961), the last man to be judicially killed in Ireland. Born in Newry, Co. Down. He was convicted of the murder of nineteen-year-old Pearl Gamble, also from Newry, and was hanged at Crumlin Road Jail, Belfast, on 20 December 1961. **Ciarán Deane**

McGoldrick, Hubert (1897–1967), decorator and STAINED-GLASS artist. Born in Dublin; studied at the Metropolitan School of Art. In 1913 he joined the ecclesiastical stained-glass firm of Earley in Dublin until in 1920 he became a member of AN TÚR GLOINE, the co-operative studio workshop, where he worked until its dissolution in October 1944. He is at his best when replacing his generally eclectic style with a narrative lyricism, as in his first *Sorrow and Joy* window (1920) at Gowran, Co. Kilkenny, *St Brigid* (1922) at Fairymount, Co. Roscommon, and *Dawn* (1927) for a private house in Singapore. **Nicola Gordon Bowe**

MacGonigal, Maurice (1900–1979), painter. Born in Dublin; educated at Synge Street CBS and apprenticed to his uncle Joshua Clarke, a STAINED-GLASS manufacturer, receiving encouragement from his cousin HARRY CLARKE. In 1917 he joined FIANNA ÉIREANN and later the IRA. He participated in raids and attacks, including that on the LORD LIEUTENANT, Lord French, outside CHRIST CHURCH CATHEDRAL, Dublin. Arrested in 1920, he was interned for a year in Ballykinler Camp, Co. Down. After his release he left the IRA and went back to the Clarke studios, also taking classes at the Metropolitan School of Art, where in 1924 he won a Taylor Scholarship.

After a stay with the van Stockum family in the Netherlands in 1927 he returned to Ireland inspired with the idea of landscape painting expressing a sense of national identity. He did some of his finest work in the west of Ireland during the 1930s—landscapes laid quickly on the canvas, '*en plein air*', with a fluid command of colour and paint-handling. He also painted at this time superb figure studies, such as *Dockers* (1934, now in the HUGH LANE Gallery) and sets for the 1936 ABBEY THEATRE production of *The Silver Tassie* by SEAN O'CASEY. He was commissioned to paint a large mural for the Irish pavilion at the 1939 New York World Trade Fair depicting Ireland's contribution to American history. He exhibited regularly at the ROYAL HIBERNIAN ACADEMY, 1924–78, serving twice as keeper. He was appointed professor of painting in 1947, a position he retained for thirty-three years. He also taught at the National College of Art, where he was professor of painting, 1954–69. A retrospective exhibition was held at the Hugh Lane Municipal Gallery of Modern Art, Dublin, in 1991 (see p. 95). **Peter Murray**

McGowan, Kieran (1943–), businessman. He joined the INDUSTRIAL DEVELOPMENT AGENCY (IDA) in 1967 when it was still part of the Department of Industry and Commerce; he was chief executive from 1990 to 1998. During his tenure the IDA was successful in attracting FOREIGN DIRECT INVESTMENT to Ireland, particularly from the American technology industry. This played an important role in the transition of the ECONOMY. In February 2001 he became president of the IRISH MANAGEMENT INSTITUTE, having been its chairman since 1998. He is chairman of the Expert Advisory Group on National Spatial Strategy, set up by the Department of Environment and Local Government in May 2000. **Jim Power**

McGinty. *Thom McGinty, street mime and actor, in the role that gave him his popular name, 'the Diceman', as a motionless mime advertising a games shop. [Derek Speirs/Report]*

MacGowran, Jack (1918–1973), actor and theatre director. Born in Dublin; educated at Synge Street CBS. He began acting at the GATE THEATRE in 1944, later acting and directing at the ABBEY THEATRE until 1954, becoming associated with the works of SAMUEL BECKETT from 1958 and filming an influential *Krapp's Last Tape* (1961). **Christopher Morash**

McGrath, Paul (1959–), soccer player. Born in London. One of Ireland's most popular sporting personalities, his name is synonymous with the euphoria generated by the Republic of Ireland's participation in the 1988 European championship finals and the two succeeding World Cup finals. He qualified easily, as one of the best centre-backs in football at the summit of his career, although JACK CHARLTON frequently deployed him as a midfielder. He left Manchester United after a dispute with Sir Alex Ferguson and went on to have a successful career with Aston Villa. His exceptional athleticism enabled him to prolong his career after recurring problems with his knees prevented him from training in the conventional manner. **Peter Byrne**

McGrath, Raymond (1903–1977), architect, artist and designer. Born in Gladesville, New South Wales; educated at the University of Sydney; he moved to England in 1926 and studied at the University of Cambridge. He carried out the *art deco* renovation of Finella, a private house in Cambridge, 1927–9, and interiors of Broadcasting House, London, from 1930 onwards, directing a similarly talented team. Other work in England includes St Anne's Hill, Chertsey (1936–7), a radially planned International-Style residence. He was senior architect with the OFFICE OF PUBLIC WORKS, Dublin, 1940, principal architect, 1948–68, responsible for interior work at DUBLIN CASTLE, ÁRAS AN UACHTARÁIN, Irish embassies, the Cenotaph on Leinster Lawn (1950), John F. Kennedy Memorial Concert Hall (unrealised), and the RHA Gallagher Gallery (1973–4, completed in the late 1980s by ARTHUR GIBNEY and Partners). Among his publications are *Twentieth Century Houses*, 1934 and *Glass in Architecture and Decoration*, 1937. **Raymund Ryan**

MacGreevy, Thomas (1893–1967), poet, literary and art critic, and administrator. Born in Tarbert, Co. Kerry, into a family of farmers and schoolteachers; educated at TCD, where he studied politics and history. He is best known for his strikingly original modernist poetry and for being one of the art critics who championed Irish modernist art and artists between the wars. He was a prolific writer, publishing more than 350 articles, seven monographs, and a collection of poetry, *Poems* (1934). He was director of the NATIONAL GALLERY OF IRELAND, 1950–63. **Susan Schreibman**

Mac Grianna, Seosamh (1900–1990), writer, under the pen-name Iolann Fionn. Born into a family of poets and storytellers in Rannafast, Co. Donegal, at a time of linguistic and cultural change; educated at St Eunan's College, Letterkenny, and St Columb's College, Derry. He trained as a teacher in St Patrick's College, Dublin, from which he graduated in 1921. He became involved in the armed struggle and was interned as a republican for fifteen months. He began a teaching career but, with his poetic and independent character, soon discovered that his vocation did not lie there. He started writing in the early twenties, and his creative period lasted some fifteen years. He wrote essays, short stories, travel and historical works, a famous autobiography, MO BHEALACH FÉIN, and a novel, as well as translating many books. He was imbued with a strong, oral traditional culture from his childhood, and this permeated his writings, particularly in the early years. Increasingly, however, he became more analytical and critical as he examined the changing face of the Irish-speaking districts and the emergence of an Anglicised Ireland with no loyalty to, or sympathy with, a heroic and cultured past. He was the greatest GAELTACHT writer of his time, whose work had developed considerably before his health broke in the mid-1930s. **Nollaig Mac Congáil**

McGuckian, Medbh (1950–), poet. Born in Belfast; educated at QUB. She has been writer-in-residence there and at TRINITY COLLEGE, Dublin, and visiting fellow at the University of California, Berkeley. She has published seven main collections of new poetry: *The Flower Master* (1982), *Venus and the Rain* (1984), *On Ballycastle Beach* (1988), *Marconi's Cottage* (1991), *Captain Lavender* (1994), *Shelmalier* (1998), and *Drawing Ballerinas* (2001). Through her use of sensuously associative, dislocating imagery she explores new possibilities for political thinking. The private themes of personal relationships and the work of writing poetry act as a commentary on the public themes of conflict in Northern Ireland and within cultural establishments. In all these, the freeing up of gender issues is a central concern. **Catriona Clutterbuck**

McGuinness, Catherine (1934–), lawyer and judge. Born in Belfast; educated at TCD. She worked as a teacher, a freelance writer and a parliamentary officer for the LABOUR PARTY before being called to the bar in 1977, becoming a senior counsel in 1989. She was a judge of the Circuit Court, 1994–6, and of the High Court, 1996–2000; as a barrister and as a Circuit Court judge she was regarded as an expert in FAMILY LAW. In 2000 she became the second woman to be appointed to the SUPREME COURT in the Republic. She chaired the NEW IRELAND FORUM (1983–4) and the Kilkenny Incest Inquiry (1993) and on three occasions was elected to SEANAD ÉIREANN for the University of Dublin constituency. **Neville Cox**

McGuinness, Frank (1953–), dramatist and lecturer. Born in Buncrana, Co. Donegal; educated at UCD, where he is Faculty of Arts writer in residence. His plays have been acclaimed for their mutual interrogation of sexual and national identities. OBSERVE THE SONS OF ULSTER MARCHING TOWARDS THE SOMME (1985) movingly and powerfully examined the dual allegiances of Northern Protestants in the FIRST WORLD WAR; it won the Evening Standard Award for Best New Play. *Someone Who'll Watch Over Me* (1992) won the New York Critics' Award for its intimate portrayal of three Beirut hostages locked in inner conflict. He has produced versions of Ibsen, Chekhov, Lorca, and Brecht in a contemporary idiom. **Anthony Roche**

McGuinness, Martin (1950–), politician. Born in the Bogside, Derry; educated by the CHRISTIAN BROTHERS. An active republican since the start of the 'TROUBLES' in 1969, he was second in command of the IRA in Derry in 1972 and in July of that year was part of an IRA delegation flown to London for secret talks with the Secretary of State for Northern Ireland, William Whitelaw. In the aftermath of the 1981 HUNGER STRIKES he was one of the younger group of northern republicans who wrested control of the movement from the old Dublin leadership; together with GERRY ADAMS he fostered the development of a political and electoral strategy. He was elected to the NORTHERN IRELAND ASSEMBLY, 1982–6, but abstained, in line with SINN FÉIN policy. During the early 1990s he was a channel in secret discussions between representatives of the British Conservative government and the IRA leadership. Following the 1994 IRA ceasefire, which he helped to secure, he became Sinn Féin's chief negotiator but was critical of John Major's insistence on decommissioning.

In the 1997 British general election McGuinness won the Mid-Ulster seat from Rev. William McCrea of the DUP. He led Sinn Féin in the multi-party talks of 1997–8 and helped win his party's support for the resulting BELFAST AGREEMENT (1998). Elected to the new Northern Ireland Assembly in June 1998, he was appointed Minister of Education in the power-sharing Executive in December 1999. **Eamon Phoenix**

McGuinness, Norah (1903–1980), illustrator and painter of landscapes and still lifes. Born in Derry; trained at the Metropolitan School of Art, Dublin, and in London and Paris. She began her career as an illustrator but soon turned to painting, adopting a semi-Fauvist and, later, a part-Cubist technique. During the 1930s, while in London, she was a member of the avant-garde 7 & 5 Society and the London Group. Returning to Ireland in 1939, she became one of the most progressive painters of her generation, her work always conveying freshness and vitality. She was a member of the Dublin Painters' Society and, in 1943, chairwoman of the IRISH EXHIBITION OF LIVING ART. **S. B. Kennedy**

McGuinness, Paul (1951–), entrepreneur. Born in Germany; educated at TCD. After television and film work and a brief period managing the folk-rock band Spud he saw the young U2 perform at the Project Arts Centre, Dublin, in 1978. After he met the band they agreed to let him manage them. His business acumen and ambitious drive were essential to U2's global success, both in securing increasingly lucrative record deals and in turning the four musicians into a corporate entity. Having earned €1,015 million under the aegis of McGuinness's company Principle Management, U2 are Ireland's most successful cultural export. Fiercely protective of U2, McGuinness has also involved himself in more general cultural affairs and served on the board of the ARTS COUNCIL. **Mick Heaney**

MacHale, John (1791–1881), bishop. Born in Tobbernavine, Tirawley, Co. Mayo; educated at ST PATRICK'S COLLEGE, Maynooth, and ordained in 1814. Professor of dogmatic theology at Maynooth, 1820–25, he publicly and outspokenly criticised the established church and the government's neglect of poverty in Ireland, often writing his public letters under the name Hierophilos. As Coadjutor Bishop of Killala, 1825–34, and Archbishop of Tuam, 1834–81, the first since penal times whose entire education and training had been in Ireland, he confronted issues surrounding the poverty of the people, FAMINE relief, vocational shortages, and evangelical Protestant missionaries. A political agitator, he supported O'CONNELL's Repeal campaigns as well as the campaigns for tenant right and the abolition of tithes; he denounced SADLIER and KEOGH following their defection from the Independent Irish Party in 1852. In education, unlike many of his episcopal colleagues, such as MURRAY of Dublin, he opposed the introduction of the national school system. He opposed the Charitable Donations and Bequests Act and the Queen's Colleges, criticised Newman's appointment as rector of the CATHOLIC UNIVERSITY, and strongly opposed Papal infallibility at the First Vatican Council (1870). He clashed with PAUL CULLEN and the ULTRAMONTANISTS on educational matters as well as on nationalist and political issues, taking no part in the NATIONAL ASSOCIATION and offering protection to republican national clerics such as PATRICK LAVELLE. **Ciarán O'Carroll**

McIlroy, Jimmy (1931–), soccer player. Born in Lambeg, Co Antrim. A supreme stylist who was one of the most accomplished players of his generation, he made fifty-five appearances for Northern Ireland after moving from Glentoran to Burnley. He was largely responsible for the club's most successful period, culminating in a First Division championship success in 1960. He scored 115 goals in 440 games for Burnley before leaving in 1963. He combined with DANNY BLANCHFLOWER to form the axis of an exciting Northern Ireland team. **Peter Byrne**

Mac Intyre, Thomas (Tom) (1931–), poet and playwright. Born in Co. Cavan; educated at UCD. His poems are terse, imagistic, and gnomic, with their stylistic roots in the compressed Irish poetry of the ninth to the twelfth centuries, and having sex and love as their themes. Excepting the early *Eye-Winker, Tom Tinker* (1972) and *Kitty O'Shea* (1990), his plays are anti-naturalistic, relying on a kind of imagism-montage and on collaboration with actors and director to produce a theatre experience in the European mode rather than a 'well-made' play in the English and American idioms. Prominent among his theatre works are *The Great Hunger* (1983–6, based on the KAVANAGH poem), *The Bearded Lady* (1984), *Rise Up, Lovely Sweeney* (1985, based on 'BUILE SHUIBHNE'), *Dance for Your Daddy* (1987), and *Snow White* (1988). Among his notable poetry collections are *I Bailed Out at Ardee* (1987) and *Fleur de Lys* (1991). Though primarily a poet, he has published short stories, *Dance the Dance* (1969) and *The Harper's Turn* (1982), a novel, *The Charollais* (1969), and non-fiction prose, *Through the Bridewell Gate* (1971), a record of the Arms Trial, as well as versions from the Irish in *Blood Relations* (1972). He is a member of AOSDÁNA. **Theo Dorgan**

Mackau (McCoy), Admiral Armand (died 1855), naval officer. Born into a family who were always in close touch with their McCoy relations in Galway; educated at the IRISH COLLEGE in Paris, where he became a close friend of Napoleon Bonaparte's brother, Jérome. With him he joined the navy at a critical moment in the war with England, and was continuously involved in French naval affairs. As a dashing but calculating gunboat commander in the Bay of Biscay and the Mediterranean, then, after the peace, captain first of frigates, then ships of the line, and insisting on systematic hydrographic work, he made his name well known. In 1843, while serving as commander of France's Mediterranean fleet, he was made Minister of the Marine, in four years transforming the navy from sail to steam, preparing the way for the launch of Europe's first iron-clad battleship in 1859. He improved seamen's pay, abolished humiliating punishments, and prepared the law to end slavery in French colonies. **John de Courcy Ireland**

McGuckian. *The Belfast poet Medbh McGuckian, whose work has given a voice to private concerns and domestic worlds. [Gallery Press]*

McKeever, Jim (1931–), Gaelic footballer. Born in Co. Derry. He played his club football with Newbridge and Ballymaguigan and was an outstanding college star in the late 1940s. His first senior game for Derry was in 1948, and he captained the team when they won their first Ulster championship in 1958. His inter-county career spanned fourteen years; and despite never having won an all-Ireland medal he is widely recognised as an exceptional midfielder and the finest player to represent Derry in Gaelic football. **Jack Mahon**

McKelvey, Frank (1895–1974), painter of portraits and landscapes. Born in Belfast, where he spent most of his career; trained at Belfast College of Art, where he won several awards, including the Taylor Scholarship, 1918. He established himself as a portraitist in Belfast in the 1920s, working in an academic manner, and thereafter painted many eminent people in the city. As a landscapist he worked in the tradition of PAUL HENRY, J. H. CRAIG, and CHARLES LAMB, though his work is less romantic than theirs; with them he dominated the inter-war period. Characteristically, he concentrated on capturing the essential visual effect of the scene. **S. B. Kennedy**

Macken, Walter (1915–1967), actor, playwright, and novelist. Born in Galway. He began writing, directing, and acting with TAIBHDHEARC NA GAILLIMHE; in the 1940s he acted in the ABBEY THEATRE and on Broadway. His writing for theatre recalls the tragicomedy of SEAN O'CASEY, including *Mungo's Mansion* (1946), *Vacant Possession* (1948), *Home is the Hero* (1952), and *Twilight of the Warrior* (1955). His noted fictional works include *Rain on the Wind* (1950), *Seek the Fair Land* (1959), *The Silent People* (1962), and *The Scorching Wind* (1964). He became artistic manager of the Abbey Theatre in 1966. **Joley Wood**

McKenna, Daniel (1892–1975), soldier. Born at Maghera, Co. Derry; he joined the IRISH VOLUNTEERS in 1915 and became commandant of South Derry IRA during the WAR OF INDEPENDENCE, 1919–21. As deputy divisional commander in Derry by December 1921 he accepted the ANGLO-IRISH TREATY and later joined the FREE STATE ARMY with other Ulster IRA officers brought south in September 1922. He served mainly in the Cork–Waterford area, was Deputy Quartermaster-General, Director of Supply and Transport, Director of Cavalry, and finally Chief of Staff, 1940–49. **Patrick Long**

McKenna, John (1880–1947), flute-player. Born in Tarmon, Co. Leitrim. His repertory and his robust, rhythmic and breathy flute-playing are acknowledged as representing the 'north Leitrim style' on the flute. An emigrant to America in 1911, he made thirty 78 r.p.m. records between 1921 and 1936, which left an indelible imprint both on Co. Leitrim musicians (such as Packie Duignan and Mick Woods) and on Irish music in general. **Desi Wilkinson**

MacKenna, John (Juan) (1771–1814), Chilean general. Born in Clogher, Co. Tyrone; educated at the Royal Academy of Mathematics, Barcelona. He joined the Spanish army and left for Peru in 1796. He did valuable work as a military engineer in Chile and was appointed governor of Osorno. In 1810 he joined Carrera's revolution and was made commander-in-chief of artillery and engineers. He fell out with Carrera and sided with his rival, BERNARDO O'HIGGINS, who defeated Carrera in 1813; MacKenna became second in command. A military revolution restored Carrera to power in 1814, and MacKenna was banished to Mendoza. He died in a duel in Buenos Aires. **David Kiely**

McKenna, Siobhán. *The stage and screen actor Siobhán McKenna in her last role, as Mommo in the Druid Theatre's production of Tom Murphy's* Bailegangaire, *1985. [Amelia Stein]*

McKenna, Siobhán (1923–1986), actor. Born in Belfast; educated at UCG. She began acting at the TAIBHDHEARC NA GAILLIMHE in 1940 and achieved international fame for playing the title role in SHAW's *St Joan* (1954). Her last role was as Mommo in the DRUID THEATRE's production of TOM MURPHY'S BAILEGANGAIRE (1985). **Christopher Morash**

MacKenna, Stephen (1872–1934), journalist and translator. Born in Liverpool, of Irish parents; he worked as a journalist in London, Paris (where he befriended SYNGE), and Dublin. An intellectual republican, he was reportedly excused service in the 1916 RISING because of the poor health that dogged him for most of his life. Alienated from FREE STATE politics, he left Ireland for London in 1922 and devoted himself to the completion of a task begun in 1908, a translation into English of the *Enneads* of Plotinus (1917–30), which remains a monument to his scholarship and his lucid yet emotive style. **Terence Brown**

McKenna, Stephen (1939–), painter. Born in London; trained at the Slade School of Fine Art, and later taught at Canterbury College of Art. He now lives and works in Co. Carlow and in Italy. A leading post-modernist painter, he lists among his influences Poussin, Cranach, and, especially, de Chirico. He is committed to borrowing, quoting, and paraphrasing, producing a rich, enigmatic result in his own recognisable idiom. His subjects range from ordinary-seeming but strange landscapes and seascapes to typical Italian architectural interiors opening onto urban or rural scenes. His work is exhibited widely throughout the world, and he is also a gifted and perceptive writer on art. He is a member of AOSDÁNA. **Dorothy Walker**

McKenna-Lawlor, Susan, née McKenna (1935–), astrophysicist. Born in Dublin; educated at UCD, DIAS, and the University of Michigan. Emeritus professor at the National University of Ireland, Maynooth, she is a member of the Senate of the university, guest professor at the Chinese Academy of Sciences, and founder and managing director of Space Technology Ireland Ltd. She has participated in space experiments launched by the European Space Agency, National Aeronautics and Space Administration (United States), Intercosmos (Russia), ISAS (Japan), CSSAR (China), and two Shuttle missions. As Principal Investigator she carried full scientific and administrative responsibility for Ireland's EPONA experiment on the European Space Agency's Giotto mission, which encountered Halley's Comet (1986), made the first historic fly-by of Earth (1990), and encountered Comet Grigg-Skjellerup (1992). She also as team leader provided the national instrument LION for the European Space Agency's Solar Heliospheric Observatory and acted as co-investigator for experiments flown on the Cluster (four-spacecraft constellation), Mars Express, Venus Express, SMART (lunar), and Rosetta (Comet Wirtanen) missions. She participated in NASA's Skylab, Solar Maximum, WIND, and Gravity Probe B (Relativity) missions; with Intercosmos in respect of Mars 96 and the Phobos mission to Mars and its moons (two spacecraft) and the Mars 96 mission. She has published more than a hundred academic publications on scientific and technical subjects and on the history of Irish SCIENCE. She received the Irish Person of the Year Award, 1986, Tsiockovsky gold medal for Outstanding Contributions to Cosmonautics, 1988, honorary citizenship of San José, California,

McKenna, Stephen. Plans and Ashes *(1991), diptych by Stephen McKenna. Fragments of the* Forma Urbis *(left front), a street plan set up in the Forum of Classical Rome, provide a focus for themes and images of Italian townscape. [Irish Museum of Modern Art; courtesy of the artist]*

for technological achievement, 1991, Woman of Europe Award, 1994, and Book Award of the International Academy of Astronautics, 1998. **Michael Ovchinnikov**

Mackey, Mick (1912–1982), hurler. Born in Castleconnell, Co. Limerick. Also a talented footballer, he dominated 1930s HURLING and is credited with turning Limerick into a hurling power. He won all-Ireland championships in 1934, 1936, and 1940. Physically he was very powerful, but he also possessed a light touch, which allowed him to amass huge scoring tallies. His career overlapped that of CHRISTY RING, and the two enjoyed a great rivalry as well as a great friendship. **Donal Keenan**

McKittrick, David (1949–), journalist. Born in Belfast. He has reported on Northern Ireland since 1971, beginning as a reporter for the *East Antrim Times*. He joined the IRISH TIMES in 1973 as a reporter in Belfast, becoming Northern editor in 1976 and London editor in 1981. He worked briefly for BBC Northern Ireland, 1985–6, before joining the *Independent* (London) in 1986; he has since worked as the paper's Irish correspondent. Widely recognised for the scope of his knowledge and the balance of his reporting on Northern Ireland, he contributes regularly to overseas newspapers and journals. His many awards include the Christopher Ewart-Biggs Memorial Prize for the promotion of peace and understanding in Northern Ireland, 1989 and 2001, Correspondent of the Year, 1999, IPR Feature-Writer and Journalist of the Year, 1999, and Orwell Prize for Journalism, 2000. He has published *Endgame in Ireland* (1994), *The Fight for Peace* (with Éamon Mallie, 1996), *Lost Lives* (with Séamus Kelters, Brian Feeney and Chris Thornton, 1999), and *Making Sense of the Troubles* (with David McVea, 2000). **Ciarán Deane**

Macklin, Charles (c. 1700–1797), actor, playwright, and THEATRE manager. Born Charles McLaughlin in Culdaff, Co. Donegal. He was a legend in eighteenth-century theatre for his short temper (he once killed a fellow-actor) and for his longevity. He struggled for the first half of his long career; his breakthrough came when he played Shylock in 1741, creating a vogue for a more naturalistic style of acting and prompting Alexander Pope to write: 'This is the Jew | That Shakespeare drew.' He also wrote comic plays, including *Love à la Mode* (1759) and *The True-Born Irishman* (1762), revised by BRIAN FRIEL as *The London Vertigo* (1990). **Christopher Morash**

McLaughlin, Thomas Aloysius (1896–1971), physicist and electrical engineer. Born in Drogheda; educated at UCD and UCG. He prepared the scheme for the hydro-power station at Ardnacrusha on the River SHANNON, designed and constructed by Siemens-Schuckert, 1925–9, and was the first managing director of the Electricity Supply Board (see p. 346). [see SHANNON SCHEME.] **Ronald Cox**

MacLaverty, Bernard (1942–), novelist and short-story writer. Born in Belfast and educated at QUB. His short-story collections,

Maclise. An Interview between Charles I and Oliver Cromwell *(1836), a history painting by Daniel Maclise. Cromwell (right), accompanied by Ireton and Fairfax, asks Charles (left, with his children James, Duke of York, and Princess Elizabeth) to sign away his authority. [National Gallery of Ireland]*

the first of which was *Secrets and Other Stories* (1977), combine comedy and tragedy in depicting often marginalised characters. His novels feature difficult or sensitive relationships. His first novel, *Lamb* (1980), tells of the tragic relationship between a borstal warder and an inmate. *Cal* (1983) explores the love between a young terrorist and his victim's wife. *Grace Notes* (1998) represents a more lyrical turn in MacLaverty's work, exploring issues of music, art, and identity through the story of a composer's return to Belfast. **John Brannigan**

McLaverty, Michael (1904–1992), writer. Born in Carrickmacross, Co. Monaghan, and moved to Belfast as a boy; educated at QUB. A teacher by profession, he spent childhood holidays on RATHLIN ISLAND, which, with Belfast and Co. Down, inspired his lyrical short stories of children and the dispossessed and his first novel, *Call My Brother Back* (1939). Seven more novels followed; but McLaverty's essential gift was for the short story. Two early volumes, *The White Mare* (1943) and *The Game Cock* (1947), together with *Collected Short Stories* (1978), contain his best work. **Sophia Hillan**

McLean (or MacLaine), James (1724–1750), highwayman. Born in Co. Monaghan. He went to London where he was successively a grocer and a chandler, but following the death of his wife in 1748, he took to the road with an accomplice and compatriot named Plunkett, becoming a popular hero, particularly among women. His victims included Horace Walpole. He was captured in July 1750; his trial was a sensation, and a military escort was required to transport him to and from court. He allegedly received some 3,000 visitors on his first day in jail. He was hanged in London on 3 October 1750. **Ciarán Deane**

Maclear, Thomas (1794–1819), astronomer. Born in Newtownstewart, Co. Tyrone; trained at Guy's Hospital and St Thomas's Hospital, London. A member of the Royal College of Surgeons (1851), he practised in Bedford. He became engrossed in ASTRONOMY and set up his own observatory, achieving professional status. In 1831 he was elected a fellow of the Royal Society and appointed HM Astronomer at the Royal Observatory, Cape of Good Hope, where his duties included a geodetic survey and the measurement of an arc of the meridian in South Africa. He was knighted in 1860. Noted for his firm directorship and hard work, he served until his retirement in 1870. **M. T. Brück**

MacLennan, Alastair (1943–), performance artist. Born in Scotland; studied in Dundee, 1960–65, and Chicago, 1966–8. He has lived in Belfast since 1975 and is professor of fine art at the University of Ulster. He is known for performances of long duration and performance installations, which he calls 'actuations'. From the seminal work *Days and Nights* (1981), a 144-hour non-stop actuation, to *No Nemesis* (2000), his Zen-informed practice has been constant. His concerns include ethics, aesthetics, religious and political bigotry, inclusive tolerance, oppositional or consensual means of political or social improvement, death, decay, mutation, and transformation. An enthusiastic and influential artist and educator, in 1989 he joined the innovative European performance art group Black Market International. In 1997 he represented Ireland at the Venice Biennale. **Liam Kelly**

Mac Líacc, Muircheartach (died 1014 or 1016), poet. In a number of ANNALS he is styled 'ardollamh Éirenn' ('Ireland's chief professor of poetry') at the time of his death. While he is unlikely to have been the author of much of the work attributed to him, a small number of poems may be his; these include a poem on the twelve sons of BRIAN BÓRÚ, 'Dá mac déc Cennéitig cháid'. Poems on the BATTLE OF CLONTARF and the death of Brian, such as 'A chinn choradh caidhe Brian' ('O Kincora, where is Brian?'), are also attributed to him. **Séamus Mac Mathúna**

Mac Liammóir, Mícheál (1899–1978), designer, actor, diarist, and playwright. Born Alfred Willmore in London; he was a child actor with Sir Herbert Beerbohm Tree and studied at the Slade School of Fine Art, where he enjoyed a platonic friendship with a fellow-student, Máire O'Keeffe, with whose encouragement he reinvented himself as an Irishman. After her death in 1927 he returned to acting with his brother-in-law ANEW MCMASTER and met his lifelong partner, HILTON EDWARDS, with whom he founded the Dublin GATE THEATRE (1928) (see p. 497). He acted in and designed sets and costumes for most Gate productions for the next thirty years before achieving overnight fame with his one-man show *The Importance of Being Oscar* (1960), based on the life of OSCAR WILDE. He wrote twelve original plays in Irish and English, of which *Ill Met by Moonlight* (1946) and *Prelude in Kazbek Street* (1973) remain of interest, and seven volumes of autobiography. **Richard Pine**

Maclise, Daniel (1806–1870), painter. Born in Cork, the son of a discharged British soldier, a shoemaker. From 1822 he drew from the newly arrived collection of plaster casts of the Vatican marbles at the Cork Institute (now in the Crawford Art Gallery). He was patronised by the antiquarian Richard Sainthill and the folklorist T. CROFTON CROKER and first came to public notice in 1825, when he lithographed a portrait he had drawn of Sir Walter Scott on a visit to Cork, which led to local commissions for portrait drawings. He also toured the south of Ireland, making drawings of picturesque views. Throughout his career he treated Irish subjects, such as *Snap Apple* (1833), and provided book illustrations of Irish subjects. In 1827 he went to London and in 1828 studied at the Royal Academy, gaining the Gold Medal for History Painting in 1831. During the 1830s he developed a highly literary form of history PAINTING, indebted to Shakespeare, the gothic revival, and Netherlandish art. He was deeply involved in literary circles, notably that of *Fraser's Magazine*, for which he made lithographic portraits, and Charles Dickens, whose books he illustrated, and had a wide circle of literary acquaintances. In the mid-1840s his career centred on commissions for murals for the Houses of Parliament, London, heavily influenced by French and German mural art. His Irish romantic side was most evident in his *Marriage of Strongbow and Aoife* (1854) at the National Gallery of Ireland (see p. 475). His work at the Houses of Parliament culminated in two gigantic murals, *The Meeting of Wellington and Blücher* (1861) and *The Death of Nelson* (1865), which show his pessimistic reaction to the destruction of war. Through engravings these had a wide circulation; however, official interest in such vast decorative schemes waned, and the work was discontinued. In his last years he returned to the literary and poetic subjects of his youth; he also painted a number of fine portraits and worked extensively as a book illustrator, for which his strong draughtsmanship was sell suited. **John Turpin**

Maclise as an illustrator. His first illustrated book was CROKER's *Fairy Legends of Ireland* (1825). Later in London he produced a range of portrait drawings of Carlisle, Coleridge, O'Connell, and other personalities for *Fraser's Magazine*. His finest achievement as an illustrator was MOORE'S IRISH MELODIES (1846), for which he contributed some 160 drawings. He was a lover of Moore's work, and this volume was his tribute to the poet. He invented decorative borders for every page and provided a coherent relationship between text and illustrations. His other notable illustrations were for Dickens's *The Chimes* (1845), whose title page is playful and imaginative, with figures of goblins forming the letters, as in a medieval manuscript. **Patricia Donlon**

McLoone, Martin (1950–), academic critic. Born in Derry; educated at UCD. He lectures in media studies at the University of Ulster and has edited symposia on the media and cultural identity in Northern Ireland. *Irish Film: The Emergence of a Contemporary Cinema* (2000) is a major development of a subject pioneered by KEVIN ROCKETT. **Richard Pine**

MacLysaght, Edward (1887–1986), historian and genealogist. Born in Somerset as E. Lysaght; educated at the University of Oxford. He settled in Co. Clare with his parents in 1909. In Dublin he formed friendships with EDWARD MARTYN, GEORGE RUSSELL, and MAUD GONNE MACBRIDE. In 1917 he was a representative at the IRISH CONVENTION and advocated DOMINION STATUS for Ireland. In 1919 he published *The Gael*, based on his own experiences and his sympathy with the executed leaders of the 1916 RISING. Following his detention by the British army in Dublin, and warned that he was on the BLACK AND TANS' black-list, he moved with his family to France. He edited a journal, *An Scuab*, and wrote a novel, *Cúrsaí Thomáis* (1927). In 1939 he published *Irish Life in the Seventeenth Century*, based on his doctoral thesis. In 1943 he was appointed to the staff of the NATIONAL LIBRARY OF IRELAND and in the same year became Chief Genealogical Officer (later Chief Herald), after the handing over of the Office of Arms by the British government. Describing himself as 'an ignoramus in HERALDRY', he nevertheless made a great contribution to that subject and in 1957 published *Irish Families: Their Names, Arms and Origins*, which was followed by two supplementary volumes. He also initiated research on claims for recognition as 'CHIEFS OF THE NAME' and set up a system based on primogeniture for doing so. He was simultaneously Keeper of Manuscripts at the National Library, where he saw the number of MANUSCRIPTS grow from 894 to 9,000. He retired in 1954 and served as chairman of the IRISH MANUSCRIPTS COMMISSION until 1973. His autobiography, *Changing Times: Ireland since 1898* (1978), gives a full account of his life and work. **Fergus Gillespie**

MacLysaght. *Edward MacLysaght, historian and genealogist. He was head of the Genealogical Office, 1943–54; his publications include* Irish Families: Their Names, Arms and Origins *(1957). [Peter Tynan O'Mahony]*

McMahon, Bernard (1775–1816), nurseryman. Having settled in Philadelphia, he established a flourishing nursery business, patronised by botanists and explorers as well as by local gardeners. He published the first book devoted to gardening in an American setting, *The American Gardener's Chronicle* (1806). Thomas Jefferson entrusted him with the seeds and plants from the Lewis and Clarke expedition, the first to cross the North-American continent. Lewis and Clarke found the Oregon grape, the first of a new genus of highly ornamental shrubs, which was named Mahonia in his honour. **John Joe Costin**

MacMahon, Bryan (1909–1998), teacher, short-story writer, and playwright. Born and educated in Listowel, Co. Kerry, where he taught for nearly fifty years. He began publishing in the BELL. His first short-story collection, *The Lion Tamer* (1948), was followed by a novel, *Children of the Rainbow* (1952), and twelve further books and plays, including a translation of *Peig* by the Blasket author PEIG SAYERS. His work reveals a warm engagement with all aspects of rural life. **Peter Costello**

MacMahon, Heber (1600–1650), Catholic bishop and representative of the militant COUNTER-REFORMATION. Born in Farney, Co. Monaghan; educated at the IRISH COLLEGE, Douai, and LOUVAIN, where he was ordained in 1625. After serving as vicar-general in the diocese of Clogher he was appointed Bishop of Down and Connor in 1642 and attended in that capacity at the SYNOD of Kells, which supported the 1641 REBELLION. In 1643 he was translated to Clogher, an appointment urged by the Confederate Supreme Council, of whose clerical faction he was a leading member. A trusted friend of Owen Roe, for whom he had recruited mercenaries for Continental service, he opposed the truce in 1643 and the treaty with Ormond in 1646, after which his opponents tried unsuccessfully to appoint him ambassador to France. He condemned the truce with Inchiquin in 1648. In 1649 he was taken prisoner at Charlemont. After escaping he was a party to the agreement between O'Neill and Ormond. After O'Neill's death MacMahon was the compromise choice as general of Ulster. Lacking any military skill, he ignored his officers' advice and engaged a Cromwellian force at Scarrifhollis on 21 June 1650. Wounded in the defeat, he was imprisoned at Enniskillen and put to death on 17 September. **Charles Ivar McGrath**

MacMahon, Jacobo (died 1887), naval officer. In 1839 he entered the Spanish navy as a midshipman and during the next thirty-nine years served in forty-two ships, experiencing the Spanish navy's revolutionary switch from sail to steam. He won distinction for his conduct in the mid-century Carlist wars. He commanded Spain's first iron-clad steam frigate, the *Tetuán*, and was promoted to commodore in 1868. Commander of Spain's Mediterranean fleet, he was awarded the Grand Cross of Naval Merit. In a long spell in command of the headquarters of Spain's Atlantic fleet at El Ferral, he made a long pioneer study of the changes in naval warfare likely with the recent invention of the torpedo, being one of the first of the world's admirals to see its significance. Probably the most outstanding Spanish naval leader in the nineteenth century, throughout his career he maintained contact with his relatives in Ireland. Shortly before his death he was responsible for ordering a ship of a new design, the *Destructor*, to protect other ships from fast torpedo boats, the first of many 'torpedo boat destroyers' in all the world's navies. [see MACKAY, ARMAND.] **John de Courcy Ireland**

MacMahon, Tony (1939–), accordion-player and television presenter. Born in Ennis, Co. Clare; he learnt MUSIC in the family home, influenced by JOE COOLEY and Seán Reid. Teacher training in Dublin introduced him to Bill Harte, JOHN KELLY, and BREANDÁN BREATHNACH; travel in America brought him together with SÉAMUS ENNIS. While playing in Dublin he met SEÁN Ó RIADA, for whom he performed in *The Playboy of the Western World*. While playing in London in 1966 he was recorded on *Paddy in the Smoke*, after which he presented the traditional music television series 'Aisling Gheal' and 'Ag Déanamh Ceoil'. On radio he initiated 'The Long Note' in 1974 and later on television 'The Pure Drop' and 'Come West along the Road'. He was a blunt ideologue of TRADITIONAL MUSIC, greatly concerned with authenticity, and his recordings, particularly on airs and in dance music with the CONCERTINA-player Noel Hill, evince great emotional intensity and arresting dynamics. His drama *The Word* (2000) is a synthesis of musicianship, spirituality, and identity. **Fintan Vallely**

MacManus, Francis (1909–1965), writer and broadcaster. Born in Kilkenny; educated at St Patrick's College, Dublin, and UCD. From 1948, when he abandoned teaching, he was director of talks and features at Radio Éireann. He contributed regularly to the *Catholic Standard* and occasionally to the *Capuchin Annual* and the BELL. *Stand and Give Challenge* (1934), his first novel in a trilogy, deals with the eighteenth-century poet DONNCHA RUA MAC CONMARA; the others are *Candle for the Proud* (1936) and *Men Withering* (1939). A second trilogy, set in the fictitious Dombridge, Co. Kilkenny, comprising *This House Was Mine* (1937), *Flow On, Lovely River* (1941), and *Watergate* (1942), considers hunger for land, emigration, and local conflict. Clerical dilemmas form the topic of *The Greatest of These* (1947), while the autobiographical *The Fire in the Dust* (1950) exposes the writer's home county's hypocritical response to healthy SEXUALITY. Among his other writings are two biographies, *Boccaccio* (1947) and *Saint Columban* (1963), and a travel book, *Seal ag Ródaíocht* (1955).

His contribution to radio was considerable. Chief among his innovations was the well-informed and accessible THOMAS DAVIS Lectures Series; he edited two associated collections of essays, *The Years of the Great Test* (1967) and *The Yeats We Knew* (1965). His novels assume the liberal, orthodox form of European Catholic realist fiction exemplified by Bernanos and Claudel and later adopted by JOHN BRODERICK; they confront mid-twentieth-century Ireland's destructive puritanism while avoiding overtly sexual description. **Mary Thompson**

McManus, Terence Bellew (1823–1861), Young Irelander. Born in Co. Monaghan. He became a shipping agent. In Liverpool he represented the REPEAL Association and then the YOUNG IRELAND Confederation. A lieutenant of WILLIAM SMITH O'BRIEN at the Ballingarry affray in July 1848, he was transported to Van Diemen's Land. Escaping in 1851, he died in poverty in California; the huge demonstration at his Dublin funeral on 10 November 1861 encouraged FENIANISM. **Richard P. Davis**

McMaster, Anew (1894–1962), actor-manager. Born in Birkenhead. He was an established West End actor when, in 1925, he formed his Intimate Shakespeare Company, indefatigably touring Ireland until the early 1960s. At various times his company included MÍCHÉAL MAC LIAMMÓIR and HILTON EDWARDS (who were introduced by McMaster) (see p. 497), MILO O'SHEA, and Harold Pinter. **Christopher Morash**

Mac Mathúna, Ciarán (1925–), music collector and broadcaster. Born in Limerick. He worked first with the PLACE-NAMES Commission, and in 1954 he joined Radio Éireann as a scriptwriter, then progressed to collecting solo instrumental music and songs at house sessions and other gatherings. The results were broadcast until 1970 as 'Ceolta Tíre' and also as 'A Job of Journeywork'. His voice became synonymous with the music revival, his material eagerly listened to by players for whom there was often little other choice of source material. 'The Humours of Donnybrook' was his first television series, with 'Reels of Memory' his archive programme in the 1970s; but he is best known for the classic radio series 'Mo Cheol Thú', broadcast every Sunday morning from 1970. A member of the Cultural Relations Committee of the Department of Foreign Affairs, he has also been a central figure in the Merriman Summer School since 1970. In 1990 he was awarded honorary doctorates by the NUI and the University of Limerick. **Fintan Vallely**

Mac Mathúna, Séamus (1939–), traditional musician and MUSIC administrator. Born in Cooraclare, Co. Clare; learnt song and whistle from Paddy Breen and others at 'AMERICAN WAKES' and HOUSE-DANCES. He was COMHALTAS CEOLTÓIRÍ ÉIREANN's Co. Clare secretary, 1959–61, worked on BREANDÁN BREATHNACH's *Tacar Port* collection, and acted as CONRADH NA GAEILGE's regional organiser in Cos. Cork and Kerry, 1966–9. A full-time worker with CCÉ since then, he has done much of its archive recording and has been its Timire Ceoil (music organiser) since the post was created in 1970. **Fintan Vallely**

Mac Meanman, Seán (1886–1962), writer. Born in An Ceann Garbh, Co. Donegal. A teacher, ardent republican and Irish-language enthusiast, his works, written in rich idiomatic Irish, are full of the history, life and lore of his native area. His aim in writing was to acquaint the new Ireland with the fast-disappearing Irish-speaking world. **Nollaig Mac Congáil**

MacMurrough, Dermot, Anglicised name of Diarmaid Mac Murchú (1110–1171), King of Leinster. He rose to power in the 1130s and in 1151 sensationally abducted Derbforgaill, wife of

Tigernán Ó Ruairc, King of Bréifne. She was returned the following year. By 1156 the Northern UÍ NÉILL king, Muirchertach Mac Lochlainn, was dominant in Ireland, with Dermot's support. However, Mac Lochlainn's dominance was precarious, and he was overthrown by an alliance of Ruaidhrí Ó Conchobhair, King of Connacht, and Ó Ruairc. In 1166 Mac Lochlainn was killed, and Ó Conchobhair, unassailable Overlord of Ireland, expelled Dermot from his KINGSHIP. Dermot travelled to Britain and the Continent to seek aid in reclaiming his kingdom. HENRY II allowed him to recruit Norman-Welsh adventurers, chief among them RICHARD FITZ GILBERT or 'Strongbow', who eventually married Aoife, Dermot's daughter. MacMurrough inadvertently reaped the whirlwind for, following his death in 1171, the Anglo-Normans proceeded to extend their conquests throughout Ireland, with lasting consequences. **Elva Johnston**

MacMurrough Kavanagh, Art, Anglicised name of Art Mac Murchú Caomhánach (1357–1416/17), King of Leinster. He was inaugurated 'King of Leinster' in 1375, using a title revived by previous leaders of the MacMurrough family, much to the unease of the Dublin administration, which had put to death several of his predecessors. Within Irish society Art was a king; his sub-kings accompanied him on his raids throughout Leinster, and praise-poems were written in his honour. He dominated the ANGLO-NORMAN settlers of Leinster, extracting 'black rent' in Castledermot and New Ross and seeking an annual fee from Dublin. Through his wife, the Anglo-Norman heiress Elizabeth Calf, he claimed the important barony of Norragh in Co. Kildare. He was the principal focus of RICHARD II's attentions during his expedition of 1394–5 to Ireland. Though initially submitting to him, Art renounced his fealty on Richard's departure, successfully resisting him in 1399 and managing to retain his supremacy in Leinster until his death. **Susan Foran**

McNab, Theo (1940–), painter. Born in Dublin; self-taught. His paintings explore experiences of space and light. In his work he combines mathematical ratios, often reflecting astronomical or seasonal cycles, with a personal aesthetic achieved through expressive, translucent layers of paint. His work moves between abstraction and exterior landscape or interior room-like evocations, which convey varying moods of psychological tension. He has exhibited internationally and at the DOUGLAS HYDE Gallery, Dublin, 1987. He was professor of fine art at the NCAD, 1988–2000. **Suzanne McNab**

MacNamara, Brinsley, pseudonym of John Weldon (1890–1963), novelist, playwright, and short-story writer. Born in Delvin, Co. Westmeath. As a young man he was a member of the ABBEY THEATRE company. His first novel, *The Valley of the Squinting Windows* (1918), won him notoriety. A study of provincial small-mindedness, it caused grave offence in his home village. He followed this exercise in aggressive realism with further attacks on Irish society and its values, including *The Clanking of Chains* (1920). He wrote comedies for the Abbey stage as well as short stories; but the *succès de scandale* enjoyed by his first novel has limited his reputation to that of an outspokenly realistic analyst of provincial life. **Terence Brown**

McNamara, Francis (Frank) (1931–), MUSIC teacher and priest. Born in Clara, Co. Offaly; educated at ST PATRICK'S COLLEGE, MAYNOOTH, UCD, the Royal Academy of Music, and the Royal College of Music, London. An authority on Gregorian chant and the music of the High Renaissance, he was the founding director of the Irish SCHOLA CANTORUM in 1970. His exceptional gifts as a teacher (organ, compositional techniques, music history and church music) were profoundly influential in the development of music education in Ireland. Former pupils include the present director of the Schola Cantorum, Shane Brennan, the director of sacred music at St Patrick's College, Maynooth, and the professor of music at the University College, Dublin, Harry White. **Éamonn O'Keeffe**

Mac Mathúna. *As Radio Éireann broadcaster Ciarán Mac Mathúna was a key figure in the traditional music revival. He is seen here at the RTÉ studios with a bust of Seán Ó Riada. [RTÉ Stills Library; 463/37]*

McNamara, Gerald (1865–1938), actor and playwright. Born in Belfast. He was a leading light in the Ulster Theatre (founded 1902). His works, mostly unpublished, are reprinted in a thesis by Kathleen Danaher (University of Delaware, 1984) and include *Suzanne and the Sovereigns* (1907), *The Mist Does Be on the Bog* (1909), and *Thompson in Tir-na-nOg* (1912). His plays delight in punctuating Orange mythology and the vogue for 'peasant comedy'; the comic conflation of time zones, a fondness for burlesque and puckish humour are reminiscent of FLANN O'BRIEN. His plays, though somewhat dated, were considered challenging satires. **Tess Maginess**

'Mac na Míchomhairle', a late seventeenth-century anonymous romantic tale, probably composed in south-west Ulster. With its burlesque mood and mock-heroic language it constitutes a learned reaction against the contemporary northern revival of heroic prose genres. Remodelling the same FOLK-TALE found in 'Laoi Chab an Dosáin', it also incorporates love-*aisling* verse and motifs. **Seosamh Watson**

MacNeice, Louis (1907–1963), poet. Born in Belfast, son of a Church of Ireland rector; he spent his childhood in Carrickfergus but was later educated in England and studied classics and philosophy at the University of Oxford. There he became a friend of the poets W. H. Auden and Stephen Spender, with whom he came to be publicly associated. His subsequent career was largely in England, first as a classics teacher in Birmingham, 1929–36, and Bedford College, London, then, after the breakdown of his marriage and a time in America, as producer and writer for the BBC, 1941–61, where his radio plays included the classic *The Dark Tower* (1946). He established himself as a poet with his second book, *Poems* (1935), which was followed by *The Agamemnon of Aeschylus* (1936), a landmark in modern verse translation; *Letters from Iceland* (1937), an inventive travel book written with Auden; and his masterpiece, AUTUMN JOURNAL (1939). After the outbreak of war he wrote a vivid memoir of childhood and youth, posthumously published as *The Strings are False* (1965), and a study of W. B. YEATS (1941). After *Plant and Phantom* (1941), *Springboard* (1944), and *Holes in the Sky* (1948) his poetic output slackened until the marvellous late harvest of *Visitation* (1957), *The Solstices* (1961), and *The Burning Perch* (1963). In 'Snow' he speaks of the 'drunkenness of things being various'. MacNeice is one of the most various, prolific and influential Irish poets of the twentieth century, with a great impact on later poets from the North of Ireland. **Hugh Haughton**

MacNeill, Eoin (1867–1945), scholar and politician. Born in Glenarm, Co. Antrim; educated at the Royal University. He was a founder of the GAELIC LEAGUE in 1893 and editor of the *Gaelic Journal*. In 1908 he was appointed professor of early Irish history at UCD. He was chairman of the council that formed the IRISH VOLUNTEERS in 1913, later becoming chief of staff. Although opposed to the 1916 RISING, seeing little hope of success, he was arrested after the surrender and sentenced to penal servitude for life. Released in the 1917 amnesty, he was elected MP for NUI. He supported the ANGLO-IRISH TREATY of 1921 and was Minister for Education in the FREE STATE government from August 1922 to November 1925. During his term of office the administration of primary, secondary, and technical education was co-ordinated under a single government department, the Department of Education. While his ministry is mostly associated with curricular reforms that gave pride of place to the IRISH LANGUAGE, to Irish MUSIC, history and literature, he also espoused a vision of EDUCATION that would lead to 'equality of education' for all. He did not, however, match his vision with the structural reform of the system necessary to make this vision a reality, and it was to be another forty years before equality of access was realised in the introduction of free second-level education. Forced to resign his ministry following criticism of his role in the Boundary Commission, he lost his seat in the general election of 1927. He then became chairman of the IRISH MANUSCRIPTS COMMISSION. His major works are *Phases of Irish History* (1919) and *Celtic Ireland* (1921). **Áine Hyland**

MacNeill, Hugo (1900–1963), soldier. Born in Howth, Co. Dublin; he was a member of FIANNA ÉIREANN before joining the IRISH VOLUNTEERS in 1917. Commissioned in the FREE STATE army in 1922, he served in Dublin during the CIVIL WAR, 1922–3. He became Adjutant-General, 1924–5, and Assistant Chief of Staff, 1925–7. He was a member of the military mission to the United States, 1926–7, becoming head of the Temporary Plans Division on his return. He was officer commanding the CURRAGH Camp, 1928–30, becoming commandant of the Military College in 1930. He was Assistant Chief of Staff again, 1932–7 and 1940–41, officer commanding the 2nd Division, 1941–6, and finally officer commanding Eastern Command, 1946–51. **Patrick Long**

McNeill, Janet (1907–), writer. Born in Dublin; educated at the University of St Andrews. Returning to Ireland, she worked as a secretary for the BELFAST TELEGRAPH, 1929–33, and in the 1950s began writing. With more than thirty children's novels to her name, she has a commanding position in Irish CHILDREN'S LITERATURE. She wrote instantly accessible stories, garnered with a quirky sense of humour for younger readers of everyday people and events, dusted with an element of magic. She also wrote about believable real boys in her Specs McCann series and in her best-known adventure story, *The Battle of St George Without* (1966). In a sequel, *Goodbye Dove Square* (1969), we see them grow and struggle with urban stress and the claustrophobia of life in a high-rise block of flats. **Patricia Donlon**

Macneill, John (1793–1880), civil engineer. Born in Dundalk. He was superintendent of the southern division of the Holyhead road, Wales, under Thomas Telford. He measured road traction parameters using a dynamometer and devised an instrument for indicating the state of repair of roads. In the late 1830s, with CHARLES VIGNOLES, he selected all the main railway routes in Ireland and was the first person to use wrought-iron latticed girders for BRIDGE construction, his most notable achievement being the BOYNE VIADUCT at Drogheda. He was consulting engineer and engineer to many railway companies. He was made a fellow of the Royal Society (London), in 1838, was professor of civil engineering at TRINITY COLLEGE, Dublin, 1842–52, and was knighted in 1844. **Ronald Cox**

MacNeill, Máire (1904–1987), folklorist. Born in Dublin. After working as secretary of the Irish FOLKLORE COMMISSION, 1935–49, she went to live in America, where she completed *The Festival of Lughnasa* (1962), the most significant scholarly achievement of the commission. **Mícheál Briody**

Macnémara family (fl. eighteenth century), French naval officers. The eighteenth century saw a remarkable influx into the French navy of Irish Macnamaras, who have left many relics in the port of Rochefort, near Cognac, most notably the elegant eighteenth-century Hôtel Macnémara. They were mostly descendants of an Irish émigré, John MacNamara, who came to Rochefort in 1697. Jean-Baptiste, having put four English ships of the line to flight in his ship, *Apollon*, became Lieutenant Général de la Marine, with the Grand Cross of the Order of St Louis, and later successfully transported to Canada, through the English blockade, the French soldiers who made a forlorn defence of Québec. His brother, Claude-Mathieu, served in nineteen naval campaigns, including two major engagements; he married the widow of Thomas Nugent, Earl of Westmeath, who had property in the West Indies, which Claude-Mathieu visited. Another Macnémara was a distinguished naval doctor during the American War of Independence at Dunkerque, the principal port from which France sent fleets of raiders, many of them Irish, to try to weaken England's war effort. Jean-Baptiste had three sons, all of whom became naval officers: Jean, who died on active service in the Seven Years' War in Martinique; Claude, killed the same year in the great naval battle off Les Cardinaux (Quiberon Bay); and Henry-Pantaléon, killed in 1791 by his revolutionary crew in the Indian Ocean. **John de Courcy Ireland**

MacNeven, William (1763–1841), chemist and physician. Born at Ballynahowna, Co. Galway; received a HEDGE SCHOOL education before moving to Continental Europe and graduating at the University of Vienna in medicine in 1783. On returning to

Ireland in 1784 he set up in practice and was elected a member of the ROYAL IRISH ACADEMY in 1785. Banished from Ireland in 1798 for his political activities, he lived in Switzerland before going to America in 1805. He held professorships in obstetrics, CHEMISTRY, and materia medica. He was a founder of the Duane Street Medical School and the New York Athenaeum and was a leader in the introduction of European ideas on chemistry to the New World, associatively being considered the father of American chemistry. **Susan McKenna-Lawlor**

McNulty, Daniel (1920–1996), organist, composer, and teacher. He worked in Dublin throughout his life. His compositions can be divided into three periods. The early and late periods concentrated on sacred choral works, while the middle years produced orchestral and instrumental music almost exclusively. In 1968 he composed the first of five Masses, initiating a return to the composition of sacred CHORAL MUSIC. These Masses are perhaps the best known of McNulty's works (which also includes two concertinos for piano and orchestra) and are regularly sung throughout Ireland as part of the Sunday liturgy. **David Mooney**

Maconchy, Elizabeth (1907–1994), musician and composer. Born in Hertfordshire to Irish parents, she moved to Ireland after the FIRST WORLD WAR; in 1923 she entered the Royal College of Music, London, studying composition with CHARLES WOOD and Vaughan Williams. She went on to become one of the leading British composers of the early twentieth century. Her works range from opera to orchestral and vocal works, but her main expression was in chamber music, including thirteen string quartets written in continuous succession from 1933 to 1983. **John Page**

McParland, Peter (1931–), soccer player. Born in Dundalk, Co. Louth. A fearless winger who could also operate effectively at centre-forward, he was among the biggest successes in Northern Ireland's World Cup odyssey in 1958, scoring five times on the team's way to the quarter-finals of the championship. He was involved in one of the great FA Cup final controversies when a collision with the Manchester United goalkeeper, Ray Wood, left Wood with a fractured jaw. He scored twice as Aston Villa won the trophy for a seventh time in 1957. **Peter Byrne**

McPeake family, a family of traditional musicians in Belfast. In 1907 Frank McPeake was taught the UILLEANN PIPES by JOHN O'REILLY, a blind travelling piper from Co. Galway. His son Francis learnt also, and with that a family tradition was established. Throughout the 1950s and 60s the McPeakes gained a growing recognition, particularly for their recording of 'Will Ye Go, Lassie, Go' (a version of the Scottish song 'Braes of Balquiddar'). Another generation, Francie McPeake and his children, remain influential in Belfast as teachers and performers. **Desi Wilkinson**

McPherson, Conor (1971–), playwright and director. Born in Dublin. He began directing his own plays while a philosophy student at UCD, jointly founding Fly by Night Theatre Company. These early plays, including *The Good Thief* (1994) and *This Lime Tree Bower* (1995), established his characteristic style, based on monologues delivered by the male characters. His storytellers are only retrospectively aware of the implications of their narratives, obliquely raising ethical questions about actions and their consequences. *The Weir* (1998) was a further evolution of this form, bringing his monologists together in the setting of a pub to tell tales of loss; it won an Olivier Award, 1998, and was voted one of the best Irish plays of the century in an IRISH TIMES poll. *Dublin Carol* (2000) and *Port Authority* (2001) continue to develop his exploration of the monologue. He also directed and wrote the screenplay for *Saltwater* (2000). **Christopher Morash**

MacNeill. *Máire MacNeill, folklorist and author of* The Festival of Lughnasa *(1962) at work in the Irish Folklore Commission. [Courtesy of Department of Irish Folklore, University College, Dublin]*

McQuaid, John Charles (1895–1973), archbishop. Born in Cootehill, Co. Cavan. He was ordained in the Holy Ghost Fathers in 1924 and became president of Blackrock College, Co. Dublin, in 1931. Consulted by DE VALERA on Catholic social teaching during the drafting of the CONSTITUTION of Ireland (1937), he was appointed Archbishop of Dublin in 1940 (see p. 171). He oversaw the huge institutional expansion of the church in the spreading Dublin SUBURBS, establishing twenty-six new parishes and building thirty-four new churches and sixty-seven secondary schools. The number of clergy in the diocese almost doubled during his episcopate. He founded a network of Catholic social service organisations, reflecting his view that the church, rather than the state, was the appropriate vehicle for the administration of SOCIAL WELFARE. His suspicion of the state was most marked in his stern opposition to the MOTHER AND CHILD SCHEME (1951). His management style was authoritarian but superbly efficient; doctrinally, he was a conservative with a strong Marian devotion. He had an ill-disguised lack of sympathy for ECUMENISM and the reforms of the Second VATICAN COUNCIL (1962–5). He promulgated and renewed a prohibition on Catholics attending TRINITY COLLEGE, Dublin, for most of his episcopate. Externally rigorous, he was privately compassionate and charitable. McQuaid was perhaps the most forceful and influential of the Irish Catholic bishops at the apogee of Catholic power in Ireland. **Fergal Tobin**

Macran, Henry Stewart (1867–1937), philosopher. Born in Dublin; educated at TCD and the University of Oxford. He was professor of moral philosophy at Trinity, 1901–34. An enthusiastic proponent of German idealist philosophy, he published *Hegel's Doctrine of Formal Logic* in 1912; he also wrote on Greek musical theory. **Ian Leask**

MacRory, Joseph (1861–1945), cardinal. Born in Ballygawley, Co. Tyrone; educated at ST PATRICK'S COLLEGE, Maynooth. He was ordained in 1885 and in the same year founded Dungannon Academy, a Catholic boys' secondary school. Professor of Sacred Scripture and Hebrew at Maynooth, 1889, and vice-president of the college, 1912, he co-founded the *Irish Theological Quarterly* in 1906. He was appointed Bishop of Down and Connor, 1915, Archbishop of Armagh, 1928, and cardinal, 1929. **Fergal Tobin**

MacSharry, Ray (1938–), politician. Born in Sligo; educated at Summerhill College, Sligo. He was elected to DÁIL ÉIREANN for Fianna Fáil in 1969 for the Sligo-Leitrim constituency. He was a loyal supporter of CHARLES HAUGHEY, nominating him for the party leadership in 1979. He served as Minister of State at the Department of Finance and Public Service, Minister for Agriculture, TÁNAISTE, and Minister for Finance in 1982. He returned as Minister for Finance in 1987, introducing drastic cutbacks in public spending to correct large budget deficits. He was elected to the European Parliament in 1984 and in 1989 became EU Commissioner for Agriculture and Rural Development. He made many reforms to the COMMON AGRICULTURAL POLICY (CAP). **Martin Clancy**

Mac Síomóin, Tomás (1938–), writer. Born in Dublin; educated at UCD. He spent periods of research in the Netherlands and the United States, was awarded a doctorate in biology from Cornell University, then taught biology in the College of Technology, Kevin Street (now DIT), Dublin. A lifelong political and Irish-language activist, he also spent many years in journalism with the newspaper *Anois* and the magazine COMHAR. He has published several well-regarded short stories but is best known for his poetry: *Damhna agus Dánta Eile* (1974), *Codarsnaí* (1981), *Cré agus Cláirseach* (1983), and *Scian* (selected poems, 1989). With Douglas Sealy he edited and translated MÁIRTÍN Ó DIREÁIN's *Tacar Dánta/Selected Poems* (1984). **Antain Mag Shamhráin**

Mac Suibhne, Toirealach (c. 1818–1916), uilleann piper, known as 'an Píobaire Mór'. Born in Gweedore, Co. Donegal, he came from a family of pipers and was reputedly as much a figure of FOLKLORE as a piper. He played at the World Fair in Chicago in 1893. **Maeve Ellen Gebruers**

MacSweeney, Seán (1935–), painter. Born in Dublin. He is a quintessential Irish landscape painter; his studies of the coast of Co. Sligo, where he lives and works, reveal a consistent vision and love of the land where it meets water, whether the ocean or the bog pool. His use of oil paint is rich and generous, and his work is deservedly popular. A retrospective exhibition was held at the RHA, Dublin, 1999. He is a member of AOSDÁNA. **Dorothy Walker**

MacSwiney, Mary (1872–1942), ideologue. Born in London, a sister of TERENCE MACSWINEY; educated at Queen's College, Cork. She was dismissed from her teaching post in 1916 for her political activities. After her brother's death on HUNGER STRIKE in 1920 she became TD for Cork. She played a prominent role in the shadow Republican government that existed between the Treaty and FIANNA FÁIL's entry into DÁIL ÉIREANN in 1927 but was never reconciled to this development and opposed the political structures of the FREE STATE and its successor until her death. **John Horgan**

MacSwiney, Terence (1879–1920), republican, writer, and politician. Born in Cork; educated at the RUI, and trained as an accountant. He helped found the Cork Celtic Literary Society in 1908 and later joined the GAELIC LEAGUE and IRISH VOLUNTEERS. Imprisoned in 1916 and 1917, he was elected to the first DÁIL ÉIREANN. Elected Lord Mayor of Cork in 1920, he was arrested and sentenced to two years' imprisonment. He went on HUNGER STRIKE and died at Brixton Prison, London, on 24 October 1920. **Seán Farrell Moran**

McSwiney, Veronica (1940–), pianist. Born in Dublin; studied PIANO with J. J. O'REILLY at the Municipal College of Music, Dublin (now DIT Conservatory of Music and Drama), and also studied in Salzburg with Bruno Seidlhofer and in London with Dennis Matthews and Ilona Kabos. A multiple prize-winner at the Dublin FEIS CEOIL, she played her first concerto with the RTÉ Symphony Orchestra at the age of fourteen. She has performed with leading orchestras in Britain, on the Continent, and in the United States; she was the first Irish artist to be invited to tour the Soviet Union for Goskonzert. She has recorded the nocturnes of JOHN FIELD (1972) and regularly adjudicates at international competitions. **Ite O'Donovan**

McTier, Martha, née Drennan (1742–1837), writer of letters. Born in Belfast, eldest child of a 'New Light' Presbyterian minister and sister of WILLIAM DRENNAN. In 1773 she married Sam McTier (died 1795), a Belfast chandler, who became president of the Belfast Society of UNITED IRISHMEN in 1791. She was herself involved with the movement, writing letters for her husband and small pieces for newspapers, and was a friend of THOMAS RUSSELL. Her politics were less radical than those of her brother, but she was a strong supporter of political reform and CATHOLIC EMANCIPATION and, like him, opposed to the Union. Their forty-three-year correspondence (1776–1819) is a major source for the political and social history of the period. She also shared her brother's literary interests, and her letters are written with considerable wit and style. They are characterised, however, by robust common sense and contain much bracing criticism and strongly worded advice. Childless herself, she was devoted to the interests of her brother and his family and was largely instrumental in persuading a cousin to leave her fortune to William. She lived for many years at Cabin Hill, Co. Down, and died in Belfast. **Jean Agnew**

MacWeeney, Alen (1939–), photographer. Born in Dublin. For many years he has been photographing TRAVELLERS, although he has found his subjects difficult to befriend. His social-documentary approach brings an intelligence to the way we perceive the travelling people and what is relevant about them. MacWeeney's work has appeared in *Life* and the *New York Times* as well as numerous books. He divides his time between Dublin and New York. [see PHOTOGRAPHY.] **John Minihan**

McWilliam, F. E. (1909–1992), sculptor. Born in Banbridge, Co. Down; studied at Belfast College of Art and Slade School of Fine Art, London. Henry Moore became a lasting friend. On receiving a Slade scholarship he visited Paris. He joined the Royal Air Force in 1940 and was on the staff of the Slade School,

1947–68. He received many commissions, including portraits, and created *Princess Macha* (1957) for Altnagelvin Hospital, Derry. A member of the Royal Academy (London), he was awarded an honorary doctorate of literature by QUB in 1964. His *Women of Belfast* series, commemorating victims of terrorist bombs, was created 1972–3. Retrospective exhibitions were held at the ULSTER MUSEUM, 1981, and the Tate Gallery, London, 1989. His work is represented in many institutions, including the Museum of Modern Art, New York, and National Portrait Gallery and Tate Gallery, London. **Theo Snoddy**

McWilliam. Princess Macha *(1957–8, bronze) by F. E. McWilliam outside Altnagelvin Hospital, Co. Derry. The subject links the new hospital and ancient Ireland; Macha reputedly founded the first hospital at Eamhain Mhacha in 300 BC. The dove seated on her left hand is a symbol of St Colmcille who built Derry's first infirmary at his monastery in the sixth century. [Irish Arts Review]*

Maamtrasna murders, notorious murders committed in Co. Galway in 1882, which led to the convictions of eight men. On 18 August 1882, a local man—probably John Casey—hired a group of men to murder an alleged sheep-stealer at Maamtrasna, Co. Galway. In the process they also killed the alleged thief's wife, mother, daughter and son. In search of scapegoats, the authorities withheld evidence and manipulated witnesses to secure the convictions of eight men. Three were sentenced to death; the remaining five had their death sentence commuted to penal servitude for life. On the eve of execution, Patrick Joyce and Patrick Casey confessed their guilt in a written deposition to a magistrate but avowed the innocence of the third condemned man, Myles Joyce. The LORD LIEUTENANT, Earl Spencer, refused to grant a stay of execution. A crown witness subsequently retracted his evidence and declared Myles Joyce and four of the five surviving prisoners to be innocent; they were not released until 1902. **Ciarán Deane**

Madden, Anne (1932–), artist. Born in London of Irish and Anglo-Chilean parents; trained at Chelsea School of Art, London. Following her marriage in 1958 to the artist LOUIS LE BROCQUY she moved to France. Her poured paintings (1960s) refer to rock formations of the BURREN, Co. Clare. Other works include the human-scale elegiac *Megalith* series (1970s), the *Openings* series (1980s), and the *Odyssey* and *Icarus* sequences (1990s). She represented Ireland at the Paris Biennale, 1965. Her work has been exhibited at the ULSTER MUSEUM, Belfast (1972), Foundation Maeght, France (1983), Arts Council Retrospective, Dublin (1991), and HUGH LANE Municipal Gallery of Modern Art, Dublin (1997). Her major painting, *Empyrius* (1999), is on the vaulted ceiling of the International Contemporary Art Centre of Carros, France; the main gallery there is named in honour of Madden and Le Brocquy. She returned to Ireland in 2000. She is represented in international and Irish public collections. A member of AOSDÁNA, she is the author of *Louis Le Brocquy: Seeing His Way* (1993). **Dorothy Walker**

Madden, Deirdre (1960–), novelist and short-story writer. Born in Toombridge, Co. Antrim; educated at TCD and the University of East Anglia. Her fiction typically explores with delicacy and compassion the impact on women's lives of political change, violence, and secrecy, particularly in Northern Ireland. She has received numerous awards, including the Rooney Prize, 1987, following the publication of her first novel, *Hidden Symptoms* (1986). In 1997 *One by One in the Darkness* won the Listowel Book of the Year Award. She was writer fellow at TCD, 1996–7. **Rachel Sealy Lynch**

Madden, R. R. [Richard Robert] (1798–1888), historian and administrator. Born in Dublin, son of a silk manufacturer. He practised medicine in London before 1833, when he accepted administrative appointments in Jamaica, West Africa, Western Australia, and Ireland. Writing poetry for the NATION, he also published a history of the UNITED IRISHMEN (1843–6), a history of the PENAL LAWS (1847), and a history of Irish Periodical Literature (1867). **Richard P. Davis**

Madden, Samuel (1686–1765), writer and philanthropist. Born in Dublin; educated at TCD. He was ordained a Church of Ireland clergyman and was awarded a doctorate in divinity in 1723, obtaining a parish in Co. Fermanagh. Through the DUBLIN SOCIETY he made funds available to encourage the development of various trades; he also contributed generously to the Physico-Historical Society, founded in 1744. He wrote extensively, often satirically, on economic, educational and legal reform issues. The poem for which he is best known, 'Boulter's Monument', was published in 1745 with the assistance of Samuel Johnson. **Brian Galvin**

Maelísa úa Brolcháin (died 1086), poet. Born near Culdaff, Co. Donegal; he lived in Armagh and died while on PILGRIMAGE to LISMORE. The ANNALS mention his death with honour. He was related to families of UÍ NÉILL and Clann Shínaigh. His corpus of poetry is deeply spiritual, mainly short personal prayers and hymns such as 'Deus Meus Adiuva Me', still sung in church. The longest, 'Ocht n-Éric na nDualach', preaches the dangers of the eight deadly sins. His name is associated with a *homilarium* and with the famous poem 'Crínóc', addressed to a hymnal in the form of a love poem. **Muireann Ní Bhrolcháin**

Máel Muire mac Céileachair (died 1016), scribe. He was one of the principal scribes of the Book of the DUN COW, his *probatio pennae* (scribal name) occuring twice in the manuscript. He appears to have belonged to a distinguished family of scholars and clerics with strong connections to the monastery of CLONMACNOISE. He was killed by marauders in the stone church there in 1106. **Séamus Mac Mathúna**

Máel Muru Othna (died 887), poet and historian. He was a member of the monastery of Othain at Fahan, Co. Donegal. An early poem recording the origin and wanderings of the Gael before coming to Ireland, 'Can a mbunadus na nGáedel' ('Whence the origin of the Gael?'), is ascribed to him. **Séamus Mac Mathúna**

Máel Ruáin of Tallaght (died 792), founder of the monastery of Tallaght (Co. Dublin) and one of the leading Irish churchmen of his day. He was much involved in the anchoritic reform movement of the CÉILÍ DÉ or 'culdees', which centred on his church. Among other works produced by this reform were two MARTYROLOGIES, one prose, the other metrical, both of which commemorate Máel Ruáin on 7 July, the day of his death. The metrical text, which also mentions him in both prologue and epilogue, extols him as 'the splendid sun of the island of the Gaeil.' He is also commemorated in the STOWE MISSAL, the earliest surviving Irish text of its kind and likewise a product of the anchoritic reform. Despite the many references to him, little is known of his background; his genealogy assigns him to the ULAIDH. **Pádraig Ó Riain**

Máel Sechnaill II (died 1022), mac Domnaill, King of the Southern UÍ NÉILL. He claimed the HIGH-KINGSHIP following the battle of TARA in 980. During his reign he struggled for supremacy with BRIAN BÓRÚ. He did not participate in the BATTLE OF CLONTARF (1014); but Brian's death left him as effective King of Ireland until his death on Cró-Inis on Lough Ennell. **Edel Bhreathnach**

magazines, journals and periodicals. The middle ground between the book and the NEWSPAPER has been occupied by a huge variety of periodicals since the days of the early pamphlets, broadsides, almanacs, chapbooks, learned journals, topical periodicals, and critical reviews. Magazines for a more general audience appeared in the nineteenth century; this development intensified in the twentieth century with a proliferation of titles, both general and specialised, aimed at the mass market. A growing range of magazines now competes with the imported (mainly British) titles that account for approximately three-fifths of all magazines sold.

In the twentieth century, notable publications included GEORGE RUSSELL's *Irish Spectator*, central to the LITERARY REVIVAL; the LEADER (1900–70), an offbeat journal of ideas founded by D. P. MORAN; *Dublin Opinion* (1924–70), which specialised in light but often potent humour; the BELL; and *Hibernia* and its successor, the PHOENIX. The monthly MAGILL has been the leading current affairs magazine since 1977. In Northern Ireland *Fortnight* (1970–) has long sought to promote rational political debate.

The *RTÉ Guide* is Ireland's largest-selling magazine; leading women's magazines are *Woman's Way* and *IT Magazine*; while the ultra-traditional *Ireland's Own* celebrated its centenary in 2002. The weekly *An Phoblacht* (formerly *Republican News*) is the newspaper of SINN FÉIN. Other English-language periodicals of note include BÉALOIDEAS (folklore studies); religious publications such as the *Irish Catholic*, *Church of Ireland Gazette*, and *Furrow*; the rock culture magazine *Hot Press*; *Business and Finance*; and the *Irish Farmers Journal*. The main emigrant newspapers are the *Irish Post* (1970–) in Britain, the *Irish Echo* (1928–) and *Irish Voice* (1987–) in New York, and the *Irish Echo* (1988–) in Australia. **David Quin**

magdalens, penitent prostitutes removed from society to institutions such as the Magdalen laundries. The Magdalen homes in Ireland originated with the eighteenth-century Female Penitentiary Movement in England, which set up its first home for prostitutes, Whitechapel Magdalen Hospital, in London in 1758. The first Irish home, the Dublin Magdalen Asylum, opened its doors (to Protestant women only) in Lower Leeson Street in 1767. A Catholic Magdalen home opened in Cork in 1809, and others were subsequently opened throughout the country.

At first the homes were largely run by lay people and were intended as a short-term refuge; however, following the arrival from France of the Good Shepherd Sisters in 1848 the temporary shelters became long-term or permanent institutions, whose inmates were discouraged from leaving and sometimes detained illegally for life. As the number of prostitutes fell, the definition of 'fallen women' was extended to include unmarried mothers, wayward or abused girls, and the mentally handicapped. Inmates laboured in the laundries attached to the convents and were subjected to harsh living and working conditions.

The Magdalen homes continued to operate almost unnoticed until the 1990s: the last Magdalen laundry closed its doors in Gloucester Street, Dublin, from where it had serviced the Seán MacDermott Street Convent of the Sisters of Our Lady of Charity, in October 1996. **Ciarán Deane**

Magee, William Connor (1821–1891), Anglican bishop. Born in Cork; educated at TCD. He ministered in both Ireland and England and gained a reputation for principled and evangelical preaching. He shared the dislike of the Irish bishops for the DISESTABLISHMENT proposals but, unlike them, was prepared to treat with the government, arguing that disestablishment would result in a 'lay tyranny'. Bishop of Peterborough, 1868–91, and Archbishop of York, 1891, he died in London within months of his enthronement at York. **Kenneth Milne**

Magill, a monthly current affairs journal published in Dublin, with a circulation in the 20,000s. Established by VINCENT BROWNE in 1977, it combines strong investigative stories with often well-written features and analysis. Gene Kerrigan, who later moved to the *Sunday Independent*, was its outstanding writer in its early period; its editors have included Brian Trench, COLM TÓIBÍN, FINTAN O'TOOLE, John Waters, and Emily O'Reilly. **David Quin**

Maginn, William (1794–1842), journalist and humorist. Born in Cork; a language prodigy, he was educated at his father's school and at TCD, being awarded a doctorate of laws in 1819. In the same year he became a mainstay of *Blackwood's Magazine*. After marrying and moving to London in 1824 he became a Grub Street regular, editing the *Standard*, writing leading articles for other newspapers, and contributing to magazines under dozens of pseudonyms, 'Ensign Morgan O'Doherty' being the most famous. His quixotic politics were radical-Tory, with unusual sympathies for the underclasses. *Whitehall*, a novel, was published in 1827, and in 1830 he helped start *Fraser's Magazine*, in which Thackeray's and Carlyle's early work appeared. After a duel in 1836 with the disgruntled subject of a bad review he drifted away from *Fraser's*, which was then edited by his friend FRANCIS MAHONY. *Miscellaneous Writings* (five volumes, 1855–7) and *Homeric Ballads* (1850) were collected after his death, following his release from a debtor's prison. Known as 'the Doctor', he was widely admired for learning and wit and deplored for irregular habits arising from drink. Sir ROBERT PEEL assisted the family after his death, in recognition of services to the Tory party. **David Latané**

Maginnis, Kenneth (Ken) (1938–), politician. Born in Co. Tyrone; trained as a teacher at Stranmillis College, Belfast. A former member of the B Specials, he was a major in the part-time ULSTER

DEFENCE REGIMENT for eleven years. In 1981 he unsuccessfully contested the Fermanagh-South Tyrone by-election against an H-Block candidate but won the seat in 1983 because of a split nationalist vote, retaining it until his retirement in 2001. As security spokesman for the ULSTER UNIONIST PARTY he repeatedly called for stronger action against the PROVISIONAL IRA. A former supporter of BRIAN FAULKNER, he always advocated power-sharing at local and STORMONT level. He forged contacts with Dublin politicians, attending the inauguration of President MARY ROBINSON in 1990, although critical of the definition of the national territory in the CONSTITUTION OF IRELAND. While sceptical of the IRA's 1994 ceasefire, he was the first UUP politician to engage publicly with SINN FÉIN. Viewed as a moderate within the UUP, he strongly supported the BELFAST AGREEMENT (1998). He was created a life peer in 2001 as Lord Kilclooney. **Eamon Phoenix**

magistrates, resident and stipendiary. Stipendiary magistrates were first appointed in the late eighteenth century in Dublin and subsequently in disturbed rural areas. They were responsible for issuing warrants, hearing minor cases, and directing the police. From 1836 resident magistrates were appointed throughout the country. No longer directly linked to the police, they were to reside in their districts and set an example to local magistrates. Replaced by district justices in the IRISH FREE STATE, resident magistrates performed all the judicial duties of the magistracy in Northern Ireland from 1935. **Virginia Crossman**

'Magna Carta Hiberniae', a name given to a version of Magna Carta approved by the minority government of Henry III shortly after the death of JOHN in October 1216 and extended to Ireland. Sealed by the Papal legate, Guala, and the regent, William Marshal, it was purportedly transferred to Dublin in February 1217, one of the earliest examples of the transmission of English law to Ireland, securing for the ANGLO-NORMAN magnates the same rights and liberties as their counterparts in England. The wording was altered to suit the LORDSHIP of Ireland: 'Ireland' was substituted for 'England', 'Irish church' for 'Church of England', 'Liffey' for 'Thames', and 'Dublin' for 'London'. It was transcribed into the fourteenth-century compiled manuscript known as the Red Book of the Irish Exchequer, from which transcripts were made by H. F. Berry and others before the destruction of the Public Record Office in 1922. **Susan Foran**

MAGNI: see ULSTER FOLK AND TRANSPORT MUSEUM; ULSTER MUSEUM.

Magrath, Cornelius (Corney) (1736–1759), giant. Born in Silvermines, Co. Tipperary. He had grown to a height of 214 cm (7 ft) by his sixteenth year. He entered the employment of Bishop Berkeley, who experimented with quack medicine and was widely credited with Magrath's great size. In 1752 he moved to Cork, where he was persuaded to exhibit himself, later travelling to England and the Continent. He died at the age of twenty-three after a fall. Medical students from TRINITY COLLEGE, Dublin, attended his wake, spiked the mourners' whiskey with laudanum, and stole his body. He was dissected by Dr Robinson, professor of anatomy, and his skeleton is preserved in the Anatomy School; it measures 219 cm (7 ft 2.25 in.). **Ciarán Deane**

Magrath, Miler (c. 1523–1622), pluralist and opportunist. Born in Co. Fermanagh. A Franciscan friar, after some years in

Magrath, Cornelius. Portrait of Cornelius Magrath *by Pietro Longhi (1757) inscribed 'True portrait of the Giant Cornelio Magrat the Irishman; he came to Venice in the year 1757; born 1st January 1737 he is 7 feet tall and weighs 420 pounds'. [Ca'Rezzonico, Venice]*

Rome he was appointed Bishop of Down and Connor. In 1567 he conformed to the CHURCH OF IRELAND and was successively appointed Bishop of Clogher and Archbishop of Cashel, a position he held for the rest of his long life. He harried Catholic priests while intriguing with Catholic rebels. Not until 1580 did the Papacy formally deprive him of the see of Down and Connor. He added the Anglican diocese of Waterford and Lismore to his charge in 1582, holding it until 1607. He was a skilled political go-between, and his knowledge of the native Irish world was valuable to the English government. He neglected his several dioceses, which languished spiritually, while acquiring a reputation for avarice and nepotism. **Fergal Tobin**

Maguire, Brian (1951–), painter. Born in Bray, Co. Wicklow; studied at Dún Laoghaire Technical School and the National College of Art. He is best known as painter and teacher for his work with the inmates of institutions such as PRISONS and mental HOSPITALS and with other marginalised groups. His paintings frequently take the form of portraits or figures in institutional settings. Exhibitions include 'Short Stories' (Hendriks Gallery, Dublin, 1984), 'Brian Maguire Paintings, 1982–87' (DOUGLAS HYDE Gallery and Orchard Gallery, Dublin, 1988), 'Behind Bars Public and Private' (Tallaght, Co. Dublin, 1991), 'Prejudicial Portraits' (Triskel Arts Centre, Cork, 1992), 'Body Politic' (Kerlin Gallery, Dublin, 1996), 'Violence in Ireland' (Lucia Douglas Gallery, Washington, 1997), and a retrospective exhibition at the HUGH LANE Municipal Gallery of Modern Art, Dublin, 1999. He represented Ireland at the São Paulo Bienal, 2000; works made in Brazil were subsequently acquired by the IRISH MUSEUM OF MODERN ART. A member of AOSDÁNA, in 2000 he was appointed head of fine art at the National College of Art and Design. **Peter Murray**

Maguire, Cúchonnacht Óg (died 1609), prominent Ulster lord and facilitator of the FLIGHT OF THE EARLS (1607). A member of the ruling Maguire family of Co. Fermanagh, he was a confidant of HUGH O'NEILL, Earl of Tyrone, and RORY O'DONNELL, Earl of Tyrconnell. Following the end of the NINE YEARS' WAR in 1603, renewed conspiratorial practices occurred in Ireland when the Crown authorities embarked on a campaign of persecution. Arrested by Lord Deputy Chichester in 1606 and questioned about rumours of impending revolt, Maguire departed Ireland 'without leave' shortly afterwards, only to return a year later, in disguise and at great personal risk, on a feigned fishing expedition with the ship that was to convey O'Neill and O'Donnell to the Continent in September 1607. He later accompanied the earls to Rome, perishing a short time later from disease. **John McCavitt**

Maguire, Hugh (1926–), violinist. Born in Dublin into a musical family; trained at the Municipal College of Music and the Royal Academy of Music, London, followed by a period of study with Georges Enesco in Paris. One of the most distinguished musicians to have come from Ireland, he was leader of the Bournemouth Municipal (Symphony) Orchestra, 1953–6, London Symphony Orchestra, 1956–62, Allegri Quartet, 1968–76, and Melos Ensemble, 1977. He was also co-leader of the Orchestra of the Royal Opera House, Covent Garden, 1983–91. He is professor at the Royal Academy of Music, London, and director of string studies at the Britten-Pears School since 1979. **John Page**

Maguire, Seán (1924–), traditional fiddler. Born in Co. Cavan, a son of the whistle and piccolo-player Johnnie Maguire. A legendary figure for fifty years, he applies classic bowing and intonation with Scottish sensibility to Irish MUSIC. He first broadcast on radio at the age of fifteen and won the OIREACHTAS competition in 1949. Thus led to professionalism, he performed with many CÉILÍ BANDS, including Malachy Sweeny's and Johnny Pickering's, and with his own ensemble toured Britain and the United States. He has produced many albums, most recently *The Master's Touch*. **Fintan Vallely**

'Maguire Seven', a name given to an Irish family living in London, together with a family friend, who were falsely convicted of charges relating to explosives in 1975. Annie Maguire, her husband, Patrick Maguire, and her brother Seán Smyth each served ten years. Their two sons, Patrick and Vincent, served four and five years, respectively. Annie Maguire's brother-in-law Giuseppe Conlon, who had travelled to London from Belfast after his son Gerard Conlon (one of the 'GUILDFORD FOUR') had been falsely accused of involvement in IRA bombings, died in prison in 1980. A family friend, Patrick O'Neil, served eight years. The convictions were overturned in 1991 following a lengthy campaign to clear their names. **Martin Clancy**

Mahaffy, Sir John Pentland (1839–1919), academic, clergyman, and author. Born in Vevey, Switzerland; educated privately and at TCD and ordained in 1864. A fellow, senior fellow and professor of ancient history in his alma mater, he achieved the provostship in 1914. He won distinction and renown as a scholar and author in the classics, philosophy, and history. A staunch unionist, he became embroiled in controversy with the GAELIC LEAGUE. A famed wit and conversationalist, he was an influence both on OSCAR WILDE (who travelled with him in Greece) and on OLIVER ST JOHN GOGARTY. He was knighted in 1918. **Terence Brown**

Maher, Alice (1956–), artist. Born in Co. Tipperary; educated at the University of Limerick, then studied at Crawford College of Art, Cork, and Belfast College of Art, and won a Fulbright Scholarship to San Francisco Art Institute, 1986–8. A sculptor, painter, and draughtswoman, among her most impressive works are her large-scale charcoal drawings of women's hair, sometimes executed directly onto a wall. Her sculptures are witty, sharp and subversive and often tiny in scale, occasionally accompanied by a related painting. She is a member of AOSDÁNA. **Dorothy Walker**

Mahon, Charles (1800–1891), adventurer, mercenary, and politician; during his adult life he referred to himself as 'the O'Gorman Mahon' (O'Gorman was his mother's surname). Born in Ennis, Co. Clare; educated privately and at TCD. A member of the CATHOLIC ASSOCIATION, he was elected to the British Parliament for Co. Clare in 1830 but in 1831 lost his seat on charges of bribery. He was called to the bar in 1834 but did not practise, choosing instead to travel. In France he befriended Talleyrand and became acquainted with King Louis-Philippe. Having travelled in Africa, Asia, and South America, he returned to Ireland to represent Ennis in Parliament, 1847–52. He moved again to France in 1853 and from there to Russia, where he was a lieutenant in the Tsar's international bodyguard. He served in the Turkish and Austrian armies, became a general in the Uruguayan army, and an admiral in the Chilean navy in the war against Spain. He fought for the Union side in the American Civil War, then returned to Paris to serve as a colonel in the regiment of chasseurs serving Napoléon III. In 1867 he moved to Berlin, where his remarkable gift for friendship brought him the acquaintance of Bismarck.

He returned to Ireland in 1871, becoming a delegate to the HOME RULE Convention (1873), a supporter of PARNELL and an opponent of BUTT. He was re-elected for Co. Clare, 1879–80, and represented Co. Carlow, 1887–91. His fellow MP for Clare (a two-seat constituency) was CAPTAIN O'SHEA, whom he claimed to have introduced to Parnell. Subsequently he was an anti-Parnellite in the split in the IRISH PARTY following the O'Shea divorce. **Ciarán Deane**

Mahon, Derek (1942–), poet. Born in Belfast; educated at RBAI and TCD. After travelling in Canada and the United States and teaching briefly in Belfast he moved to London in 1971, where he worked as a literary journalist for fifteen years. His first book, *Night Crossing* (1968), was followed by *Lives* (1972), *The Snow Party* (1975), *Poems, 1962–78* (1979), and *The Hunt by Night* (1982), establishing him, with MICHAEL LONGLEY and SEAMUS HEANEY, as a leading member of the generation of poets to put Northern Ireland on the literary map during the 'TROUBLES'; 'On a Disused Shed in Co. Wexford' was recognised as a major work in modern Irish writing. *Antarctica* (1985), a bleak harvest of terminal lyrics, followed; but for the next decade Mahon's energies went into translation: *De Nerval's Chimeras* (1982), two brilliantly theatrical adaptations of Molière, *High Time* (1985), *School for Wives* (1986), *Selected Poems of Philippe Jaccottet* (1988), and *The Bacchae* (1991). After a period as writer in residence at the New University of Ulster and Trinity College, Dublin, he moved to the United States, working as writer in residence at various universities, including New York University, then returned to Dublin in 1995. In the 1990s came two ambitious, moving sequences, *The Hudson Letter* (1995), a representation of personal and cultural crisis in New York, and *The Yellow Book* (1997), an ironic reflection on decadence in Dublin and the previous *fin de siècle*, combining autobiography and cultural critique. *Collected Poems* (1999) confirmed him as a major twentieth-century lyric poet. He was joint-editor (with PETER FALLON) of *The Penguin Book of Contemporary Irish Verse* (1990). *Journalism* (edited by TERENCE BROWN, 1996) is a selection of essays and reviews. His *Collected Poems* were published in 1999. **Hugh Haughton**

Mahony, Francis Sylvester (1804–1866), writer. Born in Cork; educated in France. He was expelled from his teaching position in Clongowes Wood College; ordained at Lucca but subsequently left his parish in Cork, thenceforth earning his living as a journalist. His pen-name, Father Prout, first appeared in *Fraser's Magazine* in 1831, and a volume of his humorous poetry, *The Reliques of Father Prout* (which includes his famous 'The Bells of Shandon'), was published in 1836. In Rome as a foreign correspondent he wrote satirical sketches (under the pseudonym Don Jeremy Savonarola), collected in *Facts and Figures from Italy* (1841). He settled in Paris in 1848, writing for the *Globe* till his death. **A. Norman Jeffares**

mail conveyance (road and rail). Mails were carried on horseback by postboys before the Irish Post Office began regular mail coach services on principal routes in 1789. Following the opening of the DUBLIN AND KINGSTOWN RAILWAY, the first mail trains began operating in 1835; when the Great Southern and Western Railway reached the outskirts of Cork in 1849, a fast mail train was introduced, carrying first and second-class passengers with a journey time of seven hours. 'Travelling post offices' (TPOs) were introduced on the Dublin–Cork night mail in 1855 and on day services in 1861. When sorting officers were withdrawn from Cunard transatlantic services in 1868, a fast mail train with sorting personnel began running between Queenstown (Cobh), Co. Cork and Dublin; with the selection of the port for mail services between Britain and North America, thus saving a day, additional mail trains from Dublin were introduced.

The outbreak of the FIRST WORLD WAR saw an end to these services. Mail trains between Dublin and Belfast were introduced in 1865, but the TPO service ceased with the establishment of the IRISH FREE STATE in 1923. TPOs were introduced on other lines but were withdrawn as road communications improved. The final TPO, between Dublin and Cork, ended in 1994, though mail continues to be carried by regular passenger train. **Bernard Share**

Main Guard, the, Clonmel, Co. Tipperary, built in 1675 as the Palatinate Court House (until 1715) by the first Duke of Ormond, it is among the earliest Irish transitional classical civic buildings. A plaque on the façade bears the duke's coat of arms. In its original form, a five-bay street arcade carried on massive sandstone drum-columns supported an upper pedimented storey with cornice, which contained the court chamber. Converted into shops and dwellings c. 1810, in the early twenty-first century the Main Guard was restored to its original dignified form as the dominant architectural feature at the junction of the town's two principal streets. **Brian Lalor**

Makem, Sarah (c. 1898–1985), traditional singer. Born near Keady, Co. Armagh. She had a repertoire of some five hundred pieces, representing Irish, English and Scottish influences as well as contemporary popular song. A direct singer, she set out her phrases, in the words of David Hammond, 'like a storyteller, aware of the inherent drama.' Never a public singer, she earned iconic status through the use of her 'As I Roved Out' as a signature tune on BBC radio. Her songs are recorded on an LP, *Sarah Makem*, and in a short film of her life by David Hammond, also titled *Sarah Makem*. **Fintan Vallely**

Makem, Tommy: see CLANCY BROTHERS AND THOMAS MAKEM.

Malachy. Anglicised name of Maolmhaodhóg (1094–1148), a prominent reformer of the twelfth-century Irish church. He is traditionally associated with the church of Armagh, of which he was archbishop, 1132–6. Facing strong opposition from unreformed clergy there, however, he resigned in 1136 to become Bishop of Down. He undertook two journeys to the Continent, on the first of which he was promoted resident Papal legate in Ireland and on the second of which he fell ill, dying at the Cistercian monastery of Clairvaux, where he was buried. He was the first Irish saint to be formally canonised by the Papacy, following a petition from the monks of Clairvaux. **Marie Therese Flanagan**

Malahide (*Mullach Íde*), Co. Dublin, a coastal town 16 km (10 miles) north of Dublin and 8 km (5 miles) from Dublin Airport; population (2002) 11,616. Its safe harbour made it a useful base for the VIKINGS. Malahide Castle, home to the Talbot family for 800 years, was originally a three-storey tower-house erected by the Norman knight RICHARD TALBOT, Lord of Malahide, after 1175; with its 26 ha (64-acre) demesne, the castle has been under the care of Dublin County Council since 1976. In the eighteenth and early nineteenth centuries Malahide was a thriving industrial centre, producing silk, cotton, salt, and cod-liver oil. The coming of the railway in 1844 encouraged its development as a residential and resort town. The Grand Hotel was built in 1835, while seaside holiday homes were built for the wealthy at St James's Terrace and Killeen Terrace.

The town has grown rapidly since the 1970s, despite relatively poor connections with the city, though an electric rail service has recently been provided. It is now a fashionable residential area with a high level of amenity, including a new marina providing berths for 300 yachts. Despite the pressures of growth, the village has retained its character and has been a winner of the NATIONAL TIDY TOWNS COMPETITION. **Ruth McManus**

Malin Head, Co. Donegal, at the tip of INISHOWEN PENINSULA, the most northerly point of the Irish mainland. Settlement began in NEOLITHIC times, both PLACE-NAMES and archaeology testifying to the antiquity and continuity of human habitation in the area; Inishowen is particularly rich in Early Christian monuments. Malin Head is the site of a weather station, established by the British Admiralty in 1870 and later operated by the British Meteorological Office until 1939, when it was taken over by the Irish service. Lloyd's of London was first to use the headland for maritime observation, recording shipping movements from the Tower of Ballyhillin, a signal tower commissioned by the Admiralty in 1805. In 1902 the tower was superseded by a wireless station, with a 46 m (150-ft) radio mast built by the Marconi Company for ship-to-shore communication. The Post Office took over the operation of this station in 1910. Inishowen and Malin Head were intimately associated with the establishment of the Coastguard, a response to the large amount of revenue—£150,000 in 1822 alone—lost to the British Treasury from smuggling in the area. Look-outs were constructed around the peninsula, with stations at Malin Head and Bunagee. Malin Head is also important as an ORDNANCE SURVEY datum, from which altitudes relative to sea level are determined. In complement, the raised shoreline of Malin Head, formed 6,000 years ago, records the highest sea level attained in Ireland during the present interglacial period. **Colman Gallagher**

Mallet, John William (1832–1912), engineer. Born in Dublin, son of the engineer Robert Mallet; received early private lectures in chemistry from John Apjohn and entered TCD in 1849. After the award of a doctorate from the University of Göttingen and a BA from Trinity College he emigrated to the United States in 1853 and served as professor of chemistry in a number of leading universities. His marriage to an Alabama woman committed him to the Confederate cause, and he became superintendent of the Confederate Ordnance Laboratories, to be remembered as 'very useful in the manufacture of gunpowder.' His scientific achievements can be divided between his work on meteorites and terrestrial minerals and his determination of densities and also of molecular and atomic weights; fellow of the Royal Society (1873); president of the American Chemical Society (1882). **Susan McKenna-Lawlor**

Mallon, Mary, 'Typhoid Mary' (1869–1938), cook and typhoid carrier. Born in Cookstown, Co. Tyrone; emigrated to the United States at the age of fifteen. In 1906, when the household of Charles Henry Warren in Long Island, New York, was struck by typhoid fever, investigators determined that the cook, Mary Mallon, was the source. Tests showed that, though she herself was quite healthy, she carried high concentrations of infectious typhoid bacilli. Detained in a hospital on the East River, Manhattan, until 1910, she was released on condition that she avoid working with food; but in 1915, when typhoid struck at Sloane Maternity Hospital, Mallon was found to be working in the kitchen, under the alias Mrs Brown. Demonised in the popular imagination as 'Typhoid Mary', she was sent back to the hospital on the East River, where she lived alone until her death, convinced that she had done nothing wrong. **Kevin Kenny**

Mallon, Seamus (1936–), politician. Born in Markethill, Co. Armagh; trained as a primary teacher at St Joseph's College, Belfast, becoming a school principal. Prominent in the CIVIL RIGHTS campaign of the 1960s, he joined the SDLP and was elected to both the 1973–4 power-sharing Assembly and the 1975 Convention. The collapse of the SUNNINGDALE AGREEMENT was a blow to his career, but in 1982 he was appointed to Seanad Éireann by CHARLES HAUGHEY, resulting in his disqualification from the NORTHERN IRELAND ASSEMBLY, 1982–6 (which the SDLP boycotted). As his party's spokesperson on law and order from 1982 he was highly critical of the British government's handling of the controversial RUC shootings in Co. Armagh while vigorously condemning the PROVISIONAL IRA's campaign. In 1986 he was elected to the British House of Commons for Newry and Armagh in a by-election precipitated by the Unionists after the ANGLO-IRISH AGREEMENT. A staunch supporter of JOHN HUME during the Hume-Adams talks, he warned the IRA in August 1994 that they must end violence 'totally and permanently.' As the SDLP's chief negotiator in the talks leading to the BELFAST AGREEMENT he became Deputy First Minister of Northern Ireland, 1998–9 (see p. 791). He resigned dramatically in July 1999 to protest against the refusal of the ULSTER UNIONIST PARTY to form an Executive but resumed the position on its establishment that December. In 2001 he did not seek reappointment as Deputy First Minister and was succeeded by MARK DURKAN. **Eamon Phoenix**

Mallon, Seamus. *Seamus Mallon campaigning in the 1986 British by-election; he won the seat for Newry and Armagh. [Derek Speirs/Report]*

Mallow (*Mala*), Co. Cork, a market and industrial town on the River BLACKWATER, 32 km (20 miles) north of Cork; population (2002) 7,109. Mallow's origins were in the late sixteenth century, when the Earl of Desmond built a castle to control the river crossing. After his rebellion ELIZABETH I granted Mallow to the Lord President of Munster, and it passed by marriage to English colonists. In 1612 JAMES I gave the town its first charter, and another castle was built to strengthen its defences. In the 1640s Mallow was the site of several battles, culminating in its capture by CROMWELL in 1650. It subsequently became an important market town and transport hub; but in the eighteenth and early nineteenth centuries the 'Rakes of Mallow' became its chief claim to fame (or notoriety). The tepid mineral-water springs were the original attraction for visitors, but the town became associated with the uninhibited carousing of wealthy Anglo-Irish gentry. Even today Mallow is associated with HORSE-RACING and HUNTING, though these are only pale reminders of the Rakes' excesses. In 1841 the population was 6,900; it then began a prolonged decline, to 4,500 by 1901, but has recovered over the past fifty years. Mallow has a large sugar-beet processing industry as well as services. Increasingly, however, its proximity to Cork and good transport connections are facilitating commuting to the city. **Kevin Hourihan**

Malone, Andrew E., pseudonym of Lawrence Patrick Byrne (1888–1939), drama critic and journalist. *The Irish Drama* (1929) criticised the ABBEY THEATRE for its loss of vision. Parallel to Harold White in music, he was probably the most influential critic of his time. **Richard Pine**

Malone, Edmund (1741–1812), scholar. Born in Dublin; educated at TCD and the Inner Temple, London. He practised law until 1777, when he moved to London, establishing himself as a private scholar. *An Attempt to Ascertain in Which Order the Plays Were Written* (1778) began his career as a pre-eminent Shakespearian; his first edition of Shakespeare's works appeared in 1790. A friend of EDMUND BURKE and of James Boswell, his twenty-one-volume edition of Shakespeare's works appeared posthumously, helped to publication by Boswell's son. **Terence Brown**

Malone, J. B. [John] (1914–1990), hill-walker, author, and way-marked trail pioneer. Born in England of Irish parents, he settled in Dublin in 1931 and began a lifelong exploration on foot of his beloved Dublin and WICKLOW MOUNTAINS, keeping meticulous records of all his excursions. By 1938 his enthusiasm had earned him a regular column in the *Evening Herald*. During the years of the Second World War he served in the Defence Forces, where he learnt draughtsmanship; he subsequently became a map-maker for the Department of Posts and Telegraphs. He wrote three guide books for walkers and wrote and appeared in early television programmes about the countryside. He also wrote *Know Your Dublin: A Visual Guide* (1969), a book on the history of Dublin's

Malone, J. B. *Memorial stone to J. B. Malone overlooking Lough Tay at Luggala, Co. Wicklow, placed along one of his favourite walking trails, the Wicklow Way. [Walking World Ireland; photo: Eoin Clarke]*

buildings and streets. He is perhaps best known for his central role in the establishment of WAY-MARKED WALKING TRAILS and in particular the Wicklow Way. **Michael Fewer**

Malton, James (c. 1764–1803), artist. Born in London, son of the architectural draughtsman and writer on perspective Thomas Malton (1726–1801); with his father he moved to Dublin in 1785. He worked as a draughtsman in the office of JAMES GANDON for three years from 1781, when Gandon began work on the CUSTOM HOUSE, but was dismissed from this position because of 'irregularities'. His *Picturesque and Descriptive View of the City of Dublin* (1799) is a valuable and informative record not only of life in late eighteenth-century Dublin but, most especially, of the ARCHITECTURE of the city, then at its most splendid. His twenty-five views of Dublin, from which engravings were made, were taken in 1791 and completed on his return to London shortly afterwards. He produced them as aquatints from plates prepared by him from his own drawings, sold in sets between 1792 and 1799 and published in volume form in 1799. He also produced views of the city as watercolours, individually drawn and painted by him, ten of which are in the NATIONAL GALLERY OF IRELAND. His drawings are very accurate, except for some small details, probably because his perspectives were produced in London rather than on the spot in Dublin. **Patricia McCarthy**

mammals. Ireland has fewer wild terrestrial mammal species (twenty-eight) than Britain (forty-nine). This is a result of the difficulties during post-glacial colonisation. There are three recognised Irish endemic sub-species: the Irish HARE, the Irish STOAT, and the Irish OTTER, which can be distinguished from species elsewhere. The Irish hare is a sub-species of the arctic hare. Irish otters are darker than British and Continental otters. The Irish stoat has an irregular back-belly line, which probably results from the fact that it very rarely goes white in winter. Straight back-belly lines are found in Irish stoats, more commonly in the south. Irish stoats also exhibit a distinct size cline, those in the south being much bigger than those in the north. The rabbit, house mouse, and common rat are significant pest species. Other common native mammals are the wood mouse, pygmy shrew, badger, and fox. Hedgehogs are not so common as in Britain.

There are at least thirteen introduced wild mammals: brown hare, rabbit, bank vole, grey and red squirrel (reintroduced), wood mouse, house mouse, both species of rat, American mink, and fallow and sika deer. Most populations of red deer are also introduced, but there are also protected populations of native Irish red deer. The Irish ELK became extinct 10,000 years ago; six Irish terrestrial mammals have become extinct since then: the red squirrel, musk rat (introduced and then trapped out), brown bear, wild cat, wolf, and wild boar. It is assumed that the last four species were hunted to extinction. **D. Patrick Sleeman**

Manannán mac Lir, the mythical Lord of the OTHERWORLD, who had a special affinity with the sea, in which he reputedly lived. Much of the imagery in the texts displays his intimate knowledge of, and identification with, the ocean. Weapons such as his shield and his knife, which he held in a bag known as the Crane Bag, which also contained precious objects belonging to TUATHA DÉ DANANN, contributed to the image of the divine being. Literature of the tenth or eleventh century included him as a member of Tuatha Dé Danann; in later literature he appears as a trickster. Tradition also associates him with Oileán Mhanann (the Isle of Man). **Ríonach uí Ógáin**

mammals. *Male red stag. Native red deer (Cervus elaphus) have been in Ireland since the last cold period, approximately 10,500 years ago. A fully grown stag can stand 120 cm (48 in.) high at the shoulder and can weigh up to 190 kg (420 lb). [Seán Ryan]*

Man of Art: see FEAR DÁNA.

Manchester, the Irish in. Manchester in north-west England provided some of the most vivid icons of the Irish emigrant experience. It was the first English city to industrialise; by 1841 there were 30,304 Irish residents, 12.5 per cent of the total. The juxtaposition of great wealth, urban squalor, and a fast-growing working-class population provoked heated controversy. In 1832 Dr James Philips Kay published a pamphlet that argued that Irish immigrants provided a bad example to native workers, spending the minimum on housing and food and dissipating what they saved on alcohol. He quoted in full a report on 'Little Ireland', a small Irish-dominated district characterised by intense pollution and bad housing. The pamphlet helped establish the enduring stereotype of the Irish immigrant as a drunken, poverty-stricken inhabitant of poor housing.

By 1851 FAMINE REFUGEES boosted the Irish population to 45,136 (15.2 per cent). They settled in all parts of the city, but most were relatively poor and there were several Irish residential clusters. Thanks to a broader and more stable economic base, a more inclusive tradition of civic leadership, and a less numerous influx, local attitudes towards the immigrants, though still displaying traditional anti-Catholic and anti-Irish prejudices, never reached the intensity of Merseyside or Clydeside.

The year 1867 provided three hero figures and a national anthem. Timothy Deasy and THOMAS KELLY, head of the FENIAN MOVEMENT, were apprehended in the city but were rescued from a prison van. During the operation a police sergeant was shot dead, and on 23 November three Irishmen—William Allen, Michael Larkin, and Michael O'Brien—were hanged. A groundswell of sympathy elevated them to the pantheon of national heroes as the 'MANCHESTER MARTYRS', while the song 'God Save Ireland', composed by T. D. Sullivan and based on a slogan shouted at their trial, became the *de facto* Irish national anthem.

Ironically, Manchester also produced Irish political operators working shrewdly within the system. Daniel McCabe, born in Stockport to Irish parents and brought up in Manchester, was for more than thirty years a Liberal and Irish Nationalist councillor. He served an unprecedented two terms as Lord Mayor, 1913–14, and was knighted by both the Vatican and George V.

Irish immigration declined after 1861 but accelerated in the 1940s and 50s. Labour shortages enabled Irish men to break into skilled employment, and the expansion of health and welfare services opened new opportunities for Irish women. Few Irish emigrants of the 1980s came to Manchester, because of the decline of its traditional industries. By 1991 the Irish comprised only 4.9 per cent, and it was an ageing population, though there were many more of Irish descent. It is a remarkably well-led and organised community, with a dense network of social, cultural, welfare, and sporting organisations. In March 1996 the first Irish Festival was held, suggesting that the Manchester Irish were achieving the difficult balancing act of entering the mainstream of local life while preserving their distinctiveness. **Mervyn Busteed**

Manchester Martyrs, the popular description given to three Fenian activists who were publicly hanged in Manchester. The activists, William Philip Allen, Michael Larkin, and Michael O'Brien, were hanged before a crowd of some 10,000 people on 23 November 1867. They had all allegedly participated in the rescue of the Fenian leaders, Col. THOMAS J. KELLY and Timothy Deasy, in September 1867 at Salford, Lancashire, in the course of which a police sergeant, Charles Brett, had been killed. The executions became a rallying point for anti-British propaganda in Ireland and temporarily united all shades of Irish nationalist opinion against some aspects of government policy. **Oliver P. Rafferty**

Mangan, James Clarence (1803–1849), poet. Born in Dublin, son of a grocer. He worked as a clerk from the age of fourteen; ten years later he forsook the secure tedium of office employment for the perils of freelance existence as a writer. He wrote for Dublin journals, to which he also contributed poems, frequently translations from the German. He was employed by the ORDNANCE SURVEY, 1833–9, which brought him into contact with a brilliant circle of scholars. In this milieu he drew on the Irish poetic tradition to produce English versions of Irish-language poetry. His prose writings were often fantastic and extravagant, mixing whimsy, verbal play, and pyrotechnics with romantic and GOTHIC modes of feeling.

A poet of the 'romantic agony', Mangan affected the style and behaviour of what came to be called the *poète maudit*, achieving legendary status in his lifetime as a figure who might have stepped from his own overheated imagination. He was prolific, often contributing to the journals under pseudonyms (one of them, 'Clarence', he added to his own given name). His verse, with its sonorous refrains and iterative symbolism, has been seen by critics to anticipate the experimentalism of Edgar Allan Poe, while his creations of landscapes of the mind can be read as proto-symbolist in the French manner of Baudelaire and Rimbaud. His dispersal of selfhood in translations, pseudo-translations, and the literary alter egos implied in the use of pseudonym has also allowed critics to see him as a modernist *avant la lettre* and as the first Irish poet to deal with the alienation felt by many in the modern world. In this context JOYCE's regard for his Dublin predecessor is frequently cited as evidence for his anticipatory originality.

In the 1840s Mangan was associated with and contributed to the NATION, the Young Irelanders' paper. As a result, poems and translations that may have had their emotional source in Mangan's heightened sense of personal injury and self-pity (which he reveals in an autobiographical fragment composed shortly before his death) were read as nationalist effusions that responded to the grim conditions of FAMINE Ireland. One such poem, 'DARK ROSALEEN', became his best-known work, its blend of idealised eroticism and sanguinary intensity offering to subsequent patriots a peculiarly potent inspiration.

Mangan died of cholera, to which a constitution weakened by alcohol abuse and an unsettled life made him an easy victim. **Terence Brown**

Maning, Frederick Edward, the 'Pakeha Maori' (1812–1883). Born in Co. Dublin. In 1824 he went with his family to Van Diemen's Land (Tasmania) and in 1833 set out to explore New Zealand. He befriended the Maori people, who soon installed him as Pakeha Maori (naturalised stranger); he married a Maori woman and adopted the customs of her people. He was appointed a British judge and published *Old New Zealand*, a record of Maori life (see p. 781), and *The History of the War in the North with Heke in 1845*. He became ill in 1881 and died in London while seeking a cure. **David Kiely**

Mannix, Daniel (1864–1963), churchman and nationalist. Born in Charleville, Co. Cork; educated at ST PATRICK'S COLLEGE, Maynooth. Ordained at Maynooth in 1890, he became professor of theology, 1894, and president of the college, 1903, in which office he was host to the visit of Edward VII the following year. Sent to Melbourne as coadjutor bishop in 1912, he became archbishop in 1917, holding the office until his death. He opposed attempts to introduce conscription in Australia during the FIRST WORLD WAR and was a vocal supporter of Irish NATIONALISM. Granted the freedom of the city of New York in 1920, he was refused leave to land in Ireland the same year, his ship being intercepted by the Royal Navy. A crucial figure in the institutional development of twentieth-century Australian Catholicism, he established 108 parishes and more than 150 primary schools. **Fergal Tobin**

Mant, Richard (1776–1848), bishop. Born in Southampton; educated at the University of Oxford. CHURCH OF IRELAND Bishop of Killaloe, 1820–23, and Down, Connor, and Dromore, 1823–48, he was a noted preacher, author, and hymn-writer. His view that worship should be conducted in an architecturally worthy setting is expressed in the influence he exerted on church-building in Belfast and beyond. His two-volume *History of the Church of Ireland from the Reformation to the Revolution* (1840) is still consulted. **Kenneth Milne**

mantle, Irish, a garment, generally rectangular, worn by all in the Middle Ages as a protection, both day and night. It was made in many versions: *rug* (tufted), *caddow* (a different tufted weave),

Mangan. *Memorial by Oliver Sheppard to James Clarence Mangan (1901) in St Stephen's Green, Dublin, with 'Róisín Dubh' as the Spirit of Poetry below. [Mark Joyce]*

lined, and *blanket*. The more expensive were finished with a curled wool effect, produced by the insertion of jogs of felt or by shearing. Irish mantles were exported from at least 1482, being in demand throughout Europe because of inclement weather and because SUMPTUARY LAWS limited the use of fur garments to the wealthy. Though the heavy mantle began to be replaced by the CLOAK in late sixteenth-century Ireland, mantles were still worn in the eighteenth century; the term *cadó* or *cadogha*, describing a blanket or wrap, survived in Irish into the twentieth century. [see ST BRIGID'S MANTLE.] **Mairead Dunlevy**

manuscripts, early. The earliest Irish manuscripts survived as enshrined relics of SAINTS, cared for in MONASTERIES or by families of hereditary keepers. The eleventh and twelfth-century vernacular manuscripts were in the hands of the learned families. Examples of the former are the CODEX USSERIANUS PRIMUS, the CATHACH, the Book of DURROW and Book of KELLS, the Stowe Missal, the Book of Mulling and Book of DIMMA, and the DOMHNACH AIRGID. The enshrined books are naturally religious books (GOSPELS and Psalters), and many of them are renowned for their distinctive decorative style, based on a combination of classical detail, such as INTERLACE, the trumpet and spiral of older Celtic ornament, and Germanic animal designs. Beginning with the modest initials of the Cathach, which are unique in the European experience and already sacrifice the legibility of the letters to artistic achievement, the process comes to its peak in the opening pages of the Gospels in the Book of Kells. At the same time decorated initials are used to increase the general legibility of the text by their function as punctuation. The Irish had to learn their Latin, so punctuation and the division of words (which they pioneered) assumed considerable importance.

The eighth century saw the highest development of the insular Gospel book, with the Book of Durrow and the Echternach Gospels probably early in that century and the Book of Kells and the Macregol Gospels towards the end. In the tenth century there are still fresh ideas, as in the Gospel book known as the Garland of Howth, where the human figure assumes more prominence. Later decoration, however, is heavily influenced by these early designs and lacks the inspired originality of the earlier period; but even in the twelfth century the Cormac Psalter can astonish by the brilliance of its colouring. While Irish design had a profound effect on the decoration of Carolingian books, it was always subordinate to legibility. [see BOOK SHRINES; HANDWRITING AND SCRIPT.] **William O'Sullivan**

'marching season'. *An Orange Order parade in Belfast, July 1970, commemorating William III's victory in the Battle of the Boyne, 1690. The various sashes identify the lodges to which the Orangemen belong. [Popperfoto]*

manuscripts, illuminated, decorated books handwritten on vellum and produced during the Middle Ages. Insular manuscripts (those made in Ireland and Britain before the ninth century) combine Celtic, Germanic, Pictish, and Late Antique elements. The earliest Irish manuscripts introduce simple Mediterranean motifs of a fish and cross (as in the CATHACH), a *chi-rho* monogram—the first two letters of the Greek Khristos = Christ, are chi 'x' and rho 'p'—(as in the CODEX USSERIANUS), and red dots. The Book of DURROW, usually dated to the late seventh century, presents decorative GOSPEL frontispieces that in different variants appear in later insular books: a Gospel *incipit* (opening words) is enlarged to a decorated initial and prefaced by an Evangelist symbol and a *carpet page* (a full-page ornamental design). Other manuscripts include either symbols or portraits of the Evangelists, or a combination of both.

Starting with the Book of Durrow, smaller initials emphasise particular texts, with special treatment given to Matthew 1:18 (the *chi-rho* initial). Decoration and the use of colour increase in the eighth and ninth-century manuscripts, reaching a peak in the Book of KELLS (see p. 523). Monochrome pen-and-ink illustrations also appear, as seen in the Book of ARMAGH's Evangelist symbols. Alongside large-format books, pocket Gospel books with frontal portraits of the Evangelists were produced for private or missionary use, such as the Book of DIMMA and Book of Mulling. Some manuscripts extend the standard scheme of illuminated frontispieces by depicting New Testament scenes. Two such manuscripts, now in Sankt Gallen, Switzerland, and Turin, Italy, represent the spread of Irish art to the Continent.

The Irish style of illumination survived, despite the incorporation of Scandinavian zoomorphic and interlacing motifs, as exemplified by the twelfth-century initials in the Corpus Missal or Cormac's Psalter, and continued in the fourteenth-century initials of encyclopaedic compilations, such as the Book of BALLYMOTE and Book of Lecan. With the introduction of new monastic orders, foreign influences intensified, and many manuscripts were imported or commissioned from abroad: for example, a richly decorated Psalter was copied in 1397 for Christ Church Cathedral Dublin.

After the twelfth century, manuscripts were no longer solely produced in monastic scriptoria but were executed for lay patrons by scribes from the 'learned families'. The LIFE OF COLM CILLE with a portrait of the saint was made at the behest of a Donegal chieftain in 1532, while in the late sixteenth century the Burke family commissioned a book that contains Passion scenes as well as family portraits. Images of royal and town officials in contemporary dress feature in the late fourteenth-century Waterford charter roll, an example of a non-ecclesiastical manuscript production. Despite the arrival of printing, in 1640 HOLY CROSS ABBEY celebrated its revival with a manuscript whose miniatures display Renaissance influences. [see INTERLACE.] **Małgorzata Krasnodębska-D'Aughton**

manuscripts abroad. Ireland's turbulent past has led to the almost complete destruction of its early manuscripts, the exceptions being some of the few that were enshrined as the relics of SAINTS. We have to look to England, France, Germany, Italy, and Switzerland for manuscripts that were carried abroad by wandering scholars and pilgrims. Over the centuries these men continued to resort to certain sites with a long tradition of Irish contacts. Bobbio, COLUMBANUS's foundation in northern Italy, preserved an important collection, dating from the seventh to the eleventh centuries. Those of particular Irish interest are now divided between Milan, like the Orosius, perhaps the oldest surviving manuscript (after the CATHACH) in Irish script; Turin, which holds the remnants of an eighth-century Irish Gospel book; and Naples, which has early grammatical texts. Similarly at Sankt Gallen in Switzerland, in a house that grew up on the site of the Irish saint's hermitage, there is an early Gospel book and grammatical manuscripts. Reichenau, whither the Sankt Gallen manuscripts were moved in the tenth century during the Hungarian invasion, was also popular with Irish scholars, as was Würzburg in Germany, the scene of St CILLIAN's martyrdom. The ninth-century Sankt Gallen catalogue contains a section for books in Irish script. England, despite its own great losses, managed to preserve some important examples of early manuscripts deriving from the evangelisation of Northumbria by the Columban monks of IONA, such as the Durham Gospels; because the Irish taught the English to write, there is some uncertainty about the origin of some of these manuscripts. Later accessions, like the Macregol Gospels from Birr and the Madurnan Gospels from Armagh, were probably gifts; the latter is known to have been given to Canterbury by King Æthelstan.

The sixteenth and seventeenth centuries saw a fresh wave of Irish EMIGRATION and the establishment of new houses on the Continent, particularly at Rome, Paris, SALAMANCA, and LOUVAIN. While Salamanca has given its name to a well-known codex of Irish saints' lives, Louvain, a foundation of the Irish FRANCISCANS, is unquestionably the most important for the transfer of manuscripts. In the first half of the seventeenth century it came to specialise in Irish history and hagiography, leading not only to the accumulation of older manuscripts but also to new works in Irish, such as the Annals of the FOUR MASTERS and the Martyrology of Donegal. These manuscripts are now divided between the Irish Franciscan House of Studies in Killiney, Co. Dublin, UCD, and the Royal Library in Brussels. [see IRISH COLLEGES IN CONTINTENTAL EUROPE.] **William O'Sullivan**

marches possibly represent some of the oldest Irish music. They occur in a number of metres, including 4/2, 9/8, 6/8, 2/4, 3/4 and 4/4 time. One of the earliest noted is 'The Irishe March' from 'My Ladye Nevells Booke' (1591), arranged by William Byrd. Several marches in 6/8 time have made the transition to dance music in the form of the double JIG. Despite a brief popularisation by SEÁN Ó RIADA, marches are seldom played by today's musicians. **Jimmy O'Brien Moran**

'marching season', a term widely applied to the period each year during which a variety of loyalist organisations parade in public places in Ulster. The tradition began with the formation of the VOLUNTEERS in 1778 and has continued annually since then without a break. The first coat-trailing march, designed to antagonise Catholics, was probably at Lisnagade by Co. Armagh Volunteers in 1792. When the ORANGE ORDER was formed in 1795 the brethren decided to march every 12 July to commemorate the BATTLE OF THE BOYNE. Though PARADES were banned periodically under the Party Processions Act (1832), marches continued, in defiance of the law. The 'marching season' begins in March and builds up steadily to a climax each summer. In 1992 there were 2,744 parades and demonstrations, 2,498 of them described by the police as loyalist. Parades by the 'loyal orders' include local lodge church parades, Junior Orange parades (particularly on Easter Tuesday), district parades known as 'mini-Twelfths' in late June and early July, commemorations to mark the Battle of the Somme, pre-Twelfth church parades, Twelfth of July parades (in which about 100,000 people take part), the APPRENTICE BOYS' marches on 12 August and 18 December, and the ROYAL BLACK PRECEPTORY parades on the last Saturday in August. **Jonathan Bardon**

Marconi. *Guglielmo Marconi, in his Radio Laboratory on board his yacht* Elettra. *In 1899 Marconi made the first live wireless report on a sports event, the Kingstown (Dún Laoghaire) Regatta, Co. Dublin, from aboard a steamboat to the* Irish Daily Express *in Dublin. [Marconi PLC]*

Marconi, Guglielmo (1874–1937), Italian-Irish electrical engineer, generally credited as the inventor of radio communications. Born in Bologna into a wealthy family; his mother, Annie Jameson, was the daughter of ANDREW JAMESON of the Dublin WHISKEY-DISTILLING family of Daphne Castle, Co. Wexford. He spent much of his early childhood in England with his mother and his older brother. As a teenager he studied physics at the technical institute in Livorno. Marconi carried out his early radio experiments at his father's estate, the Villa Grifone near Bologna. Using a Ruhmkorff induction coil as a transmitter and a Branly-Lodge coherer connected to an earthed aerial as a receiver, he was successful in sending a signal over a hill to a point 1.5 km (1 mile) away.

Though many others have claimed credit for the invention, there is no established record to support the other candidates before Marconi's historic 'WIRELESS TELEGRAPHY' Patent No. 12,039 of 2 June 1896.

Marconi formed the Wireless Telegraph and Signal Company on 22 July 1897, with a capital of £100,000. The first live wireless report on a sports event was made in July 1899 when Marconi transmitted a commentary on the Kingstown (Dún Laoghaire) Regatta from aboard a steamboat to the *Irish Daily Express* in Dublin, which summarised it in successive evening editions. In 1900 he took out the historic British Patent No. 7,777 for tuned wireless telegraphy. On 12 December 1901 he was successful in transmitting the letter S a distance of 3,300 km (2,000 miles) across the Atlantic Ocean from Cornwall to Newfoundland. In 1905 a high-powered station was set up by Marconi at Clifden, Co. Galway, which from October 1907 provided the first reliable transatlantic telegraphy service.

He also established stations at Crookhaven, Co. Cork, Letterfrack, Co. Galway, Rosslare, Co. Wexford, Malin Head, Co. Donegal, Ballybunion and Valentia, Co. Kerry. Marconi shared (with Karl Ferdinand Braun) the 1909 NOBEL PRIZE in Physics for important developments in radio communications. In 1929 the Italian government granted him the hereditary title of Marchese; the following year he was elected president of the Royal Italian Academy. **Gerard McMahon**

Marcus, David (1924–), writer and editor. Born in Cork; educated at UCC and the KING'S INNS. He worked as a barrister in Dublin before turning to an influential career as an editor, beginning with *Poetry Ireland* (a supplement to *Irish Writing*), 1948–54. After working in London he returned to Dublin as literary editor of the *Irish Press*, where he introduced a page for young writers. He also edited many collections and translated MERRIMAN's *Midnight Court*. His novels draw in part on his Jewish background; his *Oughtobiography* was published in 2001. **Peter Costello**

Marcus, Louis (1936–), documentary film-maker. Born in Cork; his early career in the 1960s included films for GAEL-LINN. His most accomplished productions have been on Irish history—*An Tine Bheo* (1966), on the 1916 RISING; *The Heritage of Ireland* (1978), a television series; a biography of PATRICK PEARSE, *Revival: Pearse's Concept of Ireland* (1979); and *Famine* (1995)—but among his more than fifty documentaries there have been programmes on contemporary Irish life, sport, and entertainment, such as *The Entertainers* (1987). A leading participant in the campaign for an indigenous Irish CINEMA, he wrote an influential series of articles in the IRISH TIMES, 1967, and was a member of the ARTS COUNCIL and chairman of BORD SCANNÁN NA HÉIREANN. **Kevin Rockett**

Maria Duce ('under Mary's leadership'), a right-wing and anti-Semitic Catholic movement founded in 1942 by a Holy Ghost priest, Dr Denis Fahey (1883–1954). He occupied the most extreme wing of CATHOLICISM at the time, putting forward the view that there was one proper social order, willed by God. The movement campaigned for the state to formally recognise the Catholic Church as the one true church, claiming that article 44 of the CONSTITUTION of Ireland, which at that time acknowledged the 'special position' of the Catholic Church, did not go far enough. In 1949 Maria Duce began petitioning for a constitutional amendment, but its proposals were never debated in the Dáil or Seanad, nor was it ever fully supported by the hierarchy. In 1954 the bishops demanded that the movement change its name to one not associated with sacred persons; under its new name, An Fhírinne ('the truth'), it survived until the early 1960s. Under both names it published its views in the periodical *Fiat*. **Ciarán Deane**

marine engines. The firm of HARLAND AND WOLFF established a marine engine works in Belfast in the 1870s. The *Oceanic* (1899) had four-crank triple-expansion STEAM ENGINES, with a 94-in. (239 cm) bore low-pressure cylinder. The *Laurentic* (1909) had triple screws, with wing shafts driven by triple-expansion engines exhausting into a direct-coupled low-pressure turbine on the central shaft, an arrangement used also in the TITANIC (1911). In 1913 Harland and Wolff began a long association with Burmeister and Wain, developing a direct-coupled four-stroke marine diesel engine. Together they developed very large two-stroke and four-stroke single-acting and double-acting engines, culminating in the two-stroke opposed-piston engines built extensively from the 1940s to the 60s. The Harland and Wolff engine works were closed in the 1980s. **Ronald Cox**

maritime archaeology. Diving on Irish shipwrecks dates back as far as the seventeenth century; but until recent decades more attention has been paid to more accessible inland waters than to the surrounding seas. CRANNÓGS have been investigated since the late nineteenth century; and LOG-BOAT finds, many of them associated with the crannógs, have been documented and studied. Stone and metallic artefacts numbering in the thousands were recovered and documented during dredging for navigational improvements on the River SHANNON in the 1840s.

In recent years maritime archaeology has developed within the broader field of archaeology, rather than as a specialist area. Modern developments are often dated to the investigation of two SPANISH ARMADA wrecks in 1968 and the recording of a considerable quantity of ship's timbers from the Dublin VIKING excavations. The discovery of further Armada wrecks led to the legal protection of the National Monuments Act (1930) being extended to underwater archaeological sites in 1987. During the 1980s, sports divers tended to concentrate on shipwreck sites and archaeologists on inland sites, such as crannógs and ancient fording points. In 1990 these groups came together to form the Irish Underwater Archaeological Research Team; soon afterwards the HERITAGE COUNCIL began financing archaeologists to train and equip themselves as divers; and in 1995 amateur divers from the Research Team searched for and found the remains of a ninth-century bridge at CLONMACNOISE. By 2000 maritime archaeology had emerged as a profession, a major interdisciplinary scientific project had been carried out in BANTRY BAY, maritime sites and monuments registers and state archaeological diving units had been set up, the DISCOVERY PROGRAMME had embarked on an investigation of the archaeology of lake settlement, and the Centre for Maritime Archaeology at the University of Ulster had produced its first batch of postgraduate students. [see BOATS, ANCIENT; WETLANDS ARCHAEOLOGY.] **Deirdre O'Hara**

maritime history. The population of Ireland is descended from people who arrived by sea. There is evidence that early settlers did not abandon seafaring but extended the populated part of the country by pushing from favourable spot to favourable spot along the shoreline and up rivers in primitive boats. Marine archaeology on rivers, LAKES and coast has shown, by the recovery of many boats from prehistoric times and later, that shipping activity was extensive. Trade by shipping with the Roman world and Continental Europe continued throughout the Middle Ages, when the legend of ST BRENDAN's voyage, which in the 'NAVIGATIO SANCTI BRENDANI' became one of the most widely copied of medieval tales, testifies to a spirited seafaring tradition (see p. 774).

The VIKING settlement gave Ireland its first seaport towns, such as Dublin, Waterford, and Wexford, as well as new shipbuilding techniques; and Irish Vikings sailed as far as Greenland and Newfoundland. ANGLO-NORMAN settlers expanded the Viking ports and gave them charters, which enabled them to develop regular trading relations with English ports, such as Chester and Bristol, and also with Continental ports, such as Bordeaux in France and Porto in Portugal, throughout the Middle Ages. A survey of European merchant shipping c. 1540 credits Irish ship-owners with having very up-to-date ships, and certainly Irish seamen were quick to take advantage of the great North Atlantic fisheries that were then opened.

The TUDOR conquest from the sixteenth century severely restricted the further development of native-owned shipping. HUGH O'NEILL not only saw the importance of Irish commercial and fishing fleets but also considered the possibility of an Irish navy. His ultimate military failure led to a prolonged period of some three centuries in which Irishmen flocked abroad and, in considerable numbers, entered the navies or took service in the merchant fleets of various European countries. After O'Neill's death the majority of his personal household took service in the important navy of the Kingdom of Naples, closely associated with Spain. Other Irishmen went to Portugal, the pioneer country of European geographical discovery, and many sailed in an area of north-western South America later taken over by the Dutch.

While Irish seamen continued to serve in large numbers under the Spanish, Portuguese, and Dutch flags, it was France above all that benefited in the seventeenth and eighteenth centuries from a steady influx of Irish seamen. Irishmen continued to serve France at sea well into the nineteenth century, when ARMAND MACKAU was Minister of Marine, 1843–7, and Admiral Cary (O'Casey) also, 1848–9. Irish names are still common in the French navy: Commander Gabriel O'Byrne was the great French submarine ace of the FIRST WORLD WAR, and an Admiral O'Neill only recently retired. In North America there were no fewer than ninety Irishmen serving in the ships that, under the French Admiral de Grasse in 1782, carried out the naval campaigns culminating in the Battle of the Virginia Cape, which liberated the recently formed United States from British rule. The story of how the United States Navy developed to be the largest in the world is full of Irish names.

By the late seventeenth century Irish merchant shipping had successfully re-established itself, and Irish ships were regularly trading to North America, the West Indies, the Mediterranean, ports all over Western Europe, and Russia. Irish ship-owners' enterprise in opening up regular trade with ports in Russia is no doubt partly responsible for an influx of Irish seamen into the Russian navy, when one Admiral Crown (Cronin) played a leading part in foiling Napoleon Bonaparte's ambitions to conquer all Europe. Another Irish officer two generations later was in communication with Irish insurgents about sending a Russian squadron to the west of Ireland to help them, while Admiral Baillie, a native of Co. Cavan, has long been recognised as one of the greatest frigate captains of the Napoleonic era, serving Russia on the Black Sea, Mediterranean, and Adriatic.

In the nineteenth century a number of Irishmen served in the Chinese imperial navy, notably a master-gunner named Mellows from Waterford, while JOHN AND CORNELIUS COLLINS from Carrigaline, Co. Cork, are remembered in Japan for some fifteen years of meticulous training that led directly to Japan's hitherto insignificant navy becoming one of the most formidable. In South America WILLIAM BROWN of Foxford, Co. Mayo, founded the Argentine navy.

In the Adriatic also in the eighteenth, nineteenth, and early twentieth centuries Irishmen played a conspicuous part in the foundation and growth to formidable proportions of the Austrian navy, from Admiral Parks of Co. Longford, its first commander-in-chief, to GOTTFRIED VON BANFIELD, who won from the Austrian government every medal a naval officer could win.

A large proportion of the crews of British warships—in some years up to a quarter—were Irish from the middle of the eighteenth century onwards, and Irishmen were prominent in the naval mutinies of Spithead and the Nore in 1796 and in several individual cases in which frigates and other warships were handed over to the French or Spanish enemy by Irish seamen mutinying against inhuman treatment. Among innumerable Irishmen who won distinctions in the last two centuries in the British navy were JOHN MACBRIDE, who rose from ordinary seaman to admiral commanding the vital Plymouth naval base by sheer ability, when most promotion was by patronage; Sir FRANCIS BEAUFORT, inventor of the wind scale and the greatest hydrographer of all time; EDWARD BRANSFIELD, who rose to command a ship in which he was the first person to see Antarctica; and Charles David Lucas (died 1914), who in 1854 in the CRIMEAN WAR was the first winner of the British decoration for supreme gallantry, the VICTORIA CROSS.

Among Irish inventors and scientists who changed the course of maritime history were JOHN PHILIP HOLLAND, designer of the first truly reliable submarine, JOHN JOLY, marine geologist and radiologist, and Sir CHARLES PARSONS, inventor of the revolutionary marine steam turbine.

During the nineteenth century almost every Irish port had its own merchant fleet; Arklow, the last, transferred its fleet to the Netherlands in 2001. Belfast saw the founding of what was to be the world's greatest shipyard, that of HARLAND AND WOLFF, in 1862, and ships were built in a score of other Irish towns. Annagassan, Co. Louth, was long known for the quality of its largely seafaring population; in the 1860s and 70s no fewer than twenty-five ships were owned in this village, almost every inhabitant being either at sea or part-owner in a share system of one or more of the local ships. Annagassan has often been quoted as a prime example of the Irish maritime tradition that twentieth-century Ireland allowed to die.

ARTHUR GRIFFITH was the only one of the Irish state's founders to declare that for real prosperity, Ireland must have a strong maritime economy. His successors throughout the twentieth century ignored this important observation; they and the great majority of the Irish intelligentsia have turned their backs on the sea and its huge possibilities. At the beginning of the twenty-first century the only Irish merchant ships were cross-channel ferries, while the Naval Service that was improvised in the EMERGENCY of 1939 is too small to give full protection to the fishing fleet. One area of progress was the establishment by the Government of CHARLES HAUGHEY of the Department of the Marine and the very active Marine Institute, founded to study and improve the marine services. [see UNDERWATER ARCHAEOLOGY.] **John de Courcy Ireland**

maritime rescue. The Irish Coast Guard, a division of the Department of Marine and Natural Resources, is the national marine emergency organisation. There is a full-time staff of approximately sixty-five people at four sites—Dublin, Malin Head, Co. Donegal, Valentia Island, Co. Kerry, and Cork—and 700 volunteer workers at fifty-two sites. The Marine Rescue Co-ordination Centre is in Dublin; there are also marine rescue sub-centres at Malin Head and Valentia Island.

The fifty-two Coast Guard coastal units, at strategic sites around the coast, all operated by volunteers, have a capability and range of equipment, depending on location, that includes radio communications, breeches-buoy rescue gear, cliff rescue gear, and support boats and vehicles. The Coast Guard operates two civilian helicopters on contract out of SHANNON AIRPORT and DUBLIN AIRPORT. For co-ordination purposes the Coast Guard also has access to the resources of the ROYAL NATIONAL LIFEBOAT INSTITUTION lifeboats, eight Community Inshore Rescue Service boats, and two

Air Corps search-and-rescue helicopters based at Waterford Airport and Finner Camp, Co. Donegal. **Fiacc OBrolchain**

Markievicz, Countess Constance, née Gore-Booth (1868–1927), republican socialist. Born in London into the Gore-Booth family of Lissadell, Co. Sligo; educated at home and later attended art college in Paris. She married the painter Casimir Markievicz but rejected artistic circles for Irish NATIONALISM. Having joined INGHINIDHE NA HÉIREANN and SINN FÉIN, she went on to form FIANNA ÉIREANN. She fought in the 1916 RISING as an officer of the IRISH CITIZEN ARMY, but her death sentence was commuted because of her sex. She became the first woman elected to the House of Commons (1918) but did not take her seat. Minister for Labour in the first DÁIL ÉIREANN, she was president of CUMANN NA MBAN (1917–26). She rejected the ANGLO-IRISH TREATY, and fought and was imprisoned during the CIVIL WAR. Active in Sinn Féin until the formation of FIANNA FÁIL, she was re-elected to Dáil Éireann in 1927 but died before taking her seat. **Margaret Ward**

Markievicz. *Portrait of the republican activist Constance Markievicz by B. Szankowski, painted in 1901 while she and her husband Count Casimir Markievicz were living in Paris. [Hugh Lane Municipal Gallery of Modern Art]*

Markree Castle Observatory (1831–1902), was established on his estate near Collooney, Co. Sligo, by EDWARD JOSHUA COOPER. It housed the world's most powerful achromatic telescope, with a 343 mm (13.5-in.) lens and other splendid equipment. Observations resulted in the discovery by Andrew Graham in 1848, based on Cooper's calculations, of a new minor planet, which was named *Metis*. A catalogue of 60,066 stars down to the twelfth magnitude, many previously unknown, together with an appendix containing information on a further seventy-seven stars, all within 3° of the ecliptic, was published in four volumes (1851–6). William Dobreck became director in 1874 and studied binary stars and planets. When Albert Mart was appointed director in 1883 the emphasis shifted to meteorological observations, with some publication of ephemerides (for observations of the Moon and planets). Frederick Henkel, appointed in 1898, was the last incumbent until the closing of the observatory in 1902. **Susan McKenna-Lawlor**

Marmion, Joseph (Columba) (1858–1923), spiritual writer. Born in Dublin; educated at UCD. Ordained in 1881, he was a curate in the parish of Dundrum, Co. Dublin, then professor of philosophy at Holy Cross College until 1886, when he entered the Benedictine abbey of Maredsous at Denée, near Dinant, Belgium. He was elected abbot in 1909, an office he held until his death. He acquired a wide reputation as a preacher of retreats and a spiritual writer; some followers considered him a saint and claimed favours and miracles worked through his intercession. He was the author of several spiritual classics, including *Christ, the Life of the Soul* (1917). He was beatified on 3 September 2000. **Mark Tierney**

marriage. Article 41 of the CONSTITUTION of Ireland (1937) refers to the institution of marriage as the foundation of the FAMILY and pledges the state 'to guard [it] with special care … and protect it against attack.' At the time the Constitution was drafted, however, Ireland had the lowest incidence of marriage of any society for which reliable records are available: one-third of men and over a quarter of women in the 1930s never married.

The pattern of late marriage and high proportions never marrying had emerged in the second half of the nineteenth century and became extreme in the early twentieth century. Marriage rates rose sharply during the 1960s, reaching a peak at almost 23,000 in 1974, the highest number in the twentieth century. The number declined steadily from 1980, falling below 16,000 in 1993 but with a resurgence to over 18,500 between 1997 and 1999.

Alongside the changing numbers of marriages, the social role of marriage has changed. Until the 1960s marriage was the main gateway to sexual activity and procreation: pre-marital sexual relations and child-bearing outside marriage were socially unacceptable. By the 1990s it had lost that role: pre-marital sexual relations had become commonplace, and a third of all births were outside marriage. In addition, the incidence of marital breakdown had been rising and was part of the reason for the abolition of the constitutional ban on DIVORCE in 1995 (see p. 919).

The influence of marriage on the role of women has also changed. In the early 1960s only 5 per cent of married women were counted as active in the labour force (though it is likely that a further 20–25 per cent were economically active in family farms and businesses). By the end of 2000, 58 per cent of married women aged twenty-five to fifty-four were active in the labour force. **Tony Fahey**

marriage bar, the requirement that women leave paid EMPLOYMENT on getting married. Such a requirement emerged in many countries, including the Republic, in the 1930s in response to high UNEMPLOYMENT. It applied mainly to women's white-collar occupations, in both the public and the private sector, rather than to lower-level industrial or service occupations. In many countries the marriage bar waned in the 1950s when labour shortages became widespread; in Ireland, where labour surpluses have been larger and more long-standing than in most countries, it persisted until the 1970s—except for primary teachers, for whom the marriage bar was lifted in 1957 in response to a temporary shortage of teachers. The marriage bar was abolished in the public sector in 1973, and

DISCRIMINATION in employment on grounds of sex was made generally illegal in 1977. **Tony Fahey**

marriage, Early Irish. Eighth-century Irish law recognised three main types of sexual relationship: formal marriages, informal marriages, and unauthorised relationships, such as elopement and rape. A formal marriage involved a betrothal before witnesses and the payment of a bride-price. The contribution of the woman's family to the marriage fund determined her legal position within the marriage. Normally both partners would make an equal contribution and have equal rights. If one of the partners did not or could not fulfil the terms implied in a marriage, it could be dissolved. Informal marriages were especially suitable for concubines. Polygyny was allowed in early Ireland, and the offspring of betrothed concubines were legitimate. The Irish maintained their practices concerning DIVORCE, polygyny, and incestuous relationships, which by the eleventh century were considered contrary to Christian teaching by outsiders and which formed one of the pretexts for the ANGLO-NORMAN intervention. **Bart Jaski**

Marsden, William (1754–1836), orientalist. Born in Co. Wicklow. He entered the East India Company in 1770, serving as government secretary at Sumatra (now in Indonesia). Returning to London, he joined the Admiralty in 1795, rising to the post of first secretary. His *History of Sumatra* (1783), *Dictionary and Grammar of the Malayan Language* (1812), and *Numismatica Orientalia* (1823–5) are significant works of oriental scholarship. A founding member of the Royal Irish Academy in 1785, he presented his coin collection of over 3,000 rare eastern coins to the British Museum in 1834. **Brian Lalor**

Marsh, Narcissus (1638–1713), bishop and provost of TRINITY COLLEGE, Dublin. Born in Hannington, Wiltshire; educated at the University of Oxford. Appointed provost of Trinity College, Dublin, in 1678, he found the students 'rude and ignorant' and the town 'lewd and debauched'. He was nevertheless a notable leader of the college, advancing the construction of several of its finest buildings and promoting the use of Irish. He took up a bishopric and eventually became Archbishop of Armagh. He established in Dublin the remarkable public LIBRARY now known as MARSH'S LIBRARY, which remains intact and open to visitors. In a lecture in 1683 to the newly founded Philosophical Society he advocated a new science, the 'Doctrine of Sounds'. This venture into scientific discourse includes the oldest known instance of the use of 'Acousticks' in its modern sense, and he also coined the word 'microphone' (by analogy with 'microscope'). **Denis Weaire**

Marshall, Rhona (1902–1993), musician. Born in Birr, Co. Offaly; she studied at the RIAM with Edith Best and MICHELE ESPOSITO. A recitalist and broadcaster in Dublin and with Radio Éireann in the 1920s, 30s and 40s, she performed Mozart violin and piano sonatas with JAROSLAV VANĚČEK. She taught at the RIAM, 1926–85, and was professor of piano from 1948. **Éamonn O'Keeffe**

Marsh's Library, Dublin, the oldest public LIBRARY in Ireland. It was built in 1701 by Archbishop NARCISSUS MARSH to a design by Sir WILLIAM ROBINSON, a plain GEORGIAN brick building beside ST PATRICK'S CATHEDRAL. The interior, with its dark oak bookcases and three elegant wire 'cages', where readers were locked with rare books, has remained unchanged for 300 years. There are four main collections, consisting of 25,000 books relating to the sixteenth, seventeenth, and early eighteenth centuries. There are Bibles and prayer books, books on MEDICINE, law, SCIENCE, MUSIC, travel, and mathematics, classical literature, and a collection of oriental books; there are also books relating to Irish history printed in the last hundred years. The library has approximately three hundred MANUSCRIPTS, the most important being a volume of the Lives of the Irish Saints dating from c. 1400. **Muriel McCarthy**

Marsh's Library. Marsh's Library *(1898) by Walter Osborne, depicting studious readers in the oak-panelled interior of Ireland's first public library. [Hugh Lane Municipal Gallery of Modern Art]*

martello towers, circular or oval stone or brick gun-batteries, erected around the coast from 1804 as a response to an expected Napoleonic invasion. The most characteristic form is a tapering drum approximately 10.5 m (35 ft) in diameter, with a string-course and battered parapet. The entrance was at first-floor level, some 3 m (10 ft) from the ground, with a corbelled machicolation above. Internally the building, with walls about 2.4 m (8 ft) thick, was divided into the powder and shot magazine in the lower chamber and a residential barrack quarter at entrance level. The roof carried a pivoting 24-pounder cannon on a tressel, under the command of a master-gunner and capable of traversing 350°, with a range of 1.6 km (1 mile).

Thirty-nine martello towers are still standing (of a possible fifty), with a concentration in the areas of DUBLIN BAY, Wexford Harbour, Cork Harbour, Bantry Bay, the SHANNON Estuary, Galway Bay, and LOUGH FOYLE. The martello tower at Sandycove, Dublin, now called the JAMES JOYCE Tower, is celebrated for its association with ULYSSES. **Brian Lalor**

martial law, explicitly imposed in Ireland from March 1798 to 1806, in the aftermath of the 1916 RISING, in four Munster counties in December 1920, and in four border counties from January 1921. The suspension of civil law and its replacement with military law and courts was in all these instances a response to rising tensions or open rebellion. Arguably, the provisions of various INSURRECTION and COERCION ACTS in the nineteenth century also amounted to martial law. **Neal Garnham**

Martin, Thomas Augustine (Gus) (1935–1995), teacher and critic. Born in Ballinamore, Co. Leitrim; educated at UCD. As a schoolteacher he was joint-founder of the Association of Teachers of English, an indication of his lifetime commitment to the encouragement of enthusiasm and excitement in the classroom. *Soundings* (1969) and *Exploring English* (with James Carey, 1967) were seminal textbooks for generations of students, as were his contributions to Teilifís Scoile, RTÉ's schools television in the 1960s. He became lecturer in English at UCD, 1965, and professor of ANGLO-IRISH LITERATURE and drama from 1979 until his death, occupying a central position in academic and literary circles as director of the YEATS International Summer School, Sligo, 1979–81, chairman of the ABBEY THEATRE, 1985–9, founder of the JAMES JOYCE Summer School, 1987, general editor of the collected works of JAMES CLARENCE MANGAN, and a senator, representing NUI, 1973–81. His archival coup was the repatriation from New York of the papers of PATRICK KAVANAGH, whose biography Martin was writing when he died. His chief works are *James Stephens* (1977) and *W. B. Yeats* (1983); his posthumous essays, *Bearing Witness* (1996), demonstrate the range and ecumenism of his literary interests. **Richard Pine**

Martin, Con (1934–), soccer player. Born in Dublin. He began as a Gaelic footballer with his native county, winning a Leinster championship title in 1942. Soon afterwards he was found to be in breach of the rule that prevented members of the GAA from playing soccer, and was suspended. Thereafter he applied himself exclusively to soccer and after three seasons with Drumcondra joined Glentoran in the Irish League. It was from this base that he travelled to Spain and Portugal for the Republic of Ireland's first post-SECOND WORLD WAR tour, finishing as an emergency goalkeeper in a 1–0 win over Spain. When he left Glentoran in 1947 he joined Leeds United as a centre-back. At a time when Republic of Ireland players also qualified for Northern Ireland, he won six caps for the Northern team to add to his twenty-five appearances for the Republic. **Peter Byrne**

Martin, Sir James (1893–1981), inventor. Born in Co. Down. In his early career he was involved in the design and manufacture of aircraft and in founding the Martin-Baker Aircraft Company. After the SECOND WORLD WAR he concentrated on solving the problem of baling out from high-speed aircraft by means of an ejection seat. On 24 July 1946 Bernard Lynch from Co. Meath, a former member of the Air Corps, was the first to use the Martin-Baker seat in a live test. In subsequent tests he made successful ejections at 675 km/h (420 m.p.h.) at heights of up to 9,145 m (30,000 ft). The Martin-Baker seat has saved thousands of lives. **Donal MacCarron**

Martin, John, 'Cornelius the Irishman' (c. 1549–1575), cabin boy and alleged heretic. Born in Cork; following the death of his father, his mother married a tailor named Cornelius, and the family moved to Padstow, Cornwall. When Cornelius died, Martin and his mother, who became blind, were reduced to begging. He joined John Hawkins's expedition as a cabin boy but was soon demoted to the lower rank of sweeper. Following the defeat of Hawkins he was taken prisoner by Spanish colonial authorities in 1568. He eventually established himself as a barber-surgeon with a family in the Guatemalan village of La Trinidad. The agents of the Inquisition caught up with him and brought him to Mexico City in 1574, where he was accused of abandoning his Catholic faith. He was garrotted and his body burnt at the auto-da-fé. **Ciarán Deane**

Martin, Mary (1892–1975), founder of the Medical Missionaries of Mary. Born in Dublin, the eldest of twelve children of a wealthy merchant family; educated at Sacred Heart Convent, Leeson Street, Dublin, and Holy Child College, Harrogate, Yorkshire. She served as a voluntary aid nurse during the FIRST WORLD WAR; on returning to Dublin she qualified as a midwife. Working in Nigeria in 1921, she was shocked by the squalid conditions she found there. Drawn to the religious life, which she was convinced should be combined with medical work, she entered a congregation in Ireland in 1923 but left in 1925. After some years of illness she was permitted to found the Medical Missionaries of Mary in 1936, which pioneered the involvement of Catholic religious women in medical work; she herself was professed a nun in 1938. The order runs hospitals in Ireland, the United States, Italy and Spain, and throughout Africa. She was awarded the Florence Nightingale Medal of the International Committee of the Red Cross, 1963. **Fergal Tobin**

Martin, Philip (1947–), pianist, composer, and teacher. Born in Dublin; studied with MABEL SWAINSON, Franz Reizenstein, Lennox Berkeley, and Richard Rodney Bennett. A recipient of the Macfarren gold medal, he also received the UK-US Bicentennial Arts Fellowship, 1980, and gave master classes at Tanglewood Summer School. A teacher at the Birmingham Conservatoire, he is a member of AOSDÁNA and a fellow of the Royal Academy of Music, London. His orchestral works include *Beato Angelico* (1990), *Piano Concerto No. 2* (1991), and *Harp Concerto* (1993); chamber works include *Serendipity* (1993), *Soundings* (1995), *Ye That Pine and Ye That Play* (1995), and *Suite for Solo Cello* (1997); vocal works include *Thalassa* (1991–2), *Echoes under the Stones* (1992), and *Miracles* (1996). **Éamonn O'Keeffe**

Martin, Richard (Humanity Dick) (1754–1834), animal rights campaigner. Born in Dublin; educated at the University of Cambridge. He was member of the Irish Parliament for Jamestown, Co. Leitrim, 1776–83, and Lanesborough, Co. Longford, 1798–1800; following the ACT OF UNION, for which he voted, he was member of the British Parliament for Galway, 1801–12 and 1818–26. Known as 'the King of Connemara' from the great extent of his estates, which consisted of some 80,000 ha (200,000 acres) surrounding Ballynahinch Castle, Co. Galway, he was regarded by his tenants as a benevolent landlord. His act of 1822 for the protection of cattle from cruelty was the first legislation for animal protection and subsequently provided the precedent for the framing of similar legislation for the prevention of cruelty to children. In 1824 he was one of the founder-members of the Royal Society for the Prevention of Cruelty to Animals. He supported many other humanitarian causes, CATHOLIC EMANCIPATION, the abolition of the death penalty for forgery, and the provision of legal aid for those charged with capital offences. George IV dubbed him 'Humanity Martin'. **Brian Lalor**

Martin, Violet: see ROSS, MARTIN.

Martyn, Edward (1859–1923), dramatist. Born in Loughrea, Co. Galway. His father died in 1860, and Martyn was raised by his mother, a devout Catholic. Educated at Beaumont College,

Windsor and Oxford, he returned to run the family estate at Tulira Castle. He jointly founded and financially underwrote the IRISH LITERARY THEATRE, offering the Ibsenite *The Heather Field* in 1899 (see p. 1045). In 1900 he contributed *Maeve and The Tale of a Town*, which Yeats and Moore rewrote; Martyn refused to let his name be used, and withdrew. In 1914 he jointly founded the IRISH THEATRE COMPANY; he also founded the PALESTRINA CHOIR at the Pro-Cathedral, Dublin in 1902 and co-founded the FEIS CEOIL in 1896. **Anthony Roche**

martyrologies. The Irish martyrological tradition, in its surviving form, begins c. 830—perhaps in response to a decree of the SYNOD of Aachen (817)—with the compilation at Tallaght (Co. Dublin) of two texts, one prose (the Martyrology of Tallaght), the other verse (the MARTYROLOGY OF ÓENGUS). The exemplar came from LINDISFARNE in Northumbria, via IONA and BANGOR. The next phase of martyrological activity followed the Synod of Clane (1162), beginning with the compilation c. 1168 of the Martyrology of Gorman, followed by the Commentary on the Martyrology of Óengus, the Drummond and Turin Martyrologies. With the revival in learning in the second half of the fourteenth century many new copies were made of earlier texts, especially of the Martyrology of Óengus, which survives in more MANUSCRIPTS than any other such text. The latest martyrology of any note was that of Donegal, which MÍCHEÁL Ó CLÉIRIGH prepared for publication in 1630. **Pádraig Ó Riain**

Martyrology of Óengus, composed c. 830 by Bishop Óengus of Tallaght (Co. Dublin) in *rinnaird* metre, mainly out of the Martyrology of Tallaght. It is one of the very earliest metrical martyrologies and comprises 365 quatrains, sometimes of a high poetic standard, to which were added a prologue and epilogue. A commentary was written on the text c. 1170–74, probably at Armagh, and this accompanies the Martyrology in all surviving copies. **Pádraig Ó Riain**

martyrs (1200–1700). Most of those who have been accounted martyrs for their religion in Ireland died in the century and a half between 1550 and 1700. These deaths often occurred during or as a result of periods of political or military upheaval, such as the DESMOND REBELLIONS in the 1570s and 80s or the warfare of the 1640s and early 50s. In the eyes of the authorities those who were prosecuted to the death in these circumstances, either by normal judicial procedures or by MARTIAL LAW, were guilty of treason. Senior Catholic prelates, such as Dermot O'Hurley, Archbishop of Cashel (hanged in 1584), Richard Creagh, Archbishop of Armagh (died by poisoning in the Tower of London in 1586), and OLIVER PLUNKETT, Archbishop of Armagh (hanged in 1681 and canonised in 1975), were accused of political disloyalty, as were many clergy of lesser rank, as well as lay people, who were victims of the regime. Though they may not have suffered overt religious persecution, the status of martyr was conferred on them through their being publicly perceived as having died at the hands of those who hated their faith. This was the case also with Protestants who were killed at the outbreak of the rebellion of 1641, and Catholics who perished in the Cromwellian campaign of 1649.

The cult of martyrdom arose through popular veneration and also in the written records or MARTYROLOGIES, compiled to glorify the memory of the dead. Among the more prominent contemporary Catholic martyrologists were David Rothe and Henry Fitzsimon, while the work of Sir John Temple, *The Irish Rebellion* (1646), was an Irish equivalent of John Foxe's *Book of Martyrs* (1563). For both Protestant and Catholic communities in seventeenth-century Ireland a crucial element in the forging of separate confessional identities was the burnishing of the cults of their martyred co-religionists. **Colm Lennon**

Mary: cult and apparitions. The Virgin Mary has a special place in Irish literature and culture. The earliest reference to her is from c. AD 600; from the Middle Ages there is a growing proliferation of religious verse, sermons, prayer, and legends. We find artistic representations in MANUSCRIPT illustrations and on late medieval wayside crosses, sometimes as the 'Three Marys'. Devotional forms included the Rosary, the Brown Scapular of Our Lady of Mount Carmel, and the Little Office or Hours of Our Lady (a shorter version of the Breviary, common in Europe from the twelfth century). Afterwards devotions were introduced by clergy educated abroad during the Penal Times. *Muire* (Mary) is found in numerous place-names, the names of flora, and many churches, both Catholic and Protestant. There are wells and places of PILGRIMAGE, the most ancient being Our Lady's Island, Co. Wexford, from the early Middle Ages. The main place of pilgrimage since the late nineteenth century is KNOCK, Co. Mayo, site of an apparition on 21 August 1879 consisting of three figures on the gable wall of the parish church: Mary, St Joseph, and St John. Interest in all other apparitions, including moving statues, such as that at Ballinspittle, Co. Cork, from 1985, has in every case rather quickly waned. **Christopher O'Donnell**

Mason, Patrick (1951–), theatre director and manager. Born in London; educated at the University of London. He began working as a vocal coach and then as a director at the ABBEY THEATRE, Dublin, 1977, becoming artistic director, 1994–9. His visual flair revolutionised the Abbey's production style. He received a Tony Award for *Dancing at Lughnasa* (1992). **Christopher Morash**

masonic dress. The chief item of masonic regalia is the apron, symbolising the protective leather garment once worn by stonemasons. In the early eighteenth century plain aprons were worn, usually made of lambskin; but as the century progressed it became fashionable to wear highly decorated ones, hand-painted or embroidered with the symbols of FREEMASONRY. By the 1840s regulations about regalia had been established by the Grand Lodge of Freemasons of Ireland; and the Master Mason's apron has remained virtually unchanged since. It is of white lambskin edged with sky-blue watered-silk ribbon, trimmed with silver braiding, metallic tassels, and three silk rosettes. Lodge officers wear a sky-blue collar or silver chain, from which is suspended the jewel of office. Officers of the Grand Lodge wear their aprons and collars trimmed in gold braid, with the addition of gauntlets. Gilt chains and jewels of office are worn for this rank. **Alex Ward**

'Mason's Apron, The', a traditional REEL tune, also known as 'The Masson Laddie', 'Lady Carbury', 'The Mason's Cap', 'Gallagher's Reel', 'Wake Up, Susan', and 'Carton's Reel'. One of the earliest printed versions of the tune appears in the late eighteenth-century Scottish collection of TRADITIONAL MUSIC by James Aird. It can also be found in most major collections of traditional Irish music. The American accordion-player John J. Kimmel recorded the tune in 1915 on a 78 r.p.m. record; since then it has been extensively recorded by other musicians, such as Paddy Killoran and SEÁN MAGUIRE. **Maeve Ellen Gebruers**

Massey, William Ferguson (1856–1925), New Zealand politician. Born in Limavady, Co. Derry, son of a tenant farmer. In

Massey. *William Ferguson Massey (centre) was Prime Minister of New Zealand, 1912–25. He liked to portray himself as a man of the land and was commonly known as 'Farmer Bill'. [Hocken Library, Uare Taoka o Hakena, University of Otago, Dunedin; neg. no. 4226/27]*

1870 he emigrated to New Zealand with his family. A successful farmer, he was elected president of the Auckland Agricultural Association. He entered Parliament in 1894 and in 1903 became leader of the Conservative Party. He was Prime Minister in 1912, heading the first Conservative government for twenty-two years. A fervent supporter of the British Empire, he pledged New Zealand's loyalty during the FIRST WORLD WAR. He was awarded many honorary degrees and received the freedom of several cities, including London, Edinburgh, and Glasgow. **David Kiely**

Massy, Anne L. (1867–1931), marine scientist and pioneer conservationist. Born in Co. Wicklow. She gained a worldwide reputation as an expert in the classification of molluscs, particularly the Cephalopoda, the group containing octopus and squid. From 1901 to 1930 she was employed by the Fisheries Service to identify the molluscs collected in research voyages by the vessels *Helga I* and *Helga II,* as well as on expeditions to all the oceans. An expert ornithologist, she was one of the founders of the Irish Society for the Protection of Birds, the first nature conservation organisation to be established in Ireland. **Christopher Moriarty**

Master M'Grath, a champion greyhound. From Lurgan, Co. Armagh, he won the Waterloo Cup for coursing greyhounds in 1868, 1869, and 1871. He is celebrated in ballad, in the town's coat of arms, in the windows of a Lurgan church, and in two statues, one outside the joint-owner, Lord Lurgan's Brownlow House, where M'Grath is buried, and the other two miles north of Dungarvan, Co. Waterford, at Ballymacmague Crossroads. **Ciarán Deane**

Masterson, Patrick (1936–), philosopher. Born in Dublin; educated at the University of LOUVAIN, where he was awarded a doctorate in 1962. He has held various academic positions at UNIVERSITY COLLEGE DUBLIN, including registrar (1983–6) and president (1986–93). Vice-chancellor of the National University of Ireland (1987, 1988), he was president of the European University Institute, Florence (1994–2001). Masterson is internationally known for his *Atheism and Alienation: A Study of the Philosophical Sources of Contemporary Atheism* (1971). **Fionola Meredith**

matchmaking. Matchmakers (*spéicéirí*) were—and for some still may be—intrinsic to the process of MARRIAGE in Irish folk tradition. Professional matchmakers, who received payment for their services, were sometimes employed by families to strike an optimal deal with the intended party. Matchmaking underlines the importance of marriage, especially in an agricultural community, where a social stigma was attached to those who were unmarried. Irish literature, especially of the nineteenth and twentieth centuries, features the matchmaker as a figure of social power in society, negotiating the exchange of land, dowries, and wealth. **Anne O'Connor**

maternity and child care services. The foundations of the Republic's present maternity services were controversial and are steeped in a historical debacle associated with NÖEL BROWNE and the Coalition Government of 1948–51. The MOTHER AND CHILD SCHEME controversy was followed by a period of negotiation and compromise, which produced the Maternity and Infant Care Scheme under the Health Act (1953); this was superseded by the Health Act (1970). Eligibility for maternity services was means-tested until the Health (Amendment) Act (1991) extended eligibility to all women, in line with the extension of eligibility for all hospital services.

At present the Mother and Infant Care scheme provides for limited free pregnancy-related general practitioner care for the mother during pregnancy and for six weeks after CHILDBIRTH, while free care is also provided for the infant for the first six weeks. The scheme is based on the principle of choice of doctor; under this scheme the general practitioner has the right to refuse to accept any patient, and the free health care is confined solely to pregnancy-related ailments. The National Health Strategy, published in November 2001, increased the period of cover for infants to twelve months, including a total of six free GP visits for the infant and also including general childhood illnesses. It also recommended the establishment of a working party to draw up a responsive, high-quality plan for maternity care and to report in 2003.

In Northern Ireland the Peel Report (1970) recommended 100 per cent HOSPITAL confinement; this led to the increased availability of hospital beds. Ten years later the Baird Report (1980) emphasised the need for women to give birth in specialist units, leading to the closure of many GP and midwife-led units. The Report of the Northern Ireland Maternity Unit Study Group (1994) recommended that women should have the right to choose the form of maternity care they want and that they should be provided with full and accurate information to facilitate informed choice. It supported the development of midwife-led units at acute hospitals but rejected independent midwife or GP units remote from acute hospital services.

The Hayes Report (2001), produced by the Acute Hospitals Review Group, recommended that women be afforded as much choice as possible in relation to delivery and emphasised that childbirth is a natural event. The report recognised the value of midwife-led units but supported their provision only where the support of OBSTETRIC, paediatric, and anaesthetic services was available. It stated that everyone should be within one hour's travel of a consultant-led maternity unit and acknowledged the danger of a concentration of services in a smaller number of units, as centralisation might provide for a less woman-centred service. [see CHILDBIRTH; MIDWIFERY; NON-MARITAL BIRTHS.] **Patricia Kennedy**

Mathew, Theobald (1790–1856), priest and temperance crusader. Born in Thomastown, Co. Tipperary; he was expelled from ST PATRICK'S COLLEGE, Maynooth, and joined the Capuchin order. He was posted to Cork in 1814, but his career was obscure until 1838, when he agreed to lead an anti-drink society. His preaching of teetotalism as a panacea for Ireland's socio-economic problems won massive support in the difficult years around 1840, with millions taking the pledge. The crusade was losing momentum before the GREAT FAMINE as Mathew became distracted by financial and church problems. In 1849–51 he campaigned in the United States. **Elizabeth Malcolm**

Mathews, Aidan Carl (1956–), poet, playwright, short-story writer, and novelist. Born in Dublin; educated at UCD, TCD, and Stanford University, California. He won IRISH TIMES and PATRICK KAVANAGH Awards before his first poetry collection, *Windfalls*, was published in 1977; a second, *Minding Ruth*, followed in 1983. Turning to fiction, he produced two volumes of short stories, *Adventures in a Bathyscope* (1988) and *Lipstick on the Host* (1992), and a novel, *Muesli at Midnight* (1990). His plays include *Exit/Entrance* (1990). After a long poetic silence he published *According to the Small Hours* (1998), a collection that displays his gift for narrative in poems that balance the corporeal and the mystical. **David Wheatley**

Maturin, Charles (1780–1824), writer. Born in Dublin; educated at TCD and ordained in the Church of Ireland in 1803. After spending three years as a curate in Loughrea, Co. Galway, he was appointed to a curacy in St Peter's, Dublin, where he served until his death. His play *Bertram* (1816) brought fame and temporary financial relief; but he is remembered today for the novel *Melmoth the Wanderer* (1820), a sprawling gothic masterpiece, published as the campaign for CATHOLIC EMANCIPATION accelerated. Like his novel *Women* (1818) and his sermons, *Melmoth* repeatedly exhibits an appalled fascination with both Catholicism and Calvinism. **Richard Haslam**

Maude, Caitlín (1941–1982), poet and traditional singer. Born in Casla, Co. Galway; educated at UCG. She taught at schools in Cos. Kildare, Mayo, and Wicklow. As a member of the Dublin Irish-speaking community she was active in many campaigns, including the establishment of the IRISH-MEDIUM primary school Scoil Santain in Tallaght, Co. Dublin. An accomplished actor, she played the leading role in Máiréad Ní Ghráda's AN TRIAÍL (1964) and jointly wrote the drama *Lasair Choille* with MICHAEL HARTNETT; she also wrote prose and poetry. A superb SEAN-NÓS singer, her sole album, *Caitlín* (1975), is a classic in the genre. **Ciarán Ó Coigligh**

Maunsel and Company (1905–25), Dublin publishers, later Maunsel and Roberts. On its inception it took over the publication of W. B. YEATS's periodical *Samhain* from Sealy, Bryers and Walker and *The Abbey Theatre Series* of plays from that institution. Maunsel held the dramatic and other rights of these plays both in Ireland and the United States and also published some seventy other Irish plays. The firm also published the leading writers of the LITERARY REVIVAL, including Yeats, GEORGE MOORE, Lady AUGUSTA GREGORY, and J. M. SYNGE. In 1907 a London publisher recommended to JAMES JOYCE that he send the manuscript of *Dubliners* to Joseph Hone of Maunsel's. Its managing director, George Roberts, had earlier expressed an interest in publishing Joyce, but after protracted negotiations the sheets of the planned edition were pulped in September 1912, prompting a vituperative response from the author in *Gas from a Burner*. **Bernard Share**

mausolea. As defined by the architectural historian MAURICE CRAIG, a mausoleum is 'a funerary structure having the character of a roofed building and large enough to stand up in, or at least having that appearance.' Such monuments were usually built of stone and tend to be ponderous and solid in design. Found in many Irish graveyards, these impressive monuments vary in scale; but their guiding principle was a desire to 'set yourself apart from the rest of humanity.' Most of them belonged to families of great wealth or social status; and by being laid to rest above ground rather than in it there was the hope of being in a better state of readiness for the resurrection. There was more than a touch of vanity about the mausoleum, in contrast to the plain headstones of the QUAKERS and other denominations.

Among the outstanding examples of mausolea in Ireland are those belonging to the members of the landed gentry, such as the Barrys of Castlelyons, Co. Cork, and the Dawson family of Dartrey, Co. Monaghan. The Dartrey mausoleum, in the hilly lakeland of the Cavan-Monaghan border, encloses a sculpture by Joseph Wilton in memory of Lord Dartrey's first wife, who died in 1772. The monument at Castlelyons is a pedimented structure of brick and stone, with an ornamental wrought-iron gate and a staircase that give access to the vault below. Another remarkable example is the lavishly decorated tomb of the Murland family at Clough, Co.

Master M'Grath. *Statue of Master M'Grath at Dungarvan, Co. Waterford, erected by admirers and friends of James Galway (joint-owner with Lord Lurgan). The champion greyhound won the Waterloo Cup three times. [Irish Coursing Club]*

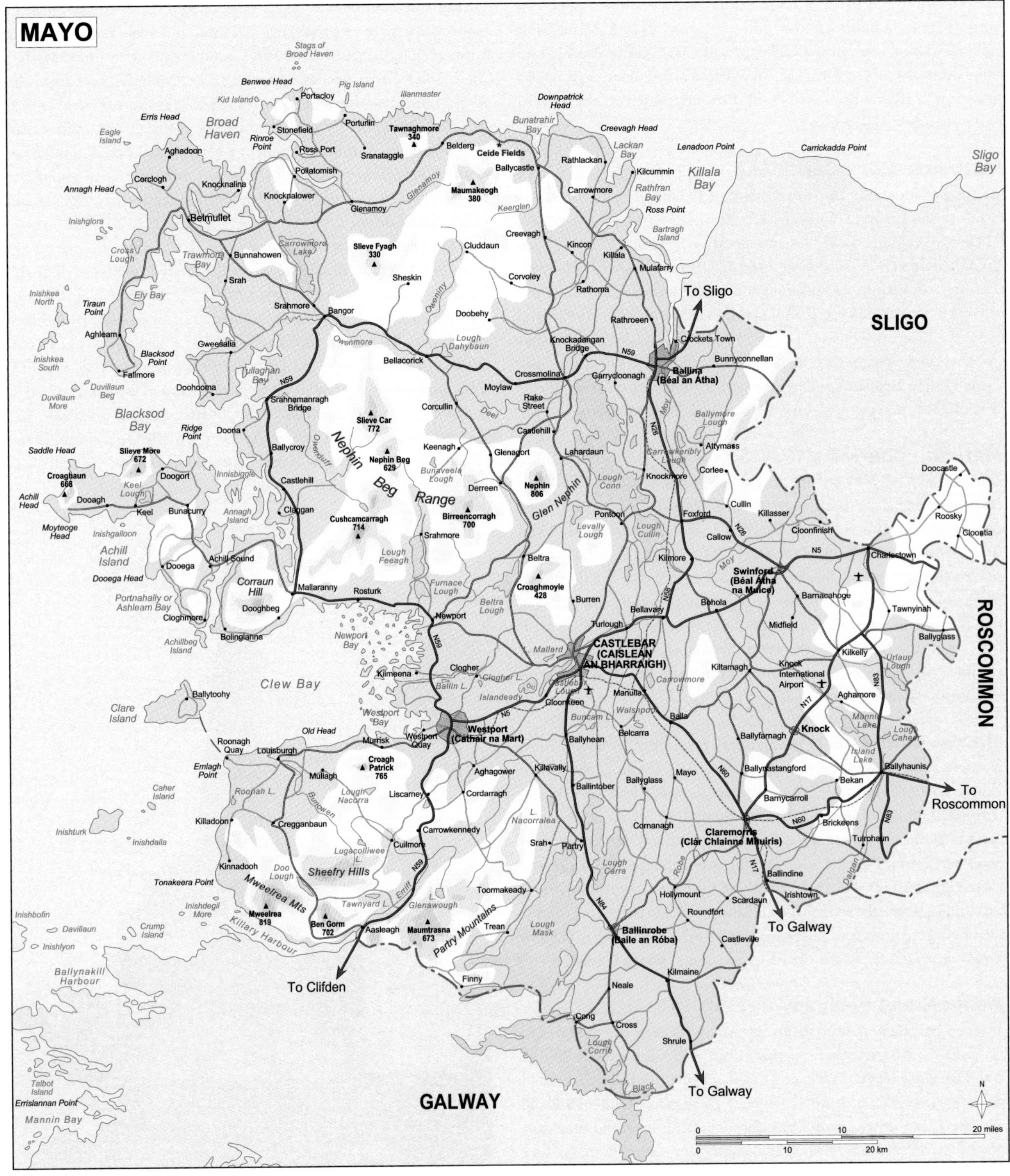

Down. This large mausoleum was built in a pseudo-baroque and neo-classical style in 1860 and stands rather incongruously behind a modest Presbyterian church. Equally dramatic is the granite pyramid at Kinnity, Co. Offaly, which stands aloof above a small churchyard. One of the largest is the stone-built obelisk at Stillorgan, Co. Dublin, designed by Sir EDWARD LOVETT PEARCE as the burial place of Lady Allen. Though never used as a burial place, it became an impressive landmark in the Stillorgan demesne.

Nineteenth-century urban cemeteries also boast many mausolea, often smaller than those on private estates but nonetheless impressive, such as the classical monument to THOMAS DRUMMOND in Glasnevin Cemetery, Dublin, and the neo-Egyptian tomb of Thomas Gresham in Mount Jerome Cemetery, Dublin.

Although the concept of the mausoleum derives from Egyptian and Roman practice, important families in medieval Ireland were also buried inside churches and abbeys. The tradition of burial even in ruined churches persisted for many centuries. **Peter Pearson**

Mawby, Colin (1936–), choral conductor and composer. Born in Portsmouth; educated at Westminster Cathedral Choir and the Royal College of Music, London. As a conductor he has worked with the London Mozart Players, Wren Orchestra, and BBC

Singers. He came to Ireland as Choral Director of RTÉ (1981–95) and was responsible for the creation of the RTÉ Chamber Choir which evolved into the National Chamber Choir of which he was director until 2002. His output includes nineteen Masses, five song-cycles, and a children's opera. He has been commissioned by RTÉ, Westminster Cathedral, Liverpool Cathedral, and the Royal School of Church Music. His chamber works include *Triptych for Organ* (1996); vocal works include *Festival Mass* (1987), *Mass of the Holy City* (1993), *In Memoriam Aloys Fleischmann* (1994), *Johnstown Choir Book I and II* (1996, 1997), *Prayer of Forgiveness* (1997), *A Modern Medieval Carol* (1997), and an opera, *The Quest* (2000). **Éamonn O'Keeffe**

Maxton, Hugh: see MCCORMACK, W. J.

Maxwell, William Hamilton (1794–1850), novelist and writer on military and sporting life. Born in Newry, Co. Down; educated at TCD. Among his many popular works was *Wild Sports of the West* (1832). **Terence Brown**

May, Frederick (1911–1985), composer. Born in Dublin; studied at the RIAM under LARCHET, graduated from TCD in 1931, and studied with Gordon Jacob and Ralph Vaughan Williams at the Royal College of Music, London, and with Egon Wellesz in Vienna. Director of music at the ABBEY THEATRE, Dublin, he was a founder of the MUSIC ASSOCIATION OF IRELAND, 1948, and wrote and broadcast on musical matters. His orchestral works include *Scherzo for Orchestra* (1933), *Suite of Irish Airs* (1933), and *Lyric Movement* (1937); chamber works include *String Quartet in C minor* (1936); vocal works include *18 Irish Songs* (1930) and *Songs from Prison* (1941). He also composed the incidental music for *Mogu* (PADRAIC COLUM), and Shakespeare's *Coriolanus*. **Éamonn O'Keeffe**

May Day, a traditional festival falling on 1 May (coinciding with the Celtic festival of BEALTAINE), the least Christianised of the QUARTER DAYS. *Bealtaine* is thought to derive from 'brilliant fire'. Myriad popular beliefs attend May Day, concerning the ancestral supernatural world and the magico-religious, from the gathering of the May morning dew to enhance beauty to the magical theft of neighbours' luck. The time for HIRING-FAIRS, it is preoccupied with the protection of the familiar. Flowers were picked to welcome the summer and an altar decorated in honour of Our Lady. Children collected decorations for the May Bush, and the FESTIVAL was marked by dancing, MUSIC, ritual fighting, bonfires, and MUMMING. [see CALENDAR CUSTOMS; IMBOLG; LUNASA.] **Stiofán Ó Cadhla**

Mayne, Rutherford, pseudonym of Samuel Waddell (1878–1967), actor and playwright. Born in Japan; trained as an engineer. He contributed work to the ULSTER LITERARY THEATRE and the ABBEY THEATRE, among others; he was also a trustee of the Lyric Theatre, Belfast. He worked for the Land Commission both before and after the Treaty, and his experience there informs some of the social and political tensions in his play *Bridgehead* (1934). Earlier and popular plays were set variously in Co. Down and other parts of rural Ulster. Standing out among these, *The Troth* (1909) exemplifies that radical social conscience that has always flickered in Ireland, testing the fruits of SECTARIANISM against the potential to be found in common unity. [see WADDELL, HELEN.] **Sam Burnside**

Maynooth (*Maigh Nuad*), Co. Kildare, a university town; POPULATION (2002) 10,845. Its unique character is formed by the opposition of the demesne of CARTON HOUSE and the grounds of ST PATRICK'S COLLEGE at opposite ends of the main street. Granted to Maurice Fitzgerald in 1176 by RICHARD FITZ GILBERT (STRONGBOW), the town grew around the Fitzgerald castle. As Earls of Kildare, the Fitzgeralds were immensely powerful until the rebellion of Silken Thomas in the 1530s. In the conflicts of the 1640s the castle was left ruinous. In the late 1730s the nineteenth Earl of Kildare remodelled Carton House to designs by RICHARD CASTLE and also sought to redevelop Maynooth as a model village, with a wide main street and a market square. In the 1790s the Duke of Leinster was influential in having the ROYAL CANAL pass just south of Maynooth, followed later by the Midland Great Western Railway; he also encouraged the establishment of the Roman Catholic College of St Patrick (1795), the government-sponsored seminary, where students for the Catholic priesthood would avoid the influence of revolutionary philosophies on the Continent. The college developed around the eighteenth-century Stoyte House, with later buildings by A. W. PUGIN and J. J. McCarthy. In 1966 it was decided to admit lay students, which resulted in a new phase of building. Maynooth now accommodates both St Patrick's College and a constituent college of the National University of Ireland.

Because of its proximity to Dublin, the town grew rapidly since the 1960s and by 41 per cent between 1991 and 1996. In 1981 the railway station was reopened for a suburban service, while the opening of the Leixlip–Kilcock motorway in 1994 has allowed long-distance through traffic to bypass the town as well as facilitating transport to Dublin. **Ruth McManus**

Maynooth grant, an act of Parliament (June 1845) under the PEEL ministry to make permanent the British government's annual grant to the Catholic seminary of ST PATRICK'S COLLEGE, Maynooth, and to increase the endowment nearly threefold, with additional funds for building. The bill was part of Peel's reorganisation of higher education in Ireland but was designed primarily to win support from Catholic clergy, who were typically effective advocates of REPEAL agitation. Conservatives in England considered the bill to be state support of Popery, and opposed it. **Richard D. Floyd**

Mayo, County (*Contae Mhaigh Eo*)

Province:	CONNACHT
County town:	Castlebar
Area:	5,398 km² (2,084 sq. miles)
Population (2002):	117,428
Features:	Lough Conn
	LOUGH MASK
	Mweelrea Mountains
	Partry Mountains
	River Deel
	River Moy
Of historical interest:	BALLINTOBER ABBEY
	CÉIDE FIELDS
	Killala round tower
Industry and products:	Fishery
	Livestock
	Peat production

Petula Martyn

County Mayo is bordered by Cos. Sligo, Roscommon, and Galway and to the west and north by the Atlantic Ocean. Co. Mayo contains a number of major metamorphosed uplands, separated by

CLEW BAY: the Nephin Beg range to the north, Nephin (806 m, 2,644 ft), the Sheeffry Hills and Mweelrea Mountains to the south, and the Partry Mountains to the south-east. A band of poorly drained drumlin topography extends north-eastwards across the county from Clew Bay. CROAGH PATRICK, south of the bay, where tradition says ST PATRICK spent forty days in prayer and fasting, is the site of an annual PILGRIMAGE climb on the last Sunday of July. The bronze *Famine Ship* (1997) by John Behan at Murrisk, at the base of the mountain, commemorates the GREAT FAMINE. Lough Conn and Lough Carra, south-west of Ballina, and Lough Mask in the south of the county are important trout-fishing lakes. Average farm size in 1991 was 16.2 ha (40 acres). The grazing of mountain sheep and the production of beef and suckler cows are the predominant agricultural activities, with dairying of some importance in the Moy Valley and in the vicinity of Ballinrobe in the south. On the north coast, 35 km (22 miles) west of Ballina, there is an extensive NEOLITHIC field system, the CÉIDE FIELDS, with an impressive interpretative centre. 11 km (7 miles) north-east of Claremorris is an important Marian shrine at **Knock**. Connacht (Knock) Airport, which can accommodate international aircraft, is 25 km (16 miles) north of **Claremorris**. The town of **Westport** was planned by JAMES WYATT (1780); Westport House, designed by Richard Castle, has a zoo and recreational park in its grounds. Co. Mayo has several inhabited islands, of which CLARE ISLAND in Clew Bay and Inishturk are of greatest importance. ACHILL ISLAND, the largest Irish ISLAND, is linked to the mainland by a bridge. **Mary E. Cawley**

mazurka, a Polish dance popular throughout Europe in the nineteenth century, adopted as a couple dance in Co. Donegal. Today the dance survives solely in the form of the couple dance *La Varsoviana*, though the tune type remains popular with certain fiddlers, such as Francie Mooney. Tunes are generally not known by individual titles. The mazurka is in 3/4 time; it differs from the WALTZ in tempo and accent. **Liz Doherty**

Méabh. *Cairn at the top of Knocknarea, Co. Sligo, 55 m (180 ft) in diameter and 10 m (32 ft) high, reputed to be the tomb of the Iron Age Queen Méabh of Connacht. [Dúchas, The Heritage Service]*

Méabh. As recorded in 'TÁIN BÓ CUAILGNE', Méabh, Queen of Connacht, led her armies against the ULAIDH; her purpose in this undertaking was to seize the sacred bull of Cuailgne. The seat of her kingdom was Cruachain (RATHCROGHAN), Co. Roscommon, a significant centre in the Iron Age period. Méabh's sexual appeal and activities are emphasised in the literature, where she is purported to have had 'one man in the shadow of another.' Among her lovers was the famous warrior Fearghus mac Róich of the Ulaidh. She was proud of her sexual conquests and had several husbands, among whom was the mythical King of Ulster, Conchobhar mac Neasa. Her sexual role contributed to her perception as divine goddess. Love and SEXUALITY are united in this divine being, in keeping with the concept of love as expressed in early Irish literature, that is, without the more modern emotional and psychological connotations. In her relationships with her lovers Méabh is the controlling, dominant one.

She is also a mother-goddess figure, the personification of the land, with warlike traits, and it is she who commands the armies that move against the Ulaidh. These traits are also documented in association with other Celtic goddesses. Méabh's supernatural power is illustrated by the fact that her very appearance can mean that the Ulaidh lose two-thirds of their fighting strength. The image of Méabh depicted in the Táin contributed to the development of further dramatic narratives about her, in which her jealousy and power are emphasised and her goddess function is reduced. [see MYTHOLOGY.] **Ríonach uí Ógáin**

Meade, E. T. (1854–1914), writer. Born in Bandon, Co. Cork. She worked in the British Museum, London, and was editor of the girls' magazine *Atalanta*. One of the most prolific of writers for girls of the late nineteenth and early twentieth centuries, she published an estimated 220 novels. She wrote on a range of themes, with an eye to changes in fashion and with an intensity that is sometimes romantic, sometimes melodramatic. She developed the school-story genre with such titles as *A World of Girls* (1886) and *The Rebel of the School* (1902). She also wrote several stories on the theme of the 'wild Irish' girl and the futile attempts of her English contemporaries to tame her, including *Wild Kitty*, *Light o' the Morning*, and *A Wild Irish Girl*. **Patricia Donlon**

Meade, Michael (c. 1814–1886), builder and developer. Entering business in Dublin in the 1840s, he was a prolific constructor of Catholic churches (including the first phase of Queenstown (COBH) CATHEDRAL, Co. Cork, 1868) and a public works contractor (FOUR COURTS extensions, Dublin, 1858; Ennis Asylum, Co. Clare, 1863). His Dublin churches include Donnybrook (1863), adjacent to his development in Aylesbury Road, where the best house was his own (now St Michael's College), built 1860. His son and partner Joseph Michael Meade (1839–1900), who was an alderman and later lord mayor, is remembered for his conversion of the early eighteenth-century mansions of Henrietta Street, Dublin, to tenements. Both men are commemorated by sumptuous monuments in Glasnevin Cemetery. **Frederick O'Dwyer**

Meagher, Lory (1899–1973), hurler. Born in Tullaroan, Co. Kilkenny, into a nationalist family with a strong tradition in the GAA. Encouraged by his father, Henry Joseph Meagher, a founder-member of the GAA, he developed his skills as a young child and showed early potential. Alongside his brothers, Willie and Henry, he played in the all-Ireland final of 1926, which they lost. But his team won the championships of 1932, 1933, and 1935. A Heritage Centre commemorating him was opened in his native village in 1994. **Donal Keenan**

Meagher, Thomas Francis (1823–1867), Young Irelander. Born in Waterford, son of a wealthy merchant and REPEAL MP; educated at Clongowes Wood College and Stonyhurst College, Lancashire. His 'Sword Speech' precipitated the YOUNG IRELAND split with O'CONNELL in 1846. Transported to Van Diemen's Land in 1849 for participating in the 1848 RISING, he escaped to the United States in 1852. After practising journalism he led an Irish Brigade for the Union in some of the bloodiest battles of the American Civil War. He mysteriously drowned in the Missouri on 1 July 1867 while Acting Governor of Montana. **Richard Davis**

Meaney, Colm (1953–), actor. Born in Dublin; trained at the ABBEY THEATRE before making his television debut in the British police series 'Z Cars'. In 1982 he emigrated to the United States, where he became a regular in 'Star Trek' (1987–93) while also playing in *Die Hard 2* (1990), *Dick Tracy* (1990), and *Come See the Paradise* (1990). Though he appeared in *The Dead* (1987), his best-known Irish roles are in the RODDY DOYLE adaptations: *The Commitments* (1991), *The Snapper* (1993), and *The Van* (1996). **Kevin Rockett**

meat. Meat has always been a popular and status-defining feature of the diet. Outside the contemporary norm, access to meat, in either fresh or salted form, varied with economic standing, season, region, and the strength or otherwise of the commercial industry in producing for the home and export markets.

The introduction of farming in the NEOLITHIC Period (c. 4000 BC) brought domesticated cattle, sheep or goats, and pigs, which could be exploited for meat and secondary meat products. By the early Middle Ages (fifth to twelfth centuries) a farming system was established that valued cattle and sheep for their secondary produce, while pigs were reared specifically for the table. Pig-meat was consumed fresh, either boiled or roasted, but more frequently salted and in various offal-based preparations. The consumption of beef, fresh and salted, from both young bullocks and the spent milch cow was limited to the upper classes, while its general high status was maintained by the fact that cattle were important units of capital of the wealthy, kept predominantly for their dairy produce and ultimately their hides. Nonetheless, the large consumption of fresh meat, beef and offal was a defining feature of the diet of the native Irish aristocracy until well into the sixteenth century.

Throughout the following century the production of beef for export was developed. The industry boomed from the middle of the seventeenth century, facilitated by the growth of transatlantic trade, and Cork became an important port specialising in the production of cured beef. Although the fortunes of the industry fluctuated, it saw good times during the French wars (1793–1815). As a by-product of the industry, perishable offal and off-cuts, in particular blood-serum beef pudding and tripe, became available at a cheap price, giving the dietary pattern of the urban poor a particular local character in areas associated with cattle slaughter, curing, and export. In towns, access to fresh meat markets made available a variety of meat to those of means.

By contrast, in rural areas the high market value of beef in inland and export trade affirmed its high status as a luxury food that frequently entered the diet of the wealthy and occasionally into that of the strong farmer. As a result, mutton and pork were more dominant in satisfying the craving for fresh meat, while quantities of salted beef were also to hand. With little export trade in mutton, together with the fact that the carcase could be consumed quickly without the need to salt a surplus, its consumption made economic sense, and it became popular throughout the eighteenth century. During the same period the increased availability of POTATOES as fodder for pigs made pig-meat readily available. The consumption of pork, fresh offal off-cuts and puddings in the days after the winter slaughter, together with ham and bacon, characterised the diet of the self-sufficient farmer until well into the twentieth century. For festive occasions, in the absence of fresh red meat a farmyard fowl was a celebratory indulgence. For the poor, meat was consumed only on particular festive days: Christmas, Easter, and Shrove Tuesday. Their meat intake could be augmented with small meats—rabbits, hares, game, and songbirds—and in some areas a pair of kids was also kept.

Meagher, Thomas Francis. *Thomas Francis Meagher (second from right) and William Smith O'Brien (seated) under guard at Kilmainham Gaol, Dublin, before being deported to Van Diemen's Land, Australia. [Courtesy of Kilmainham Gaol Museum]*

In towns, the growth of the factory bacon-curing industry throughout the nineteenth century and its expansion in the second half of the century, most importantly in Cork, Limerick, Waterford and Belfast, brought a variety of fresh and salted ('corned') offal and off-cuts to an urban populace of very modest means. At the same time a general improvement in living standards, together with the importing of cheap meat, in particular fatty American bacon, gave the poor easier access to meat and meat products.

Fresh meat was routinely both boiled and roasted, using a variety of utensils that were both reflective of and determined by social status, while salted meat was always boiled.

Today, fresh, cured and processed meats are consumed daily and are often eaten at every meal. Pig-meat remains the most popular, followed by poultry, beef, and sheep-meat. The consumption of red meat is compromised by questionable and often contradictory reports about the health risks associated with the eating of meat and animal fats. However, the export industry in red meat is vibrant, with well over half the product going to the export market, though the increased growth in factory slaughter, butchering and processing is threatening the future of the small abattoir and the local craft butcher. **Regina Sexton**

Meath, County (*Contae na Mí*)

Province:	LEINSTER
County town:	NAVAN
Area:	2,338 km^2 (903 sq. miles)
Population (2002):	133,936
Features:	RIVER BOYNE
Of historical interest:	Boyne Valley
	DOWTH
	Kells monastic site
	KNOWTH
	NEWGRANGE
	SLANE CASTLE
	TARA
Industry and products:	CARPETS
	Cement
	CLOTHING
	FURNITURE
	Livestock
	MINING

Petula Martyn

County Meath, a county dominating the east-central lowlands, is a landscape of rich limestone glacial drift, drained by the waters of the River Boyne as it flows eastwards to Drogheda. The county, which originally embraced an east and a west Meath, was created in 1297 out of two of the historic early KINGDOMS in Ireland, Mide and Brega. For centuries Co. Meath has been one of the premier grassland regions, fattening cattle for the Dublin markets. Its cultural significance reaches far back into the past with the NEOLITHIC passage-grave complex at Brú na Boinne, including DOWTH, Knowth, and NEWGRANGE. The Hill of TARA, among the most important archaeological and symbolic sites in Ireland, is in the centre of the county; by the eighth century the King of Tara became the metaphorical 'high king' of Ireland. The Boyne Valley contains a wealth of archaeological and architectural remains, including PASSAGE TOMBS, henges, motte-and-baileys, castles, and country mansions. The lordship of Meath was granted by HENRY II to HUGH DE LACY, one of the ANGLO-NORMAN conquerors who came to Ireland in 1169; he established his headquarters at **Trim**, which became an important town guarding the western edges of the English PALE. The Irish Parliament met in Trim several times in the Middle Ages, and the town's extensive medieval architectural remains are testimony to its former significance. Meath is also the site of the BATTLE OF THE BOYNE (1690). The southern parts of the county have some of the largest grazier farms in the country, where hundreds of small farms were created by the Land Commission in the 1940s for migrant families from the west. Today a large proportion of the population of the countryside and small towns in the south of the county commute to Dublin. **Navan** (population 3,415), with the largest lead-zinc mines in Europe, is the county town. **Patrick Duffy**

meat industry (twentieth century). The origins of modern MEAT factories were in the 1920s, when Matt Lyons began shipping beef quarters and lamb carcases from Co. Leitrim to England. The first purpose-built plant for slaughtering cattle was erected in the 1930s; and this trade expanded to exports to the United States in the 1950s. In 1947 Ireland had a quota to supply 225 tons of beef per week to Britain. It was not until the mid-1950s that a market for lamb opened in France and some other Continental countries.

The first purpose-built factory for beef exports was established in 1952 by a Swedish company at Grand Canal Street, Dublin. By 1970 the Republic's meat factories were exporting 1.7 million tonnes of beef to the Continent, and this more than doubled, to 4.5 million tonnes, in 1975, two years after Ireland became a member of the EEC. In 2000 exports from the Republic were 495,000 tonnes of beef (worth £1,100 million), 117,000 tonnes of pig meat (worth £220 million), and 49,000 tonnes of sheep meat (worth £145 million). Poultry exports were worth £125 million.

The Beef Tribunal (1992–3) investigated the relationship between FIANNA FÁIL and the beef industry between 1987 and 1988 and notably one meat factory owner, Larry Goodman, then the largest owner of beef-processing plants in Europe. It was the longest TRIBUNAL in the country's history, running for 226 days, with 475 witnesses being heard. The 1,400-page final report by Mr Justice LIAM HAMILTON found no evidence to suggest that either the then Taoiseach, CHARLES HAUGHEY, or the Minister for Industry and Commerce, ALBERT REYNOLDS, was personally close to Larry Goodman, or that Goodman had any political associations with either of them or with Fianna Fáil; however, the tribunal did draw attention to malpractices in some meat factories, and the EUROPEAN UNION imposed fines of £110 million on Ireland for breaches of its regulations. The European Commission fined the Department of Agriculture £69 million for irregularities in the beef intervention system and for breaking rules on beef tendering procedures.

Meat factories in Northern Ireland evolved from municipal abattoirs operated by county councils. At the end of the 1960s there were sixteen such abattoirs, two of which were municipal. In 2001 there was only one municipal meat factory, in Newtownards, Co. Down; another ten factories, all approved by the European Union for the production of meat for export, were in private ownership, exporting to forty countries. Eight of these were owned by four companies. In 2000, meat factories in Northern Ireland slaughtered 1,182,000 cattle and sheep.

Beef exports from both parts of Ireland were seriously affected from the end of 2000 by a significant drop in the consumption of beef on the Continent. This was because of the spread of bovine spongiform encephalopathy (BSE) in cattle as well as an epidemic of foot and mouth disease in Britain during 2001, which spread to Northern Ireland and some border areas of the Republic. **Margaret Donnelly**

medals, military. Medals that may be awarded by the DEFENCE FORCES are: the Military Medal for Gallantry; the Distinguished Service Medal; the Service Medal (Permanent Defence Force and Reserve Defence Force); the Emergency Service Medal; the UNITED NATIONS Peacekeeper's Medal; the Military Star; and the Good Conduct Medal (discontinued in 1990).

The Military Medal for Gallantry and the Distinguished Service Medal are awarded in recognition of any act of exceptional bravery, gallantry, courage, leadership, resource, or devotion to duty.

The Service Medal is awarded to personnel of the Permanent Defence Force and the Reserve Defence Force for specified durations of service.

The Emergency Medal was awarded for service during the years of the SECOND WORLD WAR (1939–45).

The United Nations Peacekeeper's Medal is awarded to personnel who have served with a UN force or a UN-mandated force.

The Military Star is awarded posthumously to personnel who died as a result of hostile action by an opposing force while on service abroad.

Medals that may be awarded by other organisations are UN medals for personnel who serve a tour of duty with a UN mission,

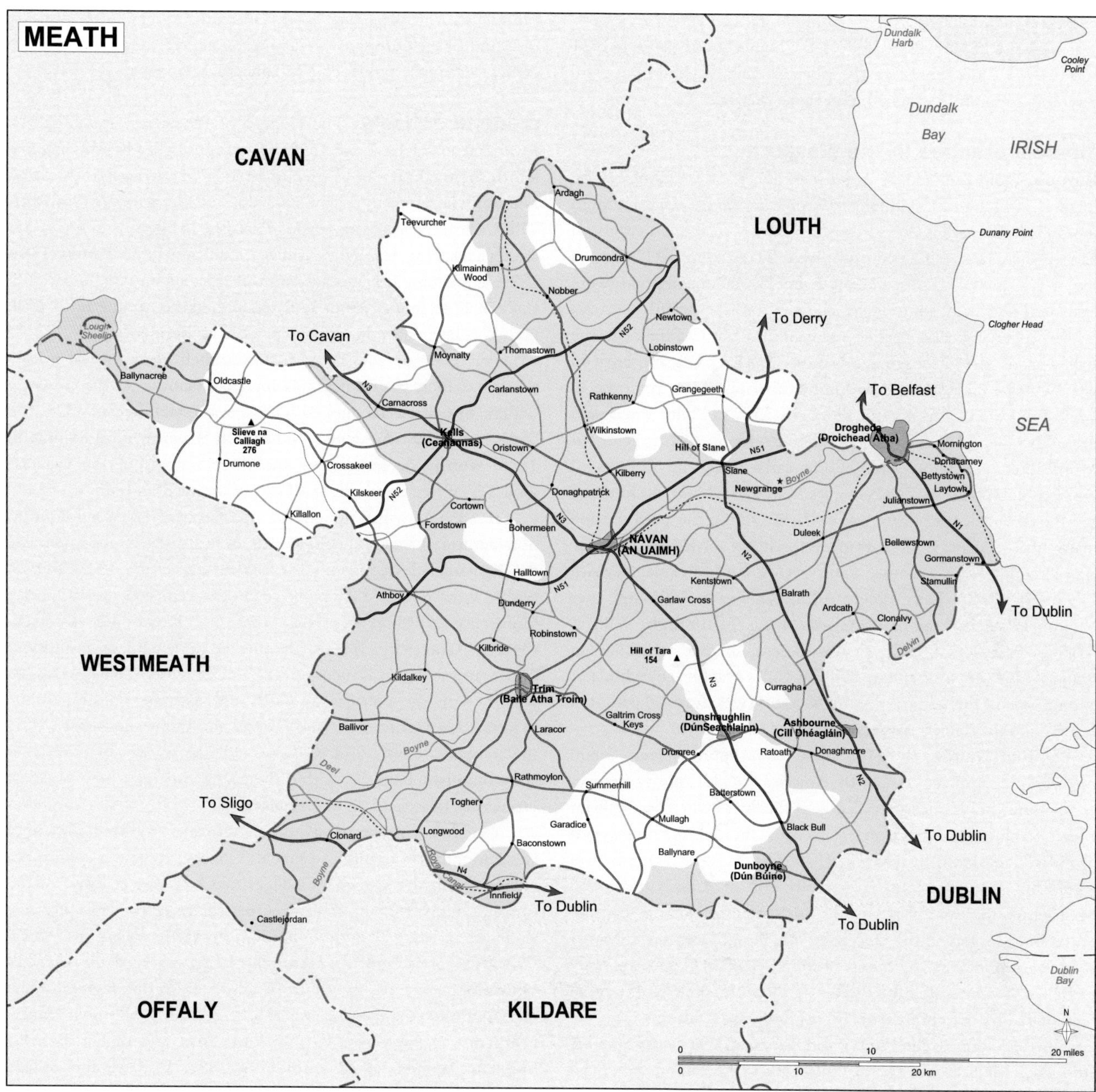

European Union medals for service with an EU mission, and medals for service with non-UN forces operating under UN mandate. **Paul Connors**

media audiences. Broadcast media audiences are measured by two different ratings systems. The Joint National Listenership Research Committee calculates the audience for radio, based on the stations heard by listeners on the day before the survey date (regardless of length of time spent listening). An average of 89 per cent of all adults listen to radio during weekdays. In the first six months of 2000, RTÉ radio stations held 55 per cent of this listenership, with Radio 1 having 31 per cent, 2FM 28 per cent, and Lyric FM 3 per cent. This figure increased to 56 per cent in the second part of 2000. The commercial station Today FM gained 14 per cent of the listenership in 2000; local stations gained the remaining 55 per cent, with Highland Radio, Radio Kilkenny and Radio Kerry gaining more than 60 per cent of the available listenership. More younger listeners (aged fifteen to thirty-five) listened to 2FM and Today FM, while a greater proportion of older listeners (aged thirty-five and more) listened to RTÉ Radio 1, Lyric FM, and local stations. Radio listenership is higher outside the Dublin region, averaging 90 per cent of all adults. RTÉ morning talk shows, news and afternoon music shows are the most popular programmes.

A. C. Nielsen measures the television audience through their ratings system, based on the percentage of all television viewing in private households. RTÉ 1 obtained the largest share of the available viewing audience in 2000, attaining a 39.4 per cent share of the average weekday evening audience (6–11:29 p.m.). This is followed by the second RTÉ station, Network 2, which had a share of 13.9 per cent, and TG4, with 2 per cent. UTV and HTV had a programme share of 11.8 per cent, followed by TV3, which gained a share of 8.3 per cent. British television stations (BBC1, BBC2, Channel 4, and SC4, excluding UTV and HTV) obtained a total programme share of 15.7 per cent. Satellite stations held an 11.7 per cent share of viewership, with Sky 1, Sky News, Eurosport and MTV dominating. These figures illustrate a decline in the numbers watching RTÉ stations and a rise in those watching TV3 from the previous year's figures. Slightly more women than men watched television, with older people watching more than younger viewers. The majority of viewers were from the higher social classes (ABC1 and C2DE). Quiz shows, serials, sports programmes and films were the most commonly watched. **Bernadette Grummell**

medical practice in the diaspora

Europe. From the Middle Ages, Irish doctors were familiar with medical thinking in Continental Europe. *Lilium Medicinae*, written in 1303 by Bernardus de Gordon, a professor in the University of Montpellier, was translated into Irish by Andrew O'Hickey, a Co. Clare physician. Several other books and manuscripts were translated into Irish, some of which date from the twelfth century.

Irish students also studied medicine on the Continent; some stayed there and filled prestigious posts. Niall Ó Glacáin, born in Co. Donegal in 1600, became professor of physic in Toulouse in 1629. John O'Higgins became chief physician to Philip V of Spain in 1718. Gerard Fitzgerald became professor of medicine at Montpellier and wrote one of the early books on diseases of women, published in 1758. Georges Mareschal (Marshall) founded the Royal Academy of Surgery in Paris. During the penal period many Irish students studied at medical schools abroad and particularly at Montpellier, Rheims, Paris, LOUVAIN, and Prague. Bernard O'Connor of Co. Kerry graduated at Rheims in 1691 and later became physician to Jan Sobieski, King of Poland. William MacNeven from Co. Galway was director of medical studies in Prague, 1754–84; his nephew William James MacNeven, who later became one of the leaders of the 1798 REBELLION, was also educated in Prague and Vienna. **Davis Coakley**

United States. By 1775 there were approximately 3,500 medical practitioners in North America. The majority remain anonymous, occasionally recalled anecdotally, as when Sir William Osler recounted how an Irish doctor came through the backwoods of Canada to attend his birth in 1849. Others were established in prominent positions: John B. Murphy, son of Anne Grimes and Michael Murphy, who met in the Wisconsin wilderness, became professor of surgery in the University of Chicago, surgeon to Mercy Hospital, founded by the Sisters of Mercy. Robert Foster Kennedy of Belfast was neurologist to Bellevue Hospital, New York, commemorated by the eponymous Foster Kennedy syndrome.

In 1786 John Archer, son of an Ulsterman, was the first graduate of the Medical College of Philadelphia, the earliest American medical school, founded in 1765. He became a member of Congress for Maryland. The Irish-born Matthew Thornton (1714–1803), a signatory of the Declaration of Independence, practised medicine at Londonderry, New Hampshire. SAMUEL CLOSSY (1724–1786) of Dublin gave the first course in anatomy at King's College, New York. John Crawford, born in Ireland in 1746 and settled in Baltimore, postulated a *contagium vivum* as the cause of fevers and was among the first in America to vaccinate against smallpox. John Mackay, a surgeon's mate, was the first European to live in what is now British Columbia, 1785–87. W. J. MacNeven (1763–1841) and THOMAS ADDIS EMMET, distinguished UNITED IRISHMEN and medical graduates, sought refuge in America; the latter's son John Patten Emmet (1796–1842) graduated in medicine from the College of Physicians and Surgeons, New York. Henry Newell Martin (1848–1896) of Newry, Co. Down, was appointed professor of biology at Johns Hopkins University, Baltimore, and taught there for seventeen years. Charles McBurney, son of Irish emigrants, who took a medical degree in New York, described the vitally important point of maximum tenderness, 'McBurney's point', in acute appendicitis.

By the 1900s America was emerging as a progressive medical centre; many Irish graduates who formerly sought further tuition in Continental Europe elected to study at one or other American clinics, and many remained permanently. **J. B. Lyons**

medical schools. The College of Physicians, established by royal charters of 1667 and 1692, was a licensing body; teaching was left to the medical school established in 1711 in TRINITY COLLEGE, Dublin, whose greatly expanded School of Physic opened in 1801. The College of Surgeons, arising from the Schools of Surgery, was always a teaching establishment and accumulated three charters (1784, 1829, and 1885). The apothecaries were formed into the Guild of St Luke in 1745, and an act of 1791 established the Apothecaries' Hall, giving its licentiates the right to practise and prescribe.

For many decades there also flourished a number of private schools, which prepared pupils for examination by the licensing bodies. In Cork a 'recognised school' was established in 1828, and the Royal Belfast Academical Institution began medical training in 1835, worthy precedents for the three schools in the Queen's Colleges of Belfast, Cork, and Galway founded in 1845.

In 1855 Newman bought the Apothecaries' Hall school for his non-statutory CATHOLIC UNIVERSITY OF IRELAND. To accommodate the Newman developments the Royal University, an examining body with power to confer degrees, replaced the Queen's University in 1879. In 1908, when the Royal was dissolved, Queen's University, Belfast, became an independent institution; Newman's school was incorporated in University College, Dublin, which, with the colleges in Cork and Galway, constituted the National University of Ireland. Under the Universities Act (1997) the Dublin, Cork, and Galway colleges were established as autonomous universities within the framework of a new National University of Ireland. **C. S. Breathnach**

Queen's University Medical School. The Medical School was a foundation faculty of Queen's College, Belfast, a constituent college (with the Queen's Colleges of Cork and Galway) of the Queen's University in Ireland. Opened in 1849 with fifty-five students, it reached a peak of 364 in 1881, when the Royal University of Ireland, an examining body, replaced the Queen's University. Students, mostly from Ulster, took the degrees or the qualifications of other licensing bodies; nearly all took clinical instruction at the ROYAL VICTORIA HOSPITAL and Belfast specialist hospitals. Women could enrol from 1889. In 1908 the college became Queen's University; the medical school, growing and strengthening, soon became the largest in Ireland. **Peter Froggatt**

medical treatises in Irish. More than a hundred Irish MANUSCRIPTS that are almost entirely medical in content have survived into modern times. Dating from the fifteenth to the seventeenth centuries, they comprise just over 16,000 pages of text and are the most important written source for the history of MEDICINE in Ireland and Gaelic Scotland during that period. The three largest collections are those of the ROYAL IRISH ACADEMY (thirty-three manuscripts), TRINITY COLLEGE, Dublin (twenty-eight), and the National Library of Scotland, Edinburgh (twenty-two). The treatises contained in these manuscripts are written in EARLY MODERN IRISH, a standard literary language cultivated by the learned classes of both Ireland and Scotland.

Throughout this period medicine was a hereditary profession, practised by more than twenty learned families, some of whom maintained schools where training was provided for members of their own and other families. Particularly prominent were the families of Mac an Leagha, Mac Caisín, Mac (or Ó) Duinnshléibhe,

Mac (or Ó) Maoil Tuile, Ó Bolgaidhe, Ó Caiside, Ó Callanáin, Ó Ceannabháin, Ó Conchobhair, Ó Cuileamhain, Ó Fearghusa, Ó hÍceadha, Ó Leighin, Ó Nialláin, and Ó Siadhail. For the most part, the manuscripts were written by members of these and other medical families. They consist in the main of translations or adaptations of Latin works that expound the Graeco-Arabic learning taught in European medical schools from the twelfth century to the seventeenth. Cosmopolitan in origin and wide-ranging in subject matter, they deal with pathology, anatomy and physiology, diagnosis and prognosis, diet and regimen, SURGERY, OBSTETRICS, and pharmacology. Major works translated include the *Lilium Medicinae* of the French physician Bernard of Gordon (died c. 1320), translated by Andrew O'Hickey, the *Rosa Anglica* of John of Gaddesden (died c. 1349), translated by Nicholas O'Hickey, and the *Cirurgia* of the Italian surgeon Petro de Argellata (died 1423). While most of the medical manuscripts have been catalogued, only a handful of the texts they contain have been published. [see POETIC FAMILIES IN MEDIEVAL IRELAND.] **Aoibheann Nic Dhonnchadha**

medicine. Early medicine in Ireland has been described as 'a mixture of FOLKLORE, doubtful facts and mixed pagan and Christian superstitions.' Medical practice in medieval Ireland was a family affair: each medical family had its hereditary appointment and its book containing notes on diseases and their cures. The O'Hickeys were physicians to septs living in what is now Co. Clare, the Fergusons held sway in Co. Mayo, the Dunlevys in Co. Donegal. This system ensured the dispersal of medical care throughout the country. The better-educated doctors had access to Greek and Latin manuscripts and other compilations.

In 1718 the 'voluntary HOSPITALS' were initiated by six surgeons who opened the Charitable Infirmary in Cook Street (moving later to Jervis Street), Dublin. The term 'voluntary hospitals' was applied to a system suited primarily for the poor; their staffs charged no fees, the patients paid nothing, or whatever small amount they could afford after discussion with the almoner. The same principle was adopted by DR STEEVENS' HOSPITAL (1733–1987), Mercer's Hospital (1734–1983), and other institutions usually governed by Protestant groups. St Vincent's Hospital (1834–) was founded by the Sisters of Charity and the Mater Misericordiae Hospital (1861–) by the Sisters of Mercy. The North Charitable Infirmary, Cork (1744), and St John's Hospital, Limerick (1780), also belonged to the 'voluntary system' and were generally more lavishly staffed than the county infirmaries established by the state after 1765 (see p. 503).

Before the development of complex and aseptic SURGERY the well-to-do were treated in their homes. The Medical Charities Act (1851) established a dispensary system throughout the country, staffed by dispensary medical officers to treat the poor either at the dispensary or in their homes. The post of DMO was keenly sought after, offering the security of a small salary and the promise of a pension. This system was replaced by the General Medical Service, of wider application, in 1972.

JOHN MCDONNELL was the first person in Ireland to operate under anaesthesia, using ether, on 1 January 1847. His son, ROBERT MCDONNELL, is credited with the administration of the first successful blood transfusion, in February 1870. His patient, suffering from loss of blood from post-childbirth haemorrhage, was fortunate that her blood was compatible with that of the donor, her husband. With the discovery of blood groups and Rh factor, transfusion became commonplace. Henry Stokes, surgeon to the Meath Hospital, Dublin, became aware of its utility while in the British army medical corps during the FIRST WORLD WAR, and on his return to

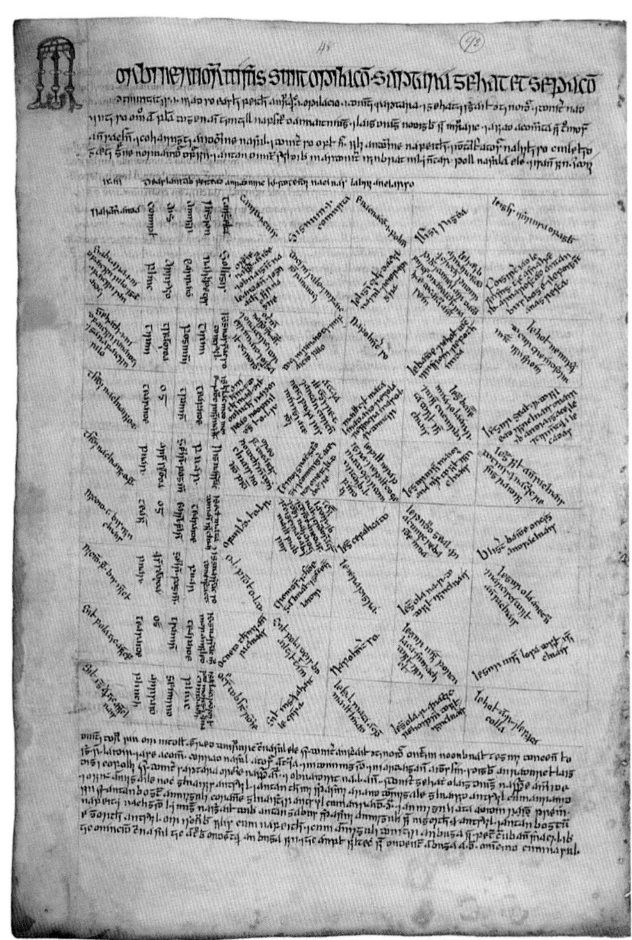

medical treatises. The Book of the O'Lees, *also known as* the Book of Hy Brasil, *fifteenth century, with translations of Latin text on medicine and tables of diseases showing name, stage, cures, etc. This folio deals with diseases of the face (morbi neurorum visus). [Royal Irish Academy]*

civilian practice he encouraged the development of facilities for its use. The Blood Transfusion Service, which eventually resulted, accepted voluntary donors only, enjoying an exemplary record until a reliance on imported blood products in the 1980s led to infections with HIV and hepatitis C.

X-rays, discovered by Röntgen in 1895, were used by R. Bolton McCausland on 23 March 1896 at Dr Steevens' Hospital to find a needle embedded in a woman's hand and remove it. The 'skiagrams' of the patient's hand were taken by Prof. Barrett at the Royal College of Science on 16 March. **J. B. Lyons**

medicine, alternative, a name given to a wide range of unorthodox medical practices that has earned wide acceptance since at least the late 1960s. In Ireland its use is not confined to the 'green' middle classes, as it tends to be elsewhere, but is widely dispersed. Practitioners attribute the phenomenon variously to Ireland's traditional faith in FOLK MEDICINE, including herbal remedies, and to what is purportedly inquisitive, anarchic, or spiritual in the Irish temperament. **John Wakeman**

medicine, developments in. The MANUSCRIPTS kept by hereditary medical families were verbatim translations into Irish from Latin; and the founders of the Dublin College of Physicians and Dublin Philosophical Society towards the close of the seventeenth century were imbued with classical scholarship. Thomas Molyneux (1661–1733) is now remembered for his benefactions and PATRICK DUN (1642–1713) for his disputed will, which led to the foundation of the king's professorships in TCD and its associated teaching HOSPITAL, Sir PATRICK DUN'S, in 1800. The Medico-Philosophical Society, founded by John Rutty (1609–1775), met from 1756 to 1784; but the eighteenth century was remarkable for the establishment of county infirmaries and voluntary hospitals, leading to the 'golden age' of JOHN CHEYNE, ROBERT GRAVES, Robert Adams (1791–1875), WILLIAM STOKES, and DOMINIC CORRIGAN, commemorated for their clinical acumen in the assessment of cardio-pulmonary and endocrine disorders.

These giants of the nineteenth century cast a long shadow into the first half of the twentieth. Electrocardiography and radiology were slowly integrated in clinical investigation in the teaching hospitals and private practice after 1900; but it was not until mid-century that the development of antibiotics dramatically altered the outlook in infectious diseases. The fourth quarter of the twentieth century saw the introduction of many new methods that widely broadened clinical investigation and also led to increasing specialisation. Ultrasonography, computed tomography and functional magnetic-resonance imaging (MRI) complement the ability to examine and repair the internal surfaces of the various systems using flexible fibre-optic endoscopes in the conscious patient. **C. S. Breathnach**

medicine, folk, can be traced back to the Celtic god Dianceacht, a *lia* or doctor who supposedly healed with herbs and magic. In the Middle Ages, doctors were honoured members of chieftains' households, and their MANUSCRIPTS had long lists of therapeutic plants and their uses. Doctors trained in Continental medical schools began to practise as early as the sixteenth century, but many people continued to rely on herbal remedies and magical charms and rituals. Some folk healers became famous, such as BIDDY EARLY in Co. Clare, whose supposed powers were said to come directly from the FAIRIES. Such healers continued to be sought out and to some extent still are. Much FOLKLORE about herbal remedies has also survived; and tokens are still left at holy wells to invoke healing or other benefits. In recent years the therapeutic use of herbs has acquired a more clinical basis with the rise of holistic medicine. **John Wakeman**

medieval food, early. With the arrival of CHRISTIANITY in Ireland in the fifth century, the monastic church, once settled and well established, encouraged the merits of learning and literacy. As a result, a wide range of early medieval texts offer a detailed picture of the dietary spectrum. Dairy produce and cereals were now the everyday staples. The former was consumed in the form of fresh milk, sour milk, thickened milk, colostrum, curds, flavoured curd mixtures, BUTTER, and soft and hard cheeses. The existence of several varieties of named soft and hard cheeses in this period is of particular note. Cereals, most commonly oats and barley and a little rye, together with more prestigious and high-ranking wheat, were used in the production of flat BREADS, and it is also likely that leavened wheat loaves were prepared. Various wet preparations—porridge, gruel, meal pastes, and pottages—and combinations of cereal, milk, FRUIT, and nuts, were also eaten. Additional condiments included hen and goose eggs, honey, fish, butter, curds, seaweeds, apples, and a root vegetable—possibly skirret—together with different types of onion, garlic, and kale. A wide range of wild foods, notably watercress and wild garlic, brought additional relish.

The availability and variety of food varied in accordance with season, region, and economic standing. With regard to season, dairy produce dominated the late spring and summer diet, while the autumn and winter months were characterised by cereal foods and saved domesticated and wild fruits. The scarcity of winter fodder, together with the fact that hay-making was not practised at this time, resulted in an autumn or winter culling of non-breeding, spent or male stocks of cattle and pigs, bringing quantities of flesh and salted meat to the diet of the more economically secure. As cereal stocks ran low, the lean months of late winter and spring were characterised by a reliance on hardy brassicas and stored alliums. Butter and salted meat bulked out the diet of the affluent; indeed butter, meat, and wheaten bread are isolated in the historical sources as the foods of the wealthy and the choice for festive days.

Historical sources also detail the wider socio-economic functions of food items as they circulated in society in the form of rents and taxes. There is specific detail of the food and hospitality provided by the nobility and their retinues as they made their annual circuit. There are accounts of special diets for different groups: children while on fosterage were fed soft fare, including porridge, milk, curds, and eggs; the convalescing sick were given a specific bread ration, together with plant foods valued for their healing properties (possibly celery and onion); the penitential monastic communities ate bread, meal pastes, thin gruels, and an early form of muesli.

The establishment of Norse towns such as Dublin, Wexford, Waterford, Cork and Limerick from the tenth century onwards developed the concept of a market economy and the effect of this on food production, and these towns may also have looked more closely at the sea as a food resource. The fact that many boating terms and more specifically the Irish words for cod (*trosc*) and ling (*langa*) were borrowed from Old Norse suggests that a taste for sea fish, whether fresh or salted, was developed under Norse influence. The Irish word for a bean (*pónaire*) is also a Norse borrowing; and while the cultivation of pulses predated Norse influence, the word-borrowing might be indicative of the introduction of better-yielding varieties by the new settlers or their increased emphasis on bean cultivation. The excavations of medieval Dublin indicate that a variety of meats, including beef, pig, and occasionally horse, were eaten, while sheep and goats seem to have been kept for their milk. A wide variety of herbs and vegetables, notably wild celery, wild cabbage, radish, fennel, hedge mustards, and several brassica species, brought additional taste to the diet. Cereals, including wheat, barley, and oats, were eaten, and there is some evidence for the cultivation of peas. A broad range of fruits was prevalent, with the remains of apple, blackberry, bilberry, cherry, plum, sloe, and strawberry found in soil, pit, and faecal material. It is interesting to speculate on the effects the Norse settlers, with their emphasis on trade and fishing, had on the dietary patterns of the rest of the population. No doubt influence was exerted in both directions, but it is also highly probable that the towns developed a particular pattern based on the fusion of the new with the old. **Regina Sexton**

medieval food, late. The twelfth-century ANGLO-NORMAN conquest and the subsequent Norman settlements brought dietary changes and developments in certain social quarters, particularly in the eastern regions of Norman influence. Both before and in tandem with the Anglo-Norman developments, the new monastic orders from the twelfth century onwards were active in diversifying the range of ingredients, specifically in broadening the range and variety of kitchen garden and orchard cultivars. The monastic ethos not only demanded a constant supply of field and garden produce to supply the brethren and lay guests but also had the concerns of fast days in mind. These factors, when combined with a recognition of the medicinal value of certain plant foods tended in the physic garden, led to a systematic and sustained attention to arable and vegetable cultivation.

Furthermore, this emphasis on the produce of the fields was facilitated by the Anglo-Norman innovations in arable AGRICULTURE. Improved plough technology and the implementation of a crop rotation system incorporating nitrogen-fixing pulses brought improvements in the cultivation of wheat in eastern and southern regions. Indeed the success of wheat cultivation in the period is clearly evident in the quantities of grain that supplied the market emanating from both monastic and manorial lands. On the table these advances were manifest in the increased use of wheaten loaves, which varied in quality from heavy wholemeal types to finer loaves of white bolted flour; the production of these loaves in quantity was made possible by the introduction of the built-up oven in the period.

Certain varieties of animals, birds, and fish were also introduced at this time: domesticated duck and white-fleeced sheep; pike and mute swan; rabbits, pheasants, pigeons, and fallow deer. These new introductions were managed for the table, with game items such as rabbit and pheasant, in addition to the young pigeon squabs, providing an important source of fresh meat throughout the year.

Changes in cooking styles and types of dishes and an alignment of the palate to the medieval European norm became prevalent in areas of direct Norman influence. Meat and fish pies and pasties were eaten, while both meat and fowl were distinctively flavoured with garlic and spices. Church, manorial and trade records testify to the importing and use of luxury goods: almonds, spices, honey and sugar, pepper, figs, and rice. Verjuice, an acid liquid made from sour grapes or crab apples, was also used in cookery.

However, a familiarity with and use of these new ingredients was limited to the wealthy in areas of Norman influence and settlement. The ingredient therefore became a mark of wealth, location and cultural outlook, while ease of access to these exotic ingredients differentiated urban and rural diets. The use of these expensive ingredients also characterised feast and fast days, with a tendency to use spice to celebrate special and festive days, while almonds were used in the preparation of almond milk, used as a substitute for milk during Lent and days of abstinence. It was regularly employed in the preparation of dishes of white fish and stockfish. In areas of Norman influence the dietary staples of the less affluent, in particular the manorial tenants and workers, centred on pea and bean meals, which were used in the preparation of BREADS and pottages. As pea and bean crops were used in rotation, a legume-rich food regime emerged as a by-product of the increased cultivation of wheat. Maslin loaves, of mixed wheat and rye meal, also became a feature of these regions.

Rapid economic growth during the thirteenth century encouraged the growth of towns and trade, especially along the south and south-east coast. Here the elite merchant aristocracies, bolstered by considerable trade profits, had access to oven-baked wheaten bread together with imported spices and exotic FRUITS that could be used in dressing meat, fowl, and fish dishes. Honey was also imported to supplement home supplies. Their secure economic standing set their tables apart and expressed their practical and aspirational links to England and Continental Europe to set fashions and influence life-style.

Feeding into these trade developments was the emergence of a viable commercial fish industry in salted cod, ling, cured herring, and pickled salmon; and while much of this produce was destined for export markets, the prevalence of fish in the home diet grew accordingly. Indeed salted white fish and herring were medieval staples, dominating the diet during Lent and days of abstinence.
Regina Sexton

medieval games. The evidence for games in medieval Ireland is plentiful. Board games were popular, as evidenced by the literature of the period. Archaeological evidence provides early medieval gaming-boards and their pieces, fashioned mainly from wood or animal bone and often elaborately decorated. The most famous find is the BALLINDERRY game-board, found in a BOG in Co. Westmeath in 1933, probably dating from the tenth century. The saga literature, the ANNALS, and the early legal material contain countless references to three specific board games: *ficheall*, *brandubh*, and *buanbhach*. These games probably existed before the VIKING invasions of the eighth and ninth centuries and survived, particularly in rural areas, throughout the Middle Ages. *Ficheall* was eclipsed in the later Middle Ages by chess, which the term later came to denote, despite its independent origins.

Field sports were also popular in medieval Ireland. Early references to games resembling the modern sport of HURLING are found throughout the saga literature, as well as descriptions of various other games played with sticks, balls, hoops, and holes. These games, together with other entertainments, such as horse and dog racing, were the main attractions at annual FESTIVALS and assemblies held throughout the country in the early Middle Ages. The ANGLO-NORMANS and in turn the English brought their own games to

medieval games. *Clonca, Co. Donegal, sixteenth-century grave slab of Magnus Mac Orristin, carved by Fergus Mac Allan, with foliated cross, sword, hurley and ball, the earliest known representation of the game of hurling. [Dúchas, The Heritage Service]*

Ireland from the twelfth century onwards, ultimately introducing the more enduring medieval games and pastimes, such as chess, backgammon, and playing-cards, as well as field games such as HANDBALL and quoits. [see GAELIC ATHLETIC ASSOCIATION.] **Angela Gleason**

medieval inscriptions. Unlike their OGHAM counterparts, inscriptions in conventional SCRIPT dating from the OLD AND MIDDLE IRISH periods (seventh to twelfth centuries) tend to be found at the sites of known ecclesiastical establishments, such as CLONMACNOISE and Gallen (both Co. Offaly), Glendalough, Co. Wicklow, and Armagh; and the people whose names are recorded on them can often be identified from the historical record, thus allowing accurate dating. Rectangular slabs are more common in this period than the standing stone of the ogham, but these later inscriptions are also to be found on the base, shaft and arms of crosses (such as the famous MONASTERBOICE cross of Muiredach) as well as on metal objects, in particular shrines (such as the shrine of the CATHACH OF COLM CILLE and that of the Bell of Armagh). The standard inscription records the name of the person commemorated, often in a formula of the type $\overline{Or}$ *do X*, 'a prayer for X', or $\overline{Or}$ *ar anmain X*, 'a prayer for the soul of X' ($\overline{or}$ being an abbreviation for *oróit*, 'prayer'), or *Bendacht for (anmain) X*, 'a blessing on (the soul of) X'; they may also record the name of the secular or ecclesiastical authority, or both, who commissioned the work or under whose auspices it was carried out. Sometimes the name of the artificer himself is recorded. Inscriptions range in extent from a single name to several lines of text, but because they date from a period in which the language is richly documented in manuscript, their linguistic interest is much less significant than that of their ogham forerunners. The degree of overlap between the two traditions is minimal. Occasionally one finds both ogham and conventional script on the same stone, and the earliest conventional inscription has some affinity with ogham morphology; for the most part, however, the conventional inscriptions represent a new beginning, inspired, no doubt, by the work of the monastic scriptoria. [see BOOK SHRINES; GRAVE SLABS; HIGH CROSSES.] **Damian McManus**

medieval metalwork. *Bronze panels with animal interlace are set between bands of silver on the Cross of Cong, early twelfth century, with enamel glass and rock-crystal bosses. The base of the cross is held in the mouth of an animal, with further heads below attaching the staff of the cross. [National Museum of Ireland]*

medieval land ownership and tenure. In the period up to 1200 most land was owned by individual farming freemen. Their title was absolute rather than feudal. (Lordship in Ireland was secured by grants of cattle.) However, the laws of inheritance restricted disposals of land. Normally all the sons inherited equally; if there were no sons, any daughters took a life interest, but thereafter the land reverted to the father's (three-generation) kin. If that kin died out the land was redistributed among wider kin-groupings. These kinsmen could protect their right to inheritance by vetoing most alienations of land. However, the church received many donations, and substantial numbers of monastic farmers worked land under its auspices. Certain lands in each territory were set aside for the local king and his officials. Some less prosperous freemen rented land. There were also semi-free tenant-farmers with limited rights. Mountainous, uncleared and unproductive lands were probably unowned and accessible to all as COMMONAGE. **Neil McLeod**

medieval metalwork. Irish metalwork in the later IRON AGE was characterised by a range of personal ornaments and horse fittings in plain cast bronze with engraved and cast curvilinear decoration, occasionally inlaid with red enamel. Gold was used sparingly, and silver was (seemingly) unknown.

Through contact with late Roman Britain in the fourth and fifth centuries, new techniques and forms were introduced first into the British and later the Irish Celtic repertoire. These included the use of silver, the tinning of bronze, and a range of new dress ornaments, including *latchets*, hand-pins, and the so-called penannular BROOCHES. The use of multi-coloured inlays of enamel and millefiori glass, especially on the elaborated terminals of penannular brooches, was a particular Irish development of the fifth and sixth centuries. Brooch terminals also became the focus of elaborate curvilinear designs in *champlevé* (reserved) enamel. Workshop debris and surviving examples show that brooches and, more particularly, hanging bowls with related ornament were also manufactured in Pictland and in Britain (where most survive from pagan Anglo-Saxon burials of the sixth and seventh centuries).

The earliest pieces of ecclesiastical metalwork—small tomb-shaped RELIQUARIES from Clonmore, Co. Tyrone, and Bobbio, Italy—date from c. 600. Comprising sheets of tinned bronze engraved with late Iron Age La Tène devices, they exhibit none of the influences from Germanic jewellery that were to change the character of Irish metalwork during the seventh century. These included a wider range of techniques—chip-carving, gilding, the use of gold filigree, stamped foils, and multi-coloured glass studs—as well as new forms, including belt buckles, drinking-horn terminals, and harness fittings, and new designs, in particular geometrical patterns and ribbon and animal INTERLACE. The Irish Kingdom of DÁL RIADA, which extended into Scotland, was an important centre in transmitting these new techniques to Ireland. Excavations in Ireland and Scotland have revealed evidence for fine metalworking in the form of crucibles, clay moulds and millefiori rods at both secular and ecclesiastical sites.

Gilding, metal inlays, and studs of glass, enamel and amber were combined to produce a polychrome effect, which is evident also in contemporary MANUSCRIPT illumination. The finest pieces were produced in the late seventh and eighth centuries and comprise both secular dress ornaments, such as the TARA BROOCH, and ecclesiastical objects, such as reliquaries (for example the MOYLOUGH BELT SHRINE) and liturgical vessels (for example the ARDAGH CHALICE and DERRYNAFLAN paten). A particular feature of seventh and eighth-century Irish metalwork was the eschewing of complex castings in favour of multipartite castings, assembled on a core of wood or metal, the elements pinned rather than soldered in place. Much of this metalwork was recycled and adapted as dress fasteners by the Vikings in the ninth and early tenth centuries and was deposited in pagan Viking graves.

During the ninth and tenth centuries polychrome inlays were replaced by amber and metal studs, and plain silver surfaces were favoured. Silver circulated in greater quantities, as a result of Viking trade and late Anglo-Saxon taste, and plain silver 'thistle' and bossed penannular brooches replaced earlier forms. The penannular brooch was finally abandoned in favour of the short-lived kite-brooch, which in turn was superseded by the bronze ringed pin, which became the universal dress-fastener in the eleventh century.

Some secular pieces of metalwork of eleventh and twelfth-century date are known (sword fittings and drinking-horn terminals); but the majority consist of ecclesiastical objects: bell shrines, BOOK SHRINES, and CROZIERS. Objects with inscriptions are known from the early eleventh century and enable individual patrons, craftsmen and distinct regional styles of metalworking to be distinguished.

Changes in church and lay patronage and in the liturgy, culminating in the ANGLO-NORMAN invasion of 1169–71, led to the replacement of native metalworking techniques and forms with imports. The absence of datable metalwork between c. 1150 and 1350 makes it difficult to determine the rate and extent of this replacement. Apart from seal matrices, there is little that is characteristically Irish before the middle of the fourteenth century. The survival of late medieval metalwork has been uneven: it consists in the main of repairs to earlier reliquaries of Irish SAINTS for Irish patrons, while the products of metalworkers in the towns who were working in the English tradition are unknown. The shrine of St Patrick's Tooth (dated by its inscription to between c. 1350 and 1375) and the Shrine of the STOWE MISSAL (1371–81) are examples of the repair of earlier reliquaries carried out by English and Irish patrons, respectively. They are characterised by the use of parcel-gilt silver with engraved ornament, combined with *repoussé* die-stamped figures with enamel inlay and set with semi-precious stones.

In the fifteenth century a confident local gothic style emerged, which produced reliquaries, liturgical objects, and jewellery, often characterised by silver filigree and inlaid rock crystal and coloured stones. The Limerick Mitre and Crozier (1418), made for Cornelius O'Dea, Bishop of Limerick, and the Ballylongford Cross (1479), made for the Franciscan Friary of Lislaghtin, Co. Kerry, are examples of liturgical objects in cast gilt silver executed in the gothic style by Irish craftsmen. The Dunvegan Cup (1493), a ceremonial drinking cup made as a gift for John Maguire, Lord of Fermanagh, is a rare survival of a piece of secular plate. **Raghnall Ó Floinn**

Adomnán. *Aerial view of the abbey on the island of Iona, showing the rectilinear earthwork surrounding the later abbey, which originally surrounded the early Irish monastic settlement. Adomnán was the ninth abbot. [Royal Commission on the Ancient and Historical Monuments of Scotland; Crown copyright]*

medieval missionary activity. Christian missionary activity is ultimately rooted in Christ's command to go forth into the world, to teach all nations and baptise (Matthew 28:19). In fact baptism often occurred first and teaching afterwards. Missionary activity was in most instances a lengthy process, which required as a minimum an attitude of tolerance by the secular leadership of the target population. The highlight of Irish missionary activity was the seventh century, two centuries after the coming of CHRISTIANITY to Ireland, which had produced committed Christians. The sources are generally more informative about successful missionary activity than about failure; this is evident with regard to COLM CILLE and the Picts in ADOMNÁN's 'Life of Columba'. Missionary activity by medieval Irish Christians is related to the Irish ascetic ideal of *peregrinatio pro Christo*, the voluntary lifelong exile in the name of Christ. It normally entailed the overcoming of language barriers (which is only exceptionally referred to in the sources). One may distinguish missionary activity undertaken on the personal initiative of an individual and commissioned missionary activity. The earliest representative of the former, Colmán or COLUMBANUS (died 615), is said to have worked briefly as a missionary in Gaul before settling in the Vosges and to have contemplated missionary activity among the Slavs before going to the Lombards c. 612. Commissioned missionary activity is evident especially in Northumbria in the second third of the seventh century. Before becoming King of Northumbria in 633, Oswald had spent many years in exile among the DÁL RIADA of Scotland and there learnt Irish. As King he invited and supported missionaries from the monastery of IONA, first Aodhán, later Fionnán and Columbanus, who held a bishopric on LINDISFARNE. Bede reports that the king acted as an interpreter for the Irish clerics, who, together with other unnamed Irish, impressed their congregations not only by preaching but also by exemplary humble and pious living. Little is known about St CILLIAN, who died in Franconia as a martyr in 687 or 689. Another prominent Irishman abroad was VIRGILIUS, who died in 784 as Bishop of Salzburg. **Michael Richter**

medieval oral culture. Early medieval Ireland entered a literate world when it was Christianised during the fifth and sixth centuries. Nevertheless, the majority of the population, including the aristocracy, were non-literate, resulting in a distinctive blending of literacy with a vibrant oral culture. This took two forms. Written texts, such as sermons or saints' lives, could be read aloud to a non-literate audience; and professional performers entertained social gatherings with recitation, music, and gesture. The most prominent of these professionals were the FILÍ or poets. Often literate, they bridged the gap between literacy and orality. They underwent an intensive course of study, after which they were expected to compose independently as well as to know the contents of the sagas. The *filí* had an important social function, particularly during the STORYTELLING season, which was bracketed by SAMHAIN (Hallowe'en) and BEALTAINE (MAY DAY). They performed in the aristocratic hall, where the chief was surrounded by his followers, and were well rewarded by their patrons; indeed they used the threat of satire to enforce generous payment. Performers of lower status catered for the needs of ordinary people. Unfortunately very little is known of them, and their traditions are mediated to us through the eyes of a literate elite. **Elva Johnston**

medieval settlements. The twelfth and thirteenth centuries were a period of population and economic growth throughout Europe. During this period existing settlements grew in size, and new towns and villages were created. Many of these villages declined and were eventually deserted in the centuries after c. 1300, for a variety of social and economic reasons. EARTHWORKS representing the remains of the houses, boundaries, gardens, and streets of deserted medieval villages are a common feature of the landscape in Britain and Continental Europe and, to a certain extent, in Ireland as well.

The century or so after the arrival of the ANGLO-NORMANS in 1169 saw the colonisation of many parts of eastern Ireland by large numbers of mostly English peasants from western Britain. The Anglo-Norman lords encouraged these colonists to come to Ireland, as they were needed to help work their newly conquered lands, which were divided into ESTATES known as *manors*. It is generally held that many of these English peasants created new villages at a number of manorial centres in eastern Ireland, though there is much debate about the size and development of these settlements over time. Some of these agricultural villages were given urban constitutions and rights as an enticement to settlers; these villages are known as *rural boroughs*, to distinguish them from true towns.

Unlike those of many other countries, the earthworks of deserted medieval villages are rare in Ireland. Today only the remains of a church site and often a motte CASTLE can be seen at these deserted medieval centres. Excavation has shown, however, that medieval peasant houses and streets do occur in the flat fields around these sites. It seems that the reason earthworks do not exist at most of these deserted village sites today is that these settlements were abandoned during the troubles of the fourteenth century, far earlier than in other countries, and it may be that many medieval villages were not inhabited long enough for extensive earthworks to form. **Kieran O'Conor**

medieval stained glass. In the Middle Ages important windows were glazed, though little glass has survived. Grooves to hold the window and holes for supporting bars can be seen cut into stone window-frames in churches and CASTLES, and there are several medieval references to glassworkers in Dublin. Window glass is likely to have been manufactured in Ireland before the seventeenth century, but there is no evidence from before that date. The same words were used to describe the glassmaker and the glazier, so we cannot tell whether any Irish craftsmen manufactured glass. Before the thirteenth century some of the small church windows may have been glazed with stained glass, but most are likely to have been shuttered or covered with greased paper or LINEN, as documented in England; paper and cloth were stretched across English windows into the late Middle Ages and often painted to look like diamond-shaped panes.

The large windows of the new churches in the thirteenth century were glazed. Though none of the windows has survived, useful samples of glass have been recovered from excavations at St Canice's Cathedral, Kilkenny, Kells Priory, Co. Kilkenny, and St Saviour's Priory, Limerick. The glass is mainly *potash glass*, prone to laminating on contact with dampness in the air and soil (unlike *soda glass*). A seventeenth-century account of St Canice's Cathedral describes the fourteenth-century east window of the choir as filled with translucent variegated glass depicting the life, passion, resurrection and ascension of Christ. Another account states that Cromwellian soldiers broke all the windows and carried away every bit of glass.

By comparison with similar English material, the glass from excavations can be dated to the thirteenth or early fourteenth century, the fifteenth century, and some to the sixteenth century. Most of the glass that survives is *grisaille*, of a pale green or grey colour, onto which patterns were painted in broad brush-strokes in red or brown paint and infilled with cross-hatching. Red and blue were the most common colours used with thirteenth-century grisaille glass, with emerald green becoming more popular in the fourteenth century. Grisaille windows were popular in the thirteenth and fourteenth centuries, and grisaille glass was used in borders around pictorial panels, which usually occupied up to half the window. The shortage of excavated glass implies that the windows were generally removed for reuse rather than vandalised during or after the REFORMATION. Pictorial panels were especially valuable, and fragments are rare. **Josephine Moran**

medieval towns. The origin of town life in Ireland is unclear in detail. Towns evidently existed by the tenth century, but the exact status of settlements before that time is a matter of debate. The first stirrings of urban life are found in the second half of the seventh century. The description of Kildare in Cogitosus's Life of BRIGID makes it clear that it was a sizeable settlement by c. 650. Derry is described in 697 by ADOMNÁN of IONA as a *portus*, which may mean that it was a trading place, while Dalkey Island appears to have functioned in the seventh century as an *emporium* or port of trade. Such settlements were characterised by the presence of specialists whose primary work was not food production, by evidence for long-distance trade, and by a population density higher than that of neighbouring settlements. Though these attributes are later regarded as characterising towns, the seventh and eighth-century *emporia* and ports of trade were not towns in the strict sense of the word.

During the ninth and tenth centuries the role of the church in urban development increased. Annual FAIRS became a feature of life at ecclesiastical settlements such as Lusk, ARMAGH, and Dunshaughlin. Documentary and archaeological evidence reveals an increase in the number of dwelling-houses and workshops found at major church sites, while kings increasingly favoured such sites for their residences. At Armagh the documentary evidence indicates the presence outside the ecclesiastical core of large residential precincts, with rows of houses and streets. Excavations at CLONMACNOISE have uncovered the remains of one such street, flanked by houses and workshops, immediately west of the ecclesiastical zone. The structural features consist of round houses, rectangular outhouses or workshops, boundary fences, a boat-slip, and paved surfaces; there is evidence for a range of craft-working activities, including bronze-smithing, gold-working, iron-working, comb-making, and the manufacture of jet bracelets.

It is not known whether the ninth and tenth-century trend towards urbanisation was purely indigenous or not. The form of the buildings and yard areas at Clonmacnoise is essentially native and traditional. Nonetheless, it cannot be without significance that the period was one of urbanisation throughout Western Europe, and it is likely that influences filtered into Ireland from the Carolingian and Anglo-Saxon worlds.

The form taken by urban development in the vicinity of church sites was almost certainly influenced by the Scandinavian settlements established during the ninth and tenth centuries. Permanent VIKING bases were set up from about the middle of the ninth century. The term used for such bases in Irish documentary sources is *longphort*, which appears to mean 'fortress for ships'. That at Dublin was established in 841 and lasted until 902, when its occupants were expelled. Nothing, however, is known about its form or appearance.

An important phase of town development began in 914 with the arrival of a large Scandinavian fleet at Waterford. Dublin was re-established in 917, Limerick was founded in 922, and Cork and Wexford were initiated about the same time. Excavations at Fishamble Street, Dublin, have shed considerable light on the form of these tenth-century towns. A regular street plan was uncovered, with houses arranged along the frontage. The houses stood within narrow property plots, which stretched back from the street to the enclosing earthen defences. All the buildings were wooden, with post and wattle as the most common form of construction. More than two hundred houses have been recovered from Viking Age Dublin; all were of rectangular plan with typical measurements of 7.5 by 5.4 m (25 by 18 ft). From the range of artefacts it is clear that the majority of townspeople were traders, craftsmen, and artisans. The earliest archaeological evidence so far from Waterford and Wexford is of eleventh-century date, while the Hiberno-Scandinavian remains discovered at Cork and Limerick date from the twelfth century.

On the eve of the ANGLO-NORMAN CONQUEST (1169–70) Ireland possessed five port towns and perhaps fifteen towns in the interior. The latter are sometimes referred to as *monastic towns*, because of their location beside church sites. The ANGLO-NORMANS changed this pattern by establishing urban networks consisting of cities, towns, boroughs, and villages. The urban network formed in eastern and southern Ireland during the late twelfth and thirteenth centuries has endured to the present. At first the Anglo-Normans expanded existing urban settlements, such as Dublin, Kildare, and Waterford; by 1180, however, the first new Anglo-Norman town was established at Drogheda. During the following century about sixty towns were initiated. Most proved to be successful, but some, such as Rindown, Co. Roscommon, were abandoned by the 1340s. Roscommon, founded in 1282, was the last Anglo-Norman town foundation in Ireland. It was established close to the frontier with native Ireland, and it appears to have been abandoned within a decade.

Though the traditional urban house, built of post and wattle, continued in use at Wexford and Waterford until c. 1300, new techniques of house-building were introduced by the Anglo-Normans. Timber-framed buildings, stone-built houses, and structures of stone

medieval trade. *Pottery jugs and a piggybank (front right) found at excavations at Wood Quay and Winetavern Street, Dublin. The piggybank and brown jug (left) are from Dublin, while the remaining are evidence of trade contacts with England and France. The large jug (right) came from Bristol and the centre pair from the Saintonge region around Bordeaux. [National Museum of Ireland]*

medieval wall painting. Armed Knight on Horseback, *one of the figures that make up the medieval wall paintings at St Brigid's Abbey (thirteenth century), Clare Island, Co. Mayo. [Dúchas, The Heritage Service]*

and wood were constructed in the towns. Archaeological excavations at Carrickfergus, Drogheda, Dublin, Galway, Kilkenny, and Waterford indicate that the thirteenth century was a period of economic growth and physical expansion for towns. By contrast, from c. 1310 there is evidence for contraction. Parts of towns were abandoned, and in some instances the archaeological layers move directly from c. 1350 to c. 1550, with perhaps a thin layer of sod in between. Architecturally, however, it is clear that the fifteenth century was a period of urban renewal. Urban expansion occurred again in the sixteenth century, particularly after the dissolution of the MONASTERIES (1536–41). An interesting but little-studied phase of urban development occurred at the very end of the Middle Ages, c. 1500, when a number of new towns, including Cavan, Granard, and Sligo, were developed and patronised by native Irish lords. [see ADMINISTRATIVE DIVISIONS; MEDIEVAL SETTLEMENTS.] **John Bradley**

medieval trade, largely controlled by merchants in the towns on the south and west coasts, with Dublin and Carrickfergus the main centres on the east coast. Wine, imported in large quantities from France and Spain, and salt, from Spain, Portugal, France, and England, were the principal imports. Iron and iron goods, such as nails and tools, were also imported, though there was also a native iron industry, which had an export trade. Pottery, soaps, and dyes were other significant imports. In contrast to the manufactured or luxury items that came into the country, the main exports were raw materials, principally wool, LINEN, and hides. Wool, the predominant export in the Middle Ages, was sent both in its raw state and as coarse manufactured items, such as friezes, blankets, and rugs. Hides from cows, sheep, and calves were sent to England but more particularly to the Continent. Fur from foxes, wolves, and martens was also in demand on the Continent. In the seventeenth century, in response to market conditions in England, the export of live cattle and barrelled beef replaced hides as the main export, though hides remained significant.

Irish trade was largely conducted in ships chartered from English or Continental owners, though the number of Irish-owned vessels increased in the seventeenth century. The substantial fishing industry, concentrated on the south and west coasts, was also largely in the hands of foreign boats, though local lords and merchants who controlled the HARBOURS and markets collected substantial revenue. Foreign trade generated considerable profits, reflected in the life-style of the merchants and the prosperity of the port towns. While much of this wealth was in ANGLO-NORMAN hands, the native Irish were not excluded, as is evident from the names of prominent merchants of the period. **Liam Irwin**

medieval wall painting. Wall paintings are paintings that embellish the walls and ceiling-vaults of buildings; but painting can decorate any structural component of an architectural space, such as the carved stone and window reveals (Kells Priory, Co. Kilkenny, and at Clare Island Abbey, Co. Mayo—the first painting scheme). For the most part the evidence from Ireland is fragmentary. Wall painting remains have been recorded at approximately sixty sites, occurring in both ecclesiastical and secular contexts. Certain of these paintings are better known because of their relatively complete survival or because they were recorded by earlier scholars. Further evidence for wall painting comes from archaeological excavations (CLONMACNOISE, TINTERN ABBEY, and Kells Priory). Identification can be difficult, because of later lime-wash applications and the action of micro-organisms and other deterioration products covering the paintings. Medieval wall paintings afford great insights into the study of materials and technology, iconography, costume, and dating and are therefore of interest to many people, including art historians, archaeologists, architects, material scientists, and conservators.

The paintings are generally applied to one or more lime-plaster layers but can also be applied to a thin preparation layer directly on the wall support or an adjoining carved architectural detail. The decoration can include incised designs. The standard palette included yellow, red and brown ochre, green earth, lime white, and charcoal or bone black. More costly pigments, such as cinnabar, lapis lazuli, lead white, and gold, have been identified at a few sites. Pigments were painted onto a *fresco* (wet plaster layer) or a lime-wash layer directly above the dry plaster application (*lime-painting*) using lime-water. Certain pigments could be added (mixed with a different, normally organic, binding medium) once the surface was dry (*secco additions*).

Irish medieval wall paintings generally range in date from the ROMANESQUE period (Cormac's Chapel, CASHEL, consecrated in 1134) (see p. 165) to the fifteenth century. The Clonmacnoise fragment was excavated from a seventh-century site. The subjects depicted are diverse. Consecration crosses, boats and imitation ashlar masonry pattern are common representations. HUNTING scenes are recorded at Urlanmore Castle, Co. Clare (now collapsed), HOLYCROSS ABBEY, Co. Tipperary, and Clare Island Abbey (in both painting phases). St Michael weighing the souls is represented at Clare Island Abbey and Ardamullivan Castle, Co. Galway. The martyrdom of St Sebastian is to be found at ABBEYKNOCKMOY, Co. Galway, and Ballyportry Castle, Co. Clare. The Crucifixion was represented at Clare Island Abbey and Abbeyknockmoy (now lost). The Trinity was the main subject at St Audoen's, Dublin (completely deteriorated), and partially survives at Abbeyknockmoy. Other religious figures, SAINTS and bishops are recorded at a number of sites. The later painting scheme at Clare Island Abbey is unique among extant Irish medieval wall paintings, in that it includes representations of secular activities, such as a CATTLE RAID, musicians, fishermen, falconry, and a variety of animals, both mythological and real; some of the representations, however, though apparently secular, have a religious symbolism. **Karena Morton**

medieval wood-carving. Wood was the most widely used raw material for fuel, structures, and artefacts during the Middle Ages. Our best evidence for medieval wood-carving derives from recent urban archaeological excavations, in particular those of VIKING Age and medieval Dublin and Waterford. The evidence suggests that medieval wood-carvers carefully selected the appropriate wood for each task. Using hand-tools such as axes, adzes, chisels, and gouges, they made such domestic equipment as lathe-turned and carved bowls, churns, troughs and buckets, spades, spoons, spatulas, pins, and tool handles. Artistic decoration was occasionally added to certain objects, such as gaming-pieces and boards, knife handles, and boxes, using techniques and art styles that illustrate the diverse national and cultural influences on medieval Ireland. **Aidan O'Sullivan**

Medlicott, Henry Benedict (1829–1905), geologist. Born in Loughrea, Co. Galway; educated at TCD. In 1851 he was appointed to the staff of the Geological Survey of Ireland. In 1853 he transferred to the GEOLOGICAL SURVEY OF ENGLAND AND WALES, and in 1854 he joined his eldest brother as an officer of the Geological Survey in India. After five months with that survey he was appointed professor of geology at the Rurki College of Civil Engineering, but he rejoined the Indian Survey in 1862 and was director from 1876 until his retirement in 1887. He was the author of several studies concerning the geology of India, including *A Manual of the Geology of India* (with W. T. Blanford, 1879). **Jean Archer**

Meehan, Paula (1955–), poet. Born in Dublin; educated at TCD and Eastern Washington University. Her poetry collections, for which she has received several prizes, include *Return and No Blame* (1984), *Reading the Sky* (1986), *The Man Who Was Marked by Winter* (1991), *Mysteries of the Home* (1996), *Pillow Talk* (1996), and *Dharmakaya* (2000). She has also written two plays, *Mrs Sweeney* and *Cell*. Her lyrical, highly personal work has earned both critical and popular acclaim. She is a member of AOSDÁNA. **Heather Clark**

megalithic tombs are characteristic of NEOLITHIC farming communities in all the lands of Europe's Atlantic coastline, from Portugal in the south to Scandinavia in the north. The principal component is a burial chamber usually constructed of *megaliths* (large unhewn stones) and covered with a mound of earth or stones. Though there is a wide variety of tomb types, certain similarities in form and content are apparent between regions. These monuments were used for collective burial over a long period, and the remains interred in them, both cremated and buried, were accompanied by grave-goods, including stone implements and pottery vessels.

The megalithic tombs of Ireland display a considerable diversity of size and form. Some 1,572 tombs have been identified, and these are divided into four principal types, distinguished especially by their architecture and, to a certain extent, by their distribution patterns and associated artefacts: COURT TOMBS (411 examples or 26 per cent), PORTAL TOMBS (180 examples or 11 per cent), PASSAGE TOMBS (236 examples or 15 per cent), and WEDGE TOMBS (532 examples or 34 per cent). In addition there are a further 213 monuments (14 per cent) that, because of the nature of the surviving evidence, must remain unclassified. The four classes are not mutually exclusive, and the points of similarity between the different types are best explained by contact between the builders of the various traditions. The custom of building these monuments persisted in Ireland for about 2,000 years, from c. 4000 to 2000 BC. The precise genesis of the Irish tombs, and indeed of the wider European tradition, is still a matter of debate, as is the role played by these monuments in the cohesion of the societies that built and used them.

Behind all these magnificent monuments were societies with very clear views on life and death, on the world and their place in it. The recurrent architectural forms point to a settled way of life and a firm social structure—not that these were static or bound by convention, for the very diversity of the monuments emphasises the regional and local nature of the styles employed. The evidence demonstrates that although they relate to the disposal of the dead we need not assume that this was their primary purpose, and it may be that not all of them functioned in the same way or were built for the same reasons. The most extraordinary feature of the tombs is that they were as much 'monuments for the living' as 'monuments for the dead'. The collective nature of the burials does suggest that some importance was attached to the continued links between ancestors and the living and that this played a significant role in how societies viewed themselves and the world (see pp. 247, 777, 887). **Paul Walsh**

Mellifont Abbey, Co. Louth, the first CISTERCIAN monastery in Ireland, established in 1142 at the instigation of ST MALACHY of Armagh as part of a broader move towards reform of the Irish church. At first the community comprised a mixture of French and Irish monks, trained at the mother-house of Clairvaux. The abbey buildings also demonstrate French influence, representing the earliest known example of integrated monastic planning in Ireland. The octagonal lavabo (c. 1210), the chapter-house (c. 1220), and the late medieval gate-house remain partly intact; the foundations of the other buildings have been exposed by archaeological excavation. Ultimately Mellifont became head of an affiliation of over twenty Irish Cistercian foundations. **Rachel Moss**

Meehan. *Paula Meehan, poet and playwright. Themes of relationships and enduring love motivate much of her writing. [John Minihan]*

Mellifont, Treaty of, the treaty that brought the NINE YEARS' WAR (1594–1603) to a conclusion. Having threatened the existence of English rule in Ireland with his famous victory at the BATTLE OF THE YELLOW FORD (1598), HUGH O'NEILL, Earl of Tyrone, saw his ambitions thwarted following his defeat at Kinsale (1601). Though he was denied victory, his tenacity in withstanding English armies for a further sixteen months proved the key to the propitious terms he was ultimately granted. Far from suffering death and the disappropriation of his family lands for treason, he suffered a slight proprietorial penalty. The financial costs of the war effort had drained the English exchequer. Combined with the imminent death of ELIZABETH I and the expected accession of James Stuart (widely suspected in England of being sympathetic to O'Neill), O'Neill was offered surprisingly favourable terms. **John McCavitt**

Melodies of Buched's House: see ESNADA TIGE BUCHAD.

melodrama. Though much derided and seldom studied, Irish melodramas—or simply 'Irish plays', as they were called—were profoundly influential in the formation of Irish cultural identity. The origins of the Irish play go back to the late eighteenth century, when the demand for stage spectacle led playwrights such as JOHN O'KEEFFE to write plays with picturesque settings, frequent changes of scene, extensive use of music and song (based on traditional airs), and a plot with a reconciliatory happy ending. Within this *mise-en-scène* certain stock characters appear: the *raisonneur* priest; the kindly LANDLORD, and his opposite, the villainous middleman; the head-strong 'colleen'; and, emerging later in the tradition, the trickster STAGE-IRISHMAN, whose verbal blunders (or 'Irish bulls') never mask his quick wit or his essential goodness. Though the term 'melodrama' did not come into widespread use until the 1820s, its basic components existed by the 1780s.

By the 1840s the English playwright John Buckstone could write *The Green Bushes* by matching these components with standard plots, usually involving spectacular escapes and mistaken identity. The master of the form was DION BOUCICAULT, whose plays THE COLLEEN BAWN (1860), *Arrah-na-Pogue* (1864), and *The Shaughraun* (1874) became the standard by which subsequent Irish plays were judged. Towards the end of the nineteenth century Edmond Falconer's *Peep-o-Day* (1861), Hubert O'Grady's *The Famine* (1886), and J. W. Whitbread's *Wolfe Tone* (1898) pushed the form in a more overtly political direction by using subject matter from recent Irish history, playing down the traditional reconciliatory ending. This politicisation continued in later Irish melodramas, including P. J. Bourke's *When Wexford Rose* (1912), popular until the 1920s.

Irish melodramas emerged at a time when the THEATRE world was dominated by touring. Consequently, they exported an enduring image of Irishness around the world, fostering a reputation for wit and engendering sympathy for opposition to English rule. As a global phenomenon, Irish plays were ideally suited to film adaptation, and many of the earliest Irish films were taken directly from plays, particularly *The Colleen Bawn*, eventually displacing them from Irish stages by the mid-1920s. However, since the 1960s the vibrant theatricality of Irish melodrama has been rediscovered, and there have been recent successful revivals of Boucicault's plays at the ABBEY THEATRE. **Christopher Morash**

mental health. There has been a dramatic shift over the past three decades from a mental health service based on large psychiatric HOSPITALS to one that is more integrated with general hospitals and where a largely out-patient service is provided to people living at home or in residences in the community. The number of people resident in psychiatric hospitals has declined from a maximum of 20,000 in the 1970s to just under 4,000 in 1999. Legislation provides for the detention of those with a mental disorder who are a danger to themselves or others. In the Republic, procedures are based on the Mental Treatment Act (1947). New legislation will ensure that legal safeguards are in accordance with those required under the EUROPEAN CONVENTION ON HUMAN RIGHTS. The Inspector of Mental Hospitals inspects all psychiatric hospitals and units each year and publishes a report on the findings. In Northern Ireland the relevant legislation is the Mental Treatment Order (1986), which established a Mental Health Commission to protect the rights of detained patients. **Ruth Barrington**

Mercator, Gerardus (Latinised name of Gérhard Kremer) (1512–1594), cosmographer and cartographer. Born at Rupelmonde, Flanders; educated at the University of LOUVAIN. The most famous European cartographer of his age, he spent most of his career under the patronage of the Duke of Cleves at Duisburg, Germany, publishing a globe, sheet maps of Europe, the world, and various individual countries, and finally a complete world atlas. Three different and increasingly detailed versions of Ireland appeared successively in his map of Europe (1554), his separate map of Britain and Ireland (1564), and a set of five maps devoted to Ireland in his general atlas (1595). In each instance Mercator was able to find better and more up-to-date sources than had been used by any previous Continental publisher. **J. H. Andrews**

Mercier, Paul (1958–), playwright, director, and screenwriter. Born in Dublin. He is the founder and artistic director of Passion Machine (1984), a theatre company that has proved to be one of the most innovative in its playing style and content and in its approach to widening the theatre's audience. He has written ten plays for the company and directed a majority of their productions. The best of his earlier work includes *Wasters* (1985) and *Studs* (1986). *Buddleia* (1995), *Kitchensink* (1996), and *Native City* (1998) formed the 'Dublin Trilogy', which was a success during the 1998 Dublin Theatre Festival. **Eamonn Jordan**

Mercier, Vivian (1919–1989), professor and critic. Born in Dublin and raised in Clara, Co. Offaly; educated at TCD. He taught at City College, New York, 1948–65, and held professorships at the University of Colorado, 1965–74, and University of California, 1974–87. He wrote ground-breaking articles on BECKETT during the 1950s. *Beckett/Beckett* (1977) brought out the Anglo-Irish Protestant legacy in its subject's life and writings. *The Irish Comic Tradition* (1962) did much to establish the field of Irish studies and was pioneering in its joint treatment of the two traditions in Irish writing. *Modern Irish Writing: Sources and Founders* (1994) was published posthumously. **Anthony Roche**

Merriman, Brian (c. 1750–1805), poet. Born near Ennistimon, Co. Clare. At an early age he and his family moved to the environs of Lough Graney in the parish of Feakle. His education most probably consisted of a good grounding in English grammar and in mathematics; one source states clearly that he was ignorant of Greek and Latin. He kept a successful school of mathematics near Lough Graney and also farmed a seven or eight-acre rented holding. He married Cáit Ní Choileáin c. 1783; they had two daughters. He seems to have been a successful and progressive farmer, as he won two spinning-wheels as prizes from the Linen Board for his crop of flax in 1796. Towards the end of the eighteenth century he moved with his family to Limerick and again maintained a mathematics school in Old Clare Street. He died suddenly on 27 July 1805.

Merriman owes his fame to the highly original and innovative poem of 1,026 lines he composed in 1780 called 'Cúirt an Mheán Oíche' ('THE MIDNIGHT COURT'). It is probable that he participated from his youth in the vibrant literary culture of Cos. Clare and Limerick of his day, but he was not moved to take an active part in this culture until encouraged by the coming together of a court of poetry in Ennis in 1780. His poem is an analysis of the patterns of MARRIAGE and MATCHMAKING in the second half of the eighteenth century and ranges over the SEXUALITY of male and female, priest and layman, married and unmarried. If the tradition of his own illegitimacy is to be believed, it is likely that this circumstance was the main personal motivation of the poet; but the fact that he was not married at the then comparatively old age of thirty is also to be taken into consideration. **Liam P. Ó Murchú**

Mesolithic period (c. 7000–4000 BC), the term usually used to denote that part of the Stone Age from the end of the late glacial period to the transition to farming. The communities living at this time usually followed a way of life based on gathering, hunting, and fishing in an environment that was not significantly different from today's in CLIMATE but where much of the landscape was covered in forests. Much of the wild FAUNA and FLORA at that time would also be similar to what still exists in certain parts of Europe.

In Ireland the Mesolithic Period represents the earliest known phase of human settlement and is normally divided into two phases: an Early Mesolithic, which appears to have lasted until c. 5500 BC, and a Later Mesolithic. The archaeological record of this period is usually recognised through assemblages of stone tools. Frequently, and particularly in parts of the north and east of Ireland, these tools are made from flint, but in other areas, such as parts of the midlands, chert was used, while elsewhere rhyolite and quartz were used as raw materials. Because of the acidic nature of much of the SOILS and other deposits, the expected bone tools have not usually been preserved. From the occurrence of numerous AXES, including polished stone axes made from a series of materials, such as baked mudstones and shales, it is presumed that much of the equipment used in the Mesolithic Period was made from wood.

The early phase of the Irish Mesolithic Period is best characterised by the assemblages from MOUNT SANDEL, Co. Derry, and LOUGH BOORA, Co. Offaly. At these sites large numbers of narrow, parallel-sided small blades, often struck with a punch from prepared cores, were recovered. These sharp-edged blades could be used as tools, but frequently portions of the blades were retouched (chipped) into a series of distinctive forms, called *microliths*. Similar and related forms of microliths of this date can be found in much of Western Europe. In Ireland they were usually elongated triangles, blunted back rods, and narrow, needle-shaped points. They could be used in *composite tools*, as insets in wooden or bone tools, such as knives and graters, or as the edges and barbs on weapons such as arrows. These tools are often accompanied by other tools, such as axes.

For a number of reasons, the stone tool technology of the Early Mesolithic Period was gradually abandoned and replaced by something distinctly insular. The composite-tool technology was replaced by one based on the production of a series of larger, robust blade and blade-like flake tools, which appear to have been produced through the use of large hammer-stones. The most characteristic tools of this period are the *butt-trimmed* forms, which include the leaf-shaped *Bann flakes* and distinctive tanged pieces, which, together with a series of related tool types, probably served as knives and other general-purpose tools. They were usually accompanied by a series of picks, borers, and large notched pieces. Excavations at Ferriter's Cove, Co. Kerry, and other sites, such as Moynagh Lough, Co. Meath, have shown that many other forms, such as pebble tools and ground-stone spearheads, were also used at this period.

Merriman. *Cover image by Brian Bourke from* The Midnight Court *by Brian Merriman, translated by Frank O'Connor [O'Brien Press Ltd, © Brian Bourke]*

Throughout the Mesolithic Period the environment was changing, from a Continental to a warm, wetter Atlantic type of climate, with a change in forest cover from the open woodlands of birch, Scots pine and hazel to one dominated by oak, elm, and alder. At the same time there was a rise in sea level, while LAKES began to fill in and BOGS develop. In spite of these changes there were certain constants in Ireland's ecology. There were a few large land mammals (such as wild pig and bear), while few of the freshwater fish found in Continental Europe occurred in Irish waters. It would appear that in Ireland the migratory species of salmon and eels played an important role in the economy of the Mesolithic Period, as would the resources around the coast. It is not surprising, therefore, that few upland hunting sites are known, or that coastal sites—though from the latest phases of the period—are known, from Dunaff Head, Co. Donegal, to Ferriter's Cove, Co. Kerry. Similarly, many sites are known from lakes, such as Lough Derravaragh, Co. Westmeath, and are found in significant numbers at important points on rivers such as the BANN, for example at Newferry and Culbane, where it is probable that extensive use was made of fish traps.

Perhaps the most important fact about the Irish Mesolithic Period is not that people managed to get to Ireland but rather that they adapted to such a distinct environment. [see MIDDENS; PREHISTORIC FOOD.] **Peter Woodman**

Methodist Church. *Detail from Maria Spilsbury's* John Wesley Preaching in Ireland *(c. 1815). Wesley is depicted preaching near Spilsbury's Co. Wicklow home; her fairhaired son Jonathan can be seen left of Wesley. [Wesley's Chapel and Leysian Centre]*

'Messe ocus Pangur Bán': see PANGUR BÁN.

metal technology in prehistory. Metal technology arrived in Ireland c. 2400 BC, leading to the exploitation of local COPPER, of which important deposits occur in Cos. Cork, Kerry, Tipperary, Waterford, and Wicklow, with lesser quantities in other counties. Subsequently the importing of tin from Cornwall allowed the making of objects from bronze, an alloy of copper and tin. In the early centuries of the BRONZE AGE, flint objects (such as arrowheads) and metal were in contemporaneous use.

The early construction from bronze of simple flat axe-heads and daggers cast in open one-piece moulds gave place with time to the casting of socketed and hollow objects employing two-piece moulds with cores of clay or wax. Among the tools and implements devised were axes, chisels, sickles, rapiers, daggers, and spearheads, as well as decorative pins and disks. A gold-working centre in the SHANNON Basin was established and as expertise evolved and spread, Irish craftsmen developed such products as LUNULAE, dress fasteners, complex lock rings, and gorgets (gold collars unique to Ireland). Gold could associatively be cast, hammered, soldered, and twisted to produce sophisticated objects that were often embellished with incised and *repoussé* work. Only Athens is said to surpass the collection of the NATIONAL MUSEUM OF IRELAND in the richness of its prehistoric gold collection. Much of this gold was imported to supplement local sources.

The addition of lead to bronze c. 900 BC and ever-increasing technological mastery in the use of clay moulds allowed the realisation of such sophisticated cast products as 'side-blow' and 'end-blow' TRUMPETS. Rigorous control over the casting process was necessary here, as very regular thin walls had to be fashioned in order to achieve success. The manufacture of large items, such as buckets and cauldrons, followed improvements in necessary techniques of sheet-metal working, riveting, and soldering. Large varieties of weapons were manufactured, including halberds, spears, swords, and shields, as well as a wide repertoire of knives. A plethora of tools, including chisels, gouges, punches, tweezers, and sickles, was also produced.

There is no clear dividing line in Ireland between the phasing out of the Late Bronze Age and the start of the succeeding Early IRON AGE. In general, the very slow spread of the use of iron technology in the country is attributable to the fact that the smelting of iron is a much more difficult process than the smelting of copper. Also, until a technique had been developed for hardening and toughening the resulting metal so as to produce a keen edge, iron would not have been perceived as superior to good bronze as a medium. The method introduced for hardening iron was by *carburisation* (repeated hammering of the red-hot bloom in contact with charcoal so as to provide inclusions of carbon). The incentive to develop such technology despite its inherent difficulties was provided by the fact that necessary ores (limonite and haematite) as well as the wood for charcoal were available in abundance.

There is some suggestion that iron was worked in Ireland before 500 BC and that contact with iron-using communities abroad took place in the centuries before the close of the millennium. The evidence for this, however, is rather slight. There is a paucity of iron objects dating from the period of transition from bronze to iron, and the information that can be derived from those finds that exist is incomplete. Some of the greatest achievements in Irish bronze working can, on the other hand, be readily traced to the transition period. The bridle bits and scabbard plates then produced were especially fine, suggesting by their elegant, abstract, Continental (La Tène type) decoration that these were the accoutrements of an elite warrior society. A variety of methods was employed to provide this ornamentation, including *repoussé*, incision, engraving, and etching techniques. The Iron Age continued uninterrupted in Ireland until the fifth century, when the coming of CHRISTIANITY and other influences brought the era now designated 'prehistoric' to an end. **Susan McKenna-Lawlor**

meteorology. The first systematic observations of the weather in Ireland using meteorological instruments are attributed to WILLIAM MOLYNEUX of TRINITY COLLEGE, Dublin. Only small fragments of the series for the two-year period 1684–6 survive. Many other dedicated individuals performed weather observations during the eighteenth and early nineteenth centuries, notably JOHN RUTTY and RICHARD KIRWAN, both of Dublin.

Organised meteorology, aimed at practical objectives, originated from the needs of shipping and was facilitated by the invention of the electric telegraph in the middle of the nineteenth century. In the early 1860s the 'storm warnings' issued by Vice-Admiral Robert Fitzroy (1805–1865) of the British navy—precursors of the shipping forecasts of today—were based on daily weather reports telegraphed from a network of forty observing stations established for the purpose around the British and Irish coasts. One of these was Valentia Observatory in Co. Kerry.

All weather forecasts for use within Ireland were supplied from London until 1936, when the growing needs of transatlantic AVIATION led to the establishment of a national Meteorological

Service. For more than a decade this new body was concerned exclusively with aviation forecasting, but in 1948 it assumed responsibility for the weather forecasts broadcast by Radio Éireann. In 1952 the Meteorological Service began to supply forecasts to the daily NEWSPAPERS, and by 1961 it was able to co-operate with RTÉ in presenting the daily weather forecast on television.

Today the Meteorological Service—operating under the name 'Met Éireann' since March 1996—has a staff of approximately 240, with its head office and Central Analysis and Forecast Office at Glasnevin, Dublin. It maintains offices at the main airports and a further network of nine weather observing stations at strategic sites around the country. A wide range of geophysical and specialised meteorological observations is carried out at Valentia Observatory. **Brendan McWilliams**

Methodist Church, a nonconformist denomination deriving from the system of faith and practice initiated by JOHN WESLEY. Originating in the middle of the eighteenth century under the leadership of Wesley, Methodism began as part of a wider evangelical revival within the Church of England. Criticised by more conventional clerics, Wesley travelled throughout Britain, preaching outdoors, forming local societies and using lay preachers to spread his message of justification by faith and Christian perfection. He first ordained preachers in 1784, and the first annual Conference took place in 1744. Wesley visited Ireland twenty-one times, establishing an annual Irish Conference in 1782. Many divisions followed his death; in Ireland, the Wesleyan Methodists became an autonomous church, while the Primitive Methodists retained their Anglican links. These groups were united in 1878. British splits were mended in 1932. [see PRIMITIVE WESLEYAN METHODISTS.] **Myrtle Hill**

Mexico, the Irish in. The legendary role of the SAN PATRICIOS in the Mexican-American War has overshadowed both the presence of earlier Irish immigrants in 'New Spain' and the prominent role some of them played in Mexico's transition from Spanish colony to independent state. While the story of the Irish in Mexico, as in Spain, is one of rapid and often complete cultural assimilation, some immigrants paid a high price for involvement in revolutionary political activities or for falling foul of New Spain's rigid religious orthodoxy.

JOHN MARTIN from Cork was among the earliest recorded settlers of Irish birth. Having reached New Spain as a crewman aboard the fleet of the English slave merchant John Hawkins, he was put ashore and was captured by the Spanish in 1568. Though he eventually settled and married in Guatemala, then part of New Spain, his behaviour, combined with previous English residence and service, aroused the suspicions of the Inquisition. Arrested in 1574 and brought to Mexico City for interrogation under torture, he admitted participating in Protestant services while remaining a Catholic at heart. This was a fatal mistake: his life would probably have been spared had he convinced the Inquisitors that he believed in the doctrines he practised. On 6 March 1575 he was garrotted and his body burnt at the stake.

By the seventeenth century, Irish-born missionaries begin to appear in New Spain's records. Michael Wadding of Waterford, a JESUIT teacher and mystic and first cousin of the famed Franciscan friar LUKE WADDING, ministered to the Mexican Indians of Sinaloa province, 1619–26, and was a professor and rector of several colleges in New Spain, 1626–44 (his name Hispanicised to Gódinez); he died in 1644 in Mexico City. It was not until 1681 that the first edition of his *Practice of Mystical Theology*, an enduring work celebrated as a commonsense manual of spiritual life, was published in Puebla, Mexico.

The FRANCISCAN friar John Lamport of Co. Wexford (his name Hispanicised to Juan Lombardo), a contemporary of Wadding's, served on the missions in Zacatecas province. His younger brother William (Guillén Lombardo), a former Spanish soldier who had won notoriety as a womaniser, reached Mexico in 1640, fleeing scandal at the Spanish Court. In New Spain he quickly came to the attention of the Inquisition for alleged plans to free Mexico's oppressed Indians and black slaves and to declare himself king. He escaped from the Inquisition's cells and became a folk hero for his bold defiance of the authorities. Recaptured (after being found in bed with the Viceroy's wife), he was burnt at the stake on 19 November 1659. Because of his early espousal of the rights of native Mexicans he is recognised as a pioneer of national independence.

In July 1821, towards the end of Mexico's independence struggle, a Spanish general landed in New Spain with orders to quell the insurgency. As Spain's last Viceroy-designate, General Juan Dumphi O'Donojú of Sevilla, the son of Kerry and Tipperary emigrants, grasped the fact that the imperial cause was lost, and on 24 August 1821 he signed the Treaty of Córdoba, recognising Mexico's autonomy. In October 1821, a month after receiving the rebel leader Iturbide in the Viceregal palace, O'Donojú died. This unexpected turn of events settled the emissary's place in Mexican history: instead of answering a furious call to Spain, where he would probably have faced a firing squad, he was honoured with a state funeral and burial in the National Cathedral. [see ARGENTINA, IRISH IN; CARRIBEAN, IRISH IN.] **Brian McGinn**

Mexico. Portrait of a Young Man in Armour *(1620) by Peter Paul Rubens, believed to be William Lamport, one of the first people to espouse the rights of native Mexicans. [Putnam Foundation, Timken Museum of Art, San Diego]*

Mhac an tSaoi, Máire (1922–), poet. Born in Dublin but spent long periods in Corca Dhuibhne, Co. Kerry; studied modern languages and Celtic studies at UCD and the Institut des Hautes Études, Paris. She worked at the School of Celtic Studies, Dublin, editing classical Irish verse in scholarly journals and *Dhá Sgéal Artúraíochta* (1946). She also worked abroad with the Department of Foreign Affairs and on the *English-Irish Dictionary* edited by Tomás de Bhaldraithe (1958). With her husband, CONOR CRUISE O'BRIEN, she wrote *A Concise History of Ireland* (1972). She was deeply influenced by her uncle, MONSIGNOR PÁDRAIG DE BRÚN. *Margadh na Saoire* (1956) is the first significant female voice in twentieth-century IRISH-LANGUAGE poetry; the acclaimed poem 'Ceathrúintí Mháire Ní Ógáin' is an honest, powerful, passionate and sensual depiction of a doomed relationship. Her poetry draws heavily on the native poetic tradition, from classical poetry to the oral poetry of the GAELTACHT, both in form and subject matter, and is invariably technically sophisticated. Her later collections, *Codladh an Ghaiscígh* (1973), *An Galar Dubhach* (1980), and the collected *An Cion go dtí Seo* (1987), reflect a wise, worldly, mature aesthetic and philosophical development. **Gearóid Denvir**

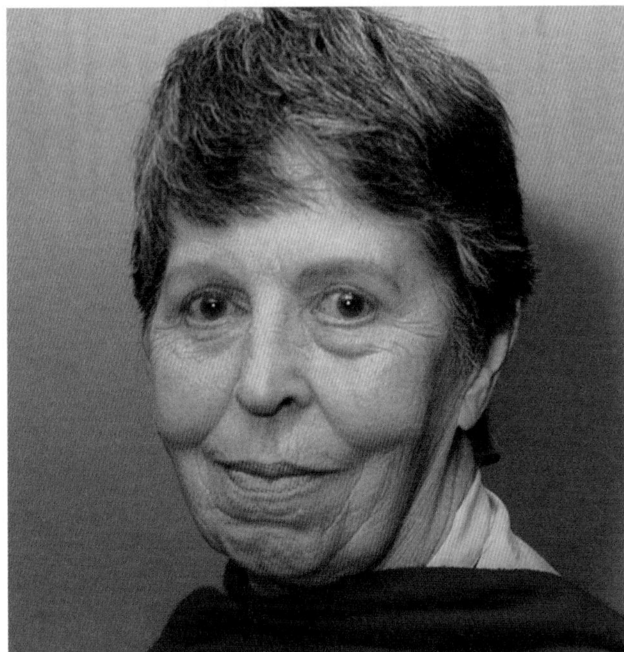

Mhac an tSaoi. *Máire Mhac an tSaoi, one of the leading poets in Irish; her work is informed by a scholarly understanding of the Gaelic tradition. [RTÉ Stills Library; 0798/002]*

Miami Showband, formed in 1962 by Tom Doherty, their manager, and originally starring Dickie Rock (see p. 885). The personnel changed over the years, but the band's popularity endured, and it toured successfully throughout Ireland, Britain, and the United States. On 31 July 1975, as five of the six members were returning to Dublin from a dance in the Castle Ballroom, Banbridge, Co. Down, a party of UVF gunmen wearing British army uniforms flagged down the minibus in which they were travelling. Two of the UVF men were killed when a bomb intended for the band exploded prematurely; the rest of the UVF party then opened fire on the band members, three of whom were killed on the spot: Fran O'Toole, Brian McCoy, and Tony Geraghty. Steven Travers was critically injured, and Desmond McAlea managed to flee. The sixth member, Ray Miller, was not travelling with the band on the night. **Ciarán Deane**

Microdisney, rock group, formed in Cork in the late 1970s. The principal members were Cathal Coughlan and Seán O'Hagan. They slowly transformed themselves from angry young men inspired by punk rock into angry older men adept at creating genuinely subversive pop songs. The band split up because of a lack of public interest, releasing along the way two of the best Irish albums ever, *The Clock Comes Down the Stairs* (1985) and *Crooked Mile* (1987). O'Hagan went on to form the highly rated High Llamas, while Coughlan formed the superbly bitter Fatima Mansions before carving out a hardly successful but creatively fulfilling solo career. **Tony Clayton-Lea**

microscopy. The light microscope was a European invention at about the beginning of the seventeenth century. The most notable nineteenth-century Irish microscopist, MARY WARD, was the first woman to write a book on the subject, *Microscope Teachings* (1864). The world-renowned Dublin optical instrument manufacturing firm of THOMAS and HOWARD GRUBB made quality microscopes. The electron microscope, invented in Germany in 1933, became available in Ireland in the 1950s. The Irish Society for Electron Microscopy was established in 1977 and later evolved into the Microscopical Society of Ireland, which caters for all forms of microscopy. **William Reville**

middens, ancient dumps of domestic refuse. The term is frequently associated with shell middens, which are mainly formed by the discarding of large numbers of shells from shellfish used as food or bait; these shells then provided a matrix in which other materials, such as artefacts, animal bones, and debris from hearths, can be found. Though often associated with the MESOLITHIC PERIOD, most of the hundred or so shell middens known in Ireland belong to later periods and can date from as late as the nineteenth century. The middens can vary from 1 m (3 ft) to more than 100 m (330 ft) in length and can be up to 2 m ($6\frac{1}{2}$ ft) in thickness. **Peter Woodman**

middlemen, an integral part of the system of letting land from the late eighteenth century. They leased land from landowners for a certain period and in turn let it to small farmers, who were usually yearly tenants or tenants-at-will. Middlemen were known for charging the maximum rent the small farmer could afford, and were prepared to evict when rents were not paid. During the GREAT FAMINE, however, their numbers were drastically reduced, as they were unable to obtain the rents from their tenants. Many were themselves dispossessed as a result or, to avoid this, evicted their tenants with a view to farming the land themselves. [see LANDLORDS AND THE LANDLORD SYSTEM.] **David S. Jones**

Middleton, Colin (1910–1983), landscape and figure painter. Born in Belfast; educated at Belfast College of Art. Apprenticed to his father as a damask designer, he briefly took over the business in 1935. In the mid-1930s, as a painter, he turned to surrealism, the first Irish artist to do so. Thereafter his work grew ever more eclectic, embracing a bewildering array of artistic styles, so that it is impossible to categorise him. He first came to prominence with the early Living Art exhibitions in Dublin. Possessed of a superb technical fluency that manifested itself with great elegance, Middleton's work is passionately human in content. **S. B. Kennedy**

Midgley, Harry (1892–1957), trade unionist and politician. Born in Belfast; he left school at the age of twelve and at fourteen became an apprentice joiner in the shipyard of Workman Clark. He appears to have become interested in politics early in life and joined the Independent Labour Party when he began work in the shipyard. He gravitated towards CONNOLLY with regard to trade unionism but did not support his nationalist politics. After service in the 36th (Ulster) Division during the FIRST WORLD WAR he returned to Belfast and became a full-time union official and was active in the Labour Party. He was defeated in the general election of 1921, in which he stood as an anti-partitionist, but served as a Labour member of the Northern Ireland Parliament, representing Dock, 1933–8, and Willowfield, 1941–7. In 1942 he broke with the NORTHERN IRELAND LABOUR PARTY and formed the short-lived Commonwealth Labour Party. During the SECOND WORLD WAR he was Minister of Public Security and later Minister of Labour, resigning in May 1945. He joined the Unionist Party in 1947 and became a member of the ORANGE ORDER; he subsequently became Minister of Education. **John Patrick Lynch**

Midleton (*Mainistir na Corann*), Co. Cork, a service and manufacturing town 23 km (14 miles) east of Cork; population (2002) 3,875. Midleton was the site of a CISTERCIAN MONASTERY founded in 1182, and the town was established c. 1670 by Sir John Brodrick. The site is half way between Cork and Youghal, in fertile farmland on the Owenacurra estuary in the north-east corner of Cork Harbour. With these advantages Midleton rapidly became an important market and industrial centre. In the 1820s two distilleries were set up and within ten years were together producing 2.7 million litres (600,000 gallons) of WHISKEY. The town still contains the largest whiskey distillery in Ireland and also a Heritage Centre devoted to the history of DISTILLING and whiskey. By the early nineteenth century Midleton also had two large breweries, malt-houses, and mills. Its prosperity resulted in the building of new houses, streets, schools, and churches; the town is still dominated by its wide, straight Main Street. In 1841 Midleton's population was 4,600; it fell to 3,400 in 1901 but recovered during the twentieth century. Its proximity to Cork results in many commuters travelling daily to the city, though it retains a strong independent identity. **Kevin Hourihan**

Midnight Court, The. *The Midnight Court* or, in the original Irish, *Cúirt An Mhéan Oíche,* is a poem of 1026 lines composed by BRIAN MERRIMAN, a Co. Clare poet, in the year 1780. It takes the form of a debate on the question of marriage: a prologue is followed by three impassioned speeches, and the debate ends when the OTHERWORLD judge, Aoibheall, gives her opinions on what has been discussed, and delivers a decisive anti-male judgment.

Merriman clearly set out to be innovative in his Cúirt. His reworking of inherited metrical forms, his combination of the most colloquial language with more literary forms, and his adaptation of various literary genres bear the marks of a highly original mind. The ostensible reason for the court session of the title is the need to discuss and resolve the problem of a lack of marriageable men for a teeming female population. But at certain junctures the arguments tend to turn on the poet himself. Thus while Merriman's criticism of the mercenary nature of the arranged marriage may have been genuine on his part, it is also probable that some doubts expressed about his paternal origins and the fact that, while writing at the age of thirty he was still unmarried, are two major factors to be considered in any attempt to discover the poet's motivation in composing a work of sustained comic effect, punctuated by passages of acute social and psychological analysis.

One of the many ironies of the Midnight Court is that, despite its Rabelaisian tenor, it can be shown that Merriman used as a compositional model a series of highly devotional seventeenth-century poems attributed to one Murchadh Riabhach Mac Namara, who may have had an ancestral connection with Merriman's forebears. **Liam P. Ó Murchú.**

midwifery and midwives. A licensed midwife is a practitioner who is allowed by law to manage normal pregnancy without the aid of doctors. The midwife has an important role in health counselling and education, not only during the antenatal period, the delivery and care of the new-born baby and the post-natal period but also within the FAMILY and the community.

Formal education for midwives can be traced back to 1774, when Dr David McBride, a lecturer in TRINITY COLLEGE, Dublin, was appointed to begin midwifery training at the ROTUNDA HOSPITAL, Dublin. It was not until 13 September 1918 that the Central Midwives Board was established to regulate midwifery education and practice in the Republic. An Bord Altranais (the Irish NURSING Board) was established in 1950. Midwifery education has evolved from a six-month certificate course to a two-year post-registration higher or postgraduate diploma. The report of the Commission on Nursing (1998) recommended the piloting of a direct-entry midwifery programme; this was begun in June 2000. [see CHILDBIRTH; MATERNITY AND CHILDCARE SERVICES.] **Mary A. Kelly**

migration, the movement of people from one place of residence (such as a region or country) to another. Migration, fertility and mortality are the principal components of population movement. Migration may be internal or international, and inward or outward.

Irish EMIGRATION (outward international migration) reached catastrophic levels during and after the GREAT FAMINE of the 1840s. It is estimated that in 1991 there were 1.143 million Irish-born people living in Britain, the United States, Australia, and Canada. During the twentieth century emigration from the Republic has been of greater significance than that from Northern Ireland, and net migration has consistently had a much greater influence on population change than natural increase (the number of births minus deaths). Consequently, Northern Ireland experienced a steady growth in population, whereas the population of the Republic declined until 1961; since then it has experienced almost uninterrupted growth. This was especially high during the 1970s and 1990s. From 1991 to 1999 net migration amounted to 62,600 in the Republic (344,700 immigrants and 282,100 emigrants) and 14,300 in Northern Ireland (168,500 emigrants and 154,200 immigrants). The number of those seeking political asylum in the Republic increased significantly, from 362 in 1994 to 4,626 in 1998.

Emigration is highest among those in their late teens and early twenties. Some migrate to further their education; this is especially true of Northern Ireland migrants to Britain. In addition to migration to and from the traditional countries of destination and origin there is increasing migration (especially from the Republic) to and from Continental Europe, with movements of greater distances caused principally by employment considerations. Internal migration too is highest among teenagers, especially the unmarried and the economically active, and declines with advancing years. Shorter mobility in urban areas reflects changes in residence and marital status, with movement of longer distances caused by employment considerations. Immigrants are generally older, often comprising families and retired people. In general, the decision to emigrate for the poorly educated is influenced by 'push' and for the better-educated middle-class is influenced by 'pull' factors. **Damien Courtney**

migratory labour, a process that began in the eighteenth century in response to changes in agricultural technology in Ireland

and Britain. Substantial farmers sought to minimise their expenditure on farm hands by hiring seasonal labourers, while small farmers drew on their families and neighbours rather than having to feed a household of farm workers all year round. The new hiring pattern served to encourage the development of networks among potential workers, and this facilitated the continuation of seasonal MIGRATION by establishing information networks on job opportunities.

While accounts of Irish people migrating within Ireland or to England for work in the eighteenth century suggest that the numbers were not great, the slack created by a generally uneven demand for labour in Ireland was taken up by growing demands for seasonal workers in England. In view of the fact that all that was required of workers was that they have a strong back and a willingness to work, the areas of employment were determined by the availability of work. In the eighteenth and early nineteenth centuries, therefore, seasonal workers were primarily in AGRICULTURE, while in the later nineteenth and twentieth centuries they tended to be in employments connected with construction.

Seasonal work provided an opportunity for tenants and smallholders to maintain their subsistence base while increasing household earnings. This was facilitated by the seasonal pattern of male labour requirements in POTATO culture (tatie hokers), in which the preparation of the ground and planting were done in February, March, and April, and the crop could then be left untended until harvest time, as late as October or November. During the late eighteenth and early nineteenth centuries changes in potato technology with the introduction of the 'lazy bed' system further reduced labour requirements during the growing season. Women and children maintained the subsistence holdings during the recurrent absence of the men, or sought casual work, or begged, nearer their homes. This pattern shifted substantial amounts of FAMILY decision-making to women during the extended periods of men's absence.

The system of combining subsistence with seasonal migration, which had been stable for almost a century, was fatally disrupted by the onset of the GREAT FAMINE in the 1840s. Following the Famine there was a permanent reduction in potato productivity, which meant that permanent migration of the entire family or the consolidation of holdings were the only viable solutions. Seasonal harvest labourers now worked abroad until they had saved a desired sum of money to buy the tenancy of a farm or additional LAND. Alternatively, seasonal labourers might work to repay debts contracted before leaving family farms in the spring, whether obligations to the LANDLORD, the tithe proctor, or the moneylender.

Migrant workers who travelled to Britain came from the areas where capitalised farming was first prevalent, in eastern Leinster and south-eastern Munster; these in turn were replaced by migrant workers from adjoining counties. For such a pattern to develop, a ready supply of labour was necessary, and this was ensured by an increasing population throughout the country, combined with a general narrowing of employment opportunity. The areas from which seasonal migrants departed for Britain in 1841, therefore, the year of the first attempt to make a census count of seasonal labourers, were once regions of local harvest migration. The 1841 census count of migrants, taken from May to August, shows that the migration was overwhelmingly male, with six men for every woman. According to the information by county, Connacht males had the highest propensity to migrate seasonally (3.4 per cent), and those of Co. Mayo the highest in the province (5.2 per cent). Ulster harvesters were next (1.5 per cent), with the preponderance coming from Co. Donegal (3.2 per cent) and the smallest number from Co. Down (0.8 per cent). Dublin people had a surprisingly high propensity to migrate (2.3 per cent); it may be that the majority of those who would become relatively permanent migrants were from there, though seasonal demands for labourers in construction work in England may have attracted Dubliners.

It is difficult to ascertain what became of seasonal migrants in their later life; they were, after all, people who left very little evidence when they moved on. One source of fragmentary information is the 'Missing Friends' column that appeared in the *Pilot*, a Boston newspaper that published advertisements in which Irish immigrants sought to find relatives and friends in North America. Data from the advertisements for more than 31,000 people sought during the first thirty-two years of the column's existence, 1831–63, bears out the belief that many of those sought had worked in England or Scotland before emigrating. The majority of those for whom a port of departure was reported left from Liverpool, despite lower fares from Irish ports. These may have been the more prosperous migrants who chose to purchase a safer and more predictable journey, but it is equally likely that they were already working in Britain. [see CONSTRUCTION WORKERS IN BRITAIN; DIASPORA; HIRING FAIRS.] **Ruth-Ann Harris**

Míl, with his relatives and followers, the Milesians, the legendary ancestors of the Irish people, having come from Spain. The mythical warrior Míl was never in Ireland but his sons and relatives arrived there at dates ranging from 1498 to 1029 BC (depending on the account), and attempted to take Ireland from TUATHA DÉ DANANN. Having eventually landed in Co. Kerry, they defeated the Tuatha Dé Danann but were forced back to sea again by the power of the druids. Éireamhóin, the Milesian leader, one of the four surviving sons of Míl, sailed clockwise around Ireland and landed at the BOYNE estuary. The Milesians then finally conquered Tuatha Dé Danann. **Ríonach uí Ógáin**

Military Archives, CATHAL BRUGHA Barracks, Dublin, the place of deposit for the records of the Department of Defence, the DEFENCE FORCES and the ARMY Pensions Board under the National Archives Act (1986). The function of the archive is to collect, preserve and make available material relating to the history and the development of the Defence Forces from the formation of the IRISH VOLUNTEERS in November 1913 to the present day, including overseas service with the UNITED NATIONS from 1958. Major collections include the Collins Papers, 1919–21; Liaison Documents (the British evacuation and Truce); CIVIL WAR Operations and intelligence reports; Captured Documents (IRA), 1922–4; Army Crisis, 1924; Volunteer Force Files; Emergency Defence Plans, 1939–46; Military Intelligence, 1939–46; Office of the Controller of Censorship; INTERNMENT Camps and Department of Defence files from that period; and Directorate of Operations, AIR CORPS and Naval Service. The archive also holds more than 800 collections of private papers. The collection known as the Bureau of Military History, 1913–21, comprising 1,773 witness statements, 334 sets of contemporaneous documents, photographs (including action sites of the 1916 RISING), press cuttings and voice recordings, compiled in the 1950s, is now available. **P. B. Brennan**

Military College, a constituent element of the DEFENCE FORCES Training Centre in the CURRAGH, Co. Kildare. It comprises four distinct schools: the Command and Staff School, Infantry School, Cadet School, and UNITED NATIONS Training School, Ireland. The Military College contributes to the development of Defence Forces doctrine and leadership training and conducts courses of instruction for officers and NCOs of the Defence Forces.

military archives. *Soldiers from the 25th Rifle Battalion saving turf during the Emergency in 1942. Turf was the principal source of domestic fuel during the Second World War. [Hanley Collection-Military Archives, Cathal Brugha Barracks]*

Cadet School. Established in 1928, the Cadet School is a constituent school of the Military College. It conducts the standard cadet course for ARMY and equitation entrants to the Defence Forces of the Republic. Additionally, AIR CORPS and NAVAL Service cadets undergo elements of the standard cadet course before reporting to their service schools for specialist training and completion of their cadetships. The standard cadet course is a progression through three seven-month stages of training. Throughout this training there is a common thread of leadership development and the fostering of loyalty, self-discipline, and a sense of duty.

Infantry School. The function of the Infantry School, which is part of the Military College, is to develop the professional knowledge, skills and understanding of its students in order to prepare them to fill various appointments within the Defence Forces and in international forces and missions. The school is charged with the development of infantry tactical doctrine up to battalion level. It also provides career courses for junior officers up to the rank of commandant and for junior and senior NCOs. Through its Infantry Weapons Wing the school develops skills in the support weapons organic to the infantry battalion. The school also assists in the research and development of military equipment for use in the Infantry Corps (see p. 47).

Command and Staff School. Established in 1930 by officers who had earlier taken part in a military mission to the United States, the Command and Staff school is part of the Military College. Its mission is to develop the professional knowledge and understanding of its students in order to prepare them for command and staff appointments at senior levels within the Defence Forces and in international forces and missions. Command and staff courses are residential and of one academic year's duration. Such courses are the cornerstone of the education of senior officers in all modern armies. The school is also responsible for staff courses and seminars and advising on the development of doctrine in the Defence Forces.

United Nations Training School, Ireland. Established in 1993 with the aim of ensuring that the training of Defence Forces personnel for peace support operations would be of the highest standards. It draws on the exceptional range of experience gained by Irish peacekeepers throughout the world. The school's mission is to study peacekeeping doctrine and to conduct training courses and seminars on peacekeeping in preparation for service with, but not exclusively with, the United Nations. The school also conducts a number of courses for students from foreign armies. **Paul Connors**

military engineering. Military engineering has been altering the Irish landscape from earliest times. Periods of political instability are reflected in protective fortifications, from prehistoric Emain Macha (NAVAN FORT) in Armagh to the fortified posts constructed by the British army in the same county during the 1990s. The construction and reduction of fortified towns kept military engineers busy through the ages. Seventeenth-century wars brought advanced engineering techniques to Ireland from Britain and the Continent, most notably at the SIEGES OF LIMERICK, 1690–91, when the city's fortifications were enhanced by French engineering expertise and Irish labour, forcing the Dutch and English engineers of the Williamite force to engage in elaborate siege works and bridging operations (see p. 287). From 1922 the military engineers of independent Ireland have been busy in reconstruction following the CIVIL WAR, in fortifications and land-mine protection on UN peacekeeping missions, and in alleviating civil emergencies at home through BRIDGE construction, firefighting, and WATER supply. **James Burke**

Military History Society of Ireland, founded in January 1949 by a group of enthusiasts, military and academic, with the aim of furthering the study of WARFARE in Ireland and of Irishmen at war; it now has a membership of more than 800. The society's first president was Sir Charles Petrie, a noted historian of the JACOBITE period. Its journal, the *Irish Sword* (1949–), published twice yearly, has become the most frequently quoted source for Irish military history. Each year the society provides a series of seven lectures and arranges two summer field trips. Overseas tours to places of Irish military interest have taken members to the United States, Turkey, South Africa, and numerous destinations on the Continent. In 1983 the society affiliated to the International Commission for Military History under the title Irish Commission for Military History; this caused a broadening of the terms of reference to include the wider study of military history, though the emphasis remains on Ireland and Irishmen. **Dónal O'Carroll**

Military Medal for Gallantry, recipients of.

Ainsworth, Capt. Adrian (1955–). Awarded the Military Medal for Gallantry with distinction in 1983 for displaying exceptional bravery in al-Tiri, Lebanon, on 8 April 1980, when, under sustained hostile fire, he went to the aid of a grievously wounded comrade and brought him to safety.

Bracken, Lt Anthony (1956–). Awarded the Military Medal for Gallantry with distinction in 1983 for displaying exceptional bravery in al-Tiri, Lebanon, on 8 April 1980, when, under heavy fire, he went to the aid of two injured comrades and brought them to safety.

Browne, Pte Anthony (1940–1960), killed in action at Niemba in the Congo on 8 November 1960. Awarded the Military Medal for Gallantry with distinction in 1961 for creating an opportunity during the ambush for an injured comrade to escape by drawing attention to his own position though he had a reasonable opportunity to escape himself.

Coventry, Pte Paul (1968–). Awarded the Military Medal for Gallantry with merit in 1997 for displaying exceptional bravery in al-Jurn, Lebanon, on 29 September 1992, when, during a serious confrontation with armed elements, he exposed himself to hostile fire in order to render assistance to a wounded comrade.

Daly, Pte Michael (1957–). Awarded the Military Medal for Gallantry with distinction in 1983 for displaying exceptional bravery in al-Tiri, Lebanon, on 8 April 1980, when, under sustained hostile fire, he went to the aid of a grievously wounded comrade and brought him to safety.

Jones, Sgt Michael (1957–). Awarded the Military Medal for Gallantry with distinction in 1983 for displaying exceptional bravery in al-Tiri, Lebanon, on 8 April 1980, when, under sustained hostile fire, he went to the aid of two injured comrades and brought them to safety.

Lynch, Comdt Michael (1942–). Awarded the Military Medal for Gallantry with distinction in 1985 for showing exemplary loyalty and courage in undertaking and successfully completing a dangerous mission in the mountains east of Beirut, Lebanon, on 25 September 1982.

Metcalfe, Cpl Thomas (1963–). Awarded the Military Medal for Gallantry with merit in 1983 for an act of exceptional bravery on 25 July 1981, when, at Port Laoise Prison, Co. Laois, he rescued a comrade trapped on a blazing rooftop. **Paul Connors**

Military Museum, established in the late 1920s as part of the education and training establishment being centred in the CURRAGH Camp, Co. Kildare. Now based in the Military College, its collection includes a range of hand-guns, small arms, and light and medium sub-machine guns, a collection fully representative of the evolution of the hand-gun and the modern military rifle; the collection also includes memorabilia of the SECOND WORLD WAR period. Sir ALFRED CHESTER BEATTY presented a world-class collection of Japanese swords and muskets to the museum in 1953. **B. L. Donagh**

Military Police Corps, formed in 1923, the law enforcement service of the DEFENCE FORCES, responsible for the investigation of crimes and misdemeanours in the military and for assisting in the maintenance of good order and discipline. It derives its authority from the Provost-Marshal, who is appointed under the Defence Act (1954) 'for the prompt suppression of all offences.' To assist the Provost-Marshal in carrying out these duties, a military police company is established in each brigade area, under the command of an assistant provost-marshal. Personnel of the corps are recognisable by their distinctive red beret. **E. D. Doyle**

militia, a civilian reserve that could be mobilised for emergency local military duties. The first Irish militia was raised in 1666. A solely Protestant force, it was replaced by a Catholic militia in 1685. During the WILLIAMITE WARS another Protestant militia was raised. These early militias were loosely organised, but the MILITIA ACT (1715) regulated the force and required county commissioners to select Protestants to train in companies. This force was mobilised during invasion scares, but the legislation lapsed after 1776. From 1778 the VOLUNTEERS fulfilled the militia's wartime home defence role (see p. 437). In 1793 a radically new militia was raised that included Catholics as privates and required full-time service. At first these men were levied by parish ballot; the conscription-like nature of the ballot was resented and sparked serious rioting in Ulster and elsewhere. Because of perceived dangers of disaffection, militia regiments served outside their home counties. However, concerns remained. In a notorious incident in 1797 four Catholic privates of the Monaghan militia were shot before their comrades for taking the oath of the UNITED IRISHMEN. The militia contained almost 30,000 men in 1798. Though proving generally reliable during the rebellion, militiamen were later encouraged to volunteer for overseas service. In 1811 legislation allowed interchange between English and Irish militia regiments. The Irish militia was disbanded in 1816 but re-established in 1854. It amalgamated with other militias in the United Kingdom in 1881 and was replaced by the Territorial Army in 1908. **Allan Blackstock**

Militia Act (1793), a radical departure from previous legislation, permitting Catholics to serve as privates. The act required men to be raised in quotas by parish ballots, though there was provision for the rich to pay for substitutes to serve in their stead. In places, severe rioting accompanied the ballots. Poor southern Catholics were enraged by what they saw as a dilution of recent Catholic relief measures, while northern Presbyterians contrasted compulsion with the independence of the VOLUNTEERS. **Allan Blackstock**

Millar, Sidney (Sid) (1934–), rugby footballer. Born in Ballymena, Co. Antrim. He played thirty-seven times at prop from 1958 to 1970. He toured Australia and New Zealand with the 1959 British Lions team, playing in three Tests, played four Tests in South

Africa in 1962, and played in two more there in 1968. He was national coach from 1972/3 to 1974/5 and a national selector. He coached the 1974 Lions team in South Africa and managed the 1980 tourists there. He was president of the IRFU in 1995/6 and has been a member of the International Rugby Board since 1993. **Karl Johnston**

Millbrook Observatory (1866–84), established near Tuam, Co. Galway, by JOHN BIRMINGHAM, a landlord and mill-owner. Using a 114 mm (4.5-in.) refractor, he had early success in discovering a recurrent nova, T Coronae, in 1866. Thereafter he undertook a revision of Skjellerup's Red Star Catalogue in 1872. On the discovery of some forty-nine red stars he decided that the new catalogue should contain not only a revision of Skjellerup's work but a complete list of all known red stars. The resulting catalogue of 658 objects was published by the Royal Irish Academy in 1877. On 22 May 1881 he discovered a remarkable deep-red variable in Cygnus, since named after him. He also published papers on sun-spots, meteor showers, and the transit of Venus in 1874. **Susan McKenna-Lawlor**

millenarianism, the Christian belief that the kingdom of God on earth will be established through a series of dramatic events, centred around a cataclysmic struggle between the forces of good and evil. Though millenarian teaching had existed for centuries, the tumultuous era of the French Revolution increased anxieties and made many in Ireland susceptible to Doomsday beliefs. Before the 1798 REBELLION political prophecies circulated by the UNITED IRISHMEN heightened apocalyptic fears; and between 1817 and 1825 the prophecies of PASTORINI, foretelling the destruction of PROTESTANTISM, gained acceptance in districts afflicted with rural violence. From the early nineteenth century, SECTARIANISM has accompanied Irish millenarian movements. **Tom Kelley**

Milligan, Alice (1866–1953), poet. Born in Omagh, Co. Tyrone; educated at a private school in Omagh before attending Methodist College, Belfast, 1879–86, and the Ladies' Department of King's College, London, 1886–7, which she left to become a governess at Derry Ladies' Collegiate School. From 1888 to 1891 she lived in Dublin, studying Irish; in 1893 she joined the Irish Literary Society, publishing poems and articles in periodicals, often under the pseudonym 'Iris Olkyrn' or 'I.O.' In 1895 she became president of Belfast branch of the Irish Women's Association; she was also a member of the Belfast branch of the GAELIC LEAGUE and the Henry Joy McCracken Literary Society. From January 1896 to March 1899 she engaged in her most noted achievement, editing with ETHNA CARBERY *Shan Van Vocht*, a journal dedicated to alleviating the disunity of NATIONALISM in the post-PARNELL era. From 1904 she worked as a travelling teacher for the Gaelic League, and a collection of her verse, *Hero Lays*, was published in 1908. The death of her parents in 1916 made her increasingly dependent on others, and she lived with relatives in England before returning to Omagh in 1932. As one of the greats of the Irish literary revival she was awarded an honorary doctorate in literature by the NUI in 1941. One of the inspirational figures of the Irish Literary Revival, she died in obscurity. **Diane Urquhart**

Milligan, Terence (Spike) (1918–2002), comedian and writer. Born in India to an Irish father and English mother. In a career often blighted by depression he was amazingly prolific as entertainer and author, beginning with BBC radio's ground-breaking comedy 'The Goon Show' (1951–60), with Harry Secombe, Peter Sellers, and (for the first few series) Michael Bentine. A film, television and

WHEN I WAS A LITTLE GIRL.

When I was a little girl
In a garden playing,
A thing was often said
To chide us delaying:

When after sunny hours,
At twilight's falling,
Down through the garden walks
Came our old nurse calling.

"Come in! for it's growing late,
And the grass will wet ye!
Come in! or when it's dark
The Fenians will get ye!"

Then, at this dreadful news,
All helter-skelter,
The panic-struck little flock
Ran home for shelter.

And round the nursery fire
Sat still to listen,
Fifty bare toes on the hearth,
Ten eyes a-glisten.

To hear of a night in March,
And loyal folk waiting,
To see a great army of men
Come devastating.

An army of Papists grim,
With a green flag o'er them,
Red-coats and black police
Flying before them.

But God (Who our nurse declared
Guards British dominions)
Sent down a deep fall of snow
And scattered the Fenians.

"But somewhere they're lurking yet,
Maybe they're near us";
Four little hearts pit-a-pat
Thought "Can they hear us?"

Then the wind-shaken pane
Sounded like drumming;
"Oh!" they cried, "tuck us in,
The Fenians are coming!"

Four little pairs of hands
In the cot where she led those,
Over their frightened heads
Pulled up the bedclothes.

But one little rebel there,
Watching all with laughter,
Thought "When the Fenians come
I'll rise and go after."

Wished she had been a boy
And a good deal older-
Able to walk for miles
With a gun on her shoulder.

Able to lift aloft
That green flag o'er them

Milligan, Alice. *Manuscript of* When I Was a Little Girl *by Alice Milligan, poet, dramatist, and novelist. She jointly founded and edited the literary journal* Shan Van Vocht. *[Courtesy of University College, Dublin, Archives Department]*

stage performer, he also wrote several volumes of humorous memoirs and a number of novels, including *Puckoon* (1965), set in Ireland in the 1920s. He was awarded an honorary knighthood in 2001. **Stephen Dixon and Deirdre Falvey**

milling. In Ireland the large-scale mechanisation of grain milling began in the middle of the eighteenth century, when, between 1758 and 1797, a government bounty on flour brought to Dublin provided the impetus for widespread structural and technological changes in the grain-milling industry. Unlike many other industries, virtually all the processes involved had already been mechanised, which encouraged the concentration of production in increasingly large units. The Irish flour mill was one of the first in Europe to expand vertically, with extra storeys provided both for more processing plant and additional storage; this development predates the multi-storey cotton mills of Richard Arkwright (1732–1792) in the later eighteenth century.

In the eighteenth and nineteenth centuries every medium-sized town had its own flour and meal mill to serve the local community. Excellent examples of the pioneering eighteenth-century multi-storey flour mill can be seen at Slane, Co. Meath (1768), Millbrook, outside Oldcastle, Co. Meath (1777), and Croom, Co. Limerick

(1788). Impressive nineteenth-century milling complexes are also widespread, such as the Lee Mills, Cork (built 1825–32), and Birr Mills, Co. Offaly (c. 1820). [see INDUSTRIAL ARCHAEOLOGY; INDUSTRIAL DEVELOPMENT; INDUSTRIAL REVOLUTION.] **Colin Rynne**

Milne, Ewart (1903–1987), poet. Born in Dublin, of Anglo-Irish parentage; educated at Christ Church Grammar School, Dublin. He fought on the republican side in the SPANISH CIVIL WAR. An effective writer of light verse, he published fourteen volumes of verse between 1938 and 1976. **Terence Brown**

Minchin, George (1845–1914), physicist. Born on Valentia Island, Co. Kerry; educated at TCD. He collaborated with G. F. FITZGERALD, Oliver Lodge and other Maxwellians and helped forge the new paradigm of physics. From 1875 he taught at the Royal Engineering (Indian) College, Coopers Hill, and later worked at the University of Oxford. His work included the invention and development of photo-electric cells (selenium photocells and sensitised chemically coated platinum plates), the invention of a very sensitive trap-door electrometer, and studies in magnetic field theory. His textbooks included the influential *Statics*. He was elected to fellowship of the Royal Society in 1895. **Norman McMillan**

mineral resources. Ireland is plentifully endowed with mineral resources and a MINING heritage, with copper-mining established more than 4,000 years ago and gold used in the BRONZE AGE to create artefacts that are now national symbols. Between the second and sixteenth centuries iron, copper, alum, lead, and silver were exploited. In the seventeenth and eighteenth centuries England became the principal market for Irish iron, because of the lower cost of charcoal smelting in Ireland. With the INDUSTRIAL REVOLUTION in England there was a resurgence in Irish copper, gold, and silver exploitation, alongside the development of new industrial resources, such as lead, manganese, barytes, slate, and coal.

From the end of the nineteenth century, however, mining declined until reinvigorated by Government measures, culminating in the discovery of lead-zinc at Abbeytown, Co. Sligo, and copper at Ballyvergin, Co. Clare, in the 1950s. The discovery of the Tynagh, Co. Galway, zinc-lead-silver ore body heralded a phase of substantial discoveries from the 1960s, including zinc-lead at Silvermines, barytes at Ballynoe—then the world's fifth-largest deposit—and the Gortdrum copper-silver-mercury deposit (all Co. Tipperary). The exploitation of the large high-grade zinc-lead deposit at Navan, Co. Meath, and the discovery of the Galmoy, Co. Kilkenny, and Lisheen, Co. Tipperary, 'Irish type' zinc-lead deposits have made Ireland the world's seventh-largest producer of zinc and tenth-largest producer of lead. Other important mineral resources include talcum, calcite, dolomite, aggregates, and fireclay, together with value-added products such as alumina and industrial diamonds. Ireland is today an important exploration territory, both onshore and offshore, with natural gas and oil the prime targets. [see BRONZE AGE COPPER MINING; INDUSTRIALISATION.] **Colman Gallagher**

miniature painting. The origins of miniature portrait PAINTING in Ireland are found in the work of enamellists. The technique of painting in metallic oxides on an enamel surface was a northern European one, probably brought to Ireland by French goldsmiths and enamellists; there is evidence that the leading enamellist Christian Friedrich Zincke (1683/5–1767) may have worked in Ireland. Zincke created a prototype for the enamel portrait that consisted of an almost full-face head and shoulders or half-length composition, sometimes with drapery, which imitated full-scale oil portraiture. The Irish enamellist NATHANIEL HONE adopted Zincke's technique. Rupert Barber (1719–1772) was trained in the craft of enamelling in London in the 1730s and returned to Dublin, where he was established as a painter of enamel portraits.

Irish miniaturists contributed to the technical development of miniature painting in the 1740s with the introduction of watercolour-on-ivory painting. Hone was one of the first miniaturists to overcome the problems of painting on ivory by introducing linear brush-strokes of watercolour paint mixed with gum arabic, which helped the watercolour to adhere to the ivory. Some of the leading miniaturists in England were of Irish birth: Nathaniel Hone, Luke Sullivan (1705–1771), and THOMAS FRYE (c. 1710–1762).

During the 1750s Dublin became an established centre of miniature painting. This was made possible by the establishment of West's Academy (c. 1746), which became the DUBLIN SOCIETY's Drawing School. At least forty-one Irish miniaturists are known to have been educated there. They were taught drawing and were then apprenticed to a miniaturist. Gustavus Hamilton (c. 1739–1775), James Reily (c. 1740–1780/8), Daniel O'Keeffe (1740–1787), John Comerford (c. 1770–1832), George Place (c. 1763–1805), John Ramage (c. 1748–1802), Walter Robertson (c. 1760–1821), and Charles Forrest (c. 1753–1787) were among those who attended the schools and helped to establish Dublin as a centre for the art.

Visiting miniaturists influenced stylistic development. The English miniaturist Samuel Collins (1735–1768) painted larger portraits on ivory and was the first to fully exploit the potential of the ivory surface by painting in delicate brush-strokes and washes of colour, which allow the ivory surface to show through. Horace Hone (1754/6–1825/7) developed his own individual style, using loosely applied linear brush-strokes of curving parallel lines. He had a highly fashionable clientele, which relied on the patronage of the Viceregal court. He may have taught Sampson Towgood Roch (1759–1847), whose neatly drawn and elegant portraits were popular in Ireland and England.

ADAM BUCK (1759–1833) was an exceptional miniaturist who was influenced by classical Greek and Roman art. His miniature portraits are painted in muted colours and linear brush-strokes. Buck and Comerford began to paint small whole-length portraits in watercolour on card, a development of the watercolour-on-ivory miniature. During the 1790s the English miniaturist GEORGE CHINNERY (1774–1852) was working in Dublin; he had a great influence on Comerford, whom he encouraged to paint larger miniatures in more freely applied brush-strokes in imitation of oil portraiture.

All miniaturists travelled for commissions, and many Irish miniaturists spent periods in England (London and Bath), India, the United States, and Canada. John Ramage and Walter Robertson were among the first to bring miniature painting to North America. Many distinguished visiting miniaturists worked in Ireland and played a part in the technical and stylistic development of miniature painting, notably Peter Paul Lens (c. 1714–c. 1750), François-Xavier Vispre (c. 1730–c. 1794), Daniel Ziegler (1716–1806), and the American HENRY PELHAM (1749–1806) (see pp. 138, 623). **Paul Caffrey**

Minihan, John (1946–), photographer. Born in Dublin but spent his childhood in Athy, Co. Kildare. For almost thirty years he worked as a staff photographer with the *Evening Standard* in London, while Athy became the subject of his magisterial black-and-white study of life in an Irish country town, *Shadows from the Pale* (1996). His perceptive and sympathetic photographs of writers have been shown internationally, at the Centre Georges Pompidou, Paris, 1986, and the National Portrait Gallery, London, 1988. Among his publications are *Samuel Beckett* (1995) and *An Unweaving of Rainbows* (1998), on contemporary Irish writers. A retrospective exhibition was held at the National Photographic Archive of the NATIONAL LIBRARY OF IRELAND in 2000 (see pp. 79, 1019). [see PHOTOGRAPHY.] **Brian Lalor**

mining. Mining has always been a marginal industrial activity in Ireland, which is poor in such natural resources as ferrous and non-ferrous metals, iron ores, copper, lead, and readily accessible coal reserves. The entire country had only seven small coalfields, which, unlike those of Britain, were difficult and expensive to work, while most Irish coal was anthracitic, unsuitable for basic tasks such as powering steam engines and manufacturing town gas. Nonetheless important mining areas, based mainly on the extraction of copper ores, grew up in Cos. Cork, Waterford, and Wicklow.

At Allihies, Co. Cork, Bunmahon, Co. Waterford, Glendasan, Co. Wicklow, Silvermines, Co. Tipperary, and Clonlig and Whitespots, Co. Down, there are important archaeological remains associated with former copper and lead mines. Stone for building and clay for the manufacture of ceramics (pottery, brick, tile and terracotta) were also extensively quarried throughout Ireland. Irish stone, such as Cork red marble and slate from Valentia Island, was even exported to Britain. An innovative water-powered marble sawing works developed by William Colles near Kilkenny in 1732 operated marble saws, the first known in Europe since the Roman period. [see INDUSTRIAL REVOLUTION; MINERAL RESOURCES.] **Colin Rynne**

Mise Éire (1959), actuality film directed by GEORGE MORRISON and produced by GAEL-LINN to commemorate the years of revolution in early twentieth-century Ireland. Using old newsreel and black-and-white still montages with a voiceover, the film recounts the events of those turbulent years. The score, consisting of SEÁN Ó RIADA's application of unique and rich orchestration to traditional Irish airs stirred the public's imagination and turned Ó Riada into a household name. **Peadar Ó Riada**

missions, the installation of several priests in a Catholic parish for a few weeks, preaching several times daily and hearing confessions. The parish missions grew out of an attempt on the part of the Irish Catholic Church to revitalise itself in the middle of the nineteenth century and more particularly to combat proselytism by English Protestant Bible Societies. Ireland was facing a 'SECOND REFORMATION' during and after the GREAT FAMINE. The parish missions provided a kind of Catholic doctrinal *blitzkrieg*, and were immensely popular with the people. Archbishop PAUL CULLEN of Dublin invited a number of religious orders newly established in Ireland, such as the Vincentians (better known as the Congregation of the Missions), Redemptorists, and Passionists, to undertake these parish missions. Father VLADIMIR PECHERIN, a convert from Russian Orthodoxy, was one of the best-known preachers. The immediate result was a 'Devotional Revolution' in Ireland between 1850 and 1875. **Mark Tierney**

missions, foreign. Born of the missionary zeal of St Patrick, the Irish church, from its foundation, sent missionaries to pagan tribes in Britain and Continental Europe. Modern foreign missions arose from historical processes in Europe; the scramble for Africa led to an explosion of Protestant foreign missions from Britain. The Qua Ibo Mission from the Presbyterian church in Northern Ireland flourished in Nigeria in the late nineteenth century and into the twentieth century. Church of Ireland missionaries were part of the Anglican Church Mission Society. There were similar movements in other denominations.

miniature painting. *Miniature portrait of the architect James Gandon (1799) by Horace Hone, with Gandon's masterpiece, the Custom House, in the background. [National Gallery of Ireland]*

In the decades before and after CATHOLIC EMANCIPATION in 1829 Catholic seminaries were established in Ireland to send missionaries to the Irish diaspora, to re-establish the church in Britain, and to establish it in the Americas and Australasia. At the same time Irish missionaries began to work in pagan lands. Early Catholic foreign missionaries joined missionary societies founded in Europe at this time, such as the Society of African Missions, the White Fathers, the Holy Ghost Fathers, and the Mill Hill Missionaries.

Catholic missionary societies in Ireland stemmed from the national seminary of ST PATRICK'S COLLEGE, Maynooth, in the early twentieth century. Father John Blowick founded the Maynooth Mission to China in 1916. In 1932 a group of Maynooth volunteers in Nigeria, led by Father Pat Whitney, founded St Patrick's Missionary Society. Congregations for women followed: the Columban Sisters, the Holy Rosary Sisters, the Medical Missionaries of Mary, and the Missionary Sisters of St Francis. Viatores Christi and the Volunteer Missionary Movement sponsored lay missionaries throughout the world. In the 1960s almost 10,000 Irish missionaries, religious and lay, worked overseas. Since then the number has fallen steadily, and Irish foreign missions are in decline. [see BRITISH EMPIRE, IRISH IN.] **Pádraig Ó Máille**

Mitchel, John (1815–1875), Young Irelander. Born near Dungiven, Co. Derry, son of a Unitarian minister; educated at TCD. A solicitor, he wrote editorials for the NATION, later establishing the more radical *United Irishman*. In May 1848 he was transported for treason-felony, but in 1853 he escaped from Van Diemen's Land to the United States. While editing newspapers he published his famous JAIL JOURNAL (1854). A slavery advocate, during the American Civil

War he supported the confederacy. Shortly before his death he was twice elected MP for Tipperary. **Richard P. Davis**

Mitchell, Alexander (1780–1868), civil engineer. Born in Dublin; educated at Belfast Academy. Blind from the age of twenty-three, he was a brick-maker and builder at Ballymacarret, Co. Down, 1800–32. He invented and patented the screw-pile foundation, 1833, used throughout the world for marine structures, such as LIGHTHOUSES and piers. **Ronald Cox**

Mitchell, George Francis (Frank) (1912–1997), geologist and archaeologist. Born in Dublin; educated at TCD, which he entered in 1930 to study modern literature, but an altercation with SAMUEL BECKETT, one of his teachers, caused him to transfer to natural science. In 1934 he became a first-class moderator with a gold medal, and he joined the staff of the Department of Geology. The COMMITTEE FOR QUATERNARY RESEARCH in Ireland appointed him to work alongside Knud Jessen (1884–1971), who visited Ireland in 1934 to train scientists in the techniques of POLLEN ANALYSIS. This experience gave Mitchell's work its lifelong orientation, and he devoted himself to research in Ireland's glacial and post-glacial history and to archaeology. He was a fine field scientist, producing many research papers and popular books. Within Trinity College he was elected to fellowship in 1944 and was later the college's highly efficient Registrar, 1952–66; a chair in quaternary studies was created for him in 1965. He was elected to fellowship of the Royal Society (London), 1973, and was president of the ROYAL IRISH ACADEMY, 1976–9. Many other bodies bestowed their presidency on him, including the Dublin Naturalists' Field Club, 1945–6, ROYAL SOCIETY OF ANTIQUARIES OF IRELAND, 1957–60, ROYAL ZOOLOGICAL SOCIETY OF IRELAND, 1959–62, and AN TAISCE, 1991–3. **Gordon L. Herries Davies**

Mitchell, Susan (1866–1926), poet and editor. Born in Carrick-on-Shannon, Co. Leitrim. She worked for the Irish Homestead and Irish Statesman and was noted for her parodies and witty verse portraits of luminaries of the LITERARY REVIVAL as in *Aids to Immortality of Certain Persons in Dublin: Charitably Administered* (1908). **Terence Brown**

Mizen Head, Co. Cork, the most southerly point of the Irish mainland. The Mizen Peninsula projects into the Atlantic Ocean between Dunmanus Bay and Roaringwater Bay. The peninsula is geologically complex, its spine consisting of old red sandstone and its lower, landward hills composed of Carboniferous grits. The area was famous for the nineteenth-century mining of both copper and barytes. The BRONZE AGE copper workings on the slopes of MOUNT GABRIEL, the peninsula's highest hill, testify to the former position of the Cork Copper Belt as the most important source of European copper after Cornwall; indeed many of the workings were later operated by Cornish miners, who established small communities in the area until c. 1851. The population of the peninsula was especially badly affected in the GREAT FAMINE; the wood-engravings in the *Illustrated London News* in February 1847 depicting starvation and death in the area brought the full horror to the world. Many of the peninsula's roads, commissioned by the BOARD OF WORKS as a famine relief measure, which employed 1,300 men in the Mizen Peninsula alone, are a lasting memorial to the disaster.

Mizen Head is known to mariners for its signal station, built on Cloghane Island in 1909 and linked to the mainland by the elegant MIZEN HEAD BRIDGE. The station was finally lit by electricity in 1959 but was automated in 1993. However, in 1994 the 'Mizen Vision' visitor centre was established in the station. The cliffs around the station are of interest as important nesting areas for seabirds. **Colman Gallagher**

Mizen Head Bridge, Co. Cork, a footbridge designed by M. Noel Ridley of London and erected in 1909 by the COMMISSIONERS OF IRISH LIGHTS to provide access to the lighthouse. It spans 52 m (172 ft) at a height of 46 m (150 ft) above the sea and is one of the oldest surviving reinforced-concrete structures in Ireland. [see CONCRETE STRUCTURES.] **Ronald Cox**

Mo Bhealach Féin (1940), an autobiographical novel by SEOSAMH MAC GRIANNA. Written in the mid-1930s and prompted by the success of the BLASKET autobiographies and O'FLAHERTY's *Two Years*, it gives an artistic GAELTACHT writer's personal reaction to an anglicised, urbanised post-revolution Ireland and the world in general and represents the author's writing at its best. **Nollaig Mac Congáil**

Modest Proposal, A, the most celebrated of JONATHAN SWIFT's pamphlets and perhaps the most admired example of irony in the English language. A ferocious indictment of English economic and political repression and Irish neglect alike, the pamphlet proposes the nurturing of infants for human consumption as a remedy for Irish social ills. Often read out of context, it is best understood as a despairing response to Swift's attempts to offer practical solutions to the economic problems of Ireland in the 1720s in works such as *A Proposal for the Universal Use of Irish Manufacture* (1720) and the DRAPIER'S LETTERS (1724–5). **Ian Campbell Ross**

Moeran, E. J. [Ernest John] (1894–1950), composer. Born in Middlesex to an Irish father and English mother; studied at the Royal College of Music, London, and later with John Ireland and Delius. He collected folk music in Norfolk. From 1924, aware of his Celtic heritage, he made regular visits to Ireland, and his music reflects an Irish influence. A prolific composer, his works include orchestral rhapsodies, a symphony and sinfonietta, two concertos, CHAMBER MUSIC, PIANO MUSIC, numerous songs and CHORAL MUSIC, CHURCH MUSIC, and folk-song arrangements. **Ite O'Donovan**

Moher, Cliffs of, a range of sea cliffs stretching 8 km (5 miles) north of Liscannor Bay, Co. Clare. Rising 196 m (643 ft) above the sea, they create one of the most dramatically contrasted landscapes in Ireland, being backed by a gentle plateau of grassland. Built of Namurian flagstones, shales, and grits, the cliffs are the youngest element of the Carboniferous Clare Plateau. Enormous vertical joints through strata of differing strength give rise to the characteristic vertical profiles of the cliffs, the jointing pattern guiding the path of marine erosion to produce spectacular sea-stacks. The flagstones are famous as building stone, having an intricate pattern of worm casts formed when the rocks were still part of the sea floor.

The cliffs are a popular tourist destination and part of the BURREN Way footpath between Liscannor and Doolin, with access also from the cliff-top visitor centre. The Moher Tower on Hag's Head originated as a signal tower during the Napoleonic War, having a panorama encompassing the ARAN ISLANDS and the coastlines of Connemara and Co. Kerry. O'Brien's Tower was constructed as a belvedere in the nineteenth century by Cornelius O'Brien, a local LANDLORD and successor to DANIEL O'CONNELL as MP for Clare in the British House of Commons. He also had the castle near Liscannor built in 1865, though paid for by his tenants. The cliffs themselves support many seabirds, including razorbills, puffins, guillemots, shags, kittiwakes, and fulmars, with wheatears and choughs living atop. The cliff-top FLORA includes the sea pink, bell heather, heaths, and sea campion, as well as the rarer roseroot, heath pearlwort, and musk stork's bill. **Colman Gallagher**

Molaise. Of the numerous SAINTS named Molaise (a pet form of the name Laisréan)—there are over forty thus named in the list of saints—two were especially important. These were Molaise of DEVENISH on LOUGH ERNE, for whom Lives were written in Latin and Irish, and his namesake at Leighlin (Co. Carlow), who was made the subject of a Latin Life and was also patron saint of the diocese of Leighlin. Their feast-days are 18 April (Leighlin) and 12 September (Devenish). **Pádraig Ó Riain**

Molana Abbey, Co. Waterford, site of the ancient monastery of Dairinis. During the twelfth century the monastery adopted the rule of the Augustinian Canons-Regular. The patron of the Augustinian foundation is thought to have been Raymond le Gros fitz William, an associate of STRONGBOW. Surviving remains include the ruins of a pre-Norman nave, with long early thirteenth-century choir. Opening off the north of the choir is a two-storey domestic building, possibly the prior's lodging. Following Dissolution, the abbey and its lands were granted to WALTER RALEIGH and later passed to RICHARD BOYLE. [see ABBEYS.] **Rachel Moss**

Molesworth, Robert (1656–1725), politician, courtier, and patron of philosophers. Born in Dublin; educated at TCD. He was a member of the Irish House of Lords, Privy Councillor and a member of the British Parliament, but he is best known as the host of a remarkable intellectual circle in Dublin that included HUTCHESON, TOLAND, and MOLYNEUX. His own writings, which were widely regarded as anti-clerical, stressed the supposed link between political and economic liberty. **Ian Leask**

Molloy, Matt (1947–), traditional flute-player. Born in Ballaghaderreen, Co. Roscommon; he was influenced by the whistle-player Jim Donoghue and had won several awards by the time of his migration to Dublin to work as an engineer. His playing circle included leading figures among regional players, but professionally he played with LIAM O'FLYNN, Tommy Peoples and PADDY MOLONEY at the Old Shieling Hotel and with DÓNAL LUNNY in sessions. He joined the BOTHY BAND in 1974 and then the CHIEFTAINS in 1979. His solo albums of 1976, 1981, and 1988 established him as a unique stylist and a musician hugely inspirational to younger players; his music bar in Westport contributed to his iconic status. **Fintan Vallely**

Molloy, M. J. [Michael Joseph] (1913–1994), playwright. Born at Milltown, Co. Galway. His plays were for many years a staple of the ABBEY THEATRE, beginning with *The Old Road* (1943); his masterpiece is *The King of Friday's Men* (1948). He wrote to the end of his life, though in later years his work was considered old-fashioned. His interest in FOLKLORE was the subject of a book written in later life that he withdrew to revise but remains unpublished. His best work can be compared to that of SYNGE, though it is more mournful and elegiac. **Peter Costello**

'Molly Maguires', a shadowy organisation of Irish mine-workers active in the anthracite region of Pennsylvania in the 1860s and 70s. The Molly Maguires were accused of killing at least sixteen mine owners and bosses, miners, and public officials, as well as carrying out numerous beatings and acts of industrial sabotage. There were two distinct waves of violence. The first, during and directly after the American Civil War (1861–5), involved resistance to conscription as well as labour issues. The second, in the summer of 1875, followed the collapse of a powerful trade union movement that united Irish, English, and American-born workers in peaceful opposition to their employers, led by Franklin B. Gowen. Like the trade union, the Molly Maguires wanted better wages and living conditions; unlike them, they used violent methods, apparently derived from pre-famine RIBBONISM and WHITEBOY agrarian protest tactics. When they went on trial in the late 1870s, most of the prosecutors (including Gowen) were railway or mine company attorneys; Irish Catholics were excluded from juries, and mere membership of the ANCIENT ORDER OF HIBERNIANS was construed as evidence of guilt. Convicted on the evidence of informers and an undercover Pinkerton detective, James McParlan (a native of Co. Armagh), twenty men were hanged. [see JONES, MARY HARRIS; UNITED STATES, IRISH IN.] **Kevin Kenny**

Molaise. *Oak carving of St Molaise or Laisréan, dating from the thirteenth or fourteenth century. Its early history is unclear, but it was housed in the church on Innishmurray during the nineteenth and early twentieth centuries. [National Museum of Ireland]*

Molly Malone, heroine of 'Cockles and Mussels', or 'Molly Malone' (c. 1880), a 'comic song' by James Yorkston of Edinburgh. Its popularity in Dublin led to a myth of authenticity, now personified by a bronze figure with fish barrow (Jeanne Rynhart, 1988) at the foot of Grafton Street; it has become an unofficial Irish RUGBY anthem as well as being a popular party chorus. **Fintan Vallely**

Molyneux, William. William Molyneux, *philosopher and political theorist, by Robert Home, one of a series of eight portraits commissioned by Trinity College in 1782 and put up in the Theatre in 1788. [Board of Trinity College, Dublin]*

Moloney, Mick (1944–), singer, banjo-player, writer, teacher, and commentator. Born in Co. Galway; he was a leading performer and organiser among ballad groups in the 1960s. He was a member of the Johnstons, a seminal group; with the collector SEÁN CORCORAN he managed the 95 Folk Club before emigrating to the United States in 1973. A contributor to countless tours, concerts and festivals there, he founded the Folklife Center in Philadelphia in 1977 and was artistic director for Irish-American arts tours such as 'The Green Fields of America'. He has appeared also in television presentations of TRADITIONAL MUSIC and has presented radio programmes in America. A consultant to the series 'Bringing It All Back Home', he researched many film documentaries involving Ireland and Irish MUSIC in America, as well as producing a doctoral thesis on 'Irish Music in America'. **Fintan Vallely**

Moloney, Paddy (1938–), orchestrator, uilleann-piper, and whistle-player. He studied pipes with LEO ROWSOME and played in several ensembles before joining CEOLTÓIRÍ CHUALANN in 1960. He founded the CHIEFTAINS in 1963, producing and arranging the MUSIC for their tours and albums. Managing Claddagh Records from 1968 onwards, he went professional with his band in 1975, his musical vision determining the Chieftains' collaboration with performers in the POPULAR MUSIC world. He has written scores for stage, CINEMA, and BALLET. In 1988 he was awarded an honorary doctorate by the University of Dublin (TCD). **Fintan Vallely**

Molony, Helena (1888–1967), nationalist, trade unionist, and actor. Born in Dublin. She joined INGHINIDHE NA HÉIREANN in 1903 and edited its journal, *Bean na hÉireann*, 1908–11. She took part in a number of ABBEY THEATRE productions between 1911 and 1922. As a member of the IRISH CITIZEN ARMY she participated in the 1916 RISING. Opposing the ANGLO-IRISH TREATY, she was involved in left-wing and republican politics throughout the 1920s and 30s. She was general secretary of the IRISH WOMEN WORKERS' UNION, 1915–16, was employed as organiser by the union until her resignation on health grounds in 1941, and was elected the second woman president of the IRISH TRADES UNION CONGRESS, 1936. **Rosemary Raughter**

Molyneaux, James, Lord (1920–), politician. Born in Crumlin, Co. Antrim; educated locally. Wounded while serving with the RAF in the SECOND WORLD WAR, he became prominent in Orangeism, which paved the way for his election as Ulster Unionist MP for South Antrim, 1970–83, and Lagan Valley, 1983–97. An unremitting opponent of the SUNNINGDALE AGREEMENT (1973), he replaced Harry West as leader of the Unionist Party in 1979. Though he co-operated with IAN PAISLEY in the United Ulster Unionist Coalition against power-sharing, he broke with him over the 'loyalist strike' led by Paisley in 1977. Under Molyneaux's shrewd if somewhat lacklustre guidance the UUP adopted a more independent stance in the British House of Commons; he persuaded the Labour Party government of James Callaghan to give Northern Ireland more MPs in 1979. He saw off the challenge of the DUP in the 1980s and, under Enoch Powell's influence, favoured integration with Britain rather than devolution. He was shocked by the ANGLO-IRISH AGREEMENT (1985) and briefly joined the DUP in a widespread campaign of civil resistance. He gave a guarded welcome to the DOWNING STREET DECLARATION (1993) but saw the IRA ceasefire of 1994 as 'destabilising'. Following the Frameworks Document (1995) he faced mounting internal opposition. He resigned in 1995 and was granted a life peerage two years later. **Eamon Phoenix**

Molyneux, William (1656–1698), philosopher, scientist, and member of Parliament for TRINITY COLLEGE, Dublin. He translated Descartes's *Meditations*, wrote treatises on optics, and was a founder-member of the Dublin Philosophical Society. Politically, he is best known for a celebrated natural rights defence of Irish autonomy, *The Case of Ireland's Being Bound by Acts of Parliament in England Stated* (1698). The book's initial force—still felt by Grattan in 1782—was such that it was condemned by the British House of Commons and burned by the hangman.

Philosophically, Molyneux is best known for drawing attention to a central issue in early modern thinking: the extent to which ideas depend on basic physical contact. The so-called Molyneux Problem—originally directed to the English philosopher John Locke in 1688—postulated a man who was blind from birth and able to distinguish by touch a sphere and a cube. If the man were suddenly granted sight, Molyneux asked, could he differentiate the two without first touching them? That is, could sight alone operate in conjunction with an innate spatial understanding to work out which was which? Locke, following Molyneux himself, answered negatively: we must learn to 'see' three dimensions; the formerly blind man would have to use touch as well as sight. BERKELEY went even further, suggesting that the question would be meaningless unless the man could relate what he now saw to what he had always felt. In Continental Europe, Voltaire, Condillac, and Diderot produced further varieties of the negative answer, but Leibniz suggested that the exact principles of geometrical reason could furnish a qualified positive answer. Nineteenth-century psychologists gave the question a new twist with their 'post-Kantian' controversy about whether spatial knowledge is learnt or innate. **Ian Leask**

Monaghan, County (*Contae Mhuineacháin*)

Province:	ULSTER
County town:	MONAGHAN
Area:	1,291 km^2 (498 sq. miles)
Population (2002):	52,772
Features:	Lough Egish
	Lough Muckno
	River BLACKWATER
	River Finn
	Slieve Beagh
Of historical interest:	Clones monastic site
	Hope Castle
	Tullyrain RING-FORT
Industry and products:	Agricultural equipment
	Cattle
	CEREALS
	Furniture and wood products
	LACE-making
	LINEN
	Meat, milk and mushroom processing
	POTATOES

Petula Martyn

County Monaghan is one of the southern border counties of Ulster. Co. Monaghan's boundaries were formalised in the later sixteenth century, during the native PLANTATION of 1589, when the MacMahon leadership recognised ELIZABETH I's authority. The characteristic drumlin topography is underlaid by ancient Ordovician and Silurian sandstones and shales in the east and by the northern edge of the midland Carboniferous limestone belt in the west. Traditionally rural and only lightly urbanised, Co. Monaghan witnessed some of the highest pre-FAMINE population densities anywhere in Ulster, due largely to the prevalence of the domestic linen industry; despite the additional income this provided it also witnessed some of the highest Famine mortality and EMIGRATION rates. This ushered in a prolonged period of population decline and economic stagnation, which lasted until the inter-war period of the twentieth century. **Lindsay Proudfoot**

Monaghan (*Muineachán*), county town of Co. Monaghan and cathedral town of the Catholic diocese of Clogher; POPULATION (2002) 5,737. It is a strategically sited 'gap town' controlling the Blackwater valley, one of the historically important routes from Leinster into south Ulster. In the later Middle Ages it was a stronghold of the MacMahons, Lords of Oriel, who built a FRANCISCAN friary here in 1462, destroyed by the English in 1589. The modern town dates from the PLANTATION period, when the village that had grown up under the protection of the English fort founded c. 1602 was replanned and incorporated as a borough in 1613 under the patronage of Sir Edward Blayney. Little survives from this period. Most of the remaining historical buildings date from Monaghan's early nineteenth-century prosperity as a corn, tillage, and LINEN market, serviced by the ULSTER CANAL. The town plan is irregular, centred on the Diamond (central square), Church Square, and Market Street. Notable buildings include the eleventh-century ROUND TOWER, a late medieval chapel, the Courthouse (1829), St Patrick's (Church of Ireland) parish church (1836), St Macartan's Seminary (1840), and St Macartan's (Catholic) Cathedral (1867). **Lindsay Proudfoot**

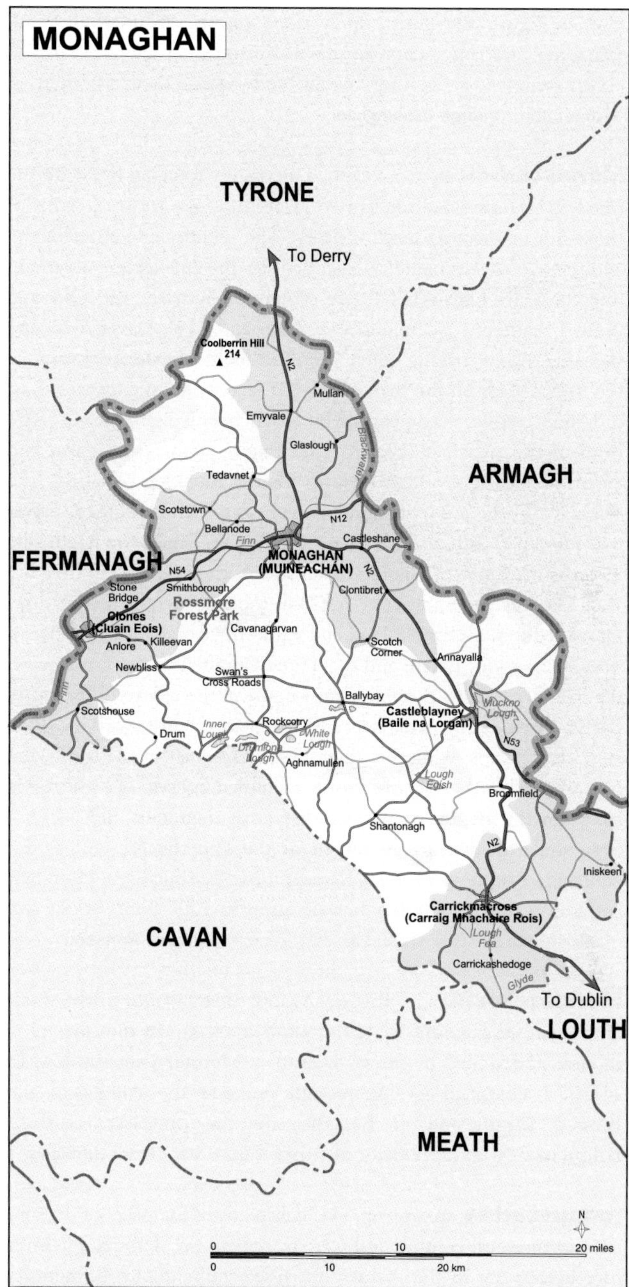

Monaincha, a ruined monastery and medieval PILGRIMAGE centre 3 km (2 miles) east of Roscrea, Co. Tipperary. The now dry bog-island of Inis Loch Cré was first recorded as the retreat of local saints: Crónán of Ros Cré, Molua of Clonfertmolua, and Canice of Aghaboe. About 800 it became a CÉILÍ DÉ centre, with Elair, anchorite and scribe, possibly leading a dissenting group from Ros Cré. Its asceticism attracted such notable penitents as Flaithbheartach, abbot and ex-king, and Maolphádraig Ó Drugáin of Armagh. GIRALDUS CAMBRENSIS recorded the site as Insula Viventium, the island on which no one could die; this story travelled around Continental Europe, eventually being recorded in the Book of BALLYMOTE as Inis na mBeo, the thirty-first wonder of the world. It remained Munster's most famous place of pilgrimage;

on one Sunday in June 1611 the Lord Deputy complained that over 15,000, 'and some say many more', gathered there. In the 1790s Loch Cré was drained and the church site on the main island walled. The surviving monuments include an exquisite twelfth-century Hiberno-ROMANESQUE church with later additions and a clothed figure of Christ on a HIGH CROSS. As Harold Leask remarked, 'no other church ruin in Ireland is so attractive in site completeness, interesting detail and appearance as that at Monaincha.' **George Cunningham**

Monasterboice, Co. Louth, a monastery founded by St Buithe (died 521), renowned for its two great sandstone HIGH CROSSES of the ninth or possibly tenth century. The identity and dates of the Muiredach whose name is inscribed on the smaller cross remain uncertain. Its high-relief figure sculpture illustrates the Old and New Testaments: Adam and Eve, Cain and Abel, David defeating Goliath, Moses striking water from the rock, and the adoration of the (four) Magi on the shaft of the east face, with an expansive Last Judgment above, accompanied by St Michael weighing souls. The head of the west face bears a Crucifixion, with resurrection and ascension, while the shaft beneath has the mocking of Christ, the 'Raised Christ', and Christ giving the keys to Peter and the Gospels to Paul. The south arm has Pilate washing his hands; the north side includes the hand of God and Paul and Anthony breaking bread.

The west cross, at over 7 m (23 ft) the tallest in Ireland, features David, Moses, a possible Paul and Anthony, Abraham's Sacrifice, a possible Samson, Elijah, and the Three Children in the Furnace on the east face, with a possible Christ figure at the centre of the head. Back to back, on the west face, are the crucified Christ with mocking and arrest panels, while the shaft illustrates Christ in the tomb, the baptism, and further unsatisfactorily identified figures. The south side has John the Baptist scenes. Further cross fragments and a cross-decorated sun-dial are preserved in the churchyard, which also contains a GRAVE-SLAB (*Ōr do Ruarcan*), two late medieval churches, and a now topless ROUND TOWER burnt in 1097 with 'books and many treasures.' [see MEDIEVAL INSCRIPTIONS.] **Peter Harbison**

Monasterevin, Co. Kildare. Moore ABBEY, south of the town (and once the home of JOHN MCCORMACK), is the site of a monastery founded by the sixth-century Munster saint Eimhín. In 1178/79 Diarmaid Ó Díomasaigh founded the Abbey of the Blessed Virgin and St Benedict for the CISTERCIANS from Baltinglass. Nothing remains of either foundation. **Peter Harbison**

monasteries sprang up like daisies over the face of Ireland around the sixth century and were to remain the dominant centres of religious life in the country for half a millennium. Sometimes grouped into *paruchiae* or families, they presented a very different form of church organisation from the episcopal system so widespread elsewhere in Europe. St Enda's monastery on Árainn (Inishmore, ARAN ISLANDS) is often credited with being among the first, but more important was St Finnian's at Clonard, Co. Meath, which became a veritable nursery of further monastic founders, many of whose monks were later to leave Ireland on voluntary PILGRIMAGE and bring the GOSPEL message to parts of Britain and Continental Europe. The monasteries were often founded by a family, which ensured that its members subsequently ruled as abbots, who were more important than the bishops and who performed all the necessary spiritual functions of baptism, Mass, and funerals. But the monasteries were also fosterers and educators, teaching a language not their own (Latin) to facilitate knowledge of the Scriptures; their *scriptoria* illuminated MANUSCRIPTS, their workshops produced religious vessels in precious metals, and their monks wrote nature poetry, preserved ancient Irish (partially pagan) lore, stored grain, dispensed hospitality, wrote history and the biographies of their founders—and even acted as warriors to defend their monastery against others.

The monastery of NENDRUM, Co. Down, may provide us with some idea of the physical appearance of such monasteries. It consists of three concentric enclosed areas. The innermost *sanctum* would have contained a church with a *plateola* (open space) in front, perhaps surrounded by monks' quarters. The second enclosure may have comprised the scriptorium, craft workshops, accommodation for monastic dependants, etc., and the outermost one farming activities. Until c. 800 almost all structures and monuments would have been of wood; perhaps VIKING raids encouraged the gradual increase in the use of stone, and HIGH CROSSES and ROUND TOWERS became common from the ninth or tenth century; but domestic buildings—sometimes even arranged in streets—were always in wood. Other island monastic sites include SCEILG MHICHÍL, Co. Kerry, and INISHMURRAY, Co. Sligo.

The original monastic ideal, as outlined in the founder's *rule*, was to live a life of asceticism and prayer. Laxity crept in, and the CÉILÍ DÉ movement tried to restore the purity of monastic life c. 800; but lay control and simony later held such sway that, after 1100, Hildebrandine church reformers strove to subdue the monasteries by setting up a DIOCESAN SYSTEM to provide the necessary church services. With the exception of those monasteries that were revitalised by the Augustinians, many were drained of resources and declined, bringing to a virtual close 600 years' tradition of fostering a culture and the arts that were so different from anything on the Continent. By then, centres of pilgrimage had developed, their venerated relics now preserved by hereditary keepers. After 1200 it was the CISTERCIANS, Dominicans, Augustinians, and FRANCISCANS who continued the monastic way of life in Ireland, though in a very different form (see p. 213). [see CÉILÍ DÉ; EASTER CONTROVERSY; MANUSCRIPTS; MEDIEVAL ECONOMY; MEDIEVAL METALWORK; SCRIPT.] **Peter Harbison**

monasticism. MONASTERIES originated in Egypt in the fourth century and soon spread to other desert areas, such as Palestine: the 'flight from the world' proclaimed a more dedicated discipleship and a surer path to God. Monasticism took two forms: *eremitic* (solitaries gathering only for liturgy) and *coenobitic* (life in community), both later found also in Ireland. This eastern, desert pattern was adapted to Western Europe by Cassian in southern Gaul in the fifth century. This 'desert period', familiar to readers of Cassian's writings, remained the monastic ideal propagated through its hagiography: Athanasius, Jerome, and Palladius. It can be seen in the ideal monasteries of ADOMNÁN's 'Vita Columbae' and the 'Navigatio Sancti Brendani'; and it inspired many later 'reforms', such as the CÉILÍ DÉ movement. These echoes, so contrasting with later Benedictinism, have led many to imagine elaborate connections between Ireland and 'the East'. The first mention of monasticism in Ireland is in Patrick's CONFESSIO, but it is not until the later sixth century that we have evidence for actual monasteries (such as BANGOR) and founders gathering disciples in places that were becoming important centres of economic activity, the religious-administrative expression of particular dynasties, as well as places of learning and asceticism. By the seventh century there were many important monasteries in Ireland, as well as Irish monks abroad, such as COLM CILLE on IONA—the focus of a *familia* of monasteries in Ireland and Britain—and COLUMBANUS on the Continent. This monasticism was not much affected by the standardisation of monasticism on the Benedictine model in the ninth century and was replaced only with the arrival of the CISTERCIANS in the twelfth century. **Thomas O'Loughlin**

monastic schools. As most of our evidence for learning in the Early Christian period is church-related or monastery-related, there is a tendency to see monastic schools *per se* as early medieval schools. However, Western MONASTICISM had an academic agenda from the outset: the monastery was a place where *disciplina* was learnt from elders about the praise of God and the pursuit of wisdom. As a place of wisdom, the monastery had to assist its monks to grow in the 'fear and knowledge of God' by understanding the two creations: the natural creation (the Universe) and the gracious new creation (Jesus Christ). Study, therefore, had a central place; and the book they held to be the guide to both creations, the Scriptures, played a unique role. But access to the book was obtained through language (specifically Latin), and so its study (grammar) was seen as the portico to wisdom; and as Latin was a foreign language in Ireland, its importance accordingly increased. Because both the creation and the book revealed God, the study of order in the creation and its coded reflection in the book demanded study, as witnessed in the Irish textbook *De Ordine Creaturarum*. This involved their perception of the classical *quadrivium* as being based on number; so the study of numbered realities, such as the heavens, or the numbers used in Scripture, became a tool of theological discovery, as in the Irish *Liber de Numeris*. A practical expression of this interest in numbered order is the concern with the dating of Easter.

The monastery was a place were *discipuli* or students came to learn. It had to pass on its learning to those following, hence the quantity of surviving teaching materials—patristic summaries, text-books, teachers' notes, and classroom dialogues—and also the energy expended in assembling libraries and copying books. In Cassiodorus's *Institutes* Irish monks found a rationale for this range of study, along with a list of works for their ideal library. **Thomas O'Loughlin**

Monck, William Henry Stanley (1839–1915), lawyer and amateur astronomer. Born in Skirk, Co. Laois; educated at home and TCD, where he studied divinity and law. He was called to the bar in 1873 and was appointed chief registrar in bankruptcy in the High Court. He returned to academic life in 1878 and became professor of moral philosophy in TCD. He contributed many well-informed articles and letters to astronomical journals. In August 1892 he and Stephen M. Dixon made the first photo-electric observations of planets and stars, using equipment provided by G. M. MINCHIN and G. F. FITZGERALD. In 1894 Monck suggested the existence of two classes of yellow stars, the *dwarfs* (dull and near) and the *giants* (bright and remote). **Ian Elliott**

Monck's Observatory (1888–1915), established at 16 Earlsfort Terrace, Dublin, by the lawyer William H. S. Monck. In 1892, with G. F. FITZGERALD and GEORGE MINCHIN and using an Erck 191 mm (7.5-in.) refractor, he succeeded in making the first photo-electric measurements of starlight, anticipating by some fifteen years the work of Joel Stebbins in the United States. He later increased the efficiency of the apparatus and made further measurements of stellar radiation at DARAMONA OBSERVATORY in 1895. He next considered the connection between the proper motion of stars and their spectra, demonstrating the correct order, in contradiction to the established temperature sequence, and came close to antici-pating by ten years the work of Hertzsprung in constructing the Hertzsprung-Russell diagram. **Susan McKenna-Lawlor**

Monasterboice. *Muiredach's Cross (east face). The Last Judgment spans the horizontal arms of the cross, with (in the panels below) St Michael weighing souls, Adoration of the Magi, Moses striking the rock, David and Goliath, Adam and Eve with Cain and Abel, and two cats. [Dúchas, The Heritage Service]*

money bill dispute, a conflict in 1753 between the Irish Parliament and executive over the disposal of a revenue surplus. It echoed the issues of the sole right controversy of 1692 but also reflected a conflict of competing factions in the Irish House of Commons. Though a solution was reached in 1756, the incident continues to be cited as a point of origin for the decline in the relationship between the British government and the Irish Protestant elite. [see PARLIAMENT 1200–1800.] **Neal Garnham**

Monsell, J. R. (born 1877), illustrator and writer. Born in Co. Kerry; after his father's death he moved to Limerick, where he and his sister Elinor were brought up by their uncle; when she won a scholarship to the Slade School of Fine Art, London, he also moved to London. With no known formal art education, by 1900 he was working as a magazine and book illustrator. He worked in a range of styles and was clearly influenced by Caldecott in his vibrant, fluid line drawings, best seen in his own books, such as *The Hooded Crow* (1926) and *Balderdash Ballads* (1934). There are elements of caricature in his style, which gives us the villainous *Buccaneers* (1908) and *The Unlucky Golfer* (1904). Interested in HERALDRY, he designed heraldic jackets for several books by his wife, Margaret Irwin. **Patricia Donlon**

Montague, John (1929–), poet and fiction writer. Born in New York, reared in Co. Tyrone by two aunts; educated at UCD and Yale University. He is one of Ireland's most established and prolific poets. His experience of being separated from his parents and his brothers was to form the background to much of his work, particularly the sequence poem *The Rough Field* (1972). Similar political and familial preoccupations were to recur in later work, especially in a second long sequence poem, *The Dead Kingdom* (1984). The joys of love and the pains of separation are matter for many of his poems; *The Great Cloak* (1978) is a trance-like study in marital breakdown and rediscovered eroticism. His poetry addresses both personal experience and national themes with a linguistic objectivity and formal experimentalism learnt from American writers such as William Carlos Williams and Charles Olson. Its consciousness of mythic and magical perspectives (as in *A Slow Dance*, 1975) also indicates a debt to W. B. YEATS. The cool intensity of the best of his lyrics, however, with their hesitant yet compelling rhythms, makes them poems of individual power.

Montague lived in France and lectured in the United States until his return to Ireland in 1972. He was appointed to an academic post at University College, Cork, where he retired as an associate professor of English. His *Collected Poems* appeared in 1995. His fiction includes *Death of a Chieftain* (1964), *The Lost Notebook* (1987), *An Occasion of Sin* (1992), and *A Love Present* (1997). In 1998 he was appointed first holder of the Ireland Chair of Poetry. **Alison Walsh**

Montez, Lola (c. 1818–1861), stage name of Marie Dolores Eliza Rosanna Gilbert, dancer. Her date and place of birth are disputed: claims have been made both for Limerick (1818) and Grange, Co. Sligo (1821). The daughter of an army officer who died young, she was educated in Scotland and England. She defied her mother's plans for a conventional marriage and eloped to Ireland at sixteen with a Lieutenant James. They divorced five years later. In June 1843 she first appeared as a professional dancer in London, under the name 'Lola Montez, Spanish dancer'. Her performance was not a success; she was recognised by some in the audience as Mrs James. However, her career prospered on the Continent. She became celebrated for her erotic 'Tarantula' dance and for her love affairs; her lovers included Liszt. In 1847 her performances in Munich captivated King Ludwig of Bavaria, whose lover she became and who made her Countess of Landsfeld. Fleeing Bavaria after the deposition of Ludwig in the revolution of 1848, she moved to the United States. She remarried, but her second husband died. She performed in the east, 1851–3, before moving to California, where she married P. P. Hull. This marriage ended in divorce in 1859, following which she returned to New York. In the meantime she had toured Australia in 1855 and 1856.

Lola Montez was a *femme de scandale* and one of the most famous women in the world. She died of pneumonia in New York, barely forty years old, on 17 January 1861. **Fergal Tobin**

Montgomery, Viscount Bernard (1887–1976), British general. Of Ulster descent, Montgomery became the most prominent British field commander of the SECOND WORLD WAR. As commander of the 3rd Division he performed well in the Battle of France and then held important appointments in the defence of southern England. In August 1942 he took over the 8th Army from General Auchinleck, who had checked the earlier Axis advance and defeated Rommel's forces at the Second Battle of al-Alamein. After fighting with considerable skill in north Africa and Italy he returned to England as land commander for the invasion of Europe. The success of the landings owed much to his flair for organisation, but his subsequent conduct of operations was controversial, particularly his failure to secure Caen. Relations with his American allies deteriorated sharply, and his plan to seize the lower Rhine with airborne forces ended with serious losses at Arnhem. He was opposed to Eisenhower's 'broad front' offensive into Germany, but he successfully led his army group in the Rhine crossings in 1945. On 4 May 1945 the German armies in the north surrendered to him on Lüneburger Heide (Lüneburg Heath). **T. G. Fraser**

Montgomery, Henry (1788–1865), Presbyterian minister. Born in Killead, Co. Antrim. Ordained in 1809, he was headmaster of the English school in the Royal Belfast Academical Institution. He was an Arian (denying the full Trinitarian nature of God) and a non-subscriber to the Westminster Confession of Faith. In the 1820s a bitter debate within Irish PRESBYTERIANISM saw the defeat of Arians and non-subscribers by their orthodox Trinitarian opponents under the leadership of HENRY COOKE. Montgomery reacted to this defeat by forming the Remonstrant Synod of Ulster in 1829. A LIBERAL in politics, he supported CATHOLIC EMANCIPATION but opposed REPEAL. **Fergal Tobin**

Monto, colloquial name in Dublin patois, current during the nineteenth and early twentieth centuries, for the vicinity of Montgomery Street, Dublin, then an extensive brothel and tenement quarter, celebrated as Nighttown in the Circe episode of ULYSSES. The numerous British army regiments garrisoned in the city, as well as local clientele, kept busy a population of prostitutes numbering at least a thousand (in 1868 there were 132 brothels in the city). Prostitution in Dublin was unregulated by police control, a situation at the time unique in Ireland or Britain, as remarked on in the 1903 edition of *Encyclopaedia Britannica*. FRANK DUFF, a vigorous lay missionary, together with members of the Legion of Mary, which he had founded in 1921, successfully campaigned for the closure of the Monto brothels, which ceased to operate following police raids in 1925. **Brian Lalor**

Mooghaun, a late BRONZE AGE HILL-FORT near Ennis, Co. Clare. Enclosing 11 ha (27 acres), it is defended by three separate lines of defence, each consisting of large stone ramparts up to 11 m (36 ft) wide and 2.5 m (8 ft) high. Excavation has shown that it was built and occupied in the period 1050–900 BC, evidently the work of a strong, wealthy and cohesive society. It was the great central site of an important regional chiefdom that occupied an area of 450 km^2 (175 sq. miles) and may have had a population of 10,000 or more. The hill-fort was intended as a symbol of power and affluence that could be recognised and shared by the whole community. However, only a small group charged with its maintenance occupied the hilltop, living in circular houses. They practised mixed farming, which included the rearing of pigs, cattle, sheep, and horses and the large-scale cultivation of cereals. While its defences appear very impressive, the hill-fort is far too large to have been defended effectively against concerted tactical assault; it is probable that it was intended as a symbolic barrier. A large hoard of Bronze Age gold was found nearby in the nineteenth century. [see GOLD, PREHISTORIC.] **Eoin Grogan**

Moone, Co. Kildare, an early, possibly Columban monastery best known for its tall and slender ninth-century HIGH CROSS, reconstructed from three fragments in 1893 and recently moved into the ruined medieval church on the site. Animals decorate the shaft, and Christ dominates one side of the head. The base is noted for its flat, graphic carvings: Adam and Eve, the sacrifice of Isaac, Daniel in the lions' den, the three Hebrew children in the furnace, the flight into Egypt, the loaves and fishes, the Crucifixion, apostles, Paul and Anthony, and an apocalyptic beast. Fragments of a second cross with central hole and symbolic animal sculpture are displayed nearby. **Peter Harbison**

Moone. *The base of the west face of Moone High Cross, depicting the Twelve Apostles. The naïve yet graphically accomplished style of the carving is unique among high crosses. [Dúchas, The Heritage Service]*

Mooney, Martin (1964–), poet. Born in Belfast and raised in Newtownards, Co. Down; educated at QUB. His collections include *Brecht and an Exquisite Corpse* (1992), *Escaping with Cuts and Bruises* (1992), *Grub* (1993), and *Bonfire Makers* (1995). His poems have appeared in numerous anthologies. **Heather Clark**

Mooney, Ria (1903–1973), actor, director, manager, and teacher. Born in Dublin; educated at the Metropolitan School of Art. She began acting with the ABBEY THEATRE company in 1924, notably in O'CASEY's *Plough and the Stars* (1926) (see p. 801). She left in 1943 to produce new plays at the GAIETY THEATRE. In 1948 she returned to the Abbey, where she directed up to twelve productions annually until 1963. **Christopher Morash**

Moore, Brian (1921–1999), novelist. Born in Belfast; educated at St Malachy's College. He served as an air raid warden in Belfast during the SECOND WORLD WAR, worked for the British Ministry of Transport in Algiers and Naples, 1943–5, and was employed by a UN relief agency in Warsaw, 1946–7. In 1948 he emigrated to Canada and settled in Montréal, where he became a successful journalist and writer of pulp fiction. His first literary novel, *Judith Hearne* (1955), retitled THE LONELY PASSION OF JUDITH HEARNE, was a critical success on both sides of the Atlantic. *The Feast of Lupercal* (1957) and *The Luck of Ginger Coffey* (1960) followed before he went to live in New York in 1959, the recipient of a Guggenheim fellowship. He moved to California in 1965 and spent the rest of his life there, making frequent visits to Ireland. His twenty-one novels deal with EMIGRATION and displacement, family ties and the search for identity, and the quest for meaning in a post-Christian world. Among his major early novels are *An Answer from Limbo* (1962), which conveys his disillusionment with the commercialisation of New York literary life, and *I Am Mary Dunne* (1968), in which he brilliantly captures the feelings and neuroses of a female protagonist. Always an experimenter in theme and style, he determined never to write a similar novel twice. In the 1970s and 80s his work varied from a Borges-style fable, *The Great Victorian Collection* (1976), to a metaphysical thriller, *Cold Heaven* (1983), and the historical *Black Robe* (1987). His later novels were thrillers, with a spiritual or metaphysical content, written in a spare, cinematic style. Three of these marked a return to settings that he experienced as a young man: *The Colour of Blood* (1987) is set in Poland; *Lies of Silence* (1990) is the novel of the Northern Ireland 'TROUBLES' that he said he would never write; and *The Statement* (1995) deals with the guilt of members of the collaborationist French Catholic Church during the Second World War. His last novel, *The Magician's Wife* (1997), is set in Algeria and deals with the ethical blindness of European colonial power as well as the presumed fanaticism of Islam. He won several literary prizes in Britain and was twice awarded the Governor-General's Award, Canada's highest literary honour. *The Lonely Passion of Judith Hearne* and three other books have been filmed. **Jo O'Donoghue**

Moore, Christy (1945–), singer, musician, and songwriter. Born in Newbridge, Co. Kildare; he left for England in the late 1960s, where he learnt his trade in the folk clubs. On his return to Ireland in 1971 he recorded *Prosperous* (released in 1972), which led to the formation of PLANXTY with DÓNAL LUNNY, ANDY IRVINE, and LIAM O'FLYNN. He was a founder-member of MOVING HEARTS in 1981; since then he has largely performed solo, mixing traditional, contemporary, and comic songs, often with strong political comment. He retired from public performance in 1998 and published his memoirs as *One Voice: My Life in Song* (2000). **Pat Ahern**

Moore, David (1807–1879), botanist. Born in Dundee, Scotland, where he learnt botany and gardening. From 1828 he was foreman of the TRINITY COLLEGE Botanic Garden in Dublin and from 1834 botanist to the ORDNANCE SURVEY of Cos. Antrim and Derry. During his curatorship of the BOTANIC GARDENS at Glasnevin, Dublin, he gained an international reputation for the extent of its plant collections. He raised orchids from seed to flowering stage, and made the first formal record of potato blight, on 20 August 1845. He recorded the mosses and liverworts of Ireland and, with A. G. MORE, wrote *Cybele Hibernica* (1866), an inventory of the native flowering plants and ferns. **Donal Synnott**

Moore, Sir Frederick William (1857–1949), horticulturist. Born in Dublin, where his father, DAVID MOORE, was keeper of the BOTANIC GARDENS at Glasnevin; educated in Dublin and Hannover, and trained in horticulture at Ghent and Leiden. On the death of his father he became curator of the Botanic Gardens at Glasnevin at the early age of twenty-two. He greatly developed the plant collections, especially the conifers, alpines, tropical orchids, palms, and cycads, and improved horticultural standards. Under his care Glasnevin came to be regarded as one of the finest botanic gardens in the world. He was knighted in 1911 for his services to horticulture. **Donal Synnott**

Moore, Gary (1952–), guitarist. Born in Belfast. He was first heard in the Dublin progressive rock band SKID ROW in the late 1960s. He soon joined THIN LIZZY, but not before playing with other notable groups, Granny's Intentions and Dr Strangely Strange. In 1979 Moore and Phil Lynott had a hit with 'Parisienne Walkways'; but his international breakthrough really came only in the early 1990s with a succession of finely wrought blues albums, including *Still Got the Blues for You* (1990). **Tony Clayton-Lea**

Moore, George. George Moore *(1879), pastel on canvas, by Édouard Manet. An influential and controversial nineteenth-century novelist, Moore was associated with W. B. Yeats and Lady Gregory in the Irish Literary Revival. [Metropolitan Museum of Art, H. O. Havemeyer Collection, Bequest of Mrs H. O. Havemeyer (29.100.55); photograph © 1990 Metropolitan Museum of Art]*

Moore, George (1852–1933), writer. Born in Moore Hall, Ballyglass, Co. Mayo, the first child of George Henry Moore, Catholic LANDLORD and member of Parliament, and Mary Blake Moore, daughter of Maurice Blake of Ballinafad. At the age of nine he went to St Mary's College, Oscott, near Birmingham, but at fifteen he was sent home as a hopeless case. In 1870, on the death of his father, he inherited an estate of 5,000 ha (12,000 acres). At twenty-one he went to Paris to study painting, but he did not succeed and took up writing instead, publishing Baudelarian poems, *Flowers of Passion* (1877), and a blank-verse tragedy, *Martin Luther* (1879), before being called home by the LAND WAR. Putting an agent in charge of his estate, he planned to make a living in London as a writer. His first success, characteristically controversial, was the Zolaesque *A Mummer's Wife* (1885), which was banned, like subsequent novels, by circulating libraries, followed by *A Drama in Muslin* (1886), an impassioned yet estranged book about landlordism. He had to wait until 1894 and the publication of *Esther Waters* to enjoy critical and popular success. Attracted to the Irish Literary Theatre by YEATS, he served as script doctor for EDWARD MARTYN's *The Heather Field* (1899) and *Bending of the Bough* (1900) and collaborator with Yeats on *Diarmuid and Grania* (1901). In 1901 he moved to 4 Upper Ely Place, Dublin, from where he observed the social and literary scene until 1911, publishing stories that influenced JOYCE (THE UNTILLED FIELD, 1903), a stream-of-consciousness novel, *The Lake* (1905), and an autobiographical trilogy, *Hail and Farewell* (1911, 1912, 1914), a farewell to defeated landlordism and an over-the-top attack on triumphant Catholicism.

Moore's last twenty years were spent at Ebury Street, London, close to artist friends in Chelsea. Of many pleasing late works the most enduring are the stories about characters not destined for heterosexual life, *Celibate Lives* (1927). Moore's own sexual sensibility was lively, polymorphous, and voyeuristic. His most lasting attachment was to Lady Maud Cunard, whose daughter Nancy may have been Moore's sole child. But his only constant love was his art. Having produced more than sixty titles, in January 1933 he gave up work on *A Communication to My Friends*, saying, 'I have written enough,' and died days later.

No turn-of-the-century literary figure of equivalent stature has been so forgotten. For readers of another century Moore is an artist of autobiography, an anti-nationalist champion of individual freedom, an experimentalist in narrative forms, and a Nietzschean who believed that only in aesthetic terms is life justified. **Adrian Frazier**

Moore, Michael (c. 1640–1726), scholastic philosopher and cleric. Born in Dublin; educated at the University of Paris. He taught rhetoric and philosophy in Paris until 1686, when he returned to Ireland to become Vicar-General of the Archdiocese of Dublin. Though the evidence is not conclusive, it seems he was also appointed as first Catholic provost of TRINITY COLLEGE, Dublin, in 1689. Having apparently offended JAMES II, however, he returned to the Continent, shortly before the defeat of the JACOBITES, and eventually became rector of the University of Paris. Philosophically, he is best known for his opposition to the growing influence of Descartes: in works such as *De Existentia Dei* (1692) and *Vera Sciendi Methodus* (1716) he argued for the continuing relevance of medieval systems of physics and metaphysics derived from Aristotle. **Ian Leask**

Moore, Paddy (1909–1951), soccer player. Born in Dublin. In a short-lived international career he won just nine caps, scoring the winner on his first appearance against Spain in front of 100,000 spectators in Barcelona in 1931. It was in a World Cup tie against Belgium at Dalymount Park in 1934 that he took his place in history as the first player to score four times in an eventful 4–4 draw. He was the first of Ireland's football superstars to fight an unrelenting battle with ALCOHOLISM in a manner that would earn him a place in the folklore of the sport. **Peter Byrne**

Moore, Thomas (1779–1852), poet. Born in Aungier Street, Dublin, son of a grocer; educated at Samuel Whyte's Academy, Grafton Street, and TCD, being among the first Catholics to attend the university. His political education began at home, his parents inculcating in him a lifelong idealisation of HENRY GRATTAN and the Volunteers. At Trinity, despite friendships with Edward Hudson and ROBERT EMMET, he was not actively involved with the United Irishmen. *Odes of Anacreon* (1800) was his passport to the fashionable houses of London. In 1804 he spent several months in Bermuda in an Admiralty post. Light, vaguely licentious collections of verse preceded numerous satires in the Whig cause, invariably advocating CATHOLIC EMANCIPATION.

His reputation rests largely on the *Irish Melodies* (ten numbers, 1808–34). His filigree verses, suffused with loss and melancholy, were set to music adapted by Sir JOHN STEVENSON from EDWARD BUNTING's collection of traditional airs. Often drawing on events in Irish history and legend, they crystallised an iconography for later generations, conferring tragic dignity and respectability on Irish culture; they were popular also in translation throughout Europe. With the success of the Oriental verse romance *Lalla Rookh* (1817), Moore's fame was rivalled only by that of Scott and Byron. In 1818 he was held responsible for his Bermudan deputy's embezzlement, and he went into exile on the Continent until 1822, after which he turned increasingly to prose. In 1824 he was complicit in the burning of Byron's memoirs; in recompense he wrote in 1830 a celebrated biography of his friend. *Memoirs of Captain Rock* (1824) and biographies of RICHARD BRINSLEY SHERIDAN (1825) and EDWARD FITZGERALD (1831) attested to an intellectual commitment to Irish affairs

Disaffection with party politics after Emancipation led to more idiosyncratic works, including religious controversy and a problematic four-volume *History of Ireland* (1835–46). In 1811 Moore married Elizabeth Dyke, an actor; they moved to Wiltshire in 1817 and together endured the deaths of their five children. Moore declined to enter Parliament in 1832 but welcomed a controversial Civil List pension three years later. In his last years he suffered from mental ill health, and he died at home on 26 February 1852. His widow presented his library to the ROYAL IRISH ACADEMY in 1855. His letters and journals, posthumously edited by his friend Lord John Russell, the Prime Minister, are a valuable if uncritical record of the daily interactions and vicissitudes of early nineteenth-century literary and political life. **Ronan Kelly**

Moore's *Irish Melodies*, a ten-volume series of the musical works of THOMAS MOORE, begun in 1808, with an additional supplement in 1834. It was so commercially and critically successful that it established Moore as the national poet. Drawing on other published material, principally the music collection of EDWARD BUNTING, private manuscripts, and certainly an amount of material accumulated in important musical friendships with people such as Edward Hudson, Moore was to publish 124 songs, with 126 related airs. *Irish Melodies* was widely and immediately celebrated, with many of its songs enduring to the present day, some in fact now perceived as part of the traditional repertoire. **Glenn Cumiskey**

Moran, D. P. [David Patrick] (1869–1936), journalist and Gaelic Leaguer. Born in Waterford and worked in London. He came to prominence by ridiculing nationalist rhetoric, social climbing, and the 'CELTIC TWILIGHT' and by equating Irishness with Catholicism and Gaelicism (*The Philosophy of Irish Ireland*, 1905). In 1900 he founded a Dublin weekly, THE LEADER. His ingenious scurrility and advocacy of industrial development won a following among Catholic activists and businessmen. His scepticism about political NATIONALISM (which led him to criticise the IRISH PARTY and SINN FÉIN) reduced his influence after 1906, but he retained a devoted readership until his death, and *The Leader* survived until 1971. **Patrick Maume**

Moran, Dermot B. (1953–), philosopher. Born in Dublin; educated at UCD and the University of Yale. He is professor of philosophy (chair of logic and metaphysics) at the University College, Dublin. As editor of the *International Journal of Philosophical Studies*, a position held since 1993, Moran has been a central figure in attempts to overcome the worldwide split between 'analytical' and 'Continental' philosophy. He has also produced important scholarly work such as *The Philosophy of John Scotus Eriugena* (1989), and *Introduction to Phenomenology* (2000). **Fionola Meredith.**

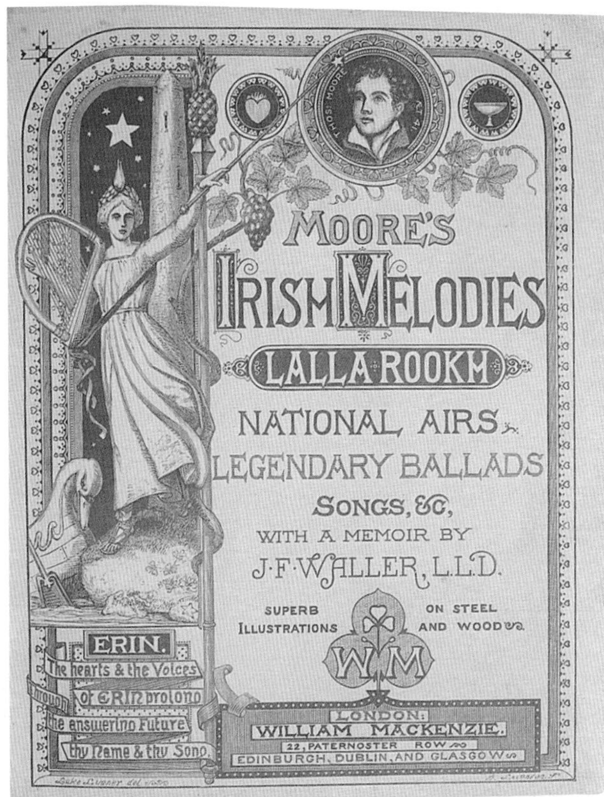

Moore's Irish Melodies. *Title page of* Moore's Irish Melodies. *The figure of Music (left) with a harp inspires Moore with her wand, against a background of a round tower, symbol of the glories of the past. [Antique Prints; photo: Denis Mortell]*

Moran, Dylan (1972–), comedian, actor, and writer. Born in Navan, Co. Meath. In his early twenties the languid, surreal storyteller drifted into stand-up COMEDY in Dublin, and a meteoric rise to fame followed. He won the Perrier Award at the Edinburgh Fringe in 1996 and appeared in two series of 'How Do You Want Me?' for BBC television in 1998 and 1999 as an Irish photographer trapped in a hostile English village. In 2000 he played an irascible bookseller in 'Black Books', written by himself and Graham Linehan. In the mid-1990s he wrote a regular column for the IRISH TIMES. **Stephen Dixon and Deirdre Falvey**

Moran, Kevin (1956–), soccer player. Born in Dublin. A pivotal personality in the success of the Republic of Ireland team under JACK CHARLTON, he found success in soccer on the rebound after an unproductive spell with Bohemians had persuaded him to concentrate on GAELIC FOOTBALL in the mid-1970s. He won all-Ireland medals with Dublin in 1976 and 1977 before Manchester United signed him at a time when he was playing soccer in the Leinster Senior League with UCD. As an old-fashioned stopper centre-back he built a successful career at Old Trafford, and on his departure in 1988 he had a spell with Sporting Gijon in Spain. When he finished his career at Blackburn Rovers he had accumulated seventy-one caps. **Peter Byrne**

Moravian Church, an episcopal and liturgical church, known as Unitas Fratrum ('unity of brothers'), which stems from the followers

Moriarty. *Joan Denise Moriarty, dancer, choreographer, and dance director. She opened her first school in 1934, which subsequently developed into Irish National Ballet.* [Irish Examiner]

of the fifteenth-century Czech reformer Jan Hus. JOHN CENNICK, an evangelist, came to Dublin and founded the first congregation there in 1749, as well as preaching all over the northern counties. A full-scale Moravian settlement was built at Gracehill, near Ballymena, Co. Antrim, now the mother church. Five Moravian congregations remain, all in Northern Ireland. **Gabrielle Brocklesby**

More, A. G. [Alexander Goodman] (1830–1895), naturalist. Born in London; educated at the University of Cambridge, where ill health prevented him taking his degree. A stimulator and adviser of a generation of Irish naturalists, his main interest was in Irish plants, which began on boyhood visits to Co. Galway. He published *Cybele Hibernica* (1866) with DAVID MOORE. He became an assistant in the NATURAL HISTORY MUSEUM in 1867 but in 1887 retired because of ill health. He was also interested in Irish FLORA and FAUNA, especially MAMMALS, birds, and fishes. **D. Patrick Sleeman**

Morgan, Dermot (1952–1998), comedian and satirist. Born in Dublin; studied English at UCD before becoming a teacher. He began sending COMEDY sketches to RTÉ in the early 1980s and soon became a full-time writer and performer, developing such memorable characters as Father Trendy in 'The Live Mike'. In 1990 Morgan and the writer GERARD STEMBRIDGE created 'Scrap Saturday', a satirical radio series that nettled the establishment and ran for several successful seasons. He played the title role in the successful television series *Father Ted* (1995–8) but died of a heart attack the day after the final scenes of the third series had been recorded. **Stephen Dixon and Deirdre Falvey**

Morgan, George (1912–1979), rugby footballer. He scored a try on his debut against England at Lansdowne Road in 1934 and then played in every international match for Ireland up to the outbreak of the SECOND WORLD WAR. He toured South Africa with the 1938 British Lions team, captained by Sammy Walker of Instonians, and played in the third Test at Cape Town, when the tourists won, 21–16. **Karl Johnston**

Moriarty, Joan Denise (1912–1992), dancer, choreographer, and dance director. Her place of birth is unknown (probably Mallow, Co. Cork); she studied ballet with Marie Rambert and Irish dancing with the Liverpool Branch of the GAELIC LEAGUE, becoming champion Irish stepdancer of Great Britain in 1931. She also won the Munster Open Championship in Solo War Pipes in Killarney in 1933. Opening her first dance school in Mallow in 1934, she founded the amateur CORK BALLET COMPANY in 1947, Irish Theatre Ballet in 1954, and Irish Ballet Company in 1973, renamed Irish National Ballet in 1983. She choreographed eighty-seven ballets, including PLAYBOY OF THE WESTERN WORLD (1978), which involved a unique collaboration with the CHIEFTAINS. She also choreographed THE TÁIN (1982) and *Reputations* (1981), the first ballet commissioned by RTÉ television. She was awarded an honorary doctorate by the National University of Ireland in 1979, a Harveys of Bristol Theatre Award, 1982, and a People of the Year Award, 1983. **Carolyn Swift**

Mormons. Missionaries of the Church of Jesus Christ of Latter-Day Saints, commonly known as Mormons, first came to Ireland in 1840. They faced considerable opposition from LANDLORDS, some of whom threatened to evict tenants associating with them. 150 full-time missionaries (most of whom are American) proselytise in pairs. The present membership stands at about 7,000. [see CALLIS, CHARLES A.] **Gabrielle Brocklesby**

Morphy, Garret (fl. 1673–1716), portrait painter. He is first documented in 1673 working in London, where he was a pupil of Edmund Ashfield. Before 1688 he travelled around the north of England painting the local gentry; after 1694 he was mainly in Ireland. Stylistically his work displays a knowledge of mainstream portraiture of the period as practised in both France and England. His importance lies in his position as the first known Irish-born portrait painter in modern times. More than eighty portraits by Morphy have been found, though only three are signed. **Jane Fenlon**

Morris, Frederick (1929–), lawyer and judge. Born in Kilkenny; educated at UCD and the KING'S INNS. He was called to the bar in 1952 and became a senior counsel the same year. He was appointed a judge of the High Court in 1990 and president of the High Court in 1998. He served on the Bar Council for ten years and was a member of the tribunal on personal injuries compensation. **Neville Cox**

Morris, Michael, Lord Killanin (1914–1999), journalist and sports administrator. Born in London; educated at the Universities of Paris and Cambridge. He spent a number of years in China during the 1930s as a correspondent for the *Daily Mail*, and served in the British army during the SECOND WORLD WAR. He was elected president of the OLYMPIC Council of Ireland in 1950; in 1952 he was appointed to the International Olympic Committee and in 1972 was appointed its sixth president. During his eight-year term of office he oversaw an extensive reform of the Olympic movement, including the expansion of the IOC and the relaxation of the rule on amateurism. **Brian Galvin**

Morris, Séamus (died 1948), naval officer. Born in Galway into one of the town's oldest maritime families. In 1916 he and his brother fought in the naval battle of Jutland or Skager Rak against the German High Seas Fleet; his brother was killed but Séamus survived. In command of a cruiser after the war, he heard of Black and Tan atrocities at home and, having verified them, felt he must resign his commission and end what promised to be a successful career. He wrote, without receiving a reply, to each Irish government after the British withdrawal urging the creation of a small coastal defence fleet and a strong merchant fleet. When the SECOND WORLD WAR began and the Government realised that its declaration of neutrality would be invalid if Ireland had no naval force to defend its coasts, he was asked to improvise a navy. This he did, in spite of numerous obstacles, and he successfully commanded it, clearing hundreds of sea mines from coastal waters and detaining suspicious ships. He also helped found the Maritime Institute of Ireland. **John de Courcy Ireland**

Morrison, George (1922–), film director and archivist. Born in Tramore, Co. Waterford. He is best known for two feature-length actuality films, *Mise Éire* (1959) and *Saoirse?* (1961), both with a score by Seán Ó Riada, which used archival film unseen for forty years or more to present the struggle for independence up to the outbreak of the CIVIL WAR in 1922. He later made documentaries on more conventional subjects, contributed photographs to books on Irish history and produced his own—*Emergent Ireland*. **Kevin Rockett**

Morrison, James (1893–1947), fiddle-player and teacher. Born in Drumfin, Co. Sligo. He was one of the touchstones of the Co. Sligo style of TRADITIONAL MUSIC. Already a respected musician and teacher before he emigrated to America in 1915, his recording career, both as a soloist and with others, spanned a period of fifteen years after 1921. These recordings remain influential today, making 'the professor', as he came to be called, a significant figure in traditional music. **Desi Wilkinson**

Morrison, Sir Richard (1767–1849), architect. Born in Co. Cork into one of Ireland's architectural dynasties, son of John Morrison, who practised mainly in the south of Ireland, and father of WILLIAM VITRUVIUS MORRISON (1794–1838); studied ARCHITECTURE at the Dublin Society schools, then under the direction of HENRY AARON BAKER. He set up practice in Clonmel, Co. Tipperary, and published *Useful and Ornamental Designs in Architecture* (1793), one of the few pattern books produced by architects in Ireland at this time. Just before his move to Dublin c. 1800 he built the County Courthouse, Clonmel; this building, together with Sir PATRICK DUN'S HOSPITAL in Dublin, shows the influence of GANDON on his work. He established a successful country house practice, from modest villas to mansions; among these are Castlegar, Co. Galway, and Cangort Park, Co. Offaly. As architect to TRINITY COLLEGE he built Botany Bay and the Anatomy House and encased the upper storeys of the Old Library in granite.

William Vitruvius Morrison joined the practice in 1809, and father and son collaborated on Kilruddery, Co. Wicklow, Ballyfin, Co. Laois, FOTA HOUSE, Co. Cork, and Baronscourt, Co. Tyrone. A founder-member of the ROYAL INSTITUTE OF THE ARCHITECTS OF IRELAND in 1839, Morrison was knighted in 1841. **Patricia McCarthy**

Morrison, George Ivan (Van) (1945–), singer. Born in Belfast. He was playing guitar, saxophone and HARMONICA by the age of thirteen, encouraged by his father, a keen collector of JAZZ and blues records. At the age of twelve Morrison had already played

Morrison, Van. *Van Morrison, one of Ireland's best-known and most successful singer-songwriters. Eschewing musical trends he has recorded a body of nearly thirty solo albums. [Hot Press]*

in semi-professional country and skiffle bands. He left school at sixteen to turn professional, joining a showband, the Monarchs, who by 1963 were embracing soul and R&B and touring Scotland and England. A subsequent trip to Germany resulted in the band splitting up, whereupon Morrison returned to Belfast, where he formed Them, an uncompromising, fierce R&B band. Following two hit singles, 'Baby, Please Don't Go' (1965)—which included the garage band classic 'Gloria' on the B side—and 'Here Comes the Night' (1965), the group broke up. Shortly afterwards Morrison moved to America, where he released what can be regarded as his best album, *Astral Weeks* (1968). Following such a landmark record would prove difficult for the majority of artists, but throughout the decades Morrison has released albums that have vied with it for supremacy: *Moondance* (1970), *St Dominic's Preview* (1972), the superb live album *It's Too Late to Stop Now* (1974), *Veedon Fleece* (1974), *Into the Music* (1979), *Inarticulate Speech of the Heart* (1983), *Irish Heartbeat* (with the CHIEFTAINS) (1988), and *Avalon Sunset* (1989). Throughout this period Morrison roamed from one musical style to another: rock, late-night jazz, country, folk, pop, traditional, and soul, investing his work with a deeply questioning, spiritual nature. An occasionally introspective style, which vacillated between gruff and meditative, ensured that his work could not be ignored. The 1990s were perhaps his least creatively successful period, though his popularity as a live attraction increased. In February 1994 he was honoured at the Brit Awards for his outstanding contribution to MUSIC, while in 1996 he was made a member of the Order of the British Empire for his services to music. His albums of the late 1990s, *The Healing Game* (1997) and *Back on Top* (1999), sold even better than his earlier recordings. Morrison remains one of rock music's giants, his body of work from Them onwards among the most admired and important in the canon. **Tony Clayton-Lea**

Morrison, William Vitruvius (1794–1838), architect. Born in Clonmel, Co. Tipperary, second of the four sons of the architect RICHARD MORRISON, who encouraged his early talent for drawing and entrusted him, at the age of fifteen, with the gothicising of Ballyheigue Castle, Co. Kerry. In 1821 he visited the Continent, spending some months in Rome and studying the ruins at Paestum. He worked independently of his father from c. 1825, designing the classical courthouses at Tralee and Carlow (both 1828). He was a pioneer of the revival of Tudor architecture, which he had studied in England; his houses in that style include Hollybrooke, Co. Wicklow (c. 1831), Clontarf Castle, Dublin (1836), and Ballygiblin, Co. Cork (c. 1837). His later years were plagued by ill health with the return of an old condition in 1836 that eventually paralysed him. A member of the ROYAL IRISH ACADEMY, he corresponded with GEORGE PETRIE on antiquarian matters. **Frederick O'Dwyer**

Morrissy, Mary (1957–), writer. Born in Dublin. Her collection of short stories, *A Lazy Eye*, was published in 1993. Her novels are *Mother of Pearl* (1995) and *The Pretender* (2000). She received several literary awards, including the Hennessy Award and the Lannan Literary Prize. **Elizabeth Drew**

Morrow brothers, illustrators. **Albert Morrow** (1863–1927) was born in Comber, Co. Down; trained at the Government School of Art and in 1882 won a scholarship to South Kensington School of Art, London. He worked for the *English Illustrated Magazine*, *Bits*, and *Good Words* and produced illustrations in a sketchy and linear style for Percy Westerman's *The Mystery Ship* (1920) and Rider Haggard's *The Ancient Allan* (1920). **George Morrow** (1869–1955) was born in Belfast; educated at Belfast Model School and the Government School of Art and apprenticed as a sign-painter. The best known of the Morrow brothers, he began contributing to *Punch* in 1906, eventually becoming art editor in 1923. He illustrated many books and was best known for his humorous drawings in *George Morrow: His Book* (1920), *More Morrow* (1921), and *Some More* (1928). His children's illustrations were lively and graphic and led to many commissions, including E. V. Lucas's *Swollen-Head William* (1914), Swift's *Gulliver's Travels* (1932), and *A Nursery Geography* (1925). He also illustrated Wyke-Smith's *The Marvellous Land of Sneags* (1927), which is credited with having inspired Tolkien to write *The Hobbit*. **Jack Morrow** (1872–1926) was born in Belfast. Like the rest of his family, he was involved with the ULSTER LITERARY THEATRE; he was elected a member of the Belfast Art Society in 1902 and designed stage sets and costumes while running a painting and decorating business. He was imprisoned in Mountjoy Jail, Dublin, in 1919 and contributed cartoons to the *Republic* and *Irish Review*. **Edwin Morrow** (1877–1952) was born in Belfast; trained at the Government School of Art, from where he won a scholarship to South Kensington School of Art, London. He contributed sketches to the *Bystander*, *London Opinion*, and *Punch*; he also illustrated F. J. Bigger's *The Northern Leaders of '98* (1906). **Norman Morrow** (1879–1917) was born in Belfast; educated at the RBAI and Government School of Art. He contributed political cartoons to the *Belfast Critic*, *Republic*, and *Graphic* and weakly drawn sketches for the *Bystander*. **Patricia Donlon**

Moss, R. J. [John] (1847–1934), chemist. Born in England; studied at the School of Pharmacy, London. He was elected to the ROYAL IRISH ACADEMY in 1874, appointed keeper of the minerals and chemical analyst of the ROYAL DUBLIN SOCIETY in 1875, and made registrar of the society some three years later. With his skill as a glass-blower and knowledge of rare gases he carried from 1914 the heavy work load of running the IRISH RADIUM INSTITUTE until his retirement (1921). His last paper, in 1926, concerned a chemical examination of Irish prehistoric metallurgical crucibles. **Susan McKenna-Lawlor**

Mosse, Bartholomew (1712–1759), surgeon and philanthropist. Born in Co. Laois, son of the Rector of Maryborough (Port Laoise); served his apprenticeship in Dublin and received his licence as a barber-surgeon in 1733. In 1738 he was commissioned as a British army surgeon in Minorca; by the time of his return to Dublin he had decided to specialise in MIDWIFERY. He travelled to the Continent to study practices there and in 1740 received a licence to practise midwifery. In 1745, with his own money, he founded the Dublin Lying-In Hospital in George's Lane (South Great George's Street), the first maternity HOSPITAL in Ireland and the first practical school of OBSTETRICS in the world.

The hospital proved a huge success, and in 1748 Mosse leased lands for a new hospital. Thanks to his tireless efforts and fund-raising, work began on a new hospital in 1751. The ROTUNDA HOSPITAL, designed by RICHARD CASTLE, was opened in Rutland Square (Parnell Square) in 1757, with Mosse as Master. He died in debt two years later, having committed his personal resources to the project. The Rotunda Hospital remains at the same site today and is a major teaching hospital in which the first Caesarean section in Ireland was performed (see p. 942). **Martin Clancy**

Mother and Child Scheme (1947–51), a public health scheme intended to improve the HEALTH SERVICES available to pregnant women and young children at a time when mortality rates were unacceptably high; the scheme was also to be part of the gradual establishment of a comprehensive national health service. Proposals for the scheme were made in a white paper in 1947, and a legislative base was provided. Responsibility for implementing the scheme fell to the Minister for Health, NÖEL BROWNE, who was appointed in 1948 at the age of thirty-two without any previous political experience. The proposals were bitterly opposed by the medical profession, which persuaded the hierarchy of the CATHOLIC CHURCH that they contained measures that threatened the moral well-being of women and girls. The hierarchy lobbied the Government against the scheme, and Browne's fellow-ministers were not prepared to support him. Browne resigned, but before doing so he made the correspondence between the bishops and the Government available to the press. The extent to which the Government appeared to take its instructions from the Catholic bishops caused an outcry and a continuing political crisis. **Ruth Barrington**

Mother and Child Scheme. *Father Frank Browne's copy of the brochure describing the Mother and Child Scheme, for which he provided the cover photograph. [Irish Picture Library, Father Browne Collection]*

motorcycling. Though there were no serious attempts at the large-scale production of motorcycles in Ireland, a number of smaller manufacturers produced what were essentially modified bicycles fitted with proprietary engines, including the Tredagh and Celtic, built in Drogheda and Dublin, respectively.

To cater for the increasing numbers of motorcyclists the Motor Cycle Union of Ireland was formed in 1902, becoming the world's first national governing body in motorcycle sport. The first president was JOHN BOYD DUNLOP, inventor of the pneumatic tyre; the first event was a social run from the PHOENIX PARK, Dublin, to BRAY, Co. Wicklow. As the availability of machines increased, interest in motorcycle sport grew, and Irish riders competed successfully at home and abroad. Many became household names, such as the road racers REG ARMSTRONG, Ralph Bryans (Ireland's first world champion), JOEY DUNLOP, and STANLEY WOODS. The trials scene was dominated by Sammy Miller of Belfast. World championship events were organised in road racing trials and motocross, and today international races are run on the North-West course near Coleraine, Co. Derry, and at Dundrod, outside Belfast. In the early twenty-first century Ireland had Gordon Crockard (motocross) and Jeremy McWilliams (road racing) competing and winning at world championship level. **Don McClenahan**

motoring. The internal-combustion engine made its Irish debut at the Shandon Bells Bazaar in Cork in April 1896; the car was a Benz Velo, driven by the London dealer Harry Hewetson. The same year Prof. John Shaw Brown of Dunmurry, Co. Antrim, bought an iron-shod Serpollet Steamer. The first regular Irish motorist was Dr John Colohan of Dublin, who had driven extensively on the Continent in the early 1890s and imported a Benz Velo after the passing of the Locomotives on Highways Act (1896) had raised the speed limit from 6.5 to 19 km/h (4 to 12 miles per hour). Ireland made a significant contribution to motoring in 1889 with the establishment in Dublin of the world's first pneumatic tyre factory by JOHN BOYD DUNLOP and HARVEY DU CROS. Irish interest, and British industry, were immensely boosted by Selwyn Edge's success in the 1902 GORDON BENNETT CUP on his Dunlop-tyred Napier, which resulted in the first major British race being held in Ireland, the 1903 Gordon Bennett Cup.

Among the early Irish motorists were Lord Iveagh (of the GUINNESS FAMILY), R. J. Mecredy and J. C. Percy (of *Irish Motor News*, which was founded in 1900), Sir HORACE PLUNKETT, Bill Peare (who built Ireland's first garage, in Waterford), and Sir William Goff (who, with Hercules Langrishe, was a founder-member of both the Automobile Club of Great Britain and the Irish Automobile Club). Some of these drivers participated in the first organised motor tour to Killaloe, Co. Clare, in 1900. The Irish Automobile Club celebrated its foundation in 1901 with a 1,000-mile (1,600 km) Tour of Ireland, which attracted sixteen entrants, including the English racer Charles Jarrott.

Though the Ford Motor Company assembled cars in Cork from 1922, there were only a few attempts at car manufacture in Ireland. The most successful was that of the Chambers brothers, who built some 500 cars between 1904 and 1928 in Belfast, where a handful of Fergus cars were also produced in 1915–21 by Joe Ferguson (brother of the tractor manufacturer HARRY FERGUSON, who was an early advocate of four-wheel drive). The former motorcycle racer John Crossle began manufacturing championship-winning sports cars and single-seater racing cars in Co. Down in 1957, while David Sheane of Co. Wicklow produced championship-winning formula vee single-seaters between 1976 and 2000. The most notorious Irish-manufactured car was the De Lorean, a two-seater sports car with gull-wing doors, aimed principally at the American market. The first car with its unique brushed stainless steel skin was produced in Dunmurry, Co. Antrim, in 1981, and by the end of the year 7,000 had been produced. But a slump the following year in the American market brought about the spectacular demise of the company. Its founder, the flamboyant John De Lorean, was tried for defrauding his research partnership of almost £5 million but was subsequently acquitted. **Brendan Lynch**

motor sport. The first major motor race in Ireland, the 1903 GORDON BENNETT CUP event, took place on a circuit based around Athy, Co. Kildare. Hostility to the automobile had prevented the race being held in England, and a strong Irish lobby led to a special act of Parliament that enabled the race to be held here. It attracted pioneer drivers, such as René de Knyff and Fernand Gabriel of France, winners of the early Continental city-to-city races, and the first American team to compete in Europe. The race was won by the Belgian Camille Jenatzy, the first person to reach a speed of a mile a minute and 100 km/h (62 miles per hour) in a car.

In the 1920s and 30s the Tourist Trophy races at the Ards circuit near Belfast regularly drew crowds of a quarter of a million and leading drivers such as the legendary Italian Tazio Nuvolari and British record-breakers Malcolm Campbell and KAYE DON. The Irish GRAND PRIX series, held in the PHOENIX PARK, Dublin, from 1929 to 1931, also featured the European champion Rudolf Caracciola, the leading Italians Achille Varzi and Giuseppe Campari, and the 'Bentley Boys': Tim Birkin, Glenn Kidston, and Sammy Davis. International races were also held in Cos. Cork and Limerick; other road races took place at Ballyclare, Bangor, Bray, Skerries, and Tallaght. Speed events were also held on sand at Duncannon, Inch, Portmarnock, Rosslare, Tramore, and Magilligan.

Racing resumed after the SECOND WORLD WAR with the revival of the Tourist Trophy event at Dundrod, Co. Antrim, where such world champions as Alberto Ascari, Juan Manuel Fangio, and Giuseppe Farina competed. The 1950 Tourist Trophy brought Stirling Moss his first international success; he also won at the Curragh, while England's first world champion, Mike Hawthorn, scored an early success in 1951 on the Wicklow circuit. Road races were also held at Dunboyne, while the Mondello Park circuit at Naas, Co. Kildare, which opened in 1968, featured the future world champions James Hunt and Alan Jones and early successes for the subsequent champions Emerson Fittipaldi and Ayrton Senna.

Irish drivers also distinguished themselves abroad. Harry Robinson scored Dublin's first success when he won the 1911 Boulogne hill climb. Sir HENRY SEGRAVE, who was brought up in Cos. Wicklow and Tipperary, became one of the world's leading record-breakers before his death in 1930. HUGH HAMILTON of Omagh won his class in the 1932 German Grand Prix and 1933 Italian Coppa Acerbo before dying of a heart attack in the 1934 Swiss Grand Prix. Joe Kelly and Desmond Titterington drove for the works Jaguar sports car team in the 1950s, while John Watson and EDDIE IRVINE were both runners-up in the Formula 1 World Championship; the team founded by EDDIE JORDAN of Dublin is now a serious Grand Prix contender. Other post-war drivers to progress to Grand Prix racing were Kenneth Acheson, Tommy Byrne, Martin Donnelly, David Kennedy, Damien Magee, and Derek Daly, who finished tenth in the 1980 World Championship.

Mount Errigal. *A winter view of the quartzite cone of Errigal (1999), Co. Donegal, a dominant feature of the local landscape. [Bord Fáilte]*

Irish drivers were also to the fore in international rallying. Cecil Vard of Dublin was a consistent Monte Carlo Rally front runner in the early 1950s, while Ronnie Adams and Frank Bigger of Belfast won the event in 1956, a feat repeated by PADDY HOPKIRK in 1964. Rosemary Smith of Dublin won the 1966 Tulip Rally, while Ronan Morgan of Dublin became a successful international rally navigator. **Brendan Lynch**

Motor Tour, Irish. Ireland's first organised motor tour took place in July 1900, when the Shannon Development Company organised a trip from Dublin to Killaloe, Co. Clare, to mark the opening of its riverside hotel. Eleven cars participated; drivers included Ireland's first motorist, Dr John Colohan, the proprietors of the *Irish Motor News*, R. J. Mecredy and J. C. Percy, and a leading Dublin motor agent, Hugh Hutton. Special trains brought large crowds from Limerick to witness their arrival. The Irish Automobile Club celebrated its inauguration with a 1,600 km (1,000-mile) Tour of Ireland in 1901, which attracted sixteen drivers, including a party of six from England. **Brendan Lynch**

Moulden, John (1941–), traditional singer, collector, researcher, and publisher. A founder-member of the Belfast Folk Song Club, 1963, and Ulster Folk Song Society, 1965, he has made Ulster song his life through the Ulstersongs agency. A rigorous writer on this subject, he has contributed to many journals and books, his most important work being the editing and indexing of the *Sam Henry Collection* (1979). **Fintan Vallely**

Mount Brandon, Co. Kerry, a peak north of Dingle on the DINGLE PENINSULA. At 953 m (3,127 ft) it is the highest peak in Ireland outside MACGILLYCUDDY'S REEKS. The mountain is associated with ST BRENDAN the navigator: according to tradition, he prayed here before beginning his voyage across the Atlantic with other monks. The remains of a stone oratory, a holy well and penitential stations are near the summit. The Saints' Road, leading there from the west side along a relatively gentle slope, is used for an annual pilgrimage on 29 June. Brandon's east side is much more rugged, with cliffs dropping precipitously to a line of glacial lakes. The nearby Connor Pass affords fine views. **Kevin Hourihan**

Mount Errigal, a peak in the Derryveagh range of north-west Co. Donegal, close to Gweedore. The highest mountain in the county, at 752 m (2,466 ft) above sea level, it stands in almost total isolation, dropping to near sea level on three sides. Made of erosion-resistant quartzite, it has weathered into a bare cone shape with steep scree slopes near the summit, typical of similar mountains, such as CROAGH PATRICK. The mountain ranges of the region are oriented north-east to south-west, part of the Caledonian trend that links them with the highlands of Scotland and on into Scandinavia, and are representative of the oldest mountains in Ireland. The area has been subjected to intense geological folding and faulting and later modification by glacial processes. Altan Lough, nearby, and the U-shaped valley of the Poisoned Glen (so named because the abundance of a poisonous variety of spurge made it unsuitable for grazing) show the power of these mountain glaciers. Glenveagh National Park (14,000 ha, 35,000 acres) is on the eastern side of the Derryveagh range and is centred on the long, deep glacial trough of Glenveagh Valley. **Joseph Brady**

Mount Gabriel, Co. Cork (408 m, 1,339 ft), a mountain in the Mizen Peninsula, the setting for intensive copper-mining in the later stages of the early BRONZE AGE, c. 1700–1500 BC. Some thirty-two mine workings have been identified along its slopes, uniquely preserved in a blanket bog environment. The mines consist of small inclined openings driven into surface exposures of copper mineralisation to a depth of up to 12 m (40 ft). They were worked by fire-setting in combination with stone hammers and wooden implements. The mineralised rock was sorted by hand outside the mine entrances and subsequently smelted either on the mountain or in adjacent settlements. [see MINERAL RESOURCES.] **William O'Brien**

Mount Leinster, the highest peak in the Blackstairs Mountains in Cos. Carlow and Wexford, at 796 m (2,610 ft). Formed of granite, these hills have steep western faces but gentler eastern sides and are easily climbed. A cairn on Mount Leinster's summit marks the traditional burial place of Cucorb, King of Leinster, who was killed by Feidlimidh Reachtmhar in the first century AD. **Kevin Hourihan**

Mount Sandel, Co. Derry, site of an important settlement on the edge of a 30 m (100 ft) escarpment that overlooks the upper reaches of the Bann Estuary near Coleraine. For more than a hundred years this area has produced numerous MESOLITHIC artefacts; as a result, a number of excavations have explored the Mesolithic occupation of the area. That of 1973–7 recovered numerous blades, microliths, AXES, and other objects that characterise the Irish early Mesolithic Period and are associated with a series of radiocarbon dates that occur mostly in the period 7000–5500 BC. The excavations showed that settlement had centred on a number of near-circular huts, up to 6 m (20 ft) across, that were outlined by a series of stake holes. It is probable that no more than one hut was erected at a time.

Scatters of waste from the making of tools and a series of large pits, possibly for storage, were found around the huts. A number of pits and hearths produced concentrations of burnt bones, showing that salmon, trout and eels, as well as some sea fish, had been caught. Bones of wild pig and hares as well as some bird bones were also found, together with concentrations of hazel nutshells and other seeds, such as apple and water lily, from which it appears that the site had been used at various seasons of the year. **Peter Woodman**

Mountmellick embroidery, a white embroidery originally devised by Johanna Carter in Mountmellick, Co. Laois, between 1830 and 1840, popular in the late nineteenth and early twentieth centuries. Worked on white satin jean cloth with thick cotton threads, the designs were based on local FLORA and had a raised appearance; the traditional Mountmellick had a knitted cotton fringe. **Alex Ward**

Mourne Mountains, Co. Down, the most attractive mountain range in Ulster, commemorated in PERCY FRENCH's famous song 'The Mountains of Mourne'. They are steeper than the rounded hills of Co. Wicklow, as they are younger, being characterised by the largest Tertiary granite outcrop in Ireland. The Western Mournes barely rise above 600 m (2,000 ft) and are covered with a roof of Silurian shale, leading to spectacular views southwards over CARLINGFORD LOUGH and the Cooley Peninsula. The High Mournes are granite intrusions, reaching as high as Slieve Donard (1,100 m, 3,600 ft), that have been largely stripped of their shale roof. GLACIATION has resulted in a diversity of steep peaks, cliffs, corries and deep valleys along the Annalong and Kilkeel Rivers. More than a million people live within 50 km (30 miles) of the Mournes, which are heavily used by recreationists. The region, which includes the Crom and Silent Valley reservoirs for Belfast, 50 km (30 miles) to the north, is one of the most vulnerable mountain landscapes in Ireland and has been designated an area of outstanding natural beauty. **Patrick Duffy**

Mourne Mountains. *Winter view of the Mourne Mountains, Co. Down. The range, covering some 200 km^2 (80 sq. miles) of unspoilt mountain and moors, was designated an area of outstanding beauty in 1986. [Northern Ireland Tourist Board Photographic Library]*

mouth organ: see HARMONICA.

Movilla Abbey, Co. Down, founded in the sixth century by St Finnén. Augustinian canons were introduced some time after 1135. The remains of one medieval church survive, incorporating fabric from the thirteenth century, with fifteenth-century additions at the west end. Inside the church is an Early Christian grave-slab, the only surviving visible remnant of the early foundation. Throughout the Middle Ages the ABBEY was an important landowner in the area and may have been a centre of production for thirteenth-century foliate coffin lids, a collection of which is preserved at the site. [see ABBEYS.] **Rachel Moss**

Moving Hearts, a music group formed in 1981 by CHRISTY MOORE (vocals, guitar, and BODHRÁN), DÓNAL LUNNY (bouzouki and keyboards), Declan Sinnott (guitar), Davy Spillane (UILLEANN PIPES), Keith Donald (alto saxophone), Eoghan O'Neill (bass), and Brian Calnan (drums). It mixed TRADITIONAL MUSIC with elements of JAZZ and rock. Moore was replaced in 1982 by Mick Hanly, who in turn was replaced by Flo McSweeney. Live appearances included the Montreux Jazz Festival; recordings include *Moving Hearts* (1982), *Dark End of the Street* (1983), and *The Storm* (1984). **Pat Ahern**

Moxon type, an IRISH PRINTING TYPE. In 1675 ROBERT BOYLE, Earl of Cork, indicated his wish 'that the Bible and Common Prayer Book be translated into Irish and printed in the vulgar character.' He had a new font of Irish type cast by the London foundry of Joseph Moxon, modelled on the earlier popular typefaces of the Irish FRANCISCAN press in LOUVAIN. The type was used for the first time in 1680 by the London printer Robert Everingham to print a fourteen-page Catechism booklet and later by the same printer for the second edition of William Ó Domhnuill's translation of the New Testament and in 1685 for WILLIAM BEDELL's translation of the Old Testament. The remaining punches represent the earliest known type to have been produced in England. [see BIBLE IN IRISH, THE.] **Dermot McGuinne**

Moylough Belt-Shrine, a belt-reliquary found in a BOG at Moylough, Co. Sligo, in 1945; it is now in the NATIONAL MUSEUM. It is one of the finest expressions of the eighth-century flowering of Irish metalworking, consisting of four hinged segments made of pairs of copper-alloy plates, formerly tinned, bound along their upper and lower edges with metal binding-strips. One of the segments ends in a large false buckle and the adjacent one in a counterplate. Each is elaborately decorated. The segments are further enriched with rectangular settings and cruciform medallions with stamped silver foils and enamel. The buckle and counterplate are decorated with cast ornament, stamped silver, enamel, and cast-glass imitation gemstones. The motifs include animal patterns, animal and bird heads, and trumpet and spiral scrollwork. The design of the object is a *skeuomorphic* representation (in material other than that originally used) of an elaborate jewelled belt, complete with stiffeners, of a type similar to examples known from sixth and seventh-century Continental Germanic graves. There is no doubt that it was constructed to preserve the leather strips that are sandwiched between the metal plates, and that these are the remains of the belt of a holy person. Miraculous saints' belts are known in early Irish tradition, one in particular being associated with the female Saint Samhthann. [see BOOK SHRINES; MEDIEVAL METALWORK; RELIQUARIES.] **Michael Ryan**

Moynihan, Maurice (1902–1999), civil servant. Born in Tralee, Co. Kerry; educated at UCC. He joined the DEPARTMENT OF FINANCE in 1925. In 1932–3 he was private secretary to ÉAMON DE VALERA, and in 1936–7 he chaired the committee supervising the draft CONSTITUTION OF IRELAND (1937). In 1937 he became Secretary of the Department of the TAOISEACH and established close working relations with de Valera and also with JOHN A. COSTELLO. He resigned in 1961 and became Governor of the CENTRAL BANK, a post he held until 1969. After his retirement he published *Currency and Central Banking in Ireland* (1975) and *Speeches and Statements by Éamon de Valera* (1980). **Deirdre McMahon**

Mulcahy, Jeremiah Hodges (died 1889), painter. Born in Limerick; he set up a school there in 1842, closing it when he went to Dublin in 1862. He painted landscapes, many of gentlemen's houses and demesnes, of which *Curragh Chase* (1834), now in the NATIONAL GALLERY OF IRELAND, is a fine example. *A View near Killarney* (1866) is a rare late work with freer brushwork. Towards the end of his life he painted some portraits. He became a member of the ROYAL HIBERNIAN ACADEMY and exhibited there, 1843–78. **Anne Crookshank**

Mulcahy, Michael (1952–), artist. Born in Cork, and grew up in Co. Waterford; trained at the Crawford School of Art, Cork, and the NCAD, Dublin. One of a group of strong New Expressionist painters prominent in the 1980s, he has travelled extensively in Europe, India, Australia, Papua New Guinea, and, particularly, north and west Africa, where he has lived and worked with indigenous peoples. He has also lived in Korea and studied calligraphy with a Buddhist monk. He now lives in Paris but returns frequently to Ireland. He is a member of AOSDÁNA. **Dorothy Walker**

Mulcahy, Richard (1886–1971), revolutionary and politician. Born in Waterford; educated at Mount Sion and Thurles CBS. He worked in the Irish Post Office and joined the IRB, the GAELIC LEAGUE and the IRISH VOLUNTEERS. He took part in the 1916 RISING at Ashbourne, Co. Meath, and was afterwards interned in Wales. Elected to DÁIL ÉIREANN in 1918, he was a TD from then until 1961, apart from the periods 1937–8 and 1943–4. A good administrator, he was chief of staff of the IRA during the WAR OF INDEPENDENCE and was close to Collins. He took the pro-Treaty side in 1921 and played a leading part in defeating the anti-Treaty forces, supporting the policy of executions. He resigned as Minister for Defence over the Curragh Mutiny in 1924, becoming Minister for Local Government in 1927. He joined the BLUESHIRTS in 1932 but soon repented. He was leader of FINE GAEL, 1944–59, and Minister for Education, 1948–51 and 1954–7; he declined to be Taoiseach in favour of JOHN A. COSTELLO in 1948, facilitating the formation of the first Coalition Government. He retired in 1959, an important if understated figure in Irish public life. **Tom Garvin**

Muldoon, Paul (1951–), poet. Born in Portadown and grew up near the Moy, Co. Armagh; educated at QUB, where his tutors included SEAMUS HEANEY and EDNA LONGLEY. His first full-length collection, *New Weather* (1973), appeared while he was still a student. Having worked for the BBC in Belfast until the mid-1980s, he became professor of creative writing at Princeton University. He was elected professor of poetry at Oxford, 1999. The most important of his early books was his fourth, *Quoof* (1983). Its long poem 'The More a Man Has the More a Man Wants' is a fragmented, hallucinatory journey through the nightmare phantasmagoria of early 1980s Northern Ireland, with a backdrop of hunger strikes and political assassination. Though he emigrated to the United States in 1987, his poetry has not left Ireland; America provides new opportunities to understand his home ground. When, in *Madoc* (1990), the poet Robert Southey establishes his ideal community in Ulster, Pennsylvania, tacit political allegory becomes possible. America allows no refuge from the violence of Northern Ireland but an opportunity to view it from a different angle. As Seamus Heaney has stated, Muldoon is a poetic radical, 'rewriting the rules of the game' and, gradually, creating the taste by which his works will be celebrated. He received the Sir Geoffrey Faber Memorial Award in 1991 and the T. S. Eliot Award in 1994. *Moy Sand and Gravel* won a Pulitzer Prize in 2003. **Tim Kendall**

Mulkerns, Val (1925–), writer. Born in Dublin. Her short-story collections include *Antiquities* (1978), *An Idle Woman* (1980), and *A Friend of Don Juan* (1988). Among her novels are *A Time Outworn* (1951), *The Summerhouse* (1984), and *Very Like a Whale* (1986). **Elizabeth Drew**

Mullaghmast, Massacre of (c. March 1578), the treacherous murder of more than forty of the leading members of the O'Mores of Laois by Sir Francis Cosby, commander of English forces in Queen's County (Co. Laois), and Robert Hartpole, Sheriff of Carlow. Summoned to a small fort on the Kildare-Laois border, ostensibly to negotiate their support against other families in the region, the O'Mores were disarmed on their arrival and summarily put to the sword. Even amid the bloody wars of the midlands the atrocity was regarded as shocking. It may have led to Cosby's own killing in an ambush at Glenmalur, Co. Wicklow, in 1580 and was commemorated in a remarkable piece of local folklore written down in the early eighteenth century. The written account of the massacre is preserved in the ROYAL IRISH ACADEMY. **Ciaran Brady**

Mullarney, Máire, née McCormick (1921–), educationalist. Born in Co. Wicklow; educated at Loreto Convent, Bray, Co. Wicklow, and Loreto (Europa) Convent, Gibraltar. She trained as a nurse at the Royal City of Dublin (Baggot Street) Hospital. The lengthy overseas absences of her father with the British colonial service left her mainly under the influence of her mother and her aunt, who, together with books, were her real educators. She has campaigned on a wide range of issues: in favour of FAMILY PLANNING, against corporal punishment, against Irish as an obligatory school subject, in favour of Esperanto. A proponent of home education, she put forward her views in *Anything School Can Do You Can Do Better* (1983) and implemented them with her eleven children who were all educated at home. She has also published *Esperanto for Hope* (1988), *Early Reading* (1990), and an autobiography, *What About Me?* (1992). **Áine Hyland**

Mullen, Karl (1926–), rugby footballer. Born in Courtown, Co. Wexford. Having taken over as captain, in 1948 he guided Ireland to the first Triple Crown since 1899 and the only Grand Slam. Under his captaincy Ireland retained the Triple Crown in 1949, subsequently going on to win the 1951 championship. He captained the 1950 British Lions team in New Zealand and Australia, playing in three Tests. He won twenty-five caps between 1947 and 1952. **Karl Johnston**

Mullin, Brendan (1963–), rugby footballer. Born in Israel. Ireland's most-capped centre, with fifty-five caps won between 1984 and 1995, until 2003 he was Ireland's top try-scorer in international rugby, with seventeen tries. He played for Ireland in three World Cups, in 1987, 1991, and 1995, when the match against France in Durban marked his last international appearance. He toured Australia with the victorious 1989 British Lions team, playing in the first Test. **Karl Johnston**

Mullingar (*An Muileann gCearr*), principal town and county town of Co. Westmeath; population (2002), 8,833. There is little evidence of settlement until the manor was assigned to the ANGLO-NORMAN Petit family; it was granted borough status in 1201. In the Middle Ages it was a market and service centre, trading in livestock, wool, and linen yarn. Its site on the road to the west gave rise to a coach-making industry, and a turnpike road built in the 1730s improved the connection with Dublin. The ROYAL CANAL (1806) saw the introduction of passenger boat services as well as goods traffic, while the arrival of the Midland Great Western Railway line from Dublin in 1848 further benefited the livestock trade. The town's proximity to Dublin (approximately one hour's drive) encouraged rapid growth and expansion in the late 1990s. While there has been a marked increase in commuting to Dublin, there is also considerable local employment, including a number of TRANSNATIONAL CORPORATIONS. Mullingar is now building on its tourism potential, based primarily on proximity to the midland lakes. **Ruth McManus**

Mullingar Choral Society, founded in 1968 by Father FRANK MCNAMARA. Following the first performance in March 1969 (Fauré *Requiem*), the membership expanded and the choir gave regular concert performances and participated in choral festivals in Cork and in Wales, winning prizes on a number of occasions. Through the 1980s and 90s the choir continued its development and widened its repertoire to include many major choral works. In 1996

Muldoon. *Paul Muldoon, a poet of great verbal dexterity and technical range, he won the Pulitzer Prize for* Moy Sand and Gravel *in 2003. [Camera Press Ireland]*

it won the Pilib Ó Laoire Trophy at the CORK INTERNATIONAL CHORAL AND DANCE FESTIVAL. The choir directors have been McNamara (1968–80), Shane Brennan (1980–92), John White (1992–9), and Fergus O'Carroll. **Ite O'Donovan**

Mullins, George (fl. 1756–1775/6), artist. Probably born in Dublin; studied at the Dublin Society Schools. He worked first in Waterford, painting trays and snuff-box lids. On his return to Dublin he married the sister-in-law of HUGH DOUGLAS HAMILTON. Awarded premiums from the DUBLIN SOCIETY in 1763 and 1768, he produced four large landscapes, representing the times of the day, for Marino, country seat of the first Earl of Charlemont (1768). He took on THOMAS ROBERTS as lodger and apprentice. He went to London in 1770 and exhibited at the Royal Academy until 1775 and also showed works at the Society of Artists in Ireland. He executed landscape and subject pictures. **Brendan Rooney**

Mulready, William (1786–1863), artist and illustrator. Born in Ennis, Co. Clare; he went to London as a child and trained at the Royal Academy School. He began illustrating at an early age and was a prolific illustrator who produced numerous vignettes. Newbury published one of the landmarks in the history of colour printing, *The Butterfly's Ball and the Grasshopper's Feast* (1807), with hand-coloured pictures based on Mulready's pen-and-brush drawings. This sold 20,000 copies within a year and was followed by several sequels, including *The Peacock's At Home* and *The Lion's Masquerade*, all with pictures by Mulready. **Patricia Donlon**

Mulroy Bay, Co. Donegal, a complex, fully marine deep-water inlet extending inland for 19 km (12 miles). It comprises two large sheltered bodies of water, Northwater and Broadwater, linked to each other and then to the open sea by a long channel in which strong currents (3–5 knots) run. The bay is a candidate special area of conservation. Significant habitats include rapids, underwater cliffs, eel-grass, and the calcareous pink alga maerl. It supports a number of rare species at their northern limits in Ireland and is a breeding-site for common seals. Well-developed, important mariculture operations include mussels, scallops, and salmonids. **Julia Nunn**

Mulvany, George Francis (1809–1869), artist. Born in Dublin, son of the genre painter and writer Thomas James Mulvany. A mediocre portrait painter, he is best known for his full-length portrait of DANIEL O'CONNELL (now in Limerick Art Gallery) wearing a cloak and gesturing with his left hand. His real claim to fame is in becoming the first director of the NATIONAL GALLERY OF IRELAND, which opened in 1864. He bought some seventy pictures, including many baroque masters, such as a superb Jordaens, and also a number of German panels. **Anne Crookshank**

Mulvany, John Skipton (1813–1870), architect. Fourth son of Thomas James Mulvany; apprenticed to William Deane Butler. In 1833 he completed his articles and exhibited at the ROYAL HIBERNIAN ACADEMY for the first time. By 1836 he was designing for the DUBLIN AND KINGSTOWN RAILWAY; his main works were the stations at Dún Laoghaire (1839) and Blackrock (1841). He designed many private houses in the Dublin suburbs as well as two Dún Laoghaire yacht clubs, the Royal St George (1842) and Royal Irish (1847). His masterpiece is the Egypto-Grec terminus of the Midland Great Western Railway at Broadstone, Dublin (1846–50), now a bus depot; he also designed the Galway terminus and hotel and Athlone station. His influences were eclectic but mostly classical: Mullingar Asylum (1847), however, was gothic. He was extensively employed in designing villas for QUAKER business families, including the Perrys, Goodbodys (of Clara), and Malcomsons (of Portlaw and Clonmel). **Frederick O'Dwyer**

Mulvany, William Thomas (1806–1885), industrialist. He worked as an engineer with the BOARD OF WORKS and played an important role in the development of the canal system. At the age of forty-three he moved to Germany to develop the coal industry. He set up the Shamrock Mine at Gelsenkirchen in 1856 and the Hibernia mine at Herne in 1857; he also founded the Erin Mining Company, which was taken over by the Prussian state in 1882. He is credited with being the leading industrialist of the Ruhr district at the end of the nineteenth century. Among his other legacies are the ironworks at Duisburg, the Rhein-Weser-Elbe Canal, the Midland Canal, the Dortmund-Ems Canal, and the Düsseldorf Stock Exchange. He is remembered in street names in Düsseldorf and several other towns, and there is a bust of him at the head office of Veba, the transnational company whose lineage can be traced directly from the Hibernia Mine. **Ciarán Deane**

mummers. The tradition of performing 'mummers' plays' is popular in many parts of Ireland and takes place at Christmas time in northern, eastern, and south-eastern parts of the country. Groups of people dress up, often in locally made straw costumes, and travel around the district performing a folk drama, usually consisting of rhymes, represented as spoken by well-known historical characters, such as Mussolini or Napoleon Bonaparte, or characters from Irish history, such as DANIEL O'CONNELL or ST PATRICK. Other figures, Beelzebub or Jack Straw, also feature. All the characters introduce themselves in rhyme, and the play normally involves the killing and resuscitation of the hero. Music, dancing, and collecting money are an integral part of the mummers' plays. [see CALENDAR CUSTOMS; FOLK-LIFE; WREN BOYS.] **Ríonach uí Ógáin**

Munnelly, Tom (1944–), singer and scholar. Born in Dublin. He began recording traditional songs in the field in 1964 and from 1969 to 1971 catalogued some 1,750 manuscripts for the IRISH FOLKLORE COMMISSION while acting as research assistant to D. K. Wilgus, professor of Anglo-American folksong at the University of California, Los Angeles. A founder of the Folk Music Society of Ireland, in 1971 he was appointed the first song collector for the National Traditional Music Collection Scheme established by the Department of Education under BREANDÁN BREATHNACH, moving with this to the Department of Irish Folklore, UCD, in 1975. He has lectured on traditional song to the majority of folklore and folk music bodies in Ireland, has taken part in numerous international ballad conferences, and has contributed to many journals on the subject of songs and singers, particularly those of the travelling people. He moved to Co. Clare in 1978, was chairman of SCOIL SAMHRAIDH WILLIE CLANCY, 1984–91 (see p. 1064), and founded the Folklore and Folk Music Society of Clare in 1982. In 1981 he was appointed to the Arts Council's Irish Traditional Music Advisory Committee (chairman, 1988–93); he was a member of the ARTS COUNCIL, 1985–8. In 1990 he founded and was chairman of the Clare Festival of Traditional Singing and in the same year founded Lahinch Folklore School. He has indexed all the oral poetry in the first 2,000 volumes of the Main Manuscripts Collection of the Department of Irish Folklore, UCD, and since 1971 has recorded some 1,600 field tapes of songs and folklore—the largest and most comprehensive collection of traditional songs compiled by a single person. Among his other work has been the publication of *The Mount Callan Garland*, a book and tapes of the songs of the Co. Clare performer TOM LENIHAN. **Fintan Vallely**

Munro, Henry (died 1798), linen-draper, freemason, VOLUNTEER, and UNITED IRISHMAN. Born in Lisburn, Co. Antrim. He became military commander of the United Irish army of Co. Down; he was not the first choice for this position, but the arrest of the adjutant-general, Rev. William Steel Dickson, left the county command structure in disarray, and Munro took over after the rebel victory at the BATTLE OF SAINTFIELD. He was a good choice, being a popular man, well known through his trade, and having some previous military experience in the Volunteers. At the BATTLE OF BALLYNAHINCH he came in for criticism for not sanctioning a night attack. His eventual deployment of his force on two fronts showed some tactical skill, and his conduct during the battle displayed considerable personal courage, as he remained on the field to the last, trying to rally his fleeing men. After the battle he hid in a farmhouse but was betrayed to the YEOMANRY and taken to Lisburn for court-martial. He was ordered to be hanged and decapitated before his own door; he showed great fortitude by first settling accounts with his creditors. His last words were 'Tell my country I have deserved better of her.' **Allan Blackstock**

Munro, Robert (died 1680), soldier. The eruption of revolt in Ulster in 1641 had led to a concerted attempt to dispossess the Protestant settlers in the province, leading to the massacre, or expulsion, of the vast majority of the planter population in the north. Arriving in Ireland at the head of a Scottish army in 1642, Munro soon made inroads into areas captured by the Catholic insurgents, his forces often exacting a merciless retribution for the massacre of Protestants. His success in re-establishing a viable Protestant military presence in Ireland was greatly jeopardised by his defeat by OWEN ROE O'NEILL at the BATTLE OF BENBURB in 1646, the most catastrophic military defeat of Protestant arms in Ireland, following which Protestant domination was temporarily in the balance. **John McCavitt**

Munster

Munster	Cúige Mumhan
Counties:	Clare, Cork, Kerry, Limerick, Tipperary, Waterford
Major towns:	Cork, Limerick, Waterford
Rivers:	Bandon, Blackwater, Lee, Shannon, Suir
Highest point:	Carrauntouhill 1,038 m
Population 1991 Census	1,009,533
Population 2002 Census	1,101,266

Munster (*Cúige Mumhan*). Our first glimpse of Munster comes through PTOLEMY's map, dating from c. AD 100. Ptolemy's Munster is dominated by the 'Iverni': these are probably identical with the historical Érainn, who were scattered in a wide belt across the centre of Munster. During the fourth and fifth centuries weakening Roman authority in Britain was seized on by Irish adventurers, raiders, and settlers; in this project Érainn peoples seem to have been heavily involved, along with the DÉISE from south-east Munster. Érainn dominance dissolved, particularly from the sixth century. About this time a federation of dynasties, known as the EOGHANACHTA, claimed the kingship of Munster, establishing their rule in Cashel. The early medieval provincial kingdom comprised the modern province of Munster along with Osraighe (roughly Co. Kilkenny). Cashel produced several able rulers, including Cathal mac Finguine (died 742), the most dominant political figure of his day. A century later Feidlimid mac Crimthainn (died 847), bishop and king, carried war to the UÍ NÉILL kings of TARA, gaining their temporary submission.

Following the reign of Feidlimid, Eoghanachta power declined in the face of internal instability, VIKING activities, and Uí Néill ambitions. In 859 the Eoghanachta were forced to accept the humiliating alienation of Osraighe from Munster. Despite resurgences Eoghanachta power collapsed, and Munster passed to the overlordship of DÁL GCAIS, who rose to power from a small kingdom in east Clare. In BRIAN BÓRÚ they produced a King of Munster who became ruler of Ireland; thus the KINGSHIP of Tara, for long the proud possession of Uí Néill, became irrelevant. Now the provincial kings would vie for primacy. Brian's descendants, the O'Briens, were prominent in these struggles. Of these, Muirchertach Ua Briain (died 1119) was arguably the most impressive; the great reforming SYNOD of Cashel in 1101 was held under his auspices. However, the O'Briens and Munster were ultimately eclipsed by the powerful O'Connor kings of Connacht. This eclipse was short-lived, for the O'Connor overkings of Ireland and the kings of Munster dismally failed to snuff out the threat of the Anglo-Norman adventurers who arrived in Ireland in 1169. **Elva Johnston**

Geography. The southernmost and the largest of the provinces, with an area of 24,126 km^2 (9,315 sq. miles), comprising Cos. Clare, Cork, Kerry, Limerick, Tipperary, and Waterford and with a POPULATION of 1,101,266 (2002), an increase of 6.5 per cent over the previous census (1996), equal to 28.1 per cent of the population of the Republic. Only Co. Tipperary is landlocked. The population grew substantially by migration during the period 1996–2002, with an average net inward migration of 5.5 per 1,000 population; Co. Clare registered the largest increase, at 10.4 per cent. The province contains three of the largest urban areas in the country, the cities of Cork, Waterford, and Limerick.

The name of the province is believed to derive from that of the goddess Mumha. Before the arrival of the ANGLO-NORMANS it was divided into a number of *tuatha* or clan territories, the most important of which were Thomond and Desmond. Traditionally these dated from the year 248, when Oliol Olum, King of Munster, divided his territory between his two sons, giving Desmond (south Munster) to Eoghan and Thomond (north Munster) to Cormac, with the border running through the SLIABH LUACHRA mountains. With the Anglo-Norman conquest, control passed to the O'Briens, Earls of Thomond, Fitzgeralds, Earls of Desmond, and Butlers, Earls of Ormond. The present-day county structure and boundaries date only from the late sixteenth century, when the process of shiring was completed, though it had begun soon after the arrival of the Anglo-Normans.

The provincial structure has no administrative function. Counties are grouped into regional authorities that sometimes cross traditional provincial boundaries: Munster includes the Mid-West Region (Clare, Limerick, and North Tipperary) and South-West Region (Cork and Kerry). **Joseph Brady**

Murdoch, Iris (1919–1999), novelist and philosopher. Born in Dublin to Irish parents; became a philosophy tutor at Oxford, 1948–63, writing *Sartre* (1953) and *Metaphysics as a Guide to Morals* (1992). Best known for her many emotionally complex novels, she explored philosophical concepts such as freedom in *Under the Net* (1954) and other early novels, *Flight from the Enchanter* and *The Bell*. Subsequent novels include two set in Ireland, *The Unicorn* (1963) and *The Red and the Green* (1965). While goodness in a random world remained a pervasive topic, humour and the depiction of character developed in her later fiction, such as *The Black Prince* (1973) and *The Sea, the Sea* (1978) which won the Booker Prize. **A. Norman Jeffares**

Murnaghan, Sheelagh (1924–1993), politician. Born in Dublin. After practising as a barrister in Belfast she was elected to the Northern Ireland Parliament for Queen's University in 1961, the only Liberal to have been elected to that assembly, and she retained her seat until 1969. She campaigned for proportional representation, fair employment legislation, the appointment of an ombudsman, and the equitable allocation of council houses. She served on the Northern Ireland Community Relations Commission, 1969–72, and thereafter chaired National Insurance and Industrial Relations Tribunals. **Jonathan Bardon**

Murphy, Cornelius (Con) (1914–2002), rugby footballer. Born in Dublin. He made his debut against England at Twickenham in 1939 and went on to play against Scotland and Wales that year, before the SECOND WORLD WAR intervened. When the championship resumed in 1947 he captained Ireland against France and England at Lansdowne Road, and although Ireland won the latter match 22–0, he was dropped. He won five caps at full-back and is the only player to have represented Ireland before and after the war. **Karl Johnston**

Murphy, Delia (1902–1971), ballad-singer. Born in Claremorris, Co. Mayo. She performed and recorded songs learnt at childhood HOUSE-DANCES and from her student days in Galway. 'The Spinning-Wheel' and 'Three Lovely Lassies from Bannion', recorded in 1939, became household favourites, as did 'Dan O'Hara'. Her life is documented in *I'll Live Till I Die* by Aidan O'Hara (1997). **Fintan Vallely**

Murphy, Dervla (1931–), travel writer. Born in Lismore, Co. Waterford. At the age of thirty, following the death of her invalid mother, she was able to fulfil a long-held wish to travel and write.

Her first book, *Full Tilt* (1965), describes an exhilarating journey from Ireland to India by bicycle. Since then, places she has visited and written about, either alone or with her daughter, include Nepal, Ethiopia, India, Baltistan, Madagascar, and Cameroon. She has also written on other subjects, such as race relations in England, in her outstanding *Tales from Two Cities* (1987). *A Place Apart* (1978), an examination of the problems of Northern Ireland, won the Ewart-Biggs Memorial Prize. She endured difficulties in the toughest terrain not only with stoicism but with a combination of enjoyment and compassion, touched by humour and eccentricity. However, the early sense of innocence and discovery that marks her accounts of wandering around the hills of Baltistan with her five-year-old daughter or perching in the Peruvian highlands has increasingly been exchanged for more sombre attitudes towards a changing world. *The Ukimwi Road* (1993) deals with the devastating problems of Africa, ravaged by AIDS, drought, corruption, and economic mayhem. Her journey through Rwanda in 1996, meeting people traumatised by the massacres, left her with a conviction that came surprisingly from someone so liberal: that the death penalty should be used on the perpetrators of genocide. In her recent travels through Laos she laments the destruction of a fragile culture by the introduction of Western values. **Peter Somerville-Large**

Murphy, Dervla. *Travel writer, Dervla Murphy, with the bicycle she used in cycling from Ireland to India, as described in her first book,* Full Tilt *(1965). [John Minihan]*

Murphy, James Cavanagh (1762–1814), writer and architect. Born in Cork. He is best known for his book on the royal church at Batalha, Portugal (1795), and was also the author of *Travels in Portugal* (1796), with which can be associated thirty-six watercolours later acquired by the NATIONAL LIBRARY OF IRELAND. A note with the watercolours shows that he had been befriended by the DEANE family, with whom he may have had architectural training. Though he is recorded at the DUBLIN SOCIETY's Drawing School in 1775, his only known work as an architect was the execution of GANDON's portico to the House of Lords (1786). He was in Spain from 1802 to 1809; his masterpiece, *The Arabian Antiquities of Spain*, appeared in 1815. **Michael McCarthy**

Murphy, Jimmy (1895–1924), racing driver. Born in San Francisco of Irish parents. He became one of America's best-loved sports figures and had a dance named after him, the 'Jimmy Murphy foxtrot'. He scored his first win at Beverly Hills in 1921 and then became the first American to win a European grand prix when he triumphed in the French Grand Prix at Le Mans. He also won the 1922 Indianapolis 500 and was American champion in 1922 and 1924. He was killed in what was to be his retirement race at Syracuse at the end of 1924. **Brendan Lynch**

Murphy, John (1753–1798), priest and rebel officer. Born in Tincurry, Co. Wexford; ordained in 1779, he studied in Seville, 1780–85. Curate of Boolavogue, Co. Wexford, 1785–98, he was probably a UNITED IRISHMAN and became an important rebel commander in 1798. Captured afterwards, he was hanged in Tullow. **Daniel Gahan**

Murphy, Noel (1937–), rugby footballer. Born in Cork. His debut international could hardly have been more auspicious when, at Lansdowne Road in 1958, Ireland beat Australia 9–6 to record their first victory against an overseas touring team. Between 1958 and 1969 he won forty-one international caps, and he is also the British Lions' most-capped flanker. He captained Ireland on five occasions and scored four international tries. He played in eight Test matches for the British Lions, on the tours to New Zealand and Australia in 1959 and again in 1966, and was coach to the 1980 British Lions team in South Africa. He was a national selector, 1975/6–79/80 and 1993/4–94/5, was national coach, 1977/8–79/80, and national team manager, 1992/3–94/5. He was president of the IRFU, 1998/9. **Karl Johnston**

Murphy, Pat (1951–), film director and scriptwriter. Born in Dublin. She has made three feature films: the formally experimental *Maeve* (jointly directed with John T. Davis, 1982), which deals with a feminist's return to her native Belfast, where she clashes with her former boy-friend; *Anne Devlin* (1984), which concerns the woman who worked with ROBERT EMMET as he plotted the rising of 1803; and *Nora* (2000), which explores the relationship between NORA BARNACLE and her partner, JAMES JOYCE. **Kevin Rockett**

Murphy, Richard (1927–), poet. Born in Co. Mayo; educated principally at boarding-schools in England and the University of Oxford. A childhood divided between England, the Anglo-Irish demesne of his grandparents and Ceylon (Sri Lanka)—where his father, in the British colonial service, was mayor of Colombo—influenced poetry that explores issues of identity and is richly redolent of place. Though much of his finest and most playful verse is contained in *High Island* and *The Price of Stone*, he remains best known for his early volumes *Sailing to an Island* (1963) and *The Battle of Aughrim* (1968). *Sailing to an Island* includes his turbulent and gripping sea narrative 'The Cleggan Disaster'. *The Battle of Aughrim*, which centres on 'the last decisive battle in Irish history,' holds the Anglo and Irish sides of his ancestry in elegant equilibrium. *Collected*

Poems (2000) shows the detached style of the earlier poems yielding to the more personal and moving work of his later years. His prose memoir, *The Kick* (2002), provides an impressionistic account of an adventurous life. **Dennis O'Driscoll**

Murphy, Robert (1806–1843), mathematician. Born in Mallow, Co. Cork; educated at the University of Cambridge. During his short life he emerged from poverty in Ireland to great fame as a mathematician. Forced to leave Cambridge with his debts unpaid, he lived in London from 1836, working at the University of London. He wrote textbooks on algebra and electricity and performed research in mathematical analysis. He is best known for Murphy's Formula; less well known is his work establishing the foundation for breakthroughs made by more famous mathematicians and for his important work in the creation of modern algebra. **Leo Creedon**

Murphy, Seamus (1907–1975), sculptor. Born near Mallow, Co. Cork; attended school in Cork. At the age of fifteen he was apprenticed to the stonemason John Aloysius O'Connor at St Patrick's Art Marble Works. Urged by his schoolteacher and friend DANIEL CORKERY, who recognised his talent, he studied full-time for a year at the Crawford School of Art, after which he attended night classes. He was awarded the Gibson Travelling Scholarship in 1931; the same year he carved a *Madonna and Child* in polished limestone, which was exhibited at the RHA. He studied at the Académie Colarossi, Paris, 1932–3, together with the Irish-American sculptor ANDREW O'CONNOR. The following year he set up his own studio and stone-yard at Blackpool, Cork. Over the next four decades he specialised in carving memorials, gravestones, and religious or commemorative SCULPTURE, becoming renowned for his sympathetic approach to stone-carving and for the quality of his lettering (see p. 270). Many of his headstones are in St Finbarr's Cemetery, Cork. His *Virgin of the Twilight*, shown at the 1942 Munster Fine Art and the 1943 RHA exhibitions, is in Fitzgerald Park, Cork. He designed the Church of the Annunciation (1945) at Blackpool. His statue of St Gobnait in Coolea, carved in limestone in 1950, is one of his finest works. In Coolea he also carved the gravestone of SEÁN Ó RIADA. **Peter Murray**

Murphy, Seán, Gaelic footballer. Born in Co. Kerry. He won all-Ireland minor and junior medals in 1949 and was quickly elevated to the senior team. In 1953 he won his first all-Ireland championship and earned the accolade of one of the finest defenders of his generation. He won two further medals in 1955 and 1959 and was chosen as Footballer of the Year in 1959 after a performance in the all-Ireland final that is regarded as one of the great individual displays of all time. **Donal Keenan**

Murphy, Suzanne (1946–), singer. Born in Limerick, she began singing lessons with VERONICA DUNNE in 1973, studying at the Municipal College of Music (now DIT Conservatory of Music and Drama) for three years. During this time she toured the country with Irish National Opera and sang in the 'We Four' pop group. In 1976 she joined Welsh National Opera as principal soprano; she went on to sing the main roles in productions such as *Rigoletto* and *La Traviata*. Her contract ended in 1983, and since then she has kept close ties with Welsh National Opera as well as appearing with opera companies on the Continent and in the United States. **Geraldine Guiden**

Murphy, Suzanne. *Suzanne Murphy, a distinguished lyric dramatic soprano with Frank Patterson. She has performed internationally as an opera and concert artist, including roles as Violetta* (La Traviata), *Tosca, and Lady Macbeth. [RTÉ]*

Murphy, Thomas (Tom) (1935–), dramatist and novelist. Born in Tuam, Co. Galway; educated by the CHRISTIAN BROTHERS until 1950 and subsequently trained and taught as a metalwork teacher. His plays have been crucial in articulating the confusion that has attended Ireland's transition from a traditional to a modern society; his marginalised characters verbally assail the institutions and mentality of class, poverty, and masculinity while remaining existentially alone. His first play, the one-act *On the Outside* (written jointly with Noel O'Donoghue, 1959), won first prize at the North Cork Drama Festival; two years later his full-length debut *A Whistle in the Dark* won the All-Ireland Amateur Drama final in Athlone; having been rejected by the Abbey, it was staged by Joan Littlewood at the Theatre Royal, Stratford East, in London. Murphy spent the 1960s in London; but it was at the new Abbey and Peacock Theatres in Dublin that important productions of *Famine* (1968) and *A Crucial Week in the Life of a Grocer's Assistant* (1969) were staged. He returned to Ireland in 1970. Many of his plays have been premiered at the Abbey, from *The Morning after Optimism* (1971) to *The House* (2000). He was also writer in association with the DRUID THEATRE, Galway, in the mid-1980s; its production of BAILEGANGAIRE featured SIOBHAN MCKENNA as Mommo in her final role (see p. 674). Murphy's novel *The Seduction of Morality* was published in 1994. A member of the board of the ABBEY THEATRE, 1972–83, and writer in association there, 1986–9, he has received numerous awards for his writing and honorary doctorates from the University of Dublin, 1998, and National University of Ireland, Galway, 2000. **Anthony Roche**

Murphy, Thomas (Tommy) (1921–1985), Gaelic footballer. Born in Graiguecullen, Co. Laois. He earned the nickname 'the Boy Wonder' when he made his senior debut for Laois at the age of sixteen. Although he never won an all-Ireland title, he gained national and international respect for the quality of his football during a great career with one of the game's less successful counties. He won four Leinster senior championships with Laois and was a member of the Leinster team that won the Railway Cup in 1940 and 1945. **Donal Keenan**

Murphy, William (1824–1872), religious agitator. Born in Castletown Conyers, Co. Limerick, eldest son of a schoolteacher. The family converted to Protestantism and were allegedly persecuted to some extent. Murphy quickly showed a talent as a Protestant Scripture-reader and joined the Old Irish Society and then the Irish Church Mission before moving to Birmingham in the 1860s. He became a national figure as a result of the widely reported violence that accompanied his lectures from 1867 onwards, representing a virulent strain of popular anti-Catholicism. He instigated disturbances throughout England over the next five years. He is often connected with the anti-Catholic and semi-pornographic text *The Confessional Unmasked*. He died at the age of forty-eight of a pulmonary disease, though he was commonly represented as dying from injuries received during a beating by Irish Catholics at Whitehaven a year earlier. He subsequently became an ORANGE hero as the 'Martyr Murphy'. His memory could evoke violent passions, and a small riot accompanied his final journey to the Birmingham cemetery in 1872. **Alexander Peach**

Murphy, William Martin (1844–1919), founder of Independent Newspapers. Born in Bantry, Co. Cork. A building contractor, he developed a business empire containing railways and tramlines in Ireland, Britain, and Africa, Clery's department store, and the Imperial Hotel, Dublin. He bought the *Irish Catholic* and *Irish Independent* in 1904, introducing popular JOURNALISM to Ireland based on HARMSWORTH's model in England. A HOME RULE MP, 1885–92, and patron and ally of T. M. HEALY, he despised the Irish Party leadership and the DUBLIN CASTLE administration as bunglers. His newspapers' criticisms of Redmondism inadvertently strengthened SINN FÉIN. The authoritarian paternalism with which he handled labour relations made him the leader of the Dublin employers' attempt to crush the IRISH TRANSPORT AND GENERAL WORKERS' UNION DUBLIN 1913 LOCK-OUT strike. He was excoriated by W. B. YEATS for opposing the HUGH LANE gallery. **Patrick Maume**

Murray Ó Laoire, architects, a partnership of Hugh Murray and Seán Ó Laoire. Murray (1949–) was born in Limerick; studied at UCD and Rice University, Houston, Texas. Ó Laoire (1946–) was born in Dublin; studied at UCD and the University of California, Los Angeles. Both taught at DIT; established Murray and Ó Laoire Associates in Limerick, 1979; offices were later established in Dublin, 1981, Moscow, 1992, and Warsaw, 1999. Their architecture is characterised by urban design concerns and attention to technology in context. Projects in Limerick include the Milk Market (restoration), and King John's Castle visitor centre (1992), a brave insertion of a twentieth-century structure in a medieval setting. Arthur's Quay park and tourist information pavilion, Limerick, was awarded the RIAI Gold Medal, 1989–91. Other work includes buildings for the University of Limerick and Limerick Institute of Technology. The Green Building in TEMPLE BAR, Dublin (1994), harnesses environmentally responsible materials, natural ventilation, solar and wind power, and underground hot water sources. Other projects include Dublin Docklands and Coombe-New Market Framework Plans, residential area plans for Pokrovsky Hills, Moscow, Osiedle Kampinos, Warsaw, Stolichny Bank, Moscow, and the Irish pavilion at Expo 2000, Hannover. **Raymund Ryan**

Murray, Ann (1949–), singer. Born in Dublin, she studied at the Royal Northern College of Music (Manchester) with Frederick Cox and quickly established close links with English National Opera. She first appeared with the ENO at the Royal Opera House in Covent Garden singing the title role in HANDEL's *Xerxes and Ariodante* and subsequently in productions of *Così fan tutte* and *Idomeneo*. She has also appeared at La Scala in Milan and with the Vienna State Opera and Bavarian State Opera, which in 1998 awarded her the title Kammersängerin. Her recital appearances have taken her to the Munich and Salzburg festivals and to the United States, where she has appeared with the Berlin Philharmonic and the Chicago Symphony Orchestra. She performs in Britain at major festivals, such as the Edinburgh Festival, and at the BBC Proms. **Geraldine Guiden**

Murray, Daniel (1768–1852), Catholic churchman. Born in Sheepwalk, near Arklow, Co. Wicklow; educated at SALAMANCA. Ordained in 1790, he was a curate in his native Arklow in 1798 and barely escaped with his life when English soldiers murdered his parish priest. He was appointed Coadjutor Bishop of Dublin, 1809, and archbishop, 1823. A supporter of DANIEL O'CONNELL, he was nonetheless a moderate in politics. He maintained good relations with the British administration in Ireland and was once offered a seat on the Privy Council, which he refused. He supported the non-denominational system of national education introduced in 1831; likewise, he accepted the QUEEN'S COLLEGES on their establishment in the 1840s. On these and other questions he was opposed by a growing number of more assertive Catholics, both lay and clerical. The Queen's Colleges were formally condemned at the SYNOD OF THURLES (1850). **Fergal Tobin**

Murray, James (1788–1871), physician and chemist. Born in Derry; studied MEDICINE at Edinburgh, graduating in 1807, and in 1808 set up a medical practice in Belfast. In 1812 he took out a patent for milk of magnesia, a remedy he had developed for stomach acidity, and he subsequently set up a manufacturing plant in Belfast to produce it. He served as resident physician to three lord lieutenants, was knighted in 1831, and appointed Inspector of Anatomy for Ireland. He experimented to see whether the waste products from his factory could be used as fertilisers and is associatively credited with the first production of superphosphate. His related company did not thrive, and three years later he sold his patent to an English competitor. **Susan McKenna-Lawlor**

Murray, Ruby (1935–1996), singer. Born in Belfast. Beginning as a child singer, she became one of the most popular singers in Britain during the 1950s. In 1955 she had five singles simultaneously in the British top twenty, a feat bettered only by Madonna thirty years later. A bona fide popular star with her own television show, Murray—like many of her era—ceased to be as prominent once the Beatles arrived. She lived out her occasionally troubled later career in England, still performing in cabaret. **Tony Clayton-Lea**

Murray, T. C. [Thomas Cornelius] (1873–1959), playwright. Born in Macroom, Co. Cork. By profession a teacher, he wrote many plays of the kind that came to be typical of the ABBEY THEATRE's repertoire in the early decades of Irish independence, dealing with the passions and traumas of country life in a realist fashion. His best-known works are *Maurice Harte* (1912) and *Autumn Fire* (1924), the former a tragedy of rural clerical ambition, the latter a drama of inter-generational sexual conflict that has been compared to EUGENE O'NEILL's *Desire under the Elms*. **Terence Brown**

Museum of Country Life, opened in 2001 at Turlough Park, Castlebar, Co. Mayo, as part of the NATIONAL MUSEUM OF IRELAND, the first branch of the museum outside Dublin. It comprises a purpose-built gallery and store as well as Turlough Park House, a neo-GOTHIC manor-house designed by THOMAS NEWENHAM DEANE in 1865. The museum houses the Irish Folklife Division of the National Museum, and the Irish Folklife Collection is exhibited. This collection comprises approximately 50,000 items, encompassing those connected with traditional life including domestic activity, agriculture, transport, trades, crafts, religion, FESTIVALS, customs, as well as film and photographic archive.

The Irish Folklife Division was established as a fourth division of the National Museum in 1974. The systematic collecting of folk artefacts had begun in 1949 with the appointment of A. T. LUCAS to the staff of the Irish Antiquities Division. Previously the collection of folk artefacts had been haphazard, though it had been given increased emphasis under Adolf Mahr, director of the National Museum, 1927–39, under whom the first temporary exhibition of FOLKLIFE material was opened in conjunction with the Irish FOLKLORE COMMISSION in 1937. In the 1960s and 70s the collection was stored in the ROYAL HOSPITAL, Kilmainham, Dublin. To permit the restoration of the Royal Hospital as a conference centre (later as the IRISH MUSEUM OF MODERN ART), the collection was moved to a vacant former reformatory, St Conleth's, in Daingean, Co. Offaly, where it remained until most of it was moved to Co. Mayo during 2001. [see ULSTER FOLK AND TRANSPORT MUSEUM.] **Séamas Mac Philib**

Museum of Irish Industry, established in 1845 (as the Museum of Economic Geology) to house the growing collections of the GEOLOGICAL SURVEY OF IRELAND and the Irish Topographical Survey. It occupied a Georgian house at 51 St Stephen's Green, Dublin, where a chemical laboratory was later established. Here important analytical work, including that on SOILS to determine their agricultural value, was subsequently carried out for various government agencies. In 1847, under the aegis of its director, Sir ROBERT KANE, the museum diversified to include displays on industrial raw materials—both organic and inorganic—and their products and manufacturing methods, and in 1853 it was restyled the Museum of Irish Industry. In 1854 the museum assumed some of the educational role of the ROYAL DUBLIN SOCIETY, which meanwhile continued to hold popular lectures for the general public. Within the museum, professors provided a technical scientific curriculum in BOTANY, CHEMISTRY, geology, physics, and zoology for fee-paying students.

In 1867 the museum was reorganised, its educational role being taken over by the ROYAL COLLEGE OF SCIENCE FOR IRELAND. Many of its displays were transferred to the NATURAL HISTORY MUSEUM. Panels of Irish marbles and limestones in the foyer of the building, now occupied by the OFFICE OF PUBLIC WORKS, are all that remain of the original displays. **Patrick N. Wyse Jackson**

museums and galleries. Paramount among Irish art institutions is the NATIONAL GALLERY OF IRELAND in Merrion Square, founded in 1854, a distinguished collection of Continental and Irish art, containing also the national portrait collection and the YEATS museum. The Millennium wing was opened in 2001. The HUGH LANE Municipal Gallery of Modern Art in Parnell Square has important collections of nineteenth and twentieth-century Continental and Irish Art. The NATIONAL MUSEUM OF IRELAND in Kildare Street, Dublin, has comprehensive collections of antiquities, decorative arts, military history, FOLK LIFE, zoology, and GEOLOGY.

Murray, Ruby. *A native of Belfast, Ruby Murray first topped the charts as a teenager with hits including 'Heartbeat' and 'Mr Wonderful'. [Rex Features Ltd]*

The CHESTER BEATTY LIBRARY, at its new site within DUBLIN CASTLE, has outstanding collections of manuscripts and rare books of Islamic, Chinese, Japanese and European origin. The IRISH MUSEUM OF MODERN ART occupies the former ROYAL HOSPITAL at Kilmainham, Dublin, Ireland's premier seventeenth-century building. Dublin Civic Museum, in South William Street, is devoted to the history of the city. Literary material is held at the Dublin Writers' Museum in Parnell Square, and the Pearse Museum in Rathfarnham is devoted to the life of PATRICK PEARSE. KILMAINHAM GAOL Museum deals with the history of the prison. TRINITY COLLEGE, Dublin, contains the Douglas Hyde Gallery for contemporary art exhibitions, the Weingreen Museum of Biblical Antiquities, and the Geological Museum. There is a Classical Museum in the UNIVERSITY COLLEGE, DUBLIN.

The James Mitchell Museum of Geology is in the National University of Ireland, Galway. Cork Public Museum is in Fitzgerald Park, and the Crawford Gallery is in Emmet Place. Apart from Limerick City Museum in Castle Lane, Limerick has the HUNT MUSEUM, distinguished prehistoric and medieval collections of the late John Hunt, recently rehoused in the restored Custom House.

County museum services are found in South Tipperary, Kerry, and Donegal. The Model Arts and Niland Gallery is situated on the Mall in Sligo. The ULSTER MUSEUM, Belfast, and Armagh County Museum are now part of the Museums and Galleries of Northern Ireland (MAGNI). Belfast also has the Ormeau Baths Gallery, devoted to contemporary art exhibitions. Local authority museums in Northern Ireland are found in Enniskillen, Co. Fermanagh, Downpatrick, Co. Down, Lisburn, Co. Antrim, and Craigavon,

Co. Armagh. In Derry, historical material is exhibited in the Tower Museum and the Harbour Museum, while the Orchard Gallery runs a lively series of contemporary art exhibitions. **Martyn Anglesea**

music. From the BRONZE AGE to the digital age, indigenous musical life in Ireland has been susceptible to the consequences of population mobility and technological developments in Europe and, latterly, America.

Though people lived in Ireland over 9,000 years ago, the first evidence of musical activity dates from surviving Bronze Age horns and hand bells (c. 1000 BC). These, and the later IRON AGE trumpas (c. 100 BC), show a high degree of technical sophistication (see pp. 178, 757). The persistence of Celtic culture from the middle of the first millennium BC to the seventeenth century suggests that pre-Christian vocal music may have consisted of praise and war songs and the use of the lyre. The Fenian or OSSIANIC lay emerged in the twelfth century and continued in popularity for many centuries and later informed the course of cultural Romanticism through Macpherson's publications (1760s). From the seventh century new Roman liturgical practices were probably introduced and co-existed with the Celtic rite, while the ANGLO-NORMAN conquest of the twelfth century introduced the Use of Sarum.

Alongside other medieval instruments, such as the *tiompán* (a plucked string instrument) and *píopaí* (war bagpipes), the distinctive Irish HARP held the highest status during the native Irish aristocratic period, which ended in the seventeenth century. It was used for accompanying singers and reciters in the bardic tradition and also formed part of the Celtic liturgy (see pp. 475, 1079). The music of the harper-composer TURLOUGH CAROLAN bears the influences of Vivaldi, Corelli, and GEMINIANI. At the BELFAST HARP FESTIVAL (1792) EDWARD BUNTING notated music of the remaining native harpers, a collection that informed subsequent compositions and arrangements, most famously MOORE'S IRISH MELODIES (1808–34).

It was with the fragmentation of the native Irish aristocracy after 1601 that the modern period of traditional music began, with the lower classes being the main performers and creators. European melodic instruments (FLUTE and violin) became standard and co-existed with the bellows-blown UILLEANN PIPES. New dance genres (REEL and hornpipe) were introduced from Britain, alongside the established JIG, and English-language songs were disseminated through ballad sheets. Irish traditional dance and vocal music has remained an oral tradition, and while solo improvisation is a characteristic feature, a variety of group performance settings can be referred to, such as CÉILÍ bands, the paraclassical CEOLTÓIRÍ CHUALANN (1960s), the BOTHY BAND (1970s), and pub sessions. Regional styles, such as the Donegal fiddle tradition, still exist, and the tradition is promoted through a variety of organisations, such as COMHALTAS CEOLTÓIRÍ ÉIREANN and the annual WILLIE CLANCY SUMMER SCHOOL (see p. 1064).

From 1500 to 1800 the Penal Laws had a devastating effect on sacred and secular musical culture. The Reformation terminated the Celtic monastic tradition and inaugurated a predominantly Protestant sponsorship of sacred music, based in the Dublin cathedrals. However, later reforms and the CECILIAN movement of the nineteenth century proved an invigorating context for Catholic sacred choral music. The eighteenth century saw many developments in musical infrastructure and performance which was mostly centred in Dublin and stemmed from London, for example, a ballad opera tradition flowed from the performance of *The Beggar's Opera* (1728) and a choral tradition from the premiere of HANDEL'S *Messiah* (1742).

The main opportunities for eighteenth-century musicians existed in the metropolitan churches and cathedrals, with the notable exception of JOHN FIELD, who made a vital contribution to European romantic pianism. The nineteenth century was dominated by Italian grand opera, with MICHAEL BALFE, WILLIAM WALLACE, and Julius Benedict composing in English. A number of orchestral and opera composers attempted to incorporate traditional music in the norms of classic-romantic style, most notably HAMILTON HARTY and C. V. STANFORD. However, the complexity of this problem, compounded by the homogenising influence of nationalism, can be seen in the career of SEÁN Ó RIADA.

Performances of orchestral music were severely neglected until the twentieth century, when the RTÉ Symphony Orchestra and ULSTER ORCHESTRA emerged as fully professional orchestras. The continuity of art music is bolstered by national and international competitions and festivals such as the FEIS CEOIL, CORK INTERNATIONAL CHORAL AND DANCE FESTIVAL, and the Sonorities festival (Belfast).

Subsequent to the arrival of English touring companies in the nineteenth century, the twentieth century saw the development of the DUBLIN GRAND OPERA SOCIETY, which engendered regular performances, the OPERA THEATRE COMPANY, which travels throughout the country, and the WEXFORD FESTIVAL OPERA, which has an international reputation for promoting lesser-known works. A number of initiatives for younger musicians also exists, such as the Irish and Ulster Youth Orchestras, Irish Youth Choir, and National Children's Choir. The ARTS COUNCIL supports organisations such as MUSIC NETWORK, which promotes musical performance throughout the country.

At present there are more than a hundred active composers registered with the Contemporary Music Centre, writing in a multiplicity of 'styles' and for a variety of forces, including digital-technological. With a few exceptions, however, most of these composers remain unknown to the general public, and it is mostly through competitions, commissions, and third-level sponsorship that opportunities for the performance of original composition exist.

American techno-cultural values have influenced urban and rural popular musical tastes since the 1920s, as evidenced by the glamorous SHOWBANDS, the singing styles of Irish country-and-western stars, the blues guitar playing of RORY GALLAGHER, and the high-octane RIVERDANCE. The preferred music of the teenage population is the media-driven chart music, a phenomenon promoted by RTÉ radio and television since the 1980s. Ireland has contributed many talents to the international scene, including VAN MORRISON, U2, DIVINE COMEDY, and the 'Boy Bands'. JAZZ in Ireland is represented internationally by LOUIS STEWART and the Cork Jazz Festival. **Michael Murphy**

music, ballet. The composition of ballet scores by Irish composers began with the founding of ballet companies in the middle of the twentieth century, the most significant groups being the Dublin Ballet Club, CORK BALLET COMPANY, Irish Theatre Ballet, Irish Ballet Company, and Irish National Ballet. The earliest Irish ballet score, *Puck Fair* (1941), was written by ELIZABETH MACONCHY for the Dublin Ballet Club, and from this time on significant numbers of Irish composers have been commissioned to write ballet scores for Irish dance groups. The close relationship between composer and dancer is illustrated by the fact that JOAN DENISE MORIARTY appointed the composer ALOYS FLEISCHMANN as her vice-chairman when she founded Irish National Ballet in 1954. Fleischman himself wrote a number of ballets, including *The Golden Bell of Ko* (1948), *An Cóitín Dearg* (1951), *The Planting Stick* (1957), and *Táin* (1981). Other notable composers of ballets include SIR HAMILTON HARTY (*The Seal Woman*, 1956; *Prisoners of the Sea*, 1961), Éamonn Ó Gallchobhair's *The Singer* (1935) and *The Twisting of the Rope* (1939), A. J. POTTER (*Careless Love*, 1960; *Full Moon for the Bride*, 1974), SEÁN Ó RIADA (*Devil to Pay*, 1962; *Billy the Music*, 1974), JOHN BUCKLEY (*Diulta Renunciation*, 1979), and GERALD BARRY (*Trespass*, 1996).

Ballet companies in Ireland have constantly struggled for funding and have had an insecure existence, the Irish National Ballet being the last to close, in 1991. A new dance organisation, the Institute of Choreography and Dance (formerly Firkin Crane), opened in Cork in 2000. **Deborah Kelleher**

music, electronic. Ireland's position on the periphery of musical life in Europe, and the lack of the necessary facilities, delayed the origination of electronic music until the 1970s. The first Irish composition to include electronics was GERARD VICTORY's *Compensations*, for cor anglais and tape, commissioned by and performed at the DUBLIN FESTIVAL OF TWENTIETH-CENTURY MUSIC in 1970. Few other composers in the 1970s ventured to use electronics, with only two—ROGER DOYLE and Paul Hayes—going on to produce a substantial body of work in the medium. Both have concentrated on electronic music throughout their careers, writing predominantly for tape. The use of electronics became more widespread in the 1980s, though again few composers consistently explored the medium. The most significant of these is MICHAEL ALCORN, who, as well as establishing the music studio at Queen's University, Belfast, has been particularly influential through his promotion of new musical technologies. Dónal Hurley and Michael Holohan have also made significant use of electronics in their compositions. Advances have been made since 1990, especially in education. Almost all university music departments now contain studios, many offering specific courses in electro-acoustic composition and technology. The principal concern of electro-acoustic composers today is the need to develop a wider audience, a concern that has been addressed by the formation of the Irish Electro-Acoustic Music Association, 1996, and the Crash Ensemble, 1997, much of whose repertoire incorporates electronically produced sound. **Adrian Scahill**

music, performers. Ireland's wealth of traditional performers is recorded at least as far back as 1185 with GIRALDUS CAMBRENSIS's comment, 'I find among these people commendable diligence only on musical instruments, on which they are incomparably more skilled than any nation I have seen.' Traditional musicians, especially harpers, enjoyed a prestige next only to BREHONS, the legal scholars, until colonisation by England broke up Irish culture, and musicians lost their status. There are only a few performers, such as the harper TURLOUGH CAROLAN, about whom much is known today. Irish TRADITIONAL MUSIC is passed on through oral transmission, and certain performers are recognised not only for their ability but also for their influence. One such performer was PÁDRAIG O'KEEFFE (1888–1963), a fiddler who passed on his technique and tunes to hundreds of people in the SLIABH LUACHRA area around the Cork-Kerry border. Into the twentieth century traditional music has continued to thrive and has begun to show influences from popular culture. Performers such as DÓNAL LUNNY, Davey Spillane and the band MOVING HEARTS have achieved international fame with their fusion of traditional and contemporary music styles.

Western European art music. By the middle of the eighteenth century Dublin was becoming the second city in the British Isles, and it is from this time that notable Irish performers of classical music begin to emerge. The influence of foreign teaching—a characteristic of Irish MUSICAL EDUCATION that remains up to the present—also appears at this time. The baritone MICHAEL KELLY was taught by the Italian Rauzzini in Dublin before moving to Italy to study with Finaroli and Aprilo. One of his most notable achievements was the creation of the role of Don Basilio in Mozart's *Le Nozze di Figaro*. The pianist JOHN FIELD was initially taught by his grandfather and subsequently moved to London to study with Clementi. In the early nineteenth century Field was regarded as the most celebrated pianist in Europe after Beethoven stopped playing. Two Irish singers achieved successful international careers in the early twentieth century. JOHN MCCORMACK is still regarded as one of the finest tenor voices in history and had a remarkable career in the United States. MARGARET SHERIDAN was described by Puccini as 'the ideal Mimi and the only Butterfly.' Moving further into the twentieth century, Irish performers continued to make their mark on the international stage, relying on foreign study to complete their training. JOHN O'CONOR was taught by J. J. O'REILLY at the Municipal College of Music (now the DIT Conservatory of Music and Drama) before studying at the Vienna Hochschule with Dieter Weber. Following first prizes in the Beethoven International Piano Competition, 1973, and Bosendorfer Competition, 1975, he had a successful international performing and recording career. The contralto BERNADETTE GREEVY studied singing with Jean Nolan in Dublin before continuing her studies at the Guildhall School and privately in London. She has a distinguished career on the concert platform and operatic stage and is recognised as a notable interpreter of Mahler. The mezzo-soprano ANN MURRAY studied with Nancy Calthorpe at the College of Music before concluding her studies in Manchester. Since then she has appeared in every significant opera house in the world and has

music, performers. *Michael Kelly, musician and composer, musical director of the Garrick Club, London, in a mezzotint by Charles Turner after a painting by James Lonsdale (1777–1839). [National Gallery of Ireland]* an extensive discography. The twenty-first century is already producing a new generation of Irish performers. Finghin Collins (1977–) studied with John O'Conor at the ROYAL IRISH ACADEMY OF MUSIC and is now taught by Dominique Merlet. A first prize-winner of the Clara Haskill International Piano Competition in Vevey, he is already developing an international performing profile. The soprano Orla Boylan (1971–) was taught by Mary Brennan at the DIT Conservatory of Music and Drama before continuing her training in Milan. She has already appeared in leading roles in opera houses in Europe, most notably debuting as Mimi in Graz. Ireland's three largest music institutions—the DIT Conservatory of Music and Drama, Royal Irish Academy of Music and Drama, and Cork School of Music—have developed performance degree courses within the last ten years. These third-level qualifications, combined with a groundswell of interest in the establishment of an Irish Academy of Performing Arts involving music and the other arts, are the first step towards providing talented young performers with the option of completing their training within the country.

Contemporary popular music. Without doubt, Ireland's best-selling performers have come from contemporary POPULAR MUSIC. Bands such as U2, Boyzone, Westlife, the CRANBERRIES and the Corrs and the solo artists SINEAD O'CONNOR, ENYA, and VAN MORRISON have sold countless millions of recordings and have placed themselves firmly in the vanguard of popular world performers. Although much of their musical influence stems from international pop culture, certain artists, such as the Corrs and Sinead O'Connor, acknowledge the importance of their traditional roots in their sound. **Deborah Kelleher**

musical-instrument makers. The earliest Irish musical instruments, dating from c. 1000 BC and named lurer, are bronze TRUMPETS (see p. 178). During the Middle Ages, Ireland was influenced by a Continent-wide Celtic culture, in which the main instruments were the harp, bagpipes, and a stringed instrument named the *tiompán*. The oldest known Irish HARP is the TRINITY COLLEGE harp, the soundbox of which is carved from a solid piece of willow, typical of all true Irish harps.

There is evidence of music in ecclesiastical establishments from the twelfth century, including the use of pipe-organ, sackbuts, cornetts, and viols from the sixteenth century. Many organ-builders working in Ireland were from abroad; these included Thomas Bateson (1570–1630), George Harris, Lancelot Pease, Renatus Harris (1652–1724), and John Baptist Cuvillie (died 1728). Eighteenth-century organ-builders included John Byfield, Ferdinand Weber (1715–1784), and William Castles Hollister (died 1802). WILLIAM TELFORD (1809–1885) was undoubtedly Ireland's foremost organ-builder in the nineteenth century. There are records of forty-two instrument-makers working in Ireland during the late eighteenth and early nineteenth centuries. Ferdinand Weber and John Hammond were expert harpsichord-makers, while William Southwell contributed greatly to the development of the pianoforte.

Thomas Perry was the greatest Dublin violin-maker of the late eighteenth century. An exhibition of ancient instruments in the South Kensington Museum, London, in 1872 included a cither-viol by Perry dated 1767 and a violin dated 1768; he also made cellos and basses. Some of his instruments are now in the NATIONAL MUSEUM. The firm later became known as Perry-Wilkinson. Other violin-makers included Edward Keenan, John Carroll, George Ward, Thomas Molyneux, Thomas Dunne, and John Macintosh. The greatest harp-maker in the eighteenth century was John Egan. Guitars were made by William Gibson, Claget, and Wilson.

Johann Bernhard Logier came to Ireland in 1790 as a band-master; from 1813 he manufactured bugles, trumpets, horns, trombones, and drums. In 1810 Joseph Haliday added keys to the bugle, an instrument that enjoyed great popularity. The flageolet or English flute was manufactured in Dublin by Andrew Ellard, John Dollard, and Wilkinson Corcoran, who shared premises at Essex Quay in the early part of the nineteenth century. Thomas Flanagan worked in Cork as a flute-maker, 1787–1820.

Numerous instrument-makers, of both classical and traditional instruments, continue to work in Ireland today. The tradition of organ-building has been continued by Kenneth Jones, Trevor Crowe, and others; Cathal Gannon was renowned as a harpsichord-maker; while Jim McKillop is an important violin-maker. **Ite O'Donovan**

musical instruments, ancient, c. 1000 BC–AD 700. More than 150 musical instruments survive in Ireland from prehistoric times. These include the great collection of BRONZE AGE horns that were cast in the era c. 1000 BC, many *crothalls* or hand-bells, wooden horns, and the earliest known member of the bassoon family. Most noteworthy are the finest surviving middle IRON AGE *trumpas* from c. 100 BC and a horn that has been dated to AD 700. Recent studies on original and reproduction instruments show that these instruments are very advanced, acoustically and musically. The highest level of bronze-casting, sheet-metal working and wood-carving was achieved by craftsmen and musicians in their time. The prehistoric musical instrument collection of Ireland is of great importance as an indicator of prehistoric and later music and craft knowledge, offering an insight into the origins of Irish music and its influence on other musical traditions, confirmed by their successful reintroduction into present-day world music (see p. 178). [see LOUGHNASHADE.] **Simon O'Dwyer and Maria Cullen O'Dwyer**

'Musical Instruments of the Ancient Irish', a series of lectures by EUGENE O'CURRY, published as a substantial segment of his printed work in 1873. Devised from manuscript sources, it develops a history of music in early Ireland and analyses scales and modes and the verse structure of songs. He deduces descriptions of a variety of instruments—plucked and bowed strings, TRUMPET and reed forms, and percussion types. His objective was to provide diverse interest for players, as well as core material for composers, though in the society music of his day he felt that both groups ignored the indigenous Irish music, which for him was particularly appealing. **Fintan Vallely**

music archives and collections. The principal music archives in Ireland are those of the university libraries, the NATIONAL LIBRARY OF IRELAND, MARSH'S LIBRARY, and the collections held in the libraries of Christ Church and St Patrick's Cathedrals, Dublin. In addition to these are the libraries of the RIAM, ROYAL IRISH ACADEMY, LINEN HALL LIBRARY, and the Representative Church Body Library. Major collections of sacred music, both manuscript and printed, are held in the cathedral libraries (including eighteenth and nineteenth-century anthems and services), TRINITY COLLEGE Library, and Marsh's Library; major collections of secular music are held in the National Library, Trinity College Library, and the Royal Irish Academy.

Trinity College Library possesses the Ebenezer Prout Collection, containing examples of nineteenth-century music, and the Townley Hall Collection, containing examples of Neapolitan opera of the late eighteenth century, popular music of the eighteenth and nineteenth centuries, and an early copy of *Messiah*. The National

Library possesses the Joly Collection, containing eighteenth-century opera and examples of eighteenth- and nineteenth-century songs and dances, and the Plunkett Collection, containing keyboard music of the eighteenth and nineteenth centuries and examples of traditional dance music printed in the eighteenth century.

In Northern Ireland the main music collections are those of the library of Queen's University, Belfast, and the Linen Hall Library. In Queen's the main sources are the published and unpublished works of HARTY, some BUNTING manuscripts, and works by contemporary British composers. The Linen Hall Library (which was partly responsible for the publishing of Bunting's *Ancient Music of Ireland*) contains nineteenth-century operas, cantatas, and oratorios. **Éamonn O'Keeffe**

Music Association of Ireland, established in 1948 to unite the various music groups that existed at the time. The main objectives included the establishment of a NATIONAL CONCERT HALL and the improvement of MUSIC EDUCATION by placing music on the school curriculum. The association was responsible for the debut concerts of many of Ireland's finest soloists, including JOHN O'CONOR and BERNADETTE GREEVY. While it has lost some of its importance in recent years, it continues to support and promote music education. **Geraldine Guiden**

music associations. There are several music associations in Ireland, covering all areas of music. TRADITIONAL MUSIC is represented by COMHALTAS CEOLTOIRI ÉIREANN, and Cumann Cheoil na Tíre. The Post-Primary Music Teachers' Association monitors educational developments for music, while the MUSIC ASSOCIATION OF IRELAND undertakes music programmes for primary and secondary schools. Light classical music is represented by the Association of Irish Musical Societies, which aims at improving the standard of music theatre by providing an adjudication and awards scheme, workshops, library, and annual competition. Associations devoted to specific instrument groups include the Irish Association of Brass and Military Bands, Irish Pipe Band Association, Association of Irish Choirs, and Irish Association of Youth Orchestras. Associations devoted to running annual competitive events include the FEIS CEOIL Association, which runs a festival of classical music in Dublin for all instruments and ages, involving approximately 7,500 competitors each year; and feiseanna in Arklow, Cork, Sligo, and Derry. The representative body for composers of contemporary music is the Association of Irish Composers. **Deborah Kelleher**

music competitions

National. The majority of pre-professional competitions are found in the competitive feiseanna. These are public, graded competitions for students and amateur musicians. Competitors are adjudicated publicly by trained professionals. In most cases the adjudicators are Irish, but in some of the larger feiseanna, such as the FEIS CEOIL in Dublin, the adjudicators are distinguished foreigners. The events are supported financially by competitors' fees, ticket sales, and corporate sponsorship. The main general music feiseanna and festivals are the FEIS CEOIL (Dublin), Arklow Music Festival, Feis Maitiú (Cork), Feis Sligigh, and Feis Dhoire Cholmcille (Derry). These feiseanna are regarded as training grounds for pre-professionals, and most, if not all, of the most distinguished performers have at one point competed in these events. Competitive events for traditional music are represented by Slógadh, a schools competition for singing and dancing, and An toireachtas, for traditional singing and instrumental playing. Certain competitions specialise in one facet of music, such as the Mostly Modern/IMRO Young Composers' Competition and the Telecom Éireann School Choirs Competition.

International. A number of competitions welcome participation from competitors outside Ireland. The juries in these cases comprise international members. Many of these events are aimed at pre-professionals, the object being to create connections between music in Ireland and music in the rest of the world. Examples are the International Military Band Competition and the CORK INTERNATIONAL CHORAL AND DANCE FESTIVAL. Ireland possesses some international competitions for young professionals, which are devoted to a specific instrument and provide substantial cash prizes and engagements for winners. Two of the most prominent of these are the DUBLIN INTERNATIONAL PIANO COMPETITION and VERONICA DUNNE International Singing Competition. **Deborah Kelleher**

music criticism and journalism. One of the most established traditions of music criticism and journalism in the daily press has been developed within the IRISH TIMES. Chief classical music critics in recent times have included CHARLES ACTON, who held the post from 1955 to 1987. His writings for the paper included more than 6,000 concert reviews, articles, and interviews—including interviews with Olivier Messiaen and Yehudi Menuhin, among others. While he never failed to provide technical and stylistic commentary in his reviews, he was also renowned for employing an extremely readable, often poignant style of writing. This is epitomised

Musical Instruments, ancient. *A reproduction of the Celtic Iron Age Loughnashade trumpet being played in the 'S' position (see page 178). [Prehistoric Music Ireland; photo: Astird Neumann]*

in a review of a performance of Holst's *Planets* given by the RTÉSO in which Acton wrote how he watched the performance 'through a haze of tears of emotion and beauty' (*Irish Times*, 20 February 1983). Acton was succeeded by Michael Dervan. Since Dervan's accession, as with the majority of Irish newspapers, the printed edition of the paper has generally not reflected the growth in classical music as an entertainment medium. However, the music criticism element of the paper has been augmented electronically by a substantial page within the *Irish Times* web site. Entitled 'Michael Dervan's Classical Music', the section consists of a weekly column covering articles, reviews and national listings. Most daily papers encompass music criticism and journalism to some degree. Since 1986 the post of chief classical music critic at the SUNDAY TRIBUNE has been held by the musicologist Ian Fox, who is widely recognised as a highly informed critic. The *Sunday Tribune* includes a considerable classical music section in its Artlife supplement, which consists of a main feature and various reviews. Details of pertinent web pages are also provided, as well as a section entitled Musical Notes, which lists selected events and news. **Emma Costello**

music education. Ireland's music education system owes much of its structure and content to nineteenth-century British models. The importing of many aspects of the British schools curriculum, with its emphasis on Western art music, has remained a strong influence in both school-based and instrumental-based instruction.

The most recent curriculum designed for use in primary schools (1971) is largely based on singing, with strong emphasis on the use of tonic sol-fa. However, this comprehensive and forward-looking model is rarely implemented successfully, because of the lack of specialist teaching at primary level. The second-level curriculum has undergone enormous change in recent years, to produce two courses for the Junior Certificate and Leaving Certificate examinations: the former promotes a broadly based listening programme, supported by performance studies, and is designed to include pupils of all abilities; the latter has recently been redesigned to allow progression from the revised junior syllabus. Pupils are prepared in performance, composition, and listening skills, with options for electives in each strand.

Music education at third level provides a variety of options, with courses on offer at more than ten institutions. Recent developments have included specialisms in performance, composition, historical studies, ethnomusicology, and music technology. Many institutions offer degrees in music in conjunction with other subjects. Instrumental and vocal tuition has not relied so heavily on state-sponsored institutions, with much of this instruction provided by private teachers. In Northern Ireland, the Education and Library Boards provide an impressive peripatetic teaching scheme to serve schools.

Though no national performing school yet exists, much success has been achieved by the larger music schools: the CORK SCHOOL OF MUSIC, the Ulster College of Music (Belfast), the DIT Conservatory of Music and Drama and the RIAM (Dublin).

Until recently, traditional music was taught outside the institutional system, apart from academic courses at third level. Since the 1960s an increase in popularity, coupled with increased musicological research in this area, has resulted in the inclusion of traditional music as a performance subject in many second-level and third-level institutions.

Assessment plays an integral role in both performance and academic study. The grade-based British system has flourished in Ireland, with the establishment of several Irish examination boards that evaluate classical and traditional performance. A strong competitive spirit has resulted in numerous and frequent MUSIC COMPETITIONS and festivals, which have been the training ground for many of Ireland's most successful performers.

Research and debate on music education has been largely neglected until recently. The establishment of new forums for debate has enhanced awareness of the problems that affect the Irish system, in particular the Music Education National Debate, which was initiated in 1994 by Frank Heneghan under the auspices of the Dublin Institute of Technology. **David Mooney**

'Music for Middlebrows', a popular radio programme presented by Des Keogh, first broadcast on RTÉ radio in the late 1960s. The show was aimed at an audience who appreciated classical music but might not have been particularly learned about it. The last show was broadcast in 1999. **Geraldine Guiden**

music-hall and popular song. Song performance was part of everyday life before the electronic reproduction of music; this is demonstrated vividly in JOYCE'S ULYSSES, in particular the 'Sirens' episode. Most Irish towns had their music-halls, such as the Alhambra in Belfast and Dan Lowry's in Dublin; concert rooms, smoking-rooms and domestic recitals provided the more refined music-lovers with popular songs in the nineteenth and early twentieth centuries. The vogue for STAGE-IRISH songs, comic and sentimental, was widespread throughout Britain and Ireland for most of the nineteenth century and beyond. Such notables as SAMUEL LOVER trod the boards of the music-halls, singing their own compositions and portraying stage-Irish characters. Few song-making thespians were more popular than WILLIAM PERCY FRENCH, many of whose songs retain their popularity to the present day. **Tom Munnelly**

music history and performance. The earliest references to art music in Ireland are to be found in the religious domain. With the unique Celtic Christian rite was an attendant vibrant musical tradition, which, considering the constant intercourse between Irish and Continental MONASTERIES, may be assumed to have followed a similar model to that in European monastic sites. However, the lack of notated sources before 1000 makes it impossible to clarify the true nature and function of music in the Celtic liturgical rite. Nevertheless, several visiting monks documented the situation. GIRALDUS CAMBRENSIS's accounts of his visits of 1183 and 1185 note the significant use of the harp in liturgical music (possibly a small eight-stringed instrument), specifically as the decorative upper part in two-part organum.

In the ensuing period, until the defeat of the Irish at Kinsale in 1601, the HARP assumed a primary role in Irish high art. This position symbolises the connection between the ethnic and art tradition at the time, the passing of which would mark the initial fissure between the Irish tradition, which was perceived to be a progressively more rebellious influence, and the art music tradition of Europe and, more importantly, England.

The effect of the REFORMATION in Ireland was essentially to end the monastic tradition of music and to develop music for the purpose of Protestant worship in the churches and particularly the cathedrals. The subsequent importation of vicars-choral and organists from England led to a more consistent use of choral music, and to the instalment of some notable figures. Thomas Bateson, the organist of CHRIST CHURCH CATHEDRAL, Dublin, from 1609 to 1630, was one of the first organists to provide music himself for the cathedral, while in ST PATRICK'S CATHEDRAL, Dublin, Daniel Roseingrave and his son, Ralph, both held the position of organist and added many of their own compositions to the cathedral's liturgy.

Throughout the eighteenth century the strong influence of English music led to the building of concert venues in Dublin, including the Great Musick Hall in Fishamble Street in 1741, in which HANDEL's *Messiah* was first performed in April 1742. The performance of music for the benefit of CHARITABLE ORGANISATIONS, including hospitals, became an important aspect of Dublin's musical life, supported by a moral Ascendancy outlook. The development of opera in Ireland was significantly marked by the first performance of *The Beggar's Opera* at the SMOCK ALLEY THEATRE in 1728. This initiated a thriving tradition of ballad opera. In 1764 the first chair of music in Ireland was founded at TRINITY COLLEGE, Dublin, and with the continuous arrival of talented European musicians, including FRANCESCO GEMINIANI, Matthew Dubourg and Johann Kusser [COUSSER], the musical status of Dublin was greatly enhanced.

By the end of the century the Ascendancy had created a sense of art music that was unmistakably English and European in character. This high art aspiration was vividly contrasted by the attempts to collate and integrate the wider Irish musical culture in the antiquarian motivation of the BELFAST HARP FESTIVAL of 1792. In the three collections of EDWARD BUNTING's *General Collection of the Ancient Irish Music*, Bunting's intention is to preserve for the future the orally transmitted Irish tradition, providing at the same time possibilities for the integration of Irish music into the Ascendancy high art culture. With the coming into force of the ACT OF UNION in 1801 the tradition of patronage gradually gave way to a new and more politicised musical landscape. The publication of THOMAS MOORE's melodies between 1808 and 1834 brought Bunting's preservation of Irish music to a new point of departure. The national aspirations of an increasingly powerful section of Irish society found voice in the work of Moore and, later, THOMAS DAVIS. With the opening of the THEATRE ROYAL in 1821 the performance of grand opera included such works as *The Bohemian Girl* by Michael Balfe and *Maritana* by WILLIAM WALLACE, but the combination of modal Irish melody with the complexity of a romantic operatic tonal idiom was a marriage of conflicting ideas and not particularly successful.

The rise of amateur music was a particular aspect of the nineteenth century, mostly organised in Dublin by ROBERT PRESCOTT STEWART, professor of music at Trinity College, and the Robinson family (Francis Robinson founded the Sons of HANDEL in 1810, possibly the first choral society in Ireland). In fact the foundation of the RIAM in 1848 was largely the result of the efforts of the Robinson family. During this period the work of composers such as FIELD, STANFORD and HAMILTON HARTY promoted the art music cause, but generally from outside Ireland. With the foundation of the feis ceoil in 1897 the desire to promote Irish traditional music became an annual event in competition form, attempting to gauge the development and transmission of Irish music.

The foundation of the National University of Ireland in 1908 led to the establishment of a music department and chair of music at University College, Dublin, in 1914 (there had been a chair of music in Cork since 1908). This enhanced educational aspect of music gradually filtered into Irish life and helped to formalise the status of music. With the formation of the state in 1921 and the creation of the state radio station, Radio Éireann, the transmission and professional performance of music became directly connected with the organisation. The Radio Éireann Symphony Orchestra was formed in 1948, from an earlier professional station ensemble dating from 1926. The orchestra was expanded to form the RTÉ Symphony Orchestra in 1961 and further restructured to create

music history and performance. Fishamble Street, Dublin, *watercolour by Flora Mitchell shows the site of Richard Castle's New Musick Hall (left) opened in 1741. On 13 April 1742 it presented the first performance of Handel's* Messiah. *[National Gallery of Ireland]*

the present NATIONAL SYMPHONY ORCHESTRA of Ireland in 1990 (see p. 911). Alongside this group there is the RTÉ CONCERT ORCHESTRA (formerly known as the Radio Éireann Light Orchestra), another professional group that fulfils the needs of RTÉ in studio work, as well as concerts and recordings. In Northern Ireland the ULSTER ORCHESTRA evolved in 1981 from a combination of the BBC Northern Ireland Orchestra and the Ulster Orchestra and is another professional group directly linked to a broadcasting institution. The IRISH CHAMBER ORCHESTRA has added a new dimension to professional chamber music; it is based in Limerick as part of the ARTS COUNCIL Plan for Regional Development. The NATIONAL YOUTH ORCHESTRA of Ireland and the Ulster Youth Orchestra are recent and valuable additions to musical education, providing vital experience for young musicians.

With the formation of the DUBLIN GRAND OPERA SOCIETY in 1941 there began a regular series of operatic productions, now under the auspices of Opera Ireland, with the chorus formed by the professional National Chamber Choir. Smaller touring opera companies, such as OPERA THEATRE COMPANY and formerly Irish National Opera have brought opera to a wider regional audience.

The role of the composer in twentieth-century Ireland has involved a problematic relationship between a vibrant traditional music and the increasingly fragmented European art music tradition. The creation of the Contemporary Music Centre has done much to champion the work of composers by archiving, commissioning, and publishing their works. The performance and recording of contemporary Irish music has been an important facet of the constitution of professional groups and directly led to a twentieth-century music festival in Dublin, a development paralleled by the Sonorities festival at Queen's University, Belfast. **John Page**

music in Irish periodical literature. Many of the journals, magazines, reviews, newsletters and newspapers from the mid-eighteenth century onwards are important sources of information on the musical life of Ireland and, in particular, of Dublin. *Faulkner's Dublin Journal* (1735–1825) and the *Dublin News-letter* give detailed accounts of HANDEL's visit to Dublin in 1742. Other journals of importance include the *Dublin Gazette* (1705–1832), *Pue's Occurrences* (1731–63), *Saunders' News-Letter* (1745–1879), *Dublin Evening Post* (1732–1875), and the *Freeman's Journal* (1763–1924); later in the eighteenth century we find the *Hibernian Journal* (1773–1820) and *Dublin Chronicle* (1787–93). The *Belfast Newsletter and General Advertiser* (1737–69 and 1792–6) provides reports of the Belfast Harp Festival of 1792.

Literary journals, such as the *Dublin Penny Journal* (1831–7), flourished in the 1830s. The *Irish Penny Journal* (1840) includes articles by GEORGE PETRIE and JOHN O'DONOVAN. With the foundation of the Dublin Society in 1731 and the ROYAL IRISH ACADEMY in 1785 more scholarly journals appeared. These establishments published proceedings and transactions, which occasionally presented articles on music. University publications include the DUBLIN UNIVERSITY MAGAZINE (1833–77), the most familiar long-running literary journal in Ireland. *Studies*, launched by University College, Dublin, in 1912, includes many articles by W. H. GRATTAN FLOOD. In Cork, ANNIE PATTERSON contributed to the *Ivernian Society Journal* (launched 1908), while the *Cork University Record* (1944–) includes articles by ALOYS FLEISCHMANN.

Church music is regularly referred to in many historical journals. The *Irish Ecclesiastical Record* (1864–1968) and LYRA ECCLESIASTICA (1879–84), journal of the Cecilian Society, provide the most comprehensive material in this area. HEINRICH BEWERUNGE, W. H. Grattan Flood, Rev. W. J. WALSH and Rev. G. O'Neill made regular contributions. Bewerunge and Flood also contributed to the *Irish Monthly* (1873–1954) and *New Ireland Review*. **Ite O'Donovan**

Music Ireland (1986–1991), a music magazine. It covered classical, contemporary, JAZZ and TRADITIONAL MUSIC, as well as interviews with Irish and international artists, reviews, special reports, news, and a full listing of concerts and events throughout the country. There were interviews with many soloists poised at the beginning of their careers, such as the pianists BARRY DOUGLAS and HUGH TINNEY, and with contemporary composers, including JOHN BUCKLEY and KEVIN O'CONNELL. The last issue featured an interview with Philippe Cassard, who won the GPA DUBLIN INTERNATIONAL PIANO COMPETITION in 1988. **Geraldine Guiden**

Music Network, an organisation set up by the ARTS COUNCIL in 1986 to develop music throughout Ireland. It acts as an agent for performers of classical, traditional and JAZZ music, and also works closely with promoters nationally, subsidising tours by Irish and international performers. An invaluable information service is another facet of Music Network. Publications include the *Directory of Musicians in Ireland* and the *Irish Music Handbook*. **Geraldine Guiden**

musicology. Until the middle of the twentieth century, musicology in Ireland was largely devoted to studies in the field of Irish TRADITIONAL MUSIC. The work of EDWARD BUNTING, beginning in 1792, laid the foundations for other historians and collectors, such as GEORGE PETRIE. During the earlier part of the twentieth century, members of the Irish Folk Song Society, particularly DÓNAL O'SULLIVAN and Charlotte Milligan Fox, were responsible for continuing scholarship into traditional music. Periodicals such as *Ceol* (1963–86) and *Irish Folk Music Studies* (1971–) were instrumental in presenting the research of many scholars. The establishment of the Irish World Music Centre at the University of Limerick was a milestone in ethnomusicology. Under the direction of MÍCHEÁL Ó SÚILLEABHÁIN, research into traditional music is continued at postgraduate level, alongside the study of music of other cultures.

The documentation of general Irish musicology can be traced back to the middle of the nineteenth century. Despite the dearth of scholarly activity in music, articles on a variety of musicological topics were to be found in periodicals, debating the current condition of music in Ireland. In particular, the work of HEINRICH BEWERUNGE on the theories and editions of plainchant gained widespread recognition. ALOYS FLEISCHMANN's *Music in Ireland* (1952) was the first important broad-spectrum musicological publication. Fleischmann was a seminal figure in Irish musicology, with a wide range of interests, as attested by his final, posthumous, publication, *The Sources of Irish Traditional Music* (1996). Since the 1970s the contribution of university departments of music has been responsible for the increase in and diversification of musicological research, with several masters' and doctoral courses on offer. Festivals of music begun by the universities, such as the Sonorities and Early Music events at Queen's University, Belfast, have provided important performance platforms, alongside musicological research and composition. The wide range of activity conveys the international scope of musicology in Ireland, including historical musicology, ethnomusicology, theory and analysis, source studies, editing, performance practice, and feminist musicology, mirroring developments in other European countries and North America. The active Irish chapter of the Royal Musicological Association, established at the University of Ulster in 1987, has provided an important forum for new scholarship. The publication of *Irish Musical Studies* (1990–) and the establishment in 1995 of the first international musicological conference at Maynooth are both considered milestones, as they reinforce the commitment to and recognition of musicology as an active discipline alongside performance and education. **David Mooney**

music publishing. Historically, music printing and publishing in Ireland have been more concerned with satisfying demand for Irish and other music than with the promotion of works by indigenous composers. Though the first record of music printing specifically in Ireland dates from 1686, conspicuous activity did not begin until the 1720s. From 1723 JOHN AND WILLIAM NEALE of Dublin published collections of instrumental and vocal music and, in 1724, the earliest collection of Irish music. Activity then rose exponentially, reaching a peak in 1820, when more than twenty music printers, publishers and sellers operated in Dublin. Of particular note were the Rhames family (1750–1810), J. B. Logier (1809–46), and Edward (and later James) M'Cullagh (1821–51), while Goulding and Company (1803–16) of London had Dublin outlets (see p. 1089). After 1840 business dramatically declined, with Samuel Pigott (later Pigott and Company) to the fore, continuing until 1968 as a publisher of Irish songs, part songs, and instrumental works. MICHELE ESPOSITO formed a short-lived publishing enterprise with Sir Stanley Cochrane (financed by the latter), CE editions, 1915–35. From the early 1920s Walton's and AN GÚM served the burgeoning demands of post-independence Ireland by publishing

Muslims. *Children at the Islamic Cultural Centre, Clonskeagh, Dublin, celebrate the Eid festival, 2000, marking the end of Ramadan, a month when Muslims fast throughout the day and eat only after night prayers. Feasts and family get-togethers are the highlights of the celebrations. [Gerry O'Dea]*

much Irish music, particularly arrangements (a practice continued by numerous other publishers up until recent times). The Contemporary Music Centre (founded in 1986) publishes a limited amount of works by Irish composers. **Philip Graydon**

music venues. In Dublin, the development of concert music after 1700 shifted the focus away from the Protestant cathedrals and precipitated the establishment of venues such as the Crow Street music hall (opened in 1731) and the Great Musick Hall in Fishamble Street (see p. 759). The latter held the premiere of HANDEL's *Messiah* in 1742. The ROTUNDA Room (opened in 1767) was also prominent, while outdoor concerts were principally held at the gardens in Great Britain Street. The ANTIENT CONCERT ROOMS, Great Brunswick Street (reconstructed in 1843), was the city's principal concert hall until 1916, while opera featured at the theatres in Smock Alley, Aungier Street (actually in Longford Street), and at the THEATRE ROYAL Hawkins Street. Until the opening of the NATIONAL CONCERT HALL in Earlsfort Terrace in 1981 the city lacked a suitable concert hall, necessitating the use of a variety of venues (such as the GAIETY THEATRE). Latterly the ROYAL DUBLIN SOCIETY's exhibition hall and the Point Theatre have become particularly prominent, as have the more intimate surroundings of the Bank of Ireland Arts Centre, Foster Place, and the HUGH LANE MUNICIPAL GALLERY OF MODERN ART. The Helix at Dublin City University opened in 2002 as a centre for performing arts.

In Belfast, the Exchange Rooms in Waring Street was the main venue from the 1770s until the later nineteenth century, while the Music Hall in May Street (opened in 1840) was the first purpose-built concert hall. Since 1862 the Ulster Hall was the primary venue for orchestral concerts until the building of the Waterfront Hall in 1997 (see p. 789). The Harty Room and Elmwood Hall at Queen's University are used for chamber recitals.

From the eighteenth century, Cork's most prominent venues were the Assembly House (which held concerts well into the nineteenth century), the Assembly Rooms, and then the City Hall (burned down in 1920). Nowadays, most prominent are the present City Hall (built 1926) and the Opera House, opened in 1888 and rebuilt in the late twentieth century.

In Limerick, the University Concert Hall was built in 1993. **Philip Graydon**

Muslims. There are no accurate statistics on the size of the Muslim community in Ireland. The first trickle of immigrants arrived in the early 1950s, and for many years the community was quite small. There was a dramatic increase in the Muslim population in the 1990s with the arrival of refugees from war-torn Bosnia, Kosovo, and Somalia, as well as asylum-seekers and workers from various Islamic countries. It is estimated that by 2002 there were some 15,000 Muslims in Ireland. In 1976 the Dublin Islamic Society set up its first mosque in Harrington Street, which moved to the South Circular Road in 1983. The Islamic Cultural Centre in Clonskeagh, Dublin, was opened by President MARY ROBINSON in 1996. The mosque at the centre has a capacity of more than 1,000, making it one of the largest in Europe. Mosques were also opened in Belfast (1980), Galway (1981), Co. Mayo (1986), Limerick (1994), and Cork (1995). The first state-funded Muslim national school was opened in 1990, and a second one opened in 2001. Both schools are in Dublin. There are no state-sponsored Muslim schools in Northern Ireland. **Yahya al-Hussein**

Muspratt, James (1793–1886), chemical manufacturer. Born in Dublin. In 1818 he set up a factory to produce prussiate of potash, used in the preparation of Prussian blue pigment. In 1822 he emigrated to England and began the manufacture of soda in Liverpool, using the Leblanc process. He briefly entered into partnership with Josias Gamble, formerly of Enniskillen, to produce soda near St Helens, Lancashire. By the 1840s his was the largest soda factory in Britain. His family greatly expanded the business around Widnes, and he is considered to be the founder of the British alkali industry. **Rod Gow**

Muspratt, James Sheridan (1821–1871), chemist. Born in Dublin, a son of the chemical manufacturer James Muspratt; studied chemistry in Glasgow, London, and Giessen, Germany. Later he went to America, where he engaged in business studies and observed the burgeoning chemical industry. He carried out significant work on the sulphites, on toluidine and nitro-aniline. In 1848 he founded the Liverpool College of Chemistry. From 1854 to 1860 he was working on his book *Chemistry, Theoretical, Practical and Analytical as Applied and Relating to the Arts and Manufactures*. He also worked on a *Dictionary of Applied Chemistry*, but it was not completed until after his death. **Susan McKenna-Lawlor**

My Bloody Valentine, rock group. Formed in Dublin in 1984, the band was influenced by the Scottish group Jesus and Mary Chain and the Australian group Birthday Party. Two albums on the Creation label, *Isn't Anything* (1988) and *Loveless* (1991), contained extremely influential guitar-based music that still resonates. The group was a band in name only from the mid-1990s; the prime motivator, Kevin Shields, temporarily joined the English rock band Primal Scream in 2000. **Tony Clayton-Lea**

'My Lagan Love', a popular song, first published in 1904 in *Songs of Uladh*. The words are by JOSEPH CAMPBELL, set by HERBERT HUGHES to a Co. Donegal version of a traditional air. **Maeve Ellen Gebruers**

Myles na gCopaleen: see O'BRIEN, FLANN.

Mythological Cycle, a cycle of EARLY IRISH TALES dealing with the adventures of the GODS AND GODDESSES of Ireland. Chief among these is 'CATH Maige Tuired' ('The Battle of Moytirra'), which tells how TUATHA DÉ DANANN defeated the shadowy and malevolent Fomoiri (Fomhóire) at Moytirra, Co. Sligo (near Lough Arrow). This saga is a rich source of information on the pagan gods of the Irish, some of which have their counterparts in Wales and among the Continental Celts, while some of the narrative is arguably a reflex of Indo-European myth.

Another tale, 'Cath Maige Tuired Cunga' ('The Battle of Moytirra at Cong'), recounts the victory of Tuatha Dé Danann over the FIR BOLG, who are said to have preceded them as invaders of Ireland. Love and enchantment mark 'Tochmarc Étaíne' ('The Wooing of Étaín'), a trilogy dealing with the relationship of the god Midir with the beautiful Étaín. In the first tale Midir marries Étaín, but his first wife transforms her into a pool of water. The water becomes a worm, and the worm a beautiful fly. The fly is swallowed by an Ulsterwoman, who becomes pregnant, and Étaín is reborn as her daughter. In the second tale Étaín is married to Echaid, King of Ireland. Midir comes to woo her, but she declines to leave Echaid. In the third tale Midir wins her from Echaid in a board game. Echaid seeks to recover her but unwittingly takes his own daughter by her. He sleeps with his daughter, and she in turn gives him a daughter, who was to become the mother of Conaire the Great, King of Ireland. **Tomás Ó Cathasaigh**

mythology. *A detail from the Táin wall mosaic by Desmond Kinney (c. 1976) at the Setanta Centre, Dublin, depicting the brown bull of Cooley and the white bull of Connaught locked in battle. [courtesy of the artist, Solomon Gallery and Tyndall Hogan Hurley]*

mythology. Mythological tales and mythology are intrinsic aspects of the Irish cultural inheritance and tradition, arguably containing some of the most imaginative and dramatic forms of narrative in that tradition. They depict a host of events and characters that vibrantly express the native imagination. This body of mythological material is based on oral tradition and also on literature; some has survived in FOLKLORE to the present day. Many mythological tales are also closely related to historical events and characters and have developed and changed over centuries of narration and transcription. The tales and accounts contain a rich combination of GODS AND GODDESSES, symbols and ritual, including a central theme of sacred association and OTHERWORLD power and connection.

At an early stage in its development the mythological material was preserved by druids and bards, who were the custodians and creators of what was to become epic lore; in the seventh century FILÍ or professors of native learning were appointed the official guardians of this corpus. The results of their work bear testimony to the conservative nature of Irish tradition and language. Material from oral tradition was written down as early as the sixth century, but little survived until after the eleventh century.

Within the realm of mythological narrative there are three main cycles of tales: the KING CYCLE, the ULSTER CYCLE, and the FIONN CYCLE. An important part of the repertoire of the *filí* comprised tales of the supernatural, and these have sometimes been described by scholars as belonging to the MYTHOLOGICAL CYCLE, though this classification is not precise, as the three main cycles also contain a great deal of narrative of the supernatural. Many of the mythological texts have preserved pre-Christian beliefs. The development of the mythological cycles was greatly influenced by the medieval text of the LEBOR GABÁLA ÉRENN (Book of the Taking of Ireland), a narrative concerning various invasions of Ireland that draws on historical, pseudo-historical, and mythological material, and by DINNSEANCHAS, the lore of places, consisting of twelfth-century accounts and versification that seek to explain PLACE-NAMES throughout Ireland, frequently by means of mythological tales associated with them. Both these and similar texts were essential to the repertoire of medieval poets and reflect the central role of narrative in the psyche of early Irish society. **Ríonach uí Ógáin**

Northern Ireland
(see page 787). In Segregation *(1989) by Rita Duffy the opposing religious communities are separated by an androgynous figure in clerical black, and the troubles of a divided community pass through the generations. [Courtesy of Crawford Municipal Art Gallery, Cork]*

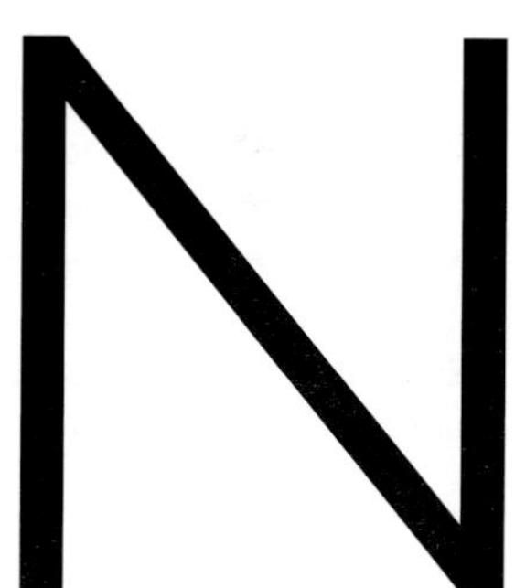

Naas (*An Nás*), Co. Kildare, county town of Co. Kildare, with county council offices, courthouse, Garda divisional headquarters, county hospital, and military barracks; population (2002), 18,312. Naas was originally a residence of the kings of Leinster, whose *dún* was probably replaced by an ANGLO-NORMAN motte when the town was granted to Maurice Fitzgerald in 1176. The town boasted three monasteries in the Middle Ages, none of which survives. In 1316 Naas was burnt and plundered by ROBERT BRUCE. In the later Middle Ages the town walls enclosed fortified stone houses, such as the mid-fifteenth-century St David's Castle.

With its position 32 km (20 miles) from Dublin on the main road to Cork, Naas was a traffic bottleneck until the opening of a motorway that bypasses the town. Its closeness to Dublin and the quality of its connections ensures its continued growth; the population increased by 26 per cent between 1991 and 1996. Many of the new residents work in local high-technology industries or commute to Dublin. There are three racecourses nearby—Punchestown (see pp. 501, 502), the CURRAGH, and Naas—while Mondello Park, 8 km (5 miles) north-west of the town, is Ireland's main motor-racing circuit. **Ruth McManus**

Nagle, Honoria (Nano) (1728–1784), educationalist. Born at Ballygriffin, near Mallow, Co. Cork, into a prosperous Catholic family; educated in Paris. In 1754 she established the first of seven schools for poor Catholic children. Though technically illegal, they flourished. An inheritance in 1757 permitted her to expand. She established her own teaching congregation, the Presentation Order, in 1776, achieving Papal recognition in 1802; it became one of the most important teaching congregations in Ireland. **Fergal Tobin**

Nairn, George (1799–1850), artist. A landscape, portrait, animal and horse painter, his work is of considerable quality. He exhibited at the ROYAL HIBERNIAN ACADEMY but rarely signed his works, and many are no doubt attributed to other artists. His horse paintings were influenced by John Ferneley, who visited Ireland at this time. **Anne Crookshank**

names (personal). The earliest native sources are OGHAM inscriptions (fifth to seventh centuries); the main medieval sources are ANNALS, genealogies, and martyrologies. Surnames—defined by the transition of *Mac X* and *Ó X* from their literal meanings 'son of X' and 'grandson of X', respectively, to a more general 'descendant of X'—are attested from the tenth century. Personal names consist of one element (for example Conn, literally 'leader') or two; in the latter case the inherited Indo-European compound type (for example OLD IRISH Cóemgen, 'of fine birth', Modern Irish Caoimhín, anglicised Kevin) was gradually replaced by corresponding phrases of noun plus genitive or adjective, for example Cú Chatha, 'hound of battle' (versus compound Cathchú, 'battle-hound'). There are also numerous borrowed names at all periods, such as Colmán from Latin Columba or COLUMBANUS, Seán (earlier disyllabic Seaán) from Norman-French Jehan, and Siobhán, from Norman-French Jehanne. **Jürgen Uhlich**

Nangle, Rev. Edward (1799–1883), evangelical clergyman. Born in Kildalkey, Co. Meath; educated at TCD. Inspired by the ideas of the SECOND REFORMATION, in 1834 he founded a missionary settlement at Dugort on ACHILL ISLAND, Co. Mayo. His aim of converting Catholics was promoted through a comprehensive system of schools, land reclamation, a printing press, an orphan asylum, and a hospital. An aggressive controversialist, he encountered hostility from the Catholic hierarchy, who, during the GREAT FAMINE, charged him with SOUPERISM. In 1852 he left the mission, and thereafter it declined. **Thomas Kelley**

Napier, Phillip (1965–), artist. Born in Belfast; studied at Belfast School of Art and also at Falmouth and Manchester. A highly original sculptor and installation artist, he has created telling political installations, using a variety of media and commonplace objects, as well as sound. He teaches at the National College of Art and Design, Dublin. He represented Ireland at the São Paulo Bienal, 1994, and won the Glen Dimplex Award. **Dorothy Walker**

Napoleon in song.

> The French are on the sea, says the Shan Van Vocht,
> They'll be here without delay, says the Shan Van Vocht,
> Then Ireland shall be free from—the centre to the sea,
> And Hurrah for Liberty, says the Shan Van Vocht.

The UNITED IRISHMEN made every effort to enlist the aid of France in the REBELLION OF 1798. The Irish hoped that Napoleon Bonaparte would not only play his part as a liberator from English rule but would also transform the lot of the people living on the land who were suffering under the injustices of the landlord class.

> Beidh an talamh gan cíos ón bhliain seo amach.
> The land will be without rent from this year out.

Napoleon assumed the position in song previously held by Bonny Prince Charlie, the Royal Blackbird, and was given the title of the Green Linnet in the ballad of the same name. There are numerous ballads written of battles won and lost, of the lovers parted or slain on the plains of Waterloo, as well as several discussions on the invasion of Russia, the retreat from Moscow, and his exile on the island of Saint Helena. The songs relating the deeds of Napoleon Bonaparte are still frequently sung at sessions today, with titles such as 'Grand Conversation on Napoleon', 'Napoleon's Farewell to Paris', 'Bonny Bunch of Roses', 'Mantle of Green', 'My Love at Waterloo', 'Bonny Light Horseman', and 'Isle of Saint Helena'. [see JACOBITE POETRY.] **Frank Harte**

Nary, Cornelius (1658–1738), religious writer. Born near Naas, Co. Kildare; he received his clerical education in Paris. On returning to Ireland he served in St Michan's parish in Dublin. The most notable writer among early eighteenth-century Catholics, he is chiefly remembered for his contributions to denominational controversy. However, he also made a more general contribution to scholarship with his *New History of the World*, prepared a translation of the New Testament, and wrote devotional and pastoral works. **C. D. A. Leighton**

Nation, the, a nationalist journal (1842–1900). Published in Dublin as the voice of Young Ireland, the *Nation* was founded by THOMAS DAVIS, JOHN BLAKE DILLON, and CHARLES GAVAN DUFFY. After Davis's death JOHN MITCHEL became assistant editor to Duffy, but in 1847 he left after political differences. On 29 July 1848 the *Nation* was suppressed because of its revolutionary articles. In 1849 Gavan Duffy was allowed to relaunch it, but it never again had the same flair or impact. Under A. M. SULLIVAN as editor, 1855–77, the paper's tone was constitutional nationalist. It merged temporarily with the *Irish Catholic*, from 1891 to 1896, and closed down in 1900, merging with the *Irish Weekly Independent.* **Brigitte Anton**

national anthems. The singing of a recognisable national anthem is a product of the eighteenth century. The first published national anthem proclaiming loyalty to the British monarch, 'God Save the King', came in 1744 (although both music and lyrics are older), receiving its first public performance at Drury Lane Theatre, London, in 1745. It grew in popularity and by 1819 was widely recognised at the national anthem of Great Britain and Ireland. As a statement of loyalty to the Crown, the singing of 'God Save the King' (or 'God Save the Queen') became a central part of functions at DUBLIN CASTLE and other events in Ireland throughout the nineteenth century. Together with the Union Jack and other symbols of identity, for the followers of the unionist cause it became a cornerstone of their belief.

'God Save the King' remained the official anthem of Ireland until after the foundation of the Irish Free State in 1922. Nationalists sought to challenge the legitimacy of British rule by rejecting 'God Save the King' and adopting their own anthem. From 1867 T. D. Sullivan's 'God Save Ireland', originally written as a celebration of the MANCHESTER MARTYRS, became the unofficial anthem of Irish NATIONALISM, developing a political legitimacy when it was adopted as the anthem of the Irish Party. From c. 1914 the IRISH VOLUNTEERS chose the more militant 'The Soldier's Song' as their unofficial anthem. Written in 1907 by PEADAR KEARNEY, with music by Patrick Heeney, it would officially become the national anthem of the Irish Free State from 1926, generally sung in Irish as 'AMHRÁN NA BHFIANN'. The first four bars followed by the last five are the Presidential Salute. Its militaristic sentiments have led to some suggestions that it should be replaced. 'God Save the King/Queen' has remained the official anthem of Northern Ireland. **Mike Cronin**

National Anti-Poverty Strategy, a policy devised by the Government in 1997 to build on the work of the Combat Povery Agency. The policy aimed to build on the Combat Poverty Agency's work by formulating a series of specific targets for the reduction of poverty levels and social exclusion. The strategic aims of the National Anti-Poverty Strategy fell into five categories: educational disadvantage, UNEMPLOYMENT, income adequacy, disadvantaged urban areas, and rural poverty. The very rapid ECONOMIC GROWTH of the late 1990s had produced great fears that Ireland was rapidly becoming a much divided society. To attempt to prevent this development, overall targets were developed for educational disadvantage, unemployment, and income adequacy. Early school leaving (before the Junior Certificate) was to be eliminated, and the retention rates to Leaving Certificate levels were to be 90 per cent by 2000 and 98 per cent by 2007. These targets have almost been met. The rate of unemployment

THE ACHILL MISSIONARY HERALD,

And Western Witness.

No. 105.] ACHILL ISLAND, MARCH 25, 1846. [VOL. IX.

Nangle. *Masthead of the* Achill Missionary Herald, *with a wood-engraving of the settlement established by Edward Nangle at Dugort. The buildings of the community are still intact more than 170 years later. [Council of Trustees of the National Library of Ireland]*

on the LABOUR FORCE SURVEY basis was to be reduced from 11.9 per cent in April 1996 to 6 per cent by 2007, and the rate of long-term unemployment from 7 per cent to 3.5 per cent by 2007. Again these targets are being achieved, and this raises the whole issue of reaching new, higher goals and the sustainability of such goals. The NATIONAL ECONOMIC AND SOCIAL FORUM and the Combat Poverty Agency have been given specific responsibilities for monitoring the performance of the National Anti-Poverty Strategy. **Geoffrey Cook**

National Archives, Dublin, established in June 1988 through the amalgamation of the State Paper Office (established 1702) and the Public Record Office of Ireland (established 1867). The National Archives is primarily responsible for the records of Government departments, the courts, and some state bodies; it also has legal responsibility for the parish records of the CHURCH OF IRELAND before DISESTABLISHMENT (1870). Access to these records is available at the reading room of the National Archives in Bishop Street, Dublin. The holdings of the National Archives date primarily from the nineteenth and twentieth centuries, though some records date from the thirteenth century. The destruction of the Public Record Office—then housed in the FOUR COURTS building—during the CIVIL WAR resulted in the loss of most of its holdings (see p. 533). From the Public Record Office the National Archives inherited, among other collections, those relating to LOCAL GOVERNMENT and to education, together with records of the courts and probate registries and records of defunct bodies, including CENSUS commissions. More recent accessions of private provenance have been acquired from business firms, solicitors' offices, and estate offices. From the State Paper Office the National Archives inherited the records of the Chief Secretary's Office, formerly housed in DUBLIN CASTLE. **Aideen M. Ireland**

National Association, a political association with the goal of achieving DISESTABLISHMENT of the CHURCH OF IRELAND, improved tenant rights, and free and equal education for all classes irrespective of religion. Founded on 29 December 1864 under the leadership of JOHN BLAKE DILLON, it was promoted by PAUL CULLEN, Archbishop of Dublin, but did not win the support of Archbishop JOHN MACHALE of Tuam. The election of GLADSTONE in 1868 led to the achievement the following year of the goal of disestablishment. **Ciarán O'Carroll**

National Botanic Gardens: see BOTANIC GARDENS.

National Chamber Choir, founded in 1991. Directed by COLIN MAWBY until 2002, it performs regularly on television and radio, as well as live performances with the NATIONAL SYMPHONY ORCHESTRA, RTÉ CONCERT ORCHESTRA, and IRISH CHAMBER ORCHESTRA. In 1995 the National Chamber Choir became choir-in-residence at Dublin City University, which secured its future and enabled the choir to concentrate on its education programme for schools. The choir is funded by RTÉ and the ARTS COUNCIL and also has grants from OPERA IRELAND and the Department of Education. **Geraldine Guiden**

National Concert Hall (NCH), Earlsfort Terrace, Dublin, officially opened on 9 September 1981. Its opening was an event of great significance and the result of considerable effort, over many years, to establish such a venue for the orchestras, choirs and performers flourishing in Ireland. The main auditorium was formerly the examination hall of University College, Dublin, and originally part of the exhibition building by Alfred Gresham Jones for the 1865 Dublin International Exhibition. The organ was built and installed by Kenneth Jones in 1991. Since its inception the NCH has, through its Celebrity Concert Series, played host to many international orchestras and soloists (see p. 911). **Geraldine Guiden**

national costume. The CELTIC REVIVAL and the political developments of the late nineteenth century created a demand for a distinctive national dress style. Men such as Francis Bigger and Lord Ashbourne interpreted in Irish wool and colours—saffron and green—the kilts worn by their fellow-Celts in Scotland. Wealthy women satisfied this need by wearing DUN EMER hand-embroidered Irish poplin outfits of *brat* (cloak), tunic, and headwear, based on what was believed to have been worn by Irish women in the early historic period. A more acceptable national dress style for the less wealthy was the red petticoat, a version of that worn in Ireland since the sixteenth century, while some men adopted the swallow-tail coat and knee breeches, based on eighteenth-century styles, worn by farmers into the twentieth century. [see CELTIC TWILIGHT; LITERARY REVIVAL.] **Mairead Dunlevy**

national debt, the accumulated public borrowing of the state. The main justification for the building up of such a debt is the financing of public investment projects, the return on which would pay for the investment without having to raise future tax rates. This debt reached record levels in the Republic in the 1980s, with general Government gross public debt amounting to 116 per cent of GDP in 1987, a figure far above the OECD average and one considered unsustainable, and therefore dangerous, by many economic commentators. This figure was reduced dramatically in the 1990s, reaching a level of less than 40 per cent in 2000, well below the OECD average. The main reason for this was the sustained high growth of GDP in the 1990s. In the early years of the twenty-first century the Republic was in the enviable position of running substantial budget surpluses, with the option therefore of reducing even further the national debt, when expressed as a percentage of GDP. Some commentators believe that this ratio should be further reduced in order to give the Republic more flexibility in the event of a serious decline in the international environment. **John O'Hagan**

National Economic and Social Council, established by the Government of the Republic in 1973 as an independent research and advisory body representing the main social and economic interests in society. Until 1997 its membership consisted mainly of representatives of the trade unions, employers' and business associations, farmers' organisations, and the Government; since 1998 community and VOLUNTARY ORGANISATIONS have also been represented. Since the mid-1980s the NESC has been the main forum for the exchange of views out of which the process of 'SOCIAL PARTNERSHIP' has developed. The NESC has published a series of reports: *A Strategy for Development, 1986–1990* (1986), *A Strategy for the Nineties: Economic Stability and Structural Change* (1990), *A Strategy for Competitiveness, Growth and Employment* (1993), *Strategy into the 21st Century* (1996), and *Opportunities, Challenges and Capacities for Choice: Overview, Conclusions and Recommendations* (1999). Each of these reports provided the framework for the negotiation of a national agreement on pay, tax reductions, and other policy issues. The NESC, NATIONAL ECONOMIC AND SOCIAL FORUM, and National Centre for Prosperity and Partnership all now fall within the National Economic and Social Development Office. **Niamh Hardiman**

National Economic and Social Forum, an independent research and advisory body established by the Government of the Republic in 1993. Members include representatives of the Government, the traditional social partners (employers and unions), and a third strand representing interests traditionally outside the consultative process, such as women, the unemployed, the disadvantaged, people with a disability, youth, the elderly, members of the travelling community, and environmental interests. The Forum was intended to complement the NATIONAL ECONOMIC AND SOCIAL COUNCIL by involving broader interests in consensus-building on economic and social policy; the restructuring of the NESC in 1998, which extended its representation to community and VOLUNTARY ORGANISATIONS, to some extent took over this function. Since then the Forum's work has concentrated on evaluating the implementation of policies dealing with EQUALITY and social inclusion. The NESC, NESF and the National Centre for Prosperity and Partnership (NCPP) all now fall within the National Economic and Social Development Office (NESDO). **Niamh Hardiman**

national economic planning, the setting of a target for the growth of the economy over a series of years. Quantitative estimates are made of what might happen to particular industries and sectors if the global expansion is achieved. The figures are normally accompanied by a list of policy measures intended to help fulfil the plan. This type of planning reached its high point in the Republic in the 1960s. The first PROGRAMME FOR ECONOMIC EXPANSION ran from 1959 to 1963 with great success, while the second covered the years 1964–70 but was abandoned in 1968. The Third Programme for Economic and Social Development was introduced in 1969 and officially ran until 1972. There have been no similar plans since then, though in 1977 a new Government department, the Department of Economic Planning and Development, was formed. In 1978 this department published a white paper on economic and social development, covering the period 1977–80, but the department was abolished in 1979. Similar planning was undertaken in Northern Ireland but did not have the same impact on policy debate. National economic planning in a looser sense has continued to the present. The SOCIAL PARTNERSHIP agreements in the South since 1987 are a form of planning, at least in fixing wage increases for a number of years. The Programme for Prosperity and Fairness (2000) covered not only pay arrangements but also agreed targets in relation to social inclusion schemes and other aspects of economic and social policy. **John O'Hagan**

National Folk Theatre of Ireland: see SIAMSA TIRE.

National Gallery of Ireland, Dublin, established 1854. The idea for the gallery stemmed from the Dublin Great Exhibition of 1853, which had been financed by the railway magnate WILLIAM DARGAN and had included an exhibition of paintings. Public subscriptions, raised in commemoration of Dargan's generosity, were placed at the disposal of the Irish Institution; a building was erected on Leinster Lawn, Merrion Square, and the gallery opened to the public in 1864 (see p. 967). The building was designed by Francis Fowke (1823–1865), an engineer in the Science and Art Department, London, who based his plans on those submitted earlier by CHARLES LANYON. The building has since been extended (in 1903, 1968 and 2002), so that it is now four times its original size.

The first director was the painter GEORGE MULVANY, 1809–69; but it was his two successors, Henry Doyle, 1869–92, and Walter Armstrong, 1892–1914, who laid the foundations of the collection with many astute purchases, as both were knowledgeable and perceptive connoisseurs. HUGH LANE was director, 1914–15; other twentieth-century directors included Robert Langton Douglas, 1916–23, THOMAS BODKIN, 1927–35, George Furlong, 1935–50, THOMAS MCGREEVY, 1950–63, JAMES WHITE, 1964–80, Homan Potterton, 1980–88, and Raymond Keaveney. The gifts and bequests of paintings that have most significantly enhanced the collection were those of the Milltown family (1902), Hugh Lane (1904–15),

National Library. *Reading Room of the National Library of Ireland, designed in 1885 by Sir Thomas Deane the Younger. [Council of Trustees of the National Library of Ireland; LROY 27,777]*

ALFRED CHESTER BEATTY (1950–51), and ALFRED BEIT (1988). The bequest of GEORGE BERNARD SHAW (1950) of a third of the royalties from his estate has provided the gallery with a substantial continuous income, which is employed mainly for the purchase of works of art (see p. 983). Caravaggio's *The Taking of Christ* has been on loan to the gallery from the Jesuit order since its discovery in Dublin in 1993.

The gallery now houses about 2,500 oil paintings, 5,000 drawings, and a similar number of prints (mainly portrait and topographical). The number of sculptures is relatively small. Highlights among the collection (which is notable for Italian baroque paintings and minor Dutch masters) are paintings by Fra Angelico, Mantegna, Titian, El Greco, Rubens, Rembrandt, Vermeer, Murillo, Velásquez, Poussin, Claude, Goya, Chardin, Reynolds, and Gainsborough. Among the drawings are examples by Raphael, Rembrandt, Poussin, Watteau, Cézanne, Picasso, and a group of Turner watercolours. The collection of Irish paintings is extensive and representative and ranges from the eighteenth century (with JAMES BARRY, HUGH DOUGLAS HAMILTON, NATHANIEL HONE, THOMAS ROBERTS, GEORGE BARRETT, and WILLIAM ASHFORD) to the twentieth century (WALTER OSBORNE, WILLIAM JOHN LEECH, RODERIC O'CONOR, NATHANIEL HONE THE YOUNGER, GEORGE RUSSELL, SARAH PURSER, MAINIE JELLETT, PAUL HENRY, and JOHN BUTLER YEATS). JACK B. YEATS is particularly prominent and is the focus of the recently established 'Yeats Museum'. **Homan Potterton**

nationalism as a political movement appears in modern form during the last half of the eighteenth century. The aim of the UNITED IRISHMEN was to unite Catholic, Protestant, and Dissenter in a single nation, but this was not achieved. It was intended that the ACT OF UNION would create a British identity in Ireland, but this was successful only in respect of Protestant opinion. In the early nineteenth century O'CONNELL successfully mobilised opinion around REPEAL and Catholic grievances, but his appeal was limited to Catholics. PARNELL created a mass political movement by concentrating on the issue of self-determination, ownership of the land, and civil rights for Catholics. By the beginning of the twentieth century Irish landlordism had been destroyed, most Catholic grievances had been redressed, and a measure of HOME RULE seemed inevitable. The emergence of Ulster UNIONISM countered the nationalist assertion that it represented all those who lived in Ireland, and relations between nationalism and unionism deteriorated after the third Home Rule Bill was introduced in 1912. Nationalism had been primarily constitutional up to this (though Fenianism advocated and practised the use of physical force), but the unionist challenge and the threat of partition radicalised opinion. REDMOND'S decision to support the British war effort in 1914 was popular but alienated more militant nationalists and led to the 1916 RISING. Though unrepresentative of nationalist opinion at the time, SINN FÉIN subsequently benefited from the executions of the leaders and the threat of CONSCRIPTION. This weakened Redmond and constitutional nationalism while providing the basis for Sinn Féin's electoral victory in 1918 and the justification for the WAR OF INDEPENDENCE. The Treaty in 1922 established the IRISH FREE STATE, though disagreement among the Sinn Féin elite led to civil war, which was won by the pro-Treaty forces. CONSTITUTIONAL NATIONALISM re-established its dominance after 1923, forcing FIANNA FÁIL to accept the new state's legitimacy.

National Museum. *A pine settle bed, closed (top) and open (bottom), from Garrycastle, Co. Offaly, dating from the middle of the nineteenth century. Its original grain has been repeatedly overpainted. [National Museum of Ireland]*

Nationalism remained an important feature of independent Ireland, reflected in legislation, in the enactment of the CONSTITUTION OF IRELAND (1937), and the declaration of a republic in 1949. The long-running conflict in Northern Ireland (especially since 1969) reinforced nationalist opinion but also led Irish governments to successfully negotiate with Britain on the status of Northern Ireland. This led to the ANGLO-IRISH AGREEMENT (1985) and the BELFAST AGREEMENT (1998), both of which changed the dynamics of the conflict. At the end of the twentieth century nationalism retains an enduring influence on Irish opinion. Despite membership of the EUROPEAN UNION, significant social change, and the amendment of articles 2 and 3 of the Constitution, nationalism remains the most powerful influence on opinion in the Republic and among Catholics in Northern Ireland. [see UNIONISM.] **Brian Girvin**

National Library of Ireland, Dublin. The library was established under the Dublin Science and Art Museum Act (1877), but its origins can be traced to the library of the ROYAL DUBLIN SOCIETY, which had been founded in 1731. In 1877 a substantial portion of the RDS library was bought by the state to become the founding collection of the new National Library. Since then the library has maintained an active policy of acquiring heritage items and other materials; today its holdings comprise some 6 million items, including books, newspapers and periodicals, official publications, MANUSCRIPTS, maps, photographs, prints, drawings, political memorabilia, literary correspondence, and ephemera. The main library building in Kildare Street, Dublin, including the domed Reading Room, opened to the public in 1890. Adjoining the library, at numbers 2–3 Kildare Street (former premises of the Kildare Street Club), is the Department of Manuscripts and the Genealogical Office, incorporating the Heraldic Museum. The library's collection of some 300,000 photographs is housed at the National Photographic Archive in Meeting-House Square, Temple Bar, Dublin (see pp. 947, 1039). **Colette O'Flaherty**

National Museum of Ireland, Dublin. The Mechanics' Institutes Drawing Schools and later the Government Schools of Design, in conjunction with a general zest for learning, created a need for a public museum in Dublin in which works of art or plaster casts of the best international works could be displayed. The government was made aware that the only publicly financed museums then in Ireland belonged to private societies. The Dublin Science and Art Museum was established by statute in 1877 and immediately began to collect contemporary works internationally as well as collections from the cradles of civilisation: the Mediterranean and Indo-European cultures. The collection of the ROYAL DUBLIN SOCIETY was transferred to the new museum from 1883. When the collection of the ROYAL IRISH ACADEMY was amalgamated, from 1890, the museum became the major repository of Irish archaeological treasures. The new museum then incorporated the NATURAL HISTORY MUSEUM, which had been opened in 1857.

The study of FOLK LIFE or Irish country life led to the development of a separate curatorial division, which has been housed since 2001 in the purpose-built MUSEUM OF COUNTRY LIFE at Turlough Park, Castlebar, Co. Mayo. The Art and Industrial Division's displays opened in the former Collins Barracks, Benburb Street, Dublin, in 1997 as the Museum of Decorative Arts and History, while the Antiquities Division as the Museum of Archaeology and History remains in Kildare Street and the Natural History Museum in Upper Merrion Street (see p. 947). **Mairead Dunlevy**

national parks. *Glenveagh National Park, Co. Donegal. Formally opened in 1986, it is the largest of Ireland's six national parks, covering some 16,500 ha (40,000 acres). [Gareth McCormack]*

national parks, established with the intention of conserving indigenous plant and animal communities. Each of the six national parks has a distinctive scenic landscape. KILLARNEY National Park, Co. Kerry, is known for its oak and yew woods as well as the variety of its lake and mountain scenery (see p. 1057). Glenveagh National Park, Co. Donegal, has a castle and luxuriant gardens, providing a striking contrast to the wilderness of the surrounding countryside. The 2,000 ha (5,000-acre) Connemara National Park, Co. Galway, on the slopes of the Twelve Pins, is renowned for its expanses of western blanket bog and is rich in wild flowers and birds. WICKLOW MOUNTAINS National Park, Co. Wicklow, also includes large areas of mountain blanket bog, which provide a protected ENVIRONMENT for wildlife and rare orchids; it has a core area of 3,700 ha (9,000 acres), centred on GLENDALOUGH. The BURREN National Park, Co. Clare, has a distinctive karst landscape (see p. 143). Mayo National Park has recently been designated, again for ecological reasons. All the national parks are under the care of the National Parks Section of the HERITAGE SERVICE.

While many forest and country parks (such as Glenarrif, Castlewellan, and Tollymore) have been established in Northern Ireland to promote awareness of PEATLAND CONSERVATION and associated issues, including the Peatlands Park in Co. Tyrone, there are as yet no national parks. A regional park of some 1,700 ha (4,200 acres) has been developed along some 21 km (13 miles) of the Lagan valley near Belfast. [see ARBORETA.] **Ruth McManus**

national pay agreements, a series of annual agreements negotiated in the Republic from 1970 to 1980 governing the rates of pay increases and of settlements above or below the norm. These developed from the wage 'rounds' dating from the late 1940s, some of which had featured explicit national-level agreements. By the late 1960s increasing industrial conflict, notably a lengthy dispute by maintenance craftsmen in 1969, caused many people to accept the need for greater co-ordination in pay movements. The first national pay agreement (1970) was influenced by a report of the tripartite National Industrial and Economic Council and was negotiated through the Employer-Labour Conference. Seven agreements were negotiated between 1970 and 1978. In 1979 and 1980 they were termed 'national understandings' and included a commitment by the Government to reductions in tax and increases in spending. Employers grew dissatisfied with the inflationary consequences of wage settlements and with increasing industrial conflict, particularly in the public sector; they pressed for reform of the institutions and legislation governing industrial relations. Pay bargaining reverted to decentralised wage rounds between 1981 and 1987; however, neither employers nor unions abandoned a preference for centralised agreement, provided suitable terms could be agreed. The FISCAL CRISIS of the 1980s prompted attempts to develop a consensus on the country's problems, within which a new approach to national pay agreements could be negotiated. [see NATIONAL ECONOMIC AND SOCIAL COUNCIL; SOCIAL PARTNERSHIP.] **Niamh Hardiman**

National Pensions Reserves Fund, established in April 2001. In addition to the proceeds of the privatisation of Eircom, at least 1 per cent of GNP will be deposited in the fund each year until 2055. After 2025 the Government may begin to make withdrawals from the fund to partially finance the projected rising costs of social welfare and public service pensions. Over time the fund will become the largest investment institution in the country. It is intended to take account of the projected ageing of the population: with the advance funding of future pension liabilities, the need to raise taxes in the coming years or to reduce pension benefits is forestalled. This is best achieved if the fund's assets are invested so as to maximise long-run returns, subject to appropriate risk management. The NATIONAL TREASURY MANAGEMENT AGENCY has been given the task of managing the fund, under the supervision of an independent commission appointed by the Minister for Finance. At least in the beginning the fund will be invested almost entirely in overseas assets, predominantly in international equity markets. **Philip R. Lane**

National Ploughing Championship. *J. Henebry of Co. Kilkenny competing in the National Ploughing Championship in Athenry, Co. Galway, February 1934. The championship is the biggest event of the agricultural calendar. [National Ploughing Association]*

National Ploughing Championship, the biggest social and promotional event of the agricultural calendar, generally held at a different venue each year. From the mid-1990s it has attracted an attendance of more than 100,000 over the three days of the competitions. Organised by the National Ploughing Association, the event requires at least 120 ha (300 acres) of land for the ploughing competitions and a huge village of trade stands and livestock exhibitions.

The first national championship, held in Athy, Co. Kildare, in 1931, grew out of a debate between J. J. Bergin of Co. Kildare and Denis Allen of Co. Wexford whether Kildare or Wexford ploughmen were the best. (Wexford won.) Early events were for horse ploughing; tractor ploughing began to dominate from 1949, when the event was held in Drogheda. Bergin, who was president of the National Ploughing Association until 1958, was also one of the founder-members of the World Ploughing Championship in 1952. Seán O'Farrell of Co. Kilkenny became the association's first managing director in 1958, a post he held until his death in 1973, when he was succeeded by Anna May McHugh (*née* Brennan). The World Ploughing Championship has been held in Ireland in 1954, 1973, 1981, and 1996. The most successful ploughman has been Martin Kehoe of Co. Wexford, who won the national senior title twelve times in a row, 1987–98, and also won the world title on several occasions. **Paddy Smith**

National Soil Survey of Ireland, a Government agency established in 1959 as part of An Foras Talúntais (the Agricultural Institute) to map soil distribution in the Republic. The first map report, for Co. Wexford, was published in 1964; this was followed by further county reports published in the *Soil Survey Bulletin*. These provided information on soil types, their distribution, and their physical and chemical properties. The greatest value of these publications lay in the discussion of the suitability of soils for particular agricultural uses. The National Soil Survey also published a generalised soil map of Ireland and reported on peatlands. It was disbanded in 1989. **Patrick N. Wyse Jackson**

National Symphony Orchestra (NSO). With the foundation in 1926 of 2RN (later Radio Éireann), a station orchestra was established. Starting with a piano trio, the infant orchestra was gradually expanded from twenty-eight players in 1937 to more than forty (1942–8). Conductors from the Army School of Music (which had been founded in 1923) included James Doyle and MICHAEL BOWLES (1941–8), who promoted a regular series of fortnightly public symphony concerts. The orchestra was reorganised in 1948 as the Radio Éireann Symphony Orchestra with sixty-two players (many of whom came from abroad), based in the Phoenix Hall in Dame Court, Dublin. It was renamed the RTÉ Symphony Orchestra in 1964 and the National Symphony Orchestra in 1991. Principal conductors who worked with the orchestra include ALBERT ROSEN, COLMAN PEARCE, BRYDEN THOMSON, Kasper de Roo, JANOS FÜRST, George Hurst, Alexander Anissimov, and the present principal conductor, Gerhard Markson. The orchestra has recording contracts with the Naxos and Marco Polo labels (see p. 911). **Geraldine Guiden and Ite O'Donovan.**

National Tidy Towns Competition, inaugurated by BORD FÁILTE ÉIREANN in 1958 to tackle the Republic's chronic litter problem and to encourage the renovation of its neglected small towns. The committees that had been set up to contribute to the spring festival of AN TÓSTAL were recruited as tidy towns committees. In the inaugural competition, which was won by Glenties, Co. Donegal, there were fifty-two entries. A panel of assessors, including architects, landscape architects, and town planners, visits towns (without notice) during the judging season. Marks are awarded for effort, tidiness, presentation of buildings, presentation of natural amenities, appearance of approach roads, and presentation of immediate residential areas. Prizes are awarded in various categories according to population, and the winners attend a reception hosted by the previous winning town.

Much local effort is expended on the competition, and there is considerable rivalry between neighbouring towns, though there has been some controversy over judging decisions. Overall, the competition has had a very positive effect on the appearance of towns and villages. It led to a boom in the sales of hanging baskets, window-boxes, and bedding plants, resulting in a prettifying effect that is not always appropriate to the character of local architecture. In 1994 the Tidy Towns competition was transferred to the Department of the Environment. For all the apparent success of the competition, both rural and urban Ireland still have a chronic litter problem.

In 1998 the Heritage Service of the then Department of Arts, Heritage, Gaeltacht and the Islands inaugurated the Heritage Towns scheme, which required that street furniture and other features of designated towns reflect the town's historical importance, that buildings of historical interest be restored and conserved, and that inappropriate development not be permitted in historically sensitive areas. The Heritage Act (1995) provided further guidelines on conservation and tourism development. **Alannah Hopkin**

National Treasury Management Agency, established by the National Treasury Management Agency Act (1990) to borrow money for the exchequer and to manage the national debt on behalf of the Minister for Finance. It was set up as a result of the substantial growth of the national debt during the 1980s and the difficulty in recruiting and retaining experienced debt management staff. **Jim Power**

National Trust for Ireland: see TAISCE, AN.

National Union of Journalists (NUJ), a British trade union with approximately 4,000 members in Ireland and the largest journalists' union in the world. The first professional body for journalists, the (British) Institute of Journalists (1884), included proprietors among its members; the NUJ, founded in 1907 for employees alone, was established in Ireland in 1909. In 1947 agreement between the NUJ and Dublin newspaper managements brought in the eight-hour working day and minimum rates of pay. The only serious attempt to set up a separate Irish body was the Irish Journalists' Association (1907), which lasted about twenty years. To enhance Irish autonomy within the NUJ the Irish Area Council was replaced by the Irish Executive Council in 1993. An important issue in recent years has been the growing casualisation in the industry. **Eddie Holt**

National Women's Council of Ireland, a national representative organisation for women. It has 152 affiliated organisations, covering a wide spectrum of women's organisations involved in community development in rural and urban areas, TRADE UNION, professional and business activities and the provision of services, as well as lobbying and campaigning on specific issues. Together these organisations comprise 300,000 women throughout the Republic; the council is structured through a national conference of affiliates, which formulates policy, and an Executive Council, which implements agreed policy.

The origins of the council lie in the establishment by the Government of the COMMISSION ON THE STATUS OF WOMEN, chaired by Dr Thekla Beere, which reported in 1972. The report drew attention to DISCRIMINATION and inequalities experienced by women in society. Its recommendation that a body representative of women's interests be set up was implemented by the Government with the establishment of the Council for the Status of Women in 1972; in 1995 the council adopted the new name National Women's Council of Ireland. Financed from a combination of Government grant and private and voluntary funds, the council operates as an independent organisation of women's interests, based on establishing a delicate balance in its policies between the concerns and interests of a broad range of women's organisations. Today it plays a central role in representing women's interests in a range of policy forums at national, regional and local level. In 1996 it achieved a place in the negotiating process involved in establishing the core elements of economic and social policy in multi-annual national agreements.

The council has established four panels, dealing with social affairs, education, health, and work, through which affiliates act as a resource to the council in this process. The council is also involved in research, policy analysis, and the critical evaluation of social development and social change from the standpoint of women. Its stated aim is the creation of a society in which all women and men can participate with equal effectiveness as full citizens and in which the independence of women is determined by right. **Ursula Barry**

National Youth Orchestra of Ireland, a pre-professional symphony orchestra for young people, founded in 1970. It is a symphony orchestra of 100 players aged eighteen to twenty-three; NYOI under-18s provides training for players aged thirteen to seventeen. Players audition annually to gain and retain places. In 1998 the orchestra toured in America and in 1999, under the conductor Alexander Anissimov, gave performances in Limerick, Dublin and Belfast of Mahler's 2nd Symphony (*The Resurrection*). In 2000 the orchestra appeared with the conductor En Shao in Symphony Hall, Birmingham, the Konzerthaus, Berlin, and the Concertgebouw, Amsterdam, featuring Stravinsky's *The Rite of Spring*. **John Page**

native woodlands. Some 10,000 years ago, at the end of the last Ice Age, the improved physical ENVIRONMENT permitted the re-establishment of woodlands, and by about 8,000 years ago the country was virtually clothed in woods. Sessile (Irish) oak dominated free-draining infertile upland SOILS along the western and eastern seaboard, together with Scots pine, birch, mountain ash, and holly. In the more fertile soils of the Central Plain, pedunculate (English) oak dominated, in association with yew, hazel, and elm. In waterlogged areas close to rivers and lakes, alder and willow prevailed.

native woodlands. *Native oak forests once covered most of Ireland, but little survived later than the seventeenth century, as a result of land clearance, shipbuilding, and iron-smelting. [Coillte]*

Subsequent CLIMATE change, but most importantly human impact, reduced the extent of these woodlands. The early settlers in Ireland were hunter-gatherers, but by 6,500 years ago agriculture had made serious inroads. By the beginning of the last millennium the development of metal tools and the plough had transformed Ireland from an essentially wooded country into a pastoral landscape.

Today people generally associate native woodlands with oakwoods, because many of the surviving woodlands are dominated by oak, especially sessile oak; however, this probably results from human management in recent centuries, favouring oak at the expense of other trees and shrubs. If left to themselves in the future, it is likely that these oakwoods would become more diverse. They remain important reservoirs of bio-diversity, especially for rare plants and birds. Initiatives such as the People's Millennium Forests project and the Forest Service's native woodland scheme aim to redress centuries of neglect and over-exploitation. [see ARBORETA; FORESTRY; FORESTRY ENGINEERING; LAND; NATIONAL PARKS.] **Declan Little**

Natural History Museum, Dublin, a section of the NATIONAL MUSEUM OF IRELAND. Founded in 1792, the museum moved to its present building in Upper Merrion Street in 1857; it became part of the National Museum in 1877 (see p. 947). Recent renovations have restored the building as a beautiful cabinet museum displaying biodiversity. There is a comprehensive display of Irish FAUNA, including the extinct giant DEER; on the upper floors are magnificent exhibitions of animals from around the world, with many rare species and superb Blaschka glass models of sea anemones. The museum is an important research resource, with scientific collections of more than 2 million specimens. [see ELK.] **James P. O'Connor**

naturalists abroad. No fewer than five Irishmen recorded the natural history of Jamaica, including Sir HANS SLOANE, whose botanical specimens formed part of the nucleus of the British Museum. Patrick Browne (born 1720 in Co. Mayo) was a correspondent of Linnaeus and wrote a *Natural History of Jamaica*. William Harris (born 1860 in Enniskillen) was Superintendent of Public Parks and Plantations and then Government Botanist in Jamaica. William Fawcett (born 1851 in Arklow) was director of the Botanic Gardens in Jamaica and jointly wrote a Jamaican Flora. William Hancock (born 1847 in Lurgan) visited Jamaica, Mexico and Guatemala and collected plants. Thomas Coulter (born 1793 in Dundalk), a botanist, doctor, and mining manager, worked in South America, Mexico, and California; his many discoveries include *Pinus coulteri*, *Romneya coulteri*, *Erigeron coulteri*, and a series of cacti. John Palliser (born 1817 in Waterford) organised an expedition of botanists and zoologists to western Canada, 1857–59. John Macoun (born 1831), an Ulsterman, botanist to the Geological Survey of Canada, collected many prairie plants new to science; his report on South Seskatchuan led to the cultivation of wheat crops there. Rev. William HINCKS, of the eminent Cork family, was professor of botany in Toronto, 1854–71. John Adams (born 1872 in Ballymena), an expert on algae and fungi, was Dominion Botanist in Ottawa. Bryan P. Beirne (born 1918 in Rosslare), an entomologist, was professor of pathology at Simon Fraser University in British Columbia. JOHN BALL, with J. D. Hooker of Kew Gardens, collected in South America, the Rocky Mountains, and Morocco. James Logan, from Lurgan, was WILLIAM PENN's secretary and a correspondent of Linnaeus, who honoured him in naming the plant family Loganiaceae; he organised the highly regarded Junto Library for Benjamin Franklin. Thomas Antisell (born 1817 in Dublin), a FENIAN sympathiser, fled to New York after the failed rising of 1848; he botanised in California and Arizona and is remembered in *Astragalus antiselli*. William Emilius Praeger (born 1863 in Belfast), a brother of ROBERT LLOYD PRAEGER, became professor of botany at Kalamazoo College, Michigan, in 1905. Rev. E. A. Armstrong (born 1900 in Belfast), a recognised authority on bird behaviour, travelled widely in South, Central, and North America, Iceland, Europe, and China. Apart from his scientific ornithology he was a distinguished folklorist, hagiographer, Biblical scholar, and Shakespearean scholar. HENRY CHICHESTER HART (born 1847 in Dublin) was also a Shakespearean scholar; he was naturalist to the *Discovery* on the British Polar expedition of 1875–6, reporting on the plants. [see ARBORETA; BOTANIC GARDENS; EXPLORERS.] **Donal Synnott**

naval forces

Marine Service. From the end of the CIVIL WAR in 1923 to the outbreak of the SECOND WORLD WAR in 1939, the Free State and Éire possessed no naval force. In accordance with the ANGLO-IRISH TREATY (1921), the British navy patrolled the Irish coast, while fisheries protection was carried out by the Department of Agriculture. On the outbreak of war the Marine Service was established. Six British-built torpedo boats, together with a fisheries protection auxiliary ship and an armed trawler, were the main vessels of the service, while the disused British naval dockyard on Haulbowline Island in Cork Harbour was reactivated as the naval headquarters. After the war the Marine Service was formally disbanded and in 1946 the Naval Service was established.

Naval Service. Established in March 1946 as the successor to the Marine Service. Headquarters, operations, support, and training elements are based at Haulbowline Island, Co. Cork. Its operational area extends 200 nautical miles (370 km) from the coast, covering an area of 342,000 km^2 (132,000 sq. miles). It has a fleet of eight ships and an enlistment of approximately 1,000 men and women. Its primary role is the maritime security of the state, which it fulfils by maintaining a naval presence in territorial waters; but its principal day-to-day task is fisheries protection, with more than 90 per cent of its operations carried out within Ireland's exclusive fishery zone. Its involvement in the prevention of drug-smuggling, as part of a joint task force with the GARDA SÍOCHÁNA and the REVENUE COMMISSIONERS, has increased significantly. The Naval Service also assists other state agencies in search and rescue, pollution control, and maritime surveillance, and its diving unit assists the authorities in such activities as search and recovery and explosive ordnance disposal.

An Slua Muirí. The naval component of the Second-Line Reserve, established in 1947 as the successor to the Maritime Inscription of the SECOND WORLD WAR. It comprises four companies, based in Dublin, Cork, Limerick, and Waterford, and numbers approximately 300 men and women. It is equipped with a number of motor vessels suitable for river patrol, as well as sail training craft, and provides operational, logistical, and administrative support to the Naval Service. **Hugh Tully**

Navan (*An Uaimh*), Co. Meath, the largest town and county town of Co. Meath, at the confluence of the Rivers BOYNE and Blackwater; population (2002) 3,415. While Navan's recent growth is linked to its position on the commuter fringes of Dublin, its medieval importance was as a ford. It became a borough under the patronage of Jocelyn de Angulo c. 1176, while its first charter was granted by Edward IV of England in 1469. Its rich hinterland of flat grassland gave Navan its importance as a market town. From 1729 a coach road linked the town to Dublin. From 1850 Navan was connected to Drogheda by rail, with a direct connection to Dublin in

Navan Fort. *The prehistoric royal site of Navan Fort, Co. Armagh, a multi-occupation enclosure dating from the Iron Age. Visible are two smaller monuments of the complex, Site A (centre left), and Site B (centre right). [Northern Ireland Tourist Board Photographic Library]*

1862; these lines closed to passengers in 1959 and 1947, respectively. The factory of Navan Carpets was founded in 1938; the town is also a centre of furniture manufacture. In 1970 lead-zinc deposits were discovered near the town, and Tara Mines (now owned by the Finnish firm Outokumpu) are the largest lead-zinc mines in Europe, employing more than 600 people. **Ruth McManus**

Navan Fort (Eamain Macha), Co. Armagh, one of the late prehistoric provincial 'royal sites' of Ireland (the others being TARA, Co. Meath, RATHCROGHAN, Co. Roscommon, and Knockaulin, Co Kildare). It is an IRON AGE sanctuary, a circular earthwork enclosure some 290 m (950 ft) in diameter encircling a drumlin 2.5 km ($1\frac{1}{2}$ miles) west of Armagh. The English name 'Navan' derives from the first element of the name of the site in early written sources, Emain Macha. *Emain* may mean 'twins'; and Macha was the goddess of the region. The site is portrayed in early literature, chiefly the ULSTER CYCLE, as the headquarters and sacred place of Conchobhar and his warriors, who defend the kingdom of the ULAIDH against various enemies from the south and west. It is also associated with the exploits of the hero CÚ CHULAINN, who led the defeat of MÉABH's Connacht army by the Ulstermen in the central epic of the Ulster Cycle, 'TÁIN BÓ CUAILNGE'. Some scholars have suggested that the tales contain a genuine memory of a prehistoric time (synchronised by medieval chroniclers with the two centuries before the birth of Christ), when the kingdom of the Ulaidh was ruled from Emain Macha. Much of the early literary material associated with the monument, however, appears to be mythological in origin.

The circular earthwork 900 m (2,900 ft) in circumference delimiting the sanctuary is a large bank with an internal ditch. It is not centred symmetrically on the hill: on the west the earthwork runs across the top of the hill, whereas on the east it drops to the lower slopes, some 13 m (40 ft) below. The earthworks are best preserved on the south and west; elsewhere the hollow along the line of the ditch and the remains of the downslope bank survive. Two smaller monuments stand on the summit of the hill, enclosed by the earthworks: on the east is a ploughed-down ringwork, designated Site A, and on the west is a large mound some 5 m (16 ft) high and 50 m (165 ft) in diameter, called Site B. Both monuments were excavated in the 1960s, while small-scale excavations have recently concentrated on archaeological features on the hilltop revealed by geophysical surveys.

The excavation of Site B revealed a sequence of complex archaeological structures. In the Late BRONZE AGE a shallow ditch some 45 m (150 ft) in diameter was dug on the hilltop. A ring of large isolated posts was enclosed by the ditch, suggesting that the monument had a ceremonial purpose. Later, in the Iron Age, perhaps c. 200 BC, the first of a series of large circular wooden buildings was constructed. In the foundation slot for one of the latest examples the skull of a BARBARY APE was found. The final dramatic event took place in 95 BC (according to tree-ring dating), when a huge circular building, 40 m (130 ft) in diameter, formed of rings of sizeable oak posts, was erected over the remains of the earlier structures. A cairn of limestone boulders 2.5 m (8 ft) high was piled inside the wooden building, which was set on fire and the remains covered with a deep layer of turves 2.5 m (8 ft) high to complete the mound of Site B, which survived intact until excavation began in 1963. More recently, in 1997, a trial excavation in the enclosure recovered a large charred timber from the bottom of the ditch. Tree-ring dating showed that it had been felled in the period 100–90 BC, suggesting for the first time that Navan Fort itself had been built in the same decade as the large mound that it encloses.

Immediately east of Navan Fort is the lake called LOUGHNASHADE, in the margins of which four bronze horns were found in 1798. Unfortunately the landscape between Navan Fort and the lake has been removed by the intrusion of a large limestone quarry.

Navan Fort lies at the heart of a complex of unusual monuments. HAUGHEY'S FORT, 1 km ($\frac{1}{2}$ mile) to the west, is the site of a triple-ditched Bronze Age hill-fort. At the foot of the hill crowned by Haughey's Fort a smaller, circular bank encloses an artificial pond known as the King's Stables. Trial excavation showed that it was made at the beginning of the Late Bronze Age, c. 1000 BC, contemporary with Haughey's Fort. [see CELTIC ART; CELTS; DENDROCHRONOLOGY.] **Christopher J. Lynn**

Navigatio. *Woodcut from the Augsburg* Sankt Brandans Seefarht, *a printing by Anton Sorg in 1746 of* Navigatio Sancti Brendani Abbatis, *a ninth-century manuscript, describing a seven-year voyage undertaken by Brendan and his fellow-monks across the Atlantic. [Council of Trustees of the National Library of Ireland]*

Navigatio Sancti Brendani Abbatis ('Voyage of St Brendan the Abbot'), a Latin prose tale of about 12,000 words. Ireland's best-known contribution to medieval literature, this was among the most frequently copied of medieval texts and has been the subject of translations and imitations from the Middle Ages to the present day. Brénainn or Brenaind (Latin Brendenus or Brendinus) was born of the Alltraige sept in west Munster and died c. 577 AD in or near Clonfert, Co. Galway; the *Navigatio* was probably written c. 800. The story, an adaptation of a voyage episode from an older *Vita Brendani* (though departing considerably from its source), is an allegory of the monastic life, which describes Brendan's seven-year voyage on the ocean in a hide boat in search of the *Terra Repromissionis Sanctorum* ('promised land of the saints'). It is a work of great sophistication, subtly blending descriptions from real ocean voyages of *peregrinatio* with Biblical motifs as well as episodes based on the lives of the desert fathers. Its voyage, centring on recurrent visits to a series of islands and ocean locations for the feasts of the monastic calendar over a period of seven years, emphasises the cyclical character of the monastic life and liturgy. A tendency to read the tale as describing a real voyage, perhaps to North America, is testimony to the author's creation of a story of great verisimilitude: the tale is an eschatology concerned with theological revelation of the 'last things' and has no historical reality. **Jonathan Wooding**

navvies: see CONSTRUCTION WORKERS IN BRITAIN.

Neale, John and William (fl. 1805), father and son, eighteenth-century instrument-makers and music publishers working in the musically rich Christ Church area of Dublin, serving both the classical and the TRADITIONAL MUSIC tradition. Their publication *A Collection of the Most Celebrated Irish Tunes* (1724) was the first publication in Ireland of exclusively traditional music. It is notable for containing numerous pieces attributed to CAROLAN. **Glenn Cumiskey**

Neeson, Liam (1953–), stage and screen actor. Born in Ballymena, Co. Antrim. He worked at the LYRIC PLAYERS' Theatre, Belfast, and the Project and ABBEY THEATRES, Dublin. His feature film debut was in *Excalibur* (1981). Most of his work has been in the British and American film industries, most successfully in *Schindler's List* (1993) and in Ireland in the title role in *Michael Collins* (1996). His return to the stage in *Anna Christie* won him a Tony award, 1993. **Kevin Rockett**

Nelson, Havelock (1917–1996), conductor, composer, and pianist. Born in Cork; studied at the RIAM. He co-founded the DUBLIN ORCHESTRAL PLAYERS in 1939 and in 1947 joined the BBC in Belfast as an accompanist and broadcaster; he founded the Studio Symphony Orchestra and Studio Opera Group in 1950. He was made an officer of the Order of the British Empire for his services to music, 1966, and was awarded an honorary doctorate from Queen's University, Belfast, 1977, and honorary fellowship of the RIAM, 1985. **Geraldine Guiden**

Nelson Pillar, Dublin, a Doric column erected in Sackville Street (now O'Connell Street) in 1808 to honour Vice-Admiral Horatio Lord Nelson (1758–1805), killed at the Battle of Trafalgar. Nelson had no connection with Ireland but was a hero of the Napoleonic wars. Designed by William Wilkins and FRANCIS JOHNSTON, the 40.2 m (134-ft) fluted Wicklow granite column stood on a massive rectangular plinth, with a Portland stone figure of Nelson by THOMAS KIRK raised on a capstan-shaped drum above the capital (see p. 805). The Pillar, as the chief monument of the street, became in time the main public transport terminus and a popular meeting-place; an internal spiral staircase gave access to a viewing platform above the capital. On 7 March 1966, the fiftieth anniversary of the 1916 RISING (the headquarters of which were in the adjacent GPO), the Pillar was blown up by a republican splinter group and the upper half of the column was destroyed; the remainder was subsequently removed. Nelson's mutilated head is in the Dublin Civic Museum (see p. 805). **Brian Lalor**

Nenagh (*An tAonach*), Co. Tipperary, county town of North Tipperary; population (2002) 6,115, an increase of 8.3 per cent since 1996. Its Irish name, meaning the assembly place, recalls its role as the site of one of the public assemblies of Ormond. Previously part of the O'Brien kingdom of Limerick, it passed to the ANGLO-NORMAN Butlers c. 1200. The O'Briens regained control in the middle of the fourteenth century and retained it for almost 200 years. The Butlers built the great castle after 1217, which was demolished after the Williamite siege in 1690, though significant ruins remain. This was a pentagonal fortress, notable for its circular donjon, still extant. Abbey Street contains remains of what was once one of the most important Franciscan friaries in Ireland, founded in 1250.

The town prospered after 1838, when Co. Tipperary was divided into two ridings and Nenagh became the administrative centre for the North Riding. It was primarily a market town, providing services for an agricultural hinterland, but, in keeping with its administrative function, it also had a courthouse, town hall, market house, a substantial military barracks, and a jail with an impressive Governor's House—an octagonal limestone building in GEORGIAN style. Associated industries, such as brewing, corn processing, coachbuilding, and iron works, were also important. Today transnational industries, such as Procter and Gamble, which employs more than 600 people, play an important role in the employment structure of the town as do public services, such as the Revenue Commissioners. Nenagh is also an important tourism gateway, providing access to LOUGH DERG, an important fishery and water amenity, and to the surrounding countryside. **Joseph Brady**

Nendrum, a monastery founded on Mahee Island in STRANGFORD LOUGH, Co. Down, by St Mochaoi some time in the fifth century. It is celebrated as one of the best examples of an early Irish monastic layout, having three roughly concentric enclosures. The innermost, with thick stone wall, contains a church with *antae* as well as the stump of a ROUND TOWER and can be interpreted as the monastic sanctuary. A rectangular building in the middle enclosure produced *trial-pieces* of slate and was dubbed the 'MONASTIC SCHOOL' by H. C. Lawlor, who excavated and partially restored the site (not entirely satisfactorily) in 1922–4. The outermost ring may have had enclosed tilled land and gardens. The annals list bishops, abbots, and *erenaghs* of the monastery. GRAVE-SLABS, pottery, and small finds are displayed in a small site museum; other finds, including a bronze bell and a runic inscription, are in the Ulster Museum, Belfast. **Peter Harbison**

Neolithic period (c. 4000–2400 BC). The introduction of farming, the Neolithic way of life, meant not only the introduction of non-native species of cultivated plants and herded animals but also, as a consequence, the development of a more diverse material culture, such as stone AXES for woodland clearance and *ards* (stone points for simple ploughs) for tillage. In addition, grinding-stones for the processing of cereal grain and pottery for cooking were introduced.

The date and nature of the beginnings of farming are much debated. Evidence from POLLEN ANALYSIS shows a decline in the number of trees and an increase in the number of plants now known to be weeds of agriculture, such as ribwort plantain and docks, before 4000 BC but with no definite evidence for farming settlements. Possible cereal-type pollen before this date has been questioned on grounds of identification and context, but recent dating of (non-native) cattle bones from the Ferriter's Cove late mesolithic site and Kilgreaney Cave to at least 4500–4100 BC raises the possibility of early contact with Neolithic groups.

From 3800 BC onwards the evidence for extensive Neolithic settlement in Ireland is indisputable. Sub-fossil pollen indicates a large-scale clearance of trees, including the famous decline in elm, possibly linked to a climatically triggered outbreak of tree disease (with people assisting in its spread) and an increase in weeds of agriculture. Clear archaeological evidence for settlement in various forms appears: house sites, field systems, and MEGALITHIC TOMBS, with these monuments a possible focus for settlement; in some instances there is evidence for pre-tomb occupation, as for example at KNOWTH, Co. Meath. While a great deal of our knowledge is still dependent on results from a few long-term field projects, such as those in the BOYNE VALLEY, LOUGH GUR, and CÉIDE FIELDS, the quantity of evidence is now increasing.

The best evidence for field systems is still the network of co-axial fields, covering over 1,000 ha (2,500 acres), discovered under blanket bog at Céide in northern Co. Mayo, laid out before 3200 BC, apparently for cattle pasture. Limited excavation has so far revealed little evidence for the nature of settlement sites associated with these field systems. While no other field systems of a similar scale have yet been found in Ireland, at least two other areas of Neolithic fields are known: at Rathlacken, also in Co. Mayo, and at Roughaun Hill, Co. Clare. Megalithic tombs (COURT TOMBS and WEDGE TOMBS) are associated with both sites, as are possibly contemporary hut sites at Rathlacken. Other known pre-bog field systems in the west may yet prove to be Neolithic. It is not clear whether this evidence indicates a more general partitioning of the Neolithic landscape.

In advance of many modern developments, areas of the country with few standing monuments have been stripped of old pasture to reveal a great number of sites and buried ancient landscapes, many dating from the Neolithic Period. Of particular significance has been the discovery of traces of a number of substantial timber houses, mainly rectangular, with internal sub-divisions. Archaeological analysis of many of these sites is continuing, but at Tankardstown, Co. Limerick, two rectangular houses dating from c. 3800 BC were discovered, one of which has produced good evidence (in the form of burnt grain and bone) for an agricultural economy based on cereal-growing and animal husbandry. Emmer (an 'ancient' wheat) and probably barley were grown, and bone evidence indicates cattle, pig, and sheep or goat husbandry; this evidence is in line with that found at other sites, although (apart from the late Neolithic and Beaker site outside NEWGRANGE) the bone evidence is relatively meagre. It is probable that the proportion of different animals reared and crops grown varied from place to place, depending on SOIL, topography, and CLIMATE, which would also have varied over time as woodland was cleared. With regard to animals, it is not yet clear whether they were reared only for their meat or whether secondary products, such as milk, hides, and wool, were the important by-products they later became. These people—perhaps living in unenclosed hamlets of one or two houses or in more concentrated settlements around hilltop sites such as Donegore Hill, Co. Antrim, or near passage grave cemeteries—were clearly settled farmers, but they continued to gather wild plants, such as hazel nuts, blackberries, and (at Tankardstown) wild apples. The combination of evidence for gathering at Neolithic sites with that of pastoralism does not mean that these people were nomadic, as some researchers have argued: they were simply exploiting the bountiful harvest of fruit and nuts from trees and shrubs that developed around the edges of cleared woodland and fields. Some areas (such as CARROWMORE, Co. Sligo) have produced evidence for temporary occupation, from which particular resources were exploited (upland sites for summer pasture and coastal sites for marine resources).

Much less is known about the later Neolithic settlement and agriculture. Certainly pollen analysis (for example from Lough Sheeauns, Co. Galway) would indicate woodland regeneration towards the end of the period. Communities may have been pulling back from marginal agricultural areas in a period of less extensive farming, possibly because of population decline, or to a concentration in areas better suited to intensive farming or perhaps perceived to be the home of ancestors, for example the Boyne Valley, where new monuments, such as HENGE MONUMENTS, were constructed. The cultivation of naked barley, emmer, and possibly bread wheat continued, while cattle, pigs, and (to a lesser extent) sheep or goats were husbanded. By this time the Neolithic Period was merging into the early BRONZE AGE. [see PREHISTORIC FOOD.] **Michael Monk**

Ne Temere (1908), a Papal decree widely though inaccurately perceived as requiring the children of mixed marriages to be baptized as Catholics, was in fact primarily concerned with the requirement that all marriages, even mixed marriages, be celebrated before a Catholic priest. This indirectly enforced the pre-existing requirement of the Catholic Church that all the children be raised Catholics. Previously, since the decree of Trent *Tametsi* (1563) did not apply to mixed marriages in many places, including Ireland, the requirement that the children be raised as Catholics could be evaded by marrying outside the Catholic Church, a marriage which was recognised as valid, but unlawful, in canon law. The decree was abrogated and most of its prescriptions absorbed into the 1917 code of canon law. **Michael Mullaney**

neutrality, a cornerstone of the foreign policy of the independent Irish state since the outbreak of the SECOND WORLD WAR, its immediate origins lying in the collapse of collective security arrangements during the 1930s. The conduct of the Government policy between 1939 and 1945 was distinctly pro-Allied. Neutrality proved popular with the public and has enjoyed multi-party support ever since. The post-war failure to come to an agreement on Northern Ireland forestalled the possibility of membership of NATO, though the state remained resolutely anti-communist during the early years of the Cold War. Admission to the UNITED NATIONS in 1955 saw the state adopt a more independent line, and over the following decades the DEFENCE FORCES participated in peace-keeping missions under the auspices of the United Nations. Neutrality was not a major issue in the discussions leading to Ireland's membership of the EEC, though SEÁN LEMASS was prepared to make concessions on the issue if they were considered necessary. The debate regarding perceived dangers to Ireland's neutrality arising from the proposed adoption of a common foreign and security policy by member-states of the EUROPEAN UNION provoked renewed controversy, which proved instrumental in the initial rejection of the Treaty of Nice in a referendum in 2001, although it was passed in a subsequent vote in 2002. [see IRELAND, REPUBLIC OF.] **Gabriel Doherty**

Nevin, Thomas E. (1906–1986), experimental physicist. Born in Bristol; following a first-class honours degree in experimental and mathematical physics at UCD he won a scholarship for research in molecular spectroscopy at Imperial College, London, 1929–31. He returned to University College, Dublin, in 1931 as a lecturer, later becoming professor of experimental physics and head of the department, 1952–76. His full-spectral analysis of the O_2^+ and MnH molecules remains among the most authoritative and complex works of its type. He was also active in involving University College, Dublin, in early collaborative experiments in cosmic ray and fundamental particle physics. **Alex Montwill**

new departure, a plan of action that brought about an alliance between Fenians, agrarian radicals, and parliamentarians. Worked out in 1878 by MICHAEL DAVITT and JOHN DEVOY, it enabled the various parties to participate jointly in an open and aggressive campaign for land reform, leading to the establishment of peasant proprietorship. Dubbed the 'new departure' by Devoy, this alliance made possible the LAND WAR and propelled CHARLES STEWART PARNELL into the leadership of both the parliamentary and popular movements in Ireland. **Donald Jordan**

'New English', a term coined in the 1620s to designate the English community who had settled in Ireland since the 1550s. They were distinguished from the older English community in Ireland, who designated themselves 'OLD ENGLISH' in the early seventeenth century, primarily on grounds of religion. The Calvinistic PROTESTANTISM of the New English precluded their assimilation into the existing, and overwhelmingly Catholic, Old English colonial community. Under Lord Deputy Chichester, 1605–16, the New English gained a stranglehold over the offices of the central government, the royal army in Ireland, and the established CHURCH OF IRELAND. They displaced the Old English community from political influence and power and took possession of as much as 40 per cent of the land of Ireland by the time of the 1641 REBELLION. CROMWELL's reconquest of Ireland, and the WILLIAMITE SETTLEMENT, greatly strengthened the New English community and resulted in what became known as the PROTESTANT ASCENDANCY. [see ANGLO-IRISH SOCIETY.] **Henry A. Jefferies**

Newfoundland, the Irish in. The island and British colony of Newfoundland received Irish immigration from c. 1680. Indentured fishermen, first from Dublin and later from Co. Waterford, customarily established fishing stations in *Talamh an Éisc* ('the land of fish') for a summer season. In 1776 ARTHUR YOUNG reported that more than 5,000 passengers left Waterford alone for Newfoundland. Increasingly they overwintered, and after 1790 few went home.

By 1800 there were about 9,000 permanent Irish inhabitants in Newfoundland. Between 1811 and 1816 a larger wave of immigration came, largely from the ports of Waterford and New Ross. Immigration virtually ended by 1836. It has been argued that no other European emigration to the New World came from such a specific region to such a specific target region over such a long period: 90 per cent came from within a 48 km (30-mile) radius of Waterford to settle in coastal communities within 97 km (60 miles) of the principal port, St John's. By 1836 Newfoundland had 37,115 Irish inhabitants, making it one of the largest concentrations of Irish immigrants in rural British North America.

In Newfoundland almost all the Irish were Catholics, and the church became the most influential social and cultural institution. Irregularly enforced Penal Laws continued until 1779, when liberty of conscience was proclaimed. In 1784 Catholicism was formally established by the Franciscan missionary James Louis O'Donel of Knocklofty, Co. Tipperary. In April 1800 news of the UNITED IRISHMEN's rising inspired a mutiny among Irish soldiers in the British garrison at St John's. O'Donel enjoined his congregation to remain peaceful, gaining the respect of British rulers. In 1806 a Benevolent Irish Society was formed to address the needs of the poor and to provide a fraternal society for the rising Irish middle class. After 1829, when the Franciscan priest Michael Anthony Fleming became bishop, Irish Catholics were less deferential to British rule. Fleming supported DANIEL O'CONNELL, advocated HOME RULE for Newfoundland, and cultivated Irish social and political aspirations. The number of priests was increased from thirteen to thirty-six, and the Presentation Sisters from Galway and Sisters of Mercy from Dublin were invited to St John's to establish schools for Irish children. Fleming built a large ROMANESQUE cathedral and decorated it with works by the Irish neo-classical sculptor JOHN HOGAN. In 1876 the Irish CHRISTIAN BROTHERS established schools for boys.

Newfoundland received self-government in 1855. Confederation with Canada took place in 1869, when many Irish inhabitants voted against union, fearing a loss of autonomy. Thereafter Newfoundland embarked on self-development in fisheries, mines, and pulp and paper, but prosperity often proved elusive.

Newgrange. *Interior of the passage tomb at Newgrange, built c. 3000 BC. The passage is illuminated by the sun at the winter solstice; the event lasts for approximately seventeen minutes at dawn from 19 to 23 December. Orthostat C10 (left) is decorated with a three-spiral motif, an example of the enigmatic Boyne Valley art. [Dúchas, The Heritage Service]*

Until the 1930s significant numbers of Irish Newfoundlanders migrated to Boston, but a substantial Irish community remained. Following a referendum, federation with Canada took place in 1949. There was a resurgence of interest in Newfoundland's Irish heritage in the 1970s, and since then a more recent Irish immigrant community has thrived and developed. **John Edward FitzGerald**

Newgrange, a PASSAGE TOMB in the BOYNE VALLEY, Co. Meath. Dating from c. 3000 BC, it is one of the most famous prehistoric monuments in Western Europe. It consists of a roughly oval mound, 11 m (36 ft) high and 79–85 m (260–80 ft) in diameter. It is bounded by a kerb of ninety-seven contiguous slabs, many of which are decorated, the most notable being the entrance stone at the south-east. Here a passage 19 m (62 ft) long leads to a polygonal chamber with three recesses opening off it in cruciform fashion. The chamber is roofed by a magnificent corbelled vault some 6 m (20 ft) high. Many stones in the tomb are profusely decorated with MEGALITHIC art. The almost vertical quartz facing with interspersed granite boulders above the tomb front is a modern feature, constructed following extensive excavations in the 1960s and 70s. Directly above the entrance the so-called roof-box allows the rays of the rising sun to shine directly into the back chamber for a few days at the time of the winter solstice (21 or 22 December). Beside the mound are three smaller passage tombs. Newgrange is surrounded by twelve stones, the remains of a later great circle (see p. 366). **Paul Walsh**

New Ireland Forum (1983–4). Concluding that 'the state of Anglo-Irish relations was little short of disastrous,' GARRET FITZGERALD, when TAOISEACH, implemented JOHN HUME's proposal that a forum of constitutional politicians 'committed to a new Ireland would together define what we really wish this new Ireland to be.' FitzGerald's insistence that all participants renounce violence ensured the exclusion of Provisional SINN FÉIN; but the refusal of unionist parties to have anything to do with it meant that the forum was essentially a conference representing 90 per cent of nationalists in Ireland. It opened in Dublin Castle on 30 May 1983; after almost a year of discussions, twenty-eight private sessions, thirteen public sessions, and fifty-six meetings of the FIANNA FÁIL, FINE GAEL, LABOUR PARTY, and SDLP leaderships it issued a report of its findings in May 1984. Three solutions were offered: 'a unitary state, achieved by agreement'; a federal arrangement; and a joint-authority solution giving the British and Irish governments equal responsibility for ruling Northern Ireland. All three solutions were rejected by Margaret Thatcher in her notorious 'out ... out ... out' interview. The forum was a powerful educative force in the Republic, revealing to many the deep complexity of the situation north of the border. **Jonathan Bardon**

Newman type, an Irish printing type. Mindful of the particular requirements involved in the planned publication of EUGENE O'CURRY's lectures at the press of the newly established CATHOLIC UNIVERSITY OF IRELAND, its rector, John Henry Newman, approved the preparation of an IRISH PRINTING TYPE in 1857. GEORGE PETRIE, working closely with O'Curry, studied early Irish manuscripts in preparing the initial drawings for what the editors of the university journal *Atlantis* described as possibly 'the most perfect, if not the first perfectly correct, Irish type ever cut.' This design, which returned to the more angular minuscule letter-forms for reference, proved to be most popular and was a source of influence for most of the Irish typefaces that were to follow. **Dermot McGuinne**

New Music Hall, Dublin. On 13 April 1742 the first performance of *Messiah* by HANDEL took place in the 'New Musick Hall' in Fishamble Street, Dublin. The hall, which in its day was a popular concert venue, no longer stands; a hotel named after the composer now stands on an adjoining site. Every year on 13 April, since 1989, OUR LADY'S CHORAL SOCIETY gives an open-air commemorative performance of choruses from *Messiah*, including the great 'Hallelujah Chorus' (see pp. 471, 759). **Geraldine Guiden**

Newry (*An tIúr*), Co. Down, a city and seaport occupying a strategic crossing on the Newry River at the head of CARLINGFORD LOUGH; population (1991) 21,633. Newry controls the ancient route into mid-Ulster by way of the historic frontier zone between the Mourne and Camlough mountain ranges. The town originated around the CISTERCIAN abbey established by Muireartach Mac Lochlainn in 1156–7, and JOHN DE COURCY built a castle here during his advance into Ulster in 1177. Thereafter Newry remained under Irish control. The abbey thrived and at the Dissolution was granted to the Bagenal family. Newry played a strategic role during the NINE YEARS' WAR and was incorporated as a borough in 1613, but it remained 'a collection of mud cabbins' until the early eighteenth century, having been burnt by SCHOMBERG in 1689. The turnpiking of the Belfast road (1700), the transfer of the Custom House from Carlingford in 1726, and the construction of the Newry Canal (begun 1731), all encouraged the town's spectacular growth in the later eighteenth century. In 1777 ARTHUR YOUNG described Newry as 'exceedingly flourishing and very well built.'

By 1780 the town was Ireland's fourth-largest port, and in 1835 it had trade worth £960,000. Further improvements to the Newry Ship Canal in 1830–50 (closed 1974) and the completion of rail links to Portadown (1852) and Armagh (1865) secured Newry's position as an important port and LINEN market. Since PARTITION the town's fortunes have depended on the state of cross-border trade and (more recently) the relative strength of the English and Irish currencies. In recent years redevelopment and bomb damage have significantly eroded the town's built heritage. It was conferred with the status of 'city' by Elizabeth II in 2002, during her Golden Jubilee celebrations. **Lindsay Proudfoot**

Newry Navigation, the first CANAL project to be completed in Ireland. The Newry Canal was begun in 1731 to open up access to the Tyrone coalfields, some 8 km (5 miles) from the western shore of Lough Neagh. The coal was to be taken by the canal to Newry and thence by coaster to Dublin, the main market. The 30 km ($18\frac{1}{2}$ miles) waterway, linking the Upper BANN near Portadown with a tidal lock at Newry, was a considerable engineering feat for the time. The first coal cargo arrived in Dublin on 19 March 1742. A passenger service from Portadown to Newry was introduced in 1813, and in 1829 the canal was passed from government control to local interests. Following the completion of the Dublin–Belfast rail link in 1852, goods traffic, which had been buoyant, declined. The last commercial movement recorded was in 1936, and in 1949 the Northern Ireland government issued a warrant for its abandonment. **Bernard Share**

Newsletter, a daily newspaper published in Belfast. The oldest daily paper in Ireland and the first newspaper in Ulster, it was founded in 1737 by Francis Joy, a local papermaker. It became a daily in 1855, having hitherto been biweekly. At first a Protestant 'patriot' journal, it supported free trade and the repeal of POYNINGS' LAW. Henry Joy, grandson of Francis, became proprietor in 1782; he was a VOLUNTEER who supported changes in the constitutional relationship between Ireland and Britain. After 1795, under its new owner, George Gordon, the paper became more conservative and gratefully accepted a government subsidy. Throughout the nineteenth and twentieth centuries and up to the present it has remained a Protestant unionist paper, but it has taken a more liberal line in the last decade. It was owned by Century Newspapers before being bought by the Mirror Group in 1998. It now has a circulation of approximately 34,000. **Eddie Holt**

newspapers, evening. Though many cities and towns had their own evening newspapers before the age of mass transport, evening papers are now in decline, particularly because of the news and commercial competition from radio and television. The Independent Group's *Evening Herald* (1891–) is Dublin's sole surviving evening newspaper since the demise of the *Evening Press* (1954–95); the *Evening Mail* survived from 1823 to 1962. The BELFAST TELEGRAPH (now also owned by INDEPENDENT NEWS AND MEDIA) remains Northern Ireland's best-selling newspaper. The *Evening Echo* (1882–), published in Cork by the IRISH EXAMINER group, is the only evening paper in Munster. [see NEWSPAPERS AND JOURNALS.] **Eddie Holt**

newspapers, Northern Ireland. There are three daily newspapers in Northern Ireland. The NEWSLETTER (founded 1737) is the oldest English-language newspaper in the world; nowadays it is read mainly by unionists. The IRISH NEWS (founded 1892) is now read overwhelmingly by nationalists. The BELFAST TELEGRAPH (1870) boasts a readership that matches neatly the denominational ratio of the population while having an editorial stance that is liberal unionist in tone. In addition there are approximately forty local newspapers, mainly weeklies, ranging from such long-established papers as the *Derry Journal* (nationalist) and *Londonderry Sentinel* (unionist) to more recent contenders, such as the *Andersonstown News* (Belfast) (see p. 1078). [see JOURNALISM.] **Bill Rolston**

newspapers, provincial. The earliest Irish provincial papers served pro-British interests. By the middle of the nineteenth century increased literacy, improved technology and reduced tax on papers led to an explosion of titles. In 1850, sixty-eight newspapers were published outside Dublin; by 1880 there were 127. This mushrooming provincial press was influential in the spread of NATIONALISM, and its editors were often important local political figures. In the twentieth century the number of titles decreased (in 1950 there were seventy-one in the Republic) but average circulations multiplied. Predictions that the introduction of local commercial radio would devastate the provincial press have proved untrue; there are now almost a hundred titles throughout Ireland. Founded in 1766, the *Limerick Chronicle* is the longest-lived provincial paper. The contemporary provincial press has been attractive to domestic groups, most notably the Independent Group, and foreign media interests such as Scottish Radio Holdings. **Eddie Holt**

newspapers, Sunday. A high readership of Sunday papers continues to sustain a wide choice of Irish and British titles. Top of the middle market is the *Sunday Independent* (1906–), the oldest of Dublin's Sunday papers (circulation over 300,000). FIANNA FÁIL's *Sunday Press* (1949–95) had sales of 400,000 in the 1960s but closed with the demise of the IRISH PRESS GROUP, while the *Sunday Review* (1957–63), owned by the IRISH TIMES, lasted for only six years. The tabloid *Sunday World* (1973–), launched by the businessmen Hugh McLaughlin and Gerry McGuinness, has a circulation of over 300,000; the Independent Group bought a controlling share of the paper in 1978.

New Sunday titles appeared in the 1980s. The *Sunday Journal* (1980–82), aimed at farmers, was taken over by Joe Moore of the insurance company PMPA but closed within two years. Hugh McLaughlin's *Sunday Tribune*, launched in 1980, was dragged down in 1982 by the collapse of his tabloid *Daily News*; the title was bought, mainly by the journalist VINCENT BROWNE and the businessman TONY RYAN, and relaunched in 1983. The Independent Group took control in 1992, and the paper now has a circulation in the 80,000s. The *Sunday Business Post* (1989–) was launched by four journalists, mainly as a financial weekly; in 1997 it was taken over by Trinity Holdings, and its circulation has risen to approximately 50,000. In 1996 the *Title* was launched as a Sunday sports paper, but it merged with *Ireland on Sunday* (1997–). In 2000 the paper was taken over by Scottish Radio Holdings and in 2001 by Associated Newspapers; it has a circulation in the mid-50,000s. In Northern Ireland the *Sunday News* (1965–93), owned by the *Newsletter*, with a readership proportionate to the sectarian split, closed in the wake of the launch of *Sunday Life* (1988–) by the BELFAST TELEGRAPH. The *Sunday Times* (London) opened an office in Dublin in 1996 and now has a circulation of almost 90,000 in the Republic; more than one in three Sunday papers sold in the Republic is a British import. **David Quin**

newspapers, tabloid. Irish tabloid papers have had mixed fortunes. The *Evening Mail* was turned tabloid by its new owners, the IRISH TIMES, in 1960, but the experiment was a costly failure and the paper closed two years later. The early *Sunday Tribune* was tabloid for a brief period but reverted to broadsheet. The *Daily News* collapsed after fifteen issues. The attempt in 1987 to squeeze the IRISH PRESS into a tabloid mould led to a drastic fall in circulation, while the tabloidisation of the *Evening Herald* in the 1980s did not transform its fortunes.

On the other hand, the *Sunday World* (1973–), combining the sharp-edged style of a British tabloid with Irish content, has thrived for three decades. The hybrid *Irish Star* (1988–), jointly owned by United Newspapers and the Independent Group, has successfully combined Irish content with the qualities and content of its British mother paper. The *Mirror* and *Sun* also have Irish editions. The market share of the tabloid British Sundays and dailies in the Republic (over 50 per cent and over 30 per cent, respectively) may be attributed in part to their sports coverage, celebrity gossip, and generally less inhibited style and content. In recent years 'contamination' by British tabloids has been blamed for a decline in journalistic standards, including invasion of privacy and trivialisation. British imports, mainly tabloids, account for more than one in four daily papers sold in the Republic. **David Quin**

newspapers and periodicals (eighteenth to twenty-first centuries) 1763 to 2002. Ephemeral reading matter in Ireland is closely associated with the rise of LITERACY in English, with politics, and with the growth of the railways. Religious books, chapbooks, cheap novels and broadsheets existed during the early modern period, but the oldest newspaper, the NEWSLETTER, published in Belfast, dates from only 1737, while the *Freeman's Journal* was published in Dublin from 1763. Between 1800 and 1850 more than 150 periodicals were founded, but most had a brief existence, almost a quarter of them surviving for only a year. Most were identified with a political outlook. One weekly, the NATION—first published in 1842 as a vehicle for YOUNG IRELAND—had a subscription ranging between 4,000 and 7,000 during its early years. By 1850 there were an estimated sixty-eight provincial newspapers. While in 1841 less than half the population aged five and above could read, by 1911 this figure had reached 88 per cent. Rapid expansion of the rail network provided the means for distributing periodicals; later, motor transport supplemented rail carriages. By 1879 there were several Dublin newspapers with national circulations and probably 120 provincial papers, with most becoming even more politicised. Many of the periodicals depended on reprinting reports that had first appeared elsewhere and on lengthy accounts of public affairs. During the final years of the nineteenth century, many newspapers began to give greater emphasis to social events; about the same time, an Irish-language press emerged, though its circulation remained small. After partition (1920–22) the press in both parts of the country became more parochial and in Northern Ireland became virulently political. By the 1960s, however, there was competition from radio and especially from television. This, combined with the availability of British publications and the absorption of some periodicals, such as the BELFAST TELEGRAPH, into international chains, meant that newspapers became less partisan, adopted visually arresting formats, and prominently featured entertainment, sports, and social events. The press remains an important medium of communication in the twenty-first century, and its circulation and influence remain significant. **Alan O'Day**

newspapers and the law. Newspapers in the Republic operate under publishing laws introduced in the middle of the twentieth century in an authoritarian and conformist society. Censorship laws were used in a draconian fashion during the SECOND WORLD WAR. In libel cases the burden of proof is on the defendant, any apology can be construed as an admission of culpability, and no

New York. *Premises of the American Irish Historical Society, 991 Fifth Avenue, New York, founded in Boston in 1897. The society's library houses the most complete private collection of Irish and Irish-American history in the United States. [American Irish Historical Society]*

distinction is made between accidental and malicious libel. In 1987 the National Newspapers of Ireland (NNI) began a campaign for reform of the libel laws. Both the Law Reform Commission (1991) and the Commission on the Newspaper Industry (1996) have recommended changes; in 2001 FINE GAEL was the first party to urge reform, but successive governments have turned a deaf ear. **David Quin**

Newtownabbey (*Baile na Mainistreach*), Co. Antrim, a mainly Protestant suburban district on the northern fringe of greater Belfast, administered as a separate borough; population (1991) 56,811. The borough includes the outer residential suburbs, light industry, and warehousing of the M2 motorway corridor, heading north from Belfast, together with the town of Ballyclare and adjacent rural areas. **Lindsay Proudfoot**

Newtownards (*Baile Nua na hArda*), Co. Down, a town on the edge of the tidal flats at the head of STRANGFORD LOUGH; population (1991) 23,869. Newtownards was founded during the Middle Ages and is mentioned as a borough in 1333. The modern town dates from the division of the barony of Upper Clandeboye between Con O'Neill, James Hamilton, and Hugh Montgomery in 1605. Montgomery acquired Newtownards and settled fellow-Scots there, a hundred houses being built by 1609; the town was incorporated in 1613. The seventeenth-century town was centred on Castle Place, where the market cross, raised by Sir James Montgomery in 1635, still stands. In 1770 the town centre shifted east when the present Market House was built and Conway Square laid out as a commercial and administrative piazza by Mr Stewart. Under the patronage of Robert Stewart (later Marquis of Londonderry) Newtownards prospered during the eighteenth and nineteenth centuries as an agricultural and LINEN market. Today the town functions as a retail centre and dormitory suburb of Belfast. **Lindsay Proudfoot**

Newtown Butler, Battle of (1689), the first significant Williamite success in an open engagement with JACOBITE forces in the war of 1689–91. An Englishman, Colonel William Wolseley, led the Protestant Enniskillen force of about 2,000 men, while Viscount Mount Cashell commanded a Jacobite force of about 4,000. The battle was preceded by an unsuccessful Jacobite attempt to take Crom Castle and by a skirmish between Jacobite dragoons and Enniskillen horsemen. On 31 July Mount Cashell set fire to Newtown Butler, Co. Fermanagh, and took up a defensive position south of the village on a wooded hill behind a bog traversed by a narrow causeway, on the southern end of which he placed his artillery. Wolseley's infantry advanced over the sun-dried bog, withstood the volleys fired at them, and captured the artillery position, thereby allowing their cavalry to cross the causeway. Mount Cashell's forces broke in panic. The battle lasted thirty minutes. The ensuing rout was worsened by the Enniskillen soldiers' superior knowledge of the countryside, which resulted in many Jacobites being killed by their pursuers or drowned in LOUGH ERNE. The battle broke the Jacobite attempt to capture Enniskillen and turned the tide of the war in Ulster in favour of the Williamites. **Charles Ivar McGrath**

new towns. Though suggested in Abercrombie's Sketch Development Plan (1941), new towns became part of the development strategy for Dublin only when the Wright Report (1967) advocated that most growth be contained within four new towns: Blanchardstown, Lucan, Clondalkin, and Tallaght. The proposed towns were long and linear, separated by green belts and able to grow westwards, and together would accommodate approximately 350,000 people. They would be self-contained in EMPLOYMENT and services but integrated in a regional TRANSPORT system. Reduced to three centres, the new towns took shape in the 1970s in Blanchardstown, Lucan-Clondalkin, and Tallaght and now have populations of approximately 40,000, 45,000, and 65,000, respectively. In form they bear little resemblance to what was suggested; they never developed an independent existence, because of proximity to Dublin and lack of services. Now, with town centres in Tallaght and Blanchardstown, it is hoped that they will develop a distinct urban identity.

Development at Shannon began in 1961, the intention being to capitalise on the opportunities provided by the airport free-trade zone. Its present population of 7,800 exceeds its target of 6,000.

In the early 1960s it was decided that the best means of relieving HOUSING and traffic pressure on Belfast and of promoting growth in the south and west of Northern Ireland was to create a new urban centre encompassing Lurgan and Portadown. Craigavon was built after 1966, using a linear planning design, and has become a centre of economic development outside Belfast, with a population of approximately 53,000. [see BUCHANAN REPORT.] **Joseph Brady**

New York, the Irish in. New York state comprises 128,402 km^2 (49,576 sq. miles) in the eastern United States. Its political capital is Albany, but its cultural and economic centre is the city of New

York. The census of 1990 recorded 2,968,411 people of Irish and 'Scotch Irish' birth or descent living in New York state, 19 per cent of whom lived in New York city. Ties with Ireland solidified in the eighteenth century. Large land grants in the northern part of the state were made to Irish officers in the British military who recruited immigrants from Ireland to settle counties that eventually included Orange, Ulster, Green, and Sullivan. Irish mercantile houses set up branches in New York city, which was a leading exporter of flax seed and importer of finished linen products in Ulster's transatlantic trade. On the eve of the American Revolution a diverse population of Irish Anglicans, Presbyterians, Huguenots, Quakers, and Methodists lived in New York city and state. Restrictions on Catholic residents were lifted, beginning in 1784.

The number of Irish immigrants significantly increased after the end of the Napoleonic wars. THOMAS ADDIS EMMET and William James MacNeven emerged as community leaders for an estimated 12,000 Irish people living in New York city in 1816. The construction of the Erie Canal absorbed 3,000 Irish labourers as early as 1818. Likewise, an extensive network of turnpikes and railways and a water pipeline system served to disperse the Irish throughout the state. Cheaper fares to Canada meant that many immigrants crossed into the United States by way of New York's northern boundary. By mid-century there were Irish districts in Buffalo, Rochester, Syracuse, Utica, Albany, Schenectady, and Troy.

When the influx of FAMINE REFUGEES levelled off, the 1855 state census found that 28 per cent of New York city's population had been born in Ireland, making it the most Irish city in America. Thereafter chain migration directed the movement in specific ways, Cork, Kerry, and Galway emigrants to Manhattan; Donegal, Mayo, Leitrim, and Longford to Brooklyn. By 1890, 275,000 people of Irish birth lived in these adjacent cities, with 320,000 second-generation Irish-Americans. Many of the clergy and religious staffing local Catholic parishes and institutions were recruited from Ireland.

In the twentieth century, most newcomers emigrated directly to and settled in New York city, particularly in the late 1920s and the 1950s. The proportion of the Irish in America living there doubled, from 17 per cent in 1900 to 34 per cent in 1960, even as their proportion of the urban total dropped from 8 per cent to 1.5 per cent. With an Irish stock population that was still larger than that of Dublin or Belfast, New York city remained one of the major growth centres in the Irish DIASPORA. Every cultural and political movement in Ireland since the second half of the nineteenth century had its New York equivalent. Steamships, then air travel, accelerated the possibilities for cultural interchanges, tourism, and return migration. By the beginning of the twenty-first century, innovations in communication virtually eliminated the spatial distance between Ireland and New York, with significant ramifications for the circulatory movement of capital, labour, politics, scholarship, and the arts. **Marion R. Casey**

New Zealand, the Irish in. Irish emigration to New Zealand was essentially a post-famine phenomenon, shaped by the availability of state financial assistance and the existence of close historical links with eastern Australia. The colony received large numbers of immigrants from Victoria and New South Wales during the gold rushes of 1861–8. However, the most important phase of Irish settlement took place between 1871 and 1885, when the central government embarked on a scheme of assisted IMMIGRATION and public works; thereafter the pace of Irish immigration slackened. The Irish-born accounted for almost a fifth of New Zealand's foreign-born population at their highest point in 1881.

New Zealand's Irish population came from two principal regions. The north-eastern counties of Antrim, Down, and Derry were consistently a major source, their prominence reflecting the Ulster bias of New Zealand's recruitment activities in Ireland. Yet the inflow also featured substantial contributions from localities with strong Australian ties in Cos. Galway, Kerry, Cork, Clare, Limerick, and Tipperary. Once established, these links were perpetuated by the constant flow of information, nominated passages and remittances to relatives and friends at home. According to the most recent estimates, Protestants comprised about two-fifths of all Irish emigrants to New Zealand before the FIRST WORLD WAR. The religious breakdown differed from region to region, with the west coast of South Island (75:25) and the province of Canterbury (37:63) at opposite ends of the spectrum. Whatever their religious affiliation, most newcomers came from a rural, small-farming background in Ireland. They were older than their compatriots arriving in the great emigration ports of Liverpool, New York, Montréal, and Sydney, and many had served an extended colonial apprenticeship elsewhere. Recent research has drawn attention to the crucial role played by Old World social ties, state-assisted passage, and family or community connections with earlier immigrants in influencing patterns of Irish mobility.

The Irish experience in New Zealand was diverse, dynamic, and rural as much as urban. Though there were moments of tension, the surviving evidence suggests that immigrants made a

OLD NEW ZEALAND

A Tale of the Good Old Times, together with a History of the War in the North of New Zealand against the Chief Heke in the Year 1845 as told by an Old Chief of the Ngapuhi Tribe, also Maori Traditions

BY A PAKEHA MAORI

FREDERICK EDWARD MANING

WHITCOMBE AND TOMBS LIMITED

New Zealand. *Title page of* Old New Zealand *by Frederick Edward Maning (1948), decorated with a Maori-inspired mask. [Board of Trinity College, Dublin]*

relatively easy accommodation with new realities. The expansion of agriculture, the low pressure of population on land, the provision of state assistance for immigration, and the absence of entrenched native-born elites created favourable conditions for economic advancement and ensured that most newcomers enjoyed modest gains within a generation. As a pioneer group, the Irish-born and their descendants played an important role in shaping New Zealand's economy and society; but their actions also made them participants in the British imperial system and subject to its underlying ideology. The expatriate population adopted a moderate stance on homeland issues until shock waves from the 1916 RISING fuelled sectarian animosities. New Zealand holds the dubious distinction of having unsuccessfully prosecuted an Irish Catholic Bishop of Auckland, James Liston, on a charge of sedition when he appeared to question the worth of the Anglo-Irish Treaty of 1922 (see p. 700). **Lyndon Fraser**

Niall Glúndub, King of TARA, 916–919. Son of ÁED FINDLIATH of Cenél nEoghain; he married Gormlaith, daughter of FLANN SINNA. Having subdued north Connacht and Ulster by 914, he was checked in Meath and submitted to the powerful Flann. Supporting the latter against his own sons, he succeeded to the kingship of Tara. Niall revived the important Aonach Tailteann (Teltown Fair), which had long lain dormant. He campaigned against the Norsemen but was defeated and slain near Dublin in 919. He was followed as King of Cenél nEoghain by his nephew Fergal son of Domnall and as King of Tara by Donnchad son of MÁEL SECHNAILL. **Ailbhe Mac Shamhráin**

Ní Chuilleanáin. *Eiléan Ní Chuilleanáin, poet and founder of the literary review* Cyphers, *is one of Ireland's foremost poets. [Macdara Woods]*

Niall of the Nine Hostages, Anglicised name of Níall Noígíallach, regarded as the ancestor of a number of royal dynasties in the north-west and the midlands. The UÍ NÉILL ('the descendants of Niall'), who dominated early medieval Irish politics, were ruled by the King of TARA. Niall reputedly lived in the early fifth century and was supposedly slain in the English Channel, or in Scotland. According to legend he derived his name from the hostages he had taken from the five Irish provinces and the Scots, British, Saxons, and Franks. His son Laoghaire is associated with the activities of St PATRICK. **Bart Jaski**

Ní Chathasaigh, Máire (1956–), harper. Born in Bandon, Co. Cork; educated at UCC. She is noted for having developed a variety of new techniques, particularly in relation to ornamentation. She has performed throughout the world, is much sought after as teacher and adjudicator, and has won many prestigious awards. Her first recording, *The New-Strung Harp*, was the first HARP album to concentrate on traditional dance music; she has since recorded a number of albums with the guitar-player Chris Newman. Her books, *The Irish Harper, volumes 1–2*, were published in 1991 and 2001. **Maeve Ellen Gebruers**

Nichol, Erskine (1825–1904), Scottish painter of genre subjects, landscapes, and watercolours. Born in Leith; studied at the Trustees' Academy, Edinburgh, under Sir William Allen and Thomas Duncan and became drawing master at Leith Academy. He visited Ireland between 1846 and 1850, working for the Department of Science and Art. He executed works exploring Irish life and character in a humorous manner, employing more caricature and satire than in his painting of similar Scottish themes. *An Ejected Family* (1853) is one of the few surviving paintings depicting poverty-stricken Ireland in the wake of the GREAT FAMINE; like most of Nichol's Irish subject pictures, it was executed on his return to Scotland. Following his return to Edinburgh he paid annual visits to Ireland. **Marie Bourke**

Nicholl, Andrew (1804–1886), topographical artist. Born in Belfast; apparently self-taught, and apprenticed to the Belfast printer H. D. Finlay, 1822–9. Having spent the years 1830–32 in London, he was a founder-member of the Belfast Association of Artists, 1836; his brother William was also a founder. Influenced by Turner, his work included numerous watercolour flower pieces and landscapes of the northern coast. He produced illustrations for periodicals and taught drawing both in Dublin and London. He departed for Ceylon (now Sri Lanka) c. 1745, where he became a teacher of landscape painting, scientific drawing, and design in Colombo. He illustrated Sir James Emerson Tenant's book on Ceylon (1860). Returning in 1849 or 1850, he lived between Dublin, London, and Belfast. He wrote for various periodicals and exhibited regularly at the Royal Academy (London) and ROYAL HIBERNIAN ACADEMY. He was elected a member of the RHA in 1870. **Brendan Rooney**

Nicholson, Asenath (1794–c. 1858), missionary and walking traveller. Born in Vermont, USA. She became fascinated by the cheerfulness and patience of the Irish immigrant poor in New York and in 1844 travelled to Ireland to study the people in their home environment. She avoided cities and the society of the well-off and delighted in spending her time in the countryside among the poor, reading to them from the Bible. She spent a year travelling extensively through Ireland, mostly on foot and alone, often covering as much as 32 km (20 miles) in a day and, though wearing 'india-rubber shoes', frequently suffering from blistered feet. When the GREAT FAMINE struck she returned to Ireland to work among the poor, buying and distributing food and Bibles, finally returning to the United States in 1852. **Michael Fewer**

Ní Chuilleanáin, Eiléan (1942–), poet. Born in Cork; educated at UCC and the University of Oxford. She lectures in Renaissance English at TRINITY COLLEGE, Dublin. She has published six main collections of new poetry: *Acts and Monuments* (1972), *Site of Ambush* (1975), *The Rose Geranium* (1981), *The Magdalen Sermon* (1990), *The Brazen Serpent* (1994), and *The Girl Who Married the Reindeer* (2001). She maps the human psyche through her poetic method of allowing abstract and concrete meanings to occupy the same space. In the same way adjacent dimensions of time and space are shown to be in continuously shifting, rather than fixed, relation to one another. Her poems' attention to these adjustments allows the buried voices in culture to speak, especially those of women. A focus of her more recent work is the sacred in history. This allows her to explore the potential for new life within the conditions of secrecy and suffering. **Catriona Clutterbuck**

Ní Dhomhnaill, Maighréad (1952–), traditional singer. Born in Kells, Co. Meath; her father, Aodh Ó Domhnaill, played flute, sang, and collected songs for the FOLKLORE COMMISSION in his native Rannafast, Co. Donegal. Her mother, from Gurteen, Co. Sligo, was also a singer and was involved in *claisceadal* song. Performing from childhood with her sister Tríona and brother Mícheál, Maighréad sang with them and Dáithí Sproule as Skara Brae in 1972 and with DÓNAL LUNNY's band up to 1998; she made her definitive solo album with him in 1991 and another with her sister Tríona in 1999. Her repertoire is based on songs gleaned from her father's collection and the extensive repertoire of her aunt, Neilí Ní Dhomhnaill. **Fintan Vallely**

Ní Dhomhnaill, Nuala (1952–), poet. Born in Lancashire, and raised from the age of five in Corca Dhuibhne, Co. Kerry; educated locally, in Limerick, and at UCC, where she was an influential member of the INNTI group of poets. She lived in the Netherlands and Turkey, returned to Ireland in 1980 and lived for a while in Corca Dhuibhne, Co. Kerry, later settling in Dublin. Well known for her poetry readings, she has travelled widely on the Continent and in the United States. Her poetry, though strongly grounded in a modernist mindset, draws its creative force from the symbolic universe of the IRISH LANGUAGE and tradition. Her first book, *An Dealg Droighin* (1981), illustrates the decay within all, which must be cleansed through the creative process to facilitate psychic healing. *Féar Suaithinseach* (1984) describes a lost innocence, obscured by overgrown weeds symbolising modern society, which she seeks to regain. *Feis* (1991), deeply influenced by Jungian psychology, is a highly structured, intense, internal IMMRAM or journey of individuation, from the dark hag-poems of the first section, 'Cailleach', to the joyous celebration of the final section, 'Spéirbhean'. *Cead Aighnis* (1998), with its emphasis on psychic loss and its striving for wholeness through repossession, builds on the previous work. Writing exclusively in Irish, she claims that 'the Irish poems are my babies,' and therefore untouchable; she has, however, collaborated with other poets by providing cribs for translating her work. The main editions in English are *Selected Poems* (1986), *Pharaoh's Daughter* (1990), *The Astrakhan Cloak* (1992), and *The Water Horse* (1999). **Gearóid Denvir**

Ní Dhomhnaill, Nuala. *Nuala Ní Dhomhnaill with her daughter Selale. While working solely in Irish she has collaborated with other poets in translations of her work. [Nuala Ní Dhomhnaill]*

Ní Dhonnchadha, Máire Áine (1919–1991), traditional singer. Born at An Cnoc, near Spiddle, Co. Galway; won a scholarship to training college, qualified as a primary teacher in 1941, and taught in Dublin and Galway. She was awarded a gold medal at the OIREACHTAS in 1950 and performed at the Edinburgh Festival in 1958 and the Irish-French Society's Festival of St Fiacre in Meaux, France. With Claddagh Records she recorded *Deora Aille*, *Traditional Music of Ireland*, and *Claddagh Choice*. **Liam Mac Con Iomaire**

Ní Dhuibhne, Éilís (1954–), writer. Born in Dublin; trained as a folklorist and archivist. Her writing engages in a range of cultural excavations. The short stories in *Blood and Water* (1988), *Eating Women Is Not Recommended* (1991), and *The Inland Ice and Other Stories* (1997) reinvent and appropriate FOLKLORE sources. *The Pale Gold of Alaska*, a collection of short stories, was published in 2000. *The Bray House* (1990), her first novel in English, is a chilling science fiction story that deploys traditional myths, particularly of Sí or OTHERWORLD women, within an environmental parable. Her second novel, *The Dancers Dancing* (1999), interweaves the coming-of-age narratives of four girls away from home for the first time in 1970s Donegal. **Gerardine Meaney**

Nielsen, Mike (1961–), JAZZ musician. Born in Sligo, son of the trumpeter Carl Nielsen; studied classical guitar with John Feeley before winning a scholarship to the leading American jazz school, Berkley College of Music, Boston, in 1982. He has played in varied line-ups, from guitar soloist with orchestra to guitar duo and larger jazz ensembles. He has featured in recordings with the American saxophonists Pat La Barbera and Dave Liebman and in a performance of his own Concerto for Jazz Guitar with the National Concert Orchestra, and released a trio album, a duo album with TOMMY HALFERTY, *In Two* (1997), and a solo album, *Solo at Garden City* (2000). Nielsen displays virtuoso ability and uses a classical guitar finger-plucking technique to achieve a distinctive sound. **Brian Trench**

Niemba ambush, Congo, West Africa. On 8 November 1960 a patrol consisting of eleven Irish soldiers, part of the UNITED NATIONS peacekeeping mission in the Congo (now Democratic Republic of Congo, formerly Zaire), set out from their base at Niemba to repair a makeshift bridge. They were ambushed by a force of several hundred local tribesmen; after a prolonged engagement nine of the UN soldiers, including the patrol commander, Lieutenant Kevin Gleeson, were dead. Most of the casualties were from arrow wounds. Two men, Private Thomas Kenny and Private Joe Fitzpatrick, survived in the jungle until they were found the following day, Kenny being particularly badly wounded. Trooper Anthony Browne, who displayed conspicuous bravery, was posthumously awarded the MILITARY MEDAL FOR GALLANTRY, the first person to receive this award. His body was not recovered until 1961. **Paul Connors**

Ní Fhoghludha, Áine (1880–1932), poet. Born in Ring, Co. Waterford; educated at UCC. She was active in CUMANN NA MBAN in Co. Tipperary; after 1916 her political activities cost her her teaching post. Her only collection is *Idir na Fleadhanna* (1922). **Diarmuid Breathnach and Máire Ní Mhurchú**

Ní Ghlinn, Áine (1955–), poet and children's author. Born in Co. Tipperary; educated at UCD. She worked for many years as a print and broadcast journalist, mainly in Irish-language media. She has published three collections of poetry: *An Chéim Bhriste* (1984), *Gairdín Pharthais* (1988), and the bilingual collection *Unshed Tears/Deora Nár Caoineadh* (1996), which deals with themes of emigration and child sexual abuse. She has also published fiction for young children and teenage non-fiction. **Máirín Nic Eoin**

Ní Ghráda, Máiréad (1896–1971), teacher, literary editor, and dramatist. Born in Kilmaley, Co. Clare; educated at UCD. A member of the GAELIC LEAGUE and CUMANN NA MBAN, she was imprisoned for her political activity. A pioneering writer and editor of women's and children's programmes in the early days of 2RN (later Radio Éireann), she was the first woman radio announcer in Ireland. As editor with the publishing house Browne and Nolan she produced many standard works for schools, as well as being a prolific dramatist. Her work in theatre culminated in the acclaimed production of AN TRIAIL (1964). **Eoghan Ó hAnluain**

Night of the Big Wind. On the night of Sunday 6 January 1839 an intense storm moving eastwards just north of Ireland caused extensive damage throughout the country. During the night it is estimated that about ninety people died (half of them at sea), many buildings were demolished, and extensive areas of forest were destroyed. The strength of the wind increased towards the centre of the storm, with speeds on the north coast averaging 36 m/s (80 miles/h) and gusts possibly over 45 m/s (100 miles/h). The central pressure of the storm at its height is estimated to have been about 925 hPa (925 mbar). Undoubtedly this storm was extreme in Irish circumstances, but the lack of warning and the fact that it occurred on the Epiphany (The Coming of the Magi) and at night also contributed to its lasting reputation. **Gerald Mills**

Ní Laoghaire, Máire Bhuí (1774–c. 1849), poet. Born in Ballingeary, Co. Cork, into the Clann Bhuí branch of Uí Laoghaire, whose former patrons were the MacCarthys of Muskerry. At eighteen she eloped and married Séamas de Búrca, a horse-dealer from Skibbereen. The couple settled near Keimaneigh, where they had six sons and three daughters. She composed love poems, devotional and humorous verse, elegies and laments but is best known for her political poetry, which conveys a vigorous hope for CATHOLIC EMANCIPATION. Her support for Repeal is unequivocal, and PASTORINI becomes her undisputed authority for the millenarian message she imparts in 'Tá Gaedhil Bhocht Cráidhte' and 'Cath Chéim an Fhiaidh', a graphic account of a skirmish between local rebels and the YEOMANRY. While it seems she was not literate, Ní Laoghaire represented a new generation of poets whose compositions were rooted in oral tradition. Her poems were orally transmitted and continue to be recited and sung, particularly in her native Co. Cork. **Meidhbhín Ní Úrdail**

Nimmo, Alexander (1783–1832), civil engineer. Born in Kirkcaldy, Fife, Scotland; educated at the Universities of St Andrews and Edinburgh. He carried out surveys of Irish bogs, 1811–14, and of the coastline, including new piers completed or under construction, many designed by him. He was engineer in charge of the Western District, 1822–32, and designed Wellesley Bridge (SARSFIELD BRIDGE), Limerick. **Ronald Cox**

Nine Years' War (1594–1603), the defining moment in English attempts to conquer Ireland for the first time. For much of the conflict such an outcome was far from apparent. Indeed the war is just as remarkable for being punctuated by a series of English military embarrassments, such as the defeat at what became known as the 'Ford of the Biscuits' (1594), where an English supply column was routed. Rebel Irish forces led by HUGH O'NEILL, Earl of Tyrone, and RED HUGH O'DONNELL had further successes, such as those at the Battle of Clontibret (1595) and the Battle of the Curlew Mountains (1599). The most dramatic rebel victory occurred at the BATTLE OF THE YELLOW FORD (1598), when a royal army over 4,000 strong was virtually annihilated, being reduced to 1,500 men. For a time, English control in Ireland, such as it was, teetered on the brink of extinction. With O'Neill unable to press home his military advantage because of a lack of siege skills in reducing the walled towns, the prospects of an ultimate victory for the rebel forces took a decided upturn with the arrival in 1601 of experienced Spanish soldiers at KINSALE. Previous rebel military victories had relied to a large extent, though not exclusively, on ambuscade and hit-and-run tactics; at Kinsale, O'Neill's army was forced to attempt an entirely conventional military battle, with the decided disadvantage of having undergone a prolonged march along the entire length of Ireland in winter conditions. As it turned out, O'Neill's disastrous defeat at Kinsale frustrated his aspirations of defeating the royal forces outright. Despite this, he managed to hold out against the determined onslaught of Crown forces for a further sixteen months (see p. 596). During this time a series of royal garrisons were planted in Ulster, while a lethal campaign of starvation and extermination was unleashed against the population in rebel-held territories, leading to the reported deaths of tens of thousands. In the end the English army was unable to defeat O'Neill outright. The war had cost the Crown coffers the enormous sum of £2 million, while the imminent death of ELIZABETH I in 1603 changed the political complexion of the war. Senior English military and official figures, fearing that the ascension of JAMES I to the throne would offer O'Neill an opportunity to seek a rapprochement with the English Crown, concluded the war by agreeing to the TREATY OF MELLIFONT in 1603. **John McCavitt**

Niníne Éces (fl. 700), poet. He probably belonged to the Uí Echdach northern KINSHIP group, which had lands to the south and west of Armagh and produced many distinguished scholars and ecclesiastics. The Patrician hymn 'Dóchas Linn Naomh Pádraig' is based on an early poem addressed by Niníne to ST PATRICK, 'Admuinemmar nóeb-Pátraicc' ('We invoke holy Patrick'). **Séamus Mac Mathúna**

Ní Riain, Nóirín (1951–), *sean-nós* singer. Born in Lough Gur, Co. Limerick; she has made the performance of spiritual songs of Irish and other traditions her life study. Her MA dissertation 'Traditional Religious Song in Irish' was followed by numerous recordings, most notably that of 1989 with monks from Glenstal Abbey, Co. Limerick. Her publications include *Stór Amhrán* (1988), a collection of traditional songs, and *The Gregorian Chant Experience* (1997). **Fintan Vallely**

Ní Scolaí, Máire (1910–1985), singer, collector and broadcaster of Irish folk song. Born in Dublin; moved to Galway, where she taught, sang, and acted; she later travelled extensively, singing at concerts and making broadcasts. The best of her recordings have been reissued by GAEL-LINN. **Liam Mac Con Iomaire**

Ní Uallacháin, Pádraigín (1950–), researcher and singer. Born in Drogheda, Co. Louth. She has long collected the songs of her ancestral south Ulster, releasing two solo recordings, *An Dara Craiceann* (1995) and *An Dealg Óir* (2002); she has been granted a fellowship by the Northern Ireland Community Relations Executive and Queen's University to record and publish the remainder. She has published two albums of children's songs, *A Stór 's a Stóirín* (1994) and *When I Was Young*, with Len Graham (1996). **Lillis Ó Laoire**

Nobel Prize, the leading international award for outstanding achievement. The prize has been presented since 1901 under the will of the Swedish chemist and inventor of dynamite, Alfred Nobel. It is awarded annually in the categories of physics, chemistry, medicine, literature, and world peace; a further prize, for economics, was added from 1969. A committee of Swedish academics awards five categories, while the peace prize is selected by members of the Norwegian Parliament. The prize is accompanied by a substantial financial presentation. Irish Nobel laureates have been in the fields of literature, peace, and the sciences, with awards being made to W. B. YEATS (1923, literature); GEORGE BERNARD SHAW (1925, literature); ERNEST WALTON (1951, joint winner with Ernest Cockcroft, physics); SAMUEL BECKETT (1969, literature); SEAN MACBRIDE (1974, joint winner with Eisaku Sato, peace); Mairead Corrigan and Betty Williams (1976, peace); SEAMUS HEANEY (1995, literature); JOHN HUME and DAVID TRIMBLE (1998, peace). [see MARCONI, GUGLIELMO.] **Brian Lalor**

Nolan, Christopher (1965–), writer. Born in Mullingar, Co. Westmeath; brain damage at birth left him physically disabled, but

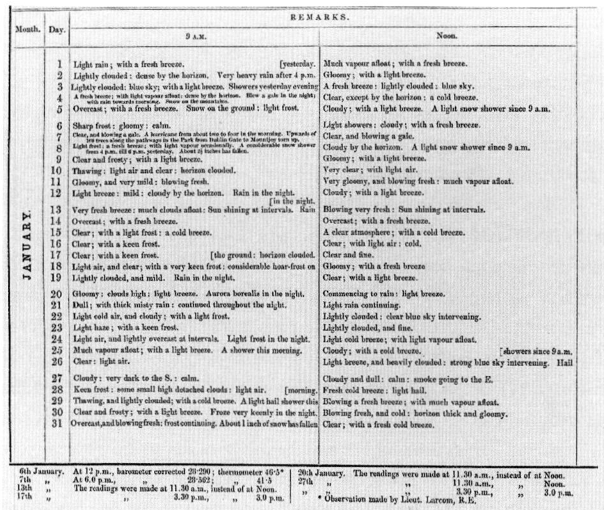

Month.	Day.	REMARKS. 9 A.M.	REMARKS. Noon.
JANUARY.	1	Light rain; with a fresh breeze. [yesterday.	Much vapour afloat; with a fresh breeze.
	2	Lightly clouded: dense by the horizon. Very heavy rain after 4 p.m.	Gloomy; with a light breeze.
	3	Lightly clouded: blue sky; with a light breeze. Showers yesterday evening	A fresh breeze: lightly clouded: blue sky.
	4	A fresh breeze; with light vapour afloat: dense by the horizon. Blew a gale in the night; with rain towards morning. Snow on the mountains.	Clear, except by the horizon: a cold breeze.
	5	Overcast; with a fresh breeze. Snow on the ground: light frost.	Cloudy; with a light breeze. A light snow shower since 9 a.m.
	6	Sharp frost: gloomy: calm.	Light showers: cloudy; with a fresh breeze.
	7	Clear, and blowing a gale. A hurricane from about two to four in the morning. Upwards of [illegible] trees along the pathways in the Park from Dublin Gate to Mountjoy torn up.	Clear, and blowing a gale.
	8	Light frost: a fresh breeze; with light vapour occasionally. A considerable snow shower from 4 p.m. till 6 p.m. yesterday. About 2½ inches has fallen.	Cloudy by the horizon. A light snow shower since 9 a.m.
	9	Clear and frosty; with a light breeze.	Gloomy; with a light breeze.
	10	Thawing: light air and clear: horizon clouded.	Very clear; with light air.
	11	Gloomy, and very mild: blowing fresh.	Very gloomy, and blowing fresh: much vapour afloat.
	12	Light breeze: mild: cloudy by the horizon. Rain in the night.	Cloudy; with a light breeze.
	13	Very fresh breeze: much clouds afloat: Sun shining at intervals. Rain [in the night.	Blowing very fresh: Sun shining at intervals.
	14	Overcast; with a fresh breeze.	Overcast; with a fresh breeze.
	15	Clear; with a light frost: a cold breeze.	A clear atmosphere; with a cold breeze.
	16	Clear; with a keen frost.	Clear; with light air: cold.
	17	Clear; with a keen frost. [the ground: horizon clouded.	Clear and fine.
	18	Light air, and clear; with a very keen frost: considerable hoar-frost on	Gloomy; with a fresh breeze
	19	Lightly clouded, and mild. Rain in the night.	Clear; with a light breeze.
	20	Gloomy: clouds high: light breeze. Aurora borealis in the night.	Commencing to rain: light breeze.
	21	Dull; with thick misty rain: continued throughout the night.	Light rain continuing.
	22	Light cold air, and cloudy; with a light frost.	Lightly clouded: clear blue sky intervening.
	23	Light haze; with a keen frost.	Lightly clouded, and fine.
	24	Light air, and lightly overcast at intervals. Light frost in the night.	Light cold breeze; with light vapour afloat.
	25	Much vapour afloat; with a light breeze. A shower this morning.	Cloudy; with a cold breeze. [showers since 9 a.m.
	26	Clear: light air.	Light breeze, and heavily clouded: strong blue sky intervening. Hail
	27	Cloudy: very dark to the S.: calm.	Cloudy and dull: calm: smoke going to the E.
	28	Keen frost: some small high detached clouds: light air. [morning.	Fresh cold breeze: light hail.
	29	Thawing, and lightly clouded; with a cold breeze. A light hail shower this	Blowing a fresh breeze; with much vapour afloat.
	30	Clear and frosty; with a light breeze. Froze very keenly in the night.	Blowing fresh, and cold: horizon thick and gloomy.
	31	Overcast, and blowing fresh: frost continuing. About 1 inch of snow has fallen	Clear; with a fresh cold breeze.

6th January. At 12 p.m., barometer corrected 28·290; thermometer 46·5*
7th " At 6.0 p.m., " 28·362; " 41·5
13th " The readings were made at 11.30 a.m., instead of at Noon.
17th " " 3.30 p.m., " 3.0 p.m.

20th January. The readings were made at 11.30 a.m., instead of at Noon.
27th " " 11.30 a.m., " Noon.
" " 3.30 p.m., " 3.0 p.m.
* Observation made by Lieut. Larcom, R.E.

Night of the Big Wind. *Observations by Captain Lacroom in his meteorological journal record the storm of 6 January 1839. Some gusts were possibly over 45 m/s (100 miles/h). [Board of Trinity College, Dublin]*

nevertheless he was educated at TCD. He published *Dam Burst of Dreams* (1981) at the age of sixteen and in 1987 his autobiography, *Under the Eyes of the Clock*, which won the Whitbread Award. **Joley Wood**

Nolan, J. J. [John] (1888–1952), experimental physicist. Born in Omagh, Co. Tyrone; educated at UCD. In 1917 he was awarded a doctorate of science on published work on the electrification of water. With his brother, PATRICK J. NOLAN, he set up a laboratory to research atmospheric electricity at University College, Dublin, which established an international reputation on atmospheric ions and aerosols, with practical applications to pollution, smoke and fog detection still cited in current literature. He held the chair of experimental physics at University College, Dublin, 1920–52, and was elected president of the ROYAL IRISH ACADEMY, 1949. In 1947 he advised the DE VALERA Government on the establishment of the DUBLIN INSTITUTE FOR ADVANCED STUDIES. **Alex Montwill**

Nolan, Patrick J. (1894–1984), experimental physicist. Born in Omagh, Co. Tyrone; educated at UCD. In 1914 he won a travelling studentship to the University of Cambridge, where he was involved in pioneering alpha scattering experiments under Ernest Rutherford and J. J. Thomson, which led to the discovery of the atomic nucleus. He returned to University College, Dublin, in 1920 as lecturer and became professor of geophysics in 1953. His research interests were centred on atmospheric electricity, on which subject he and his brother J. J. NOLAN became international authorities. Elected to the ROYAL IRISH ACADEMY in 1947, he was later vice-president. He was awarded the BOYLE MEDAL by the ROYAL DUBLIN SOCIETY in 1971 and was awarded an honorary doctorate of science by TRINITY COLLEGE, Dublin. **Alex Montwill**

Nollekens, Joseph (1737–1823), sculptor. Born in London; apprenticed to Peter Scheemakers in 1750. Having been awarded numerous premiums from the Society of Arts, he went to study in Rome in 1762. He received the patronage of a number of Grand Tourists. He returned to England in 1770, was elected an associate of the Royal Academy in 1771 and a member the following year, exhibiting at the academy regularly until 1816. Though he is best known for his consistently neo-classical portrait busts, his Irish works include the Leslie Monument at St Malachy's Church, Hillsborough, Co. Down, and the memorial to the family of Dr Welbore Ellis in CHRIST CHURCH Cathedral, Dublin. During his career he amassed a considerable fortune, which he bequeathed to three friends. **Brendan Rooney**

non-marital births. Social sanctions against child-bearing outside marriage were severe up to the middle of the twentieth century, sustained in part by strict religious injunctions against pre-marital sexual relations. In the early 1960s fewer than 2 per cent of births in Ireland were outside marriage; from then on, public attitudes began to change. The Abortion Act (1967) in England contributed to a softening of traditional Catholic hostility to non-marital child-bearing, as this hostility came to be represented as an added pressure on pregnant single women in Ireland to seek an abortion in Britain. Following a recommendation from the COMMISSION ON THE STATUS OF WOMEN in 1972 the Government introduced an unmarried mother's allowance in 1973, which further eased the situation of unmarried mothers. By 1980 the proportion of births outside marriage was still low, at 5 per cent of all births, but thenceforth it increased rapidly and by 1999 had risen to 32 per cent. Non-marital child-bearing is now most common among younger mothers: virtually all births to teenage mothers and two-thirds of births to mothers aged twenty to twenty-four are outside marriage, while fewer than 10 per cent of births to mothers aged thirty to thirty-four are outside marriage. Little is known about the pattern of relationships between the fathers and mothers of children born outside marriage, though the indications are that certain proportions are in quasi-marital relationships at the time of birth, and many others marry or enter quasi-marital relationships at some point following the birth of the child. **Tony Fahey**

Norse. *A runic inscription on a cross shaft fragment at Killaloe, Co. Clare, which reads '[Th]urgrim risti [kr]us thina' (Thurgrim carved this cross), as well as an ogham inscription, 'Bendacht [ar] Torogr[im]' (A blessing on Thurgrim). [Dúchas, The Heritage Service]*

Non-Subscribing Presbyterian Church, the liberal wing of the Irish Presbyterian tradition, dating from its refusal in 1910 to impose a compulsory subscription to the Westminster Confession of Faith on its ministers and elders. The church now has 3,500 members, all of them in Northern Ireland. **Gabrielle Brocklesby**

Nore, River, a river approximately 140 km (87 miles) in length that drains a catchment area of 2,500 km^2 (965 sq. miles). It rises in Co. Tipperary, drawing its headwaters from streams in the Slieve Bloom and Devilsbit Mountains. Its course is easterly at first but turns south-easterly near Mountrath, Co. Laois, to flow through Co. Kilkenny, until it meets the River BARROW near New Ross, Co. Wexford. Flowing over limestone, the channel is relatively narrow but increases in width downstream. There is a significant level of tillage west of the river, but grassland farming is more important; to the east of the river there is a predominance of mixed livestock enterprises. The river flows through the town of Kilkenny, where Kilkenny Castle was built on a good site overlooking the river after 1172. Further south it flows through Thomastown, a medieval walled town, and on to Inistioge, by which point it has widened to about 30 m (100 ft). Here an eighteenth-century bridge of ten arches spans the river, and the village is also noted for its charming tree-lined square and the ruins of an early thirteenth-century Augustinian priory. The river is tidal below this point and is navigable, though only at high water, for the next 30 km (20 miles). Salmon fishing is an important activity, as is trout fishing, especially upstream of Thomastown. **Joseph Brady**

Norris, David (1944–), lecturer, Joycean scholar, senator, and campaigner for gay rights. Born in Dublin; educated at TCD. He has lectured in English literature at Trinity College, Dublin, since 1968. First elected to SEANAD ÉIREANN in 1987, he was re-elected in 1989 and has held his seat since. In 1988 he secured a ruling from the EUROPEAN COURT declaring that Irish laws criminalising homosexual acts contravened the EUROPEAN CONVENTION ON HUMAN RIGHTS, though it was 1993 before the law was changed. He is the recipient of various awards, including the Diplôme d'Honneur from the Centre for the Study of Sexual Minorities, Paris, and the gold medal of the Brazilian Academy of Letters, 1997. He is Irish trustee of the International Joyce Foundation and chairman of the JAMES JOYCE Cultural Centre. **Ciarán Deane**

Norse language and influence. Irish was influenced by the language of the Norsemen, who, if the ANNALS are to be believed, had established permanent settlements around the Irish coasts before AD 985. They gave Irish many seafaring terms: their *hábora*, rowlock, gave the Irish *ábhar*; their *akkeri*, anchor, became Irish *acaire*; *dorg*, fishing-line, became Irish *dorú*; *styri*, rudder, became Irish *stiúir*. Their interest in commerce is reflected in the number of words assimilated into Irish. Norse *mál*, tax, gave Irish *mál*; *mangari*, pedlar, became Irish *mangaire*; *markaðr*, market, gave Irish *margadh*. We must thank them too for *bjórr*, beer, Irish *beoir*, for *vindauga*, window, Irish *fuinneog*, for *lopt*, loft, Irish *lochta*, for *baunir*, bean, Irish *pónaire*, and for many other homely words. They left us some place-names: for example *Ueig-fjorðr*, 'fjord of Ueig', became Wexford; *Ueðra(r)-fjorðr*, 'ram fjord' or 'windy fjord', became Waterford; *Uíkar-ló*, 'meadow of the bay', became Wicklow. The Norsemen had been completely assimilated into Irish culture long before the emergence of EARLY MODERN IRISH and the introduction of English and French after 1169. **Diarmaid Ó Muirithe**

Norse place-names. The number of place-names of Norse origin is comparatively small—surprisingly so in view of the more than two centuries (from c. 795 onwards) during which the speakers of that language, the VIKINGS, had direct dealings with Ireland, first as raiders and then as settlers. (This is in contrast to the marked Norse influence on the place-names of the northern and western islands and highlands of Scotland.) Most Norse names occur on or near the eastern and southern coasts. The Norse name (if such it be) furthest from the sea appears to be *Leixlip* (possibly from Norse *Laxhlaup*, 'salmon leap'), Co. Kildare. Some of the names are wholly Norse, such as *Waterford*, *Wexford*, and *Wicklow*, while others are translations, in whole or in part, of Irish names; the most celebrated of the latter is *Dublin*, Norse *Dyflin* (from Old Irish *Dublinn*). **Nollaig Ó Muraíle**

North Bull Island, Dublin, a flat island 5 km (3 miles) long and rising 6 m (20 ft) above high water that arose from the sea when harbour works at the mouth of the River LIFFEY from the eighteenth century onwards interrupted sediment flows in DUBLIN BAY. The island, noted for its sand-dune and saltmarsh ecosystem, is now a UNESCO world biosphere site as well as Ireland's first bird sanctuary, declared in 1930. It has a resident population of twenty-two (1996) as well as two golf courses; the Royal Dublin Golf Club claims to be the second-oldest in Ireland, having been founded in 1885. Access other than by a timber bridge is by a causeway, added in 1964–5, which many people fear will lead ultimately to the silting up of the flats between the island and Dollymount shore, an overwintering site for the 3,000 Brent Geese from Arctic Canada, and feeding ground for up to 30,000 waders. **Stephen A. Royle**

Northern Fiddler, The (1979), a book by Allen Feldman and Éamonn O'Doherty. An artistically conceived ethnography, it documents the scope, details and personality of the FIDDLE music of Cos. Donegal and Tyrone, using graphic images, personal interviews, and repertoire. O'Doherty's introduction establishes the historical framework for the MUSIC in Ireland; Feldman's sociological overview places the musicians in a changing society. The book's thirty-two drawings and sixty-one photographs are by O'Doherty (see p. 559); the 191 pieces of music were transcribed by ANDREW ROBINSON from recordings made by the authors and Natalie Joynt. The research and writing were undertaken between 1977 and 1979, with grants from the ARTS COUNCIL OF NORTHERN IRELAND. The published tunes—REEL, JIG, highland, strathspey, MARCH, air, hornpipe, barn dance, and mazurka—show the strong influence of Scotland in Donegal music's sound, while the text demonstrates, in Feldman's words, 'the single-minded commitment of a few gifted musicians deeply involved in a classical consciousness of form and style.' Twenty-five players were recorded, thirteen in Co. Donegal, twelve in Co. Tyrone, most of them born at the end of the nineteenth century, which renders their orally acquired, socially functional music an important bridge into the era of recording transmission and genre-specific listening. The book carries tune notations taken from JOHN AND SIMON DOHERTY, Con Cassidy and Danny O'Donnell of Co. Donegal, and John Loughran, Peter Turbit and John McKeown of Co. Tyrone. John Doherty's influential recording *Bundle and Go* was compiled from the project's tapes. The original drawings, photographs and recordings are now in the Irish TRADITIONAL MUSIC ARCHIVE, Dublin. **Fintan Vallely**

Northern Ireland

Area: 14,160 km^2 (5,241 sq. miles)
Population: 1,685,257 million (2001)
Population, Local Government districts (2001): Antrim 48,366; Ards 73,244; Armagh 54,263; Ballymena 58,610; Ballymoney 26,894; Banbridge 41,392; Belfast 277,391; Carrickfergus 37,659; Castlereagh 66,488; Coleraine 56,315; Cookstown 32,581; Craigavon 80,671; Derry 105,066; Down 63,828; Dungannon 47,735; Fermanagh 57,527; Larne 30,832; Limavdy 32,422; Lisburn 108,694; Maherafelt 39,780; Moyle 15,933; Newry & Mourne 87,058; Newtownabbey 79,995; North Down 76,323; Omagh 47,952; Strabane 38,248
Capital: Belfast
Counties: Antrim, Armagh, Derry/Londonderry, Down, Fermanagh, Tyrone
Provinces: Ulster (part of)
Geographic features: Belfast Lough, Carlingford Lough, Lough Erne, Lough Foyle, Lough Neagh, Strangford Lough; Glens of Antrim, Mourne Mountains, Sperrin Mountains; River Bann, River Blackwater, River Erne, River Foyle, River Lagan; Giant's Causeway
Historical interest: Armagh Cathedral, Carrickfergus Castle, Derry City walls, Downpatrick Cathedral, Navan Fort (Eamhain Macha)
Industry and products: Aerospace/ Shipbuilding, Agriculture and Food, Clothing and Textiles, Computers and Information Technology, Tourism

Joseph Brady

Created as a region of the United Kingdom by the Government of Ireland Act (1920), coming into being in May 1921. Its origins are to be found in the crisis of 1912–14, when Northern unionists, supported by the Conservative Party, were prepared to resist the establishment of a parliament in Dublin by force of arms if necessary. By the late spring of 1914 both the Conservative opposition and the Liberal government were concluding that the PARTITION of Ireland was the obvious solution, but neither was able to convince their Irish allies. When the third HOME RULE Bill was enacted in September 1914, the Prime Minister, Asquith, made it clear that there would be amending legislation to make special provision for Ulster. A crucial step was taken by the ULSTER UNIONIST COUNCIL following the 1916 RISING, when it was agreed to accept partition and that Cos. Monaghan, Cavan and Donegal should not be included.

Following the 1918 general election the Ulster Unionists found themselves in a position vastly more favourable than they had been in on the eve of the war. More than half the members of the House of Commons were Conservatives (still calling themselves Unionists), very sympathetic to Northern Protestant aspirations. Abstentionist SINN FÉIN had supplanted all but six Nationalist MPs, led by JOSEPH DEVLIN; what ARTHUR BALFOUR described as 'the blessed refusal of Sinn Féiners to take the OATH OF ALLEGIANCE in 1918' allowed Ulster Unionists to work out an arrangement to suit themselves, at leisure and with the minimum of interference. That arrangement was the Government of Ireland Act (1920), whose provisions were drawn up by a Cabinet committee chaired by WALTER LONG, a former leader of the Irish Unionist MPs. In the House of Commons, Unionists asserted that they were making a 'supreme sacrifice' in accepting the terms, but it was they who decided on devolution, for, as Captain Charles Craig said, 'without a parliament of our own constant attacks would be made upon us,

Northern Ireland. *Unionist supporters of the peace agreement outside the Europa Hotel, Belfast, 18 April 1998, where David Trimble MP, leader of the UUP, was meeting the Ulster Council to decide the party's position on the Belfast Agreement; the Grand Opera House is on the left. [Leon Farrell/Photocall Ireland]*

and constant attempts would be made ... to draw us into a Dublin parliament.' The decision of the Ulster Unionist Council in 1916 to ask for no more than six counties still stood. A devolved parliament representing all nine counties of Ulster would have a very fragile Unionist majority, as CRAIG further explained: 'A couple of members sick, or two or three members absent for some accidental reason, might in one evening hand over the entire Ulster parliament and the entire Ulster position.'

When elections were held for the new Northern Ireland Parliament in May 1921, the Unionists won forty of the fifty-two seats in the Northern Ireland House of Commons. Their position was by no means impregnable, however. Northern Ireland had a violent birth. During the late spring of 1920 the Anglo-Irish War had edged into Ulster, and furious intercommunal violence erupted, particularly in Belfast, Derry, and Lisburn. George V opened the Northern Ireland Parliament in June 1921, at considerable personal risk; and the IRA truce the following month did not operate north of the new border. The ANGLO-IRISH TREATY of December 1921 also posed a mortal threat: article XII provided for a BOUNDARY COMMISSION, which nationalists assumed would award Derry, Newry, and swathes of Cos. Fermanagh and Tyrone to the IRISH FREE STATE. The most intense period of violence was during the first six months of 1922, when in Belfast alone 236 people were killed. The IRA's hope was that Northern Ireland would become so destabilised that it could not survive. The government in Belfast, however, took resolute action to counter its opponents. The ROYAL ULSTER CONSTABULARY, modelled on the ROYAL IRISH CONSTABULARY, was created in April 1922 as an armed force; in the same month the adoption of special powers enabled suspects to be held without trial; on occasion, the assistance of the British army could be called upon; above all, the rapid expansion of the Special Constabulary so increased the level of policing that there was a constable for every six families by June 1922.

The Unionist government had an unexpected stroke of good fortune at the end of June 1922: the bombardment of the FOUR COURTS in Dublin signalled the start of the CIVIL WAR, and it was not long before IRA activists had pulled back to take part in it. Peaceful conditions had almost completely returned by 1923. The Civil War also postponed the implementation of the Boundary Commission until 1924. Because the Free State had only one representative, only trifling BORDER changes were recommended. The leaked report was suppressed, and as a result Craig was triumphantly successful in ensuring that Northern Ireland would cede 'not an inch.'

By the end of 1925, therefore, Northern Ireland seemed secure. Following the orgy of intercommunal violence between 1920 and 1922 there was not a single sectarian murder between 1923 and 1933. Nationalists had little choice but to accept that they would be marooned within a Unionist-controlled region of the United Kingdom for some time to come, and their elected representatives began to end their boycott of local authorities and of the Northern Ireland Parliament. This seemed to be a particularly appropriate moment for the Unionist government to ensure future stability by magnanimity towards the Catholic minority; but the opportunity was not taken.

Though they did little to assuage them, neither Craig nor his colleagues had created the intercommunal tensions that plagued Northern Ireland from the outset. Such divisions were remarkably parallel to those that manifested themselves after the FIRST WORLD WAR in the states emerging from the collapsed Austro-Hungarian, Russian, Turkish, and German Empires. Of these only Austria had a fairly homogeneous population; all were to suffer from bitter divisions between citizens with clashing cultural traditions and aspirations. In Northern Ireland the fact that a third of the population was so hostile to the state that it hoped for its downfall would have taxed the ingenuity of any government. Protestants believed that Catholics were aiming for nothing less than the destruction of the state; Northern Catholics felt that they had been abandoned by the Free State and Éire government, and that they had suffered a marked deterioration in their position as a result of partition and the new constitutional arrangements. Mounting criticism in the British press from the autumn of 1921 had left Ulster Unionists feeling embattled and isolated. The opportunity was not taken to attempt to cajole Catholics into accepting the status quo, however reluctant. When Nationalists began to take their seats in the Northern Ireland Parliament they found it a disheartening experience. Local government boundaries were adjusted by blatant GERRYMANDERING following the abolition of proportional representation in 1922; Catholic schools were not as well funded as state schools; and there were numerous instances of members of the government positively discouraging Catholics from entering the public service.

The healing of wounds was inhibited by unexpected economic difficulties. As Northern Ireland came to birth, significant shifts in the pattern of world trade severely affected Ulster's staple export industries. This protracted depression, intensifying after the Wall Street crash of 1929, not only made it impossible to bring Catholics back into the shipyards, mills, workshops, and factories from which they had been expelled in 1920 but also left many Protestants without work. Between 1931 and 1939, 27 per cent of the insured work force was unemployed. Deprivation levels rose; when compared with six British cities, Belfast had the lowest infant mortality rate in 1901 but in 1938 the highest; maternal mortality actually rose by a fifth between 1922 and 1938; and the mortality rate from tuberculosis was 20 per cent higher in Northern Ireland than in Britain. The byzantine financial provisions of the Government of Ireland Act left the Unionist government with little room for manoeuvre, and in many areas—notably that of HOUSING—it failed to adhere to its policy of staying 'step-by-step' with Britain in welfare legislation.

The SECOND WORLD WAR exposed the shortcomings of an ageing Unionist administration that had become indolent, complacent, unheeding, and tolerant of petty corruption. Craigavon died in 1940, and his successor, JOHN ANDREWS, proved equally incapable of organising efficient war production and protecting citizens from air attack. In the worst of three German air raids nearly a thousand people lost their lives during the BELFAST BLITZ on the night of 15/16 April 1941. Sir BASIL BROOKE was fortunate in ousting Andrews in 1943, when the tide of war had changed and the region had become a significant arsenal of victory.

Allied gratitude to Northern Ireland while Éire had remained neutral ensured an unhesitating reaffirmation of Northern Ireland's constitutional position in the IRELAND ACT (1949) and a reluctance on London's part to look more closely at how the Unionist government operated. During the quiet years after the war, living standards rose steadily, in part because the British Treasury was prepared to underwrite the additional costs involved in providing health and other welfare services. However, this greatly increased expenditure was to set a time bomb ticking that would eventually explode in 1968–9. Most of the new dwellings and services were provided by local authorities, which failed to ensure the fair allocation of jobs and council houses.

In 1963 TERENCE O'NEILL became Prime Minister, the first to state clearly that reconciliation was a central part of his programme. Despite genuine conciliatory gestures, however, O'Neill eventually created intense frustration by his inability to deliver thoroughgoing reform; at the same time, more and more loyalists were convinced he was conceding too much. Assisted by televised reports of direct action abroad, a powerful CIVIL RIGHTS MOVEMENT emerged predominantly on the Catholic/Nationalist side. By 1969 Northern Ireland was in a state of near-revolutionary crisis, leading to the fall of O'Neill in April and the placing of the British army on the streets in mid-August.

Welcomed by Catholics at first, the soldiers were soon regarded as agents of the STORMONT regime, particularly after the Prime Minister, BRIAN FAULKNER, introduced INTERNMENT in August 1971. Virtually all prisoners arrested were from the Nationalist community. The outcome was an increase in violence (particularly on the part of the PROVISIONAL IRA), intimidation, and intercommunal conflict (see p. 1081). The British government imposed DIRECT RULE in March 1972 and soon afterwards formulated a policy that was to be pursued for the next three decades: Northern Ireland was to have a form of self-government restored to it, on condition that power was shared between Protestant and Catholic

Northern Ireland. *Waterfront Hall, Belfast, opened in 1997 as a national and international centre for concerts, arts and entertainment as well as a venue for business and sports events. [Northern Ireland Tourist Board Photographic Library]*

representatives and that there should be some recognition of an 'Irish dimension'. The first experiment in power-sharing devolution was torpedoed by the majority of voters in February 1974 and by the ULSTER WORKERS' COUNCIL STRIKE in May. While further efforts to find political solutions ran into the sand, Northern Ireland was becoming the most continuously disturbed part of Western Europe since the end of the SECOND WORLD WAR. If the voters of Northern Ireland could not agree on a constitutional compromise, then those in power in London and Dublin would have to impose their own. That view was strengthened by the upsurge in support for Sinn Féin during and after the 1981 HUNGER STRIKES, and it was put into effect in the ANGLO-IRISH AGREEMENT (1985)—a treaty subsequently registered with the UNITED NATIONS, which gave the Republic an enhanced consultative role in Northern Ireland. Unionists were outraged and conducted a protracted campaign against this 'diktat'. The Provisional IRA, finding that the agreement included acceptance by Dublin of a British presence in part of Ireland, continued its campaign of bombings and shootings with the aid of arms from Libya.

An alarming upsurge in paramilitary violence in the early 1990s revitalised behind-the-scenes attempts to end the violence by agreement. The outcome was the IRA 'cessation' of 1 September 1994, followed by the loyalist ceasefire in October and a dramatic improvement in the quality of life for all citizens. Despite a temporary resumption of the IRA campaign in 1996, punishment beatings and shootings, and bitter disputes over contentious parades, notably at DRUMCREE, the NORTHERN IRELAND PEACE PROCESS was never halted. Following seemingly interminable discussions and a high level of involvement by leaders of the British, Irish, and American governments, the BELFAST AGREEMENT (1998) won the acceptance of most political parties and the main paramilitary organisations.

It took time to activate the new institutions, in particular the Northern Ireland Assembly, and the agreement was constantly imperilled by intercommunal tension and disagreements over the decommissioning of arms and over police reform. Nevertheless, Northern Ireland entered the twenty-first century as a much safer and more prosperous region than it had been a decade earlier. It was widely observed that Parliament Buildings had never been as lively, busy and accessible as when the Assembly was in session (see p. 791). In short, if the institutions set up in 1998 were to fall, public pressure for them to return would not be long in coming. [see NORTH-SOUTH ECONOMIC LINKS; NORTHERN IRELAND HOUSING EXECUTIVE.] **Jonathan Bardon**

Northern Ireland, establishment of. The establishment of Northern Ireland was foreshadowed in the debates over some form of Ulster exclusion during the HOME RULE debates in 1912–14 and in DAVID LLOYD GEORGE's proposal in 1916 to retain six Ulster counties under the British Parliament. During the 1918 general election the Conservative party secured from Lloyd George a pledge not to submit 'the six counties of Ulster to a Home Rule parliament against their will.' The Cabinet Committee on the Irish Question, which reported on 4 November 1919, recommended a form of PARTITION, whereby there would be a parliament in Belfast for the nine counties of Ulster and one in Dublin for the rest of Ireland. A Council of Ireland with twenty representatives from each parliament would provide a mechanism for Irish unity through consent. Fearing that a nine-county parliament would leave the Unionists with too slim a majority, JAMES CRAIG worked successfully to convince the Cabinet to confine the proposal to six counties; he was supported in this by influential Conservatives, notably ARTHUR BALFOUR, who believed six counties would provide a more homogeneous division. This formed the basis of the Cabinet decision of 24 February 1920 that 'Northern Ireland' was to consist of Cos. Antrim, Armagh, Derry, Down, Fermanagh, and Tyrone, including the cities of Belfast and Derry. It was opposed by EDWARD CARSON, for whom it was a betrayal of Southern loyalists; but other unionists welcomed it as providing a guarantee of a permanent majority. Nationalist members, such as JOSEPH DEVLIN, opposed it for the same reason. Despite the opposition of unionists in Cos. Donegal, Cavan, and Monaghan, the terms of the bill were endorsed by the ULSTER UNIONIST COUNCIL.

With the enactment of the Government of Ireland Act on 23 December 1920, the Unionists could begin to prepare for their new parliament and government. In January 1921 the Ulster Unionist Council voted that Craig should be prime minister, Carson having demurred. The following May, Unionists won forty of the fifty-two seats for the Northern Ireland parliament, which was opened by George V on 22 June. Even so the position of Northern Ireland was not quite secure, with Lloyd George putting pressure on CRAIG in the course of his negotiations with SINN FÉIN. Northern Ireland's position was tenaciously defended by ANDREW BONAR LAW. The Anglo-Irish Treaty signed on 6 December 1921 permitted the parliament of Northern Ireland to vote itself out of the jurisdiction of the proposed IRISH FREE STATE, which it did on 7 December 1922. **T. G. Fraser**

Northern Ireland: constitution. Northern Ireland's constitutional status as a devolved government and administration within the United Kingdom was established by the Government of Ireland Act (1920). Powers not transferred included those relating to the Crown, the making of peace or war, armed forces, foreign treaties, COINAGE, weights and measures, LAND ANNUITIES, the Post Office, Customs and Excise, and income tax. Because of these reserved powers, twelve members were elected to the House of Commons in London.

The devolved Parliament consisted of the Crown (represented by the Governor), the Senate, and the House of Commons. The Governor gave, in the monarch's name, the Royal Assent to bills and had the power to summon, prorogue, or dissolve the Parliament. Twenty-four senators were elected by the House of Commons and were joined by the Lord Mayor of Belfast and the Mayor of Derry. Legislative authority rested with the fifty-two-member House of Commons, from whose ranks the Government of Northern Ireland was drawn. The Executive Committee, or Cabinet, was headed by the Prime Minister and comprised the heads of the following departments: Finance, Home Affairs, Labour and National Insurance, Education, Agriculture, Commerce, Health, and Local Government. From 1921 to 1972 (when the Northern Ireland Parliament was suspended) the constitution was the only example of devolved government within the United Kingdom and therefore attracted some scholarly interest. Any possible lessons for Scotland and Wales tended to be vitiated by the sectarian nature of politics and the fact that the government never changed hands. The BELFAST AGREEMENT (1998) provided for the repeal of the Government of Ireland Act, setting Northern Ireland on a different constitutional foundation. **T. G. Fraser**

Northern Ireland Assembly. Not long after it had imposed DIRECT RULE in 1972, the British government planned an Assembly elected by proportional representation and the formation of an Executive with power shared between Catholic and Protestant representatives. The first Assembly was elected on 28 June 1973, and despite the opposition of a majority of Unionists, an overall majority there approved the SUNNINGDALE AGREEMENT. The power-sharing Executive fell, however, in May 1974, and the British government closed down the Assembly in July.

A second Assembly—arising out of the plan by the Secretary of State for Northern Ireland, James Prior, for 'rolling devolution'—was elected on 20 October 1982. Though nationalists fought the election, they refused to take part in the proceedings. As a consequence the 'Prior' Assembly was merely a Unionist talking-shop, and few noticed when it was wound up in 1986.

A third Assembly was created by the BELFAST AGREEMENT (1998). The result of the first elections on 25 June 1998 was: ULSTER UNIONIST PARTY twenty-eight; SOCIAL DEMOCRATIC AND LABOUR PARTY twenty-four; DEMOCRATIC UNIONIST PARTY twenty; SINN FÉIN eighteen; ALLIANCE PARTY six; United Kingdom Unionist Party five; Progressive Unionist Party two; Northern Ireland Women's Coalition two; Others three. Eighty of the 108 members of the Assembly were in favour of the Belfast Agreement. **Jonathan Bardon**

Northern Ireland Assembly. *The Assembly in session at Stormont, the unionist benches in the bottom foreground, the nationalists directly opposite. Deputy First Minister Seamus Mallon (left, standing) is speaking. First Minister David Trimble sits opposite. [Pacemaker]*

Northern Ireland Civic Forum, established under the BELFAST AGREEMENT (1998), with its first meeting in October 2000. It consists of an independent chairman and sixty voluntary nominees, appointed originally for three years, from among various sections of 'civil society' (seven business, seven trade union, eighteen voluntary and community, five churches, four arts and sport, four culture, three agriculture and fisheries, two education, two community relations, two victims, and three each nominated by the First Minister and Deputy First Minister). Reporting to the Office of the First Minister and Deputy First Minister, the forum's role is to advise the Executive and the Assembly on economic, social and cultural matters.

Its inclusion among the new institutions represented a significant gain for the Northern Ireland Women's Coalition in the negotiations leading to the Belfast Agreement, embodying their ideological commitment to a 'new politics' of participatory democracy and active citizenship and an intention that nationalist-unionist rapprochement should not marginalise other issues, nor the civic and community leaderships that had secured influence under direct rule. As a result, the forum had a mixed reception from local party elites. Despite initial proposals from some quarters that it be established as a neo-corporatist second chamber, akin to Seanad Éireann, parallels are to be found rather in a new style of consultative body recently established in Dublin, Edinburgh, London, and elsewhere. **Richard Jay**

Northern Ireland Civil Rights Association: see CIVIL RIGHTS; COALISLAND TO DUNGANNON MARCH; DERRY CIVIL RIGHTS MARCH.

Northern Ireland Economic Council (NIEC), an independent advisory body set up in 1997 by the Secretary of State for Northern Ireland. Following the establishment of the Northern Ireland Assembly in 1998, the NIEC reports to the First Minister and Deputy First Minister. The NIEC has a wide remit in providing independent advice on the development of ECONOMIC POLICY. It performs this role through a range of publications, covering the issues of health and social care priorities, research and development, ECONOMIC DEVELOPMENT, linkages and inward investment, local economic development, the improving of schools, and the regional economic and policy impacts of European monetary union. The council has fifteen members, all of whom are appointed by the First Minister and Deputy First Minister. There are five independent members, one of whom is the chairperson; five members represent trade union interests and are nominated by the IRISH CONGRESS OF TRADE UNIONS; and five represent industrial and commercial interests and are nominated jointly by the Confederation of British Industry and the Chamber of Commerce and Industry. The NIEC has a small staff of economists and administrators. **Douglas Hamilton**

Northern Ireland Equality Commission. The Northern Ireland Equality Commission was established under the Northern Ireland Act (1998) and took over the functions previously exercised by the Commission for Racial Equality for Northern Ireland, the Equal Opportunities Commission for Northern Ireland, the FAIR EMPLOYMENT COMMISSION, and the Northern Ireland Disability Council. The commission's task is to use its powers to enforce both specific Northern Ireland equality legislation on disability, fair EMPLOYMENT, fair treatment and race relations, and UK equality legislation on sex discrimination, race relations, disability DISCRIMINATION, and equal pay, as well as the specific duties regarding equality and fair treatment in policy-making placed on public authorities by the Northern Ireland Act. The commission's objectives are to promote equality of opportunity in employment practices and in economic and social policy and to promote awareness of equality of opportunity. The commission's first chairperson is Joan Harbison (former chairperson of the Commission for Racial Equality for Northern Ireland). The commission may be seen as the social and economic counterpart of the Northern Ireland Human Rights Commission. [see DISCRIMINATION.] **Eithne McLaughlin**

Northern Ireland Heads of Government

1921–40	Sir James Craig
1940–43	John Miller Andrews
1943–63	Sir Basil Stanlake Brooke
1963–9	Terence Marne O'Neill
1969–71	James Dawson Chichester-Clarke
1971–2	Arthur Brian Deane Faulkner
1972–98	Direct rule from London
1998–2001	David Trimble/Seamus Mallon
2001–	David Trimble/Mark Durkan

Northern Ireland Housing Executive. The unfair allocation of council HOUSING by local authorities was a major grievance of the CIVIL RIGHTS MOVEMENT; and in the Downing Street Declaration (1969) both the Northern Ireland and British governments pledged themselves to set up a central housing body. The Northern Ireland Housing Executive, which began to operate in March 1971, faced formidable problems: decades of public housing neglect (the government was described by a minister as 'the largest slum landlord in Europe'); 4,670 households forced to move as a direct result of the violence in the summers of 1969 and 1971; and 22,000 tenants in public housing on rent and rates strike. In Northern Ireland as a whole 20 per cent of the total housing stock was still officially unfit in 1974. The executive's main work was done in the mid-1980s, when it spent approximately £100 million a year; the result is that Northern Ireland has some of the finest and most visually pleasing public housing in Ireland or Britain. **Jonathan Bardon**

Northern Ireland Labour Party (NILP), established in 1924, based on the old Belfast Labour Party. Throughout its existence most of its activity remained confined to its city of origin. Attempts to stress the primacy of social and economic issues did not hide difficulties created by its lack, before 1949, of a stated policy on partition; members' capacity to express varying views on the subject provided cause for continuing strains and defections. Early electoral successes were overturned by the abolition of proportional representation in local government (1922) and parliamentary elections (1929), though a brief revival followed the SECOND WORLD WAR. Its decision in 1949 to support the existing constitutional position split the party but eventually enabled it to attract the protest votes of Protestant workers disaffected by economic malaise during the later 1950s. Attempts in the 1960s to attract cross-community support through the advocacy of some reform met with moderate success, until internal disputes, and the communal polarisation of the later 1960s, led to desertions by increasing numbers of Protestants and Catholics. With the new ALLIANCE PARTY offering a centrist alternative, the NILP's precipitate decline had made it irrelevant long before it was wound up in the early 1980s. [see LABOUR PARTY.] **Alan Scott**

Northern Ireland peace process. Northern Ireland was dominated by chronic political violence from the late 1960s onwards. While security responses from the British government contained the conflict, basic grievances and aspirations among nationalists and unionists remained unsatisfied. Seven British government political initiatives to secure agreement between moderate nationalists and unionists in the period 1973–90 ended in failure.

The peace process, beginning in the early 1990s, took a different approach. It was based on the principle of inclusion, attempting to involve all parties to the conflict in the hope that a comprehensive accord could be reached. The development of the process relied on a strong relationship between successive British and Irish governments and their mutual interest in lessening violence and securing a long-term agreement that would receive the support of majorities in both communities, thus undermining the legitimacy of political violence. The President of the United States, Bill Clinton, was another strong supporter of peace initiatives.

The process was also dependent on the willingness of the main loyalist and republican paramilitary organisations to announce a ceasefire, which they did in 1994. Secret talks between the governments and the paramilitary organisations gradually led to more formal negotiations, involving most of Northern Ireland's political parties. These culminated, after many setbacks, in the BELFAST AGREEMENT (1998), which received 70 per cent support in a subsequent Northern Ireland REFERENDUM (see p. 788). The agreement was comprehensive, paving the way for a new devolved NORTHERN IRELAND ASSEMBLY, institutional links with the Republic and with the devolved assemblies of Scotland and Wales, the release of prisoners, and police and judicial reform. Many unionists, however, felt that the process favoured nationalists and were suspicious of their reluctance to engage in disarmament.

The peace process did not mark an end to sectarian hatred or violence; instead it was a series of compromises that allowed conflicting parties to share power in a less violent environment. **Roger MacGinty**

Northern Ireland political collection: see LINEN HALL LIBRARY.

Northern Ireland Railways (NIR), a state authority set up by the Transport Acts (1966 and 1967), having operated as Ulster Transport Railways between those dates. The establishment of NIR allowed what remained of the railway system to escape the influence of the road bias consistently exhibited by its predecessor, the Ulster Transport Authority; but it inherited a truncated, run-down network, shorn of its freight business and with track, rolling stock and stations in poor repair. NIR nevertheless pursued a positive policy, reconnecting the Belfast termini that had been severed by the closure of the Belfast Central Line, upgrading track and signalling, and acquiring new equipment. In this it had to contend from the 1970s to the 1990s with the activities of paramilitaries, who were responsible for the widespread destruction of buildings and rolling stock.

In 1995, together with Ulsterbus and Citybus, NIR came under a common board of management, which adopted the service name Translink. The stated aim was to co-ordinate road and rail services, but a fear was expressed that the bias would once more incline in favour of road. This fear would appear to have been justified by the publication by Translink in March 2000 of a report recommending the investment of £183 million over ten years to address safety-related issues on NIR and the response of the responsible minister that such financing was not available, while at the same time the establishment of a task force to review the future, if any, of the rail network was announced. This new threat provoked strong reaction from a wide political and public spectrum, Translink stressing, with particular reference to the upgraded Enterprise service, that investment had a positive effect on passenger numbers. In the event, however, a radical change of policy towards rail transport was reflected in the reopening of the shorter route from Belfast to Derry, the upgrading in 2002 of the Belfast–Bangor commuting line, and in the same year the placing of an order for twenty-three new train sets, the largest single procurement by a Northern Ireland railway undertaking. **Bernard Share**

Northern Ireland Social and Political Archive (ARK), a resource on the worldwide web that provides access to a range of material on the social and political life of Northern Ireland. It was set up to facilitate public involvement in the new political life of Northern Ireland by building a bridge between the wider community and the research information held in institutes of higher education. A joint initiative of Queen's University, Belfast, and the University of Ulster, it is aimed at schoolchildren, policy-makers, academics, voluntary and community groups, journalists, and any citizen with an interest in social issues in Northern Ireland. It consists of a number of linked resources, including the following:

The Northern Ireland Life and Times Survey is a resource for anyone interested in the social attitudes of people living in Northern Ireland. An annual survey, begun in 1998, it asks questions on a wide range of social issues. The range of topics varies from year to year. However, questions on community relations and political attitudes are included each year, allowing for time-series analysis, which is important in a rapidly changing political environment. Life and Times participates in the International Social Survey Programme, in which the same set of questions on a particular theme is asked in approximately forty countries each year. Background information, tables of results, questionnaires, publications, and the data to download are freely available on the web site.

Conflict Archive on the Internet (CAIN) is an encyclopaedic web site providing a wide range of information and source material on the 'TROUBLES' in Northern Ireland from 1968 to the present day. Information is divided into three sections: background to the conflict (such as abstracts on organisations, bibliographies, and chronologies), important events of the conflict (such as the CIVIL RIGHTS campaign, INTERNMENT, and the ULSTER WORKERS' COUNCIL STRIKE), and central issues (such as politics, elections, and violence). It also provides information on society and politics in the region. Extensive collections of photographs and murals are also maintained on the site.

The Online Research Bank (ORB) provides a searchable bibliography and summaries of research relating to social policy. A range of academic and government research is featured, as well as material from voluntary organisations.

Surveys On Line provides results and questionnaires from other influential Northern Ireland social surveys in the same manner as that of the Northern Ireland Life and Times web site.

The Survey Analysis Unit provides technical support for groups that have the need, but not the resources or skills, to carry out secondary analyses of large-scale survey data. **Paula Devine**

Northern Ireland Statistics and Research Agency (NISRA), established in 1996 as Northern Ireland's official statistics organisation. With its head office in Belfast and a staff of over 250, the agency carries out social research and publishes vital statistical information. The data provided by the agency is used in the formation of policy in many government departments, such as Education, Health, and Agriculture. The NISRA is also responsible for the registration of births, deaths, marriages, and adoptions. [see CENTRAL STATISTICS OFFICE.] **Myra Dowling**

Northern Ireland Tourist Board (NITB), established by the Northern Ireland Development Tourist Traffic Act (1948). Its original remit included the registering of catering establishments and assisting in the development of amenities and services that would promote tourist traffic; it is now part of the Department of Enterprise, Trade, and Investment. Its annual budget was approximately £13.5 million in 2001. The board has three divisions: Marketing, Corporate Policy, and Investment. It is responsible for the inspection of accommodation and the granting of permits to operate, and publishes recommended lists of where to stay. It also handles advertising, research, and product development and offers an advisory service to the industry.

Northern Ireland has never been an easy place to market as a tourist destination, being physically similar to its bigger neighbours, the Republic and Scotland. In 1958 the NITB listed the problems with TOURISM as follows: the shortness of the holiday season, lack of coaches, poor access to attractions, including the GIANT'S CAUSEWAY, inadequate signposting, litter, and a shortage of hotels and restaurants. By 1969 the board was dealing with problems of infrastructure and had established an overseas marketing campaign. Tourist trips had increased in number from 633,000 in 1959 to 1,080,000 in 1967.

The civil disturbances of the early 1970s led the NITB to cease advertising in overseas markets other than Britain. In 1975 it began a sales drive aimed at Dutch and German tourists, portraying Northern Ireland as a destination for outdoor activity holidays. The recession of the early 1980s coincided with wide media coverage of the HUNGER STRIKES; but this time the NITB carried out an intense programme of overseas marketing aimed at maintaining its market position. By 1990 numbers had reached 1.15 million, overtaking the 1967 peak for the first time.

The NITB has been criticised for ignoring Northern Ireland's political violence in its publications. While most commercial guidebooks offered the visitor information on what to expect (including security checks and the presence of armed soldiers) and on which areas were best avoided, the NITB remained silent on the matter, concentrating instead on the beautiful unspoilt countryside that awaited the visitor. During 2001 a new all-Ireland tourism company, Tourism Ireland, established by the North-South Ministerial Council, took over all the NITB's external and overseas offices, with the exception of the Dublin office. [see BORD FÁILTE.] **Alannah Hopkin**

Northern Ireland Women's Rights Movement, formed in 1975, principally to campaign for the extension to Northern Ireland of the Sex Discrimination Act. Its membership was dominated by Communist Party and trade union activists. The organisation resembled the civil rights movement rather than non-hierarchical, woman-only feminist groups. It produced a Women's Charter, campaigning for parity of rights with British women while remaining neutral on the constitutional link. In 1980 it opened a women's centre in Belfast, set up Rent-a-Creche, and provided space for 'unity meetings', though republican feminists remained separate. It co-ordinated International Women's Day events throughout the 1990s under the auspices of the Downtown Women's Centre. **Margaret Ward**

north-south economic links. The most significant formal economic links between the Republic and Northern Ireland are those dealt with under the auspices of the north-south co-operation and implementation bodies established under the BELFAST AGREEMENT (1998). Six implementation bodies are provided for: Waterways Ireland, the Food Safety Promotion Board, the Trade and Business Development Body, the Special EU Programmes Body, the North-South Language Body, and the Foyle, Carlingford, and Irish Lights Commission. In addition there were six matters for co-operation through the mechanism of existing bodies in each jurisdiction:

Nugent. Count Laval Nugent *(1873) in a portrait by three artists, Michele Canzio, Tommaso Darin, and Francesco Beda. [Pomorski i Povijesni Muzej Hrvatskog Primorja Rijka]*

TRANSPORT, AGRICULTURE, EDUCATION, HEALTH, ENVIRONMENT, and TOURISM. It appears that the broadest implementation body, the Trade and Business Development Body, will concentrate on trade promotion between the two regions and on matters relating to indigenous firms on both sides of the border, rather than on the more controversial matters relating to attracting foreign investment. The specific areas of implementation include devising new approaches to cross-border business development in research, training, marketing, and quality improvement, promoting north-south trade and supply chains, and supporting business by making recommendations to increase competitiveness in such areas as the availability of skills, telecommunications, information technology, and 'e-commerce'. **John W. O'Hagan**

Nowlan, David (1936–), drama critic. Born in Dublin; educated at TCD. He was been senior drama critic of the IRISH TIMES, 1979–2001 (where he was also medical correspondent, 1969–87, and managing editor, 1989–), a post in which, with the recent exception of FINTAN O'TOOLE, he has been the most influential commentator on the theatre in Ireland. **Richard Pine**

Nua-Nós, a contemporary music ensemble. Formed in 1990 and conducted by Dáiríne Ní Mheadhra, the group premiered numerous works by Irish contemporary composers as well as performing Irish premieres of works by Contintental composers, such as Gruber, Schnittke, and Shostakovich, and have broadcast on RTÉ Radio and BBC Radio Ulster. One of the last appearances by the ensemble was in 1994 at a week-long festival, organised by RTÉ, celebrating the works of Irish composers. Nua-Nós specialised in performing the works of GERALD BARRY, recording a CD of his music in Canada in 1993. **Geraldine Guiden**

Nugent, Count Lavall, von Westmeath (1777–1862), Austrian field-marshal. Born in Ballinacor, Co. Wicklow. He joined the Austrian engineer corps, serving as lieutenant and then captain, distinguishing himself in the Napoleonic wars, 1800–5. Promoted to general chief of staff in 1809, he led the conquests of Croatia, Istria, and the Po region. He commanded the Austrians in Naples in 1816 and was made a prince of the Holy Roman Empire and a magnate of Hungary. He became a field-marshal in 1849. At eighty-two he was present as a volunteer at the Battle of Solferino (1859). **David Kiely**

Nuinseann, Uilliam, also known as William Nugent (1550–1625), poet. He was sent to England with his brother Christopher under the protection of the Earl of Sussex in 1559; he attended the University of Oxford but returned to Ireland in 1573 without graduating. Sonnets in English attributed to him have not survived. He composed two poems in Irish on the death of Cúchonnacht Óg Mag Uidhir in 1608 and another poem for GIOLLA BRIGHDE Ó HEÓDHUSA when he joined the Franciscan order in 1607. His poems of exile reflect a growing sense of Irishness, caused both by physical absence and by the Renaissance recovery of the classical concept of *patria*. **Mícheál Mac Craith**

nursing. The introduction of statutory registration bodies between 1918 and 1919 led to considerable advances in the practice and status of general nursing and MIDWIFERY. In 1950, in the light of expanding health services and important social and scientific changes affecting the practice of MEDICINE, the Government of the Republic replaced these bodies with An Bord Altranais (the Nursing Board). Later statutes changed the role and constitution of the board; and nursing also became subject to EU directives. Nursing was comprehensively examined by a Government commission that reported in 1998, its recommendations becoming the basis of public policy.

Nursing careers offer a choice between general, psychiatric and mental handicap nursing, consisting of a mixture of clinical and theoretical instruction, which involves links between training HOSPITALS and higher education institutions. During 2001 there were approximately 50,000 nurses on the register, a large proportion of them employed in the public service.

In Northern Ireland the regulation of the nursing profession is the responsibility of the National Board for Nursing, Midwifery and Health Visiting, the main training centres being the School of Nursing and Midwifery at Queen's University, Belfast, and the School of Nursing and Midwifery at Altnagelvin Area Hospital, Derry. **Joseph Robins**

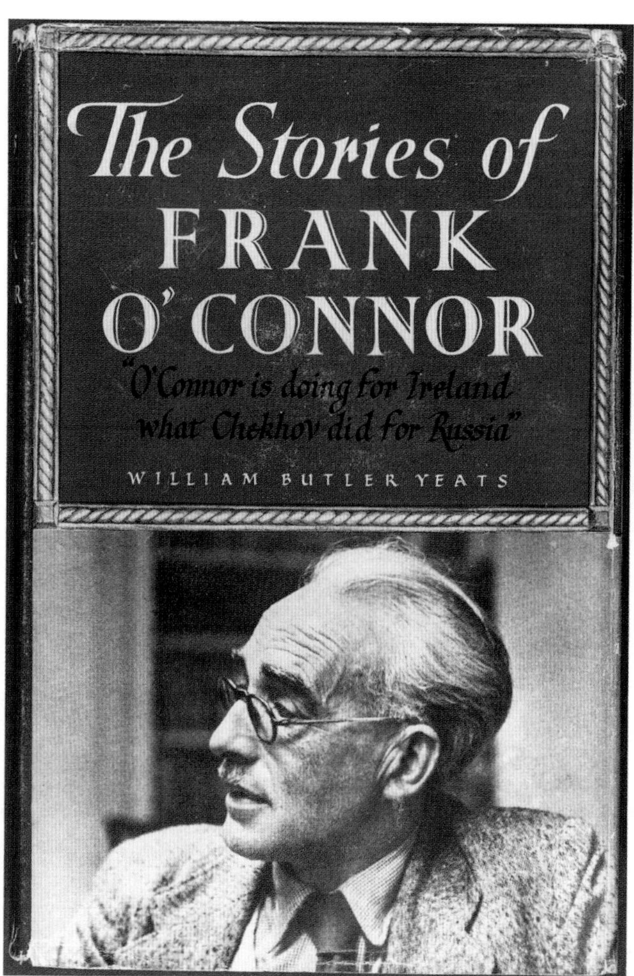

O'Connor, Frank
(see page 805). The jacket of Frank O'Connor's first retrospective collection of short stories, edited by W. B. Yeats. O'Connor was one of Ireland's best-known short-story writers of the middle of the twentieth century. [Courtesy of Lilly Library, Indiana University, Bloomington, IN/ © Mark Faurer, Courtesy Gallery 292, NYC]

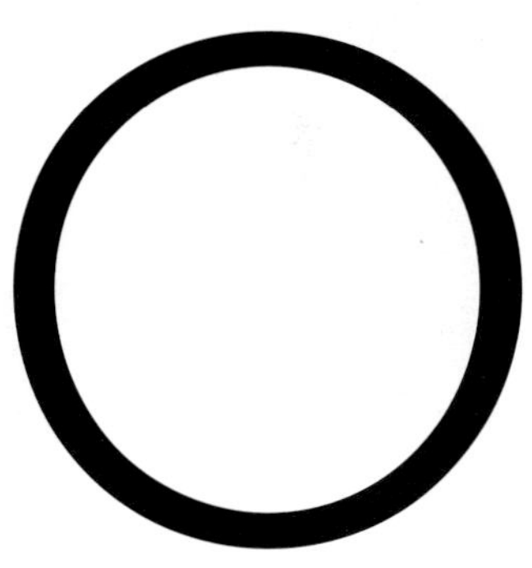

Oath of Abjuration. By an English act of 1702, extended to Ireland, office-holders were called on to swear that James Stuart (The Old Pretender, son of JAMES II) had no claim to the British thrones. A stir was raised in 1709, when those priests who remained legally in Ireland were required to take this oath. Only thirty-three out of over a thousand did so. This rendered the presence of the rest in the country illegal. However, the mass refusal meant that imposition of the oath was impossible. **C. D. A. Leighton**

Oath of Allegiance. Proposals to allow Catholics to declare their allegiance to the Hanoverian dynasty were long stymied by the JACOBITISM of Catholics and the desire of Protestants to tack theological statements onto the proposed oaths. An act of the Irish Parliament, probably noting the provisions then being made for Catholics in QUÉBEC, provided an oath in 1774. Bishops and laity divided acrimoniously over the acceptability of this oath, but by 1778 opposition to it had ceased. **C. D. A. Leighton**

O'Boyle, Seán (1908–1979), song collector and broadcaster. Born in Belfast; educated at QUB. He collected songs from Aodh Ó Duibheannaigh in Rannafast, Co. Donegal, 1937–45, which were published with notation in *Cnuasacht de Cheoltaibh Uladh* (1944). He collected a hundred items of Ulster folk music for the BBC, 1952–4, many of which were broadcast in the series 'As I Roved Out'. His publications include *The Irish Song Tradition* (1976) and the posthumous *Ogham: The Poet's Secret* (1980). **Pádraigín Ní Uallacháin**

Ó Briain, Muircheartach (c. 1050–1119), King of Munster and High King of Ireland. He first came to notice in 1075 as governor of the Hiberno-Norse city of Dublin. By 1084 he was associated with his father, Toirdhealbhach, in the kingship of Munster; he succeeded him in 1086 but had to struggle to secure his position. By 1096 he was master of Munster, Leinster, and Connacht; from then on he campaigned to bring the whole of Ireland under his sway. His main opponent was Domnall Mac Lochlainn, King of CENÉL NEOGHAIN. He came closest to achieving his goal in 1101, when he completed a triumphant circuit around Ireland and presided over the SYNOD of Cashel; however, he never quite succeeded in dominating the north. Dynamic, modernising, subtle, and outward-looking, he was also active in the politics of Scotland, the Isle of Man, and Wales, for which he incurred the wrath of Henry I of England and a trade embargo in 1102. He was patron of the church reform movement but his power was waning by the SYNOD OF RÁTH BHREASAIL (1111). He was deposed following illness in 1114 and died at Lismore, Co. Waterford, in 1119. **Anthony Candon**

O'Brien, Edna. *Since the publication of Edna O'Brien's first novel,* The Country Girls *(1960), she has remained a controversial figure in Irish writing. [John Minihan]*

O'Brien, Catherine (1881–1963), stained-glass artist. Raised in Newmarket-on-Fergus, Co. Clare, then studied in Dublin under WILLIAM ORPEN at the Metropolitan School of Art. SARAH PURSER invited her in 1906 to join AN TÚR GLOINE, her Dublin stained-glass co-operative, and enabled her to study stained glass in England and France. Early panels attracted critical notice, as did her leatherwork. Over thirty-four years An Túr Gloine became her life and livelihood as she steadily produced windows, such as those for Kinsale, Co. Cork, and Coolcarrigan, Co. Kildare. In 1940, after Purser's retirement, she managed the studio until it closed in January 1944, when she bought it out. **Nicola Gordon Bowe**

O'Brien, Charlotte Grace (1845–1909), writer and social reformer. Born in Cahirmoyle, Co. Limerick, daughter of WILLIAM SMITH O'BRIEN, who was exiled when she was three. Raised at Cahirmoyle and Dromoland, she began to be politically active in 1880. A supporter of PARNELL, she also opened an emigrant home in Queenstown (Cobh), Co. Cork, campaigned for improved ship-board conditions, and championed emigrant rights. **Anne Colman**

O'Brien, Conor Cruise (1917–), writer, historian, academic, and politician. Born in Dublin; educated at TCD. He served with the Department of Foreign Affairs and was Dag Hammarskjöld's UNITED NATIONS representative in the former Belgian Congo in 1960, an experience that became the basis of *To Katanga and Back* (1962), which established his international reputation. Following academic appointments in Ghana and the United States he served as Minister for Posts and Telegraphs, 1973–7, when he vigorously opposed the campaign of the PROVISIONAL IRA. His then unfashionable but increasingly influential views on the Northern Ireland question had been outlined in his semi-autobiographical *States of Ireland* (1972). Following electoral defeat in 1977 he devoted himself to letters and journalism, producing notable works on the Israel-Palestine conflict and on EDMUND BURKE. Always suspicious of the intersection of literature with nationalist politics, he has never hesitated to give his writings a keen polemical edge. [see GUBU.] **Terence Brown**

O'Brien, Denis (1958–), businessman. One of Ireland's best-known young entrepreneurs, he was chairman and chief executive officer of the Esat Telecom Group, which he founded. He sold the company to British Telecom in 2000 and set up the E-Island group. He is chairman and chief executive officer of Communicorp, which controls the Dublin radio station 98 FM, and chairman of the organising committee for the Special Olympics in Ireland in 2003. **Jim Power**

O'Brien, Dermod (1865–1945), portrait and landscape painter. Born at Foynes, Co. Limerick, a grandson of WILLIAM SMITH O'BRIEN; studied painting in Paris, Antwerp, and London. Returning to Dublin in 1901, he became a prominent figure, serving as president of the ROYAL HIBERNIAN ACADEMY, 1910–45, the Irish Agricultural Wholesale Society, and vice president of the ROYAL IRISH ACADEMY OF MUSIC. He was an academic painter, but his style loosened when he was painting familiar scenes, such as the SHANNON, the LIFFEY, and DUBLIN BAY. Until 1920 he lived periodically at his family home at Cahirmoyle, Co. Limerick; his depictions of farming and family life there are among his most sensitive works. **Anne Millar Stewart**

O'Brien, Edna (1936–), novelist and short-story writer. Born in Tuamgraney, Co. Clare; educated at the Pharmaceutical College, Dublin. She left Ireland for London in 1959. THE COUNTRY GIRLS (1960), the first in a trilogy of novels offering a frank semi-autobiographical account of a young Irish woman's sexual development, was banned in Ireland. Other fiction, including *August Is a Wicked Month* (1965), *A Pagan Place* (1970), *The High Road* (1988), *The House of Splendid Isolation* (1994), and *In the Forest* (2002) followed a predominantly though not exclusively realist tradition. Pre-empting many concerns of the WOMEN'S MOVEMENT, O'Brien has been seen as both pioneering and controversial for her treatment of female sexuality, incest, and adultery. **Eve Patten**

O'Brien, Fitz-James (1828–1862), writer. Born in Co. Cork and raised in Co. Limerick; educated at TCD. He left for London in 1849, squandered his inheritance, and sailed for America in 1851. In New York he maintained a bohemian life by churning out fiction, poetry, plays, and journalism. During the American Civil War he joined the Union Army and died of wounds in April 1862. His literary reputation rests on a handful of skilfully executed and sometimes menacing fantasy stories, including 'Seeing the World' (1857), 'The Diamond Lens' (1858), 'The Wondersmith' (1859), and 'What Was It?' (1859). **Richard Haslam**

O'Brien, Flann, pen-name of Brian O'Nolan (1911–1966), novelist and columnist. Born in Strabane, Co. Tyrone; educated at Synge Street CBS, Dublin, Blackrock College, and UCD. His first literary personae were those of Brother Barnabas and Count O'Blather in UCD college magazines; in these early pieces

O'Brien's wit and satire can be enjoyed in nascent form. His vision is at once comic and seriously rebellious, taking its cue from JAMES JOYCE's increasing emphasis on style and form; he has therefore been labelled a post-modern writer. His first novel, AT SWIM-TWO-BIRDS (1939), is a brilliantly subversive work, with the characters of the story wresting control of the narrative from their 'author', thus attacking notions of novelistic as well as other forms of 'authority'. In a specifically Irish context the playful commingling of genres by placing characters from Old Irish epics and cowboys from popular fiction registers wonderfully the diversity of cultural reference available in a supposedly backward and narrow Ireland. O'Brien's next work, *The Third Policeman*, could not find a publisher in 1940 and was published posthumously in 1967. While the author's comic and absurdist spirit is very much in evidence, there is a darkness present in the novel too. *An Béal Bocht* (1941) (published in English as *The Poor Mouth* in 1964) demonstrated O'Brien's ability to wield his satirical axe in relation to Irish. This is a magnificent satire on the state of the language in post-independent Ireland, which investigates the gap between official attitudes to the language and the realities. In this novel, as in his previous work, O'Brien's focus is on style itself as he mercilessly parodies the work of writers such as TOMÁS Ó CRIOMHTHAINN. In 1940 the IRISH TIMES asked him to contribute a humorous column, 'Cruiskeen Lawn', which he did under yet another pseudonym, Myles na gCopaleen (taken from a DION BOUCICAULT character); a selection of these columns was brought together in *The Best of Myles* (1985). Two late novels, *The Hard Life* (1961) and *The Dalkey Archive* (1964), while displaying signs of the comic and subversive genius of the earlier work, are somewhat laboured and obvious in comparison with them. However, all O'Brien's writing offers a genuinely funny and quirky view of Irish life. **Derek Hand**

O'Brien, Kate (1897–1974), novelist, playwright, and essayist. Born in Limerick; educated at Laurel Hill Convent and UCD. After a brief marriage she lived mostly in England, 1920–50, apart from a year in Spain as a governess, 1922–3. A successful play, *Distinguished Villa* (1926), began her writing career. Her novels include *Without My Cloak* (1931), *The Ante-Room* (1934), *Mary Lavelle* (1936), banned in Ireland, *Farewell Spain* (1937), banned in Spain, THE LAND OF SPICES (1941), banned in Ireland, and *That Lady* (1946). She lived in Roundstone, Co. Galway, from 1950 and published *Teresa of Avila* (1951), *The Flower of May* (1953), and *As Music and Splendour* (1958). She returned to England in 1960, where she died.

O'Brien wrote from within a Catholic middle-class consciousness yet was subtly critical of it. Her education gave her cultural access to the Continent, enhanced by her period in Spain. The experience of her books being banned in both Ireland and Spain in the 1930s alerted her to the fact that freedom, personal and intellectual, could not be taken for granted. The romance, plot, and style of some of her novels allowed her to be dismissed by critics for a time; now she is regarded as a complex and perceptive feminist writer whose best work, including her travel and historical writing,

O'Brien, Flann. *Flann O'Brien (pen-name of Brian O'Nolan) at Clifton Avenue, Monkstown, Dublin. Novelist, newspaper columnist, and master of many voices, he wrote his* Irish Times *'Cruiskeen Lawn' column under the name of Myles na gCopaleen.* [Irish Times]

O'Brien, Kate. *The feminist writer Kate O'Brien began her literary career in 1926 with a successful play,* Distinguished Villa, *which ran in London for three months. [Prof. L. Reynolds Collection/Ireland of the Welcomes]*

challenges the restrictions of censorship and explores the difficulties of self-determination for women in the creative, sexual, intellectual, and political aspects of life. **Riana O'Dwyer**

O'Brien, Máire Rua (c. 1615–c. 1686). Born in Co. Clare. She married three times. Her second husband was Conor O'Brien of LEAMANEH CASTLE, Co. Clare, who was killed in 1651 fighting against the Cromwellian forces. Following his death she petitioned the government to secure the family property for her sons. She subsequently married John Cooper, a Cromwellian soldier and land speculator, a marriage that also helped protect the O'Brien lands in Co. Clare from forfeiture in the 1650s. Máire Rua is best known for the FOLKLORE associated with her name, which depicts her as a ferocious and lustful woman. She is said to have refused to receive the mortally wounded Conor at Leamaneh, saying, 'We want no dead men here,' and to have immediately travelled to Limerick and demanded a Cromwellian soldier as a husband. She was also reported to have murdered John Cooper and to have had several other husbands, who also died in suspicious circumstances. In fact there is a gap of several years between Conor O'Brien's death and her marriage to John Cooper; she made her will as Mary Cooper in June 1686 and probably died shortly thereafter. **Mary O'Dowd**

O'Brien, Matthew (born 1837), marine engineer and hero of the American Civil War (1861–6). He was brought to North America at the age of six; he trained as a merchant ship engineer in New Orleans. Like many of the hundreds of Irish seamen who joined the navy of the Confederacy, he saw in the possibility of a victory for the North not freedom for slaves but loss of local self-government and financial subjugation. The Confederate naval authorities fitted out a series of commerce-raiders to destroy the North's overseas trade. He was third engineer in the first of these, the *Sumter*, and after a successful voyage he became second engineer in the most notorious of these vessels, the *Alabama*, which destroyed millions of dollars' worth of Northern shipping and its cargoes. When, after its sinking by the *Kearsage* following a cruise as far as Indonesia, he was appointed to the raider *Shenandoah* as chief engineer (under the Irish-born Captain Waddell), he enhanced his reputation in its extremely successful raiding cruise around the world. **John de Courcy Ireland**

O'Brien, Murrough, first Earl of Inchiquin (1614–1674), soldier and politician, eldest son of Dermod O'Brien, sixth Baron Inchiquin. He embarked on a military career, serving with the Spanish army in Italy. In 1640 he obtained the Vice-Presidency of Munster through the patronage of his father-in-law, Sir William St Leger, Lord President of Munster. He became governor of the province and had important military success against the Confederates in 1642. The withdrawal of a large part of his army to England after the 1643 cessation, coupled with his lack of confidence in the king and the refusal to grant him the Presidency of Munster, led to his defection to Parliament in August 1644. His immediate expulsion of the Catholic inhabitants of Cork, Kinsale and Youghal and particularly his massacre of all the defenders of the Rock of Cashel in September 1647 gave him a notorious reputation and the nickname Murchadh na dTóiteán ('Murrough of the Burnings'). Despite his military victories he was neither trusted nor rewarded by Parliament, and in April 1648 he rejoined the royalist side, forming a new alliance with the Confederates. When he could no longer muster support against the Cromwellian reconquest in 1650 he went into exile on the Continent. He returned to Ireland in 1663 after the restoration of his estates, though he was again denied the political prize of the Presidency of Munster, and lived in retirement until his death. **Liam Irwin**

O'Brien, Oliver (1922–2001), organist and choir director. Born in Dublin, son of VINCENT O'BRIEN; he studied piano at the READ SCHOOL and organ with William Watson; graduated from UCD in 1948. He held many important posts, including professor of music at Carysfort College of Education, 1948–87, director of OUR LADY'S CHORAL SOCIETY, 1948–79, and director of the PALESTRINA CHOIR at the Pro-Cathedral, Dublin, 1946–78, where he was also organist, 1946–76. In 1976 he was awarded the knighthood of St Gregory by Pope Paul VI and in 2001 was elected president of the JOHN MCCORMACK Society of Ireland. His compositions include choral arrangements and church music. **Ite O'Donovan**

O'Brien, Paddy (1922–1991), traditional musician. Born in Newtown, Co. Tipperary. He is responsible for revolutionising the technique used for interpreting TRADITIONAL MUSIC on the two-row button ACCORDION. His approach was greatly influenced by the styles of the great Sligo FIDDLE players of the 1920s and has been widely copied and developed by subsequent generations of accordionists. He is also renowned for his distinctive compositions, which have been published in *The Compositions of Paddy O'Brien*. **Martin Dowling**

O'Brien, Vincent (1871–1948), organist and choir director. Born in Dublin; studied piano with his father and organ with Sir ROBERT STEWART at the RIAM. From 1885 he held posts as organist and choir-director at Rathmines, Dominick Street, and Clarendon Street, where he revived the music of Palestrina. In 1902 he became director of the newly founded PALESTRINA CHOIR at the Pro-Cathedral, Dublin. He trained many singers, including MARGARET SHERIDAN, JAMES JOYCE and JOHN MCCORMACK, whom he accompanied on a world tour in 1913. He founded the Dublin Oratorio Society, 1906, and was first music director at 2RN (Radio Éireann), 1926–41, and of OUR LADY'S CHORAL SOCIETY, 1945–8. He was awarded an honorary doctorate by the National University of Ireland in 1932. **Ite O'Donovan**

O'Brien, Michael (Vincent) (1917–), horse trainer. Born in Churchtown, Co. Cork. He began as an amateur jockey, taking up HORSE training in 1943. He moved to Ballydoyle House, Co. Tipperary, in 1951. He has trained winning horses for all the principal national hunt races, including the Grand Nationals of 1953 (Early Mist), 1954 (Royal Tan), and 1955 (Quare Times). His horse Cottage Rake won the Cheltenham Gold Cup in three successive years, 1948–50; another, Knock Hard, won in 1953. On the flat he trained a record twenty-seven Irish classic and sixteen English classic winners. Some of his more famous horses were Hatton's Grace, winner of the Champion Hurdle three times, 1949, 1950, 1951; Nijinsky, which won the British Triple Crown (2,000 Guineas, Derby and St Leger) in 1970, ridden by Lester Piggot; and Alleged, twice winner of the Prix de l'Arc de Triomphe, 1977 and 1978. He retired in 1994. His versatility in both national hunt and flat racing is unmatched, and marks him as one of the twentieth century's finest trainers anywhere—many would say the very best of all. **Ciarán Deane**

O'Brien, Vincent. *Nijinsky, ridden by Lester Piggott, is led by its trainer, Vincent O'Brien, into the winner's enclosure at Ascot, July 1970, following its victory in the King George VI and Queen Elizabeth Diamond Stakes. [Inpho Photography]*

O'Brien, William (1852–1928), nationalist, agrarian campaigner, journalist, and author. Born in Mallow, Co. Cork. He was editor of PARNELL's newspaper, *United Ireland*, and a leading activist in the PLAN OF CAMPAIGN. In 1898 he founded the UNITED IRISH LEAGUE, which achieved through the Irish LAND ACT (1903) comprehensive land purchase for tenant-farmers. After 1903 he vigorously pursued a policy of conciliation with non-Catholic interests and bitterly opposed PARTITION. He was a member of Parliament almost continuously from 1883 to 1918 and founder and leader of the All-for-Ireland League, 1909–18. **Philip J. Bull**

O'Brien, William Smith (1803–1864), nationalist and political agitator. Born in Dromoland, Co. Clare, into a landed Protestant family; educated at the University of Cambridge. A supporter of CATHOLIC EMANCIPATION in 1828, he was MP for Ennis, 1826–31, and Limerick, 1835–48. He joined the Repeal Association in 1844, led it on O'CONNELL's imprisonment that year, but left in 1846. Joint-founder of the Irish Confederation in 1847, he favoured peaceful tactics but on the arrest of the YOUNG IRELAND leaders led an unsuccessful rebellion at Ballingarry, Co. Tipperary, 23 July 1848. His sentence of death was commuted to transportation for life. Pardoned in 1856, he returned to Ireland but abstained from politics thenceforth (see p. 705). **Carla King**

Ó Broin, Éimear (1927–), conductor. Born in Dublin, educated at UCD, studied conducting at the Paris Conservatoire (premier prix in 1952), also attending the classes of Olivier Messiaen. He was assistant conductor of the RTÉ Symphony Orchestra 1955–70. In 1957 he took part in a conducting course for young conductors organised by the London Philharmonic and shared the highest award with Colin Davis. In 1958 the BBC broadcast two of his concerts in Dublin, and he went on to work with some of the best-known orchestras in Europe. **Geraldine Guiden**

Ó Bruadair, Dáibhí (c. 1625–1698), the last of the great bardic poets. Born in Co. Cork; he was well read in Latin and English and in KEATING's FORAS FEASA AR ÉIRINN (Compendium of knowledge about Ireland), of which he makes extensive use in his poetry. His concern, for the most part, is with the downfall of aristocratic Gaelic Ireland. In his celebrated satirical reflection on the pathetic state of the nation, 'Créacht do Dháil Mé' (1652), he ridicules both the native and the Cromwellian upstarts who have assumed authority. In 1660 he moved to Co. Limerick, where he wrote official verse for his patrons, the Bourkes of Cahirmoyle. By the mid-1670s he was lamenting his lot and wishing he were an ignoramus like the rest: 'Is mairg nach bhfuil ina dhubhthuata.' By the 1680s he was mourning the neglect and decay of the native tradition in 'D'aithle na bhFileadh n-Uasal'. The long historical poem 'Suim Purgadóra bhFear nÉireann' concerns itself with the sufferings of the Catholic Irish during the period 1641–84. In 1687 he celebrated the succession of JAMES II in 'Caithréim an Dara Séamuis', and he celebrated SARSFIELD's Ballyneety ambush in 'Caithréim Phádraig Sáirséal'. After the TREATY OF LIMERICK and the flight of the WILD GEESE he vented his anger, sadness, and frustration at his own state and that of the country, laying much of the blame for the disaster on the conniving and sinfulness of the native Irish. His voice is not just a commentary on the political situation but an apocalyptic cry in the wilderness for the fall of a great civilisation, in language reminiscent of that of Jeremiah and Hosea. **Tadhg Ó Dúshláine**

observatories, private. The nineteenth and early twentieth centuries were a particularly brilliant period for Irish ASTRONOMY. In the prevailing zeitgeist of enlightened interest in the SCIENCES, academics and dilettantes of various backgrounds founded a number of observatories throughout the country, including those of BIRR CASTLE, CRAWFORD, DARAMONA, FETHARD, GORE'S, MARKREE, MILBROOK, MONCK's, and SHERRINGTON. These were often equipped, at considerable expense, with instruments of the highest quality. Despite the vagaries of climate natural to an island at a relatively high northern latitude, the results obtained contributed materially to astronomical research. **Susan McKenna-Lawlor**

Observe the Sons of Ulster Marching towards the Somme (1985), a play by FRANK MCGUINNESS dealing with the predominantly Protestant 36th (Ulster) Division of the British army, who were massacred in the Battle of the Somme (1916) during the FIRST WORLD WAR. Acclaimed for its insight into unionist culture, the play marked a shift in the theatrical exploration of Irish identity. **Christopher Morash**

obstetrics, developments in. Three books tell the story over three centuries: James Wolveridge's *Irish Midwives' Handmaid* (1671), William Montgomery's *Signs and Symptoms of Pregnancy* (1837), and Fleetwood Churchill's *Essays on Puerperal Fever* (1849). Epidemics of puerperal fever (infection after delivery) carried a high

Observe the Sons of Ulster. *Scene from the premiere of Frank McGuinness's play* Observe the Sons of Ulster Marching towards the Somme *at the Peacock Theatre, Dublin, 1985. [Amelia Stein]*

mortality and did not spare BARTHOLOMEW MOSSE's ROTUNDA HOSPITAL, founded in 1745. Mosse's example was followed by the establishment of 'lying-in hospitals' in Belfast (1793), Cork, Galway and Limerick, and the Coombe Hospital (1829) and National Maternity Hospital (1894) in Dublin. It was not until the discovery of sulphonamide drugs that puerperal fever was overcome in 1935. From 1950 an organised blood transfusion service reduced maternal mortality to close to nil.

In 1966 Kieran O'Driscoll and Declan Meagher advocated drugs to stimulate the uterus and so avoid prolonged labour in first deliveries in the 'active management of labour'. The popularity of epidural regional anaesthesia after 1970 doubled the rate of instrumental deliveries. Foetal monitoring increasingly suggested the advisability of elective delivery. In the Rotunda Hospital the proportion of deliveries by Caesarean section rose from 3.6 per cent in 1950 to 12.9 per cent in 1989, when it was 9.9 per cent in the Coombe Hospital and 5.9 per cent in the National Maternity Hospital. Assisted reproduction became available from 1980.

The successful care of premature infants by ROBERT COLLIS made neonatal intensive care units a necessity in every maternity hospital. Newborn exchange transfusion for Rhesus incompatibility was eliminated with the introduction of gamma globulin in the 1960s. The perinatal death rate fell from a national average of 37.5 per 1,000 births to 12.2 per 1,000 over the last three decades of the twentieth century. [see CHILDBIRTH.] **C. S. Breathnach**

O'Byrne, Fiach mac Hugh (died 1597), son of Hugh O'Byrne, Lord of Ranelagh. He was already the dominant lord in Co. Wicklow before his father died in 1579. The English administration in Dublin found him difficult to control, because of his adventurous character and the wild and inaccessible nature of his territory. In 1580 he joined Viscount BALTINGLASS in rebellion, largely because Thomas Masterson, seneschal for Co. Wicklow, used martial law to terrorise the Irish into submission. O'Byrne routed a sizeable English army under Lord Deputy Grey at GLENMALUR on 25 August 1580. Though the rebellion failed, O'Byrne survived. He actively supported HUGH O'NEILL and his allies in the NINE YEARS' WAR. In 1595 his wife was captured by the English and condemned to death by burning; to save her life O'Byrne submitted, but he resumed his rebellion in 1596. He was captured and killed by English forces in Glenmalur on 8 May 1597. **Henry A. Jefferies**

O'Byrne, Gabriel (1878–1914), French naval officer. Born in western France to a family that had emigrated from Co. Wicklow early in the nineteenth century; he studied at the Jesuit College at Sarlat and at the Naval College. He served first in big battleships, winning a reputation for daring and for imaginative competence. In 1908 he volunteered to serve in submarines, the development of which the French navy had pioneered. Having served as second in command of two submarines, in 1910 he was made commander of the *Aiguille* and in 1912 given special promotion to *capitaine de frégate* (commander) to captain the new submarine *Curie*. The first submarine to break into a hostile base was the *Curie* early in the FIRST WORLD WAR, when he took the submarine past innumerable obstacles at the then unheard-of depth of 18 m (59 ft) into the Austrian naval base at Pula on the Adriatic. But the *Curie* was spotted before it could fire a torpedo, and he was wounded and captured, dying in captivity. **John de Courcy Ireland**

Ó Cadhain, Máirtín (1906–1970), writer, academic, and language activist. Born in Spiddle, Co. Galway; he won a scholarship to St Patrick's College, Dublin, where he spent the years 1924–6. His first teaching appointments were on the island of Dinish, and in Camas, where he was principal until February 1932. During this period he began a lifelong collection of FOLKLORE and materials relating to the Irish dialects of Co. Galway. He accepted another principalship, in Carnmore National School, Co. Galway, but was dismissed in June 1936 after he led a group of Galway republicans to the WOLFE TONE Commemoration in Bodenstown, Co. Kildare. He was one of the founders of Muinntir na Gaedhealtachta and was central to the campaign to move families from Connemara to estates acquired by the Government in Co. Meath, during the 1930s.

He had been an officer in the IRA and was a member of its Army Council in 1938. He was twice interned, between September and December 1939 and for a longer period between April 1940 and July 1944. On his release he settled permanently in Dublin. *Idir Shúgradh agus Dáiríre*, his first volume of short stories, had been published in 1939, and another volume, *An Braon Broghach*, appeared in 1948. He had secured employment as a translator in Rannóg an Aistriúcháin in March 1947 and continued to work there until becoming a lecturer in TRINITY COLLEGE, DUBLIN, in February 1956. He published prodigiously during this period and also contributed a weekly column to the IRISH TIMES between 1953 and 1956. *Cré na Cille*, a revolutionary novel in language, form, and subject, was published in November 1949 and was to reap the praise of critics and public alike. He also wrote another novel, *Athnuachan*, which won Duais an Chlub Leabhar in 1951 but was not published until 1995.

His third volume of short stories, *Cois Caoláire* (1953), marked a new departure in his writing. While some stories continued to be set in Cois Fharraige and other districts of Connemara, the emphasis shifted to a more existential examination of the individual, rather than seeking to relate the individual's narrative within a community setting. The publication of short stories in *An tSraith ar Lár* (1967) confirmed that Ó Cadhain could accomplish delicate studies of conscience and character with masterful and at times blistering prose. Trinity College made him associate professor in the School of Irish and Celtic Languages in 1967, and he was elected to a full professorship in 1969. **Dónall Ó Braonáin**

Ó Cadhla, Labhrás (1889–1961), *sean-nós* singer. Born at Scartnadriny, Co. Waterford. He spent his working life as a teacher of Irish. He was a highly skilled exponent in the style of his home area, Sliabh gCua; his singing made use of subtle rhythmic variations and tasteful ornamentation. He had a large repertoire of songs, which were almost exclusively local in their origins; a collection of these is to be found on *Labhrás Ó Cadhla: Amhráin ó Shliabh gCua*. **Peter Browne**

Ó Caoimh, Eoghan (1656–1726), poet and scribe. Active in Cork and Kerry literary circles, he was a prolific copyist of the works of GEOFFREY KEATING. Following the death of his wife in 1707 and one of his sons in 1709 he studied for the priesthood; he was ordained in 1717 and became parish priest of Doneraile, Co. Cork. He was involved in these later years in a poetic dispute with the local poet SEÁN CLÁRACH MAC DOMHNAILL. **Máirín Nic Eoin**

O'Casey, Sean (1880–1964), dramatist and autobiographer. Born John Casey in Dublin, 30 March 1880; attended St Mary's and St Barnabas' national schools, though mostly educated at home by his widowed mother because of his poor sight. He left school at fourteen to work, first as a labourer on the RAILWAYS, 1902–11, also teaching Irish, writing political JOURNALISM, poetry, and ballads, and acting in amateur productions. In 1906 he adopted an Irish form of his name, Seán Ó Cathasaigh, before hybridising it as Sean O'Casey in plays submitted to the ABBEY THEATRE. He was involved with LARKIN in the DUBLIN LOCK-OUT OF 1913 but resigned from the IRISH CITIZEN ARMY in 1914, opposing its takeover by what he regarded as middle-class nationalists, an outlook that shaped the view of 1916 in his play *The Plough and the Stars* (1926). His first three plays submitted were rejected by the Abbey, 1920–22, but the fourth, *On the Run*, was accepted in November 1922, with the title changed to *The Shadow of a Gunman*. His plays offered a new urban realism in place of the usual rural fare, a unique blend of comedy and tragedy, strong character parts for a new generation of Abbey actors (many of them recruited from the more popular QUEEN'S ROYAL THEATRE), a strong vein of authentic Dublinese, and the dramatisation of recent turbulent political events: the Anglo-Irish War in *The Shadow of a Gunman*, the Civil War in *Juno and the Paycock* (1924), and the 1916 RISING in *The Plough and the Stars*. His plays attracted full houses and saved the Abbey from bankruptcy; but the satire of PEARSE's blood sacrifice and the realistic treatment of Dublin life in *The Plough and the Stars* caused riots; and his next play, an expressionist treatment of the FIRST WORLD WAR, *The Silver Tassie* (1928), was rejected by YEATS, Lady AUGUSTA GREGORY, and LENNOX ROBINSON. O'Casey was already living in London; the rejection of *The Silver Tassie* made for an irreparable breach with Ireland and its national theatre. He continued to write plays, in an increasingly experimental mode, the most successful being his treatment of the Lock-Out, *Red Roses for Me* (1942). His later plays are regarded as a falling off and have never been fully tested in performance. Beginning with *I Knock at the Door* (1939) he published six volumes of vivid, highly coloured autobiography, whose authenticity has been questioned but whose prose narrative of the early decades of Dublin in the twentieth century has proved hugely influential on later writers. [see ABBEY TRILOGY.] **Anthony Roche**

Ó Caside, Tomás (an Caisideach Bán) (fl. 1750), poet and writer. Born and reared near Castlerea, Co. Roscommon; he entered the Augustinian convent at Ballyhaunis but left before ordination and spent some time travelling around Ireland. He was kidnapped and sold to a French army official and was an armed trooper in the French army, c. 1733–4. Afterwards he served in the Prussian army before returning first to England and eventually to Ireland to continue his rambles around the country. The date and place of his death are unknown. **Ciarán Mac Murchaidh**

Ó Catháin, Darach (1922–1987), traditional singer. Born in Máimín, Co. Galway; moved with his family to Ráth Cairn, Co. Meath, in 1935, where he worked with a local farmer before emigrating to England. He won Oireachtas SEAN-NÓS competitions and recorded five songs with SEÁN Ó RIADA and Ceoltóirí Chualann on the LP *Reacaireacht an Riadaigh*. His solo recording is the LP *Darach Ó Catháin*. **Liam Mac Con Iomaire**

occupational segregation. Two analytical types have been identified: *horizontal segregation* (the tendency for women and men in a particular society to hold qualitatively different kinds of occupation) and *vertical segregation* (the tendency for men to occupy positions at the top of the occupational hierarchy). Horizontal segregation limits the application of DISCRIMINATION LEGISLATION. Occupations in which at least two-thirds of those involved are men include farming; labouring; producing, making, and repairing; administration; executive and managerial occupations; and proprietors. Clerical work is predominantly done by women; women are also predominant to a slightly lesser extent among service workers, shop assistants, and bar workers. Professional and technical work is generally less horizontally segregated (53 per cent female). However, horizontal segregation persists in particular areas: the majority of primary teachers (79 per cent) are women, while the majority of university lecturers (72 per cent) are men. In positions of authority, men are disproportionately represented in both areas, constituting 52 per cent of primary school principals and 95 per cent of university professors. This reflects the widespread existence of vertical segregation, with men constituting 72 per cent of executives, administrators, managers, and proprietors. Vertical segregation is even more obvious in senior management positions: men occupy between 91 and 97 per cent of such positions in the public and the private sector. These inequalities are not, of course, peculiar to Ireland. **Pat O'Connor**

Ó Ceallaigh, Uilliam Buí (died 1381), son of Donnchadh Muimhneach, chief of Uí Maine. He is best known for a great

O'Casey. *Sean O'Casey with Ria Mooney as the prostitute in the 1926 Abbey Theatre production of* The Plough and the Stars. *O'Casey inscribed the photograph 'Be clever maid and let who will be good.' [G. A. Duncan]*

Christmas feast he held in 1351 for all the bardic learned classes of Ireland, poets, brehons, historians, musicians, and men of lesser arts. The event is recorded both in the Annals of CLONMACNOISE and in a poem by GOFRAIDH FIONN Ó DÁLAIGH, who was one of the guests. The poem enthusiastically describes Ó Ceallaigh's limewashed stone castle as dominating the streets of temporary huts erected for those invited, and the feast may have been in the nature of a housewarming. **Katharine Simms**

ocean wave energy. The amount of energy in the ocean waves off the west coast of Ireland is, in winter, among the greatest on Earth. As they approach the shore, waves lose much of their energy through friction with the sea-bed. Spectacular as they may be, there is less power in storm seas crashing along a shoreline than in the corresponding rollers passing seemingly effortlessly in deep water offshore. The 'available' deep-water resource off the Irish coast is estimated to be more than 35 gigawatts—far more power than the total installed electrical generating capacity of Ireland—and it is everlasting. [see COASTAL EROSION; ENERGY.] **William Dick**

Ó Cearnaigh, Nioclás (c. 1802–c. 1865), poet. Born in the Dundalk area of Co. Louth. His poems 'Triamhain na Máthara' and 'Thar Sáile Anonn' are admired; he attributed others to famous poets. He was reviled for inventions in *The Prophecies of SS. Columbkille …* (1856). A member of the OSSIANIC SOCIETY and the Hibernian Gaelic Society (Drogheda), his is a lone voice from Co. Louth during a bleak period. **Diarmuid Breathnach and Máire Ní Mhurchú**

Ó Conaill, Seán. *Seán Ó Conaill of Cill Rialaig, Ballinskelligs, Co. Kerry, a renowned storyteller who inspired Séamus Ó Duilearga, folklore collector. [Courtesy of the Department of Irish Folklore, University College, Dublin; M0018,374-377]*

Ó Cianáin, Tadhg (died c. 1609), writer. Member of a learned family linked to the Maguires of Fermanagh, he was the author of an account of the FLIGHT OF THE EARLS written in Rome in 1609. He was among the earls' retinue, and his narrative describes at first hand the journey and subsequent fate of HUGH O'NEILL, RORY O'DONNELL, CÚCHONNACHT ÓG MAGUIRE, and their followers. They left Co. Donegal in September 1607 and travelled to Rome through the Low Countries, France, Switzerland, and the Italian states. Ó Cianáin may have died in Rome without completing the narrative. **Bernadette Cunningham**

Ó Cíobháin, Pádraig (1951–), writer. Born near Ballyferriter, Co. Kerry; educated at UCC. He is the author of three novels and three collections of short stories, all noted for their consciously textured use of language, their attention to details of place, and their dramatic exploration of themes of identity and belonging. **Máirín Nic Eoin**

Ó Cléirigh, (Tadhg) Mícheál (c. 1590–1643), historian. Born in Kilbarron, Co. Donegal; a trained historian in the Gaelic tradition, he joined the Irish Franciscans at St Anthony's, Louvain, in 1623 as a lay brother. He worked throughout Ireland from 1626 to 1637 transcribing MANUSCRIPTS on Irish SAINTS' lives and Irish history. His best-known work is the *Annals of the Kingdom of Ireland* (Annals of the FOUR MASTERS). He also compiled the *Martyrology of Donegal*, revised the LEBOR GABÁLA ÉRENN, compiled genealogies of Irish saints and kings, and a dictionary, *Foclóir nó Sanasán Nua*. **Bernadette Cunningham**

Ó Coileáin, Seán (c. 1754–1817), poet and scribe. Born in West Carbery, Co. Cork, he lived on the Continent while studying for the priesthood before returning to Midhe Ros (Myross), Co. Cork, where he subsequently established a school. Though noted for his rather rakish life-style, he was respected as a scholar, his transcripts being sought by MÍCHEÁL ÓG Ó LONGÁIN in particular. There is also evidence that he was preparing an Irish–English dictionary. Eleven of his manuscripts survive. Some ten poems are attributed to him, including 'Machnamh an Duine Dhoilíosaigh', which contemplates the fate of Timoleague Abbey, and the AISLING 'An Buachaill Bán'. **Meidhbhín Ní Úrdail**

Ó Coisdealbha, Seán (Johnny Chóil Mhaidhc) (1930–), oral poet and dramatist. Born in Indreabhán, Co. Galway. His poems and dialogues, well known in oral tradition, are selected in *Buille faoi Thuairim Gabha* (1987). His plays, mainly on folk themes, include *An Tincéara Buí* (1962), *Ortha na Seirce* (1962), *Pionta Amháin Uisce* (1975), *An Crústóir* (1985), and *An Mhéar Fhada* (1995). **Gearóid Denvir**

Ó Conaill, Peadar (1755–1826), scholar, schoolmaster, and scribe. Born in Carne, near Kilrush, Co. Clare. He travelled extensively and transcribed for Chevalier O'Gorman and Charles O'Conor of Belanagare and collaborated at length with Theophilus O'Flanagan at TRINITY COLLEGE, Dublin. He also received the patronage of Dr Simon O'Reardon of Limerick. He compiled a manuscript Irish–English dictionary, now in the British Library. More than forty of his manuscripts survive, many unsigned. **Éilís Ní Dheá**

Ó Conaill, Seán (1853–1931), small farmer, fisherman, and storyteller. Born in Cill Rialaig, Ballinskelligs, Co. Kerry; he received no schooling. He was the first major storyteller that SÉAMUS Ó DUILEARGA worked with; it was while collecting from him that Ó Duilearga was inspired to begin his lifelong devotion to the collection of the FOLKLORE of Ireland (see p. 406). **Mícheál Briody**

Ó Conaire, Pádraic (1882–1928), writer, best known as the first prose modernist in Irish. Born in Galway, he had the advantage of being born in a city in which much Irish was spoken, and he tasted the rough side of life from an early age. He was orphaned by the time he was eleven and was sent to live with his uncle in Ros Muc in the heart of Connemara; but he was treated as an outsider by his rich relatives and he observed the ordinary life of the rural poor. His secondary education enabled him to get a position in the British civil service in 1899. London was one of the centres of the LITERARY REVIVAL, and he involved himself in the cultural life of the exiles. It was while he was in London that he started writing seriously, and it was here he did his best work. *Nóra Mharcuis Bhig agus Sgéalta Eile* (1909) contains some of his best stories. His strength is his unflinching clarity of vision, expressed in simple language. He created a world of his own, whether the physical setting is Connemara, the streets of London, or Biblical Palestine. It is a world of harshness and little hope, occasionally elevated by personal kindness and the goodness of chance. His only worthwhile novel, DEORAÍOCHT (1910), testifies to all his strengths and weaknesses. A tale of a young Irishman who is crippled while in exile in London, it is both bleak and darkly humorous, grimly realistic while teetering on the brink of fantasy. Apart from the occasional flash of a genuine short story, he turned to dross after this. He fled home to Ireland in 1914, drinking and wandering; his last years were dogged by poverty and ill health. He collapsed on the street in Dublin and died shortly afterwards, leaving some fine writing and many legends behind him. **Alan Titley**

Ó Conaire, Pádraic. *Pádraic Ó Conaire was the first prose modernist in Irish; the work for which he is best known was written in London during the Irish Literary Revival. [RTÉ Stills Library; 0057/014]*

Ó Conaire, Pádraig Óg (1893–1971), cultural activist and popular and prolific writer. Born in Ros Muc, Co. Galway; attended PATRICK PEARSE's school, Scoil Éanna, in Dublin, then worked as translator, teacher, journalist, and broadcaster. His best work, such as *Éan Cuideáin* (1936), *Ceol na nGiolcach* (1939), and *Déirc an Díomhaointis* (1972), exhibits a rural proletarian focus, a romantic style, and a rich, idiomatic use of language and creates authentic vignettes of nineteenth and twentieth-century Connemara life. **Breandán Ó Conaire**

Ó Conchobhair, Cathal Crobhdhearg (1189–1224), King of Connacht, son of TOIRDHEALBHACH (died 1156) and brother of Ruaidhrí (died 1198), both high kings of Ireland. An early opponent of ANGLO-NORMAN encroachment, Cathal Crobhdhearg ('red-handed') later became skilled in negotiating his dynasty's survival; he is the ancestor of both the O'Connor Roe and O'Conor Don. **Seán Duffy**

Ó Conchobhair, Toirdhealbhach (1106–1156) King of Connacht. His greatest achievement was to make Connacht a first-rate political power. He subjugated Dublin, a crucial step on the way to pre-eminence. He endorsed reform in the Irish church, campaigning successfully to win for Connacht an archbishop's see. His early dominance was such that he is referred to as King of Ireland on the Cross of Cong (AD 1124–1136) and in a mandate of Henry I of England (1121) (see p. 712). His sway was more limited after 1131, but his political legacy was developed by his son Ruaidhrí after 1166. **Colmán Etchingham**

Ó Conchobhair, Toirdhealbhach (died 1266), King of Connacht, 1249–50. His father, Aodh (died 1228), and grandfather, CATHAL CROBHDHEARG (died 1224), were both kings of Connacht. Toirdhealbhach was active against the ANGLO-NORMANS of Connacht during the reign of his uncle, Féilim, resulting in his imprisonment in the castle of Athlone in 1246. By 1247 he was leader of a failed campaign against the Anglo-Normans under the command of the sheriff, Jordan d'Exeter. In 1249 the Justiciar, John fitz Geoffrey, led an army into Connacht against Aodh, son of Féilim, who was in revolt, and replaced Féilim with Toirdhealbhach. Toirdhealbhach proved unable to restrain his men, who attacked Athenry against his wishes on 8 September 1249 and were defeated by Jordan d'Exeter. In 1250 Féilim returned to Connacht with the support of the CENÉL NEOGHAIN and expelled Toirdhealbhach. Accepting the stronger claimant, Féilim was re-instated by the Anglo-Normans as king. Toirdhealbhach died in 1266 in the monastery of Knockmoy, Co. Galway. **Susan Foran**

Ó Conghaile, Micheál (1962–), writer and publisher. Born in Galway; educated at UCG. The publishing house Cló Iar-Chonnachta, which he established in 1985, is now one of the most successful publishers of IRISH-LANGUAGE books and traditional songs. His fiction, which ranges in style from the realist to the absurd, explores various aspects of contemporary GAELTACHT and urban life and has met with widespread critical acclaim. He has received many awards for his work, including OIREACHTAS and Listowel Writers' Week awards for his novel of homosexual youth *Sna Fir* (1999). His publications include a collection of poetry, two short-story collections, a study of Connemara social history, and many edited volumes. **Máirín Nic Eoin**

Ó Conluain, Proinsias (1919–), broadcaster and researcher. Born near Benburb, Co. Tyrone. His documentaries for Radio Éireann and RTÉ covered songs, balladry, and the lives of such personalities as CARL HARDEBECK, Henry Morris, SAM HENRY, FRANCIS O'NEILL, Robert Cinnamond, and EDDIE BUTCHER. A founder-editor of *Dúiche Néill*, journal of the O'Neill Country Historical Society, he has also written on the status of SEAN-NÓS singing in the OIREACHTAS competitions. **Fintan Vallely**

O'Connell, Daniel (1775–1847), political leader. Born near Cahersiveen, Co. Kerry; educated at Saint-Omer, Douai, and London. After early success as a barrister he became increasingly involved in politics and was active from his early thirties onwards in the campaign for CATHOLIC EMANCIPATION. Though he gained popularity with fellow-Catholics for his opposition to the VETO, it was not until he jointly founded the CATHOLIC ASSOCIATION in 1823 and became its chief spokesman that he began to dominate nationalist politics. O'Connell's suggestion that the association open its ranks to anyone who could pay a subscription of one penny a month (the CATHOLIC RENT) transformed this body into a mass political organisation that was without precedent in Europe. His stunning victory in the Clare election in 1828 led directly to the attainment of Catholic Emancipation, which earned him the title of 'the Liberator'. In Parliament he and like-minded Irish MPs eventually allied themselves with the WHIGS to obtain social legislation for Ireland by means of the Lichfield House Compact. His ultimate goal was repeal of the ACT OF UNION, and this became the focus of his final years. The REPEAL MOVEMENT that he led after 1842 culminated in his arrest and brief imprisonment in 1844. On his release it became increasingly apparent that his once-formidable physical and mental powers were on the wane. His last days were clouded by quarrels with former YOUNG IRELAND allies, which split the nationalist movement.

O'Connell ranks among the greatest figures of modern Irish political history. His skills as a lawyer, orator, political organiser and parliamentarian, together with his legendary charisma, earned him the admiration of millions of contemporaries, who looked upon him as 'Ireland's uncrowned monarch'. Subsequent generations of nationalists, particularly physical-force separatists, were more ambivalent, praising his organisational skills while criticising his opposition to armed rebellion as a means of achieving Irish self-government. He also had a major influence on the emergence of European Christian democracy (see p. 402). **Gary Owens**

O'Connell, Eilis (1953–), sculptor. Born in Derry; educated in Cork, where she attended Crawford School of Art, graduating in 1974; the following year she studied at Massachusetts College of Art, Boston. Influenced by David Smith and Richard Serra, her early works were mainly welded steel. She later used a wide variety of materials, for example stainless-steel wire woven into large conical forms. Her sculptures combine physical presence with a sense of the history of materials and construction techniques. A founder-member of the National Sculpture Factory, Cork, in 1988 she was commissioned by the ARTS COUNCIL to make *The Great Wall of Kinsale*, a controversial public sculpture in Corten steel. She moved to England in 1990 and received public sculpture commissions in Cardiff, Milton Keynes, and London. In Bristol she designed *Pero's Footbridge* (1999), erected at St Augustine's Reach. In 1999 the Arnolfini Gallery in Bristol presented a ten-year retrospective of her work. She is a member of AOSDÁNA. **Peter Murray**

O'Connell, Kevin (1958–), composer. Born in Derry. He began composing at a young age, winning the RTÉ MUSICIAN OF THE FUTURE Composer's Prize while he was still in university. In 1984 he completed his first commission, which was for BBC Radio 3, and this led to further commissions from the ULSTER ORCHESTRA, IRISH CHAMBER ORCHESTRA, Derry City Council, and various soloists, with much sponsorship coming from the ARTS COUNCIL. He was commissioned to compose a test piece for the 2000 Guardian DUBLIN INTERNATIONAL PIANO COMPETITION. **Geraldine Guiden**

O'Connell, Martin (1963–), Gaelic footballer. Born in Co. Meath. He began his career with Meath in 1982, when the county was enduring a barren period, but by the time he retired at the end of 1996 Meath was the most feared team in the game. Although he played briefly as a forward, it was at wing-back that he flourished. He won all-Ireland championship medals in 1987 and 1988 and was still going strong when a new Meath team won the title in 1996. He was chosen as Footballer of the Year in 1996 and also won four All-Star awards. **Donal Keenan**

O'Connell, Maura (1959–), singer. Born in Ennis, Co. Clare. She made her name as a member of DÉ DANANN during the late 1970s and early 80s. From 1983 she pursued a successful solo career from her base in Nashville, Tennessee, though she performs periodically in Ireland. Her intelligent blend of Irish traditional singing and American folk musical styles—notably bluegrass—has won her many fans throughout the world. She remains a diverse, mostly interpretative singer. Her albums include *Just in Time* (1986), *A Real-Life Story* (1990), and *Blue Is the Colour of Hope* (1993). **Tony Clayton-Lea**

O'Connell, Michael (Mick) (1937–), Gaelic footballer. Born on Valentia Island, Co. Kerry. He played for Kerry in the 1950s, 60s and 70s and during that time won four all-Ireland championships. He first played for Kerry at senior level in 1956 and won a Munster championship in 1958. A year later he was promoted to Kerry captain and won his first all-Ireland. His extraordinary fitness and stamina, allied with his superb fielding and kicking, made him the most respected player of his generation, and when he retired in 1972 his legendary status was confirmed. **Donal Keenan**

O'Connor, Andrew (1874–1941), sculptor. Born in Worcester, Massachusetts, the son of a Scottish stone-carver; his mother was from Co. Antrim. He first emerged as a sculptor-carver at the Chicago World's Fair in 1891, and by 1894 he was in London in the studio of the painter John Singer Sargent. On his return to America he worked with the sculptor D. C. French, through whom he obtained the commission (in 1900) for his celebrated earliest public work, the Vanderbilt Memorial Doors on St Bartholomew's, New York. He was later patronised by the architect Cass Gilbert. He was in Paris, 1905–14 and c. 1926–31; in Paxton, Massachusetts, 1914–c. 1926, and between London and Dublin (where he died), 1931–41. He exhibited widely in America (where he also executed a number of public monuments) and at the Paris salons. His recumbent *Victim* (Merrion Square, Dublin) was conceived as part of a war

O'Connell, Daniel. O'Connell Centenary Celebrations *(1875) by Charles Russell, reveals the nationalist fervour of the commemoration of the birth of O'Connell, 6 August 1875, in Sackville Street (O'Connell Street), Dublin, with banners of O'Connell, Erin with her wolfhound, and Brian Bórú. The monument dominating the street, Nelson Pillar, was blown up by the IRA in 1966. [National Gallery of Ireland]*

memorial (c. 1920–30), as was his *Christ the King* (1926)—originally titled *Triple Cross* and conceived as a memorial to the dead of the FIRST WORLD WAR—erected in Haig Terrace, Dún Laoghaire, in 1978. Many of his plaster maquettes, including the equestrian *Lafayette* (c. 1920), are in the Hugh Lane Municipal Gallery of Modern Art, Dublin, to which they were presented by the sculptor. He worked in the lyrical and naturalistic style favoured by his contemporaries in America and France, such as Rodin. **Homan Potterton**

O'Connor, Arthur (1763–1852), United Irishman. Born in Mitchelstown, Co. Cork; educated at TCD and called to the bar in 1788. As MP for Philipstown, 1791–6, his radicalism led to prominence in the UNITED IRISHMEN and editorship of the *Press*, the organisation's main newspaper. A close associate of LORD EDWARD FITZGERALD, he was arrested in Margate, England, on 28 February 1798 when illegally seeking passage to France. Acquitted of high treason and imprisoned in the Tower of London and Fort George, Inverness-shire, until 1802, he emigrated to France and was appointed a general in the army. **Ruan O'Donnell**

O'Connor, Feargus Edward (1794–1855), Chartist leader. Born in Connorville, Co. Cork, a nephew of ARTHUR O'CONNOR; educated at TCD and called to the bar. He became MP for Co. Cork, 1832–5, supporting DANIEL O'CONNELL. He emerged as a leader of the English Chartist movement in 1837 and became its most popular speaker. He owned the *Northern Star* of Leeds and continually expressed Irish grievances and sought Irish support. His 'physical force' standpoint alienated moderate Chartist leaders, but in 1841, after a year's imprisonment in York, he became CHARTISM's undisputed leader. After the failure of the second Petition (1842), Chartism began to lose its impetus. He became MP for Nottingham in 1847, presenting to Parliament the unsuccessful 1848 Petition following the Kennington Common meeting, which he masterminded. His Land Plan also failed. By 1850 he was already displaying signs of madness; he was declared insane in 1852 and admitted to an asylum, where he died. **Marjorie Bloy**

O'Connor, Frank, pseudonym of Michael O'Donovan (1903–1966), writer. Born in Cork; educated at local schools, briefly taught by DANIEL CORKERY, otherwise self-educated; interned during the CIVIL WAR. He began to publish in the 1920s, with GEORGE RUSSELL and W. B. YEATS as mentors; director of the ABBEY THEATRE in the 1930s; first poetry editor of the BELL, founded by his friend SEAN O'FAOLAIN, in the 1940s. Widely regarded as one of the masters of the realistic SHORT STORY in the twentieth century, and as the most important translator of Irish poetry into English, he also wrote novels, literary history and criticism, autobiography, biography, drama, travel books, and extensive socially critical journalism. Collections of short stories include *Guests of the Nation* (1931), *Bones of Contention* (1936), *Crab Apple Jelly* (1944), *The Common Chord* (1947), *Traveller's Samples* (1951), *Stories* (1952), *Domestic Relations* (1957), *More Stories* (1954), *Collection 3* (1969), and *Collected Stories* (1981). Collections of poems translated from Irish include *The Wild Bird's Nest* (1932), *The Midnight Court* (1945), *Kings, Lords and Commons* (1959), *The Little Monasteries* (1963), and *The Golden Treasury of Irish Poetry* (1967, with David Greene). O'Connor's fiction deals especially with war experiences, childhood, priesthood, the death of traditional culture and provincial domestic life and is notable for its handling of narrative voice. *An Only Child* (1961), his autobiography covering his early life in a poor district of Cork, is a classic of the genre. He lived variously in Cork, Dublin, England and the United States and was awarded an honorary doctorate by the University of Dublin, 1962 (see p. 795). **Ruth Sherry**

O'Connor, James Arthur (1792–1841), painter. Born in Dublin, son of an engraver and print-seller; he may have attended the DUBLIN SOCIETY Schools or have been self-taught. A romantic landscape painter sensitive to nature, he executed drawings and watercolours intended as studies for his oils. He first exhibited in Dublin in 1809. He travelled to London in 1813 with GEORGE PETRIE and FRANCIS DANBY; on his return he painted picturesque views and received commissions, 1818–19, to depict country estates in the west of Ireland, such as Westport, Co. Mayo. In 1822 he emigrated to England, exhibiting in London between 1822 and 1840, and on the Continent in 1826, where his career was more successful. His style changed to a romantic tone in later work, coinciding with an unsettled period in his life. O'Connor's romanticism is revealed in *A Thunderstorm: The Frightened Wagoner* (1832), now in the NATIONAL GALLERY OF IRELAND, a magnificent landscape showing mysterious and terrifying elements in nature using dramatic treatments of light. **Marie Bourke**

O'Connor, Pat (1943–), film director. Born in Ardmore, Co. Waterford; studied film in Toronto and then worked in RTÉ. He came to prominence with an acclaimed television adaptation of WILLIAM TREVOR's short story about sexual repression in rural Ireland in the 1950s, *The Ballroom of Romance* (1981), for which he won a British Academy award (see p. 903). His first feature film, *Cal* (1984), was set in Northern Ireland; his other Irish films include *Fools of Fortune* (1990), set among the ANGLO-IRISH in rural Ireland during the WAR OF INDEPENDENCE; an adaptation of MAEVE BINCHY's coming-of-age novel *Circle of Friends* (1995); and BRIAN FRIEL's play *Dancing at Lughnasa* (1998). He has also made non-Irish mainstream commercial films, such as *Stars and Bars* (1988), *The January Man* (1989), *Inventing the Abbotts* (1997), and *Sweet November* (2001). **Kevin Rockett**

O'Connor, Sinead. *One of Ireland's most controversial rock singers, Sinead O'Connor has inspired with her distinctive vocal range and shocked with her provocative attitudes. [Bill Cooper, Bilcop Photography]*

O'Connor, Sinead (1966–), singer. Born in Dublin. Her thoroughly distinctive vocal range, coupled with her provocative attitude, has sharply divided both critics and fans. Her debut album, *The Lion and the Cobra* (1988), was a genuinely intriguing debut but was nothing compared with her follow-up album, *I Do Not Want What I Haven't Got* (1990). A cover version of Prince's 'Nothing Compares 2 U' was the flagship single release. In 1990, at the Garden State Arts Centre in New Jersey, she gave considerable offence by refusing to go on stage after the playing of the American national anthem—her protest against a wave of 'politically correct' censorship then sweeping America. In 1992 she ripped up a photograph of the Pope on American television, causing international criticism. All this controversy was supplemented by a series of interviews that showed the singer to be as fraught in her private life as her public life hinted. A third album of cover versions, *Am I Not Your Girl?* (1993), was a creative and commercial sidestep, while her fourth, *Universal Mother* (1994), found only a dwindling number of fans. An appearance in NEIL JORDAN's film of *The Butcher Boy* (1997) saw her as an Irish Virgin Mary. This role proved all the more ironic when she was ordained a Catholic priest by the Tridentine Bishop Michael Cox in a ceremony at Lourdes in April 1999. In 2000 she released her fifth studio album, *Faith and Courage*. **Tony Clayton-Lea**

O'Connor, Tony (1943–), philosopher. Born in Cork; educated at UCC. Since 1976 he has been lecturer in philosophy at University College, Cork. Central in the dissemination of CONTINENTAL THOUGHT IN IRELAND, O'Connor has published *Discourse and Power* (1997) and edited *Social Philosophy* (1997). **Fionola Meredith**

O'Connor, T. P. [Thomas Power] (1848–1929), journalist and nationalist leader, popularly known as 'Tay Pay'. Born in Athlone; educated at Queen's College, Galway. As a freelance journalist he wrote the caustic *Life of Lord Beaconsfield* (1876). Elected to the British Parliament in 1880, he supported PARNELL and in 1883 became president of the Irish Nationalist League. He founded two radical newspapers, the *Star* (1887) and *Sun* (1893); the literary *T. P.'s Weekly* (1902), and other weeklies. He became a member of the Privy Council, 1924, and 'Father of the House of Commons'; he published *The Parnell Movement* (1886) and *Memoirs of an Old Parliamentarian* (1929). **David Quin**

O'Conor, Charles Owen, known as the O'Conor Don (1838–1906), politician and author. Born in Dublin. He was MP for Co. Roscommon, 1860–80, and appointed High Sheriff of Co. Sligo, 1863. He was actively involved in efforts to reform taxation, education, and landlord-tenant relations. He was a member of several royal commissions, including the Bessborough Commission (1880) on land reform, from whose report he dissented, writing a minority report of his own. He also served as president of the ROYAL IRISH ACADEMY and of the Society for the Preservation of

O'Conor, Roderic. Red Rocks near Pont-Aven *(1898) by Roderic O'Conor, one of a number of seascapes exploring the Breton coastline in which the natural red rock formations were painted in heightened vibrant shades of crimson and orange. [AIB Art Collection, courtesy of Sister Theophane O'Conor]*

the Irish Language. His writings include *The O'Conors of Connaught* (1891). **Brian Galvin**

O'Conor, John (1947–), pianist and teacher. Born in Dublin, where he studied at the College of Music (now DIT Conservatory of Music and Drama) with J. J. O'REILLY. He won both the Beethoven Prize in 1973 and the Bosendorfer Prize in 1975 in Vienna (where he was studying with Dieter Weber), helping to secure his future as a performer. He is renowned for his Beethoven interpretations and has recorded the complete sonatas, and the concertos and solo music of JOHN FIELD. In 1994 he was appointed director of the RIAM, where he has taught since 1976. He has performed as a soloist in Europe, the United States, and Japan and gives the annual Wilhelm Kempff masterclasses in Positano, Italy. In 1988 he founded the DUBLIN INTERNATIONAL PIANO COMPETITION, and is a frequent jury member on competitions such as Leeds'. **Geraldine Guiden and Richard Pine**

O'Conor, Roderic Anthony (1860–1940), painter. Born in Milton, Co. Roscommon; educated at Ampleforth College, Yorkshire. He studied at the Metropolitan School of Art and RHA, Dublin, and attended the Académie Royale des Beaux-Arts, Antwerp, 1883–4. He left Ireland in 1886, studied with Carolus Duran in Paris, and exhibited a portrait in the 1888 Salon. In 1889/90 he painted impressionist-influenced landscapes at Grez-sur-Loing, south of Paris. He lived in Brittany from 1891 to 1904 and became a member of Paul Gauguin's circle of international artists known as the School of Pont-Aven. He painted portraits of Breton peasants and expressive seascapes; his Breton landscapes from 1892 to 1894 show a van Gogh influence, with rich colour contrasts and a direct approach. He returned to Paris in 1904 and painted still lifes, nudes and portraits in his studio in Montparnasse. He exhibited exclusively in group exhibitions, including the RHA, 1883 and 1885, Salon des Indépendants, 1889–1908, Salon d'Automne, 1903–35, Galerie le Barc de Boutteville, 1894 and 1895, and La Libre Esthétique in Brussels, 1898 and 1905. In 1933 he moved to Nueil-sur-Layon in Maine-et-Loire; he died there in 1940 and is buried in the local cemetery. **Roy Johnston**

Ó Corcráin, Brian (fl. 1600), poet and prose writer. An associate of EOCHAIDH Ó HEÓDHUSA, his name appears on four occasions between 1586 and 1603 in the Elizabethan fiants alongside members of other Co. Fermanagh learned families who received Crown pardons. Seven poems are ascribed to him in the Book of O'Conor Don; he enjoyed the patronage of the Maguires and is thought to be the author of 'Eachtra Mhacaoimh an Iolair', an Irish version of a French romantic tale. Having given jury service in 1603, he served in 1609 as a juror for the plantation commissioners in Enniskillen and was himself subsequently granted land in the barony of Clanawley. **Máirín Nic Eoin**

Ó Criomhthainn, Tomás (1854–1937), pioneer Blasket Island writer. He was a farmer-fisherman whose major works are the highly accomplished island journal *Allagar na hInise* (1928, 1977, 1999) and his renowned autobiography, AN TOILEÁNACH (1929), both of which are important personal, sociological, and literary documents. His occasional journalism, published in *Bloghanna ón mBlascaod* (1997), and collections of folklore and toponymy, *Seanchas ón Oileán Tiar* (1956) and *Dinnsheanchas na mBlascaodaí* (1937), also merit attention. Encouraged and supported by Brian Ó Ceallaigh and ROBIN FLOWER, and with little or no formal tuition in his native language, Ó Criomhthainn combined his innate personal talents, mental acuity and imaginative awareness with the rich oral traditions of GAELTACHT culture and succeeded in creating modern, sophisticated literary texts that vividly depict many facets of Blasket Island life. Other Blasket authors followed in his wake, notably MUIRIS Ó SÚILEABHÁIN and PEIG SAYERS, and the demise of communal life on the Great Blasket in 1953 lent an increased historical significance to the work of this 'island school'. **Breandán Ó Conaire**

Ó Criomhthainn. *Tomás Ó Criomhthainn, farmer-fisherman and Blasket Island writer, photographed at the age of seventy. [Courtesy of the Department of Irish Folklore, University College, Dublin; photo: Carl von Sydow]*

Octennial Act (1768), a law requiring elections to be held in Ireland every eight years. It formed part of the programme of the LORD LIEUTENANT, Townsend, for generating Irish support. It differed from its British equivalent, which stipulated elections every seven years, as the Irish Parliament usually met only every two years. **Neal Garnham**

Ó Cuirnín, Ádhamh (fl. fifteenth century), scribe. A member of a hereditary learned family of north Connacht, in 1418 he penned more than twenty folios of the Great Book of Lecan for GIOLLA ÍOSA MAC FIR BHISIGH, *ollamh* to Uí Fiachrach. He is also identified as the scribe, perhaps c. 1425, of the Gaelic manuscript known as John Beaton's Broad Book (now in the National Library of Scotland, Edinburgh). **Nollaig Ó Muraíle**

O'Curry, Eugene (1794–1862), scholar and scribe. Born at Doonaha, Co. Clare. He worked for a time in a lunatic asylum in Limerick. Employed as a researcher for the Topographical Department of the Ordnance Survey, 1835–42, he worked in collaboration with JOHN O'DONOVAN. A self-taught authority on manuscript material, he made many notable transcripts, including DUALTACH MAC FHIRBHISIGH's Book of Genealogies, the Book of Lismore, Book of Lecan, Book of O'Conor Don, Book of the DUN COW, Cocad Gaedal re Gallaib, Leabhar Breac, Tripartite Life of St Patrick, and three martyrologies. He compiled a catalogue of Irish manuscripts in the library of the ROYAL IRISH ACADEMY, 1843–4, and transcribed texts for the Irish Archaeological Society and the Celtic Society. He assisted O'Donovan with his edition of the annals of the FOUR MASTERS (1848–51). In 1849 he catalogued the Irish manuscripts in the British Museum and visited the Bodleian Library in Oxford. He also collaborated with PETRIE on *The Ancient Music of Ireland* (1855). His edition of 'Cath Maige Léna' was published in 1855. In 1853 he was elected a member of the RIA; in 1854 he was appointed to the chair of archaeology and Irish history in the CATHOLIC UNIVERSITY. He delivered a series of twenty-one lectures, 1855–6, later published as *Lectures on the Manuscript Materials of Ancient Irish History* (1861); a further series of lectures was published posthumously as *On the Manners and Customs of the Ancient Irish* (1873). On behalf of the BREHON LAW Commission he worked (together with O'Donovan) on an edition of the *Ancient Laws of Ireland*. He died suddenly in Dublin and is buried in Glasnevin Cemetery. **Éilís Ní Dheá**

Ó Dálaigh, Aonghus Fionn (fl. 1590), Aonghus son of Amhlaoibh Ó Dálaigh, poet. He lamented the first Earl of Clancare (died 1596) and the latter's son (died 1587/8) but was nicknamed Aonghus na Diadhachta ('of the Divinity') for his religious poems (which have been edited by Lambert McKenna). He ran a poetic school in Duhallow, Co. Cork, where he died. **Katharine Simms**

Ó Dálaigh, Aonghus mac Cearbhaill Bhuidhe (fl. 1309), *ollamh* to Aodh, King of Connacht. He is known only through his poems, especially 'Tomhus Muir Chruachna i gCluain Fhraoich', on his patron's palace. His patronymic links him to the Bréifne branch of Ó Dálaigh poets. **Katharine Simms**

Ó Dálaigh, Aonghus mac Dáire (fl. 1580), poet. This member of the learned family of Ó Dálaigh lived at Palace in north Co. Wexford and was chief poet to the O'Byrnes of Wicklow. He is most celebrated for his provocative poem 'Dia libh, a laochruidh Gaoidhiol' (God be with you, Irish heroes), in which he incites his patrons to resist English expansionism. Both this poem and another poem in song metre addressed to FIACH MAC HUGH O'BYRNE after a successful raid on an English garrison have been cited by the historian Brendan Bradshaw as evidence for the emergence and articulation of a decidedly national political ideology in late sixteenth-century Ireland. Ó Dálaigh received Crown pardons in 1598 and in 1601. **Máirín Nic Eoin**

Ó Dálaigh, Aonghus Rua (died 1617), poet. Known as 'Aonghus na nAor' (Aonghus of the satires) and 'an Bard Rua' (the red poet); his most famous composition is the satire 'An t-each díola nach díol damh' on the prominent families of Ireland, excoriating their miserly mentality. He was known also as an exponent of satirical extempore quatrains in the Gaelic tradition of Scotland. Some sources claim he was murdered. **Michelle O Riordan**

Ó Dálaigh, Cearbhall (fl. 1620). Folklore recalls Cearbhall Ó Dálaigh as a great lover. Eleanor Kavanagh, a historical character, allegedly eloped with Cearbhall against her father's wishes. He seems to have been the son of another Cearbhall Ó Dálaigh, who is mentioned in the fiant lists of 1597 and 1601. **Mícheál Mac Craith**

Ó Dálaigh, Cearbhall (1911–1978), lawyer. Born in Bray, Co. Wicklow; educated at UCD, graduating in Celtic Studies, and studied law at KING'S INNS. He was a senior counsel, 1945, ATTORNEY-GENERAL, 1946–8 and 1951–3, a SUPREME COURT judge, 1953, Chief Justice, 1961, and a member of the European Court of Justice, 1972. He was an agreed candidate for President of Ireland in 1974. As President he referred an Emergency Powers Bill, aimed at IRA activities, to the Supreme Court in 1976 (which found it to be constitutional). This referral was denounced by the Minister for Defence, Patrick Donegan, and Ó Dálaigh resigned in protest. **Tom Garvin**

Ó Dálaigh, Donnchadh Mór (died 1244), 'a master of poetry who never has been excelled and never will be' (Annals of Connacht). His reputation for religious poetry was so high that several seventeenth and eighteenth-century compositions were fathered on him; but poems preserved in the fourteenth-century Book of Uí Maine are probably genuine. In 'Gabham Deachmhaidh ar nDána' he pledges to address a tithe of all his professional eulogies to God. Very few of his secular poems survive, the most striking being his lament for his dead son, Aonghus, 'Ar Iasacht Fhuaras Aonghus' ('I obtained Aonghus on loan'). **Katharine Simms**

Ó Dálaigh, Gofraidh Fionn (died 1387), 'master of Ireland in poetry' (Annals of Ulster). Educated by Mac Craith poets of Thomond, his earliest patron was Conchobhar Ó Briain (died 1328), but others included Ó Domhnaill, Ó Ceallaigh, Clann Charthaigh and Munster sub-chieftains and the first three Earls of Desmond. Addressing Maurice, the first earl, Gofraidh stated: 'In the foreigners' poems we promise that the Irish shall be driven from Ireland, in the Irishmen's poems we promise that the foreigners shall be routed across the sea.' Religious verse and tracts on composing poetry are also attributed to him. **Katharine Simms**

Ó Dálaigh, Lochlainn Óg (fl. 1550 or later), poet. Perhaps as many as five individuals who flourished around the same time are covered by this name. At least one of them was a friar, whose composition on the expulsion of the friars from Multyfarnham, 'Uaigneach ataoi, a theagh na mbráthar,' is among his better-known poems. **Michelle O Riordan**

Ó Dálaigh, Muireadhach Albanach (fl. 1220), poet. A member of one of the great poetic families of Ireland, he was born in Co. Meath in the latter decades of the twelfth century. He received the traditional training of a professional bardic poet and worked in that capacity for the O'Connors of Sligo. The annals tell us that in 1213 he murdered a tax-collector of the O'Donnells of Donegal, who were overlords of the region. He was forced to flee for his life, first of all to the Burkes of Connacht and soon afterwards to the O'Briens of Thomond. He was not safe until he reached Scotland, where he worked for the Earls of Lennox near present-day Dumbarton. After the death of his patron he embarked on a pilgrimage to the Holy Land, probably on the coat-tails of the Fifth Crusade (1217–21). He returned to Ireland and may have been friendly with CATHAL CROBHDHEARG Ó CONCHOBHAIR, a brother of the last HIGH KING of Ireland, Ruaidhrí Ó Conchobhair. His attempt to gain forgiveness from the O'Donnells seems to have been spurned, and he returned to Scotland, where he died some time after 1230. His descendants continued a poetic tradition that lasted to the beginning of the nineteenth century. We can piece this story together from the twenty or so poems that survive and have been attributed to him. Some are purely professional poems, but the most interesting are those that are deeply personal. One of these is on the death of his wife; another is an appeal to the Blessed Virgin to reward him with Heaven for the excellence of his verse. A strong personality beats across the centuries from his poetry and is only accentuated by the strictures of the traditional metres within which he worked. He has been described as one of the most fascinating characters in Irish literature. **Alan Titley**

Ó Dálaigh, Tadhg Camchosach (fl. 1375), poet. The best-known poem attributed to this poet is the one he wrote on departing from Ireland as a friar, 'Dá ghrádh féin d'fhághbhas Éirinn'. Poems for Niall Mór Ó Néill and other members of that family are attributed to him. **Michelle O Riordan**

Ó Dálaigh, Tadhg mac Diarmada (fl. 1618), poet. Among the compositions attributed to him are an elegy on the death of Dermot O'Sullivan (died 1618). He may have been the 'Odalie' who was O'Sullivan Beare's representative to his kinsman Eoghan Óg during their opposing conflicts with the English in south-west Cork. **Michelle O Riordan**

Ó Danachar, Caoimhín: see DANAGHER, KEVIN.

O'Dea, Jimmy (1899–1965), comedian. The archetypal Dublin comedian, he was famous for his characterisation of the witty, contemptuous market trader 'Biddy Mulligan, the Pride of the Coombe', in sketches written by Harry O'Donovan. Their first collaboration, *We're Here* (1928), was at the QUEEN'S ROYAL THEATRE. For the rest of his career the diminutive O'Dea was justly regarded as Ireland's finest comedian, often displaying a subtlety and poignancy that transcended the variety stage (see p. 222). Well known through touring and films, including *Penny Paradise* (1938) and *Let's Be Famous* (1939), in 1959 he was the King of the Leprechauns in Disney's *Darby O'Gill and the Little People*. **Stephen Dixon and Deirdre Falvey**

Ó Direáin, Máirtín (1910–1988), poet. Born at An Sruthán Beag, Árainn, Co. Galway. He left the island at eighteen to work as

Ó Direáin. *A native of the Aran Islands, Máirtín Ó Direáin was one of the principal twentieth-century poets writing in Irish; his work depicts the desolation and cultural impoverishment of everyday life. [Courtesy of RTÉ Stills Library/photographer unknown]*

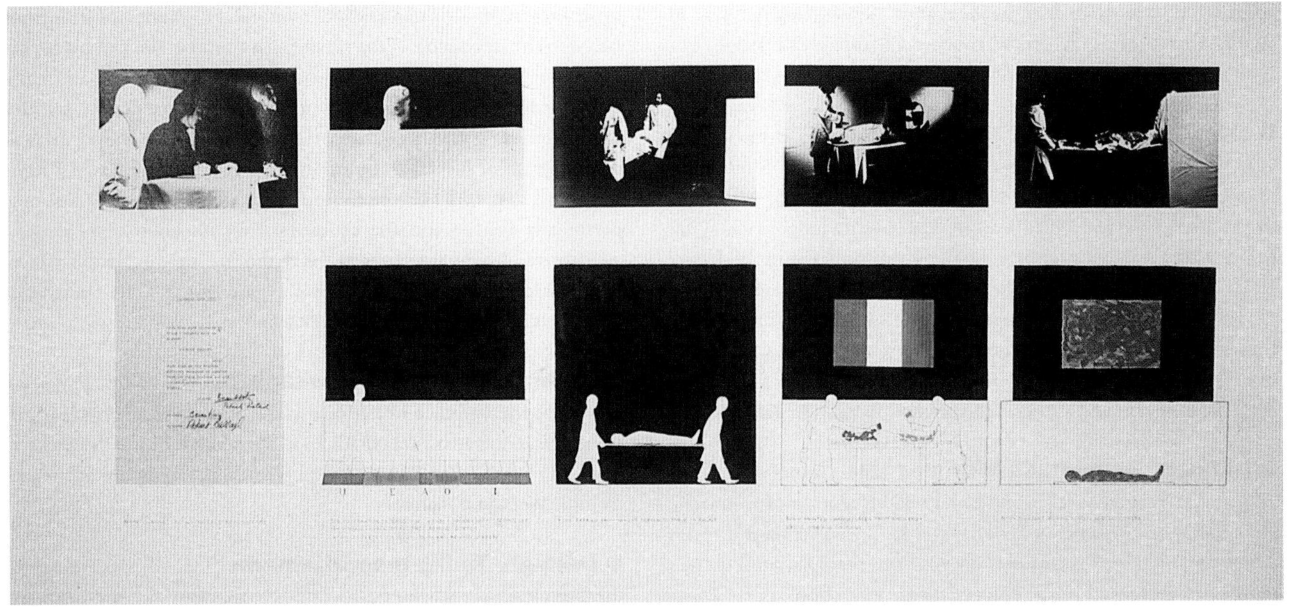

O'Doherty, Brian. Name change *(1972), a mixed-media collage, by Patrick Ireland (Brian O'Doherty), documenting the artist's performance, during which he changed his name to Patrick Ireland as a protest against the Bloody Sunday killings in Derry on 20 January 1972. [Brian O'Doherty]*

a clerk with the Department of Posts and Telegraphs in Galway; there he became involved with TAIBHDHEARC NA GAILLIMHE and also published essays and SHORT STORIES in various literary magazines and newspapers. He moved to Dublin in 1938 to take up a post as a civil servant in the Department of Education. He began to move in literary circles and on 23 December published his nativity poem 'Réalt na hOíche' in the IRISH PRESS. The collections *Coinnle Geala* (1942) and *Dánta Aniar* (1943), both published at his own expense, were significant developments: apart from their thematic appeal, they marked a distinct break with the forms and metres of traditional poetry in Irish. It was with the publication of the selected poems, *Rogha Dánta* (1949), however, that his reputation began to be firmly established. Though working full-time, he continued to publish regularly, and further collections followed: *Ó Mórna agus Dánta Eile* (1957), *Ár Ré Dhearóil* (1962), *Cloch Choirnéil* (1966), *Crainn is Cairde* (1970), *Ceacht an Éin* (1979), *Béasa an Túir* (1984), and *Craobhóg Dán* (1986). The collection *Feamainn Bhealtaine* (1961) presented him as an accomplished essayist, and his contributions to literary journals were a significant addition to a burgeoning literary criticism in Irish. While his major literary work was in poetry, he also published short stories, literary and critical essays, and a play. Two selected anthologies—*Máirtín Ó Direáin, Dánta, 1939–1979* (edited by Eoghan Ó hAnluain, 1980) and *Máirtín Ó Direáin, Tacar Dánta/Selected Poems* (edited by Tomás Mac Síomóin and Douglas Sealy, 1984)—mark his importance as one of the principal twentieth-century poets in Irish. Ó Direáin's accessible but subtle and finely wrought body of work articulates a sense of erosion of personal, social and humane values and a deep sense of desolation, uprootedness, and spiritual and cultural impoverishment, which he saw as inherent in much of contemporary life. Even in his darkest poems of exploration into the human psyche he evoked a universal response in his abiding quest for authenticity and truth. The National University of Ireland conferred an honorary doctorate on him, and he was awarded the Ossian-Preis in Paris in 1977 and many other literary prizes. **Éanna Mac Cába**

O'Doherty, Brian, also known as Patrick Ireland (1930–), artist and writer. Born in Ballaghaderreen, Co. Roscommon; graduated in medicine from UCD, 1952. While a student he exhibited at the IRISH EXHIBITION OF LIVING ART and the ROYAL HIBERNIAN ACADEMY. He studied visual perception at the Experimental Psychology Laboratories, Cambridge, and in 1957 was awarded a Smith Mundt fellowship to Harvard University. He settled in the United States, pursuing parallel careers as artist, writer, and film-maker. He was art critic with the *New York Times*, 1961–4, and editor of *Art in America*, 1971–4; his films include *Hopper's Silence* and *Barbara One to Three*. He was director of visual arts programmes at the National Endowment for the Arts, 1969–76.

His art is often concerned with labyrinths, mazes, visual signs and codes and frequently employs the OGHAM alphabet. From 1973 characteristic works have included 'rope drawings'—installations using the entire gallery space—ink drawings, and paintings. He exhibited at Documenta, 1977, Rosc, 1977, the Venice Biennale, 1980, the Charles Cowles Gallery, 1980, and Leo Castelli Gallery, 1982. Retrospective exhibitions have been held at the Smithsonian American Art Museum, New York, 1985, Elvehjem Museum of Art, Madison, Wisconsin, 1993, and PS1 Institute of Contemporary Art, 1994. His installation *One Here Now* was shown at the Sirius Art Centre, Cobh, Co. Cork, 1996–7.

In 1972, following the BLOODY SUNDAY shooting of unarmed civil rights demonstrators in Derry, O'Doherty undertook to sign his work 'Patrick Ireland' until the British military presence was removed from Northern Ireland. His publications (as Brian O'Doherty) include *American Masters: The Voice and the Myth* (1974) and *Inside the White Cube* (2000) and two novels, *The Strange Case of Mlle P* (1992) and *The Deposition of Father McGreevy* (2000). **Peter Murray**

O'Doherty, Sir Cahir (1587–1608), Lord of Inishowen. Dynastic rivalries saw O'Doherty siding with the English during the NINE YEARS' WAR (1594–1603). When the war ended he pursued a policy of accommodation with the newly dominant Crown administration in Ireland, seeking to become a member of the household of the Prince of Wales. Given this background, his death in rebellion in 1608 is somewhat surprising. The explanation for this extraordinary turn of events owed much to persistent provocation by Sir George Paulet, the governor of Derry. Following one incident, when

Paulet reportedly assaulted O'Doherty, the youthful Lord of Inishowen plotted his revenge. He seized Derry in April 1608, putting Paulet to the sword, though generally sparing the rest of the English colonists. His forces ultimately rose to almost a thousand men. By July 1608 the rising had ended as suddenly as it had begun, with O'Doherty's death during a skirmish at Kilmacrenan, Co. Donegal, a comparatively small-scale revolt by the standard of the Nine Years' War; O'Doherty's rebellion nevertheless had far-reaching implications. The relatively minimal plantation plans that had been agreed in the wake of the FLIGHT OF THE EARLS were abandoned in favour of a much more ambitious project. **John McCavitt**

O'Doherty, Éamonn Feithín (1918–1998), psychologist, logician, and philosopher. Educated at Rome and Cambridge, graduating in Celtic studies; ordained a priest in 1943, later becoming a monsignor. From the age of thirty-one until his retirement in 1981 he was professor of logic and psychology at University College, Dublin, where he created one of Ireland's first departments of empirical psychology, and set up the Department of Social Science. He acted as assistant to Jan Lucasiewicz, whose two-page initial sketch of Aristotle's Syllogistic he kept framed on his office wall. He maintained a lifelong interest in philosophical as well as empirical psychology, and logic, and published on the psychology of religion and religious life. **Thomas A. F. Kelly**

O'Doherty, Kevin Izod (1823–1905), Young Irelander. Born in Dublin. He joined the Repeal Association, eventually becoming involved with the radical YOUNG IRELAND movement. He wrote for the NATION and helped to found the *Irish Tribune*. After the 1848 RISING he was sentenced to ten years' TRANSPORTATION to Tasmania. In 1853 he helped to organise the escape of JOHN MITCHEL to the United States. After his release he returned to Ireland in 1844 and married MARY EVA KELLY ('Eva of the *Nation*'), before returning to Australia and establishing a successful medical practice in Brisbane. He entered politics and was elected to both houses of the Australian legislature, 1877–85. He returned to Ireland and was elected MP for North Meath in 1885, but by 1888 he was again in Australia, where he died in poverty. **Brian Galvin**

Ó Doibhlin, Breandán (1931–), priest, writer, and critic. Born in the Muintir Loinigh area of Co. Tyrone; educated at ST PATRICK'S COLLEGE, Maynooth, and Rome, where he was ordained in 1955. He was professor of modern languages (French) at Maynooth, 1958–96, and had a long involvement with the Irish College, Paris, but is best known as a novelist (*Néal Maidine agus Tine Oíche*, 1964, *An Branar Gan Cur*, 1979), literary critic (*Aistí Critice agus Cultúir*, 1974, *Aistí Critice agus Cultúir II*, 1997), translator (mainly from French literature but also the Book of Isaiah and the new Roman Catholic Catechism), and dramatist. He was also the chief motivator of young critics involved with IRISLEABHAR MHÁ NUAD, and compiler of a unique thesaurus of Irish, *Gaoth an Fhocail* (1998). **Antain Mag Shamhráin**

Ó Doirnín, Peadar (1700–1769), poet and scribe. Born in Co. Louth, and taught in Forkill, Co. Armagh. He was essentially a love poet, whose poems, in particular 'Úrchnoc Chéin Mhic Cáinte' and 'Uilleagán Dubh Ó', were sung. His poem 'Mná na hÉireann' was set to music by SEÁN Ó RIADA in 1969. Two collections of his poems (edited by Breandán Ó Buachalla and Seán de Rís) were published in 1969. He died in his schoolhouse in Forkill in 1769 and is buried close by in Urney graveyard. **Pádraigín Ní Uallacháin**

Ó Dónaill, Niall (1908–1995), lexicographer. Born in the Rosses, Co. Donegal; educated at UCD. He translated many works into Irish, and wrote a history of the Rosses, *Na Glúnta Rosannacha* (1952). His essay 'Forbairt na Gaeilge' (1951) argued a compelling case for the standardisation of written Irish from a modernising, urban viewpoint. He edited the principal Irish–English dictionary, *Foclóir Gaeilge-Béarla* (1978), and was joint-editor of the revised edition of the standard Irish grammar, *Graiméar Gaeilge na mBráithre Críostaí* (1999), published after his death. His contributions to the ideology, lexicography and grammatical explication of the modern written language played a defining role in the twentieth-century history of Irish. **Liam Mac Mathúna**

Ó Donnchadha an Ghleanna, Séafraidh (c. 1620–1678), poet. Head of his branch of the O'Donoghue family, he managed to retain his lands at Glenflesk, Co. Kerry, at the time of CROMWELL. He was skilful in both bardic verse and the increasingly prevalent stressed metres. A full inventory and edition of his poetry has yet to appear (see p. 270). **Seán Ó Cearnaigh**

O'Donnell, Daniel (1961–), singer. Born and educated at Kincaslough, Co. Donegal. He began his career in the early 1980s as a backing singer for his sister, Margo. O'Donnell is a leading exponent of the musical genre known as 'country and Irish'. He regularly tops the British country music charts, and though he has not officially released any records in America, imported albums have sold remarkably well in Irish-populated areas. In 2002 he was made an honorary member of the Order of the British Empire for his services to the music industry. **Tony Clayton-Lea**

O'Donnell, 'Red' Hugh (c. 1571–1602), military leader during the NINE YEARS' WAR (1594–1603). O'Donnell is famed for the quality of his military leadership and for his exploits in escaping from DUBLIN CASTLE. Kidnapped as a youth under the orders of Lord Deputy Perrot in 1587 so that leverage could be exercised on the great families of the north, O'Donnell was to languish in Dublin Castle until 1591, when he effected an intrepid escape from Bermingham Tower. Harbouring a deep antipathy towards the growing power of the English Crown in Ireland, he was to the fore in seeking to confront it by force. While his ally HUGH O'NEILL, Earl of Tyrone, was less willing to commit himself openly to the rebel cause in the early stages of the war, O'Donnell played a prominent role in the conflict from the start and in Irish military successes, not

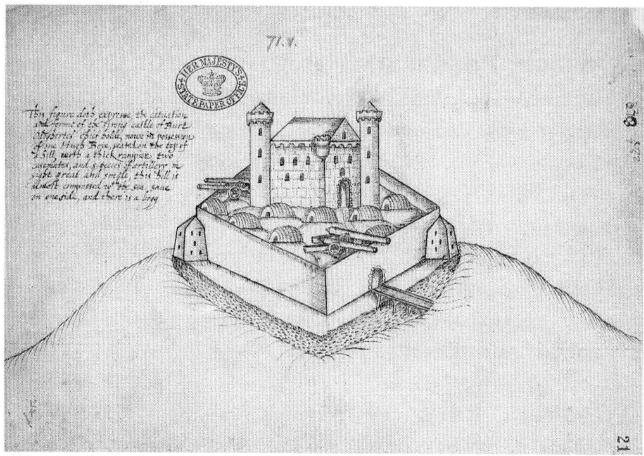

O'Doherty, Cahir. Drawing of Burt Castle *(1601), with descriptive notes on the natural defences. Overlooking Lough Swilly, it was the fortress of Sir Cahir O'Doherty, Lord of Inishowen. [Public Record Office, London; MPFI/335]*

least at the BATTLE OF THE YELLOW FORD (1598). Though he was ultimately defeated at the BATTLE OF KINSALE (1601), O'Donnell's forced march along virtually the entire length of Ireland in an attempt to establish liaison with his Spanish allies earned great contemporary admiration. Following the catastrophic defeat at Kinsale and the departure of Spanish forces in its aftermath, O'Donnell travelled to Spain in 1602 in a desperate bid to rally further Spanish assistance, where he died. Such was his perceived menace to English interests in Ireland that it was widely rumoured at the time that he was poisoned by a hired assassin. **John McCavitt**

O'Donnell, Manus (c. 1490–1564), Lord of Tyrconnell, 1537–55. Eldest son of Hugh Dubh O'Donnell, Lord of Tyrconnell, 1505–37; he became Lord of Tyrconnell in July 1537, having first ruled as his father's deputy while he went on a pilgrimage to Rome in 1510. In 1539 Manus joined CONN BACACH O'NEILL, Lord of Tyrone, in a vain attempt to restore the Earldom of Kildare to the nephew of Lady ELEANOR FITZGERALD, whom he had recently married. However, in June 1540 he submitted to HENRY VIII. Unusually for an Irish lord, he is credited with literary compositions. He dictated a version of 'BETHA COLAIM CHILLE' to a scribe; some bardic poetry is also attributed to him. In 1555 he was obliged to surrender his lordship to his son, Calbhach. He died at Lifford on 9 February 1564. **Henry A. Jefferies**

O'Donnell, Mary E. (1954–), poet and writer. Born in Monaghan; educated at NUI, Maynooth. She has published three collections of poetry: *Reading the Sunflowers in September* (1990), *Spiderwoman's Third Avenue Rhapsody* (1993), and *Unlegendary Heroes* (1998). Her poetry has been praised for its elegance of structure and for its celebration of sensuality, childhood, love, motherhood, and femininity. A collection of short stories, *Strong Pagans* (1991), was followed by three novels: *The Light Makers* (1992), *Virgin and the Boy* (1996), and *The Elysium Testament* (1999). She is a member of AOSDÁNA. **Elaine Sisson**

O'Donnell, Nicholas (Nick) (1925–1988), hurler. Born in Co. Kilkenny. Having won an all-Ireland medal with Kilkenny as a substitute in 1947, he moved to Enniscorthy to work, and declared for Wexford. He won three all-Ireland championships, in 1955, 1956, and 1960, and enjoyed the honour of being team captain on two of those occasions. He was named Hurler of the Year in 1960. **Donal Keenan**

O'Donnell, Peadar (1893–1986) novelist and socialist. Born in Meenmore, Co. Donegal. He commanded an IRA brigade there, 1921–2, and was imprisoned during the CIVIL WAR. He edited *An Phoblacht* in the late 1920s and was a member of the IRA Army Council, 1925–34. His arguments against the payment of land annuities to Britain became FIANNA FÁIL policy in 1932. He formed the Republican Congress in 1934. He edited the BELL, the influential literary magazine, from 1946 to 1954. Two of his six novels, *Islanders* (1928) and *The Big Windows* (1955), are classic depictions of rural life. **Peter Hegarty**

O'Donnell, Rory, first Earl of Tyrconnell (1575–1608). Together with HUGH O'NEILL, Earl of Tyrone, he took part in the FLIGHT OF THE EARLS (1607). A younger brother of RED HUGH O'DONNELL, famed rebel leader during the NINE YEARS' WAR (1594–1603), he succeeded as chieftain of the O'Donnells in the later stage of the conflict, following his elder brother's death in Spain in 1602. He maintained his family alliance with the O'Neills and took a leading role in renewed conspiratorial practices before the Flight. He was intensely aggrieved by harassment from Crown officials in his private affairs and alarmed by a policy of persecution embarked on by the royal authorities. Liaising with discontented elements among the Catholic OLD ENGLISH in Ireland, he became the focus of much government suspicion. On the verge of being arrested he found temporary salvation in taking flight to the Continent, only to perish a year later from disease in Rome. **John McCavitt**

O'Donnell and Tuomey, architects, Dublin, established in 1988, a partnership of Sheila O'Donnell (1953–) and John Tuomey (1954–); both educated at UCD, O'Donnell also at the Royal College of Art, London. O'Donnell has been a studio lecturer at UCD since 1981, and was a visiting critic at Princeton University, 1987. Both worked with Stirling Wilford and Associates, London, 1976–80, Tuomey worked with the OFFICE OF PUBLIC WORKS, Dublin, 1981–7 (where he worked on the laboratory at Abbotstown and the courthouse in Smithfield, Dublin), has been a studio lecturer at UCD since 1980, and was a visiting critic at Princeton University, 1987, 1993, and at Harvard University, 1988–9. The practice has won six AAI Downes Medals: for the Irish Film Centre, Eustace Street, Dublin (1988), the Living in the City project, Parliament Street, Dublin (1990), the Irish pavilion (with BRIAN MAGUIRE paintings) at Leauwarden, Friesland (1992), the Gallery of Photography, Temple Bar, Dublin (1997), the multi-denominational school at Ranelagh, Dublin (1999), and the Furniture College, Letterfrack, Co. Galway. They were members of the City Architecture Studio, 1984, and Group 91 (which produced the TEMPLE BAR FRAMEWORK PLAN, 1991). Projects inspired by the landscape have included Blackwood Golf Centre, Clandeboye, Co. Down. **Raymund Ryan**

O'Donoghue, Bernard (1945–), poet and academic. Born in Cullen, Co. Cork. He teaches medieval English in Oxford and has published a study of SEAMUS HEANEY. His poems, which frequently recall his native county, are collected in *Poaching Rights* (1987), *The Weakness* (1991), *Gunpowder* (1995), winner of the Whitbread Book of the Year Award, and *Here Nor There* (1999). **Terence Brown**

O'Donoghue, Hugh (Hughie) (1953–), painter. Born in Manchester of Irish parents; graduated in fine art from Goldsmiths College, London. He now lives and works near Thomastown, Co. Kilkenny, one of the most important painters working in Ireland. The twelve vast canvases of his most important work, the hugely impressive *Episodes from the Passion*, are on a Renaissance scale of ambition and achievement; his prints on the subject are equally ambitious and impressive. O'Donoghue has also completed several series of works based on his father's experiences in the SECOND WORLD WAR. He is a member of AOSDÁNA. **Dorothy Walker**

O'Donovan, Gerald (1871–1942), priest and novelist. Born in Co. Down; educated at Cork, Galway, and Sligo. He entered ST PATRICK'S COLLEGE, Maynooth, and in 1895 was ordained a priest for the diocese of Clonfert. He was an energetic administrator in Loughrea, Co. Galway, and was involved in the creation of the new cathedral. A supporter of the GAELIC LEAGUE and the CO-OPERATIVE MOVEMENT, he fell out with his superiors. He left the priesthood and Ireland and worked in publishing in London, where he was the intimate friend of Rose Macaulay and published a series of corrosive novels, beginning with *Father Ralph* (1913). **Peter Costello**

O'Duffy, Eoin. *Eoin O'Duffy addressing a meeting of the Blueshirts at Bandon, Co. Cork, c. 1934. The Blueshirts were a fascist-style response to Fianna Fáil's victory in the general election of 1932. [Getty Images/Hulton Archive]*

O'Donovan, John (1806–1861), scholar. Born in Attateemore, Co. Kilkenny; educated at Hunt's Academy, Waterford. Contemplating the priesthood, he attended Latin classes in Dublin, 1823–7. Two years working part time for JAMES HARDIMAN trained him in the use of state papers and traditional Irish sources. He spent brief periods teaching Irish to THOMAS LARCOM and doing scribal work for Myles John O'Reilly, a collector of manuscripts. From 1830 to 1842, except for a short break in 1833, he worked for the topographical department of the ORDNANCE SURVEY, travelling the country in difficult conditions and sending in a series of letters, often humorous, that are an important contribution to Ireland's lore and literature. From 1832 he contributed articles to the *Dublin Penny Journal* and *Irish Penny Journal*. He was called to the bar in 1847.

In the early 1840s he edited texts for the Irish Archaeological Society; in 1845, in spite of scruples, he published *A Grammar of the Irish Language* for St Columba's College, Rathfarnham, Co. Dublin, a new Church of Ireland boarding-school. In 1847 he published *Leabhar na gCeart*, or *The Book of Rights*. In the same year he was elected a member of the ROYAL IRISH ACADEMY and in 1848 was presented with its Cunningham Gold Medal. He had long been interested in translating and editing the 'Annals of the FOUR MASTERS', and its six volumes appeared in 1848–51; his notes fill more than half the 4,170 pages. In 1849 he became professor of CELTIC LANGUAGES in Queen's College, Belfast.

O'Donovan and his brother-in-law EUGENE O'CURRY were the greatest Irish scholars of their day. They were appointed joint-editors for the transcription and translation of the old Irish law texts but did not live to see their work published. O'Donovan died of rheumatic fever on 10 December 1861 and is buried in Glasnevin Cemetery, Dublin. **Diarmuid Breathnach and Máire Ní Mhurchú**

O'Donovan Rossa, Jeremiah (1831–1915), nationalist. Born in Rosscarbery, Co. Cork. His Phoenix Society was incorporated in the IRB in May 1859. He became the business manager of the Fenian newspaper, and was arrested in 1865. His mistreatment in prison became a *cause célèbre*. Amnestied in 1871, he went to New York, where he organised the 'skirmishing fund' in 1875, became the head centre of the IRB in 1877, and helped direct a terrorist campaign in Britain and Ireland in the years 1881–7. He was buried in Dublin, and his funeral was a rallying point for advanced NATIONALISM. [see PEARSE, PATRICK.] **Oliver P. Rafferty**

O'Dowd, Nace (1931–1987), Gaelic footballer. Born in Ballinacarrow, Co. Sligo. He captained the Sligo minor team in 1948 and 1949, leading them to their first provincial success in 1949. In 1950 he became a regular on the Sligo senior team and served it in many positions over the years: defence, midfield, and in the forward line. Though he never won a provincial senior medal he played consistently for Connacht between 1951 and 1959, winning three Railway Cup medals (1951, 1957, and 1958), the last two at full-back. A player of exceptional talent and flexibility, he is a hero of Sligo football. **Jack Mahon**

O'Driscoll, Dennis (1954–), poet and critic. Born in Thurles, Co. Tipperary; educated at the Institute of Public Administration and UCD. His collections of verse include *Kist* (1982), *Hidden Extras* (1987), *Long Story Short* (1993), and *Quality Time* (1997). His poems are markedly attentive to daily life in a world of institutions, and time's depredations are wittily and movingly observed. A selection of his prose writings, *Troubled Thoughts: Majestic Dreams*, was published in 2001. **Terence Brown**

Ó Dubhagáin, Seán Mór (died 1372), historian and poet of Uí Maine (east Galway and south Roscommon). He is the author of several historical and topographical poems; others may have been in sections of the Book of Uí Maine (formerly called the Book of Ó Dubhagáin), now lost. He is also mentioned as having been a teacher to the scribe Adam Ó Cianáin. He spent the last seven years of his life in the monastery of Rindown, Co. Roscommon. **Nollaig Ó Muraíle**

O'Duffy, Eimar (1893–1935), novelist. Born in Dublin; educated at Stonyhurst College, Lancashire, and UCD. His principal literary achievement is the Cuandine trilogy—*King Goshawk and the Birds* (1926), *The Spacious Adventures of the Man in the Street* (1928), and *Asses in Clover* (1933)—a sustained satirical attack on the bourgeois materialism of post-independence Ireland. Remarkably inventive in his juxtaposition of Irish mythology with mundane reality, O'Duffy has often been compared to FLANN O'BRIEN and JAMES JOYCE. Other work of interest includes *The Wasted Island* (1919, revised 1929), a fictionalised account of the years leading up to the 1916 RISING. **Derek Hand**

O'Duffy, Eoin (1892–1944), soldier, policeman, politician. Born in Co. Monaghan. He commanded Monaghan Brigade IRA in the WAR OF INDEPENDENCE, 1919–21, and was briefly imprisoned. As deputy Chief of Staff he persuaded the Ulster IRA to accept the ANGLO-IRISH TREATY, December 1921. He was Chief of Staff of the Free State army in early 1922. After brief CIVIL WAR service, July–August 1922, he became Commissioner of the GARDA SÍOCHÁNA, returning to the military in 1924–5 as temporary Inspector-General during the Army Crisis. After 1932, he led the rightwing BLUESHIRTS and a Francoist Irish Brigade in the SPANISH CIVIL WAR. **Patrick Long**

Ó Duilearga, Séamus (1899–1980), folklorist and Celtic scholar. Born James Hamilton Delargy in Cushendall, Co. Antrim. On the staff of UCD, 1923–72, he was professor of folklore from 1946. His visit to the Nordic and Baltic regions in the summer and autumn of 1928 helped lay the foundation for the systematic and scientific collecting of Irish folklore undertaken, under his direction, by the Irish Folklore Institute, 1930–35, and especially its successor, the IRISH FOLKLORE COMMISSION, 1935–70. During this trip, of less than six months' duration, he deepened his knowledge of folkloristics under the tutelage of Carl William von Sydow and acquainted himself with various Scandinavian languages, and his visits to the folklore archives of the region inspired him to emulate and to surpass the collecting work of Nordic and Baltic folklorists. Throughout his later career he maintained close contacts with folklorists in those countries of northern Europe that he visited as a young man, particularly with Sweden. His magnum opus, *Leabhar Sheáin Í Chonaill* (1948), records folklore from Co. Kerry; his directorship of the Irish Folklore Commission, 1935–70, was undoubtedly his greatest achievement (see p. 406). [see Ó CONAILL, SEAN.] **Mícheál Briody**

Ó Duinn, Proinnsías (1941–), conductor and composer. Born in Dublin, he studied at DIT, CMD and RIAM. He was appointed Principal Conductor of the Icelandic Symphony Orchestra 1963–4 and subsequently of the Symphony Orchestra of Ecuador (1966–71), and also lectured at the University of Popayan (Columbia). He returned to Ireland as RTÉ's Choral Conductor 1974–78 and was Principal Conductor of the RTÉ CONCERT ORCHESTRA 1978–2002. **Richard Pine**

O'Dwyer, Robert (1862–1949), first professor of Irish music at UCD, a post he occupied from 1914 to 1939. He was an active promoter of Irish music; his most important composition, *Eithne*, an Irish-language opera in three acts, was premiered in 1910. **David Mooney**

O'Faolain, Eileen, née Gould (1902–1988), writer. Born and educated in Cork, she was married to SEAN O'FAOLAIN. Overshadowed by PATRICIA LYNCH, her output is almost exclusively in the area of fantasy and fairy-tale, together with retellings of Irish myths and sagas. Her books, published between 1940 and 1959, provided children of the time with stories that were based in their own world. The stories were written for her daughter JULIA, who regularly features in them, as in *Miss Pennyfeather in the Springtime* (1946), *Miss Pennyfeather and the Pooka*, and *The Children of Crooked Castle* (1945). All her tales have a strong element of fantasy and magic, a magic that is frequently wrought through and by animals, as in *The Little Black Hen* (1940), *The King of the Cats* (1941), and *The White Rabbit's Road*. A superb storyteller, she was attuned to the language and lore of the *seanchaí*. **Patricia Donlon**

O'Faolain, Julia (1932–), writer. Born in London, daughter of SEAN O'FAOLAIN and EILEEN O'FAOLAIN, and raised in Dublin; she lives in London. Her fiction deals with personal dilemmas in different cultural and historical settings, often from women's point of view. *Women in the Wall* (1975) and *The Judas Cloth* (1992) are historical novels; *The Irish Signorina* (1984) narrates in explicit terms a foreigner's experience of contemporary Italian life, intertwined with a private past. *No Country for Young Men* (1980) is an account of Irish revolutionary history as seen from a revisionist viewpoint. Her latest novel, *Ercoli e il Guardiano Notturno* (1999), published in Italian, is about the Italian communist leader Palmiro Togliatti. **Marie Arndt**

O'Faolain, Sean (1900–1991), writer. Born in Cork as John Whelan, son of an RIC man; educated at UCC and Harvard University. He fought in the WAR OF INDEPENDENCE and took the Republican side in the CIVIL WAR. After teaching in London he returned permanently to Ireland in 1933. He travelled frequently on the Continent, mainly in Italy, and in the United States. He came to oppose the literary ideals of his early mentor, DANIEL CORKERY, preferring Continental writers, such as Maupassant and Chekhov, whom he acclaims in *The Short Story* (1948), where his theory of the SHORT STORY—his preferred literary form—is outlined. His fiction is largely set in Ireland. His first collection of short stories, *Midsummer Night Madness* (1932), deals mainly with the War of Independence; IRA characters are louts, not fighting heroes. His novel *Bird Alone* (1936) was banned by the Censorship Board.

Many strong women feature in his fiction. Later collections, such as *I Remember! I Remember!* (1961), portray the repressed Catholic urban middle class in independent Ireland, a topic he often discussed in articles, especially in the BELL, the journal he founded and edited, 1940–46. His cultural history, *The Irish* (1947, revised edition 1981), and his biography of DANIEL O'CONNELL, *King of the Beggars* (1938), are thinly disguised critiques of politics in contemporary Ireland. Though admiring DE VALERA as a leader, O'Faolain deplored his anti-intellectual politics. His autobiography, *Vive Moi!* (1964), reveals his desire for moral and intellectual freedom with an international outlook, which was hindered by his persistent attachment to his Irish roots (see p. 127). **Marie Arndt**

Ó Faracháin, Roibeard (1909–1984), poet and critic. His poetry has strong religious and nationalist overtones and often contains Irish prosodic patterns. He and AUSTIN CLARKE jointly founded the Dublin Verse-Speaking Society, from which evolved the Lyric Theatre. He was also controller of programmes at Radio Éireann and a director of the ABBEY THEATRE. **Mary Thompson**

O'Farrell, Mary (Sister Genevieve) (1923–2001), educator. Born in Tullamore, Co. Offaly; joined the Daughters of Charity of St Vincent de Paul in 1941 and reluctantly trained as a teacher at the University of Manchester and Sedgeley Park College of Education. In 1958 she was appointed vice-principal of a newly opened girls' school in Belfast, St Louise's Comprehensive College on the Falls Road. She was totally opposed to the ELEVEN-PLUS selection process and determined that the quality of education available at St Louise's would be of the highest standard. Despite the 'TROUBLES' and the location of the school in a volatile and deprived area of Belfast, she succeeded during her tenure as principal, 1963–88, in maintaining impressively high education levels. Many went on to university, the first of their families to do so. In 1978 she was made an officer of the Order of the British Empire. On her retirement she continued to campaign for improvements in public education. She was a member of the Senate of Queen's University, the Northern Ireland Curriculum Council, and the Northern Ireland Standing Commission on Human Rights. St Louise's Comprehensive College is the largest single-sex school in Europe. **Myra Dowling**

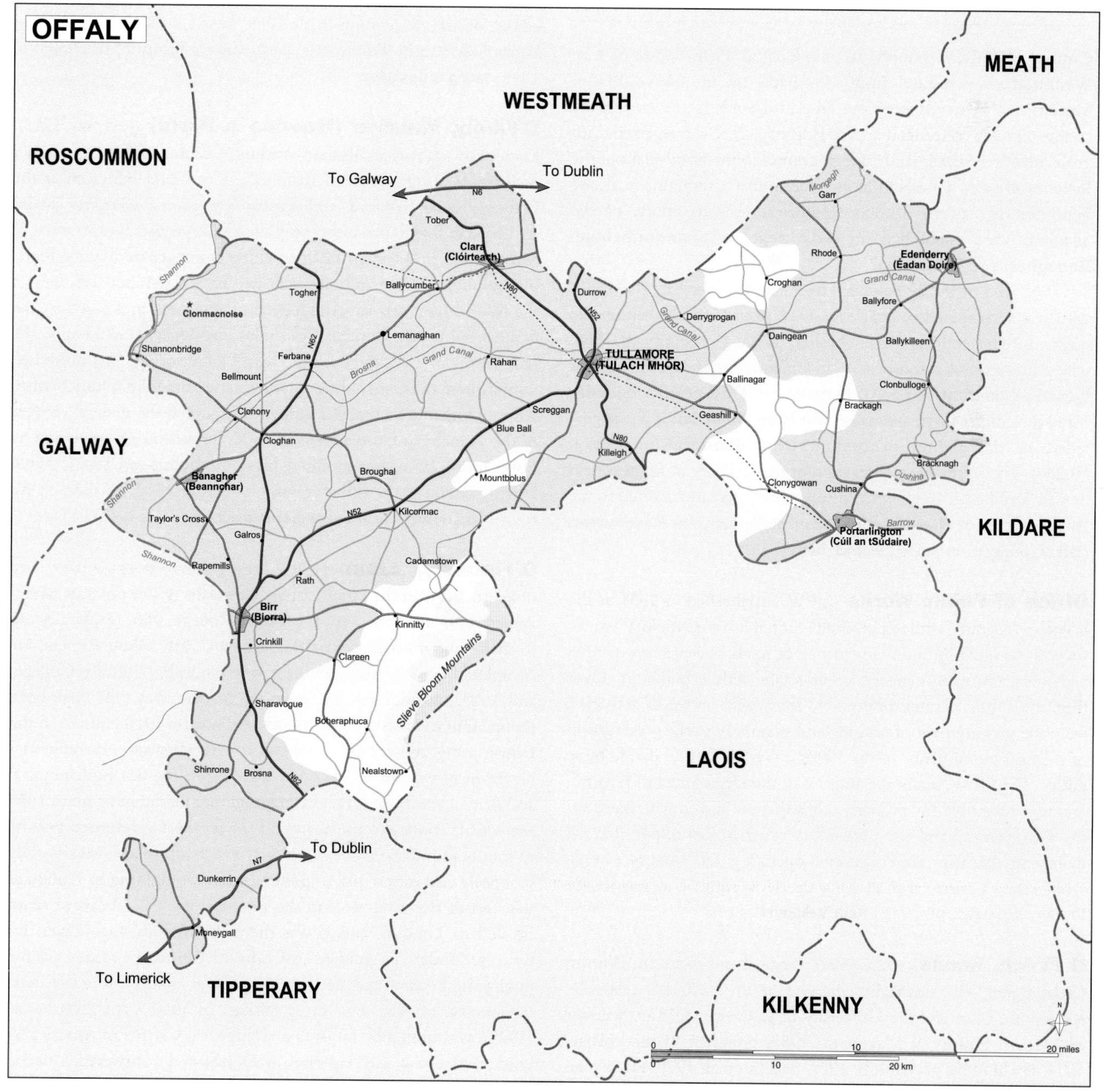

Offaly, County (*Contae Uíbh Fhailí*)

Province:	LEINSTER
County town:	Tullamore
Area:	2,000 km^2 (772 sq. miles)
Population (2002):	63,702
Features:	River Brosna
	River SHANNON
	Slieve Bloom Mountains
Of historical interest:	Cloghan Castle
	CLONMACNOISE
	DURROW monastic site
	Gallen monastic site
Industry and products:	BREWING
	DISTILLING
	Engineering
	Food-processing
	Peat production
	TEXTILES

Petula Martyn

County Offaly, a county in the Central Plain south of Co. Westmeath, is separated from Co. Laois by the Slieve Bloom Mountains. It extends from the raised boglands in the east of the county known collectively as the Bog of ALLEN, interspersed with great 'islands' of Esker lands, and continues to the flood-plain of the River SHANNON. Grassland farms predominate, though cereals are important in eastern districts. Historical crossing-points of the Shannon were established on esker ridges at **Shannonbridge**, **Banagher**, and **Portumna**.

The land of Offaly belonged to the O'Connor Faly (Uí Failí), who was accustomed to attack the PALE from fastnesses within the boglands. The county was established as King's County in 1556, when the area was confiscated and planted at the same time as Queen's County (Co. Laois). Philipstown (**Daingean**) was designated the county town and named for King Philip, but it was superseded in the eighteenth century by **Tullamore** (population 10,260). The south-western portion of the territory of Ely was held by O'Carroll until 1620, when it was confiscated and granted to the Parsons family of Norfolk, whose main settlement was Parsonstown (**Birr**) (population 3,573). **Patrick Duffy**

Office of Public Works (OPW), established in 1831 as the BOARD OF WORKS, with responsibility for public infrastructural works, such as the building and maintenance of roads, CANALS, HARBOURS and piers, BRIDGES, drainage systems, and public buildings. Over time the OPW became responsible for a wide range of activities, from the procurement of printing and stationery to the preservation of national monuments. In the 1990s it was decided to divide these duties. The OPW, under the auspices of the Department of Finance, is now responsible for property, construction and procurement for the Government and the public service; it is also responsible for managing the state art collection, operating the DUBLIN CASTLE Conference Centre, and advising the Government in relation to Dublin Zoo. [see DÚCHAS.] **Ruth McManus**

Ó Fiaich, Tomás (1923–1990), cardinal and historian. Born in Crossmaglen, Co. Armagh; educated at ST PATRICK'S COLLEGE, Maynooth, UCD, and the University of Louvain. He was Professor of Modern History at Maynooth, 1959, president of the college, 1974, Archbishop of Armagh, 1977, and cardinal, 1979. He was an authority on the early Irish church, especially its evangelising role in early medieval Europe. His time at Armagh coincided with some of the worst years of the 'TROUBLES'. He was vociferous in his denunciation of paramilitary violence and also of the state's mistreatment of prisoners. Politically, his was an almost impossible balancing act: his south Armagh roots, of which he was very proud, made him an object of unionist suspicions. A man of great charm and erudite wit, he died in Toulouse while en route to Lourdes (see p. 169). **Fergal Tobin**

Ó Fiannachta, Pádraig (1927–), priest, scholar, and poet. Born near Dingle, Co. Kerry; educated at ST PATRICK'S COLLEGE, Maynooth, and UCC. Appointed professor of Old Irish at Maynooth in 1959 and professor of Modern Irish in 1981, he has been parish priest of Dingle since 1993. His creative output includes poetry (*Ponc*, 1970; *Rúin*, 1971; *Deora Dé*, 1988; *Léim an Dá Mhíle*, 1999), autobiographical novels (*An Chomharsa Choimhthíoch*, 1957; *Ag Siúl na Teorann*, 1984), and literary criticism (*Léas ar Ár Litríocht*, 1974; *Léas Eile ar Ár Litríocht*, 1982). He is joint-editor of the ROYAL IRISH ACADEMY's *Dictionary of the Irish Language*, editor of the annual Maynooth lecture series *Léachtaí Cholm Cille* since 1970, and editor of the Maynooth Irish Bible (1981). He established An Díseart, the Celtic Educational and Cultural Institute, in Dingle in 1996. **Tadhg Ó Dúshláine**

O'Fihely, Maurice (Maurice a Portu) (c. 1460–1513), Franciscan scholar, archbishop, leading Scotist, and founding father of 'Irish Writing'. Born in Baltimore, Co. Cork; educated at the Universities of Oxford and Padua. He joined the Franciscans c. 1475 and was professor of philosophy at the Universities of Milan, 1488, and Padua, 1491, reaching eminence in divinity, logic, philosophy, and metaphysics. Known as 'Flos Mundi' (Flower of the World), he was superintendent of the press in Venice to the famous publishers Bonetus Locattelus and Octavianus Scotus, the first Irishman to influence the world of printing. He published numerous works, including commentaries on John Duns Scotus, whose works he edited. An influential figure at the general chapter of the Franciscan Conventuals in 1506, he was highly esteemed by Pope Julius II, who appointed him Archbishop of Tuam, 1506. Having attended the fifth Lateran Council in 1512, he died on his return to Galway. **Juan José Pérez-Camacho**

O'Flaherty, Liam (1896–1984), short-story writer and novelist. Born in the Aran Islands, Co. Galway; his obvious talents gained him admission to Rockwell College, Co. Tipperary, to study for the missionary priesthood of the Holy Ghost Fathers. He completed his education at Blackrock College, Clonliffe College, and UCD, abandoning his vocation on the way. He had been involved in the IRISH VOLUNTEERS but in early 1916 enlisted in the British army and served in the FIRST WORLD WAR. He suffered a severe head wound in 1917 and was hospitalised for both physical and mental conditions. He was released into his father's care in 1920 and set off at once to travel around the world. He returned in time to jointly found the first COMMUNIST PARTY of Ireland with Roddy Connolly and others and to participate in the fighting in Dublin at the start of the CIVIL WAR in the summer of 1922. To avoid arrest he fled to London, and it was there that friends encouraged his writing. Under the guidance of Edward Garnett, a reader for the publishing house Cape, he began to publish rapidly a series of short stories and novels. The most famous of these, THE INFORMER (1925), was filmed by his distant relative JOHN FORD in America. A visit to Moscow and a period in Hollywood completed a hectic period in his life, and by the middle of the 1930s he was almost written out. The novel *Famine* (1937), his finest piece of extended prose, in effect closed his writing career, though he continued to work in a desultory and less effective manner. In the 1920s he was involved with PÁDRAIC Ó CONAIRE in an IRISH-LANGUAGE THEATRE group in Dublin. He lived on the Continent and in America until 1946, when he returned to live in Ireland. He died in Dublin at a time when his books were again being reissued regularly and younger CRITICS were reassessing him. A collection of his short stories in Irish was published as *Dúil* (1953). **Peter Costello**

O'Flaherty, Roderic (1629–1718), landlord and scholar. Born in his father's castle at Moycullen, Co. Galway, heir to a vast estate in Connacht; educated in Alexander Lynch's school in Galway. He remained a devout Catholic throughout his life, which led to the seizure of his estates and his reduction to a life of poverty. His major work was *Ogygia, seu Rerum Hibernicarum Chronologia* (1685), a history of Ireland in Latin published in London. His *Chorographical Description of West or h-Iar Connacht*, written in English in 1684 but not published until 1846, gives a first-hand account of geography and natural history. **Christopher Moriarty**

O'Flanagan, Kevin (1919–), athlete. Born in Dublin. As a soccer international he scored on his debut for the Republic of Ireland in the 3–3 draw with Norway at Dalymount Park in 1937 and would remain as the youngest to do so until ROBBIE KEANE eclipsed his record sixty-one years later. With the suspension of international competition during the SECOND WORLD WAR he was deprived of some of his best years, but in 1947, at a time when he was alternating between SOCCER with Arsenal and RUGBY with London Irish, he became the first to represent Ireland in soccer and rugby with his selection for a rugby game against Australia, his only cap in that code. **Peter Byrne**

Ó Flannghaile, Tomás (1846–1916), teacher and poet. Born in Ballinrobe, Co. Mayo; educated at St Wilfred's, Manchester. He helped launch the IRISH TEXTS SOCIETY and edited MICHEÁL COIMÍN's *Laoi Oisín i dTír na nÓg* (1896) and DONNCHA RUA MAC CONMARA's *Eachtra Ghiolla an Amaráin* (1897). *For the Tongue of the Gael* (1896) is a selection of essays. **Diarmuid Breathnach and Máire Ní Mhurchú**

Ó Flatharta, Antaine (1953–), dramatist. Born in Lettermullen, Co. Galway; he has been a full-time writer since 1981. He writes in both Irish and English, and some plays are almost macaronic in their switching between the two languages. The plays are gritty, realistic illustrations of the GAELTACHT life not shown in tourist brochures; his characters tend to be wanderers or outsiders who dream great unfulfilled dreams. His plays, performed in Ireland, England, and America, include *Gaeilgeoirí* (1986), *Imeachtaí na Saoirse* (1986), *Grásta i Meiriceá* (1990), *Grace in America* (1993), *Blood Guilty* (1995), and *An Solas Dearg* (1998). He has also written scripts for film and television and a children's book, *The Prairie Train* (1998). **Gearóid Denvir**

Ó Flatharta, John Beag (1958–), singer. He sings in a 'country music' style, and also in the more traditional unaccompanied style associated with his native Connemara. Throughout the 1980s he was the lead singer with a popular group, Na hAncairí. The songs document social and political issues of concern to the people of Connemara, such as emigration or local events, including boat-racing. **Ríonach uí Ógáin**

Ó Floinn, Tomás (1910–1997), teacher and school inspector, essayist and critic. Born in Stradbally, Co. Waterford; he became an assistant secretary in the Department of Education. He published modern versions of Old Irish poetry and prose texts, including *Athbheo* (1955), *Athdhánta* (1969), and *Aisling Mhic Conglinne* (1980). *Cion Fir* (1997) is a comprehensive collection of his literary essays. **Aisling Ní Dhonnchadha**

O'Flynn, Críostóir (Críostóir O'Floinn) (1927–), writer and journalist. Born in Limerick; educated at TCD. A versatile man of letters, he has written poetry, plays, novels, stories and journalism in both Irish and English. All his work is marked by a clarity of style and by a sharp humour. His best work in English may be the collection of stories *Sanctuary Island* (1971) and his play *The Order of Melchizedek*, produced by the ABBEY THEATRE in 1967. Along with an earlier version in Irish, *Cóta Bán Chríost* (1966), they showed his ability to move with ease in and out of the two languages, adapting and reshaping as he saw fit. *Mise Raifteirí an File* (1974) is a play that moves between the life of RAIFTEARAÍ, the nineteenth-century poet, and the cultural wars at the time of the Irish revival and beyond. It showed his stagecraft at its most imaginative and subtle, while making a strong statement about the place of art in society. *There Is an Isle* (1998) is a memoir of growing up and of education. **Alan Titley**

O'Flynn, Liam (1945–), uilleann piper. Born in Kill, Co. Kildare. He was introduced to the UILLEANN PIPES by Tom Armstrong, studied under LEO ROWSOME, and was later influenced by WILLIE CLANCY and SÉAMUS ENNIS. He was a founder-member of Planxty in 1972 with CHRISTY MOORE, DÓNAL LUNNY, and ANDY IRVINE.

Ogham. *The Brandon Monument, Arraglen, Co. Kerry, shown during excavation. The ogham inscription is carved along both edges and across the top; it reads 'Rónán the priest son of Comgán.' [Prof. John Waddell, Department of Archaeology, National University of Ireland, Galway]*

Orchestral work includes SHAUN DAVEY's *The Brendan Voyage* and *The Relief of Derry Symphony;* musical collaborations include those with John Cage, ENYA, Mark Knopfler, Elmer Bernstein, the Everley Brothers, Kate Bush, and SEAMUS HEANEY. **Pat Ahern**

ogham, an unusual script employing tally-like scores rather than conventional letters. Ogham inscriptions date approximately from the fifth to the seventh centuries and are the earliest written source in Irish. Approximately 330 such inscriptions have been found in Ireland, two-thirds of them in the southern counties of Kerry, Cork, and Waterford. They have also been found in areas of the Irish DIASPORA of the period: Wales, Devon and Cornwall, the Isle of Man, and Scotland (those of Scotland differing from all others in that they are not written in Irish). The inscriptions are usually cut along the edge of standing stones (of various sizes and shapes), as opposed to slabs. Those in Britain (excluding Scotland) are frequently complemented by an equivalent in Latin written in conventional script on the face of the stone, and these provide a contemporary key to the ogham characters, which is supplemented in the (much later) manuscript tradition in Ireland.

The inscriptions are commemorative in nature and confine themselves to a record of the person's name, often accompanied by that of his father (in all but one case—in Wales—the name is that of a male) and occasionally by a tribal affiliation. They therefore constitute an important source of information on Irish PERSONAL NAMES; and though their grammatical accidence is very limited they do provide us with a unique insight into linguistic developments in Primitive Irish, a period of the language otherwise recoverable only by comparative reconstruction. In particular they span the period during which the language dropped the inherited Indo-European inflectional endings and replaced them with a distinctive series of initial mutations and variation in consonantal quality.

The ogham inscriptions have occasionally been described as 'pagan' and contrasted with the later Christian tradition of the manuscript record. None of the arguments for this view, however, stand up to scrutiny. The stones on which they are inscribed frequently bear crosses, some of which can be shown to be older than the accompanying inscription; and one inscription records the name of a priest, using an Early Christian Latin loanword. [see GRAVE SLABS.] **Damian McManus**

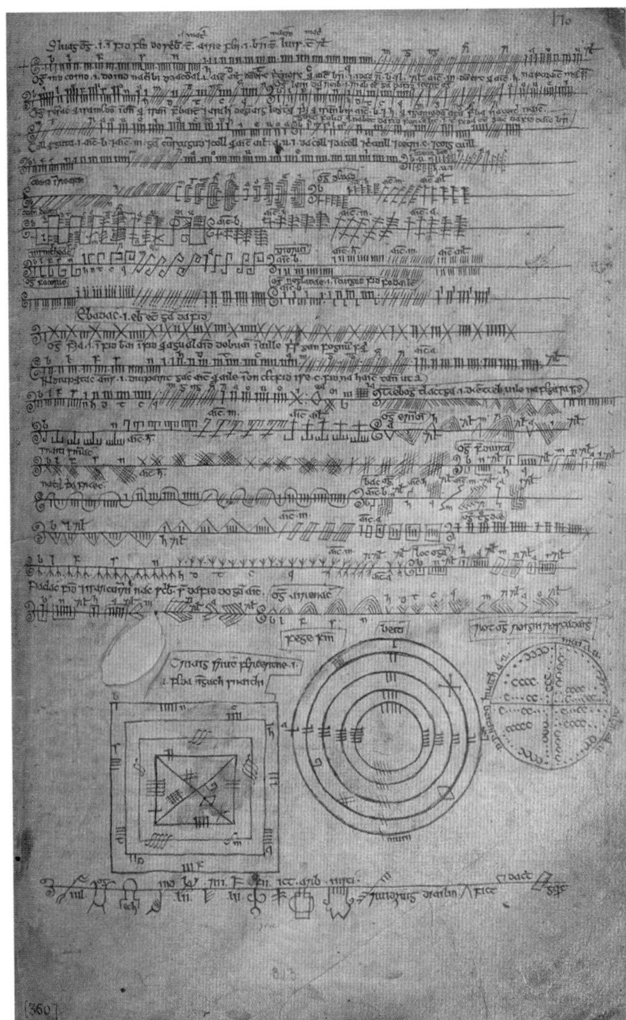

Ogham. The Book of Ballymote, *which documents genealogical and quasi-historical literature from late medieval Connacht, showing folio 170R, on which ogham script is translated. [Royal Irish Academy]*

Ogilby, John (1600–1676), theatre manager, cartographer, and dancer. Born in Edinburgh. He travelled to Dublin with Thomas Wentworth, Earl of Strafford, who appointed him first Master of the Revels in Ireland, 1638. He managed the WERBURGH STREET THEATRE, 1635–41, returning after the RESTORATION to build and manage SMOCK ALLEY THEATRE, 1662–9. **Christopher Morash**

Ó Gnímh, Fear Flatha (fl. 1602–c. 1640), poet to the Clandeboye O'Neills in Co. Antrim. Though he was granted a Crown pardon in 1602, his poetry laments the breakdown of the native order and Irish acquiescence in the face of dispossession and encroaching Anglicisation. His best-known poem, 'Mo thruaighe mar táid Gaoidhil!' (My pity for the plight of the Gaeil!), composed shortly after the launch of the ULSTER PLANTATION in 1609–10, offers a fatalistic outlook on Ireland's political and cultural situation. That he could adapt to socio-political change, however, is demonstrated by his use of the bardic practices of dynastic and genealogical validation to support the territorial claims—under English law—of one of the largest Scottish landowners in Co. Antrim, Sir RANDAL MACDONNELL, who became first Earl of Antrim in 1620. It is also evidenced by his ability to include Martha Stafford, daughter of the English official Sir Francis Stafford and wife of Sir Henry O'Neill, within the framework of traditional Irish encomium. A disparaging reference to him as 'file an tslúaigh' (poet of the masses) by a contemporary poet writing some time before 1638 would suggest that Ó Gnímh may also by this time have adapted his style to cater for a non-élite audience. **Máirín Nic Eoin**

Ó Gormáin, Muiris (c. 1714–1794), scribe. Born probably in Co. Monaghan. He taught at schools in Cos. Armagh, Cavan, and Dublin; among his patrons were John Fergus, Thomas Leland, CHARLES O'CONOR, CHARLES VALLANCEY and CHARLOTTE BROOKE. Possibly a parish clerk, he also traded in books and manuscripts. Given to drink, he died in poverty in Dublin; his manuscripts filled five sacks. **Diarmuid Breathnach and Máire Ní Mhurchú**

O'Grady, Desmond (1935–), poet. Born in Limerick; educated at UCD and Harvard University, where he was awarded a doctorate in Celtic and comparative studies. While teaching in Rome he befriended Ezra Pound, whom he cites (with JAMES CLARENCE MANGAN) as an early formative influence. His many volumes include *The Dying Gaul* (1968), *A Limerick Rake* (1978), *The Headgear of the Tribe* (1979), and *Alexandria Notebook* (1989), as collected in *The Road Taken: Poems, 1956–1996. Trawling Tradition: Translations, 1954–1994* displays a Poundian ambition, with versions of classical,

Arabic and a wide range of modern European poets. He is a member of AOSDÁNA. **David Wheatley**

O'Grady, Geraldine (1932–), violinist. Born in Dublin to a musical family, she studied at the Paris Conservatoire with Jean Fournier (premier prix). She was guest leader of the Radio Éireann Symphony Orchestra 1960–63, when she resigned to pursue a solo career which has made her one of the best-known Irish musicians abroad, playing principally with the late Havelock Nelson as accompanist. She taught at the RIAM 1970–74 and 1985–2002. **Richard Pine**

O'Grady, Standish (1846–1928), writer. Born in Castletown Bearhaven, Co. Cork; educated at TCD and in 1872 was called to the bar, which he later abandoned to pursue his interest in ancient Irish history and mythology. Concerned that his young readers might be unfamiliar with the great hero legends, he wrote a series based on the FIONN CYCLE: *Finn and his Companions* (1892), *The Coming of Cuculain* (1894), *The Gates of the North* (1901), and *The Triumph and Passing of Cuculain* (1920). He produced a number of adventure stories extolling the virtues of loyalty, bravery, and honesty, among them *Lost on Du-Corrig* (1894), *The Chain of Gold* (1895), and *Ulrich the Ready* (1896). **Patricia Donlon**

Ó Grianna, Séamus (1889–1969), writer, under the pen-name 'Máire'. Born into a family of poets and storytellers in Rannafast, Co. Donegal; attended local primary school until the age of fourteen. He spent several years at home and as a seasonal worker in Scotland. He attended an Irish summer college in 1910 and taught for a while for CONRADH NA GAEILGE. He trained formally as a teacher in St Patrick's College, Dublin, 1912–14, and taught mostly in Co. Donegal until 1920. He became involved with political matters and was interned as a republican during the CIVIL WAR. He worked subsequently as a translator for AN GÚM, in the CIVIL SERVICE, and on Irish dictionaries in the Department of Education. He expressed bitterness with Irish-language politics, however, and in 1966 joined the 'Language Freedom Movement'. His prolific literary output, spanning more than fifty years and including novels, short stories, essays, autobiography, and his famous *Rann na Feirste*, is a romantic and nostalgic celebration of his native place, its rich oral tradition, poetic speech, colourful characters, local lore, and varied landscape. He was the most influential of the Donegal school of regional writers and the GAELTACHT writer most widely read and imitated by native speakers and learners of Irish during the twentieth century. **Nollaig Mac Congáil**

O'Hagan, John (1822–1890), judge and political activist. Born in Newry, Co. Down; educated by the Jesuits at Hardwicke Street, Dublin, and TCD, graduating in 1842. In 1844 he travelled through the southern counties in the company of CHARLES GAVAN DUFFY (for whom he later acted as counsel), recording his experiences in a diary. The following year he went on a walking tour of Ulster with Gavan Duffy and two seasoned pedestrians, John Martin and JOHN MITCHEL; his lively and informative descriptions of his experiences appeared in the *Irish Monthly* in 1912 and 1913 under the pen-name 'Slieve Gullion'. He was called to the bar in 1845, became a Queen's Counsel in 1865, and later a judge, and was appointed in 1881 by the then Prime Minister, GLADSTONE, the first Judicial Commissioner of the Irish Land Commission. **Michael Fewer**

O'Hagan, Susan (1802–1909), domestic servant and centenarian. For ninety-seven years she was in domestic service with the Hall family of Lisburn, Co. Antrim, from the age of ten to her death at the age of 107. **Ciarán Deane**

O'Halloran, Sylvester (1728–1807), surgeon. Born in Cahirdavin, Co. Clare; following instruction abroad, he practised surgery in Limerick. Skilled in eye surgery and the treatment of head injuries, he published books on these subjects. His suggestion that a register of surgeons be kept inspired the creation of the Royal College of Surgeons in Ireland. He also published a general history of Ireland. **J. B. Lyons**

O'Hanlon, Count Redmond (died 1681), chieftain and highwayman. The estates of the O'Hanlons were confiscated during the Cromwellian wars in the 1650s. In about 1670 he became leader of a group of outlaws who roamed Cos. Tyrone and Armagh. DUBLIN CASTLE put a price of £200 on his head. He was killed by his foster-brother, Arthur O'Hanlon, at Eightmilebridge, Co. Down, and his head was placed on a spike over Downpatrick Jail. **Ciarán Deane**

O'Hara, Maureen, stage name of Maureen Fitzsimmons (1920–), film actor. Born in Dublin; she began performing on radio as a child and appeared with the Abbey Players as a teenager. Her first leading role in a film was in *My Irish Molly* (1938), which led to a career in Hollywood, where she soon played Esmerelda in *The Hunchback of Notre Dame* (1939). It was the female lead in JOHN FORD's *How Green Was My Valley* (1941) that made her a star; of her fifty films her most famous part was as the fiery 'colleen' in another Ford film, *The Quiet Man* (1952). **Kevin Rockett**

Ó hÉanaí, Seosamh (1919–1984), traditional singer. Born in Carna, Co. Galway; won a scholarship to Coláiste Éinde, Galway, but spent only two years there, moving to Glasgow in 1947 and working as a labourer on building sites in Scotland and England. He

Ó hÉanaí. *Seosamh Ó hÉanaí,* sean-nós *singer and storyteller. He spent most of his life in England as a labourer and in the United States as a lift operator, throughout which time he worked with the leading traditional musicians of his era. [Lensmen and Associates]*

won a gold medal at the OIREACHTAS in 1955 and performed in the Damer Hall, Dublin, in 1958, where his 'Caoineadh na dTrí Muire' won wide acclaim. He returned to Dublin in the early 1960s, performed at the Newport Folk Festival with the CLANCY BROTHERS in 1965, then emigrated permanently to the United States in 1966, where he achieved some prominence through his television appearance on the 'Merv Griffin Show'. In 1980 he was appointed part-time teacher in Irish FOLKLORE at Wesleyan University, Middletown, Connecticut, and later to a similar position at the ethnomusicology Department of the University of Washington, Seattle. In 1982 he was presented with the National Heritage Award for Excellence in Folk Arts by the National Endowment for the Arts. He died in Seattle and is buried in his native Carna. **Liam Mac Con Iomaire**

O'Hehir, Mícheál (1920–1997), broadcaster and sports commentator. Born in Dublin; educated at UCD. Ireland's most famous sports broadcaster, renowned for his unique voice and descriptive style, he made his debut broadcast for Radio Éireann in 1938, having previously worked for the *Irish Independent*. His sports commentaries on GAA games and HORSE RACING were the focal point for local community listening. His most famous commentaries include the 1947 all-Ireland senior football final between Kerry and Cavan played in New York, the 1968 Australian trip by Meath senior footballers, and his commentaries on the Aintree Grand Nationals. **Bernadette Grummell**

Ó hEidhin, Mícheál (1938–), musician, teacher, and schools music inspector. Born at Rossaveel, Co. Galway, into a musical family. Graduating first in science, he studied music at UCC under ALOYS FLEISCHMANN, did choral development with Pilib Ó Laoghaire in Co. Cork, worked as music inspector for Co. Galway VEC, and initiated COMHALTAS CEOLTÓIRÍ ÉIREANN's teaching diploma in 1980. His publications for schools include *Cas Amhrán*, *Amhráin do Choláistí* and *Ceol don Chór*; he has also been music director for the RTÉ programmes 'Bring Down the Lamp' and 'Comórtas—Cabaret'. An adjudicator for OIREACHTAS competitions and for SLÓGADH since its inception in 1969, he was also instrumental in setting up a grades syllabus in traditional music for Comhaltas Ceoltóirí Éireann and the RIAM in 1998. **Fintan Vallely**

Ó hEithir, Breandán (1930–1990), journalist and novelist. Born in Kilronan, Inishmore, Co. Galway; educated at Coláiste Éinde, Galway, and UCG. He was Irish-language editor of the IRISH PRESS, 1957–63, served for two periods as editor of the magazine COMHAR, and worked as a sports commentator, reporter and scriptwriter for RTÉ television, where he received particular recognition for his work with the current affairs programme 'Féach'. His novel *Lig Sinn i gCathú* (1976), translated into English by the author as *Lead Us into Temptation* (1978), is a racy narrative of student life in Galway in the late 40s and met with widespread critical and popular acclaim. His picaresque novel *Sionnach ar Mo Dhuán* (1988) was more ambitious but less successful and sparked off a lively debate on the subject of realism in Irish-language fiction. **Máirín Nic Eoin**

Ó hEódhusa, Eochaidh (c. 1560–1612), member of a family of hereditary poets from Ballyhose, Co. Fermanagh, *ollamh* ('poet-official') to successive Maguire chieftains, including Aodh Még Uidhir (died 1600), author of some fifty extant compositions. English documents show him to have lived at Ballyhose, 1585–91; he subsequently moved to lands at Currin, near Ballinamallard, granted to him by Maguire in virtue of his office and alluded to in his poem 'T'aire riot, a rí ó nUidhir'. He was allotted a plantation grant of 210 acres at Clanawley, 1610–11, which suggests an accommodation with the new order.

He trained as a poet in Munster. In 'Atám I gcás idir dhá chomhairle' he ponders whether he should break off his studies in Thomond to return to Maguire's household. His special relationship with Maguire is celebrated in 'Connradh do cheanglas re hAodh', which recalls how Ó hEódhusa came to undertake to append a quatrain in Aodh's honour to all his compositions. Among his later poems for this patron are the inaugural ode 'Suirgheach sin, a Éire ógh', the poem on the rights of his office, 'Mór an t-ainm ollamh flatha', and the elegy 'Fada re hurchóid Éire'. Compositions to other patrons comprise approximately half the surviving total attributed to him, including addresses to RED HUGH O'DONNELL ('Díol fuatha flaitheas Éireann'), TURLOUGH (Toirdhealbhach) LUINEACH Ó NÉILL ('An sluagh sidhe so i nEamhain'), and various of the O'Byrnes in Leinster. Among noteworthy poems composed after Maguire's death in 1600, 'Mór theasda dh'obair Óivid' celebrates the accession of James I, 1603, while 'Beag mhaireas do mhacraidh Gaoidheal', composed after the FLIGHT OF THE EARLS, is marked by a deeply felt gloom concerning the Irish cause. Ó hEódhusa was an outstanding eulogist whose verse shows consistent compositional perfection, originality of expression and imagery, and thematic versatility. **Pádraig A. Breatnach**

Ó hEódhusa, Giolla Brighde (died 1614), a member of a family who were hereditary poets to the Maguires of Fermanagh. He travelled to Douai to study for the priesthood and entered the Franciscan order in LOUVAIN in 1607, where he took the name Bonaventura. In 1611 he produced the first printed work of the Catholic COUNTER-REFORMATION in Irish, a catechism published in Antwerp, influenced in content by Canisius and Bellarmine. Ó hEódhusa was innovative in adding verse summaries of the catechism's main teaching. He also produced one of the first grammars of Irish, *Rudimenta Grammaticae Hiberniae*, unpublished until 1968. **Mícheál Mac Craith**

O'Herlihy, Dan (1919–), actor. Born in Wexford. He worked at the ABBEY and GATE THEATRES, Dublin, appearing in more than seventy plays, including the premiere of SEAN O'CASEY's *Red Roses for Me*. He made his first film appearance in *Hungry Hill* (1946), and shortly afterwards he appeared in the influential *Odd Man Out* (1947), set in Northern Ireland. Emigrating to the United States, he appeared in a wide variety of films, including Luis Buñuel's *The Adventures of Robinson Crusoe* (1952), *The Virgin Queen* (1955), *The Cabinet of Dr Caligari* (1962), as Franklin Roosevelt in *MacArthur* (1977), and in *The Dead* (1987). **Kevin Rockett**

Ó hIfearnáin, Liam Dall (c. 1720–1803), poet. Born in Lattin, Co. Tipperary. While many stories of the poet survived in the folk tradition of his native district, few definite facts about his life are known. Tradition has it that he was an accomplished fiddler, and that he was blind for most if not all of his life. Close on forty of his compositions have survived; some twenty of these were edited by Risteárd Ó Foghludha in *Ar Bruach na Coille Muaire* (1939). The songs beginning 'Ar bruach na Coille Muaire' and 'I ngleanntaibh séimh' are two of his best-known works. **Breandán Ó Conchúir**

Ó hIfearnáin, Mathghamhain (fl. 1585), Tipperary poet. The opening line of his famous lament for diminishing patronage, 'Ceist! cia do cheinneóchadh dán?' (Pray, who would buy a poem?), has become a catch-phrase for philistinism, both in its sixteenth-century and subsequent manifestations. The poem describes the poet's attempt to sell his compositions throughout Munster; he concludes that he would be better off making combs. His advice to his son in 'A mhic, ná meabhraigh éigse' (Son, do not cultivate poetry) is offered in the context of the decline of local patronage in the form of the Fitzgeralds of Desmond. He demonstrates the new pragmatics of the poetic class, however, when he advises his son that, if he should persist and become a poet, he should seek English rather than Irish patrons. His clear perception of political change is also illustrated in his allegorical contribution to IOMARBHÁGH NA BHFILEADH. **Máirín Nic Eoin**

O'Higgins, Ambrose (Ambrosio) (c. 1720–1810), Viceroy of Peru. Born near Dangan Castle, Co. Meath; educated at Cádiz. He went to South America, first to Buenos Aires, then to Lima, where he worked for a time as a pedlar. He joined the Spanish engineer corps and gained rapid promotion, emerging as Count of Bellenar and, in 1788, Marquis of Osorno, with the Governor-Generalship of Chile. He spent the following eight years developing the country's resources, accomplishing much for Spain. He was Viceroy of Peru, 1796–1801, the highest rank in the Spanish colonial service. **David Kiely**

O'Higgins, Bernardo (1778–1842), Chilean leader. Born at Chillán, a son of AMBROSIO O'HIGGINS; educated in England and Spain. He returned to Chile in 1802. In 1810 he joined the revolution against Spain and in 1813 was made commander of the patriot army. Defeated by royalist troops in 1814, he fled to Argentina but returned to help defeat the Spanish. He was made supreme director of Chile and in 1818 proclaimed its independence. He tried to liberalise the country but alienated both the Catholic clergy and the aristocracy. Deposed in 1823, he spent the rest of his life in exile in Peru. **David Kiely**

O'Higgins, Brian (1882–1966). Born in Kilskeer, near Kells, Co. Meath. He played an active part in the cause of Irish freedom and the promotion of the IRISH LANGUAGE throughout his life. He was an active member of CONRADH NA GAEILGE and fought with the GPO garrison during the Easter Week RISING OF 1916. He was later elected a member of the first Dáil, in which he represented West Clare. He wrote under the name of Brian na Banban and was one of the most prolific writers of patriotic ballads during the whole period of the struggle for independence. His songs lampooning the authorities on their lack of knowledge of the Irish language were particularly effective.

'Tis Irish here and Irish there
In every nook and corner,
They'd jeer to death a man who'd dare
To imitate the foreigner.
'Tis a grádh instead of my ducky dear,
A stór in place of Popsy,
And a rúin mo chroidhe are the words I hear
Instead of my mopsy wopsy.

He took the Republican side in the CIVIL WAR, and for years he published the *Wolfe Tone Annual*, which perpetuated the ideals and the memory of Irish patriots. He was widely known for his greeting cards, which contained a verse set in a Celtic design. He continued writing ballads and verse up until his death. **Frank Harte**

O'Higgins, Kevin (1892–1927), revolutionary and politician. Born in Co. Laois; educated at ST PATRICK'S COLLEGE, Maynooth, and UCD. He was jailed in 1918 for agitation. Elected TD for Laois,

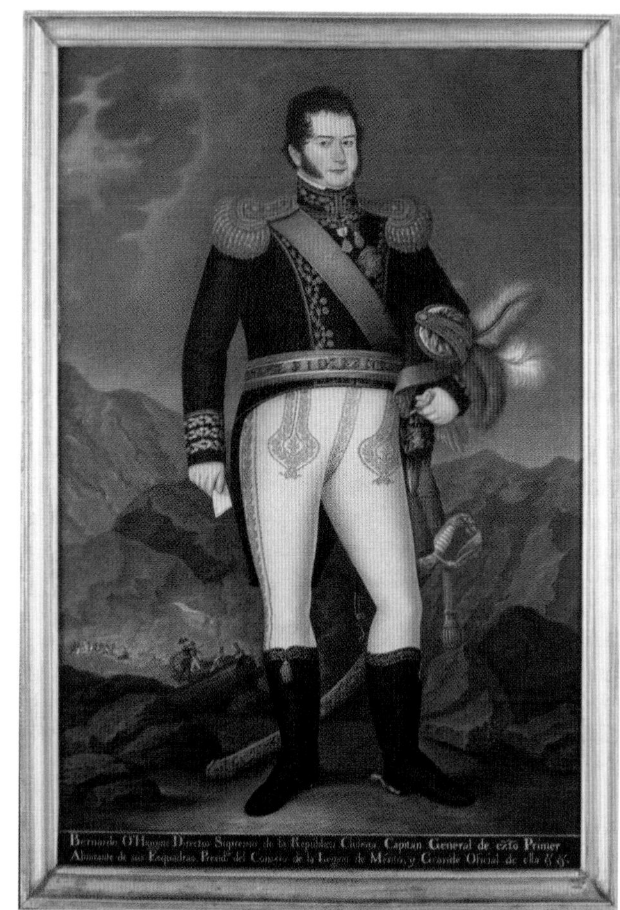

O'Higgins, Bernardo. Bernardo O'Higgins *(1820) by José Gil de Castro y Morales. O'Higgins became the revolutionary leader of Chile in 1813 and is regarded as the father of Chilean independence. [Museo Histórico Nacional, Chile]*

he became deputy Minister for Local Government, supported the Treaty in 1921, and became Minister for Home Affairs in 1922. He supported the policy of executions with great reluctance, and was responsible for the establishment of an unarmed police force and for restrictive drinking hours. He was assassinated in July 1927 by an IRA group operating at random, an event that forced FIANNA FÁIL to recognise the FREE STATE. **Tom Garvin**

Ó hUaithnín, Seon (c. 1688–c. 1722), poet. Born in Kilshanny, Co. Clare. A JACOBITE supporter, he was arraigned for what was considered a 'treason' song. Seventeen of his poems survive, giving interesting insights into the social and political life of his time. He was a member of the Regiment of Limerick in Spain in 1721. **Eoghan Ó hAnluain**

Ó hUid, Tarlach (1917–1990), writer. Born in London, from a unionist background. His writings largely deal with the discovery of his Irishness; this is most obvious from his novel *An Bealach chun a' Bhearnais* (1949), where the main character is a black descendant of the Irish transported under CROMWELL to the New World. His autobiographical works *Ar Thóir mo Shealbha* (1960) and *Faoi Ghlas* (1985) are both useful documentary accounts. His editorship of the newspaper *Inniu*, 1979–84, was marked by rigorous and exacting standards of writing and language. **Alan Titley**

Ó hUidhrín, Giolla na Naomh (died 1420), poet. He composed the celebrated topographical poem beginning 'Tuilleadh feasa ar Éirinn óigh' ('Further information about virginal Ireland'). Covering the southern half of Ireland, it complements an incomplete earlier work of the same nature by SEÁN MÓR Ó DUBHAGÁIN. Perhaps a native of present-day Co. Offaly, nothing more is known of him than that the ANNALS describe him at his death as a 'learned historian'. **Nollaig Ó Muraíle**

Ó hUiginn, Maoilsheachlainn (na nUirsgéal) (fl. fifteenth century), hereditary bardic poet. He addressed patrons who flourished in Connacht and Ulster during the early to middle fifteenth century. He was nicknamed 'na nUirsgéal' ('of the apologues') from his habit of inserting learned tales into his eulogies as examples or vehicles of compliment. **Katharine Simms**

Ó hUiginn, Pilib Bocht (died 1487), a hereditary bardic poet. Son of Conn Crosach Ó hUiginn, he became an Observantine Franciscan friar and left a legacy of many religious poems in the bardic style, mostly eulogies of saints, including St Francis, St Dominic and the Blessed Virgin Mary. **Katharine Simms**

Ó hUiginn, Tadhg Dall (1550–1591), poet. Despite his premature death at the age of forty-one, Tadhg Dall, son of Mathghamhain Ó hUiginn, was one of the most prolific and best-recorded of the late sixteenth-century bardic poets. He came from an old-established poetic family in Co. Sligo, celebrated for their schools, and had access to a wide range of books. In one poem he states that an early patron, William Burke, used to read books aloud to him, the poet himself being blind. A feature of his poems is the illustrative anecdotes he includes from both Irish and Continental sources. His patrons, apart from a single poem to Aodh Ó Broin of Co. Wicklow, were all from the north-west of Ireland, the rulers of Tír Conaill, Tír Eoghain, and Fir Manach, the Mac Suibhne GALLOGLASS chiefs, and many Irish and OLD ENGLISH nobles of Connacht. His brother, Maolmhuire Ó hUiginn, also a poet, was a cleric in Rome and was appointed Archbishop of Tuam but died in Antwerp on his way back to his see. Traditionally Tadhg Dall is said to have been murdered by members of the O'Hara family, whom he had satirised. He left an under-age son and heir, Tadhg Óg, who became a poet in his turn and inherited his estates in Doheran, Coolrecuill, and other lands in the parishes of Achonry and Kilmactigue, Co. Sligo. **Katharine Simms**

tOileánach, An (1929), autobiography of the Blasket Islander TOMÁS Ó CRIOMHTHAINN. It provides a unique personal record of one man's life and that of an island community, since departed. It is distinguished by an ability to vividly depict island scenes and personalities, supported by a masterly command of language, vocabulary and dialogue and informed by a strong faith. It describes a life dominated by the sea and enlightened by a sense of humour, irony, and drama. **Breandán Ó Conaire**

Oireachtas: see GOVERNMENT OF IRELAND.

tOireachtas, An, an annual festival of TRADITIONAL MUSIC and song. The GAELIC LEAGUE held its first Oireachtas or assembly in the Rotunda, Dublin, in May 1897, a one-day festival attended by more than a thousand people that was to grow into a ten-day event, with competitions in music, song, and literature, now also an important annual social and cultural event. It was held in Dublin for the first sixteen years, then in Galway in 1913, Killarney in 1914, and Dundalk in 1915. In 1916 the competitions were cancelled but the festival was resumed in Waterford in 1917, Killarney in 1918, Cork in 1919, and Dublin again in 1920. Because of political turmoil the Oireachtas planned for Killarney in 1921 and for Dublin in 1922 had to be abandoned, while the 1923 festival was replaced by a performance of the opera *Sruth na Maoile* by Geoffrey M. Palmer, with words by Father Tomás Ó Ceallaigh, in the GAIETY THEATRE, Dublin. After a successful Oireachtas in Cork in 1924 the festival was discontinued indefinitely because of lack of funds and a decline of interest in traditional cultural events in the early turbulent years of the state. In 1939 CONRADH NA GAEILGE revived the Oireachtas in its traditional form in Dublin; in 1974 it was brought out of Dublin again; and in 1999 a new structure was introduced, whereby half the festival is held in Dublin in early summer and the other half at a venue outside Dublin in the late autumn or early winter.

The Oireachtas continues to promote Irish literature, drama, art and music through exhibitions and competitions, the most popular of which are those in SEAN-NÓS SINGING, culminating in the competition for the prestigious Corn Uí Riada. While the music competitions have declined in competitive significance with the rise of the fleadhanna ceoil from the 1950s onwards, the annual *sean-nós* singing competition at the Oireachtas, with the co-operation of Raidió na Gaeltachta since its inception in 1972, has done much to promote this art form. **Liam Mac Con Iomaire**

Oisín, son of the legendary FIONN MAC CUMHAILL, one of the Fianna veterans. In 'Acallam na Senórach' he is portrayed as surviving until the era of St PATRICK; subsequently he is the main narrator of OSSIANIC POEMS AND TALES. He was conceived when his mother was in the guise of a deer, hence his name (diminutive of *os*, 'deer'). Presented as a young warrior in early texts, in later literary and oral lore he functions as an aged narrator of an idyllic pagan past. Irish and Scottish oral tradition explained his longevity by his sojourn in TÍR NA NÓG, the Land of Youth. **Máirtín Ó Briain**

Oisín and Niamh, heroes of a story in the FIONN CYCLE. Niamh is a beautiful woman who is in love with the hero Oisín, son of FIONN MAC CUMHAILL and Sadhbh, of TUATHA DÉ DANANN, and asks him to come with her to TÍR NA NÓG (the Land of Youth). He spends several hundred years there but is overcome with a longing to see his home and return to Ireland. In the literary version of the tale Niamh returns with Oisín on a white horse. He had been warned not to set foot on Irish soil; when he falls from his horse he immediately becomes a very old man. **Ríonach uí Ógáin**

O'Keeffe, Daniel (Dan) (1907–), Gaelic footballer. Born in Fermoy, Co. Cork. He was Kerry's goalkeeper from 1931 to 1948. The extraordinary length of his career is said to have been a result of his athleticism and meticulous approach to his craft. He won seven all-Ireland senior championships, a record that lasted until 1986. His record of fourteen Munster championship medals still stands. He played in thirteen all-Ireland finals, the last of them the 1947 final played at the Polo Grounds in New York. **Donal Keenan**

O'Keeffe, John (1747–1833), playwright. Born and educated in Dublin. By 1764 he had begun working at the SMOCK ALLEY THEATRE under Henry Mossop as actor and writer. His first play was produced in Ireland in 1767, but most of his literary output (farces, comedies, and pantomimes) was produced while he was living in England from 1781. *Tony Lumpkin in Town* (1778) established a lasting friendship with the manager George Colman. His most successful play was *Wild Oats* (1791). Though evidently loyal to the Crown, he often displays a detectable sympathy for

Catholic Ireland through themes, allusions, characters, or setting. A collection of more than sixty plays was published in 1798 and an autobiography, *Recollections*, in 1826. **Carolyn Duggan**

O'Keeffe, Pádraig (1887–1963), FIDDLE-player and traditional music teacher. Born in Gleanntán, Cordal, Castleisland, Co. Kerry. His career as a musician and teacher has left an indelible mark on the music of the SLIABH LUACHRA area. His playing was skilled and tasteful, and accounts from his pupils show that he was a sensitive teacher who thought deeply about his music. His playing can be heard on *The Sliabh Luachra Fiddle Master: Pádraig O'Keeffe*. **Peter Browne**

O'Kelly, Alanna (1955–), artist. Born in Gorey, Co. Wexford; trained at the NCAD, afterwards undertaking postgraduate research work in Helsinki. She was research assistant at the Slade School of Fine Art, London, 1985–7. She works with traditional and non-traditional art media, including audio, voice and performance work. Her work is often inspired by the rituals, beliefs and histories of rural Ireland, particularly of the nineteenth century. Performances, installations and exhibitions include *St John's Night Fire Paths* (1983), an outdoor night piece at Marlay Park, Rathfarnham, Co. Dublin; *Still Beyond the Pale* (1986), Slade School of Fine Art, London; *Chant Down Greenham* (1987), a performance work that toured to New York, Boston, and Toronto; *The Country Blooms ... A Garden and a Grave* (1992), Irish Museum of Modern Art, Dublin; and *Deoraíocht* (1997), San Francisco Art Institute. She represented Ireland at the São Paulo Bienal, 1996, with the video installation *A Beathœ*. **Peter Murray**

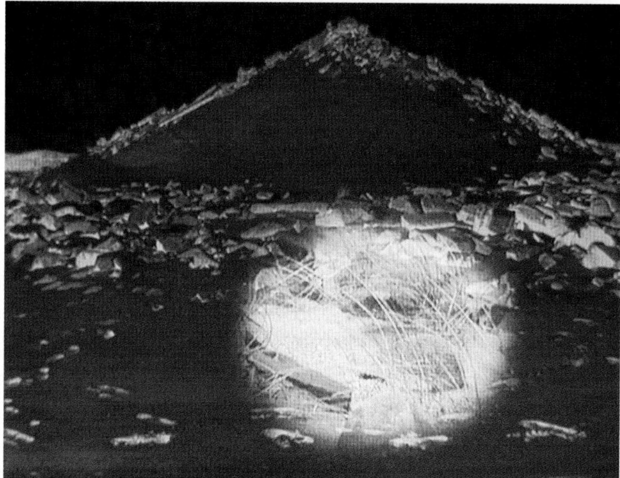

O'Kelly, Alanna. Sanctuary—Wastelands *(1994), a video projection installation in which O'Kelly uses the image of a desolate hillside to invoke the tragedy of the Great Famine. [Irish Museum of Modern Art; courtesy of the artist]*

O'Kelly, Aloysius (1853–c. 1941), painter and illustrator. Born in Dublin, a brother of the Fenian and MP James J. O'Kelly; emigrated to London in 1861. He studied at the École des Beaux-Arts in 1874 with Jean-Léon Gérôme and later with Léon Bonnat. An eclectic, highly skilled and politically motivated artist, he was one of the first Irish artists to go to Brittany, from the mid-1870s. He returned to the west of Ireland in 1880 as artist for the *Illustrated London News*, for which he documented the Land War, and he painted in Connemara in the early 1880s. In the mid-1880s he went to Cairo, then to Sudan to document the war with the Mahdi. In 1895 he emigrated to New York. During his life he exhibited at the major French, British, Irish and American public and private exhibition venues. A retrospective exhibition was held in the Hugh Lane Municipal Gallery of Modern Art, Dublin, in 1999. **Niamh O'Sullivan**

O'Kelly, Gerald Edward, Count O'Kelly de Gallagh (1890–1968), diplomat. Born at Portumna, Co. Galway; educated at the RUI. He travelled commercially in the Far East and America before the FIRST WORLD WAR. He joined the diplomatic service in 1919, was Irish representative at Brussels in 1921 and first Irish minister to France in 1929. In 1935 he retired to start a wine business in France but returned to the diplomatic service in 1948 as chargé d'affaires in Lisbon. He retired again in 1955 and was named honorary counsellor to the Lisbon legation, serving there until his death. **David Kiely**

O'Kelly, Seán T. (1882–1966), revolutionary and politician. Born in Dublin; educated at O'Connell Schools, where he attempted to organise a strike against the teaching of Irish. Orphaned, he spent much of his youth at Rosmuc, Co. Galway. He joined the GAELIC LEAGUE in 1898, becoming manager of *An Claidheamh Soluis*, and later the IRB. A founder-member of SINN FÉIN in 1905, he was elected to Dublin City Council in 1906. He was staff captain to PEARSE in the 1916 RISING and afterwards interned. Elected Sinn Féin TD for College Green, Dublin, in 1918, he remained a DÁIL deputy until 1945, when he was elected second President of Ireland. As Ceann Comhairle of the first Dáil he attended the Paris Peace Conference in 1919 and diplomatic gatherings in Rome and Washington. A member of the Knights of Columbanus and close to DE VALERA, he opposed the Treaty in 1921 and helped to found FIANNA FÁIL in 1926. He became Minister for Local Government and Public Health in 1932 and abolished the ratepayers' franchise limitation for local elections. He was Minister for Finance, 1941–5, and President of Ireland, 1945–59. **Tom Garvin**

O'Kelly, Seumas (c. 1875–1918), journalist and writer. Born in Loughrea, Co. Galway; educated at St Brendan's College, Loughrea. In his late teenage years he edited the *Midland Tribune* (Birr), the *Southern Star* (Skibbereen) in 1903, and the *Leinster Leader* (Naas) in 1906. He was a supporter of Griffith and SINN FÉIN. Among plays performed by the Theatre of Ireland and the ABBEY THEATRE were *The Matchmakers* (1907), *The Shuiler's Child* (1909), and *The Parnellite* (1917). His novels include *The Lady of Deerpark* (1917). He is remembered for his short story 'The Weaver's Grave'; the collection *Waysiders* (1917) is typical of his illusive yet concise style. He died in the offices of Griffith's newspaper *Nationality* during disturbances on the third night after Armistice Day. **Colin Graham**

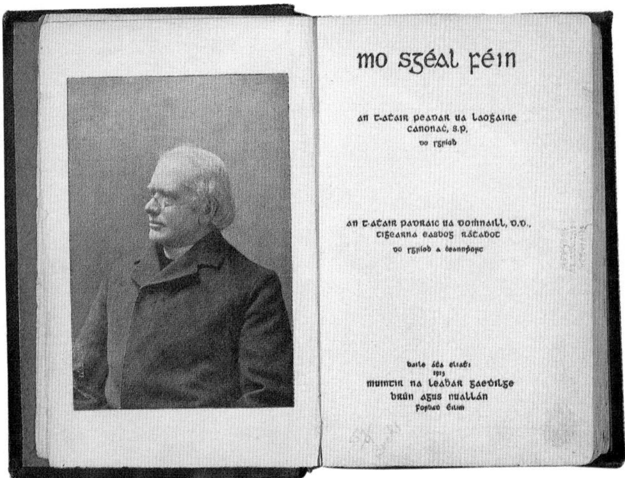

Ó Laoghaire. *Frontispiece and title page of Peadar Ó Laoghaire's autobiography,* Mo Sgéal Féin *(1915). A leading figure of the Irish revival, his output was prolific: he wrote more than 500 works in his twenty-seven-year career. [Council of Trustees of the National Library of Ireland; Ir592 044]*

Ó Laighléis, Ré (1953–), writer. Born in Sallynoggin, Co. Dublin. Formerly a teacher and dramatist, he has been a full-time writer since 1992 and has won numerous literary prizes. He has been acclaimed for his realistic treatment of contemporary issues in both Irish and English, particularly with regard to young people's lives. His most popular titles include *Ciorcal Meiteamorfach* (1991), *Ecstasy agus Scéalta Eile* (1994), and *Gafa* (1996). **Aisling Ní Dhonnchadha**

Ó Laoghaire, Peadar (1839–1920), priest and author. Born at Liscarrigane, near Macroom, Co. Cork; educated at ST PATRICK'S COLLEGE, Maynooth; parish priest of Castlelyons, Co. Cork, from 1891. Following the founding of the GAELIC LEAGUE in 1893 he began writing, at the age of fifty-four, and contributed anecdotes to *United Ireland* before embarking on SÉADNA (1904), the first major creative work of the language revival, originally published in serial form in IRISLEABHAR NA GAEDHILGE and elsewhere from 1894. It is set as a story within a story and is a reworking of a FOLK-TALE of a shoemaker who sells his soul to the Devil in return for thirteen years of access to a purse of plenty. With it Ó Laoghaire ensured the success of contemporary rather than yesteryear language as the staple medium of Irish prose—*caint na ndaoine* ('the people's language'), as he styled it.

Séadna was followed by some 500 works—an average of one a fortnight for twenty-seven years. Often bowdlerised versions of earlier tales (such as those of Bricriu, Eisirt, and Guaire), they ranged in content from loose retellings (such as *Aesop a Tháinig go hÉirinn* and *Don Chíchóté*) to translation of the Bible. Apart from *Séadna*, he is best known for his autobiography, *Mo Sgéal Féin* (1915).

The dominant literary figure of the Irish revival, ascendant in his own lifetime and for a generation afterwards, Ó Laoghaire had trenchant views on style, translation, and grammar. Both the quasi-naïve language and the subject matter he favoured had a debilitating effect on the work of lesser writers; the inevitable reaction has still not quite waned. **Liam Mac Mathúna**

Olcott, Sidney (1873–1949), screenwriter and director of silent films. Born John Sidney Alcott in Toronto of Irish parents. He entered the film industry in 1904 as an actor and in 1907 became the Kalem Company's first director. The subject of a famous copyright case for his unauthorised production of a film version of *Ben-Hur* (1907), he was the first major director to shoot films on location. During trips to Ireland in 1910–14, usually in collaboration with the actor and screenwriter Gene Gauntier, he made the first fiction films shot in the country, adapting DION BOUCICAULT's *The Colleen Bawn* (1911), *Arrah-na-Pogue* (1911), and *The Shaughraun* (1912), while also making films on emigration, comedies, and original historical dramas, such as the 1798 story *Rory O'More* (1911) and *Bold Emmet: Ireland's Martyr* (1914). He also made the first feature-length life of Christ, *From the Manger to the Cross* (1913), shot in Palestine. A pioneer of documentaries and westerns, in 1915 he joined Famous Players and directed a number of films featuring Mary Pickford, before retiring in 1927 after making *The Claw.* **Kevin Rockett**

'Old English', one of a number of contemporary as well as historical terms for the descendants of the ANGLO-NORMAN adventurers who came to Ireland in the twelfth century. By historical convention the term is applied to the beginning of the seventeenth century as a means of differentiating the descendants of the original, and largely Catholic, Anglo-Norman settlers from the 'NEW ENGLISH' and almost exclusively Protestant settlers who proliferated following the Elizabethan conquest in 1603. The Old English were predominantly resident in the PALE and in southern and western coastal towns, such as Waterford, Cork, and Galway. They were traditional rivals of the majority native Irish population, and a shared Catholic faith since the REFORMATION did little to mould a common identity for a prolonged period. **John McCavitt**

O'Leary, Daniel Florence (1801–1854), soldier of fortune. Born in Cork, son of a prosperous merchant. In 1817 he enlisted with Simón Bolívar and in 1819 helped to free Colombia from Spain. By 1824 Bolívar had liberated Venezuela, Ecuador, and Peru, and O'Leary was his principal assistant, with the rank of brigadier-general. After Bolívar's death in 1830 O'Leary was exiled, but in 1833 he returned to Venezuela and became a diplomat, serving in London, Paris, Madrid, and the Vatican. In 1841 Britain appointed him consul at Caracas and in 1843 consul-general in Bogotá, where he died. **David Kiely**

O'Leary, David (1958–), soccer player. Born in London. He made the first of his sixty-eight appearances for the Republic of Ireland on one of the most intimidating stages of all when, at eighteen, he played against England at Wembley. It caught the mood of a spectacular career in which he made more than 700 appearances—a club record—during his twenty years at Arsenal. A dispute with Jack Charlton saw him in effect exiled from the national team for two-and-a-half years. Recognised as a talented central defender with exceptional pace and positional sense, he went into management at the end of his playing career and, in his first season with Leeds United, revitalised one of the slumbering giants of English football. **Peter Byrne**

O'Leary, Jane (1946–), composer and pianist. Born in Hartford, Connecticut; attended Vassar College and Princeton University, where she studied under Milton Babbitt, and moved to Ireland in 1972. In 1976 she founded CONCORDE, a contemporary music ensemble, which she directs. Her early works are written in a serial idiom, strongly influenced by Babbitt and Webern. From her *String Quartet* (1983) onwards she departed from this strict, abstract style to compose in a more melodic and lyrical manner, often drawing inspiration from poetry. She has received many commissions and awards and is a member of AOSDÁNA. **Adrian Scahill**

O'Leary, John (1830–1907), Fenian. Born in Tipperary; educated at TCD. Imprisoned as both a YOUNG IRELANDER and a Fenian, he was the editor of the Fenian newspaper, the *Irish People*, 1863–5. On his release from prison he settled in Paris. Although opposed to both the 'NEW DEPARTURE' and the LAND LEAGUE, he nevertheless continued to concern himself with advanced nationalist affairs but became increasingly disillusioned with Fenian activities. In later life he concentrated his energies on literature, though he remained as a prototype of an old republican hero. His was an early and significant influence on W. B. YEATS (see p. 1159). **Oliver P. Rafferty**

O'Leary, Liam (1910–1992), actor, director, and archivist. Born in Youghal, Co. Cork. One of the founders of the Irish Film Society in 1936, he worked as a theatre director before producing documentaries in the 1940s, the most important of which is the first Irish party political film, *Our Country* (1948), made for CLANN NA POBLACHTA. He also acted in films—in the thriller *At a Dublin Inn* (1948) and as a missionary priest in *Men Against the Sun* (1953). He worked at the National Film Archive, London, 1953–65, and published *Silent Cinema* (1965). Previously he had written the first Irish book on the cinema, *Invitation to the Film* (1945); he also wrote about the director REX INGRAM, 1980. A documentary on his life, *At the Cinema Palace: Liam O'Leary* (1983), was made by DONALD TAYLOR BLACK. **Kevin Rockett**

Ó Liatháin, Annraoi (1917–1981), short-story writer, novelist, editor, actor, and broadcaster. Born near Portumna, Co. Galway. He joined the CIVIL SERVICE in 1936. He was editor of *An Glór*, 1941–2, president of CONRADH NA GAEILGE, 1950–52, and in 1964 was appointed to the staff of the Irish–English dictionary (1978) edited by Niall Ó Dónaill. His books include *Luaithreach an Bhua* (1969), *Gleann an Leasa* (1973), and *Nead na gCreabhar* (1977). **Aisling Ní Dhonnchadha**

ollamh, the highest grade in a number of hierarchically organised professions and crafts, most commonly that of poets. The term is explained by D. A. Binchy as a superlative of the word *oll*, 'beyond, transcending', and by others as an agentive from the adjective *oll*, 'great, mighty'. [see CLASSICAL IRISH POETRY.] **Damian McManus**

Ó Longáin, Mícheál Óg (1766–1837), scribe and poet. Born in Carrignavar, Co. Cork, into the Uí Longáin scribal family. He was appointed local secretary of the UNITED IRISHMEN and worked as a courier for the movement, 1797–9. Three of his sons, Peadar, Pól, and Seosamh, were also accomplished scribes. He wrote approximately 350 compositions in verse. He was one of the most productive of the later professional scribes, compiling more than 150 manuscripts. He also worked as a labourer, teacher and translator to supplement his income. **Meidhbhín Ní Úrdail**

Olympia Theatre, Dublin, designed by John J. Callaghan and opened in 1879 in Dame Street as the Star of Erin Music Hall by the impresario Dan Lowrey. It was later renamed the Empire Palace Theatre, then the Olympia Theatre, in deference to growing nationalist public opinion. It is a Victorian theatre with boxes, a dress circle, and gods, seating 1,300 patrons in an intimate, French rococo auditorium. Throughout its existence it has played host to MUSIC HALL and variety acts as well as plays, a regular Christmas PANTOMIME, and, since the 1980s, popular music. **Christopher Morash**

Olympic Games. With the exception of 1936, Irish athletes have competed at all Olympic Games since 1896. Prior to 1922, they either represented the United Kingdom, of which all Ireland was then a part, or in many cases the United States, where the Irish diaspora distinguished itself in sports. Since partition and independence, the Irish Free State/Republic of Ireland has sent a team to all succeeding games, beginning with Paris in 1924. Athletes from Northern Ireland have competed either for the Irish or the British teams, according to individual choice. Pat O'Callaghan (hammer 1928, 1932) has the unique record of being the only Irish athlete to have retained an Olympic title in that time. **Fergal Tobin**

1896–1922	
Gold	
1896 Athens	John Pius Boland, Tennis singles; Tennis doubles
1900 Paris	John Flanagan, Hammer Throw; Denis St George Daly, John George Beresford, Great Britain Polo team
1904 St Louis	John Flanagan, Hammer Throw; Pat Flanagan, U.S. tug of war team; Thomas F. Kiely All-Around (Decathlon precursor); Martin J. Sheridan, Discus Throw
1906 Athens	John Flanagan, Hammer Throw; Cornelius 'Con' Leahy, High Jump; Peter O'Connor, Hop Step Jump; Martin J. Sheridan, Shot Putt; Martin J. Sheridan, Discus Throw
1908 London	Tim Ahearne, Hop Step Jump; Edward Barrett, City of London Police tug-of-war team; Joseph Edmund Deakin, Three-man team race over three miles; John Flanagan, Hammer Throw; John Hayes, Marathon (representing U.S.); Robert Kerr, 200 m; George Corneluis O'Kelly, Heavyweight freestyle wrestling; Martin J. Sheridan, Discus Throw; Martin J. Sheridan, Discus Throw, Greek Style;
1912 Stockholm	Kennedy McArthur, Marathon; Pat McDonald, Shot Putt; Matt McCrath, Hammer Throw
1920 Antwerp	Frederick Whitfield Barrett, Polo; Pat McDonald, 56 lb Weight Throw; Noel Mary Purcell, Great Britain Water Polo team; Patrick J. Ryan, Hammer Throw
Silver	
1900 Paris	Patrick J. Leahy, High Jump; Harold Sigerson Mahony, Tennis singles; Harold Sigerson Mahony, Tennis mixed doubles
1904 St Louis	John J. Daly, 2,500 m Steeplechase; John Flanagan, 56 lb Weight Throw
1906 Athens	Cornelius 'Con' Leahy, Hop Step Jump; John McGough, 1,500 m; Peter O'Connor, Long Jump; Martin J. Sheridan, Throwing the Stone; Martin J. Sheridan, Standing High Jump; Martin J. Sheridan, Standing Long Jump
1908 London	James Clark, Tug of war; Denis Horgan, Shot Putt; Cornelius 'Con' Leahy, High Jump; James Cecil Parker, Tennis men's doubles; Matt McCrath, Hammer Throw
1912 Stockholm	Mathias 'Matt' Hynes, Tug of war; Pat McDonald, Shot Putt, two hands aggregate

1920 Antwerp	Patrick Flynn, 3,000 m Steeplechase; Frank Hegarty, 8,000 m cross country; Patrick J. Ryan, 56 lb Weight Throw

Bronze

1900 Paris	Patrick J. Leahy, Long Jump; Harold Sigerson Mahony, Tennis doubles
1904 St Louis	James Mitchell, 56 lb Weight Throw
1908 London	Edward Barrett, Heavyweight freestyle event; Robert Kerr, 100 m; Martin J. Sheridan, Standing Long Jump; Cornelius 'Con' Walsh, Hammer Throw; Hardness Lloyd, John McCann, Percy O'Reilly and Auston Rotherham, Polo

Irish Free State; Éire/Ireland; Irish Republic

Gold

1928 Amsterdam	Pat O'Callaghan, Hammer
1932 Los Angeles	Pat O'Callaghan, Hammer; Bob Tisdall, 400 m hurdles
1956 Melbourne	Ronnie Delany, 1,500 m
1992, Barcelona	Michael Carruth, Boxing
1996 Atlanta	Michelle Smith, Swimming—400 m freestyle; 400 m individual medley; 200 m butterfly

Silver

1952 Helsinki	John McNally, Boxing
1956 Melbourne	Fred Teidt, Boxing
1980 Moscow	David Wilkins and Jamie Wilkinson, Sailing
1984 Los Angeles	John Treacy, Marathon
1992 Barcelona	Wayne McCullough, Boxing
2000 Sydney	Sonia O'Sullivan, 5,000 m

Bronze

1956 Melbourne	Fred Gilroy, Tony Byrne, John Cauldwell, Boxing
1964 Tokyo	Jim McCourt, Boxing
1980 Moscow	Hugh Russell, Boxing
1996 Atlanta	Michelle Smith, Swimming—200 m individual medley

Northern Ireland

Gold

1964 Innsbruck	Robin Dixon (Lord Glentoran), Bobsleigh
1972 Munich	Mary Peters, Pentathlon
1988 Seoul	Stephen Martin, Hockey; James Kirkwood, Hockey

Jim Sheridan/Tom McSweeney

Omagh (*An Ómaigh*), county town of Co. Tyrone and the second-largest town (after Derry) in the north-west of Ireland; population (estimated) 20,000. The town possibly grew from an abbey founded here in 792. In the late fifteenth century it was fortified by Mac Art O'Neill as a defence against the English, to whom it passed following the PLANTATION OF ULSTER in 1609.

The present town dates from the eighteenth century, a disastrous fire in 1743 having destroyed all but two houses. By the middle of the nineteenth century it had taken on its role as a market and assize town, with a barracks and county jail. Today it retains its role as a market town and regional centre. Employment is varied, with public and agricultural services, including those concerning livestock and dairy products, the largest sources of employment. There is also some light industry, including textile manufacture. Tourism is an important industry. The ULSTER-AMERICAN FOLK PARK is an outdoor museum that tells the story of eighteenth and nineteenth-century emigration to America, while the Ulster History Park presents the history of human settlement in Ireland over the last ten thousand years. The OMAGH BOMBING of August 1998 was one of the worst terrorist attacks of the 'Troubles' (see p. 877). **Joseph Brady**

Omagh bombing (15 August 1998). A 135 kg (300 lb) car bomb was planted in the centre of Omagh, Co. Tyrone, on a busy Saturday afternoon during the town's Civic Week, killing twenty-eight people (nineteen adults, nine children and nine-month-old

Olympic Games. *Ronnie Delany crossing the finish line to take the gold medal in the 1,500 m race at the 1956 Olympic Games in Melbourne. He was the first Irish athlete in twenty-four years to win a gold medal. [Inpho Photography]*

unborn twins) and injuring 310; a twenty-ninth victim died three weeks later. It was the largest loss of life during the TROUBLES. The bomb was planted by members of the 'Real IRA', a dissident group opposed to the ceasefire and the BELFAST AGREEMENT (1998) supported by other republicans. A series of fatally inaccurate warnings was given, which resulted in people being moved towards the device. The event had a profound impact on both sides of the border (several victims were from Co. Donegal) and in fact strengthened the determination to apply the arrangements made in the Belfast Agreement, together with a tightening of anti-terrorism legislation in the Republic. Though the 'Real IRA' suspended military action in the wake of the bombing, it subsequently resumed operations, though with little success. The organisation, along with its political counterpart, the 32-County Sovereignty Movement, remains a bastion of diehard REPUBLICANISM. By 2002 only one individual had been convicted in connection with the Omagh bombing. **Keith Jeffery**

O'Mahony, John (1816–1877), Fenian. Born in Kilbeheny, Co. Limerick. After the failure of the 1848 RISING he lived for several years in Paris before settling in New York. The founder of American Fenianism, he was also a noted Irish scholar and translated GEOFFREY KEATING'S FORAS FEASA AR ÉIRINN. Unbendingly devoted to his principles, he died in abject poverty. **Oliver P. Rafferty**

O'Malley, Desmond (1939–), politician. Born in Limerick; educated at UCD and the Incorporated Law Society and became a solicitor. A nephew of DONOGH O'MALLEY, he took his DÁIL seat in Limerick East in 1968, which he held until his retirement in May 2002, first for FIANNA FÁIL and since 1986 for the PROGRESSIVE DEMOCRATS. Parliamentary Secretary to JACK LYNCH, 1969–70, and Minister for Justice, 1970–73, he introduced no-jury courts to deal with terrorist offences. He was Minister for Industry, Commerce and Energy, 1977–9, and Industry, Commerce and Tourism, 1979–81. He opposed CHARLES HAUGHEY energetically and was involved in several attempts to depose him as party leader. O'Malley was expelled from Fianna Fáil in 1985 for dissenting on the CONTRACEPTION issue and soon afterwards became leader of a new party, the Progressive Democrats. In an unprecedented step, Fianna Fáil entered COALITION with the new party in 1989, and O'Malley became Minister for Industry and Commerce. In 1992 the Progressive Democrats precipitated a general election by pulling out of the coalition, and Fianna Fáil formed a new coalition with the LABOUR PARTY. O'Malley retired as party leader and contested the European Parliament in 1994 but was defeated by Pat Cox. An important dissident figure within Haughey's Fianna Fáil, O'Malley symbolised the growing dissent within what had been de Valera's monolithic party. **Tom Garvin**

O'Malley, Donogh (1921–1968), politician. Born in Limerick; educated at UCG and became an engineer. He was elected FIANNA FÁIL TD for East Limerick in 1961, a position he held until his death. He was Parliamentary Secretary to the Minister for Finance, 1961–5, Minister for Health, 1965–6, and Minister for Education, 1966–8. In an extraordinary and irregular coup, in September 1966, and without prior agreement of his Government colleagues, he introduced free education for secondary school children, thereby breaking a political log-jam that had blocked such a move for at least a decade; this was possibly the most important shift in the Republic's educational policy in the twentieth century and may have been the parent of the economic boom of the 1990s, as it made possible the education of large numbers of young people from poorer backgrounds in a way that was not previously possible. He also introduced free school bus transport for rural areas. His attempt to merge the University of Dublin (TRINITY COLLEGE) and UNIVERSITY COLLEGE, Dublin, was unsuccessful. **Tom Garvin**

Omagh. *The people of Omagh, Co. Tyrone, gather to observe a minute's silence one week after the bomb that exploded on 15 August 1998, killing twenty-nine people. [Photocall Ireland]*

O'Malley, Ernest (Ernie) (1897–1957), revolutionary and writer. Born in Castlebar, Co. Mayo; educated at UCD. Partly inspired by the 1916 RISING, he became a leading member of the IRA during the WAR OF INDEPENDENCE and, as an anti-Treatyite, during the CIVIL WAR. After the revolution he travelled widely and wrote extensively, including two celebrated literary accounts of his IRA adventures, *On Another Man's Wound* (1936) and *The Singing Flame* (1978). **Richard English**

O'Malley, Grace (Gráinne Ní Mháille, also colloquially known as Gráinne Mhaol) (died c. 1603). Born in the early sixteenth century into a seafaring family whose territory lay on the west coast of Co. Mayo. She married twice. Her first husband was Dónall O'Flaherty from west Galway, with whom she had three known children. Her second husband was Richard an Iarainn Burke, a prominent member of the Burke family of Co. Mayo, with whom she had a son, Theobald, who later became Viscount Mayo. Though she never held the position of chief, she was recognised by the English administration as a formidable power in west Connacht. She is best known for her activities as a sea captain. In 1576 she offered the Lord Deputy, Sir HENRY SIDNEY, the use of three galleys and 200 fighting men. Two years later she and her second husband came into conflict with the English forces in Connacht, and she was imprisoned for a short time in Limerick Castle and later in DUBLIN CASTLE. After her husband's death in 1583 she continued to command ships and men. In 1593 she travelled to London, where she petitioned ELIZABETH I for land for her sons and for her rights as a widow from her husbands' property. No record of her meeting Elizabeth has survived, but the queen appears to have granted her requests. This did not, however, prevent her from offering assistance to the northern chiefs in their war against Elizabethan forces in the late 1590s. There is no contemporary reference to her in Irish sources, but later FOLKLORE transformed her into 'Granuaile' (presumably a corruption of her name), a pirate queen who sailed the seas around Ireland in search of booty (see pp. 205, 875). **Mary O'Dowd**

O'Malley, Mary (1954–), poet. Born in Connemara; educated at UCG. She taught for eight years at the University of Lisbon before returning to Ireland in 1982. Part of a wave of younger women poets who emerged in the mid-1980s and early 90s, she carries a particular distinction in that she has achieved an authoritative voice and sustained lyric vision throughout several volumes: *A Consideration of Silk* (1990), *Where the Rocks Float* (1993), and *The Knife in the Wave* (1997). Her poems explore the nexus where unassimilated energies and emblems of feminine voice meet the culture of the west of Ireland. **Jody Allen Randolph**

O'Malley, Tony (1913–2003), painter. Born in Callan, Co. Kilkenny; largely self-taught but spent several seasons working with the artists of St Ives, Cornwall, before giving up his banking career in his late forties to become a full-time painter. His early paintings of the 1960s are powerful elegies on the untimely death of his friend and mentor Peter Lanyon. He suffered from TUBERCULOSIS and in the 1970s and 80s spent the winter in the benign climate of the Bahamas, where the tropical colours of flora and fauna dispersed the dark mourning of his 1960s palette. In later years his painting became more and more colourful, a testimony to his blithe and courageous spirit. With his wife, the painter Jane O'Malley, he lived and worked in Callan, Co. Kilkenny. From the 1990s he made painted timber constructions and produced large-scale prints with the Graphic Studio, Dublin. *Hawk and Quarry: In Memory of Peter Lanyon* (1964) is in the Crawford Gallery, Cork. He was a *saoi* of AOSDÁNA. **Dorothy Walker**

Ó Maolchonaire, Flaithrí (c. 1560–1629), priest and translator. Born into a professional learned family at Cluain na hOíche, Co. Roscommon; joined the Franciscan order in Salamanca. He translated Jeronimo de Ripalda's catechism into Irish, 1593. He was Papal legate at Kinsale, returning to Spain with RED HUGH O'DONNELL after his defeat. Appointed provincial of the Irish FRANCISCANS in 1606, he prevailed on Philip III of Spain to establish a college for Irish Franciscans in Louvain. He was appointed Archbishop of Tuam by Pope Paul V in 1609. He published *Desiderius* (1616) in Louvain, an Irish translation of a Catalan original but containing substantial additions encouraging Irish Catholics to persevere in the faith. **Mícheál Mac Craith**

Ó Maolmhuaidh, Proinsias (c. 1614–1685). Ordained in St Isidore's College in Rome; his catechism in Irish, *Lucerna Fidelium*, was published by the PROPAGANDA FIDE press in 1676. His *Grammatica Latino-Hibernica* (1677), the first published grammar of Irish, came from the same press; it was used by Edward Lhuyd in his *Archaeologica Britannica* (1707). **Mícheál Mac Craith**

O'Meara, Eugene (1815–1880), botanist and clergyman. Born in Wexford; educated at TCD. A founder-member of the Dublin Microscopical Club, he distinguished himself as an expert on the diatoms, one of the major groups of microscopic algae. His first publications were catalogues of the diatoms of the POWERSCOURT Demesne and of Co. Dublin; thereafter he described a number of new species from various parts of Ireland. In 1875 he published the first part of a monumental *Report of the Irish Diatomacea*. **Christopher Moriarty**

O'Meara, Frank (1853–1888), artist. Born into a medical family in Carlow; studied art in the atelier of Carolus-Duran in Paris, c. 1872–6. He moved to the Forest of Fontainebleau and settled at the village of Grez-sur-Loing, c. 1875–87, painting from nature. In spite of a short career and a limited output, O'Meara exerted a subtle influence on his Irish, British, Swedish, and American contemporaries, who included JOHN LAVERY, Robert Louis Stevenson, Carl Larsson, and William Stott of Oldham. His canvases generally contain the single figures of women in an autumnal landscape setting, combining aspects of French realism with an elegiac pre-Raphaelite mood. He exhibited paintings in Paris, London, Liverpool, and Glasgow, but his name was scarcely known in Ireland during his lifetime. He painted briefly in Étaples in 1887; suffering from ill health, probably TUBERCULOSIS, he returned home, dying in Carlow in 1888. A significant body of his work is in the Hugh Lane Municipal Gallery of Modern Art, Dublin. **Julian Campbell**

Ó Míocháin, Tomás (fl. 1776), poet and teacher. Born near Quin, Co. Clare. He lived for a time near Milltown Malbay and subsequently moved to Ennis, where he taught school. He was the founder of a school of poetry based there. He is remembered for some rousing songs commemorating the American War of Independence. **Diarmaid Ó Muirithe**

O'More, Rory (c. 1592–c. 1666), grandson of a deposed leader of the O'More sept of Queen's County (Laois). He inherited ESTATES in Cos. Kildare and Armagh that had been awarded by the Crown to his grandfather and father. In 1641 he approached Lord Maguire urging that the Anglo-Scottish crisis offered the Irish a chance to regain lost estates by force. He played a subordinate role in executing this plot, being one of the leaders tasked with taking DUBLIN CASTLE on 23 October 1641. He evaded arrest after the betrayal of the attempted coup. Through his marital connections to some of the leading families of the PALE and by his persuasive speech at the Knockcrofty meeting he facilitated the subsequent alliance of the Pale nobility with the Ulster insurgents in November 1641. In 1643 he was stripped of his military command in King's County (Offaly) and the adjacent half of Queen's County (Laois). A marginal figure thereafter, by 1652 he was serving on Inishbofin, one of the last Irish outposts. He escaped before the final surrender of the island and remained in hiding in Ireland until at least 1666. **Pádraig Lenihan**

O'Morphi, Marie-Louise (1736–1815), mistress of Louis XV of France. Born in Rouen to Irish parents. Her father was a shoemaker who died when she was young, leaving her mother, Margaret Murphy, to care for five daughters. Margaret moved to Paris, where Marie-Louise drew the attentions of the infamous Casanova, who in turn introduced her to the court painter François Boucher. She posed for some of the most erotic nudes in the history of art, and became Boucher's lover. At seventeen she became the king's mistress, which prompted Madame de Pompadour to arrange O'Morphi's marriage to an elderly army officer. During the Reign of Terror she

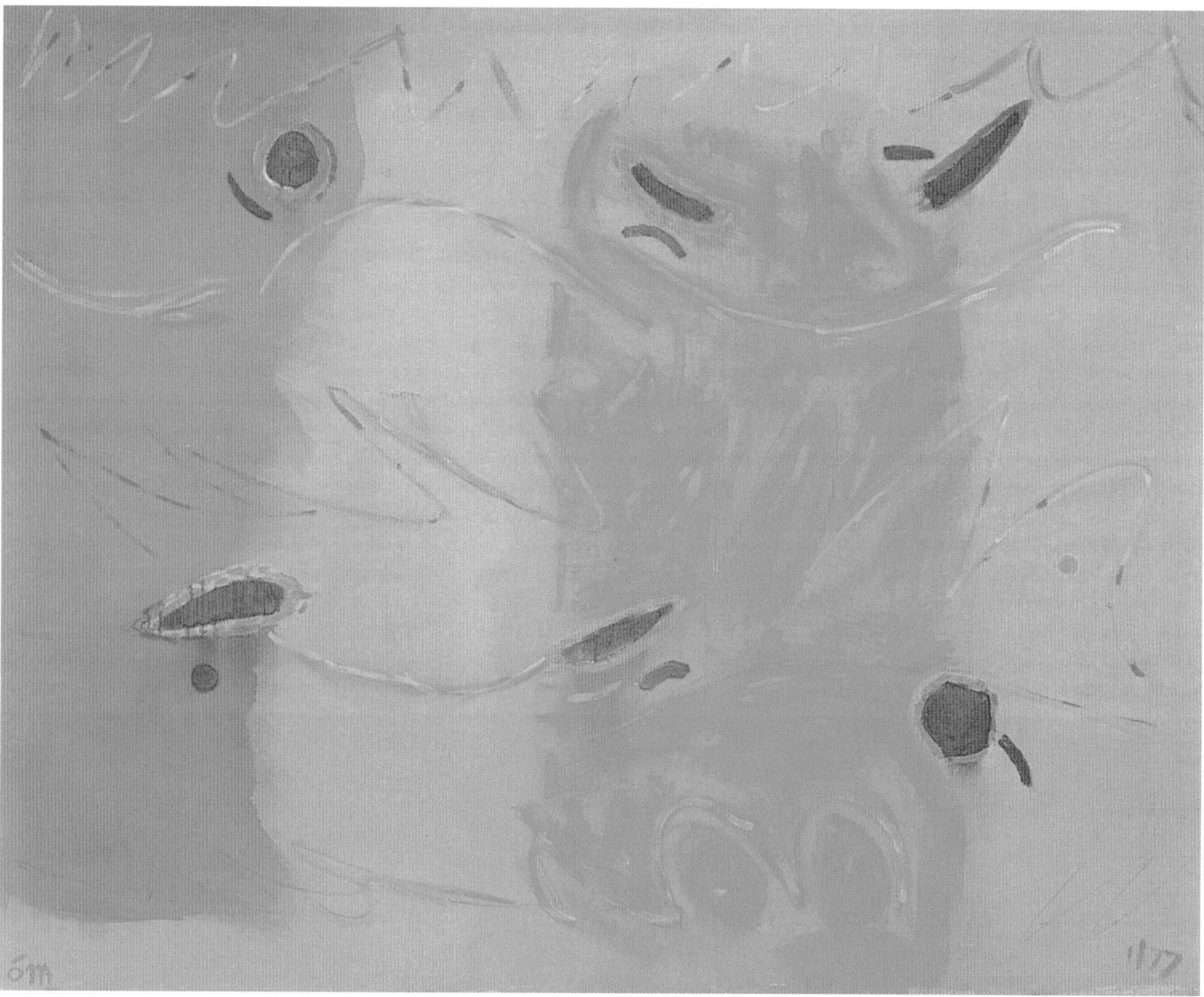

O'Malley, Tony. Arawak Beach *(1979) by Tony O'Malley, a work in which he maximises the use of light and colour to celebrate the images of a tropical paradise, producing a work that delves beneath the surface of literal expression. [AIB Art Collection]*

was imprisoned for two years. She had three children by Louis, but she was separated from each of them at birth. **Ciarán Deane**

Ó Muireadhaigh, Lorcán P. (1883–1941), historian and song collector. Born in Carlingford, Co. Louth; educated at ST PATRICK'S COLLEGE, Maynooth, 1901–8, and ordained a priest in St Paul, Minnesota, 1910. Each summer from 1910 to 1918 he returned from the United States to Omeath, Co. Louth, to collect folk-tales and songs from the last Irish-speakers of the area; more than 300 pieces were recorded on cylinders. He published *Ceolta Óméith* (1920), *Amhráin Chúige Uladh* (1927), and *Amhráin Chúige Uladh* (1937). He was one of the few collectors with the foresight to publish songs with notation. Much of his collection was published in 2001; the cylinder recordings have not survived. His manuscripts are in St Patrick's College, Maynooth, and the Ó Fiaich Library, Armagh. He died at the age of fifty-eight and is buried in Dunleer, Co. Louth. **Pádraigín Ní Uallacháin**

Ó Muirgheasa, Enrí (1874–1945), folklorist and music collector. Born Henry Morris in Farney, Co. Monaghan. He became a national school teacher and, in 1921, schools inspector. A founding member of Louth Archaeological Society, he edited and published much Ulster song; his collections include *Céad de Cheoltaibh Uladh* (1915), *Amhráin Airt Mhic Cubhthaigh* (1916), *Duanaire na Midhe* (1933), *DháChéad de Cheoltaibh Uladh* (1934), and *Dánta Diadha Uladh* (1936), with regrettably few tunes. **Lillis Ó Laoire**

Ó Muirthile, Liam (1950–), poet, dramatist, and prose author. Born in Cork; educated at UCC, where he was one of the 'INNTI' poets. A former radio and television journalist, his collection *Tine Chnámh* (1984), a dramatic version of which was produced in 1993, demonstrated his poetic voice, later developed in *Dialann Bóthair* (1992) and *Walking Time agus Dánta Eile* (2000). Two collections from his literary journalism in the IRISH TIMES have been published. A novel, *Ar Bhruach na Laoi* (1995), the plays *Fear an Tae* (1995) and *Liodán na hAbhann* (1999) and the prose allegory *Gaothán* (2000) reflect Cork as a source and illustrate a growing experimentation with genre and bilingualism. **Seán Ó Cearnaigh**

Ó Murchadha, Seán (na Ráithíneach) (1700–1762), poet and scribe. Born in Carrignavar, Co. Cork; he earned his living on the family farm, writing poetry and transcribing manuscripts in his spare time. He was accustomed to writing his poems in a pocket-sized notebook. In 1938 one of these notebooks was discovered in the attic of a house in Dana, near Ware, Massachusetts, containing his own poems as well as those of other poets from the period 1719–44, a total of 145 poems. This collection formed the basis for Tadhg O'Donoghue's 1954 edition of the poet's work. **Breandán Ó Conchúir**

Ó Murchú, Labhrás (1939–), music organiser. Born at Cashel, Co. Tipperary. He was a clerical officer with South Tipperary County Council, then CONRADH NA GAEILGE's organiser in Dublin, 1965–8. A teacher of CÉILÍ DANCING, he joined COMHALTAS CEOLTÓIRÍ ÉIREANN in the late 1950s. In 1968 he was elected president for the first of two three-year terms; he was then appointed as full-time director—the first salaried executive position in TRADITIONAL MUSIC. He has been a FIANNA FÁIL member of Seanad Éireann from 1997; as joint Fianna Fáil spokesperson on the arts, culture and the GAELTACHT his major achievement was the drafting of the first report on Irish traditional music (1998), a document challenged on its release as unrepresentative. Within CCÉ he initiated the development of the Cultúrlann; its head office and cultural centre in Monkstown, Co. Dublin, opened in 1974. Having disputed the right of the IRISH MUSIC RIGHTS ORGANISATION to claim royalties on traditional music, he subsequently negotiated a licence with it in 1998 in return for substantial funds for CCÉ. **Fintan Vallely**

Ó'n Cháinte, Fear Feasa (fl. 1600), Cork poet. His patrons included members of the MacCarthy and O'Keeffe families. He took part in IOMARBHÁGH NA BHFILEADH (the contention of the poets), and his poetry reflects the social changes of the period, particularly the decline in patronage and the popular indifference to bardic art. **Máirín Nic Eoin**

Ó Neachtain, Joe Steve (1942–), oral poet, writer, dramatist and actor. Born at An Chré Dhubh, Co. Galway. He published *Fead Ghlaice* (1988) and *De Dhroim Leice* (1990), poetry drawing mainly on oral tradition, and a short-story collection, *Clochmhóin* (1998). He also wrote a popular radio serial, 'Baile an Droichid' (1987–97), a sell-out play, *Níor Mhaith Liom Do Thrioblóid* (2000), and a prize-winning novel, *Scread Mhaidne* (2002). **Gearóid Denvir**

Ó Neachtain, Seán (c. 1650–1729), scribe and author. From the Barony of Athlone, Co. Roscommon; forced to move, he settled in Co. Meath and ultimately in Dublin, where he taught school. He could write with feeling (as in his well-known love-poem 'Rachainn fán gCoill Leat') and solemnity (as in his elegy on Edmund Byrne, Archbishop of Dublin). Above all, he could compose with witty originality, incorporating socio-linguistic sensitivities in both poetry, such as the burlesque 'Cath Bearna Chroise Brighde', and the partly autobiographical prose tale 'Stair Éamuinn Uí Chléire', reflecting the regional and social differences of his day. 'Cath Bearna Chroise Brighde' sees Irish-speaking potato-eaters from Tallaght in south Co. Dublin pitted against English-speaking bean and cereal-fed opponents from Fingall in the north of the county, while other poems poke fun at some of the clergy, whose Irish was permeated with English vocabulary and idiom. With 'Stair Éamuinn Uí Chléire' Irish teetered on the brink of creating an urban literature,

O'Morphi. *Marie-Louise O'Morphi, mistress of King Louis XV of France, by the court painter François Boucher, who specialised in depicting the elegant superficiality of the French court with a startling sensuality. [Munich, Alte Pinakothek]*

but the work remained in a half-way house between medieval romance and the modern novel. **Liam Mac Mathúna**

Ó Neachtain, Tadhg (1671–c. 1752), scribe and scholar. Born in Dublin, son of SEÁN Ó NEACHTAIN; educated by his father, who had a lasting influence on him. He was the centre of a circle of some twenty-six Irish scholars, who came from both Dublin and further afield. They were a hive of intellectual activity, busy exchanging and copying manuscripts and compiling dictionaries, genealogies and histories. A prolific scribe, he composed many poems, which while erudite and competent lack a creative flair. Of more lasting merit is his interaction in a diary-like compilation with events of the day, particularly as recorded by the newspapers. His *Eólas ar an Domhan*, though largely a derivative textbook on world geography, shows a keen awareness of contemporary social change, noting for instance that Irish was being abandoned for English, though people were still adhering to the Catholic religion. **Liam Mac Mathúna**

O'Neill, Arthur (1734–1818), harper and raconteur. Born in Dungannon, Co. Tyrone. He lost his sight at an early age and was sent to learn the HARP under Owen Kennan of Augher. At fifteen he began a career as an itinerant musician, and he travelled extensively around the country. Most of his life story was dictated to a scribe appointed by EDWARD BUNTING during O'Neill's stay in Belfast between 1808 and 1813. He gave Bunting many tunes, as well as being one of his chief sources of information on harpers and harping. His memoirs can be read in *Carolan: The Life, Times and Music of an Irish Harper* by DÓNAL O'SULLIVAN. **Maeve Ellen Gebruers**

O'Neill, Cathal (1931–), architect. Born in Dublin; educated at UCD and Illinois Institute of Technology. He worked in the offices of Ludwig Mies van der Rohe and Harry Weese, Chicago, and in 1961 established his own practice in Dublin. He was professor of architecture at UCD, 1973–96, and undertook the renovation of the Masonic Boys' School, Clonskeagh, for the School of Architecture (1981); he also designed the Chaplaincy Building. He has an evolving ecological agenda and has produced Travellers' housing in Co. Limerick and Co. Laois, offices and laboratories for the Environmental Protection Agency, Monaghan (1996) and UCD (2000–2), and Ballyedmond House, Midleton, Co. Cork (2001). **Raymund Ryan**

O'Neill, Conn Bacach (c. 1484–1559), Lord of Tyrone, 1519–59, and first Earl of Tyrone, 1542–59. Son of Conn Mór O'Neill, Lord of Tyrone, 1483–93, and Alice Fitzgerald, daughter of GERALD FITZGERALD, EIGHTH EARL OF KILDARE, he succeeded his brother, Art Óg, as Lord of Tyrone in 1519. He maintained close relations with GERALD FITZGERALD, NINTH EARL OF KILDARE, his cousin, and joined his son in rebellion, 1534–5. He joined MANUS O'DONNELL, Lord of Tyrconnell, in a vain attempt to restore the Earldom of Kildare to its young heir in 1539. However, in September 1542 HENRY VIII made O'Neill Earl of Tyrone as part of the SURRENDER AND REGRANT agreements that aimed to integrate Ireland peacefully in the Tudor polity. The earl's grasp on power faltered as he grew old, and after much warfare his youngest 'legitimate' son, Seán (SHANE O'NEILL), took control of Tyrone in 1558; the earl took refuge with the Bishop of Meath at Ardbraccan, where he died early in 1559. **Henry A. Jefferies**

O'Neill, Daniel (Dan) (1920–1974), painter of figures, landscapes, and genre scenes. Born in Belfast; an electrician by trade, he briefly attended Belfast College of Art before studying under Sidney Smith, but otherwise was self-taught. He quickly developed an expressionist technique and strong romanticism, with imagery, often laden with pathos, evoking such universal themes as love, life, and death. In 1949 he visited Paris and was influenced by Rouault, Vlaminck, and Utrillo; there followed a number of atmospheric works, including *Place du Tertre* (1949), *The Blue Skirt* (1949), *Knockalla Hills, Donegal* (1951), and *Birth* (1952), on which his reputation largely rests. His later work, generally brighter in colour, is less successful. **S. B. Kennedy**

O'Neill, Eugene Gladstone (1888–1953), playwright. Born in New York, son of the Irish actor James O'Neill (c. 1846–1920). The elder O'Neill was an accomplished and versatile actor who had, as his son put it, 'the good bad luck' to find a hugely successful role in *The Count of Monte Cristo*, which he played for thirty years, dissipating his talent. Eugene O'Neill would later claim to have been impressed by the ABBEY THEATRE's American tour of 1911; he began writing plays in 1913, joining the Provincetown Players in 1916. His first full-length play, *Beyond the Horizon*, appeared on Broadway in 1920, winning the first of his four Pulitzer Prizes. Much of O'Neill's work is autobiographical, drawing on his Irish-American Catholic background. This is particularly true of *Long Day's Journey into Night* (1941, staged 1956), which had an impressive production at the Abbey Theatre in 1959, with RIA MOONEY as Mary Tyrone. O'Neill was awarded the NOBEL PRIZE for Literature in 1936. **Christopher Morash**

O'Neill, Francis (1848–1936), traditional flute-player, collector and publisher. Born in Tralibane, Co. Cork; sailed around the world before being shipwrecked and brought to America, where he joined the Chicago police force and rose through the ranks to become chief of police, 1901–5. From the 1880s he was also collecting music from the many Irish traditional musicians living in Chicago and from printed and manuscript sources. In 1903 he produced *O'Neill's Music of Ireland: Eighteen Hundred and Fifty Melodies*, the largest collection of Irish music ever published. This was followed by five other collections and two important studies, *Irish Folk Music: A Fascinating Hobby* (1910) and *Irish Minstrels and Musicians* (1913). His publications, mostly still in print, were ground-breaking in preserving Irish dance music and had a great impact on the course of the music in the twentieth century. **Nicholas Carolan**

O'Neill, Hugh, Earl of Tyrone (1550–1616), rebel leader during the NINE YEARS' WAR (1594–1603) and participant in the FLIGHT OF THE EARLS (1607). Despite his involvement in such turbulent episodes, it is notable that O'Neill's advancement in his early career owed much to royal patronage, which led to his being created in the first instance Baron of Dungannon and later Earl of Tyrone. He sought both to benefit from the support of the English Crown and to limit its influence in Ulster, the last bastion of Irish society, and his career was often characterised by ambivalence. Even his active participation in the early years of the Nine Years' War has been the source of much debate. What is beyond doubt is that his generalship during that conflict was critically important in dictating the complexion of the war. Securing a series of resounding victories against Crown forces, none more so than at the BATTLE OF THE YELLOW FORD (1598), where he annihilated the royal army, O'Neill almost succeeded in eradicating English hegemony in Ireland. With the arrival of a Spanish army at Kinsale in 1601 this seemed all the more likely; but the disastrous outcome of the BATTLE OF KINSALE put paid to his aspirations of an outright victory over the English.

O'Neill, Daniel. Western Landscape *(1951) by Daniel O'Neill. It depicts, with surreal overtones and without sentimentality, central elements of the rural landscape: a ruined dwelling, a holy well with image of a saint, and an isolated cottage. [AIB Art Collection; © 2002. All rights reserved, DACS]*

Brought to terms with the TREATY OF MELLIFONT (1603), he was rendered temporarily vulnerable, a factor later manifested at the time of the Flight of the Earls (1607), when he escaped to the Continent with Rory O'Donnell, Earl of Tyrconnell, fearing arrest by the English authorities. Despite living in exile for the rest of his life, O'Neill continued to be an important participant in Irish politics. Persistent rumours of his imminent return to Ireland were a significant factor in stunting the development of the PLANTATION OF ULSTER in its early stages. **John McCavitt**

O'Neill, Martin (1952–), soccer player. Born in Kilrea, Co. Derry. A former Gaelic footballer, he enjoyed an outstanding career in England after moving from Distillery to Nottingham Forest in 1972. An inventive midfielder, he provided much of the skill in the Northern Ireland team that reached the finals of the 1982 World Cup. That experience stood him in good stead when he went into management, and he succeeded against all the odds in keeping Leicester City in the Premiership. Victory in the League Cup final attracted the interest of bigger clubs, and he transformed Celtic to the point where they broke Rangers' dominance in Scottish football. **Peter Byrne**

O'Neill, Moira, pseudonym of Agnes Skrine, née Higginson (1865–1955), poet. Born in Cushendun, Co. Antrim. After her marriage she lived in Canada, then returned to Cushendall, Co. Antrim. She is best known for her collections of dialect poems based on her interpretation of the customs, ways and sayings of the rural inhabitants of the region, most notably *Songs of the Glens of Antrim* (1901). Her work was very popular, and her *Collected Poems* were published in 1933. She was the mother of MOLLY KEANE, the novelist. She later settled in Co. Wicklow, where she died. **Robbie Meredith**

O'Neill, Onora (1941–), philosopher. Born in Aughafatten, Co. Antrim; educated at the University of Oxford and Harvard University. She taught at Columbia University, 1970–77, and the University of Essex, 1977–92, and since 1992 has been principal of Newnham College, Cambridge. She has produced a unique and celebrated interpretation of the work of Kant, avoiding the formalism usually associated with him and instead developing a 'community-based' ethics. She has published *Acting on Principle* (1975), *Faces of Hunger* (1986), *Constructions of Reason* (1989), and *Bounds of Justice* (2000). **Ian Leask**

O'Neill, Owen Roe, anglicised name of Eoghan Rua Ó Néill (c. 1590–1649), soldier, victor of the BATTLE OF BENBURB (1646). Commissioned as an officer in the service of Spain in 1606, he became a highly experienced senior officer, eventually taking command of his own regiment. When the 1641 REBELLION broke out in Ireland he endeavoured to return at the earliest opportunity to the land of his birth, which he had left as a child. As a nephew of the Earl of Tyrone, his homecoming was considered highly symbolic. Leading a band of some 200 Irish veterans of the Continental wars, he returned to Ulster to take command of the rebel forces that had seized much of the province from the control of Protestant settlers. Bringing to bear a highly professional military approach, he is credited with transforming the military fortunes of the rebel forces. His biggest success occurred at the BATTLE OF BENBURB (1646), when his army of 5,000 men comprehensively defeated a larger settler army commanded by ROBERT MONRO. Inflicting some 2,000–3,000 casualties on his opponents, with his own dead and wounded numbered at less than 300, O'Neill temporarily held the fate of Ulster, possibly Ireland, in his grasp. Rather than pursuing the expulsion of the settler forces from Ulster, he is widely regarded as having mistakenly directed his army south. Becoming embroiled in the divisive politics of the Irish Confederation, based in Kilkenny, O'Neill's talents were dissipated by the internecine rivalries between Old English and native Irish Catholics. **John McCavitt**

O'Neill, Sir Phelim (1605–1653), one of the leaders of the 1641 REBELLION in Ulster. O'Neill's involvement has taxed the understanding of historians, as his family had benefited from the PLANTATION OF ULSTER in 1610. Brought up in the PALE, such was the manner in which he had integrated with planter society that he had been appointed a justice of the peace and was socially familiar with the Protestant planter class; indeed he had used the pretext of a dinner invitation to the home of Sir Toby Caulfield, a prominent planter, to seize the important fort at Charlemont, Co. Armagh, and launch the revolt. Such were the complexities of the issues involved in the so-called rebellion that O'Neill affirmed that he had not taken arms against the king but was taking steps to neuter the machinations of parliamentary supporters in Ulster. Despite the fact that O'Neill never intended the rising to degenerate into an assault on the Protestant settlers in Ulster, the reality was that thousands were promptly either massacred or evicted from their settlements. O'Neill gave way to the military expertise of OWEN ROE O'NEILL, whom he had helped persuade to return to Ireland. On the collapse of the rising, Sir Phelim was tried and put to death. **John McCavitt**

Ó Néill, Séamus (1910–1981), novelist, short-story writer, playwright, and poet. Born in Clough, Co. Down; educated at QUB and later UCD and Innsbruck. He taught history at Carysfort College, Blackrock, Co. Dublin. His best-known works are two novels, *Tonn Tuile* (1947) and *Máire Nic Artáin* (1959), which explore bourgeois life and mixed marriage, respectively. **Seán Ó Cearnaigh**

O'Neill, Seán (1940–), Gaelic footballer. Born in Co. Down. In 1960, at the age of twenty, he was one of the inspiring figures who created history and helped Down to win the all-Ireland title; he helped them to retain it the following year. Playing in a variety of positions in the attack, he was one of the great finishers of his time. He added a third all-Ireland in 1968, the year in which he was honoured as Footballer of the Year. **Donal Keenan**

O'Neill, Shane (Seán Ó Néill) (1530–1567), known as Seán an Díomais (Shane the Proud), one of the most powerful Irish chieftains in the sixteenth century. A product of vicious internecine factionalism in the north, he became 'the O'Neill' in 1559. In his rise to power he displayed ruthlessness combined with no small degree of cunning. He exhibited similar characteristics in extending his sway throughout much of Ulster. At odds with the O'Donnells of Tír Chonaill, he embarked on a killing spree during the summer of 1564, leaving 4,500 dead. The Scots settlers in Co. Antrim, the MacDonnells, also felt his wrath, with 600 killed at the Battle of Glenshesk in 1565. Like many of his contemporaries, Shane rode on the back of the burgeoning Tudor state in Ireland only to end up challenging it. He is most famously remembered for his visit to ELIZABETH I's court, where he addressed the monarch dressed in traditional Irish attire and speaking Irish. Conceived as a diplomatic mission to resolve differences between O'Neill and the Crown, his trip to court witnessed hard bargaining on both sides in an attempt to reach a *modus vivendi*, O'Neill, for his part, wishing to be elevated to the Earldom of Tyrone, an English title. Agreement was not reached. His visit caused quite a stir, the English looking at him 'with such wonderment as if he had come from China or America.' An extremely powerful military leader, he ultimately earned himself the searing enmity of the English Crown, the O'Donnells, and the MacDonnells. At war again with the O'Donnells in 1567, he suffered a spectacular reverse at the Battle of Farsetmore, his army virtually annihilated. In desperate straits, he opted to negotiate with the MacDonnells of Antrim, a fatal decision. With memories of Glenshesk still vivid, Shane had his throat cut. **John McCavitt**

O'Neill, Terence, Lord O'Neill of the Maine (1914–1990), politician. Born in Co. Antrim; educated at Eton College, Windsor. He served in the British army throughout the SECOND WORLD WAR and in 1946 became MP for Bannside in the STORMONT parliament. After serving as Minister of Finance for seven years he succeeded Brookeborough as leader of the Unionist Party and Prime Minister. He attempted to improve relations between unionists and nationalists in Northern Ireland and stressed

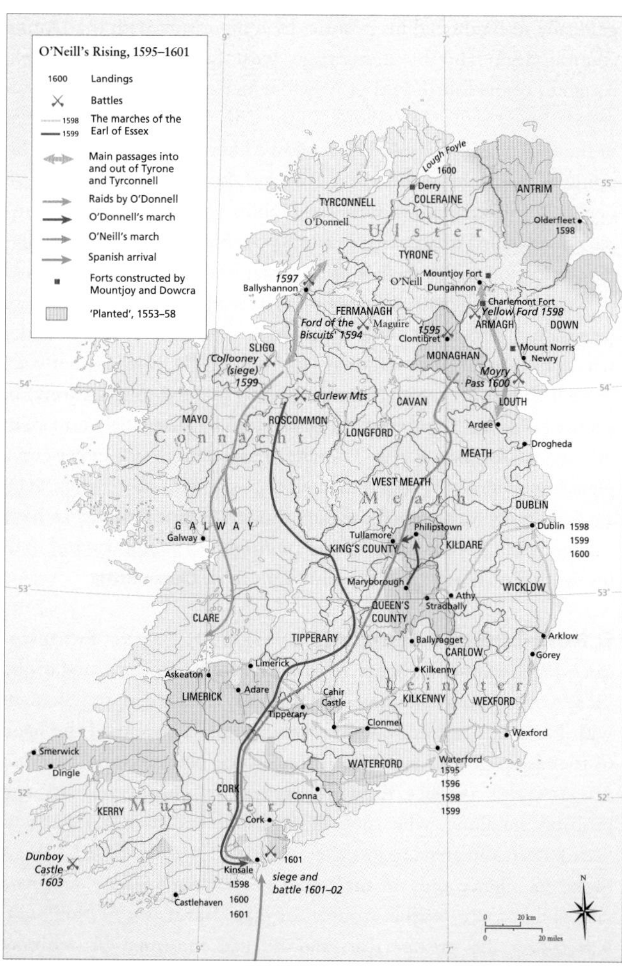

the need for greater economic co-operation with the Republic. In January 1965, in a move that brought much criticism from right-wing unionists, he met the Taoiseach, SEÁN LEMASS, at Stormont. At the same time pressure for internal reform was being exerted by the Northern Ireland Civil Rights Association, forcing O'Neill to face opposition from two directions simultaneously.

Tensions increased after the RUC clashed with demonstrators at a civil rights march in Derry in October 1968. A series of reforms were introduced, but these raised expectations of further change on the one hand and unionist fears on the other. In a television address on 9 December 1968 O'Neill famously declared that 'Ulster stands at the crossroads,' and he appealed to the general public to support his policies. The appeal appeared successful at first: in December 1968 an 'I back O'Neill' campaign run by the BELFAST TELEGRAPH brought 150,000 responses, while *Sunday Independent* readers voted O'Neill their man of the year. Tension again increased, however, as a result of events surrounding a march from Belfast to Derry organised by PEOPLE'S DEMOCRACY when the RUC failed to protect the marchers when they were attacked by loyalists at BURNTOLLET BRIDGE. In a Stormont general election on 24 February 1969 O'Neill failed to see off his unionist critics, and on 28 April he resigned as Prime Minister. He became a life peer as Lord O'Neill of the Maine in 1970 and died in June 1990. **Gordon Gillespie**

O'Neill, Turlough Luineach (c. 1530–1595), Ulster chieftain, son of the sometime tánaiste to CONN BACACH O'NEILL, Niall Conallach (died 1544). He spent his early career under the shadow of SHANE O'NEILL, whom he sometimes supported (in his assassination of the young Baron of Dungannon) and whom he frequently deserted. Following Shane's killing he seized the O'Neillship and gradually strengthened his position by temporising with the Dublin administration and by a marriage with Lady Agnes Campbell, daughter of the fourth Earl of Argyll, which gave him access to several thousand Scots mercenaries. In the early 1570s the depredations of the Earl of Essex in east Ulster allowed him to further advance his claims as protector of the native Irish in Ulster, but he continued to negotiate for recognition with the Dublin administration and completed a detailed treaty with Lord Deputy Sidney in 1576. Dublin's preoccupation with rebellion in Munster in the early 1580s allowed O'Neill to consolidate his position in Ulster, but he was willing to negotiate a settlement with Lord Deputy PERROT in 1585 under which he agreed to a temporary division of Tír Eoghain between himself and HUGH O'NEILL (with Hugh to succeed to its entirety) in exchange for his elevation to the peerage and a substantial permanent inheritance for his son Art. Though the agreement was never completed by patent, O'Neill remained at peace with the Crown even as Hugh grew more rebellious; and though he was reported to have resigned the O'Neillship in favour of Hugh in 1593, it was not until his death that Hugh formally laid claim to it. **Ciaran Brady**

O'Neill-Lemass meeting (1965). SEÁN LEMASS, TAOISEACH since 1959, knew that better relations with Britain were vital to the success of his economic strategy. That must include a rapprochement with Northern Ireland; but Brookeborough flatly refused the hand of friendship Lemass had offered on several occasions. So different was TERENCE O'NEILL from his predecessor that it was he, and probably he alone, who took the initiative and invited Lemass to STORMONT. On arriving just after noon on 14 January 1965 Lemass broke his silence only in the toilets of Stormont House when he said: 'I'll get into terrible trouble for this.' But it was O'Neill who was taking the greater risk; and he had informed his Cabinet colleagues only that morning. The ministers smiled bravely for the cameras after a cordial lunch. When he returned to Dublin, Lemass told waiting reporters: 'I think I can say that a road-block has been removed.' That evening on television O'Neill justified the meeting, observing that North and South 'share the same rivers, the same mountains, and some of the same problems.' The meeting was little more than an ice-breaker, and discussion concentrated on possible North-South economic co-operation. **Jonathan Bardon**

O'Nolan, Brian: see O'BRIEN, FLANN.

On the Study of Celtic Literature (1867), a series of lectures delivered in 1865–6 in the University of Oxford by the English poet and critic Matthew Arnold. Drawing on the writings of the French critics and scholars Henri Martin and Ernest Renan and on his limited knowledge of Welsh literature in translation, he propounded an influential version of Celticism. In this the Celt was both celebrated and diminished as one possessed of 'natural magic' but 'always liable to react against the despotism of fact.' This characterisation of Celtic peoples as mystically inspired yet ineffectual took deep root in late nineteenth-century literary culture in Britain and Ireland. **Terence Brown**

opera. The earliest reference to opera in Ireland dates from 1661, when John Ogilvy was licensed 'to represent Comedyes, Tragedyes and Operas' in Dublin. However, in seventeenth- and eighteenth-century Ireland (as in England) the term 'opera' could refer to any theatrical performance including music, usually comprising plays with a high proportion of songs. Very little opera was performed in Ireland in the early eighteenth century, despite the presence of many foreign musicians; nevertheless, the period did see *The Island Passion* with music by Daniel Purcell and Jeremiah Clarke, among others, at the Theatre Royal, SMOCK ALLEY—now considered to be the first true opera performed in the country. Dublin remained impervious to the contemporaneous vogue for Italian opera, prevalent in London, and it was not until the success of John Gay's *The Beggar's Opera*, in March 1728, that the spread of ballad opera, and later English comic opera, began in earnest. While Dublin companies performed in provincial towns on occasion, Belfast and Cork were the only other important centres, with ballad and comic operas forming the mainstay of activity there in the later eighteenth century also. However, from 1760 visiting companies from Britain and the Continent presented serious operas in Italian and English at the Smock Alley and CROW STREET theatres (the former presenting GIORDANI's *L'eroe cinese*, the first Italian opera seria to be performed in Ireland) and, from 1820, at the THEATRE ROYAL, Hawkins Street.

The remainder of the nineteenth century largely saw the cultivation of Italian grand opera (Bellini, Donizetti), and grand opera in English, including *The Bohemian Girl* (1845) and *Maritana* (1845) by the Irish expatriates MICHAEL BALFE and WILLIAM VINCENT WALLACE, respectively, and *The Lily of Killarney* (1862) by Julius Benedict. Belfast, which was enjoying a flowering of musical activity, saw the replacement of an earlier theatre with the Theatre Royal in 1871 and the building of the GRAND OPERA HOUSE in 1895 (rebuilt 1980).

By the early twentieth century, public operatic experience was largely dependent on the visits of, for example, the Carl Rosa, Moody-Manners, and O'Mara companies to Dublin, Belfast, Cork, and other centres. Regular seasons of opera date only from 1941, with the establishment of the DUBLIN GRAND OPERA SOCIETY, based at the GAIETY THEATRE, Dublin. The WEXFORD FESTIVAL OPERA,

opera. *Majella Cullagh (left) as Clarice and Colette McGahon as Lisetta in The Opera Theatre Company's production of Josef Haydn's* Life on the Moon, *Dublin, 1997. [Opera Theatre Company; photo: Tom Lawlor]*

founded in 1951 by T. J. WALSH, features lesser-known works and has enjoyed international critical acclaim. Smaller, touring companies such as Irish National Opera (1965), its successor OPERA THEATRE COMPANY (1986), and OPERA NORTHERN IRELAND (1985) have been instrumental both in providing opportunities for young singers and in popularising the standard repertoire. Despite this level of national and local activity, Dublin remains a capital city without an opera house.

It is perhaps not surprising that few Irish composers have succeeded in this medium, given also the uneven record of opera performance. CHARLES STANFORD's *Shamus O'Brien* (1895) is more notable for its stage-Irishisms than for any intrinsic artistic merit, while Butler's *Murgheis* (1903) and O'DWYER's *Eithne* (1910) represent a conscientious, if only partly successful, attempt to fuse late romantic harmonic practice with the national tradition. Since the 1950s a number of operas have been written, including works by JAMES WILSON (*Twelfth Night*, 1969), GERARD VICTORY (*Chatterton*, 1971), and GERALD BARRY (*The Intelligence Park*, 1981–90). **Philip Graydon**

Opera Ireland: see DUBLIN GRAND OPERA SOCIETY.

Opera Northern Ireland, established 1985, a company that concentrated on performing lesser-known productions, using alternative venues. It received most of its funding from the ARTS COUNCIL OF NORTHERN IRELAND and was also involved in educational schemes, visiting schools and putting on workshops for pupils. It ceased to function in 1999 and its funding was transferred to OPERA THEATRE COMPANY, based in Dublin. **Geraldine Guiden**

Opera Theatre Company (OTC), a company that performs a more unusual and adventurous repertoire than is usually heard. It was founded in 1986 by James Conway. The company aims to employ Irish singers as much as possible, and plays smaller venues, touring extensively and making opera more accessible. It runs an educational scheme, in which the company visits schools and the pupils are involved in every aspect of the production. The works are specially commissioned by OTC and funding is provided in part by the ARTS COUNCIL OF NORTHERN IRELAND. **Geraldine Guiden**

Operational Programmes for Tourism, jointly financed cross-border schemes that set targets for the number of overseas visitors, TOURISM income, and domestic EMPLOYMENT. The programmes were set up to remedy a lack of investment in tourism in the 1980s. In 1987 £25 million was invested in tourism in the Republic; under the first programme, 1989–93, a total of £380 million from public and private sectors was invested in tourism-related services, including marketing and training. A further £707 million was spent in the second programme, 1994–9. The European Regional Development Fund contributed £378 million to the first programme, and EU agencies have contributed a further £369 to the second one. **Alannah Hopkin**

Opik, Ernst Julius (1893–1985), astronomer. Born in Kunda, Estonia; educated at the University of Moscow. Having held various posts internationally, he was research associate at ARMAGH OBSERVATORY from 1948 until 1981. He was acting director of Armagh Observatory from 1974 to 1976. Among his many contributions to ASTRONOMY were his determination of the distance to the Andromeda nebula in 1922, his suggestion in the 1950s that it would be worthwhile searching for craters on Mars (discovered by spacecraft in 1965), and his studies on the source of stellar energy. He edited the *Irish Astronomical Journal* from 1950 to 1981. He was the recipient of a number of gold medals, including the Smith

Medal (1960) of the National Academy of Sciences, Washington, the Leonard Medal (1968) of the Meteoritical Society International, the Kepler Anniversary Medal (1972) of the American Association for the Advancement of Science, and the Gold Medal of the Royal Astronomical Society (1975). **John McFarland**

optics. The first treatise on optics in English, WILLIAM MOLYNEUX's *Dioptrica Nova* (1692), discussed the relations between sight and touch, later taken up by GEORGE BERKELEY in his *Essay towards a New Theory of Vision* (1709). Considerable work in optics was done by Irish scientists during the nineteenth century. WILLIAM ROWAN HAMILTON predicted conical refraction and made optics a science based on general principles. William MacCullagh (1809–1847) developed a model of the 'ether' (the postulated universal substance thought necessary for the transmission of light but not detectable by experiment); GEORGE F. FITZGERALD explained this by proposing that objects shrink along their direction of motion. JOHN TYNDALL studied the diffusion of light by particles and explained that the sky is blue because sunlight is scattered by the atmosphere; his demonstration of the conduction of light through a curved stream of water led to the development of fibre optics. THOMAS GRUBB and his son HOWARD GRUBB were renowned Dublin manufacturers of TELESCOPES; Thomas Grubb helped WILLIAM PARSONS, third Earl of Rosse, to build the largest telescope in the world at Birr, Co. Offaly, which Parsons used to discover the spiral shape of some galaxies. Research in optics today concentrates on opto-electronics, particularly the use of lasers in communications. **William Reville**

Opus Dei, an organisation describing itself as 'a personal prelature of the Catholic Church', founded by Father José María Escrivá in Spain in 1928 and introduced to Ireland in 1947. Members seek deepened spirituality through their daily lives and work. Though explicitly forswearing any form of secrecy, Opus Dei has frequently been accused of organising secret networks of professional people in support of conservative Catholic causes. **Fergal Tobin**

O'Rahilly, Michael Joseph, otherwise 'The O'Rahilly' (1875–1916), republican. Born in Ballylongford, Co. Kerry; he emigrated to the United States in 1898. Returning to Ireland in 1909, he became a member of the Central Executive of the GAELIC LEAGUE and a founder-member of the IRISH VOLUNTEERS. He was not a member of the IRB and so was excluded from the counsels of those planning the 1916 RISING. He agreed with EOIN MACNEILL's view that the order for the rising should be stopped, and he delivered the countermanding instructions to Limerick; but when, on returning to Dublin, he realised that it had gone ahead he joined the GPO garrison and fought throughout the week. He died bravely, leading a break-out from the beleaguered garrison on Friday 28 April. YEATS's ballad 'The O'Rahilly' (1937) immortalised his name. **Fergal Tobin**

O'Rahilly, T. F. [Thomas Francis] (1883–1953), Celtic scholar and author. Born in Listowel, Co. Kerry; educated at the School of Irish Learning, Dublin, and Royal University of Ireland. He was professor of Irish at TCD, research professor of Gaelic languages at UCC and UCD, and first director of the School of Celtic Studies at the DUBLIN INSTITUTE FOR ADVANCED STUDIES. While his theory that varieties of P-Celtic preceded Q-Celtic dialects in Ireland is not widely accepted, he is still considered a major contributor to IRISH-LANGUAGE scholarship and Irish studies. His keen interest in history is exemplified by his seminal work *Early Irish History and Mythology* (1946); other notable publications are *Dánta Grádha: An Anthology of Irish Love Poetry (A.D. 1350–1750)* (1926), *Irish Dialects, Past and Present* (1932), and *The Two Patricks: A Lecture on the History of Christianity* (1942). He also founded and edited the journal *Gadelica*, 1913. **Myra Dowling**

Ó Raifeartaigh, Lochlainn S. (1933–2000), theoretical physicist. Born in Dublin; graduated in physics and mathematical science from UCD before being awarded a doctorate in theoretical physics by the University of Zürich, 1960, under the supervision of WALTER HEITLER. He was a member of the Institute of Advanced Studies at Princeton University, New Jersey, 1967–8, and senior professor at the DUBLIN INSTITUTE FOR ADVANCED STUDIES from 1968. Among theoretical physicists of his epoch in Ireland he enjoyed the greatest international recognition; in 2000 he was awarded the prestigious Wigner Medal. His most prominent contributions are the celebrated no-go theorem (1965), concerning the mass spectrum of fundamental particles, and a mechanism for the spontaneous breaking of supersymmetry (1975). He made many other important contributions to the theory of elementary particle physics, in the areas of gauge field theories and solitons, supersymmetry, and Kac-Moody and W algebras. He published 147 scientific works, including one monograph. **Tigran Tchrakian**

oral and aural tradition. With regard to TRADITIONAL MUSIC, tradition is popularly equated with a body of knowledge or set of practices sanctioned by time; but most students apply the test of oral transmission. Purely oral transmission is now unusual: many singers and musicians find material in books, on records, and on radio or television. This is not a disqualification, for, once learnt, the piece is practised and performed without reference to the source from which it was heard. This allows fluidity in the manner of performance while preserving continuity of style, form, and instrumentation. Though embracing modern elements, such music remains rooted in the past. **John Moulden**

Orange Order. In September 1795, during the protracted sectarian warfare in south-central Ulster, the PEEP O' DAY BOYS and their Protestant allies routed DEFENDERS at the Diamond in Armagh. The victorious loyalists marched into Loughgall, and there, in the house of James Sloan, the Loyal Orange Institution was founded. This was a defensive association of lodges (modelled on those of the Masonic Order) pledged to defend 'the King and his heirs so long as he or they support the PROTESTANT ASCENDANCY.' At first the order was a parallel organisation to the Defenders—it was oath-bound, used passwords and signs, and was confined to one sect—and its membership comprised mainly weaver-farmers. The immediate outcome was an intensification of the sectarian conflict and the expulsion of some 7,000 Catholics from Co. Armagh. Orangemen enlisted in the YEOMANRY in great numbers, and in the following years the officers, members of the gentry, joined the order. WHIG governments in the 1830s were alarmed by affrays arising from Orange demonstrations and ordered an inquiry. A 4,500-page report by a select committee in 1835 was damning, and the outcome was that the Grand Orange Lodge of Ireland dissolved itself in 1836. Largely deserted by the upper classes though it was, the organisation continued to flourish in Ulster. In 1870 William Johnston of Ballykilbeg succeeded in getting the Party Processions Act (1832) repealed. Members of the order played a leading role in the formation of the Irish Unionist Party in 1886 and of the ULSTER UNIONIST COUNCIL in 1905.

Today the Orange Order is the largest Protestant organisation in Northern Ireland, with about 100,000 active members (including women's and junior branches), and its annual Twelfth of July demonstrations take place at around twenty venues, the climax of a long 'MARCHING SEASON'. Since the beginning of the DRUMCREE confrontation in 1995 membership of the order has grown, as Orange MARCHES have become increasingly contentious (see pp. 651, 692, 1097). **Jonathan Bardon**

Orange Order outside Ireland. Though strongest in Ulster, the Orange Order spread from the early nineteenth century to all parts of the BRITISH EMPIRE. Soldiers who served in Ireland in 1798 were among the first to take Orangeism beyond Ireland; but it was the emigrant flow from the north that replenished and enhanced the order. As well as relying on Irish emigrants, Orangeism also attracted indigenous support, especially in England. The first English lodge emerged in the late 1790s in Manchester and the first Scottish one in Maybole, Wigtownshire. By 1807 a centralised English Orange institution had come into being. In the 1830s Lancashire had seventy-seven lodges and Yorkshire thirty-six, while Scotland had thirty-nine. These early lodges, like their counterparts in Ireland, had an overwhelmingly working-class membership.

Orangeism in Britain and Ireland was impeded in the 1820s by legislation against secret oaths and against MARCHES. It was condemned by a Select Committee report in 1835 and was voluntarily liquidated; but this meant that the movement passed back from London to its working-class roots, where it continued to prosper, especially in northern England and in Scotland. By the 1840s the order was noted for its social conservatism and fierce anti-Catholicism. These facts, and FAMINE IMMIGRATION, accounted for its significant growth in the middle of the century. A further boost was provided in the 1860s and 70s by FENIANISM and Irish NATIONALISM, while its political message of empire LOYALISM and UNIONISM gave Orangeism a role in popular conservative politics in the three decades before 1914. Orange parades grew significantly after 1850: in 1876 between 60,000 and 80,000 people turned out in Liverpool to cheer 7,000–8,000 marchers; in 1878 some 90,000 Scottish Orangemen publicly celebrated the Twelfth of July, with 14,000–15,000 in Glasgow alone. Regions such as Cumberland and the north-east also became more significant at this time.

These were also years of growth in the Canadian Orange Order. Military lodges were appearing in the Maritime Provinces by the early 1800s, and by the 1820s there were two core regions of Orangeism in Canada: New Brunswick and Ontario. Ontario in particular prospered thereafter, as Irish Protestants were the largest group of arrivals in these pre-famine decades. In 1829 Ogle R. Gowan, whose father, a Co. Wexford landlord, had been a founder-member of the Irish Grand Lodge, emigrated to Canada and almost immediately oversaw the formation of the Grand Lodge of British North America. He was unscrupulous in using the order to further his career in local and state politics. By 1870 there were 930 lodges in Ontario alone, but the lodge tradition had spread across the Prairie states and even to Vancouver. Orange sources claim that Canada's movement had a million members at one time, though historians estimate that approximately 70,000, spread between 1,450 lodges, is a more accurate picture. In Canada, as in Africa, indigenous peoples saw the utility of joining a movement that gave access to favours: lodge no. 99, for example, was based in the Mohawk reservation of Tyendinaga and has had only two white members since its inception in 1848.

Antipodean Orangeism was later in arriving and less significant when it did. The first Australian lodge was opened in Sydney in 1845, and the city soon had eight. The order eventually reached all six Australian colonies. New Zealand's first lodge proceedings were in 1842, following the emigration of James Carlton of Co. Wicklow, a former district master. A Grand Lodge meeting in 1867 shows that the order must have achieved significant strength in New Zealand by that time. The marching tradition was adhered to in Australia and New Zealand, but less so than in other places. Orange demonstrations in Victoria in the 1890s drew a negative reaction from Catholics. Charges of municipal corruption, including favouritism in the allocation of jobs, were levelled at Australian Orangemen, as with their Canadian and Irish counterparts.

Orange Order. Orange Order Series: Portadown, 1991, *one of a series of photographs by the artist Paul Seawright exploring aspects of Protestant culture, and seeking out the Order's ideology and symbols, here evident in the uniform of an Orange band. [Courtesy of the artist and Kerlin Gallery, Dublin]*

In the twentieth century the Orange Order withered in most places outside Ulster, except for Scotland; and even there it was outmanoeuvred by more extreme Protestant organisations, such as John Cormack's Protestant Action in Edinburgh, or else saw its members slip away with declining Irish immigration and generally lower levels of religiosity. The ACT OF UNION (1801) also reduced the political relevance of the movement, especially in Britain. Today Orangemen continue to parade in Canada, Australia, New Zealand, and Britain, but their membership is much reduced from its high point in the nineteenth century. **Donald MacRaild**

Orange regalia. From its inception in 1795, members of the ORANGE ORDER have worn collars and sashes, both at their private meetings and at public demonstrations (see pp. 316, 692). These regalia bear emblems that evoke the stories dramatised during the rituals of three distinct but related Orange societies: the Orange, Royal Arch Purple, and Royal Black Institutions.

Of the three organisations through which an Orangeman may successively pass, the Orange Order has the simplest regalia. Its emblems, worn on a collar or sash (usually orange-coloured), depict the Crown, the Bible, and WILLIAM III. They evoke the order's central activity, which is to celebrate the memory of William III as a defender of a Bible-based, evangelical Christianity.

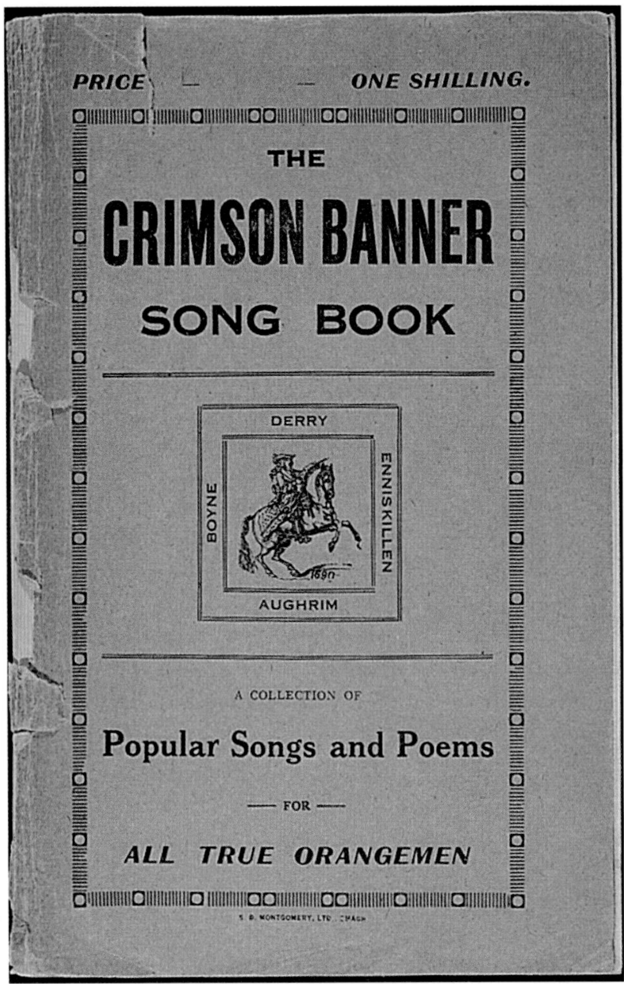

Orange song. *The ballad form is shared by loyalist and nationalist singers, often using the same tunes. Orange heroes and traditions are celebrated in* The Crimson Banner Song Book. *[Board of Trinity College, Dublin]*

The Royal Arch Purple Chapter is open only to Orangemen, and its emblems are mainly found on Orange Order regalia. The Royal Arch Purple has an exuberant initiation ritual dramatising the journey of Moses through the wilderness, and its emblems—among them the arch, ladder, and star—refer obliquely to this ritual.

The Royal Black Institution is open only to Royal Arch Purplemen. It has eleven degrees of membership, each with an initiation ceremony telling a Bible story; its emblems, worn on black collars and sashes, evoke these stories. The second degree, called 'Royal Scarlet', dramatises the story of Joshua and the Battle of Jericho; its emblems, therefore, show trumpets and the Ark of the Covenant. The fifth, 'Royal White' degree tells of David's battle with Goliath; its emblems include five stones and a sling. The highest degree is the 'Red Cross', whose emblem speaks of the death and resurrection of Christ. **Anthony Buckley**

Orange song, often used loosely to describe loyalist songs. There are relatively few Orange songs. The oldest, 'Lisnagade', concerns a battle over a disputed march route—a pervasive theme. Others remember 1690, express fear that the massacres of 1641 may recur, mirror Orange ritual, ridicule Catholic belief and practice, and praise Orange heroes. Many themes and attitudes show continuity with English constitutional and anti-Catholic songs of the sixteenth and seventeenth centuries. The main body is printed in semi-official songbooks; the latest, *The Orange Lark* and *Lilliburlero*, have the imprimatur of the Ulster Society, but there are many songs locally made for local use and seldom published.

A feature of these songs is the number of tunes shared with republican songs or unexceptionable traditional songs. The borrowing has been two-way; and artistically (in poetic and musical form and in singing style) Orange songs and their singers stand squarely within the Irish song and singing traditions, though the songs' content places them at a political extreme. Singing at lodge events is now unusual, but formerly this practice included other traditional songs as well as Orange ones. Recent songs, more loyalist than Orange, tend to use the tunes of COUNTRY-AND-WESTERN songs. **John Moulden**

Ó Rathaille, Aogán (c. 1670–1729), JACOBITE poet. Born, according to tradition, at Scrahanaveele in the SLIABH LUACHRA district of Co. Kerry. His life and poetry reflect the political fortunes of the local landholding families, especially the MacCarthys. An early poem (c. 1699–1700) laments the dispossession of Captain Eoghan Mac Carthaigh when the estate of the Jacobite Sir Nicholas Browne, Viscount Kenmare, on which Mac Carthaigh held lands on lease, was confiscated after the BATTLE OF THE BOYNE. The poem 'Créachta Crích Fódla' also reflects the upheaval and displacement associated with this period; it was followed by other poems of cultural breakdown and geographical dislocation in which the personal and political are juxtaposed to great dramatic effect.

While successfully employing elegiac, panegyric and satirical forms, Ó Rathaille is best known for his development of the political AISLING, his most celebrated examples being 'Mac an Cheannaí' and the exquisite 'Gile na Gile', which scholars have related to the period 1708–9, when hopes of a Jacobite rebellion ran high. His poem to Sir Valentine Browne (who was reinstated on the Kenmare estates on the death of his father, Sir Nicholas Browne, in Ghent in 1720) expresses deeply felt anger that he was ever obliged to seek favours from a non-native family who would ultimately prove to be a source of bitter disappointment. The event that spurred the writing of this poem was probably Browne's refusal to re-establish the poet on the traditional Ó Rathaille leasehold. Ó Rathaille made a copy of KEATING's FORAS FEASA AR ÉIRINN in Drumcolliher, Co. Limerick, in 1722, but by 1726 he was back again on the Kenmare estate, now living in greatly reduced circumstances. In the death of Raghnall Mac Carthaigh, 1729, Ó Rathaille saw the end of an era, and themes of death and desolation are pursued further in his final poem, 'Cabhair ní ghairfead', in which he ponders his own fate in the light of the downfall of the native lords, 'na flatha fá raibh mo shean roimh éag do Chríost' (in MICHAEL HARTNETT's translation, 'the lords my elders served before the death of Christ') (see p. 270). **Máirín Nic Eoin**

oratorio, a large-scale vocal and instrumental work based on sacred or Biblical material. The establishment of oratorio performances in Dublin originated in eighteenth-century charity performances, the proceeds of which financed the establishment of eight Dublin hospitals in the mid-1700s. HANDEL's *Messiah* was the culmination of two series of concerts that began on 13 December 1741. It was given on 13 April 1742 in the Musick Hall, Fishamble Street, and marked the first of many successes (see p. 759). The reasons for this were twofold: the erection of the Musick Hall, Fishamble Street, allowed for the performance of large sacred works that were unsuited to public theatres; and contemporary Dublin concert audiences were from a prosperous society. Oratorio performances differed from those of modern times in two ways: they were performed without performance cuts, and usually included a full concerto between the oratorio parts. Furthermore, the oratorio chorus of the period was much smaller (twelve singers) than its later counterpart. The 1759–60 concert series saw thirty-three performances of large-scale choral works, including oratorio. The large number of performances was not unusual, as they were less extensively prepared than in more recent times. The founding of various choral societies from the nineteenth century, including the University of Dublin Choral Society (established 1837), OUR LADY'S CHORAL SOCIETY (see p. 471), Tallaght Choral Society, the CULWICK CHORAL SOCIETY, and Dún Laoghaire Choral Society, ensured the regular performance of Handel's oratorios as well as those of Bach and later composers. In more recent times the music departments of most universities sponsor regular performances of oratorios. The term 'oratorio' is now generally applied to any large-scale vocal and instrumental work based on religious, moral or Biblical themes. Murray Wylie's Irish premiere of the Jerusalem Passion, given in Wesley College, Dublin, in 1997, is one such example. *Messiah XXI* (1999) by Frank McNamara is a controversial modern reworking of Handel's masterpiece, featuring the addition of contemporary procedures derived from rock and gospel sources. At this time also CHRIST CHURCH BAROQUE and the Cathedral Choir gave the first authentic period performance of *Messiah* in recent times. **Paul J. Kerr**

orchestral music. The requirements of ensemble music for civic ceremonies and theatre in the sixteenth, seventeenth, and eighteenth centuries, the establishment of music societies and amateur bands in the eighteenth and nineteenth centuries, and the development of broadcasting in the twentieth century all contributed to the development of Irish orchestras. The earliest surviving records include those of the Dublin City Musicians (1561). Theatre orchestras flourished, and from 1736 benefit concerts for charitable purposes were held in various venues. Important eighteenth-century societies include the Dublin Academy of Music, founded in 1727 'for the cultivation of music by the great masters,' and the amateur Anacreontic Society, founded in 1740 for the promotion of instrumental music programmes. Dublin's fashionable gardens, especially the ROTUNDA Gardens from 1749, were important venues for music performance.

Musical societies played an important role during the nineteenth century. Francis Robinson founded the SONS OF HANDEL in 1810; his son Joseph founded the Antient Concerts Society (1834–63) and the Dublin Musical Society (1876–94). Other societies included the Amateur Musical Society (founded 1852), the Philharmonic Society (1826–66), the New Philharmonic Society (1872), MICHELE ESPOSITO'S DUBLIN ORCHESTRAL SOCIETY (1899–1914), and the Dublin Philharmonic Society (founded 1927). In Belfast, the Classical Harmonists' Society (1851) and Belfast Musical Society (1872) joined forces in 1874 to become the Belfast Philharmonic Society.

Indoor promenade concerts began at the Round Room in the Rotunda in July 1840. Theatre orchestras continued to flourish in the principal towns, and military bands (from 1806), temperance society bands (from 1838), and trade union bands contributed to Irish musical life. The report of the Irish Artisans' Exhibition (1887) mentions thirty amateur bands in Dublin.

Orchestral music in Ireland before the twentieth century was essentially organised for individual events, with some notable exceptions, such as the Anacreontic Society in Belfast from 1814 to 1866. It was only with the establishment of the BBC Northern Ireland Orchestra in 1924 that permanent professional orchestras became part of Irish musical life. In 1981 the orchestra was amalgamated with the ULSTER ORCHESTRA, previously known as the City of Belfast Orchestra, in an attempt to provide for a larger repertoire, including the commissioning of works from Irish composers.

In the Republic the establishment of a permanent professional orchestral group dates from 1926, with the formation of a Radio Éireann station chamber ensemble. From these beginnings the Radio Éireann Symphony Orchestra developed in 1948. It became the RTÉ Symphony Orchestra in 1961; in 1990 it expanded further to become the NATIONAL SYMPHONY ORCHESTRA of Ireland, based in the NATIONAL CONCERT HALL in Dublin (see p. 911). The Radio Éireann Light Orchestra was also established in 1948. It is known now as the RTÉ CONCERT ORCHESTRA. Its primary function was to provide RTÉ with a studio-based group of just twenty-two players. Since 1978, however, with the appointment of PROINNSÍAS Ó DUINN as principal conductor, the orchestra has developed into a diverse group, performing concerts, undertaking tours, working with OPERA IRELAND, and producing commercial recordings.

In addition to the national radio station orchestras, the New Irish Chamber Orchestra was founded in 1970 by André Prieur. In 1994, with support from the ARTS COUNCIL, the ensemble was renamed the IRISH CHAMBER ORCHESTRA and became resident at the University of Limerick. Important amateur orchestras have included Ferruccio Grossi's Irish Musical Arts Society (late 1940s) and Terry O'Connor's Dublin String Orchestra. The DUBLIN ORCHESTRAL PLAYERS (founded 1939) and DUBLIN BAROQUE

O'Reilly, Anthony. *Anthony O'Reilly, chairman and chief executive officer of Independent Newspapers and Waterford Wedgwood. Capped for Ireland and the British Lions in international rugby, he was an accomplished sportsman before entering business. [Photocall Ireland]*

PLAYERS (founded 1966) enjoy continued success. The NATIONAL YOUTH ORCHESTRA OF IRELAND was founded in 1970, and regional and youth orchestras have flourished in the late twentieth century. **John Page and Ite O'Donovan.**

Order of St Patrick. The Most Illustrious Order of St Patrick was founded by George III in 1783 as a counterpart of the (English) Order of the Garter and the (Scottish) Order of the Thistle. Its membership was originally limited to fifteen knights, apart from the sovereign, but was increased to twenty-two in 1833. It was never awarded outside members of the peerage. The LORD LIEUTENANT of the day was always *ex officio* grand master of the order, though not a member. The grand master's insignia, the so-called 'Irish CROWN JEWELS', were stolen from DUBLIN CASTLE in 1907 and never recovered. After the foundation of the Irish Free State in 1922 only four new appointments to the order were made; three of these were members of the British royal family. In 1927 the Attorney-General determined that, as a purely Irish order, all matters relating to it were solely the concern of the Government of Ireland; and while British governments did not agree with this ruling, moves to revive the order came to nothing. The last surviving knight, the Duke of Gloucester, died in 1974. **Micheál Ó Comáin**

Order of St Patrick: regalia. The regalia of the 'Most Illustrious Order of St Patrick' (1783–1934) consisted of a 'St Patrick's blue' (sky-blue) mantle of Irish silk, a sky-blue sash, a collar, star, and badge. The eight-pointed star, worn on the left breast, was in cut or faceted silver with an enamel centrepiece, incorporating 'St Patrick's cross', shamrock, three imperial crowns, the order's motto, *Quis separabit?* (Who will separate [them]?), and the foundation date, MDCCLXXXIII. The collar, in gold and enamel, alternated harps and roses, linked by knots. The collar badge, also in enamel and gold, was similar to the central medallion of the star. [see CROWN JEWELS, IRISH.] **Alex Ward**

Ordnance Survey, the official department, part military and part civilian, established in 1791 to produce a topographical map of Britain at a scale of 1 inch to the statute mile (1:63,360) within the framework of a scientific triangulation. In 1824 the Ordnance Survey was given the very different task of mapping the boundaries and calculating the acreage of every townland in Ireland as an aid to standardising local taxation. As published by counties at 6 inches to the statute mile (1:10,560) in 1833–46, the new map provided a comprehensive portrait of the Irish landscape, useful not just for official valuation but also in planning roads, RAILWAYS and other engineering works and as an aid to the management of landed property. Its success in Ireland led to the mapping of Britain at a similar scale, and during the 1850s the government gradually developed a policy of mapping both countries at as many different scales as the public would find useful, a programme completed with a new field-by-field survey of Ireland at 1:2,500 in 1887–1914. All these maps needed periodic revision, and the Ordnance Survey was also faced with a growing demand for thematic maps of various kinds. Its work was continued after 1922 by two new CARTOGRAPHIC departments, based in Dublin and Belfast, both of which retained the name Ordnance Survey. [see BOARD OF WORKS.] **J. H. Andrews**

Ó Reachtabraig, Antaine: see RAIFTEAR.

O'Reilly, Sir Anthony (Tony) (1936–), businessman and rugby player. Born in Dublin; educated at UCD (civil law) and the University of Bradford (agricultural marketing). His international rugby career began when he was nineteen. He played for fifteen years, during which time he scored a record eighteen tries for the British Lions and was capped for Ireland twenty-nine times. He worked for the H. J. Heinz Company, 1973–2000, becoming the first non-family chairman in 1987. Much of his huge personal wealth derives from his media interests, most notably as chairman and chief executive of the INDEPENDENT NEWS AND MEDIA GROUP. He is one of the founders of the Ireland Fund, a charitable organisation that promotes peace and cultural development in Ireland, North and South, and it was for his work with this organisation that he was awarded a knighthood in 2001. **Myra Dowling**

O'Reilly, J. J. (1905–1983), teacher and composer. Born in Dublin, he taught piano at the Municipal College of Music in Dublin in the 1950s and also worked as a composer. Among his works is 'Remembrance: Nocturne for Milan Horvat' (Horvat was principal conductor of the Radio Éireann Symphony Orchestra, 1953–8) and the tone poem, 'Oluf' (1954), also premiered by Horvat. **Geraldine Guiden**

O'Reilly, John Boyle (1844–1890), poet and Fenian. Born in Dowth, Co. Meath. He joined the British army in order to recruit soldiers to FENIANISM. Arrested in 1866, he escaped from Dartmoor. Rearrested, he was imprisoned in Australia from where he also escaped, in 1869. A noted poet and a public figure in Boston, where he edited and jointly owned the *Pilot*, in later life he became completely disillusioned with Fenianism, saying that it was as great a humbug as Mormonism. [see CLANN NA GAEL.] **Oliver P. Rafferty**

O'Reilly, John Joe (1918–1952), Gaelic footballer. Born in Cornafean, Co. Cavan, a member of a famous football family. He was an all-round athlete of great ability, but football was always his priority. An army officer, he was appointed Cavan captain in succession to his brother, Tom, in 1946. He had already played in three all-Ireland finals but had lost each time. However, in the 1947 final, played at the Polo Grounds, New York, he led Cavan to success. The team defended its title in 1948 and was beaten in the 1949 final by Mayo. O'Reilly played in six finals before his death at the age of thirty-four. **Donal Keenan**

organic agriculture, a system of LAND use and FOOD production that avoids the use of synthetic chemicals, is based on recycling to maintain fertility, and is indefinitely sustainable without causing environmental damage.

Organic agriculture was promoted first in Ireland in the mid-1970s, with a handful of smallholders producing mainly vegetables. The Irish Organic Growers' Association was formed in 1982, and the first steps in certification soon followed. The adoption of the Rural Environmental Protection Scheme in 1994 was the first element of financial support for organic production and has resulted in a large increase in the number of organic livestock-producers while having almost no effect on vegetable production. There has been a corresponding development in markets and processors. In 2000 registered organic holdings accounted for approximately 32,000 ha (79,000 acres); this represents little more than 0.5 per cent of total land farmed. It is estimated that more than 70 per cent of organic food sold in Ireland is imported.

The demand for organic produce has increased steadily, despite the fact that the organic industry has done little by way of promotion. There has been a similar increase in interest in organic

Ordnance Survey. Surveyors at Work, *engraving by a member of the Brocas family. Two surveyors hold a short chain while another uses a theodolite on a tripod, with men constructing a building nearby. [Council of Trustees of the National Library of Ireland; 2177 (TX) 1]*

gardening, which has been met by the provision of courses for amateur gardeners and the increased availability of 'organic' garden requisites. **Rod Alston**

Organisation of National Ex-Servicemen and Women (ONE), a voluntary organisation formed to advance the welfare of ex-service personnel by providing accommodation and other assistance to those in need, to foster public interest in the DEFENCE FORCES and comradeship between serving and retired personnel, and to liaise with ex-service organisations in the EUROPEAN UNION. Membership is open to former Permanent and Reserve Defence Force personnel, as well as Coast Watching, Construction Corps, Irish Red Cross, and Civil Defence. **E. D. Doyle**

organ music. Most of Ireland's leading organists have been associated with the cathedrals—in particular CHRIST CHURCH, ST PATRICK'S and the Pro-Cathedral in Dublin. Such musicians have included Daniel (died 1727), Ralph (c. 1695–1747) and Thomas (1691–1766) ROSEINGRAVE, PHILIP COGAN (1748–1833), ROBERT PRESCOTT STEWART (1825–94), Charles Herbert Kitson (1874–1944), GEORGE HEWSON (1881–1972), William Sidney Greig (1910–1983), GERALD GILLEN, PETER SWEENEY, JOHN DEXTER, and MARK DULEY (1960–).

Among Irish composers, CHARLES VILLIERS STANFORD (1852–1924), CHARLES WOOD (1866–1926), JAMES WILSON, GERARD VICTORY, Bernard Geary (1934–), DAVID BYERS (1947–), ERIC SWEENEY, JOHN BUCKLEY (1951–), GERALD BARRY, RAYMOND DEANE, EIBHLIS FARRELL, Martin O'Leary (1963–), and Donnacha Dennehy (1970–) have all written works for organ. Two large-scale concertos for organ and orchestra, by John Buckley and IAN WILSON, have also been premiered by Peter Sweeney at the NATIONAL CONCERT HALL in Dublin, which houses a four-manual instrument built and installed by Kenneth Jones in 1991.

Annual organ recital series, such as those held at St Michael's Church, Dún Laoghaire, St Patrick's Cathedral and Christ Church Cathedral, Dublin, Galway Cathedral, the Ulster Hall, Belfast, and the Church of the Assumption, Tullamore, have also brought leading world organists, as well as much of the organ's vast repertoire, to large audiences. Established in 1974 by Gerard Gillen, the Dún Laoghaire series in particular has done much to promote organ music in Ireland, having featured so far more than 150 players from nineteen countries. In addition to the various recital series, the DUBLIN INTERNATIONAL ORGAN AND CHORAL FESTIVAL, of which there have been eleven since 1980, has, under the direction of its founder-chairman, Gerald Gillen, further provided a forum for the appreciation of the organ and its music. The core of the festival is the prestigious organ-playing competition, which has been won by David Adams of Ireland, 1986, Andreas Liebig of Germany, 1988, Kevin Bowyer of Britain, 1990, Bengt Tribukait of Sweden, 1992, Neil Cockburn of Britain, 1996, Shane Douglas O'Neill of the United States, 1999, and Balint Karosi of Hungary, 2002. **Paul Collins**

Ó Riada, Seán (1931–1971), musician. Born in Adare, Co. Limerick, son of a Garda sergeant; educated at UCC. In 1953 he was appointed assistant director of music in Radio Éireann. In 1955 he resigned, but after a short period in Paris he returned to Dublin, where he began his most prolific period, making many arrangements for the Radio Éireann Singers and Light Orchestra, original compositions for the Symphony Orchestra and Chamber Orchestra, and writing for solo voice and for piano. During this time he was also director of music at the ABBEY THEATRE, Dublin. In 1959 he created the score for the film MISE EIRE. He launched CEOLTÓIRÍ CHUALANN, the first traditional Irish group. The radio series 'Our Musical Heritage' set out the parameters of the music tradition. In 1962 he moved to Co. Kerry and from there in 1963 to Coolea, Co. Cork, having been appointed assistant lecturer of music in UCC. While there he wrote his three Masses. He died in Coolea on 3 October 1971 and is buried in St Gobnait's Cemetery.

In addition to his orchestral works he made more than 700 arrangements of songs and dance music for traditional groups. He

Ó Ríordáin. *Seán Ó Ríordáin, among the most important Irish-language poets of the twentieth century. Through his writings and position as lecturer in Irish in UCC he inspired the emergence of a younger generation of Irish-language poets.* [Irish Times]

presented various lecture series, the most important being a radio series produced in the early 1960s entitled 'Our Musical Heritage' and a short series of lectures on Irish music delivered in UCC some weeks before he died; he also wrote a play, *Spailpín a Rún*, articles, essays, and some songs. There is also a body of original Irish melodies composed with the express purpose of letting them drift into the mainstream of Irish songs and melodies, the best known of these being 'Mná na hÉireann' (text by MÁIRTÍN Ó DIRÉAIN). He wrote two Masses: 'Cúil Aodha' (1965) and 'Glenstal' (1968) (see p. 679). [see SAOIRSE?] **Peadar Ó Riada**

Ó Riada Masses. Arriving in Coolea, Co. Cork, in 1963, SEÁN Ó RIADA spent the latter half of his career working on, among other things, the spiritual side of life. The greatest and most innovative work during this period was three Masses, composed at a time when the SECOND VATICAN COUNCIL was finishing its deliberations and the Catholic Church's ceremonies were reverting to the vernacular. Experimenting with new forms and settings for congregational singing in the Mass, Ó Riada founded a male choir, and placed it in the middle of the congregation.

Parts of his first Mass are sung daily all over the world today, in particular 'Ag Críost an Síol' ('Christ the Seed'). The second Mass was commissioned by the Benedictine order in Glenstal Abbey, Co. Limerick. This is a more challenging work to perform and had more room for expression, in that it was composed with daily use by the community in mind, and answers a different need from that of the first Mass. The third Mass was composed in 1969, towards the end of Ó Riada's life (he died in 1971). A Requiem, it was a Government commission, to be sung at state funerals; in particular, the future funeral of the then President, ÉAMON DE VALERA, was in mind, though de Valera served out his second term and indeed outlived Ó Riada. The Requiem has never been publicly performed. **Peadar Ó Riada**

Ó Ríordáin, Seán (1916–1977), one of the most important IRISH-LANGUAGE poets in the twentieth century. Born in Ballyvourney, Co. Cork; educated locally and in Cork, where the family moved on the death of his father in 1932. Though Irish was spoken in Ballyvourney when Ó Ríordáin was growing up, English was the language of the home, as his mother knew no Irish. This break with the past later came to symbolise a fundamental aspect of his sense of alienation from his 'true self', one of the most important themes in his poetry.

On leaving school he worked as a clerk with Cork City Council. Diagnosed with TUBERCULOSIS in 1938, he spent long periods in hospital over the rest of his life, and his illness had a central influence on his poetry. In accordance with the medical practice of the time, a room was constructed for him at the rear of the family home, separating him from his family and the outside world. This confined space is a constant metaphor for the dark interior 'mindspace' that is the locus of most of his poetry. He began writing a diary, his 'fight against death', in 1940 and continued with it until five days before he died. His mother's death in 1945, commemorated in his superb innovatory poem 'Adhlacadh mo Mháthar', affected him deeply and left him living alone in the family home. His first collection, *Eireaball Spideoige* (1952), at once grounded in Irish tradition and thoroughly modernist in sensibility and tone, revolutionised poetry in Irish. The poems, both individually and as an integrated aesthetic statement, seek to answer fundamental questions about the nature of human existence and the place of the individual in a universe without meaning. In the Ireland of the MOTHER AND CHILD SCHEME this was a courageous *non serviam*, all the more so for being written in Irish. The book was haughtily dismissed by MÁIRE MHAC AN TSAOI in two reviews as being merely 'the common scruples of conscience of an ordinary Catholic' and, moreover, as being narrated in a discourse that was non-Gaelic. These reviews upset Ó Ríordáin deeply, and he did not publish his second collection, *Brosna*, until 1964. He had spent much time during the intervening period in the Dingle Peninsula, and *Brosna* is dedicated to the people of Dunquin, where, in his celebrated poem 'Fill Arís', he claims one can find 'd'intinn féin is do chló ceart' ('your own mind and true self').

In 1965 he retired from his employment with Cork City Council on health grounds, and in 1969, at the instigation of SEÁN Ó TUAMA, he was appointed a part-time lecturer in Irish at UCC, where he seminally influenced the INNTI generation of poets. Other collections are *Línte Liombó* (1971) and the posthumous *Tar Éis Mo Bháis* (1978). From 1968 onwards he also wrote a regular and often controversial column for the IRISH TIMES. His unpublished diaries, now in the UCD library, in which most of his poetry is interspersed, reveal an original, creative, insightful, opinionated mind constantly searching for some measure of light in a dark world (see p. 963). **Gearóid Denvir**

Ormond Manor House (c. 1565), Carrick-on-Suir, Co. Tipperary, a seven-bay, two-storey-with-attic Elizabethan manor-house arranged around a courtyard. It was built by THOMAS ('BLACK TOM') BUTLER, tenth Earl of Ormond, who had spent his youth at the English court. The house abuts the fifteenth-century castle built by his ancestor Éamonn mac Risteaird Butler and is unique for the middle to late sixteenth century in its lack of defences, apart from pistol-loops flanking the projecting entrance porch. The long gallery on the first floor, which runs the full length of the façade, has decorative stucco, including portrait medallions of ELIZABETH I and Edward VI. A carved chimneypiece in the gallery, dated 1565, bears a Latin inscription that shows it was made for Thomas Butler, Earl of Ormond and Orrery. **Brian Lalor**

Ormsby, Frank (1947–), poet, editor and anthologist. Born in Enniskillen, Co. Fermanagh; educated at QUB. As editor of the *Honest Ulsterman*, 1969–89, he played an important role in encouraging new writing in Northern Ireland. Since 1971 he has taught English at the Royal Belfast Academical Institution. His poetry, which includes *A Store of Candles* (1977), *A Northern Spring* (1986), and *The Ghost Train* (1995), explores family relationships, marriage, and 'the values of art in times of violence.' He edited *A Rage for Order: Poetry of the Northern Ireland Troubles* (1992) and *The Collected Poems of John Hewitt* (1991). **Patricia Horton**

Ó Rócháin, Muiris (1944–), music administrator. Born in Dingle, Co. Kerry. He has written on music for such journals as DÁL GCAIS and TREOIR. An associate of BREANDÁN BREATHNACH in Dublin from 1967, he moved to Milltown Malbay, Co. Clare, in 1970, where he proposed the establishment of SCOIL SAMHRAIDH WILLIE CLANCY in 1973; he has been its charismatic director during its considerable development since. **Fintan Vallely**

Ó Rodaigh, Tadhg (1623–1706), poet. Born in Co. Leitrim. He did not have a prodigious output and only a few of his poems survive. Existing evidence in the surviving poetry of his contemporaries suggests that he was well respected for his learning, and for his ability to advise and teach poets. **Ciarán Mac Murchaidh**

O'Rourke, Brian (died 1591), Lord of Leitrim. He became chief of the O'Rourkes in 1566. He fought other leading O'Rourkes and the officials of the English Crown in Connacht to maintain his authority. In 1588 he gave shelter to up to a thousand survivors of the ill-fated SPANISH ARMADA, and asked in vain for their assistance against the English forces in Ireland; the succour he gave to the Armada survivors was acknowledged by a letter from Philip II of Spain but earned him the enmity of the English. In November 1589 English forces drove O'Rourke from his lordship, and he had to take refuge in Tyrconnell. In February 1591 he went to seek assistance from James VI of Scotland, but, for a sum of money, the Scottish king handed him to the English. He was tried for treason against the English Crown and was put to death after he was judged to have abused his early release by engaging in PIRACY against Spain in the Americas. **Henry A. Jefferies**

O'Rourke, Fran (1951–), philosopher. Born in Portlaoise, Co. Laois; educated at UCG and the Universities of Vienna, Cologne, Munich, and Leuven. A senior lecturer in UCD, O'Rourke has a

Ormond Manor House. *Ormond Manor House, Carrick-on-Suir, Co. Tipperary, built by Thomas Butler, tenth Earl of Ormond, some time after 1565, the best surviving example of an unfortified sixteenth-century manor-house in Ireland. [Dúchas, The Heritage Service]*

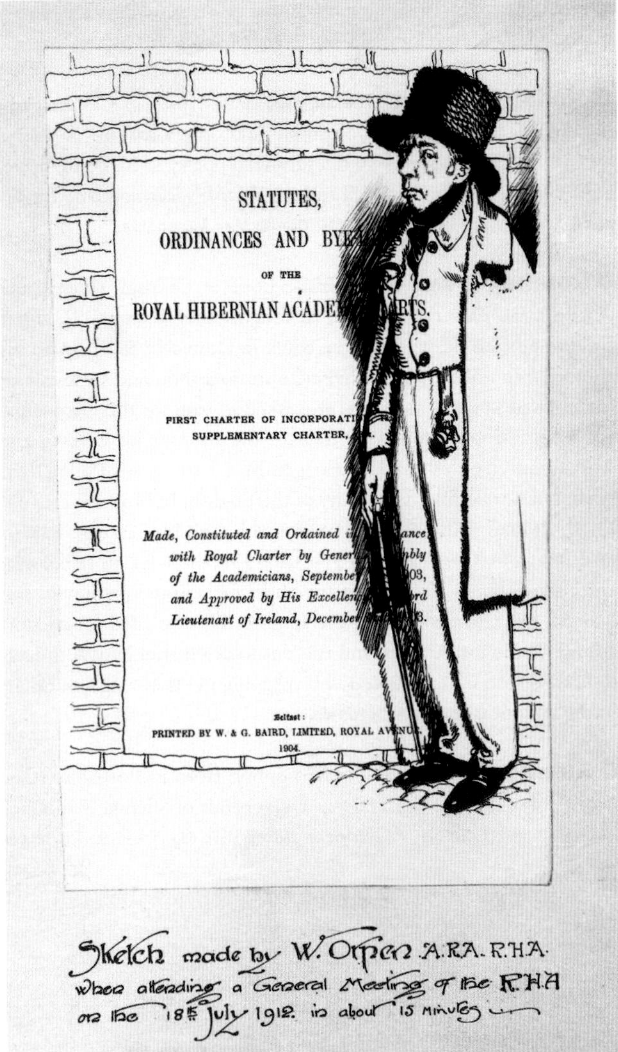

Orpen. *Self-portraits are a theme in William Orpen's work, and he frequently produced caricatures, often self-deprecating, of himself in his letters and casual sketching. [Irish Architectural Archive]*

reputation as a first-rank scholar of philosophy. He has published *Pseudo-Dionysius and the Metaphysics of Aquinas* (1992) and edited *At the Heart of the Real* (1992). **Fionola Meredith**

O'Rourke, Mícheál (1948–), pianist. He studied at the Municipal College of Music, Dublin, with ELIZABETH COSTELLO and subsequently in London, Paris, and Antwerp. He has performed in Russia (where he premiered the Britten and Lutoslawski concertos), the United States, China, and the Middle East. In recognition of 'outstanding Chopin performances' he was awarded the Chopin Medal at Zelazowa Wola. His repertoire includes all the major classical, romantic, and twentieth-century concertos. He has played at many international festivals, including the Chopin Festival (Paris) and White Night Meetings (Leningrad). His recordings include the complete works of John Field (1996). **Ite O'Donovan**

Orpen, Sir William (1878–1931), artist. Born in Stillorgan, Co. Dublin; trained at the Metropolitan School of Art and Slade School of Fine Art, London, and exhibited with the New English Art Club. Having moved to London, he returned to Ireland regularly from 1902 to 1914 to teach life classes at the Metropolitan School. He was a highly influential teacher, his students including SEÁN KEATING and PATRICK TUOHY. His book *An Onlooker in France, 1917–1919* (1921) recalls his years as a war artist. In 1924 he published *Stories of Old Ireland and Myself*. He became an associate member of the ROYAL HIBERNIAN ACADEMY in 1904 and a member in 1909, resigning in 1915. Knighted in 1918, he was elected a member of the Royal Academy, London, in 1919. One of the most successful artists of his generation, he was admired for his consummately painted society portraits; these and his many self-portraits reflect his Slade training in the French realist tradition. His subject paintings, such as *The Mirror* (1900), now in the NATIONAL GALLERY OF IRELAND, reveal his admiration for the Dutch and Spanish Old Masters. The female nude was another favourite subject. Exceptional in his *œuvre* is the enigmatic *The Holy Well* (1915) and related works; painted in an opaque style, it comments on burgeoning NATIONALISM. His commitment to an academic approach was continued in Ireland by his students, who became dominant figures in the RHA and the National College of Art. **Róisín Kennedy**

Orr, James (1770–1816), bard. Born near Ballycarry, Co. Antrim, son of a weaver. A 'weaver poet' who joined the UNITED IRISHMEN and fought in the BATTLE OF ANTRIM (1798), he composed in formal English and in the ULSTER SCOTS DIALECT. In the former his best-known poem is 'The Irishman', while that in his native dialect, 'Death and Burial of an Irish Cottier', is a realistic and affecting piece. **Terence Brown**

Orr, Philip (Phil) (1950–), rugby footballer. Born in Dublin. His first international was at Parc des Princes in Paris in 1976, and, remarkably, he won his first forty-nine caps in succession. He made his final appearance for Ireland in the World Cup quarter-final at the Concord Oval in Sydney, when Ireland lost, 33–15. He is Ireland's most capped prop forward, making fifty-eight appearances between 1976 and 1987. He toured New Zealand with the British Lions in 1977, playing in the first Test at Wellington, and was called out as a replacement on the 1980 tour of South Africa but failed to make the Test teams. **Karl Johnston**

Orthodox churches. No Orthodox parish existed in Ireland before 1969. A small number of Russian émigrés arrived shortly after the 1917 Revolution, among them Nicholas Couriss, later to be Ireland's first resident Orthodox priest. Several hundred Orthodox, including Greek and Greek Cypriots, had settled in the country by the early 1950s. In 1969 a parish was established by the Russian Church Abroad with Father Nicholas as priest, and a number of Irish people were received into the church. From 1971 to 1973 he was assisted by Father Michael Beaumont, a UCD lecturer and priest of the Moscow Patriarchate. Father Nicholas died in 1977, and with him the house chapel.

The first Greek church in Ireland, St Mary's, was consecrated in 1981 in Mary Street, Dublin. In 1986 the building was declared unsafe, and a mendicant period followed. A permanent building at Arbour Hill, Dublin, was consecrated in 1994. The Greeks have house chapels in Limavady, Co. Derry, Monasterevin, Co. Kildare, and Cork.

Oriental Orthodoxy has been represented since 1995 by the Coptic Church, with its church centre at Herbert Road, Bray. The late 1990s saw an influx of people from eastern Europe, and in 2000 the Romanian Church came into being, with its own priest. From 2001 Sunday worship has taken place in Belvedere College chapel, Dublin, by courtesy of the Jesuit order. The Russian Church (Moscow Patriarchate) now has its own church at Harold's Cross, while the Russians Abroad have monthly Liturgies at Stradbally, Co. Laois, and a new chapel in Belfast. **Godfrey O'Donnell**

Osborne, Patrick (fl. 1768), stuccodore. Of unknown background and dates, he is noted in particular for his bridging of the formal and technical gulf between the fluid Irish rococo style of decoration and the more formal Irish Adamesque variation of neo-classicism. This transition is best expressed in his most fully documented decoration, that at Castletown Cox, Co. Kilkenny, where the bill for his work survives. Through his work there, and through his only other documented work, the Cork Mayoralty House (1768), later part of the Mercy Hospital, his name is firmly linked with the work of the architect DAVIS DUCART. His hand, or at least his designs, features also at what was Baron Tracton's villa of Neptune, Dublin. **Seán O'Reilly**

Osborne, Walter (1859–1903), artist. Born in Dublin, son of the animal painter William Osborne; studied at the RHA schools, 1876–81, and at the Royal Academy, Antwerp, 1881–3. His life was dedicated to his painting; he soon came to be regarded as the most brilliant young artist of his generation, but his career was cut short by his early death. Genre subjects painted in the open air in Antwerp and in villages in Brittany and England in the 1880s are characterised by an intense scrutiny and realism. Returning to Ireland in 1892, Osborne represented Dublin street and market scenes, suburban gardens, and open landscapes. He also painted in Galway, and visited Spain. He established himself as Ireland's leading portrait painter, by which he earned his living. He was equally gifted in his tender studies of women and children and his lively animal studies. His careful and textured style of the 1880s developed into a more fluid, 'painterly' style in the 90s, finally evolving into natural impressionism at the turn of the century. A dedicated exhibitor of works throughout his career, Osborne showed at the RHA as well as the Royal Academy and New English Arts Club, London. His portrait *Mrs Noel Guinness and Her Daughter* won a bronze medal at the World Fair in Paris in 1900. Following his death from pneumonia in 1903, a memorial exhibition of his works was held in Dublin (see p. 697). **Julian Campbell**

O'Scanlon, Timoteo (1772–1831), naval officer and maritime historian. Born in Spain to a family of Irish origin, all his life he was closely associated with the Irish emigrant population. He spoke Spanish, English, Italian, and French, and during his chequered career he found time to complete university courses in Latin and chemistry, as well as being one of the Spanish navy's earliest and most brilliant hydrographers. He served in ships of various types under some famous admirals in the Napoleonic wars and became official inspector of the condition of warships at the naval base at Cartagene. During the Napoleonic occupation of Spain he hid and personally added to the navy's collection of charts. He denied accusations of collaboration with the French invaders, received the High Order of St Hermenegilde, and died a captain and harbour-master of Puerto Salou on Spain's north Mediterranean coast. Shortly before his death he published the first European dictionary of maritime terms, which the Spanish naval authorities retain in circulation as an immense work of accurate scholarship, still invaluable to researchers. **John de Courcy Ireland**

Oscar recipients. The 'Oscar' statuette of the American Academy of Motion Picture Arts and Sciences was designed by a Dubliner, Cedric Gibbons (1893–1960), supervising art director of some 1,500 MGM films, with direct responsibility for 150 of them; he himself won the award eleven times. Other Irish-born award-winners were GEORGE BERNARD SHAW for his own adaptation of his play *Pygmalion* (1938), Greer Garson for *Mrs Miniver* (1942), and BARRY FITZGERALD for best supporting actor in *Going My Way* (1944). Following the resurgence of Irish film-making in the 1980s, Daniel Day-Lewis and BRENDA FRICKER won Academy Awards for their performances in *My Left Foot* (1989), while the director NEIL JORDAN won the award for best original screenplay for *The Crying Game* (1992). In the technical grades, the make-up artist Michelle Burke won three Academy Awards, including one for *Quest for Fire* (1981) and *Bram Stoker's Dracula* (1992), and the production designer Josie McAvin won an award for *Out of Africa* (1985). **Kevin Rockett**

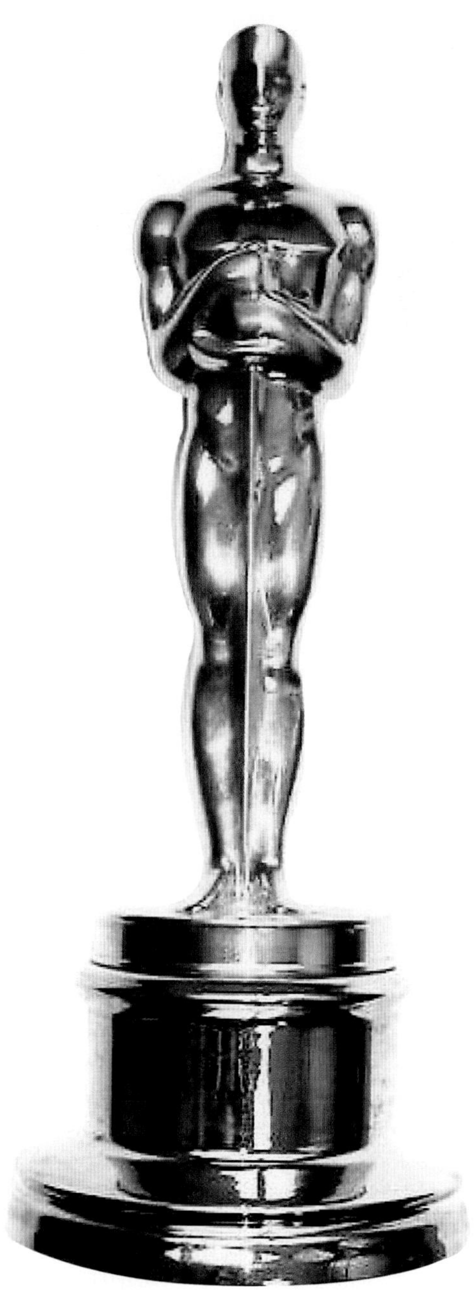

Oscar. *The Academy Award 'Oscar' statuette of a gilded male figure holding a sword, which has become a symbol of the film industry, was designed by the Dubliner Cedric Gibbons. [© AMPAS]*

Ó Searcaigh. *Cathal Ó Searcaigh, poet, noted for the sensuality of his writing and the blending of Eastern and Western influences. [John Minihan]*

Ó Sé, Seán (1936–), singer. Born in Ballylickey, Co. Cork. He sang with Blarney CÉILÍ BAND before being invited by SEÁN Ó RIADA to join CEOLTÓIRÍ CHUALANN (1961–8). Television work includes 'An Ghaoth Aneas'. He spent most of his working life as a teacher, retiring as principal of Knocknaheeny National School, Cork. **Pat Ahern**

Ó Seaghdha, Pádraig ('Conán Maol') (1855–1928), customs officer, journalist, and author. Born in Co. Kerry. He wrote historical fiction and plays and in 1898 was the first winner of OIREACHTAS prizes for short stories, published as *An Buaiceas* (1903). While retaining certain aspects of the FOLKTALE narrative tradition, these stories were written in a distinctive and refined literary style. **Aisling Ní Dhonnchadha**

Ó Searcaigh, Cathal (1956–), poet. Born in Cloghaneely, Co. Donegal; educated at the NIHE, Limerick, and NUI, Maynooth. He lived in London and Dublin, where he worked for RTÉ for a period, then returned to the small farm on which he was raised. He also travels widely, particularly in the East. His poetry draws much of its inspiration from his native place, which reverberates throughout the work, grounding the poet in a cognitive landscape that gives him a metaphor for interrogating and ultimately mapping the greater world beyond. The poems are strongly lyrical, intensely emotional, often spiritual (with an Eastern influence), and at times strongly sensual, particularly in their celebration of HOMOSEXUALITY. His principal collections are *An Bealach 'na Bhaile/Homecoming* (1993), *Out in the Open* (1997), and *Ag Tnúth leis an tSolas* (2000). **Gearóid Denvir**

O'Shea, Jack (1957–), Gaelic footballer. Born in Cahersiveen, Co. Kerry. He played his early club football for St Mary's, Cahersiveen. He won two under-21, one minor and seven senior all-Ireland medals in a long career with Kerry. There was controversy when he was not selected for the Gaelic Football Team of the Millennium, having been selected for the Team of the Century in 1984. He was a highly skilled player with remarkable athletic prowess and is widely acknowledged as one of the best midfield players in the history of Gaelic football. **Jack Mahon**

O'Shea, Katharine, née Wood (1845–1921), wife of CHARLES STEWART PARNELL. Born at Glazenwood, Essex; in 1867 she married CAPTAIN W. H. O'SHEA. As they grew apart, appearances were maintained. Shortly after O'Shea's election to Parliament as HOME RULE candidate in 1880 she and Parnell met, and they settled into a semi-covert but highly domesticated relationship. She was an emissary of Parnell in his dealings with GLADSTONE. Her husband's divorce proceedings precipitated Parnell's fall in December 1890. After her divorce she married Parnell, less than four months before his death. An isolated and increasingly impecunious figure, she survived Parnell by thirty years, dying at Littlehampton, Sussex, on 5 February 1921. She had two children with O'Shea and three with Parnell. **Frank Callanan**

O'Shea, Milo (1925–), actor. Born in Dublin. He worked at the ABBEY THEATRE before appearing in the film *Talk of a Million* (1951). His career as a screen actor developed in the 1960s when he played Leopold Bloom in ULYSSES (1967) and thereafter appeared in *Sacco and Vanzetti* (1971), *The Verdict* (1982), *The Purple Rose of Cairo* (1985), *Only the Lonely* (1991), and *The Playboys* (1992). **Kevin Rockett**

O'Shea, Tony (1947–), photographer. Born on Valentia Island, Co. Kerry; educated at UCD. He has been published widely in magazines and newspapers in Ireland and abroad. His work appears in *Walking along the Border* (1988) and *Dubliners* (1990). **Martin Clancy**

O'Shea, Captain William Henry (1840–1905), politician. Born in Dublin; educated at TCD. He was elected HOME RULE MP for Clare in 1880. He supported PARNELL in his campaign for leadership of the IRISH PARTY and for a time ignored the love affair between his wife, Katharine, and Parnell. In 1882 he helped to negotiate the KILMAINHAM TREATY between Parnell and GLADSTONE. The decline in his political fortunes caused increasing strain on the relationship with Parnell; in 1889 he sued for divorce, citing Parnell as co-respondent and severely damaging his reputation. **Brian Galvin**

O'Siadhail, Micheal (1947–), poet. Born in Dublin; educated at TCD and the University of Oslo. He was assistant professor at the Dublin Institute for Advanced Studies, 1980–87, before leaving to become a full-time writer. His study *Modern Irish* was published in 1991. His collections of poetry include *An Bhliain Bhisigh* (1978), *Runga* (1980), *Cumann* (1982), *Hail! Madam Jazz* (1992), *A Fragile City* (1995), and *Our Double Time* (1998). **Peter Sirr**

Ó Siochfhradha, Pádraig ('An Seabhac') (1883–1964), teacher, civil servant, editor, senator, and author. Born in Dingle, Co. Kerry. He was an organiser for the GAELIC LEAGUE, 1905–22, and editor for the Gaelic League and later for the Educational Company of Ireland. He was active in various cultural and literary groups and collected and published much FOLKLORE, including *An Seanchaidhe Muimhneach* (1932). He wrote modern versions of old tales, such as *An Ceithearnach Caolriabhach* (1910), and also published *Laoithe na Féinne* (1941). *An Baile Seo 'Gainne* (1913) is a collection of SHORT STORIES, written in finely crafted language, that present entertaining sketches of rural life. He is best remembered for *Jimín Mháire Thaidhg* (1921), a humorous novel for young people. **Aisling Ní Dhonnchadha**

Ossianic poems and tales, so named from Ossian, a Scottish form of the name OISÍN used in the middle of the eighteenth century by James Macpherson. Fionn, Caoilte and Oisín are presented as narrators of poems found in the twelfth-century BOOK OF LEINSTER. Poems (also called lays and ballads) in syllabic metres about the mythical life, lore and exploits of the FIANNA came into vogue in that century. Subsequent tradition assigns the role of main narrator of this increasingly popular cycle of poems to Oisín, hence the modern designation Ossianic lays. St PATRICK acts frequently as an interlocutor in them. They contain a great variety of themes and subject matter and were appreciated all over the medieval and modern Gaelic-speaking areas of Scotland, Ireland, and the Isle of Man. The Book of the Dean of Lismore, compiled in Scotland in the sixteenth century, and the seventeenth-century DUANAIRE FINN contain important early anthologies of ballads.

Whereas many Irish manuscripts written in the eighteenth and nineteenth centuries contain substantial compilations of ballads, transmission in Scotland was almost exclusively by oral means, and significant collections of lays were made there in the same period. Some of these poems were sung; a number of them survived in the repertoire of traditional singers in Gaelic Scotland up to the twentieth century. Prose tales, literary and oral, were also a prominent part of the tradition. The story of the aged, desolate Oisín and his somewhat uneasy relationship with St Patrick was popular in Irish and Scottish folklore. **Máirtín Ó Briain**

Ó Súileabháin, Muiris (1904–1950), writer. Born on the Great Blasket Island, Co. Kerry; educated to primary level. In 1928 he joined the GARDA SÍOCHÁNA. While stationed in Connemara he wrote his celebrated autobiography FICHE BLIAIN AG FÁS (1933), with encouragement and assistance from the English classical scholar and Marxist George Thomson, a close friend. Inspired by TOMÁS Ó CRIOMHTHAINN's AN TOILEÁNACH, Ó Súileabháin's book was widely acclaimed as a younger man's account of island life and as a valuable cultural and social document. It was subsequently translated into seven languages. He retired from the Gardaí in 1934 and began to publish articles and stories in newspapers and magazines. Among his unpublished work is *Fiche Bliain fé Bhláth*, a sequel to his first book. He drowned while swimming on 25 May 1950. **Stephen Newmann**

Ó Súilleabháin, Amhlaoibh (1783–1838), diarist. He owes his place in literary history to the diary or *cín lae* (a term he coined) that he kept in Callan, Co. Kilkenny, from 1827 to 1835. He was engaged in a range of literary tasks, collecting and transcribing manuscripts, as well as writing poetry and romantic tales. He was a local O'Connellite leader, collecting the 'O'Connell rent' and making a speech at a monster CATHOLIC EMANCIPATION meeting in 1828. In that year he led the Catholic side in a vicious struggle against Protestant control of the charitable Callan dispensary. His diary, *Cín Lae Amhlaoibh Uí Shúilleabháin*, provides background to these and many other historical developments and contemporary practices; it is unrivalled in Irish as a source of information on the *mentalité* of the Catholic middle class. Ó Súilleabháin travelled regularly to Dublin, was well read in the learning of his day, and was influenced by contemporary intellectual currents. Originally from Co. Kerry, he never lost his attachment to that area, though he had left it at the age of six. He owed this allegiance, his involvement in Irish learning, and his early career as a schoolmaster to his father. His later career as a shopkeeper may have derived from his wife's wealth (see p. 293). **Proinsias Ó Drisceoil**

Ó Súilleabháin, Diarmaid (1932–1985), writer. Born in Eyeries, Beara Peninsula, Co. Cork; qualified as a national teacher at St Patrick's College, Dublin. He taught and lived for many years in Gorey, Co. Wexford. Dramatist, poet, short-story writer and republican, he achieved greatest distinction as an innovative and crusading novelist. He was keen to infuse literature in Irish with modernist thinking, and his work is highly influenced by French existential literature in particular. A prolific writer of fourteen books, including eleven novels, as well as numerous articles and pamphlets, two of his most important works are *An Uain Bheo* (1968) and *Maeldún* (1972). **Seosamh Ó Murchú**

Ó Súilleabháin, Eoghan Rua (1748–1784), poet. Born in the SLIABH LUACHRA area of Co. Kerry. While conscious of his own special status as a poet, he was forced by the circumstances of his time to earn a living as a wandering teacher and a *spailpín* (itinerant labourer). This accounts for periods spent in various places in Cos. Cork and Limerick, as well as in Co. Kerry. He also spent some time in the British navy aboard the *Formidable*; one of his English

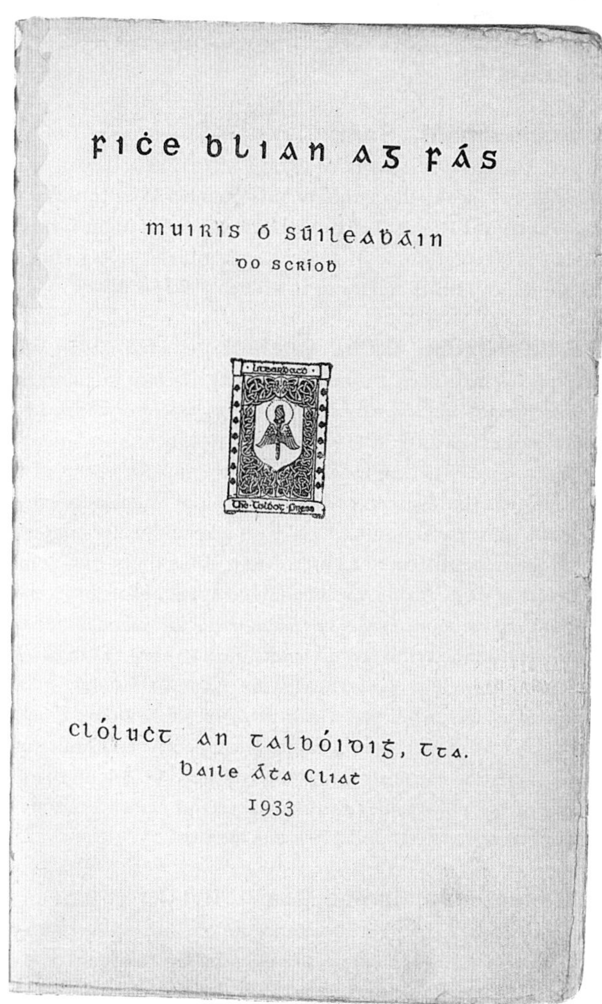
Fiċe Blian ag Fás

Muiris Ó Súileabáin
do scríob

Clólucṫ an Talbóidiġ, Tta.
Baile Áta Cliat
1933

Ó Súileabháin. *Muiris Ó Súileabháin's acclaimed autobiography,* Fiche Bliain ag Fás *(1933), describes his years growing up on the Great Blasket Island, Co. Kerry; it was translated into English as* Twenty Years a-Growing. *[Council of Trustees of the National Library of Ireland; Ir 89162 OS18]* compositions, 'Rodney's Glory', celebrates a victory under Admiral Rodney over the French fleet in 1782. Ó Súilleabháin's image as a rakish poet earned him a place until recently in folk memory, while the fact that he wrote his poems to some of the finest of the classic Irish airs ensured that his songs would live on into the present day in Irish-speaking communities in Munster, especially some of his AISLING or vision poems, with their extraordinary metrical virtuosity. Editions of his work were published by PATRICK DINNEEN in 1901 and 1923 and by Risteárd Ó Foghludha in 1937 (see p. 270). **Breandán Ó Conchúir**

Ó Súilleabháin, Micheál (1950–), pianist and composer. Born in Clonmel, Co. Tipperary; he studied with SEÁN Ó RIADA, and was awarded a doctorate by QUB in 1987. A lecturer at UCC, 1975–93, he established parity of esteem for traditional and classical music. In 1994 he was appointed professor of music at the Irish World Music Centre, University of Limerick. He introduced and taught postgraduate courses, some unique in Ireland, including ethnomusicology, ethnochoreology, MUSIC EDUCATION, and music therapy, as well as performance degrees in chant, contemporary dance, TRADITIONAL MUSIC, and traditional dance. His sometimes controversial conviction that traditional music should mediate with other types of music is evident in his ten albums and in his television series 'A River of Sound' (1995). He was assistant editor on ALOYS FLEISCHMANN'S SOURCES OF IRISH MUSIC project (1999). **Lillis Ó Laoire**

Ó Súilleabháin, Seán (1903–1996), folklorist. Born in Tuosist, Co. Kerry. Archivist of the IRISH FOLKLORE COMMISSION, 1935–70, he was also the author of numerous books and articles; his magnum opus is *A Handbook of Irish Folklore* (1942). An unassuming scholar, his dedication as an archivist, often under trying circumstances, leaves all Irish folklorists in his debt. **Mícheál Briody**

Ó Súilleabháin, Tadhg Gaelach (c. 1715–1795), poet. Sixty poems have been attributed to Tadhg Gaelach in eighteenth and nineteenth-century manuscripts, and his lament on the death of Eiléan de Barra in Cork in 1753 is the first to which a date and place can be ascribed. The language of his poetry displays aspects of the Múscraí and DÉISE dialects, while the content of his religious poems suggests a clerical education. Much of his religious poetry originated in the Dungarvan-Waterford area. Most of his thirty-two secular poems are of Co. Cork provenance. His compositions are in accented verse and are baroque in style. His religious poetry was published frequently in the nineteenth century under the title *Timothy O'Sullivan's Pious Miscellany*. The post-TRIDENTINE Catholic Church in the south-east of Ireland played a role in these publications. They in turn increased the spread of his religious poetry in manuscripts, largely under the patronage of Bishop Murphy of Cork, in the first quarter of the nineteenth century. Manuscript evidence points to his death between 1791 and 1796. **Úna Nic Éinrí**

Ó Súilleabháin, Tomás Rua (1785–1848), poet. Born in Derrynane, Co. Kerry. A schoolmaster, he was a friend and admirer of DANIEL O'CONNELL, whose triumphs he recorded in some of his songs. His compositions were taken down by Séamus (Dubh) Ó Fiannachta and published in *Amhráin Thomáis Ruaidh* (1914). **Breandán Ó Conchúir**

O'Sullivan, Cornelius (1841–1907), chemist. Born in Bandon, Co. Cork; attended evening classes taught by professors from Queen's College, Cork, in a scheme designed to bring science to rural areas. Awarded a scholarship to the Royal School of Mines, London, in 1862, he studied chemistry under August Hofmann and in 1865 followed him to Berlin University. He later became head brewer at the Bass brewery in Burton upon Trent, Staffordshire, where he put brewing on a scientific basis through the introduction of exact methods of analysis. He never forgot his roots and returned to Bandon each year to fish; he set up a scholarship for students there and was an ardent supporter of HOME RULE. He is now credited with being, through his research work, the founder of modern biochemistry. **Susan McKenna-Lawlor**

O'Sullivan, Dónal (1893–1973), music collector. Born in Liverpool to parents from Co. Kerry. He entered the civil service in London, and supported the GAELIC LEAGUE from his youth. Having moved to Ireland after the FIRST WORLD WAR, he was editor of the *Journal of the Irish Folk Song Society* from 1920, publishing BUNTING's first two volumes (1927–39). A lecturer in foreign affairs at Trinity College, Dublin, 1949–65, and director of folk music studies at University College, Dublin, 1951–62, he wrote the entry on folk music in Grove's *Dictionary of Music and Musicians* (1954), as well as *Irish Folk Music and Song* (1952), *Songs of the Irish* (1960), and other works. His major work was *Carolan: Life and Times of an Irish Harper* (1958). His exclusion of FRANCIS O'NEILL from his article in Grove's *Dictionary* was thought elitist. **Lillis Ó Laoire**

O'Sullivan, Gilbert, stage name of Raymond O'Sullivan (1946–), singer. Born in Waterford; he moved to London during his childhood. Between 1970 and 1975 he had twelve British top twenty hits, including 'Nothing Rhymed' (1970), 'Alone Again (Naturally)' (1972), and 'Clair' (1972). He possesses a superb songwriting talent that has produced many classic pop songs. A High Court battle against his former manager and record company in the early 1980s made legal history when all the singer's master tapes and copyright reverted to him, a decision with immense repercussions for the British music-publishing world. **Tony Clayton-Lea**

O'Sullivan, Maureen (1911–1998), film actor. Born in Boyle, Co. Roscommon. She made her debut in the JOHN MCCORMACK feature *Song o' My Heart* (1929) but is remembered mainly as Jane to Johnny Weissmuller's Tarzan in the film series. On her marriage to the director John Farrow she retired from films; one of their seven children is the actor Mia Farrow. She later worked in television and on Broadway and eventually returned to films, appearing late in life in *Hannah and her Sisters* (1986), *Peggy Sue Got Married* (1986), and *Stranded* (1987). **Kevin Rockett**

O'Sullivan, Seán (1906–1964), portrait painter. Born in Dublin; trained at the Metropolitan School of Art, Dublin, and studied lithography in the Central School of Arts and Crafts, London, and painting in Paris. A superb technician and draughtsman, his portrait drawings provide a veritable 'who's who' of Irish political and cultural life and include MAUD GONNE MACBRIDE, JAMES JOYCE and ÉAMON DE VALERA. He exhibited regularly at the RHA and was made a full member in 1931. O'Sullivan believed that a portrait should reveal how the artist feels about his sitters, each of whom must be portrayed 'as dispassionately as a piece of still life' (see p. 576). **Síghle Bhreathnach-Lynch**

O'Sullivan, Seumas, pen-name of James Sullivan Starkey (1879–1958), poet and editor. Born in Dublin; educated privately and at Wesley College. His early poetry appeared in the *Irish Homestead*, *United Irishman*, and *Celtic Christmas*; his first book of poetry, *The Twilight People*, was published in 1905. His *Verses: Sacred and Profane* appeared in 1908 and *The Earth-Lover and Other Verses* in 1909. He edited the *Dublin Magazine* from 1923 until his death in 1958. As editor he promoted talents of the fading Irish LITERARY REVIVAL, such as YEATS and RUSSELL, alongside younger writers such as BECKETT, LAVIN, O'FLAHERTY and others from beyond Ireland's shores. **Joley Wood**

O'Sullivan, Thaddeus (1948–), film director and cameraman. Born in Dublin. Following his early career as an experimental film-maker with *A Pint of Plain* (1975) and *On a Paving Stone Mounted* (1978), he made mainstream commercial cinema and television films, including the well-regarded *December Bride* (1990), an adaptation of the novel by SAM HANNA BELL; *Nothing Personal* (1995), about loyalist violence; and *Ordinary Decent Criminal* (2000), based on the life of the Dublin criminal MARTIN CAHILL. **Kevin Rockett**

O'Sullivan Beare, Philip (fl. sixteenth to seventeenth century), author and historian. Born in Cork some time in the 1590s, a nephew of Dónal O'Sullivan Beare, whom he followed into exile in Spain; educated at Santiago de Compostela. Though primarily interested in scholarship, he embarked on a military career, receiving a commission in the Spanish navy from Philip II. His most famous work, *Historiae Catholicae Iberniae Compendium* (1621), is a highly partisan history of Ireland with a central role for his own family and their role in the Elizabethan wars. His *Zoilomastix* (1625) contains valuable lists of Irish clergy and doctors on the Continent as well as a sustained attack on the writings of GIRALDUS CAMBRENSIS and RICHARD STANIHURST. He also produced a life of St PATRICK, *Patritiana Decas* (1629), a polemic against the writings of ARCHBISHOP USSHER, and some unpublished hagiography. His date of death—perhaps some time in the 1630s—is unknown. **Liam Irwin**

Otherworld (Irish *an Saol Eile*), seen in FOLKLORE as a real place, inhabited by the spirits of the dead and also by a host of supernatural beings, ranging from the FAIRIES to individual supernatural personages, including hags such as CAILLEACH BHÉARRA, the Devil, and the BANSHEE. The fairies (*síóga*) are communal supernatural beings, cohabiting the Earth with human beings.

Folklore about spirits, both good and evil, is rich and widespread. *Revenants* (the spirits of people returning from the dead) come back for a variety of purposes and in various guises, taking human, animal, or other forms. Famous spirits, such as 'Petticoat Loose', a renowned evil spirit who is said to have killed her unbaptised child and died unrepentant, haunted particular places in the south of the country, especially Cos. Tipperary and Waterford; according to tradition, she was ultimately banished and exorcised by priests.

Ghosts and spirits were fêted in folk song and ballads. Fear of the Otherworld and of the unknown is evident in much of the folk tradition, and great attention was given to various protective practices, both religious and secular. To ward off danger, people carried objects to which supernatural powers were ascribed, such as holy water, a black-handled knife, or red thread. Ambiguity concerning the supernatural was tolerated, encapsulated in the saying 'God is good, but the Devil isn't bad either.' **Anne O'Connor**

O'Toole, Fintan (1958–), critic. Born in Dublin; educated at UCD. He has been a committed commentator on cultural politics and the politics of culture since 1980, when he became theatre critic of

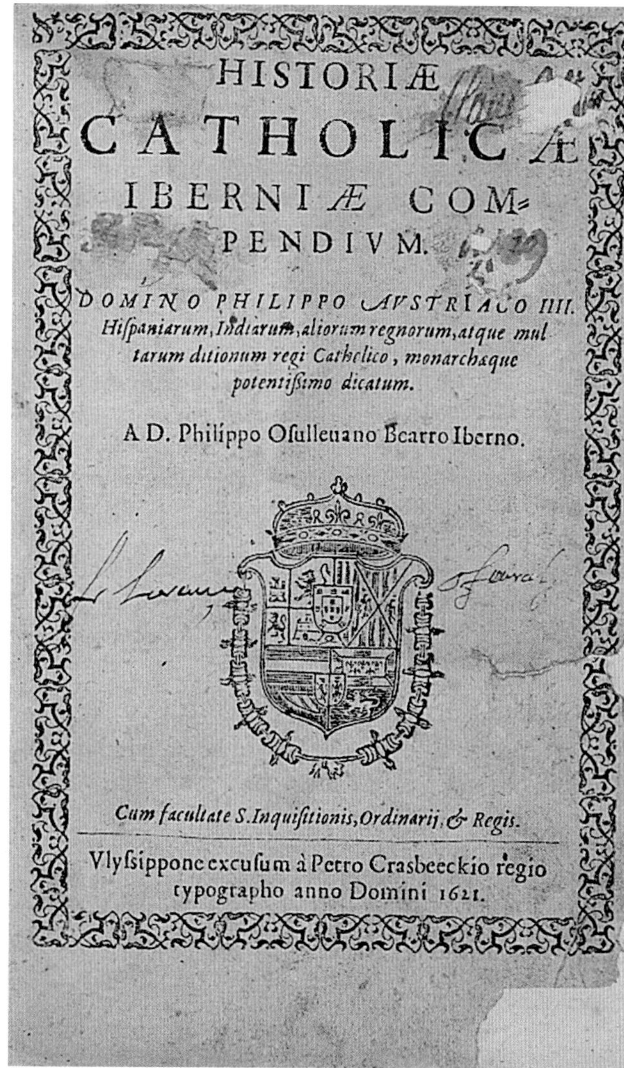

HISTORIÆ CATHOLICÆ IBERNIÆ COMPENDIVM.

DOMINO PHILIPPO AVSTRIACO IIII. Hispaniarum, Indiarum, aliorum regnorum, atque multarum ditionum regi Catholico, monarchæque potentissimo dicatum.

A D. Philippo Osulleuano Bearro Iberno.

Cum facultate S. Inquisitionis, Ordinarij, & Regis.

Vlyssippone excusum à Petro Crasbeeckio regio typographo anno Domini 1621.

O'Sullivan Beare. *Title page of O'Sullivan Beare's* Historia et Catholicae Iberniae Compendium *(1621), his history of Ireland, in which he gives pride of place to the role of his own family. [Board of Trinity College, Dublin]*

In Dublin, and subsequently as a journalist with the *Sunday Tribune* (of which he was arts editor, 1984–6), *Magill* (which he edited, 1986–7), and the IRISH TIMES, where he has written a column since 1988 and became senior drama critic, 2001. In addition to several journalistic books, this commitment is evident in *The Politics of Magic: The Work and Times of Tom Murphy* (1987) and *A Traitor's Kiss: The Life of Richard Brinsley Sheridan* (1997). **Richard Pine**

O'Toole, Laurence, anglicised name of Lorcán Ó Tuathail (1128–80), Archbishop of Dublin. Son of Muirchertach, King of northern Leinster (Uí Muiredaig dynasty), he was child-hostage with his overlord, DERMOT MACMURROUGH. Educated at Glendalough, he became abbot in 1153. Elected archbishop in 1162, he introduced the Augustinians to CHRIST CHURCH, Dublin. He developed a working relationship with the ANGLO-NORMANS from 1171, which unravelled when his dynasty was dispossessed. As envoy for RUAIDHRÍ Ó CONCHOBHAIR he came into conflict with HENRY II of England. Created papal legate, he secured his temporalities. He followed Henry to France, seeking further negotiations, but died at Eu. Accorded a Latin 'Life', he was canonised in 1226. **Ailbhe Mac Shamhráin**

O'Toole, Peter (1932–), actor. Born in Leeds. He made his film debut in *Kidnapped* (1960) and became an international star after appearing in *Lawrence of Arabia* (1962), for which he won a British Academy award. Other acclaimed roles were in *Becket* (1964), *The Lion in Winter* (1968), *Goodbye, Mr Chips* (1969), *The Ruling Class* (1972) and *My Favourite Year* (1982). In 1990 he played the lead in the successful London run of *Jeffrey Bearnard is Unwell*. **Kevin Rockett**

otter, found all over the country where a suitable habitat is available. The lustrous pelt is darker in the Irish sub-species; it may have white patches on its coat, especially on the throat. It lives in rivers and lakes and on the seashore, eating fish and various invertebrates; in a salt-water habitat it must bathe regularly in fresh water. It lies up in a *holt* (a burrow usually underneath a tree on the bank of a river) and sometimes visits badgers' burrows near the seashore. Hunted until recently, both for sport and for its pelt, it is now fully protected. **D. Patrick Sleeman**

Ó Tuairisc, Eoghan (1919–1982), writer. Born Eugene Watters in Ballinasloe, Co. Galway. Author of poetry, plays, short stories, novels, literary essays, and translations, he is best known for his literary output in Irish. His novels *L'Attaque* (1962) and *Dé Luain* (1966) deal with historical events of 1798 and 1916, respectively, while his long poems 'Aifreann na Marbh' and 'The Week-End of Dermot and Grace' (1964) address in dramatic form many of the social and moral issues raised by the use of nuclear power. His episodic novel *An Lomnochtán* (1977), described by himself as 'a portrait of the artist as a young chiseller,' met with widespread critical acclaim, as did the diary of poems *Dialann sa Díseart* (1981), written jointly with his second wife, the writer Rita Kelly. **Máirín Nic Eoin**

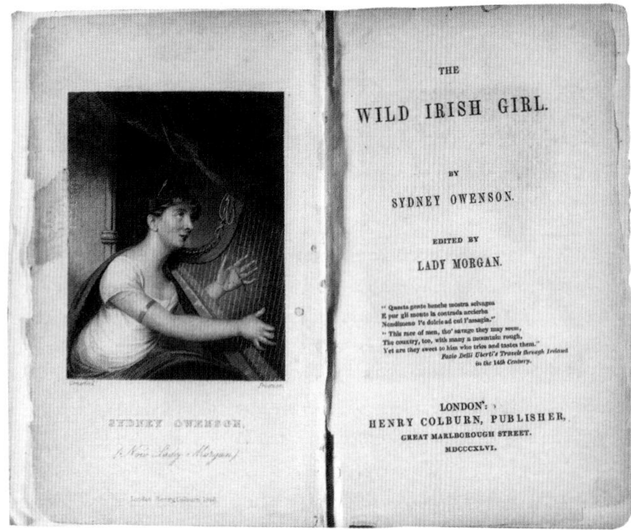

Owenson. The Wild Irish Girl *(1806) by Sydney Owenson (Lady Morgan), espousing nationalist sentiment, is one of the founding texts in the discourse of Irish nationalism. The frontispiece of Owenson, from a painting by John Comerford, depicts her as a romantic heroine; she was in fact an accomplished harpist and singer. [Council of Trustees of the National Library of Ireland IR82379m15]*

Ó Tuama, Seán (1926–), poet, dramatist, critic, and professor of modern Irish literature at the University College, Cork. Born in Cork; educated at UCC. His anthology *Nuabhéarsaíocht, 1939–1949* (1950) drew critical attention to the work of contemporary poets in Irish, as does the later anthology *Coiscéim na hAoise* (1991), which he jointly edited with LOUIS DE PAOR. His original writings include the poetry collections *Faoileán na Beatha* (1962), *Saol fó Thoinn* (1978) and *An Bás i dTír na nÓg* (1988) and the plays *Gunna Cam agus Slabhra Óir* (1967) and *Molony agus Drámaí Eile* (1966). He has had a profound influence as critic and teacher, especially for his examination of Irish love poetry in *An Grá in Amhráin na nDaoine* (1960) and *An Grá i bhFilíocht na nUaisle* (1988), his edition of CAOINEADH AIRT UÍ LAOGHAIRE (1961), and his interpretations of the work of AOGÁN Ó RATHAILLE and SEÁN Ó RÍORDÁIN in *Filí faoi Sceimhle* (1978). **Eoghan Ó hAnluain**

Otway, Caesar (1780–1842), clergyman, editor, and travel writer. Born in Co. Tipperary; graduated from TCD in 1801. After ordination as a CHURCH OF IRELAND minister he jointly founded in 1825 (and edited until 1831) an anti-Catholic periodical, the *Christian Examiner and Church of Ireland Magazine*. Chiefly remembered today for publishing in the *Christian Examiner* early pieces of writing by WILLIAM CARLETON, he also wrote polemical religious tracts, such as *A Letter to the Roman Catholic Priests of Ireland* (1814), and Irish travelogues, such as *Sketches in Ireland* (1827), *A Tour in Connaught* (1839), and *Sketches in Erris and Tyrawly* (1841). **Richard Haslam**

Our Lady's Choral Society, a dynamic and popular choir, founded in Dublin in 1945. Since its inception the choir has retained close ties with both the NATIONAL SYMPHONY ORCHESTRA and the RTÉ CONCERT ORCHESTRA. As well as its many recital and recording engagements the choir performs HANDEL's *Messiah* every Christmas; on 13 April each year it performs choruses from *Messiah* at the site of the New Musick Hall in Fishamble Street, Dublin, where the work had its first performance in 1742. The choir is directed by PROINNSÍAS Ó DUINN (see p. 471). **Geraldine Guiden**

Ouseley, Gideon (1762–1839), Methodist preacher. Born in Dunmore, Co. Galway. Having undergone a religious conversion following an accident that left him partially blind, he became an itinerant preacher and in 1798 was appointed by the METHODISTS as Irish-speaking missionary. His evangelical zeal, fervent anti-Catholicism, and emotional preaching drew large crowds and inspired many local revivals. **Myrtle Hill**

Owenson, Sydney, Lady Morgan (c. 1776–1859), writer. A daughter of the actor-manager Robert Owenson, in 1812 she married the physician Sir Charles Morgan. A professional writer from a young age, she wrote novels, travels, poetry, art history, and political journalism. She made a career of public controversies, attacking variously TORY critics, French royalism, Italian absolutism, and the Catholic Church in England. One of her earliest publications is an attack on John Wilson Croker's anonymous strictures on the Dublin stage; Croker in turn denounced her most influential novel, *The Wild Irish Girl* (1806), which was responsible for inaugurating the language and imagery of romantic Ireland. **Claire Connolly**

Phoenix Park
(see page 869).
The Phoenix Park, Dublin, encompassing an area of 712 ha (1,762 acres). The Wellington Testimonial (1817) is at bottom left, Dublin Zoo straddles the lakes, right, and Áras an Uachtaráin is at top centre.
[Imagefile]

P

paganism. We know nothing about the organisation of Irish paganism, though it has been the subject of much debate. St PATRICK, who flourished in the fifth century, is our earliest witness to conditions in pre-Christian Ireland; frustratingly, however, his generally fascinating writings do not tell us very much about Irish paganism. CHRISTIANITY did not take firm root until the sixth century; significantly, it is arguable that Diarmait mac Cerbaill (died 565) was the last pagan King of TARA. He was certainly the last to celebrate the pagan festival known as Feis Temro (the feast of Tara). Despite the triumph of Christianity it is clear that many of the legendary figures that appear in Irish narratives have pagan origins, particularly the TUATHA DÉ DANANN and such heroes as CÚ CHULAINN and FIONN MAC CUMHAILL. Furthermore, early medieval Irish culture was an amalgam of Christian and native, ultimately pagan, traditions. [see BOA ISLAND; IDOLS; PRE-CHRISTIAN IRELAND.] **Elva Johnston**

Pain, James (1779–1877) and **George Richard** (1793–1838), architects. Born in London, sons of a builder and grandsons of a writer on architecture; studied under Nash and travelled to Ireland to supervise his design for Lough Cutra Castle, Co. Galway (1811). James then settled in Limerick and George in Cork. They worked together as well as separately, with great stylistic versatility, and were prolific throughout the south of Ireland. Their first commission in Cork was for the Jail (1818), a design worthy of George Dance, with a central massive Greek Doric portico. They built many country houses in the style of Nash throughout the south, such as Mitchelstown Castle (1823) and Dromoland Castle (c. 1826). James was appointed architect to the BOARD OF FIRST FRUITS for Munster, 1820s–40s; George acted as his assistant. Their Protestant churches, though modest in scale, have great picturesque gothic qualities, such as that of Castletownshend, Co. Cork (1826). George was the architect on his own of two important Catholic churches in Cork, the Capuchin Church of the Holy Trinity (1832), with an elegant soaring Gothic portico, and St Patrick's Church (c. 1836), a strong design with deep Corinthian portico and towering lantern, as well as the North Cathedral (Cathedral of St Mary and St Anne), since altered. Cork Courthouse (1835), by both, is a magnificent yet simple classical masterpiece with an immense Corinthian portico. **Eve McAulay**

painting, seventeenth century to the present day. William Carey wrote in 1826: 'Ireland had some native artists, and was occasionally visited by straggling adventurers of the brush from London.' This was once assumed to be so, but recent research has revealed that the opposite is true. An impressive number of Irish-born painters made their careers in England and beyond. Hugh Howard (1675–1738) went from Dublin to England in 1688, to Holland in 1697, and c. 1708 to Rome. CHARLES JERVAS of Dublin (c. 1695–1739) studied under Kneller in London and then in Rome, finally establishing himself in London as Principal Painter to the King. THOMAS FRYE (1710–62), born apparently near Dublin, was in London by 1735 and was one of the pioneers of mezzotint engraving (see p. 895). Another Dublin-born painter, NATHANIEL HONE (1718–1784), was in England by 1742 and incurred the enmity of Sir Joshua Reynolds. HUGH DOUGLAS HAMILTON (1739–1808) was in London by 1764 and went to Rome and Florence in 1778. JAMES BARRY of Cork was taken to London by his mentor, Edmund Burke, in 1764. Burke also paid for Barry to go to Italy (see p. 60). Back in London, Barry's uncompromising attitude led to the distinction of his being the only painter ever to be expelled from the Royal Academy (in 1799). Another Dublin painter, Thomas Hickey (1741–1824), having worked in London and Bath in the 1770s, went by way of Portugal to India, arriving in Calcutta in 1787 and ending his days in Madras. In the meantime he accompanied Lord Macartney's diplomatic mission to China, 1792–4. Rev. Matthew William Peters (1741–1814), of a Dublin family, studied under Thomas Hudson in London in the 1750s. Taking holy orders in 1781, he was appointed chaplain to the Royal Academy.

A number of Irish-born miniature painters achieved success in England, including Rupert Barber (1736–1772), Horace Hone (1756–1825), ADAM BUCK (1759–1833), and Sampson Towgood Roche (1759–1847). Sir MARTIN ARCHER SHEE rose from obscure origins in Dublin to become president of the Royal Academy in London. WILLIAM MULREADY, from Ennis, Co. Clare, and DANIEL MACLISE, from Cork, both became renowned nineteenth-century Royal Academicians. Sir FREDERICK BURTON (1816–1900), from Co. Clare, was appointed director of the National Gallery, London, in 1874. Sir JOHN LAVERY (1856–1941) emigrated from Belfast by way of Glasgow and Gréz-sur-Loing to become an influential society painter, with homes in London and Tangier. Painters such as JACK BUTLER YEATS of Sligo and PAUL HENRY, originally from Belfast, made the west of Ireland their focal point and arguably created a national tradition of landscape painting. LOUIS LE BROCQUY, born in Dublin in 1916, is probably Ireland's most distinguished living painter; he has worked for many years in the south of France. WILLIAM SCOTT (1913–1989), brought up in Enniskillen, Co. Fermanagh, the most internationally important twentieth-century painter to emerge from the North of Ireland, has worked in London and St Ives, Cornwall. **Brian Lalor**

'Pairlement Chloinne Tomáis', a prose satire that attacks 'Clann Tomáis', the landless labourers of Gaelic Ireland. The author was probably from Co. Kerry and may have been an O'Dinneen. The narrative tells how Clann Tomáis originated from an unnatural union of Beelzebub's great-grandson and a human woman and so multiplied on the earth that they could not be restrained. The main events in the story are two imaginary sessions of the churls' parliament on Crusline Hill, Co. Kerry, in 1632 and 1645. These dates are projections, since the work probably dates from c. 1615. Clann Tomáis are given absurd names like Mathghamhain Ó Meacanáin ('Mahon O'Parsnip') and Raghnait Ní Mheigealláin ('Renny O'Bleat') and are ruthlessly but eloquently ridiculed for their boorish pretensions. 'Pairlement Chloinne Tomáis', a fusion of the burlesque tales of Gaelic Ireland with the European genres of the *parlement* and estates satire, gave rise to many imitations. The first work to be based on 'Pairlement Chloinne Tomáis' was the second book of 'Pairlement Chloinne Tomáis' itself. This was probably written in Co. Westmeath in the early years of the reign of Charles II; it satirises the small craftsmen and minor tradespeople who had done well out of the Cromwellian confiscations. **Nicholas J. A. Williams**

Paisley, Rev. Ian Richard Kyle (1926–), religious and political activist. Born in Co. Armagh; son of a Baptist minister with a strictly religious upbringing, he was educated in Ballymena, then at South Wales Bible College. An effective preacher and communicator, he established and headed the FREE PRESBYTERIAN CHURCH of Ulster. As its Moderator he was to the fore in opposing the ecumenical movement and the political liberalism he associated with it, both philosophies for him embodying a threat to PROTESTANTISM. A vehement opponent of TERENCE O'NEILL's mild reformism, he succeeded him as MP for Bannside in 1970 and was elected to the British House of Commons for North Antrim in 1971, during which year he established the DEMOCRATIC UNIONIST PARTY. Following the imposition of direct British rule of Northern Ireland, he consistently advocated a return to regional government but resisted power-sharing arrangements. A supporter of the ULSTER WORKERS' COUNCIL STRIKE in 1974, which brought down the 'Sunningdale' Executive, his attempt to emulate it in 1977 was a failure. In 1979 he was elected to the European Parliament on a strong popular vote, his party reaching its electoral zenith in the later 1970s and early 80s. His co-ordination of opposition to the ANGLO-IRISH AGREEMENT (1985) with the ULSTER UNIONIST PARTY emphasised the depth of pan-unionist opposition to the deal, though co-operation between the two parties soon broke down. He was elected to the Northern Ireland Forum in 1996 and to the NORTHERN IRELAND ASSEMBLY in 1998, where his party aimed to bring an end to the BELFAST AGREEMENT (1998). **Alan Scott**

Pakenham, Edward Arthur Henry, sixth Earl of Longford (1902–1961), theatrical producer and playwright. Educated at the University of Oxford. He was an ebullient personality who, in 1931, unexpectedly saved the GATE THEATRE, Dublin, from bankruptcy by buying all outstanding shares in the company. However, he differed with MÍCHEÁL MAC LIAMMÓIR and HILTON EDWARDS and in 1936 formed his own company, LONGFORD PRODUCTIONS, also based at the Gate, which toured the country, presenting his own translations of classical Greek drama as well as his original plays and those of his wife, Christine Longford. *Yahoo* (1933), in which Edwards played JONATHAN SWIFT, is generally regarded as his best play. **Christopher Morash**

Palatines, Protestant refugees from the Rhineland palatinate who were settled in Ireland in 1709. Of the original 821 families, by 1720 only 185 remained. They settled on estates in Cos. Kerry, Tipperary and Wexford and, most importantly, at Rathkeale, Co. Limerick, where they farmed land on extremely favourable leases. They resisted assimilation and maintained their distinct language and customs. Their fervent PROTESTANTISM was revived by their encounter with METHODISM. Most left Ireland in the 1760s for North America, where they played a strategic role in the development of American Methodism; those who remained were integrated into the population at large, as the surnames Switzer, Guerin and Teskey attest. **Kevin Herlihy**

Pale, or English Pale, a term first used in Ireland in 1495 to denote the fortified lowland region around Dublin that was subject to English rule. During the fifteenth and early sixteenth centuries the area that remained under effective English control, the 'Maghery' (*machaire*) or innermost district of the Pale, had become equated with

Paisley. *Moderator of the Free Presbyterian Church of Ulster, Ian Paisley has been a stern defender of Evangelical Protestantism and Unionism, and has represented the constituency of Bannside for over thirty years. [Popperfoto]*

the greater part of the medieval shires of Dublin, Kildare, Meath, and Louth. Though some inhabitants of the Maghery were Irish, the majority were exemplars of English civility, their language, customs, social hierarchy, agricultural practices, legal system, and government closely resembling those of their counterparts in lowland England. Beyond this English heartland lay the *marches* or borderlands of the Pale, defended by castles and pales. A locally paid and recruited force defended the Pale community from the 1470s until the mid-1530s.

The adoption of the term and concept of a 'pale' in Ireland originated with Sir Edward Poynings, who served as deputy lieutenant of the Calais Pale before his appointment in a similar capacity in Ireland in 1494. The following year he instigated the first co-ordinated steps to enclose the 'four obedient shires', apparently with a view to creating a true pale, that is, a defensive ring of fortifications around a precisely delineated area. Poynings' Parliament in 1495 legislated for 'diches to be made aboute the Inglishe pale.' Inhabitants of the marches were ordered to build a double rampart and ditch 1.8 m (6 ft) high along the boundary of the Maghery and more ditches between the marches and the Irishry. However, unlike the Calais model, the Pale in Ireland was a shifting medieval frontier whose borders coincided with geographical, cultural, administrative, political, and military boundaries between English and Irish regions in Leinster that became increasingly obsolete with the advance of the Tudor conquest. **Mary Ann Lyons**

Palestrina Choir, a choir of men and boys founded and endowed by EDWARD MARTYN in 1902 and constituted as the choir of St Mary's Pro-Cathedral, Dublin. The choir continues to preserve the church's rich heritage of plain-chant and polyphony within the new liturgical norms of the SECOND VATICAN COUNCIL. Between 1980 and 1994 it travelled to many European cities and in 1995 visited the United States and Canada. JOHN MCCORMACK was a member of the choir in 1904. Directors have been VINCENT O'BRIEN (1902–48), OLIVER O'BRIEN (1948–78), Seán Ó hEarcaigh (1978–82), Ite O'Donovan (1982–95), Joseph Ryan (1996), Orla Barry (1996–2002) and Blánaid Murphy (2002–). **Ite O'Donovan**

Palladius, fifth-century bishop. Our sole informant is Prosper of Aquitaine's reliable Chronicon (431): 'Pope Celestine ordained Palladius sending him to the Irish believers in Christ as their first bishop.' He may be the deacon who instigated the visit of Germanus of Auxerre to Britain to combat Pelagianism in 429. Of his work in Ireland we know nothing, but he probably ministered to Christian captives. Later writers, such as Muirchú, anxious to respect the Papal agent yet wishing to present PATRICK as the first bishop, imagined Palladius failing in his task and being succeeded by Patrick: hence the dating of Patrick's arrival as 432. **Thomas O'Loughlin**

Pallas Castle, Co. Galway, a very fine example of a TOWER-HOUSE with later extensions, bawn, and gate-house; it was in existence in 1574 and belonged to Moyler McHenry (Burke). It is four storeys high, with intramural stairs and a bartisan at battlement level. There is a rectangular gate-house in the middle of the bawn wall at the opposite side of the enclosure to the tower. Angle-towers in the same wall as the gateway provided flanking fire with bartisans on the other angles of the bawn. **David Sweetman**

pampooties, a name (of unknown origin) sometimes given to rawhide shoes with a single sole, called *bróga úrleathair* (rawhide shoes) on the ARAN ISLANDS, where they were worn until recent decades (see p. 1117). Made from a single piece of hide, a pair would last about a month. They were the last remnants of a tradition of wearing rawhide shoes in Ireland, which began at least in the Early Christian period, c. AD 200–500. **Anne O'Dowd**

Pangur Bán, subject of 'Messe ocus Pangur Bán' ('Me and White Pangur'), a delightfully witty Old Irish poem of eight quatrains, in heptasyllabic lines, written c. 800. Its speaker is a scholar, perhaps a monk, who shares his cell with a white cat called Pangur; and a comparison of the scholar's joyful pursuit of knowledge with the cat's sporting after mice is sustained throughout. The poem is known from a single copy in a codex (now in the monastery of St Paul at Unterdrauberg, Austria) of miscellaneous Irish, Greek, and Latin material written by an Irishman, possibly the poem's author and probably when he was in Europe. Best known in English in ROBIN FLOWER's translation, the poem has recently been translated by PAUL MULDOON. **Máirín Ní Dhonnchadha**

Pangur Bán. *Imogen Stuart's sculpture group* Pangur Bán *(1981), includes the scholar, the cat chasing mice under a bench, and the poem on the wall relief. [University College, Dublin (AVC); courtesy of the artist]*

pantomime. Though the term was first used in Greece in the second century, the conventions of today's pantomime can be traced back to eighteenth-century England. Pantomime has been hugely popular in Ireland since *Bluff King Hal*, a variation on the Harlequinade, appeared at Dublin's first THEATRE ROYAL in 1851. The theatre burnt down in 1880, but two subsequent theatres of the same name, 1897–1934 and 1935–62, were home to Dublin's most acclaimed pantomimes; some 258,000 people saw the 1944 production of *Mother Goose*, starring Noel Purcell and Eddie Byrne. In an earlier production of *Mother Goose*, at the QUEEN'S ROYAL THEATRE (1844–1969), Jack Judge first sang his song 'TIPPERARY' in 1912, and JIMMY O'DEA made his panto debut there in *Cinderella* in 1923. The OLYMPIA THEATRE, Dublin (formerly Dan Lowry's Music Hall), continues to stage annual pantomimes, as does the GAIETY THEATRE. Favourite performers of the past have included Cecil Sheridan, Jack Cruise, Danny Cummins, Cecil Nash, and MAUREEN POTTER; the leading pantomime artist today is the multi-talented Twink (Adele King). **Stephen Dixon and Deirdre Falvey**

Papal agression: see RUSSELL, LORD JOHN.

parades. Public parades have been a common feature of Irish life for 500 years. Parades can be expressions of power, prestige, political identity, community, and enjoyment; they can be both carnivalesque and commemorative, include but also exclude people. Parades play an important role in public expressions of politics. In the late Middle Ages parades were principally of a civil or religious nature, such as 'Riding the Franchises' and the guilds' parades in Dublin. ST PATRICK'S DAY, Our Lady's Day and commemorations of the BATTLE OF THE BOYNE and the SIEGE OF DERRY all developed as commemorative days from the eighteenth century onwards. These became prominent in the North and the focus for civil disorder.

Party Procession Acts prohibited parading from 1832 to 1845 and again from 1850 to 1872. Parading increasingly became associated with Ulster UNIONISM through the ORANGE ORDER, the APPRENTICE BOYS OF DERRY, and marching bands (see p. 651). After partition, legislation and policing in Northern Ireland led to an expansion of this tradition, while parades representing NATIONALISM were prohibited or restricted. In the South, military parades, or parades with military participation, were common, particularly during the years of the SECOND WORLD WAR; the 1916 RISING was commemorated by a military parade in Dublin up to 1972. In Northern Ireland, Twelfth of July parades became events of state, with the Prime Minister and senior Unionist politicians making speeches. Parades by the Royal Black Institution, held on the last Saturday of August, and the Apprentice Boys of Derry, held on Easter Monday and on the nearest Saturday to 12 August, also increased. During this time, for a variety of reasons, the ANCIENT ORDER OF HIBERNIANS went into decline.

The 'right to parade' has been an important issue in Northern Ireland, and civil disorder has remained common at parades. When CIVIL RIGHTS marchers took to the streets from 1967, expressions of territoriality became more marked. A few of the parades by the loyal orders were seen as crossing boundaries, and conflicts over parade routes increased. Controversies became particularly prominent in 1985 and 1986 as the policing of certain 'traditional' parades was changed and unionists reacted to the ANGLO-IRISH AGREEMENT. In the 1990s residents' groups opposing loyal order parades became prominent, and the number and intensity of the disputes became greater, resulting in serious civil disorder. None has been more symbolic of divisions than that of DRUMCREE, near Portadown, Co. Armagh. Approximately 3,500 parades take place in Northern Ireland annually. In the weeks preceding 12 July, flags are put up, and on the night before, bonfires are lit. The Orange Order holds around twenty large parades on the Twelfth, preceded by hundreds of local 'feeder' parades. While parades are regarded as 'traditional', research into routes, politics, the bands, and the flags carried has shown that great changes have taken place in what is a diverse range of events. [see PARADES AUTHORITY.] **Dominic Bryan**

Paris type, an IRISH PRINTING TYPE. Partly with a view to fostering the use of their native language among the seminarians of the Irish College in Paris, a font of Irish type was acquired from Holland by the Paris foundry of Loyson. It was used for the first time in 1732 by the local printer Jacques Guerin to print the English–Irish Dictionary compiled by Conchúr Ó Beaglaoich. In the introduction it is indicated that Ó Beaglaoich arranged for the provision of the type in an effort to harmonise the Irish style with the Roman as much as possible. The result, possibly based on

Ó Beaglaoich's own handwriting, was a cursive, script-like type that differed significantly from any of its predecessors. **Dermot McGuinne**

Park, Audrey (1936–1995), violinist. Born in Ayr, Scotland; joined the RTÉ Light Orchestra in 1955, becoming deputy leader in 1957; transferred with her violist husband Archie Collins to Cork as members of the RTÉ STRING QUARTET 1967–71; Leader of RTÉLO 1971–79, when she became leader of the RTÉ Symphony Orchestra, a position she held until her death. **Richard Pine**

Parke, Dorothy (1904–1990), teacher and composer. Born in Derry; studied piano with Ambrose Coviello and composition with Paul Corder at the Royal Academy of Music, London. She returned to Belfast and became a renowned piano teacher. She also composed and arranged songs and piano pieces for children, many of which were used as competition pieces. Her instrumental compositions include a violin sonata (1929), *Improvisation on 'The Snowy-Breasted Pearl'* (1955) for piano and orchestra, and *Tunetime: Six Pieces for Piano* (1971). Her song compositions include *By Winding Roads: Fifteen Songs* (John Irvine) (1950) and *Wee Hughie* (1980). **Ite O'Donovan**

Parke, Thomas Heazle (1857–1893), explorer; the first Irishman to cross Africa. Born at Kilmore, Co. Roscommon. In 1875 he entered the College of Surgeons, Dublin, where he obtained his medical degree. He served as a surgeon with the British army in Egypt during Arabi's revolt in 1882 and in 1884 accompanied the expedition to relieve General Gordon, who was besieged by the Mahdi in Khartoum. Two years later he was chosen by Henry Stanley to accompany him on his mission to rescue Emin Pasha (Eduard Schnitzer), who had succeeded Gordon as governor of Equatoria. The expedition took nearly three years, from March 1887 to December 1889, and involved sailing 1,600 km (1,000 miles) up the river into dense equatorial jungle. After journeying through the unknown Ituri rain-forests, Parke and Arthur Jephson discovered the peaks of the Ruwenzori Range, the legendary 'Mountains of the Moon'.

Emin Pasha was found safe and well at Lake Albert. The expedition crossed Africa and reached Zanzibar. Of the 800 who started from Banana Point at the mouth of the Congo only 200 survived the appalling journey; that more did not perish was largely due to the medical skills of Parke, who would become widely known as 'the man who saved Stanley.'

Though Parke accepted the prevailing imperial attitudes, he was a humane and likeable man, highly regarded for his dedication and his medical skill. With a ghost writer, his friend Dr John Knott, he wrote a sanitised account of his African trip, *My Personal Experiences in Equatorial Africa* (1891), which became a best-seller. His recently discovered journals and letters are written in a more vivid style. He received gold medals from the British Medical Association and the Royal Geographical Society. Worn out by his African experiences, he died on 10 September 1893 at the age of thirty-five and was buried in Drumsna, Co. Leitrim. His statue, rifle in hand, stands in front of the NATURAL HISTORY MUSEUM in Upper Merrion Street, Dublin; on the pedestal he is shown sucking poison from a comrade's wound. Inside the museum a small case contains the weather-stained uniform he wore crossing the African continent. [see BRITISH EMPIRE, IRISH IN.] **Peter Somerville-Large**

Parke, Thomas Heazle *Surgeon-Major Thomas Heazle Parke, the first Irishman to cross Africa, on a mission to rescue Emin Pasha, governor of Equatoria. The expedition lasted three years (1887–9). [Royal College of Surgeons in Ireland, Stoker Donation]*

Parker, Dehra, née Kerr-Fisher (1882–1963), politician. Born in India. In 1901 she married Lieutenant-Colonel Robert Spencer Chichester. She organised nursing units for the ULSTER VOLUNTEER FORCE during the third HOME RULE crisis, was made a member of the Order of the British Empire in 1918 for her war work, and was a vice-chairwoman of the Ulster Women's Unionist Council, 1918–30. She was also a justice of the peace and a member of Magherafelt Rural District Council and Magherafelt Board of Guardians (chairwoman, 1924–7). In 1921 she was elected Unionist MP for Londonderry in the Parliament of Northern Ireland. Widowed in 1921, she married Rear-Admiral Henry Parker in 1929 and in the same year stepped down from her parliamentary seat in favour of her son-in-law JAMES CHICHESTER-CLARK. She returned to politics following Chichester-Clark's death in 1933 and remained MP for South Londonderry until 1960. A stalwart unionist, she was Parliamentary Secretary for Education, 1937–44, and Minister of Health and Local Government, 1949–57. A capable orator with a wry wit, she was the most prominent woman MP in Northern Ireland. Made a dame commander of the Order of the British Empire in 1949, she retired from politics in June 1960 because of ill health. **Diane Urquhart**

Parker, Stewart (1941–1988), playwright. Born in Belfast; educated at QUB. Parker writes with a sense of his distinctive Northern Protestant heritage. He has written plays for radio, such as *The Iceberg* (1975), and for television, such as *Lost Belongings* (1987), a reworking of the DEIRDRE legend. He is best known for his work in theatre, especially *Northern Star* (1984), which deals with the 1798 REBELLION, and *Pentecost* (1987), his last play, commissioned by FIELD DAY, set during the ULSTER WORKERS' COUNCIL STRIKE of 1974; Parker claimed it presented a 'working model of wholeness' for a divided society. POPULAR MUSIC is an omnipresent feature of his work. **Wesley Hutchinson**

Parker type, an IRISH PRINTING TYPE. The first font of Irish type known to have been cut and cast in Ireland was that produced by the Irish Letter Foundry of Stephen Parker. It was prepared in 1787 and advertised in the *Dublin Chronicle* as 'a complete Fount of beautiful Irish Character commended by the Royal Irish Society.' It was modelled directly on a type that appeared in Paris about fifty years earlier. It was first used in 1788 for sections of the *Transactions of the Royal Irish Academy*; in the following year it was used for setting *Reliques of Irish Poetry* by CHARLOTTE BROOKE, but because of its largeness it was not widely employed for setting text. [see PARIS TYPE.] **Dermot McGuinne**

Parkinson, Siobhán (1954–), writer. Born in Dublin; educated at TCD. Her first book, *The Leprechaun Who Wished He Wasn't* (1993), bears many of the author's hallmarks: irony, an original outlook on life, an acute ear for dialogue, and a sympathy for the preoccupations of young people. She handles sensitive topics with dexterity and compassion. *All Shining in the Spring* (1995) came from her personal experience: the need to explain to her son the untimely death of his baby brother. Her novels for young adults have won acclaim. *Sisters—No Way!* (1996) is an inventive, compelling and funny flip-over book that narrates the story from the differing viewpoints of two young women thrown together by the remarriage of their parents; it was Bisto Book of the Year, 1996–7. *The Moon King* (1999), an innovative book based on an abused child's fantasy and real world, won both the Bisto Merit Award and a place on the IBBY honour list for 2000. **Patricia Donlon**

Parliament, 1200–1700. The earliest recorded parliament in Ireland was held at Castledermot, Co. Kildare, in 1264, though it was still in an embryonic state, and membership was confined to the lords; only gradually were representatives of commoners admitted. Organisation and procedure were modelled on and tended to follow English precedents. The presence of the lower clergy in what was in effect a house of their own was a distinctive feature in Ireland. By the fifteenth century the Parliament passed legislation, levied taxes and heard petitions; by 1460 it had reached a sufficient stage of self-confidence to assert that only its laws could be binding in Ireland. Its manipulation by powerful chief governors, especially the Earls of Kildare, and the support given to Yorkist pretenders, led to the enactment in 1494 of the serious limitation of its power known as POYNINGS' LAW. Under this measure, no parliament could be held in Ireland without the prior permission of the King and his Privy Council in England, and all proposed legislation had similarly to be approved in advance. The lower clergy lost their role in 1536–7, and Gaelic lords first attended in 1541.

The Catholic and overwhelmingly OLD ENGLISH domination was challenged in 1613 with the creation of forty new boroughs in Ulster, designed to boost Protestant representation. While this stratagem was successfully challenged, it was a portent of inevitable change, which became evident in the increased Protestant membership in 1634 and 1640–41. Abolished under CROMWELL, the Irish Parliament was restored in 1661–6 as a completely Protestant body, whose legislation permanently secured the CROMWELLIAN LAND SETTLEMENT in the interests of Protestant solidarity. The brief reversal to Catholic control in the JACOBITE Parliament of 1689 was permanently ended in the 1690s when the Ascendancy-dominated and exclusive character of the eighteenth-century phase was firmly established. **Liam Irwin**

Parliament, 1692–1800, the legislative authority in Ireland before the ACT OF UNION. The Irish Parliament met for the first time on 18 June 1264 at Castledermott and for the last time in the Parliament House, Dublin, on 2 August 1800. The only parliament with the medieval structure of King (represented by the Lord Lieutenant), Lords, and Commons, the Irish Parliament developed in parallel with the English Parliament, and in the eighteenth century it adjusted contemporary British practices to Irish conditions. Before 1692 its meetings were erratic and peripatetic. The Parliament (which until 1782 required all legislation to have the prior approval of the Irish and English Privy Councils) passed POYNINGS' LAW at a Parliament that met at Drogheda in 1494. Ireland did not receive its county structure or its full complement of constituencies before the Revolution of 1688. Thereafter there were 150 double-member constituencies, thirty-two counties, eight county boroughs (cities), 117 boroughs, and the University of Dublin, making a total of 300 members. By 1692 the thirty-two counties had taken on their modern form and were administrative units as well as parliamentary constituencies. Their electorate was the FORTY-SHILLING FREEHOLDERS, including those holding leases for life. If not otherwise qualified, all Protestants, regardless of denomination, were eligible throughout the century, while Catholics were ineligible from 1727 to 1793 and there is a grey area before 1727. From 1692 until after the Union no Catholic could sit in Parliament, though they could wield a certain degree of political influence through their enfranchised Protestant tenants. All eight county boroughs (Carrickfergus, Cork, Drogheda, Dublin, Galway, Kilkenny, Limerick, and Waterford) were medieval; their electors combined the characteristics of county electorates and boroughs. They were broadly based and had comparatively large electorates, and their MPs were usually closely involved with the constituency. The electorate of the 117 boroughs was restricted to members of the established church, and in 1747 an act was passed confirming that residence by burgesses was unnecessary, thereby divorcing the corporation of a town from any political participation and in many instances diminishing its social and economic development. Though towns such as Cork and, particularly, Belfast developed in spite of these restrictions, there were also landlords who built model villages and encouraged economic development—Castlewellan, Co. Down, and Monivea, Co. Galway, for example.

As corporations were self-perpetuating, even the Catholic Enfranchisement Act (1793) had little immediate effect. However, the Act of Union (1800) automatically reformed the electoral system: by disfranchising eighty-five boroughs outright, it switched its emphasis from the boroughs to the counties, with Dublin and Cork retaining two members each and the remaining county boroughs, twenty-six of the larger towns, and the University of Dublin one each. Compensation of £1.26 million was paid to those who had previously controlled the disfranchised boroughs, who genuinely regarded them as property to be bought, sold, or bequeathed.

Despite its narrow foundation, the legacy of the Irish Parliament was impressive, though its ambitions were always beyond its resources, and local jealousies made their impact on a small society. Irish Parliaments laid the foundation of the road system and oversaw and supported the construction of a CANAL system, sometimes more in expectation than to meet present need, but in the NEWRY CANAL, completed in 1741, they encouraged the construction of the first commercial canal in Ireland. They gave the first grant to education, though like later grants in Ireland and elsewhere it had the

Parnell, Charles Stewart *Floral tributes (including one from the Irish of New York) in the form of harps, a Celtic cross, and a round tower decorate the grave of Charles Stewart Parnell in Glasnevin Cemetery, Dublin. A granite boulder from his home, Avondale, Rathdrum, Co. Wicklow, now marks his grave. [Irish Picture Library]*

ulterior motive of proselytism. The Dublin Society (later ROYAL DUBLIN SOCIETY), to which many members belonged and which supported recurrent grants, held its early meetings in the committee room of the newly constructed Parliament House, while Parliament Square in TRINITY COLLEGE, Dublin, records their generosity to that institution. Social gatherings of Dublin society were held in the ROTUNDA, the proceeds going to the support of the first maternity hospital in Ireland, opened in 1745. Among the more interesting experiments was the attempt to set up the county infirmaries, while the inspectorate system, which they developed for prisons, later provided a basis for British factory and industrial legislation. They were enthusiastic town planners, and the centre of Dublin has largely remained as they planned it, and their taste is seen in many of the city's public buildings. [see ADMINISTRATIVE DIVISIONS; GEORGIAN PERIOD.] **E. M. Johnston-Liik**

Parliament Act (1911), a watershed in the constitutional relationship between the British House of Commons and House of Lords. It arose after the Conservative-dominated Lords rejected Lloyd George's 'people's budget' of 1909. The Lords' power of veto over legislation initiated in the House of Commons was reduced to a delaying power: one month in the case of money bills and two years for other bills. Its adoption meant that the House of Lords could no longer veto a HOME RULE Bill. **Thomas Hennessey**

Parliament House (1729), College Green, Dublin, designed by Sir EDWARD LOVETT PEARCE, the leading and most talented architect of Palladianism in Ireland (see p. 437). The original building of 1729 has been subsumed into a larger complex that somewhat mutes the dramatic effect and purity of Pearce's design. The Parliament House was fronted by a three-sided colonnaded Ionic piazza, behind which the bicameral legislature (the first purpose-built bicameral parliament house in the world) was located, the House of Commons chamber entered axially from the piazza, with the Lords' chamber accessed from the right-hand colonnade (see pp. 454, 863). A Corinthian portico on the east was added by JAMES GANDON in 1785 as an entrance for the Lords' chamber and a further, smaller portico created by Robert Park to the west. The curved blind quadrant screens were added by FRANCIS JOHNSTON in 1803 following the acquisition of the building by the Bank of Ireland, the ACT OF UNION having made the Parliament House redundant. The original tapestries by Jan van Beaver of the SIEGE OF DERRY and the BATTLE OF THE BOYNE still hang in the Lords' chamber. **Brian Lalor**

Párliament na mBan, an imaginative catechetical work compiled at the end of the seventeenth century by Father Dónall Ó Colmáin, parish priest of Glanmire, Co. Cork, who had been educated on the Continent. Essentially a series of sermons on the seven deadly sins and the four cardinal virtues, it is similar in both language and style to works of the Continental Catholic Reformation and the English recusants in particular, imaginatively framed within the notion of a parliament of women, convened to address the dire moral state of the nation. The opening day is taken up with procedural matters and the status of women and contains much bawdy humour, as old as Aristophanes, mediated through the *Senatulus* of Erasmus. The succeeding homiletic material is of the stock in trade of the period, rich in Biblical reference, quotations from the Fathers of the church and classical authors, and the homely everyday imagery and illustrative examples of the medieval preacher. [see MIDNIGHT COURT; PAIRLEMENT CHLOINNE TOMÁIS.] **Tadhg Ó Dúshláine**

Parnell, Catherine Maria (Anna) (1852–1911), artist and political activist. Born in Rathdrum, Co. Wicklow, a sister of CHARLES STEWART PARNELL; educated by governesses and at the Royal Hibernian Academy of Art. From 1877 to 1880 she worked in the United States for the LAND LEAGUE and Famine Relief Fund.

From January 1881 to August 1882 she took charge of the LADIES' LAND LEAGUE in Ireland. From 1882 she lived mainly in England, where she wrote *The Tale of a Great Sham*, a searing indictment of the Land League. She died in a drowning accident in Devon. **Dana Hearne**

Parnell, Charles Stewart (1846–1891), statesman. Born at Rathdrum, Co. Wicklow, the seventh child of John Henry Parnell and Delia Tudor Stewart (daughter of an American naval hero, Commodore Charles Stewart). After three-and-a-half undistinguished years at Magdalene College, Cambridge, Parnell for a period lived the life of a member of the Wicklow gentry. In 1874, at the age of twenty-seven, he abruptly resolved to enter HOME RULE politics and was elected for Meath the following year. Mastering a somewhat faltering and diffident manner, he came rapidly to prominence. In the House of Commons he was the most coldly provoking of the 'Obstructionists'. In Ireland he gathered together a broad nationalist coalition, which extended to supporters of the LAND LEAGUE and the more enlightened Fenians (the 'New Departure'). He was elected leader of the IRISH PARTY in May 1880.

As he emerged from six months' imprisonment in KILMAINHAM GAOL, Dublin, in May 1882, his strategy was shaken by the PHOENIX PARK MURDERS. He raised the Irish question to a pitch that led Gladstone to introduce the first Home Rule Bill in 1886. At the Special Commission in 1889 the letters to the *Times* implicating Parnell in the Phoenix Park murders were shown to have been forged by Richard Pigott.

The O'Shea divorce case opened the last act of Parnell's life. Repudiated by GLADSTONE and deserted by a majority of the Irish Party, he fought furiously to reassert his leadership. The exhausting pace of the campaign in Ireland taxed his fragile constitution. Parnell, whom James Joyce was to characterise as 'strong to the verge of weakness,' fought on. In June he married KATHARINE O'SHEA, with whom he already had three daughters. He died at Brighton on 6 October 1891 at the age of forty-five. **Frank Callanan**

Parnell, Frances (Fanny) (1848–1882), poet, political writer, and activist. Born in Rathdrum, Co. Wicklow, a sister of CHARLES STEWART PARNELL; educated by governesses. From 1869 to 1874 she lived in Paris. In 1874 she went with her mother to live on the Stewart estate in Bordentown, New Jersey. In 1880 she wrote *The Hovels of Ireland*, a scathing attack on the Irish landed gentry. She worked for the Famine Relief Fund in New York. In October 1880 she set up the first branch of the Ladies' Irish National LAND LEAGUE in New York. **Dana Hearne**

Parnell, Thomas (1679–1718), clergyman and poet. Born in Dublin; educated at TCD. He was appointed Archdeacon of Clogher in 1706 and Vicar of Finglas in 1716. A frequent visitor to London, he became a member of the Scriblerus Club and was friendly with JONATHAN SWIFT and with Alexander Pope, who edited his poems for publication after his death. Parnell translated Homer's 'Battle of the Frogs and Mice' and wrote satires and devotional poetry. He is remembered today primarily for his poetic 'Essay on the Different Stiles of Poetry' and for some entertaining occasional verse. **Andrew Carpenter**

Parsons, Hon. Charles Algernon (1854–1931), engineer and scientist. Born in London, son of WILLIAM PARSONS, THIRD EARL OF ROSSE; educated by tutors at BIRR CASTLE, at TCD, and the University of Cambridge, and apprenticed at the Elswick Works of Sir W. G. Armstrong at Newcastle-upon-Tyne. He joined Clarke Chapman as a partner in 1884, patenting the world's first steam-turbine-driven ELECTRICITY generator. He established his own company in 1889 to push turbine development more aggressively, initially for electricity supply. In 1897, after four years' research, he demonstrated the potential of steam turbines for ship propulsion with his *Turbinia* at the Spithead Naval Review. In 1905 the Royal Navy adopted turbines for its future warships, an example followed by navies from the United States to Japan. The two 35,000 HP turbines of the Cunard liner *Mauretania* (1907) were the largest in existence, and it held the Blue Riband for the speediest Atlantic crossing until 1929. He ran several successful businesses, licensing others to use his patents but avoiding costly litigation, which ruined many inventors. He inherited from his father an interest in optical instruments. From 1890 he supplied most of the moulded mirrors used in searchlights. In 1921 he acquired the optical instrument manufacturer Ross Ltd and the Derby Crown Glass Company. In 1925 the firm of HOWARD GRUBB, which made large astronomical TELESCOPES, was rescued from insolvency by him. Not all projects were commercially profitable, such as his acoustic amplifier and attempts at synthesising diamonds, which absorbed much effort. In the development of his many inventions he displayed physical courage, great determination in the face of reverses, and always a meticulously scientific approach. He was elected a fellow of the Royal Society in 1898, knighted in 1911, and in 1927 was the first engineer to be awarded the Order of Merit. **W. Garrett Scaife**

Parsons, Sir Laurence, second Earl of Rosse (1758–1841), politician in GRATTAN'S PARLIAMENT. A disciple of HENRY FLOOD, for whose legacy to establish the first chair of Irish at TRINITY COLLEGE, Dublin, he had to fight as executor. He pursued a fiercely independent line in Parliament, 1782–90; his denouncement of government corruption, English ministers' view of the Irish, and Irish nationhood generally influenced WOLFE TONE, who later referred to him as 'one of the very, very few honest men in the Irish House of Commons.' His strong opposition to corruption led him to expose the bribery used to push through the ACT OF UNION, which he vehemently opposed, as well as to refuse a knighthood, which he was offered as an inducement to support the government. His later appointment as Joint Postmaster-General of Ireland ironically led to the building of the edifice where the realisation of Irish nationhood was to be eventually proclaimed (the GPO). **Lord Rosse**

Parsons, Laurence, fourth Earl of Rosse (1840–1908), astronomer. Both the 72-inch and the smaller TELESCOPE at Birr were somewhat unwieldy, without any mechanism to drive them. He devised and built a water clock to drive the smaller and later a mechanism for driving the 72-inch, though the latter's mounting made it more difficult to operate. He therefore concentrated on the smaller 36-inch telescope, which he developed with an independent observer's bucket. Although this worked so well that it became accepted as standard practice, it is essentially for measuring the heat of the Moon that he is best known. He built an instrument on which the 36-inch telescope could focus the lunar radiation and produced temperature graphs whose accuracy was recognised only long after his death. **Lord Rosse**

Parsons, Mary (née Field), Countess of Rosse (1813–1885), photographer. Born in Yorkshire. She married WILLIAM PARSONS, and at BIRR CASTLE from 1836 she embarked on a vigorous scheme of remodelling and extending parts of the building. In 1854 she took up PHOTOGRAPHY, experimenting with new techniques and creating what is believed to be the oldest surviving darkroom in the world. The darkroom at the castle, little altered since she left it, has acted as a time capsule, preserving the equipment used in the early days of the photographic process (see p. 870). **Susan McKenna-Lawlor**

Parsons, William, third Earl of Rosse (1800–1867), astronomer. In the 1840s he designed and built a TELESCOPE with a reflector of 72 inches, which was then, and was to remain for more than seventy years, the largest in the world. The engineering feat was considerable, as he had to design and make everything himself, from the giant reflector, whose ideal alloy he had first to work out, to the foundry he set up in the bottom of the moat to cast it in and the huge ingenious machine he then had to invent to polish it. When completed, the telescope was able to gather more light, and hence to see further into space, than had ever been possible before. With its immense light grasp it was able to show the star systems or galaxies in detail. This enabled him to make what was perhaps his most fundamental discovery: that many of the galaxies were spiral in shape. He published all his discoveries and freely shared his knowledge with all those who came to Birr to see so far into space. **Lord Rosse**

partition, the process and the result of dividing Ireland into two distinct political entities in 1920. Since the ACT OF UNION (1800), resistance to demands for Irish self-government had been fiercest among Ulster unionists. Partition had been dismissed as unworkable, but by 1914 discussions centred on the exact area to be excluded from HOME RULE and the question of its permanence. Proposals to exclude Ulster's entire nine counties were discarded following the Government of Ireland Act (1920), which established devolved governments in Northern and Southern Ireland, the former consisting of six counties separated by a 499 km (310-mile) boundary from the remaining twenty-six. The ANGLO-IRISH TREATY recognised Northern Ireland and the new Irish Free State, pending a decision by a BOUNDARY COMMISSION, which was expected to transfer territory to the South. However, the commission's limited findings were suppressed in 1925, leaving the BORDER unaltered. Partition had become entrenched earlier by a customs barrier in 1923, and the CONSTITUTION OF IRELAND (1937) restated territorial claims by the South. Division was deepened later by the declaration of a republic (1948) and by the Ireland Act (1949), which guaranteed the North's constitutional position in the United Kingdom. Both smuggling and paramilitary activity have demonstrated the border's porosity. Particularly after 1969, it was a symbol of the evil of partition to nationalists and of the integrity of the United Kingdom to unionists. However, it lost some practical significance within the context of European integration and since the BELFAST AGREEMENT (1998) has assumed more of a constitutional than a territorial dimension. The territorial claims by the Republic were replaced with aspirations to unity by the referendum of 1998. **K. J. Rankin**

Partnership for Peace (PFP), a security programme that was launched in 1994, the aim of which is to promote peace and stability in Europe through co-operation and common action. The PFP process expands and intensifies political and military co-operation throughout Europe, thereby increasing stability, which in turn diminishes threats to peace and builds strengthened relationships by promoting a spirit of practical co-operation and commitment to democratic principles. There are forty-five member-states in the partnership. These consist of the nineteen NATO members and twenty-six partner countries. The partnership succeeds in drawing

Parsons, Charles. *The* Turbina, *Charles Parsons' first experimental steam-turbine vessel, launched on 2 August 1894, photographed by Alfred J. West, slicing through the North Sea at 65 km/h (35 knots). [Irish Picture Library]*

together the countries of the Euro-Atlantic and Euro-Asia in one organisation working together. Membership includes Russia, all the former Soviet Republics, the former Warsaw Pact countries, and all the major European neutrals, Switzerland, Austria, Finland, Sweden, and Ireland. On 1 December 1999 Ireland joined the PFP and the European Atlantic Partnership Council, which is the political roof of the organisation. The Irish Government sees the PFP as having a significant role to play in co-operation and planning for UN-authorised Petersberg tasks. Joining the PFP enhanced Ireland's ability to contribute to future Petersberg Task missions, particularly in the areas of peacekeeping, humanitarian operations, search and rescue operations, co-operation in environmental protection, and marine matters. **Paul Connors**

partnerships. Since the late 1980s there has been a shift away from traditional models of hierarchical government to more flexible forms of regulation that stress facilitative governance. This involves partnership between public-sector organisations and private business, with an increasing role being provided for third-sector civic society groups. In the partnership approach, the quest for national and local development and social welfare is no longer viewed as a matter for governments or their subordinate agencies alone: instead it is increasingly seen as a collaborative effort involving new and flexible political, administrative, and participatory arrangements involving a range of options, such as public-private partnerships and, more recently, tripartite public-private-civic society partnerships.

The Irish Government has pursued a consensus (partnership) approach to national development since 1987, when it agreed the Programme for National Recovery with what are now called the social partners (originally confined to representatives of the main employer groups, the TRADE UNIONS, and other important economic interest groups). National partnership agreements have underpinned all subsequent national development programmes. Each subsequent national programme has been tailored both to building on the economic dimensions of the preceding programme and to fitting EU policy requirements (particularly in the areas of competition and social policy). The later national partnerships have built on the earlier programmes by broadening both the focus and the representation of the partnership model at both national and local levels. From the mid-1990s onwards a range of local area-based partnership initiatives has been introduced that have combined targeted economic and social objectives with increased representation from civic society. **Brendan Bartley**

party system. The Republic has a multi-party system. The mould of the party system was set in the period 1916–23. Rooted in the conflict over the ANGLO-IRISH TREATY (1921) and in the CIVIL WAR that ensued, the now residual differences between FIANNA FÁIL and FINE GAEL reflect different approaches to the nationalist agenda. The struggle for independence and the nature of the secession that occurred sidelined left-right issues and contributed to the minority status of the LABOUR PARTY and to the ease with which, at different times, each of the two main parties has allied itself with the Labour Party while at the same time competing with it for votes. By creating a state that was highly homogeneous in religion, PARTITION also meant that issues related to religion and church-state relations found little or no place in the party system.

Change in this inherited party system has been inexorable but gradual. Despite the efforts and expectations of the Labour Party on the centre-left and the PROGRESSIVE DEMOCRATS on the centre-right, the mould has neither been broken nor replaced by an alternative alignment; instead it has worn thin, the thinness being manifest in declining rates of party attachment among voters and in reduced policy differences between the parties. The exigencies of coalition reinforce a process in which competition between parties has more to do with performance, with leadership, and with candidates in the constituencies than with ideological or other cleavages. In order of size of vote in the general election of 2002 the party strengths were: Fianna Fáil 41.5 per cent, Fine Gael 22.5 per cent, Labour Party 10.8 per cent, SINN FÉIN 6.5 per cent, Progressive Democrats 4 per cent, and GREEN PARTY 3.9 per cent. **Richard Sinnott**

Paschal controversy: see EASTER CONTROVERSY.

passage tombs. The Irish passage tombs are among the most elaborate and the most spectacular MEGALITHIC TOMBS in Europe. The characteristic element of these monuments is a round mound, usually surrounded by a kerb of large stones, enclosing a burial chamber that is entered through a passage. The tombs vary from simple sites with circular or polygonal chambers to elaborate monuments with long passages and multiple burial chambers. Many have side and end recesses opening off a central chamber, resulting in a cruciform plan. The passages are generally roofed with horizontal lintels, whereas the chambers are often surmounted by corbelled vaults, which in some instances (such as at NEWGRANGE and KNOWTH) can be quite elaborate.

Unlike the other tomb types, passage tombs are usually found in groups or *cemeteries*, and many are situated in prominent positions on hilltops or ridges. There are four major cemeteries in Ireland: the BOYNE VALLEY and LOUGHCREW in Co. Meath, and CARROWMORE and CARROWKEEL in Co. Sligo. It is difficult to estimate the total number of passage tombs in the country, as there are many unopened round hilltop cairns and it is possible that some of these may contain tombs. Some 236 probable or definite sites have been recorded; their distribution is mostly confined to the northern and eastern parts of the country, and almost half occur within the four major cemeteries. The orientation of the tombs varies, though many sites face in an easterly direction.

A distinctive feature of a number of tombs is the presence of incised or picked ornament on many of the stones, both internally and externally. This megalithic 'art' is non-representational or abstract in form and includes curvilinear and angular designs, with

passage tombs. *Kerbstone 5 at Knowth passage tomb in the Boyne Valley, Co. Meath. The spiral with flanking crescent designs as well as the sequence of smaller circular markings above, may depict phases of the moon. [Dúchas, The Heritage Service]* circles, spirals, arcs, serpentiform lines, lozenges, and triangles being the more common motifs. Sometimes they appear to have been carved at random on the surface of the stones, while others were placed in positions that were hidden as soon as the structures were completed. In a number of tombs they are combined in elegant designs ingeniously adapted to the shape of the stones, and within the Brú na Bóinne cemetery in particular the style achieves a visual grandeur that appears to have been intentionally created to enhance the architectural impact of the monuments. At Knowth certain designs were confined to different parts of the tomb. There is no simple code that will explain the meaning of this megalithic art but, like ROCK ART, it clearly had a sacred and ritual significance.

Cremation was the predominant practice in passage tombs, and the remains were often placed in large stone basins accompanied by personal ornaments, such as beads, pendants, bone and antler pins, enigmatic stone and chalk balls, and a special type of round-bottomed pottery named *Carrowkeel ware*, after one of the four cemeteries. The grave-goods of the Irish passage tombs seem to be distinctively native, and yet the architecture shares many structural and artistic characteristics with the broad family of similar graves of Continental Europe, especially those in Iberia and Brittany. Some of the simpler tombs in the west at Carrowmore have produced radiocarbon dates suggesting use in the early fourth millennium BC, but the high point of the passage tomb tradition at Brú na Bóinne is generally dated to the centuries just before 3000 BC. **Paul Walsh**

Pastorini: see RIBBONMEN.

patchwork. Though patchwork has been made in Ireland since the eighteenth century, it was mostly produced during the nineteenth century, when, with EMBROIDERY and dressmaking, it formed part of the curriculum for girls in national schools. Surviving patchwork bed-covers reflect the quality and diversity of Irish silks, cottons and poplins and also the ingenuity and thrift of poorer households, where remnants, including even flour bags, were routinely recycled. The shirt-making industries of Belfast and Derry and the regional preference for Turkey red flannel provided the basis for many pieced bed-covers.

The craft almost disappeared after the 1920s, when mass-produced bedding became widely available. The KILKENNY DESIGN WORKSHOPS rekindled interest through a touring exhibition of Irish patchwork in 1979; this led to the establishment of many patchwork guilds and international recognition for contemporary patchwork-makers, such as Irene MacWilliam of Belfast, Rita Scannell of Cork, and Evelyn Montague of France, working in Ireland since 1972. **Valerie Wilson**

Patrick, bishop and missionary. He lived probably in the fifth century; our information about him comes entirely from his two short writings in Latin, and the temptation to use seventh-century and later HAGIOGRAPHY to fill this out should be avoided. Patrick tells us that he came from Britain, the son of rural Roman gentry who were also clergy, and was captured and taken into slavery in Ireland. After six years he escaped, and later he believed himself called to evangelise the Irish. He tells us of his mission in Ireland, of opposition from other Christians, presumably in Britain, and of his views of his work and its success. We have no dates, but the later fifth century would fit all the evidence. The traditional arrival date (since the seventh century) of 432 is an attempt to integrate his mission with the dated mission of Palladius in 431. Patrick implies that CHRISTIANITY arrived in Ireland only with his mission; however, we know that there were already Christian communities before then, so he probably worked in regions not yet touched by Christianity. While later tradition would see him as the sole apostle of the Irish, he perceived himself as the final Christian preacher, whose proclamation at the earth's end would usher in the Last Days. His date of death, 17 March, is attested from the seventh century, and this is evidence that he established a viable community that preserved his memory as their founder.

While we know little of Patrick's life, we know more about him than about any other person from Ireland or Britain at the period, and he is the only ancient captive who escaped and whose story has survived. Later sources link him with Armagh, but this reflects seventh-century concerns rather than his own time, and it is from that later situation that his cult as the sole missionary belongs. Since then his memory has become an important element in forming an Irish cultural identity and has been reconstructed for different groups. In the post-REFORMATION period it became disputed ground between various Christian denominations (see pp. 255, 959). [see CONFESSIO; ST PATRICK'S DAY; ST PATRICK'S DAY AND THE DIASPORA.] **Thomas O'Loughlin**

Patrick. *Medieval stonecarving of the saint with mitre, book, and staff, trampling on a snake, at the well named after him, Patrickswell, Co. Limerick. [Bord Fáilte]*

'Patriots' (eighteenth century), a name given to the minority of Irish Protestants who combined the principles and convictions of civic humanism, which placed a weighty emphasis on political virtue and improvement, of Protestantism, and of Whiggery, as enshrined in the 'Glorious Revolution'. The main popularisers of that ideology in Ireland in the late seventeenth and early eighteenth centuries were WILLIAM MOLYNEUX and JONATHAN SWIFT; its primary spokesmen during the mid-eighteenth century and later were CHARLES LUCAS, HENRY FLOOD, and HENRY GRATTAN. **James Kelly**

pattern (from 'patron'), a vernacular religious and secular assembly on the day designated for commemorating the patron saint of an area. A ceremony takes place around a holy well (of which there are thought to be about 3,000 in Ireland), where pilgrims do 'rounds' (*deiseal* or sunwise circumambulations of the Stations of the Cross) for special intentions or seek a cure in the waters by applying it to the body or drinking it, while reciting a mixture of traditional and formal prayers. Patterns were formerly marked by a combination of demonstrative religion and intense celebrations. **Stiofán Ó Cadhla**

Patterson, Annie (1868–1934), activist, composer and, academic. Born in Lurgan, she studied at the RIAM and was the first music graduate of the Royal University. Her concern for the

'peace lines'. *Peace lines at Short Strand in east Belfast, built to separate nationalist and loyalist areas, a compelling image of a divided community. [Frankie Quinn]*

wellbeing of traditional music led her to co-found both the FEIS CEOIL and AN TOIREACHTAS. She became organist at St Anne's, Shandon, in Cork and lecturer in Irish music at UCC, 1924–34. Her compositions include three operas. [see MARTYN, EDWARD.] **Richard Pine**

Patterson, Francis (Frank) (1938–2000), singer. Born in Clonmel, Co. Tipperary; studied singing in Dublin with HANS WALDEMAR ROSEN. A prizewinner at Dublin FEIS CEOIL, he travelled to London, the Netherlands, and Paris, where he studied with Janine Micheau. He performed as a soloist with the principal orchestras of Ireland, Continental Europe, and the United States. Particularly acclaimed as an evangelist in performances of Bach, he made a total of thirty-six recordings in six languages. He received numerous awards, including the knighthood of St Gregory and honorary doctorates (see p. 751). **Ite O'Donovan**

Patterson, Glenn (1961–), novelist. Born in Belfast, where he returned after living in England, and was writer in residence at Queen's University, where he teaches creative writing. He has published four novels: *Burning Your Own* (1988), following which he was awarded the Rooney Prize for Irish Literature, *Fat Lad* (1992), *Black Night at Big Thunder Mountain* (1995), and *The International* (1999). His fiction notably avoids received wisdom on the 'TROUBLES' and proffers, through his often misfit characters, imaginative possibilities of alternative ways of life and feelings. Patterson is at the forefront in developing a securely urban consciousness in Northern fiction and is widely credited with providing the most accurate and compassionate portraits of modern Belfast. **Aaron Kelly**

Patterson, Ottilie (1932–), jazz musician. Born in Newtownards, Co. Down; trained as an art teacher in Belfast. She became the singer with Chris Barber's Jazz Band in 1955 when the band was a leading representative of the British jazz revival. With an alto range and a blues-belter style based on Bessie Smith, she particularly suited Barber's band, which went under the title 'jazz and blues band' for a time. Barber and Patterson had some commercial success with singles but nothing like that enjoyed by the band from 1959 and 'Petite Fleur' onwards with Monty Sunshine (clarinet) as soloist. She recorded with the blues legend Sonny Boy Williamson in 1963. **Brian Trench**

Paulin, Tom (1949–), poet and critic. Born in Leeds, raised in Belfast; educated at Hull and Oxford. He taught at the University of Nottingham and is now G. M. Young lecturer at Hertford College, Oxford. He made frequent appearances on television discussion programmes. His eight books of poetry include *Selected Poems, 1972–1990*, *The Wind Dog* (1999), and *The Invasion Handbook* (2002). A former director of FIELD DAY, he has adapted plays by Sophocles and Aeschylus, edited two poetry anthologies, and written studies of Thomas Hardy and William Hazlitt and three collections of critical essays. An acerbic, morally earnest political poet, he frequently deploys Ulster dialect in stark, linguistically surprising lyric evocations of Northern culture. **Jonathan Allison**

'peace lines', a name given in Northern Ireland to walls specifically erected in order to separate neighbouring Protestant and Catholic communities with a history of sectarian conflict. The term was coined in 1969 by the British army to describe the position it had taken up between the Falls Road and Shankill Road, Belfast, and then came to be applied to the barriers erected following further rioting. In most instances these walls replaced street barricades built by local communities.

The first walls were constructed primarily of corrugated metal sheets and barbed wire. While they were meant to be provisional, continuing episodes of violence created a situation of long-term conflict, which was tackled by the British government in the form of increasingly fortified and landscaped structures. The peace lines were financed and built under the authority of the Security Policy and Operations Division of the Northern Ireland Office and by other agencies, such as the NORTHERN IRELAND HOUSING EXECUTIVE, often in consultation with the Police Service and community groups.

Fifteen districts in Belfast are divided by peace lines. While these are primarily in the inner city and feature semi-permanent walls, there are examples both outside Belfast and of temporary usage. There is a peace line in Derry, between the Fountain and Bogside areas; and similar barriers have also been used at the Lower Ormeau Road, Belfast, and in Portadown, as a result of the civil disturbances connected with the annual parades of the ORANGE ORDER. **Margrethe Lauber**

Peace People, a movement that grew out of the emotional response to the death of the three Maguire children in Belfast on 10 August 1976, killed by a PROVISIONAL IRA getaway car that was being chased by the security forces. Two local women, Mairead Corrigan (the children's aunt) and Betty Williams, and a journalist, Ciarán McKeown, founded the movement, which sponsored a series of massive rallies in Northern Ireland and elsewhere, characterised by a high level of cross-community support, especially among women. Corrigan and Williams were awarded the 1976 NOBEL PEACE PRIZE. The organisation's declared character as a 'non-violent movement towards a just and peaceful society' embodied a reaction against both republican and loyalist violence as well as an implicit rejection of traditional nationalist and unionist party politics. The mass popular support of the early days fell away as the movement struggled to transform itself into a more activist organisation. While the other two founders left the movement, Mairéad Corrigan (Corrigan-Maguire after her marriage in 1981) remained active in an organisation that continues to work with peace-oriented community groups and schemes bringing together Catholic and Protestant young people. [see NOBEL PRIZE; NORTHERN IRELAND PEACE PROCESS.] **Keith Jeffery**

Peacock, Joseph (c. 1783–1837), artist. Nothing is known about his training, but from 1809 he was exhibiting in Dublin, and he was a founder-member of the ROYAL HIBERNIAN ACADEMY. He painted a few portraits but is best known for his genre scenes, particularly those such as *Donnybrook Fair* and *The Patron, or Festival of St Kevin at the Seven Churches, Glendalough* (1813), now in the ULSTER MUSEUM. The latter is a very lively picture, full of contrasts, from the tent full of the gentry having refreshments to the scene in

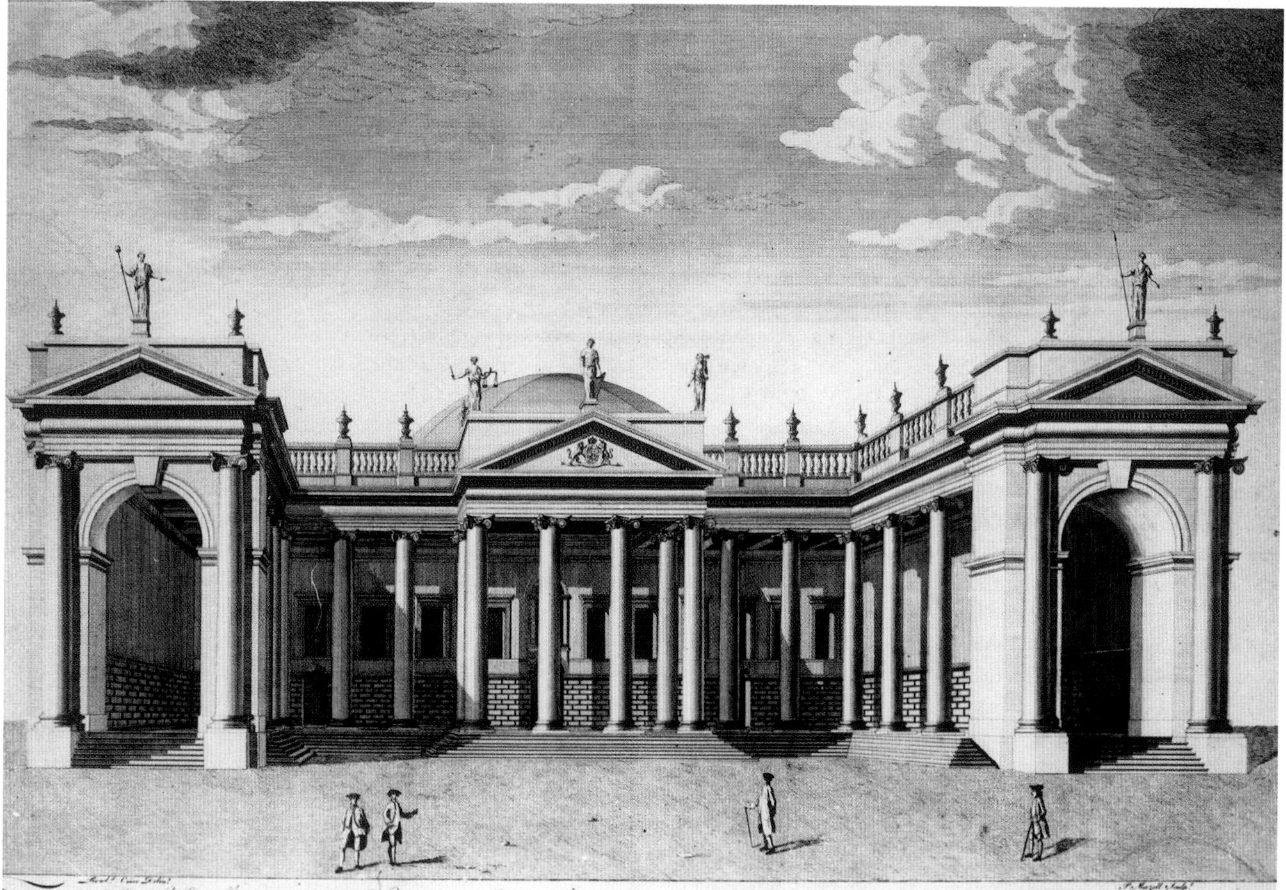

Pearce, Edward Lovett. *Dublin's first great Palladian building, the Parliament House in College Green (now the Bank of Ireland), designed by Sir Edward Lovett Pearce, 1728–39, in an engraving published by Bernard Scalé, 1767. [Irish Architectural Archive]*

Pearse, Patrick. *c. 1905, showing (back row, from left) William Pearse, Henry Clifton, Patrick Pearse, E. Ní Niocoil, Mr Geoghegan, (front row) Edward Sheridan, Professor Mary Hayen, Mrs Sheridan, Mrs Geoghegan. [Pearse Museum, Dublin]*

the background of a faction fight; there are dealers selling hardware, pottery, toys, and hats, and a blind fiddler playing for a singer selling broadsheets, all seen against the mountainous background of Glendalough with its ROUND TOWER. **Anne Crookshank**

Pearce, Colman (1938–), conductor and composer. Born in Dublin; following his music degree at UCD he studied conducting in Hilversum and Vienna. He was principal conductor of the RTÉ Symphony Orchestra, 1981–3, principal guest conductor of the Bilbao Symphony Orchestra, 1984–7, and principal conductor and music director of the Mississippi Symphony Orchestra, 1987–99, and is now staff conductor with the NATIONAL SYMPHONY ORCHESTRA of Ireland. In the 1970s he formed the chamber group Ulysses Ensemble with whom he gave many concerts at 'Summer Music at Carroll's' of which he was music director. He has recorded many works by Irish composers for the Marco Polo label. His own compositions include the song cycle *Summerfest* (1993), *Robinson the Cat* (1998), and *Anagram for Chamber Ensemble* (2000). **Michael Murphy**

Pearce, Sir Edward Lovett (c. 1699–1733), architect. The son of a major-general in the British army who was a first cousin of Sir John Vanbrugh, architect of Blenheim Palace, Oxfordshire, he received a commission as captain in a regiment of dragoons, and in 1723–4 he travelled in Italy and France, studying architecture and annotating his copy of Palladio's *I Quattro Libri*. He may have studied architecture with Vanbrugh, whose drawings Pearce acquired after his cousin's death. Pearce's drawings indicate that he made a number of designs for English clients. By 1726 he was established in Dublin, and the following year he was elected MP for Ratoath. In 1730 he succeeded Thomas Burgh as Surveyor-General and in 1732 received a knighthood.

With the PARLIAMENT HOUSE in College Green, begun 1729 (now the Bank of Ireland), Pearce was responsible for designing Dublin's first great Palladian building; other works include BELLAMONT FOREST, Cootehill, Co. Cavan, Cashel Palace, Cashel, Co. Tipperary, and numbers 9–12 Henrietta Street, Dublin. His style owes little to Vanbrugh's baroque and leans more towards the Palladianism of Lord Burlington, in whose circle he associated in London. His early death was a great loss to Irish architecture. **Patricia McCarthy**

Pearse, Patrick (1879–1916), revolutionary, writer, and educator. Born in Dublin; educated at RUI and called to the bar, but did not practise. He had a deep interest in Irish culture, language, and history. He joined the GAELIC LEAGUE and became editor of its paper, AN CLAIDHEAMH SOLUIS, advocating a revival of IRISH LANGUAGE and culture. He founded the bilingual school Scoil Éanna (St Enda's) at Rathfarnham, Co. Dublin, in 1908. He published a number of works in Irish and English and became widely known as a visionary speaker, especially for his eulogy for JEREMIAH O'DONOVAN ROSSA in 1915. He joined the IRB in 1913, serving on its Supreme Council, and was director of military organisation of the IRISH VOLUNTEERS. During the 1916 RISING he served as commander-in-chief of insurgent forces and as president of the PROVISIONAL GOVERNMENT. He was shot by firing squad in KILMAINHAM GAOL on 3 May 1916 (see p. 897). **Seán Farrell Moran**

Pearse, William (1881–1916), sculptor, teacher, and revolutionary. Born in Dublin, younger and devoted brother of PATRICK PEARSE; educated at the Metropolitan School of Art, where he studied under OLIVER SHEPPARD. A close ally of his brother in the founding of St Enda's School in 1908, he taught art and produced and acted in school plays. Small expressionist figure-sculptures by him are in the Pearse Museum, Rathfarnham, Co. Dublin, and St Andrew's Church, Westland Row, Dublin. He was with his brother in the GPO during the 1916 RISING and was shot by firing squad in KILMAINHAM GAOL on 4 May. **Patrick Cooke**

Pearson Collection. Since the late 1970s the conservationist, artist, and writer Peter Pearson (1955–), born in Dún Laoghaire, Co. Dublin, while actively campaigning against the demolition of historic buildings in Dublin and around Ireland, amassed a collection of architectural artefacts and other material from the eighteenth, nineteenth and early twentieth centuries. There are thousands of individual items, ranging from woodwork, plasterwork, ironwork, and bricks to period shop-fronts. They form an invaluable index to the building skills and anonymous craftsmanship of their periods. Such fragments are often all that is left of important buildings, such as Frascati House, Blackrock, Co. Dublin, the childhood home of EDWARD FITZGERALD. It is important to Pearson that the collection reflects the circumstances in which it has evolved: for example, blackened plaster medallions embody the gradual process of dereliction, fire and finally demolition of the late eighteenth-century Rosemount House, Clonskeagh, Dublin, in 1984. In addition Pearson has also collected thousands of paper ephemera, such as bill-heads and heterogeneous everyday articles.

It is ironic that this collection, which preserves significant cultural heritage, has itself developed through individual effort, without state support. The collection is being fully catalogued but at presents exists mostly in storage. Pearson's long-term plan is to see his collection permanently housed and publicly displayed. Pearson's publications include *The Heart of Dublin* (2000) and *Between the Mountains and the Sea* (1998). **Sarah Durcan**

peasant society. Peasants have been defined as 'persons who, owning or controlling land and resources, produce primarily agricultural crops for their own subsistence, but who also produce a surplus product, a portion of which is appropriated, directly or indirectly, by representatives of a larger economic system.' While scholars have applied the term to agricultural populations in various parts of the world over several thousand years, its application to Ireland has been largely confined to the period from the seventeenth to the twentieth century. Though there is a substantial literature on the history of the Irish land system, and though the term 'peasant' has been sporadically used, systematic application of the comparative literature on peasants has been limited.

The term has been applied to the hierarchically organised rural society of 1700–1845, with its great estate (or BIG HOUSE) at the top and beneath it, in descending order, agents or middlemen, wealthy tenant farmers, small farmers, cottiers and casual day-labourers, and defines peasants as 'a class ... of small producers on land who, with the help of simple equipment and the labour of their own families, produce mainly for their own consumption, and for the fulfilment of their duties to the holders of political and economic power.' Literary sources provide an insight into landlordism, the lives of the peasantry, and agrarian secret societies and sees the end of the cottier system in the 'thrust towards modernity.'

Ireland can be seen as very much a part of the enormous transformation resulting from the rise of world capitalism and the impact of modernisation generally on peasant societies, the nature of peasant collective action, including obstacles to and facilitators of such action, and the variations in type of peasant systems, including class differences. The impressive succession of regional movements punctuating every decade between 1760 and 1840 indicates the capacity of Irish peasants for effective political action without external assistance and the evolution from family-size tenancies to family farms and a variant of ranch-style units and, regarding the potential for conflict between poorer and middle peasants, suggests that there is a significant difference between the pre-famine and post-famine situations.

A debate on the applicability of a 'peasant model' sprang up around reappraisals of the anthropological work of Arensberg and Kimball in Co. Clare, hinging on interpretations of the degree of local autonomy that small farmers retained and the degree to which and point at which their economy and culture were drawn into the expanding world of market relations. The 'peasant model' has been characterised as involving a subsistence family economy, stem family arrangements and a highly localised cultural and co-operative system, and Hannan has argued that only a 'peasant model' could 'adequately represent or help to explain the complexities of small farm community life' in the west of Ireland in the 1920s and 30s. Hannan underemphasised the degree to which Irish farmers were sensitive to the market: the farmer of the west of Ireland was 'to a considerable degree influenced by external market forces,' while nevertheless retaining important local survival strategies. A steady process of social differentiation (class formation) was taking place with the disappearance of the smallest land-holdings, and, he believed, family-labour farms showed considerable resilience and persistence. **Séamas Ó Síocháin**

peat-fired locomotives. Lack of native coal supplies and in particular the severe shortages of the war years, 1939–45, led O. V. S. Bulleid, who became chief mechanical engineer of CIÉ in 1949, to experiment with a peat-burning main-line locomotive. It operated for some time on goods trains on the Cork line, but with Bulleid's departure in 1958 and the changeover to diesel power the project lapsed. BORD NA MÓNA introduced three turf-burning locomotives in 1949 on their extensive bog system, but they proved uneconomical and were withdrawn, though one survives in operational order at Stradbally, Co. Laois. **Bernard Share**

peatland conservation. With their connotations of poverty, Ireland's BOGS were long seen at best as a source of fuel, at worst as a blight. By the mid-1980s, 30 km^2 ($11\frac{1}{2}$ sq. miles) of bog were disappearing annually, mainly from the mechanised cutting of peat for domestic fuel and electricity generation. Consequently, only 2,200 km^2 (850 sq. miles) of an original 11,788 km^2 (4,550 sq. miles) of peatland remain undisturbed, of which only 270 km^2 (104 sq. miles) are legally protected. Each year 4 million tonnes of milled peat is produced for ELECTRICITY generation, domestic heating and horticultural compost.

However, peatlands are increasingly recognised as a priceless cultural-environmental inheritance, a defining element of Ireland's natural ENVIRONMENT. Increased environmental awareness and exposure through TOURISM, amid changing agricultural and energy demands, have transformed peatlands into natural assets that improve the more nature is left unimpeded. Peatlands are now afforded protection under the Wildlife Act (1976) and the Flora Protection Order (1987). Between 1982 and 1991 'areas of scientific interest' were identified by the NATIONAL PARKS and Wildlife Service, and a survey in 1992 identified 'natural heritage areas', to be afforded legal status. However, a peatland conservation strategy did not emerge. With degradation worsening, the IRISH PEATLAND CONSERVATION COUNCIL was formed in 1982 to protect remaining peatlands through habitat and wildlife conservation and education.

Ireland retains the largest growing peatlands in Europe, their importance recognised in the European Parliament resolution of 1983 on the Protection of Irish Bogs. In 1992 the EU Habitats Directive identified 176 peatlands in Ireland that will form part of 'Natura 2000', a European network of special areas of conservation. **Colman Gallagher**

Pecherin, Vladimir (1807–1885), Redemptorist priest. Born in Ukraine; he converted from Orthodoxy to Catholicism and was ordained in 1843, spending many years preaching parish missions in England and Ireland. In 1855, during a mission at Kingstown (Dún Laoghaire), he presided over the burning of 'evil' books. A group of Protestants, led by a Methodist minister, alleged that he had burned a Bible in the pyre, for which he was brought to trial but sensationally acquitted. **James H. Murphy**

Peel, Sir Robert (1788–1850), politician. Born in Lancashire; educated at the University of Oxford. He was Tory MP for Cashel in 1809 before moving to an English seat. Chief Secretary for Ireland, 1812–18, he was Home Secretary, 1822–30, and Leader of the House of Commons, 1828–30; he served as Prime Minister, 1834–5 and 1841–6. He combined coercion of nationalists with conciliating of moderate Irish opinion, and responded to the GREAT FAMINE with an effective relief programme of public works and price controls. However, this was soon overwhelmed by the scale of the catastrophe. The repeal of the CORN LAWS split the Tory party and enabled opponents to drive him from office in June 1846. **William Anthony Hay**

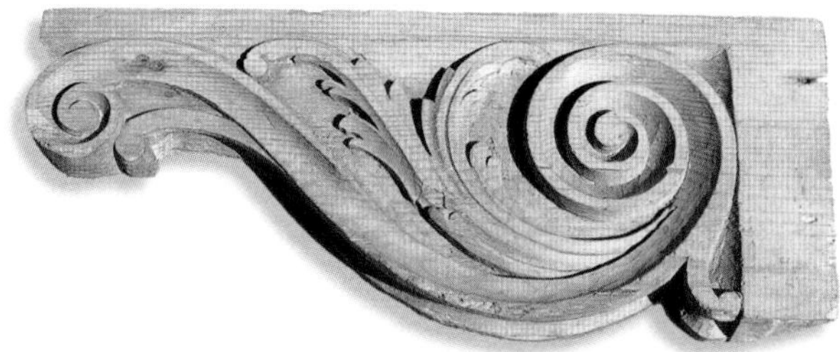

Pearson. *Wooden stair-bracket from Allenton House (eighteenth century), Old Bawn, Co. Dublin, from the Pearson Collection of architectural artefacts from eighteenth, nineteenth, and early twentieth-century buildings. [Sarah Durcan]*

'Peeler and the Goat, The', a satirical song by Darby Ryan (c. 1775–1855) lampooning ROBERT PEEL's new police force. A drunken policeman arrests a goat during the mating season; the ensuing dialogue demonstrates the political polarities in Ireland of the time. Ryan, from Bansha, Co. Tipperary, was educated in a HEDGE-SCHOOL and was well read in BIG HOUSE libraries. He wrote many local place-praise songs; 'The Peeler and the Goat' was written following his wrongful arrest during the TITHES agitation. The song was first sung from horseback in Bansha and spread rapidly throughout Ireland, taking on local place-names, even arriving in Australia and the United States on broadsheet. It has been performed widely by traditional, ballad, and classical singers up to modern times. **Fintan Vallely**

Peep o' Day Boys. Drunken affrays among farmer-weavers in the vicinity of Markethill, Co. Armagh, between gangs calling themselves the Nappach Fleet, the Bawn Fleet, and the Bunkerhill Defenders had become openly sectarian by 1786. The combatants regrouped, Protestants becoming the Peep o' Day Boys (so called because they rose at dawn to tear the LINEN webs, smash the looms and burn the homes of their Catholic neighbours) and Catholics the DEFENDERS; and for the next decade and more, sectarian warfare raged throughout the county. Members also went in for a form of intimidation known as 'placarding', with notices such as this one: 'Now teak this for Warnig, For if you Bee in this Contry Wednesday Night I will Blow your Soul to the Low hils of hell And Burn the House you are in.' 'Peppered legs' was an antecedent of modern kneecapping with a firearm. At first the organisation experienced little opposition, as many Peep o' Day Boys had been armed rank-and-file members of the VOLUNTEERS. The Defenders, using similar tactics, checked their progress in south Armagh, however. Peep o' Day Boys were the principal founders of the ORANGE ORDER, and did not maintain a separate organisation after 1795. **Jonathan Bardon**

Pelham, Henry (1749–1806), cartographer and miniaturist. Born in Boston, Massachusetts; he was raised by his widowed mother and his half-brother, the painter John Singleton Copley (1738–1815), who gave to him his artistic training. His fine royalist map of Boston under siege (1777) was published after he fled the New for the Old World. As an émigré he spent two years on the London art scene before settling in Co. Clare c. 1779; in 1787 he moved to Co. Kerry, where he was for eleven years agent to the Lansdowne estates. He surveyed both counties: his grand jury map of Co. Clare was engraved in 1787 but his map of Co. Kerry (1800), remained unpublished. He was a keen antiquarian, whose descriptions and illustrations of OGHAM stones were published in vol. 6 of CHARLES VALLANCEY's *Collectanea de Rebus Hibernicis* (1770–1804). He died on Bear Island, Co. Cork, where he was assistant engineer for the island's fortifications. **Jean Archer**

Penal Laws, a series of discriminatory laws passed by the Irish Parliament following the Williamite victory of 1691. The defeat of the JACOBITE cause left Ireland at the mercy of the New English Protestant interest. The immediate context in which the Penal Laws were enacted was the series of pro-Catholic proposals carried by the so-called Patriot Parliament of 1689, where the Jacobites had held the upper hand before their military defeat. These measures, together with the heightened confessional tensions created by the war—whose wider European dimension was a struggle between Catholic France and Protestant England and the Netherlands—left the Irish Parliament of the 1690s with little taste for accommodation with the defeated.

The principal penal laws were as follows. In 1692 an act encouraged Protestant settlement in Ireland. The 1695 act was designed to stop Catholics sending children abroad for their education. The 1697 act aimed to banish 'all papists exercising any ecclesiastical jurisdiction and all regulars of the popish clergy,' declaring that 'all popish archbishops, bishops, vicars-general, deans, jesuits, monks, friars, and all other regular popish clergy shall depart out of this kingdom before the 1st day of May, 1698, and if any of said ecclesiastical persons shall after that day be in this kingdom, they shall suffer imprisonment, and remain in prison until transported out of his Majesty's dominions ...' Remaining clergy had to register with the authorities and were subject to other restrictions. A further act of 1697 forbade marriage between Protestants and Catholics.

The Act to Prevent the Further Growth of Popery (1704) forbade Catholics to purchase land. They were confined to leasehold interests and were prevented from taking leases for more than thirty-one years. They could not inherit land from Protestants. On the death of a Catholic landowner the estate was to be divided equally between his sons. Further acts prohibited Catholics from practising law, sitting in Parliament, or holding public office and voting. The 1704 act also introduced the SACRAMENTAL TEST into Ireland, whereby those assuming public office were obliged to take communion under the auspices of the CHURCH OF IRELAND: this measure was aimed principally at Dissenters—especially the Presbyterians of Ulster—against whom the Penal Laws were also directed, though generally less vigorously than against Catholics.

The Penal Laws were intended to break the political power of Irish Catholics. No attempt was made at the mass conversion of Catholics. Despite their formal ferocity, they were not rigorously enforced; there was no sustained campaign of persecution; and from the 1720s onwards the structures and institutions of the Catholic Church began to recover. Catholic landowners were the principal target, in an age when ownership of land and the possession of political influence were inextricably linked. By forcing partible inheritance on Catholic estates, the laws persuaded many Catholic landowners to conform to the Church of Ireland. But their effect was hardly felt outside this class. They did little to stop the development of a vigorous mercantile middle class among Catholics, especially in the south-east of the country.

A series of minor enactments against Catholics continued until 1755, but by then the tide had turned. The death of the Old Pretender (James Stuart, son of JAMES II) in 1766 and the formal recognition of the Hanoverian monarchs of Britain by the Papacy ended any residual Jacobite threat. Relief acts passed in 1778, 1782, 1792 and 1793 swept away most of the Penal Laws. **Fergal Tobin**

Penn, William (1644–1718), founder of the state of Pennsylvania. Son of William Penn, an admiral of the Parliament's fleet in the English Civil War; educated privately in London and at the University of Oxford, matriculating in 1660. At Oxford he was influenced by Thomas Loe, a leading QUAKER, and in 1661 he was expelled for not conforming to the Church of England. After some years on the Continent he went to Ireland in 1665. While victualler of a naval squadron off Kinsale he lived on his father's estate at Shanagarry, Co. Cork. He attended a Quaker meeting in Cork led by Loe and became a Quaker, suffering intermittent bouts of imprisonment as a consequence. In March 1681 he became proprietary and governor of Pennsylvania, named after his late father, a colony that was remarkable for its religious toleration. **Henry A. Jefferies**

pensions, a form of income provided to income-earners (mainly employees and self-employed) when they retire, or have to retire early because of incapacity, and to their dependants when the income earner dies. Most income earners in Ireland are compulsorily insured for basic pensions under social insurance that gives entitlement to flat-rate pensions (not related to previous income) in return for the payment of contributions, which finance the pensions. Cover is maintained during periods out of the work force (if sick or unemployed, for example). Pension rights are also fully protected by EU regulations if a person goes to another EU country to work for a period, and similarly by bilateral agreements with other countries, such as Australia and the United States. Those who fail to qualify for a pension under social insurance are eligible for a corresponding pension under tax-financed social assistance, entitlement to which is subject to a means test. Pension payments may be supplemented by allowances, including those for a qualified adult (usually the spouse) and child dependants. A NATIONAL PENSION RESERVE FUND has been established to set aside assets for partly financing state pensions from 2026 onwards. This is to meet the substantial increase in pension costs arising from the ageing of the population. Workers may also be covered for pensions under occupational and personal pension schemes, which supplement or, in the case of some public servants, are a substitute for social-insurance pensions. Contributions to these schemes and the returns on their investment are not taxed. Tax is paid on the pensions when they become payable, with the exception of the lump sum, which is tax-free up to the amount of 1.5 times final salary. The Pensions Board regulates the operation of occupational schemes to ensure that entitlements are safeguarded. Up to half those in the work force are members of occupational or personal pension schemes. The Pensions Board has estimated that up to 70 per cent need such cover to maintain a reasonable link with their present standard of living when they become pensioners. Personal retirement savings accounts are being introduced to make it easier for people to arrange supplementary pension cover, and employers will be required to facilitate this for their employees. Scheme assets, which are set aside in pension funds, are the equivalent of more than half of GDP. They are a major source of investment in Ireland, and Irish pension funds also hold substantial assets abroad. **Gerry Mangan**

Pentecostal churches. The origins of the Elim Pentecostal Movement go back to 1915, when a young Welshman, George Jeffreys, ran an evangelistic crusade in Co. Monaghan. The movement spread, and the church later became known as the Elim Pentecostal Church. Despite its emphasis on the Bible as the word of God, it met with great resentment from the mainstream churches. Other Pentecostal groups include the Apostolic Church and the Assemblies of God. There are more than 15,000 members of Pentecostal churches, both North and South. **Gabrielle Brocklesby**

People's Democracy (1968–9), a CIVIL RIGHTS group established by students of Queen's University, Belfast, after the DERRY CIVIL RIGHTS MARCH of October 1968. Its early protest marches attracted large-scale participation by students of all political affiliations and none. The lack of formalised machinery and definition of membership, however, meant that policy decisions could easily be reversed, leaving it open to influence by more politically committed adherents. A largely 'new left' group capitalised on end-of-term university absences to press through a contentious decision to march from Belfast to Derry. The march, beginning on 1 January 1969, was attacked by loyalists at BURNTOLLET, outside Derry, which reactivated communal tensions. Eight candidates in the 1969 STORMONT election, standing on its civil rights platform, secured more than 4 per cent of the vote, but no seats. Though it established a number of branches outside Belfast during 1969, its growing radicalism alienated moderate support and brought it increasingly into conflict with the more cautious Northern Ireland Civil Rights Association. Mounting violence during 1969 saw leadership of the Catholic community pass gradually out of its shrinking sphere of influence, and by November it was reduced to a membership of committed social radicals, with a much diminished public profile. [see CIVIL RIGHTS MOVEMENT.] **Alan Scott**

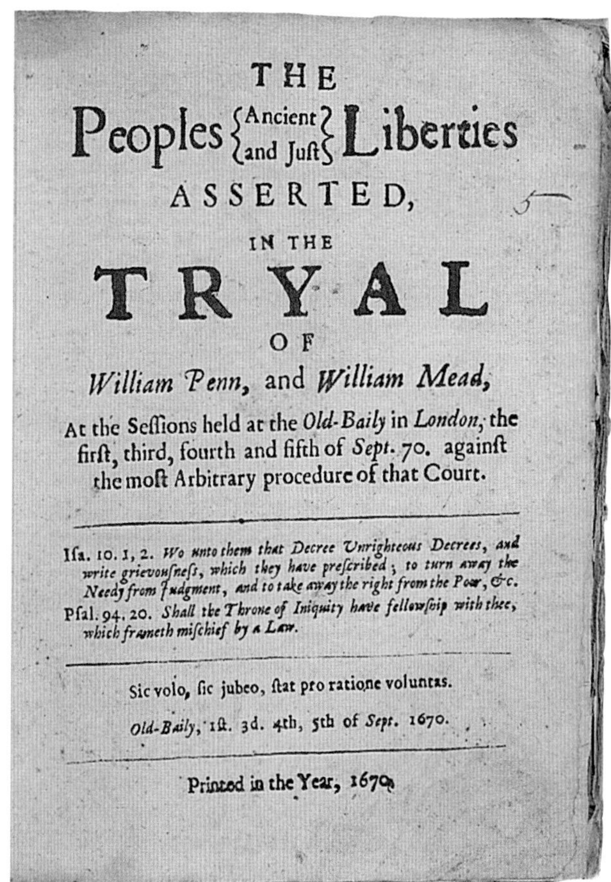

THE

Peoples {Ancient / and Juſt} Liberties

ASSERTED,

IN THE

TRYAL

OF

William Penn, and *William Mead*,

At the Seſſions held at the *Old-Baily* in *London*, the firſt, third, fourth and fifth of *Sept*. 70. againſt the moſt Arbitrary procedure of that Court.

Iſa. 10. 1, 2. *Wo unto them that Decree Unrighteous Decrees, and write grievouſneſs, which they have preſcribed; to turn away the Needy from Judgment, and to take away the right from the Poor, &c.*
Pſal. 94. 20. *Shall the Throne of Iniquity have fellowſhip with thee, which frameth miſchief by a Law.*

Sic volo, ſic jubeo, ſtat pro ratione voluntas.

Old-Baily, 1ſt. 3d. 4th, 5th of *Sept*. 1670.

Printed in the Year, 1670.

Penn. *Title page of* The People's Liberties Asserted in the Tryal of William Penn and William Mead *(1670), their written account of their trial at the Old Bailey for a tumultuous assembly to 'the Disturbance of the Peace'. [Board of Trinity College, Dublin]*

Performing Rights Society, an association of composers, authors, and publishers of musical works, established in England in 1914. It administers the performing rights of its members by granting licences and collecting and distributing royalties. Many Irish artists were members of the society before the establishment of the IRISH MUSIC RIGHTS ORGANISATION in 1989. **Anthony McCann**

Perrot, Sir John (c. 1527–1592), President of Munster and Lord Deputy of Ireland. A highly connected courtier rumoured to be a son of HENRY VIII, he served effectively in Munster during the closing stages of the first DESMOND REBELLION (1568–73). Having long campaigned for the office, he returned to Ireland as Lord Deputy in 1584, determined to revive and develop the policy of 'composition' pioneered by Sir HENRY SIDNEY in the 1570s. Learning from Sidney's mistakes, he planned to delegate the implementation of composition in Connacht to a commission of lawyers, to resolve the constitutional doubts of the PALE by summoning a parliament, and to devote intense personal attention to Ulster. He made remarkable progress in the early years of his administration, concluding unprecedented agreements with the O'Neills in Co. Tyrone and the Scottish MacDonnells in Co. Antrim. But plans to extend composition to Munster earned him the hostility of the newly arrived planters there and their influential supporters at court, while in his dealings in the Pale he gravely underestimated the alienation of the community that had occurred under GREY DE WILTON. His irascible personality and his refusal to be distracted from his reforms by rumours of Spanish invasion also contributed to his difficulties and hastened his recall. In 1588 he was arraigned, tried and found guilty on wholly spurious charges of treason. It is probable that ELIZABETH I planned his pardon before his death, but it is clear that a conspiracy of powerful forces at court had been determined to destroy him. **Ciaran Brady**

Perrot, John (died c. 1671), Quaker zealot. Born in Ireland. By 1656 he had joined the Quakers and was preaching in Limerick. In 1657, with a fellow-Irishman, John Lowe, he travelled to Rome with the aim of converting the Pope. On their arrival they began preaching against the Catholic Church, and they were soon arrested. Lowe died under the tortures of the Inquisition; Perrot was thrown into a mental asylum. He was released in 1661, but his zeal remained undiminished, and he travelled throughout Britain and Ireland, preaching to large crowds. In 1662 he emigrated to Barbados with his family. He died, heavily in debt, in Jamaica. **Ciarán Deane**

Peter of Ireland (Petrus de Ibernia) (fl. 1239–1265), philosopher. Of probable ANGLO-NORMAN birth, he may have studied at both Oxford and Paris. A lecturer in logic and natural philosophy at the University of Naples, he almost certainly introduced his young student Thomas Aquinas to Aristotle and his Arabic commentators, 1239–45. A decade later he was part of a Jewish-Christian group studying the *Guide for the Perplexed* of Maimonides. Commentaries survive from the late 1250s to early 1260s on Aristotle's *De Longitudine et Brevitate Vitae* and *Peri Hermeneias* as well as a *Determinatio Magistralis* on design in nature (published at Louvain in 1993 and 1996). **Michael Dunne**

Petrie, George (1790–1866), antiquarian, scholar, and collector of traditional music. Petrie's work with the ORDNANCE SURVEY sent him throughout Ireland and facilitated his noting of the tunes and songs that led to his collection. He offered material to EDWARD BUNTING and THOMAS MOORE; he also published widely in the popular and academic press on ancient Irish music and related topics, and founded and contributed to the *Irish Penny Journal*. In 1851 he founded the Society for the Preservation and Publication of the Melodies of Ireland, whose only publication was vol. 1 of *The Petrie Collection of the Ancient Music of Ireland* (1855). The bulk of Petrie's collections was edited by Sir CHARLES STANFORD and published as *The Complete Collection of Irish Music as Noted by George Petrie* (1902–5), which comprises almost 1,600 tunes. **Colin Hamilton**

Petrie type, an IRISH PRINTING TYPE. The planned publication of *The Annals of the Kingdom of Ireland* (Annals of the FOUR MASTERS) led to the production of an Irish printing type that was the first to be modelled on the round half-uncial style of lettering. The artist, archaeologist and antiquarian GEORGE PETRIE, working closely with EUGENE O'CURRY, studied manuscripts and Early Christian stone and metal inscriptions in preparing what was to become a particularly well-designed type. It made its first appearance in 1835 in the advance copies of *The Ordnance Survey of County Londonderry*. It was used almost exclusively by M. H. GILL at DUBLIN UNIVERSITY PRESS and to great effect in the printing of the *Annals*. **Dermot McGuinne**

Pettit, Philip (1945–), philosopher. Born in Ballygar, Co. Galway; educated at NUIM and QUB. He has held appointments at Queen's University, Belfast; UNIVERSITY COLLEGE, Dublin; Trinity Hall, Cambridge; the University of Bradford; the Australian National University; and Princeton University. He is best known for using insights from analytical philosophy of mind as the basis for political theory; the broadly conceived republicanism that results aims to provide an alternative to traditional liberal notions. His publications include *Judging Justice* (1980), *The Common Mind* (1993), *Republicanism* (1997), and *A Theory of Freedom* (2001). **Ian Leask**

Petty, Sir William (1623–1687), medical doctor, surveyor, and author. Born in Hampshire; studied at the universities of Caen, Utrecht, Leiden, Amsterdam, Paris, and Oxford. Appointed a fellow of Brasenose College, Oxford, in 1649, he became professor of anatomy there two years later. In 1652 he was made physician-general to the army in Ireland and quickly acquired a reputation for effective administration. He was given the task of measuring and mapping the ESTATES that were to be confiscated under the CROMWELLIAN LAND SETTLEMENT. Known as the DOWN SURVEY (because the information was marked down on maps, unlike the preliminary civil survey), this was later expanded by him to produce the first atlas of Ireland (1685). He acquired large estates in Cos. Kerry and Limerick but denied charges of corruption arising from his survey work. Despite losing his political appointments at the RESTORATION, he was looked on favourably by CHARLES II, who gave him a knighthood in 1662 for his work with the Royal Society, of which he was a founder-member. He concentrated on his scientific research and publication for the remainder of his life and was the first president of the Dublin Philosophical Society. In 1677 he married Elizabeth Fenton, who was created Baroness Shelburne after his death (Petty had twice refused a peerage for himself). He was a prolific author of demographic, statistical, and economic studies, most notably the *Treatise of Taxes and Contributions* (1662), a pioneering analysis of the origin of wealth, and *The Political Anatomy of Ireland* (1672), which was both descriptive and prescriptive. **Liam Irwin**

Phelan, Patrick (Paddy) (c. 1912–), hurler. Born in Co. Kilkenny. He played for Leinster as a goalkeeper before he first played for Kilkenny and played in ten consecutive inter-provincial finals, winning four titles. However, having begun his career as a goalkeeper, it was as an outfield defender that he enjoyed his greatest years as a hurler. He played in seven all-Ireland finals between 1932 and 1940 and was a member of the winning team on four occasions: 1932, 1933, 1935, and 1939. **Donal Keenan**

Philadelphia, the Irish in. Irish immigrants have come to Philadelphia for centuries. Ten per cent of the original QUAKER settlers in 1681 were Irish, while thousands of Ulster Protestants arrived in the 1700s. By 1790, 28 per cent of Philadelphia residents were Ulster Protestants, including many Revolutionary War leaders. The Catholic Irish first came as indentured servants to early Quakers, with more coming by the time of the GREAT FAMINE in the 1840s; by 1860 they made up 16 per cent of the population. Early Irish institutions, such as the Friendly Sons of St PATRICK (established 1771), included both Protestant and Catholic elites, but these friendships soon gave way to anti-Catholic tensions in the early nineteenth century. As greater numbers of unskilled Catholic immigrants arrived they competed with African-American labourers, which led to bitter race riots. Controversies within the Catholic Church led to the appointment in 1830 of Bishop Francis Patrick Kenrick, who encouraged a separatist mentality for Philadelphia Catholics that would last until the SECOND VATICAN COUNCIL. His objections to using the King James (Authorised Version) Bible in public schools, as well as competition by Irish people for jobs, provoked the nativist riots of 1844, during which Irish homes, churches, and a seminary were burnt and eighteen people were killed. The riots cemented sectarian hostilities and precipitated the creation of a strong parochial school system.

Despite such widespread nativism, the Irish had greater opportunities than in other cities. Increasing industrialisation created jobs in Philadelphia's many brickyards, railways, and factories. Irish women found employment as domestic servants and as textile workers, later becoming nurses, teachers, and shop assistants. In addition, Philadelphia's large land area and inexpensive terrace houses allowed the Irish to own their own homes, encouraging dispersal into several districts instead of crowding into ghettos.

The Philadelphia Irish led several national causes. From the UNITED IRISHMEN of the 1790s to Northern Aid (Noraid) in the 1980s the city was a centre of Irish revolutionary activity in America. The first nationalist meeting in America, the National Repeal Convention, was held there in 1842, followed by the first national Fenian convention in 1863. Irish Philadelphians revived the national temperance movement with the foundation of the Catholic Total Abstinence Union in 1866. They were also heavily involved with the Knights of Labor, founded in Philadelphia in 1869; it later became America's largest union, under the Irish-American Terence Powderly.

Unlike other cities, Philadelphia lacked a strong Democratic Party, not electing its first Irish Catholic mayor, James H. J. Tate, until 1962. As a result, instead of becoming political bosses many Irishmen were active in the powerful building and contracting trades, playing an influential role in changing the city's landscape.

By 1890 Philadelphia's Irish-born population was the second-largest in the country, at 110,935. They were the city's largest foreign-born group until 1910 and remained prominent throughout the twentieth century. In 1990 people of Irish birth and descent made up 22 per cent of Philadelphia's metropolitan population—its second-largest national group. The community continues to be active and fosters connections with Ireland, strengthened by a dynamic TRADITIONAL MUSIC scene and involvement in Irish causes. **Meaghan Dwyer**

Philips, Katherine, née Fowler (1631–1664), poet, playwright and letter-writer. Born in London. Though a royalist who had published cavalier lyrics in Henry Vaughan's *Poems* (1651), she married a Welsh Cromwellian adventurer, James Philips, in 1648. While her husband awaited the outcome of an Irish land claim she moved to Dublin in 1662, founding an influential Platonic 'Society of Friendship', among whose members she was known as 'the Matchless Orinda'. Members of the society included powerful figures in the viceregal court, and Philips was introduced to ROGER BOYLE, Earl of Orrery, who encouraged her to write a verse tragedy in rhyming couplets, a form admired by CHARLES II. She subsequently translated Corneille's *Pompey*, which was staged in the SMOCK ALLEY THEATRE with Boyle's support (1663), becoming the first professional production in English of a play by a woman. She was translating Horace when she died from smallpox in 1664. **Christopher Morash**

Phillips, Molesworth (1755–1836), explorer. Born in Swords, Co. Dublin. In 1776 he became a lieutenant in the Royal Marines and sailed in the *Resolution* on Captain James Cook's third voyage. On 14 February 1779, with a detachment of nine marines, he accompanied Cook to Kealakakua Bay, Hawaii, to recover a stolen boat. When King Kalaniopu agreed to go with Cook as a hostage, a hostile crowd attacked; Cook and seven marines were killed. Phillips was wounded but swam to a boat and escaped. On returning to England he was promoted captain. In 1796 he retired to Co. Cork, but he returned to England in 1799. He died of cholera in London, 1836. **Peter Somerville-Large**

Phoenix (1982–), a fortnightly magazine published in Dublin. It was launched by John Mulcahy, former editor and proprietor of *Hibernia*; it justifies the '*Hibernia* reborn' intimation of the title by offering a similar mixture of hard information, investigative articles, scandal and gossip, business and finance stories, and a satirical section. Featuring anonymous stories, it has appealed to readers for financial support to meet a small number of substantial judgments for libel. It has a circulation of more than 20,000. **David Quin**

Phoenix Park, Dublin, one of the world's largest enclosed city parks, covering almost 712 ha (1,762 acres) on the north bank of the River LIFFEY. The site passed into the possession of the Crown from the Knights Hospitallers after the dissolution of the monasteries under HENRY VIII and was later turned into a deer park by CHARLES II. It was opened to the public in 1747 by the Viceroy, Lord Chesterfield, who laid it out and planted elms and thorns. An early use was as a duelling ground. Chesterfield erected the Phoenix Monument as the centrepiece of Chesterfield Avenue, the main thoroughfare (though the park's name is probably a corruption of *Fionnuisce*, a reference to a clear stream). The avenue is lit by gas lamps, and the gates at its entrance have recently been restored. Within the parkland there are many different land uses, including sports grounds for polo, CRICKET, football, HURLING, and, until recently, HORSE-RACING. There are many important buildings and institutions in the park: the Magazine Fort, the Zoological Gardens, the People's Garden, ÁRAS AN UACHTARÁIN (the President's residence), Ashtown Castle, the residence of the United States ambassador, the headquarters of the GARDA SÍOCHÁNA, and the ORDNANCE SURVEY. Imposing features are the Wellington Testamonial (1817), a 62 m (205-ft.) obelisk, the Phoenix Column (1747), and the Papal Cross; but otherwise the park is surprisingly lacking in monuments. The park was the site of the murder of Lord Frederick Cavendish by the INVINCIBLES (1882), the centenary celebrations of CATHOLIC EMANCIPATION (1929), the EUCHARISTIC CONGRESS (1932), and the visit by Pope John Paul II attended by 1.3 million people (1979) (see p. 851). **Joseph Brady**

Phoenix Park murders. On 6 May 1882 the new Chief Secretary for Ireland, Lord Frederick Cavendish, arrived in Dublin; the same day he and the Under-Secretary, Thomas Burke, were assassinated outside the Viceregal Lodge (now ÁRAS AN UACHTARÁIN) in the PHOENIX PARK by a previously unknown group, the Irish National INVINCIBLES. The incident had three immediate consequences: the bargain known as the 'KILMAINHAM TREATY' assumed controversial proportions; GLADSTONE's intention to dispense with COERCION was scuttled, with a new, stronger measure being implemented; and detectives trailing CHARLES STEWART PARNELL discovered that he was living with KATHARINE O'SHEA, a fact they drew to the attention of the Home Secretary.

Five of the assassins—Joseph Brady, Thomas Caffrey, Daniel Curley, Michael Fagan, and Timothy Kelly (then nineteen years old)—were hanged in KILMAINHAM GAOL in May and June 1883 (see p. 928), having been informed on by a fellow-conspirator, James Carey, who received a Queen's pardon. Carey was murdered en route to Cape Town by another Invincible, Patrick O'Donnell. Eight of the plotters served lengthy jail sentences, while O'Donnell was hanged at Newgate Jail, London (see p. 527). **Alan O'Day**

photography, early. The first recorded Irish photographer was a Belfast engraver, Francis S. Beattie, who announced in the *Northern Whig* on 6 August 1840 that he had made a 'photogenic drawing' of the Long Bridge. This process, an account of which had been published in England by W. H. Fox Talbot in 1839 and which was later renamed the calotype, produced a paper negative from which positive photographic prints could be made. In the same year in Paris, Louis Daguerre unveiled his daguerrotype process, which fixed a positive image onto a polished metal plate. Beattie had written to the Belfast *Newsletter* in September 1839 regarding his successful experiments with both techniques, and by December he was advertising daguerrotypes of Belfast scenery and buildings. His portrait daguerrotypes, first produced in 1841, attracted the attention of Richard Beard, a London coal merchant who had bought the patent rights for daguerrotypes in England and Wales and also opened Europe's first commercial photographic portrait studio in London in March 1841. Beattie was offered the post of operator of Beard's proposed Dublin studio but declined (no doubt aware that Beard's patent rights did not extend to Ireland) before selling his engraving business to open his own studio in Belfast in October 1842. The first photographic studio in Ireland opened in Dublin in October 1841, apparently as part of the chain of such premises that Beard licensed in various cities. In February 1842 the ownership passed to its operator, a Frenchman, the Chevalier Doussin-Dubreuil.

The infancy of Irish photography is marked by its extreme transience. The country's second studio opened in Dublin in November 1841; within a year, however, its owner moved to Glasgow. Beattie's business disappeared from the Belfast directories for 1843 and 1846 but reappeared in 1850. In 1844 Dubreuil apparently went bankrupt following a fierce trade war with Horatio Nelson's 'New Daguerrotype Rooms'; shortly after this, Prof. Leon Gluckman opened his 'Daguerrotype Portrait Institution' in Dublin, the most long-lived of the early Irish studios, thought to be responsible for the series of portraits (many obviously fabricated) of imprisoned Young Irelanders in 1848.

The invention of the simpler and faster wet-collodion process by Frederick Scott Archer in 1851 made both the daguerrotype and the calotype obsolete and opened the field to increasing numbers of professional and amateur photographers. By 1860 sixty new studios had opened in Dublin. Belfast doubled its complement during the same period, from six to twelve. This commercial expansion was underpinned by the growing popularity of portrait photography, especially after the availability from 1861 of the much cheaper *carte-de-visite*. Commercial scenic photography also grew in prominence at this time, with firms offering prints of scenery, ruins, and cityscapes, often as fashionable stereoscopic views. One of the leading Irish makers and retailers of these images was John Fortune Lawrence, whose trade was taken over by his brother William, who founded Dublin's and probably Ireland's most successful early photographic business in his mother's toy shop in Sackville Street (O'Connell Street) in 1865.

The wet-collodion process introduced photography to the professional and landed classes, enabling women such as MARY PARSONS, Countess of Rosse, to make significant artistic and technical contributions. Wet collodion was superseded by the invention of a gelatin-based dry-plate process by Richard Leach Maddox in 1878. This freed the medium from the need to bring darkroom and chemicals to the field of operation as well as greatly simplifying the process, preparing the market for its true popularisation. In America in 1885 George Eastman introduced a roll-film holder that fitted the standard plate camera, and in 1889 the first Kodak box camera was produced, with the capacity for taking 100 circular pictures, which were returned with the camera to the makers for processing. Sold under the inspired slogan 'You press the button, we do the rest,' this sold in its thousands in Ireland for 5 guineas (£5.25) before being overtaken in 1900 by the famous Kodak 'Brownie' box camera, through which the 'snapshot' era began.

The transportability of dry-plate equipment made possible the professional photographing of Ireland. From 1880 people such as Robert French, chief photographer to William Lawrence, traversed the country, photographing its sights for publication as postcards and views (see p. 913). A similar business was undertaken in Ulster by R. J. Welch, his former assistant W. A. Green, and, somewhat later, A. R. Hogg (see pp. 15, 205, 229). The same years saw an enormous expansion in amateur photography and the mushrooming of local and national photographic societies, such as the Photographic Society of Ireland (re-formed 1879) and the Ulster Amateur Photographic Society (1885).

The development of the halftone block in the 1890s allowed photographs to be printed directly with type, offering new opportunities for professional and amateur alike to show their work. The near-contemporaneous introduction of the hand-held camera encouraged documentary photography of political events, such as labour disputes (1907 and 1913), the Home Rule crisis, and the 1916 RISING. The commissioning of official photographers by such firms as HARLAND AND WOLFF, the shipbuilders, led to populated images of commerce and trade becoming more common (see p. 1053). At the same time, photography was more widely used in advertising.

The next stage in the development of photography was marked by the first showings of moving pictures, perfected by the Lumière brothers in Paris in 1895. The Belfast demonstration in November 1896 attracted the attention of a local hotel-owner, John Walker Hicks, who set up in business under the stage name 'Professor Kineto'. On 19 April 1900 theatre-goers in Belfast saw his moving images of VICTORIA entering Dublin earlier the same day, a remarkable achievement for the period, sealing Hicks's reputation as the leading Irish pioneer of cinematography and film-making. [see VOLTA PICTURE PALACE.] **Vivienne Pollock**

photography, twentieth century. During the twentieth century photography developed rapidly from a specialist interest to an activity accessible to the average person. This era saw the emergence of a variety of treatments of the medium, including documentary, photojournalism and commercial photography, as well as photography as a unique art form in itself. Ireland did not differ greatly from other countries in this respect, and a strong amateur and professional photographic culture existed from the outset. There were many studios producing both portraiture and commercial images, as well as a number of organisations and societies for the enthusiast.

From a historical viewpoint, the collection of the NATIONAL LIBRARY OF IRELAND attests to the strong photographic heritage in Ireland. With about 300,000 images, representing various genres and subjects, the collections housed in the National Photographic Archive in Temple Bar, Dublin, provide a large body of photographic work

photography. *The Birr Castle camera rooms of Mary, Countess of Rosse, Co. Offaly, with early photographic equipment. Little altered since the mid-nineteenth century, it is one of the oldest surviving darkrooms in the world. [Irish Picture Library]*

taken in Ireland during the nineteenth and twentieth centuries. Most of the collections are historical in nature, but the archive also holds some contemporary material and maintains an active policy of collection.

Many of the collections are of commercial images and photographs that were originally intended for use in the postcard trade, such as the Lawrence Collection, the majority of which were taken by Robert French between 1870 and 1914. Similarly, the Eason and Valentine Collections represent images of the country during the first half of the twentieth century. The Poole Collection, taken by the studios of A. H. Poole, comprises portraiture as well as extensive documentary records of social and economic conditions in the south-east of the country between 1884 and 1954 (see p. 628). The Keogh Collection, by the Keogh Brothers of Dorset Street, Dublin, covers the period 1915–30 and is of particular interest as it includes many of the political events and figures of that era. The Wiltshire Collection, taken by Elinor Wiltshire, depicts Dublin in the 1950s and 60s. Other collections of note are the work of amateur photographers. The photographs of Dr J. J. Clarke document turn-of-the-century Dublin and are remarkable both in their photojournalistic approach and in how they capture the spirit of Joycean Dublin. The Clonbrock Collection gives an insight into life on the estate of the Dillon family in Co. Galway between 1860 and 1930. The O'Dea Collection represents the specialist interest of the railway enthusiast James P. O'Dea, whose photographs chronicle the RAILWAYS of Ireland between 1937 and 1966. Other important historical photographers have included FATHER FRANK BROWNE and Nevill Johnson. Father Browne created up to 42,000 photographs, which make up an astonishing document of his travels during his long lifetime (see pp. 743, 929). He is most famous for having captured the TITANIC on film before it set sail for New York. Johnson's images concentrate on Dublin in the 1950s.

In Northern Ireland an archive of almost 500,000 photographs from 1983 to the present has been assembled by the BELFAST EXPOSED group. The group's primary function is to promote awareness and debate in the community through the use of photography. Also in Belfast is the photographic magazine *Source*, first published in 1992 by Photo Works North, an organisation formed to promote photography in Northern Ireland. The magazine features reproductions of photography, reviews, and comment on photography in Ireland and Britain. It is now jointly published with the Gallery of Photography, Dublin, and receives funding from both Northern and Southern ARTS COUNCILS as well as the EUROPEAN UNION.

Perhaps one of the biggest challenges to Irish photography in the twentieth century was its weak status among Ireland's cultural and artistic establishment, compared with the position in other countries. There are a number of historical and cultural reasons for this. In the South the search for an intrinsically national cultural identity in the period following independence resulted in an emphasis being put on the more established art forms. The comparative strength of the literary tradition compounded this phenomenon. A less than favourable economic atmosphere and, more broadly, a traditional reluctance on the part of the art world to accord photography the status of visual art have also played a part in the lack of official support of the medium, both North and South.

Until the 1990s there was no degree course for photography in Ireland, though this has since been remedied with the introduction of a course in the Dublin Institute of Technology. It was not until

photography. The Wheel of Death, Camilla and George, Portadown *by Victor Sloan from his series,* Circus *(1991), an example of his creative manipulation of the original photographic image through drawing, painting, and the use of mixed media on the negative or print. [Courtesy of the artist]*

1978 that the Arts Council first granted a bursary to a photographer. In the same year the Gallery of Photography opened. Funded by the Arts Council and Dublin City Council, this specialist gallery space has done much to improve the profile and the output of photography in Ireland. Originally at Wellington Quay, the gallery moved to its purpose-built premises in Temple Bar in 1995. It exhibits works by both Irish and overseas photographers and sells a wide range of books and publications on photography. The gallery also has its own darkrooms and regularly holds seminars and workshops. It is perhaps largely due to this development that many Irish photographers have achieved widespread recognition in the international arena.

Since the late 1990s photography has played an ever-increasing role in the indigenous art world. It has become an important component in the artistic process as well as occupying more space in galleries and museums. Latterly, much prominence has been given to fine art photography. As the use of the photographic medium by artists has increased, so too has the presentation by photographers of their work in an overtly artistic context. Within this arena the distinctions between terms such as visual art, lens-based art, and photography are gradually becoming less important.

Artists and photographers such as VICTOR SLOAN, SEÁN HILLEN, PAUL SEAWRIGHT, WILLIE DOHERTY, and DAVID FARRELL are all internationally acclaimed for their work, in which the North of Ireland has been a common theme (see p. 837). Other photographers who have won widespread recognition include KARL GRIMES, who has been concerned with exploring the modalities of life using physical and natural motifs, and ANTHONY HAUGHEY, whose work has encompassed commentary on identity, place and peripherality.

One of the strongest driving forces behind photography in Ireland has been the tourist industry and, by extension, the documentation of the Irish landscape and people. One of the best-known contributors in this genre was JOHN HINDE, whose studios achieved huge success manufacturing postcards of idyllic colour-tinted views of rural Ireland, in which representations of the landscape and the people were often contrived and unrealistic. Despite their apparent artifice, the aesthetics of Hinde's images did much to shape perceptions of Ireland among natives and visitors alike. More recently, photographers such as LIAM BLAKE, Tom Kelly, and FERGUS BOURKE have added to and updated visual representations of the Irish landscape. Moreover, there has been a large degree of social documentary in both urban and rural settings by such photographers as Bill Doyle, Tony Murray, and TONY O'SHEA.

With some notable exceptions, Ireland's print media do not regularly devote a lot of space to photo-journalism. Consequently, the Gallery of Photography and the Press Photographers' Association have seen the need to hold regular exhibitions of press photography and photo essays. Significant contributions have been made in the area of press photography by such stalwarts as COLMAN DOYLE, who worked with the IRISH PRESS for more than forty years, and JOHN MINIHAN, who worked as a press photographer in London with the *Evening Standard*. Minihan is also known for his portraiture of famous writers, and has also exhibited in his own right (see p. 79). The work of the photo-journalist Derek Speirs has been noteworthy for its social consciousness. In the area of sports photography BILLY STICKLAND has excelled, while such photographers as TOM LAWLOR, AMELIA STEIN, and ROD TUACH have produced an important body of work in the area of music, theatre, and film in addition to their own projects (see p. 800). **Martin Clancy**

physics, experimental and mathematical. Among early contributors to what was once called natural philosophy, WILLIAM MOLYNEUX and NARCISSUS MARSH are notable seventeenth-century exponents. The first university chair in physics in Ireland may be considered to be the Erasmus Smith professorship of natural and experimental philosophy at TRINITY COLLEGE, Dublin, 1724, first held by RICHARD HELSHAM. Thereafter the university maintained an extensive collection of physical instruments, but the chair was not again filled with distinction until the period of HUMPHREY LLOYD's researches in OPTICS and terrestrial magnetism in the middle of the nineteenth century. At the same time WILLIAM ROWAN HAMILTON, working at DUNSINK OBSERVATORY as professor of ASTRONOMY, emerged as the world's leading mathematical physicist. He and Lloyd collaborated on what was regarded as a triumphant vindication of the wave theory of light: the prediction and discovery of conical refraction. Later holders of the Erasmus Smith chair included G. F. FITZGERALD and ERNEST WALTON. Most of Fitzgerald's best students went abroad, including THOMAS RANKEN LYLE.

Notable nineteenth-century physicists associated with Queen's College, Galway, were JOSEPH LARMOR and GEORGE JOHNSTONE STONEY. The early success of THOMAS PRESTON, and the return of J. A. McLelland from research with J. J. Thomson in Cambridge, established at University College, Dublin, a strong line of research in atomic spectroscopy and ionised gases, involving P. J. NOLAN, J. J. NOLAN, and THOMAS NEVIN, which still survives. In the twentieth century Queen's University, Belfast, maintained a distinguished school of theoretical atomic physics. Among other institutions, the Dublin Philosophical Society was an early forum for scientific debate, and the ROYAL COLLEGE OF SCIENCE was briefly of importance, with, for example, William Barrett working in metallurgy and magnetism.

In the 1930s the Taoiseach, ÉAMON DE VALERA, invited ERWIN SCHRÖDINGER to come to Dublin and eventually become director of the School of Theoretical Physics at the new DUBLIN INSTITUTE FOR ADVANCED STUDIES. This reflected de Valera's lifelong devotion to mathematics and mathematical physics. It was an inspired initiative, in that the institute continued to attract leading theoretical physicists, such as WALTER HEITLER and CORNELIUS LANCZOS, winning a worldwide reputation and helping to foster a strong national tradition in the study of relativity, exemplified by ARTHUR WILLIAM CONWAY and JOHN LIGHTON SYNGE and in recent times by LOCHLAINN Ó RAIFEARTAIGH, who was awarded the international

Wigner Prize in 1999 for his outstanding work in relativity and particle physics. It also contributed through its Geophysics section to the establishment of Ireland's rights on the Continental Shelf. However, public support for experimental science remained paltry, so that Ernest Walton never succeeded in establishing in Dublin the line of research in Cambridge that earned him the NOBEL PRIZE. Subsidies from the EUROPEAN UNION and the economic boom produced substantial funding at the end of the twentieth century, engendering a lively debate on the case for joining CERN and other international physics projects. **Denis Weaire**

piano in traditional music. For some, the piano's rhythmic drive is the essence of the music of CÉILÍ BANDS; for others, this harmonic instrument is the quintessential symbol of Western art music, with its associated middle-class ideals. This dichotomy can be traced back to the early twentieth century, when the piano moved from the domestic sphere of the parlour to the public podium. The piano was used in printed music collections from BUNTING's time onwards. However, it was through its use in Irish-American dance-halls and on 78 r.p.m. recordings of Irish music that it truly became popular. Not only was the piano acoustically suitable in these settings but it also brought with it an air of prestige and helped to mediate between tradition and modernity.

As céilí bands flourished, many leading players were women, which is not surprising, given the fact that the piano was for a long time regarded primarily as a female instrument. Today many accompanists continue to give a high profile to the piano. COMHALTAS CEOLTÓIRÍ ÉIREANN features it in accompaniment and solo competitive categories. In the SEISIÚN, more portable accompaniment instruments, such as the guitar and bouzouki, have challenged the piano's dominance, but it remains popular. **Aibhlin Dillane**

piano music. The piano was introduced to Ireland towards the end of the eighteenth century, displacing the harpsichord by the early decades of the nineteenth century. The flourishing state of music in Dublin at that time is reflected in the quality of contemporary piano music, particularly that of PHILIP COGAN. The fashion for sets of variations and rondos on both popular and folk airs produced many examples, those of Timothy Geary being extremely popular and of some merit. The early Dublin compositions of JOHN FIELD, the foremost figure in Irish piano music, were also in this idiom. Field's emigration lessened the impact he had on music in Ireland; he had, however, a dual influence on piano music in general: he pioneered an expressive and intimate playing style that departed from the prevailing virtuoso approach, and he created an original form, the *nocturne*, which established the tradition of the single-movement piano piece. Salon music became more prevalent in the nineteenth century, and the ensuing deterioration in the quality of Irish piano music is symptomatic of the general musical decline of the period. An abundance of piano music has been written in the twentieth century, with the works of BRIAN BOYDELL, JOHN BUCKLEY, RAYMOND DEANE, PHILIP MARTIN, and JANE O'LEARY being of particular note. The commissioning of works in recent years by the DUBLIN INTERNATIONAL PIANO COMPETITION has provided wider exposure to Irish piano music, and the publication of these and other piano works by the CONTEMPORARY MUSIC CENTRE is an important factor in the continuing promotion of Irish piano music. **Adrian Scahill**

piccolo. Practically unknown in traditional music before the twentieth century, the piccolo came to the fore in the classic recordings of Irish music made in America between 1922 and 1934, mainly in ensemble recordings—where it could be easily heard above the other instruments—but also in duets and a few solos. A few players after this period made it their speciality, notably John Doonan, born of Irish parents in Newcastle, Northumberland, who released two recordings of solo piccolo in 1972 and 1978. **Colin Hamilton**

Pigott forgeries, forged documents attempting to blacken the name of CHARLES STEWART PARNELL. Richard Pigott (1828–1889), a Dublin newspaper editor, sold documents, including a letter apparently written by Parnell, appearing to condone the murder of the Under-Secretary, Thomas H. Burke. The material was used by the *Times* to link Parnell with criminal activity. The exposure of the forgery on 21 February 1889 proved a turning-point for the Special Commission on Parnellism and Crime. **Carla King**

Pike Theatre, Dublin (1953–60), a tiny 55-seat theatre in Herbert Lane built by Carolyn Swift and her husband, Alan Simpson. Resembling (in Swift's words) 'a weird cross between Covent Garden Opera House and a doll's house,' it played a central role in the revitalisation of Irish theatre. In 1954 it premiered BRENDAN BEHAN's first major play, THE QUARE FELLOW, and in 1955 gave BECKETT's WAITING FOR GODOT its first Irish production. An unsuccessful attempt to prosecute the Pike over a production of Tennessee Williams's *The Rose Tattoo* in 1957 resulted in a landmark court case. **Christopher Morash**

Pike. *The arrest of Alan Simpson, director of the controversial play* The Rose Tattoo *by Tennessee Williams. [Photograph from the* Irish Press, *24 May 1957, at the Pike Theatre. Irish Press PLC]*

pilgrimage, part of religious life in Ireland since at least the sixth century. COLM CILLE was the first of many Irish people recorded as having gone on *peregrinatio*, which often involved permanent voluntary exile for the sake of God and the soul. But the activities of these wandering Irish *peregrini* were curtailed on the Continent in 813, though Rome and, to a lesser extent, Santiago de Compostela remain goals for Irish pilgrims today.

Pilgrimage within Ireland had no Irish Chaucer to chronicle it and was an activity more practised than written about. As a result, while it was doubtless an important part of Christian life in early medieval Ireland we can only reconstruct it from a few literary scraps and references in the ANNALS to the deaths of pilgrims at particular places. CLONMACNOISE was the first instance we know of, in 606, but Glendalough and ARMAGH were to follow before the turn of the millennium. Pilgrimage reached a peak in Ireland, as it did elsewhere in Europe, in the twelfth century, when many places were recorded as pilgrimage sites, including two still active today. The oldest of these, CROAGH PATRICK, probably continued the tradition of a pagan

LÚNASA festival at the beginning of harvest. The second, LOUGH DERG, also came to be associated with St PATRICK; it is the only well-documented place of early Irish pilgrimage, because those who came there from outside the country—from as far away as Catalunya and Hungary—wrote accounts of their efforts to experience the same vision of purgatory that a Welsh knight, Owain, claimed to have seen in a cave on one of the lake's islands c. 1140. The ascetic nature of the pilgrimage and the prescribed prayers and activities there may well continue medieval practice. As a result of 'drink and debauchery,' however, the Catholic Church closed many other pilgrimage sites in the nineteenth century; today KNOCK represents an organised and acceptable alternative. Annual PATTERNS at holy wells represent old pilgrimage traditions at local level. **Peter Harbison**

Pilkington, Laetitia (c. 1708–1750), writer. Best known for her account of an imperious SWIFT in the *Memoirs* (1748–54), Pilkington herself remains the 'scandal' memoirist, the 'most profligate whore in either kingdom', in Swift's phrase. The *Memoirs* is certainly a work of breathless self-defence, but there is also a sense of her desperation, that of a woman notoriously separated from her husband, with duns and rakes prowling at the door. Virginia Woolf's description seems the more apt: a 'very extraordinary cross between Moll Flanders and Lady Ritchie, between a rolling and rollicking woman of the town and a lady of breeding and refinement.' **Moyra Haslett**

Pine, Richard (1949–), critic. Born in London; educated at Westminster School and TCD. He worked at RTÉ, 1974–99, in music and public affairs. Chairman, Media Association of Ireland, 1986–8; secretary, Irish Writers' Union, 1988–90; a governor of the RIAM from 1989; director of the Durrell School, Corfu, from 2000. As a freelance lecturer he has been influential in developing the concept of interdisciplinary Irish studies. He is a pioneering proponent of OSCAR WILDE's Irishness in two books and a profound critic of BRIAN FRIEL's drama (1990 and 1999). He has written histories of the GATE THEATRE (1978, 1984) and, with Charles Acton, the RIAM (1998), and two books on Lawrence Durrell. **Anthony Roche**

Píobairí Uilleann, Na, an organisation for the promotion of uilleann piping and pipemaking, founded in October 1968 at Bettystown, Co. Meath. With some fifty pipers participating and BREANDÁN BREATHNACH as chairman, the club made an important contribution to the instrument's revival, organising classes and public events. By 2000 a large national and international membership had developed, and the function of the club had changed, also providing contact services and co-ordinating piping events. Publications include books, CDs, and videos, as well as a quarterly bulletin, *An Píobaire*, and an annual journal, *Ceol na hÉireann/Irish Music*. **Jimmy O'Brien Moran**

Pioneers, the (Pioneer Total Abstinence Association of the Sacred Heart), established in Dublin on 27 December 1898 by a Co. Wexford Jesuit, Father James Cullen, who devised the 'heroic offering' in which people pledged to abstain from ALCOHOL for life. It became the country's most successful Catholic lay movement, its Jesuit directors vigorously decrying the pervasive Irish drink culture. Its golden jubilee in 1949 attracted 90,000 people to Croke Park, Dublin. Membership reached a peak at nearly half a million in the 1950s, after which it went into decline (see p. 19). [see ALCOHOL ABUSE; DISTILLING; ETHER DRINKING.] **Diarmaid Ferriter**

pipe bands. Pipe bands are organised by two associations: the Irish Pipe Band Association in the Republic and the Royal Scottish Pipe Band Association (Northern Ireland Branch). The RSPBA (NI) has a membership of nearly 100 bands, divided into four sections (Fermanagh, Antrim, Down, and Mid-Ulster), while the IPBA caters for about fifty bands, divided into five branches (Leinster, South-East, Munster, Connacht, and North-West). Both organisations have colleges of piping and drumming and enter examinations set by the RSPBA.

Pipe band contests first took place in the North in 1912. In 1945 Pipe Band Leagues were formed in the North and the South; since then, on alternate years, they have jointly organised the all-Ireland pipe band, solo piping, and drumming championships. The Field-Marshal Montgomery Band (Carryduff) has won the all-Ireland championship eleven times; the Fintan Lalor Pipe Band (Dublin) and Robert Armstrong Memorial Band (Belfast) nine times; Ballycoan (Purdysburn) seven times; Cullybackey five times; and Macneillstown (Portglenone) four times.

In 1950 the Northern League joined the Scottish Pipe Band Association, which had been formed in 1930 to supervise contests. Championships were first held in 1951. In 1953 the RSPBA (NI) brought the European championship to Belfast and in 1956 and 1962 hosted the world championship. Band competitions consist of six grades. Bands from Northern Ireland have won every grade at some period, the most notable being the Field-Marshal Montgomery Band, which has won the grade 1 world championship on two occasions. Drum-majors have dominated in all grades, winning the championship many times, while drummers have won all the grades in world solos, the senior title having been achieved on four occasions. **Wilbert Garvin**

pipe-makers. It is now generally accepted that the Irish bellows-blown pipes were developed from the older 'pastoral' pipes c. 1750–60. The earliest and best-known Irish pipe-makers of this period are James Kenna of Munster and later near Mullingar, where in 1770 he advertised that he had been making Irish pipes for twenty years. John Egan is a name ascribed to the maker of various early surviving sets that are marked 'Egan' and obviously of a date c. 1780. William Kennedy of Tandragee, Co. Armagh, was making Irish pipes by 1783. The term *union pipes* became the accepted name in the 1790s, perhaps with the addition of the regulators.

Timothy Kenna, son of James (died c. 1837), moved from Mullingar to Dublin in 1812, when he advertised a 'perfected instrument'. He was possibly responsible for the addition of the bass regulator, as well as other innovations. Contemporary with him in Mullingar was another great maker named Colgan. Maurice Coyne of Dublin followed as the best maker of the 1840s. Michael Egan worked from c. 1840 (in Liverpool) to c. 1860 (in New York). John Coyne is believed to have worked in the 1850s. Denis Harrington of Cork was a master who disappeared c. 1860, possibly to Australia.

The brothers Billie and Charlie Taylor of Drogheda and Philadelphia, who worked from the 1870s to the mid-1890s, invented the wide-bore concert pitch (D) chanter that is heard most today. This was as a result of their search for a louder instrument to suit the venues of their day. Many of their design concepts were later adopted by Willie Rowsome and, later, his brother Leo. The term *uilleann pipes* ('elbow pipes') came into use in the early twentieth century, possibly by false etymology.

The majority of wide-bore D pipes played today are based on the work of LEO ROWSOME. Lovers of the older, lower-pitched (B flat) instruments try to emulate the work of Kenna, Coyne, Egan, Colgan, and Harrington. Some 150 makers are now producing pipes. Their instruments for the most part have wide-bore chanters, after the work of the Taylors and the Rowsomes; only a few modern makers base their work on the legacy of the master makers of the first half of the nineteenth century (see p. 1063). [see MUSICAL INSTRUMENT MAKERS.] **Ken McLeod**

piracy, a complex problem in early modern Ireland, varying according to time and place. For much of the sixteenth century coastal raiding and plunder appear to have been widespread along the west coast, where the O'Malleys and O'Flahertys employed fleets of small vessels in short-distance, opportunistic activity. GRACE O'MALLEY was one of the leading promoters of this type of enterprise during the 1570s and 80s, arousing concern among officials about her support for rebellions against English rule. By the early seventeenth century such localised plunder was overlaid by organised, long-distance piracy, predominantly English in origin. This was based on a regular pattern of enterprise, involving as many as twenty ships in some years, which visited the coastal communities of Munster to dispose of plundered cargoes in exchange for provisions and other services. But the economic and social impact of this pirate trade was short-lived. The decline of the deep-sea pirate community in the 1620s was followed by the appearance of Turkish pirates, who raided vulnerable coastal settlements in search of captives; during 1631 more than a hundred people were carried off after a raid on Baltimore, Co. Cork, by Algerian pirates.

Piracy remained a problem for the rest of the seventeenth century, but its significance was steadily reduced, especially after the 1640s and 50s, which experienced a resurgence of maritime plunder under the guise of privateering. By the 1680s and 90s organised piracy had been contained in local waters, though Irish recruits, including ANNE BONNEY from Cork, continued to serve aboard pirate ships operating from bases in North America and the Caribbean. **John Appleby**

piracy. *Grace O'Malley, popularly known as 'Granuaile', is reputedly buried on Clare Island, Co. Mayo, at the abbey that bears this O'Malley coat of arms. [Dúchas, The Heritage Service]*

Pirrie, William James, Viscount (1847–1924), shipbuilder. Pirrie was made a 'gentleman apprentice' in 1862 in HARLAND AND WOLFF, formed the previous year. In 1874 he became a partner in the firm, and since both EDWARD HARLAND and GUSTAV WOLFF became active Unionist politicians, Pirrie in practice presided over the firm, though he did not become chairman until 1895 (see p. 1145). A flamboyant and innovative businessman, he was chairman when the firm on successive occasions launched the world's biggest ships, including the *Oceanic*, the *Olympic*, and the ill-fated TITANIC. He was a Unionist Lord Mayor of Belfast in 1896–7, but from 1905 he was a Liberal, and his workforce had no liking for his support for HOME RULE. After the 1916 RISING he became a Unionist again and was made a senator in the first Northern Ireland Parliament. During the final year of the FIRST WORLD WAR he superintended merchant shipbuilding as Comptroller-General. He was made a baron in 1906 and a viscount in 1921. Pirrie was probably the richest man in Ireland and was certainly the country's most extravagant host. He was secretive and autocratic as chairman, however, and bequeathed grave financial problems to the firm on his death. **Jonathan Bardon**

Place, Francis (1647–1728), antiquarian and artist. Born in Dinsdale, Co. Durham; entered Gray's Inn, London, but left to study under the Bohemian topographical artist Wenceslaus Hollar. He produced a large number of etchings. Having toured England and the Netherlands during the mid-1670s, drawing and making prints, he settled in York and was living there c. 1675. His extensive travel between 1677 and 1701 included walking tours of the Isle of Wight and France. He arrived in Drogheda in 1698 and toured Ireland, via Dublin and Kilkenny. He produced numerous illustrations, portraits, and panoramic views, predominantly in pen and ink; his landscapes were expertly executed (see p. 1126). He departed from Waterford in 1699. **Brendan Rooney**

place-name lore. Names identify and distinguish topographical features. The earliest inhabitants of Ireland naturally named the most prominent items in the landscape; later arrivals generally accepted these established names. As the population density increased, even the minor gaps in the toponymic map were gradually closed.

Much lore grew up in relation to place-names, and this was formalised in the distinctive verse and prose form called DINNSEANCHAS ('place lore'), which flourished mainly in the eleventh to fifteenth centuries. Notable exponents of this genre were SEÁN MÓR Ó DUBHAGÁIN (died 1372) and Giolla na Naomh Ó hUidhrín (died 1420). The first serious study of Irish toponymy was undertaken by P. W. JOYCE (died 1914); despite its defects, his work is still of real value. Most recent books merely rehash Joyce's work; the serious student must turn to scholarly writings in such specialised journals as *Dinnseanchas*, *Northern Ireland Place-Name Bulletin* (two series) and *Ainm*, and to occasional articles in foreign journals such as *Studia Celtica*, *Nomina* and *Names*. Much of the best and most comprehensive modern research relates to Ulster.

The earliest names may have been bestowed by the MESOLITHIC, NEOLITHIC, and BRONZE AGE inhabitants, and this older substratum underlies the modern toponymy. However, the introduction of the IRISH LANGUAGE was of crucial significance. Later linguistic arrivals had minimal impact. A handful of Norse names dot the east and south coastlands. The ANGLO-NORMAN impact in the Pale was reduced in the thirteenth century, when many of the *-town* names were converted to *Baile*. The colonists and their descendants tended to accept the existing Irish toponymy, as did the planters in Ulster, so that even today the great bulk of townland names are of Irish provenance. In recent centuries some LANDLORDS tried to Anglicise the immediate vicinity of their demesnes, but with limited success. However, the twentieth century saw a marked trend towards the Anglicisation of street names: such infelicities as Finsbury Park (in Churchtown, Dublin) are now all too common.

Many Irish names are descriptives, for example Mullaghmore (Mullach Mór, 'great summit'). Others signify ownership or association, for example Craggykerrivan (Creag Uí Chiardhubháin, 'Ó Ciardhubháin's rock'). Still others are commemoratives, for example Termonbarry (Tearmann Bhearaigh, 'St Bearach's sanctuary'). Quite a few have a basis in FOLKLORE, for example Beaufort (Lios an Phúca, 'ring-fort of the púca'), or in history, for example Spanish Point (Rinn na Spáinneach), or in social geography, for example Ballinahown (Buaile na hAbhann, 'milking-place by the river').

Since the twelfth century English officials have transliterated Irish place-names; the resultant forms are frequently highly corrupted. Thus Glenavy is derived from Lann Abhaigh, 'little church', and Ballinacarrow from Baile na Cora, 'townland of the weir'. The interpretation of Irish place-names demands a rigorous investigation of evidence stretching back in some instances more than 1,200 years. **Breandán Mac Aodha**

place-names. Most place-names in all parts of Ireland are, in linguistic terms, Irish. (There is a continuing and inconclusive debate about how many, and which, may be of pre-Celtic origin, though adapted and modified by speakers of Irish.) Place-names in an English-language context are generally written in an Anglicised orthography that is a fairly thinly disguised rendering of the original Irish form.

The largest category of place-names of which there is a comprehensive written record is that of the more than 63,000 townlands. Further up the pyramid are the names of some 2,420 civil parishes, 324 baronies, thirty-two counties, and four (earlier five) provinces. In addition there are scores of thousands of *microtoponyms*, many still unrecorded and in imminent danger of being lost for ever, particularly with the decline of Irish. (Names in this category are most numerous in areas where Irish is, or was until recently, spoken.) Some names can be traced back almost two millennia, while many more—often, at least partly, of Latin origin—date from the Early Christian centuries. The VIKINGS, who raided and later settled Ireland in the ninth and tenth centuries, have left a comparatively small number of NORSE PLACE-NAMES, mainly in areas on and near the eastern and southern coasts. Few clearly Norman-French names survive; but English, naturally, has had a notable impact on nomenclature, especially in the former 'English PALE'. Nevertheless this has given rise to fewer purely English names than one might have expected; only one county, Dublin, has a majority of non-Irish (i.e. mainly English) townland names. In the eighteenth century LANDLORDS added another onomastic layer by applying Continental names to BIG HOUSES and ESTATES.

In the nineteenth century the ORDNANCE SURVEY researched and standardised (in Anglicised form, rarely translated) administrative place-names. Most of these names passed through the hands of the great linguistic scholar and historian JOHN O'DONOVAN, who, between 1834 and 1841, personally visited many of the parishes to collect evidence on the place-names of each locality. Among the things reflected in Ireland's enormously rich place-name heritage are natural features, FLORA and FAUNA, land divisions, settlement patterns (both secular and ecclesiastical), ways of life (and death), land clearance and cultivation, historical events, and religious or mythological matters. By including family names and personal names, some place-names may also preserve the memory of families and individuals of whom there is no longer any trace in the places they once inhabited. [see ADMINISTRATIVE DIVISIONS.] **Nollaig Ó Muraíle**

plague. While we know from the early annalists that Ireland suffered outbreaks of plague during the sixth and seventh centuries, it would appear that this form of contagious infection went into abeyance during the eighth century. The BLACK DEATH, a devastating pandemic of bubonic and pneumonic plague, passed to humans by fleas carried by the black rat, arrived in Ireland in 1348; by 1350, when the worst of the crisis was over, the population may have been reduced by as much as a third. More than a dozen further nationwide epidemics were recorded between 1350 and 1540. Plague, as a catch-all term for a variety of contagious diseases, took a heavy toll among civilian and military personnel during the wars of the sixteenth century. It again struck Ireland during the early 1650s and, combined with the impact of warfare and failed harvests, led to a sharp rise in mortality. **Patrick Fitzgerald**

Plan of Campaign. Initiated in 1886, its primary object was to organise tenant farmers on selected estates in withholding rents until reductions were conceded by the LANDLORDS. The ESTATES selected were often those of economically more vulnerable landlords, thus increasing the chance of favourable precedents. Its two most active leaders were WILLIAM O'BRIEN and JOHN DILLON, with PARNELL himself holding aloof. It was aggressively confronted by the Unionist government, earning for its CHIEF SECRETARY the epithet 'Bloody BALFOUR'. The split in Parnell's movement in 1891 undermined its viability. **Philip J. Bull**

planning process. In the Republic, while legislation exists from the 1930s, the present system is based on the LOCAL GOVERNMENT (Planning and Development) Act (1963), as amended and augmented by seven later acts and numerous regulations. Planning is managed by 114 local authorities—twenty-nine county councils, five city councils, five borough councils, and seventy-five town councils—by means of a development plan, which must be formally reviewed every five years in a process that involves public participation. The plan creates the framework for development and usually sets out a spatial zoning for land use. All developments require planning permission and must be in accordance with this plan, but it is possible in limited circumstances for the authority to vary it for specific projects. The investigation of development applications is one of the functions of the planning authority; its decisions can be appealed to An Bord Pleanála, an independent body that replaced the system of ministerial appeal in 1976. The 2000 act was designed to consolidate existing legislation and streamline the process. The concept of sustainable development is to underpin development, but restrictions on the rights of objectors to planning decisions have proved controversial.

Development planning in Northern Ireland is highly centralised. After 1973, as a consequence of the 'TROUBLES', the Department of the Environment became the sole planning authority. Only a limited role was given to district councils, though they must be consulted during the preparation of a development plan. The process is managed by the Planning Service, a state agency that prepares development plans for the various districts that set out detailed policies and specific proposals for the development and use of land. It also manages planning applications. There is an independent planning appeals commission for applicants, but not for third parties. **Joseph Brady**

planning regions. Formal regional planning in both the Republic and Northern Ireland dates from the 1960s, when plans were commissioned for Belfast (Sir Robert Matthew), the mid-west (Nathaniel Lichfield and Associates), Dublin (Miles Wright and Partners), and the Republic as a whole (Colin Buchanan and Partners). The EU 'nomenclature of territorial units for statistics' (NUTS) is a means whereby the European Union defines a hierarchical system of regions, used as the basis for deciding eligible areas for structural funds, with regions classified from NUTS1 (very large) to NUTS5.

During the 1970s regional planning in the Republic became associated with industrial planning by the INDUSTRIAL DEVELOPMENT AUTHORITY (IDA) for eight regions. The Shannon Free Airport Development Company had responsibility for the ninth, the Mid-West Region, and Gaeltarra Éireann (subsequently replaced by Údarás na Gaeltachta) for the GAELTACHT. Regional development organisations, with broad co-ordination roles, were established in 1969, disestablished in 1987, and reinstated as eight regional authorities in 1994. The regions (NUTS3 level) were regrouped into two NUTS2 regions in 1999—the Border, Midlands and West Region, and the Southern and Eastern Region—and regional assemblies were established. The former has EU objective 1 status and the latter transitional objective 1 status.

The Northern Ireland Development Programme, 1970–75, was followed by a Regional Physical Development Strategy, 1975–95, based on twenty-six district council areas, rather than counties. The Education and Library Service is organised into five regions. Based on EU and GDP criteria, Northern Ireland is a transitional objective 1 and NUTS2 region. **Mary E. Cawley**

Plantation of Antrim and Down (1603). The plantation of Cos. Antrim and Down originated with the difficulties of Conn O'Neill, lord of much of north Down, who remained a prisoner in Carrickfergus after the ending of the NINE YEARS' WAR in 1603. Hugh Montgomery, a Scottish courtier, secured O'Neill's release in return for the promise of a large tract of land. Another royal favourite, James Hamilton, exerted pressure to benefit from lands on offer. To complicate matters further, Sir ARTHUR CHICHESTER, Lord Deputy of Ireland, with private interests already in the area, prevailed upon Montgomery and Hamilton to allow him to take a share in the rich rewards on offer. Further lands in Cos. Antrim and Down were acquired by similarly dubious practices, including the exploitation of a legal stratagem involving proxy land dealings, with Montgomery, Hamilton, and Chichester once again prominently involved. Whatever about its uncertain legal status in the early stages, there can be no doubt that these private enterprises greatly assisted Crown policy in sponsoring the effective settlement of English and Scots in Cos. Antrim and Down. The geographical proximity of Scotland greatly facilitated this process, though the leasing of lands by Chichester to a series of acquaintances, mostly army officers who had served under his command, also boosted the English presence in the area. Stipulations in the land grants that fortified dwellings be erected presaged a central aspect of the later official plantation of much of the rest of Ulster in 1610. **John McCavitt**

Plantation of Munster. Following the second DESMOND REBELLION (1579–83), ELIZABETH I confiscated the rebels' lands and, after a protracted process of survey and planning, granted 298,653 acres (120,000 ha) to thirty-five 'UNDERTAKERS' recruited from England to establish a plantation in Munster. The grantees received seigniories of up to 12,000 acres (4,850 ha) each and in turn undertook to clear the land of its Irish inhabitants and replace them with English settlers. The plantation formally got under way in September 1587, but its progress was hampered by litigation, as local people struggled to hold on to their land, succeeding in recovering some 28,000 ha (70,000 acres). Some planters settled English tenants and invested in their new estates; most, however, simply retained the local Irish people as tenants and made only a tentative start in transforming southern Ireland into a 'new England', as the Crown intended. The plantation was quickly overthrown in 1598 by Irish rebels under JAMES FITZGERALD, whom HUGH O'NEILL promoted to a revived Earldom of Desmond. Many of the settlers were stripped and were directed to return to England unceremoniously; others were mutilated and killed. However, after the NINE YEARS' WAR the plantation was re-established. Eleven seigniories, including that of WALTER RALEIGH, changed hands, and RICHARD BOYLE emerged as the leading figure in the revived plantation. By 1611 there were an estimated 14,000 settlers in the plantation; by 1641 there were 22,000, a significant English community, which played an important part in the transformation of Munster's society and economy (see p. 915). **Henry A. Jefferies**

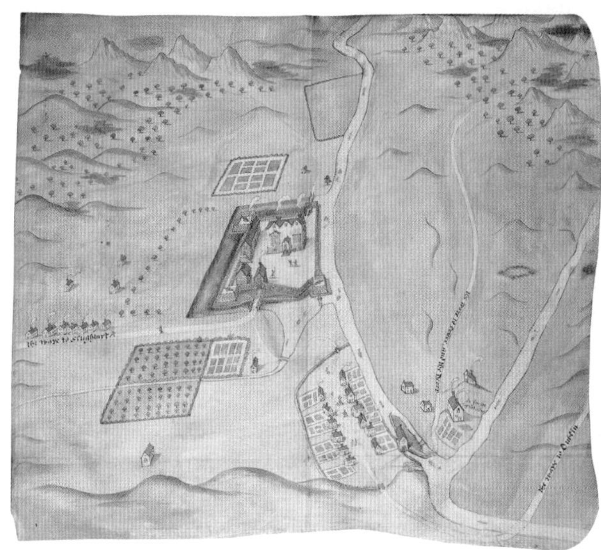

Plantation. *The fort and village of Omagh, Co. Tyrone, c. 1611. Depicted are a moated and fortified plantation manor-house, formal tree-planting and laid-out village with water-mill, essential elements in the establishment of new communities in Ulster. [Board of Trinity College, Dublin]*

Plantation of Ulster (1609). Despite its name, the scheme drawn up and implemented during 1609 and 1610 comprised only six of the nine counties of Ulster: Armagh, Tyrone, Fermanagh, Coleraine (Derry), Cavan, and Donegal. The remaining counties (Antrim, Down, and Monaghan) had been the subject of settlement initiatives in the period 1603–7. The plantation originated in the aftermath of the FLIGHT OF THE EARLS in 1607, when HUGH O'NEILL, Earl of Tyrone, and RORY O'DONNELL, Earl of Tyrconnell, fled to the Continent in suspicious circumstances. Convinced that treason had been planned, the Crown authorities took steps to confiscate the lands of O'Neill and O'Donnell and their associates. At first, guided by the Lord Deputy of Ireland, Sir ARTHUR CHICHESTER, a relatively small-scale settlement of Protestant colonists was planned. This intention was abandoned following the rebellion of Sir CAHIR O'DOHERTY in 1608. A further series of confiscations ensued. But the plantation was to increase not only in scope but also in scale. The native inhabitants of the affected areas, those known as the 'deserving' Irish, were to find that their proposed stake in the revised settlement was to be greatly reduced, which provoked considerable discontent. The primary beneficiaries of the plantation project, English and Scottish settlers, as well as the CHURCH OF IRELAND, were to be allocated almost three-quarters of the confiscated lands. The English and Scottish 'UNDERTAKERS' were assigned lands on favourable terms. The amount allocated was 400, 600, or 800 ha (1,000, 1,500, or 2,000 acres), on which they were expected to settle twenty-four British males per thousand acres. Various conditions were also laid down with regard to buildings, also scaled according to the amount of land granted, with those granted 2,000 acres expected to build a castle on the lands; a period of three years was allowed for fulfilment. However, continuing political uncertainty in Ireland militated against large numbers of Protestant settlers arriving by the time this period had elapsed. Subsequent migration resulted in a settler population of some 40,000 in Ulster by 1640. **John McCavitt**

plantations: see TUDOR PLANTATIONS.

planxty, a tune written in honour of a patron, particularly associated with the harper-composer TURLOUGH CAROLAN. Unlike much of the contemporary HARP repertoire, the planxty had no corresponding text. They are lively, spirited pieces in various time signatures (6/8 being the most common); there are no other unifying features in structure or style. [see MOORE, CHRISTY.] **Liz Doherty**

plasterwork. At the Ormond Manor House, Carrick-on-Suir, Co. Tipperary, some fine Elizabethan stuccowork of c. 1568 survives, incorporating heraldic medallions and portrait busts. At BUNRATTY CASTLE, Co. Clare, foliate stuccowork of c. 1619 adorns the chapel ceiling, and some fragments remain in the great hall. Such survivals are rare, and few complete Irish secular interiors survive from before the late seventeenth century, making it hard to generalise on the quality of early stuccowork. Undoubtedly any fine work was carried out by artisans from abroad. This must be the case with the remarkable ceiling in the chapel of the ROYAL HOSPITAL, Kilmainham, Dublin, which dates from the mid-1680s. This compartmented, coved and panelled ceiling (surviving in the form of a 1902 replacement) is profusely decorated in fruit, flowers, and vegetable ornament. The exaggerated ornamentation has transformed its Jonesian geometrical form in the realms of the baroque.

Domestic stuccowork before the mid-1720s consisted at its best of old-fashioned (by English standards), heavily moulded classical forms (as at Beaulieu, Co. Louth), sometimes with heraldic additions (as at STACKALLEN, Co. Meath). With the arrival of neo-Palladianism in the 1720s and 30s came bold cornices, covings, and geometrical compartmented ceiling flats (as at CASTLETOWN, Co. Kildare, and BELLAMONT FOREST, Co. Cavan). Mouldings were crisper and had good floral detail and even the occasional baroque flourish found on ceiling roses or friezes (as at Castletown). The subsequent consciously 'antique' Renaissance-inspired interiors of the 1720s (such as 9 Henrietta Street, Dublin) were in turn replaced from 1739 onwards by the vigorous Continental late baroque figural stuccowork of the LAFRANCHINI BROTHERS. These strongly modelled allegorical ceilings (as at CARTON, Co. Kildare, and 85 St Stephen's Green, Dublin) gave way in the 1740s to lively rococo ensembles dominated by acanthus foliage interwoven by occasional *putti* (as at Russborough House, Blessington, Co. Wicklow, and Tyrone House, Dublin). In the 1750s the most significant baroque or rococo stuccowork was that carried out in the chapel of the ROTUNDA HOSPITAL, Dublin, by BARTHOLOMEW CRAMILLION. This French artist has also been credited with several pictorial rococo ceilings, which illustrate a variety of narrative styles (such as Mespil House and La Touche Bank, Dublin). Under the influence of Cramillion and Lafranchini, there developed a number of individuals and workshops who carried out foliate rococo ceilings throughout Ireland until the mid-1770s. With the shift of fashion towards neo-classicism in the 1770s, stuccowork, dominated by the workshop of MICHAEL STAPLETON, interpreted the published designs of Adam, Rose, Richardson, and others. Native vigour prevailed, however, and Irish neo-classical ceilings are frequently densely filled and curiously imbued with a rococo rhythm (as at Belvedere House, Dublin, and Lucan House, Co. Dublin).

After 1800 the middle-class building boom relied mainly on mould-made plasterwork. A notable exception in the second and third decades of the nineteenth century is the work of Christopher Moore, whose exuberant and detailed stuccowork sometimes has a mid-eighteenth-century flavour (as at Carton and at Ballyfin, Co. Laois) (see pp. 543, 603). **Christopher Moore**

Playboy of the Western World, The (1907), a play by J. M. SYNGE. The playwright's masterpiece, it caused disturbances on its first performance, its detractors claiming that it traduced the people of Co. Mayo as drunkards, liars, and thugs at a time when a national theatre should have been depicting a sturdy folk ready to assume the responsibilities of self-government. The plot reworked a story that Synge had heard on the ARAN ISLANDS. In his version Christy Mahon fears he has killed his father with the blow of a spade, and he runs away to Co. Mayo, where repeated tellings of his deed bring him acclaim from villagers, who long for a hero figure. He wins the hand of Pegeen Mike, daughter of the local publican, only to lose her when his revived father appears and destroys his credibility. Christy is driven out, and Pegeen voices the social consensus: 'There's a great gap between a gallous story and a dirty deed.' **Declan Kiberd**

Playboy of the Western World (1962), a composition by SEÁN Ó RIADA, first released as the score of the film directed by Brian Desmond Hurst. He used a small orchestra of traditional and folk musicians, including whistles, FLUTE, and PIPES, violins and viola, and two button ACCORDIONS, with percussion consisting of BODHRÁN and BONES. Based on traditional and some original pieces, the unusual arrangements and use of these instruments was unique at the time. Ó Riada later developed the score as MUSIC for a BALLET of the same title by JOAN DENISE MORIARTY. **Peadar Ó Riada**

plays, historical and mythological. Beginning in the early seventeenth century, playwrights attempting to create a distinctively Irish dramatic form frequently turned towards history, legend, and myth. Indeed the first Irish play, James Shirley's ST PATRICK FOR IRELAND (1639), uses the legends surrounding St Patrick. Later attempts to create an indigenous drama—including Charles Shadwell's *Rotherick O'Connor* (1719) and William Philips's *Hibernia Freed* (1722)—stage semi-legendary moments in Irish history. Shadwell's play uses the VIKING invasions of the eleventh century to explore Ireland's complex (and, for Anglo-Irish writers, problematic) history of conquest. George Edmond Howard returned to the same material in 1773 with *The Siege of Tamor*, as did JAMES SHERIDAN KNOWLES with *Brian Boroimhe* [Bórú] (1811), which was still being successfully performed in the 1870s. At the same time Irish melodramas often found subject matter in history. From the late nineteenth century until the 1920s there was a popular sub-genre of melodramas dealing with the UNITED IRISHMEN and ROBERT EMMET.

The example of Wagner's exploration of Germanic mythology, and the excitement generated by the rediscovery of Irish MYTHOLOGY as part of a wider project of cultural nationalism, led to a flowering of mythological plays in the early twentieth century, of which ALICE MILLIGAN's *Last Feast of the Fianna* (1900) is an early example. From GEORGE RUSSELL's *Deirdre* (1902) to SYNGE's *Deirdre of the Sorrows* (1910) the mythological play was an important form in the early years of the LITERARY REVIVAL. However, with the increasing dominance of naturalistic theatre, and the growing mistrust of all forms of heroic posturing in the aftermath of the CIVIL WAR, by the 1930s W. B. YEATS was one of only a few remaining playwrights using the form. Yeats's mythological plays tower above those of his contemporaries: from *The King's Threshold* (1904) to *The Death of Cuchulain* (1939) they transcend the florid language and wooden characterisation of their predecessors. The history play, however, continues to thrive; Brian Friel's TRANSLATIONS (1980) and *Making History* (1988) and Frank McGuinness's OBSERVE THE SONS OF ULSTER MARCHING TOWARDS THE SOMME (1985) have continued a vital re-imagination of the Irish past. [see ABBEY THEATRE; FIELD DAY.] **Christopher Morash**

Plummer, Henry Crozier Keating (1875–1946), astronomer and mathematician. Born in Oxford, son of the astronomer W. E. Plummer; educated at the University of Oxford, where he graduated in mathematics and physics. After a year as lecturer in mathematics at Owen's College, Manchester, and a year as demonstrator at the Clarendon Laboratory, Oxford, he joined the staff of Oxford University Observatory in 1901. He went to DUNSINK OBSERVATORY in 1912 as Andrews professor of astronomy and carried out research on variable stars with the 15-inch Roberts reflector. In 1913 he suggested that the variability of certain stars was due to pulsations; this idea was later developed by A. Eddington. In 1921 he was appointed professor of mathematics at the Artillery College, Woolwich, London, where he wrote several textbooks. He was elected a fellow of the Royal Society, 1920, and was president of the Royal Astronomical Society, 1939–41. **Ian Elliott**

Plunkett, Edward, eighteenth Baron Dunsany (1878–1957), writer. Born in London. He succeeded to estates in Co. Meath, where he lived after the ANGLO-BOER WAR. He was a contemporary of the writers of the LITERARY REVIVAL but did not share their NATIONALISM, and befriended the poet FRANCIS LEDWIDGE. He was acquainted with H. G. Wells, MARY LAVIN, and OLIVER ST JOHN GOGARTY. His writing draws on MYTHOLOGY and fantasy, making him a precursor of such writers as Tolkien. He produced hundreds of plays and articles and fifty-five volumes of prose, including *Gods of Pegana* (1905), *Tales of Wonder* (1916), and *The King of Elfland's Daughter* (1924). **Joley Wood**

Plunkett, George Noble, Count (1851–1948), politician. Born in Dublin. Director of the NATIONAL MUSEUM of Ireland, 1907–16, he was dismissed following the execution of his son, JOSEPH MARY PLUNKETT, for his role in the 1916 RISING. In 1917 he was put forward by a group of SINN FÉIN supporters to contest the North Roscommon by-election; his unexpected victory over the Redmondite candidate signalled the changing political climate in the country. He was Minister for Foreign Affairs in the first DÁIL ÉIREANN and an abstentionist member, 1922–7. His title was a Papal honour. **T. G. Fraser**

Plunkett, Grace: see GIFFORD, GRACE.

Plunkett, Sir Horace Curzon (1854–1932), agricultural pioneer. Born in Sherborne, Dorset, third son of the seventeenth Baron Dunsany; educated at the University of Oxford. He founded the Irish Co-operative Movement in 1889. He was a member of the CONGESTED DISTRICTS BOARD and Unionist MP for South Dublin, 1892–1900. He formed the Recess Committee to urge the establishment of a Department of Agriculture and Industries, becoming the department's first acting head in 1900, resigning in 1907. In 1904 he published *Ireland in the New Century*. In 1917 he was chairman of the Irish Convention and was nominated to the Senate in 1922. During the CIVIL WAR his house, Kilteragh, Foxrock, Co. Dublin, was burned down, and he moved to Surrey. **Carla King**

Plunkett, Horace. *Cartoon of 'Cathleen Ní Houlihan' and Horace Plunkett, a pro-union MP serving South Dublin from 1892 to 1900, by Grace Plunkett (Grace Gifford). [Council of Trustees of the National Library of Ireland]*

Plunkett, James, pen-name of James Plunkett Kelly (1920–), writer. He grew up in working-class Dublin, the setting for much of his fiction. He published short stories in the BELL in the 1940s, encouraged by SEAN O'FAOLAIN, and collected them in *The Trusting and the Maimed* (1955). His radio play about JAMES LARKIN, *Big Jim*, was produced in 1954; but he is best known for his historical novel *Strumpet City* (1969), which sets life in early twentieth-century Dublin against a backdrop of national uprising. *Farewell Companions* (1977) and *The Circus Animals* (1990) continued to represent the same themes of class, NATIONALISM, and religion in later settings. **John Brannigan**

Plunkett, Joseph Mary (1887–1916), poet and revolutionary. Born in Dublin, son of COUNT GEORGE NOBLE PLUNKETT; educated at Belvedere College, Stonyhurst College, Lancashire, and UCD. He published a poetry collection, *The Circle and the Sword* (1911), and was joint-founder with THOMAS MACDONAGH, PÁDRAIC COLUM and JAMES STEPHENS of the *Irish Review*. With MacDonagh and EDWARD MARTYN he was a founder of the Irish Theatre in 1914. A member of the IRB and IRISH VOLUNTEERS, he was a signatory of the PROCLAMATION OF THE IRISH REPUBLIC in 1916 and served as director of military operations for the RISING. He was court-martialled and shot by firing squad on 4 May 1916, having married GRACE GIFFORD in KILMAINHAM GAOL the night before. **Elaine Sisson**

Plunkett, Hon. Katherine (1820–1932), painter and centenarian. Born in Kilsaran Rectory, Co. Louth, daughter of the Bishop of Tuam. She lived for most of her life in Ballymascanlan, near Dundalk. In her eighties she presented the NATIONAL MUSEUM with a volume of 1,200 plants she had painted from nature; it is now in the herbarium of the National Botanic Gardens. She died at the extraordinary age of 112, making her the oldest Irish person whose age can be authenticated. **Ciarán Deane**

Plunkett, Oliver (1625–1681), Catholic archbishop and martyr. Born at Loughcrew, near Oldcastle, Co. Meath; he travelled to Rome in 1647 to study for the priesthood with Father Scarampi, the Papal envoy to the CONFEDERATION OF KILKENNY, who helped finance his studies. Unable to return to Ireland after his ordination in 1654 because of the Cromwellian persecution, he was appointed a lecturer in the Collegio PROPAGANDA FIDE, Rome, in 1657, where he remained until his appointment as Archbishop of Armagh in 1669. He immediately began an energetic reorganisation of the Irish church and the imposing of discipline. Despite his expressed concern that there were too many secular priests in Ireland, he ordained large numbers for his own archdiocese and was at pains to ensure that they were both well educated and obedient. A notable feature of his primacy was his friendship with many prominent Protestants, both lay and clerical. His strained relations with the Franciscans, the largest and most influential of the regular orders in Ireland, predated his arrival in Ireland, when he had advocated a limitation on their numbers; his resolution in 1671 of a long and bitter dispute between them and the Dominicans in favour of the latter further soured relations, and members of the order were to give evidence against him at his trial. Plunkett was the main Irish victim of the Popish Plot. Arrested in 1679 and taken to London after an abortive trial in Dundalk, he was charged with high treason for allegedly plotting a French invasion. Despite his clear innocence, he was convicted and was hanged in July 1681. Plunkett was beatified in 1920 and canonised in 1975. **Liam Irwin**

'Poem Book of Fionn': see DUANAIRE FINN.

poems on the DART. Poems have been displayed in the DART (the Dublin Area Rapid Transit system) since January 1987. For its first decade the scheme used the rubric 'Poems on the DART', but since then the posters, moved to the bulkheads of the carriages, have been styled 'Poets' Corner'. The first poems to be put up were W. B. YEATS's 'Beautiful Lofty Things', with its reference to 'Maud Gonne at Howth station waiting a train', and a ninth-century nature poem in Irish, alongside a translation by THOMAS KINSELLA. Three Nobel laureates—SEAMUS HEANEY, Derek Walcott, and Joseph Brodsky—have read their poems in the carriages; Heaney, Craig Raine, and others have written poems expressly for the venture. **Jonathan Williams**

poetic families. Schools of language and literature that flourished in medieval Ireland c. 1200–1600 used a standardised literary dialect known as Classical or EARLY MODERN IRISH. The teachers and masters were the FILÍ, who produced grammatical treatises expounding the norms of the literary style, which were used as textbooks and so secured the primacy of the standardised dialect in the formal syllabic poetry produced by the graduates of the schools. These masters are known to us now as bardic poets and their poetry as bardic poetry or *filíocht na scol* (poetry of the schools); in general they are referred to in Irish sources as the *aos dána* (artists).

Subjects suitable for classical compositions included the usual list associated with 'court' poetry: praise poetry (the largest category of surviving material), religious poems, poems of reconciliation with an angry patron (a stereotyped form of the genre), and praise of the dwellings of the chief. Many families kept collections of poems in DUANAIRÍ or poem books.

It is not clear exactly how the schools evolved, how they were organised, or how they were maintained. Generally they survived under the auspices of local political patronage, through association with the ecclesiastical school system, perhaps on the income accumulated by the successful poet, and perhaps on scholars' fees. The school year began at Michaelmas (29 September) or in November and finished on the feast of the Annunciation (25 March). A scholar might travel around Ireland and Scotland to avail of the teaching of various masters; this added to his prestige as well as to his contacts. An intensive course of six or seven years covering all branches of literature was followed. Several varieties of metre were learnt and practised, suitable examples were used as standard formulas, tales and sagas were learnt by heart, and official histories and genealogies were taught.

As with many medieval institutions, the profession and craft of poetry and of teaching in the schools became hereditary. Chronicles and ANNALS depict the continuity of the professions of poetry, law, medicine, religion, and other crafts in the often scant information conveyed in obituary notices. The title OLLAMH was used in respect of those who achieved the highest status among their peers and who, in the later period, seemingly enjoyed a regular reciprocal arrangement with a chief in the formula 'X, ollamh to Y.'

The seventeenth-century scholar DUBHALTACH MAC FHIRBHISIGH listed the most prominent of the families involved in teaching and the composition of poetry. Among them are Uí Dálaigh, Uí Uiginn, Clann an Bhaird (Mac an Bhaird), Clann Chon Midhe (Mac Con Midhe), Uí Eodhusa, and Uí Gnímh; Clann Bhruaideadha (Mac Bruaideadha) were listed among those whose speciality was history. The *filí* flourished in a system of composition and reward, and the eulogistic function they exercised was part of the aristocratic economy of the era.

The most prominent of the learned families associated with the classical poetry of medieval and early modern Ireland is that of Uí Dálaigh. They were linked with the schools specifically from the mention of their supposed progenitor, Cúchonnacht na Scoile (died 1139), 'chief professor of poetry at Clonard'. Originating in the midlands, poets of this surname emerged in each province, all traditionally regarded as descendants of Aonghus, a grandson of Cúchonnacht na Scoile. Various branches of the sept appear in thirty-six entries of the Annals of the FOUR MASTERS between 1139 and 1589.

The Connacht family of Ó hUiginn appear in no fewer than thirty-three entries in the Annals of the Four Masters between 1315 and 1536. The best-known of the name is the sixteenth-century poet TADHG DALL Ó HUIGINN, who dedicated poems to the prominent leaders of his time, including Mac Suibhne, Ó Ruairc, Ó hEadhra, Ó Domhnaill, and Ó Néill. His brother Maol Muire was Archbishop of Tuam. The earliest example of an edition in print of a poem from the schools is that of a composition by PILIB BOCHT Ó HUIGINN (died 1487), in the form of a broadsheet dated 1571.

Clann an Bhaird were originally a Connacht family, but by the sixteenth century their closest political association was with the O'Donnells of Tír Chonaill. In the Annals of the Four Masters the name Mac an Bhaird occurs from 1173 (Maelísa, a bishop).

Compositions in the style of the schools are attributed to members of Clann an Bhaird down to the middle of the seventeenth century. Twenty-two entries in the Annals of the Four Masters spanning some 400 years give an idea of the cultural continuity possible in medieval and early modern Ireland.

Another prominent Ulster family was Clann Chon Midhe. Originating in the midlands, this family was settled in what is now Co. Tyrone, becoming known as poets to O'Neill of Tyrone. The Annals of the Four Masters mention members of this family in ten entries in the half millennium between 1095 and 1582. The Uí Eodhusa produced poets noted in the Annals of the Four Masters from 1350 to 1618. The family became associated with Fermanagh's leading sept, Maguire. The best-known of them are the sixteenth-century poet EOCHAIDH Ó HEODHUSA (died 1613) and his kinsman GIOLLA BRIGHDE (in religion Bonaventure) Ó HEODHUSA (died 1618).

Clann Bhruaideadha were of Munster origin. Though principally involved with *seanchas* or history, they emerge in the annals as a family of poets towards the end of the sixteenth century, dedicating poems to members of the O'Dea, O'Quinn and MacGorman families and later to the O'Briens, Earls of Thomond. The earliest attribution of a classical poem to a member of this family, Seán Buí Mac Bruaideadha, is dated to the late fourteenth century.

The family of Ó Gnímh appear towards the end of the sixteenth century and in the early decades of the seventeenth as poets associated with the O'Neills of Clandeboye in the person of two poets in particular, Brian Ó Gnímh and FEAR FLATHA Ó GNÍMH. Fear Flatha is the author of a moving composition on the 'death of poetry', 'Tairing Éigse Fhuinn Gaoidheal', in which he mentions in particular his contemporary Eochaidh Ó hEodhusa and in general the principal families of poetry. **Michelle O Riordan**

poetry in English. Irish poetry in English took root in the seventeenth and eighteenth centuries as a consequence of the conquest and the development of a distinctive form of the language, termed HIBERNO-ENGLISH. From this period come many anonymous ballads—'The Wearing of the Green' and the ORANGE SONG 'LILLIBURLERO' among the most famous—that make this verse form ubiquitous in the poetic tradition. Polite letters offered much occasional verse from within the ranks of the Anglo-Irish Ascendancy; an increasing appreciation of such poets as WILLIAM DUNKIN, THOMAS PARNELL, and LAETITIA PILKINGTON suggests that JONATHAN SWIFT and OLIVER GOLDSMITH were not isolated figures in the period.

Changes in European taste, in which the OSSIANIC craze played its part, made Ireland in the nineteenth century a site of romantic feeling, and in this context THOMAS MOORE achieved renown with his *Irish Melodies*. The nineteenth century also saw antiquarian interest in the Celtic past develop into a nationally minded celebration of Irish civilisation. English-language versions of saga material evoked a heroic prehistory in the works of SAMUEL FERGUSON. Others, such as J. J. CALLANAN and JAMES CLARENCE MANGAN, allowed English-language verse to bear the imprint of Irish prosody, while translation from Irish became a popular activity, vested with national significance.

It was W. B. YEATS who, in his poetry and in his critical writings, deliberately sought to invoke a distinctive Anglo-Irish poetic tradition. His own immense achievement as a poet and as prime mover in the LITERARY REVIVAL meant that it was no longer possible to consider Irish poetry in English as merely English verse with an Irish accent, for Yeats had self-consciously made Ireland—its history, MYTHOLOGY, FOLKLORE, and topography—the basis of a lifelong inspiration. Subsequent Irish poets writing in English inevitably felt his presence as intimidating precursor. AUSTIN CLARKE chose, in Yeats's shadow, to concentrate on aspects of Irish historical experience that Yeats had largely ignored, including the Hiberno-Romanesque period of Celtic Christianity, making his verse seem more distinctively Irish than Yeats had done. PATRICK KAVANAGH, by contrast, eschewed history, mythology, and Irish-language tradition in his anti-romantic portrayal of rural life, which had so inspired Yeats and the poets of the revival. A later generation of Irish poets writing in English found it possible to take the Yeatsian achievement for granted and to develop themes and styles appropriate to an individual rather than an explicitly national vision. In the poetry of THOMAS KINSELLA Dublin is made the setting for a drama of racial and personal conscience reminiscent of JAMES JOYCE's fiction. Women poets such as EILÉAN NÍ CHUILLEANÁIN, EAVAN BOLAND, and MEDBH MCGUCKIAN have registered female experience as a poetic theme.

Poetry in English is written by poets from all parts of Ireland and in its variety and energy it reflects a country increasingly at ease with its dual-language inheritance. From the 1960s, poetry by poets born in Northern Ireland has in particular enjoyed international attention; among these are MICHAEL LONGLEY, DEREK MAHON, PAUL MULDOON, and SEAMUS HEANEY. Their work bears witness to a period of violence but also reflects a commitment to aesthetic values as a prevailing aspect of the Irish experience. **Terence Brown**

Poetry Ireland/Éigse Éireann, the national poetry society of Ireland, founded by JOHN F. DEANE in 1978. Based in Dublin Castle, it publishes a quarterly journal, *Poetry Ireland Review*, and a bi-monthly newsletter, *Ireland News*. Poetry Ireland, which is a clearing house for anything pertaining to poetry in Ireland, organises poetry readings countrywide and, through its education department, administers the Writers in Schools Scheme. Its extensive poetry library includes the collections of AUSTIN CLARKE and JOHN JORDAN. The poet THEO DORGAN was director of Poetry Ireland, 1985–2000, and the GREAT BOOK OF IRELAND (1989), a collaboration between Poetry Ireland and Clashganna Mills Trust. **Brian Lalor**

poets: see FILÍ.

Pogues, the, rock group, formed in the early 1980s by Shane MacGowan, Peter 'Spider' Stacey, and Jem Finer. Blending TRADITIONAL MUSIC with punk rock, their debut album, *Red Roses for Me* (1984), introduced a major songwriting talent in MacGowan, whose disciplined lyrics in songs such as 'Dark Streets of London' and 'Streams of Whiskey' combined the rawness of Brendan Behan with a metropolitan poetic sensibility. *Rum, Sodomy and the Lash* (1985), produced by Elvis Costello, was even better. From an Irish viewpoint the gradual introduction of Philip Chevron (the former guitarist of RADIATORS FROM SPACE) and Terry Woods (formerly of SWEENEY'S MEN) contributed to the line-up. Loved by expatriate Irish in London and beyond, the band was nevertheless loathed by some traditional music purists. A raucous duet with the DUBLINERS, 'The Irish Rover' (1987), only added to the debate. The Pogues reached their commercial and creative zenith with the release of the poignant hit single 'Fairy Tale of New York' (1987) with Kirsty McColl and the album from which it came, *If I Should Fall from Grace with God* (1988). By this time MacGowan's heavy drinking had begun to have a deleterious effect on the collective creative talent of the band. Both *Peace and Love* (1989) and *Hell's Ditch* (1990) featured fewer MacGowan songs. By 1991 the Pogues had ceased to function with MacGowan as vocalist, releasing a couple of albums, *Waiting for Herb* (1993) and *Pogue Mahone* (1995), to decreasing interest. A solo career for MacGowan beckoned with a band called the Popes; *The Snake* (1994) and *The Crock of Gold* (1997) were well received. **Tony Clayton-Lea**

Pogues. *The Pogues, a rock group formed in the early 1980s: (standing left to right) James Fearnley, Peter Stacey, and Shane MacGowan, (kneeling left to right) Andrew Ranken and Jem Finer. They are acclaimed for their music, described as a hybrid of punk and Irish traditional music. [John Minihan]*

poitín (poteen), illicit home-made spirit. Poitín has been distilled in various ways for several centuries. The first levy imposed on it was introduced in 1661 but was completely ignored. In 1760 a new law made it necessary for all distillers to have a licence; and poitín-making has been illegal ever since. Its distillation, however, was not considered a CRIME by the rural community. In the early nineteenth century it was made with malt, but this was inconvenient and increased the risk of detection, and the use of raw grain was introduced instead. As the growing of grain declined, however, other ingredients were used, including sugar, POTATOES, and apples. Poitín was most commonly made in the west and north-west; it was sold locally and transported to market towns, where it was often consumed in SHEBEENS. The illegal distillation of poitín continues today, but its consumption is no longer commonplace. [see ALCOHOL CONSUMPTION.] **Ciarán Deane**

polar exploration. The involvement of Irishmen in polar exploration largely arises from their recruitment into the Royal Navy and the British merchant service. The Corkman EDWARD BRANSFIELD, who rose from the deck, was a merchant seaman before he was pressed into the Royal Navy, while the naval career of Sir ERNEST SHACKLETON was in the merchant service because of his family's lack of means. THOMAS CREAN made a name for himself in Antarctic exploration through his recruitment into the Royal Navy. The story of nineteenth-century Arctic exploration, dominated by the tragedy of Sir John Franklin's expedition, is filled with the names of Irish sailors, beginning with FRANCIS CROZIER, who perished in the expedition, and highlighted by ROBERT M'CLURE, the discoverer of the North-West Passage. [see BRITISH EMPIRE, IRISH IN.] **Peter Somerville-Large**

Police Service of Northern Ireland (PSNI): see ROYAL ULSTER CONSTABULARY.

policing. Modern policing dates from 1814, when ROBERT PEEL, then CHIEF SECRETARY FOR IRELAND, introduced the Peace Preservation Force. A separate Irish Constabulary was formed in 1822, which absorbed the Peace Preservation Force in 1836 to become a national police force, though separate municipal police existed in some cities. In 1867 the Irish Constabulary was given the prefix 'Royal' as a result of its action in containing civil unrest. Policing in this pre-1922 period was shaped by Ireland's relationship with Britain, in that policing tended to conform to the colonial model. However, by the beginning of the twentieth century and until the WAR OF INDEPENDENCE the RIC had become more socially integrated and was no longer colonial in its style.

The RIC was disbanded in 1922 on PARTITION, the ROYAL ULSTER CONSTABULARY replacing it in the North and the GARDA SÍOCHÁNA in the South. The Garda purposely established itself as a civil police force on the liberal model, encouraging close contact with the community and establishing consent from the public, and refusing to be armed. The RUC fared differently. The illegitimacy of the Northern state to nationalists affected both the RUC's policing role and its social composition. It was forced to develop a public order role in civil unrest and never met its quota of one-third Catholic membership; meanwhile Protestants tended to appropriate the force as their own. The RUC never succeeded in overcoming these problems, despite instances of reform since 1969, which culminated in 2002 in the replacement of the RUC by the PSNI (Police Service of Northern Ireland). **John Brewer**

political culture normally refers to the core values of a community. These are a product of the community's history, providing it with distinctive attitudes and behaviour; its normative character allows it to persist over time. In the Republic the political culture is homogeneous and consensual, whereas in Northern Ireland there are two political cultures, which internalise distinctive and conflicting values. In the Republic the traditional characteristics are Catholicism, NATIONALISM, proprietorialism, PATRIARCHY, and authoritarianism; these were institutionalised in legislation and in the CONSTITUTION OF IRELAND (1937) and remain influential. Change has taken place gradually since the 1970s, but the political culture has been modified rather than transformed. Political culture is now more pluralist and secular and less irredentist than heretofore, but the core values of nationalism and RELIGION continue to influence opinion and behaviour. **Brian Girvin**

political poetry in Irish, seventeenth century. The Irish bardic poet from c. 1200 to c. 1600 was for the most part the official political apologist for his feudal lord. According to O'Donovan's celebrated definition, 'he was often a public official, a chronicler, a political essayist.' Political poetry in the strict sense, however, inspired by and reflecting the cultural and social turmoil of the period, chronicles the defeat of Gaelic Ireland after the BATTLE OF KINSALE (1601), through the tribulations of the century and the development of the allegorical AISLING.

The historical conditions of the time caused the poets to turn to the poetry of Job, the Psalms, Jeremiah, and Isaiah in particular as exemplars for their own predicament in the cultural and religious upheaval that followed the REFORMATION. Many of the themes and motifs that appeared at the end of the Middle Ages in French poetry in particular reappear throughout European literature of this period of religious and political unrest and can be traced back to the Bible: God's anger at people's sin as an explanation for their suffering; Ireland depicted as the Whore of Babylon; and an emphasis on the author's personal suffering. Stylistically too the common European baroque is all-pervasive and rhetorical hyperbole much in evidence. Much of this poetry too has a definite structure, which reflects the devotional and meditative practices of the period, including a dramatic opening, often containing a composition of place, followed by a detailed analysis of the question in hand, often by means of an application of the senses, and finishing with a definite conclusion, usually in the form of a request or prayer. In all probability this significant structural development in Irish poetry was mediated through the devotional practices of the Irish Continental college movement.

From the beginning of the seventeenth century an uneasy sense of foreboding pervades the work of the later bards. EOCHAIDH Ó HEODHUSA expresses his concern for the young Hugh Maguire in his poem 'Fúar Liom an Adhaighsi dh'Aodh' in terms of pending apocalyptic doom, while EOGHAN RUA MAC AN BHAIRD's frequent use of the word *anbhuain* (angst) portends a similar sense of unease and urgency. The note of personal anxiety becomes a cry *de profundis* at the fate that has befallen the nation in the poetry of GEOFFREY KEATING ('Óm sgeol ar Ardmhagh Fáil ní chodlaim oidhche') and the Biblical meditations that chronicle Ireland's woes at the time of the Cromwellian campaign, 'An Síogaí Rómhánach' and 'Deorchaoineadh na hÉireann' (1648).

Towards the end of the seventeenth century DÁIBHÍ Ó BRUADAIR muses in heart-rending terms on the fall of the great race: 'D'aithle na bhFileadh n-Uasal' bemoans the decline of native learning, while 'Suim Purgadóra bhFear nÉireann' details the suffering of his countrymen during the years 1641–84.

By the close of the seventeenth century poetry was to turn to Messianic aspiration; and the efforts of the last of the great Irish poets, AOGÁN Ó RATHAILLE, regarded as the father of the fully developed aisling, expresses the hope for the salvation of the Gaeil in the darker days of the 'hidden Ireland', even after all expectation of foreign help had long since disappeared. His finest aisling, 'Gile na gile', transcends the exigencies of place and time and testifies to the resilience, hope, dignity, pride, and independence of the human condition. [see JACOBITE POETRY.] **Tadhg Ó Dúshláine**

political street art in Northern Ireland. The practice of painting political murals on the walls of inner-city housing in Belfast and other Northern Ireland towns dates from the early 1900s and took place in working-class loyalist areas in the weeks preceding the July–August 'MARCHING SEASON', during which the BATTLE OF THE BOYNE is commemorated. It has no parallel in any other part of the island. The Boyne and its victor, William of Orange, gave the early muralists their principal subject, that of King William on a prancing white horse crossing the river, a subject borrowed from the iconography of the banners carried during Orange marches, in turn derived from seventeenth-century historical engravings of the event. Bobby Jackson's 1920s murals of the Boyne and the SIEGE OF DERRY at the Fountain, Derry, mirror the subjects of the two great tapestries by the HUGUENOT weaver Jan van Beaver that hang in the House of Lords chamber of the PARLIAMENT HOUSE, Dublin.

Public murals are an ephemeral art form and are frequently either painted over and disappear or are retouched annually. Over the initial seventy-year period up to the 1980s the loyalist mural-painters came from the trades of house and coach painters, and the amateurism of these practitioners continues to determine the prevailing standard of all subsequent work, irrespective of political affiliation. It was not until the emergence of a nationalist mural-painting tradition following the HUNGER STRIKES of 1981 that new subject matter and more overt political language began to appear on Northern walls. This change led in turn to an invigoration and expansion of the loyalist mural tradition. Since that time a small number of professionally trained artists have joined the ranks of the still largely untutored muralists. What began as a purely demotic art form gradually expanded its canvas to include almost any accessible surface, utilising a much wider repertoire of imagery, symbols, and slogans than had previously been considered. Murals and street art became territorial markers rather than purely cultural emblems or celebrations of heritage. Garden walls, pavement kerbs, street surfaces, the blank gable ends of local authority housing blocks were all enlisted in an ever-expanding range of public political statements and engagements. Even the international language of traffic signs came into use in the creation of bogus examples displaying paramilitary imagery. Comment on local and everyday events also became commonplace as the subject matter for murals.

political street art. Petrol Bomber *(1994), photo-realist political mural at Rossville Street, Derry, by the 'Bogside artists', showing a boy with gas mask and petrol bomb during the Battle of the Bogside, 1969. [Bogside Artists; photo: Bill Rolston, from* Drawing Support, *2]*

The loyalist tradition that began with King William and the Siege of Derry expanded its visual repertoire to include a wide range of symbolism utilising the Union Jack, the RED HAND OF ULSTER, heraldic devices, and a map of Northern Ireland. Added to these graphics came imagery of armed loyalist fighters in paramilitary attire with texts asserting the Britishness or independence of Ulster. The loyalist range of imagery is focused on Ulster topics and symbolism, with excursions abroad in references to the heroism and sacrifice on the battlefields of the FIRST WORLD WAR and a fellowship with Israel. The appearance of OLIVER SHEPPARD's figure of the 'Fall of CUCHULAINN' (1911), portrayed as 'defender of Ulster from Irish attack', is based on the original sculpture that now stands in the GPO in Dublin, the Valhalla of NATIONALISM (see p. 1090). This same Cú Chulainn image appears with equal frequency on nationalist murals.

Nationalist murals share many basic approaches and formats with the loyalist versions: heraldic and religious symbols, maps (of Ireland in this instance), cartoons, armed and masked paramilitaries in action, slogans, and texts, the latter frequently, as in loyalist murals, reiterating popular ideological quotations (see p. 901). The point where nationalist murals show an awareness missing in their loyalist counterparts is in harnessing the graphic language of nineteenth-century and particularly late twentieth-century fine art, and in references to liberation struggles around the world. Imagery from the German expressionist Kate Kollwitz (Lecky Road, Derry), variations on Edvard Munch's *The Scream* and superb photo-realism (both at Rossville Street flats, Derry), the aptly political contemporary American artist Leon Golub (Bancroft Park, Newry), and the Spanish Paolo Genovese (Crossmaglen, Co. Armagh) have merged with traditional mural language to vastly invigorate what was essentially a static and naïve visual tradition. The internationalising of the republican position is conveyed by suggested fellowship with liberation struggles, with the PLO (Palestine), Nicaragua, ANC (South Africa), and Native Americans. BOBBY SANDS is seen with CHE GUEVARA and Lenin (Cable Street, Derry).

Even more subject to a limited life span than the public mural art of the streets are the paper ephemera of conflict. Beginning in 1968, the year in which the 'TROUBLES' intensified, the LINEN HALL LIBRARY in Belfast began to systematically collect works on paper (posters, hand-bills, leaflets, stickers, commemorative publications, and memorabilia) produced by the many strands of public opinion in Northern Ireland and by 2002 had amassed a collection of more than a quarter of a million items dating from 1966 onwards. This archive is unparalleled in its tracking of the imagery of political struggle in Ireland and complements the content of the wall murals in a vastly increased range of subjects and imagery, suggesting a wider diversity of concerns than is implied by the territorially and ethnically fixated murals. Slogans as close and as opposed as *Smash Stormont* and *Smash Sinn Féin*, each accompanied by appropriate imagery (a crumbling building, a Union Jack), or *It's right to say no* and *Give bigotry the red card*, are typical of the terse language and immediacy of the poster art of the conflict. The level of widespread and passionate public engagement in the political evolution of Northern Ireland is nowhere more tangibly recorded than in its street art, represented by its muralists and poster-makers. **Brian Lalor**

polka, a dance originating in Bohemia that became popular throughout Europe; it was introduced to Ireland towards the end of the nineteenth century. A simple, rhythmic tune in 2/4 time, the polka, along with the slide, remains a common tune for SET-DANCING and is associated in particular with Cos. Cork and Kerry. **Liz Doherty**

Pollaphuca Reservoir, an artificial lake on the River LIFFEY at Blessington, Co. Wicklow, created by the damming of the Pollaphuca gorge in 1940. With an area of 1,200 ha (2,900 acres) and a maximum depth of 31 m (100 ft), it is the largest reservoir in Ireland. Designed for the production of electric power, to supply domestic water to Dublin and its suburbs, and to control FLOODING in the Liffey, it has also provided an immense amenity area for water sports, fishing, and nature conservation. **Christopher Moriarty**

pollen analysis or palynology, the study of pollen grains (modern and fossil) of flowering plants and conifers and the spores of ferns, mosses, algae, and fungi. Pollen grains and spores of many plant families differ morphologically and can be identified microscopically, in many instances to species level, by their distinct shape, size (approx. 10–100 μm), sculpturing, and number of apertures. Of fundamental significance to the science of pollen analysis is the fact that pollen and spores are produced in relatively large quantities and are distributed away from the site of production (predominantly by wind or insects). Pollen and spores are extremely resistant to decay under anaerobic conditions and in suitable sedimentary environments can survive for thousands of years. Furthermore, the pollen composition within the sedimentary matrix reflects the vegetation of the area around the site of preservation at the time of deposition.

Vertical cores extracted from lake and bog sediments rich in fossil pollen and spores are the main source of material for analysis. Individual sediment samples along the length of the core are treated with highly corrosive chemicals, which serve to remove unwanted debris, such as carbonates, cellulose, and minerogenic particles, while concentrating the pollen, which is unaffected by the chemicals. The residues containing the pollen and spores are mounted on glass slides in a suitable medium, and all pollen and spores are identified and counted until a pollen sum high enough to ensure statistical reliability (approx. 700 grains or more) is achieved. The proportions of different pollen types present in each sample are usually expressed as a percentage of total terrestrial pollen for that sample and are depicted graphically in a *pollen diagram*. Since peat and lake muds accumulate over time, this data can be interpreted in terms of past vegetation around the site.

One of the most frequently used applications of pollen analysis is the study of vegetation history and environmental change over time. In most instances changes in the vegetation of an area recognised in pollen diagrams are due to CLIMATE change or human impact on the landscape. In Ireland, vegetation history from late glacial times to the present has been particularly well documented in pollen diagrams, which record the development of woodlands as the FLORA responded to climatic amelioration at the end of the last Ice Age and the initiation and spread of peatlands. In addition, detailed, high-quality site-specific pollen analysis has been particularly useful in the detection of long-term human impact on Holocene (of the last 11,500 years) environments. Coupled with accurate RADIOCARBON DATING, pollen analysis has made it possible for the nature and duration of prehistoric farming events in areas of prime archaeological significance to be reconstructed, in many instances for the first time. [see DENDROCHRONOLOGY; NEOLITHIC IRELAND.] **Karen Molloy**

Ponsonby family. Originating with Sir John Ponsonby, who accompanied OLIVER CROMWELL to Ireland in 1649, successive generations of Ponsonbys rose to positions of eminence in politics, the law, and the military in Ireland and Britain over several centuries. Among the most notable were John Ponsonby (1713–1789), the political UNDERTAKER, Speaker of the Irish House of Commons, and long-time leader of the powerful Ponsonby interest; George Ponsonby (1755–1817), briefly Lord Chancellor of Ireland and leader of the WHIG Party in the British Parliament; and the reclusive Sarah Ponsonby, who set up home at Llangollen with LADY ELEANOR BUTLER. **James Kelly**

pooka (Irish *púca*), a spirit who assumes the form of a horse-like creature, which was said to take mortals away on nightmare rides at night, leaving them home exhausted by dawn. Particular places are associated with the manifestation of this troublesome spirit; one such is POLLAPHUCA (*Poll an Phúca*, the hole or pool of the Púca), Co. Wicklow. Children were told not to eat berries or other fruit after Hallowe'en (*Oíche Shamhna*), as the pooka went about on that night, spoiling all wild fruits. **Anne O'Connor**

Pool and Cash (fl. 1770s–1790s), engravers. As students in the Dublin Society's Architectural School, Robert Pool and John Cash were taught by THOMAS IVORY. They published *Views of the Most Remarkable Public Buildings, Monuments and Other Edifices in the City of Dublin* (1780), the first such comprehensive record of Dublin and its ARCHITECTURE since Brooking's map of 1728. The buildings included are mostly from after 1760 and are dominated by the work of Ivory and THOMAS COOLEY; they reflect the growing sense of a powerful and independent city. Pool and Cash's engravings were much copied after their publication. The Pigeon House Hotel (1793–8) on the South Bull, Dublin, has been attributed to Pool. **Eve McAulay**

Pooley, Thomas (1646–1723), portrait painter. Born in Suffolk, the son of a Dublin attorney; he received his legal education at Gray's Inn, London, and began his artistic training, probably in London, c. 1670. His earliest known portraits, of the Southwell family and their relatives, were painted in 1674. He came to Ireland in 1676 in the train of the Earl of Essex and soon established himself as the principal portrait painter to the establishment in Dublin. Several of his portraits, painted in the manner of Lely and Kneller, are now in the great hall of the ROYAL HOSPITAL, Kilmainham, Dublin. **Jane Fenlon**

Poor Laws. In 1833 a Commission was appointed to inquire into the condition of the poorer classes in Ireland. Evidence of the nature of widespread poverty was taken from a cross-section of eighteen parishes, resulting in the most comprehensive report on the social conditions of the Irish poor in the pre-GREAT FAMINE period. The commissioners were opposed to a Poor Law for Ireland, favouring a system of voluntary assistance.

The Irish Poor Law Act of 1838 set up a national administrative system for the relief of the destitute poor in Ireland. The day to day running of the WORKHOUSE was controlled by elected Poor Law Guardians while the Poor Law Commissioner and his assistants determined workhouse policy at national level. Ratepayers in each of the 163 Poor Law districts (unions) paid a tax (a poor rate) that contributed to the upkeep of paupers in the workhouse. The Poor Law Commission was the central policymaking and regulatory structure responsible for the administration of the Poor Law in Ireland. The Dublin-based Poor Law Commissioner and his assistants sought to ensure that the 163 Poor Law unions and their board of guardians acted in a uniform manner in their administration of relief.

The Irish Poor Laws offered non-statutory relief to the destitute, as part of a carefully worked-out strategy for peace in Ireland. Anybody who wanted could enter the workhouse and avail of food, shelter, medical attention, rudimentary education, apprenticeship, and seasonal work, as well as religious services. On 31 December 1840 there was a total of 5,648 people in the workhouse and a total of 10,910 relieved during the year. By 31 December 1846, heading for the worst year of the Famine, there were 96,437 people in the workhouse with a total of 243,933 seeking assistance during 1846. The workhouse was not designed to cope with such numbers and as a result many of the destitute perished. To offset these crises the Poor Law Extension Act was passed in 1847. Relief to the poor in the form of food was now available outside the workhouse but those who owned a quarter acre of land had to relinquish it in order to avail of poor relief. As a further response to the crises of the Famine and the prevalence of disease, auxiliary workhouses were built and fever hospitals were established to take care of the sick poor.

In an effort to reduce the number of paupers in the workhouse over 4,000 young girls were assisted to emigrate to Australia in 1848. This initiated a period of widespread, predominately female, assisted pauper EMIGRATION to North America. [see GREGORY ACT.] **Dympna McLoughlin**

poplin. Irish poplin, of silk warp and worsted weft, was a hard-wearing fabric with corded surface and lustrous silk finish, woven in various weights, weaves, and patterns. The traditional poplin industry prospered in the early nineteenth century; VICTORIA's coronation train was of Dublin poplin woven with symbols of the Union in white and gold. Irish furnishing poplins (harder-wearing fabrics woven with silk warp and cotton or LINEN weft) were used in the royal courts of Europe in the nineteenth century.

Market-conscious Dublin poplin-weavers constantly tried to improve the fabric by reducing its weight. Its durability became even less attractive in the late nineteenth century; but in 1903 the Dublin

popular music. *Dickie Rock and the Miami Showband, performing on 4 May 1968. One of the most popular showbands of the 1960s, between 1963 and 1977 they had eight top ten hits. [Michael O'Reilly]* houses introduced a new line: poplin ties and scarves, sold in clubs throughout the BRITISH EMPIRE and the United States. The sumptuary rulings for clergy at the SECOND VATICAN COUNCIL sounded the death knell for the Dublin poplin industry. **Mairead Dunlevy**

popular music. The origins of Irish popular music are to be found in New York in the 1920s. The early recording industry realised that a particularly Irish music was commercially viable, and groups such as the Flanagan Brothers began to record TRADITIONAL MUSIC for the Irish-American market. They became Ireland's pioneering pop stars. The music, though grounded in traditional techniques, was heavily influenced by American show business and by exposure to various international sounds. With the practical need to be audible in the larger dance halls of New York, louder instruments were introduced, creating not only vaudeville groups like the Flanagans but also the large-scale CÉILÍ BANDS. When all these new sounds reached Ireland by way of 78 r.p.m. records, Irish musicians began to make similar music at home. Home-grown céilí bands achieved considerable popular status and reigned until their displacement by the showbands—very often the same people adapting to the new demands of dancers.

The arrival of the showbands is more usually regarded as the beginning of Irish pop. When they first took control of Irish entertainment, their only competition was the céilí bands. The showbands, with their suits and dance routines, played successfully to huge crowds all over Ireland. The music itself was almost entirely a matter of 'covering' hits from the British top thirty. There was little room for creativity or individuality; but with the ballrooms constantly full, the showbands relentlessly played the latest material. The bands were usually of high calibre, but their dominance on the music scene seemed for a time both stifling and unbreakable.

The worldwide musical impact of the 1960s was therefore slow in coming. An alternative emerged, however, when small groups of musicians sought out new venues in which to play music more in tune with the times. In Belfast groups like Them were at the heart of a rhythm-and-blues boom, and their lead singer, VAN MORRISON, went on to international success. In Dublin the beat group scene grew up around a series of small venues. The approach of groups like the Greenbeats was to play music of their own together with well-chosen covers of material by the stalwarts of American rhythm and blues and the Beatles. It was all a reaction against the showband phenomenon, and it provided a more 'hip' focus for the more sophisticated young person. This was a period that produced, among others, RORY GALLAGHER, PAUL BRADY, Van Morrison, and the early THIN LIZZY.

By the 1970s there was another generation of young musicians with yet another approach. Both the showbands and the beat scene were still lingering when groups like HORSLIPS emerged. Coming from a background that combined graphic design, poetry, advertising, and glam rock, they invented a fusion of traditional music and seventies rock, known as 'Celtic rock'. Horslips were to prove a cultural force, taking their music into the heart of the showband world and playing the same venues. There they found a loyal following, particularly among rural youth, long starved of a glamour that seemed more connected to the outside world. Horslips made the further important decision to remain in Ireland, and to organise everything themselves; they were therefore Ireland's first 'indie' band and an influence on later bands like the RADIATORS and U2. By this time artists such as Rory Gallagher were achieving success beyond Ireland, Thin Lizzy were appearing on 'Top of the Pops', and Van Morrison was being hailed as one of the most influential figures in music.

It was a trinity that remained unchallenged until a new wave of bands emerged at the end of the 1970s and in the early 80s with a completely different set of influences. Taking their cue from punk and new wave, bands like the UNDERTONES and the BOOMTOWN RATS headed for the charts, and the Dublin band U2 went on to virtually dominate the global rock scene. There were many other bands that enjoyed limited success at this time, but Ireland's reputation for original rock and pop remained high.

Ireland's pop successes since the mid-1990s have come in the 'boy band' category. In many ways this is a throwback to the showband era, with the emphasis clearly on maximum sales, and musical originality seemingly irrelevant. The success of Boyzone and Westlife has been unprecedented; but there are many other musicians with altogether different ambitions, with DIVINE COMEDY, ASH, GAVIN FRIDAY, and SINEAD O'CONNOR among those who continue to follow a more individual artistic path. **John Kelly**

popular music and the diaspora. Though the Irish DIASPORA is most commonly associated with TRADITIONAL MUSIC, first and second-generation Irish have also been a formidable force in rock and pop since the late 1960s. Shane MacGowan of the POGUES is probably the most well-known example of how the Irish musical inheritance can find its way into the charts. MacGowan, brought to London from Co. Tipperary at a young age, hitched a Behanesque love of ballads and beer to the amphetamine rush of punk rock, resulting in a potent hybrid somewhere between the DUBLINERS and the Sex Pistols. The Sex Pistols' front man, John Lydon (Johnny Rotten), was also of Irish lineage, and anti-establishment anthems such as 'Anarchy in the UK' (1976) and 'God Save the Queen' (1977) were not far from distorted Irish rebel songs. Meanwhile, in the early 1980s in Manchester the Smiths' lead singer, Morrissey, opted for a more erudite Wildean approach but one that was no less insurrectionary, as evidenced by the classic album *The Queen Is Dead* (1986). Also in Manchester, the drug-inspired lyrics of Happy Mondays' front man, Shaun Ryder, suggested a psychedelic FLANN O'BRIEN, while Liam and Noel Gallagher of Oasis revelled in an aggressive approach to rock and roll that expressed their Irish roots. Other acts have identified with their Irish ancestry in less audacious ways: Radiohead, Jarvis Cocker of Pulp, and Elvis Costello have all variously married the lyricism and melancholia of Irish music with an Anglocentric sensibility. In America, Kurt Cobain of Nirvana had an Irish father; and though the singer may never have listened to Irish traditional music, there lay beneath his band's punk ferocity an uncanny affinity with the Irish-American folk standards of the early twentieth century, apparent on the posthumous album *Unplugged in New York* (1994). **Peter Murphy**

population: statistical profile. A comprehensive CENSUS OF POPULATION has been undertaken regularly in Ireland since the 'Great Census' of 1841 and separately in the Republic and Northern Ireland since 1926. The most recent census in the Republic was in 2002; the most recent in Northern Ireland was that of 2001. In 1841, shortly before the GREAT FAMINE, the population of the twenty-six counties that now constitute the Republic was approximately 6.5 million, almost four times the population of the future Northern Ireland. Subsequently there was a marked decrease in both parts of Ireland, reflecting the impact of the Famine and a high rate of EMIGRATION. Between 1841 and 1901 the population declined by approximately 50 per cent in the area that is now the Republic and by 25 per cent in what is now Northern Ireland.

Table 1: Population by sex, 1841–2002

	Republic (thousands)			Northern Ireland (thousands)		
	Male	Female	Total	Male	Female	Total
1841	3,223	3,306	6,529	800	849	1,649
1851	2,495	2,617	5,112	698	745	1,443
1861	2,169	2,233	4,402	668	729	1,396
1871	1,993	2,061	4,053	647	712	1,359
1881	1,912	1,958	3,870	621	684	1,305
1891	1,729	1,740	3,469	590	646	1,236
1901	1,610	1,612	3,222	589	647	1,237
1911	1,590	1,550	3,140	603	648	1,251
1926	1,507	1,465	2,972	608	649	1,257
1936	1,521	1,448	2,968	631	663	1,294
1946	1,495	1,460	2,955	638	676	1,314
1951	1,507	1,454	2,961	668	703	1,371
1961	1,417	1,402	2,818	694	731	1,425
1966	1,449	1,435	2,884	724	761	1,485
1971	1,496	1,483	2,978	755	781	1,536
1981	1,729	1,714	3,443	757	786	1,543
1986	1,770	1,771	3,541	768	805	1,574
1991	1,753	1,772	3,526	783	824	1,607
1996	1,800	1,826	3,626	816	853	1,669
2001	—	—	—	821	863	1,685
2002	1,945	1,972	3,917	—	—	—

Central Statistics Office/Northern Ireland Statistics & Research Agency

The Republic's population continued to decline for much of the twentieth century. Between 1901 and 1961 it decreased by 12 per cent; it then increased by close to 30 per cent between 1961 and 1996. However, the 2002 census total of 3.9 million was approximately 40 per cent lower than that recorded for 1841. In Northern Ireland the population increased throughout the 1900s, rising by more than a third between 1901 and 1996. Nonetheless, the Northern population estimate for 1996 (1.7 million) was only slightly higher than the corresponding figure for 1841.

Approximately 25 per cent of the population in the Republic is aged fifty or more, compared with just under 28 per cent in Northern Ireland. More than 25 per cent of the Republic's population is in the ten to twenty-four age range, compared with 22 per cent in Northern Ireland.

Table 2: Estimated population by age and sex, 1999

	Republic (thousands)			Northern Ireland (thousands)		
	Male	Female	Total	Male	Female	Total
0–4	133.8	125.6	259.4	61.7	58.7	120.4
5–9	138.3	131.7	270.0	66.4	63.4	129.7
10–14	153.5	146.3	299.9	69.1	65.6	134.8
15–19	176.1	166.9	343.0	65.1	62.0	127.2
20–24	158.8	156.1	314.9	58.5	55.0	113.5
25–29	146.4	144.4	290.8	65.5	61.5	127.1
30–34	130.5	134.0	264.6	65.4	66.4	131.9
35–39	131.0	134.9	265.9	61.8	64.2	126.0
40–44	125.3	126.6	251.8	54.1	55.9	110.0
45–49	117.3	117.1	234.4	49.2	49.6	98.7
50–54	109.6	106.8	216.3	47.5	49.1	96.6
55–59	84.9	82.8	167.8	40.8	42.6	83.4
60–64	71.7	72.6	144.3	34.8	37.7	72.5
65–69	62.3	65.5	127.8	29.4	35.2	64.6
70–74	49.7	61.0	110.7	24.7	32.4	57.1
75–79	37.0	51.9	88.8	18.5	28.2	46.8
80–84	20.4	33.9	54.2	9.9	18.1	28.0
85+	12.6	27.5	40.1	6.1	17.5	23.6
Total	1859.1	1885.6	3744.7	828.6	863.2	1691.8

Central Statistics Office/Northern Ireland Statistics & Research Agency

Portadown (*Port an Dúnáin*), Co. Armagh, a manufacturing and marketing town, traditionally associated with the LINEN industry; population (1991) 21,299. The town was founded in the early seventeenth century at a ford on the River Bann. Its first bridge was built in 1702, the second in 1768, and the third in 1838. Like Lurgan, since 1965 Portadown has formed part of the new town of Craigavon. Scene of a notorious massacre in the 1641 REBELLION, Portadown developed as a brown linen market during the eighteenth century but really prospered only from the 1840s, when it became the principal junction of Ulster's four main RAILWAYS, linking Belfast, Dublin, Newry, Armagh, and Omagh. Most of the town's surviving historical buildings date from this nineteenth-century boom. In recent years Portadown has suffered from the general decline in Ulster's traditional textile industries, the difficulty of sustaining replacement foreign investment, and the persistence of deep sectarian divisions among its population. **Lindsay Proudfoot**

portal tombs, the smallest, though often the most visually imposing, of Irish MEGALITHIC TOMBS. The 180 examples have a distribution broadly similar to that of COURT TOMBS, with which they share comparable burial rites and finds; there is a scattering along the eastern seaboard, and similar monuments occur in Wales and Cornwall. The classic portal tomb consists of a single short chamber formed by two tall portal-stones, two side-stones, and a back-stone. Sometimes a stone between the portals closes the entry. The chamber is covered by a roof-stone, often of great size, which slopes down from the front towards the rear, as at POULNABRONE, PROLEEK, and BROWNE'S HILL. **Paul Walsh**

Porter, Leslie (1881–1917), racing driver. Born in Belfast. The first Irishman to compete in a major Continental event, he crashed his Wolseley car in the 1903 Paris–Madrid race, killing his mechanic, the former motorcycle racer Willie Nixon. He finished fourth in the 1908 Tourist Trophy race. He was killed in the FIRST WORLD WAR in a flying accident in France. **Brendan Lynch**

Port Laoise, county town of Co. Laois; population (2002) 3,482, with a further 9,000 in its immediate environs. The town originated in the PLANTATION of Laois and Offaly under Mary Tudor. On a tributary of the River Barrow, the site was probably chosen for its centrality and its proximity to a large garrison. Named Maryborough in honour of the queen, it was given a charter of incorporation in 1570 by ELIZABETH I. It retained its garrison

portal tombs. *The Poulnabrone portal tomb, Burren region, Co. Clare, c. 2500 BC, the finest example of a portal tomb in Ireland. Two entrance stones (1.8 m/6 ft) mark a rectangular chamber and are covered by a large capstone of limestone. [Dúchas, The Heritage Service]* function and developed as the assize town for the county. The courthouse was built in 1782, while the jail dates from 1830; this was extended in 1911 and has recently become a national high-security prison. It also developed as an important market town, a role enhanced by its position as an important road and rail junction. Following independence, the town took on its historical name.

While it continues to provide services to its hinterland, both national and international manufacturing industry are important to the local economy. New offices to house a large component of the then Department of Agriculture, Food and Forestry were opened in 1996. Port Laoise's centrality has also led to its development as a regional hub for postal services. The town has suffered from traffic congestion in recent years; the building of an inner relief road had the effect of shifting the focus of the town to either side of this road. However, it has benefited greatly from the completion of a motorway-standard bypass that was opened in 1997. **Joseph Brady**

Portlock, Joseph Ellison (1794–1864), geologist. Born in Gosport, Hampshire. He was commissioned into the Royal Engineers in July 1813. He served in Canada from 1814 until 1822, and soon after his return to England he was appointed to assist Colonel THOMAS FREDERICK COLBY (1784–1852) with the ORDNANCE SURVEY of Ireland. He took charge first of the triangulation survey of Ireland and then of the scheme to compile a detailed memoir descriptive of each parish in Ireland. The Memoir Project was abandoned, but his 1843 report on the geology of Co. Derry and adjacent regions is a classic of Irish geology. In 1843 he returned to the general duties of his corps, and in 1857 he retired with the rank of major-general. **Jean Archer**

Portrait of the Artist as a Young Man, A (1916), the first novel by JAMES JOYCE, serialised in the *Egoist* (1914–15). Through the character of Stephen Dedalus, the autobiographical story traces Joyce's life from early childhood until the eve of his departure from Ireland in 1904. There is a careful patterning of sympathy and irony towards Stephen throughout the novel. The story traces his rebellious relationships with his family and with women, his schooling, his possible vocation for the Catholic priesthood, and his literary ambitions. In the final chapter he famously sets forth his aesthetic theory (a mixture of Aristotle and Aquinas) of the impersonality of art. Throughout, the novel's structure echoes the myth of Icarus, son of Daedalus, who flew too near the Sun, burning his wings; Stephen's flights of imagination suffer similar downfalls, and the novel is structured around his hesitant growth to maturity. Stephen's attempt to escape all forms of conventional social and intellectual authority—family, nation, religion, and empire—is left unresolved. The novel ends with his diary before his departure and his avowed tactic of 'silence, exile and cunning'. It is both an intriguing portrait of the young Joyce and a calculatedly ironic depiction by the mature Joyce of his naïve younger self. The novel further secured Joyce's reputation as an exceptional experimental writer and prose stylist. A much earlier version, describing Stephen's college years and lacking the ironic detachment of the final book, was published posthumously as *Stephen Hero* (1944). **John Nash**

ports. The VIKINGS, and later the ANGLO-NORMANS, settled around river estuaries and natural harbours, as at Dublin, Waterford, Cork, and Limerick. There is abundant archaeological evidence that wooden quays existed at these sites in the Middle Ages; but goods were generally transferred to shore in small boats from larger vessels moored offshore. To proceed upriver, arriving vessels often deposited ballast material at river mouths and on departure obtained ballast from other sites. The uncontrolled nature of this practice led to the establishment in the eighteenth century of Ballast Boards at the main ports of Dublin, Belfast, and Cork and later the appointment of Harbour Commissioners to regulate shipping, collect dues, and develop the ports. Much of the basic development took place in the nineteenth and early twentieth centuries and consisted of the provision of quay walls and wet and dry docks and the straightening and deepening of approach channels. As the size of shipping increased, quay walls were rebuilt to provide deep-water berths, and port activities moved further downriver.

SHIPBUILDING is often associated with ports, the prime example being the HARLAND AND WOLFF shipyards in Belfast. Dublin, Belfast, Cork, and Waterford developed extensive facilities during the late twentieth century for containerised goods and passenger and vehicle ferries (see pp. 239, 525, 1135). **Ronald Cox**

Portumna Castle, Co. Galway, a fine example of a fortified house, built by the fourth Earl of Clanricarde c. 1618, which clearly shows a move away from defence towards the aggrandisement of a residence. The large three-storey rectangular block with square tower at each angle is similar to Co. Cork fortified houses and is more of a grand house like that of BURNCOURT, Co. Tipperary, but without the high gables and chimney-stacks. An imposing entrance leads to a large hall over a basement. It was defended by a machicolation and gun-loops in the angle-towers for flanking fire. It has an inner and outer bawn, now in formal gardens. **David Sweetman**

postal services. Daily postal service in Ireland began in 1635. A General Post Office for England, Scotland, and Ireland was established in 1657; local service expanded with the legalisation of penny posts in 1765. After becoming independent in 1784, the Irish Post Office was reintegrated in a United Kingdom postal administration in 1831. Following partition, separate postal bodies served the Irish Free State and Northern Ireland. **K. J. James**

post-colonialism, a term employed by literary historians and critics and by cultural theorists with reference to Irish literary production. This is taken to be crucially affected by Ireland's historical experience of subjection to English colonisation and British imperialism. Nineteenth and twentieth-century literature in English in particular is read as participating in and reflecting a process of subjection, revolution, and decolonisation. In this model of Irish historical experience, parallels with other colonised countries are frequently drawn. The foundation text of this theoretical tendency is the Algerian writer Franz Fanon's *The Wretched of the Earth* (translated 1967), while the writings of the Palestinian critic Edward Said, especially *Orientalism* (1978), are also influential. DECLAN KIBERD's *Inventing Ireland* (1995) is a pioneering attempt to provide a comprehensive overview of Irish writing from such a viewpoint. THE FIELD DAY ANTHOLOGY OF IRISH WRITING (1991) was also significantly influenced by the view that 'Ireland has been colonised through conquest and invasion several times and in several ways.' **Terence Brown**

potato and potato cookery. The means by which the potato was introduced to Ireland remain unclear, though legend assigns the honour to Sir WALTER RALEIGH. The first record of potato cultivation is from a lease of 1606 relating to the granting of lands to Scottish settlers in Co. Down, while the first recorded potato recipe (that of a spicy potato pie) comes from a source dated to 1666.

At first the potato was grown as a garden curiosity, and its consumption was largely confined to the wealthy classes. The transition from garden to field is attributed to several factors. The potato is ideally suited to Ireland's wet conditions and SOIL types; it was also easily adapted to the prevailing system of ridge cultivation. In its early existence the potato was adopted as a supplement to a grain-strong diet and also proved an invaluable fall-back in times of shortage. As its cultivation spread throughout the first half of the eighteenth century from Munster into Connacht and Leinster, it was used increasingly as the winter FOOD of the poor. By the second half of the eighteenth century the dietary function of the potato was augmented as a result of changing market forces and an unprecedented population explosion. From the 1760s onwards the cultivation of cereals expanded in response to growing British markets, and the potato, as an excellent cleansing crop in rotation, assumed an importance not only in facilitating the growth of arable AGRICULTURE but also in its increased presence at local markets where prices were competitive.

The potato supported and encouraged the population boom of the late eighteenth century (from approximately 2.5 million in 1767 to about 4 million in 1781 and about 4.4 million in 1791). Demographic changes saw a repeated subdivision of holdings, together with a spread of settlement into previously unsettled areas of poor and marginal lands. The potato responded well to both movements. If well manured, it gave excellent returns; it has been estimated that an acre (0.4 ha) of well-managed potatoes was sufficient to meet the yearly dietary demands of a family of six. Its merits as an invaluable reclamation crop brought settlement to hill, mountain and bogland, and, once established, the potato flourished in these seemingly unfavourable conditions. A mushrooming of smallholdings was especially associated with the west and south-west coast, where a particular regional dietary pattern developed among the small poorer farmers based on potatoes supplemented with shore foods: periwinkles, limpets, whelks, and seaweeds, such as carrageen, dulse, and sloke.

The second half of the eighteenth century was the high point for the potato, with several varieties under cultivation. The one of greatest merit was the 'Irish apple', which was valued for its keeping quality and its highly flavoured mealy flesh. By the early nineteenth century two additional varieties, the 'cup' and the 'lumper', were gaining. A clear hierarchy in quality and preference held, with the Irish apple considered the most superior, followed by the cup and finally the lumper. By virtue of its high quality, the Irish apple commanded the best market price; and as the population continued to grow to record levels (from 6.8 million in 1821 to 7.8 million in 1831) the poor and labouring classes concentrated increasingly on the cultivation of the cup and the lumper.

On the eve of the GREAT FAMINE, however, the lumper, a prolific cropper, was almost the universal food of the poor and distressed UNDERCLASS, whose numbers had reached approximately 3 million. Their dangerous reliance not simply on one food but on one variety, which was highly susceptible to potato blight (*Phytophthora infestans*), made inevitable the dire consequences of the arrival of this fungal disease in 1845 (see p. 520).

The impoverished and monotonous diet of the poor in the years immediately before the Great Famine is exemplified by the simple manner of potato cookery. Lumpers, a thick, waxy, creamy potato variety, were simply boiled, drained, and eaten communally from a basket, sack, or cloth. Depending on the time of year, two or three potato meals were taken each day, with daily individual consumption varying from 3.2–6.4 kg (7 to 14 lb). Boiled potatoes were supplemented with a restricted variety of foods. Herrings were cheap fare, and shore foods brought additional taste to the coastal diet, while buttermilk or simply salted water were the most common accompaniments. MEAT, most usually salted pig meat, was an occasional indulgence and was taken as a 'kitchen' or relish to the potato. Perhaps the best illustration of pre-famine poverty was the fact that a 'dry potato' (a floury variety) was considered holiday fare. In late summer this repetitive pattern of potato consumption was disrupted, as the poor, who had exhausted their stock of old potatoes, were left without food until the new season's crop became available. For some, oatmeal was the fall-back; but for others the waiting month of July, variously known as 'Hungry July' and 'July of the Cabbage', was a time of hardship and want.

In marked contrast, the wealthy classes consumed the potato as but one item in an otherwise diverse diet, and its treatment benefited from easy access to complementary ingredients. Apart from the more conventional methods of cooking, the potato was popularly used in the preparation of potato pudding. This was a dish composed of mashed potatoes of a floury variety mixed with liberal amounts of BUTTER, sugar, cream, and eggs, with additional flavourings, most commonly nutmeg, candied orange, or lemon, and white wine or brandy. The finished dish resembles and tastes like a moist sweet cake, and it was routinely served as part of the first or second course at dinner. Moving further down the social scale, in particular among the self-sufficient comfortable farming community, potatoes were taken with a restricted range of additional vegetables—cabbage, onions, and turnips—together with butter or meat, especially pig meat. The prevalence of the potato as a fodder in the late eighteenth and early nineteenth centuries advanced and augmented the pig economy, with the result that pig meat became the most widely available and cheapest of meats. Pig numbers soared (to approximately 1.4 million in 1841), and, not surprisingly, meals of potatoes with bacon or ham with an accompanying vegetable were a feature of the middle-class diet, especially for festive occasions. A similar advantageous relationship grew up between the potato and the fowl yard, where the size of flocks—turkeys, geese, ducks, and hens—fed and thriving on potatoes was striking.

For those of moderate means, potato bread and mashed potato dishes were prevalent. 'Champ' was a simple creamed dish of potatoes mashed with milk or cream and mixed with seasonal greens. Equally popular was 'colcannon' (*cál ceannann*)—mashed potatoes mixed with kale or white cabbage, along with the occasional addition of turnips or parsnips. From the early eighteenth century colcannon was the supper dish for HALLOWE'EN, which, as the vigil of All Saints' Day, was a meatless fast day. The rituals surrounding its consumption demanded that individual bowls of colcannon be distributed among the party. The top of the mash was hollowed out with the back of a spoon and filled with butter. For those whose material wealth did not rise to ownership of individual bowls, the colcannon was eaten communally from a pot. Potato bread was made by combining mashed potatoes with flour and milk. Grated potatoes were used in the preparation of 'boxty' (*bacstaí*), a notable feature of the diet in some northern and western counties. Potato apple-cakes were popular in the apple-growing regions of Co. Armagh.

The potato continued to play an important part in the post-famine diet, though it would not resume its former dominance in the life rhythms of the rural poor, except in the most impoverished areas of the west. The middle to late nineteenth century brought the 'champion', a new potato variety. Though highly vulnerable to blight, it was hugely popular, because of a preference for its floury flesh. By the 1890s it has been estimated that the cultivation of champions represented 80 per cent of the total area devoted to the potato crop, though they too fell victim to blight in the late nineteenth century. The increased acceptance by farmers of the merits of spraying with 'bluestone' (copper sulphate), widespread by the early years of the twentieth century, introduced an additional sense of food security. And while the status of the potato had changed, it remained an indispensable item in the make-up of meals of all classes, thereby giving a distinctive character to Irish foodways. In the twentieth century Ireland gained an international reputation for the development of new varieties. In cooking, floury varieties remain the most prized. [see FOOD OF THE BLASKETS; FOOD, POST FAMINE; MOORE, DAVID.] **Regina Sexton**

Potter, A. J. (Archie) (1918–1980), composer. Born in Belfast; studied at the Royal College of Music, London, with Ralph Vaughan Williams, 1936–8. He served in east Asia and west Africa during the Second World War and returned to Ireland in the late 1940s. In 1951 his *Missa Brevis* won the Festival of Britain Prize (Belfast), and in 1952–3 he won the Radio Éireann Carolan Prize. From 1952 to 1973 he taught singing and composition at the RIAM. His compositions for the Radio Éireann Light Orchestra include *Overture to a Kitchen Comedy* (1950), *Concerto da Chiesa* (1952), and *Variations on a Popular Tune* (1955) (12-note row). *Sinfonia de Profundis* (1969) was written for the RTÉ Symphony Orchestra. **Ite O'Donovan**

Potter, Maureen (1925–), comedian and actor. Born in Dublin. The multi-talented Potter was all-Ireland junior Irish dancing champion at seven and three years later played a fairy with JIMMY O'DEA in PANTOMIME. Billed as 'the Pocket Mimic', she toured Britain and the Continent as a child with Jack Hylton's troupe, resuming what became a thirty-year association with O'Dea when she returned to Ireland. A brilliant dancer and sketch comedian, she presented her own shows, such as 'Gaels of Laughter', in the 1970s. Switching late to straight theatre, she appeared in *School for Scandal* at the Gate (1989), and *Juno and the Paycock* at the Olympia (1990). **Stephen Dixon and Deirdre Falvey**

pottery, country. The manufacture of pottery declined in Ireland during the late Middle Ages but revived with the settlement of English potters c. 1650. Potteries are known to have been working before 1700 in Cos. Antrim, Cork, Down, Monaghan, and Wexford, as well as in Dublin. Early country pots were often intended for table use and so were finely potted, whereas those made after c. 1800 were usually employed in the dairy or kitchen and so became more utilitarian. Surviving pots are typically plain, black or brown-glazed redwares, but some bear regionally distinctive *sgraffito* (scratched design) and slip-trailed decoration. The last major manufacturer, at Coalisland, Co. Tyrone, ceased work during the 1950s. [see CRAFTS AFTER 1945.] **Peter Francis**

Potts, Tommy (1912–1988), fiddle-player and variously plumber, fireman, and rent-collector. Born in Dublin; educated at Bolton Street Technical School. His idiosyncratic aesthetic sense and the experimental sensibility with which he approached TRADITIONAL MUSIC led to much argument over the importance of his fiddling. His playing may be heard on the recording *Liffey Banks* (1972). **Anthony McCann**

Poulnabrone, Co. Clare, a PORTAL TOMB in the BURREN in which two tall stones form the entrance to a stone-lined chamber covered by a single large capstone. The chamber was archaeologically excavated in 1986–8 and it was revealed that the tomb had been used sporadically for the burial of disarticulated human remains between 3800 and 3200 BC. At least twenty-two individuals—sixteen adults and six children, male and female—were represented. Items of special significance were deposited with the dead: a bone pendant, two quartz crystals, a polished stone axe, flint and chert implements, a bone pin, and sherds of pottery. **Ann Lynch**

Power, Albert (1881–1945), sculptor. Born in Dublin; at the Metropolitan School of Art he was a pupil of JOHN HUGHES, OLIVER SHEPPARD, and WILLIAM ORPEN. In 1912 he established himself as a monumental mason, specialising in ecclesiastical work, notably St Joseph's Church, Ballinasloe. He accepted commissions for portrait busts of literary and political figures, most successfully the heads of W. B. YEATS and MICHAEL COLLINS (see p. 461). His many monuments include the statue of PÁDRAIG Ó CONAIRE in Eyre Square, Galway. His exhibited work includes the admired *Leenane Trout* (1944). Power is valued as a stone-carver working in native stone and presenting national figures in an unheroic idiom. **Judith Hill**

Power, Richard (1928–1970), novelist. Born in Dublin; educated at TCD. He spent some time on the ARAN ISLANDS; his book on his experience, *Úll i mBarr an Ghéagáin*, appeared in 1959. The islands also supplied the backdrop for his first novel in English, *The Land of Youth* (1964), a historical saga set before and after the WAR OF INDEPENDENCE. *The Hungry Grass* (1969), published the year before his premature death, is a compassionately realistic study of the loneliness of a rural priest. **Terence Brown**

Power, Tyrone (1797–1841), actor and playwright. Born in Kilmacthomas, Co. Waterford. He was the first actor to specialise in Irish roles, playing with a pronounced Irish accent. Popular in Ireland, England, and America, he also wrote plays, including *O'Flannigan and the Fairies* (1836). The film actor Tyrone Power (1914–1958) and TYRONE GUTHRIE were his great-grandsons. **Christopher Morash**

Powerscourt, Enniskerry, Co. Wicklow, a house by RICHARD CASTLE, built (1731–40) for Richard Wingfield, later first Viscount Powerscourt, in one of the most celebrated landscape settings of all eighteenth-century country houses. The impressive entrance front, of central block with flanking wings and extended screen walls culminating in obelisks, has a pedimented central breakfront, with busts of Roman emperors in roundels set between pilasters. The garden front, which is terminated by curved bows surmounted by domes, faces over descending terraces with statuary, to an ornamental lake. The gardens were created by Daniel Robertson in the 1840s for the sixth viscount and by Alexander Robertson in the 1850s for the seventh. The rugged uplands of the WICKLOW MOUNTAINS, culminating in the GREAT SUGAR LOAF, end the superb vista from the terraces of the gardens. The interior of the house, including much of its furnishing, was destroyed by a fire in 1974. Powerscourt estate, originally of 14,500 ha (36,000 acres), includes the Powerscourt waterfall, at 122 m (400 ft) the highest in Ireland. **Brian Lalor**

Poynings' Law (1494), the ninth act introduced by Sir Edward Poynings, Lord Deputy of Ireland, at a parliament at Drogheda in December 1494. It declared that henceforth no parliament could be held in Ireland without the king's prior consent, and no bills could be introduced other than those already approved by the king and his council in England. Its aim was to ensure that the Irish Parliament never again acted independently or contrary to the wishes of the Crown of England, as had happened in 1487, when the Earl of Kildare secured the coronation of the pretender LAMBERT SIMNEL. Though introduced to meet a specific set of circumstances, it continued to be used throughout the following three centuries for purposes far beyond those originally intended and was to have repercussions in Irish parliamentary history down to the eighteenth century; it was finally repealed in 1782. **Susan Foran**

Praeger, Robert Lloyd (1865–1953), naturalist, author and librarian. Born in Belfast; educated at QUB, qualifying as an engineer in 1886. He was a leading member of the BELFAST NATURALISTS' FIELD CLUB in its study of the natural history and antiquities of the north-east. In 1893 he moved to Dublin, where he worked at the NATIONAL LIBRARY, eventually succeeding T. W. Lyster as director in 1920. He was a founding editor, with G. H. CARPENTER, of the monthly *Irish Naturalist* (1892–1924), and also established the Irish Field Club Union to advance the study of Ireland's natural history. Throughout his long and active life his energies as a botanical field-worker drove him to explore little-known areas of the midlands and west, including many ISLANDS. He undertook a remarkable survey of plant distribution during the 1890s and published his findings as *Irish Topographical Botany* (1901). Many articles and books followed, including *A Tourist's Flora of the West of Ireland* (1909) and his major work of reference, *The Botanist in Ireland* (1934).

Praeger was an influential member of the ROYAL IRISH ACADEMY and served as its president, 1931–4. Under its auspices he organised and edited the first CLARE ISLAND SURVEY (1909–11). His studies in plant taxonomy were published as *An Account of the Genus Sedum* (1921) and *An Account of the Sempervivum Group* (1932). In 1937 he published his classic account of the Irish landscape, *The Way that I Went*, a work that made his name known to a general readership and that continues to ensure his popular reputation. He was a founder-member and first president of AN TAISCE in 1948 and held office with many other societies, including the presidency of the ROYAL ZOOLOGICAL SOCIETY OF IRELAND and the Dublin Naturalists' Field Club. **Seán Lysaght**

Praeger, (Sophia) Rosamond (1867–1954), sculptor and illustrator. Born in Holywood, Co. Down; educated at Sullivan School, Holywood, Government School of Art, Belfast, and Slade School of Fine Art, London. She divided her time between sculpture and illustration, writing and illustrating twelve children's books. Public recognition came c. 1914 with the success of *The Philosopher*, a sculptural child study. She worked in a variety of media, modelling in clay and plaster, casting in bronze, and carving in stone. In 1902 she was elected vice-president of the Belfast Art Society; in 1930 the society became the Ulster Academy of Arts, and Praeger was included among the twelve founder-academicians, being elected president 1940/41. Queen's University, Belfast, awarded her an honorary degree; in 1943 she was made a member of the Order of the British Empire and was appointed to the advisory committee of CEMA. **Catherine Gaynor**

Praeger as illustrator. Her early work appears in *Cheery Times for Merry Youngsters* (1894), *A Sunshiny Holiday* (1896) by Barbara Inson, *As Happy as a King* by the then unknown Edith Nesbit, and her own book of verses, *A Visit to Babyland* (1896). There followed *The Adventures of the Three Bold Babes* (1897), and Praeger's distinctive voice and quirky humorous style had emerged. In a sequel, *Further Doings of the Three Bold Babes* (1898), we meet one of her most breathtakingly original creations in the Sea-serpent, an enormous creature clad in shamrocks instead of scales. She collaborated with her brother ROBERT LLOYD PRAEGER, providing finely drawn sketches for *Open-Air Studies in Botany and Weeds: Simple Lessons for Children* (1913), while *The Child's Picture Grammar* (1913) is another example of her taking a difficult subject and

Praeger, Rosamond. *Illustration by Rosamond Praeger from* Further Doings of Three Bold Babes *(1898), featuring one of her brilliant illustrations of the Sea-serpent, clad in shamrocks instead of scales, forming himself into a tubular bridge so that the 'three babes' may pass across the water. [Longmans, Green and Company]*

producing a book that is both instructive and entertaining. She excelled at mirroring the everyday world of wealthy Edwardian society, which she portrays accurately and sensitively in *How They Went to School* (1903), *How They Came Back from School*, *How They Went to the Seaside* (1909), *Wee Tony* (1913) *and the Naughty Ninepins* and *Wee Tony and (Me) Baby Writes a Book*. Largely overlooked today, Praeger's illustrative work is difficult to find, despite the fact that many of her books went into several printings in Belfast, London, New York, and Bombay. **Patricia Donlon**

Pratt, John Jeffreys, second Earl Camden (1759–1840), LORD LIEUTENANT of Ireland. He succeeded his father as Earl Camden in 1794. Following the FITZWILLIAM affair he was appointed Lord Lieutenant for Ireland and pressed to have his step-nephew, ROBERT STEWART, Viscount Castlereagh, named CHIEF SECRETARY. He was replaced in June 1798 because of his inability to handle the 1798 REBELLION. **Patrick Geoghegan**

pre-Christian religions. Pre-Christian religions in Ireland have been the subject of conjectures that range from matriarchy to occult mystery; scholarship and speculation have coexisted uneasily. However, it is certain that many forms of religious belief flourished in Ireland. The country was a racial palimpsest from prehistoric times, as different peoples established themselves. However, these peoples were non-literate, and we can only make educated guesses about the nature of their beliefs. It is clear that the NEOLITHIC tomb-builders, who have left such impressive monuments to their material culture in the BOYNE VALLEY, had a strong sense of the importance of the landscape and valued astronomical knowledge; yet we cannot hope to reconstruct their beliefs. Their metaphysical world is intangible (see pp. 777, 860).

The beliefs of the CELTS, who eventually dominated Ireland, are less intangible, though evidence for them is indirect. PAGANISM only survived transformed by the pens of early medieval Christian writers, who amalgamated Christian and native elements. The heroes and magical beings that inhabit their written worlds owe something to pre-Christian religions. For instance, the names and abilities of TUATHA DÉ DANANN, a sorcerous OTHERWORLDLY and immortal people, suggest that many of them were once pagan divinities. Similarly, heroes such as FIONN MAC CUMHAILL may once have had divine or semi-divine status. Yet names and the suggestion of divine abilities do not make GODS; and we have no clear idea of the relations between the various pagan gods of Celtic Ireland, or whether they were ever worshipped in a systematic way.

Extrapolation is possible. It is highly likely that the druids, who survived as a pitiful and low-status remnant in early medieval Ireland, were originally a pagan priesthood, similar to that which classical writers describe as existing among the British and Continental Celts. However, St PATRICK, whose genuine fifth-century writings offer a valuable glimpse into pre-Christian Ireland, does not obviously mention the druids, nor does he give the impression that Irish paganism, relatively speaking, was either particularly well organised institutionally or particularly hostile towards CHRISTIANITY: indeed one of the most interesting features of the Christianisation of Ireland during the fifth and sixth centuries is its peaceful nature. There appear to have been no martyrs. Irish paganism in institutional form, whether it comprised one RELIGION or many competing sets of beliefs, seems to have simply faded away. It has been convincingly suggested that this was because Irish Christianity proved accommodating to the aspirations of the pagan elites. Early medieval Christianity was intensely local and heavily influenced by local practice. Irish Christianity, therefore, was able to absorb native practices while remaining clearly Christian. One of the best examples is the prevalence of belief in the efficacy of holy wells. The Irish landscape is dotted with them; and through them the old pagan forces, living in the springs and streams, flowed into the deep sea of Christian religion. The pre-Christian religions did not simply vanish: they were transformed. [see BOA ISLAND; CORLECK; IDOLS.] **Elva Johnston**

prehistoric food. Archaeological excavation shows that Ireland has been inhabited from c. 7000 BC. The earliest MESOLITHIC inhabitants exploited a landscape that was considerably at variance with that of today in CLIMATE, appearance, and resources. To begin with, the climate was dryer and the landscape was heavily forested with a mixture of coniferous and deciduous trees, in particular hazel and Scots pine. Given the complexities of GLACIATION and the emergence of the country's island status, Ireland had a limited range of plant, animal, and fish species that could be exploited for food.

The earliest communities hunted wild pig, and possibly hare, while the woodlands provided small game birds, such as thrush, woodpigeon, woodcock, and capercaillie. In summer, migratory fish species, in particular salmon, trout, and eels, provided additional protein, and there is evidence to suggest a strong reliance on plant foods in season, with a particular emphasis on wild apples, wild raspberries, and hazelnuts. It is possible that meat, bird, and fish were cooked on stakes before an open fire or in shallow pits filled with heated stones. But if the summer and autumn months provided relatively good and diverse supplies of food, the challenge lay in providing for the winter and early spring months, and therefore it is likely that some food was preserved and stored. Hazelnuts, by their nature, are easily stored, while FRUITS were possibly dried and stored in baskets. It is also probable that fish was preserved by smoking towards the end of its season of plenty.

Marine resources played an extremely important role in both the early (7000–6000 BC) and later Mesolithic diet (c. 5500 BC onwards). The bone chemistry from skeletons recovered from coastal sites suggests an almost complete reliance on seafood, with little food of land origin entering the diet. Fish, such as whiting, wrasse, and tope, possibly caught from boats with long lines or nets, was eaten together with shellfish, notably limpets, periwinkles, and whelks. In line with earlier practice, fish may have been roasted before an open fire or boiled in shallow water-filled pits. This was a community of fishers, hunters, and gatherers, adept in maximising the potential of resources in different localities in accordance with seasonal changes.

The NEOLITHIC PERIOD (c. 4000–2000 BC) saw the introduction of AGRICULTURE; and people with knowledge of the cultivation of crops and the management of farm animals introduced what in time would become the dietary staples. Domesticated cattle, sheep, or goats and pigs were introduced, together with two main cereal crops: a naked free-threshing species of barley, and einkorn and emmer wheat. It has also been suggested that red deer were deliberately reintroduced at this time, as they became extinct in Ireland at the end of the Ice Age. The transitional period between the introduction of agriculture and the development of the requisite skills to make it effective saw a continued reliance on the resources of the wild, as evidenced by the range of flint hunting equipment and the find of wild apples on one Neolithic site, where they were possibly dried for winter use.

Cereals could be simply crushed or ground into meal for the preparation of wet foods such as gruel and porridge or made into dough and baked as flat BREADS. The prehistoric type of cattle (not unlike the Kerry cow) supplied meat and meat off-cuts, while the prehistoric sheep type, similar to the Soay breed, was kept for its fleece and milk. It is likely that early farming communities relied on perishable items of dairy produce: milk, sour milk, and curd dishes. However, the production of storable dairy produce in the form of BUTTER and CHEESE may have been a much later innovation, perhaps coming to Ireland through contact with the Roman world.

The BRONZE AGE (c. 1800 BC onwards) and the IRON AGE (c. 800 BC onwards) are characterised by clear evidence of different social ranks, all of which have implications for the diet. *Fulachta fia* or cooking-pits, an outdoor system for boiling meat by means of heated stones placed in a large water trough, become prevalent at this time. Similarly, the use of cauldrons for cooking appears for the first time; and given that these, when their place of origin is identified, are associated with the wealthiest sites, it seems that boiled flesh, as opposed to spit-roasted meat, may have been considered superior. In the saga literature, which idealises a warrior society, roast and particularly boiled flesh are the foods of elaborate aristocratic feasting.

Diversification of the cereal economy may have been influenced by contact with Roman Britain in the PRE-CHRISTIAN period. It is believed that oats were introduced at this time, while there is also a greater emphasis on bread wheat. Domesticated fowl were probably also introduced from the Roman world. [see FOOD OF THE BLASKETS.] **Regina Sexton**

Prendergast, Kathy (1958–), sculptor. Born in Dublin; studied at the NCAD and Royal College of Art, London. She works with a wide range of materials, creating both objects and environments that are essentially poetic and layered in meaning. Surprising juxtapositions of scale and unexpected combinations of elements lend her work surrealist qualities. A restrained atmosphere of powerful yet harnessed emotion pervades her work. She won the Best Young Artist award at the Venice Biennale, 1995, and is a member of AOSDÁNA. Her drawing *City Map* was exhibited at the Tate Gallery, London, 1998, and the Drawing Center, New York, 1999. There is a collection of her work at the Albright Knox Art Gallery, Buffalo, New York. **Suzanne McNab**

Presbyterianism. Most Presbyterians came to Ireland from Scotland with the PLANTATIONS, and then mostly to Ulster, where by 1640 they outnumbered the Anglicans by five to one. They brought with them the Scottish Kirk's tradition of political dissension, which made them objects of suspicion to the Anglican Ascendancy and resulted at first in limitations on worship. These restrictions led in part to heavy involvement by Presbyterians in the revolt of the UNITED IRISHMEN and encouraged early EMIGRATION to the United States. They also brought with them covenantal theology, a mixture of Calvinist notions of the 'elect' and John Knox's ideas that linked reformed theology with support for the supremacy of Parliament against monarchical absolutism. Presbyterianism has therefore always been political.

It has also always been anti-Catholic. Its critique of Catholicism was theological, in that it is wrong doctrinally, and constitutional, in that it is absolutist in its understanding of power. These beliefs shaped Ulster religion and politics and led to fierce opposition to HOME RULE. The Presbyterian Church in Ireland was indefatigable in its support for PARTITION and the ULSTER COVENANT. Present-day Presbyterianism still subscribes to the Westminster Confession, which states that the Pope is the 'Antichrist' and the Catholic Church the 'Whore of Babylon', though this is no more than a historical anomaly.

With its stress on local church democracy, the voting power of local congregations in regional presbyteries and in the General Assembly and its support for the principle of the priesthood of all believers, Presbyterianism has had a tendency to schism, and there are several denominations. Early disputes featured subscription to confessional statements, creating Subscribing and NON-SUBSCRIBING denominations, and conflict between 'Old light' and 'New light' theology, creating reformed denominations, and EVANGELICAL and non-evangelical denominations. The FREE PRESBYTERIAN CHURCH was established in the 1950s (see p. 853).

The largest denomination by far is the Presbyterian Church in Ireland. It has kept its all-Ireland structure and presence, though its geographical distribution reflects the patterns of plantation society, being strongest in the north-east. Following partition, many Presbyterians in the South moved north; through years of assimilation and intermarriage the numbers in the Republic have dwindled. There are 562 congregations in Ireland, only 17 per cent of them in the Republic. But Northern Ireland is not a stronghold, for the Presbyterian Church in Ireland is subject to the general drift away from mainstream Protestant religion that is occurring in Northern Ireland. While Presbyterianism generally is the largest Protestant denomination in Northern Ireland, its numbers are falling. In the 1998 social attitudes survey 21.2 per cent of the sample identified themselves as Presbyterian, compared with 24.5 per cent in 1991. This partly reflects SECULARISATION among the young (and most mainstream Protestant churches are increasingly aged in their congregations) and also the growth of fundamentalist, charismatic, and neo-Pentecostal churches. **John Brewer**

Presbyterianism. *Rev. Ruth Patterson, the first Irish Presbyterian woman minister. Ordained on 2 January 1976, she is director of Restoration Ministries, a non-denominational charitable trust promoting peace and reconciliation in Northern Ireland. [Richard Leslie Stuart]*

Presbyterian thought. PRESBYTERIANISM combines rigorous morality with anti-hierarchical radicalism. Like other REFORMATION movements (such as Hussites, HUGUENOTS and Puritans), Presbyterians found themselves at logger-heads with the old monarchies of Europe. Unlike their Scottish brethren (who successfully resisted the Crown's episcopalian church organisation), Irish Presbyterians, concentrated in Scottish-settled Ulster, remained a minority under Anglican supremacy. At the time of the PENAL LAWS Irish Presbyterians shared many civic disabilities with Catholics.

During the eighteenth century the democratically minded tendency within Presbyterianism was fanned into political radicalism. Famously, the UNITED IRISHMEN had their strongest support in the Ulster Presbyterian milieu, though mistrust between Catholics and Presbyterians at grassroots level was never wholly overcome. The time of the flourishing United Irish movement also witnessed the foundation of the ORANGE ORDER. After the failure of the United Irish rising, Presbyterians withdrew from a radical into a more conservative (orangist and unionist) position.

A significant contribution of Presbyterianism to Irish cultural awareness is its emphasis on the non-episcopal roots of Irish CHRISTIANITY. Mistrustful of Anglican and Catholic interpretations, which placed St PATRICK's introduction of Christianity (Rome-endorsed or Rome-inspired) under the auspices of a bishop-led church hierarchy, Presbyterians tended to stress the importance of the CÉILÍ DÉ and monastics in the country's primitive Christian life. **Joep Leerssen**

Presidents of Ireland

25 June 1938–24 June 1945	Douglas Hyde (Fianna Fáil)
25 June 1945–24 June 1959	Seán T. O'Kelly (Fianna Fáil)
25 June 1959–24 June 1973	Éamon de Valera (Fianna Fáil)
25 June 1973–17 Nov. 1974	Erskine Childers (Fianna Fáil) (died in office)
19 Dec. 1974–22 Oct. 1976	Cearbhall Ó Dálaigh (Fianna Fáil) (resigned)
3 Dec. 1976–2 Dec. 1990	Patrick J. Hillery (Fianna Fáil)
3 Dec. 1990–12 Sep. 1997	Mary Robinson (Labour Party) (resigned)
11 Nov. 1997–	Mary McAleese (Fianna Fáil)

Preston, Thomas (1585–1655), Confederate officer. In 1605 he was commissioned as a captain in Henry O'Neill's regiment in the Spanish Netherlands. The climax of his career in the Netherlands came in 1635 when, now commanding his own regiment, he formed part of the small garrison that defended Louvain for eleven days against vastly superior French forces. This was the start of a period of heavy attrition, and, having fallen under strength, Preston's regiment was disbanded in 1636. Preston was commissioned in December 1642 as general of the Leinster provincial army of the Catholic Confederates. He proved to be skilful in siege warfare; such actions, between December 1642 and May 1643, include those at Borris, Birr, Fort Falkland (near Banagher), Ballinakill, and, above all, Duncannon (January–March 1645). However, he was an incompetent battlefield commander. Defeats at Ross (March 1643) and Dungan's Hill (August 1647) betray recurrent flaws: committing himself to battle unnecessarily, poor deployment of cavalry, and a loss of control during the actions. At Dungan's Hill at least 3,000 of the Leinster infantry were slain, as against forty or so English.

Preston was characteristically indecisive in choosing whether to side with the Ormondists or the followers of the Nuncios during the factional power struggles of 1646–8. During the Cromwellian conquest (1649–52) Preston, by now Viscount Tara, served as governor of Waterford and, later, Galway. In neither instance can his conduct of the defence in conditions of blockade and epidemic disease be faulted. Subsequently he was allowed by Parliament to embark soldiers for the Spanish service. **Pádraig Lenihan**

Preston, Thomas (1860–1900), physicist. Born in Ballyhagan, Co. Armagh; educated at TCD. A protégé of GEORGE FRANCIS FITZGERALD, he became professor of natural philosophy at University College, Dublin, and a fellow of the Royal University, where he performed his experiments. A fellow of the Royal Society, he was the author of outstanding textbooks on heat and light. He discovered the Anomalous Zeeman Effect, which he recorded photographically in 1897; this was important in the later development of the quantum theory of atoms. **Denis Weaire**

Prevention of Terrorism Act (PTA), a British statute giving the police extended powers to deal with suspected terrorists. The Prevention of Terrorism (Temporary Provisions) Act (1974) was introduced following the bombs in BIRMINGHAM pubs in November 1974 that killed twenty-one people and injured 169. The act provided the police with extended powers of arrest and detention and gave them new powers to control the movement of people entering and leaving Britain and Northern Ireland, gave the Secretary of State the power to issue an exclusion order banning a person from living in any part of the United Kingdom, and provided for the proscription of certain organisations and made the display of support for them illegal. The Home Secretary, Roy Jenkins, described the powers as 'draconian' and agreed that 'in combination, they are unprecedented in peacetime.' The legislation was amended and extended on a number of occasions and was further expanded and made permanent in the Terrorism Act (2000).

The act has had a profound effect on Irish people travelling between Ireland and Britain and also on the resident Irish population in Britain. At ports and airports travellers to and from Ireland have been required to proceed through special channels, where the police and certain other officials have unfettered discretion in stopping and questioning travellers. Millions of people have been stopped and questioned about the purpose of their travel. In the early days of the act's operation an examination could continue for up to seven days. In 1984 certain limits were placed on the process: an examination may proceed for up to one hour, after which time the person must be told of their rights and a formal record made of the examination. Between 1984 and 1999 more than 4,000 people were questioned for more than an hour but not detained.

A person can be detained at any time during the examination without any reasonable suspicion, but if after twelve hours there is no reasonable suspicion the person must be released; if there is suspicion it is up to the examining officer whether the person is released or further detained. A person can also be detained following an arrest under the act. Between 1984 and 1999 almost 2,000 people were detained in connection with Northern Ireland matters; only 3 per cent were charged with an offence.

Most of those stopped, examined, arrested, or detained under the Prevention of Terrorism Act were not suspects in the normal sense of the word, in that they were believed to be involved in illegal acts: in effect they were being drawn into the net because they were Irish or had Irish connections and were therefore members of a suspect community. **Paddy Hillyard**

priests, Catholic, eighteenth and nineteenth century. The Bishops Banishment Act (1697) resulted formally, in 1698, in the expulsion of the regular orders from Ireland, but the act of 1704, requiring the registration of the secular parochial clergy, had the unintended consequence of giving them a form of legal protection. During the penal era priests were trained, generally after ordination, in one of thirty colleges conducted by both regular and secular clergy on the Continent, and a good number of them remained abroad. The forcible closure of most of these colleges at the time of the French Revolution, and the creation of ST PATRICK'S COLLEGE at Maynooth in 1795 and of diocesan colleges at Carlow, Kilkenny, Navan, Waterford, Tuam, and Wexford, resulted in a continuous expansion of the priesthood serving the Catholic Church in Ireland and the huge Irish diaspora overseas, in Britain, the United States, and the far corners of the British Empire. The clergy enjoyed considerable status and authority among their parishioners, though clerical involvement in politics—earnestly desired by laymen like O'CONNELL in the nationalist cause—always risked a backlash from both reactionaries and revolutionaries. [see IRISH COLLEGES IN CONTINTENTAL EUROPE; LOUVAIN.] **Sheridan Gilley**

Primitive Wesleyan Methodists: see METHODIST CHURCH.

printing in Irish. Compared with other CELTIC languages, particularly Welsh and Breton, printed publications in Irish from the sixteenth century onwards were scarce. This was both a consequence and a cause of the long-term decline of Irish: a strong print culture would have conferred greater prestige on the language, while a larger language community would in turn have constituted a larger market for printed material. This scarcity was principally due to the fractured religious history of the country and the consequent failure of any church to carry through religious reform in the vernacular, accompanied by printed catechisms and other religious texts.

Printed publications in Irish can for convenience be divided into three broad phases. The first represents the initial efforts of the churches to promote the aims of the Protestant and Catholic REFORMATIONS. The established Anglican Church produced the first printed book in Irish, a catechism, in 1571, and translations of the New and Old Testaments during the seventeenth century. Catholic presses in Continental Europe, particularly that of the Franciscans at LOUVAIN, produced devotional works during the seventeenth and early eighteenth century. Few of these books had more than one edition, and their print runs were relatively small.

The second phase, from the middle of the eighteenth century to the GREAT FAMINE, saw works produced in response to a growing bilingual literacy consequent on the expansion of the economy. They differed from the earlier publications in being printed largely in roman type, as opposed to Gaelic type, often containing prefaces in English, frequently being printed in provincial towns, such as Cork and Limerick, and sometimes running into many editions. Among Catholic books, Bishop Gallagher's *Sermons*, first printed in 1736, had fourteen editions by 1820, while the *Pious Miscellany* of TADHG GAELACH Ó SÚILLEABHÁIN had twenty editions in the first half of the nineteenth century. The 1820s and 30s also saw large-scale printing projects undertaken by a series of Protestant evangelical societies, which financed schools to teach reading in Irish and distributed large numbers of primers, editions of the Bible, and religious tracts.

The rapid decline of Irish in the post-famine decades was paralleled in its printed production, which was almost non-existent. The establishment of language revival organisations, particularly the GAELIC LEAGUE, at the end of the century led to a third phase in PUBLISHING, which can be described as revivalist. This aimed at the creation of a new reading public in Irish and supplying that public with as wide a variety of texts as possible. This project was consolidated after independence with the establishment of a state publisher, AN GÚM, in 1926 and the creation of a large market for schoolbooks in Irish. Since the 1940s the existence of a small but enthusiastic reading public, mainly outside the traditional Irish-speaking areas, combined with a system of state subsidy, has led to the foundation of a number of smaller publishing houses as well as many NEWSPAPERS AND JOURNALS. **Niall Ó Ciosáin**

prints and print-makers

Seventeenth to nineteenth centuries. Until the development of photomechanical printing processes in the late nineteenth century, print-making was the main technique for reproducing graphics. Prints produced in and relating to Ireland before the twentieth century were largely reproductions of oil portraits, watercolour topographical scenes, social and political caricatures, prints for industrial and commercial design, illustrations in works of fiction, plates in scientific and medical studies, and illustrations in NEWSPAPERS.

Copperplate engraving was taught at the DUBLIN SOCIETY's schools from 1756, prints of industrial and commercial designs being most encouraged. The flourishing late eighteenth-century PUBLISHING and printing trade employed copperplate engravers in both bookplate design and book illustration. Engravers prepared plates for prints of map surveys and copperplate designs for map cartouches.

The 'Irish School' in London included the artist and engraver William Kilburn (1745–1818), whose botanical plates were published in the *Flora Londinensis*; John Brooks (fl. 1730–1756), whose mezzotint engravings included the BATTLE OF THE BOYNE and the SIEGE OF DERRY; the mezzotint portraitist James Macardle (1728/9–1765); the mezzotint engraver of art works James Egan (1799–1842); and William Nelson Gardiner (1766–1814), engraver of book illustrations. Captain William Baillie (1723–1810) was distinguished as a collector and as an amateur engraver and etcher of copperplates, widely known for his series *Prints and Etchings after Rembrandt, Teniers, G. Dou, Poussin and Others* (1792).

Copperplate etching made possible the rapid and timely production of political and personal caricature prints, most numerous between 1780 and 1820. Teams of young women in workshops coloured the prints. James Sidebotham and his colleague and rival

prints. Self-Portrait *(1760) by Thomas Frye (c. 1710–1762), mezzotint. The tonality of the mezzotint technique made it ideal for the reproduction of oil portraits. [National Gallery of Ireland]*

William McCleary were Dublin caricature-etchers and publishers in the early 1800s, noted for their copying of James Gillray's personal caricatures. In the 1790s Hanna Humphrey, who published prints relating to Britain and Ireland, employed Gillray and published his prints, including his political caricatures relating to Ireland; she employed George Cruickshank to assist and then take over from him. In the 1840s Cruickshank's steel plates, using mixed engraving and etching, illustrated W. H. MAXWELL's *History of the Irish Rebellion in 1798* (see p. 974). In satirical caricature the Irishman John Doyle (1797–1868) worked in England as 'H. B.', his lithographic prints relating to contemporary political events.

Examples of nineteenth-century scientific exploration and recording of FLORA include the drawings and lithographs of Robert David FitzGerald (1830–1892) for his *Australian Orchids* (1875–82) and the drawings and lithographs of WILLIAM HENRY HARVEY (1811–1866) for his *Flora Capensis* (1859–65).

Nineteenth-century topographical prints include the etchings and engravings of generations of the BROCAS FAMILY (early 1700s to 1873) (see p. 841) and the aquatints of THOMAS SAUTELLE ROBERTS (c. 1760–1827), JONATHAN FISHER (died 1809), Francis Jukes, and JAMES MALTON. Portrait prints include the line-and-stipple engravings of Patrick Maguire (fl. 1790–1820) and Henry Brocas Senior (1762–1837), the etchings and engravings of John Kirkwood (died 1853), and the lithographs of James Henry Lynch (died 1868) and Henry O'Neill (1798–1880). From the 1860s wood-engraved prints, such as those in the *Illustrated London News*, ensured graphic newspaper coverage of events in Ireland. **Elizabeth M. Kirwan**

Nineteenth to twenty-first centuries. From the end of the nineteenth century, with the advance of photographic reproduction processes, reproductive print-making was threatened by the new technology, though the use of wood engraving and lithography to illustrate popular journals lasted into the early twentieth century. Original print-making began to achieve popularity among artists only when these media had virtually ceased to have a commercial application.

The history of Irish artists' print-making begins in France and Britain. From the 1880s many Irish artists who had studied abroad, in Antwerp or Paris, experimented briefly in print-making, usually with etching, though these initiatives rarely represented a significant departure in their artistic practice. WALTER OSBORNE in Antwerp in the 1880s made some tentative genre etchings, while in Brittany RODERICK O'CONOR during the period 1893–8, influenced by the Pont-Aven artist Armand Seguin (1869–1903), produced a suite of superb post-impressionist landscape etchings. There are many other examples of artists who produced a body of prints early in their career and then abandoned the medium, such as WILLIAM CONOR and SEÁN O'SULLIVAN, both trained as lithographers.

An important development in the growth of Irish print-making was the establishment in London of the Society of Wood Engravers (1920), with three Irish artists—ROBERT GIBBINGS, E. M. O'Rorke-Dickey (1894–1977), and Mabel Ansley (1881–1959)—as founder-members, ELIZABETH RIVERS being later invited to join. Gibbings, a prolific print-maker, travel writer, and proprietor of the Golden Cockerel Press, was among the most consistent print-makers of the early twentieth century. Working in wood engraving or woodcut, these artists established what was to be the prevailing and virtually only mode of Irish print-making during the first half of the twentieth century. Prints for book illustration were central to their area of interest, rather than single-sheet editioned prints for exhibition. In Dublin, ESTELLA SOLOMONS, influenced by Whistler, worked in small architectural etchings of the city, while HARRY KERNOFF, the most prolific of print-makers, over a lengthy period produced a body of small figurative woodcuts of widely varying quality, his earliest prints being the most accomplished. He issued three collections of his woodcuts in book form, in 1942, 1944, and 1951.

prints. *Woodcut (c. 1930) by Harry Kernoff (1900–1974). Symbols of the labour movement, a heroic worker and the dawn, are combined with great force in this early print. [Private collection]*

In 1960, influenced by the establishment of artists' print studios on the Continent and in North America, the Graphic Studio, Dublin, was established by the publisher Liam Miller (1924–1987, founder of the DOLMEN PRESS), the painter Leslie McWeeney (b. 1936), ELIZABETH RIVERS (who represents a link to the Society of Wood Engravers), and PATRICK HICKEY. While Rivers' work continued in the vein of delicate wood engravings for books, Hickey, who had trained at Urbino in Italy, introduced modern movement concepts of European print-making to Ireland and is the seminal figure in the development of Irish print-making throughout the second half of the twentieth century. Most of the leading original print artists of the period, including Mary Farl Powers (1948–1992) and PATRICK PYE, were members of the Graphic Studio. From 1988 the Black Church Print Studio, also in Dublin, provided a further outlet for print-makers such as John Kelly and Andrew Folan, while other co-operative studios, the Seacourt Print Studio in Belfast and Cork Printmakers, indicated the increasing centrality of print as a medium for younger artists. **Brian Lalor**

Prior, Thomas (1682–1751), lawyer and landowner. Born in Rathdowney, Co. Laois; educated at TCD. Among his intimate friends were BERKELEY, SWIFT, and Lord Chesterfield. A founder-member of the Physico-Historical Society, he was involved with BARTHOLOMEW MOSSE in founding the ROTUNDA LYING-IN HOSPITAL. His article 'A list of absentees of Ireland ... with observations on the present trade and conditions of that kingdom' was considered subversive, as he was critical of the absentee landlords and published their names and incomes. As a benefactor he endeavoured to promote the welfare of Ireland through every branch of husbandry and manufacture, acting as secretary to the Dublin Society (later ROYAL DUBLIN SOCIETY) from its inception. Following the renovation of the RDS members' rooms in 1994 the largest and most elegant was renamed the Thomas Prior Room; it displays a marble bust of Prior by JOHN VAN NOST. There is also a monument to his memory in CHRIST CHURCH CATHEDRAL with the inscription 'This monument was erected to Thomas Prior Esq. ... to honour the memory of that worthy patriot, to whom his veracity, actions and ... endeavours in the service of his country have raised a monument more lasting than marble.' **Dervilla Donnelly**

prisons. The BREHON LAW relied on fines and other non-custodial forms of punishment; imprisonment was limited to holding hostages pending payment of a fine. Prisons in Ireland began as local institutions maintained by landed proprietors and gentry in their own houses. Local authorities, specifically the GRAND JURIES, were responsible in 1800 for forty-one city and county jails and 112 bridewells (where petty offenders and debtors were held in transit to county prisons). Until 1856 the TRANSPORTATION of offenders to penal colonies in Australia and other distant places vied with imprisonment as the primary method of punishment.

A move towards a central prison authority was first evident in the 1780s, when the LORD LIEUTENANT was authorised to establish a prison inspectorate and a penitentiary for convicts whose sentence had been commuted to imprisonment. Prison regimes closely followed English practice, with solitary confinement to avoid contamination by association. The end of transportation left some four thousand prisoners stranded in a newly created category of penal servitude, promoting further steps towards centralisation and experiments in prison reform. A Board of Directors of Irish Convict Prisons was created, chaired by the noted reformer and skilled administrator Sir William Crofton. He took a radical step in championing rehabilitation as the goal of imprisonment and created a 'progressive four-stage system' to reintegrate prisoners as members of society. Prisoners in convict prisons progressed through an initial period of solitary confinement to labour at public works while housed in a traditional prison. Training for a trade while confined in an 'intermediate prison' followed and, finally, conditional release under police supervision. The apparent success of this system influenced prison policy in the United States and Continental Europe.

The Crofton revolution, however, was short-lived. Deteriorating prison conditions and a campaign of public protests led to the creation of a General Prisons Board in 1877, financed from the imperial exchequer. Grand juries retained the authority to hear prisoners' complaints and report abuses. The board oversaw a rapid consolidation of prisoners into twenty-three institutions by 1921: one convict prison, one convict and local prison, fourteen local prisons, five bridewells, one inebriates' reformatory, and a borstal for young offenders.

After 1922 the Prison Board was absorbed into the Department of Justice, then abolished in 1928, with prisons coming under direct ministerial control. An independent prison authority remained in Northern Ireland. The number of prisoners dwindled in both the Republic and Northern Ireland. Prison facilities also deteriorated, and prison policy did not advance. Neither system was prepared for the increase in prison numbers associated with rising CRIME rates after 1960 and the strains of accommodating prisoners claiming political status during the 'TROUBLES'. A committee of inquiry into the penal system in the Republic recommended that imprisonment be the punishment of last resort, with the re-establishment of an independent Prison Board and a cap on the prison population. After a gap of ten years many of these recommendations were adopted, but so far no policy has succeeded in containing the size of the prison population.

In Northern Ireland the 'TROUBLES' strained the capacity of the prison system and placed prison policy at the heart of the conflict. Internees were first afforded 'special category' status, housed separately, and allowed to organise themselves, much like prisoners of war; this status was later extended to all those convicted by the DIPLOCK COURTS. An attempt to retract this status led to the 'dirty protest' and HUNGER STRIKES as the will of the paramilitaries to assert prisoner-of-war status conflicted with that of the STORMONT authorities to treat them as ordinary criminals. [see KILMAINHAM GAOL.] **David Rottman**

private health insurance. By 2001 approximately 1.5 million people in the Republic were covered by private medical insurance, mainly under the aegis of the Voluntary Health Insurance (VHI) Board, established by statute in 1957. Since 1994 the VHI Board has been exposed to competition, and other bodies in the health insurance field now include BUPA (Ireland) and a number of small schemes linked to occupational groups. The VHI Board offers limited schemes for people resident in Northern Ireland, where a number of British commercial bodies also offer services. **Joseph Robins**

Proclamation of the Irish Republic (1916). Drafted mainly by PATRICK PEARSE and JAMES CONNOLLY, the Proclamation was addressed to the people of Ireland from the PROVISIONAL GOVERNMENT of the Irish Republic 'established' by the RISING of 1916. It was signed by THOMAS J. CLARKE, SEÁN MAC DIARMADA, THOMAS MACDONAGH, Patrick Pearse, ÉAMONN CEANNT, James Connolly and JOSEPH PLUNKETT; all seven were shot by firing squad following the collapse of the rising. A thousand copies of the proclamation were printed on a flatbed press in Liberty Hall on the afternoon of Easter Sunday, 23 April. The printers were Christopher Brady, Michael Molloy, and William O'Brien. The first copy was taken by CONSTANCE MARKIEVICZ, who read it aloud to a small crowd on the steps outside; the first official reading was by Pearse outside the GENERAL POST OFFICE in O'Connell Street the following day. **Fergal Tobin**

POBLACHT NA H EIREANN.

THE PROVISIONAL GOVERNMENT

OF THE

IRISH REPUBLIC

TO THE PEOPLE OF IRELAND.

IRISHMEN AND IRISHWOMEN: In the name of God and of the dead generations from which she receives her old tradition of nationhood, Ireland, through us, summons her children to her flag and strikes for her freedom.

Having organised and trained her manhood through her secret revolutionary organisation, the Irish Republican Brotherhood, and through her open military organisations, the Irish Volunteers and the Irish Citizen Army, having patiently perfected her discipline, having resolutely waited for the right moment to reveal itself, she now seizes that moment, and, supported by her exiled children in America and by gallant allies in Europe, but relying in the first on her own strength, she strikes in full confidence of victory.

We declare the right of the people of Ireland to the ownership of Ireland, and to the unfettered control of Irish destinies, to be sovereign and indefeasible. The long usurpation of that right by a foreign people and government has not extinguished the right, nor can it ever be extinguished except by the destruction of the Irish people. In every generation the Irish people have asserted their right to national freedom and sovereignty; six times during the past three hundred years they have asserted it in arms. Standing on that fundamental right and again asserting it in arms in the face of the world, we hereby proclaim the Irish Republic as a Sovereign Independent State, and we pledge our lives and the lives of our comrades-in-arms to the cause of its freedom, of its welfare, and of its exaltation among the nations.

The Irish Republic is entitled to, and hereby claims, the allegiance of every Irishman and Irishwoman. The Republic guarantees religious and civil liberty, equal rights and equal opportunities to all its citizens, and declares its resolve to pursue the happiness and prosperity of the whole nation and of all its parts, cherishing all the children of the nation equally, and oblivious of the differences carefully fostered by an alien government, which have divided a minority from the majority in the past.

Until our arms have brought the opportune moment for the establishment of a permanent National Government, representative of the whole people of Ireland and elected by the suffrages of all her men and women, the Provisional Government, hereby constituted, will administer the civil and military affairs of the Republic in trust for the people.

We place the cause of the Irish Republic under the protection of the Most High God, Whose blessing we invoke upon our arms, and we pray that no one who serves that cause will dishonour it by cowardice, inhumanity, or rapine. In this supreme hour the Irish nation must, by its valour and discipline and by the readiness of its children to sacrifice themselves for the common good, prove itself worthy of the august destiny to which it is called.

Signed on Behalf of the Provisional Government,
THOMAS J. CLARKE.
SEAN Mac DIARMADA. THOMAS MacDONAGH.
P. H. PEARSE. EAMONN CEANNT.
JAMES CONNOLLY. JOSEPH PLUNKETT.

Proclamation. *The founding document of the Irish Republic, read by Patrick Pearse from the portico of the GPO on 24 April (Easter Monday) 1916. There are twenty-five known surviving copies in public and private collections. [Camera Press Ireland]*

Programme for Economic Expansion (1959–63). In response to the economic stagnation of the 1950s a comprehensive review of the ECONOMY in the Republic was undertaken, with proposals for change presented to the Department of Finance in the report *Economic Development* (1958); these were translated into a statement of policy objectives and measures in the *Programme for Economic Expansion* (1958). This applied particularly to manufacturing, with encouragement of exports and foreign participation a central aim, a clear reversal of earlier policy. To counteract the dearth of investment it was proposed that public investment be channelled into more directly productive purposes, that foreign investment be sought, and that private investment be encouraged and guided by an integrated development programme. It was estimated that implementing the programme would result in a 2 per cent annual growth in real national income. Over the period of the programme the economy grew at 4 per cent per annum, considerably above that projected and anything experienced since independence. It is widely believed that 1958 marked a watershed in Irish ECONOMIC

DEVELOPMENT and that *Economic Development* and the *Programme for Economic Expansion* played a leading role in this. **John W. O'Hagan**

Progressive Democrats, a political party formed by former FIANNA FÁIL and FINE GAEL politicians in 1985. In his foundation address the first leader, DESMOND O'MALLEY, committed the new party to 'breaking the mould of Irish politics and giving a real alternative to the CIVIL WAR parties.' The party is ideologically on the right, but in the Irish context is radical on some important social issues. In February 1987, in its first general election, the party won fourteen seats with 12 per cent of the national vote. In the general election of June 1989 this was reduced to 6 per cent of the vote and six seats; nevertheless the party entered a Coalition Government with Fianna Fáil with three ministers. In November 1992 these ministers resigned from the Government, and an election followed. The immediate cause of the election was a clash over evidence given by the Progressive Democrats and Fianna Fáil leaders to a public inquiry into possible malpractices in the beef industry. The parties had also differed sharply over the administration of industrial development policy and about the wording of a REFERENDUM question on ABORTION. The Progressive Democrats increased their seats to ten but lost office. The party was the first to have a woman leader, MARY HARNEY, who was also the first woman TÁNAISTE. In the 1997 general election the Progressive Democrats were reduced to 5 per cent of the vote and four seats but again joined Fianna Fáil in government. In the 1999 local election its support was 2.9 per cent. The party did not contest the 1999 European Parliament elections. [see TRIBUNALS.] **Neil Collins**

Proleek, Co. Louth, site of two MEGALITHIC TOMBS, the western tomb one of the most imposing PORTAL TOMBS in Ireland. Two tall, well-matched stones 2.25 m ($7\frac{1}{2}$ ft) high support, with the aid of a third upright, a massive granite roof-stone estimated to weigh at least 30 tonnes. Some 80 m (250 ft) to the east are the remains of a WEDGE TOMB gallery. **Paul Walsh**

Pro-Life Amendment Campaign (PLAC), a group whose principal aim was the insertion of an amendment in the CONSTITUTION OF IRELAND that would recognise the absolute right to life of every unborn child from conception. It expressed the fear that Ireland's membership of the European Union would lead to changes in socio-moral attitudes and that abortion might be legalised. The campaign was formally launched on 27 April 1981, much of the planning and research having been carried out by the Council of Social Concern, a group formed by the Knights of St Columbanus, a lay Catholic organisation that actively works to defend and uphold Catholic moral teaching. In Ireland it has concentrated its efforts on matters of sexual morality, pornography, CONTRACEPTION, ABORTION, and DIVORCE. Its members are professional men who, through participation in voluntary organisation and civic action, seek to defend Catholic Church teaching from any liberalising legal and social changes. The medical patrons of the Pro-Life Amendment Campaign included senior gynaecologists and obstetricians. The campaign was supported by numerous Catholic organisations. While being opposed by the Anti-Amendment Campaign, the PLAC gained the support of both FIANNA FÁIL and FINE GAEL for an amendment that was approved by the electorate in 1983: 'The State acknowledges the right to life of the unborn, and with due regard for the equal right to life of the mother, guarantees in its laws to respect and as far as it is practicable, by its laws to defend and vindicate that right.' [see SPUC.] **Evelyn Mahon**

promontory forts, a combination of one or more earth or stone ramparts on a coastal headland or inland spur, the greater part of which is naturally defended by a cliff, with the fort completing the fortification on the landward side. The enclosed area, though often reduced by COASTAL EROSION, may reach several hectares in area and is frequently accessible by a causeway that breaches the rampart. Despite their often inhospitable setting, mainly along the indented Atlantic seaboard, many of the approximately three hundred surviving monuments exhibit evidence of seasonal or permanent occupation and occasionally reoccupation up to the late Middle Ages. They are broadly divided into two categories, one consisting of larger, complex, and strategically sited examples, which may be dated to the later Prehistoric Period by analogy with inland HILL-FORTS and fortified headlands in other countries. While they may have been built primarily for defence, there is evidence of a closer relationship between a second category of smaller and more numerous promontory forts and the Irish RING-FORT. [see EARTHWORKS, LINEAR; LATER BRONZE AGE SETTLEMENT.] **Markus Casey**

Propaganda Fide, Congregation of, the Congregation for the Propagation of the Faith. Established by Pope Gregory XV in 1622, this was the department of the Vatican administration with responsibility for Catholic missions in non-Catholic countries. Ireland was unusual in coming under its aegis, as the majority of its population had remained Catholic and the medieval Catholic hierarchy of bishops had survived the REFORMATION. In the nineteenth century, especially after 1850, during the Irish archiepiscopates of PAUL CULLEN, Propaganda Fide presided over the creation of an Irish ecclesiastical empire throughout the Irish diaspora in North America and Australasia. In 1908, as one of his far-reaching administrative reforms proposed in 1906, Pope Pius X abolished its jurisdiction in Ireland (and in the churches of the Irish DIASPORA in Britain, the United States, and Canada, and in the Netherlands and Luxemburg), though it retained its authority in Australia and New Zealand. **Sheridan Gilley**

prophecies and prophetic visions, a feature of OLD IRISH literature. Such special powers are ascribed to members of the druidic caste, poets, and SAINTS. In the 'TÁIN', Fedelm the seer tells MÉABH of the imminent destruction of the Connacht hosts; in Muirchú's Life of Patrick, Lóegaire's druids foretell the coming of the saint. The first book of the Life of COLM CILLE concerns especially the saint's miracles of prophecy; he predicts the fate of kings and clerics and the outcome of battles and voyages. As with other literatures, prophecies were invariably written long after the events they claim to presage. **Ailbhe Mac Shamhráin**

prose fiction in English. Literary history has often identified MARIA EDGEWORTH'S CASTLE RACKRENT (1800) as the first self-consciously Irish novel; scholarship, however, shows that *Castle Rackrent*'s involvement with a social theme, its concern with national character, its deployment of a fictional method deriving from the told tale, and its taste for the fantastic were anticipated by other ASCENDANCY writers, who published a considerable body of fiction in the eighteenth century. Irish prose fiction in English might more properly be said to have originated with WILLIAM CHAIGNEAU'S picaresque *The History of Jack Connor* (1752) or THOMAS AMORY'S THE LIFE OF JOHN BUNCLE, ESQ. (1756–66), with its often fantastic narrative.

Castle Rackrent, in its regional focus, was an influence on the Walter Scott of the Waverley novels; historical fiction in nineteenth-century Ireland exhibits a debt to Scott, as in JOHN BANIM'S *The Boyne Water* (1826), while a taste for a literature that dealt in national character had one of its most popular manifestations in SYDNEY OWENSON, Lady Morgan's *The Wild Irish Girl* (1806) (see p. 850). WILLIAM CARLETON'S TRAITS AND STORIES OF THE IRISH PEASANTRY (1833) satisfied English curiosity about Irish rural life in the period before the Great Famine.

It is possible that the disturbed conditions of nineteenth-century Ireland prevented the emergence of a bourgeois realism in prose fiction (though SOMERVILLE AND ROSS came close to a fully achieved work of realism in 1894 with THE REAL CHARLOTTE); it may also be that, in as much as a fictional tradition emerged, it took the extremism of GOTHIC imagining as a generic resource in preference to realism, as in the work of CHARLES MATURIN, SHERIDAN LE FANU, and BRAM STOKER; or it reckoned Irish distinctiveness an occasion for STAGE-IRISH humour and drollery, as in the work of CHARLES LEVER and SAMUEL LOVER.

GEORGE MOORE in THE UNTILLED FIELD (1903) allowed his realistic eye to inspect the deficiencies of Irish rural life. JAMES JOYCE performed a similar task for urban experience in DUBLINERS (1914), which launched his career in prose fiction. Combining, in its exacting fashion, realism and symbolic technique, this collection of short stories was the first entry in an œuvre of remarkable experimentation. Joyce's work, particularly ULYSSES (1922) and FINNEGANS WAKE (1939), seemed to exhaust the possibilities of the European and English novel, making Joyce's successor in fictional experiment, SAMUEL BECKETT, the bleakly comic prose poet of negation, particularly in the TRILOGY (1951–3).

By contrast to such works of high modernism and postmodernism, independent Ireland produced a series of short-story writers, among them FRANK O'CONNOR, SEAN O'FAOLAIN, and MARY LAVIN, who employed realistic methods to explore the disillusionment and frustrations of the post-revolutionary period (see p. 795). FLANN O'BRIEN'S AT SWIM-TWO-BIRDS (1939) and *The Third Policeman* (posthumously published, 1967) showed that the fantastic and the gothic still appealed to a post-Joycean imagination.

Irish prose fiction in the middle and late twentieth century was marked by the increasingly diverse experiences it sought to register in a variety of forms—though realism remained a dominant mode. Northern Ireland life and exile from its confines were the basis of BRIAN MOORE'S extensive œuvre, while the complex experience of women in a changing Ireland was inaugurated as a vital theme in the early novels of EDNA O'BRIEN. Novelists no longer felt any need to treat explicitly national themes, as can be seen in JOHN BANVILLE'S scientific tetralogy. Increasingly, urban life became the theme, as in the work of RODDY DOYLE. **Terence Brown**

protectionism. The Republic's protectionist period had its basis in the class politics of the early 1930s, as support for the first FIANNA FÁIL Government came from small farmers and urban workers. While the large beef and dairy farmers of the period would have favoured FREE TRADE, industrial protection was seen as a way of stimulating EMPLOYMENT. It succeeded in this until the 1950s, when protectionism saw the Republic excluded from the European post-war boom. Balance-of-payments crises, which led to fiscal contraction, followed from the continuing necessity to import capital equipment and a broad range of consumer goods. The various infant-industry arguments that provide theoretical support for industrial protection are inappropriate to Ireland, as the economies of scale necessary to allow a take-off into export activity could never be attained within the small Irish market. **Frank Barry**

Protestant Ascendancy, a term that entered the political

Pro-life. *The Society for the Protection of Unborn Children (SPUC) holding a vigil in Dublin, 27 December 1981. [Derek Speirs/Report]*

lexicon in the 1780s when it was appealed to by defenders of the *status quo*, who aspired to preserving the existing constitution in church and state. Popularised in the 1790s and the early nineteenth century by those most opposed to the concession of political rights to Catholics, it was given a more respectable gloss at the end of the century by W. B. YEATS. Subsequently appealed to by historians to define both the era and the social elite that dominated Irish society for a century and a half after the BATTLE OF THE BOYNE, its particular origins demand that it be used more circumspectly. [see ANGLO-IRISH SOCIETY; 'BIG HOUSE'.] **James Kelly**

Proud, Malcolm (1952–), harpsichordist and organist. Born in Dublin; having graduated from the University of Dublin in 1973, he studied harpsichord at Copenhagen Conservatory and with Gustav Leonhardt at the Sweenlinck Conservatory, Amsterdam. In 1982 he won the International Harpsichord Competition in Edinburgh and taught at the RIAM, 1983–6. He gives regular performances in Ireland, on the Continent, and in the United States. He has made recordings of Bach, Byrd, Couperin (1985), and Purcell (1994). **Ite O'Donovan**

proverbs (Irish *seanfhocail*). 'Man cannot live by beans alone!'—heard recently in a Belfast supermarket—demonstrates the essential nature of the proverb: durability and flexibility. The inspiration for this example, as for many throughout the Christian world, is the Bible; others current in Ireland have been recorded in classical writings.

Proverbs give advice in a succinct and memorable way, partly because of metre, contrast, humour, alliteration, or rhyme ('Ash green, fit for the queen'); they often preserve archaic words and dialect. They are usually only one sentence long, but the great majority are metaphorical ('Never sell your hen on a wet day'), which enables them to be applied in a wide range of situations. Some proverbs are related to other short, fixed forms of oral tradition, such as blessings, curses, and riddles ('What four things is an Irishman afraid of?'—'A cow's horn, a horse's hoof, a dog's snarl, and an Englishman's laugh'). Nowadays proverbs, or adaptations of them, are extensively used in promotions and newspaper captions ('Safety first,' 'No place like work').

Despite their international nature, brief explanations ascribing a local origin to widespread proverbs are common. While it is likely that a few were created in Ireland (such as 'If the rowan tree is tall, even so it is bitter on the top'), it is easier to identify variants that are particularly Irish, such as *'Aithníonn ciaróg ciaróg eile'* ('A beetle recognises another beetle'). Other proverbs have persisted in Ireland in a certain form or have died out elsewhere (such as 'Live horse, and eat grass').

There is a great uniformity of proverbs throughout Ireland, and a great overlap between those in Irish and English, with the same sixty-one of the 106 commonest European proverbs found in both languages. Proverbs are often quoted in Irish by English-speakers, many of whom would be unaware that English versions of such often-quoted proverbs as *'Níl aon tinteán mar do thinteán féin'* ('There's no fireside like your own fireside') also exist. The GAELIC LEAGUE organised proverb competitions, while proverbs in English were disseminated in VERE FOSTER copybooks.

While primarily an oral genre, proverbs have often been developed as a literary form, such as the TRIADS from approximately the ninth century. This style—where two, three or more things are compared—is a particular feature of Irish proverbs, in both literary and oral tradition. An example from literary tradition is *'Trí uara ná tairiset fri tráig ocus fri tuile: uair gene, uair choimperta, uair scartha anma duine'* ('Three times that stay not for ebb tide nor for flood: the time of birth, the time of conception, the time the soul departs'), while an example existing in oral tradition is *'Súil, glúin, agus uilleann—na trí neithe is frithre i gcolainn an duine'* ('Eye, knee, and elbow—the three most sensitive parts of the human body'). The style is also found in comparatively recent English-language proverbs in Ireland ('Love and a cough cannot be hid').

The Department of Irish Folklore, UCD, holds a massive collection of proverbs. **Fionnuala Carson Williams**

provincial presidencies, established during the reign of ELIZABETH I in an effort to increase the power of the Crown in areas controlled by local magnates. They were modelled on similar administrative structures in the north of England and in Wales and were promoted by SIDNEY as part of his plan for the pacification of Ireland. The introduction of the presidency in Munster in 1570 was a factor in the rebellion of JAMES FITZMAURICE FITZGERALD. This gave undue emphasis from the beginning to the military character of the presidency there, which was to last for the rest of the Tudor period. The Connacht presidency, established in 1569, functioned more like its English and Welsh counterparts. Each lord president was both a military leader and a civil administrator. In the exercise of his executive and judicial functions he was assisted by a provincial council (nominated by the Lord Deputy), two judges, a clerk of the council, and numerous lesser officials. While he was empowered to exercise martial law if necessary, his main duty was to expand and administer the common law through a prerogative jurisdiction. He had commissions to hear and determine both civil and criminal cases. Most of the Tudor appointees were English military men, but in the more peaceful conditions of the early seventeenth century local noblemen were granted the office. Having reverted to being military positions in the 1640s and removed in the 1650s, the presidencies were restored under CHARLES II, only to be abolished in 1672. **Liam Irwin**

Provisional Government of Southern Ireland (16 January to 6 December 1922), the Government established under article 17 of the ANGLO-IRISH TREATY (1921) to administer Southern Ireland from the ratification of the Treaty until the foundation of the IRISH FREE STATE. Membership of the Provisional Government overlapped with the revolutionary government of Dáil Éireann, not recognised by the British, and it was disowned by anti-Treaty republicans. Its first chairman was MICHAEL COLLINS. The Provisional Government drafted the Constitution of the Irish Free State (1922) and won the Collins-DE VALERA Pact election the same year. Following Collins's death in August, W. T. COSGRAVE became chairman; he went on to become first President of the Executive Council (government) of the Irish Free State. **Fergal Tobin**

'Provisional IRA' ('Provos'), formed in early 1970 by dissidents who had split from the IRA after it decided to give at least token recognition to the partitionist parliaments in Belfast and Dublin. The founding core of the movement were especially strongly represented in the urban Catholic ghettoes of Northern Ireland, where the IRA had manifestly failed to provide protection against loyalist attacks in the summer of 1969. From 1970 the Provisionals made most of the running in the republican campaign against British rule in Northern Ireland, developing into the most sophisticated and formidable terrorist organisation in the Western world. Its initial strategy was to pursue a broadly based military campaign, including mass demonstrations among the nationalist population; but after this failed to secure any great success, in the mid-1970s the Provisionals reformed themselves into a tight cellular structure and settled down for a 'long war' of attrition, characterised by specific bombing attacks on RUC and army bases as well as civilian targets, such as government offices, railways, factories, hotels, and shops, together with attacks on security force and para-security personnel, including judges, prison officers, and civilian employees of the security forces. They also sought to bring the war to the British with attacks and bombings in Britain and on British military targets on the Continent. In the early 1980s a clear political dimension to the campaign emerged following the electoral mobilisation of nationalist public opinion during the HUNGER STRIKES of 1980–81. The political wing of the movement, SINN FÉIN, headed by GERRY ADAMS, who had played a leading role in Belfast in the early 1970s, began to challenge the SDLP as the main nationalist party in Northern Ireland. The balance in what was called the 'Armalite and ballot-box strategy' increasingly shifted towards the political side, with Sinn Féin becoming involved in talks with representatives of the British government. In August 1994 the Provisional IRA announced a complete cessation of military operations, but it resumed action in February 1996, before once again calling a ceasefire in July 1997. This move followed Sinn Féin's decision to participate in elections for both Dáil Éireann and the new Northern Ireland legislative assembly (see pp. 827, 926). **Keith Jeffery**

'Provisional Sinn Féin': see SINN FÉIN.

Psychological Society of Ireland, established in 1970, the professional body for psychologists. It plays a leading role in the setting of professional standards, developing public policies, advising the Government and employers on the development of psychological services, and the accreditation of university courses. It publishes the

Provisional IRA. *Members of the IRA in the Ardoyne area of Belfast, Easter 1997. A mural depicting the leaders of the 1916 Rising and the Easter lily, symbol of the Rising, is on the wall behind the crowds. [Kelvin Boyes Photography]*

Irish Journal of Psychology (1971–) and also the *Irish Psychologist*. In conjunction with the University of Ulster it operates a postgraduate diploma course in clinical psychology. The society, which has a membership of 1,340, has been successful in recruiting both academic and professional psychologists, so avoiding the gulf that often separates these groups in other countries. **Maureen Gaffney**

psychology, the science of mind and behaviour. Like other branches of science, it searches for underlying principles in behavioural and mental processes, including perception, memory, thought, the functioning of the brain, and intergenerational relationships. Clinical psychologists study and treat what is variously termed abnormal behaviour, psychopathology, or simply psychological problems, working mainly in multi-disciplinary teams in the mental health service. Counselling psychologists work mainly as psycho-therapists, helping people to deal with life problems. Educational psychologists deal with learning disability, specific learning problems, and the school environment. Organisational or occupational psychologists apply the principles of psychology to performance in the workplace and other personnel issues.

Both as a discipline and as a profession, psychology is well developed in Ireland, despite its relatively late arrival in the second half of the twentieth century. Queen's University, Belfast, awarded the first degree in psychology in 1949, that of bachelor of education (reflecting the fact that psychology was then studied as a subject within education); the first BA in psychology proper was awarded in 1955. In 1958 QUB appointed the first professor of psychology in Ireland, Dr George Seth. By the late 1980s psychology was organised as a separate school in the university.

The same evolution from a sub-set of a larger discipline to an independent scientific discipline was apparent in the Republic. Until the late 1950s the study of psychology took place within the discipline of philosophy, itself strongly influenced by the Catholic Church. University College, Dublin, established a chair of logic and psychology as early as 1909. In 1958 Father Feichin O'Doherty, professor of logic and psychology at UCD, established the first course in psychology in the Republic, a postgraduate diploma. In 1964 the first undergraduate degree course in psychology at University College, Cork, was also established by a priest, Prof. Peter Dempsey, a former lecturer in philosophy. It was rumoured at the time that the Bishop of Cork and Ross, and Governor of the college, Dr Cornelius Lucey, objected to the new degree course, considering psychology a branch of theology, and agreed to the new course only if it were entitled applied psychology. Nonetheless, from the beginning, psychology courses in the Republic were structured to reflect the strong empirical base of psychology and its practical application in the fields of child development, health, education, and industry. In 1964 an undergraduate degree course in psychology was set up in TRINITY COLLEGE, Dublin, by Prof. Derek Forrest and in 1971 in University College, Galway, by Prof. Martin McHugh. Later the

University of Ulster established courses in psychology at Coleraine, Magee, and Jordanstown colleges.

The organisation and study of psychology as a discipline and as a profession is strongly influenced by the scientist-practitioner model. Unlike the situation in some other countries, where the teaching of psychology is still strongly influenced by philosophy and psychoanalysis, most undergraduate psychology courses provide a general training in the main areas of the discipline, such as cognitive, biological, developmental, abnormal, and social psychology. Because of the strong emphasis on the scientific basis of psychology, training in research, experimental, and statistical methods is a central component of courses. Many academic psychologists have established an international reputation in their specialist field of research, despite the dearth of funds for postgraduate research. The increased research funds recently allocated by the Government are a significant advance. The funds becoming available under the Higher Educational Authority's Programme for Research in Third-Level Institutions, from the Health Research Board and from the Research Council for the Humanities, will provide psychologists with the long-awaited opportunity to produce a higher volume of high-quality research.

Psychologists work in very diverse employments. Of the total membership of the Psychological Society of Ireland, approximately a third are employed in education, mainly at third level, more than a quarter in health, and about a fifth each in disability services and in private practice. The majority of psychologists working in the health service are clinical psychologists.

Clinical psychologists generally work as part of a multidisciplinary team, with all age groups and in a variety of clinical settings: in-patient, out-patient, clinic, and community. The range of their work is equally diverse: assessment, treatment, research, evaluation, and consultancy. A significant feature is the concentration of psychologists who work in the area of learning disability. Ireland traditionally had a high rate of learning disability (then known as mental handicap), perhaps related to the traditional later age of marriage and large families, leading to a higher risk of mental handicap, particularly Down's syndrome. However, both the Catholic Church and VOLUNTARY ORGANISATIONS also had a strong commitment to caring for those with such disabilities; as a result, services for those with learning disabilities are highly developed and innovative.

Educational psychologists mainly work for the National Educational Psychological Service Agency, under the aegis of the Department of Education and Science. Eighty psychologists are employed at present by this service (to increase to 200 by the end of 2003), which provides a consultative and support service to first-level and second-level schools. It works principally with teachers and guidance counsellors but in some circumstances provides a direct service to children with special difficulties. The regional organisation of the educational service closely parallels health board areas, to allow for full collaboration with the clinical services. **Maureen Gaffney**

Ptolemy (Claudius Ptolemaeus) (c. 90–168), Greek astronomer resident in Alexandria. His treatise on geography (c. AD 150) consists mainly of tabulated latitudes and longitudes for towns, river-mouths, bays, and promontories throughout the known world, nearly all of them derived from more or less inaccurate estimates of terrestrial distance and direction, rather than from astronomical observations. The oldest surviving maps based on Ptolemy's tables date only from the thirteenth century; the earliest printed versions appeared in 1477 and became in the next half century a major influence on European cartography. For Ireland, Ptolemy gave co-ordinates for about fifty places, most of them with names that are otherwise unknown. **J. H. Andrews**

Ptolemy's map of Ireland. Claudius Ptolemaeus compiled his *Geographia* c. AD 150, and in book II he provides the earliest surviving PLACE-NAME evidence for Ireland. He did not provide maps but rather lists of places and map references from which maps could be drawn. Some fifty-three names are provided for Ireland and its ISLANDS. The sources of his information were various, including Marinus of Tyre (early second century), who took much of his information from Philemon (early first century) and probably merchants, and the material has been severely corrupted in transmission. The difficulties are formidable: the earliest manuscript dates from the thirteenth century, and there is no reliable modern edition of Ptolemy for Western Europe; not only have the names been corrupted but in some instances it has been suggested that the order of the names has been inverted; and, unlike other parts of Europe, which were part of the Roman Empire, there is no corroborative evidence from other contemporary sources. Nevertheless some names are identifiable, for example *Iouernia* 'Ireland', *Bououinda* 'Boyne', *Auteinoi* 'Úaithni' (tribal area in North Co. Limerick). A striking fact, however, is that relatively few of the tribal names survived, even to the seventh or eighth centuries, when substantial records begin to appear. **Paul Russell**

Public Dance Halls Act (1935), enacted after a campaign against the 'evils of all-night dancing,' seeking to confine dances to halls licensed for the purpose. In 1935 and 1936 there was a spate of court cases arising from the act; in areas such as Co. Clare, where the practice of holding house dances was deeply rooted, the effect of the legislation was particularly noticeable in its destruction of long-established patterns of rural social life. **Helen Brennan**

public expenditure. Any overview of public expenditure in Ireland must take into account the pronounced swings of the last three decades of the twentieth century. A rapid fiscal expansion in the late 1970s culminated in a public expenditure share of GROSS DOMESTIC PRODUCT equal to 50 per cent in the mid-1980s and very large budget deficits; repeated attempts at correction in the 1980s finally bore fruit in the late 1980s and 90s. The effect has been to move the Republic's public expenditure share and composition from levels typical of the EUROPEAN UNION in the early 1980s to starkly lower levels early in the twenty-first century. Favourable demographic circumstances (a young POPULATION and increasing participation in the labour force) explain much of this, but as social structure and aspirations move closer to EU averages, some reversion can be expected.

In 2000, total public expenditure was approximately 33 per cent of Gross Domestic Product, of which 30 per cent was current expenditure and 3 per cent capital expenditure. All the principal components were significantly lower than previous levels and EU averages, and continued rapid growth in GDP has so far allowed cash expenditure to expand while shares declined.

Important outlays and shares include (1) the provision of goods and services by the Government (such as law, health, and education), at about 14 per cent of GDP, which includes wages of public employees (8 per cent of GDP); (2) social transfers (such as SOCIAL WELFARE payments and PENSIONS), at about 10 per cent of GDP in 2000, down from 12 per cent in 1995, which in turn was down sharply from levels seen in the 1980s and early 90s; (3) interest payments, at about 2 per cent of GDP, one of the sharpest swings over the last twenty years, as the vicious cycle of high interest rates and high debt was reversed; (4) subsidies, at about 1 per cent of GDP, a continuing decline, reflecting the rationalisation or sale of state-owned enterprises; and (5) capital expenditure, at 3 per cent of GDP, somewhat closer to average EU levels than the other components, severely curtailed in the 1980s but in 2000 reflecting attempts to correct severe INFRASTRUCTURE deficiencies.

A comparison with Northern Ireland is complicated by the different levels of government involved as well as the high level of expenditure on security in the North. The public sector accounts for about 18 per cent of EMPLOYMENT in the Republic but 28 per cent in Northern Ireland. Through the link with the British exchequer, Northern Ireland avoided the large swings experienced in the Republic; sources of compositional differences with the Republic include the higher level of UNEMPLOYMENT and the better public infrastructure. **Kevin Carey**

Northern Ireland. Public expenditure, and the public sector more widely, is central to the Northern Ireland economy and dominates its economic performance and prospects. Public expenditure stood at £6 billion in 2001; the annual subvention from the British treasury (the difference between the amount spent by government in Northern Ireland and the revenue raised through taxes etc.) accounts for between 25 and 30 per cent of Gross Domestic Product. In other words, the Northern Ireland economy is far from self-sustaining, its standard of living maintained by annual injections of public expenditure from Britain. This degree of dependence on public expenditure is extremely high by European standards. Much of it is the result of the continuing legacy of political and violent conflict over many decades, but, importantly, it also reflects the poor performance of the privately owned manufacturing and service sectors. Approximately 40 per cent of those employed work directly in the public sector, in health care, education, security, and other services. Moreover, many jobs in the private sector are dependent on the incomes of those employed in the public sector, while the lives of many more are sustained by a range of publicly financed social welfare benefits. **Douglas Hamilton**

public utility societies, a specialist form of combined limited dividend company and friendly society, first provided for under the Housing (Ireland) Act (1919), which empowered local authorities to promote and assist any public utility society that supplied houses for the working class. Similar societies had been operating in England from c. 1901. Rev. David Henry Hall was responsible for the registration of St Barnabas' Public Utility Society in January 1920, the first operational public utility society in Ireland. It built almost 200 houses in the 1920s, raising funds by issuing loan stock and shares. The residents bought their houses over a number of years through a tenant-purchase scheme.

Public utility societies were encouraged to undertake building operations to supplement the provision of houses by local authorities. Dublin City Corporation had a close relationship with many of the public utility societies; most of them built on land leased from the city, often on the fringes of the local authority estates, beginning with the leasing of land at Marino to the Dublin Commercial Public Utility Society from 1925. Societies were formed throughout the country to avail of special provisions under the Housing (Building Facilities) Act (1924) and the Housing Act (1925), while a further spate of registrations was associated with grants made available under the Housing (Financial and Miscellaneous Provisions) Act (1932). By the end of 1933 there were 125 registered public utility societies, making a significant contribution to Ireland's housing stock in both urban and rural areas. **Ruth McManus**

Public Dance Halls Act. *John Kavanagh and Brenda Fricker in a scene from* The Ballroom of Romance *(1982), based on a short story by William Trevor. As a consequence of the Public Dance Halls Act (1935), dance halls were built throughout the country to curb the public's enjoyment of all-night House Dances. [© K. G. Trodd/Irish Film Archive of the Film Institute of Ireland]*

publishing. Book publishing in its contemporary sense is, in Ireland, a relatively recent phenomenon: as late as the 1960s the functions of printer, publisher, and bookseller continued to be combined, reflecting the scale of such operations as influenced by a limited reading public. The first book printed or published in Ireland was the *Boke of Common Prayer* of the established church (Dublin, 1551), while the earliest Belfast publications date from 1697. From 1551 to 1680 the KING'S PRINTER held a virtual monopoly on publishing, and publications were almost exclusively made up of religious and classical texts or official edicts. A broadside religious poem in Irish was published in Dublin in 1571, while the first book of Catholic teaching in Irish, *An Teagasg Críosdaidhe* (Antwerp, 1611), was written by a member of the Irish Franciscan College at LOUVAIN. Together with Rome and other Continental centres, Louvain was a primary source of publishing in Irish during this period.

The growth of Dublin as a commercial centre in the early years of the eighteenth century with the onset of relative political and social stability led to a concomitant increase in printing and publishing, stimulated by the fact that the English Copyright Act (1709) was not extended to Ireland. Irish printers and publishers produced numerous editions of London titles, both authorised and pirated, many of which were sold well below the English price, as no royalties were paid. For this reason Irish authors sought to have their books published in London, establishing a practice that was to endure, if for different reasons, into the twenty-first century. There was strong reaction, however, from the British trade, and from 1739 attempts were made, only partially successful, to ban the sale of Irish editions in Britain, a development that JONATHAN SWIFT described as 'absolute oppression'. He expressed himself on these and other social issues in anonymous political pamphlets, a branch of the publishing industry that was to flourish, sustained by both political and religious polemic, well into the nineteenth century and particularly in Dublin and Belfast. The reprint trade reached its peak in the 1780s and 90s, with a substantial export trade to North America and elsewhere.

An important development in the eighteenth century was the establishment of DUBLIN UNIVERSITY PRESS in 1739, while Swift's publisher, GEORGE FAULKNER, was the outstanding figure in a prospering trade. Publishing also consolidated itself at this time in other cities and towns, particularly the import and export centres of Cork, Derry, Limerick, and Waterford. The economics of publishing to a limited literate audience, predominantly of the landed and professional classes, meant that many titles were published by subscription and in some instances through co-operation between several printers or publishers, printing not being undertaken until a viable subscribers' list had been generated. Print runs were short, typically between 500 and 1,000 copies. Until the end of the eighteenth century Catholic printers and publishers, among them the enterprising Patrick Wogan, laboured under the restrictions imposed by the PENAL LAWS, but increased in both numbers and influence as these were relaxed.

With the ACT OF UNION (1800) publishing and the allied trades went into a decline, and many tradesmen emigrated, particularly to Philadelphia, where they consolidated the foundations of the American book trade. The extension of the Copyright Act to Ireland killed the reprint business, and publishing was thereafter largely concentrated on cheap popular reprints and devotional tracts. With the growth of the nationalist movement, and particularly the influence of YOUNG IRELAND, the industry began to revive, with native printers and publishers such as JAMES DUFFY and M. H. GILL and Scottish immigrants such as James McGlashan and Alexander Thom active in Dublin. Publishing, however, continued to cater largely for an urban, English-speaking audience, with even religious titles directed towards the largely Irish-speaking rural population being produced in English; professional scribes jealously guarded their function of copying devotional texts originally published in Irish in the 1700s in such Continental centres as Louvain, Paris, and Rome. On the other hand, Protestant proselytising bodies were recognising the advantage of publishing in Irish, though adherents of such Bible Societies were locally stigmatised. Scholarly publishing in Irish received an early impetus from CHARLOTTE BROOKE's bilingual *Reliques of Irish Poetry* (1789) and came fully into its own with the appearance of JOHN O'DONOVAN's seven-volume edition of the Annals of the FOUR MASTERS (1848–51).

Improved communications, in particular the development of the RAILWAYS, posed an ever-increasing threat to the Irish industry from London publishing, with many Dublin booksellers and publishers finding it expedient to establish commercial links, while Irish authors benefited from possibilities of enhanced distribution. This factor was to militate against the development of native publishing until well into the twentieth century. The LITERARY REVIVAL in the latter part of the nineteenth century did, however, offer a renewed impetus to domestic publishing with the establishment of imprints such as MAUNSEL and CUALA INDUSTRIES (see p. 1157); though W. B. YEATS, the key figure, continued to publish in both Dublin and London.

The political events of the early twentieth century and the difficult birth of the new state had a severe impact on the publishing industry in the South, a situation exacerbated by the punitive Censorship of Publications Act (1929), which compounded the difficulties of an industry already operating in a depressed economic climate and, subsequently, in the shadow of world war. While firms such as Browne and Nolan, Gill and the TALBOT PRESS continued to publish, it was not until the 1950s that a revival began to make itself felt, when Liam Miller's DOLMEN PRESS grew from modest beginnings to serve as a standard-bearer for a number of new imprints (see p. 1032).

In 1970 seven publishers formed themselves into the trade association CLÉ, with new Belfast imprints, such as Appletree and Blackstaff, participating in the general Renaissance. New technology improved the economics of small operations and short print runs, while support by Government agencies and aggressive marketing enabled the industry to exploit the Irish DIASPORA as a vital extension of the limited domestic market. University presses in Belfast, Cork, and Dublin (with the notable exception of TRINITY COLLEGE) developed a serious publishing role, while publishing in Irish, concentrated at first in the Government agency of AN GÚM, also showed marked development, though most titles necessitated subsidy from Bord na Leabhar Gaeilge, while the ARTS COUNCIL similarly supported publications of artistic merit in English.

While the industry continued to expand (with 995 new titles published in 2000 and 8,352 titles in print), it had historically been male-dominated. In 2001 a report *Women in Publishing* concluded that there were few women in positions of ownership and that in general women were undervalued and underpaid, but this situation is steadily being rectified.

As in many other countries, the publishing of textbooks for schools and universities provided the principal commercial base of the publishing industry in Ireland. From its foundation the Dublin University Press printed and published a majority of the textbooks required for the college courses; but it was not until the eighteenth century that educational publishing, with the advance of the English language, became significant. Chapbooks and tracts were distributed throughout the country by itinerant chapmen, with series such as the sixpenny 'Burton Books', reprinted in Dublin, Limerick, and Cork.

The establishment of the Commissioners of National Education in Ireland in 1831 created a demand for elementary textbooks that publishers, including Alexander Thom, hastened to supply. His texts, such as *Books of Lessons for the Use of Schools* (1862), were also exported to Australia and elsewhere, as were the VERE FOSTER copybooks, which remained in use in Ireland until the 1920s. The Scottish firm of Blackie opened a Dublin branch in 1870, its premises being taken over in 1910 by the newly established Educational Company of Ireland, which, with other companies, such as Browne and Nolan, C. J. Fallon, and M. H. Gill and Son, set out to modernise the schoolbook trade and to replace British imports. These companies also established significant markets for educational books in Africa and the West Indies, where Irish missionaries were founding schools, and in Australasia. By the mid-1980s an independent report established that more than 90 per cent of books used in primary and secondary schools were published in Ireland. [see BIBLE IN IRISH; DUNLAP, JOHN; PRINTING IN IRISH.]
Bernard Share

Pugin, A. W. N. [Augustus Welby Northmore] (1812–1852), architect. Born in London; as a young man he developed an interest in medieval architecture from his father, an illustrator. After periods as a stage carpenter and furniture-maker he began architectural practice in 1835. A convert to Catholicism, he espoused the cause of authentic gothic revival architecture, both in his writings and in his (mostly ecclesiastical) designs. Most of his Irish work is in Co. Wexford: the chapel of St Peter's College (1838), Enniscorthy Cathedral (begun 1843), and churches at Gorey (1839), Barntown (1844), and Tagoat (1845). He also designed Killarney Cathedral (begun 1842), extensions to ST PATRICK'S COLLEGE, Maynooth (1845), convents in Waterford (1841) and Birr (1846) and, with Patrick Byrne, the chapel of Loreto Abbey, Rathfarnham, Co. Dublin (1839). **Frederick O'Dwyer**

Pugin and Ashlin, the architectural partnership of Edward Welby Pugin (1834–1875) and GEORGE COPPINGER ASHLIN (1837–1921). After A. W. N. PUGIN died, his practice was continued by his son Edward, who developed a penchant for French gothic. In 1860 Ashlin formed a partnership with Edward Pugin to run an Irish practice, with an office in Dublin. Their first projects were a church in the city, SS. Augustine and John, and another in Cork, SS. Peter and Paul, both polychromatic essays in Ruskinian gothic. Their work was predominantly ecclesiastical, with further churches in Dublin and Co. Dublin—Donnybrook (1863), Monkstown (1865), Glasthule (1866), and Harrington Street (1868)—as well as a number of smaller parish churches, mostly in Cos. Wexford and Cork. Their masterpiece is ST COLMAN'S CATHEDRAL, Cobh, awarded in 1867 but not completed until 1919. The architectural partnership broke up in 1868, Ashlin continuing to practise under his own name and later with Thomas A. Coleman as partner. **Frederick O'Dwyer**

Punch, John (1603–1672), Franciscan philosopher and theologian, leading 'non-orthodox' Scotist. Born in Cork; he studied philosophy at the University of Cologne and theology at the University of Louvain, where he joined the Franciscan order. He taught philosophy and theology at the Irish College of St Isidore, Rome. He was a contributor to the 1639 edition of *John Duns Scotus's Works*, co-ordinated by LUKE WADDING. In 1648 he left Rome for France, where he first taught in Lyon, later in Paris. His works, in particular his *Philosophy Courses* (1642), demonstrate a remarkable independence of thought in his interpretation of Duns Scotus. Involved in political controversies with Richard Bellings, he remained faithful to the nuncio GIANBATTISTA RINUCCINI. **Juan José Pérez-Camacho**

Purcell, Seán, Gaelic footballer. Born in Tuam, Co. Galway. Although remembered primarily as a forward of outstanding ability, he was equally comfortable at the centre of the defence or in midfield in a career in which he won six Connacht championships and was the prime mover behind Galway's all-Ireland success in 1956. He formed a legendary partnership with Frankie Stockwell, and they were affectionately named the 'Terrible Twins'. **Donal Keenan**

Purser, Sarah (1848–1943); painter in oils and pastels, designer, art activist, and patron. Born in Dún Laoghaire; educated at a Swiss finishing school and trained in Dublin and Paris (Académie Julian). She exhibited, 1872–1930, in Dublin, Belfast, Cork, London, Liverpool, Paris, Brussels, and Boston, showing genre, landscape, flowers, portraits, and STAINED GLASS. She was immediately successful with her brisk technique and Parisian mode, as in *Le Petit Déjeuner* and *Woman with a Child's Rattle*, and developed a lucrative portrait practice. She was elected a full member of the RHA in 1924. In 1899 she helped organise the first exhibition of foreign modern art in Ireland and reviewed it for the *Art Journal* (London). She published on art in Ireland, 1900–28; organised a NATHANIEL HONE and J. B. YEATS exhibition in 1901; founded AN TÚR GLOINE in 1903;

Purser. Woman with a Child's Rattle *(1885) by Sarah Purser. Inscribed 'à M. Julian Sturgis hommage respectueux!', it is a portrait of his wife Mary Maud. [National Gallery of Ireland]*

supported HUGH LANE's activities from 1908; was a governor of the NATIONAL GALLERY OF IRELAND from 1911; jointly founded the Friends of the National Collections of Ireland in 1924; and led moves to recover the Hugh Lane Bequest pictures. **John O'Grady**

Pursuit of Diarmaid and Gráinne: see TÓRUIGHEACHT DHIARMADA AGUS GHRÁINNE.

Pye, Patrick (1929–), artist. Born in Winchester, and has lived in Dublin since 1932. He began painting in 1943 under the direction of OISÍN KELLY at St Columba's College, Rathfarnham, Co. Dublin, then studied at the National College of Art and Design, Dublin, and the Jan van Eyck Academy, Maastricht. He works in various media, including tempera, etching, and stained glass; his work is represented in Glenstal Abbey, Co. Limerick, Loughrea Cathedral, Co. Galway, and the Church of the Resurrection, Killarney, Co. Kerry. He has also published *Apples and Angels* (1981) and *The Time Gatherer* (1991). Pye's work is primarily concerned with Christian iconography. He is a member the ROYAL HIBERNIAN ACADEMY and of AOSDÁNA. **Alison FitzGerald**

Pyle, Hilary (1936–), curator and critic. Born in Dublin; educated at TCD and the University of Cambridge. She was a lecturer in UCC before becoming curator (and creator) of the Yeats Museum at the NATIONAL GALLERY OF IRELAND, resulting from her pioneering work on the life and work of JACK YEATS (1971, 1992–4). She is also the biographer of JAMES STEPHENS (1965) and SUSAN MITCHELL (1998). **Richard Pine**

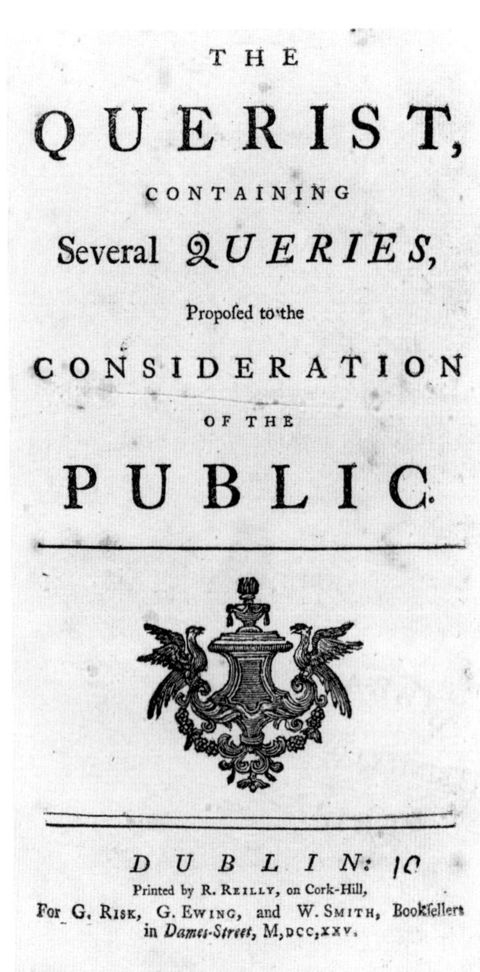
THE

QUERIST,

CONTAINING

Several *QUERIES*,

Propoſed to the

CONSIDERATION

OF THE

PUBLIC.

DUBLIN:

Printed by R. Reilly, on Cork-Hill,

For G. Risk, G. Ewing, and W. Smith, Bookſellers in *Dames-Street*, M,DCC,XXV.

Querist *(see page 908).* The Querist *(part 1, 1735) by George Berkeley, published in Dublin, 1735–52, a tract in which problems of economics, philosophy, and society are discussed as a series of 900 rhetorical, sometimes tongue-in-cheek questions. Question no. 100: 'Whether it would not be more reasonable to mend our state than to complain of it; and how far this may be in our own power?' [Board of Trinity College, Dublin]*

Quakers, popular name for members of the Religious Society of Friends, whose origins lie in the political and religious turmoil of seventeenth-century England. The message of the founder, George Fox, based on the teaching of Jesus, was that there is 'that of God' in every person. The emphasis is on a personal spiritual experience in a search for God, and not in the acceptance of statements of creed or corporate doctrine. From this follow the central attributes or 'testimonies' of Quakerism: civil and religious freedom and equality, regardless of race, sex or creed; pacifism and mediation; simplicity of life-style; truthfulness; and service to humanity. In Ireland the society, brought to the country by William Edmundson, spread among Cromwellian settlers, and the ideas and life-style quietly led to its acceptance by the community. Later this was strengthened by a neutral, pacifist stance in 1798 and the helping of famine victims in the 1840s.

Today the society is an autonomous body with 1,600 members throughout Ireland and twenty-five established Meetings (congregations), more representative now of Ireland's population than at any time in the past. Each Sunday, Friends worship silently in open meeting, waiting on the Holy Spirit to move those assembled to speak in its name. Many members express their faith in practical ways: in education, prison reform and conflict resolution, ECUMENISM, and social reform. The original beliefs are fundamental to the search for spiritual truth, though the interpretation in the meeting for worship is often firmly fixed in the twenty-first century. [see PENN, WILLIAM; RUTTY, JOHN; SHACKLETON, ABRAHAM.] **J. Glynn Douglas**

Quare Fellow, The (1956), a play by BRENDAN BEHAN. Drawing on his own experiences as a political offender and of prison in both Ireland and England, it deals with the period in Mountjoy Jail just before the hanging of the unseen 'quare fellow' for murder and the effect the tension has on both the inmates and the staff. First produced at the PIKE THEATRE, Dublin, it is Behan's most considerable dramatic work. **Peter Costello**

quark, a word adopted for an elementary particle by the physicist Murray Gell-Mann in 1964 (taken from a typically obscure passage, 'Three quarks for Muster Mark,' in JOYCE's *Finnegans Wake*). At the time of their conception, quarks were thought to be of three varieties. **Denis Weaire**

quarter days, the four principal FESTIVALS of the popular year: SAMHAIN (HALLOWE'EN), IMBOLC (ST BRIGID'S DAY), (1 February) (see p. 150), BEALTAINE (MAY DAY), and LÚNASA (1 August). These festivals come from an older Celtic division of the year into four quarters, in line with seasonal shifts, but still feature to a greater or lesser extent in the vernacular calendar. They mark the transition from one season to another and usually begin on the eve of the festival: in Irish *Oíche Nollag* ('Christmas Night') refers to the night before Christmas Day. There is a considerable amount of vernacular discourse surrounding each of these festivals. **Stiofán Ó Cadhla**

Québec, the Irish in. Though Irish people may have constituted as much as 5 per cent of the population of New France, large-scale Irish settlement in Lower Canada began only after 1815. Both Montréal and Québec were host to large Irish communities, especially following the GREAT FAMINE, while smaller rural communities were established before the Famine. In 1871 Irish people constituted more than 10 per cent of the total population of the province.

In early nineteenth-century Ireland the combination of rapid population growth and a lack of political and religious freedom, as well as a deteriorating economy, led to greater EMIGRATION. As British North America's leading port, Québec handled the majority of this stream. From 1816 to 1860 more than a million immigrants passed through Québec; these were almost all from either Ireland or Britain, with the Irish consistently averaging more than 60 per cent of the total. Up to the mid-1830s many of these were Ulster Protestants; thereafter, especially during the Great Famine, 80–90 per cent were Catholics from the south and west of Ireland. Several hundred orphans arrived with the immigrants at the GROSSE ÎLE quarantine station and were adopted by both Irish and French-Canadian families (see p. 153).

First settling in both urban and rural areas, Irish immigrants tended to concentrate in the cities of Montréal and Québec as the century progressed, constituting at least a quarter of each city's population by the middle of the century. While the province's Irish population was two-thirds Catholic in 1871, in the cities of Montréal and Québec the proportion exceeded 80 per cent. Several place-names in Québec bear witness to this settlement: Armagh, Coleraine, Kildare, Kilkenny, Shannon. According to the 1996 census, people of Irish origin (313,660) constitute 4.4 per cent of the population of the province of Québec (7,138,795); more than half of these are French-speakers.

The Irish in Québec were conspicuous for their impact on labour relations in the nineteenth century. There were disturbances between employers and Irish labourers on the Lachine and Beauharnois canals in the 1840s. Famine immigrants set up a powerful ship labourers' union at the port of Québec that endured well into the twentieth century. Wages earned during seasonal migrations to ports in the southern United States enabled many Irish families in Québec to survive the winter months.

The Irish were also significantly active on Québec's political scene and in the arts. The position of mayor was filled by Irishmen in both Montréal and Québec, and the province elected two Irish premiers, Edmund James Flynn (1847–1927) and Daniel Johnson (1915–1968). Montréal and Québec were also host to Canada's leading Fenian circles. THOMAS D'ARCY MCGEE was a leading architect of Confederation but was assassinated by Fenian agents in 1868. In the arts, Émile Nelligan is considered a major voice in French-Canadian literature. **Robert J. Grace**

Queen's Colleges Act (Colleges (Ireland) Act) (1845), the statute that established colleges at Belfast, Cork, and Galway, intended to satisfy Catholic requests for access to university education and

Quakers. *Limerick Meeting-House, the fourth established in Limerick since the end of the seventeenth century and the third built during the 1980s and 90s, furnished with benches from former meeting-houses. [Brian C. Grubb, M.R.I.A.I.]*

thereby undercut nationalist demands for repeal of the ACT OF UNION. To satisfy Protestants it placed restrictions on theological instruction, a feature that prompted opposition from the Catholic hierarchy. DANIEL O'CONNELL condemned the 'godless colleges', thereby widening the breach between him and the YOUNG IRELANDERS. **Gary Owens**

Queen's Royal Theatre, Dublin, built in 1844 on the site of the earlier Adelphi Theatre (1829–44) in Great Brunswick Street (Pearse Street). It was not successful until J. W. Whitbread became manager in 1884, transforming the Queen's into the 'Home of Irish Drama', presenting Irish MELODRAMAS, some of which he wrote himself. The auditorium was remodelled in 1909, and the theatre continued to present melodramas, notably those of P. J. Bourke, until the 1920s, when it became a variety theatre. When the ABBEY THEATRE burnt down in 1951 the Abbey company performed in the Queen's until 1966. The theatre was demolished in 1969. **Christopher Morash**

Querist, The (1735–52), an economic treatise by the philosopher GEORGE BERKELEY. Its title derives from the rhetorical style: an unbroken succession of 'leading' questions. *The Querist* attempts to unravel the various elements of Ireland's economic stagnation: the pauperisation of the native population, the anti-Irish protectionism prevalent in Britain, and the landlord system with its absentee landlords. The treatise is an early harbinger of Anglo-Irish 'PATRIOTISM' in demonstrating that, despite political divisions, Ireland forms a single economy and that the Anglo-Irish elite had more in common with the country's native population than it had with England (see p. 906). [see PATRIOTS.] **Joep Leerssen**

querns, stone hand-mills for grinding corn. Three main types have been identified. The earliest is the *saddle quern*, known since the NEOLITHIC PERIOD, which consists of a lower stone with a slightly concave section, the grinding being undertaken with a smaller rubbing-stone. The IRON AGE saw the introduction of the *beehive quern*, which was rotated by hand and consisted of two roughly circular stone discs, the upper one dome-shaped. These were followed in the Early Historic Period by flatter, thinner *rotary querns*; the upper stone had a central perforation, through which the corn was introduced, and a hole for the insertion of a turning-handle. **Michelle Comber**

Quin Friary, Co. Clare, a Franciscan friary founded c. 1433 by Mac Con MacNamara. The friary was constructed on the foundations of the great thirteenth-century castle built by THOMAS DE CLARE, the Anglo-Norman invader of Thomond; sections of the castle's curtain-wall are incorporated in the fabric of the church and claustral buildings, and three of the four original bastions are still visible. A good example of fifteenth-century Franciscan planning, Quin has a particularly well-preserved cloister arcade lying to the north of the church and some interesting medieval tombs, one of which, on the south wall of the chancel, incorporates an unusual stucco Crucifixion. [see ABBEYS.] **Rachel Moss**

Quinn, Aidan (1959–), Irish-American actor. Born in Chicago. He made his stage debut in Dublin but came to prominence in the American feature film *Desperately Seeking Susan* (1985), which was followed by appearances in *The Mission* (1986), *Stakeout*, (1987), and *The Lemon Sisters* (1989). Returning to Ireland frequently, he appeared in the adaptation of SHANE CONNAUGHTON's *The Playboys* (1992) and as Harry Boland in NEIL JORDAN's *Michael Collins* (1999). With his brothers, the cameraman Declan Quinn and director Paul Quinn, and his actor sister Kathleen Quinn, he played the lead in the emigrant story *This Is My Father* (1998). **Kevin Rockett**

Quinn, Bob (1939–), film director and writer. Born in Dublin. He worked in RTÉ before emerging as the most interesting independent film-maker of the 1970s with his first experimental fiction film, *Caoineadh Airt Uí Laoire* (1975), and the more conventional narrative *Poitín* (1978), featuring CYRIL CUSACK. His prescient silent feature *Budawanny* (1987), later developed in *The Bishop's Story* (1994), examines what happens when a priest and his housekeeper have a child. He is a member of AOSDÁNA. **Kevin Rockett**

Quinn, Edel (1907–1944), lay missionary. Born in Kanturk, Co. Cork. She joined the Legion of Mary in 1927 and had hoped to become a nun but developed TUBERCULOSIS and was unable to proceed. After a year and a half in a sanatorium she volunteered for Legion work in east Africa, where she established the organisation in Kenya, Uganda, Tanganyika, Nyasaland, and Mauritius. The tuberculosis recurred in 1941. Though much weakened, she resumed her work in 1943, but died at Nairobi the following year. **Fergal Tobin**

Romanesque
(see page 939). *The twelfth-century west doorway of Clonfert Cathedral, Co. Galway, showing Irish Romanesque at its most developed: a gabled hood with representations of human heads above an arcade surmounts the arched doorcase with six orders of complex decoration. [Bord Fáilte]*

R

racism can be seen as an ideology or as a set of practices. As an ideology it involves a set of beliefs or prejudices that legitimate discriminatory behaviour and stereotype and devalue others on the grounds of their (presumed) biological, racial, or cultural background. Racism in Ireland can be seen as reflecting a racially homogeneous construction of Irishness, combined with a lack of acceptance of 'otherness'. The main identifiable targets for racism are TRAVELLERS, black Irish people, and (in the 2000s) immigrants and asylum-seekers. Racist practices can occur at an individual or an institutional level; at an individual level they may take the form of verbal or physical abuse. The admission of only sixty Jewish refugees to Ireland between 1933 and 1946 can be seen as emanating from institutionalised racism. The present treatment by the state of asylum-seekers has been severely criticised by senior legal and humanitarian figures and can also arguably be seen as institutionalised racism. [see DISCRIMINATION.] **Pat O'Connor**

Rackard, Bobbie (1927–), hurler. Born in Killane, Co. Wexford, a member of a famous hurling family. He won two all-Ireland medals with the county alongside his brothers, Nicky and Billy. He was an emergency full-back in the 1954 final when Nick O'Donnell was injured. Although Wexford lost that final, the team returned with Bobbie at right-full-back to win the title in 1955, and retained the Liam McCarthy Cup the following year. **Donal Keenan**

Radcliffe, Thomas, third Earl of Sussex (1526–1583), Lord Deputy of Ireland. An ambitious and highly placed Tudor aristocrat, he was appointed Lord Deputy in 1556 and approached the government of Ireland with clear but narrow preconceptions. Ireland's chronic instability, he believed, was the result of the corrosive influence of the great rival factions that had divided the country and rendered it susceptible to foreign intervention. The Geraldines, followers of the Fitzgeralds of Kildare, were the most dangerous of such factions, and he set about destroying them through direct confrontation and the extension of favour to their enemies. But he both underestimated the influence of the Geraldines and oversimplified the causes of Ireland's instability. The Geraldines struck back by securing the support of another factional intriguer, the rising young Elizabethan favourite Lord Robert Dudley, while Sussex's increasingly costly military operations in the midlands and in Ulster alienated the loyal community of the English PALE, who were forced to bear the burden of his substantially increased garrison. His failure to suppress SHANE O'NEILL, whose claims to the earldom of Tyrone he had unreasonably opposed on the grounds of O'Neill's Geraldine connections, combined with an inquiry into serious allegations against the conduct of his army in the Pale, led to his physical collapse, his replacement by a caretaker government, and his eventual resignation in 1565, though thereafter he continued to intervene, not always objectively, on matters of Irish policy. **Ciaran Brady**

Radiators from Space, rock group. Ireland's first bona fide punk rock band, Radiators from Space were formed in 1977. Their debut album, *TV Tube Heart* (1977), was of its time: a collection of guitar-driven, high-energy attacks on various topics, notably the placebo effect of the media. In 1979, as the Radiators, they released their second and final album, *Ghostown*, a shamefully overlooked classic Irish rock record. **Tony Clayton-Lea**

radiocarbon dating, developed in the late 1940s by the American scientist Willard Frank Libby and first applied to archaeological problems in the early 1950s. It is popular because of its widespread application. Radiocarbon—the radioactive isotope ^{14}C of the element carbon—is constantly produced high in the atmosphere under the influence of cosmic radiation. The dating method is based on the fact that all living matter maintains an equilibrium in ^{14}C by exchange with the atmosphere during its lifetime; after death this exchange ceases and the radiocarbon decays at a constant rate (the *half-life*, conventionally 5,568 years, after which half the original radiocarbon has disappeared). When the amount of radiocarbon in a sample is measured, its radiocarbon age can be established. *Conventional radiocarbon dating* estimates the amount of ^{14}C by measuring the radioactive decay over twenty-four or forty-eight hours; *accelerator mass spectrometry (AMS) dating* measures the amount of ^{14}C directly.

Radiocarbon dates are quoted in radiocarbon years BP ('before the present', by convention 1950), with a standard deviation, for example '1500 $\pm$40 BP.' The real radiocarbon age of the sample lies with 68.3 per cent certainty within the range of the measured radiocarbon age plus or minus one standard deviation, that is, between 1540 and 1460 BP, with 95.4 per cent certainty within the range 1580–1420 BP, and with 99.7 per cent certainty within the range 1620–1380 BP.

Because of fluctuations in the production rate of ^{14}C in the atmosphere, and because the conventional half-life is incorrect (in fact 5,730 years), radiocarbon ages cannot be directly compared with calendar dates. Calibration curves based on the high-precision dating of single tree-rings of known age are used to convert radiocarbon ages to calendar dates. Because of the statistical nature of the radiocarbon result, the calibrated date is expressed as a range of calendar dates and is conventionally designated 'cal. BC' or 'cal. AD' to distinguish it from a historical date or absolute date based on DENDROCHRONOLOGY.

Libby processed the first Irish samples c. 1951; an influential series of dates was produced in TRINITY COLLEGE, Dublin, 1958–60. The growth in the use of radiocarbon dating during the 1960s and 70s had a revolutionary impact on interpretations of past time-scales and processes. It has largely replaced cross-referencing to Mediterranean chronologies, which had dominated archaeological interpretation. The widespread occurrence of bone and charcoal in archaeological sites provides the main source of absolute dates in archaeology today. [see POLLEN ANALYSIS.] **A. L. Brindley**

Radio Telefís Éireann (RTÉ), the public-service broadcaster. Public-service BROADCASTING is regulated by the Broadcasting Authority Act (1960), as amended in 1976, 1993, and 2001. The acts endow the RTÉ Authority with the responsibility for establishing and maintaining public broadcasting services. The 1976 act specifies that RTÉ's programming policy must be responsive to the interests and culture of the whole community and must have particular concern for the IRISH LANGUAGE; it must uphold democratic values and be fair and impartial in its programmes; and it must have regard to the desirability of promoting understanding of other countries. The 1993 act requires RTÉ to spend some of its programming budget on productions made by independent production companies.

The RTÉ Authority is appointed by the Government for a five-year term. The relevant minister also has important powers with regard to financing, including deciding on the level of the licence fee and the amount of advertising time allowed. Advertising and other commercial income, at 67 per cent, contributes more to RTÉ's finances than the licence fee. The minister also had the power under the act, until 1994, to act as censor.

The passing of the Broadcasting Authority Act in 1960 and the establishment of the RTÉ Authority as a public-service broadcaster brought new life into broadcasting in the Republic, which had been limited to one radio station broadcasting for a limited number of hours each day. In 1961 RTÉ began transmitting television programmes; in 1978 a second television channel (now Network 2) was introduced; while in 1996 an Irish-language channel (now TG4) began broadcasting. Programming policy has been characterised by a strong sense of public service, reflected in news and current affairs programmes. It has also been characterised by a recognition of the need to compete for audiences with richer British stations and, since 1998, with commercial television (TV3). The need for success in this competition is reinforced by RTÉ's dependence on advertising for over half of its revenue. The consequences of this competitive situation include a recognition, firstly, that in order to compete successfully, programmes have to be as good in quality as British programmes; and, secondly, since it is impossible, given resources, to fill the schedules with such programmes, that importing programmes is a necessity; indeed, imported programmes have tended to fill half of the schedule. However, home-produced programmes have consistently been among the most popular of all programmes transmitted. These include talk shows, home-produced serials, current affairs, and the main evening news.

With the establishment of the RTÉ Authority, radio services also expanded. In 1968, day-long radio transmission began on Radio 1, which now offers a twenty-four-hour traditional public-service programming mix. In 1972 the Irish-language station Raidió na Gaeltachta was established. Recognising the preferences of younger audiences for a mainly music channel and the extent to which they listened to pirate radio, 2FM began transmission in 1979, which contributed to the significant 'repatriation' of Irish audiences from foreign—mainly British—to Irish stations. Listeners to classical music began to be catered for in the mid-1980s with a limited service, which expanded in 1999 to a classical music and arts channel, Lyric FM.

With the licensing of private commercial broadcasting services in the 1988 Act, RTÉ radio stations have had to compete with one national commercial radio station (Today FM) as well as with local and community radio. In 2000 RTÉ had a 49 per cent share of the national radio daytime listening audience, with commercial broadcasting, especially local radio, attracting the remainder.

The state continues to support the concept of public-service television. In general, it recognises the need to support programming through the licence fee in the face of commercial broadcasting from both within and outside the state. In the television market, audiences are fragmenting as ever more channels become available. RTÉ television holds over half the prime-time audience share nationally. Further fragmentation may be expected with the introduction of 200 digital channels. [see ANGELUS; CENSORSHIP.] **Mary Kelly**

Radio Telefís Éireann and music. Listeners have been served by RTÉ, the national BROADCASTING station, since the radio station (originally named 2RN) was established in 1926, followed by television in 1961. Popular and folk music is broadcast by Radio 1, 2FM, and Raidió na Gaeltachta. In 1999 the first twenty-four-hour classical music radio station, LYRIC FM, was launched. RTÉ television (incorporating RTÉ1, Network 2, and TG4) has some weekly programmes dedicated to popular and folk music, such as 'Sult', 'No Disco', and '2TV', and frequently presents operas, ballets, and classical music competitions, such as the RTÉ MUSICIAN OF THE FUTURE. RTÉ also supports a number of performing groups, including the NATIONAL SYMPHONY ORCHESTRA, RTÉ CONCERT ORCHESTRA, RTÉ Philharmonic Choir, Cór na nÓg, and VANBRUGH STRING QUARTET. These groups broadcast for the station and also undertake concerts in Ireland and abroad. [see RTÉ MUSICIAN OF THE FUTURE.] **Deborah Kelleher**

Rahan, Co. Offaly, an early monastic site traditionally associated with Bishop Camelacus, author of a Latin hymn in praise of St PATRICK. The remains include earthworks and three stone churches. The largest church dates mainly from the eighth century but incorporates a twelfth-century chancel. The chancel was flanked by two small chambers of uncertain function and has a sculpted chancel arch and decorated circular window, reset in the east gable. To the north-east is a single-cell church, rebuilt in the fifteenth century, which incorporates a late ROMANESQUE door and large, well-cut blocks from an earlier structure. **Rachel Moss**

Raiftearaí, popular name of Antaine Ó Reachtaire (1779–1835), poet. Born in Killedan, near Kiltimagh, Co. Mayo. Blinded by smallpox in childhood, and illiterate, he became a wandering minstrel, spending most of his time in south Co. Galway. His poems and song deal with contemporary events, such as the agrarian unrest associated with the WHITEBOYS and RIBBONMEN, and the campaigns of O'CONNELL. 'An Cíos Caitliceach' refers to the 'CATHOLIC RENT', the subscription of a penny a month paid to the CATHOLIC ASSOCIATION, and invokes the prophecies of PASTORINI as the authority for its central message of Catholic empowerment, while 'Bua Uí Chonaill' celebrates O'Connell's victory in the Clare election of 1828. Songs in praise of women, such as the popular 'Máire Ní Eidhin' or 'An Pabhsae Gléigeal', are extensions of the love-song. One of his most memorable songs is 'EANACH DHÚIN', a powerful lament for those drowned in a boating accident at Annaghdown on LOUGH CORRIB in 1828. He also wrote humorous verse and poems on historical themes and engaged in a vicious contention with two other poets, the brothers Marcas and Peatsaí Ó Callanáin, from Craughwell, Co. Galway. Raiftearaí's songs and poems were collected and published by DOUGLAS HYDE in 1903 and have recently been re-edited by Ciarán Ó Coigligh in *Raiftearaí: Amhráin agus Dánta* (1987). **Ciarán Ó Coigligh**

railway engineering. The first RAILWAY system in Ireland was the DUBLIN AND KINGSTOWN RAILWAY, opened in 1834 and linking Dublin with Kingstown (Dún Laoghaire), a distance of 10 km (6 miles). All main-line railways now use a gauge of 5 ft 3 in. (1.6 m), which was first used on the Dublin–Belfast line and was a compromise between the British gauge of 1.435 m (4 ft $8\frac{1}{2}$ in.), which had been used on the Dublin and Kingstown Railway, and 1.88 m (6 ft 2 in.), which had been used by the ULSTER RAILWAY.

Irish railways benefited from the contribution of many of the great railway pioneers, including CHARLES VIGNOLES, WILLIAM DARGAN, JOHN MACNEILL, and Isambard Kingdom Brunel, who was associated with the tunnelling and viaduct work at Bray Head, Co. Wicklow. Three Irish developments of particular engineering significance were the ATMOSPHERIC RAILWAY that ran from Kingstown (Dún Laoghaire) to Dalkey, 1844–54, the Listowel and Ballybunion Lartigue monorail, 1888–1924, and the DRUMM BATTERY TRAINS, 1932–49. **Dermot W. O'Dwyer**

Radio Telefís Éireann. *The National Symphony Orchestra on stage at the National Concert Hall, Dublin, which has been the orchestra's home since its opening in 1981. In addition to its subscription series, the orchestra's schedule features its Horizon contemporary music season, summer season, and national tours. [RTÉ Music]*

railway gauges. Early railway development saw the use of a variety of gauges, from the 1.435 m (4 ft $8\frac{1}{2}$ in.) of the DUBLIN AND KINGSTOWN RAILWAY (which was to become the British, Continental European and North American standard) to the 1.88 m (6 ft 2 in.) of the ULSTER RAILWAY.

JOHN MACNEILL, engineer of the Dublin and Drogheda Railway, advocated a gauge of 1.57 m (5 ft 2 in.) for the proposed through line between Dublin and Belfast. When the Ulster Railway protested to the Board of Trade in London, a major-general was despatched to adjudicate on the issue. His method was to average the narrowest gauge then in popular favour, 1.52 m (5 ft), and the widest, 1.68 m (5 ft 6 in.). As a result, under an act of 1846, 1.6 m (5 ft 3 in.) became the compulsory Irish standard gauge, to be replicated in three Australian states under the influence of an Irish engineer, Wentworth Shields. Some NARROW-GAUGE RAILWAY lines, generally with a gauge of 0.91 m (3 ft), were subsequently constructed as an economy measure in rural areas. **Bernard Share**

railways. As early as 1826 authorisation had been sought for a railway between Limerick and Waterford; but this scheme was too ambitious for the time, and it was not built for another twenty years. There were more immediate prospects of success in the Dublin area, and the DUBLIN AND KINGSTOWN RAILWAY opened in 1834. On 19 May 1836 an act of Parliament established the Ulster Railway Company, with powers to build a 58 km (36-mile) line from Belfast to Armagh. In that year the British government set up the Drummond Commission to inquire into railway development in Ireland in the light of economic and military considerations, and several projects were put on hold for two years pending its report. This concluded that the sparse and scattered population, allied to lack of INDUSTRIAL DEVELOPMENT, would justify no more than two trunk routes, Dublin–Belfast and Dublin–Cork, with branches to Limerick and Galway. Popular opinion, or 'railway mania', dictated otherwise, and soon every town of any size was demanding a rail connection. The commission had also recommended government investment in rail development, but this was not to come to pass until 1945, by which time more than 150 private undertakings, many enjoying no more than a fugitive existence, had been formed.

In 1840 DANIEL O'CONNELL was successful in piloting through the British Parliament a bill to authorise the Dublin and Drogheda Railway, which opened in 1844. The Dublin and Belfast Junction Railway was authorised in 1845, and though it never reached either city it provided a connection at Drogheda between the Dublin and Drogheda Railway and the ULSTER RAILWAY at Portadown, the barrier of the River BOYNE having been bridged in 1853, and through services to Belfast beginning in 1855. In 1876 the three companies, together with the Irish North-Western Railway, were amalgamated to form the Great Northern Railway (Ireland) or GNR.

While the route north had encountered little local opposition, that proposed to the south and west was seen as trespassing on the territory of the Grand Canal Company. There were powerful British interests backing this scheme, however, with Robert Peel (Chief Secretary for Ireland, 1812–18, and subsequently Prime Minister) seeing it as a means of both relieving unemployment and reducing the growing agrarian agitation, particularly acute in Co. Tipperary. The involvement of the successful London and Birmingham Railway established a precedent for a link between the railway interests of the two countries, which remained until independence and beyond.

The first sod of the Dublin and Cashel Railway, as it was originally called, was turned in December 1845; by 3 July 1848 the line had reached Limerick Junction and a connection with the Waterford and Limerick Railway. On 18 October 1849 a train from the Dublin terminal of Kingsbridge (now Heuston Station) arrived at a temporary platform at Blackpool on the outskirts of Cork, having covered the 264 km (164 miles) of what was by then known as the Great Southern and Western Railway (GSWR) in $5\frac{1}{2}$ hours.

Work on the expanding railway network continued against the grim background of the GREAT FAMINE; despite this, and inter-company rivalries and land acquisition disputes, track length increased from 105 km (65 miles) in 1844 to more than 580 km (360 miles) four years later. As a nationwide system took shape, its demographic and economic consequences became apparent: in the aftermath of the Famine a first trip on a train was for many their last in Ireland, as the railways carried thousands of emigrants to the transatlantic ports of Queenstown (Cobh), Galway, Derry (for Moville), and others. Those who remained saw local industries put out of business by competing goods, largely imports from Britain, transported cheaply by rail. The traffic, however, was not all one way. The third major system after the GSWR and GNR, the Midland Great Western Railway (MGWR), served the prosperous midland cattle country, and this export traffic remained a staple of the line until it was superseded by road transport in the 1950s.

By 1860 most of the network was in place, though over the following sixty years it was to add a further 3,200 km (2,000 miles), reaching its maximum of some 6,000 km (3,750 miles) by 1920. By 1891 the five Dublin terminals had been linked by rail, making possible the through carriage of mails landed at Dún Laoghaire to all parts of the country. (Belfast terminals were not to be similarly linked until 1994, with the opening of the William Dargan Bridge across the River Lagan.) This progress was achieved against the background of increasing social and political unrest. With private investors, the majority of them British, reluctant to support Irish projects, the British government was obliged to offer grants and guarantees for new lines, many of which were built as light, narrow-gauge railways with the intention of reducing costs.

The railways had from the outset been constrained by low population density and limited freight potential and competed keenly for business, not only among themselves but with the canal interests. The Railway and Canal Traffic Act (1854) sought to control restrictive practices, followed by similar legislation in 1873 and 1894. In 1906 a commission was appointed to report on the under-utilisation of the railway system as a whole, but its leisurely deliberations were overtaken by the outbreak of the FIRST WORLD WAR and a consequent, if temporary, increase in traffic.

Irish railways, unlike those of Britain, did not come under government control until after the 1916 RISING, when an Irish Railway Executive was established to manage all the railway companies, a measure that remained operative until 1921. Easter Week, during which no trains operated in or out of Dublin, marked the onset of the years of political unrest, culminating in the CIVIL WAR, which were to severely affect railway fortunes. Not only did they suffer structural damage but, with wages and costs having risen substantially as a result of wartime conditions—the former by 300 per cent—their economic future appeared anything but promising. With the signing of the Treaty in 1921 and the subsequent PARTITION of the country, these difficulties were compounded by the effects of the new border, Belfast and Derry in particular being deprived of much of their former economic hinterland, while the GNR became subject to the attentions of the Customs and Excise Service in both jurisdictions, as several of its routes criss-crossed the new frontier.

railways. *A late nineteenth-century photograph of the twelve-arch viaduct dominating the estuary of Ballydehob, Co. Cork, the major engineering achievement of the Skibbereen and Schull Light Tramway, a rail service which opened in 1886 and closed in January 1947. [Council of Trustees of the National Library of Ireland; LROY 10264]*

The Railways Act (1924) brought about the amalgamation of those companies operating exclusively within the Irish Free State. So serious were the economic prospects that the largest company, the GSWR, had given notice of its intention to close down, but it now became the major partner in the new Great Southern Railway (GSR). Cutbacks and rationalisation of the system followed, accelerated by the depression of the 1930s and the ECONOMIC WAR with Britain. The GSR nevertheless undertook an ambitious programme of equipment renewal, culminating in 1939 in the construction at its Inchicore Works, Dublin, of three Queen class 4-6-0 express steam locomotives, the largest and most powerful ever to run in Ireland. They had little opportunity to show their paces, however, before the war years of 1939–45 almost brought the railway system to a standstill because of a lack of coal supplies. What trains did run were packed; and since no petrol was available for private motoring, the railways experienced a brief renaissance, regaining traffic lost to road transport in the 1930s.

North of the new border the railways had similarly suffered from competition with roads; by 1933, the year of a major strike that hastened their decline, there were some seven hundred buses on the roads, owned by fifty small operators. The Second World War, in which Northern Ireland was fully involved, saw the system stretched to the limit of its capabilities, but this increased activity served only to mask a serious situation that, with the ending of hostilities, governments north and south found themselves forced to address.

Under the Transport Act (1944) the GSR and the Dublin United Transport (formerly Tramways) Company merged to form CÓRAS IOMPAIR ÉIREANN (CIÉ). In 1949 the Milne Report recognised that, for the size of the population, the country was over-endowed with a road and rail network, with travel per head of population the lowest in Europe. The Transport Act (1950), arising from this report, brought CIÉ into the state sector. In the North, a White Paper of 1946 recommended the merger of the railway system with the Northern Ireland Road Transport Board, a proposal given effect by the Transport Act (1948), which established the Ulster Transport Authority (UTA). **Bernard Share**

railways, industrial. Limited mineral resources and the small scale of heavy industry meant that industrial railways in Ireland have been few in number, though large ports, such as Belfast and Derry, operated their own systems. In 1872 Samuel Geoghegan, chief engineer of the GUINNESS BREWERY, Dublin, designed an internal NARROW-GAUGE RAILWAY system connecting the two working levels, 8 m (26 ft) apart, with a spiral tunnel. The brewery was also connected to Kingsbridge (Heuston) Station by a standard-gauge tramway; this closed in 1965, and the narrow-gauge system ten years later. When the Ardnacrusha hydro-electric SHANNON SCHEME was being constructed in 1925 the German contractors installed a large railway system with 110 locomotives and 3,000 wagons operating on 0.6 m (2-ft) and 0.9 m (3-ft) gauges. On the completion of the undertaking the system was dismantled and shipped back to Germany.

Minor industrial lines have from time to time served quarries. In 1906–7 a line was built across bogland near Clifden, Co. Galway, to the MARCONI wireless telegraph station, subsequently destroyed in the CIVIL WAR. In 1786–7 RICHARD LOVELL EDGEWORTH reclaimed large tracts of bogland on his estate in Co. Longford, making use of portable wooden railways. Today by far the most extensive industrial lines are those of BORD NA MÓNA, which has laid more than 960 km (600 miles) of permanent lines and more than 300 km (180 miles) of temporary track to carry turf to midland power stations. A section of this system in Co. Offaly has been developed as a tourist railway. **Bernard Share**

railways, narrow-gauge. To extend the railway system to sparsely populated areas where the expense of standard-gauge lines could not be justified, the Tramways (Ireland) Act (1883) and its successors facilitated the construction of railways with a gauge of 0.91 m (3 ft), of which some 1,000 km (600 miles) were constructed, largely in Cos. Donegal, Kerry and Mayo but also in Cos. Antrim and Clare. Most, including some standard-gauge lines in remote areas, were built under the 'BALFOUR Act' of 1889, and some—notably the Londonderry and Lough Swilly Railway and the County Donegal Railway—were quite extensive. In the face of competition from roads, however, most did not survive until the Second World War, when the few remaining enjoyed a brief renaissance. In post-war struggles for survival the Londonderry and Lough Swilly converted entirely to bus transport, while the West Clare converted to diesel engines in its latter years in an unsuccessful attempt to stave off closure. **Bernard Share**

Ralahine Agricultural and Manufacturing Co-operative Association, an early CO-OPERATIVE association, founded in 1831 on the estate of John Scott Vandeleur at Ralahine, near Bunratty, Co. Clare. The association was organised by an Englishman, Thomas Craig. Vandeleur hoped that his novel scheme would discourage his tenants from joining agrarian secret societies. A commune of fifty-two tenants was established. Its purpose was to acquire common capital and provide mutual assistance; it was governed by a committee of nine, elected twice yearly. By agreement, the estate and the property were to remain Vandeleur's at a rent of £700 per year until the commune could afford to buy it. The scheme received international attention but collapsed two years later when Vandeleur's gambling debts forced him to flee the country. His creditors seized the estate. Thomas Craig's *History of Ralahine* was translated into several European languages. **Ciarán Deane**

Raleigh, Sir Walter (c. 1552–1618), planter. A poor country gentleman from Devon, he pursued a military career, seeing service in the DESMOND REBELLION (1579–83), most infamously in the massacre of hundreds of Spanish and Italian prisoners at SMERWICK, Co. Kerry. From 1581 he was the favourite of ELIZABETH I, who lavished offices and lands on him; she granted him 17,000 ha (42,000 acres) in the PLANTATION OF MUNSTER in 1586, and he invested heavily in his plantation seigniories. He is reputed by tradition to have planted the first POTATO in Ireland, in the garden of his house at Youghal, Co. Cork. By contrast, his colonial ventures in Virginia and Guiana (modern Venezuela) were expensive failures. He was imprisoned for a while by Elizabeth in 1592 for courting one of her maids of honour; he never regained her favour. He played a distinguished part in the raid by the second Earl of Essex on Cádiz (1596), but it brought him no financial advantage. His estates in Munster were devastated in the NINE YEARS' WAR, and in 1602 he sold them to RICHARD BOYLE, clerk of the Munster Council, for £1,500—a small fraction of their value. In November 1603 Raleigh was convicted of plotting against JAMES I and was condemned to death, but the sentence was commuted to life imprisonment. However, in October 1618 the death sentence was carried out after he was judged to have abused his early release by engaging in piracy against Spain in the Americas. **Henry A. Jefferies**

Ramage, Hugh (1875–1938), chemist. Born in Buckinghamshire; studied at the ROYAL COLLEGE OF SCIENCE OF IRELAND under WALTER HARTLEY. During the eight years in which they worked co-operatively in Dublin, Ramage and Hartley jointly published fourteen papers on the spectrographic analysis of minerals. In parallel, Ramage was the sole author of several papers concerning the spectra of rare elements and on the electric spark. In 1899 he left Ireland for Cambridge, where he studied the distribution of metallic elements in animal and vegetable tissues. He became principal of the Norwich Technical Institute in 1902 and held that position until his retirement in 1930. **Susan McKenna-Lawlor**

Rambaut, Arthur Alcock (1859–1923), astronomer. Born in Waterford, a nephew of W. H. Rambaut (1822–1893), astronomer at Birr and Armagh; educated at the Royal School, Armagh, and TCD, where he excelled in mathematics and physics. In 1882 he was appointed assistant to ROBERT S. BALL at DUNSINK OBSERVATORY; his transit circle observations were published in three catalogues. With the gift of a 15-in. reflector from Isaac Roberts of Crowborough, Sussex, research at Dunsink was switched to stellar photography. In 1892 Rambaut was appointed Andrews professor of astronomy; in 1897 he moved to the Radcliffe Observatory, Oxford, where he erected and used a twin telescope made by HOWARD GRUBB consisting of a 24-in. photographic reflector and an 18-in. visual refractor. He took part in two solar eclipse expeditions, to Vadsø (Norway) in 1896 and Plasencia (Spain) in 1900. He was elected a fellow of the Royal Society in 1900. **Ian Elliott**

Ranch War (1906–10), a name given to a campaign among the landless poor, principally in the midlands and west, for the redistribution of grazing land to relieve population congestion. A residue of the main land issue resolved in 1903, its objective was unachievable. There was no consensus about the potential recipients of redistributed land. Grazing was one of the most profitable areas of AGRICULTURE, and the issue was deeply divisive within nationalism, many graziers being leading supporters of the IRISH PARTY. Its method, cattle-driving, involved cruelty and viciousness. The only positive achievement was a Royal Commission on Congestion, designed rather to buy time for a Liberal government hoping to placate Irish allies and a nationalist leadership needing to show action on what was an unresolvable issue. **Philip J. Bull**

rape crisis centres, first established in the 1970s as women-centred, community-based organisations to meet the needs of survivors of sexual violence. There are now eighteen rape crisis centres in the Republic, which vary in size, in the level of statutory support received, and in the range of services offered (such as individual counselling for women and men, crisis lines, outreach services in sexual assault units, and the provision of education and training, both at home and overseas). Typically their objectives are to provide support and counselling for those who have experienced rape, sexual abuse, or other forms of sexual violence, to undertake research and raise public awareness, and to campaign for specialised services and for legislative changes (such as separate legal representation for victims in all circumstances). A network of rape crisis centres exists, providing support, information, and training for its members and representing survivors' interests at regional and national level. Most of those contacting rape crisis centres are women, though the proportion of male calls to the Dublin Rape Crisis Centre has doubled in the past ten years. Child sexual abuse, rape, and adult sexual abuse were the most common reasons for contacting this centre, the great majority of these crimes being committed by people known to the victim but with convictions occurring in only a small minority of instances. **Pat O'Connor**

Ratass, Co. Kerry, the monastery selected as the episcopal see of Kerry at the SYNOD OF RÁTH BHREASAIL (1111), though by 1117 this privilege had passed to ARDFERT. One church survives at the

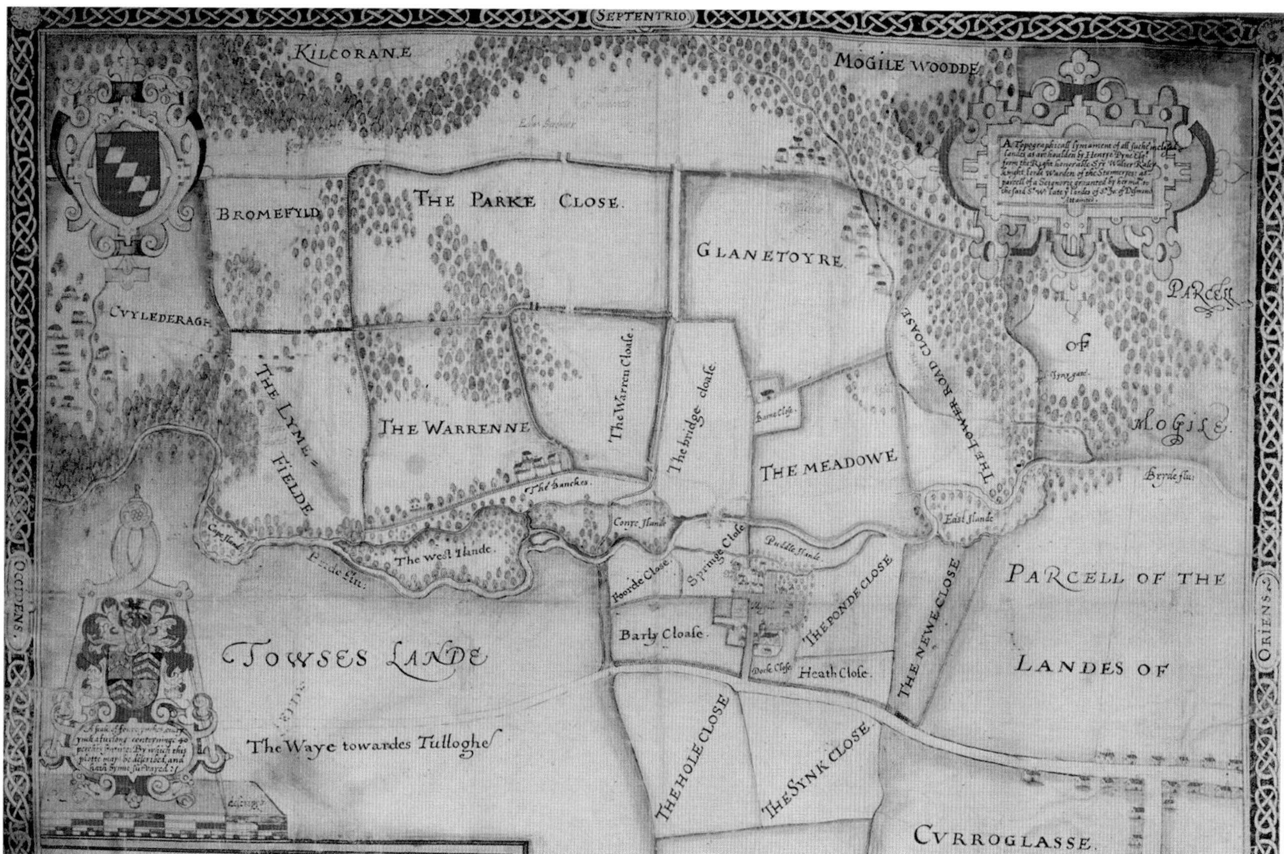

Raleigh. *Mogeely, Co. Cork (1598), the earliest known Irish estate map, watercolour on vellum, possibly drawn by John White of Virginia, an associate of Walter Raleigh, depicting part of the lands forfeited by the Earls of Desmond during the Plantation of Munster. [Council of Trustees of the National Library of Ireland; Ms. 22,028]*

site. The nave, which dates from the tenth or eleventh century, is constructed from large, well-cut blocks and has *antae* projecting from the western face. The west door has inclined jambs and a large lintel and is framed by a raised architrave. The chancel is a twelfth-century addition. Extensive repairs were carried out on the building in the seventeenth century. **Rachel Moss**

rates, property taxes, customarily applied to both private houses and non-domestic or business property. Taxes based on domestic property have been hugely controversial. In the Republic they were abolished, to popular acclaim, in 1978; several attempts to reintroduce taxes on domestic property have foundered on political grounds, despite the almost universal support of economists and research groups for such taxes.

Rates on domestic property still apply in Northern Ireland. There the rating system consists of two elements: a district rate fixed by each district council to meet the cost of the services it provides, such as street cleaning and leisure facilities, and a regional rate struck by the Department of Finance and Personnel to help pay for services such as education, roads, and water. In the fixing of the regional rate a distinction is made between domestic and non-domestic ratepayers, the former being given a reduction in the rate poundage, known as the domestic rate aid-grant. There is also a housing benefit scheme, which enables domestic ratepayers on low incomes or on income support to apply for assistance towards payment of their rates. **John W. O'Hagan**

Ráth Bhreasail, Synod of (1111), one of the reforming synods of the Irish church in the twelfth century, presided over by MUIRCHEARTACH UA BRIAIN, King of Munster and HIGH KING. It established a national diocesan structure governed by bishops and defined the boundaries of twenty-six territorial dioceses, divided into two provinces (Armagh and Cashel), with Armagh the primatial church. A number of other decrees are mentioned but not recorded. The site of Ráth Bhreasail is not certain: possibly in Co. Tipperary but more likely near Banteer, Co. Cork. **Anthony Candon**

Rathcroghan, a complex of more than fifty archaeological monuments on elevated ground north-west of Tulsk, Co. Roscommon. Its focus is Rathcroghan Mound, a broad, flat-topped circular mound; geophysical survey has shown that it is a human-made monument with a complex history, with several prehistoric enclosures entombed within it. Dáithí's Mound, to the south, is a burial mound with enclosing bank and internal ditch and a tall pillar-stone at its centre. The site called Relignaree (*Reilig na Rí*, 'cemetery of the kings'), once believed to be a burial ground, is one of a series of early historic or medieval RING-FORTS; it contains a SOUTERRAIN and several house sites. On sloping ground to the south-west are the intriguing embankments called the Mucklaghs, two LINEAR EARTHWORKS that had some ritual purpose. Rathnadarve (*Ráth na dTarbh*, 'fort of the bulls') is a large example of a ring-fort. Nearby Rathbeg is a ring barrow with two encircling banks, each with an internal ditch. Rathmore, north-west of Rathcroghan cross-roads, is an example of a ringwork, a high-status settlement of the Middle Ages.

Rathcroghan is the Cruachain of old, one of several important ROYAL SITES. In early literature it features as a royal settlement and the place where the epic TÁIN BÓ CUAILNGE began; it was also a place of assembly. Its magico-religious importance is attested by its association with MÉABH, goddess of sovereignty, and the existence there of an entrance to the OTHERWORLD, Oweynagat (*Uaimh na gCat*, 'cave of the cats'), once a centre of considerable mythological activity and whose inhabitants included the Morrígan, an ancient goddess of BATTLE. **Conor Newman**

Rathgall, Co. Wicklow, site of four roughly concentric stone enclosures, the innermost likely to be medieval or later in date. Excavation yielded evidence of intensive use in the Late BRONZE AGE (c. 1000–500 BC). Within a circular ditched enclosure with an external bank, the foundation of a circular structure 15 m (50 ft) in diameter was found. Inside this was an oval pit that contained the burnt bones of an infant, accompanied by a small penannular gold ring. A series of large open-air hearths and a deep funnel-shaped storage pit were also found, as well as a large scatter of pottery fragments and other items. An area of intense high-status occupation was discovered nearby; a large number of clay mould fragments, together with two clay crucibles, showed that bronzeworking had been practised. Mixed with the occupation material were animal bones, QUERN stones, and numerous pottery fragments, as well as artefacts of bronze and gold and a large quantity of glass beads, several amber beads, and bracelet fragments of lignite or jet. An object of great potential importance is a circular bronze mount with traces of mercury gilding on one surface.

Close by was a circular ditch, 16 m (52 ft) in diameter, which enclosed a central cremation deposit in a stone-lined pit dug into an area of intense burning; this was in turn enclosed by a packed U-shaped concentration of stake-holes. Another cremation was contained within a coarse pot that stood upright in a shallow pit. In another part of this enclosure a pit was found that contained three bronze artefacts: a chisel, a spearhead, and part of a sword blade.

Later occupation of the site is demonstrated by an iron smelting-pit and a decorated bronze mount of the second century AD. Traces of a large rectangular house, fragments of imported green glazed pottery and two silver coins of the thirteenth and fourteenth centuries are indications of late reoccupation. Outside the HILL-FORT, on the southern slopes, there was considerable evidence of activity contemporary with that on the hilltop. **Barry Raftery**

Rathlin Island, Co. Antrim, a limestone-and-basalt island of 13.8 km^2 ($5\frac{1}{2}$ sq. miles), Northern Ireland's only inhabited island. Rathlin was traditionally attributed to Ireland rather than Scotland because, like the rest of Ireland, it has no snakes. At Brockley, Stone Age axes were made from porcellanite formed from volcanic intrusions. In the eighth century Rathlin was plundered by the VIKINGS. In 1306 ROBERT BRUCE, while seeking refuge on Rathlin, was reputedly inspired to try again for the Scottish crown by observing a spider's indefatigable efforts to spin a web. In 1575 WALTER DEVEREUX, Earl of Essex, slaughtered the entire population of 600 during the process of colonisation, and there was mass slaughter again in 1642, in the wake of the 1641 REBELLION. The island used to belong to the Gage family; their restored property, now a visitors' facility, dominates the harbour.

There are three LIGHTHOUSES on Rathlin. MARCONI's assistant carried out early radio transmissions across water from Rathlin to Ballycastle on the mainland. The island has significant bird life; in the west the townland of Kebble, with its guillemots, razorbills, fulmars, shearwaters, and puffins, is a nature reserve.

As with all Irish islands, Rathlin's population has dramatically declined, having been 1,010 in 1841 (before the GREAT FAMINE) and 368 in 1901; its present population of about 100 is dispersed throughout the island, with a cluster around the harbour of Church Bay. The island has shops, a guesthouse, a pub, a post office, a primary school, and two churches. There was considerable investment in the 1990s, including harbour works, a wind and diesel-generated ELECTRICITY scheme, and a roll-on/roll-off ferry from Ballycastle operated by the Scottish company Caledonian MacBrayne. This easier crossing of the turbulent Rathlin Sound has helped the TOURISM industry, which, with farming and fishing, principally supports the population. **Stephen A. Royle**

Rathmines and Rathgar Musical Society (R & R), an amateur musical society founded in Dublin in 1913 by C. P. Fitzgerald to produce operatic, choral, and other musical works. Its first production, *The Mikado* by Gilbert and Sullivan, was at the QUEEN'S ROYAL THEATRE in 1913, but from 1914 it has performed at the GAIETY THEATRE, where it has since had an unbroken run, with two productions each year, alternating Gilbert and Sullivan with musical comedy. There have also been presentations at the NATIONAL CONCERT HALL since 1983. An amateur society but enjoying the support of professional musical directors, producers, and choreographers, it has become a recognised training ground for young singers and actors; its Irish premieres have included *My Fair Lady*, *Fiddler on the Roof*, *Gigi*, and *Camelot*. **Ite O'Donovan**

Raymond, Anthony (1675–1726), scholar. Born in Ballyloughrane, near Listowel, Co. Kerry; educated at TCD. Ordained a minister in the CHURCH OF IRELAND, 1699, he was Vicar of Trim from c. 1705. A friend of SWIFT, he was notable for his lack of animosity towards Catholics. He maintained close contact with the Ó NEACHTAIN circle of Irish scholars in Dublin, exchanging manuscripts of historical significance. He bitterly attacked the credentials of Dermod O'Connor, a competing translator of KEATING's FORAS FEASA AR ÉIRINN. Though he never succeeded in publishing his own projected history of Ireland, his affirmation of the activities of Dublin's Irish scholars, who had to operate on the periphery of an otherwise uncaring society, was highly valued by them. **Liam Mac Mathúna**

RDS: see ROYAL DUBLIN SOCIETY.

Rea, Stephen (1946–), actor. Born in Belfast. He came to international prominence for his performance in *The Crying Game* (1992). He has appeared in a number of NEIL JORDAN films, including *Angel* (1982), *The Company of Wolves* (1984), *Michael Collins* (1996), *The Butcher Boy* (1997), *In Dreams* (1999), and *The End of the Affair* (1999), while he has also played in *Life Is Sweet* (1991), *Bad Behaviour* (1993), *Prêt-à-Porter* (1994), and *Trojan Eddie* (1996). He is a founding director of the FIELD DAY Theatre Company. **Kevin Rockett**

Read School for Instruction in Pianoforte Playing, a PIANO school in Harcourt Street, Dublin, founded in 1915 by Patricia Read. Read, herself a student of Albanesi at the Royal Academy of Music, London, had taught at the Leinster School of Music before opening her own establishment, which employed as many as seventeen teachers, including Rhoda Coghill, WALTER BECKETT, LILY HUBAN, MABEL SWAINSON, Eithne O'Sharkey, and Noreen O'Neill. The school taught all levels, from beginners up to advanced pupils training for the musical profession, providing supplementary classes in the theory of music, aural training, harmony, and composition. It closed in the mid-1950s. **Deborah Kelleher**

Real Charlotte, The (1894), a novel by SOMERVILLE AND ROSS. Written in 1890–93, their third novel depicts the struggle for land among a primarily Protestant population in the early 1890s. The text overturns romantic expectations while demonstrating the complexity of the Irish Anglican world-view. It received mixed reviews for its 'sordid' nature but was acclaimed by Andrew Lang and W. B. YEATS. Somerville and Ross considered it their best work; it reigns as the foremost document in Irish literature of an imaginative reconciliation of the Irish Anglican inheritance with the developments of a secularised Irish world. **Julie Anne Stevens**

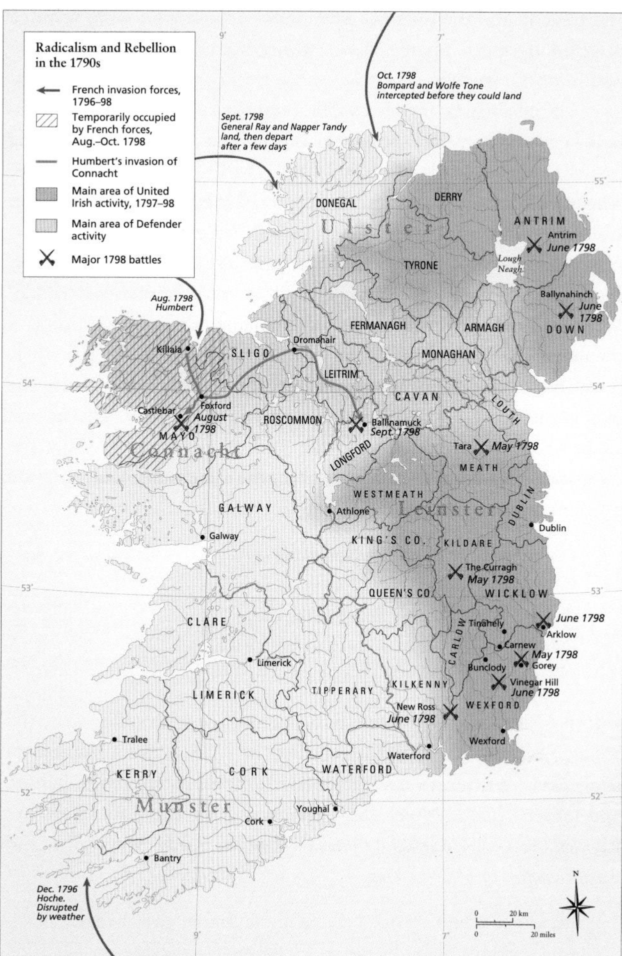

Reavy, Ed (1898–1988), traditional musician. Born in Maudabawn, Co. Cavan. Resident in Philadelphia for his entire adult life, he is regarded as one of the most prolific and original composers of TRADITIONAL MUSIC in the twentieth century. In the 1920s he made a number of recordings, and his FIDDLE style bears the influence of the Sligo style, which predominated in New York at that time. An influential volume of his tunes, *Where the Shannon Rises*, was published by his nephew, Joseph Reavy, in 1971. Today his tunes are common currency among traditional musicians on both sides of the Atlantic. **Martin Dowling**

Rebellion, 1641, a name given to the protracted conflict that began in 1641 associated with the massacre of Protestants in Ulster, the surprising union of OLD ENGLISH and native Irish Catholics, and the Cromwellian onslaught against the insurgents in the later stages of the conflict. The rebellion erupted in the first instance in Ulster, when rebel Catholic elements surprised Protestant settlers; in the ensuing hostilities large numbers of settlers were killed. The number of deaths was inflated by contemporary and subsequent Protestant writers as some hundreds of thousands. Modern research calculates the number of deaths to be 12,000, out of a total Protestant population in Ulster at the time of 40,000—a massacre by any standards. The rebellion soon spread to other areas when the native Irish of Ulster were joined in revolt by their Old English co-religionists. For a time, such was the success of the revolt that the Protestant dominance of Ireland was in danger of being eradicated, not least when OWEN ROE O'NEILL led the insurgents in Ulster to a famous victory at the BATTLE OF BENBURB in 1646, when the primary Protestant army in Ireland was annihilated. Political and cultural differences between the native Irish and the Old English are widely considered to have been a primary cause of the failure of the insurgents. What began as an event associated with the massacre of Protestants was to end with the equally notable massacres wrought by the armies of OLIVER CROMWELL, who landed in Ireland in 1649. The slaughter of the inhabitants of Drogheda and Wexford are as indelibly imprinted on the psyche of Irish Catholics as the previous massacres in Ulster are on Protestants. [see DEPOSITIONS.] **John McCavitt**

Rebellion, 1798, the first attempt to establish an independent Irish republic. The rebellion was organised by the Society of UNITED IRISHMEN. Founded by THEOBALD WOLFE TONE and other young radicals in Belfast in 1791, the society became revolutionary and republican after it was suppressed in 1794. The United Irishmen were largely inspired by French revolutionary ideals, and after a French attempt to land troops in 1796 had failed, the leaders of the movement, most notably Lord EDWARD FITZGERALD, initiated a rising on 23 May 1798, during which they hoped to seize first Dublin and then the rest of the country. The arrest of Fitzgerald (who died in prison on 4 June) and other leaders in the days before the outbreak foiled their plans, and in a situation of great confusion, rebel forces mobilised in only three regions: in Cos. Meath, Kildare, and Wicklow (23 May), Co. Wexford (26 May), and Cos. Antrim and Down (7 June). Government forces, under the direction of JOHN PRATT, Earl Camden (1759–1840) as Viceroy, and Lieutenant-General GERARD LAKE (1744–1808) as commander-in-chief, were able to deal with each of these regional rebellions separately: Cos. Kildare, Meath, and Wicklow by 30 May (the Battle of Gibbet Rath), Cos. Antrim and Down by 13 June (the BATTLE OF BALLYNAHINCH), and Co. Wexford by 21 June (the BATTLE OF VINEGAR HILL). The rebellion in Leinster was over as a serious conventional struggle after Vinegar Hill, but smaller actions took place in various parts of the province for months afterwards, in Co. Wicklow especially. The French government sent a small expedition to aid the rebels; it landed at Killala, Co. Mayo, on 22 August, two months too late. The French force, under General Jean Humbert, gathered considerable local support and marched towards Dublin, but, having won a few small battles, the soldiers were surrounded and defeated at Ballinmuck, Co. Longford, on 8 September. WOLFE TONE, who had spent the previous three years in France working on behalf of the United Irishmen, was captured on a French ship in LOUGH SWILLY, Co. Donegal, on 12 October, and died from a self-inflicted wound in a Dublin prison cell on 19 November.

The rebellion would inspire fierce polemics over ensuing generations and in the late twentieth century was the subject of intense debate among historians over the question of its causes. Both the centennial of the rebellion in 1898 and its bicentennial in 1998 were marked by large public commemorations. **Daniel Gahan**

Rebellion of 1798 in song. Irish traditional songs are indeed the expression of the people and in many cases the unwritten history of the people. They contain all their feelings of love, laughter, and tragedy and the political aspirations of those who were not in a position to speak openly at that time, because of the oppressive nature of the society.

An old almanac prophecy said about the year 1798 that it would have 'a wet winter, a dry spring, a bloody summer, and no king'. During that summer upwards of 30,000 Irish rebels would lose their lives. The revolution was initiated by the Presbyterians in the north of Ireland, and through their organisation, the Society of UNITED IRISHMEN, the movement spread throughout the country. However, the conflict was mainly confined to Ulster and Leinster, where Co. Wexford bore the brunt of the fighting. The rebels, or Croppies, as they were called, were finally defeated at the BATTLE OF VINEGAR HILL.

The Belfast NEWSLETTER of 1798 sarcastically summed up the efforts of the ill-equipped rebels by saying: 'Nobody will set out again to catch cannonballs on the end of pitchforks.' While the songs of the Orange YEOMANRY reflect the same sentiment, they are by their nature triumphalist:

> O Croppies, ye'd better be quiet and still,
> Ye shan't have your liberty, do what ye will;
> As long as salt water is found in the deep,
> Our foot on the neck of the Croppy we'll keep,
> Derry down down, Croppies, lie down.

But those in power write the history, and those who suffer write the songs, and so it was with the rebellion of 1798. A great number of songs were written to commemorate the various atrocities, battles, and leaders. In the North they were written in memory of HENRY JOY MCCRACKEN, General HENRY MUNRO, Rody McCorley, and BETSY GRAY.

> An Ulster man it's proud I am, from the Antrim glens I come,
> And though I labour by the sea I followed fife and drum,
> I heard the tramp of marching men, I saw them fight and die,
> And, my boys, I do remember well how I followed Henry Joy.

> All you good men who listen, just think of the fate
> Of the brave men who died in the year ninety-eight,
> No doubt poor old Ireland would be free long ago
> If her sons were all rebels like Henry Munro.

In the rest of the country the songs were written to commemorate the massacre in Dunlavin, Co. Wicklow, 'The Bold Belfast Shoemaker', BAGENAL HARVEY, EDWARD FITZGERALD, Father JOHN MURPHY, and THEOBALD WOLFE TONE. Many of the songs that are sung today commemorating the rebellion of 1798 are not contemporary but were written at a later date to commemorate the centenary of the rebellion in 1898. Songs were written at this time by JOHN KELLS INGRAM, P. J. McCall, Robert Dwyer Joyce, William Rooney, John Keegan Casey, and THOMAS DAVIS. These songs would provide the inspiration for the various uprisings that would follow, culminating in the EASTER RISING in Dublin in 1916, which set in motion the struggle that would establish an independent Irish republic.

> Though Fitzgerald died, sure we fought them still,
> And we shouted Vengeance on Vinegar hill,
> Knowing our flag would again be flown,
> If France gave ear to the prayers of Tone.

> He came, was beaten, we bear him here,
> From a prison cell on his funeral bier,
> And Freedom's hope shall be buried low
> With his mouldering corpse 'neath the winter snow.

> Hush, one said o'er the new-set sod,
> Hope shall endure with our faith in God,
> And God shall only forsake us when
> This grave is forgotten by Irishmen.

[see REPUBLICAN AND REBEL SONG.] **Frank Harte**

Reddin, Tony (1919–), hurler. Born in Mullagh, Co. Galway. Despite his place of birth, it was with Tipperary that he enjoyed his great successes on the hurling field. His agility and vision made him the most difficult keeper to beat for goal. He won three all-Ireland medals in his career, the first coming when he was thirty, in 1949. He and the team went on to make it three-in-a-row in 1950 and 1951. A regular with Munster in the inter-provincial series, he won five of those championships before bringing his career to an end in 1957. **Donal Keenan**

Red Hand of Ulster, a symbol originating in the coat of arms of the O'Neills, later Earls of Tyrone. A right hand was a common heraldic motif, perhaps representing the hand of God. From the seventeenth century onwards the red hand was widely accepted as a symbol of Ulster and was incorporated in the coat of arms of the province, in school and sports club badges, and in trade marks. In the twentieth century the red hand was more widely used as a political symbol by unionists than by nationalists, and from 1925 it appeared in the coat of arms of the Northern Ireland government. From the 1960s loyalist paramilitaries almost always adopted it, though the Ulster Freedom Fighters preferred a clenched red fist. **Jonathan Bardon**

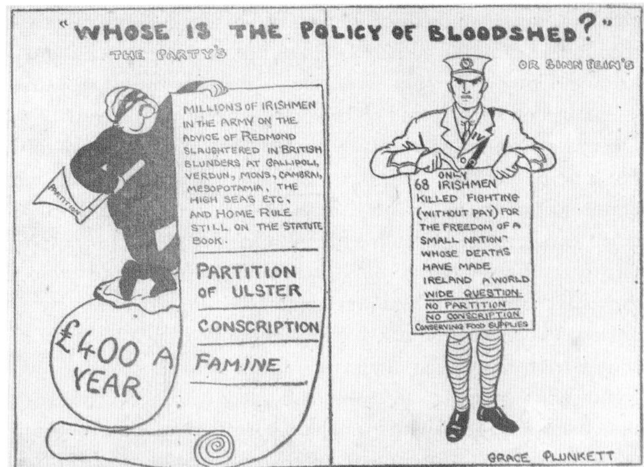

Redmond, John. *A cartoon by Grace Plunkett attacking John Redmond's support for the British war effort during the First World War. The panel on the right refers to nationalists killed during the 1916 Rising. [Stephen Lalor collection]*

Redmond, John (1856–1918), political leader. Born in Ballytrent, Co. Wexford, eldest son of William Archer Redmond; educated at TCD. A clerk in the British House of Commons when his father was an MP, he came under the spell of CHARLES STEWART PARNELL, resigned his post and was elected to Parliament, 1881–1918, succeeding on Parnell's death to the leadership of the minority faction, 1891, and chairman of the reunited party, 1900–18. Though never an agrarian radical, he took part in the LAND WAR (1879–82) and PLAN OF CAMPAIGN (1886–91), suffering a short term of imprisonment, 1888. On becoming party chairman in 1900 he shouldered the delicate task of balancing the diverse elements and personalities within the national ranks. He was respected by British and Irish politicians, but his dream of a unified self-governing

Ireland was shattered in the years after 1912 and his reputation sank from 1916, in part because of his enthusiastic support for the British war effort (see p. 391). **Alan O'Day**

Redmond, William (Willie) (1861–1917), politician. Born in Ballytrent, Co. Wexford, younger brother of JOHN REDMOND; educated at Clongowes Wood College, Co. Kildare. He was commissioned in 1914 and served in the FIRST WORLD WAR as a company commander. In 1917 he passionately addressed Parliament on behalf of Irishmen in the British army, demanding self-government within the British Empire. On 7 June he was killed in the attack on Wytschaete; at the time of his death, he was MP for East Clare. **T. G. Fraser**

reel, the most popular tune type in the Irish tradition. Introduced from Scotland in the eighteenth century, it is in common time and consists largely of a quaver movement, with an accent on the first and third beat of each bar. Typically the tunes are in two parts, with each part repeated (AABB), though 'single' (AB) and extended (AABBCC etc.) tunes are also found. The reel is also the most common tune type borrowed from other traditions today (for example Scotland, Cape Breton, and Québec). As a dance the reel is common in a solo competitive form and is also required for a variety of group dances. **Liz Doherty**

Reeves, Percy Oswald (1870–1967), enamellist and metalworker. Born in Staffordshire; studied metalwork, jewellery, and enamelling at Birmingham School of Art before teaching at Southport and then qualifying as an art master at the Royal College of Art, London, in 1900. In 1903 he left the employment of Alexander Fisher, the English arts and crafts enamellist, to inaugurate metalwork classes at Dublin Metropolitan School of Art. He was an accomplished teacher there until his retirement in 1937, achieving success with his own important commissions as well as with those of his students. He was the articulate honorary secretary of the ARTS AND CRAFTS SOCIETY OF IRELAND. **Nicola Gordon Bowe**

referendums. Article 6 of the CONSTITUTION OF IRELAND states that 'all powers of government, legislative, executive and judicial, derive, under God, from the people, whose right it is to designate the rulers of the State and, in final appeal, to decide all questions of national policy, according to the requirements of the common good.' Extensive recourse to direct democracy in deciding important political questions is a unique feature of Irish politics. Since the adoption of the Constitution in 1937 there have been twenty-four referendums, on such issues as the ELECTORAL SYSTEM (1959 and 1968), membership of the European Economic Community (1972) and subsequent EU treaty revisions (1987, 1992, and 2001), the position of the state on 'moral' issues, such as the special position of the Catholic Church (1972), ABORTION (1983 and 2002), access to abortion information and services outside the state (1992), DIVORCE (1986 and 1995), access to bail (1997), and removal of the death penalty (2001).

In Northern Ireland, referendums have been used less frequently: so far there have been three. The first so-called 'Border Poll', in 1973, was on the question of Northern Ireland's continued incorporation in the United Kingdom as against a united Ireland. 57.5 per cent of the electorate voted to remain part of the United Kingdom and 0.6 per cent voted for a united Ireland, while 41.3 per cent did not vote. The second was part of a United Kingdom referendum on continued participation in the European Economic Community (52 per cent in favour). In 1998 a referendum on the

referendums. *The counting of votes in the 1995 divorce referendum at the Royal Dublin Society premises, Dublin. More than a million voters decided to lift the legal ban on divorce. [Photocall Ireland]*

BELFAST AGREEMENT was held concurrently in Northern Ireland and the Republic. The turn-out in Northern Ireland was 81.1 per cent, with 71.1 per cent voting for the agreement; in the Republic the turn-out was lower, at 55.6 per cent, with 94.4 per cent in favour of the agreement. [see APPENDIX.] **Maura Adshead**

Reflections on the Revolution in France (1790), a book by EDMUND BURKE. It began as a letter to a French deputy, Charles Jean François Depont, and evolved into a rebuttal of Richard Price's sermon *A Discourse on the Love of Our Country.* Maintaining its bifocal vision, it argued that speculative politics inspired by ENLIGHTENMENT THOUGHT threatened political stability. Burke contrasted the utopianism of French governments with the ancient constitution of England, relying on the wisdom of traditional leaders. He interpreted the 'Glorious Revolution' of 1688 as defending English liberties against Stuart despotism and famously repudiated the revolutionaries' treatment of Marie Antoinette as 'unchivalrous'. He saw politics as embedded in civil society and predicted a military dictator restoring order in France. A masterpiece of rhetoric, the book prompted responses from Thomas Paine, MARY WOLLSTONECRAFT, Joseph Priestley, and Sir James Macintosh. **Michael Brown**

Reformation, fifteenth to sixteenth centuries, a movement for the reform of religious life and institutions begun in Germany in the early sixteenth century and introduced into Ireland by the English administration in the 1530s. Unlike their Continental counterparts, the English and Irish Reformations were not so much popular, doctrinally driven upsurges as a changing of ecclesiastical management at the behest of HENRY VIII. He substituted his authority for that of the Pope in the English and Irish churches while retaining Catholic dogma. The RELIGIOUS ORDERS were dissolved, and all monastic possessions were vested in the Crown. Shrines and places of PILGRIMAGE were shut down, and some minor liturgical alterations were made.

While the impact of these changes in Ireland was stunted by the limited reach of the Dublin administration, there was general acquiescence among senior clergy and leading lay figures. The process of introducing radical PROTESTANTISM by decree in the reign of Edward VI, 1547–53, was truncated by the brief restoration of Papal supremacy and Catholicism under Mary, 1553–8; but ELIZABETH I settled the issue of the Irish state religion with the Act of Supremacy and Act of Uniformity (1560). From then until 1870 the established ecclesiastical system in Ireland enshrined a moderate form of Protestantism, to which all subjects of the Crown had to subscribe.

The implementation of the new beliefs and practices was hampered, however, by the structural weakness of the old church institution that was taken over by the state agents of reform. With few exceptions, church livings were poor and unattractive to educated, career-minded clerics; church buildings were neglected and often ruinous; and educational facilities, vital for the training of ministers, failed to develop. Part of the problem lay in the inaccessibility of church revenue and patronage to state church agents. Through the alienation of property by ecclesiastical personnel and direct grants of monastic lands, local gentry had acquired extensive rights to TITHE income and the nomination of clergy. Their lack of sympathy for the new RELIGION, turning eventually into outright hostility, led them to direct these resources towards an alternative, quasi-underground system, staffed by seminary-trained Catholic clergy. The problem of a shortage of suitably educated Protestant ministers was addressed with the foundation of TRINITY COLLEGE, DUBLIN, in 1592; but the dominant cultural thrust of the CHURCH OF IRELAND was towards evangelisation within an English-speaking milieu. Little or nothing was done to ensure that the Reformation would be preached in Irish, thus putting the majority of the population beyond its reach.

The result of the stalled effort to promote the Reformation in Ireland was that there were two separate denominational groups in early seventeenth-century Ireland, each with its own evolving identity. There was a Protestant minority, comprising mostly newcomers from England, in the newly planted areas, such as Ulster, Munster, and the midlands, while the Catholic majority, more confident as a result of the work of COUNTER-REFORMATION agents, continued to dominate town life and most areas of the countryside. The character of the Irish Reformation was by then established as an elitist, English movement, though with a distinctively Irish heritage. The emphasis was not so much on the conversion of the majority as on the consolidation of Protestantism among the official and planter classes, which increasingly held state power. Originating in and contributing to a period of intensive political, economic, and cultural changes, the Irish Reformation produced the phenomenon of a Protestant minority dominating a largely Catholic country that was to be a feature of Irish history down to the modern period. **Colm Lennon**

Reformation, seventeenth to twenty-first centuries. The founding of TRINITY COLLEGE, Dublin, in 1592 marked a more systematic approach to Reformation in Ireland, but by then the majority of the population was becoming committed to Catholicism. In response to their minority position, Irish Protestants developed their own distinctive identity. Not only were the articles of the CHURCH OF IRELAND more puritan than their English counterparts but the engagement of Protestants in debate with Catholic opponents brought ideological certitude. In particular, JAMES USSHER, Anglican Archbishop of Armagh, propounded the legitimacy of Irish PROTESTANTISM as the true successor to the pristine CHRISTIANITY of the Patrician era. Another important dimension was added with the arrival of substantial numbers of Scottish Presbyterians as settlers in Ulster.

The turmoil of the 1640s steeled the resolve of Irish Protestants and forged greater self-identity among Ulster Presbyterians. After the Cromwellian regime of the 1650s, which introduced a large number of Protestant newcomers as settlers on confiscated land, a consolidated Protestant interest emerged. This bonded the older and newer Protestants within the Anglican mainstream as the politically and economically privileged, while dissenting Protestants, mainly PRESBYTERIANS, were excluded from power and position within the state, along with Catholics. After the brief but explosive upheaval of the JACOBITE campaign in Ireland, the Protestant interest was further consolidated and protected by the PENAL LAWS against dissenters, including Presbyterians and the more recently arrived HUGUENOTS.

Behind the protective wall of the Penal Laws the Protestants showed little inclination to embark on a campaign of converting Catholics and Dissenters to Anglicanism, once their landed and civic position was secured. The Presbyterian community experienced internal organisational difficulties, but the gradual relaxing of religious and social restrictions benefited that confession as well as Catholicism. METHODISM arose in Ireland in the middle of the eighteenth century and achieved impressive growth as an Anglican reform movement but also as a separate Protestant Church in the following century.

The early nineteenth century was marked by a revitalisation of the Protestant churches under the auspices of a movement known as the SECOND REFORMATION. A campaign of proselytism among Catholics proved a relative failure, however, and served to heighten sectarian tensions at a time when the Catholic Church was undergoing what has been called a 'devotional revolution'. With the proportional decline of the Church of Ireland population in the middle of the nineteenth century, a political campaign for disestablishment and disendowment culminated in 1869–70, when the Church of Ireland was detached from the state and became self-supporting.

In spite of DISESTABLISHMENT, a more coherent Protestantism emerged in the twentieth century. Now the term 'Protestants' was more commonly taken to refer to those of the reformed faiths, and not just to Anglicans. Presbyterians and Anglicans had been brought closer by their shared evangelicalism of the nineteenth century. Between the Protestant churches internally, and between them jointly and the Catholic Church, the growth of the ecumenical movement in the later twentieth century has been extremely significant. Separate worshipping communities of Lutherans, BAPTISTS, and EVANGELICALS are also numbered within the broad movement of reformed religions in Ireland. **Colm Lennon**

refugees: see IMMIGRATION.

Regan, John (1905–1988), dancer, choreographer, and dance director. Born in Mallaranny, Co. Mayo; trained with Cecchetti and Legat before dancing with Diaghilev's, de Basil's, Woizikowski's, and Balanchine's Ballets Russes, as well as Nijinsky's Warsaw Ballet, the Markova–Dolin Ballet, and the Georgian State Dancers. He founded the International Ballet Company in London, 1937, while his series 'Ballet for Beginners' ran on BBC Television for over four years. Returning to Ireland in 1977, he founded the Limerick School of Classical Ballet, Mid-West Ballet Workshop, and, in 1982, Theatre Omnibus, then a dance company. His choreography includes *Romeo and Juliet*, *The John Field Suite* and *Death and the Maiden*, in which he performed the mime role of Death at the age of eighty. **Carolyn Swift**

Regency Crisis (1789), a crisis arising out of the Irish Parliament's vote in February 1789 that the Prince of Wales be asked to assume the powers of regent, though the British Parliament was still considering the matter. A potential constitutional conflict was averted by George III's recovery from insanity. **Neal Garnham**

regional development, the development of regions in output, income, UNEMPLOYMENT and EMPLOYMENT, dependence, population density, and quality of life. The level of regional development can be defined and measured in a number of ways, including the level of any of the aforementioned areas. The most widely used measures are income and output measures. Within Ireland there is a high degree of variation with regard to output measures. For example, in 1998 output measured as regional gross value added (GVA) per capita relative to the national average regional GVA per capita of the combined Dublin and Mid-East regions was 119.3 per cent, while that of the Midlands region was only 67.7 per cent.

The gap between the East region (Dublin plus the Mid-East) and the weaker regions is growing. This is illustrated by the change in difference between that region and the weakest region. In 1981 the gap was just short of 35 per cent; in 1998 it increased to over 52 per cent. This implies that there is a process of divergence from the national average.

The relative position of Northern Ireland within the United Kingdom has improved only slightly over the past thirty years, from 75.4 per cent of national GROSS DOMESTIC PRODUCT per capita in 1974 to 77.5 per cent in 1999, which is almost the same GDP per capita as that recorded for the Midlands region of the Republic. Over recent years the relative position of Northern Ireland has worsened, so that one can speak of divergence relative to the UK average.

Differences between the regions are much smaller when regional development is measured in terms of disposable income per capita. In 1997, in the index of regional disposable income per capita relative to the national average disposable income, the highest index was to be found in the East region (111.2 per cent), while the lowest index was found in the Midlands region (88.8 per cent). In this case the gap between highest and lowest is 22.4 per cent. **Edgar Morgenroth**

regionalisation. The Irish state comprises only two tiers of government: central and local. Central government dominates public life, while LOCAL GOVERNMENT is extremely weak. Arguably, Ireland's classification by the EUROPEAN UNION as a single region for the purposes of 'objective 1' regional aid further postponed the development of regional political and administrative structures—a situation that changed following the boom in the economy in the 1990s. In November 1998 the Government divided the country into two regions for statistical purposes, arguing that there was still a case for maintaining objective 1 status in the newly created Border, Midland and Western (BMW) region. Brazening out significant opposition from political parties, long-time campaigners for devolution, would-be members of the new regions and a cynical European Commission, the Government succeeded. The new regions have no governmental powers or functions. **Maura Adshead**

regional policy. There has been an active regional policy in the Republic since the foundation of the state. The tariff measures of the 1930s had a regional policy aspect, as had grant policies from the 1950s. The need for more balanced spatial development requires a greater emphasis on regional development policies. The regionalisation arrangements negotiated by the Republic with regard to the EUROPEAN UNION's Agenda 2000 discussions resulted in the designation of two regions for the purposes of EU structural funds: the Border, Midlands and West objective 1 region and the Southern and Eastern objective 1 region in transition. To achieve a greater regional convergence in economic circumstances, the central consideration is increasing the attractiveness of poorer regions for investment in industry, TOURISM, and natural resources.

The approach in Northern Ireland to regional balance is what is termed a 'hub, corridor and gateway' approach, which aims to develop essential transport corridors, a compact and thriving metropolitan core centred on Belfast, a strong north-west regional centre based on Derry, a polycentric network of strong regional towns

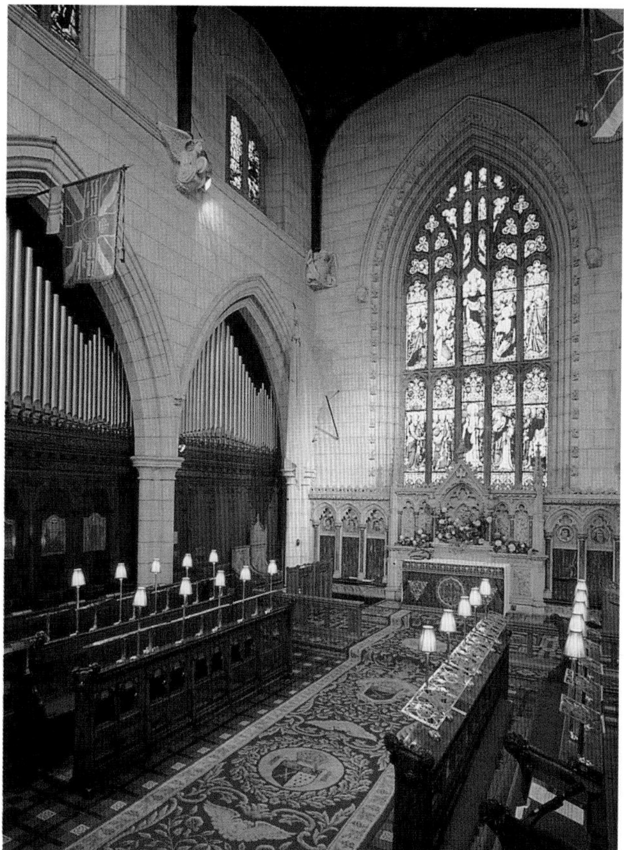

Reformation. *St Columb's Cathedral, Derry, the first post-Reformation cathedral to be built in Ireland; its architectural style is known as 'Plantation gothic'. [Derry Visitor and Convention Bureau]*

with a reinforced role as the main services centres for urban and rural communities, and a vibrant rural community. **John W. O'Hagan**

regional tourism authorities, established in 1963 to provide a network of tourist information offices in the Republic, covering regions defined by the Government. Six of the seven TOURISM regions—Dublin, South-East, South-West, West, North-West, and Midlands East—are administered by regional tourism authorities; the seventh—Shannon—is administered by the tourism division of Shannon Development, a state agency working on the integrated economic development of the Shannon region. The regional tourism authorities promote tourism in their area through promotional publications and are the principal contact at local level for all those involved in tourism. They operate marketing advisory services for their members and co-operate in the production of regional tourism development plans; they also help with product development and with grant applications. The authorities operate the national network of tourist information offices, which provide information and booking services.

The seven authorities and the counties they cover are as follows: Dublin Tourism; South-East Tourism (Carlow, Kilkenny, Waterford, Wexford, and south Tipperary); Cork-Kerry Tourism (Cork and south Kerry); Shannon (Clare, north Kerry, Limerick, south Offaly, and north Tipperary); Ireland West Tourism (Galway, Mayo, and Roscommon); North-West (Cavan, Donegal, Leitrim, Monaghan, and Sligo); and Midlands East (Kildare, Laois, Longford, Louth, Meath, north Offaly, Westmeath, and Wicklow). The regional tourism authorities operate in consultation with BORD FÁILTE ÉIREANN, which has a representative on each board. The regional tourism organisations in Northern Ireland are Belfast Visitor and Convention Bureau, Derry Visitor and Convention Bureau, Fermanagh Lakelands, Causeway Coast and Glens, and South-East Region, all of which operate in liaison with the NORTHERN IRELAND TOURIST BOARD.

In 2000 the six regional tourism authorities received £1.67 million from Bord Fáilte. (Shannon Development has separate financing arrangements.) The rest of their income is earned principally from membership fees, together with booking fees for accommodation and the sale of publications and souvenirs. The authorities offer annual membership to local authorities and to associations and individuals involved in the tourist industry. They have developed and operate several visitor centres, including the Dublin Writers' Museum, Malahide Castle, the SKELLIG Experience, BUNRATTY CASTLE and Folk Park, and THOOR BALLYLEE. Each regional tourism authority publishes an annual report. **Alannah Hopkin**

Rehan, Ada (1860–1916), actor. Born Ada Crehan in Limerick; she emigrated to the United States at the age of five and began acting at fourteen. She joined the company of the prestigious American manager Augustin Daly in 1879, the year in which he opened Daly's Theatre on Broadway, New York. Rehan laid the foundation stone for Daly's London theatre in 1891, where she had considerable success in the role of Katharina in *The Taming of the Shrew*. She was a principal player in Daly's company until his death in 1899, after which her popularity declined. She gave her final performance in 1905. **Christopher Morash**

Reid, Christina (1942–), playwright. She has written a number of formally different award-winning plays that deal with Belfast communities struggling with issues of violence, SECTARIANISM, sex, and class. Her best-known plays are *Tea in a China Cup* (1983), *Did You Hear the One About the Irishman?* (1985) and *Joyriders* (1986). **Eamonn Jordan**

Reid, Forrest (1875–1947), novelist and critic. Born in Belfast; educated at the University of Cambridge. A deft elegist of male youth and adolescence, his best fiction concerns the conflicts and attachments that characterise these twilight years. In addition to the Tom Barber trilogy—*Uncle Stephen* (1931), *The Retreat* (1936), and *Young Tom* (1944)—important novels include *Brian Westby* (1934) and *Peter Waring* (1937). He also wrote two acclaimed autobiographical works, *Apostate* (1926) and *Private Road* (1940), and several critical studies, including a monograph on W. B. YEATS (1915). **Desmond O'Rawe**

Reid, J. Graham (1945–), playwright. Born in Belfast. He first came to prominence with *The Death of Humpty Dumpty* (1979), a play that examines the relationship between power and violence through the character of a schoolteacher left paralysed after an assault. His reputation is strongest as a 'TROUBLES' playwright. The 'Billy' and 'Ties of Blood' series of television plays, 1982–5, dealt with daily life within loyalist communities. Reid's strength as a playwright has been his ability to dramatise vicious and virtuous human instincts concealed beneath the political rhetoric of Northern society. **Michael McAteer**

Reid, Meta Mayne (1905–1991), writer. Born in Woodlesford, Yorkshire, of Irish parents; educated at the University of Manchester. She lived and worked in Belfast, where she wrote and published twenty-four books for children between 1952 and 1980. Her first book, *Phelim and the Creatures* (1952), the story of a seahorse that lives in LOUGH NEAGH and an old man living in a nearby cave, has a cast of talking animals and magic deeds. She wrote her best stories about the planters of Ulster in the period 1789–1810: *The Two Rebels* (1969), *The Plotters of Pollnashee* (1973), *Beyond the Wide World's End* (1972) and *The Silver Fighting Cocks* (1966). One of her last books was for younger children, *The Noguls and the Horse* (1976), which describes the traumatic effect on a girl of a terrorist bomb. **Patricia Donlon**

Reid, Nano (1905–1981), painter. Born in Drogheda; trained at the Metropolitan School of Art, Dublin. Apart from a brief period of study in Paris and London she lived all her life in her native town and in Dublin and painted the locality and inhabitants of her surroundings. One of the strongest painters of her generation, her subject matter included an uninhibited treatment of people, places, and animals. She used paint with direct, spontaneous freedom within a restricted green-brown colour range. In 1950 she and NORAH MCGUINNESS were the first artists to represent Ireland at the Venice Biennale. Her *Gypsy Encampment* is in the ARTS COUNCIL collection. **Dorothy Walker**

Reid, Thomas Mayne (1818–1883), pseudonym of Thomas Mayne, soldier and novelist. Born in Ballyroney, near Banbridge, Co. Down. He served as a captain in the American army in the Mexican War; he then enjoyed huge success in the 1850s with his adventure yarns for boys, *The Rifle Rangers* and *The Scalp Hunters*. **Nicholas Allen**

Reilly, John (1926–1969) traditional singer and tinsmith. Born in Carrick-on-Shannon, Co. Leitrim. A Traveller, he moved mainly around Leitrim and Roscommon. Although unlettered, he had a large repertoire of ancient ballads, some of medieval origin. Part of his repertoire was recorded by TOM MUNNELLY of University College, Dublin, and D. K. Wilgus of the University of California, Los Angeles. CHRISTY MOORE performs several of his songs. He received little recognition from the musical establishment or media in his impoverished and brief lifetime. **Tom Munnelly**

Reilly, John Joe (1918–1952), Gaelic footballer. Born in Cornafean, Co. Cavan, a member of a famous football family. An all-round athlete of great ability, Gaelic football was always his priority. An army officer, he was appointed Cavan captain in succession to his brother Tom in 1946. He had already played in three all-Ireland finals but had lost each time. However, in the final played at the Polo Grounds, New York, in 1947 he led Cavan to success. The team defended its title in 1948 and was beaten in the 1949 final by Mayo. He played in six finals before his death at the age of thirty-four. **Donal Keenan**

religion. In contemporary Ireland 'religion' refers to the ways in which people and groups relate to a sense of the transcendent, to God or to some spirit or life force greater than themselves. It is essentially a social and communal phenomenon: people are members of churches, such as the CATHOLIC CHURCH, the CHURCH OF IRELAND, or the Presbyterian Church. In a wider sociological sense religion has been defined both substantively, as beliefs and practices of recognisable groups, and functionally, in its consequences. Recent analyses have attempted to distinguish institutional religion from 'invisible', 'folk', 'implicit', and 'customary' religion, as well as other forms of relating to the transcendent. With the recent decline in adherence to institutional religion there has been a growing awareness of individual 'spirituality'. **Michael Hornsby-Smith**

religious lay societies. The CATHOLIC ASSOCIATION, founded by DANIEL O'CONNELL in 1824, was directly political in character, but as a movement for national renewal it lies behind the TEMPERANCE crusade of the Cork Capuchin Father THEOBALD MATHEW, begun in 1838, which attracted about 5 million adherents, had a strongly devotional dimension, and laid the spiritual groundwork for O'Connell's Repeal Association of 1840. Mathew's work was resumed by the PIONEER TOTAL ABSTINENCE ASSOCIATION of the Sacred Heart, established by the Jesuit Father James Cullen in 1898; the association attracted hundreds of thousands of members. The preaching of Catholic Parish Missions was begun by the Vincentians in 1842.

The most important lay society in modern Ireland with a definite social purpose, the SOCIETY OF ST VINCENT DE PAUL, founded in Paris by Antoine-Frédéric Ozanam in 1833 for the care of the poor, was established in Dublin in 1845. The 'DEVOTIONAL REVOLUTION' in nineteenth-century Ireland inspired the creation of scores of sodalities, confraternities and 'third orders' intended for the sanctification of their members, with mass membership, often under the aegis of the religious orders in the towns: the Dominicans, Jesuits, Vincentians, Carmelites, Augustinians, and Franciscans. The Dominicans in Dublin had responsibility for the Rosary Confraternity, the White Star League, and the Holy Name Sodality, founded by Father Joseph Slattery in 1884. Pre-eminent among lay devotions were those to the Sacred Heart of Jesus, encouraged by the *Irish Messenger of the Sacred Heart of Jesus*, and the Marian piety that inspired FRANK DUFF in 1921 to create the lay-run Legion of Mary. A grotto dedicated to Our Lady of Lourdes at Inchicore, Dublin, in 1925 attracted thousands of pilgrims. There were local cults of a Dutch Passionist priest. Blessed Father Charles Houben of Mount Argus, who died in 1893; of a reformed alcoholic Dublin labourer, MATT TALBOT, who died in 1925, and was declared venerable in 1976, and now enjoys a cultus beyond Ireland; and of the Jesuit Father John Sullivan, who died in 1933. The climax of the devotional movement was the gathering of a million people for the Mass celebrated at the EUCHARISTIC CONGRESS in the Phoenix Park, Dublin, in 1932; but these forms of piety, with the institutions that sustained them, underwent a very considerable decline in the last quarter of the twentieth century. **Sheridan Gilley**

religious magazines, 1900–2001.

The great majority of religious magazines in Ireland are Catholic, as might be expected. The *Irish Ecclesiastical Record* (1864–1968), founded by CARDINAL PAUL CULLEN, published mostly literary and historical material, though always with an ecclesiastical connection. Also long-lived was the *Irish Monthly* (1873–1954), established by Father Matthew Russell, who contributed many essays in literary biography. At first it serialised novels by upper-class Catholics, but during the LITERARY REVIVAL it published YEATS, WILDE, and MOORE, among others; later it reverted to the confessional mode of *Catholic Ireland*, which it had replaced. The *Catholic Bulletin* (1911–39) was in its early years a vehicle for important articles on Catholic social teaching by PETER COFFEY. In favour of censorship, and opposed to the ANGLO-IRISH TREATY, it became increasingly extreme and isolated.

Of periodicals devoted entirely or partially to Catholic theology, one of the oldest is the Jesuit journal *Studies* (1912–), still intellectually influential. The scholarly *Irish Theological Quarterly* is published at ST PATRICK'S COLLEGE, Maynooth. The *Furrow*, a monthly also published in Maynooth, deals with social as well as theological issues, as do two Dominican publications, *Doctrine and Life* and *Spirituality*, a comparative newcomer.

There are many religious magazines aimed at a general readership, with features, news, illustrations, readers' letters, and in some instances stories. Among the best-known are *Reality*, *Outlook*, *Intercom* (published by the bookshop chain Veritas), and the *Sacred Heart Messenger* (which has a monthly circulation of 180,000). Scarcely less popular than the *Messenger* are two magazines devoted to the work of missionary societies, the *Far East*, published by the St Columban Missionaries, and *Africa*, published by St Patrick's Missionary Society. Many popular magazines, some long established, are devoted to the work of other missionary societies and such special-interest groups within the church as the PIONEER TOTAL ABSTINENCE ASSOCIATION, which publishes the monthly *Pioneer.*

The Catholic dioceses publish magazines of their own, as do the CHURCH OF IRELAND dioceses, and many are of considerable sophistication. There are also two national magazines associated with the Church of Ireland, the twice-yearly *Search*, containing theological essays and reviews, and the *Church of Ireland Gazette*, an independent weekly that carries news and features on theology and church history. The *Methodist Newsletter*, a more considerable magazine than its title suggests, is a monthly, while the *Presbyterian Herald* appears ten times a year; both are published in Belfast. The *Congregationalist* is a quarterly. The Religious Society of Friends (QUAKERS) has a 'news journal' called the *Friendly Word*. The Lutheran Church publishes a small newsletter in German, *Gemeindebrief*, and the Unitarian Church a monthly *Calendar*; both have short articles as well as news.

A growing interest in ECUMENISM is reflected in some of the more thoughtful journals and was prominent in the short-lived *Céide*, an independent 'review from the margins' published in Co. Mayo. It seeks to promote 'a critical dialogue involving religion and society, the arts and the sciences,' while maintaining 'a close affinity with those on the religious, social, economic and political margins of our society.' **John Wakeman**

religious orders (female)

Thirteenth to seventeenth centuries. Most communities of nuns in thirteenth-century Ireland became Augustinian Arroasian. At first their mother house was Clonard, Co. Meath (founded c. 1144), but this declined in the fourteenth century, and by 1383 the abbacy had transferred to Odra, Co. Meath. The most important houses included the Abbey of St Mary de Hogges, Dublin (founded c. 1146), the Priory of St Mary at Gracedieu, near Lusk, Co. Dublin (founded c. 1190)—both Arroasian—and the Augustinian abbey at Killone, Co. Clare (founded c. 1189). There were CISTERCIAN houses at Derry and Ballymore, Co. Westmeath. The Franciscan nuns (Order of St Clare) had six houses in Ireland in 1316 but only three in 1384–5 (probably at Carrick-on-Suir, Co. Tipperary, Youghal, Co. Cork, and Fooran, Co. Westmeath). Mixed communities existed in at least three Augustinian priory-hospitals of the Fratres Cruciferi, in the monastery-hospitals of the Benedictine monks at Waterford and Cork, and in fifteenth-century Franciscan Third Order Regular houses. Nuns resident in the Cistercian abbeys at Mellifont, Inishlounaght, and JERPOINT were probably expelled c. 1228. A large number of these houses, particularly those within the Pale, were closed as part of a general suppression campaign of the Henrician REFORMATION in the 1530s and 40s. Many were abandoned before the suppression (St Mary's Abbey of Augustinian nuns, Clonard, the Arroasian house at Calliaghstown, Co. Meath, and St Mary's in Derry); others evaded suppression until later in the sixteenth century or beyond. Notwithstanding the revival and establishment of congregations of female religious during the seventeenth-century COUNTER-REFORMATION, in 1731 only nine nunneries in Ireland are recorded.

Some female religious communities provided welfare services for the poor of the district. The convent at Gracedieu, Co. Dublin, had a school for girls from the Old English community. After the

religious orders. *Anne Margaret Cusack, widely known as the Nun of Kenmare, founded the Sisters of St Joseph of Peace in 1884. [Council of Trustees of the National Library of Ireland; R.18250]*

suppression, daughters of wealthy Catholic families were sent abroad for their education or to be professed as nuns. The first convent on the Continent that catered specifically for Irish women was the Bom Sucesso convent in Lisbon, founded by the Dominicans in 1639.

In the seventeenth century there were sporadic attempts to found new female religious congregations in Ireland. One of the best-known was the Poor Clare convent founded by members of the Dillon family in Dublin in 1629; it later moved to Bethlehem on the shores of Lough Rea, and then to Galway. During the reign of JAMES II, Irish nuns from the Benedictine convent of Ypres in Belgium established two convents in Channel Row (now North Brunswick Street) and Great Ship Street, Dublin; the latter, which was supported by Frances Jennings, Duchess of Tyrconnell, had a school for girls of gentry families. Neither convent survived the religious and political turmoil of the 1680s. **Mary Ann Lyons**

Eighteenth to twenty-first centuries. A number of communities of women—Dominicans, Carmelites, Augustinians, and Poor Clares—survived the PENAL LAWS. The Poor Clares undertook the care of orphans from 1806, though they were enclosed, as were the Ursulines, who taught schoolgirls and were brought to Cork by a wealthy laywoman, NANO NAGLE, in 1771. It was Nagle, however, who founded in 1775 the Sisters of Charitable Instruction of the Sacred Heart of Jesus, later the Sisters of the Presentation—the first of the new active religious orders of women, popularly called nuns, though not properly so, who became a primary element in the transformation of Irish Catholicism. Though the Presentation order adopted solemn vows and enclosure in 1805, the new uncloistered pattern was followed by MARY AIKENHEAD's Irish Sisters of Charity in 1815; by the Loreto Sisters, created in 1820 by FRANCES BALL (on the model of the Mary Ward Sisters); by the Sisters of Mercy, founded by CATHERINE MCAULEY in 1831; and by MARGARET AYLWARD's Sisters of the Holy Faith, established in 1867. These founders were strong-minded women, usually of independent means. Other new orders, like the Brigidines of Kildare and Leighlin (founded 1807), remained local or diocesan. The largest orders were the Mercy and Presentation, and most of the new convents were established in Leinster and Munster, recruiting largely from the sort of middling urban or farming families who furnished vocations to the priesthood. There was also a large nineteenth-century influx into Ireland of modern active orders from England and the Continent, mostly from France, including the Faithful Companions of Jesus, the Sisters of the Sacred Heart, the Sisters of St Joseph of Cluny, La Sainte Union, the Daughters of Charity of St Vincent de Paul, and the Sisters of St Louis. Some of them specialised in particular tasks: the Bon Secours, the Little Company of Mary, and the Little Sisters of the Assumption nursed the sick, the Sisters of the Good Shepherd and of Our Lady of Charity primarily conducted reformatories, and the Sisters of Nazareth and the Little Sisters of the Poor ran homes for the aged and destitute; but it was more common for convents to embrace a wide range of responsibilities. Their work was mainly in the area of poor schools and select schools of the middle and upper classes, and then in HOSPITALS, often in connection with WORKHOUSES, but it also embraced orphanages, the training of teachers, the visitation of the poor and outdoor relief, and the whole machinery of philanthropy, while their particular forms of prayer and devotion in their convents and chapels gave a new dimension to Irish religious life. The Sisters of Charity established the first Catholic hospital, St Vincent's, Dublin, in 1834. A minority of convents, of which the most notable were the Carmelites, maintained or reverted to their original contemplative character, and they also increased in number in the later nineteenth century. From 120 sisters in eighteen houses in six orders in 1800 the membership of the women's orders had grown to 8,000 by 1900, in thirty-five orders with 368 convents. These statistics exclude the larger population of sisters in daughter-houses (and granddaughter-houses) founded from Ireland by Irish emigrants throughout the BRITISH EMPIRE and North America. The institutions inherited from the nineteenth century flourished until the 1960s, but despite attempts at renewal, the decline of the orders since has mirrored a wider weakening of attachment to religion, and of the forms of piety and of distinctive external dress and behaviour as badges of identity that also sustained them. **Sheridan Gilley**

religious orders (male). Though Benedictine, Cistercian, and Canons Regular foundations proliferated in medieval Ireland, it was the friars (Dominicans, FRANCISCANS, Carmelites, and Augustinians) who survived the REFORMATION. The Dominicans, Franciscans (both Observant and Capuchin), and Augustinians established colleges, some with novitiates, at Lisbon, Louvain, Rome, Prague, Capranica, near Viterbo, Bar-sur-Aube, and Boulay in Lorraine. Despite their exile or imprisonment under the Banishment Act (1697), the friars returned to Ireland and flourished, but their numbers and discipline were considered unsatisfactory, and Rome itself decided to limit their recruitment by closing their Irish novitiates in 1751. The controversial Congregation of Canons Regular of St Patrick, established in 1646, failed in its effort to reassert its claims to rights of the medieval Canons Regular of St Augustine. The JESUITS, who, though few in number, had been active in Ireland from the late sixteenth century, ran Irish Colleges in Rome, Poitiers, Tournai, Lisbon, Santiago, Salamanca, and Seville but were formally dissolved in 1773. They were restored in 1814. Their colleges at Clongowes Wood and Tullabeg were founded in 1814 and 1818, respectively, and they conducted University College, Dublin, from 1883. Among the works of the older orders in the nineteenth century deserving a special mention was the temperance crusade of the Cork Capuchin FATHER THEOBALD MATHEW; it was an important part of DANIEL O'CONNELL's campaign for national renewal. The first and largest of the teaching orders of Brothers, the CHRISTIAN BROTHERS, suggested by St John Baptist de la Salle's Brothers of the Christian Schools, was founded by EDMUND RICE in Waterford in 1802. Its schools spread throughout the world wherever the Irish had settled and in Ireland itself had a remarkable influence on the formation of a nationalist political elite. The Patrician Brothers (the Congregation of the Brothers of St Patrick) were founded by Bishop Daniel Delany in Tullow, Co. Carlow, in 1808. The Vincentians, Holy Ghost Fathers, Oblates of Mary Immaculate and Marists from France, Redemptorists from Austria, the Netherlands, and Belgium, and Passionists from England and Italy established large and flourishing houses in Ireland in the nineteenth century. As well as making a heavy investment in EDUCATION the orders were instrumental from the 1840s in the promotion of missions and retreats and the organisation of lay sodalities, confraternities and guilds with a pious or charitable purpose, a special importance attaching to the Jesuit propagation of devotion to the Sacred Heart of Jesus, especially through the *Irish Messenger of the Sacred Heart of Jesus*. The chief contemplative male order, the Cistercians, established the Abbey of Mount Melleray from the mother house of Melleray in Brittany in 1833 and Mount St Joseph, Roscrea, Co. Tipperary, in 1878. **Sheridan Gilley**

Religious Society of Friends: see QUAKERS.

reliquaries, medieval. Relics take the form of parts of the body of a saint, objects associated with a holy person, or objects that have touched relics. Relics of the SAINTS were highly prized in the early Irish church as a focus of devotion and PILGRIMAGE or as a form of validation of the importance of a religious house or of the legitimacy of its claims. Oaths were sworn on relics; they went on circuit when dues were to be collected; and their presence solemnised important political occasions, including battles. The earliest Christian relics in Ireland were those brought by the first missionaries. Armagh, significantly, from early times had relics of SS. Peter and Paul.

The earliest reliquaries may have been simple stone boxes, such as the one found at Dromiskin, Co. Louth. However, the most common seem to have taken the form of small gabled tombs or churches, often covered in, or inlaid with, metal; these are generally known as *house-shaped* shrines. The earliest Irish shrines of this form (there are many Continental correlatives) are the fragmentary seventh-century ones from Clonmore, Co. Armagh, and Bobbio, Italy. There are two complete later examples, also preserved in Italy: in the Civic Museum in Bologna (ninth century) and in the Church of Abbadia San Salvatore in Tuscany (eighth or ninth century). The latter still contains corporeal relics and is remarkably like the Emly Shrine, now in Boston. An insular eighth or ninth-century example from Norway, now in Copenhagen, is also associated with corporeal relics; an inscription on it indicates that a Norse woman called Ranvaik owned it at one time. Fragments of Irish shrines of eighth or ninth-century date are frequently met with in Viking-age graves in Norway.

In Ireland, books associated with saints were also enshrined; the notion probably originated in the Roman liturgical practice of carrying the sacred book for the Mass readings in a metal case. The earliest book reliquary is the eighth or ninth-century example from Lough Kinale, Co. Longford. There is a record of a tenth-century shrine for the Book of DURROW, and in the early eleventh century the Book of KELLS was stolen and later recovered with its metal ornaments torn off (this probably refers to a reliquary rather than a cover). In the eleventh century, shrines were renovated (for the Gospel of St MOLAISE), or made, at Kells (for the CATHACH of COLM CILLE) and at CLONMACNOISE (for the STOWE MISSAL) (see pp. 105, 305). A shrine of silver was made for the Book of DIMMA in the twelfth century.

Reliquaries sometimes took the form of the object enshrined. Perhaps the most famous is the early twelfth-century shrine of ST PATRICK'S BELL. The Shrine of St Lachtín's Arm clearly signalled in its form that it held a relic of the saint's arm. The CROSS OF CONG was made in the early twelfth century to enshrine a portion of the True Cross (see p. 712). Relics were often enshrined under the joint patronage of leading churchmen and kings; from the eleventh century onwards inscriptions record this and often also the names of

reliquaries. Shrine of St Lachtín's Arm *(c. 1120), comprising wood covered with bronze plates with patterns of interlace inlaid with silver and rows of ornate stones. The arm, reputedly of St Lachtín, is preserved in a case of yew inside the shrine. [National Museum of Ireland]* the craftsmen. Many early reliquaries were lost in the Reformation and in the wars of the seventeenth century. Some survived because they were in the possession of hereditary keepers, descendants of once-powerful families that had held quasi-religious office in ancient monasteries. Only one major shrine of the early Irish church is still associated with the home area of the saint whose relics it contains: the twelfth-century Shrine of St Manchán, normally kept in the parish church of Boher, Co. Offaly. [see BOOK SHRINES.] **Michael Ryan**

Remembrance Day. *Terrified victims flee the Provisional IRA bomb that exploded without warning as people gathered at the war memorial in Enniskillen, Co. Fermanagh, on 8 November 1987 for the annual Remembrance Day service, killing eleven people and injuring sixty-three. [Pacemaker]*

Remembrance Day bombing, a PROVISIONAL IRA bombing attack on Sunday 8 November 1987 at the war memorial in ENNISKILLEN, Co. Fermanagh, just before the ceremony was about to begin. The bomb killed eleven people and injured sixty-three. Though clearly aimed at the military and police personnel participating in the service, the choice of venue and occasion was a grievous error of judgment and demonstrated how out of touch the Provisionals were with any opinion beyond that of militant REPUBLICANISM itself. On the same day a second bomb, placed close to the scene of the remembrance ceremony at Tullyhommon, Co. Fermanagh, failed to detonate. The Enniskillen bombing, which the Provisionals admitted was a mistake, was widely condemned in Britain and the Republic, where the Taoiseach, CHARLES HAUGHEY, expressed his 'anger and revulsion.' Temporarily, at least, the attack undermined republican support in the area; at the next council elections SINN FÉIN lost four of its eight seats in Co. Fermanagh. An appeal fund to help the victims raised over £600,000, some of which was put towards a 'Spirit of Enniskillen' bursary, which supports cross-community work among young people. [see WILSON, GORDON.] **Keith Jeffery**

'Remonstrance of the Irish Princes' (1317), a letter to Pope John XXII from Dónal O'Neill, King of CENÉL NEOGHAIN, probably in 1317 during Edward Bruce's invasion of Ireland. O'Neill, claiming to act on behalf of the under-kings, magnates and people of Ireland, lists a series of grievances against the English colonists, whom he accuses of having disregarded the conditions of the bull LAUDABILITER, a copy of which he encloses. He recounts a series of well-known crimes and injustices committed by the colonists against the Irish in an attempt to vindicate the transfer of Ireland from English control to the lordship of Edward Bruce. He hoped to counter English diplomatic lobbying at the Papal curia and gain Papal sanction for the invasion. While the document recounts the specific sentiments of O'Neill and his allies, it nonetheless provides an invaluable understanding of later medieval Irish national consciousness. It survives only in a Scottish manuscript. **Susan Foran**

Renehan, Laurence J. (1798–1857), priest and historian. His research interest lay in music and Irish ecclesiastical history, and he spent holidays travelling in Europe copying manuscripts. He was president of ST PATRICK'S COLLEGE, Maynooth, 1845. He was the author of *Grammar of Gregorian and Modern Music* (edited by Richard Hackett, 1865), regarded as a significant contribution to church music reform in Ireland before the founding of the Irish Society of St Cecilia in 1878, and he also published *A Choir Manual of Sacred Music, A Requiem Office Book, A History of Music* (edited by Daniel McCarthy, 1858), and *Collections on Irish Church History* (two volumes, edited by Daniel McCarthy, 1861, 1873). **Deborah Kelleher**

Rennie, John (1761–1821), civil engineer. Born in Prestonkirk, East Lothian; educated at the University of Edinburgh. He was first a millwright and then a civil engineer, building bridges, CANALS, docks, and HARBOURS. He was consulted on the ROYAL CANAL, engaged on the CUSTOM HOUSE Dock, Dublin, 1815–21, and engineer for HOWTH HARBOUR, 1809–19, and DÚN LAOGHAIRE HARBOUR, 1817–21. **Ronald Cox**

Renouf, Louis Percy Watt (1887–1968), marine zoologist. Born in Birmingham; educated at the University of Cambridge. On being appointed professor of biology at University College, Cork, in 1922, he visited LOUGH HYNE, near Skibbereen, Co. Cork, and was entranced by the lough's rich FAUNA. He established the first field laboratory there in 1928 and impressed numerous visiting groups with the potential of the site, including J. A. KITCHING and F. J. EBLING, who made Lough Hyne famous for marine ecology. Ireland's only marine nature reserve, Lough Hyne contains 60 per cent of the recorded marine flora of Ireland and Britain, along with a variety of fauna, including goby, three-spined stickleback, clingfish, and blenny. **Trevor Norton**

Renunciation Act (1783), a British act that acknowledged the exclusive rights of the Irish Parliament and courts to create and administer the law in Ireland. It underlined the intention of the repeal of the DECLARATORY ACT and enabled its principal sponsor in Ireland, HENRY FLOOD, to achieve a new public and political standing. **Neal Garnham**

Repeal movement. Though many opposed the ACT OF UNION (1800) from its inception, it was not until the 1830s that a campaign was begun to rescind it and to restore a version of the Irish Parliament. DANIEL O'CONNELL founded the Precursor Society in 1838 with Repeal as its ultimate objective, followed in 1840 by the Loyal National Repeal Association, whose structure resembled that of the CATHOLIC ASSOCIATION and featured a 'Repeal rent', modelled on the successful 'CATHOLIC RENT'. Members were linked through their local officers to the central committee in Dublin. O'Connell proclaimed 1843 'Repeal year', which would see self-government established, and through more than thirty 'monster meetings' around the three southern provinces sought to show that Repeal enjoyed overwhelming popular support and could not be refused. Whereas British politicians had earlier bowed to pressure tactics over the issue of CATHOLIC EMANCIPATION, there was no willingness to do so with Repeal, a proposal that seemed to jeopardise the existence of the United Kingdom. The British government banned a meeting at Clontarf, Dublin, in October and arrested O'Connell and a group of colleagues on a charge of conspiracy. Following their conviction and imprisonment in 1844 they tried to revive the Repeal campaign, but without success. **Gary Owens**

republicanism. Irish republicanism in the twentieth century was the heir to an insurrectionary tradition that included the UNITED IRISHMEN of the 1790s, the YOUNG IRELAND movement of the 1840s, the FENIANS in the 1860s, and the IRISH REPUBLICAN BROTHERHOOD, which planned the 1916 RISING. The PARTITION of Ireland in 1920–21 created the context for successive splinterings of the movement, beginning with the CIVIL WAR.

ÉAMON DE VALERA left the anti-Treaty SINN FÉIN in 1926 to found FIANNA FÁIL and entered Dáil Éireann in 1927. Embracing a majoritarian strategy and a socio-economic programme based on self-reliance and PROTECTIONISM, Fianna Fáil became the dominant political party of the Irish state. Dissident republicans coalesced around an IRA Army Council, claiming a mandate from the second DÁIL (1919). They were committed to a physical-force strategy to end partition and a policy of abstaining from the two parliaments in Ireland. Periodic military activities proved completely ineffectual, such as the bombing campaign in England, 1939–40, and the abortive 'BORDER CAMPAIGN', 1956–62. However, republicans maintained a marginalised culture of resistance based on prison experiences, commemorations, and conflict with army and police. Attempts to broaden republican strategy in a socialist direction failed to win wider democratic support in the 1930s and again in the 1960s, though republicans played an active role in the CIVIL RIGHTS MOVEMENT in Northern Ireland.

The outbreak of the conflict in Northern Ireland in 1969 was to revitalise and popularise the republican movement among Northern nationalists. It split again with the emergence of the PROVISIONAL IRA as a communal defence force in 1971; thereafter it went on the offensive, engaging in a prolonged three-cornered conflict with the British government and loyalists lasting almost thirty years. In the wake of the HUNGER STRIKES, Sinn Féin began to develop a significant political strategy in Northern nationalist communities alongside the military campaign. With the BELFAST AGREEMENT (1998) it has entered parliamentary politics in both jurisdictions and has asserted its commitment to 'taking the gun out of Irish politics.' Dissident groups, such as Republican Sinn Féin, the Continuity IRA, and the 'Real IRA', retain little support but continue to give priority to armed struggle as a means of achieving Irish reunification.

Critics of Irish republicanism emphasise its history of political failure, its tendency to split, its elitist and militarist aspects, and its quasi-theological preoccupation with the abstraction of 'the Republic'. The Northern Ireland conflict revitalised the historical debate over the role of armed struggle and political violence. This debate has not only emphasised divisions between CONSTITUTIONAL NATIONALISM and republicanism but has spawned intense disagreement over the nature and continuity of the Irish republican tradition itself. The negotiation of the Belfast Agreement was facilitated by the re-creation of an uneasy coalition between various strands of nationalism and republicanism in response to a changing political situation. In the wake of the agreement, Sinn Féin has become an important participant in mainstream electoral politics in both parts of Ireland.

Republicans have proved highly successful at mobilising urban working-class and rural support in Catholic communities in Northern Ireland; yet they face many difficult strategic choices in

republicanism. *Title page of* The Soldier's Song, *written by Peadar Kearney in 1907. It officially became the anthem of the Irish Free State in July 1926. [Council of Trustees of the National Library of Ireland; LOP 203]*

consolidating political accommodation in Northern Ireland and in transcending the divisive legacy of the conflict and communalist politics. Advocates of the republican ideal generally face even greater challenges, as well as opportunities, arising from globalisation and the emergence of transnational entities such as the EUROPEAN UNION. Republicanism in the twenty-first century will have to re-address the question of what self-determination means, as well as the appropriate territorial parameters of democratic politics in the face of transnational corporations and bureaucracies, which give priority to market rights over citizenship rights. **Liam O'Dowd**

republican and 'rebel' song. Ireland's colonial history has ensured the politicisation of its culture, including music and song. From the seventeenth century, bards, pipers, musical instruments, broadside ballad printers, singers, and song-writers have been intermittently subject to legal sanction; the Special Powers Act (1922), among other things, prohibited gramophone records. Historical and social context radically transform the meaning of a song. In the middle of the twentieth century 'The Wind that Shakes the Barley' (about the 1798 rising) or 'Kevin Barry' (about the young medical student hanged during the War of Independence) might function in the South as a nostalgic fireside song whereas in the North it would be a song of resistance.

From the end of the eighteenth century an organically developing canon of republican and rebel songs told a history of Ireland's struggle against English oppression. Included are songs of solidarity among volunteers, of the atrocities of the enemy, of campaigns to release or improve the conditions of prisoners, of great, often humorously told escapes; but the core of the tradition is the 'hero-martyr

republican and 'rebel' song. *'Hero-martyr ballad' commemorating the execution of two of the Phoenix Park Murderers (1882); the illustration was re-used from other ballad-sheets. [Courtesy Kilmainham Gaol Museum]*

ballad'. These remember named individuals who died for the cause: croppies, freedom-fighters, volunteers, leaders, or—subverting the enemy's language—'felons' and 'unrepentant Fenians'. The 'memory of the dead' serves as an example for those who live on and for future generations 'to follow their footsteps.' The songs are at once historical and contemporary, conflating past and present rebellion, heroes, and enemies. The roll of honour in song links the deceased volunteer by name to predecessors over centuries of struggle, predominantly the RISINGS OF 1798 AND 1916.

Continuity is maintained in the face of change—stylistic, political, and cultural. Versions of songs first appearing as late eighteenth and nineteenth-century broadside ballads and in the NATION endure in songbooks, recordings, and performances of the twentieth century. Devotional Catholic imagery enters, and leaves, the tradition in the course of the twentieth century. Developments beginning to emerge in the rebel song tradition during the protracted 'TROUBLES' in Northern Ireland, and especially since the HUNGER STRIKES, include a recognition of women's role in REPUBLICANISM and an acknowledgment of past omissions; evidence of class-consciousness and a concern for economic conditions as an impetus to action; an international dimension, placing Ireland's struggle in the context of other resistance movements; and a shift away from the formulaically brave, unquestioning subject to one who is more reflective and emotionally vulnerable.

At the present time, for many republicans the music that expresses their politicised culture is Irish TRADITIONAL MUSIC. Overt political expression is as likely to be in songs of more mainstream culture, such as those of CHRISTY MOORE, DOLORES KEANE, the North American Hiphop Band, Seanchaí, Bob Marley, and Peter Tosh. **May McCann**

Republic of Ireland: see IRELAND, REPUBLIC OF.

Reserve Defence Force. The DEFENCE FORCES have a First-Line and Second-Line Reserve. The First Line consists of former regular officers and enlisted personnel who are placed on the reserve for specific periods after they leave the Defence Forces. Members of the First-Line Reserve are liable to be called up as required. In recent years, however, no members of the First-Line Reserve have been called up, and the reserve function is to all intents and purposes carried out by the Second-Line Reserve, which comprises two organisations, the FCA (army reserve) and AN SLUA MUIRÍ (Naval Service reserve). **Paul Connors**

Restoration. In 1660 CHARLES II was restored to the English throne. The most important development of his reign was the fusion of the older Protestant settlers and the Cromwellian planters in Ireland into a new and all-powerful Ascendancy landed class. This united front, together with the threat of armed revolt by more radical elements, ensured that no significant restoration of Catholic land could be implemented. The exclusively Protestant Parliament, elected on the Cromwellian electoral franchise, successfully limited the attempt, through the Court of Claims, to restore innocent Catholics. Their share of land was reduced by two-thirds from what it had been in 1641. In general the period was one of tacit religious toleration, with no attempt to enforce conformity to the restored established church. Suspicion of Dissenters remained, however, and the 'Popish Plot' scare led to the execution of the Catholic Primate, OLIVER PLUNKETT, in 1681. Trade restrictions introduced by the English Parliament damaged the economy, and the administration remained chronically short of money. [see ANGLO-IRISH SOCIETY; PROTESTANT ASCENDANCY.] **Liam Irwin**

Revenue Commissioners, the state agency responsible for the administration of the Customs and Excise regime as well as smaller *quit rent* and forfeiture offices. First appointed in the seventeenth century, the commission consisted of seven members until 1789, when nine commissioners were named. The commissioners—who administered a large number of government employees—were the subject of parliamentary inquiries in 1758, 1783, and 1795. In the nineteenth century the Irish customs and excise service was amalgamated with that of the United Kingdom. Following PARTITION, the Revenue Commissioners retained responsibility for customs and excise. They also administer the taxation system. **K. J. James**

Reynolds, Albert (1932–), businessman and politician. Born in Co. Sligo; educated at Summerhill. An energetic businessman, he was involved in dance halls, newspapers, a cinema, and pet foods. He became FIANNA FÁIL TD for Longford in 1977 and supported CHARLES HAUGHEY for the leadership in 1979. Afterwards he became Minister for Posts and Telegraphs, then Minister for Transport and Power. On Fianna Fáil's returning to power in 1987 he became Minister for Industry and Commerce, and was Minister for Finance, 1988–91. He replaced Haughey as party leader and TAOISEACH in 1992. He presided uneasily over the Coalition Government of Fianna Fáil and the PROGRESSIVE DEMOCRATS, and relationships deteriorated over the revelations of the 'Beef Tribunal', at which he and DESMOND O'MALLEY gave contradictory testimony. The coalition broke up and in 1993 Fianna Fáil lost nine seats, many to the LABOUR PARTY. A new coalition, of Fianna Fáil and the Labour Party, was formed. Reynolds was heavily involved in efforts to end the violence in Northern Ireland, and the 'DOWNING STREET DECLARATION' was agreed in 1993, with an IRA ceasefire following in 1994. Reynolds was then forced to resign over the BRENDAN SMYTH extradition case and the appointment of Harry Whelehan to the Presidency of the High Court—a bizarre end to a short but effective tenure as Taoiseach. **Tom Garvin**

Reynolds, James Emerson (1844–1920), chemist. Born in Booterstown, Co. Dublin. He set up his own small chemistry laboratory, and his first paper was published when he was only seventeen. He was awarded a licentiate in medicine by the Royal College of Physicians and Surgeons, Edinburgh, 1865, but decided to devote himself to chemistry. He was appointed Keeper of Minerals at the NATIONAL MUSEUM, 1867. Subsequent appointments included professorships of chemistry at the ROYAL DUBLIN SOCIETY, Royal College of Surgeons, and TRINITY COLLEGE, Dublin, and also Public Analyst. Resigning from Trinity College in 1903, he worked at the Royal Institution, London, and was a vice-president of the Royal Society. **Susan McKenna-Lawlor**

Reynolds, Osborne (1842–1912), scientist and engineer. Born in Belfast, where his father was principal of Belfast Collegiate School; educated at the University of Cambridge. At the age of twenty-six, he was appointed to the chair of engineering at Owens College (later Victoria University), Manchester. He tackled some of the principal practical engineering issues of his time but also studied the scientific principles underlying engineering processes and developed fundamental theories to explain them. As a result his work is still relevant to many areas of scientific and engineering investigation; for example, a critical value of the Reynolds number identifies the transition from regular to turbulent fluid flow. **P. Frank Hodnett**

RHA: see ROYAL HIBERNIAN ACADEMY OF ARTS.

Rhind, Ethel Mary (c. 1879–1952), designer and opus sectile and stained-glass artist. Born in Bengal; educated at Derry High School and trained at the Metropolitan School of Art, Dublin. In 1908 she joined AN TÚR GLOINE, the stained-glass co-operative, on the strength of her opus sectile mosaic work. She was unique in Ireland in producing notable work of fine design in this medium in a specifically Celtic Revivalist idiom such as at St Brendan's Cathedral, Loughrea (1929–33), and St Enda's, Spiddle, Co. Galway (1918–28). Two of her tapestry designs, *A Viking Ship* and *Smuainteach*, were woven at the DUN EMER GUILD. **Nicola Gordon Bowe**

RIA: see ROYAL IRISH ACADEMY.

Ribbonmen, a later name for the DEFENDERS in the nineteenth century. A secret and oath-bound Catholic organisation, it was strongest in the 'linen triangle' of south-central Ulster but also extended to north Leinster, Dublin, and parts of Connacht and to Irish communities in Britain. Ribbonmen were both revolutionary and sectarian and—like many English industrial workers at the time—strongly influenced by millennial prophecies, especially those of Pastorini, the pseudonym of an eighteenth-century Catholic bishop, Charles Walmesley, who foretold, in his *General History of the Christian Church* (1771), the violent destruction of Protestant churches in 1825. Cheap editions of Pastorini circulated freely as the year of doom approached; when it passed quietly, 1844 was fixed as the new date on which the 'locusts from the bottomless pit' (the Protestants) would meet their end. One Ulster Ribbon oath included these words: 'I will Aid and Support Our holy Religion by Destroying the Heriticks and as far as my power & property will Go not one Shall be excepted …' The defeat of some 400 Ribbonmen in Co. Derry on 26 July 1813 was celebrated in the ORANGE ballad 'The Battle of Garvagh'. The British government tended to blame Ribbonism for much unexplained crime in the first half of the century. **Jonathan Bardon**

Rice, Edmund. *New Street, Waterford, where Edmund Rice established his first school for boys in 1802, as photographed by Father Browne, SJ. [Irish Picture Library, Father Browne Collection]*

Rice, Edmund Ignatius (1762–1844), educator, founder of the Irish CHRISTIAN BROTHERS and Presentation Brothers. Born in Callan, Co. Kilkenny. He amassed a fortune in trade in Waterford, but following the death of his wife in 1789 he became increasingly involved in pious and charitable pursuits. Following the example of NANO NAGLE, he established a religious community of laymen dedicated to teaching poor boys. Collaborating with O'CONNELL, FATHER THEOBALD MATHEW, and CHARLES BIANCONI, he was a central figure in the modernisation of Irish society. He was beatified by Pope John Paul II in 1996. **Daire Keogh**

Rice, Peter (1935–1992), structural engineer. Born in Dundalk; educated at QUB and Imperial College, London. He joined Ove Arup and was resident engineer on the Sydney Opera House. His structural engineering commissions included the Pompidou Centre in Paris, the Houston Art Museum, Bari Stadium, and Kansai Airport terminal. He was an innovator, designer, and mathematician, interested in the use of materials and the exploration of new techniques and combinations in his structures. **Ronald Cox**

Richard II (1367–1400), King of England; grandson of Edward III and son of Edward, Prince of Wales. After securing a truce with France, he turned his attention to Ireland and mounted the largest expedition to reach Irish shores in the Middle Ages. He landed in Waterford in October 1394 and secured the submission of Irish chiefs throughout the country. His tenuous hold over power in England forced him home in 1395, and his settlement for Ireland foundered with the failure of the ANGLO-NORMAN colony to enact the reforms he had initiated. With the death of John of Gaunt in 1399, on 1 June he once again landed in Waterford, with a smaller army, but this time failed to secure submissions from the Leinster Irish. His expedition was cut short by the revolt of the future Henry IV, forcing Richard to return home, where he was deposed. **Susan Foran**

Richard, Duke of York (1411–1460), claimant to the English throne through his descent on both sides from Edward III (through Lionel, Duke of Clarence, and Edmund, Duke of York) and the most powerful landowner in England. Heir-presumptive to the throne, 1447–53, in 1415 he succeeded his uncle Edward as Duke of York and in 1425 inherited his Irish lordships of Ulster, Connacht, Trim, and Leix. He was Governor of France and Normandy, 1436–7 and 1440–45. In 1447 he was appointed Lieutenant of Ireland, a post he held for most of his remaining life. He arrived at Howth in July 1449, securing submissions from Irish chiefs. He won widespread popularity among the Yorkist-dominated ANGLO-NORMAN government and in August 1450 returned to England to face the political crisis that had erupted. In England he was engaged in disputes with the Lancastrian faction in what was to become known as the Wars of the Roses.

He returned to Ireland in 1459 as a fugitive from the Lancastrian victory at the Battle of Ludford Bridge. The English parliament of November 1459 attainted him of treason, stripping him of all his offices and lands; but at a parliament at Drogheda in 1460 he was confirmed as Lieutenant and protected from English jurisdiction by the declaration of 1460, which made it a treasonable offence for anyone to challenge his authority. From his Irish sanctuary he prepared his return to England, where he was killed in battle at Wakefield, Yorkshire, on 30 December 1460. **Susan Foran**

Richard family (fl. eighteenth century), a dynasty of French gardeners and botanists of Irish origin. Claude Richard I went to France as a refugee after the BATTLE OF THE BOYNE. His son Claude Richard II (1705–1784) assembled and acclimatised many rare plants collected from overseas exploration; c. 1750 he was appointed Jardinier-Fleuriste du Roy and given the brief to create a new flower garden at the Trianon, Versailles. He was the first in France to cultivate species requiring particularly light acid soil, such as rhododendrons. Claude's son Antoine Richard (1735–1807) was appointed Jardinier-Botaniste at the Trianon in 1767; it was he who planted it, incorporating a collection of exotic species acclimatised successfully by his father and himself. [see GARDEN DESIGN.] **John Joe Costin**

Richards, Shelah (1903–1985), actor and producer. Born in Dublin; educated at Alexandra College. She joined the ABBEY THEATRE in 1924, where she played Rosie Redmond in the premiere of O'CASEY's *The Plough and the Stars*. She formed her own production company at the OLYMPIA THEATRE. In 1962 she joined RTÉ television as a drama producer. **Christopher Morash**

Richmond Hospital, popular name for a group of state-financed hospitals connected with the Dublin House of Industry, founded in 1773. By 1813 there were four units: fever (the Hardwicke), surgical (the Richmond), acute and chronic (the Whitworth), and insane asylum, together with an associated medical school, all in or near North Brunswick Street, Dublin. Innovations include the first Irish operation under full anaesthetic in 1847. Many great names of Dublin medicine learnt or practised in the hospitals, notably WILLIAM STOKES and Sir DOMINIC CORRIGAN. In 1987 the Richmond became part of the new Beaumont Hospital. **Tony Farmar**

riddles (Irish *tomhais*), though not universal, are popular in many societies and foster certain modes of thinking. Those in Ireland fit into the general European tradition, where the question is often formulaic and the answer usually one word ('Patch upon patch without any stitches, riddle me that and I'll buy you some breeches.'—'A cabbage'). Generally an everyday item—an egg, smoke, tongs, a cow—is described in an ambiguous or fanciful way, with puns, rhythm, rhyme, and other stylistic devices (*'Tháinig éan gan chleite faoi bhéal leice, tháinig éan gan bhéal agus d'ith sé éan gan chleite.'—'Tonn.'* ('A featherless bird came under a stone, a mouthless bird came and ate the featherless bird.'—'A wave.')

Riddles need the active participation of more than one person but no particular skill, other than cultural insight. Within set rules they challenge and often deliberately confuse ('Londonderry, Cork, and Kerry, spell that without a k.'—'T, h, a, t!').

A few FOLK-TALES and narrative songs hinge on riddles, where overcoming such mental barriers is often linked to successful courtship. Some riddles are transparently related to PROVERBS ('Why does a dog turn around twice before he lies down?'—'Because one good turn deserves another!'), and many employ proverbial similes, for example *'chomh hard leis an spéir'* ('as high as the sky') and 'as black as ink.'

Though essentially transmitted orally, riddles have existed in Ireland for centuries. Posing riddles was once part of an evening's entertainment; sometimes this became a contest. In Irish-speaking districts, riddling contests were held well into the twentieth century. While the use of riddles as adult entertainment has dwindled (though it is not dead), a sub-genre, the joking riddle, connected with conflict and trauma, is now prolific. Such topical riddles can act as a safety valve and are obviously short-lived.

Conventional riddles ('What goes up the chimney down but can't go down the chimney up?'—'An umbrella') remain popular with children, who at a critical age are attracted to word-play. Among children particularly they often go in cycles and spread rapidly into various languages, like the 'elephant' cycle that began in the 1950s ('How do you get four elephants into a Mini?'—'Two in the front and two in the back!'). Older children exchange graphic riddles, where an object is sketched from an unusual angle.

Trick riddles, or anti-riddles, where the answer can never be guessed, are relatively new, as are alternative answers for classic riddles. In addition to word of mouth, riddles are nowadays circulated in Christmas crackers. Though many riddles in the past had international connections, the internet is now an additional means whereby riddles are communicated globally, and this is having a strong effect on the repertoire in Ireland.

The Department of Irish Folklore, UCD, holds a massive collection of riddles; since much of this collection was carried out by children, obscene and suggestive riddles—a significant type among some adults—are probably under-represented. **Fionnuala Carson Williams**

Rightboys, a movement mainly dedicated to reducing TITHE payments, originating in Cork in 1785; by 1787 it had spread throughout Munster and into Leinster. Its assemblies prevented the collection of tithes and also threatened LANDLORDS and clergy. Those sworn in were mostly Catholics, but there was some support from local gentry, especially for tithe reform. The movement was eventually ended by the new powers of the Police Act (1787) but raised questions about the position of the CHURCH OF IRELAND. **Eoin Magennis**

Ring, Christy (1920–1979), hurler. Born in Cloyne, Co. Cork. Playing with Cloyne and later with Glen Rovers, he was a fierce competitor. He was not a big man, but worked extremely hard to build up his strength and became a very powerful player with wonderful skills. He scored some spectacular goals and was still playing at a high level at the age of forty-seven. In a quite extraordinary career with Cork that began when he was nineteen, he won eight all-Ireland medals, four National League medals, and an exceptional total of eighteen inter-provincial championships with Munster. He later became a respected coach. Few will argue with the contention that he was the greatest hurler of all time. **Donal Keenan**

ring-forts, the physical remains of protected farmsteads of the Early Historic Period, consisting of a roughly circular space surrounded by a bank and outer fosse or simply by a rampart of stone. They are also known by the terms *ráth*, *dún*, *lios*, rath, and fort; stone examples are called cashel (*caiseal*) or caher (*cathair*). They are the commonest type of archaeological monument in Ireland, with more than 45,000 known examples.

Ring-forts were constructed mainly during the seventh, eighth and ninth centuries AD—a narrow date range disputed by some. In many instances excavation has revealed a complex and prolonged sequence of occupation at each site, commonly with a circular house and additional out-buildings consistent with the needs of a single-family farming unit and their retainers. From their dispersed distribution and the predominantly rural nature of Early Historic society it is accepted that ring-forts represent the Irish version of a common European settlement pattern known as *einzelhöfe* (dispersed individual farmsteads). Despite some evidence for tillage and manufacturing within excavated sites, ring-fort dwellers were principally cattle farmers, and dairying was their chief economic pursuit. In addition, the number of cows held by each person was an important determinant of their status. Ring-forts were not built to resist the lightning CATTLE-RAIDS that were endemic during the Early Historic Period in Ireland.

The enclosed space or living area of ring-forts is on average 33 m (110 ft) in diameter, with diameters of 20–44 m (65–145 ft) accounting for the great majority of sites. Cashels, or stone-built ring-forts, tend to be smaller than earthen ones. Some examples, called *platform ring-forts*, have their interior raised above the level of the surrounding countryside. A ring-fort's entrance usually consisted of an undug causeway across the fosse leading to a gap in the banks, protected by a gate, while platform sites had a ramped entrance. The entrance was usually in the east or south-east portion of the ring-fort, regardless of the aspect of the site. Ring-forts are usually enclosed and defended by a single bank; these *univallate* ring-forts account for more than 80 per cent of sites in most areas. Because the contemporary law tracts describe a king's principal dwelling as a large univallate ring-fort, some notion is obtained of the lofty status of *bivallate* and (extremely rare) *trivallate* sites. These *multivallate* sites, which tend not to have a larger living area than univallate examples, constitute about 20 per cent of the ring-forts in many areas. This is itself evidence for a consistent and widespread settlement hierarchy, which must mirror a similar social stratification.

The mean density of ring-forts in Ireland is 0.55 per square kilometre. The regions of highest density are north Munster, east Connacht, north-west Leinster, and east Ulster. Areas of very high density are centred on Sligo Bay, the BURREN (Co. Clare), central Co. Limerick, and east of LOUGH NEAGH. Areas of low density are north-west Ulster, most of central and south Leinster, and the western extremities of Cos. Donegal, Mayo, and Galway. Ring-forts are not evenly spread across the landscape, even where conditions permitted. In areas of mean density, a single square kilometre containing four ring-forts is not unusual; in areas of high density, groups of up to nine ring-forts are known.

Ring-forts are not found in areas that cannot support farming communities; but throughout most of Ireland where ring-forts are found they usually display a preference for sloping or hilly terrain. The builders took advantage of even the slightest undulation in the local landscape to provide a sloping site for their farmsteads. In choosing such a site they avoided the heaviest lowland clays, improved drainage, and enhanced the view available. Meeting, as they did, the needs of a cattle-rearing population, ring-forts were sited in areas of good-quality SOIL and so have a distribution broadly similar to contemporary dispersed farming patterns.

Ring-forts and ecclesiastical sites display a complementary distribution. At a small scale this is reflected in the upland-lowland settlement dichotomy demonstrated by the high density of ecclesiastical enclosures throughout the midlands, where ring-forts are uncommon. At a larger scale, church sites are often shown to be at the margins of a ring-fort grouping. Similarly, ring-forts were not closely linked to arteries of communication, as were church sites.

In areas where ring-fort morphology has been examined in relation to topography and other locational factors, the distribution pattern suggests one roughly similar settlement model. Within environmentally favoured areas this model provides a four-fold classification of ring-forts and the likely status of the individual that would have inhabited each site. High-status bivallate enclosures with a smaller than average interior diameter—approximately 29 m (95 ft)—were the most centrally sited within territories and ring-fort groupings, an attribute of royalty and other high-status individuals in early Irish law. In contrast, large, well-defended ring-forts, approximately 47 m (155 ft) in diameter, often with internal divisions, were consistently established at strategic boundary sites. In early Irish law the lord with lowest status seems to have functioned as a military leader in inter-territorial conflicts; this suggests a peripheral site for such an individual and a link with these larger, strategically sited enclosures. Smaller ring-forts—approximately 28 m (92 ft) in diameter—with slight defences are found throughout Ireland in groupings commonly in association with high-status bivallate ring-forts. The occupants of these small sites clearly lay at the other end of the social scale, and the sources describe younger, landless clients established on land units of 14 ha (35 acres) rented from lordly grades with surplus land. This places the farmsteads of this lowest class of freemen in close proximity to the more prominent members of Early Historic society. Typical univallate ring-forts with average diameters are more evenly spread throughout the countryside. This type of ring-fort is associated with the economically and spatially independent large farmer of 28 ha (70 acres), who is described in early law tracts as holding land in his own right (see pp. 334, 493, 1035). [see EARTHWORKS; HILL-FORTS; MEDIEVAL SETTLEMENTS; SOUTERRAINS.] **Matthew Stout**

Ringsend cars, one-horse public vehicles, peculiar to Dublin, operating in the late eighteenth century between the city centre and what was then the popular sea-bathing resort of Ringsend. Lacking springs and consisting of a seat suspended between the shafts on a leather strap, they were anything but comfortable. They were succeeded by the equally individual 'noddy', so called because of its backward-and-forward oscillating movement. It held two passengers and a driver, or 'noddy boy', who, owing to his position, sat somewhat indelicately almost in the lap of his fares. Both vehicles ran on two wheels. **Bernard Share**

Rinuccini, Gianbattista (1592–1653), Archbishop of Fermo and nuncio to the CONFEDERATION OF KILKENNY. Rinuccini has frequently been blamed for sowing dissent among the Confederate Catholics, but divisions between the clergy and the Supreme Council had already opened up before Rinuccini's mission in Ireland (October 1645 to February 1649). The council had ignored clerical demands in order to conclude a definitive agreement with the king's governor in Ireland, JAMES BUTLER, EARL OF ORMOND, in July 1646. Rinuccini gave leadership to a hitherto unassertive clerical interest in rejecting the treaty and seizing control of the

Confederation. The basis of his formal power and informal influence lay partly in his office as Papal nuncio, partly in the funds he brought from Rome, and not least in his energy and his determination to secure the position of the Catholic Church in Ireland.

His prestige suffered from the military disasters of 1647, and in May 1648 the Supreme Council concluded a truce with MURROUGH O'BRIEN, Lord Inchiquin, parliamentary leader in Munster, who had declared for the royal cause the previous month. Rinuccini, in a re-enactment of his 1646 strategy, excommunicated all those who in any way subscribed to the truce. However, on this occasion a broader section of war-weary Irish Catholic opinion recognised the need for some settlement with the royalists. Rinuccini fled Kilkenny and decided to leave Ireland in October after the Confederate general assembly censured him as a divisive influence. He left in February 1649, a month after the Catholic Confederation was subsumed in a pan-royalist alliance headed by the Duke of Ormond.

Rinuccini's opponents claimed that Pope Innocent X rebuked him on his return to Rome for his second excommunication decree: *'Temerarie te gessisti'* ('You acted rashly'). Apart from this unsubstantiated claim, there is no evidence that Rinuccini's actions were repudiated at Rome. **Pádraig Lenihan**

Riordan, Maurice (1953–), poet. Born in Lisgold, Co. Cork; educated at UCC and McMaster University, Canada. His published collections of verse include *A Word from the Loki* (1995) and *Floods* (2000). His poetry tellingly combines domestic concerns with scientific and mythic perspectives. **Terence Brown**

Rising, 1848, reluctantly led by WILLIAM SMITH O'BRIEN after the British Parliament suspended *habeas corpus* in early July (see p. 705). Failing to obtain support in Kilkenny and Carrick, O'Brien and other YOUNG IRELAND leaders, opposed by the Catholic clergy, struggled for a week to raise insurgents in the north Tipperary triangle of Mullinahone, Killenaule, and Ballingarry. O'Brien's refusal to commandeer food lost support. On 29 July his ill-equipped forces unsuccessfully besieged forty-six well-armed RIC men ensconced with child hostages in a house near Ballingarry. Two insurgents died from police fire. Despite some action elsewhere, the rising was in effect over. **Richard P. Davis**

Rising, 1867, unsuccessful Fenian attempt at a revolution. Following an earlier confused and abortive attempt in February, which was roundly condemned by the Catholic Church, the Fenians staged a rising on the evening of 5 March. Some initial success at Stepaside and Glencullen, Co. Dublin, was soon brought to an end by the police at Tallaght, the result being the arrest in the early hours of 6 March of some 200 Fenians. Sporadic outbreaks in Cos. Cork, Limerick, and Tipperary scarcely amounted to a revolution, and such insurgency as did occur was quickly curtailed by the Crown forces. **Oliver P. Rafferty**

Rising, 1916 (24 April–1 May 1916). As early as the spring of 1915 a secret Military Council within the IRISH REPUBLICAN BROTHERHOOD had planned to mount a rising before the end of the FIRST WORLD WAR. Largely under the leadership of THOMAS CLARKE and SEÁN MAC DIARMADA, it included PATRICK PEARSE, THOMAS MACDONAGH, and JOSEPH PLUNKETT; in January 1916 it succeeded in co-opting JAMES CONNOLLY. The committee infiltrated the leadership of the IRISH VOLUNTEERS without the knowledge of its Chief of Staff, EOIN MACNEILL, who discovered that a rising was to be launched on Easter Sunday, 23 April. MacNeill confronted Pearse but was reassured that the plans included a shipment of arms to arrive from Germany. But when ROGER CASEMENT was captured coming ashore from a German submarine in Co. Kerry on the preceding Friday and the arms ship AUD was discovered by the British and scuttled in Cork Harbour on Sunday, MacNeill sent orders for the cancellation of the rising. Despite this, the Military Council called on its supporters to proceed on the Monday.

Originally planned as a national insurrection, the rising was almost inevitably limited to the Dublin area following the arms debacle and the confusion over orders. On the Monday morning approximately 1,600 Volunteers led by Pearse and some 200 members of the IRISH CITIZEN ARMY led by Connolly took over a number of strategic sites in the city, establishing a headquarters in the GENERAL POST OFFICE in Sackville Street (O'Connell Street). Pearse proclaimed the Irish Republic, declaring the insurgents a PROVISIONAL GOVERNMENT (see p. 897). Despite extensive planning, they failed to capture Dublin Castle or the principal transport sites in the city. It is arguable that the military strategy, largely devised by Plunkett and Connolly, was not intended to sustain a long-term conflict. Vigorous and deadly street fighting could not forestall the inevitable, and by the middle of the week British forces, reinforced from elsewhere in Ireland and equipped with artillery, turned the tide in their favour.

Outside Dublin, other risings failed to materialise, with the exception of minor conflicts in Cos. Meath, Wexford, Cork, and Galway. On Saturday 29 April, Pearse agreed to surrender 'to prevent the further slaughter of Dublin Citizens.' By then the casualties numbered some 500 dead and more than 2,500 wounded. Most of the casualties were civilians. A secret military tribunal court-martialled the leaders of the rising, and fifteen were shot by firing squad between 3 and 12 May: Pearse, MacDonagh, Clarke, Plunkett, Edward Daly, WILLIAM PEARSE, Michael O'Hanrahan, JOHN MACBRIDE, ÉAMONN CEANNT, Michael Mallin, Con Colbert, SEÁN HEUSTON, Thomas Kent, Mac Diarmada, and Connolly. ÉAMON DE VALERA and CONSTANCE MARKIEVICZ, with many others, had their death sentences commuted. Public reaction to the rising moved from initial disapproval to a swing in favour of its intentions following the execution of the leaders. More than 2,000 men and women were imprisoned, but all were released by the summer of 1917. [see PROCLAMATION OF THE IRISH REPUBLIC.] **Seán Farrell Moran**

Ritchie, Jean (1922–), song-collector and traditional singer. Born in Kentucky; she has been widely recorded, and her book *Singing Family of the Cumberlands* (1955) describes her early life and family background. In 1952–3 she received a Fulbright Scholarship to research British and Irish song tradition; this produced some of the earliest recordings of many important Irish singers, and these, together with photographs of the performers by her husband, George Pickow, comprise a valuable record, now housed at the Hardiman Library, NUIG (see pp. 258, 357). **John Moulden**

river and ferry transport. Before a modern road system evolved, rivers provided essential facilities for the movement of both people and goods, though natural hazards and tidal considerations limited traffic until the eighteenth century, when serious attempts were made to improve navigation. In 1715 an act was passed to facilitate the linking of the River LIFFEY, Rye Water, River BOYNE, Murragh River and River Brosna to provide a through route between Dublin and the River SHANNON, but the scheme proved a costly failure. Also, in 1715, the provision of a through navigation on the Shannon between Limerick and Carrick-

Rising of 1916. *Children forage in the rubble of William's Row off Middle Abbey Street, Dublin, after the 1916 Rising, during which 500 people were killed, and over 100 buildings destroyed. Evident is the damage to J. W. Elvery & Co. Ltd, Waterproof Manufacturers. [Getty Images/ Hulton Archive]*

on-Shannon had been authorised, though work did not begin until 1755. The Limerick Steam Navigation Company was established in 1767; responsibility for the still uncompleted waterway changed hands several times thereafter between the Directors-General of Inland Navigation, the OFFICE OF PUBLIC WORKS, and the Shannon Commissioners, with the OPW again the responsible authority from 1846. Passengers in 1840 numbered 18,544, while in 1847 goods traffic, at 121,000 tons, reached its peak, most of it concentrated between Limerick and the GRAND CANAL at Shannon Harbour.

The Inland Steam Navigation Company, formed in 1829, operated services until the involvement of the RAILWAYS on the river put them out of business. Regular passenger services ceased in 1861 but were revived in 1897 by the Shannon Development Company, which operated six steamers between Athlone and Killaloe. The railways encouraged the development of tourist traffic, and circular tours were operated from Dublin that included a river trip from Banagher to Killaloe. Steamer services did not survive the FIRST WORLD WAR, and it was forty years before the Shannon again saw a passenger vessel. Towns on the Shannon Estuary that had been linked to Limerick since 1829 also lost their passenger service in 1914, attempts to revive the traffic in 1922 proving a failure.

Many other waterways were developed for both passenger and goods traffic in the eighteenth and early nineteenth centuries, including the Barrow–Nore–Suir system, the Munster BLACKWATER, the Boyne, and the Bann. The first lake steamer, the *Marchioness of Donegal*, entered service on LOUGH NEAGH in 1821, and when the ULSTER CANAL was completed twenty years later WILLIAM DARGAN brought a wooden paddle steamer through it to LOUGH ERNE, where it operated a passenger service. This was succeeded by others promoted by railway interests. In Cork the Citizens' River Steamers Company operated routes on the harbour from 1844 to 1890, from 1850 in competition with the Cork, Blackrock and Passage Railway, while the British Admiralty ran ferry services from its base at Haulbowline to several points on the mainland.

Minor ferry services operated in the nineteenth century on many rivers and estuaries; in recent times those across the Shannon Estuary, Waterford Harbour, Cork Harbour, and STRANGFORD LOUGH have been developed to carry vehicles. Several islands are served by ferries, that from Galway to Árainn having its origin in a regular steamer service inaugurated in 1891 by the CONGESTED DISTRICTS BOARD. **Bernard Share**

'Riverdance', a dance spectacular that began as a seven-minute interval entertainment in the 1994 EUROVISION SONG CONTEST, directed for RTÉ by Moya Doherty. With BILL WHELAN's music, choral singing by ANUNA, choreography by MICHAEL FLATLEY, and performed by Flatley and Jean Butler, backed by a long line of dancers arranged by Mavis Ascott, it was so successful that Doherty and John McColgan re-created it as a two-hour stage show. 'Riverdance: The Show' opened at the Point Theatre, Dublin, in 1995, travelled to London in 1996, and has since had three separate companies constantly touring the world. **Carolyn Swift**

'Riverdance'. *Created as intermission entertainment during the 1994 Eurovision Song Contest, 'Riverdance' integrated traditional and modern music and dance and became a global commercial success. [Used by kind permission of Abhann Productions Ltd; photograph by Joan Marcus, 2000]*

Rivers, Elizabeth (1903–1964), painter. Born in England; studied at Goldsmiths College, London, before winning a scholarship in 1926 to the Royal Academy schools, where she studied under Sickert. In 1931 she studied with André Lhôte in Paris and the following year was part of Wertheim Gallery's 'Twenties Group'. She lived on the ARAN ISLANDS in the second half of the 1930s, exhibiting at the ROYAL HIBERNIAN ACADEMY; her book *Stranger in Aran* was published in 1946, and in 1952 Waddington Galleries published a portfolio of her wood engravings of life on the islands. During and after the war she lived in London, exhibiting at the New English Art Club and the Royal Academy. Returning to Ireland, she assisted EVIE HONE with designs for STAINED-GLASS windows and in the 1950s exhibited wood carvings, wood engravings, and PAINTINGS. Her painting *Noah's Ark* is in the Irish Museum of Modern Art. [see PRINTS AND PRINTMAKERS.] **Peter Murray**

road engineering. Early plank roads dating from 150 BC, discovered in Corlea and Derraghan bogs, Co. Longford, may be considered engineering works. The trackways linking TARA with the four provinces were of earth and gravel, weaving their way around hills and bogs and through forests, linking the fords on major rivers. By 1700 this network of roads had developed into an 11,000 km (7,000-mile) system that had doubled in length by 1925.

Gravel, found in abundance throughout Ireland, was the predominant road surfacing material until mechanical stone-crushers and steamrollers were introduced at the end of the nineteenth century. Bituminous surfaces were the solution to the problems of dust and mud brought about by motorised vehicles. The appointment of county surveyors in 1834 and the foundation of the Institution of Civil Engineers of Ireland in 1835 brought a scientific approach to road engineering and the classification of roads. Following the traffic census of 1925 the development of the road network accelerated, with designated trunk roads receiving special attention. The first motorway was opened in 1963, between Belfast and Lisburn. The National Roads Authority was established in 1994. By 2000 there were in Ireland approximately 450 vehicles per 1,000 population. **Ronald Cox**

Roberts, Hilda (1901–1982), artist. Born in Dublin into a prosperous QUAKER family; enrolled at the Metropolitan School of Art in 1919, where she studied under PATRICK TUOHY and SEAN KEATING. While a student she illustrated Lorimer's *Persian Tales*, published by Macmillan. After two years at the London Polytechnic she returned to Dublin to study sculpture under OLIVER SHEPPARD. She won two Taylor scholarships and the RDS California Prize in 1925 and spent the following year in Paris. In 1929 and 1931 she exhibited, mainly portraits of friends and Mayo country people, at the Dublin Painters' Gallery. Her most famous portrait, that of GEORGE RUSSELL, was shown in New York in 1930. In 1932 she married Arnold Marsh, a headmaster; thereafter her painting career was largely set aside as she raised a family and taught art at Newtown School, Waterford. **Peter Murray**

Roberts, John (1712–1796), architect and builder. Born in Waterford, son of an architect; he went to London as a young man to 'improve himself' before returning home to the family business. He and his wife, Mary Sautelle, had twenty-four children, of whom two, THOMAS ROBERTS and THOMAS SAUTELLE ROBERTS, became landscape painters. His principal buildings in Waterford are the two cathedrals, CHURCH OF IRELAND (1774) and Catholic (1792), the Town Hall (1783), and the Leper Hospital (1785). Among the domestic works attributed to him are the Gibbsian forecourt of Curraghmore (1750s), Tyrone House, Co. Galway (1779), and Moore Hall, Co. Mayo (1795). His descendants include the architect and public works commissioner Samuel Ussher Roberts (1821–1900) and Field-Marshal Earl Roberts (1832–1914). **Frederick O'Dwyer**

Roberts, Thomas (1748–1778), landscape painter. Born in Waterford, son of the architect JOHN ROBERTS; trained at the DUBLIN SOCIETY Schools from 1763, winning premiums both during his student days and afterwards. On leaving the schools he worked with GEORGE MULLINS, first in Waterford and then in Dublin until 1768. He exhibited at the Society of Artists, 1765–77. The greatest landscape painter of the eighteenth century, he seems often to have painted series of pictures for his aristocratic patrons, which sometimes include the patron's house; but more often he depicts the demesnes, and never cultivated farmland. He includes figures, usually sportsmen—shooting, hunting, or fishing—or farm labourers, and often horses. The landscapes are usually imaginary. More than any other painter he portrayed the moist atmosphere of Ireland, its blue distances, its sudden storms, its rare severe frosts, its lakes, waterfalls, and occasional bursts of sunshine. He painted with a minute technique—his leaves look more like those of a miniature painter—but this does not affect the general composition. In 1775 he was in London painting two landscapes for Sir Watkin Williams Wynn and in 1776 in Bath, where he went for his health, as he did in 1777 to Lisbon, where he died. **Anne Crookshank**

Roberts, Thomas Sautell (c. 1760–1827), artist. Born in Waterford, son of JOHN ROBERTS and a brother of THOMAS ROBERTS, taking the name Thomas on his brother's death; trained in the DUBLIN SOCIETY Schools. He became a landscape painter and finished some of his brother's works but after 1800 developed a more romantic style, his rivers sparkling with his understanding of water. He also painted fine storm scenes. He worked as a watercolourist, producing a series of Irish views, some of which he exhibited in Dublin in 1801. Only a dozen of this series were issued as aquatints. Few oils survive, and none of his horse portraits or his landscapes with architecture. **Anne Crookshank**

Robertson, William (c. 1770–1850), architect and antiquarian. He worked in Kilkenny, practising latterly from a house of his own design, Rose Hill (1830). In 1797 he exhibited drawings of Kilkenny Castle and Kilkenny College at the Royal Academy from a London address. He rebuilt the castle (from 1826), designed a new county jail (1808), and had a country-house practice: Gowran Castle (1816–19) and extensions to Woodstock, Co. Kilkenny (1804), and Gracefield, Co. Laois (1817, after a plan by John Nash). He designed the city jail in Cork (1818–24). He is sometimes confused with his contemporary Daniel Robertson, who also worked in south Leinster. **Frederick O'Dwyer**

Robinson, Andrew (1948–), viola da gamba player, teacher, lutenist, and conductor. Born in Dublin; educated at TCD, and was a student of JOSEPH GROOCOCK, JOHN BECKETT, and José Velasquez. He performs in and directs several period-instrumental groups, including the Dublin Viols, and also tutors at the RIAM and on Orpheon Early Music courses. In 1993 he became the founding director of Maoin Cheoil an Chláir, the traditional and classical music school in Ennis, Co. Clare, where he and his wife, the recorder player Jenny Robinson, spent five years. His setting of Tomi Ungerer's story ZERALDA'S OGRE has been performed by the RTÉ CONCERT ORCHESTRA. **Deborah Kelleher**

Robinson, Joseph (1816–1898), composer, arranger, teacher, and conductor. He founded the Society of Ancient Concerts in 1834 and the Dublin Musical Society in 1876. Closely associated with the RIAM, working there as professor of singing and conductor of the orchestra, he was elected a vice-president in 1893. A prolific composer and arranger, he was described by CHARLES VILLIERS STANFORD as 'both by culture and ability one of the best musicians of our time.' In 1847 he conducted the first performance outside Germany of Mendelssohn's *Antigone*. **Deborah Kelleher**

Robinson, Esmé Stuart (Lennox) (1886–1958), writer. Born in Douglas, Co. Cork. He was closely associated with the ABBEY THEATRE, where he worked as a playwright, manager, and director. He wrote more than twenty plays for the Abbey, including *Patriots* (1912), *The Whiteheaded Boy* (1916), *The Big House* (1926), *The Far-Off Hills* (1928), *Drama at Inish* (1933) and *Church Street* (1934). Regarded as an important playwright though not of the first rank, he was particularly successful at comic portrayals of small-town life. Though his work has generally gone out of fashion (except with amateur groups), *The Whiteheaded Boy* enjoys periodic revivals. **S. E. Wilmer**

Robinson, Mary, née Bourke (1944–), lawyer, human rights activist, and politician. Born in Ballina, Co. Mayo; educated at TCD, KING'S INNS, and Harvard University. A member of Seanad Éireann, 1969–89, she became known for her legal work in many constitutional cases before both Irish and European courts during the 1970s. She became Reid professor of LAW at Trinity at the age of twenty-five. She joined the LABOUR PARTY in 1977 and, despite resigning her membership in 1985 in protest at the ANGLO-IRISH AGREEMENT, she accepted the party's nomination for the presidential election in 1990. The campaign was successful and she became Ireland's first woman President. During her term she actively used the office to support the work of community groups and develop links with the Irish DIASPORA. She resigned from the office of President in September 1997 to take up appointment as United Nations Commissioner for Human Rights, 1997–2002. **Brian Galvin**

Robinson, Thomas (died 1810), artist. Born in Westmorland, some time before 1770; apprenticed to George Romney, then living in London. He used to sign his pictures *T. Robinson of Windermere*. He came to Dublin in 1790 but probably moved to Ulster in the early 1790s, where he was patronised by Bishop Percy of Dromore and painted his *Battle of Ballinahinch* (1798) (see p. 67). He had a large practice painting the northern gentry and such industrialists as William Ritchie, founder of the Belfast shipyards (now in the ULSTER MUSEUM). He was not financially successful, however, and in 1808 returned to Dublin, where he exhibited. **Anne Crookshank**

Robinson, Thomas Romney (1793–1882), astronomer. Born in Dublin; entered TCD in 1805 supported by subscriptions to his book, *Juvenile Poems* (1806), graduating in 1810. Having formed close links with JOHN BRINKLEY, director of DUNSINK OBSERVATORY,

Robinson, Mary. *Mary Robinson at her inauguration as first woman President of Ireland, Dublin Castle, 3 December 1990, surrounded by Government ministers and officials; included are (left to right) the Taoiseach, Charles Haughey, outgoing President Patrick Hillery, the former Taoisigh, Jack Lynch and Garret FitzGerald, and Chief Justice Tom O'Higgins. [Photocall Ireland]*

he made significant contributions to the development of reflecting TELESCOPES through involvement with Lord Rosse's 6-ft telescope at BIRR CASTLE and the Great Southern (Melbourne) Telescope. He compiled a star catalogue, *The Places of 5,345 Stars Observed from 1828 to 1854 at the Armagh Observatory*, for which he received the Gold Medal of the Royal Society. He was the inventor of a well-known wind gauge, the Robinson cup-anemometer. He was also responsible for the act of Parliament that prevented trains passing within 700 yards of Armagh Observatory because of the detrimental effect of the tremors on his telescope measurements. He was summoned to England to prevent similar disturbances at Greenwich Observatory and Oxford Observatory (see p. 24). **John McFarland**

Robinson, Timothy (Tim) (1935–), cartographer and writer. Born in Yorkshire; educated at the University of Cambridge. *Stones of Aran: Pilgrimage* (1985) was a notable contribution to an Irish tradition of island literature; it was followed by *Stones of Aran: Labyrinth* (1995), *Setting Foot in Connemara* (1996), and *My Time in Space* (2001). An essayist of distinction, he combines ecological, scientific, and visionary perspectives in his writings. **Terence Brown**

Robinson, Sir William (c. 1643–1712), architect. Apparently descended from a Yorkshire family. In 1671 he succeeded Captain John Paine as 'surveyor-general of all fortifications, buildings etc. in Ireland.' By 1675 he was also Clerk of the Ordnance and had carried out repairs and works at DUBLIN CASTLE, Phoenix House, and Chapelizod House. Under the patronage of the LORD LIEUTENANT, the Duke of Ormond, he designed the ROYAL HOSPITAL, KILMAINHAM (1680–87), the first classical public building in Dublin. He played a prominent role in the redesign of Dublin Castle after the fire of 1684, though only one range of State Apartments was built during his incumbency. He also designed the infirmary of the ROYAL HOSPITAL (1684), the east window of St Mary's Church (1700), and MARSH'S LIBRARY (1703). He held numerous other official posts, which brought him considerable wealth. Elected to Parliament in 1693, he was briefly jailed a decade later for misrepresenting the national debt. A subsequent scandal in 1706 over the alleged misappropriation of funds for army clothing forced him to move to London, where he died in 1712. Robinson's cashier, Thomas Putland, who seems to have engineered the fraud, subsequently tried to expropriate his estate. **Frederick O'Dwyer**

Robinson, William (1838–1935), garden designer. He trained at the NATIONAL BOTANIC GARDENS in Glasnevin, Dublin. In 1861 he moved to London, where he joined the Royal Botanic Gardens in Regent's Park. From there his life both as a gardener and as a writer was to have an enormous influence on the design of both contemporary and later gardens. The term 'Robinsonian' is used to describe gardens influenced by his ideas. He propounded alternatives to the then formal garden layouts and preached informality, which is still a favoured taste. He encouraged the placing of perfectly hardy exotic plants where they could thrive or grow without further care and also encouraged the mimicking of nature, with bulbs planted in grass or mixed borders of native and exotic plants, shrubs, and perennials. **John Joe Costin**

Robinson Keefe Devane, architects, established in Dublin in 1880 by J. L. Robinson (1847–1894) and directed by subsequent generations of the Robinson and Browne families, becoming Robinson Keefe Devane in 1958 with the participation of ANDREW DEVANE. Notable work includes Dún Laoghaire Town Hall

(1890–95, extended by MCCULLOUGH MULVIN and Robinson Keefe Devane, 1996), Dublin Gas Company offices, D'Olier Street, Dublin (1928), and the College of Catering, Cathal Brugha Street, Dublin (1936), noted for its geometrical detailing and massing. Their work in the middle of the twentieth century included many churches, such as Corpus Christi, Griffith Avenue, Dublin, and Galway Cathedral (1957–65), designed by John J. Robinson. Other work includes the elegant raised office building for P. J. Carroll Ltd at Grand Parade, Dublin (1962–4), designed by P. J. Robinson, the Guinness Storehouse, Dublin (with Imagination, London), and the *Irish Independent* printing works (see p. 515), Citywest industrial estate, Co. Dublin (designed by David Browne). **Raymund Ryan**

Roche, Adrienne (Adi) (1955–), anti-nuclear campaigner. Born in Clonmel, Co. Tipperary. She became active in the anti-nuclear movement in 1978 and in 1986 left her job with Aer Lingus to take up full-time work with the Campaign for Nuclear Disarmament. She initiated the Chernobyl Children's Project in 1990 to help children suffering from the radioactive fall-out that followed the explosion in the Chernobyl nuclear reactor, Belarus, in 1986. The project has brought hundreds of children to Ireland for medical treatment and recuperation; it also provided supplies and general humanitarian aid to hospitals and orphanages in the contaminated areas of Belarus and western Russia. Her book *Children of Chernobyl* (1996) was a best-seller, and she was declared European Person of the Year, 1996. She unsuccessfully contested the presidential election of 1997. **Ciarán Deane**

Roche, Anthony (1951–), academic and critic. Born in Dublin; educated at TCD and the University of California. He has taught in the United States and since 1990 at UCD, where he is chairman of the Department of Drama Studies and edited *Irish University Review*, 1998–2003. His exceptional appreciation of Irish drama is evident in *Contemporary Irish Drama from Beckett to McGuinness* (1994). He also served as chairman of the Irish Writers' Union, 1993–4. **Richard Pine**

Roche, Billy (1949–), playwright, actor, director, and screen-writer. Born in Wexford. His first success was with his novel *Tumbling Down* (1986); this was followed by three plays that came to be known as the 'Wexford Trilogy' presented in London, comprising *A Handful of Stars* (1988), *Poor Beast in the Rain* (1989), and *The Belfry* (1991). These were followed by *Amphibians* (1992), *Cavalcaders* (1993), and *On Such as We* (2001). He also wrote the screenplay for *Trojan Eddie* (1995). Roche's urban consciousness is heavily influenced by popular music as well as the structures and rhythms of myth and legend. **Eamonn Jordan**

Roche, Sir Boyle (1743–1807), soldier and politician. Born in Dublin to a prosperous family of Norman extraction. He joined the British army at an early age and served in the American War, distinguishing himself at the capture of Moro Fort, Havana. He returned to Ireland and entered Parliament, where he represented Gowran, Co. Kilkenny, 1777–83, Portarlington, Co. Laois, 1783–90, Tralee, Co. Kerry, 1790–97, and Old Leighlin, Co. Carlow, 1798–1800. An opponent of CATHOLIC EMANCIPATION and a supporter of the ACT OF UNION, he was celebrated for the many 'bulls' in his parliamentary speeches. On one occasion he announced that 'the cup of Ireland's misery has been overflowing for centuries and is not yet half full.' On another occasion he asked 'why we should do anything for posterity, for what has posterity ever done for us?' His main political achievement was to block the admission of Catholics to the franchise, in connection with the Volunteer Convention of 1783. For his constant support of the government he was awarded a pension, appointed chamberlain to the Viceregal court, and in 1782 created a baronet. **Ciarán Deane**

Roche, Eamonn (Kevin) (1922–), architect. Born in Dublin and raised in Mitchelstown, Co. Cork; educated at UCD. He worked with MICHAEL SCOTT and with Eero Saarinen and Associates, Michigan, 1950 (principal associate in design, 1954), and established Kevin Roche, John Dinkeloo and Associates in Hamden, Connecticut, 1966. He won the Pritzker Prize, 1982, and the Gold Medal of the American Institute of Architects, 1993. His design for the Oakland Museum, California (1962–9), consists of four city blocks terraced as galleries and roof gardens. For the Ford Foundation, New York, he designed a beautifully detailed office atrium at a metropolitan scale (1963–8). Other work includes the headquarters of the Knights of Columbus, New Haven, the Nations Plaza, Atlanta, the Fine Arts Center at the University of Massachusetts, Amherst, the Creative Arts Center, Wesleyan University, Connecticut, Central Park Zoo, New York, and the Museum of Jewish Heritage, New York. An exhibition of his work was held at the Douglas Hyde Gallery, Trinity College, Dublin, in 1983. **Raymund Ryan**

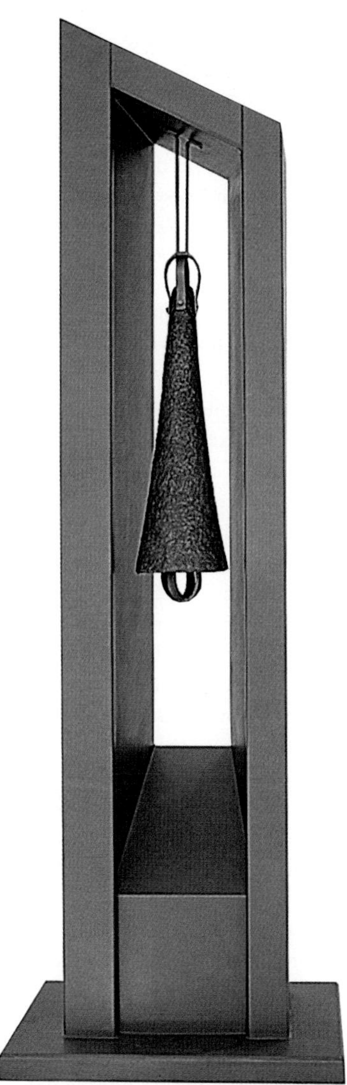

Roche, Vivienne. Viapori Bell *(1991), 2.36 m ($7\frac{3}{4}$ ft) bronze-and-steel sculpture by the Cork sculptor Vivienne Roche, presented by the Friends of the Crawford Gallery to the Crawford Gallery. [Courtesy of Crawford Municipal Art Gallery, Cork]*

Roche, Stephen (1959–), cyclist. Born in Ranelagh, Dublin. He turned professional in 1981, competed in his first Tour de France in 1983, and won the white jersey for best newcomer. 1987 marked the pinnacle of his career: he became the first Irish man to win the Giro d'Italia, the Tour de France, and the World Road Race Championship. He returned to Ireland to an ecstatic welcome from more than 250,000 fans and was made a Freeman of Dublin. **Séamus Shortall**

Roche, Vivienne (1953–), artist. Born in Cork; studied sculpture at Crawford College of Art and the School of the Museum of Fine Arts, Boston. In addition to carrying out commissions for public sculptures in Sneem, Co. Kerry, University College, Cork, St Patrick's Park, Dublin, and the Dental Hospital at Trinity College, Dublin, she has been represented in many exhibitions, including 'Edge to Edge', which toured Scandinavia, 1990–91. Her most recent exhibition, 'Tidal Erotics', was shown at the Hugh Lane Municipal Gallery of Modern Art, Dublin, and Sirius Arts Centre, Cobh, Co. Cork, in 1999. She is best known for her brightly painted welded-steel works installed in town centres, parks, and other public areas. Recent bronze sculptures represent a move into a more personal idiom and a specific aesthetic that derives in part from her travels in Scandinavia; for public sculpture commissions, however, she still works predominantly in steel. She was commissioned to create *Sea Garden* at the ferry terminal at Ringaskiddy, Co. Cork, in 1994, and in 1999 won the commission for a sculpture for the new Jack Lynch Tunnel under the River Lee in Cork. In 1989 she was a founder of the National Sculpture Factory in Cork. She served as a member of the ARTS COUNCIL, 1993–8, and was elected a member of AOSDÁNA in 1996. **Peter Murray**

rock art (also known as *petroglyphs*), motifs inscribed on the surface of rock outcrops and, more occasionally, on isolated boulders or STANDING STONES and the structural stones of monuments. It forms part of a varied tradition that occurs widely in Atlantic Europe. The designs are pecked onto rock surfaces, which are often flat or gently sloping.

Irish rock art is characterised by a limited number of abstract motifs: cup-marks, circular motifs, straight-line motifs, and a small number of unclassifiable types. Cup-marks are hollowed-out circular areas. Circular motifs are most often in the form of a cup-and-ring, a cup-mark surrounded by between one and nine concentric rings. Penannular rings also occur around cup-marks; and rings can also occur without cup-marks. Sometimes associated with the various forms of circular motif are radial grooves that run from the centre of the motif outwards, or from the outermost ring outwards. Less common are straight-line motifs, such as combinations of parallel lines. On the rock surface, motifs may be linked or closely spaced, giving the impression of a composition, or may be isolated (see pp. 118, 777, 860).

Though rock art is traditionally dated to the BRONZE AGE (2400–600 BC), the overlapping between its motifs and those found on MEGALITHIC PASSAGE TOMBS has led to a reassessment of the dating. The present interpretation is that these two art styles are related and overlap. This would suggest that rock art began to be inscribed in the NEOLITHIC Period, before 3000 BC. Rock art is occasionally found incorporated in early Bronze Age monuments, for example on the underside of CIST roof-slabs.

Rock art occurs widely and is known from more than a hundred sites. Particular centres are the south-west, the DINGLE PENINSULA and IVERAGH PENINSULA (Co. Kerry), with a notable complex at Derrynablaha, about 12 km ($7\frac{1}{2}$ miles) north-east of Sneem; west Cork; and the Inishowen Peninsula (Co. Donegal); smaller concentrations occur elsewhere.

While there is considerable regional variation, there are definite patterns to the location of rock art. It occurs from 15 to 360 m (50–1,200 ft) above sea level but most often in what can be described as intermediate areas between upland and lowland. Sites are frequently on rocky slopes, with a wide field of view, overlooking potential settlement areas or routeways through the landscape. A majority of the sites are within 50 m (165 ft) of water, usually either a river or a lake. In most instances they are accessible, and the motifs may represent the accretion of activity at different times, rather than being the result of one episode. In the Iveragh Peninsula the sites are in the upper reaches of river valleys; here and elsewhere some of the more complex rock art is at sites at higher altitudes. This pattern of distribution may indicate sites that were important in marking routes of movement or boundaries; rock art may therefore have marked places that were important in the prehistoric social landscape, associated with the fertility of the land, patterns of movement or sacred places, or as markers of territory. **Gabriel Cooney**

Rockett, Kevin (1949–), film historian and academic. Born in Dublin; educated at the University of Ulster, Coleraine. The leading authority on Irish cinema and the Irish in international cinema, he is joint author (with LUKE GIBBONS and John Hill) of *Cinema and Ireland* (1987), *Still Irish: A Century of the Irish in Film* (1995), *The Companion to British and Irish Cinema* (with Emer Rockett, 1996) and *Neil Jordan: A Search for Origins* (2002) and editor of *The Irish Filmography: Fiction Films, 1896–1996* (1996). He has received the Film Institute of Ireland Award for Contribution to Irish Film, 2001, and is a lecturer in film studies in Trinity College, Dublin. **Emilie Pine**

Rocque, John (c. 1705–1762), surveyor and cartographer. Probably born in France, of HUGUENOT parents; he settled in London as a young man, becoming well known for his large-scale maps of English towns and counties. An unusual feature of his maps is that all the main cartographic processes—fieldwork, drawing, and engraving—were done under his own supervision, giving his work a characteristic appearance unlikely to be mistaken for anyone else's. He maintained an office in Dublin from 1754 to 1760, publishing plans of the city to various scales and formats, one of which, *An Exact Survey of the City and Suburbs of Dublin* (1756), was large enough to distinguish every building and enclosure. He also published plans of Thurles, Kilkenny, and Cork, together with county maps of Cos. Armagh and Dublin in four sheets each. His manuscript estate maps for the Earl of Kildare established a tradition of estate surveying that was continued by his pupil Bernard Scalé. **J. H. Andrews**

Rodgers, W. R. [William Robert] (1909–1969), poet. Born in Belfast; educated at QUB and Presbyterian College; ordained 1935. He was Presbyterian minister at Loughgall, Co. Armagh, until 1946, when he left the church to work for the BBC in London with his friend LOUIS MACNEICE. Having first encountered modern poetry in 1938, he published *Awake! and Other Poems* (1940) and *Europa and the Bull* (1952) but little thereafter. In 1966 he took a university post in California, where he died. He has been described by MICHAEL LONGLEY as a latter-day metaphysical poet; his work is both erotic and erratic, marked by word-play and a gallivanting rhetoric that gave a new linguistic licence to writing in Ulster. **Hugh Haughton**

Roe, Michael (1954–), racing driver. Born in Naas, Co. Kildare. A talented driver, he won the 1976 Irish Formula Ford

Championship and the 1978 British Formula Ford Festival. After distinguishing himself in formula 3 he went to America, where he won the 1984 Can-Am Sports Car Championship with a record number of wins and fastest laps. **Brendan Lynch**

Rolfe, Nigel (1950–), artist. Born in the Isle of Wight; trained at Farnham School of Art and Bath Academy of Art. He moved to Ireland in 1975. He taught at Yale University, Connecticut, 1986–91, and has been visiting critic at the University of Pennsylvania School of Art and Chelsea School of Art and external examiner in fine art at Goldsmiths College, London, Brighton Polytechnic, and the National College of Art and Design, Dublin. He works in performance, video art, sculptural installation, and photography. Renowned throughout the art world as a pioneering performance artist and teacher, he lectures in many art schools in Europe and North America and is a member of AOSDÁNA. **Dorothy Walker**

Rolfe. Red Sculpture *(1989) documents a work by Nigel Rolfe, who makes living sculptures with his body in controlled and ritualistic performances. [Irish Museum of Modern Art; courtesy of the artist]*

Romanesque, the artistic and architectural style current in Europe during the eleventh and twelfth centuries, employed in Ireland from the end of the eleventh century to the early part of the thirteenth. In metalwork, ARCHITECTURE and SCULPTURE it is characterised by a unique blend of traditional forms with contemporary European trends, commonly termed *Hiberno-Romanesque*. The greatest survivals of the style are in ecclesiastical architecture. Many patrons of the style, such as Cormac Mac Carthaigh, DERMOT MACMURROUGH, and Turlough O'Connor, were of high status and appear to have used the 'new' architectural idiom to reflect their power and, in some instances, their support of the contemporary church reform.

Hiberno-Romanesque architecture is typified by small, one or two-cell churches, usually found in a monastic rather than a parochial setting. A number of early CISTERCIAN abbeys, such as JERPOINT, Co. Kilkenny, and BALTINGLASS, Co. Wicklow, also incorporate elements of the style. The majority of churches are distinguished from earlier building traditions by the incorporation of round-headed portals and chancel arches, nearly always accentuated by sculpture. In the use of architectural sculpture and the clear definition of architectural spaces they reflect the essence of European Romanesque. However, they are conservative in their diminutive size and simplicity of plan, and certain buildings also retain particular features of the earlier Irish building tradition. Examples of this include the steep-pitched stone roofs at Killaloe, Co. Clare, Cormac's Chapel at Cashel, Co. Tipperary, and Kilmalkedar, Co. Kerry, and trabeate doorways at Aghowle, Co. Wicklow, and Banagher, Co. Derry. The portal, usually in the western gable of the church, provided the focus for sculptural embellishment. The west portal at CLONFERT CATHEDRAL (see p. 909), Co. Galway, is one of the finest examples of Romanesque sculpture in the country. It incorporates mainly decorative motifs, such as INTERLACE and animal heads, probably inspired by contemporary metalwork. Other motifs typical of the style in Ireland include chevron or zigzag ornament and human heads with interlaced hair and foliage. Particularly good examples of sculpture survive at Killeshin, Co. Laois, GLENDALOUGH, Co. Wicklow, Tuam, Co. Galway, Killaloe, Co. Clare, and Rahan, Co. Offaly. The figurative sculpture depicting Biblical or allegorical scenes that defines much European Romanesque sculpture is rare, though examples are found at ARDMORE, Co. Waterford, Maghera, Co. Derry, and Kilteel, Co. Kildare. A number of HIGH CROSSES erected during the period also incorporate large-scale figures.

Early works suggest that the Romanesque style may have been introduced to Ireland by English craftsmen. At St Flannan's Oratory, Killaloe (c. 1090), the portal is comparable to work in the east of England, while Cormac's Chapel at Cashel (c. 1127–34) has affinities with contemporary sculpture in the west of England. A number of schools of sculptors appear to have worked in Ireland throughout the period, with clear affinities visible in a number of groups of buildings. The best known of these is the so-called 'School of the West', whose work is represented at Clonfert and a number of ABBEYS west of the Shannon. Their work, dating from the first half of the thirteenth century, is most readily characterised by stylised foliage ornament, and marks the end of the Hiberno-Romanesque style and the transition to the gothic. **Rachel Moss**

romantic tales in Irish. From the end of the Middle Ages a new narrative genre in Irish became popular, the work of a secondary class of writers who—though competent stylists—were concerned only with adventure and willingly indulged in anachronism and geographical confusion. Though much of the nomenclature and characterisation was drawn from earlier heroic stories, these 'romantic' tales were rambling, picaresque, and light in sentiment. Through being read aloud from MANUSCRIPTS, some of the tales passed into oral tradition and sprouted several variants. The most popular of these tales, and quite typical of the genre, was the EACHTRA (adventure) of CONALL GULBAN, written in Co. Donegal in the sixteenth century. Conall was in fact a historical person, son of the great HIGH KING Niall, who lived a thousand years before. In compiling the text, however, the anonymous author jumbled together genuine tradition of Conall with much blatant invention of his own; Conall is even represented as kidnapping a beautiful Leinster princess called Eithne while his father is away on a crusade. The young woman having been in turn stolen from him, Conall sails abroad and searches much of Europe for the warrior who took her. After many gripping episodes he finds him, overcomes him in single combat, and regains Eithne. Learning that his father and the German Emperor are sorely pressed by the Saracens, Conall goes to their defence and performs prodigious feats of arms before routing the enemy. [see NIALL OF THE NINE HOSTAGES.] **Dáithí Ó hÓgáin**

Roman world contacts. The Roman conquest of Britain in AD 43 brought advanced Mediterranean civilisation to the IRISH SEA basin, engaging Ireland in a cultural exchange that would influence profoundly the development of early medieval Irish society. Ironically, most of the long-term effects, such as LITERACY, CHRISTIANITY, aspects of dress, and improved agricultural techniques, are not manifest in the historical record until after the collapse of Roman Britain in the early fifth century.

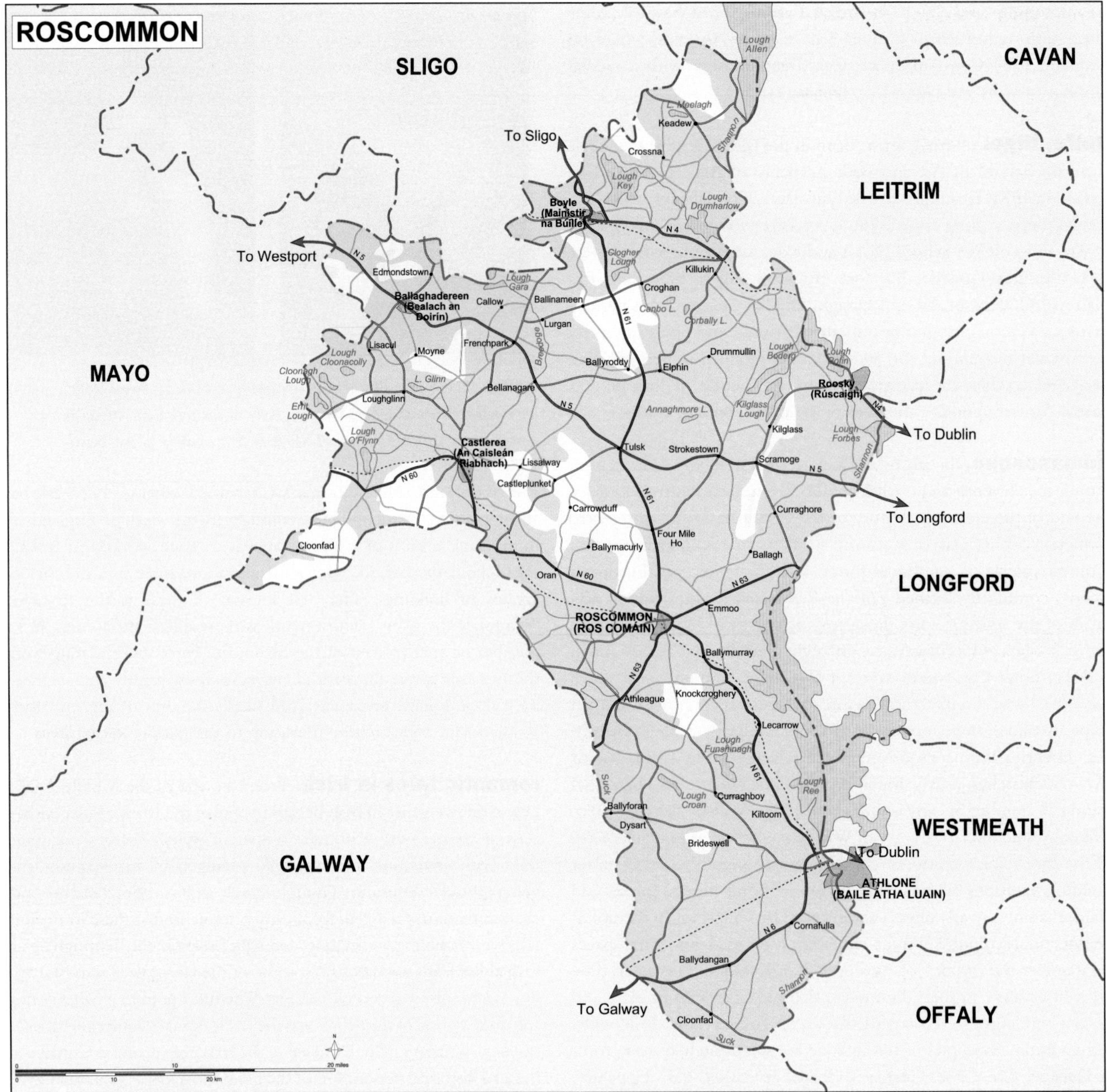

To protect and develop its strategic and economic interests, imperial Rome gathered considerable geographical and cultural information about Ireland from traders, the accuracy of which is testified in a map of Ireland compiled by Claudius Ptolemaeus (PTOLEMY) in the middle of the second century. Agricola, commander of the 20th Legion and third Governor of Britain, is reputed to have estimated that Ireland could be subdued with one legion; but such calculations were firmly in the realms of speculation, and Ireland remained outside the Roman world. However, the possibility of punitive raids or even strategic support of central figures in Irish military politics cannot be ruled out and would accord well with Roman foreign policy elsewhere.

Roman material in Ireland falls into two broad chronological groups: that of the first and second centuries and that of the fourth and early fifth centuries. The former, including a group of Brigantine burials on LAMBAY ISLAND, Co. Dublin, and a glass cinerary urn burial from Stonyford, Co. Kilkenny, tells of social displacement in Britain and exploratory trade contacts with Ireland. The later group, comprising some large coin and hack-silver hoards (chopped-up pieces of church and domestic silverware), may represent a combination of payment to Irish mercenaries who served in the imperial army, payment to strategic allies and booty from Irish raids on Britain, which were endemic in the fourth and fifth centuries. Roman material has also been found at some of the so-called 'royal' sites, including TARA, Knockaulin, and the Rock of CASHEL, as well as at NEWGRANGE, where the range and distribution of material parallels that in the Roman world and its frontier zone. The promontory fort of Drummanagh, Co. Dublin, may have been a type of trading post.

Despite neighbouring Roman Britain and Gaul, and mimicking aspects of its political structures, religions, and art styles, Irish society in general appears to have benefited relatively little from such proximity before c. AD 300. Indeed some Irish POLLEN records for the period suggest a collapse in agriculture during the first three centuries AD, whether or not coincidental with the demise of some of the 'royal' sites. Conversely, the collapse of Roman Britain spelt opportunity for Ireland, not just through raids but also through full-scale colonisation of parts of western Britain. Through such developments Ireland was introduced to literacy and to the Christian religion. **Conor Newman**

Rome and Ireland, 1200–1700. The framework for church-state relations in late medieval Ireland was established by the Papal bull LAUDABILITER, which purported to grant the LORDSHIP of Ireland to the English kings, provided they promoted ecclesiastical reform. The *de facto* position, however, was that within the nationally and politically divided Irish church in the late Middle Ages the Papacy provided directly to benefices within the native Irish dioceses, while the English kings presented to church posts within Anglo-Ireland. This compromise was shattered by HENRY VIII's break with Rome in 1536 and subsequently the official Protestantisation of the church in Ireland. The service of a Roman episcopate for the residual Catholic community was disrupted for several decades until the early seventeenth century, when resident bishops gradually returned to all the Catholic dioceses. Among their tasks was the propagation of the Catholic renewal and reform as decreed by the Council of Trent; and eventually an alternative to the state church was established, owing allegiance to Rome while remaining outside the law.

Despite the schism of the 1530s, the Papacy came to recognise the unilateral declaration of the kingdom of Ireland by the English king; but the excommunication by the Pope of ELIZABETH I in 1570 rendered the position of her Catholic subjects extremely problematic. Eventually a *modus vivendi* was achieved in relations between the Vatican and London, whereby, for most of the seventeenth century, the legitimacy of the English monarchs as rulers of Ireland was recognised in return for religious toleration for the Catholic population. **Colm Lennon**

Rome type, an IRISH PRINTING TYPE. In 1625, when the Irish Franciscan College of St Isidore was established in Rome, many of its early community who had come from LOUVAIN sought to continue their interest in publishing texts in Irish. With the support of the polyglot printing press of the Sacred Congregation of the Propagation of the Faith (PROPAGANDA FIDE), an Irish type was prepared by John the Teuton, modelled on those used at the Irish Franciscan press at Louvain. It was first used in 1676 for the publication of *Lóchrann na gCreidmheach* (Guiding Light of the Faithful) by Francis Molloy. The font was taken to Paris in 1799 and was the subject of J. J. Marcel's *Alphabet Irlandais*, before being reclaimed by the Vatican in 1815, where the punches and matrices still remain. **Dermot McGuinne**

'Rónan's Slaying of a Kinsman': see FINGAL RÓNÁIN.

Rooney, David (1962–), illustrator. Born in Galway; trained at the NCAD, becoming a freelance scraperboard illustrator. The artist's work developed from the strong line drawings, though of a not-yet-defined character, of the early Art Decó books to the powerful, evocative, and skilled suite of illustrations for the Folio Society's 2000 edition of the classic *Lorna Doone*. In between he has produced a steady range of work, mostly pencil drawings and scraperboard illustrations. He revels in unusual perspectives, such as figures seen from above, through a mirror, caught in the flash of a camera, or through the narrow aperture of a monastic scriptorium. Since the late 1980s his work has been seen regularly in the pages of the IRISH TIMES. **Patricia Donlon**

Ros, Amanda McKittrick, (1860–1939), novelist and poet. Born in Drumaness, Co. Down; educated at Marlborough Training College, Dublin. Her melodramatic and singular style, outdoing Euphues (a sixteenth-century florid romance by John Lyly) in its verbosity, was the subject of considerable mirth, with a parodic Amanda Ros Club formed in London. Her books include *Irene Iddlesleigh* (1897), *Delina Delaney* (1898), *Poems of Puncture* (1912), *Fumes of Formation* (1933), and an unfinished novel (completed by her biographer, Jack Loudan), *Helen Huddleston* (1969). Her most memorable creation is the gothic Lady Matie Maynard. A highly coloured personality, she conducted frequent diatribes against the 'donkeosity' of critics and lawyers. **Tess Maginess**

Roscommon, County (*Contae Ros Comáin*)

Province:	CONNACHT
County town:	Roscommon
Area:	2,463 km^2 (950 sq. miles)
Population (2002):	53,803
Features:	Curlew Mountains
	Lough Ree
	River SHANNON
	River Suck
Of historical interest:	Boyle Abbey
	Clonalis House
	Donamon Castle
	RATHCROGHAN
	Roscommon Castle
Industry and products:	AGRICULTURE
	Engineering
	Food-processing
	Metal industry

Petula Martyn

County Roscommon, occupying the area between the River SHANNON and a tributary, the River Suck, bordered by Cos. Mayo, Sligo, and Leitrim. The north of the county is formed of old red sandstone in the Curlew Mountains and depleted coal-bearing Upper Carboniferous measures at Arigna, the southern part of Lower Carboniferous measures. DRUMLIN topography, interspersed with peat, dominates in the west and adjoins the Shannon and Suck. There are several lakes, notably Lough Allen and Lough Ree on the eastern boundary and Lough Gara and Lough Key in the north. The average farm size in 1991 was 20 ha (49 acres). The production of beef and suckler cows dominates in the north and lowland sheep in the south. Clonalis, home of the O'Conor Don family, is at **Castlerea** in the west. The ancient site of Cruachan, near **Tulsk**, 20 km (12 miles) east of Castlerea, appears in early epics as the seat of Ailill mac Máta, King of Connacht, and his wife, MÉABH, who is credited with instigating the cattle raid of Cooley (TÁIN BÓ CUAILGNE). The county town, **Roscommon** (population 1,630), is 18 km (11 miles) south of Tulsk, and **Boyle** (population 1,641) is 26 km (16 miles) north. Elphin (population 713), 10 km (6 miles) north of Tulsk, gives its name to the diocese that includes most of Cos. Roscommon and Sligo. **Mary E. Cawley**

Roseingrave family, organists. Daniel Roseingrave (died 1727) was organist at Gloucester (1679–81), Winchester (1682–92), and Salisbury (1692–8) before moving to Dublin in 1698 as organist in the two Dublin cathedrals. One son, Thomas (1690–1766), born in Winchester, was a chorister in ST PATRICK'S CATHEDRAL, studied at Trinity College, Dublin, from 1707, and in 1710 was sent to study with Domenico Scarlatti in Italy. He returned to London in 1713 and championed Scarlatti's harpsichord music. From 1725 to 1737 he was organist at St George's Church, Hanover Square, London; he returned to Dublin in 1749. His opera *Phaedra and Hippolytus* was performed in Fishamble Street Musick Hall in 1753. Daniel's other

Rotunda. *An early twentieth-century photograph of medical students from many countries outside the Rotunda Hospital, Dublin, with newborn babies. Founded in 1757, the Rotunda is the world's oldest maternity hospital. [Courtesy of the Rotunda Hospital, Dublin]*

son, Ralph (1695–1747), born in Salisbury, succeeded Daniel as organist at St Patrick's Cathedral in 1719 and Christ Church in 1727. He composed anthems and two service settings. **Ite O'Donovan**

Rosen, Albert (1924–1997), conductor. Born in Vienna; studied piano, conducting, and composition at Charles University, Prague, and the Vienna Academy of Music. By 1965 he was director of the Smetana Theatre, Prague. He was principal conductor of the RTÉ Symphony Orchestra from 1968 to 1981, when he became principal guest conductor and later Conductor Laureate. He had a successful international career in Britain, the United States, and Australia, including the British premiere of Rimsky-Korsakov's *Christmas Eve* with English National Opera in 1988. He contributed greatly to opera in Ireland, conducting at the WEXFORD FESTIVAL OPERA, 1964–94, and the DUBLIN GRAND OPERA SOCIETY from 1969. **Ite O'Donovan**

Rosen, Hans Waldemar (1904–1994), conductor. Born in Leipzig; studied at the State Music Academy and at the Universities of Leipzig and Innsbruck. His early career was as an opera and choral conductor and music critic. In 1948 he was appointed director of Cór Radio Éireann and in 1953 of the RTÉ Singers, with whom he broadcast regularly and made numerous European tours, regularly attending the Swetzingen and Tützing festivals. He had close personal contact with Richard Strauss, Sibelius, and other celebrities and was awarded the White Rose by the Finnish government. **Ite O'Donovan**

Rosenstock, Gabriel (1949–), poet and translator. Born in Kilfinnane, Co. Limerick; educated at UCC, where his collection *Suzanne sa Seomra Folctha* (1973) heralded the 'INNTI' group of poets. He works as an editor with AN GÚM. He is highly influential through both his own prolific work—of which *Rogha Rosenstock* (1994) is a selection—and his eclectic *Translations into Irish*. **Seán Ó Cearnaigh**

Ross, Martin, pen-name of Violet Martin (1862–1915), writer. Born in Co. Galway, daughter of James Martin of Ross House, a branch of the Anglo-Norman Martins of Connacht; educated at home. In 1872 the family moved to Dublin, where the eldest brother, Robert Martin, wrote pantomimes for the GAIETY THEATRE. In 1885 she worked in London as amanuensis for her relative, the playwright William G. Wills. In 1886 she met her second cousin EDITH SOMERVILLE, and they collaborated on a 'shilling shocker' called *An Irish Cousin* (1889). The ironic perspective of their ensuing novels, *Naboth's Vineyard* (1891), THE REAL CHARLOTTE (1894), and *The Silver Fox* (1898), dealt with land issues and was sharpened by *fin-de-siècle* self-consciousness. In 1888 she returned to Co. Galway. Like her second cousin LADY AUGUSTA GREGORY, she collected folklore and studied Irish, but she preferred comedy to social realism. Her acute ear for HIBERNO-ENGLISH is illustrated in *A Patrick's Day Hunt* (1902), written entirely in dialect.

After her brother's death in 1905 she became increasingly interested in politics. The collected essays *All on the Irish Shore* (1903) and *Some Irish Yesterdays* (1906) include commentary on Irish affairs. In 1912 she travelled to Belfast to witness the signing of the ULSTER COVENANT. Her involvement in the Munster Women's Franchise League, of which she was vice-president in 1913, was eclipsed by her commitment to unionism. She also corresponded with the moderate nationalist MP Stephen Gwynn. Her love of farce and of politics is demonstrated in the artful parodies in her writing, including a satirical view on Irish matters in the deceptively simple IRISH R.M. STORIES. In 1906 she moved to Co. Cork; but the black humour of her writing manifests the spirit of the west of Ireland. **Julie Anne Stevens**

Rosse, Earls of: see PARSONS.

Rosserk Friary, Co. Mayo, the best-preserved example of a friary of the Third Order of Franciscans and a good example of

Franciscan friary design. The large double *piscina* is decorated with carved angles and a unique carving of a ROUND TOWER. The east window is filled with particularly good tracery. [see ABBEYS.] **Rachel Moss**

Rosserrily Friary, Co. Galway, one of the best-preserved examples of medieval Franciscan architecture in the country. There is some confusion over the date of its foundation, but the earliest standing remains date from the late fifteenth century. The monastery comprises a church with a typical slender tower and rood-loft beneath. The conventional buildings include a kitchen with fireplace, fish tank, and adjoining bakery. The refectory in the north-east range preserves a reader's desk. The Earls of Clanricarde, who were granted the friary at the Dissolution, protected the friars, so that they returned to the friary seven times between 1538 and 1753. [see ABBEYS.] **Rachel Moss**

Ross Island, Co. Kerry, site of a copper mine on the Killarney Lakes (see p. 1057), possibly the first place where metal was made in Ireland. Mining began here during the first period of copper use in Ireland, the final NEOLITHIC-Beaker period, c. 2400 BC. Though badly damaged by subsequent mining, these early BRONZE AGE mines survive as large cave-like openings within a copper-rich stratum of the surrounding limestone. They were worked by fire-setting and the use of stone hammers and bone tools. A work camp from this period, used for both domestic habitation and the processing of copper, has been discovered. The copper minerals were hand-sorted with the use of stone hammers and anvils before being reduced to metal in simple pit furnaces. The discovery of Beaker pottery in this mine camp is an important connection with those culture groups generally believed to have introduced copper metallurgy to Ireland at the end of the Neolithic Period. Copper and bronze objects made from the distinctive Ross Island metal were exchanged widely within Ireland between 2400 and 1800 BC. **William O'Brien**

Rosslare Harbour, Co. Wexford, a major ferry and container port. Timber jetties erected in 1873 and 1882 were replaced in 1906 with a RAILWAY viaduct and a new jetty in concrete and steel. The harbour was completely rebuilt and enlarged, first in the late 1960s and again in the 1990s. **Ronald Cox**

Rothwell, Richard (1800–1868), romantic painter. Born in Athlone; attended the Dublin Society Schools, 1814–20, and exhibited at the RHA, 1826–66. In 1829 he moved to London, where he worked in the studio of Sir Thomas Lawrence, who called him the 'Irish prodigy'. He executed portraits, subject pictures, and landscapes and developed a rich colour sense with a technique involving thick impasto, glazes, and deep reds. He exhibited successfully at the Royal Academy, but following a trip to Italy, 1831–3, he found it difficult to regain his career. He became restless, moving between London, Dublin, Belfast, and other towns. One of his most appealing pictures, *The Young Mother's Pastime* (now in the NATIONAL GALLERY OF IRELAND), illustrates the soft, vibrant skin colours for which he was renowned. Excessive use of bitumen ruined many of his pictures. **Marie Bourke**

Rotunda Hospital, Dublin. BARTHOLOMEW MOSSE (1712–1759) qualified as a surgeon in Dublin in 1733. Concerned at the poor quality of MIDWIFERY offered by traditional 'handywomen' and surgeons, in 1740 he visited the Hôtel Dieu in Paris to study methods for training midwives and surgeons. In 1745 he founded the Dublin Lying-In Hospital, the first maternity training hospital in Ireland. This was so successful that he planned a New Lying-In Hospital, which was opened in 1757 and survives as the Rotunda Hospital (a name derived from the circular entertainment complex opened beside the hospital for fund-raising through plays and musical performances, now comprising the Ambassador concert venue and the GATE THEATRE).

Obstetrical management in the eighteenth and nineteenth centuries concentrated on using manipulative procedures and the use of forceps when the pelvic capacity was reduced because of rickets associated with malnutrition. The earliest reported successful caesarean section in Ireland was performed on a woman of short stature in 1889 at the Rotunda; but caesarean section continued to carry an unacceptably high risk of maternal mortality from infection and haemorrhage until antibiotics, blood transfusion, ergometrine and safe anaesthesia became generally available in the wake of the Second World War. **Alan Browne**

round towers. The Irish round towers form a corpus of unique and singularly beautiful architectural monuments, constructed between the tenth and thirteenth centuries as the belfries of stone churches and found only on ecclesiastical sites. They are generally sited some distance to the north-west or south-west of the west entrance of the church for which they were constructed, with the tower door conventionally facing the church. Referred to in the ANNALS as *cloigtheach* (bell-house), they may also have had secondary functions as treasuries for church plate, shrines, and manuscripts and occasionally acted as places of refuge, for which they were remarkably ill-suited: the towers are not defensive structures. The earliest annalistic mention of a round tower is that of Slane, Co. Meath, c. 950; the latest is that of Annaghdown, Co. Galway, in 1238.

The towers, of which about seventy-four of a possible hundred still stand, intact in whole or in part, are in their most typical form a free-standing tapering tube of locally quarried stonework, terminated by a conical stone cap, and averaging in height from 20 to 30 m

round towers. *Kilmacduagh, Co. Galway, founded by St Colmán MacDuagh c. AD 600. The eleventh-century tower stands close to the east gable of the roofless twelfth to fifteenth-century cathedral. At a height of 34 m (112 ft) it is the tallest surviving round tower in Ireland; it has a noticeable lean of almost 50 cm (20 in.) from the perpendicular. [Brian Lalor]*

(65–100 ft), with the tallest, Kilmacduagh, Co. Galway, standing at 34 m (112 ft), though that of Fertagh, Co. Tipperary, would have stood at 35 m (115 ft) when its cap was intact. The average diameter at the base is 15 m (49 ft). The entrance door, generally 2–3 m ($6\frac{1}{2}$–10 ft) above ground level, is the only form of access, internal lighting being provided by occasional small windows in the drum of the tower, with four axially placed larger windows on the bell-floor, beneath the cornice of the cap. As there is no evidence for hung bells in this period in Ireland, it is assumed that hand-held bells, of which many survive, were used with a timber striker. Access to the bell-floor would have been by a series of ladders, rising between the timber (or occasionally stone) floors.

Round towers of more complex or experimental form are found, principally in Leinster, and date from the twelfth century. Of these, St Kevin's Church at Glendalough, Co. Wicklow, has a later attached round tower, forming the belfry of the oratory. Temple Finghin in CLONMACNOISE, Co. Offaly, is a late and altogether more advanced treatment of the round tower form, where the tower is engaged as an integral part of the church structure. Other than a small number of isolated examples in Scotland and the Isle of Man—areas of Irish ecclesiastical influence—round towers are found only in Ireland, where they are widely distributed from TORY ISLAND, Co. Donegal, in the north to Kinneigh, Co. Cork, in the south. The architectural origins of the towers most probably derive from ecclesiastical buildings in Continental Europe, but no confirmed precedent has been identified. **Brian Lalor**

round towers. *St Kevin's Church, Glendalough, Co. Wicklow; the stone-roofed belfry is a late adaptation of the concept of the free-standing round tower. [Brian Lalor]*

Rowan, (Archibald) Hamilton (1751–1834), United Irishman. Born in London into a family from Co. Down. He settled in Co. Kildare in 1784, having lived in France and America. He gravitated from the VOLUNTEERS to the Northern WHIG Club in Belfast in 1790 and the more radical Dublin Society of UNITED IRISHMEN in November 1791. Though convicted of sedition in January 1794, he escaped from custody in Newgate Prison, Dublin, and travelled to France. His abhorrence of revolutionary violence disposed him to eschew further illegal republican activities, and he soon emigrated to America. He and his family moved to Hamburg in 1800, and he was pardoned by the British authorities in 1803. This rare concession aroused the suspicions of former associates, and his autobiography was poorly received. The Rowans lived from 1803 in Killyleagh, Co. Down, and in Dublin. **Ruan O'Donnell**

rowing. There has been competitive rowing in Ireland since the 1830s. In 1899 the Irish Amateur Rowing Union was set up to organise and control the sport. A national championship, for men's senior eights, was inaugurated in 1912, which City of Derry won. Today thirty-nine national championships are held annually, for men and women, in events ranging from the senior eight to the junior single scull. Some seventy-five clubs throughout Ireland are affiliated to the Irish Amateur Rowing Union. Dublin, with five of the country's most successful clubs—Neptune, Dublin University Boat Cub, UCD, Garda Síochána, and Commercial—is the main rowing centre, challenged by Belfast, Galway, Limerick, and Cork.

Henley Royal Regatta in England was a target since 1870 for Irish clubs seeking international competition. Representative international rowing for Ireland came in 1948, when an all-Ireland eight was sent to the OLYMPIC Regatta in Henley. The Irish Amateur Rowing Union joined the International Rowing Federation (FISA) that year and since then has competed in world championships and Olympic regattas. At the world championships in 1975 Seán Drea won Ireland's first medal, a silver in the men's single sculls. Niall O'Toole won Ireland's first title, in Vienna in 1991, in the men's lightweight single sculls; and in Lucerne in 2001 three further championships were won by Ireland: the women's lightweight single sculls (Sinéad Jennings), the men's lightweight single sculls (Sam Lynch), and the men's lightweight coxless pair. Irish rowing has twice achieved fourth place in the Olympic Games. **Micheal Johnston**

Rowley, Richard, pseudonym of Richard Valentine Williams (1877–1947), poet. Born in Belfast; educated at Sullivan Upper School, Holywood, Co. Down. His collections *The City of Refuge* (1917) and *City Songs and Others* (1918) memorably evoke Belfast and its industrial landscapes. In 1918 he moved with his family to Newcastle, Co. Down, where the MOURNE MOUNTAINS and their people became his principal subject. **Terence Brown**

Rowsome, Leo (1903–1970), player and maker of UILLEANN PIPES. A central figure in the revival of TRADITIONAL MUSIC, he was the third generation involved with the instrument. He revived the DUBLIN PIPERS' CLUB in 1936 and with his brother Tom became a founder of COMHALTAS CEOLTÓIRÍ ÉIREANN in the 1950s. An award-winner at the FEIS CHEOIL of 1921, he taught pipes in the Dublin Municipal School of Music, published the twentieth century's first tutor for the instrument in 1936, and made many recordings, including an LP, *Rí na bPíobairí*. His son Leon (died 1994) was also a musician and PIPE-MAKER; his daughter Helena is a piper; his grandson Kevin is a pipe-maker and award-winning piper. **Fintan Vallely**

Royal Black Preceptory, common name of the Imperial Grand Black Chapter of the British Commonwealth, the most senior and elite Orange organisation. It was introduced to Ireland from Scotland in the 1830s, and the Grand Black Chapter of Ireland was formally instituted in 1846. Like the ORANGE ORDER, 'the Black' is a secret society dedicated to upholding PROTESTANTISM and the Union. Its basic ritual, derived from the feudal theory of knighthood, involves the Sovereign Grand Knight conferring the status of knighthood on prospective members, who undertake to defend the reformed faith. It has 536 preceptories in Ireland as well as a substantial membership overseas. Its main demonstration is staged on the last Saturday of August, when 30,000 members parade, while it also sponsors the colourful Sham Fight at Scarva, Co. Down, on 13 July. The former Unionist leader JAMES MOLYNEUX was its Sovereign Grand Knight, 1972–98, reflecting its links with UNIONISM. **Eamon Phoenix**

Royal Botanic Gardens: see BOTANIC GARDENS, BELFAST.

Royal Canal. Following the construction of the GRAND CANAL, proposals were revived for a rival northern route, and in 1789 parliamentary grants of £66,000 were added to the £134,000 already promised by subscribers to the Royal Canal Company. Work proceeded slowly, and it was not until 1796 that the first section, to Kilcock, Co. Kildare, was opened. The canal reached Mullingar in 1806 and the western end of the summit level three years later, after which the company's financial affairs became the subject of a government investigation. In 1813 the company was dissolved and the project handed over to the Directors-General of Inland Navigation, to be completed at public expense. The remaining 38 km (24 miles), involving twenty-one locks, thirty-eight bridges, forty tunnels, and several harbours, were completed and the canal opened for through traffic between Dublin (Broadstone terminus) and Tarmonbarry on the Shannon on 1 May 1817. It was never profitable, however, and in 1845 it passed into the ownership of the Midland Great Western Railway. The last passenger service operated in November 1849. From a peak tonnage of 112,000 in 1847 trading dwindled steadily, until by 1946 only two boats were operating. The Royal Canal closed completely in 1960, but thanks to the efforts of a group of enthusiasts it was reopened from Blanchardstown, Co. Dublin, to Mullingar in 1990 as the first stage in a projected complete restoration. **Bernard Share**

Royal College of Science for Ireland (RCSI), established in 1867, after several years of deliberation, through the reorganisation of the teaching roles of the MUSEUM OF IRISH INDUSTRY and the Dublin School of Science Applied to Mining and the Arts. It was to offer higher technical education through courses in agriculture, applied science, chemistry, engineering, geology, natural sciences, and physics. Unlike other third-level teaching establishments at the time, the college placed a strong emphasis on practical laboratory training; it also trained agricultural instructors for government duty, and science teachers for secondary schools. Members of the staff included the physicist WALTER HARTLEY, the zoologist A. C. Haddon, and the geologist GRENVILLE COLE, all of whom were internationally recognised authorities in their fields.

During its first forty-three years the college occupied 51 St Stephen's Green, Dublin, where its laboratories and facilities gradually became inadequate and cramped. In 1911 it moved to a purpose-built complex in Upper Merrion Street designed by Sir Aston Webb and Thomas Manley Deane. In 1922 the college was closed for security reasons; in 1926 its teaching role was transferred to University College, Dublin, which occupied the premises until 1990. In the 1990s the building was remodelled for use as part of Government Buildings. **Patrick N. Wyse Jackson**

rowing. *The Trinity College rowing team, competing against University College, Dublin, on their way to victory in the Bórú Vodka Gannon Cup boat race on the River Liffey, Dublin, 25 March 2000. They won by half a length. [Sportsfile]*

Royal Cork Institution (RCI). The Cork Institution for the Diffusion of Knowledge owed its existence to Rev. Thomas Dix Hincks (1767–1857), Unitarian minister, and was inaugurated during a lecture series given by him in 1803. The background was the lively middle-class interest in 'useful knowledge', particularly in the sciences. On 20 March 1807 the institution was incorporated by charter, becoming the Royal Cork Institution. Its patrons, proprietors and members included the Co. Cork landed gentry as well as such notables as William Crawford, William Beamish, Cooper Penrose, and James Roche, the banker. In 1807–8 its revenue from substantial subscriptions and a parliamentary grant totalled £4,200. There were courses of public lectures in chemistry (EDMUND DAVY was a lecturer, 1813–26), electricity, botany, and agriculture. The first volume of the *Munster Farmer's Magazine*, edited by Hincks, was published in 1812 by a committee of the RCI. The institution was connected with the local medical schools, and lectures on anatomy were given. In 1809 a site was acquired at Ballyphehane for a botanic garden; but with the withdrawal of government funding in the late 1820s the 'Botanic' became St Joseph's Cemetery. As a chartered body, the institution received all government publications. It had a good scientific reference library and museum, as well as a collection of scientific instruments. It had temporary premises in South Mall (opposite the present Imperial Hotel); from 1832 its permanent home was in the Old Custom House, now the Crawford Gallery.

Though the RCI loomed large in the intellectual life of the city and lasted to 1861, struggling to maintain its usefulness as a teaching body, it gradually shrank to the dimensions of a private cultural society, being succeeded in that respect by the CORK CUVIERIAN SOCIETY, then being made redundant in its main rationale by Queen's College, Cork (now University College, Cork), founded in 1849. [see HINCKS, EDWARD.] **John A. Murphy**

Royal Dublin Society (RDS). The Dublin Society for the Improvement of Husbandry, Manufacturing and Other Useful Arts was founded on 25 June 1731 by fourteen men at a meeting in the rooms of the Philosophical Society in TRINITY COLLEGE: Judge Michael Ward, Sir Thomas Molyneux, Thomas Upton, JOHN PRATT, Richard Warburton, Arthur Dobbs, Rev. Dr John Whitcomb, Dr William Stephens, Dr Alexander Magnaten, Dr John Madden, Dr Le Hunte, Mr Walton, THOMAS PRIOR, and William Maple. While all are regarded as founder-members, it is generally agreed that the moving spirit was Thomas Prior, and it was his inspiration and dedication that directed the society during its early years.

The society was founded to promote by practical means the development of AGRICULTURE, INDUSTRY, SCIENCE, and art. For the first thirty years of its existence it relied largely on private subscriptions. In 1820 the society became the Royal Dublin Society after Lord Sidmouth informed the society that George IV would be pleased to become a patron. Between 1731 and 1767 meetings of the society were held in a number of buildings, among which were rooms in the House of Lords, College Green. In 1814 the society bought LEINSTER HOUSE, Kildare Street, from the Duke of Leinster for £10,000 and a ground rent of £600 (which was subsequently redeemed); and this remained its home for over a hundred years.

From the 1760s the society was patronised extensively by the Irish Parliament as an efficient and ready-made conduit for promoting technical education and ECONOMIC DEVELOPMENT. By 1800, with the benefit of parliamentary aid, it had financed and was operating a school of art (1740s), a museum (1793), and botanic gardens (1795). By the nineteenth century its small private library, established in 1731, had become one of the largest research libraries in Dublin. In the 1830s, following the ACT OF UNION, the British government developed a long-term strategy for Ireland that involved changes in land tenure and the established church and in the development of a national system of education. The RDS was already involved in science education through a professorial system and its public lectures. In 1835 it experienced a crisis of public confidence, and the government seized the opportunity to impose certain changes, under a threat of the withdrawal of all grants. For ten years nothing significant happened; then the government decided to nationalise the art school, the botanic gardens, the museums, and the library, and the society was persuaded that this step was in the public interest. The truncated RDS was left to run its agricultural shows and conduct its scientific proceedings. From 1854 its remit was to organise and supervise the system of scientific education in a manner directed towards the working class.

In 1861 the RDS asked for a grant in aid to complete the NATURAL HISTORY MUSEUM and to acquire land for agricultural shows. In 1866 a new charter was granted, and the accounting of public and private funds was separated. In 1875 the vice-president of the Committee of the Council on Education, Lord Sandon, stated that 'the time has come when the wants of the community at large have outgrown the usefulness of private societies.' His proposal was to make the RDS a predominantly agricultural institution and the ROYAL IRISH ACADEMY a scientific and literary one. Following a meeting in London, the suggestion was made that the RDS and RIA might amalgamate. Complexities concerning the private and public ownership of the two bodies posed difficulties in dividing the assets between the RDS, the RIA, and the state; what resulted was years of argument and dissent. But the issues were eventually resolved, with the RDS library becoming the National Library, the Art School and Botanic Gardens transferred to public ownership, and the collections of the RDS and RIA housed in the new Dublin Science and Art Museum (later the NATIONAL MUSEUM), both bodies having rights of nomination to a supervisory role in all these institutions. A supplemental charter was granted on 20 May 1888.

The legacy the RDS left behind in Kildare Street is a significant one. Leinster House is surrounded by most of Ireland's great cultural institutions: the NATIONAL LIBRARY, the NATIONAL GALLERY, and the NATIONAL MUSEUM. The juxtaposition of government and culture is an important one and a constant reminder to those in power of the fundamental significance of heritage, art and learning to the spiritual and intellectual well-being of a modern state.

Criticism of the limited facilities available for the spring and winter agricultural shows in the Kildare Street premises caused by encroaching buildings on Leinster Lawn—that of the Natural History Museum from 1856 and National Gallery from 1859—led to the move of the expanding shows to a site in Ballsbridge used previously as a showground by the Royal Agricultural Society (which later merged with the RDS). The construction of buildings on the Ballsbridge site began in 1880 and included the re-siting of the former Agricultural Hall (1858) from Kildare Street.

The first of the RDS Horse Shows was held on Leinster Lawn in 1868, with the object of improving the breeding of HORSES. The move to Ballsbridge saw the introduction of a permanent jumping course in 1881 and an increase in the number of entries. The show became established as a significant contributor of income to the society's private funds; a new social season developed around the racing calendar and the Dublin Horse Show and exists to this day. The most prized trophy competed for by international teams is the competition for the Aga Khan Cup, which is the highlight of the show. For the society the success of the Ballsbridge venture was especially satisfactory, as it was achieved without reliance on government grants and repudiated those administrators who had concluded in 1877 that the society was moribund.

In the early twenty-first century the society's lands at Ballsbridge house the largest events complex in Ireland, with a turnover of €9 million. The gross annual expenditure is €2.5 million, which includes the promotion of its foundation activities. The break with government, despite the doubts and misgivings of some, had a liberating influence on the society. Women were admitted as associates in 1877, though until 1921 they were excluded from attending general meetings or exercising voting rights. The first woman member of the Council, Dr Mary Hutton, was elected in 1929; the first woman president, Prof. Dervilla Donnelly, was elected in 1989. In 1998 a publication of the treasures of the RDS appeared. This project was led by JAMES WHITE, former Director of the National Gallery, and comprised a summary catalogue of the works of art in the society's collection. A millennium project was a substantial enhancement of the BOYLE MEDAL award, which for more than a hundred years has been given for excellence in scientific achievement. The society provides a meeting place for large conferences and has renovated many of its existing buildings to yield a more suitable environment for international conventions. The RDS remains dedicated to the advancement of agriculture and other branches of industry and of science and art. Its whole operation rests on the voluntary work of its members. It is now fully dependent on its own resources, not having received any state assistance since 1900; this independence is used for the benefit of the society's traditional purpose, the advancement of the prosperity of Ireland. **Dervilla Donnelly**

Royal Flying Corps (RFC), the original British air force, formed in April 1912. In September 1913 it undertook a long-distance flight with six aircraft from its recently established base at Montrose in the east of Scotland to participate in British army exercises in Munster. The flight was undertaken in stages, and eventually four aircraft arrived at the base at Rathbane, Co. Limerick. As a precaution against a forced landing in the North Channel, inflated cylindrical air-bags were fitted to the aircraft. The aircraft were constantly in use and provided the ground forces with invaluable information, presaging the demise of cavalry in a scouting capacity. During that year an Instructor's Flying School was also begun at the CURRAGH, Co.

Royal Dublin Society. Panorama of the Kildare Street buildings of the Royal Dublin Society *by Sir Thomas Deane the Younger (1885). Leinster House (now the seat of Dáil Éireann) stands at the centre of the complex, the National Museum to the right (foreground), and the National Library to the left, with (behind Leinster House) the National Gallery and (right) the Natural History Museum. Merrion Square is to the top right, with Dublin Bay behind and Howth on the horizon. [National Museum of Ireland]*

Kildare. On 1 April 1918 the Royal Flying Corps and the Royal Naval Air Service were amalgamated to become the Royal Air Force, which played a limited role in the WAR OF INDEPENDENCE, its scope being confined to patrolling and to VIP and AIR MAIL services, necessitated by the closure of roads and rail links. Some combat operations were carried out, particularly when the IRA attacked force-landed aircraft, which was a common occurrence. The RAF was short of aircraft and spares and in general not integrated in the activities of Crown forces. Its aircraft operated mainly from aerodromes that had been established from 1917 onwards. **Donal MacCarron**

Royal Geological Society of Ireland (1831–90), founded on 29 November 1831 as the Geological Society of Dublin 'for the purpose of investigating the mineral structure of the earth, and more particularly of Ireland.' The first president was Bartholomew Lloyd (1772–1837); many distinguished geologists were members, though membership never exceeded 200. A journal was published from 1833, and in March 1864 the society became the Royal Geological Society of Ireland. From the 1870s the membership declined and there were financial problems, and the society's last recorded meeting was on 5 February 1890. The journal contains many pioneering papers descriptive of Irish regional geology by such notable authorities as M. H. CLOSE, R. J. GRIFFITH, J. B. Jukes, and G. H. KINAHAN. Of international importance is PATRICK GANLY's paper of 1856 introducing a fundamental method for determining the orientation of strata. The society's surviving papers are in the Geology Department of TRINITY COLLEGE, Dublin. **Jean Archer**

Royal Hibernian Academy of Arts (RHA). In 1821 a charter of incorporation was granted by the LORD LIEUTENANT to a group of Dublin artists who had petitioned for the establishment of an academy, but it was not until 1823 that this process was complete, with financial assistance from the Royal Irish Institution. There were to be fourteen academicians, ten associates, a president, a secretary, and a treasurer, as well as professors and honorary members. WILLIAM ASHFORD, a landscape painter, was elected the first president, being succeeded by FRANCIS JOHNSTON, architect, who built Academy House in Abbey Street at his own expense in 1826. This building also contained space for the academy's school, as well as a Council Room, a library, and apartments for the Keeper. After Johnston's death his widow added an additional gallery for the exhibition of SCULPTURE.

The first exhibition took place in 1826, and in 1832 the British government granted £300 to the academy, to be paid annually, subject to reports. Sales of works were enhanced by the purchase of prizes by the Royal Irish Art Union Lottery from 1839 to 1847. With the economic depression resulting from the Great Famine the academy fell into financial disarray. In 1856 a campaign to reform its finances, led by the secretary, MICHAEL ANGELO HAYES, resulted in a bitter public controversy. The divisions paralysed the academy, and no exhibition was held in 1857. At the request of the academy the British government conducted an official inquiry, which suggested that the school be discontinued in view of the existence of the RDS School of Art. The academy drew up a new charter, allowing for up to thirty members, which was approved in 1861. Its grant was paid from 1860 by the Department of Science and Art, subject to an annual inspection of the school.

In the second half of the nineteenth century the academy prospered, reaching a high point in the 1880s, when sales were supported by the revived Art Union. Thomas Jones, the president, paid for the building of a new Life School. The Albert Prize was instituted out of the surplus of the Prince Consort Memorial Fund to encourage the students of the school. The 1890s were a period of decline, especially in attendance at the school—to which women were admitted from 1893. An official report by W. de Abney in 1901 recommended closure. To revive the academy's fortunes new premises were sought near the cultural institutions in Kildare Street. An official inquiry into the academy (1906), chaired by Lord Plymouth, was divided in its conclusions on whether the schools should be closed or a new premises acquired. When DERMOD O'BRIEN became president in 1910 he dramatically improved the financial efficiency and profitability of the academy.

During the 1916 RISING, Academy House was destroyed, with its records, collections, and current exhibition; the government provided compensation, and the Abbey Street site was sold. The Life School continued in rented rooms, but it and the £300 grant ceased in 1940. From 1917 the academy exhibitions were held in the gallery of the Metropolitan School of Art, Dublin. Exhibitions were not financially successful in the difficult early years of the Irish Free State. Many efforts were made to secure a permanent site, and in 1939, 15 Ely Place, Dublin, and the adjoining gardens were bought. The academy continued unsuccessfully to seek government grants to build a gallery there. Because of the student disturbances at the National College of Art the academy moved its exhibition in 1970 to DUBLIN CASTLE and then to the National Gallery of Ireland until 1984. New premises were paid for by Matthew Gallagher to the designs of RAYMOND MCGRATH, with building starting in 1970. The Gallagher Gallery in Ely Place, while still unfinished, was first used by the academy in 1984, and its annual exhibitions have been held there since 1985. **John Turpin**

Royal Hospital, Kilmainham, Dublin, by far the largest early classical public building in Ireland (see p. 135). Erected from 1680 by order of the Viceroy, the Duke of Ormond, it was designed by Sir WILLIAM ROBINSON, architect and Surveyor General. Built in the former lands of the Knights Hospitallers of St John of Jerusalem, it consists of a quadrangle surrounded by three arcaded two-storey ranges of accommodation for retired soldiers, with the Master's residence, dining hall, and chapel comprising the fourth, north side of the square. A tower with spire marks the centre of the northern range. The chapel FURNITURE and the *tympana* (overdoors) of the axial entrances to the courtyard have baroque woodcarving by Jacques Tarbary, while the heavy foliated compartmental ceiling of the chapel (now a partial replica) is a rare example of Carolean PLASTERWORK. The Royal Hospital was converted to accommodate the IRISH MUSEUM OF MODERN ART in 1991, and its seventeenth-century formal gardens and outlying buildings have been restored. **Brian Lalor**

Royal Institute of the Architects of Ireland (RIAI), the representative professional body for architects in Ireland. Founded in 1839, it is one of the oldest architectural organisations in the world. Its objectives are the promotion of ARCHITECTURE and of high standards of conduct and practice and the development of architectural education. A class in architectural study established in 1867 led to the founding of the first School of Architecture in Ireland at the NUI in 1909; the RIAI continues its educational activities at second level, third level, and postgraduate level today. A newsletter, first published in 1972, has developed into the monthly magazine *Irish Architect*.

In 1932 the RIAI instituted a Gold Medal award for excellence in architectural design, awarded for an outstanding building over a three-year period; it also has awards for HOUSING, conservation, and restoration, and an annual Irish Architecture Awards system. It has represented Ireland in the International Union of Architects since 1948 and in the Architects' Council of Europe since 1963. Through its publications, standard contract forms (first published 1910), and client support systems the RIAI provides a service to architects, the public, and the building industry. **John Graby**

Royal Irish Academy (RIA), Ireland's premier learned body. It was founded in 1785, with the Earl of Charlemont as first president. Its royal charter, granted the following year, declared its aims to be the promotion and investigation of the sciences, polite literature, and antiquities, as well as the encouragement of discussion and debate between scholars of diverse backgrounds and interests. Unusually for the time, the academy placed greater emphasis on the sciences, by giving eleven seats on its Council to scientists and ten to representatives of the humanities. At the annual general meeting, members elect the president and members of the Council (including the honorary secretary and treasurer), who conduct the academy's business, organise conferences, arrange discourses, and oversee research, with the assistance of a permanent staff of forty. In addition to the approximately 285 members there are also more than fifty distinguished honorary members, who in the past have included J. W. von Goethe, Jakob Grimm, MARIA EDGEWORTH, Albert Einstein, and Max Born.

The academy was housed first at 114 Grafton Street, Dublin (adjoining the ROYAL DUBLIN SOCIETY at the time), but its ever-increasing collection of antiquities was one reason why it moved in 1851 to its present more spacious premises at 19 Dawson Street, a fine mid-eighteenth-century house built by Lord Northland. The Reading Room and Meeting Room were added at the rear in 1852–4. In anticipation of the British Association coming to Dublin in 1857, WILLIAM WILDE organised a new display for the museum objects and prepared three parts of a catalogue over the following five years, before the whole collection was transferred in 1890 to the new Dublin Science and Art Museum (now the NATIONAL MUSEUM), with the academy retaining custody under certain conditions. This material included some of the country's best-known treasures, such as the CROSS OF CONG, the TARA BROOCH, and the ARDAGH CHALICE, some of which had been donated to the academy, others bought through subscriptions from the individual members.

Wilde was one of the many distinguished personalities who contributed to the academy's reputation in the humanities during the nineteenth century; others were GEORGE PETRIE, the 'founder of Irish archaeology', and EDWARD HINCKS, who made significant progress in the decipherment of Egyptian hieroglyphics and cuneiform script. The sciences too have always played a vital role in the academy's research interests. Mathematics and physics have been areas of particular strength, especially during the nineteenth century, when Sir WILLIAM ROWAN HAMILTON made significant advances in OPTICS and dynamics and, through his discovery of quaternions, in algebraic theory. Hamilton's collected works have been published under the aegis of the academy, the first volume appearing in 1931 and the final one in 2000. The editors of the first volume were J. L. SYNGE, whose work on relativity was particularly influential, and A. W. CONWAY, who also specialised in relativity. Ireland's only scientific Nobel laureate, ERNEST WALTON, was one of the academy's most distinguished physicists, while the quantum theoretician ERWIN SCHRÖDINGER (1887–1961) was an honorary member, temporarily domiciled in Dublin, who introduced Ireland to modern physics through his academy lectures of 1939–40.

From the academy's inception its library has been a major research tool for those studying aspects of Irish history, archaeology, language, and culture. Unique features include the invaluable collection of seventeenth to nineteenth-century pamphlets bequeathed by the Dublin merchant Charles Haliday and the library of THOMAS MOORE, donated by his widow. The library also contains a very valuable and wide-ranging collection of internationally important periodicals, as well as a great number of monographs, with a particular emphasis on Irish material. Even more important are its MANUSCRIPTS, including the famous CATHACH of COLM CILLE. Indeed the library holds the largest collection of Irish manuscripts in a single repository, prime among those being the Book of the DUN COW (c. 1100), the later medieval LEABHAR BREAC, and the Book of BALLYMOTE (see p. 818), as well as original manuscript volumes of the Annals of the FOUR MASTERS. The academy's encouragement in preserving such manuscripts, and the employment of scribes to copy others later, led to a flowering in Irish studies that built on the foundations laid in its early years by the election of Irish scholars, notably CHARLES O'CONOR of Belanagare. Subsequent generations rediscovered and interpreted the contents of these manuscripts through ground-breaking work undertaken in association with the academy by such scholars as EUGENE O'CURRY and JOHN O'DONOVAN, while the academy was also the focus of twentieth-century international interest in OLD IRISH language and literature through scholars of the calibre of Rudolf Thurneysen, Kuno Meyer, and Carl Marstrander. The academy's continuing interest in Irish studies is further reflected in its publications over the years, including a series of manuscript facsimiles, the Todd Lecture series, the journal *Ériu* (which the academy took over from the School of Irish Learning in 1926), the *Atlas of Ireland* (1979), and the *Dictionary of the Irish Language* (1913–76). The academy's own outstanding journals began with the *Transactions* (1787–1907), augmented in 1836 by the *Proceedings*, which are now published in three separate sections: mathematics; biology and environment; archaeology, Celtic studies, history, linguistics, and literature. Other periodicals include the *Irish Journal of Earth Sciences* and *Irish Studies in International Affairs*. The academy has also produced many monographs of its own on a variety of subjects, among them the *New Survey of Clare Island*, updating its very thorough base-line study of 1909–11 (see p. 205).

A number of important projects are undertaken in Academy House, including the almost complete *New History of Ireland*, *Foclóir na Nua-Ghaeilge*, *Dictionary of Irish Biography* (for completion c. 2005) and *Dictionary of Medieval Latin from Celtic Sources*, as well as the *Irish Historic Towns Atlas* (of which eleven of the projected forty-four fascicles have so far been published). The work of the academy's Social Science Research Council led to the creation in 1999 of the Irish Research Council for the Humanities and Social Sciences. Since 1965 some twenty national committees in a variety of disciplines have been created to bring together scholars from all over Ireland to discuss matters of common interest at the highest level. The academy has links with sister institutions in other countries and is the Irish representative on most international learned associations, as well as being a participant in a number of international research projects. It also contributes policy advice to the Government, which finances the academy through the Higher Education Authority. **Peter Harbison**

Royal Irish Academy of Music (RIAM), founded in 1848 as the Irish Academy of Music, adopting its present name in 1872. The first classes were in the ANTIENT CONCERT ROOMS, Great Brunswick Street (Pearse Street), Dublin, transferring to 18 St Stephen's Green in 1856 and then to Westland Row in 1871. A Board of Governors was established in 1889 to administer the fund arising from the Coulson Bequest. The Academy administered the Municipal School of Music from its foundation in 1890 until 1905.

Royal Irish Academy. *The Meeting Room of Academy House in Dawson Street, Dublin, home of the Royal Irish Academy, Ireland's leading scholarly institution. The Meeting Room was added after the Academy took over the original eighteenth-century house in 1851. [Royal Irish Academy]*

The local centre examinations system was established in 1894. The twentieth century saw continued expansion, particularly influenced by MICHELE ESPOSITO, 1882–1928, and JOHN F. LARCHET, 1920–55. The academy has offered diplomas since 1930 and degree courses, in association with Trinity College, Dublin, and Dublin City University, since 1990. **Ite O'Donovan**

Royal Irish Constabulary (RIC), established as the County Constabulary in 1822, reformed in 1836 and renamed the Irish Constabulary. Based in hundreds of barracks throughout Ireland, this armed and well-trained force was an effective instrument of the DUBLIN CASTLE authorities, receiving the epithet 'Royal' for its role in suppressing the FENIAN rising of 1867. It bore the brunt of the IRA's campaign of 1919–21 before being disbanded in 1922, when it was replaced in the Irish Free State by the unarmed GARDA SÍOCHÁNA and in Northern Ireland by the ROYAL ULSTER CONSTABULARY (since 2002 the Police Service of Northern Ireland, PSNI). **Brian Griffin**

Royal Irish School of Art Needlework (1874–1915), set up in Dublin by Countess Cowper in emulation of the London School (established 1872); its twenty members were directed by Baroness Pauline Prochazka, needlewoman and watercolourist. After her departure in 1886 the school foundered until it was rescued in 1894 by Geraldine, Countess of Mayo (whose husband, the seventh Earl of Mayo, founded the ARTS AND CRAFTS SOCIETY OF IRELAND the same year). Radically reorganised on a self-supporting financial and optionally educational basis in Clare Street, Dublin, it flourished until 1915 under its manager, Hannah Beresford, who supervised finely executed, often distinguished designs, which included plain work, copies and originals, fashionable and artistic, made for exhibition and on commission. **Nicola Gordon Bowe**

Royal National Lifeboat Institution (RNLI), a voluntary organisation that operates the coastal life-saving service in both Britain and Ireland, founded in 1824 by Sir William Hillary. It provides a twenty-four-hour search and rescue service in waters up to 80 km (50 miles) from the coasts of Britain and Ireland. Forty-nine lifeboats are stationed around Ireland at thirty-nine harbours, with one inland station on LOUGH ERNE, Co. Fermanagh. Many stations have two vessels, an inshore and an offshore lifeboat. Crews total approximately 800 volunteers, the only full-time workers being the mechanics on offshore vessels. The annual running costs of the lifeboat service, approximately €5 million, are raised by subscription and fund-raising activities.

On average the service launches a lifeboat 6,200 times a year and rescues more than 6,300 people. One of the most famous rescues was that carried out by the Ballycotton, Co. Cork, lifeboat on 11 February 1936, when the Daunt Rock light-vessel, with its crew of eight, broke from its moorings. When the lifeboat set out the seas were so mountainous that spray covered the local lighthouse, at a height of 60 m (195 ft). The lifeboat did not return to its station for three days, during which time its crew had only three hours' sleep and little food; all members of the light-vessel's crew were saved. **Fiacc OBrolchain**

royal sites, a specific group of monuments and places associated in documentary sources with the medieval institution of KINGSHIP, such as INAUGURATION SITES, burial sites, and assembly sites. Irish medieval kingship was modelled in part on Germanic and Late Antique traditions. Its sacral dimension derived from mythological aspects of its rather obscure prehistoric roots. It is not surprising, therefore, that so many Irish royal sites are in fact prehistoric religious complexes, burial grounds whose mounds served as assembly points, *forradha* (inauguration mounds), dwelling-places of tribal deities, and symbols of ancestral ownership. Rather than describing their original function, therefore, the prefix 'royal' refers instead to their role in early medieval politics.

A number of royal sites are distinguished in literature as having enjoyed quasi-regional importance in IRON AGE times, namely Teamhair (Hill of TARA, Co. Meath), Emain Macha (NAVAN FORT, Co. Armagh), Cruachain (RATHCROGHAN, Co. Roscommon), Dún Ailinne (Knockaulin, Co. Kildare) (see p. 493), Caiseal (CASHEL, Co. Tipperary), and Uisneach (Co. Westmeath), the traditional centre of ancient Ireland. Archaeological investigations at some of these sites have revealed combinations of recurring architectural motifs, suggesting conformity to a general pattern. It is also clear that they are in reality complexes of ceremonial and burial monuments whose material decline in the first few centuries AD paved the way for their becoming symbolically important during the political re-organisation of early medieval Ireland. **Conor Newman**

Royal Society of Antiquaries of Ireland (RSAI), established in 1849 by Rev. James Graves as the Kilkenny Archaeological Society 'to preserve, examine and illustrate the ancient monuments of the history, language, arts, manners and customs of the past as connected with Ireland.' After two changes of name it assumed its present title on 14 January 1890, having moved from Kilkenny to Dublin in 1868. The *Journal of the Royal Society of Antiquaries of Ireland* is published annually. **Ciarán Deane**

Royal Ulster Constabulary (RUC). On 31 May 1922 the RUC was formed by the Northern Ireland Parliament, closely modelled on the ROYAL IRISH CONSTABULARY. Like its predecessor, the force was armed; and one-third of the places were reserved for Catholics. By the beginning of 1925 the force had a strength of 2,990, consisting of 2,449 Protestant members and 541 Catholics. Nearly half the force—1,435—were former members of the Special Constabulary. The violence during August 1969 demonstrated the inability of the RUC to handle civil disorder unaided and its unacceptability in the eyes of Catholics, which led to reforms, contained in the Police Act (1970), designed to bring the force into line with others in the United Kingdom. The policy of 'Ulsterisation' (increasing local personnel in security operations) from the late 1970s led to an increase in the force to 8,496 full-time, 2,862 full-time reserve and 1,217 part-time reserve members by March 1999. The policing of Orange parades and of protests against the ANGLO-IRISH AGREEMENT (1985) enhanced the RUC's reputation for impartiality, and members and their families suffered from loyalist intimidation and attacks. By 2000 a total of 303 members had been killed, almost all by militant republicans, since the beginning of the 'TROUBLES'. A committee on policing, chaired by Chris Patten, reported in January 2000 and recommended a change in the name of the force to Police Service of Northern Ireland (PSNI), the adoption of a new human rights ethos, a reduction to 7,500 full-time members, and the recruitment of equal numbers of new Protestant and Catholic members. [see RUC BOOK OF REMEMBRANCE.] **Jonathan Bardon**

Royal Victoria Hospital, Belfast, successor to the Belfast General Dispensary (1792) and Fever Hospital (1797). After changes in name, site, and administration it was granted a royal charter in 1899, moved to its present site in 1903, was nationalised in 1948, and became a trust hospital in the health service reorganisation of 1993. Substantially rebuilt, it has more than 700 beds; with specialist maternity, children's, and dental hospitals it comprises the Royal Group, with a total of some 1,000 beds. It began clinical lectures in 1826, was the exclusive local general teaching hospital until 1908, by the late nineteenth century accommodated some 200 students during the winter sessions and 150 during the summer sessions, and remains the principal teaching hospital in Northern Ireland, with most of the clinical academic and regional speciality units. Its high reputation has been further enhanced throughout the medical exigencies of the recurring civil disturbances. **Peter Froggatt**

Royal Zoological Society of Ireland. The Zoological Society of Ireland was founded by a small group under the chairmanship of the Duke of Leinster at a meeting in the ROTUNDA HOSPITAL, Dublin, on 10 May 1830. By 1831 the Duke of Northumberland had arranged for land to be donated from the PHOENIX PARK for the establishment of the ZOOLOGICAL GARDENS, which officially opened on 1 September 1831; Dublin Zoo is therefore the third-oldest public zoo in the world (preceded only by that of Paris, 1828, and London, 1829). The first general meeting of the society was held in November 1832; the first president was Philip Crampton, elected in 1833. The name of the society was changed to Royal Zoological Society of Ireland in 1838, when VICTORIA was invited to become patron of the zoo in the year of her coronation.

Royal Ulster Constabulary. *Members of the Royal Ulster Constabulary in riot gear at the funeral of an IRA volunteer, Finbarr McKenna, in Belfast, 6 May 1987. [Derek Speirs/Report]*

In 1983 the society, in conjunction with University College, Cork, opened FOTA WILDLIFE PARK on Fota Island, Co. Cork, to mark the 150th anniversary of the founding of Dublin Zoo, the aim being to provide a more natural approach to animal welfare; all animals were originally supplied by the society. The last decade of the twentieth century was a period of growth and development for the society, with the implementation of a development plan (1993–2005) for Dublin Zoo. To facilitate this plan the management of the society was reorganised in 1993, with the establishment within the Council of a smaller Executive and Development Committee that could quickly and more effectively assist the director in the expansion of the zoo. [see CAIRBRE.] **Peter Wilson**

RTÉ: see RADIO TELEFÍS ÉIREANN.

RTÉ concert orchestra, founded in 1948 as the Radio Éireann Light Orchestra, a salon ensemble of twenty-two players, principally for broadcasting purposes, conducted in its formative years by Dermot O'Hara and EIMEAR Ó BROIN. It toured the smaller towns of Ireland whose halls could not accommodate the RTÉ Symphony Orchestra. Its stature has grown steadily, reflected in its change of title and increased concert responsibilities; it now numbers forty-five players. It is acknowledged internationally as one of the most versatile broadcasting orchestras in the world; it won the Nordring Radio Prize on three occasions and has worked with stars such as Liberace, Elmer Bernstein, Carl Davis, and the Bolshoi and Kirov Ballet companies. It has toured in North America and Europe and is the resident orchestra for OPERA IRELAND. Its principal conductor 1978–2002 was PROINNSIAS Ó DUINN. **Richard Pine**

RTÉ Musician of the Future Festival, a biennial event. Founded by its director, Jane Carty, in 1976, and sponsored by RTÉ, the festival now incorporates five competitions: Musician of the Future, Singer of the Future, Composer of the Future, RTÉ Ensemble Prize, and Poet of the Future. The jury includes international performers who also give master classes during the event. The prize fund is in excess of €30,000, and concert and broadcast engagements are also awarded to winners. Competition age limits vary between fifteen and thirty. Previous winners include HUGH TINNEY, MÁIGHRÉAD MCCRANN, and FINGHIN COLLINS. **Deborah Kelleher**

RTÉ Philharmonic Choir, one of Ireland's largest vocal ensembles. Founded in 1985, the choir, in addition to maintaining a busy concert schedule, has also made a number of recordings, including BALFE's *Bohemian Girl*, Verdi's *Aïda*, and GERARD VICTORY's 'Ultima Rerum'. MARK DULEY, director of music at Christ Church Cathedral, has been chorus master of the choir since 1995. **Deborah Kelleher**

RTÉ String Quartet. In 1957 RTÉ responded to requests from citizens in Cork for a greater musical presence in the city by forming a string quartet resident in Cork which, in addition to its broadcasting and concert activities, would also contribute to musical life through a connection with the CORK SCHOOL OF MUSIC and, latterly, UCC, where the current RTÉ VANBRUGH STRING QUARTET are artists-in-residence. **Richard Pine**

RUC: see ROYAL ULSTER CONSTABULARY.

RUC Book of Remembrance, a series of manuscript volumes containing the names of the 415 members of the ROYAL ULSTER CONSTABULARY killed on duty. Begun in 1977, it now consists of five volumes. Written on calfskin vellum, illuminated with muted variants of blue, green, and brown watercolour and heightened with gold, it is the work of the calligrapher Sam Somerville. Each entry has an opening containing the member's name, rank, and date of death on the left-hand page and on the right a map and short text describing the fatal incident. The binding, by George Kirkpatrick, incorporates the RUC badge, using a variety of coloured leather onlays and tooling. **Timothy O'Neill**

Ruddock, John Alexander (1924–), musician. Born in Carlow; educated at TCD. In 1967 he founded the Limerick Music Association to engage international artists for concerts around Ireland; in more than 750 events, these have included Vladimir Ashkenazy, Beaux Arts Trio, and Takaks Quartet. In 1986 he was appointed to the first board of the NATIONAL CONCERT HALL and was awarded a Knight's Cross by the Austrian government; in 1991 the Hungarian government awarded him the medal Pro Cultura Hungarica, and in 1997 he was awarded a doctorate by the University of Limerick. **Deborah Kelleher**

rugby football. Though the inaugural general meeting of the Irish Rugby Football Union took place at 63 Grafton Street, Dublin, on 5 February 1880, the union celebrated its centenary in 1974. This apparent inconsistency is due to the fact that Ireland's first international match—against England at Kennington Oval, London—was played on 15 February 1875, at a time when there were two governing bodies, the Irish Football Union in Dublin and the Northern Football Union in Belfast, which between them selected the early national teams, before the two groups amalgamated in 1880. But handling-ball games in one form or another had been played in Ireland for many years before the formation of the two unions. It has been claimed that the ancient game of *caid*, which existed largely in Munster, was played by the Celtic nations.

Long before the two unions that would become the IRFU were formed, Trinity College, Dublin, played a role in the development of rugby in Ireland. The rugby club in Trinity was formed in 1854 (though the game was played there long before its official formation); the only older club in the world is that of Guy's Hospital, London. Charles Burton Barrington of Glenstal, Co. Limerick, who had attended Rugby School before going to Trinity, was an outstanding all-round sportsman, and with Richard M. Wall he drew up a list of rules that had a considerable influence on the developing game.

After losing that first international match to England in 1875, Ireland lost again to the same team later that year, on 13 December, at the Leinster Cricket Club's ground at Rathmines, Dublin, both matches being between twenty-a-side teams. From then on it was fifteen a side, and Ireland lost the following eight games in succession. Ireland's first win against Scotland was in Belfast on 19 February 1881; the first victory over England was at Lansdowne Road, Dublin, on 5 February 1887 and against Wales at the same venue on 3 March 1888. Ireland's first match against France, at Lansdowne Road on 20 March 1909, also resulted in a win.

Since those early years Ireland has won six Triple Crowns (victory over the other three original 'home' countries—England, Scotland, and Wales—in the same season), in 1894, 1899, 1948, 1949, 1982, and 1985, and just one Grand Slam (victory over all other teams in the championship, i.e. the Triple Crown plus France and, since 1999, Italy), in 1948. But despite this modest record it has produced many of rugby's greatest players and, since the touring team's first fully representative inception in 1910, has made a huge contribution to the British Lions team (a selection of the best players from the four 'home' countries), in players, captains, coaches, and managers.

The IRFU administers the game through its four provincial branches, which compete in interprovincial championships from senior to under-age and schools levels. On the international stage Ireland competes at senior, A, under-age, schools, youths, students, and university levels while also regularly touring overseas, especially in more recent years. Ireland has competed in all four Rugby World Cup campaigns, reaching the quarter-finals in 1987, 1991, and 1995, but was knocked out by Argentina at the pool stages in 1999. The Senior Cup competitions in each of the provinces were long the zenith at club level but were overtaken in popularity by the All-Ireland League, the first all-Ireland competition, inaugurated in the 1990/91 season, and more recently by the European Cup and Shield campaigns, in which the provinces compete.

The advent of the professional game in 1995 brought its own problems, as a spate of top Irish players left to join English clubs. But by contracting players at provincial and national levels the IRFU stopped that drain, and with notable success, as Ulster won the European Cup in 1999, and Munster reached the final the following year and again in 2002, losing both times. The IRFU is also attracting more young players to the game, through its team of full-time regional development officers and youth development officers, who operate throughout the country through the provincial branches. **Karl Johnston**

rundale, a system of agricultural organisation that facilitated rapid population growth in poorer landscapes of pre-famine western Ireland, having antecedents in traditional Irish landholding practices of the Middle Ages. It is characterised by clusters of houses surrounded by open-field farmland, in which each family held scattered portions of cultivated land, which may periodically have been redistributed. It is associated with surrounding grazing COMMONAGE and perhaps upland summer pastures. Most such holdings were rearranged in land reform schemes by LANDLORDS or the CONGESTED DISTRICTS BOARD in the later nineteenth and early twentieth century. [see CLACHANS; BOOLEYING.] **Patrick Duffy**

rural development, generally understood as ensuring the economic and social well-being of rural communities. Two phases of rural development policy can be identified, the first in the 1960s and 70s and the second emerging in the late 1980s. In the 1960s, declining agricultural incomes and DEPOPULATION were serious problems. Farm diversification and agri-tourism were promoted as important instruments of rural development. In addition, a policy of dispersing foreign-owned transnational companies to rural areas was adopted. Rural depopulation trends were reversed during the 1970s, and agriculture benefited from the COMMON AGRICULTURAL POLICY following membership of the EEC. However, recession brought the decline of industries in rural areas. The effects were disastrous. UNEMPLOYMENT was high and depopulation resumed. Nonetheless, rural development faded as a policy objective. Its re-emergence in the late 1980s must be seen within an evolving EU framework. A perceived failure of the common agricultural policy and the advent of the single European market required a new strategy to develop lagging regions in order to secure economic and social cohesion. The EU Commission provided funds for schemes

rugby. *David Humphreys of Ireland being tackled by Frank Belot of France during a Six Nations rugby international on 19 March 2000 in Paris. Ireland won with a score of 27 points. [Sportsfile]*

that were to be integrated between sectors and that would involve greater regional and local participation in their preparation and implementation. Today rural development schemes are area-based, taking place within a defined locality. Critics have questioned the tenuous future of what are essentially pilot programmes. **Sally Shortall**

rural landscape and rural settlement patterns. These are regionally varied and reflect past differences in the organisation of society and in its economic exploitation of the natural ENVIRONMENT. Most settlement is relatively recent, dating from the radical transformations of the countryside during and after the GREAT FAMINE. By 1911 Ireland's population had almost halved, and a far greater proportion lived in Dublin and Belfast. The loss of farm labourers, the shift to pastoralism, and increasing EMIGRATION and rural-urban MIGRATION emptied large parts of the countryside and created today's typical pattern of isolated, dispersed farm settlement. Only in remote upland and western areas, such as Cos. Kerry and Donegal, did the pre-famine pattern of numerous farm clusters or CLACHANS survive, but subsequently these too have declined. Elsewhere, in the south-east heartland of the Anglo-Norman colony, nucleated villages of medieval origin have survived, such as Kilmessan, Co. Meath. These were an imported settlement form, however, and the modern rural landscape consists of scattered farms supported by a dense network of small market towns, such as Rathfriland, Co. Down, and Augher, Co. Tyrone. More than 750 of these towns were founded, rebuilt, or extended at the instigation of their LANDLORD proprietors between 1700 and 1845. In recent years both parts of Ireland have been plagued by ribbon development on the outskirts of towns and by a rash of bungalows built in ostentatious and inappropriate styles, which have added nothing to the countryside's visual amenity. **Lindsay Proudfoot**

rural utopian communities, villages established by culturally distinctive minority groups that adhere to distinguishing linguistic, religious, or material cultural practices. In Ireland the two most important groups were the MORAVIANS and the PALATINES. The Moravians were an enlightened Protestant sect that was relatively numerous in Co. Antrim in the middle of the eighteenth century, where JOHN CENNICK established more than 200 religious societies and the model village of Gracehill, Co. Armagh (1746). The Palatines were German Protestant refugees from the Rhineland, 3,000 of whom settled after 1709 mainly in Co. Limerick, where they established various settlements, including Killiheen, Ballingrane, and Courtmatrix. By the early nineteenth century they had virtually disappeared as a separate cultural group.

Arthur Vandeleur, a landlord, was greatly influenced by Robert Owen's socialism and established a community on his property at Ralahine, Co. Clare, with the aid of Thomas Craig of Manchester, a follower of Owen. The RALAHINE AGRICULTURAL AND MANUFACTURING CO-OPERATIVE ASSOCIATION began in 1831, with rules emphasising mutual assistance, common capital, and the mental and moral development of its members. The community failed in 1833 when Vandeleur became bankrupt and the new owners refused to recognise the community's legitimacy.

Rev. EDWARD NANGLE established a Protestant settlement, the Achill Mission Estate, at Dugort on ACHILL ISLAND in the 1830s. He reclaimed large tracts of land and built strong stone slated houses; he also established a hospital, orphanage, printing press, church, and schools. His EVANGELISM inevitably brought conflict with the Catholic authorities. Other groups include the Bible-based Cooneyites, variously known as the Two-by-Twos and Nameless House Church, founded by William Irvine, said to be from Co. Tipperary. Their first convention was held in Ireland in 1903; despite not building settlements or churches they have spread their beliefs throughout the world. [see SHACKLETON, ABRAHAM.] **Lindsay Proudfoot**

Russell, George William, widely known as 'AE' (from his pen-name Æ, originally Æon) (1867–1935), poet, mystic, editor, writer, and artist. Born in Lurgan, Co. Armagh; trained at the Metropolitan School of Art. Employed by Pim's (drapers), Dublin, he subsequently worked as banks organiser for the IRISH AGRICULTURAL ORGANISATION SOCIETY before becoming editor of the *Irish Homestead*, 1905–23. He was a leading figure in the Dublin Theosophical Society from 1888/9 until 1908, when he formed his own Hermetic Society. He became vice-president of the Irish National Theatre Society in 1902, a position he still held when, in 1904, this became the Abbey Theatre Company. A mentor to many young writers, he was also an outspoken opponent of the employers during the 1913 DUBLIN LOCK-OUT (*To the Masters of Dublin*, 1913) and key negotiator in the IRISH CONVENTION, 1917–18 (*Thoughts for a Convention*, 1917). He declined an invitation to become a senator of the Irish Free State but accepted the editorship of the *Irish Statesman* (1923–30). He made two tours of the United States: the first in 1930 to raise money for the *Irish Statesman*, the second in 1934 to lecture on rural policy.

He was variously a mystic (*The Candle of Vision*, 1919; *Song and its Fountains*, 1932), an expert on agricultural economics (*The Building up of a Rural Civilisation*, 1910), a poet, whose poetry tends to vague abstraction, suggesting mystical raptures (*Collected Poems*, 1935), a minor dramatist (*Deirdre*, 1902), an authority on Eastern religions, a significant symbolist painter and theatre designer, a political theorist (*The National Being*, 1916; *The Avatars*, 1933), a social thinker whose opinions were sought by the Irish, British, and American governments, and one of the foremost mentors and critics of the LITERARY REVIVAL (*Some Irish Essays*, 1906; *Imaginations and Reveries*, 1915). The degree to which he impressed his contemporaries can be gauged by his appearances in GEORGE MOORE's *Hail and Farewell* (1911–14), W. B. YEATS's *Autobiographies* (1938), SEAN O'CASEY's *Inishfallen, Fare Thee Well* (1949), and FRANK O'CONNOR's *My Father's Son* (1968). **Peter Kuch**

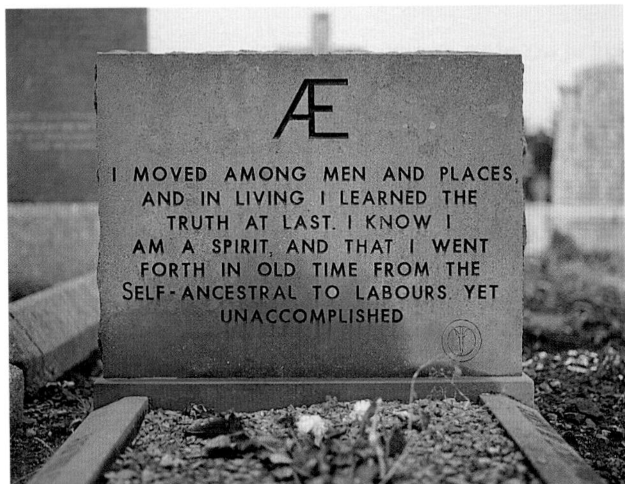

Russell, George. *One of the leading literary and artistic figures of early twentieth-century Dublin, George Russell, known as AE, is buried in Mount Jerome Cemetery, Dublin. [Mark Joyce]*

Russell, Lord John (1792–1878), politician. Born in London, son of the sixth Duke of Bedford, a former Irish LORD LIEUTENANT. Member of Parliament for Bandon Bridge, Co. Cork (1826–30), he supported conciliation throughout his career. Home Secretary and Leader of the House of Commons, 1835, he introduced the first Irish POOR LAW in 1838. As Prime Minister from 1846 he responded to Famine less effectively than Sir ROBERT PEEL, and charged relief costs to Irish ratepayers. His charges in 1850 against Pope Pius IX of 'papal aggression', in response to the Pope's reappointment of an English Catholic episcopacy, cost Irish support and led to his government's defeat. **William Anthony Hay**

Russell, Miko (1915–1994), tin-whistler, singer, and flute-player. Born in Doolin, Co. Clare. He was influenced primarily by the community he grew up in. His father, Austin, was a SEAN-NÓS singer; his mother, Annie, played the 'German' CONCERTINA. His brothers Gussie and Packie played FLUTE and concertina. Russell's musical style had a unique sparse beauty, and his engaging personality and deep knowledge of local FOLKLORE made him an epic figure in the world of traditional music. Equally at home at the fireside and on a festival stage, he can be heard on the recording *Ireland's Whistling Ambassador*, and his life and personality are documented in a video by Bill Ochs. **Desi Wilkinson**

Russell, Thomas (1767–1803), revolutionary. Born in Dromahane, Co. Cork, a member of the Church of Ireland. After serving in India as an officer in the British army he was posted to Belfast in 1790. A chance meeting with THEOBALD WOLFE TONE led to a lively friendship based on their enthusiasm for political reform and Catholic Emancipation; they were both founder-members of the UNITED IRISHMEN in 1791. Having resigned his commission, Russell travelled on foot through Ulster, making geological and botanical observations but also talking to working people. He was appointed librarian of the LINEN HALL LIBRARY in Belfast in 1794 and wrote for the *Northern Star*. He was imprisoned from 1796 to 1802 and released on condition that he live abroad. He met ROBERT EMMET in Paris and they planned the ill-fated 1803 Rising. Russell was commander of the insurgent forces in Ulster but received little support from his former associates; he was arrested, tried, and hanged at Downpatrick on 21 October 1803. **Jean Agnew**

Russell, Sir William Howard (1820–1907), war correspondent. Born at Jobstown, Co. Dublin. He reported 'shocking' scenes of the GREAT FAMINE for the *Morning Chronicle* (London). Reporting for the *Times* from 1841, he publicised the mismanagement of the CRIMEAN WAR, helping to bring down the British government of Lord Aberdeen and inspiring the work of Florence Nightingale. Known for his invention of the term 'thin red line', describing British infantry at BALAKLAVA, he founded the *Army and Navy Gazette*, 1860, and wrote *The War from the Landing at Gallipoli to the Death of Lord Raglan* (1855–6). **David Quin**

Russian crown jewels. In 1920 the first Dáil Éireann agreed to accept a portion of the Russian crown jewels as security for an interest-free loan of $25,000 to the Soviet Union. Harry Boland brought the jewels to Ireland, but in the aftermath of the Treaty he entrusted them to his family, with instructions that they be given to ÉAMON DE VALERA when he came to power. They were duly delivered to de Valera in 1932 but subsequently lay forgotten in Government offices until P. J. McGilligan, Minister for Finance in the first inter-party Government (1948–51), rediscovered them. They were returned to the Soviet Union, and the loan was repaid. **Ciarán Deane**

Rutty, John (1697–1775), physician and chemist. Born in Wiltshire of Quaker parents; educated in Dublin and London and at the University of Leiden. He settled in Dublin as a physician. A lifelong student of medicine, natural history, and chemistry, he also read spiritual books. He lived sparingly, often giving his services free to the poor. He published several major texts, including *Mineral Waters of Ireland* (1757); this brought him into dispute with Dr CHARLES LUCAS. JOHN WESLEY noted that he was 'held in high repute for his professional skills, as a writer, naturalist and highly spiritual member of the Society of Friends.' **D. Thorburn Burns**

Ryan, Cornelius (1920–1974), war correspondent. Born and educated in Dublin, he became an American citizen in 1951. He covered the SECOND WORLD WAR in Europe and the Pacific and chronicled the events in his books *The Longest Day* (1959), *The Last Battle* (1966), and *A Bridge Too Far* (1974). **Joley Wood**

Ryan, Florence (1939–), pianist and teacher. Born in Dublin; studied piano with Dina Copeman at the RIAM, later with Ginette Doyen and Carlo Zecchi, and was among the last students of Edwin Fischer. She credits ELIZABETH HUBAN as her greatest musical influence. A renowned performer, she has played regularly with the RTÉ Symphony Orchestra, specialising in performances of Mozart. A piano teacher at the Municipal College of Music, Dublin, for many years, she now teaches at the Leinster School of Music. **Ite O'Donovan**

Ryan, Hugh (1873–1931), chemist. Born in Nenagh, Co. Tipperary: he took first place and a gold medal at Queen's College, Galway, in 1897. At the University of Berlin he worked on sugar chemistry under Hermann Emil Fischer. Appointed professor of chemistry at the Royal University of Ireland and subsequently at University College, Dublin, he carried out research on glucosides, peat, and natural dyes, among other areas. On the outbreak of the FIRST WORLD WAR he took on consultancy work for the NOBEL Explosive Company. Invited by the Free State Government in 1924 to take up the newly created post of State Chemist, he worked assiduously to build up the State Laboratory. **Susan McKenna-Lawlor**

Ryan, Seán (c. 1952–1985), traditional musician. Born in Nenagh, Co. Tipperary. He won numerous awards in solo and duet competitions. During the 1960s he appeared frequently on television and radio. His playing was marked by a steady and relatively unsyncopated rhythm and long and controlled bow strokes, with an emphasis on crisply fingered embellishment. He also composed nearly 250 tunes, many of which had already become standards of the traditional repertoire by the 1970s. **Martin Dowling**

Ryan, Thomas Anthony (Tony) (1936–), businessman and entrepreneur. Born in Tipperary; educated at Northwestern University, Chicago. He joined AER LINGUS in 1956 and held various senior positions. In 1975 he left to set up Guinness Peat Aviation, which became an international success until a failed flotation in 1992 caused its collapse; it was subsequently taken over by the General Electric Company. He is chairman of RYANAIR, formed in 1985, which became Europe's largest low-fare airline, and has received three honorary doctorates from Irish universities. **Martin Clancy**

Russell, William Howard. *Sir William Howard Russell, war correspondent. Reporting for the* Times *(London) in 1841, he publicised the mismanagement of the Crimean War, and is pictured here in his Crimean outfit. [NI Syndication]*

Ryanair, an airline founded by TONY RYAN in 1985. It offered significant reductions in fares on routes between Ireland and Britain; however, over-ambitious expansion led to increasing losses, which by 1990 had accumulated to €25 million. A new management under Michael O'Leary rationalised the network and introduced a 'no frills' policy, abandoning complimentary in-flight services, still common on traditional airlines, while continuing to drive promotional fares downwards. The airline recorded a modest profit in 1991; it went from strength to strength during the following decade and by 1995 carried more passengers on the crucial Dublin–London route than any other airline. By 2002 it was carrying more than eleven million passengers a year; it recorded a profit of €150 million for the financial year and had hubs in London-Stansted, Brussels-Charleroi, and Frankfurt-Hahn in addition to its original Dublin base. Its market capitalisation of more than €5 billion made it one of the largest airlines in Europe. Ryanair was arguably the most spectacular Irish business success story during the 'CELTIC TIGER' period of the late 1990s. **Fergal Tobin**

Rynd, Francis (1801–1861), surgeon. Born in Dublin; educated at TCD. He became surgeon to the Meath Hospital, Dublin, and is remembered as the first doctor to administer a subcutaneous injection, which he did in 1844, using an instrument designed by himself. **Robert Mills**

Spanish Armada *(see page 1010). Gold and silver treasure, including coins and jewellery, from the* Girona, *a galleass of the Spanish Armada, which foundered on 30 October 1588, at Lacada Point, Co. Antrim. [Ulster Museum. Photograph reproduced with the kind permission of the Trustees of the National Museums and Galleries of Northern Ireland]*

S

Sabine, Sir Edward (1788–1883), explorer. Born in Dublin. Commissioned in the Royal Artillery, 1800, he served in Gibraltar and Canada and took part in the Niagara frontier campaign in 1814. Returning to England in 1816, he studied astronomy and terrestrial magnetism. Created a fellow of the Royal Society in 1818, he was appointed official astronomer with Arctic expeditions captained by Ross and Parry. Between 1821 and 1823 he made a number of voyages to conduct pendulum and magnetic experiments off the coasts of Africa, America, and the Arctic. After 1827 he left the army to take up research, particularly on terrestrial magnetism; he supervised the establishment of magnetic observatories in territories throughout the British Empire. **Peter Somerville-Large**

Sacramental Test, enacted into Irish law in 1704, requiring all office-holders under the Crown to take Communion in the established church. Part of a larger penal act aimed at the Catholic population, this clause was in fact intended to curb the power of Protestant Dissenters, especially Presbyterians in Ulster. In the short term it had little effect, as most offices were already monopolised by Anglicans; but it did eventually exclude Dissenters from urban corporations. Attempts to repeal the test failed in 1719 and 1733, but in 1780 it was removed as part of wider reformist measures. **Neal Garnham**

Sadleir, John (1814–1856), solicitor and politician. MP for Carlow, 1847–53, and for Sligo thereafter, he supported Lord JOHN RUSSELL until the 1851 conflict over 'Papal aggression'. He briefly took office under Lord Aberdeen in 1852. His suicide in 1856 exposed decades of fraud that led the *Times* to call him 'a national disgrace'. **William Anthony Hay**

Sadler family, artists. The first recorded member of this family is **William Sadler** (died 1788), born in England, known as a mezzotint scraper and for one chalk drawing of the actor J. B. Kemble. His son **William Sadler II** (c. 1782–1839) was the painter of many small genre scenes and topical events, often on mahogany or copper. Topographically his landscapes are poor; he had a passion for scenes of fires and battles (see p. 1111). At his best in a large work, such as *The Battle of Waterloo*, which is based on contemporary accounts, he attempted to portray the scene of the battle at about 1:30 in the afternoon. It is painted on canvas and gives a clear, vivid view of the horror of the scene as well as its magnificence. The work of his son, **William Sadler III** (born 1808), is little known. He may have continued to make versions of his father's small pictures; however, his only known work is a straightforward panorama of Fermoy, Co. Cork, clearly and simply painted. **Anne Crookshank**

sailing. Many Irish sailors have circumnavigated the world in cruising yachts; the first to do so was Conor O'Brien, in his yacht *Saoirse* in 1922, who made important oceanographic observations.

The oldest yacht club in the world, the Royal Cork Yacht Club, based at Crosshaven in Cork Harbour, traces its history back to 1720, from the start of yachting as a sport by British naval officers based at Haulbowline Island, Cobh. Under the name of the Waterboys they began a system of complicated manoeuvring in yachts, which is regarded as the forerunner of sailing as a competitive sport. A central concept in modern competitive sailing, one-design racing, was introduced in DUBLIN BAY by Thomas Middleton and his supporters through the water wag class, a dinghy sailing boat, in 1887. The class is still in existence, making it the oldest one-design competitive class in the world still actively racing since the year it started. One of the toughest international races is the FASTNET YACHT RACE, from Cowes on the south coast of England, for which the turning mark is the FASTNET ROCK, Co. Cork. In 1990–91 an Irish team for the first time entered a round-the-world yacht race, the Whitbread Race, with the 25 m (82-ft) maxi-yacht *NCB Ireland*. [see MARITIME HISTORY.] **Tom MacSweeney**

sail training. In the late 1970s sail training began using the ASGARD, the gaff ketch designed by Colin Archer used in the HOWTH GUN-RUNNING of 1914. For the first fifteen years the scheme was run mainly by Captain Eric Healy, who oversaw the building and commissioning of *Asgard II*, a purpose-built 30 m (98-ft) brigantine. *Asgard II* takes approximately 500 young people to sea each year and is a popular entrant in the annual Tall Ships events. There are sail training schemes in most yacht clubs, catering for young people who want to learn dinghy sailing. The Irish Sailing Association is the supervisory body for the many commercial sailing schools operating around the coast and on the Shannon lakes. **Fiacc OBrolchain**

St Aengus, Burt, Co. Donegal, a rural Catholic parish church designed by LIAM MCCORMICK in 1965 and superbly sited on rising ground. Its circular plan, a radical departure from the basilical form of all previous Irish church architecture, owes its inspiration to the IRON AGE fort of the Grianán of Aileach on the nearby hillside. Above the external wall of rubble masonry, the ribbed asymmetrical copper roof rises into a pierced spire in a gentle curve. Internally the enveloping circular space is lit by a clerestory band, while a shaft of light descends on the sanctuary from within the lantern of the spire. The smaller circle of the interior is tangential to the outer circle, allowing sacristy, baptistery, and confessionals to be inserted within the space between the arcs of the two circles. St Aengus was awarded the RIAI Triennial Gold Medal in 1971 and was voted 'Building of the Century' in a poll conducted by the *Sunday Tribune* in 1999, a rare harmony of professional esteem and popular regard (see p. 665). **Brian Lalor**

St Brigid's Cross, a cross woven from rushes, traditionally made on or before 1 February, the feast-day of St Brigid. It takes the form of a central square from which four arms of equal length extend. Legend says that Brigid made the cross while nursing a dying pagan, thereby converting him to Christianity before his death. Used as the symbol of RTÉ television when it began broadcasting in 1961, St Brigid's cross is one of the few folklore items to survive into the twenty-first century. Straw versions and plastic replicas are sold in supermarkets, and hang in the windscreens of cars (see pp. 743, 1117). **Martin Clancy**

St Brigid's Day, a traditional FESTIVAL falling on 1 February (anciently known as IMBOLC), named after BRIGID, the fifth-century Abbess of Kildare. St Brigid's Cross, woven out of rushes, is still used to bring luck to the home. *Brat Bhríde* (St Brigid's mantle) was left outdoors on the eve and kept to relieve women in labour, cure barrenness, or protect virginity. The *Brídeoga* or 'Biddies', a procession of young people, carried an effigy of the saint from door to door. The day was marked by PILGRIMAGES to the many holy wells dedicated to her, many of which were thought to cure sterility, such as that of Brideswell, Co. Roscommon (see p. 150). **Stiofán Ó Cadhla**

St Brigid's mantle, a fragment of an Irish woollen mantle with a curled or tufted nap, regarded as having belonged to BRIGID, the sixth-century saint. The earliest documentary reference to it is from 1347, when the mantle is listed among the treasures of the Cathedral of St Donation, Bruges. [see MANTLE, IRISH.] **Mairead Dunlevy**

St Colman's Cathedral, Cobh, Co. Cork, cathedral of the Catholic diocese of Cork, Cloyne and Ross (see p. 54). Designed by EDWARD PUGIN and GEORGE ASHLIN, it is among the most remarkably sited and successful Gothic Revival buildings. Begun following a competition in 1867, it was not completed until 1918, at a vastly increased cost relative to the original modest estimates. Constructed on a sloping site, the building stands on a boldly modelled arcaded terrace, from which the 91 m (300-ft) spire rises to dominate the town and harbour. French Gothic in inspiration, St Colman's is built of limestone with granite dressings, its exterior enhanced by buttresses and abundant sculptural embellishment. Internally, the soaring nave and sanctuary are lit by expanses of glass by Meyer of Munich, while the sanctuary walls are fretted with diaper patterns and sculptural reliefs of great richness. **Brian Lalor**

Saintfield, Battle of (1798), a brief but bloody affair that opened the Co. Down phase of the United Irish rebellion of 1798. On Saturday 9 June a rebel force, probably totalling several thousand, took control of Saintfield, Co. Down, after burning the house of a loyalist family called McKee, killing all the occupants. Acting under various local leaders, the rebels sprang a devastating ambush on an advancing column of about 350 soldiers and yeomen, commanded by Colonel Staplyton of the York Fencible Infantry. The rebels chose their ground skilfully, trapping Staplyton's column at a place where they had to pass sloping wooded ground and high hedges, giving the United Irish pikemen a decisive advantage. Staplyton lost almost sixty men in severe hand-to-hand fighting before he rallied his men and brought cannon into play, causing numerous casualties. He then prudently retreated; and though he did not admit defeat, Saintfield was seen as a United Irish victory. **Allan Blackstock**

Saint-Gaudens, Augustus (1848–1907), sculptor. Born in Dublin to a French father and an Irish mother; when he was six months old the family emigrated to the United States, settling eventually in New York. Saint-Gaudens trained as a cameo-cutter and attended classes at the Cooper Union Art School; he also studied under Leutze at the National Academy of Design. In 1867 he was in Paris, attending the École des Beaux Arts and receiving tuition from François Jouffroy. During the 1870s he travelled between France, Italy, and the United States, carving cameos and copying classical sculptures, often for American patrons. In a reaction to the conservatism of the National Academy of Design he joined the Tile Club; he was also a joint-founder of the Society of American Artists.

sailing. *Fleet racing off the Co. Cork coast, where annual sailing events, such as Ford Cork Week, attract sailors from around Ireland and overseas to enjoy top-level competition. [David Branigan, Oceansport]*

His first large public sculpture, a memorial to the naval commander David Glasgow Farragut, was unveiled in Madison Square Park, New York, in 1881; subsequent commissions included the Abraham Lincoln Memorial (1884–7) in Lincoln Park, Chicago, the Puritan (1883–6), in Springfield, Massachusetts, the Shaw Memorial (1884–97) in Boston Common, and a colossal statue of Diana (1886–91) commissioned as a weathervane for the tower of Madison Square Garden, New York. In 1891 Saint-Gaudens settled in Cornish, New Hampshire. Among his later works were the Sherman Monument (1892–1903), New York, and the PARNELL Monument (unveiled 1911) in O'Connell Street, Dublin. Saint-Gaudens is perhaps best known for his coin designs for the US Treasury, carried out between 1905 and 1907. **Peter Murray**

St James's Brass and Reed Band, Dublin, established in 1800, though earlier references to a band in St James's parish exist. The thriving local tanners' trade provided many of the early members, though the band was not exclusively linked to any particular craft. Originally a typical brass band, its present name was adopted in 1877. The band has historic associations, particularly with the 1916 Rising, and has played at many important national events. It was the first civilian band to broadcast on 2RN (1926), the precursor of RTÉ, and it continues to perform and tour regularly. **Adrian Scahill**

St Leger, Sir Anthony (1496–1559), Lord Deputy of Ireland, 1540–47, 1550, and 1553–6. A successful courtier who, as one of the 'gentlemen pensioners', enjoyed a particularly close personal relationship with HENRY VIII; he inherited all the problems that had plagued his deposed predecessor, LORD LEONARD GREY. His proposed solution was a brilliant initiative whereby the native Irish lords were supposed fictionally to have been conquered and to be pardoned and reconstituted as nobles by the new Irish monarchy established in the person of Henry VIII by statute in 1541. This policy of 'surrender and regrant', fuelled by rewards and the lavish distribution of monastic lands, proved immensely successful in its early stages, as leading figures, such as O'Neill and O'Brien, agreed to terms; but St Leger's open-door policy soon encountered the opposition of the Ormondists (followers of the Duke of Ormond) and of English officials in Dublin, both of whom expected preferential treatment; and his position was rapidly undermined during the prolonged political instability that followed the death of Henry VIII in 1547. In the early 1550s St Leger made a number of desperate efforts to defend his position through the dissolution of ST PATRICK'S CATHEDRAL, Dublin, and the initiation of a colonising enterprise in the midlands. But these actions—together with his failure to stem the intensifying migration of the Scots of the Isles to Ulster, and revelations of extensive abuses in his administration of royal finances—led to the establishment of an inquiry and his dismissal in disgrace in 1556. [see SCOTTISH SETTLEMENT IN IRELAND.] **Ciaran Brady**

St Patrick: see PATRICK.

St Patrick for Ireland (1639), a mythological play by James Shirley, resident playwright at the WERBURGH STREET THEATRE. The first play on an Irish subject written for an Irish theatre, Shirley's version of St PATRICK's evangelisation of Ireland employs spectacular processions, ending with a pagan magician being swallowed by the ground. **Christopher Morash**

St Patrick's Bell, an iron hand-bell of standard type but atypical construction. Its name—*Clog an Aidheachta,* 'Bell of the Testament'—is first recorded in 1044 and must reflect a belief that

PATRICK willed the bell to his successors. Together with a crozier attributed to Patrick, and the Book of ARMAGH, it was one of the insignia of the Armagh abbacy. A shrine made c. 1100 bears the names of Abbot Dónal, of the Ó Lochlainn high king, and of the keeper of the bell, Ó Maoilchalainn. The Uí Maoilchalainn (later Mulhollands) retained almost continuous possession of the bell and shrine until the early nineteenth century; both are now in the NATIONAL MUSEUM, Dublin. [see RELIQUARIES.] **Cormac Bourke**

St Patrick's Cathedral, Dublin, built by Archbishop John Comyn as a collegiate church, dedicated in 1192. Following a disagreement with the Dean and Chapter of CHRIST CHURCH, Archbishop Henry de Londres advanced the church to cathedral status in 1213 and began to rebuild it on a grander scale. The oldest parts of the fabric date from the thirteenth and fourteenth centuries. JONATHAN SWIFT was dean from 1713 to 1745. During the nineteenth century the cathedral underwent major restoration. It was enacted as the national cathedral of the CHURCH OF IRELAND in 1872. **Rachel Moss**

St Patrick's College, Maynooth, set up by an act of the Irish Parliament passed at the request of the Catholic bishops for the training of diocesan priests. Officially the Roman Catholic College of St PATRICK, it was located on land given by the Duke of Leinster from his estate in Co. Kildare, some 25 km (15 miles) west of Dublin, where the foundation stone was laid by the LORD LIEUTENANT on 20 April 1795. It received an annual parliamentary grant (much increased, amid great controversy, in 1845) until 1870, when this was abolished under the Irish Church Act (1869).

Despite its official status, the college's clerical trustees and managers acted with much independence of mind, and it soon acquired a reputation as a nursery of priests conspicuous for their religious conservatism and political liberalism. The pontifical charter granted in 1900 enabled Maynooth to confer degrees in ecclesiastical subjects; at about the same time its students began sitting examinations of the Royal University of Ireland in arts and science. In 1910 it became a 'recognised college' of the new National University of Ireland. Since 1795 some 10,000 candidates for the priesthood have studied at Maynooth.

In 1966 the college began admitting lay students, first members of lay religious orders (brothers and nuns), then, in 1968, ordinary young men and women, who by 1977 outnumbered seminarians and religious. In 1997 a legal separation was made between St Patrick's College and the National University of Ireland, Maynooth, on a new campus, though some buildings and other facilities continue to be shared. **C. J. Woods**

St Patrick's Day (17 March), a holy day in the liturgical calendar. In the middle of the nineteenth century such Irish-American groups as the ANCIENT ORDER OF HIBERNIANS sponsored

St Patrick's Bell. *St Patrick's Bell, showing (left) the bell (19.3 cm) and (right) the shrine (26.7 cm). Made some time between the sixth and the eighth centuries, the bronze-coated iron bell (left) was traditionally believed to have been used by St Patrick. The backplate of the shrine (right), c. 1100, with interlocking cross decoration, bears an inscription around the margins stating that it was made by Condulig Ua hInmainen and his sons for Domhnall Ua Lochlainn, King of Ireland (1094–1121). [National Museum of Ireland]*

parades on St Patrick's Day to demonstrate the self-discipline and contribution of Irish emigrants, though parades had been held since the late eighteenth century. Over time St Patrick's Day festivities have become more inclusive events, a day when 'everyone is Irish.' Since the mid-1970s American-style parades have been organised in Irish cities. **Lawrence W. McBride**

St Patrick's Day and the diaspora. In the middle of the seventeenth century ST PATRICK'S DAY was formalised by the Vatican as a day of religious observance and celebration, and during the eighteenth century it became a common feature of Irish life. With the spread of Irish people throughout the world, in the pre-famine decades and after, St Patrick's Day moved with them. The day was formally marked for the first time in Boston in 1737 by the Charitable Society of Boston, while the first New York parade was staged in 1766. These original celebrations were organised by members of the elite Protestant Irish population in America and centred on Irish men serving in the British army. From the early nineteenth century, with increased numbers of Catholic immigrants, the nature of the celebrations was transformed and they became centred, as they are today, on public parades organised by such bodies as the ANCIENT ORDER OF HIBERNIANS. American parades now take place throughout the country and are massive in scale. The New York parade includes 150,000 marchers, watched by a crowd of 1.5 million, while the parade in Savannah, Georgia, first staged in 1824, attracts 400,000 spectators. Other countries with large numbers of Irish immigrants also developed the tradition of marking St Patrick's Day. In Canada, Australia, New Zealand, South Africa, and Argentina, the Irish community staged parades, celebratory dinners, and church services from the early nineteenth century. In Montserrat the legacy of the Irish diaspora is marked by the only public holiday on 17 March outside Ireland.

St Patrick's Day performed a vital function for Irish people overseas in allowing them an opportunity to publicly declare their cohesion as an immigrant group in their new home; it also allowed them to display their support for the nationalist community in Ireland. Though the day is now dominated by commercial interests, and often viewed as one based on the sentimentality of green beer, shamrock, and LEPRECHAUNS, St Patrick's Day is still the most important day in the calendar for the Irish diaspora. **Mike Cronin**

St Patrick's Tooth, The Shrine of: see FIACAIL PHÁDRAIG.

St Ruth, Charles Calmont, Marquis de (c. 1650–1691), French general. He led the Irish soldiers of Mountcashel's Brigade in Savoy, 1690, and was placed in command of the JACOBITE army for the Irish campaign of 1691. He arrived in Limerick in May 1691, together with a French convoy carrying limited quantities of arms, ammunition and supplies. He was the most popular leader of the Irish soldiers and the only foreign officer whose departure from the scene was genuinely regretted in Ireland. It was he, therefore, who led the army which confronted the Williamite forces during the siege of Athlone (June 1691) and the BATTLE OF AUGHRIM (12 July 1691).

Among his peers, his command of the Jacobite army met with a mixed response. Certainly on his arrival he vigorously prepared for the forthcoming campaign, putting French engineers to work on the fortification of the principal strongholds, placing 10,000 soldiers in garrisons and consigning 21,000 to the field. However, his decision to change his troops continuously at Athlone led to five hundred deaths, compared with only thirteen on William's side; the Earl of Tryconnell later maintained that if St Ruth had followed his advice the Battle of Aughrim would have been unnecessary. It was during this engagement that St Ruth met his death, when a cannon-ball from the Williamite battery tore off his head. The spot where he is traditionally believed to have fallen is marked by a whitethorn bush, while on the southern slope of Aughrim Hill there are traces of an old burial ground in which it is said his body was first buried before it was removed to Athenry (see p. 562). **Rosemary Richey**

saints. At first sight, Ireland's saints (most of whom are thought to have lived in the period 500–650) outnumber those of all other parts of Christendom. In fact there are relatively few original Irish saints, the majority being either products of localising tendencies or Christian versions of pre-Christian ancestral cults.

The proliferation of pet forms of saints' names led to the local fragmentation and consequent multiplication of cults. The name Colm is the most striking example of this development. Borne by the founder of Iona, COLM CILLE (Latinised 'Columba'), this name generated a substantial number of diminutive and pet forms, including Colmán, Colla (Coille), Comma (Coimme), Conna (Coinne), Canna (Cainne) and Camma (Caimme), all of which can be further extended by the use of prefixes (*Mo-* or *Do-*) and suffixes (e.g. *-óg*, *-ín*, *-án*). Being one of Ireland's most important saints, Colm Cille's cult spread to almost every corner of the country. However, because of strong localising tendencies, most churches associated with his name no longer recall the saint. Noted examples are Terryglass (Colm), Inishcealtra (Caimín), Roscommon (Comán), and Kilkenny (Cainneach). The canonisation of saints did not become customary until the twelfth century, and so none of the early Irish saints has been canonised.

Among the numerous pre-Christian cults that have come to be identified as saints are those of BRIGID of Kildare, GOBNAIT of Ballyvourney, Co. Cork, Molaga of Timoleague, Co. Cork, and Molua of Killaloe, Co. Clare. **Pádraig Ó Riain**

St Stephen's Singers. Originally founded as a madrigal group, the choir was established in University College, Dublin, in 1967 by Audrey Corbett (conductor from 1967 to 1971), and from 1968 to 1971 it won prizes for madrigal singing at the FEIS CEOIL. In 1970–71 the St Stephen's Singers received the National Trophy for mixed voice choirs at the Cork Choral Festival. Chosen in 1971 to represent Ireland in the international competition 'Let the People Sing', the choir tied with Hungary for first place. Also in 1971 the St Stephen's Singers issued an album, entitled 'Sing Joyfully'. Later conductors have included GERARD GILLEN and Margaret O'Sullivan. **Adrian Scahill**

Sáirséal agus Dill, publishers. Founded by Seán Sáirséal Ó hÉigeartaigh in 1946, it was soon to become the leading publisher of modern writing in Irish. Publishing to high and innovative editorial and production standards, Sáirséal agus Dill helped, within a few years, to foster a new generation of writers. The publication of MÁIRTÍN Ó CADHAIN's CRÉ NA CILLE (1949) firmly established the company's credentials. It had a long association with Ó Cadhain and other prolific writers, including SEÁN Ó RÍORDÁIN and DIARMAID Ó SÚILLEABHÁIN. The company was sold in the early 1980s and now publishes as Sáirséal Ó Marcaigh. [see PUBLISHING.] **Seosamh Ó Murchú**

Salamanca, site of a famous Spanish university from the Middle Ages, attended by Irish students from the 1570s. In 1592 the College of St PATRICK was established with the financial assistance of Philip II to train Catholic priests for Ireland, in response to the opening of

TRINITY COLLEGE, Dublin. It became the largest Irish seminary in Europe, sending some 500 priests to Ireland, England, and Scotland in the space of a hundred years. Though at least a third of its student body was drawn from the native Irish, it was administered in the main by OLD ENGLISH Jesuits. Following the expulsion of the Jesuits from Spain in 1767, it was taken over by the Irish diocesan clergy. It was a rallying point for the Irish exile community in Spain and continued as an Irish cultural centre throughout the eighteenth century but was closed during the SPANISH CIVIL WAR in 1936. [see IRISH COLLEGES IN CONTINENTAL EUROPE; LOUVAIN.] **Gráinne Henry**

Sally Gap (a corruption of 'Saddle Gap'), one of the main passes in the WICKLOW MOUNTAINS, connecting the coastal lowland of east Co. Wicklow with the plains of Leinster west of the mountains. Part of an extensive granitic plateau at an altitude of about 530 m (1,740 ft), the Sally Gap is overlooked by the peaks of Kippure, Djouce, Tonduff, and Corrig. During the last GLACIATION the area was an extensive snowfield that fed many of the valley glaciers that flowed out of the mountains, including those that occupied the Liffey, Dargle, Annamoe, and Cloghoge valleys. Now, as well as being the source of the River Liffey, the Sally Gap is an important area of blanket bog that supports a wide variety of flora, including heather, cross-leaved heath, bog cotton, deer grass, bog asphodel, and bilberry; it is also an important habitat for wild birds, including snipe, meadow pipit, skylark, red grouse, dipper, grey wagtail, peregrine falcon, and merlin.

The Sally Gap became important in the first millennium as a trade route linking the distant plains of Leinster with Britain by way of the ports of Wicklow and Arklow. Goods carried through it included not only high-value materials and artefacts bound for the royal houses of Leinster but also, especially in VIKING times, slaves. Though the valleys below the Sally Gap, especially the Liffey valley, experienced increased population pressure from the eighteenth century until the GREAT FAMINE, the area is now largely a wilderness, much of it within the Wicklow Mountains National Park. **Colman Gallagher**

Salmon, George (1819–1904), mathematician and theologian. Born in Dublin, he was brought up in Cork; he graduated from TCD in 1838 and was elected a fellow in 1841. From 1841 until 1866 he held a college tutorship, during which time he wrote four influential textbooks on higher geometry, including the frequently republished *Treatise on Conic Sections* (1848). In 1866 he was elected professor of divinity and thereafter devoted himself to theology. His later books include *The Infallibility of the Church* (1888). He served as provost of Trinity College, Dublin, from 1888 until his death. **Rod Gow**

Samhain. HALLOWE'EN derives from the ancient festival of Samhain and is one of the QUARTER DAYS, marking the first day of winter. Oíche Shamhna (November Eve) is especially identified with spirits, OTHERWORLD activity, and divination. Apples, nuts, and POTATO-based foods, such as stampy, boxty, and colcannon, are eaten, and children dress up and go from house to house collecting apples and nuts. Barm brack *(bairín breac)*, a type of fruit cake, contains various objects associated with divination, especially regarding marriage. Many games are played, for example attempting to bite an apple floating in water. People believed that evil spirits were abroad and so took measures to protect themselves, their property and livestock: measures against evil forces included the sprinkling of holy water on animals and crops. Children are warned against picking and eating certain FRUITS that have the spit or faeces of the POOKA (*púca*) on them. Bonfires are a prominent feature of Hallowe'en. [see BEALTAINE; IMBOLC; LÚNASA.] **Ríonach uí Ógáin**

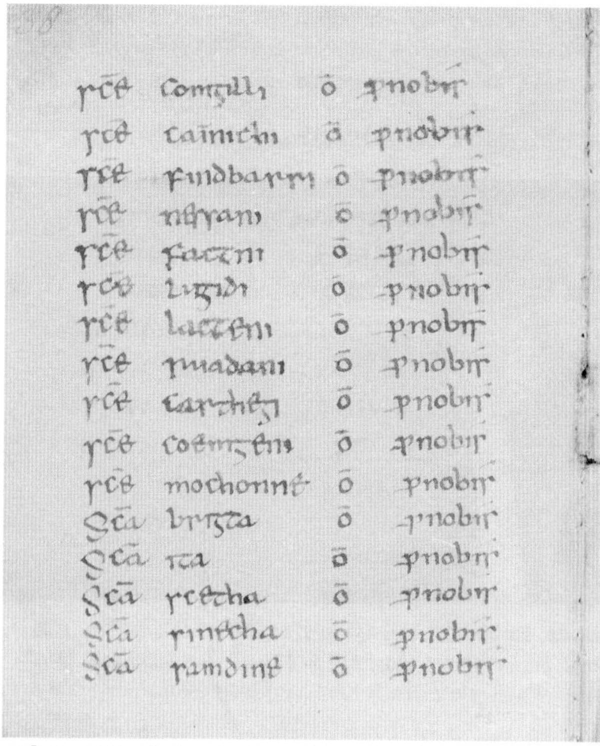

saints. *Folio 30r from the Stowe Missal, the earliest surviving example of a liturgy. Its author is unknown, but it spent some time in a private library of the Dukes of Buckingham at Stowe, Buckinghamshire, in the 1800s. This page lists various saints, among them St Finbarr (third from top) and St Brigid (fifth from the bottom). [Royal Irish Academy]*

samplers. The earliest known Irish needlework sampler is one made in Wexford in 1622. Seventeenth and eighteenth-century samplers were made as a record of needlework stitches and techniques; later they became a decorative means of teaching the alphabet and linen-marking skills to girls aged seven and upwards in national schools. The middle of the nineteenth century produced vivid 'Berlin woolwork' samplers, using the new colourfast aniline dyes. Punched card was the background for many of the sentimental texts and mourning samplers of the late Victorian period. Today, sampler kits based on traditional patterns are available through mail order and specialist suppliers. **Valerie Wilson**

Sands, Robert (Bobby) (1954–1981), hunger-striker and MP. Born in Rathcoole, Belfast. Sands was the first, and the best known, of the ten republican HUNGER-STRIKERS who died in the campaign of 1980–81 for 'political status' in the 'H blocks' of the Maze Prison. The commanding officer of the PROVISIONAL IRA prisoners, he began his fast on 1 March 1981. At regular intervals other prisoners, chosen from a range of home districts to achieve maximum emotional impact, joined the strike. The self-sacrificial ethos of the protesters found an echo in the Catholic-dominated theology of Irish NATIONALISM, and the refusal of Margaret Thatcher's government in London to make any concessions alienated much moderate opinion. Early in April, Sands' campaign received a substantial boost when he was elected MP in a by-election for the border constituency of Fermanagh and South Tyrone. On 5 May he died after sixty-six days without food. The widespread nationalist support that the H-Block campaign secured was further marked by the election of two hunger-strikers to Dáil Éireann in the June general election. In general, the electoral successes associated with the campaign powerfully reinforced the advocates of a more political strategy within the republican movement. **Keith Jeffery**

Sands, Bobby. *A street sign in Tehran, Iran, commemorates Bobby Sands, the hunger-striker and MP for Fermanagh-South Tyrone, who died on 5 May 1981. [Patsy McGarry,* Irish Times*]*

Sands family, a family folk music group from Mayobridge, Co. Down, performing together since 1967. They have released sixteen albums and toured internationally, most notably in eastern Europe. The group includes Tommy, Colum, Ben, and Anne Sands and formerly also Eugene (died 1975). Tommy, Colum, and Ben maintain solo careers as singer-songwriters; Tommy presents 'Country Céilidh' on Downtown Radio, and Colum presents 'Folk Club' and 'Shifting Sands' on Radio Ulster. Colum also runs Spring Records from a studio in Rostrevor, Co. Down, which released *The Sands Family Collection* in 1993. **Anthony McCann**

San Francisco, the Irish in. The Gold Rush transformed San Francisco from a small trading village into a booming commercial port city. Irish immigrants poured into the city with thousands of others, drawn by stories of instant wealth. While most did not strike it rich in gold, the Irish thrived in San Francisco, attaining economic, social, and political success much earlier than in the east. By 1880 a third of the population, including many leading citizens, were Irish.

Several factors made the Irish experience in San Francisco unique. Rapid growth, the lack of an established culture, and the influx of immigrants from all over the world created an extremely fluid society. Also, nearly half the Irish came from eastern cities, where they had become acculturated to American ways. More importantly, large numbers of Chinese labourers made Irish (as well as German) immigrants seem less threatening to native-born Americans, and provided them with a common target of nativism. As a result, while they were not completely immune to prejudice, the Catholic Irish had a greater feeling of confidence and acceptance, without lingering memories of hostility to pass down to future generations. This confidence was evident in the rapid rise of the Irish in banking, railways, and city life. The engineer Jasper O'Farrell designed San Francisco's distinctive street grid; the property mogul John Sullivan helped to found the city's leading bank, the Hibernia Savings and Loan Society (established 1859). This institution enabled many working-class Irish to buy their own houses in several neighbourhoods within the Mission District, preventing overcrowding into a ghetto. Irish businessmen were active philanthropists, donating millions to the city and the Catholic Church for establishing churches, schools, and charitable organisations. In addition, a quarter of public school teachers by 1910 were Irish, the most famous of whom was the educator and women's rights advocate Kate Kennedy (1829–1890).

The Irish dominated San Francisco politics for more than a century, electing the first Irish-born mayor, Frank McCoppin, in 1867, almost twenty years before New York (1880) or Boston (1884). Yet San Francisco's Irish political machines were just as open to charges of corruption, most notably by the 1856 Vigilance Committee and the People's Party of the late 1860s. By the 1870s a fifth of voters were Irish, making them the most significant voting group. Working-class Irish helped elect the powerful but short-lived Workingmen's Party (1877–8), led by Denis Kearney, the 'sandlot orator'. This party's slogan was 'The Chinese must go', demonstrating Irish workers' fears for their jobs on the docks and in construction.

San Francisco clings tightly to its Irish roots. Its St Patrick's Day parade celebrated its 150th anniversary in 2002, while its Irish paper, the *Irish Herald*, is the oldest on the west coast. Despite widespread suburbanisation after the Second World War, the Mission District remains a centre of Irish culture and is home to many Irish immigrants. Since 1973 the United Irish Cultural Center has helped San Francisco's second-largest white national community (10 per cent of the population in 1990) to maintain their Irish identity and their connection with Ireland. **Meaghan Dwyer**

San Patricios, los (Battalion of ST PATRICK), an artillery battalion composed of foreigners that fought for MEXICO against the United States in the war of 1846–8. It engaged in all the principal battles of the war. At Churubusco, US forces captured or killed 60 per cent of the battalion in combat; fifty of those captured were deemed guilty of desertion during a time of war and were put to death by order of US court martial. During US occupation of the capital the Mexican army reconstituted the battalion, but President Herrera dissolved it after the US evacuation of 1848.

Irish influence is evident from the unit's name, but the assessment of that influence has been a source of controversy since the battalion's formation; in fact the Irish component was probably not more than 40 per cent. At first, American reaction cited the battalion as another example of Irish-American disloyalty, claiming that its Irish members had deserted from the US army. Mexican historians and popular memory, on the other hand, have respected the battalion's courage and questioned the justice of the US court martial. Recently American historians have argued that Irish members of the battalion, even had they deserted, could not have been 'disloyal' to the United States, as most of them were recent immigrants, who knew little English and had little in common with American culture. Instead the United States betrayed them: army recruiters offered them citizenship and steady pay for military service, only to have them serve under abusive nativist officers. Mexican commanders during the war also demonstrated their awareness that many Irish did not consider the United States their home by producing leaflets soliciting their service, emphasising their shared Catholic faith and oppression by Protestant countries. **David Michaelsen**

Saoirse? (1961), an actuality film using historic documentary footage, directed by George Morrison and produced by GAEL-LINN, with music by SEÁN Ó RIADA. The score consolidated Ó Riada's reputation, based on his earlier successful and unique form of orchestration, using both original material and traditional airs and formats, in the film MISE ÉIRE (1959). **Peadar Ó Riada**

Sarsfield, Patrick, first Earl of Lucan (c. 1655–1693), soldier. The date and place of his birth are unknown, and details of his childhood, education, and early military service are sketchy. He is first mentioned in army registers in 1678, when his regiment was disbanded. His military reputation was established at the Battle of Sedgemoor (1685), where the Duke of Monmouth, the illegitimate son of CHARLES II, was defeated in his attempt to seize the throne. A grateful JAMES II made Sarsfield lieutenant-colonel of a cavalry regiment. In 1688 he took part in the attempt to stop the invasion of WILLIAM III and then joined James in exile. When the war began in Ireland in 1689 he was promoted to brigadier and given command of a cavalry regiment. After the defeat at the BOYNE he was instrumental in rallying the dispirited JACOBITES and encouraging them to fight on. His raid on the Williamite artillery cavalcade at Ballyneety, Co. Limerick, in August 1690 further enhanced his reputation, though he took no direct part in the defence of Limerick. Leader of the war faction of the Jacobites, he strongly rejected any overtures for negotiation with William. His *volte-face* in agreeing to GINKEL's terms in October 1691 appears to have resulted from a loss of nerve; and his limited political skills were shown in the careless drafting of the religious liberty clause in the TREATY OF LIMERICK. He resumed his military career on the Continent and died from wounds received at the Battle of Landen (1693). [see LIMERICK, SIEGE OF.] **Liam Irwin**

Sarsfield Bridge, the principal bridge over the River SHANNON at Limerick, opened in 1835 as Wellesley Bridge. The designer, ALEXANDER NIMMO, was greatly influenced by Perronet's Pont Neuilly in Paris. The main bridge has five arches with a span of 21.3 m (70 ft) and arch profiles designed to aid the flow of water under the bridge. **Ronald Cox**

'Sash My Father Wore, The', an ORANGE SONG commending former brethren for defending liberty; probably based on 'The Hat My Father Wore'. Usually only the chorus is sung, often provocatively in public. **John Moulden**

Saunderson, Colonel Edward (1837–1906), politician. Born in Ballinamallard, Co. Fermanagh. He began his political career, in the family tradition, as a Liberal and was MP for Co. Cavan between 1865 and 1874. He disliked many of the reforms of GLADSTONE's first administration, however, and was outraged by the activities of the Land League. He joined the ORANGE ORDER in 1882 and was elected as a Conservative for North Armagh in the pivotal general election of 1885. He brought Conservatives and Liberal Unionists together to form the Irish Unionist Party in 1886 and led this rather loose group until his death. His impassioned denunciations of HOME RULE and his outspoken support for the Orange Order earned him the nickname of the 'Dancing Dervish'. His unbending defence of landlord interests encouraged defections in the Ulster unionist camp to the farmers' champion, T. W. Russell, and to the INDEPENDENT ORANGE ORDER. **Jonathan Bardon**

Save the West, a movement formed in 1963, prompted by the accelerating destruction of the western smallholder class and the region's rural economy. The campaign's central message was that the only way to stave off the decline of the west was through the mobilising of local community groups, which would design and implement development plans for their areas, combined with grants, loans, and subsidies to smallholders from the Government. The campaign depended heavily on the leadership of a Co. Donegal priest, Father James McDyer (1911–1987) of Glencolumbkille. He firmly believed the solution to problems of western decline was to be found in local initiatives. While the campaign garnered considerable support, its success was limited. It remained very dependent on Father McDyer, and when he retired the campaign quickly disintegrated.

However, the problem of rural decline in the west continued. In the 1990s a group of small farmers in Co. Galway approached their bishops to express concern about the decline in rural communities. The bishops of Connacht and Co. Donegal subsequently set up an organisation called Developing the West Together, whose central message was very similar to that of Save the West. It called for local community activity, combined with regionally directed strategies by the Government. Following a recommendation made in a report by Developing the West Together, a statutory body, the Western Development Commission, was established in 1999. Its remit is to promote the economic and social development of the western region. [see RURAL DEVELOPMENT.] **Sally Shortall**

Saville Inquiry. In Northern Ireland the Widgery Report, summing up the conclusions of the British government inquiry into the events of BLOODY SUNDAY, is still the subject of controversy. In January 1998 the British Prime Minister, Tony Blair, set up a new tribunal of inquiry, chaired by Lord Saville of Newdigate, to inquire into 'the events of Sunday, 30th January 1972, which led to the loss of life in connection with the procession in Londonderry on that day, taking account of any new information relevant to events on that day.' The work of this tribunal, which has the same legal powers as the High Court, is continuing. **Maura Adshead**

Saw Doctors, the, pop group. Formed in 1988 in Tuam, Co. Galway, within two years the group had become one of the most popular bands in Ireland. Combining rock with a peculiarly Galwegian view of things, the Saw Doctors' brand of roots and rock divided the critics, but their debut album, *If This Is Rock and Roll, I Want My Old Job Back* (1991) topped the charts. Their keynote song remains 'I Useta Love Her' (1990). **Tony Clayton-Lea**

Sayers, Peig (1873–1958), oral storyteller and autobiographer. Born and educated at Dunquin, Co. Kerry; employed as a household

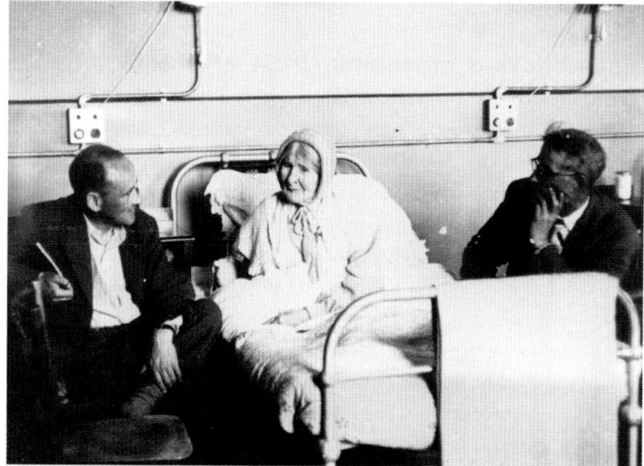

Sayers. *Peig Sayers, last of the major storytellers from the Great Blasket Island, Co. Kerry, c. 1958, blind in Dingle Hospital, with Seán Ó Ríordáin (left) and her son Mícheál Ó Gaoithín (right). [Ionad an Bhlascaoid Mhóir; photo: Tomás Ó Muircheartaigh]*

and farm servant from c. 1886. She wished to emigrate but could not raise the cost of the passage to America. She married Pádraig Ó Gaoithín of the Great Blasket, raising their ten children there, though six of them were lost to childhood diseases and one in adulthood to a cliff fall. In old age she moved to the mainland.

Literate in English but not in Irish, she was among the finest storytellers. Greatly respected by Irish scholars and folklorists, she had a large repertoire, including both international tales and the principal Irish hero-tales not usually recited by women. She dictated her life story, published as *Peig: A Scéal Féin* (1936) and *Machnamh Seana-Mhná* (1939), to her son Míchéal Ó Gaoithín, who collected further biographical materials in *Beatha Pheig Sayers* (1970). It is probable that there was some editing or bowdlerisation of the material between composition and publication to accommodate these texts to ideological expectations in a period that idealised rural life and GAELTACHT traditions; nevertheless they make a singular contribution to social history in general and in particular to Irish autobiography and to our understanding of life, especially of women's lives, in an isolated subsistence society. [see FLOWER, ROBIN; Ó CRIOMHTHAINN, TÓMAS; Ó SUILEABHAIN, MUIRIS.] **Patricia Coughlan**

Scaife, Brendan Kevin Patrick (1928–), engineer. Born in London to Irish parents; studied electrical engineering at the University of London and researched the effect of high pressures on dielectric materials under H. Tropper. A scholar at the Dublin Institute for Advanced Studies under ERWIN SCHRÖDINGER, he subsequently collaborated with H. Fröhlich at the University of Liverpool. In 1961 he joined the Engineering School at TRINITY COLLEGE, Dublin, and in 1972 was appointed to the chair of engineering science. His dielectrics research group gained an international reputation and gave the Graduate School of Engineering Studies a strong impetus. In 1992 he was awarded the BOYLE MEDAL of the RDS. His published works include *Principles of Dielectrics*. **W. Garrett Scaife**

Scallon, Rosemary, née Brown, also known as Dana (1951–), singer and politician. Born in Derry. She won the EUROVISION SONG CONTEST in 1970 with the song 'All Kinds of Everything' (by Lindsay and Smith). In 1990 she moved to Alabama and in 1992 began a broadcasting career with the conservative Catholic television channel EWTN (Eternal Word Television Network). In 1997 she unsuccessfully contested the Irish Presidential election, and in 1999 she was elected a member of the European Parliament for Connacht-Ulster. **Myra Dowling**

Scandinavian museums, Irish artefacts in. Many items of Irish or probable Irish origin are preserved in Nordic museums, having been brought to Scandinavia either in VIKING times or in the nineteenth century. The most sizeable collections of the former are in Norwegian museums—in Oslo, Bergen, Stavanger, and Tromsø in particular—and consist of smaller items of largely religious metalwork taken from Irish MONASTERIES in about the ninth century that crossed the North Sea either as loot or as goods traded at markets such as Kaupang on the Oslo fjord. The same applies to the 'CROZIER' head and possibly also other items from Helgö in the Statens Historiska Museum in Stockholm. During the nineteenth century a considerable collection of prehistoric and medieval bronze objects was obtained by the National Museum of Denmark in Copenhagen through exchange with the ROYAL IRISH ACADEMY, or by purchase from a Dublin dealer, J. H. Underwood. An ivory crozier head from Aghadoe, Co. Kerry, formerly in Stockholm, is now in Hannover. **Peter Harbison**

Scanlon, James (1952–), sculptor and STAINED-GLASS artist. He studied at Crawford School of Art, Cork. Sculpture commissions include Sneem, Co. Kerry, 1989, the Sculptured Courtyard at University College, Cork, 1993, and the Ark Children's Centre, Temple Bar, Dublin; other examples include Woodfield House, Limerick, the Cathedral of St Mary and St Anne, Cork, and the Consilium Building, Brussels. He has exhibited widely and received many international awards and represented Ireland with a stained-glass panel at the Garden Festival, Japan, 1990. He is a member of AOSDÁNA. There is a collection of his work at the Crawford Gallery, Cork (see p. 1014). **Suzanne McNab**

Sceilg Mhichíl (also called Great Skellig Rock), Co. Kerry, an island monastery and PILGRIMAGE site comprising at least six BEEHIVE HUTS, two stone-roofed oratories, and cross-decorated stones on a platform 170 m (560 ft) above sea level, reached by stone steps, and with an eerie hermit's oratory on the South Peak. Associated with a St Finian and dedicated to the Archangel Michael, the island was plundered by VIKINGS in 824, and an abbot of Sceilg is recorded as having died in 882. [see SKELLIGS.] **Peter Harbison**

'Scéla Cano Meic Gartnáin' ('Story of Cano, son of Gartnán'), a composite tale that has been dated to the second half of the ninth century but probably underwent further expansion and modification during the Middle Irish period. It relates the exile in Ireland of the Scottish noble Cano son of Gartnán and of his love affair with Créd, wife of Marcán and daughter of GUAIRE AIDNE. Cano refuses her love until he becomes King of Scotland, thereafter limiting himself to an annual tryst with her. While going to such a tryst he is attacked by Colco, son of Marcán; seeing him injured, the distraught Créd dashes her head on a rock, killing herself and shattering the 'life-stone' he had given her as a token. As a result, Cano dies three days later. **Ruairí Ó hUiginn**

'Scéla Mucce Meic Dathó' ('the story of Mac Dathó's Pig'), a tale that, like 'FLED BRICRENN', revolves around a contest for the hero's portion of a pig at a feast. The contest between the warriors of Ulster and Connacht, who have come to claim the wonderful hound of the Leinster hospitaller Mac Dathó, is brought about through the machinations of Mac Dathó's wife. The Ulster champion, Ceat mac Mághach, claims the status as pre-eminent warrior in the gathering, dismissing all other pretenders by dint of boast and verbal acumen. He is forced to yield, however, at the arrival of the Ulsterman Conall Cearnach carrying the head of Ceat's brother. The contest finally results in a general brawl, in which the Ulstermen triumph but Mac Dathó's hound is killed. This particularly vivid tale may have more than a hint of satire on the heroic ethos in general. **Ruairí Ó hUiginn**

scenic design. Irish theatre was primarily an actor's theatre until the middle of the eighteenth century, when audiences began to demand an ever-increasing level of spectacle. A print of 1758 shows the Crow Street Theatre, Dublin, with an extended forestage running around the auditorium, on which a horse-race is being staged. Catering to such tastes, playwrights responded with new theatrical forms, such as JOHN O'KEEFFE's *The Giant's Causeway* (1770), which promised audiences 'an elegant View of the Giant's Causeway, the Dargle, and the Waterfall of Powerscourt.' By the 1820s plays were using translucent scenery and gaslight to create elaborate stage reproductions of idealised landscapes.

The reaction against these forms of stage spectacle happened as much by necessity as by intention. W. B. YEATS, one of the founders of the ABBEY THEATRE, was interested in new forms of scenic design, experimenting in 1910 with Edward Gordon Craig's innovative system of moving screens. However, financial constraints and small stage spaces meant that in practice the Abbey increasingly reused conventional box set interiors, while the long-serving Abbey lighting designer Seaghan Barlow lit almost every play with the same amber wash. At first the response to such austere simplicity was enthusiastic; by the 1920s, however, there was a growing sense of boredom with the lack of scenic transformation.

When MICHEÁL MAC LIAMMÓIR and HILTON EDWARDS founded the GATE THEATRE in Dublin in 1928 they showed that it was possible to create visually interesting performances with limited means. Favouring stylised sets, often with elaborate neo-Celtic detailing, and strong colours in their lighting designs, Edwards and Mac Liammóir were for many years the leading Irish scenic artists. It was not until MICHAEL SCOTT's 1966 Abbey Theatre came into operation that there was scope for younger scenic artists to exercise their abilities. This would become evident in Bronwen Casson's towering, abstract, and suggestive forest for TOM MURPHY's *The Morning after Optimism* (Abbey Theatre, 1971). Later work by Consolata Boyle, Frank Flood, and others established an expectation among audiences that even a theatre with a strong tradition of the spoken word must also be visually challenging and innovative. **Christopher Morash**

Scharff, R. F. [Robert Francis] (1858–1934), naturalist. Born in Leeds; educated in England, Scotland, Germany, and Italy. He became keeper of the NATURAL HISTORY MUSEUM, Dublin, in 1890; from then until his retirement in 1921 he dealt with a wide variety of zoological groups, including seals, birds, fishes, turtles, leeches, and tapeworms. He attended many international zoological gatherings and took a leading role in many of the scientific societies in Dublin. He published several books on zoogeography and was a proponent of land bridges to explain distributions. **D. Patrick Sleeman**

Schola Cantorum, established by the Catholic hierarchy in 1970 and based in St Finian's College, Mullingar, under the direction of Father FRANK MCNAMARA. Five-year scholarships are awarded to musically talented boys, who receive specialised musical instruction in parallel with their secondary education. Tuition concentrates on piano and organ, though other instrumental instruction is provided. In 1984 Shane Brennan, a former pupil of the Schola, became director. The success of the Schola is evident not only in the influence of its graduates in CHURCH MUSIC but equally so in music EDUCATION. **Adrian Scahill**

'Scholars' Primer': see AURAICEPT NA NÉCES.

scholasticism, a characteristic logical and analytical method employed in academic disciplines, such as philosophy, theology, law, medicine, and science, according to which arguments for and against a position are presented and assessed before a conclusion is proposed. The origins of scholasticism can be traced to the twelfth century, and it was heavily influenced by Aristotle.

It must be presumed that scholasticism in Ireland began after the ANGLO-NORMAN CONQUEST and the arrival of the Continental RELIGIOUS ORDERS and Anglo-Norman clerics. Because of the failure to found a university in Ireland, students in the Middle Ages had to travel to universities in England or on the Continent. On their return they would have taught what they received, and in the manner in which they received it. In this way scholasticism in Ireland extended itself to all aspects of public life, including sermons,

Scandinavian museums. *Bronze enamelled escutcheon with millefiori decoration in the form of a squatting figure, from the so-called Buddha Bucket (late seventh century), found in the Viking ship burial of Oseberg, an example of Irish metalwork plundered during Viking raids in Ireland. [© University Museum of Cultural Heritage, University of Oslo, Norway]*

legal documents, teaching, and medical texts, in both Irish and English.

The scholastic method and textbooks were used in TRINITY COLLEGE, Dublin, for the first two centuries from its establishment in 1592. With the foundation of Carlow College in 1793 and the Roman Catholic College of St Patrick (later St Patrick's College), Maynooth, in 1795, a renewed scholasticism manifested itself in Catholic higher education. A Department of Scholastic Philosophy was established at Queen's University, Belfast, in 1909. In the new National University of Ireland (established in 1908), departments of philosophy presented strong neo-scholastic influences from such centres as Louvain and the Gregorian University, Rome. While the influence of scholasticism declined after the 1960s, most philosophy departments still include courses presenting scholastic thought. **Michael Dunne**

Schomberg, Friedrich Herman, Duke of (1615–1690), Dutch general. Born in Heidelberg. A German Protestant mercenary of international reputation; his career included time in the Dutch, Swedish, and French service. He became a Marshal of France in 1675, but resigned after the revocation in 1685 of the Edict of Nantes (1598), which had guaranteed religious freedom to

Huguenots. In 1688 William III appointed him general for the invasion of England, for which he received £100,000 and the title of duke. In command of the 14,000-strong army that landed at Bangor, Co. Down, he captured Carrickfergus and protected the surrendering Jacobites from his soldiers and the local Protestant community. He marched south to Dundalk and camped in a damp, low-lying area, and the failure of the English regiments to obey his orders for preparing quarters resulted in the death of about 6,000 men from disease. Excessive caution and a lack of supplies meant there was no further significant activity until the siege of Charlemont in May 1690. William III blamed him for not finishing the war quickly, and his advice for the 1690 campaign was rejected by the king on his arrival in Ireland. Schomberg was killed at the Battle of the Boyne when he went to rally the Huguenot regiments. He is buried in St Patrick's Cathedral, Dublin, where there is an inscription to him composed by Swift. **Charles Ivar McGrath**

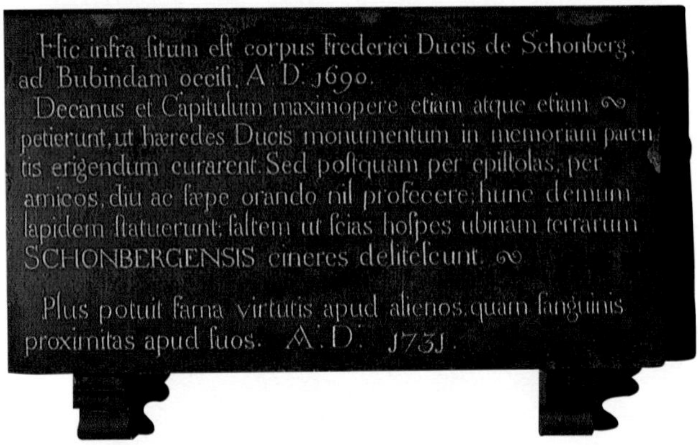

Schomberg. *Monument to Marshal Friedrich Schomberg in the choir of St Patrick's Cathedral, Dublin, erected by the Dean and Chapter, with an inscription written by Jonathan Swift. [St Patrick's Cathedral; photo: Denis Mortell]*

school effectiveness. The issue of school effectiveness has been a controversial one in research and policy debates. Research in the United States and Britain in the 1960s suggested that differences between schools made little substantive difference to educational attainment by pupils, with family background the main influence on achievement. This view was challenged by subsequent research, which suggested that schools can make a difference in how pupils perform. With regard to policy, school 'league tables' for ranking schools by examination results have been adopted in Britain, an approach that has received little support in Ireland. Research on second-level schools in the Republic suggests that schools differ significantly in relation to a range of outcomes, both academic and non-academic. Schools vary in examination performance, levels of absenteeism and drop-out, stress levels, and self-image among pupils.

Differences between schools in relation to outcomes are related to two sets of factors. Firstly, schools differ in their pupil intake. The issue of competition between schools has received little attention; however, there is evidence of active selection on the part of parents, especially those from professional backgrounds. As a result, schools vary significantly in the social background and ability mix of their pupils, which has obvious consequences for levels of performance. Secondly, schools differ in relation to policy and practice, including choice of subjects, ability grouping, and disciplinary climate. In general, pupils tend to do better in schools with a more flexible approach to subject choice and ability groups, with a 'strict but fair' disciplinary climate, where there are positive relations between teachers and pupils, and where teachers hold high (but realistic) expectations of their pupils.

In Northern Ireland, research indicates that primary and second-level schools vary in their effectiveness, as measured by examination performance and achievement tests. Some, but by no means all, of the difference between second-level schools is related to the allocation of pupils in the different types of school (grammar schools and secondary schools) in accordance with the eleven plus ability tests carried out at the age of eleven, and abolished in 2002. **Emer Smyth**

Schrödinger, Erwin Rudolf Josef Alexander (1887–1961), theoretical physicist. Born in Vienna; educated at the University of Vienna. He held university posts at Vienna, Jena, Stuttgart, Wrocław, Zürich, Berlin, Oxford, and Graz. In 1933 he won the Nobel Prize for physics for his discovery of new forms of atomic theory and the applications of them. He was an opponent of Nazism, and his life was disrupted when Hitler came to power. He was invited by the Taoiseach, Éamon de Valera, to a senior professorship at the newly established Dublin Institute for Advanced Studies. He lived and worked in Dublin from 1939 to 1956, during which time he published seven books and about seventy-five articles on the natural sciences and the philosophy of science. His 'Schrödinger equation' revolutionised scientific thought and indeed the philosophy of science; it became the basis for the quantum-mechanical treatment of problems in atomic and molecular physics and in chemistry. Schrödinger became an Irish citizen in 1948 but eventually returned to Vienna, where he died. **Charles Mollan**

science. While the term essentially means 'knowledge', it now implies the discipline of drawing objective conclusions from observations and, wherever possible, of testing the conclusions by experiment. The application of the 'scientific method' has served humanity in two ways. First is the purely philosophical ideal of revealing how the material universe works; the second lies in the comforts and benefits enjoyed by modern society through advances in medicine and agriculture, the harnessing of energy, and the development of new materials. While in general both are considered to be branches of science, there is an increasing tendency to restrict the use of the term 'science' to the philosophical side, with the application of science to invention and the solving of day-to-day problems being known as 'technology'.

The Greek philosopher Aristotle (384–322 BC) is widely regarded as the first known scientist. There was little scientific progress in the Western world over a period of nearly 2,000 years, between Aristotle's time and the Renaissance. Learned people by and large relied on the written word, rather than making direct observations. In Ireland an element of astronomical knowledge may be seen about 5,000 years ago in the design of Newgrange and other prehistoric monuments (see p. 777). A remarkable exception to the principle of depending on written sources was seen in the work of Augustine in the years around AD 655.

On the Continent the fifteenth and sixteenth centuries saw the beginning of the Renaissance and the flourishing of such true scientists as Leonardo da Vinci, Copernicus, and Galileo. In Ireland, medicine, mathematics, and botany began to be studied in Trinity College, Dublin, in the seventeenth century, while in Galway one remarkable individual, Roderic O'Flaherty, set down scientific observations on the topography of western Connacht.

The later years of the seventeenth century saw the beginnings of the promotion of systematic scientific study in Ireland or by Irish people. Pre-eminent was Robert Boyle, a founder of modern chemistry. In 1684 WILLIAM MOLYNEUX founded the Dublin Society for the Improving of Naturall Knowledge, Mathematicks and Mechanicks; it survived for only twenty-four years but was succeeded in 1731 by the Dublin Society, later the ROYAL DUBLIN SOCIETY. Set up for the promotion of the sciences, among other things, it concentrated on the application of science to the improvement of industry and agriculture. The ROYAL IRISH ACADEMY, founded in 1785, aimed to redress the imbalance by encouraging studies in pure science. While Trinity College expanded its scientific teaching, the Royal Dublin Society and the ROYAL CORK INSTITUTION both employed scientists to undertake research and to give public lectures. The Queen's Colleges, established in the middle of the nineteenth century, replaced these private societies as institutions for research.

Two important foundations of the twentieth century were the experimental physics branch of the DUBLIN INSTITUTE FOR ADVANCED STUDIES and An Foras Talúntais—later replaced by TEAGASC—for agricultural research. Towards the end of the twentieth century a number of technical institutes were upgraded to university status, and at the beginning of the twenty-first century greatly increased funding for research was made available by the Government. **Christopher Moriarty**

science and scientists. While Ireland is renowned for its abilities in the arts, particularly literature, its scientists have not received much recognition; it has therefore come as a surprise to many that Ireland has taken so easily and successfully to the scientific and technological age. Ireland has in fact a fine historical record in science. Such acclaimed scientists as ROBERT BOYLE, JOHN TYNDALL, Sir WILLIAM THOMSON and ERNEST WALTON are not always credited as being of Irish birth, though in every instance their Irish background was of importance to their personality and achievements. Also Irish were such important engineers as JOHN PHILIP HOLLAND, who built submarines, CHARLES PARSONS, who invented the steam turbine engine, and HARRY FERGUSON, who developed the tractor. All used opportunities offered outside Ireland that were not available at home, which is one reason why they are not always recognised as being Irish. There were others who achieved at home, including NICHOLAS CALLAN, who invented the induction coil, WILLIAM PARSONS, third Earl of Rosse, who built enormous telescopes, and GEORGE JOHNSTONE STONEY, who named the electron. More recently Irish scientists have competed successfully for international research funds, though it was not until the end of the twentieth century that governments realised the need to support science adequately as an essential step to continuing economic success. Significant funds were eventually made available, and the best of Irish scientists can now stay at home, while both emigrated scientists and talented people not of Irish birth can be attracted to the modern technological state that is Ireland today. **Charles Mollan**

scientific illustration. The earliest views of the GIANT'S CAUSEWAY are landmarks in geological illustration. In 1694 a crude engraving after a drawing by Christopher Cole illustrated an article in the *Philosophical Transactions of the Royal Society.* In 1740 a pair of gouache paintings on vellum by the obscure but talented SUSANNA DRURY won the £25 premium of the Dublin Society. The long series of watercolours of 113 views of the Co. Antrim coast painted by the young ANDREW NICHOLL in 1828 stress the way in which the basalt lavas overlie the white chalk. While principally a topographical and antiquarian draughtsman, GEORGE VICTOR DU NOYER illustrated PORTLOCK's *Geological Report on Londonderry, Tyrone and Fermanagh* (1843).

scientific illustration. *A meticulous botanical illustration of a cultivated hybrid of* Sarracenia *by Lydia Shackleton (1828–1914), who was commissioned to record living plants at the National Botanic Gardens, Glasnevin (1884–c. 1907). [National Botanical Gardens, Dublin]*

Ireland's outstanding work of ornithological illustration is the series of 170 large watercolours painted between 1840 and 1868 by Richard Dunscombe Parker (1805–1881), now in the ULSTER MUSEUM. In BOTANY, MARY DELANY began producing her famous cut-out flower collages in the 1770s. ANNE ELIZABETH BALL collected and painted seaweeds and fungi; many of her drawings are at the NATIONAL BOTANIC GARDENS, Glasnevin, Dublin.

The most prolific Irish botanical illustrator of the late nineteenth century was LYDIA SHACKLETON (1828–1914) of Co. Kildare. The collections at Glasnevin include about 1,500 of her watercolours. Alice Jacob (1862–1921) also produced work for Glasnevin. Edith Osborne, Lady Blake (1845–1926), whose husband, Sir Henry Blake, served as Governor of the Bahamas, Newfoundland, Jamaica, Hong Kong, and Ceylon, travelled with him to all these places and recorded plants and insects. Hardly any of her work has been published; most of it is privately owned, but the British Museum (Natural History) in London has 195 of her paintings of Jamaican lepidoptera. The naturalist ROBERT LLOYD PRAEGER employed MATILDA KNOWLES as his illustrator. Two eminent botanical artists working in Ireland today are Wendy Walsh in Dublin and Raymond Piper in Belfast. **Martyn Anglesea**

scientific instrument-makers. The earliest surviving Irish-made commercial instruments are surveying equipment. The first

Irish-born instrument-maker about whom anything substantial is known is the Deputy Surveyor-General Gabriel Stokes (1682–1768) of Dublin. The largest group of surviving instruments from the later eighteenth century are surveyors' compasses, engraved with makers' or retailers' names, for example Lynch, Mason, Spear, Spicer, Buckley, Walker, and YEATES. All these firms are known to have produced a variety of items. For much of the nineteenth century the instrument-making and retailing trade in Dublin grew with new developments in science. The family firms of Mason, Spear, Spencer, and Yeates continued in business, manufacturing instruments invented by such scientists as JOHN JELLETT and JOHN JOLY, among others. Pride of place goes to THOMAS and HOWARD GRUBB, whose TELESCOPES, made in their factory in the Dublin suburb of Rathmines, were sold to the principal observatories throughout the world (see p. 53). The greatest telescope of all was the 'Leviathan', built by WILLIAM PARSONS at BIRR CASTLE, Co. Offaly (see p. 1037). **A. D. Morrison-Low and Christopher Moriarty**

scientific instrument-makers. *An inclining-plate sundial made by Seward of Dublin, dating from the middle of the eighteenth century. It could be used in more than one latitude by adjusting the dial against an attached degree scale. [National Museum of Ireland]*

scientific surveys. By the end of the nineteenth century the broad outlines of distribution of the major plant and animal groups in Ireland had been discovered. This was largely the result of individual effort by specialists and amateur naturalists working in isolation or as part of informal networks. The statistical surveys of counties commissioned by the Dublin Society in the late eighteenth and early nineteenth centuries included observations on the natural history and geology of the areas concerned but merely itemised the more interesting animal and plant life and features already found. The Ordnance Survey of Cos. Antrim and Derry in the 1830s included surveys of the geology, botany, and zoology of the counties. The surveyors included DAVID MOORE, later director of the BOTANIC GARDENS at Glasnevin, and the artist (and later geologist) GEORGE DU NOYER. The ambitious pilot survey of the parish of Templemore, Co. Derry, published by the Ordnance Survey was not extended. Only the geological work was continued; and the GEOLOGICAL SURVEY OF IRELAND continues to produce updated maps of the solid geology and related topics.

The recolonisation of the Indonesian island of Krakatoa following its virtual destruction by a volcanic eruption in 1883 was of great interest to biologists all over the world and led to an interest in ISLANDS, in how quickly they were colonised by plants and animals, and the relationship between size of island and number of species. The CLARE ISLAND SURVEY, 1911–15, organised by the ROYAL IRISH ACADEMY, was headed by the naturalist ROBERT LLOYD PRAEGER. He had worked out a *modus operandi* during an earlier survey of LAMBAY ISLAND, Co. Dublin, 1908–9. A wider range of specialists was assembled for the Clare Island Survey than the relatively small number of mostly local specialists who had worked on Lambay. The FAUNA and FLORA as well as the archaeology and folk life of Clare Island and the surrounding seas and adjoining mainland were described in sixty-eight reports published in three volumes by the Royal Irish Academy (see p. 205). Some 1,253 animals and 583 plants, mostly from the more difficult and less-worked groups, were new to Ireland; of these, 109 animals and eleven plants proved new to science. The Lambay survey had added more than eighty species to the Irish list, of which five animals were new to science. A modern survey of Clare Island by the Royal Irish Academy, begun in 1990, involved a wide range of specialists. A comparison of the results with those of the earlier survey gives a unique insight into changes in the life and ENVIRONMENT of a relatively small inhabited island after almost a century.

An English party advised by A. C. Haddon surveyed the fauna and flora of Valentia Harbour in 1895–6, greatly adding to knowledge of the Irish marine fauna. This knowledge has been expanded by the work of the Fisheries Division. Among the earliest vegetation surveys were those conducted by Praeger and R. Pethybridge on the mountains of south Co. Dublin, 1905, and Pethybridge's unpublished survey of Howth Head. MATILDA KNOWLES of the NATIONAL MUSEUM undertook a pioneering survey of the coastal lichen flora of Howth in 1913. A survey of the vegetation and of the flora and fauna of NORTH BULL ISLAND in Dublin Bay was carried out in 1977 by biologists from Trinity College and University College, Dublin; the results were published by the ROYAL DUBLIN SOCIETY.

The Central Fisheries Board has surveyed the flora and fauna of inland waters over several decades. A number of societies specialising in plant and animal groups have conducted network surveys and produced atlases of distribution; this work has been especially successful for vascular plants, bryophytes, lichens, and coastal algae and for the major animal groups, such as mammals and birds, as well as for the larger insects and other invertebrates, such as earwigs and woodlice. It was facilitated by the active participation of amateur naturalists and professional biologists in the universities, Government departments and state institutions, and museums. Members of the Botanical Society of the British Isles have concluded a resurveying of the vascular plants for their *Atlas 2000* project. An Foras Forbartha conducted valuable coastal and other habitat surveys in the 1960s and 70s.

The Forest and Wildlife Service in the Republic and the Department of the Environment in Northern Ireland continue to monitor flora and fauna. Conservation legislation and international commitments in relation to rare species and sites of scientific importance have prompted official support for more extensive surveys, now often commissioned by the appropriate Government departments. Soil and grassland surveys have been carried out by An Foras Talúntais (succeeded by TEAGASC). The NATURALISTS' FIELD CLUBS in Belfast and Dublin have surveyed the flora of their hinterlands and published the results. The Belfast club resurveyed the flora of the north-eastern counties of Antrim, Down, and Derry; uniquely, this was the second updating of the flora of that area that had been written by Samuel A. Stewart in 1898. A first update was written by Praeger and W. R. Megaw in 1938. A flora of Dublin's inner city—the area between the ROYAL and GRAND CANALS—was produced by the Dublin club in 1984; this was extended to the county and the results published as a flora in 1998.

In the 1930s Prof. Knud Jessen of Copenhagen was invited to Ireland to advise on and help with investigations of the flora of glacial and post-glacial deposits. A COMMITTEE FOR QUATERNARY RESEARCH was formed, including geologists, zoologists, botanists, and archaeologists, and the visit led to training in Copenhagen for Irish workers and a scheme of organised work. The survey of glacial and interglacial deposits was extended by FRANK MITCHELL in particular and is continued by a number of university departments.

Outlets for the publication of survey work have been provided by the *Irish Naturalist*, *Irish Naturalist's Journal*, *Scientific Proceedings of the Royal Dublin Society*, *Proceedings of the Royal Irish Academy*, *Bulletin of the Irish Biogeographical Society*, and *Glasra: Contributions from the National Botanic Gardens*. **Donal Synnott**

Scoil Acla, a summer school established c. 1910 on ACHILL ISLAND, Co. Mayo, to promote piping, music, singing, and dancing as part of the national cultural revival. It was resumed in 1985 with similar objectives but with an emphasis on SEAN-NÓS SINGING and TRADITIONAL MUSIC, expressed through classes, recitals, and dances. **Fintan Vallely**

Scoil Samhraidh Willie Clancy, the first of the modern summer schools for TRADITIONAL MUSIC, begun in Milltown Malbay, Co. Clare, to commemorate the musical legacy of the uilleann-piper WILLIE CLANCY. Its object is to pass on these skills to a wide variety of learners. The biggest of the summer schools, its idea was initiated by the piper himself in response to the interest of visiting musicians during his lifetime. Established in the year of his death by a local teacher, MUIRIS Ó RÓCHÁIN, and SÉAMUS MAC MATHÚNA of COMHALTAS CEOLTÓIRÍ ÉIREANN, it has been running since 1973 with a programme of instrumental and SET-DANCING classes and recitals and lectures dealing with the major styles within traditional music. The teaching emphasises the oral, the local, and the regional; the thousand and more students are augmented by large numbers of music aficionados and players from Ireland and abroad who attend for the opportunity to play and for the ambience of a dedicated traditional music community (see p. 1064). **Fintan Vallely**

Scotch-Irish (also Scots-Irish), term of eighteenth-century American origin that came to be applied to the significant body of Irish Presbyterian emigrants who settled in colonial America. The assumption underlying the label is that these settlers, though having come from Ireland, were originally of Scottish stock. It has been variously estimated that between 60,000 and 250,000 settlers from Ulster emigrated to colonial America in the century before the American Revolution. The fact that at least a quarter of these were Protestants but not Presbyterian, and that almost certainly a greater proportion were of predominantly English or Welsh lineage, demonstrates the difficulties associated with the use of this term. The extent to which it was used and could be considered representative of the self-identity of these eighteenth-century settlers is an issue of debate among historians. The term was used by individual Ulster Presbyterian settlers in colonial America; but it would appear to have been more frequently applied to these settlers by others, particularly by colonial governors and the planter elite, and often in a pejorative way. Certainly there is evidence that many Protestant settlers from Ireland were comfortable with being identified in eighteenth-century America simply as Irish.

What seems clear, however, is that the influx of impoverished Irish Catholics during the years of the GREAT FAMINE stimulated the cultivation of a self-conscious Scotch-Irish identity. Those who perceived themselves as Scotch-Irish wished primarily to dissociate themselves from more recent Irish Catholic immigrants but also to distinguish themselves and their forebears from those of English Puritan stock.

The high point of the celebration of Scotch-Irish heritage and culture was reached at the end of the nineteenth century. The publication of Frederick Jackson Turner's influential 'frontier thesis' in 1893 coalesced with growing public concern over the issues of immigration and national identity. In 1889 the Scotch-Irish Congress met for the first time; during the following years its proceedings stridently proclaimed the leading role of the Scotch-Irish in the winning of independence from England and their centrality to what has been called the 'militant expansive movement in American life.' The quintessential Scotch-Irishman became a figure like that of Davy Crockett, the Tennessee Congressman whose exploits as a frontiersman were legendary and who claimed ancestors whose martial credentials stretched back to the defence of Derry's walls in the siege of 1689. The evolution of this kind of Scotch-Irish stereotype and its enduring popularity in Southern Appalachian America and in Ulster ensured its regular reinforcement in popular literature. Recent academic writing on the subject has been directed towards revising the particularist and stereotypical depiction of the historical experience of Ulster Presbyterian settlers and their descendants. **Patrick Fitzgerald**

Scotland, links with. Geography has facilitated Irish-Scottish connections at all times, especially between northern Ireland and western Scotland. At several junctures in historical times this has involved serious political interaction, including population movement. There is archaeological evidence to hint that this intercourse was established in the prehistoric period; more recent interconnections, from the PLANTATION OF ULSTER to the INDUSTRIAL REVOLUTION and down to the present day, are simply the continuation of a long-established pattern.

The earliest connection for which we have documentary accounts relates to the Gaelic kingdom of DÁL RIADA. The traditional account tells of an expedition, led by the three sons of Erc, from Irish Dál Riada (in modern Co. Antrim) to found a kingdom in Scotland (in what is now Argyll) c. AD 500. This account is doubtless a schematic representation of a complex process, comparable to similar accounts of the coming of the Anglo-Saxons to England. But it is tempting to view Scottish Dál Riada in the context of Irish colonisation elsewhere in Britain—in Cornwall, Wales, Anglesey, the Isle of Man, and perhaps Galloway—in the sub-Roman period. Certainly there is no evidence for Gaelic-speakers in Scotland before the period of Dál Riada.

In the sixth century this Gaelic enclave among the British peoples of Pictland and Strathclyde consisted of three main kindreds: Cenél nGabráin in Kintyre and Knapdale, Cenél Loairn in Mid and Upper Argyll (modern Lorne), and Cenél nÓengusa in Islay and Jura. Their principal palace and stronghold was at Dunadd (near the present-day Crinan Canal). We learn of some of their expeditions and battles, which included defeats as well as victories, from references in Irish ANNALS, whose Scottish entries were based mainly on a lost Iona chronicle. Other written sources include the remarkable Senchus Fer nAlban ('Account of the Men of Alba'), which purports to detail the military contributions required of the various families of Dál Riada. For the rest we have to rely on archaeology (most notably at Dunadd) and on the evidence of place-names, where recurrent Gaelic name-forming elements (such as *cill*, 'church') can help us judge the extent of Gaelic penetration. Place-names of the 'New Ireland' type, incorporating old names for Ireland (Ériu, Banba, Elca, and Fótla, as found in Auldearn, Banff, Elgin, and Athol, respectively), also tell a story. The overall picture is a fragmentary and in some ways conflicting one, in which the Gaelic kingdom appears at times to succumb to its Pictish neighbours; but Scotland north of the Forth and Clyde eventually became thoroughly Gaelicised, so that the united kingdom of the Picts and the Gaelic Scots that emerged in the ninth century was known as Scotia (or Scottia), not Pictavia.

During this period the Irish connection was not lost. Accounts of the Convention of Druim Cett (575) present it as a debate about the relationships between the kings of the northern UÍ NÉILL, the Irish Dál Riada, and the Scottish Dál Riada. In 637 Domnall Brecc, King of the Scottish Dál Riada, participated disastrously in the battle of Magh Rath. The picture is clearer in the case of the church, especially with regard to IONA, were Uí Néill influence was consistently exerted to control and promote COLM CILLE's foundation. Other Irish saints have also left traces of their activities in Scotland. When Columban influence spread to Pictland and Northumbria, Iona became the lynch-pin of an ecclesiastically based cultural province uniting Ireland with northern Britain, to whose confidence and resources the Book of KELLS bears eloquent testimony.

The ninth-century Norse raiders and settlers drove a wedge between Scotland and Ireland in the short term, severing ecclesiastical and political connections. But as they became integrated into Scottish and Irish society their presence encouraged links of new sorts throughout the Irish Sea area, including the Isle of Man. When eventually the Norwegian power to control events in the south became attenuated it was the Gaelic-Norse dynasty of Somerled that filled the vacuum in the late Middle Ages. The result was the Lordship of the Isles, centred on the southern Hebrides and having strong links to northern Ireland. During the Scottish Wars of Independence period the ambitions of the BRUCES raised the possibility, during Edward Bruce's campaigns (1315–18), that one family might rule Ireland and Scotland. Intercourse between the two countries was also strengthened throughout the later Middle Ages by the presence in Ireland of Scottish mercenaries (the *gallóglaigh* or 'GALLOGLASS'), some of whom settled permanently in Ireland (such as Clann Suibhne or MacSweeneys). Moreover, the learned order of professional poets, historians, lawyers, and doctors moved fairly freely between Ireland and Scotland and regarded the two as forming a single Gaelic cultural province. References in Scottish court records to the presence of Irish harpers testifies further to the mobility of entertainers between Scotland and Ireland.

The eclipse of the Lordship of the Isles (confiscated by the Crown in 1493) permitted the Campbell Earls of Argyll to become the principal political force in Argyll and the western seaways, and they duly became involved in northern Irish affairs in the later sixteenth century. The fall of the Lordship also affected Ireland, in that considerable numbers of Scottish Gaels from the old Clan Donald territories moved into Ulster in the sixteenth century. The destabilising potential of this intercourse was eventually curbed by the aspirations of James VI and I to unite and rule as one the three kingdoms in the realm. Accordingly, one of the aims of the Ulster Plantations was to drive a new wedge between Gaelic Scotland and Ireland.

The intrusion of a new sort of Scottish settler, the Protestant Lowland planter, undoubtedly altered the political map for ever. Nevertheless, as religious differences came to the fore and became politicised in the course of the seventeenth century, new sorts of Scottish-Irish interfaces emerged. During the CIVIL WAR, Campbell forces were sent to Ireland to subdue Co. Antrim, and a force of Antrim MacDonalds led by Alasdair mac Colla played an important role in the Montrose campaigns in Scotland. The royalist link, centred especially on the loyalty of the descendants of Clan Donald and their satellites and allies to the Stuart kings, continued to manifest itself intermittently in the JACOBITE period, down to the 1745 rising in Scotland of 'Bonnie Prince Charlie', grandson of JAMES II, and to attract a limited Irish following and a more widespread sense of solidarity.

Thereafter Irish-Scottish intercourse became more sporadic, though never non-existent. There were Catholic missions from Ireland to the Highlands in the eighteenth century, and Presbyterian missions to Ireland from Scotland in the nineteenth. And informal links were generated that occasionally surface in literature or through the intertwining of the lives of individuals, by means of such diverse agencies as military garrisons, such activities as horse-trading and whisky-smuggling, the communication of Irish and Scottish fishermen pursuing the same shoals, and the pursuit of seasonal or permanent work as a respite from famine or poverty. **William Gillies**

Scotland, the Irish in. Large-scale Irish emigration to Scotland in modern times began during the 1790s, as thousands fled the country to escape the violence or the authorities. During the nineteenth century the Scottish manufacturing industry expanded rapidly, at a time when Ireland was experiencing severe economic difficulties and population pressures. As a result, many Irish workers moved to Scotland to improve their social and economic condition. In 1841 there were approximately 126,000 people of Irish birth in the country, or 4.8 per cent of the population; by 1851 the number had risen to approximately 207,000 (7.2 per cent). Fifty years later Irish immigrants numbered approximately 205,000 (4.6 per cent). Thereafter Irish emigration to Scotland declined markedly: in 1951 the total Irish-born population was just under 90,000. Today there are only approximately 50,000 people of Irish birth living in Scotland, though there are more than a million who are of Irish descent.

Most of the Irish people who went to Scotland during the nineteenth century were from Ulster. While the majority were Catholic, a sizeable minority (between a quarter and a third) were Protestant. They settled mostly in the principal industrial towns, such as Glasgow, Dundee, Paisley, Greenock, Ayr, and Kilmarnock, and in the mining districts of Lanarkshire, Ayrshire, and the Lothians. The majority found employment in unskilled and semi-skilled occupations.

Irish immigration transformed the Catholic Church in Scotland. In the late 1780s there were approximately 30,000 Catholics in the country; by 1914 there were more than 520,000, of whom most were Irish or of Irish descent. At first the church struggled to cope with the influx. However, strong Catholic communities eventually emerged in areas of significant Irish settlement. Moreover, the Catholic Irish had a strong sense of national identity, and were enthusiastic supporters of the movements for REPEAL and HOME RULE.

Protestant Irish immigrants integrated easily into Scottish society, as their culture and religious beliefs were the same as those of the majority of the native population. The Catholics, however, encountered considerable hostility from Protestant ministers and sections of the middle class on account of their nationality, religion, and politics and because they were seen as a burden on the poor rates and the cause of most of the social problems that afflicted urban life. However, outside those parts of the Lanarkshire and

Ayrshire coalfields where the immigrants were employed as strike-breakers there was little open hostility from Scottish workers towards the Catholic Irish in nineteenth-century Scotland: the only major sectarian incidents were the 'Orange and Green' clashes between Protestant and Catholic Irish immigrants. Furthermore, Irish Catholics participated in strikes, trade unions, and temperance activities and in political and labour movements alongside Scottish workers. It was not until the inter-war period, when Scotland was experiencing economic depression and a crisis in national identity, that there was significant working-class opposition to the Catholic Irish community. After 1945 hostility from within Scottish society towards Catholics of Irish descent continued, though by the late twentieth century it had declined considerably (see p. 1012). **Martin Mitchell**

Scott, Michael (1905–1989), architect. Born in Dublin; articled with Jones and Kelly and began practice in 1928, also touring the United States as an actor with the Abbey Players. In the forefront of the Modern Movement in Ireland, he designed the County Hospitals at Port Laoise, Co. Laois, and Tullamore, Co. Offaly, in the mid-1930s, his own home, 'Geragh', at Sandycove, Co. Dublin, 1937–8, and the Irish pavilion at New York's World Fair, 1939, and was awarded the freedom of the city of New York. Busáras, Store Street, Dublin (1946–53), is Scott's stylish masterwork, influenced by Le Corbusier; it accommodates national bus services around the ground-floor pavilion and offices of the Department of Social Welfare in perpendicular blocks above (see p. 525). Donnybrook Bus Garage (1946–51) has long-span concrete shells designed with the Anglo-Danish engineer Ove Arup. Scott established Scott Tallon Walker (with RONALD TALLON and ROBIN WALKER) in 1974. An increasing Miesian influence is seen in the ABBEY and PEACOCK THEATRES (1958–66), with Ronald Tallon. Scott was joint-founder of the Rosc international art exhibitions, 1967; he was awarded an honorary doctorate by the University of Dublin, 1970, and the Royal Gold Medal for Architecture of the Royal Institute of British Architects, London, 1975. **Raymund Ryan**

Scott, Patrick (1921–), artist. Born in Kilbrittain, Co. Cork; attended the School of Architecture, UCD. He worked as an architect in the practice of MICHAEL SCOTT while continuing his work as an artist; in 1960 he gave up architecture to devote himself full time to painting. In 1958 he was selected for the Guggenheim Exhibition at the Museum of Modern Art, New York, which acquired one of his paintings. He represented Ireland at the Venice Biennale in 1960, having previously held exhibitions in Dublin and London. He has designed many tapestries and has also designed theatre sets; he is renowned for his serenely beautiful gold-leaf paintings on raw linen. He is a member of AOSDÁNA. **Dorothy Walker**

Scott, W. A. [William Alphonsus] (1871–1921), architect. Born in Dublin; educated at St Finian's Seminary, Navan, and the Metropolitan School of Art, Dublin. As the foremost exponent of 'arts and crafts' architecture and a leading figure in the Celtic Revival, he was the most significant Irish architect of the early twentieth century; from 1911 until his death he was professor of architecture at UCD. His works include the town halls of Enniskillen, Co. Fermanagh, and Cavan; churches at Spiddle, Co. Galway, and Lough Derg, Co. Donegal; St Mary's College, Galway, and furnishings for Loughrea Cathedral, Co. Galway, and the Honan Chapel, Cork. **Paul Larmour**

Scott, William (1913–1989), painter. Born in Greenock, Renfrewshire, to an Irish father who returned to Enniskillen when Scott was a child. He grew up in Co. Fermanagh, attended Belfast School of Art, and moved to London in 1931, where he studied at

Scott, William. Blue Still Life with Knife *(1971) by William Scott. Scott pares down and adjusts the simple arrangement of kitchen objects, with the knife centred in the blue ground of the painting. [AIB Collection/Estate of William Scott RA, archive no. 204]*

the Royal Academy. He spent some time painting in France just before the SECOND WORLD WAR, then came to Dublin, where he was refused a teaching post at the National College of Art because of his lack of knowledge of Irish; he returned to London. He visited New York in 1953 and was impressed with the scale and power of the abstract expressionist painting he saw there by such artists as Rothko, Pollock, and de Kooning. He was the first artist to bring back to London a first-hand account of this new art, which subsequently had a worldwide influence. His own painting, however, remained quite distinctive, based on domestic utensils in an elegant abstract form of still life. He represented Britain at the Venice Biennale in 1958 and the São Paulo Biennale in 1961. He had a retrospective exhibition at the Tate Gallery, London, in 1972. His work is in important art galleries throughout the world. **Dorothy Walker**

Scottish settlement in Ireland. Scottish involvement in Ireland, stretching back to the Middle Ages, predominantly affected northern areas of the country. In the thirteenth century Scottish mercenary forces, known as 'GALLOGLASS', were hired by Irish chieftains to boost their military capabilities. While some of the galloglass settled in Ireland, the Scots generally did not establish any demographic control of a significant area.

An important development that altered future Scottish involvement occurred in the fourteenth century with the marriage of Margery Bisset, the ANGLO-NORMAN heiress to two-thirds of the Glens of Antrim, to John Mór MacDonnell, Lord of the Isles. By the sixteenth century the MacDonnells had consolidated their grip on much of Co. Antrim, while Scottish settlers had expanded further south into parts of Co. Down. In addition, marriage alliances saw Scottish links with the powerful O'Neills of Tyrone and O'Donnells of Tyrconnell.

With the expansion of Tudor rule in the sixteenth century, Crown officials became increasingly concerned about further penetration by the Scots in Ireland. The REFORMATION had further complicated matters, as the Scots settlers and their kinsmen in the Scottish Isles had remained Catholic. Several efforts were made to uproot the Scots in Ulster by force, meeting only with transient success. In the end, by 1586, when this was recognised as an impossible task, the Crown authorities adopted a policy of granting the Scots legal right to the territories they occupied in an attempt to bind them to allegiance to the English Crown. If this was the expectation, the events of the NINE YEARS' WAR (1594–1603) were to prove that it was misplaced. The MacDonnells of Antrim played a leading role in supporting the military campaigns of HUGH O'NEILL, Earl of Tyrone. Indeed, supply routes through Scotland played an important part in facilitating O'Neill's war effort.

After 1603 the complexion of Scottish settlement changed dramatically, not least because of the accession of James VI of Scotland to the English throne as JAMES I. This was particularly manifested at the time of the PLANTATION OF ULSTER in 1610. Scots settlers were granted 33,000 ha (81,000 acres), almost exactly the same amount as that granted to Englishmen. The Scottish planters were almost exclusively Protestant, largely from the Lowlands rather than the Isles, a significant departure from previous experience. The viability of the Plantation of Ulster in the seventeenth century owed much to the fact that the Scottish settlers were more successful in fulfilling their settlement conditions than their English counterparts. Later the inclination of Charles I to insist on Anglicanism as the orthodox religion in his kingdoms led to persecution of the nascent Scots Presbyterian church in Ulster, precipitating a degree of emigration back to Scotland in the 1630s. At the time of the 1641 REBELLION the strong Scottish connections in Ulster resulted in a Scottish Covenanter army being hurriedly despatched to assist the settlers in Ulster, an important element in sustaining the plantation at a time when it was vulnerable. [see SCOTCH-IRISH; SCOTLAND, LINKS WITH.] **John McCavitt**

Scouler, John (1804–1871), surgeon and naturalist. Born in Glasgow; graduated in medicine in 1827. He served as ship's surgeon on voyages of exploration to the Columbia River, 1824–5, and to the Cape, Mauritius, India, and Macao, 1827–8. On these he kept journals and collected plant, animal, and geological specimens. In 1833 the ROYAL DUBLIN SOCIETY appointed him professor of geology, zoology, and botany. Poor health forced him to retire in 1854, and he returned to Glasgow. While in Dublin he donated plants to the BOTANIC GARDENS. The plant genus *Scouleria* and the mineral scoulerite were named in his honour. **Christopher Moriarty**

scouting. The Scout Association of Ireland (SAI) was founded in 1908 in accordance with the principles laid down by Robert Baden-Powell in England. The Catholic Boy Scouts of Ireland (CBSI) was founded by Father Ernest Farrell in 1927 and is now the largest of the three scouting organisations. There is also a separate Scout Association in Northern Ireland (SANI). These three organisations have a combined total membership of more than 40,000. The CBSI and SAI are jointly represented in the World Scout Conference by the Federation of Irish Scout Associations. FIANNA ÉIREANN, a nationalist scouting organisation, was founded by BULMER HOBSON and CONSTANCE MARKIEVICZ in 1909. **Brian Galvin**

script. The MANUSCRIPT tradition in Ireland began with the need to copy Biblical books and service books to supply new churches and communities. The books had first come with the earliest Christian missionaries and were written in the scripts current in the late Roman Empire: a round formal *uncial*, and a *half-uncial* with distinct ascenders and descenders.

The oldest surviving Irish manuscripts date from the end of the sixth century and include the Springmount Bog writing tablets (now in the NATIONAL MUSEUM OF IRELAND), the CODEX USSERIANUS PRIMUS Gospel book fragment (TRINITY COLLEGE Library), and the CATHACH (ROYAL IRISH ACADEMY). All three show the main characteristics of what is commonly called *insular script*, namely fully rounded letter-forms and distinctive wedge-shaped serifs and terminals. The script was written with a quill, which had its point cut off in a chisel edge. The scribe held the edge of the pen more or less parallel to the writing lines and maintained this angle constantly; this pen angle gave a thick downstroke and a thin horizontal line, resulting in majestic, solid LETTER-FORMS. The letters were always written close together, generally touching, with a small space between the words, giving the strong horizontal appearance to the writing characteristic of insular majuscule manuscripts. This script evolved in the MONASTERIES of Ireland, Scotland, and Northumbria, achieving its full development c. 700 in the books of DURROW and LINDISFARNE and, arguably, its finest manifestation a century or so later in the Book of KELLS.

The characteristic serifs were formed by a thin leading-in or approach stroke, completed by a separate angular stroke to the shaft. Like all formal scripts, the letters were composed of separate components drawn from the top down. The *o*, for example, was formed by two separate strokes, first the left half, then the right. What may appear to be a rather cumbersome method of writing became with practice smooth, regular, and surprisingly swift; it has been estimated that it took about thirty minutes to write each of the text pages of the Book of Durrow.

The rise of the MONASTIC SCHOOLS in the seventh century can be linked to the development of the *insular minuscule* script, which in appearance is more angular than the majuscule, though the letter-forms are largely the same. The pointed appearance resulted from the pen being held at an angle of 35–45° to the ruled writing lines; held like this, the chisel-edged pen produces vertical and horizontal strokes of equal thickness, with the verticals ending in a point on the line. One effect of the shift of pen angle was a much more economical script in words per line; another advantage was that it could be written minutely without loss of legibility. The development of the *minuscule* or lower-case letter-forms was an important Irish contribution to the written language of the West.

The two earliest surviving examples of insular minuscule are the ANTIPHONARY OF BANGOR (680–92) and ADOMNÁN's Life of COLM CILLE (before 713). The latter is finely written in two-column pages and is representative of hundreds of non-liturgical books, now lost, produced in the monastic scriptoria. The oldest examples of small minuscule are found in the pocket GOSPELS, a number of which survive from c. 800. They were designed for personal use rather than liturgical display and were of small size: the Book of Mulling's vellum leaves, for example, measure only 165 by 120 mm ($6\frac{1}{2}$ by $4\frac{3}{4}$ in.) and have approximately forty-four lines in two columns per page. The utilitarian nature of the minuscule ensured its survival. From the outset it was used extensively for scholarly as much as for liturgical purposes; it was particularly suitable for making marginal notes and adding interlinear GLOSSES—a favourite activity of Irish scribes and scholars through the ages.

The half-uncial insular majuscule and minuscule survived side by side for hundreds of years. The half-uncial was used for large Gospel books and psalters and the minuscule for less formal texts. Sometimes the two scripts were used together, as in the Psalter of St Caimín, a fragmentary copy of Psalm 118 written c. 1100. The verses of the psalm are written in a fine majuscule hand, each section beginning with a large initial filled with blocks of colour. The entire text is surrounded by a commentary in Latin, with some glosses in OLD IRISH, all written in a neat spiky minuscule very similar to the script in the two copies of the Liber Hymnorum produced about the same time. But the majuscule was going out of use, to be replaced by a more formal version of the Irish minuscule in larger format. Its last appearance may be in some archaic Irish texts in Ms. Rawlinson B 502, written c. 1130, where the scribe for several pages writes the main text in majuscule, adding the commentary in minuscule, until, without warning, in the middle of a page he gives up the majuscule completely and continues in large-format minuscule. The older script was to disappear from use for almost seven hundred years, to return in the nineteenth century in the typefaces of GEORGE PETRIE, once again presenting old Irish texts in the publications of the Irish Archaeological Society.

From the beginning, insular minuscule had been used for writing in Irish. The finest early example of the script is that of FERDOMNACH, who wrote the Book of ARMAGH in 807. Because it has a complete New Testament, a large proportion of the text is in Latin, but it is also the oldest manuscript to contain examples of connected Irish prose narrative. By the twelfth century the minuscule had become standardised and remained virtually unchanged until the seventeenth century. The Book of the DUN COW (Lebor na hUidre) is the oldest surviving book completely written in Irish and the earliest of the great medieval codices, the 'one-volume libraries', which, together with the law tracts and the medical manuscripts, represent the written culture of Ireland in the later Middle Ages. Through its CLONMACNOISE connections, the Book of the Dun Cow may represent the last link with the monastic scriptoria.

Individual scribes varied greatly in their skill, as can be seen in the hands of the thirty-nine individuals who made the entries in the Annals of Inisfallen between 1092 and 1326. By the second half of the fourteenth century the names of a number of professional scribes are known from signed examples of their work, and their hands have been discovered in manuscripts throughout the country. Sighraid Ó Cuirnín (died 1388) re-inked parts of the Book of the Dun Cow. GIOLLA ÍOSA MÓR MAC FIR BHISIGH, head of a famous learned family and school in Co. Sligo, wrote a clear, well-spaced minuscule in the Book of Lecan and in parts of the Yellow Book of Lecan. The Book of BALLYMOTE, a manuscript of more than 500 pages, was begun and partly written at least for Tomaltach Mac Donncha by three scribes (Solamh Ó Droma, Robert Mac Síthigh, and Maghnus Ó Duibhgeannáin) before 1397 (see p. 818). The Leabhar Breac, a manuscript belonging to the learned family of Mac Aogáin, was written entirely by Murchadh Ó Cuindlis, a professional scribe who also worked for Mac Fir Bhisigh. From marginal notes by Ó Cuindlis it is possible to calculate that he averaged one two-column page per day; if he copied for five hours he would have written about 180 words an hour.

The changes in society as a result of wars and plantations and the decline of native Irish civilisation after the FLIGHT OF THE EARLS in 1607 brought about a noticeable change in manuscript production and writing style. The script in the Annals of the FOUR MASTERS, written in the 1630s, is in form the same minuscule that the compilers read in their medieval exemplars, but the appearance of the letter-forms is different, as the pointed quills they used for writing could not imitate the thick-and-thin strokes of the edged pen; some variation in line thickness could be produced by pressure, but this was rarely consistent. Throughout the seventeenth and eighteenth centuries manuscripts continued to be written, always on paper, in spare, unadorned minuscule without serifs. This script provided the model for most of the Irish typefaces that were produced from the seventeenth century onwards. So close was the link between language and script that it was most unusual to see Irish written or printed in any form but minuscule. The end of an era came in 1880 with the death of Seosamh Ó LONGÁIN, the last of the hereditary scribes. He spent many years working for the Royal Irish Academy, transcribing texts and making line-for-line copies of some of the great medieval codices for lithographic reproduction.

The rediscovery of the edged pen and the revival of insular majuscule in the writing of English owes a debt to Edward Johnson (1872–1944), who pioneered the scientific study and practice of calligraphy in England in the early twentieth century; the contemporary Irish scribes Myra Maguire, Tim O'Neill, Frances Breen, and Denis Brown all acknowledge his influence on their individual interpretations of traditional hands. [see LETTER-FORMS AND HANDWRITING.] **Timothy O'Neill**

Scriptures, Cross of the, CLONMACNOISE, a HIGH CROSS formerly standing in front of the Cathedral at Clonmacnoise, now in the nearby interpretative centre. It is called the Cross of the Scriptures because it was equated with 'Cros na Screaptra' mentioned in the Annals of the FOUR MASTERS for 1060. Carved from a single block of sandstone and reaching a height of 3.9 m (13 ft), including the separate base, it is perhaps the most elegant of Irish high crosses; it is also unique among them in that the ring stands out from the cross. Much-defaced inscriptions on the shaft name King Flann and

Scullabogue. *George Cruikshank's gruesome illustration from William Maxwell's* History of the Irish Rebellion in 1798 *(1852), based on eyewitness records of a massacre of Protestants by 1798 rebels at Scullabogue, Co. Wexford. [Royal Irish Academy]*

Colmán. Flann assisted the Abbot of Clonmacnoise, Colmán, in building the cathedral in 909; but if the Colmán of the inscription were the sculptor rather than the abbot, the cross can only be dated generally to the years of Flann's rule, 879–916.

The cross deserves its name, because many of the scenes carved on both cross and base illustrate Biblical subjects, concentrating on the passion, death and resurrection of Christ, with the Crucifixion occupying the head of one face and the Last Judgment the other. However, a number of panels on the narrow sides and some on the broad face have defied generally acceptable identification. **Peter Harbison**

Scullabogue massacre, an atrocity committed by insurgents during the REBELLION OF 1798. On the morning of 6 June 1798, at Scullabogue, Co. Wexford, six miles from New Ross, about 100 loyalists or suspected loyalists, some of them children and almost all non-combatants, were shot and burnt to death prior to the rebel attack on New Ross. The killings were most probably instigated by rebels fleeing from the early stages of the battle. **Daniel Gahan**

Scully, Seán (1945–), artist. Born in Dublin; left Ireland at the age of four and grew up in England; educated at Central School, Croydon College of Art, London, University of Newcastle upon Tyne, and Harvard University, Massachusetts. He moved to New York in 1975 and taught at Princeton University, New Jersey. He became famous for his distinctive abstract painting using a striped motif. He remained faithful to the abstract mode throughout the period of figurative new expressionism in the 1980s but combined the striped motif with a vigorous expressionist mode of painting that was unique; he later developed a second motif of luminous abstraction in the form of a chequerboard. Scully's work is represented in art galleries and both private and corporate collections throughout the world, and there have been one-man exhibitions in most of the principal galleries. His work includes large-scale oil paintings, paintings on metal, watercolours, pastels, and prints, in all of which his artistic skills are at an equally high creative level. **Dorothy Walker**

sculpture, 1600–2000. The Elizabethan wars took their toll on the quality of stone sculpture in Ireland, which devolved into a naïve folk art in the early decades of Stuart rule. But the new landlords, such as CHICHESTER in Carrickfergus and ROGER BOYLE in Youghal and Dublin, continued the earlier tradition of family tomb-sculpture, and BASIL BROOKE boosted his ego with a swaggering fireplace in DONEGAL CASTLE. Standing in splendid isolation is the mid-seventeenth-century muscular Christ figure at Athcarne, Co. Meath, with strong overseas (perhaps Dutch) echoes.

In the eighteenth century many masterpieces were created by foreign craftsmen, such as William Kidwell (1662–1736), who carved the exuberant baroque effigy of Donogh O'Brien at Kilnasoolagh, Co. Clare, and two Englishmen of Dutch parentage, JOHN VAN NOST the younger (died c. 1780), famous for his naturalistic busts, and Simon Vierpyl (1725–1810), whose classical carvings superbly enhance the CASINO at Marino, Dublin (see p. 183). These masters inspired Irish followers, many of whom were trained in the DUBLIN SOCIETY's schools from the 1740s onwards. Its pupils also included fine wood-carvers, such as John Houghton (died 1761) and Richard Caulfield (1731–1809), who also produced remarkably sculpted furniture. It was in stone carving, however, that the new generation excelled, with CHRISTOPHER HEWETSON (c. 1739–1798) executing the fine Baldwin memorial in Trinity College and John Hickey (1759–1795) the giant monument to David La Touche in Delgany, Co. Wicklow. Outstanding in architectural sculpture was EDWARD SMYTH of Navan, Co. Meath (c. 1749–1812), whose riverine heads on Gandon's CUSTOM HOUSE, Dublin, were famous even in his own day.

The classic dignity of eighteenth-century funeral sculpture continued into the middle of the nineteenth century, gaining in realism particularly in monuments to those who lost their lives in battles far away on land or sea. A touch of Victorian sentimentality came to the fore in nineteenth-century sculpture in the round, in works by THOMAS KIRK (1781–1845), JOHN HOGAN, trained in Cork, and Sir THOMAS FARRELL (1827–1900), while JOHN HENRY FOLEY produced ennobling public statuary that gave an aura of dignity to his sitters. Architectural sculpture had its last great vogue in the latter half of the nineteenth century, ranging from the decorative to the hilarious, as in the O'Shea brothers' carvings on the old Kildare Street Club in Dublin.

The rise of nationalism in the second half of the nineteenth century led to the production of sculpture of varying quality, such as the many 'Maid of Erin' statues commemorating the centenary of 1798, and its shadow inspired the heroic figures of OLIVER SHEPPARD, such as *The Death of Cuchulainn* in the GENERAL POST OFFICE, Dublin (see p. 1090). Fresh impulses came from across the Atlantic in memorials created by three Irish-American sculptors: AUGUSTUS ST GAUDENS (1848–1943), who created the Parnell monument in O'Connell Street, Dublin; JEROME CONNOR, who was responsible for the *Lusitania* memorial in Cobh, Co. Cork; and ANDREW O'CONNOR (1874–1941), famed for his *Christ the King* memorial in Dún Laoghaire. From the middle of the twentieth century the towering presence of OISÍN KELLY made itself felt on both large and small scales, as in his *Last Supper* at Knockanure, Co. Kerry. IMOGEN STUART, Michael Biggs, and KEN THOMPSON have distinguished themselves in, among other things, religious sculpture and church furniture (see p. 854). Their feel for carved lettering was led by SEAMUS MURPHY, who produced fine busts and public monuments (see p. 270), as did ALBERT POWER.

The second half of the twentieth century has seen the emergence of a host of other sculptors, many working to commissions often channelled through the Sculptors' Society of Ireland. They have produced lively and imaginative works, both abstract and figurative, in a great variety of media and sites—MICHAEL WARREN in wood, DEBORAH BROWN in plastics, and CONNOR FALLON, EDWARD DELANEY, and JOHN BEHAN in a variety of metals—all demonstrating that sculpture is now one of the most vibrant, if often insufficiently appreciated, art forms in the country. [see FURNITURE; HIGH CROSSES.] **Peter Harbison**

SDLP: see SOCIAL DEMOCRATIC AND LABOUR PARTY.

sea-fishing. In 1998 total sea-fish landings in the Republic were 278,000 tonnes, worth £152 million at first point of sale, with more than 6,000 fishermen engaged on board fishing vessels. Landings in Northern Ireland were approximately 20,000 tonnes, worth a further £20 million and employing 1,100 fishermen. There were approximately 1,300 vessels greater than 10 m in length, in addition to an unknown number of smaller craft, engaged in fishing for shellfish. The principal harbours by value of fish landed are Killybegs, Co. Donegal, Castletown Bearhaven, Co. Cork, Rathmullan, Co. Donegal, Howth, Co. Dublin, and Greencastle, Co. Donegal.

The seafood industry provides employment for 14,800 people and is a significant source of income in coastal regions beyond the fringe of cities and towns. A rapid expansion began in the 1950s, when substantial Government funds were made available for developing the infrastructure. Harbour improvements, navigation aids, the provision of subsidised training courses, and, above all, grant and loan facilities for the purchase of vessels contributed to sustained development. By the end of the twentieth century large deep-sea vessels had greatly expanded the scope of the fishery by moving to more distant waters. While trawling remained the mainstay of the fin-fish industry, line-fishing became widely used for the capture of fish over rough ground.

The catch comprises approximately a hundred species. Ten of these—including herring, megrim, mussel, crab, oyster, prawn, and newer species, such as albacore and horse mackerel—constitute 60 per cent of the catch. Familiar species such as whiting, cod, and haddock ranked some distance behind the top ten. The official catch data for 1999 showed Dublin Bay prawn, horse mackerel, mackerel, albacore, and angler to be the most valuable species, earning €10–20 million.

The consumption of seafood in Ireland is low compared with other European countries but has been growing rapidly to a level of 8.8 kg per person. This increase is due in part to promotion and to the greater availability of fresh fish as well as to a greater awareness of health benefits and the expanding range of consumer-ready fish products. The retail market is estimated to be worth approximately €120 million per annum. **Fiacc OBrolchain and Christopher Moriarty**

Scully. *Sanda (1992) by Seán Scully, a leading contemporary abstract painter. Scully's work is characterised by a distinctive and energetic use of striped and chequered motifs. [Hugh Lane Municipal Gallery of Modern Art, courtesy of the artist]*

Seanad Éireann: see GOVERNMENT IN IRELAND.

Sean-Nós Cois Life, a festival of traditional singing in Dublin, begun in 1992. It emphasises tuition in Irish through exposure to renowned performers of SEAN-NÓS SINGING from all Irish-speaking areas. SEAN-NÓS STEP-DANCING is also a component. From 1993 it has presented the honorary award Gradam Shean-Nós Cois Life to those who have contributed substantially to *sean-nós* singing. **Glenn Cumiskey**

***sean-nós* singing,** orally transmitted songs in *amhrán* metre in Irish-speaking communities. Most airs are modal. Unrequited love is a major theme in songs, some of which date from the sixteenth century, echoing medieval European traditions of courtly love. They include such items as 'Dónall Óg', 'An Droighneán Donn', 'Caisleán Uí Néill', 'Bean Dhubh an Ghleanna', and 'Bean an Fhir Rua'. Local catastrophes, as as RAIFTEARAÍ's 'EANACH DHÚIN', and political *aislingí* also feature. The voice is usually solo and unaccompanied, lacks overt dynamics, and may have a certain nasal intonation, though a wide range of timbres exists. Styles vary regionally and individually, the ornate west Galway style being highly valued. The OIREACHTAS is the most prestigious forum, also shaping the genre's maintenance and development throughout the twentieth century and largely responsible for its recognition as a valid artistic expression. The coveted Corn Uí Riada is the supreme accolade. SEOSAMH Ó HÉANAÍ is the most renowned twentieth-century singer, first brought to national prominence by the Oireachtas. **Lillis Ó Laoire**

***sean-nós* step-dancing.** The term *sean-nós* (old-style) as applied to step-dancing is relatively recent, dating only from the 1970s, and is a borrowing from the term applied to singing. It has come to be used to describe styles of dancing that are outside the canon of the COIMISIÚN LE RINCÍ GAELACHA but particularly that of Connemara. Originally called *an bhataráil* (the battering), this style is characterised by its use of *timeáil* (timing). The percussive effect is produced by using the heel and toe; other typical flourishes include stamping, kicking the floor with the tip of the toe with either foot to the rear of the starting position, and a variety of side-step patterns. Occasionally some dancers make use of gently swinging or raised arm movements, which may be a reflection of the absence of formal dance teaching in this tradition. **Helen Brennan**

Seawright, Paul (1965–), artist. Born in Belfast; educated at the University of Ulster and West Surrey College of Art and Design. His early photographic series, *Sectarian Murder, the Orange Order and Police Force*, is an inquiry into the politicised landscape and organisations of Northern Ireland (see p. 837). He has since moved away from an overtly Irish context to explore peripheral urban spaces, undistinguished borders whose banal subject matter is belied by the formal beauty of the photographic compositions. He received the Glen Dimplex Artists' Award, 1997, and Ville de Paris Artist Award, 1999. **Fiona Kearney**

Second Reformation, a name given to the efforts of evangelical clergymen to advance the mass conversion of Catholics during the first half of the nineteenth century. Though it was spearheaded by high-ranking Anglican clergymen, missionary societies played a central role in distributing Bibles and other devotional material in Irish. They included the Association for Discountenancing Vice (1792), the Hibernian Bible Society (1806), the Sunday School Society (1809), the Religious Tract and Book Society (1810), and the Irish Society (1818). Its promoters also engaged in bitter public controversy and established several colonies for converts, the most significant at ACHILL ISLAND under REV. EDWARD NANGLE; while never very successful, it left a legacy of heightened sectarian tensions. After the Great Famine the Catholic Church regrouped and regained ground through a vigorous programme of parish missions. [see ALTAR CONTROVERSY.] **Thomas Kelley**

Second Vatican Council: see VATICAN COUNCIL, SECOND.

Second World War (1939–1945). The war affected the two parts of Ireland very differently. As part of the United Kingdom, Northern Ireland was committed to participation; its ports and airfields played a vital role in the defence of Britain's Atlantic sea routes, while its manufacturing industries contributed to war production in both the military and civilian fields. Northern Ireland was also an important training ground for British and (after 1942) American forces, and this military presence acted as an insurance against a possible Axis attack on neutral Ireland. German bombing did considerable damage, including the BELFAST BLITZ of April and May 1941, which caused more than 900 deaths and widespread destruction. Despite nationalist alienation from the Northern state, there was little anti-war agitation, and sporadic IRA efforts to make mischief proved ineffectual.

Éire, by contrast, stuck to its long-declared policy of NEUTRALITY, despite the weakness of its DEFENCE FORCES and its reliance, in effect, on British air and sea power to protect it. Given the memory of the WAR OF INDEPENDENCE, the continuing grievance of partition, and the threat of republican insurrection, DE VALERA had no other choice, and his approach was supported even by most of his bitterest political opponents. In the invasion fever that followed the fall of France in June 1940, a call to arms produced a remarkable public response, resulting in a quadrupling of ARMY numbers within months, though acute shortages of equipment were not so easily overcome. This consensus on the importance of neutrality made it easier for de Valera to crack down on the IRA, which increased its armed action within the state and attempted to build links with Nazi Germany. By 1942 the IRA was a spent force, most of its activists interned and its links with Germany broken.

The state enjoyed similar success in the other direct threat to neutrality it faced, that posed by Axis espionage. Through a combination of efficient counter-intelligence and close co-operation with British agencies, none of the dozen German agents sent to Ireland between 1939 and 1943 achieved anything worthwhile. Similarly, tight surveillance and diplomatic pressure on Axis and pro-Axis diplomats reduced their opportunities for gathering intelligence against Britain, though the presence of a clandestine wireless transmitter in the German legation caused great difficulties until its eventual surrender into Irish custody in December 1943.

Irish neutrality was bitterly denounced in both Britain and the United States, where President Roosevelt urged Irish participation on Britain's side long before his own country was prepared to enter the war. Neutrality caused acute difficulties in Anglo-Irish relations, particularly from June 1940 to July 1941, when German invasion was a real possibility. The British Prime Minister, Churchill, at first made a vague offer of post-war Irish unity in return for participation in the war against Germany but then sought to use economic as well as political pressure to force a change. Such action, however, only strengthened de Valera's position domestically, and it harmed British trade. Ireland served as an important supplier of manpower to British industry and to the armed forces, while Dublin also sought to soften the impact of neutrality through covert co-operation with

Britain in matters such as intelligence, weather information, and even joint planning to repel any German attack; but Churchill remained bitter. Neutrality was also much resented in Washington, where it was seen as a hypocritical and dangerous policy that threatened Allied security.

By 1945 neutrality was seen in Ireland as the true vindication of the SOVEREIGNTY won in 1921, while the standing of Northern Ireland within the United Kingdom was boosted by its contribution and suffering in the war effort. Historians remain divided on whether the Second World War widened or merely confirmed the gulf between the two Irish states. [see EMERGENCY, THE.] **Eunan O'Halpin**

sectarianism. In its most general manifestations, sectarianism is a form of prejudice and abuse of power based on religious intolerance. It has parallels with RACISM and other forms of prejudice but with religion, rather than skin colour or culture, as the marker of group difference.

Sectarianism has deep roots in history; present-day examples include conflicts between Christianity and Islam and between Hindus and Muslims. In Ireland its roots go back to the REFORMATION, when England became a Protestant state and the bulk of the Irish population remained loyal to Catholicism; over time the labels 'Catholic' and 'Protestant' became more fully identified with conflicting national affiliations. In Northern Ireland the terms have become inaccurate general labels for an amalgam of social identifications on each side of a communal divide; in particular there is mutual reinforcement between religious affiliation and the underlying political divide between unionists and nationalists. There is considerable sociological evidence for the importance of RELIGION as a boundary marker when Protestant denominations are aggregated and compared with Catholics. 'Catholic' and 'Protestant' as nominal religious affiliations are highly correlated with voting behaviour, national identification, political ideology (NATIONALISM V. UNIONISM), residence, schooling, unemployment, choice of marriage partner, a variety of social and political attitudes, and propensity to engage in certain forms of sport and voluntary activity. Until recently also the two communities were characterised by significant differences in FERTILITY rates and in propensity to emigrate.

The institutionalisation of communal division acts as a powerful socialising force, shaping beliefs and practices at individual and group level. While communal division provides fertile ground for sectarianism, it is not synonymous with it, though it may be in part the result of past sectarian practices. Other divisions, such as those of sex, class, and age, retain their importance but are frequently experienced and viewed through the lens of sectarian affiliation.

More specifically, sectarianism may be understood as a set of beliefs and practices that represent and reproduce communal division in a particularly antagonistic and prejudicial form. These ideas and practices may derive from deliberate intention or reflection, or alternatively they may be largely tacit or taken for granted. Conscious sectarianism involves negative stereotyping of individuals where the perceived characteristics of a particular community are ascribed to every individual within it. DISCRIMINATION against, and intimidation and murder of, people simply because they are members of the other community are examples of sectarianism as conscious practice; examples of more tacit forms of sectarianism include the quasi-automatic use of cues to 'tell the difference' between Catholics and Protestants in everyday social interaction. While such practices may have malign consequences, they may also serve to facilitate communication, ensuring that certain contentious subjects are avoided and that different rules are observed for intercommunal, as opposed to intracommunal, interaction. The ignoring of communal division, however well-intentioned, may also involve tacit sectarianism. The failure to actively advertise jobs within each community may lead to the preservation of communal inequalities in the labour market, thereby promoting indirect discrimination.

Sectarian division may rest on cultural affinity with one's community and with a desire to live separately from the other group. But voluntary segregation also presupposes intercommunal relationships. Here sectarianism always involves prejudice, either in thought or deed, or both. It typically represents the communities in Northern Ireland as engaged in a 'zero-sum conflict', where gains by one community are seen to inevitably mean losses for the other. Power differentials are crucial to the significance of sectarianism, as are attempts to empower one community at the expense of the other. While in Northern Ireland religion continues to serve as a communal marker, actual religious beliefs and practices are seldom a point of contention. For a minority, however, the religious practices and beliefs of the other community are the core problem, in that they are perceived as blasphemous and even non-Christian.

In the Republic, sectarianism is no longer fuelled by unionist-nationalist divisions, though it may persist in cross-border unionist-nationalist relationships. The privileging of one religion over others in state legislation and practices may be considered sectarian in its consequences. In both Northern Ireland and the Republic it seems likely that sectarianism would be reduced by a successful political resolution of the Northern Ireland conflict. Moreover, IMMIGRATION and multi-culturalism are beginning to challenge the primacy of traditional forms of Protestant and Catholic sectarianism in both jurisdictions. **Liam O'Dowd**

sectarianism. *Interior of the Church of the Immaculate Conception, Leitrim, Castlewellan, Co. Down, after a sectarian arson attack on 1 July 1998. [Pacemaker]*

sects. Membership of the 'sect' form of religious organisation is exclusive, confined to a minority, and typically depends on high and demonstrable levels of religious commitment, in contrast to the 'church', where membership is inclusive of the majority and demands little by way of entry qualifications. A wide variety of sects exists, from the 'world-affirming' to the 'world-rejecting'. The early Christian church was sect-like in character, while the Catholic Church in the early years of the Irish state was a virtual monopoly church. In practice both churches and sects may evolve into denominations in a religiously plural society. In Northern Ireland the organisation of all social, economic, cultural, and political life around the religious, sect-like differences of different groups, with limited opportunities for social interaction between them, reflects a centuries-long process of SECTARIANISM. **Michael Hornsby-Smith**

secularisation, the supposed declining power and influence of religion in the modern world in consequence of various social, cultural, economic, and technological changes associated with modernisation. Sociologists point to the multi-dimensional character of secularisation and distinguish social, organisational, and individual aspects. There is general agreement that individual forms of religion, in the form of beliefs and practices, may well survive, while the principal aspect of secularisation is the declining social significance of RELIGION. In Ireland until the early 1990s it was still possible to claim, on the grounds of survey findings, that there was little evidence of declining religious beliefs and practices within birth cohorts; in the early twenty-first century it would be difficult to maintain this claim with the collapse of clerical authority following recent scandals. **Michael Hornsby-Smith**

Sedulius Scotus. Latinised name of Siadhail (fl. 848–874), a leading member of the Irish colony at Liège in the middle of the ninth century. At the centre of Carolingian political and cultural life he wrote a treatise on governance (*Liber de Rectoribus Christianis*). Some knowledge of Greek is to be found in his writings, particularly in his poems (*Carmina*). Commentaries survive on the grammarians Eutyches, Priscian, and Donatus (the *Ars Minor* and *Ars Maior*), on the letters of St Paul, and on the Gospel of St Matthew. He also produced a florilegium of ancient and Christian authors (*Collectaneum*) as well as a book of proverbs (*Proverbia Graecorum*). **Michael Dunne**

Sefton, Catherine: see WADDELL, MARTIN.

Segrave, Henry O'Neill De Hane (1896–1930), racing driver. Born in Baltimore, Maryland, to an Irish father; he lived in Wicklow and Portumna, Co. Galway, from 1898 until 1917. In the FIRST WORLD WAR he survived being shot down. He achieved his first motor racing success in 1920 at the Brooklands track in England and won the 1923 French Grand Prix for Sunbeam, the first time a British car won an international grand prix. After winning the 1924 San Sebastián Grand Prix and the Grand Prix de Provence in both 1925 and 1926 he turned his attentions to record-breaking. In 1926 he established a new world land speed record of 245 km/h (152.33 miles/h) at Southport. At Daytona Beach, Florida, on 29 March 1927 he became the first person to drive at 322 km/h (200 miles/h), and he was knighted in 1929 after extending the record to 372 km/h (231.44 miles/h) in his Golden Arrow machine. He won the 1929 European Speedboat Championship at Venice but was killed on 30 June 1930 when his boat, *Miss England II*, crashed at Windermere, Lancashire, after setting a new water speed record of 159 km/h (98.76 miles/h). His unfulfilled ambition was to add the air speed record to his other titles, and before his death he designed the super-streamlined Segrave Meteor plane. The Segrave Trophy was instituted in his memory in 1930 for the most outstanding possibilities of transport by land, air, or water, and each year a wreath-laying ceremony is held in his memory on Windermere. [see MOTOR SPORT.] **Brendan Lynch**

seisiún: see SESSION.

seismology at Rathfarnham Castle. In 1913 Rathfarnham Castle, at Rathfarnham, Co. Dublin, dating mainly from 1585, was bought by the Society of Jesus for use as a house of studies. In 1915 Father William O'Leary was transferred there from the JESUIT college at Mungret, near Limerick. Born in 1869, he had joined the Jesuit order in 1886. Mungret was one of three Jesuit colleges (the others being Stonyhurst College, Lancashire, and Riverview, near Sydney, Australia) that set up seismological observatories following the San Francisco earthquake of 1906, with the encouragement of Father H. V. Gill, an authority on earthquakes. O'Leary had been in charge of the Mungret observatory, which seems to have contained two commercial Mainka-type seismographs (E–W and N–S), though few records now exist, and the source and the fate of the instruments are unknown.

At Rathfarnham, O'Leary installed in 1917 what was the world's largest inverted-pendulum seismograph in a new observatory. The bob consisted of about 1,800 kg (1.5 tons) of octagonal iron plates, and the rod was about 2 m (6.5 ft) long in a pit below the floor. Three steel rods (rather than wires) supported the pendulum through the disk at the base of the shaft. On a platform above the bob, an intricate system of levers separated the movement into two orthogonal components and recorded them through glass styli on smoked paper on a drum driven by clockwork. Time marks were recorded electrically. The period of the pendulum was about 16 seconds, and it had air dampers. It has been said that O'Leary built it with his own hands, but in view of the size and complexity, especially of the recording gear, this must be an exaggeration. It is likely that most parts, if not all, were built by the firm of GRUBB, then the foremost instrument and TELESCOPE makers in Dublin, though no records are known to exist, and there are no makers' marks.

Under the care of various members of the Jesuit community this apparatus gave daily records for many years, and for about fifty years Rathfarnham was in effect the centre for seismology in Ireland. Grubb also built parts for a photographically recording three-component seismograph (two horizontal, one vertical) designed by O'Leary in 1913. Though a foundation pillar was installed at Rathfarnham and the instrument assembled, there is no record of its being completed or used. Possibly by then it was too late, as O'Leary had left Ireland in 1919 to direct the Riverview College observatory, which still has a precision clock designed, patented, and constructed by him. He also had patents for a free-pendulum clock, granted in 1918. He died in Australia in 1939.

Many recordings are kept at the DUBLIN INSTITUTE FOR ADVANCED STUDIES. The 'big O'Leary' continued in use, but a commercial Milne-Shaw seismograph was bought in 1932. This used a horizontal pendulum, representing the boom of a yacht, 0.4 m (1.3 ft) long, with a mass of approximately 0.5 kg (1.1 lb). Its outer end was supported by two fine steel wires from the top of a massive pillar, near the base of which a pin at the inner end of the boom rested in an agate cup. This instrument had electromagnetic damping and photographic recording. A World-Wide Standard Seismograph Station was opened at Valentia Island, Co. Kerry, in 1962. The Rathfarnham observatory closed in 1967. The Milne-

Shaw instrument was removed elsewhere, and the observatory and other instruments were allowed to decay and were later vandalised. The remains of the 'big O'Leary' were dismantled in 1976 and most of the parts transferred to the National Science Museum, Maynooth. **Adrian Somerfield**

Semple family, architects. George Semple (died 1782) was a renowned engineer in Georgian Dublin. He designed St Patrick's Hospital, Essex Bridge, and the spire of ST PATRICK'S CATHEDRAL, was an adviser to the Corporation of Dublin, and published treatises on *The Art of Building in Water* and *Hibernia's Free Trade.*

As a tradesman John Semple (died 1784), brother of George, worked on the King's Hospital School ('Bluecoat School') and the CUSTOM HOUSE, Dublin, while his son, John Semple senior (1763–1840), worked on Trinity College Chapel and the King's Inns Library. As a member of the grand jury (city government), John senior benefited from public works contracts. He used the city guild structure to achieve patronage and advancement, becoming a sheriff's peer and member of the House of Sheriffs and Commons, and led right-wing corporate opposition to CATHOLIC EMANCIPATION. His certification of the HA'PENNY BRIDGE suggests ability as an engineer, though his structural proposals for the Custom House stores were controversial. With the construction of the Mansion House rotunda for the reception of George IV in 1821, and subsequent appointment as Architect to the Corporation, Semple's reputation was restored.

Having been made Archbishop of Dublin, and following his appointment as treasurer of the BOARD OF FIRST FRUITS, the militant Protestant WILLIAM MAGEE appointed Semple to the newly created post of Architect for the Ecclesiastical Province of Dublin. Semple's churches reflect a collaboration of architect and theologian in their references to Irish early Christian architecture, echoing 'SECOND REFORMATION' Episcopal claims to Patrician origin. In St Mary's Chapel of Ease (the 'Black Church'), Dublin, the corbelled vault recalls the vault of St Kevin's church at Glendalough, while its catenary form suggests Magee's professorship of mathematics and membership of the Science Committee of the ROYAL IRISH ACADEMY.

Semple built more than twenty-five churches during Magee's archiepiscopacy, 1822–31. The simple churches at Grangegorman and Tipperkevin were followed by the more developed gothic-revival churches at Whitechurch, Kilternan, Ballysax, Morristownbiller, and Donnybrook, all using his archetypal formula of pseudo-stone arches, buttresses, string courses, and pointed doorways, features that recur at Clonygowan, Cloneyhurke, and Thomastown and in the naves of St Selskar's and Mountmellick. Experiment in detail characterises Feighcullen, Tallaght, and Monkstown, while catenary theory informed the plaster vault of Rathmines and the corbelled stone vaults of Graigue, Abbeyleix, and the Black Church.

With Magee's death, Semple's architecture entered decline. Kinneagh, Kilanne, Redcross, Mountrath, and Taghadoe show little originality, while the stone arches at Inch parody the structural triumph of the Black Church.

Service as High Sheriff failed to halt the decline of John Semple junior (1801–1882). With his father's practice of John Semple and Son replaced at the Board of First Fruits, he languished as Engineer to the Piped Water Establishment until his ignominious dismissal by the reformed Town Council in 1842. As an architect, he designed Carysfort Royal School at Macreddin and added to Wexford and Carlow jails. Bankruptcy in 1849 saw the loss of his Regency villas at Seaview Terrace and Belgrave Square; and his death in 1882 ended 150 years of Semple ubiquity in Dublin.

Other Semples included the stuccodores Patrick and Edward (fl. 1760), and William (died 1813), carpenter and celebrated treasurer of Dublin Freemasons. **Cormac Allen**

Semple. *St Mary's Chapel of Ease (the 'Black Church'), St Mary's Place, Dublin, characteristic of John Semple's pared-down gothic style, the west façade distinguished by a series of receding planes framing the door. [Irish Architectural Archive; photo: Owen McCann]*

Senchán Torpéist (fl. seventh century), poet and genealogist. He is the subject of a number of legends, one of which credits him with the rediscovery of the epical text 'Táin Bó Cuailnge', which the poets had given away in exchange for a work of Latin learning, *The Encyclopaedia of Isidore of Seville.* **Tomás Ó Cathasaigh**

Serglige Con Culainn ('The wasting sickness of Cú Chulainn'), one of the early medieval tales of the ULSTER CYCLE. It concerns CÚ CHULAINN's debilitating lovesickness, his journey to the OTHERWORLD, his love affair with the Otherworld woman Fand, and the intervention of his wife, Emer, to foil her rival. The tale survives in two early MANUSCRIPTS and is an interweaving of both OLD IRISH and later MIDDLE IRISH materials. It is noteworthy for its poetic descriptions of the Otherworld as a realm of beauty and sinless bliss and for its interesting depiction of the women's speech in their debate over the hero. **Joanne Findon**

service sector, usually defined as consisting of everything that is not included in the agricultural and industrial sectors. This definition is so all-embracing that it includes an enormous diversity of economic activities, from public services such as education to private services such as hairdressing and from high-technology traded services such as telecommunications to relatively low-technology non-traded services such as baby-sitting. The distinctions between market and non-market services and between traded and non-traded services are particularly important in Ireland. The services sector accounted for approximately 63 per cent of output in the Republic in the late 1990s and approximately 75 per cent of output in Northern Ireland. Marketed services (such as hotels and catering, retailing, and BANKING) accounted for a higher proportion of total output in the South (43 per cent, as opposed to 40 per cent), meaning that non-market services (such as education, health, police, and defence) accounted for a much higher proportion of total output in the North (29 per cent, as opposed to 15 per cent). Services that are traded are defined as those that are exposed to international competition. TOURISM in both parts of Ireland is an important traded service industry, generating substantial EMPLOYMENT. In recent years, because of technological advances, many banking and insurance services have become exposed to international competition, and the establishment of the INTERNATIONAL FINANCIAL SERVICES CENTRE in Dublin is a reflection of this. **John W. O'Hagan**

Services, Industrial, Professional and Technical Union (SIPTU), the largest TRADE UNION in Ireland, with more than 200,000 members in almost every industry and the public service. It originated in a merger in 1990 between the IRISH TRANSPORT AND GENERAL WORKERS' UNION, previously the largest union, and the Federated Workers' Union of Ireland. Both unions had been founded by JAMES LARKIN. The ITGWU was established in 1909 as an alternative to British unions, with a particular emphasis on organising unskilled workers. It had a marked syndicalist orientation at first; this had abated by 1922, and under the leadership of William O'Brien membership increased rapidly. Personal as well as political differences with O'Brien caused Larkin to set up the Workers' Union of Ireland in 1923; but the WUI never rivalled the ITGWU in size, range of membership, or influence within the rest of the trade union movement. The merger of these two unions was part of the general process of trade union rationalisation that had been taking place from the 1970s, and many smaller unions had previously transferred their engagement to the ITGWU. But this was no takeover; hence the new name. **Niamh Hardiman**

session. With its origins in the term 'jam session', associated with JAZZ, this term has been used in Irish TRADITIONAL MUSIC circles since at least the late 1950s. A session typically comprises musicians or singers, or both, and (occasionally) storytellers. It usually has a leader or leaders—generally the senior or dominant musicians; but essentially it is informal. Since the late 1960s the session usually (though not always) takes place in a pub. The term is used also to describe gatherings of singers who prefer solo, unaccompanied songs. **Desi Wilkinson**

set-dancing. The early nineteenth century saw the introduction to Dublin of the 'first set of quadrilles'. These were essentially ballroom dances; but the popularity of a dance measure knows no social barriers, and these dances moved gradually from the ballrooms of 'polite society'—generally by way of the dancing-masters or local dancing enthusiasts—to the country houses and crossroads of rural Ireland as well as to towns. By the late nineteenth century they had penetrated the entire country. Far from simply adopting these new dances with their original form and musical accompaniment, however, the Irish dance tradition absorbed the sets and made of them something new, in their figures, musical tempo, and stepping. The transformation wrought on the quadrilles was produced by a combination of factors—the adoption of JIG and REEL measures, which had the effect of increasing the tempo; the application of the Irish 'travelling' steps and the subtly ornamental features of the solo jig and reel steps in place of the 'marching' step of the quadrilles; and the cross-fertilisation of the new imports with the older jig and reel group dances—resulting in a new and identifiably Irish phenomenon. Among the most popular of the sets were the MAZURKA (which became the *mazolka* in Co. Monaghan, the *mazorka* in Co. Donegal, the *myserks* in Co. Clare, and the *mesarts* in Co. Kerry) and the lancers, which was danced from Antrim to Wexford and from Mayo to Meath. Certain sets became associated with particular districts, such as the Caledonian in Co. Clare, while other sets adopted the name of the area in which they were danced, such as the Cashel and Ballycommon sets of Co. Tipperary. The passing of the PUBLIC DANCE HALLS ACT (1935), emigration, and other demographic changes and the powerful influence of international 'pop music' in the 1950s virtually wiped out the sets in all but a few areas; since the early 1980s, however, there has been a tremendous revival of set-dancing, with thousands of enthusiasts thronging the many workshops that are held throughout the year. **Helen Brennan**

Severin, Timothy (Tim) (1940–), explorer. Born in Tonbridge, Kent; since 1970 he has lived at Timoleague, Co. Cork. He has made a speciality of following myths as well as historical evidence for ancient voyages to explore the borderline between fact and fiction. Since his 'BRENDAN Voyage' in 1977, when he and a select crew faced the Atlantic Ocean in a leather boat, he has researched other ancient sailing vessels and re-created the experiences of legendary sailors. The 'Sindbad Voyage', from Oman to China, was conducted on an Arab sailing ship, while a crew of a reconstructed *Argo* rowed 2,400 km (1,500 miles) in 1984 to re-create the legendary voyage of Jason. Other seagoing experiments include the 'Ulysses Voyage' in 1987 and an investigation into traditional methods of whale-hunting (*In Search of Moby Dick*, 1999). Land journeys have traced places associated with Genghis Khan and with the Crusaders. Severin has been awarded the Founders' Medal of the Royal Geographical Society and the Livingstone Medal of the Royal Geographical Society of Scotland. **Peter Somerville-Large**

sexuality. Sexuality to an extent is socially constructed. In the early part of the twentieth century the Catholic Church dominated and informed the discourse on sexuality in Ireland. Kinship and reproduction rather than sexuality were central concerns. Reproduction was dominated by kinship and subsistence demands. In rural Ireland the stem family system facilitated high rates of FERTILITY within MARRIAGE which co-existed with low rates of marriage and high rates of celibacy. CENSORSHIP laws ensured that alternative discourses on sexuality were not promoted. Now, however, with CONTRACEPTION, sexual behaviour can be separated from reproduction and this has generated competing discourses on sexuality. A traditional discourse as produced by the church is no longer hegemonic. A progressive discourse focuses on empowering people to operate in the world in which they find themselves and to avoid sexually transmitted diseases and unwanted pregnancies. A liberal viewpoint centres on experiencing, exploring, and understanding sexuality, creating conditions for sexual freedom and emancipation. Finally, a radical viewpoint underlies a feminist critique of patriarchal heterosexuality. It challenges the dominant definition of what is sexually normal and acceptable. This approach has helped to promote gay and lesbian sexuality. In more recent times there has also been a focus on institutional sexual abuse and paedophilia, which reveals aspects of past intimate lives that until recently remained secret, hidden, and unknown. **Evelyn Mahon**

Seymour, Dermot (1956–), painter. Born in Belfast; educated at the University of Ulster. Earlier paintings of detailed images render commonplace subjects in unlikely juxtaposition; the titles of his paintings are sardonic comments on life in Northern Ireland. He now lives in Co. Mayo and paints in a figurative, quasi-photorealist style. He has exhibited widely in Ireland and abroad, with solo exhibitions in Dublin, London, Berlin, and New York and a retrospective exhibition at Model Arts Centre, Sligo, 1997. He is a member of AOSDÁNA. **Suzanne McNab**

Shackleton, Abraham (1696–1771), teacher. Born in Yorkshire. In 1726 he opened a school in Ballitore, Co. Kildare, designed along QUAKER principles but open to all denominations. Ballitore School attracted a talented pool of students, including EDMUND BURKE, who remained a close friend of the Shackleton family throughout his life. PAUL CULLEN was a student at a later period, as was the botanist W. H. HARVEY. **Kevin O'Neill**

Shackleton, David (1923–1988), plantsman, born in Dublin. One of the most influential Irish gardeners of the late twentieth century, he created a garden at Beech Park, Clonsilla, Co. Dublin, where he grew a remarkable range of plant species and cultivated varieties. He achieved particular success in growing *Celmisias* in raised beds. By his vigilance he rescued many rare and endangered plants from extinction. He enriched Irish gardens by his constant search for new and better plants and by distributing good plants to good gardeners. Beech Park became a mecca for plant enthusiasts and a trial ground for new plants and for experiments in growing difficult subjects. **Donal Synnott**

Shackleton, Sir Ernest (1874–1922), explorer. Born in Kilkea, Co. Kildare. When he was six his family moved to Dublin, where his father practised as a doctor. In 1884 the family moved to England, where Shackleton was educated at Dulwich College, London. He was teased at school for his Irish accent but would lose contact with the land of his birth; his later patriotism was patriotism for England. At sixteen he joined the merchant service, his family's lack of means preventing him from joining the officer class of the Royal Navy. In 1901 he joined Captain Robert Scott on the National Antarctic Expedition, and together with Scott and Dr Edward Wilson he made extensive land journeys on the continent before turning back. It has been said that Scott's decision to invalid him back to England changed his life.

In 1907 Shackleton led his own expedition to Antarctica, with the purpose of reaching the geographical South Pole and magnetic South Pole. Though he and his men reached the summit of Mount Erebus and the magnetic pole, the South Pole itself eluded them, and he prudently turned back; he told his wife he would rather be a live donkey than a dead hero. However, his expedition had sledged to within 156 km (97 miles) of the pole, surpassing Scott's efforts by 580 km (360 miles). He was knighted in 1909. In 1914, after the outbreak of the FIRST WORLD WAR and two years after Scott perished, Shackleton set off once more for the Antarctic with a crew of twenty-eight men in the *Endurance* (whose name was derived from his family motto, *Fortitudine vincimus*—By endurance we conquer). Though he failed in his objective of crossing the continent from the Weddell Sea to the Ross Sea, this expedition—recorded by the American Frank Hurley in a brilliant series of photographs, now in the possession of the Royal Geographical Society, London—is the one by which he is remembered. After the *Endurance* was embedded in ice in the Weddell Sea, the crew was marooned on Elephant Island, from where Shackleton and a crew that included THOMAS CREAN set off for the whaling station on South Georgia Island, 1,300 km (800 miles) away, in an open boat. This rescue operation has been called 'one of the greatest boat journeys ever accomplished.' When he returned to retrieve his men, not one of them had died. The boat is preserved in his old school.

Shackleton, Ernest. *The* Endurance, *Ernest Shackleton's exploration vessel on his expedition to the Antarctic, 1914–16, embedded in the frozen Weddell Sea, 1,300 km (800 miles) from its intended base, in a photograph by the expedition's photographer, Frank Hurley. [Collins Press]*

Scott's death may have made him better known, but without doubt Shackleton's qualities of leadership were unsurpassed. 'Sometimes I think I am no good at anything but being away in the wild with men,' he wrote to his wife in 1919. The qualities he valued were optimism, patience, physical endurance, idealism, and courage. His attention to detail, sometimes described as 'fussiness', went far in securing the safety of his crews. It has been said that polar exploration appealed both to his poetic turn of mind and to his aspiration to secure a position of fame in the class-riven world of his time. In 1921 he sent off again for his beloved Antarctica in the *Quest*. He died of a heart attack on 5 January 1922 at South Georgia, where he is buried. His last words to the doctor who attended him were 'What, do you want me to give up now?' **Peter Somerville-Large**

Shackleton, Lydia (1828–1914), botanical artist. Born in Lucan, Co. Dublin, a member of a celebrated QUAKER family; trained at the Dublin Metropolitan School of Art. Housekeeper for her brother Joseph at the family flour-mill, she was commissioned by FREDERICK

MOORE to illustrate the orchid, peony, hellebore, and other collections at the NATIONAL BOTANIC GARDENS, Glasnevin, some of them flowering in cultivation for the first time. She began the work in 1884 and continued until failing eyesight forced her to stop c. 1907. She has left more than 1,500 watercolour illustrations in the Glasnevin archive, many of them of superb quality (see p. 967). **Donal Synnott**

shanachie (*seanchaí*), a traditional storyteller. A distinction is often made between the *scéalaí*, who told long, multi-episode international FOLK-TALES as well as Irish hero-tales, and the *seanchaí*, who specialised in shorter lore. The number of gifted *scéalaithe* in a community was probably always quite restricted, but many individuals might narrate lore of a less demanding nature, whether historical, religious, or mythological. In traditional society, in recent centuries at least, there were no professional storytellers, though accomplished *scéalaithe* might receive presents in recognition of their services to the community. **Mícheál Briody**

'Shankill Butchers', the name given to a gang of freelance murderers associated with the UVF, based in the Shankill Road area of Belfast, responsible for nineteen killings in north and west Belfast between November 1975 and February 1977. The gang's leader, Lenny Murphy, had been involved in loyalist paramilitary activities from the beginning of the 'TROUBLES', with a reputation for gratuitous violence. The gang's victims were usually abducted by car and tortured and mutilated with butcher's knives or meat-cleavers before being killed, hence their notorious nickname. Though most of their targets were innocent Catholics, selected merely on sectarian grounds, the gang killed a number of Protestants also, aiming to reinforce Murphy's position within his own community. In March 1976 Murphy was arrested and subsequently jailed for possessing arms, but the gang continued to operate until 1977. After his release from prison in 1982 Murphy was killed by the PROVISIONAL IRA, apparently acting on information provided by loyalists, for whom the maverick killer had become a serious liability. **Keith Jeffery**

Shannon Airport. Several sites 'suitable for land-planes and seaplanes on a transatlantic service' were considered before the Government took the decision, on 14 August 1936, to establish a base at Rineanna, Co. Clare. Work began in October, but the first land-plane, an AIR CORPS Anson, did not touch down until 18 May 1939. In the meantime controversy had arisen as to whether the sea-plane base should be proceeded with; in the event, though some construction took place, Rineanna never saw flying-boat services.

After 1945 Shannon became an important staging post, as the generation of aircraft then operating required refuelling facilities to achieve the Atlantic crossing, and its renowned restaurant operated twenty-four hours a day. Its sales and catering manager, Brendan O'Regan, established the world's first duty-free shop and, with the airport subsequently threatened with overflying by the new generation of jets, promoted the duty-free industrial zone, a new town (Shannon, Co. Clare), and a strong local TOURISM infrastructure. Under a bilateral agreement of 1945 between Ireland and the United States, all transatlantic services were obliged to serve Shannon in each direction, a condition that, though later modified, remains a source of controversy and political infighting. Popular with airlines for flight training because of its low traffic densities, Shannon has retained its role through commercial vicissitudes both as a major airport and as an air navigation services and training centre. [see FOYNES; IRISH COFFEE.] **Bernard Share**

Shannon–Erne Waterway: see BALLINAMORE AND BALLYCONNELL CANAL.

Shannon Navigation. The River Shannon is navigable from Lough Allen to the sea at Limerick. It is also connected by canal with LOUGH ERNE and by the GRAND and ROYAL CANALS with Dublin. Work began in 1755 under Thomas Omer on improving the navigation, with locks and bypass canals at Meelick and Athlone. Commissioners were appointed in 1831 and surveys of the navigation carried out by Thomas Rhodes. A combined drainage and navigation improvement scheme was undertaken in the 1840s, with much dredging and new locks designed to accommodate passenger steamers. The 30 m (100-ft) fall at Ardnacrusha is used for the hydro-electric SHANNON SCHEME (1925–9). The Shannon Navigation is also much used by pleasure craft. **Ronald Cox**

Shannon, River, the longest river in Ireland, rising east of Sligo Bay at Shannon Pot on Tiltibane, and flowing south for a distance of 358 km (222 miles). Together with its tributaries, the Shannon dominates the drainage system of the central lowlands. It is linked to Dublin by the GRAND and ROYAL CANALS. Over much of its course the river flows sluggishly and has no recognisable valley. It has a long history of FLOODING and is surrounded by extensive BOGS and marshlands, which include the 'callows' (*caladh*, river-meadow), now regarded as environmentally sensitive areas. At the other extreme the Shannon is particularly susceptible to low water levels during periods of drought, mainly because of drainage to underground flow systems. One of the river's most significant features is the series of LAKES along its course, the largest of which are Lough Allen, Lough Ree, and LOUGH DERG; their presence is generally ascribed to the solution of the Carboniferous limestone that, though concealed beneath glacial deposits, underlies much of the central lowland. Other theories of their formation consider the role of subsidence and glacial meltwaters.

There are some interesting changes in gradient along the length of the river, which falls only 17 m (56 ft) over a distance of 160 km (100 miles) to Lough Derg. In the last 26 km (16 miles), from Lough Derg to tide-water level at Limerick the river falls by more than 30 m (100 ft); this drop has been used to generate hydro-electricity at the SHANNON SCHEME at Ardnacrusha, constructed between 1925 and 1929. Downstream from here is the striking Killaloe gorge, which has been cut into resistant rocks, probably as a result of glacial diversion. The river becomes tidal 3 km (2 miles) above Limerick, 80 km (50 miles) from the open sea. The estuary is a drowned river valley fringed on each side by sand and mud banks and vast expanses of alluvial flats. Some of this land has been reclaimed and provides good pasture. **R. A. Charlton**

Shannon Scheme. In 1924 a plan to harness the 30 m (100-ft) fall in the River Shannon between Killaloe and Limerick to generate ELECTRICITY was put forward by THOMAS MCLAUGHLIN. Under the Shannon Electricity Act (1924) a contract for the construction of a hydro-electric power station and associated works was awarded to the German firm Siemens-Schuckert. The works consist of a small dam on the river south of Killaloe that diverts part of the river flow down a 12.6 km (8-mile) intake canal to a 30 m (100-ft) dam at Ardnacrusha. Penstocks lead the water through the dam to four turbines, each linked to a generator. The capacity of the station was 86 MW but this was increased to 110 MW in the 1990s. The scheme was handed over to the Electricity Supply Board in October 1929, and by 1936 it was supplying 87 per cent

of the electricity requirements of the Republic (see pp. 346, 578).
Ronald Cox

Shaw, Fiona (1958–), actor. Born in Cork; attended the Royal Academy of Dramatic Art, London. She quickly established herself as an intense, intelligent and adventurous performer. Important roles have included *The Waste Land* (filmed 1985), a controversial London production of Beckett's *Footfalls*, 1994, and *Medea* at the ABBEY THEATRE, 2000. She also works extensively in film and television.
Christopher Morash

Shaw, George Bernard (1856–1950), writer. Born in Dublin to Protestant parents of what he called the 'downstart' class. He did not attend university but started work at sixteen as a clerk in a land agent's office. He left Ireland for London in 1876 and was to live in England for the rest of his life. After an unsuccessful start as a novelist (five novels written in five years, all of them rejected for publication), he eventually established himself as a journalist, reviewing art, music, and (outstandingly) theatre for the *Saturday Review*. A convert to socialism in the 1880s, he became a leading member of the Fabian Society, and his political commitment informed all his writing. His first plays, published in 1898 as *Plays Pleasant and Unpleasant*, inspired by the example of Ibsen, aimed to challenge conventional theatrical representation, forcing audiences to rethink their social and political attitudes. Though some of them have since become very popular (such as *Arms and the Man* and *You Never Can Tell*), at the time they were mostly considered too avant-garde for production; the notorious *Mrs Warren's Profession* was banned by the censor.

After 1898, when he married Charlotte Payne-Townshend, an Irishwoman of independent means, and his play *The Devil's Disciple* had been successfully produced in America, Shaw did not need to work at paid journalism. In the new century he wrote three plays that he himself regarded as among his major works: *Man and Superman* (1903), JOHN BULL'S OTHER ISLAND (1904), and *Major Barbara* (1905). In these he perfected the dialectical method of his comedy of ideas, by which, on the basis of a sketchy comic plot, social, political, and metaphysical issues are argued out: creative evolution (the concept that human beings are continually evolving towards greater self-awareness), national identity, the relations between power and progressive politics. These plays, and many others, produced at the Court Theatre, London, in a series of repertory seasons (1904–7) established Shaw as a playwright.

Though *John Bull's Other Island* was at first turned down for production in the ABBEY THEATRE in 1904, the Abbey's production in 1909 of *The Shewing-up of Blanco Posnet* (which had been banned in England) provided the starting-point for a greater degree of involvement with the Abbey and a close friendship with LADY GREGORY (see p. 235). In 1905, largely at the insistence of his wife, Shaw had spent a holiday in Ireland, and this was to become an almost yearly event, with extended periods of the summer spent in Cos. Cork and Kerry, most often at Parknasilla. He supported the Abbey with help and advice, and after 1916, when *John Bull's Other Island* was at last produced there, many of his plays entered its repertory.

After achieving one of his outstanding popular successes with *Pygmalion* in 1914, Shaw alienated many people in Britain by his critical view of the FIRST WORLD WAR. He was prepared to risk public odium also in 1916 in his defence of the 1916 RISING (though he was wholly opposed to separatism) and his efforts to save ROGER CASEMENT from execution. The outstanding product of his disillusionment with the war was *Heartbreak House* (written 1917, published 1919), a tragi-comic diagnosis of the failures of Western European culture.

Shaw, George Bernard. George Bernard Shaw *(1927) by Paul Troubetzkoy, outside the National Gallery of Ireland, Dublin. The author of fifty-two plays, including* Saint Joan, *he won the Nobel Prize for Literature in 1926. He bequeathed one-third of the royalties from his estate to the National Gallery. [Pat O'Dea, Bord Fáilte]*

In the immediate post-war period Shaw's stock seemed to have fallen; *Back to Methuselah* (1921), his five-play cycle expounding his doctrines of creative evolution, seemed passé and unproduceable. But with *Saint Joan*, completed in 1923 on what proved his last visit to Ireland and produced in 1924, he once again achieved success, and his renewed reputation was confirmed by the award of the NOBEL PRIZE in 1926. Shaw's fame not only as playwright but as public guru continued to grow in the latter part of his life, in spite of his politically obtuse support for Stalin, Mussolini, and Hitler. While later plays, such as *The Apple Cart* (1929), *Too True to Be Good* (1932) and *Geneva* (1938), were only moderately successful, he was much fêted and quoted on extensive world travels in the 1930s. He remained active through the last decade of his life, in spite of the loss of his wife in 1943 and increasing restrictions in his movements; his last completed work, the puppet play *Shake versus Shav*, was written the year before his death in 1950 at his home in Ayot St Lawrence, Hertfordshire.

Though Shaw's academic reputation has declined, some dozen of his fifty-two plays continue to hold the stage, and the larger-than-life persona of GBS manages to reach a wide readership through the characteristic wit and iconoclastic energy of everything he wrote. **Nicholas Grene**

Sheares, Henry (c. 1753–1798), UNITED IRISHMAN. Born in Goldenbush and raised at Glasheen, Co. Cork; educated at TCD. He proceeded to an officership in the 51st Foot. On gravitating to the bar in 1790, his life became closely connected with that of his younger brother, JOHN SHEARES. He presided at several United Irish meetings in Dublin in 1793–4 but kept a low profile until March 1798, when he assisted in the developing conspiracy. His arrest on 21 May led to a treason trial on 13 July and his hanging outside Newgate Prison, Dublin, the following day. **Ruan O'Donnell**

Sheares, John (1766–1798), UNITED IRISHMAN. Born in Glasheen, Co. Cork; he attended TCD in 1783 and was called to the bar in 1789. He visited revolutionary France with his brother, HENRY SHEARES, in 1792, and witnessed the execution of King Louis before returning home in January 1793. He joined the United Irishmen in mid-1793 and quickly rose to prominence, writing several inflammatory documents and articles in the nationalist *Press*. Arrests of other conspirators thrust him to high authority in March 1798, but his own arrest on 21 May resulted in his hanging for high treason on 14 July. **Ruan O'Donnell**

shebeen (*síbín*), an unlicensed drinking establishment. The word originally meant a vessel of 2.3–3.5 litres (2–3 quarts) used for measuring grain, later for measuring drinks, and hence for any small or rudimentary public house. The use of the word has spread from Ireland to Scotland and South Africa. **Ciarán Deane**

Shee, Martin Archer (1769–1850), artist. Born in Dublin, a member of an impoverished Catholic gentry family; attended the DUBLIN SOCIETY schools, where he won many prizes. In 1788 he went to London, where he made his distinguished career. He attended the Royal Academy school and was influenced by Reynolds and Gilbert Stuart. Apart from portraits he painted a number of subject pictures and was a brilliant painter of children. His full-length pictures of men are his best work, well composed and painted. He became president of the Royal Academy in 1830, the only Irish painter to achieve this distinction. **Anne Crookshank**

Sheehan, Canon Patrick Augustine (1852–1913), priest and novelist. Born in Mallow, Co. Cork. Sheehan's novels, originally written for an American audience, became immensely popular and made him a leading spokesman for Irish Catholicism but brought suspicion from less intellectual colleagues. Their dream of rural society guided by paternalistic priests is haunted by a sense of powerlessness before the moral and intellectual challenges of modernisation. His most popular novels are *My New Curate* (1900) and *Glenanaar* (1905). Though inclined to sermonise, Sheehan's novels are given interest by the discreet, tortured self-questioning in such accounts of priestly life as *Luke Delmege* (1901) and *The Blindness of Dr Gray* (1909). **Patrick Maume**

Sheehan and Barry, architects and interior designers. The practice was established in Dublin in 1981 by David Sheehan and Desmond Barry, both educated at UCD, with Denis Looby and David Averill, both educated at DIT. Among their most celebrated conservation projects, underpinned by an archaeological sense of scholarly attention to the historical fabric, are STACKALLEN HOUSE, an early eighteenth-century mansion in Co. Meath; Cashel Palace, Cashel, Co. Tipperary, by EDWARD LOVETT PEARCE; Newman House, St Stephen's Green, Dublin, and Ardbraccan House, Co. Meath, both by RICHARD CASTLE; Corbalton Hall, Co. Meath, by FRANCIS JOHNSTON; and Ayesha Castle, Dublin, by Sandham Symes. Of major significance are individual restorations of historic interiors, such as the Apollo Room and piano nobile at Newman House (see p. 603). A further intervention is Gilltown, Co. Kildare, the re-creation of a classical villa from surviving eighteenth-century structures, while other conservation projects are ecclesiastical, including the reordering of St Patrick's Pro-Cathedral, Dundalk, by Thomas Duff. **Brian Lalor**

Sheehy, Jeanne (1939–1999), art historian. Born in Dublin; educated at UCD, TCD, and Paris. A ground-breaking writer on WALTER OSBORNE (1970) and in *The Discovery of Ireland's Past: The Celtic Revival* (1980), she lectured in art history at Oxford Polytechnic (now Oxford Brookes University) from the late 1970s. **Richard Pine**

Sheehy, Michael (Mikey) (1954–), Gaelic footballer. Born in Tralee, Co. Kerry. As part of the great Kerry team of the 1970s and 80s he was their scorer-in-chief from frees and from play. He scored a famous goal in the 1978 all-Ireland final when cheekily chipping the ball over the Dublin goalkeeper, Paddy Cullen. He won eight all-Ireland medals in his career. **Donal Keenan**

Sheehy Skeffington, Francis (1878–1916), socialist, pacifist, and journalist. Born Francis Skeffington in Bailieborough, Co. Cavan; educated at UCD, where he formed a friendship with JAMES JOYCE, who portrayed him in *Portrait of the Artist as a Young Man*. He revived the Literary and Historical Society in 1897. In 1903 he married HANNA SHEEHY and adopted her name. They worked on various radical causes, and he wrote for the IRISH CITIZEN. During the 1916 RISING he was arrested while attempting to stop looting and was summarily shot. **Seán Farrell Moran**

Sheehy Skeffington, Hanna, née Sheehy (1877–1946), feminist and republican activist. Born in Kanturk, Co. Cork; educated at the Royal University. Joint-founder of the Irish Women's Franchise League (1908), she campaigned for votes for women in HOME RULE Ireland. She was imprisoned in 1912 after a window-smashing protest. She carried supplies during the 1916 RISING. Following the murder of her husband, Francis Sheehy Skeffington, she obtained a judicial inquiry. She travelled to the United States to publicise the murder and to gain support for an Irish republic and was received by President Woodrow Wilson. On her return to Ireland in 1918 she joined SINN FÉIN; she edited the IRISH CITIZEN until 1920. She opposed the Constitution of Ireland (1937). An unsuccessful independent candidate for Dáil Éireann in 1943, she remained a prominent figure in feminist and republican circles, nationally and internationally. **Margaret Ward**

sheela-na-gig, female exhibitionist figures whose original function was to alert the faithful to the dangers of the sin of lust. (The origin of the term is unknown.) They, and related male carvings, are found on medieval European churches, particularly those along PILGRIMAGE routes. The emphasis on the genitalia, which are usually enlarged, related to the church's teaching that sinners were punished in Hell through the bodily organs by which they had offended.

In Ireland, exhibitionist figures are almost exclusively of females posed in a manner that displays and emphasises the genitalia. The earliest appear to be associated with ROMANESQUE buildings; most carvings are later, occurring mainly within areas of ANGLO-NORMAN SETTLEMENT. The earliest carvings are on churches, usually as a single figure set in isolation on a gable wall, or near a door or window. Later they appear on town walls and on TOWER-HOUSES, where they seem to have functioned as protective carvings. The change in meaning from figure of lust to protective icon appears to relate to changes brought about by Irish cultural resurgence and its influence on the Anglo-Norman colony during the later Middle Ages. **Éamonn P. Kelly**

Sheil, Richard Lalor (1791–1851), politician. Born in Drumdowney, Co. Kilkenny; educated at Stonyhurst College, Lancashire, and TCD. After a brief career as a playwright he concentrated on the law while becoming involved in the campaign for CATHOLIC EMANCIPATION. With his erstwhile political opponent DANIEL O'CONNELL he founded the CATHOLIC ASSOCIATION and, following Catholic Emancipation, sat for various Irish seats in Parliament. He eventually allied himself with the WHIGS, a connection that brought him government appointments that included an ambassadorship to Florence. **Gary Owens**

Sheppard, Oliver (1865–1941), sculptor. Born in Cookstown, Co. Tyrone, and grew up in Dublin, where his father was an artisan-sculptor. He attended the Metropolitan School of Art, 1884–8, and the RHA life drawing school. He received a scholarship to the Royal College of Art, London, 1889–91, where he studied under Édouard Lanteri, and subsequently studied at the Académie Julian, Paris, and in Italy. He taught at Leicester School of Art, 1892–3, Nottingham School of Art, 1894–1902, and the Dublin Metropolitan School of Art, 1902–37. He exhibited regularly at the RHA from 1891 to 1941 and was a full member from 1901 and professor of sculpture. He was a founder-member of the Royal Society of British Sculptors and exhibited at the Royal Academy and on the Continent. He was a friend of W. B. YEATS and GEORGE RUSSELL, and his work was deeply influenced by the Celtic Revival, as in *Niamh and Oisín* (1895), *Inis Fáil* (1900), and his masterpiece, *The Death of Cuchulain* (1911–12), which was chosen by ÉAMON DE VALERA in 1935 as the national monument to the 1916 RISING and placed in the GPO in O'Connell Street, Dublin (see p. 1090). He had great success in public sculpture with his large-scale bronze memorials to the 1798 REBELLION in Wexford (1904) and Enniscorthy (1908); he also created the public memorials to JAMES CLARENCE MANGAN in St Stephen's Green, Dublin (1909), and to WILLIAM REDMOND in Wexford (1930). He was a prolific modeller of portrait busts and reliefs, notably those of medical men and political figures, such as the bust of PATRICK PEARSE (1936) in DÁIL ÉIREANN. He also made prize medals for Trinity College, Dublin. He was highly regarded as a teacher of sculpture and was the dominant influence in Dublin up to his retirement. **John Turpin**

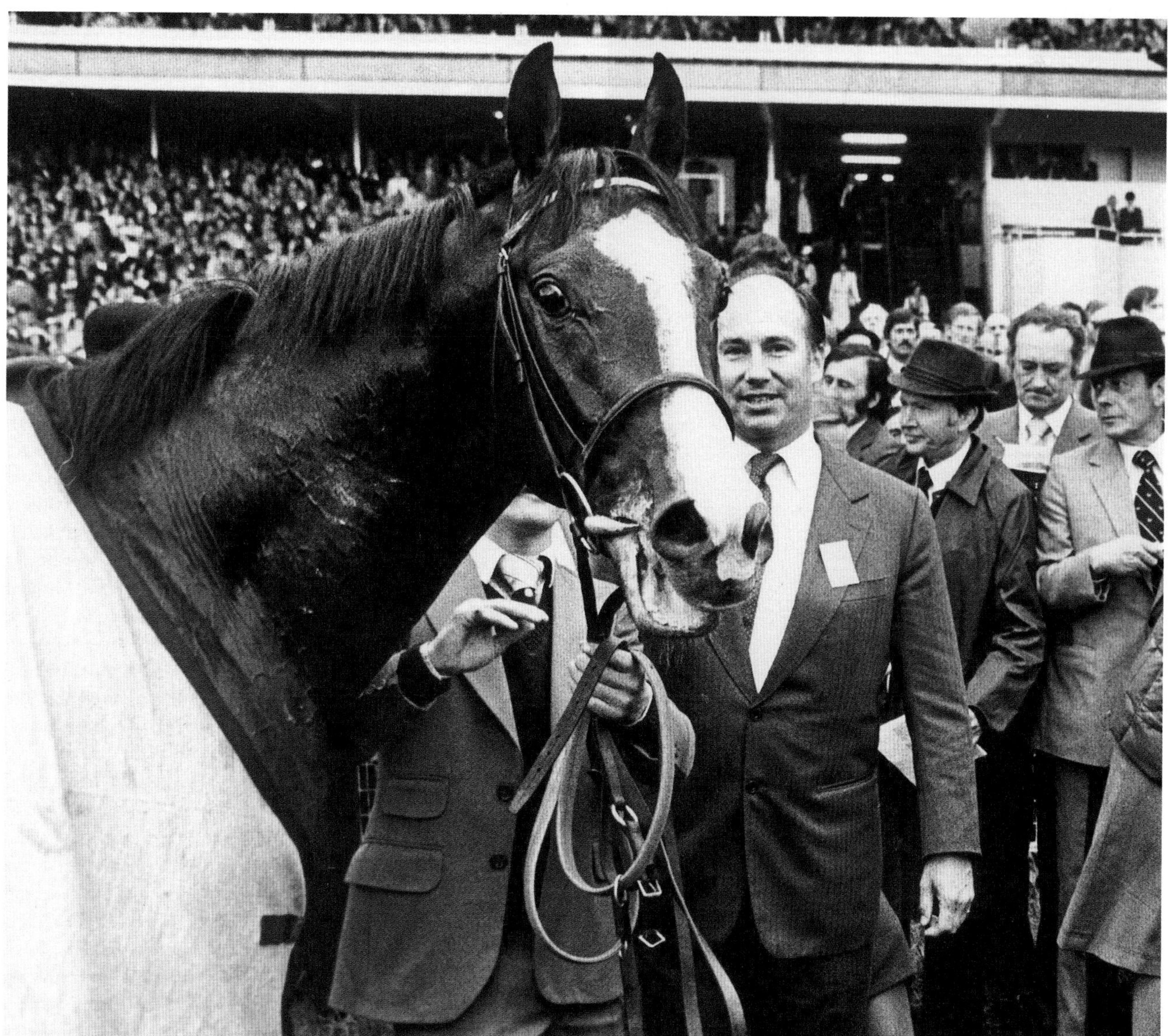

Shergar. *One of Ireland's greatest racehorses, Shergar, with his owner, Prince Karim Aga Khan, in 1981, having won the Irish Derby. Shergar was kidnapped in 1983 and has never been recovered. [Derek Speirs/Report]*

Shergar (1978–1983?), a racehorse. Born in 1978, he belonged to the fourth Aga Khan and was trained by Michael Stoute. His many racing victories included the Epsom Derby, the Irish Derby, and the King George VI and Queen Elizabeth Stakes. He was retired to Ballymany Stables, Co. Kildare, but was kidnapped from there on 9 February 1983 by, it is believed, the PROVISIONAL IRA. A ransom was demanded but the money was never paid, and Shergar must be presumed dead. **Ciarán Deane**

Sheridan, Frances, née Chamberlayne (1724–1766), novelist and dramatist. Born in Dublin. She wrote her first novel at fifteen. After marriage to THOMAS SHERIDAN the Younger she helped support her family by writing. Her sentimental novel *Memoirs of Miss Sydney Biddulph* (1761–7) was greatly admired in its day; a harsh indictment of contemporary attitudes to women's conduct, it is today established as among the very finest eighteenth-century novels. The long-popular *Nourjahad* (1767) is an accomplished oriental tale. Sheridan's plays include the successful *The Discovery* (1762) and the unfinished *A Journey to Bath*—an important influence on the work of her son, RICHARD BRINSLEY SHERIDAN. **Ian Campbell Ross**

Sheridan, Margaret. *The soprano Margaret Sheridan, famed for her performances in the great opera houses of Europe. Toscanini, conductor and director of La Scala, Milan, dubbed her 'Empress of Ireland'. [G. A. Duncan]*

Sheridan, Jim (1949–), film director and writer. Born in Dublin. His career began in the 1970s as a theatre director and playwright; eight of his plays have been produced, mainly during his period as chairman of the Project Arts Centre, Dublin. Artistic director of the Irish Arts Centre, New York, in the 1980s, he briefly studied film at New York University before adapting, with the producer Noel Pearson, CHRISTY BROWN's autobiography, *My Left Foot* (1989), which won two Academy Awards (for Daniel Day-Lewis and BRENDA FRICKER). RICHARD HARRIS featured in his next film, *The Field* (1990) (see p. 197), which was followed by *In the Name of the Father* (1993). He was also the scriptwriter for the children's film *Into the West* (1992) and, with the director, Terry George, of *Some Mother's Son* (1996); with George he jointly wrote the Northern Ireland ceasefire film *The Boxer* (1997), which he also directed. **Kevin Rockett**

Sheridan, Margaret (1889–1958), soprano, later known as Margaret Burke Sheridan. Born in Castlebar, Co. Mayo; her success at the FEIS CEOIL led to study at the Royal Academy of Music, London, with William Shakespeare, 1909–11, and later in Italy with Alfredo Martino (with financial support from Guglielmo Marconi). She made her debut in *La bohème* in Rome, 1918, and sang the title role of *La Wally* for her first performance at La Scala, 1920. After hearing her in *Madama Butterfly* in Milan, Puccini coached her in 1923 for the title role in *Manon Lescaut*, which became her most famous part. She retired in 1936 and returned to Ireland, where she established a singing school. **Adrian Scahill**

Sheridan, Noel (1936–), painter and performance artist. Born in Dublin, son of the actor Cecil Sheridan; attended Synge Street CBS before working at Independent Newspapers. He wrote revues for the Trinity Players and collaborated with the actor John Molloy on *Tete at Eight*, which toured to New York in 1963. He settled in New York and became a painter, supporting himself by working at a variety of jobs, including as a guard at the Museum of Modern Art. In 1967 he exhibited abstract paintings at the Dawson Gallery, Dublin, and three years later became director of the Experimental Art Foundation, Adelaide, Australia, specialising in performance and conceptual art. He returned to Ireland in 1980 as director of the National College of Art. He is a member of AOSDÁNA. **Peter Murray**

Sheridan, Richard Brinsley (1751–1816), playwright, politician, orator, and theatre manager. Born in Dublin, son of THOMAS SHERIDAN, manager of SMOCK ALLEY THEATRE, and FRANCES SHERIDAN, novelist and playwright. He left Ireland at the age of eight, was educated at Harrow School, Middlesex, and rejoined his family in Bath in 1770, where he met Elizabeth Linley, a singer and famous beauty. He created a sensation by eloping with (and eventually marrying) her, events he transmuted into his first play, *The Rivals* (1775), which was a huge success at Covent Garden Theatre, London. In quick succession he wrote an afterpiece, *St Patrick's Day* (1775), and an operatic play, *The Duenna* (1775), and in 1776 he bought David Garrick's half-share in Drury Lane Theatre, becoming its manager and writing one of its most valuable properties, *The School for Scandal* (1777). In the same year he wrote *A Trip to Scarborough*, which, like his remaining works, was an adaptation, in this case of Vanbrugh's *The Relapse*. *The Critic* (1779), is based on Buckingham's *The Rehearsal*; and *Pizzaro* (1779) was adapted from August Kotzebue.

His two most successful plays, *The Rivals* and *The School for Scandal*, are among the great comedies in English, dexterously manipulating ideas of truth, illusion, and reputation in a virtuoso subversion of theatrical convention. However, Sheridan always wrote quickly and for money, and from 1780, when he was elected member of Parliament for Stafford, his interest in theatre declined. Joining Fox's WHIG Party, he became a rival, and later opponent, of EDMUND BURKE. He rose rapidly through Fox's Cabinet; in 1787 his five-hour speech supporting the impeachment of Warren Hastings, Governor-General of India, established his reputation as an orator. Though he was an intimate friend of the Prince Regent, Sheridan always lived beyond his means, and he incurred enormous debts rebuilding Drury Lane Theatre in the 1790s. When the theatre was burnt in 1809 he could no longer avoid his creditors. He lost his parliamentary seat in 1811 and in 1813 was arrested for debt, and he died, impoverished but respected, in 1816.

Though he left Ireland as a child, Sheridan's attack on Hastings and his public support for American independence made him a popular figure in his native country. His status as an Irish writer was confirmed when THOMAS MOORE published *Memoirs of the Life of the Right Honourable Richard Brinsley Sheridan* (1825). **Christopher Morash**

Sheridan, Thomas (1719–1788), actor, theatre manager, educator, and biographer. Born in Quilca, Co. Cavan, son of the educator and classicist Thomas Sheridan (1687–1738); educated at TCD. He first acted in the SMOCK ALLEY THEATRE in 1743, becoming its most influential manager in 1745. His attempts at theatrical reform provoked riots in 1747 and 1754. After 1754 he acted occasionally, teaching elocution and pursuing a controversial project to reform the English language and educational system, publishing *British Education: Source of Disorders* (1756). He was the biographer and posthumous editor of JONATHAN SWIFT, who was his godfather. RICHARD BRINSLEY SHERIDAN was his son. **Christopher Morash**

Sherkin Island, Co. Cork, 2 km ($1\frac{1}{4}$ miles) off the coast. It has an area of 612 ha (1,500 acres); the highest point is Slievemore, 112 m (367 ft) above sea level. It is the second-largest island in Roaringwater Bay and Long Island Bay and has a population of over 100. Much of the island is rough grazing and heathland, with some woodland and scrub developing. The main grazing animals are cattle, with farming, fishing, and TOURISM the main sources of income. The island has a church, post office, primary school, hotel, and public house, as well as two national monuments, the Franciscan abbey and Dún na Long Castle. There is a daily ferry to and from the fishing village of Baltimore on the mainland. The island has a rich FLORA: of the 592 flowering plants and ferns found on the islands of Roaringwater Bay, 483 of these can be found on Sherkin. It and the other islands and the bays are now recognised as among the most important of Ireland's heritage areas and have been designated a special area of conservation. **Matt Murphy**

Sherkin Island Marine Station, on the north-west corner of SHERKIN ISLAND, Co. Cork, founded in 1975 by Matt and Eileen Murphy. The purpose of the station is to establish baseline data on the FLORA and FAUNA along the coast, as well as to educate

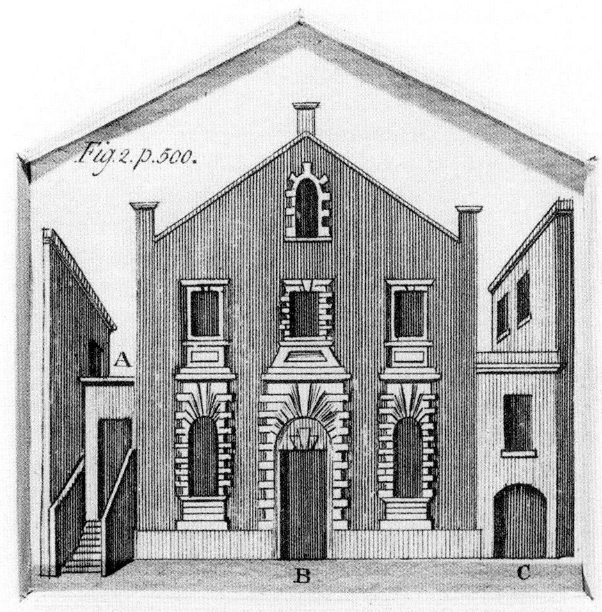

Sheridan, Thomas. *Engraving in* Gentleman's Magazine, *London, June 1789), of the Smock Alley Theatre, Dublin where Sheridan first performed and subsequently served as manager. [National Gallery of Ireland]*

adults and children on the ENVIRONMENT. The main projects carried out are the rocky shore survey, in which data is recorded annually at 146 sites from Cork Harbour to Bantry Bay, and the phytoplankton survey, in which phytoplankton populations at various stations in Roaringwater Bay and south of Sherkin are monitored. Other projects include work on birds, otters, butterflies, moths, insects, rock-pools, seaweeds, sponges, macro-fauna, zooplankton, and terrestrial flora. The station has also kept daily weather data since 1972.

The aim of the station, which is staffed by volunteer biologists, is to educate by means of its quarterly environmental newspaper, *Sherkin Comment*, and its other publications, as well as through school visits by Audrey Murphy. The station's environmental conference is held annually in Cork; approximately thirty other conferences and workshops have been held over the years. It has an extensive library as well as reference collections, seaweed and flora herbaria, and more than 10,000 natural history photographs and slides. **Matt Murphy**

Sherrington Observatory (1877–90), established near Bray, Co. Wicklow, by Dr WENTWORTH ERCK. He equipped it with both a 191 mm ($7\frac{1}{2}$-in.) and a 381 mm (15-in.) reflector, each on a personally designed mount. Erck is believed to have been the first to note the proper motion of the Great Red Spot on Jupiter with respect to the general surface of the planet. He made more than 1,900 measurements of forty selected binaries between 1873 and 1888. He also made regular observations of sun-spots between 1869 and 1888 and published many papers on observational astronomy and astronomical instrumentation. After his death the Clark refractor passed to WILLIAM MONCK. **Susan McKenna-Lawlor**

Shields, Hugh (1929–), collector of TRADITIONAL MUSIC and researcher. Born in Belfast; educated at TCD, where he became senior lecturer in French. He has collected and published extensively on traditional music in Ireland and France from the 1950s, with a particular emphasis on Ulster. His best-known works are *Shamrock, Rose and Thistle: Folk Singing in North Derry* (1981), *Narrative Singing in Ireland: Lays, Ballads, Come-All-Yes and Other Songs* (1993), and *Tunes of the Munster Pipers: Irish Traditional Music from the James Goodman Manuscripts* (1998). **Maeve Ellen Gebruers**

Shiels, George (1886–1949), playwright. Born in Ballymoney, Co. Antrim; he emigrated to Canada, then returned home following an accident that left him disabled. The ULSTER LITERARY THEATRE staged his first work; between 1921 and 1948 the ABBEY THEATRE produced more than twenty of his plays, including *Bedmates* (1922) and *The Rugged Path* (1940). He used his knowledge of Ulster's rural community to create a body of largely realistic work that moved from easy humour to grey and sometimes black satire and from easy entertainment to sporadic insight. His vision became bleaker as he grew older; his view of his fellow-humans can be defined as either pragmatic or caustic. **Sam Burnside**

shillelagh, a blackthorn or oak cudgel, named after the Co. Wicklow village of Shillelagh, which used to have extensive oak woodlands surrounding it. The shillelagh was the favourite weapon used in nineteenth-century faction fights. **Ciarán Deane**

shipbuilding. Cork shipbuilding yards were the most extensive in Ireland during the first half of the nineteenth century, building mainly wooden vessels. Marine STEAM ENGINES were built as early as 1829 in Dublin; and an iron-hulled vessel was built at Cork in 1844. The Dublin Dockyard Company, established in 1901, survived until the 1960s. At that time shipyards at Rushbrooke in Cork were extensively modernised and extended.

By far the largest concentration of shipbuilding was at Dargan's Island (now Queen's Island) in Belfast Harbour. Here, from 1861, HARLAND AND WOLFF became shipbuilders to many of the world's shipping companies and the Royal Navy. Their yards constructed large ocean-going liners, such as the ill-fated TITANIC (1911) and later the *Canberra* (1960) (see p. 1053). For the British navy they built warships such as the *Belfast* (1939) and the aircraft-carrier *Formidable* (1940). With the completion in 1969 of the Building Dock, supertankers, bulk carriers, and offshore oil platforms were constructed. **Ronald Cox**

shipping, commercial. Ireland's economic dependence on commercial shipping is considerable, with more than 95 per cent of its traded goods passing through the country's ports. More than 50 million tonnes are handled by twenty-three commercial ports, 20 million tonnes passing through Dublin alone. The enormous growth in the ECONOMY from 1990 meant that Dublin Port in particular had to adapt rapidly, with eighteen ferry and roll-on/roll-off sailings daily, as well as substantial container traffic. BELFAST PORT handled more than 17 million tonnes of goods in 2000, Cork 10 million tonnes, and Waterford 2 million tonnes. The majority of Ireland's daily traffic goes to Holyhead and Liverpool, with regular sailings to Rotterdam, Le Havre, and other Continental ports. Labour relations problems, a feature of port operations in past decades, have declined in recent years, as increased trade has meant that mechanisation is no longer a threat to employment. In recent years the ports have changed from being state-owned to becoming commercial port companies, with greater independence and responsibility for infrastructure development.

Ireland's principal merchant fleet, Irish Shipping Ltd, closed in 1984 as a result of the shipping slump and controversial Government decisions. Today, largely for tax reasons, very few ships are registered in Ireland; Arklow Shipping Ltd, the last Irish shipping company of any size, has recently re-registered its vessels in the Netherlands. **Fiacc OBrolchain**

shipwrecks. There are documentary records of 9,724 wrecks around the Irish coast. Sites and monuments registers are biased towards documented events of the late eighteenth and nineteenth century and tend not to record the many shipwrecks that must have occurred in earlier periods: no Norse wreck sites are recorded, for example. One of the five wrecks from the VIKING era found at Skuldelev in Denmark was built in Dublin in the eleventh century; and hundreds of Viking ship timbers have been found in the excavations at Wood Quay and Winetavern Street, Dublin. The only evidence so far of a medieval shipwreck consists of single timbers brought up in nets in DUBLIN BAY and Waterford, though there is a considerable amount of historical evidence for frequent and hazardous maritime travel and trade during this period.

Between twenty-six and twenty-eight ships of the SPANISH ARMADA were wrecked off the Irish coast in the stormy autumn and winter of 1588. Though cannon reputed to be from an Armada wreck were salvaged in Broadhaven Bay, Co. Mayo, in the seventeenth century, the remains of only six of the fleet have been found. Two of them were excavated in 1968: the Neapolitan galleass *Girona* and the *Santa María de la Rosa*. The *Girona* was carrying the crews of two other sunken vessels when it sank at Lacada Point, Co. Antrim, with the loss of 1,300 lives. Large quantities of jewellery, gold and silver plate and coins were retrieved from the site, as well as a couple of small cannon, but none of the ship's structure remained (see p. 956). Some of the hull, including the mast step, was found under the ballast mound of the *Santa María de la Rosa* in Blasket Sound, Co. Kerry; little of the muskets, shot, lead ingots, and pewter plate removed from the site has survived, however, apparently because of inadequate conservation. A Venetian merchant ship, *La Trinidad Valencera*, being used as an invasion transport when it was wrecked in Kinnigoe Bay, Co. Donegal, was excavated in 1971. Finds included many items of rigging, part of the planking, a range of ship's equipment and ordnance, including two large siege guns, two Venetian guns, a bronze swivel gun, gun carriages, and gunnery and navigation equipment. The site at Streedagh Strand, Co. Sligo, where the remains of *La Juliana*, *La Lavia*, and *Santa María de la Visión* were found in 1985 has not been excavated, because of legal arguments between the state and the discovery team. Three bronze guns have been removed from the site, and the 12 m (40-ft) rudder of *La Juliana* was observed before being covered again by shifting sands.

A number of Dutch and English East Indiamen are known to have come to grief on the Irish coast during the seventeenth century, but none of these sites has been identified. The attempted French invasions of the late 1790s resulted in at least three shipwrecks in Irish waters, all of which have been found. The remains of the *Impatiente*, off MIZEN HEAD, Co. Cork, and the *Amitié*, at Ardglass, Co. Down, survive as scatters of cannon and other artefacts in rocky, storm-tossed gullies. By contrast, the *Surveillante*, scuttled off Whiddy Island on its arrival in a leaky condition, comprises quite extensive structural remains, complete with cannon, lying on a silty bottom. This site was revealed following side-scan sonar sweeps of Bantry Bay, Co. Cork, in the aftermath of the *Betelgeuse* disaster and was excavated in 1999. A pottery scatter at 8 m (26 ft) in Glandore Harbour has been dated to the late seventeenth century and the site provisionally identified as that of the *Mary* of Boston, which sank in January 1804. Later the same month the *Aid*, carrying oil paintings as well as antiquities from Pompeii and Herculaneum, was wrecked off Wicklow Head; part of the cargo was salvaged and auctioned. In 1987 a team from Trinity College, Dublin, found and excavated a wooden wreck of the same period in shallow water in the vicinity of the reported site. Timber planking was recorded, thirty-five artefacts, mostly ferrous, were removed for conservation, and some cut stone was identified as ballast, but there was no evidence of any remaining cargo.

Unknown sites provisionally dated to the late eighteenth century include a wooden wreck found during pipeline construction off the Shellybanks in DUBLIN BAY and cannon scatters off the Looe Rock, Co. Cork, in Derrynane Harbour, Co. Kerry, and off the Little Skellig. The Derrynane cannon are thought to be associated with the smuggling activities of Maurice 'Hunting Cap' O'Connell, an uncle of DANIEL O'CONNELL. In 1796 a Guinea trader, reputed to have contained ivory and gold dust, was dug up by a local landowner on Tyrella Beach, Co. Down. Remains of a vessel dated to the late nineteenth century were discovered in a search for this ship and were partially excavated in 1996. Isambard Kingdom Brunel's *Great Britain* ran aground on the same beach on its first voyage in 1851. The cargo of the emigrant ship *Tayleur*, wrecked in 1854 with the loss of about 400 lives off LAMBAY ISLAND, Co. Dublin, en route to the Australian goldfields, represented a mid-nineteenth-century time capsule before the site was discovered and looted. Material removed included willow-pattern plates, leather shoe parts, and carved wooden chair backs; slate grave-stones and mantelpieces remain buried under the silt and collapsed iron plating.

The excavation in 1995 of the site where the *Taymouth Castle* was wrecked in 18 m (60 ft) of water off Cushendun, Co. Antrim, on its journey to Singapore in 1867 revealed valuable details of its cargo of beer, pottery, spirits, and building materials. In 1875 the ironclad *Vanguard* was rammed in mist off the Co. Wicklow coast by another ship in its squadron and sank within an hour. The wreck is lying in 42 m (140 ft) of water in good condition and was due to be surveyed in 2000. In 1915 the German vessel *Libau*, masquerading as the Danish vessel AUD, was scuttled by its captain in Cork Harbour when it was apprehended by the British navy with a cargo of guns and ammunition for the Irish Volunteers. Its remains, and those of its cargo, lie in 34 m (110 ft) of water and are quite extensive, though scattered, having been depth-charged as an obstruction to navigation. Also in 1915 the Cunard liner LUSITANIA was torpedoed by the German submarine *U20* and sank in 90 m (300 ft) of water off the Old Head of Kinsale. The site is protected by an underwater heritage order and has been surveyed in recent years under licence by remotely operated video as well as by divers. The relatively intact remains of the LEINSTER, a mail packet torpedoed by the German submarine *U123* in October 1918, lie in 30 m (100 ft) of water about 6 km (4 miles) east of the KISH LIGHTHOUSE. Many of the 501 lives lost were military personnel. [see GEOPHYSICAL SURVEY; MARITIME ARCHAEOLOGY.] **Deirdre O'Hara**

shirts. By the middle of the eighteenth century, Irish men, even of modest means, expected to own more than twenty shirts. This, and an increase in demand for ARMY shirts, meant that by the 1780s ready-made shirts had to be available. These were sewn by seamstresses for shops and by children in the houses of industry. By c. 1850 Arnott's of Cork employed approximately 450 people in making shirts alone. The Derry shirt factories claimed to be the first of their kind, introducing sewing-machines to the industry about the same time. By 1904 William Tillie employed 80,000 factory workers and out-workers in the Derry-Strabane-Inishowen region in producing machine-made and hand-made shirts. [see CLOTHING, LINEN.] **Mairead Dunlevy**

shopping centres, purpose-built developments providing a range of shops and consumer services. Such centres were first developed in the 1960s at Newtownbreda in Belfast and at Stillorgan in Dublin to provide shopping facilities for expanding suburban populations; since then they have developed in towns of all sizes throughout the country. In the Republic more than 0.9 million m^2 (10 million sq. ft) of shopping space has been developed, with centres becoming larger. They range from small local centres selling frequently required goods—such as food and newspapers—to district-level centres anchored by a large supermarket with a range of smaller shops, and regional-scale centres of c. 23,000 m^2 (over 250,000 sq. ft). These have been developed in the Dublin western overspill towns, at Blanchardstown, Liffey Valley (Clondalkin), and the Square (Tallaght), as well as in the city (such as Jervis Centre), and elsewhere (such as Golden Island, Athlone); they frequently contain large clothes shops, department stores, supermarkets, and a wide range of shops competing directly with the traditional town centre.

Shopping centres in towns have been developed as part of urban regeneration schemes, for example in Galway, Longford, Carlow, and Newry, often being established in designated areas and receiving tax relief. Entertainment facilities, such as multiplex cinemas, are increasingly being incorporated in shopping centres to enhance their attraction. Newer forms of shopping developments include 'retail parks', which contain large warehouse-type retail outlets selling bulky goods, such as DIY goods, furniture, and carpets, and 'designer villages' that contain tourist-oriented shops, often selling clothing and craft goods at discounted prices. **Tony Parker**

short story. As a literary form, the short story has obvious roots in oral tradition. It has tended to flourish in borderland societies, wherever a vibrant FOLKLORE is challenged by the onset of literary codes. The American mid-west and provincial Russia and France in the late nineteenth century produced many masterly versions, as did Ireland through that period and for much of the twentieth century. FRANK O'CONNOR, in an influential study, *The Lonely Voice* (1962), argued that at its most potent it expressed the experiences of a 'submerged population group'. If the novel fitted itself to a made society, he implied, the short story was better calibrated to the isolated figures of a society still in the making. O'Connor's own tale of gunmen on the run in the War of Independence, 'Guests of the Nation', is a classic illustration of this thesis; so also are such strong collections as GEORGE MOORE'S THE UNTILLED FIELD (1903) and JAMES JOYCE'S DUBLINERS (1914). While O'Connor, like DANIEL CORKERY, drew heavily on narrative devices of the STORYTELLING tradition, IRISH-LANGUAGE masters of the form, such as PÁDRAIC Ó CONAIRE and MÁIRTÍN Ó CADHAIN, tended to be determinedly literary, as was LIAM O'FLAHERTY, whose *Dúil* (1953) is arguably the best collection of all. The form enjoyed immense prestige in the middle decades of the twentieth century as the quintessential Irish literary genre. SEAN O'FAOLAIN (who also wrote a critical study of it) and Frank O'Connor used the mode to strike a realist note, first sounded by Moore and Joyce, against the high Yeatsian romanticism of the LITERARY REVIVAL.

Later exponents, such as MARY LAVIN, BENEDICT KIELY, JAMES PLUNKETT, and EDNA O'BRIEN, found a ready audience in overseas magazines, such as the *New Yorker*; but within Ireland too the form enjoyed great popularity, being suitable for radio broadcasts and single-page publication in newspapers. Even as independent Ireland appeared to stabilise and settle, the short story remained strong, though (as if in further confirmation of O'Connor's thesis) it was notable that its finest exponents, such as JOHN MCGAHERN and WILLIAM TREVOR, now tended to concentrate more on the marginal figures of the new society, whether remnants of Anglo-Ireland or disillusioned veterans of the independence struggle. Critics also began to notice that many of the radical narratives of Irish modernism, from Joyce's ULYSSES through BECKETT's TRILOGY and FLANN O'BRIEN's AT SWIM-TWO-BIRDS (1939) down to Ó Cadhain's CRÉ NA CILLE (1949), were often little more than collections of anecdotes and short stories in the appearance of an experimental novel. If most of the greatest Irish poems, like Yeats's 'Meditations in Time of Civil War' or MONTAGUE's 'The Rough Field', were really sequences of short lyrics, then many of the major novels appeared to be disguised collections of shorter narratives. Equally, many ostensible collections of stories, like *Dubliners* or Ó Conaire's *Seacht mBua an Éirí Amach*, were seen to contain many of the embryonic elements of a modern novel. It was as if Irish writers were collectively attempting to splice short story and novel in the development of a new genre, for which there is yet no name. **Declan Kiberd**

show-jumping. *Eddie Macken, one of Ireland's leading international showjumpers, on Fan Pascal competing in the Kerrygold Challenge at the Dublin Horse Show, 8 July 1998. [Inpho Photography]*

show-jumping. Ireland is the birthplace of show-jumping, the first event having taken place on Leinster Lawn, Dublin, in 1868. Its progress was confirmed in 2000 with a world record ten Nations Cup team wins at the RDS, Dublin. In 1926 an army side contested Ireland's first Nations Cup at the ROYAL DUBLIN SOCIETY's grounds at Ballsbridge. Coached by Col. Paul Rodzianko of Russia, they achieved twenty-two cup wins throughout the world during the 1930s. ARMY officers such as Ged O'Dwyer and Dan Corry became national heroes; so did such civilian riders as Iris Kellett, first winner of the Queen's Cup, and Séamus Hayes, first winner of the Hickstead Derby after the war. Hayes joined Diana Conolly-Carew, Col. William Ringrose, and the legendary Tommy Wade on the first joint army-civilian team to win the Aga Khan Cup in 1963. Other leading riders in the 1960s were Col. Ned Campion, Tommy Brennan, Ada Matheson, and Larry Kiely.

The 1970s team of Eddie Macken, Con Power, Paul Darragh, and James Kernan won three Aga Khan Cups in a row (1977–9). Macken, on Boomerang, took every major Grand Prix in the world and a record four consecutive Hickstead Derbies. John Ledingham won it three times since. Winners of the 1990s included Col. Gerry Mullins, Trevor Coyle on Cruising, Jessica Kurten, and the European champion Peter Charles. The Irish team of Charles, Kurten, Kevin Babbington, and Dermot Lennon won the 2001 European championship. With more than 7,000 members and 500 show days, the Show-Jumping Association of Ireland celebrates its fiftieth anniversary in 2004. **Michael Slavin**

Sí: see FAIRIES.

Siabhradh Mhic na Míochomhairle: see MAC NA MÍCHOMHAIRLE.

Siamsa Tíre, the National Folk Theatre of Ireland, founded in Tralee, Co. Kerry, in 1974 by its choreographer and director, Father Pat Ahern, evolving from an experiment in 1964 to interest young people in native music and traditions. It was awarded the European Prize for Folk Art in 1974. Establishing a network of folk theatre training workshops throughout north Kerry, the group built its own theatre in Tralee Town Park in 1991, while continuing to tour around the world. Since 1985 it has had a nucleus of professional performers, augmented by the original large amateur group; it has recently merged contemporary with traditional dance in works based on Irish MYTHOLOGY, such as *Clann Lir* (1999). Oliver Hurley became artistic director in 2000. **Carolyn Swift**

Sidney, Sir Henry (1530–1586), Lord Deputy of Ireland, 1565–71 and 1575–8. Having assumed the Viceroyalty with considerable previous experience of Ireland, 1556–9, and a highly creditable reputation as an administrator in Wales, Sidney determined to initiate a programme of extensive administrative and legal reforms, including the revival of judicial circuits, the establishment of provincial councils in Munster and Connacht, the reform of the central courts, and the introduction of a series of improving statutes. His hopes of enforcing his policies, however, were frustrated both by criticism at court from the influential Earl of Ormond and the former Lord Deputy, THOMAS RADCLIFFE, EARL OF SUSSEX, and by ELIZABETH I's command that he first see to the destruction of SHANE O'NEILL. It was not until 1568, therefore, that he secured a mandate to summon an Irish Parliament and to establish provincial councils. But these plans too were disrupted by the rebellion of the FITZGERALDS and the BUTLERS in Munster in 1569, whose suppression consumed the rest of his first term in office.

Reappointed in 1575, Sidney essayed a radically new approach towards Irish reform, which sought to secure the acceptance in the Irish LORDSHIPS of English forms of landholding and inheritance through the use of a powerful local garrison, which would fix and enforce rents and services between LANDLORD and tenant and

Siamsa. *Siamsa Tíre, the National Folk Theatre of Ireland, stages performances based on folk traditions, featuring both professional and amateur actors. This is a scene from the 1991 production of* Labhraí Loingseach, *The Story of the King who had Horse's Ears. [Bord Fáilte]*

collect an annual tax from both parties by way of commission. This policy of 'composition' was attractive to several elements in the lordships but inevitably aroused the hostility of the professional military caste, whose role as protectors of the lords it threatened to make redundant. Growing instability in the provinces—together with the sharply expressed opposition of the English of the PALE and of the Crown's own lawyers to this policy of taxation without representation and Sidney's steep budgetary overrun—led to his recall under a cloud in 1578. **Ciaran Brady**

Sigerson, George (1836–1925), physician, historian, and poet-translator. Born outside Strabane, Co. Tyrone; studied neurology in Paris before attending Queen's College, Cork. He subsequently taught at the CATHOLIC UNIVERSITY, Dublin, and UCD. In 1893 he became second president (after DOUGLAS HYDE) of the National Literary Society. Apart from influential anthologies and translations of Irish poetry, his main intellectual contribution was probably his continual opposition, from within cultural nationalism, to theories of national purity. His works include *The Poets and Poetry of Munster* (1860), *Modern Ireland* (1868, 1869), and, most famously, *Bards of the Gael and Gall* (1897, enlarged 1907). He became a Free State senator in 1922. **Brian Cliff**

Sign of the Three Candles, the printing and PUBLISHING house established in 1916 as the Candle Press by Colm O Lochlainn (1892–1972). The name, echoing that of the publishing and bookselling business of the Three Candlesticks in High Street, Dublin, 1730–50, was derived from one of the TRIADS: 'Three candles light up every darkness: Truth, Nature and Knowledge'; it became the Sign of the Three Candles when O Lochlainn moved to Fleet Street in 1926. His work first attracted widespread attention with his *Dublin Civic Week Handbook* (1927), and his concern for standards of design and production is evident in his more than a hundred book titles and a wide range of ephemeral productions. He won the silver medal of the ROYAL DUBLIN SOCIETY and the silver and bronze medals of Aonach Tailteann for BOOKBINDING, but perhaps his greatest achievement was his involvement in the design of IRISH PRINTING TYPES. **Bernard Share**

silk. While silk was worn in Ireland from at least the early Middle Ages, it was not woven here until the early seventeenth century. The HUGUENOTS later improved the industry through the investment of capital and developing the manufacturing system. In the eighteenth century Irish weavers produced a wide variety of silks in different weights, weaves, and designs; but they had difficulty in competing with the splendour of imported French brocades and with English silks, which were free of duty. The Irish Parliament gave grants to encourage the industry, and the Dublin Society's Irish Silk Warehouse, established c. 1764, assisted weavers and promoted silk fashions. Though the production of brocades was affected by new modes in cotton in the late eighteenth century, the industry continued into the nineteenth century. **Mairead Dunlevy**

Silken Thomas: see FITZGERALD, THOMAS, TENTH EARL OF KILDARE.

Simmons, James (1933–2001), poet. Born in Derry; educated at Campbell College, Belfast, and the University of Leeds. He was founding editor of *The Honest Ulsterman* in 1968. From his first collection, *Ballad of a Marriage* (1966), he favoured the lyric form. *Poems, 1956–1986* introduces the vernacular style of a fiercely independent mind. He was elected to AOSDÁNA and founded Poet's House, Islandmagee, in 1989. The final years of his life were spent in Falcarragh, Co. Donegal. **Nicholas Allen**

Simms, George Otto (1910–1991), churchman and scholar. Born in Dublin; educated at Cheltenham College and TCD. He was ordained in the Church of Ireland in 1936, appointed Bishop of Cork, Cloyne and Ross, 1952, Archbishop of Dublin, 1956, and Archbishop of Armagh, 1969. He was one of the world's leading authorities on the Book of KELLS, on which he wrote and lectured extensively. An ecumenist, he responded actively to the thaw in Catholic attitudes following the Second Vatican Council (1962–5). He retired in 1980 but continued to play a role in the Church of Ireland, chairing the Liturgical Advisory Committee, whose work produced the *Alternative Prayer Book* (1984). **Fergal Tobin**

Simnel, Lambert (c. 1475–1522), pretender to the English throne. Born in Oxford. Margaret, Duchess of Burgundy, sister of the late Edward IV, trained the boy to impersonate her imprisoned nephew Edward Plantagenet, Earl of Warwick, whose claim to the throne was stronger than that of the Lancastrian Henry VII. Early in 1487 she sent him to Ireland, where his cause was embraced by the ANGLO-NORMAN community, largely Yorkist in sympathy, and on 24 May he was crowned in CHRIST CHURCH CATHEDRAL, Dublin, as Edward VI, of England, Ireland, and France. Supported by 2,000 German soldiers sent by Margaret and by Maximilian, the Holy Roman Emperor, 4,000 Irish soldiers, and some English Yorkists, the pretender invaded England but was heavily defeated at the Battle of Stoke (16 June 1487). He was captured but was subsequently pardoned as harmless and survived as a servant in Henry VII's court. [see WARBECK, PERKIN.] **Henry A. Jefferies**

Simpson, Maxwell (1815–1902), organic chemist. Born in Beech Hill, Lisnadill, Co. Armagh; educated at TCD, where he studied medicine. He attended lectures in CHEMISTRY at University College, London, and worked in Thomas Graham's laboratory. In 1845 he returned to Dublin. Having finished his medical degree, he became a lecturer at the 'Original' School of Medicine in Peter Street. He studied chemistry in Marburg, Heidelberg, and Paris. Working in his own laboratory in Wellington Road, Dublin, he was the first chemist to synthesise the organic compound succinic acid from inorganic starting materials; he was also the first to establish that the acidity of organic acids arises from the presence of the carboxylic group –COOH. His working life spanned a major portion of the period when modern chemistry was being developed in Europe and in America. His own contributions were recognised by his election as a fellow of the Royal Society, his appointment as vice-president of the Chemical Society, and the award of honorary degrees from the University of Dublin and the Queen's University of Ireland. In 1872 he was appointed professor of chemistry in Queen's College, Cork. **William J. Davis**

Singer, Paul (1911–), financier. Born in Bratislava; educated at Lausanne (where he received a doctorate in political science), Paris, and the London School of Economics. He joined his father's finance company, eventually becoming a director. The company failed in 1953, and Singer moved to Ireland with his family. In February 1954 he launched Shanahan's Stamp Auctions with Desmond and Diana Shanahan, auctioneers, of Dún Laoghaire, Co. Dublin. Thousands of small investors were attracted through newspaper advertising and by media accounts of Singer's extravagant and charismatic personality, as well as his undoubted expertise as a philatelist. The company collapsed on 25 May 1959, with assets of between £400,000 and £450,000 and liabilities totalling approximately £2 million. Singer was twice tried by jury on charges of fraud but was acquitted after a three-year legal battle. Desmond Shanahan was sentenced to fifteen months' imprisonment with hard labour at the Central Criminal Court in 1960. **Ciarán Deane**

Single European Act (signed 1986, ratified 1987), the first substantial modification to the founding treaties of the EUROPEAN UNION. When negotiated and ratified, the Single European Act was regarded as a rather modest reform of EU institutions and decision rules; in fact it was part of a substantial transformation of the European Union, which led in turn to a series of other treaties. The Single European Act encompassed a mixture of institutional and policy change. The core of the act was the commitment to achieving a single market in the European Union by January 1993. It unleashed a major change in the European economy and in the regulation of economic exchange among European states. It brought the European Union into the nooks and crannies of European states and made it more visible than it had ever been in the past.

To complete the internal market, the European Union had to make it easier to pass laws, and this it did with the extension of weighted voting. This made it more difficult for any one state to block EU developments. The treaty also made provision for a stronger policy on cohesion, which was of major benefit to Ireland. In the act, the European Parliament was given more power, and foreign policy co-operation was codified in treaty form. Few commentators realised the historical significance of the Single European Act at the time; it was only with hindsight that its real importance became apparent. **Brigid Laffan**

Single European Market. During the 1980s it came to be recognised that many barriers existed to intra-European FREE TRADE, one of the cornerstones of the policy of the EUROPEAN UNION. These include customs formalities, nationalistic procurement policies on the part of member-governments, and differing technical standards in member-states. The single European market aimed to eradicate these remaining barriers (optimism about how rapidly this could be achieved led to its designation as the '1992' programme). It is now accepted that only a short distance along the road to a single market has been travelled; this can be seen, for example, in the difficulties created by the Government in the Republic in order to prevent the importing of new cars from Britain, or the disparity in wine prices between Ireland and France. The Republic is nonetheless thought to have gained more from the single European market than many other European countries, because of the stimulus the policy provided for both intra-EU and inflows of American investment, from which Ireland has gained disproportionately. **Frank Barry**

Sinn Féin

1905–70. Sinn Féin was founded in 1905 as a broad grouping of nationalists favouring total separation from Britain, rather than HOME RULE. It became the principal party promoting independence after the 1916 RISING. Sinn Féin established a genuinely mass party, with strong roots in local communities and a pervasive organisational network. In the general election of 1918 it won seventy-three of Ireland's 105 seats but refused to attend the London Parliament, forming instead a separatist legislature, DÁIL ÉIREANN.

Following the ANGLO-IRISH TREATY, which ended the WAR OF INDEPENDENCE, Sinn Féin split into two: CUMANN NA NGAEDHEAL, and a group retaining the name Sinn Féin. In 1926 ÉAMON DE VALERA led a defection from the party and formed FIANNA FÁIL. In the general election of 1927, Fianna Fáil obtained forty-four seats and the rump Sinn Féin five. Subsequently the party remained small and ineffective. In 1957 it won four seats, its only electoral success since 1927, but its members refused to sit in the Dáil.

A further split in 1970 led to the creation of 'Provisional Sinn Féin' and 'Official Sinn Féin'. Ostensibly the reason for the division was the policy of abstention. Sinn Féin refused to recognise the parliaments in Dublin and Belfast; differences on this issue, however, masked a split between those favouring traditional methods of resistance and military campaigns and those who espoused a longer-term strategy increasingly expressed in the Marxist terms that had become popular among radical movements throughout the world in the 1960s. The Provisionals were predominantly from Northern Ireland and tutored by the renewed conflict there.

1970 to the present. 'Official Sinn Féin' was the name given to Sinn Féin after a split in 1970 led to the formation of the breakaway 'Provisional Sinn Féin'. It changed its name to Sinn Féin the Workers' Party in 1977, then to the WORKERS' PARTY in 1982. Provisional Sinn Féin is now accepted as Sinn Féin. The party is noted for its support for the PROVISIONAL IRA and gained significant electoral impetus from its association with the HUNGER STRIKES among republican prisoners in Northern Ireland in 1981. A leading Sinn Féin member described his party's electoral strategy as one 'with an Armalite [automatic rifle] in one hand and the ballot box in the other.' The party contests elections in both Northern Ireland and the Republic; in 1986 it abandoned its policy of abstention in relation to the OIREACHTAS. In 1997 it gained 2.6 per cent of the votes for Dáil Éireann and elected one TD; in the 1999 local election its support was 3.5 per cent; in the 1999 European Parliament election in the Republic 6.1 per cent of the vote was not enough to give the party a member of the European Parliament.

In Northern Ireland, Sinn Féin almost equalled the vote of the UUP candidate for the European Parliament, at 17.3 per cent, and narrowly failed to win a seat. At the 2002 general election the party increased its Dáil representation to five. It also has fifty-seven LOCAL GOVERNMENT councillors in the Republic, four members in the London House of Commons, eighteen members of the NORTHERN IRELAND ASSEMBLY, and 118 Northern Ireland local councillors. Sinn Féin contributes two members of the Northern Executive. The president of the party since 1983 is GERRY ADAMS, a negotiator for and supporter of the BELFAST AGREEMENT as well as abstentionist MP for West Belfast. He is credited with a central part in brokering the IRA ceasefire in 1994. Sinn Féin combines left-wing politics with staunchly republican views; its support is strongest in working-class areas where its activists are prominent in promoting local community interests. Its association with the IRA has led other Dáil parties to refuse to consider Sinn Féin as potential coalition partners. **Neil Collins**

SIPTU: see SERVICES, INDUSTRIAL, PROFESSIONAL AND TECHNICAL UNION.

Sirius, a paddle steamer. In 1838, under its captain, Richard Roberts, a Corkman of a famous seafaring family, the Irish-owned *Sirius* succeeded in making the first crossing of the Atlantic Ocean solely on its STEAM ENGINE. The English ship *Great Western*, associated with the famous engineer Brunel, had not, as many expected, been able to reach New York before the *Sirius*. Roberts was lionised in New York, and before long the news of his voyage, spreading rapidly, convinced people everywhere that a new door had been opened for the history of sea transport. Within twenty years the Atlantic had claimed the life of Roberts in a storm, as well as the *Sirius* in a typical westerly gale off the coast of Co. Cork, near Ballycotton. **John de Courcy Ireland**

Sirius. *The Cork Steam Ship Company's 700-ton, 320-horsepower* Sirius, *built in 1837, in a print after a drawing by George Atkinson Jr. In 1838 the* Sirius *made the first crossing of the Atlantic Ocean solely under steam power. [Getty Images/Hulton Archive]*

Sir Patrick Dun's Hospital (1814–1986), Grand Canal Street, Dublin, built as a teaching hospital for TRINITY COLLEGE with funds that had accrued from a bequest of Sir PATRICK DUN (died 1713), who had served as president of the College of Physicians on several occasions. Several famous physicians and surgeons served on the staff, including Edward Halloran Bennett, James Macartney, and Robert W. Smith. Margaret Huxley, appointed lady superintendent of nurses in 1884, was a pioneer of modern NURSING in Dublin. It was a busy general hospital, and in 1961 it became one of the Dublin Federated Voluntary Hospitals; it closed in 1986 and its services were transferred to the new St James's Hospital. **Davis Coakley**

Sirr, Major Henry Charles (1756–1841), army officer and, from 1796, town major of Dublin, controlling the city's police. Feared and despised by his opponents but respected by loyalists, he specialised in covert counter-insurgency activities and was personally involved in arresting Lord EDWARD FITZGERALD and ROBERT EMMET. He was also an antiquarian and art collector. **Allan Blackstock**

Sirr, Peter (1960–), poet and editor. Born in Waterford; educated at TCD, where he researched the poetry of PÁDRAIC FALLON. His work is marked by its urban subject matter, fluid syntax, hospitality to experiment, and influence of American poetry (O'Hara, Ashbery, Schuyler). His five collections of poetry are *Marginal Zones* (1984), *Talk Talk* (1987), *Ways of Falling* (1991), *The Ledger of Fruitful Exchange* (1995), and *Bring Everything* (2000). He was an editor of the cultural review *Graph* and works in Dublin as director of the Irish Writers' Centre. **David Wheatley**

Sisters of Mercy, an order of nuns founded by CATHERINE MCAULEY in Dublin in 1831. The congregation developed from the House of Mercy that McAuley established in 1827. The community was not cloistered, and the rule allowed for great flexibility. McAuley and her first companions ran a poor-school and a refuge

Skelligs. *View of Little Skellig Rock from Sceilg Mhichíl, off the coast of Co. Kerry. The monastic dwellings known as clocháns or beehive huts are visible in the middle foreground. The stones projecting from the roof of the beehive in the foreground were used to secure a covering of thatch or sods. [Dúchas, The Heritage Service]*

for unemployed women, as well as caring for the sick poor. These services were replicated all over the English-speaking world, once the expansion of the congregation got under way. Communities were established in England (1839), Newfoundland (1842), the United States (1843), Australia (1846), New Zealand (1849), Argentina (1856), and South Africa (1897). **Séamus Enright**

Sitric Silkbeard, Anglicised name of Sigtryggr Silkiskeggi (died 1042), son of Olaf Cuarán, King of Dublin, 989–1036, and Gormlaith. He married Sláine, daughter of BRIAN BÓRÚ, who later defeated his forces in the BATTLE OF CLONTARF (1014). He was the first to mint coins in Ireland, 995, and founded CHRIST CHURCH CATHEDRAL following a pilgrimage to Rome in 1028 (see p. 217). **Seán Duffy**

Sive (1959), a play by JOHN B. KEANE. It was premiered by the Listowel Drama Group and established Keane as a playwright. It deals with a young woman who aspires to independence and education but whose family belong to a traditional Ireland of MATCHMAKING and ties to the land. **Christopher Morash**

Skeffington, Sir William (died 1535), Lord Deputy of Ireland, 1530–32, 1534–5. Remembered rather for the momentous events in which he played a part than for his role in bringing them about, Skeffington was a professional soldier who had held the senior position of Master of the Ordnance before being appointed Lord Deputy of Ireland. Intended to serve as a brake on the overweening power of GERALD FITZGERALD, ninth Earl of Kildare, rather than a direct challenge to the Geraldines as a whole, he failed to establish his authority during his first term of office and was recalled in response to Fitzgerald allegations of partiality towards the BUTLERS of Ormond. Following Fitzgerald's summons to London and his arrest in 1534, Skeffington was again appointed Lord Deputy, but his delay in assuming office allowed the rebellion of Fitzgerald's son, SILKEN THOMAS, to spread. He re-established royal authority by the successful siege of Maynooth (1535), where his refusal of mercy to the surrendered garrison persuaded many of the Fitzgeralds' allies to submit while giving rise to the term 'pardon of Maynooth' as a proverbial symbol of English perfidy. **Ciaran Brady**

Skelligs, Co. Kerry, two uninhabited rock pinnacles 16 km (10 miles) from the mainland. Little Skellig Rock is a bird sanctuary, containing the world's third-largest colony of gannets—about twenty thousand pairs. SCEILG MHICHÍL (also called Great Skellig Rock) is notable for its possibly ninth-century Christian remains, principally BEEHIVE HUTS, situated 170 m (560 ft) above sea level, where the land is flat enough for buildings. **Stephen A. Royle**

Skid Row, rock group. Formed in 1967 by Brendan 'Brush' Shiels, the group—together with THIN LIZZY and Taste—placed Ireland on the international rock music map. Early members of the band included both GARY MOORE and PHIL LYNOTT. The band's mixture of blues, psychedelia, and progressive rock proved simultaneously individual and difficult to market, but they recorded two influential Irish rock albums, *Skid* (1970) and *34 Hours* (1971), before they split up in the early 1970s. **Tony Clayton-Lea**

'Skin-the-Goat', the nickname given to James Fitzharris, one of the cab drivers who drove some members of the secret society the Irish National INVINCIBLES to the PHOENIX PARK, Dublin, on 6 May 1882, where they murdered the CHIEF SECRETARY, Lord Frederick Cavendish, and the Under-Secretary, Thomas H. Burke. He was later arrested and sentenced to penal servitude for life for his part in the assassination; he was released after serving fifteen years of his sentence. A tombstone erected to his memory marks his grave in Glasnevin Cemetery, Dublin. His name is frequently mentioned in literary circles because of his inclusion in JOYCE'S ULYSSES. His name crops up when Mr Bloom and Stephen enter the cabman's shelter, where it is pointed out to Stephen that the keeper of the shelter is reputed to be 'Skin-the-Goat Fitzharris', the former Invincible, who drove the assassins in his cab to the Phoenix Park. **Frank Harte**

Slane Castle, Slane, Co. Meath, a house incorporating an earlier castle, built in the Gothic Revival style by James Wyatt c. 1785. It is noted for its two-storey circular ballroom. The layout of the village may be by FRANCIS JOHNSTON. Slane has been the site of large open-air rock concerts since 1981. The grounds form a natural amphitheatre, and the owner, Lord Henry Mount Charles, saw Slane's potential as a venue. The first concert, in 1981, with THIN LIZZY (supported by U2), was attended by 18,000 people; the 1982 concert by the Rolling Stones attracted more than 50,000 and established Slane as Ireland's principal rock venue of the 1980s. **Mick Heaney**

Slaney, River, a river with its main source high up in a glacially carved hollow on the western side of Lugnaquilla Mountain, Co. Wicklow. At first it follows a steep course to the GLEN OF IMAIL, then travels around the western side of the WICKLOW MOUNTAINS before swinging to the east near Tullow. It flows between the Wicklow and Blackstairs Mountains through the Slaney Gap, an impressive steep-walled granite gorge upstream from Kilcarry Bridge that acts as a connecting link between the lowlands of Cos. Carlow and Wexford. It continues its journey across the fertile Co. Wexford lowlands towards its mouth at Wexford Harbour. The lower reaches are canalised for approximately 32 km (20 miles). The Slaney is noted as one of the few Irish rivers with a run of spring salmon. **R. A. Charlton**

Slattery, John (Fergus) (1949–), rugby footballer. Born in Dún Laoghaire, Co. Dublin. He made his debut in the 8–all draw with South Africa at Lansdowne Road in 1970 and won his first twenty-eight caps in succession until injury interrupted his career in 1976, but he was back for Ireland's last two matches the following year. He took over as captain in 1979 and led the team seventeen times in all, before handing over to CIARÁN FITZGERALD at the start of the successful 1982 championship. His last match was against France in Paris in 1984, and by then he, WILLIE DUGGAN, and John O'Driscoll had played nineteen times together in Ireland's back row—a world record for official matches between the IRB countries. He is Ireland's most-capped flanker, with sixty-one appearances

Slane. *Crowds mass on the lawns of Slane Castle (left), which form a natural amphitheatre, at a Robbie Williams concert (1999). The Castle has hosted rock concerts since 1981 when U2 played support to Thin Lizzy. [Bill Cooper (Bilcop Photography)]*

between 1970 and 1984. He toured Australia and New Zealand with the 1971 British Lions team, being selected for the third Test but not playing, because of injury, and South Africa with the 1974 Lions, playing in all four Tests. **Karl Johnston**

Slattery's of Dublin, a pub in Capel Street that played a leading role in the preservation of traditional music and became a focus for the resurgence of that music. Formerly a music-hall, it was owned in the 1960s by Paddy Slattery. There was a growing audience at that time for TRADITIONAL MUSIC, usually played by groups consisting of guitarists and a singer, an instrumental format at odds with previous traditional practice. Of the several sessions on different evenings, the most successful one, the Tradition Club, was begun in 1967 by SEÁN CORCORAN and Mary McGannon. Tom Crean, Kevin Conneff and Finbar Boyle ran it until 1988, presenting the music as it had traditionally been performed, emphasising solo melody instruments and unaccompanied singers. Famous musicians who made their first Dublin appearance there included MIKO RUSSELL, GEORDIE HANNA, and Phil Murphy, while musicians resident in Dublin, such as JOHN KELLY and Joe Ryan of Co. Clare and SÉAMUS ENNIS, also performed regularly. **Finbar Boyle**

Slaughter, Stephen (1697–1765), portraitist. Born in London; trained at Kneller's academy. He probably lived in Paris for a number of years, where he painted a portrait of Patrick Ross, but he was back in London by 1733. The following year he made a visit to Ireland, where the Lord Mayor of Dublin sat for him. He was busily employed in London between 1735 and 1743 but then returned to Dublin, where he stayed, except for a short absence, until 1748. He painted numerous members of the gentry, clergy, and aristocracy. He was appointed Keeper and Surveyor of King's Pictures in 1744, a position he retained until his death. **Brendan Rooney**

Sleator, James Sinton (1885–1950), artist. Born in Co. Armagh; studied art in Belfast and afterwards at the Metropolitan School of Art, Dublin, where he was a pupil of WILLIAM ORPEN. In 1914 he worked in Orpen's London studio; the following year he taught at the Metropolitan School and exhibited at the RHA for the first time. In the 1920s he worked in France and Italy before settling in London. He moved back to Dublin in 1941, succeeding DERMOD O'BRIEN four years later as president of the RHA. A quiet and retiring man, he was a sensitive colourist and a fine academic artist, as shown by his portraits and still-lifes. **Peter Murray**

Sliabh Luachra, a district in Cos. Kerry and Cork with its own distinctive musical tradition; its outer boundaries are not clearly defined but the centre lies along the Cork–Kerry border and includes the town of Castleisland as well as smaller towns and villages, such as Scartaglen, Ballydesmond, Knocknagree, Rathmore, and Gneeveguilla. The main instruments associated with the area are the FIDDLE and the ACCORDION; the style of music is characterised by the playing of *slides* (single JIGS with localised variations in rhythm) and POLKAS, as well as distinctive versions of tunes that are well known nationally. Dancing has always been strong in the region also. Large-scale EMIGRATION in the 1940s and 50s led to the absence of many good players, but in recent years there has been a revival of interest in the style and tunes of Sliabh Luachra, and some local music FESTIVALS have helped to maintain this interest. **Peter Browne**

Sligo, County (*Contae Shligigh*)

Province:	CONNACHT
County town:	SLIGO
Area:	1,795 km^2 (695 sq. miles)
Population (2002):	58,178
Features:	BENBULBIN
	Clydagh River
	Lough Arrow
	Lough Gara
	Lough Gill
	Ox Mountains
	River Moy
Of historical interest:	CARROWKEEL
	Carrowmore
	Inishmurray monastic site
	Sligo Abbey
Industry and products:	Dairy farming
	Fishing

Petula Martyn

County Sligo, bounded by Cos. Mayo, Leitrim, and Roscommon. Distinctive limestone plateaus, their highest point at Truskmore (643 m, 2,110 ft), lie to the north-east. The Precambrian Ox Mountains extend south-west into Co. Mayo, and the uplands of the Curlew Mountains border Co. Roscommon. Lough Gill lies south-east of the town of Sligo, with Lough Arrow and Lough Gara further south. Farms are small—19.1 ha (47 acres) on average in 1991; the production of beef and suckler cows dominates, with sheep on the uplands, while dairying is of some importance in the south. The landscape extending from Sligo Bay to Co. Leitrim provided inspiration for W. B. YEATS (who is buried in Drumcliff churchyard in the shadow of BENBULBIN) and his brother, the artist JACK B. YEATS. INNISHMURRAY, 9 km (6 miles) off the north-west coast (named after St Muireadhach of Killala), contains the remains of an Early Christian monastery founded by MOLAISE, recorded in the Annals as being destroyed during a VIKING raid in 807. South-west of Sligo at Carrowmore is the largest cemetery of MEGALITHIC TOMBS in Ireland, the oldest predating NEWGRANGE by 700 years. Ballymote (population 1,396), 26 km (16 miles) south of Sligo, contains the ruins of an early fourteenth-century De Burgo castle, where part of a celebrated literary codex, the Book of BALLYMOTE, was compiled by the Duignans and others c. 1400. Six km (4 miles) south-east is Keshcorran, a limestone upland with seventeen caves, which features in the literary legends of CORMAC MAC AIRT and Diarmaid and Gráinne. Six km (4 miles) south-east of Keshcorran at CARROWKEEL is an important PASSAGE TOMB cemetery. **Mary E. Cawley**

Sligo (*Sligeach*), the largest town and county town of Co. Sligo, situated where the Garavogue River enters Sligo Bay from Lough Gill, between Knocknarea to the west and BENBULBIN and Truskmore to the north; population (2002) 18,429. Sligo is a rail terminus, and there is a small airport at Strandhill, 11 km (7 miles) to the west. It is also a cathedral town for the Catholic diocese of Elphin and the CHURCH OF IRELAND diocese of Elphin and Ardagh. Extensive lands here were granted to the ANGLO-NORMAN baron Maurice Fitzgerald in 1235. He built a castle (1245), none of which remains, and founded a Dominican friary (1253). The choir, part of the nave of the original thirteenth-century church, the fifteenth or sixteenth-century high altar, the remains of the cloister arcade, the

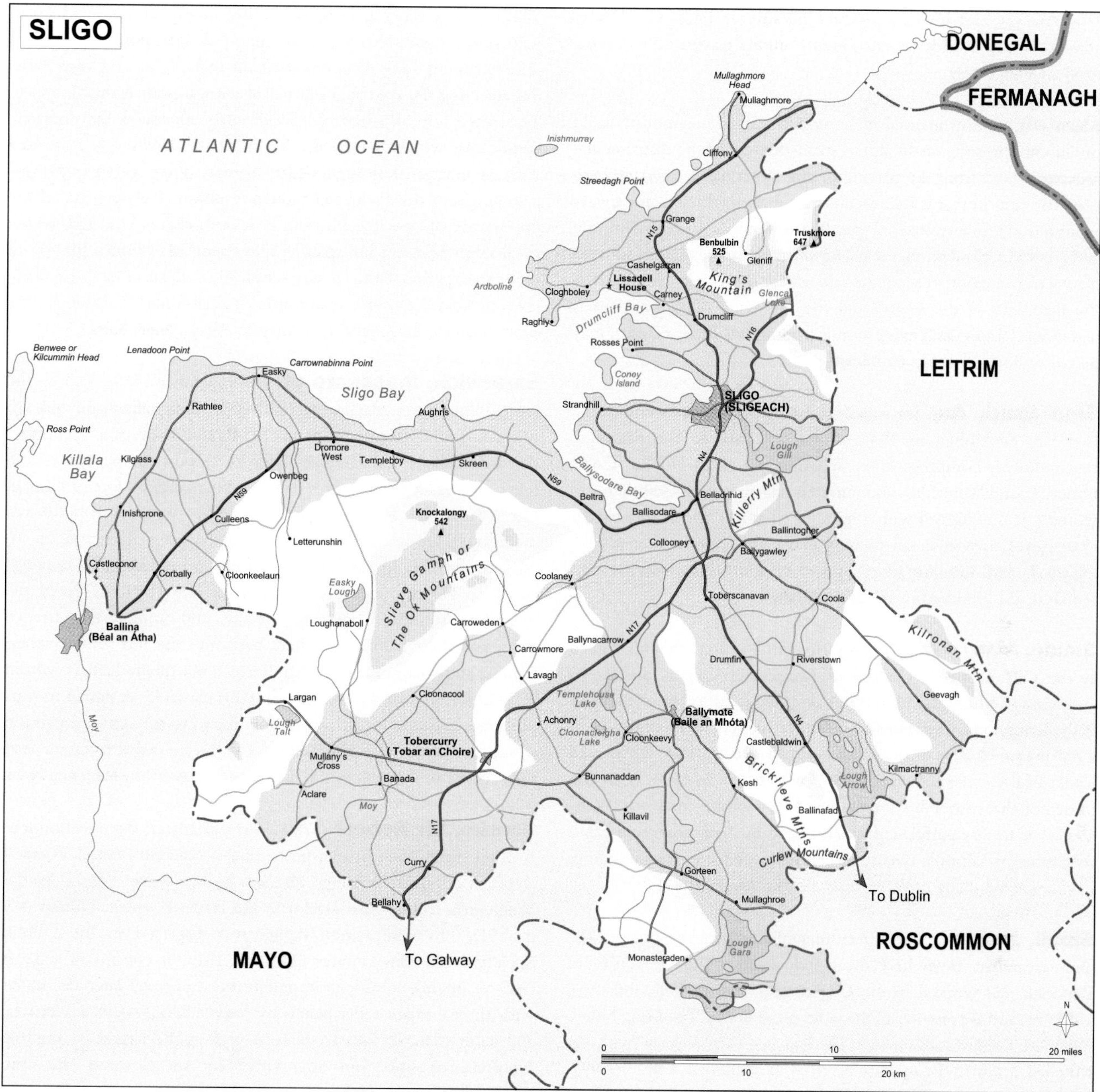

sixteenth-century O'Crean tomb and the seventeenth-century O'Conor Sligo monument are of particular interest. Most of the main streets were laid out in the seventeenth century; the second half of the nineteenth century, when overseas trade expanded, saw further urban development. The Town Hall (1860s) is by Hague. Houses of note in the vicinity are Lissadell House (1830s), home of the GORE-BOOTH family, and Hazelwood House by RICHARD CASTLE (c. 1731), formerly home of the Wynnes, now part of a factory complex. There is an Institute of Technology and two hospitals north of the town, with St Angela's College of Education 6 km (4 miles) to the east. There is an industrial estate at Finisklin to the west. The seaside resort of Rosses Point, 9 km (6 miles) to the north-west, has a championship links GOLF course. **Mary E. Cawley**

Sloan, Victor (1945–), photographer. Born in Dungannon, Co Tyrone; studied at Belfast College of Art and Leeds College of Art and Design. His work is characterised by his treatment of photographs with etchings, drawings, and mixed media to produce images that portray the complexities of Northern Ireland society (see p. 872). His work has been exhibited extensively and is held in collections throughout the world, including the Imperial War Museum, London, Arts Council of Northern Ireland, National Museum for Film, Photography and Television, Ulster Museum, and Museum of International Contemporary Art, Brazil. **Martin Clancy**

Sloane, Sir Hans (1660–1753), physician and collector. Born at Killyleagh Castle, Co. Down. In his youth he collected plants from around STRANGFORD LOUGH. Moving to London in May 1689 after fifteen months as physician to the Governor of Jamaica and collecting specimens of 800 plant species, he set up a successful medical practice. In 1727 he was elected president of the Royal Society. His natural history collection formed the foundation of the British Museum; his manuscripts, containing letters from the greatest physicians of his time, form one of the most valuable sources for English medical history. **Martyn Anglesea**

Slógadh, a competition for young people in drama, music, and dancing, organised by GAEL-LINN since 1969. It encourages both

TRADITIONAL and POPULAR MUSIC; because of high standards in adjudication its awards are rated highly among players of traditional music. **Fintan Vallely**

slow air, an instrumental piece, which may or may not be based on an existing song air. It differs from the rest of the instrumental repertoire (and from the playing of airs in Scotland, Shetland, and Cape Breton) in that it follows no strict metre (which is not always indicated in transcriptions). Typically the slow air is performed solo and as an independent piece; recent practice, however, has allowed for the introduction of accompaniment (controversially, as it restricts the flexibility of the metre) and the following of the air with a dance tune. Individual expression is paramount; the execution may be either florid or stark. **Liz Doherty**

Slua Muirí, An, the naval component of the Second-Line Reserve, established in 1947 as the successor to the Maritime Inscription. It comprises four companies, based in Dublin, Cork, Limerick, and Waterford, and numbers approximately 300 men and women. It is equipped with a number of motor vessels suitable for river patrol, as well as sail-training craft, and provides operational, logistical, and administrative support to the NAVAL SERVICE into which it was absorbed in 2002. **Hugh Tully**

Smale, Alan (1954–), violinist. Born in Torquay, Devon; studied at the City of Leeds College of Music and later at the Royal Academy of Music, London. On becoming joint leader of the then RTÉ Symphony Orchestra in 1977 he moved to Dublin and in 1984 became leader of the RTÉ CONCERT ORCHESTRA. Appointed leader of the NATIONAL SYMPHONY ORCHESTRA in 1994, he is also leader of the Irish Film Orchestra. As a member of CONCORDE, 1977–98, he has performed much music by Irish composers; as a soloist he specialises in twentieth-century repertoire. His recordings have included many contemporary works. **Adrian Scahill**

Small, Jackie (1946–), instrumentalist, set-dancer, broadcaster, and researcher. Born in Galway; educated at the University of Limerick. He worked in the Department of Irish Folklore, UCD, 1983–91, and as presenter of the radio programme 'The Long Note', 1988–90. Publications include *The Piping of Patsy Touhey* (with Pat Mitchell, 1986) and *Ceol Rince na hÉireann*, volumes 4 and 5 (1997, 1999). **Anthony McCann**

'small open economy'. At its most basic level, the theory of the small open economy assumes that an ECONOMY such as the Republic's should be viewed as equivalent to a 'perfectly competitive firm' operating on the world market. This implies that all prices (in foreign-currency terms) are determined on world markets and are unaffected by Irish demand and supply conditions, and that Irish cost conditions determine output and EMPLOYMENT, while Irish demand conditions simply affect the external trade balance. The theory first gained currency in Ireland in the 1970s as a reaction to the view that INFLATION could be broken down into domestic and foreign components. The theory of the small open economy suggested instead that all inflation was imported, either through high inflation abroad or through movements in exchange rates. The more radical implication of the theory, that an expansion in Irish demand would leak out through the balance of payments rather than stimulating Irish employment, became prominent in the early 1980s as the failure of the expansionary-demand strategy of the Lynch/O'Donoghue administration of the late 1970s became apparent. While it is correct to emphasise that supply or cost and competitiveness conditions are more important than domestic demand in determining long-term employment and output, this view erred in neglecting the role of goods that were not internationally traded. The prices of non-tradable goods are influenced by domestic conditions, which is why the boom of the 1990s was associated with an inflation rate higher than in most other countries participating within the European monetary union. Recognition of the importance of non-tradables also provides a channel through which fiscal expansion can influence employment and output, though in the Irish experience the adverse supply-side effects of having to raise taxes to service a fiscal expansion have been found to dominate the short-term expansionary demand-side effects. **Frank Barry**

Smerwick, massacre of (10 November 1580). During the second DESMOND REBELLION (1579–83), 600 Italian and Spanish soldiers under the command of Bastiano di San Giuseppi, despatched by Pope Gregory XIII in support of the GERALDINE rebels, barricaded themselves in James Fitzmaurice's fort of Dún an Óir at Smerwick Harbour, Co. Kerry. After two days of bombardment by English cannon the fort proved pregnable, and on 10 November 1580 the garrison surrendered to Lord GREY DE WILTON, the Lord Deputy, in the expectation of mercy. He accepted the defenders' submission unconditionally, and immediately herded them and their Irish accomplices back into the fort without their armour and weapons and put to death all but fifteen leaders, whom he held for ransom. In orchestrating this massacre, designed to suppress the Catholic threat and to put an end to foreign intervention in support of the Geraldine rebels, Grey, a staunch Protestant, had the support of ELIZABETH I. [see SPENSER, EDMUND.] **Mary Ann Lyons**

Smirke, Sir Robert (1780–1867), architect. Born in London. A pupil of Sir John Soane, he became a successful Greek Revival architect of public buildings. His only known work in Ireland is the Wellington Testimonial (1820) in the PHOENIX PARK, Dublin (see p. 851). His competition design was displayed in the Dublin Society's rooms in Leinster House in 1815. It consists of a 62 m (205-ft) obelisk in Wicklow granite on a pedestal later decorated with three bronze relief panels by Joseph Kirk, THOMAS FARRELL and JOHN HOGAN. Nearly twice as high as the largest monolithic Egyptian obelisk, and augmented by its elevated site, the Wellington Testimonial has become a Dublin landmark. **Judith Hill**

Smith, Henry John Stephen (1826–1883), mathematician. Born in Dublin, he was brought up in England; he graduated from the University of Oxford in 1849 and was elected a fellow of Balliol College. He was appointed professor of geometry at Oxford in 1860. His main work was in algebra and number theory, and he is remembered by the concept of the Smith normal form of a matrix. In April 1883 the French Academy posthumously awarded him its prestigious prize for his essay on the sums of squares of integers. **Rod Gow**

Smith, Paul (1935–1996), novelist. Born in Dublin. He worked on the Continent, in Australia, and in North America, and did some design work for the ABBEY and GATE THEATRES. *The Countrywoman* (1962) and *'Stravaganza!* (1963) gained him critical acclaim. He received the American Irish Foundation Literary Award, 1978, and was a member of AOSDÁNA. **Joley Wood**

Smithson, Harriet (1800–1854), actor. Born in Ennis, Co. Clare. She first appeared in the Crow Street Theatre, Dublin, in

1815, playing Lady Teazle in SHERIDAN's *School for Scandal*. Her first London appearance was at Drury Lane in 1818, after which she acted with Edmund Kean and Charles Kemble. Her greatest success was her passionate, unrestrained playing of Ophelia opposite William Macready's Hamlet. Her romantic interpretation of the role caused a sensation in Paris in 1827; one critic claimed that she 'revealed Shakespeare to France.' She retired from the stage in 1833 after marrying the composer Hector Berlioz; their tempestuous marriage ended in 1840. **Christopher Morash**

Smock Alley Theatre, Dublin. When the theatre opened in Smock Alley (now West Essex Street), Dublin, on 18 October 1662 it was the first purpose-built RESTORATION theatre. With a proscenium arch and large forestage, it had an intimate auditorium, 12 by 20 m (40 by 65 ft), holding a pit and three galleries, the lowest centred on a Viceregal box for the LORD LIEUTENANT. The original Smock Alley actors were frequently officers in nearby DUBLIN CASTLE regiments; however, this eventually changed, and many leading actors of the eighteenth century made their debut on its stage, including SPRANGER BARRY, PEG WOFFINGTON, and THOMAS SHERIDAN, who managed the theatre, 1745–54. Equally important to Dublin's cultural life were visiting performers, including David Garrick, who first played Hamlet in Smock Alley in 1742. During Sheridan's tenure there were serious riots in Smock Alley in 1747 and 1754. The last, instigated by members of the PATRIOT movement during a production of Voltaire's *Mahomet*, was partly provoked by Sheridan's friendly ties with Dublin Castle.

Increasing competition led to Smock Alley's closure in 1788. In 1815 the theatre was converted into the Church of SS. Michael and John, which was deconsecrated in 1990 (see p. 987). **Christopher Morash**

smokeless zones. Urban air pollution comes from many sources, such as industry and motor vehicles; but the control of smoke from domestic fuel has been recognised as a priority. Belfast has had smoke controls for more than thirty years, but the absence until recently of natural gas as an alternative fuel limited their effectiveness. More stringent controls recently introduced will lead to significant improvements in Belfast and other designated towns. The Republic was slower to respond to urban air pollution, and it was only in 1990 that the sale and distribution of bituminous solid fuel was banned in the Dublin region. This followed episodes in the 1980s when pollution levels reached ten times the winter average, with consequent risks to public health. The ban was extended to Cork in 1995 and to Arklow, Drogheda, Dundalk, Limerick, and Wexford in 1998. Galway, Waterford, Naas, Leixlip, and Celbridge were included in 2000, and it is intended to extend this list as required. Within a short time of the introduction of the ban in Dublin, fewer than 3 per cent of households were using bituminous coal, while 38 per cent used smokeless solid fuel and a further 27 per cent used natural gas. Recent results show that air quality has improved in the controlled towns; attention has now shifted to the growing problem of emissions from motor vehicles. **Joseph Brady**

Smurfit, Michael (1936–), businessman. Educated at St Mary's College, Dublin, and Clongowes Wood College. He began his career with his father's corrugated box business when it was a small family firm, becoming chief executive and director of Jefferson Smurfit Ltd in 1977. The company has since developed into a transnational corporation involved in printing, packaging, and financial services. An acquisition in 1994 was the biggest in Irish corporate history and made the Smurfit Group (bought out in 2002 by Chicago-based merchant bankers) one of the world's largest firms in the paper industry. Smurfit served as chairman of Telecom Éireann, 1979–91, and of the Racing Board, 1985–90. **Brian Galvin**

Smyllie, Robert (1894–1954), editor of the IRISH TIMES, 1934–54. Born in Glasgow, son of a well-known Scottish journalist; the family moved to Sligo when he was an infant. During the FIRST WORLD WAR he was interned while on holiday in Germany from TCD. He joined the *Irish Times* in 1919 and reported on the Versailles Peace Treaty. He was a staunch supporter of the Allies during the SECOND WORLD WAR; ebullient and eccentric, he repeatedly tried to thwart wartime press CENSORSHIP. Despite his Protestant unionist background he enjoyed an amicable personal relationship with ÉAMON DE VALERA, which helped him obtain scarce wartime newsprint. **Eddie Holt**

Smyth, Brendan. *Father Brendan Smyth during a hearing for his sentencing, 1993, after pleading guilty to seventy-four charges of sexual and indecent assault on children. He received a twelve-year prison sentence. [Eamonn Farrell/Photocall Ireland]*

Smyth, Brendan (1927–1997), priest. Born in Belfast; educated at the Gregorian University, Rome, and ordained into the Norbertine Order, 1951. Previously jailed in Northern Ireland for sexual offences, in 1993 he received a twelve-year prison sentence after pleading guilty to seventy-four charges of indecent and sexual assault on children over a period of thirty-five years. The case not only damaged the Catholic Church in Ireland but also had serious political and legal repercussions. In 1994 the scandal caused by the Attorney-General Harry Whelehan's failure to process an RUC extradition warrant for Smyth eventually precipitated the resignation of both the Taoiseach, ALBERT REYNOLDS, and Whelehan, the newly appointed President of the High Court, leading to the collapse of the Government. Smyth died after four years in prison. **Brian Galvin**

Smyth, Edward (1744 or 1745–1812), sculptor. Born in Co. Meath, where his father may have been a stone-cutter. He was apprenticed to Simon Vierpyl and carved chimneypieces and executed plaster decoration for the builder Henry Darley. He showed early promise in 1771 by winning the competition for a statue of CHARLES LUCAS for the Royal Exchange (now City Hall), Dublin. His potential was fully realised when GANDON employed him in 1781 to execute decorative stone carving on the CUSTOM HOUSE, Dublin: he contributed the colossal figure of Commerce for the cupola, skyline statues, and the pediment relief; but his masterpieces were the coats of arms and the river-god keystones, largely undamaged in the fire of 1921. He is celebrated for infusing drama and character into these natural allegories without detracting from their decorative role within the architectural scheme. He continued to work with Gandon, producing, notably, the skyline statues on the House of Lords, the trophies (now restored), and the well-regarded figure of Moses for the FOUR COURTS and caryatids for the KING'S INNS. Though his portrait busts and funerary monuments were less accomplished, Smyth, who was succeeded by his son, John, is an important figure in the Irish stone-carving tradition. **Judith Hill**

soccer. Since its introduction in 1878, association football or soccer has filled an important social role in Ireland. John M. McAlery, a Belfast merchant, is credited with fostering the sport in Ireland after watching a game in Edinburgh. Cliftonville, founded in Belfast a year later, was the first Irish club, and the Irish Football Association was founded in the city shortly afterwards. It was another three years before soccer was played in Dublin. Serious problems soon surfaced in the relationship between Belfast and Dublin, which had co-existed uneasily for a number of years, and the growing climate of separatism in the South led to the Leinster Football Association seceding from the Irish Football Association in 1921 to form the Football Association of the Irish Free State, later renamed the Football Association of Ireland.

If the new body hoped to ingratiate itself with the GAELIC ATHLETIC ASSOCIATION, which had always perceived soccer as a 'garrison sport', it had the opposite effect. To its original objections the GAA added the accusation that the infant organisation was partitionist; and the ban on its members playing or attending soccer matches would remain for the next fifty years. The slur of being less than wholly Irish was resented by the Southern body, which, shortly after the Irish Free State left the British Commonwealth in 1948, banned its players from representing Northern Ireland in international competitions. It was not until the introduction of the Inter-City Cup in the 1940s, featuring teams from both sides of the border, that the bitterness of the split began to subside; but despite occasional attempts at reconciliation, the division would endure. In spite of this, the Irish Football Association in Belfast, by now closely aligned with the English, Scottish, and Welsh associations, continued to prosper, with Linfield the dominant club, after increasing sectarian tension had forced Belfast Celtic to disband in 1949.

In common with the other 'home' countries, Northern Ireland declined to participate in the World Cup until the preliminaries of the 1950 championship, but eight years later they reached a significant milestone when, under the captaincy of DANNY BLANCHFLOWER, they qualified for the finals in Sweden. That remained as the pinnacle of Irish soccer achievement until 1982, when they again reached the finals, this time in Spain. BILLY BINGHAM, an influential member of the team twenty-four years earlier, was now in charge and, helped by a memorable win over the host country at Valencia, led them to a place in the last eight of the competition. Enough of that team survived to enable them to qualify for the finals again in Mexico in 1986; with their elimination from that championship, Northern Ireland went into decline as a force at the top level.

The nearest the Republic of Ireland team came to qualifying in that period was in 1965, when they were beaten in a play-off by Spain for a place in the championship, won by England the following year. With the amendment of the international soccer federation's eligibility rules, enabling players to represent the country of their ancestors, the team's fortunes began to climb in the 1970s, when, under the managership of JOHN GILES, the requisite format for success was established. But it was not until 1986, when JACK CHARLTON became the first manager from outside Ireland, that all the components came together to form a world-class team. Charlton, a member of England's successful team in 1966, brought to his new role a heightened sense of pragmatism. Within two years Ireland qualified for the finals of the 1988 European championship in Germany. Ray Houghton's winning goal against England at Stuttgart would be the catalyst for a remarkable development in the game in the Republic, and over the next fourteen years soccer became the fastest-growing sport in the country. The odyssey of the team's first appearance in the World Cup finals in Italy in 1990 captivated the public in remarkable fashion and ended only in a 1–0 defeat by the host country in the quarter-finals. By the 1994 World Cup finals in the United States the framework of that talented team was beginning to break up, but a victory over Italy was some consolation for failure to reach the last eight. It would fall to MICK MCCARTHY, captain of the 1990 team, to succeed Charlton as manager; and in spite of the disappointment of losing out in play-off ties for the finals of the 1998 World Cup and the European championship two years later, his achievement has been to sustain the Republic of Ireland team's high rating in the world of international football. His side qualified for the World Cup finals in Japan and South Korea in 2002, beating Saudi Arabia and drawing with Cameroon and Germany (the eventual runners-up) in the first round before losing on penalties to Spain in the second after a 1–1 draw. A row between McCarthy and the captain, ROY KEANE, resulted in Keane being sent home before the first match. McCarthy resigned in October 2002 and was succeeded by Brian Kerr. **Peter Byrne**

social class. In Ireland, class distinctions are thought of as quintessentially English: the popular impression is that rigid social class demarcation was left behind with the ending of landlordism and the demise of the ANGLO-IRISH ASCENDANCY. However, the term 'class' does not imply snobbishness or deference: instead it refers to the manner in which one's position in the labour market determines one's life chances. In Ireland, educational opportunities, income, health, and even mortality are strongly related to class position. Such inequalities show no signs of declining. Such advantages are also transmitted between generations.

In understanding the manner in which class inequalities are reproduced, it is necessary to distinguish between absolute and relative opportunity. While the class structure in Ireland was extremely stable from the founding of the state until 1960, subsequently a dramatic transformation was observed. This involved the contraction of farming, a reduction in unskilled manual work, and an increase in white-collar work. Substantial opportunities for upward social mobility were created. As a consequence, the professional and managerial class is drawn from diverse backgrounds. The rising tide had indeed raised all boats; however, the pattern of relative advantage remained stable, and the unskilled manual class increasingly constitutes a self-recruiting bloc. Irish society is far from being meritocratic. The operation of class processes in Ireland provides a perfect example of the principle of 'the more things change, the more they remain the same.' **Christopher T. Whelan**

Northern Ireland. In sociology there are two competing conceptualisations of social class: the Marxist and the Weberian. Within the Marxist paradigm the determinant of class is the control (or lack of control) of economic capital. Marxism has difficulties explaining the position of the middle classes. The best-known attempt in sociology is that of Erik Olin Wright, whose scale attempts to differentiate between workers, 'servicers' of capitalist

soccer. *Packie Bonner's historic save during the penalty shoot-out against Romania at Genoa, 25 June 1990, which secured Ireland's place in the World Cup quarter-finals against Italy. [Inpho Photography]*

interests, and controllers or owners of capital. The alternative paradigm, which originated from the work of Max Weber, also recognises the importance of market wealth for determining class position but broadens the conception of 'valued goods' to include the possession of marketable skills or abilities that are characteristic of the middle class.

Reflecting its peripheral location and relatively high rates of UNEMPLOYMENT and poverty, the class distribution in Northern Ireland, in comparison with England or other large European or North American countries, shows a smaller upper middle class and a larger proportion of the population in semi-skilled and unskilled manual strata. The relationship between RELIGION and class has been a political issue in Northern Ireland, with Catholics showing a lower class profile than non-Catholics. This has changed in recent years, mainly because of structural changes in the ECONOMY that have led to a decline in Protestant-dominated sectors. At present the class distributions of employed Catholics and Protestants show few differences, though Catholic rates of unemployment remain higher. **Robert Miller**

Social Democratic and Labour Party (SDLP), the most effective voice of the Catholic population in Northern Ireland since PARTITION, founded on 21 August 1970 by a coalition of political figures who had been prominent in the CIVIL RIGHTS struggle of the late 1960s. Led first by the West Belfast MP GERRY FITT and including the independent MPs JOHN HUME and Ivan Cooper, as well as the former Nationalist Austin Currie, it channelled the demand of the rising Catholic middle class for political participation and soon eclipsed the old rurally based Nationalist Party. The SDLP presented itself as a non-sectarian left-of-centre party, wedded to power-sharing and strong north-south links, with eventual Irish unity conditional on Unionist consent. It also established close links with the Dublin political establishment. It withdrew from STORMONT in July 1971 and, following the introduction of INTERNMENT in August 1971, sponsored a civil disobedience campaign. After the introduction of DIRECT RULE in 1972 the SDLP helped to negotiate the SUNNINGDALE AGREEMENT. With 22 per cent of the vote in its first election, 1973, it held four seats in the short-lived power-sharing Executive of 1974 but suffered from the ensuing vacuum.

In 1979 Fitt resigned over policy differences, enabling Hume as leader and main ideologue as well as a member of the European Parliament to forge vital contacts in Dublin, Brussels, and Washington. The party welcomed the ANGLO-IRISH AGREEMENT (1985) and Hume's peace initiative with GERRY ADAMS after 1988, which resulted in the IRA ceasefire of 1994. It helped to negotiate the BELFAST AGREEMENT (1998), securing four posts in the Executive, with its deputy leader, SEAMUS MALLON, becoming Deputy First Minister. In 2001 MARK DURKAN was elected leader of the party after Mallon's resignation and became Deputy First Minister. **Eamon Phoenix**

Socialist Women's Group, formed in 1975 by feminists connected with Queen's University, Belfast, together with women from left-wing groups who hoped this development would encourage male socialists to consider FEMINISM seriously. Some were members of the NORTHERN IRELAND WOMEN'S RIGHTS MOVEMENT who disagreed with that movement's acceptance of male members and its refusal to adopt a position on the constitutional status of Northern Ireland. The Socialist Women's Group developed an analysis of female oppression in the context of the unresolved national question, its manifesto stressing a link between anti-imperialist politics and the struggle for WOMEN'S LIBERATION. It emphasised the building of a working-class women's movement and sold its journal, *Women's Action*, at factory gates and from door to door.

It joined the Trotskyist left in united fronts, established a branch in Andersonstown, Belfast, and worked with women from west Belfast in the Relatives' Action Committee, campaigning for the restoration of political status for republican prisoners. Arguing for feminism in the early years of Socialist Women's republican politicisation proved an uncomfortable experience. In 1976 members split from the Northern Ireland Women's Rights Movement on whether to give support to the Peace Movement or to the Troops Out Movement. The Socialist Women's Group was dissolved in 1977, believing its socialist-feminist programme deterred recruits and alienated women from the wider community. **Margaret Ward**

social justice. The SOCIETY OF ST VINCENT DE PAUL, the Simon Community, and the Combat Poverty Agency are three of the more visible and active advocates of social justice in Ireland. They respond in practical ways to the plight of the disadvantaged and also contribute to debates on public policy regarding social and economic matters. The Christian churches and other religious groups also have a long history of involvement in justice issues; in the past this was seen primarily in their involvement in health care, education, and the care of the poor.

The Catholic community has responded to issues of poverty, DISCRIMINATION, and injustice through such agencies as the Irish Commission for Justice and Peace and the 'Justice Desk' of the Conference of Religious of Ireland (CORI). The Irish Catholic Bishops' Conference has published three significant works in recent decades that reflected in a systematic way on the reality and causes of injustice in Irish society. *The Work of Justice* (1977) used the Scriptures to establish that the doing of justice is an essential demand of Christian witness; it also employed the notion of 'social sin' in reference to the fact that injustice, greed, and hatred can become enshrined in the social structures and fabric of society. This contribution also rejected any attempt to see religion as a purely private matter. *Work Is the Key* (1992), published at a time of widespread unemployment and economic stagnation, dealt with the negative impact of UNEMPLOYMENT on human dignity; it argued that all in society are obliged to work together to create 'an economy that needs everyone.' The bishop's most recent publication on the theme of social justice, *Prosperity with a Purpose* (1999), addressed a radically changed social and economic scene; here the bishops dealt with the challenges created by Ireland's new-found wealth, including the reality of persistent poverty and disadvantage in the midst of prosperity, and the responsibility of society towards those in the developing world. **Pádraig Corkery**

social mobility. The mainstream of research into social mobility relies on the analysis of social survey data, in which mobility is measured by comparing the present occupational status of respondents with the occupational standing of their parents a generation before (intergenerational mobility) or with themselves when they entered the labour market (intragenerational or career mobility).

Social mobility in Ireland has been well documented for more than a generation, with the first comprehensive national study covering both North and South carried out in the 1970s and full replications for the South in 1995 and for the North in 1996. The original mobility data has been subjected to rigorous comparative analysis. Both parts of Ireland fall within a general pattern of mobility that is common to all industrialised countries. The features of this pattern are a strong tendency to remain at the same level as that at origin and for most mobility to be relatively 'short-range'; upward mobility exceeding downward mobility, because of ECONOMIC DEVELOPMENT; and mobility out of a shrinking agricultural sector. With regard to 'openness', Northern Ireland falls close to the average for European societies; in the analysis of the 1970s data the Republic is found to be less open, but this may have changed in the last decade. [see CLASS; SOCIAL CLASS; UNDERCLASS.] **Robert Miller**

'social partnership', the consensus-building negotiation of economic and social policy in the Republic between the Government and the main economic interests in society, dating from the mid-1980s and extending to representatives of community and VOLUNTARY ORGANISATIONS from 1997. The policy documents of the NATIONAL ECONOMIC AND SOCIAL COUNCIL provided the basis of national framework agreements on pay, tax, welfare, and other policy issues. The social partnership agreements were the Programme for National Recovery (1987), Programme for Economic and Social Progress (1990), Programme for Competitiveness and Work (1993), Partnership 2000 for Inclusion, Employment and Competitiveness (1997), and Programme for Prosperity and Fairness (2000). The process originated as a response to the severe economic and fiscal difficulties of the 1980s. The perceptions and expectations of the TRADE UNION movement had been transformed during the period of high UNEMPLOYMENT and decentralised pay bargaining of the early 1980s; these agreements therefore differed from their predecessors of the 1970s in several ways. Firstly, the terms of the pay agreements were quite moderate, and control over enterprise-level bargaining was more stringent in most sectors during the 1990s. Secondly, strike levels were low. Thirdly, tax reductions increased disposable income to a greater extent than the pay terms themselves. Fourthly, the scope of the agreements was widened to include a growing range of social policy issues, a development explicitly recognised by the broadening of participation in the talks since 1997.

Social partnership has been credited with an important role in the policy successes of the 1990s and beyond, particularly by facilitating the conversion of steady ECONOMIC GROWTH into an unprecedented rise in EMPLOYMENT. The changed economic circumstances of the early 2000s saw some divergence between the preferences of unions and employers; many hoped nevertheless that a new form of social partnership might be devised to meet the new challenges. [see NATIONAL PAY AGREEMENTS.] **Niamh Hardiman**

social services. The twentieth century and particularly the post-war period in Europe saw increasing involvement in social policy by governments in economically developed countries. This is reflected in increasing expenditure on the provision of social services, such as HEALTH, EDUCATION, HOUSING, social security, and personal social services (social work or social care). Whatever the detail of policies in the different social areas and the laws and regulations that enforce them, the actual provisions made reflect the influence of political choices. This explains the differences between countries in expenditure, range of risks covered, quality of services, and the very definition of what constitutes the welfare state. Social services support social institutions that unite concern with the objectives of social policy with the development and administration of particular statutory and voluntary organisations. Debates about the appropriate role of the state, market, and family suggest that Ireland has what is called a mixed economy of welfare. This is distinguished by the tiered character of social service provision and the significance of the market in liberal welfare states, such as Ireland. **Ann Lavan**

social welfare. Social welfare redistributes resources from those receiving an income to those who are ill, retired, unemployed, or involved in full-time caring. It encompasses *social insurance* (financed by contributions from employees and employers), means-tested *social assistance*, and universal *child benefit* payments (both financed by taxes). The Poor Relief (Ireland) Act (1838) introduced the first statutory system of social welfare in Ireland; the National Insurance Act (1911) introduced the first compulsory social insurance scheme.

Social welfare expenditure in the Republic was approximately €8 billion in 2001, representing about 10 per cent of GROSS NATIONAL PRODUCT; this figure is low by the standards of EU countries. Expenditure in Northern Ireland was approximately £3.5 billion, or 11 per cent of GNP. The main social welfare expenditure categories in the Republic were the aged (approximately 24 per cent), widows, widowers, and one-parent families (19 per cent), illness, disability, and caring (15 per cent), UNEMPLOYMENT supports (15 per cent), and child-related payments (10 per cent). In recent years rates of social welfare payments have risen faster than INFLATION but more slowly than the growth in average earnings. The debate on SOCIAL PARTNERSHIP policy is likely to shift away from large tax decreases (in return for pay moderation) and towards increases in social expenditure, which encompasses expenditure on HEALTH and EDUCATION as well as social welfare. **Francis O'Toole**

Social Welfare, Commission on, established by the Government in 1983 to review the social welfare system and to make recommendations; the commission comprised twelve members, chaired by John Curry. Its report, published in 1986, opted for a reformed system of social insurance and social assistance, rather than more radical change. It recommended that the coverage of social insurance be as comprehensive as possible, to include groups then not fully covered, such as the self-employed and part-time workers, and this policy was subsequently implemented. It also recommended the rationalisation of various aspects of the social welfare system, including the means test and payment rates, also mostly carried through into policy. It placed the greatest emphasis, however, on the inadequacy of the basic weekly payment to many of those depending on social welfare, particularly the lowest rates for those relying on the means-tested safety net. The commission set out the minimum income that it regarded as adequate and recommended that priority be given to bringing the lowest rates up to that level. This came to be seen as a benchmark against which the evolution of rates was assessed, though it was more than a decade before the real value of all payments reached this minimum level. **Brian Nolan**

Society for the Protection of Unborn Children (SPUC), a group launched in 1980 to oppose the legalisation of ABORTION. It had connections with the American organisation that, subsequent to *Roe v. Wade* (1973), had launched a campaign to an amendment to the Constitution of the United States that would declare the foetus to be a human person. The Irish branch of SPUC

social justice. *Sisters for Justice, championing the rights of Travellers, march in Dublin in protest against the Criminal Justice Bill, 10 March 1984. [Derek Speirs/Report]*

was active in providing anti-abortion speakers to schools. It formed the PRO-LIFE AMENDMENT CAMPAIGN, which advocated that the CONSTITUTION OF IRELAND should guarantee the unborn child an absolute right to life from the moment of conception. On foot of the anti-abortion constitutional amendment of 1983 it obtained an injunction against the Open Door Counselling and Well Woman Centre. The injunction was upheld in the Hamilton judgment (1986), which ruled that it was now illegal to provide information in Ireland that would facilitate abortions in England. Later that year SPUC obtained an injunction against three students' unions for publishing in their student handbooks the addressees and phone numbers of British abortion clinics. In 1992 the European Court of Human Rights ruled that Ireland was in breach of the Convention of the Rights of Man, as the ban on abortion information put the health of Irish women at risk because it could lead to late abortions and deprive women of post-abortion check-ups; but in 1992 this was legally interpreted as permitting abortion in the 'X' CASE. While SPUC wanted such an interpretation precluded, three abortion-related referendums in 1995 failed to do so. The Regulation of Information (Services Outside the State for Termination of Pregnancies) Act (1995) was subsequently enacted. [see ABORTION; REFERENDUMS.] **Evelyn Mahon**

Society of Dublin Painters, an exhibition society founded in 1920 by PAUL and GRACE HENRY, JACK B. YEATS, and others as a place where young, avant-garde painters could show their works, the other bodies—principally the RHA—being strictly reactionary in mood. It was at first limited to ten members; this was increased to twelve in 1932 and to eighteen in 1934. Each member was entitled to hold a one-person exhibition every year, while group exhibitions of members' works were held in the spring and autumn. The society embraced no theory or aesthetic, members being free to work in their own manner. It was notable for the large number of women painters who were associated with it—EVIE HONE, MAINIE JELLETT, LETITIA HAMILTON, Harriet Kirkwood, NORAH MCGUINNESS, NANO REID, ELIZABETH RIVERS, and Mary Swanzy, among others—who were an important force in twentieth-century Irish art (see p. 565). The 'Dublin Painters' were at their most radical in the 1920s, but in general they represented the progressive aspect of Irish painting until the advent of the LIVING ART exhibitions in 1943. The society was disbanded in 1969. **S. B. Kennedy**

Society of St Vincent de Paul (SVP), a Catholic international VOLUNTARY ORGANISATION whose members seek to relieve social need through direct person-to-person contact. Founded by Antoine-Frédéric Ozanam in Paris in 1833, the society was established in Ireland in 1844 and by the late 1990s had a membership of 9,000 in more than 1,000 conferences (branches). Under the patronage of St Vincent de Paul, the society situates itself within the tradition of Catholic social teaching but is open to Christians of any denomination. It is best known for its work of visiting the needy in their homes, in hospital, or in prison and providing them with financial assistance; it therefore offers a short-term safety net for those in situations of acute distress, which complements state support schemes. The society also seeks to promote self-sufficiency through such means as advice and counselling, a budgeting service, educational grants, and support in preparing for and seeking jobs. It runs family resource centres, hostels for the homeless, DRUGS projects, social housing projects, and summer projects. It has committed itself to identifying the root causes of poverty and social injustice and to working to eliminate them. As a SOCIAL PARTNER recognised by the Government it is a member of the NATIONAL ECONOMIC AND SOCIAL COUNCIL and the NATIONAL ECONOMIC AND SOCIAL FORUM. With a budget of approximately £17 million in the late 1990s, it is one of the largest and best-known voluntary social organisations in Ireland. **Peadar Kirby**

soils. Most Irish soils are formed from glacial or post-glacial deposits, rather than from underlying solid rock. They generally reflect the varied origin, texture, and chemical reaction of these deposits, and their geographical distribution is complex. Irish soils can be grouped into ten major classes, called *great soil groups*, according to their soil profile. Soils of the same type behave similarly and are strongly associated with relief or topographical situation. Soils within each group have the same kind and sequence of horizons in the soil profile, and therefore those falling within each group have similar potential for land use.

Gleys are soils with impeded drainage that develop under conditions of permanent or intermittent waterlogging and are commonly not suitable for cultivation unless artificially drained. They are frequently used for pasture and are considered relatively productive forest soils. Gleys are the most common mineral (as distinct from organic) soil type in Ireland, covering much of Cos. Antrim, Cavan, Monaghan, Roscommon, and Leitrim, as well as parts of Cos. Laois, Limerick, Kerry, Meath, Kilkenny, Carlow, west Wexford, and east Clare.

Brown earths are relatively mature mineral soils possessing a rather uniform profile, with little differentiation into horizons. They usually possess loamy textures and desirable structure and drainage characteristics. They are generally good arable soils: with good management they can support high-quality grassland and are also ideally suited to a wide range of forest tree species. Brown earths are common in the well-drained areas of Cos. Wexford and Waterford and parts of Cos. Down, Derry, Longford, Louth, and north Meath.

Brown podzolics are a more intensely leached variety of the brown earths; the upper horizons are therefore more depleted of base and other constituents, often forming a sub-surface horizon of strong red-brown or yellowish-brown colour (principally leached iron oxides), and they are more degraded generally and more acidic than the brown earths. They closely resemble the brown earths in productive capacity and behaviour and are good forest soils. They are very common over much of the bedrock of old red sandstone in Cos. Cork and Kerry and on the lower flanks of the Wicklow Mountains.

Grey-brown podzolics are inherently associated with leaching throughout their development. These soils usually form over limestone-dominated sub-soil (mostly glacial till) and are usually moderately acidic to neutral. They are good all-purpose soils under Irish conditions and are used for the production of a wide range of crops. Grey-brown podzolics are widespread in the midlands and east, as well as in east Galway and north Tipperary.

Podzols are soils that have been intensely leached. They form on acidic parent materials and are poor agricultural soils. Iron pans often develop in podzols, causing the drainage in the surface layer to be very poor. In their unreclaimed state they usually have a cover of semi-natural vegetation; where management is poor following reclamation they revert easily. In most instances the nature and terrain associated with these soils is such that mechanical reclamation and cultivation are not feasible; they are therefore devoted mostly to rough grazing or forestry. Podzols often occur in association with blanket bog and often have a thin layer of peat on their surface. They occur extensively in the mountains of Co. Mayo, in the valleys of west Cork and Kerry, in south Waterford, and around Lough Gill in Co. Sligo.

Lithosols are skeletal, stony soils, often of an organic nature, overlying, in most instances, solid or shattered bedrock. The shallow stony soils in parts of Connemara, those along the Donegal and south Galway coasts and those present in high mountain areas are classified as lithosols. They have a very limited potential for AGRICULTURE, because of depth limitations, and can be used only for extensive grazing, or FORESTRY in some areas.

Basin peats in the midlands take the form of peat-filled hollows or depressions in which the surface of the peat rises from the margins to the centre, forming a dome. The formation of peat began almost immediately following the last Ice Age, about 10,000 years ago. Midland basin bogs tend to be deeper than blanket peats. Basin peat occurs extensively in Cos. Offaly, Laois, Westmeath, Kildare, and Meath, as well as east Galway, east Mayo, and Roscommon, generally in hollows and in flat, poorly drained areas.

Blanket bog is acid peat up to about 3 m (10 ft) in thickness that completely envelops level to gently undulating ground. *Blanket peats* occur mainly in the west (Connemara, west Mayo, and Donegal) but also in the WICKLOW MOUNTAINS. Though they can be several metres deep, their surface configuration is closely related to the underlying topography, and they therefore cover the landscape like a blanket. They are very difficult to drain and have a low agricultural value.

Rendzinas are dark-coloured, shallow soils usually formed over limestone bedrock. They can be up to 50 cm ($1\frac{1}{2}$ ft) deep but are

Solomons. *Family photograph at the silver wedding anniversary of Maurice and Rosa Solomons in Dublin, 1903, showing (left to right, standing) Maurice, Edwin, Rosa; (sitting) Bethel, Sophie, Estella. Bethel became master of the Rotunda Hospital and Estella a member of Cumann na mBan; a noted portrait-painter; her studio on Brunswick (Pearse) Street was a safe-house for revolutionaries. [Dr Michael Solomons]*

often less. Drainage is always free to excessive. Where they are deep enough they are valuable agricultural soils and can be used for a wide range of crops; otherwise rock outcrops and broken topography render them suitable only for extensive grazing. They do not occur extensively but are to be found in parts of Co. Galway and in the Burren, Co. Clare.

Regosols have poorly developed horizons and are therefore considered immature. They are formed from river and lake deposits where there has not been enough time for distinct horizons to develop and are also found on young deposits, such as aeolian sands. [see CLIMATE; GEOLOGY; LAND; WATER.] **Robert Meehan**

soil survey: see NATIONAL SOIL SURVEY.

Soiscéal Molaise, a BOOK-SHRINE believed to have once contained a GOSPEL book associated with ST MOLAISE of Devenish, dated by an inscription to between 1001 and 1011. It is decorated with cast gilt silver plates and gold filigree, the front face bearing a cross and symbols of the four Evangelists. **Raghnall Ó Floinn**

'Soldier's Song': see AMHRÁN NA BHFIANN.

Sollas, William Johnson (1849–1936), geologist. Born in Birmingham; educated at the Royal School of Mines and the University of Cambridge. In 1879 he was appointed professor of GEOLOGY and zoology at University College, Bristol, and between 1883 and 1897 he was professor of geology and mineralogy at Trinity College, Dublin. While in Dublin he also held the post of petrologist to the GEOLOGICAL SURVEY OF IRELAND and published an important paper on the distribution of eskers (1896). The author of many papers and several books, he led an expedition in 1896 to Funafuti in the South Pacific to test rival theories on the origin of coral reefs; his findings were inconclusive. After 1897 he was professor of geology at the University of Oxford. **Jean Archer**

Solomons, Estella (1882–1968), painter and printmaker. Born in Dublin; studied art at the ROYAL HIBERNIAN ACADEMY Schools and the Dublin Metropolitan School of Art. She was a member of CUMANN NA MBAN, and her studio was a centre for literary and political activists, many of whom sat for her. She became an associate of the Royal Hibernian Academy in 1925 and an honorary member in 1966. Her etchings feature in several books, including *The Book of St Ultan* (1920) and *The Glamour of Dublin* (1918, 1928). **Sinéad McCoole**

Somerville, Edith Œnone (1858–1949), writer and artist. Born in Corfu; educated at home in Castletownshend, Co. Cork, and briefly at Alexandra College, Dublin, and studied art in London, Germany, and France. She published comic illustrations in English magazines. In 1886 she met her second cousin, Violet Martin, and they began a collaborative writing career as Edith Somerville and MARTIN ROSS, writing witty and often satirical travelogues, essays, stories, and novels. Somerville illustrated many of their works. THE REAL CHARLOTTE (1894) received critical acclaim; popular success came with *Some Experiences of an Irish R.M.*, first published in *Badminton Magazine*, 1898–9. *Further Experiences of an Irish R.M.* and *In Mr Knox's Country* appeared in the illustrated magazines *Strand* and *Graphic* as well as more serious periodicals, such as *Blackwood's*.

An accomplished sportswoman and activist for women's rights, Somerville was master of the West Carbery Foxhounds, 1903–8, and president of the Munster Women's Franchise League, 1913. After Martin's death in 1915 she continued to publish most of her fiction under their joint names; she believed Martin communicated with her on these texts through automatic writing. One exception was *An Enthusiast* (1921), loosely based on the life of HORACE PLUNKETT. *The Big House of Inver* (1925) became a landmark study of the demise of the ANGLO-IRISH ASCENDANCY. In 1932 she was awarded an honorary doctorate of letters by the University of Dublin. The same year she published an account of her and Martin's great-grandfather, Charles Kendal Bushe, in *An Incorruptible Irishman*. In 1933 she became a founder-member of the IRISH ACADEMY OF LETTERS and in 1941 was awarded the Gregory Medal. She published until the last year of her life, and is buried alongside Martin in Castlehaven parish church, Castletownshend. **Julie Anne Stevens**

Somerville. *Illustration by Edith Somerville, one of three wash drawings from 'In the State of Denmark', published as a serial in* The Ladies' Pictorial, *1893. Somerville and Ross are portrayed searching their Danish phrasebook for 'bread and butter, a thing which riper knowledge has shown does not exist in Denmark in the readymade slice.' [Queen's University, Belfast; Special collections]*

Somerville-Large, Peter (1928–), travel writer. Born in Dublin; educated at TCD. He has been variously a lecturer at the Royal Military Academy in Kabul, Afghanistan, a gold miner in Australia, and a journalist. His many books on Irish topics include *The Coast of West Cork* (1972), *From Bantry Bay to Leitrim: A Journey in Search of O'Sullivan Beare* (1974), *The Irish Grand Tour* (1982), and *The Irish Country House: A Social History (*1995), and *An Irish Childhood* (2002). Foreign travel books include *Tribes and Tribulations* (1967) on the Yemen and, on Iran, *Caviar Coast* (1968). **Brian Lalor**

Something Happens, rock group, formed in Dublin in the mid-1980s. The group's initial influence was REM, but they soon matured into one of Ireland's most original and innovative guitar bands. They released their debut *Been There, Seen That, Done That* in 1988. They followed this with *Stuck Together with God's Glue* (1990), an album that has since regularly cropped up in lists of best Irish albums of all time but never succeeded commercially. **Tony Clayton-Lea**

song-collectors. Song-collecting began in Ireland with CHARLOTTE BROOKE and her *Reliques of Irish Poetry* (1789). Though EDWARD BUNTING is best known for his collecting of HARP music, he also engaged Patrick Lynch to collect the words of Irish songs for him. Bunting's successor, GEORGE PETRIE, included songs in Irish while showing a disdain for English lyrics. This policy was to be imitated for almost a century by his followers, particularly P. W. JOYCE. Nevertheless, Joyce's *Old Irish Folk Music and Song* (1909) is a rich repository from the nineteenth-century field. Notable among twentieth-century collectors were A. M. FREEMAN, whose west Cork songs appeared in the *Journal of the Folk Song Society*, 1920–21, and Eileen Costello (1870–1962), whose *Amhráin Mhuighe Seola* (1923) documents east Galway song. ÉNRÍ Ó MUIRGHEASA (1874–1945) published an important body of song texts from Ulster in *Céad de Cheoltaibh Uladh* (1915) and *Dhá Chéad de Cheoltaibh Uladh* (1934).

The collection of songs in English was comparatively erratic. Such songs appeared randomly in the works of commentators on life in Ireland, such as SAMUEL LOVER, WILLIAM ALLINGHAM, and Patrick Kennedy. From its inception in 1935 the Irish FOLKLORE COMMISSION (and its successor, the Department of Irish Folklore, UCD) briefed collectors to gather songs in both languages. However, it was SAM HENRY of Coleraine who published the largest collection of songs in English, in his 'Songs of the People' column in the *Northern Constitution*, 1923–39, published in book form in 1990. The importance of Ireland's heritage of traditional song in English was brought to academic attention by the collector HUGH SHIELDS. The Department of Irish Folklore, the IRISH TRADITIONAL MUSIC ARCHIVE, and other bodies and individuals continue collecting today. **Tom Munnelly**

songs of the *Nation*. The NATION was the weekly newspaper founded in 1842 by THOMAS DAVIS, JOHN BLAKE DILLON, and CHARLES GAVAN DUFFY. It was the voice of the Young Ireland movement, its object being to educate the people, rouse the national spirit, and foster the idea of Irish nationality, regardless of creed, as originally proposed by THEOBALD WOLFE TONE. John Blake Dillon was the editor of the paper, but its most talented contributor was Thomas Davis, a native of Mallow, a barrister and a Protestant. The paper was distributed throughout the country, and the ballads written by Davis and others praising the heroes of the past and looking forward to a time when Irishmen would control their own destiny were taken up and widely sung by the people. These songs and poems were later issued in a collection called *The Spirit of the Nation*. Many of Thomas Davis's songs are still sung wherever singers gather today: 'The West's Awake', 'A Nation Once Again', 'My Land', 'Tone's Grave'.

> That chainless wave and lovely land
> Freedom and nationhood demand—
> Be sure the great god never planned
> For slumbering slaves a home so grand.
>
> But hark, a voice like thunder spake:
> The West's awake, the West's awake
> Sing, oh! hurrah! Let England quake,
> We'll watch till death for Erin's sake!

Frank Harte

song styles. Regional differences of style in SEAN-NÓS SINGING have been described as 'a very florid line in Connacht, contrasting with a somewhat less decorated one in the south and, by comparison, a stark simplicity in the Northern songs.' This description concentrates on only one dimension, *melisma*—the amount of melodic ornament used—and ignores other stylistic factors: changes of vocal quality; variation of the melody by changing pitch or splitting notes; and, especially in the North, variations of tempo and the introduction of stops—rhythmic rather than melodic ornament. It also ignores the tonal and rhythmic variation to be found in Connemara singing. In addition, regional accent and dialect also condition every performance before regional style can be considered. Probably the most distinctive singing style is that of members of the Travelling community. It is typically high-pitched and hard-edged, far back in the throat and nasal; its most obvious features are tone, accent, and an exaggerated glottal stopping at phrase endings. However, some settled singers have the same characteristics. It is likely that an individual voice will be recognised before an unknown one is placed in its regional setting. Few firm distinctions can be made; this is an area ripe for study. [see TRAVELLERS.] **John Moulden**

song types. Song types are bounded only by the imagination of the songmaker, and this is unlimited. The Department of Irish Folklore, UCD, uses hundreds of working headings for Irish song types, with many more sub-groups. The love song predominates in both Irish and English, those presenting an idealised portrait of the woman being the most numerous. Love and political poetry combine in the AISLING, the vision-song, in which the beautiful 'sky-woman' represents Ireland. Many of these songs contain a beauty that retains a hold on tradition long after most political songs—which by their nature are ephemeral—have disappeared. From the early seventeenth century to the present, political comment was voiced in song, many being 'journalistic' and partisan. Satire is particularly favoured and frequently most effective. Important events find comparatively little resonance in song lore, which prefers the tangible microcosm to the grand sweep of history. The countless songs on EMIGRATION almost always concentrate on the sadness of the individual. (Many such songs were written by poets who had never left their own parish.)

Until recently, most events within the experience or imagination of the local songmaker—from murder to the loss of a hen—would be circulated in the song lore of the area; in particular, sporting events would be commemorated in verse. Recent collecting has unearthed hundreds of such songs. Analysis, only now revealing the kaleidoscopic variety of traditional song types, demonstrates a (suspected) preference for romantic and comic songs and an (unsuspected) quantity of narrative songs. **Tom Munnelly**

Sons of Handel, a large choral group, founded c. 1790, exclusively for the performance of ORATORIO. The activities of the group are closely associated with those of the Irish Musical Fund Society (founded 1787), which gave an annual concert commemorating HANDEL most years until 1820 and only twice thereafter; the Sons of Handel made their first appearance at such concerts in 1795. Performances independent of the charity appear to have taken place only between 1822 and 1824. Though it is not clear who founded the group, the conductors Jonathan Blewitt and Francis Robinson were particularly associated with it. It was succeeded by the Antient Concerts Society (1834–63). **Philip Graydon**

Soundpost: Ireland's Musical Magazine, a bimonthly journal published by the MUSIC ASSOCIATION OF IRELAND between 1981 and 1985. The first issue, that of April–May 1981, was edited by Honor Ó Brolcháin; Michael Dervan and Bernard Harris became joint editors from no. 6, with Dervan continuing as sole editor for nos. 20–23. The varied content included news, research, interviews, and reviews and provided regional coverage of music in Ireland. The magazine drew attention to both established and rising musical talent, and especially to composers, adventurously publishing studies and scores of their music. **Adrian Scahill**

Souter. Buon Divertimento *(1958), an early painting conveying Camille Souter's appreciation for the physical properties of paint; though abstract, it represents her response to extended periods in Italy during the 1950s. [Courtesy of the artist]*

souperism, the exchange of spiritual allegiance for material benefits of one kind or another, typically soup during famine. Allegations of souperism were made against promoters of the SECOND REFORMATION, especially in Munster and Connacht during the GREAT FAMINE, where food was scarce and conversions most frequent. Recent scholarship suggests that proselytism generated much suspicion, and, therefore, charges of souperism were probably exaggerated. As conditions improved, religious converts (known as jumpers) returned usually to their original faith, thus reflecting the great temptations of all concerned. [see ALTAR CONTROVERSY.] **Thomas Kelley**

Souter, Camille (1929–), painter. Born Betty Holmes in England, and brought by her parents to Dublin in early childhood; educated at Glengara Park School, where she enjoyed sports and art rather than the academic curriculum. Having completed her schooling as the Second World War ended, she moved to London and enrolled as a trainee nurse in Guy's Hospital. Her interest in painting was triggered by visits to a retrospective exhibition of the work of Pierre Bonnard (died 1947). She taught herself the disciplines of painting during a period of convalescence following a bout of TUBERCULOSIS and returned to Dublin in the early 1950s a dedicated professional painter. A grant from the Italian government allowed her to spend a period working in Italy, during which she refined the techniques that have informed all her subsequent work. Her preferred medium is oil on paper, in which she has been steadily productive without being prolific. A retrospective exhibition of her work in Sligo and Dublin in 2001 confirmed her position as one of the most important and influential contemporary painters. **Gerry Dukes**

souterrains, artificial underground or semi-subterranean structures found in association with EARLY HISTORIC settlements, including RING-FORTS. They were constructed either by tunnelling or by digging and roofing an open trench and can be of dry-stone or timber construction. Common features include *drop-holes* between levels, *creeps* or restricted passages, *guard-chambers* or niches, sill-stones, ventilation shafts, drains, and floor paving. Souterrains appear to have had a dual function, providing both storage and refuge. Cool and very often dry, they were ideal storage areas, especially for foodstuffs; some features were clearly defensive, while early documentary information refers to their use as refuges. **Michelle Comber**

South Africa, the Irish in. South Africa did not attract mass Irish immigration in the nineteenth century. Nonetheless, selective Irish settlement did occur. The 1820 settlers included 350 Irish people, who were sent to the semi-arid Clanwilliam region of the Northern Cape. After protests they were later moved to the Eastern Cape. A party of 352 Irish people sailed from Cork in 1823, but this settlement also proved problematic. From then on Irish immigration was patchy and *ad hoc*. About 15,000 emigrants received assisted passage to the Cape between 1820 and 1900. This included the shipload of 163 Irishwomen who were brought out to the Eastern Cape in 1857 with the intention that they would marry former German mercenaries. Some did, but most went into domestic service in King William's Town or Grahamstown.

In the 1890s gold-mining attracted about 1,000 Irishmen to Johannesburg. Many of these were advanced Irish nationalists, who joined the Boer forces when war broke out in 1899. By the beginning of the twentieth century some 18,000 first-generation Irish people were living in South Africa.

The Irish were a minority of a minority of a minority: a minority of the English-speaking minority of the white minority population. The numbers of Irish settlers may not have been great; but because they tended to concentrate in certain areas and occupations they gave the impression of being greater in number than they were. Poor Irish urban settlements were to be found in Newlands and Woodstock in Cape Town, near the docks in Port Elizabeth, around the Kynoch explosives factory at Umbogintwini, south of Durban, and in the Fordsburg suburb of Johannesburg in the Transvaal Republic. Occupations that attracted Irish people included the railways and the colonial police forces, a quarter of the latter being composed of Irishmen. As well as the Witwatersrand gold mines, Irishmen were to be found on the Kimberley diamond fields. Ulstermen were particularly prominent in the retailing business, in chain stores such as that of Cuthberts (from Dungiven, Co. Derry), R. H. Henderson (from Co. Armagh), and John Orr (from Benburb, Co. Tyrone). A fair number of Irish adventurers were also to be found in the wilder areas of the sub-continent. Among these were Michael Hogan, the privateer and slave-smuggler; Sarah Heckford, the eccentric itinerant trader; and big-game hunters such as Gervase Bushe and Richard Orpen. A host of Irish farm names reflect the fact that some settlers did work the African soil, including farms called the Curragh, the Dargle, Home Rule, Killaloe, and Phoenix Park.

In the professional occupations there were many notable Irish doctors and lawyers, the most famous being William Porter, the Cape's attorney-general. The Cape Colony and Natal also had prominent Irish politicians, two of whom, Thomas Upington from Cork and Alfred Hime from Kilcoole, Co. Wicklow, were prime ministers. The churches could boast a strong Irish presence; this was especially so in the Catholic dioceses of the Eastern Cape, which for many decades was dominated by Irish bishops. These included Bishops Devereux from Co. Wexford, MacSherry from Co. Armagh, Moran from Co. Wicklow, and Ricards from Co. Wexford. The first resident Catholic bishop in South Africa was Bishop Patrick Griffith from Limerick.

The British imperial presence brought with it regiments made up of Irishmen, one of which, the 83rd Regiment, helped capture the Cape Colony in 1806 and another, the 27th Regiment, Natal in 1842. Before 1899 eight such regiments were stationed in South Africa: the 5th (Royal Irish Lancers), 6th (Inniskilling Dragoons), 8th (King's Royal Irish Lancers), 27th (Inniskilling Fusiliers), 83rd, 86th, 88th (Connaught Rangers), and 103rd (Dublin Fusiliers). Some thirty thousand Irishmen fought in the British army in the ANGLO-BOER WAR of 1899–1902. In addition there were several Irish militia forces, such as the Cape Town Irish Rifles (1885–90); and Irishmen were prominent in the Cape Mounted Rifles.

The creation of the Union of South Africa and the rise of Afrikaner nationalism led to a dramatic decline in Irish immigration. [see BRITISH EMPIRE, IRISH IN.] **Dónal P. McCracken**

Southern, Rowland (1882–1935), marine scientist. Born in Lancashire; studied chemistry in Bolton. Appointed to the City Analyst's laboratory, Dublin, in 1902, he became a member of the ROYAL IRISH ACADEMY in 1908. He worked in the NATURAL HISTORY MUSEUM from 1911 and was transferred to the fisheries branch as assistant inspector in 1919. He made a major contribution to the knowledge of the polychaete FAUNA of Ireland and subsequently pioneered limnological studies in LOUGH DERG, 1920–23, followed by work on trout in the Liffey. He was the principal author of *Angler's Guide to the Irish Free State*. **Christopher Moriarty**

Southerne, Thomas (1660–1746), playwright. Born in Oxmantown, Dublin; educated at TCD and the Middle Temple, London. A popular writer, he collaborated with Dryden and was a friend of SWIFT, Pope and Gay. He was renowned in his day for his comedies, especially his adaptations of the Aphra Behn novels *The Fatal Marriage* (1694) and *Oroonoko* (1696). His works brought him much wealth but little lasting reputation; they have been criticised for lacking the talent and comedy for which they were once famous but remain testaments to their period. **Joley Wood**

southern unionism. In 1885 Irish Conservatives and Liberals created the Irish Loyal and Patriotic Union (Irish Unionist Alliance from 1891) to resist HOME RULE. Despite some working-class support it was dominated by LANDLORD and professional elites. It had little electoral success, its importance lying in publicity work and contacts among the British elite. More sophisticated and less sectarian than Ulster unionism (increasingly distinct after 1905), it was divided between advocates of co-opting moderate nationalists through reform and those who saw concessions as treason. This was exacerbated by the revival of home rule and Ulster unionist acceptance of PARTITION; after 1918 the IUA split between moderates and diehards. [see UNIONISM IN INDEPENDENT IRELAND.] **Patrick Maume**

southern United States, the Irish in the. The Irish of the southern states are often overlooked in Irish-American history. Only 10 per cent of the Catholic Irish who went to America settled there, and they are believed to have been completely assimilated into Southern society. However, the Irish have a long and distinct history in the South, beginning with the 'SCOTCH-IRISH' or Ulster Protestant EMIGRATION of the colonial period. Many of these emigrants of the 1700s migrated from New York or Pennsylvania to the wilderness back-countries of Virginia, Georgia, and the Carolinas, or arrived there directly as indentured servants. Many of these early settlers, already known for their anti-British sentiment, became enthusiastic participants in the American Revolution. Others came in the early 1800s to settle in Kentucky and Tennessee, becoming the country's first 'Indian-fighters' and producing such American heroes as President Andrew Jackson (1767–1845), the son of Ulster Presbyterians (see p. 295).

The Catholic Irish dominated Southern immigration between the GREAT FAMINE and the American Civil War, settling in such cities as Savannah, New Orleans, Charleston, and Baltimore; by 1850 New Orleans was America's second-largest port of entry, after New York. There was also a significant Irish MIGRATION from Northern states, attracted by job opportunities on the railways, canals, and docks. Considered less valuable than slaves and less dangerous than free blacks, the Irish were the perfect workers for the antebellum urban South. In addition, fears of competition from free blacks made many Irish solidly pro-slavery.

The South produced harsh conditions for the Irish, both physically and socially. Outbreaks of yellow fever in New Orleans (with ten thousand epidemic deaths in 1853), Savannah, and other cities claimed thousands of lives, while Catholicism and active involvement in politics left the Irish open to nativist hostility during the 1850s 'Know-Nothing' period. They quickly established benevolent and communal societies to help them combat both. The Southern Catholic Church rallied the Irish at local level and also produced several national leaders, most notably Bishop John England (1786–1842) of Charleston and Cardinal James Gibbons (1834–1921) of Baltimore.

Like the Revolution for the Scotch-Irish, the Civil War proved to be the test of Irish loyalty in the South. Fears of job competition from free blacks increased the support of the Irish for slavery, while they likened the Southern secession to the Irish struggle for freedom from England. The bravery of Irish regiments, such as the Jasper Greens of Savannah and the Montgomery Guard, earned the Irish respect and acceptance.

Irish immigration to the South slowed to a trickle after the American Civil War. A poor economy and Jim Crow's discriminatory laws did not offer much for new immigrants, while the Irish already there almost completely blended with the dominant white society out of necessity. However, Southern culture retains many Irish and Scotch-Irish elements, particularly in rural Appalachian customs, country and bluegrass music, and clog dancing. In addition, the Irish-American communities of many Southern cities continue to celebrate their roots; Savannah's ST PATRICK'S DAY parade is the third-largest and one of the oldest in the United States, while Scarlett O'Hara, the heroine of *Gone With The Wind* (1935), created by Margaret Mitchell of Atlanta, is one of the most beloved figures of American fiction. **Meaghan Dwyer**

sovereignty, a multi-faceted concept, usually understood as encompassing internal sovereignty on the one hand, and external sovereignty, on the other. Internal sovereignty requires the presence of a supreme political authority—a government—within a defined territory, with a monopoly over the legal means of coercion. This connotes the right to make laws and to enforce such laws with force if necessary. External sovereignty is based on recognition by other states and participation as a sovereign state in the international system. Though sovereignty retains a powerful image in domestic and international politics, it has been subject to erosion, transfer, and pooling. The EUROPEAN UNION has had substantive and specific effects on state sovereignty in Europe. In the European Union, legal sovereignty has been transferred to a European system of law and judicial review that is independent of, though not separate from, national legal orders. All member-states have two constitutions: the national CONSTITUTION and the EU constitution, in the form of treaties. In addition, political sovereignty has been shared in Europe. All the member-state governments and public administrations are embedded in a system of public policy-making that produces policies and programmes that affect the lives of all citizens. Popular sovereignty, exercised through elections, remains predominantly national. **Brigid Laffan**

space exploration. Ireland's first involvement in space SCIENCE occurred in the early 1970s, when a co-operative experiment was carried out with the National Aeronautics and Space Administration (United States) to expose solid-state nuclear track detectors on the Moon during the *Apollo 16* and *17* missions. This resulted in the first measurements of heavy cosmic ray nuclei made outside the Earth's magnetosphere. The first Irish experiment selected in 1980 for launch by the European Space Agency was the EPONA INSTRUMENT for the Giotto mission to Comet P/Halley and subsequently to another, older comet, Grigg Skjellerup. The two sets of data provide significant insights into how atomic nuclei can be accelerated to unexpectedly high energies in cometary environments.

In 1984, in co-operation with the European Space Research and Technology Centre in the Netherlands, Irish scientists launched a large array of nuclear detectors on NASA's Long-Duration Exposure Facility. This was deployed in Earth orbit by the *Space Shuttle* and collected a statistically significant sample of cosmic actinides. In 1988 the Russian Space Agency launched the first Irish experiment to fly on a Russian spacecraft, the *Phobos* mission to Mars and its moons. The instrument, called SLED, measured energetic particles in a range that had never previously been investigated at Mars.

The SOHO mission, designed to study the Sun, was launched by the European Space Agency in 1995. The Irish instrument on board, called LION, continuously monitors solar activity. This data provides insights into such topics as the early formation of the Solar System and the nature of space weather.

Cluster II is a constellation of four spacecraft flying in orbital configurations that allow different regimes of the close Earth environment to be studied in three dimensions. On board each of these spacecraft is the imaging energetic particle spectrometer (RAPID), part of the hardware and software for which was designed in Ireland. Ireland also contributed to the design and construction of the WAVES instrument flown on board NASA's WIND spacecraft. A further instrument developed in Ireland for China's *Double Star* mission consists of two spacecraft designed to support the Cluster observations, called the Neutral Atom Detector Unit (NUADU).

In the space agencies of the world there is now an increased interest in designing missions to study the basic laws of physics. The first of these, a NASA spacecraft *Gravity Probe B* (also called the Relativity Mission), is designed to test two important predictions of Einstein's general theory of relativity. An Irish instrument is designed to monitor the influence of ambient high-energy particles and thereby allow successful realisation of the objectives of the mission. Ireland is also a participant in the European Space Agency's *Rosetta* mission, which (after an eight-and-a-half-year journey that attained a maximum distance from the Sun of about 800 million kilometres) will, after some reconnaissance, land a fully instrumented scientific laboratory, LANDER, on the nucleus of comet Wirtanen in 2012. Material drilled out from a depth of about 20 cm (8 in.) below the surface of the comet's nucleus will be analysed on board the LANDER by the Cometary Sampling and Composition Experiment (COSAC), in which Ireland participates. This experiment is designed to detect the presence, among other chemical signatures, of the pre-biotic building-blocks of life. Mission-critical instruments designed and built in Ireland for the *Rosetta* mission, the electrical support system (ESS), will be used to accomplish the release and push-off of the LANDER. The ESS will also perform the critical tasks of handling the command streams to, and the data streams from, the international instruments operating on the nucleus of the comet. **Susan McKenna-Lawlor**

Spain and Ireland (1200–1700). Ireland had established trading links with northern Spanish ports from the Middle Ages, and Irish communities were established in Spanish territories, particularly Galicia in north-west Spain and the Spanish Netherlands. From the sixteenth century the Irish enjoyed the same rights as Spaniards in obtaining political and military appointments: they acquired properties in Spanish territories, and Irish officers were admitted into the sacred ranks of the military orders of Santiago, Alcántara, and Calatrava. Thousands of Irishmen found employment with the armies of Spain. Following the collapse of the Confederate army, 22,531 Irish soldiers emigrated to Spain between 1641 and 1654.

In the sixteenth and early seventeenth centuries there were close cultural and political ties between Ireland and Spain. Under Philip II, Spain regarded itself as the defender of the COUNTER-REFORMATION in Europe, and successive Irish nobles, both native Irish and Anglo-Irish, appealed to Spain for military help against the encroachment of English political authority. Spain offered asylum to Catholic recusants and political exiles from Ireland as well as England and Scotland. Factions emerged as Ulstermen, Munstermen, OLD ENGLISH, and native Irish sought support for their own causes. The spirit of Catholic reform in Spain prompted the growth of Catholic schools and colleges, such as that at SALAMANCA, which were attended by many Irish men and women up to the eighteenth century. The political links between Ireland and Spain declined with the emergence of French hegemony in Europe. **Gráinne Henry**

Spanish Armada. Philip II of Spain sent a great *armada* or fleet of 130 warships to England in May 1588, hoping to depose the Protestant ELIZABETH I and restore the Catholic Church there. The Armada's commander, the Duke of Medina-Sidonia, was directed to sail to the Spanish Netherlands and take on board a Spanish army for the invasion. Using an ingenious crescent formation to defend itself, the Armada succeeded in sailing up the English Channel, despite the best efforts of the English fleet, under the command of Lord Howard of Effingham. On 27 July the Armada docked at Calais. However, by sending eight fire-ships into the harbour, Howard forced the Spanish ships to leave Calais precipitately and in disorder. Wracked by storms and unable to restore the crescent formation, the Armada was obliged to abandon its mission and head for home by a hazardous route around the north of Scotland and west of Ireland, However, Atlantic storms caused more than twenty-five ships to founder on the north and west coast of Ireland. Thousands of Spaniards lost their lives, though some 3,000 were succoured by Irish lords in Ulster and north Connacht. Material excavated from the wrecks of some Armada ships is on display in the ULSTER MUSEUM, Belfast (see p. 956). [see SHIPWRECKS.] **Henry A. Jefferies**

Spanish Civil War. The Spanish Civil War (1936–9) was fought between supporters of the Second Republic, mainly secularists, communists, and Catalan and Basque nationalists, and their 'nationalist' opponents, mainly royalists, Carlists, conservatives, and the sub-fascist Falange—a typically post-French Revolution set of opposites. Irish opinion, strongly Catholic, favoured the nationalists; the Government was officially neutral. In 1934 EOIN O'DUFFY led a party of some 600 former BLUESHIRTS to support the nationalist cause, though they saw no action. Some 200 socialists and left-wing republicans formed the Connolly Column, led by Frank Ryan, which fought as part of the International Brigade. They distinguished themselves at the Battle of Jarama (February 1937), where their casualties included the poet CHARLES DONNELLY. [see BLUESHIRTS; MILNE, EWART.] **Fergal Tobin**

Spearman, David (1937–), mathematician. Born in Dublin; educated at TCD, graduating in mathematics and experimental science in 1958 and in 1961 awarded a doctorate by the University of Cambridge for a thesis on problems in pion physics. Following positions at University College, London, the Conseil Européen pour la Recherche Nucléaire (CERN), Geneva, and the Universities of Illinois and Durham, he was appointed university professor of natural philosophy in Trinity College, Dublin, in 1966. There he led research in theoretical elementary particle physics and served as vice-provost, 1991–7. He has also written on many of the principal Irish mathematicians and physicists. He became the fiftieth president of the ROYAL IRISH ACADEMY in 1999. **Christopher Moriarty**

Special Criminal Court, provided for under article 38 of the CONSTITUTION OF IRELAND and established under part V of the Offences Against the State Act (1939) to deal with seditious and terrorist crimes. It generally comprises one District Court judge, one Circuit Court judge and one High Court judge. The Director of Public Prosecutions has the power to transfer a case to the Special Criminal Court when he feels that the ordinary courts will not secure the effective administration of justice and where this is necessary for the preservation of public peace and order. This occurred notably in the prosecution of those accused of complicity in the murder of the journalist VERONICA GUERIN in 1996. The operation of this court has been criticised as representing a limitation on human rights; it is the only court in Ireland that sits without a jury. The present Special Criminal Court was established in 1972. [see 'DIPLOCK COURTS'.] **Neville Cox**

Speed, John (1552–1629), historian and cartographer. Born in Cheshire; he worked as a tailor in London before turning in middle age to the practice of history and cartography, as exemplified in his atlas, *The Theatre of the Empire of Great Britaine* (1611–12). With Ireland newly conquered and Scotland now sharing a monarchy with England, Speed's aim was to map the whole of JAMES I's dominions. For England and Wales he adapted the county maps of earlier surveyors and for Scotland a compilation by the Flemish cartographer GERARD MERCATOR. Ireland was represented by one national map and four provincial maps, all of them based mainly on previously unpublished data that included surveys of the southern provinces by ROBERT LYTHE and of central and eastern Ulster by Francis Jobson. Part of Speed's scheme in the *Theatre* was for each regional map to include one or more large-scale inset plans of important towns; in Ireland he chose Dublin, Cork, Limerick, and Galway, the first of which he claimed to have surveyed himself. **J. H. Andrews**

Spire, the. Dublin. Following the destruction in 1966 of NELSON PILLAR which had been, since 1808, the principal monument of O'Connell St, Dublin, considerable public discussion took place on the merits of a replacement, and what form such a monument might take. Two open competitions were held, the Pillar Project in 1988, the outcome of which was inconclusive, and a second competition in 1998. The winning submission in the latter, by English architect Ian Ritchie and called the Spire, is a 120 m stainless steel cone (3 m at base, 0.15 cm at the top) the upper twelve meters of which is illuminated. It was erected in 2003 by Dublin City Council on the site of the 40.2 m Nelson Pillar and is the sole monument on the street without political, historical, or ideological associations. **Brian Lalor**

speleology, the scientific exploration and study of caves. Caves are mainly developed in Carboniferous limestone, particularly in Cos. Cavan, Clare, Fermanagh, Kerry, Leitrim, and Sligo, though caves in older limestones in Cos. Donegal and Dublin are known. They are formed through the solution of the limestone by slightly acid water passing through fractures. Many caves in the BURREN developed since the Ice Age ended 12,000 years ago. However, radiometric dating of stalactites in other caves shows that many are more ancient, the oldest surveyed being more than 350,000 years old.

Caves contain a range of depositional features, including sediments, stalagmites, and stalactites. Exploration sponsored by the ROYAL IRISH ACADEMY in the nineteenth century discovered interesting fossils of extinct bears, hyenas, mammoths, and other animals; recent analysis of these has yielded scientifically important data regarding the animal colonisation of Ireland after the Ice Age. Modern study of Irish caves began in the 1930s, conducted by groups from Bristol University, and continues to the present day through the Speleological Union of Ireland. Hundreds of caves have been surveyed, and new ones are still being found. The longest cave system, Pollnagollum-Pollelva in Co. Clare, is approximately 14 km ($8\frac{1}{2}$ miles) in extent. [see STELFOX, ARTHUR.] **Patrick N. Wyse Jackson**

Spenser, Edmund (1552–1599), poet, colonist, and Elizabethan official. Born in London; attended Merchant Taylors' Grammar School and Pembroke Hall, Cambridge, as a scholarship boy. He wrote 'THE FAERIE QUEENE' (1596), sonnets, and pastoral and philosophical poems. Appointed secretary to Lord LEONARD GREY, Lord Deputy of Ireland, he accompanied him on many military expeditions, witnessing the massacre of Papal forces at SMERWICK, Co. Kerry (1580). He supported Grey's draconian approach and was granted 1,200 ha (3,000 acres) at Kilcolman, Co. Cork, in the PLANTATION OF MUNSTER (see p. 124). He held administrative posts, acquiring wealth and the rank of 'gentleman', and enjoyed the friendship of WALTER RALEIGH. ELIZABETH I's favourable reception of *The Faerie Queene* brought Spenser recognition as the age's finest poet. His harsh tract *A View of the Present State of Ireland* (1596) eloquently exemplifies Elizabethan attitudes to Ireland, expressing

Spanish Civil War. *Frank Ryan (second from left) with members of the International Brigade which fought in the Spanish Civil War. [Michael McInerney/RTÉ Stills Library; 0219/092]*

hostility to Irish culture and society and disapproval of the Norman English, now assimilated in that society. When HUGH O'NEILL's rebellion overwhelmed Munster, Spenser's house was burnt and he fled to Cork, then to London, where he died. **Patricia Coughlan**

Speranza: see WILDE, LADY JANE.

Spillane, Patrick (Pat) (1955–), Gaelic footballer. Born in Co. Kerry. He won nine All-Star awards during a career that lasted from 1975 to 1991. One of the most dedicated footballers in history, he overcame a career-threatening knee injury at the start of the 1980s to add three all-Ireland medals to the five already won, before injury struck again. He shares the record of eight medals with four of his team-mates from the great Kerry team of that era: Páidí Ó Sé, Ger Power, Denis 'Ogie' Moran, and MIKEY SHEEHY. **Donal Keenan**

sports and games outside Ireland. Sport has been one of the crucial social and cultural forms that assisted in the creation of modern Australia. The British, as the majority, and the Irish, as the largest minority, had vital roles in this process; the tension between these groups became the most dynamic inter-immigrant relationship in this development and prevented Australia from emerging as a solely British-oriented society. The system of Catholic schooling, dominated by the Irish, has been one of the most important vehicles for the promotion of sport and has ensured a significant cultural contribution to the character, nature, and status of sport in Australia. Contrary to popular belief, Australian rules football is not a direct descendant of GAELIC FOOTBALL, though both developed in sporting rebellion against the domination of British cultural influences; but the game in Australia has proved attractive to aspects of the Irish character, and its similarities with the Irish version are noteworthy. This was explicitly recognised with the famous Australia v. Meath football challenges of 1967–8, an attempt to give both games an international dimension. By the late 1990s a compromise form of rules for touring Australian and Irish international teams proved popular among adherents of both codes.

Irish immigrants have traditionally taken to BOXING, both as participants and as spectators. Les Darcy, during his short reign in Australia, and the American champions John L. Sullivan and 'Gentleman' Jim Corbett, among many, helped build self-esteem among Irish immigrant communities. Dan O'Mahony of Ballydehob, Co. Cork, emigrated to the United States, where he won the world

sports and games. *Supporters of Glasgow Celtic Football Club throng the stadium at Celtic Park, Glasgow, festooned in the club colours of green and white, reflecting the Irish roots of the club, founded in 1888 by an Irish monk, Brother Walfred. [First Press Publishing]*

heavyweight wrestling championship in 1934, one of his throwing styles becoming known as the 'Irish whip'. In Britain, Irish names have long been predominant among those who have held British and world boxing titles, one of the most famous in the 1930s being Benny Lynch, born in Glasgow of Co. Donegal parents, another in the 1990s being Pat Clinton, originating from the uniquely Irish diaspora village of Croy, near Coatbridge, outside Glasgow, also a member of the Irish community in Scotland.

In the United States, Irish immigrants and their offspring have made an impact on baseball, the national game. In the nineteenth century most players were of British, German, or Irish origin. Baseball was a popular sport in the north-eastern cities where Irish immigrants settled, and many second-generation Irish played, usually on teams sponsored by saloons or political clubs, thus displaying a capacity to integrate into indigenous culture while maintaining a sense of Irishness. Early in the twentieth century Irish immigrants had such an impact on baseball that eleven of the sixteen management posts in the American and National Leagues of 1915 were filled by Irish people.

The GAELIC ATHLETIC ASSOCIATION has been important to many late nineteenth and twentieth-century Irish immigrants. Gaelic sports have experienced a measure of success in many of the countries where Irish emigrants have settled, with the United States, Canada, Australia, England, and Scotland witnessing the greatest success stories of Gaelic football. In London, MICHAEL COLLINS and Sam Maguire both involved themselves with local GAA clubs early in the twentieth century (see p. 421). Today organised Gaelic football competitions in these countries, as well as teams developing in a number of Continental countries, reflect the wish of immigrants to maintain important aspects of their identity beyond Ireland. HURLING too has been one of the GAA sports that has been part of the heritage of Ireland's emigrants, and it can record sustained or temporary histories all over Britain, on the eastern seaboard of the United States, in Australia, New Zealand, South Africa, and Argentina.

Though not adhering to specifically Irish sporting pursuits, the Irish contribution to the American basketball club Boston Celtics is widely recognised, as is that of the 'Fighting Irish' football club of the University of Notre Dame, Indiana, in the National Collegiate Athletic Association.

Despite such broadly Irish achievements, the Irish who emigrated to the west of Scotland possibly created in the late nineteenth century the most enduring and successful of Irish immigrant sporting communities. Celtic Football Club was founded to help feed poor Irish immigrants in the east end of Glasgow, to help them raise their self-esteem, and to help a despised minority integrate into Scottish society and to maintain a national and cultural focus. By the 1960s and 70s Celtic had become one of the greatest teams in world football and by the twenty-first century was regularly attracting crowds of 60,000. As one of the most outstanding institutions of the Irish sporting diaspora, Irishness is celebrated and can be witnessed today at Celtic matches through the songs, colours, and flags of its army of supporters. **Joseph M. Bradley**

sports journalism, an increasingly important element in print as well as broadcast media. By the beginning of the twentieth century sport already accounted for approximately 4 per cent of editorial space; by the beginning of the twenty-first century the average was approximately 20 per cent. In the 1930s the fledgling IRISH PRESS made sports reporting, most notably of Gaelic games, a pronounced feature. Since the 1960s and the rise of television, print coverage of sports events has added background features, columns, colour writing and analysis to sports news and match reports. Notable sports writers include Con Houlihan, whose thrice-weekly back-page column in the *Evening Press* became an institution in 1970s journalism; the former Republic of Ireland international soccer player EAMON DUNPHY, whose insider knowledge and pugnacious writing have featured in the *Sunday Tribune*, the *Sunday Independent*, and latterly the IRISH EXAMINER; Tom Humphries of the IRISH TIMES; David Walsh, now writing for the *Sunday Times*; and the former professional cyclist Paul Kimmage. The importance of sports journalism crosses the tabloid-broadsheet divide, but no sports-only newspaper has yet succeeded. The *Title* (1996), Ireland's first weekly sports paper, merged with *Ireland on Sunday* when the latter was launched in 1997. **Eddie Holt**

SPOT satellite image of Dublin, a picture taken from 822 km (510 miles) above the Earth. Each pixel is equivalent to 20 m (65 ft) on the ground. The image, which uses 'false colours' to differentiate land use, shows how geography has been important to the city's development. From early times, four important trade routes focused on the LIFFEY ford (Áth Cliath), close to which a monastic settlement developed. In the early ninth century the VIKINGS used the river to establish a raiding base; a century later they founded the city on high ground on the south bank, near the 'black pool' (Dubhlinn) where they berthed their boats.

The mountains to the south shelter the city from the prevailing winds but can also on occasion facilitate the development of stagnant air over the city, concentrating air pollution. Expansion to the north is limited by the airport (whose runways can be clearly seen), as a development-free corridor is required for safety reasons, though suburban development has jumped this barrier to such places as Swords, Malahide, and Portmarnock. Dublin is constrained, therefore, to expand to the west, a strategy adopted in 1967, when, following the Wright Report, it was decided to build three 'new towns' in Blanchardstown, Clondalkin, and Malahide.

Trade has always been an important activity, and the extensive docks, mainly on the north bank, are clearly visible. Much of this land was reclaimed in the twentieth century as the port moved eastwards from the river banks. The suburbanisation of industry and changing shipping technology left a great deal of derelict land in the docklands, but under the Dublin Docklands Authority there has been extensive commercial and residential development in recent years. The bay is prone to silting, and constant efforts are required to maintain the shipping channel. The South Wall was built in the eighteenth century, followed by the Great North Wall on the north side, completed in 1825. These BULL WALLS created a tidal scour that helped keep the channel clear as well as facilitating the rapid development of NORTH BULL ISLAND. Dún Laoghaire harbour was developed in its present form in the nineteenth century to provide a safe alternative to Dublin in bad weather.

The built-up area is largely a twentieth-century creation; more than 85 per cent of housing in Dublin dates from after 1919. It is generally a low-density city, and this changes little from centre to suburbs. The river is an important social divide, with the south-eastern sector most favoured by the better off. The north city, especially Sackville Mall (O'Connell Street), was once the most fashionable area, but by the end of the eighteenth century fashion had turned towards the south-eastern city; the townships of Pembroke and Rathmines-Rathgar, which were middle-class in composition, continued this southward trend. The high status of this sector was maintained during the twentieth century, while local authority housing to the west and south-west established a west-east social gradient. North of the Liffey, for a variety of historical reasons, the social map is more fragmented, but the coastal areas, especially Howth, are among the most desired locations. **Joseph Brady**

Spratt, Geoffrey (1950–), lecturer and conductor. Born in London; educated at the University of Bristol and joined the staff of UCC as lecturer in 1976, where he founded the university choir and orchestra. He conducts the Irish Youth Choir, which he founded in 1982, and was director of the CORK INTERNATINAL CHORAL AND DANCE FESTIVAL, 1987–93. He became director of the CORK SCHOOL OF MUSIC in 1992 and has since held the position of chairman of Cork Orchestral Society. He is widely recognised for regular performances of Bach and Mozart with the Orchestra of St Cecilia. His publications include *Honegger* (1986) and *Music of Arthur Honegger* (1987), and he has made several choral recordings. **Adrian Scahill**

Spring, Richard (Dick) (1950–), politician. Born in Tralee, a son of Dan Spring TD; educated at TCD and KING'S INNS. Elected to Dáil Éireann for the LABOUR PARTY in 1981, he was appointed a junior minister on his first day and in 1982 succeeded Michael O'Leary as party leader. He inherited a divided party but one that was going into power with FINE GAEL. Tánaiste and Minister for the Environment, 1982–7, and Minister for Energy, 1983–7, he was closely involved in the NEW IRELAND FORUM (1984–5) and the ANGLO-IRISH AGREEMENT (1985). He defeated militant and anti-coalition tendencies in the Labour Party but withdrew the party from the coalition Government in 1987 over the budget. His choice of MARY ROBINSON as presidential candidate in 1990 was a coup. The Labour Party under his leadership won a record thirty-three seats in 1992, and Spring became Tánaiste in a Coalition Government with FIANNA FÁIL. He was Minister for Foreign Affairs, 1993–7, with an important contribution to the NORTHERN IRELAND PEACE PROCESS. He resigned as party leader in 1997 (see p. 27). **Tom Garvin**

Spring Rice, Mary Ellen (1880–1924), nationalist. Born in Foynes, Co. Limerick, daughter of Lord Monteagle of Brandon.

SPOT. *Dublin Bay and hinterland recorded by the French* SPOT *satellite in 1969, showing urban growth and natural geographical features [ERA Maptec]*

She was active in the GAELIC LEAGUE and a friend of its founder, DOUGLAS HYDE, campaigning for Irish to be taught in national schools in her area. She supported the IRISH VOLUNTEERS and in 1914 accompanied ERSKINE CHILDERS on the gun-running voyage of the ASGARD, helping to arrange the unloading of the arms in Howth, Co. Dublin. **Brian Galvin**

SPUC: see SOCIETY FOR THE PROTECTION OF UNBORN CHILDREN.

squash. Irish Squash, the body responsible for the development and control of squash in Ireland, can trace its beginnings to 1935, when there were few courts and players. Squash reached its peak from the early 1970s to the mid-1980s. Recently there has been renewed growth, especially in schools and at over-age level. Many players have represented Ireland with distinction. Jonah Barrington won the British Open, then regarded as the unofficial world title, on six occasions between 1967 and 1973. Donald Pratt, Willie Hosey, and David Gotto, who holds the world record for the greatest number of international caps (122), have a fine record. Derek Ryan is a professional player on the world circuit and reached number 7 in 1999. Geraldine Barniville, Mary Byrne (world 16), and Rebecca Best (world 7) were also outstanding. Madeleine Perry has recently become a professional (world 33). Fitzwilliam Lawn Tennis Club has played a leading role in the development of the game, bringing the world's best players to the Irish Open throughout the 1970s. In 2000 the club rejuvenated the Irish Open, which became a world-ranking event for the first time and attracted all the leading players. **Tom Cantwell**

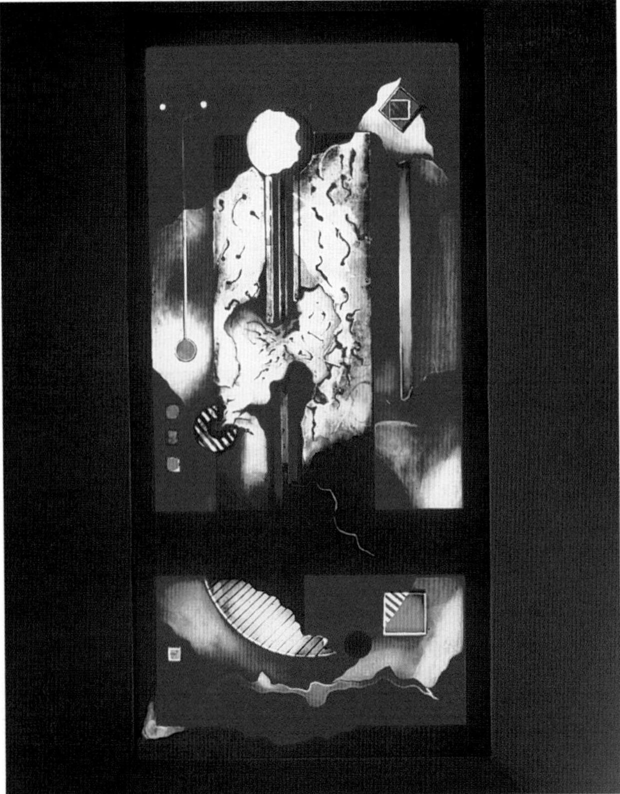

stained glass. Study No. 2 for Miro *(1985, 52 by 27 cm (20 by 11 in.)) by James Scanlon, an innovative piece comprising four layers of coloured and etched glass, in which the artist eschews the traditional practice of leading. [Hugh Lane Municipal Gallery of Modern Art; courtesy of the artist]*

Stack, Austin (1879–1929), republican and politician. Born in Tralee, Co. Kerry; educated by the Christian Brothers. Active in the GAA, he became a member of the IRB in 1908. Joining the IRISH VOLUNTEERS, he commanded the Kerry Brigade and was arrested for his role in the attempted arms landing by ROGER CASEMENT. He served as a member of the first Dáil Éireann and held various ministerial posts between 1919 and 1922. He fought against the ANGLO-IRISH TREATY, was captured, and in 1923 went on hunger strike. In 1926 he was a central figure in the founding of FIANNA FÁIL. **Seán Farrell Moran**

Stackallen House, Co. Meath, built c. 1712 or possibly earlier for Gustavus Hamilton, later first Viscount Boyne, a general in the army of WILLIAM III. Originally called Boyne House, it is a rare survival of a major classical country house from the early eighteenth century. Substantially seventeenth century in style, it is a sober three-storey L-shaped block with two adjoining pedimented fronts, of seven bays on the entrance façade and nine bays on the garden front. The verticality is offset by a pair of bold string courses and heavy entablature. The steep roof with projecting eaves is sprocketed. Internally, the dominant feature of the house is the great staircase, which rises to a landing with heavy figurative PLASTERWORK, displaying Hamilton's crest as a centrepiece. **Brian Lalor**

stage-Irishman, a derogatory stereotyping of Irish people, a character not confined to the stage, and not always a man. Such stereotyping of Irish people in literature goes back to GIRALDUS CAMBRENSIS, who in the twelfth century portrayed them as barbarians who should be colonised for their own good. Three centuries later, similar calumnies were promulgated for similar reasons in the Anglo-Saxon Chronicles. Thereafter the stereotype became more contemptuous than vicious. Irishmen were portrayed as boastful, drunken, and belligerent, speaking a grotesque parody of HIBERNO-ENGLISH. (Captain Macmorris in Shakespeare's *Henry V*: 'By Chrish law, 'tish ill done. The work ish give over, the trumpet sound the retreat. By my hand I swear, and my father's soul, the work ish ill done, it ish give over. I would have blowed up the town, so Chrish save me law, in an hour …')

Further characteristics were added in English plays of the seventeenth and eighteenth centuries, including a propensity to illogical statements known as 'Irish bulls' (perpetuated in the Irish jokes and cartoons beloved of *Punch* and similar journals). Even Irish playwrights, RICHARD BRINSLEY SHERIDAN among them, contributed to the caricature, though FARQUHAR and others subverted it with portraits of blundering Irishmen who nevertheless outwit cunning English rogues. Irish peasants proliferated in plays and fiction of the nineteenth century, usually as buffoons, like LOVER's Handy Andy and many of the characters in the stories of SOMERVILLE AND ROSS.

All this changed at the beginning of the twentieth century with the growth of the independence movement and the LITERARY REVIVAL, which led to serious research into Irish MYTHOLOGY and FOLKLORE, language, and literature. Rural Ireland tended to be idealised as an unspoiled pastoral world. Anything smacking of stage-Irishry was vilified, with the result that SYNGE's *Playboy of the Western World* (1907), unfashionably realistic in portraying the imperfections of the rural communities of Co. Mayo, at first caused riots in Dublin. The play is now regarded as a masterpiece; and the growth in national self-confidence has also brought a more relaxed attitude to the colonialist caricatures of the past. **John Wakeman**

Staigue, Co. Kerry, on the IVERAGH PENINSULA. Staigue Cashel is possibly a high-status settlement of the EARLY HISTORIC period. It consists of a roughly circular interior surrounded by a massive dry-stone rampart. Its entrance is on the south, while the interior of the rampart is marked by a terrace reached by several flights of steps, with further flights leading to the top of the wall. Two mural chambers are contained within the thickness of the rampart. Encircling the fort is a flat-bottomed fosse with external bank. [see RING-FORTS.] **Michelle Comber**

stained glass. So far, none of the stained-glass fragments, panels, or windows documented in Ireland indicate evidence of indigenous production before the eighteenth century. By then three of the leading glass-painters in England were Irish-born or Dublin-trained: Thomas Jervais, Richard Hand, and James Pearson, each of whom followed contemporary convention by translating painterly cartoons onto glass. This treatment continued into the nineteenth century, notably with George M'Allister and Michael O'Connor (who moved his thriving business to London in 1845); the fifty or so smaller glaziers faced strong competition from the large English and German workshops. In 1853 the collaboration of the influential English Gothic Revival architect A. W. N. PUGIN with John Hardman and Company in Birmingham led to the setting up of a church decorating depot in Dublin and, by 1864, the establishment of Earley and Powell, one of half a dozen competent stained-glass studios in Ireland. Their style was eclectic, proficient, and more or less reliant on depicting fashionable imagery as well as importing the raw materials of their craft.

Ireland is best known for its windows of unique quality and character produced during the early twentieth-century Celtic revival. These emulated Irish medieval architecture, sculpture, and metalwork and evoked ancient heroic myths and monastic legends while technically being inspired by European gothic stained glass and the prevailing English arts and crafts ideology expounded by Christopher Whall.

Between 1903 and 1955, taught first by Whall's disciple A. E. CHILD at the Metropolitan School of Art, Dublin, HARRY CLARKE, working from his family studio, and the artists based at AN TÚR GLOINE, the Dublin stained-glass co-operative, made outstanding panels and windows. WILHELMINA GEDDES, perhaps the most powerful exponent from AN TÚR GLOINE, moved to London in 1925, where she taught EVIE HONE, whose deeply religious, semi-abstract windows would inspire the next generation, notably Patrick Pollen and PATRICK PYE.

In the late 1970s MAUD COTTER and JAMES SCANLON, trained as sculptors in Cork, offered inventive three-dimensional forms and fresh approaches based on an understanding of tradition, while in the 1980s Peter Young made miniature narrative windows using fused techniques. Donna Coogan is among those who have since developed this approach in small, symbolic panels. **Nicola Gordon Bowe**

standing stones. Next to RING-FORTS and BURNT MOUNDS, standing stones are probably the most numerous type of monument in Ireland, with particular concentrations in the south-west (where they are called *galláin*) and north (called *dalláin*), areas rich in other megalithic monuments. Among the most spectacular are the great granite pillars in Co. Kildare (such as Punchestown and Longstone). Standing stones served many and varied functions through the ages: as prehistoric burial markers, commemorative monuments, and indicators of routes or boundaries. Others may be the sole survivor of more elaborate monuments, for example STONE CIRCLES, STONE ALIGNMENTS, or MEGALITHIC TOMBS. Not all are ancient: some were erected as scratching-posts for cattle. **Paul Walsh**

Stanford. *Sir Charles Villiers Stanford, composer and teacher, c. 1900. He wrote music in many genres, including a substantial body of organ and choral music. [Getty Pictures/Hulton Archive]*

Standún, Pádraig (1946–), priest and novelist. Born near Castlebar, Co. Mayo. While an understanding of cultural and economic issues affecting disadvantaged Irish-speaking districts underlies much of his work, he is best known for his fictional exploration of problems of an ethical nature. His popular first novel *Súil le Breith* (1983)—the subject of the film *Bodawanny* by BOB QUINN—anticipated much subsequent debate on the issue of CLERICAL CELIBACY; later works deal either in a disturbingly realist or a tragi-comic manner with such problems as domestic violence and rural disintegration. **Máirín Nic Eoin**

Stanford, Sir Charles Villiers (1852–1924), composer and teacher. Born in Dublin; educated at Henry Tilney Bassett's school. Though intended for the legal profession, he became a choral scholar at Queen's College, Cambridge, in 1870, and had the distinction of becoming organist of Trinity College, Cambridge, in 1873 while still an undergraduate. He studied in Leipzig and Berlin while on periods of leave from Trinity. In 1883 he became professor of composition and orchestral playing at the newly opened Royal College of Music, London, and was elected professor of music at Cambridge in 1887, holding both posts until his death. Stanford was prolific in all musical forms, which include *Festival Overture* and *The Veiled Prophet of Khorassan* (1877), settings of Irish poems, *An Irish Idyll* (1901) and *Cushendall* (1910). His treatment of traditional melodies has received sharp criticism; only his CHURCH MUSIC,

CHORAL MUSIC, and songs have maintained their position in the repertory. His lasting achievement was as a teacher of composition: the revival of composition in twentieth-century Britain owed much to his tuition. **Adrian Scahill**

Stanihurst, Richard (1547–1618), physician and writer. Born in Dublin, son of the Speaker of the Irish Parliament; educated at the University of Oxford and at Lincoln's Inn, London. In 1570 he returned to Dublin with Edmund Campion, his mentor, inspirer, and friend. After Campion's execution he moved to the Netherlands. He became adviser to Spanish policy-makers in Brussels and Madrid. Renowned as a physician, he practised alchemy with the Earl of Kildare and later in El Escorial, Spain, 1591–5. His ever-changing views moved his ideal from an Anglo-Norman expansion of the PALE, through cultural development of Gaelic Ireland, to a Spanish-supported unified Catholic Ireland. He was a supporter of the Spanish succession in England and of the Continental IRISH COLLEGES. From 1595 he was O'Neill's agent in Brussels. He took holy orders in 1602. After O'Neill's defeat he retired to scholarly and spiritual activities. He corresponded with leading humanists throughout Europe, including his nephew, JAMES USSHER. A very prolific author, he published *Harmonia* (1570), an early work on Porphyry's philosophy; 'Description of Ireland' (in Holinshed's *Chronicles*, 1577); a translation of Virgil's *Aeneid* into English hexameters (1582); *De Rebus in Hibernia Gestis* (1584) on Ireland's past; *De Vita Sancti Patricii* (1587); some devotional works; and *Brevis Praemunitio pro Futura Concertatione cum Jacobo Usserio* (1615), an answer to his nephew's attacks on the papacy. **Juan José Pérez-Camacho**

Stapleton, Michael (c. 1740–1801), master-builder and stuccodore. First mentioned in 1774, he appears in Dublin directories from 1776 onwards. He ran a workshop renowned for its neo-classical PLASTERWORK; a friend (and executor) of ROBERT WEST, he was a Catholic and therefore not a guild member. A large collection of his drawings and engravings survive (now in the NATIONAL LIBRARY OF IRELAND). These suggest that he designed some of the stucco compositions but also relied on the published works of Robert and James Adam, George Richardson, Joseph Rose, and Stuart and Revett. It is known that he worked with Thomas Penrose, who was one of JAMES WYATT's Irish architectural agents. He is associated with the stuccowork in Belvedere House, Great Denmark Street, Dublin (1778–80), Lucan House (1774–6), and Mount Kennedy House (1782–4). In each of these the handling of the neo-classical plasterwork suggests a variety of hands and his mixed range of sources. **Christopher Moore**

Stardust disaster (1981), a fire that claimed the lives of forty-eight people. On the night of 13/14 February 1981 the Stardust nightclub at Kilmore Road, Artane, Dublin, was full of young people enjoying a St Valentine's night disco. Two burning seats were discovered at 1:40 a.m. in a closed-off balcony area. An attempt to extinguish the fire failed, and it spread rapidly across the ceiling tiles and walls. A stampede ensued, and the venue filled rapidly with noxious fumes. Many of those trying to escape were confronted with locked fire exits and barred windows. In addition to those who died, more than 200 young people suffered from burns, smoke inhalation, and trauma. The Fire Services Act (1981), introduced as a consequence of the disaster, puts the onus for fire safety in a premises on the person having control over the premises, as well as designating each local authority a fire authority.

On 5 July 1982 a tribunal of inquiry concluded that the fire had probably been started deliberately. The owners of the Stardust were severely criticised, while Dublin City Council and the Department of the Environment were censured for failing to enforce fire safety regulations. **Ciarán Deane**

Starkie, Enid (1897–1970), academic. Born in Killiney, Co. Dublin, a sister of WALTER STARKIE; educated at home, at Alexandra College, Dublin, and the Universities of Paris and Oxford. She sacrificed her musical potential to pursue an academic career, being awarded a scholarship to Somerville College, where she became reader emeritus in French. She was challenging in attitude, behaviour, and dress; her refusal to conform to the role her upper-middle-class grooming and education had fitted her for is recorded in her autobiographical book, *A Lady's Child* (1941). Her academic output is notably biographical, revealing an interest in the canonical authors—thus, Flaubert—as well as the tormented and those who transgressed, such as Baudelaire, Gide, and Rimbaud. **Jacqueline A. Hurtley**

Starkie, Walter (1894–1976), academic and writer. Born in Ballybrack, Co. Dublin; educated at home, locally, and at Shrewsbury School, England. A promising violinist, he studied at the RIAM and graduated from the University of Dublin. He joined the Dominions and Colonial Office in London before working with the Young Men's Christian Association in Italy in 1919. Made a fellow of TCD in 1924, he occupied the chair of Spanish and lectured in Italian. He contributed to the *Irish Statesman* and made radio broadcasts, became active in the ROYAL DUBLIN SOCIETY, and was a director of the ABBEY THEATRE, 1927–42. He published on Benavente (1924) and Pirandello (1926) and was an established travel writer, with *Raggle-Taggle* (1933), *Spanish Raggle-Taggle* (1934), *Don Gypsy* (1936), *In Sara's Tents* (1953), and *The Road to Santiago* (1957). *The Waveless Plain* (1938) was partly autobiographical; *Scholars and Gypsies* (1963) covered his childhood and youth. He was the first representative of the British Council in Spain, 1940–54, and spent the latter part of his career teaching at a number of American universities. **Jacqueline A. Hurtley**

Stars of Heaven, rock group. Formed in the mid-1980s, the Stars of Heaven took as their blueprint American urban roots music. The band were vehemently unlike U2 in their approach to rock music: no rhetoric, no poses. Inevitably, there was more critical kudos than sales after they released two marvellous records, *Sacred Heart Hotel* (album, 1986) and *Before Holyhead* (mini-album, 1987). A compilation album, *Unfinished Dreaming* (1999), retrospectively demonstrated the band's many talents. The lead songwriter-singer, Stephen Ryan, went on to form the equally revered Revenants. **Tony Clayton-Lea**

state-sponsored bodies, defined in the Republic's administration as 'autonomous public bodies, other than universities, neither temporary in character nor purely advisory in function.' They may be statutory corporations deriving their authority directly from the statute used to create them, such as IARNRÓD ÉIREANN and the Electricity Supply Board; alternatively they may be set up as public or private companies where their establishment was envisaged by legislation but not directly provided for. Most of the staff of state-sponsored bodies come from outside the CIVIL SERVICE, though either the Government or a Government minister is responsible for appointing directors or council members to their executive boards. **Maura Adshead**

Statistical and Social Inquiry Society of Ireland, founded in 1847 to encourage the scientific study of Ireland's economic and social environment, using the most modern analytical techniques available, both by theoreticians and by policy-makers. Through its journal and proceedings it quickly became, and remains, a respected forum for specialist debate on development issues, providing a link between the academic and administrative worlds. **Eunan O'Halpin**

Status of Women, Commission on the. The first Commission on the Status of Women, established in 1970 by the Taoiseach, Liam Cosgrave, and chaired by Dr Thekla Beere, was required 'to make recommendations on the steps necessary to ensure the participation of women on equal terms and conditions with men in the political, social, cultural and economic life of the country.' Among its recommendations, published in 1972, were the abolition of the 'MARRIAGE BAR', which prevented women in the public service remaining in employment on marriage, and the awarding of equal pay for work of equal value, which became law through the Equal Pay Act (1974).

The second Commission on the Status of Women, established in 1990 by the Taoiseach, CHARLES HAUGHEY, and chaired by Ms Justice Mella Carroll, examined the progress made since the first commission and found that women continued to earn 70 per cent of male rates of pay, despite the Equal Pay Act. However, the significant social changes that had taken place since the report of the first commission were reflected in the recommendations of the second: a referendum on DIVORCE and ABORTION legislation, an improvement in supports for child care, and the implementation of separate tax assessment for married couples. **Alison Walsh**

Staveley, Colin (1942–), violinist. Born in Dublin, studied at the RIAM, and was a member of the EEC Youth Orchestra and leader of the UK National Youth Orchestra in 1959. He was co-leader of the Royal Philharmonic Orchestra and leader of the BBC Welsh Symphony before returning to Dublin as leader of the RTÉSO 1974–79. He resigned to pursue a freelance career in the UK. **Richard Pine**

steam engines. Advances in engineering research in England during the seventeenth and eighteenth centuries led to Thomas Newcomen's atmospheric steam engine (1712), which set the scene for a technology that developed over the next two centuries. With James Watt's separate condenser (1769) the use of expanding steam and rotary motion meant that steam engines became the prime movers of the industrial revolution. Richard Trevithick pioneered the use of high-pressure steam, and the locomotive age became a reality.

In Ireland the first such 'fire engine' was erected at Castlecomer Collieries, Co. Kilkenny, in 1740. The DUBLIN AND KINGSTOWN RAILWAY (1834) was one of the world's earliest passenger lines. CHARLES PARSONS of Birr, Co. Offaly, constructed the world's first steam turbo-generator in 1884. A few nineteenth-century stationary engines survive in Ireland; good examples can be seen at Midleton Distillery, Co. Cork, the Straffan Steam Museum, Co. Kildare, and the ULSTER MUSEUM, Belfast. Trevithick's 'third model' (1797) can be seen at Straffan. Parsons' 1884 turbine is in TRINITY COLLEGE, Dublin.

There have been several manufacturers of steam engines in Ireland. Notable were the LOCOMOTIVE works of the Great Southern Railway (Inchicore, Dublin), Midland Great Western Railway (Broadstone, Dublin), and Great Northern Railway (Dundalk). The north of Ireland was well represented by the marine engine works at HARLAND AND WOLFF and the mill engine makers Victor Coates, both in Belfast. The *Queen Maeve*, an express passenger locomotive built at Broadstone, now at the ULSTER FOLK AND TRANSPORT MUSEUM, and a 'house-built' beam engine by Victor Coates, now at the School of Engineering, UCD, are two fine surviving examples. **William Dick**

Steelboys: see HEARTS OF STEEL.

Steele, Sir Richard (1672–1729), playwright. Born in Dublin; educated at the University of Oxford but took no degree. At school he met Joseph Addison and was to work with him throughout his career. He edited the *Gazette*, 1707–10, then founded the *Tatler*, 1709–11, in which Addison and SWIFT appeared. He later founded the *Spectator* (with Addison), 1711–12, and then the *Guardian*, 1713. His first book, *The Christian Hero* (1701), led to three successful stage farces—*The Funeral* (1702), *The Lying Lover* (1704), and *The Tender Husband* (1705)—but he is best known for his comedy *The Conscious Lovers* (1723). **Joley Wood**

Stein, Amelia (1958–), photographer. Born in Dublin; educated at the Dublin Institute of Technology, where she qualified as an ophthalmic optician. Best known for her work in theatre and the music industry, she was photographer in residence at the National Theatre (ABBEY and Peacock), 1994–5, and has also worked with Druid Theatre Company, Rough Magic Theatre Company, Project Arts Centre, WEXFORD FESTIVAL OPERA, and Dublin Theatre Festival, as well as the National Theatre and Royal Shakespeare Company in London (see pp. 674, 800). Her music industry work includes album covers and portraits for Elvis Costello, the CRANBERRIES, and DOLORES KEANE. More personal projects include Triúr Ban (1986), an exhibition and publication in collaboration with the poet NUALA NÍ DHOMHNAILL and the dancer-choreographer Cindy Cummings; In Living Memory (1989), an exhibition and publication, with poems by FRANK MCGUINNESS; and Palm House (2001), a collection of images from the BOTANIC GARDENS in Dublin. She has exhibited both nationally (Rubicon Gallery, Gallery of Photography) and internationally (Open Eye Gallery, Liverpool; Jerusalem Theatre, Israel). **John Minihan**

Stelfox, Arthur Wilson (1883–1972), naturalist. Born in Belfast; educated at Campbell College, Belfast, trained as an architect, and obtained associateship of the Royal Institution of British Architects in 1909, but practised little. He worked in the natural history division, NATIONAL MUSEUM OF IRELAND, from 1920 to 1948. A member of the ROYAL IRISH ACADEMY (1919) and honorary fellow of the Linnean Society (1947), he refused offers of honorary degrees. He undertook major studies on non-marine molluscs of Britain and Ireland, on bees, wasps, ants, and sawflies, together with work on the identification of bone fragments in cave deposits. His main work was making a vast collection of parasitic hymenoptera, many new to science. Much of this collection is in the Smithsonian Institution in Washington. **Frank Winder**

Stelfox, Dawson (1958–), mountaineer. Born in Belfast; educated at QUB. An architect by profession, Stelfox attributes his interest in the great outdoors to his grandfather, ARTHUR STELFOX. He began climbing in the Mourne Mountains with his father. He was part of the Northern Ireland expedition to Iran in 1977 and subsequently conquered many of the world's most important summits, in Europe, South America, and the Himalayas. In 1993 he led the first Irish expedition to Mount Everest and became the first Irishman to reach the summit. **Martin Clancy**

'Stella': see JOHNSON, ESTHER.

Stembridge, Gerry (1958–), director and writer. Born in Limerick. He is best known as a writer and director of comedy, especially in the 1980s for the satirical RTÉ radio show 'Scrap Saturday' and the television show 'Nighthawks'. He has also written numerous stage productions, including *Lovechild*, which won the Stewart Parker Award (1992), *Ceausescu's Ear* (1993), and *The Gay Detective* (1996). He made his feature film debut with *Guiltrip* (1995), a drama about domestic violence, while his second film, *About Adam* (2000), a popular success, depicted the seduction of three sisters by a mysterious stranger. His topical RTÉ television production *Bad Day at Blackrock* (2001) dealt with prejudice towards immigrants in a small town. **Kevin Rockett**

step-dancing. Competitive Irish step-dancing is taught primarily in schools under the auspices of AN COIMISIÚN LE RINCÍ GAELACHA. The teachers in these schools are required to pass a set of examinations under the headings of teaching, theory, music, and dancing. Candidates must be proficient dancers, must have a reasonable knowledge of traditional dance music, and are required to assimilate in detail the thirty group dances that form the canon of the commission's repertoire of dances published under the title *Ár Rincí Foirne*. Step-dancing teachers are also trained by Comhdháil na Múinteoirí Gaelacha. This division occurred in 1969 as a result of policy differences, largely concerned with the perceived under-representation of practising dancers on the commission's governing body.

Stevenson. *The composer Sir John Stevenson by George Joseph (1764–1846). A chorister in Christ Church Cathedral and later St Patrick's Cathedral, he wrote the piano accompaniment for Thomas Moore's* Irish Melodies. *[National Gallery of Ireland]*

The emphasis on competitive rather than social dancing is the *raison d'être* of the modern step-dancing schools. Dancers compete at one of four levels, depending on their ability and their performance in previous competitions. Adjudicators use a marking scheme under the headings timing, carriage, construction of steps, and execution. Classes in Irish step-dancing are now available in Britain, the United States, Canada, New Zealand, Australia, and South Africa. **Helen Brennan**

Stephens, James (1824–1901), nationalist. Born in Kilkenny; educated at St Kieran's College. A participant in the 1848 RISING, he was wounded at the Ballingarry affray, after which he fled to France. With THOMAS CLARKE LUBY he founded the IRISH REPUBLICAN BROTHERHOOD in Dublin in March 1858; he was arrested in November 1865 but escaped. Deposed as leader of the IRB in December 1866, he spent most of the next twenty-five years in France and the United States; he returned to Dublin in 1891 and died in Blackrock. **Brian Griffin**

Stephens, James (c. 1882–1950), novelist and poet. Born in Dublin; he spent the years 1886–96 as a boarder in the Meath Protestant Industrial School for Boys. He took up employment as a solicitor's clerk and was 'discovered' by GEORGE RUSSELL, who was impressed by Stephens's early pieces published in ARTHUR GRIFFITH's *Sinn Féin*. With Russell's encouragement he became a central figure of the LITERARY REVIVAL. The year 1912 marked a high point in his career with the publication of two of his most important novels, *The Charwoman's Daughter*, which dwells on the conditions of the Dublin tenements, and THE CROCK OF GOLD, an experimental and irreverent blend of fantasy, philosophical speculation, and acute social commentary that anticipates the fiction of JAMES JOYCE, EIMAR O'DUFFY, and FLANN O'BRIEN. During a two-year sojourn in Paris he published a realist collection of short stories, *Here Are Ladies* (1913), and a further prose fantasy, *The Demi-Gods* (1914). He accepted the post of registrar of the NATIONAL GALLERY, Dublin, in 1915. His journal of the 1916 RISING was published as *The Insurrection in Dublin* (1916). Later books, such as *Reincarnations* (1918), *Irish Fairy Tales* (1920) and *In the Land of Youth* (1924), bespeak a developing interest in the Irish language, myth and FOLKLORE, yet are marked by his own idiosyncratic style and interests. Poetry collections include *Insurrections* (1909), *Songs from the Clay* (1915), and *Kings and the Moon* (1938). In the 1930s he became a popular literary broadcaster for the BBC in London. **P. J. Mathews**

Stephenson, Sam (1933–), architect. Born in Dublin; studied at DIT. He established Stephenson Gibney Associates (with ARTHUR GIBNEY), Dublin, 1960, and Sam Stephenson Associates, Dublin, 1975. He designed the Irish pavilion at Expo 70, Osaka, Japan, and the company's own offices in Bride Street, Dublin. Controversial urban interventions included the ESB offices in Fitzwilliam Street, Dublin (1968, Stephenson Gibney), which entailed the demolition of a row of GEORGIAN houses, the CENTRAL BANK, Dame Street, Dublin (1976), and the Civic Offices, Wood Quay, Dublin (1982), all awarded through competition. He was awarded the RIAI Gold Medal, 1977–9, for the Currency Centre, Sandyford, Co. Dublin. Subsequent projects in Ireland and Britain exploit more historicist imagery. **Raymund Ryan**

Sterne, Laurence (1713–1768), novelist. Born in Clonmel, Co. Tipperary; Sterne, whose mother was Irish, spent only his childhood in Ireland, following the postings of his father, an army officer. For long an obscure Anglican clergyman in rural Yorkshire, Sterne achieved extraordinary celebrity with his comic masterpiece *The Life and Opinions of Tristram Shandy, Gentleman* (1759–67) and *A Sentimental Journey* (1768). Though his Irish connections appear slight, Sterne's influence has been felt by many Irish novelists, from Richard Griffith and HENRY BROOKE to FLANN O'BRIEN and SAMUEL BECKETT. JOYCE considered Sterne his 'fellow-countryman' and, attempting to describe *Work in Progress*, asked, 'Did you ever read Laurence Sterne?' **Ian Campbell Ross**

Stevenson, Sir John Andrew (1761–1833), composer. Born in Dublin, he was the first Irish-born choir-boy of CHRIST CHURCH CATHEDRAL (in contravention of the 1380 Statutes of Kilkenny). His musical life was centred around the cathedrals, both as chorister and vicar-choral of ST PATRICK'S CATHEDRAL, 1783–1823, and vicar-choral of Christ Church, 1800–23. In 1791 he received an honorary MusD from the University of Dublin. Predominantly a composer of vocal music, he received prizes for his glees and catches and composed several operas. He also composed theatrical and church music; but he is best remembered for his symphonies and his accompaniments to MOORE'S IRISH MELODIES. **Adrian Scahill**

Stewart, Louis (1944–), JAZZ musician. Born in Waterford. Self-taught, Stewart played for three years in showbands before turning exclusively to jazz. He was associated with JIM DOHERTY and NOEL KELEHAN, playing at the Fox Inn in Co. Meath in the late 1960s. At the Montreux festival in Switzerland in 1968 he was nominated outstanding European soloist, together with the British saxophonist Alan Skidmore. He quickly became, and has remained, Ireland's most highly rated jazz musician.

Despite claiming no ambitions to be a leader, Stewart has maintained trios or quartets that have often provided a training ground for younger musicians but have also featured long-time associates such as Peter Ainscough (drums) and Jim Doherty. He has formed strong musical associations with individual musicians and has recorded one or more albums with several of them, including the English bassist Peter Ind, the Scottish guitarist Martin Taylor, and the Norwegians Per Husby (piano) and Knut Mikalsen (guitar). An album recorded with Mikalsen's group, Good News (1986), received top rating from the influential American jazz magazine *Downbeat*. From the 1990s Stewart has frequently worked with the German guitarist and guitar-maker Heiner Franz, who has also reissued some earlier Louis Stewart releases. The first album in Stewart's own name was produced in 1975; later releases include *Out on His Own* (1977). The more recent albums feature Franz and Stewart in duets and quartet settings and include *I Wished on the Moon* (1999).

Stewart has an individual style, generally using a soft tone and developing long melodic lines. He draws on an extensive repertoire of material, mainly from the 1930s to 60s, but is also a composer, his own work being featured on *Milesian Sources* (1978). **Brian Trench**

Stewart, Robert, Viscount Castlereagh (1769–1822), politician. Born in Dublin, he spent his childhood on his father's estate, Mount Stewart, near Newtownards, Co. Down; educated at Armagh and the University of Cambridge. He became a member of Parliament for Co. Down in 1790, when he stood as an independent WHIG and reformer. He visited Paris in 1791 and saw the effects of the French Revolution; this may have influenced his decision to drop opposition politics and support the government, though his previous supporters sneered at him as the 'rising Robert'. His political career was boosted when Lord Camden, his step-uncle, became LORD LIEUTENANT in 1795, and in 1796 he was given the title Viscount Castlereagh. He was one of Camden's closest advisers during the crisis years before 1798 and was personally active as a county magistrate against the UNITED IRISHMEN.

Stewart, Louis. *Jazz musician and composer, Louis Stewart has been an influential figure in jazz music in Ireland; in 1988 he was awarded an honorary doctorate in music by the University of Dublin. [John Minihan]*

Castlereagh became CHIEF SECRETARY FOR IRELAND in 1798; his main and most famous role was to guide the proposed Union between Ireland and Britain through the Irish Parliament. At first he seriously underestimated the opposition, though the measure eventually passed in 1800, an event in which Castlereagh took great pride, not least because his strong parliamentary performances rebutted criticisms that he was a bad speaker with an aloof personality. He resigned when George III refused to allow CATHOLIC EMANCIPATION to follow the Union, but his abilities were recognised in London, and he held increasingly senior positions, culminating in his appointment as Foreign Secretary in 1812. His star reached its height in 1815, when he played a crucial role at the Congress of Vienna, which re-drew the map of Europe after the defeat of Napoleon Bonaparte.

Castlereagh was a complex, sensitive, and private man. In 1822 the burdens of work saw the return of an earlier mental breakdown, and he committed suicide by slitting his throat. **Allan Blackstock**

Stewart, Sir Robert Prescott (1825–1894), composer, conductor, and teacher. Born in Dublin, he was a chorister of

CHRIST CHURCH CATHEDRAL and became organist both there and at TCD, 1844, and later at ST PATRICK'S CATHEDRAL, 1852. Conductor of the Choral Society in Trinity, 1846, he received his MusB and MusD there in 1851, becoming professor of music in 1861. He also taught at the RIAM, becoming a professor in 1871. He conducted the Dublin Philharmonic Orchestra, 1873, and the Belfast Harmonic Society, 1877. His compositions (most of which he destroyed) include glees, CHURCH MUSIC, and ORGAN MUSIC. **Adrian Scahill**

Stickland, William (Billy) (1955–), photographer. Born in Dublin; educated at TCD. One of Ireland's best-known sports photographers, he was Irish Press Photographer of the Year in 1990 and won first prize in the sports section of the World Press Photography competition the same year. He has five times been awarded first prize by the Press Photographers' Association of Ireland. Publications include *Hoping for Heroes* (1998), on Irish sports people. He is the founder of the INPHO sports photographic agency. **Myra Dowling**

Stiff Little Fingers, punk-rock group. Formed in Belfast in 1977, the group came to prominence with the release of their debut single, 'Suspect Device' (1978). While other punk bands sang of anything other than politics, Stiff Little Fingers agitated the listener with polemics. To many the result was fiercely exciting punk rock music; to others it was manipulative and politically coercive. Their keynote song remains 'Alternative Ulster' (1978), a stirring example of Northern punk music. **Tony Clayton-Lea**

stoat, Irish, found only in Ireland and the Isle of Man. It differs from stoats elsewhere by usually having an irregular back-belly line. It is small in the north of Ireland and large in the south, showing a size cline. It eats rabbits, rodents, birds, and even fish. Though preferring woodland habitats, it will make dens in rat holes and rabbit burrows. **D. Patrick Sleeman**

Stock Exchange, Irish, Anglesea Street, established in Dublin in 1793. It provides markets for equities, Government and corporate bonds, and investment funds. The securities listed on the exchange are of six main types: domestic Irish equities, overseas equities, Government bonds, bonds or fixed-interest stocks issued by companies or local authorities, UCITS and investment funds, and specialist securities. The Irish Stock Exchange has three main markets: the Official List, which is the main market, the Developing Companies Market, and the Exploration Securities Market. The market in Government bonds is also regulated by the exchange. More than 1,450 securities are now traded by the exchange.

The Irish Stock Exchange is a limited company, with a board of eleven directors. The board comprises an independent chairperson, three co-opted directors representative of wider market interests, and seven directors elected by member-firms. **Jim Power**

stockings. The cottage industry in hand-knitted stockings is known from the late sixteenth century and gave EMPLOYMENT in rural Ireland into the early twentieth century. Machine-knit stockings became possible when Rev. William Lee of Nottinghamshire invented a frame for knitting stockings in 1589. London developed a monopoly in this industry; to break it, the Earl of Orrery introduced frame-knitting to Cork in 1682, and the Viceroy, the Earl of Tyrconnell, introduced it to Dublin in 1687. Irish hosiers were formed into a guild by a royal charter of 1688; other framework centres were established in Waterford and Balbriggan. To encourage the industry the Dublin Society granted premiums for inventions in this trade in the 1740s. The hosiery industry continued at Balbriggan until c. 1980. **Mairead Dunlevy**

Stoker, Abraham (Bram) (1847–1912), writer. Born in Dublin; educated at TCD. He worked as a civil servant before moving to London in 1879 as acting manager to the celebrated Shakespearean actor Henry Irving. While he published fiction from the early 1870s onwards, the novel for which he is now remembered, the popular supernatural thriller DRACULA, did not appear until 1897. His other novels include *The Snake's Pass* (1890), *The Mystery of the Sea* (1902), *The Jewel of Seven Stars* (1903), *The Lady of the Shroud* (1909), and *The Lair of the White Worm* (1911). **Nicholas Daly**

Stokes, Dorothy (1898–1982), music teacher. Born into a medical family in Dublin; was taught by Margaret O'Hea and MICHELE ESPOSITO at the RIAM, becoming a student teacher there at thirteen. She joined the staff in 1928, was director of the RIAM Orchestra, 1941–7, and was appointed professor in 1951. A stalwart in the Students' Musical Union, she instigated many concerts, particularly a series of Gilbert and Sullivan operettas, and formed a string orchestra, which won twice at the FEIS CEOIL. A respected accompanist and singing coach, she remained at the academy until her death. **Adrian Scahill**

Stokes, Sir George Gabriel (1819–1903), mathematical physicist. Born in Skreen, Co. Sligo; graduated as 'senior wrangler' (first in mathematics) from the University of Cambridge, 1841. He was Lucasian professor of mathematics at the University of Cambridge, 1849–1903, fellow of the Royal Society, 1851, secretary, 1854–85, and president 1885–90; he was made a baronet in 1889. He made important contributions to studies of the motion of fluids and to OPTICS (he introduced the term 'fluorescence') and carried out mathematical analysis of a range of practical problems. He advised WILLIAM PARSONS, third Earl of Rosse, and HOWARD GRUBB regarding the building of their TELESCOPES. His name is carried into posterity in Stokes's Law (dealing with viscosity), the Stokes layer (a boundary between a fluid and solid), Stokes's Theorem (relating to the surface integral of the curl of a vector), Stokes's line (in spectral studies), Stokes's Conjecture (about waves of greatest height), Navier-Stokes equations (dealing with fluid motion), and the Campbell-Stokes sunshine recorder, as well as in the stokes, a unit of viscosity. **Charles Mollan**

Stokes, Margaret M'Nair (1832–1900), antiquarian. Daughter of the physician WILLIAM STOKES. She made a singular contribution to Irish architectural studies in editing the posthumous publication of the third Earl of Dunraven's *Notes on Irish Architecture* (1875–7) and in her own work, *The High Crosses of Ireland* (1898), which remained unfinished at her death. She was an honorary member of the RIA and RSAI. **Brian Lalor**

Stokes, Whitley (1763–1845), physician, author, and founder of a distinguished academic and intellectual dynasty. Born and educated in Waterford; he became a fellow of TCD in 1788. His friendship with WOLFE TONE and membership of the UNITED IRISHMEN caused his suspension from the college in 1798; Tone later described him as 'the very best man I have ever known.' He became professor of medicine at the Royal College of Surgeons in Ireland and regius professor of physic at Trinity College, Dublin. As well as medical treatises on respiration, children's diseases, and contagion he wrote an attack on Paine's *Age of Reason* and on Malthus in *Population and Resources of Ireland*. In 1814 he financed the printing of an English–Irish dictionary. He was succeeded in the Trinity post by his son WILLIAM STOKES, author, with ROBERT GRAVES, of *Diseases of the Chest*. His grandson, WHITLEY STOKES, was a distinguished scholar. **Tony Farmar**

Stokes, Whitley (1830–1909), Celtic scholar, philologist, and legal administrator. Born in Dublin, son of the heart specialist WILLIAM STOKES; educated at TCD and the Inner Temple, London. He was called to the English bar in 1855 and practised for six years before undertaking legal work for the colonial administration in India. While in Dublin he studied Early Irish and comparative philology under Prof. R. T. Siegfried. With John Strachan he published *Thesaurus Paleohibernicus* (1901–03), more than 1,200 pages of Old Irish glosses from manuscripts dating from before the eleventh century, from Continental as well as Irish libraries. Among his other numerous publications were *Togail Troí* (1881), *Tripartite Life of St Patrick* (1887), and *Lives of the Saints from the Book of Lismore* (1890). He also edited and translated Cornish and Breton texts and undertook critical reviews of the works of other scholars. In his legal career in India he drafted much of the Code of Civil and Criminal Procedure, while his study of Sanskrit led to the publication of the *Hindu Law Books* in 1865. He was made a member of the Most Exalted Order of the Star of India in 1879. **Ciarán Deane**

Stokes, William (1804–1878), physician. Born in Dublin, son of WHITLEY STOKES (1763–1845); studied medicine in Dublin and at the University of Edinburgh. Physician to the Meath Hospital, he is commemorated by the eponymous CHEYNE-Stokes breathing and Stokes-Adams syndrome. While still a student he published the first treatise in English on the stethoscope; he is also the author of textbooks on diseases of the chest and of the heart. **J. B. Lyons**

Stokes, William. *William Stokes, physician to the Meath Hospital, Dublin, and leader of the Dublin school of anatomical diagnosis, which emphasised the clinical examination of patients. [Royal College of Physicians of Ireland]*

'Stolen Railway'. In 1863 work began on the Parsonstown (Birr) and Portumna Bridge Railway, linking Birr, Co. Offaly, with the east bank of the Shannon at Portumna, Co. Galway, but the contractor became bankrupt, and the 19 km (12-mile) line did not open for traffic until 5 November 1868. An agreement was made with the Great Southern and Western Railway to work the line, but disputes ensued, and traffic ceased in 1878. The railway was heavily in debt, notably to the Public Works Loan Commissioners, and when in 1883 that body disclaimed all further responsibility, the other creditors set about removing the whole system piecemeal, the station at Portumna Bridge disappearing in a single night. **Bernard Share**

stone alignments, often called *stone rows* (in order not to prejudge whether they were meant to be aligned on something), comprising a number of STANDING STONES erected in a line, forming a distinctive category of prehistoric monument. Two main types can be distinguished. The first, found all over the west of Ireland but with a concentration in Cos. Cork and Kerry, comprise up to six stones, typically about 2 m (6 ft) in height. The second represents a tradition that is localised in mid-Ulster, comprising numerous small stones often found in association with cairns and STONE CIRCLES, as at the famous site of Beaghmore, Co. Tyrone. All these monuments appear to date from the second millennium BC. [see ASTRONOMY, PREHISTORIC.] **Clive Ruggles**

stone circles, more correctly called *stone rings* (since many are far from being exactly circular), built in many parts of Ireland. They typically consist of a ring of STANDING STONES, usually well separated but sometimes crowded together, surrounding an open space, which it is tempting to see as a sacred space demarcated for the purposes of ritual. Impressive examples include Ballynoe, Co. Down, BELTANY, Co. Donegal, and Grange, Co. Limerick, the last of which comprises no fewer than 113 stones surrounding a space over 45 m (150 ft) in diameter. At some sites the stones are set into an earthen bank; other variants include the remnants of the circle surrounding the passage tomb at NEWGRANGE, Co. Meath.

The tradition of building stone circles may span a considerable period, from the Later NEOLITHIC PERIOD (c. 3000 BC) to the Middle BRONZE AGE some 2,000 years later. A distinctive form of stone circle is found in considerable numbers in Cos. Cork and Kerry, characterised by the presence of a single *axial* or *recumbent* stone set on its side and two tall uprights, known as *portals*, on the opposite side. The remaining stones are placed symmetrically about the axis through the centre of the axial stone and the centre of the portals. The diameter of these *axial stone circles* rarely exceeds 10 m (33 ft), and the number of stones varies from nineteen to five, the five-stone circle being a diminutive form in which the axial stone and portals are barely distinguishable. The larger axial stone circles show a remarkable consistency in their orientation, the axial stone always being found on the south-west or west side of the circle.

The other main concentration of stone circles is in mid-Ulster. Here they are often of small stones and are found in association with STONE ALIGNMENTS and cairns. At a number of sites there are complex settings of several circles and rows, good examples being Beaghmore and Copney, Co. Tyrone, and Aughlish, Co. Derry. Recent excavations at Copney have revealed three circles with complex interior arrangements of stones, patterned radially in one case and concentrically in the other two. **Clive Ruggles**

Stoney, Bindon Blood (1828–1909), civil engineer. Born in Co. Offaly, brother of GEORGE JOHNSTONE STONEY; educated privately and at TCD. He published a seminal work on the theory of strains in girders and was Assistant Engineer of Dublin Port, 1856–61, and Chief Engineer, 1862–98. He used 350-ton concrete blocks to form the deep-water Alexandra Basin; he also rebuilt Grattan Bridge and O'Connell Bridge. **Ronald Cox**

Stoney, George Johnstone. *Physicist and mathematician, George Johnstone Stoney, best known for introducing the scientific term 'electron' in 1861. [Irish Picture Library]*

Stoney, George Johnstone (1826–1911), physicist. Born near Birr, Co. Offaly; educated at TCD, but failed the fellowship examinations. He was professor of natural philosophy at Queen's College, Galway, 1852–7, secretary of the Queen's University, 1857–82, fellow of the Royal Society, 1861, and first BOYLE MEDALLIST of the ROYAL DUBLIN SOCIETY, 1899. He is best known for introducing the term 'electron' to science in 1891; he was studying the mathematics of the splitting of lines in spectra, and in the process he proposed the term for a charge associated with atomic bonds. After the mass and charge of what were originally called 'corpuscles' were determined by Sir J. J. Thomson (1856–1940) in 1897, these negatively charged fundamental particles were renamed electrons. Stoney had wide interests, publishing on OPTICS, molecular physics, the kinetic theory of gases, and music. **Charles Mollan**

Stopford Green, Alice (1847–1929), nationalist and historian. Born in Kells, Co. Meath. During the ANGLO-BOER WAR she challenged the British establishment, supporting Boer prisoners, especially those on St Helena, which she visited in 1900. She returned to Ireland in 1918, becoming a senator in 1921. She was active in the African Society. **Stephen A. Royle**

Stormont, seat of Northern Ireland's devolved Parliament, 1932–72, replacing the Presbyterian Assembly's College, Belfast, where both houses of the Northern Ireland Parliament had met since 1921. The grandiose Parliament Building, erected on the Cleland estate in east Belfast, was designed by Sir ARNOLD THORNLEY in the Greek classical style. It is built of Portland stone on a plinth of Mourne granite and is reached by a broad processional avenue, almost a mile long. The building is fronted by an imposing statue of Sir EDWARD CARSON in characteristically defiant pose, while Northern Ireland's first Prime Minister, Viscount Craigavon, is buried nearby. Stormont was opened by the Prince of Wales in November 1932 and quickly became a symbol of and synonym for Unionist ascendancy. The Nationalist opposition boycotted the opening and often abstained from attending the Parliament, accepting the role of official opposition only in 1965.

In the same grounds are Stormont House, the former residence of the Speaker of the Northern Ireland Parliament, and Stormont Castle, once the official residence of the Northern Ireland Prime Minister and since 1972 used by the Secretary of State for Northern Ireland.

The last sitting of the Northern Ireland Parliament took place on 28 March 1972, when it was prorogued by the British government and DIRECT RULE introduced. Stormont was used again for the power-sharing Assembly of 1973–4, the Convention (1975–6), and the Assembly of 1982–6. In July 1998 it became the home of the new NORTHERN IRELAND ASSEMBLY and Executive established under the BELFAST AGREEMENT (1998), which was negotiated in the adjoining Castle Buildings. **Eamon Phoenix**

storytelling. Stories are still related spontaneously in domestic, work, and recreational settings in Ireland, though storytelling no longer plays as prominent a role in everyday life as it once did. Nowadays more formal, public storytelling, as practised by professional or semi-professional storytellers, is growing in popularity, but it tends to concentrate on the humorous and the quaint, to the detriment of other genres, and consequently gives an incomplete picture of the function of storytelling.

In the past, and indeed today, stories were not told simply to entertain but had many other functions, reflected in the variety of lore told. In traditional society, formal storytelling usually took place in the *teach airneáin* (house frequented by night visitors). From November to May men would resort after the day's work to a particular house in the townland; after an exchange of news the entertainment would begin, consisting of long FOLK-TALES, songs, and other shorter lore. SÉAMUS Ó DUILEARGA argued that the *teach airneáin* was the mainstay of traditional storytelling, particularly of the telling of long folk-tales; however, though large-scale, more formal storytelling, dominated by men, was undoubtedly a feature of many areas during the late nineteenth and early twentieth centuries, it may well be that this type of *teach airneáin* is a relatively late development (see p. 407). Much small-scale, informal storytelling also took place in domestic and other settings, some of it in mixed company as well as in exclusive male or female gatherings. Only a generation or two ago, *bothántaíocht* or *cuartaíocht* (house visiting) was still quite common in many rural and indeed urban areas; but stories might be told at many other venues throughout the year, such as turf-cutting, workshops, spinning sessions, WAKES, boolies, and in pubs.

Folklorists in the past, by concentrating on formal storytelling, invariably distorted the picture in favour of men. Though far fewer folk-tales were recorded from women than from men, women did narrate folk-tales and played an important role in socialising young people towards acquiring folk-tales. Men had a preference for certain types of folk-tale, especially those involving heroic exploits; and because the collectors of the FOLKLORE COMMISSION collected such tales in great numbers, and in general collected mainly from men, and as all the full-time collectors were men, women have been assigned a lesser role. But there is no doubt that women told stories of various types and that they appreciated each other as storytellers, however men viewed their skills.

The variety of tales and lore told nowadays is not as great as in former times, and venues for storytelling are more restricted, partly because the pace of life is less conducive to storytelling and because people rely on other media for entertainment, moral and social instruction, and intellectual stimulation. Folk-tales are rarely told nowadays except to professional folklorists (and to children, of course); but a new genre, the modern urban legend, is very pervasive. [see BOOLEYING.] **Mícheál Briody**

Stowe Manuscripts, so called after the house of their collectors, the Marquess and Duke of Buckingham. They were bought by the British government in 1883 and divided between the ROYAL IRISH ACADEMY and the British Museum. The RIA acquired most of those of Irish interest, including important manuscripts in Irish collected by CHARLES O'CONOR, as well as the Stowe Missal (see p. 961). **William O'Sullivan**

Strabane (*An Srath Bán*), Co. Tyrone, a town and bridging point at the junction of the Finn and Mourne rivers; population (1991) 11,670. Strabane faces its 'twin' town, Lifford, Co. Donegal, across the river. The town was laid out c. 1608, during the PLANTATIONS, by the Earl of Abercorn, around Turlough Art O'Neill's earlier castle, which he also rebuilt. Proposed as a borough in 1611 and incorporated in 1613, Strabane had a population of 600 by 1630, a sessions and market house, a 'fair stone castle', and a school. The town remained in the Abercorns' possession, and under their patronage it developed as a regional market by the early nineteenth century. The Lifford bridge was rebuilt in 1775, and the Strabane Canal, linking the town to the navigable stretches of the River Foyle, was completed in the 1790s. Plans were drawn up for extensions to the town in the 1750s and again in 1802.

Strabane remained relatively prosperous during the later nineteenth century, when much of the surviving historical fabric was built, but experienced a significant loss of trade after PARTITION. In the post-war period it has experienced further prolonged economic decline and, despite recent government and community initiatives, remains an unemployment black-spot. **Lindsay Proudfoot**

Strangford Lough, Co. Down, a large, fully marine sheltered lough 14 km ($8\frac{1}{2}$ miles) east of Belfast. It is linked to the IRISH SEA by the Narrows, a channel with currents of up to 8 knots. Recognised as one of the most diverse sea loughs in Ireland, it has many statutory conservation designations, including marine nature reserve and candidate special area of conservation. Significant habitats include those of underwater horse-mussel beds and intertidal eelgrass. More than two thousand species have been recorded, many rare or not found elsewhere in Northern Ireland. It is an important breeding site for common and grey seals. Mariculture operations include mussels, oysters, and scallops. [see LOUGH HYNE.] **Julia Nunn**

street and town directories. Published from the eighteenth century onwards, town directories are a useful source of information on society and the economy. The coverage is most comprehensive for Dublin and Belfast, but many directories have a local focus. In Dublin the *Treble Almanack* developed as a compendium of the *Gentleman and Citizen's Almanack* (1729), the *Dublin Directory* (1752), and the *English Registry* and provided information on communications, lists of merchants and traders, and, from the 1780s, a street map of the city. Shaw's *New City Pictorial Directory* (1850) provided perspective drawings of streetscapes but in only one edition. More durable, the *Post Office Dublin Directory* (1832) and *Thom's Irish Directory and Official Almanack* (1844) provided increasingly comprehensive listings of public and commercial life. For Dublin and its nineteenth-century townships the name (and occasionally the occupation) of householders and the valuation of each property, organised by street, were listed; included also were alphabetical lists of the upper classes and merchants and guides to industries, organised by location. A detailed city map was included until early in the twentieth century. After 1927 THOM'S DIRECTORY listed commercial activities in the main towns. From 1959 separate Dublin and commercial directories were published in alternate years; the directory is again published annually, with street listings now covering the principal cities. Appearing first in 1852, the *Belfast and Province of Ulster Directory* was published regularly during the nineteenth century and is now published annually as the *Belfast and Northern Ireland Directory*. **Joseph Brady**

Strong. *Eithne Strong, a prominent figure in the revival of Irish-language literature from the 1940s, she is widely acclaimed for her poetry. [RTÉ Stills Library: 0798/049]*

Strong, Eithne (1923–1999), writer and poet. Born in Glensharrold, Co. Limerick. She published short stories and novels but is most acclaimed for her poetry, in English and Irish, in which interpersonal relationships are explored with a searing honesty. Her collection *Spatial Nosing: New and Selected Poems* was published in 1993. **Máirín Nic Eoin**

Strongbow: see FITZ GILBERT, RICHARD.

Stuart, Francis (1902–2000), novelist. Born in Townsville, Queensland, Australia, of Ulster parents; educated at Rugby School, Warwickshire. In 1920 he married Iseult Gonne, daughter of MAUD GONNE. He fought on the Republican side in the CIVIL WAR. His early collection of poetry, *We Have Kept the Faith* (1924), was much

Stuart, Francis. *Born in Australia and educated in England, the novelist Francis Stuart gained notoriety for broadcasting Nazi propaganda from Berlin during the Second World War. He would later allude to this period in his novel* Black List, Section H *(1971). [Irish Press PLC; photo: Sean Larkin]*

admired by YEATS. Ten novels were written in the 1930s, two of which—*Pigeon Irish* (1932) and *The Coloured Dome* (1932)—received wide critical acclaim. He accepted a lecturing post in Berlin during the SECOND WORLD WAR; his decision to broadcast Nazi propaganda to Ireland from 1942 to 1944 dogged him till his death. Two post-war novels, *The Pillar of Cloud* (1948) and *Redemption* (1949), are generally regarded as among his finest work. His best-known novel, *Black List, Section H* (1971), is a fictional autobiography and can be read as an attempt by the author to confront, at an imaginative remove, the actions and choices of his life. It brings together many of the major themes of his work. Like many of Stuart's protagonists, the central character is not an outcast, in that he actively chooses to live at a tangent from social norms; his life is lived at an intense pitch, in the hope that a moment of revelation or redemption may be achieved. Of Stuart's later work, the increasingly experimental novels *Memorial* (1973) and *Hole in the Head* (1977) are considered the most successful. **Derek Hand**

Stuart, Gilbert (1755–1828), portraitist. Born in North Kingston, Rhode Island. He accompanied the Scottish artist Cosmo Alexander on tours of the southern colonies in 1769 and Scotland in 1770. On his return to Newport he received important commissions. In London, 1775–87, he entered Benjamin West's studio. He exhibited at the Royal Academy from 1787 and retained his English and American clientele. From 1787 to 1793 he was in Dublin, probably evading creditors; Irish portraits include JOHN FITZGIBBON, first Earl of Clare. In 1793 he returned to America, leaving behind many unfinished works. In New York and Philadelphia he produced exceptional portraits, including two of George Washington. He moved to Washington in 1803 and then to Boston, where he remained until his death in 1828. **Brendan Rooney**

Stuart, Imogen (1927–), sculptor. Born in Berlin; studied for five years with the sculptor Otto Hitzberger in Bavaria and attended the Academy of Fine Arts in Munich. She first came to Ireland in 1949. She works in stone, metal, wood, clay, and stained glass. Liturgical commissions include work for the cathedrals of Armagh, Galway, and Longford in addition to a number of churches designed by LIAM MCCORMICK in Co. Donegal. Her work is represented in ST PATRICK'S COLLEGE, Maynooth, University College, Dublin, Stillorgan Shopping Centre, Dublin, and Market Square, Cavan. She has exhibited annually at the ROYAL HIBERNIAN ACADEMY since the 1950s and is a member of the RHA and of AOSDÁNA (see p. 854). **Alison FitzGerald**

suburbs, generally defined as residential areas at some distance from a city's central and business area. While suburbs have been a feature of cities throughout history, they grew rapidly in the nineteenth century as the wealthy sought to escape the noise and crowding of developing industrial centres. In the twentieth century most city authorities looked to suburban sites to solve their HOUSING problems, and large public housing estates were created. In Belfast, for example, almost half the population of the urban area could be classed as suburban by the 1990s. The spatial extent of towns increased, as suburbs were generally developed at low densities, with fewer than ten people per hectare in Cork and Limerick at 5 km (3 miles) from the city centre. INDUSTRY recognised the benefits of suburban sites, where land was cheaper and accessibility better than in the increasingly congested city centres, and industrial estates proliferated. To these have been added SHOPPING CENTRES, retail warehouses, and business parks, facilitating a 'suburban life-style'.

Suburban living has led to increased commuting, as EMPLOYMENT remains anchored in the city centre. For the Republic it was estimated that by the mid-1990s more than 10 per cent of employees in Dublin, Cork, and Limerick commuted more than 15 km ($9\frac{1}{2}$ miles) per day. Since only a small proportion of this is by public transport—22 per cent in the greater Dublin area and less than 10 per cent in Cork, Limerick, Galway, and Waterford—this has raised questions about the sustainability of cities and led to demands that future growth be within existing urban areas. **Joseph Brady**

suffrage movement: see WOMEN'S SUFFRAGE MOVEMENT.

Sugar Loaf, Great (501 m, 1,644 ft) and Little Sugar Loaf (342 m, 1,122 ft), two quartzite peaks in north-east Co. Wicklow, more akin to the landscape of the west of Ireland. The former is an important site for hill-walkers, who are rewarded with extensive views of Dublin to the north and Co. Wicklow's mountains and valleys to the west. **Patrick Duffy**

'Suibhne's Frenzy': see BUILE SHUIBHNE.

suicide. Male suicide rates, especially young male suicide rates, are increasing in Ireland. Improved data-gathering accounts for no more than 40 per cent of the increase. Explanations such as the decline in religious practice, the increased use of street DRUGS, and increased pressure in the educational system are not compatible with the actual trends. In fact suicide is highest in rural areas, where religious practice has remained strongest, and lowest in Dublin, where drug abuse is highest, with students having a relatively low suicide rate. Explanations such as married women's increased participation in paid EMPLOYMENT and increased family instability are also insufficient, as suicide is very much less common among young women aged fifteen to twenty-four. There is no evidence that mood disorders are increasing, though some young men may be unable or unwilling to obtain access to psychological support services. Suicide has been linked with cultural unease about the position and status of men as breadwinners in a society where there is an increasing demand for cheap, flexible female labour, trends that are common in many Western societies. This explanation is also insufficient, as the total male suicide rate is only 23 per 100,000 (i.e. 504 suicides in 1998, of which 120 were young men aged fifteen to twenty-four). The National Suicide Research Foundation (established in 1995) found the highest rate of attempted suicide among fifteen to twenty-four-year-olds, women's rate being 409 per 100,000, compared with 318 for men. Attention has been concentrated on actual suicides, which have a much lower rate, but where the gender trend is in the opposite direction. **Pat O'Connor**

Suir, River, a river approximately 184 km (114 miles) in length that rises in the Devilsbit Mountains, Co. Tipperary, and flows southwards through CAHER until it dramatically changes direction south of Newcastle to flow first to the north and then east, until it reaches the sea at Dunmore East, Co. Waterford (this is because it is constrained to follow an east–west geological trend). The channel widens gradually downstream, though it remains relatively shallow, until it reaches a width of 60 m (200 ft) at Carrick-on-Suir. From this point the river is tidal.

The catchment area is predominantly agricultural, and in the lowlands of the Suir and its tributaries—the Anner and the Tar—dairy farming is the main economic activity. The river is an important fishery and holds important stocks of wild brown trout (see p. 25). Among the many towns along its route are Thurles and Caher. A rocky island in the river provided the site for the thirteenth-century castle around which Caher grew. Clonmel is an ANGLO-NORMAN town, dating from the first decades of the thirteenth century. Carrick-on-Suir was also developed as an Anglo-Norman settlement and the ORMOND MANOR HOUSE, built in the mid-sixteenth century by Black Tom Butler, tenth Earl of Ormond, is of national importance (see p. 843). However, it may have its origins in a raiding base established by the VIKINGS in the ninth century. Both these towns are on the floodplain of the river and have experienced severe flooding in recent years. Downstream of Waterford the Suir joins the River Barrow at Cheekpoint, from where the wide Waterford Harbour leads to the sea (see p. 1026). **Joseph Brady**

Sulivan, Laurence (c. 1713–1786), colonial administrator. Born in Ireland, probably the illegitimate son of Philip O'Sullivan of Co. Cork. He joined the East India Company in 1741, was elected to the board of directors in 1755, and from then until his death some thirty years later, except for an interval of six years, 1772–8, was chairman and the company's leading figure. He also held a seat in the British Parliament from 1762 to 1774. During the years of his directorship he and his fellow-directors had to sustain wars in Asia, devise means of government in newly conquered Indian provinces, and cope with the demands of the British government and Parliament. He wrote in his memoirs that his power over the company was 'absolute' in the years 1757–63. **Ciarán Deane**

Sullivan, A. M. [Alexander Martin] (1830–1884), politician and journalist. Born in Bantry, Co. Cork; educated locally. He edited the NATION from 1855 to 1877 and was one of the founders of the IRISH PARTY, 1870. MP for Louth, 1874–80, and Meath, 1880–81, he was called to the bar in 1876 and to the English bar in 1877. He published various books on history, such as the nationalist classic *The Story of Ireland* (1870). **Brigitte Anton**

Sullivan, T. D. [Timothy Daniel] (1827–1914), nationalist. Born in Bantry, Co. Cork, brother of A. M. SULLIVAN. A journalist and politician, he was MP for Westmeath, 1880–85, for Dublin, (College Green), 1885–92, and Co. Donegal, 1892–1900, as well as Lord Mayor of Dublin, 1886–7. He is best known as the author of 'God Save Ireland', first published by his brother in the NATION in 1867 to commemorate the MANCHESTER MARTYRS. It became the unofficial national anthem of nationalist Ireland for fifty years. **Fergal Tobin**

Sullivan, W. K. [William Kirby] (1822–1890), chemist and university administrator. Born in Dripsey, Co. Cork; educated by the CHRISTIAN BROTHERS. He later studied chemistry in Justus von Liebig's famous laboratory in Giessen. He worked as a chemist successively at the Museum of Irish Industry (where he succeeded ROBERT KANE), Newman's CATHOLIC UNIVERSITY, where he was appointed professor of chemistry in 1854, and the Royal College of Science. His main work was in chemical analysis (he was the first to describe the iron test for phosphates, which became a standard procedure) and in mineral and industrial investigations. He was particularly concerned with the utilisation of one of Ireland's natural resources, peat, and the production of sugarbeet. He followed ROBERT KANE as second president of Queen's College, Cork, in 1873; the selection of a former member of the Catholic University made at least one of the Queen's Colleges more acceptable to the Catholic bishops. Under his presidency the college prospered, new laboratories were built, and more staff were recruited. The student body also grew, from less than 200 in 1873 to 402 in 1882.

Sullivan had many interests outside SCIENCE. He was an active member of the YOUNG IRELAND movement, escaping arrest in 1848 only because he was ill with rheumatic fever. His book *Celtic Studies* (1863) dealt with philology. His three-volume work on pre-Christian Irish culture (1873), an edited version of EUGENE O'CURRY's celebrated lectures on manuscript materials in Irish history, became as outstanding an achievement as his work in science and technical education. **William J. Davis**

sumptuary laws, passed throughout Europe between 1300 and 1700 to ensure the preservation of class distinctions, whereby only those of a specific rank could wear the more expensive garments, fabrics, embroidery, and decoration. It was claimed that this also reduced the import of costly foreign products, so protecting home industries. Sumptuary laws passed in Ireland from 1297 to 1682 were intended similarly to protect industries, both British and Irish, but they were also more complicated in Ireland, as clothing styles communicated not only one's class but also one's political affiliation. **Mairead Dunlevy**

Sunningdale Agreement (1973). In October 1972 the British government published a green paper, *The Future of Northern Ireland*, which envisaged an 'Irish dimension' and representatives of the nationalist community being given executive power. This was followed in March 1973 by a white paper that proposed an Assembly, from which a cross-community government would be drawn, and mechanisms for CROSS-BORDER CO-OPERATION. In the Assembly elections the SOCIAL DEMOCRATIC AND LABOUR PARTY secured nineteen seats, the ALLIANCE PARTY eight, and the Northern Ireland Labour Party one. Unionist Party candidates who supported the white paper could win only twenty-four seats, while an alliance of Unionist parties opposed to it won twenty-six. Faulkner became Chief Executive, with GERRY FITT of the SDLP as Deputy Chief Executive.

On 6 December 1973 Edward Heath convened a conference at Sunningdale Park, a civil service college in Berkshire, attended by representatives of the Irish Government, the Unionist Party, the SDLP, and the Alliance Party. The principal agreement was that a

Council of Ireland would be established, consisting of seven members each from the Irish Government and the Northern Ireland Executive, with power of 'executive action' in eight areas. Faulkner failed to secure the endorsement of the ULSTER UNIONIST COUNCIL, and in May 1974 the ULSTER WORKERS' COUNCIL strike forced the Executive's resignation, wrecking the agreement. **T. G. Fraser**

Supreme Court, the supreme court of appeal in the state, established by the Courts (Supplemental Provisions) Act (1961). The Chief Justice and seven other judges may sit as a three, five, or eight-judge court, in two or more divisions and at the same time; when the Supreme Court is dealing with constitutional matters it must sit as either a five-judge or an eight-judge court. It decides on the constitutionality of legislation (under article 26 of the Constitution) and must consider whether the President of Ireland has become permanently incapacitated (article 12.3.1°). Generally it will hear appeals only on a point of law, but when the Court of Criminal Appeal is abolished it will take over its work. **Neville Cox**

surgery. Before the eighteenth century, surgery in Ireland was performed by various practitioners, including members of the Guild of Barber-Surgeons, founded under a charter from Henry VI in 1446. The modern era of surgery came with the foundation of the Royal College of Surgeons in Ireland in 1784. Many of the HOSPITALS that still provide surgical services were established in the eighteenth and nineteenth centuries, including voluntary hospitals and county and WORKHOUSE infirmaries; many were run by religious nursing orders, especially the Sisters of Charity and Sisters of Mercy.

surgery. An Operation in a Dublin Drawing Room *(1817), watercolour by an unknown artist, recording abdominal surgery, a procedure that few survived. The inscription (bottom right) reveals that this patient did not survive: 'N. Power Operated on 20 July Died this 11 August 1817.' [Meath Hospital Foundation]*

Irish surgeons who achieved international status for their work include ABRAHAM COLLES in orthopaedics and anatomy, Sir Peter Freyer and Terence Millin in urology, and Denis Burkitt for his eponymous lymphoma and work on dietary fibre. The first general anaesthetic in Ireland was given in 1847 by JOHN MACDONNELL (1796–1892), who also performed the surgery, while in 1868 John Maconchy of Co. Down was the first surgeon to operate using Lister's method of antisepsis. ROBERT MCDONNELL (1828–1889) gave a blood transfusion in 1870. Sir Thornley Stoker (1845–1912) pioneered abdominal surgery and neurosurgery in Dublin. The first X-rays were used in 1896 at DR STEEVENS' HOSPITAL, Dublin.

The twentieth century saw the expansion of surgical services (county and regional hospitals) and the development of surgical specialisations. Several older hospitals were amalgamated, and the Republic was divided into eight health board regions in 1970, while Northern Ireland was divided into four health regions in 1948. Specialist hospitals were established (paediatrics, orthopaedics) and specialist units for ear, nose, and throat (ENT), cardiac surgery, neurosurgery, urology, vascular surgery, and plastic surgery were developed. Transplant surgery began in Ireland in the 1960s with kidney transplants; pancreas and heart transplants have been performed since the 1980s. **Pierce A. Grace**

surrender and regrant, a conciliatory policy for incorporating the Irish LORDSHIPS into a newly configured Anglicised kingdom of Ireland, initially implemented during Sir ANTHONY ST LEGER's first term as Lord Deputy of Ireland, 1540–44. The elevation of the lordship to the status of a kingdom by act of Parliament in 1541 created the constitutional framework for this policy, uniting the country's inhabitants in a single community of subjects under the unilateral jurisdiction of the Crown. Native Irish lords were induced to hold their lands of the king, who had to forgo many of the Crown's ancient but unrealisable feudal rights to those lands in return for their full recognition of his sovereignty. The entire process was transacted through individual agreements negotiated by St Leger with individual lords, but in every instance it involved three indentures. In the first, the lord bound himself to recognise the King of England as his liege lord, to apply for a royal grant of his lands and for a peerage, to attend Parliament, and to reject Papal jurisdiction. He then undertook to renounce his Irish title in return for an English peerage, to accept, assist, and obey in the adoption of English customs, language, and laws, to encourage tillage, build houses, and Anglicise socio-economic structures within his lordship, to render military service, and to pay Crown rents. He then received a charter granting him the lands of his lordship to hold from the Crown by knight service in perpetuity. The third stage involved arbitration on the lord's rights and obligations in respect of his vassals, tenants, and other landowners with a view to resolving disputes arising from conflicting claims. Each settlement was rendered legally binding following the enrolment of these indentures in Chancery; not all settlements, however, reached the final stage of enrolment. Surrender and regrant was revived by Sir HENRY SIDNEY, Lord Deputy in the 1560s, and was adopted intermittently down to the early seventeenth century. **Mary Ann Lyons**

Sutherland, Peter (1946–), politician. Born in Dublin; educated at UCD and King's Inns. A member of Fine Gael, he was ATTORNEY-GENERAL in Coalition Governments, 1981–2 and 1982–4. His period in office was dominated by a protracted extradition case and the constitutional prohibition on ABORTION, the wording of which he advised the Government to reject. After a term as member of the European Commission with responsibility for competition policy, 1985–9, he became a director of several large companies. As director-general of the General Agreement on Tariffs and Trade (now the WTO, World Trade Organisation) he supervised a new trade agreement between the United States and the European Union. He is joint chairman of BP Amoco and European chairman of the Trilateral Commission. **Brian Galvin**

Swift. *Ten-pound note (in circulation 1978–2002) featuring a portrait of Jonathan Swift, together with the coat of arms of Dublin, against the background of a letter by Swift, dated 11 April 1735, in which he expressed his intention to found a mental hospital by bequest. [Central Bank of Ireland]*

Swainson, Mabel (1928–) pianist and teacher. Born Boyle, Co. Roscommon; studied at the READ SCHOOL, taught there until its closure and at the RIAM 1985–7 and the Leinster School 1982–. Head of Piano at the SCHOLA CANTORUM 1970–84. Her former pupils include PHILIP MARTIN and HUGH TINNEY. **Richard Pine**

Swastika Laundry, a laundry business founded in 1912, with headquarters at Northumberland Road, Ballsbridge, which traded in Dublin until 1989. The laundry chimney at Northumberland Road, as well as the delivery vans and depots, were emblazoned with a Nazi-style swastika (though its use long predated the Third Reich), and its visibility throughout the SECOND WORLD WAR and after was possibly the sole benign public display in Europe of the symbol, evidence of the measure of Southern Irish isolation during those years. **Brian Lalor**

sweathouses, a form of traditional sauna, mainly used for the treatment of rheumatism. They were usually circular, dry-stone corbelled chambers, about 1.5 m (5 ft) in internal diameter, dug into terraces above stream-beds and entered through a very narrow low passageway. Turf fires were lit within the structure to provide a heated interior. Users entered and stayed inside sweating for a number of hours; they then bathed in the nearby stream. The great majority of Irish sweathouses are found in western Ulster and north-eastern Connacht. While the tradition of sweathouses could be medieval, the remains of those that survive are clearly of eighteenth, nineteenth, and possibly early twentieth-century date. Sweathouses continued to be used in places until the late 1940s. **Kieran O'Conor**

Sweeney, Eric (1948–), composer. Born in Dublin, he lectured at DIT Conservatory of Music and Drama and TCD, was Choral Director at RTÉ 1978–81, and is now Head of the Music Department at Waterford Institute of Technology. He has represented Ireland at the International Rostrum of Composers on five occasions. He has received commissions from the Royal Philharmonic Orchestra, DUBLIN BAROQUE PLAYERS, CONCORDE, and Young European Strings, and his output includes two symphonies, concertos, and many chamber and vocal works. He was a member of the ARTS COUNCIL 1989–93 and is a member of AOSDÁNA. **Richard Pine**

Sweeney, Matthew (1952–), poet. Born in Co. Donegal; educated at Freiburg. Publishing his first collection, *A Dream of Maps*, in 1981, Sweeney became one of the most prolific poets of his generation. His other volumes include *A Round House* (1983), *The Lame Waltzer* (1985), *Blue Shoes* (1989), *Cacti* (1992), *The Bridal Suite* (1997), and *A Smell of Fish* (2000) and are marked by a taste for nonchalant and zany narrative. He has also written extensively for children. *Emergency Kit* (1996) is an anthology jointly edited with Jo Shapcott; *Beyond Bedlam* (1997) is an anthology jointly edited with Ken Smith, devoted to the poetry of mental disturbance. He lives in London. **David Wheatley**

Sweeney, Peter (1950–), organist. Born in Dublin, he studied at the College of Music (now DIT Conservatory of Music and Drama, where he now lectures) and in Geneva with Lionel Rogg. He appears regularly with the NATIONAL SYMPHONY ORCHESTRA and RTÉ CONCERT ORCHESTRA and was director of the DUBLIN INTERNATIONAL ORGAN AND CHORAL FESTIVAL for six years. He was organist at CHRIST CHURCH CATHEDRAL, Dublin, 1980–91. He enjoys a busy international career as a soloist and has premiered works by Tavener, BOYDELL, BUCKLEY, and IAN WILSON. **Richard Pine**

Sweeney's Men, an influential folk band formed in 1966 by ANDY IRVINE, Johnny Moynihan, and the songwriter Joe Dolan. Theirs was an innovative mixture of Irish, Scottish, and English songs, combined with American folk material; they are credited with being the first to introduce the bouzouki to Irish music. Irvine and Moynihan remain important figures on the folk scene, Irvine having been a founder-member of Planxty and Patrick Street, and he continues to tour. They recorded two albums: *Sweeney's*

Men (1968) and the more experimental *The Tracks of Sweeney* (1969). Dolan was replaced in 1967 by Terry Woods, later to join Steeleye Span and the POGUES, and Irvine left in 1968, to be replaced by HENRY MCCULLOUGH, later of the Joe Cocker Band and Wings. **Tom Sherlock**

Swift, Jonathan (1667–1745), poet and satirist. Born in Dublin; educated at Kilkenny College and TRINITY COLLEGE, Dublin. Like most TCD students and fellows, Swift went to England in 1689 during the JACOBITE period. In 1691 he became secretary to the distinguished retired diplomat Sir William Temple at Moor Park, Farnham, Surrey; while there he met the young ESTHER JOHNSON, who, as 'Stella', was to remain a close friend for life. He also began his career as a writer with a series of Pindaric Odes—his least successful works. Satire rather than panegyric was to be Swift's forte.

Ordained in the Church of Ireland in 1695, he was appointed curate at Kilroot, near Larne, Co. Antrim, a Presbyterian stronghold. His dislike of Presbyterians—and of Catholics, whom he had experienced in triumph in the Jacobite Dublin of his youth—found expression in his first major work, *A Tale of a Tub* (1704), a sparkling satirical attack on 'the Abuses and Corruptions in Learning and Religion'; his targets were not only the official churches, which had corrupted primitive Christianity, but also the 'Modern' writers of his day—hacks, prepared to write anything for money. Swift aimed to alert readers 'of Wit and Taste' to the excesses of religious fanaticism and to warn them of the intellectual and moral dangers of the world of 'Modern' writers.

During the period 1699–1710 he became a significant figure in the Church of Ireland, and he was sent to London to petition the government for relief of ecclesiastical taxes. Though originally a supporter of the WHIGS, he changed allegiance to the Tories in 1710 when Harley and Bolingbroke took power. For the next three years he was a close confidant of these two politicians and was at the centre of English political and literary life. He contributed to the *Tatler* and was a founder-member of the Scriblerus Club with his friends Alexander Pope, John Arbuthnot and John Gay. Harley recruited him to write propaganda for the Tory government. His essays in the *Examiner* and his masterly *The Conduct of the Allies* (1711) raised political journalism to heights never known before. He also wrote an intimate JOURNAL TO STELLA, describing his daily life. But the rivalry between Harley and Bolingbroke led to the collapse of the ministry, and Swift's reward for loyal service was not the English bishopric he believed he deserved but the position of Dean of ST PATRICK'S CATHEDRAL, Dublin (see p. 966).

He returned to Dublin in 1713 a disillusioned man; but within six years, roused by the injustices in the relationship between England and Ireland, he took up his pen on the Irish side with such success that he became known as the 'Hibernian Patriot'. His *Proposal for the Universal Use of Irish Manufacture* (1720) urged the Irish people to boycott English goods, while THE DRAPIER'S LETTERS urged them not to accept the new coinage imposed on them by the English government. Infuriated by the behaviour of greedy absentee LANDLORDS, Swift ironically proposed the ultimate solution for the 'Irish problem' in A MODEST PROPOSAL (1729): that Irish children should be served up as food.

During the 1720s and 30s Swift wrote many pamphlets and presided over a circle of Dublin wits and poets. Much of his best verse dates from this time, particularly the ironic 'Verses on the Death of Dr Swift' and the vituperative attack on the corruption of the Irish Parliament, 'The Legion Club'. In addition he conceived and wrote GULLIVER'S TRAVELS (1726), the most challenging satire of the age. The 1720s also saw the death of Esther Johnson and of ESTHER VANHOMRIGH ('Vanessa'), a younger woman whom Swift had met in London, who loved him passionately and who had moved to Ireland to be near him. Though Swift was a respected figure in Dublin, his private life invited speculation. In the late 1730s his health began to fail, and he died in 1745.

Swift is undoubtedly the greatest satirist yet born in Ireland. He often used the device of a fictional author whose description of human affairs from a novel viewpoint alerts the reader to the self-deceptions and hypocrisies of ordinary life. He aims to make us see our follies and so amend our ways; but the brilliant surface and the black humour of his work have ensured its popularity, despite its underlying moral purpose. The questions he poses about the nature of human reasoning and the extent of self-deception remain as relevant today as they were in the eighteenth century. **Andrew Carpenter**

Swift, Patrick (1927–1983), artist and writer. Born in Dublin; studied at the National College of Art, Dublin, and Académie Grande Chaumière, Paris. He returned to Dublin in 1951, where he worked alongside Lucien Freud. Having travelled in France and Italy, 1952–4, he moved to London in 1955 and became associated with the Soho literary and artistic scene, and in 1959 he jointly founded the magazine X. In 1962 he moved to Portugal, where he continued to paint but did not exhibit regularly; he was linked stylistically with British artists such as Freud and BACON. While not in favour of abstraction, neither was he a traditional academic. He focused on still life and repeatedly on images of trees and studies of foliage. His later works became larger and more expressive but reveal his continued concern with such subjects. **Daire O'Connell**

Swift's Hospital (St Patrick's Hospital), Dublin. Soon after it opened in 1703 the Dublin Workhouse in St James's Street could accommodate no more 'miserable lunaticks exposed to hazard of others as well as themselves.' Against this background, JONATHAN SWIFT decided to leave his estate for the construction of a new hospital (see p. 1027). His poem 'Verses on the Death of Dr Swift' (1731) records that in his will

> He gave the little wealth he had,
> To build a house for fools and mad:
> And showed by one satiric touch,
> No nation wanted it so much.

The hospital, opened in 1758 in St James's Street, was built along the lines of Bethlem Hospital in London. Its ranges of cells, measuring 2.4 by 3.7 m (8 by 12 ft), radiated from a central block, women to the west, men to the east. In 1778 the ranges were extended, and in 1899 St Edmundsbury in Lucan was bought for convalescent care. Nursing and medical staff were provided from 1961 in the psychiatric unit of St James's Hospital, and in 1985 out-patient and day-care services were begun in the Dean Swift Centre of the revamped St Patrick's. **C. S. Breathnach**

swimming. The earliest evidence of competition swimming in Ireland is from Ulster in the late eighteenth century, while the earliest written record of swimming in Leinster relates to the Forty-Foot, Sandycove, Co. Dublin, in 1849. Sandycove Swimming Club was founded in 1882, and two years later Clontarf Swimming Club came into being. Both these clubs were on DUBLIN BAY, and all swimming was in the sea.

The Irish Amateur Swimming Association was formed at a

meeting in Fisher's Restaurant, Belfast, in 1893. At the first general meeting after the FIRST WORLD WAR, in May 1919, it was decided to introduce a 91 m (100-yard) championship and a diving championship for women, though Pembroke Ladies' Swimming Club, Dublin, had been in existence since 1908. The first national championships were held in 1941 at Blackrock Baths, Co. Dublin, as were the championships of subsequent years, until they eventually moved indoors.

Among the most famous swimmers of the twentieth century were Donncha O'Dea, the first man to break the one-minute record for the 100 m (110-yard) free-style, and Gary O'Toole, who won a silver medal in the breast stroke at the European championships. Michelle Smith was the dominant figure in women's swimming for many years.

At the beginning of the twenty-first century there were 10,500 active swimmers in Ireland, including competing and non-competing. The interest in competitive swimming is generally on the increase, with clubs being formed all over Ireland. There are 132 clubs affiliated to the Irish Amateur Swimming Association, which now operates under the name Swim Ireland. **Jim Sherwin**

Swiss Cottage, Caher, Co. Tipperary (c. 1810), a *cottage orné*, attributed to John Nash, built for Richard Butler, twelfth Baron Caher, later Earl of Glengall. The two-storey garden pavilion in the Caher demesne on the banks of the River SUIR is roofed by billowing thatch, with latticed windows and rustic balconies and porches, and has pretty reception rooms and small bedrooms. The Dufour wallpaper *Rives du Bosphore* decorating the music room depicts idyllic Orientalist scenes on the Bosphorus. The *cottage orné* concept was inspired by Marie Antoinette's enthusiasm for a rustic idyll, where the grandees can imagine themselves, however briefly, as herdsmen and dairymaids, without the inconvenient requirement for sweated labour. The Swiss Cottage, a perfect example of nineteenth-century ornamental parkland architecture, was restored in 1989, its interiors reinterpreted by the fashion designer SYBIL CONNOLLY. **Brian Lalor**

Synge, Francis Millington (1923–1983), geologist. Born in Dublin, a grandnephew of JOHN MILLINGTON SYNGE; educated at TCD and the Universities of Oslo and Uppsala. A superb draughtsman, he was cartographer in the University of Aberdeen, 1949–57. As a postgraduate student he had offered a stimulating interpretation of the Pleistocene drifts of the Trim region, Co. Meath; and Pleistocene history was now his prime interest. From 1957 to 1963 he was a geologist with the GEOLOGICAL SURVEY OF IRELAND, mapping drift deposits in his own inimitable style. Frustrated at the Geological Survey's failure to develop a publications programme, he resigned in 1963 to accept research posts in Queen's University, Belfast, 1963–4, and the Universities of Leicester, 1964–6, and Aberdeen, 1966–9. In 1969 he returned to Dublin to join a revitalised Geological Survey as senior geologist and head of the Quaternary Division. Much of his later research dealt with changing shorelines, and his links with Scandinavia remained strong. He was a gentle, quiet, and reserved man, and tales relating to his devotion to his science are legion. **Gordon L. Herries Davies**

Synge, John Lighton (1897–1995), mathematician and theoretical physicist. Born in Dublin; educated at TCD, graduating in mathematics and experimental physics, with a Large Gold Medal. Having held posts at Trinity College, Dublin, the University of Toronto, Ohio State University, and the Carnegie Institute of

Synge, J. M. John Millington Synge 1903 *by Harold Oakley, a striking portrait of the playwright, one of several early twentieth-century artists and writers who looked to the west of Ireland for inspiration and for an 'authentically' Irish subject matter. [Hugh Lane Municipal Gallery of Modern Art]*

Technology, he was senior professor of theoretical physics at the DUBLIN INSTITUTE FOR ADVANCED STUDIES, 1948–72. A fellow of the Royal Society, London, from 1943, he was president of the ROYAL IRISH ACADEMY, 1961–4. He was awarded the Tory Medal of the Royal Society of Canada, 1943, the BOYLE MEDAL of the ROYAL DUBLIN SOCIETY, 1972, and honorary doctorates from St Andrew's University, Edinburgh, Queen's University, Belfast, and the National University of Ireland. He published more than 200 scientific papers and eleven books, including two epoch-making books on relativity.

Synge was the most distinguished Irish mathematician and theoretical physicist since Sir WILLIAM ROWAN HAMILTON. All his writings are characterised by his extraordinary geometrical insight and clarity of expression. An important theorem bearing his name, published in 1936, is acclaimed as 'one of the most beautiful results in global differential geometry of the twentieth century.' **Petros Florides**

Synge, John Millington (1871–1909), playwright. Born in Rathfarnham, Co. Dublin, into an Anglo-Irish family of Protestant clergy and professional men. He lost his father at an early age and was raised by his deeply evangelical mother, who taught that all strong language and exaggerations were sins against God, for which the sinner would one day have to account—hence perhaps the playwright's later love of the colourful phrase. As a student at TRINITY COLLEGE, Dublin, he won prizes for proficiency in Irish, then a subject taken by future Church of Ireland ordinands, who were expected to preach to rural congregations in their vernacular. Despite poor health the young Synge was a keen cyclist and hill-walker in Co. Wicklow. An intense study of Darwin's evolutionary theory destroyed his religious belief; he thereafter substituted a faith in the 'kingdom of Ireland' for faith in the 'kingdom of God.' His agnosticism led to many clashes with his mother and the rejection of his marriage proposals by Cherrie Matheson, a member of the Plymouth Brethren; but these experiences heightened his sense of the Pagan-Christian conflict that is such a feature of Irish cultural tradition.

He was a keen violinist and a composer. He played in the RIAM orchestra and might, but for his extreme shyness, have chosen a career as a musical performer. He composed scores for such traditional lyrics as 'EIBHLÍN, A RÚN'. Ultimately in his literary art he sought many musical effects, scoring entire scenes of his plays 'Andante' and 'Allegro', as in orchestral composition. He spent many months after graduation in Germany, where his musical studies continued, and in Paris, where he attended lectures on Celtic culture by Henri d'Arbois de Jubainville. He made a study of Breton culture from the writings of Anatole Le Braz. In 1896 W. B. YEATS was so enthused by Synge's learning and conversation that on their first meeting he urged him to go to the ARAN ISLANDS and 'express a life that has never found expression.' Synge's first visit was in 1898, and he returned in the summers of 1899–1902, gathering the stories and lore that would feed many of his great plays. His main aim, however, was to perfect his Irish, at which he had excelled at Trinity; it was this that provided the substratum of the Hiberno-English dialect that became his perfected dramatic medium. On the Aran Islands and later in Co. Kerry and on the BLASKET ISLANDS he listened closely to people who were still thinking in Irish while using English words, and he made copious notes of the results, with phrases that greatly energised his plays. As GEORGE MOORE once joked, Synge was responsible for the discovery that if one translated Irish word for word into English, the result was poetry.

Synge's was essentially a genius for translation; he was one of the first artists to recognise that more may be added than lost in such a manoeuvre. He translated from the CLASSICAL IRISH POETRY and prose of GEOFFREY KEATING as well as from the folk lyrics of the west of Ireland, in the process forging a 'bilingual wave' between Irish and English. Though he was later accused of being a 'faker of peasant speech,' his idiom at its best was more subtle and expressive than either standard Irish or standard English—so much so that YEATS seriously contended in *Samhain*, the journal of the Literary Theatre, that the dialect should not be the sole preserve of a literary movement but should also be the language in which such activities as university lectures, newspaper editorials, and church sermons were written. This call fell on deaf ears.

The objectivity that Synge derived from the use of dialect was technical. Earlier writings, such as *Vita Vechia* (1895) and *When the Moon Has Set* (1901), suffered from a cloying subjectivity and ill-defined moodiness; but once he had found the objective correlative of rural life and the language in which to render it, there was no limit to his powers. *The Shadow of the Glen* (1903) allowed him to explore his own loneliness in the plight of an unhappily married woman, Nora, and an unnamed wandering tramp, with whom she leaves her home in an Irish rewriting of Henrik Ibsen's famous play *A Doll's House*. *Riders to the Sea* (1904) has claims to being the most perfect one-act tragedy of the twentieth century; its depiction of the grave dignity of Aran life in the face of a warring Nature seems almost Greek in its purity of outline. *The Well of the Saints* (1905) studies what happens when two blind beggars are cured but find the visible world hateful: it is a profound meditation on the disastrous effect of the artist's clarity of vision in everyday life. Its stark opening scene, with two tramps talking at a crossroads, and its closing frame, in which the tramps walk off in hope of deliverance by a God in whom they do not really believe, anticipate Beckett's WAITING FOR GODOT. Synge's master-drama, THE PLAYBOY OF THE WESTERN WORLD (1907), is a further exploration of the gulf between imagination and reality; and here once again the artist-figure is expelled by a society incapable of self-renewal. The fate of Christy Mahon was prophetic of Synge's own, for the play was denounced as a STAGE-IRISH libel on the Irish people; yet the violence of the protesters was, as Yeats complained, the only real insult. In Pegeen Mike, Synge re-created the image of a strong Celtic womanhood first celebrated in Irish saga. The part was specially written for his fiancée, Molly Allgood (Máire O'Neill).

He went on to produce an anti-heroic version of the legend of the sons of Uisneach, *Deirdre of the Sorrows* (staged posthumously in 1910). Intended as a further vehicle for his beloved, it also allowed a dying author to put the words of his own epitaph onto the lips of DEIRDRE as she weeps over the grave of her dead partner, Naisi. Synge removed the supernatural, otherworldly elements from the tale, making it more psychologically credible as a story of how exhausted and pressured people behave on the verge of death. The lovers, faced with an open grave, lapse into the very bickering that their return from a wandering life in Scotland was intended to avoid.

Synge's own relations with Molly Allgood are memorialised in their letters; but the couple were never married. He died of Hodgkin's disease in 1909, and his poems were published in 1911. Yeats, who worked on that edition, was greatly influenced by Synge's attempt to challenge the rather mawkish lyricism of the later nineteenth century with a more harsh, surgical, and monosyllabic art. Synge's dramatic themes and techniques exercised a profound influence not alone on BECKETT but on such recent playwrights as MARTIN MCDONAGH, TOM MURPHY, BRIAN FRIEL, and MARINA CARR; but the linguistic possibilities opened up by his dialect remain largely unexplored and under-exploited, except by the Kerry playwright GEORGE FITZMAURICE. **Declan Kiberd**

synods, meetings of the Irish church held during the twelfth century that attempted to bring the church into line with the European norm. The first was held at Cashel in 1101, presided over by MUIRCHEARTACH Ó BRIAIN, then at the height of his power. The decrees of Cashel were concerned with the freedom of churches from lay interference and exactions, clerical immunity (from prosecution in secular courts), clerical celibacy, church sanctuary, and Irish marriage practices. At this synod Cashel itself was given to the church by Ó Briain, thus depriving his dynasty's rivals, the EOGHANACHT of Cashel, of their traditional capital. The next synod, that of RÁTH BHREASAIL, held in 1111, established a diocesan structure governed by bishops. A local synod held at Uisneach (Co. Westmeath) made minor adjustments. The third major synod was held at Kells and Mellifont in 1152 and modified the structure to create four provinces—Armagh, Cashel, Tuam, and Dublin—instead of two (Armagh and Cashel), reflecting changed political circumstances. Cardinal John Paparo brought *pallia* for four archbishops from the Pope. Armagh retained the primacy. Additional legislation dealt with simony, the payment of TITHES, and Irish marriage practices. The Second Synod of Cashel (1172) was held against the backdrop of ANGLO-NORMAN CONQUEST. The church supported the intervention of HENRY II of England in Ireland. Decrees of the synod show the church still struggling to conform to European norms. [see THURLES, SYNOD OF; WHITBY, SYNOD OF.] **Anthony Candon**

Tyrone *(see page 1086). Glenelly Valley, with its majestic glacial landscape, in the heart of the Sperrin Mountains, Co. Tyrone. [Northern Ireland Tourist Board Photographic Library]*

T

tabloid newspapers: see NEWSPAPERS, TABLOID.

Taibhdhearc na Gaillimhe, an IRISH-LANGUAGE theatre in Galway, established in 1928 and driven principally by Liam Ó Briain; MÍCHEÁL MAC LIAMMÓIR became its first producer. Many noted producers and actors began their career there or worked with the company, including SIOBHÁN MCKENNA, Michael Lally, Frank Dermody, WALTER MACKEN, and CAITLÍN MAUDE; playwrights whose work has been produced include EOGHAN Ó TUAIRISC, MÁIRÉAD NÍ GHRÁDA, CRIOSTOIR O'FLYNN, BRENDAN BEHAN, and ANTAINE Ó FLATHARTA. Since the 1960s the names of Seán and Máire Stafford have been inextricably linked with the theatre. Productions include original Irish plays, translations from many languages, opera, pantomime, and summer shows. **Muireann Ní Bhrolcháin**

táin bó (cattle raid). The cattle-raid tales of early Irish literature usually describe the gathering of cattle by a female figure, such as Flidais. They are often connected with the Cattle Raid of Cooley, as in 'Táin Bó Fraích' ('Fraech's Cattle Raid'). In this convoluted tale Fraech woos Findabair, daughter of Medb and Ailill. They oppose the union, and Ailill attempts to have Fraech killed by a water monster. His OTHERWORLD mother revives him, and he travels abroad to find his existing wife and cows. He returns to Ireland to take part in the Cattle Raid of Cooley. **Muireann Ní Bhrolcháin**

'Táin Bó Cuailnge' ('Cattle Raid of Cooley'), generally held to be the centrepiece of the ULSTER CYCLE. It tells of a foray made by MÉABH, queen of Connacht, into Ulster to seize the Donn Cuailnge, the supernatural bull of Ulster. Her progress northwards is impeded by the actions of the youthful Ulster warrior CÚ CHULAINN, who is not afflicted by the debilitating illness that afflicts the Ulstermen each year at SAMHAIN. In the ranks of the Connacht army are some exiled Ulster warriors who had earlier left their province in protest at a breach of faith by their king, Conchobhar. The army is led by the great Fearghus mac Róich, paramour of Méabh and a former King of Ulster. In a substantial interlude to the main narrative the exiles relate to Méabh the *macgnímrada* (boyhood deeds) of Cú Chulainn, who has single-handedly killed so many of her soldiers. Cú Chulainn further delays her advance by engaging her champions, including his own foster-brother Fear Diadh, in single combat at a ford, emerging victorious each time. The Ulstermen finally recover from their sickness and defeat the forces of Connacht in battle. The Donn Cuailnge fights with the equally supernatural Connacht bull, the Findbennach of Aí, killing it and scattering fragments of its body throughout Ireland (see p. 762). Reaching Ulster, its heart breaks from its exertions and it dies.

Táin bó ('cattle raid') is a generic designation and is found in the title of at least nine other tales. The pre-eminent status of Táin Bó Cuailnge may be partly due to its length: it is by far the longest of the Ulster sagas. Several other sagas are linked to it. Medieval tradition lists some twelve *remscélae* or 'fore-tales', which purport to tell how the circumstances leading to the events of Táin Bó Cuailnge came about, or how certain characters became involved in it. Though not always listed among the remscélae, 'Longas mac nUislenn' ('The Exile of the Sons of Uisliu') is closely related to the events of 'Táin Bó Cuailnge', as it recounts how certain of the Ulster warriors find themselves allied with the Connacht forces in their march against Ulster. **Ruairí Ó hUiginn**

Taisce, An, a voluntary organisation founded in 1948 to promote the conservation and management of the Republic's natural and built ENVIRONMENT in a manner that is sustainable. An Taisce fosters the view that Ireland's environment is a vital asset, the conservation of which is central to our well-being. It supports national and international efforts to ensure that our global environment is managed wisely. It publishes reports, books, and a magazine, *Living Heritage*. It is a prescribed body under the Planning Acts, which means that it must be consulted on a variety of planning and related matters. In Northern Ireland, similar conservation of the natural and built environment is undertaken by the National Trust. **Anne-Marie Cunningham**

Taking of Ireland, The: see EXPUGNATIO HIBERNICA.

Talbot, Matthew (Matt) (1856–1925), TEMPERANCE advocate. Born in Dublin; educated briefly at primary level. Working as a labourer on the Dublin docks, he quickly developed a serious ALCOHOL addiction. He took the pledge and began a recovery based on prayer, fasting, sacraments, solitude, and self-mutilation. Following his death he became a model for alcoholics in recovery. In 1975 the Catholic Church declared him 'Venerable'. There is a commemorative figure of Talbot at City Quay, Dublin; the Talbot Memorial Bridge is named jointly in his honour and that of merchant seamen of the Second World War period. Talbot's remains are enshrined in Our Lady of Lourdes church, Seán MacDermott Street, Dublin. **Diarmaid Ferriter**

Talbot, Richard, Earl of Tyrconnell (1630–1691), JACOBITE soldier. An 'OLD ENGLISH' Catholic from Co. Meath, he served as a cornet in the Confederate army, being wounded at Drogheda during the Cromwellian siege. He joined the royalist army in Flanders, where he met James, Duke of York, becoming lieutenant-colonel in York's regiment. Imprisoned in London in 1655 for plotting the assassination of CROMWELL, he escaped and at the RESTORATION returned to England, where his influence with York secured beneficial modifications to the Irish land settlement. Following the accession of York as JAMES II in 1685 he was made an earl and oversaw the Irish Catholic revival. In 1686 he became army commander and began a policy of Catholicisation, which increased in scope when he became Lord Deputy in 1687. Though it was rumoured that he might submit to WILLIAM III, he was created duke by James

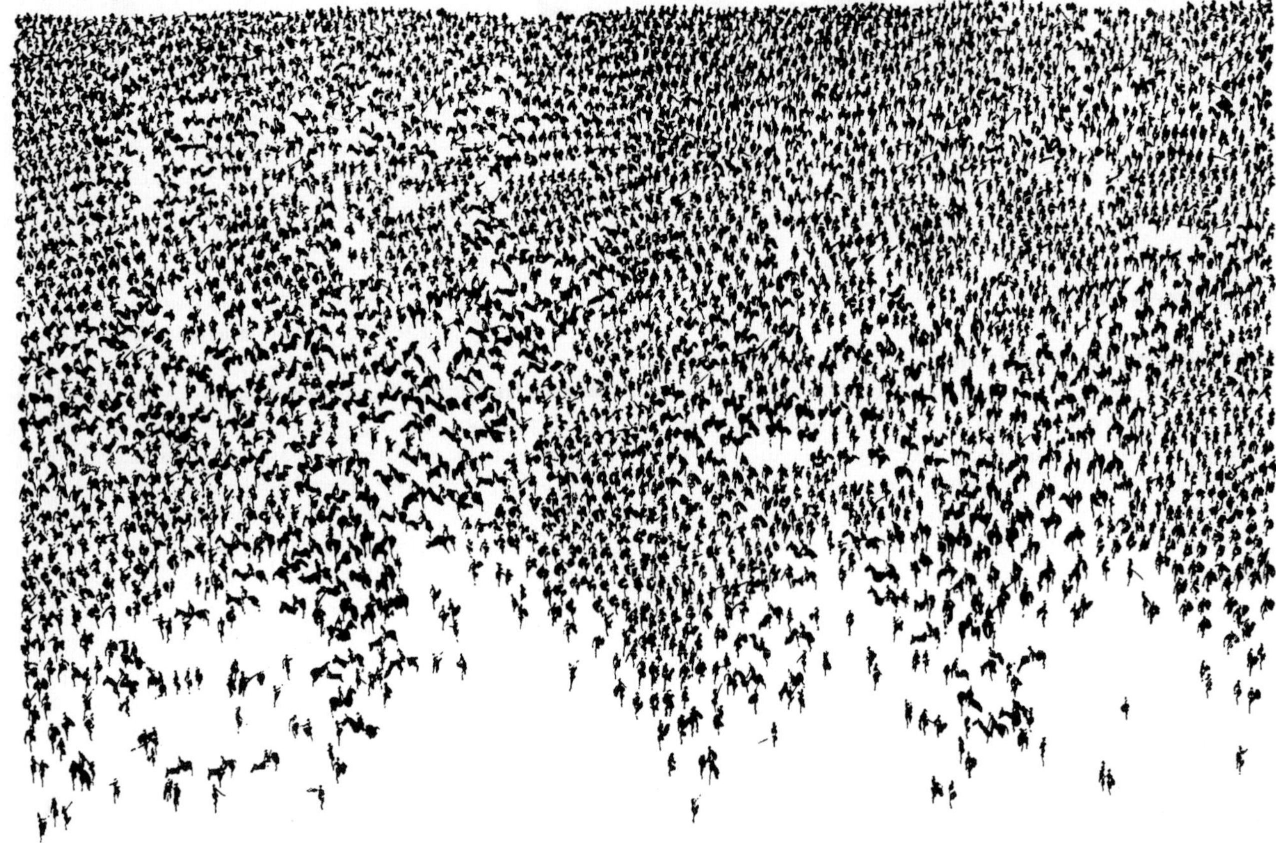

Táin. The Massing of the Army *by Louis Le Brocquy, one of the greatest Irish graphic works of the twentieth century, from a series of brush drawings created to illustrate Thomas Kinsella's acclaimed translation of the mythological epic 'Táin Bó Cuailgne', published in 1969 by Dolmen Press. [Louis Le Brocquy]*

following the latter's arrival in Ireland in 1689. At the BATTLE OF THE BOYNE he commanded the main fighting. He favoured negotiations following the defeat, though the defence of Limerick renewed his confidence. Following his absence during the winter, his authority was undermined by discontent within the Jacobite camp. In 1691 SAINT-RUTH disregarded Tyrconnell's orders to retreat to Limerick and suffered a decisive defeat at AUGHRIM. However, the promise of more French aid led Tyrconnell to favour continued resistance, despite a desire among Jacobites for peace terms. His death from a stroke in August was a blow for the war party; the final capitulation followed in October. In the early eighteenth century Tyrconnell's name remained a Protestant catch-word for arbitrary government. **Charles Ivar McGrath**

Talbot Press, Dublin (1913–90), founded as an offshoot of the Educational Company of Ireland by William Fitzsimmons and W. G. Lyon. Its policy was to publish books about Ireland and books by Irish writers. It was a significant force in PUBLISHING through a difficult period, producing some 200 titles between 1913 and 1922 and some 500 between 1922 and 1970. When MAUNSEL AND COMPANY ceased trading in 1925 the Talbot Press took over some of its titles, notably the works of SYNGE and PEARSE and other leading figures of the LITERARY REVIVAL. It also consistently published titles in Irish, among them the landmark Irish–English dictionary (1927) of PATRICK DINNEEN, published for the IRISH TEXTS SOCIETY. **Bernard Share**

Tallaght, monastery of. Tallaght (Co. Dublin) is called one of Ireland's 'two eyes' in the ninth-century TRIADS of Ireland (the other being Finglas, Co. Dublin). This was doubtless because of its leading role in the reform movement of the late eighth century, also known as the anchoritic or CÉILÍ DÉ ('culdee') reform. The exact date of Tallaght's foundation is not recorded, but its founder and first abbot, MÁEL RUÁIN, died in 792. It was therefore one of the many new churches founded in the period 750–850. The church's reputation otherwise rests on the productions of its very active scriptorium, which included two MARTYROLOGIES and, very probably, a missal. By 900 the church becomes much less visible in the ANNALS. **Pádraig Ó Riain**

Tallentire, Anne (1949–), performance and installation artist. Born in Co. Armagh; studied at the School of Visual Art, New York, and Slade School of Fine Art, London. Since 1984 she has lived and worked in London, lecturing at Central Schools and St Martin's College of Art. Originally a painter, she now works with a wide variety of media, in gallery and non-gallery contexts, exploring issues of memory, language, and identity. She has presented performances and exhibitions internationally, including a video installation in *0044*, 1999–2000, shown at the PS1 Institute for Contemporary Art, New York, Albright-Knox Museum, Buffalo, and the Crawford Gallery, Cork. She represented Ireland at the Venice Biennale, 1999, with a video installation, *Instances*. From 1993 she has worked collaboratively with the artist John Seth while continuing independent projects. **Peter Murray**

Tallon, Ronald (1927–), architect. Born in Dublin; studied at UCD. He worked with the OFFICE OF PUBLIC WORKS, 1950–56, inspired by the later work of Mies van der Rohe. He became a senior partner with Scott Tallon Walker in 1974. He designed the RTÉ studios at Donnybrook, Dublin, for which he received the RIAI Gold Medal, 1959–61; the GEC factory at Dundalk, which also received the RIAI Gold Medal, 1962–4; the ABBEY THEATRE, Dublin, 1958–66; P. J. Carroll factory, Dundalk, 1967–9 (see p. 41); Bank of Ireland head office, Baggot Street, Dublin, 1968–78; Goulding Summerhouse, Enniskerry, Co. Wicklow; and the Dublin Civic Offices, Wood Quay, 1992–5 (see p. 1122). **Raymund Ryan**

tánaiste. The medieval title *tánaiste rí* ('second to the king') was used for the heir-apparent, who was usually a close relative of the chief (TAOISEACH). As part of his office he ruled a territory as a sort of governor, which he had to relinquish to the next heir-apparent if he himself succeeded to the kingship. The institution was known to the English as *tanistry*. The title is also that of the deputy head of the Irish Government, introduced in the Constitution of Ireland (1937). **Bart Jaski**

Tandragee, Co. Armagh, site of a solemn-eyed IDOL with horned helmet and wide-open mouth, the most striking of the pre-Christian carvings at Armagh Cathedral. Its right hand is clasped over a protuberance on the left arm, a gesture possibly identifying this idol as the silver-armed god Nuad or the mythical Ulster god-hero Conall Cearnach. **Helen Lanigan Wood**

Tandy, (James) Napper (1740–1803), United Irishman. Born in Dublin. He was a prominent figure in city politics in the 1780s and 90s. An early Jacobin enthusiast, he was an officer in the Volunteer artillery corps, which was among the first to invite Catholic recruits. Founding chairman of the Dublin Society of UNITED IRISHMEN in November 1791, he was frequently in trouble from his anti-government pronouncements. In 1792 he was one of several United Irish leaders implicated in negotiations with the revolutionary DEFENDERS. He swore their oath at Castlebellingham, Co. Louth, and was forced to go on the run, fleeing first to Philadelphia and then to Paris in 1798. Appointed to the rank of general in the French army, he revisited Rutland Island, Co. Donegal, with the *Anacreon* on 16 September 1798; on finding that Humbert's expedition had been defeated at Ballinamuck, he left for the Continent. He was illegally extradited from Hamburg to England on 27 October 1799 and sentenced to death in Ireland five months later. His release was a French precondition for signing the Peace of Amiens in March 1802; he was deported to Bordeaux, where he settled and died the following year. **Ruan O'Donnell**

Taoiseach ('chief'), title of the head of the Government, introduced by ÉAMON DE VALERA in the CONSTITUTION OF IRELAND (1937). It reflects de Valera's wish to underline the Irish character of the state as well as the increased authority his constitution conferred on the office. [see TÁNAISTE.]

Taoisigh

21 July. 1937–18 Feb. 1948	Éamon de Valera (Fianna Fáil)
18 Feb. 1948–13 June 1951	John A. Costello (Fine Gael)
13 June 1951–2 June 1954	Éamon de Valera (Fianna Fáil)
2 June 1954–20 Mar. 1957	John A. Costello (Fine Gael)
20 Mar. 1957–23 June 1959	Éamon de Valera (Fianna Fáil)
23 June 1959–16 Nov. 1966	Seán Lemass (Fianna Fáil)
16 Nov. 1966–14 Mar. 1973	Jack Lynch (Fianna Fáil)
14 Mar. 1973–5 July 1977	Liam Cosgrave (Fine Gael)
5 July 1977–12 Dec. 1979	Jack Lynch (Fianna Fáil)
12 Dec. 1979–30 June 1981	Charles Haughey (Fianna Fáil)
30 June 1981–9 Mar. 1982	Garret FitzGerald (Fine Gael)
9 Mar. 1982–14 Dec. 1982	Charles Haughey (Fianna Fáil)

14 Dec. 1982–10 Mar. 1987	Garret FitzGerald (Fine Gael)
10 Mar. 1987–11 Feb. 1992	Charles Haughey (Fianna Fáil)
11 Feb. 1992–15 Dec. 1994	Albert Reynolds (Fianna Fáil)
15 Dec. 1994–26 June 1997	John Bruton (Fine Gael)
26 June 1997–	Bertie Ahern (Fianna Fáil)

tapestry-making. The first known attempt to weave tapestries in Ireland was in Kilkenny in 1525, when weavers from Flanders worked for Piers Butler, second Earl of Ormond, and his wife, Margaret Fitzgerald, daughter of the Earl of Kildare. The second attempt was in the late seventeenth century, when tapestry-weavers, probably also from Flanders, received government assistance to work in Dublin. The third was from 1727, when Robert Baillie, with the encouragement of the Irish Parliament, brought tapestry-weavers from England, France, and Flanders to weave large tapestries and furnishings for the new PARLIAMENT HOUSE. Two tapestries were completed under the supervision of Jan van Beaver in 1732 and are the earliest Irish tapestries to survive. Van Beaver trained two apprentices, Richard Pawlett and Daniel Reyley, who continued to weave tapestry portraits and pictures and settee and chair covers until the late 1760s.

In the early twentieth century the DUN EMER GUILD wove tapestries as seat covers and pictures in Celtic Revival, medieval, and contemporary art styles. In the later twentieth century the artists LOUIS LE BROCQUY and PATRICK SCOTT designed works that were woven in tapestry. [see VAN DER HAGEN, WILLIAM.] **Mairead Dunlevy**

Tara, Co. Meath. At 155 m (500 ft) above sea level, the Hill of Tara commands a panoramic vista of the north Central Plain. The name Tara (Irish *Teamhair*, Old Irish *Temair*) means, variously, a lofty height and the meeting place of darkness and light. The remains of twenty-five monuments are visible; many more have been discovered by GEOPHYSICAL SURVEY and aerial photography. The names of the monuments probably date from at least later prehistory and are preserved in the eleventh-century DINNSEANCHAS. The complex is a prehistoric necropolis but has acquired the reputation in early documentary sources as seat of the so-called HIGH KINGS of Ireland.

The oldest visible monument is the passage tomb of Dumha na nGiall (Mound of the Hostages), dating from the third millennium BC and excavated in the 1950s. The passage is divided by sill-stones into three compartments, originally filled with cremated bones and a rich grave assemblage of pottery, beads, and pins. There is a decorated stone on the left-hand wall. Two propitiatory burials were placed behind the orthostats; one contained a NEOLITHIC pot filled with cremated bone, an antler pin, and a bone bead necklace. These and the burial chamber were covered with a cairn of stones and a mantle of soil. The Lia Fáil (Stone of Destiny), a phallic-shaped white granite stone, stood near the passage tomb but was re-erected on the Forradh in 1824. During the earlier BRONZE AGE thirty-nine cremation burials were interred in the soil mantle, and further burials were placed in the passage. The only inhumation in the mound was that of a young man with a necklace of jet, amber, bronze, and faience, at his feet a dagger and a bronze awl.

Later in the third millennium the Teach Midchuarta (Banquet Hall), a cursus-like enclosure and avenue, was on the northern flank of the hill. It is more than 200 m (650 ft) long, its banks curving westwards and gapped at irregular intervals. There is a medieval reference to a terminal bank at the northern end, and slight evidence of another at the southern end. Immediately south of this a huge oval pit or timber circle, 210 m (690 ft) in maximum diameter, was erected. It comprised a wide fosse, on each side of which are more than three hundred regularly spaced pits. It probably dates from c. 2500 BC and is contemporary with two other HENGE MONUMENTS nearby, namely Ráth Mhéabha (MÉABH's rath) to the south and another in Riverstown, 1 km to the west.

There are more than twenty-five barrows and ring-ditches of various forms on Tara, many probably dating from the Bronze Age. Stray finds of tools and weapons are further evidence of second-millennium activity around Tara. Two large gold torcs of Bronze Age date were found c. 1810. Some of the barrows were deliberately incorporated intact in the fabric of the larger specimens. Bowl barrows were incorporated in both the northern and southern *claonfhearta* (sloping trenches) and in Ráth Ghráinne (Gráinne's Fort) and the Forradh (the 'royal' seat). The Forradh is the inauguration mound of Tara. A revival in monumental religious architecture at Tara took place during the IRON AGE, as evidenced by Ráth na Rí (Fort of the Kings), a hengiform enclosure of 1,000 m (3,300-ft) circumference encircling the crown of the hill and radiocarbon-dated to approximately the first century BC. The internal ditch is V-sectioned and 3 m (10 ft) deep. Ráth Laoghaire, immediately to the south of Ráth na Rí, is a *bivallate* (double-banked) circular enclosure, approximately 125 m (410 ft) in diameter. It has a more military character and compares with sites such as Ringlestown Rath (to the south-west) and Ráth Lugh (to the north-east). A bivallate linear earthwork to the west, stretching for at least 1.5 km (1 mile), defends Tara's western flank. Ráth na Seanad (Rath of the Synods) represents the fourth use of this spot: twice a burial ground and once a series of wooden enclosures. Excavations in the 1950s revealed quantities of Romano-British material, suggesting a date between the later first and fourth centuries AD. The authenticity of some of the pagan sacral kings of later Iron Age Tara is not in doubt. Others, such as the third-century CORMAC MAC AIRT, credited with a great building revival, remain nebulous. It is their exploits, however, that comprise the core of the huge corpus of medieval literature associated with Tara.

Like most of the great 'royal' sites, by the sixth century Tara was in decline. Becoming a pawn in the political rivalries of early medieval Ireland, it came under the control of Síl nÁedo Sláine, whose territory (the kingdom of Bregha) once stretched from modern Ardee to the River LIFFEY. Teach Chormaic (Cormac's House), a bivallate ring-fort, is probably the latest earthwork on Tara and, in conjoining the Forradh, the inauguration mound of Tara, proclaims the aspirations of those who built it some time during the early Middle Ages. The fact that Tara appears not to have seen large-scale settlement at this time, however, reveals as much again. In fact a new royal residence had been established a few kilometres to the south on the shores of Loch Gabhair (LAGORE) beside the important monastery of Dunshaughlin (Domhnach Seachnaill). It was from here, for over two centuries, that the kings of Southern Breagha reigned. **Conor Newman**

Tara Brooch, a ring brooch of a type sometimes called *pseudo-penannular*, discovered in 1850 at Bettystown, Co. Meath; it is now in the NATIONAL MUSEUM. (It has no connection with TARA: the name was given to it by a dealer.) Frequently misdescribed, the brooch is made of cast-silver gilt and has a diameter of 87 mm (3.4 in.). It takes the form of a completely closed ring, on which a composite pin swivels freely. The ring expands for about half its circumference, and on the obverse it has cast compartments, which were designed to hold filigree panels, some now lost. The head of the pin is similarly decorated. The reverse bears cast gilt ornament

Tara. *Hill of Tara, Co. Meath, the ancient seat of power in Ireland. On top of the Forradh, 'Royal Seat' (centre), is one of the most important monuments, the Lia Fáil (Stone of Destiny), said to be the inauguration stone of the kings of Tara; Teach Cormac, a bivallate ring-fort, conjoins the Forradh. [Dúchas, The Heritage Service]*

in imitation of faceted, deeply cut engraving. The brooch mimics the earlier penannular form in the layout of its decorative panels. However, as the pin cannot make a full 360° rotation, it could not function as a true locking brooch—hence, probably, the elegant knitted-wire guard chain attached to the side. In its closed ring and such features as the beasts that break out in relief from the margins, the brooch traces elements of its design to Germanic and Anglo-Saxon disc-brooches of the seventh century.

The front of the brooch carries very high-quality filigree ornament of animal patterns, serpents, and abstract motifs on the front and on the pinhead. Amber and polychrome glass imitation gemstones decorate both main faces. There are important cast-relief embellishments in the form of fish-tailed beasts and bird heads on the margins of the ring and the pinhead. The principal ornament of the reverse consists of patterns of entwined animals, and trumpet scrolls and spirals in a style close to that of the Lindisfarne Gospels, the Hunterston Brooch from Ayrshire, and the door furniture from DONORE, Co. Meath. Christian influence is present in the art of the brooch, for example the frieze of birds on the back along the narrow part of the ring, which is derived from similar bird processions on the canon-table arcades of illuminated Gospel books. The art style of the brooch emerged from the close interaction of the peoples of northern Britain (including the Angles of Northumbria) and Ireland during the period of close ecclesiastical and political contact in the seventh and eighth centuries. The Tara Brooch is one of the first major Irish products of the great INSULAR ART to survive and probably dates from the later seventh or earlier eighth century. **Michael Ryan**

Tara, kingship of. According to medieval writers, Tara was the seat of the pre-Christian kingship of Ireland. The first reliable information about the institution comes from about the seventh century, when the kings of Tara were the acknowledged overkings of the UÍ NÉILL, the most powerful dynasty in Ireland at the time. The Uí Néill were named after NIALL OF THE NINE HOSTAGES, who supposedly lived in the fifth century. Among his alleged descendants four dynasties dominated the rest: CENÉL CONAILL and CENÉL EOGHAIN (kings of Aileach) in the north, and Síl nÁedo Sláine (kings of Brega) and Clann Cholmáin (kings of Mide) in the midlands. These four competed for the kingship of Tara, until c. 730 Cenél nEoghain and Clann Cholmáin subjugated their other rivals. Until the tenth century their kings alternately held the kingship of Tara. They also claimed the suzerainty over the kings of Connacht and of Airghialla, who descended from Niall's kinsmen but had relinquished their claims to the kingship of Tara. This meant in effect that the kings of Tara claimed to rule the northern part of Ireland, and they sought to extend their hold over the rest of the country. The kings of Tara could call themselves kings of Ireland if they also subjugated the kings of Ulster, Leinster, and Munster. MÁEL SECHNAILL (846–862) was the first to achieve this, and a number of his successors were equally successful. Internal rivalry and losses against the VIKINGS and others weakened the Uí Néill in the tenth century, and they were unable to stop the emergence of new rival dynasties. In 1002 Máel Sechnaill II (980–1022) had to submit himself to BRIAN BÓRÚ, King of Munster. After 1022 the kingship of Tara became the meaningless prerogative of the weakened kings of Mide.

An elaborate tradition tells of centuries of rivalry among the provincial kings for the kingship of Tara and Ireland. In the sixth century the Uí Néill took it for themselves, but they vacated the place after it had been cursed by the Irish SAINTS between 560 and

565. This tradition is both supported and contradicted in the medieval literary sources. It has many unreliable aspects, and it is hard to tell truth from fiction and propaganda. It is likely that Tara had once been an important cult site, but its real significance before the seventh century remains unclear. After the kingship of Tara had lost its meaning it came to be regarded as the HIGH-KINGSHIP of Ireland and even the national monarchy of the past. **Bart Jaski**

Tate, Nahum (1652–1715), poet and playwright. Born in Dublin; educated at TCD. He adapted and translated the work of others; his notorious happy-ending version of *King Lear* held the stage until the 1850s. He was appointed Poet Laureate in 1692 and collaborated on *A New Version of the Psalms* in 1696. **Joley Wood**

tax amnesty, a general pardon for those who admit to having minimised their tax liability by illegal means. Limited amnesties have been a recurrent feature of recent tax history in the Republic, but the most important instances were the broadly based amnesties of 1988 and 1993. The former, which was accompanied by credible threats of intensified enforcement of penalties for evasion, contributed significantly to the fiscal turnaround in that year. The latter, which concentrated on achieving the disclosure of offshore bank deposits, raised less revenue but allowed many evaders to regularise their tax affairs—for what was subsequently widely felt to have been an unduly low price. [see TRIBUNALS.] **Patrick Honohan**

taxation, eighteenth to twentieth centuries. In the eighteenth century the expanding tax regime in Ireland included Crown rents on confiscated lands, *quit rents* on forfeited property, Customs and Excise duties, and a tax on hearths. Additional levies included a stamp duty, a window tax (introduced in 1799), and *ad hoc* poll taxes. After 1801 differential taxation existed within the United Kingdom; though customs rates were made uniform in 1823, excise duties on spirits remained lower in Ireland until harmonisation in 1858. Income tax was introduced later in Ireland than in Britain, in 1853, and a number of other levies were not applied in Ireland. Estate duties were also introduced in 1853. Local rates included assessments on LAND by GRAND JURIES, municipal governments, and POOR LAW unions. Taxation was a cause of protest in late-eighteenth-century Ireland; the country's share of revenue and expenditure of the United Kingdom also provoked widespread debate throughout the nineteenth century. After PARTITION the IRISH FREE STATE adopted its own tax regime, while Northern Ireland continued to be integrated in the United Kingdom's system. **K. J. James**

taxation, twentieth and twenty-first centuries. While taxation in Northern Ireland remained essentially determined by British legislation, and British traditions remained influential in tax policy in the Republic also, the latter's tax regime has become quite distinctive. The structure and level of taxation in the Republic has evolved more under the pressures of populist politics than of ideology. At the end of the twentieth century the bulk of revenue came from four sources: personal income tax accounted for more than a third and a broad expenditure-based value-added tax for rather less, while excises (mainly on sales of alcohol, motor vehicles, petrol, and tobacco) and corporation tax accounted for a further one-sixth each.

The share of GNP collected rose rapidly in the 1960s and especially in the 1970s and until 1984, at which point both were considered unsustainably high, though large areas remained lightly taxed, including residential property, income from agricultural production and exports, and expenditure on food and clothing. After 1984 the emphasis shifted to a rationalisation and lowering of the higher rates, with some expansion of the tax base. By 2000 the marginal tax rate on the highest incomes had fallen to 48 per cent, down from 67 per cent in the mid-1980s, though the complexity of the tax and SOCIAL WELFARE systems meant that some at lower incomes were still faced with extremely high marginal rates over some ranges.

Tax incentives, especially for property development and for exports, have long been an important feature. The latter have been effective in ensuring a steady stream of direct investment in manufacturing facilities by foreign firms, especially American firms able to book sizeable profits as being from their Irish operations but which are really attributable to intellectual property, in fields such as pharmaceuticals, proprietary soft drinks, and computer hardware and software. To comply with EU directives, export tax relief was recast in 1979 as a low (10 per cent) rate of corporation tax applicable to manufacturing and certain internationally traded services. Though criticised for their distorting effects, these incentives are now so deeply embedded in the economic environment that no government has been willing to take the risk of dismantling them. Instead, to help ensure compliance with further EU directives requiring the removal of sectoral discrimination in tax rates by 2003, the rates of corporation tax for all sectors converged to the low rate of 12.5 per cent. **Patrick Honohan**

Taxation, Commission on, established to defuse growing unease about the fairness, level, and efficiency of the tax system. Established in March 1980, the widely respected Commission on Taxation produced five reports between 1982 and 1985. The first of these defined the debate on tax policy for years to come by proposing efficiency as the principal objective, to be achieved through a flat rate of income tax on a broad base supplemented by a surcharge on expenditure out of higher incomes. Special incentives and measures to enhance equality would be the task of expenditure policy. Though some of its recommendations were implemented, the main thrust never found general acceptance. **Patrick Honohan**

Taylor, Dennis (1949–), snooker player. Born in Coalisland, Co. Tyrone. He turned professional in 1971 and won the Irish snooker championship six times. He became world champion in 1985, beating Steve Davis in one of the most exciting and closely fought finals in the competition's history. **Myra Dowling**

Taylor, Geoffrey (1900–1956), poet and anthologist. Born Geoffrey Phibbs in Norfolk; educated at Haileybury, Hertfordshire. The family home was at Lisheen, Co. Sligo. He published two collections of experimental verse in the 1920s; as poetry editor of the BELL he gave encouragement to a younger generation of Irish poets. **Terence Brown**

Taylour, Fay (c. 1908–1983), speedway racer. Born in Birr, Co. Offaly. She won events in Australia, New Zealand, and South Africa before returning to win the first Leinster Trophy motor race at Skerries, Co. Dublin, in 1933. She also won the first women's race at the Donington Park circuit in England in 1935. **Brendan Lynch**

TCD: see TRINITY COLLEGE, DUBLIN.

teachers' unions. The development of teachers' unions must be seen in relation to the general institutional structure of the

telescopes. The Great Telescope, *watercolour by Henrietta Crompton, depicting work on the 'Leviathan', at Birr, Co. Offaly; Lord Rosse directs the conveyance of the Great Speculum. Completed in 1845, it was for more than seventy years the largest telescope in the world. [Irish Picture Library]*

educational system. The Irish National Teachers' Organisation, which represents primary teachers in the Republic and Northern Ireland, was established in 1868 to unify the existing local teachers' associations. The Association of Secondary Teachers in Ireland, which represents 16,000 second-level teachers, was established in 1909. The Teachers' Union of Ireland represents second-level teachers in vocational, community, and comprehensive schools, as well as those working in third-level institutions. Historically, teachers' unions have been highly influential in policy formulation and are formally represented in a number of policy forums, such as the National Council for Curriculum and Assessment, as well as structures for social partnership. They have been particularly important in influencing modes of assessment and school evaluation.

In Northern Ireland, second-level teachers are represented by four different unions: the Association of Teachers and Lecturers, the National Association of Head Teachers, the National Association of Schoolmasters and Union of Women Teachers, and the Ulster Teachers' Union. **Emer Smyth**

Teagasc: see AGRICULTURAL ADIVSORY SERVICES.

tearmann (sanctuary, from Latin *terminus*), the lands around an early Irish church in which rights of sanctuary (usually from secular authority) were claimed or enforced. Theoretically the tearmann was exempt from secular jurisdiction. Sanctuary within the tearmann was supported in canon law and in the vernacular law tracts. **Elva Johnston**

'Tecosca Cormic' ('Cormac's Instructions'), a 'wisdom-text' in OLD IRISH. It is cast in the form of a dialogue in which the legendary King of TARA, CORMAC MAC AIRT, instructs his son on various aspects of human behaviour and especially on the conduct appropriate to kings and lords. The advice is generally high-minded, stressing justice, truth, and moderation. The king must be wise and learned, generous to the poor, and protective of the weak; he must observe the law in all its aspects, and he must subdue evil-doers. The text contains some valuable information on early Irish law, though it is marred by a thoroughly misogynistic section on women. **Tomás Ó Cathasaigh**

telescopes. In the nineteenth century Ireland led the world in the building of large telescopes, thanks to the skill of the gifted engineers THOMAS GRUBB and WILLIAM PARSONS, Earl of Rosse. Grubb acquired an international reputation for his optics and precision clock drives. He made large telescopes for the most important observatories in the world (see p. 53); from 1834 he built telescopes for the principal Irish OBSERVATORIES, including ARMAGH OBSERVATORY, MARKREE CASTLE OBSERVATORY (where thousands of new stars and the asteroid Metis were discovered), DUNSINK OBSERVATORY (where his telescope is still in use today), and CRAWFORD OBSERVATORY (recently restored). Another important telescope was that at William Edward Wilson's DARAMONA OBSERVATORY in Co. Westmeath; among the first electrically controlled telescopes in the world, it produced some of the earliest successful photographs of galaxies and nebulae.

During the same period Parsons established BIRR CASTLE OBSERVATORY in Co. Offaly and introduced new technology in the making of astronomical mirrors. In 1845 he built the largest telescope of the day, the 1.83 m (72-in.) 'Leviathan', with which he discovered the spiral arms in galaxies. The largest operational telescope in Ireland today is the 914 mm (36-in.) reflector established at Kingsland Observatory in Co. Roscommon in 2002. **Éamonn Ansbro**

Telesis Report (1982), a radical reappraisal of the Republic's industrial policy. Telesis was an American consultancy firm led by Ira Magaziner, and its report was one of five on industrial policy commissioned by the NATIONAL ECONOMIC AND SOCIAL COUNCIL. Among the report's recommendations for change were a new emphasis on developing internationally trading indigenous companies and skilled sub-supply firms, and the scaling down of grants to foreign companies. It also recommended that the Government should play a more active role in the formulation of industrial policy. In response, the IDA stated that it was difficult to expand existing enterprises and to encourage indigenous firms, as they lacked entrepreneurs. However, the Government partially followed the Telesis advice when, some years later, it divided the IDA into two agencies: IDA Ireland, to concentrate on foreign direct investment, and FORBAIRT, to concentrate on developing INDIGENOUS INDUSTRY. Later, Forbairt merged with CÓRAS TRÁCHTÁLA and the company training section of FÁS to become Enterprise Ireland. An umbrella body, Forfás, was established as a policy adviser and co-ordination board for industrial development and science and technology. **Paul Sweeney**

Telford, William (1809–1885), organ builder. Birthplace unclear, though his family came to Dublin from Warwickshire. In 1830 he established an organ-building and pianoforte 'manufactory' at Bride Street, before moving to 109 St Stephen's Green. It provided organs for nine cathedrals, collegiate halls and churches, twenty-two convents, monasteries and asylums, and nearly 100 parish churches, while attracting some international recognition. He was awarded the ROYAL DUBLIN SOCIETY's gold medal three times. The oldest surviving instrument (from 1838) and the most important (a pair with matching spires, installed in twin Wexford churches, of the Assumption and the Immaculate Conception (Robert Pierce, 1851)), show Telford to have been a craftsman of exceptional achievement and consummate artistry. **Philip Graydon**

Tellin, Ignatius (1623–1699), Jesuit scholar. Born in the diocese of Armagh. He joined the Jesuits in 1642 and held the chairs of mathematics in the prestigious Jesuit Roman College, 1655–6, and of philosophy and theology in Ingolstadt and Venice. He published three books on physics and philosophy. His mathematical lectures are preserved in manuscript form. **Juan José Pérez-Camacho**

temperance and total abstinence. The first Irish anti-drink societies appeared in the late 1820s. These early societies were dominated by urban middle-class Protestants and were directed against the consumption of spirits by the working class; Catholic total abstinence societies began to emerge during the 1830s. Father THEOBALD MATHEW's Cork society was the most successful of these in the early 1840s, with a membership running into millions. The movement reoriented itself after the GREAT FAMINE. Well-organised middle-class societies attempted to secure prohibition through parliamentary lobbying. While they did not succeed, licensing laws were tightened and were enforced more rigorously, partly as a result of their efforts. The various churches also conducted their own influential anti-drink campaigns. Most Protestant denominations became teetotal. The Catholic Church always preached temperance rather than total abstinence, but in the 1890s it produced a powerful teetotal society, the PIONEER TOTAL ABSTINENCE ASSOCIATION of the Sacred Heart, which by the early twentieth century had approximately half a million members in Ireland, as well as many thousands abroad (see p. 19). Although Irish people have acquired a reputation as heavy drinkers, during the nineteenth and twentieth centuries the country experienced some of the most successful anti-drink campaigns seen in the Western world. [see ALCOHOL ABUSE; TALBOT, MATTHEW.] **Elizabeth Malcolm**

Temple Bar, Dublin. The recent renewal of the Temple Bar area was innovative, as it envisaged the creation of a district with a distinctive character. The street takes its name from Sir William Temple, whose house once stood here, but the name has also become a generic term for the area from Fishamble Street to Westmorland Street and from Dame Street to the River Liffey. Relatively unaffected by the work of the WIDE STREETS COMMISSIONERS, the area retained its character of short and narrow streets and was in decay by the 1950s as the city's commercial core contracted. CIÉ bought property in the area, intending to build a much-needed central bus station; in the interim it rented property cheaply on short leases for a variety of fringe activities. A successful campaign to retain and develop this character led to the Temple Bar Area Renewal and Development Act (1991) and the establishment of Temple Bar Properties Ltd. This company's goal was the development of a cultural, residential, and small-business precinct within a flexible and adaptable framework. Following a competition, the plan proposed by Group 91, a consortium of eight architectural practices, was chosen. The built environment was transformed by the reintroduction of cobblestones, the creation of public spaces, including a new street, the pedestrianisation of the core area, and the attraction of a residential population. A vibrant entertainment district has been created with a growing residential population, though concern exists about the dominance of the entertainment sector and large pubs and the displacement of fringe cultural activities. This development should be compared with the renewal of the Smithfield area on the opposite side of the Liffey, the 'HARP' project. **Joseph Brady**

Temple Bar Framework Plan. An extensive zone between Dame Street and the Liffey, including an area on the other side of the river beyond Ormond Quay, was threatened by a proposed multi-storey transport interchange in the mid-1980s, designed by Skidmore Owings and Merrill of Chicago. A competition for an architectural framework plan was won in 1991 by Group 91, a consortium of eight architectural practices: SHAY CLEARY, GRAFTON ARCHITECTS, Paul Keogh, MCCULLOUGH MULVIN, MCGARRY NÍ ÉANAIGH, O'DONNELL AND TUOMEY, Shane O'Toole, and DEREK TYNAN. The plan proposed the retention of most existing buildings, giving priority to pedestrian access, the creation of three new squares, two of which have been realised (the third replaced by Cow Lane and two internal courts), the introduction of new cultural institutions, and the volumetric manipulation of urban blocks as new residential prototypes. The key buildings, also by Group 91 practices, fuse internationalist and contextual responses. The area is now home to the IRISH FILM CENTRE, Gallery of Photography, the National Photographic Archive of the National Library of Ireland, the Project, many bars and restaurants, while the original target of 3,000 residents was reduced to approximately 2,000. **Raymund Ryan**

Temple Bar. *The Temple Bar quarter, Dublin (in the process of redevelopment), bounded on the north by the River Liffey and on the south by Dame Street, with in the centre Meeting House Square, surrounded by the principal cultural institutions of the area, the National Library's Photographic Archive (top), the Ark Children's Centre (right), and Gallery of Photography (bottom). [Courtesy of Temple Bar Properties]*

Templeton, John (1766–1825), naturalist. Born in Cranmore, near Belfast. He developed an interest in natural history from boyhood and had the private means to pursue this in adult life. He published little but corresponded with the leading naturalists of the day, and his many discoveries in Ireland were included in the works of others, such as Dillwyn, Sowerby, Turner, and Hooker. His knowledge of the major plant and animal groups was said to rival that of any individual in Europe. Surviving manuscripts include a 'Journal' (1806–1825), 'Catalogue of Native Plants of Ireland', and part of a 'Hibernian Flora' with watercolour illustrations by the author. **Donal Synnott**

Tenant League, formed in August 1850 in response to the agrarian crisis caused by the GREAT FAMINE. Its objectives were to improve the condition of tenants by legislating for customary rights and establishing the 'THREE FS': fair rent, fixity of tenure, and free sale. CHARLES GAVAN DUFFY was the most prominent of the founder-members. Despite early promise it fell victim to political intrigue, clerical hostility, and Gavan Duffy's departure for Australia, and folded in 1858. Nevertheless it articulated concerns that were successfully taken up by the Land League in the 1880s. **Fergal Tobin**

tenant right (also known as the ULSTER CUSTOM, because of its widespread practice in that province), essentially the right of free sale, one of the 'THREE FS' (fair rent, fixity of tenure, and free sale) demanded by agrarian reformers in the nineteenth century. It meant that a tenant could sell his interest in a holding, including the value of any improvements he had made, subject to the landlord approving the purchaser. It became law under the Land Law (Ireland) Act (1881). **Fergal Tobin**

tennis. Joshua Pim won Wimbledon singles titles in both 1893 and 1894, having been a finalist in 1891 and 1892. In April 1896 JOHN PIUS BOLAND (later an Irish Party MP) travelled to Athens to the first OLYMPIC GAMES of the modern era and returned as the men's singles and doubles champion. There were suggestions that he had gone to Athens on holiday and casually entered the tennis events at the Olympics; whatever motivated him, he remains Ireland's only Olympic tennis champion. George McVeagh played in the Davis Cup for Ireland, 1933–7, and Cyril Kemp was all-conquering in Irish tennis in the period immediately after the Second World War.

Many people look on the 1980s as the great days of Irish tennis, when Matt Doyle and Seán Sorensen lifted Ireland into the World Group of the Davis Cup. Doyle, a relaxed Irish-American who touched fifty in the world rankings, and Sorensen, a left-handed player from Cork, took on McEnroe, Fleming, and Teltcher in a famous moral victory at the RDS grounds in Dublin in 1983.

Today up to 50,000 men and women are members of 200 tennis clubs throughout the country; and this is both the defining strength and the weakness of the sport. Tennis remains a recreational sport to its roots, yet the club structure continues to be the base from which will be drawn the successors to the present twelve-strong contingent of professional Irish players who continue in their slow if unrelenting struggle through the world rankings: Kelly Liggan at 220 is now the highest-ranked Irish woman ever. Owen Casey represented Ireland in Seoul, Barcelona, and Atlanta and began a still active Davis Cup career in 1988. **Des Allen**

territorial boundaries, an important feature of early and medieval Irish politics, marking divisions between *tuatha* (local petty kingdoms), *mórthuatha* (regional mesne-kingdoms), and *cúigí* (provincial over-kingdoms). A degree of fluidity is often assumed with regard to boundaries, as KINGDOMS of all grades could expand or contract; and while old petty kingdoms were sometimes subsumed into larger realms, offshoots of expanding dynasties could establish new political units. Nonetheless it is probable that boundaries were fixed—at least for certain periods—and that natural features, such as rivers, mountains, or forests, were taken as boundary markers. It seems that boundaries were consciously protected: a tendency for BATTLE sites to cluster in border areas has been noted. Similarly, lands close to boundaries were not uncommonly donated to the church as a means of creating buffer zones, while *rídhála*—important royal meetings, such as that convened at Terryglass in 737—were sometimes held in such marchlands. **Ailbhe Mac Shamhráin**

Teskey. *Donald Teskey's cover illustration for Marita Conlon-McKenna's* Under the Hawthorn Tree, *which explores a child's experience of the Famine. [© The O'Brien Press Ltd, Dublin]*

Teskey, Donald (1956–), artist and illustrator. Born in Rathkeale, Co. Limerick; educated at Wesley College, Dublin, and Limerick School of Art and Design. He has been a full-time artist since 1979, having his first solo show in 1980 in the Lincoln Gallery, Dublin, and regular solo shows in Dublin and London. He was a part-time lecturer in the Dublin Institute of Technology and the National College of Art and Design, 1984–99. He began illustrating children's books in 1990 and has also produced some designs for postage stamps. His work is varied to suit the subject matter, with sweeping black brush strokes or delicate line drawings full of movement and character. Books he has illustrated include *Wildflower Girl* by MARITA CONLON-MCKENNA (1991), *Moon Cradle* edited by Donlon and Glas (1991), and *All Shining in the Spring* (1995) by SIOBHÁN PARKINSON. **Patricia Donlon**

Texas, the Irish in. Following the independence of MEXICO from Spain in 1821, Coahuila y Texas was the most vulnerable of its northern states to the influx of American squatters. Fear of the Americanisation of Texas led to the recruitment of European settlers, especially Catholic Irish; and two pairs of Irish merchants were contracted as *empresarios* (agents) to establish mixed Irish and Mexican settlements. In 1830 John McMullen and James McGloin established the town of San Patricio de Hibernia on the Nueces River, and in 1834 James Power and James Hewetson founded Refugio on the site of the old Spanish mission a few miles inland from the port of El Copano. The Mexican government offered generous land grants to encourage settlement, each family receiving 1,800 ha (4,400 acres) of pasture and 72 ha (177 acres) of arable land.

The Irish families that settled in San Patricio were mostly recruited from New York, Philadelphia, and New Orleans, while others came directly from Co. Tipperary. The Irish in Refugio—mostly small tenant farmers—were brought directly from Co. Wexford and other southern counties. Two ships, the *Prudence* (with eighty-one listed passengers) and the *Heroine* (with seventy-one adult passengers), sailed in the spring of 1834 from Liverpool to New Orleans, where they encountered a cholera epidemic that killed some of the passengers of the *Prudence*. Many others died from cholera and through shipwreck of the schooners taking them to the Texas coast.

The survivors acquired their land grants during the period 1834–5 but were soon engulfed in the war between Texas and Mexico (1835–6). At first San Patricio sided with Mexico, while Refugio stood for Texan independence. Following the destruction of the two settlements by the Mexican army, commanded by General Urrea, both communities fought for Texas. Some of the Irish who enlisted in the Texan army were killed alongside American volunteers at the massacres of Goliad and at the Alamo in March 1836. Others, including Thomas O'Connor, nephew of James Power, fought in the decisive battle of the war, under Sam Houston, at San Jacynto in April 1836. Texan independence was won.

The Irish colonists faced an insecure future, threatened by attacking Comanches and Mexican bandits, until 1845, when families evacuated from the war zone in 1836 returned to their burnt-out homesteads. Thomas O'Connor had stayed all through the war and its aftermath and began to build up a ranching estate that was eventually to make him the 'cattle king' of Refugio. At his death, in 1887, he had amassed 200,000 ha (500,000 acres) and

100,000 head of cattle, much of the land having formerly been in the possession of fellow-colonists; it remains in the family to the present time. In 1934 oil was discovered on the O'Connor estate. Irish families owned a third of all ranches and inherited the Hispanic ranching tradition in the coastal bend area of south Texas. From the 1840s, Irishmen were also prominent as judges, merchants, and bankers in Corpus Christi, Victoria, and San Antonio. **Graham Davis**

textiles. During the eighteenth and nineteenth centuries the principal textile industries (in order of importance) were LINEN, wool, and cotton. The linen industry was heavily concentrated in the Lagan Valley, with considerably smaller pockets of activity in Cos. Cork and Louth. Co. Cork was the main centre of the WOOLLEN industry by the second half of the nineteenth century. The cotton industry, from promising eighteenth-century origins in Belfast, Cork, and Dublin, was supplanted from the 1820s onwards by the Belfast linen industry and thereafter became a marginal industry in the rest of Ireland.

Important archaeological sites associated with these industries include Allman's cotton mill at Overton, near Bandon, Co. Cork, completed in 1802; Laurence Atkinson's woollen mills at Celbridge, Co. Kildare, dating from 1805; and Malcolmson's cotton mill and industrial village at Portlaw, Co. Waterford, established in 1826. The best-preserved buildings, motive power, and original plant are at Benburb, Co. Tyrone, site of a complete linen-weaving factory of c. 1870, with power looms ranging in date from c. 1890 to the 1940s, an industrial STEAM ENGINE, and an associated *beetling* mill, a process that imparted a sheen to the finished cloth. [see INDUSTRIAL ARCHAEOLOGY; INDUSTRIAL REVOLUTION.] **Colin Rynne**

textiles (archaeological evidence). Specific conditions account for the survival of textiles in the ground. In Ireland, mainly damp, anaerobic conditions in BOGS allow wool and silk to survive but little LINEN, as cloth made from vegetable fibre seems vulnerable to decay.

The earliest evidence is from Killymoon, Co. Tyrone, where differing pieces of good-quality plain-weave wool cloth, spindle whorls, and gold 'tress-rings' dating from c. 1000 BC were found. A large plain-weave cloth from c. 800 BC, with an exceptionally fine woven and tasselled horsehair ornament laid on it, was wrapped around bronze tools deposited in Cromaghs Bog, Co. Antrim. IRON AGE finds include plain-weave wool cloth from Lough Gara, Co. Sligo, and a wool MANTLE and leather CLOAK dating from the second to fourth centuries with a male bog burial at Baronstown West, Co. Kildare. Early medieval sites that produced textile finds from the seventh to ninth centuries include DEER PARK FARMS, Co. Antrim, Lagore crannóg, Co. Meath, Moynagh Lough, Co. Meath, and Church Island, Co. Kerry.

The largest find, of more than 2,000 items, is from Hiberno-Norse Dublin, including fine wool twills with Scandinavian patterning, tablet-woven silver and gold braids, imported compound-weave silks, and lightweight wool and silk caps and scarves. VIKING Age textiles were also found in Waterford. ANGLO-NORMAN sites in Dublin, Waterford, and Cork produced mainly wool and fewer silk pieces in differing weaves. Fragments of expensively dyed cloth of shaggy wool pile from early sixteenth-century Drogheda were perhaps part of an Irish MANTLE. In the late sixteenth or early seventeenth century ninety-five textiles, ranging from velvets and silks to coarse wools from a Dublin tailor's workshop, were dumped in Bridge Street and recovered in twentieth-century archaeological excavation. Good evidence for sixteenth and seventeenth-century

textiles. *The Shinrone Dress, a woollen gown found in a bog in Shinrone, Co. Tipperary, in 1843, one of the best examples of ancient textiles found in Ireland. Dating from the late sixteenth or early seventeenth century, it is a tailored open-style gown, with bodice open to the waist, under which a smock would have been worn. [National Museum of Ireland]*

rural clothing came from bogs in Cos. Derry, Donegal, Kerry, Mayo, Sligo, and Tipperary. **Elizabeth Wincott Heckett**

textiles, printed. While a fondness for bright colours and a developed knowledge of dyeing are recorded of the ancient Irish, the technique of printing textiles is not immediately associated with Ireland. One significant development in this process, however, did take place in Ireland. The technique of printing LINENS from engraved metal plates now referred to as *toiles de Jouy* was first developed and advertised in 1752 by Francis Nixon of Drumcondra, Co. Dublin, several years before Oberkampf established the famous French factory (see p. 600). Since then the printing of fabrics has been carried on by several firms, though one of the most established, that of Glendenning in Lurgan, Co. Armagh, closed at the end of the twentieth century. **Hilary O'Kelly**

textiles, woven. Unlike cotton, the weaving of silk was an established industry in Ireland but never became synonymous with the country in the way that wool and LINEN did. Ireland gained an early reputation for warm, waterproof wools, particularly the shag-lined rug traded on the Continent over several hundred years. Similarly linen, exported since the fourteenth century, had by the nineteenth century an established reputation for household, underwear, and SHIRT cloths. Apart from this reputation, Ireland's identity in history and economy is closely bound up with the vicissitudes of wool and linen. Successfully exporting until the middle of the seventeenth century, the industry was then undermined by deliberate intervention. Attempts to revive it failed until the late nineteenth century, when the production of woven cloth was boosted as part of the encouragement of cottage industries. After independence, state agencies promoted more standardised cloth production, using machine-spun yarn, in favour of homespun. In 1951 the National College of Art and Design, Dublin, established the Department of Spinning, Dying and Weaving to preserve a traditional craft and to promote weaving as part of the national economy. **Hilary O'Kelly**

Thackeray, W. M. [William Makepeace] (1811–1863), English novelist. Born in Calcutta; educated at the University of Cambridge. His first novel, *The Luck of Barry Lyndon* (1844), tells the tale of an eighteenth-century Irish adventurer. Thackeray toured Ireland in 1842; *The Irish Sketchbook*, published the following year, gave offence to Irish opinion with its unrelenting descriptions of pre-FAMINE poverty. **Terence Brown**

thatching. A wide range of materials has been used in the past to thatch roofs, including cultivated straw (of wheat, oats, rye, and barley); flax and, rarely, potato stalks were also used. Wild growths include rushes, water reed, various wild grasses (such as moor and marram grass), and heather. Suitable thatching straw is now difficult to obtain, and imported water reed has grown in favour. In much of Connacht and Ulster the thatch overlies a bed of heather or tough lea sod.

Three distinct methods of applying thatch are used. The most common is 'pinned thatch', in which bundles of thatch are secured to the roof with the aid of willow or hazel rods, briars, or splints of bog fir. In exposed coastal districts of the west and north the thatch is generally held in position with a network of ropes. In east Leinster and Munster handfuls of straw are thrust into the base layer, which in turn is stitched to the roof timbers. **Críostóir Mac Carthaigh**

That Petrol Emotion, rock group. Formed in Derry in 1984 by John O'Neill following the break-up of the UNDERTONES, the group developed their own nationalist political argument through thinly coded pop songs. Their finest moment was the single 'Big Decision' (1987). Towards the later part of their career the group dispensed with their political agenda, but they remain perhaps the only band to write credible songs about the political situation in Northern Ireland during the latter half of the 1980s. John and Damian O'Neill joined the re-formed Undertones in 2000. **Tony Clayton-Lea**

theatre. Unlike POETRY and MUSIC, theatre has no ancient Irish prehistory. The chieftains of pre-conquest Ireland did maintain an entourage of performers, ranging from the OLLAMH (professor of poetry) to the *cleasamhnach* (trickster). However, there is little to suggest that early Irish performances employed the definitive theatrical element of personification, where the performer adopts a role, as opposed to narrating a story. Consequently, the first Irish play, the liturgical *Visitatio Sepulcri*, comes from the centre of Norman power, Dublin, in the late fourteenth century; and other records of medieval theatre are concentrated in Dublin and Kilkenny. Similarly, in 1635 the Lord Lieutenant, THOMAS WENTWORTH, built the first Irish theatre in Werburgh Street, Dublin, adjacent to DUBLIN CASTLE. It was here that the first Irish play dealing with Ireland, James Shirley's ST PATRICK FOR IRELAND (1639), was staged. When the next important theatre, SMOCK ALLEY THEATRE, was built after the restoration in 1662, it too was only a few hundred yards from Dublin Castle, on whose patronage it would remain dependent for some time.

In the years after the wars of the 1690s the Irish theatre gradually began to expand from its limited base. Tours by the Dublin companies established theatres in Cork, Belfast, Waterford, and Limerick in the 1730s, expanding theatre's geographical coverage. Similarly, attempts to write distinctively Irish plays, including Charles Shadwell's Rotherick O'Connor (1720), inaugurated the exploration of Irish myth and ancient history on the stage. And yet one of the controlling forces of Irish theatre culture had already begun to assert itself: the magnetic proximity of the London theatre world. From the early eighteenth century onwards there was a steady haemorrhage of actors and playwrights from Dublin to London, where the rewards of a life in the theatre were greater. Nonetheless Irish theatre in the eighteenth century was vibrant, providing one of the few public places in which a reasonable cross-section of society—from the Lord Lieutenant to shopkeepers and artisans—could sit together while issues of loyalty, justice, and identity were debated in forms ranging from neo-classical TRAGEDY to COMEDY, of which THOMAS SHERIDAN'S THE BRAVE IRISHMAN (1743) is a notable example. Towards the end of the century the theatre combined the new taste for stage spectacle with the emerging romanticisation of Irish landscape to produce plays such as JOHN O'KEEFFE'S *The Poor Soldier* (1782). With its music, idealised rural setting, and stock characters, this play points the way towards Irish MELODRAMA, which was to dominate the stage until the early twentieth century in extraordinarily popular plays such as DION BOUCICAULT'S THE COLLEEN BAWN (1860).

The demand for elaborate scenery created a need for larger theatres to accommodate the burgeoning number of English and American touring companies. The result was a boom in theatre construction throughout the nineteenth century. Some of these theatres have been lost, among them the THEATRE ROYAL, DUBLIN; others remain, including the THEATRE ROYAL, WEXFORD, the GAIETY and OLYMPIA THEATRES, Dublin, the THEATRE ROYAL, WATERFORD, the GRAND OPERA HOUSE, Belfast, and the EVERYMAN PALACE, Cork. The number of late nineteenth-century theatres testifies to a thriving theatre culture; however, few of the plays on these stages were Irish. Responding to this situation, W. B. YEATS, LADY AUGUSTA GREGORY and EDWARD MARTYN founded the Irish Literary Theatre, subsequently the ABBEY THEATRE, in 1899. Emphasising dramatic writing rather than stage spectacle, the early Abbey nurtured an extraordinary outpouring of seventy original plays over the next decade, inspiring a parallel movement in Belfast, the ULSTER LITERARY THEATRE. Among the Abbey's early productions were J. M. SYNGE'S darkly comic plays of rural life and YEATS'S experiments with Irish tragedy, combining esoteric ritual and mythology. In 1904 Yeats's patron Annie Horniman provided the funds to establish the theatre in Abbey Street, Dublin, from which it took its name.

While Synge would always be popular, audiences increasingly showed a preference for rural comedies over Yeats's theatrical explorations. Consequently, while SEAN O'CASEY'S corrosive demythologisation of recent Irish history in his ABBEY TRILOGY would provoke a passionate response (and a riot in the case of *The Plough and the Stars* in 1926), the Abbey for the most part ceased to challenge audiences in the 1930s and 40s. Though the GATE THEATRE, founded in 1928, brought a modernist sensibility to SCENIC DESIGN, Irish theatre did not regain its vitality again until the late 1950s.

The reinvigoration of the 1950s came from a number of sources. The seeds of a broadly based theatre culture were being sown by the burgeoning AMATEUR AND COMMUNITY THEATRE movement, co-ordinated by the DRAMA LEAGUE OF IRELAND. JOHN B. KEANE'S SIVE was first performed by amateurs, as was TOM MURPHY'S early work. Equally, small experimental theatres, such as the PIKE in Dublin (premiering BECKETT and BEHAN) and the LYRIC PLAYERS in

theatre. *Interior of the Theatre Royal, Waterford, which forms part of Waterford City Hall. In 1876 the west wing of the City Hall—formerly a Georgian playhouse—was converted into a modern theatre. [Waterford County Council Archives]*

Belfast (which staged BRIAN FRIEL's early work) were exploring new theatrical forms. So, when the new Abbey Theatre building opened in 1966 (the original having been destroyed by fire in 1951) Irish theatre was already moving towards its late twentieth-century form.

Underlying much recent Irish theatre is a scepticism that a single theatre can represent a nation. This was evident in the content of plays such as FRANK MCGUINNESS's OBSERVE THE SONS OF ULSTER MARCHING TOWARDS THE SOMME (1985); it is equally evident in a tendency among younger playwrights to construct plays from conflicting parallel monologues. At the same time there has been a diversification of the structure of the Irish theatre world, as theatre companies have proliferated outside the traditional theatre centres. Among these are the DRUID in Galway and FIELD DAY in Derry, which premiered Friel's TRANSLATIONS in 1980 (see p. 674). Specialised physical theatre, community, and theatre-in-education companies have come into existence, and theatre training is professionalised as never before. As these forces converge there is an excitingly diverse new generation of dramatists, including MARINA CARR and CONOR MCPHERSON, and a boom in theatre construction unparalleled since the nineteenth century. **Christopher Morash**

theatre architecture. While Ireland has not developed an indigenous form of theatre architecture, there have been periods of intensive theatre construction. In 1662 the SMOCK ALLEY THEATRE, Dublin, was the first purpose-built public proscenium theatre in Ireland (see p. 987); in the middle of the eighteenth century there were new theatres in Cork, Limerick, Belfast, and Waterford. Except for the outer walls of Smock Alley, none of these theatres survives; however, there are a number of theatres still in use from the building boom of the nineteenth century, when managers responded to the influx of touring companies; these include the THEATRE ROYAL, WATERFORD, THEATRE ROYAL, WEXFORD, OLYMPIA and GAIETY THEATRES, DUBLIN, GRAND OPERA HOUSE, BELFAST, and EVERYMAN PALACE, Cork.

The non-indigenous nature of theatre architecture became problematic during the Irish Renaissance of the late nineteenth century, with its purist quest for authenticity in Irish culture. Even the ABBEY THEATRE was converted by JOSEPH HOLLOWAY in 1904 from an existing theatre, the Mechanics' Institute, and it retained many of the features of a small nineteenth-century theatre until it was destroyed by fire in 1951. The first major theatre with a fan-shaped auditorium came late in the wider development of theatre architecture, with MICHAEL SCOTT's replacement for the Abbey in 1966. In the closing decades of the twentieth century the Abbey was followed by a burgeoning number of new theatre spaces, some retaining a proscenium arch, while others, like the Project in Dublin, have turned to flexible 'black box' configurations. **Christopher Morash**

theatre companies. With the opening of the Smock Alley Theatre, Dublin, in 1662 it became customary for theatres—at least in Dublin—to have a resident company organised around a leading actor. The actor-manager was the leading figure in eighteenth-century theatre, playing leading roles and distributing the remaining parts among the rest of the company. At a time when plays were frequently revived, members of the audience (who often watched the same play more than once) became discerning judges of the collective work of a company, with whose quality the theatre's fortunes rose or fell. It was not until the end of the eighteenth century that the first theatre managers who were not actors emerged, heralding a new order in which, by the middle of the nineteenth century, few theatres had a permanent company. Instead, producer-managers brought in touring companies or else cast individual plays around a visiting star.

Though the Irish Literary Theatre (later the ABBEY THEATRE) first operated in this way, after 1902 it began to function as a permanent company. Unlike earlier companies, the Abbey had no single leading actor, instead working collectively (though not without internal acrimony). It continued to operate in this manner until the end of the twentieth century, when the growing authority of the artistic director led to a tendency to cast plays individually. By contrast, the GATE THEATRE under MÍCHEÁL MAC LIAMMÓIR and HILTON EDWARDS (founded in 1928), was in some respects a throwback to the earlier theatre companies, in that the company's founders invariably took the leading roles (as well as usually directing and designing) (see p. 497). After their retirement in the late 1970s, however, the Gate ceased to have a permanent company, and it is now based around a permanent artistic director, Michael Colgan, who hires directors for each new production, which is cast individually. The same is true of the LYRIC THEATRE in Belfast and, increasingly, of the Abbey.

While there has been a convergence of practice with the three largest theatre companies, there has been an unprecedented proliferation of smaller theatre companies since 1980. This has been stimulated by the practice of the ARTS COUNCILS, North and South, of directing funds towards theatre companies rather than individual productions. Indeed the FIELD DAY THEATRE COMPANY, which flourished in the 1980s, was formed originally to permit its founders, STEPHEN REA and BRIAN FRIEL, to finance a production of Friel's TRANSLATIONS (though its cultural project subsequently became more all-embracing). By contrast, the DRUID THEATRE COMPANY, Galway, and Blue Raincoat, Sligo, resemble the traditional model of a group of theatre artists based in their own theatre building, working collectively from a shared artistic philosophy. Other companies specialise in children's theatre, theatre in education, or community theatre; most, by necessity, are touring companies, lacking their own permanent premises. Given that Arts Council funding is vital to the existence of almost all theatre, as long as present funding practices exist the theatre company will continue to be the basic unit of theatrical organisation. **Christopher Morash**

theatre, geographical distribution. The first professional theatre in Ireland was in WERBURGH STREET, Dublin, 1635, followed by the SMOCK ALLEY THEATRE, 1662. Though there was theatrical activity in Kilkenny from the fourteenth century onwards, it was not until the 1730s that regular theatrical performances began to take place elsewhere, as rival Dublin companies toured south to Kilkenny, Limerick, Waterford, and Cork and north to Newry, Belfast, and Derry. These early tours drew the template for theatrical geography for two centuries. With the development of a RAILWAY network in the first half of the nineteenth century there was a consolidation of theatre along the east and south-east coasts, on an axis running through Belfast, Dublin, and Cork. English touring companies crossed the IRISH SEA, played at stops along the circuit, and then sailed back to Liverpool. Ireland's major nineteenth-century theatres—the GRAND OPERA HOUSE in Belfast, the GAIETY THEATRE in Dublin, and the EVERYMAN PALACE in Cork—are the products of this geography.

The domination of the touring companies in effect cut off the west of Ireland from a continuous theatre culture, so that towns such as Galway and Derry saw only intermittent professional performances. This situation was alleviated somewhat by the 'fit-up' companies—smaller groups of itinerant actors of variable skills—who roamed the entire country. The real change came in the early 1930s, when hundreds of small AMATEUR AND COMMUNITY THEATRE companies were formed in towns and villages all over Ireland. In the early 1980s changes in the policies of the ARTS COUNCILS, north and south, made funds available for new regional professional companies, which were able to build on the basis of the audiences and actors established by the amateur movement. There are now professional companies in Galway (DRUID), Cork (Corcadorca), Waterford (Red Kettle), Sligo (Blue Raincoat), and elsewhere. At the beginning of the twenty-first century the greatest concentration of theatrical activity is still in Dublin; however, unlike previous centuries, there are now active theatre cultures in most large communities. **Christopher Morash**

theatre, the Irish in American. The Irish have been a formidable presence on stage and behind the scenes of theatre in the United States. Theatre and politics have been an explosive combination for the Irish: Irish NATIONALISM was frequently a topic of drama in the United States, and Irish-Americans often protested against stereotypes of the Irish on stage. In addition, the history of Irish contributions to American theatre chronicles the rising social status of the Irish and their descendants in the United States.

In the colonial period, Irish characters were already familiar on the American stage. *The Disappointment* (1767) featured an early American example of the stereotypical STAGE IRISHMAN—a fun-loving and hard-drinking character. Irish influence on American theatre increased throughout the nineteenth century. John Brougham, a graduate of Trinity College, Dublin, arrived in New York in 1842. Many of his plays included historical figures, including DANIEL O'CONNELL. Around the same time several performers of Irish descent, such as Dan Emmett, helped establish and popularise the 'minstrel show', a black-face performance style catering to white working-class male audiences in the urban north. The close proximity of Irish and African-Americans in some urban settings was the basis of Irish familiarity with, and hostility towards, African-Americans; the denigration of African-Americans in this popular entertainment helped the Irish establish a white identity for themselves among the American working class.

By the late 1800s first and second-generation Irish-American actors and theatrical professionals dominated the American theatre. DION BOUCICAULT, who came to New York in 1853, used Ireland's struggle for independence as a setting and theme for his historic melodramas. THE COLLEEN BAWN (1860) dealt with the fraught relationship between tenants and landlords; *The Shaughraun* (1874) followed the adventures of an escaped Fenian. Though Boucicault was careful to present English and Irish characters sympathetically, the political themes of his plays nevertheless fuelled Irish-American nationalism.

Edward Harrigan, an actor and writer with Irish roots, performed in minstrel shows before he began to offer parodies of Boucicault's plays in the 1870s. After pairing with Tony Hart (Anthony Cannon) in 1871, he wrote and performed in a series of musical comedies about Dan Mulligan, an Irishman who gambles, drinks and fights but is also compassionate and steadfast. *The Mulligan Guard Ball* (1879), *Mulligan's Silver Wedding* (1880), *Cordelia's Aspirations* (1883) and other plays in this series captured the rivalries and bonds between Irish-Americans and other immigrant groups, depicted Irish-Americans' political contests and leadership, and also offered a humorous view of Irish-American upward mobility, particularly the aspirations of women. In these ways American theatre increasingly focused on Irish IMMIGRATION and assimilation in a distinctly American setting, as opposed to Boucicault's attention to Irish history.

In the late nineteenth and early twentieth century Irish-American theatre became intensely political in several ways. The Irish role in American urban politics became a theme of many plays, including E. W. Townsend's *McFadden's Row of Flats* (1897). And when Irish-American nationalists turned to cultural concerns in the 1890s they began to attack the caricatures of the Irish on stage. Protests against the stage Irishman in the United States date back to at least the 1840s, when several angry Irishmen were thrown out of a performance of TYRONE POWER's *O'Flannigan and the Fairies*; but the uprising against the stage Irishman, led by the GAELIC LEAGUE and the ANCIENT ORDER OF HIBERNIANS, reached a crescendo around the beginning of the twentieth century. Activists objected to images of lascivious maids, ape-like men, and backward peasants. The largest protest of this period was against the ABBEY THEATRE's American tour of THE PLAYBOY OF THE WESTERN WORLD by Synge in 1911.

The 1911 Abbey tour helped launch the little theatre movement in the United States, such as the Provincetown Players, a company that included EUGENE O'NEILL, son of an Irish immigrant and actor, James O'Neill. *Long Day's Journey into Night*, which had its premiere in 1956, featured an Irish-American family. Like other Irish-American playwrights of the early twentieth century, O'Neill grappled with the tension between individual autonomy and loyalty to family or church. Several Irish-American authors of this period turned away from Irish topics: George Kelly, for example, wrote comedies about the theatrical world and elite society, including *The Show-Off* (1924) and *Reflected Glory* (1936).

The theatre has been both a source of distinctive Irish identity and a means of assimilation; it has been both insulting and inspiring to Irish-American political activists. **M. Alison Kibler**

theatre, the Irish in British. There has been a close relationship between the theatre worlds of Ireland and England—and, more narrowly, between Dublin and London—since the end of the seventeenth century, when a generation of actors and writers nurtured by the SMOCK ALLEY THEATRE, Dublin, achieved success on the London stage. WILLIAM CONGREVE, THOMAS SOUTHERNE, and GEORGE FARQUHAR all had their first experience of the theatre in Dublin before moving to the more lucrative theatre world of London. Farquhar in particular inaugurated a specific tradition of Irish writing for the London stage. His most popular creation, Sir Harry Wildair in *The Constant Couple* (a part created by the Irish actor Robert Wilks) is ostensibly English; but Wildair has the witty irreverence usually associated with STAGE-IRISH characters, and this allows him to view the follies of English culture from an outsider's point of view. Of course, not all Irish plays for the London stage belong in this coded tradition; nonetheless, in the eighteenth century, when the English stage was dominated by Irish actors (PEG WOFFINGTON, James Quin, Henry Mossop, SPRANGER BARRY, and THOMAS SHERIDAN) and Irish writers (CHARLES MACKLIN, Arthur Murphy, Hugh Kelly, Richard Cumberland, OLIVER GOLDSMITH, and RICHARD BRINSLEY SHERIDAN), an Irish point of view created a position from which the English theatre could engage in social critique.

The coded tradition of Irish writing and acting for the London theatre would re-emerge briefly and impressively in the work of OSCAR WILDE and GEORGE BERNARD SHAW at the end of the nineteenth century. In the interim, however, a more overt form of stage-Irishness developed. A growing taste for spectacular stage designs, presenting sublime landscapes and picturesque poverty in plays with conciliatory endings, first helped to establish the English popularity of Irish plays like JOHN O'KEEFFE's *The Poor Soldier* (1782). By the 1840s the conventions of what became known as the 'Irish play' were firmly established, so that it was possible for an English writer like John Buckstone to write one of the most popular Irish plays of the nineteenth century, *Green Bushes* (1845). Irish writers also contributed to the burgeoning Irish MELODRAMA; the most successful of these, DION BOUCICAULT, had a string of successes in the English theatre, with VICTORIA going to see THE COLLEEN BAWN (1861) three times.

theatre. *Poster announcing one of the seminal events in Irish cultural history, a prelude to the founding of the Abbey Theatre and the Literary Revival. [Council of Trustees of the National Library of Ireland]*

When the reaction against the Irish play came, in the form of the Irish Literary Theatre (later the ABBEY THEATRE), it too was embraced by English theatre-goers. Founded in 1899 by W. B. YEATS, LADY AUGUSTA GREGORY, and EDWARD MARTYN, the company first played London in 1903 to rave reviews, at first under the auspices of the Irish Literary Society of London. Within a few years, tours took them to Manchester, Leeds, Liverpool, Hull, Newcastle, and Cardiff, while a visit to Glasgow in 1907 would inspire the foundation of the Scottish National Players. By 1914 it was clear that the old economic patterns continued to persist, in spite of a rapidly changing political scene, as leading performers from the early Abbey, such as SARA ALLGOOD, left Ireland for the larger theatrical market of London. In the 1920s an increasingly puritanical strain in Irish culture gave artists another reason for leaving, most notably SEAN O'CASEY, who moved to England after *The Plough and the Stars* was met with riots in 1926.

The resources of the London theatre—in audiences, performance space, actors, directors, and designers—continued to attract Irish theatre people throughout the second half of the twentieth century. Most Irish directors, designers, and actors work regularly in England, and some—from PETER O'TOOLE to FIONA SHAW—have had a predominantly English career. Similarly, many Irish plays since 1950 have had their premiere in London: BRENDAN BEHAN's *The Hostage* (1959), the English translations of SAMUEL BECKETT's major works, TOM MURPHY's *A Whistle in the Dark* (1961), and FRANK MCGUINNESS's *Mutabilitie* (1997). Since the late 1980s there has been a tendency for young Irish playwrights to be commissioned to write new work for London venues such as the Tricycle Theatre, the Bush Theatre, or even the Royal Court, as has happened with Billy Roche's Wexford Trilogy (1988–1993), SEBASTIAN BARRY's *The Steward of Christendom* (1995), CONOR MCPHERSON's *The Weir* (1997), and MARTIN MCDONAGH's Leenane Trilogy (1996–7, which transferred to London shortly after a Galway opening). Surprisingly, the rapid growth and increased funding of the theatre community in Ireland since 1990 has not reversed this trend, as English audiences continue to embrace plays whose concerns are uncompromisingly centred on the neighbouring island. **Christopher Morash**

theatre, medieval. The theatre of medieval Ireland resembled that of other European countries in that it was either liturgical or an expression of civic pride. Outside the English-speaking centres of population there was a diverse and widespread Irish performance culture, but it had little impact on the urban forms of medieval theatre and lacked the element of personification that defines theatre.

The earliest surviving Irish play is the *Visitatio Sepulchri*, from the second half of the fourteenth century, when it was probably performed in the church of St John the Evangelist, near CHRIST CHURCH CATHEDRAL, Dublin. Written in Latin and probably sung, it is a liturgical drama ritually re-enacting the visit to the Sepulchre of the Three Marys. Also from Dublin and dating from the late fourteenth or early fifteenth century is *The Pride of Life*, a morality play written in HIBERNO-ENGLISH. As with the *Visitatio*, there is no direct evidence of *The Pride of Life* having been performed, though it was certainly intended for performance, possibly outdoors.

A late body of medieval drama originated in Kilkenny, where an Anglican reformer, John Bale, while Bishop of Ossory, 1552–3, staged three original plays—*God's Promises, Johan Baptystes Preachynge*, and *The Temptacyon of Our Lorde*—all of which were performed outdoors at the town's market cross. While Bale's reforming liturgical dramas are in one respect something of an anomaly, in another respect they form part of a long, but now largely lost, tradition of public pageants and performances in both Dublin and Kilkenny during the late Middle Ages. In both places there was an annual procession through the streets on feasts such as Corpus Christi, when plays dealing with Biblical subjects were performed as an expression of civic pride. For Dublin a unique and detailed record of these processions for 1498 exists in the city's Great Chain Book. However, in the upheavals of the early seventeenth century the practice was discontinued, and the last records from Kilkenny date from 1639. **Christopher Morash**

Theatre Royal, Dublin, designed by Samuel Beazley and opened in January 1821 in Hawkins Street, just north of Trinity College. The Theatre Royal was the most important Dublin theatre of the middle of the nineteenth century. It was an ornate theatre, with a horseshoe-shaped 3,800-seat auditorium and deep stage. When it opened it boasted the latest in theatre technology: an elaborate fly system, traps, and (from 1823) gas lighting. During the Repeal campaign of the 1830s there were frequent disturbances in the theatre; on one occasion a box-keeper died after being thrown down a flight of stairs. Under the management of J. W. Calcraft the theatre moved up-market in the 1840s, frequently presenting opera but returning to plays after the extraordinary success of BOUCICAULT's *The Colleen Bawn* in 1861. It burnt down in February 1880; a second theatre, 1897–1934, and a third, 1935–62, subsequently occupied the same site, becoming a cine-variety theatre in its final incarnation. **Christopher Morash**

Theatre Royal, Waterford. In 1876 the demand for touring venues that brought the GAIETY and EVERYMAN PALACE into existence led to the conversion of the west wing of the City Hall, Waterford, into a theatre. The result was a typical small Victorian theatre, with a horseshoe-shaped 650-seat auditorium and three rows of tiered galleries. It was renovated in 1996 (see p. 1043). **Christopher Morash**

Theatre Royal, Wexford, built in 1832 and the oldest theatre in Ireland still in use. For some years the fate of this 555-seat theatre was in doubt; however, after being taken over by the WEXFORD FESTIVAL OPERA it underwent extensive restoration work in 1961 and again in 1972. Though the stage is not large by opera house standards, at 8.4 by 7.8 m (28 by 26 ft), the excellent acoustics and the intimacy of the small, raked auditorium make it a well-loved venue. **Christopher Morash**

theological education. The Irish Universities Act (1908) precluded state grants 'for the provision or maintenance of any theological or religious teaching or study,' and this prohibition remained in force until this act was superseded by the Universities Act (1997). Theological education at university level was therefore available only if privately financed, and for a long time this meant in practice that degrees in theology in the Republic could be obtained only at ST PATRICK'S COLLEGE, Maynooth, and TRINITY COLLEGE, Dublin, though there was a privately financed professorship in theology at University College, Cork. Third-level education in theology was also available at the seminaries and theological colleges of the various denominations, as were religious studies at the teacher education colleges.

Since 1927 degrees have been granted by Queen's University, Belfast, though theological teaching has been done not at the university itself but at the Theological Colleges. These are constituted constituent colleges of the university's Institute of Theology, which operates like a school within the Faculty of Humanities. In recent decades, affiliation to Maynooth, Trinity or Queen's has enabled students at other institutions to take degrees, as has recognition of courses by the National Council for Educational Awards in the Republic. Kimmage Mission Institute and All Hallows, Dublin, also offer degree courses in theology and related disciplines, such as philosophy. The Milltown Institute of Philosophy and Theology, in addition to affiliation to the National Council for Educational Awards, is empowered by Papal charter to grant degrees in these subjects. Religious studies is now a degree subject in the teacher education colleges by virtue of the recognition or affiliation of these institutions by the universities. The Irish School of Ecumenics is an affiliate of Trinity College.

Whereas at one time theology was studied mainly, if not exclusively, by ordinands, the majority of students are now lay. This is partly because of the decrease in the number of candidates for ordination but is attributable also to the fact that there are now opportunities for lay people that formerly did not exist. These include not merely the traditional university faculties and their affiliates but also some of the higher education institutes. Also, though the 1908 Act forbade state funding, this prohibition was not taken to apply to such forms of subvention as county council grants or the remission of third-level fees. Theology graduates who do not enter the ministries are mainly, though not at all exclusively, to be found among the ranks of religion teachers.

It remains to be seen whether the absence in the 1997 Act of a ban on funding theology will result in its introduction in all the universities to which that statute applies. One view is that the constitutional prohibition on endowment would preclude the provision of denominational theology. This is open to challenge, but in any case it is unlikely that in present circumstances a university or other institution of higher learning would wish to introduce a denominational course. There are plans for the further development of centres for Catholic theology by the Western Theological Union and the Newman Institute, Ballina. **Patrick Hannon**

Therapy?, rock group. Formed in the late 1980s, Therapy? cite STIFF LITTLE FINGERS and the UNDERTONES as two of their formative influences. Despite changes in composition, the band, fronted by Andy Cairns, has continued to play its uncompromising music and is considered to be one of the best hard-rock bands to have come out of Ireland. Two early mini-albums, *Babyteeth* (1991) and *Pleasure Death* (1992), contain some of the group's finest moments. **Tony Clayton-Lea**

Thin Lizzy, rock group. Founded in Dublin in 1970 by Phil Lynott (1949–1986), Eric Bell, and Brian Downey, the trio quickly released a debut single, 'I Need You' (1970), followed by two albums, *Thin Lizzy* (1971) and *Shades of a Blue Orphanage* (1972). The band appeared significant because of their innate musicianship, their intense relationship with Ireland, and the fact that Lynott, their lead singer, was of Brazilian-Irish parentage—a rarity in Dublin during the 1950s and 60s. By 1972 the band had moved to London, recording material for a third album, *Vagabonds of the Western World* (1973). The single 'Whiskey in the Jar' (1973), a rock version of the traditional song, reached the British top ten, beginning a successful ten-year run of fourteen top forty hit singles. In 1974 the group experienced a series of personnel changes, which was not settled until the arrival of Brian Robertson and Scott Gorham, heralding the band's golden period. 'Jailbreak' (1976), 'Johnny the Fox' (1976), 'Bad Reputation' (1977), and *Live and Dangerous* (1978) saw the group cross over internationally. From the 1980s, however, the band was experiencing difficulties. Despite albums such as *Black Rose* (1979), *Renegade* (1981), and *Thunder and Lightning* (1983) selling well, the band's personnel changes were indicative of internal conflict. Lynott released a solo album, *Solo in Soho* (1980), followed by *The Phillip Lynott Album* (1982), neither of which was commercially successful. In the summer of 1983 Lynott split up the band. His drug habit was taking its toll, and in 1985 he suffered a collapse; following several days in a coma he died of heart failure, exacerbated by pneumonia. A celebration of his life and music, the Vibe for Philo, takes place annually in Dublin. **Tony Clayton-Lea**

Thin Lizzy. *Phil Lynott, lead singer of the 1970s rock group Thin Lizzy, during their concert at the Wembley Arena, London, 22 June 1978. [Universal Pictorial Press and Agency Ltd]*

Thomas, Adrian (1947–), composer, lecturer, and broadcaster. Born in Cornwall; educated at the University of Nottingham and Krakow Conservatory. He joined the school of music at Queen's University, Belfast, in 1972, was HAMILTON HARTY professor of music there from 1985 to 1996, and was on secondment to the BBC as Radio 3's head of music, 1990–93. He has been head of the department of music at the University of Cardiff since 1996. **Philip Graydon**

Thomas, Sir (Alfred) Brumwell (1868–1948), architect. Born in Surrey, son of an architect. He won the principal competition for Belfast City Hall in 1897 with a design in the baroque revival style, much influenced by the works of Wren. It was completed in 1906 at a cost of more than £360,000, double the original estimate; knighted for his work, he nevertheless had to sue for the final instalment of his fee. He returned in 1925 to build the War Memorial and Garden of Remembrance in its grounds, finished by the City Surveyor after a further dispute in 1927. After Belfast he designed several town halls in England. **Frederick O'Dwyer**

Thomas, General George (1756–1802), the 'Rajah from Tipperary'. Born in Roscrea, Co. Tipperary. He joined the British navy in 1781, deserted at Madras, and became a mercenary. In 1787 he entered the service of the Begum Sumru of Delhi, who appointed him commander of her army. Later he served Appa Rao, the Muhratta governor of Meerut, upon whose death in 1797 Thomas made himself rajah. His territory grew, and he offered to conquer Punjab for the British. He made enemies of the Sikhs, who finally deposed him in 1802 with French aid. Escorted to the British frontier, he died of fever in Bengal. **David Kiely**

Thompson, Hugh (1860–1920), illustrator. Born in Coleraine, Co. Derry, son of a tea merchant; educated at Coleraine Model School, otherwise, apart from a few classes at the Government School of Art, largely self-taught. He was apprenticed in the art department of the publisher Marcus Ward, under the supervision of the designer John Vinycomb. In 1883 he went to London to seek work, eventually becoming an illustrator with the *English Illustrated Magazine*, where he produced a wide range of work notable for its delicacy, humour, and atmosphere. Much in demand, he illustrated some seventy books, particularly such classics as Goldsmith's *The Vicar of Wakefield* (1890), Austen's *Pride and Prejudice* (1894), and *Tales from Maria Edgeworth* (1903); he also produced work for contemporary authors, including J. M. Barrie, Austin Dobson, and Stephen Gwynn. His nostalgic and almost whimsical illustrations for Gaskell's *Cranford* had a considerable following of illustrators, who became known as the 'Cranford School'. **Patricia Donlon**

Thompson, Kenneth (Ken) (1946–), sculptor. Born in Cork; educated in England at Worth and Downside Abbey. Inspired by the work of Eric Gill and the arts and crafts tradition, he took up stone-carving and lettering in Liverpool in 1969. Following an introduction by Henry Moore he spent two years in Carrera, Italy, on a scholarship before settling in 1975 in Ballintober, Co. Cork. In 1975 he was bequeathed SEAMUS MURPHY's tools and unfinished commissions. Among Thompson's public commissions are the *Air India Disaster Monument* at Ahakista, Co. Cork (1986), eight bas-relief panels and a Portland stone figure of *St Patrick as Pilgrim* for Westport, Co. Mayo (1989), and a second monumental figure of St PATRICK, completed in 2002, for the shores of LOUGH DERG. His *Innocent Victims* (1996) is outside Westminster Abbey, London, while in Westminster Cathedral stands his monument to Cardinal Hume (1999). Thompson's work is often related to places of worship, notably his Stations of the Cross in St Brigid's Church, Belfast (1994), and in the Church of St Thomas Moore, Cheyne Row, London (2002). As well as carving figurative sculptures, lettered gravestones, plaques, sundials, and monuments, Thompson is an accomplished wood-engraver. **Peter Murray**

Thompson, Samuel (Sam) (1916–1965), playwright. Born in Belfast; left school at fourteen and went to work as a painter in the HARLAND AND WOLFF shipyard. Though he may be regarded as a playwright who failed to achieve his potential (he died at the age of forty-nine), he is an important and humane voice in Ulster theatre. His first and best-known stage play, *Over the Bridge* (1960), drew heavily on his own experience. Speaking out of one community, Thompson looked at life as a socially conscious Belfast working man; his work contributed to a tradition that has long sought to overcome sectarian divisions. **Sam Burnside**

Thompson, Sydney Mary (1847–1923), geologist. Born in Belfast. A member of Belfast Field Club, and stimulated by the work of Percy Kendall, she, with MARY ANDREWS and a few others, carried out research on the local glacial deposits, especially in the collecting and naming of the erratics of the drift with a view to determining the direction of ice-flow. Her reports (as secretary of the committee) were published in the Club's *Proceedings*. **Geoff Warke**

Thompson, William (1775–1833), radical economist and early socialist. Born in Co. Cork. Between 1807 and 1822 he developed lectures at the Royal Cork Institution to promote universal education. His recommendations ignored, he moved to England and collaborated with Jeremy Bentham, the utilitarian philosopher, and Robert Owen, founder of the Co-operative movement. *An Inquiry into the Principles of the Distribution of Wealth* (1824) was recognised as a critique of capitalism. With ANNA WHEELER he published *Appeal of One Half of the Human Race* (1825), advocating equality between men and women. *Practical Directions for the Establishment of Communities* (1830) outlined proposals for a system of communes in Ireland. On his death in 1833 he left his wealth to co-operative societies. [see RALAHINE AGRICULTURAL AND MANUFACTURING CO-OPERATIVE ASSOCIATION.] **Margaret Morse**

***Thom's Directory*.** The brainchild of the immigrant Scottish printer and publisher Alexander Thom (1801–1879), *Thom's Irish Almanac and Official Directory* first appeared in 1844. Though it never paid for itself during his lifetime it was an immediate success and is still published annually. The 1904 edition was a source of factual material for JAMES JOYCE's novel ULYSSES. [see STREET AND TOWN DIRECTORIES.] **Bernard Share**

Thomson, Bryden (1928–1991), conductor. Born in Ayr, Scotland; he studied at the Royal Scottish Academy of Music. In 1966 he became associate conductor of the Scottish National Orchestra and in 1968 principal conductor of the BBC Northern Orchestra, which under him was renamed the BBC Philharmonic Orchestra. Between 1977 and 1985 he was music director of the ULSTER ORCHESTRA and between 1984 and 1987 he was Principal Conductor of the RTÉ Symphony Orchestra with whom he performed a remarkable cycle of Bruckner symphonies. A charismatic and popular conductor, he did much to advance the reputation of both the Ulster and RTÉ Orchestras. **Emma Costello**

Thomson (or Thompson), Elizabeth (fl. seventeenth century), consort of Emperor Sidi Muhammad of Morocco and mother of Emperor Muli Ishmael. Born in Cork into a rich merchant family, she eloped to Spain to marry Eugenio O'Shea, a wine merchant and ship-owner in Cádiz, who came from an old Cork family. Her ship was captured en route to Cádiz by a Moroccan corsair, and she was sold into the harem at the imperial palace. She eventually converted to Islam and became the favourite consort of Sultan Sidi Muhammad and mother of two sons. The assassination of the sultan and the outbreak of civil war led her to flee to Alicante in Spain. When her eldest son, Moulay Yazid, succeeded his father, she returned to the Imperial Palace in Marrakesh. **Ciarán Deane**

Thomson, Sir Charles Wyville (1830–1882), naturalist. Born in Linlithgow, Midlothian; educated at the University of Edinburgh. He was appointed lecturer in BOTANY at the University of Aberdeen at the age of twenty and professor the following year. His career in Ireland began in 1851 as professor of natural history at

Queen's College, Cork. His next post was professor of mineralogy and GEOLOGY at Belfast, changing in 1860 to the professorship of natural history—a post he held for ten years. He also held the chair of botany at the Royal College of Science, Dublin, 1868–70. While professor of natural history at the University of Edinburgh, 1870–80, he directed the expeditions of the research ship *Challenger*. **Christopher Moriarty**

Thomson, Sir William, Baron Kelvin of Largs (1824–1907), physicist. Born in Belfast; graduated from the Universities of Glasgow and Cambridge, 1845. He was professor of natural philosophy at Glasgow, 1846–99; knighted in 1866 for his contribution to the successful transatlantic telegraph cable; created Baron Kelvin of Largs in 1892; president of the Royal Society, 1890–95. He used his immense talents in practical ways, helping to develop the second law of thermodynamics (the absolute scale of temperature is named after him), inventing advanced scientific instruments, and improving the navigational compass. **Charles Mollan**

Thoor Ballylee, a sixteenth-century de Burgo fortified tower in Co. Galway. The tower was bought by W. B. YEATS in 1917 so that he could keep in close contact with his friends LADY AUGUSTA GREGORY and EDWARD MARTYN, who lived at nearby Coole and Tullira, respectively. Yeats commissioned the architect WILLIAM A. SCOTT to restore the tower and to design furniture for it, and he occupied it with his family intermittently between 1919 and 1926. The building gave the name for his collection of poems entitled THE TOWER (1928). It was restored and reopened in 1965, the centenary of Yeats's birth. **Ciarán Deane**

Thornley, Sir Arnold (1870–1953), architect. In private practice in Liverpool, he was awarded the commission for the Northern Ireland Parliament House in 1921, much to the chagrin of the Irish profession, who were not invited to compete. Originally there were to be flanking blocks of public offices, designed by the London architect Ralph Knott; in the event the whole was combined into a single structure, Parliament Buildings at STORMONT, entrusted to Thornley and erected in 1927–32. Faced in Portland stone on a Mourne granite plinth, the style is neo-classical, with an Ionic temple front, surmounted by an attic storey decorated with neo-Grec details and sculpture. Thornley was knighted in 1933. **Frederick O'Dwyer**

Three Fs: see ULSTER CUSTOM.

Threlkeld, Caleb (1676–1728), preacher, physician, and herbalist. Born in Cumberland; he settled in Dublin in 1713. He combined his learning in medicine with an enthusiasm for walking and plant-collecting and is remembered above all for his book *Synopsis Stirpium Hibernicarum* (1726). Primarily a catalogue of wild flowers, especially those growing near Dublin, with observations on their medicinal value, it is also a work of considerable literary merit and diverts into observations on politics and philosophy. It includes the Irish names of plants, mostly derived from a now lost manuscript. **Christopher Moriarty**

Thurles, Synod of (1850). The synod opened in Thurles, Co. Tipperary, on 22 August 1850—the first Catholic episcopal synod since 1642. Chaired by Archbishop of Armagh and Apostolic Delegate PAUL CULLEN, the episcopal bench was fraught with divisions on educational issues. By a majority vote the Queen's Colleges were condemned, while the establishment of a CATHOLIC UNIVERSITY was promoted. Less contentious were the resolutions passed dealing with the administration of the sacraments, the life and character of the clergy, the duties of clerics, and the administration of ecclesiastical property. **Ciarán O'Carroll**

Thomas, George. *A portrait of George Thomas, known as the 'Rajah from Tipperary', from William Francklin's* Military Memoirs of G. Thomas *(1803). [By permission of the British Library: V18062]*

Thurston, Katherine Cecil, née Madden (1875–1911), writer. Born in Cork, daughter of Paul Madden, Mayor of Cork and a friend of PARNELL. In 1901 she married the writer Ernest Temple Thurston, but the marriage was not a success and they divorced. A popular novelist, she was associated with Ardmore, Co. Waterford, where she spent most of her life. The influence of her work on later writers, such as KATE O'BRIEN, is clear. Her best-known work was *John Chilcote M.P.* (1904), a huge success in the United States, filmed in 1905; later novels include *The Gambler* (1906) and *The Fly on the Wheel* (1908). **Tina O'Toole**

'Tidings of Cano, Son of Gartnán': see 'SCÉLA CANO MEIC GARTNÁIN'.

'Tidings of MacDathó's Pig': see 'SCÉLA MUCCE MEIC DATHÓ'.

Tidy Towns Competition: see NATIONAL TIDY TOWNS COMPETITION.

Tievebulliagh, Co. Antrim, a conspicuous peak 4.5 km (3 miles) west-south-west of Cushendall and site of a NEOLITHIC porcellanite quarry. Porcellanite was the most important source for stone axes in the Neolithic Period; more than 10,000 porcellanite axeheads are known. It was quarried at two landscape sites: Tievebulliagh and

Brockley, RATHLIN ISLAND. The results of quarrying are visible on a small area of exposed outcrop. Excavation revealed evidence of a definite production sequence. Porcellanite axeheads were distributed very widely in Ireland and also occur in Britain. **Gabriel Cooney**

tillage farming. The most suitable land for tillage is largely confined to the south and east. In addition to having the highest incidence of suitable soils, these areas also have the most suitable CLIMATE, with lower rainfall, higher temperatures, and more hours of sunshine than the west and north. The main regions of arable use are the south-east, mid-east, and south-west. The distribution of highly specialist tillage farms is concentrated in these areas. The highest incidence of specialist tillage farms is in parts of north Co. Dublin, Cos. Louth, Meath, and Kildare, and some dispersed districts of east Cork and Wexford.

The last quarter of the twentieth century saw significant changes in Irish farming, and tillage farming has benefited from such technological change, probably more so than any other sectors of AGRICULTURE. Ireland consistently achieves the world's highest yields in major cereal crops.

Because of the very small amount of land coming on the market, the proportion of rented-in land is an important feature of Irish farming. Tenure of land is more of an issue for tillage farmers; and though renting occurs on farms of all sizes, it is much more likely on large farms, and even more so on tillage farms. In an intensive tillage county such as Co. Dublin, where the predominant crops are winter wheat, potatoes, and vegetables, almost 35 per cent of all farms have land rented, with 30 per cent of these renting their entire farming unit. Nationally, 36.5 per cent of specialist tillage farms have large areas rented, on average 40 ha (100 acres), whereas almost 30 per cent of specialist dairy farmers also have some land rented, though the average area is much smaller, at 12 ha (30 acres).

Increased mechanisation has been a vital component of the modernisation of farming, and nowhere more so than in tillage farming. Tillage farming has reached a stage where the shortage of labour and its cost are driving a new era of mechanisation. On the conventional one-pass system there are bigger ploughs, power harrows, and seed drills, while an alternative system is looking at minimal-cultivation systems, commonly referred to as 'eco-tillage'. Cereal crops account for approximately 7 per cent of the total area farmed and approximately 80 per cent of the total tilled area.

Ireland is limited to a 'national base area' of 345,000 ha (850,000 acres) of eligible crops for which arable aid may be claimed. In 2000 there were 15,866 applicants for arable aid, and 337,688 ha of the national base area was utilised. All cereal crops and 'set-aside' produced on eligible land command an arable aid premium of €382 per hectare (€154 per acre). Forage maize (commonly referred to as maize silage) is eligible for a payment of €363 per hectare (€147 per acre), and this has been the driving force in increasing the area of maize from 3,055 ha (7,500 acres) in 1993 to 12,415 ha (30,000 acres) in 2000. Total arable aid payments are worth approximately €121 million annually to tillage farmers.

In Northern Ireland the agricultural census for 2000 showed 4,000 farmers growing 41,000 ha (100,000 acres) of cereals and 6,000 ha (15,000 acres) of potatoes, with the Republic growing a little over 283,000 ha (700,000 acres) of cereals in the same year. Average area per farm under tillage crops is quite small in Northern Ireland: there are just under 107 farmers growing 50 hectares or more of cereals or potatoes. Cos. Down and Derry are the most intensive tillage counties, having more than 27,000 ha (67,000 acres) of the total tillage crops. **Derek O'Donoghue**

Timahoe, Co. Laois, site of a monastery founded in the seventh century by St Mochua mac Lonáin. The earliest surviving remains are those of the twelfth-century ROUND TOWER, which incorporates an unusual ROMANESQUE sculpted doorway decorated with interlaced human heads and chevron ornament. The O'More family refounded the monastery in the later Middle Ages. After Dissolution, the fifteenth-century church was converted into a castle, the remains of which can be seen to the north-west of the tower. **Rachel Moss**

Timoney, Séamus (1926–1991), mechanical engineer and entrepreneur. Born in Galway; educated at UCD. He worked with Alvis before returning to UCD in 1954; from 1979 until shortly before his death he was professor of mechanical engineering. He published widely on high-specific-output diesel engines and the use of ceramics in engines and was also the recipient of many awards and distinctions. In 1971, with his brother, he established an engine research facility in Dublin, Timoney Technology, which designed specialist vehicles, including airport fire tenders. Timoney is commemorated by the Timoney Postgraduate Research Award. **Ronald Cox**

Timoney, Thérèse (1949–), violinist. Born in Dublin, she was a member of the RTÉ Symphony Orchestra and led the New Irish Chamber Orchestra 1980–93. One of the most distinguished Irish musicians working internationally, she is leader of the RTÉ CONCERT ORCHESTRA, leader and co-director of Christ Church Baroque and co-leader of the Hanover Band. In 1990 she gave the premiere of the violin concerto by her husband JOHN KINSELLA. **Richard Pine**

Tinney, Hugh (1958–), pianist. Born in Dublin; educated at TCD and studied piano with MABEL SWAINSON, Louis Kentner, Bryce Morrison, and Maria Curcio. He made his performance debut in 1983 at the Purcell Room, London. He has won many awards, including RTÉ MUSICIAN OF THE FUTURE 1976, Ettore Pozzoli International Piano Competition, 1983, Benson and Hedges Threshold Award, 1984, and Paloma O'Shea International Piano Competition, 1984. Recognised as an international performer, he is one of Ireland's most accomplished musicians. **Emma Costello**

Tintern Abbey, Co. Wexford, founded by William Marshal of Pembroke c. 1200 and colonised from Tintern Major, Wales. The earliest ruins of the church date from c. 1300, with further additions from the middle of the fifteenth century. Following Dissolution, the abbey and its lands were granted to Sir Anthony Colclough, who converted the buildings for domestic use; it remained in the Colclough family until 1958. In recent years the abbey has been cleared of post-medieval fabric and restored to its CISTERCIAN form. **Rachel Moss**

tin whistle, perhaps the commonest instrument in TRADITIONAL MUSIC today, used widely in an introductory and educational role. The whistle became common after mass production in the nineteenth century made it cheap and readily available. Long considered a toy or a children's instrument, it has carved out a secure place in modern traditional music. Original whistles were made from tinplate and had a wooden fipple and a conical bore. From the 1950s they were more likely to have a parallel bore and plastic mouthpiece. At present there are makers producing expensive brass, silver, and wooden whistles, which are believed by some to have a superior tone and response. **Colin Hamilton**

tin whistle. *A boy busking on the steps of No. 22 St Stephen's Green, Dublin. A stalwart of traditional music, the tin whistle is also one of the most popular children's instruments. [Derek Speirs/Report]*

Tipperary, County (*Contae Thiobraid Árann*)

Province:	MUNSTER
County town:	NENAGH (North Tipperary)
	CLONMEL (South Tipperary)
Area:	4,255 km^2 (1,644 sq. miles)
Population (2002):	140,281
Features:	Galty Mountains
	LOUGH DERG
	River NORE
	River SUIR
	Silvermines
Of historical interest:	CAHER CASTLE
	HOLYCROSS ABBEY
	ROCK OF CASHEL
Industry and products:	Agricultural produce
	Dairy farming
	Horse-breeding

Petula Martyn

County Tipperary, the only non-maritime county in Munster. Drained by the Rivers SUIR and SHANNON, Co. Tipperary has a rich agricultural heritage with a strong CO-OPERATIVE tradition. Dairying is the predominant activity in the fertile Golden Vale, with some sheep farming evident in the upland areas of the Galty, Silvermines, Arra, and Knockmealdown Mountains. Deriving from this strong link with the land, a Rural and Business Development Institute has been established in Thurles.

The main towns are **Clonmel**, **Nenagh**, **Roscrea**, **Cashel**, **Tipperary**, and **Thurles**. Clonmel, the county's main industrial centre, possesses a wide range of activities but specialises in BREWING and pharmaceuticals. Cashel, once the seat of the kings of Munster, possesses the ruins of a medieval cathedral, ROMANESQUE church, and ROUND TOWER. The ROCK OF CASHEL dominates the townscape. Other historic sites in Co. Tipperary include CAHER CASTLE and HOLYCROSS ABBEY (see p. 167). Two significant voluntary bodies, the GAELIC ATHLETIC ASSOCIATION (1884–) and Muintir na Tíre (1931–), originated in Co. Tipperary.

Uniquely, since 1839 Co. Tipperary has been divided into two administrative counties, North Tipperary (formerly called North Riding) and South Tipperary (South Riding). The GARDA SÍOCHÁNA Training College is at Templemore. **Raymond O'Connor and John Crowley**

'Tipperary', a song written in 1912 by the English songwriters Jack Judge and Harry Williams, which became one of the most popular British army marching songs of the FIRST WORLD WAR. The choice of Tipperary as the place nostalgically remembered in the song was prompted by the demands of the lyric, as neither Judge nor Williams had any previous connection with Co. Tipperary. It was first performed at a PANTOMIME in the Gaiety Theatre, Dublin. [see FIRST WORLD WAR SONGS.] **Brian Lalor**

Tír na nÓg ('the Land of the Young People'), a mythical land associated with OISÍN, a character in the FIONN CYCLE, who accompanied a beautiful woman there. After 300 years he longed to return to Ireland. Though warned not to stand on Irish soil, he inadvertently did so and thereby became an old man. **Ríonach uí Ógáin**

Titanic, a luxury liner of the White Star Line, built in Belfast in the shipyards of HARLAND AND WOLFF and, at the time of its launch on 31 May 1911, the world's largest vessel (see p. 1053). Harland and Wolff also built two sister ships of similar size, the *Olympic* (1911) and the *Britannic* (1915), the former remaining in service on the North Atlantic until 1935, the latter sank in the Aegean Sea in 1915.

The *Titanic*, designed under the direction of WILLIAM JAMES PIRRIE, was 269 m (883 ft) in length and had a displacement of 66,000 tons. Two massive triple-expansion reciprocating STEAM ENGINES and a low-pressure turbine were fed with steam from twenty-nine coal-fired boilers. The engines transmitted power through large drive-shafts to three screw propellers, enabling the ship to reach speeds of up to 25 knots. Near midnight on 14 April 1912, while on its first voyage, from Southampton to New York, the *Titanic* struck an iceberg at 41° 46′ N, 50° 14′ W. Prompt action by an officer of the watch prevented a head-on collision, but the damage sustained caused the liner to sink; and though there were 706 survivors, 1,517 lives were lost.

The *Titanic* disaster has been the subject of several books and films, including *Titanic* (1953) directed by Jean Negulesco, *A Night to Remember* (1958) directed by Roy Baker, and *Titanic* (1997) directed by James Cameron. The wreck has been found on the ocean floor at a depth of 3 km (2 miles) and many artefacts recovered. There are numerous memorials, including a fine statue in Belfast, dedicated in 1920, depicting two mermaids claiming a victim from the sea. **Ronald Cox**

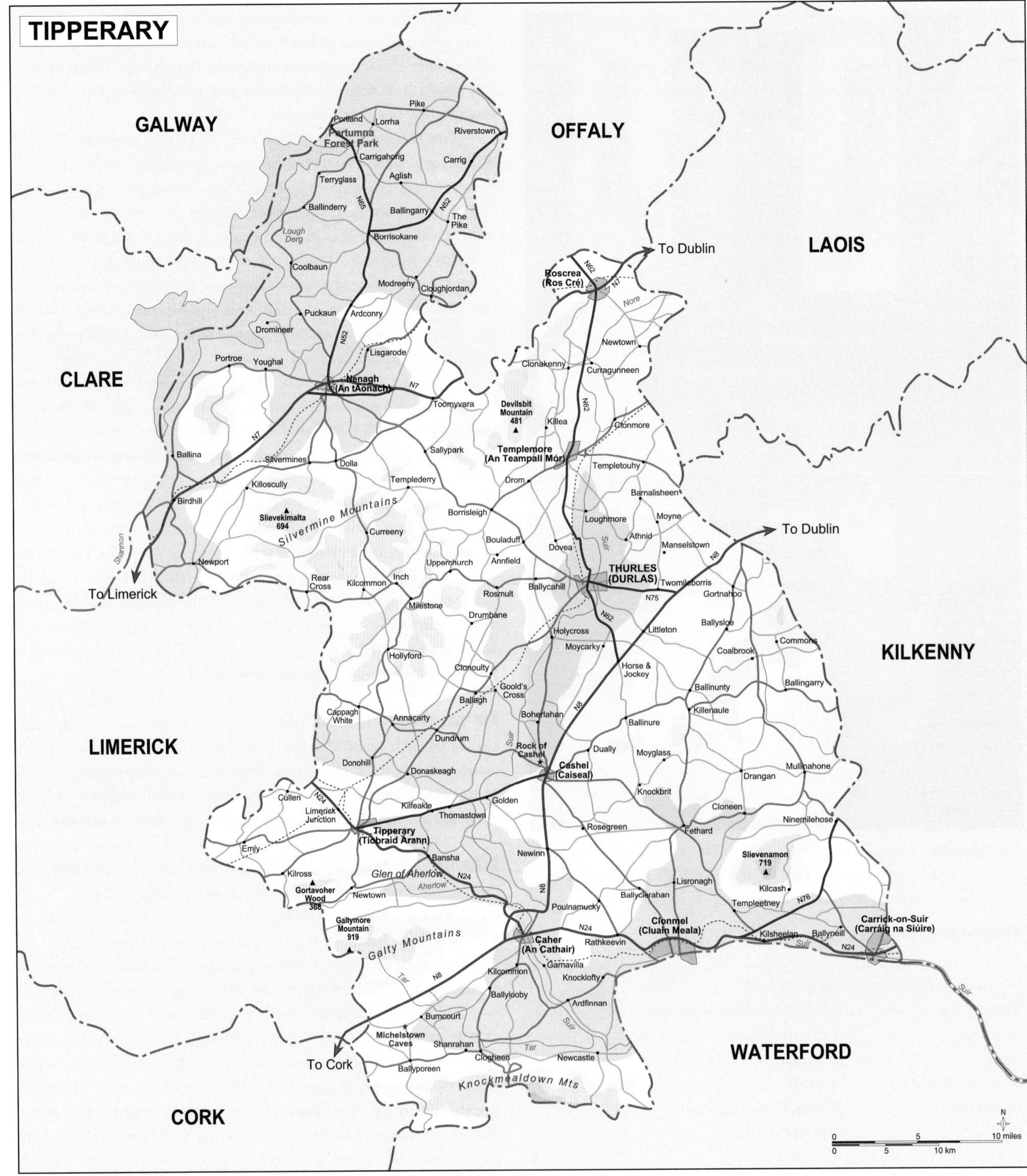

tithes, a church levy on agricultural produce and livestock. From the Middle Ages the church had demanded a levy on agricultural produce and livestock, sometimes collected in kind. By the seventeenth century this had become a tax payable by all denominations to the clergy of the established CHURCH OF IRELAND, legally binding on all producers. Resentment over tithes, especially felt by Catholics and Dissenters, contributed to the Whiteboy and other agrarian violence of the eighteenth century. The 1830s saw a widespread refusal to pay tithes, leading to violent incidents, litigation, and rural disturbance, with many Protestant clergy losing much of their income. The Tithe Rentcharge (Ireland) Act (1838) converted the tithe into a rent charge payable by landlords. [see AGRARIAN PROTEST.] **Kenneth Milne**

Tithe War. Tithes were a tax—notionally one-tenth of earnings—levied on people of all denominations for the support of the clergy of the established CHURCH OF IRELAND. Resistance to payment had been sporadic among Catholics since the 1760s; but in the period of heightened expectation following CATHOLIC EMANCIPATION (1829) the sense of grievance turned to outright resistance. The 'Tithe War' started in Graiguenamanagh, Co. Kilkenny, in October 1830 when the cattle of the parish priest—a relation of Bishop JAMES WARREN DOYLE—were distrained for non-payment. A campaign of non-payment spread throughout south Leinster and Munster; eventually twenty-two of the thirty-two counties were involved. Though formally a campaign of passive resistance, it inevitably turned violent; the use of police and soldiers to distrain goods and livestock resulted in serious clashes. Fourteen people were killed at Newtownbarry (Bunclody), Co. Wexford, in 1831. In all, more than 43,000 decrees were issued against defaulters, while Lord Gort claimed in 1832 that the anti-tithe campaign had by then resulted in 1,179 robberies, 723 attacks on houses, 568 burnings, 401 burglaries, 280 cattle maimings, 242 homicides, 203 riots, and 161 assaults. The withdrawal of police and soldiers from tithe enforcement duties in 1833 took most of the heat out of the situation, but the tithe question itself was not settled by legislation for another five years. **Fergal Tobin**

Titley, Alan (1947–), writer and critic. Born in Cork; educated at St Patrick's College, Dublin. He taught in Nigeria after qualification, was appointed lecturer in Drumcondra in 1974 and head of department in 1981. Novels include *Méirscrí na Treibhe* (1978), set in Africa, a linguistic *tour de force* exploiting the richness of the Irish tradition; *Stiall Fhial Feola* (1980), a Beckettian satire set in Dublin; and the historical *An Fear Dána* (1993), which exploits the richness of the bardic tradition. His play *Tagann Godot* (1992) out-becketts BECKETT. Other publications include *Eiriceachtaí agus Scéalta Eile* (1987), *Fabhalscéalta* (1995), *Leabhar Nóra Ní Anluain* (1998), and collected essays, *Chun Doirne* (1996). He was awarded a doctorate for *An tÚrscéal Gaeilge* (1991), the definitive work on the novel in Irish. **Tadhg Ó Dúshláine**

tochmarc (wooing). Wooing tales in early Irish literature describe the hero's pursuit of his chosen bride. Typically, many obstacles prevent his achievement of this goal. The acquisition of a wife is essential to the heroic biography of king and hero. In 'Tochmarc Emire' ('the Wooing of Emer') from the ULSTER CYCLE of tales, CÚ CHULAINN's quest for Emer, daughter of Forgall Monach, is hampered by her father's insistence that he train in the OTHERWORLD. Forgall hopes for Cú Chulainn's death, but the hero returns to marry his bride and kill his father-in-law. **Muireann Ní Bhrolcháin**

Tod, Isabella (1836–1896), suffragist. Born in Edinburgh; she moved to Belfast in the 1860s. Self-educated, she earned some independent income from journalism. A philanthropist, she was a committee member of Belfast Women's Temperance Association, vice-president of the British Women's Temperance Association, 1877–92, and vice-president of the Irish Women's Total Abstinence Union, 1893–6. Her overriding interest, however, was women's rights. She campaigned for equal educational provisions, the repeal of the Contagious Diseases Acts, married women's property rights, and suffrage, organising the first Irish suffrage society in Belfast in 1871. From the introduction of the first Home Rule Bill (1886) her commitment to unionism transcended all other interests. She addressed meetings, wrote articles, and was the only woman member of the executive committee of the Ulster Liberal Unionist Association. She also established the Ulster Women's Liberal Unionist Association in 1888 and was one of the main organisers of the *conversazione* held before the unionist convention of 1892. She was the most prominent Irish feminist of the late nineteenth century, but her presence on the predominantly male unionist political stage is also of considerable significance. [see FEMINISM.] **Diane Urquhart**

Todhunter, John (1839–1916), man of letters. Born in Dublin; educated at TCD, graduating in MEDICINE in 1871. He was professor of English literature at Alexandra College, Dublin, 1870–74. Living in London from 1874, he published several minor volumes of

Titanic. *Starboard stern view of the* Titanic *in Belfast Lough with tugs, 2 April 1912, on the first phase of its fateful voyage. [Harland and Wolff Collection, Ulster Folk and Transport Museum; photograph reproduced with the kind permission of the Trustees of National Museums and Galleries of Northern Ireland]*

poetry, notably the Irish heroic *The Banshee and Other Poems* (1888), criticism, *A Study of Shelley* (1880), and drama, such as *A Sicilian Idyll* (1890), much admired by the young W. B. YEATS. He was a member of the Rhymers' Club in the 1890s. **Nicholas Allen**

togail ('destruction'), an EARLY IRISH TALE TYPE describing the destruction and death of famous saga characters in liminal, OTHERWORLDLY settings. The highly atmospheric 'Togail Bruidne Da Derga' ('Destruction of Da Derga's Hostel') is the second-longest tale in MIDDLE IRISH, encompassing the entire biography of the legendary King of TARA Conaire Mór. Conaire's reign is methodically destroyed by his disobeying and infringing the taboos put on him by his birdman-guardian and father. Giving a wrong judgment, he is doomed, ending his life in the blazing hostel, his decapitated head begging for water. **Muireann Ní Bhrolcháin**

Tóibín, Colm (1955–), novelist and journalist. Born in Enniscorthy, Co. Wexford; educated at UCD. He has published four novels—*The South* (1990), *The Heather Blazing* (1992), *The Story of the Night* (1996), and *The Blackwater Lightship* (1999)—and several works of non-fiction, including: *Walking Along the Border* (1987), *Homage to Barcelona* (1990), *The Sign of the Cross: Travels in Catholic Europe* (1994), *The Irish Famine* (1999), *Love in a Dark Time* (2002), and *Lady Gregory's Toothbrush* (2002). He also edited *The Kilfenora Teaboy: A Study of Paul Durcan* (1996) and *The Penguin Book of Irish Fiction* (1999). He writes in a spare, economical style about characters who are typically at odds with their social and family origins. Each of his central protagonists is forced to confront crises and anxieties—marital breakdown, social change, political conflict, AIDS—which compel them to re-examine the terms of their relationship with history, family, place, and community. **Liam Harte**

Toksvig, Signe (1891–1983), novelist and diarist. Born in Denmark; with her family she emigrated in 1905 to the United States, and in 1916 she graduated from Cornell University. In New York she worked on the magazine *Vogue* and the *New Republic*, where she met, and later married, the Irish literary critic FRANCIS HACKETT. They lived in Ireland, 1926–37, principally in Newtown Mount Kennedy, Co. Wicklow. Her candid diaries, which record cultural and social life in Ireland, published as *Signe Toksvig's Irish Diaries* (1994), present, uniquely for the period, a view of Irish society as observed from the critical viewpoint of an atheistic outsider. Her other writings include a biography, *Hans Christian Andersen* (1933) and *Eve's Doctor* (1937). **Brian Lalor**

Toland, John (1670–1722), controversialist. Probably born near Clonmany, Inishowen, Co. Donegal, into a Catholic family; studied at the Universities of Glasgow, Edinburgh, and Leiden. Having converted to the Church of Ireland, he helped to man the barricades in Glasgow in 1688 in support of WILLIAM III. In his most notorious book, *Christianity Not Mysterious* (1696), he argued that CHRISTIANITY should be a rational religion and that mystery was used by clerics to consolidate their power over their flock. The predominantly Episcopalian Irish Parliament ordered the book to be burnt by the hangman, and he fled Dublin to return to London. It is likely that JONATHAN SWIFT based *A Tale of a Tub* on this controversy. On friendly terms with William III, Toland was entrusted with the task of bringing to Queen Sophie Charlotte in Hanover the Act of Succession (1700), which guaranteed the Protestant succession to the crown of England. He debated many issues at the royal court in Hanover with the philosopher Gottfried Wilhelm Leibniz. His *Letters to Serena* (1704) marks the first use of the term 'pantheist'. He travelled extensively around Protestant Europe and has been proposed as a central figure in the spread of FREEMASONRY in early eighteenth-century Europe. Much of his writing shows a venting of spleen against the Catholic Church. He also displayed venom towards the Church of England, regarding much of its activity as no more than 'Protestant Popery'. He was sympathetic towards persecuted religious minorities, such as HUGUENOTS and Jews; his *Reasons for Naturalising the Jews* (1714) was one of the earliest pleas for an end to anti-Semitism. He may be regarded as the founder of comparative religion: he subjected the main Christian religions to the same type of scrutiny as Judaism and Islam. He also investigated the religion of PRE-CHRISTIAN Ireland and the early Irish Christian church (particularly the CULDEES) in *Nazarenus* (1718) and *A History of the Druids* (1720). Despite his close connections with many senior political figures in England, he died in poverty. A pioneer of polemic pamphletic journalism, he was regarded by Locke as the first freethinker. He is now regarded as a person of seminal importance in the transmission of ideas in the ENLIGHTENMENT. **Philip McGuinness**

Toleration Act (1719), Irish legislation exempting Presbyterians from the strictures of the Act of Uniformity (1666). In fact these strictures had long been inoperative, and the measure was actually promoted by opponents of Protestant dissent as a means of circumventing potentially more generous legislative action. **Neal Garnham**

Tomelty, Joseph (1911–1995), playwright, novelist, and actor. Born in Portaferry, Co. Down; educated locally. In 1940 he was a joint founder of the Ulster Group Theatre in Belfast, for which he wrote and acted. His popular comedies exhibited a sure control of the northern vernacular. In 1947 he created for BBC Northern

Tone. *Aquatint engraving of Margaret Tone with her sons Matthew (left) and Theobald (right), 1778, an early portrait of the United Irishmen. Matthew (unbreeched above on left) was hanged in September 1798 following the Battle of Ballinamuck; Theobald committed suicide in prison in November of the same year. [National Museum of Ireland]*

Ireland the popular radio serial 'The McCooeys', which dramatised the life of a Belfast working-class family without indicating whether the family was Catholic or Protestant. His play *All Souls' Night* is an atmospherically tragic evocation of fishing life in his native county. Tomelty's career as actor and dramatist was ended by a motor accident in 1954. **Terence Brown**

Tone, Theobald Wolfe (1763–1798), United Irishman. Born in Dublin, son of an Anglican coach-maker; educated at TCD, where he excelled. He pursued legal studies and became a barrister in 1789. For several years he attempted to make his way in the legal profession and appeared determined to gain a place in the establishment. When he became secretary to the CATHOLIC ASSOCIATION his opinions changed, and his *Address on Behalf of the Catholics of Ireland* (1791) established him firmly in the opposition camp. In 1791 he was instrumental in founding the Society of UNITED IRISHMEN; in 1795, after the organisation was banned, he exiled himself to the United States and then to France, where he worked tirelessly for three years to engineer a French invasion of Ireland in support of a republican revolution. He was captured in LOUGH SWILLY, Co. Donegal, following the unsuccessful REBELLION OF 1798, and died from a self-inflicted wound in prison in November of that year. Largely forgotten in the early nineteenth century, he became the central martyr figure in Irish revolutionary NATIONALISM in the late nineteenth and twentieth centuries. **Daniel Gahan**

torcs, prehistoric neck rings made from rods or strips of twisted metal. During the early stages of the late BRONZE AGE gold torcs of various types and sizes were produced. *Ribbon torcs* are made of strips of twisted gold; *bar torcs* are made by twisting bars of varying cross-section. By hammering out flanges from the corners of the bar, flange-twisted torcs, such as the pair from TARA, were produced. IRON AGE torcs of tubular form and ribbon form are also known. [see BROIGHTER; GOLD, PREHISTORIC.] **Mary Cahill**

Tories, a term derived from the Irish *tóraí* (bandit), first used to describe outlaws in seventeenth-century Ireland. It had political connotations, given that such outlaws included former Confederates and royalists in the 1650s and, later, dispossessed native Irish nobility. In the eighteenth century the term became interchangeable with 'rapparee' (Irish *ropaire*, violent robber, or *rapaire*, rapier, half-pike), first applied to irregular Irish JACOBITE soldiers in 1689–91. The first use of the term 'Tory' in English politics was during the exclusion crisis of 1679–81, when it was used as a derisive reference to those who supported the right of succession of the Catholic James, Duke of York (the future JAMES II). By the 1690s 'Tory' and 'WHIG' had become the accepted names for the two political parties in England. English Tories believed in the principle of passive obedience, though they accepted that the 'Glorious Revolution' was a regrettable necessity; they believed that the established church was in greater danger from Protestant dissent than from Catholicism. English Toryism was often identified with Jacobitism and opposition to the Hanoverian succession of 1714, after which the party went into decline. The first use in Irish politics occurred in 1703–4. Irish Tories were more reticent than English Tories, because any association with Jacobitism was political suicide in Ireland. The Irish Tories also went into decline after 1715. The term was revived in English politics in the 1760s and continues to be applied to the British Conservative Party and to the conservative element in former colonies, such as Canada. **Charles Ivar McGrath**

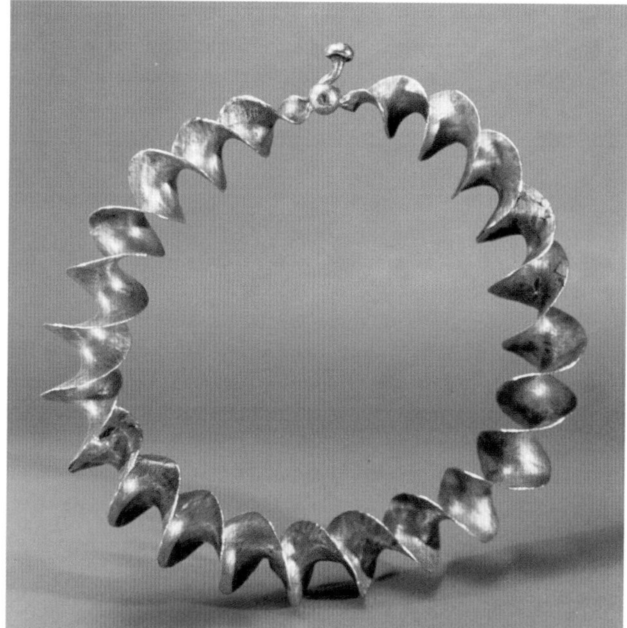

torc. *A Late Bronze Age gold ribbon torc, 1200–1000 BC, created by beating an ingot of gold into a strip about 1 mm ($\frac{1}{32}$ in.) thick, with the twisted gold ribbon narrowing towards the ends and closed by unadorned interlocking knobs. [National Museum of Ireland]*

tort, a civil wrong, other than breach of contract, giving rise to a claim for unliquidated damages. For a tort to be committed, the wrongdoer must have caused damage to the claimant under some recognised head of liability (such as negligence, nuisance, or defamation) by failing to live up to the required standard of care, and the harm suffered must be reasonably foreseeable. Certain torts may also be crimes. Since 1988 the JURY has been removed from most tort actions, though there are certain exceptions, notably the tort of defamation. [see LAW, BRANCHES OF.] **Neville Cox**

'Tóruigheacht Dhiarmada agus Ghráinne' ('The pursuit of Diarmaid and Gráinne'), a famous tale of the FIONN CYCLE, popular in oral tradition and available in manuscript sources from the seventeenth century onwards. It recounts the pursuit of Diarmaid and Gráinne by Diarmaid's commander, Fionn, elderly leader of the FIANNA and Gráinne's betrothed. Gráinne forces Diarmaid to abandon his comrades by placing him under *geasa* (a form of social bond or injunction), but the pair eventually become lovers, and the tale becomes a narrative of escape from the strictures of martial and patriarchal authority. **Máirín Nic Eoin**

Tory Island, Co. Donegal, an island of 3.2 km^2 ($1\frac{1}{4}$ sq. miles) off the north-west corner of Ireland, 14 km ($8\frac{1}{2}$ miles) from the mainland across the turbulent Tory Sound. Its name (*Toraigh*) reflects the 'towers' or pinnacles of the dramatic landscape of the island's eastern edge. It has been occupied since neolithic times; its most prominent archaeological remains are an eleventh-century Round Tower and a *tau* (T-shaped) cross, surviving from COLM CILLE's monastery, sacked by the English in 1595. Tory also has an early nineteenth-century lighthouse.

The population fell from 399 in 1841 (before the Great Famine) to 335 in 1901 and 169 in 1996. Isolation is a problem, particularly in winter, when the island can be cut off for long periods. In the 1970s HOUSING began to be provided for islanders on the mainland, and it seemed that Tory might be abandoned. However, some islanders, supported by the local priest, pressed instead for investment in the island to improve conditions. Public housing was provided, an improved ferry service lessened problems of isolation, and a small hotel was built. Harbour improvements have also been made. Now TOURISM is important, and population decline has lessened. Tory has two villages, East Town (An Baile Thoir) and West Town (An Baile Thiar). The former has the harbour and all services: school, shops, hotel, café, generating station, church, and offices of the co-operative, an important organisation in the management of the island economy.

Tory is notable for its cultural heritage; it is Irish-speaking, and it retains the tradition of one of its citizens being regarded as the 'king'. A more recent cultural tradition has been the development of the Tory Island naïve school of painting. A number of islanders paint in this style, and there is a gallery. The instigator was DEREK HILL, an English painter who made annual visits from the 1950s; he was awarded honorary citizenship of Ireland in 2000 in recognition of his contributions to Irish art. **Stephen A. Royle**

Tóstal, An, 'Ireland at Home', a national festival organised by the Irish Government from 1953 with the aim of giving an earlier start to the tourist season. The idea failed to flourish after the 1950s and disappeared everywhere except in Drumshanbo, Co. Leitrim, where it continues, largely as a TRADITIONAL MUSIC festival. Though An Tóstal failed, the festival idea caught on, generating many events that are carried on today, including the Dublin Theatre Festival. **Ciarán Deane**

Tottenham, Charles (1685–1758), politician. Born at Tottenhamgreen, near New Ross, Co. Wexford. He represented New Ross in the Irish Parliament from 1727 until his death. He earned the nickname 'Tottenham in His Boots' when he dramatically interrupted a sitting of the Parliament after riding all the way from Co. Wexford, arriving just in time to defeat a vote that would have forced Ireland to hand over surplus tax revenue to the English government. He was appointed sheriff of Co. Wexford in 1737. **Brian Galvin**

Touhey, Patrick J. (Patsy) (1865–1923), uilleann piper. Born in Loughrea, Co. Galway; his parents emigrated to America when he was three. He began to learn the pipes some years after the death of his father, his teachers including the piper and pipemaker Billy Taylor. He worked as a professional piper for thirty-seven years. An excellent and popular player, he left a legacy of some fifty-eight recordings, many of which were individually recorded on the Edison Phonograph. **Jimmy O'Brien Moran**

tourism, 1800–2001. The World Tourism Organisation defines a tourist as 'a person travelling to and staying at least one night in a country other than his or her country of usual residence … for leisure, business or other purposes.' This definition extends beyond holidaymakers, as business travellers and other categories of visitors are all customers for tourism services.

Ireland has attracted visitors ever since the romantic movement fostered enthusiasm for unspoilt scenery in the late eighteenth century. Early visitors spread the fame of its scenery by publishing accounts of their travels; but travel for purposes of education (the 'grand tour'), health (visiting spas or sea-bathing), and gazing on nature was strictly a privilege of the rich. The spread of the RAILWAYS in the second half of the nineteenth century made travel less expensive. VICTORIA's visit in 1861, when she travelled to Killarney, did much to spread the fame of Ireland as a scenic destination. The RAILWAY companies built large hotels in Killarney, Co. Kerry, Galway, Mulrany, Co. Mayo, Killaloe, Co. Clare, Dún Laoghaire, Co. Dublin, and elsewhere, aimed primarily at wealthy travellers.

The outbreak of the First World War in 1914 and the 1916 RISING and its aftermath combined with an ailing economy to slow the development of tourism. After 1922 there was a growing number of middle-class holidaymakers, generally seeking a family break near the sea during July and August. The less affluent used the railway for a day trip to the nearest resort—hence the early popularity of resorts such as Ballybunion, Co. Kerry, Bangor, Co. Down, Bray, Co. Wicklow, Skerries, Co. Dublin, Tramore, Co. Waterford, and Youghal, Co. Cork. The years immediately after the Second World War brought an influx of visitors, principally from Britain, where food rationing continued. The NORTHERN IRELAND TOURIST BOARD (NITB) was set up in 1948, and BORD FÁILTE ÉIREANN emerged in its present form in 1955. Both organisations set about encouraging investment in accommodation, engaging in marketing campaigns to attract more visitors, and ensuring that high standards were established and maintained.

The new industry was greeted at first with suspicion in a conservative society. The influx of strangers was seen as a threat to the prevailing religious and moral ethos, while the concept of holiday-making was alien to the majority of the farming community. The improvement in the economy in the late 1950s and early 60s, together with the introduction of paid holidays, made summer breaks a possibility for lower-income families. In Northern Ireland the holiday destination was generally determined by religious affiliation: Co. Donegal (Catholic) or the north Antrim coast (Protestant). Visitors from Britain, many of whom had Irish connections, added to the numbers seeking a traditional seaside summer fortnight; there were the added attractions of GOLF and ANGLING in uncrowded locations. The number of visitors to the Republic in 1956 was 805,000. In the early 1960s cheaper transatlantic travel led to an increase in the number of American visitors, many of whom preferred to tour Ireland by coach on an all-inclusive package holiday. This suited the growing hotel industry, and Americans were encouraged to travel outside the busy months of July and August.

The outbreak of the 'Troubles' in 1969 had an adverse effect on tourism in both the Republic and Northern Ireland, particularly in the British market. The NITB began to concentrate on the Dutch and German market in 1975, while Bord Fáilte concentrated on people of Irish descent in Britain and North America. When the cost of holidays in the sun fell dramatically in the late 1960s, the traditional seaside holiday market declined. However, the introduction of roll-on/roll-off ferries from Britain in 1968 and 1969 helped to increase car traffic. This coincided with an improvement in both the standards and the organisation of BED AND BREAKFAST ACCOMMODATION, a flexible option that was particularly suited to visitors touring by car. A programme of festivals, the introduction of Shannon cruises and horse-drawn caravans, and the publication of Ireland's first guide to eating out all helped to broaden the country's appeal as a destination.

While growth in tourism had been slow but steady in the first half of the 1970s, it picked up in 1976, only to be slowed again by worldwide recession, the Gulf War, higher fuel prices, and continued unrest in Northern Ireland. In spite of increased advertising in the European market and the introduction of direct ferries from France and flights from the Continent, the decline in the number of visitors continued until 1984. In that year real growth of 5 per cent was achieved, with foreign exchange earnings from tourism reaching £591 million. Research suggested that the Republic could double

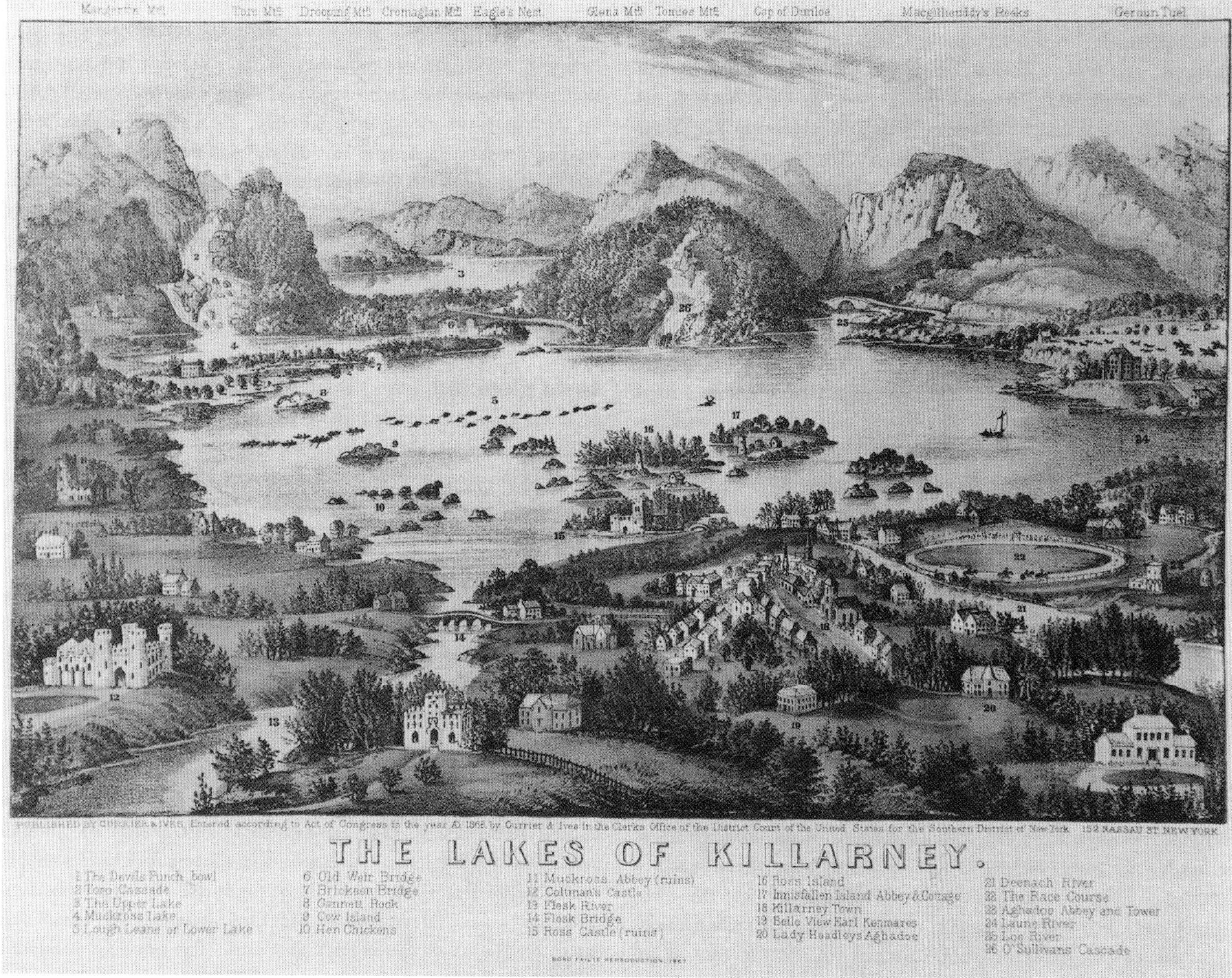

tourism. *An early tourist view of the Lakes of Killarney, published by Currier and Ives, New York (1868), depicting the noted sights of the region. [Muckross House Research Library (Hilliard collection)].*

both numbers and income; this aim became a central component of the Programme for National Recovery (1988). The OPERATIONAL PROGRAMME FOR TOURISM, 1994–9, provided for an investment of £652 million in development, marketing, and training. As a result of these initiatives the number of overseas visitors grew from 2.3 million in 1988 to 6.4 million in 2000, while income grew from £841 million in 1988 to £2,502 million in 1999. The number of employees in tourism rose from 67,600 in 1988 to 127,000 in 1998 and continues to rise. The figures for Northern Ireland have been steadily increasing since the 1980s; in 1999 the number of visitors totalled 1.17 million.

From the point of view of business and the provision of jobs, the development of tourism over recent years is undoubtedly a success story. Both the Government and the industry emphasise the benefits of tourism to the Irish people. Improved roads, new golf courses, angling facilities, walking trails, indoor pools, museums, heritage centres, festivals and other cultural events created for the tourist can also be enjoyed by those living locally. But the trebling of numbers over a relatively short period, and the presence of over 6 million visitors in a country with a total population of 5.25 million, has its cost. In 2001 there was growing criticism of the tourist industry for making a priority of increased numbers rather than aiming for growth in selected markets, a tactic that would attract fewer but higher-spending visitors.

Tourism is seen by many as a threat to the natural ENVIRONMENT. Traditional free access to cliff paths and the seashore has been cut off in places by golf courses or by farmers. Badly designed clusters of holiday homes, which often stand empty for ten months of the year, mar the landscape, particularly in the west. The very popularity of Ireland as a tourist destination is eroding the existence of the elements that attract visitors in the first place; empty roads, unspoilt and unpeopled scenery, empty beaches, and quiet bars with friendly local people are becoming ever harder to find. While tourism has been important for the growth of the economy, there is a lack of impartial research into its negative social and environmental effects, which are seldom mentioned by industry or Government reports. **Alannah Hopkin**

Tourism Brand Ireland, a name given to a new symbol and advertising campaign launched in 1996 jointly by BORD FÁILTE ÉIREANN and the NORTHERN IRELAND TOURIST BOARD to develop a new all-Ireland marketing strategy, based on extensive consumer research. The new emblem consists of a representation of two dancers with arms outstretched forming a circle, and a small stylised shamrock in one corner. The Minister for Tourism, Sport and Recreation, Dr James McDaid, objected to the new device and requested that it be changed back to the original shamrock, while the Ulster Unionist leader David Trimble objected to the use of 'Gaelic' imagery. The device was modified shortly after its launch, which was followed by an international advertising campaign. **Alannah Hopkin**

Tower, The (1928), a collection of poems by W. B. YEATS, widely reckoned to be his most impressive volume of verse. The book contains twenty-one poems, some of which are sequences of poems. It takes its title from the second poem in the collection, set in THOOR BALLYLEE, the Norman keep in Co. Galway that Yeats had bought in 1917 as his Irish residence. The poem sets the tone for much of the book in its philosophical and emotionally charged engagement with the inexorable facts of aging and death. During the violence of the CIVIL WAR, Yeats and his family spent the summer of 1922 at Thoor Ballylee, on which he reflects in 'Meditations in Time of Civil War,' which makes the opening section of the book a powerful evocation of the disturbance and violence of recent European and Irish history. *The Tower* gives full poetic expression to Yeats's philosophy of history, first propounded in *A Vision* (1925), which he had developed in co-operation with his wife through experiments in automatic writing and spiritualist communication. This involved complex theories of historical cycles and moments of violent annunciation, which found mythic expression in poems such as 'Leda and the Swan' and 'Two Songs from a Play'. Less sublime, more earthy energies are evoked in the book in 'A Man Young and Old' and 'The Gift of Harun Al-Rashid', while 'Among School Children' is a nostalgic brooding on youth, age, and the transcendence of time that only bodily delight can afford. **Terence Brown**

tower-houses, the most numerous type of CASTLE found in Ireland, with almost 1,200 standing remains. They have been described both as poorly defended stone towers and as fortified houses, and they were the typical residence of the Irish, those of English extraction, and planters. Many attempts have been made to push their origin back into the fourteenth century, but the main impetus for their building appears to have been a £10 grant, under a statute of Henry VI of 1429, to every man in the PALE (Cos. Louth, Meath, Dublin, and Kildare) who wished to build a castle. According to the statute they had to be more than 20 feet by 16 feet (6 m by 5 m) and 40 feet (12 m) high. As a result, numerous small tower-houses were built in the Pale in the fifteenth century. Most are three to four storeys high, with stone vaults over the ground floor and projecting angle-towers containing stairs and *garderobes* (latrines). They were protected by a defended *bawn* (courtyard) wall. The entrance was protected by a *machicolation* (projecting stone box) immediately above, from which missiles could be dropped on attackers. Inside the doorway in the roof of the lobby or in the floor of the chamber above was an opening called a *murder-hole*, from which missiles could be dropped on attackers. The doorway to the stairs was also often protected by a murder-hole. Immediately over the stone-vaulted ground floor in these simple tower-houses was the hall and above that the private chambers of the owner. Retainers were housed mainly in ancillary wooden buildings within the bawn.

In the early fifteenth century, tower-houses in the east of the country appear to have had no fireplaces and to have depended on braziers for heat. The architecture of the tower-house appears to owe its origin to the HALL-HOUSE and in particular to later examples, such as those at Dunmoe, Co. Meath, Delvin, Co. Westmeath, and Kindlestown, Co. Wicklow. The hall-house in its later stage of development in the fourteenth century has many features in common with the tower-house.

Tower-houses in the rest of the country are more sophisticated, especially those in Cos. Clare, Cork, Galway, Limerick, and Tipperary. Here most tower-houses date from the sixteenth century and are more commodious, having more chambers and large fireplaces. The famous BLARNEY CASTLE in Co. Cork is a good example. Most late tower-houses of the midlands and west have upper chambers with large windows, often with fine carved details on the stonework. Some fireplaces have dates and the initials of the original owners. Some later tower-houses were built in two phases, and most are protected by *bartisans* (small projecting stone chambers on the corners at the upper levels to protect the angles) and large well-defended bawns, often with gate-houses and flanking towers.

In summary, most of the tower-houses of the east and particularly in the Pale are simple and early, while those in the midlands and the west are later and more complex. **David Sweetman**

town planning, often paired with regional or country planning, an attempt to ensure the orderly use of urban land to promote its efficient and equitable functioning. As a distinct discipline it draws from engineering, ARCHITECTURE, geography, and sociology and is central to the process of development. Ireland was visited by many of the great names in planning early in the twentieth century, but enthusiasm was greatest in Dublin and, to a lesser extent, in Cork. Geddes and Unwin advised that Dublin's HOUSING needs be met by garden-city suburbs, and their influence is clear in the Marino scheme and later suburban developments. The first comprehensive town plan for Dublin, that of Abercrombie and associates in 1922, resulted from a competition promoted by Geddes and the Civics Institute of Ireland (then the Housing and Town Planning Association of Ireland). The Town and Regional Planning Act (1934) was largely ineffectual, but a number of advisory plans were produced for Cork, Galway, Limerick, and Waterford, though none was fully implemented. A planning scheme for Dún Laoghaire was published in 1936, while Abercrombie, Kelly and Robertson produced a sketch development plan for Dublin in 1941, which was used as a general development framework. The Local Government (Planning and Development) Act (1963) put town and regional planning on a legislative footing. Belfast was the main focus of planning concern in Northern Ireland; reports were prepared in 1945 and 1952, but little accomplished. The Matthew strategy for the Belfast region (1964) did much to engender debate on the role of planning in Northern Ireland. **Joseph Brady**

Townsend, John Sealy (1868–1957), physicist. Born in Galway; educated at TCD. The first Wykeham professor at the University of Oxford, he was knighted and made a fellow of the Royal Society and a Chevalier de la Légion d'Honneur. He entered the University of Cambridge as one of its first two PhD students (with Ernest Rutherford) under J. J. Thomson. There he made the first direct measurement of the electron charge by a method that was later improved in the United States by R. A. Millikan. He continued his research on electrons in gases at the University of Oxford and participated in the discovery of the Ramsauer-Townsend Effect. **Denis Weaire**

Townshend, George, fourth Viscount and first Marquis (1724–1807), soldier and politician. He enjoyed a successful military career before his appointment as LORD LIEUTENANT of Ireland in 1767. Though he outmanoeuvred the opposition of vested interests to secure the augmentation of the Irish military establishment and an OCTENNIAL ACT in 1768, the refusal of the 'UNDERTAKERS' to approve a 'Privy Council' money bill in 1769 cast the die for his administration. Choosing, unlike his predecessors, to live in Ireland, he oversaw the transfer of the initiative in forging a majority in the House of Commons from the undertakers to DUBLIN CASTLE and, in the teeth of fierce opposition, set the pattern of government in Ireland for a generation. **James Kelly**

trackways, a general term to describe structures used for crossing BOGS. The largest are of transversely laid planks up to 4 m (13 ft) wide (at CORLEA, Co. Longford, of IRON AGE date); the longest is 1.75 km (1 mile) in length (Annaghcorrib, Co. Galway). Most of the trackways are simple structures of brushwood and roundwoods used to create a walkway for crossing the wetter areas of the bog. These sites show the use of the landscape in the past as well as providing evidence of woodland management and woodworking. They were built from c. 3500 BC onwards, with most dating from the BRONZE AGE. **Conor McDermott**

Tracy, Joe (1873–1959), racing driver. Born in Waterford. A quiet but determined driver, he was the most successful early American racing motorist. He became the only Irish driver to participate in the GORDON BENNETT CUP when he was picked to represent the United States in the 1905 race. He was second in the Havana 100-mile race in 1905 and third in the Vanderbilt Cup, and he set the record Vanderbilt lap the following year before retiring from racing after injuring a spectator. He undertook fuel economy research for the US government during the First World War and later became a leading figure in the American veteran car movement. **Brendan Lynch**

trade, geography of. Trade provides one measure of the degree of interaction and interdependence between countries. The CENTRAL STATISTICS OFFICE produces detailed monthly analyses of trade in goods between the Republic and the rest of the world, though a number of years must be viewed to determine trends. While there are limitations to this data, it provides information on the nature of the commodities traded, the volume of goods, and their estimated value. The information for Northern Ireland is much more limited, as until recently its trade was not disaggregated from the UK total. Data for 2000 showed that 64 per cent of its imports came from outside the EUROPEAN UNION, while 58 per cent of EXPORTS went to the European Union.

An examination of imports and exports for the Republic shows the declining importance of Britain, especially since joining the European Union. The figure for exports is now approximately 22 per cent (20.4 per cent in 2000, 22.1 per cent in 2001), compared with 50.5 per cent in 1972. Britain remains the principal, but much-reduced, source of imports, supplying over the past few years between 30 and 33 per cent. The importance of Northern Ireland as an export market has also declined (7.2 per cent in 1983, 1.9 per cent in 2001). That the Irish economy acts as a gateway to EU markets is seen in the fact that intra-EU trade has consistently accounted for over 60 per cent of exports (62.3 per cent in 2000, 61.9 per cent in 2001). As a source of imports the European Union has declined in importance, from 72 per cent in 1973 to 59.2 per cent in 2001 (55 per cent in 2000). This reflects the growing importance of the United States as a source of raw materials for the chemical, electrical, and electronic industries. Imports from the United States have stood at 15 to 16 per cent in recent years (16.3 per cent in 2000, 15.2 per cent in 2001), compared with less than 7 per cent on Ireland's accession to the European Union. Similarly, Japan was far more important as a source of imports than any EU country with the exception of Britain, and only Britain and Germany exceeded Singapore. Materials for further production,

tower-houses. *One of the best-preserved tower-houses, that of Aughnanure, Co. Galway, built by the O'Flahertys in the fifteenth century on an island in Lough Corrib, with intact bawn walls and moat. [Dúchas, The Heritage Service]*

mostly to fuel export-oriented industry, usually account for between 60 and 64 per cent of all imports, with a strong concentration on computer and electronic components. Within the European Union the core countries of Germany (12.7 per cent in 2001), France (6.1 per cent), Belgium (4.8 per cent), the Netherlands (4.6 per cent) and Italy (3.6 per cent) are Ireland's most important export markets. While the relative importance of these countries varies from year to year, these have remained the focus of exports since accession.

Outside the European Union, the United States is an important export market, with 17 per cent of the total in recent years. The value of both imports and exports of goods has risen steadily, and the Republic has shown a trading surplus, estimated at €35 million in 2001, every year since 1985—an unprecedented run. The world economic downturn may change this trend, at least in the short term.

The composition of trade has also changed. In 2001 some 93.7 per cent of exports were classified as industrial, with only 3.9 per cent classified as agricultural; fifty years ago more than 80 per cent of all exports were of livestock. **Joseph Brady**

trade banners. Trade banners evolved out of the flags and banners carried by guild members in the pageantry of riding the city franchise. This survived up to c. 1821. Banners for the evolving TRADE UNIONS were produced from the 1830s; the largest and most splendid were made in the 1860s and 70s. To show the antiquity of the trades, banners were painted with the ancient arms or the patron saint of the guild; others were painted with the symbols of the new Ireland. The tradition waned after about 1900. **Mairead Dunlevy**

trade unions, among the most significant organisations with all-Ireland membership: almost all unions in Ireland are affiliated to the IRISH CONGRESS OF TRADE UNIONS. The politics of national independence coloured the development of the trade union movement during the twentieth century. At first most unions were British and mainly organised skilled craft workers, particularly in the industrialised north-east and in Dublin. Unskilled workers became more organised in the early twentieth century, especially after the establishment of the IRISH TRANSPORT AND GENERAL WORKERS' UNION in 1909. Divisions between British and Irish unions did not directly mirror attitudes to political independence, and all remained affiliated to the Irish Trades Union Congress after 1922. Nevertheless some differences were manifested, not only on national issues but also on the conduct of industrial relations: Irish unions tended to be rather more sympathetic to co-operative involvement with the governments of the Irish Free State and the Republic. This division led to a split in the trade union movement between 1945 and 1959. It faded from the 1960s onwards, though its residual influence is still evident in the somewhat more critical response of unions of British origin to NATIONAL PAY AGREEMENTS and SOCIAL PARTNERSHIP. [see SERVICES, INDUSTRIAL, PROFESSIONAL AND TECHNICAL UNION.] **Niamh Hardiman**

tradition, an important concept in many academic disciplines as well as in common discourse, often seen as the bedrock of collective identity and the guarantor of cultural authenticity. As a result, a static notion of tradition tends to dominate. Anthropology, FOLKLORE studies, and sociology were founded on the opposition between tradition and modernity. To the innovation and flux of modern societies was contrasted the conservatism and stability of traditional societies. Opposing the negative ENLIGHTENMENT perspective on tradition, romanticism revalued it; and, because of the latter's influence on the development of folklore scholarship, tradition became and remained the central concept in folklore research until the 1960s.

Most approaches to the study of tradition emphasise its 'pastness', looking backwards to models for human behaviour. But tradition is also future-oriented, and the creation of the future should be seen as the aim of tradition, rather than the simple preservation of the past. Connotations of antiquity, of respect, and of duty adhere to the idea of 'tradition', yet in every generation a selection process takes place whereby old cultural material is rejected, adapted or reinterpreted and new material integrated. The process is similar to that by which artistic canons are made. The scholarly notion that some traditions are actually invented (proposed by Eric Hobsbawm and Terence Ranger) is useful but implies that some traditions are unproblematically 'authentic'.

The idea of Gaelic tradition as central to Irishness is a product only of the nineteenth and early twentieth centuries and reflects essentialist concepts such as that of the *volksgeist* ('national spirit'), which predate romanticism but reached their apogee during it. Disenchantment with a contemporary urban high and popular culture, seen as inauthentic and of foreign origin, meant that only the social stratum most removed from modernity, the peasantry, could have inherited the national spirit. The glories of an authentically national high culture were in the past but were reachable through a peasant tradition that, owing to its supposed conservatism, had preserved medieval aristocratic traditions intact. This argument rested on the belief that oral traditions faithfully transmitted knowledge from the distant past.

The more interesting recent debates on tradition in Ireland have taken place in TRADITIONAL MUSIC circles. Traditionalists are seen as stultifying the music, while modernisers cut themselves off from the source of the genuine tradition. In fact for several generations traditional music has been intersecting with the culture industries and with formal MUSIC EDUCATION. This in fact is true of the folk tradition today as much as it is of 'high' and 'popular' culture in general, all of which converge in the culture industries, largely losing their previous association with specific social groups. **Diarmuid Ó Giolláin**

traditional music. 'Traditional music' and 'folk music' are synonymous. In 1954 the International Folk Music Council adopted the following definition:

> Folk music is the product of a musical tradition that has been evolved through the process of oral transmission. The factors that shape the tradition are (i) continuity, which links the present with the past; (ii) variation, which springs from the creative impulse of the individual or the group; and (iii) selection by the community.

This definition remains substantially accurate in relation to traditional music in Ireland, which has at its base, vocally and instrumentally, the solo performer. Items in the present repertoire are seldom older than the eighteenth century, earlier accounts being sparse and frequently sketchy. Dissemination is still primarily oral, and the acceptance of new compositions into the tradition remains a matter of natural selection. Popular trends and innovations at the present time are no guarantee of their absorption into the traditional repertoire. Because people's experience of their music until comparatively recently was largely limited to their own area, regional styles flourished; electronic media created access to a much wider range of musical influences, with a consequent erosion of indigenous styles. Amazingly, the twenty-first century begins with more people performing Irish traditional music than at the beginning of the twentieth century. **Tom Munnelly**

traditional music archives. Archives of traditional music include those of the BBC, Belfast; CAIRDEAS NA BHFIDLÉIRÍ; Coleman Heritage Centre; COMHALTAS CEOLTÓIRÍ ÉIREANN; Cullinane Archive Collection of Irish Dance; Department of Irish Folklore, UCD; IRISH TRADITIONAL MUSIC ARCHIVE, Muckross House, Killarney; UCC; NUIG; Queen's University, Belfast; RTÉ; ULSTER FOLK AND TRANSPORT MUSEUM; and University of Limerick. **Glenn Cumiskey**

traditional music: Arts Council officers. The need for such positions was recognised in 1975 by the poet MICHAEL LONGLEY within the ARTS COUNCIL OF NORTHERN IRELAND. The poet and musician CIARÁN CARSON was appointed to the first such position, holding it until 1998. He was succeeded by the fiddle-player and historian Martin Dowling. In the Republic the fiddle-player PADDY GLACKIN held the first such post with the Arts Council from 1985 to 1990. He was succeeded by Dermot McLaughlin, also a fiddle-player. The post has since been subsumed into the work of a music officer, a post held by Maura Eaton from 1998 to 2001. **Desi Wilkinson**

traditional music awards. The earliest awards for traditional music were the competitive OIREACHTAS and FLEÁ CHEOIL prizes. In later years the Fiddler of Dooney and Fiddler of Oriel competitions were instituted in Cos. Sligo and Monaghan, respectively. In 1980 the Seán O'Boyle Award was begun as a bestowed honour, the first recipient being CHARLES ACTON. Gradam SHEAN-NÓS COIS LIFE was begun in 1993 and is presented annually to someone who has greatly contributed to the promotion of SEAN-NÓS SINGING. The National Traditional Music Awards began life as the AIB Traditional Music

Awards in 1995, with TG4 taking over the sponsorship in 1998 and creating an additional prize for the Young Musician of the Year. The Irish Music Magazine Awards were begun in 1999, and the Young Traditional Musician of the Year Award, sponsored by the Harcourt Hotel and the music shop Celtic Note, were begun the same year. **Maeve Ellen Gebruers**

traditional music broadcasting. Following the practice of its precursor, 2RN, from its inception in 1928, RTÉ has pursued a policy of playing and promoting TRADITIONAL MUSIC and song. Raidió na Gaeltachta, since its inception in 1972, has been to the forefront in this area, spearheaded by Máirtín Ó Fátharta, while TG4, since it began broadcasting in 1996, has presented regional styles of traditional music and song in such series as 'Geantraí' and 'Síbín'. UTV and BBC have produced significant programmes on both radio and television from the 1960s; while some local radio stations have promoted the music in specialist programmes, with Clare FM being the leader in the field for many years. SEÁN Ó RIADA's pioneering work with CEOLTÓIRÍ CHUALANN was encouraged by RTÉ with such radio programmes as 'Reacaireacht an Riadaigh' and 'Fleadh Cheoil an Raidió'. SÉAMUS ENNIS, Seán Mac Réamoinn, PROINSIAS Ó CONLUAIN, and CIARÁN MAC MATHÚNA collected important early material for Radio Éireann, while Tony MacMahon's 'Bring Down the Lamp' and 'The Long Note' and television programmes such as 'Come West Along the Road' encouraged fresh thinking. Julian Vignoles' 'The High Road' took this work further from 1997. Harry Bradshaw has transferred much of RTÉ's collected material to new formats, while Peter Browne has made invaluable documentary programmes on the lives of famous musicians. Peter Browne, Ian Lee, and Cathal Goan have produced high-quality CDs of archive material, thereby making it available to later generations. **Liam Mac Con Iomaire**

traditional music collection. Serious music collection began with the financing of EDWARD BUNTING to notate tunes at the BELFAST HARP FESTIVAL (1792). The event united political idealism and the preservation of indigenous music, endangered by hostile colonial domination. Until Bunting published his *Ancient Irish Music*, publication was concerned with the transmission of utilitarian music rather than the preservation of an artefact. WALKER's *Historical Memoirs of the Irish Bards* (1786) had already set a 'national' agenda in music, and BROOKE's *Reliques of Irish Poetry* (1789) the idea of preservation. The ideological connection was maintained in the titles of subsequent publications: O'Farrell's *'National' Music* (1804), HARDIMAN's *Irish Minstrelsy* (1831), Conran's *National Music of Ireland* (1848), ALLINGHAM's *Folk Melodies of Ireland* (1852), PETRIE's *Ancient Music of Ireland* (1855), Levey's *Dance Music of Ireland* (1858), Joyce's *Ancient Irish Music* (1873), O'CURRY's manuscript deductions in *Musical Instruments of the Ancient Irish* (1873), and Hoffman's *Music of Ireland* (1877). The unpublished collections involved identity also, notably the efforts of the Hudsons (mid-1800s) and Grier (1883). Goodman alone (1860s) appeared to be interested in the endangered music of his locality as such, but O'NEILL (1903) strongly linked nationality and culture, as did HARDEBECK (1908) and Roche (1911 and 1923). Patriotic zeal and antiquarian obsession have thus been synergistic keys to—if not motivators of—the survival of the core printed body of traditional music. The ideology of the GAELIC LEAGUE may have provided a mould that shaped this as something other than the mere vehicle for entertainment that no doubt it predominantly was; but in doing so it provided a reason to preserve and promote that which through trivialisation would have fallen to obsolescence. Its agenda also facilitated repopularisation in the late twentieth century, which in turn led to intensive study of the music. **Fintan Vallely**

traditional music. *A music session at Ennis, Co. Clare, with (left to right) Michael Falsey, Bobby Casey, Junior Crehan, Seán Reid, Andy Conroy, Pat Mitchell, and John Kelly. [Irish Traditional Music Archive]*

traditional music composition. The individual composers of the great body of tunes handed down from the twentieth century by means of oral transmission, early sound recordings and published manuscript are now lost to history. However, with the rapid growth of the traditional music culture as a whole, many of the compositions of important composers of the 1950s and 60s, such as SEÁN RYAN, ED REAVY, and PADDY O'BRIEN, folded themselves into the traditional repertoire. The composition of dance tunes is now widespread. Though most musicians compose tunes only rarely, a growing number are cultivating this process and directing their creative energies towards the full melodic possibilities of the structure of dance tunes, moving beyond the rhythmic emphasis and repetitiveness traditionally perceived to be required for dancing. While composition has flourished, criticism and teaching of modern tune-making can hardly be said to exist. In a largely unspoken process of selection, a minority of tunes possessed of that special combination of playability and aesthetic interest gradually gain popularity, while the great majority of new compositions languish in printed collections, on commercial CDs, or in the repertoires of isolated practitioners. **Martin Dowling**

traditional music education. Recent decades have seen a massive growth in the number of young people playing traditional music. Instruction was previously given within families or small communities without reference to any formal teaching; progress was marked informally and, with the introduction of the fleadhanna cheoil by COMHALTAS CEOLTÓIRÍ ÉIREANN in the 1950s, by success in competitions. With dramatically increased participation, tuition has grown both in scope and formality. An important development in the 1990s was the formulation of structured curriculums for traditional music. The first, introduced by the London College of Music in 1998, features eight grades and higher diplomas in teaching and performance. A similar curriculum subsequently developed by the ROYAL IRISH ACADEMY OF MUSIC is used by Comhaltas Ceoltóirí Éireann. In contrast to other music curriculums, these feature aural skills appropriate to the historic nature of transmission. The London College of Music system is popular in Northern

Ireland and is employed by the Andersonstown Traditional and Contemporary Music School and the ARMAGH PIPERS' CLUB as well as by local branches of Comhaltas Ceoltóirí Éireann. **Martin Dowling**

traditional music education facilities. Traditional music is included, to varying extents, in the syllabus of the Junior Certificate and Leaving Certificate and, in Northern Ireland, for both the GCSE and A-Level examination. At third level, traditional music forms part of the curriculum in a number of music degree courses. The Music Department of UCC employs specialist staff in the area and encourages traditional music performance as part of the BA and BMus courses. NUIM, UCD, NUIG, TCD and QUB all offer some elements of traditional music, as do the Cork School of Music, Waterford and Tralee Institutes of Technology, St Patrick's College, Dublin, and Mary Immaculate College, Limerick. The NUI and Dublin Institute of Technology have provided undergraduate degree courses from 2001, and SIAMSA TÍRE and the Institute of Technology, Tralee, offer a degree in traditional music studies. A BA course in Irish music and dance began at the Irish World Music Centre, University of Limerick, in 2002. This was established as a postgraduate research centre with special interests in traditional music and dancing.

A number of post-Leaving-Certificate courses, in traditional music are available, for example 'Ceoltóir' at Senior College, Ballyfermot, and 'Northern Rhythms' in Donegal. Various teacher training courses are also offered, such as TTCT by COMHALTAS CEOLTÓIRÍ ÉIREANN in Monkstown, Co. Dublin. In 1997 the London College of Music began the first grade exams in Irish traditional music, as an equivalent to the classical music system; this was followed in 1998 by a grade exam syllabus operated jointly by the ROYAL IRISH ACADEMY OF MUSIC and Comhaltas Ceoltóirí Éireann. The bulk of instrumental and dance training is done privately, by Comhaltas Ceoltóirí Éireann and by specialist schools, such as An Gael-Acadamh in Connemara and the Pipers' Club in Ulster. Commercial music schools, such as the new Walton's School of Music in Dublin, also offer instruction in traditional music. **Liz Doherty**

traditional music families. Traditional music has many perceived 'great families', some with the resources to operate as CÉILÍ BANDS, others with only one or two significant players. Some of these have become household names, others are quietly influential, while some small number may have practised music for generations, though the great majority are of the 'revival' years. The conditions that made possible the passing on of music that created the great dynastic names such as ROWSOME, KELLY, and GLACKIN can be reproduced today by modern recording technology anywhere in the world; but parental and sibling teaching, approval, effort, and incentive guide the formation of all the great and widely known families in traditional music, among them the O'Briens, O'Connors, McKeons, Potts, Mulligans, McKennas, and Cassidys of Dublin, McSherrys of Belfast, O'Briens of Portglenone, Shannons and Custys of Co. Clare, Lewises of Co. Mayo, Nugents of Co. Tipperary, Ó Domhnaills of Kells and Rannafast, O'Briens of Co. Tipperary, Murphys of Sliabh Luachra, Smiths of Co. Mayo, Vallelys of Armagh, Ó Raghallaighs of Rathmolyon, Mac Gabhanns of Dunshaughlin, and Ó Grádas and Ó Riabhaighs of Co. Cork. **Fintan Vallely**

traditional music groups. The emergence in the early twentieth century of céilithe sponsored by the GAELIC LEAGUE saw groups of traditional musicians formed to provide music for social dancing. Traditional music had previously been seen largely as a solo art—though musicians had undoubtedly played together informally. Radio provided an impetus for the development of ensemble playing, and groups such as the AUGHRIM SLOPES CÉILÍ BAND, BALLINAKILL CÉILÍ BAND, and Belhavel Trio gained a nationwide audience through broadcasts on Radio Éireann. Céilí bands such as the Kilfenora, TULLA, Gallowglass, and MCCUSKER BROTHERS established a significant live audience.

The emergence of showbands and ballad groups in the 1960s saw CÉILÍ BANDS decline in popularity. Ballad groups such as the CLANCY BROTHERS and the DUBLINERS established an international audience for their identifiably Irish music throughout the 1960s. In the same decade Seán Ó Riada's CEOLTÓIRÍ CHUALANN was significant in developing a new form of group playing that featured FIDDLES, UILLEANN PIPES, TIN WHISTLE, FLUTE, ACCORDION, BODHRÁN, and harpsichord in arrangements of traditional tunes. The CHIEFTAINS, formed around some of the core players of Ó Riada's group, released their first recording in 1963, and they continue to bring Irish music to an international audience. Planxty, formed in 1972, combined the bouzouki and mandolin arrangements of DÓNAL LUNNY and ANDY IRVINE with the charismatic vocal presence of CHRISTY MOORE and the uilleann piper LIAM O'FLYNN. The BOTHY BAND, formed in 1974, was based around a melodic core of fiddle, flute, and pipes, underpinned by a formidable rhythm section of guitar, bouzouki, and keyboards.

Many of these new groups had an understanding of contemporary POPULAR MUSIC and culture, and their arrangements often reflected this. DÉ DANANN, led by the fiddle player FRANKIE GAVIN, have featured various singers, including DOLORES KEANE, Mary Black, MAURA O'CONNELL, and Eleanor Shanley. A revitalised recording industry in the 1970s and 80s helped develop the market for this music, and many bands—not all of them Irish—were formed, including the BOYS OF THE LOUGH, Inchiquin, Na Filí, Pumpkinhead, Le Chéile, Aileach, Stockton's Wing, Oisín, General Humbert, Ceoltóiri Laighean, Shaskeen, Na Caisidigh, Any Old Time, Cherish the Ladies, MOVING HEARTS, Relativity, Nightnoise, Puck Fair, Skylark, Arcady, Moving Cloud, ALTAN, the Sharon Shannon Band, Buttons and Bows, Meristem, Lá Lugh, Dervish, Nomos, Solas, Cran, Lúnasa, Coolfin, and Danú. **Tom Sherlock**

traditional music instrument-makers. A large body of artisans is engaged in instrument-making for traditional music as a full-time occupation; for others it is a part-time occupation or a labour of love. The total number has been estimated to be about 130. There are guitar-makers in several places, accordion-makers in Cos. Limerick and Clare, and makers of tin whistles in several places, including Dublin. Many of the instruments used in TRADITIONAL MUSIC are nevertheless made abroad, particularly the internationally used instruments, such as the ACCORDION, banjo, TIN WHISTLE, guitar, mandolin, and piano. Some Italian and French accordion-makers have begun to make specialist instruments for Irish music, such as the Máirtín O'Connor accordion. Apart from a couple of bouzouki-makers in Dublin and Galway, the indigenous instruments, such as the uilleann pipes, concert flute, HARP, and BODHRÁN, which were in short supply up to the 1970s, are the ones most commonly produced in Ireland. The FIDDLE, which is both universal and indigenous, is also well represented among Irish instrument-makers; and there are several reputable bagpipe-makers. While many of these instrument-makers are self-taught, others have been apprenticed—usually in an informal way—to older instrument-makers. This is particularly true in the case of the UILLEANN PIPES. Reed-making for the pipes is often considered a separate process;

some skilled workers are in demand as reed-makers alone. Because of the worldwide demand for instruments, many of the skilled craftsmen making them are working abroad, particularly in the United States, Britain, France, and Germany. **Desi Wilkinson**

traditional music instruments. Any instrument can be played in a manner that suggests an Irish style or accent. The UILLEANN PIPES, FIDDLE, FLUTE, and TIN WHISTLE are viewed as central to the tradition. The Highland pipes are not used in many ENSEMBLES, but they are long established and were certainly the precursor of the uilleann pipes. The HARP has been in use for centuries, but because of its serious decline in the nineteenth century and its size it is outside the mainstream at present. Other instruments assumed importance during the twentieth century, among them the ACCORDION (all types), CONCERTINA, mandolin, and tenor banjo. For rhythmic accompaniment the BODHRÁN is perceived as most authentic, with the guitar and the bouzouki being the dominant harmonic instruments, having superseded the piano and electric keyboard, providing backing in many groups and bands. Jew's harps and BONES are also heard, with didgeridoo and djembe drum achieving some fringe avant-garde popularity in the later 1990s. **Desi Wilkinson**

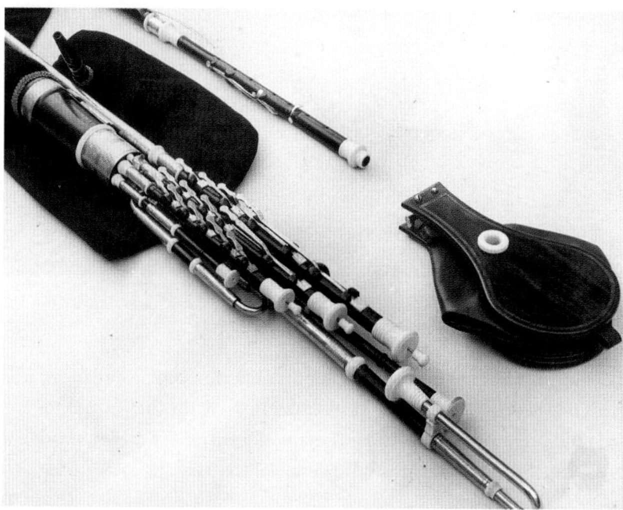

traditional music. *Uilleann pipes in the key of B made by Geoff Wooff, 1988, after a set made by Coyne in the first half of the nineteenth century, using ebony, ivory, and nickel silver, with sterling silver keys. The bellows are of South American rosewood, with pearwood inlay over stitching. [Na Píobairí Uilleann; photo: Geoff Wooff]*

traditional music instruments and dance in paintings. Paintings and other representations of traditional music, instruments and dance are rare before the nineteenth century. A harper and a player of warpipes depicted in Derricke's *Image of Ireland* (1581) are among the earliest images of indigenous music-making. HIGH CROSSES and isolated later medieval sources sometimes show musicians and instruments, but these are often symbolic rather than necessarily reflecting actual practice. Portraits of CAROLAN and of other harpers with their instruments exist from the eighteenth century. In the nineteenth century traditional musicians sometimes feature in paintings of rural life; despite their often romanticised settings, these underline the prominence of the UILLEANN PIPES in Irish music at that time. The much rarer paintings of Irish dancing (such as Trevor Fowler's *Children Dancing at a Crossroads*, now in the NATIONAL GALLERY) provide glimpses of dance practices before the GAELIC LEAGUE reforms of the late nineteenth century (see pp. 404, 475, 568). **Barra Boydell**

traditional music ornamentation. The most important element of traditional ornamentation is idiosyncratic flair. The style of influential players (including recording artists and teachers) is naturally copied by learners. However, throughout the nineteenth century and arguably long before, certain techniques and embellishments have been passed on as definitive. Uilleann piping (and highland bagpiping) fingering ornamentation has been particularly influential on all the instruments used. Though the techniques are different on the ACCORDION and the FIDDLE, for example, the ornaments are increasingly given the same names. Tutor books now available for all instruments tend to standardise the basic ornaments as *rolls*, *cuts*, *crans*, and *triplets*. The 'roll' is played by sounding a given note briefly, 'cutting' the note above it and then 'tipping' the note below, before returning to the given note. Some preferred styles are heavily ornamented, others sparsely so. **Desi Wilkinson**

traditional music publishing. Given the fact that traditional music is still essentially an oral tradition, the appearance of collections of tunes has had more significance as an indication of academic and amateur interest than as an indication of the level of musical literacy of the bulk of traditional musicians. Many tune collections appeared after NEALE's *Collection of the Most Celebrated Irish Tunes* (1724), but until recently the only one to have any significance for the practising traditional musician was *The Dance Music of Ireland: 1,001 Gems* (1907) by FRANCIS O'NEILL. The work of such well-known collectors as EDWARD BUNTING, GEORGE PETRIE, P. W. JOYCE, and JAMES GOODMAN, among others, provides a valuable insight into the world of Irish music in the nineteenth century.

Works of commentary and analysis have been scarce at all periods. JOSEPH COOPER WALKER's *Historical Memoirs of the Irish Bards* appeared in 1786, and only a handful of works appeared throughout the nineteenth and twentieth centuries, with Francis O'Neill's *Irish Folk Music* (1910) and *Irish Minstrels and Musicians* (1913) occupying an important place. BREANDÁN BREATHNACH's *Folk Music and Dances of Ireland* was a seminal work, as was Tomás Ó Canainn's *Irish Traditional Music* and CIARÁN CARSON's *Pocket Guide to Irish Traditional Music*. FINTAN VALLELY's *Companion to Traditional Music* (1999) was the major assembly of information on the revival period of traditional music. The 1980s saw a huge increase in the publication of popular material, the bulk of it in the form of tutors for various instruments and collections of tunes. Breandán Breathnach's *Ceol Rince na hÉireann*, issued in three volumes after 1963, has become the definitive collection of modern times, its most recent volumes, 4 and 5, being edited by JACKIE SMALL. **Colin Hamilton**

traditional music summer schools, an established and expanding series of annual events and one of the most pleasurable ways of acquiring the skills of traditional music. They combine instrumental, SET-DANCING, and song repertory classes with lectures and socialising. The first of the schools was Scoil Acla (1960) in Achill Island, Co. Mayo; but the modern prototype is SCOIL SAMHRAIDH WILLIE CLANCY, held annually since 1973 at Milltown Malbay, Co. Clare. Now a national event, it commemorates the town's best-known UILLEANN PIPER, WILLIE CLANCY. More recent events include the South Sligo Summer School at Tubbercurry; Joe Mooney Summer School, Drumshanbo, Co. Leitrim; Michael Davitt Summer School, Ballaghaderreen, Co. Roscommon; 'Blas' at the University of Limerick; the Keadue Harp Festival, Co. Roscommon; Scoil Éigse (an integral part of Fleá Cheoil na hÉireann); and Cairdeas na bFhidléirí at Glencolumbkille, Co. Donegal. **Desi Wilkinson**

traditional music. *Éamon Cotter leads a flute class at the Scoil Samhraidh Willie Clancy, held annually at Milltown Malbay, Co. Clare. [Fintan Vallely]*

traditional music, transmission of, the methods by which style and repertoire are passed on within a generation and between generations. Fundamental to this is the *oral* or *aural* method, the music being passed on by singing or playing for a learner, who picks up 'by ear'. *Graphic systems* of notation were first used in Ireland for CHURCH MUSIC from the twelfth century, in order to standardise religious singing. Dance tunes were noted first in Ireland in JOHN AND WILLIAM NEALE's *Collection of the Most Celebrated Irish Tunes* (1724); EDWARD BUNTING preserved the repertoire played at the BELFAST HARP FESTIVAL (1792); and the nineteenth century produced many collections of dance music and songs. Playing from such scripts does not guarantee the accurate reproduction of rhythm, ornamentation, and dynamics, however, and listening to players of traditional music is still a necessary component of learning. Members of the TRAVELLER community were important *physical transmitters* and retainers of song and music too in the pre-recording age. Moving from place to place, they could absorb the repertoire of different localities and pass it on to other regions (see p. 1074).

Early *mechanical recordings* became critical to the transmission of music after the process was invented in the late 1880s and made some other methods largely redundant. Seventy-eight r.p.m. discs store a physical representation of sound patterns indefinitely and can guarantee reproduction as accurate as the ear of the learner. *Electronic recording*, from 1947 onwards, hugely improved the quality of transmission; the invention of cheap cassette tape in the 1960s increased and democratised the potential for learning and repertoire expansion. *Digital transmission*, from the 1980s onwards, now makes the high-fidelity preservation of music and song possible; but because a high proportion of its content is studio manipulation, it is still necessarily used also in conjunction with the oral and the graphic. The oral has thus remained central to all methods of traditional music transmission. **Fintan Vallely**

traditional music tune titles. These follow no particular pattern but refer to all areas of human life. Some are straightforward, such as the timeless 'Give Us a Drink of Water', while others are quirky, such as 'Wallop the Spot'—possibly a reference to dancing. The 'Home Ruler' may be a reference to 'The Woman of the House' (another title) or to the period of political agitation for HOME RULE (late 1800s). Older tunes refer to places, people, and happenings, usually local: 'The Humours of Lissadell', 'The Black-Haired Lass', 'The Blackthorn Stick', 'The 'Rights of Man', 'The Foxhunt', 'Rolling on the Rye-Grass'. Many have bilingual titles, such as 'Cailleach an Airgid' or 'The Hag with the Money'. Older tunes, such as this one, often had words to them ('dance songs'). Modern tune titles, such as 'Robert Emmet's Flying Rocket' (Cathal McConnell) and 'The Doberman's Wallet' (FRANKIE GAVIN) tend to be either epic, obscure, or humorous (or all three) and in general are less reflective of local place and community than the bulk of earlier tunes. **Desi Wilkinson**

traditional music tune types. The most familiar tune types are the REEL (4/4 time), the *double* JIG (6/8), and the HORNPIPE (4/4). The *slip jig* or *hop jig* (9/8), the *single jig* (6/8 and 12/8), the *march* (2/4 and 4/4), and the SLOW AIR (often a musical rendering of a song) are common. Some areas are known for specific genres, the *slide* (6/8 and 12/8) and POLKA (2/4) being popular in Co. Kerry and the south-west and the *highland* (4/4) peculiar to Co. Donegal and the North. More popularly recognised Continental tune types, such as MAZURKA, WALTZ, and PLANXTY, also exist. **Desi Wilkinson**

tragedy. The first post-Restoration English tragedies were both written for the SMOCK ALLEY THEATRE, Dublin: ROGER BOYLE's *The Generall*, and KATHERINE PHILIPS's *Pompey* (both 1663). However, the first successful Irish tragedian, JAMES SHERIDAN KNOWLES, appeared at the tail end of the vogue for verse tragedy. His *Virginius* (1820) elicited comparisons with Shakespeare and was performed by the leading tragic actors of the period, William Macready and Edwin Forrest. Knowles's work was part of a brief flowering of Irish verse tragedy in the early nineteenth century, which included CHARLES MATURIN's *Bertram* (1816), RICHARD LALOR SHEIL's *The Apostate* (1817), JOHN BANIM's *Damon and Pythias* (1821), and GERALD GRIFFIN's *Gisippus* (1842).

The dominance of MELODRAMA in the second half of the nineteenth century marginalised tragedy, until the form was developed by the writers associated with the ABBEY THEATRE in their effort to create 'a Theatre where beautiful emotion and profound thought … might have their three hours' traffic once again.' W. B. YEATS in his mythological plays, such as *On Baile's Strand* (1904), began a long exploration of the tragic form that would lead him to translate Sophocles' *Oedipus* (1928) and *Oedipus at Colonnus* (1934). JOHN MILLINGTON SYNGE, for his part, wrote one of the great short tragedies in English, *Riders to the Sea* (1904), inaugurating a move towards 'peasant tragedy' that included T. C. Murray's *Birthright* (1910). In the aftermath of the Civil War, SEAN O'CASEY described as tragedies the three plays of his ABBEY TRILOGY: *The Shadow of a Gunman* (1923), *Juno and the Paycock* (1924), and *The Plough and the Stars* (1926). Collectively, they constitute a landmark of modern tragic writing (see p. 2).

Since the middle of the twentieth century the concept of tragedy has become more problematic. However, certain central features—the move towards an inevitable death, accompanied by a moment of recognition—can be found in much recent Irish dramatic writing, including TOM MURPHY's *A Whistle in the Dark* (1961), BRIAN FRIEL's *Faith Healer* (1979), and MARINA CARR's *By the Bog of Cats* (1998). Similarly, there has been a continuous use of the tragic form in plays dealing with the conflict in Northern Ireland, beginning with St John Ervine's *Mixed Marriage* (1911). This in turn has awakened interest in producing distinctively Irish translations of classical Greek tragedy, including TOM PAULIN's *The Riot Act* (1985), based on Sophocles' *Antigone*, and SEAMUS HEANEY's *The Cure at Troy* (1990), a version of Sophocles' *Philoctetes*. **Christopher Morash**

Traits and Stories of the Irish Peasantry (1830), a combination of folklore and melodrama by WILLIAM CARLETON. A second series followed in 1833; these stories, including 'Wildgoose Lodge' and 'The Poor Scholar', show a considerable advance in dramatic power and narrative skill. A collected edition was produced in 1842–4, with the addition of two further stories and an autobiographical introduction, now celebrated as Carleton's best non-fictional prose. His experimentation with dialect and narrative voice in *Traits and Stories* and his handling of narrative suspense are among Carleton's most significant legacies. **Margaret Kelleher**

Tralee (*Trá Lí*), county town of Co. Kerry; population (2002) 6,332, with a further 14,030 in the immediate hinterland. The town is at the head of Tralee Bay, where the River Lee reaches the sea (and from which it derives its name). At the north-east corner of the DINGLE PENINSULA, it is an important gateway town providing access for the thousands of tourists who visit Dingle each year. While there is evidence of earlier occupation, the town dates from the ANGLO-NORMAN period, when John Fitzthomas built a castle there after 1216; a Dominican priory followed in 1243. A market town grew up around the castle, but both town and castle suffered in the seventeenth century as a result of rebellion and siege.

Tralee prospered in the eighteenth century, and many fine examples of GEORGIAN architecture survive, while the classical courthouse dates from 1830. The workhouse, opened in 1844 and the largest in the country, played an important role in relief during the GREAT FAMINE. It became a hospital in 1932 and more recently has been renovated as the offices of the county council. While tourism is an important economic activity, many people are employed in local and transnational industries. The Kerry Group, now one of the world's largest suppliers of food ingredients, is particularly important. There is an Institute of Technology, and access to Britain and the Continent is facilitated by the airport at nearby Farranfore. Tralee is also the base of SIAMSA TÍRE, Ireland's National Folk Theatre, and is the venue for the annual Rose of Tralee festival. **Joseph Brady**

tramway systems. Ireland's first horse tram began operation at Fintona, Co. Tyrone, in 1854. In 1872 services were inaugurated in Dublin, Belfast, and Cork, with Galway following in 1879 and Derry in 1897. The latter two systems, each of one route only, were never converted to electric traction, and both closed in 1919. Services in Cork had ceased even earlier—in 1875—but a new electric system was inaugurated in 1898, operating until 1931,

Traits and Stories. *A portrait of William Carleton by John Slattery (fl. 1846–58) shows him as a successful professional writer. Carleton's literary career is a vivid reflection of the divisions and tensions in early nineteenth-century Ireland. [National Gallery of Ireland]*

when competition from buses put it out of business. Horse trams also operated between Warrenpoint and Rostrevor, Co. Down, 1877–1915, while minor electric services included the GIANT'S CAUSEWAY, the Bessbrook and Newry (1885–1948), and the Hill of Howth, Co. Dublin (1901–59), the last tram service to operate in Ireland, widely lamented if only for its unrealised tourist potential.

The distinction between steam trams and RAILWAYS is anomalous, but those operating between Dublin and Lucan (1888–1900) and between Dublin and Blessington (1888–1932), with the track laid largely at the roadside, could properly be described as tramways. The former was converted to electric traction and operated as part of the Dublin United Tramway Company's system until 1940. Steam trams also ran in Portstewart, 1882–1926, and through the Clogher Valley, Co. Tyrone, 1887–1942, though this system described itself in its later years as the Clogher Valley Railway.

The advent of the motor bus in the 1920s heralded the eclipse of the tram as the dominant public service vehicle, with the last Dublin route closing in 1949 and that of Belfast in 1954. Increasing traffic congestion in Dublin prompted a renewal of interest in fixed-rail urban transport, and two lines of a long-planned light rail system, branded Luas ('speed'), were due to become operative in late 2003, with further extensions projected. **Bernard Share**

translation into and from Irish. Translators in Irish have been active for over a thousand years. The earliest recorded instances of translation are to be found in the GLOSSES of sacred and secular texts that were kept in the monasteries of Milan, Würzburg, Sankt Gallen, Karlsruhe, Turin, Vienna, Bern, Leiden, and Nancy. The translations were of Greek or Latin words and phrases, which helped to explain them to the Irish teacher or student in his native language. Irish monastic presence on the Continent was extensive from the sixth century onwards, and Irish monastic scholars made a well-documented contribution to the reorganisation of the educational system in Merovingian and Carolingian Europe. The first vernacular translation of Dares Phrygius's *De Excidio Troiae Historiae* was made in Ireland in the tenth century and was known in Irish as *Togail Troí*. The Irish translation of Nennius's history of the Britons and the Picts, *Historia Brittonum*, is generally attributed to Giolla Caemháin, recorded in the ANNALS as having died in 1072. Irish translations of Statius's *Thebaid*, Virgil's *Aeneid* and Lucan's *Pharsalia* from this period appear to be the oldest vernacular translations of these texts in Europe. The translators of late medieval Ireland were either attached to monasteries or were members of leading bardic families.

Latin was the main source language for many of the translations, and a wide variety of text types was translated. The Irish versions of medico-philosophical texts, such as Johannes Anglicus's *Rosa Anglica* and Bernard of Gordon's *Lilium Medicinae*, enjoyed wide circulation in medieval Ireland. The translation of devotional literature was also widespread.

The Tudor conquest was to have far-reaching linguistic consequences for Irish; but at first the REFORMATION's emphasis on the importance of preaching the Gospel to people in their own language led to a strong emphasis on translation into Irish. The first printed book in Irish was a translation by John Carswell of the Book of Common Order, published in April 1567 in Edinburgh as *Foirm na nUrrnuidheadh*. ELIZABETH I ordered type to be made so that books could be printed in Irish; as a result, in 1602 the New Testament appeared in a printed Irish translation. Three translators were responsible: William Daniel, a senior fellow of TRINITY COLLEGE, Dublin; Nicholas Walsh; and Fearganainm Ó Domhnalláin. William Daniel also translated the BOOK OF COMMON PRAYER into Irish, the translation appearing in 1609. In 1640 the translation of the Old Testament was completed under the supervision of WILLIAM BEDELL, a former provost of Trinity College and Protestant Bishop of Kilmore. The chief translators were Muircheartach Ó Cionga and Séamas de Nógla. The translation was not published, however, until 1685.

The activity of the Protestant churches in IRISH-LANGUAGE translation was a source of concern in Catholic circles, and in 1611 a printing press was acquired by the College of St Anthony, the Irish college in Louvain, then part of the Spanish Netherlands. The main purpose was to produce printed literature in Irish, including translations. In 1616 FLAITHRÍ Ó MAOLCHONAIRE produced *Sgáthán an Chrábhaidh*, a translation of *Spill de la Vida Religiosa*, a religious work originally composed in Catalan. Translation into Irish in the seventeenth century was increasingly the work of translators belonging to Continental religious orders, such as the Franciscans based in the Irish Colleges of Louvain, Rome, and Prague. The translation activity was one of the factors contributing to the simplification and modernisation of Irish in the early modern period. The first English translation of an Irish-language poem is to be found in the Addenda to the *Calendar of State Papers Relating to Ireland* (1601–3); the translator was a clergyman, Meredith Hammer.

Written translation from Irish was a relatively rare event in the seventeenth century, but the eighteenth century was markedly different, with a demand from antiquarian scholars close to the new ASCENDANCY for materials relating to Ireland's past. These scholars usually spoke only English, and the pressure was now for material to be translated into English rather than into Irish, particularly as Irish was absent from the official public life of the country. The major translation event of the early eighteenth century was the publication in 1723 of Dermod O'Connor's English translation of GEOFFREY KEATING's influential history of Ireland, FORAS FEASA AR ÉIRINN. The revival of interest in CELTIC LANGUAGES and literature occasioned by James MacPherson's *Fragments of Ancient Poetry Collected in the Highlands of Scotland and Translated from the Gaelic or Erse Language* (1760) led to even greater demands for Irish–English literary translation. CHARLOTTE BROOKE, in her *Reliques of Ancient Irish Poetry* (1789), sought to respond to this demand.

The early nineteenth century witnessed continued growth in Irish–English translation through the efforts of translators and editors such as SAMUEL FERGUSON, J. J. Callanan, JAMES HARDIMAN, Mathew Moore Graham, JAMES CLARENCE MANGAN, and GEORGE SIGERSON. The most influential collections of translations in the nineteenth century were two volumes produced by DOUGLAS HYDE. In *Beside the Fire* (1890), containing translations of Irish FOLK-TALES, Hyde decided not to use standard British English in his translations but the English vernacular of the Irish countryside; he adopted a similar approach to the English prose translations of Irish poems in *Abhráin Grádh Chúige Connacht/The Love Songs of Connacht* (1893). These translations were important founding texts for the end-of-century literary renaissance.

Though translation into Irish was practised throughout the late eighteenth and early nineteenth centuries, it was not until the second half of the nineteenth century that serious efforts were made to produce translations again in Irish. In 1877 the founders of the Society for the Preservation of the Irish Language declared one of their aims to be the production of a modern Irish literature, whether original or in translation. The establishment of the GAELIC LEAGUE in 1893 gave further impetus to the movement for translation into Irish. The leaders of the 1916 RISING and of the IRISH FREE STATE were strongly influenced by the thinking of the league, and in 1922

DÁIL ÉIREANN decreed that all legislation should be available in both Irish and English. This move led to the establishment of the translation section of Dáil Éireann, Rannóg an Aistriúcháin, which would play a crucial role in the 1940s and 50s in the moves to standardise the spelling and grammar of Irish.

In 1928 a scheme was initiated for the translation of literature in other languages into Irish; by 1937 a total of 214 works had been translated by translators working for the Publications Branch of the Department of Education, AN GÚM. Though the standard of translation was high, the predominance of English as a source language and the limited success of the scheme with the book-buying public led to the policy being discontinued after the Second World War.

The end of the twentieth century witnessed a rapid increase in the number of translations into Irish from languages other than English. Among the more prominent translators were GABRIEL ROSENSTOCK (German), BREANDÁN Ó DOIBHLIN (French), Máire Nic Mhaoláin (Italian), and Aodh Ó Canainn (Spanish). The 1980s saw the beginning of a new trend towards translating contemporary Irish-language poets into English with the publication of the landmark bilingual collection *The Bright Wave/An Tonn Gheal* (1986).

Translation down through the centuries has remained an important source of cultural renewal and linguistic development for Irish, but excessive or indiscriminate translation has not been without its perils for the language. **Michael Cronin**

Translations (1980), a historical play by BRIAN FRIEL, written for the FIELD DAY THEATRE COMPANY. Set in an Irish-speaking community on the eve of the Great Famine, the play's exploration of identity and linguistic loss made it an instant classic. **Christopher Morash**

translations and adaptations from Latin. The language of the Christian church, Latin, became immensely influential in Ireland from the time of St PATRICK in the fifth century. It was the principal language of church activity, including literary activity. By the sixth century the vernacular language had already been adopted in the church for literary purposes. In the eighth century a broad range of material was being written in Irish: tales, poetry, homilies, LAWS, ANNALS, and genealogies. Translations or adaptations of Latin works in the tenth and eleventh centuries reflect demand in a changing society for texts in Irish relating to Greek and Roman history. In the tenth century a biography of Alexander the Great ('Scéla Alaxandair'), based mainly on the fifth-century Paulus Orosius' *Historiarum Adversus Paganos*, was in circulation.

Soon afterwards the story of the destruction of Troy, 'Togail Troí', was composed. The earliest version was based closely on *De Excidio Troiae Historia*, a fifth or sixth-century work attributed to Dares Phrygius. The closeness of 'Togail Troí' to the *Historia* is evident from correspondences in structure and content, as well as Latin phrases and forms taken over by the Irish author. Early in its development, material not found in the *Historia* was added, including long passages describing battle scenes. In the eleventh or twelfth century more material was added, turning the Irish version of the story into a substantial work. The alliterative rhythmical style seen in the 'Togail' is found in later translations, such as 'Imtheachta Aeniasa' (based on the *Aeneid*), 'Togail na Tebe' (the *Thebaid*), and 'In Cath Catharda' (Lucan's *Pharsalia*). **Uáitéar Mac Gearailt**

transnational corporations. The strategy of attracting FOREIGN DIRECT INVESTMENT into the economy is reflected in the high share of manufacturing employment in foreign-owned companies: almost half of the Republic's manufacturing jobs are in these companies, compared with approximately 20 per cent in Britain, France, Italy, and the Netherlands. Northern Ireland's share is just slightly above the UK average. Ireland's low rate of corporation tax gives these companies an incentive to engage in 'transfer pricing' (manipulating the prices reported for intra-firm trade), which distorts Irish GDP statistics. GNP statistics, however (which net out the profits these firms report as having been earned in Ireland), are probably not much affected. Until the 1990s transnational corporations established in the Republic paid very little corporation tax, as a nil tax rate had been levied on the exporting activities in which they are largely engaged. This exemption was removed at the insistence of the EUROPEAN UNION, and by the late 1990s the corporation tax revenue from these companies amounted to roughly 10 per cent of total income tax revenue. Other positive benefits, besides the direct and indirect employment effects, are the relatively highly skilled and highly paid jobs they offer and the fact that they engage intensively in research and development. One adverse effect of dependence on these firms, however, roughly half of which are American, is that Ireland is now less likely to find itself able (as it was in the 1950s and 60s) to follow policies in the international arena that do not coincide with US interests. **Frank Barry**

transplantation to Connacht. Following the Cromwellian reconquest of Ireland, a large-scale confiscation of Irish land was undertaken, both for financial gain and for the future security of the Protestant interest. This directly affected only a small minority, as full pardon on submission was given to the majority of the Catholic population. The Act for the Settling of Ireland (1652) specified that those of the propertied classes who had fought in the Confederate war were to be punished on a scale appropriate to their guilt; this ranged from loss of life and estate for a few to varying degrees of dispossession for the rest, who would be compensated with a grant of lesser acreage west of the Shannon. A survey of all land ownership and occupancy was followed by measurement and mapping of the confiscated areas. A special court determined degrees of guilt and consequent entitlement to reallocation, while the process of distributing the land was in the hands of five commissioners. The logistical and administrative problems were overwhelming; but the fundamental flaw was the lack of sufficient land to implement the scheme. In June 1657 the plan was deemed to be complete, with a freezing of the situation at that date and in effect a tacit acceptance of its failure. Of the approximately 3,000 Irish Catholic landowners, nearly two-thirds were given land in Connacht or Co. Clare, but the majority of these were transplanted within those areas, and only 770 were moved from elsewhere in Ireland. [see DOWN SURVEY; TRANSPORTATION.] **Liam Irwin**

transport. In early Ireland the transport of goods and people was effected principally through animal carriage along an early road network, as well as by coastal travel on sailing vessels. The road system expanded in the eighteenth century, becoming the responsibility of GRAND JURIES in 1765. Turnpike trusts, in which some of these roads were vested, were abolished in 1857; by then Ireland boasted a network of coaches, roads, and navigational canals. Construction of the NEWRY CANAL began in the 1730s; many subsequent inland waterways proved unprofitable, especially with the advent of railway travel from 1834 (see p. 913). Sea connections with England were enhanced by a Dublin–Liverpool steam service in the 1820s. After partition the Irish Free State and Northern Ireland assumed responsibility for their separate transport infrastructures. The second half of the twentieth century saw increasing use of private cars and

transport, horse-drawn. *An engraving by John Harris the Younger from an original by Michelangelo Hayes, one of a series depicting Charles Bianconi's transport network. The 'bians' carried mail and goods in the middle while passengers sat at the sides. [National Gallery of Ireland]*

public coach transport, the establishment of AER LINGUS in 1936, and the contraction of the rail network throughout Ireland. [see BIANCONI, CHARLES; CANALS.] **K. J. James**

transport, bus. From the earliest days the RAILWAYS had subsidised road services from railheads to areas of tourist interest, such as those operated by the Midland Great Western Railway from Galway to Connemara from 1851. Motorised bus services were attempted from 1906 but met with little success until after the FIRST WORLD WAR, when, in the absence of any licensing system, numerous private operators took to the road. Dublin's first route was inaugurated in 1919 by the Clondalkin Omnibus Company, using a wooden body from a horse-drawn vehicle on a 5-ton chassis. The company was taken over in 1926 by the Irish Omnibus Company, which entered into an agreement with the Great Southern Railway, then prohibited by law from operating road services. The Dublin United Tramway Company ran its first buses in 1925, progressively converting its tram routes from 1932. Between 1933 and 1936 it acquired, or put out of business, all the private operators in the city under the terms of the Transport (Compulsory Acquisition) Act (1933); an act of 1932 had already prohibited the operation of scheduled services except under licence. The sole private operation was that of St Kevin's Bus Service to Glendalough, which continues to operate. In 1934 the Irish Omnibus Company was taken over by the Great Southern Railway and wound up, thus greatly reducing private involvement in public transport for a generation, though small undertakings succeeded in maintaining services in rural areas, such as those of Cos. Kilkenny, Waterford, and Tipperary.

In 1929 the Great Northern Railway began bus operations with a town service in Drogheda and thereafter pursued a policy of acquiring small private operators under the 1933 act. In 1935 its routes and vehicles operating in the North were taken over by the newly formed Northern Ireland Road Transport Board, which itself became part of the ULSTER TRANSPORT AUTHORITY in 1948. Many other railways operated bus services to cover gaps in their systems and as replacements for uneconomic services. With the formation of CÓRAS IOMPAIR ÉIREANN in 1945, road services in the Republic came under state authority, from 1987 operating as Bus Átha Cliath in Dublin and as Bus Éireann elsewhere. From the 1960s onwards Bus Éireann faced competition from long-haul private operators catering in particular for weekend traffic to and from Dublin. These 'charter' services were of dubious legality, but no action was taken to impose restraints because of the complex contractual arrangements resorted to by the operators to circumvent the legislation.

In 1999, in an attempt to alleviate Dublin's acute traffic problems, Bus Átha Cliath began the introduction of reserved bus lanes under the title of quality bus corridors. In 2000, under the National Development Plan, full or partial privatisation of the city services was under active consideration, while other cities, such as Cork, Limerick, and Galway, were seeking accelerated investment in transport. **Bernard Share**

transport, horse-drawn. The marked improvement in Ireland's roads in the early part of the eighteenth century, allied to a rising POPULATION, encouraged the development of transport, both private and public. While the poorer classes continued to travel on horseback or on foot, gentlemen's carriages were increasingly in evidence. Imports from Britain were substantially displaced by native carriage-building, which attained, especially in Dublin, a high standard of production and finish, employing some two thousand people by the end of the century. One Dublin coach-builder, John Hutton, was to survive in business, through many changes in transport modes, until 1925. By the end of the eighteenth century a stage-coach network linked most large towns with the capital, a twice-weekly service between Dublin and Kinnegad, Co. Westmeath, having been inaugurated as early as 1718. In 1742 a Dublin–Belfast service was introduced, leaving Dublin on Mondays and Belfast on Thursdays, with a journey time of three days in winter and two in summer, though the service was not reliably operative until 1788. Other routes were more immediately successful; but coach travel was both slow and expensive, both because of the dilatory manner of changing horses at the stages and the high level of manpower involved. In the early years of the nineteenth century the Dublin–Limerick journey took twenty-one hours—more than two days, with overnight and meal stops—and that to Cork thirty-one hours. There were, however, express or 'flying' coaches, such as that which in the 1750s was covering the distance between Dublin and Kilkenny—117 km (73 miles)—in one day.

In 1784 the Irish Post Office was established, followed in 1789 by the introduction of mail-coach services. These, however, were confined to the principal routes—by 1811 fewer than a dozen—and they supplemented rather than displaced the steadily increasing stage-coach services. The first mail coaches accommodated five passengers, four inside and one outside, while later models carried more than twenty. Even after their introduction, however, travel remained both expensive and unpredictable; in areas lacking a coach service the traveller was at the mercy of local post-chaise proprietors and their frequently dirty and dangerous vehicles. Such conveyances, however, were widely availed of, as evidenced by the frequently reprinted *Post-Chaise Companion*.

By the beginning of the nineteenth century many towns still lacked a public service, while others were only minimally linked: Clonmel, for example, was served by the Dublin–Cork mail but had no connections to Limerick, Wexford, or Waterford. Transport in the cities, Dublin in particular, had developed in tandem with the national network. The capital provided and supported a service of hackney-coaches on the British model, first officially regulated in 1703, when their number was limited to 150 and the horses that drew them were required to be $14\frac{1}{2}$ hands high. There were also one-horse conveyances peculiar to the city, known as RINGSEND CARS. The 'jingle', a four-wheeler that rattled like the bells of a wagon-team, was succeeded by the jaunting-car, common in all parts of the country and still surviving as a tourist attraction, notably in Killarney.

The opening of the CANALS to passenger traffic from 1780 served to stimulate competition from road interests, but it was not until July 1815 that the rivalry was seriously consolidated by CHARLES BIANCONI. His initiative, in effect a transport revolution, had significant economic consequences, for as communications between different localities were extended the resources of the country were opened up. By 1843 Bianconi was operating a hundred vehicles of all types, travelling at between 8 and 9 miles per hour and carrying from four to twenty passengers at a rate of $1\frac{1}{2}$ pence a mile. His 'bians' were hugely popular and prompted several rival concerns to set up, though none were as successful. One of these, Purcell of Dublin, operated almost exclusively on radial routes from the capital, whereas Bianconi's strength lay largely in his cross-country services and in his willingness to co-operate with, rather than oppose, other modes of transport—first the canals and then the RAILWAYS. His 1842 timetable, for example, listed a daily car from Galway at 9:00, connecting at Ballinasloe at 14:30 with the Grand Canal service to Dublin, and quoted combined car and boat fares.

While the coming of the railways spelt the end of horse-drawn transport as a national infrastructure, horse power remained a feature of private and urban life. In 1859 there were four horse-drawn omnibus routes serving the Dublin area, and horse tramways were a feature of other cities from 1871 until they were replaced by electric traction. Horse transport, in many shapes and forms, enjoyed a brief and bizarre revival during the years of the Second World War, when, for example, a stage-coach service, complete with post-horn, operated between Adare and Limerick. **Bernard Share**

transport and tourism: statistics. In 1998 there were more than 138,500 new car registrations in the Republic, two-thirds more than in 1990. In Northern Ireland there were more than 62,000 new registrations, approximately a fifth more than in 1990. Ford was the most popular make of car, accounting for 11 per cent of new cars registered in the Republic and 14 per cent of Northern Ireland registrations.

Table 1: New private cars registered for the first time, 1990–98

	Republic	Northern Ireland
1990	83,420	52,596
1991	68,533	39,096
1992	67,861	38,199
1993	60,792	40,573
1994	77,773	43,820
1995	82,730	43,958
1996	109,333	46,576
1997	125,818	52,468
1998	138,538	62,138

More than 600 people were killed in road accidents in 1998, 7 per cent less than in 1990. In 1998 the number of road accident deaths in the Republic, 458, was approximately 4 per cent lower than in 1990; the corresponding total in Northern Ireland, 160, was approximately 14 per cent lower. Between 1990 and 1998 the number of road accident deaths per 100,000 population was consistently lower in Northern Ireland than in the Republic.

Table 2: Road accident deaths, 1990–98

	Republic		Northern Ireland	
	deaths	per 100,000 population	deaths	per 100,000 population
1990	478	13.7	185	11.6
1991	445	12.6	185	11.5
1992	415	11.7	150	9.2
1993	431	12.1	143	8.7
1994	404	11.3	157	9.5
1995	437	12.1	144	8.7
1996	453	12.5	142	8.5
1997	472	12.9	144	8.6
1998	458	12.4	160	9.5

Between 1994 and 1999 there was a 65 per cent increase in the number of visits to the Republic and a 28 per cent increase in the number of visits to Northern Ireland. In the Republic the totals for holiday and business visits both increased by more than 80 per cent. In Northern Ireland there was an increase of 11 per cent in holiday visits and a 29 per cent increase in business visits. **Central Statistics Office/Northern Ireland Statistics & Research Agency**

transport maps and guides. The development of the road network in the early eighteenth century led to an increase in travel and the nascent tourist traffic, but travellers still had to rely on inaccurate or inadequate maps or route guides, offering little more than tables of distances, such as Watson's *Gentleman's and Citizen's Almanack*, issued annually from 1733. The publication of Taylor and Skinner's *Maps of the Roads of Ireland* (1778) was a major advance, with its accurate, detailed maps and with distances in both Irish and English (statute) miles. The subsequent rapid development of passenger services prompted the publication of *The Post-Chaise Companion or Traveller's Directory* (1784), a detailed guide and gazetteer that ran to several editions.

With the coming of the RAILWAYS the major competing companies recognised the value of tourist traffic, particularly from Britain, and either produced their own guides or were actively involved in publications such as W. F. Wareman's *Three Days on the Shannon* (1852), which, according to its dedication to the directors of the Midland Great Western Railway, was 'originated by their enterprise and patronage.' In 1912 a series of cigarette cards issued by the Gallaher tobacco company of 'Views in North of Ireland' carried the offer of a free return ticket to Portrush on surrender of a complete set of twenty-five. Artists such as PAUL HENRY, WILLIAM ORPEN, and Norman Wilkinson produced posters advertising Ireland, largely for British railway companies. Such publications and promotions virtually disappeared with the development of private motor transport and the state organisation of TOURISM. **Bernard Share**

transport preservation. Northern Ireland has been markedly in advance of the Republic in this field. In 1954, with steam traction and tramways close to extinction, the nucleus of a collection was assembled at Queen's Quay station, Belfast, transferring to more suitable accommodation at Witham Street in 1961. Perhaps its most notable rescue was that of GSR LOCOMOTIVE no. 800, *Meadhbh*, built in 1939, the largest and most powerful steam locomotive built in Ireland. The collection grew to include road, tramway, and rail vehicles, many of them, such as the FINTONA HORSE TRAM, unique. In 1995 it was transferred to a purpose-built transport gallery at the ULSTER FOLK AND TRANSPORT MUSEUM in Cultra, near Holywood, Co. Down. One of its locomotive acquisitions, the former GNR no. 85, *Merlin*, is on extended loan to the Railway Preservation Society of Ireland, based at Whitehead, Co. Antrim, which since 1964 has restored and operated vintage locomotives and rolling stock on tours throughout the remaining railway system, with the co-operation of the operating companies. Other Northern preservation initiatives include the narrow-gauge Londonderry and LOUGH SWILLY Railway, Derry, and the Downpatrick Railway Project.

In the Republic, attempts by a small group of enthusiasts from 1942 onwards to establish a tram museum failed to attract support, and it was the 1970s before the Transport Museum Society of Ireland acquired a highly unsuitable site at Kilruddery, near Bray, Co. Wicklow. Many items were vandalised or otherwise destroyed. The National Transport Museum, still devoted largely to trams, is now at Howth Castle, Co. Dublin. Railway preservation has equally lagged behind that of other countries, but recently restoration projects have been begun involving the former WEST CLARE RAILWAY, Cavan and Leitrim Railway, and Tralee and Dingle Railway, among others.

Waterways preservation dates in effect from 1954, when the Inland Waterways Association of Ireland was formed to counter a threat to the CANAL system with the forthcoming termination of freight traffic. Since then derelict lines have been restored and access reopened to several sites on the Shannon system, culminating in the restoration of the BALLINAMORE AND BALLYCONNELL CANAL. With the growth of leisure boating, further restorations are envisaged, including that of the ULSTER CANAL. Private owners have undertaken the renovation of many former canal barges and other craft. **Bernard Share**

transportation, eighteenth and nineteenth centuries. The transportation of convicts from Ireland began as a political measure. During the Cromwellian period, rebel soldiers, 'TORIES', and some priests were sent to Barbados as indentured workers; the number transported between 1641 and 1660 may have been as high as 50,000. English statutes authorising the exile of 'vagabonds' were also applied by Cromwell's commissioners. In July 1669 there were about 8,000 Irish in Barbados and 4,000 in the other West Indian plantations. However, their numbers did not increase, the planters complaining of their idleness and their proclivity to assist the French, who were vying with the English for dominance in the area.

From the early eighteenth century, transportation to the American colonies was instituted as a means of dealing with lesser offenders. Following the English statute of 1703, Irish legislation authorised transportation as a reprieve for those sentenced to death for stealing less than two cows or ten sheep, or for felonies worth not less than £1, or for harbouring tories or rapparees. The sheriffs of each county arranged with merchants to ship the accused off after providing a bond. Later Irish statutes made transportation the mandatory punishment for certain offences and established a formal procedure for the listing and delivery of convicts and the levying of funds by local authorities.

Transportation was increasingly resorted to by the courts from the 1720s, and more than 13,000 Irish men and women had been sent to the American colonies by 1776. Restrictions imposed by several colonial legislatures were overturned by the Crown. When transatlantic transportation ceased, as a result of opposition, the Irish Parliament substituted port works; but the municipal authorities declined to provide the facilities. Prisoners sentenced to hard labour swelled the already overcrowded and insecure Newgate, KILMAINHAM, and other county jails; this led to the decision in 1784 to revive transatlantic transportation. Nine shipments of Irish convicts were duly despatched to North America and the West Indies.

Problems arose when the colonists rejected the new arrivals, which culminated in a political row when the Governor of Newfoundland shipped convicts back to Portsmouth in 1789. This, together with a fiasco in the Leeward Islands in 1790, persuaded the Home Office to make space on its transports to New South Wales. The Irish authorities had been requesting this since 1786, but the Home Office declined to provide assistance. The first transport, the *Queen*, sailed from Cork for Sydney on 14 April 1791 with 133 male and twenty-two female convicts, arriving on 26 September.

From 1791 to 1867 approximately 40,000 convicts were transported from Ireland to Australia and a further 8,000 or more Irish-born from England. Almost a quarter of all convicts sent to Australia were Irish. Early nineteenth-century nationalist writing on the Irish convicts represented them as heroes or martyrs. A one-in-ten statistical analysis of all convicts made in 1965 concluded that no neat division could be made between Irish and English; nevertheless it revealed that Irish women convicts were less likely than English and particularly Scottish women to have been previous offenders. Their average age was twenty-seven, older than most English women and Irish men, and two-thirds were single. Most women transported for animal-stealing during the 1830s and 40s were Irish first offenders from the countryside. Irish males were on average two years older than English convicts, and a higher proportion were married. There were relatively few juvenile offenders. One-fifth came from Dublin and Cork, of whom about half had previous convictions. Of the remainder, most came from the countryside and were first offenders. Petty theft accounted for most urban convictions, while most rural convictions were for animal-stealing and the theft of food, cooking utensils, or clothing. Reflecting the events of 1798 and the agrarian disorder of the 1830s and 40s, most of the convicts transported for illegal possession or theft of firearms—making pikeheads, swearing illegal oaths, posting threatening notices, etc.—were Irish. There was also a high proportion of violent crime: more than half the convicts sent to eastern Australia for assault were Irish, and most of the Irish convicted of murder or manslaughter came from rural areas.

Recent research has dealt with the educational levels and work skills of Irish convicts rather than their criminality. Of the 2,210 women transported between 1825 and 1840, 70 per cent of the Irish women were rural-born, 94 per cent of them sentenced to terms of seven years. They were less likely to have had previous convictions than their English counterparts, and were more literate and more skilled. Irish and English urban convicts came from similar socio-economic conditions, but the higher proportion of Irish rural offenders reflected the agrarian conditions of the late eighteenth and early nineteenth centuries.

Statistical studies obscure changing social and economic conditions. The shipments from 1791 to 1798 consisted largely of urban petty offenders from Dublin and Cork, but with some DEFENDERS; from 1798 to 1803 many were supporters of the UNITED IRISHMEN. Estimates of their number have ranged as high as 800, but 500 is a more likely figure. From 1803 to the early 1820s there was a return to the urban emphasis of the first phase. The surge in crime after 1815 led to increased use of the statutes. Deteriorating economic conditions and agrarian protest from the late 1820s to the 1840s resulted in the transportation of mostly rural offenders, including members of agrarian terrorist organisations. In the early 1830s some people committed crimes in order to be transported.

The last Irish convicts sent to Australia were the approximately 1,000 transported to Fremantle between 1853 and 1867. The first arrived in August 1853 on the *Phoebe Dunbar* and the *Robert Small*, some after years in Irish prisons for famine-related offences. The final arrivals, on the *Hougoumont* in January 1868, were sixty-two Fenians, among them JOHN BOYLE O'REILLY, convicted of mutiny and sentenced to be shot. In early 1869 local sympathisers got him aboard the American whaler *Gazelle* at Bunbury, and on 16 April 1876 the six remaining military Fenians escaped on the *Catalpa*, an American whaler despatched for the purpose. **Bob Reece**

transportation, sixteenth and seventeenth centuries. The concept of exporting the troublesome military retainers of Irish chieftains to ease the problems of the English government had its origin in the sixteenth century. From 1586 onwards, large numbers of native Irish were recruited to serve in Flanders. A movement that may be more accurately described as transportation occurred in the years between 1609 and 1614. By May 1614 the Lord Deputy, CHICHESTER, claimed he had sent 6,000 'disaffected Irishmen to the wars in Sweden.' While he insisted that only those who volunteered should be enlisted, it would appear that a wide range of malefactors were in fact shipped to Sweden. Undoubtedly many had little real choice. The primary motive was to clear the 'idle swordsmen' and KERN, who were likely to destabilise the country, particularly from the newly planted Ulster counties.

Transportation, as a palliative for the government, re-emerged in the early 1650s as CROMWELL sought to impose his control over the country. The primary destination on this occasion was the Caribbean, to which free indentured servants from Ireland had been migrating for decades. Between 1652 and 1657 probably between 5,000 and 10,000 Irish men, women and children were transported to Montserrat, Barbados, and Jamaica, among them military prisoners, able-bodied vagrants, and 'TORIES'. After several Catholic priests were sent to Barbados the island's colonial governor complained so vehemently that the Council of State, in May 1657, ordered an end to such transportation. **Patrick Fitzgerald**

Travellers, or the travelling people, an indigenous minority group numbering approximately 25,000 in the Republic and 1,500 in Northern Ireland, with substantial communities in Britain and North America. Their family structure, employment patterns, mobility, and language are distinctive and combine to ensure their survival among a largely hostile majority. On the margins of mainstream Irish society, Travellers enjoy a vibrant cultural life of their own, with the family at its core.

Irish folk belief insists that Traveller-mainstream relations have only recently deteriorated from a mutually beneficial peaceful co-existence, but all contemporary records indicate mainstream hostility. Artistic expression, from SYNGE's *The Tinker's Wedding* (1907) to films such as *Into the West* (1992) and *Snatch* (2000)—in which Travellers invariably symbolise forces opposing bourgeois values—tell us more about their authors than they do about Travellers themselves.

Post-independence official policy began with the *Report of the Commission on Itinerancy* (1963), which promoted 'absorption into the community.' Subsequent reports (1983 and 1995) advocate recognition and accommodation in place of assimilation; but anti-Traveller prejudice remains a pervasive, and largely unquestioned, fact of Irish life. In 1999 a Mayo county councillor, John Flannery, who suggested that Travellers should be electronically tagged, was acquitted of incitement to hatred; in 2000 the Clare county manager, William Moloney, attempting to implement accommodation plans, was subjected to vandalism and death threats from settled people.

State-employed specialists (such as social workers and health visitors), non-governmental community development bodies, and numerous all-Traveller pre-schools, primary classes, training centres, and development courses address Travellers' perceived needs. With the passing of the Race Relations Order (1997), Northern Ireland became the first jurisdiction to recognise Travellers' ethnicity and to offer them protection from DISCRIMINATION. The Republic followed with the Employment Equality Act (1998) and Equal Status Act (2000); in 2000 Britain amended the Race Relations Act to include Irish Travellers.

Irish Travellers insist that they are not GYPSIES but (like Gypsies) have no standard theory about 'where they came from.' Non-Travellers, by contrast, tend to treat historical origins and cultural legitimacy as synonymous and have engaged in a great deal of speculation—but no systematic research—into their origins. Perhaps the most widely held view is that Travellers descend from the rural poor dispossessed at the time of the GREAT FAMINE; yet there are tens of thousands of Irish Travellers in the United States whose forebears emigrated there, as Travellers, in the middle of the nineteenth century. This hypothesis is also contradicted by fundamental differences between Traveller and mainstream core values and practices, giving rise to amply documented hostility, and by the fact that many common Irish surnames do not occur among Travellers. Travellers consciously contrast themselves to the rural community: their umbrella term for non-Travellers (including urban ones) is 'country people'.

An alternative view of the origins of the travelling community suggests that little is known of the ancient Irish peoples whose remains, including Newgrange, predate the arrival of the Celts—themselves a loose confederation of peoples. The tenacity of Travellers' language, and the fact that so much of its etymology cannot be traced, is also cited.

Historically, Travellers have been largely invisible among the poor, and mobile, Irish. Dismissed as an occupational or social sub-group, they appear under a variety of ambiguous descriptions, usually as a problem to be solved, as in the Act for the erection of Houses of Correction and for the punishment of Rogues and Vagabonds, Sturdy Beggars and other lewd and idle persons (1634). The POOR LAW Enquiry Report (1836) clearly differentiates 'beggars and vagrants who habitually roam the countryside and with no fixed abode' from other mobile groups, such as drovers and seasonal agricultural labourers. More recent terms have included 'itinerants' and 'traders', expressing majority unease at Travellers' characteristic mobility while recognising its economic nature.

British sources are equally unclear. Nothing is known of the proportion of Travellers affected by the deportation of Irish vagrants from England in 1413, or under the Act for the more effectual Transportation of Felons and Vagabonds (1743). The identification problem is compounded by their being known as 'tinkers' (tinsmiths), a term also applied to Scots Travellers, which describes an occupation not exclusive to these groups.

Irish Traveller language is known to academics (but not to Travellers themselves) as Shelta. It is divided into two distinct but mutually intelligible dialects: Gammon (whose speakers cluster in the south-east) and Cant. Speakers of the two dialects differ in other ways also; bearing different surnames, with different kinship patterns and social control mechanisms, they rarely intermarry. Scholarly investigation of this language reached a peak in the nineteenth century; subsequent treatment continues to speculate on the etymology of Traveller-specific vocabulary (supposedly deliberately scrambled Irish) while ignoring characteristic grammar, syntax, and phonics, all of which combine to render Travellers' English uniquely distinctive. This form of English is Travellers' vernacular, but Cant or Gammon is effortlessly switched to as a 'protection language' when circumstances require; it is also used in the home, and all Travellers acquire it in infancy. By unobtrusively slipping words of their own language into an otherwise HIBERNO-ENGLISH sentence, speakers can convey messages without those overhearing even realising that they are doing so. The descendants of Irish Travellers who emigrated to the United States in the middle of the nineteenth century continue to speak it, and dialects on each side of the Atlantic remain mutually intelligible.

Cant: Needesh granny ah minceirs luba I toree.

American Cant: Ya needjaish grannee a lubba I thaaree.

Irish: Ní thuigeann tú focal a deirim.

English: You don't understand a word I say.

Virtually all Irish Travellers are Catholics; church rituals surrounding the transitions of life and death are intrinsic elements of Travellers' culture. The *Report of the Commission on Itinerancy* (1963) lists thirty-five surnames that account for 70 per cent of the families in their census; ten surnames alone account for 40 per cent. McDonagh and Ward, the two most common surnames among Cant-speakers, and O'Connor (or Connors) and O'Brien (or Brien), the two most common Gammon ones, account for 13 per cent and 11 per cent, respectively, of the total Traveller population. While Travellers' surnames overlap with those of the general population, their numerical and geographical distribution do not. Cash, Cawley, Lawrence, Maughan, and Mongan are distinctively Traveller surnames, while many common mainstream surnames are rare or non-existent among Travellers.

The Traveller family, synonymous with identity and with every aspect and stage of life, is a social, economic, and educational unit linked with other such units through marriage. The individual, and the nuclear family, are components of much larger wholes, within which they achieve meaning and security. Every family member, including the disabled, is cherished, while arranged marriages ensure that even the shy and plain-looking find partners and form families of their own. The aged are revered, and the youngest members are treated with warmth by a wide range of aunts, uncles, and cousins. Irish Travellers appear to have the world's highest incidence of both cousin and sibling set marriage (i.e. two brothers marrying two sisters), a pattern that goes back generations and has produced a social structure of extraordinary complexity and resilience. Travellers' weddings are lavish affairs, bringing together hundreds of relatives to socialise, celebrate, and 'draw down' (arrange) new weddings.

The fact that 'Travellers' is what the group calls itself indicates the importance attached to mobility, which is both purposeful and a cultural value in itself. More than half the Traveller population continues to live in mobile dwellings; but whatever the type of accommodation, social ties remain based on kinship, not geographical proximity. Weddings, funerals, PATTERNS, and certain annual FAIRS bring people together from all over Ireland, and from Britain, while many travel hundreds of miles a week in connection with work or family visits. Travellers' geographical mobility should be understood as one aspect of a broad pattern of flexibility: the freedom to respond to opportunities, and to family obligations, when they arise.

Travellers cultivate occupational flexibility and self-employment, both of which are linked with mobility, supplying goods and services to the majority population. In the nineteenth century tinsmithing was a characteristic skill (whence the synonymous use of 'tinker' with 'Traveller'), but it was never the only one: horse-dealing and recycling were equally important then and, in modernised forms, remain so. Scrap collection, market trading, the resale of second-hand goods, and tarmacking are now the main occupations; Travellers also offer services such as tool-sharpening, spray-painting farm outbuildings, tree surgery, and lawnmowing. They work with members of their families as equal partners, and all family members are economically active, including children, who, by minding younger siblings, free the adults. Non-Travellers commonly perceive Travellers as inherently dishonest, even as a criminal subculture, a perception fuelled by sensational media treatment. The great majority of Travellers' encounters with the law are in fact for minor offences, such as begging and trespass.

Irish Travellers were once associated with the bow-top waggon, a light horse-drawn cart with a semicircular covering, often ornately carved and beautifully painted, and with the canvas shelter tent of similar shape; but with motorisation nomadic Travellers shifted to caravans. This occurred at about the same time as the general rural-to-urban transition of the Irish population. Travellers now cluster in towns, often in appalling conditions, giving rise to health problems and tension with non-Traveller neighbours. Since the 1960s local authorities have actively penalised the nomadic life-style, not least through the systematic blocking of traditional campsites and a refusal to implement state guidelines on accommodation. Some provision has been made: 1,152 families in the Republic are on legal sites with some basic facilities, 380 in purpose-built all-Traveller housing schemes, and another 2,110 in standard local authority housing, while 1,093 are illegally camped, with no facilities. No figures are available for those who privately build or buy their own houses or who purchase land on which to camp. The greatest number of Travellers live in and around Dublin, but there are places with a far higher ratio of Travellers to non-Travellers, notably Rathkeale, Co. Limerick (about half Traveller), and Tuam, Co. Galway (about a third).

Despite the transition to motorised transport, the horse retains a central role in Travellers' life and symbolism. Horse fairs, particularly that of BALLINASLOE in October, are the social highlights of the year. Travellers are associated with a distinct breed of multi-coloured pony, known internationally as the 'Irish tinker'.

Travellers' preferred way of dealing with conflict is to move away from it—yet another function of geographical mobility. Where confrontation between Travellers is inevitable it ideally takes the form of a 'fair fight', a strictly refereed bare-fisted BOXING match between selected representatives of each side, witnessed (and avidly wagered on) by other Travellers. Boxing is a popular sport; Francis Barrett, a Galway Traveller, represented Ireland at the 1996 OLYMPIC GAMES and carried the Irish flag at the opening ceremony. In recent years imposed settlement and increased competition for scarce resources have led to an explosive rise in intra-Traveller violence, much emphasised by the media, involving weapons and pitched battles. Where conflict occurs with non-Travellers, Travellers continue to withdraw, a fact that has contributed to their general non-involvement in political action on their own behalf. Notable exceptions have been Nan Joyce, who ran for Dáil Éireann; Ellen Mongan and Martin Ward, elected town commissioners; and a number of individuals who have successfully challenged pub licence renewals on the grounds of discrimination. **Sinéad ní Shúinéar**

Travellers and prejudice. Until very recently, Government policy was concerned with assimilation rather than fostering pluralism. Research has found a high level of prejudice and DISCRIMINATION against Travellers: 93 per cent would not accept a Traveller into their family; 73 per cent would not accept a Traveller as a friend; 44 per cent would not accept them as a member of their community; and 40 per cent would be annoyed at the possibility of an official halting site in their neighbourhood. Local authorities have a statutory obligation to meet the accommodation needs of Travellers, but only 4 per cent of those units of Traveller-specific accommodation that were to be made available by 2000 have been provided; in 1998, 24 per cent of Travellers were living in unserviced sites or by the side of the road. Traveller life expectancy is twelve years below the national mean, with slightly over 1 per cent being aged sixty-five or older (compared with over 11 per cent of the total POPULATION). **Pat O'Connor**

Travellers. *Cover of* Voice of the Traveller, *with the boxer Francis Barrett and his mother, Noreen. Barrett competed in the 1996 Atlanta Olympic Games, the first Traveller to represent Ireland. [Courtesy of the* Voice of the Traveller *and Noreen Barrett]*

Travellers' music. Irish Travellers carry a vibrant traditional culture, which remains comparatively unknown outside the travelling community. Lack of access to electronic media ensured that the oral transmission of ancient songs and music survived among them later than among settled people. The Co. Wexford UILLEANN-PIPER John Cash (1832–1909) was famous in his day, while the music of the brothers JOHNNY DORAN (1908–1950) and Felix Doran (1915–1972) from Co. Wicklow remains vastly influential. Music-collecting among Travellers has uncovered a rich vein of ancient song. The most celebrated Traveller singer was Margaret Barry of Co. Cork, who performed in Ireland, Britain, and North America. The songs of JOHN REILLY were brought to popular attention by artists such as CHRISTY MOORE and the Waterboys, while the FUREY BROTHERS and the piper PADDY KEENAN are internationally known Traveller musicians. Jim Carroll and Pat Mackenzie recorded Traveller singers in London for more than fifteen years; copies of some three hundred of these tapes are in the IRISH TRADITIONAL MUSIC ARCHIVE, Dublin. Extensive recordings of Traveller singers may also be found in the Department of Irish Folklore, UCD, which houses tales recorded from such notable Traveller-storytellers as Ooney Power. Pavee Point, the Travellers' Culture and Heritage Centre in Dublin, is archiving and publishing materials related to Traveller traditions. **Tom Munnelly**

Travellers' music. *James Collins playing the accordion at the Travellers' Arts Festival at Pavee Point, North Great Charles Street, Dublin. [Derek Speirs/Report]*

Travellers outside Ireland. There is a visibility paradox in relation to members of the Irish Traveller community abroad. Local populations, unaware of Traveller markers such as accent and surname, simply class them together with other Irish, and many, perhaps most, Irish Travellers outside Ireland are not readily identifiable as such by those around them. On the other hand, Travellers who assert their identity—especially those who form large communities, whether mobile or permanent—are doubly exotic, both as Irish and as 'GYPSIES', and attract a great deal of attention. Scholarly interest in Irish Travellers began abroad, in the 1880s, when word lists were collected from Travellers in Argyllshire, Southampton, London, and Liverpool, as well as Poughkeepsie and Philadelphia. Figures for the Traveller population—15,000 for Britain, 30,000 for the United States—are speculative: only those Travellers who are conspicuous are identified as such, and mobile families may be counted several times, or not at all. No information is available on their presence anywhere outside Britain and the United States, apart from anecdotal references to uncles in Australia and—increasingly—working trips within the EUROPEAN UNION.

Irish Travellers in Britain are essentially a continuum with Traveller communities in Ireland itself: individuals and families frequently travel between the two countries in connection with set events (such as FAIRS and PATTERNS) and family affairs. Like other Irish emigrants, some gradually come to see Britain as their base, but Ireland remains the point of reference; even British-born dead are returned to family cemeteries. Travellers in Britain are in competition with local Gypsies for work and for camping space. This, in a social system wary both of the Irish and of mobile populations, has led to their serving as the 'ultimate whipping boys'. They tend to live separately from English Travellers—incognito in rented accommodation, or on all-Irish sites—and to seek safety in numbers when travelling.

The majority of today's Irish-American Travellers trace their ancestry to named individuals who emigrated in the middle of the nineteenth century. Once there, communication with Ireland virtually ceased. The many cultural traits they share with Travellers in Ireland (such as the group name itself, language, and kinship patterns) must therefore have been firmly established before the split. There are several distinct, long-established Irish-American Traveller communities, each named after an area with which they were once associated but to which they are not confined. The world's largest concentration of Irish Travellers is Murphy Village, South Carolina, with a population of more than 2,000. Like other Traveller enclaves on both sides of the Atlantic, this serves as a base for mobile self-employment.

Irish-American Travellers differ in some important respects from Irish Travellers in Ireland and Britain, notably in distances travelled and visible economic success and in bearing different surnames. Their Catholicism, matched weddings at an early age, and emphasis on in-family education as opposed to schooling—all traits shared with Travellers at home—set them apart from, and sometimes at odds with, their American neighbours. **Sinéad ní Shúinéar**

travel writers on Ireland (nineteenth and twentieth centuries). The first half of the nineteenth century is dominated by the travel 'sketch', with its emphasis on anecdote and comic detail, the most notable example being W. M. THACKERAY's *The Irish Sketchbook* (1843). The Great Famine and political unrest led to a relative decline in travel writing on Ireland in the second half of the nineteenth century, but the twentieth century was to witness a significant revival, travellers often dealing with Ireland as a pre-modern refuge in industrialised Europe. The exponential growth in TOURISM, the political conflict in Northern Ireland, and the new romanticism of the 1960s generation led to sustained interest in Ireland as a destination for travel writers from many countries and languages, including Ireland itself. John Gibbons, H. V. Morton, HEINRICH BÖLL, KATE O'BRIEN, PETER SOMERVILLE-LARGE, DERVLA MURPHY, and Nicolas Bouvier are among the twentieth-century writers to produce accounts of Irish journeys. **Michael Cronin**

travel writers on transport. From the stage-coach era onwards, foreign visitors have recorded their impressions of Ireland's TRANSPORT amenities. In the 1770s the English visitor ARTHUR YOUNG observed that there were 183 four-wheeled and 115 two-wheeled carriages in Limerick, compared with a total of four of all descriptions forty years previously. In 1796 the Frenchman LA TOCNAYE found the Dublin coach over-booked, an experience repeated by the novelist W. M. THACKERAY in 1842 when he attempted to travel from Killarney to Tralee. In 1836 the Scot Robert Graham had taken the mail car from Galway to Oughterard. 'It is a one horse concern,' he recorded in his diary, 'and carries four passengers. We changed horses at a small inn having done the six miles in one hour ...'

The earliest account of CANAL travel was by the visiting founder of Methodism, JOHN WESLEY, who noted in his diary for 22 June 1785: 'It is a most elegant way of travelling, little inferior to that of the Tracksjuyts in Holland.' La Tocnaye also found that 'the Canal boats are very comfortable, being indeed very like those of Holland, but the cost here is nearly double.' Less impressed was the novelist Anthony Trollope, who in his novel *The Kellys and the O'Kellys* (1848) compared the Ballinsasloe service very unfavourably with travel by coach. The principal operator in that field, CHARLES BIANCONI, was interviewed by Robert Graham in 1835 and by a German traveller, Johann Kohl, in the 1840s. Graham also reported on his experiences of travel on the River Shannon and, very shortly after its opening, on Ireland's first railway, the DUBLIN AND KINGSTOWN RAILWAY. He had the advantage of having patronised the Liverpool to Manchester railway, England's pioneer line, but even so was not over-impressed with the new transport mode. 'It is a great saving of time,' he concluded, 'but for luxury in the long run I should consider it as falling far short of ordinary travelling with horses.' **Bernard Share**

Treaty ports. The ANGLO-IRISH TREATY (1921) provided that 'harbour and other facilities' at specified places be provided during peacetime to the British government by the Irish Free State, with the possibility of additional facilities being employed in time of war or strained international relations. The ports of Bearhaven, Co. Cork, Queenstown, Co. Cork, and LOUGH SWILLY, Co. Donegal were so designated, with guarantees of coastal defence facilities in their environs. In addition, minimum stocks of fuel oil were to be maintained at Haulbowline, Co. Cork, and Rathmullan, Co. Donegal. These provisions were the subject of detailed scrutiny during the Treaty debates, with those opposed to the Treaty arguing that they represented an unwarranted restriction on the state's freedom of action and left it vulnerable to attack in time of war.

The facilities were maintained at a low state of readiness during the 1920s and 30s, but the British government consistently objected to their transfer. In 1938, however, as a result of altered political and military circumstances, their negotiated return was a central feature of the ANGLO-IRISH AGREEMENT. In any event, the fall of France in 1940 undermined the strategic value of the ports, though it served to enhance the possession by the British navy of facilities at Belfast and Derry. **Gabriel Doherty**

Trench, William Steuart (1808–1872), land agent and writer. Born near Portarlington, Co. Laois, son of a Church of Ireland dean; educated at TCD. He became an agent for various large estates in Cos. Monaghan, Kerry, and Offaly. He published a novel, *Ierne* (1871), but is remembered today for writing *Realities of Irish Life* (1868), an absorbing autobiography that gives an agent's-eye view of the causes and effects of the GREAT FAMINE, mass emigration, and rural agitation; it also includes anthropological reflections on the Protestant religious revival of 1859. **Richard Haslam**

Treoir, journal of COMHALTAS CEOLTÓIRÍ ÉIREANN, edited from its inception in 1968 by LABHRÁS Ó MURCHÚ. Originally published every two months, it has been quarterly since 1978. Though concentrating on branch activities, fleadhanna ceoil, and articles of musical and historical interest, it also includes obituaries of leading musical figures in local communities and consistently maintains a cultural nationalist tone. A feature of the magazine is the inclusion of transcriptions of songs and tunes in the traditional idioms for the purpose of transmission. Regular contributors have included BRYAN MACMAHON, PADDY TUNNEY, and SÉAMAS MAC MATHÚNA. The journal is a valuable historical and social document in the world of traditional music. **Anthony McCann**

Tressell, Robert, pseudonym of Robert Noonan (1870–1911), socialist and novelist. Born in Dublin. His posthumously published novel *The Ragged Trousered Philanthropists* (1914) is an immensely popular account of working-class life. **Terence Brown**

Trevelyan, Sir Charles (1807–1886), administrator. As Assistant Secretary to the Treasury, 1840–59, he had responsibility for relief during the GREAT FAMINE. Motivated by evangelical dogmatism and liberal economic theory, he sought to minimise state activity and compel self-reliance, despite great loss of life. He defended his policy in *The Irish Crisis* (1848). **Peter Gray**

Trevor, William, pen-name of William Trevor Cox (1928–), novelist and short-story writer. Born in Mitchelstown, Co. Cork; educated at TCD. He worked as a teacher and sculptor before becoming a writer. His first novel, *A Standard of Behaviour*, appeared in 1958. He writes with urbanity and assurance, spiced with the irony of the contrast between eccentrics (often unpleasant) and apparently normal society; *The Old Boys* (1964), which won the Hawthornden Prize, *The Love Department* (1966), and *Mrs Eckdorf in O'Neill's Hotel* (1968) are good examples of this. *The Children of Dynmouth* (1976), which won a Whitbread Prize, gives us Timothy Gedge, and *Other People's Worlds* (1980) gives us Francis Tyte, both memorable characters.

Trevor's treatment of political change and violence in Ireland is impressive, notably in *The Silence in the Garden* (1988). He uses the setting of the BIG HOUSE effectively, with *Fools of Fortune* (1983) winning him a second Whitbread Prize. He is a master of the short story, of which 'The Ballroom of Romance' (televised successfully) and 'Beyond the Pale' are excellent examples (see p. 903). His collection *Angels at the Ritz* won the Royal Society of Literature Prize in 1978. His *Collected Stories* appeared in 1992; like his novels, they set his cleverly complex plots in both England and Ireland. His many plays for television, radio, and the stage include *The Elephant's Foot*, *The Old Boys*, and *Scenes from an Album*. In *A Writer's Ireland* (1984) he explores the influence of Ireland's landscape on its literature with skill and sensitivity, reminding us of Trevor's evocative recapturing of memories of his youth in Co. Cork. Later publications include his autobiography, *Excursions in the Real World* and *Collected Studies* (1993), *Felicia's Journey* (1994), *The Hill Batchelors* (2000), and *The Story of Lucy Gault* (2002). **A. Norman Jeffares**

Trevor. *The novelist and short-story writer William Trevor at his home in Devon. Trevor writes with the same assured authority of English as of Irish experience. [John Minihan]*

triads. The arranging of ideas in groups of three is common in CELTIC literature. The main Irish collection, Trecheng Breth Féne, 'a triad of judgments of the Irish', was compiled in the ninth century. It contains 214 triads (with some tetrads, duads, and single items) on geographical, social, religious, mythological, and legal topics. **Fergus Kelly**

Triail, An (1964), a play by MÁIRÉAD NÍ GHRÁDA. It deals with the crisis of an unmarried mother, her social ostracisation and consequent SUICIDE. It was notable at the time for its social criticism and its expressionistic style. First produced in Damer Hall, Dublin, 1964, it was produced in English as *The Trial* in the Eblana Theatre, Dublin, 1965. **Eoghan Ó hAnluain**

trial or motif pieces, designs carved or incised on pieces of bone, stone, wood, or leather, believed to have been casual sketches, apprentices' exercises, or finished patterns intended to be reproduced in metal by casting or impressing. They are peculiar to Ireland and to VIKING Dublin in particular, though a few are known from Viking York and London. **Raghnall Ó Floinn**

tribunals. The Tribunals of Inquiry (Evidence) Act (1921), as amended by the Tribunals of Inquiry (Evidence) (Amendment) Acts (1979 and 1997), provides for the establishment of a tribunal of inquiry, pursuant to a resolution passed by both houses of the Oireachtas, to investigate a matter of urgent public interest. This legislation was the subject of an unsuccessful constitutional challenge in the Supreme Court, where the parties concerned claimed that the chairperson's status as a judge was contrary to the separation of powers.

Tribunals of inquiry in Northern Ireland, set up under the same principal act, are created by a resolution of both houses of Parliament and entrust to a judge or other appointed person the task of inquiring into some recent scandal or disaster in the public interest, one example being the Widgery Tribunal, appointed in 1972 to investigate the killing of unarmed demonstrators in Derry on 'BLOODY SUNDAY'. Under the Tribunals and Inquiries Act (1992) the Lord Chancellor can make procedural rules for inquiries created by individual statutes for a specific purpose. The chairperson of such a tribunal, while often in practice drawn from the judicial bench, is not in this context fulfilling a judicial role. [see SAVILLE INQUIRY.] **Neville Cox**

Tribunals, Beef and Moriarty. The received wisdom in Ireland is that the misuse of office and a marked want of probity have increased since the 1970s. These opinions have been largely formed by a spate of widely publicised tribunals of inquiry into political misdeeds. In 1994 the Tribunal of Inquiry into the Beef Industry was established to investigate allegations (made first in a British television programme) of irregularities in the administration of state export credit guarantees on consignments of beef to Iraq. In its conclusions the tribunal drew attention to alarmingly close relations between certain Government officials and agricultural interests but made no suggestion of personal gain by any politician involved. This was not so in 1997, when the McCracken Tribunal (named after the senior judge in charge), set up to examine payments to politicians by BEN DUNNE, former head of Dunnes Stores, the largest Irish-owned retail chain, revealed a 'golden circle' of senior politicians who had all benefited from Dunne's largesse. The main target of the judge's findings was CHARLES HAUGHEY, leader of FIANNA FÁIL for thirteen years, nearly nine of these as TAOISEACH, who had been attracting attention by the manner in which he financed an estate outside Dublin, a number of racehorses, a yacht, and an island, all on a DÁIL deputy's salary. Other politicians were also exposed; but the chief consequence was the establishment of a further tribunal of inquiry (this time under Judge Moriarty) with a much broader remit, to probe into Haughey's business dealings over a period of three decades, rather than the four or so years scrutinised by Judge McCracken. Despite these revelations, most political commentators conclude that the series of tribunals during the 1990s signify an increased awareness of political corruption rather than an increased incidence of it. **Maura Adshead**

Tricolour, the, popular name of the national flag of the Republic of Ireland. Tricolour flags, in varying patterns, first appeared c. 1830 and more widely at gatherings of the Irish Confederation in the early months of 1848; they subsequently became associated with physical-force NATIONALISM and as a result were less popular than the traditional national flag of green with a yellow harp. Under the influence of the IRB the insurgents of 1916 gave precedence to the Tricolour, and it was widely used during the War of Independence. It became the *de facto* flag of the Irish Free State in 1922 and is declared to be the national flag in the Constitution of Ireland (1937). **Gary Owens**

Tridentine movement, a conservative movement within the Catholic Church based on the teachings of the Council of Trent (1545–63) and named after Trento (Latin *Tridentum*) in northern Italy, site of the Council. One of the Council's aims was to unify liturgical practice in the Western church; this was achieved in 1570 by Pope Pius V when he issued the Roman Missal and ordered that only this rite be used. The modern Tridentine movement is dedicated to ensuring that this form of the Mass is maintained; it is believed that the use of Latin helps preserve a correct theological understanding of the Mass. Adherents regard the reforms of the SECOND VATICAN COUNCIL as revisionist, and the movement is essentially a reaction against such reforms. Pope John Paul II, while fully endorsing the Second Vatican Council's liturgical changes, also believed that there should be a place in the church for those who wished to use the pre-conciliar rites, provided they acknowledged the Missal of Pope Paul VI as the church's official liturgy. In October 1984 permission was granted for a more widespread use of the Tridentine rite. It is difficult to estimate the membership in Ireland. The main place of worship is St Audoën's (High Street, Dublin), where approximately 400 people attend Mass every week. **Suzanne Mulligan.**

Trilogy, the, by SAMUEL BECKETT. Written in French during a period of intense productivity between May 1947 and January 1950, the trilogy of novels *Molloy*, *Malone Meurt* and *L'Innommable* is considered to be among Beckett's finest work. *Molloy* received critical acclaim from such critics as Georges Bataille and Maurice Nadeau when it was published by Éditions de Minuit in 1951. It was quickly followed by *Malone Meurt* in the same year and *L'Innommable* in 1953. An English translation of *Molloy*, by Beckett and Patrick Bowles, was published by Olympia Press, Paris, and Grove Press, New York, in 1955. Finding it easier to translate alone than to revise another's work, Beckett translated *Malone Dies* and *The Unnamable* himself, producing versions that are also revisions of the original text. *Malone Dies* was published by Grove Press, New York, in 1956 and by John Calder, London, in 1958. *The Unnamable* was published by Grove in 1958, and in 1959 John Calder published the three novels together as a trilogy.

Molloy is a first-person narrative written in two parts, the first in Molloy's voice, the second in that of Jacques Moran. It opens with Molloy's pronouncement, 'I am in my mother's room. It's I who live there now,' and progresses to describing a circular narrative regarding the stiff-legged Molloy's unsuccessful journey to see his mother. The second part of the novel opens with Jacques Moran obeying the instructions of the mysterious Youdi by embarking with his son on a journey to 'see about Molloy.' *Malone Dies* continues Beckett's preoccupation with mutating identities through the character of Malone, who may be a reincarnation of Molloy. The ancient Malone writes a misanthropic narrative about a boy, Sapo, who is also Macmann. Both novels explore the difficulty of narrative progression and the impossibility of self-knowledge through a text that is acutely conscious of its own fictionality. Beckett's narrative, which begins to fragment at the end of *Malone Dies*, is further destabilised in *The Unnamable*. Spoken in the first person, the novel raises questions about the subjectivity of the speaking voice and the paradoxical obligation of speaking in order to be silent. The attenuated prose of *The Unnamable* demonstrates Beckett's increasingly austere style in the later prose and drama. Remarkable for its formal innovation and philosophical inquiry, the trilogy remains one of the most important prose works of the twentieth century. **Derval Tubridy**

Trimble, David (1944–), lawyer and politician. A lecturer in Queen's University who was a VANGUARD Convention member, 1975–6, he joined the ULSTER UNIONIST PARTY and was elected to the House of Commons for Upper Bann in 1990. He was a prominent critic of the Hume-Adams talks and of the British government's willingness to 'publicly negotiate with terrorists.' His triumphalist behaviour in July 1995, when he was televised walking hand in hand with IAN PAISLEY at the conclusion of an ORANGE march down the Garvaghy Road in Portadown, won warm approval from many rank-and-file Unionists. In August 1995

Trimble, David. *David Trimble makes his way to the Europa Hotel, Belfast, to put the Belfast Agreement to the Ulster Unionist Council, 18 April 1998. The agreement was accepted by a 2:1 majority. [Photocall Ireland]*

he was elected leader of the Unionist Party in the third ballot after the resignation of JIM MOLYNEUX. Thereafter he demonstrated that he was prepared to take risks for UNIONISM that his predecessor was not. He was the first Unionist leader to visit Government Buildings, Dublin; he addressed a fringe meeting of the British Labour Party in 1996; he engaged in talks with Edward Kennedy in the United States; and he entered into the multi-party talks that resulted in the BELFAST AGREEMENT (1998). In July 1998 he was elected First Minister by the NORTHERN IRELAND ASSEMBLY, and in December, with JOHN HUME, he received the NOBEL PEACE PRIZE. Frustration over delays in decommissioning arms caused Trimble to pull his party out of the Assembly in July 1999, and the restoration of devolution had to wait until 1 December. The same issue led to a return to DIRECT RULE between February and May 2000 and again in 2002. **Jonathan Bardon**

Trimble, Joan. *The composer, pianist, and newspaper-owner Joan Trimble in her study. In 1967 she took over the* Impartial Reporter *(Enniskillen), one of Ireland's oldest independent newspapers, managed since its launch in 1825 by successive generations of the Trimble family. [Impartial Reporter]*

Trimble, Joan (1915–2001), composer. Born in Enniskillen, Co. Fermanagh; trained at the RIAM and TCD and studied piano with Arthur Benjamin and composition with Ralph Vaughan Williams at the Royal College of Music. An honorary fellow of the RIAM, she also received an honorary degree from Queen's University, Belfast. Professor of piano at the Royal College of Music, London, 1959–77, she enjoyed a successful career as part of a piano duo with her sister, Valerie, for whom Arthur Benjamin wrote 'Jamaican Rumba'. She rose to prominence as a composer in 1938 with the publication of *Buttermilk Point, Humours of Carrick* and *The Bard of Lisgoole* for two pianos, and the song 'Green Rain'. Other compositions include *Phantasy Trio* (winner of the Cobbett Prize, 1940) and *Blind Raftery*, an opera commissioned by the BBC. **Emma Costello**

Trim Castle, Co. Meath, the largest and earliest ANGLO-NORMAN castle in Ireland. The first fortification was a *ringwork* (earth-and-timber castle) built by HUGH DE LACY in 1172. It was burnt down in 1175, and shortly afterwards the first stone castle was built, which included the bawn walls and west gateway. The keep was constructed in at least three phases, from c. 1177 to 1204. Excavations in the mid-1990s revealed elaborate stone inner defences with a drawbridge and a mantlet wall dating from the middle of the thirteenth century at the entranceway to the keep; the remains of a great aisled hall were also uncovered in the north-east section of the outer ward. **David Sweetman**

Trinity College, Dublin, sole college of the University of Dublin, founded by ELIZABETH I in 1592 on lands originally belonging to the Augustinian Priory of All Hallows (suppressed in 1538) and the oldest seat of learning in Ireland. It was established as

> the College of the Holy and Undivided Trinity near Dublin whereby knowledge and civility might be increased by the instruction of our people there, whereof many have heretofore used to travail into ffrance Italy and Spaine to gett learning in such foreign universities, whereby they have been infected with poperie and other ill qualities, and soe become evil subjects.

No building survives from the original foundation: in fact the earliest buildings, the residential Rubrics, date from no earlier than 1701. THOMAS BURGH's Old Library was begun in 1712; its Long Room, enhanced by DEANE AND WOODWARD's addition of a timber barrel vault (1860s), is the finest secular interior in Ireland (see p. 39).

The eighteenth century was the great age of Trinity, during which it acquired its present form as an exemplary complex of classical public architecture and during which it had a remarkable body of celebrated scholars among its staff and students (see p. 437). RICHARD CASTLE's Doric temple Printing House (1734) and Dining Hall (1740s) were followed in Front Square by the Theatre and Chapel by Sir WILLIAM CHAMBERS (1780s). The great west façade to College Green is by Theodore Jacobson (1752) (see p. 437). The Provost's House by John Smyth (1759) is a Palladian town house with opulently decorated interiors. The nineteenth century saw the addition of another major building with Deane and Woodward's Venetian Gothic Museum Building (1852). Twentieth-century additions include the Berkeley Library (1970) and Arts Building (1980), both by AHRENDS, BURTON AND KORALEK.

Founded as a Protestant college, it admitted Catholics and Dissenters until the early seventeenth century, when restrictions were placed in 1637 against attendance by Catholics. These were not lifted until the CATHOLIC RELIEF ACT (1793), 150 years later. The Catholic hierarchy opposed attendance at Trinity on account of its Anglican orientation. This position lasted well into the twentieth century, with 'the ban' on attendance by Catholic students not lifted until 1970. In 1904 Trinity was the first of the historic universities in Britain and Ireland to admit women. Famous graduates include GEORGE BERKELEY, JONATHAN SWIFT, and OLIVER GOLDSMITH, while illustrious names continue for succeeding centuries in the humanities, medicine, mathematics, and the sciences, to include the NOBEL PRIZE winners ERNEST WALTON for physics (1951) and SAMUEL BECKETT for literature (1969). **Brian Lalor**

Trinity College harp ('Brian Bórú harp'), the oldest surviving Irish harp and the model used for the state emblem, which appears on the COINAGE and on Government documents. Traditionally associated with BRIAN BÓRÚ (died 1014), it dates in fact from the late fourteenth century. Made from high-density wood and strung with brass wire, it is decorated with incised geometrical patterns and carvings of animals and was originally set with precious stones. Its design is typical of the long line of Irish harps produced in various sizes over a period of 800 years, until the middle of the nineteenth century. This harp had a long and colourful history; as late as 1745 it was played in the streets of Limerick by the celebrated harper ARTHUR O'NEILL. **Gráinne Yeats**

Trinity College Harp. *Dating from the late fourteenth century, the Trinity College Harp is the oldest surviving Irish harp, erroneously associated in the past with Brian Bórú (died 1014). It is made from willow and has twenty-nine strings. [The Board of Trinity College, Dublin]*

trí rainn agus amhrán, a verse form consisting of three syllabic stanzas followed by a fourth in *amhrán* (stressed) metre; the form may derive partly from the English (fourteen-line) sonnet and partly from the older Irish practice of adding an *amhrán* to a syllabic poem (of any length). Some 102 examples survive, dating from c. 1675 to 1860. Perhaps the form arose independently in different places: of the eight examples from before 1700, seven come from Munster; thereafter groups originate in east Connacht and in Dublin, but the great majority belong to the wide cultural unit of south Ulster and north Leinster. **Colm Ó Baoill**

Triumphs of Cellach: see CAITHRÉIM CHELLAIG.

Triumphs of Cellachán Chaisíl: see CAITHRÉIM CHELLACHÁIN CHAISIL

Triumphs of Turlough: see CAITHRÉIM THOIRDHEALBHAIGH.

Trócaire, the official overseas development agency of the Irish Catholic bishops. Established in 1973, it saw itself as having a mandate to tackle the causes as well as the effects of underdevelopment in the world's poorer countries. It allocates 70 per cent of its resources to development projects in developing countries, 20 per cent to education and lobbying in Ireland, and 10 per cent to responding to emergencies. In its project spending it is unique among Irish development agencies in seeking to ensure a balance between the three regions of Asia, Africa, and Latin America. Unlike other Irish development agencies, which support volunteers working in developing countries, Trócaire allocates its development funds entirely to local organisations and emphasises the need for local contributions to promote the continuity of projects. It has field offices in Honduras, Kenya, Angola, Somalia, Rwanda, and Mozambique. Among the projects it supports are leadership training, health and welfare schemes, the promotion of human rights and combating of racism, community development and support for small industries, and the advancement of women. In the first twenty-five years of its existence Trócaire spent some £120 million on 6,000 projects in more than sixty countries. Its extensive programme of development education and publication has had a significant impact in raising awareness in Ireland about development issues, both through the educational system and among the wider public, and it has campaigned on such issues as international debt, the arms race, and human rights violations. Public donations constituted more than 70 per cent of Trócaire's income in 1998/99, with half coming from its annual Lenten campaign. **Peadar Kirby**

Trollope, Anthony (1812–1882), writer. Born in London; educated at Harrow and Winchester Schools. He worked as a clerk in the General Post Office, London, from 1834. He found employment in 1841 as a Post Office official in Ireland, where he wrote and set his first novel, *The Macdermots of Ballycloran* (1847), met his future wife, and, according to his *Autobiography* (1883), began at last to live a happy life. Further Irish-placed novels include *The Kellys and the O'Kellys* (1848), *Castle Richmond* (1860)—published a year after he left Ireland—and the unfinished *The Landleaguers* (1883);

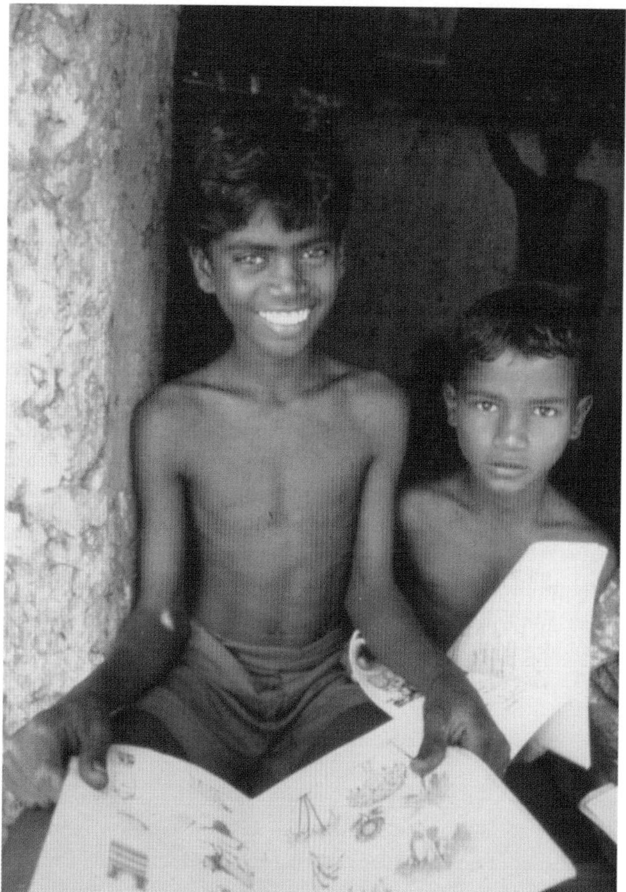

Trócaire. *Kuppamal (left), a freed bonded labourer from Tamil Nadu in India, at school. In 2001, Trócaire highlighted the issue of bonded labour as part of their campaign against slavery. [Trócaire]*

the last two display his growing political conservatism about Irish affairs. Ireland and Irish characters also feature in a considerable number of his other novels and in some of the shorter fiction. **Richard Haslam**

Trotter, John Bernard (1775–1818), political activist and walker. Born in Newry, Co. Down; graduated in law from the University of Dublin in 1795, after which he engaged in writing and politics. Family connections and his many anti-Union pamphlets brought him to the attention of Charles James Fox, who in 1806 employed him as private secretary. A founder-member of the Dublin Harp Society, he aspired to the culture and traditions of the English while seeking a measure of parliamentary independence for Ireland. He led a chequered life, sometimes apparently well off and at other times incarcerated in a debtor's prison, often profuse in his hospitality while at the same time being hounded by creditors. He was a prolific writer and a walking traveller. One year after his somewhat mysterious death in destitution in Cork his best-known work, *Walks through Ireland in 1812, 1814 and 1817 in a Series of Letters*, was published. **Michael Fewer**

'Troubles', the (1916–1923). Historians have found considerable problems in nomenclature for the period covering the final stages of British administration in Ireland. The years 1916–23 encompass a series of dramatic events: the 1916 RISING and the EXECUTIONS and internment following it, the failure to achieve any Irish consensus on a HOME RULE settlement, the abrupt collapse of the IRISH PARTY, the rise of the SINN FÉIN coalition and the reorganisation of the IRISH VOLUNTEERS, and the establishment of DÁIL ÉIREANN and the Dáil government in 1919 and 1920, with the whole climaxing in the guerrilla warfare of January 1919 to July 1921, the signing of the ANGLO-IRISH TREATY in December 1921, and the CIVIL WAR of 1922–3 in the South. There has been some reluctance to use the term Irish Revolution for these events: supporters of the Anglo-Irish Treaty who presided over the establishment of a conservative government in the twenty-six counties recoiled from any notion of revolution, while republicans viewed the revolution as having been cut off in mid-stream in 1921 and then reversed by the Free State administration. Any social and economic content in an Irish revolution long preceded the political crisis from 1912 onwards. The term Anglo-Irish War, which has been widely used by historians, has been applied only to the years 1919–21 and to the south and west; and the British government never admitted the existence of a war. The term War of Independence, popular with traditional nationalists, cannot be applied to the six counties of the north-east and should encompass a much longer period than 1919–21. To bypass such problems of definition the term 'Troubles' is frequently used (as has again been the case in the Northern crisis since 1969). It is also often applied to the early 1920s in the six counties, where it became synonymous with sectarian violence as well as the widespread challenge to civil administration. Indeed the term has been widely used by such writers as SEAN O'CASEY and J. G. Farrell and has been taken up throughout the population to denote any generalised violence and breakdown of authority in Ireland, thus making the term both democratic and exclusively Irish. A beguiling euphemism, the term nonetheless represents an evasion of vital questions relating to the means by which Irish independence was won. To use 1916 as the starting-point for the period is to play down the significance of the Ulster Crisis (1912–13) and the beginning of the FIRST WORLD WAR in transforming Irish opinion. These years are best understood in the context of a long-term breakdown of British rule in Ireland from Parnellite times. **Michael A. Hopkinson**

'Troubles', the (from 1969), a name given to the serious violence, concentrated principally in Northern Ireland, that began in the summer of 1969 and may have ended with the ceasefires of the 1990s. At the root of the problem is a fundamental disagreement between nationalists and unionists over the constitutional position of Northern Ireland, the former seeking its inclusion in a united Irish state comprising the whole of Ireland, the latter desiring to remain part of the United Kingdom. But the conflict has been exacerbated by socio-economic factors, such as high levels of unemployment and the associated social deprivation, as well as religious ones, with sectarian animosities fuelling much antagonism. The violence developed when a CIVIL RIGHTS campaign in the late 1960s, seeking to raise the position of Northern Ireland's Catholics (who comprised a third of the population), was opposed by Protestant loyalists, defending their traditional supremacy. Violent clashes put such a strain on the police that in August 1969 the British army was deployed, at first in Belfast and Derry, to help keep the peace.

The first phase of the Troubles, from 1969 to c. 1977, was typified by large-scale civil commotion, with rioters attacking both the security forces and the opposing community. Accompanying this came the emergence of well-armed and organised paramilitary organisations, most notably the PROVISIONAL IRA, which for most of the Troubles has been perceived as the principal opponent of the security forces. Republican groups, such as the Provisional IRA, the Official IRA (which called a ceasefire in 1972), and the IRISH NATIONAL LIBERATION ARMY, have also attacked security force targets, symbols of the British connection, personnel such as judges and prison officers, and economic and infrastructural installations. A bombing campaign that began in the early 1970s was sustained throughout the whole period after rioting became more intermittent in the mid-1970s. Republican groups have sought to take the war to Britain and British military targets on the Continent, while loyalists have planted bombs in the Republic. Particularly in the early years of violence there were numerous loyalist paramilitary organisations; most enduring and attracting most support were the ULSTER VOLUNTEER FORCE and the ULSTER DEFENCE ASSOCIATION. Sectarian assassination was the terror tactic principally employed by loyalists, notably the 'SHANKILL BUTCHERS' between 1975 and 1977.

After the mid-1970s both the republicans and the security forces settled down into a 'long war' of attrition, with the latter putting much effort into intelligence and covert operations against the terrorists. During the early 1990s loyalist paramilitary groups for the first time became responsible for more killings than republicans. Both the Provisionals and the main loyalist groups called a ceasefire in 1994 (though the Provisionals resumed military operations from February 1996 to July 1997), up to which time more than 3,200 people had died since 1969, 950 of whom were members of the security forces, and more than 25,000 had been injured. The largest number of casualties occurred up to 1976, after which the annual average of fatalities was about 100.

The original campaign for civil rights having been met with extensive reforms, the reduction of violence in Northern Ireland depends on the establishment of a settlement that accommodates the legitimate political and national aspirations of both nationalists and unionists. **Keith Jeffery**

Troy, Dermot (1927–1962), singer. Born in Wicklow; studied voice with MICHAEL O'HIGGINS at the RIAM. He made his debut as

'Troubles'. *A hoarding on a Belfast church, 22 December 1974, illustrating the death toll of the Troubles, which had reached over 3,200 by the ceasefires of the 1990s. [Getty Images/Hulton Archive]*

a tenor as Tamino in an RIAM production of *The Magic Flute*. Winner of the *Irish Independent* Caruso competition in 1952, he joined the Glyndebourne chorus two years later. He also sang with Covent Garden Chorus, London, where his roles included Vasek in *The Bartered Bride* and David in *Die Meistersinger*. In 1958 he became principal lyric tenor with the Mannheim Opera House, and four years later he joined the Hamburg State Opera and performed the role of Lensky in *Eugene Onegin*. He was on the path to an international career before his premature death at the age of thirty-five. **Emma Costello**

Troy, John Thomas (1739–1823), bishop. Born in Castleknock, Co. Dublin; he went to Rome at the age of fifteen to enter the Dominican order and was ordained in 1762. He became prior of St Clement's in Rome in 1772 but was recalled to Ireland in 1776 to become Bishop of Ossory. On moving from Ossory to become Archbishop of Dublin in 1786 he became in effect the leader of the Catholic Church in Ireland. His zeal in advancing the interests of the Catholic laity was moderated by his need to check a militancy linked to the revolutionary ideas and politics of the era. **C. D. A. Leighton**

trumpets, Bronze Age. Bronze horns are among the more distinctive metal products of the Irish late BRONZE AGE, with some 120 examples, mostly found in BOGS as single finds or in hoards. They are principally found in the Cork-Kerry region and in north-east Ireland, the largest find consisting of twenty-six examples in the DOWRIS HOARD from Co. Offaly. There are two principal forms: those blown through an aperture in the side and those blown through a mouthpiece at one end. These slender curving horns are often decorated at the bell end, usually with ribs, grooves, bosses, and conical spikes. Some have ring attachments for a carrying-chain or leather strap. Their fabrication in two-piece clay moulds was a considerable technical achievement. Experiments have shown that these horns can produce a varied rhythmic sound, and different types can be played in harmony. Interpreted as war trumpets and ritual clarions, they may have had a variety of ceremonial uses. **William O'Brien**

Tuach, Rod (1945–), photographer. Born in Dublin; educated at the High School, Dublin. He has worked extensively in the theatre, including the ABBEY and the GATE as well as with the Focus and FIELD DAY theatre companies. He has also worked in the film industry, most notably in a stills documentary on the making of *The Field* (1990). He has exhibited widely, both in Ireland and abroad. Solo exhibitions include Foto Festival, Turnhout, Belgium (1996) and Source Foxford Gallery (2002). Group shows include Contemporary Irish Photography, Guinness Hop Store, Dublin (1987), Fêtes Irlandaises at the Montréal World Trade Centre (1992), and RHA Dublin (2001). He is a member of AOSDÁNA. **Myra Dowling**

Tuatha Dé Danann, represented in medieval traditions as the masters of Ireland before the coming of the sons of Míl, the mythical ancestors of the dynasties that ruled Ireland in the historical period. Immortal, magical, and capable of changing shape, they are the main characters in several sagas, their role fluctuating between the human and the divine. Undoubtedly many personalities of Tuatha

Dé Danann were originally pagan gods; this is certainly true of LUGH, MANANNÁN MAC LIR, Óengus, and the DAGDA. They are imagined to have retreated to OTHERWORLD dwelling-places with the coming of the sons of Míl but make frequent appearances in the ordinary world or entice humans into their domains. These could be found within mounds, under lakes, or over the sea. The most important dwelling-place of Tuatha Dé Danann was Brú na Bóinne (the MEGALITHIC cemetery of the BOYNE VALLEY, Co. Meath). **Elva Johnston**

tuberculosis. The tuberculosis mycobacterium causes a group of diseases, including scrofula, lupus, and meningitis, but the term is generally used to refer to pulmonary tuberculosis (consumption or phthisis), commonly called TB (for 'tubercle bacillus'). Like other viral diseases, it affects especially those whose immune system is depressed. Archaeological evidence suggests that tuberculosis was uncommon in Ireland before the seventeenth century. Urban living conditions worsened, and more than 750,000 Irish people died in the tuberculosis epidemic of the nineteenth and twentieth centuries; by 1900 it was responsible for one death in six. As in Continental Europe, the disease thereafter began a steady decline, apart from wartime, until by 1954 it caused only 800 deaths, many fewer than are caused by heart disease or cancer.

Attempts to tackle tuberculosis, notably those led by Lady Aberdeen in the 1900s and NÖEL BROWNE in the 1940s, concentrated on sanatorium care, which removed the public source of infection and gave the patient's immune system the best chance to control the disease; but until the introduction of the *bacillus Calmette-Guérin* (BCG) vaccine and antibiotics, reactivation was always possible. The tendency of family members to infect one another led to the long-held belief that tuberculosis was hereditary. The disease was also associated with poverty and, in the final stages, an inexplicable euphoria. It was often young adults, of all classes, who were affected. Emigrant studies suggested (wrongly) that Irish people were especially vulnerable to the disease.

The worldwide incidence of tuberculosis has increased in recent years; however, the Irish death rate from TB remains constant. **Tony Farmar**

Tuckey, James Kingston (1776–1816), explorer. Born in Mallow, Co. Cork; joined the Royal Navy in 1793 and was wounded in an engagement at Amboina in the Moluccas. In 1802 he was sent to Port Phillip, New South Wales, on the *Calcutta* to found a colony; he published an account of this voyage in 1805. In 1806, on his return journey, he was captured by a French ship and spent the next eight years as a prisoner of war in Verdun. During this time he married a fellow-prisoner and wrote *Maritime Geography and Statistics*, published in 1815 after his release. In 1816 he led an expedition to the Congo, where he died of fever on 4 October 1816. His *Narrative of an Expedition to Explore the River Zaïre* was published posthumously in 1818. **Peter Somerville-Large**

Tudor, Joseph (died 1759), landscape painter. He lived in Dame Street, Dublin, and in the 1740s the DUBLIN SOCIETY awarded him five premiums for landscape painting. He was admitted to the Guild of St Luke in 1755. His landscapes were very much in the idiom of WILLIAM VAN DER HAGEN. He designed scenery for SMOCK ALLEY THEATRE, Dublin, and executed work for the supper at DUBLIN CASTLE to celebrate the birthday of George II. A number of his paintings were engraved. He produced six views of Dublin, which proved very popular in print form, and may also have painted altarpieces. He received prestigious patronage. **Brendan Rooney**

Tudor plantations, one of the policies adopted for 'reforming' Ireland. Colonisation appealed to Tudor governments, as they hoped that colonies would serve as models of civility and reformed religion for the 'wild' Irish, as strategic outposts for fending off foreign invasion, and as centres of administrative and military control. Colonisation also offered opportunities for landless younger sons from England to acquire ESTATES and provided an outlet for what was perceived to be England's excess population. Plantation schemes tended to be promoted by Lord Deputies and English Secretaries of State driven by a desire for profit and aggrandisement.

The first plantation was that of the O'More and O'Connor territories of Laois and Offaly. Initial allotments were made to leaseholders in the vicinity of the newly established Crown forts called Governor and Protector in 1549. In the 1550s the area was shired as Queen's County and King's County (after Queen Mary and her Spanish consort Prince Philip) and the forts renamed Maryborough (now Port Laoise) and Philipstown (Daingean). However, raids by the dispossessed Irish resulted in few settlers remaining in the early 1560s. In 1563 the LORD LIEUTENANT, the Earl of Sussex, made forty-four grants to NEW ENGLISH soldiers, fifteen to the OLD ENGLISH, and twenty-nine to native Irish parties, though the latter steadily diminished as a result of confiscation and indebtedness. The foundations of this plantation were shaky, as it proceeded without an adequate survey, the support of the Earl of Kildare, or the issuing of permanent freehold grants, and the English soldier-settlers proved ill-suited to farming. The extent of its failure was manifest by the mid-1570s, when the plantation yielded less than a twentieth of the cost of its maintenance.

The attempted colonisation of eastern Ulster by private schemes headed by Sir Thomas Smith and his son Thomas (north Down and the Ards) and WALTER DEVEREUX, Earl of Essex (Co. Antrim) in 1571–5 ended in failure. The large-scale PLANTATION OF MUNSTER was facilitated by the confiscation of rebel land stretching from Limerick to Cork following the second DESMOND REBELLION (1579–83) (see p. 915). Thirty-five 'UNDERTAKERS' were granted 120,000 ha (298,653 acres); but incompetent land surveying resulted in protracted litigation. Some undertakers merely extracted rent from their Irish tenants, while others introduced settlers and new methods of husbandry and invested in their estates. The plantation population reached 3,030 in 1592, but in October 1598, during the NINE YEARS' WAR, the Munster seigniories were repossessed by former owners under the leadership of James fitz Thomas Fitzgerald, causing many settlers to flee to England. After 1601 the colony was re-established and steadily prospered. Some historians regard the Irish plantations as prototypes for English colonisation in America. **Mary Ann Lyons**

Tudor rebellions. Rebellions against Tudor rule in Ireland can be divided into two useful (though ultimately artificial) categories. The first were the numerically large and frequent occurrences of low-level campaigns of resistance against the intrusions of English soldiers, administrators, and adventurers into native Irish localities, where confrontation took place at the outset and was sustained for decades thereafter. Such were the rebellions of the O'Byrnes in Co. Wicklow, the O'Carrolls in Ossory, and, most notably, the long-drawn-out guerrilla campaign of the O'Mores in Laois and the O'Connors in Offaly against the introduction of a plantation in their territories from the 1550s on. The second were the numerically smaller but more serious revolts led by figures whose military power and political influence stretched beyond their own localities and posed a far greater challenge to English rule in Ireland as a whole. Such were the rebellions of the FITZGERALDS of Kildare (1534–6), the wars of SHANE O'NEILL (1559–67), the first DESMOND REBELLION (1568–73), the Butler revolt (1569–70), the second Desmond rebellion (1579–83), and the rebellion of HUGH O'NEILL, Earl of Tyrone, and HUGH O'DONNELL, which became known as the NINE YEARS' WAR (1594–1603).

A certain irony underlies these challenges to Tudor governance, in that they were headed by those who already had, or were avidly seeking, recognition as figures of authority and legitimacy within that regime. The Kildare, Butler, and Desmond revolts were conducted by ancient Anglo-Irish families keen not to reject but to consolidate and advance their place in English rule in Ireland, while the wars of Shane O'Neill, who wanted to be made Earl of Tyrone, and Hugh O'Neill, who actually was, were fought to defend their political authority while it was being transformed and legitimated under English law. Ideological influences have sometimes been adduced to account for these great lords' defiance of English government: their dislike of the religious REFORMATION and their nascent sense of an Irish national identity. More evidence exists for the former than for the latter; but such apologias (which usually came late) were at best intended to encapsulate or perhaps obscure more complex material and cultural problems that lay at the heart of the process of Anglicisation in Ireland. First among such problems was demilitarisation—the requirement that the lords disband the great private armies they had employed to enforce their authority and collect the rents and taxes due to them.

The dissolution of the military castes inevitably presented serious tactical and political difficulties to the lords. But such difficulties were increased by the fact that the armies were not mere excrescences on Irish society but products of the essential characteristics of the social system itself. Because property in land—freehold and leasehold—was not held individually but corporately by the kinship group, which held complete responsibility for its management, redistribution, and inheritance, the collection of rents and services by the lords was of necessity a fluid, flexible affair subject to constant renegotiation and bargaining, which required a far more constant intervention and supervision by the lords than the rigid legal and fiscal procedures recognised by English law permitted. Initial English attempts to secure the transformation of local Irish fiscal practices into acceptable English forms simply by securing the agreement of the lords themselves failed through the sheer inability of the lords to enforce them. But a more sophisticated approach—the policy of 'composition', developed by English administrators in the 1570s—entailed a degree of sustained intervention in the LORDSHIPS that at once deepened the hostility of the military men, discomfited the lords, and disappointed some of the freeholders in each lordship. It nevertheless scored some success in Connacht and Thomond; but the inability of the Crown to sustain its own initiatives after the crucial opening stages served only to divide the lordships into supporters and opponents of tenurial reform, to undermine the authority of the lords, and to provoke a form of civil war that issued ultimately in rebellion. **Ciaran Brady**

Tulla Céilí Band, one of the more famous TRADITIONAL MUSIC dance ensembles. With a continuous existence from the early 1940s, it was formalised in Minogue's pub, Tulla, Co. Clare, in 1946. It included Bert McNulty, Paddy Canny, P. Joe Hayes and Aggie White on FIDDLE, Seán Reid on pipes, JOE COOLEY on ACCORDION, Jack Murphy and Paddy and James O'Donoghue on flute, and Teresa Tubridy on PIANO. Later WILLIE CLANCY played with them, and then the drummer Jack Keane. They broadcast on Radio Éireann and became one of the best-known bands in the country, also playing

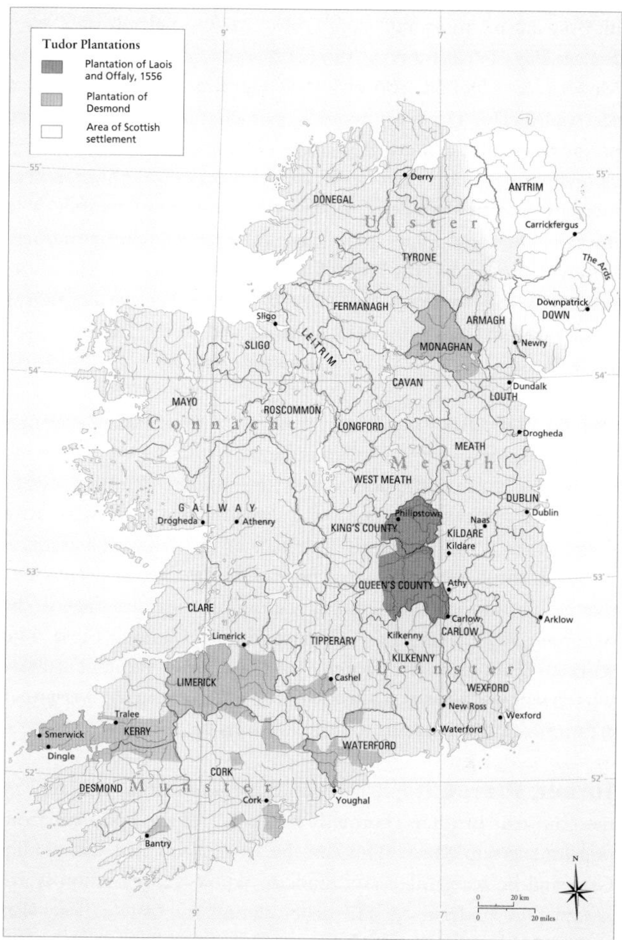

emigrant venues in Britain and the United States, carrying on through the terminal decline of céilí dancing to recover with the SET-DANCING revival of the 1980s. They won three all-Ireland FLEÁ CHEOIL titles and made several recordings, most recently with MARTIN HAYES in 1997. **Fintan Vallely**

Tunney, Paddy (1921–), health inspector, singer, lilter, dancer, and writer. Born in Glasgow; raised in Pettigoe, Co. Donegal. He is a highly regarded and influential source singer (as was his mother, Brigid Tunney, from whom he acquired much material), renowned for his versions of 'big' songs of the unaccompanied tradition, such as 'Mountain Streams Where the Moorcock Crows' and 'Moorlough Mary'. His publications include the autobiographical *The Stone Fiddle: My Way To Traditional Song* (1979) and *Where Songs Do Thunder: Travels in Traditional Song* (1991). *A Wild Bee's Nest* (1992) is regarded as his definitive recording. **Anthony McCann**

Tuohy, Liam (1930–), soccer player. Born in Dublin. A protégé of Paddy Coad, a celebrated player and coach of Shamrock Rovers in the 1940s and 50s, he did much to maintain the club's image as the most successful in the League of Ireland. After a spell with Newcastle United he returned to oversee Rovers' record sequence of six FAI Cup victories, ending in 1969. In an age when the Republic of Ireland was spoiled for choice in left-wingers he won only six caps, but in a two-year spell as manager his influence was profound. He resigned in 1973 because of pressure of business but later returned to manage the Republic's under-age teams. **Peter Byrne**

Tuohy, Patrick J. (1894–1930), artist. Born in Dublin; studied at the Metropolitan School of Art under ORPEN, who considered him one of his most able pupils. His arresting portrait of a *Mayo Peasant Boy* (1912), now in the Hugh Lane Municipal Gallery of Modern Art, Dublin, shows that at eighteen he was already an accomplished portrait-painter. He painted many of the leading personalities of the new Irish state—politicians, military, gentry, clergy, writers, and actors—portraying his subjects with directness, intensity, and an absence of flattery. Characteristic of his style is an insistence on tonal values and the use of unusual colour harmonies. Tuohy is also known for his brilliant pencil portraits of personalities related to the contemporary theatre. A member of the ROYAL HIBERNIAN ACADEMY, in 1927 he emigrated to the United States, where he died three years later. **Rosemarie Mulcahy**

Túr Gloine, An ('the Tower of Glass'), a co-operative STAINED-GLASS studio founded in Dublin in January 1903 by the writer and art patron EDWARD MARTYN and the painter SARAH PURSER. Inspired by the teachings of the English arts and crafts artist Christopher Whall and by the emphasis on revivalist applied arts at the reconstituted Metropolitan School of Art, it was determined that each artist should be entirely responsible for every stage in the designing and making of a window. Eminent among those who worked there until its closure in 1944 were MICHAEL HEALY, WILHELMINA GEDDES, EVIE HONE, ETHEL RHIND, CATHERINE O'BRIEN, and HUBERT MCGOLDRICK. **Nicola Gordon Bowe**

Turner, Pierce (1950–), singer. Born in Wexford; educated by the Christian Brothers. Formerly a member of the Irish-American pop-funk group Major Thinkers, he has collaborated with Philip Glass and he is regarded as a musician whose unique vision is not always fully understood. His debut album, *It's Only a Long Way Across* (1986), clearly stated his credentials: oddly beguiling and idiosyncratic but with a strong Celtic sensibility. He remains one of Irish rock's genuine insurgents. **Tony Clayton-Lea**

Turoe. *The Turoe Stone, Loughrea, Co. Galway, a granite boulder 1.68 m (5½ ft) total height, carved in the La Tène style c. 250–150 BC. The function of the monument is unknown. [Dúchas, The Heritage Service]*

Turner, Richard (c. 1798–1881), ironfounder. Born in Dublin. In 1834 he established Hammersmith Iron Works at Ballsbridge, Dublin, specialising in wrought-iron conservatories. His work includes the Belfast Palm House (1840), Kew Palm House, London (1848), the Great Exhibition Buildings (London, 1851, Dublin, 1853), and the central portion of the Curvilinear Range at the NATIONAL BOTANIC GARDENS, Glasnevin, Dublin (1848). **Ronald Cox**

Turner de Lond, William (fl. 1767–1826), painter. Born in London. He travelled in France and extensively in Italy before 1821, in which year he exhibited twenty-four paintings in Limerick, alongside works by the BROCAS brothers, William Sadler, Joseph Samuel Alpenny, Richard Wilson, and others. Pictures in the exhibition included Irish and Italian scenes, and religious subjects. His street scenes in oils include *The Entry of George IV into Dublin*, a view of the courthouse and quays in Limerick, and *The Market Place, Ennis*. He also painted views of Killarney and executed illustrations for publication. He lived for some time in Scotland, painting in Edinburgh. **Brendan Rooney**

Turnerelli, Peter (1774–1839), sculptor. Born in Belfast; educated in Dublin but moved to London in 1792 and became a pupil of Peter Francis Chenu and also studied at the Royal Academy. He enjoyed enormous success, boasting an international clientele. He visited Dublin in 1812. Appointed Sculptor to the Queen in 1814, he produced monuments and portraits. His works include the High Altar in the Pro-Cathedral, Dublin, a monument to Robert Burns (1816) in Dumfries, a statue of DANIEL O'CONNELL, and busts of JOHN PHILPOT CURRAN and HENRY GRATTAN (1812). He exhibited in Dublin in 1834 and 1835. Despite his success, he endured poverty. After his death in Dublin the contents of his gallery and studio were auctioned. **Brendan Rooney**

Turoe Stone, near Loughrea, Co. Galway, a rounded, oval-sectioned boulder of fine-grained granite standing 1.2 m (4 ft) above present ground level. Its total length is 1.86 m (6 ft), and its basal section tapers to a blunt point. It was moved to its present site in the nineteenth century from the vicinity of a possible Iron Age site at Feerwore. The upper 78 cm ($2\frac{1}{2}$ ft) of the stone has been carved with curvilinear decoration in false relief, bounded by an engraved band of poorly produced linear-step ornament. The curvilinear ornament, which has been carved with considerable expertise and grace, is laid out in four distinct panels, two D-shaped and two roughly triangular, which suggests that the organisation of the design was based on a rectangular-sectioned prototype.

There are three other decorated stones in Ireland that are probably more or less contemporary. The type is unknown in Britain; the closest parallels occur in Brittany, where several hundred examples are found. There they vary from tall cylindrical examples to those that are low and rounded. The great majority are plain, but a few are embellished with curvilinear and linear patterns, in several instances bounded by bands of linear-step ornament. The Breton stones are occasionally rectangular in section, calling to mind the fourfold arrangement of the Turoe ornament. Earlier studies of the Co. Galway stone saw a direct relationship between it and the Breton carvings, a view that was enhanced by the presence in the two regions of linear-step ornament. The curvilinear ornament on the Turoe Stone, however, is of entirely insular inspiration, displaying

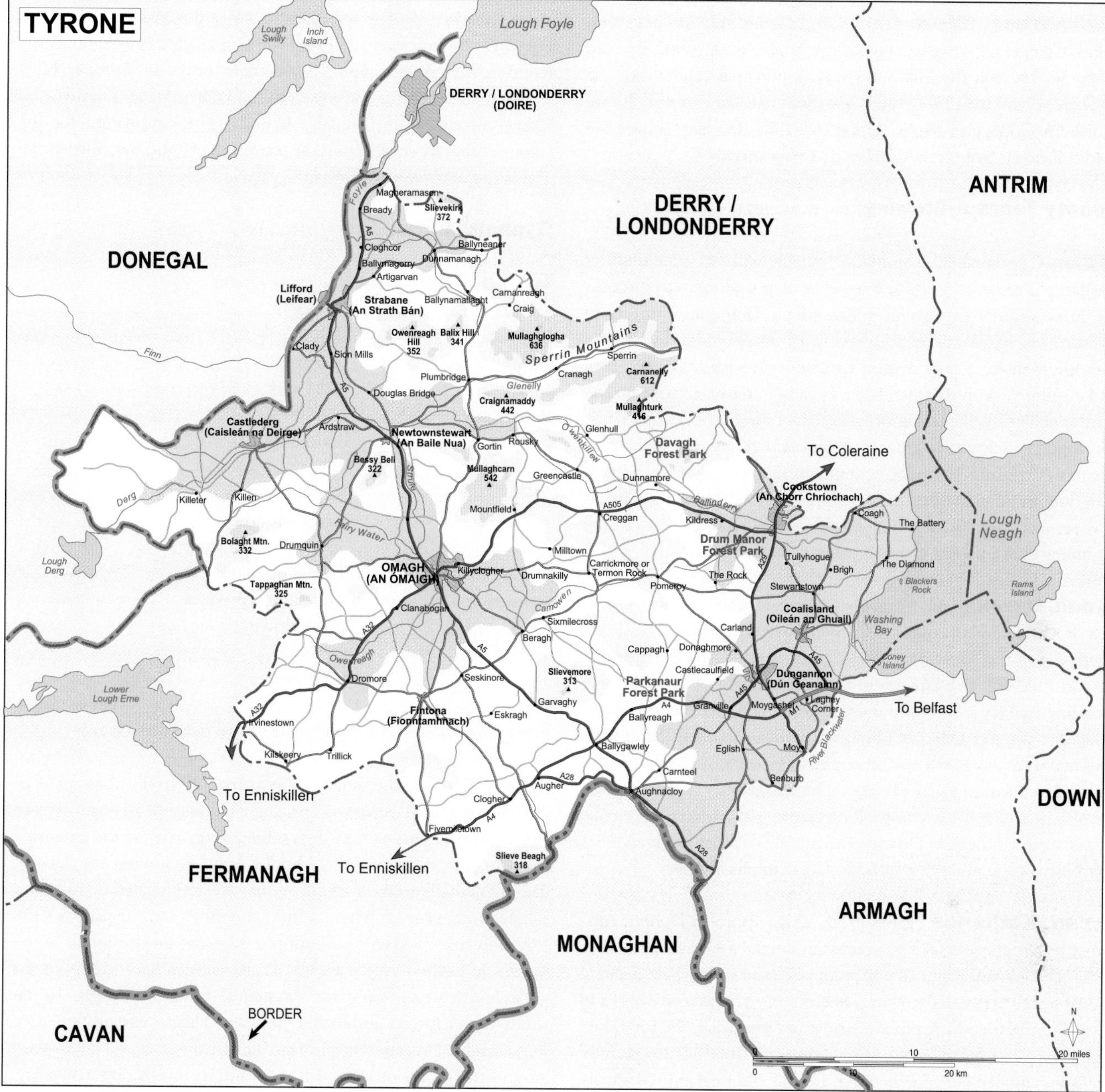

stylistic links with native as well as British metalwork. It is therefore a matter of debate to what extent, if any, the Turoe carving was influenced by carvings in Brittany. The possibility that locally produced timber carvings played a part in the development of the Irish stones has been suggested. **Barry Raftery**

Tuskar Rock Lighthouse. Tuskar Rock lies directly in the path of shipping approaching ROSSLARE HARBOUR. The lighthouse is a tapering bell-bottomed granite tower some 34 m (111 ft) high. Lit in 1815, it was one of the first to be completed following a reorganisation of the LIGHTHOUSE service in 1810. **Ronald Cox**

Tussaud, Madame Marie, née Grosholtz (1761–1850), artist. Born in Bern, Switzerland. She became drawing mistress to the family of Louis XVI and then a celebrated wax modeller in Paris. For four years at the beginning of the nineteenth century, 1804–8, she lived in Ireland. Her Grand European Cabinet of Figures opened at the Shakespeare Gallery in Exchequer Street, Dublin, in 1804, with a suitably chilling display of topical figures from the French Revolution and Terror, including the late royal family as well as Marat and Robespierre (still on display in Madame Tussaud's in London), many of the faces cast from heads of the guillotined. Contemporary Irish political figures, such as HENRY GRATTAN, modelled from life, were also included in the display, which she brought to Belfast, Cork, Kilkenny, and Waterford. **Brian Lalor**

Tweedy, Hilda, née Anderson (1911–), feminist and consumer rights activist. Born in Co. Monaghan; educated at the University of London. In 1941 she initiated a 'housewives' petition', which sought Government action on the production and distribution of essential goods. She was a founder-member of the IRISH HOUSEWIVES' ASSOCIATION, joint honorary secretary, 1942–51, and chairwoman, 1959–62. She was chairwoman of the ad hoc Committee on the Status of Women, established in 1968, represented the IHA on the National Commission on the Status of Women, 1969–72, and was first chairwoman of the Council for the Status of Women, established 1972. In 1990 she was awarded an honorary doctorate by the University of Dublin. **Rosemary Raughter**

Twelvetrees, Clyde (1875–1956), cellist. He studied with Julius Klengel in Leipzig and taught at the RIAM 1902–19 and 1945–56. He was the Hallé Orchestra's principal cellist from the 1921/2 season to 1937/8 and was also a teacher at the Royal Northern College of Music during that time. He later joined the Radio Éireann Symphony Orchestra. **Emma Costello**

Twenty Years a-Growing: see FICHE BLIAIN AG FÁS.

Tynan, Co. Armagh, probably identifiable with the monastery of Tuidhnigha recorded in 1072. Fragments of at least six HIGH CROSSES are preserved. Two, now in Tynan Abbey Demesne, came from Glenarb nearby—one, on an island, with spiral-bossed decoration, the other, above a well, with a Crucifixion and possible SS. Paul and Anthony. A third cross, from Tynan churchyard, now on the terrace of Tynan Abbey, has decorated flat bosses. The Village Cross (perhaps two separate fragments), probably standing near its original site, has Adam and Eve and a hemispherical boss. A shaft with interlace and an *orans* figure (in a praying posture) flanked by beasts was recently identified in the churchyard, which also has a ring fragment built into the gatepost. **Peter Harbison**

Tynan, Derek (1954–), architect. Born in Dublin; studied at UCD and at Cornell University with Colin Rowe. He was an assistant professor at the University of Virginia, 1981–2, design tutor at UCD, 1982–92, and director of the Urban Design Unit, National Building Agency, 1986–9, and founded his own practice in Dublin, 1990. He was a member of Group 91 (which proposed the TEMPLE BAR FRAMEWORK PLAN) and other Urban Projects, such as dockland housing at Clarion Quay (1998–). The Printworks at Temple Bar, Dublin, is a mixed-use complex integrating old and new elements; it was awarded the AAI Downes Medal, 1995. Other work includes the North Gate multiplex CINEMA, Cork. **Raymund Ryan**

Tynan, Katharine (1861–1931), writer. Born in Dublin; educated in Drogheda. Her first volume of poetry, *Louise de La Vallière* (1885), established her as an important poet, and she became a central figure in the LITERARY REVIVAL. She met W. B. YEATS in 1885 and they became friends. A prolific writer and journalist, she published more than 160 volumes of poetry and prose. After her marriage in 1893 she divided her time between Ireland and England. Gradually surpassed by other Irish talents, her best work is probably her four volumes of memoirs. **Robbie Meredith**

Tyndall, John (1820–1893), physicist. Born in Leighlinbridge, Co. Carlow; educated by a local teacher, John Conwill. He was employed first by the ORDNANCE SURVEY, but his main employment was from 1854 at the Royal Institution of Great Britain in London. There he developed his researches on diamagnetism and glaciology, and he became the most famous popular lecturer of his day. His major research fields were infra-red transmission in the atmosphere, meteorology, and bacteriology. He was a pioneer worker, in parallel with Pasteur, in the discovery of bacterial infection and on measures for controlling it. His many inventions included the fireman's respirator, the fibre optic, the infra-red analyser, and the nephelometer. It was through his glacial researches that he ventured high into the mountains, and he was one of the first enthusiasts for alpine exploration.

His most famous public lecture was his 'Belfast Address' in 1873 to a meeting there of the British Association for the Advancement of Science. His then scandalous views on SCIENCE and RELIGION—he was an agnostic and a devoted protagonist of Darwin's evolutionary theory—were circulated throughout the world in newspaper reports. Mountain peaks in Europe, New Zealand, and America and towns in the United States, Canada, and Alaska are named in Tyndall's honour. The explanation for the colour of the sky comes from the scattering of light, described as the Tyndall effect. **Norman McMillan**

'Typhoid Mary': see MALLON, MARY.

Tyrone, County (*Contae Thír Eoghain*)

Province:	ULSTER
County town:	OMAGH
Area:	3,263 km^2 (1,220 sq. miles)
Population (1991)*:	144,000
Features:	LOUGH NEAGH
	River BLACKWATER
	River Foyle
	River Mourne
	Sperrin Mountains
Of historical interest:	Tullaghoge Fort
Industry and products:	Agricultural produce
	Glass-blowing
	LINEN
	Printing

Petula Martyn

* last year of census by county, [see NORTHERN IRELAND.]

County Tyrone, the largest of Northern Ireland's counties. Co. Tyrone originated as part of Tír Eoghain, 'land of Eoghan' (son of NIALL OF THE NINE HOSTAGES), subsequently part of the extensive UÍ NÉILL possessions in the Middle Ages. Following the Earl of Tyrone's rebellion, most of the county was confiscated in 1608 and subsequently planted. Much of the modern settlement pattern dates from this time, and its distribution reflects the diverse relief. In the north and north-west the ancient Pre-Cambrian Sperrin Mountains encircle the Strule valley and the county town of Omagh. To the south-west a lower, undulating sandstone plateau extends into Co. Fermanagh. The most fertile land lies to the east and south-east, around the shores of LOUGH NEAGH and in the Blackwater valley. Despite limited exploitation of the east Tyrone coalfield from the sixteenth century, Co. Tyrone was and remains one of the most rural and agricultural counties in Northern Ireland. Like Co. Fermanagh, it has been characterised by high levels of rural deprivation, lack of social amenity, and political violence, whose effects have been only partly allayed by regional planning initiatives since 1973 (see pp. 359, 1031). **Lindsay Proudfoot**

Tyrrell, Charles (1950–), painter. Born in Trim, Co. Meath; studied at the NCAD. He lives and works on the Beara Peninsula, Co. Cork. At first he produced large, stained, colour field abstract paintings; his work gradually became more complex in geometrical structure. In more recent paintings, linear forms interplay and are overlaid with richly coloured expressive brushwork. Tension is created between the interaction of opposites: cool void and active paint-filled forms. He has exhibited widely in Ireland and abroad, was awarded the jury's Special Mention at the International Festival of Painting, Cagnes-sur-Mer, 1981, and is a member of AOSDÁNA. **Suzanne McNab**

U2. *(from left) 'Bono' (Paul Hewson), 'the Edge' (David Evans) Larry Mullen, and Adam Clayton, the four members of Ireland's most successful rock group. Its influence reaches beyond music, with the band dedicated to various charities and global issues.* [Hot Press]

U2, rock group. Formed in Dublin in 1976, the group consists of 'Bono' (PAUL HEWSON, 1960–), 'the Edge' (David Evans, 1961–), Adam Clayton (1960–), and Larry Mullen (1960–). They are Ireland's most successful rock band and one of the most successful in the world. Founded by Mullen at Mount Temple School, Dublin, the band was known first as Feedback and then Hype; in 1978 they settled on U2 (suggested by Steve Averill of RADIATORS FROM SPACE as a name that could be translated into virtually any language). They won a talent contest in Limerick the same year; it was after this that U2 came to the attention of their future manager, PAUL MCGUINNESS, who oversaw the release of the band's debut EP, *U2: 3* (1979), the main track of which was 'Out of Control'. A further four singles were released in 1980—'Another Day', '11 O'Clock Tick Tock', 'A Day Without Me', and 'I Will Follow'—each of which was critically lauded but sold poorly. When U2 released their debut album, *Boy* (1980), and its successor, *October* (1981), neither made any huge commercial impact, despite the critical plaudits. The band's third studio album, *War* (1983), and a live album, *U2 Live: Under a Blood-Red Sky* (1983), proved to be their breakthrough records, particularly in the American market. By the time of the release of *The Joshua Tree* (1987), U2 had broken through internationally. *Rattle and Hum* (1988) was released in tandem with the film of the same name, while *Achtung Baby* (1991) was followed by *Zooropa* (1993) and then *Pop* (1997). Following the release of the band's first compilation album, *The Best of 1980–1990* (1998), a new studio album was released, *All That You Can't Leave Behind* (2000). In the same year the four members and the manager, McGuinness, were made honorary freemen of Dublin. Despite reservations by some critics, U2 remain one of the most popular arena rock bands since the 1980s. Remarkably for a band of their standing, each new album is not a retread of the previous one. **Tony Clayton-Lea**

Úallach ingen Muinecháin (Úallach daughter of Muinechán), designated one of the 'wonderful *cailleach*s' of the people of Corca Dhuibhne, Co. Kerry, in an introduction to the OLD IRISH poem 'AITHBE DAMSA BÉS MARAI'. She is described as *banfhile Herend,* 'woman-poet of Ireland,' in her death notice in the annals of Innisfallen (AD 934); she and her work are otherwise unknown. **Máirín Ní Dhonnchadha**

Úa Lothcháin, Cúán (died 1024), chief poet of Ireland at the time of his death. His work deals with the prestige of TARA and the prerogatives of kings. The achievements of his patron, MÁEL SECHNAILL (died 1022), ruler of the southern UÍ NÉILL kingdom of Mide and sometime King of Ireland (980–1002 and 1014–22), feature in his poetry, as does the legendary lore of places and rivers in Mide and elsewhere. The poet was murdered in Tethba; the perpetrators of this crime allegedly putrefied and died immediately afterwards. The annalists referred to this remarkable retribution as *fert filed* (a poet's miracle). **Máirtín Ó Briain**

Ua Maoileoin, Pádraig (1913–2002), writer and editor. Born in Com Dhíneol, Co. Kerry, a grandson of TOMÁS Ó CRIOMHTHAINN; member of the GARDA SÍOCHÁNA for some thirty years; editor in the Department of Education and researcher for Ó Dónaill's Irish-English dictionary. His celebrated creative work includes the novel *Bríde Bhán* (1968), *De Réir Uimhreacha* (1969), based on his experiences in the Garda Síochána, and the fable *Fonn a Níos Fiach* (1978), which bears comparison with Hemingway's *The Old Man and the Sea*. He was editor of the new edition of Ó Criomhthainn's AN TOILEÁNACH (1973) and *Allagar na hInise* (1977) and of Peig Sayers's *Machnamh Seanmhná* (1980). He was awarded an honorary doctorate by the NUI in 1999 for his lexicographical and literary work. **Tadhg Ó Dúshláine**

UCD: see UNIVERSITY COLLEGE, DUBLIN.

UDA: see ULSTER DEFENCE ASSOCIATION.

UDR: see ULSTER DEFENCE REGIMENT.

uilleann pipes ('elbow' pipes—but before the twentieth century called the 'union pipes'). The uilleann pipes are unique among bagpipes for their sensitive tonal quality and their complexity. A 'full' set of pipes consists of a bag, bellows, *chanter*, three *drones* (tenor, baritone, and bass), and three *regulators* (tenor, baritone, and bass). It is a relatively quiet indoor instrument. The player sits while playing, the bag under one arm and the bellows under the other, while the end of the chanter is 'stopped' on the thigh. The drones and regulators are fixed in a common *stock* and lie across the player's thigh. The drones can be switched on or off with a key, while the regulators, which sound only when their keys are depressed, are played with the side of the hand to give a simple accompaniment to the chanter. The chanter and regulators have conical bores and double-headed reeds, while the drones have cylindrical bores and single reeds. The chanter can be played solo; the drones can be added and, for greater variety, the regulators, as simple harmony or to accent the rhythm of the music.

The chanter has a range of two octaves and can be fitted with keys to be fully chromatic. The facility to close or open the end of the chanter at will adds greatly to the versatility of the instrument, enabling the piper to employ different fingering techniques, which mirror perfectly the requirements of Irish music—a tighter or more staccato style for the lively dance music and an open or more legato style for the plaintive airs. The piper also uses a range of specific piping ornaments to add colour and rhythm to the music.

The pipes are available in a range of pitches. A 'concert' set is in the key of D—the pitch normally used when playing with other instruments. For solo piping the tone of the 'flat' pipes is preferred by many players—normally in C sharp, C, B, or B flat. Uilleann pipes are a difficult instrument to learn, tune and balance and to maintain in good playing order.

The uilleann pipes were developed during the second half of the eighteenth century; by the early part of the nineteenth century this development was complete. Such was their later decline, however, that by the beginning of the twentieth century it seemed they would become mere museum specimens. Pipers' clubs set up in Cork (1898) and Dublin (1900) lasted only a few years. An association to further piping, Cumann na bPíobairí Uilleann, was formed in 1944; this was later subsumed into COMHALTAS CEOLTÓIRI ÉIREANN.

A significant step forward took place in 1968 when a players' association, NA PÍOBAIRÍ UILLEANN, was formed, on the initiative of BREANDÁN BREATHNACH, to promote the playing of the pipes, to collect and preserve the music of the pipes, and to promote their manufacture and servicing. This new organisation provided the vision and impetus required, and since its formation there has been a tremendous upsurge of interest. Na Píobairí Uilleann have produced a wide range of books, recordings, and videos devoted to the instrument, as well as a web site, making information about it widely available (see pp. 579, 1063). **Wilbert Garvin**

Uí Néill, the dominant dynasties in the northern half of Ireland from the seventh to the twelfth centuries, descendants of NIALL OF THE NINE HOSTAGES. Their origin is obscure. Official genealogies, produced in the eighth century, credit Niall with numerous sons, from whom were descended the northern and southern Uí Néill; this construct probably masks a highly complex evolution. Some Uí Néill dynasties, including Cenél Cairbre and Cenél Laoghaire, possibly originated from larger entities, which held territories throughout the midlands to Connacht and which fragmented in the sixth and seventh centuries. The southern Uí Néill, Clann Cholmáin and Síl nÁedo Sláine, were 'officially' descended from Diarmait mac Cerbaill (died c. 565). However, they may have been related to the northern CENÉL CONAILL and to the CRUITHNI, Laighin, and ULAIDH, from which Uí Néill wrested the east and north midlands. The north-western dynasties, CENÉL CONAILL and CENÉL NEOGHAIN, could probably rightfully claim to be the original Uí Néill.

While Uí Néill propagandists claimed the Kingship of TARA and the Kingship of Ireland from time immemorial, their kings rarely achieved dominance of the whole country before the eighth century. Uí Néill emerged at the beginning of the eighth century as a relatively cohesive entity of two dominant dynasties, Clann Cholmáin and Cenél nEoghain, supported by a military alliance with another northern federation, the Airghialla. From c. 700 the kingship of Ireland was dominated by Uí Néill and Munster kings, with kings of Connacht and Leinster contending from the eleventh century. Among the illustrious kings of Uí Néill were Domnall Midi (died 763), MÁEL SEACHNAILL I (died 863), and Máel Seachnaill II (died 1022), FLANN SINNA (died 917), NIALL GLÚNDUB (died 919), Muirchertach mac Néill (died 942), and Muirchertach Mac Lochlainn (died 1166). COLM CILLE, founder of IONA (died 597) (see p. 1112), and ADOMNÁN, ninth Abbot of Iona and author of the VITA COLUMBAE (died 704), belonged to Uí Néill. **Edel Bhreathnach**

Ulaidh: see ULSTER.

Ulster

Ulster	Cúige Uladh
Counties:	Antrim, Armagh, Cavan, Derry, Donegal, Down, Fermanagh, Monaghan, Tyrone
Major towns:	Bangor, Belfast, Craigavon, Lisburn, Londonderry
Rivers:	Foyle, Bann (Ulster), Lagan, Erne
Highest Point:	Slieve Donard 850 m
Population (NI 2001 Census)	1,685,267
Population (Ulster 2001/2 Census)	1,931,838

Ulster (*Ulaidh*), an overkingdom that, throughout most of the historical period, occupied only the eastern portion of the modern province of Ulster, to which it gave its name (Middle Irish *Uladh* + Old Norse *ster*). Overkingdom and modern province were perhaps roughly conterminous before the dawn of the historical period; it seems that rulers of Ulaidh (originally a tribal designation, Uluti, arguably identifiable with the Voluntii of Ptolemy's map) once held sway throughout the north of Ireland. Such ancient greatness is echoed in the Middle Irish epic 'TÁIN BÓ CÚAILNGE', in which Conchobhar mac Neasa, legendary King of Ulaidh, rules the province from Emain Macha (NAVAN FORT). From the fifth century, Ulaidh influence in the north-west declined with the expansion of Connachta dynasties—forebears of Uí Néill. Its kings remained powerful in the north Irish Sea area, striving to maintain lordship over the Isle of Man and the DÁL RIADA realm in Argyll. They were strong challengers for the Kingship of Tara—at least until the fall of Congal Clóen, defeated at Mag Roth in 637. Thereafter they contracted into the north-east, lordship being fitfully maintained over some CRUITHIN kingdoms by the Dál Fiatach dynasty. By the twelfth century the ruling line had adopted the surname Mac Duinnshléibhe. **Ailbhe Mac Shamhráin**

Geography. The northernmost of the provinces, with an area of 22,133 km^2 (8,546 sq. miles). The province is divided between the jurisdictions of Ireland and the United Kingdom. Six counties comprise Northern Ireland: Cos. ANTRIM, ARMAGH, DERRY, DOWN, FERMANAGH, and TYRONE; together they contain an estimated population of 1,697,800 (2001) in an area of 14,121 km^2 (5,452 sq. miles). Northern Ireland has a well-developed and self-contained urban system. The remaining counties of CAVAN, DONEGAL and MONAGHAN have a population of 246,571 (2002), an increase of 5.3 per cent on the previous census. This is 6.3 per cent of the population of the Republic, in a land area of 8,012 km^2 (3,093 sq. miles). The population is predominantly rural, and urban areas tend to be small, with a population of 8,109 in Letterkenny and 5,737 in Monaghan. Today these three counties are part of the Border regional authority, which includes Cos. SLIGO, LEITRIM, and LOUTH.

Ulster as a territorial unit predates the modern counties, which were not created until late in the sixteenth century. At one time the province excluded much of Co. Cavan but extended as far south as Louth. Eamhain Macha (NAVAN FORT) became the provincial capital. Of great importance is the ULSTER CYCLE, a collection of epic tales centred on CÚ CHULAINN. By the fourth century AD Ulster had broken into the smaller territorial units of Tír Chonaill (covering most of Co. Donegal), Tír Eoghain (containing most of modern Tyrone and Derry), Oriel (which included Cos. Monaghan, Louth, and Armagh), and ULAIDH (which incorporated the north-eastern counties). Though the ANGLO-NORMANS penetrated along the east coast, the traditional overlords of the O'Neills and O'Donnells retained sway until the PLANTATION OF ULSTER early in the seventeenth century. [see URBANISATION.] **Joseph Brady**

ulster coat, a caped travelling-coat with numerous pockets, first made and sold in 1866 by McGee and Company of High Street, Belfast. It was made of frieze (a napped and curled woollen cloth that was remarkably weatherproof) and was popular around the world until the advent of enclosed motor travel. **Elizabeth McCrum**

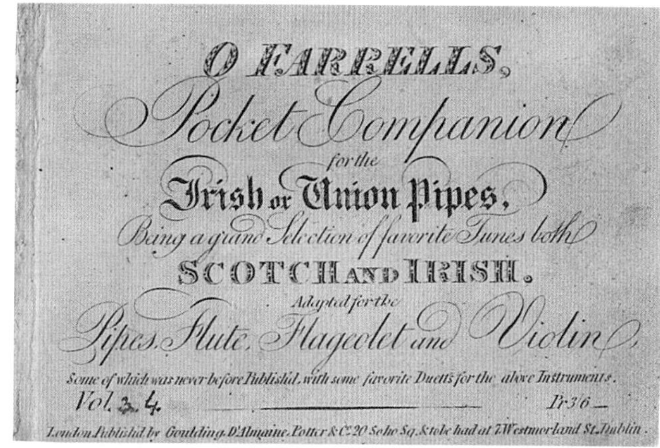
O FARRELLS,
Pocket Companion
for the
Irish or Union Pipes,
Being a grand Selection of favorite Tunes both
SCOTCH AND IRISH.
Adapted for the
Pipes, Flute, Flageolet and Violin.
Some of which was never before Publishd. with some favorite Duetts for the above Instruments.
Vol. 3. 4. Pr 3/6
London Publishd by Goulding, D'Almaine, Potter & Co. 20 Soho Sq. & to be had at 7 Westmorland St. Dublin.

uilleann. *Music for pipes published in London in the early nineteenth century. [Antique Prints, Dublin; photo: Denis Mortell]*

Ulster-American Folk Park, an outdoor museum near Omagh, Co. Tyrone, dedicated to the history and material culture of emigrants from Ulster to the New World in the eighteenth and nineteenth centuries. It regularly organises events devoted to the traditional music of the 'SCOTCH-IRISH' in America, and throughout the 1990s it organised the largest festival of bluegrass music in Ireland. With growing interest in history and cultural diversity throughout Europe and America, the park continues to host conferences and events exploring transatlantic cultural themes. Recent events have included a meeting of the Ulster-American Heritage Symposium and a cross-cultural music festival called 'Music on the Move'. **Martin Dowling**

Ulster Canal, the canal link between LOUGH NEAGH and LOUGH ERNE. First proposed by the Directors-General of Inland Navigation in 1814, it was not completed until 1841. The principal contractor was WILLIAM DARGAN. The work involved twenty-six locks; to cut costs, these were built to smaller dimensions than normal—one, the narrowest in the country, was only 3.7 m (12 ft) wide—which greatly affected its potential as a commercial waterway. Structural defects led to its closure for eight years, but when it reopened in 1873 the water supply was still inadequate, and in 1877 only forty boats passed through it. Traffic increased slightly in the 1880s and 90s, but receipts were not covering maintenance costs. Transferred from the BOARD OF WORKS to the Lagan Navigation Company, it still failed to show a profit, and when it was divided by PARTITION in 1921 it was allowed to fall into disuse, the last movement taking place in October 1929. It was officially closed in 1931. Its reopening as a tourist amenity, following the success of the BALLINAMORE AND BALLYCONNELL CANAL, is under consideration. **Bernard Share**

Ulster Covenant (1912). Unionist and TORY resentment at the Liberal government's determination to push through HOME RULE for Ireland found its voice in the Dublin lawyer EDWARD CARSON and the British Conservative leader BONAR LAW, both of whom had in their own way attempted to raise the political stakes. Bonar Law had expressed his opinion that there were things stronger than parliamentary majorities and had unsuccessfully attempted to sway the king into refusing royal assent to the bill. To demonstrate the strength of opposition to home rule, the ULSTER UNIONIST COUNCIL launched a series of mass demonstrations, beginning in Enniskillen, Co. Fermanagh, on 18 September 1912 and culminating in 'Ulster Day', 28 September 1912, when all men who could prove birth in Ulster were invited to sign the Solemn League and Covenant. The title of the document harked back to the Covenant of 1643 between Scotland and England, a heady mix of political expediency and religious certainty; Ulster's version also recalled the centrality of religious freedom to the maintenance of civil liberties and tied this

Ulster Cycle. The Death of Cuchulain *(1911) by Oliver Sheppard, installed in the General Post Office, Dublin, in 1945 as a memorial to the dead of 1916. A central figure in the Ulster Cycle, Cú Chulainn is the greatest hero of Irish folklore. [Brian Lynch, Bord Fáilte]*

to the very continuance of the British Empire. Its stated objective was to register all unionists over the age of sixteen, whether or not they were voters or members of the Unionist Party.

In an emotionally charged atmosphere, many signed in their own blood, pledging to keep Ulster part of the United Kingdom by whatever means necessary and to refuse to recognise the authority of any parliament forced on them. Women signed their own declaration. Altogether 471,414 people signed either the Covenant or the declaration—over 30,000 more women, in fact, than men. **Roddy Hegarty**

Ulster custom. Tenants in most parts of Ulster acquired customary rights, which varied from estate to estate. By the time the Ulster Tenant Right Association was being set up in 1847 (which became part of the IRISH TENANT LEAGUE in 1850) the 'Ulster custom' was being defined as the 'three Fs': *free sale* (the right of an outgoing tenant to sell his interest in the holding to the incoming tenant, partly in compensation for improvements made to the farm), *fair rent* (rent below market value as a reward for reliability and good husbandry), and *fixity of tenure* (no eviction provided the rent was paid). An exact definition proved almost impossible; GLADSTONE confided to his diary in September 1869 that 'it is like trying in algebra to solve a problem of two unknown quantities with only one equation.' The Ulster custom was given the force of law in the Landlord and Tenant (Ireland) Act (1870) and the Land Law (Ireland) Act (1881). **Jonathan Bardon**

Ulster Cycle, or *Rúraíocht*, a substantial body of hero tales in Irish literature, some of which also exist in oral tradition. Tradition places the Rúraíocht around the period of Christ's birth. Formerly, of the three cycles the Ulster Cycle was held in highest esteem, mostly because it portrayed ideal heroes in an aristocratic society and thereby an idealised code of behaviour. The tales depict a people known as the ULAIDH (hence the modern province of Ulaidh or Ulster), who lived in the eastern part of Ulster and were known as descendants of the mythical Ulster characters; in medieval literature they are often called Clann Rudhraighe. (Though the corpus was sometimes described as relating to the 'Red Branch Knights', this is a misinterpretation of the word *rudhraighe*, which means a rightful occupier and seems to have no connection with the word *rua*, 'red'.)

The principal story is that of 'TÁIN BÓ CUAILNGE' (The Cattle Raid of Cooley), of which the earliest known version dates from the eleventh century, though certain elements existed in manuscript form as early as the seventh century. Much of the Ulster Cycle was probably part of the oral tradition before that time. A number of other tales directly related to the TÁIN predate this major narrative; some of these earlier tales, or 'pre-tales', contain accounts of the history and background to the saga. The tale of 'Táin Bó Cuailnge' is most probably a combination of older tales of the Ulaidh and illustrates many aspects of heroic lives from within their own culture. The emphasis is largely on heroic traits, warriors, and nobility. The entire tale is a complex, multi-episodic story that has been preserved for the most part in literary sources, with many versions, changes and developments regarding the creation and introduction of various characters. Some episodes of the Táin were recounted in oral tradition until very recently, but these appear to have stemmed originally from written sources.

Though the title of the Táin suggests an epic description of a cattle raid, the tale itself emphasises the warriors, the fighting, and the supernatural. The bulls, however, play an essential role in the narrative, especially in the form of symbolism. In one of the 'pre-tales' the narration recounts that two of the bulls had been rivals, in another form, in a previous existence. The full tale of the Táin hardly features in recent oral tradition, and though it is difficult to date its disappearance from oral narrative, it may have occurred at the end of the Middle Ages. Themes of rivalry, dispute and heroic exploits are constantly found throughout the Rúraíocht narratives; these characteristics apply both to the Ulaidh as a warring group and to the individual personages among them.

In addition to the Táin there are numerous other narratives in the Ulster Cycle. Tales of DEIRDRE and the sons of Uisneach also feature prominently in the Ulster Cycle. The principal characters in the Rúraíocht are the ruler Conchobhar mac Neasa; the most celebrated and stalwart hero, CÚ CHULAINN, who, along with Conall Cearnach, is renowned for his physical strength and is also the former King of the Ulaidh; and Fearghus mac Róich, who abandons Ulster for MÉABH of Connacht. Sencha mac Ailella plays a peace-keeping role, while the character Bricriu is noted for causing a great deal of strife. Another character who features prominently in the Rúraíocht is the powerful druid Cathbhadh. Although, by definition, the tales are primarily associated with Ulster, the Ulster Cycle was also held in high esteem outside Ulster. **Ríonach uí Ógáin**

Ulster Cycle, transmission. The surviving corpus of Ulster tales comprises more than ninety compositions, ranging from extensive sagas such as 'TÁIN BÓ CUAILNGE', 'FLED BRICRENN', 'Tochmarc Emire', 'Mesca Ulad', and shorter tales such as 'Aided Óenfir Aífe', 'Longas mac nUislenn', and 'SCÉLA MUICE MEIC DATHÓ', to poems and briefer items of DINNSEANCHAS (place lore). The earliest strata of the tales may belong to the seventh century; others are dated to the eighth and subsequent centuries. The process of composition endured until at least the eighteenth century. In addition to fresh compositions, older tales were continually being copied in MANUSCRIPTS, sometimes faithfully but in other instances with substantial changes in language and content. In quite a number of instances older tales were rewritten completely. Late compositions, such as 'Tóruigheacht Ghruaidhe Griansholus' or 'Tóruigheacht na hEilite le Coin Culainn', written in south-east Ulster in the period 1680–1720, represent the final creative phase of the cycle in the manuscript tradition. In mood and tenor these romantic compositions are at some remove from earlier tales and are closer in spirit to tales of the Fionn Cycle.

In addition to the written tradition, a number of tales have been recorded since the end of the nineteenth century from oral recitation, the most prominent being versions of 'Foghlaim Con Culainn' and 'Oidheadh Chonlaoich mhic Con Culainn', EARLY MODERN IRISH versions of the earlier tales 'TOCHMARC Emire and Aided Óenfir Aífe', respectively. Medieval tradition had the ancient Ulster warriors as contemporaries of Christ. Under their king Conchobhar mac Neasa they reside at Emain Macha (NAVAN FORT, Co. Armagh). The society portrayed is a pagan warrior aristocracy. Bravery, honour and generosity are the values held most dearly. Boasting is not considered a vice, provided the deed matches the boast. Single combat is the most common method of battle. The youthful CÚ CHULAINN is the supreme hero of the Ulstermen and embodies most of the virtues of the perfect warrior. Other prominent warriors are Fearghus mac Róich, Conall Cearnach, Celtchar mac Uthidir, and Laoghaire Buadhach; the druid Cathbadh and the mischievous Bricriu also play important roles. Many of the characters in the tales have supernatural attributes, which suggests that they may originally have been pagan deities. In many tales the Ulstermen are confronted by the warriors of Connacht under their warlike queen MÉABH, who shows attributes associated with the goddess of sovereignty. It has been suggested that the enmity depicted between the people of Connacht and Ulster in this literature may reflect an actual conflict between the two provinces that took place in prehistoric times. **Ruairí Ó hUiginn**

Ulster Defence Association (UDA), the largest loyalist paramilitary organisation in Northern Ireland, founded in 1971 out of loyalist vigilante groups. To a certain extent it has tried to encourage a common working-class cause across the sectarian divide, for example with the New Ulster Political Research Group in the late 1970s and its political offshoot, the Ulster Democratic Party, from the late 1980s. In 1981 its then commander, Andy Tyrie, described the UDA as a 'counter-terrorist organisation' while denying any direct involvement in military operations. At the outset it had a membership of more than 30,000 and played a major part in the success of the ULSTER WORKERS' COUNCIL STRIKE of 1974. In more recent years the mass membership has deliberately been replaced by much smaller, and more controllable, numbers.

The Ulster Freedom Fighters, a markedly sectarian terrorist group associated with the UDA since 1973, has claimed responsibility for numerous attacks on Catholics, ostensibly in retaliation for assaults on loyalists. In the early 1990s the UFF was especially active; its attacks included the shooting of five Catholics in a bookmaker's shop in Belfast in February 1992 and the killing of six Catholics and a Protestant in a bar at Greysteel, Co. Derry, in October 1993. Though the UFF was included in the 1994 loyalist ceasefire, in August 1999 and 2002 a leading member, Johnny Adair, released under the BELFAST AGREEMENT, was sent back to jail for fomenting violence. The Ulster Democratic Party played a leading role in securing support for the agreement but failed to get representatives elected to the Assembly. Its leaders were unable to prevent some UDA members resorting to violence again; the UDA was once again proscribed, and the party collapsed in 2001. **Keith Jeffery**

Ulster Defence Regiment (UDR), a locally raised, mostly part-time military unit created in 1970 to provide disciplined military reinforcement for the BRITISH ARMY IN NORTHERN IRELAND. Though intended to be a cross-community replacement for the almost wholly Protestant B SPECIAL police reserve, the initial proportion of Catholics in the force—18 per cent—soon fell almost completely away, and in the eyes of many nationalists it came to be seen as a sectarian body, an attitude reinforced by the worryingly large number of UDR personnel implicated in loyalist activity—seventeen, for example, having been convicted of murder. Its main tasks included patrolling and mounting vehicle check-points. It was never used for riot control duties. The regiment reached its maximum size of nearly 9,000 in 1972; over its twenty-two-year life some 40,000 men and women (colloquially known as 'Greenfinches') passed through its ranks. It was always a prime target for republican paramilitaries: 197 members and 47 former members were killed between 1970 and July 1992, when it was merged with the regular army Royal Irish Rangers to form the Royal Irish Regiment, part of which continued to provide security cover in Northern Ireland. **Keith Jeffery**

Ulster Folk and Transport Museum, established in 1958 to interpret the way of life and traditions, past and present, of the people of Northern Ireland (see pp. 15, 1145). A large site was acquired at Cultra, Co. Down, on the south side of Belfast Lough. 'Vernacular' buildings were removed from places throughout Ulster and re-erected in the open-air museum, and a model of Ulster society of c. 1900 was created, emphasising social harmony and continuity of tradition. The explicit aim was to show that many aspects of life were shared by Ulster people, despite religious and political divisions.

This approach has been reworked following two major developments. In 1967 the museum acquired a large collection of artefacts relating to the history of TRANSPORT in Ireland, which, as products of international mass technology, could not be set convincingly in

Ulster Defence Association. *Led by masked figures carrying truncheons, women members of the association patrol in Belfast, 1972. The UDA is the largest loyalist paramilitary group in Northern Ireland. [Popperfoto]*

a model of small-scale folk society; and the increasing emphasis on archival collections in the museum meant that material relating to religious and political divisions was collected, which also required interpretation. The museum now interprets local history and popular culture. In 1998 it became part of the MUSEUMS AND GALLERIES of Northern Ireland (MAGNI), which has made possible further developments, including work on environmental history and biodiversity. **Jonathan Bell**

Ulster Literary Theatre, Belfast (1902–34), founded by Bulmer Hobson and Lewis Purcell, modelling itself on the Irish Literary Theatre but quickly establishing a distinctive regional identity. 'Our talent is more satiric than poetic,' claimed its journal, *Uladh* (1904–5); and this was evident in plays such as GERALD MACNAMARA's *Thompson in Tír-na-nÓg* (1912). Between 1904 and 1930 the theatre produced forty-seven original plays, most of which were either political satires or rural comedies or tragedies, usually with a satirical edge. The lack of a permanent building contributed to its dissolution in 1934. **Christopher Morash**

Ulster Museum. The origins of the Ulster Museum stem from the collections owned by the Belfast Museum (opened in 1833) run by the Belfast Natural History Society, later the Belfast Natural History and Philosophical Society, and the Belfast Public Art Gallery and Museum (opened in 1888). In 1891 the Belfast Corporation accepted responsibility for the Grainger Collection of antiquities and natural science, and in 1909 they acquired the collections of the Belfast Natural History and Philosophical Society. This prompted the Belfast Corporation to rehouse the Belfast Art Gallery and Museum in a new Neo-Classical building by James Cummings Wynnes, whose original plans were only partially completed, due to financial constraints, when the museum opened in the Botanic Gardens in 1929.

In 1961 the Belfast Museum and Art Gallery, as the institution was then known, was transferred from the jurisdiction of the Belfast Corporation to a new Board of Trustees, becoming the Ulster Museum, a national institution. The collections had continued to expand to such an extent that the government undertook to complete the 1929 building. An architectural competition was staged, and the winning entry, Francis Pym's modern poured concrete extension, was opened in 1972.

The Ulster Museum houses an immense array of material including a nationally and internationally significant collection of fine and applied art from the seventeenth century to the contemporary. The history collections include Irish archaeology and historical material from earliest times to the present day, collections from Egyptian and Classical cultures, treasures from the *Armada*, and ethnography. The natural sciences are represented by geology, botany, and zoology. Exhibitions and gallery displays are continually changed to provide the visitor with an insight into the diversity and importance of the collections. **Kim Mawhinney**

National Museums and Galleries of Northern Ireland (MAGNI). In the 1970s the Ulster Museum took responsibility for Armagh County Museum, then the only other public museum in the province. Finally, in 1998, an amalgamation took place as the National MUSEUMS AND GALLERIES of Northern Ireland (MAGNI), uniting the Ulster Museum, Ulster Folk and Transport Museum at Cultra, ULSTER-AMERICAN FOLK PARK, near Omagh, and Armagh County Museum under a single board of trustees and one chief executive. A recent development has been the Odyssey Centre at Queen's Quay, Belfast, now known as Whowhatwherewhenwhy or 'W5'. **Martyn Anglesea**

Ulster Orchestra. Formed in 1966 and amalgamated with the BBC NORTHERN IRELAND ORCHESTRA in 1981. One of the most successful and distinguished orchestras in the UK, its chief conductors have included BRYDEN THOMSON, Vernon Handley, Yan Pascal Tortelier, Dmitri Sitkovetsky and, from 2001, Thierry Fischer. It performs regularly at Belfast's Waterfront Hall and at QUB, and throughout Ireland, and since 1979 has recorded extensively, including the works of HARTY. It broadcasts a twelve-week schedule per year for BBC Radio 3 and Radio Ulster, and has a wide-ranging programme of international touring. **Richard Pine**

Ulster Railway. Under an act of 3 March 1836 the Ulster Railway Company was granted powers to build a 58 km (36-mile) line from Belfast to Armagh. Construction, to a gauge of 1.88 m (6 ft 2 in.), began the following year, and the first section, from Belfast to Lisburn, was opened on 12 August 1839. Seagoe, a mile outside Portadown, was reached in 1842, by which time authority for the Portadown–Armagh section had lapsed and a new act was required, obtained in 1845. By this time the Dublin and Drogheda Railway, which planned to link with the Ulster Railway on a through route to Belfast, was laying rails to a gauge of 1.57 m (5 ft 2 in.), leading to a dispute that eventually produced the Irish standard gauge.

The first passenger train reached Armagh on 1 March 1848, and the line was subsequently extended to Clones via Monaghan, with the company contributing to the cost of the Clones–Cavan line. A line from Portadown to Omagh and connecting there with the Londonderry and Enniskillen Railway opened in 1861, thus establishing a through-link between Belfast and Derry. On 1 April 1876 the Ulster Railway became part of the Great Northern Railway (Ireland). **Bernard Share**

Ulster Scots dialect, a dialect of English. When O'Neill and O'Donnell took ship in 1607 for Rome and Spain, James I planted the lands they had abandoned with Scots and English. The language of the descendants of the Scots planters is often confused with northern Hiberno English, which is a mixture of Irish and English or Irish and Scots. Ulster Scots is of an even more archaic kind than the language spoken in Scotland itself. It is still to be heard in parts of the Ards Peninsula, Co. Down, in a strip that runs up the east coast of Co. Antrim and, with the exception of Rathlin Island, in the north-eastern glens from Ballycastle to just north of Carnlough, where northern Hiberno English is spoken, and follows the coast to east Donegal's Laggan area. The following is part of a conversation recorded near Cullybackey, in west Antrim, in the 1960s:

> The next thang [thing] A knowed ma yann [one] fit [foot] slapped [slipped] ann [in] behann the athar yann an doon A went aan ma groof [belly] ann the coo [cow] shairn [shit]. That wasnae aa. Wheen A spraaghled [sprawled] aboot traayin tae get up, shae [shoe] nor fit cud A putt undher me. At laast A gaut on ma baakside an airsed ower tae A gaut o haul [hold] o yann o thos pailin posts forninst the laant [flax] dam. A was chaakin [shaking] wae the coul, and claaried [smeared] wae coo dung frae heel tae thraaple [throat]. A thoght [thought] Raab wud navver come. At last A hard his wheeple [whistle] ann the whuns [whins, furze]. 'Jammie, is thaat you?' Sez aai: 'Whaa dae ye think it wud be? A hae broke ma leg.' 'Naw,' sez he. 'Is the whusky aa raght?'

Diarmaid Ó Muirithe

Ulster Transport Authority. In 1948, with the RAILWAYS in a parlous state, the Northern Ireland government created a state-owned body to take over the assets of the Northern Ireland Road

Transport Board, the Belfast and County Down Railway, and the Northern Counties Committee of the London, Midland and Scottish Railway. This involved acquiring some 550 km (340 miles) of railway, ninety LOCOMOTIVES, 440 carriages, 3,000 wagons, 998 buses, and 924 lorries. The authority was inhibited from acquiring the assets of the four systems then operating on both sides of the BORDER.

From the start the new body was oriented towards road transport, a position strengthened by the Benson Report (1962), which saw no need for rail services, with the exception of the Belfast commuter lines and the cross-border route of the Great Northern Railway. By then wholesale closures had already taken place, including the entire Belfast and County Down Railway, with the exception of the Bangor line.

In 1953 the UTA was represented on the board set up jointly by the Dublin and Belfast governments to rescue the GNR from financial disaster, and when its assets were split in 1958 between the two state transport companies the UTA acquired 280 route-km and a quantity of rolling stock, including eighty-three locomotives. The Benson Report prompted a review of inland transport as a whole, leading to the establishment of the Northern Ireland Transport Commission. This new body was to take over the UTA's rail assets, while new undertakings were to be responsible for road passenger and road freight services. The railways, in spite of some expenditure on new diesel engines, continued to be run down, with the entire Portadown–Derry main line closing in 1965, against strong local opposition. All rail freight services were also withdrawn. New Transport Acts of 1966 and 1967 created two separate limited companies, NORTHERN IRELAND RAILWAYS and Ulsterbus; these, together with the UTA, became subsidiaries of the Northern Ireland Transport Holding Company. By this time, however, the effects of the anti-rail bias that existed from government level downwards had decimated the system, while failing to effect the transfer of traffic to road services. **Bernard Share**

Ulster Unionist Convention (1892). Irish unionists had been somewhat embarrassed by the ferocity of their own supporters in Belfast during the summer of 1886. When the threat of HOME RULE loomed again during the general election campaign of 1892, northern unionists were determined to present their views in a dignified manner. On the plains of Stranmillis in Belfast a large temporary building was erected for the Ulster Unionist Convention, covering one acre and containing a third of an acre of glass in the roof. Special trains brought 12,000 delegates to the hall on Friday 17 June 1892; they entered the hall by twenty-eight doors and walked up eight aisles to take their numbered seats. Slogans around the hall included *Quis Separabit?* (Who will separate?), *Keep our noble Kingdom whole*, and, surprisingly, *Erin-go-Bragh*—the 1798 slogan *'Éirinn go brách'* (Ireland for ever). The CHURCH OF IRELAND Archbishop of Armagh began the proceedings by asking God to send down 'Thy Holy Spirit to guide our deliberations for the advancement of Thy Glory, the safety of the Throne, and the integrity of the Empire.' Then, led by a choir, all sang the versified Psalm 46, 'God is our refuge'. 'Men of the North—I say—We will not have Home Rule!' the Duke of Abercorn declared at the conclusion of his speech. When the meeting broke up, some 300,000 people came into the BOTANIC GARDENS to hear speeches from three different platforms. The organisers allowed no bands or PARADES, and the event passed off peacefully. **Jonathan Bardon**

Ulster Unionist Council (UUC). By the beginning of the twentieth century, northern unionists felt in need for their own organisation; and the party had been suffering desertions to T. W. Russell's land reform movement and the INDEPENDENT ORANGE ORDER. In December 1904 it was agreed to create a council 'for bringing into line all Local Unionist Associations in the Province of Ulster, with a view to consistent and continuous political action.' Launched officially in March 1905 with 200 members, the UUC swiftly reinvigorated loyalism throughout the province. Party machinery was streamlined, and unionist associations were formed or reformed. Stronger links were forged with the ORANGE ORDER. The council's work was assisted by the resolution of the land question, talk of 'devolution' among members of the government, and the Liberal landslide of 1906. By the time HOME RULE had moved to centre stage again in 1912 the UUC was ready to put into effect an ambitious programme of resistance to all plans to set up a Dublin parliament. The council was enlarged five times between 1911 and 1944, by which time it had become unwieldy. Despite some changes in 1946, it eventually had 1,000 members, with 300 on the standing committee. By the end of the century membership had been reduced to 600. Normally this governing body of the ULSTER UNIONIST PARTY meets once a year to elect the party leader and officers, but additional meetings became more frequent after the BELFAST AGREEMENT (1998) (see p. 1077). **Jonathan Bardon**

Ulster Unionist Party (UUP), Northern Ireland's largest party. It has its origins in the ULSTER UNIONIST COUNCIL, its ruling body, which was formed in 1905 as a cross-class alliance to galvanise Protestant opposition to HOME RULE. An amalgam of local constituency associations, members of Parliament, and ORANGE delegates, it was led by Sir EDWARD CARSON, 1911–21, and JAMES CRAIG, Northern Ireland's first Prime Minister, 1921–40. From 1921 to 1972 the Unionist Party provided the government of Northern Ireland with up to forty of the fifty-two seats in the STORMONT House of Commons; but in the late 1960s it split irreparably over TERENCE O'NEILL's reformist policy, losing support to the centrist ALLIANCE PARTY and right-wing DEMOCRATIC UNIONIST PARTY. DIRECT RULE (1972) and the subsequent SUNNINGDALE AGREEMENT (1973) further divided the party into those who followed BRIAN FAULKNER into the 1974 power-sharing experiment and those who favoured majority rule or objected to the proposed Council of Ireland.

In January 1974 the Ulster Unionist Council rejected Faulkner's leadership, his successor, Harry West, joining with the DUP and VANGUARD to help overthrow the Executive in May 1974. Under JAMES MOLYNEUX's leadership after 1979 the UUP adopted a more pragmatic, even integrationist, stance, securing extra Northern Ireland seats while retaining its electoral ascendancy over the DUP. It opposed the ANGLO-IRISH AGREEMENT (1985), forcing a series of by-elections in protest. While sceptical of the Hume-Adams initiative of 1993–4, it did not reject the DOWNING STREET DECLARATION (1993). Molyneux was replaced in 1995 by DAVID TRIMBLE, a perceived hard-liner, who led his party into the multi-party talks resulting in the BELFAST AGREEMENT (1998). The UUP executive endorsed the agreement by fifty-five votes to twenty-three, though Trimble, as Northern Ireland's First Minister, faced continuing opposition. **Eamon Phoenix**

Ulster Volunteer Force (UVF) (1913–20), a paramilitary organisation set up by the ULSTER UNIONIST COUNCIL in January 1913 to provide armed backing for their campaign against HOME RULE. With the help of many retired and reserve British army officers (Field-Marshal Earl Roberts lent his support) the UVF developed into a formidable body. Up to 100,000 men enlisted, and a complete command structure was set up, with every contingency

Ulster Volunteer Force. *Members of the Ulster Volunteers, the unionist paramilitary force, in training at a remote location in Ulster, 1914. [Getty Images/Hulton Archive]*

provided for. There was an intelligence branch and a transport committee, and the Ulster Women's Unionist Council recruited 40,000 women for nursing and other duties. A fund of over £1 million was raised to compensate wounded members or bereaved dependants. In April 1914 the organisation imported some 25,000 rifles and 3 million rounds of ammunition, bought in Germany, and by the early summer of 1914 it looked as if hostilities might occur between the Ulster Volunteers and the rival (though much less well-armed) nationalist IRISH VOLUNTEERS. But when war with Germany broke out in August 1914, both paramilitary bodies pledged themselves to support the British war effort. In Ulster, 30,000 Ulster Volunteers joined up almost *en masse* and in effect became the 36th (Ulster) Division, which suffered terrible casualties on the first day of the Battle of the Somme, 1 July 1916.

In July 1920 the UVF was briefly revived in the wake of serious public disorder in Belfast, but its personnel were mostly incorporated in a new part-time Special Constabulary. **Keith Jeffery**

Ulster Volunteer Force (UVF) (1966), a loyalist paramilitary organisation, invoking the name of the body originally set up in 1913, founded in 1966 at a time of Protestant working-class discontent with TERENCE O'NEILL's liberalising policies. In June 1966 a young Catholic was shot dead; the best-known UVF leader, Gusty Spence, was convicted of the crime. The organisation was estimated to have reached a strength of 1,500 by 1972, and during the mid-1970s it carried out a large number of sectarian assassinations, some committed by the dissident SHANKILL BUTCHERS. Other killings were perpetrated under the cover-name of the Protestant Action Force, including the shooting of three members of the MIAMI SHOWBAND in July 1975 (see p. 885). In the early 1980s the force was badly affected by informers, though ten years later a particularly violent dissident element emerged in the Portadown area, led by Billy Wright, who was later killed by an INLA gunman in the Maze Prison. One of the most notorious UVF attacks occurred in June 1994 when six Catholics were shot dead in a bar in Loughinisland, Co. Down, as they watched the Republic of Ireland team play in a World Cup SOCCER match. While a political wing, the Volunteer Political Party, emerged briefly in 1974, a more durable party associated with the UVF, the Progressive Unionist Party, was launched in 1978. In 1994 the PUP, led by Hugh Smyth, together with Gusty Spence, played a central role in brokering a ceasefire by the Combined Loyalist Military Command. **Keith Jeffery**

Ulster Workers' Council strike, a general strike that began on 14 May 1974 in protest against the power-sharing Executive and the proposed Council of Ireland contained in the 'SUNNINGDALE AGREEMENT' of December 1973. The UWC, a co-ordinating body composed of loyalist politicians and paramilitaries, shrewdly concentrated its attention on restricting electricity production, though with widespread intimidation it also closed down most industrial concerns. Over the fourteen days of the strike electricity output was reduced to 10 per cent of normal, and at times there were twelve-hour power cuts. The government examined various possibilities to counter the action, but the British army concluded that it could not run the main power station without the co-operation of the civilian control room operators, who threatened to withdraw if the army came in. After ten days the telephone system began to break down as the GPO's stand-by generators ran out of butane. A wild idea to take power from a nuclear submarine moored in Belfast Lough was dismissed as impractical. When the army finally took over oil depots during the weekend of 26–27 May and began distributing fuel, the UWC threatened a complete electricity stoppage. To meet the real possibility of pumping-works shutting down and raw sewage spilling onto the streets, arrangements were made to organise decontamination squads. Since road haulage was at a standstill, the government also prepared plans for food distribution. But on 28 May the Executive resigned, and the strike was called off. **Keith Jeffery**

tUltach, An (1942–), a monthly literary magazine, founded by Lorcán Ó Muireadhaigh (1883–1941). Its principal aim was and is the promotion of a modern literature in Irish in Ulster. It has played an important role in developing and cultivating such a literature and in the development of LITERARY CRITICISM IN IRISH. **Dorothy Ní Uigín**

ultramontanism, the doctrine of central Papal supremacy. It had its origins in a movement within the Catholic Church, originating in France, promoting Papal authority over local episcopal jurisdiction, in opposition to Gallicanism. The term (from *ultra montes*, 'beyond the mountains', referring to the Alps, beyond which lay Rome) was applied to advocates of Papal infallibility, as defined by the First Vatican Council in 1870. Ultramontanists argued that only a centralised Papacy could protect and lead the church against oppressive civil laws and unorthodox theologies. PAUL CULLEN was the leading ultramontanist prelate in nineteenth-century Ireland. **Ciarán O'Carroll**

Ulysses, a novel by JAMES JOYCE, written in Trieste, Zürich and Paris between 1914 and 1921, serialised in the *Little Review*, 1918–20, and published by a small bookseller, Shakespeare and Company, Paris, in 1922. It was banned for obscenity in the United States and Britain until 1933. Set in Dublin on 16 June 1904, it tells the story of the relations between Stephen Dedalus (the autobiographical hero of A PORTRAIT OF THE ARTIST AS A YOUNG MAN), Leopold Bloom, and Bloom's wife, Molly. This 'modern epic' is a gentle parody of Homer's *Odyssey*: the traditional heroic qualities of Odysseus (Ulysses) are ironically transferred to the passive and pacifist Leopold Bloom, a newspaper advertisement canvasser who spends the day walking the streets. Bloom is of Jewish descent and is a marginalised figure in early twentieth-century Dublin. The first half of the story is told largely through a combination of conventional third-person narrative and innovative 'stream of consciousness', giving the reader access to the inner thoughts of Stephen and Bloom. In the second half of the book, where Bloom befriends

Stephen, this technique is replaced by an array of different styles, including those of a popular romance, a dramatic text, and an elaborate pastiche of the development of English prose styles. The novel returns to the 'stream of consciousness' technique in the final chapter, which is an explicit rendition of Molly's thoughts as she lies in bed at the end of the day—in which she has been unfaithful. The effect of this stylistic odyssey is to render as much of the modern world as possible while cataloguing the breakdown of literary forms. The unresolved crux of the novel is the state of the Blooms' marriage and their relationship with Stephen, who acts as a potential surrogate for their dead son.

Ulysses is now widely regarded as the most important novel of the twentieth century, radically transforming the genre, and one of the great artistic productions of modernism. Among the many qualities for which it has been praised are the sympathetic humanity with which it chronicles the intimate lives of its main characters, its liberal championing (unusual among modernist writing) of the 'ordinary man', its determination to map 1904 Dublin in meticulous detail, its commentary on the patriarchal, nationalist and imperial ideologies of the time, the virtuosity of its narrative techniques and the brilliance of its linguistic excess, its often ironic restatement of Western literary traditions, and its comic exuberance. [see BLOOMSDAY; GOGARTY, OLIVER ST JOHN; MARTELLO TOWER.] **John Nash**

underclass, a class beneath the usual social scale consisting of the most disadvantaged people. Perceptions that poverty has become more concentrated in urban local authority HOUSING, and has taken on a qualitatively different character, have led to concerns about the emergence of behaviour and values leading to a vicious circle of deprivation. However, poverty in Ireland is not concentrated in urban 'black spots'. Furthermore, the strikingly high poverty rate observed for such households is largely a consequence of low levels of EDUCATION and high levels of UNEMPLOYMENT and exclusion from the labour market. Housing policy has contributed to a process of 'residualisation', whereby those with the highest level of resources move out of social housing. The remaining residents are fatalistic, perceive little opportunity in the labour market, and see their localities as troubled by various expressions of anti-social behaviour. However, there is little evidence that this leads to kinds of behaviour that significantly exacerbate the existing difficulties. **Christopher T. Whelan**

Under-Secretary for Ireland, the principal administrative officer under the CHIEF SECRETARY, responsible for the routine workings of the Irish administration up to 1922. The post became more important under the ACT OF UNION (1800) because of the frequent absences of the CHIEF SECRETARY and the unification of the civil and military departments of his office in 1819. By the 1860s the position had become a CIVIL SERVICE rather than political appointment. Active Under-Secretaries, such as William Gregory, 1812–30, THOMAS DRUMMOND, 1835–40, and ANTONY MACDONNELL, 1902–8, had significant influence over policy. [see PHOENIX PARK MURDERS.] **Peter Gray**

undertakers, participants in an eighteenth-century system of political management (first referred to in 1695) by which the English-appointed LORD LIEUTENANT entrusted government business in Parliament to leading political magnates, who in return received preferment to high office, influence in policy-making, and disposal of patronage. Party factionalism overshadowed the developing system until the TORY collapse in 1714. Leading undertakers, including WILLIAM CONOLLY and HENRY BOYLE, governed as Lords Justices in

Ulster Workers' Council. *Escorted by the British Army, workers attempt to break the two-week strike called in protest at the Sunningdale Agreement, May 1974. The strike resulted in widespread power cuts and the breakdown of other services. [Belfast Telegraph Newspapers Ltd]*

the Lord Lieutenant's absence during the long recesses between two-yearly parliamentary sessions. The system was replaced after 1767 with that of direct management by a resident Lord Lieutenant. **Charles Ivar McGrath**

Undertones, the, rock group. Formed in Derry in 1974, the Undertones came to prominence through their classic debut single, 'Teenage Kicks' (1978). The song catapulted them from Derry to London and from there to wider success. Always the critics' favourites, the group received scant commercial reward; they split up in 1983 shortly after the release of *The Sin of Pride*, possibly their most fully formed album. Following the split the brothers Seán and Damian O'Neill formed THAT PETROL EMOTION, while Feargal Sharkey had a reasonably successful solo career. The Undertones (without Sharkey) re-formed in 2000. **Tony Clayton-Lea**

underwater archaeology, a modern sub-discipline of archaeology, the scientific study of those material remains of past cultures that are submerged in oceans, lakes, rivers, and estuaries, or any other body of water. Underwater archaeology was first developed in Ireland by amateur divers in the 1980s but in recent years has emerged as a highly specialised and fully professional discipline. Using a range of modern diving equipment and remote sensing devices, archaeologists have recently surveyed and excavated ancient ships and boats, CRANNÓGS and lake-dwellings, inter-tidal fish traps, riverine bridges, and other stone and wooden features associated with settlement, defence, economy and TRANSPORT on water. [see MARITIME ARCHAEOLOGY.] **Aidan O'Sullivan**

unemployment. Historically, unemployment has been a serious problem in Ireland. Even during relatively favourable economic conditions during the 1960s and 70s unemployment was higher in Ireland than in most other European countries. It soared during the recession of the 1980s, reaching over 17 per cent of the labour force in 1986. It fell somewhat during the brief employment boom of 1989–90 but increased again to almost 16 per cent in 1993. Since then the booming economy, which generated unprecedented EMPLOYMENT growth, meant that unemployment fell rapidly, to less than 5 per cent in 2000, with the result that Irish unemployment is now well below the European average, and the labour market is at near full-employment levels. Mass unemployment during the 1980s and early 90s was characterised by a high incidence of long-term unemployment (defined as unemployment for one year or more): in 1989, 65 per cent of the unemployed had been unemployed for one year or more, almost 10 per cent of the labour force, one of the highest rates of long-term unemployment in Europe. The long-term unemployed suffer particularly severe educational, skill and other labour market disadvantages, with the result that they have great difficulty in obtaining work. Nevertheless, long-term unemployment fell sharply in the last years of the twentieth century, to about 2.5 per cent of the labour force in 1999. Young people tend to suffer much higher rates of unemployment than adults, mainly because of the difficulty in gaining a foothold in the world of work. Unemployment among those aged under twenty-five rose to over 27 per cent of the young labour force in 1993 but fell back to single figures in the late 1990s. **Philip O'Connell**

unemployment training. The national training and employment authority is An Foras Áiseanna Saothar (FÁS), set up under the Labour Services Act (1987). It reports to the Minister for Enterprise, Trade and Employment. Its functions include training and retraining; recruitment and EMPLOYMENT schemes; placement and guidance services; assistance to community groups and workers' co-operatives; and advice to those leaving or returning to Ireland. Financed by the Irish state and the EU Community Support Framework, it was set up during a period of high unemployment. It has had to refocus its activities during the present period of low unemployment. It now aims to anticipate and provide training to meet skills shortages; to focus on those who are disadvantaged in the labour market, including those with poor educational qualifications, with disabilities or in long-term unemployment. Under the EU Employment Guidelines, every person under the age of twenty-five who has been six months on the live register of the unemployed is referred to FÁS, interviewed and offered employment or training (this is being extended to over-25s who are unemployed for up to twelve months). In 1998, 88,585 people completed FÁS courses, the majority of these (54,444) being involved in community employment schemes with a training component. Through training support schemes, FÁS also facilitated the training of 27,546 employees. FÁS has been criticised for its limited attempts to facilitate the re-integration of middle-aged married women into paid employment [see DISABILITY; DISCRIMINATION; NATIONAL WOMEN'S COUNCIL.] **Pat O'Connor**

uniforms: Air Corps. Apart from essential gear required for flying, Air Corps uniforms followed the army pattern until the introduction of a blue uniform for all ranks in 1997. In 1935 a light-blue dress uniform was made available for officers. In 1999 a mess dress for officers was introduced. Silver-grey rank insignia are worn on the cuffs and sleeves. **F. Glenn Thompson**

uniforms: Army. The origins of army uniforms lie in a report by the IRISH VOLUNTEERS in 1914 recommending a suitable green serge; and green has remained, with shade variations, to the present. In 1922 dark-green uniforms appeared in public, consisting of a soft cap, high-collared tunic, and breeches. Officers wore a lighter shade. The introduction of the Vickers helmet in 1928 gave a slightly German appearance. The Volunteer Force of 1934 wore greyish-green, based on the uniform of CASEMENT's Irish Brigade. A dress uniform was introduced between 1932 and 1935 for the Mounted Escort, bands, and officers of the various corps and services. The years of the SECOND WORLD WAR brought a British-pattern helmet and a lighter-green tunic with roll collar, and an open-necked tunic for officers. In 2000, camouflage uniforms were introduced.

In 1922 rank insignia were worn on the cuffs and caps in the form of coloured bands and diamonds, respectively. From the following year insignia were worn on the left arm, or on the shoulder straps by officers. In addition, general officers wore gold-lace bars on the collar; in 1924 these were replaced, and red stripes were introduced for other ranks. Officers wore bronze bars and diamonds set on coloured cloth mounts on the shoulder straps. General officers wore the same components but embroidered in gold thread on a scarlet base. Collar badges were introduced for the various corps and services; these were in silver for officers and brass for other ranks. The design of many of these badges has survived to the present day. In the 1950s a winged chevron was introduced, and this gave way to a revised table of insignia. The bar was replaced by a diamond, and commandants and colonels received crossed swords. General officers received gold-embroidered crossed swords on a scarlet base.

Over the years numerous medals with their corresponding ribbons have been awarded to members of the DEFENCE FORCES, for gallantry, merit, Emergency service (1940–46), and latterly for service with the UNITED NATIONS. **F. Glenn Thompson**

uniforms: Garda Síochána. Dark-blue was associated with Garda uniforms until 1992, when all ranks received a lighter shade, almost identical to the officer's pattern. A distinctive black mess dress was made available for officers in the 1920s. Helmets with metal fittings were replaced with peaked caps in 1957. Rank insignia are now worn on shoulder straps by all ranks. **F. Glenn Thompson**

uniforms: Naval Service. The navy-blue uniforms of the Naval Service follow the general pattern worn by the majority of the world's navies. Rank insignia are worn on the cuffs by officers and senior ratings and on the sleeve by other ranks. A formal dark-blue mess dress for officers, consisting of a cap, mess jacket, trousers, and white waistcoat, is worn when the occasion requires. **F. Glenn Thompson**

unionism. While a desire to maintain the Union of 1801 existed for much of the nineteenth century, unionism really came together in the first two HOME RULE crises. In 1891 southern unionists formed the Irish Unionist Alliance, while in 1892 the Ulster Convention foreshadowed the creation of the ULSTER UNIONIST COUNCIL in 1904–5. The council, which brought together unionist associations and clubs with the ORANGE Institution, organised opposition to the third Home Rule Bill under the leadership of Sir EDWARD CARSON and Sir JAMES CRAIG between 1912 and 1914. In 1916 the council conceded that any exclusion from a Dublin parliament would be on the basis of the six counties of Antrim, Armagh, Derry, Down, Fermanagh, and Tyrone. By 1919–20 Craig and other unionist leaders concluded that the best they could achieve was the creation of a six-county Northern Ireland with a home rule parliament in Belfast, at the cost of sacrificing unionists elsewhere in Ireland. Under Craig's premiership, 1921–40, unionism dominated Northern Ireland's political life. It attracted the support of the bulk of the Protestant population, but it was always a broad coalition of interests, and there were regular challenges from independent unionists, such as Tommy Henderson, the long-serving MP for Shankill. Northern Ireland's role in the SECOND WORLD WAR meant that the two decades after 1945 saw unionism

unionism in independent Ireland. *Orangemen commemorate the twelfth of July at Rossnowlagh, Co. Donegal. Contingents from Cos. Donegal, Cavan, Monaghan and Leitrim join those from other counties of Ulster in the only 'Twelfth' march in the Republic. [Colman Doyle]*

at its strongest. The ULSTER UNIONIST PARTY remained almost exclusively Protestant, strongly aligned with the Orange Institution.

Under the leadership of TERENCE O'NEILL from 1963, attempts were made to change the tone, if not the substance, of unionist politics by reaching out to the Catholic community. But his meetings with the TAOISEACH, SEÁN LEMASS, in 1965 provoked critics within the party. By 1966 Rev. IAN PAISLEY was also becoming a vocal public critic. O'Neill's response to the CIVIL RIGHTS MOVEMENT in 1968 brought to the surface tensions simmering within unionism, notably with his two key ministers, WILLIAM CRAIG and BRIAN FAULKNER. When an election was called for 24 February 1969, unionism split into pro and anti-O'Neill factions. The results were unsatisfactory from O'Neill's viewpoint, and he was strongly challenged in his constituency of Bannside by Ian Paisley. On 28 April 1969 he resigned, to be succeeded by JAMES CHICHESTER-CLARK.

Chichester-Clark attempted to steer unionism through the challenges of the breakdown in public order in August 1969, but his standing in the Protestant community never really survived the policing recommendations of the HUNT COMMITTEE. In March 1971, faced with a deteriorating security situation, he resigned.

His successor, Brian Faulkner, brought with him a reputation as a moderniser who had introduced new industries in the 1960s. Unionists also looked to him as someone who had confronted the IRA campaign of 1956–62; but his introduction of INTERNMENT in August 1971 proved disastrous. In March 1972 the British government suspended the Northern Ireland Parliament, in effect ending unionism's five decades of exclusive power. By then, unionism had fractured. In September 1971 Paisley and Desmond Boal formed the Democratic Unionist Party, which proved to be a durable challenger to established unionism. In 1972 William Craig formed Ulster VANGUARD, a right-wing unionist grouping that organised strikes and rallies against direct rule. In December 1973 Faulkner agreed to the SUNNINGDALE SETTLEMENT, but this was rejected by the Ulster Unionist Council, and the new assembly fell in the face of the ULSTER WORKERS' COUNCIL STRIKE. Faulkner formed the short-lived Unionist Party of Northern Ireland, and the leadership of the Ulster Unionist Party was assumed by Harry West. The initiative steadily passed to JAMES MOLYNEAUX, MP for South Antrim, who was strongly supported by the former Conservative politician Enoch Powell, now Unionist MP for South Down. Molyneaux became leader in 1979 and steadily rebuilt the party. The ANGLO-IRISH AGREEMENT of 1985 came as a bitter blow to unionists of all shades, and for a time Molyneaux and Paisley seemed to form a united front against it.

In September 1995 the Ulster Unionist Party elected DAVID TRIMBLE to succeed Molyneaux. Trimble led his party into the negotiations that culminated in the BELFAST AGREEMENT of 10 April 1998. But important members of his party, including Jeffrey Donaldson, who had been part of the negotiating team, did not follow him. Trimble held his ground in a series of closely contested meetings of his party's executive and council. The Democratic Unionists and Robert McCartney's United Kingdom Unionist Party were also strongly opposed to the agreement, further emphasising the divided views of unionism. In the elections for the new NORTHERN IRELAND ASSEMBLY, Trimble's Ulster Unionists won twenty-eight seats, while the Progressive Unionist Party, which also supported the agreement, secured two. The Democratic Unionists won twenty, the United Kingdom Unionists five, and independent unionists opposed to the agreement three. With some of Trimble's Assembly party known to be uncomfortable with the agreement, unionism as a political movement seemed split down the middle. [see SOUTHERN UNIONISM.] **T. G. Fraser**

unionism in independent Ireland. Southern ex-Unionists (predominantly Protestant) accepted the new Irish state while retaining pro-British attitudes; TRINITY COLLEGE, Dublin, flew the Union Jack and played 'God Save the King' on ceremonial occasions into the 1940s. In the 1920s proportional representation produced several independent ex-Unionist TDs; the COSGRAVE government nominated prominent ex-Unionists to the Senate in recognition of their social and economic importance but disregarded their protests at 'de-Anglicising' legislation. The rise of FIANNA FÁIL, whose economic nationalism incorporated sectarian populism, drove most ex-Unionists into FINE GAEL, though independent representatives in DÁIL ÉIREANN and local councils survived in border counties into the 1960s. The dwindling of unionist nostalgia is symbolised by the transformation of the IRISH TIMES from a predominantly Protestant and pro-British organ into a more broadly based liberal paper during the 1940s. After the demise of those brought up under the Union, SOUTHERN UNIONISM survived only among eccentrics and as a border offshoot of Ulster unionism. **Patrick Maume**

'Union of Líadain and Cuirither': see 'COMRAC LÍADAINE OCUS CHUIRITHER'.

United Arts Club, Upper Fitzwilliam Street, Dublin, one of the country's most venerable private cultural institutions. It was founded in 1907 by Ellie Duncan, later first curator of the Municipal Gallery of Modern Art. Among its early members were LADY GREGORY, CONSTANCE MARKIEVICZ, W. B. YEATS, JACK B. YEATS, as well as most of the principal intellectual figures of the period. Duncan hosted the first post-impressionist exhibition in Ireland (Roger Fry's pioneering 1910 London exhibition) at the club's premises in 1911, which showed, to a lacklustre public response, the works of van Gogh, Matisse, Cézanne, Gauguin, and others. The club continues to support the arts and in 1990 instituted the Markievicz Medal for excellence awarded annually to emerging young practitioners. **Brian Lalor**

United Irish League, founded by WILLIAM O'BRIEN in January 1898. It sought the ownership of their farms by tenants and the eclipse of factional divisions in national politics. The IRISH PARTY was reunited in 1900 but without the reform and rejuvenation that the league had sought. Land purchase was in effect completed by the Irish Land Act (1903) (the 'Wyndham Act'). O'Brien's support for conciliation with the former LANDLORD class led to his alienation from the movement he had founded, and the league's role was subsequently reduced to that of political machine for the parliamentary party. **Philip J. Bull**

United Irishmen, a society dedicated originally to the reform of the Irish constitution and later to republican revolution. The Society of United Irishmen was founded in Belfast in November 1791 by a small group of young radicals, most of them Protestant, including THEOBALD WOLFE TONE, WILLIAM DRENNAN, THOMAS RUSSELL, and Samuel McTier. It was dedicated to reform of the Irish constitution, including the granting of the franchise to Catholics. It soon spread to Dublin and remained an active though small part of political life until 1794, when, in a time of strong conservative reaction, it was banned. In response, the United Irishmen became a secret society, dedicated to republican revolution and independence, and appealed to a broad spectrum of Irish society—Presbyterians and Catholics in particular. Through Tone especially, the society established contact with revolutionary France; a French attempt at invasion failed in December 1796. United Irish leaders, including EDWARD FITZGERALD, initiated a rebellion in May 1798; the rebellion collapsed after a few weeks of fighting but resulted in the deaths of thousands, including Tone and Fitzgerald, and in the destruction of the movement. In subsequent generations the ideals of the United Irishmen would frequently be espoused by nationalists; the name itself would be used in a variety of organisations and publications, symbolising, as it did for many, a non-sectarian NATIONALISM that was very much the product of the late eighteenth century. **Daniel Gahan**

United Nations. The Republic of Ireland became a member of the United Nations in 1955. Three years later, in 1958, the DEFENCE FORCES provided troops in the form of unarmed observers to their first UN mission, UNOGIL in Lebanon. Since then the Defence Forces have had a continuous presence on UN peacekeeping missions. The main missions to which Ireland has contributed are ONUC (Congo, 1960–64), UNFICYP (Cyprus, 1964–), and UNIFIL (Lebanon, 1978–2001). However, during the 1990s Defence Forces peacekeepers served in many parts of the world. Since the 1980s Defence Forces personnel have served in Central America (Costa Rica, Honduras, El Salvador, Guatemala, and Nicaragua), Bosnia, Kosovo, Cambodia, Iran, Iraq, Afghanistan, Kuwait, Namibia, Western Sahara, Somalia, Haïti, and East Timor.

The extensive Irish participation in peacekeeping is regarded very positively both by the Government and by the Defence Forces, so much so that, in September 1993, when the Government restated the roles of the Defence Forces, it defined one of them as being 'to participate in United Nations missions in the cause of international peace.' Ireland's participation in peacekeeping operations has promoted a positive image of Ireland and its Defence Forces within the international community, at the United Nations, and among all sides in mission areas

Defence Forces service with the United Nations and UN-sponsored overseas missions. The following is a selection of some of the many missions to which the Defence Forces have contributed since 1958.

Congo, United Nations Mission in. The peacekeeping mission under the name Organisation des Nations Unies au Congo (ONUC), which began on 14 July 1960 and ended on 30 June 1964, was the first UN mission to which Ireland contributed military units. The objective was to bring peace and order to a huge country that had until recently been a Belgian colony and had been granted independence at short notice, without a credible infrastructure to sustain it. In the four years of ONUC a total of 6,191 Irish soldiers participated, of whom twenty-six lost their lives while on service. Despite the small size of the Defence Forces, Ireland contributed six infantry battalions, two infantry groups and two armoured units over the four-year period.

Cyprus, United Nations Force in. The United Nations Force in Cyprus (UNFICYP) was established with a mandate 'to use its best efforts to prevent a recurrence of fighting and as necessary, to contribute to the maintenance of a buffer zone between the lines of the Cypriot National Guard and Turkish Cypriot forces.' Ireland's involvement with UNFICYP began in 1964, when an infantry battalion was deployed with the force. Over the intervening years Irish soldiers have continued to serve with the mission in a variety of appointments. Irish commitment to UNFICYP has

United Nations. *Members of the 86th Infantry Battalion on review, the forty-third rotation of units to Lebanon since Irish involvement in the UNIFIL peacekeeping mission began in 1978. [Public Relations Section, Defence Forces, Ireland]*

been reduced in recent years in line with a UN reduction programme.

East Timor, United Nations Transitional Authority in. The bloodshed and widespread destruction in East Timor that followed the referendum on independence from Indonesia in August 1999 resulted in the establishment of the International Force, East Timor (INTERFET). This Australian-led force began operations in East Timor on 20 September 1999 with the aim of restoring peace and security. In February 2000 the mission was handed over to the United Nations Transitional Authority in East Timor (UNTAET). Since October 1999 the Defence Forces have contributed a platoon of troops to INTERFET and the UNTAET. The first two platoons were supplied from the Army Ranger Wing. The Irish platoon is attached to a New Zealand battalion near Suai on the south coast of East Timor.

Kosovo Force (KFOR). On 10 June 1999 the UN Security Council adopted resolution 1244, which authorised the establishment and deployment of an international security presence in Kosovo, an autonomous region in the Federal Republic of Yugoslavia. The force, KFOR, is structured around a substantial NATO core and is commanded by a NATO general. The Defence Forces contribute a transport company group of approximately 100 personnel to KFOR. The Irish unit's mission is to provide a general lift capability to the force.

Lebanon, United Nations Interim Force in. Following the Israeli invasion of Lebanon in 1978, the United Nations Interim Force in Lebanon (UNIFIL) was established to supervise the withdrawal of Israeli forces and to restore peace to the area. Following the final withdrawal of Israeli forces in May 2000 the UNIFIL mission has been reorganised and scaled down. In 2001 three contingents, the Irish, Finns, and Nepalese, withdrew from the mission in accordance with the UN's plans. During the twenty-three years with the mission the Defence Forces rotated an infantry battalion with UNIFIL every six months as well as providing approximately 100 personnel to UNIFIL headquarters in Naqura and the Force Mobile Reserve in Qana. Throughout its time in Lebanon the Irish battalion was headquartered in the vicinity of the village of Tibnin. During the time of the Israeli occupation the Irish battalion carried out its mission by means of checkpoints, observation posts, extensive patrolling, and maintaining a presence in many of the villages within its area of operations. The Irish battalion also provided humanitarian assistance to a variety of worthy causes, such as Tibnin Orphanage, and conducted medical clinics in local villages. The Defence Forces lost forty-seven of its personnel while serving with UNIFIL, and a permanent monument to them was left in Tibnin when the last Irish battalion withdrew at the end of 2001.

Somalia, United Nations Operations in. In August 1993 the Defence Forces sent troops to serve with the United Nations mission in Somalia (UNOSOM II). This was the first peace enforcement, as distinct from peacekeeping, mission to which Ireland contributed troops and required new legislation to allow for Irish troops to participate. The Defence Forces' contribution to the mission consisted of a transport company based in Baidoa and personnel in the force headquarters. During Ireland's involvement with the mission 177 personnel served with No. 1 and No. 2 Transport Companies.

Yugoslavia Stabilisation Force (SFOR). As a result of the Dayton Peace Agreement, concluding the war between Croatians,

Serbs and Muslims in the former Yugoslav republic of Bosnia-Herzegovina in 1995, a UN-sponsored NATO-led force, IFOR (Implementation Force), was established in December of that year. On 20 December 1996 authority was transferred from IFOR to another NATO-led force, SFOR (Stabilisation Force). Its mission was to deter hostilities, stabilise Bosnia-Herzegovina, and assist in the consolidation of peace. Since 1997 the Defence Forces have committed a military police component, consisting of fifty personnel, to this force. The Irish troops form the headquarters element and one of the platoons of the International Military Police Company at SFOR headquarters in Sarajevo. **Paul Connors**

United Nations force commanders. The Defence Forces have provided a number of commanders of UN peacekeeping forces.

Callaghan, Lieutenant-General William (1921–). Born in Co. Cork; commissioned in 1940. He served throughout the Southern Command and in 1971 took command of the 2nd Infantry Battalion, Dublin. In 1979 he was promoted to brigadier-general and in 1980 became Adjutant-General of the DEFENCE FORCES, with the rank of major-general. He served with the United Nations in Congo, Cyprus, and UNTSO. He was appointed force commander of UNIFIL in February 1981 and was promoted lieutenant-general. In 1986 he was appointed Chief of Staff of UNTSO; he completed his tour of duty in June 1987.

Mac Eoin, Lieutenant-General Seán (1910–1998). Born in Co. Louth; commissioned in the Infantry Corps in 1931. He commanded the 12th Infantry Battalion during the years of the SECOND WORLD WAR. He served as commandant of the Military College, 1957–60. In 1960 he was appointed Chief of Staff and in 1961 was the first Irish officer to be selected as a UN force commander when he took command of 20,000 soldiers in the Congo. He returned to Ireland in March 1962 and resumed the post of Chief of Staff.

Minehane, Major-General Michael (1933–). Born in Co. Cork; commissioned in the Infantry Corps in 1953. He commanded the 21st Infantry Battalion (FCA) in 1979 and served in a variety of appointments at Defence Forces headquarters. He was promoted brigadier-general in 1991 and appointed general officer commanding Southern Command. He served with the United Nations in the Congo and Cyprus, commanded the 51st Battalion in Lebanon in 1981, and served as a military adviser to the Irish delegation to the Conference on Security and Co-operation in Europe (CSCE) in Vienna in 1989. He was appointed force commander of the United Nations Force in Cyprus with the rank of major-general in 1992.

Quinn, Major-General James (1918–1982). Born in Roscrea, Co. Tipperary. He was commissioned in the Infantry Corps in 1939, and during the years of the SECOND WORLD WAR he served with the 12th Infantry Battalion. He was promoted colonel in 1959; he then served in the Military College, was director of training, and in 1972 was appointed officer commanding Curragh Command. He saw service with the United Nations in the Congo and Cyprus before being appointed assistant chief of staff in 1976. He was selected as commander of the United Nations Force in Cyprus six months later, a post he held until 1981.

Stapleton, Lieutenant-General David (1937–). Born in Clonmel, Co. Tipperary. He was commissioned in 1957 and held a variety of appointments in the Supply and Transport Corps. He graduated from the British army Staff College before being posted to the MILITARY COLLEGE. He was also first president of the Representative Association of Commissioned Officers in 1991. He was promoted major-general in 1995 as Quartermaster-General of the Defence Forces and in 1998 was appointed Chief of Staff, with the rank of lieutenant-general. His service overseas included the Congo, Middle East, Lebanon, and Namibia. In 1997 he was appointed commander of the UN Disengagement Observer Force (UNDOF) on the Golan Heights.

Vize, Major-General John (1942–). Born in Wicklow; commissioned in the Infantry Corps in 1962. He spent much of his career in the Curragh area and served in a variety of appointments, including the Cadet School and the 3rd Infantry Battalion. He was appointed commandant of the United Nations Training School on promotion to colonel in 1995 and was made a brigadier-general in 1998. His service abroad includes Cyprus, Lebanon, and Cambodia. He was selected as commander of the UN Mission in Kuwait, an appointment he took up in December 1999, with the rank of major-general. **Paul Connors**

United Nations Training School (Ireland), one of the constituent schools of the MILITARY COLLEGE, established in 1993. Its object is to study peacekeeping doctrine and to conduct training courses and seminars on peacekeeping in preparation for service with the United Nations, drawing on the experience gained by Irish peacekeeping soldiers in various parts of the world. The school also conducts courses for students from foreign armies. **Paul Connors**

United Nations Veterans' Association, Irish, founded in 1989 for Irish citizens adversely affected, physically or psychologically, by United Nations service; it also maintains a memorial to overseas dead. A registered charity, the association aims to provide an advice and counselling service and to encourage and assist research into members' problems and their treatment. **E. D. Doyle**

United States, the Irish in the. While popular legend holds that mass EMIGRATION from Ireland began with the GREAT FAMINE of the 1840s, large-scale emigration was under way as early as the 1720s. An estimated 200,000 Irish emigrants went to America in the eighteenth century, three-quarters of them Protestant. An estimated 14–17 per cent of the white population of the United States in 1790 was of Irish origin, most of them Ulster Presbyterians. Remarkably, of the 44 million Americans who claimed 'Irish' as an ethnicity in the US census of 1990, roughly half were Protestant, a figure that can be attributed mainly to early arrival.

The history of Irish America before the 1820s is that of a mainly Protestant group settled in Pennsylvania and the southern back country. At least 6 million Irish men, women and children crossed the Atlantic in the century thereafter, almost 1 million between 1815 and 1845, about 2 million between 1846 and 1855 alone, and 3.5 million in the post-famine era, 1856–1921. Because some 90 per cent of these emigrants were Catholic, the history of the American Irish has been told almost exclusively as a Catholic matter; the story of Protestant Irish-Americans, especially since 1800, remains largely untold.

The Irish-born population of the United States reached its peak in 1890 at 1.87 million. In that year there were also 2.92 million second-generation Irish-Americans (born in America but with one or both parents born in Ireland), making a total of 3.8 million. The second generation reached its highest level in 1900, at 3.37 million, though the Irish-born population had fallen to 1.6 million by this time, making a total of just under 5 million (500,000 greater than the entire POPULATION of Ireland at that time). Irish immigration thereafter was relatively slight, with peaks in the 1950s and 80s.

Labour and social mobility. Measured by the indices of almshouse admissions, disease, housing, and criminality, Irish immigrants in the period 1830–80 were the poorest and most disadvantaged social group in antebellum America, apart from Native Americans and African-Americans. Most Irish-American men worked as labourers and most women (among those who worked outside the home) as domestic servants or garment workers. Yet by the early twentieth century the occupational status of Irish-Americans matched the national average and greatly exceeded that of other recent immigrants. Irishmen of the second generation and beyond now worked disproportionately in the highly skilled, heavily unionised and better-paid trades. In heavy industries, such as iron, steel, and mining, they dominated blue-collar managerial posts, while the lowest-paid manual labour was carried out by newly arrived Slavs, Hungarians, and Italians. Even though the immigrant generation continued to cluster disproportionately in unskilled labour in 1900, the remainder of the twentieth century was marked by steadily increasing social mobility for the American Irish.

Not the least of the reasons for Irish-Americans' social advancement was their involvement in organised labour. Ostracised in the antebellum era by native-born labour leaders, the American Irish formed their own labourers' unions or adapted to American conditions the traditions of secrecy and violence they had known in Ireland, as with the 'MOLLY MAGUIRES'. By the last two decades of the nineteenth century, however, they had become significant participants in the American Trade Union movement. In 1900 Irish immigrants or their descendants held the presidency of more than 50 of the 110 unions in the American Federation of Labor, the most powerful labour federation. Irish-American influence in the labour movement reached its height in the middle of the twentieth century, just as that movement as a whole was reaching its own peak of historical power (see p. 569).

Politics. While organised labour was among the most important vehicles of Irish-American social advancement, the situation with regard to politics is less clear-cut. Irish-Americans' advancement in politics, especially at the municipal level, outstripped their socio-economic progress until at least the middle of the twentieth century. The Democratic Party actively courted the Irish from the 1830s onwards. By the early 1870s the Irish had taken over Tammany Hall, the Democratic political organisation in New York; and three powerful Irish political bosses, 'Honest John' Kelly, Richard 'Boss' Croker, and Charles Francis Murphy, controlled Tammany, and hence the city, with only minor interruptions from 1871 to 1924. The Irish also dominated politics in Brooklyn, BOSTON, CHICAGO, SAN FRANCISCO, Buffalo, Jersey City, Albany and Kansas City during this period. The political bosses were notorious for their corruption, dispensing favours in return for votes and in many instances taking full advantage of their position to amass a considerable fortune. The political machines paid people to vote; they registered and voted for all sorts of people who were not qualified; and they destroyed the ballots of their opponents. They used the Irish-dominated police force and gangs of 'plug-uglies' to prevent voters from entering the polling booths and to intimidate labour and socialist parties.

The success of the Irish machines rested on their ability to perform functions and to meet needs that were inadequately met by the existing social and political structure, especially in the realms of welfare and business. They gave material assistance to the needy in the form of cash and jobs, collecting their votes in return; they awarded contracts to utility and transport companies in return for bribes and campaign contributions; and they provided a sizeable pool of patronage jobs for their constituents. Whether the machines fostered upward social mobility is questionable. Non-Irish constituents were typically excluded from the more tangible benefits; and, even for the Irish, the jobs provided by the political machine (firefighters, police, and clerks) or by their corporate allies (mainly construction work) were typically working-class or lower middle-class, perpetuating existing patterns of largely blue-collar employment, rather than providing upward mobility. For several generations, however, the unique style of the Irish bosses, with their personal attention to each constituent's needs, countered or concealed these deficiencies. The art of city politics in the Irish style was perfected in New York by George Washington Plunkitt, in Boston by James Michael Curley, and in Chicago by Richard Daley, the last of the great city bosses. Daley's reign, from 1955 until his death in 1975, was very much an Indian summer, however, as a combination of New Deal welfare schemes and 'new ethnic' insurgency had undermined most of the machines in the 1930s. Tammany Hall was toppled in 1933 by a coalition led by Fiorello La Guardia.

It is fitting that a product of Tammany Hall, Alfred E. Smith, was the first Irish-American politician to break through on the national stage. After serving three terms as Governor of New York state he sought the Democratic nomination for the presidency in 1924, only to face virulent anti-Catholic opposition. He secured the nomination in the face of similar opposition in 1928 but was easily defeated by the Republican candidate, Herbert Hoover. Smith was the first Catholic to be nominated as a presidential candidate; the second, JOHN F. KENNEDY, would go on to win the presidency in 1960, laying to rest more than a century of anti-Irish bigotry (see p. 575).

Religion. The details of America's anti-Irish Catholic crusade—from Maria Monk and the burning of the Ursuline convent in Charlestown, Massachusetts, in 1834 to the conspiracy theories of Samuel F. B. Morse and the rise of the Know-Nothing Party in the 1850s—are well documented. What is less well understood is the extent of anti-Catholicism in the twentieth century. From the early nineteenth century to at least 1960, Catholicism was condemned as un-American, largely on the grounds of its hierarchical and authoritarian character. In the light of this discrimination it is hardly surprising that the Catholic Church became arguably the most important institution in Irish-American life. At the heart of every urban community lay the parish church, the one structure in America that immigrants from Ireland were sure to recognise.

The American Catholic Church grew rapidly in the nineteenth century, in line with massive Irish and German immigration; by 1850 it had become the largest Christian denomination in the United States. Dominated by the Irish, American Catholicism assumed an authoritarian and combative style that is exemplified by its pre-eminent leader in the middle of the nineteenth century, Archbishop John Hughes of New York. An emigrant from Co. Tyrone, he was a formidable anti-nativist polemicist and a staunch proponent of clerical authority and devotional orthodoxy. By 1900 two-thirds of American Catholic bishops were of Irish birth or descent, including those of the most important dioceses: New York, Baltimore, Boston, Philadelphia, Detroit, St Paul, and San Francisco. The first American cardinal was John McCloskey of New York, born in Brooklyn, who was selected in 1875; the next leader of American Catholicism was James Gibbons, who served as Archbishop of Baltimore from 1878 and as cardinal from 1886 until his death. Other influential Irish-American church leaders were Bishop John Ireland of St Paul, Minnesota, and Bishop John Keane of Richmond, both of them Irish-born and liberal, and their American-born conservative opponent, Michael Corrigan, who replaced McCloskey as Archbishop of New York in 1885. The liberals and conservatives engaged in a series of battles over such issues as education and labour, with Gibbons and the liberals generally emerging triumphant. By the end of the century, not only did the Irish control the church but Catholicism was the central ingredient of Irish-American identity.

During the Progressive Era (1900–17), Irish-American Catholic theologians were in the vanguard of social reform. Inspired by the Papal encyclical on social and labour questions, *Rerum Novarum* (1891), Monsignor John Ryan called for a variety of reforms to improve the conditions and wages of workers and to regulate the power of business. His position drew increasing attack from conservative Irish-American Catholics, however, one measure of which was the enormous popularity of FATHER CHARLES COUGHLIN, the 'radio priest', whose early calls for social justice descended into rabid anti-Semitism before he was finally silenced during the Second World War. In the meantime the New Deal had enacted a series of reforms broadly compatible with Ryan's vision of social justice.

The Catholic Church retained its powerful position at the heart of Irish-American history in the decades after the Second World War, though not to the extent of the previous century. Irish-Americans continued to dominate the upper echelons of the Catholic Church in the post-war era, the principal figure during the Cold War being the deeply conservative Cardinal Francis J. Spellman. Spellman's successors in New York were two more Irish-American conservatives, Terence Cooke, who became cardinal in 1969, and John O'Connor, who became cardinal in 1985. At the other end of the political spectrum were Cardinal Richard J. Cushing of Boston and Cardinal Timothy Manning. As late as 1970 more that half the American bishops and 34 per cent of priests had an Irish background, at a time when Americans of Irish descent made up less than 20 per cent of American Catholics.

John F. Kennedy's victory in 1960, combined with the liberal reforms of the Second Vatican Council (1962–5), led to much greater acceptance of Catholicism in the United States. The reforms alienated many Irish-American Catholics, however, mainly those to the right but some on the left as well. The ensuing crisis of religious identity was exacerbated by the impact of post-war suburbanisation, which undermined the inner-city parish and its system of parochial education. Then, in the 1980s and 90s, the teachings of the church on matters of sexuality and abortion alienated many young Irish-Americans, especially recent arrivals from Ireland. As in Ireland—if not to the same extent—the historical link between Irishness and Catholicism was coming into question. Combined with the effects of material success and suburbanisation, the result was a situation in which most Irish-Americans by the late twentieth century placed their primary emphasis clearly on the American rather than the Irish side of the hyphen. [see ARGENTINA; CANADA; CARIBBEAN; DISAPORA; MEXICO; SOUTHERN UNITED STATES.] **Kevin Kenny**

United States, the, Irish writing in. The tradition of Irish-American literature in the United States parallels the experience of the Irish in America. While Irish emigrants have crossed the Atlantic to the North American continent since the 1600s, the dominant legacy of the Irish in America dates from the GREAT FAMINE (1845–50). The prominent features of that migration—the transfer of millions of young Catholic men and women to the cities and developing industries of a society and culture that was predominantly Protestant and often hostile to the newcomers—is reflected in their literature. As the Irish Catholic community settled into the fabric of the United States, its progress can be tracked by what the writers within the culture chose to record and often what they ignored.

The first Irish-American writer of influence was Mary Anne Sadlier. An immigrant who made her way from Ireland to Montréal and thence to New York, she married into a publishing family, raised six children, and produced more than a dozen novels about Ireland and Irish America between 1850 and 1870, many of them serialised in the *Tablet* (New York) and *Pilot* (Boston). Her widely read novels read like advice manuals, warning unsuspecting, innocent immigrant women of the dangers of Protestant, capitalist America and its emphasis on money, status, and vanity. Virtually unknown in the twenty-first century, her work merits recognition as a record of daily immigrant life and an immigrant's perception of American culture in the nineteenth century.

As the twentieth century dawned and immigrants raised families and settled into American life, writers turned towards stories of assimilation, sacrifice, and compromise. The literature of the post-famine generations also reflects the expansion of the Irish beyond the East Coast. One of the more prominent writers of this era was Finley Peter Dunne, a journalist whose satirical column chronicling the life of Martin Dooley in the Bridgeport area of Chicago in the 1890s is notable for its vernacular and its voice from within the American Irish community as it converts itself from struggling working class to self-conscious respectability. Dunne captured the pattern of immigrant speech without patronising or ridicule. Dooley's working-class observations on American life exposed the irony in national political controversies as well as the tension within the immigrant community as the first-generation Irish stand aside for their more ambitious American children and grandchildren to climb the socio-economic ladder to middle-class respectability as teachers, bishops, lawyers, politicians, and entrepreneurs. According to some literary critics, this hard-won status in the first quarter of the twentieth century deflected writing within the Irish-American community away from self-examination. Writers such as F. Scott Fitzgerald and John O'Hara did not write about the Irish-American condition directly, but their tenuous status as new or marginal members of the middle class surfaced in their writing through themes of alienation and acceptance. It was not until the 1930s and later that Irish-American writers felt more comfortable exposing the fault lines of the Irish-American community. James T. Farrell's *Studs Lonigan* (1932), EUGENE O'NEILL's *Long Day's Journey into Night* (1941, first performed 1956) and Mary Curran Doyle's *The Parish and the Hill* (1948) drew on personal experience to expose the conflicts between traditional immigrant and Catholic culture and modern American society through the lens of the family. While nineteenth-century writers such as Sadlier lauded the family as a safe haven in a hostile world, twentieth-century writers present the family as both prison and cocoon, from which second and third-generation national minority cultures emerge, complete with contradictions and questions about Irish-American Catholic identity. The period following the Second World War produced works that dealt with the evolution of the American Irish as they became fully integrated into mainstream American culture.

From the nineteenth century onwards each succeeding generation dealt with its own issues of migration, whether from old country to new, from working class to middle class, or from city district to suburbs. With each transition there are losses and gains as the community moves further away from its immigrant heritage and its reliance on the church and on politics for power, recognition, and security. By 1960 the Irish-American community had achieved its pinnacle of political, religious and social success with the election of

JOHN F. KENNEDY to the White House. In the decades that followed, writers such as William Kennedy, Edwin O'Connor, Alice McDermott, Elizabeth Cullinan and Mary Gordon, among others, took the opportunity to look back to where they came from and take the measure of Irish-American identity and what remained of the core of its culture as the new century approached. **Linda Dowling Almeida**

United States Navy Air Arm. US naval air stations were established at Queenstown (Cobh), Whiddy Island, Co. Cork, Wexford and LOUGH FOYLE, Co. Derry, from early in 1918, manned by 3,000 personnel. Air operations from these stations began in September, and seven German submarines were attacked before the Armistice was agreed in November 1918. A US Navy kite-balloon station was also established at Bearhaven, Co. Cork, in 1918. **Donal MacCarron**

United States Presidents of Irish descent. Of the forty-two men who have held the office of President of the United States, at least thirteen had substantive Irish ancestry. (It has been suggested that at least eighteen had some Irish ancestry.) Many other European nationalities are represented in the genealogies of American presidents; but in proportion to Ireland's size, and even to the scale of Irish emigration to America, this is a pronounced over-representation. No fewer than eleven presidents had ancestral roots among the Ulster Presbyterians who emigrated in large numbers to America in the century before 1815.

Andrew Jackson, 1829–37. Conceived in Ireland but born in America in 1767. His ancestral homestead is at Boneybefore, near Carrickfergus, Co. Antrim (see p. 295).

James Knox Polk, 1845–9. His great-great-grandfather, Robert Pollock, or Polke, emigrated to Maryland in the 1680s from Co. Donegal (though his family held lands near Coleraine, Co. Antrim).

James Buchanan, 1857–61. His father, John Buchanan, emigrated from Rathmelton, Co. Donegal, to Pennsylvania in 1783. The family also held lands in Co. Tyrone, and the ancestral home is at Deroran, near Omagh.

Andrew Johnson, 1865–9. His grandfather, Andrew Johnson, emigrated to America from Mounthill, near Larne, Co. Antrim, c. 1750.

Ulysses Simpson Grant, 1869–77. His mother was the granddaughter of John Simpson, who emigrated to Pennsylvania from Ulster c. 1760. The ancestral home is at Dergenagh, near Dungannon, Co. Tyrone.

Chester Alan Arthur, 1881–5. He was the son of William Arthur, born at Dreen, near Cullybackey, Co. Antrim, in 1796, and emigrated to America in 1816.

Grover Cleveland, 1885–9, 1893–7. His maternal grandfather, Abner Neal, emigrated from Ulster to America during the 1820s.

Benjamin Harrison, 1889–93. His mother, Elizabeth Irwin, was descended from two great-grandfathers, James Irwin and William McDowell, who emigrated to America from Ulster during the first half of the eighteenth century.

William McKinley, 1897–1901. He was the great-great-grandson of James McKinley, who emigrated from Conagher, near Ballymoney, Co. Antrim, in 1743.

Theodore Roosevelt, 1901–9. His mother, Martha Bulloch, had Presbyterian and Huguenot ancestors who had emigrated from Larne, Co. Antrim, during the early eighteenth century.

Woodrow Wilson, 1913–21. His paternal grandfather, James Wilson, was born at Dergalt, near Strabane, Co. Tyrone, and emigrated to America in 1807.

US presidents of Irish descent. President Woodrow Wilson *(1917) by John Singer Sargent. This commission was proposed by Sir Hugh Lane as part of art-related war efforts. Following Lane's death, the Board of Guardians and Governors of the National Gallery of Ireland fulfilled the terms of his will, commissioning the portrait and paying £10,000 to the Red Cross. [National Gallery of Ireland]*

John Fitzgerald Kennedy, 1961–3. The president whose Irish roots were most celebrated by his fellow-Americans; his paternal great-grandfather, Patrick Kennedy, emigrated to Boston in 1848 from Dunganstown, Co. Wexford (see p. 575).

Ronald Reagan, 1981–9. Among his paternal great-great-grandparents may be Thomas O'Regan of Ballyporeen, Co. Tipperary. **Patrick Fitzgerald**

University College, Dublin (UCD), a college whose origins may be traced back to the CATHOLIC UNIVERSITY OF IRELAND, which opened in 1854 with John Henry Newman as rector. Its medical school in Cecilia Street made progress from the start. The management of its liberal arts school in St Stephen's Green was transferred to the Jesuits in 1883 and, under the name of University College, had remarkable success. Among its most famous students was JAMES JOYCE; several of his contemporaries became nation-builders of independent Ireland. The Irish Universities Act (1908) established the college as a constituent college of the National University of Ireland, and it soon became the largest university institution in the country. As a result of rapid expansion in numbers, accommodation in Cecilia Street, St Stephen's Green, and Earlsfort Terrace became cramped. In 1926 the transfer of the College of Science, with its buildings in Merrion Street, and the Albert Agricultural College in Glasnevin brought temporary alleviation of the problem. Because of chronic overcrowding and lack of proper facilities, in 1964 the college began moving to its new site at Belfield, Mount Merrion, now the largest university campus in Ireland. The Universities Act (1997) conferred independent university status on the college. **Dónal McCartney**

Untilled Field, The (1903), by GEORGE MOORE, a collection of stories about the state of Ireland. Six were published in Irish as *An tÚr-gort: Sgéalta* (1902)—an unwelcome contribution to the Irish language revival because of the book's anti-clericalism. A projected title, *Ruin and Weed,* captures its pessimistic thesis: anti-modernist Irish Catholicism is to blame for the country's emigration, desolation, and poverty. As an integrated set of stories, in a style of literary realism with a polemical thesis about the soul of a country, Moore's collection was evidently JOYCE's model for DUBLINERS. **Adrian Frazier**

'Urard mac Coisse's stratagem': see 'AIREC MENMAN URAIRD MAIC COISSE'.

urban government. The responsibility for urban government in the eighteenth century was shared by municipal corporations (where these existed), parish vestries, and manor courts. In most places these bodies were inactive, failing to provide even the most basic services, such as cleaning and lighting the streets. In 1828 towns lacking such services were empowered by act of Parliament to elect commissioners, whose powers to maintain and improve the local INFRASTRUCTURE were gradually increased as the century progressed. Municipal corporations, most of which were exclusive, self-perpetuating oligarchies, were abolished in 1840 in all but ten of the larger towns, where elected councils with limited powers were established. Under the LOCAL GOVERNMENT (IRELAND) ACT (1898) municipal corporations and town commissions were replaced by borough and urban district councils; under the Local Government Act (2001) the latter became town councils. **Virginia Crossman**

urbanisation. There is no universally accepted definition of a town. In addition, as towns often exceed their legal boundary, urban statistics must be interpreted cautiously. In the Republic the convention has been to define a town as a 'population cluster' of 1,500 people or more. In 1900 only 28 per cent of the POPULATION was urban; and although this increased steadily it was not until 1966 that more than 50 per cent lived in towns and cities. Urbanisation has continued; by the time of the 1966 census there were 2.108 million people in towns (58 per cent). This is a low figure by EU standards.

Most Irish towns are small: there are only seven urban areas with a population of 25,000 or more, twenty-one with 10,000 or more, twenty-nine with between 5,000 and 10,000, and twenty-seven with between 3,000 and 5,000, while forty-eight towns have a population between 1,500 and 3,000. In 1971 only ten towns had a population greater than 10,000. Ireland has a *primate urban system*—generally seen as undesirable—where the largest urban centre has a multiple of the population of the next-largest centre. The greater Dublin area had a population in 1996 of 952,692 (26 per cent of the population of the Republic), compared with Cork at 179,952 (5 per cent), which in turn was twice as large as Limerick (2 per cent).

Dublin contains more than 45 per cent of the urban population, but spatially much of Ireland remains rural. Only in the Dublin, mid-east and south-western regions is there a majority of urban dwellers, while in the border area, midlands and west more than two people in three are rural. The metropolitan area of Dublin includes towns such as Bray (26,215), Swords (30,989), Naas (18,312), Malahide (11,616), and Leixlip (15,143), bringing the population of the area to approximately 1.1 million—more than 30 per cent of the population of the Republic and more than 50 per cent of all town-dwellers. This region has suffered from a lack of strategic PLANNING since the 1970s; efforts have been made to reduce Dublin's dominance, but with limited success. Despite regional development policies, much new industry prefers the Dublin region. Government policy has concentrated on the decentralisation of the CIVIL SERVICE and, latterly, of the public service generally. At present about half of all civil service jobs are outside Dublin; further significant decentralisation, including that of state agencies and state-sponsored bodies, is planned.

The towns of Northern Ireland can be viewed as a distinct urban system; moreover, different definitions are used in the compiling of data. Belfast is the dominant city, with a population of approximately 279,000 in its built-up area and perhaps 730,000 in its regional hinterland—just over 46 per cent of the population (1991). It too is a primate city. The second city, Derry, has a population of 72,334 (1991). The BORDER has had the effect of limiting Derry's growth by cutting off its western hinterland and preventing it developing into the regional city for the north-west. Newtownabbey (57,103), Bangor (52,437) and Lisburn (42,110) come next in the hierarchy and, with Newtownards (24,301), Carrickfergus (22,885), and Antrim (20,878), form the main towns in the Belfast region. Important regional centres are Ballymena (28,717), Newry (22,975), Lurgan (21,905), Portadown (21,299), and Coleraine (20,721). At the last CENSUS there were six towns with a population greater than 25,000 (including Belfast), eighteen between 10,000 and 25,000, and twenty-eight between 2,500 and 10,000. **Joseph Brady**

urban origins and morphology. The oldest sites of urban development in Ireland are associated with Early Christian MONASTERIES or VIKING AGE seaports. In the eleventh and twelfth centuries some Early Christian monasteries became centres of learning and art, with administrative and economic functions; they represent the roots of such modern towns as Derry, Armagh, Downpatrick, Kells, Kildare, Cashel, and Tuam. In Armagh and Kells the monastic origin is reflected in the layout of the streets, which follow the circular alignment of the former monastic enclosures. The contemporary Viking towns served a trading network that reached as far east as Novgorod; they included Dublin, Wexford, Waterford, Cork, and Limerick, as well as smaller sites such as Arklow and Wicklow. It is possible to trace the layout of the Viking town in the present-day streets of Dublin around Castle Street and its extension, High Street.

The ANGLO-NORMAN conquest and colonisation in the second half of the twelfth century led to a century of new town foundations in those areas where the conquest was successful, which excluded the whole of the north-west. These towns were established as boroughs by the grant of a charter. Dublin received its first charter, modelled on the law of Bristol, in 1171. The majority of modern Irish towns have their origin in these medieval boroughs, with the greatest density in the east and south-east. As a result of archaeological research and documentary evidence, fifty-six boroughs have been identified for medieval Ireland. Some of these boroughs were superimposed on Early Christian monastic sites, and all the Viking towns were promoted to borough status; but most of the new foundations were established around feudal castles (such as those of Carrickfergus, Athlone, Trim, and Kilkenny), regional markets (such as Navan and Clonmel), or ports (such as Galway,

Youghal, and New Ross). These towns were laid out regularly, with the main street serving as the market-place. A stone wall with mural towers and gate-houses surrounded the new towns (see p. 336).

The English reconquest of Ireland in the sixteenth century was followed by the plantations, which initiated the founding of a large number of new towns, particularly in Ulster (see p. 877). These were regularly planned, with an open space in the centre, generally referred to as the Diamond. The eighteenth and early nineteenth-century landlords built a total of 750 estate towns and villages, such as Westport, as part of the improvements on their estates. In the nineteenth century a very small number of railway towns was established, such as Portadown, and resort towns, such as Bray.

The main changes in existing towns followed Catholic Emancipation in the early nineteenth century and the development of a Catholic quarter, consisting of the parish church, schools, and monastic buildings. In the second half of the twentieth century a number of satellite towns with purely residential functions were built around the cities of Dublin and Belfast. **Anngret Simms**

urban renewal. By the 1980s the inner suburbs of many cities suffered from problems of urban decay, having lost population and INDUSTRY to the suburbs, while the 'TROUBLES' in the North were an additional factor there. In the Republic it was recognised that state intervention was necessary, the result being the Urban Renewal Act (1986). Areas were designated in Dublin, Cork, Waterford, Limerick, and Galway within which tax incentives were available both to developers and to occupiers. By the end of the first scheme, in 1994, designated areas had been established in thirty-five towns. In addition to its designated areas, Dublin had two special projects. The Custom House Docks Development Authority was given wide-ranging planning powers and financial incentives to develop the docklands, especially as a centre for financial services; in 1996 the designated area was extended to both sides of the River Liffey east of Butt Bridge, an area of approximately 530 ha (1,300 acres), under a reconstituted Dublin Docklands Development Authority (see p. 525). The TEMPLE BAR area was designated in 1991 as a cultural, tourism and small-business quarter.

The second urban renewal scheme concentrated on areas where dereliction was most severe. Criticism of a lack of involvement by local communities and issues relating to the quality of some developments led to the introduction of 'integrated area plans' in the Urban Renewal Act (1998). These attempt to ensure a holistic approach, involving not only the built environment but also the social and economic impact of the schemes. By 1999 plans had been approved for forty-three urban areas, and an additional scheme, the Townscape Restoration Scheme, had been announced for smaller towns.

In Northern Ireland the Department of the Environment has responsibility for urban renewal through one of its divisions, the Urban Regeneration Group, and its regional offshoots. This has a wide remit and is responsible for the regeneration of Belfast, Derry, and regional towns (see p. 789). Efforts are concentrated on deprived areas and on the regeneration of vacant or underdeveloped land. HOUSING renewal is a priority, as is the renewal of town centres. Various policy initiatives are employed, particularly public-private partnerships. The Laganside Development Corporation was established in 1989 and is now redeveloping a 200 ha (500-acre) corridor along the River Lagan to provide housing, commercial and leisure activities. **Joseph Brady**

Ussher, (Perceval) Arland (1899–1980), essayist and critic. Born in London of an Irish family; educated at TCD and the University of Cambridge. He passed his subsequent life in Ireland. He published an English translation of MERRIMAN's *Cúirt an Mheán Oíche* ('THE MIDNIGHT COURT') in 1926, with a preface by W. B. YEATS. *The Face and Mind of Ireland* (1949) was an insightful study of the Irish *mentalité*, while *Three Great Irishmen* (1952) offered acute assessments of the work of SHAW, YEATS, and JOYCE. He dedicated his later life to philosophical and psychoanalytical reflection. **Terence Brown**

Ussher, Henry (1741–1790), meteorologist and astronomer. Born in Dublin; educated at TCD. As first Andrews professor of astronomy, Ussher was responsible for planning and equipping DUNSINK OBSERVATORY; he chose the site and paid particular attention to meteorological factors in the design of the Meridian Room, where transits of stars were observed using a 4-in. telescope by Jesse Ramsden and regulator clocks by John Arnold. In 1788 the fourteen-year-old FRANCIS BEAUFORT spent five months at Dunsink learning the elements of astronomy and meteorology. An important legacy of Ussher's tenure at Dunsink is a daily diary of systematic weather records from July 1786 to May 1790. **Ian Elliott**

Ussher, James (1581–1656), scholar and Church of Ireland Archbishop of Armagh. Born in Dublin; he was among the first students of TCD, 1591. He was professor of divinity at Trinity College, 1607–21, and vice-provost, but he declined the provostship. He proclaimed the Articles of the Church of Ireland in 1615. Bishop of Meath from 1621 to 1625, he was Archbishop of Armagh and Primate of All Ireland, 1625–56. A brilliant and meticulous scholar, he excelled in history, chronology, and theology. Described as a 'miracle of learning', he was a reluctant administrator and politician. Educated in the Ramist humanism (after the French follower of Copernicus, Petrus Ramus) of Trinity College, Dublin, he felt in constant threat of a Spanish-supported native rising. He used his scholarship as a weapon against the Catholic COUNTER-REFORMATION. He visited England regularly to carry out research in libraries, finally moving there in 1640. He corresponded with Catholics and Protestants throughout Europe and the East to discover, purchase, consult and copy books and manuscripts, and created a library of more than 10,000 volumes, now preserved in Trinity College. He was the earliest known Irish supporter of the Keplerian view of the universe; assisted by England's leading scholars, he employed modern astronomical knowledge of eclipses to calibrate his Biblical chronology, based on a literal interpretation of the Bible, and Scaliger's Universal Calendar (as corrected by Thomas Lydiat). His dating of the creation to 4004 BC became very popular. He resolved the Ignatian question and was a pioneer of the study of the early Irish church. Though a royalist and a believer in the Protestant episcopal structure of the church, he was close to Puritan views and was respected by all in British politics. His *Whole Works* were published by C. R. Elrington (1847–64), but numerous manuscripts are still unpublished. **Juan José Pérez-Camacho**

UVF: see ULSTER VOLUNTEER FORCE.

Valentine. *The casket below a side chapel altar in the Carmelite church, Aungier Street, Dublin, contains the remains of St Valentine, patron saint of lovers. [Denis Mortell]*

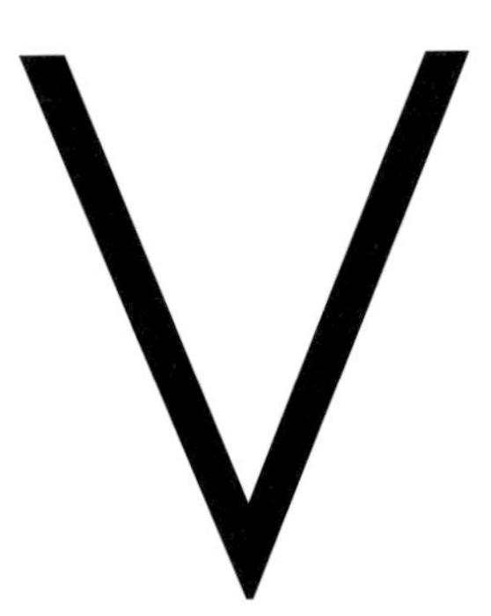

Valentine (died c. 269), saint and martyr. His feast day, 14 February, is popularly associated with lovers and the giving of cards and tokens; the tradition may derive from the Roman mid-February feast of the Lupercalia, and the date was believed in the Middle Ages to be the occasion on which birds mated. Two Valentines are listed in the Roman martyrology: a bishop of Terni and a priest martyred on the Flamian Way. Catholic Church authority favours the latter Valentine, whose relics were granted to Father John Spratt of Whitefriars' Street church (now the Carmelite church in Aungier Street), Dublin, by Pope Gregory XVI and transferred there in 1835. His remains are contained in a casket displayed beneath a side altar dedicated to the saint. **Brian Lalor**

Vallancey, Charles (1725–1812), engineer and antiquarian. Born probably in Flanders to an Anglo-French family; educated at Eton College, Windsor. He embarked on a career as an army engineer and cartographer. His earliest map was of Gibraltar (1750); his most celebrated is the military map of the south of Ireland (begun 1776) and the general map of Ireland (finished 1787, the year in which he also copied the DOWN SURVEY in a Paris library). His works include Queen's Bridge (Mellows Bridge), Dublin (1764–8), and improvements to the harbour defences in Cork, where he was stationed, 1790–96. A keen antiquarian, he was active in the Dublin Society and the ROYAL IRISH ACADEMY. His writings include translations of French engineering works and studies of antiquities and of Irish etymology (on which he had some fanciful ideas). He constantly complained about money and lack of promotion but was eventually appointed chief engineer of the Irish establishment (1794) and rose to the rank of general (1803). He was elected a fellow of the Royal Society, London, 1786. **Frederick O'Dwyer**

Vallely, Fintan (1949–), lecturer, flute player, songwriter, and writer. Born in Tullygarron, Co. Armagh. With music on both sides of his family, he started playing the whistle and later took up the flute and the pipes. He has recorded two albums of traditional flute music and in 1986 wrote and published the first manual for the Irish traditional flute. He is Ireland's leading theorist and writer on TRADITIONAL MUSIC, and his writings on the subject have been many, varied, and influential. Significant items he has written or edited are *The Blooming Meadows: The Soul of Traditional Music* (1998), *Crosbhealach an Cheoil: The Crossroads Conference Papers* (1999), and the encyclopaedic *Companion to Irish Music* (1999). Motivated by uninformed media reaction to the 'RIVERDANCE' phenomenon and to the television programmes 'River of Sound' and 'Bringing It All Back Home', he played a leading part in organising the conference Crosbhealach an Cheoil (1996), at which musicians and singers came together to debate change and continuity in traditional music, and articulated a broadly based practitioner's consensus on the nature and form of the music. He also writes in a lighter vein, his sense of humour finding expression in a satirical journal and in comic songs that tackle the various secular and sacred cows of Irish life. **Terry Moylan**

Vallely, J. B. [John Brian] (1943–), painter and musician. Born into a Co. Armagh family with strong cultural involvement in sport and language. He studied art in Belfast and Edinburgh and travelled in Spain, Morocco, France, and Italy. He took up the UILLEANN PIPES, studying the playing of WILLIE CLANCY, SÉAMUS ENNIS, and LEO ROWSOME, eventually setting up the ARMAGH PIPERS' CLUB in 1966. A prolific artist, his work depicts musicians, dancers, sports, and Celtic mythology. A forty-year retrospective presented by Armagh District Council in 2000 displayed his progression from myth and spirituality to engagement with music performance. His music themes chronicle the emergence of traditional music from the shadowy mid-twentieth century to the optimism of the revival years. His work appears in many publications, in particular *A Work of Art* (2000). **Fintan Vallely**

Vanbrugh String Quartet, founded in 1986 as quartet-in-residence at RTÉ. The players are also artists-in-residence at University College, Cork, and founded the West Cork Chamber Music Festival in 1996. The members of the quartet are Gregory Ellis and Keith Pascoe (violins), Simon Aspell (viola) and Christopher Marwood (cello). In 1988 they won the London International String Quartet Competition, and in 1995 they were awarded Ireland's National Entertainment Award for Classical Music. Their broad discography includes a critically acclaimed recording of the complete Beethoven quartets (1997). Their 1999 recordings of quartets by E. J. Moeran and John MacCabe were nominated for Gramophone Awards. **Emma Costello**

van der Hagen, William (fl. 1720–1745), landscape painter. Probably a member of a family of peripatetic painters, he began by painting coastal scenes and panoramic views in England. He travelled to Gibraltar and Messina and was first recorded in Dublin in September 1722, remaining there for the rest of his life. He painted scenery for SMOCK ALLEY THEATRE and altarpieces for St Michan's Church, Dublin, and St Patrick's Cathedral, Waterford. In 1728 he was commissioned to provide landscape designs for six tapestries for the Irish House of Lords, of which just two were executed. Well known for topographical views and architectural capricci, he was an important influence on subsequent generations of Irish landscape painters (see p. 29). [see PARLIAMENT HOUSE.] **Brendan Rooney**

van Dessel, Michael (1899–1974), organist. Born in Belgium; studied at the Malines Institute, from where he graduated with distinction in 1923. He came to Dundalk, Co. Louth, to take up the post of organist at ST PATRICK'S CATHEDRAL, which he held until his death. He was also musical director of the CYMS Musical Society and Dundalk Musical Society. An adjudicator in the FEIS CEOIL, 1944, he was examiner for the Department of Education music examinations, 1964–73. He founded the Dundalk Municipal Choir, 1966. He composed several Masses and other religious works, including *Missa in Honorem Mariae Virginis*, which in 1968 was broadcast by RTÉ throughout Europe. **Emma Costello**

Vaněček, Jaroslav (1920–), violinist. Born in Bratislava; studied violin at the Prague Conservatory. He enjoyed a successful solo career, travelling throughout Europe before coming to Ireland in 1948. He was professor of violin and viola at the RIAM. He also taught at the Municipal College of Music, Dublin, and established a school of violin at Belfast College of Music. More than any other single teacher, he is responsible for training a cadre of string players in Ireland whose sound was evident in the RTÉ Symphony Orchestra and The Irish and New IRISH CHAMBER ORCHESTRAS. In 1952 he returned to London and became professor of violin and viola at the Royal College of Music. He is recognised as one of Europe's most accomplished violinists, both as a soloist and as a teacher. **Emma Costello**

Vane-Tempest-Stewart, Charles S. H., seventh Marquis of Londonderry (1878–1949), politician. He was chairman of the standing committee of the ULSTER UNIONIST COUNCIL, 1912–14, and Minister for Aviation, 1919–21, but turned down a Cabinet post in London in 1921 to become the first Minister of Education in Belfast. 'Religious instruction in a denominational sense during the hours of compulsory attendance there will not be,' he declared as he steered his Education Bill (1923) through Parliament. His attempt to create integrated state elementary schools met with fierce criticism from both the Catholic and Protestant churches. When his act was amended to compel Bible teaching, he resigned in 1926. **Jonathan Bardon**

Vane-Tempest-Stewart, Edith, Marchioness of Londonderry (1878–1959), political activist. Born in Lincolnshire; in 1889 she married CHARLES VANE-TEMPEST-STEWART, Lord Castlereagh and later seventh Marquis of Londonderry. She was active in Conservative and Unionist politics as vice-president of the Ulster Women's Unionist Council, 1919–59, and president of the Women's Advisory Committee of the Northern Counties National Union of Conservative and Unionist Associations and of North Down and Newtownards Women's Unionist Association. During the FIRST WORLD WAR she led the Women's Volunteer Reserve, until she established the Women's Legion in 1915. Acknowledged as the last great Tory hostess, she ran a weekly political club from 1915 and from 1924 was a political confidante of Ramsay MacDonald. In the late 1930s she supported her husband in his attempts to improve relations between Britain and Nazi Germany. **Diane Urquhart**

Vanguard (1972–8), a pressure group within UNIONISM formed as 'Ulster Vanguard' in February 1972 by WILLIAM CRAIG, the former hard-line Minister of Home Affairs. It was dedicated to the preservation of the Northern Ireland Parliament, stronger measures against the IRA, and resistance to a united Ireland. Drawing strong support from the loyalist paramilitaries, it staged a series of rallies in 1972 at which Craig, complete with motorcycle escort provided by the paramilitary Vanguard Service Corps, reviewed men in military formation. Craig's remark at Ormeau Park, Belfast, that 'if the politicians fail, it will be our duty to liquidate the enemy' brought nationalist protests that Vanguard was a fascist movement. It held a massive protest meeting at STORMONT against the introduction of DIRECT RULE but lost support in May 1972 when it hinted at an independent Northern Ireland. In March 1973 it became a formal political party, the Vanguard Unionist Progressive Party, under Craig's leadership, securing 11 per cent of the vote and seven seats in the Assembly elections of that year. Vanguard rejected the SUNNINGDALE AGREEMENT but in the Northern Ireland Convention of 1975 split over Craig's idea of a voluntary coalition with the

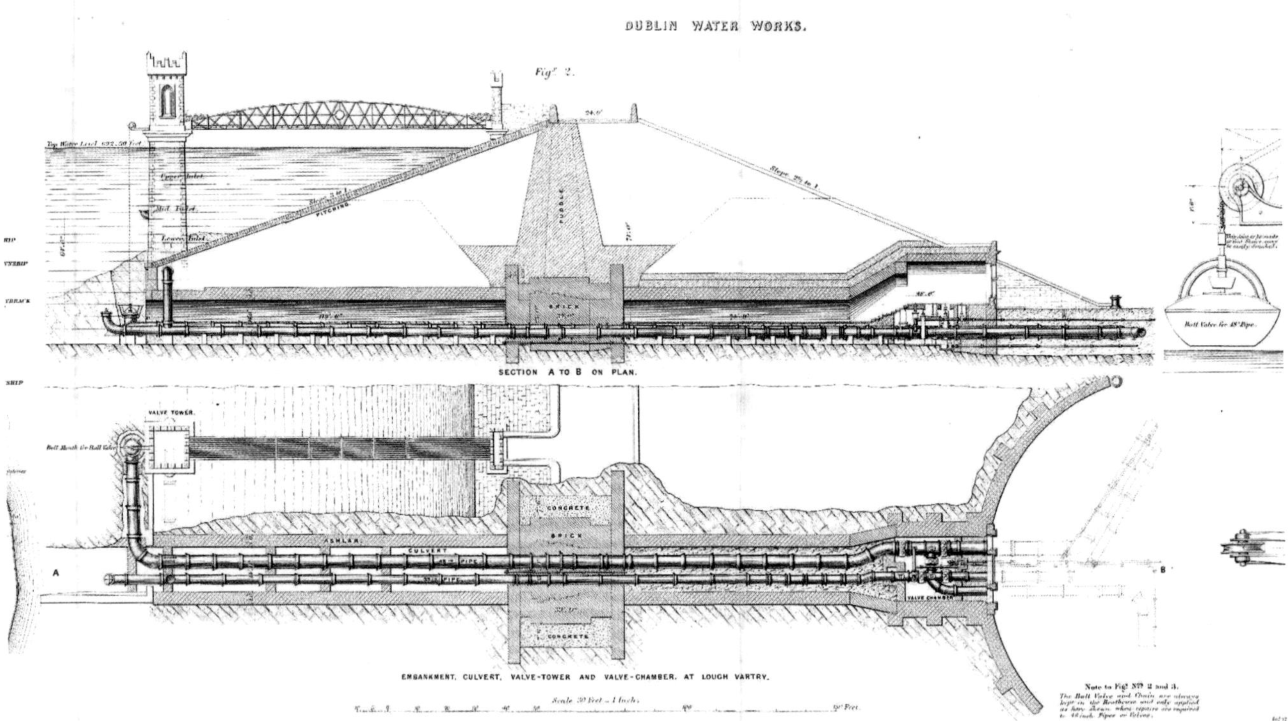

Vartry. *The plans of Dublin's first public water supply, Vartry Waterworks, completed on 15 July 1868; the entire city, together with the townships of Pembroke and Blackrock, was supplied with water from the Vartry River, Co. Wicklow. [Institution of Engineers of Ireland]*

SDLP, a majority of its members breaking away under Ernest Baird to form the United Ulster Unionist Movement. DAVID TRIMBLE, the future UUP leader, supported Craig's proposal. By 1978 Vanguard had dissolved, with Craig returning to the Ulster Unionist Party. **Eamon Phoenix**

Vanhomrigh, Esther (1688–1723), called 'Vanessa', JONATHAN SWIFT's companion. Born in Dublin, daughter of a merchant whose wealthy widow moved her family to London. She met Swift in London and fell in love with him; 'Vanessa' was his nickname for her. When Swift was given the deanery of ST PATRICK'S CATHEDRAL, Dublin, in 1713, she followed him to Ireland, settling on her father's estate at Celbridge, Co. Kildare. Her presence near Dublin was a source of embarrassment and almost led to his estrangement from ESTHER JOHNSON ('Stella'). The relationship between Swift and Vanessa is described by Swift in his poem 'Cadenus and Vanessa', which recounts the love and friendship between an ageing and reluctant dean and an eager young woman. She died of tuberculosis, leaving none of her substantial estate to Swift. Only after she died did Swift circulate his poem. **Ciarán Deane**

van Nost, John (the Elder) (c. 1660–1712), sculptor. Born in Mechelen, Belgium. Foreman to Arnold Quellin, 1653–86, he took over his business; his work shows the influence of the earlier Gibbons-Quellin style. He was the leading sculptor of the day, his earliest work in England dating from 1692. The most important surviving work commissioned from the firm is the equestrian statue of George I (1717) erected on Essex Bridge, Dublin, in 1722, which was a landmark in the city until it was removed in 1753; later erected in the garden of the Mansion House, Dawson Street, it was removed for storage following the destruction of other symbols of British rule. THOMAS BODKIN acquired it in 1937 for the Barber Institute, Birmingham, where it now stands. **Anne Kelly**

van Nost, John (the Younger) (c. 1712–1780), sculptor. Born in London, son of JOHN VAN NOST THE ELDER; apprenticed to Henry Scheemakers. He worked in Dublin from c. 1750. He created a series of plaster busts of classical writers, commissioned by MRS MARY DELANY and her husband, and taught at the Dublin Society's Figure Drawing School. The Guild of Weavers (Dublin) commissioned a statue of George II (1750, later destroyed) for their building in the Coombe; he also produced an equestrian statue of George II for Dublin Corporation (1758), erected in St Stephen's Green, which was destroyed by dynamite in 1937. He made the lead figures of Justice and Mars (1753) on the gateways of the Upper Yard, DUBLIN CASTLE, and a life-size statue of George III as a Roman emperor (1765), originally for the Royal Exchange and now in the NATIONAL GALLERY OF IRELAND. **Anne Kelly**

Vartry reservoirs. The first major public water supply to Dublin was provided by impounding the flow of the Vartry River near Roundwood, Co. Wicklow. The lower reservoir was formed in 1865 by the construction of an earthen dam 500 m (1,640 ft) long, with puddle-clay core, which carries the road between Roundwood and Wicklow along its crest. The water treatment works are below the lower dam. Treated water is conveyed first in a rock tunnel and thence by pipeline aqueduct to reservoirs at Stillorgan, Co. Dublin. An upper reservoir at Roundwood was completed in 1925. [see POLLAPHUCA RESERVOIR.] **Ronald Cox**

Vatican Council, Second (1962–5), the most recent of the General Councils of the Roman Catholic Church. It was called by Pope John XXIII in order to promote a process of '*aggiornamento*' or renewal in the church and to enable it to come to terms with the modern world and engage in dialogue with it after two centuries of bitter resistance to the forces unleashed by the French Revolution and the ENLIGHTENMENT. The principal achievement of the council was the theological shift of emphasis in its understanding of the nature of the church, from an emphasis on its hierarchical nature with the Pope at its apex to that of the 'people of God' as pilgrims on the move, all of whom have their own gifts to contribute to the church's mission. Other teachings of the council, such as the collegiality of the bishops and the greater participation of the laity in the church's liturgy, flow from this. Inevitably, after four centuries of an earlier Tridentine and static model of the church and a process of 'creeping infallibility' since the First Vatican Council (1869–70), there have been conflicts between those who regret the loss of the old certainties and the centralisation of power in the Vatican and those who wish to promote the new model. The papacy of John Paul II is likely to be seen in many respects as having encouraged the forces of reaction in the church and the increasing power of the Vatican relative to the bishops. At the conclusion of the Council in 1965 the Archbishop of Dublin, JOHN CHARLES MCQUAID, told Irish Catholics that the council would change little. Apart from liturgical reform and a greater awareness of Third World issues, the reforms have had limited impact. **Michael Hornsby-Smith**

Vaughan, James (Jimmy) (1964–), musician. Born in Dublin; educated at TCD, where he graduated with the Mahaffy Award for Composition, 1986, and studied piano with DOROTHY STOKES, with Norma Fisher, and at the Accademia di Santa Cecilia in Rome. Twice winner of the RTÉ MUSICIAN OF THE FUTURE competition, he taught piano at the University of Vienna, 1989–98. He was also assistant to the conductor of the Vienna State Opera. Since 1998 he has been assistant to Riccardo Muti at the Teatro alla Scala, Milan. He has travelled widely in his capacity as conductor's assistant and also as a freelance musician. He is probably best known in Ireland as accompanist to BERNADETTE GREEVY. **Emma Costello**

veto controversy, a decades-long dispute linked to the issue of CATHOLIC EMANCIPATION. It was hoped that by giving the British government the power to reject the appointment of Catholic prelates of whom it disapproved, emancipation would be more palatable to Protestant and parliamentary opinion. DANIEL O'CONNELL represented the views of the majority of Irish Catholics in his opposition to the veto. By the 1820s the veto had become a dead issue, and it was not part of the final emancipation terms. **Gary Owens**

viaducts. The relatively gentle topography of Ireland presented few problems for the RAILWAY-builders; but occasionally viaducts were required when crossing wider valleys and estuaries. The earliest stone arch viaduct is that at Balbriggan, Co. Dublin (1844), on the Dublin–Belfast line. Craigmore, Co. Down (1855), on the same line, is the highest in the country. Of special interest is the viaduct spanning the Boyne estuary near Drogheda (1855), which incorporates major bridge spans. A notable iron arch viaduct exists at Chetwynd (1851) near Cork, while concrete viaducts are to be found near Wellingtonbridge, Co. Wexford (1906), and at Bleach Green, Co. Antrim (1932). **Ronald Cox**

Vicar of Wakefield, The (1766), a novel by OLIVER GOLDSMITH. It is full of disguises, remarkable for its portrayal of a likeable, good character in the kindly vicar, whose unworldliness Goldsmith treats with gentle irony. Appalling misfortunes disrupt the idyllic pastoral contentment of the family's ordered Christian life, and Goldsmith holds our attention as his admirably told story moves through disaster, anti-climax, and even absurdity. Mini-comedies, such as Moses selling his horse for worthless spectacles, and the Vicar's wife's hopes for her daughters, blend with Goldsmith's eminently sensible philosophical reflections and perhaps his autobiographical experiences in the adventures of George Primrose. The novel ends very effectively with the vicar's faith in humanity tested and proved. **A. Norman Jeffares**

Viceroy: see LORD LIEUTENANT.

Victoria (1819–1901), Queen of Great Britain and Ireland and, from 1876, Empress of India. Born in London. She is sometimes known in Ireland as 'the Famine Queen', from having presided as monarch over the period of the GREAT FAMINE. She visited Ireland four times during her sixty-four-year reign: in 1849, when she landed at Cobh, Co. Cork, bestowing on the town the name Queenstown (which it retained until 1922); 1853, when she opened WILLIAM DARGAN's Irish Industrial Exhibition on Leinster Lawn, Dublin; 1861, when her visit to KILLARNEY contributed to the growth of the tourist industry; and 1900, on which occasion MAUDE GONNE and JAMES CONNOLLY organised a 'Patriotic Children's Treat' for 40,000 poor children, in opposition to the official celebration of the queen's visit in the PHOENIX PARK on the same day. JOHN HUGHES's Victoria monument (1907) at LEINSTER HOUSE was removed in 1948 (ostensibly to provide space for car parking), and the figure of Victoria (following fifty years in storage)

Victoria Cross. *The Victoria Cross awarded to Private William Coffey of Co. Limerick, 34th (Cumberland) Regiment of Foot (King's Own Royal Border Regiment). [Regimental Museum of The Border Regiment and The King's own Royal Border Regiment; photo: David Truesdale.]*

was re-erected in Bicentennial Plaza, Sydney, Australia, in 1998. [see INGHINIDHE NA HÉIREANN.] **Brian Lalor**

Victoria Cross. Britain's premier gallantry award, the Victoria Cross, was instituted by VICTORIA in 1856 (but made retrospective to 1854, when the CRIMEAN WAR began, to mark the gallantry of soldiers and sailors in that war). Charles Davis Lucas from Poyntzpass, Co. Armagh, won the first Victoria Cross when he threw a burning shell overboard from the *Hecla* during an operation in the Åland Islands, thereby saving many lives; he eventually became an admiral. Luke O'Connor, from Elphin, Co. Roscommon, won the British army's first Victoria Cross while serving with the 23rd Regiment (Royal Welch Fusiliers) at the Battle of the Alma, where, though wounded, he took charge of the regiment's colours. A sergeant at that time, O'Connor retired as a general.

Over the next eighty-nine years many more Irishmen were to win the Victoria Cross. Of 1,354 awarded (to 1,350 individuals, three of whom earned a bar, or second award, together with America's Unknown Warrior of the First World War), at least 218 were born in Ireland or of Irish parentage. Representing more than 16 per cent of all Victoria Crosses awarded, this figure is proportionately greater than for any other nation.

Irishmen won the first VCs of the twentieth century (John Barry, from Kilkenny), of the First World War (Maurice Dease, from Co. Meath), and of the Royal Air Force in the Second World War (Donald Garland, from Co. Wicklow), while the sons of Irish parents also provided the first Canadian-born VC (Alexander Dunn of the Light Brigade) and the first South African VC (Joseph Crowe, whose father was from Ballybay, Co. Monaghan). The last Irish recipient was James Magennis of Belfast, who was awarded it for placing mines on the hull of a Japanese cruiser off Singapore in July 1945. [see BRITISH EMPIRE, THE IRISH IN THE.] **Richard Doherty**

Victory. *Gerard Victory, composer and director of music at RTÉ, 1967–82. Composing in a broad range of musical genres, he has written pieces inspired by the lives and writings of such literary figures as Jonathan Swift, Thomas Hardy, William Blake, Oscar Wilde, and James Joyce. [RTÉ]*

Victory, Gerard (1921–1995), composer. Born in Dublin; educated at UCD and TCD. From 1948 he worked with RTÉ, where he held the post of director of music, 1967–82. He was president of UNESCO's International Rostrum of Composers, 1981–3. Awarded the Order of Arts and Letters by the French government and the Order of Merit by the German government (both 1975), he was one of the organisers of the DUBLIN FESTIVAL OF TWENTIETH-CENTURY MUSIC, 1970–84. He became interested in serial composition in the 1950s and 60s; he composed more than 200 works, including eight operas, four symphonies, two piano concertos, music for films and plays, and the cantata *Ultima Rerum*. **Emma Costello**

Vignoles, Charles Blacker (1793–1875), civil engineer. Born near Enniscorthy, Co. Wexford; educated privately under Charles Hutton. His early years were spent in the British army. From 1825 he was a civil engineer, working on railway and canal surveys, tunnels, and cast-iron BRIDGES. He designed and supervised the construction of the DUBLIN AND KINGSTOWN RAILWAY (opened 1834) and numerous other railways in Europe and South America, as well as the large suspension bridge across the Vistula at Kiev. He was professor of civil engineering at University College, London, 1841–3, was elected a fellow of the Royal Society (London), 1855, and was president of the Institution of Civil Engineers, 1870–71. **Ronald Cox**

Viking cemeteries, Islandbridge and Kilmainham, Dublin. Furnished graves offer the clearest archaeological evidence for the presence of VIKINGS in Ireland (see p. 333). Uncovered between 1846 and 1934, the finds from the Islandbridge and Kilmainham areas, west of Dublin, together constitute the largest collection of Viking grave-goods found outside Scandinavia, though few were archaeologically investigated. It is now known that these finds represent at least two separate burial grounds, one at the monastic site of Cill Mhaigneann (in the grounds of the ROYAL HOSPITAL, Kilmainham), another to the west of present-day Islandbridge. These cannot be viewed in isolation from smaller cemeteries from College Green (on the site of the Thingmote) and Parnell Square, along with some single-grave finds. Together these burials indicate a more dispersed Viking settlement in the Dublin area.

Male and female burials are represented, the former typically including a sword, spear, and shield, while female burials contained oval brooches and other personal ornaments. Much of the weaponry and the oval brooches were imports from Scandinavia; but Insular grave-goods (ringed pins, brooches and mounts) are also represented. Together the finds underline the essentially Norwegian character of the Dublin Vikings. Cremation and burial were both practised, and a minimum of forty (possibly as many as seventy) male and at least seven female graves are represented. The majority date from within a century of the foundation of Dublin in 841. **Raghnall Ó Floinn**

Vikings. The Vikings or Norsemen were invaders from Scandinavia who were active as raiders, traders, and settlers in the coastal areas of northern Europe and beyond from the ninth to the eleventh century. They travelled overseas in their longships and gained a reputation as fierce warriors. An initial phase of raiding was often followed by settlement, as happened in western Scotland, eastern England (the *Danelaw*), and Normandy. Small expeditions raided the Irish coast in the period 795–830. Their main targets were the rich MONASTERIES, where they looked for church treasures, tradable goods, livestock, provisions, and people to sell as slaves. In later decades larger expeditions were launched, against which the Irish kingdoms could scarcely defend themselves.

From the 840s onwards the Vikings established bases at favourable sites on the coast and on rivers and lakes. Of these, Dublin became the most important and developed into one of the most prosperous Viking settlements in the west. The leaders of the large Viking fleets of the 840s and 850s were regarded as kings by the Irish. One of them, Ívarr (died 873), was also active in Scotland and possibly England. He became the founding father of the dynasty that ruled Dublin until the eleventh century.

The Vikings at first caused considerable damage to economic, cultural and religious life, but with their settlement they became involved in Irish political and economic affairs. Their leaders intermarried with Irish royalty and served as mercenaries in the Irish struggles for power. They especially frustrated the ambitions of a number of kings and would-be kings of TARA in the ninth and tenth centuries, and incidentally speeded up the development of a new political order in Ireland. The Irish managed to expel the Dublin Vikings in 902, but the descendants of Ívarr returned in 914 and resettled Dublin in 917, after defeating the Irish. From there they launched their campaigns to conquer Northumbria and hold the kingship of York, while their compatriots plundered the Irish. This situation lasted until 952, when Northumbria was finally lost to them. Viking ambitions in Ireland were crushed in the battles of Tara in 980 and CLONTARF in 1014. From this time onwards the most powerful Irish kings were keen to exploit the economic and military resources of the Ostmen, to the point where controlling Dublin became tantamount to controlling Ireland. When the ANGLO-NORMANS came to Ireland in the late twelfth century they turned the former Viking settlements into their main harbours and strongholds.

The Viking contribution to Ireland was two-sided; their destruction and disruption is balanced by their economic contributions. A number of Viking settlements developed into the main towns of Ireland, including Dublin, Cork, and Limerick. The place-names *Waterford*, *Wexford*, *Carlingford,* and *Strangford* all contain the NORSE PLACE-NAME element *fjord*, while *Arklow* and *Wicklow* contain the element *ló*, meaning 'meadow' (see p. 1126). A number of Norse words, mainly connected with trade and seafaring, were borrowed into Irish, demonstrating their influence on the Irish in these matters. The archaeological record shows that Irish goods ended up in Scandinavia, while the Vikings left hoards with coins, ingots, jewellery, and other precious objects in Ireland, both of their own manufacture and brought from their raids elsewhere. Remains of their settlements, especially those in and around Dublin, have been extensively excavated (see p. 333). [see SCANDINAVIAN MUSEUMS.] **Bart Jaski**

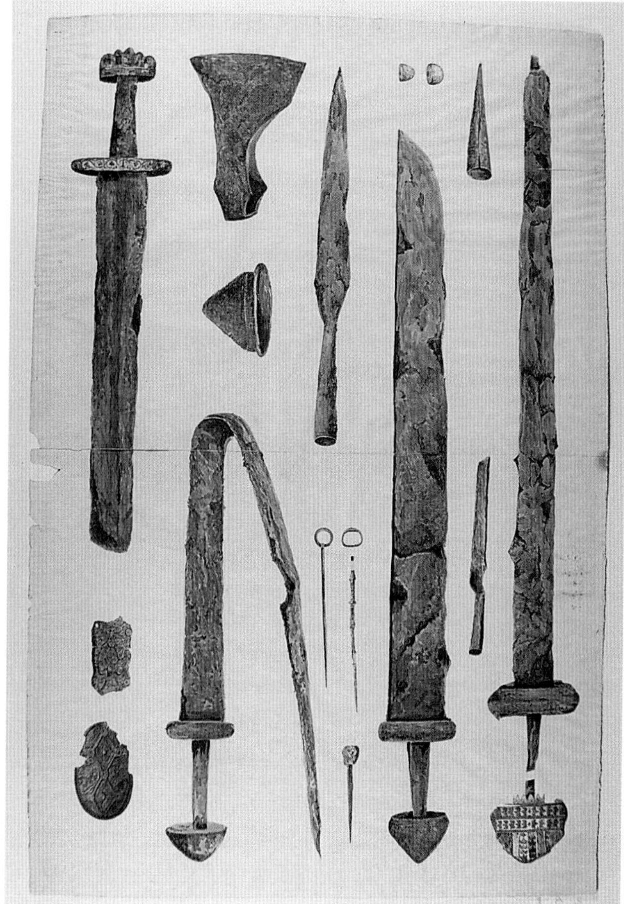

Vikings. *One of a series of watercolours prepared by James Plunket (1847) to record Viking artefacts, among them swords and spearheads, found during excavations of Viking graves at Islandbridge and Kilmainham, Dublin. [National Museum of Ireland]*

Vinegar Hill, site of an important insurgent campsite in Co. Wexford in 1798. Overlooking Enniscorthy, the hill, capped by the ruins of a windmill, affords a sweeping view of central Co. Wexford. A number of loyalists were put to death here during the rebellion. In the Battle of Vinegar Hill, 21 June 1798, General Lake drove a large rebel army from the summit and the adjacent town. Loyalists held a commemorative march to the hilltop on the anniversary of this battle for several decades afterwards. **Daniel Gahan**

violence against women. Women's organisations have been to the fore in drawing attention to the reality of violence against women, providing support services and lobbying to have protective legislation implemented. In 1976 WOMEN'S AID established the first women's refuge in the Republic, followed shortly afterwards by the setting up of the Dublin RAPE CRISIS CENTRE in 1979. The first legislation dealing specifically with rape, the Criminal Law (Rape) Act (1981), followed a restrictive definition of rape; in 1990 the act was amended to finally recognise rape in marriage and to introduce a wider category of offences. After many years of vigorous campaigning by women's organisations, the Domestic Violence Act (1996) was introduced, a breakthrough in the criminalisation of violence and abuse in intimate relationships. Following a report from a National Task Force on Violence Against Women established in 1997, national and regional task forces now have the role of co-ordinating research and policy implementation, drawing together Government departments, statutory agencies, and VOLUNTARY ORGANISATIONS.

Reported levels of violence against women continue to rise. In 1998 and 1999 rape and sexual assault were the only crimes that increased in the Republic—by 37 per cent and 13 per cent,

Vinegar Hill. Battle of Vinegar Hill fought 1798 *(c. 1880), one of William Sadler II's energetic depictions of the 1798 Rebellion. Overlooking Enniscorthy, Co. Wexford, Vinegar Hill was one of the key battle sites of the rising. [National Library of Ireland PD.3176 TX6]*

respectively; in 1999 the number of reported incidents of domestic violence increased by 20 per cent. Telephone help lines run by Women's Aid and the Rape Crisis Centres deal with tens of thousands of calls each year. Meanwhile the provision of services remains underfinanced and inadequate: there are fewer than twenty refuges in the Republic, while 5,000 women unsuccessfully sought refuge places in 2000. Research commissioned by Women's Aid suggests that one in five women in the Republic have experienced abuse, that domestic violence has become increasingly sexualised, and that the lack of independent income and HOUSING options continue to trap women in situations of violence and abuse. Implementation and enforcement of the legislation are now the central issues for women's organisations. **Ursula Barry**

Virgilius of Salzburg, Latinised name of Fearghal (died 784). Virgilius came from Ireland, or possibly IONA, to the court of the Frankish major Pippin in the early 740s. It is assumed that through his circle the *Collectio Canonum Hibernensis* came first to the Franks and he was one of the sources of inspiration for the royal anointing of Pippin in 751. Soon after his arrival Virgilius was denounced by Boniface to Pope Zacharias, without any consequences, for teaching the heretical ideas of the global shape of the Earth. Within the decade he transferred to the court of the Bavarian duke. At an unknown date, but presumably not long after his arrival, he became Bishop of Salzburg and in this position the leading adviser of the last independent Duke of Bavaria, Tassilo III, who was to become the arch-enemy of Charlemagne. In this position he supported the duke's expansion eastwards into Slav territories and witnessed in a prominent place the foundation charter of the monastery of Kremsmünster. His possible authorship of the *Cosmographia* of Aethicus Ister has been recently disputed. He died on 27 November 784. The Salzburg Book of Confraternities (*Verbrüderungsbuch*), begun in 784, lists prominently the first fifteen abbots of Iona, ending with Sléibéne (died 767). **Michael Richter**

Virgin Prunes, rock group. Formed in the late 1970s by GAVIN FRIDAY and Derek Rowan (Guggi), the group brought an avant-garde sensibility to Irish rock. Musically and visually the band was concerned with extremes. While their records were uneven, their live shows, once seen, were never forgotten. Sometimes unpleasant but always enthralling, the Virgin Prunes were perceived as pretentious and as pioneers. Their joint leader, Guggi, is now an established and highly regarded painter; Gavin Friday is a successful solo artist, his work infused with European influences and cinematic references. **Tony Clayton-Lea**

vision: see AISLINGE.

'vision of Adomnán': see 'FÍS ADOMNÁIN'.

'vision of Mac Conglinne': see 'FÍS MEIC CONGLINNE'.

'Vita Sanctae Columbae' ('Life of St COLM CILLE'), one of the three great examples of Irish HAGIOGRAPHY, written in the late seventh century by ADOMNÁN on IONA. Written nearly a century after Colm Cille's death (9 June 597), when the saint had an established cult not only on Iona but in its related MONASTERIES in Ireland and Scotland, its purpose was to provide reading (*legenda*) for his cult and to proclaim that his intercessory power was recognised not only among his own but widely in Britain and throughout Europe and even in Rome (book III, 23). There were earlier hagiographical documents about Colm Cille on Iona, no longer surviving, which the *Vita* drew on to produce such a masterpiece of HIBERNO-LATIN prose that many treat the text simply as biography, without reckoning with the author's skill or his declared hagiographical interest. The *Vita* is episodic, without a chronological frame (though Colm Cille's death comes at its end), and these episodes are arranged as belonging in these categories: 'revelations' (book I), miracles (book II), and 'angelic visitations' (book III). This portrays Colm Cille as the perfect disciple and model of monks and so exhibits Adomnán's perception of what a Christian life requires. In this he shows his dependence on the hagiography of Athanasius, Jerome, Gregory the Great, and Gregory of Tours. While any use of hagiography for historical details of its society requires caution, the *Vita* provides us with important details on early Irish monasticism, missionary work among the Picts, and early evidence for the royal anointing ritual. **Thomas O'Loughlin**

vocal music. Ireland has in the past produced many singers of international repute. Perhaps the earliest of these to gain fame was MICHAEL KELLY of Dublin, an acquaintance of Mozart, who performed in opera houses throughout Italy and in Vienna as well as in Ireland and Britain. The libretto for one of Kelly's operas, *The Gipsy Prince* (1801), was written by THOMAS MOORE, also much renowned as a poet, musician, and singer. Among other prominent Irish singers were Henry Robinson Allen (1809–1876) from Cork, the opera and concert singer CATHERINE HAYES (1818–1861) from Limerick, Tom Karl (1846–1916) of Dublin, William Ledwidge Ludwig (1847–1923), Barton McGuckian (1852–1917), and John O'Sullivan (1877–1955) of Cork. Two singers who won particular acclaim were the tenor JOHN MCCORMACK and the soprano MARGARET SHERIDAN.

The strong Irish vocal tradition continues today, with many singers establishing themselves on the international stage. This is largely as a result of the inspiration and support of such performers and teachers as VERONICA DUNNE and BERNADETTE GREEVY. Contemporary Irish singers of note include ANN MURRAY, SUZANNE MURPHY, FRANK PATTERSON, Patricia Bardon, Cara O'Sullivan, Conor Biggs, Orla Boylan, Alison Browner, Mary Hegarty, VIRGINIA KERR, Colette McGahon, and Regina Nathan. More recently, Irish vocal performance has come to prominence with the phenomenal success, especially in the United States, of the 'Irish Tenors' (Anthony Kearns, Finbar Wright, and Ronan Tynan). **Paul Collins**

Volans, Kevin (1949–), composer. Born in South Africa; studied with Stockhausen in Cologne, 1973–81. Composer-in-residence at Queen's University, Belfast, 1986–9, and at Princeton, New Jersey, 1992, he has been resident in Ireland since 1986. He has written for orchestra, chamber ensemble, vocal and choral and electro-acoustic medium. He came to prominence as part of the 'New Simplicity' of 1970s Germany, as exemplified in *Nine Beginnings* (two pianos, 1979). He also became established as a composer with a series of pieces built on African harmonies and rhythms, including *White Man Sleeps* (1982). An arrangement recorded by the Kronos Quartet (1989) became the biggest-selling string quartet recording of all time. **Emma Costello**

Volta Picture Palace, Dublin, Ireland's first cinema. Established by JAMES JOYCE, it opened in Mary Street on 20 December 1909. With the support of four businessmen from Trieste and an agreement that he would receive 10 per cent of the profits, Joyce found premises and hired the staff. The cinema attracted good though rather superficial reviews, and the business lasted less than a year. Under the management of Francesco Novak, a Trieste bicycle-shop owner, it presented mostly Italian films to an unenthusiastic Dublin audience. It was also perceived as being an anti-Catholic establishment. **Ciarán Deane**

voluntary organisations. Voluntary organisations constitute a significant phenomenon in all contemporary societies. There are various definitions, and there are overlaps between the concept of voluntary sector and related concepts, such as charities, non-profit, non-governmental organisations, civil society and social ECONOMY sectors. One central definition of voluntary organisations states that they must be formal, independent of government, self-governing, non-profit-distributing, and have some voluntary labour. This distinguishes the voluntary sector from informal help by relatives or neighbours, from commercial companies, and from statutory agencies. However, neither statutory funding nor charging fees for services disqualifies organisations from the voluntary sector. Indeed, without state funding many would simply collapse. On this basis the

'Vita Sanctae Columbae'. *A pen drawing of Colm Cille, abbot of Iona, from a ninth-century manuscript of Adomnán's* Vita Sanctae Columbae *(c. AD 700). A few incisive lines depict the saint, his arms outstretched in prayer, standing beneath a Romanesque archway. [Stiftsbibliothek St Gallen (Cod. Sang. 555 p. 166)]*

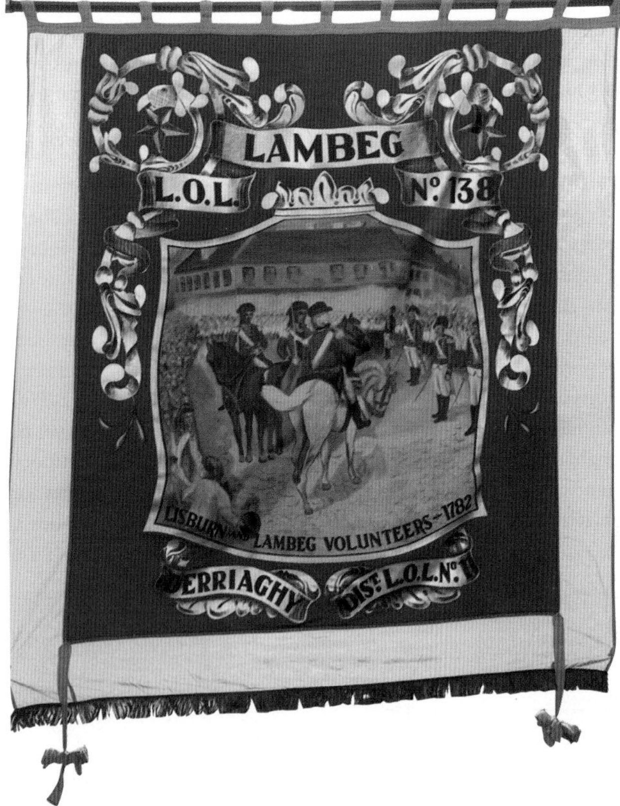

Volunteers in Ulster, (1778–93). *Modern Orange marching banner, Dunmurry (1995), depicting the Lambeg and Lisburn Volunteers of 1782. [Neil Jarman]*

Irish voluntary sector is thought to account for more than 8 per cent of GDP and 10 per cent of EMPLOYMENT. Some define the sector to include mutual benefit organisations, such as traditional CO-OPERATIVES, because, though they distribute dividends to members, they are not profit-maximising but are principally based on certain shared values. This is particularly so in some European countries, where the term is interchangeable with the 'social economy'. Others define voluntary organisation more narrowly to include service-providing organisations only, excluding associations formed specifically for bargaining, lobbying or quasi-political aims, such as TRADE UNIONS and employers' associations. Including the latter often broadens the scope to 'civil society' and emphasises the role of associations in mediating between market forces, the state, and households. **Joe Larragy**

Volunteer Force (1934–46), a militia of the ARMY established on 6 April 1934 as a reserve for the regular force. Twenty-one former Republicans had already been commissioned into the army as officers to oversee the recruiting of the Volunteer Force. In its first year £250,000 was allocated for the nationwide force with 24,000 volunteers. The Volunteer uniform was based on that of the German Casement Brigade of the FIRST WORLD WAR. At local level the force was run with the assistance of a committee known as a Sluagh. It quickly became clear that the Volunteer Force was not as successful as was first hoped. Despite the attention of two Government committees in 1936 and 1939 the force was dogged by a series of problems, principally related to insufficient financing, and recruiting began to tail off. Despite these difficulties many members achieved a high standard of training. Between March 1934 and March 1939 16,146 men joined the force. Once the Second World War began, the force was quickly subsumed into the regular army and proved its worth in the rapid expansion of 1940. The Volunteer Force was finally disestablished in 1946. **Labhrás Joye**

Volunteers, eighteenth century, a locally based amateur military force raised during the reduction in British forces caused by the American War. Unlike the MILITIA, Volunteer companies were independent, holding no official commissions and supplying their own equipment. Though primarily raised in 1778–9 to provide anti-invasion and police duties, the Volunteer movement developed a political aspect through links with 'PATRIOT' politicians, who wanted the Irish Parliament to have more independence from England. With more than 80,000 members, the Volunteers were a formidable pressure group. They helped gain 'legislative independence' in 1782 but declined thereafter; in 1792–3 attempts at revival in Dublin and in Ulster by ultra-radicals and the UNITED IRISHMEN were suppressed and all Volunteering banned (see p. 437). **Allan Blackstock**

Volunteers in Ulster (1778–93). When France joined the American revolutionaries in 1778, a Volunteer corps was formed in Belfast; enlistment was brisk after an American privateer, the *Ranger*, commanded by Paul Jones, seized a Royal Navy sloop, the *Drake*, on 13 April 1778 off the Co. Antrim coast. Though many Ulster Presbyterians sympathised with the American cause, they had no hesitation in identifying France as the traditional enemy. As Ireland was stripped of regular soldiers and the Dublin administration could not raise money to activate the militia, the Volunteer movement spread rapidly throughout the country. Approximately half the Volunteers (numbering 60,000 in 1782) were Ulstermen; and it was in the north that the popular campaign for legislative independence, launched by the DUNGANNON CONVENTION, was strongest. After the failure to get parliamentary reform in 1783–4 the movement lost prominence until it was stimulated by news of the French Revolution. Volunteers in Cos. Antrim and Down tended to be radical: Belfast Volunteers were the first in Ireland to formally invite Catholics to join them, and they largely paid for the first Catholic chapel in the town in 1784. In mid-Ulster, however, Volunteers were increasingly drawn into sectarian affrays with the Catholic DEFENDERS. The Gunpowder Act (1793) made the movement illegal, though Volunteer weapons were used by insurgents in 1798. **Jonathan Bardon**

Voynich, Ethel Lilian, née Boole (1864–1960), novelist. Born in Cork, daughter of GEORGE BOOLE; she finished her education in Berlin and travelled to Russia, where she married the Polish patriot Habdank Woynick. In 1916 they moved from London to New York, where she remained. Her most famous book, *The Gadfly* (1897), set in Italy, described by Bertrand Russell as the most exciting novel in English he ever read, was dramatised by SHAW, made into a film in Russia by A. Feinzimmer (1955) with music by Shostakovich, and made into an opera by Antonio Spadvecchia (1957), produced at Perm. Her other works include *Jack Raymond* (1901), *Olive Latham* (1904), *An Interrupted Friendship* (1910), and *Put Off Thy Shoes* (1946). **Joley Wood**

Wexford Festival Opera *(see page 1133). Cornelia Helfricht (left) as the Queen and Tereza Matlova (right) as Astaroth performing in* Die Königin von Saba *(The Queen of Sheba) by Karl Goldmark at the Wexford Festival Opera, 1999. [Wexford Festival Opera; Derek Speirs/Report]*

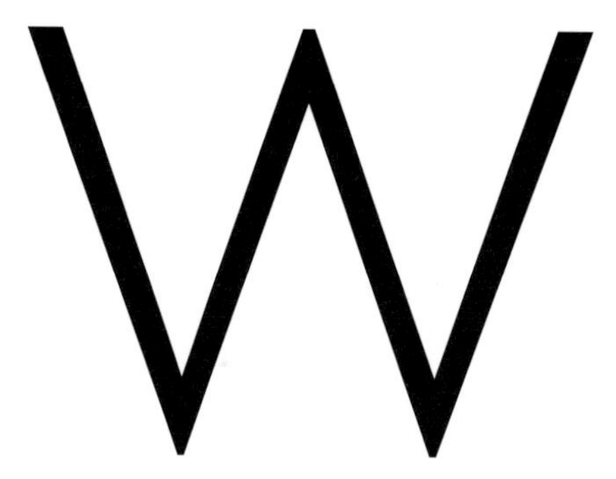

Waddell, Helen (1889–1965), medievalist and writer. Born in Tokyo to Irish parents; educated at QUB and the University of Oxford. Her work belongs simultaneously to scholarship and to literature. *The Wandering Scholars* (1927), a literary history, was instantly popular; the novel *Peter Abelard* (1933) made her a celebrity. Her translations, *Medieval Latin Lyrics* (1929) and the posthumous *More Latin Lyrics* (1976), are still frequently anthologised; she also translated, in prose, *Beasts and Saints* (1934) and *The Desert Fathers* (1936). Her rhetoric renders the past coeval with the present, drawing out 'some touch of almost contemporary desire or pain' from medieval Latin. Her scope is European but permeated with Irish references. **Jennifer FitzGerald**

Waddell, Martin (1941–), writer. Born in Belfast. He was a professional footballer with Fulham Football Club before becoming a thriller-writer. A prolific and talented author, he writes for children of all ages, from babies to young adults, with sensitivity, clarity, and an offbeat sense of humour. He began his writing career with the Otley books—adult thrillers—and became a children's author 'for amusement only.' Under the pseudonym CATHERINE SEFTON he produced some of the finest writing for children in English in the twentieth century. His warm, probing and sensitive stories, such as *In a Blue Velvet Dress* and *Emer's Ghost*, were an instant success. Though not consciously about the 'TROUBLES', many of his books are set against the backdrop of Northern Ireland and the dilemma of a divided community. His timeless, classically simple texts for picture-books have given us such titles as *The Owl Babies*, *The Park in the Dark*, and the perennial favourite *Can't You Sleep, Little Bear?* **Patricia Donlon**

Waddell, Samuel: see MAYNE, RUTHERFORD.

Wadding, Luke (1588–1657), Franciscan theologian, scholar, and historian. Born into a prominent merchant family in Waterford; educated in Latin and the classics in Waterford. Following the death of his parents when he was fourteen, he travelled to Portugal, where he studied with the Jesuits at the Irish seminary in Lisbon. He then entered the novitiate of the Friars Minor and in 1613 was ordained as a Franciscan priest. He distinguished himself as a scholar; in 1617 he became professor of theology at Salamanca and added Hebrew to his existing knowledge of Portuguese and Castilian. A year later he was chosen as theologian by Philip III for the Spanish embassy to Rome to promote the doctrine of the Immaculate Conception. Wadding remained in Rome, where he became an influential figure in Irish affairs. In 1625 he established the Irish Franciscan College of St Isidore and in 1627 the Ludovisian College for Irish secular clergy. He was responsible for securing 17 March as the feast of St PATRICK. He was made Agent and Procurator for the Catholic Confederacy in 1642 and was responsible for sending arms and money to Ireland. Pope Paul V made him Qualificator of the Holy Office. He was Consultor of the Sacred Congregation of Rites, the Propaganda and the Index and a member of the committee on Irish affairs, as well as Procurator-General and Praeses (guardian) of St Isidore's. A prolific writer, he published thirty-six books, including a history of the Franciscan order, *Annales Ord. Minorum* (1625–54), and a critical edition of the works of his fellow-Franciscan JOHANNES DUNS SCOTUS. His scholarly work on Hebrew remains highly regarded. **Martin Clancy**

Wade, Walter (c. 1740–1825), botanist. Born in Dublin into a medical family. He practised as a surgeon and midwife from 1776. In 1786 he was admitted as a licentiate of the College of Physicians. He gave public lectures in BOTANY at his house in Capel Street in 1789. In 1790 he was a member of a group that successfully petitioned Parliament to found a BOTANICAL GARDEN. The Dublin Society established the garden at Glasnevin in 1795 and the following year appointed him its first professor of botany. He published the first catalogues of the FLORA of Dublin and of Connemara and a complete list of the flora of Ireland. **Donal Synnott**

Wadham, John (1936–), jazz musician. Born in England but living in Dublin since 1953, Wadham has worked as a full-time musician, tutor, and broadcaster as well as work in theatre music, studio sessions, and many and varied jazz line-ups. He has been the drummer of choice in providing support for visiting musicians, such as Benny Carter, Zoot Sims, Ronnie Scott, and Gerry Mulligan; he has also been a keystone of local groups, from the Ian Henry Quintet of the late 1950s to the Jazz Heralds, the NOEL KELEHAN Quintet of the late 1970s, and the innovative trio with TOMMY HALFERTY and RONAN GUILFOYLE of the early 1980s. He has performed in concert and at jazz festivals in Finland, Germany, Canada, and elsewhere. On the one album in his own name, *Drums and Friends* (1978, reissued 2000), he is heard with LOUIS STEWART, the flautist Brian Dunning, and others. **Brian Trench**

Waiting for Godot (En Attendant Godot) (1949), a play by SAMUEL BECKETT. Written between October 1948 and January 1949 as a respite from the prose TRILOGY on which Beckett was embarked, it received its world premiere at the Théâtre de Babylone, Paris, on 3 January 1953. Its immediate success made the reputation of this shy, diffident expatriate who now chose to write in French. It initiated a Copernican revolution in world theatre with its minimalist approach to drama and apparent lack of plot and its combination of high philosophical discussion with broad physical farce. It was seen at the time as an existential play, with the teasing possibility that the Godot who was endlessly expected but never appeared was some version of the deity. By the beginning of the 1960s it was claimed for the Theatre of the Absurd, with no evident cause and effect in its universe and a lack of certainty about the operations of time. The play was translated into English by its author in mid-1950, and its London production emphasised non-communication, the interplay of language and silence which influenced Harold Pinter. American productions emphasised the comedic aspects in casting and playing. But from its first staging at the PIKE THEATRE, Dublin, in 1955 *Waiting for Godot* increasingly came to be seen as Irish, in a line from YEATS, SYNGE, and O'CASEY, with critics pointing to the presence of tramps and beggars in these works, to a psychic interdependence between two leading males, and to a combination of tragedy and comedy. The GATE THEATRE, Dublin, cemented the connection with a Beckett festival that staged all nineteen theatre pieces in Dublin in 1991, two years after the author's death. **Anthony Roche**

wakes. In Irish tradition the wake is central to customs surrounding death, and the practice partially continues today. Traditionally, when a person died the body was laid out to be 'waked', usually in the family home (sometimes called the 'corpse-house'), so that people could pay their respects to the dead person and to the family. The wake lasted at least one night, and after the initial prayers those present engaged socially; alcohol and tobacco were traditionally provided, and wake 'amusements' began. These games, often cathartic in nature, were condemned by church authorities, yet their practice survived well into the twentieth century. [see AMERICAN WAKE.] **Anne O'Connor**

Waldré, Vincenzo (Vincent) (1742–1814), artist. Born in Vicenza, Italy, he came to Ireland in 1787 with the Viceroy, the Duke of Buckingham. He worked as a decorator, easel painter, and architect, remembered for his decoration of St Patrick's Hall in DUBLIN CASTLE, planned during his first visit to Ireland and painted when he settled in Dublin in the 1790s. His original work has been much changed, but the three principal paintings on the ceiling survive. The central circular canvas (finished c. 1800) depicts George III supported by Justice and Liberty. The two side panels show St Patrick converting the Irish to Christianity and Henry II receiving the submission of the Irish chiefs; these were exhibited in the Society of Artists' exhibition in 1801 and 1802, respectively, though unfinished, and his widow said they were unfinished at his death. **Anne Crookshank**

Wales, the Irish in. Travel and trade between Ireland and Wales have taken place throughout the centuries. In Roman times the sea separating the two countries was a highway along which trade and exchange took place, rather than a barrier preventing contact. In the fourth and fifth centuries Irish chieftains invaded and colonised parts of south-west Wales, leaving behind evidence of their presence in numerous Irish OGHAM stones and place-names. In subsequent periods migrants crossed to Wales to escape from economic crises, as in the 1620s and during the appalling famine of 1741. Political upheavals, such as the REBELLION OF 1798, also caused some people to flee to Wales in search of safety.

However, in spite of the longevity of this movement between the two countries, most attention has concentrated on the nineteenth century. At that time industrialisation and urbanisation in Wales attracted Irish workers to the country, where they worked on the excavation of docks and the building of railways and also formed an important element of the labour force in the docks, the ironworks, and the coal-mines.

A great impetus to immigration came with the GREAT FAMINE. Relations between Irish and Welsh people were hostile, with serious anti-Irish riots on twenty occasions between 1826 and 1882. Even so, not all Irish people were an alienated and outcast minority. Some Irish workers established their own friendly societies and embraced the temperance movement, participating fully in the cult of respectability. Moreover, there was a small but significant middle class, composed of businessmen and doctors. Such people occasionally came into conflict with those other leaders of the Irish community, the Catholic clergy. Some commentators have overestimated the religious devotion of Irish immigrants at this time, but the Catholic Church undoubtedly played a central role in immigrant life. Occasionally there were tensions between the demands of Catholicism and the pull of the homeland. Despite the alienation of the famine years, integration began to take place from the mid-1880s, partly because of Welsh Liberalism's support for Irish HOME RULE and partly because of the creation of mass trade unions, which drew Irish workers into the labour movement.

Irish emigration to Wales tailed off in the middle of the twentieth century, as the Welsh economy stagnated. Among the notable developments in that century, however, was the appointment of Michael McGrath as Archbishop of Cardiff in 1935, the first graduate of the National University of Ireland to be appointed to the Catholic hierarchy in Britain. A sign of closer ties at the end of the century was the establishment of official diplomatic links in the form of the Irish Consulate-General in Cardiff in 1998. **Paul O'Leary**

Walker, Dorothy (1929–2002), art critic. Born in Dublin; educated in Paris. A member of the Board of the IRISH MUSEUM OF MODERN ART from 1990, she was president of AICA Ireland, 1980–86 and 1998–2000. *Louis Le Brocquy* (1981) was the first monograph on this significant artist; she has also written on the architect MICHAEL SCOTT and the painter PATRICK SCOTT. **Richard Pine**

Walker, Rev. George (1646–1690), governor of Derry and Church of Ireland rector of Donoughmore, Co. Tyrone. Walker raised a Protestant force at Dungannon in late 1688 and in April 1689—following the refusal of ROBERT LUNDY to participate in the preparations for resisting the JACOBITE siege—was made civil governor of Derry, with Major Henry Baker as military governor. Walker's diary, published as *A True Account of the Siege of Londonderry* (1689), is the most famous contemporary account, though it does not concur with those written by others who were in the city. Walker gives great credit to his own exploits, whereas the Presbyterian minister John Mackenzie's *Narrative of the Siege of Londonderry* (1690) portrays Adam Murray, a Scot, as the true hero of the siege; Mackenzie believed that Walker was only nominally joint governor and that he took credit for the work of Baker, who died during the siege. Walker took umbrage at the representation by Presbyterian ministers to WILLIAM III in Belfast in 1690 of the great services performed by Presbyterians at the siege. At the time of his death at the BATTLE OF THE BOYNE, Walker was bishop-elect of Derry. A monument erected to him on the walls of Derry in 1828 was blown up in 1973. **Charles Ivar McGrath**

Walker, Joseph Cooper (c. 1761–1810), antiquarian. Born in Dublin; educated at Thomas Ball's School. A founder-member of the ROYAL IRISH ACADEMY in 1786, he wrote on various antiquarian topics, including *Historical Essay on the Dress of the Ancient Irish* (1788). His most significant work was *Historical Memoirs of the Irish Bards* (1786), an account of the development of Irish poetry and music and among the earliest publications to deal with the history of Irish music. Though often subjective and emotional, it contains information not found elsewhere, especially regarding CAROLAN. The inclusion of forty-three airs also makes it one of the earliest written sources of Irish folk music. **Emma Costello**

Walker, Robin (1924–1991), architect. Born in Dunmore East, Co. Waterford; studied at UCD, Paris (working briefly with Le Corbusier), and Illinois Institute of Technology, Chicago (under the direct tutelage of Mies van der Rohe). He became a senior partner

wakes. The Aran Fisherman's Drowned Child *(1841) by Frederick W. Burton; among the mourners at the wake, a vivid depiction of a keening woman. [National Gallery of Ireland]*

with Scott Tallon Walker, 1974 (with MICHAEL SCOTT and RONALD TALLON). He also taught at UCD. His work includes the BORD FÁILTE offices, Baggot Street, Dublin (1962–6); O'Flaherty House, Kinsale, Co. Cork (1967), a concrete-framed pavilion with dramatic harbour views; the master plan for Wesley College, Dublin; the Restaurant Building, UCD (for which he won the RIAI Gold Medal, 1968–70); and the laboratories of St Columba's College, Rathfarnham. Perhaps the most philosophical of contemporary Irish architects, he retired from practice in 1982. **Raymund Ryan**

Walker, William (1871–1918), trade unionist. Born in Belfast; became an apprentice joiner in HARLAND AND WOLFF's shipyard in 1885. He was a member of the Amalgamated Society of Carpenters and Joiners throughout the 1890s, being involved in several disputes, before being blacklisted in 1901. He was appointed a full-time union officer and became president of the Belfast Trades Council the following year. Though a prominent member of the Labour Party, Walker failed on three occasions to win a Westminster seat in Belfast. He combined Ulster unionism and socialism in a manner that many found difficult to accept. His only publication, *The Irish Question* (1908), stated clearly his opposition to HOME RULE, though he criticised both nationalists and unionists for being obsessed with the location of the government of Ireland rather than its defects. Following his appointment in 1912 as an official to administer the National Insurance Act, his influence in the labour movement declined. He earned a reputation for ruthlessness in inter-union disputes and as a consequence enjoyed stormy relations with many other labour leaders. The most famous of these feuds, with JAMES CONNOLLY, stemmed from the latter's criticism of Walker's politics. Walker died at the age of forty-seven after a long illness. **John Patrick Lynch**

Wall, Mervyn Eugene Welply (1908–1997), novelist and playwright. Born in Dublin; educated at UCD. He achieved cult status with *The Unfortunate Fursey* (1946) and *The Return of Fursey* (1948), two novels about the comic adventures of a medieval monk. *Leaves for the Burning* (1952), *No Trophies Raise* (1956), and *Hermitage* (1982) are more serious works, manifesting a darkly critical view of middle-class Ireland. He also wrote two plays for the ABBEY THEATRE, *Alarm among the Clerks* (1940) and *The Lady in the Twilight* (1941). He was secretary of the ARTS COUNCIL from 1957 to 1975. **Derek Hand**

Wall, Richard (Ricardo) (1694–1778), Spanish statesman and diplomat. Born in Waterford; educated in France. He emigrated to Spain at the age of twenty-four and entered the military service. He held important diplomatic posts, helping to negotiate the Treaty of Aix-la-Chapelle (1748), which ended the War of the Austrian Succession and conferred the Duchies of Parma, Piacenza and Guastalla on the Spanish infante Philip. He was ambassador to England, 1748–52, and was instrumental in securing improved Anglo-Spanish relations. In Madrid he served as a minister of state, 1752–64, first under Ferdinand VI and later under Charles III. **David Kiely**

Wall, William Guy (1792–c. 1864), painter. Born in Dublin; trained as an artist. In 1818 he emigrated to the United States. Living in New York, he painted many views of the Hudson River, twenty-three of which were engraved and published as *The Hudson River Portfolio* (1820). A founder-member of the National Academy, he also showed at the Pennsylvania Academy and the Apollo Association. After 1828 he moved to Newport, Rhode Island. In 1834 he was in New Haven, Connecticut, and two years later in New York. He then returned to Ireland, working with a silhouette portraitist named Hubard. He returned to the United States in 1856 but was back in Ireland by 1864. His death is not recorded. **Peter Murray**

Wallace, William Vincent. *Watercolour by J. Hanshaw of the musician and composer William Vincent Wallace, who performed in Australia, Chile, Argentina, Cuba, and the United States. [National Gallery of Ireland]*

Wallace, William Vincent (1812–1865), composer. Born in Waterford, the son of a bandmaster; studied piano with W. S. Conran and organ with Haydn Corri. In 1830 he became organist at Thurles Cathedral and also professor of music at Thurles Ursuline Convent. He had a successful career as a solo violinist and made his debut as a composer at the age of twenty-two, when he performed his own violin concerto for the Dublin Anacreontic Society. He left Ireland in 1835 to conduct, perform and compose, initially in Australia, where he was nicknamed the 'Australian Paganini'; he travelled widely throughout the world. He is best known for his opera *Maritana* (1846). **Emma Costello**

Waller, James Hardress de Warrenne (1884–1968), engineer. Born in Tasmania, Australia, where his father (from Nenagh, Co. Tipperary) was farming; he studied engineering at UCG and UCC and in the United States. The elegant concrete Western Road bridge at UCC was his first commission. When in Iraq during the 1920s he saw the third-century AD Sassanian palace at Ctesiphon on the Tigris, the banqueting hall of which is a vast inverted catenary vault and one of the great achievements of Middle Eastern architecture. This provided the inspiration for his remarkable 'Ctesiphon' building system of unsupported continuous concrete vaulting, which he used in a great variety of projects around the world, in Ireland mainly as agricultural and commercial buildings, few of which survive, in Britain for the War Office during the SECOND WORLD WAR, and also in Spain, the Middle East, India, and Africa. An engineer of visionary ideals, Waller was motivated by an active social conscience, and low-cost housing and shelter structures were among his main preoccupations. **Brian Lalor**

Walsh, Brian (1918–1998), lawyer and judge. Born in Dublin; educated at UCD and KING'S INNS. He was called to the bar in 1942. He was a judge of the HIGH COURT, 1959–61, of the SUPREME COURT, 1961–90, and of the European Court of Human Rights, 1990–98; he was also president of the Law Reform Commission, 1975–81. He was regarded as the central judicial figure in a Supreme Court that made landmark judgments in a number of cases, including *Byrne v. Ireland* (in which the right to sue the state was recognised) and the Crotty case (where a constitutional amendment was required before Ireland could ratify the SINGLE EUROPEAN ACT). He is regarded as the most important judicial influence on the development of the Constitution of Ireland and the role of the Supreme Court in the history of the state. **Neville Cox**

Walsh, Maurice (1879–1964), writer of romantic and historical fiction. Born near Listowel, Co. Kerry; educated locally. His novels include *The Key above the Door* (1926), *While Rivers Run* (1928), *The Small Dark Man* (1929), *Blackcock's Feather* (1932), *The Road to Nowhere* (1934), *Green Rushes* (1935), and *And No Quarter* (1937). He also wrote short stories. John Huston's film *The Quiet Man* (1952) had its source in his work. **Terence Brown**

Walsh, T. J. [Thomas] (1911–1988), founder and artistic director of WEXFORD FESTIVAL OPERA. Born in Wexford; educated at TCD, where he qualified as a doctor in 1944. He founded Wexford Festival Opera in 1951 and was artistic director until 1966. It was during this time that the festival received international recognition. He was also the author of several books on opera in Dublin, Monte Carlo, and the French Second Empire. **Emma Costello**

Walsh, William Joseph (1841–1921), Archbishop of Dublin. Born in Dublin; educated at the CATHOLIC UNIVERSITY, Dublin, and ST PATRICK'S COLLEGE, Maynooth, and ordained in 1866. He was appointed professor of theology at Maynooth in 1867, vice-president in 1878, and president in 1880. Though a noted scholar and the leading intellectual in the Irish Catholic Church, he devoted most of his time to his interests in public affairs, especially EDUCATION. He was a committed nationalist, and his political views almost prevented him from being elected to the archbishopric of Dublin. He was nevertheless appointed to the see in 1885 but, unlike his two immediate predecessors, was not made a cardinal. Though he opposed PARNELL, in later life he became increasingly radical, supporting SINN FÉIN in 1918 and opposing the Government of Ireland Act (1920). **Oliver P. Rafferty**

Walton, E. T. S. [Ernest Thomas Sinton] (1903–1995), physicist. Born in Dungarvan, Co. Waterford; educated at Cookstown Academy, Banbridge Academy, and Methodist College, Belfast, 1915–22. With a scholarship to TCD, he proceeded to take a double honours degree in physics and mathematics, 1927. He was awarded a master's degree for work on vortices in liquids as a Fitzgerald scholar. He went to Cambridge, on a scholarship, to work on nuclear physics under Rutherford at the Cavendish Laboratory. Rutherford had produced the first disintegration of an atom using alpha particles from radium. A copious supply of different fast particles was now required, and Walton was put to work on accelerating electrons. In 1929 he was joined by J. D. Cockcroft in work on the acceleration of protons. Walton's abilities as an experimentalist contributed largely to the building of an accelerator capable of operating at up to 700,000 volts. A circuit known as the Cockcroft-Walton voltage-doubler was developed for the project. On 14 April 1932 Walton observed for the first time the artificial disintegration of lithium into two alpha particles on bombardment by highly accelerated protons. Rutherford confirmed that alpha particles had been produced and swore the experimentalists to secrecy, until an announcement was made in *Nature* on 30 April 1932. This 'splitting of the atom' made headlines and marked the birth of nuclear physics employing high-energy accelerators. The experiment also confirmed the famous Einstein equation $E = mc^2$. In 1934 Walton returned to Trinity College, Dublin, where he became a fellow and Erasmus Smith professor of natural and experimental philosophy. He became head of the Physics Department, a position he held until his retirement in 1974. He received many honours, including the Hughes Medal of the Royal Society, 1938, and honorary doctorates from four universities. In 1951 he was awarded the NOBEL PRIZE, jointly with J. D. Cockcroft, for 'pioneer work on the transmutation of atomic nuclei by artificially accelerated atomic particles.' **Philip W. Walton**

Walton. *The first person to 'split the atom,' the physicist Ernest T. Walton, jointly awarded the Nobel Prize in 1951. [Irish Picture Library]*

waltz, a dance form in 3/4 time originating in sixteenth-century Germany, Austria or Bohemia and hugely popular in Napoleonic France. It was introduced to Ireland during the nineteenth century and was included in the programme for the first CÉILÍ dance, held in London in 1897. There are many waltz tunes, but in Irish practice the dance is most often performed to the adjusted air of popular ballads, such as 'The Boston Burglar' and 'The Rocks of Bawn'. **Fintan Vallely**

Wanderings of Oisin, The (1889), a narrative poem by W. B. YEATS; written 1886–7, published 1889, substantially revised 1895. The warrior OISÍN is led by his immortal lover Niamh through various states of afterlife in TÍR NA NÓG and its islands of dancing, victory and forgetfulness until, grown tired of that world, he returns to his pagan country, only to find that St PATRICK has Christianised it. Yeats later characterised this journey as 'vain gaiety, vain battle, vain repose.' The poem is seen variously as contrasting imaginative pagan and lifeless Christian Ireland or as an allegory of Ireland under English rule. Many critics cite the poem's imaginative resources while criticising its ornateness. **Jefferson Holdridge**

Warbeck, Perkin (1474–1499), pretender to the English throne. Apparently at the instigation of an English Yorkist, John Taylor, the son of a Tournai burgess, arrived in Cork in November 1491 posing as Richard, Duke of York (1473–c. 1483), second son of Edward IV. Supported by Margaret of Burgundy, Charles VIII of France, Maximilian I, and James IV of Scotland, he won widespread support in Munster, including that of Maurice Fitzgerald, ninth Earl of Desmond. Henry VII decisively thwarted his designs, and in the spring of 1492 Warbeck departed for the French court. He returned to Ireland in 1495, when he joined the DESMOND REBELLION and participated in the unsuccessful siege of Waterford (23 July–3 August). In 1496 James IV had his cousin marry Warbeck. After a last unsuccessful attempt to garner support in Ireland in July 1497 he sailed to Cornwall in September, accompanied by a handful of Irish Yorkists. Captured by HENRY VII, he was hanged on 23 November 1499. [see SIMNEL, LAMBERT.] **Mary Ann Lyons**

Ward, Anthony (Tony) (1954–), rugby footballer. Born in Dublin. He won nineteen caps at out-half between 1978 and 1987. Much controversy about their respective talents marked his career and that of Ollie Campbell. A replacement with the 1980 British

Ward, Mary. *Photograph by Mary Parsons, Countess of Rosse, of Mary Ward, microscopist, artist, entomologist, and author, one of the first Irish woman scientists, pictured here with a Smith, Beck and Beck stereo viewer. [Irish Picture Library]*

Lions team in South Africa, he scored eighteen points (five penalty goals and a dropped goal) in the first Test at Cape Town—a joint Lions Test record he shares with Gavin Hastings of Scotland. **Karl Johnston**

Ward, Isaac W. (1834–1916), astronomer. Born in Belfast into a prominent family. Possessing an 11 mm (4.3-in.) refractor, he was the first to report, on 19 August 1885, a bright astronomical object near the nucleus of the Andromeda Galaxy, M31, with an estimated magnitude of 7; this object brightened to magnitude 5 on succeeding days and then gradually faded to invisibility over several months. With insight obtained later, this object is now interpreted as having been a supernova (S. Andromeda). Ward's ability to resolve double stars and to identify faint objects using relatively small apertures earned forty-three citings in the popular book *Celestial Objects for Common Telescopes* (1962) by T. W. Webb. He was a member of the Ulster Astronomical Society, 1890–94. **Susan McKenna-Lawlor**

Ward, Mary, née King (1827–1869), naturalist and astronomer. Born at Ballylin, Co. Offaly, a cousin of WILLIAM PARSONS, THIRD EARL OF ROSSE. She had an interest since childhood in ASTRONOMY, entomology, and MICROSCOPY. Her early publications presaged her popular masterpiece, *Microscope Teachings* (1864), which includes such topics as the circulation of the blood in young vertebrates, vision in insects, and the structure of insect scales and of feathers, all beautifully illustrated with her own drawings. A companion volume, *Telescope Teachings* (1859), also based on her own observations, includes accounts of the planets, planetary satellites, stellar clusters, and the Orion nebula. Of special interest is her set of detailed drawings of Donati's Comet at its 1858 apparition. **Susan McKenna-Lawlor**

Ware, Sir James (1594–1666), historiographer. Born in Dublin; educated at TCD. He became Auditor-General for Ireland in 1632. Committed to publishing elements of Irish history, he produced such works as *Ancient Irish Histories* (1633) and *De Scriptoribus Hiberniae Libri Duo* (1639), among many other important books. **Joley Wood**

warfare, 1200–1700. From the twelfth to the sixteenth century Irish warfare was generally a series of struggles between invaders and their settled descendants, supported by the increasing power of England and in conflict with a network of Irish lords. Military and political power in thirteenth-century Ireland was held by Irish and Norman lords intent on maintaining and extending their territorial lordships. The ANGLO-NORMAN CONQUEST had concentrated on Leinster and Meath, had over-run parts of Munster and Connacht, and in Ulster had merely established a small settlement on the eastern seaboard; it was not, therefore, a complete conquest. Military activity in resistance to external institutional changes in the centuries following the Anglo-Norman conquest tended to occur on the periphery of earlier Norman influence. In the late Middle Ages the military capacity of the more notable Irish lords, the MacCarthys, O'Briens, O'Neills, and O'Donnells, gained in strength, while some of the descendants of the Normans, though Gaelicised in language and customs, kept their English allegiance when it suited them to act as aristocratic delegates for the Crown of England.

As elsewhere, war was normally waged by freemen holding land on condition of providing unpaid military service for their overlords. From the middle to the late thirteenth century many of these lords employed mercenaries, the GALLOGLASS, and defence was entrusted to landowners, who were obliged to serve in the 'rising out' or hostings; but many commuted military service for money payments, known in England as 'scutage' and in Ireland as 'royal service'. In Irish society power was based on the relationships between the lord, his kinsmen—often at feud with him—and *uirrithe* or vassal chiefs and their kinsmen; such complexities reflected an unsettled society, a conflict of cultures, and insecurity of land titles, all of which were conducive to armed combat.

The numbers involved in a 'rising out' were small, reflecting the population level and a rural subsistence economy. In 1515, for example, a large lordship could host about 2,000 men, consisting of 500 spearmen mounted, 500 galloglass, and 1,000 KERN. The armed knight on a war-horse was rare in Ireland. There were no large-scale ironfoundries, so armoury and weaponry tended to be chain mail, pikes, spears, axes, and later hand-guns, with plate armour and heavy cannon a rarity. Fourteenth-century statutes forbidding the OLD ENGLISH to supply armour, weapons or horses to the Irish were frequently ignored.

Though Ireland was a land of war, formal battles were few; but there was much low-level conflict in border and cattle raids, minor sieges, skirmishes, and ambushes, often caused by dynastic feuds as well as the larger conflicts with the invader or would-be coloniser. Defensive sites or CASTLES are perhaps more evident in place-names than on the landscape; but surviving small TOWER-HOUSES from the fifteenth to early seventeenth centuries show how they had retained a defensive function long after the development of cannon had made the private fortress obsolete elsewhere. The Normans and their Old English descendants were mainly responsible for walled town defences, built and maintained by tolls on goods brought to market until the seventeenth century. Until the eve of the TUDOR CONQUEST the nature of Irish warfare was largely dictated by topographical and cultural divisions existing from the earlier medieval

English settlements. Notable conflicts were often castle or town sieges; the massive Geraldine keep at Maynooth fell after a ten-day assault in March 1535, after which the garrison was put to death following a breach of trust (thereafter known as the 'pardon of Maynooth')—a strong reminder of what to expect if garrisons did not yield up their fortresses. But the strongest Irish castles could not stand against heavy artillery, available to Crown forces from the early sixteenth century, as shown by the famous castle sieges at Glin, Askeaton, Kinsale and Dunboy or those of walled towns in the seventeenth century, such as Derry, Drogheda, Wexford, and Limerick (see pp. 596, 632).

The conduct of war on both sides, especially in the second half of the sixteenth century, was ruthless and barbaric; chivalric codes and the 'rules of war' went largely unobserved. Military and general history are virtually conterminous in the Elizabethan age, perhaps because religion shaped so much of Irish military history from the 1590s to the restoration of Charles II in 1660. However, between 1603 and 1641 there was comparative peace; but the next two decades experienced widespread warfare, military occupation, and land confiscation. The struggle at the end of the seventeenth century was in essence an Irish civil war, in which the victors laid the foundation of the PROTESTANT ASCENDANCY, not only in the armed forces but also in law, government, and society. **John J. N. McGurk**

'War of the Gael with the Gaill': see 'COGADH GAEDHEL RE GAILLIBH'.

War of Independence, also called the Anglo-Irish War (1919–21). The war followed the SINN FÉIN victory in the 1918 general election and the first meeting of DÁIL ÉIREANN on 21 January 1919. The initial stages consisted of localised attacks on the RIC, resulting in the police withdrawal from large areas of the south and west by the beginning of 1920. This allowed the widespread establishment of Republican courts and LOCAL GOVERNMENT and the stepping up of guerrilla warfare by IRA units. By the summer of 1920 the British writ no longer ran in large parts of the country. LLOYD GEORGE's government responded by reinforcing the police with the BLACK AND TANS and AUXILIARIES and by implementing further repressive measures. Reprisals and counter-reprisals followed, together with a series of notorious incidents in the autumn and early winter, including the seventy-four-day hunger strike of TERENCE MACSWINEY, the hanging of eighteen-year-old Kevin Barry, the murders of BLOODY SUNDAY, and the burning by the Auxiliaries of much of central Cork city. The first six months of 1921 saw a further intensification and a military stalemate. The Truce of 11 July 1921, ending the war, represented the IRA's acknowledgment of weakness in arms and ammunition and the British government's recognition of domestic and international consequences of a continuation. The fact that the Northern government had already been set up expedited the start of negotiations (see p. 555).

Traditionally the war has been depicted as a heroic victory against the odds; more recently the limited and heavily regionalised IRA activity has been stressed and the supposed symbiotic relationship between the flying columns and the community questioned; the IRA achievement in propaganda and intelligence has been emphasised. Debate increasingly centres on how necessary violence was for the gaining of a large measure of independence for the twenty-six counties that became the Irish Free State. **Michael A. Hopkinson**

Warren, Barbara (1925–), artist. Born in Dublin; studied at the NCAD, Regent Street Polytechnic, London, and with André Lhôte, Paris. She taught painting at the NCAD and is a regular exhibitor at the RHA and was elected a committee member, 1988. She has held many one-woman exhibitions, latterly at the Taylor Galleries, Dublin. She also exhibited at the Florence Biennale, 1999. Her early work was influenced by the school of Paris, the English artist Keith Vaughan, and post-war romantic Irish painting, such as that of GERARD DILLON. A strictly figurative artist, she represents still-life and landscape in coastal locations of Achill, Connemara, and Spain, depicting the observed with acuteness of perception. Sometimes remembered figures are included, to give a mood of reflective calm. She is a member of AOSDÁNA. **Julian Campbell**

Warren, Michael (1950–), sculptor. Inspired by OISÍN KELLY, his art teacher at St Columba's College, Rathfarnham, Co. Dublin, he went on to study at Bath Academy of Art and the Accademia di Belle Arti di Brera, Milan. He has exhibited widely and has received numerous commissions for site-specific sculpture throughout the world; awards include the Macaulay Fellowship, 1978, Mont

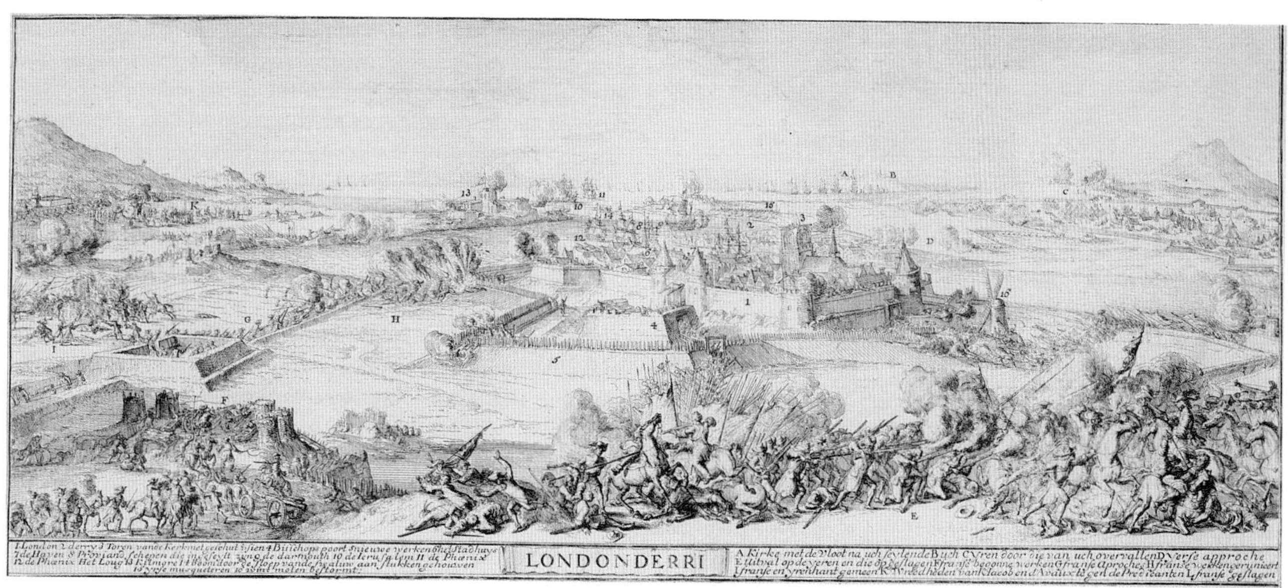

warfare. *A print of c. 1689 showing the fortified city of Derry, viewed from the east bank of the Foyle, during the 105-day siege of 1688–9. Walled in 1618, it was the last fortified city to be built in Western Europe. [National Library of Ireland R22, 652]*

Kavanagh Award for Environment Art, 1980 and 1983, Utsukushi-ga-Hara Open-Air Museum Award, Japan, 1989, and the Medalla al Mérito Artístico, Madrid, 1991. His works are technically highly skilled; he uses steel, stone, and especially wood for his sculptures, which are abstract and often large-scale. They often consist of columnar, balancing or interlocking forms that dramatically and poetically penetrate and define space and frequently appear to defy gravity. Public commissions include *Two Thrones* at Clonmel, the 1798 Memorial near Gorey, Dublin Port Authority head office, Dublin City Council offices, and the RTÉ studios, Dublin. RONALD TALLON designed Warren's studio at Gorey. **Suzanne McNab**

Warren, Raymond (1928–), composer and teacher. Born in Weston-super-Mare, Somerset; educated at the University of Cambridge, where his tutors included Berkeley and Tippett. He was professor of composition at Queen's University, Belfast, and resident composer to the ULSTER ORCHESTRA, 1966–72. From 1972 to 1994 he was professor of music at the University of Bristol. The composer of numerous operas, oratorios, and three symphonies, he played an important role in the musical life of Northern Ireland, writing works for schools and incidental music for plays at the Lyric Theatre. Many of his compositions were premiered in Belfast, including *The Passion*, *Graduation Ode*, his two symphonies, and a violin concerto. **Emma Costello**

Warrenpoint bombing. On 27 August 1979, the same day that Lord Mountbatten was killed near his holiday home, Classiebawn Castle, Mullaghmore, Co. Sligo, eighteen British soldiers, mostly from the Parachute Regiment, were killed in two explosions at Narrow Water Castle, near Warrenpoint, Co. Down. The first bomb was detonated from the Republic, about 1 km (half a mile) across CARLINGFORD LOUGH. Estimated at 230 kg (500 lb) of explosive, packed into milk churns and hidden in a trailer loaded with hay and straw, it killed six soldiers in a passing convoy. This was followed by gunfire from across the lough, but in returning fire the soldiers succeeded only in shooting dead a passing English tourist. The second bomb exploded half an hour later, with even more devastating effect. It was cunningly planted in the only area of cover available to the survivors of the first explosion, along with reinforcements who had quickly arrived on the scene. This explosion killed a further twelve soldiers, including a battalion commanding officer who had arrived by helicopter. It was the worst incident up to that time in the TROUBLES and included the largest number of British army fatalities. The synchronisation of the Mountbatten killing and the Warrenpoint bomb, though unplanned, was a publicity coup for the PROVISIONAL IRA. In striking at the Parachute Regiment, perpetrators of the BLOODY SUNDAY killings, republicans could represent the carnage as legitimate revenge; a slogan painted on a Belfast wall declared: '13 gone but not forgotten, we got 18 and Mountbatten.' **Keith Jeffery**

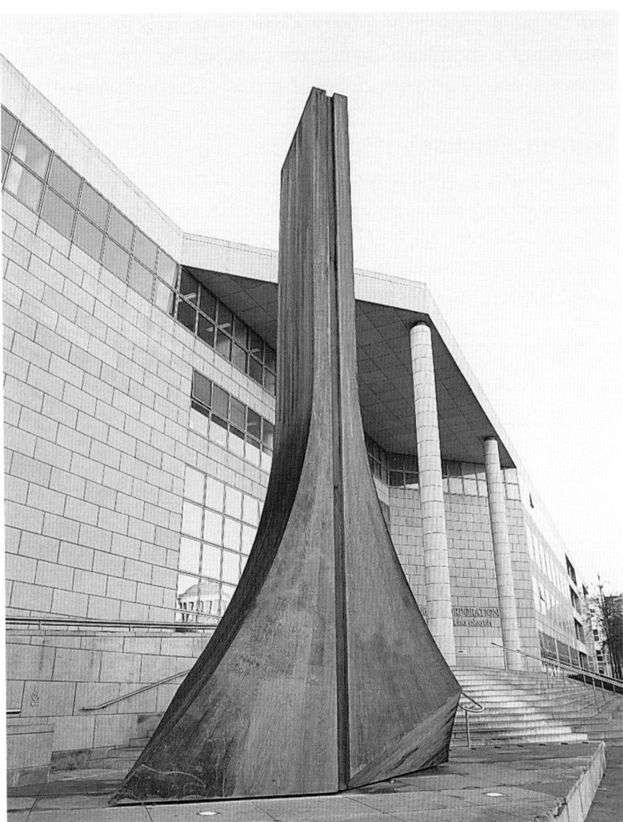

Warren, Michael. Wood Quay *(1995) by Michael Warren, inspired by the form of the prow of a Viking ship, a sculpture of red American cedar-wood on steel frame, 10 m (33 ft) in height, resting on a white Portuguese limestone podium, 17 m (56 ft) long, installed outside the Dublin Civic Offices, Wood Quay. [Dublin City Council; photo: Denis Mortell]*

Waste management as a whole poses a serious environmental problem, with the generation of waste increasing considerably in recent years. In the Republic, 80 million tonnes of waste was generated in 1998; of this, approximately 64.5 million tonnes originated from agricultural sources, mainly animal manure, the remaining 15.4 million tonnes comprising mainly industrial and municipal waste (domestic and commercial). For the same year an estimated 370,000 tonnes of hazardous waste was generated by industry (70 per cent), agriculture (10 per cent), services (10 per cent), and other sources (10 per cent), an increase of 13 per cent in two years. In Northern Ireland, the amount of household waste increased by 19 per cent over a period of ten years.

Ireland has traditionally relied on landfill as the principal method of dealing with waste. However, this one-dimensional approach is unsustainable. Rates of recycling are low by comparison with other countries. In the Republic in 1998 only 9 per cent of municipal waste was recycled. However, waste policy is now based on a hierarchy of options, with prevention the most desirable and disposal the least desirable. An extensive planning process has taken place in recent years, with an increase in the proportion of waste recycled and the diverting of materials as central parts of these plans. The EU Directive on Packaging and Packaging Waste requires targets for the recovery and recycling of packaging waste to be met over certain periods. This was incorporated in Irish law by the Packaging Regulations (1997), and subsequently REPAK was established as an approved body for facilitating industry in meeting these targets. Litter has been a problem in Ireland for many years. There has been an increased employment of litter wardens by local authorities and a corresponding increase in the number of 'on-the-spot' fines and prosecutions. **Anne-Marie Cunningham**

waste-water. Up to 1900 the collection, treatment, and disposal of waste-water or sewage was primitive or non-existent. Following the Public Health (Ireland) Act (1878) and the work of the Royal Commission on Sewage Disposal, in 1906 Dublin Corporation completed a main drainage scheme with associated primary treatment of the collected waste-water. The introduction of regular piped-water supplies made it possible for sewers to be flushed.

Partially treated waste-water is generally discharged into the sea or into rivers or LAKES; waste-water is also disposed of to septic tanks. Recent legislation and EU directives have imposed stricter requirements for treatment and disposal. **Ronald Cox**

'wasting sickness of Cú Chulainn': see 'SERGLIGE CON CHULAINN'.

water. Ireland is bounded on the north, west and south by the Atlantic Ocean; to the east lies the IRISH SEA. It has been estimated that Ireland can lay claim to almost 0.9 million km^2 (0.35 million sq. miles) of the Atlantic Continental shelf—fourteen times its land area and 14.5 per cent of the total sea-bed area of the EUROPEAN UNION. In relation to population, Ireland has by far the largest sea-bed territory in the European Community.

Ireland's coastal and offshore waters are among the highest-quality marine waters in Europe, and they host a rich and varied marine life. However, the open sea is not entirely free of contaminants, as it receives atmospheric deposition of pollutants that have been emitted into the air. The discharges from the nuclear reprocessing plant at Sellafield, Cumberland, also continue to result in contamination of the Irish marine environment. Closer to the shore, particularly in certain bays and estuaries, urban and industrial effluents give rise to varying degrees of impairment. Coastal waters with poor exchange of water can become polluted from a build-up of such contaminants as synthetic organic compounds, microbial organisms, oil, nutrients, heavy metals, radionuclides, and litter. Some estuaries are at risk from *eutrophication* (the over-enrichment of water by nutrients, particularly nitrates and phosphates), because of their low flushing rate and high nutrient content from agricultural and, in some instances, urban sources. This causes an accelerated growth of algae and other forms of plant life, produces an undesirable disturbance in the balance of organisms in the water, and can cause deoxygenation of the affected waters.

The Government of the Republic has ratified the Convention on the Protection of the Marine Environment of the North-East Atlantic (1992), whose objectives include conserving marine ecosystems and, when practicable, restoring marine areas that have been adversely affected, taking all possible steps to prevent and eliminate pollution, and enacting the measures necessary to protect the sea from the adverse effects of human activities. Ireland's sea waters, however, are generally clean, and the main environmental concern at present is the impact of fishing on target and non-target species, with concern about the stocks of particular fish. The marine environment on the Continental shelf is generally productive of fish, but the bulk of the catch has for long been taken by the fleets of other countries, and the fortunes of the Irish fishing industry have fluctuated. From the early 1960s considerable development efforts were made, including the improvement of HARBOURS, the provision of larger and better-equipped vessels, training, expansion of processing, organisation of distribution, and market development at home and abroad. Fish landings expanded dramatically, but from the mid-1970s expansion was hindered by some problems of resource supply, with the need for restrictions on fishing. Total allowable catches have been lowered for the Irish Sea, where cod stocks are below safe biological limits, and other stocks, such as those of haddock, whiting, and prawns, are severely depleted.

The seas around Ireland support large numbers of seals and dolphins, as well as a variety of whale species. In 1991 the Government declared an area within the 370 km (200-mile) limit to be a cetacean (whale and dolphin) sanctuary. Twenty-one species of cetacean have been recorded (between sightings and strandings), though only eleven are commonly sighted; common dolphins and harbour porpoises are most frequently reported. The abundance of most cetacean species is unknown, but a survey in 1995 estimated that there were approximately 36,000 harbour porpoises and 75,000 common dolphins in the 'CELTIC SEA' (St George's Channel). Strandings of cetaceans are common events on all Irish coasts but particularly along the south and west. The number of reported strandings is increasing, though this may be largely due to an increase in recording efforts. The precise reasons for stranding are unknown, but it may be largely a natural phenomenon. Interactions with fisheries, such as entanglement in nets, and high body burdens of organochlorine contaminants have also been identified as possible contributors.

water. *A jewel anemone photographed at Puffin Island, Co. Kerry. The more exposed reef faces of the west coast are home to great numbers of these anemones, with the result that they rival tropical coral reefs for sheer colour. [Nigel Motyer]*

Coastal areas are typically rich in biodiversity, and those in Ireland are particularly so, because of the wide range of habitats within a relatively small area. This richness is the result of the interaction of weather and water movements, working together to shape the rocks and sediments that produce a range of niches in which plants and animals can live. Habitats include sand dunes, salt-marshes, vegetated shingle banks, and rocky cliff habitats. However, as much of the population, including more than half the population in the Republic, live in coastal areas, both marine and coastal biodiversity are threatened by new HOUSING and other polluting activities in coastal areas.

The quality of sea bathing water is relatively good: 98 per cent of the 121 monitored sites in the Republic comply with EU requirements, while 80 per cent comply with more stringent guideline values. In Northern Ireland, 100 per cent of sixteen bathing waters comply with mandatory and guideline standards; during 2000 a further ten non-identified bathing waters were monitored, of which 90 per cent complied with the mandatory standards.

Relatively high rainfall and low population density ensure that Ireland is among the European countries with the highest availability of freshwater. This constitutes an important economic resource in the supply of drinking-water and of water for domestic, agricultural and industrial purposes. In many areas, rivers and lakes are attractive features of the landscape, helping to promote TOURISM and providing venues for recreational activities. Traditionally they also provide opportunities for game and coarse fishing; the high occurrence of salmon and trout in Irish freshwater bodies is unparalleled in most other European countries.

The River SHANNON, the longest river in the country, rises in the Cuilcagh Mountains in Co. Cavan and reaches the tide at the Shannon Estuary (the country's largest sea inlet) after flowing slowly through the Central Plain, which contains a number of other slow-flowing rivers. The rivers on the seaward side of the mountain ranges are short and flow rapidly to the sea. Ireland has approximately 4,000 LAKES, large and small, covering one-fiftieth of the total area of the country (see p. 648). Lakes are important for breeding and wintering wildfowl, and many are listed as 'special areas of conservation' (SACs). Salmon and trout are still widespread in inland waters but have been adversely affected by drainage and eutrophication in recent years. The char, which appears to be particularly sensitive to eutrophication, has been lost from a number of lakes since the beginning of the century. Coarse fish, which are non-native, now thrive in many rivers and lakes. The salmon is a listed species in the EU Habitats Directive, and Irish authorities are required to propose sites for its protection. However, despite Ireland being one of the most important sites for salmon rivers, the list and extent of the proposed sites appears extremely limited. A number of species in rivers and streams are of particular conservation importance, such as the remaining populations of the rare freshwater pearl mussel and white-clawed crayfish (see p. 25).

Eutrophication is believed to pose the most widespread threat to water quality. Some lakes and rivers are naturally eutrophic, because of their particular site and the underlying GEOLOGY; but in most instances eutrophication is a consequence of human activities that lead to increased losses of nutrients from land to water, from sources such as AGRICULTURE and sewage. Nutrient enrichment has caused a reduction in natural diversity as more productive species outbreed others. To prevent or reverse eutrophication these losses must be controlled; this is particularly necessary if the indigenous salmonid fish are to be preserved. Though measures have been taken to control the discharge of phosphorus, the risk presented by agricultural sources is still significant. In the Republic 67 per cent of monitored rivers and streams are unpolluted, 18 per cent are slightly polluted, and 14 per cent are moderately polluted; only 1 per cent (122 km) are seriously polluted. Since the early 1970s a substantial decline in the quality of river water has occurred. The bulk of the serious pollution is in streams and small rivers, where the dilution is limited.

As with rivers, eutrophication is the most serious threat to the water quality of lakes. In the Republic, 80 per cent of monitored lakes are judged to be in a satisfactory condition, 6 per cent are classed as moderately eutrophic, while the remaining 14 per cent show a strong to very high level of nutrient pollution. However, there has been an improvement in the quality of lake water, with the proportion of strongly eutrophic lakes falling from 16 to 3 per cent over ten years. This has resulted mainly from improvements in sewage treatment facilities, particularly the introduction of nutrient-removal processes.

Evidence available at present shows that there is nutrient enrichment in both LOUGH NEAGH and LOUGH ERNE and that many other rivers and lakes in Northern Ireland are also affected. This is attributed to an increase in phosphorus, derived primarily from agriculture, septic tanks, and urban sewerage systems, as well as from FORESTRY, creameries, and the food-processing industry.

Fish deaths caused by pollution are evidence of the existence of an extremely serious degree of environmental degradation. In most instances they arise from the unauthorised or accidental discharge of waste, such as silage liquors, manure slurries, and sewage, which cause rapid deoxygenation and at times direct toxicity, because of the presence of such compounds as ammonia and hydrogen sulphide. Events of this type have been relatively frequent, and in many instances the cause was found to be farm wastes. Recent education schemes, allied with enforcement measures, have led to a reduction in such pollution, but it remains a problem.

Ground-waters are particularly vulnerable to nitrate contamination, because of the high mobility of the substance in the soil and the consequent ease with which it can leach downwards through the water table. Most at risk are those ground-waters in agricultural areas where there is a high rate of application of fertilisers or animal manure. The contamination of ground-water has serious consequences for sources used as drinking-water. In the Republic, 20 per cent of monitored sites showed concentrations greater than the EU mandatory value. Ground-water resources account for about 11 per cent of public water supply in Northern Ireland, and high levels of nitrates in ground-water exist in three areas. Under the EU Nitrates Directive, these areas have been designated as 'nitrate-vulnerable zones', and farmers in these zones have to comply with restrictions aimed at reducing nitrate leaching. **Anne-Marie Cunningham**

Waterford, County (*Contae Phort Láirge*)

Province:	MUNSTER
County town:	Dungarvan
Area:	1,838 km² (710 sq. miles)
Population (2002):	101,518
Features:	Comeragh Mountains
	Knockmealdown Mountains
	Monavullagh Mountains
	River BLACKWATER
	River SUIR
Of historical interest:	Ardmore monastic site
	Curraghmore House
	Reginald's Tower
	Waterford cathedrals
Industry and products:	Beer
	Cattle
	Glass
	Paper
	Whiskey

Petula Martyn

County Waterford, a maritime county in the south-east of Ireland, with many of its principal settlements, including Waterford, Tramore,

and Dungarvan, along its indented coastline. Historically farming (dairying, sheep farming, and some cereal production) and fishing have been the predominant economic activities in the county. It has a rich tapestry of landscapes, the uplands to the north consisting of two mountain ranges, the Comeragh Mountains and Knockmealdown Mountains, while the eastern part is relatively low-lying. Lismore and Ardmore were significant monastic settlements; but the geography of settlement changed with the arrival of the Vikings. The city of WATERFORD, founded by VIKING traders at the meeting of the Rivers SUIR and BARROW, has become synonymous with the production of high-quality hand-cut glass, which remains one of the most important industries in both the city and county. The continued expansion of the port and the presence of an institute of technology have led to a more diverse industrial base.
Raymond O'Connor and John Crowley

Waterford (*Port Láirge*), historic port city on the estuary of the River SUIR; population (2002) 44,564. Waterford was established by the VIKINGS, who gave it the name Vadrefjord ('ram inlet'), c. 914. It was fortified by a stone wall in the first half of the twelfth century but was captured by the Normans after a siege in 1170. The town was reinforced, and over the next four centuries it became one of the most prosperous places in Ireland. The medieval economy was based on shipbuilding and trade, with the export of wool and hides to Flanders and elsewhere, though the neighbouring town of New Ross was a competitor. Imports of wine from south-west France were important. The medieval quays were half a mile long and capable of handling sixty ships.

Despite battles with New Ross and problems with piracy, Waterford remained the second city of Ireland in the sixteenth century. The attempt to impose Protestantism during the reign of Elizabeth I was rejected in Waterford, and the city's charters were revoked and military rule imposed. Though a new charter was granted in 1626, the seventeenth century brought warfare (including a siege by CROMWELL in 1649) and the imposition of a Protestant oligarchy on the city after 1660. This regime was responsible for transforming Waterford during the seventeenth century. The medieval walls were demolished and the city was allowed to expand. The old, congested fabric was replaced with fine GEORGIAN streets and buildings. The main dock became, in the words of the architectural historian Mark Girouard, 'the noblest quay in Europe'.

The year 1783 saw the beginning of the industry that has become synonymous with Waterford: high-quality lead crystal. The first plant was set up by the Penrose brothers, and the product was excellent, but the factory closed in 1851 because of severe excise duties and a lack of capital. Other industries survived, such as shipbuilding on the banks of the Suir; but for Waterford, like Cork to the west, the nineteenth and early twentieth centuries were a time of stagnation and decay. Its population fell from almost 40,000 in 1800 to 23,000 in 1841. By 1901 it had recovered somewhat, to 27,000, but it remained almost unchanged for the next sixty years. The modern revival of the city began with the reopening of the crystal industry as Waterford Crystal in 1947 and particularly the development of the market in the United States. The city has expanded and its population has grown continuously since 1961. The docks on the east side of the estuary have been modernised, and a new bridge across the river was opened in 1984. Waterford also benefited from URBAN RENEWAL since 1986, with the conservation of older buildings and the pedestrianisation of shopping streets, though traffic congestion remains a problem. Every year the city

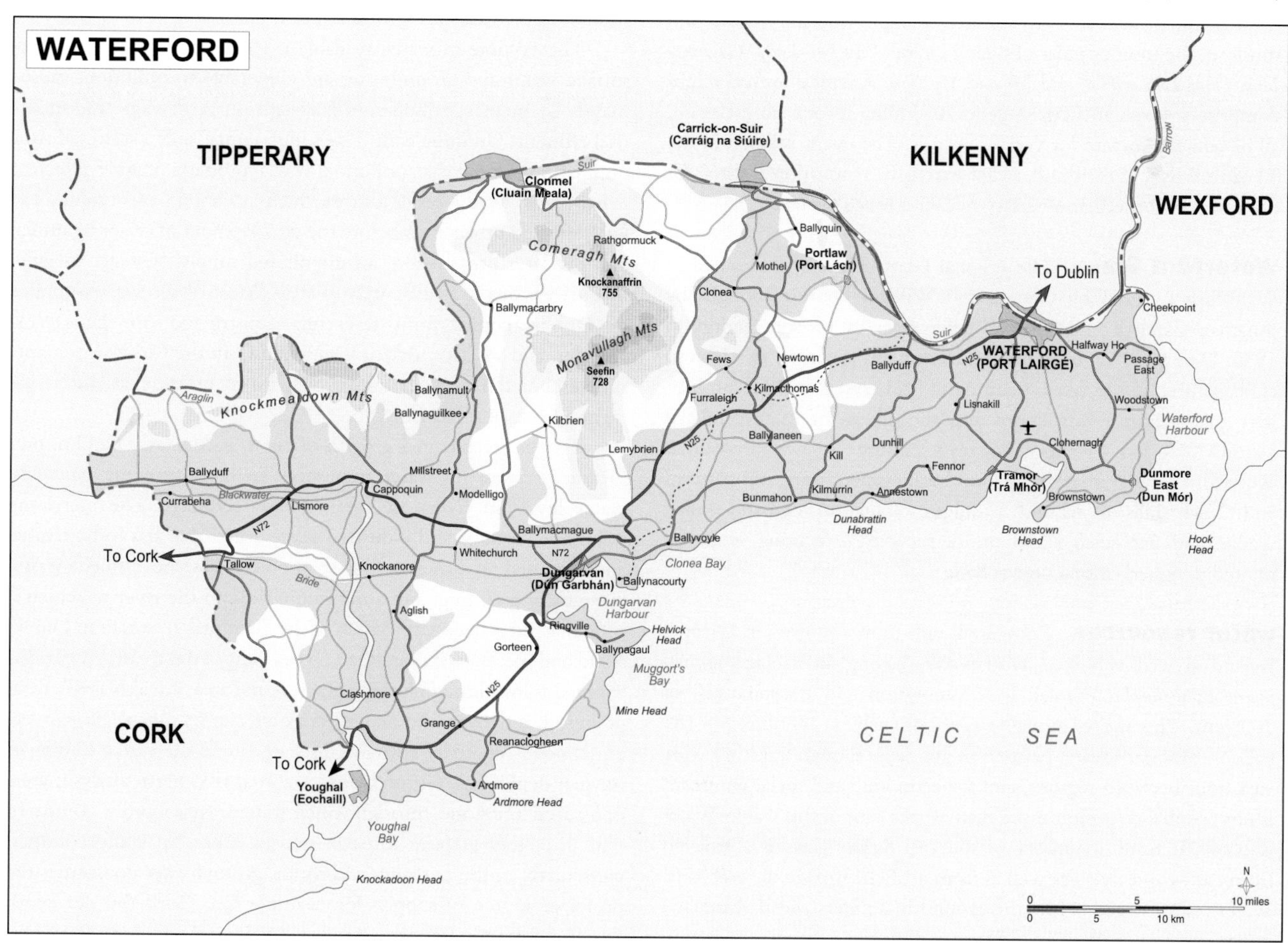

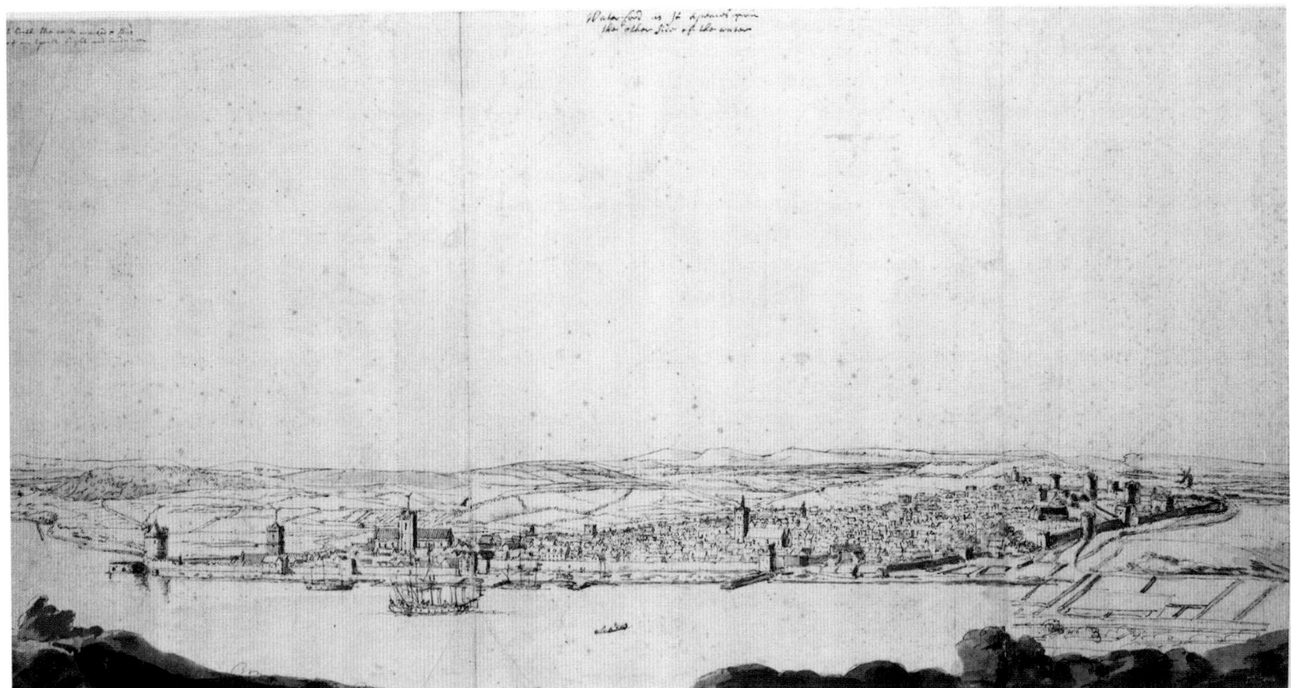

Waterford. Waterford from Across the River Suir, *ink and wash drawing on paper by Francis Place. The walled Viking and Anglo-Norman city is majestically sited on the Suir, with Reginald's Tower on the extreme left and the medieval Christ Church Cathedral the principal ecclesiastical building. [National Gallery of Ireland]*

hosts the WATERFORD INTERNATIONAL FESTIVAL OF LIGHT OPERA. **Kevin Hourihan**

Waterford Festival of Light Opera. Occurring annually in September, the festival consists of light operatic shows and musicals, the most popular of which include *My Fair Lady*, *Calamity Jane*, *Some Like it Hot*, and *Me and My Girl*. A typical festival might comprise a dozen amateur societies, including several from Britain, all of which compete for various awards. The event is based in the Theatre Royal, which underwent extensive renovation in time for the festival's fortieth anniversary in 2000. **Emma Costello**

Waterford Glass. The original Glass House was founded in Waterford in 1783 by George and William Penrose, bought by Jonathan Gatchell in 1799, and taken over by his son George in 1835. Despite its renown for the clarity and precision of virtuoso craftsmanship in the faceted cutting of lead crystal, in 1851 prohibitive taxes, export restrictions and the effects of FAMINE-related EMIGRATION led to the company's closure. It was revived as Waterford Crystal in 1947 by local businessmen, using old patterns and Czech skills, to rebuild its unique reputation for hand-skilled wedge and flat cutting and, more recently, executing work by invited designers. **Nicola Gordon Bowe**

water resources. Compared with most countries in Europe, Ireland is well endowed with water, having an average annual *precipitation surplus* (rainfall less evaporation and transpiration) of 700 mm. This makes available approximately 31,000 litres (8,189 gallons) of surface water per person per day—though there are wide variations between regions, and for economic and social reasons it is not possible to exploit more than 50 per cent of this water. Water is obtained from a number of sources. *Surface water* is abstracted from LAKES and rivers as well as from artificial storage in reservoirs. Water is also stored below the ground in aquifers and is abstracted at springs and wells. *Groundwater* is a major natural resource in Ireland, providing between 20 and 25 per cent of the supply of drinking-water. The regional distribution, size and type of aquifers varies considerably. In rural areas not served by public or group water schemes, groundwater is usually the only source, and many thousands of wells and springs are in use.

The volume of water available is affected by its quality. Both surface water and groundwater are vulnerable to pollution, caused mainly by incorrect disposal of farmyard slurry, sewage, and industrial effluent. Until the early 1960s high rainfall and a scattered rural population meant that pollution was a problem mainly affecting urban areas. Water-borne disease, such as cholera and typhus, had long affected urban areas before the development of water treatment and the later provision of an unpolluted supply of water to cities from reservoirs in nearby upland areas. Most of the water supplied to Dublin comes from reservoirs constructed on the LIFFEY, Dodder, and VARTRY. Belfast is supplied from the Mourne Scheme, supplemented by smaller reservoirs; more recently attention has turned to LOUGH NEAGH.

The unprecedented growth of cities, particularly Dublin, puts further pressure on water resources. To meet growing demands, water levels in rivers are often greatly reduced. The increasing volume of sewage and industrial waste-water that has to be treated and disposed of presents further problems, as the effluent is still potentially polluting, and a minimum flow in the river to which it is discharged is necessary. Much of the distribution system in Dublin is old and inefficient; more than 30 per cent of the treated water distributed is lost through leaking pipes. Rural areas are also at risk from pollution, and many lakes and rivers are affected by *eutrophication* (over-enrichment caused by nutrients discharged into the water, leading to oxygen depletion). Groundwater is also at risk, particularly in areas of fissured limestone, through which water travels rapidly, compared with the slow seepage through porous rocks. In some counties, particularly in the midlands and south, groundwater constitutes the principal source of supply, for example Co. Cork (90 per cent), Co. Roscommon (86 per cent), Co. Offaly (60 per cent), Co. Laois

(54 per cent), and Co. Kilkenny (52 per cent). In Northern Ireland groundwater is approximately 7 per cent of water supplied, mainly in the remoter parts of the west and north-east. Groundwater is most at risk from improperly managed land-fill sites, leaking septic tanks, and agricultural waste such as slurry and silage liquor. **R. A. Charlton**

water supply. Water supplies for domestic and industrial use are obtained from surface reservoirs, directly from rivers or lakes, or from groundwater sources. Dublin obtains its supplies from the Rivers LIFFEY, Dodder, and VARTRY, all impounded to form reservoirs, the oldest being that at Roundwood on the Vartry (1865). Belfast draws much of its water from the Silent Valley reservoirs in the MOURNE MOUNTAINS. Cork extracts supplies from the River LEE, Limerick from the River SHANNON. Most large towns obtain their supplies from rivers or lakes; smaller towns and villages are often connected to group or regional water schemes, the supplies being extracted from groundwater. **Ronald Cox**

water-wheels. Two varieties of water-wheel were used in Ireland up to recent times: the horizontal water-wheel, which had a vertical axle and did not require gearing, and the vertical water-wheel, which had a horizontal axle and was an important prime mover in eighteenth and nineteenth-century industry. Until the end of the eighteenth century nearly all water-wheels and their gearing were made of wood; gradually these components came to be replaced by cast iron. The first all-metal water-wheel erected in Ireland is believed to be that installed at Caledon, Co. Tyrone, in 1829 (reputedly by William Fairbairn of Manchester) for the Earl of Caledon, which still survives. In traditional water-wheels the motion of the wheel was transmitted to the gear wheels by means of its wooden axle, which was mechanically less efficient. In the early 1800s Thomas C. Hewes (1768–1832) of Manchester was developing what was to become known as the suspension water-wheel, in which power from the wheel was transmitted from a gear wheel on its rim. The earliest known example of such a wheel was installed at Allman's cotton mill, near Bandon, Co. Cork, in 1802. Good surviving examples of suspension water-wheels can be seen at Croom Mills, Co. Limerick (made by the Vulcan foundry of Cork in the 1840s), and the Midleton Distillery, Co. Cork (made by William Fairbairn of Manchester in 1852). [see INDUSTRIAL ARCHAEOLOGY; STEAM ENGINES.] **Colin Rynne**

Watson, John (1946–), racing driver. Born in Belfast. A single-minded driver, he survived numerous accidents and setbacks to become the first Irishman to lead the Drivers' World Championship. He won five grands prix and was runner-up in the 1982 World Championship. His climb from twenty-second to first place in the 1983 Long Beach Grand Prix made motor racing history. **Brendan Lynch**

Watts, William Arthur (1930–), botanist. Born in Dublin; educated at TCD, qualifying first in modern languages and subsequently in natural SCIENCE. In 1955 he was appointed to a lectureship in the Botany Department in Trinity College and, under the supervision of FRANK MITCHELL, embarked on studies of quaternary palaeo-ecology. In 1965 he succeeded D. A. WEBB as professor of botany, subsequently becoming professor of quaternary ecology. His work on the analysis of pollen grains and other plant remains from peat and sediments led to major advances in understanding the history of FLORA and climate in Europe and North America during and after the Ice Age. He served as provost of Trinity College, 1981–91, and president of the ROYAL IRISH ACADEMY, 1982–5. **Christopher Moriarty**

Wayman, Patrick Arthur (1927–1998), astronomer. Born in Bromley, Kent; educated at the University of Cambridge, where he was awarded a doctorate in OPTICS. After two years in the United States he joined the Royal Greenwich Observatory in 1952. In 1964 he was appointed director of DUNSINK OBSERVATORY, where he cherished its heritage and modernised the research facilities. Primarily an observer, he and his students employed telescopes at the Boyden Observatory in South Africa until the mid-1970s; a major achievement was his negotiation of Irish access to the international observatory in the Canary Islands. An abiding interest in optics led him to design new instruments and to restore old ones. He raised the profile of ASTRONOMY in Ireland and contributed significantly to the effective administration of the International Astronomical Union, of which he was general secretary, 1979–82. **Ian Elliott**

way-marked walking trails, cross-country walking routes suitable for all ages and fitness levels and designed to be walked in part or in whole in short sections. Though they often include magnificent mountain and wilderness stages, they are planned so as not to require great stamina or navigational skills, and they rarely rise above an altitude of 300 m (1,000 ft). The first such trail to be established in Ireland was the Ulster Way, an 800 km (500-mile) route instigated by Wilfrid Capper (1905–1998), who had been impressed by similar trails in England. With some interruptions it circled Northern Ireland; though the first way-marked section was opened in 1974, the route was never completed but instead became a series of separate routes. In the Republic in 1977 JOHN BRUTON TD, as parliamentary secretary to the Minister for Education, was the first politician to take positive steps to promote walking routes in furtherance of his policy of 'Sport for All' and the involvement of a greater number of the population in leisure exercise. He authorised the setting up of a committee to look into the planning of pedestrian walkways, and specifically to consider the possibility of connecting with the Ulster Way and so encourage cultural and sporting cross-border links.

In 1979 the veteran hill-walker J. B. MALONE was appointed field officer on the Long-Distance Walks Committee and he immediately embarked on setting up the Republic's first way-marked walking route, the Wicklow Way, a route he had dreamed of and planned decades before (see p. 689). The 132 km (82-mile) route, with frequent signposts, was opened in 1982. Since then a further thirty-one signposted routes have been established throughout the country, providing nearly 3,500 km (2,100 miles) of way-marked walking trails, incorporating ancient routes, droving roads, old coach-roads, FORESTRY roads, lanes, and tow-paths. Eventually it is hoped to establish a complete circuit of Ireland using linked trails.

Since the early 1980s hiking and hill-walking on and off the way-marked trails have become popular activities; by 1998 more than a quarter of a million tourists were participating in them, bringing in a revenue that year of over €137 million. **Michael Fewer**

wealth tax, annual, a tax based on the assets of citizens, with the assets valued and the tax calculated and paid yearly. An annual wealth tax was in force in the Republic for the years 1975–7 under the Wealth Tax Act (1975). Exemptions applied, and the tax was then levied at a flat rate of 1 per cent per annum on the remainder. It was introduced primarily as part of the cement in an inter-party Coalition Government involving FINE GAEL and the LABOUR PARTY,

way-marked walking trails. *Walking the Dingle Way at Slea Head, Co. Kerry, a view from one of the many designated self-guided scenic walking trails marked across Ireland. [Gareth McCormack]*

which came to power in 1973; it was abandoned after the electoral success in 1977 of FIANNA FÁIL, a party that had no political need to make gestures to the left.

Although there were 'scare stories' circulating in the mid-1970s concerning the amount of capital leaving Ireland to avoid the new tax, this was not the main difficulty. An annual wealth tax founders on the problem of valuation. The Irish wealth tax involved the valuation of all assets every year: for some items valuation was contentious, and collection and compliance costs enormous, while some important items of personal wealth could not be valued at all and were omitted from the act.

While the Labour Party government of 1974–9 in the United Kingdom seriously considered the idea of an annual wealth tax, such a tax was not introduced in Britain and Northern Ireland. **John W. O'Hagan**

Webb, David Allardice (1912–1994), botanist. Born in Dublin; in 1931 he graduated in natural sciences from the University of Dublin, where he was awarded a doctorate in marine zoology. He became assistant to H. H. DIXON, professor of botany in TCD, succeeding him in 1950 and in 1966 accepting a personal post as professor of systematic botany. *An Irish Flora*, first published in 1943, became the standard reference for the identification of Irish wild flowers; its concise style was subsequently adapted for the monumental *Flora Europaea* (1960–70s), of which he was principal editor. A world authority on the saxifrages, he was recognised in his day as the foremost expert on field botany in Ireland. **Christopher Moriarty**

wedge tombs, the last phase of the MEGALITHIC TOMB tradition and the most numerous and most widespread group. LABBACALLEE, Co. Cork, is one of the largest examples. The 532 known sites have a marked western distribution. Essentially they consist of a long burial gallery, sometimes with an ante-chamber or small closed end-chamber; they are generally broader and higher at the front, which invariably faces west. They are roofed with slabs laid directly on the side walls, which often have one or more rows of outer walling. Evidence from the small number of excavated sites suggests that they were being built between 2500 and 2000 BC. Though a truly Irish phenomenon, parallels have been sought for them in Brittany. **Paul Walsh**

weeds. The description of Ireland as the 'EMERALD ISLE' (first used by WILLIAM DRENNAN in 1795) is mainly due to its widespread grassland: approximately 11 million of its 17 million acres are covered by grassland of one kind or another. But grassland survives only as long as it is actively managed, which means either mowing or grazing a number of times each year. If these activities cease, shrubs, trees, and what are generally described as 'weeds' invade the grassland; it reverts to scrub, and eventually to woodland. Even a grass lawn, if neglected, will soon become overgrown with briars (blackberry) and the seedlings of nearby shrubs.

A weed can most conveniently be described as 'a plant out of place', and generally one that is undesirable or damaging in its wrong ENVIRONMENT. For the modern grassland farmer the most difficult weed is the broad-leaved dock. Where pastures are being reseeded, the new reseed provides the most opportune time to deal with this problem. A programmed approach is required; but the ability of seedling docks to survive many years in the soil adds to the difficulty of control.

Weeds were once a headache for the TILLAGE farmer. Different crops tend to have a characteristic weed flora associated with them. However, methods of chemical control of tillage weeds are now so successful that only fragmented weed communities can be seen in tillage fields. The weeds of tillage land have a remarkable seedling ability in relation to their size, which helps them to colonise open areas rapidly. Some weeds that do not produce much seed often produce several seed crops or generations in a single cropping year; examples are chickweed, groundsel, and shepherd's purse. Another remarkable attribute of weeds is their ability to flourish and produce young seedling plants in a wide range of soil and climatic conditions. Some of the more resilient ones, such as groundsel, chickweed, and annual nettle, require prolonged periods of sub-zero temperatures before they are killed.

Given the large proportion of CONACRE in tillage farms, and the tight margins that prevail, the control of weed beet and wild oats has been overlooked in recent years by some growers in an attempt to cut costs. The same years have seen a marked increase in the incidence of these potentially deadly yield-robbers. The successful campaign against wild oats by tillage farmers and advisory bodies in Northern Ireland has shown the value of concentrated effort on the part of the farming community in the control of unwanted species. **Derek O'Donoghue**

Wejchert, Andrzej (1937–), architect. Born in Gdańsk, Poland; educated at Warsaw Polytechnic and the Design Office of City Buildings, Warsaw, 1959–64. He won first prize in the International Master Plan Competition, UCD, 1964. He designed the Arts and Commerce Building, Administration Building (awarded RIAI Gold Medal, 1971–3), water tower and sports centre of UCD. His early work is characterised by exposed concrete and organisational grids. He and his wife, Danuta Wejchert, established A. + D. Wejchert, Dublin, 1974; they designed prefabricated schools at Ballincollig, Co. Cork, and Ballynanty, Co. Limerick, and the Access Building at AILWEE Cave, Co. Clare (which won the Europa Nostra diploma, 1980). Post-modern tendencies are seen at the Smithfield Village housing and entertainment development, Dublin, while strong geometrics mark the Sobanski Palace Complex, 1997–99, and the Media Business Centre, 2002 (both in Warsaw), as well as the Helix, a performing arts centre at DCU, Dublin, 2002. **Raymund Ryan**

Weldon, Liam (1933–1995), singer and songwriter. Born in Dublin. With his wife he ran the Pavee's Club at SLATTERY's pub in Capel Street and a singers' club in the Tailors' Hall during the 1970s. His lyrics berate injustice and defend the poor and marginalised, nowhere more strikingly than in 'The Blue Tar Road', an indictment of Dublin City Council's treatment of travelling people. With TONY MACMAHON, DÓNAL LUNNY, Tríona Ní Dhomhnaill, and PETER BROWNE he was a member of 1691, the group that evolved into the BOTHY BAND. His collected songs were issued on CD in 1999 as *Dark Horse on the Wind*. **Fintan Vallely**

welfare state. The 'welfare state' as it is known today in Western capitalist countries was developed primarily in the period after the Second World War, but the roots of many contemporary policies were planted between the 1880s and 1920s in Western Europe. Welfare states were developed to reconcile problems of production and distribution, and these responses are reflected in social rights to certain minimum standards of income, HEALTH, EDUCATION, and (in some states) HOUSING, irrespective of labour market status. In this sense all developed capitalist countries are welfare states; but there is considerable variation between countries in the type and scope of social provision and in the criteria for access to benefits and services. This reflects different political choices.

The Irish welfare state is usually categorised as a liberal welfare state. While the welfare state in Northern Ireland differs in some significant respects from that in the Republic, it also fits into the liberal welfare state category, as does the British welfare state. This implies a strong emphasis on means-testing for access to services and a generally strong role for the market, relative to the state and the family, in the provision of services. This contrasts with the social-democratic welfare state—exemplified by Sweden—where the state has a much greater role in the provision of services, and the conservative or status-based welfare state—exemplified by Germany—where there is strong dependence on the family for the provision of services. Like all other liberal welfare states, the welfare states in the Republic and in Northern Ireland are not exclusively liberal in orientation; elements of the other types of welfare states can be identified. **Julia S. O'Connor**

Wellesley, Arthur, Duke of Wellington (1769–1852), soldier and politician. Born in Dublin, a brother of RICHARD COLLEY WELLESLEY; he had a distinguished military career in India, the Iberian Peninsula, and the Waterloo campaign. Politically he was an Irish MP, 1790–5, CHIEF SECRETARY, 1807–9, and a Cabinet minister from 1819. As Prime Minister, 1828–30, he opposed CATHOLIC EMANCIPATION but in 1829 gave way rather than risk violent disorder (see p. 851). **Peter Gray**

Wellesley, Richard Colley (1760–1842), politician. Born in Dangan Castle, Co. Meath, elder brother of ARTHUR WELLESLEY, DUKE OF WELLINGTON. Created Marquis Wellesley in 1799, he was Governor-General of India, 1798–1805, before serving twice as LORD LIEUTENANT of Ireland, 1821–8 and 1833–4. He was favourable to Catholic Emancipation and hostile to Orangeism; his second term was widely regarded as a failure. **Peter Gray**

Went, A. E. J. [Arthur] (1910–1980), fishery biologist. Born in London; educated at the University of London. Inspector and scientific adviser in the Government fisheries service, he gave special attention to salmon, char, and sea trout and was a founder of the Salmon Research Trust of Ireland and the Irish Specimen Fish Committee. He was a member of the Council of the ROYAL IRISH ACADEMY, ROYAL DUBLIN SOCIETY, ROYAL ZOOLOGICAL SOCIETY OF IRELAND, and AN TAISCE and was president of the International Council for the Exploration of the Sea, 1968–71. A friendly, efficient and memorable man, he published many important scientific papers on Irish fish. **D. Patrick Sleeman**

Wentworth, Thomas, first Earl of Strafford (1593–1641), politician. Born in London, eldest son of Sir William Wentworth; educated at the University of Cambridge. A strong supporter of CHARLES I in his struggle with Parliament, he was appointed Lord Deputy of Ireland in 1632. An efficient administrator, he had an ultimately disastrous disregard for the political repercussions of his policies. He largely ignored the native Irish and appears to have regarded Ireland as a laboratory in which he could test his plans for achieving greater royal control in England. He determined to destroy the vested interests of both the OLD ENGLISH and the NEW ENGLISH, which he saw as weakening the prerogative of the king. In the Parliament of 1634 he deftly manipulated the Old English, obtaining renewal of the subsidies agreed in return for the Graces, without conceding the demand that they be enacted. He further alienated the Old English through his plans for a plantation in Connacht, which, though unrealised, ensured the permanent hostility of this politically significant group. His twin attack on lay impropriations and the Low Church theology, as expressed in the articles of 1615 of the Church of Ireland, generated strong New English hostility to him. In Ulster he aroused the ire of Scottish settlers through his attempts to eradicate Presbyterian influence in the Church of Ireland. His politically insensitive approach generated an unlikely alliance between the Old and New English representatives in Parliament, which culminated in their crucial testimony at his impeachment in 1640 and his subsequent beheading in May 1641. **Liam Irwin**

Werburgh Street Theatre (1635–41), Dublin, the first Irish theatre, established in Werburgh Street, just behind DUBLIN CASTLE. It had a pit, a gallery, and a stage box for its patron, THOMAS WENTWORTH, Earl of Strafford. The stage was well equipped, with at least two doors, a discovery space, a trap, and an upper gallery. By 1637, under the management of JOHN OGILBY, the theatre had a permanent company of professional actors fleeing the plague that had closed London theatres, and a resident playwright, James Shirley, whose ST PATRICK FOR IRELAND (1639) was premiered on its stage. The theatre was forced to close with the onset of civil war in 1641. **Christopher Morash**

Wesley, John (1703–1791), founder of METHODISM. Born in Epworth, Lincolnshire; educated at the University of Oxford. Ordained deacon in 1725 and priest in 1728, he was concerned to reform Anglicanism from within; he was influenced by Moravianism and began to preach out of doors and to form religious societies. His zeal and organisational talents ensured rapid growth in his following and the emergence of a distinct religious body that broke with the Church of England after his death in 1791. He travelled extensively throughout Britain and visited Ireland on twenty-one occasions (see p. 720). **Myrtle Hill**

West, Anthony C. (1910–1988), novelist and short-story writer. Born in Co. Down. His prose style is often described as poetic. His short stories deal with life in a rural community, linking fertile nature with the emotions of puberty. *As Towns with Fire* (1968) is a semi-autobiographical novel about a British airman in the Second World War, complete with long philosophical meditations on the meaning of life. Other work includes *River's End and Other Stories* (1958), *The Ferret Fancier* (1963), and *All the King's Horses and Other Stories* (1982). **Derek Hand**

West, Sir James Grey (1885–1951), architect. Born in Cardiff; following an apprenticeship he entered the Office of Works in London, 1904. His major designs include the Ministry of Pensions building at Acton, the RAF College at Cranwell, and the Consulate-General in Alexandria. His celebrity in Ireland rests on a single building, the Royal Courts of Justice (1928–33), at the corner of Chichester Street and May Street, Belfast. The courts are to a monumental classical design, with baroque touches, clad in Portland stone on a steel frame. West was promoted chief architect in 1934, a post he held for six years, and was knighted in 1936. **Frederick O'Dwyer**

West, Robert (died 1790), master-builder and stuccodore, from a family of Dublin stuccodores who are recorded as early as 1639. He was the first of the Irish craftsmen to imitate the ornamental rococo style of the LAFRANCHINI BROTHERS. In the 1750s he carried out fine foliate and diaperwork stucco in the Lying-In Hospital (ROTUNDA), Dublin. Like other craftsmen, he was also an entrepreneur, building houses in Dominick Street, Dublin, in the 1750s. The finest, no. 20 (1758), contains some of the most idiosyncratic and the best-known Irish stuccowork, heavily influenced by Lafranchini and CRAMILLION (see p. 543). West or his studio have been credited with a number of rococo interiors: among the finest are those at Dowth Hall, Co. Meath, and, by association, 86 St Stephen's Green, Dublin, and Dunsandle, Co. Galway. Each of these houses contains (or contained) stucco variants of French rococo *boiserie* (wainscoting) decorated with modelled vine leaves, puffs of cloud, swags, and thoroughly asymmetrical compositions, held firmly in place within a Palladian framework. **Christopher Moore**

West Clare Railway, a NARROW-GAUGE RAILWAY built under the Tramways Act (1883) by WILLIAM MARTIN MURPHY. The line between Ennis and Milltown Malbay, with a gauge of 0.91 m (3 ft), opened on 2 July 1887, being subsequently linked by a separate company, the South Clare Railway, to Kilrush and Kilkee. It acquired a poor reputation for timekeeping, being somewhat unjustly ridiculed by Percy French in his song 'Are You Right There, Michael?' which achieved wide popularity. The line closed on 1 February 1961, but a small section has been reopened as a tourist attraction. **Bernard Share**

Westmeath, County (*Contae na hIarmhí*)

Province:	LEINSTER
County town:	Mullingar
Area:	1,764 km^2 (679 sq. miles)
Population (2002):	72,027
Features:	Lough Derravaragh
	Lough Ennell
	Lough Owell
	River Deel
	River Inny
Of historical interest:	Athlone Castle
	Fore Abbey
	Tullynally Castle
	Uisneach Hill and Earthworks
Industry and products:	Dairy products
	Light engineering
	Limestone
	Metal products
	Peat production
	TEXTILES
	Trout fishing

Petula Martyn

County Westmeath, a county in the Central Plain, created out of Co. Meath in 1541. Its landscape is dominated by ranges of good grassland on well-drained eskers interspersed with extensive patches of raised bogland. This patchwork was important in shaping settlement and communications: most routeways run east to west over esker ridges, along which were established many Early Christian settlements, while villages such as **Milltownpass** and **Tyrrellspass** mark historic passages through the boglands. The county contains some large lakes, such as Lough Derravaragh (scene of the legend of 'The CHILDREN OF LIR'), Lough Owel, Lough Ennell, and Lough Ree on the River SHANNON, important for fishing and boating. **Mullingar** (population 8,833), the county town, and **Athlone** (population 7,479) are the largest towns. While Westmeath was included in the initial ANGLO-NORMAN CONQUEST, it became part of the Gaelicised region beyond the PALE reclaimed by the

MacGeoghegans and O'Melaghlins. The countryside contains many remains of mottes from the Norman settlement, the Georgian town of **Moate** (population 1,934), established by the QUAKER Clibborn family, taking its name from the Anglo-Norman period. The dense network of ruined TOWER-HOUSES testifies to the contested nature of this frontier territory in the Middle Ages. **Patrick Duffy**

Westminster, Irish representation at. Under the ACT OF UNION (1800), Ireland was granted 100 seats (out of a total of 658) in the British House of Commons. This rose to 105 in 1832 but was reduced to 103 in 1870. Ireland was at first grossly under-represented in proportion to its population, but this was reversed in the aftermath of the Great Famine. In addition, twenty-eight Irish representative peers and (until 1870) four CHURCH OF IRELAND bishops sat in the House of Lords. **Peter Gray**

wetland archaeology, a modern sub-discipline of archaeology, the scientific study of past human activities in raised BOGS, LAKES, rivers, and estuarine and coastal wetlands. The waterlogged and therefore anaerobic character of the soils of these environments means that certain types of archaeological remains that normally rot or desiccate on dry land—such as wooden structures and artefacts of wood, leather, textile, and bone—are often spectacularly well preserved (see p. 1041). Wetland archaeological investigations are often multi-disciplinary in scope, as a wide range of scientific techniques is used to extract a maximum of information from these highly informative sites. Recent wetland archaeological discoveries have included CRANNÓGS and lake-dwellings, prehistoric and historical TRACKWAYS, BOG BODIES, and settlements (such as CLONFINLOUGH, Co. Offaly), and trackways and fish traps on estuarine mudflats. **Aidan O'Sullivan**

Wettin, Ernst Heinrich (1897–1971), Prince of Saxony. Born in Germany, the youngest of three sons of the former King of Saxony, Friedrich August III of the House of Wettin. In French-occupied Germany in 1947 he made a deal with the French government whereby he would relinquish a priceless family treasure, the crown of Louis IX, in return for domicile in Ireland. The Government offered no objection, and he settled in Co. Westmeath, where he took up dairy farming. **Ciarán Deane**

Wexford, County (*Contae Loch Garman*)

Province:	LEINSTER
County town:	WEXFORD
Area:	2,352 km^2 (907 sq. miles)
Population (2002):	116,543
Features:	Blackstairs Mountains
	River SLANEY
Of historical interest:	Clonmines medieval site
	Dunbrody Abbey
	DUNCANNON FORT
	Enniscorthy Castle
	Ferns churches
Industry and products:	Fishery
	Food-processing
	Light and heavy engineering
	Livestock
	Oats, barley, POTATOES

Petula Martyn

County Wexford, a county in the south-eastern corner of Ireland, bounded by the River BARROW, the Blackstairs Mountains, and the

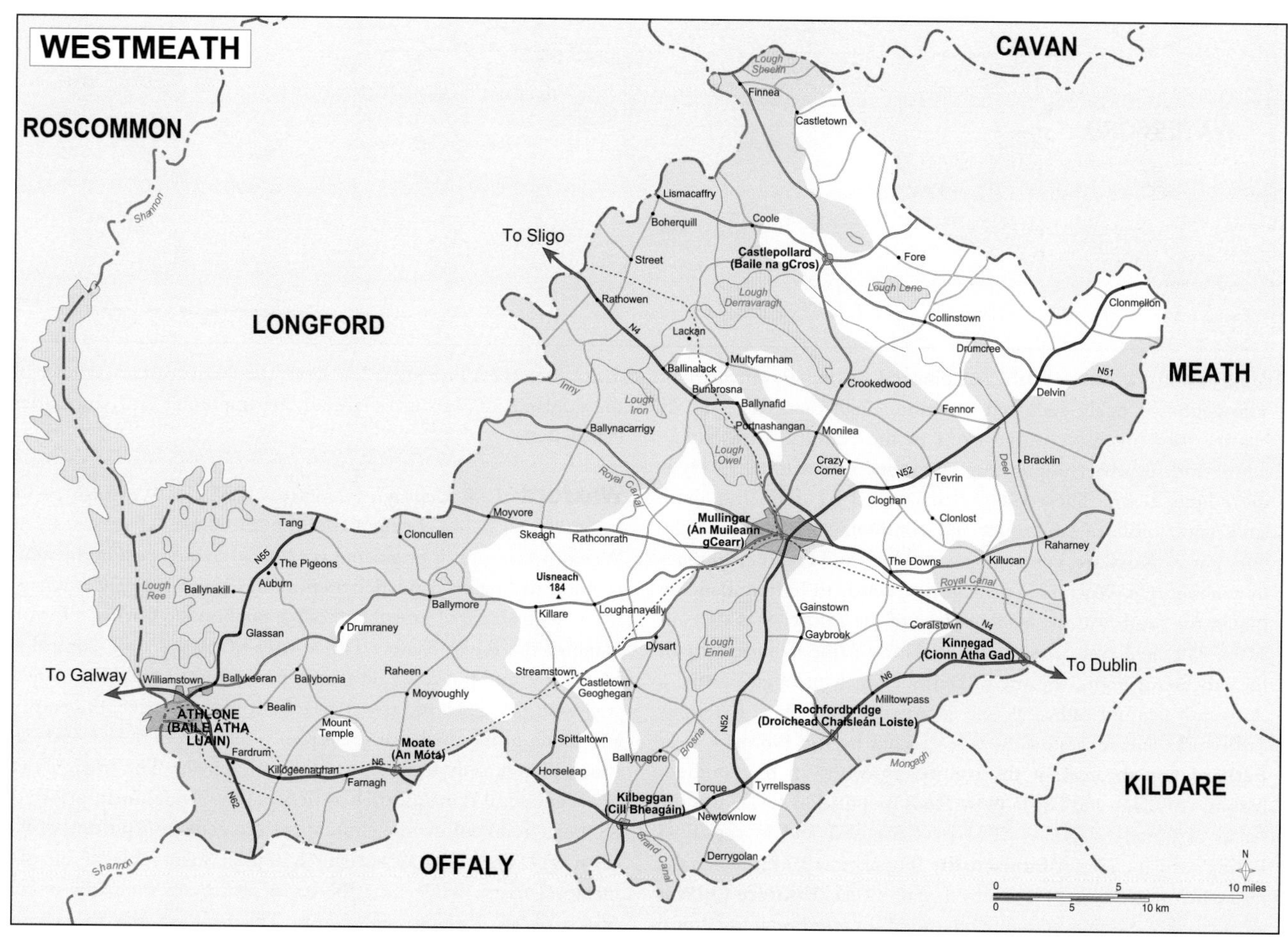

south WICKLOW MOUNTAINS and bisected by the River SLANEY. The county is richly endowed, environmentally and culturally. It has the most intensive tillage farms in the country, with barley, wheat and sugarbeet dominating. **Wexford** (population 9,443) is the county town. The coast is characterised by distinctive dune landscapes, offshore sandbanks, and continuing sea erosion. The ferry port at **Rosslare**, connecting with Wales and France, continues to symbolise Co. Wexford as the historic gateway to Ireland. Bannow Bay in the south was the landing-place of the ANGLO-NORMANS in 1169. The medieval county, with its Norse name, coincided with the diocese of Ferns, the site of Dermot MacMurrough's castle, a thirteenth-century cathedral, and an Augustinian abbey. Extensive earthworks and moated sites were erected by the Normans near **Fethard** and throughout the county, especially in the southern baronies of Bargy and Forth. **New Ross** (population 4,812) was the scene of bloody sieges in 1643 by Cromwell and in the 1798 Rising, which ended at **Enniscorthy** (population 3,742), when the insurgents were defeated at nearby VINEGAR HILL. **Kilmore Quay** is an attractive fishing village, with good examples of traditional thatched houses. The Saltee Islands off the south coast, together with the sloblands of Wexford Harbour, are important bird sanctuaries.

Patrick Duffy

Wexford (*Loch Garman*), county town of Co. Wexford; population (2002) 9,443. Lying at the mouth of the River SLANEY in Wexford Harbour, it originated as a VIKING trading post in the tenth century. Its English name derives from the Norse *Ueig-fjorðr*, 'Ueig's fjord'; its Irish name probably recalls a pool on the Garma, a former name of the River Slaney. The ANGLO-NORMANS took control in May 1169, and the town ultimately passed to STRONGBOW. A new wall with five gates and towers was built in the fourteenth century, and much of the medieval street plan is retained in the present-day town, though only fragments of the wall remain. The town is rich in ecclesiastical remains, such as those of the Augustinian priory of SS. Peter and Paul, whose churchyard also contains a portion of the town wall. The FRANCISCAN church in John Street is on the site of a medieval friary, while near the town centre are remnants of the priory of the Knights of St John. The Bullring was the site of bull-baiting until 1770 and the traditional site of a Cromwellian massacre; it has recently been redeveloped as a memorial to the 1798 REBELLION.

The present-day town has a range of manufacturing industry and is only 20 km (12 miles) from Rosslare Europort, one of the country's most important freight and passenger ports. Tourism is an important economic activity and the town is particularly noted for the annual WEXFORD FESTIVAL OPERA, which takes place in October. This is centred in the restored eighteenth-century THEATRE ROYAL and attracts an international audience. **Joseph Brady**

Wexford, Siege of (29 September to 11 October 1649). Despite the fact that Wexford was strongly fortified, the governor, Colonel David Synnott, complained of 'no resolution in the townsmen to defend the town', an attitude perhaps explicable by the hopes of religious toleration still entertained at this early stage of the Cromwellian reconquest. While negotiations were in progress, the commander of the castle adjacent to the walls surrendered his post. From here the attackers entered and captured the town, meeting resistance only in the bull ring or market square. Claims such as those in a subsequent petition by the inhabitants that Cromwell 'put man, woman and child to the sword, to very few', are exaggerated, as the town was not completely cut off, and many of the inhabitants escaped before and during the attack. The massacre of soldiers, clergy, and some civilians happened, in contrast to DROGHEDA, when soldiers exceeded their orders. Cromwell was probably being truthful when he claimed that he had not wanted to sack the town. **Pádraig Lenihan**

Wexford Festival Opera, an annual international opera festival held in Wexford in October. Having grown out of the Wexford Opera Study Group, the first festival took place in 1951 under its artistic director, T. J. WALSH, and president, Sir Compton Mackenzie. The festival's inaugural work was *The Rose of Castille* by MICHAEL WILLIAM BALFE, performed at the THEATRE ROYAL, where the main festival is still held. From 1955 the festival staged two operatic works. It now also incorporates many other recitals, concerts, and lectures. The main aim of the festival has always been to rediscover forgotten operas as well as less familiar works by famous composers. Wexford celebrated its fiftieth season in 2001 with productions of Dvořák's *Jakobín*, Flotow's *Alessandro Stradella*, and Massenet's *Sapho* (see p. 1115). **Emma Costello**

Whaley, Thomas 'Buck' (1766–1800), politician and eccentric. His fame derives primarily from his penchant for gambling. Obliged to leave Paris because of debts incurred at cards, he achieved renown by walking to Jerusalem to play ball against the city walls and by taking up other odd wagers. He devoted his later years to the preparation of a cautionary memoir of his life; but his preparedness to treat with both the pro-Union and anti-Union interests shows that he never quite embraced respectability. **James Kelly**

Whately, Richard (1787–1863), Archbishop of Dublin. He came to the Church of Ireland from a chair of political economy at the University of Oxford. Unfamiliarity with affairs of church and state in Ireland did not inhibit him from exercising with vigour the powers of his office—which he held from 1831 to 1863—to further his broad church and liberal principles. In contrast with his contemporary at Armagh, Beresford, he proved accommodating, though by no means subservient, where government policy was concerned and attracted criticism for his attitude to the CHURCH TEMPORALITIES (IRELAND) ACT (1833) and the tithe question. His leading role in the establishment of the national school system (for which he wrote some controversial textbooks), earned him particular opprobrium in some church circles. His relations with Archbishop Murray were cordial, but, though a supporter of Catholic Emancipation, he had little sympathy with Roman Catholicism, or with the Tractarians in his own church. **Kenneth Milne**

Wheatley, David (1970–), poet, critic, and editor. Born in Dublin; educated at TCD. His first collection, *Thirst*, was published in 1997; a second collection, *Misery Hill*, appeared in 2000. He won the Friend's Provident National Poetry Competition in 1994. He jointly edits *Metre* and edited *Stream and Gliding Sun: A Wicklow Anthology* (1998). **Terence Brown**

Wheatley, Francis (1747–1801), painter. Born in London; trained at Shipley's Drawing School and also with Richard Wilson. He painted mainly portraits and landscapes, exhibiting at the Society of Artists. He visited Ireland in 1767 and later, in 1779, escaped creditors by settling in Dublin for four years. He produced several important paintings in Ireland, depicting contemporary events, including *A View of College Green with the Meeting of the Volunteers on the 4th November 1779, to Commemorate the Birthday of King William* (now in the NATIONAL GALLERY OF IRELAND) and *The Irish House of Commons in 1780: Henry Grattan Urging the Claim of Irish Right*, the only contemporary depiction of the interior of the House of Commons (see pp. 437, 454). Back in London, he exhibited several paintings with Irish subjects at the Royal Academy in 1784, including Donnybrook Fair. He was elected to the Royal Academy six years later. **Peter Murray**

Wheeler, Anna, née Doyle (1785–c. 1850), socialist feminist. Born in Co. Tipperary; tutored at home and influenced by the works of Mary Wollstonecraft and the French philosophers. In 1801 she married Francis Massey-Wheeler but in 1812 fled the marital home to Guernsey. Between 1816 and 1820 she collaborated with the French Saint-Simonians, who aspired to integration and co-operation between European states. From 1820 to 1823 she assisted Robert Owen, leader of the co-operative movement, introducing him to Irish sociopolitical reformers. In 1825, with WILLIAM THOMPSON, she published *Appeal of One Half of the Human Race*, which argued for civil, domestic, and political rights for women. She continued to advocate a reformed society based on egalitarian communities. **Margaret Morse**

Whelahan, Brian (1971–), hurler. Born in Birr, Co. Offaly, into a family steeped in the game. In 1987, at the age of sixteen, he won an all-Ireland minor medal. He added a second minor title in 1989 when he also graduated to the senior team. He won two all-Ireland senior medals, in 1994 and 1998, by which time he had been joined by his brothers, Simon and Barry, in the Offaly team. He was Hurler of the Year in 1994 and 1998 and is seen as one of the greatest talents in the history of the game. **Donal Keenan**

Whelan, Bill (1950–), composer, musician, and record producer. Born in Limerick; having studied law, he opted instead for a career in music. He spent some time as resident bandleader for RTÉ, and joined the group Planxty for a short period. He has produced records for many traditional artists as well as artists from other fields. His commissioned orchestral works include 'The Ó Riada Suite' (1987), 'The Seville Suite' (1992), and 'The Spirit of Mayo' (1993); film scores include *Some Mother's Son* (1996). Collaboration with Moya Doherty for an intermission act during the EUROVISION SONG

CONTEST in 1994 led to the show 'RIVERDANCE', an arrangement of traditional dancing, which has toured the world with unprecedented success. **Jimmy O'Brien Moran**

Whelan, Leo (1892–1956), portrait and genre painter. Born in Dublin; trained at the Metropolitan School of Art. He developed a portrait style under the influence of WILLIAM ORPEN, who insisted on academic accuracy, strong composition, and a realistic approach to his sitters. Whelan established himself as a portraitist and produced many competent representations, including that of WILLIAM T. COSGRAVE. He also painted some superb interior scenes, such as *The Kitchen Window* (1926, Crawford Gallery, Cork). He regularly exhibited with the RHA and was made a full member in 1924; in 1950 he was made an honorary member of the Royal Ulster Academy. **Síghle Bhreathnach-Lynch**

Whigs, members of a British political party identified with upholding the principles of the 1688 revolution. From the 1760s, Whigs tended to oppose the use of royal prerogative and to advocate parliamentary and administrative reform and CATHOLIC EMANCIPATION. Whig governments (1782–3, 1806–7, 1830–34, 1835–41, 1846–52) were generally more favourable to Irish and Catholic claims than were their TORY rivals. The party was absorbed into British Liberalism in the 1850s, after which the term was applied to the more conservative landed elements of the Liberal Party. A parallel Irish Whig Party emerged from 1788 to 1789 combining the Ponsonby interest and PATRIOT reformers; it united with its British sister-party after the Union. **Peter Gray**

whiskey, a spirit made by distilling fermented cereals. The English word 'whiskey' is derived from an earlier Irish term, *uisce beatha*, itself a translation of the Latin *aqua vitae* ('water of life'). It is not known when whiskey was first distilled in Ireland, but it is probable that it was introduced by monks and used first for medicinal purposes; a fourteenth-century Latin treatise on aqua vitae was largely concerned with the drink's supposed healing properties. But in the early fifteenth century the annals record the death of a lord who drank too much whiskey; by 1400, therefore, and probably earlier, whiskey was being consumed for reasons of pleasure rather than health, or perhaps both. Its growing popularity is shown by the fact that in 1556 the Irish Parliament, complaining that aqua vitae was made 'universally' in Ireland and 'daily drunken', passed an act forbidding distillation without a licence.

But while governments worried that the production of whiskey wasted valuable grain, and that the drink gave courage to rebels, whiskey was not in fact widely consumed in Ireland, outside Ulster, until the late eighteenth century. Then new restrictions and taxes on DISTILLING helped foster an extensive illegal distilling industry, which flourished up to the Great Famine. POITÍN—cheap illicit whiskey—popularised whiskey-drinking throughout the country, though from the 1850s onwards the constabulary fought a long and generally successful battle to curb its production. With the decline of poitín in the late nineteenth century, large commercial distilleries were able to satisfy the increased taste for whiskey, as well as to develop lucrative overseas markets, in competition with the more powerful Scottish distillers. This competition was often fierce and, in the early twentieth century, led to the legal differentiation of 'Irish whiskey' from 'Scotch whisky'. **Elizabeth Malcolm**

Whitaker, T. K. [Kenneth] (1916–), civil servant. Born in Co. Down; educated at Drogheda CBS and graduated with BA and MScEcon from the University of London by private study. He took first place in four CIVIL SERVICE examinations, joining the service in 1934 and becoming an assistant principal officer in 1943 and principal officer in 1945. He became Secretary of the Department of Finance in 1956 at the age of thirty-nine, a promotion that ignored the custom of seniority. In part his promotion was a reaction against economic crisis and a perceived bankruptcy of the protectionist policies of Griffith and De Valera. Emigration was accelerating and growth non-existent; Whitaker believed that free trade and Government investment in productive enterprise rather than in housing and other social services was the way out. In 1958 a white paper, PROGRAMME FOR ECONOMIC EXPANSION, was published under his name—another unprecedented departure for a civil servant. The document emphasised AGRICULTURE rather than INDUSTRY as the core of the future ECONOMY; but its importance was that it publicly declared the end of the de Valera era and announced a new departure. The dismantling of the tariff system began, and in the 1960s the economy boomed for the first time since independence. In 1965 Whitaker prompted SEÁN LEMASS to arrange a meeting with the Prime Minister of Northern Ireland, Terence O'Neill, the first such public meeting since 1922. Whitaker was Governor of the CENTRAL BANK, 1969–76, and a senator; at various periods he has been chancellor of the NUI and chairman of the ECONOMIC AND SOCIAL RESEARCH INSTITUTE, the National Industrial and Economic Council, Bord na Gaeilge, and many other public bodies (see p. 339). **Tom Garvin**

Whitby, Synod of (664). The Synod of Whitby marked one stage in the EASTER CONTROVERSY that affected the Irish, Britons and Anglo-Saxons in the seventh and eighth centuries. At Whitby the Northumbrian king decided to adopt Roman practice as regards the date of Easter and the shape of the tonsure, rather than continue following the practices introduced by the Irish mission from Iona. The effect of his decision was to end IONA's close involvement in and supervision of the Northumbrian church. The Irish Bishop of Northumbria, Colmán, left Northumbria, taking with him all the Irish monks and thirty like-minded Anglo-Saxons from the monastery of LINDISFARNE. The monks were settled in newly founded monasteries in Ireland, on Inishbofin and (for the Anglo-Saxons) at Mayo. The latter continued to attract English monks and retained close links with Northumbria for well over a century, becoming known as 'Mayo of the Saxons'. **Clare Stancliffe**

White, Harry (1958–), musicologist. Born in Dublin; educated at UCD, Toronto, and TCD. He was appointed professor of music at UCD in 1993. His specialisms are the music of J. J. Fux, the cultural history of music in Ireland, and the history of MUSICOLOGY. The most prominent Irish musicologist of his time, he was national advisory editor for Ireland for the second edition of the *New Grove Dictionary of Music and Musicians* (2001), and editor of the Fux collected edition. His book *The Keeper's Recital* (1998) is a seminal publication in Irish cultural studies. He jointly instigated (with GERARD GILLEN) the *Irish Musical Studies* series, of which he is general editor, and (with Patrick F. Devine) the first Irish international musicological conference, at Maynooth, 1995. **Michael Murphy**

White, James (1913–), curator and critic. Born in Dublin; educated at Belvedere College. He worked in industry for more than thirty years, and as art critic of the *Irish Press*, before becoming curator of the Hugh Lane Municipal Gallery of Modern Art, Dublin, 1960–64, and director of the NATIONAL GALLERY OF

whiskey. *A consignment of Jameson whiskey being loaded at Dublin docks for shipment to America in 1934 after the repeal of prohibition. [© Jameson Irish Whiskey]*

IRELAND, 1964–80, where he was responsible for transforming the gallery's public image and reception. He published monographs on PAULINE BEWICK (1985) and GERARD DILLON (1997) and was decorated by the governments of France, Italy, and Germany. **Richard Pine**

Whiteboys, the classic agrarian movement of the eighteenth century, its name taken for every rural protest afterwards. There were only two outbreaks of Whiteboyism, 1761–5 and 1769–75, mainly in Cos. Tipperary, Waterford, Cork, and Kilkenny. These assemblies of farmers and tradesmen, some wearing white sheets, swore an oath of secrecy, threatening LANDLORDS and their agents and attacking their property. As Catholics they were accused of being JACOBITES, but their grievances were economic, concerned with TITHES, rents, and taxes. **Eoin Magennis**

'white-collar crime', the pursuit of profit through such occupational crimes as embezzlement for personal gain as well as corporate crime, such as bribery or breach of industrial safety regulations for the greater profitability of the corporation.

White-collar crime is very different in the Republic and Northern Ireland. One reason for this is that after 1922 the relevant laws and enforcement practices in Northern Ireland were modified and updated regularly in accordance with English law and regulations, allowing the law and its enforcement to keep pace with changes in business practices and technology. A similar process of revision did not take place in the South. The Free State absorbed wholesale the existing statute and common law accumulated during seven centuries of English rule. Until the Law Reform Commission began its work in the late 1980s, relatively little had been done to rationalise and update statute law. Nineteenth and early twentieth-century statutes defined white-collar crime in the Republic: the Forgery Acts (1861 and 1913), Falsification of Accounts Act (1875), and Larceny Act (1916). The Oireachtas made modifications to these laws without effecting fundamental change or reconciling the law with the reality of contemporary business and professional practice. Successive Governments were lax also in providing adequate staffing to prosecute the existing laws. As a result, crime statistics from the Republic are likely to greatly understate the extent of white-collar crime.

The Republic's experience of white-collar crime is most notable for the extent to which such crime became interwoven into the political system. The entrenched nature of these links was revealed when a series of official TRIBUNALS during the last years of the twentieth century and first years of the twenty-first uncovered a web of bribery of public officials who abetted and shielded tax evasion and the violation of zoning and land use regulations. The Beef Tribunal (1991–4) investigated an alleged tax evasion scheme involving EU beef subsidies. The Flood Tribunal (1998–) investigated bribery and other matters connected with the granting of rezoning and PLANNING permission for a large parcel of land in Co. Dublin. The McCracken Tribunal (1997) investigated massive payments by a prominent businessman to politicians; the Moriarty Tribunal (1997–) further pursued the pattern of payments to politicians.

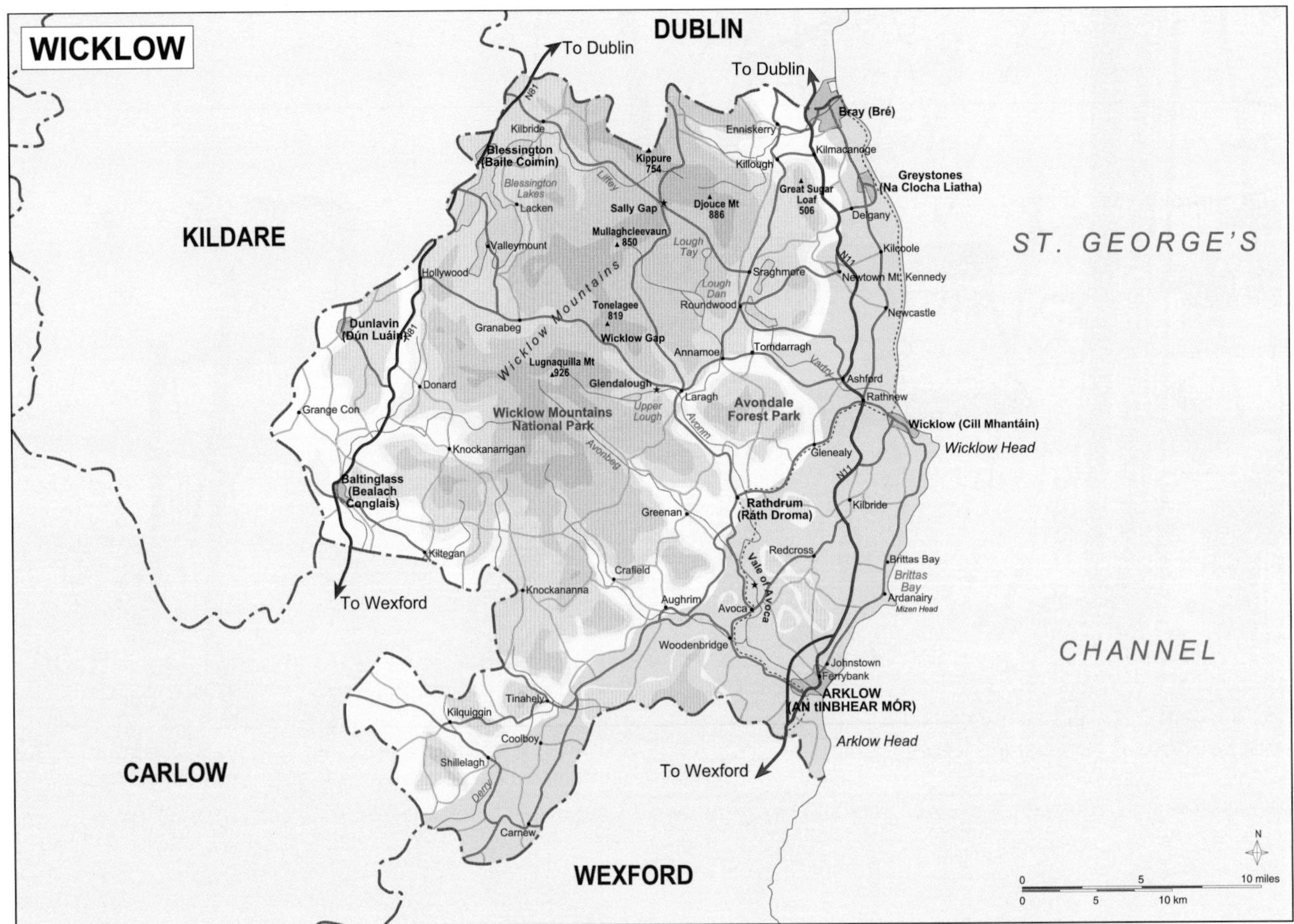

The significance of white-collar crime is often not appreciated. The financial cost probably exceeds by a great deal the costs inflicted through conventional property crimes, such as robbery, shoplifting, and burglary. One estimate (from the report of the Whitaker Committee of Inquiry, 1985) suggested that property stolen through conventional crime had a value of £34 million a year, that of white-collar crime between £200 and £1,000 million annually. An Advisory Committee on Fraud reported in 1992 that the top fifty cases being investigated by the Garda Fraud Squad involved a sum of £26 million.

The cost is not only financial: the consequences can include injury and death from unsafe business practices, as in the building industry. The main cost, however, cannot be calculated: the reduction in the trust the Irish people have in their political system and in the leading financial institutions. **David Rottman**

White Island, Co. Fermanagh, site of unique carvings found at various times in or near the wall of the surrounding church, probably of tenth or eleventh-century date. There are six complete figures, designed in three pairs, each pair a different height. All have sockets, indicating their function as supporting pillars, perhaps for the steps of a pulpit, or for an altar, wall seat, or church screen. Apart from one of the smallest figures, an exhibitionist female probably representing the sin of lust, all the other figures are solemn-eyed ecclesiastics, conveying through Christian symbols various spiritual meanings drawn from the Old and New Testaments. **Helen Lanigan Wood**

White Stag Group, a group of artists founded by the English painters Basil Rakoczi and Kenneth Hall in London in 1935. (The name is derived from a Hungarian symbol of creativity; the motif also appeared on the coat of arms of Herbrand Ingouville-Williams, an associate member of the group.) Broadly influenced by developments in PSYCHOLOGY, Rakoczi was an untrained analyst, interested in the theories of Freud and Jung. Both he and Hall were self-taught artists who believed in the fundamental importance of 'subjectivity' or self-expression.

Rakoczi and Hall came to Ireland in 1939 to avoid conscription, moving to Dublin in March 1940. The group's first exhibition, held in April 1940, comprised work by MAINIE JELLETT and others. In their next group show, in October the same year, a number of progressive Irish and foreign artists participated, including Stephen Gilbert and Jocelyn Chewett and the composer BRIAN BOYDELL. From then until 1946 group and one-man shows were held, with Nick Nicholls, Thurloe Conolly, PATRICK SCOTT, Doreen Vanston, Paul Egestorff, Ralph Cusack, and NANO REID among the contributors. An international dimension was added by the inclusion of work by contemporary British and French artists, including Pablo Picasso. Lectures on aspects of contemporary art, as well as life classes, were held regularly. The group's most ambitious undertaking was the EXHIBITION OF SUBJECTIVE ART (1944). Jellett described their work as not being 'hidebound to any particular school, or cramped by academic conventionality.'

The book *Three Painters* (1945) summarises the group's ideas: their art, like that of Klee and Picasso, is situated between abstraction at one extreme and surrealism at the other; it combines both structure and emotion but is not reliant on either alone.

After the war Rakoczi and Hall left Ireland. While ostensibly a vehicle for the careers of these two artists, the White Stag Group had a fundamental impact on the development of modernist practice in Ireland. **Róisín Kennedy**

Whittaker, Sir Edmund Taylor (1875–1956), astronomer and mathematician. Born in Birkdale, Lancashire; educated at the University of Cambridge, where he excelled in mathematics and where in 1896 he was elected a fellow of Trinity College. He moved to DUNSINK OBSERVATORY in 1906 as Andrews professor of astronomy and made a considerable impact on the scientific life of Dublin through his lectures and social contacts. At Dunsink he began a programme of systematic photographic observations of variable stars with the 15-in. Roberts reflector. In 1912 he was appointed professor of mathematics at the University of Edinburgh, where he taught until his retirement in 1946 and where he established a flourishing research school. He played a critical role c. 1938 in advising ÉAMON DE VALERA on setting up the DUBLIN INSTITUTE FOR ADVANCED STUDIES and its constituent School of Theoretical Physics. Apart from his contributions to pure and applied mathematics, his scientific books have been very influential, not least his *History of the Theories of Aether and Electricity* (1910). He was elected a fellow of the Royal Society in 1905 and knighted in 1945. **Ian Elliott**

Whittaker-Barry, William (died 1875), barrister, walking tourist, and writer. Born in Wiltshire; he came to Belfast in 1865 and embarked on a seven-week, 1,600 km (1,000-mile) circuit of Ireland on foot. He visited twenty counties, to view the scenery, to ascertain 'the habits and character of a people which ... seem ever in fact to be foreign', and to write an original, impartial description of the country. His brisk and observant account of his travels was published in 1867 under the title *Walking Tour around Ireland in 1865 by an Englishman*. He noted the denuding of the country by rural people seeking fuel, the hospitality of the poor, the lack of courtesy in the upper classes, and the uneven standard of inns. He went on to complete a walking tour of Normandy, and died in 1875 while on a walking tour in the Austrian Tyrol. **Michael Fewer**

Whyte, James Francis Xavier, Comte de Maleville (born 1730), prisoner in the Bastille. Born in Dublin. He travelled to France in his youth, joined the IRISH BRIGADE, and became a captain in the Regiment of Lally. In 1781 he began to suffer from dementia and was confined by his family to the old fortress of Vincennes. He was moved to the Bastille in 1784. On 14 July 1789 he was released by the mob and fêted in the streets; the following day he was transferred to the asylum at Charenton, where he spent the remainder of his days. **Ciarán Deane**

Whyte, Samuel (1733–1811), poet and schoolmaster. Born on board a ship and brought up in Dublin in the family of his cousin, FRANCES SHERIDAN. In 1758 he opened Whyte's Academy in Grafton Street, Dublin, a school for young men and women that became the most famous and fashionable of its day. He wrote on education and rhetoric and encouraged his pupils—girls as well as boys—to write poetry, much of which is collected, with his own work, in *The Shamrock* (1772), a handsome quarto publication. Many of Whyte's pupils went on to Trinity College, Dublin. **Andrew Carpenter**

Wicklow, County (*Contae Chill Mhantáin*)

Province:	LEINSTER
County town:	WICKLOW
Area:	2,025 km^2 (784 sq. miles)
Population (2002):	114,719
Features:	Glenmalur
	Lough Dan
	River LIFFEY
	River SLANEY
	SUGAR LOAF MOUNTAINS
	VARTRY River
	WICKLOW MOUNTAINS
Of historical interest:	BALTINGLASS ABBEY
	Baltinglass Hill Fort
	GLENDALOUGH
Industry and products:	FORESTRY
	Peat-cutting
	Quarrying

Petula Martyn

County Wicklow, the county to the south of Co. Dublin on the east coast of Ireland. Sometimes called the 'Garden of Ireland', it comprises an extensive natural ENVIRONMENT on the doorstep of a large city; part of its central upland region has been designated Wicklow National Park. The WICKLOW MOUNTAINS form a large part of the central core of the county, with a narrow coastal stretch leading southwards to Co. Wexford and on its western flanks the King's River and River LIFFEY flowing into the Co. Kildare lowlands. The mountain landscapes are best seen at POWERSCOURT and Enniskerry, the GLEN OF THE DOWNS, GLENDALOUGH, Glenmacnass, and the Vale of Avoca. The inaccessibility of most of the highlands contributed to the survival intact of the O'Byrne and O'Toole septs into the seventeenth century. They harassed Dublin throughout the Middle Ages.

The county town, **Wicklow** (population 7,007), developed as a ninth-century Norse settlement on the site of the church founded by Mantán in the fifth century. Glendalough is a spectacular valley that was the site of St KEVIN's seventh-century monastery and associated medieval PILGRIMAGE. Avondale, the eighteenth-century home of CHARLES STEWART PARNELL at **Rathdrum**, is maintained by the state. **Blessington** (population 3,147), an estate village built by Lord Hillsborough in the eighteenth century, adjoins POLLAPHUCA Reservoir, formed by the hydro-electric dam that flooded the Liffey and King's River in the early 1940s to supply water to Dublin. Nearby is Russborough House, one of Ireland's most important Georgian houses. **Patrick Duffy**

Wicklow Mountains, the largest area of continuous high ground in Ireland, part of the Leinster chain of Caledonian folding, which extends from the Blackstairs Mountains to the Dublin Mountains at Blackrock. Lugnaquilla, at 1,197 m (3,927 ft), is the highest point. Consisting largely of a granite batholith that has been unroofed to form rolling peat-covered uplands, the mountains have been severely glaciated to form valleys, corries, and melt-water gorges, all contributing to an attractive landscape of mountains, valleys, and lakes, such as GLENDALOUGH, the GLEN OF IMAAL, GLENMALUR, Glenmacnass, and the scenic corrie lakes of Lough Tay, Lough Dan, and Lough Bray. The extensive blanket peat supports several heather species, whose purple colour combines with the yellow bloom of gorse on the eastern slopes. Following the 1798 REBELLION, the British government built a fortified military road through the mountain core from the SALLY GAP to help in rooting out rebel forces; the road remains an important tourist amenity. Because of its close proximity to Dublin and the numerous minor roads that lead into the mountains, the mountain landscape of Co. Wicklow has come under enormous pressure from walkers and recreationists (see p. 689). **Patrick Duffy**

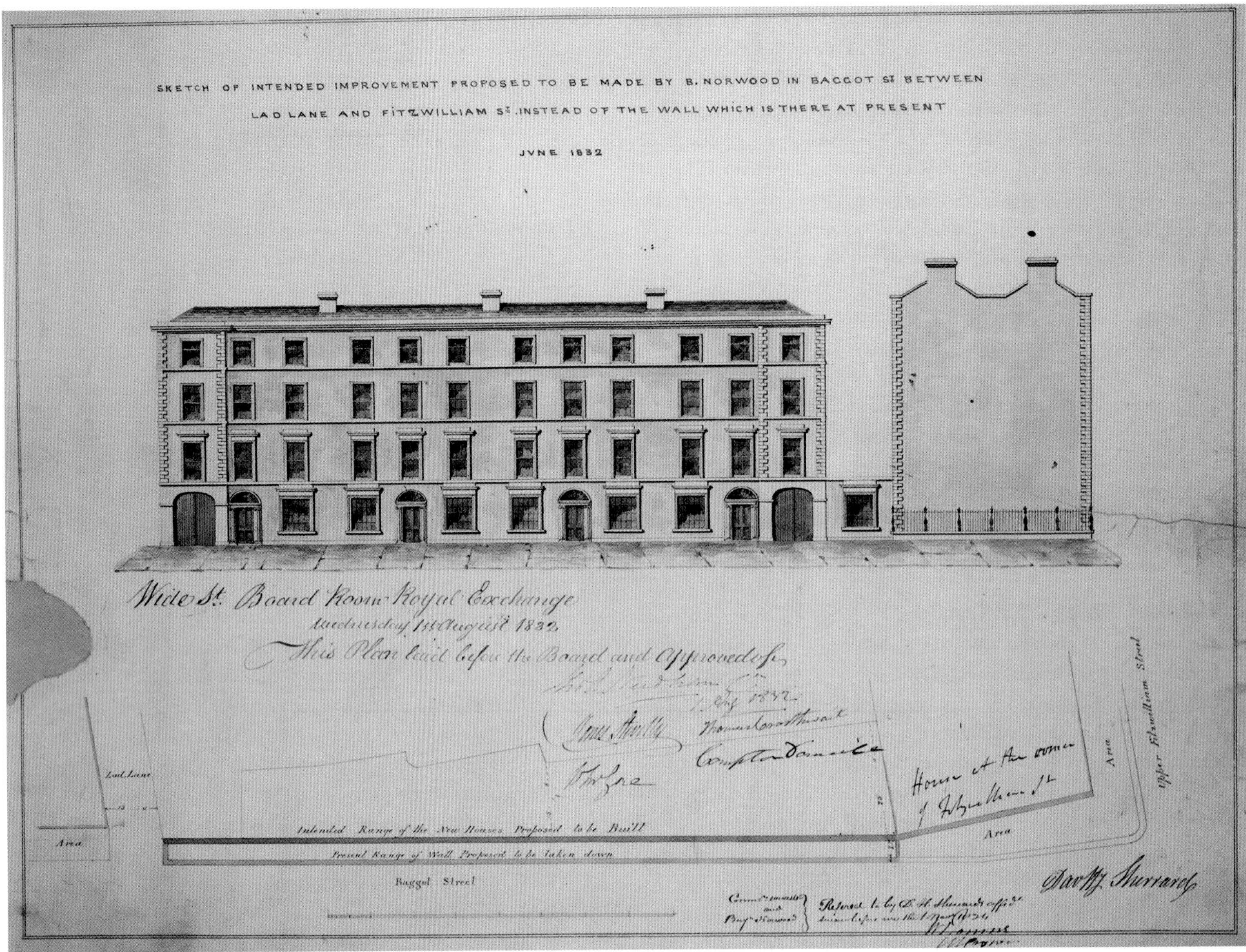

Wide Streets. *Sketch, June 1832, for the proposed elevation in Baggot Street between Lad Lane and Fitzwilliam Street to be made by B. Norwood of the Wide Streets Commission. [Dublin City Council/City Archives W5C/maps/450/1]*

Wide Streets Commissioners. The Commissioners for Making Wide and Convenient Ways, Streets and Passages were appointed by Parliament in 1757 and controlled the planning of Dublin until 1851. A commission with considerable powers was seen as the only means of solving the problem of traffic congestion in the narrow streets of the city, which had defied resolution for more than a century. The commissioners aimed to provide the city with wide, straight streets but also sought to ensure that the new streetscapes were worthy of Dublin's status as a capital city. They had considerable powers, could acquire property compulsorily (but with compensation for owners), and controlled all aspects of the design and layout of the new streets. However, many projects resulted from initiatives by interested third parties. Purchasers of plots in the new streets were expected to adhere to the general design, and the commissioners took pains to ensure compliance. By the end of the eighteenth century the city had a series of routes that linked the great buildings, the residences of the powerful, and the chief commercial areas. Parliament Street and Dame Street improved access to DUBLIN CASTLE, the PARLIAMENT HOUSE, and the Viceregal Lodge, while a new axis linked the fashionable Sackville Mall (O'Connell Street) by way of a new bridge with the new thoroughfares of Westmorland Street and D'Olier Street and thence College Green and Grafton Street. Following the extension of their jurisdiction in 1792 the commissioners played a significant role in the development of the private estates, especially those of GARDINER and Fitzwilliam. **Joseph Brady**

Wilde, Lady Jane Francesca, née Elgee (c. 1821–1896), poet, writer, translator, and wit, widely known by her pen-name 'Speranza'. Born in Dublin. Married to Sir WILLIAM WILDE and the mother of OSCAR WILDE, she was celebrated for her convivial salons in Dublin and later in London. She wrote regularly for the NATION and achieved iconic status as a nationalist poet; her article 'Jacta alia est' (1848) resulted in the suppression of the paper. Her translation of Meinhold's *Sidonia the Sorceress* influenced the pre-Raphaelites, while her Irish folk-tales provided source material for other writers, including W. B. YEATS. Her works include *Poems by Speranza* (1864), *Driftwood from Scandinavia* (1884), *Ancient Legends, Mystic Charms and Superstitions of Ireland* (1887), and *Ancient Cures, Charms and Usages of Ireland* (1890). **Noreen Doody**

Wilde, Oscar Fingal O'Flahertie Wills (1856–1900), aesthete, critic, dramatist, and poet. Born in Dublin; educated at Portora Royal School, Enniskillen, TCD, and the University of Oxford. His father, Sir WILLIAM WILDE, was a distinguished pioneer of eye and ear surgery and of antiquarianism; his mother was the poet, critic, and feminist JANE FRANCESCA WILDE ('Speranza of the *Nation*'), whose influence can be traced in Wilde's essay 'The Soul of Man under Socialism'. Their bohemian life at their home in Merrion Square introduced Wilde to an emancipated and indulgent atmosphere in which he met many of the leading artists, lawyers, and scientists of the day. A scholar of classics, at TCD his teachers included J. P. MAHAFFY and, at Oxford, Walter Pater, apostle of 'epicureanism'. His notebooks from this period (published in 1989) show both the seriousness and the depth of his scholarship. At Oxford he won the Newdigate Prize for his poem 'Ravenna' (1878). His *Poems* (1881) are on aesthetic, sexual, and republican themes, demonstrating that he had embarked on a career in London as a self-styled 'professor of aesthetics'. He was commissioned by Richard d'Oyly Carte to undertake a lecture tour of the United States and Canada in 1882 as a foil to, and advertisement for, the Gilbert and Sullivan opera *Patience*, which lampooned the aesthetic movement. On his return he married and settled down to a life of literary reviewing and lecturing to support his wife and two sons, editing *Woman's World* (1887–9) and writing fables ('The Happy Prince', 'The Selfish Giant'), which originated in his children's nursery, and essays ('The Critic as Artist', 'The Truth of Masks', 'The Decay of Lying'). He exercised a deep influence on the young W. B. YEATS with his theory of masks and his statements that 'a man should invent his own myth' and 'we are a nation of brilliant failures, but we are the greatest talkers since the Greeks.'

In 1886 he began a long-term affair with Robert Ross (who became his literary executor), and his work became increasingly concerned with HOMOSEXUALITY, with which he had flirted since Oxford. In 1889 he published *The Picture of Dorian Gray*, a highly suggestive but non-specific novella on the theme of the 'double' or 'enemy within', which created a scandal among the CRITICS, who associated it with the French 'decadence' with which Wilde had long been fascinated, while his essay 'The Portrait of Mr W. H.' openly discussed Shakespeare's alleged homosexuality. In the aesthetic, moral and political arenas Wilde challenged the British establishment's Anglocentrism and homophobia, a crusade in which he was joined by SHAW. His first two plays, *Vera* (1883) and *The Duchess of Padua* (1891), were unsuccessful, but in 1891 he scored a triumph with *Lady Windermere's Fan*, followed by *A Woman of No Importance* (1893) and in 1895—his annus mirabilis et horribilis—*An Ideal Husband* and THE IMPORTANCE OF BEING EARNEST (see p. 512). These were conventionally regarded as 'society comedies', but their darker side, exploring disloyalty, treason, greed, and self-serving hypocrisy, reveal Wilde's scepticism and his rejection of the mores of London society. (His Biblical drama *Salomé* was refused a licence in 1892 and was not staged until 1896, in Paris.)

Meanwhile his infatuation with Lord Alfred Douglas, a minor poet and the son of the Marquis of Queensberry, provoked Queensberry in 1895 to entice Wilde (with a card inscribed 'To Oscar Wilde, posing somdomite' [*sic*]) into a prosecution for criminal libel, an action that exposed the extent of Wilde's immersion in the homosexual demi-monde and led to his prosecution for acts of gross indecency, for which he was convicted and imprisoned for two years with hard labour, 1895–7. This experience led him to write his last significant work, *The Ballad of Reading Gaol* (1898). Broken physically and mentally, he drifted to Paris, where he died from meningitis.

It was at his trial that Wilde, in his own persona, voiced the apologia for homosexuality that has become a byword and has made him an iconic figure in an age of sexual liberation, attracting the attention of such writers as Havelock Ellis, Susan Sontag, and Camille Paglia. During his imprisonment he wrote a long letter to Douglas, 'De Profundis', in which he charted his personal development and his place in the evolution of nineteenth-century aesthetics and moral philosophy. Wilde's position as an artist and as a thinker in relation to both modernism and post-modernism has been better appreciated in recent decades by the development of Irish studies and gender studies and the deeper understanding of the relationship of art and politics. **Richard Pine**

Wilde, Sir William Robert Wills (1815–1876), eye and ear surgeon, cultural and scientific polymath, and prolific author. Born in Castlerea, Co. Roscommon, son of a local doctor; trained at the Royal College of Surgeons, qualifying in 1837. He travelled extensively and wrote early travel books but settled to practise in Dublin in 1840. He founded St Mark's Hospital (1841), edited, reformed and internationalised the *Dublin Quarterly Journal of Medicine*, and with his surgical textbook in 1853 became internationally acclaimed. He was assistant commissioner for the innovatory and comprehensive Irish decennial censuses, 1841–1871, for which he was knighted (1864). A precocious member of the ROYAL IRISH ACADEMY (aged twenty-four), he contributed extensively to its activities as naturalist, antiquarian, archaeologist, and folklorist. He married JANE FRANCESCA ELGEE ('Speranza'), nationalist writer and literary hostess, in 1851. He had three legitimate children: Willie (1852–1899), OSCAR (1854–1900), and Isola (1857–1867), and three acknowledged illegitimate ones. An equally energetic private life involved him in a very public civil action in 1864 brought by a former consort, Mary Travers, which harmed his reputation. In declining health, he increasingly handed his clinical work to his natural son, Henry Wilson, though remained otherwise active. **Peter Froggatt**

Wild Geese, a term in use from the early eighteenth century for the thousands of Irishmen and women who found employment with the Catholic armies of Europe from the sixteenth to the eighteenth centuries. Consisting mainly of kin and family groupings, they created Irish military communities on the Continent and formed close ties with the Irish merchant and religious communities there. At first the main employer was Spain; in the eighteenth century it was France and Austria. Traditionally the term referred to a group of Irish noblemen who, in the face of English and Protestant oppression, fled Ireland, thereby leading to the collapse of resistance to English rule. Those leaving are no longer regarded as landed elites but are recognised as coming from all classes of Irish society who were affected by the process of Tudor and later Stuart political centralisation and colonisation and the demise of the native Irish ascendancy. After the TREATY OF LIMERICK (1691) approximately 14,000 JACOBITE soldiers went to France, where they formed part of the IRISH BRIGADE, bringing its strength up to twelve regiments.

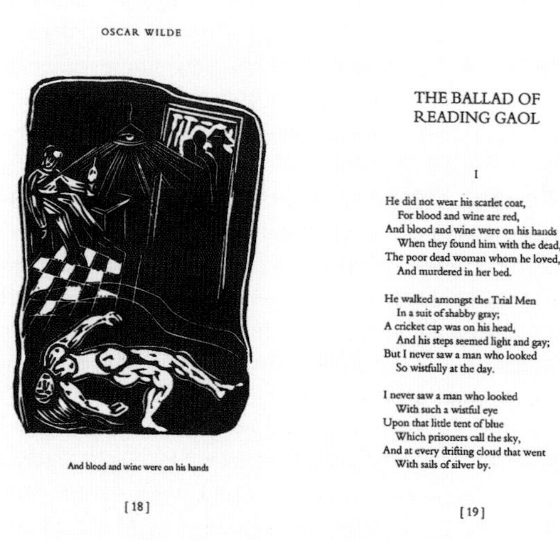

OSCAR WILDE

And blood and wine were on his hands

[18]

THE BALLAD OF
READING GAOL

I

He did not wear his scarlet coat,
For blood and wine are red,
And blood and wine were on his hands
When they found him with the dead,
The poor dead woman whom he loved,
And murdered in her bed.

He walked amongst the Trial Men
In a suit of shabby gray;
A cricket cap was on his head,
And his steps seemed light and gay;
But I never saw a man who looked
So wistfully at the day.

I never saw a man who looked
With such a wistful eye
Upon that little tent of blue
Which prisoners call the sky,
And at every drifting cloud that went
With sails of silver by.

[19]

Wilde, Oscar. The Ballad of Reading Gaol *(1898), Wilde's last major work, which reflects his prison experiences and exposes the inhumanity of the prison system. [Woodcut, Brian Lalor, 1997]*

Wilde, Sir William. *A cartoon by Spex satirising the surgeon and antiquarian Sir William Wilde. [National Library of Ireland R.12386]*

The world of the Wild Geese was predominantly COUNTER-REFORMATION Europe. Members of this group subsequently produced a cultural ideology that saw Catholicism as the inherent factor that united those of native Irish and Norman descent in one nation and tended to identify Protestant England as an enemy. This ideology and the literature that stemmed from it created an Irish identity that had a profound effect on how future generations regarded their Irishness (see p. 539). [see IRISH COLLEGES IN CONTINENTAL EUROPE.] **Gráinne Henry**

Wild Geese, women. Women began to emigrate from Ireland to the Continent in substantial numbers during and following the NINE YEARS' WAR; recurrent political and economic crises during the seventeenth and early eighteenth centuries led to further waves of women wild geese. Most left Ireland with their husband or family, but some went on their own, seeking religious asylum. Many women from upper-class families sought pensions from the King of Spain; they had to prove they were of noble birth and impeccable virtue and to provide evidence of the religious persecution that had forced them to leave Ireland. Women also became involved in business: Ellen MacCarthy, wife of Florence MacCarthy, set up a trading company in 1610 that transported beer to the Low Countries. A census from Cádiz in 1791 recorded Irish women working as domestic servants, seamstresses, nail-sellers, and even chocolate-moulders.

Women played an important economic role supplementing their husbands' income in the armies of Europe. Women's jobs in the army included washing, spinning, and weaving but could extend to selling tobacco and brandy or collecting snails and birds' nests. Most Irish women who emigrated to the Continent, however, made their living from begging, and their stay was often temporary, lasting only until the crisis in Ireland had passed. Generally, women who did stay on the Continent, whether of native Irish or OLD ENGLISH background, married Irish-born men. In this way they played a crucial part in creating overseas Irish communities in many of the cities and towns of Catholic Europe. The minority who married local men were often from merchant families, and such unions commonly merged Irish and European business interests.

The proportion of Irish women to Irish men who emigrated is difficult to ascertain without accurate records; but the evidence suggests that a large proportion of Irish emigrants were women. A group of 146 Irish people who arrived in Galicia in 1605 was made up of thirty soldiers and 116 'followers', most of whom were women and children. From a Spanish list of army widows' pensions in 1635, including widows of Irish soldiers and officers, roughly two-thirds had Irish wives.

Many Irish women were sent to the Continent to be educated. Convents such as the Abbey of Avesnes, near Arras, the White Ladies at Louvain, and the Dominicans in Lisbon had Irish students; the subjects taught included reading, writing, Latin, plain-chant, and vernacular languages, including English, Irish, Spanish, French, and Portuguese. Some Irish women became nuns and founded their own religions institutions, such as the Irish Poor Clares at Gravelines. **Gráinne Henry**

Wilkinson, George (1814–1890), architect. Born in Oxfordshire, son of a builder. He designed a number of workhouses in England before being appointed architect to the Irish POOR LAW Commissioners in 1839. Much to the annoyance of the Irish architectural profession (which organised itself into an institute in consequence), Wilkinson was charged with designing all 160 Irish workhouses. By 1843 the profession was won over by the rapidity of his programme and by his interest in Irish antiquities and geology, on which he published a book in 1845. Pensioned in 1856, he worked for the railway companies (his work including Harcourt Street Station, Dublin, 1859) before rejoining the public service in 1860 as architect to the Board of Control for constructing asylums. **Frederick O'Dwyer**

Wilks, Maurice (1910–1984), painter. Born in Belfast; attended night classes at Belfast School of Art, winning the Dunville scholarship to the day school. He first exhibited in 1933 at the Ulster Academy of Arts and was elected an associate in 1935. His mentor was the landscape painter J. Humbert Craig. He was a regular exhibitor at the RHA, 1933–49; the Victor Waddington Galleries, Dublin, also presented shows in 1944 and 1946. Exhibitions were held in Canada and the United States. Prints of his landscapes were popular in Britain, and he was a regular exhibitor at the Royal Ulster Academy. Several exhibitions were held at Anderson and McAuley's department store, Belfast. He was represented at the inaugural meeting of the Ulster Watercolour Society in 1977. Collections include the Ulster Museum and Ulster Folk and Transport Museum. **Theo Snoddy**

William III (1650–1702), Prince of Orange (1650), Governor of the Dutch Republic (1672), King of England, Scotland and Ireland

(1689). Born in the Hague, the only child of William II of Orange and Mary, sister of CHARLES II and JAMES II. A Calvinist, he was concerned for most of his life with opposing French expansionism. By birth a distant candidate in the English succession; his claim was strengthened by marriage in 1677 to Mary, eldest daughter of James II. Following the birth of a male heir to the Catholic James II in 1688, William invaded England at the invitation of leading Protestants, resulting in James's flight and William and Mary's acceptance of the crown. Slow progress in the Irish war caused William to take personal command, despite having to turn his attention away from the Continent. He landed at Carrickfergus, Co. Antrim, on 14 June 1690, visited Belfast, where he agreed to revive and increase the *regium donum* (an annual grant for the payment of Presbyterian ministers), and marched southwards. While reconnoitring at the Boyne his shoulder was grazed by a cannonball. During the battle he suffered an asthma attack while crossing the river, which forced him to dismount and proceed on foot, though once across he rallied his cavalry and led several charges. In Dublin by 6 July, he heard a *Te Deum* in ST PATRICK'S CATHEDRAL. He remained in Ireland until 5 September, first taking Waterford and then unsuccessfully besieging Limerick. Though he was never in Ireland again, the war hampered his European plans for another year, and Irish politics and religious divisions continued to occupy attention throughout his reign. 'Good King Billy' of 'glorious and immortal memory' in Ulster Protestant tradition, his name was also associated with the onset of the penal era. An equestrian statue erected outside Trinity College, Dublin, in 1701 was attacked on several occasions until finally destroyed by a bomb in 1929 (see pp. 117, 437). **Charles Ivar McGrath**

Williamite Settlement (1691). Williamite victory in 1691 restored and reinforced Protestant hegemony in Irish government, church, and society. The focal point of the settlement was the TREATY OF LIMERICK, which concluded the war, and the land confiscations. The treaty was the result of WILLIAM III's desire to free his army for the Continental war. A compromise agreement that was not well received by the Protestant Irish, who considered it too lenient towards Catholics, it soon came to represent to Catholics the perfidious nature of Protestantism. The military articles allowed 14,000 JACOBITE soldiers to go to France in 1691–2. The thirteen civil articles, which related to those who remained, were dogged by controversy, particularly the first (on the practice of Catholicism), second (on pardons and property), and ninth (on oath-taking). Ratification occurred in 1697, when a mutilated version was passed by the Irish Parliament. No article was confirmed in full: the first and ninth were excluded, the second restricted. Article 1 was already a dead letter, as the first PENAL LAWS were imposed in 1695, while the restrictions in article 2 meant that fewer Catholics could avail of it, which in principle meant that greater confiscations were possible, though in practice this did not occur to a great extent. In 1688 Catholics owned 22 per cent of the land; the confiscations reduced this to 14 per cent. Confiscations were largely confined to Jacobites who were killed, captured or under protection before the treaty or who went into exile. Conflict between William III and the English Parliament over disposal of the land resulted in the Resumption Act (1700). The confiscations were more restricted than the CROMWELLIAN LAND SETTLEMENT and did not introduce a new proprietor grouping. However, the eighteenth-century penal code broke the meaning of the treaty and further reduced Catholic land ownership and religious freedom. **Charles Ivar McGrath**

Williamite Wars, fought between the JACOBITES (followers of JAMES II) and Williamites (followers of WILLIAM III) from the 'Glorious Revolution' (1688) until the TREATY OF LIMERICK (1691). The wars had a European dimension as well as being an Irish civil war. James had abandoned England, but RICHARD TALBOT, Earl of Tyrconnell, led a Catholic administration and army for him in Ireland. JUSTIN MACCARTHY in Munster quelled Protestant resistance; in east Ulster the Protestants were led by Earl Mount Alexander but were also defeated by the Jacobites at Dromore, Co. Down, while in south Ulster and north Connacht the Williamites, led by Gustavus Hamilton, with headquarters at Enniskillen, maintained their allegiance to William, as did the city of Derry.

James landed in Ireland with French help on 12 March 1689 and, under Conrad van Rosen, began to besiege Derry (18 April–31 July), but failed. Likewise, from Enniskillen, Thomas Lloyd drove back the Jacobites at Ballyshannon and Belleek, slaughtering many in their retreat to Newtown Butler. By September his forces had taken Sligo and Boyle, Co. Roscommon. However, William's principal expedition, under SCHOMBERG, failed to advance beyond Ulster, while SARSFIELD's Jacobite army recaptured Sligo and had driven the Enniskillen men out of Connacht. The year 1689/90 ended in military stalemate.

By June 1691 William had taken charge of his armed forces in Ireland, about 37,000, made up of Dutch, English (officered in the main by Irish Protestants), French HUGUENOTS, and Danes, as well as six Ulster regiments. Louis XIV of France sent James 6,000 more soldiers—French, Wallon, and German—under Count de Lauzan. On

William III, *a mezzotint portrait engraving (1689). In 1688 William invaded England at the invitation of leading Protestants, resulting in James II's flight. Both kings fought at the Boyne in 1690, where William's army was victorious. [Getty Images/Hulton Archive]*

1 July 1690 William's celebrated victory at the Boyne gave him control of Dublin and the eastern half of the country. The outcome of the BATTLE OF THE BOYNE is still controversial. The Jacobites still held Munster and Connacht, halting the Williamite advance at Athlone (17–24 July 1691), which also stopped the fall of Limerick. But south Munster had fallen to the Williamites after the Earl of Marlborough's successes at Cork and Kinsale in September and October. Though further French help arrived with ST RUTH, William's army under GINKEL took Athlone and crossed the Shannon to go on and defeat the Jacobites at the significant BATTLE OF AUGHRIM (12 July 1691), which led to the encirclement of Limerick and the surrender of Galway, defeats that signalled the end of the war.

Surrender on terms proved seductive to the OLD ENGLISH Jacobites, who otherwise would have lost their lands; the native Irish, with nothing to lose, wished to continue hostilities, but with Sarsfield's conversion to terms in the TREATY OF LIMERICK (3 October 1691) his followers were offered free passage to France in return for their stronghold of Limerick. The departure of the Catholic soldiers is historically known as the flight of the WILD GEESE. By force of proclamation and parliamentary legislation the standing army in peacetime Ireland of about 12,000 men became for a time exclusively Protestant. **John J. N. McGurk**

William of Orange: see WILLIAM III.

Willie Clancy Summer School: see SCOIL SAMHRAIDH WILLIE CLANCY.

Wilshere, Reginald Sharman (1889–c. 1961), architect. Born in England; trained in Leicester and London, where he attended the Royal Academy School. He was decorated for bravery while serving as an engineer officer during the First World War. In 1926, after a period with Essex County Council, he took up the post of architect to Belfast Education Committee, for which he had designed twenty-six schools in a variety of styles by 1939; a further thirteen were built by the time he retired in 1954. One of the earliest, the neo-Georgian Strandtown School at Holywood, Co. Down (completed 1930), won him the Ulster Architecture Medal. His work was mostly 'moderne' yet picturesque, with many innovative features. **Frederick O'Dwyer**

Wilson, Gordon (1927–1995), peacemaker. Gordon Wilson and his twenty-year-old daughter Marie were at the war memorial in Enniskillen on Sunday 8 November 1987 for the annual wreath-laying. A bomb planted by the PROVISIONAL IRA killed eleven people, including Marie Wilson (see p. 926). Gordon Wilson that evening gave a television interview in which he described his last conversation with his daughter as they lay beneath the rubble. No words uttered in all the years of the 'TROUBLES' had such an emotional impact, and many agreed with the *Daily Mirror*'s observation that Wilson's 'Christian compassion saved a bloodbath of revenge killings from angry loyalists.' He was appointed to Seanad Éireann in 1993 on the nomination of the Taoiseach, ALBERT REYNOLDS. He met representatives of the IRA in 1993 and attended a SINN FÉIN conference in 1994 in attempts to persuade them to abandon violence; he had similar clandestine meetings with loyalist paramilitaries, with the same object. **Jonathan Bardon**

Wilson, Ian (1964–), composer. Born in Belfast; educated at the University of Ulster, where he was awarded the first doctorate in composition. He has written for orchestra, chamber ensemble, vocal, choral and electro-acoustic medium. Awards include the 1991 Composition Prize at the Ultima Festival, Oslo, for the orchestral work *Running, Thinking, Finding*, and the 1992 Macaulay Fellowship, awarded by the ARTS COUNCIL. Recordings include his first string quartet, *Winter's Edge*, recorded by the VANBRUGH STRING QUARTET (1994), and *Piano Trios* (1997). In 1993 the University of Ulster commissioned the orchestral work *Rise*, to celebrate its tenth anniversary. He is a member of AOSDÁNA. **Emma Costello**

Wilson, James (1922–), composer. Born in London; educated at TCD. Teacher of composition at the RIAM, 1971–82, he was first distinguished as a composer by his children's opera *The Hunting of the Snark* (1965). Other operas include *Twelfth Night*, which premiered at the 1969 WEXFORD FESTIVAL OPERA, *Letter to Theo* (1984), a tribute to Van Gogh, and *A Passionate Man* (1995, libretto by BRUCE ARNOLD), based on the life of Swift. He also composed numerous choral works, two symphonies, song cycles, instrumental pieces, a ballet, *Arachne*, and concertos for various instruments, including *Menorah*, for viola and orchestra. He is a member of AOSDÁNA. **Emma Costello**

Wilson, James Glen (1827–1863), landscape and marine painter. Born in Co. Down; said to have been self-taught but may have studied at the Belfast Government School of Design, 1849–51. He joined the Royal Navy in March 1852 as a ship's artist and photographer with the survey vessel *Herald* and served for seven years of its nine-year expedition to the south-west Pacific and Australia. He left the navy in 1859 and worked as a surveyor with the New South Wales Department of Lands. He died in Australia of rheumatic fever. His paintings are represented in public collections in Belfast and Sydney. **Eileen Black**

Wilson, Robert McLiam (1964–), writer. Born in Co. Donegal; educated in Belfast and Cambridge. His debut novel, *Ripley Bogle* (1989), a picaresque and semi-autobiographical black comedy set in London, Belfast, and Cambridge, was celebrated for its irreverent treatment of the 'TROUBLES'. After publishing *Manfred's Pain* in 1992 Wilson returned to a Belfast setting in *Eureka Street* (1996), a convoluted satire on the corruption and alienation of Northern society after the IRA ceasefire. Combining romance, slapstick humour, and highly poetic descriptions of Belfast with an aggressive cynicism, the novel exemplifies the stylistic extravagance that characterises Wilson's work and confirms his place in the vanguard of a younger generation of Northern writers. **Eve Patten**

Wilson, William Edward (1851–1908), astronomer. Born in Belfast; educated privately. In 1870 at the family home, Daramona, Street, Co. Westmeath, he set up an OBSERVATORY with a 12-inch telescope, later replaced by a 24-inch silver-on-glass reflector, and a laboratory. His important researches include the determination of the effective temperature of the Sun (with P. L. Gray) and the photo-electric measurement of starlight. A series of fine photographs of nebulae and star clusters taken with the 24-inch TELESCOPE were published in his 'Astronomical and Physical Researches' (privately printed, 1900). He became a fellow of the Royal Society in 1896 and was awarded an honorary doctorate by the University of Dublin, 1900. **M. T. Brück**

Windle, Sir Bertram Coghill Alan (1858–1929), anatomist and academic administrator. Born in Mayfeld, Staffordshire, he received an M.A, M.D. and D.Sc. from TCD; an M.Sc (Birmingham) and a Ph.D. (Rome). A Protestant, he was received (1883) into the Roman Catholic Church. In 1884 he was appointed professor of anatomy at Queen's College, Birmingham. As president of Queen's College, Cork, from 1904 he guided its transformation into University College. Knighted in 1911, he left Ireland to lecture in philosophy at St Michael's College, Toronto (1919). He produced books and articles on literature, archaeology, science, and morals and emphasized the church's relationship with science. **Susan McKenna-Lawlor**

windmills. The earliest recorded wind-powered mill in Ireland was at Kilscanlan, near Old Ross, Co. Wexford, which was at work in 1281. This is generally thought to have been a *post mill*, where the whole mill building is rotated about a central wooden pivot, so that the sails can face into the prevailing wind. In the early decades of the seventeenth century the type of windmill that was to become relatively common in Ireland's main grain-producing counties on the eastern seaboard made an appearance in the midlands. A good example of this type of mill at Elphin, Co. Roscommon, built by Edward Synge, Bishop of Elphin, c. 1750, has recently been restored to working order. The small tower-mill at Tacumshin, Co. Wexford, however, with its tail-pole and thatched cap, though built in 1846, retains many of the features of the early eighteenth-century examples. The Thomas Street windmill in Dublin (1790–1810) is the tallest tower-mill in Ireland. Some 250 windmills are shown on the first editions of the Ordnance Survey map, compiled between the 1830s and 1842; the great majority are in Co. Down (which accounted for more than a hundred of this total in 1834) and Co. Wexford. [see NIGHT OF THE BIG WIND.] **Colin Rynne**

wireless telegraphy. The first Irish contribution to wireless technology was that of the Maynooth priest-scientist NICHOLAS CALLAN and his development of the induction coil from the 1830s. G. F. FITZGERALD was the first physicist to comprehend the full significance of Clerk-Maxwell's announcement in 1876 of the electro-magnetic theory. Fitzgerald's contributions in three seminal papers of 1879 show that he perhaps more fully realised the significance of this theory than the inventor. Fitzgerald's uncle, GEORGE JOHNSTONE STONEY, fundamentally advanced the electro-magnetic theory in the following decade. These 'Irish Maxwellians' developed unique insights into practical wireless transmission and receiving equipment.

In 1897 the young GUGLIELMO MARCONI made his first public demonstration of ship-to-shore wireless transmissions at the Kingstown (Dún Laoghaire) Regatta. The same year he helped to form the Wireless Telegraphy Company, but by 1900 he had established his own Marconi's Wireless Telegraphy Company. He conducted the majority of his pioneering work on wireless telegraphy in Ireland, beginning in 1898 with a 12 km ($7\frac{1}{2}$-mile) wireless link for Lloyd's between Ballycastle, Co. Antrim, and RATHLIN ISLAND. On 12 December 1901 he made the first Atlantic transmission from a station at Poldu, Cornwall, with a monitoring station established in Crookhaven, Co. Cork. This station had originally been established by Marconi, together with one at Rosslare, Co. Wexford, and another at MALIN HEAD, Co. Donegal, to monitor ship-to-shore broadcasts. By 1907 Marconi had established a second transatlantic wireless station at Clifden, Co. Galway, which transmitted to a sister station in Grace Bay, Nova Scotia. Another Marconi station was built in 1912 a few miles away at Letterfrack, Co. Galway, to allow for the simultaneous receiving and transmission of wireless signals. He had established three experimental stations in Crookhaven, Co. Cork, in 1901, one in Derrygimla, Co. Galway,

Wilson, Gordon. *Senator Gordon Wilson, whose daughter Marie died in the IRA's Enniskillen bombing in 1987, at the Mansion House, Dublin. His humanity and charity, despite the loss of his daughter, had a profound impact, making him a unique spokesman for the new Ireland being forged in the aftermath of the peace process. [Derek Speirs/Report]*

and a giant station at Clifden in 1907. Perhaps spurred by the arrival of a competitor in the form of the Amalgamated Radio Telegraph Company, which established a transatlantic facility in Knockroe, near Tralee, Co. Kerry, in 1907, Marconi extended his capability in 1912 with a station in Ballybunion, Co. Kerry, transmitting to Louisberg, Nova Scotia.

Marconi's decision to develop his technology in Ireland was based on the obvious advantage presented by the country's position on the Atlantic seaboard; but from 1916 he had begun to exploit short waves for more efficient transmissions over longer distances, and this diminished the importance of Ireland's position. The Clifden facility ceased broadcasting in 1922 when Irregulars destroyed it, but by then Marconi had established a new transatlantic station in Wales.

In 1922 the BBC in England, using Marconi equipment, had demonstrated the potential for civilian broadcasting. In September 1924 station 2BE came on the air in Belfast, broadcasting from Linenhall Street with a 1.5 kW transmitter. It was perhaps inevitable that the Irish Free State would turn to Marconi to establish its broadcasting capability, and on 14 August 1923 Marconi's Wireless Company made the first radio broadcast from the Royal Marine Hotel, Dún Laoghaire. In 1924 the company established a test station in South William Street, Dublin. The Wireless Society of Ireland had been formed in September 1925 in anticipation of the great national event. William Arnold Beaty, a former Marconi maritime engineer, was appointed on 25 October as assistant engineer; then, to coincide with the Dublin Wireless Exhibition in November 1925, station 2RN came on the air, beginning a process of fundamental social change. [see ATLANTIC TELEGRAPH CABLE.] **Norman McMillan**

Wittgenstein in Ireland. Ludwig Wittgenstein (1889–1951), who initiated two revolutions in twentieth-century philosophy, was born in Vienna. In 1908 he began the study of aeronautics at the University of Manchester, where he became friendly with William Eccles from Coleraine, Co. Derry, which Wittgenstein visited about this time. He soon became involved in the work of Gottlob Frege and Bertrand Russell on logic and mathematics, an involvement that grew into the *Tractatus Logico-Philosophicus* (1921) on the limits of language. After war-time army service he taught in rural Austrian primary schools for several years. In 1929 he took up a lectureship at the University of Cambridge, where he developed the novel approach to philosophical problems exemplified in the *Philosophical Investigations* (1953). He became friendly with one of his students,

Maurice O'Connor Drury, who kept a journal of their relationship, a valuable source of Wittgenstein's views on religion and psychiatry. When Drury went on to study medicine in Trinity College, Dublin, Wittgenstein came to visit. In 1934 they stayed at Drury's brother's holiday home at Rosroe on KILLARY HARBOUR, Co. Mayo. He went to Dublin in 1936 and again in 1938. He resigned his Cambridge professorship in 1947 to be free to write. Drury, who was by then practising psychiatry at St Patrick's Hospital in Dublin, arranged for him to stay at Kilpatrick House, Redcross, Co. Wicklow. Wittgenstein became unhappy there and discussed his difficulties with Dr Norman Moore of St Patrick's. In April 1948 he went again to stay in Rosroe. In October, fears for his health persuaded him to live in Dublin at Ross's Hotel (now substantially rebuilt as the Ashling) in Parkgate Street. His Dublin work was published as *Last Writings on the Philosophy of Psychology* (1982). In May 1949 Dr T. G. Moorhead examined him in hospital. Wittgenstein left Ireland in June. A diagnosis of prostate cancer was made at Cambridge in November and he died two years later. **John Hayes**

Woffington, Margaret (Peg) (c. 1714–1760), actor. Born in Dublin, daughter of a bricklayer. She began as a child actor, first appearing at the SMOCK ALLEY THEATRE c. 1735, where she continued to appear until 1754. Acclaimed for roles including Sir Harry Wildair in FARQUHAR's *The Constant Couple*, she regularly acted opposite David Garrick and later SPRANGER BARRY. **Christopher Morash**

Wogan, John de (died 1321), Justiciar of Ireland, 1295–1308, 1309–12. Probable son of Sir Matthew Wogan and Avicia Malephant, he married Joan, heiress to Picton Castle, Pembrokeshire, thus adding her estates to his own inheritance of Wiston, Pembrokeshire. Details of his early life remain obscure. In 1295 he was appointed Justiciar of Ireland by Edward I, and he immediately set about ending the long-standing GERALDINE-DE BURGH feud. He then used the reconciled magnates to provide contingents for royal campaigns abroad. In accordance with the wishes of Edward II he successfully suppressed the Knights Templars in Ireland between February 1307 and 1308.

He is one of the best-documented justiciars of the Middle Ages, as the Justiciary Rolls for his term in office had been calendared before they were destroyed in 1922. This wealth of surviving information has fostered his reputation as the most competent and energetic of chief governors. He strengthened the resources of the Anglo-Irish colony to support the wars of Edward I and Edward II, led a number of successful expeditions into the Leinster mountains and elsewhere in a successful bid to extend royal control, and held a series of parliaments between 1297 and 1310 to deal with this increasing unrest. He seems to have retired to Pembrokeshire when he left the justiciarship in 1312. According to one source his children settled in Ireland; his son founded the Wogans of Rathcoffey, a grant originally made to John as part of a series of awards for his services to the Crown. **Susan Foran**

Wogan, Terry (1938–), broadcaster. Born in Limerick; educated at Crescent College, Limerick. He worked in the Bank of Ireland before joining RTÉ as a news-reader and continuity announcer and later as a light entertainment presenter. He presented the BBC radio programme 'Late Night Extra', 1967–9, moving permanently to England in 1969 on being given his own radio programme. His easy-going blend of charm and humour, together with his ability to identify with his audience, led him to present a number of successful BBC television shows, including 'Blankety Blank', a celebrity quiz show, 'Wogan', a prime-time chat show, the EUROVISION SONG CONTEST, and 'National Lottery Live'. He has presented 'Wake Up to Wogan' on BBC Radio 2 since 1993, was made an honorary officer of the Order of the British Empire in 1997, and has published an autobiography, *Is It Me?* (2000). **Colm O'Gaora**

Wolfe, Charles (1791–1823), poet. Born in Blackhall, Co. Kildare; educated at Winchester School (Hampshire) and TCD, and took holy orders in the Church of Ireland. He is remembered for the often-anthologised 'The Burial of Sir John Moore', published anonymously and much admired by Byron. **Terence Brown**

Wolfe, David (died c. 1579), Papal legate to Ireland. Born in Limerick, probably early in the 1520s. One of the first Irish members of the Society of Jesus (JESUITS), he studied for seven years in Rome under the guidance of Ignatius of Loyola and Francis Borgia before being professed in 1550. He was rector of the Jesuit College at Modena before being sent to Ireland in August 1560. He worked hard to see the decrees of Trent implemented as far as was practicable. ELIZABETH I was upset by his mission and complained of it to Pope Pius IV. Wolfe was captured in 1567 and was imprisoned in DUBLIN CASTLE until his escape in 1572. Fourteen months later he sought refuge in Spain. He wrote *Description of Ireland* in 1574. He was in Portugal in 1579, though it is said that he died in Ireland about that time. **Henry A. Jefferies**

Wolfe Tone: see TONE, THEOBALD WOLFE.

Wolfe Tones, a ballad group born out of the traditional music revival of the 1960s. Comprising the brothers Derek and Brian Warfield, Noel Nagle, and Tommy Byrne, the group reached the height of their success in the 1970s with a series of ballads and rebel songs. While songs such as 'On the One Road', 'A Nation Once Again', and 'My Heart Is in Ireland' ensured the success of the band among Irish audiences around the world, their fervent republicanism often got them into trouble at home, with detractors accusing them of being pro-IRA. The band always rejected any claim that they supported violence or sectarianism and continued in their original form until 2002, when the songwriter Brian Warfield retired from the group. **Martin Clancy**

Wolff, Gustav Wilhelm (1834–1913), shipbuilder and politician. Born in Hamburg; he moved to England in 1849, where he lived with his uncle, Gustav Schwabe, while attending Liverpool College. He served a five-year engineering apprenticeship with Joseph Whitworth and Company of Manchester and subsequently worked as a draughtsman. In 1857 he moved to Belfast, having been engaged by EDWARD HARLAND as his personal assistant, becoming his partner after he bought Hickson's yard in 1861. Harland and Wolff were very different characters but proved capable of working well together, Wolff's humour and wit being seen by many as an excellent foil for Harland's stern fastidiousness. While serving as members of the British House of Commons, Harland was nicknamed 'Majestic' while Wolff was known as 'Teutonic', after well-known products of their shipyard. As with his colleague, Wolff later became less involved in the shipyard, devoting his time to other business ventures—notably the Belfast Ropeworks—and politics. In June 1903 he finally retired as principal of Harland and Wolff and sold his shareholding to WILLIAM PIRRIE. He served as Conservative MP for East Belfast in 1892 and 1910, being made an honorary burgess of the city of Belfast in 1911. **John Patrick Lynch**

Wollstonecraft, Mary (1759–1797), radical English feminist writer; born in London, author of *Thoughts on the Education of Daughters* (1787) and *A Vindication of the Rights of Woman* (1792). From November 1786 to August 1787 Wollstonecraft (whose mother, Elizabeth Dickson, was from Ballyshannon, Co. Donegal) worked as governess for Lord and Lady Kingsborough at their demesne in Mitchelstown, Co. Cork, and at their town-house in Henrietta Street, Dublin. She was in charge of some of their many children, and was accused (correctly) by the Kingsboroughs of teaching revolutionary ideas to their eldest daughter, Margaret. The Kingsboroughs were hardly older than the twenty-five-year-old Wollstonecraft, and their extravagant and feckless life-style contributed to her poor opinion of the aristocracy and to her convictions on the corrupting influence of property. In Bristol to take the waters with the family, she was dismissed from her post and never returned to Ireland. [see WHEELER, ANNA.] **Brian Lalor**

women, status of, 800–1200. According to eighth-century Irish law, a woman was always under the authority of a male guardian: the head of the family (father, brother, or uncle), her husband, or, if a religious, her abbot. A woman could not inherit family property permanently, and her status depended on that of her guardian. He had to authorise her business with others, except if the terms of her marriage decided otherwise. An heiress who married a man without property acted as his guardian; but after her death the inheritance was taken by her uncles and cousins. Though women could not rule territories, they could still exercise influence by their personality. Queens were usually held in high esteem. The twelfth-century list of Irish queens, the Banseanchas, is unique in medieval Europe. In literature, figures such as Queen MÉABH in the TÁIN and St BRIGID are two examples of different roles women could assume. **Bart Jaski**

women, status of, 1200–1700. There were significant changes in Irish women's legal, political and economic status in the period from the thirteenth to the seventeenth century. Neither Irish customary law nor English law endowed women with a legal status equal to that of men, but there were notable differences between the two codes, particularly in relation to the ownership and inheritance of property. According to Irish law, women were not permitted to inherit family land. This law was not always followed in practice, and there are documentary references to women landowners; but these are increasingly rare by 1500. By contrast, under English common law a daughter could inherit her father's land, provided he had no sons; if a man had more than one daughter, the land was divided between them. A number of large ANGLO-NORMAN estates were divided in the twelfth and thirteenth centuries as a result of female inheritance. Consequently, in the later Middle Ages families tried to prevent land passing to a daughter by drawing up legal documents that *entailed* the land to male heirs only. When new English settlers arrived in the sixteenth and seventeenth centuries they were more open to female inheritance, and there is a notable increase in the number, and consequently the status, of heiresses in the seventeenth century. MARRIAGE to a wealthy heiress became the means by which many landed families expanded their estates in the eighteenth century.

The status of widows also underwent change. Under traditional Irish law a widow was entitled to the goods she had brought to the marriage, but under English law a widow was entitled to a third of her husband's estate for her lifetime as well as a proportion of his movable goods. The more favourable position of widows under

Wolff, Gustav. *Gustav Wolff (left) with W. H. Wilson, W. J. Pirrie, and Edward J. Harland (right), the four partners in Harland and Wolff between 1876 and 1885. [Harland and Wolff Collection, Ulster Folk and Transport Museum. Photograph reproduced with the kind permission of the Trustees of the National Museums and Galleries of Northern Ireland]*

English law was recognised in the Middle Ages as Irish women appealed for their rights as English widows. There was further change in the status of widows in the seventeenth century as the landed jointure or *dower* was gradually replaced by a cash annuity, and widows' control over property was thereby diminished. By the late seventeenth century also men were no longer legally obliged to leave their wives a portion of their movable goods, though most continued to do so.

The transformation of Ireland's political system from medieval LORDSHIP to centralised colonial state also changed the political access and influence of elite women. Politics in medieval Ireland was based on dynastic alliances, in which women from aristocratic families played a pivotal role. In native Irish areas elite women might marry a number of times, as their families entered into new alliances and abandoned old ones. DIVORCE was permitted in Irish law, though it was forbidden by the church. The Earls of Kildare built up their power in the fifteenth century through a series of marriage alliances that linked them to all the important political families in Ireland. In the locally based politics of lordship, women could also exercise more direct forms of political control. In Anglo-Norman lordships, such as that of the BUTLERS of Ormond, a widow could take control of the lordship while her son remained a minor. There is no record of an Irish woman chieftain, but the power of one of the most well-known native Irish women, GRACE O'MALLEY, was locally based in the west of Ireland. The centralisation of government in the course of the sixteenth century undermined the local political influence of women. With the development of court life at DUBLIN CASTLE in the 1630s and again after the restoration of CHARLES II, some elite women became politically influential figures, a role that was to be enhanced in the eighteenth century, when politics once again revolved around the creation of dynastically allied power groups.

Economically, the most significant change for women in the period was the accelerated rate of urbanisation in the seventeenth century, which created new opportunities for paid work in the cloth, retail and service industries. In rural Ireland the transition from the military-based TOWER-HOUSE to the more domestic BIG HOUSE gave elite women new roles in house and estate management as they managed staff, oversaw the erection of new buildings and the restoration of others, and bought the latest fashions in interior decoration and FURNITURE. The big house also provided local women with far more employment than did the tower-house, which mainly employed a retinue of men. [see ABDUCTION OF HEIRESSES.] **Mary O'Dowd**

Women Against Imperialism, a group formed in 1978 following a split in the Belfast Women's Collective, the dissidents arguing that feminist priorities should be issues relating to women in anti-imperialist struggle. The group helped to develop a voice for women within the nationalist community. It included working-class nationalists, English feminists, and left-wing members. Its paper, *Saor-Bhean*, covered British army harassment, the killing of children with plastic bullets, violence against women, and the campaign to repeal the Payments for Debt Act. A male-only republican social club was picketed, and pressure was put on nationalists to incorporate EQUALITY for women in their political agenda. On International Women's Day in 1979 the group organised the first picket of solidarity with women in Armagh Prison, resulting in the arrest and conviction of eleven members. Two members subsequently served prison sentences, joining the 'no-wash' protest. Protests outside Armagh Prison increased in size through support from British feminists, though this remained a controversial issue within the Irish movement. Political and personal strains led to dissolution in 1981, with some members joining SINN FÉIN and other republican organisations. Some former members were later involved in setting up the Falls Women's Centre in 1983. **Margaret Ward**

women and careers. The story of women's paid work outside the home is one of rapid change in the last decades of the twentieth century. Until recently in the Republic women's primary career was expected to be that of wife and mother. The CONSTITUTION OF IRELAND gave special protection to a woman's place in the home and emphasised the centrality of the FAMILY to Irish life. This was institutionalised in the form of the 'MARRIAGE BAR', which prevented women working in the public service after MARRIAGE, though primary school teachers were exempted from the marriage bar in 1957.

Since 1971 the participation of women in the paid labour force has increased substantially. The sharpest rise was in the proportion of married women in the work force, rising from 8 per cent in 1971 to 37 per cent in 1996. The total number of women at work increased by 212,000 between 1971 and 1996, compared with 23,000 men. The share of the labour force (41 per cent) was still below the European average of 45 per cent, a result of low participation rates among older middle-aged women. Whereas the younger age group (twenty-five to thirty-four) had similar rates to the rest of Europe (63 per cent), the participation of married women aged forty-five to fifty-four was only 37 per cent.

As usual in Western societies, women are concentrated in a much smaller range of occupations than men, and also segregated into female areas of work. More than half the female work force in the Republic falls into two groups—clerical workers and professional and technical workers—which account for only 18 per cent of those employed. It is harder for women to argue for equal pay in this situation.

Those most able to benefit from a career structure are women in managerial and professional occupations, where numbers have increased substantially. The proportion of women in administrative, executive and managerial positions rose from 5 per cent in 1971 to 24 per cent in 1996, a high proportion compared with women in other EU countries. This contrasts with only 13 per cent of male workers. However, this apparent advantage is outweighed by differentials in status and rewards. Even in the most senior jobs, women remain clustered in areas of 'expertise' rather than 'authority' and at lower levels in hierarchies. In professional services, women make up 65 per cent of employees but are overwhelmingly in the lower-paid areas of work. They are over-represented in EDUCATION and routine health care and under-represented in the law, hospital consultancy, and higher grades of the CIVIL SERVICE.

Many of the reasons for women's lack of access to better-paid jobs are the same as those in other Western societies, including the difficulties in reconciling paid work and family life (still seen as primarily women's responsibility), organisational cultures that favour men, and the socialisation of women to undervalue their capabilities. Additional obstacles for women in Ireland include a high proportion of married women workers in full-time (rather than part-time) paid work (91 per cent, compared with 76 per cent in Britain), combined with very low levels of publicly financed CHILD CARE.

In Northern Ireland there has been a much longer history of women's participation in paid EMPLOYMENT. From this higher base the proportion has also increased dramatically, to 58 per cent in 1995, substantially greater than the total in the Republic (41 per cent). However, there are differences between the two religious communities. Protestant women have higher rates of participation in economic activity than Catholic women, reflecting differences in family size and length of education. Whereas Protestant women are more numerous in finance and distribution, Catholic women echo patterns in the Republic and are more strongly represented in the 'caring' professions of teaching and health care. In 1990 Catholic women predominated among those earning the highest salaries, with 13 per cent earning more than £200 per week, compared with only 9 per cent of Protestants, but they also featured more strongly among the low-paid, 61 per cent earning less than £100 a week, compared with 53 per cent of Protestant women.

There have been remarkable changes in women's career options and achievements in recent years, but obstacles to EQUALITY of opportunity with men remain deeply entrenched. **Bronwen Walter**

women and conflict. Women's experiences, responses, and roles in situations of conflict have been diverse as well as complex. Women have played a wide variety of roles in the conflict with Britain, as revolutionaries, peace activists, refugees and volunteers as well as wives, mothers, girl-friends and sisters of republican and loyalist militants. Excluded from early male-led nationalist organisations, nationalist and republican women sometimes founded their own, including the LADIES' IRISH NATIONAL LAND LEAGUE (1881), INGHINIDHE NA HÉIREANN (1900), and CUMANN NA MBAN (1914). Feminist peace activists in the Irish Branch of the Women's International League for Peace and Freedom—opposing both state violence and physical-force NATIONALISM—organised separately from men, on the premise that women could transform male politics away from war.

Following partition, which created the Protestant Unionist government of Northern Ireland, women in Catholic and Protestant communities were structured into the conflict in different ways. However, working-class Catholic and Protestant women shared certain experiences, including loss of homes in riots, loss of male family members through violence or imprisonment, and general anxiety over the safety of children and loved ones. In the recent conflict many women became politicised by their experiences and joined or supported paramilitary projects as well as challenging a

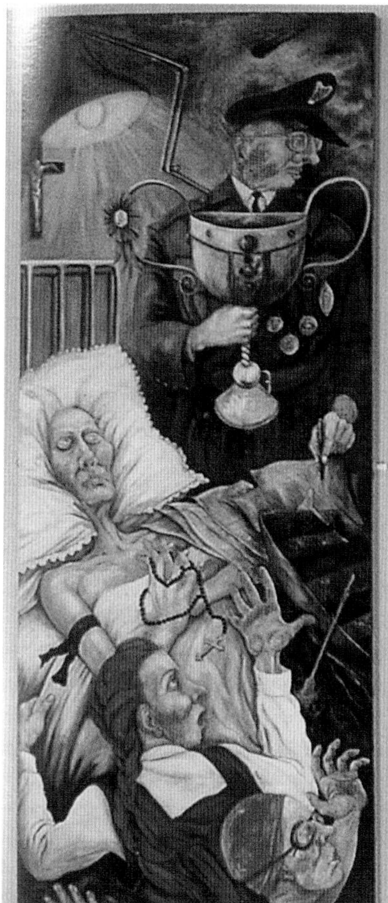

women and careers. *Rita Duffy's* Emerging from the Shamrock *(1991), rich in symbolism, explores the complex position of women in Ireland. Using the historical triptych altarpiece format, with infancy and old age represented in the wings, the work shows liberated woman walking purposefully forward, freed from traditionally dominant religious and social restraints. [Courtesy of the artist]*

wide range of government policies and practices. Women—for the most part Catholics—became active in the CIVIL RIGHTS marches (1968–9), led by such figures as BERNADETTE MCALISKEY, the Falls Road curfew (1970), the milk campaign (1971), the Relatives' Action Committee (1976), the Turf Lodge campaign (1978), and support for women prisoners in Armagh Jail (1979). **Marie Hammond Callaghan**

women and emigration. EMIGRATION from Ireland has shown an unusual relationship between men and women. More women than men left post-famine Ireland, especially in the peak years of emigration in the later nineteenth century; in the rest of Europe, by contrast, emigrants were predominantly male. Until recently the only CENSUS decades in which more men than women left Ireland were those of major British wars, when many Irish men joined the British army (1891–1901, 1911–26, and 1936–46) and years of exceptional employment decline (1951–61 and 1981–91). In the 1990s, however, men have predominated as emigrants, reflecting changed economic opportunities for women in Ireland and a more liberal social climate.

Reasons for the high proportion of women emigrants are both economic and social. After the Great Famine, farms were no longer divided between children on their father's death but were passed intact to a single son. One daughter might remain in the locality by marrying a neighbour's eldest son; but other daughters, unless they were able to find a means of acquiring a dowry, could not be supported as single adults. Additionally, the change from labour-intensive arable farming to extensive pastoral systems removed areas of women's agricultural responsibility; by the end of the nineteenth century, remaining areas of women's farm work—dairying and the raising of poultry—had also been taken over by men.

Educational differences also help to explain greater emigration among daughters than sons. In the late nineteenth century girls had higher levels of EDUCATION than boys, in part to compensate them for the lack of a land inheritance but also to improve their role as providers of remittances from abroad. Their aspirations were raised, and they were better prepared for emigration. Women have continued to achieve higher educational qualifications throughout the twentieth century.

EMPLOYMENT prospects for women were further reduced after the establishment of the Irish Free State in 1922. In accordance with a strict Catholic ideology that emphasised women's domestic role as wives and mothers, a MARRIAGE BAR was introduced in 1923 that prohibited women from remaining in public-service occupations after MARRIAGE, a restriction not lifted until 1973; this intensified the economic incentives to emigrate. In Northern Ireland, however, women's participation in the industrial labour force continued, and emigration rates for women and men were approximately equal.

Over the last 150 years socially restrictive attitudes to women encouraged a search for greater freedom outside Ireland. In addition to the limited roles endorsed by the Catholic Church—paralleled by fundamentalist Protestant ideologies in Northern Ireland—many studies of rural Ireland have pointed to the higher valuation of sons than daughters. It has been particularly difficult for certain groups to remain in Ireland, especially those who did not conform to the narrow definition of acceptable Irish womanhood, including single people, lesbians, and women who became pregnant outside marriage. The right-wing backlash of the 1980s, which led to the imposition of more stringent anti-ABORTION legislation and an initial rejection of the constitutional amendment permitting DIVORCE, confirmed and even strengthened the limiting social climate from which many continued to escape.

Women have also left at younger ages than men; this reflects both the greater ease with which girls could sever their family ties as well as their passage directly into a household structure as domestic servants. Between 1881 and 1891, 26 per cent of women emigrants but only 13 per cent of men were aged between fifteen and nineteen, while among those granted travel employment permits in the period 1943–51 the proportions were 31 per cent and 13 per cent, respectively.

The most popular destination for women in the late nineteenth and early twentieth centuries was the United States. Here the proportion of women in the emigrant population was far above that of men. In 1920 the census showed 22,161 Irish-born women employed in six large states, compared with 12,612 Irish-born men. This balance contrasted strikingly with that of immigrants in the labour force from Germany, Italy, Britain, and Sweden. However, there was a sharp shift in destination towards Britain after the mid-1920s: approximately 180,000 female emigrants went to Britain between 1926 and 1951, compared with 52,000 to the United States. Before 1921 the sex balance of Irish-born emigrants in Britain slightly favoured men, but since then women have outnumbered men, constituting 53 per cent of the emigrant population in 1991. **Bronwen Walter**

women and equality legislation. Following the Republic's membership of the European Economic Community in 1973, new legislation—the Anti-Discrimination (Pay) Act (1974) and the Employment Equality Act (1977)—provided for equal pay for work of equal value and banned discrimination in employment on the grounds of sex or marital status. Since then, case law developed steadily; but the requirement to have a 'male comparator' in equal pay claims limited the application of the legislation in female-dominated sectors of EMPLOYMENT; the pay gap has consequently been persistent and one of the widest in the European Union. The Employment Equality Act (1998) extended the grounds on which direct and indirect discrimination in employment were prohibited to include race, religion, disability, age, sexual orientation, family status, and membership of the travelling community. This law also codified sexual harassment, displacing the previous reliance on case law. In parallel, the Equal Status Act (2000) provides for protection against discrimination in the provision of services.

While the scope of the legislation is progressive, the provision for penalties, sanctions and enforcement is weak. Severe segregation in the labour market sees women concentrated in low-paid, low-status service employment, limiting the material impact of the legislation. **Ursula Barry**

women in farming. Farming is predominantly a male preserve, with land traditionally passing from father to son, yet Irish farm women are extensively involved in the family business. They typically 'marry into' their husband's farm, and the majority of farm women are therefore the wives or mothers of male farmers; it is unusual for women to own land or to farm in their own right. Nevertheless women's involvement in farm work can be substantial, particularly in the more labour-intensive farming systems and where men take up off-farm employment. Farm women often undertake the increasing burden of paperwork associated with farm businesses. However, as with household work, women's farm work is largely undervalued and ignored in official statistics. Their place in the shadows is confirmed by their lack of prominence in farming organisations and agri-business.

In recent years farm women have begun to articulate their concerns and to demand recognition, respect, and professional status for their work. Government responses to these concerns include a commitment to equality between men and women in agricultural and rural development policies and support for various schemes to improve farm women's status. Many farm women are pursuing a separate career by choosing to work off the farm or to launch farm food or agri-tourism businesses. On smaller holdings it is often women's earned income that sustains the farm family. **Patricia O'Hara**

women in medicine. After the passing of the Medical Qualifications Act (1876) women were granted access to the medical profession. However, many institutions remained closed to women. The Royal College of Physicians in Ireland became the first institution in Ireland or Britain to allow women to sit its examinations; as a result, prominent British women, such as Sophia Jex Blake, sat the licentiate examinations in Ireland. By 1890 all medical schools except that of Trinity College, Dublin, accepted female students. Some of the early medical graduates achieved success abroad, particularly in missionary work, where the presence of women was considered essential. Others, such as KATHLEEN LYNN and Ada English, were prominent in the movement for national independence. Dorothy Stopford Price gained an international reputation as an expert on childhood TUBERCULOSIS, while Louise McIlroy of Belfast became professor of gynaecology and OBSTETRICS at the Royal Free Hospital, London.

By the 1920s more than 20 per cent of medical graduates were women. This proportion did not increase substantially until the 1970s; by 1995, 65 per cent of the graduates of UCD medical school, the largest in Ireland, were women. However, at the beginning of the twenty-first century women were still under-represented in the upper echelons of the profession. **Margaret Ó hÓgartaigh**

women naturalists. Women have played an active part in the study of natural history in Ireland, with an international reputation for excellence out of all proportion to their numbers. The earliest of these women belonged to that class that could afford to engage in this activity as amateurs; yet when one examines the work done, often in isolation and without formal schooling, its quality and accuracy is remarkable.

ELLEN HUTCHINS of Ballylickey, Co. Cork, noted many rare and previously unrecorded plants. MARY WARD of Birr, Co. Offaly, was a researcher of exceptional abilities, becoming the first woman to write a book on the microscope. MARY BALL of Cobh, Co. Cork, and CYNTHIA LONGFIELD of Cloyne, Co. Cork, became internationally acclaimed entomologists. By the 1880s the teaching of nature studies in schools greatly increased the number of women whose published work is still consulted today. MAUDE DELAP of Valentia Island, Co. Kerry, and ANNE MASSY of Malahide, Co. Dublin, were marine zoologists. MATILDA KNOWLES of Ballymena, Co. Antrim, was a lichenologist, while KATHLEEN KING of Mount Merrion, Co. Dublin, studied mosses.

By the twentieth century the popularity of natural history was such that its acceptance as a subject for university education was assured; here too women played their part as skilled teachers as well as researchers. **Timothy Collins**

women and peace movements. *Monica McWilliams speaking to the press at Stormont following the signing of the Belfast Agreement, 10 April 1998, with fellow-delegates of the Women's Coalition, a cross-community political group founded on human rights, inclusion, and equality. [Derek Speirs/Report]*

women and peace movements (Northern Ireland). Women have played significant and distinctive roles in the peace movement of Northern Ireland. While their responses to the conflict varied widely, large numbers of women were motivated to join peace groups as an extension of their traditional roles in FAMILY, church, and community. Though perceived as predominantly middle-class, many women became active in the peace and reconciliation movement of Northern Ireland through largely ecumenical, church or community projects in mixed-sex and mixed-class groups. 'Protestant and Catholic Encounter' (PACE), 1969, People Together, 1974, and the PEACE PEOPLE (led by the NOBEL PRIZE-winners Mairead Corrigan and Betty Williams, with Ciarán McKeown), 1976, are some examples. Believing women to have a special interest in peace, and seeking autonomy for women in their groups, women also founded separatist peace groups, such as Women Together for Peace in Belfast, 1970, founded by Ruth Agnew and Monica Patterson, and the Derry Peace Women, 1972.

The Northern Ireland Women's Coalition, originating in the Northern Ireland Women's Rights Movement, was founded in April 1996 in an attempt to redress the imbalance between men and women in political decision-making and to draw attention to women's issues in the NORTHERN IRELAND PEACE PROCESS. **Marie Hammond Callaghan**

women and religion. The role of women in society and in the Catholic Church in Ireland underwent a dramatic change in the second half of the twentieth century. Previous generations of women—with some notable exceptions—saw their role as almost exclusively bound up with child-bearing, mothering, and home-making. While in practice women may have exercised remarkable authority in these roles, society did not accord them the rights and dignity of their male partners. The emergence of apostolic FEMALE RELIGIOUS ORDERS in the nineteenth century brought women into a new and significant role in society and in the church. Women of the standing of CATHERINE MCAULEY, NANO NAGLE, and MARY AIKENHEAD became pioneers in education, medicine, and social services. Schools and training colleges in education and NURSING offered to women a new dignity and status and virtually transformed their role. Education made it possible for women to have a career and to exercise a positive and creative role in society. The middle of the twentieth century saw a flourishing of missionary activity by women religious that extended medical, educational and social services to non-industrialised countries. Entry to the professions and equality of status and pay are now guaranteed to women by law. Women politicians and two women presidents have given women in Ireland a voice and place in economic and social policies. Women hold important positions in academic fields.

The Second Vatican Council in its decrees, while affirming the significance of women in their role as wife and mother, upheld their claim for 'equity with men before the law and in fact.' Previously Irish women who wished to have an active role in the church chose to do so within the apostolates undertaken by the female religious orders. There they exercised roles of service, having little opportunity in ministry or decision-making in ecclesial matters. The decrees of the Vatican Council emphasised the important role of the laity and in so doing gave all women, including religious women, a wider sphere of influence and ministry. Many women now serve as lay ministers, as members of parish councils, and in an advisory capacity on episcopal commissions. Many laywomen work with

VOLUNTARY ORGANISATIONS in non-industrialised countries and contribute to promoting the dignity of women. This changing role is reflected in all the main churches, and women from all churches are making important contributions in reconciliation work and ecumenical dialogue. **Consilio Rock**

Women's Aid, a VOLUNTARY ORGANISATION that supports victims of domestic violence. It was founded in 1974 at the instigation of Nuala Fennell, who wrote to the IRISH TIMES to draw attention to the problem of domestic violence and asking for support in tackling the issue. Against the background of changing legislation in the area of domestic violence, the organisation began by providing direct support to victims. Refuges for abused women were set up and, in 1994, a national twenty-four-hour help line, which receives 8,000 calls a year. The organisation expanded its remit during the 1990s to include education and development programmes, creating employment opportunities and providing medium-term accommodation for women who have been abused. In addition, Women's Aid pioneered awareness-raising programmes in the country as a whole, where, they estimate, one in five women experience domestic violence. **Alison Walsh**

women's campaign for equal rights. Embracing more than the WOMEN'S SUFFRAGE movement, the campaign also included demands to participate in local government, to have equal education, and to have restrictive legislation repealed. The Intermediate Education Act (1878), the Royal University Act (1879), and the campaign against the Contagious Diseases Acts (1869–86) produced articulate, politicised women activists. In 1896 women could become POOR LAW guardians and in 1898 achieved the LOCAL GOVERNMENT franchise. By 1899, 100,000 women in Ireland were qualified to be Poor Law electors, eighty women were elected to Poor Law Board rural councils, and four women were urban district councillors. Advances made in these areas were built upon by suffragists in the early twentieth century. **Clíona Murphy**

Women's Christmas, a traditional festival falling on 6 January (coinciding with the Feast of the Epiphany), known in Irish as *Nollaig na mBan* or *Lá Cinn an Dá Lá Dhéag* (Concluding Night of the Twelve Days of Christmas). It featured traditional fare of wine, tea, and cakes; a popular idiom says that on this night wine is made of water, silk of seaweed, and gold of grit. It has been reinvented in recent years as a women's night out. **Stiofán Ó Cadhla**

Women Graduates' Association, founded in 1902 as the Irish Association of Women Graduates and Candidate Graduates. Its efforts were instrumental in securing EQUALITY for women under the Irish Universities Act (1908). Following independence, the National University and Dublin University Women Graduates' Associations protested against discriminatory measures, such as the Juries Act (1927), the Conditions of Employment Act (1935), and the Constitution of Ireland (1937). Both organisations were involved in the formation in 1968 of an *ad hoc* committee to press for the establishment of a National COMMISSION ON THE STATUS OF WOMEN. **Rosemary Raughter**

women's movement. The Irish Women's Liberation Movement was founded in 1970. Its manifesto, *Chains or Change* (1971), sought equal pay, equal access to EDUCATION, EQUALITY before the law, the availability of CONTRACEPTION, justice for deserted wives, unmarried mothers, and widows, and a house for every family. It made effective use of a non-hierarchical, consciousness-raising style and of media events, such as the public (and illegal) importing of contraceptives by train from Belfast. There has been no subsequent mass women's movement. Radical FEMINISM surfaced with renewed vigour in 1974 with the emergence of IRISH WOMEN UNITED, whose objectives included free legal contraception and women's right to self-determined SEXUALITY. Throughout the 1970s organisations emerged from within the movement to provide services in the area of FERTILITY, support for single pregnant women and battered wives, and RAPE CRISIS CENTRES. The 1980s were years of demoralisation, with the reinforcing of the prohibition on ABORTION (1983 referendum), the rejection of DIVORCE (1986 referendum), and continuing legal struggles concerning access to information and counselling in crisis pregnancies. The 1990s saw general gains, such as the election of MARY ROBINSON as the first woman President of Ireland, the establishment of the second COMMISSION ON THE STATUS OF WOMEN (1990), and the passing of the second divorce referendum (1996). The 1990s also saw the rapid growth of local, mainly working-class women's groups concerned with women's poverty and the penetration into all the universities of women's studies courses at undergraduate or postgraduate level. **Pat O'Connor**

Northern Ireland. 'Second-wave' feminism (as distinct from the 'first-wave' early twentieth-century suffrage movements) emerged in the 1970s, developing distinctive ideological features. The first groups were the Lower Ormeau Women's Group (1973–5), Queen's University Women's Liberation Group (1974–5), and Coleraine Women's Group, (1974–8). The United Nations declaration of the International Year of Women (1975) provided a further catalyst; the NORTHERN IRELAND WOMEN'S RIGHTS MOVEMENT, Socialist Women's Group, and WOMEN'S AID were formed, and links were established with women in the Republic. Early campaigns concentrated on comparisons with women in Britain. Differences emerged regarding the continuation of the British link, as against support for a united Ireland. Abortion law reform was also contentious. The Women's Law and Research Group and Northern Ireland Women's Rights Movement lobbied for legal change while remaining neutral on the constitutional question, while the Socialist Women's Group, Belfast Women's Collective, and WOMEN AGAINST IMPERIALISM argued for a specifically anti-imperialist feminism.

In 1978 Women's Aid united women's groups throughout Ireland in the campaign to free Noreen Winchester, jailed for the manslaughter of her sexually abusive father. The protests of republican prisoners in Armagh Jail further polarised feminists. Unity meetings during the period 1979–81 united groups on certain issues, including the Action on Debt campaign and the production of a seminal issue of the journal *Scarlet Woman*. Lesbian women organised in several groups, one of which organised the All-Ireland Women's Conference in 1977.

The 1980s saw a consolidation of the movement, with the establishment of a Rape Crisis Centre and several women's centres and the funding of *Women's News* (1984) by Belfast City Council. Since the 1990s the community women's movement has developed a strong identity, with an emphasis on cross-community links. Though political differences remain, increasing political participation by women is a central challenge, partly addressed by the education work of Women into Politics, 1995, based in the Downtown Women's Centre, and the political success of the Northern Ireland Women's Coalition, 1996. **Margaret Ward**

women's suffrage movement. The first Irish women's suffrage organisation, the Northern Ireland Society for Women's

Suffrage, was established in 1871 by ISABELLA TOD. A few years later, in 1876, the Dublin Women's Suffrage Association (later the Irish Women's Suffrage and Local Government Association) was founded by ANNA HASLAM. This became the leading constitutional suffrage society, campaigning on a range of feminist issues and co-operating with suffragists in Britain and other countries. Some advances were made in the field of local politics. Women householders in Belfast achieved the municipal franchise in 1887; in 1896 women won the right to participate in the election of POOR LAW guardians and, in 1898, of rural and urban district councils on the same basis as men. However, failure to achieve the parliamentary vote fuelled impatience with constitutional methods among younger members, and in 1908 HANNA SHEEHY SKEFFINGTON and MARGARET COUSINS founded the militant Irish Women's Franchise League. A number of new constitutional societies were also established, and by 1913 fifteen societies had affiliated to the IRISH WOMEN'S SUFFRAGE FEDERATION, founded in 1911 by LOUIE BENNETT as a co-ordinating body.

However, strenuous campaigning failed to secure the inclusion of a suffrage clause in the third HOME RULE Bill, and the outbreak of war created division in the movement. While some suffragists supported the war effort, others opposed it as inimical to feminist aspirations, or on nationalist or pacifist grounds. Differences also emerged between nationalists and feminists, the former regarding independence as a precondition for political equality, the latter distrusting nationalists' commitment to women's rights. However, the aftermath of the 1916 RISING saw a rapprochement between these tendencies, with leading suffragists, such as Sheehy Skeffington, participating in SINN FÉIN organisation and propaganda efforts. The Representation of the People Act (1918) gave women over the age of thirty the right to vote in parliamentary elections. Women played a vital role in the subsequent election campaign, and CONSTANCE MARKIEVICZ was returned to the British House of Commons as its first woman member though she refused to take her seat. The franchise was extended to women over twenty-one in the Irish Free State in 1922 and in Northern Ireland in 1928. However, feminist hopes that possession of the parliamentary franchise would translate into full EQUALITY were disappointed, and the women's movement, handicapped by weak support and by internal strains, was unable to counter the anti-woman bias evident in much post-independence legislation and in the CONSTITUTION OF IRELAND. [see IRISH WOMEN WORKERS' UNION.] **Rosemary Raughter**

women's suffrage organisations. The suffrage movement in Ireland was an urban, middle-class movement. It encompassed different societies, which ranged from the militant Irish Women's Franchise League (founded 1908) to the older, non-violent Irish Women's Suffrage and Local Government Association (founded 1876) and Irish Women's Suffrage Society (founded 1873). It also included the Unionist Women's Franchise Association, the Munster Women's Franchise League, the Irish Catholic Women's Suffrage Association, and the Church League for Women's Suffrage (Anglican). The Irishwomen's Suffrage Federation contained many smaller suffrage groups.

Unlike suffragists elsewhere, Irish women did not have their own government to petition. Therefore, some joined forces with British suffragists and risked accusations of being un-nationalistic. Militant Irish suffragists were imprisoned in England and Ireland and went on hunger strike. The movement suffered because of the First World War (which undermined the English movement and its support network for Irish women) and because of the 1916 Rising and its aftermath. Irish women over the age of thirty (along with British women) received the vote under the Representation of the People Act (1918); as this was quickly followed by the War of Independence and Civil War, British legislation became irrelevant. Women in the Irish Free State received the vote from the age of twenty-one. **Clíona Murphy**

women and the trade union movement. The Women's Committee of the IRISH CONGRESS OF TRADE UNIONS is the principal representative structure for women in the male-dominated TRADE UNION movement. It provides a forum in which active women trade unionists can draw attention to women's position in EMPLOYMENT and debate policies of specific relevance to women. Important policy issues for the Women's Committee in recent years have been low pay, entitlement to maternity leave, reform of the equal pay legislation, tax allowances for the costs of CHILD CARE, and the rights of part-time workers. The introduction of legislation to protect part-time workers, in the form of the Worker Protection (Regular Part-time Employee) Act (1991), and the implementation of a statutory minimum wage in 2000 were both seen as breakthroughs for women workers.

Today, with the exception of the craft unions, women are strongly present throughout the trade union movement, particularly in public service unions and those representing retail and distribution services. Women account for 44 per cent of the membership of trade unions but, despite their increased representation among those in paid employment, are severely under-represented in the decision-making positions. Only 20 per cent of trade union officials' jobs and a small minority of leadership positions are occupied by women. Historically, there has been a radical tradition of women trade union activism, giving priority to the conditions of low-paid women workers in precarious, low-status service and manufacturing employment (see p. 601). The IRISH WOMEN WORKERS' UNION played a leading role in organising women workers and supporting women in disputes. Over recent years major industrial disputes, particularly in the public service, have predominantly involved women workers; recent examples include nurses and teachers, both of which groups have found themselves disadvantaged in a centralised industrial bargaining system that tends to reinforce historical wage and salary hierarchies. **Ursula Barry**

Wood, Charles (1866–1926), composer and teacher. Born in Armagh; studied organ with T. O. Marks at Armagh Cathedral and at the Royal College of Music, where he was winner of the Morley Scholarship for composition. Having taught at the Royal College of Music, he became lecturer at the University of Cambridge, 1897, where among his students was Vaughan Williams. He succeeded STANFORD as professor of music in 1924. Earlier compositions included much instrumental music, such as *Ode to the West Wind* (1890). Later he was increasingly active as a church music composer, producing more than thirty anthems, sixteen organ preludes, and a setting of St Mark's Passion. His sacred music, often distinguishable by its austerity, continues to be performed. **Emma Costello**

Wood, James J. (died 1928), electrical and optical engineer and inventor. Born in Kinsale, Co. Cork. He represents the link between the pioneering ages of Edison and Steinmetz, when ELECTRICITY became an industry. His family emigrated to the United States when he was eleven. In 1874 he began working for a lock company in Connecticut, then moved to the Brady Manufacturing Company, New York, rising rapidly to become superintendent and chief

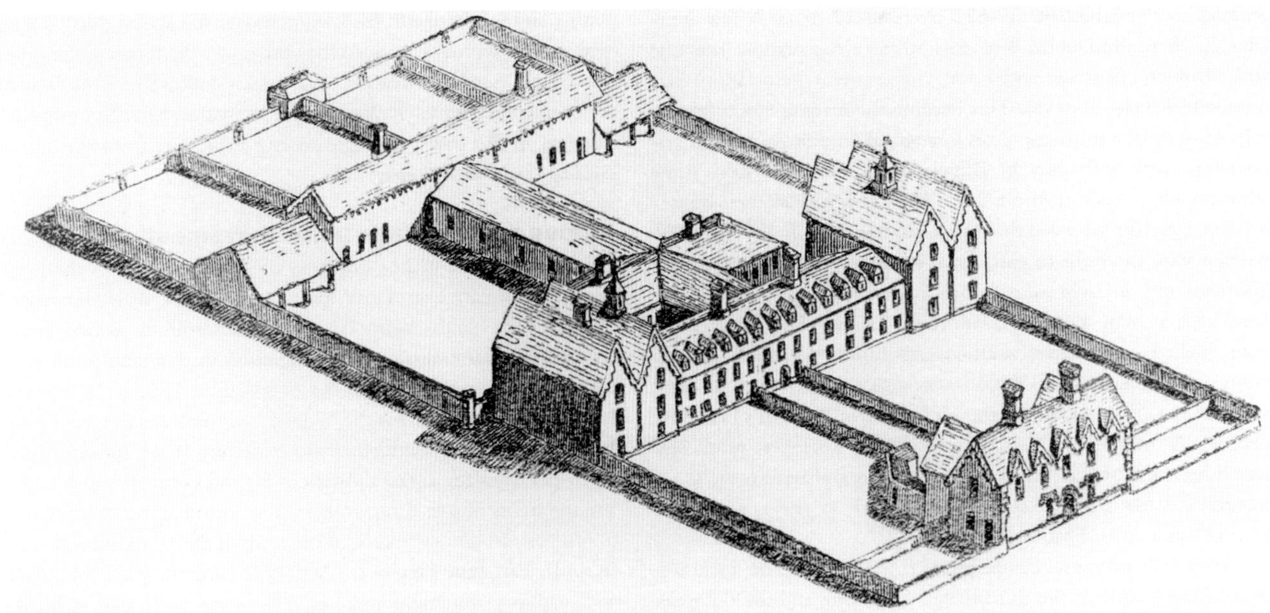

workhouses. *Schematic drawing of a workhouse, from* Ireland, Its Scenery, Characters, etc. *(1842) by Samuel Carter Hall and Anna Maria Hall. Constructed to a standard design by George Wilkinson, some 130 workhouses were erected under the Poor Relief (Ireland) Act (1838). [National Library of Ireland IR 9141h1]*

engineer. There he designed the engines used on JOHN HOLLAND's submarine and the machinery to make the main cables of the Brooklyn Bridge. He gained a mechanical engineering qualification from Brooklyn Polytechnic. From 1879 his development of a new, smaller arc lamp with increased power resulted in a design that remained in use for thirty-five years. The 'Wood system' was based on a spark-free dynamo arc lamp and was marketed by the Fort Wayne Electrical Company—later the General Electric Company—which had become famous for lighting the first floodlit baseball game. In 1902 he produced other major inventions, the stationary and revolving fans. In all, he produced 240 patents and stands, with Edison, Elihu Thomson, and E. F. W. Alexanderson among General Electric's most prolific inventors. Before his death he played a major role in the development of General Electric's refrigerator business. **Norman McMillan**

Woods, Macdara (1942–), poet and translator. Born in Dublin. Though primarily a poet, he has published translations (with the author, Redwan Abushwesha, *The King of the Dead and Other Libyan Tales*, 1977) and is a founder-editor of the magazine *Cyphers*. His extensive travels in North Africa and latterly in Italy are manifested in his work in a cosmopolitan diversity of themes and subject matter. His poems are many-layered, dense in their references, often set in the border zone between private compassion and public anger. His most recent work, much of it translated into Italian, deals with family matters and notably with the poet's relationship with his son. His collections are *Decimal D. Sec Drinks in a Bar in Marrakesh* (1970), *Early Morning Matins* (1972), *Stopping the Lights in Ranelagh* (1987), *Miz Moon* (1989), *The Hanged Man Was Not Surrendering* (1990), *Notes from the Country of Blood Red Flowers* (1994), *Selected Poems* (1996), *Knowledge in the Blood: New and Selected Poems* (2000), and *The Nightingale Water* (2000). He is a member of AOSDÁNA. **Theo Dorgan**

Woods, Robert (1865–1938), biophysicist. Born in Tullamore, Co. Offaly; studied natural philosophy at TCD, qualifying in experimental physics and medicine. Working as a demonstrator in anatomy, he realised that Laplace's Law could explain the workings of the heart, the urinary bladder, and the uterus. His theory was experimentally tested in the laboratory using cadaveric hearts and was explained in his paper of 1892, 'A Few Applications of a Physical Theorem to Membranes in the Human Body in a State of Tension'. The accuracy and broader applications of his work were not fully realised until the middle of the twentieth century. **Donal Synnott**

Woods, Stanley (1903–1993), motorcyclist. Born in Dublin. He competed in local speed events before taking on the challenge of the famous Isle of Man TT course in 1922; he finished fifth at this first attempt, winning the junior race the following year. He subsequently went on to win ten more TT races before the Second World War brought the curtain down on his career. Before that he competed all over the Continent, winning numerous Grand Prix races. He drove in a number of important car races and competed in local scramble, grass-track, speedway, and trial events until the 1960s. **Don McClenahan**

Wood's halfpence, coins minted in 1722 that led to political conflict in Ireland. Minted by a prominent Wolverhampton iron-master, William Wood, under a royal patent, they were intended for circulation in Ireland. Their introduction was opposed on political and economic grounds. Despite official pressure, even the Irish administration refused to accept them, and the value of the patent was first reduced, then cancelled entirely in September 1725. [see DRAPIER'S LETTERS, THE.] **Neal Garnham**

Woodward, Benjamin: see DEANE AND WOODWARD.

wooing (tale type): see TOCHMARC.

woollens. While some farmer-weavers wove woollens for home and local use, there were others who wove for manufacturers and who were controlled by the Weavers' Guild. From 1446 the guild guaranteed the quality, length, and width of its cloth. From about the same time its members also wove the new-style broadcloths. In an attempt to improve the quality and to encourage the weaving of new woollens, the administration brought Dutch and Walloon weavers to centres such as Kilkenny, Carrick-on-Suir, and Clonmel, both Co. Tipperary, and Chapelizod, Co. Dublin, c. 1660. There was anger that the Woollen Act (1698) restricted the export of Irish woollens, but in practice weavers continued to produce a wide variety of cloths, including the 'new draperies' of worsted or combed wool. The specialist weaver sold his woven lengths in markets and fairs and in centres such as the 'flannel hall' at Rathdrum, Co. Wicklow. The lengths were bought by urban cloth-finishers, who, through a 'wet and dry' process, stabilised the cloth so that it would retain its shape.

Because of the difficulty of competing with new-style woollen imports, the administration enabled the Dublin Society to establish the Irish Woollen Warehouse, which sold Irish fabrics made from Spanish, south Down and Wicklow wool, claimed to be equal in texture and durability to any English cloths. The introduction of cheap Manchester cottons affected the sale of fine woollens. To compete, factories were established, such as that at Ennisnag, Co. Kilkenny, c. 1810, where novel wools, such as merino, were woven. With the introduction of large water-powered factories the mass manufacture of woollens developed from the middle of the nineteenth century in many parts of the country. Typical of these large factories was that at Athlone, which employed 400 people c. 1890 and produced 15,000 m (17,000 yards) of cloth a week. **Mairead Dunlevy**

Workers' Party, a left-wing party founded in 1982 that achieved some success in the 1985 local and 1989 general elections but lost most of its members to DEMOCRATIC LEFT in 1992. Before 1982 the party had been known as Sinn Féin the Workers' Party. **Neil Collins**

workhouses. Under the Poor Relief (Ireland) Act (1838), workhouses were built in the 130 (later 163) POOR LAW unions, providing accommodation for some 100,000 paupers. The buildings were constructed to a standardised design by GEORGE WILKINSON. The regime adopted was punitive and deterrent, involving the separation of families, a limited diet, and monotonous physical labour; medical and educational facilities were added later. Rarely half full before 1845, the workhouses were overwhelmed during the GREAT FAMINE and became centres for the spread of contagious diseases. The workhouse system survived until 1921, in Northern Ireland until 1946. **Peter Gray**

work songs: see AMHRÁIN SAOTHAIR.

World War I: see FIRST WORLD WAR.

World War II: see SECOND WORLD WAR.

Wörner, Markus H. (1945–), philosopher. Born in Potsdam-Babelsberg, Germany; educated at the Universities of Bonn,

Wren boys. *Wren boys celebrate Lá an Dreoilín (Day of the Wren) near Brosna, Co. Kerry. St Stephen's Day, 26 December, has traditionally been the day for 'hunting the wren'. [Department of Irish Folklore, University College, Dublin, NO55.5]*

Oxford, and Berlin. Since 1986 he has been professor of philosophy at the National University of Ireland, Galway. He has published *Performative und Sprachliches Handeln* (1978), *Das Ethische in der Rhetorik des Aristoteles* (1990), *Glückendes Leben: Gespräche mit Aristoteles und Thomas von Aquin* (2000), and *Thomas von Aquin: Summa contra Gentiles IV* (second edition, 2001). **Fionola Meredith**

Worth, Katharine (1922–), professor and critic. Born in Newcastle-upon-Tyne; educated at the University of London. From 1978 she was first professor of drama and theatre studies at the University of London. Her ground-breaking *Irish Drama of Europe from Yeats to Beckett* (1978) related developments in Irish theatre to Continental techniques and established influential lines of continuity between the writers of the LITERARY REVIVAL and BECKETT. *Oscar Wilde* (1983) brought an informed theatrical sensibility to WILDE's drama. *Sheridan and Goldsmith* (1992) compared two Irish dramatists on the eighteenth-century London stage and contextualised their joint attack on sentimental comedy. *Samuel Beckett's Theatre: Life Journeys* (1999) drew on a lifetime's experience of viewing and directing his works. **Anthony Roche**

Worth Library, a collection of approximately 4,500 scholarly volumes, in superb contemporary bindings, bequeathed by Edward Worth (1678–1733) to DR STEEVENS' HOSPITAL, Dublin (now the head office of the Eastern Regional Health Authority), and still housed in its original, specially designed room. **Robert Mills**

Woulfe, Peter (c. 1727–c. 1803), chemist and mineralogist. Born in Co. Limerick. Most of his work was done in London. Though eccentric in habits he was distinguished, being appointed Bakerian lecturer at the Royal Society, 1756–7, elected a fellow, 1767, and awarded the Copley Medal, 1768. In his paper 'Experiments on the distillation of acids and volatile alkalis' (1767) he described (but did not illustrate) his apparatus for passing gases through liquids, 'Woulfe's bottle', which carried his name to posterity. He introduced the method of purifying phosphorus by pressing it through chamois leather, prepared picric acid from indigo by reaction with concentrated nitric acid, and investigated the composition of 'mosaic gold' (tin (IV) sulphide). **D. Thorburn Burns**

wren boys, (in this context pronounced 'wran'). On St Stephen's Day (Lá an Dreoilín, 26 December) groups of disguised musicians and dancers go from door to door, or from pub to pub, collecting alms and carrying in a bush a wren that has been killed earlier (though nowadays an imitation is used), reciting a rhyme beginning

> The wran, the wran, the king of all birds,
> On Stephens's Day was caught in the furze

—a reference to the folk belief that the martyred St Stephen was betrayed by a wren. The alms were used to buy drink for a 'wran ball', though nowadays they are frequently donated to charity. Some areas, such as Dingle, Co. Kerry, bring out wren troupes of Mardi Gras proportions; elsewhere the groups are more modest. **Tom Munnelly**

Wright, John Michael (1617–1694), portraitist. Born in London; studied in Edinburgh under George Jamesone. He visited Rome in the early 1640s and became a member of the Guild of St Luke there in 1648. He returned to England in 1656, having spent some years in France and Flanders. He visited Ireland at least once, arriving in 1679; he painted a number of Irish sitters, including Ladies Catherine and Charlotte Talbot and Robert King, second Baron Kingston. He served as steward to the Earl of Castlemaine's embassy to Pope Innocent XI, 1685–7. The accession of William III to the throne heralded a change in his fortunes, and he died in penury. **Brendan Rooney**

Wyatt, James (1746–1813), architect. Born in Burton Constable, Staffordshire. As a youth he was taken by Lord Bagot to Rome, where he studied classical architecture. He adapted the numinous spatiality of buildings like the Pantheon (Rome) and Hagia Sophia (Istanbul) to the refined sensibilities of eighteenth-century domestic architecture, designing both exteriors and interiors and closely supervising the furnishing and decoration. A precursor of nineteenth-century eclecticists, he was able to negotiate disparate styles, ranging from the chaste Heaton Hall to the fantastic Fonthill Abbey. His chief contribution to Irish architectural history is CASTLE COOLE, the great country house of the LOWRY-CORRY family in Co. Fermanagh. Among his extensive Irish commissions were work on LEINSTER HOUSE, Dublin, Westport House, Co. Mayo, Currahchase, Co. Limerick, and SLANE CASTLE, Co. Meath, for some of which his original drawings have survived. **George Mott**

Wyndham, George (1863–1913), politician. Born in London. In 1887 he was appointed private secretary to Arthur Balfour, and in 1889 was elected Conservative MP for Dover. From 1900 to 1905 he served as CHIEF SECRETARY FOR IRELAND, committed to continuing the policy of constructive UNIONISM; he is best known in Ireland for the LAND ACT (1903), partly based on recommendations of the Dunraven Land Conference. He also tried unsuccessfully to solve the Catholic University question. He resigned in 1905, because of unionist opposition to the devolution scheme promoted by his Under-Secretary, Sir ANTONY MACDONNELL. **Carla King**

Wynne, Arthur Beavor (1835–1906), geologist and artist. Born possibly in Dublin, a member of a distinguished Irish family of Welsh origin. He worked as an assistant in the General Valuation Office under Sir RICHARD GRIFFITH until the spring of 1855, when he was appointed assistant geologist on the Irish GEOLOGICAL SURVEY under Sir Henry de la Beche. Along with Jukes, DU NOYER and Kinahan he mapped large areas of Cos. Tipperary, Waterford, and Cork. He appears in a group photograph of the staff of the Irish branch of the Geological Survey taken c. 1860. In 1862 he was appointed to the Indian Geological Survey, in which he served for twenty-one years in Bombay, then in Kutch and the Punjab, publishing three memoirs, which remain the standard works on the geology of those areas. In April 1883 he resigned on health grounds, returned to Ireland, and rejoined the Irish Survey as resident officer in Dublin. Always a prolific draughtsman, between 1876 and 1904 he exhibited more than eighty landscape watercolours at the RHA, including views from all over Ireland as well as the Scottish Highlands and Islands, Wales, India, Canada, Norway, Algeria, Egypt, Sicily, and Switzerland. He was elected president of the ROYAL GEOLOGICAL SOCIETY OF IRELAND in 1889. After retirement in 1890 he lived mostly in Switzerland. **Martyn Anglesea**

'X' case. *A 'Women's Choices, Women's Voices' rally in Dublin, 14 November 1992, in support of the fourteen-year-old rape victim at the centre of the 'X' case. The case forced the Government to hold a new set of referendums, with the result that the Constitution now guarantees a right to information and travel. [Derek Speirs/Report]*

X (1961–3), a quarterly review published in London and edited by the artist PATRICK SWIFT and the South African poet David Wright (translator of *The Canterbury Tales* and Beowulf). Seven numbers were issued, containing work by ANTHONY CRONIN, PATRICK KAVANAGH, SAMUEL BECKETT, and JOHN MCGAHERN (his first appearance in print). [see LITERARY MAGAZINES.] **Brian Lalor**

'X' case, the, the controversy surrounding an injunction obtained by the ATTORNEY-GENERAL in 1992 to restrain a pregnant fourteen-year-old girl ('X') from travelling to England—with the consent and support of her parents—for an ABORTION. She was pregnant as a result of rape by an adult friend of the family. There was considerable public dismay at the action of the Attorney-General. The Government encouraged the girl's family to appeal the judgment to the SUPREME COURT and undertook to pay the legal expenses. The court ruled, in the light of the threat to the girl's life from possible SUICIDE, that the Eighth Amendment to the CONSTITUTION (1983) granted a right to abortion in the event of a real and substantial threat to the life (as distinct from the HEALTH) of the mother. A REFERENDUM proposing the removal of the possibility of suicide as grounds for abortion was rejected in 1992, while the existence of a right to travel and to information for lawful services was affirmed. In 1995 legislation was enacted to allow information on abortion services outside Ireland to be lawfully distributed. Widespread public discussion of the case clarified for many people the conditions under which they were willing to waive their moral and social reservations concerning abortion. A green paper outlining various options (including legislation and a third referendum on abortion) was produced in 1999. A third referendum was held in 2002 and the electorate rejected the proposed amendment, which would have removed the possibility of suicide as grounds for abortion. Legislation to clarify the circumstances under which abortion is legal has yet to be introduced. [see 'C' CASE; KERRY BABIES CASE; LOVETT, ANN.] **Pat O'Connor**

Yeats, W. B *(see page 1157). The poet W. B. Yeats, in a photograph by George C. Beresford, 15 July 1911. Celebrated as one of the most important figures of twentieth-century literature, Yeats is regarded as the leader of the Irish Literary Revival. [Getty Images/Hulton Archive]*

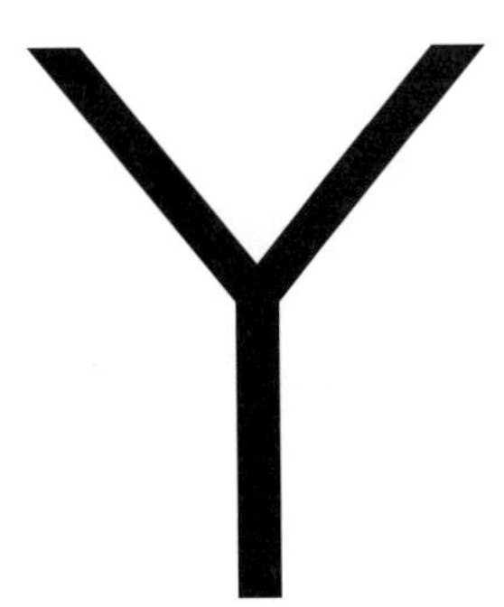

Yeates and Son, instrument-makers. Samuel Yeates (1762–1834) was an 'optician' (in the original sense of a maker of optical instruments) from 1790 until his death; the firm was continued by his second son, George Yeates, who was succeeded by his son, Stephen Mitchell Yeates, from c. 1865 until his death in 1901. The Yeates family and the Masons (also Dublin opticians) intermarried in more than one generation, and Samuel Yeates may have served his apprenticeship with Seacombe Mason (1745–1804) in Dublin. Although by the 1880s Yeates and Son sold apparatus for telegraphy, METEOROLOGY, and medical diagnosis, surviving catalogues make it clear that the government-financed educational market was an important one. **A. D. Morrison-Low**

Yeats, Anne (1919–2001), painter and stage designer. Born in Dublin, daughter of W. B. YEATS; studied at the ROYAL HIBERNIAN ACADEMY Schools, Dublin, 1933–6, and also as a pupil of Lilian Davidson (died 1954). She worked at the ABBEY THEATRE as assistant stage designer, later chief stage designer, 1936, then as a freelance designer, 1940–46. In 1941 she began to paint, holding her first one-woman show in Dublin in 1946. HILARY PYLE observed in the Rosc 1975 catalogue that Yeats was preoccupied with the human situation, particularly with the isolation of the individual. In the 1940s she worked mainly in watercolour and gouache; c. 1948–50 she incorporated wax with watercolour. Uncertainty about the permanence of the wax led her to abandon the method, and her later work is mainly in oil. In 1947 she joined the committee of the IRISH EXHIBITION OF LIVING ART. She participated in group exhibitions in the United States, the Netherlands, Germany, Scotland, and Monaco. Her work is represented in the collections of the ARTS COUNCIL, the HUGH LANE Municipal Gallery of Modern Art, Dublin, the ULSTER MUSEUM, Belfast, Sligo County Museum, TRINITY COLLEGE, Dublin, and the Yeats Museum, National Gallery of Ireland. **Martyn Anglesea**

Yeats, Elizabeth: see CUALA INDUSTRIES.

Yeats, Gráinne, née Ní hÉigeartaigh (1925–), harpist, researcher, and singer. Born in Dublin; studied piano, singing, and harp at the RIAM and *sean-nós* singing with Máighréad Ní Bheaglaíoch. She built up a repertoire of traditional songs and music and has written extensively on the history and music of the wire-strung harp and performed throughout the world. Recordings include *The Harp of Ireland* (1992), comprising some of the tunes collected by Bunting at the Belfast Harpers' Festival (1792). **Emma Costello**

Yeats, Jack Butler (1871–1957), painter and illustrator (see p. 202). Born in London, youngest child of JOHN BUTLER YEATS and brother of W. B. YEATS. A prodigy in drawing, in 1879, at the age of eight, he was taken to Co. Sligo to live with his mother's parents, the Pollexfens, and much of his imagery was formed there. He was fascinated by horses, horse fairs, and race meetings. In 1887, aged seventeen, he returned to London to join the rest of his family and to study at South Kensington under Sir Thomas Armstrong and at the Westminster School of Art under Fred Brown. Between 1888 and 1910 he worked as an illustrator for numerous papers, including the *Vegetarian*, *Lika Joko*, *Paddock Life*, *Boy's Own Paper*, and *Punch*, and for a time was the breadwinner for his father's indigent family.

In 1894 he married a fellow-artist, Mary Cottenham White, and they settled near Chertsey, Surrey. In 1897 the couple moved to Devon, and Yeats made his first experiments in oil painting. In 1898 he visited Venice; the following year he stayed for the first time with LADY AUGUSTA GREGORY in Co. Galway and also visited Paris. In 1904 he visited New York, where the collector John Quinn organised an exhibition of his watercolours. In 1905 he was commissioned by J. M. SYNGE to illustrate a series of twelve articles on the congested districts of the west of Ireland; two years later he produced hand-coloured illustrations for a limited edition of SYNGE's *The Aran Islands*. After this he illustrated exclusively for *Punch*, using the name 'W. Bird'. In 1905 he settled again in Ireland, first at Greystones, Co. Wicklow, and later in Dublin. He did not work regularly in oils until after 1905, but he was influenced by HUGH LANE's collection of French impressionist paintings, and in 1913 he was among the European artists featured in the 'New York Armory Show'.

Yeats was the most distinguished Irish painter of the twentieth century, his mature work an idiosyncratic form of expressionism, having some similarity with the late work of Lovis Corinth but with a strong literary dependence. His work had some influence on the Austrian painter Oskar Kokoschka, whom he met in Dublin c. 1950. He produced a quantity of articles and a number of books, novels, and plays, including *Life in the West of Ireland* (1912), *Sligo* (1930), *The Amaranthers* (1936), *The Careless Flower* (1947), and *In Sand* (1949). He was elected an associate member of the ROYAL HIBERNIAN ACADEMY in 1914 and a member in 1915 and in 1949 was made an officer of the Légion d'Honneur. **Martyn Anglesea**

Yeats, John Butler (1839–1922), painter and critic (see pp. 511, 1159, 1160). Born in Tullylish, near Banbridge, Co. Down, son of the Church of Ireland rector; educated at Atholl Academy, Isle of Man, and TCD, where his tutor was JOHN KELLS INGRAM. After graduating in 1862 he enrolled at the KING'S INNS to study for the bar, to which he was called in 1866, though he never practised. In 1862 his father died suddenly, leaving him a small estate near Thomastown, Co. Kildare, which provided an income of several hundred pounds a year. In 1863 he married Susan Pollexfen (1841–1900) of Sligo, and in 1865 their eldest son, WILLIAM BUTLER YEATS, was born. Determined to become a painter, he left for London early in 1867 and enrolled at Heatherley's, a private art school; in the summer his wife, son, and two daughters joined him in London, where their two youngest children, Robert Corbet Yeats and JACK BUTLER YEATS, were born. He received encouragement from two Irish artists established in London, the sculptor JOHN HENRY FOLEY and the comic illustrator RICHARD 'DICKY' DOYLE. He earned a precarious living by sending illustrations to magazines; but his ambition was to be a society portrait painter.

The family returned to Ireland in 1881, and he began to exhibit paintings at the ROYAL HIBERNIAN ACADEMY, which elected him a member in 1892. His portraits were admired, and he had no difficulty in obtaining commissions; but he was a poor businessman and made very little money. In 1887 he returned to London, leaving his family in Ireland. After his wife's death in 1900 he returned to Dublin, where in October 1901 he staged a joint exhibition with NATHANIEL HONE. The influence of HUGH LANE led to a number of commissions for portraits of literary and political figures; many of these are now in the NATIONAL GALLERY OF IRELAND.

In December 1908, at the age of sixty-nine, he accompanied his daughter Lily to New York, with the intention of taking the city by storm and attracting Irish-American patrons. He was to spend the rest of his life there, with the support of the lawyer and collector John Quinn. He quickly entered the New York artistic community, becoming friendly with the 'Ashcan School' painters, such as John Sloan and Robert Henri; but he never achieved the prestige as a portraitist that he desired, being recognised more for his fluent conversation and writing. His essays for *Harper's Weekly* were collected as *Essays, Irish and American* (1918). *Early Memories: A Chapter of Autobiography*, was published posthumously. **Martyn Anglesea**

Yeats, Lilly: see CUALA INDUSTRIES.

Yeats, W. B. [William Butler] (1865–1929), writer, poet, dramatist, and essayist, generally considered one of the greatest poets of the twentieth century. Born on 13 June 1865 in Sandymount,

NO. 1 (NEW SERIES) JANUARY 1937.

A BROADSIDE

EDITORS: DOROTHY WELLESLEY AND W. B. YEATS.
PUBLISHED MONTHLY AT THE CUALA PRESS, ONE HUNDRED AND THIRTY THREE LOWER BAGGOT STREET, DUBLIN.

COME GATHER ROUND ME PARNELLITES

Come gather round me Parnellites
And praise our chosen man;
Stand upright on your legs awhile;
Stand upright while you can
For soon we lie where he is laid
And he is underground.
Come fill up all those glasses
And pass the bottle round.

300 copies only.

Yeats, Jack B. *The first issue of the new series of* A Broadside, *published in the 1930s by the Cuala Press and illustrated by Jack B. Yeats. The broadsides were first published in 1908–15, following the founding in 1908 of the Cuala Press by Yeats's sisters, Elizabeth Corbet Yeats and Susan Mary Yeats. [Board of Trinity College, Dublin]*

Yeats, Jack B. For the Road *(1951), a late work by Jack B. Yeats celebrating a central motif throughout his oeuvre—the horse. His expressive application of paint conveys the emotion and spirit of the horse galloping towards its master at the end of a tunnel of trees. [National Gallery of Ireland]*

Dublin; educated in London at the Godolphin School and in Dublin at the Erasmus Smith High School and Metropolitan School of Art. His childhood was spent in Co. Sligo, London, and Dublin, which established the tension between country and city, periphery and centre, and coloured all his literary and political endeavours. His most successful early work is the title poem of *The* WANDERINGS OF OISIN *and Other Poems* (1889), a lengthy mystical poem based on Irish legend. The remaining poems of the volume were later collected separately, with some additions, under the title *Poems* (1895). Like many poems of the early period, they demonstrate an interest in symbolism, the occult (he was to become a member of the Hermetic Order of the Golden Dawn in 1890), and nationalism, always controversial for a Protestant Irishman. 'Who Goes with Fergus?' and 'The Lake Isle of Innisfree' proved that his early symbolism already had distinctly Irish backgrounds.

In 1889 he fell in love with MAUD GONNE, a fervent nationalist who, like Yeats, belonged to the circle of the Fenian JOHN O'LEARY. O'Leary's cultural nationalism would prove formative for Yeats in his disagreements with the more militant Gonne. His long-sustained love for her was to have enormous consequences for both his politics and his poetry; throughout his career as a nationalist poet he endeavoured with varying success to write more directly.

The section entitled 'The Rose' in *Poems* (1895) and the volume *The Wind Among the Reeds* (1899) developed Yeats's early nationalist, occult and symbolist concerns into a more complex, transcendental aesthetic. Poems such as 'The Secret Rose' from the latter volume exhibit a pre-Raphaelite influence, which was conveyed to him through his father, the painter JOHN BUTLER YEATS, and an aestheticised Celticism; yet they contain a love of country and mystery, indeed of religion, that would cause conflict between father and son. They also reflect the erotic forces inspired by Gonne, the subsequent unleashing of desire in a love affair with Olivia Shakespear, and the sad conclusion of that romance because of Yeats's continuing obsession with Gonne. Poets of the Rhymers' Club in London—Arthur Symons, Lionel Johnson, and Ernest Dowson, devotees of both French symbolism and Walter Pater's aestheticism—were also influential, because of their preoccupation with religion and sexuality. Controversies in Ireland during the 1890s, such as the Jubilee riots in 1897 and the national effort to commemorate the centenary of the 1798 Rebellion, increasingly captured and troubled Yeats's imagination.

In the early 1890s he became involved in the beginning of the Irish Literary Revival, and in 1897 he began plans for a national dramatic movement, which would lead to the founding of the ABBEY THEATRE, Dublin. *The Land of Heart's Desire* (1894), THE COUNTESS CATHLEEN (1899), the overtly nationalist and controversial *Cathleen Ni Houlihan* (1902)—in which Gonne played the title role—and *On Baile's Strand* (1904) are notable early plays. The artistic effort to engage with national affairs complemented a personal need (coupled with Gonne's continuing dismissal of his affections) to become less passive and escapist; *The Wind Among the Reeds* (1899), *In the Seven Woods* (1903), and *The Green Helmet and Other Poems* (1910) increasingly mirrored this tendency. He believed himself too timid for Maud Gonne and ruffled into a 'manly prose', as he later wrote (in 'Coole Park, 1929'). This feeling of inadequacy worsened when in 1903 Gonne married the physical-force nationalist JOHN MACBRIDE, a veteran of the ANGLO-BOER WAR, whom Yeats thought a grossly unsuitable match for her; but it also began a series of investigations into sex roles, culture, and society that would culminate in his finest writing.

The greatest change in Yeats's work is evident in the collection *Responsibilities* (1914), in which he arduously sought to establish a poetry of social responsibility. Written under the influence of Ezra Pound, whom he had met in 1909, its comparative realism and modernist colloquialism was a watershed, widely regarded as beginning his mature period. Such change was not only personal and artistic, however: the 1916 RISING had a profound effect on him, as solemnised in the poem 'Easter 1916', forcing him to revise his entrenched satire of the Catholic middle class and his disillusionment with nationalism. It also led him to compose a theory of historical change (first formulated in 'No Second Troy'), which greatly influenced his later thinking. The rising, like the succeeding War of Independence and Civil War, made him reconsider the place of violence in personal, social and even religious renewal, and readings in Nietzsche helped him to develop this philosophy.

Yeats married Georgie Hyde Lees in 1917, having earlier proposed to Maud Gonne's daughter, Iseult. His wife shared his continued, and often maligned, interest in the occult and in spiritualist experiment. Seeing that her husband was distracted on their honeymoon, she decided to fake automatic writing. Her ruse was successful, and subsequent attempts proved fruitful in the form of poetry and mystical prose. In *Per Amica Silentia Lunae* (1918) Yeats had outlined views of history and human personality that were systematised in *A Vision* (1925, revised 1937), a series of stories, treatises, and poems devising a complicated symbolic and geometrical system derived from the automatic writing and meant to illuminate the sexual-religious basis of psychological and historical change. *The Wild Swans at Coole* (1919) displays the effects of his marriage through its treatment of the feminine as the basis of culture and its meditations on love, death, and the pastoral. In *Michael Robartes and the Dancer* (1921) and THE TOWER (1928) he returned to investigate violence more fully. With *The Winding Stair and Other Poems* (1933) feminine themes of the beautiful achieve the status of religious proof that 'profound philosophy' can be born of 'terror'. Yeats's bid to unify masculine and feminine, war and peace, took him to the summit of his creative powers. Most critics agree that *The Tower* and *The Winding Stair* contain his greatest poems, reflecting his lifelong aim to hammer political and aesthetic concerns into a unity. The last collections, *New Poems* (1938) and *Last Poems and Plays* (1940), alternate, with often savage eloquence, between despair in the face of cultural decay or personal death and more transcendent visions of civilisation and the soul.

Yeats served as a senator of the Irish Free State, 1922–8, and was awarded the NOBEL PRIZE for Literature in 1923. He died in Roquebrune in the south of France, survived by his wife—who became a skilled manager of his literary estate—and his two children, Anne and Michael Yeats. His remains were brought to Drumcliff, Co. Sligo, in 1948. **Jefferson Holdridge**

Yeats, John B. John O'Leary *by John B. Yeats. O'Leary, Fenian and editor of the* Irish People, *was president of the Supreme Council of the IRB until his death in 1907. This unfinished work presents a double portrait of the defiant O'Leary. Yeats was the most significant portrait painter of the early years of the Literary Revival. [Tipperary South Riding County Museum]*

Yellow Ford, Battle of the (1598), one of the biggest military defeats of English arms in Irish history, temporarily rendering English hegemony in Ireland vulnerable. The main royal army, more than 4,000 strong, commanded by Marshal Bagenal, was engaged at several points as it marched from Armagh to the River Blackwater at a point known as Béal an Átha Buí (the Yellow Ford). Benefiting from the cover of the natural terrain as well as elaborately manufactured earthworks, the Irish forces rained a deadly fire on the advancing English columns. A mass charge delivered the *coup de grâce*; as few as 1,500 of the Crown army managed to retreat and seek sanctuary in the cathedral in Armagh. Estimates of Crown casualties vary widely; what is certain is that Bagenal and eighteen English captains lost their lives, Bagenal being criticised afterwards for taking up his position in the van of the army rather than the more secure 'main battle'. **John McCavitt**

Yelverton's Act (1782), an Irish act that modified POYNINGS' LAW. The act provided that only bills passed by the Irish Parliament, and forwarded to England, could become law in Ireland. It negated the powers of the Privy Councils, and made the HEADS OF BILLS procedure redundant. It was not opposed by the administration but was declared inadequate by the patriot HENRY FLOOD, largely for his own political ends. **Neal Garnham**

Yeats, John B. W. B. Yeats *(1898), monochrome watercolour by John B. Yeats; commissioned by Lady Gregory, the artist regarded it as the best sketch he made of his son. [National Gallery of Ireland]*

Yeomanry. Begun in 1796, the Irish Yeomanry was a part-time force of civilians who provided military service in their own localities. Their remit was to help the magistrates to combat the UNITED IRISHMEN and to assume the garrison duties of the British army if Ireland was invaded by France and the army had to move to the coast. By late 1796 the Yeomanry contained 20,000 men, organised in small, locally based units of cavalry and infantry. In rural areas the Yeomanry corps were raised and officered by landlords; in cities and towns they were often organised by trade or profession. Ultimate control lay with the Irish administration, which issued the officers' commissions and the yeomen's pay, arms, and uniform. Yeomen trained twice weekly, but they could be called out for full-time service if invasion or insurrection threatened. Most were Protestants, though some Catholics served in Leinster and Connacht. The Yeomanry has acquired a ferocious reputation, largely through popular memories of the 1798 REBELLION. Contemporaries, however, were divided about its utility: United Irish supporters criticised its brutality, while loyalists claimed it saved the country. A less well-known and possibly more important aspect was the Yeomanry's role as an anti-invasion reserve after 1798. Numbers reached a peak in 1810, at 85,000, but declined after the Napoleonic War ended in 1815. Only in Ulster, where links had developed with the ORANGE ORDER, did significant numbers remain. Largely inactive in the 1820s, the Yeomanry was disbanded in 1834. **Allan Blackstock**

Yola. Documentary evidence exists for the survival of an unusual form of English in the baronies of Forth and Bargy, Co. Wexford, where the ANGLO-NORMANS first invaded, and in Fingall, north of Dublin. RICHARD STANIHURST, writing in 1577, was the first to comment on the strange Wexford English.

> There was of late dayes one of the Péeres of England sent to Weiseford as Commissioner, to decide the controuersies of that countrey, and hearing in affable wise the rude complaintes of the countrey clownes, he conceyued [understood] here and there, sometyme a worde, other whyles a sentence. The noble man beyng very glad that vpon his first comyng to Ireland, he vnderstood so many wordes, told one of hys familiar frends, that he stoode in very great hope, to become shortly a well spoken man in the Irishe, supposing that the blunte people had pratled Irishe, all the while they iangled Englishe. Howbeit to this day the dregs of the old Chaucer English, are kept as well there as in Fingall.

The comparison with Chaucerian English is made again in 1682 when Colonel Solomon Richards reported to Sir WILLIAM PETTY on Forth speech:

> Itt's notorious that itt's the very first language brought over by Fitzstephen, and retained by them to this day. Whover hath read old Chaucer, and is at all acquainted therewith, will better understand the barony of Forth dialect than either an English or Irishman, that never read him, though otherwise a good linguist.

Chaucer appears again as late as 1824 when the rector of Tacumshane states that his workmen gave him more accurate glosses on the *Canterbury Tales* than did the writings of Dryden. But within half a century, Yola, the name given to it in its decline (meaning 'old'), was dead. Nevertheless hundreds of words from it survived to very recent times.

The following specimen of Yola is from a HURLING song composed early in the eighteenth century. A man tells the story of how his son lost the match.

> Na, now or neveare! W' cry't t' Tomeen,
> Fan Cournug yate a rishp, an Treblere pit w'eeme.
> A clugercheen gother: all, ing pile an ing heep,
> Wourlik'd an anooree, lick lhuskes o' sheep.
> Nay, now or never! We cry'd to Tomeen,
> When Cournug gave a stroke,
> and Treblere put with him (helped him)
> A crowd gathered, all in pile and in heap,
> Tumbled on one another, like flocks of sheep.

Diarmaid Ó Muirithe

yole. During the failed French maritime invasion at Bantry, Co. Cork, in 1796 commanded by General Lazare Hoche, a longboat called a 'yole' embarked on a reconnaissance mission from the *Resolue* but was captured by Captain Richard White of Whiddy Island. This was as close as any member of the invasion fleet got to Irish soil; WOLFE TONE remained on board the *Indomitable*. The yole, with accommodation for ten oars and two lugsails, measures 11.6 m by 2 m (38 ft by 6 ft 7 in). Captain White, ancestor of the Earls of Bantry, kept the boat at what became Bantry House, and it was sailed at Bantry Regatta until 1900. In 1944 it was transferred to the Maritime Museum in Dún Laoghaire, Co. Dublin, a rare survival of an eighteenth-century French naval craft. **Brian Lalor**

Young, Andrew (1919–1992), mathematician. Born in Edentown, Lancashire; educated at the University of St Andrews, where he was Harkness scholar and winner of the Carstairs and Miller Prizes. The first professor of mathematics at the New University of Ulster, Coleraine, 1968–84, he was an applied mathematician of breadth, taking in geophysics, biomathematics, numerical analysis, operations research, mathematical modelling, and approximation theory (on which he wrote forty-one papers); his work was characterised by scientific intuition and mathematical rigour. As a combatant officer in the Second World War he was wounded at the Battle of Kohima (1944) and subsequently became a pacifist. An ardent socialist as well as a QUAKER, he served in high office in universities, the Institute of Mathematics and its Applications, the Association of University Teachers, the Nursing Council, and the Abercorn Trust. **Gerald P. Shannon**

Young, Arthur (1741–1820), agricultural theorist and traveller. Born in Suffolk, England. He visited Ireland twice, in 1776 and 1777, and was appointed agent to the Kingsborough estate at Mitchelstown, Co. Cork, but was dismissed following family intrigues. *A Tour in Ireland* (1780) presents an account of his journeys as well as valuable observations on the economy, agricultural practice, and statistical information, and he is among the most perceptive and informed of eighteenth-century visitors to Ireland. Following his visit of 1787–90 to France during the Revolution he published *Travels in France* (1792), on which his reputation rests. [see WOLLSTONECRAFT, MARY.] **Brian Lalor**

Young, Sydney (1857–1937), chemist. Born in Farnworth, near Widnes, Lancashire; studied at Owen's College, Manchester, and graduated from the University of London in 1880. Appointed a lecturer at University College, Bristol, in 1882, he collaborated there with William Ramsay on research into the vapour pressure of liquids. In 1887 he succeeded Ramsay as professor of CHEMISTRY; in 1904 he was appointed to the chair of chemistry at Trinity College, Dublin, retiring in 1928. He was a leading authority on fractional distillation to purify organic chemicals and devised a way to dehydrate alcohol using benzene. His books include *Fractional Distillation* (1903) and *Stoichiometry* (1908). **Rod Gow**

Young Ireland, originally a ginger group within the REPEAL ASSOCIATION consisting of contributors to the NATION, established by THOMAS DAVIS and CHARLES GAVAN DUFFY in 1842; their 'Young Ireland' confronted O'CONNELL's more conservative 'Old Ireland'. Advocating cultural nationalism, the Young Irelanders supported non-sectarian education and, after Davis's death, independence from the WHIG government. In July 1846 O'Connell's prohibition of violence, except in defence, forced Young Ireland, led by WILLIAM SMITH O'BRIEN, from the Repeal Association. In 1847, despite the Famine, the Repeal Association confronted the seceders' Irish Confederation. The death of O'Connell in May swung nationalist opinion against Young Ireland, itself divided between Gavan Duffy and the more radical MITCHEL. The French Revolution of February 1848 temporarily reunified Young Ireland in advocating force; but Mitchel was transported without resistance in May, and the British government in early July suspended *habeas corpus* and began arrests, including that of Gavan Duffy. Smith O'Brien and other leaders attempted an insurrection in Co. Tipperary. Their failure, followed by the TRANSPORTATION or escape of the chief Young Irelanders, ended the movement (see p. 705). Influential in the United States, Canada, and Australia, some Young Irelanders joined the later Fenians or the IRISH PARTY, while their poems and prose inspired subsequent generations. **Richard P. Davis**

Young Scientists Exhibition, held annually since 1965 at the RDS, Dublin. The principal sponsor for the first thirty-three years was AER LINGUS, followed by Esat and Esat BT. The primary aim of the exhibition is to encourage awareness of the world of science among young people at secondary school level. Prizes are awarded for projects that entail original research by individuals or groups in four categories: biological, physical, social and behavioural sciences, and technology. Three levels of entries are accepted according to age groups in each category, and there are additional awards for display. The winner of the first prize is designated Young Scientist of the Year and goes on to compete—and frequently excel—in international competitions. Most of the Young Scientists of the Year have followed distinguished careers in research or industry. **Christopher Moriarty**

Zozimus *(see page 1163). Drawing of Zozimus (Michael Moran) by H. R. O'Neill (1836). Blind from birth, he made a living at an early age from reciting and creating his own popular ballads and poetry on the streets of Dublin. [National Library of Ireland R.12675]*

Z

Zafforini, Filippo (fl. 1798–1811), Italian mythological and landscape painter. An itinerant artist who worked as scene painter at the Crow Street and Peter Street Theatres, Dublin. He accomplished a notable sequence of wall paintings for the second Earl of Aldborough at Aldborough House, c. 1795, the last great aristocratic mansion to be built in Dublin before the Act of Union. The paintings have not survived. **Brian Lalor**

Zimmermann, Denis-Georges (1930–), song researcher and retired professor of English language and literature at the University of Neuchâtel. He visited Ireland annually from 1951 to 1965, preparing his pioneering *Songs of Irish Rebellion* (1966), which gives republican and Orange songs their objective historical and scholarly context; more recently he has been a valuable contributor of articles and reviews, mainly to the *Journal of the Folk Music Society of Ireland*. His main interest since 1965 has been the Irish oral prose tradition, and his important book *The Irish Storyteller* was published in 2001. **John Moulden**

Zoological Gardens, Dublin. The Zoological Society of Ireland was founded at a meeting in Dublin on 10 May 1830. By the following year the Duke of Northumberland had arranged for land to be donated from the PHOENIX PARK for the establishment of the Zoological Gardens, which officially opened on 1 September 1831; Dublin Zoo is therefore the third-oldest public zoo in the world. The first general meeting of the society was held in November 1832, when the collection was reported to include 123 species of animal: forty-seven mammals, seventy-two birds, and four reptiles. On 1 January 2000 the gardens held more than 646 species: fifty mammals, sixty-seven birds, and eighteen reptiles. In 1838 the name of the society was changed to ROYAL ZOOLOGICAL SOCIETY OF IRELAND, when VICTORIA was invited to become patron of the zoo in the year of her coronation.

The daily management of the zoo was traditionally the responsibility of the superintendent, with the more important decisions undertaken by the honorary secretary. However, Dr B. B. FERRAR brought about the most significant changes seen in the running of the gardens when he was appointed superintendent in 1911. From his time onwards the superintendent managed the zoo, while referring to the Council for final approval. The title superintendent was replaced in 1967, when Terence Murphy became the first director of Dublin Zoo.

The Zoological Gardens has had a prestigious history since its humble beginnings on 2.2 ha ($5\frac{1}{2}$ acres) of land in the Phoenix Park (see p. 851). According to the surveyors' and architects' report of 1832, the original buildings in the gardens consisted of a house, an outhouse or stable, and a small cottage. The house, which is known today as the Director's Residence, was rebuilt in 1866 and is still occupied by the director as well as accommodating the administrative centre for the zoo on its ground floor. The earliest building erected by the society was the entrance lodge of 1833 in the style of a thatched cottage. This lodge is still in use, though it no longer functions as the main entrance to the zoo.

The first permanent enclosures to be constructed by the society consisted of a granite bear pit and a carnivore house. While many of the original buildings still stand, many others have been renovated in order to better suit the needs of the animals. Nesbitt House, originally built in 1877 as an aviary, was extensively renovated in 1988 and reopened as a bat house for Indian and Egyptian fruit bats. Roberts House, opened in 1902 to house lions, has also been extensively remodelled and now functions as a walk-through aviary. Dublin Zoo holds the honour of producing the first mandrill birth in captivity, the first Himalayan bear cubs (1879), and the first litter of cape hunting-dogs (1896). The first giraffe arrived in 1844 and the first lions in 1885. The arrival of the lions Natal and Natalie laid the foundations of a world-famous breeding stock at the zoo, which produced among others the famous lion CAIRBRE, later used in the introduction to Metro-Goldwyn-Mayer films.

In 1983 the society, in conjunction with University College, Cork, opened FOTA WILDLIFE PARK on Fota Island, Co. Cork, to mark the 150th anniversary of the founding of Dublin Zoo. The aim was to provide a more natural approach to animal welfare; and all animals were originally supplied by the society.

The last decade of the twentieth century was a period of unprecedented growth for the society, with the implementation of a development programme for the zoo. This period of development and investment began in 1993 and was set to continue until at least 2005. Within the Council a smaller Executive and Development Committee were formed that could quickly and more effectively assist the director in the expansion of the zoo. The expansion involved in particular the opening of the new African Plains. While doubling the size of the zoo, this development also improves facilities for many of the larger African animals, such as the rhino, hippo, and giraffe. The new 12 ha (30-acre) development is the largest and most significant expansion in the 170-year history of the zoo.

Today Dublin Zoo is a conservation and education institution. It participates in thirty-one endangered breeding programmes as well as sixteen international and twelve regional programmes. It also acts as studbook co-ordinator for two European endangered species breeding programmes: the Moluccan cockatoo (an Indonesian parrot) and the golden lion tamarin (a South American primate), both of which are seriously endangered in their native habitats. **Peter Wilson**

Zozimus. Michael Moran, better known as Zozimus, was born in Faddle Alley, off Blackpitts in the Liberties of Dublin, c. 1794. He lost his sight a fortnight after he was born, but according to all reports he was blessed with an extraordinary memory and could learn by heart almost immediately long poems, recitations, or ballads, and these he recited or sang on the street where he sold his ballad sheets. The name Zozimus came from a fifth-century holy man who featured in a long poem about St Mary of Egypt written by a Dr Coyle. This was one of Zozimus's preferred recitations, and he recited it so often that he became known by the name of Zozimus. He was married twice, and, as he said himself, he ventured into the chariot of Venus by doing the connubials, the last

Zoological Gardens. *Golden lion tamarins, South American primates, one of the thirty-one endangered species included in the Dublin Zoo breeding programme. The Royal Zoological Society of Ireland established Dublin Zoo in the Phoenix Park in 1830. [Karen McDonnell, Zoological Society of Ireland]*

time being to the Widow Curran. His best-known song is probably 'The Finding of Moses in the Bulrushes'.

On Egypt's banks contaygious to the Nile,
The old Pharaoh's daughter went to bathe in style,
She took her dip and came unto the land,
And for to dry her royal pelt she ran along the strand.
A bulrush tripped her, whereupon she saw
A smiling babby in a wad of straw,
She took him up and said in accents mild,
Tear an ages, girls, which of yez owns the child?

Zozimus was very aware of the politics of the time and wrote several political ballads that still survive, such as those that called for the repeal of 'the vile Act of Union.' William Butler Yeats wrote an article about him in his *Celtic Twilight* called 'The Last of the Gleemen'. Zozimus died on Friday 3 April 1846 in number 15 Patrick Street, Dublin, and was buried in Glasnevin cemetery on Palm Sunday. A tombstone to his memory was erected over his grave in 1998. He had dictated his own epitaph before he died:

My burying place to me is of no concern to me,
In the O'Connell circle let it be,
And as to my funeral all pomp it is vain,
Illustrious people does prefer it plain.

Frank Harte

Subject Index

Aviation

Cartography

Children's Literature

Classical Music

Clothing

Comedy

Craft

Criticism

Dance

Diaspora

Economics

Education

Engineering

Environment

Exploration

Feminism

Film

Folklore

Food and Drink

Geography

History to 1200

History 1200–1700

History 1700–1918

History from 1918

History of Ulster

Homosexuality

Irish Family History

Journalism

Language

Law

Literature in English

Literature in Irish

Marine

Maritime History

Publishing

Religion

Science

Script

Sociology

Transport, land

Travellers

Typography

Visual Arts

Walking

General Index

Page references in *italic* indicate illustrations.

E

H

I

J

M

O

P

S

X

Y

Z